THE

CENTURY BOOK OF FACTS

A HANDBOOK OF READY REFERENCE

EMBRACING

HISTORY, BIOGRAPHY, GOVERNMENT, LAW, LANGUAGE, LITERATURE, INVENTION, SCIENCE, DOMESTIC ECONOMY, INDUSTRY, FINANCE, ART, RELIGION, EDUCATION, HYGIENE, AND USEFUL MISCELLANY.

COLLATED AND EDITED
BY
HENRY W. RUOFF, M.A., D.C.L.,
Author of "The Origin of the Family," "Leaders of Men," "The Capitals of the World," etc.

AUTHENTIC, COMPREHENSIVE, UP-TO-DATE.

The King-Richardson Company,
SPRINGFIELD, MASS.

CHICAGO. BUFFALO. SAN JOSÉ.

PREFACE.

THIS volume is designed to meet the popular demand for a book of reliable and authentic information touching our every day pursuits and requirements. It belongs to a class of publications of a cyclopedic character that are not only a very great *desideratum* but an unquestioned necessity in an age like the present,—marked, as it is, by a constantly expanding spirit of invention, progress, innovation, general enlightenment, and humane achievement, the record of which is found in a wide and diverse literature.

It has been truly said, "Of the making of books, there is no end"; nor is it desirable that there should be. The thing that *is* desirable is, that the books we are compelled to own should be the best of their class—rich repositories to which we can repair with entire confidence for new knowledge, or the refreshing of that which may have lapsed through some trick of memory. This is especially true, not only as a matter of economy in time and energy, but because of the utter futility of any effort on our part to keep abreast of the knowledge of the times, and the practical issues that concern us, in any other way. When it is remembered that the yearly output of books exceeds 30,000 volumes, and that the reading capacity of the average man is not more than 3,500 in a lifetime, even though he devote the whole of his working hours to the task of reading, the necessity and wisdom of properly and judiciously epitomizing that knowledge which is of most avail in making us into better citizens and more intelligent beings, is only emphasized.

The present work is confined exclusively to those departments of knowledge with which we are most practically and vitally concerned. Its mission is to convey useful and general information to all classes of readers, and incidentally to add something to every one's store of general culture. It is the result of a large expenditure of labor, painstaking care, judicious discrimination, and wide research. The material included has been drawn from numerous sources and authorities, and great care exercised in its collation so as to exclude everything of doubtful authenticity. Obviously the grouping of related facts into Books will be found advantageous for quick reference, as well as in giving a comprehensive view of certain fields of knowledge. The topics in the various Books are not meant to follow any specific order, but have been permitted to fall in line in such fashion as seems most likely to sustain their interest for the general reader. This seeming disorder is, however, fully met by a complete index, both direct and indirect, at the end of the volume.

The points that have been steadily kept in view are, conciseness, authenticity, comprehensiveness, range, and utility; and in these respects it is believed that this volume occupies a niche peculiarly its own.

CONTENTS.

BOOK IV.

Science, Invention, Discovery.

BOOK V.

Hygiene, Domestic Economy, Dietetics.

BOOK VI.

Finance, Industry, Transportation.

BOOK VII.

Religion, Education, Fine Arts.

BOOK VIII.

Miscellaneous Facts and Figures.

CANADIAN HOUSE OF PARLIAMENT.

Book I.

Government and Law.

Government and Law.

UNITED STATES OF AMERICA.

Constitution and Government.—A Congress representing the thirteen original colonies declared their independence of Great Britain July 4, 1776, and thereafter each colony was known as a State. As a result of the war with Great Britain, the latter acknowledged the independence of the United States November 30, 1782, and September 3, 1783, a definitive treaty of peace was concluded at Paris. The government of the United States continued under the Congress provided by the Articles of Confederation until March 4, 1789, when a constitution, which had been adopted by representatives of the different States September 17, 1787, went into effect. March 4, 1789, then, is the date of the inception of the present constitutional government of the American Union.

Ten amendments were added to the original Constitution December 15, 1791; the eleventh amendment, January 8, 1798; the twelfth amendment, September 25, 1804; the thirteenth amendment, December 18, 1865; the fourteenth amendment, July 28, 1868; and the fifteenth amendment, March 30, 1870. Amendments proposed by the Congress must be adopted by three fourths of the States, acting through their legislatures.

In the table of States hereafter given, the date of the adoption of the original Constitution by each is stated, and also the dates of the admission of States subsequent to that time, there having been thirty-two States admitted since the adoption of the Constitution, the whole number of States now being forty-five.

By the Constitution, the government of the nation is intrusted to three separate departments, the Executive, the Legislative, and the Judicial. The executive power is vested in a President, who holds his office during the term of four years, and is elected, together with a Vice-President chosen for the same term, in the mode prescribed as follows: "Each State shall appoint, in such manner as the Legislature thereof may direct, a number of electors, equal to the whole number of senators and representatives to which the State may be entitled in the Congress; but no senator or representative, or person holding an office of trust or profit under the United States, shall be appointed an elector." The practice is that in every State the electors allotted to the State are chosen by direct vote of the citizens on a general ticket, on the system known in France as *scrutin de liste*. The Constitution enacts that "the Congress may determine the time of choosing the electors, and the day on which they shall give their votes, which day shall be the same throughout the United States"; and further, that "no person except a natural-born citizen, or a citizen of the United States at the time of the adoption of this Constitution, shall be eligible to the office of President; neither shall any person be eligible to that office who shall not have attained to the age of thirty-five years, and been fourteen years a resident within the United States."

Executive.—The President is commander-in-chief of the army and navy, and of the militia in the service of the Union. The Vice-President is *ex officio* President of the Senate; and, in case of the death or resignation of the President, he becomes the President for the remainder of the term. The elections for President and Vice-President are at present held in all the States on the Tuesday next after the first Monday in November, every four years; and, on the 4th of March following, the new President-elect assumes office.

By a law approved January 19, 1886, in case of removal, death, resignation, or inability of both the President and Vice-President, the Secretary of State, and after him, in the order of the establishment of their departments, other members of the Cabinet, shall act as President until the disability of the President is removed, or a President shall be elected. On the death of a Vice-President the duties of the office fall to the President *pro tempore* of the Senate, who receives the salary of the Vice-President. The party in the majority usually elects a President *pro tempore* at the beginning of each term of Congress, or reorganization of the Senate, who acts as President of the Senate whenever the Vice-President is absent.

The administrative business of the Government is conducted by eight chief officers, or heads of Departments, denominated "Secretaries," who constitute what is popularly known as the "Cabinet," although there is no legal or constitutional provision for that designation. The Secretaries are chosen by the President, and commissioned by him after confirmation by the Senate. Each Secretary presides over his particular department, and acts under the immediate authority of the President. Each Secretary receives an annual salary of $8,000, and holds office during the pleasure of the President. The Departments, in the chronological order of their establishment, and the duties, are as follows:

Secretary of State.—The Department of State is charged with all duties appertaining to correspondence with public ministers, American consuls, and representatives of foreign powers accredited to the United States, and with negotiations of whatever character relating to the foreign affairs of the nation. The Secretary is accorded first rank among the members of the President's Cabinet. He is the custodian of treaties made with foreign states, and of the laws of the United States. He grants and issues passports, and exequaturs to foreign consuls in the United States are issued under his supervision.

Secretary of the Treasury.— The Secretary of the Treasury is charged with the management of the national finances, and prepares plans for the improvement of the revenue and the support of public credit. He controls the plans for public buildings; the coinage and printing of money; the collection of commercial statistics; the administration of the Coast and Geodetic Survey, Life-Saving, Light-House, Revenue-Cutter, Steamboat-Inspection, and Marine Hospital branches of public service, and annually submits to Congress estimates of probable revenues and disbursements of the Government.

Secretary of War.— The Secretary of War performs all duties relating to the military service; he has supervision of the United States Military Academy at West Point, of the national cemeteries, and of all matters relating to river and harbor improvements, the prevention of obstruction to navigation, and the establishment of harbor lines.

The military bureaus of the War Department constitute a part of the military establishment, and have officers of the regular army at their head, while the Secretary and his immediate assistants are civilians as a rule.

Department of Justice.— The Attorney-General represents the United States in matters involving legal questions, and gives advice and opinion, when so required by the President or by the heads of the Executive Departments, on questions of law arising in the administration of their respective offices; he exercises a general superintendence and direction over United States attorneys and marshals in all judicial districts in the States and Territories, and provides special counsel for the United States whenever required by any department of the Government.

Postmaster-General.— The Postmaster-General has the direction and management of the general postal business of the Government; he appoints officers and employees of the Department, except the four Assistant Postmasters-General, who are appointed by the President, by and with the advice and consent of the Senate; appoints all postmasters whose compensation does not exceed $1,000; makes postal treaties with foreign governments, by and with the advice and consent of the President, and directs the management of the domestic and foreign mail service.

Secretary of the Navy.— The Secretary of the Navy has the general superintendence of construction, manning, armament, equipment, and employment of vessels of war. The Secretary, Assistant Secretary, and the attachés of what is known as the Secretary's office are civilians, while the heads of all bureaus are navy officers.

Secretary of the Interior.— The duties of the Secretary of the Interior are varied; he is charged with the supervision of the public business relating to patents, pensions, public lands, and surveys, Indians, education, railroads, the geological survey, the census, Indian reservations, the Territories, the various public parks, and certain hospitals and eleemosynary institutions in the District of Columbia.

Secretary of Agriculture.— The Secretary of Agriculture is charged with the supervision of all public business relating to the agricultural industry, and he exercises advisory supervision over the agricultural experiment stations deriving support from the National Treasury; he also has control of the quarantine stations for imported cattle, and of interstate quarantine when rendered necessary by contagious cattle diseases.

Legislative.—The whole legislative power is vested by the Constitution in a Congress, consisting of a Senate and House of Representatives. The Senate consists of two members from each State, chosen by the State Legislatures for six years. Senators must be not less than thirty years of age; must have been citizens of the United States for nine years; and be residents in the States for which they are chosen. Besides its legislative functions, the Senate is intrusted with the power of ratifying or rejecting all treaties made by the President with foreign powers, a two-thirds majority of senators present being required for ratification. The Senate is also invested with the power of confirming or rejecting all appointments to office made by the President, and its members constitute a High Court of Impeachment. The judgment in the latter case extends only to removal from office and disqualification. The House of Representatives has the sole power of impeachment.

The House of Representatives is composed

of members elected every second year by the vote of citizens who, according to the laws of their respective States, are qualified to vote. In general such voters are all male citizens over twenty-one years of age. Neither race nor color affects the right of citizens. The franchise is not absolutely universal; residence for at least one year in most States (in Rhode Island and Kentucky two years, in Michigan and Maine three months) is necessary, in some States the payment of taxes, in others registration. On the other hand, many of the Western States admit to the franchise unnaturalized persons who have formally declared their intention to become citizens. Untaxed Indians are excluded from the franchise, in most States convicts, in some States duelists and fraudulent voters; in Massachusetts voters are required to be able to read English, and in Mississippi and South Carolina there are also educational restrictions. Colorado, Idaho, Utah, and Wyoming admit women to the franchise on equal terms with men. The number of members to which each State is entitled is determined by the census taken every ten years. By the Apportionment Act consequent on the census of 1900, the number of representatives is 386, distributed as follows:—

Alabama	9	Nevada	1
Arkansas	7	New Hampshire	2
California	8	New Jersey	10
Colorado	3	New York	37
Connecticut	5	North Carolina	10
Delaware	1	North Dakota	2
Florida	3	Ohio	21
Georgia	11	Oregon	2
Idaho	1	Pennsylvania	32
Illinois	25	Rhode Island	2
Indiana	13	South Carolina	7
Iowa	11	South Dakota	2
Kansas	8	Tennessee	10
Kentucky	11	Texas	16
Louisiana	7	Utah	1
Maine	4	Vermont	2
Maryland	6	Virginia	10
Massachusetts	14	Washington	3
Michigan	12	West Virginia	5
Minnesota	9	Wisconsin	11
Mississippi	8	Wyoming	1
Missouri	16		
Montana	1	Total	386
Nebraska	6		

On the basis of the last census there is one representative to every 201,860 inhabitants. The popular vote for President in 1900 was about 14,000,000, or nearly one in five of the entire population. In 1900 there were in the United States 21,329,819 males of voting age—21 years and over, including unnaturalized foreigners.

The next apportionment will be based upon the Federal census of 1910, the results of which census will be reported to the Congress assembling the first Monday in December of that year, the Congress passing an apportionment act providing the requisite number of representatives from each State, and notifying the respective States of this action. Each State will then rearrange its congressional districts for the next election, which will take place in November, 1912, and the apportionment then established in accordance with the next enumeration will hold for ten years. The apportionment at the various censuses has been as follows:—

Under	Census		Apportionment		Whole Nu'ber of Representatives
	Year	Populat'n	Year	Ratio	
Constitution	—	—	1789	30,000	65
First Census	1790	3,929,214	1793	33,000	105
Second Census	1800	5,308,483	1803	33,000	141
Third Census	1810	7,239,881	1813	35,000	181
Fourth Census	1820	9,633,822	1823	40,000	213
Fifth Census	1830	12,866,020	1833	47,700	240
Sixth Census	1840	17,069,453	1843	70,680	223
Seventh Census	1850	23,191,876	1853	93,423	233
Eighth Census	1860	31,443,321	1863	127,381	243
Ninth Census	1870	38,558,371	1873	131,425	293
Tenth Census	1880	50,155,783	1883	151,911	325
Eleve'th Census	1890	62,622,250	1893	173,901	356
Twelfth Census	1900	76,303,387	1903	201,860	386

According to the terms of the Constitution, representatives must not be less than twenty-five years of age, must have been citizens of the United States for seven years, and be residents in the States from which they are chosen. In addition to the representatives from the States, the House admits a "delegate" from each organized Territory, who has the right to speak on any subject and to make motions, but not to vote. The delegates are elected in the same manner as the representatives.

Each of the two houses of Congress is made by the Constitution the "judge of the elections, returns, and qualifications of its own members"; and each of the houses may, with the concurrence of two thirds, expel a member.

The Congress of the United States has the power to propose alterations in the Constitution, by the 5th article of the same. The article orders that the Congress, whenever two thirds of both houses shall deem it necessary, shall propose amendments to the Constitution, or, on the application of the Legislatures of two thirds of all the States, shall call a convention for proposing the amendments, which in either case shall be valid to all intents and purposes as part of the Constitution when ratified by the Legislatures of three fourths of the several States, or by conventions in three fourths thereof, as the one or other mode of ratification may be proposed by Congress.

Slavery was abolished throughout the whole of the United States by the Thirteenth Amendment of the Constitution, adopted Dec. 18, 1865. The vast change in the political and social organization of the Republic made by this new fundamental law was completed by the fourteenth and fifteenth Amendments of the Constitution, adopted in 1868 and 1870, which gave to the former slaves all the rights and privileges of citizenship.

Under an act of Congress approved Jan. 20, 1874, the salary of a senator, representative, or delegate in Congress is $5,000 per annum with traveling expenses calculated at the rate of twenty cents per mile, by the most direct route of usual travel, and similar return, once for each session of Congress. There is also an annual allowance of $125 for stationery, etc., for each member. The salary of the Speaker of the House of Representatives is, under the same Act of Congress, $8,000 per annum.

No senator or representative can, during the time for which he is elected, be appointed to any *civil* office under authority of the United States which shall have been created or the emoluments of which shall have been increased during such time; and no person holding *any* office under the United States can be a member of either house during his continuance in office. No religious test is required as a qualification to any office or public trust under the United States.

The period usually termed "a Congress" in legislative language continues for two years; as, for example, from noon, March 4, 1899, until March 4, 1901, at which latter time the term of the representatives to the Fifty-sixth Congress expires, and the term of the new House of Representatives commences; but a new Congress does not assemble, unless called together by the President in special session, until the first Monday in December following, and the organization of the House, that is, the election of the Speaker and other officers, takes place on the first assembling, whether in special session after the 4th of March of every second year, as stated, or on the first Monday in December after its term begins. While the sessions of the Senate are held contemporaneously with those of the House, its organization may continue from Congress to Congress.

There are usually two sessions of each Congress—the first or long session, which may hold until adjourned by resolution of the two Houses, and the short session, which is the closing one, and which expires on the 4th of March every second year, the new Congress beginning its term the same day.

Neither house of Congress can adjourn for more than three days at any one time without the joint action of both. In case of a disagreement of the two houses as to adjournment, the President has the right to prorogue the Congress.

The Vice-President of the United States, as before stated, is President of the Senate, but he has no vote unless there is a tie. The Senate has the sole power to try all impeachments, and it acts upon the nominations for appointment by the President; it also acts upon treaties submitted to it by the administration. The Senate may be called in extra session for these purposes by the President without the Congress being called together.

All bills for raising revenue must originate in the House of Representatives, but the Senate may propose or concur with amendments to such bills, as on all other bills.

Judiciary.—The judicial system, like the executive and legislative systems, is dual. The Federal Government maintains courts for the trial of civil causes arising out of the admiralty, patent, banking, and other laws of the United States; of certain causes between citizens of different States; and of crimes against the United States. These crimes are few in number, and the criminal jurisdiction of United States courts is comparatively insignificant, extending only to piracy, murder on the high seas, offenses against the postal and revenue laws, and the like. Almost all offenses against the person and against property are dealt with by the State courts; also all civil causes where the parties are residents of the same State, and matters of probate, divorce, and bankruptcy.

In the separate States the lowest courts are those held by Justices of the Peace, or, in towns and cities, by Police Judges. In the counties courts of record are held, some by local county officers, others by District or Circuit Judges, who go from county to county. In these courts there are usually the grand and petty jury. The highest court in each State is the Supreme Court, or Court of Final Appeal, with a Chief Justice and Associate Judges. These judges are usually elected by the people, but sometimes appointed by the Governor, with or without the Senate or Council; they usually hold office for terms of years, but sometimes practically for life or during good behavior. Their salaries vary from $2,500 to $7,500.

Of the Federal Courts the lowest are those of the districts, of which there are about sixty, each State forming one or more districts. These courts may try any case of crime against the United States not punishable with death. Above these are nine Circuit Courts, each with a Circuit Judge, with or without the local District Judge; but one or two District Judges may by themselves hold a Circuit Court. The Circuit Court Judges appoint commissioners, whose duty it is to arrest, examine, and commit persons accused of crime against the

United States, and to assist the Circuit and District Judges in taking evidence for the trial of such persons. These duties may, however, be performed by a judge or magistrate of either a State or the Federal Government. Each of the nine Justices of the Supreme Court must hold a Court in one of the nine circuits at least once every two years, and with each may be associated the Circuit or District Judge. The Supreme Court consists of a Chief Justice and eight Associate Judges, appointed by the President with the consent of the Senate. It deals with appeals from inferior courts, and has original jurisdiction in cases affecting foreign ministers and consuls, and those in which a State is a party.

Other courts with criminal jurisdiction are the Court of the District of Columbia and those of the Territories. There is also at Washington a Court of Claims.

States and Territories. — The Union comprises thirteen original States, seven States which were admitted without having been organized as Territories dependent on the Union, and twenty-five States which had been Territories. Each State has its own constitution, which must be republican in form, and each constitution derives its authority, not from Congress, but from the population of the State. In the case of the original States the colonial charters were adopted, with more or less modification, as State constitutions; the other States, before entering the Union, had constitutions already made. Admission of States into the Union is granted by special Acts of Congress, either (1) in the form of "enabling Acts," providing for the drafting and ratification of a State constitution by the people, in which case the Territory becomes a State as soon as the conditions are fulfilled, or (2) accepting a constitution already framed and at once granting admission.

Each State is provided with a Legislature of two Houses, a Governor, and other executive officials, and a judicial system. Both Houses of the Legislature are elective, but the Senators (having larger electoral districts) are less numerous than the members of the House of Representatives, while in some States their terms are longer and, in a few, the Senate is only partially renewed at each election. Members of both Houses are paid at the same rate, which varies from $150 to $1,500 per session, or from $1 to $8 per day during session. The duties of the two Houses are similar, but in many States money bills must be introduced first in the House of Representatives. The Senate has to sit as a court for the trial of officials impeached by the other House, and, besides, has often the power to confirm or reject appointments made by the Governor. In most of the States the sessions are biennial, the Governor having power to summon in extraordinary session, but not to dissolve or adjourn. State Legislatures are competent to deal with all matters not reserved for the Federal Government by the Federal Constitution, or falling within restrictions imposed by the State constitutions. Among their powers are the determinations of the qualifications for the right of suffrage, and the control of all elections to public office, including elections of members of Congress and electors of President and Vice-President; the criminal law, both in its enactment and in its execution, with unimportant exceptions, and the administration of prisons; the civil law, including all matters pertaining to the possession and transfer of, and succession to, property; marriage and divorce, and all other civil relations; the chartering and control of all manufacturing, trading, transportation, and other corporations, subject only to the right of Congress to regulate commerce passing from one State to another; the regulation of labor; education; charities; licensing, including regulation of the liquor traffic; fisheries and game laws. The revenues of the States are derived chiefly from a direct tax upon property, in some cases both real and personal, in others on land and buildings only. The prohibition upon Congress to levy direct taxes save in proportion to population, contained in the National Constitution, leaves this source of revenue to the States exclusively.

The Governor is chosen by direct vote of the people over the whole State. His term of office varies from one year (in 2 States), to four years (in 19 States), and his salary from $1,500 to $10,000. His duty is to see to the faithful administration of the law, and he has command of the military forces of the State. His power of appointment to State offices is usually unimportant. He may recommend measures but does not present bills to the Legislature. In some States he presents estimates. In all the States except Delaware, North Carolina, Ohio, and Rhode Island, the Governor has the power to veto bills, but where this power exists the Legislature, by a two thirds vote, may override the veto.

The officers by whom the administration of State affairs is carried on — the Secretaries, Treasurers, and Auditors, and in some of the States members of boards or commissions — are usually chosen by the people at the general State elections for terms similar to those for which Governors themselves hold office. In some States commissioners are appointed by the Governor.

Including Hawaii, there are now six Territories, and when the status of Porto Rico is established there will probably be seven Territories. Arizona, New Mexico, and Oklahoma have local Legislatures, the form of which has been prescribed by the Federal Government; they have powers similar to those of the States, but any of their acts may be modified or annulled by Federal statutes.

The Governor of each of the Territories, except the Indian Territory, is appointed for four years by the President, to whom annual reports are submitted. These Governors have the power of veto over the acts of Territorial Legislatures. The President appoints the Territorial Secretaries and other officials, together with Territorial judges.

Alaska and the Indian Territory have no power of self-government, the former being governed like a British crown colony, by a Governor who is not assisted by a Legislature. In the Indian Territory the native tribes are under the direct control of the Department of the Interior, but the civilized tribes, with the support of the National Government, maintain local governments of their own, with elective Legislatures and executive officers, whose functions are strictly limited to the persons and personal property of their own citizens; that is, the Indians.

The District of Columbia presents an anomalous status. It is the seat of the Federal Government. It is coextensive with and is practically the City of Washington, and embraces an area of $69\frac{1}{4}$ square miles. The District has no municipal legislative body, and its citizens have no right to vote, either in national or municipal affairs. Under an act of 1878 its municipal government is administered by three commissioners, appointed by the President. They constitute a non-partisan board, one being selected from each of the leading political parties, and the third being assigned to duty as a commissioner from the Engineer Corps of the army. All legislation relative to the District of Columbia is by the Congress.

All the legislatures, State and Territorial, have biennial sessions, except Georgia, Massachusetts, New Jersey, New York, Rhode Island, and South Carolina, which have annual sessions, beginning in January of each year, with the exception of Georgia, whose Legislature meets in October. Nearly all the present biennial sessions began in January, 1899. The States whose Legislatures meet in January, 1900, are Iowa, Kentucky, Maryland, Mississippi, and Ohio. Alabama's next biennial session begins in November, 1900, Louisiana's in May, 1900, and Vermont's in October, 1900.

HAWAII.

Constitution and Government.—The Hawaiian or Sandwich Islands, discovered by Captain Cook in 1778, formed during the greater part of the nineteenth century an independent kingdom, whose integrity was recognized by Great Britain, France, the United States, and other governments. In 1893, however, the reigning Queen, Liliuokalani, was deposed, and a provisional government formed; in 1894 a Republic was proclaimed, with a Legislature of two Houses and a President; and in accordance with a resolution of Congress of July 7, 1898, the islands were on August 12, 1898, formally annexed to the United States. Five commissioners were appointed to recommend such legislation concerning the islands as they should deem necessary and proper, and in the beginning of December the report of the Commission with its legislative proposals was transmitted to Congress. The principal Bill, providing for the erection of the islands into a Territory, to be styled the Territory of Hawaii, was enacted by the first session of the Fifty-sixth Congress, and was approved by the President, April 30, 1900. All whites, including Portuguese, all persons of African descent, and all descendants of Hawaiian race, either on the paternal or the maternal side, who were citizens of Hawaii immediately prior to the transfer of the sovereignty to the United States, are declared citizens of the United States. Prior to the transfer all Hawaiians of full age who could speak, read, and write either Hawaiian or English, had the right to vote. The number of registered electors on September 3, 1897, was 2,687.

Area and Population.—The total area of the islands is 6,640 square miles: namely, Hawaii, 4,210; Maui, 760; Oahu, 600; Kauai 590; Molokai, 270; Lanai, 150; Niihau, 97; Kahoolawe, 63 square miles. In 1896 the population numbered 109,020 (72,517 males and 36,503 females). Of the total, 31,019 were natives, 8,485 half-castes, 21,616 Chinese, 24,407 Japanese, 15,191 Portuguese, 3,086 Americans, 2,250 British, 1,432 Germans, 378 Norwegians, 101 French, 455 Polynesians, and 600 other foreigners. The population comprised 7,570 persons engaged in agriculture, 2,100 in fishing and navigation, 2,265 in the industries, 2,031 in trade and transport, 2,580 in liberal professions, 34,498 laborers, 4,310 of various occupations, and 53,726 without regular occupation. The native population (closely allied to the Maories of New Zealand) is rapidly decreasing, while the foreign element is increasing.

Commerce, Shipping, and Communications.—The islands are to a great extent mountainous and volcanic, but the soil is highly fertile and productive. Sugar and rice are the staple industries, while coffee, hides, bananas, and wool are also exported.

Steamers connect the islands with the American continent, Australasia, and China. In 1897 there were 62 registered vessels belonging to the islands, of 34,066 tons; of these, 21 of 28,510 tons were built in England. There are about 100 miles of railway in the islands of Hawaii, Maui, and Oahu. There are telegraphs in the islands of Maui, Hawaii, between Hawaii and Oahu, and round the latter island; total length, 250 miles; nearly every family in Honolulu has its telephone. In 1897 the total number of letters, etc., transmitted and received by the Post Office was 5,079,872; there were 73 post offices. Postal savings banks, 1897: depositors, 10,620; amount, $953,981. Honolulu is lighted by electricity, and has lines of tramways. The various islands will shortly be connected by telegraphic cable.

PORTO RICO.

Area, Population, Etc. — The island of Porto Rico (added to the United States by Spain in accordance with the Treaty of Paris, signed Dec. 10, 1898, and ratified by the Senate Feb. 6, 1899, and by the Queen Regent of Spain March 17), according to a recent report of the British consul (Foreign Office, Annual Series, No. 1,917, 1897), has an extent of about 3,668 square miles — 35 miles broad and 95 miles long. The population, according to an enumeration made in 1900, was 953,243.

Government.—An act providing for a civil government for Porto Rico was passed by the Fifty-sixth Congress, and received the assent of the President, April 12, 1900. Under this act a civil government was established, which went into effect May 1, 1900.

Geographical Formation.—The island is traversed from east to west by a mountain range, dividing the island into two unequal portions, by far the longest slope being on the north, so that the rivers on that coast are much the longer. From this chain several branches diverge toward the north coast, giving it a rugged appearance. The most of the population is situated on the lowlands at the sea front of the hills. For lack of roads, the interior is accessible only by mule trails or saddle paths, and it is covered with vast forests.

Rivers and brooks are numerous, forty-seven very considerable rivers having been enumerated. They are short and rapid, especially on the Caribbean slopes, which are steep and abrupt. The mountains intercept the northeast trade winds blowing from the Atlantic and wring their moisture from them, so that the rainfall of the north section is very copious. South of the mountains severe droughts occur and agriculture demands irrigation, but such work is unsystematically carried on.

The northeast coast is broken and forbidding; that of the south safer. The chief port on the north coast is the capital, San Juan. On the west is the important harbor of Mayaguez. On the south side are Guanica, Ponce, and Guayama. The island of Vieques, which lies off the east coast of Porto Rico, is 21 miles long and 6 miles wide.

Climate. — The climate is hot, but much alleviated by the prevailing northeast winds. A temperature as high as 117° Fahrenheit has been recorded, but it seldom exceeds 97° Fahrenheit in the shade during the hottest hours. At night it sinks to 68 or 69°. The rainy season lasts from August to December, and the rainfall is at times so copious north of the mountains as to inundate cultivated fields and produce swamps. The mean annual average rainfall is 64½ inches. The prevailing diseases are yellow fever, elephantiasis, tetanus, marsh fever, and dysentery.

Productions. — Porto Rico is unusually fertile, and its dominant industries are agriculture and lumbering. In elevated regions the vegetation of the temperate zone is not unknown. There are more than 500 varieties of trees found in the forests, and the plains are full of palm, orange, and other trees. The principal crops are sugar, coffee, tobacco, cotton, and maize, but bananas, rice, pineapples, and many other fruits are important products.

The principal minerals found in Porto Rico are gold, carbonates, and sulphides of copper and magnetic oxide of iron in large quantities. Lignite is found at Utuado and Moca, and also yellow amber. A large variety of marbles, limestones, and other building stones are deposited on the island, but these resources are very undeveloped. There are salt works at Guanica and Salinac on the south coast, and at Cape Rojo on the west, and these constitute the principal mineral industry in Porto Rico.

Inter-Communication. — Railways are in their infancy, and cart roads are deficient. There are 137 miles of railway, with 170 miles under construction, and 470 miles of telegraph lines. These connect the capital with the principal ports south and west. Submarine cables run from San Juan to St. Thomas and Jamaica.

Cities.—The capital of Porto Rico is San Juan Bautista, founded by Ponce de Leon. It is situated on the small island of Morro, now connected with the mainland by the San

Antonio Bridge. The district of its name contains 27,000 inhabitants. On the western end of the island Ponce de Leon built the Governor's palace, inclosed within the Santa Catalina fortifications, where also are the cathedral, town house, and theater. This portion of the city is now called Pueblo Viejo. It is an Episcopal see subordinate to the Archbishop of Santiago de Cuba. The city is strongly fortified for the defense of the entrance to the outer harbor. The interior harbor is landlocked, capacious, and safe, and is being dredged to a uniform depth of twenty-nine feet. The houses are of stone, usually one story high, and have roof gardens, from which fine marine views may be enjoyed. Almost every house has a garden in its patio or court.

Besides the capital, San Juan, there are some sixty or seventy towns and villages of considerable size in the island. Of these the most important are Ponce and Arecibo, each with a larger population than San Juan (that of Ponce being about 35,000 or 40,000, while that of San Juan is estimated at 25,000); Mayaguez (also larger than the capital) and Aguadilla, on the west coast; Farjardo and Humacao, on the east coast: Guanica and Aroyo, on the south, and Pepino and Cayey, in the interior.

Commerce.—The foreign trade of Porto Rico in 1896 amounted to $36,624,120, the imports being valued at $18,945,793, and the exports at $17,295,535. The largest trade was done with Spain, being $11,259,702, and the next largest with the United States, $6,526,029. In the year 1897 the imports from the United States were $1,988,888, and the exports to the United States $2,181,024. The imports from the United States included petroleum, ironware, dried and salted meats, textiles, and dairy products. Rice was the principal article of import from the rest of the world.

The largest article of export from Porto Rico is coffee, which is over 63 per cent. of the whole. The next largest is sugar, 28 per cent. The other exports in order of amount are tobacco, honey, molasses, cattle, timber, and hides.

PHILIPPINE ISLANDS.

These islands, ceded by Spain to the United States by the treaty signed by the Peace Commissioners, Dec. 10, 1898, and ratified by the Senate, Feb. 6, 1899, and by the Queen Regent of Spain March 17, extend almost due north and south from Formosa to Borneo and the Moluccas, embracing an extent of 16° of latitude and 9 of longitude. They are about 2,000 in number; the two largest are Luzon (area 40,024 square miles) and Mindanao; and the total area, including the Sulu Islands, is about 115,300 square miles. The population is estimated at about 8,000,000. The capital of the Philippines, Manila, has 154,062 inhabitants (1887); other towns are Laoag, 30,642; Lipa, 43,408; Banang, 35,598; Batangas, 35,587. There are about 25,000 Europeans in the islands and about 100,000 Chinese, in whose hands are the principal industries. The native inhabitants are mostly of the Malayan race, but there are some tribes of Negritos. The group is divided into three governments: Luzon, the Visayas, and Mindanao with the Sulu Islands; but in many of the islands the natives have hitherto been practically independent.

Financial and Industrial Conditions.—Silver is the basis of the currency in the Philippine Islands. There is no gold in general circulation, and has been none for more than twenty years. The Mexican dollar of a date previous to 1877 is current in the islands, and it is practically the only money in general circulation. The Spanish Government, in the summer of 1897, coined $6,000,000 of silver in a local currency, which was sent to the islands. These dollars are lighter in weight than the Mexican dollar, but the scarcity of money in the Philippine Islands caused them to be quickly absorbed. There is a local note-issuing bank, called the Banco Español Filipino, which has in circulation notes based on silver, of which there was outstanding on Sept. 30, 1898, approximately $2,500,000.

It is estimated there are in circulation $10,000,000 of subsidiary coins, the 10-cent, 20-cent, and 50-cent pieces, which have been recoined from Mexican dollars by the Spanish Government. The estimate of the Mexican dollars now in circulation, as given by one of the best-informed bankers in the islands, is from $20,000,000 to $25,000,000. This, with the $2,500,000 of notes of the Banco Español Filipino now in circulation, constitutes the currency of the islands. This would make a total of from $40,000,000 to $45,000,000, speaking roughly, for the entire islands, or, approximately, $5 per capita for the total population of the islands. It must not be overlooked that these figures are given on a silver basis, and that, therefore, in figuring on our own standard all of these figures must be cut in two. On a gold basis, the currency of the islands is, therefore, from $20,000,000 to $22,500,000, or $2.50 per capita, figuring on the total population of the islands.

Three banking institutions do the banking business of the Philippine Islands aside from that done by the large commercial houses.

which buy and sell exchange, and to a limited extent carry on the business which legitimately belongs to banking institutions. Of the three banks, the two most important are branch concerns, the third being a local institution controlled by Spaniards and natives.

There are about 25,000 Europeans resident in the islands (the total population is nearly 8,000,000), of course, not counting the troops. Some 12,000 are established in the capital, Manila, the center of the colonial government. English, Spanish, and German houses are engaged in trade, advancing money to the natives on their crops. Such business methods involve risks and necessitate large capital in the beginning, but the profits are immense. The land is fertile and productive, and lacks only intelligent cultivation. Abaca (manila hemp) is one of the chief sources of wealth of the country. Sugar cane does not give as satisfactory returns, owing largely to the ignorance of planters. The average production is 178,000,000 kilograms (175,186.96 tons), while that of Cuba is equal to 720,000,000 kilograms. The sugar goes almost entirely to Japan, England, and the United States. It is of poor quality and very cheap. The cultivation of tobacco is one of the most important industries, although it is capable of much greater development. The native coffee, although not equal to the mocha or bourbon varieties, has a fine aroma. It goes chiefly to Spain. Cocoa trees grow in abundance, and the oil is used for lighting houses and streets. The indigo is famous for its superior qualities. The inhabitants are apathetic to a degree that is noticeable even in these countries, where every one is averse to exertion. The women have long and slender fingers, remarkably fine and sensitive, and well adapted to their work. The hats and cigarette-holders they make and the articles they embroider are models of delicacy. Cotton spinning and work in bamboo are among the chief industries.

The fiber which gets its common name from the city of Manila is perennial and requires little cultivation; in fact, it does very well without any. It reaches the proportions of a tree, but its soft stem is cut with a knife, though several inches in diameter, and the decortication of the fiber is rather a matter of time and patience than of skill or hard work. About a million bales are exported annually, nearly all of it going to England or coming to this country, and our importation of the fiber has been increasing.

The sugar culture has remained in its primeval condition because the supply of labor was so great that there was no incentive to economize labor, and there was no United States at hand, as in the case of Cuba, to invest money in plantations and develop the business in accordance with modern ideas. There is no doubt that the culture of the cane can be immensely extended, and the methods of production would be modernized very rapidly if capital were directed toward the islands and there were a greater degree of confidence in their future.

The tobacco is as well known in Europe and Asia as the tobacco of Cuba is in this country; it is extensively cultivated and its manufacture is the staple business of the capital city.

Commerce.—In 1891 the Philippines' exports to Spain amounted to $22,479,000 ($18,095,595 in United States currency). In 1891 the Philippines' imports from Spain amounted to $17,126,000 ($13,786,430).

The total exports from the Philippines in 1892 consisted of 95,016 tons of hemp; 3,951,060 piculs (553,148,400 pounds) of sugar; 21,223 piculs (2,971,220 pounds) of coffee; 61,459 piculs (8,604,260 pounds) of sampanwood; 5,570 piculs (779,800 pounds) of indigo; 254,428 quintals (56,091,197 pounds) of tobacco leaf; 137,059,000 cigars. The total exports in 1892 were of the value of $33,479,000 ($23,803,569). Total value of imports, in 1892, were of the value of $27,000,000 ($19,197,000).

The imports into the Philippines from the United States in 1897 were but $94,597, the principal item being mineral oils. The exports to the United States were $4,383,740, the largest items being hemp, $2,701,651, and cane sugar, $1,199,202.

Climate.—Mr. Hilder, Assistant Secretary of the National Geographical Society, who spent nine months in the islands, says in the *Forum* that there is considerable variety in the climate, and that for the tropics it is not excessively hot. On the western side of Luzon the hot season is from March till June, May being the hottest month, when the temperature ranges from 80° to 100°. The mean temperature for the month is 84°, 2° above the summer temperature of New Orleans and 9° above the hottest month in Washington. From October to March is a cool, dry season. The northern islands are subject to terrific storms, which never pass south of 9° north latitude.

Railways and Shipping.—In a report published in Special Consular Reports, Highways of Commerce, Consul Elliott, of Manila, says that there is but one railway in the islands—from Manila to Dagupin—a distance of 123 miles. It is single track and well built, steel rails being used its entire length, the bridges being of stone or iron, and the station buildings substantial. English engines are used, which make 45 miles per hour. The Government assisted in the construction of the road by making valuable concessions of land with right of way its entire length and by guaranteeing 8 per cent. per year upon the stock of the road for a period of ninety-nine years, when it is to become State property.

SAMOAN ISLANDS.

The island of Tutuila and other small Samoan islands came into the possession of the United States, January, 1900. This island has an area of about 54 square miles, with a population of 3,800. Manua and the other islets have a united area of about 25 square miles, with about 2,000 inhabitants. Pago Pago is the only good harbor.

GUAM (LADRONES).

The Island of Guam or Guahan, the largest in the Marianne or Ladrone Archipelago, was ceded by Spain to the United States in 1898, and will probably be used as a coaling station for the United States navy. The island is about 32 miles long and 100 miles in circumference, and has a population of about 9,000, of whom about 6,000 are in Agaña, the capital. The inhabitants are mostly immigrants or the descendants of immigrants from the Philippines, the original race of the Marianne Islands having become extinct. The recognized language is Spanish, but English is also spoken. On the island there are 18 schools, and nine tenths of the islanders can read and write. The island is thickly wooded, well watered, and fertile, and possesses a roadstead.

REPUBLIC OF CUBA.

Government. — The island had been a Spanish possession ever since its discovery. After long years of bitter oppression, the United States came to the relief of the Cubans, and precipitated the Spanish-American War, which resulted in freeing Cuba from Spanish tyranny. A definite peace treaty was signed by the Peace Commission in Paris, Dec. 10, 1898, and ratified by the Senate, Feb. 6, 1899, and by the Queen Regent of Spain, March 17, 1899, whereby Spain relinquished all claim to the island of Cuba.

The armed interposition of the United States in the struggle against Spanish domination brought the island into close association with the United States Government, and, though Congress affirmed Cuban independence, the island was held in military occupation by the United States forces until the Cuban people were in a position to formulate and organize a government of their own, which was consummated on May 20, 1902, when the Republic of Cuba was formally inaugurated, and the "stars and stripes" were hauled down from the Government building at Havana and the flag of Cuba took its place.

Area and Population.—The area of Cuba is about 45,872 square miles. Ten per cent. of the area is cultivated, 7 per cent. is unreclaimed, and 4 per cent. is under forests. There are large tracts of country still unexplored. The population of the island in 1894 was given as 1,631,696, of which 65 per cent. was white, the remainder being negro. The capital, Havana, has 200,000 inhabitants; Matanzas (1892), 27,000; Santiago de Cuba, 71,307; Cienfuegos (1892), 27,430; Puerto Principe, 46,641; Holguin, 34,767; Sancti Spiritu, 32,608; Cardenas (1892), 23,680. Education was made obligatory in 1880. There are 843 public schools in the island, and Havana has a university.

Consul Hyatt, of Santiago do Cuba, in a report dated January 8, 1897, and printed in Consular Reports No. 197 (February, 1897), p. 262, says that the area of Cuba is about equal to that of the State of Pennsylvania, the length being 775 miles and the width varying from 30 to 160 miles. The productive soil, mineral wealth, and climatic conditions of the island entitle it to rank among the foremost communities of the world. The soil is a marvel of richness, and fertilizers are seldom used, unless in the case of tobacco, even though the same crops be grown on the same land for a hundred years, as has happened in some of the old sugar cane fields. The mountains are of coral formation, while the lowlands of eastern Cuba at least seem to be composed largely of fossils of sea matter from prehistoric times and are extremely rich in lime and phosphate, which accounts for their apparent inexhaustibleness.

Although founded and settled more than fifty years before the United States, Cuba has still 13,000,000 acres of primeval forests; mahogany, cedar, logwood, redwood, ebony, lignum-vitæ, and caiguaran (which is more durable in the ground than iron or steel) are among the woods.

If all the land suitable to the growth of sugar cane were devoted to that industry, it is estimated that Cuba might supply the entire Western Hemisphere with sugar. The island has already produced in a single year for export 1,000,000 tons, and its capabilities have only been in the experimental stage. The adaptability of the soil for tobacco culture has long been known. Cuba takes great pride in the quality of her coffee, and until the war the plantations were flourishing.

The land is not suitable to the cultivation of cereals, and probably no flouring mill exists on the island.

Finances.—The estimated revenue for 1897-98 was 24,755,760 pesos (a peso equals $0.965), of which 11,890,000 was from customs; ordinary expenditure, 26,119,124 pesos, of which 12,602,216 pesos was for the debt, 5,896,741 pesos for the Ministry of War, and 4,036,088 pesos for the Ministry of the Interior. The extraordinary revenue was estimated at over 80,000,000 pesos. The debt was in 1896 put at about £70,220,000, of which £10,000,000, was due to the Spanish treasury.

The interest on the debt is estimated to impose a burden of $9.75 per inhabitant.

Minerals.—According to Consul Hyatt, Cuba is capable of taking high rank in mineral wealth. Gold and silver have not been found in paying quantities. Copper was mined at Cobre by the natives before Columbus discovered the island, and there is strong proof that native copper was carried across to Florida and used by the Florida Indians hundreds of years ago. From 1828 to 1840 an average of from $2,000,000 to $3,000,000 worth of copper ore was shipped annually to the United States from these mines.

The iron mines of Cuba, all of which are located near Santiago, overshadow in importance all other industries on the eastern end of the island, constituting the only industry that has made any pretense of withstanding the shock of the present insurrection. The Juragua and Daiquiri iron companies (American), with a combined capital of over $5,000,000, now operate mines in this vicinity and employ from 800 to 1400 men, shipping to the United States from 30,000 to 50,000 tons of iron ore per month, the largest portion of which is used at Bethlehem, Steelton, and Pittsburg, Pa., and Sparrows Point, Md. The ore of these mines is among the richest in the world, yielding from 62 to 67 per cent. of pure iron, and is very free from sulphur and phosphorus. There are numerous undeveloped mines of equal value in this region.

In the Sierra Maestra range, on the southern coast of Cuba, from Santiago west to Manzanillo, within a distance of about 100 miles, are found numerous deposits of manganese, an ore indispensable in the manufacture of steel. As nearly all the manganese used in the United States comes from the Black Sea regions of Europe and a smaller quantity from the northern part of South America, it is but reasonable to suppose that the products of these near-by mines will be in great demand when the conditions are such that they can be operated in safety.

In the district of Santiago de Cuba, at the end of 1891, the total number of mining titles issued was 296, with an extent of 13,727 hectares. Of the mines reported and claimed, 138 were iron, 88 manganese, and 53 copper.

Commerce and Industry.—Railroads and other highways, improved machinery, and more modern methods of doing business are among the wants of Cuba; and with the onward march of civilization these will doubtless be hers in the near future. Cuba, like other tropical and semi-tropical countries, is not given to manufacturing; her people would rather sell the products of the soil and mines and buy manufactured goods. The possibilities of the island are great, while the probabilities remain an unsolved problem.

The number of landed estates on the island in 1891 was estimated at 90,960, of the value of 220,000,000 pesos, and rental of 17,000,000 pesos. The live stock consisted of 584,725 horses and mules, 2,485,766 cattle, 78,494 sheep, and 570,194 pigs. The chief produce is sugar and tobacco. The quantity of sugar produced in the year 1894-95 was 1,004,264 tons; 1895-96, 225,221 tons; 1896-97, 212,-051 tons. The insurrection and incendiarism in the island ruined the prospects of sugar cultivation in 1896. The tobacco crop on an average is estimated at 560,000 bales (1 bale = 110 lbs.), 338,000 bales being exported and the remainder used in cigar and cigarette manufacture in Havana. In 1896 the cigars exported numbered 185,914,000. Tobacco leaf exported in 1895, 30,466,000 lbs.; in 1896, 16,823,000 lbs. The decrease in cigar exports and decrease in leaf exports is due to decree of May 12, 1896, forbidding tobacco-leaf exports except to Spain. Cigarettes exported in 1895, 48,163,846 packets. Nearly all the tobacco and nearly half of the cigars go to the United States. About 80,000 of the inhabitants are ordinarily engaged in the cultivation of tobacco. Mahogany and other timbers are exported, as are also honey, wax, and fruits. The chief imports are rice, jerked beef, and flour. The Spanish official returns state the value of the imports from Cuba into Spain for 1896 to be 21,898,215 Spanish pesetas ($4,216,355.49), and the exports from Spain to Cuba 134,461,675 pesetas ($25,951,-003.27). In 1897 the imports of the United States from Cuba amounted to $405,326,637, and the exports from the United States to Cuba $100,456,712.

Railways.—According to a report published in Special Consular Reports, "Highways of Commerce," there are ten railway companies in Cuba, the most important being the Ferrocarriles Unidos; upward of 1000 miles of main line belong to these companies, and there are, besides, private branch lines to all the important sugar estates. The Ferrocarriles Unidos has four lines, connecting Havana with Matanzas, Batabano, Union, and Guanajay. The roads pass through the most populous part of the country and connect Havana with other lines.

The Western Railway was begun some forty years ago, and in 1891, when it was acquired by an English company, had reached Puerto de Golpe, 96 miles from Havana and 10 miles from Pinar del Rio, the capital of the province of that name and the center of the tobacco-growing district. The line has been completed to Pinar del Rio, and improvements have been made in the old part, many of the bridges having been replaced by new steel ones, the rails renewed, modern cars put on, etc.

The other companies are: Ferrocarriles Cardenas-Jacaro, the main line of which joins the towns of Cardenas and Santa Clara; Ferrocarril de Matanzas, having lines between Matanzas and Murga, and also between Matanzas and Guareiras; Ferrocarril de Sagua la Grande, running between Concha and Cruces; Ferrocarril Cienfuegos-Santa Clara, connecting those towns; Ferrocarriles Unidos de Caibarien, from Caibarien to Placetas; Ferrocarril de Puerto Principe-Nuevitas; Ferrocarril de Guantanamo.

The Marianao Railway also belongs to an English company, with headquarters in London. The original line, belonging to Cubans, was opened in 1863, but liquidated and was transferred to the present owners. The line, only 8½ miles in length, runs from Havana to Marianao, with a branch line to a small village on the coast. During 1894, over 750,000 passengers were carried, this being the chief source of revenue. The carriages are of the American type, and are fitted, as well as the locomotives, with the Westinghouse automatic brake; the rails are of steel, weighing 60 pounds per yard.

Ports, Interior Transportation, Etc.—In 1895 the port of Havana was visited by 1179 vessels, of 1,681,325 tons; in 1897, 231 vessels, of 309,758 tons, visited Cienfuegos. There are 54 ports in Cuba, of which 15 are open to commerce. There are 19 lighthouses.

Cables.—There are four cable lines connected with Cuba. The International Ocean Telegraph Company has a cable from Havana to Florida; the Cuban Submarine Company has a cable connecting Havana with Santiago de Cuba and Cienfuegos; the West India and Panama Company has a cable connecting Havana with Santiago de Cuba, Jamaica, Porto Rico, the Lesser Antilles, and the Isthmus of Panama; the Compagnie Française de Cables Sous-Marins has a line connecting Havana with Santiago de Cuba, Haiti, Santo Domingo, Venezuela, and Brazil.

The only three towns in Cuba having cable connections are Havana, Cienfuegos, and Santiago de Cuba.

Telegraphs, Telephones, Etc.—The telegraph and telephone systems in Cuba belong to the Government, but the latter is farmed out for a limited number of years to a company called the Red Telefonica de la Habana. Nearly all the public and private buildings in the city and suburbs are connected by telephone.

DECLARATION OF INDEPENDENCE.

In Congress July 4, 1776. The unanimous Declaration of the Thirteen United States of America.

When, in the course of human events, it becomes necessary for one people to dissolve the political bands which have connected them with another, and to assume, among the powers of the earth, the separate and equal station to which the laws of nature and of nature's God entitle them, a decent respect to the opinions of mankind requires that they should declare the causes which impel them to the separation.

We hold these truths to be self-evident, that all men are created equal, that they are endowed, by their Creator, with certain unalienable rights, that among these are life, liberty, and the pursuit of happiness. That to secure these rights, governments are instituted among men, deriving their just powers from the consent of the governed, that whenever any form of government becomes destructive of these ends, it is the right of the people to alter or to abolish it, and to institute new government, laying its foundation on such principles, and organizing its powers in such form as to them shall seem most likely to effect their safety and happiness. Prudence, indeed, will dictate, that governments long established should not be changed for light and transient causes; and accordingly all experience hath shown that mankind are more disposed to suffer where evils are sufferable, than to right themselves by abolishing the forms to which they are accustomed. But when a long train of abuses and usurpations, pursuing invariably the same object, evinces a design to reduce them under absolute despotism, it is their right, it is their duty, to throw off such government, and to provide new guards for their future security. Such has been the patient sufferance of these colonies; and such is now the necessity which constrains them to alter their former systems of government. The history of the present King of Great Britain is a history of repeated injuries and usurpations, all having in direct object the establishment of an absolute tyranny over these states. To prove this, let facts be submitted to a candid world.

He has refused his assent to laws the most wholesome and necessary for the public good.

He has forbidden his governors to pass laws of immediate and pressing importance, unless suspended in their operation till his assent should be obtained; and when so suspended, he has utterly neglected to attend to them.

He has refused to pass other laws for the accommodation of large districts of people, unless these people would relinquish the right of representation in the legislature—a right inestimable to them, and formidable to tyrants only.

He has called together legislative bodies at places unusual, uncomfortable, and distant from the depository of their public records, for the sole purpose of fatiguing them into compliance with his measures.

He has dissolved representative houses repeatedly, for opposing with manly firmness his invasions on the rights of the people.

He has refused, for a long time after such dissolutions, to cause others to be elected; whereby the legislative powers, incapable of annihilation, have returned to the people at large, for their exercise, the state remaining, in the meantime, exposed to all the dangers of invasion from without, and convulsions within.

He has endeavored to prevent the population of these states; for that purpose obstructing the laws for naturalization of foreigners, refusing to pass others to encourage their migration hither, and raising conditions of new appropriations of lands.

He has obstructed the administration of justice, by refusing his assent to laws establishing judiciary powers.

He has made judges dependent on his will alone for the tenure of their offices, and the amount and payment of their salaries.

He has erected a multitude of new offices, and sent hither swarms of officers, to harass our people, and eat out their substance.

He has kept among us, in times of peace, standing armies, without the consent of our legislatures.

He has affected to render the military independent of, and superior to, the civil power.

He has combined with others to subject us to a jurisdiction foreign to our constitution, and unacknowledged by our laws; giving his assent to their acts of pretended legislation,—

For quartering large bodies of armed troops among us:

For protecting them, by a mock trial, from punishment from any murders which they should commit on the inhabitants of these states:

For cutting off our trade with all parts of the world:

For imposing taxes on us without our consent:

For depriving us, in many cases, of the benefits of trial by jury:

For transporting us beyond the seas to be tried for pretended offenses:

For abolishing the free system of English laws in a neighboring province, establishing therein an arbitrary government, and enlarging its boundaries, so as to render it at once an example and fit instrument for introducing the same absolute rule into these colonies:

For taking away our charters, abolishing our most valuable laws, and altering, fundamentally, the powers of our governments:

For suspending our own legislatures and declaring themselves invested with power to legislate for us in all cases whatsoever.

He has abdicated government here, by declaring us out of his protection, and waging war against us.

He has plundered our seas, ravaged our coasts, burnt our towns, and destroyed the lives of our people.

He is, at this time, transporting large armies of foreign mercenaries, to complete the works of death, desolation and tyranny, already begun with circumstances of cruelty and perfidy scarcely paralleled in the most barbarous ages, and totally unworthy the head of a civilized nation.

He has constrained our fellow-citizens, taken captive on the high seas, to bear arms against their country, to become the executioners of their friends and brethren, or to fall themselves by their hands.

He has excited domestic insurrections among us, and has endeavored to bring on the inhabitants of our frontiers the merciless Indian savages, whose known rule of warfare is an undistinguished destruction of all ages, sexes, and conditions.

In every stage of these oppressions we have petitioned for redress in the most humble terms; our repeated petitions have been answered only by repeated injury. A prince whose character is thus marked by every act which may define a tyrant is unfit to be the ruler of a free people.

Nor have we been wanting in attentions to our British brethren. We have warned them, from time to time, of attempts by their legislature to extend an unwarrantable jurisdiction over us. We have reminded them of the circumstances of our emigration and settlement here. We have appealed to their native justice and magnanimity, and we have conjured them by the ties of our common kindred to disavow these usurpations, which would inevitably interrupt our connections and correspondence. They too have been deaf to the voice of justice and of consanguinity. We must, therefore, acquiesce in the necessity which denounces our separation, and hold them, as we hold the rest of mankind, enemies in war, in peace friends.

We, therefore, the Representatives of the United States of America, in General Congress assembled, appealing to the Supreme Judge of the world for the rectitude of our intentions, do, in the name, and by authority of the good people of these Colonies, solemnly publish and declare, That these United Colonies are, and of right ought to be, *free and independent States;* that they are absolved from all allegiance to the British crown, and that all political connection between them and the State of Great Britain, is, and ought to be, totally dissolved; and that as *free and independent States*, they have full power to levy war, conclude peace, contract alliances, establish commerce, and to do all other acts and things which *independent States* may of right do. And for the support of this declaration, with a firm reliance on the protection of Divine Providence, we mutually pledge to each other our lives, our fortunes, and our sacred honor.

JOHN HANCOCK.

NEW HAMPSHIRE.

Josiah Bartlett,
William Whipple,
Matthew Thornton.

MASSACHUSETTS BAY.

Samuel Adams,
John Adams,
Robert Treat Paine,
Elbridge Gerry.

RHODE ISLAND.

Stephen Hopkins,
William Ellery.

CONNECTICUT.

Roger Sherman,
Samuel Huntington,
William Williams,
Oliver Wolcott.

NEW YORK.

William Floyd,
Philip Livingston,
Francis Lewis,
Lewis Morris.

NEW JERSEY.

Richard Stockton,
John Witherspoon,
Francis Hopkinson,
John Hart,
Abraham Clark.

PENNSYLVANIA.

Robert Morris,
Benjamin Rush,
Benjamin Franklin,
John Morton,
George Clymer,
James Smith,
George Taylor,
James Wilson,
George Ross.

DELAWARE.

Cæsar Rodney,
George Read,
Thomas M'Kean.

MARYLAND.

Samuel Chase,
William Paco,
Thomas Stone,
Charles Carroll, of Carrollton.

VIRGINIA.

George Wythe,
Richard Henry Lee,
Thomas Jefferson,
Benjamin Harrison,
Thomas Nelson, Jr.,
Francis Lightfoot Lee,
Carter Braxton.

NORTH CAROLINA.

William Hooper,
Joseph Hewes,
John Penn.

SOUTH CAROLINA.

Edward Rutledge,
Thomas Heyward, Jr.,
Thomas Lynch, Jr.,
Arthur Middleton.

GEORGIA.

Button Gwinnett,
Lyman Hall,
George Walton.

IN CONGRESS, }
JANUARY 18, 1777. }

Ordered:

That an authenticated copy of the Declaration of Independence, with the names of the members of Congress subscribing the same, be sent to each of the United States, and that they be desired to have the same put on record.

By order of Congress.

JOHN HANCOCK, *President.*

Attest, CHAS. THOMSON, *Secy.*

A true copy.

JOHN HANCOCK, *Presidt.*

THE MECKLENBURG DECLARATION.

Some thirteen months previous to the signing of the great Declaration of Independence there was drawn up a document in Mecklenburg County, N. C., that was almost a model in wording and sentiment of the great charter of American liberty. There are different accounts of the matter, but the most reliable is this:—

At a public meeting of the residents of Mecklenburg County, in the State of North Carolina, held at Charlotte on the 20th day of May, 1775, it was

"*Resolved*, That whenever directly or indirectly abetted, or in any way, form, or manner countenanced, the unchartered and dangerous invasion of our rights, as claimed by Great Britain, is an enemy of our country—to America—and to the inherent and inalienable rights of man.

"*Resolved*, That we, the citizens of Mecklenburg County, do hereby dissolve the political bonds which have connected us to the mother-country, and hereby absolve ourselves from all allegiance to the British crown, and abjure all political connection, contract or association with that nation, which has wantonly trampled on our rights and liberties and inhumanly shed the blood of American patriots at Lexington.

"*Resolved*, That we do hereby declare ourselves a free and independent people: are and of right ought to be a sovereign and self-governing association, under the control of no power other than that of our God and the general government of the Congress. To the maintenance of which independence we solemnly pledge to each other our mutual cooperation, our lives, our fortunes, and our sacred honor."

Two other resolutions in the same document, regarding administration of the law and regulating the militia, having no present value, are omitted.

CONSTITUTION OF THE UNITED STATES OF AMERICA.

(Went into operation first Wednesday in March, 1789.)

Preamble.—We, the people of the United States, in order to form a more perfect union, establish justice, insure domestic tranquillity, provide for the common defense, promote the general welfare, and secure the blessings of liberty to ourselves and our posterity, do ordain and establish this Constitution for the United States of America.

ARTICLE I.

Section I. 1. All legislative powers herein granted shall be vested in a Congress of the United States, which shall consist of a Senate and House of Representatives.

Section II. 1. The House of Representatives shall be composed of members chosen every second year by the people of the several States; and the electors in each State shall have the qualifications requisite for electors of the most numerous branch of the State Legislature.

2. No person shall be a Representative who shall not have attained to the age of twenty-five years, and been seven years a citizen of the United States, and who shall not, when elected, be an inhabitant of that State in which he shall be chosen.

3. Representatives and direct taxes shall be apportioned among the several States which may be included within this Union, according to their respective numbers, which shall be determined by adding to the whole number of free persons, including those bound to service for a term of years, and excluding Indians not taxed, three fifths of all other persons. The actual enumeration shall be made within three years after the first meeting of the Congress of the United States, and within every subsequent term of ten years, in such manner as they shall by law direct. The number of Representatives shall not exceed one for every thirty thousand, but each State shall have at least one Representative; and until such enumeration shall be made, the State of New Hampshire shall be entitled to choose three; Massachusetts, eight; Rhode Island and Providence Plantations, one; Connecticut, five; New York, six; New Jersey, four; Pennsylvania, eight; Delaware, one; Maryland, six; Virginia, ten; North Carolina, five; South Carolina, five, and Georgia three.

4. When vacancies happen in the representation from any State, the executive authority thereof shall issue writs of election to fill such vacancies.

5. The House of Representatives shall choose their speaker and other officers; and shall have the sole power of impeachment.

Section III. 1. The Senate of the United States shall be composed of two Senators from each State, chosen by the Legislature thereof for six years; and each Senator shall have one vote.

2. Immediately after they shall be assembled in consequence of the first election, they shall be divided as equally as may be into three classes. The seats of the Senators of the first class shall be vacated at the expiration of the second year, of the second class at the expiration of the fourth year, and of the third class at the expiration of the sixth year, so that one third may be chosen every second year; and if vacancies happen by resignation, or otherwise, during the recess of the Legislature of any State, the executive thereof may make temporary appointments until the next meeting of the Legislature, which shall then fill such vacancies.

3. No person shall be a Senator who shall not have attained to the age of thirty years, and been nine years a citizen of the United States, and who shall not, when elected, be an inhabitant of that State for which he shall be chosen.

4. The Vice-President of the United States shall be President of the Senate, but shall have no vote unless they be equally divided.

5. The Senate shall choose their other officers, and also a President pro tempore, in the absence of the Vice-President, or when he shall exercise the office of President of the United States.

6. The Senate shall have the sole power to try all impeachments. When sitting for that purpose, they shall all be on oath or affirmation. When the President of the United States is tried, the chief-justice shall preside: and no person shall be convicted without the concurrence of two thirds of the members present.

7. Judgment in cases of impeachment shall not extend further than to removal from office, and disqualification to hold and enjoy any office of honor, trust, or profit under the United States; but the party convicted shall nevertheless be liable and subject to indictment, trial, judgment, and punishment, according to law.

Section IV. 1. The times, places and manner of holding elections for Senators and Representatives shall be prescribed in each State by the Legislature thereof; but the Congress may at any time by law make or alter such regulations, except as to the place of choosing Senators.

2. The Congress shall assemble at least once in every year; and such meeting shall be on the first Monday in December, unless they shall by law appoint a different day.

Section V. 1. Each House shall be the judge of the election, returns, and qualifications of its own members, and a majority of each shall constitute a quorum to do business; but a smaller number may adjourn from day to day, and may be authorized to compel the attendance of absent members, in such manner and under such penalties as each House may provide.

2. Each House may determine the rule of its proceedings, punish its members for disorderly behavior, and, with the concurrence of two thirds, expel a member.

3. Each House shall keep a journal of its proceedings, and from time to time publish the same, excepting such parts as may in their judgment require secrecy; and the yeas and nays of the members of either House on any question shall, at the desire of one fifth of those present, be entered on the journal.

4. Neither House, during the session of Congress, shall, without the consent of the other, adjourn for more than three days, nor to any other place than that in which the two houses shall be sitting.

SECTION VI. 1. The Senators and Representatives shall receive a compensation for their services, to be ascertained by law, and paid out of the treasury of the United States. They shall, in all cases, except treason, felony, and breach of the peace, be privileged from arrest during their attendance at the sessions of their respective houses, and in going to and returning from the same; and for any speech or debate in either house, they shall not be questioned in any other place.

2. No Senator or Representative shall, during the time for which he was elected, be appointed to any civil office under the authority of the United States which shall have been created, or the emoluments whereof shall have been increased during such time; and no person holding any office under the United States shall be a member of either House during his continuance in office.

SECTION VII. 1. All bills for raising revenue shall originate in the House of Representatives, but the Senate may propose or concur with amendments, as on other bills.

2. Every bill which shall have passed the House of Representatives and the Senate shall, before it become a law, be presented to the President of the United States; if he approve, he shall sign it, but if not, he shall return it, with his objections, to that House in which it shall have originated, who shall enter the objections at large on their journal, and proceed to reconsider it. If after such reconsideration two thirds of that House shall agree to pass the bill, it shall be sent, together with the objections, to the other House, by which it shall likewise be reconsidered; and if approved by two thirds of that House it shall become a law. But in all such cases the votes of both Houses shall be determined by yeas and nays, and the names of the persons voting for and against the bill shall be entered on the journal of each House respectively. If any bill shall not be returned by the President within ten days (Sundays excepted) after it shall have been presented to him, the same shall be a law in like manner as if he had signed it, unless the Congress by their adjournment, prevent its return; in which case it shall not be a law.

3. Every order, resolution, or vote to which the concurrence of the Senate and House of Representatives may be necessary (except on a question of adjournment) shall be presented to the President of the United States; and before the same shall take effect shall be approved by him, or being disapproved by him, shall be repassed by two thirds of the Senate and the House of Representatives, according to the rules and limitations prescribed in the case of a bill.

SECTION VIII. 1. The Congress shall have power:

To lay and collect taxes, duties, imposts, and excises, to pay the debts and provide for the common defense and general welfare of the United States; but all duties, imposts, and excises shall be uniform throughout the United States.

2. To borrow money on the credit of the United States.

3. To regulate commerce with foreign nations, and among the several States, and with the Indian tribes.

4. To establish an uniform rule of naturalization and uniform laws on the subject of bankruptcies throughout the United States.

5. To coin money, regulate the value thereof, and of foreign coin, and fix the standard of weights and measures.

6. To provide for the punishment of counterfeiting the securities and current coin of the United States.

7. To establish post offices and post roads.

8. To promote the progress of science and useful arts by securing for limited times to authors and inventors the exclusive rights to their respective writings and discoveries.

9. To constitute tribunals inferior to the Supreme Court.

10. To define and punish piracies and felonies committed on the high seas, and offenses against the law of nations.

11. To declare war, grant letters of marque and reprisal, and make rules concerning captures on land and water.

12. To raise and support armies, but no ap-

propriation of money to that use shall be for a longer term than two years.

13. To provide and maintain a navy.

14. To make rules for the government and regulation of the land and naval forces.

15. To provide for calling forth the militia to execute the laws of the Union, suppress insurrections, and repel invasions.

16. To provide for organizing, arming, and disciplining the militia, and for governing such part of them as may be employed in the service of the United States, reserving to the States respectively the appointment of the officers, and the authority of training the militia according to the discipline prescribed by Congress.

17. To exercise exclusive legislation in all cases whatsoever over such district (not exceeding ten miles square) as may, by cession of particular States and the acceptance of Congress, become the seat of Government of the United States, and to exercise like authority over all places purchased by the consent of the Legislature of the State in which the same shall be, for the erection of forts, magazines, arsenals, dry docks, and other needful buildings.

18. To make all laws which shall be necessary and proper for carrying into execution the foregoing powers, and all other powers vested by this Constitution in the Government of the United States, or in any department or officer thereof.

SECTION IX. 1. The migration or importation of such persons as any of the States now existing shall think proper to admit shall not be prohibited by the Congress prior to the year one thousand eight hundred and eight, but a tax or duty may be imposed on such importation, not exceeding ten dollars for each person.

2. The privilege of the writ of habeas corpus shall not be suspended, unless when in cases of rebellion or invasion the public safety may require it.

3. No bill of attainder or ex post facto law shall be passed.

4. No capitation or other direct tax shall be laid, unless in proportion to the census or enumeration hereinbefore directed to be taken.

5. No tax or duty shall be laid on articles exported from any State.

6. No preference shall be given by any regulation of commerce or revenue to the ports of one State over those of another, nor shall vessels bound to or from one State be obliged to enter, clear, or pay duties in another.

7. No money shall be drawn from the Treasury but in consequence of appropriations made by law; and a regular statement and account of the receipts and expenditures of all public money shall be published from time to time.

8. No title of nobility shall be granted by the United States. And no person holding any office of profit or trust under them shall, without the consent of the Congress, accept of any present, emolument, office, or title of any kind whatever from any king, prince, or foreign state.

SECTION X. 1. No State shall enter into any treaty, alliance, or confederation, grant letters of marque and reprisal, coin money, emit bills of credit, make anything but gold and silver coin a tender in payment of debts, pass any bill of attainder, ex post facto law, or law impairing the obligation of contracts, or grant any title of nobility.

2. No State shall, without the consent of the Congress, lay any impost or duties on imports or exports, except what may be absolutely necessary for executing its inspection laws, and the net produce of all duties and imposts, laid by any State on imports or exports, shall be for the use of the Treasury of the United States; and all such laws shall be subject to the revision and control of the Congress.

3. No State shall, without the consent of Congress, lay any duty of tonnage, keep troops or ships of war in time of peace, enter into any agreement or compact with another State, or with a foreign power, or engage in war, unless actually invaded, or in such imminent danger as will not admit of delay.

ARTICLE II.

SECTION I. 1. The Executive power shall be vested in a President of the United States of America. He shall hold his office during the term of four years, and, together with the Vice-President, chosen for the same term, be elected as follows:

2. Each State shall appoint, in such manner as the Legislature thereof may direct, a number of electors, equal to the whole number of Senators and Representatives to which the State may be entitled in the Congress; but no Senator or Representative or person holding an office of trust or profit under the United States shall be appointed an elector.

3. [The electors shall meet in their respective States and vote by ballot for two persons, of whom one at least shall not be an inhabitant of the same State with themselves. And they shall make a list of all the persons voted for, and of the number of votes for each, which list they shall sign and certify and transmit, sealed, to the seat of the government of the United States, directed to the President of the Senate. The President of the Senate shall, in the presence of the Senate and House of Rep-

resentatives, open all the certificates, and the votes shall then be counted. The person having the greatest number of votes shall be the President, if such number be a majority of the whole number of electors appointed, and if there be more than one who have such majority, and have an equal number of votes, then the House of Representatives shall immediately choose by ballot one of them for President; and if no person have a majority, then from the five highest on the list the said House shall in like manner choose the President. But in choosing the President, the vote shall be taken by States, the representation from each State having one vote. A quorum, for this purpose, shall consist of a member or members from two thirds of the States, and a majority of all the States shall be necessary to a choice. In every case, after the choice of the President, the person having the greatest number of votes of the electors shall be the Vice-President. But if there should remain two or more who have equal votes, the Senate shall choose from them by ballot the Vice-President.]*

4. The Congress may determine the time of choosing the electors and the day on which they shall give their votes, which day shall be the same throughout the United States.

5. No person except a natural born citizen, or a citizen of the United States at the time of the adoption of this Constitution, shall be eligible to the office of President; neither shall any person be eligible to that office who shall not have attained to the age of thirty-five years and been fourteen years a resident within the United States.

6. In case of the removal of the President from office, or of his death, resignation, or inability to discharge the powers and duties of the said office, the same shall devolve on the Vice-President, and the Congress may by law provide for the case of removal, death, resignation, or inability, both of the President and Vice-President, declaring what officer shall then act as President, and such officer shall act accordingly until the disability be removed or a President shall be elected.

7. The President shall, at stated times, receive for his services a compensation, which shall neither be increased nor diminished during the period for which he shall have been elected, and he shall not receive within that period any other emolument from the United States, or any of them.

8. Before he enter on the execution of his office he shall take the following oath or affirmation:—

"I do solemnly swear (or affirm) that I will faithfully execute the office of President of the United States, and will, to the best of my ability, preserve, protect, and defend the Constitution of the United States."

SECTION II. 1. The President shall be Commander-in-Chief of the Army and Navy of the United States, and of the militia of the several States when called into the actual service of the United States; he may require the opinion, in writing, of the principal officer in each of the executive departments upon any subject relating to the duties of their respective offices, and he shall have power to grant reprieves and pardons for offenses against the United States except in cases of impeachment.

2. He shall have power, by and with the advice and consent of the Senate, to make treaties, provided two thirds of the Senators present concur; and he shall nominate, and by and with the advice and consent of the Senate shall appoint ambassadors, other public ministers and consuls, judges of the Supreme Court, and all other officers of the United States whose appointments are not herein otherwise provided for, and which shall be established by law; but the Congress may by law vest the appointment of such inferior officers as they think proper in the President alone, in the courts of law, or in the heads of departments.

3. The President shall have power to fill up all vacancies that may happen during the recess of the Senate by granting commissions, which shall expire at the end of their next session.

SECTION III. He shall from time to time give to the Congress information of the state of the Union, and recommend to their consideration such measures as he shall judge necessary and expedient; he may, on extraordinary occasions, convene both Houses, or either of them, and in case of disagreement between them with respect to the time of adjournment, he may adjourn them to such time as he shall think proper; he shall receive ambassadors and other public ministers; he shall take care that the laws be faithfully executed, and shall commission all the officers of the United States.

SECTION IV. The President, Vice-President, and all civil officers of the United States shall be removed from office on impeachment for and conviction of treason, bribery, or other high crimes and misdemeanors.

ARTICLE III.

SECTION I. The judicial power of the United States shall be vested in one Supreme Court, and in such inferior courts as the Congress may from time to time ordain and establish. The judges, both of the Supreme and inferior

*This clause is superseded by Article XII., Amendments.

courts, shall hold their offices during good behavior, and shall at stated times receive for their services a compensation which shall not be diminished during their continuance in office.

SECTION II. 1. The judicial power shall extend to all cases in law and equity arising under this Constitution, the laws of the United States, and treaties made, or which shall be made, under their authority; to all cases affecting ambassadors, other public ministers, and consuls; to all cases of admiralty and maritime jurisdiction; to controversies to which the United States shall be a party; to controversies between two or more States, between a State and citizens of another State, between citizens of different States, between citizens of the same State claiming lands under grants of different States, and between a State, or the citizens thereof, and foreign States, citizens, or subjects.

2. In all cases affecting ambassadors, other public ministers, and consuls, and those in which a State shall be party, the Supreme Court shall have original jurisdiction. In all the other cases before mentioned the Supreme Court shall have appellate jurisdiction both as to law and fact, with such exceptions and under such regulations as the Congress shall make.

3. The trial of all crimes, except in cases of impeachment, shall be by jury, and such trial shall be held in the State where the said crimes shall have been committed; but when not committed within any State the trial shall be at such place or places as the Congress may by law have directed.

SECTION III. 1. Treason against the United States shall consist only in levying war against them, or in adhering to their enemies, giving them aid and comfort. No person shall be convicted of treason unless on the testimony of two witnesses to the same overt act, or on confession in open court.

2. The Congress shall have power to declare the punishment of treason, but no attainder of treason shall work corruption of blood or forfeiture except during the life of the person attained.

ARTICLE IV.

SECTION I. Full faith and credit shall be given in each State to the public acts, records, and judicial preceedings of every other State. And the Congress may by general laws prescribe the manner in which such acts, records and proceedings shall be proved, and the effect thereof.

SECTION II. 1. The citizens of each State shall be entitled to all privileges and immunities of citizens in the several States.

2. A person charged in any State with treason, felony, or other crime, who shall flee from justice, and be found in another State, shall on demand of the Executive authority of the State from which he fled, be delivered up, to be removed to the State having jurisdiction of the crime.

3. No person held to service or labor in one State, under the laws thereof, escaping into another shall, in consequence of any law or regulation therein, be discharged from such service or labor, but shall be delivered up on claim of the party to whom such service or labor may be due.

SECTION III. 1. New States may be admitted by the Congress into this Union; but no new State shall be formed or erected within the jurisdiction of any other State, nor any State be formed by the junction of two or more States, or parts of States, without the consent of the Legislatures of the States concerned, as well as of the Congress.

2. The Congress shall have power to dispose of and make all needful rules and regulations respecting the territory or other property belonging to the United States; and nothing in this Constitution shall be so construed as to prejudice any claims of the United States, or of any particular State.

SECTION IV. The United States shall guarantee to every State in this Union a republican form of government, and shall protect each of them against invasion, and, on application of the Legislature, or of the Executive (when the Legislature cannot be convened), against domestic violence.

ARTICLE V.

The Congress, whenever two thirds of both Houses shall deem it necessary, shall propose amendments to this Constitution, or, on the application of the Legislatures of two thirds of the several States, shall call a convention for proposing amendments, which, in either case, shall be valid to all intents and purposes, as part of this Constitution, when ratified by the Legislatures of three fourths of the several States, or by conventions in three fourths thereof, as the one or the other mode of ratification may be proposed by the Congress; provided that no amendment which may be made prior to the year one thousand eight hundred and eight shall in any manner affect the first and fourth clauses in the Ninth Section of the First Article; and that no State, without its consent, shall be deprived of its equal suffrage in the Senate.

ARTICLE VI.

1. All debts contracted and engagements entered into before the adoption of this Con-

stitution shall be as valid against the United States under this Constitution as under the Confederation.

2. This Constitution and the laws of the United States which shall be made in pursuance thereof and all treaties made, or which shall be made, under the authority of the United States, shall be the supreme law of the land, and the judges in every State shall be bound thereby, anything in the Constitution or laws of any State to the contrary notwithstanding.

3. The Senators and Representatives before mentioned, and the members of the several State Legislatures, and all executive and judicial officers, both of the United States and of the several States, shall be bound by oath or affirmation to support this Constitution; but no religious test shall ever be required as a qualification to any office or public trust under the United States.

ARTICLE VII.

The ratification of the Conventions of nine States shall be sufficient for the establishment of this Constitution between the States so ratifying the same.

Amendments to the Constitution.

ARTICLE I.

Congress shall make no law respecting an establishment of religion, or prohibiting the free exercise thereof; or abridging the freedom of speech or of the press; or the right of the people peaceably to assemble, and to petition the Government for a redress of grievances.

ARTICLE II.

A well-regulated militia being necessary to the security of a free State, the right of the people to keep and bear arms shall not be infringed.

ARTICLE III.

No soldier shall, in time of peace, be quartered in any house without the consent of the owner, nor in time of war but in a manner to be prescribed by law.

ARTICLE IV.

The right of the people to be secure in their persons, houses, papers, and effects, against unreasonable searches and seizures, shall not be violated, and no warrants shall issue but upon probable cause, supported by oath or affirmation, and particularly describing the place to be searched, and the persons or things to be seized.

ARTICLE V.

No person shall be held to answer for a capital or other infamous crime unless on a presentment or indictment of a grand jury, except in cases arising in the land or naval forces, or in the militia, when in actual service, in time of war or public danger; nor shall any person be subject for the same offense to be twice put in jeopardy of life or limb; nor shall be compelled in any criminal case to be a witness against himself, nor be deprived of life, liberty, or property, without due process of law; nor shall private property be taken for public use without just compensation.

ARTICLE VI.

In all criminal prosecutions, the accused shall enjoy the right to a speedy and public trial, by an impartial jury of the State and district wherein the crime shall have been committed, which district shall have been previously ascertained by law, and to be informed of the nature and cause of the accusation; to be confronted with the witnesses against him; to have compulsory process for obtaining witnesses in his favor, and to have the assistance of counsel for his defense.

ARTICLE VII.

In suits at common law, where the value in controversy shall exceed twenty dollars, the right of trial by jury shall be preserved, and no fact tried by a jury shall be otherwise reexamined in any court of the United States than according to the rules of the common law.

ARTICLE VIII.

Excessive bail shall not be required, nor excessive fines imposed, nor cruel and unusual punishments inflicted.

ARTICLE IX.

The enumeration in the Constitution of certain rights shall not be construed to deny or disparage others retained by the people.

ARTICLE X.

The powers not delegated to the United States by the Constitution, nor prohibited by it to the States, are reserved to the States respectively, or to the people.

ARTICLE XI.

The judicial power of the United States shall not be construed to extend to any suit in law or equity, commenced or prosecuted against one of the United States, by citizens of another State, or by citizens or subjects of any foreign State.

ARTICLE XII.

The electors shall meet in their respective States, and vote by ballot for President and Vice-President, one of whom at least shall not be an inhabitant of the same State with themselves, they shall name in their ballots the person voted for as President, and in distinct ballots the person voted for as Vice-President; and they shall make distinct lists of all persons voted for as President, and of all persons voted for as Vice-President, and of the number of votes for each, which list they shall sign and certify, and transmit, sealed, to the seat of the Government of the United States, directed to the President of the Senate; the President of the Senate shall, in the presence of the Senate and House of Representatives, open all the certificates, and the votes shall then be counted; the person having the greatest number of votes for President shall be the President, if such number be a majority of the whole number of electors appointed; and if no person have such majority, then from the persons having the highest numbers, not exceeding three, on the list of those voted for as President, the House of Representatives shall choose immediately, by ballot, the President. But in choosing the President, the votes shall be taken by States, the representation from each State having one vote; a quorum for this purpose shall consist of a member or members from two thirds of the States, and a majority of all the States shall be necessary to a choice. And if the House of Representatives shall not choose a President, whenever the right of choice shall devolve upon them, before the fourth day of March next following, then the Vice-President shall act as President, as in the case of the death or other constitutional disability of the President. The person having the greatest number of votes as Vice-President shall be the Vice-President, if such number be a majority of the whole number of electors appointed, and if no person have a majority, then from the two highest numbers on the list the Senate shall choose the Vice-President; a quorum for the purpose shall consist of two thirds of the whole number of Senators, and a majority of the whole number shall be necessary to a choice. But no person constitutionally ineligible to the office of President shall be eligible to that of Vice-President of the United States.

ARTICLE XIII.

1. Neither slavery nor involuntary servitude, except as a punishment for crime whereof the party shall have been duly convicted, shall exist within the United States, or any place subject to their jurisdiction.

2. Congress shall have power to enforce this article by appropriate legislation.

ARTICLE XIV.

1. All persons born or naturalized in the United States, and subject to the jurisdiction thereof, are citizens of the United States and of the State wherein they reside. No State shall make or enforce any law which shall abridge the privileges or immunities of citizens of the United States; nor shall any State deprive any person of life, liberty, or property without due process of law, nor deny to any person within its jurisdiction the equal protection of the laws.

2. Representatives shall be apportioned among the several States according to their respective numbers, counting the whole number of persons in each State, excluding Indians not taxed. But when the right to vote at any election for the choice of electors for President and Vice-President of the United States, Representatives in Congress, the executive and judicial officers of a State, or the members of the Legislature thereof, is denied to any of the male members of such State, being of twenty-one years of age, and citizens of the United States, or in any way abridged, except for participation in rebellion or other crime, the basis of representation therein shall be reduced in the proportion which the number of such male citizens shall bear to the whole number of male citizens twenty-one years of age in such State.

3. No person shall be a Senator or Representative in Congress, or elector of President and Vice-President, or holding any office, civil or military, under the United States, or under any State, who, having previously taken an oath, as a member of Congress, or as an officer of the United States, or as a member of any State Legislature, or as an executive or judicial officer of any State, to support the Constitution of the United States, shall have engaged in insurrection or rebellion against the same, or given aid and comfort to the enemies thereof. But Congress may, by a vote of two thirds of each House, remove such disability.

4. The validity of the public debt of the United States, authorized by law, including debts incurred for payment of pensions and bounties for services in suppressing insurrection and rebellion, shall not be questioned. But neither the United States nor any State shall assume or pay any debt or obligation incurred in aid of insurrection or rebellion against the United States, or any claim for the loss or emancipation of any slave; but all such debts, obligations, and claims shall be held illegal and void.

5. The Congress shall have power to enforce by appropriate legislation the provisions of this article.

ARTICLE XV.

1. The right of the citizens of the United States to vote shall not be denied or abridged

by the United States or by any State on account of race, color, or previous condition of servitude.

2. The Congress shall have power to enforce the provision of this article by appropriate legislation.

Ratification of the Constitution.

The Constitution was ratified by the thirteen original States in the following order:

Delaware, December 7, 1787, unanimously.

Pennsylvania, December 12, 1787, vote 46 to 23.

New Jersey, December 18, 1787, unanimously.

Georgia, January 2, 1788, unanimously.

Connecticut, January 9, 1788, vote 128 to 40.

Massachusetts, February 6, 1788, vote 187 to 168.

Maryland, April 28, 1788, vote 63 to 12.

South Carolina, May 23, 1788, vote 149 to 73.

New Hampshire, June 21, 1788, vote 57 to 46.

Virginia, June 25, 1788, vote 89 to 79.

New York, July 26, 1788, vote 30 to 28.

North Carolina, November 21, 1789, vote 193 to 75.

Rhode Island, May 29, 1790, vote 34 to 32.

Ratification of the Amendments.

I. to X. inclusive were declared in force December 15, 1791.

XI. was declared in force January 8, 1798.

XII., regulating elections, was ratified by all the States except Connecticut, Delaware, Massachusetts, and New Hampshire, which rejected it. It was declared in force September 28, 1804.

XIII. The emancipation amendment was ratified by 31 of the 36 States; rejected by Delaware and Kentucky, not acted on by Texas; conditionally ratified by Alabama and Mississippi. Proclaimed December 18, 1865.

XIV. Reconstruction amendment was ratified by 23 Northern States; rejected by Delaware, Kentucky, Maryland, and 10 Southern States, and not acted on by California. The 10 Southern States subsequently ratified under pressure. Proclaimed July 28, 1886.

XV. Negro citizenship amendment was not acted on by Tennessee, rejected by California, Delaware, Kentucky, Maryland, New Jersey, and Oregon; ratified by the remaining 30 States. New York rescinded its ratification January 5, 1870. Proclaimed March 30, 1870.

COPYRIGHT LAW OF THE UNITED STATES.

1. A *printed* copy of the title (besides the two copies to be deposited after publication) of the book, map, chart, dramatic or musical composition, engraving, cut, print, or photograph, or a *description* of the painting, drawing, chromo, statue, statuary, or model or design for a work of the fine arts, for which copyright is desired, must be sent by mail or otherwise, *prepaid*, addressed "Librarian of Congress, Washington, D. C." This must be done before publication of the book or other article.

The *printed title* required may be a copy of the title page of such publications as have title pages. In other cases, the title must be printed expressly for copyright entry, with name of claimant of copyright. The style of type is immaterial, and the print of a typewriter will be accepted. But a separate title is required for each entry, and *each* title must be printed on paper as large as commercial note. The title of a *periodical* must include the date and number.

2. The legal fee for *recording* each copyright claim is 50 cents, and for a *copy* of this record (or certificate of copyright) an additional fee of 50 cents is required. The *record* fee from aliens and non-residents is $1.

3. On or before the day of publication of each book or other article, two complete copies of the best edition issued must be sent, to perfect the copyright, with the address "Librarian of Congress, Washington, D. C." The postage must be prepaid, or else the publication inclosed in parcels covered by printed Penalty Labels, furnished by the Librarian. In the case of a book, photograph, chromo or lithograph, the two copies deposited shall be printed from type set in the United States, or from plates made therefrom, or from negatives or drawings on stone made in the United States, or from transfers made therefrom.

4. No copyright is valid unless notice is given by inserting in every copy published, on the title page or the page following it, if it be a book; or, if a map, chart, musical composition, print, cut, engraving, photograph, painting, drawing, chromo, statue, statuary, or model or design intended to be perfected as a work of the fine arts, by inscribing upon some portion thereof, or on the substance on which the same is mounted, the following words, viz.: "*Entered according to act of Congress, in the year——, by———, in the office of the Librarian of Congress, at Washington,*" or, at the option of the person entering the copyright, the words: "*Copyright, 18—, by——.*"

The law imposes a penalty of $100 upon any person who has not obtained copyright who shall insert the notice "*Entered according to act of Congress,*" or "*Copyright,*" etc., or words of the same import, in or upon any book or other article.

5. Any author may reserve the right to translate or dramatize his own work. In this case, notice should be given by printing the words "*Right of translation reserved*," or "*All rights reserved*," below the notice of copyright entry, and notifying the Librarian of Congress of such reservation, to be entered upon the record.

Since the phrase *all rights reserved* refers exclusively to the author's right to dramatize or to translate, it has no bearing upon any publications except original works, and will not be entered upon the record in other cases.

6. The original term of copyright runs for twenty-eight years. *Within six months before* the end of that time, the author or designer, or his widow or children, may secure a renewal for the further term of fourteen years, making forty-two years in all. Applications for renewal must be accompanied by explicit statement of ownership, in the case of the author, or of relationship, in the case of his heirs, and must state definitely the date and place of entry of the original copyright. Advertisement of renewal is to be made within two months of date of renewal certificate, in some newspaper, for four weeks.

7. The time within which any work entered for copyright may be issued from the press is not limited by law, but the courts hold that it should take place within a reasonable time. A copyright may be secured for a projected as well as for a finished work. The law provides for no *caveat*, or notice of interference—only for actual entry of title.

8. A copyright is assignable in law by any instrument of writing, but such assignment must be recorded in the office of the Librarian of Congress within sixty days from its date. The fee for this record and certificate is one dollar, and for a certified copy of any record of assignment one dollar.

9. A copy of the record (or duplicate certificate) of any copyright entry will be furnished, under seal, at the rate of fifty cents each.

10. In the case of books published in more than one volume, or of periodicals published in numbers, or of engravings, photographs, or other articles published with variations, a copyright is to be entered for each volume or part of a book, or number of a periodical, or variety, as to style, title, or inscription, of any other article. But a book published serially in a periodical, under the same general title, requires only one entry. To *complete* the copyright on such a work, two copies of each serial part, as well as of the complete work (if published separately), must be deposited.

11. To secure a copyright for a painting, statue, or model or design intended to be perfected as a work of the fine arts, so as to prevent infringement by copying, engraving, or vending such design, a definite description must accompany the application for copyright, and a photograph of the same, at least as large as "cabinet size," should be mailed to the Librarian of Congress not later than the day of publication of the work or design.

12. Copyrights cannot be granted upon trade-marks, nor upon mere names of companies or articles, nor upon prints or labels intended to be used with any article of manufacture. If protection for such names or labels is desired, application must be made to the Patent office, where they are registered at a fee of $6 for labels and $25 for trade-marks.

13. These provisions apply to citizens of the United States, British Empire, France, Belgium, Switzerland.

14. Every applicant for a copyright should state distinctly the full name and residence of the claimant, and whether the right is claimed as author, designer, or proprietor. No affidavit or formal application is required.

PATENT OFFICE PROCEDURE.

Patents are issued in the name of the United States, and under seal of the Patent Office, to any person who has invented or discovered any new and useful art, machine, manufacture, or composition of matter or any new and useful improvement thereof, not known or used by others in this country before his invention or discovery thereof and not patented or described in any printed publication in this or any foreign country, before his invention or discovery thereof or more than two years prior to his application, and not in public use or on sale in the United States for more than two years prior to his application, unless the same is proved to have been abandoned; and by any person who, by his own industry, genius, efforts, and expense, has invented and produced any new and original design for a manufacture, bust, statue, alto-relievo, or bas-relief; any new and original design for the printing of woolen, silk, cotton, or other fabrics; any new and original impression, ornament, pattern, print, or picture to be printed, painted, cast, or otherwise placed on or worked into any article of manufacture; or any new, useful, and original shape or configuration of any article of manufacture, the same not having been known nor used by others before his invention or production thereof, nor patented nor described in any printed publication, upon payment of the fees required by law and other due proceedings had.

Every patent contains a grant to the patentee, his heirs or assigns, for the term of seventeen years, of the exclusive right to make, use, and vend the invention or discovery throughout the United States and the Territories, referring to the specification for the particulars thereof.

If it appear that the inventor, at the time of making his application, believed himself to be the first inventor or discoverer, a patent will not be refused on account of the invention or discovery, or any part thereof, having been known or used in any foreign country before his invention or discovery thereof, if it had not been before patented or described in any printed publication.

Joint inventors are entitled to a joint patent; neither can claim one separately. Independent inventors of distinct and independent improvements in the same machine cannot obtain a joint patent for their separate inventions; nor does the fact that one furnishes the capital and another makes the invention entitle them to make application as joint inventors; but in such case they may become joint patentees.

No person otherwise entitled thereto will be debarred from receiving a patent for his invention or discovery, by reason of its having been first patented or caused to be patented by the inventor or his legal representatives or assigns in a foreign country, unless the application for said foreign patent was filed more than seven months prior to the filing of the application in this country, in which case no patent shall be granted in this country.

Applications.— Applications for a patent must be made in writing to the Commissioner of Patents. The applicant must also file in the Patent Office a written description of the same, and of the manner and process of making, constructing, compounding, and using it, in such full, clear, concise, and exact terms as to enable any person skilled in the art or science to which it appertains, or with which it is most nearly connected, to make, construct, compound, and use the same; and in case of a machine, he must explain the principle thereof, and the best mode in which he has contemplated applying that principle, so as to distinguish it from other inventions, and particularly point out and distinctly claim the part, improvement, or combination which he claims as his invention or discovery. The specification and claim must be signed by the inventor and attested by two witnesses.

When the nature of the case admits of drawings, the applicant must furnish a drawing of the required size, signed by the inventor or his attorney in fact, and attested by two witnesses. In all cases which admit of representation by model, the applicant, if required by the Patent Office, shall furnish a model of convenient size to exhibit advantageously the several parts of his invention or discovery.

The applicant shall make oath that he verily believes himself to be the original and first inventor or discoverer of the art, machine, manufacture, composition, or improvement for which he solicits a patent; that he does not know and does not believe that the same was ever before known or used, and shall state of what country he is a citizen and where he resides. In every original application the applicant must distinctly state under oath that the invention has not been patented to himself or to others with his knowledge or consent in this or any foreign country for more than two years prior to his application, or on an application for a patent filed in any foreign country by himself or his legal representatives or assigns more than seven months prior to his application. If any application for patent has been filed in any foreign country by the applicant in this country or by his legal representatives or assigns, prior to his application in this country, he shall state the country or countries in which such application has been filed, giving the date of such application, and shall also state that no application has been filed in any other country or countries than those mentioned; that to the best of his knowledge and belief the invention has not been in public use or on sale in the United States nor described in any printed publication or patent in this or any foreign country for more than two years prior to his application in this country. Such oath may be made before any person within the United States authorized by law to administer oaths, or, when the applicant resides in a foreign country, before any minister, chargé d'affaires, consul, or commercial agent holding commission under the Government of the United States, or before any notary public of the foreign country in which the applicant may be, provided such notary is authorized by the laws of his country to administer oaths.

On the filing of such application and the payment of the fees required by law, if, on examination, it appears that the applicant is justly entitled to a patent under the law, and that the same is sufficiently useful and important, the Commissioner will issue a patent therefor.

Every patent, or any interest therein, shall be assignable in law by an instrument in writing; and the patentee or his assigns or legal representatives may, in like manner, grant and convey an exclusive right under his patent to the whole or any specified part of the United States.

Reissues. A reissue is granted to the original patentee, his legal representatives, or the assignees of the entire interest, when, by reason of a defective or insufficient specification, or by reason of the patentee claiming as his invention or discovery more than he had a right to claim as new, the original patent is inoperative or invalid, provided the error has arisen from inadvertence, accident, or mistake, and without any fraudulent or deceptive intention. Reissue applications must be made and the specifications sworn to by the inventors, if they be living.

Caveats. A caveat, under the patent law, is a notice given to the office, of the caveator's claim as inventor, in order to prevent the grant of a patent to another for the same alleged invention upon an application filed during the life of a caveat without notice to the caveator.

Any citizen of the United States who has made a new invention or discovery, and desires further time to mature the same, may, on a payment of a fee of ten dollars, file in the Patent Office a caveat setting forth the object and the distinguishing characteristics of the invention, and praying protection of his right until he shall have matured his invention. Such caveat shall be filed in the confidential archives of the office and preserved in secrecy, and shall be operative for the term of one year from the filing thereof. The caveat may be renewed, on request in writing, by the payment of a second fee of ten dollars, and it will continue in force for one year from the payment of such second fee.

The caveat must comprise a specification, oath, and, when the nature of the case admits of it, a drawing, and, like the application, must be limited to a single invention or improvement.

Fees.—Fees must be paid in advance, and are as follows: On filing each original application for a patent, $15. On issuing each original patent, $20. In design cases: For three years and six months, $10; for seven years, $15; for fourteen years, $30. On filing each caveat, $10. On every application for the reissue of a patent, $30. On filing each disclaimer, $10. For certified copies of patents and other papers in manuscript, ten cents per hundred words; for certified copies of printed patents, eighty cents. For uncertified printed copies of specifications and drawings of patents, for single copies, or any number of unclassified copies, five cents each; for copies by subclasses, three cents each; by classes, two cents each, and for the entire set of patents issued, in one order, one cent each. For recording every assignment, agreement, power of attorney, or other paper, of three hundred words or under, $1; of over three hundred and under one thousand words, $2; of over one thousand words $3. For copies of drawings, the reasonable cost of making them. The Patent Office is prepared to furnish positive blue-print photographic copies of any drawing, foreign or domestic, in the possession of the office, in sizes and at rates as follows: Large size, 10x15 inches, twenty-five cents; medium size, 7x11 inches, fifteen cents; small size, 5x8 inches, five cents. An order for small sized copies can be filled only when it relates to the drawings of an application for patent.

The total number of applications filed at the Patent Office in sixty-one years, 1837-97, was 1,040,035; number of caveats filed, 107,415; number of original patents, including designs issued, 601,268. Receipts to December 31, 1896, $34,309,331.06; expenditures, $29,293,-672.32; net surplus, $5,015,658.74. The largest number of patents granted for an article prior to January, 1895, has been for carriages and wagons, 20,000, and for stoves and furnaces, 18,000. The next largest has been for harvesters, 10,000; lamps and gas fittings, 10,000; boots and shoes, 10,000, and packing and storing vessels, 10,000 approximately.

NATURALIZATION LAWS.

The conditions under and the manner in which an alien may be admitted to become a citizen of the United States are prescribed by Sections 2, 165-74 of the Revised Statutes of the United States.

Declaration of Intentions.—The alien must declare upon oath before a circuit or district court of the United States or a district or supreme court of the Territories, or a court of record of any of the States having common law jurisdiction and a seal and clerk, two years at least prior to his admission, that it is, *bona fide*, his intention to become a citizen of the United States, and to renounce forever all allegiance and fidelity to any foreign prince or State, and particularly to the one of which he may be at the time a citizen or subject.

Oath on Application for Admission.—He must at the time of his application to be admitted declare on oath, before some one of the courts above specified, "that he will support the Constitution of the United States, and that he absolutely and entirely renounces and abjures all allegiance and fidelity to every foreign prince, potentate, State, or sovereignty, and particularly by name, to the prince, potentate, State, or sovereignty of which he was before a citizen or subject," which proceedings must be recorded by the clerk of the court.

Conditions for Citizenship.—If it shall appear to the satisfaction of the court to which the alien has applied that he has made a declaration to become a citizen two years before applying for final papers, and has resided continuously within the United States for at least five years, and within the State or Territory where such court is at the time held one year at least; and that during that time "he has behaved as a man of good moral character, attached to the principles of the Constitution of the United States, and well disposed to the good order and happiness of the same," he will be admitted to citizenship.

Titles of Nobility.—If the applicant has borne any hereditary title or order of nobility he must make an express renunciation of the same at the time of his application.

Soldiers.—Any alien at the age of twenty-one years and upward who has been in the armies of the United States, and has been honorably discharged therefrom, may become a citizen on his petition, without any previous declaration of intention, provided that he has resided in the United States at least one year previous to his application, and is of good moral character. (It is judicially decided that residence of one year in a particular State is not requisite.)

Minors.—Any alien under the age of twenty-one years who has resided in the United States three years next preceding his arriving at that age, and who has continued to reside therein to the time he may make application to be admitted a citizen thereof, may, after he arrives at the age of twenty-one years, and after he has resided five years within the United States, including the three years of his minority, be admitted a citizen; but he must make a declaration on oath and prove to the satisfaction of the court that for two years next preceding it has been his *bona fide* intention to become a citizen.

Children of Naturalized Citizens.—The children of persons who have been duly naturalized, being under the age of twenty-one years at the time of the naturalization of their parents, shall, if dwelling in the United States, be considered as citizens thereof.

Citizens' Children Who Are Born Abroad.—The children of persons who now are or have been citizens of the United States, are, though born out of the limits and jurisdiction of the United States, considered as citizens thereof.

Chinese.—The naturalization of Chinamen is expressly prohibited by Section 14, Chapter 126, Laws of 1882.

Protection Abroad to Naturalized Citizens.—Section 2,000 of the Revised Statutes of the United States declares that "all naturalized citizens of the United States while in foreign countries are entitled to and shall receive from this Government the same protection of persons and property which is accorded to native-born citizens."

The Right of Suffrage.—The right to vote comes from the State, and is a State gift. Naturalization is a Federal right and is a gift of the Union, not of any one State. In nearly one-half of the Union aliens (who have declared intentions) vote and have the right to vote equally with naturalized or native-born citizens. In the other half only actual citizens may vote. (See Table of Qualifications for Voting in each State, on another page.) The Federal naturalization laws apply to the whole Union alike, and provide that no alien may be naturalized until after five years' residence. Even after five years' residence and due naturalization he is not entitled to vote unless the laws of the State confer the privilege upon him, and he may vote in several States six months after landing, if he has declared his intention, under the United States law, to become a citizen.

PASSPORT REGULATIONS.

Rules governing the granting and issuing of passports in the United States:

By Whom Issued.—No one but the Secretary of State may grant and issue passports in the United States.—Revised Statutes, secs. 4075, 4078.

A citizen of the United States desiring to procure a passport while he is temporarily abroad should apply to the diplomatic representative of the United States in the country where he happens to be; or, in the absence of a diplomatic representative, to the consul general of the United States; or, in the absence of both, to the consul of the United States. The necessary statement may be made before the nearest consular officer of the United States.

To Citizens Only.—The law forbids the granting of a passport to any person who is not a citizen of the United States.—Revised Statutes, sec. 4076.

A person who has only made the declaration of intention to become a citizen of the United States cannot receive a passport.

Applications.—A citizen of the United States in this country in order to procure a passport must make a written application, in the form of an affidavit, to the Secretary of State.

The affidavit must be attested by an officer authorized to administer oaths, and if he has an official seal it must be affixed. If he has no seal, his official character must be authenticated by certificate of the proper legal officer

If the applicant signs by mark, two attesting witnesses to his signature are required.

The applicant is required to state the date and place of his birth, his occupation, and the place of his permanent residence, and to declare that he goes abroad for temporary sojourn and intends to return to the United States with the purpose of residing and performing the duties of citizenship therein.

The applicant must take the oath of allegiance to the Government of the United States.

The application must be accompanied by a description of the person applying, and should state the following particulars, viz.: Age, — years; stature, — feet — inches (English measure); forehead, —; eyes, —; nose, —; mouth, —; chin, —; hair, —; complexion, —; face, —.

The application must be accompanied by a certificate from at least one credible witness that the applicant is the person he represents himself to be, and that the facts stated in the affidavit are true to the best of the witness's knowledge and belief.

NATIVE CITIZENS.—An application containing the information indicated by rule 3 will be sufficient evidence in the case of native citizens.

A PERSON BORN ABROAD WHOSE FATHER WAS A NATIVE OF THE UNITED STATES.—In addition to the statements required by rule 3, his application must show that his father was born in the United States, has resided therein, and was a citizen at the time of the applicant's birth. The Department may require that this affidavit be supported by that of one other citizen acquainted with the facts.

NATURALIZED CITIZENS.—In addition to the statements required by rule 3, a naturalized citizen must transmit his certificate of naturalization, or a duly certified copy of the court record thereof, with his application. It will be returned to him after inspection. He must state in his affidavit when and from what port he emigrated to this country, what ship he sailed in, where he has lived since his arrival in the United States, when and before what court he was naturalized, and that he is the identical person described in the certificate of naturalization. The signature to the application should conform in orthography to the applicant's name as written in the naturalization paper, which the Department follows.

THE WIFE OR WIDOW OF A NATURALIZED CITIZEN.—In addition to the statements required by rule 3, she must transmit for inspection her husband's naturalization certificate, must state that she is the wife or widow of the person described therein, and must set forth the facts of his emigration, naturalization, and residence, as required in the rule governing the application of a naturalized citizen.

THE CHILD OF A NATURALIZED CITIZEN CLAIMING CITIZENSHIP THROUGH THE NATURALIZATION OF THE FATHER.—In addition to the statements required by rule 3, the applicant must state that he or she is the son or daughter, as the case may be, of the person described in the naturalization certificate, which must be submitted for inspection, and must set forth the facts of his emigration, naturalization, and residence, as required in the rule governing the application of a naturalized citizen.

EXPIRATION OF PASSPORT.—A passport expires two years from the date of its issuance. A new one will be issued upon a new application, and if the applicant be a naturalized citizen, the old passport will be accepted in lieu of a naturalized certificate, if the application upon which it was issued is found to contain sufficient information as to the emigration, residence, and naturalization of the applicant.

WIFE, CHILDREN, AND SERVANTS.—When an applicant is accompanied by his wife, minor children, or servant, being an American citizen, it will be sufficient to state the fact, giving the respective ages of the children and the citizenship of the servant, when one passport will suffice for all. For any other person in the party a separate passport will be required. A woman's passport may include her minor children and servant under the above-named conditions.

PROFESSIONAL TITLES.—They will not be inserted in passports.

FEE.—By act of Congress approved March 23, 1888, a fee of one dollar is required to be collected for every citizen's passport. That amount in currency or postal money order should accompany each application. Orders should be payable to the Disbursing Clerk of the Department of State. Drafts or checks will not be received.

BLANK FORMS OF APPLICATION.—They will be furnished by the Department to persons who desire to apply for passports, upon their stating whether they are native or naturalized citizens or claim through the naturalization of husband or father. Forms are not furnished, except as samples, to those who make a business of procuring passports.

ADDRESS.—Communications should be addressed to the Department of State, Passport Division, and each communication should give the post office address of the person to whom the answer is to be directed.

REJECTION OF APPLICATION.—The Secretary of State may refuse to issue a passport to anyone who, he has reason to believe, desires it for an unlawful or improper purpose, or who is unable or unwilling to comply with the rules.

UNITED STATES CIVIL SERVICE.

The purpose of the Civil Service act, as declared in its title, is "to regulate and improve the Civil Service of the United States." It provides for the appointment of three Commissioners, a chief Examiner, a Secretary, and other employees, and makes it the duty of the Commissioners to aid the President as he may request in preparing suitable rules for carrying the act into effect; to make regulations to govern all examinations held under the provisions of the act, and to make investigations and report upon all matters touching the enforcement and effect of the rules and regulations. The address of the Commission is Washington, D.C.

Extent of the Service. — The number of persons regularly employed in the Executive Civil Service of the United States is about 179,000, of whom 80,334 are classified subject to competitive examination or registration under the Civil Service act and rules. The total number of persons in the classified Civil Service (by which is meant all that part of the Executive Civil Service embraced within the provisions of the Civil Service act and rules) is 83,817. Of this number 78,728 are classified by reason of designation, duties performed, or compensation, and of these 3,483 are required merely to pass a non-competitive examination or are excepted from examination (2,240 of the latter class being Indians); 5,063 are classified under regulations of the Navy Department, approved by the Commission and sanctioned by the President, and 26 are classified whose appointments are made by the President solely. The classified Civil Service does not include persons whose appointments are subject to confirmation by the Senate, or mere laborers or workmen.

Divisions of the Service.—The rules require that all that part of the Executive Civil Service of the United States which has been or may hereafter be classified under the Civil Service act shall be arranged in branches as follows: The Departmental Service, the Customs Service, the Postal Service, the Government Printing Service, and the Internal Revenue Service.

The Departmental Service includes all officers and employees who on the one hand are not appointed subject to the consent of the Senate, and on the other hand are above the grade of laborer, and who are serving in or on detail from the Departments, Commissions, and Offices in the District of Columbia, the Railway Mail Service, the Indian Service, the Pension Agencies, the Steamboat Inspection Service, the Marine Hospital Service, the Light-House Service, the Life-Saving Service, the Revenue Cutter Service, the Mints and Assay offices, the Sub-Treasuries, the Engineer Department at large, the Ordnance Department at large, the Land Office Service, and the force employed under Custodians of Public Buildings, and in the U. S. Penitentiary at Leavenworth, Kan. In addition to these are included all other employees (except laborers and persons whose appointments are subject to the consent of the Senate) whose duties are clerical or medical, or who serve as watchmen, messengers, draughtsmen, engineers, firemen, computers, or as superintendents of construction, superintendents of repairs, or foremen under the Supervising Architect of the Treasury, or who are in any branch of the Treasury Department not enumerated above. The Customs Service includes all officers and employees between the extremes before mentioned who are serving in any customs district. The Postal Service includes all similar officers and employees at free delivery post offices. The Government Printing Service and the Internal Revenue Service cover all like positions in the branches indicated by their designations.

Applications.—Persons seeking to be examined must file an application blank. The blank for the Departmental Service at Washington, Railway Mail Service, the Indian School Service, and the Government Printing Service should be requested directly of the Civil Service Commission at Washington. The blank for the Customs, Postal, or Internal Revenue Service must be requested in writing of the Civil Service Board of Examiners at the office where service is sought. These papers should be returned to the officers from whom they emanated.

Applicants for examination must be citizens of the United States, and of the proper age. No person using intoxicating liquors to excess may be appointed. No discrimination is made on account of sex, color, or political or religious opinions. The limitations of age vary with the different services, but do not apply to any person honorably discharged from the military or naval service of the United States by reason of disability resulting from wounds or sickness incurred in the line of duty.

Examinations.—The applicants to enter the services designated are examined as to their relative capacity and fitness. For ordinary clerical places in the Departmental, Customs, and Internal Revenue Services the examination is confined to orthography, penmanship, copying, letter writing, and simple arithmetic. Patent examiners are examined in physics and technics, mathematics, chemistry, and mechanical drawing. Meat inspectors are examined in letter writing, veterinary anatomy and physiology, veterinary pathology, and meat inspection. One of the tests for post office and railway mail clerks is an exercise in reading manuscript addresses. Specimen sets of questions will be furnished by the Commission upon request. Examinations are held twice a year in every State and Territory at fixed times and places. All examinations relate as nearly as possible to the duties to be performed, and, whenever practicable, include experience and practical tests. No applicant is admitted to an examination in any one of the different recognized trades, such as those in the Government Printing Office, unless he has had five years' experience in his trade, one year of which must have been as a journeyman. This information is obtained by personal questions relating to the applicant's experience at his trade and the certificates of persons who have employed him. No one is certified for appointment whose standing in any examination is less than 70 per centum of complete proficiency, except applicants whose claims for military or naval preference under Section 1,754 R. S. have been admitted. These need obtain but 65. The law also prescribes competitive examinations for promotion in the service. A certificate is given to each person examined, stating whether he passed or failed to pass. For positions in the classified service where technical qualifications are needed special examinations are held. In the Departmental Service they are held for the State Department, the Pension, Patent, and Signal Offices, Geological and Coast Surveys, Engineer Department at large, Ordnance Department at large, etc. For places which do not require technical qualifications the number of applicants is usually excessive, and only those who attain high grades have a good chance for appointment.

Excepted Places.—A number of positions are excepted from examination or are subject only to non-competitive examination. In the former class are included the following positions: Private secretaries and confidential clerks (not exceeding two) to the President or to the head of each of the eight Executive Departments; attorneys or assistant attorneys whose main duties are connected with the management of cases in court; one assistant postmaster, or chief assistant to the postmaster, of whatever designation, at each post office, and one cashier for each first-class post office when employed under the roster title of cashier only; Indians employed in the Indian Service at large, except those employed as superintendents, teachers, teachers of industries, kindergartners, and physicians. In the latter class are included the following employees in the Customs and Internal Revenue Services: One cashier in each customs district, one chief or principal deputy or assistant collector in such district, and one principal deputy collector at each sub-port or station; one employee in each Internal Revenue district who shall act as cashier or chief deputy or assistant collector, as may be determined by the Treasury Department; one deputy collector in each Internal Revenue district where the number of employees in the office of the collector exceeds four, and one deputy collector in each stamp (or branch) office.

Appointments.—Upon the occurrence of a vacancy, the appointment to fill it, if not made by promotion, reduction, transfer, or reinstatement (for all of which provision is made by the Civil Service rules), must be made by selection from the eligibles of highest grade on the appropriate register. In the Executive Departments at Washington and in the Government Printing Office appointments are apportioned among the States and Territories on the basis of population. Every appointment is made for a probationary period of six months. Whenever there are no names of eligibles upon a register for any position in which a vacancy exists, and the public interest requires that it be filled before eligibles can be provided by the Commission, such vacancy may, subject to the approval of the Commission, be filled by appointment without examination and certification until an eligible can be provided by the Commission. The number of women applying for clerical places is greatly in excess of the calls of appointing officers. The positions to which the largest nunbers of them are appointed are those of assistant microscopist in the branch offices of the Bureau of Animal Industry at the various stockyards throughout the country, and teachers, matrons, seamstresses, etc., in the Indian Service. A few receive appointments as stenographers and typewriters in the Departmental Service, and a few are appointed to technical and professional places.

Preference Claimants.—Persons who served in the military or naval service of the United States, and were discharged by reason of disabilities resulting from wounds or sickness incurred in the line of duty, are, under the Civil Service rules, given certain preferences. They are released from all maximum age limitations, are eligible for appointment at a grade of 65, while all others are obliged to obtain a grade of 70, and are certified to appointing officers before all others. Subject to the other conditions of the rules, any person who served in the military or naval service of the United States in the war of the rebellion, and was honorably discharged therefrom, or the widow of any such person, or any army nurse of said war, may be reinstated without regard to the length of time he or she has been separated from the service.

Provisions Concerning Political Discrimination, Assessments, Etc.—The Civil Service rules provide that no person in the Executive Civil Service shall dismiss, or cause to be dismissed, or make any attempt to procure the dismissal of or in any manner change the official rank or compensation of any other person therein, because of his political or religious opinions or affiliations; that no removal shall be made from any position subject to competitive examination except for just cause and upon written charges filed with the head of the department or other appointing officer, and of which the accused shall have full notice and an opportunity to make defense; and that no person in the Executive Civil Service shall use his official authority or official influence for the purpose of interfering with an election or controlling the result thereof. Such rules also provide that any person in the Executive Civil Service who shall willfully violate any provision of the Civil Service act or rules shall be dismissed from office.

The Civil Service act contains provisions forbidding any person in the service of the United States from levying upon or collecting from persons in the Executive Civil Service contributions to be devoted to political objects, the collection of such contributions by any person in any public building of the United States, or discrimination against persons who do not make such contributions or render political service. A violation of any of the provisions concerning political assessments, or their collection in a public building of the United States, is declared to be a misdemeanor, punishable by a fine not exceeding five thousand dollars, or by imprisonment for a term not exceeding three years, or by such fine and imprisonment both in the discretion of the court. The act also declares that when rules to carry its provisions into effect shall have been promulgated, "it shall be the duty of all officers of the United States in the departments and offices to which any such rules may relate, to aid, in all proper ways, in carrying said rules, and any modifications thereof, into effect."

Political Activity of Officials.—An executive order of July 14, 1896, which is still in force, warns office-holders that, while individual interest and activity in political affairs are by no means condemned, they must bear in mind that their time and labor are due to the Government, and that they should scrupulously avoid, in their political action as well as in the discharge of their official duty, offending, by obtrusive partisanship, their neighbors who have relations with them as public officials.

The Unclassified Executive Civil Service.—The portion of the Executive Civil Service which is not classified embraces the following: All officers nominated by the President and confirmed by the Senate, including members of the Cabinet, assistant secretaries, certain chiefs of bureaus, etc., in the Executive Departments at Washington, collectors, naval officers, surveyors, and appraisers in the Customs Service, collectors in the Internal Revenue Service, and first, second, and third class postmasters. Other unclassified positions are fourth class postmasters, the employees of the District of Columbia, the employees of the Library of Congress, clerks in post offices not having free delivery, mere laborers and workmen, certain positions having a compensation of less than $300 a year, and the Consular Service. Examinations for positions in the service last named are non-competitive, and conducted by a board of the Department of State.

UNITED STATES CUSTOMS DUTIES.

A TABLE OF LEADING ARTICLES IMPORTED, GIVING RATE AT ENTRY BY THE TARIFF ACT OF 1897.

N. e. s. indicates "when not elsewhere specified."

Articles.	Tariff Rate.
Alcohol, amylic, or fusel oil	¼c. ℔ lb.
Alcohol, absolute	$2.25 ℔ gal.
Barley, bushel of 48 lbs	30c ℔ bu.
Beads, glass (not strung)	35 p. c. ad val.
Beads, glass (strung)	45 p. c.
Beef, mutton and pork	2c. ℔ lb.
Beer, ale, not in bottles	20c. ℔ gal.
Beer, porter, and ale, in bottles	40 c. "
Bindings, cotton	45 p. c. ad val.
Bindings, flax	45 "
Bindings, wool	50c. ℔ lb. and 60 p. c. ad val.
Blankets	22c. ℔ lb. and 30 p. c. ad val.
Blankets, value 40c to 50c	33c. ℔ lb. and 35 p. c. ad val.
Blankets, wool, value over 50c. ℔ lb	33c. ℔ lb. & 40 p. c. "
Bonnets, silk	60 p. c. ad val.
Books, charts, maps	25 "
Bronze, manufactures of	45 "
Brushes	40 "
Butter, and substitutes for	6c. ℔ lb.
Buttons, sleeve and collar, gilt	50 p. c. ad val.
Canvas for sails	45 "
Caps, fur and leather	35 "
Carpets, treble ingrain	22c. ℔ sq. yd. & 40 "
Carpets, two-ply	18c. " 40 "

Articles.	Tariff Rate.
Carpets, tapestry Brussels	28c. ℔ sq. yd. & 40 p. c. ad val.
Carpets, Wilton, Axminster, velvet	60c. ℔ sq. yd. & 40 p. c. ad val.
Cattle (over one year old)	27½ p. c. ad val.
Cheese, all kinds	6c. ℔ lb.
Cigars and cigarettes	$4.50 ℔ lb. and 25 p. c. ad val.
Clocks, n. e. s	40 "
Clothing, ready-made, cotton, n. e. s	50 "
Clothing, linen	50 "
Clothing, silk	60 "
Clothing, wool	44c. ℔ lb. and 60 "
Coal, bituminous	67c. ℔ ton.
Confectionery, all sugar	50 p. c. ad val. (if more than 15c. ℔ lb.)
Copper, manufactures of	45 p. c. ad val.
Cotton gloves	50 "
Cotton handkerchiefs, hemmed	45 "
Cotton handkerchiefs, hemstitched	55 "
Cotton hosiery	50c. to $2 ℔ doz. pairs & 15 "
Cotton shirts and drawers	60c to $2.25 ℔ doz. pairs and 15 p. c. to 50 p. c. ad val.
Cotton plushes, unbleached	9c. ℔ sq. yd. & 25 p. c. ad val.
Cotton webbing	45 "
Cotton curtains	60 "
Cutlery, more than $3 ℔ doz.	20c. ℔ piece & 40 "
Cutlery, razors, over $3 ℔ doz.	$1.75 ℔ doz. and 20 p. c. ad val.
Cutlery, table knives	16c. each & 15 p. c. ad val.
Cutlery, table knives, over $4 ℔ doz	45 "
Diamonds (uncut, free), cut and set	60 "
Diamonds, cut, but not set	10 "
Drugs (crude, free), not crude	¼c. ℔ lb. & 10 "
Dyewoods, extracts of	⅞c. ℔ lb.
Earthenware, common	25 p. c. ad val.
Earthenware, porcelain, plain	55 "
Earthenware, porcelain, etc., decorated	60 "
Eggs	5c. ℔ doz.
Engravings	25 p. c. ad val.
Extracts, meat	35c. ℔ lb.
Firearms	$1.50 to $6 and 35 p. c. ad val.
Fish, smoked, dried	¾c. ℔ lb.
Flannels	22c. ℔ lb. and 30 p. c. ad val.
Flannels, value 40c. to 50c.	33c. " 35 "
Flax, manufactures of, n. e. s	45 "
Flowers, artificial	50 "
Fruits, preserved in their own juice	1c ℔ lb. and 35 p. c. ad val.
Fruits, apples	25c. ℔ bu.
Fruits, oranges, lemons, n. e. s	1c. ℔ lb.
Fur, manufactures of	50 p. c. ad val.
Furniture, wood	35 "
Glassware, plain and cut	60 "
Glass, polished plate, not over 16x24	8c. ℔ sq. foot.
Glass, silvered, not over 16x24	11c. "
Glass bottles, over 1 pint	1c. ℔ lb.
Gloves, men's, ladies', children's	75c. ℔ doz. pairs.
Glucose	1½c. ℔ lb.
Glue, value not over 7c. ℔ lb	2½c. ℔ lb.
Gold, manufactures of, not jewelry	45 p. c. ad val.
Hair of hogs, curled for mattresses	10 "
Hair, manufactures, n. e. s	35 "
Hair, human unmanufactured	20 "
Hams and bacon	5c. ℔ lb.
Hay	$4 ℔ ton.
Hemp cordage	2c. ℔ lb.
Hides, raw, dried, salted, pickled	15 p. c. ad val.
Honey	20c. ℔ gal.
Hoops, iron or steel, baling	5-10c. ℔ lb.
Hops	12c. ℔ lb.
Horn, manufactures of	30 p. c ad val.
Horses, mules	$30 ℔ head.
India rubber, manufactures of	30 p. c. ad val.
India rubber, vulcanized	35 "
Instruments, metal	45 "
Iron, manufactures of, n. e. s	45 "
Iron screws, ½ inch or less in length	12c. ℔ lb.
Iron, tinned plates	1½c. ℔ lb.
Ivory, manufactures of, n. e. s	35 p. c. ad val.
Jewelry	60 "
Knit goods, wool, value not over 30c. ℔ lb.	38½c. ℔ lb.
Knit goods, woolen apparel, 30 to 40c. ℔ lb.	38½c. ℔ lb.
Knit goods, woolen apparel, over 40c. ℔ lb.	44c. ℔ lb. and 50 p. c to 60 p. c. ad val.
Knit goods, silk	60 p. c. ad val.
Lard	2c. ℔ lb.
Lead, pigs, bars	2⅛c. ℔ lb.
Lead, type metal	1½c. ℔ lb.

Articles.	Tariff Rate.
Leather manufactures, n. e. s	35 p. c. ad val.
Linen manufactures, n. e. s	45 "
Linen, wearing apparel	60 "
Macaroni	1½c. ℔ lb.
Malt, barley	45c. ℔ bu.
Matches, friction, boxed	8c. per gross.
Matting, cocoa and rattan	6c. ℔ sq. yard.
Meerschaum pipes	60 p. c. ad val.
Milk, fresh	2c. ℔ gal.
Milk, condensed	2c. ℔ lb.
Molasses, n. e. s	40° to 56°, 3c. ℔ gal.
Muffs, fur	35 p. c. ad val.
Musical instruments	45 "
Nails, cut	6-10c. ℔ lb.
Nails, horseshoe	2¼c. "
Oilcloth, value over 25c.	8 to 20c. ℔ sq. yd. and 15 p. c. to 20 p. c. ad val.
Oil, olive	50c. ℔ gal. in bottles, etc.
Oil, olive, n. e. s	40c. ℔ gal.
Oil, whale and seal, foreign, n. e. s	8c. ℔ gal.
Onions	40c. ℔ bu.
Opium, liquid preparations	40 p. c. ad val.
Opium, crude and unadulterated	$1 ℔ lb.
Paintings and marble statuary	20 p. c. ad val.
Paper manufactures, n. e. s	35 "
Pepper, cayenne, unground	2½c. ℔ lb.
Perfumery, alcoholic	60c. ℔ lb. and 45 p. c. ad val.
Photograph albums	35 "
Photograph slides	45 "
Pickles	40 "
Pins, metallic	35 "
Pipes of clay, common, 40c. ℔ gross	15c. ℔ gross.
Poultry, dressed	5c ℔ lb.
Potatoes	25c. ℔ bu.
Pulp wood, for paper-makers	1-12c. ℔ lb.
Quicksilver	7c. ℔ lb.
Railroad ties, cedar	20 p. c. ad val.
Rugs, oriental	10c. ℔ sq. ft. and 40 "
Salmon, dried or smoked	¾c. ℔ lb.
Salmon, prepared or preserved	30 p. c. ad val.
Salt	12c. ℔ 100 lbs., packages; 8c. ℔ 100 lbs., bulk.
Sauces, n. e. s	40 p. c. ad val.
Sausages, other than bologna	25 "
Sealskin sacques	35 "
Silk, spun in skeins	35 "
Silk laces, wearing apparel	60 "
Skins, tanned and dressed	20 p. c. ad val.
Slates, manufactures of, n. e. s	20 "
Smokers' articles, ex. clay pipes	60 "
Soap, castile	1¼c. ℔ lb.
Soap, toilet, perfumed	15 p. c. ad val.
Spirits, except bay rum	$2.25 prf. gal.
Straw manufactures, n. e. s	30 p. c. ad val.
Sugars, not above 16 Dutch standard	95-100c. ℔ lb.
Sugars, above 16 Dutch standard	95-100c. "
Tin plates	1½c. ℔ lb.
Tobacco, cigar wrappers, not stemmed	$1.85 "
Tobacco, if stemmed	$2.50 "
Tobacco, all other leaf, stemmed	50c. "
Tobacco, unmfd., not stemmed	35c. "
Unbrellas, silk or alpaca	50 p.c. ad val.
Vegetables, natural, n. e. s	25 "
Vegetables, prepared or preserved	40 "
Velvets, silk, 75 p. c. or more silk	$1.50 ℔ lb. and 15 p. c. ad val.
Watches and parts of	40 p. c. ad val.
Wheat, bushel of 60 lb	25 "
Willow for basket-makers	20 "
Willow manufactures, n. e. s	40 "
Wines, champ., in ½ pint bottles or less	$2 ℔ doz.
Wines, champ., in bottles, ½ pt. to 1 pt.	4 "
Wines, champ., in bottles, 1 pt. to 1 qt.	8 "
Wines, still, in casks containing more than 14 p. c. absolute alcohol	50c. ℔ gal.
Woods, cabinet sawed	$1 to $2 ℔ M ft.
Wool, 1st class	11c. ℔ lb.
Wool, 2d class	12c. "
Wool, 3d class, n. e. s., above 13c. ℔ lb.	7c. "
Wool or worsted yarns, value not over 30c. ℔ lb.	27½c. ℔ lb and 40 p. c. ad val.
Wool or worsted yarns, value 30 to 40c. ℔ lb.	38½c. ℔ lb. and 40 p. c. ad val.
Wool or worsted yarns, value over 40c. ℔ lb.	38½c. ℔ lb. and 40 p. c. ad val.
Woolen or worsted clothing	44c. ℔ lb. and 60 p. c. ad val.
Woolen manufactures, n. e. s	33c. ℔ lb.

PRESIDENTIAL ELECTIONS

There is, properly speaking, no popular vote for President and Vice-President; the people vote for electors, and those chosen in each State meet therein and vote for the candidates for President and Vice-President. The record of any popular vote for electors prior to 1824 is so meager and imperfect that a compilation would be useless. In most of the States, for more than a quarter of a century following the establishment of the government, the State Legislatures "appointed" the Presidential electors, and the people therefore voted only indirectly for them, their choice being expressed by their votes for members of the Legislature. In this tabulation only the aggregate electoral votes for candidates for President and Vice-President in the first nine quadrennial elections appear.

1789. Previous to 1804, each elector voted for two candidates for President. The one who received the largest number of votes was declared President, and the one who received the next largest number of votes was declared Vice-President. The electoral votes for the first President of the United States were: George Washington, 69; John Adams, of Massachusetts, 34; John Jay, of New York, 9; R. H. Harrison, of Maryland, 6; John Rutledge, of South Carolina, 6; John Hancock, of Massachusetts, 4; George Clinton, of New York, 3; Samuel Huntingdon, of Connecticut, 2; John Milton, of Georgia, 2; James Armstrong, of Georgia, Benjamin Lincoln, of Massachusetts, and Edward Telfair, of Georgia, 1 vote each. Vacancies (votes not cast), 4. George Washington was chosen President and John Adams Vice-President.

1792. George Washington, Federalist, received 132 votes; John Adams, Federalist, 77; George Clinton, of New York, Republican (*a*), 50; Thomas Jefferson, of Virginia, Republican, 4; Aaron Burr, of New York, Republican, 1 vote. Vacancies, 3. George Washington was chosen President and John Adams Vice-President.

1796. John Adams, Federalist, 71; Thomas Jefferson, Republican, 68; Thomas Pinckney, of South Carolina, Federalist, 59: Aaron Burr, of New York, Republican, 30; Samuel Adams, of Massachusetts, Republican, 15; Oliver Ellsworth, of Connecticut, Independent, 11; George Clinton, of New York, Republican, 7; John Jay, of New York, Federalist, 5; James Iredell, of North Carolina, Federalist, 3; George Washington, of Virginia, John Henry, of Maryland, and S. Johnson, of North Carolina, all Federalists, 2 votes each; Charles Cotesworth Pinckney, of South Carolina, Federalist, 1 vote. John Adams was chosen President and Thomas Jefferson Vice-President.

1800. Thomas Jefferson, Republican, 73; Aaron Burr, Republican, 73; John Adams, Federalist, 65; Charles C. Pinckney, Federalist, 64; John Jay, Federalist, 1 vote. There being a tie for Jefferson and Burr, the choice devolved upon the House of Representatives. Jefferson received the votes of ten States, which, being the largest vote cast for a candidate, elected him President. Burr received the votes of four States, which, being the next largest vote, elected him Vice-President. There were 2 blank votes.

1804. The Constitution of the United States having been amended, the electors at this election voted for a President and a Vice-President, instead of for two candidates for President. The result was as follows: For President, Thomas Jefferson, Republican, 162; Charles C. Pinckney, Federalist, 14. For Vice-President, George Clinton, Republican, 162; Rufus King, of New York, Federalist, 14. Jefferson was chosen President and Clinton Vice-President.

1808. For President, James Madison, of Virginia, Republican, 122; Charles C. Pinckney, of South Carolina, Federalist, 47; George Clinton, of New York, Republican, 6. For Vice-President, George Clinton, Republican, 113; Rufus King, of New York, Federalist, 47; John Langdon, of New Hampshire, 9; James Madison, 3; James Monroe, 3. Vacancy, 1. Madison was chosen President and Clinton Vice-President.

1812. For President, James Madison, Republican, 128; De Witt Clinton, of New York, Federalist, 89. For Vice-President, Elbridge Gerry, of Massachusetts, 131; Jared Ingersoll, of Pennsylvania, Federalist, 86. Vacancy, 1. Madison was chosen President and Gerry Vice-President.

1816. For President, James Monroe, of Virginia, Republican, 183; Rufus King, of New York, Federalist, 34. For Vice-President, Daniel D. Tompkins, of New York, Republican, 183; John Eager Howard, of Maryland, Federalist, 22; James Ross, of Pennsylvania, 5: John Marshall, of Virginia, 4; Robert G. Harper, of Maryland, 3. Vacancies, 4. Monroe was chosen President and Tompkins Vice-President.

1820. For President, James Monroe, of Virginia, Republican, 231; John Q. Adams, of Massachusetts, Republican, 1. For Vice-President, Daniel D. Tompkins, Republican, 218; Richard Stockton, of New Jersey, 8; Daniel Rodney, of Delaware, 4; Robert G. Harper, of Maryland, and Richard Rush, of Pennsylvania, 1 vote each. Vacancies, 3. James Monroe was chosen President and Daniel D. Tompkins Vice-President.

Year of Election.	Candidates for President.	States.	Political Party.	Popular Vote.	Plurality.	Electoral Vote.	Candidates for Vice-President.	States.	Political Party.	Electoral Vote.
1824	Andrew Jackson,	Tenn.	Rep.	155,872	50,551	(*b*) 99	John C. Calhoun,*	S. C.	Rep.	182
	John Q. Adams,*	Mass.	Rep.	105,321	......	84	Nathan Sanford,	N. Y.	Rep.	30
	Henry Clay,	Ky.	Rep.	46,587	......	37	Nathaniel Macon,	N. C.	Rep.	24
	Wm. H. Crawford,	Ga.	Rep.	44,282	......	41	Andrew Jackson,	Tenn.	Rep.	13
							M. Van Buren,	N. Y.	Rep.	9
							Henry Clay,	Ky.	Rep.	2
1828	Andrew Jackson,*	Tenn.	Dem.	647,231	138,134	178	John C. Calhoun,*	S. C.	Dem.	171
	John Q. Adams,	Mass.	Nat. R.	509,097	......	83	Richard Rush,	Pa.	Nat, R.	83
							William Smith,	S. C.	Dem	7
1832	Andrew Jackson,*	Tenn.	Dem.	687,502	157,313	219	M. Van Buren,*	N. Y.	Dem.	189
	Henry Clay,	Ky.	Nat. R.	530,189	......	49	John Sergeant,	Pa.	Nat. R.	49
	John Floyd,	Ga.	Ind.	33,108 (Floyd and Wirt)	......	11	Henry Lee,	Mass.	Ind.	11
	William Wirt,	Md.	Anti-Mas'nic			7	Amos Ellmaker (*c*),	Pa.	Anti-M.	7
							Wm. Wilkins,	Pa.	Dem.	30
1836	Martin Van Buren,*	N. Y.	Dem.	761,549	24,893	170	R. M. Johnson (*d*),*	Ky.	Dem.	147
	W. H. Harrison,	O.	Whig.	736,656 (Harrison, White, Webster, Mangum)	......	73	Francis Granger,	N. Y.	Whig.	77
	Hugh L. White,	Tenn.	Whig.			26	John Tyler,	Va.	Whig.	47
	Daniel Webster,	Mass.	Whig.			14	William Smith,	Ala.	Dem.	23
	Willie P. Mangum,	N. C.	Whig.			11				
1840	W. H. Harrison,*	O.	Whig.	1,275,017	146,315	234	John Tyler,*	Va.	Whig.	234
	Martin Van Buren,	N. Y.	Dem.	1,128,702	......	60	R. M. Johnson,	Ky.	Dem.	48
	James G. Birney,	N. Y.	Lib.	7,059	......	......	L. W. Tazewell,	Va.	Dem.	11
							James K. Polk,	Tenn.	Dem.	1
							Thomas Earle,	Pa.	Lib.	..
1844	James K. Polk,*	Tenn.	Dem.	1,337,243	38,175	170	George M. Dallas,*	Pa.	Dem.	170
	Henry Clay,	Ky.	Whig.	1,299,068	......	105	T. Frelinghuysen,	N. J.	Whig.	105
	James G. Birney.	N. Y.	Lib.	62,300	......	......	Thomas Morris,	O.	Lib.	..

*Elected. (*a*) The first Republican party is claimed by the present Democratic party as its progenitor. (*b*) No candidate having a majority of the electoral vote, the House of Representatives elected Adams. (*c*) Candidate of the Anti-Masonic Party. (*d*) Elected by Senate.

PRESIDENTIAL ELECTIONS—*Continued.*

Year of Election.	Candidates for President.	States.	Political Party.	Popular Vote.	Plurality.	Electoral Vote.	Candidates for Vice-President.	States.	Political Party.	Electoral Vote.
1848	Zachary Taylor,*	La.	Whig	1,360,101	139,557	163	Millard Fillmore,*	N. Y.	Whig	163
	Lewis Cass,	Mich.	Dem.	1,220,544	....	127	William O. Butler,	Ky.	Dem.	127
	Martin Van Buren,	N. Y.	F. Soil	291,263	....	..	Charles F. Adams,	Mass.	F. Soil.	..
1852	Franklin Pierce,*	N. H.	Dem.	1,601,474	220,896	254	William R. King,*	Ala.	Dem.	254
	Winfield Scott,	N. J.	Whig	1,380,576	....	42	William A. Graham,	N. C.	Whig	42
	John P. Hale,	N. H.	F. D. (*i*)	156,149	....	..	George W. Julian,	Ind.	F. D.	..
	Daniel Webster, (*k*)	Mass.	Whig	1,670	....	..				
1856	James Buchanan,*	Pa.	Dem.	1,838,169	496,905	174	J. C. Breckinridge,*	Ky.	Dem.	174
	John C. Fremont,	Cal.	Rep.	1,341,264	....	114	William L. Dayton,	N. J.	Rep.	114
	Millard Fillmore,	N. Y.	Amer.	874,538	....	8	A. J. Donelson,	Tenn.	Amer.	8
1860	Abraham Lincoln,*	Ill.	Rep.	1,866,352	491,195	180	Hannibal Hamlin,*	Me.	Rep.	180
	Stephen A. Douglas,	Ill.	Dem.	1,375,157	....	12	H. V. Johnson,	Ga.	Dem.	12
	J. C. Breckinridge,	Ky.	Dem.	845,763	....	72	Joseph Lane,	Ore.	Dem.	72
	John Bell,	Tenn.	Union	589,581	....	39	Edward Everett,	Mass.	Union	39
1864	Abraham Lincoln,*	Ill.	Rep.	2,216,067	407,342	(*e*)212	Andrew Johnson,*	Tenn.	Rep.	212
	George B. McClellan,	N. J.	Dem.	1,808,725	....	21	Geo. H. Pendleton,	O.	Dem.	21
1868	Ulysses S. Grant,*	Ill.	Rep.	3,015,071	305,456	(*f*)214	Schuyler Colfax,*	Ind.	Rep.	214
	Horatio Seymour,	N. Y.	Dem.	2,709,615	....	80	F. P. Blair, Jr.	Mo.	Dem.	80
1872	Ulysses S. Grant,*	Ill.	Rep.	3,597,070	762,991	286	Henry Wilson,*	Mass.	Rep.	286
	Horace Greeley,	N. Y.	D. & L.	2,834,079	....	(*g*)	B. Gratz Brown,	Mo.	D. & L	47
	Charles O'Conor,	N. Y.	Dem.	29,408	....	..	John Q. Adams,	Mass.	Dem.	..
	James Black,	Pa.	Temp.	5,608	....	..	John Russell,	Mich.	Temp.	..
	Thomas A. Hendricks	Ind.	Dem.	......	....	42	George W. Julian,	Ind.	Lib.	5
	B. Gratz Brown,	Mo.	Dem.	......	....	18	A. H. Colquitt,	Ga.	Dem.	5
	Charles J. Jenkins,	Ga.	Dem.	......	....	2	John M. Palmer,	Ill.	Dem.	3
	David Davis,	Ill.	Ind.	......	....	1	T. E. Bramlette,	Ky.	Dem.	3
							W. S. Groesbeck,	O.	Dem.	1
							Willis B. Machen,	Ky.	Dem.	1
							N. P. Banks,	Mass.	Lib.	1
1876	Samuel J. Tilden,	N. Y.	Dem.	4,284,885	250,935	184	T. A. Hendricks,	Ind.	Dem.	184
	Rutherford B. Hayes*	O.	Rep.	4,033,950	....	(*h*) 185	William A. Wheeler,*	N. Y.	Rep.	185
	Peter Cooper,	N. Y.	Gre'nb.	81,740	....	..	Samuel F. Cary,	O.	Gre'nb	..
	Green Clay Smith,	Ky.	Pro.	9,522	....	..	Gideon T. Stewart,	O.	Pro.	..
	James B. Walker,	Ill.	Amer.	2,636	....	..	D. Kirkpatrick,	N. Y.	Amer.	..
1880	James A. Garfield,*	O.	Rep.	4,449,053	7,018	214	Chester A. Arthur,*	N. Y.	Rep.	214
	W. S. Hancock,	Pa.	Dem.	4,442,035	....	155	William H. English,	Ind.	Dem.	155
	James B. Weaver,	Iowa	Gre'nb.	307,306	....	..	B. J. Chambers,	Tex.	Gre'nb	..
	Neal Dow,	Me.	Pro.	10,305	....	..	H. A. Thompson,	O.	Pro.	..
	John W. Phelps,	Vt.	Amer.	707	....	..	S. C. Pomeroy,	Kan.	Amer.	..
1884	Grover Cleveland,*	N. Y.	Dem.	4,911,017	62,683	219	T. A. Hendricks,*	Ind.	Dem.	219
	James G. Blaine,	Me.	Rep.	4,848,334	....	182	John A. Logan,	Ill.	Rep.	182
	John P. St. John,	Kan.	Pro.	151,809	....	..	William Daniel,	Md.	Pro.	..
	Benjamin F. Butler,	Mass.	Peop.	133,825	....	..	A. M. West,	Miss.	Peop.	..
	P. D. Wigginton,	Cal.	Amer.	......	....	..				
1888	Grover Cleveland,	N. Y.	Dem.	5,538,233	98,017	168	Allen G. Thurman,	O.	Dem.	163
	Benjamin Harrison*	Ind.	Rep.	5,440,216	....	233	Levi P. Morton,*	N. Y.	Rep.	233
	Clinton B. Fisk,	N. J.	Pro.	249,907	....	..	John A. Brooks,	Mo.	Pro.	..
	Alson J. Streeter,	Ill.	U. L.	148,105	....	..	C. E. Cunningham,	Ark.	U. L.	..
	R. H. Cowdry,	Ill.	U'd L.	2,808	....	..	W. H. T. Wakefield,	Kan.	U'd L.	..
	James L. Curtis,	N. Y.	Amer.	1,591	....	..	James B. Greer,	Tenn.	Amer.	..
1892	Grover Cleveland,*	N. Y.	Dem.	5,556,918	380,810	277	Adlai E. Stevenson,*	Ill.	Dem.	277
	Benjamin Harrison,	Ind.	Rep.	5,176,108	....	145	Whitelaw Reid,	N. Y.	Rep.	145
	James B. Weaver,	Iowa.	Peop.	1,041,028	....	22	James G. Field,	Va.	Peop.	22
	John Bidwell,	Cal.	Pro.	264,133	....	..	James B. Cranfill,	Tex.	Pro.	..
	Simon Wing,	Mass.	Soc. L.	21,164	....	..	Charles H. Matchett,	N. Y.	Soc. L.	..
1896	William McKinley,*	O.	Rep.	7,104,779	601,854	271	Garret A. Hobart,*	N. J.	Rep.	271
	William J. Bryan,	Neb.	Dem. }	6,502,925	{	176	Arthur Sewall,	Me.	Dem.	149
	William J. Bryan,	Neb.	Peop. }		{	..	Thomas E. Watson,	Ga.	Peop.	27
	Joshua Levering,	Md.	Pro.	132,007	....	..	Hale Johnson,	Ill.	Pro.	..
	John M. Palmer,	Ill.	N. Dem.	133,148	....	..	Simon B. Buckner,	Ky.	N. Dem	..
	Charles H. Matchett,	N. Y.	Soc. L.	36,274	....	..	Matthew Maguire,	N. J.	Soc. L.	..
	Charles E. Bentley,	Neb.	Nat (*j*)	13,969	....	..	James H. Southgate,	N. C.	Nat. (*j*)	..
1900	William McKinley,*	O.	Rep.	7,207,923	849,790	292	Theodore Roosevelt*	N. Y.	Rep.	292
	William J. Bryan,	Neb.	Dem. P	6,358,133	....	155	Adlai E. Stevenson,	Ill.	Dem. P.	155
	John G. Woolley,	Ill.	Pro.	208,914	....	..	Henry B. Metcalf,	O.	Pro.	..
	Wharton Barker,	Pa.	MP (*m*)	50,373	....	..	Ignatius Donnelly,	Minn.	MP (*m*)	..
	Eugene V. Debs,	Ind.	Soc. D.	87,814	....	..	Job Harriman,	Cal.	Soc. D.	..
	Jos. F. Maloney,	Mass.	Soc. L.	39,739	....	..	Valentine Remmel,	Pa.	Soc. L.	..
	J. F. R. Leonard,	Iowa	U C (*n*)	1,059	....	..	John G. Woolley,	Ill.	U C (*n*)	..
	Seth H. Ellis,	O.	U R (*o*)	5,698	....	..	Sam'l T. Nicholson,	Pa.	U R (*o*)	..
1904	Theodore Roosevelt*	N. Y.	Rep.	7,624,489	2,541,735	336	C. W. Fairbanks,*	Ind.	Rep.	336
	Alton B. Parker,	N. Y.	Dem.	5,082,754	....	140	Henry G. Davis,	W. Va.	Dem.	140
	Thomas E. Watson,	Ga.	Pop.	117,935	....	..	Thomas H. Tibbles,	Nebr.	Pop.	..
	Eugene V. Debs,	Ind.	Soc.	402,286	....	..	Benjamin Hanford,	N. Y.	Soc.	..
	Silas C. Swallow,	Pa.	Pro.	258,787	....	..	George W. Carroll,	Texas	Pro.	..

* Elected. (*e*) Eleven So. States not voting. (*f*) Three Southern States disfranchised. (*g*) Horace Greeley died after election, and Democratic electors scattered their vote. (*h*) There being a dispute over the electoral vote of Florida, Louisiana, Oregon, and South Carolina, they were referred by Congress to an electoral commission composed of eight Republicans and seven Democrats, which, by a strict party vote, awarded 185 electoral votes to Hayes and 184 to Tilden. (*i*) Free Democrat. (*j*) Free Silver Prohibition party. (*k*) In Massachusetts. There was also a Native American ticket in that State, which received 184 votes. (*m*) Middle of the Road or Anti-Fusion People's party. (*n*) United Christian party. (*o*) Union Reform party.

THE GOLD STANDARD ACT OF 1900.

By this act the dollar consisting of twenty-five and eight tenths grains of gold, nine tenths fine, shall be the standard of value, and all forms of money issued or coined shall be maintained at a parity of value with this gold standard. The United States notes and Treasury notes shall be redeemed in gold coin, and a redemption fund of $150,000,000 of gold coin and bullion is set aside for that purpose only. The following is the text of the section carrying out this provision:—

SEC. 2. That United States notes and Treasury notes issued under the act of July 14, 1890, when presented to the Treasury for redemption, shall be redeemed in gold coin of the standard fixed in the first section of this act, and in order to secure the prompt and certain redemption of such notes as herein provided it shall be the duty of the Secretary of the Treasury to set apart in the Treasury a reserve fund of $150,000,000 in gold coin and bullion, which fund shall be used for such redemption purposes only, and whenever and as often as any of said notes shall be redeemed from said fund it shall be the duty of the Secretary of the Treasury to use said notes so redeemed to restore and maintain such reserve fund in the manner following, to wit:—

First—By exchanging the notes so redeemed for any gold coin in the general fund of the Treasury.

Second—By accepting deposits of gold coin at the Treasury or at any sub-Treasury in exchange for the United States notes so redeemed.

Third—By procuring gold coin by the use of said notes, in accordance with the provisions of Section 3,700 of the Revised Statutes of the United States.

If the Secretary of the Treasury is unable to restore and maintain the gold coin in the reserve fund by the foregoing methods, and the amount of such gold coin and bullion in said fund shall at any time fall below $100,000,000, then it shall be his duty to restore the same to the maximum sum of $150,000,000 by borrowing money on the credit of the United States, and for the debt thus incurred to issue and sell coupon or registered bonds of the United States, in such form as he may prescribe, in denominations of $50 or any multiple thereof, bearing interest at the rate of not exceeding 3 per centum per annum, payable quarterly, such bonds to be payable at the pleasure of the United States after one year from the date of their issue, and to be payable, principal and interest, in gold coin of the present standard value, and to be exempt from the payment of all taxes or duties of the United States, as well as from taxation in any form by or under state, municipal or local authority; and the gold coin received from the sale of said bonds shall first be covered into the general fund of the Treasury and then exchanged, in the manner hereinbefore provided, for an equal amount of the notes redeemed and held for exchange, and the Secretary of the Treasury may, in his discretion, use said notes in exchange for gold, or to purchase or redeem any bonds of the United States, or for any other lawful purpose the public interests may require, except that they shall not be used to meet deficiencies in the current revenues.

That United States notes when redeemed in accordance with the provisions of this section shall be reissued, but shall be held in the reserve fund until exchanged for gold, as herein provided; and the gold coin and bullion in the reserve fund, together with the redeemed notes held for use as provided in this section, shall at no time exceed the maximum sum of $150,000,000.

The legal tender quality of the silver dollar and other money coined or issued by the United States is not affected by the act.

The deposit of gold coin with the Treasurer, and the issue of gold certificates therefor, and the coinage of silver bullion in the Treasury into subsidiary silver coin are provided for.

The National Bank law is amended to permit banks to be created with $25,000 capital in places whose population does not exceed 3,000. Provision is made for the refunding of outstanding bonds at a low rate of interest, and under it bonds bearing 3, 4, and 5 per cent. interest have been refunded for bonds bearing 2 per cent.

Section 10 provides that Section 5,138 of the Revised Statutes is amended so as to read as follows:—

"Section 5,138. No association shall be organized with a less capital than $100,000, except that banks with a capital of not less than $50,000 may, with the approval of the Secretary of the Treasury, be organized in any place the population of which does not exceed 6,000 inhabitants, and except that banks with a capital of not less than $25,000 may, with the sanction of the Secretary of the Treasury, be organized in any place the population of which does not exceed 3,000 inhabitants. No association shall be organized in a city the population of which exceeds 50,000 persons with a capital of less than $200,000."

Section 12 provides for the issue of circulating notes to banks on deposit of bonds, and for additional deposits when there is a depreciation in the value of bonds. The total amount of notes issued by any National banking association may equal at any time, but shall not exceed, the amount at any such time of its capital stock actually paid in.

Every National banking association shall pay a tax in January and July of one fourth of 1 per cent. on the average amount of such of its notes in circulation as are based on its deposit of 2 per cent. bonds, and such taxes shall be in lieu of the taxes on its notes in circulation imposed by Section 5,214 of the Revised Statutes. Provision for international bimetallism is made in the final section of the act, which is as follows:—

SEC. 14. That the provisions of this act are not intended to preclude the accomplishment of international bimetallism whenever conditions shall make it expedient and practicable to secure the same by concurrent action of the leading commercial nations of the world and at a ratio which shall insure permanence of relative value between gold and silver.

LABOR LEGISLATION.

Anti-Boycotting and Anti-Blacklisting Laws. — The States having laws prohibiting *boycotting* in terms are Colorado, Illinois, and Wisconsin.

The States having laws prohibiting *blacklisting* in terms are Alabama, Colorado, Connecticut, Florida, Georgia, Illinois, Indiana, Iowa, Kansas, Minnesota, Missouri, Montana, Nevada, North Dakota, Oklahoma, Utah, Virginia, and Wisconsin.

The following States have laws which may be fairly construed as prohibiting *boycotting:* Alabama, Connecticut, Florida, Georgia, Maine, Massachusetts, Michigan, Minnesota, Mississippi, Missouri, New Hampshire, New York, North Dakota, Oklahoma, Oregon, South Dakota, Texas, Utah, Vermont, and Wisconsin.

The following States have laws which may be fairly construed as prohibiting *blacklisting:* Georgia, Michigan, New Hampshire, New York, Oklahoma, Oregon, Rhode Island, and South Dakota.

In the following States it is unlawful for any employer to exact an agreement, either written or verbal, from an employee not to join or become a member of any labor organization, as a condition of employment: California, Colorado, Idaho, Indiana, Massachusetts, Minnesota, Missouri, New Jersey, New York, Ohio, and Pennsylvania.

Eight-Hour Laws. — CALIFORNIA. — Eight hours of labor constitute a day's work, unless it is otherwise expressly stipulated by the parties to a contract. A stipulation that eight hours of labor constitute a day's work must be made a part of all contracts to which the State or any municipal corporation therein is a party. But in the case of drivers, conductors, and gripmen of street cars for the carriage of passengers, a day's work consists of twelve hours. Employment of minor children for more than eight hours per day is absolutely prohibited, except in vinicultural or horticultural pursuits, or in domestic or household occupations.

COLORADO. Eight hours constitute a day's work for all workingmen employed by the State, or any county, township, school district, municipality, or incorporated town.

CONNECTICUT. Eight hours of labor constitute a lawful day's work unless otherwise agreed.

DISTRICT OF COLUMBIA. Eight hours constitute a day's work for all laborers or mechanics employed by or on behalf of the District of Columbia.

IDAHO. Eight hours' actual work constitute a lawful day's work on all State and municipal works.

ILLINOIS. Eight hours are a legal day's work in all mechanical employments, except on farms, and when otherwise agreed; does not apply to service by the day, week, or month, or prevent contracts for longer hours.

INDIANA. Eight hours of labor constitute a legal day's work for all classes of mechanics, workingmen, and laborers, excepting those engaged in agricultural and domestic labor. Overwork by agreement and for extra compensation is permitted. The employment of persons under fourteen years of age for more than eight hours per day is absolutely prohibited.

KANSAS. Eight hours constitute a day's work for all laborers, mechanics, or other persons employed by or on behalf of the State or any county, city, township, or other municipality.

NEBRASKA. Eight hours constitute a legal day's work for all classes of mechanics, servants, and laborers, except those engaged in farm or domestic labor.

MISSOURI. Eight hours constitute a legal day's work. The law does not prevent an agreement to work for a longer or a shorter time and does not apply to laborers and farm hands in the service of farmers or others engaged in agriculture.

MONTANA. Eight hours constitute a legal day's work for persons engaged to operate or handle any first-motion or direct-acting hoisting engine, or any geared or indirect-acting hoisting engine at any mine employing fifteen or more men underground when the duties of fireman are performed by the person so engaged; also for any stationary engineer operating a stationary engine developing fifty or more horse power when such engineer has charge or control of a boiler or boilers in addition to his other duties. The law applies only to such steam plants as are in continuous operation or are operated twenty or more hours in each twenty-four hours, and does not apply to persons running any engine more than eight hours in each twenty-four for the purpose of relieving another employee in case of sickness or other unforeseen cause.

NEW JERSEY. Eight hours constitute a day's labor on any day whereon any general or municipal election shall be held.

NEW YORK. Eight hours constitute a day's work for mechanics, workingmen, and laborers, except in farm or domestic labor, but overwork for extra pay is permitted. The law applies to those employed by the State or municipality, or by persons contracting for State work.

OHIO. Eight hours shall constitute a day's work in all engagements to labor in any mechanical, manufacturing, or mining business.

unless otherwise expressly stipulated in the contract. But in case of conductors, engineers, firemen, or trainmen of railroads, a day's work consists of ten hours.

PENNSYLVANIA. Eight hours of labor shall be deemed and held to be a legal day's work in all cases of labor and service by the day where there is no agreement or contract to the contrary. This does not apply to farm or agricultural labor by the year, month, or week, to labor in factories, laundries, and renovating establishments, or to labor on street railways.

Eight hours out of the twenty-four shall make and constitute a day's labor in penitentiaries and reformatory institutions receiving support from the State, also for all mechanics, workmen, and laborers in the employ of the State, or of any municipal corporation therein, or otherwise engaged on public works; this shall be deemed to apply to mechanics, workingmen, or laborers in the employ of persons contracting with the State or any municipal corporation therein, for the performance of public work.

UTAH. Eight hours constitute a day's work upon all public works and in all underground mines or workings, smelters, and all other institutions for the reduction or refining of ores.

WISCONSIN. In all engagements to labor in any manufacturing or mechanical business, where there is no express contract to the contrary, a day's work shall consist of eight hours; but the law does not apply to contracts for labor by the week, month, or year. In all manufactories, workshops, or other places used for mechanical or manufacturing purposes, the time of labor of children under the age of eighteen, and of women employed therein, shall not exceed eight hours in the day.

WYOMING. Eight hours' actual work constitute a legal day's work in all mines and public works.

UNITED STATES. Eight hours shall constitute a day's work for all laborers, workmen, and mechanics who may be employed by or on behalf of the United States.

PENSION LAWS.

Any person who has been, since the 4th of March, 1861, disabled in the military or naval service of the United States, or in its marine corps, shall, upon making due proof of the fact, be placed on the list of invalid pensioners of the United States. No claim for pension on the part of a State militiaman, or non-enlisted person, on account of disability from wounds received in battle, shall be valid unless prosecuted to a successful issue prior to July 4, 1874.

Rates of Pension Per Month.

DISABILITIES.	Rate from July 4, 1864.	Rate from March 3, 1865.	Rate from June 6, 1866.	Rate from June 4, 1872.	Act of June, '80.*
Loss of both hands	$25 00	.....	.....	$31 25	$72 00
Total disability in both hands	.....	.....	$25 00	31 25	.....
Loss of both feet	20 00	.....	.....	31 25	72 00
Total disability in both feet	.....	.....	20 00	31 25	.....
Loss of sight of both eyes	25 00	.....	.....	31 25	72 00
Loss of sight of one eye, the sight of the other having been previously lost	.....	.....	25 00	31 25	72 00
Loss of one hand and one foot	.....	$20 00	.....	24 00	36 00
Total disability in one hand and one foot	.....	.....	20 00	24 00	.....
Any disability equivalent to the loss of a hand or foot	.....	.....	15 00	18 00	.....
Any disability incapacitating for the performance of any manual labor	.....	.....	20 00	24 00	.....
Any disability resulting in a condition requiring the regular aid and attendance of another person	.....	.....	25 00	31 25	June 4, '74. 50 00
Total deafness	.....	.....	....	13 00	.....

* Rate from June, 1880, in case the disability is permanent and requires the regular aid and attendance of another person. An applicant for increase of pension from $31.25 to $72 per month must furnish the testimony of his physician, or of two credible witnesses, to prove the extent to which he requires the aid and attendance of another person.

The same provision of law which entitles to $31.25 per month entitles to $72 per month, provided that in the latter case the disability is permanent. The loss of a leg above the knee, or an arm at or above the elbow, entitles the person so disabled to a pension of $24 per month after June 4, 1874.

The rates of $10, $12, $14, and $16 per month will be allowed in cases in which the disability bears the same proportion to that produced by the loss of a hand or foot that those rates bear to the rate of $18 per month.

Under the pension law of 1890 the soldier who is wholly incapacitated from earning a living receives the sum of $12 a month, whether the disability was contracted in the service or not; for a lesser degree of disability, $10, $8, or $6.

The first step to be taken by an applicant for a pension is to file a declaration before a court of record, or before some officer thereof having custody of its seal, setting forth the ground upon which he claims a pension. Blank forms of declaration are furnished upon request at Commissioner of Pensions office. The identity of the applicant must be shown by the testimony of two credible witnesses, who must appear with him before the officer by whom the declaration may be taken. A pensioner who may deem himself entitled to an increase of pension should file a declaration on a blank form furnished for the purpose, setting forth the ground upon which he claims such increase. A declaration for increase of pension may be taken before any officer duly authorized to administer oaths.

All invalid pensions granted under the general law will terminate at re-enlistment, or when the disabilities for which they were allowed shall have ceased.

A widow's pension will end at her re-marriage, and not be renewable should she again become a widow.

Pensions allowed to dependent mothers and sisters end at re-marriage or when dependence ceases. Pensions allowed to dependent fathers end when the dependence ceases.

The name of any pensioner shall be stricken from the roll upon his or her failure to claim a pension for three years after the same shall have become due.

To entitle a widow or children to pension, the death of the soldier does not need to have been the result of injury received or disease contracted under such circumstances as would have entitled him to an invalid pension had he been disabled.

A widow is entitled to a pension of $8 per month, no matter whether the death of the soldier was due to army service or not. In addition to this rate, she will be allowed $2 per month for each child of the officer or soldier under the age of sixteen years.

In the application of widows and children for pensions, they are not required to prove that death of husband resulted from the injury or disease on account of which his pension was granted; but, if the husband had not established his claim for an invalid pension, the widow shall prove origin and cause of the fatal disease. Widows will be required to prove their marriage to the person on account of whose service and death the claim is made; also proof of dates of birth of children by copy of church record.

A mother claiming a pension must prove the cause and date of the death of her son; her relationship; that he left no widow or minor child or children surviving; and that, if living, she would be dependent upon him for support.

A father claiming pension on account of the death of his son, upon whom he was dependent for support, must prove facts similar to those required of a mother.

The claim on behalf of minor brothers and sisters should be made by a guardian duly appointed.

In administration of the pension laws, no distinction is made between brothers and sisters of the half blood and those of the whole blood. Evidence in a claim for pension can not be verified before an officer who is engaged in the prosecution of such claim.

In claims for increase of pension, a fee of $2 will be allowed. All letters of inquiry relative to claims pending in Pension Office should give the number of the claim.

No sum of money due, or to become due, to any pensioner, shall be liable to attachment, levy or seizure, under any legal or equitable process.

Agents for paying pensions shall receive two per centum on all disbursements made by them to pensioners.

No agent, or attorney, or other person, shall demand or receive any other compensation for his services in prosecuting a claim for pension or bounty-land than such as the Commissioner of Pensions shall direct to be paid to him, not exceeding $10.

Every officer, or enlisted or hired man, who who has lost a limb, or the use of a limb, in the military or naval service of the United States, is entitled to receive, once every three years, an artificial limb or apparatus, or commutation therefor. The period of three years is reckoned from the filing of first application after March 2, 1891. The commutation allowed in case of the amputation of a leg is $75; in all other cases, $50. Applications for artificial limbs should be transmitted through the proper pension agent to the surgeon-general of the army.

JURISDICTION OF JUSTICES OF THE PEACE.

Justices of the Peace generally have jurisdiction throughout the county or township in which they are elected, and the limit of the amount is as follows: —

Alabama	$100	Mississippi	$150
Arizona	300	Missouri	250
Arkansas	300	Montana	300
California	300	Nebraska	200
Colorado	300	Nevada	300
Connecticut	100	New Hampshire	13⅓
Dakota, North	200	New Jersey	200
Dakota, South	100	New Mexico	100
Delaware	200	New York	200
District of Columbia	100	North Carolina	200
Florida	100	Ohio	100
Georgia	100	Oregon	500
Idaho	300	Pennsylvania	300
Illinois	200	Rhode Island	300
* Indiana	200	South Carolina	100
† Iowa	100	Tennessee	500
Kansas	300	Texas	200
Kentucky	50	Utah	300
Louisiana	100	Vermont	200
Maine	20	Virginia	100
Maryland	100	Washington	300
Massachusetts	300	West Virginia	300
Michigan	100	* Wisconsin	200
Minnesota	100	Wyoming	300

* By confession, $300. † By consent, $300.

United States Custom Regulations as to Baggage.—The following articles are exempt from duty: Wearing apparel and other personal effects (not merchandise), professional books, implements, instruments and tools of trade.

To ascertain what articles ought to be exempted as the wearing apparel and other personal baggage, and the tools or implements of a mechanical trade only, of persons who arrive in the United States, due entry thereof, as of other merchandise, but separate and distinct from that of any other merchandise imported from a foreign port, shall be made with the Collector of the district in which the articles are intended to be landed by the owner thereof or his agent, expressing the persons by whom or for whom such entry is made, and particularizing the several packages and their contents, with their marks and numbers; and the persons who shall make the entry shall take and subscribe an oath before the Collector, declaring that the entry subscribed by him, and to which the oath is annexed, contains, to the best of his knowledge and belief, a just and true account of the contents of the several packages mentioned in the entry, specifying the name of the vessel, of her master, and of the port from which she has arrived; and that such packages contain no merchandise whatever, other than wearing apparel, personal baggage, or, as the case may be, tools of trade, specifying it; that they are all the property of a person named who has arrived, or is shortly expected to arrive, in the United States, and are not, directly or indirectly, imported for any other, or intended for sale.

Whenever any article subject to duty is found in the baggage of any person arriving in the United States which was not, at the time of making entry for such baggage, mentioned to the Collector before whom such entry was made, by the person making entry, such article shall be forfeited, and the person in whose baggage it is found shall be liable to a penalty of triple the value of such article.

"Professional books, implements, and tools of trade, occupation, or employment," are understood to embrace such books or instruments as would naturally belong to a surgeon, physician, engineer, or scientific person returning to this country.

Jewelry that has been worn or is in use as a personal ornament may be admitted free of duty.

Duty must be demanded on all watches but one, brought into the United States by a single passenger. If all the watches are old, the passenger may choose the one to be treated as personal effects. If some are old and some new, the new are to be included among those treated as subject to duty.

The United States Supreme Court has decided that the free list includes (1) wearing apparel owned by the passenger, and in a condition to be worn at once without further manufacture; (2) brought with him as a passenger, and intended for the use or wear of himself or his family who accompanied him as passengers, and not for sale or purchased or imported for other persons, or to be given away; (3) suitable for the season of the year which was immediately approaching at the time of arrival; (4) not exceeding in quantity, or quality, or value of what the passenger was in the habit of ordinarily providing for himself and his family at that time, and keeping on hand for his and their reasonable wants, in view of their means and habits in life, even though such articles had not been actually worn.

The Law of Finding.—The law of finding, though not prescribed by statute, is well defined by precedent. It may be stated thus: The finder has a clear title against the whole world except the owner. The proprietor of a hotel or a shop has no right to demand the property or premises. Such proprietor may make regulations in regard to lost property which will bind their employees, but they cannot bind the public. The law of finding was declared by the King's bench, England, over 100 years ago, in a case in which the facts were these:—

A person found a wallet containing a sum of money on a shop floor. He handed the wallet and contents to the shopkeeper to be returned to the owner. After three years, during which the owner did not call for his property, the finder demanded the wallet and the money from the shopkeeper. The latter refused to deliver them up on the ground that they were found on the premises. The former then sued the shopkeeper, and it was held as above set forth, that against all the world but the owner, the title of the finder is perfect. And the finder has been held to stand in the place of the owner, so that he was permitted to prevail in an action against a person who found an article which the plaintiff had originally found, but subsequently lost. The police have no special rights in regard to articles lost, unless those rights are conferred by statute. Receivers of articles found are trustees for the owner or finder. They have no power in the absence of special statute to keep an article against the finder, any more than the finder has to retain an article against the owner.

QUALIFICATIONS FOR VOTING IN EACH STATE OF THE UNION.

In all the States except Colorado, Idaho, Utah, and Wyoming the right to vote at general elections is restricted to males of 21 years of age and upward. Women are entitled to vote at school elections in several States. They are entitled by law to full suffrage in the States of Colorado, Idaho, Utah, and Wyoming.

States.	Requirements as to Citizenship.	Previous Residence Required.				Persons Excluded from Suffrage.
		In State.	In County	In Town.	In Precinct.	
Alabama*	Citizen of United States or alien who has declared intention.	1 year	3 mos.	30 days.	30 days.	Convicted of treason or other felonies, idiots, or insane.
Arizona Ter.	Citizen of United States (*a*)	1 year	90 days.	10 days.	10 days.	Indians and Chinamen.
Arkansas*	Citizen of United States or alien who has declared intention.	1 year	6 mos.	30 days.	30 days.	Idiots, insane, convicted of felony, until pardoned, failure to pay poll tax.
California*	Citizen by nativity, naturalization (90 days prior to election), or treaty of Queretaro.	1 year	90 days.	....	30 days.	Chinese, idiots, insane, embezzlers of public moneys, convicted of infamous crime.†
Colorado*	Citizen or alien, male or female, who has declared intention four months prior to election.	6 mos.	90 days.	30 days.	10 days.	Convicted of crime, bribery in public office.
Connecticut*	Citizen of United States who can read English language.	1 year	....	6 mos.	....	Convicted of heinous crime, unless pardoned.
Delaware*	Citizen who shall have paid a registration fee of $1, and who is duly registered as a qualified voter.	1 year	3 mos.	....	30 days.	Insane persons and paupers, or persons convicted of felony.
Dis. of Colum.	See top of page 50.					
Florida*	Citizen of the United States	1 year	6 mos.	....	....	Idiots, duelists, convicted of felony or any infamous crime.
Georgia*	Citizen of the United States who has paid all his taxes since 1877.	1 year	6 mos.	....	....	Convicted of felony, unless pardoned, idiots, and insane.
Idaho*	Citizen of the United States, male or female.	6 mos.	30 days.	3 mos.	10 days.	Idiots, insane, convicted of felony or treason.
Illinois*	Citizen of the United States	1 year	90 days.	30 days.	30 days.	Convicted of felony or bribery in elections, unless restored to citizenship, idiots, lunatics.
Indiana*	Citizen or alien who has declared intention and resided one year in United States.	6 mos.	60 days.	60 days.	30 days.	United States soldiers, sailors, and marines, and persons convicted of infamous crime.
Iowa*	Citizen of the United States	6 mos.	60 days.	(*e*)	(*e*)	Idiots, insane, convicted of infamous crime.
Kansas*	Citizen of United States or alien who has declared intention.	6 mos.	30 days.	30 days.	30 days.	Felons, insane, rebels not restored to citizenship (*d*).
Kentucky*	Citizen of the United States	1 year	6 mos.	60 days.	60 days.	Convicted of felony, idiots, and insane.
Louisiana*	Citizen of United States (*f*)	2 years.	1 year	....	6 mos.	Idiots, insane, convicted of felony or treason, unless pardoned, with express restoration of franchise.
Maine*	Citizen of the United States	3 mos.	3 mos.	3 mos.	3 mos.	Paupers and Indians not taxed.
Maryland*	Citizen of the United States	1 year	6 mos.	....	....	Convicted of felony, unless pardoned, lunatics, persons *non compos mentis*.
Mass'chusetts*	Citizen who can read and write (*b*).	1 year	6 mos.	6 mos.	6 mos.	Paupers and persons under guardianship.
Michigan*	Citizen or alien who declared intention to become a citizen prior to May 8, 1892 (*b*).	6 mos.	20 days.	20 days.	20 days.	Indians with tribal relations, duelists, and accessories.
Minnesota*	Citizen of United States who has been such for 3 months preceding election.	6 mos.	....	....	30 days.	Convicted of treason or felony, unless pardoned, under guardianship, insane, Indians untaxed.
Mississippi*	Citizen of the United States who can read or understand Constitution.	2 years.	1 year	1 year	1 yr (*c*)	Insane, idiots, Indians not taxed, felons, persons who have not paid taxes.
Missouri*	Citizen of United States or alien who has declared intention not less than 1 year or more than 5 before election.	1 year	60 days.	60 days.	60 days.	Persons in poorhouses or asylums at public expense, those in prison or who have been convicted of infamous crimes
Montana*	Citizen of the United States (*b*)	1 year	30 days.	30 days.	30 days.	Convicted of felony, unless pardoned, idiots, insane, United States soldiers, seamen, and marines, Indians.
Nebraska*	Citizen of United States or alien who has declared intention 30 days before election.	6 mos.	40 days.	10 days.	10 days.	Convicted of felony, unless restored to civil rights, persons *non compos mentis*.
Nevada*	Citizen of the United States	6 mos.	30 days.	30 days.	30 days.	Idiots, insane, unpardoned convicts, Indians, Chinese.
N. Hampshire*	Citizen of the United States (*b*)	6 mos.	6 mos.	6 mos.	6 mos.	Insane or paupers.
New Jersey*	Citizen of the United States	1 year	5 mos.	....	....	Idiots, paupers, insane, convicted of crime, unless pardoned or restored by law.
N. M. Territory	Citizen of the United States	6 mos.	3 mos.	....	30 days.	Convicted of felony, unless pardoned, United States soldier or camp follower, Indians (*h*).

STATES.	Requirements as to Citizenship.	Previous Residence Required.				Persons Excluded from Suffrage.
		In State.	In County	In Town.	In Precinct.	
New York*....	Citizen who shall have been a citizen for 90 days prior to election.	1 year..	4 mos...	30 days.	30 days.	Convicted and sentenced to a State prison or penitentiary for felony or other infamous crime; persons who have received or offered to receive, or who have paid or promised to pay, compensation for giving or withholding votes, or who have laid any bet or wager upon the result of an election.
North Carolina	Citizen of the United States......	1 year..	90 days.	....	....	Convicted of felony or other infamous crime, idiots, lunatics, and those who deny the being of Almighty God.
North Dakota*	Citizen of the United States, alien who has declared intention 1 year and not more than 6 years prior to election, and civilized Indian‡ (*i*).	1 year..	6 mos...	....	90 days.	Under guardianship, persons *non compos mentis*, or convicted of felony and treason, unless restored to civil rights.
Ohio*..........	Citizen of the United States (*i*)...	1 year..	30 days.	30 days.	20 days.	Idiots, insane, and felons.
Okla. Territ. (*i*)	Citizen of the United States or alien who has declared intention.	6 mos...	60 days.	60 days.	30 days.	Indians having tribal relations.
Oregon*.......	White male citizen of United States or alien who has declared intention (*i*).	6 mos...	30 days.	30 days.	....	Idiots, insane, convicted of felony punishable by imprisonment in the penitentiary.
Pennsylvania*.	Citizen of the United States at least 1 month, and if 22 years old or more must have paid tax within 2 years.	1 year..	....	....	2 mos...	Convicted of perjury and fraud as election officers, or bribery of voters.
Rhode Island*.	Citizen of the United States......	2 yrs (*j*)	....	6 mos...	....	Paupers, lunatics (*g*).
South Carolina	Citizen of the United States (*l*)...	2 years.	1 year..	4 mos...	4 mos...	Convicted of felony, or bribery in elections, unless pardoned, idiots, insane, paupers.
South Dakota*	Citizen of the United States or alien who has declared intention (*i*).	6 mos.§	30 days.	10 days.	10 days.	Underguardianship, insane, convicted of treason or felony, unless pardoned, United States soldiers, seamen, and marines.
Tennessee*.....	Citizen of the United States who has paid poll tax of preceding year.	1 year..	6 mos...	....	....	Convicted of bribery or other infamous offense.
Texas*.........	Citizen of the United States or alien who has declared intention 6 months prior to election.	1 year..	6 mos...	....	(*k*)	Idiots, lunatics, paupers, convicted of felony, United States soldiers, marines, and seamen.
Utah*.....	Citizen of the United States, male or female, who has been a citizen 90 days.	1 year..	4 mos...	....	60 days.	Idiots, insane, convicted of treason or crime against elective franchise, unless pardoned.
Vermont*.....	Citizen of the United States......	1 year..	....	3 mos...	30 days.	Those who have not obtained the approbation of the board of civil authority of the town in which they reside.
Virginia*......	Citizen of the United States......	1 year..	3 mos...	3 mos...	....	Idiots, lunatics (*m*).
Washington*..	Citizen of the United States......	1 year..	90 days.	30 days.	30 days.	Idiots, lunatics, convicted of infamous crimes, Indians not taxed.
West Virginia*	Citizen of the State..............	1 year..	60 days.	....	(*k*)	Paupers, idiots, lunatics, convicted of treason, felony, or bribery at elections.
Wisconsin*....	Citizen of United States or alien who has declared intention.	1 year..	1 year..	10 days.	10 days.	Indians having tribal relations, insane, convicted of treason or felony.
Wyoming*....	Citizen of the United States, male or female.	1 year..	60 days.	....	....	Idiots, insane, convicted of infamous crimes, unable to read State Constitution.

*Australian Ballot law or a modification of it in force. † Or a person unable to read the Constitution in English and to write his name. ‡ Indian must have severed tribal relations. § One year's residence in the United States prior to election required. (*a*) Or citizens of Mexico who shall have elected to become citizens under the treaties of 1848 and 1854. (*b*) Women can vote in school elections. (*c*) Clergymen are qualified after six months' residence in precinct. (*d*) Also those under guardianship, public embezzlers, guilty of bribery, or dishonorably discharged from the United States service. (*e*) Only actual residence required. (*f*) If unable to read and write, as provided by the Constitution, then he shall be entitled to register and vote if he shall, at the time he offers to register, be the *bona fide* owner of property assessed to him in the State at a valuation of not less than $300 on the assessment roll of the current year in which he offers to register, or on the roll of the preceding year, if the roll of the current year shall not then have been completed and filed, and on which, if such property be personal only, all taxes due shall have been paid. (*g*) Or persons *non compos mentis*, convicted of bribery or infamous crime, until restored to right to vote, under guardianship. (*h*) Except Pueblo Indians, if "acequia" officers. (*i*) Women can vote in school elections. (*j*) Owners of real estate, one year. (*k*) Actual residence in the precinct or district required. (*l*) Who has paid six months before election any poll tax then due, and can read and write any section of the State Constitution, or can show that he owns and has paid all taxes due the previous year on property in the State assessed at $300 or more. (*m*) Or convicted of bribery at election, embezzlement of public funds, treason, felony, and petty larceny, duelists and abettors, unless pardoned by Legislature.

Residents of the District of Columbia never had the right to vote therein for national officers, or on other matters of national concern, after it became the seat of the general government. But from 1802 to June 20, 1874, the citizens of Washington, and from January 1, 1790, to said date, the citizens of Georgetown were entitled to vote on municipal subjects and for certain municipal officers; the citizens of the portion of the District outside of Washington and Georgetown were entitled to the same privilege from April 20, 1871, to June 20, 1874, but that suffrage was abolished in the District of Columbia and was rescinded June 20, 1874, by the act of Congress of that date.

THE STATES AND THE UNION.

THE THIRTEEN ORIGINAL STATES.

	States.	Ratified the Constitution.		States.	Ratified the Constitution.
1	Delaware	December 7, 1787	8	South Carolina	May 23, 1788
2	Pennsylvania	December 12, 1787	9	New Hampshire	June 21, 1788
3	New Jersey	December 18, 1787	10	Virginia	June 26, 1788
4	Georgia	January 2, 1788	11	New York	July 26, 1788
5	Connecticut	January 9, 1788	12	North Carolina	November 21, 1789
6	Massachusetts	February 6, 1788	13	Rhode Island	May 29, 1790
7	Maryland	April 28, 1788			

STATES ADMITTED TO THE UNION.

	States.	Admitted.		States.	Admitted.
1	Vermont	March 4, 1791	17	Wisconsin	May 29, 1848
2	Kentucky	June 1, 1792	18	California	September 9, 1850
3	Tennessee	June 1, 1796	19	Minnesota	May 11, 1858
4	Ohio	February 19, 1803	20	Oregon	February 14, 1859
5	Louisiana	April 30, 1812	21	Kansas	January 29, 1861
6	Indiana	December 11, 1816	22	West Virginia	June 19, 1863
7	Mississippi	December 10, 1817	23	Nevada	October 31, 1864
8	Illinois	December 3, 1818	24	Nebraska	March 1, 1867
9	Alabama	December 14, 1819	25	Colorado	August 1, 1876
10	Maine	March 15, 1820	26	North Dakota	November 2, 1889
11	Missouri	August 10, 1821	27	South Dakota	November 2, 1889
12	Arkansas	June 15, 1836	28	Montana	November 8, 1889
13	Michigan	January 26, 1837	29	Washington	November 11, 1889
14	Florida	March 3, 1845	30	Idaho	July 3, 1890
15	Texas	December 29, 1845	31	Wyoming	July 11, 1890
16	Iowa	December 28, 1846	32	Utah	January, 1896

STATE AND TERRITORIAL STATISTICS.

States and Territories.	Gross Area in Square Miles.*	Extreme Breadth, Miles.†	Extreme Length, Miles.	Capitals.	States and Territories.	Gross Area in Square Miles.*	Extreme Breadth, Miles.†	Extreme Length, Miles.	Capitals.
Alabama	52,250	200	330	Montgomery.	Montana	146,080	580	315	Helena.
Alaska Ter.	577,390	800	1,100	Sitka.	Nebraska	77,510	415	205	Lincoln.
Arizona Ter.	113.020	335	390	Phœnix.	Nevada	110,700	315	485	Carson City.
Arkansas	53,850	275	240	Little Rock.	New Hamp.	9,305	90	185	Concord.
California	158,360	375	770	Sacramento.	New Jersey	7,815	70	160	Trenton.
Colorado	103,925	390	270	Denver.	N. Mexico T.	122,580	350	390	Santa Fé.
Connecticut	4,990	90	75	Hartford.	New York	49,170	320	310	Albany.
Delaware	2,050	35	110	Dover.	N. Carolina	52,250	520	200	Raleigh.
Dist. of Col.	‡70	9	10	Washington.	N. Dakota	70,795	360	210	Bismarck.
Florida	58,680	400	460	Tallahassee.	Ohio	41,060	230	205	Columbus.
Georgia	59,475	250	315	Atlanta.	Oklahoma T.	§39,030	365	210	Guthrie.
Idaho	84,800	305	490	Boisé City.	Oregon	96,030	375	290	Salem.
Illinois	56,650	205	380	Springfield.	Pennsylvania	45,215	300	180	Harrisburg.
Indiana	36,350	160	265	Indianapolis.	Rhode Island	1,250	35	50	Npt. & Prov.
Indian Ter.	31,400	210	210		S. Carolina	30,570	235	215	Columbia.
Iowa	56,025	300	210	Des Moines.	South Dakota	77,650	380	245	Pierre.
Kansas	82,080	400	200	Topeka.	Tennessee	42,050	430	120	Nashville.
Kentucky	40,400	350	175	Frankfort.	Texas	265,780	760	620	Austin.
Louisiana	48,720	280	275	Baton Rouge.	Utah	84,970	275	345	Salt Lake City.
Maine	33,040	205	235	Augusta.	Vermont	9,565	90	155	Montpelier.
Maryland	12,210	200	120	Annapolis.	Virginia	42,450	425	205	Richmond.
Massachusetts	8,315	190	110	Boston.	Washington	69,180	340	230	Olympia.
Michigan	58,915	310	400	Lansing.	W. Virginia	24,780	200	225	Charleston.
Minnesota	83,365	350	400	St. Paul.	Wisconsin	56,040	290	300	Madison.
Mississippi	46,810	180	340	Jackson.	Wyoming	97,890	365	275	Cheyenne.
Missouri	69,415	300	280	Jefferson City.	Total U. S.	3,602,990	‖2,720	‖1,600	

* Gross area includes water as well as land surface. These areas are from the U. S. Census Report of 1890. † Breadth is from east to west. Length is from north to south. ‡ The District of Columbia was originally 100 square miles, but 30 miles were receded to Virginia in 1846. § Including the Cherokee Strip and No Man's Land. ‖ Breadth from Quoddy Head, in Maine, to Cape Flattery, in Washington; length from the 49th parallel to Brownsville, on the Rio Grande. This is exclusive of Alaska.

THE TERRITORIES.

TERRITORIES.	Organized.	TERRITORIES.	Organized.
New Mexico	September 9 1850	District of Columbia	{ July 16 ....1790 { March 3 1791
Arizona	February 24 1863	Alaska	July 27 1868
Indian*	June 30 1834	Oklahoma	May 2 1890
		Hawaii	June 14 1900

* The Indian Territory has as yet no organized territorial government.

STATE AND TERRITORIAL GOVERNMENTS.

STATES AND TERRITORIES.	GOVERNORS.			LEGISLATURES.			Time of Next State or Territorial Election.	Salaries of Members, Annual or Per Diem, while in Session.	TERMS OF MEMBERS, YEARS.	
	Salaries.	Length Term, Years.	Terms Expire.	Next Session Begins.	Ann. or Bien.	Limit of Session.			Senators.	Representatives.
Alabama	$5,000	4	Jan. —, 1907	Jan. 8, 1907	Quad	50 days.	Nov. 6, 1906	$4 per diem	4	4
Alaska	5,000	4	June —, 1904	......	......	......	......	......	......	......
Arizona	3,000	4	Dec. —, 1906	Jan. 16, 1905	Bien.	60 days.	Nov. 8, 1904	$4 per diem	2	2
Arkansas	3,000	2	Jan. 18, 1905	Jan. 9, 1905	Bien.	60 days.	Sept. 5, 1904	$6 "	4	2
California	6,000	4	Jan. —, 1907	Jan. 3, 1905	Bien.	60 days.	Nov. 6, 1906	$8 "	4	2
Colorado	5,000	2	Jan. 10, 1905	Jan. 2, 1905	Bien.	90 days.	Nov. 8, 1904	$7 "	4	2
Connecticut	4,000	2	Jan. —, 1905	Jan. 4, 1905	Bien.	None.	Nov. 8, 1904	$300 annum	2	2
Delaware	2,000	4	Jan. 19, 1905	Jan. 3, 1905	Bien.	60 days.	Nov. 8, 1904	$300 session	4	2
Florida	3,500	4	Jan. 1, 1905	Apr. 4, 1905	Bien.	60 days.	Nov. 8, 1904	$6 per diem	4	2
Georgia	3,000	2	June 24, 1905	June 22, 1904	Ann.	50 days.	Oct. 5, 1904	$4 "	2	2
Hawaii	5,000	4	June 13, 1904	Feb. 18, 1904	Bien.	60 days.	......	$400 annum	4	2
Idaho	5,000	2	Jan. 2, 1905	Jan. 2, 1905	Bien.	60 days.	Nov. 8, 1904	$5 per diem	2	2
Illinois	6,000	4	Jan. 11, 1905	Jan. 4, 1905	Bien.	None.	Nov. 8, 1904	$1,000 bien.	4	2
Indiana	5,000	4	Jan. 1, 1905	Jan. 5, 1905	Bien.	60 days.	Nov. 8, 1904	$5 per diem	4	2
Iowa	5,000	2	Jan. 1, 1906	Jan. 11, 1904	Bien.	None.	Nov. 8, 1904	$550 per term.	4	2
Kansas	3,000	2	Jan. 11, 1905	Jan. 10, 1905	Bien.	50 days.	Nov. 8, 1904	$3 per diem	4	2
Kentucky	6,500	4	Dec. 10, 1907	Jan. 5, 1904	Bien.	60 days.	Nov. 5, 1907	$5 "	4	2
Louisiana	5,000	4	May 1, 1904	May 9, 1904	Bien.	60 days.	Apr. 19, 1904	$5 "	4	4
Maine	2,000	2	Jan. 1, 1905	Jan. 4, 1905	Bien.	None.	Sept. 12, 1904	$150 annum	2	2
Maryland	4,500	4	Jan. 8, 1908	Jan. 6, 1904	Bien.	90 days.	Nov. 7, 1905	$5 per diem	4	2
Massachusetts	8,000	1	Jan. 6, 1905	Jan. 6, 1904	Ann.	None.	Nov. 8, 1904	$750 annum	1	1
Michigan	4,000	2	Jan. 1, 1905	Jan. 4, 1905	Bien.	None.	Nov. 8, 1904	$3 per diem	2	2
Minnesota	5,000	2	Jan. 1, 1905	Jan. 3, 1905	Bien.	90 days.	Nov. 8, 1904	$5 "	4	2
Mississippi	3,500	4	Jan. 1, 1908	Jan. 7, 1904	Bien.	None.	Nov. 5, 1907	$400 annum	4	4
Missouri	5,000	4	Jan. 1, 1905	Jan. 4, 1905	Bien.	70 days.	Nov. 8, 1904	$5 per diem	4	2
Montana	5,000	4	Jan. 4, 1905	Jan. —, 1905	Bien.	60 days.	Nov. 8, 1904	$6 "	4	2
Nebraska	2,500	2	Jan. 6, 1905	Jan. 3, 1905	Bien.	60 days.	Nov. 8, 1904	$5 "	2	2
Nevada	4,000	4	Jan. 6, 1907	Jan. 9, 1905	Bien.	50 days.	Nov. 6, 1906	$8 "	4	2
N. Hampshire	2,000	2	Jan. —, 1905	Jan. 4, 1905	Bien.	None.	Nov. 8, 1904	$200 annum	2	2
New Jersey	10,000	3	Jan. —, 1905	Jan. 12, 1904	Ann.	None.	Nov. 8, 1904	$500 "	3	1
New Mexico	3,000	4	Jan. 22, 1906	Jan. 17, 1905	Bien.	60 days.	Nov. 8, 1904	$4 per diem	2	2
New York	10,000	2	Jan. 1, 1905	Jan. 6, 1904	Ann.	None.	Nov. 8, 1904	$1,500 annum.	2	1
N. Carolina	4,000	4	Jan. 1, 1905	Jan. 4, 1905	Bien.	60 days.	Nov. 8, 1904	$4 per diem	2	2
North Dakota	3,000	2	Jan. 1, 1905	Jan. 3, 1905	Bien.	60 days.	Nov. 8, 1904	$5 "	4	2
Ohio	8,000	2	Jan. 8, 1906	Jan. 4, 1904	Bien.	None.	Nov. 8, 1904	$600 annum	2	2
Oklahoma	2,400	4	Apr. —, 1905	Jan. 10, 1905	Bien.	60 days.	Nov. 8, 1904	$4 per diem	2	2
Oregon	1,500	4	Jan. —, 1907	Jan. 9, 1905	Bien.	40 days.	June 6, 1904	$3 "	4	2
Pennsylvania	10,000	4	Jan. 17, 1907	Jan. 3, 1905	Bien.	None.	Nov. 8, 1904	$1,500 session	4	2
Porto Rico	8,000	4	Jan. —, 1905	Jan. 1, 1904	Bien.	60 days.	......	$5 per diem	1	1
Rhode Island	3,000	1	Jan. 1, 1905	Jan. 5, 1904	Ann.	None.	Nov. 8, 1904	$5 "	1	1
S. Carolina	3,000	2	Jan. —, 1905	Jan. 12, 1904	Ann.	40 days.	Nov. 8, 1904	$4 "	4	2
South Dakota	3,000	2	Jan. 1, 1905	Jan. 3, 1905	Bien.	60 days.	Nov. 8, 1904	$5 "	2	2
Tennessee	4,000	2	Jan. 15, 1905	Jan. 2, 1905	Bien.	75 days.	Nov. 8, 1904	$4 "	2	2
Texas	4,000	2	Jan. 12, 1905	Jan. 2, 1905	Bien.	None.	Nov. 8, 1904	$5 "	4	2
Utah	4,000	4	Jan. 7, 1905	Jan. 9, 1905	Bien.	60 days.	Nov. 8, 1904	$4 "	4	2
Vermont	1,500	2	Oct. —, 1904	Oct. 5, 1904	Bien.	None.	Sept. 6, 1904	$3 "	2	2
Virginia	5,000	4	Feb. 1, 1906	Jan. 13, 1904	Bien.	60 days.	Nov. 7, 1905	$4 "	4	2
Washington	4,000	4	Jan. 14, 1905	Jan. 12, 1905	Bien.	60 days.	Nov. 8, 1904	$5 "	.2	2
West Virginia	2,700	4	Mar. 4, 1905	Jan. 11, 1905	Bien.	45 days.	Nov. 8, 1904	$4 "	4	2
Wisconsin	5,000	2	Jan. 1, 1905	Jan. 11, 1905	Bien.	None.	Nov. 8, 1904	$500 annum	4	2
Wyoming	2,500	4	Nov. 8, 1904	Jan. 10, 1905	Bien.	40 days.	Nov. 8, 1904	$5 per diem	4	2

Territorial Governors are appointed by the President.

FEDERAL BANKRUPTCY ACT.

The States of the Union have insolvency laws, under which debtors conforming to the provisions of law can secure a release from debts owed in the State. Only the Federal Government can enact laws under which debtors can be discharged from their debts wherever they are owed. Among the duties of Congress is that of providing a uniform system of bankruptcy. Under this power Congress has passed four bankruptcy acts, the first in the year 1800, which law by its own terms was limited to five years, but it was repealed, nevertheless, in 1803. In 1841, the second bankruptcy act was passed, and was repealed in March, 1843. The third bankruptcy act was approved March 2, 1867, and repealed in 1878. The fourth bankruptcy act was approved July 1, 1898, and, in brief, this act constitutes the district courts of the United

States in the several States, the Supreme Court of the District of Columbia, the district courts of the several Territories, and the United States courts in the Indian Territory and the district of Alaska courts of bankruptcy. The law defines acts of bankruptcy as follows:—

Acts of bankruptcy by a person shall consist of his having (1) conveyed, transferred, concealed, or removed, or permitted to be concealed or removed, any part of his property with intent to hinder, delay, or defraud his creditors, or any of them; or (2) transferred, while insolvent, any portion of his property to one or more of his creditors with intent to prefer such creditors over his other creditors; or (3) suffered or permitted, while insolvent, any creditor to obtain a preference through legal proceedings, and not having at least five days before a sale or final disposition of any property affected by such preference vacated or discharged such preference; or (4) made a general assignment for the benefit of his creditors; or (5) admitted in writing his inability to pay his debts and his willingness to be adjudged a bankrupt on that ground.

The following described persons may become bankrupts:—

Any person who owes debts, except a corporation, shall be entitled to the benefits of this act as a voluntary bankrupt.

Any natural person, except a wage-earner or a person engaged chiefly in farming or the tillage of the soil, any unincorporated company, and any corporation engaged principally in manufacturing, trading, printing, publishing, or mercantile pursuits, owing debts to the amount of one thousand dollars or over, may be adjudged an involuntary bankrupt upon default or an impartial trial, and shall be subject to the provisions and entitled to the benefits of this act. Private bankers, but not national banks or banks incorporated under State or Territorial laws, may be adjudged involuntary bankrupts.

The act does not affect the allowance to bankrupts of the exemptions which are prescribed by State laws in force at the time of the filing of a petition in the State wherein they have had their domicile for six months or the greater portion thereof immediately preceding the filing of a petition. The law creates two offices — referees and trustees.

The act went into full force and effect upon its passage, that is, July 1, 1898, but no petition for voluntary bankruptcy could be filed within one month of that date, and no petition for involuntary bankruptcy within four months thereof. Proceedings commenced under State insolvency laws before the passage of the act were not affected by it.

THE LAW OF TRADE-MARKS.

Any person, firm, or corporation can obtain protection for any lawful trade-mark by complying with the following:—

1. By causing to be recorded in the Patent Office the name, residence, and place of business of persons desiring the trade-mark.
2. The class of merchandise and description of the same.
3. A description of the trade-mark itself with facsimiles.
4. The length of time that the said mark has already been used.
5. By payment of the required fee — $6.00 for labels and $25 for trade-marks.
6. By complying with such regulations as may be prescribed by the Commissioner of Patents.
7. A lawful trade-mark must consist of some arbitrary word (not the name of a person or place), indicating or not the use or nature of the thing to which it is applied; of some designated symbol, or of both word and symbol.

INTERSTATE COMMERCE LAW.

The Interstate Commerce Act is a law passed by Congress in 1887 for the regulation of rates and the management of interstate commerce. It applies to carriers engaged in the transportation of passengers or property wholly by railroad or partly by railroad and partly by water, from one State, Territory, or District of the United States to any other State, Territory, or District, or to or from a foreign country. It provides for the appointment of a board of five commissioners, empowered to inquire into the management of the carriers and determine the reasonableness of their rates. A carrier whose line is entirely within a State is subject to the act so far as it makes or accepts through rates on interstate commerce.

Among other things the act requires that all charges shall be just and reasonable; that charges for a shorter distance shall not exceed those for a longer distance on the same line in the same direction, when the circumstances and conditions are similar; that there shall be no unjust discrimination as between persons or classes of traffic or localities, in the charges made, or in the service rendered; that the rates charged for transportation shall be printed, filed with the Commission, and kept for public inspection at the several stations, and that the carriers shall annually make a complete exhibit of their business to the Commission.

The act makes exceptions from its provisions of the carriage of property for the United States or for any State or municipal government, or for charitable purposes, or to or from fairs and expositions, and it allows of the issuing of mileage, excursion, or commutation tickets, and admits of the giving of reduced rates to ministers of religion and free transportation to the officers and employees of the carrier, and to the principal officers of other carriers.

BUSINESS LAW AND FORMS.

Agency.—"Whatever business a man may do, he may employ another man to do for him." An agency may exist by *Implication*, *Verbally*, or by *Writings*.

By *implication* when the acts and words lead people in general to believe that the agency exists.

Verbally, whenever there is only the verbal agreement between the parties. A verbal agency permits the agent to make a contract even in cases where the contract must be in writing.

By *writings*, as notes, memoranda or formal instruments under seal.

The authority conveyed must be equal to the deed to be performed. The instrument of agency must be under seal when the conveyance requires a seal. When the business to be transacted does not require a seal, the instrument of agency need not be under seal.

Kinds.—General agents; special agents; professional agents.

A *general agent* is empowered to transact all the business of a particular kind. He may bind his principal, generally, with innocent parties so long as he keeps within the apparent scope of his authority, even if he exceeds *private* instructions.

A *special agent* is one invested with limited powers for the performance of some especial business. He cannot bind his principal whenever he exceeds his authority. Who deals with a special agent, deals at his peril, when the agent passes the limit of his power.

Professional agents, as attorneys, brokers, captains, auctioneers, factors, etc., are usually licensed by competent authority to transact a particular kind of business.

They are invested with ample power and the law holds them responsible for the proper performance of their duties.

Liabilities of Principal.—Private instructions to a general agent do not avoid the principal's liability to innocent parties. A principal is responsible for fraud on the part of the agent, if permitted while transacting his business. A principal is not bound by the acts of a special agent who exceeds his authority. A principal is not generally liable for the willful wrong done by his agent.

Forms of Powers of Attorney.—*Know all men by these presents:* That I, A. B., of . . . ., have made, constituted, and appointed, and by these presents do make, constitute, and appoint B. C., of . . . ., my true and lawful attorney, for me and in my name and stead (state purpose for which issued), giving and granting to my said attorney, by these presents, full power and authority to do and perform all and every act and thing necessary to be done in and about the premises, as fully to all intents and purposes as I might or could do if personally present, hereby ratifying and confirming all that my said attorney shall lawfully do or cause to be done by virtue hereof.

In witness whereof, I have hereunto set my hand and seal, this . . . . . . day of . . . . . . , A. D. 189 . .

A. B. [L. S.]

Sealed and delivered in the presence of B. C.

Married women, lunatics, and minors, in general, are disqualified from appointing agents, but a married woman in the State of New York, if over twenty-one years, may appoint an agent the same as though unmarried. A minor may authorize an agent to perform an act that is to his advantage, but not that is to his prejudice.

Deeds.—The grantor is the person who makes the conveyance and the grantee is the person who receives the conveyance.

A deed, being a contract, has the same essentials. In most States married women may convey real estate which they own in their own right. A partner cannot convey real estate belonging to the firm unless empowered by special authority from the partners to do so.

Consideration.—A sufficient consideration is necessary to a valid deed. (See consideration under contracts.)

Subject-matter.—The description of the land and its boundaries should be extremely accurate. The usual words of the transfer are "give, grant, sell, and convey," though any others conveying the same idea could be used. Land sold without reserving any crops at that time growing on it, conveys the crops or everything attached to the land. When a building is sold it conveys everything that belongs to it. The words "heirs and assigns" are necessary in some States to convey an unconditional title.

Forms of Deeds.—Deed with full covenants. (New York Laws of 1890.)

This indenture, made the . . day of . . . . , in the year . . . . , between A. B., of . . . . (give occupation and residence), of the first part, and C. D., of . . . . (occupation and residence), of the second part.

Witnesseth: That the said party of the first part, in consideration of .... dollars, lawful money of the United States, paid by the party of the second part, doth hereby grant and release unto the said party of the second part, his heirs and assigns forever (here describe property), together with the appurtenances and all the estate and rights of the party of the first part in and to the said premises.

To have and to hold the above granted premises unto the said party of the second part, his heirs and assigns forever.

And the said party of the first part, doth covenant with said party of the second part, as follows:—

First. That the party of the first part is seized of the said premises in fee simple, and has good right to convey the same.

Second. That the party of the second part shall quietly enjoy the said premises.

Third. That the said premises are free from incumbrance.

Fourth. That the party of the first part will execute or procure any further necessary assurance of the title to said premises.

Fifth. That the party of the first part will forever warrant the title of said premises.

In witness whereof, the said party of the first part hath hereunto set his hand and seal the day and year first above written. A. B.

In the presence of, [L. S.]

B. C.

Acknowledgment for the above.

STATE OF NEW YORK, } *ss.:*
County of ..... }

On this .. day of ...., in the year ...., before me, the subscriber, personally came A. B. (and C. B., his wife), to me known to be the person (or persons) described in and who executed the within instrument, and (severally) acknowledged that he (or they) executed the same. J. A.,

(Give official title.)

NEW YORK.—"Every conveyance unless recorded is void against a subsequent purchaser in good faith, whose conveyance shall be first duly recorded. To entitle a conveyance to be recorded it must be acknowledged by the party or parties executing the same, or shall be proved by a subscribing witness." "The acknowledgment of married women may be made, taken, and certified in the same manner as if they were sole."

OHIO.—All deeds, mortgages, etc., executed within the State of Ohio must be signed by the grantor and acknowledged before two attesting witnesses, and the said grantor must also acknowledge the same before a judge of the court of record of that State or some other competent authority.

STATE OF OHIO, } *ss.:*
County of ...., }

Be it remembered that on this .. day of ...., 189.., before me, the subscriber, a (give official title), in and for the said county, came A. B., and C. B., his wife, the grantors in the foregoing instrument, and acknowledged the signing thereof to be their voluntary act and deed for the uses and purposes therein mentioned. And the said C. B., wife of the said A. B., being examined by me separate and apart from her said husband, and the contents of the said instrument being by me made known and explained to her as the statute directs, declared that she did voluntarily sign and acknowledge the same and that she is still satisfied therewith as her act and deed.

In testimony whereof I have hereunto set my hand and affixed my official seal, the day [L. S.] and year last above written.

(Signature and title.)

The following States require no separate examination in acknowledgments by husband and wife: Connecticut, the Dakotas, Illinois, Indiana, Iowa, Kansas, Maryland, Massachusetts, Michigan, Minnesota, Mississippi, Missouri, Nebraska, New Hampshire, New Mexico, New York, Wisconsin, Wyoming, and Washington.

The following States require a separate examination: Delaware, District of Columbia, Florida, Idaho, Kentucky, Nevada, New Jersey, North Carolina, Pennsylvania, Ohio, Rhode Island, South Carolina, Tennessee, and Texas.

Common Carriers.—A common carrier is one who, for a compensation, carries the goods of anyone offering them for transportation as a regular business.

Carrier's Obligations.—He must take all goods offered, unless of a dangerous kind. He must charge one person no higher rates than another. He must take such care of the goods as a prudent man would of his own. He must carry them by the usual route and make a proper delivery of them. He must place the goods in a proper place and give notice of their arrival.

Carrier's Liabilities.—In common law they are liable for all losses "except those occasioned by the act of God or the acts of the public enemy." He is responsible for losses by theft, robbery, etc.

Railroad companies are responsible as carriers to parties sending goods by express over their lines, irrespective of the said parties' contract with the express company.

A carrier's liability begins as soon as he has accepted the goods. It ends as soon as he has carried them to their destination and has deposited them there.

The notices on their receipts whereby they seek to avoid all responsibility, are "no evidence of assent on the part of the owner," and the liability cannot be avoided that way. He may avoid almost anything by making a special contract.

He might avoid liability by notice if he could prove that the shipper had read his notice or was familiar with its terms, though there is some question about this in New York at least.

Carriers of Passengers.—They are bound to make use of all ordinary methods for the safety of their passengers. They must employ proper vehicles and competent servants. In general, they are bound to run trains on their advertised time. They are liable to passengers for the misconduct of their servants. If any person is injured through their negligence, they are liable not only for the damage that person has received, but for *prospective* damage as well. He is an insurer of his passengers' baggage. He is liable for such baggage as his passengers carry for their own personal use. He cannot avoid liability by notices, as a notice is no evidence of the assent of the owner of the baggage. The carrier may avoid liability to some extent by a special contract.

They must take each person who tenders the price of transportation and wishes to be carried. They are not obliged to take disorderly or persons of doubtful character, or those afflicted with some contagious disease. They are not responsible to their passengers for accidents where all skill and diligence has been employed. Passengers are required to submit to all reasonable rules and regulations, to show their tickets whenever asked, and to surrender their tickets whenever required.

Currency.—The National Bank Act fixes the capital required to establish a National Bank as follows: Towns of less than 6,000 inhabitants, a capital of not less than $50,000; towns of from 6,000 to 50,000, a capital of not less than $100,000; in towns of over 50,000, at least $200,000 will be required.

Each bank must deposit with the Treasurer at Washington, government bonds to the extent of at least one third its capital, as security for the notes of the bank. The government then issues to the bank ninety per cent. in notes, which, when properly filled and signed, constitute the circulation of the bank.

Such banks are required to keep on hand at least twenty-five per cent. in legal tender of its circulation and deposits.

The notes of such banks are secured to the holders, but depositors run the same risk of loss as with other banks.

Checks.—A check is an order to a bank to pay the holder a certain sum of money on presentation and without days of grace.

A check, as in the case of a promissory note, may or may not be negotiable, according to the way it is drawn.

A check given is no payment of a debt unless paid when presented.

Payment of a check may be stopped at any time before it is presented if notice is given the bank.

Every indorser of a check is liable to each following indorser as in the case of promissory notes, but for no longer time than he would have been held had he been the maker of the check.

Certificates of Deposit partake of the nature of certified checks and are used when money is deposited for a short time and no regular bank account opened.

When wishing to draw your money in person, draw the check payable to "Self" or "Cash."

Write the amount of the check both in words and figures, taking care that no blank spaces are left that could be filled to "raise" the amount of the check.

Indorsements.— The *left-hand end* of a check is the *top*.

Write the indorsement across the back, a short distance from the top.

If your name has been improperly spelled in the body of the check, indorse it exactly as written therein, then below write your name properly.

If titles are used in the body of the check, they must appear with the name in the indorsement.

In drawing a check payable to one not known at the bank you can avoid the necessity of identification by having him indorse it in your presence and you write under it, "Above indorsement correct" and sign your name.

Checks that are to be deposited are usually indorsed, "For deposit," or "For deposit to the credit of," and such indorsements may be made by clerks, and the checks deposited to the credit of their firm. For further reference see indorsements of promissory notes.

Notes.— A promissory note is an unconditional promise in writing, to pay a certain person a certain sum of money at a certain future time. The essentials are that it be certainly paid, not out of any particular fund, nor dependent upon any contingency; that it be for the payment of money only.

Five important points of a negotiable promissory note are: (1) That the date of payment be specified. (2) That the amount be plainly stated. (3) That it be paid only in lawful money. (4) That the promise be without conditions. (5) That it contain the words "order" or "bearer," or other words showing the intention to make it negotiable.

Indorsement: A note is indorsed when anything relating to it is written upon the back. The writer of the name is called the *indorser*, and the person for whose benefit it is written is the *indorsee*.

There are five kinds of indorsements: (1) *In full.* (2) *In blank.* (3) *Conditional.* (4) *Qualified.* (5) *Restrictive.*

1. *In full:* When the name of the indorsee is mentioned, when none but he can demand payment. If he wishes to transfer it he must add his own indorsement in writing. This is the usual form and shows through what hands it passes.

2. *In blank:* Indorsement in blank consists of the indorser's name alone. It is then payable to bearer, and is transferred by simple delivery from hand to hand. The indorser in full or in blank is obligated to any subsequent holder if the maker does not pay it, and the indorser is given due notice of such failure.

3. *Conditional:* When the payment is made conditional upon some uncertain event.

4. *Qualified:* When the usual form is departed from and the indorser restrains, limits, or enlarges his liability as such.

An indorsement "without recourse to me" transfers the title and releases the indorser from any liability. The exact words used do not matter if they show the intention to avoid responsibility.

When acting for another party the words "agent," "attorney," or their equivalent will release, if added to the indorsement, the said agent from personal responsibility.

5. *Restrictive:* When the indorsement restrains the negotiability to some certain person as, "Pay to John Doe only," or "Pay John Doe for my account."

Transfer.—An indorsement to *bearer* is transferred by delivery; or, if indorsed *in blank*, it can be done in the same way by the indorsee, though drawn payable to *order*.

1. *Before maturity* an innocent purchaser can enforce the collection of a note, even if it be found to have been lost, stolen, or obtained by fraud. Five things are necessary: (1) That he obtained it in good faith. (2) That he was not aware of any defect in the title of the one from whom he obtained it. (3) That it be negotiable. (4) That it was obtained for value. (5) That it was obtained *before maturity*. Should he be aware of any defect in the title at the time of obtaining it, he takes it subject to any defense that could be legally brought against it at first.

2. *After maturity:* A note may still be negotiable, but the purchaser now takes it subject to any defense originally existing.

Demand.—No demand is necessary to hold the maker. For the purpose of holding those *conditionally* liable, a demand must be made first on those *primarily* liable.

1. Notes should be presented for payment by the holder or his authorized agent.

2. Demand should be made on the maker, or, in his absence, on his authorized agent.

3. To hold indorser, the demand must be made on the very day of maturity, no sooner, no later.

4. If no place of payment is specified in the note, it must be presented at the residence or place of business of the maker, and *during regular business hours.* A personal demand is not necessary when the place of payment is specified. It is sufficient if the note be sent there in due time.

Law of Place.—When given in one State and payable in another, it will be governed by the laws of the State where payable, in the matter of interest, if the rate is not mentioned. The "law merchant" is, that the maker is bound by the laws of the place where made; the indorser by the law where indorsed; demand, days of grace, etc., by the laws where payable.

Payment.—Possession is presumptive evidence of title on paper drawn or indorsed, payable to bearer, and payment may be made to the one presenting it. Before paying, the maker should be careful that any indorsements are genuine, and that the title is properly transferred. Payment by an indorser satisfies only so far as the subsequent indorsers are concerned, for the note is not discharged until paid by the maker. After an indorser has paid a dishonored note, he may put it in circulation again.

The holder takes his title from the *first* indorser if made in blank or is a general indorsement, and the maker is protected in making payment to him.

Non-payment.—If the only parties concerned are the *original ones*, demand need not be made at maturity. The whole object of demand, protest, and notice of non-payment is to hold the indorsers or others conditionally liable.

Protest.—A protest is a formal statement made by a notary public, giving a copy or description of the note, stating that payment has been demanded and refused, giving reason of refusal, if any, and the purpose and object of the protest. The protest must be made by the notary *personally*, and duly signed and sealed.

Notice.—1. Notice should be given by the holder or some suitable person authorized to act for him. The notary may do this.

2. Notices must be served on all whom the holder wishes to make responsible for the payment. He may notify all prior parties, or only the immediate indorser, as he may wish. Each indorser should protect his own interests by notifying all parties responsible to him. Indorsers are liable, in order of their respective indorsements, to each subsequent indorser.

3. Due diligence must be exercised in giving the notice. It is best to give it the same day, but if the dishonor occurs Saturday or immediately preceding a holiday, it will be in time if given the succeeding secular day. Certain obstacles, as war, prevalence of a contagious disease, floods, or act of Providence, will be accepted as legal excuses for want of notice.

4. Any place will do, if given personally. Notice in writing may be left at the place of business or at the house of the person to be notified. When the person resides at a distance he may be notified by a letter properly addressed and mailed to the office where he receives his letters.

5. The notice may be either verbal or written, and any form that clearly conveys the idea intended will be sufficient. The note should be clearly described. It is well described when its maker, payee, date, amount, and time and place of payment are named.

Personal notice must be given when the holder and person to be notified live in the same place, unless the laws of the State do not require it. In New York and many other States written notice properly addressed and mailed is sufficient

Notice of Protest.

$587.00.

SECOND NATIONAL BANK, Utica, N. Y.,
June 23, 1894.

Take notice that the promissory note made by C. M. Taylor for $587 and interest, dated October 2, 1893, payable to your order at this bank, payable this day and indorsed by you, is protested for nonpayment, and the holder, J. B. Morrow, looks to you for the payment thereof, payment of the same having this day been demanded and refused.

Respectfully yours,
H. K. LONG,
Notary Public.

TO J. L. BROWNE.

The indorser may waive demand of payment, notice of protest, etc., at the time of the indorsement, or even at any time before maturity. The following is the usual form: "I hereby waive demand, protest, and notice of dishonor." (Signed) ——— ———.

Guaranty.—Guaranties are of two kinds, guaranty of payment and guaranty of collection.

1. Guaranty of payment absolutely guarantees that the note shall be paid at maturity

2. Guaranty of collection holds the guarantor after the holder has failed to collect of the maker.

The general rule is that the guarantor is not entitled to demand and notice of protest. The following is the usual form. "For value received I hereby guaranty the payment (or collection) of the within note. (Signed)
JOHN F. HERRICK.

Defenses.—1. Want of consideration, if total, is a perfect defense. If it is only a partial failure it will defeat recovery only to that extent.

2. Obtained through fear or compulsion. The threats and duress must be such as would cause a person of ordinary firmness of mind to apprehend danger to himself, reputation, or property.

3. Fraud. Fraud vitiates all contracts.

4. Obtained by finding or theft. This is no defense against a *bona fide* and innocent purchaser who obtains the note *before* maturity and gives a valuable consideration for it.

5. Illegal consideration. A note illegal on its face gives warning to all. A note showing on its face that it called for more than the legal rate of interest would be subject to such defense.

Notes given for "debts of honor" are void between original parties, but if indorsed and negotiated, the first indorser would be holden.

Presumptions.—1. The law presumes that the negotiable paper was given for a consideration, whether expressed or not. The contrary must be proven to constitute a defense.

2. The holder is presumed to be the owner.

3. Indorsements and transfers are presumed to be made before the paper became due.

4. The law presumes the holder to have acquired the paper in the usual course of business

5. It is conclusively presumed that the paper means precisely what it says and parol evidence will not be allowed to offset it.

A note given by a lunatic, an intoxicated person or a minor, is void.

A note given by one who cannot write should be witnessed by an uninterested person.

A person receiving a note, knowing it to be defective, has no better title than the person from whom he purchased.

A note as a gift, being without consideration, is voidable.

If the holder of a note extends the time of payment to the maker, his action releases all persons conditionally liable.

In a note containing "*we promise*," or "*we jointly promise*," the liability is a joint one, and all must be sued; "*we or either of us promise*," or "*we jointly and severally promise*," here the liability is both joint and several and either or all the parties may be sued.

In a note containing "*I promise*" and signed by two or more persons, each signer is obligated for the whole amount, and either or all may be sued.

After becoming of age a minor may ratify a note given during his minority.

Forms of Notes.

A Note Negotiable Without Indorsement.

$250. St. Louis, June 8, 1899.
Thirty days after date I promise to pay J. H. Ames, or bearer, Two Hundred and Fifty Dollars, at the Third National Bank in St. Louis, for value received. Charles Carns.

A Note Negotiable Only by Indorsement.

$200. Chicago, Nov. 26, 1899.
Three months after date I promise to pay John H. Woltering, or order, Two Hundred Dollars, value received. J. T. Norton.

A Note Not Negotiable.

$200. St. Louis, Nov. 17, 1899.
Ninety days after date I promise to pay Charles C. Collins Two Hundred Dollars, value received.
Samuel Atkinson.

A Note Bearing Interest.

$100. Baton Rouge, La., Nov. 26, 1899.
Six months after date I promise to pay R. V. Jennings, or order, One Hundred Dollars, with interest, for value received. John Q. Watson.

A Note Payable on Demand.

$150. Philadelphia, Nov. 30, 1899.
On demand I promise to pay Lamonte Whittlesey, or bearer, One Hundred and Fifty Dollars, value received. John Q. Chaffington.

A Note Payable at Bank.

$100. Cincinnati, Dec. 24, 1899.
Thirty days after date I promise to pay Thomas I. Rankin, or order, at the Second National Bank, One Hundred Dollars, value received.
Frank T. Morrison.

Principal and Surety.

$793. Newark, N. J., Dec. 28, 1899.
Sixty days after date I promise to pay Daniel O'C. Patterson, or order, Seven Hundred and Ninety-three Dollars, with interest, value received.
John G. Watterson, *Principal.*
T. R. Graham, *Security.*

Promissory Note Secured by Mortgage.

$1,000. Lansing, Mich., Dec. 1, 1899.
One year after date I promise to pay to S. H. Moore One Thousand Dollars at the First National Bank of Lansing, Mich., with interest at the rate of ten per cent. per annum, for value received.

This note is secured by a mortgage of even date herewith, on a certain tract or parcel of land situate (*describe the premises*).
(*Signed*) R. S. Marsh.

A Married Woman's Note in New York.

$400. New York, Dec. 13, 1899.
Three months after date I promise to pay Johnson, Dunham & Co., or order, Four Hundred Dollars, with interest. And I hereby charge my individual property and estate with the payment of this note. Clara C. Dickerson.

A Joint Note.

$3,000. Detroit, Mich., Dec. 12, 1899.
One year after date we jointly promise to pay E. C. Langworthy, or order, Three Thousand Dollars, value received. John C. Jennings.
Walter D. Curtis.

A Joint and Several Note.

$3,000. Detroit, Mich., Dec. 12, 1899.
One year after date we jointly and severally promise to pay E. C. Langworthy, or order, Three Thousand Dollars, value received.
John C. Jennings.
Walter D. Curtis.

A Partnership Note.

No. — Boston, Mass., Nov. 26, 1899.
One month after date, without grace, we promise to pay to the order of ourselves Two Hundred and Fifty Dollars, at any bank in Boston.
Johnson & Co.,
$250. Due Dec. 26, 1899. 209 Temple Place.

A Note Payable by Installments.

$3,000. Philadelphia, Pa., April 20, 1899.
For value received, I promise to pay Smith & Brown, or order, Three Thousand Dollars, in the manner following, viz.: One thousand dollars in one year, one thousand dollars in two years, and one thousand dollars in three years, with interest on all said sums, payable semi-annually, without defalcation or discount. Hugh Faulkner,
120 Chestnut St.

Sealed Note.

$5,000. Cleveland, O., May 8, 1899.
For value received, I promise to pay Smith & Edgar, or order, Five Thousand Dollars, in three years from the date hereof, with interest, payable semi-annually, without defalcation or discount. And in case of default of my payment of the interest or principal aforesaid with punctuality, I hereby empower any attorney-at-law, to be appointed by said Smith & Edgar, or their assigns, to appear in any court which said Smith & Edgar, or their assigns, may select, and commence and prosecute a suit against me on said note, to confess judgment for all and every part of the interest or principal on said note, in the payment of which I may be delinquent.

Witness my hand and seal, this 8th day of June, A. D. 1899. John Drew. [SEAL.]
Attest, George White.

Judgment Note.

$425 $\frac{25}{100}$.
For value received, I promise to pay to John Doe, or order, Four Hundred Twenty-five and 25-100 dollars ($425.25), three months after date; and I here nominate, constitute, and appoint the said John Doe, or any attorney-at-law of this State, my true and lawful attorney, for me and in my name to appear at any court of record of this State, at any time after the above promissory note becomes due, and to waive all processes and serv

ices thereof, and to confess judgment in favor of the holder herein, for the sum that may be due and owing hereon, with interest and costs and waiving all errors.

In Witness Whereof, I have hereunto set my hand and seal at Williamsport, Pa., this first day of June, 1899. [SEAL.] RICHARD ROE.

Indorsements.

In Blank.	In Full.	General.
L. A. Davis.	*Pay Chas. Evans or order. L. A. Davis.*	*Pay Chas. Evans. L. A. Davis.*

Qualified.	Conditional.	Restrictive.
Pay Chas. Evans or order, without recourse. L. A. Davis.	*Pay Chas. Evans or order, unless payment forbidden before maturity. L. A. Davis.*	*Pay Chas. Evans only. L. A. Davis.*

Forms of Guaranty.

Guaranty of a Note.

For value received, I guarantee the due payment of a promissory note, dated October 8, 1883, whereby John Paxson promises to pay George Andrews Eighty Dollars in three months.

ST. LOUIS, Oct. 10, 1883. PETER FABER.

General Guaranty.

I hereby guarantee payment to any person who shall accept and retain this instrument as a guaranty, for all goods which he may from time to time supply to Eugene Parsons, not exceeding at any time the sum of Five Hundred Dollars, this to be a continuing guaranty till specially revoked. Notice to be given me within ten days after its acceptance. DARBY CONGER.

ST. LOUIS, Sept. 8, 1883.

Extension of Time.

In consideration that George Andrews gives to John Paxson additional time to the extent of one month for payment of the indebtedness due him from said John Paxson guaranteed by me, I hereby continue my guaranty for due payment thereof.

January 8, 1884. PETER FABER.

Guaranty of Fidelity.

In consideration of the performance of the agreements and covenants specified in the within agreement by M. M., with my son, A. A., I do hereby bind myself to said M. M. for the true and faithful observation and performance of all the matters and things by said A. A. agreed and covenanted therein, and that he shall well and truly serve said M. M.

Witness my hand this —— day of ——, A.D.——.

P. A.

Contracts.—A contract is "an agreement for a suitable consideration to do or not to do a certain thing."

The essentials of a contract are: 1. *The Parties;* 2. *Consideration;* 3. *Subject-matter;* 4. *Asssent;* 5. *Time.* These are essential and the other elements are those that give to the contract its particular character.

1. *The Parties.*—The parties must be competent. A contract with a minor is not binding upon him for anything except necessaries, though he may hold the other party to a strict accounting. What constitute necessaries would depend upon the age, the rank, and fortune of the minor.

2. *Consideration.*—No contract is valid without a sufficient consideration. Consideration may be divided; as (A) VALUABLE; (B) GOOD; (C) INSUFFICIENT.

(A) VALUABLE CONSIDERATION is usually expressed by money or is convertible into money.

(B) A GOOD CONSIDERATION is founded on love, affection or gratitude. It will be accepted as consideration for a contract already performed, but is not good for contracts to be performed some time in the future. As a gift already made but not holding for one promised.

(C) INSUFFICIENT CONSIDERATION may be classed, as (D) GRATUITOUS; (E) ILLEGAL; (F) IMPOSSIBLE; (G) MORAL.

GRATUITOUS.—A contract based on a promise wholly gratuitous is void for want of consideration. Examples: Public subscriptions, charities, etc.

ILLEGAL.—A contract with an illegal consideration is void. A contract to commit, conceal, or compound a crime is void. Either party may avoid the contract where the consideration is illegal.

IMPOSSIBLE.—If the consideration is impossible the contract is void. The law compels no one to perform impossibilities. That the consideration was difficult would not be an excuse.

MORAL.—A moral obligation, alone, is not a sufficient consideration. A person is not legally obligated to pay for services already rendered a relative, even though he promise to do so after the services are performed. Had the person promised before the service was performed, the case would be different. The position of a parent and minor child would be an exception.

3. *Subject-matter.*—All contracts the subject-matter of which is illegal, immoral, or impolitic are void.

Contracts in restraint of trade are void even though given for a valuable consideration. A contract not to carry on a lawful business *anywhere*, whether the time be limited or not, is invalid. An agreement in partial restraint of trade, if confined within reasonable bounds, or to certain persons and given for a sufficient consideration, would be valid.

A doctor might sell his practice and agree not to practice within a certain number of miles of the place. If given for a valuable consideration, the contract would be valid. The court would decide the reasonableness of the limitation.

Contracts in general restraint of marriage are void, because against public policy. A contract not to marry a particular person would be valid. A contract not to marry until of a suitable or reasonable age is valid. The condition that a widow shall forfeit certain portions of her deceased husband's estate if she marry again may be valid, if she accepted it under those conditions.

Fraud vitiates any contract if the innocent party so wishes, otherwise the other party may be held. A contract that operates as a fraud on third parties is void. Examples: Fraudulent assignments; fraudulent sales; perversion of insolvent laws.

"Fraud consists in the employment of any kind of cunning, deception, artifice, or concealment to cheat, circumvent, or deceive another in a business matter." If both parties are equally guilty, neither has usually any redress at law. If one party is more innocent, the reverse is true. The innocent party may many times hold the other if he chooses, or himself refuse to be bound by the contract. The guilty party cannot avoid the contract on account of his own fraud if the contract is already executed.

4. *Assent.*—There can be no contract valid and binding, unless the parties assent to the same thing and in the same sense. There must be a proposition by one party and an acceptance by the other.

If the proposition and acceptance are made by mail, the contract is presumed to be completed as soon as the acceptance is mailed, and even a telegram countermanding it before the letter was received need not necessarily be allowed to avoid it.

5. *Time.*—Time enters into the contract as an essential element and is either expressed or implied. Something to be done between two certain days is not performed if done on either of those days. If the day for performance falls upon Sunday, the performing party has the privilege of performing on the next secular day.

Statute of Frauds.—By the "Statute of Frauds," which has been adopted by most States, certain contracts must be in writing. The following are those adopted by New York and most other States: "Every contract for the leasing of a longer period than one year, or for the sale of any lands, or any interest in lands, shall be void, unless the contract or some note or memorandum thereof, expressing the consideration, be in writing and be subscribed by the party by whom the lease or sale is made." Annual crops resulting from cultivation, if the price is less than fifty dollars, do not come within the meaning of the statute; as corn, wheat, oats, potatoes, etc.

In the following cases every agreement shall be void unless such agreement, or some note or memorandum thereof, be in writing and subscribed by the party to be charged therewith:

1. Every agreement that, by its terms, is not to be performed within one year from the making thereof.

2. Every special promise to answer for the debt, default, or miscarriage of another.

3. Every agreement, promise, or undertaking, made upon consideration of marriage, except mutual promises to marry.

4. Every contract for the sale of any chattels, goods, or things in action, for the price of fifty dollars or more shall be void unless,

"*First*, A note or memorandum of such contract be made in writing and subscribed by the parties to be charged thereby; or,

"*Second*, Unless the buyer shall accept and receive part of such goods or the evidences, or some of them, of such things in action; or,

"*Third*, Unless the buyer shall, at the time, pay some part of the purchase money."

In addition to being written, there must be a consideration in the contracts, as above, either express or implied.

"A party to a contract is not bound until he yields a full, free, and intelligent assent of its terms." "An offer made may be retracted any time before its acceptance."

A competent party making contract with a minor cannot hold the minor, except as before noted, but the minor can sue and recover for the nonperformance of the other party.

Contracts required to be in writing by the "Statute of Frauds," hold only the party signing if but one signs. The other has it at his option.

Damages.—"Perform your contract or pay damages." The law cannot compel the performance of a contract; it only knows a money remedy for nonperformance. In a contract for personal service which cannot well be filled by another, the sickness of the promising party will excuse nonperformance.

A court of equity may compel the performance of certain agreements: as the conveyance of real estate.

Construction. — The following rules are observed in the interpretation of contracts:

1. INTENTION.— The first care is to give effect to the intention of the parties so far as the intention was mutual and legal.

2. MEANING OF TERMS.— The terms of a contract are to be interpreted according to their usual meaning, if that seems to satisfy the intention of the parties. Technical words are interpreted according to their use in the profession, or the trade to which they belong.

Interpretation. — Certain contracts are expounded according to the usage or custom of trade when needed to explain the meaning of peculiar terms. The law of place would also enter as a factor; if the custom of the place where the contract was made differed from other places, that would give a different meaning to its terms.

The interpretation is made upon the *whole* contract and not upon its parts. The object of the parties is to be gathered from the *whole* instrument, and one clause will be interpreted by another.

Wherever one portion cannot be reconciled with the obvious intention of the parties, it will be expunged. "Effect will be given to the whole intention."

Forms of Contracts. — *A General Release.*

Know all men by these presents: That I, A. B., of . . . . . , in consideration of . . . . . , and other good and valuable considerations to me in hand paid by A. C., of . . . . . . , have remised, released and forever discharged, and by these presents do, for me, my heirs, executors and administrators, remise, release, and forever discharge said A. C., his heirs, executors, and administrators, of and from all and all manner of actions, suits, debts, dues, sums of money, accounts, reckonings, bonds, bills, specialties, covenants, contracts, controversies, agreements, promises, variances, damages, judgments, executions, claims and demands whatsoever, in law or equity, which against the said A. B. I ever had, now have, or which I, my heirs, my executors and administrators hereafter can, shall, or may have, for, upon or by reason of any matter, cause or thing whatsoever (or by reason of . . . . . .), from the beginning of the world to the day of the date of these presents.

In witness whereof, I have hereunto set my hand and seal, this . . . . . . day of . . . . . . A. D. 189 . .

(Signed) A. B. [L. S.]

Signed and delivered in the presence of

D. E.

Memorandum of Sale. — It is agreed by and between A. B. and B. E., of, etc., that said A. B., in consideration of two hundred bushels of wheat, sold to him this day by the said B. E., free of all charges or expenses, whatsoever, at . . . . . . , on or before . . . . . . , shall and will pay or cause to be paid to the said B. E., or his assigns, upon such delivery, the sum of . . . . . . dollars.

And the said B. E., in consideration of the agreement aforesaid of the said A. B., doth promise and agree, on or before the said . . . . , at his own expense, to send in and deliver to the said A. B., or his assigns, the said two hundred bushels of wheat so sold to him as aforesaid, and the said B. E. shall and will warrant the same to be good, clean, and merchantable grain.

In witness whereof, the said parties have hereunto set their hands the day and year first above written.

A. B.

In presence of B. E.

C. D.

Lease of House.—I, ... of . . . . . . , hereby lease to . . . . . . of . . . . . . , for the term of . . . . . . , to commence on . . . . . . the dwelling house (describe it) with its appurtenances, for the yearly rent of . . . . . . , to be paid . . . . . .

Said . . . . . . , agrees to pay said . . . . . , said rents at the times above specified and to surrender the premises at the expiration of the term, in as good condition as reasonable use will allow, fire and unavoidable accidents excepted.

In witness whereof, the said parties have hereunto set their hands this . . . . . . of . . . . . . , A. D. 189 . .

(Signed) —— ——.
(Signed) —— ——.

General Form of Contract.—Memorandum of an agreement made this . . . . . day of . . . . . , in the year 189 . . , between A. B., of . . . . . , as first party, and B. C., of . . . . . . , as second party,

Witnesseth: That the said first party hereby agrees to, etc., ... (Here insert first party's obligations.)

In consideration of the above being faithfully kept and performed by the said first party, the said second party, etc. (Here insert second party's obligations.)

In witness whereof, we have hereunto set our hands and seals the day and year first above written.

A. B.

In the presence of B. C.

C. D.

A seal on an instrument is usually conclusive proof that it was given for a consideration, but the laws of New York permit evidence to be submitted on rebuttal of this presumption.

Partnerships.—"A partnership is a contract between two or more competent persons for joining together their money, goods, labor and skill, or any or all of them, under an understanding that there shall be a communion of profit between them, and for the purpose of carrying on a legal trade, business, or adventure.—STORY.

Partners: Any person of sound mind and able to conduct ordinary business may enter into a partnership. An infant may be a partner, but in general he could incur no liability and might disaffirm the contract at any time. Married women can be partners only in such States as have removed their disabilities.

Partners are grouped as follows:—

Ostensible, those whose names are known and appear as partners; *nominal*, those who appear to the world as partners, but who have really no interest in the business.

Nominal partners are responsible to all creditors who gave the firm credit because of their apparent connection with it.

Dormant partners are those who do not appear to the world as partners, but are actually interested in the business. They are liable to creditors of the business. *Special* partners are those who supply a certain amount of capital, and on complying with certain requirements are not liable for debts of the firm above the amount they invest.

Relations of Partners: Mutual respect, confidence in the honesty, skill, judgment, and good business instinct of each other must be the basis of each partnership. On this account, if the partnership suffers through the neglect of any partner, he is liable to the others. He is liable in damages to the other partners for any breach of partnership contract.

No partner has any right to engage in any private business that will in any way operate to the detriment of the partnership.

The powers of all partners in ordinary cases are equal and neither can exclude the other from a share in the management of the business or from the possession of partnership property.

A partnership can only exist by voluntary contract, and no third party can be introduced into the firm without unanimous consent.

Powers of Partners: The acts of one partner bind all the rest. Each partner has power to transact any and all necessary business for the partnership. The frauds of one partner bind the firm, though the others have no knowledge of his action. The partner should transact all business in the name of the firm, otherwise he alone is liable. He has no power to bind the partnership outside the transaction of the regular business of the firm. The fraud of a partner will not bind the partnership if the third party is aware of the fraud or that the partner is exceeding his authority. Each partner is liable to third parties for partnership debts to the extent of his whole private property.

Subject-matter: By this is meant the business in which they have engaged. The essence of the contract is, that the partners are *jointly* concerned in the profits and losses, or at least the profits of some legitimate business. If the contract does not specify the manner of division, they will be supposed to be divided equally.

Articles of Co-partnership.—If the business is extensive, or the relations to continue for a great length of time, formal articles should be adopted. Any form that clearly sets forth the nature of the business, the investments of each partner, the division of the profits and losses, the powers and duties of each partner, the commencement and termination of the partnership, will answer the purpose. The partnership commences at once if no other time is specified. The laws of New York prohibit the use of fictitious names in the firm name. "& Co." cannot there be used unless it represent an actual partner. If no time is expressed for termination, the partnership is presumed to be "at will" only, and may be dissolved at any time.

Dissolution.—This may take place by acts of the parties, by judicial decree, by operation of law.

A partnership may be dissolved at any time by mutual consent. If the partnership is for any specified time it may be dissolved by one partner refusing to act with the other, or by his assigning his share to a third party. Such assignment does not constitute the third party a partner without the consent of all the others. A partnership for a certain time expires when that period is passed.

The partnership could be dissolved by judicial decree at any time for good and sufficient reasons, as unfitness or inability of a partner developed after the commencement of the partnership, or should the business be impracticable or when founded in error.

The law would operate to dissolve the partnership if one partner became insane, idiotic, or in any way incapable of performing his duties.

All right, title and interest of any partner may be sold under execution against him. The bankruptcy of one partner would dissolve the partnership unless provided for by special agreement.

After dissolution no power remains to create new obligations, and a partner could not renew a partnership note, or even indorse one to pay a prior debt of the firm. Unless provided for, to the contrary, each partner has power to collect accounts and to settle up the affairs of the business.

A notice of dissolution to all persons dealing with the firm is necessary when the retiring partner wishes to avoid further liability for debts incurred by the partnership. The retiring partner is already liable for all prior debts. To avoid responsibility, notice must be given to each person who has had dealings with the partnership. A notice published in the local paper will do for all subsequent creditors.

Wills.—No particular form of a will is required. Any words that clearly convey the idea of the testator are sufficient.

Kinds.—Unwritten or nuncupative and written. All wills must be written, except those of soldiers and sailors when in actual service, or in some States they may be allowed in extreme cases when a necessity. The parties to a will are the testator or person making the will, the donee or person benefited by the will, and the executor or person empowered to see that the provisions of the will are carried out.

Testator.—The testator must be competent. In New York, males of 18 years of age and females of 16 years of age may dispose of personal property. A married woman cannot make a valid will without the consent of her husband, except in those States where their disabilities have been removed. The testator must possess mind and memory enough to fully understand the nature and consequences of his action.

Donee.—The donees are the persons benefiting by the will.

They are called devisees when the gift is of real estate, and legatees when the gift is one of personal property.

Any person in general, capable of acquiring property by his own exertion, may be a donee. Corporations cannot take by will unless empowered to do so by their charters.

Executor.—Any person capable of making a will may be an executor.

He must see that the deceased is buried in a suitable manner; he must file a bond, offer the will for probate, make the return and inventory, collect the property, pay the debts and distribute the remainder according to the terms of the will. He must render an account of all, and file with the probate office.

Subject-matter.—Little form is necessary for disposing of personal property. A will might be accepted for disposing of personal property when parts relating to real estate would not be valid.

By common law the testator must be possessed of real estate he devises at the time the will is made. By the laws of Vermont, Massachusetts, New York, Pennsylvania and Virginia, he may devise any that he is possessed of at the time of his death, if that was evidently his intention. The laws of Maine, Ohio, Illinois, and Connecticut are similar.

Execution.—The will must be signed by the testator, or by some person acting for him at his request. When he signs or acknowledges the will he must declare it to be his last will.

It is best to have three witnesses, though some of the States require but two. The New England States and some of the Southern States require three; the Middle and Western States in general require two; Louisiana requires four witnesses. The witnesses must write their names and addresses as witnesses. New York prescribes a fine of fifty dollars for their failure to do so.

The testator must sign or acknowledge his signature in the presence of these witnesses. A codicil to be valid must be witnessed with the same formalities as the will.

A subsequent will revokes the preceding one. All witnesses should be disinterested parties.

The following States have particular provisions in their statutes concerning wills:—

New York.—No person having a husband, wife, child, or parent, shall devise more than one half of his or her estate to any charitable, literary, scientific, or kindred institution. Should a testator marry after making a will disposing of the whole of his estate, and there should be born an issue of such marriage, unless provision shall have been made for such issue, by settlement, or unless the will provides for such issue, or shows an intention not to provide for such issue, the will shall be revoked and no other evidence shall be submitted in rebuttal.

A child born after the making of a will, and not provided for by will or settlement, shall succeed to such portion of the estate as would have fallen to it had the parent died intestate.

A bequest to a witness renders the will void only so far as the witness and his bequest is concerned. He is a competent witness still.

Colorado.—A married man cannot by will deprive his wife of more than one half his estate. A married woman cannot deprive her husband of more than one half her estate without his consent in writing.

Connecticut.—No bequest can be given to

a subscribing witness, and a subsequent marriage or birth of a child revokes the will unless specially provided for therein.

District of Columbia.—Bequests to any minister, teacher, or religious sect or denomination, unless made at least one month before the testator's death, are void.

Iowa.—Disposition of homestead or other privileged property to wife and family is void.

Kansas.—A married person cannot, without the consent of the husband or wife, dispose of more than one half of his or her property.

Maine.—A posthumous child shares the same as though there was no will, unless otherwise provided for.

Massachusetts.—A bequest to a subscribing witness is void, or to the husband or wife of such witness, unless there are three other witnesses.

New Hampshire.—Bequest to subscribing witness void without there are three other subscribing witnesses.

New Jersey.—Same as Maine.

Pennsylvania.—Bequest to a charity within one month of testator's death is void.

Short Form for a Will.—I, James Dickson, of the city of Chicago, in the county of Cook, and State of Illinois, being of sound mind and memory and understanding, do make my last will and testament in manner and form following:—

First. I give and bequeath to my daughters Mary and Jane two thousand dollars each after they have attained the age of twenty years.

Second. I give and bequeath to my wife Susan all my household furniture, and all the rest of my personal property, after paying from the same the legacies already named, to be hers forever: but if there should not be at my decease sufficient personal property to pay the aforesaid legacies, then so much of my real estate shall be sold as will raise sufficient money to pay the same.

Third. I also give, devise, and bequeath to my wife Susan all the rest and residue of my real estate as long as she shall remain unmarried, and my widow; but on her decease or marriage, the remainder thereof I give and devise to my said children and their heirs, respectively, to be divided in equal shares between them.

I appoint my wife Susan sole executrix of this my last will and testament.

In testimony whereof, I hereunto set my hand and seal, and publish and decree this to be my last will and testament, in the presence of the witnesses named below, this eighth day of March, in the year of our Lord one thousand eight hundred and ninety-three.

James Dickson. [L. S.]

Signed, sealed, declared and published by the said James Dickson as and for his last will and testament, in the presence of us, who, at his request and in his presence, and in presence of each other, have subscribed our names as witnesses hereto.

John Smith, residing at Chicago in Cook County.

Peter Jones, residing at Chicago in Cook County.

Another Form of Will. *Know all men by these presents:* That I, Joseph Atkinson, of Media, in the county of Chester, and State of Pennsylvania, merchant, considering the uncertainty of this life, and being of sound mind and memory, do make, and declare, and publish, this my last will and testament.

First. I give and bequeath unto my beloved wife Mary the use, improvement and income of my dwelling house, warehouses, lands, and their appurtenances, situate in Nelson township, Chester county, State of Pennsylvania, to have and to hold the same to her for and during her natural life.

Second. I give and bequeath to my son Robert two thousand dollars, to be paid to him by my executor, hereinafter named, within six months after my decease; and I also give, devise, and bequeath to my said son Robert the reversion or remainder of my dwelling house, warehouses, lands and their appurtenances, situate in Nelson township, Chester county, State of Pennsylvania, and all profit, income, and advantage that may result therefrom, from and after the decease of my beloved wife Mary.

Third. I give, devise, and bequeath to my beloved wife Mary all the residue of my estate, real, personal, or mixed, of which I shall be seized or possessed, or to which I shall be entitled at the time of my decease; to have and to hold the same to her and her executors and administrators and assigns forever.

Fourth. I do nominate and appoint my brother James Atkinson to be the executor of this, my last will and testament.

In testimony whereof, I have to this, my last will and testament, contained on two sheets of paper, and to each sheet thereof, subscribed my name and set my seal; and to this, the last sheet thereof, I have here subscribed my name and affixed my seal, this eighteenth day of May, in the year of our Lord one thousand eight hundred and ninety-three.

James Atkinson. [L. S.]

Signed, sealed, declared and published by the said James Atkinson, as and for his last will and testament, in presence of us, who, at his request and in his presence, and in presence of each other, have subscribed our names as witnesses hereto.

THOMAS MAY, residing at Media, Pa.
JOHN NOLAN, " " " "
HENRY MANN, " " " "

Codicil to a Will.—Whereas, I, Richard Roe, of the city of Pittsburg, in the county of Allegheny and State of Pennsylvania, have made my last will and testament, in writing, bearing date the fourteenth day of February, in the year of our Lord one thousand eight hundred and ninety-three, in and by which I have given to the Pennsylvania Institution for Deaf Mutes, in the city of Philadelphia, the sum of one thousand dollars.

Now, therefore, I do, by this my writing, which I hereby declare to be a codicil to my said last will and testament, and to be taken as a part thereof, order and declare that my will is that only the sum of five hundred dollars shall be paid to the said Pennsylvania Institution for Deaf Mutes as the full amount bequeathed to the said institution, and that the residue of the said legacy be given to the person who shall be acting as treasurer at the time of my decease of the Baptist Publication Society, located in the city of Philadelphia, to be expended by the society in such manner as the officers of the said society may deem best for the interests of said society; and, lastly, it is my desire that this codicil be annexed to and made a part of my last will and testament as aforesaid, to all intents and purposes.

In testimony whereof, etc. (as in form of will).

MISCELLANEOUS FORMS.

Mortgage of Lands by Husband and Wife.—This Indenture, made the——day of——, in the year of our Lord one thousand eight hundred and——, between F. F., of the city of New York, merchant, and J. his wife, of the first part, and L. M., of said city, merchant, of the second part, *witnesseth:* That the said parties of the first part, for and in consideration of the sum of——, lawful money of the United States, to them in hand paid, the receipt whereof is hereby acknowledged, have granted, bargained, sold, aliened, released, conveyed, and confirmed, and by these presents do grant, bargain, sell, alien, release, convey, and confirm, unto the said party of the second part, and to his assigns forever, all that certain lot, etc.; together with all and singular the hereditaments and appurtenances thereunto belonging, or in any wise appertaining, and the reversion and reversions, remainder and remainders, rents, issues, and profits thereof; and also all the estate, right, title, interest, dower, possession, claim, and demand whatsoever, of the said parties of the first part, of, in, and to the same, and every part thereof, with the appurtenances: To have and to hold the said hereby granted premises, with the appurtenances, unto the said party of the second part, his heirs and assigns, to his and their only proper use, benefit, and behoof forever. Provided always, and these presents are upon this condition, that if the said parties of the first part, their heirs, executors, administrators, or assigns, shall pay unto the said party of the second part, his executors, administrators, or assigns, the sum of——, on or before the——day of——, which will be in the year——, with interest, according to the condition of a bond of the said F. F., to the said L. M., bearing even date herewith, then these presents shall become void, and the estate hereby granted shall cease and utterly determine. But if default shall be made in the payment of the said sum of money, or the interest, or of any part thereof, at the time hereinbefore specified for the payment thereof, the said parties of the first part, in such case, do hereby authorize and fully empower the said party of the second part, his executors, administrators, and assigns, to sell the said hereby granted premises at public auction, and convey the same to the purchaser, in fee simple, agreeably to the act in such case made and provided, and out of the moneys arising from such sale, to retain the principal and interest which shall then be due on the said bond, together with all costs and charges, and pay the overplus (if any) to the said F. F., party of the first part, his heirs, executors, administrators, or assigns.

In witness whereof, the parties to these presents have hereunto set their hands and seals, the day and year first above written.

Sealed and delivered in the presence of John Smith.

FRANCIS FOREST. [L. S.]
JULIA FOREST. [L. S.]

Articles of Copartnership.—Articles of copartnership made and concluded this——day of——, in the year one thousand eight hundred and sixty, by and between A. B., bookseller, of the first part, and C. D., bookseller, of the second part, both of——, in the county of——.

Whereas, it is the intention of the said parties to form a copartnership, for the purpose of carrying on the retail business of booksellers and stationers, for which purpose they have agreed on the following terms and articles of agreement, to the faithful performance of which they mutually bind and engage themselves each to the other, his executors and administrators.

First. The style of the said copartnership shall be "—— and company"; and it shall continue for the term of —— years from the above date, except in case of the death of either of the said parties within the said term.

Second. The said A. B. and C. D. are the proprietors of the stock, a schedule of which is contained in their stock book, in the proportion of two thirds to the said A. B., and of one third to the said C. D.; and the said parties shall continue to be owners of their joint stock in the same proportions; and in case of any addition being made to the same by mutual consent, the said A. B. shall advance two thirds, and the said C. D. one third of the cost thereof.

Third. All profits which may accrue to the said partnership shall be divided, and all losses happening to the said firm, whether from bad debts, depreciation of goods, or any other cause or accident, and all expenses of the business, shall be borne by the said parties in the aforesaid proportions of their interest in the said stock.

Fourth. The said C. D. shall devote and give all his time and attention to the business of the said firm as a salesman, and generally to the care and superintendence of the store; and the said A. B. shall devote so much of his time as may be requisite, in advising, overseeing, and directing the importation of books and other articles necessary to the said business.

Fifth. All the purchases, sales, transactions, and accounts of the said firm shall be kept in regular books, which shall be always open to the inspection of both parties and their legal representatives respectively. An account of stock shall be taken, and an account between the said parties shall be settled, as often as once in every year, and as much oftener as either partner may desire and in writing request.

Sixth. Neither of the said parties shall subcribe any bond, sign or indorse any note of hand, accept, sign, or indorse any draft or bill of exchange, or assume any other liability, verbal or written, either in his own name or in the name of the firm, for the accommodation of any other person or persons whatsoever, without the consent in writing of the other party; nor shall either party lend any of the funds of the copartnership without such consent of the other partner.

Seventh. No importation, or large purchase of books or other things, shall be made, nor any transaction out of the usual course of the retail business shall be undertaken by either of the partners, without previous consultation with, and the approbation of, the other partner.

Eighth. Neither party shall withdraw from the joint stock, at any time, more than his share of the profits of the business then earned, nor shall either party be entitled to interest on his share of the capital; but if, at the expiration of the year, a balance of profits be found due to either partner, he shall be at liberty to withdraw the said balance, or to leave it in the business, provided the other partner consent thereto, and in that case he shall be allowed interest on the said balance.

Ninth. At the expiration of the aforesaid term, or earlier dissolution of this copartnership, if the said parties or their legal representatives cannot agree in the division of the stock then on hand, the whole copartnership effects, except the debts due to the firm, shall be sold at public auction, at which both parties shall be at liberty to bid and purchase like other individuals, and the proceeds shall be divided, after payment of the debts of the firm, in the proportions aforesaid.

Tenth. For the purpose of securing the performance of the foregoing agreements, it is agreed that either party, in case of any violation of them or either of them by the other, shall have the right to dissolve this copartnership forthwith, on his becoming informed of such violation.

In witness whereof, we have hereunto set our hands and seals, the day and year first above written.

Sealed and delivered in presence of JOHN SMITH, FRANK ROBINSON.	A. B. [L. S.] C. D. [L. S.]

Agreement to Continue the Partnership; to be Indorsed on the Back of the Original Articles.—Whereas, the partnership evidenced by the within-written articles has this day expired by the limitations contained therein [*or*, will expire on the —— day of —— next], it is hereby agreed, that the same shall be continued on the same terms, and with all the provisions and restrictions therein contained, for the further term of —— years from this date [*or* from the —— day of —— next].

In witness, &c. [*as in General Form*].

Assignment of a Lease.—Know all men by these presents, that I, the within-named A. B., the lessee, for and in consideration of the sum of one thousand dollars, to me in hand paid by C. D., of, &c., at and before the sealing and delivery hereof (the receipt whereof I do hereby acknowledge), have granted, assigned, and set over, and by these presents do grant, assign, and set over, unto the said C. D., his executors, administrators, and assigns the within indenture of lease, and all that messuage, &c., thereby demised, with the appurtenances; and also all my estate, right, title, term of years yet to come, claim, and demand whatsoever, of, in, to, or out of the same. To have and to hold the said messuage, &c., unto the said C. D., his executors, administrators, and assigns, for the residue of the term within mentioned, under the yearly rent and covenants within reserved and contained, on my part and behalf to be done, kept, and performed.

In testimony whereof, I have hereunto set my hand and seal, this tenth day of May, one thousand eight hundred and sixty.

Executed and delivered in the presence of } A. B. [SEAL]

Assignment of a Mortgage.—Know all men by these presents, that I, A. B., the mortgagee within named, for and in consideration of the sum of sixteen hundred dollars, to me paid by C. D., of, &c., at and before the sealing and delivery hereof (the receipt whereof is hereby acknowledged), have granted, bargained, sold, assigned, and set over, and by these presents do grant, bargain, sell, assign, and set over, unto the said C. D., his heirs, executors, administrators, and assigns, the within deed of mortgage, and all my right and title to that messuage, &c., therein mentioned and described, together with the original debt for which the said mortgage was given, and all evidence thereof, and all the rights and appurtenances thereunto belonging. To have and to hold all and singular the premises hereby granted and assigned, or mentioned, or intended so to be, unto the said C. D., his heirs and assigns, forever; subject, nevertheless, to the right and equity of redemption of the within named E. F., his heirs and assigns (if any they have), in the same.

In testimony, &c. [*as in General Form of Assignment*].

Assignment of a Patent.—Whereas, letters patent, bearing date —— day of ——, in the year ——, were granted and issued by the government of the United States, under the seal thereof, to A. B., of the town of ——, in the county of ——, in the State of ——, for [here state the nature of the invention in general terms, as in the patent], a more particular and full description whereof is annexed to the said letters patent in a schedule; by which letters patent the full and exclusive right and liberty of making and using the said invention, and of vending the same to others to be used, was granted to the said A. B., his heirs, executors, and administrators, or assigns, for the term of fourteen years from the said date:

Now, know all men by these presents, that I, the said A. B., for and in consideration of the sum of —— dollars, to me in hand paid (the receipt whereof is hereby acknowledged), have granted, assigned, and set over, and by these presents do grant, assign, and set over, unto C. D., of the town of ——, in the county of ——, and State of ——, his executors, administrators, and assigns, forever, the said letters patent, and all my right, title, and interest in and to the said invention, so granted unto me: To have and to hold the said letters patent and invention, with all benefit, profit, and advantage thereof, unto the said C. D., his executors, administrators, and assigns, in as full, ample, and beneficial a manner, to all intents and purposes, as I, the said A. B., by virtue of the said letters patent, may or might have or hold the same, if this assignment had not been made, for and during all the rest and residue of the said term of fourteen years.

In testimony, &c. [*as in General Form of Assignment*].

Assignment of a Policy of Insurance.—Know all men by these presents, that I, the within named A. B., for and in consideration of the sum of ——, to me paid by C. D., of, etc. (the receipt whereof is hereby acknowledged), have granted, sold, assigned, transferred, and set over, and by these presents I do absolutely grant, sell, assign, transfer, and set over to him, the said C D., all my right, property, interest, claim, and demand in and to the within policy of insurance, which have already arisen, or which may hereafter arise thereon, with full power to use my name so far as may be necessary to enable him fully to avail himself of the interest herein assigned, or hereby intended to be assigned. The conveyance herein made, and the powers hereby given, are for myself and my legal representatives to said C. D. and his legal representatives.

In testimony, etc. [*as in General Form of Assignment*].

Assignment of Demand for Wages or Debt.—In consideration of $100 to me in hand paid by M. D., of the city of ——, the receipt whereof is hereby acknowledged, I, L.C., of the same place, have sold, and by these presents do sell, assign, transfer, and set over, unto the said M. D., a certain debt due from N. E., amounting to the sum of $150, for work, labor, and services, by me performed for the said N. E. (or for goods sold and delivered to the said N. E.), with full power to sue for, collect, and discharge, or sell and assign the same in my name or otherwise, but at his own cost and charges; and I do hereby covenant that the said sum of $150 is justly due as aforesaid, and that I have not done and will not do any act to hinder or prevent the collection of the same by the said M. D.

Witness my hand, this April 10th, 1863.

L. C.

Assignment of Account Indorsed Thereon.—In consideration of $1, value received, I hereby sell and assign to M. D. the within account which is justly due from the within named N. E., and I hereby authorize the said M. D. to collect the same.

Troy, April 10th, 1863. L. C.

INTEREST LAWS AND STATUTES OF LIMITATIONS.

States and Territories.	Interest Laws.		Statutes of Limitations.		
	Legal Rate.	Rate Allowed by Contract.	Judgments, Years.	Notes, Years.	Open Accounts, Years.
	Per ct.	Per ct.			
Alabama	8	8	20	6*	3
Arkansas	6	10	10	5	3
Arizona	6	Any rate.	5	4	3
California	7	Any rate.	5	4†	2
Colorado	8	Any rate.	10‡‡	6	6
Connecticut	6	(*j*)	‡	(*e*)	6
Delaware	6	6	20	6‖	3
D. of Columbia	6	10	12	3	3
Florida	8	10	20	5	2
Georgia	7	8	7	6	4
Idaho	7	12	6	5	4
Illinois	5	7	20	10	5
Indiana	6	8	20	10	6
Iowa	6	8	20 (*d*)	10	5
Kansas	6	10	5	5	3
Kentucky	6	6	15	15	5 (*a*)
Louisiana	5	8	10	5	3
Maine	6	Any rate.	20	6‖	6§§
Maryland	6	6	12	3	3
Massachusetts	6	Any rate.	20	6	6
Michigan	5	7	6*	6	6§§
Minnesota	6	10	10	6	6
Mississippi	6	10	7	6	3
Missouri	6	8	10	10	5
Montana	10	Any rate.	10 (*b*)	8	3
Nebraska	7	10	5‡‡	5	4
Nevada	7	Any rate.	6	6	4
N. Hampshire	6	6	20	6	6
New Jersey	6	6	20	6	6
New Mexico	6	12	7	6	4
New York	6	6††	20 (*i*)	6	6§§
North Carolina	6	6	10	3*	3
North Dakota	7	12	10	6	6§§
Ohio	6	8	5‡‡	15	6
Oklahoma	7	12	5 (*h*)	5	3
Oregon	6	10	10	6	6
Pennsylvania	6	6	5 (*f*)	6‖	6
Rhode Island	6§	Any rate.	20	6	6
South Carolina	7	8	10	6	6
South Dakota	7	12	10 (*l*)	6	6
Tennessee	6	Any rate.	10	6	6
Texas	6	10	10‡‡	4	2
Utah	8	Any rate.	8	6	4
Vermont	6	6	8	6	6§§
Virginia	6	6	20	5*	2¶
Washington	7	12	6	6	3
West Virginia	6	6	10	10	3
Wisconsin	6	10	20 (*i*)	6	6
Wyoming	8	12	5 (*k*)	5	8

* Under seal, 10 years. † If made in State; if outside, 2 years. ‡ No law and no decision regarding judgments. § Unless a different rate is expressly stipulated. ‖ Under seal, 20 years. ¶ Store accounts, other accounts, 3 years. †† New York has by a recent law legalized any rate of interest on call loans of $5,000 or upward, on collateral security. ‡‡ Becomes dormant, but may be revived. §§ Six years from last item. (*a*) Accounts between merchants, 2 years. (*b*) In courts not of record, 5 years. (*d*) Twenty years in Courts of Record; in Justice's Court, 10 years. (*e*) Negotiable notes, 6 years; non-negotiable, 17 years. (*f*) Ceases to be a lien after that period. (*h*) On foreign judgments, 1 year. (*i*) Is a lien on real estate for only 10 years. (*j*) Any rate, but only 6 per cent. can be collected at law. (*k*) And indefinitely by having execution issue every 5 years. (*l*) Ten years foreign, 20 years domestic.

Inns and Innkeepers.—*An Inn* is a public house for the lodging and entertainment of travelers for compensation, and the person who conducts such house is called an innkeeper. To enable him to obtain his compensation the law invests an innkeeper with peculiar privileges, giving him a lien upon the personal property brought into the inn by the guest, and on the other hand holds him to a strict degree of responsibility to the guest if the goods are lost or stolen.

The essential character of an inn is, that it is open for all who may desire to visit it; hence, a mere private boarding house, or lodging house, cannot, in any proper sense, be regarded as an inn; nor will a coffeehouse or restaurant come within the term. A person who entertains travelers occasionally, although he may receive compensation, is not an innkeeper, nor liable as such, provided he does not hold himself out in that character.

An Innkeeper is bound to receive all travelers and wayfaring persons who may apply to him, and to provide entertainment for them, if he can accommodate them, unless they are drunk, or disorderly, or afflicted with contagious diseases. If a person be disorderly he may not only refuse to receive him, but even after he has received him may eject him from the house.

He is further bound to exercise a high degree of care over the person and property of his guests, and is held to a strict responsibility for all loss or damage which may occur through his negligence. This responsibility extends not only to his own acts, and the acts of his servants, but also to the acts of his other guests. The liability of an innkeeper commences from the time the goods are brought into the inn or delivered to any of the innkeeper's servants; and a delivery into the personal custody of the innkeeper is not necessary in order to make him responsible. He is not liable for what are termed the acts of God, or the public enemy; nor for property destroyed without his negligence by accidental fire; and, generally, the innkeeper will be exonerated if the negligence of the guest occasion the loss in such a way that the loss would not have happened if the guest had used the ordinary care that a prudent man may be reasonably expected to have taken under the circumstances.

The strict liability of an innkeeper has been much modified by statute, particularly in regard to money and valuables, and where the innkeeper provides, in the office or some other convenient place in the hotel, an iron safe for the keeping of money, jewels, etc., and notifies his guests of that fact, and the guest neglects to avail himself of the opportunity thus afforded, the innkeeper will not be liable for the losses sustained by the guest by theft or otherwise.

A Guest, in the restricted and legal sense, is the only person who is entitled to the privilege of protection, and to entitle him to this he must have the character of a traveler, a mere sojourner or temporary lodger, in distinction from one who engages for a fixed period, and at a certain agreed rate; but if a party be in fact a wayfarer, and his visit is only transient, it matters not how long he remains, provided he retains this character. Thus, regular boarders by the week or month are not guests, nor are they entitled to the privileges of guests, and on the other hand, in the absence of an enacted statute, the landlord is not, as to them, an innkeeper, and as such entitled to a lien on their effects for his compensation.

The Law of the Road.—*General Principles.*—To prevent collisions, and to secure the safety and convenience of travelers meeting and passing each other upon the highway, a code of rules has been adopted which constitutes what is called the law of the road. These rules, originally established by custom, have, in many instances, been re-enacted and declared by statute, and are of general and uniform observance in all parts of the United States. In general, they apply to private ways, as well as public roads, and, indeed, extend to all places appropriated, either by law or in fact, for the purposes of travel.

The fundamental rule, applicable alike to all who use a traveled way, is, that every person must exercise reasonable care, adapted to the place and circumstances, to prevent collision and avoid accidents, and to this all other rules are subsidiary. No one will be entitled to redress for an injury sustained on the highway where his own negligence contributed to such injury, nor will the fact that a fellow-traveler fails to observe the law in the use of the road absolve another who is in the right from the duty of exercising ordinary care to avoid injury to himself or to prevent injury to the party who is in the wrong. At the same time, a person lawfully using a public highway has a right to assume that a fellow-traveler will observe the law and exercise ordinary care and prudence, and to govern his own conduct in determining his use of the road accordingly. This assumption he may rely on, not to justify carelessness on his own part, but to warrant him in pursuing his business in a convenient manner.

Vehicles.—It is a primary rule that vehicles meeting on a highway must bear or keep to the right. This, however, applies only to passing vehicles, for a person having before him the entire road free from carriages or other obstructions, and having no notice of any carriage behind him, is at liberty to travel upon any part of the way as suits his convenience or pleasure, and no blame can be imputed to him. But while a traveler may well occupy any part of the road if no other is using any portion of it, he must, upon all occasions of the meeting of another, reasonably turn to the right; and in all cases of a crowded condition of a thoroughfare must keep to the right of the center or traveled part of the way. A driver may, indeed, pass on the left side of the road, or across it, for the purpose of stopping at a house, a store, or other object on that side; but he must not interfere or obstruct another lawfully passing on that side; and if he does, he acts at his peril, and must answer for the consequences of his violation of duty. In such case he must pass before or wait until the person on that side of the way has passed on.

When two drivers are moving in the same direction, the one in advance is entitled to the road, provided he does not obstruct it, and is not bound to turn out for the other if there is room for the latter to pass on either side; if, however, there is not sufficient room to pass, the foremost traveler should yield an equal share of the road, on request made, if that is practicable. If it is not practicable, then they must defer passing until they reach more favorable grounds. If the leading traveler then refuses to comply with the request to permit the other to pass him, he will be answerable for such refusal. Ordinarily, when a driver attempts to pass another on a public road, he does so at his peril, and will be held responsible for all damages which he causes to the one whom he attempts to pass, and whose right to the proper use of the road is as great as his, unless the latter is guilty of such recklessness, or even gross carelessness, as would bring disaster upon himself.

The rule requiring persons meeting upon the highway to keep to the right is not imperative, however, and where a driver cannot safely turn to the right on meeting another vehicle, the law will absolve him from negligence in not attempting impossibilities; but where it is not practicable to pass to the right, either of the travelers should stop a reasonable time until the other passes ; nor will the rule apply in the winter season, when the depth of snow renders it difficult or impossible to ascertain where the center of the road is. In such cases the center of the road is the beaten or traveled track, without reference to the worked part of the road. Again, the rule does not apply when one vehicle is passing along one street and another is passing into said street from a cross street.

A traveler is bound to keep his harness and carriage in good condition, and is liable for any damage that may result from a failure to do so; he must not drive at an immoderate rate of speed, and must yield the road to a heavier or loaded vehicle.

Equestrians are not governed by the same stringent rules that apply to drivers of vehicles, and usually all that is required of them is to exercise prudent care under the existing circumstances. They need not turn out in any particular direction on meeting another horseman or a vehicle, but in crowded thoroughfares must keep to the proper side in passing, and must yield the traveled part of the road to a wagon.

Pedestrians have a right to use the carriage-way as well as the sidewalk, and drivers must exercise reasonable care to avoid injuring them, but a foot passenger in crossing the street of a city has no prior right of way over a passing vehicle; both are bound to act with prudence to avoid an accident, and it is as much the duty of the pedestrian to look out for passing vehicles as it is for the driver to see that he does not run over any one; nor does the rule requiring vehicles to keep to the right apply to carriages and foot passengers, for, as regards a foot passenger, a carriage may go on either side.

Landlord and Tenant.—*The relation of landlord and tenant* exists by virtue of a contract for the use or occupation of lands or tenements, either for a definite period, for life, or at will. It is usually created by express contract, but its existence will be implied by law whenever there is an ownership of land on the one hand and an occupation of it by permission on the other. In every such case it will be presumed that the occupant intends to compensate the owner for such use. While the relation may be inferred from a variety of circumstances, the most obvious acknowledgment is the payment of rent. If a tenant under an express contract hold over after the termination of his term, the landlord may consider him as a tenant, and, indeed, is so understood, unless he takes some steps to eject him. If the landlord receives rent from him, or by any other act admits the tenancy, a new leasing begins, and can only be terminated by a proper notice to quit.

The rights and obligations of the parties are usually considered as having commenced from the date of the lease, if there be one, and no other time has been designated as the commencement of the tenancy, or, if there be no date from the delivery of the papers, and if there be no writings, from the time the tenant entered into possession.

The Landlord is bound to protect the possession of his tenant, and to defend him against every one asserting a paramount right. Nor can the landlord do any act himself calculated to disturb the enjoyment of the tenant. He must, unless otherwise agreed, pay all taxes and assessments on the property, and all other charges of his own creation ; and if the tenant, in order to protect himself in the enjoyment of the land, is compelled to make a payment which should have been made by the landlord, he may call upon his landlord to reimburse him, or deduct the amount from the rent.

The landlord has no right of possession during the continuance of the lease, nor indeed any substantial rights in the property further than such as may be necessary to protect his reversionary interests. He may go upon the premises peaceably and during reasonable hours, for the purpose of viewing same and ascertaining whether waste or injury has been committed, and may make such repairs as are necessary to prevent waste; but he is under no obligation to make any repairs, nor does he guarantee that the premises are reasonably fit for the purposes for which they were taken. Nor can the tenant make any repairs at the expense of the landlord in the absence of a special agreement.

The Tenant is entitled to all the rights incident to possession, and to the use of all the privileges appendant to the land, and, on the other hand, is personally liable for any misuse or obstruction he may erect. He must use the premises in such a manner that no substantial injury shall be done them, and that they may revert to the landlord at the end of the term unimpaired by any negligent or willful conduct on his part. He must keep the premises in fair repair at his own expense, but is not bound to rebuild structures which have accidentally become ruinous during his occupation; nor is he answerable for incidental wear and tear, nor accidental fire, or flood.

He must further punctually pay the rent reserved, or if none have been specifically reserved, then such reasonable compensation as the premises are fairly worth. In the absence of special agreement he must pay only for the time he has had the beneficial enjoyment, but if he has agreed to pay for an entire term, as a rule nothing short of an eviction will excuse him from such payment. If he is evicted by a third person, or if the landlord annoys him by the erection of a nuisance, or renders the premises untenantable, or makes his occupation so uncomfortable as to justify his removal, he will be discharged from the payment of rent.

The rights and liabilities of the relation are not confined to the immediate parties, but attach to all persons to whom the estate is transferred, or who may succeed to the possession of the premises. A landlord may not violate his tenant's rights by a sale of the property, nor can the tenant avoid his responsibility by assigning his term. The purchaser of the property becomes, in one case, the landlord, with all his rights and remedies, while in the other the assignee of the tenant assumes all the responsibilities of the latter, but the original lessee is not thereby discharged from his obligations.

The Tenancy may be terminated in a variety of ways. If for a definite time, or conditioned on the happening of a certain event, it expires by its own limitation, and usually, when depending upon the express conditions of a lease, no notice to quit is necessary. If from year to year, or at will, a notice is always necessary. This must be in writing, and explicitly require the tenant to surrender up the premises. It must be served upon the tenant and afford the statutory notice in regard to time. A breach of any of the covenants of the lease will forfeit the tenant's rights, and when a tenancy has been terminated, by whatever cause, the landlord's right to re-enter becomes absolute.

EXEMPTION LAWS.

Alabama.—A homestead not exceeding 160 acres of land, or a lot in a city, town or village, with a dwelling house thereon, not exceeding the value of $2,000. Personal property to the value of $1,000. May be selected by the debtor. Waiver of exemption is not valid unless joined in by the wife.

Arkansas.—For single person, personal property in addition to wearing apparel $200. For head of a family, personal property to the value of $500.

For a head of a family outside of any town or city, 160 acres of land not to exceed $2,500 in value or not less than 80 acres without regard to value.

In city or town, not exceeding one acre of the value of $2,500, or not less than one fourth of an acre without regard to value.

Arizona.—The homestead of a married person or head of a family in the country, not exceeding 160 acres with improvements, not to exceed $2,500. Personal property of married person, $500 besides wearing apparel, and of a person unmarried, $200 and wearing apparel.

California.—The homestead on which debtor resides, to the value of $5,000, if he is the head of a family; if not, to the value of $1,000. Personal property exempt includes chairs, tables, desks and books, $200; necessary household and kitchen furniture, sewing machines, stoves, beds, etc.; provisions for family for three months, three cows, four hogs, two horses, oxen or mules; seed, grain, and vegetables for sowing, not above $200 in value; tools and implements of husbandry of the debtor, not exceeding the value of $1,000; the necessary instruments of a surgeon, physician, surveyor, or dentist together with their professional library and necessary office furniture; the professional library of attorneys, judges, ministers of the gospel, editors, school teachers and music teachers and their necessary office furniture; miner's cabin, not exceeding $500 of value, with all tools and gear necessary for his business, not exceeding $500. Two horses or mules with harness, and the miner's claim worked by him, and not exceeding $1,000 in value, are also exempt.

Colorado.—A homestead consisting of house and lot in town or city, or a farm of any number of acres, in value not exceeding $2,000, is exempt if occupied by a householder and head of a family, provided it has been entered on record as a homestead and so specified in the title. Personal property, including wearing apparel of the debtor and his family, pictures, schoolbooks, library, etc., and household furniture, not exceeding $100; provisions for six months, tools, implements or stock in trade, $200; one cow and calf, ten sheep and necessary food for six months; working animals up to $200; the library and implements of a professional man up to $300. The head of a family may select personal property to the value of $1,000; others, to the value of $300.

Connecticut.—There is no homestead exemption. Personal property is exempt as follows: Libraries not above $500 in value; a cow worth $150; ten sheep, not over $50 in value; two hogs, and 200 pounds of pork. Implements of trade, the horse, harness and buggy of a practicing physician, and the boat, not exceeding $200 in value, of a person engaged in fishing, and used for that purpose, are also exempt.

North and South Dakota.—A homestead consisting of not more than 160 acres, with buildings and appurtenances thereon, and personal property defined by statute, aggregating in value not to exceed $1,500, is exempted to a householder. A firm can claim but one exemption, not a several exemption for each partner. Tools and implements of a mechanic to the value of $200, books and instruments of a professional man to the value of $600, are also exempt from seizure.

Delaware.—Family pictures, family Bible, and library; lot in burial ground and pew in church; family wearing apparel and tools and implements necessary to carry on business, the whole not exceeding $75 in value, are exempt from attachment. In addition to the above the head of a family may claim $200 of personal property. In Newcastle county wages of laborers are also exempt. No homestead law.

District of Columbia.—Family wearing apparel; household furniture to the amount of $300; provisions and fuel for three months; tools or instruments necessary to carry on any trade, to the value of $200; library and implements of a professional man or artist not above $300; family pictures and library to the value of $400, and a farmer's team and other utensils to the value of $100, are exempt from attachment or sale on execution, except for servants' or laborers' wages. There is no homestead exemption.

Florida.—A homestead of 160 acres of land, together with improvements, in the country, or a residence and one-half acre of ground in a village or city, is exempted to the head of a family. Also personal property to the value of $1,000. No property is exempt from sale for taxes or for obligations contracted for its purchase or for the erection of improvements thereon. The wages of every laborer who is the head of a family are also exempt under any process of law.

Georgia.—Each head of a family, or guardian, or trustee of a family of minor children, and every aged or infirm person, or person having the care and support of dependent females of any age, who is not the head of a family, is entitled to realty or personalty, or both, to the value in the aggregate of $1,600. Said property shall be exempt from levy and sale by virtue of any process whatever, under the laws of this State, except for taxes, purchase-money, of the homestead, labor done thereon, or material furnished therefor, or for the removal of incumbrances.

Idaho.—A homestead worth $5,000 is exempted to a householder who is head of a family; either husband or wife may select the homestead. Personal property is also exempted to the value of $300. Exemption does not extend to purchase-money or to mortgages on the property.

Illinois.—A homestead valued at $1,000 is exempted to every householder who has a family; such exemption not covering liabilities for purchase-money or improvement of the homestead. After the death of a householder his family are entitled to the exemption so long as the survivor occupies it, or until the youngest child is twenty-one years of age. There are also exempted to every person wearing apparel, schoolbooks, family pictures and family Bible, and $100 worth of other property selected by the debtor. In addition to this, $300 worth may be selected by the debtor if a head of a family; but such selection cannot be made from any money or wages due; no exemption is allowed when the debt is for the wages of laborer or servant; $50 of wages is exempt to every head of a family if residing with the same.

Indiana.—There is no homestead exemption; any resident householder has exempted real or personal property, or both, to the amount of $600 on any debt founded on contract since May 31, 1879. On debts founded on contracts made previous to that date, exemption is $300. Exemption does not, in any event, affect liens for labor, purchase-money or taxes.

Iowa.—A homestead in country of 40 acres, or in town or city of one-half acre, with improvements and buildings to the aggregate value of $500, is exempted to the head of every family. If less than $500 in value, it may be increased to that amount. It is not exempted from execution for the purchase-money thereof, or for debts contracted prior to its acquirement. Upon the death of either husband or wife the homestead passes to the survivor. Professional men are allowed their libraries, instruments, etc., and a team and wagon; printers retain their presses and type to the value of $1,200. The head of a family may claim wearing apparel, tools, a gun, his library and furniture to the extent of $200 in value. The personal earnings of the debtor for ninety days preceding the execution, certain stock, with food for them for six months, a pew in church and a lot in a burying ground are also exempt. Non-residents and unmarried persons, not being heads of families, can only claim their ordinary wearing apparel and trunk necessary to carry the same to the value of $75.

Kansas.—An independent fortune is exempted in this State. A homestead of 160 acres of farming land, or of one acre within an incorporated town or city, with buildings and improvements thereon, with no limit to value. The head of every family is allowed personal property as follows: The family library, schoolbooks and family Bible; family pictures and musical instruments in use; pew in church and lot in burial ground; all wearing apparel of the family, beds, bedsteads and bedding, one cooking stove and appendages, and all other cooking utensils, and all other stoves and appendages necessary for the use of the debtor and his family; one sewing machine, spinning wheel and all other implements of industry, and all other household furniture not herein enumerated, not exceeding $500 in value; two cows, ten hogs, one yoke of oxen and one horse or mule, or in lieu of one yoke of oxen and one horse or mule, a span of mules or horses; twenty sheep and their wool; food for the support of the stock for one year; one wagon, two plows, drag and other farming utensils not exceeding in value $300; grain, meat, vegetables, groceries, fuel, etc., for the family for one year; the tools and implements of any mechanic, miner or other workman, kept for the purpose of carrying on his business, together with stock in trade not exceeding $400 in value; library, instruments and office furniture of any professional man. Residents, not the head of a family, have tools, implements and stock in trade up to $400. No personal property is exempt for the wages of any clerk, mechanic, laborer, or servant. A lien on the homestead may be created by husband and wife joining in the mortgage.

Kentucky.—To bona-fide housekeepers with a family are exempted from execution and attachment for debt: A homestead to the value of $1,000; two work beasts, or one work beast and one yoke of oxen; two cows and calves; one wagon or cart; two plows and gear; five head of sheep; provisions for family and provender for stock for one year; the tools and stock of a mechanic who is a housekeeper and has a family, not exceeding $200 in value; libraries or instruments of professional men, which may vary in value from one to seven hundred dollars; the wages of a laboring man to the amount of fifty dollars, except for house rent and necessaries.

Louisiana.—A homestead of 160 acres of land, with buildings and improvements thereon, is exempted to the head of a family, if owned and occupied as a residence, together with personal property, the whole not to exceed $2,000; all wearing apparel, implements, stock, etc., with provisions and supplies necessary for the plantation for one year. If the wife own separate property in her own right to the value of $2,000 there is no exemption.

Maine.—Homestead $500, or any lot purchased from State as a homestead; $50 furniture; $150 library; $300 team; $50 poultry; $100 sewing machine; $10 lumber; cow and heifer, ten sheep and lambs, plow, wagon, mowing machine, a two-ton boat, the flax, raw and manufactured, from one acre of ground, wearing apparel, provisions, fuel, seed, grain, provender for stock, and tools. After the debtor's death his family has the benefit of the exemptions.

Maryland.—Besides wearing apparel, books, and tools used for earning a living, there is exempt other property to the value of $100. No homestead.

Massachusetts.—Homestead, $800 (must be recorded as such); furniture, $300; sewing machine, $100; library, $50; tools and implements, $100; stock in trade, $100; boats and outfit, $100; one cow; one hog and six sheep, and wages under $20.

Michigan.—Forty acres of land, with improvements, in the country, or house and lot worth $1,500 in town; furniture, $250; library, $150; two cows, five hogs, ten sheep, team, tools, provisions, and fuel. No exemptions from execution for purchase money.

Minnesota.—Eighty acres with improvements, in country, or lot with dwelling on it, in town. Household property, $500; wagon, plows and farming implements, $300; three cows, ten hogs, twenty sheep, yoke of cattle and a horse, or, instead, a pair of horses; one year's provisions, fuel, feed for stock and seed grain. A miner's or mechanic's tools and stock in trade to $400; the library and instruments of a professional man. Wages under $50 of a laboring man, earned within the last ninety days, and where the debtor is publisher of a newspaper, his complete outfit to value $2,000, and stock $400.

Mississippi.—To householding head of family, 160 acres of land and improvements in country, or house and lot in town, either to value of $2,000. Tools and farming implements necessary for two male laborers; library and instruments of professional man to value of $250; two horses or mules or a yoke of oxen, two cows and calves, five hogs, five sheep; wagon, $100; personal property, $250; one sewing machine; provisions and provender; wages of a laborer, $100.

Missouri.—To head of family one hundred and sixty acres in the country to the value of $1,500, a lot (thirty rods) in small town to same value, or lot (eighteen rods) in city having 40,000 inhabitants, to value of $3,000. Personal property, $300. One month's wages.

Montana.—House and a quarter acre lot in town, or a farm of eighty acres, neither to exceed $2,500 in value. Personal property to the value of $1,400. No exemptions are good against a mortgage, a mechanics' lien or a claim for purchase-money.

Nebraska.—Dwelling and 160 acres of land in country, or two adjoining lots in town, value $2,000. If he has no real property, the debtor may retain personal property to value $500. Clothing, furniture, provisions, animals, tools, and other things as per statute, and sixty days' wages of laborer. Exemptions are not good against mechanics' lien, mortgage, or purchase-money.

Nevada.—Homestead, $5,000; tools, implements, and other personal property, as per statute; miner's cabin, $500.

New Hampshire.—Homestead, $500; $100 furniture; $100 tools; $200 books; $500 fuel and provisions; sewing machine, cook stove, bedding and clothing, one hog, six sheep, one yoke of oxen or one horse, and four tons of hay.

New Jersey.—Homestead $1,500, and $200 household property.

New Mexico.—Homestead, $100; $10 furniture; $20 tools; $25 provisions.

New York.—Homestead, $1,000; $250 furniture,

tools, team and other personal property; sixty days' wages.

North Carolina.—A homestead to the value of $1,000, and personal property worth $500. No exemption is good against taxes, purchase-money, or mechanics' liens.

Ohio.—Homestead is exempt to the value of $1,000; if appraised to a higher value a partition is made, or an appropriate rental is charged. Clothing and necessary furniture are exempted; tools and farming implements to value $100; $50 worth of provisions and three months' wages; one horse or yoke of cattle, harness and wagon; one cow, two hogs, six sheep, and sixty days' provender, or, instead, $65 in household property. A professional man's books, $100. When resident debtor, being head of a family, has no homestead, he may retain personal property to the value of $500, besides other exempted property.

Oklahoma.—Exemption to head of a family outside of city or town not to exceed 160 acres; and in a city or town not more than one acre; in addition thereto, certain personal effects and equipment appertaining to the various vocations. These exemptions do not apply to corporations for profit, to a non-resident, or a debtor who is in the act of removing his family from the territory, or who has absconded, taking with him his family.

To a single person: Wearing apparel, tools, apparatus and books belonging to a trade or profession; one horse, saddle and bridle or one yoke of oxen; current wages for personal service. In certain classes of debts all exemptions are invalid.

Oregon.—Musical instruments, books and pictures, $75; household effects, $300; clothing, $100, and clothing to each member of the family, $50; team, tools, instruments, library or whatever is needed in the trade or profession of debtor, $400; ten sheep, two cows, five hogs, three months' provisions and six months' provender. No exemption is good against a claim for purchase-money. No homestead.

Pennsylvania.—Clothing, books, sewing machine and $300 worth of other property. Right may be waived. No homestead.

Rhode Island.—Furniture and supplies for family, $300; tools, $200; library, $300; wages, $10; clothing; one cow and one hog; debts secured by negotiable paper. No homestead.

South Carolina.—Homestead, $1,000; this right cannot be waived. Furniture, wagons, live stock and tools, to value of $500. Homestead exemption cannot hold against an execution for the purchase-money, a lien for improvements or for taxes. Any person not the head of a family may have one third of his annual earnings exempted.

Tennessee.—Only the head of a family can have the benefit of exemptions; $1,000 homestead and a variety of personal property designated by statute, prominent items being horses, mules, oxen, cows, calves, wagon, tools, lumber, grain, provisions, beds, bedding, furniture, and $30 wages.

Texas.—Two hundred acres of land with improvements in the country, or city property to value at time of being designated as homestead (regardless of the value of after improvements) of $5,000. Furniture, farming implements, tools, books, five cows and calves, two yoke of cattle, two horses and wagon, a carriage or buggy, twenty hogs, twenty sheep, provision, provender and many other articles. The exemption of the homestead is not good against taxes, purchase-money or mechanics' lien; but in this last case the contract must have been signed by both husband and wife. On the death of a husband, the widow and children may have one year's support out of the estate, and if the property be not in such shape as to be exempted by law, enough may be sold to raise an allowance for homestead to value of $5,000 and other property $500. Any person not the head of a family may have exempted clothing, books, horse, bridle and saddle.

Utah.—Homestead, $1,000; personal property to head of the family, $700, and to each member $250. Not good against purchase-money, mechanics' lien or a mortgage.

Vermont.—Homestead, $500; growing crop, clothing, furniture, sewing machine, tools, one cow, ten sheep, one hog, three hives of bees, poultry, one yoke of oxen or two horses, fuel, provisions and provender; also the instruments and library of a professional man, $200.

Virginia.—The head of a family who is a householder has a homestead exemption to the value of $2,000, which may be in real or personal property, both or either. Also clothing, sewing machine, furniture and animals; books, $100; tools, $100. The value of the exemptions outside of the homestead is varied according to the number in family, and ranges from $50 to $500.

West Virginia.—Homestead, $1,000, where the property has been granted or devised for the purpose, to the head of a family, or where he has devoted such property to that purpose by having it so recorded. Also personal property to value of $200. Tools to mechanic, $50.

Washington.—Homestead (must be actually occupied) to the value of $1,000; clothing, books, bedding and household goods, to value of $1,500; one small boat to value of $50; two cows, five hogs, bees, poultry, fuel, and provisions. To a farmer, two horses, or two yoke of oxen, and farming implements to value of $200. To professional man, library worth $500, office furniture and fuel. To lighterman, his boats, to value of $250. To drayman, his team.

Wisconsin.—Forty acres in the country, or one quarter of an acre in town, with the dwelling thereon. Clothing, household furniture, $200; books, two cows, ten hogs, ten sheep, one horse and yoke of cattle, or a pair of horses and mules, farming tools, one year's provisions and provender. To a mechanic, tools, $200; professional man, his library, $200; a publisher or printer, his outfit for $1,500. To any head of a family, sixty days' earnings. No exemption good against a mechanic's lien or claim for purchase-money.

Wyoming.—House and lot in town or one hundred and sixty acres of land in the country, either to value of $1,500. Tools, team and stock in trade of mechanic, miner, or other person, $300. Benefit of exemption can only be claimed by a *bona fide* resident householder.

Ontario.—The exemptions from execution are, speaking generally: the beds and bedding in ordinary use by the debtor and his family; necessary wearing apparel and a list of domestic utensils necessarily incident to living, not to exceed in value the sum of $150; necessary provender for 30 days not to exceed in value the sum of $40; a cow, six sheep, four hogs, and twelve hens, in all not to exceed the value of $75; tools and implements ordinarily used in the debtor's occupation to the value of $100 or the debtor may elect to receive the proceeds of the sale of such tools up to $100.

Under the Free Grants and Homestead Act, there is an exemption from liability for any debt incurred before the issue of the patent and for twenty years from date of location, except where the land itself is mortgaged or pledged or for the payment of taxes.

Quebec.—The exemptions from execution are: beds, bedding and bedsteads in ordinary use by debtor and his family; necessary wearing apparel; one stove and pipes and a number of smaller articles; all necessary fuel, meat, vegetables, fish, flour not more than sufficient for ordinary consumption of debtor and family for thirty days and not exceeding in value $40; one cow, four sheep, two hogs and food therefor for thirty days; tools and implements or chattels ordinarily used in debtor's occupation. No real estate.

New Brunswick.—Wearing apparel; bedding, kitchen utensils; tools of trade to the value of $100 are exempted.

Nova Scotia.—Necessary wearing apparel; beds, bedding and bedsteads of debtor and his family; household utensils not exceeding in value $20; food enough for thirty days' consumption and not exceeding in value $40; one cow, two sheep, and hay and food therefor for thirty days; tools or chattels ordinarily used in the debtor's occupation to the value of $30. No real estate.

Prince Edward Island.—Necessary wearing apparel and bedding for the debtor and his family; tools and instruments of his trade or calling; $16.20 in money and his last cow are exempted from execution out of Supreme Court. Wearing apparel and bedding of debtor and his family; the tools and implements of his trade; one cook stove and one cow, in all amounting in value to $50, are exempt from process out of county court.

Manitoba.—Household goods to the value of $500; tools, agricultural implements and necessaries used by the debtor in his trade, occupation or profession, to the value of $500; homestead to the extent of 160 acres being the residence of the debtor, the buildings and improvements thereon; or the town residence of the debtor to the value of $1,500, provided that no real or personal property shall be exempt from seizure or sale under execution for the purchase price of the same. A debtor cannot waive his exemption from seizure and sale under execution.

Northwest Territories.—Necessary clothing of

the defendant and his family; furniture and household furnishings belonging to defendant and his family to the value of $500; also certain personalty exclusive of the foregoing and homestead not exceeding 160 acres; house and buildings occupied by the defendant, also the lot or lots on which same is situate according to the registered plan, to the extent of $1,500; defendant is entitled to his choice from a greater number of articles from the same class.

British Columbia.—Personal property of debtor to the value of $500 is exempt from execution. No goods or personalty, however, is exempt from seizure in respect to debts contracted in regard to the identical goods. The stock in trade of a merchant is not exempt from seizure although under $500 and they can be sold to satisfy a judgment. Registered homesteads are exempt from execution to the value of $2,500.

MARRIAGE AND DIVORCE LAWS.

Marriage Licenses.—Required in all the States and Territories except New Mexico, New Jersey, New York, North Dakota, Oklahoma, and South Carolina.

Marriage, Prohibition of.—Marriages between whites and persons of negro descent are prohibited and punishable in Alabama, Arizona, Arkansas, California, Colorado, Delaware, District of Columbia, Florida, Georgia, Idaho, Indiana, Kentucky, Maryland, Mississippi, Missouri, Nebraska, Nevada, North Carolina, Oklahoma, Oregon, South Carolina, Tennessee, Texas, Utah, Virginia, W. Virginia, Michigan.

Marriages between whites and Indians are void in Arizona, Nevada, North Carolina. Oregon, and South Carolina.

Marriages between whites and Chinese are void in Arizona, Nevada, Oregon, and Utah.

The marriage of first cousins is forbidden in Arizona, Arkansas, Illinois, Indiana, Kansas, Missouri, Montana, Nevada, New Hampshire, North Dakota, Ohio, Oklahoma, Oregon, South Dakota, Washington, and Wyoming, and in some of them is declared incestuous and void, and marriage with step-relatives is forbidden in all the States, except California, Colorado, Florida, Georgia, Idaho, Louisiana, Minnesota, Nebraska, New Mexico, New York, North Carolina, Oregon, Utah, and Wisconsin.

Marriage, Age to Contract, Without Consent of Parents.—In all the States which have laws on this subject 21 years is the age for males, and for females 21 years in Connecticut, Florida, Illinois, Kentucky, Louisiana, Ohio, Pennsylvania, Rhode Island, South Dakota, Virginia, West Virginia, and Wyoming, and 18 in all the other States having laws, except Maryland, in which it is 16 years.

Marriages, Voidable.—Marriages are voidable in nearly all the States when contracted under the age of consent to cohabit.

Divorce Laws.

Alabama.—Divorce may be obtained for the following causes: Impotency, adultery, desertion for two years, habitual drunkenness, imprisonment for two years and continued cruelty. An allowance must be made by the court, out of the husband's estate, for the support of the wife pending suit; also an allowance when the decree is made. The custody of minor children may be given to either parent, in the discretion of the court.

Arizona.—Divorce may be granted for the violation of the marriage vow; physical incapacity; willful desertion for six months; habitual drunkenness; conviction for felony; cruelty; failure by husband to provide for six months.

Arkansas.—Divorce may be granted for impotency, bigamy, adultery, conviction of felony, habitual drunkenness, willful desertion for one year, cruel and barbarous treatment. Plaintiff must reside in the State one year before bringing suit. Court may allow alimony to the wife.

California.—Divorces are granted for adultery, extreme cruelty, conviction of felony, willful desertion, neglect or habitual intemperance continued for one year. No divorce can be granted by default.

Colorado.—Divorces may be granted for adultery, impotency, bigamy, willful desertion for one year, habitual drunkenness for two years, extreme cruelty or conviction for felony or infamous crime. One year's residence in the State is required before bringing suit, except where the offense was committed in the State or while one or both of the parties resided there.

Connecticut.—Absolute divorce may be granted by the Superior Court for adultery, fraud, duress or force in obtaining the marriage, willful desertion for three years, seven years' absence without being heard of, habitual intemperance, intolerable cruelty, sentence to imprisonment for life, the commission of any crime punishable by imprisonment in the State penitentiary and any such misconduct as permanently destroys the happiness of the petitioner and defeats the purposes of the marriage relation. Three years' residence in the State is necessary before filing a petition. Either party may marry again after divorce, and the court may change the wife's name and make order for alimony and custody of the children.

North and South Dakota.—Divorce may be granted for violation of the marriage vow; willful desertion; conviction for felony; cruelty and physical incapacity.

Delaware.—Divorce may be granted by the Superior Court for adultery, impotency at the time of marriage, habitual drunkenness, extreme cruelty, desertion for three years or conviction of crime sufficient to constitute a felony. In the case of marriage by fraud or for want of age, the wife being less than sixteen, the husband being less than eighteen, at the time of marriage, absolute divorce or divorce from bed and board may be granted, at the discretion of the court. The wife receives all her real estate and such other allowance and alimony as the court may decree where the husband is proved to be in fault. Willful neglect of the husband to provide the necessities of life also forms sufficient grounds for divorce.

District of Columbia.—Divorce may be granted for violation of the marriage vow; physical incapacity; willful desertion for two years; habitual drunkenness; conviction for felony; cruelty; insanity or idiocy at time of marriage.

Florida.—Applicants for divorce must have resided two years within the State. Absolute divorces may be granted only by the Circuit Courts. Adultery, impotency, bigamy, extreme cruelty, habitual intemperance or desertion for one year are sufficient causes. Alimony may be granted to the wife by the courts, and provision for a division of property when a decree is granted.

Georgia.—Grounds for total divorce are as follows: Marriage within the prohibited degrees of affinity or consanguinity; mental or physical incapacity at the time of marriage, force, menace, duress or fraud in obtaining it; adultery, willful desertion by either party for three years; cruel treatment by, or habitual intoxication of either party; or sentence to the penitentiary for two years or over for any offense involving moral turpitude. No total divorce may be granted except by the concurrent verdict of two juries, rendered at different times of court; and when a divorce is granted, the jury rendering the final verdict determines the rights and disabilities of the parties.

Idaho.—Divorce may be granted for violation of the marriage vow; willful desertion for one year; habitual drunkenness; conviction for felony; cruelty; failure of husband to provide for one year; insanity and confinement in an asylum six years.

Illinois.—Divorce may be granted, where complainant has been a resident of the State for one year, for impotency, bigamy, adultery, desertion or drunkenness for

two years, attempt upon the life of the other by poison or other means showing malice, extreme cruelty, conviction of felony or other infamous crime. If no defense is interposed, decree may be granted on testimony of complainant alone; but examination of witnesses must be had in open court, and the judge is required to be satisfied that all proper means have been taken to notify defendant. When decree is granted, the court may restore the wife's maiden name. During pendency of suit, the court may require the husband to pay such sum as may enable the wife to maintain or defend the suit, and alimony when declared just and equitable.

Indiana.—Petitioners for divorce must be *bona fide* residents of the State for two years, and of the county at the time of, and for at least six months prior to, filing the petition; the oath of two resident freeholders being required to this fact. Decrees may issue by the Superior or Circuit Court for the following causes: Impotency at marriage; adultery (where connivance or collusion is not proven); habitual cruelty or habitual drunkenness by either party; abandonment for two years; failure by the husbund to provide for the family for a period of two years, and conviction of either party of an infamous crime at any time subsequent to marriage.

Iowa.—Divorce may be granted by the District or Circuit Court of the county in which plaintiff resides. Plaintiff must declare under oath that he or she has resided in the State for one year next preceding the filing of the petition, unless defendant is resident, and received personal service of the writ. A decree may issue against the husband for adultery, willful desertion for two years, conviction of felony subsequent to marriage, habitual drunkenness and continued ill-treatment. The husband may obtain a decree for like causes, and also when the wife at the time of marriage was pregnant by another. Bigamy or impotency at the time of marriage is also a sufficient cause to annul.

Kansas.—To obtain a decree of divorce, plaintiff must have resided in the State one year, and must bring suit in the county of residence. Decrees are granted in the Circuit Court on the following grounds: Adultery, impotency fraudulent contract, extreme cruelty, habitual drunkenness, gross neglect, abandonment for one year or conviction of felony.

Kentucky.—Before a petition can be presented for a decree of divorce, one year's continuous residence in the State is required. Jury trials are not permitted, and decrees are granted by courts having equitable jurisdiction. An absolute divorce may be granted to the party not in fault on the ground of adultery, impotency, etc., separation for five years, condemnation for felony subsequent to the marriage, force, duress or fraud in obtaining the marriage, or uniting with any religious society which requires a renunciation of the marriage contract. Habitual neglect or maltreatment on the part of the husband, or where the husband is a confirmed drunkard, may give the wife a divorce; and where the wife is proven unchaste, or pregnant by another man at at the time of marriage, the husband is entitled to divorce. The parties are free to marry again, and their personal property is restored.

Louisiana.—Sentence of either party to imprisonment in the penitentiary is sufficient ground for divorce. A decree may also be obtained by either party for adultery, habitual intemperance or cruel treatment of such nature as to render living together insupportable.

Maine.—The Supreme Judicial Court grants divorce for impotency, adultery, or for three years' willful desertion. Alimony may be allowed and dower if the husband be to blame.

Maryland.—Absolute, for adultery, three years' abandonment, or ante-nuptial misconduct of wife. Partial, for cruelty, abandonment, and desertion. Alimony and restoration of wife's property.

Massachusetts.—Unfaithfulness, incapacity, three years' desertion, cruelty, drunkenness, neglect to provide, sentence to five years' imprisonment and joining a sect which disavows marriage, are grounds for absolute divorce. Alimony is allowed, and where the husband is at fault the wife's personal property is restored.

Michigan.—Absolute divorce may be granted for incapacity at time of marriage, adultery, two years' continuous desertion, drunkenness or three years' sentence to imprisonment. A life sentence dissolves the marriage without any proceedings in court. Divorce from bed and board for cruelty and neglect to provide. Separation of property, dower, and alimony as per statute.

Minnesota.—Absolute divorce for unfaithfulness, incapacity, three years' abandonment, one year's drunkenness, cruel treatment or sentence to State's prison. Limited divorce for abuse, desertion or failure to support. Plaintiff, except where breach of faith occurred in the State, must have been one year a resident. The court may order alimony and custody of the children, and the wife regains possession of her real estate, unless decree has been obtained on account of her bad conduct.

Mississippi.—After one year's residence in the State, divorce may be obtained for impotency, adultery, bigamy, cruelty, two years' abandonment or imprisonment in the penitentiary. Alimony is allowed when the wife is the injured party, and the court awards the custody of minor children.

Missouri.—Grounds: Impotency at time of marriage, unfaithfulness, bigamy, conviction of crime, drunkenness, cruelty, and one year's desertion. Petitioner must have been one year a resident of the State. Trial without jury.

Montana.—Divorce may be granted for violation of the marriage vow; physical incapacity; willful desertion one year; habitual drunkenness; conviction for felony; cruelty.

Nebraska.—Unless the marriage took place in the State, and the plaintiff has since continuously resided therein, a residence in the county of six months next preceding the application is necessary. Divorce is granted on the grounds of impotency at the time of marriage, adultery, two years' desertion, drunkenness, cruelty, three years' sentence to imprisonment, or failure on the part of husband to support wife. The court may order alimony, and where a decree is granted on account of the husband's bad conduct the wife takes dower.

Nevada.—Plaintiff must have resided six months in the county. Grounds of divorce are physical incompetency at time of marriage, adultery, one year's desertion, drunkenness, cruelty, conviction of crime, and failure on part of husband to support.

New Hampshire.—Divorces are granted by the Superior Court for physical incompetency, adultery, drunkenness, cruelty, three years' desertion, one year's sentence to prison or adherence to a religious sect that condemns marriage.

New Jersey.—Absolute for adultery, bigamy, two years' abandonment and intolerable cruelty. Applicant must reside in the State, unless the marriage or the alleged misconduct occurred here.

New Mexico.—Divorce may be granted for violation of the marriage vow; habitual drunkenness; cruelty; failure of husband to provide.

New York.—Only for adultery will an absolute divorce be granted. Partial divorce is ordered for cruelty, desertion and neglect. Marriages are annulled for fraud or force, idiocy, lunacy or impotency at the time of marriage, or for bigamy.

North Carolina.—Only for impotency or adultery can absolute divorce be obtained. Partial divorce is granted for cruelty, desertion, or drunkenness.

Ohio.—Divorce is granted for unfaithfulness, bigamy, incapacity, cruelty, drunkenness, deception, three years' neglect and abandonment, or imprisonment in a penitentiary. Alimony may be granted; and if the decree is obtained on account of the husband's ill conduct, the wife has her separate property and her maiden name restored.

Oklahoma.—Divorce may be granted for violation of the marriage vow; physical incapacity; willful desertion one year; habitual drunkenness: conviction of felony; cruelty.

Oregon.—Plaintiff must have been a resident for one year before bringing suit. Grounds are impotency, adultery, two years' drunkenness, three years' abandonment, cruelty, conviction of felony. Plaintiff gaining the suit has a right to one third of the real estate belonging to defendant; and if a successful plaintiff be the wife, she may have a maintenance awarded her.

Pennsylvania.—Plaintiff must have been a resident of the State for one year next preceding the application. Grounds: Deception or force in procuring the marriage, impotency, adultery, bigamy, cruelty and two years' abandonment, and two years' sentence to imprisonment. Divorce will not be granted on the ground of adultery if proved to have been condoned. Even after a divorce, defendant is not allowed to marry a co-respondent. A wife may obtain partial divorce and alimony for ill treatment.

Rhode Island.—Divorce is granted for impotency, adultery, cruelty, drunkenness, neglect to support, five years' abandonment, conviction of murder or arson, presumption of death from long absence, or for defect in marriage rendering it void. Divorce may only be decreed by Supreme Court. Alimony may be ordered, and restoration of wife's separate property.

South Carolina.—Has no divorce laws.

Tennessee.—The applicant must have been a resident of the State for two years next preceding the petition. Grounds: physical incapacity at time of marriage, bigamy, adultery, two years' abandonment, conviction of crime, imprisonment in penitentiary, drunkenness, ante-nuptial immorality of wife, attempt of either party upon the life of the other. Limited divorce may be granted for cruelty, desertion, or failure to provide.

Texas.—Applicant must be really an inhabitant of the State and a resident of the county for six months previous to filing petition; grounds: adultery, three years' desertion, unendurable cruelty.

Utah.—Divorce may be granted for violation of the marriage vow; willful desertion one year; habitual drunkenness; conviction for felony; cruelty; failure of husband to provide; parties cannot live in peace and union.

Vermont.—Divorce is granted for adultery, cruelty, three years' abandonment, three years' imprisonment in penitentiary or seven years' absence without being heard of. The wife may obtain divorce where the husband, being able, fails to support.

Virginia.—Grounds: Impotency, adultery, sentence to penitentiary, guilt of either of infamous crime before marriage, the other being ignorant, notorious immorality of wife before marriage, five years' abandonment. Partial divorce for cruelty or desertion. Alimony and maintenance of children are decreed, and the care of the children is given to either party at the discretion of the court.

West Virginia.—Divorce is granted for mental or physical defect at time of marriage, unfaithfulness, three years' abandonment, sentence to penitentiary, conviction of crime before marriage, or notorious immorality of either before marriage, the other party being ignorant. Partial divorce may be obtained for cruelty or desertion. Alimony and custody of children is decreed by the court.

Washington.—Divorce may be granted for violation of the marriage vow; physical incapacity; willful desertion one year; conviction for felony; cruelty; fraud and fraudulent contract; indignities as render life burdensome; insanity lasting ten years.

Wisconsin.—Unless the parties had been married and since remained in the State, the applicant must have been for one year a resident before filing a petition. Absolute divorce is granted for impotency, adultery, one year's abandonment, five years' separation, three years' sentence to penitentiary, cruelty and drunkenness. Partial divorce for desertion, cruelty, drunkenness, or failure to provide. The court may decree alimony, and the wife regain her separate property.

Wyoming.—Divorce may be granted for violation of the marriage vow; physical incapacity; willful desertion one year; habitual drunkenness; conviction for felony; cruelty; failure of husband to provide one year; indignities as render life burdensome; vagrancy of husband.

PROPERTY RIGHTS OF MARRIED WOMEN.

Alabama.—Married women may hold all property, real and personal, acquired before and after marriage, as a separate estate not liable for the husband's debts, and it may be devised or bequeathed as by a single woman. This separate estate is liable for debts contracted by the woman before marriage, and for contracts after marriage for articles of comfort and support of family. The wife is entitled to dower of one half of husband's real estate, if he leave no lineal decendants, one third if there are any, provided she has no separate estate; if her separate estate is less than the dower interest would be, she is entitled to as much as would make it equal. Women attain their legal majority at twenty-one, but may marry without consent of their parents at eighteen.

Arizona.—Married women may carry on business and sue and be sued in their own names. All property acquired before marriage, and all afterwards acquired, by gift, grant, devise or inheritance, is separate estate, liable for her own but not for her husband's debts. She may control it and dispose of it in all respects like a single woman.

Arkansas.—Married women have absolute and unqualified right in property of every kind and are not liable for debts or contracts of the husband. But a schedule under oath, and verified by some other reputable person, must be made by the husband and wife, and filed in the recorder's office of the county where the property is. and of the county where they reside. The wife may control her property, may carry on business on her sole and separate account, may sue and be sued, may make a will and may insure her husband's life for her benefit. The widow is entitled to one third part of the estate, unless legally relinquished by her.

California.—All property acquired in any manner before marriage, or afterwards by gift, grant, inheritance or devise, is wife's separate property, controlled by her and not liable for debts of the husband. The husband's property similarly acquired is not liable for debts of the wife. All property acquired after marriage by husband or wife, except as above, shall be common property, but under the husband's control. Dower and curtesy are abolished, but the survivor takes half the common property after payment of debts and expenses of administration. A married woman may dispose of her separate estate by will without the consent of her husband and may insure her husband's life for her benefit.

Colorado.—Married women are treated in all respects, as to their property rights, as if they were single. A wife may carry on trade or business, sue or be sued, contract debts, transfer real estate, and in all ways bind her separate property, without the husband's joining. She may make a will, but cannot bequeath more than half her property away from her husband without his consent in writing. The husband cannot by will deprive his wife of over one half of his property. Dower is abolished. The husband is liable for debts of the wife contracted before marriage to the extent of the property he may receive through her, but no further.

Connecticut.—Previous to the year 1877, the husband acquired a right to the use of all the real estate of the wife during her life and if he had a child by her and survived her, then during his own life as tenant by curtesy. By the Act of May 20th, 1877, the rights of married women are materially enlarged. Any woman married after that date retains her real estate as if unmarried. She may make contracts, convey real estate, and sue or be sued in regard to any property owned by her at the time of marriage, or afterwards acquired. The estate is liable for her debts, and, jointly with her husband, for debts contracted for joint benefit of both or household expenses. The separate earnings of a wife are her sole property. Dower exists only in real estate of which the husband is possessed at the time of his decease.

North and South Dakota.—Married women may transact business in all respects the same as if unmarried. Neither husband nor wife has any interest in the separate estate of the other. The earnings and accumulations of the wife are her separate property and not liable for the husband's debts nor even for household debts contracted by her as her husband's agent. Her separate property is, however, liable for her own debts, contracted before or after marriage, if such debts are contracted on her own responsibility.

Delaware.—Married women, married since 1873, retain all real and personal property held at marriage, or since acquired from any person other than the husband, as their separate estate, and not subject to the disposal of the husband or liable for his debts. They may receive wages for personal labor, sue or be sued in respect to their own property as if unmarried; and the rents, issues, and profits of their separate estate are not controlled by the husband. The widow is entitled to one third dower of all the lands and tenements whereof the husband was seized at any time during her marriage, unless she shall have relinquished such right for and during the term of her natural life. She may be an administratrix, and the husband's life may be insured for her benefit if premium does not exceed $150.

District of Columbia.—Married women may bequeath, devise, or convey property or interest therein in the same manner as if unmarried. Real or personal property belonging to the wife at marriage or afterwards acquired is separate estate. She may sue and be sued in all matters pertaining to her property, and the husband is not liable for any contracts made by her in respect to her personal estate.

Florida.—Married women retain all real or personal property owned at marriage or acquired thereafter, and are not liable for the husband's debts. In order that it shall be free from his debts, the property must be inventoried and recorded within six months after marriage or subsequent acquirement of the property. The wife may sell and convey all real estate inherited by her the same as if she were unmarried; but her husband must join in all sales, transfers, and conveyances of her property, both real and personal. She is entitled to dower in a life estate in one third of all the real estate of which her husband was seized and possessed at his death or at any time during his life, unless she has relinquished the same; also an absolute one third of his personalty.

Georgia.—Married women retain as a separate estate all property in their possession at the time of marriage, or afterwards acquired and are not liable for any debts, defaults, or contracts of the husband. By consent of her husband advertised for four weeks she may become a free trader, in which event she is liable the same as if unmarried. The wife may not bind her estate by any contract of suretyship, either in behalf of her husband or any other person. The widow takes dower in one third of all the lands of which her husband was seized at his death; and wife and children, after the husband's death, are entitled to one year's support from his property, all other claims yielding to this.

Idaho.—All property, both real and personal, owned at marriage or afterwards acquired, by either wife or husband, remains a separate estate. All property acquired after marriage is held in common. Separate property of the wife should be inventoried with the county recorder; the husband has control of it during marriage, but cannot create a lien or encumbrance unless joined by the wife, who is examined separately. If the husband mismanages, or commits waste, the District Court may, on application of the wife, appoint a trustee to manage her separate property. Upon the death of husband or wife, half the common property goes to survivor; if no direct descendants, all goes to survivor.

Illinois.—Married women may own in their own right realty and personalty, may sue and be sued, contract and incur liabilities, the same as if unmarried; but they may not enter into or carry on any partnership business without consent of the husband, unless abandoned by him or he is incapable of giving assent. Beyond the necessaries, the husband is not liable for debts of the wife, except in cases where he would be jointly liable if the marriage did not exist. The estate of both is liable for family expenses, but the wife's separate earnings are her own. A surviving wife or husband takes one third of all the realty of the deceased, unless relinquished in due form. The husband and wife are put upon the same footing as to dower, and the estate of curtesy is abolished.

Indiana.—Married women retain all realty and personalty owned by them at marriage, or afterwards acquired, and are not liable for the husband's debts. The husband is liable for debts of the wife contracted before marriage only to the extent of the personal property he may receive from or through her, or derive from sale or rent of her lands. She may sell personal property, but she may not convey or encumber her real estate unless the husband joins. Suits against her separate estate should be brought in the name of both. A widow takes one third of her deceased husband's real estate in fee simple, free from all demands of creditors, where the estate does not exceed $10,000; where the estate is over $10,000 and under $20,000, she takes one fourth; and one fifth if it exceeds $20,000. She also takes one third of the personalty after payment of debts, and in all cases takes $500, without accounting, and may occupy the dwelling and forty acres of land for one year, rent free.

Iowa.—Married women may own in their own right real and personal property acquired by descent, gift, or purchase, may sell, convey, and devise the same, may sue and be sued, make contracts and buy goods in their own name. Wife or husband are not liable for the debts of the other before marriage, or for separate debts incurred afterwards. The wife's earnings are her own, and her note is good against her own estate. Women attain majority at eighteen, or earlier, upon marriage; a female of fourteen may marry. The surviving wife or husband is entitled to one third of the real estate of the deceased, free from all claims of creditors. If they leave no children, survivor takes one half, parents the other half.

Kansas.—Married women have the same property rights as men, and may make contracts, carry on business, sue and be sued, and sell or convey real estate precisely as their husbands; their earnings or profits are their own. A note or indorsement made by a married woman will bind her property the same as if unmarried. Homestead is absolute property of widow and children, and neither wife nor husband may bequeath more than half their property without written consent of the other. If either die intestate and without children, the entire property goes to the survivor.

Kentucky.—Married women may hold real or personal property as a separate estate free from the control of the husband or liability for his debts. By petition to the Circuit Court, in which the husband must join, she may acquire the right to transact business in her own name. Unless dower be barred, forfeited, or relinquished, she takes one third of the real estate and one half of the personal property.

Louisiana.—Married women may hold and control both real and personal property owned at time of marriage; all property or revenues of separate property acquired by either husband or wife after marriage is held in common, and is divided equally between them at dissolution of the marriage either by death or divorce. The wife may carry on a separate business, but her husband will be bound by her contracts, so long as the community of property exists; she cannot sue without the concurrence of her husband, and she cannot bind herself or her property for his debts. There is no right of dower to the wife.

Maine.—A married woman holds real and personal property, acquired in any way except from the husband, the same as if single. She may make contracts, sue and be sued, and do business in her own name; and her property may be taken to satisfy judgments against her. Her property is liable only for her own debts. She joins husband in a deed selling his property to relinquish dower. He joins with her in selling hers only when such property comes from him. A wife, being abandoned by her husband, may be allowed to take and use his personal property. Dower, life estate in one third of all husband's real property owned during coverture; one half if no children. He has same interest in deceased wife's estate.

Maryland.—Property acquired by a married woman is her own, controlled by herself, and is free from her husband's debts. She conveys by joint deed with the husband, but devises and bequeaths the same as if single. She may be sued with her husband on joint contracts made by them, and the property of both is equally liable. Dower one third, if they have children; one half, if none.

Massachusetts.—The property of a married woman is managed by herself, and is not liable for her husband's debts. She may make contracts, sue and be sued, and do business in her own name, provided a certificate is filed by her or her husband in the office of the town clerk. Contracts and conveyances between husband and wife are not allowed. Her conveyances of real estate are subject to husband's tenancy by curtesy. A wife cannot make a will affecting her husband's right to one half of the personal property or his tenancy by curtesy in her real estate, without his written consent. Dower as by common law.

Michigan.—Married women own and control property the same as if single. A wife may do business in her own name and make contracts, even with her husband. Her separate property is liable for wrongs committed by her. Widow has dower, but there is for the surviving husband no right of tenancy by curtesy.

Minnesota.—A married woman holds property in her own name. She may make contracts, and her property is liable only for her own debts. She cannot sell or convey real estate further than a mortgage for purchase-money or a three years' lease, without her husband joining her. Contracts between husband and wife are void. The surviving husband or wife keeps the homestead for life.

Mississippi.—A married woman holds property acquired in any manner, and the revenues therefrom, for her own use and free from control or liability of her husband. She may convey and encumber the same as if single, but husband joins in conveyance. She may devise and bequeath. Deed from husband to wife is void as to creditors at time of making it. A wife may not encumber her estate by mortgage or otherwise for her husband's debts; she may do business on her own account the same as if single, and is then liable for her contracts, housekeeping and family expenses. She joins her husband in conveyance of homestead, but not in that of his other property. Dower in property of which the husband dies seized.

Missouri.—A married woman controls her own property, and holds it through a trustee, free from liability for her husband's debts. She may make contracts, sign notes, and do business in her own name. She may make a will. She joins her husband in his conveyances to release dower. Her dower is one third for life of all lands owned by husband.

Montana.—A list of married woman's property filed and recorded saves it from being liable for the husband's debts, except necessaries for herself and children under eighteen. A married woman may become a sole trader by recording her intention. If she invests more than $10,000 in business she must make oath that the surplus did not come from her husband. The husband is not liable for debts contracted by her in business. She is also responsible for the maintenance of her children. A surviving husband or wife takes one half of deceased's property, if no children; one third if there are.

Nebraska.—A married woman holds her separate property free from the disposal of her husband and from liability for his debts. She may bargain, sell, make contracts, do business, sue and be sued, all so far as her separate estate may warrant; but she cannot become surety for another, not even being allowed to bind herself for her husband's debts. Property coming to the wife from the husband is not privileged as her separate property. Dower, use for life of one third of real estate owned by husband during coverture.

Nevada.—The separate property of a married woman which is controlled by herself is such as she may have owned before marriage or acquired afterwards by gift, devise, or descent. All property acquired otherwise, by either husband or wife, is common property, and under the absolute control of the husband. On the death of the husband the widow receives one half of the common property.

New Hampshire.—A married woman holds property owned before marriage or acquired afterwards, except what may come from the husband, for her own use. She may sell, convey and encumber, devise and bequeath, do business, give notes, sue and be sued. Her contracts are binding, excepting that there can be no contracts or conveyances between husband and wife, nor can the wife become security for her husband. Wife is entitled to dower.

New Jersey.—The property owned before marriage, and such as she may acquire afterwards by gift, descent, or bequest, is the sole property of a married woman and is not liable for the husband's debts. She may make contracts, but cannot sell or encumber her real estate without consent of husband. She cannot indorse notes or become security. She joins husband in his conveyances and mortgages. Dower and curtesy.

New Mexico.—The separate property of a married woman is what she owned previous to marriage, or what she may inherit. All that she acquires afterwards, and the revenues of her separate estate, go into the common property. The husband has control and management of her separate estate and the common property. There is no dower, but on decease of a husband the wife's private property is first deducted; then she receives one half of the common property, after all debts are paid. If there be no children she has a right to all the common property.

New York.—Married women may have real and personal property, buy and sell, and do business in their own names. A married woman is liable for debts contracted in her own trade or business, or when an agreement or contract has been made for the benefit of her separate property, when, by the terms of such instrument, her separate property is to be charged with the liability. Dower.

North Carolina.—A married woman's separate property is not liable for her husband's debts. She may devise and bequeath, but must have husband's consent to convey. Unless she be a free trader, she can make no contract other than for personal or family necessities or for payment of ante-nuptial debts, without the consent of her husband. She becomes a free trader, the husband assenting, by filing her intention. Common law dower and one year's subsistence.

Ohio.—The property of a married woman is not liable for her husband's debts; beyond a three years' lease or a contract for the improvement of her real estate, she cannot sell or encumber it without the consent of her husband. If a married woman engages in trade, her separate property is liable for the debts she may then contract, and she may sue and be sued the same as if single. A deserted wife must procure an order from court, by which she shall have all property rights as a femme sole. Dower in all real estate owned by husband during coverture.

Oklahoma.—Neither husband nor wife has any interest in the property of the other. Either may enter into any engagement or transaction with the other, or with any other person, respecting property which either might, if married, subject, between them, to rules which control the actions of persons occupying confidential relations. The wife may, without consent of husband, convey her separate property. Woman retains the same legal existence and personality after marriage as before, and receives the same protection of her rights as does her husband. She may hold and transfer real and personal property; may buy and sell goods, give notes or other obligations, and sue and be sued, same as if unmarried.

Oregon.—A married woman holds her property free from the control or debts of her husband. She may make contracts, buy and sell, and give notes, and her own property will be liable. The husband joins in her conveyances. She may make a will, but it must not interfere with her husband's rights of curtesy.

Pennsylvania.—The property of a married woman is held as her separate estate, but is chargeable for family necessaries ordered by her. A wife cannot make a contract or conveyance without her husband joining her. By obtaining leave from the court she may have the benefit of her own earnings. She may make a will, saving the husband's right by curtesy. She may deposit money in bank and write checks against it in her own name. Dower, one third of all real estate owned by husband during coverture.

Rhode Island.—A married woman's property is held by trustees for her separate use free from her husband's debts. She cannot make contracts or do business. She may make a will subject to husband's right by curtesy.

South Carolina.—The property of a married woman cannot be seized for her husband's debts. A married woman can bequeath, devise, and encumber her separate property. She can buy in her own name, and have conveyances made to her, and make contracts, the same as if she were single. A gift from husband to wife is not good against a creditor's claim. Dower rights.

Tennessee.—A married woman has her separate property free from the husband's control and from liability for his debts. She may encumber, convey, or devise her separate property without being joined by her husband in the deed. Widow has dower in one third of husband's real estate, and a child's share in his personalty. The husband dying intestate, leaving no heirs, the wife inherits all his property.

Texas.—The property owned by husband or wife before marriage, and what either may acquire afterwards, by gift, devise, or descent, is community property. The husband controls the common property and the wife's separate estate. The common property is liable for the debts of either, and the husband may dispose of it. At the death of either, the survivor takes one half and the children the other half of the common property. The husband joins wife in conveyance of her separate property. She joins him in conveyance of homestead. A married woman cannot do business in her own name, but she may become security for her husband by mortgaging her separate estate.

Utah.—A married woman's separate property is held, managed, controlled, and disposed of by herself. A wife may carry on business, sue and be sued, give notes and make contracts the same as if single.

Vermont.—The property of a married woman is held separate, and is not liable for her husband's debts. In conveyance of the wife's real estate the husband must join in deed. A married woman may make a will. Widow has dower in one third the real estate of which the husband died seized.

Virginia.—A married woman holds the property owned by her previous to marriage, and what she may afterwards acquire, as sole trader, free from the control of her husband, and from liability for his debts. She may make a will subject to husband's rights by curtesy. Common law dower.

West Virginia.—The property of a married woman, however acquired, except from the husband, is held for her sole and separate use. Husband must join in conveyances of real estate. Dower.

Washington.—The property owned before marriage by husband or wife, and all acquired afterwards by gift, devise, or descent to either, is separate property. All otherwise acquired is common property, subject to control of the husband. He also controls the separate property of the wife, but cannot sell or convey it without her joining in the deed. To save the separate property of the wife from attachment for husband's debts, there must be an inventory of it on record.

Wisconsin.—A married woman has all property rights the same as if single. She may buy and sell, lend and borrow, make conveyances, and have real estate conveyed to her, and all such business may be transacted between her and her husband as between strangers. She may sue alone, but in being sued she must be joined to husband. Dower, life interest in one third of all husband's realty held during the marriage. Husband has wife's realty for life.

Wyoming.—A married woman may carry on business, make contracts, keep her own earnings, hold property, real or personal, receive the rents in her own name, sue and be sued, make a will, free from any control or interference of her husband, the same as if she were single. Her property is not liable for the debts of her husband. Women in this State have the right to vote and hold office.

Canada.—In the provinces of the Dominion, generally, a married woman holds all her property and earnings, free from the control of her husband. It is liable for her debts before marriage, and her husband is not. She may manage it and bequeath it. She is entitled to dower, but there is no tenancy by curtesy. In the province of Quebec the law is modified by the French law. There all the personal property and gains of both parties are put together, and form the community property, which the husband administers. Each can bequeath only his or her interest, and the heirs of each inherit the interest of each.

THE BRITISH EMPIRE.

The supreme legislative power of the British Empire is by its Constitution given to Parliament. Parliament is summoned by the writ of the sovereign issued out of Chancery, by advice of the Privy Council, at least thirty-five days previous to its assembling. On a vacancy occurring in the House of Commons whilst Parliament is sitting, a writ for the election of a new member is issued upon motion in the House. If the vacancy occurs during the recess, the writ is issued at the instance of the Speaker.

It has become customary of late for Parliaments to meet in annual session extending from the middle of February to about the end of August. Every session must end with a prorogation, and by it all Bills which have not been passed during the session fall to the ground. The royal proclamation which summons Parliament in order to proceed to business must be issued fourteen days before the time of meeting. A dissolution is the civil death of Parliament; it may occur by the will of the sovereign, or, as is most usual, during the recess, by proclamation, or finally by lapse of time, the statutory limit of the duration of the existence of any Parliament being seven years. Formerly, on the demise of the sovereign, Parliament stood dissolved by the fact thereof; but this was altered in the reign of William III., to the effect of postponing the dissolution till six months after the accession of the new sovereign, while the Reform Act of 1867 settled that the Parliament "in being at any future demise of the Crown shall not be determined by such demise."

The present form of Parliament, as divided into two Houses of Legislature, the Lords and the Commons, dates from the middle of the fourteenth century.

The House of Lords consists of peers who hold their seats—(1) by hereditary right; (2) by creation of the sovereign; (3) by virtue of office—English bishops; (4) by election for life—Irish peers; (5) by election for duration of Parliament—Scottish peers.

The number of names on the "Roll" was 401 in 1830; 457 in 1840; 448 in 1850; 458 in 1860; 503 in 1877; and 586 in 1898. About two thirds of the hereditary peerages were created in the present century. Excluding the royal and ecclesiastical peerages, the 4 oldest existing peerages in the House of Lords date from the latter part of the thirteenth century, while 5 go back to the fourteenth and 7 to the fifteenth century. There are besides 8 peeresses of the United Kingdom in their own right, and 2 Scotch peeresses, and 18 Scotch and 62 Irish peers who are not peers of Parliament.

The House of Commons has consisted, since 49 Hen. III., of knights of the shire, or representatives of counties; of citizens, or representatives of cities; and of burgesses, or representatives of boroughs, all of whom vote together. To the House of Commons, in the reign of Edward I., 37 counties and 166 boroughs each returned two representatives; but at the accession of Henry VIII., the total number of constituencies was only 147. The additions from Edward VI. to Charles II. were almost entirely of borough members. In the fourth Parliament of Charles I., the number of places in England and Wales for which returns were made, exclusive of counties, amounted to 210; and in the time of the Stuarts, the total number of members of the House of Commons was about 500. At the union of the English and Scottish Parliaments in 1707, 45 representatives of Scotland were added; and at the union of the British and Irish Parliaments in 1801, 100 representatives of Ireland. The average number of members was then about 650.

By the Reform Bill of 1832, the number of English county constituencies was increased from 52 to 82; 56 boroughs, containing a population of less than 2,000 each, were totally disfranchised, and 31 other boroughs, of less than 4,000 each, were required to send one representative instead of two. On the other hand, 22 new boroughs acquired the right to return two members, and 24 to return one member. In Scotland the town members were increased from 15 to 23—making 53 in all, while the Irish representatives were increased from 100 to 103.

The next great change in the constituency of the House of Commons, was made by the Reform Bill of 1867-68. By this Act England and Wales were allotted 493 members and Scotland 60, while the number for Ireland remained unaltered, and household suffrage was conferred on boroughs in England and Scotland. A still greater reform was effected by the Representation of the People Act, 1884, and the Redistribution of Seats Act, 1885. The former introduced a "service franchise," extending to householders and lodgers in *counties* the suffrages which in 1867 had been conferred upon householders and lodgers in *boroughs*, and placed the three Kingdoms on a footing of equality as regards electoral qualifications; while the latter made a new division of the United Kingdom into county and borough constituencies, and raised the total number of members to 670, England receiving 6 new members, and Scotland 12.

All elections for members of Parliament must be by secret vote by ballot, an Act being passed annually to this effect.

No one under twenty-one years of age can be a member of Parliament. All clergymen of the Church of England, ministers of the Church of Scotland, and Roman Catholic clergymen are disqualified from sitting as members; all Government contractors, and all sheriffs and returning officers for the localities for which they act, are disqualified both from voting and from sitting as members. No English or Scottish peer can be elected to the House of Commons, but non-representative Irish peers are eligible.

The executive government of Great Britain and Ireland is vested nominally in the Crown; but practically in a committee of Ministers, commonly called the Cabinet, whose existence is dependent on the possession of a majority in the House of Commons.

The member of the Cabinet who fills the position of First Lord of the Treasury is, as a rule, the chief of the Ministry. It is on the Premier's recommendation that his colleagues are appointed; and he dispenses the greater portion of the patronage of the Crown.

The Cabinet officers are as follows:—

Prime Minister and Secretary of State for Foreign Affairs.
Lord President of the Council.
Lord High Chancellor.
Lord Privy Seal.
Chancellor of the Duchy of Lancaster.
First Lord of the Treasury.
Secretary of State for the Home Department.
Chancellor of the Exchequer.
Secretary of State for the Colonies.
Secretary of State for War.
Secretary of State for India.
First Lord of the Admiralty.
President of the Local Government Board.
President of the Board of Trade.
Lord Lieutenant of Ireland.
Lord Chancellor of Ireland.
Secretary for Scotland.
First Commissioner of Works.
President of the Board of Agriculture.

Local Government.—*England and Wales.*—In each county the Crown is represented by a Lord Lieutenant, who is generally also *custos rotulorum*, or keeper of the records. He usually nominates persons whom he considers fit and proper persons to be justices of the peace for his county, to be appointed by the Lord Chancellor. His duties, however, are almost nominal. There is also a sheriff, who represents the executive of the Crown, an under-sheriff, a clerk of the peace, coroners, who are appointed and paid by the County Councils, and other officers. The licensing of persons to sell intoxicating liquors, and the administration of the criminal law—except that which deals with some of the graver offenses—is in the hands of the magistrates. For the purposes of local government, England and Wales are divided into sixty-one administrative counties, including the county of London, which differ slightly in area from the geographical counties.

For each administrative county there is a popularly-elected Council, called a County Council, who co-opt a prescribed number of aldermen, either from their own body or from outside it. Aldermen are elected for six years, half of them retiring every third year. A councilor is elected for three years. The jurisdiction of the County Councils extend to (1) making of county and police rates; (2) borrowing money; (3) supervision of county treasurer; (4) management of county halls and other buildings; (5) licensing of houses for music and dancing, and of race courses; (6) maintenance and management of pauper lunatic asylums; (7) maintenance of reformatory and industrial schools; (8) management of bridges and main roads; (9) regulation of fees of inspectors, analysts, and other officers; (10) control of officers paid out of the county rate; (11) coroner's salary, fees, and district; (12) Parliamentary polling districts and registration; (13) contagious diseases of animals, and various other matters. The control of the county police is vested in a standing joint committee, composed of an equal number of magistrates and members of the County Council. The London police are, however, under the control of the Home Secretary.

The administrative counties, with the exception of the County of London, are subdivided into "County Districts," which are either Urban or, Rural, as the case may be. Generally speaking, an urban district comprises a town or a small area more or less closely populated, and a rural district takes in several country parishes. Women may be elected to District Councils, but may not sit on County Councils; and the chairman of a District Council is, unless a woman, a magistrate for the county by virtue of his office. The District Councils administer the Public Health and Highway Acts, and also exercise some powers formerly exercised by the justices out of session.

In every civil parish in a "rural district" there is a Parish Meeting, at which every parochial elector may attend and vote. In such parishes of over 300 inhabitants there is in addition a Parish Council. To these latter bodies has been transferred all the civil powers of the old Vestries, including the election of overseers, and in addition very considerable powers over charities, allotments, and other public matters. Where there is no Parish Council some of these powers, including the appointment of the overseers, are exercised by the Parish Meeting. Urban District Councils can, by petitioning the Local Government Board—which is the supreme Local Government authority—obtain part or all of the powers of a Parish Council. Only Parish Meetings may have power to adopt the Public Libraries Acts, the Baths and Washhouses Acts, the Lighting and Watching Acts, the Burials Acts, and the Public Improvements Acts.

In the County of London local government is carried on under the County Council by the Vestries, formed under the Metropolis Management Acts, which exercise powers similar but somewhat wider than urban district councils. These Vestries are elected on the same wide suffrage as district councilors. Married women, properly qualified, have votes, and may now sit on them, as well as single women.

In all the great towns, including "county boroughs," local business is administered by a municipal Corporation, which derives its authority from a charter granted by the Crown. In 1835 the municipalities of the country were completely reorganized. A municipal Corporation consists of the mayor, aldermen, and burgesses, and acts through a Council elected by the burgesses—practically by the ratepayers. The councilors serve for three years, one third retiring annually; the aldermen are elected by the Council, and the mayor, who serves for one year, also by the Council. A municipal Corporation has practically all the powers of an urban district council, in addition to the privilege of electing a mayor and corporation, and in some cases municipal boroughs have a separate commission of the peace and maintain their own police force. As to Poor Law and School Board administration, see "Pauperism" and "Instruction."

Scotland.—By the Local Government (Scotland) Act, 1894, a Local Government Board for Scotland was constituted, its President being the Secretary for Scotland. The Local Government Act, which was passed for Scotland in 1889, followed in its main outlines the English Act of the previous year. The powers of local administration in counties formerly exercised by the Commissioners of Supply and Road Trustees, were either wholly or in part transferred to the new Councils, which took over their duties and responsibilities in 1890. The Act of 1894 provided that a Parish Council should be established in every parish to take the place of the Parochial Boards, and to exercise powers similar to those of the Parish Councils in cost of administration. Such towns, having over 1,500 inhabitants, may be constituted urban sanitary districts.

The *Isle of Man* and the *Channel Islands* are not bound by Acts of the Imperial Parliament unless specially mentioned. The Isle of Man is administered in accordance with its own laws by the Court of Tynwald, consisting of the Governor, appointed by the Crown; the Council for Public Affairs, composed chiefly of ecclesiastical and judicial dignitaries appointed by the Crown, and the House of Keys, a representative assembly of 24 members chosen on a property qualification for seven years by the six "sheadings" or local subdivisions, and the four municipalities. The Channel Islands are administered according to their own laws and customs, each by a Lieut. Governor, with judicial and other functionaries; and a "States" Assembly, partly elective. Jersey has a separate legal existence. Guernsey, Alderney, and Sark have a Lieut. Governor in common, but otherwise their governments are separate.

Justice.—*England and Wales.*—The principal courts having criminal jurisdiction are the petty sessional courts, the general or quarter sessions, the courts of oyer and terminer and gaol delivery, more popularly known as "assizes," and the Central Criminal Court. Two or more justices of the peace sitting in a petty sessional courthouse, the Lord Mayor or any alderman of the City of London, or any metropolitan or borough police magistrate or other stipendiary magistrate sitting in a courthouse, constitute a petty sessional court. The courts of quarter sessions are held four times a year by the justices of the county. Similar courts can be held at other times, and are then called "general sessions." Two justices constitute a court, but usually a larger number attend. Certain boroughs have a court of quarter sessions, with similar jurisdiction to the county justices in quarter sessions assembled, in which the recorder of the borough is the judge. The assize courts are held four times a year in various towns throughout the country by "commissioners" nominated by the Crown. These commissioners are generally judges of the Queen's Bench Division of the High Court of Justice, but sometimes Queen's Counsel of good standing are appointed. The trial takes place before a single commissioner. The Central Criminal Court is the court of oyer and terminer and gaol delivery for the City of London and a large surrounding district. The sessions of this court are held at least twelve times a year, and more often, if necessary. The Recorder and the Common Sergeant, and, if the number of the prisoners makes it necessary, the judge of the City of London Court, sit on the first two days, after which they are joined by the judges of the High Court on the rota, for whom the more serious cases are reserved. A petty sessional court deals summarily with minor offenses. Cases of a more serious nature are usually investigated by a petty sessional court before being tried at the sessions or the assizes. To every session, assize, and to every sitting of the Central Criminal Court, the sheriff cites 24 of the chief inhabitants of the district, of whom not less than 12 and not more than 23 are sworn and constitute a grand jury. The grand jury examines the bill of indictment against the accused person, hears the evidence of witnesses for the prosecution, and if they think a *prima facie* case for trial is made out they indorse the bill "a true bill." All criminal trials, except those which come before a court of summary jurisdiction, take place before a judge and a petty jury of twelve men. Except on some highly technical point of procedure there is no appeal in criminal cases. No man can be tried again for the same crime after a petty jury has found him "not guilty." On a conviction the judge can, if he think fit, reserve a question of law (but not of fact) for the Court for Crown Cases Reserved. This Court is formed by five or more judges of the High Court, and can reverse, amend, or affirm the judgment. The only other method of securing the revision of a sentence is by the royal prerogative, exercised on the advice of the Home Secretary, by which a sentence can be modified or annulled. Nominally all the judges are appointed by the King, but in practice the Lord Chancellor (who is a Cabinet minister, ex officio president of the House of Lords, and goes out with the ministry) and the Lord Chief Justice are appointed on the recommendation of the Prime Minister, and all the other judges on the recommendation of the Lord Chancellor.

Scotland.—The High Court of Justiciary is the supreme criminal court in Scotland. It consists of all the judges of the Court of Session, and sits more or less frequently, as the number of cases before it may require, in Edinburgh or in the circuit towns. One judge can, and usually does, try cases, but two or more preside in cases of difficulty or importance. It is the only competent court in cases of treason, murder, robbery, rape, fire-raising, deforcement of messengers, and generally in all cases in which a higher punishment than imprisonment is by statute directed to be inflicted; and it has moreover an inherent jurisdiction to punish all criminal acts, both those already established by common law or statute, and such as have never previously come before the courts and are not within any statute.

The sheriff of each county is the proper criminal judge in all crimes occurring within the county which infer only an arbitrary punishment, and if the case is tried with a jury the High Court has no power of review on the merits. Even in cases indicted to the High Court the accused is, under the Criminal Procedure (Scotland) Act of 1887, regularly asked to plead in the sheriff court, and minor objections to the indictment can be wholly or in part disposed of there. Borough magistrates and justices of the peace have jurisdiction in petty cases occurring within the burgh or county, and in a number of minor offenses under various statutes.

Ireland.—In Ireland persons charged with crime are first brought before the petty sessions court, which must consist of at least two ordinary justices of the peace, one of whom *may be* a stipendiary—commonly called a resident magistrate. Then if the charge be trifling it may be disposed of, the prisoner, if convicted, having a right of appeal to the quarter sessions or recorder's court (according as it is in a borough or in the county), provided he is fined more than twenty shillings or sentenced to a longer imprisonment than one month (Petty Sessions Act, sec. 24). If the charge be of a more serious character it must either be dismissed or sent for trial to the quarter sessions or recorder's court, or to the assizes, as in England. There is this difference, however, between quarter sessions in Ireland and in England: in England they are presided over by an unpaid chairman, who need not be a lawyer, and who is elected by his fellow justices of the peace for the county; while in Ireland they are presided over by a paid official, who must be a barrister, whose decision on points of law binds the court, who is appointed by the Crown, and who is also judge of the civil bill court of the county, which corresponds to the English county court. The assizes are presided over by one of the common law judges of the High Court of Justice. In the quarter sessions, recorder's court, and assizes the trial is by jury in all cases save appeals from petty sessions. Under the Crimes Act witnesses and persons suspected of crime may be interrogated before a secret court of inquiry; but admissions then made are not evidence against the persons making them. Prisoners may be convicted before two resident magistrates specially appointed to hear cases under the Crimes Act, and in cases where the sentence exceeds a month, convicted persons have a right of appeal to the county chairman at quarter sessions.

Territorial Extent of the British Empire.

THE UNITED KINGDOM.

Countries.	Area in Square Miles.	How Acquired by England.	Date.	Population, 1891.
England	50,840		....	27,499,984
Wales	7,470	Conquest	1282	1,501,034
Scotland	29,785	Union	1603	4,033,103
Ireland	32,583	Conquest	1172	4,706,448
Islands	295		....	147,870
Total	120,973			37,888,439

COLONIES AND DEPENDENCIES.

Europe:				
Gibraltar	2	Conquest	1704	25,869
Malta, etc	122	Treaty cession	1814	165,662
Asia:				
India (including Burmah)	1,800,258	Conquest Transfer from East India Co.	Begun 1757 1858	287,223,431
Ceylon	25,365	Treaty cession	1801	3,008,239
Cyprus	3,584	Convention with Turkey	1878	187,000
Aden and Socotra	3,070	(Aden) conquest	1839	44,000
Straits Settlements	1,500	Treaty cession	1785–1824	506,577
Hong Kong	30½	Treaty cession	1841	221,441
Labuan	31	Treaty cession	1846	5,853
British North Borneo	31,000	Cession to Company	1877	150,000
Africa:				
Cape Colony	221,310	Treaty cession	1588, 1814	1,527,224
Natal	21,150	Annexation	1843	543,913
St. Helena	47	Conquest	1673	4,116
Ascension	38	Annexation	1815	200
Sierra Leone	15,000	Settlement	1787	300,000
British Guinea, Gold Coast, etc	339,900	Treaty cession	1872	23,455,000
Mauritius, etc	1,063	Conquest and cession	1810, 1814	392,500
British South and East Africa	1,989,247	Conquest and cession	1870–1890	14,911,000
Transv'l and Orange River Colony.				
America:				
Canada Proper	370,488	Conquest	1759–60	
New Brunswick	28,200	Treaty cession	1763	
Nova Scotia	20,907	Conquest	1627	
Manitoba	73,956	Settlement	1813	4,833,239
British Columbia, etc	383,300	Transfer to Crown	1858	
Northwest Territories	3,257,500	Charter to Company	1670	
Prince Edward Island	2,133	Conquest	1745	
Newfoundland	42,200	Treaty cession	1713	198,000
British Guiana	76,000	Conquest and cession	1803–1814	282,000
British Honduras	7,562	Conquest	1798	28,000
Jamaica	4,193	Conquest	1655	581,000
Trinidad and Tobago	1,754	Conquest	1797	205,000
Barbadoes	166	Settlement	1605	172,000
Bahamas	5,794	Settlement	1629	48,000
Bermuda	41	Settlement	1612	16,000
Other Islands	8,742		....	255,000
Australasia:				
New South Wales	310,700	Settlement	1788	1,132,234
Victoria	87,884	Settlement	1832	1,140,405
South Australia	903,690	Settlement	1836	320,431
Queensland	668,497	Settlement	1824	393,718
Western Australia	975,876	Settlement	1828	49,782
Tasmania	26,215	Settlement	1803	146,667
New Zealand	104,032	Purchase	1845	626,658
Fiji	7,423	Cession from the natives	1874	125,402
New Guinea (British)	234,768	Annexation	1884	350,000

CANADA.

Constitution and Government.—As originally constituted the Dominion of Canada was composed of the Provinces of Canada—Upper and Lower—Nova Scotia, and New Brunswick. They were united under the provisions of an Act of the Imperial Parliament passed in March, 1867, known as "The British North America Act 1867," which came into operation on the 1st July, 1867, by royal proclamation. The Act provides that the Constitution of the Dominion shall be "similar in principle to that of the United Kingdom"; that the executive authority shall be vested in the Sovereign of Great Britain and Ireland, and carried on in her name by a Governor General and Privy Council; and that the legislative power shall be exercised by a Parliament of two Houses, called the "Senate" and the "House of Commons." Provision was made in the Act for the admission of British Columbia, Prince Edward Island, the North-West Territories, and Newfoundland into the Dominion; Newfoundland alone has not availed itself of such provision. In 1869 the extensive region known as the North-West Territories was added to the Dominion by purchase from the Hudson's Bay Company; the province of Manitoba was set apart out of a portion of it, and admitted into the confederation on the 15th July, 1870. On 20th July, 1871, the province of British Columbia, and on the 1st July, 1873, the province of Prince Edward Island, respectively entered the confederation.

The members of the Senate of the Parliament of the Dominion are nominated for life, by summons of the Governor General under the Great Seal of Canada. By the terms of the Constitution, there are now 81 Senators — namely, 24 from the Province of Ontario, 24 from Quebec, 10 from Nova Scotia, 10 from New Brunswick, 4 from Manitoba, 3 from British Columbia, 4 from Prince Edward Island, and two from the Territories. Each senator must be 30 years of age, a born or naturalized subject, and reside in, and be possessed of property, real or personal, of the value of 4,000 dollars within, the province for which he is appointed. The House of Commons of the Dominion is elected by the people, for five years, unless sooner dissolved, at the rate at present of one representative for every 22,688, the arrangement being that the province of Quebec shall always have 65 members, and the other provinces proportionally according to their populations at each decennial census. On the basis of the census of the Dominion taken in April, 1891, and in accordance with a redistribution bill passed in 1892, the House of Commons consists of 213 members — 92 for Ontario, 65 for Quebec, 20 for Nova Scotia, 14 for New Brunswick, 7 for Manitoba, 6 for British Columbia, 5 for Prince Edward Island, and 4 for the North-West Territories.

The members of the House of Commons are elected by constituencies, the electors of which are supplied by franchises under the control of the several provincial assemblies, an Act having been passed to that effect in the session of 1898. The qualifications for voting at provincial elections vary in the several provinces. Voting is by ballot.

The Speaker of the House of Commons has a salary of 4,000 dollars per annum, and each member an allowance of 10 dollars per diem, up to the end of 30 days, and for a session lasting longer than this period the sum of 1,000 dollars, with, in every case, 10 cents per mile for traveling expenses. The sum of 8 dollars per diem is deducted for every day's absence of a member, unless the same is caused by illness. There is the same allowance for the members of the Senate of the Dominion.

Dominion Executive Officers.—

Governor General.
Premier and President of Privy Council.
Minister of Public Works.
Minister of Customs.
Minister of Militia and Defense.
Minister of Agriculture.
Minister of Finance.
Minister of Justice.
Minister of Marine and Fisheries.
Minister of the Interior.
Minister of Railways and Canals.
Minister without Portfolio.
Secretary of State.
Postmaster-General.

Rulers since 1867.—

Lord Monck, Governor General. 1867-1868.

Lord Lisgar, Governor General. 1868-1872.

Earl Dufferin, Governor General. 1872-1878.

Marquis of Lorne, Governor General. 1878-1883.

Marquis of Lansdowne, Governor General. 1883-1888.

Baron Stanley of Preston, Governor General. 1888-1893.

Earl of Aberdeen, Governor General. 1893-1898-.

Earl of Minto, Governor General 1898.

Each of the ministers has a salary, fixed by statute, of 7,000 dollars, or 1,400*l.* a year, with the exception of the recognized Prime Minister, who has 8,000 dollars, or 1,600*l.* and the Ministers of Customs and Inland Revenue, who have each 5,000 dollars a year. The body of ministers is officially known as the "Queen's Privy Council of Canada." The Governor General has a salary of 10,000*l.* per annum.

Provincial Government.—The seven provinces forming the Dominion have each a separate Parliament and administration, with a Lieutenant Governor at the head of the executive. They have full powers to regulate their own local affairs and dispose of their revenues, provided only they do not interfere with the action and policy of the central administration. The Lieutenant Governors are appointed by the Governor General. Quebec and Nova Scotia have each two Chambers (a Legislative Council and a Legislative Assembly) and a responsible Ministry. In New Brunswick, Ontario, Manitoba, British Columbia, and Prince Edward Island there is only one Chamber (the Legislative Assembly) and a responsible Ministry. The members of the Legislative Council of Nova Scotia number 21, and Quebec 24. The membership of the Legislative Assemblies are: Prince Edward Island 30, Nova Scotia 38, New Brunswick 41, Quebec 73, Ontario 94, Manitoba 40, British Columbia 33, and the North-West Territories 26. The North-West Territories are presided over by a Lieutenant Governor and a Legislative Assembly. The Executive Council consists (since October 1, 1897) of the Lieutenant Governor and five members, elected, as such, by the people.

Instruction.—All the provinces of the Dominion have one or more universities, and several colleges which prepare for university degrees. There are in all about 16 degree-granting bodies in the Dominion, with about 24 colleges, including denominational, medical, and other special institutions. From special official statistics of these institutions it may be estimated that they are attended by about 13,000 students, and their total annual expenditure is upwards of $700,000, while the estimated value of their endowments, buildings, land, etc., is over $16,000,000.

The expenditure for the year on public and high schools, including Government grants, was over $10,000,000. The supervision of education is under the control of the Governments of the several provinces, and the systems in use vary somewhat, but are all based on the principle of free education, the funds being supplied in nearly all the provinces by Government grants and local taxation. In British Columbia and the North-West Territories the schools are supported wholly by Government. Education is more or less compulsory in all the provinces, but the law is not very strictly enforced. In Ontario, Quebec, and the North-West Territories there are separate schools for Roman Catholics; in the other provinces the schools are unsectarian. Separate schools in Manitoba were abolished by a Provincial Act passed in 1890.

Justice.—There is a Supreme Court in Ottawa, having appellate, civil, and criminal jurisdiction in and throughout Canada. There is also an exchequer court, which is also a colonial court of admiralty, with powers as provided in the Imperial "Colonial Courts of Admiralty Act, 1890." There is a Superior Court in each province; county courts, with limited jurisdiction, in most of the provinces; all the judges in these courts being appointed by the Governor General. Police magistrates and justices of the peace are appointed by the Provincial Governments.

Religion.—There is no State Church in the whole of British North America. The Church of England is governed by twenty bishops, with about 1,000 clergy; the Roman Catholic Church by one cardinal, seven archbishops, twenty-three bishops, and about 1,500 clergy: and the Presbyterian Church in Canada, with about 1,000 ministers—formed in 1875 by the union of two formerly distinct bodies—by presbyteries, synods, and an annual assembly as in the Scotch Church, with 2,358 churches and stations. The Methodists have 1,700 and the Baptists about 500 ministers. All these bodies have one or more divinity schools. The number of members of each religious creed in the Dominion was as follows at the census of April 6, 1891:—

Roman Catholics	1,992,017	Congregationalists	28,157
Presbyterians	755,326	Miscellaneous creeds	106,739
Anglicans	646,059	No creed stated	*89,355
Methodists	847,765		
Baptists	303,839	Total	4,833,239
Lutherans	63,982		

* Including Pagans.

The following shows the numbers of the leading denominations in the several provinces according to the census of 1891:—

Province.	Roman Catholic.	Church of England.	Presbyterian.	Methodist.	Baptist.
Ontario	358,300	385,999	453,147	654,033	106,047
Quebec	1,291,709	75,472	52,673	39,544	7,991
Nova Scotia	122,452	64,410	108,952	54,195	83,122
New Brunswick	115,961	43,095	40,639	35,504	79,649
Manitoba	20,571	30,852	39,001	28,437	16,112
British Columbia	20,843	23,619	15,284	14,298	3,098
Prince Edw'd Island	47,837	6,646	33,072	13,596	6,265
The Territories	14,344	15,966	12,558	8,158	1,555

Production and Industry.—*Agriculture.*—Of the total area of Canada in 1891, there were 28,537,242 acres of improved land, out of 60,287,730 acres of occupied land. Of the improved lands, 19,904,826 acres were under crop, being 4,792,542 acres more than were under crop in 1881. The acreage under pasture in 1891 was 15,284,788 acres, an increase of 8,899,226 acres since 1881. The acreage under wheat in 1891 was 2,723,861 acres, an increase of 381,506 acres in ten years. The average yield of 1891 per acre was 15.4 bushels, an increase of 1.6 bushels per acre over the yield of 1881. There is a central experimental farm near Ottawa, and others in several of the provinces. In 1895 there were 195 ranches in the N.-W. Territories, covering an area of 904,187 acres.

Forestry.—The timber wealth of Canada is very large, and timbering one of its most important industries. The forest area is estimated at 1,248,798 square miles. The forest products of 1891 were valued at 80,071,415 dollars, of which 27,207,547 dollars were exported. The census returns show an aggregate of 2,045,073,072 cubic feet as the total cut of the year. The forest products exported to the United Kingdom in 1897 amounted in value to 14,973,292 dollars out of a total of 32,937,976 dollars. The recently introduced wood pulp industry is increasing rapidly, the exportable surplus being 741,960 dollars in 1897, chiefly going to Great Britain and the United States. The Crown forests belong to the Provincial Governments, except in Manitoba, the N.-W. Territories, and the Railway Belt (forty miles wide) in British Columbia, where they belong to the Dominion.

Fisheries.—The total value of the produce of the fisheries of Canada in 1896 was 20,407,424 dollars; in 1895, 20,185,298 dollars. The values of the principal catches in 1896 were: cod, 3,610,979 dollars; salmon, 4,009,679 dollars; herring, 2,909,744 dollars; lobsters, 2,205,762 dollars, and mackerel, 727,743 dollars. In 1896, according to provinces, the values were: Nova Scotia, 6,070,895 dollars; British Columbia, 4,183,999; New Brunswick, 4,799,433; Quebec, 2,025,754; Ontario, 1,605,674; Prince Edward Island, 976,126; Manitoba and N.-W. Territories, 745,543.

Mining.—Nova Scotia, British Columbia, Quebec, N. and W. Ontario, and part of the N.-W. Territories, are the chief mining districts of Canada. The total value of the mineral produce of Canada was, in 1897, 28,779,173 dollars; in 1896, 22,609,825 dollars. The principal product is coal, of which, in 1896, 3,745,716 tons were raised, valued at 7,226,462 dollars; in 1897, 3,876,201 tons, valued at 7,442,204 dollars. Among the other minerals produced in 1897 were gold, 6,190,000 dollars; nickel, 1,400,000 dollars; asbestos, 324,700 dollars; petroleum, 1,011,546 dollars; copper, 1,501,660 dollars; silver, 3,322,000 dollars; lead, 1,396,850 dollars; iron ore, 178,719 dollars. It is estimated that the coal-bearing area of the N.-W. Territories extends over 65,000 square miles.

Capital.—The capital of Canada was transferred in 1841 from Kingston to Montreal, and in 1849 serious riots arose resulting in the burning of the Parliament Houses on the 26th of April, over the question of compensation for those who had suffered losses during the recent rebellion. The riots were in reality caused by the hostility of the British and French inhabitants. One of the results was the establishment of two seats of government, one at Toronto and the other at Ottawa, Parliament sitting four years in each city alternately. Ottawa later on was made the capital of Canada and eventually of the Dominion.

Naturalization.—No question of naturalization arises in connection with the emigration of British subjects to Canada. Settling in the Dominion makes no more change in this respect than a removal from York, Glasgow, Swansea, or Dublin to London, and a new arrival has all the privileges of a Canadian born fellow subject. For foreigners the Canadian naturalization laws are marked by a spirit of liberality, and such persons can transact any business and hold real estate without being naturalized. By residing three years and taking the oath of allegiance they become naturalized British subjects. The oath is one of simple allegiance and does not require any offensive renunciations. Naturalization confers political and all other rights.

Money and Credit.—The Bank Acts of Canada impose stringent conditions as to capital, notes in circulation, limit of dividend, returns to the Dominion Government, and other points in all chartered and incorporated banks. In making payments every bank is compelled if required to pay a certain proportion in Dominion Government notes, and must hold not less than 40 per cent. of its cash reserve in Dominion Government notes. In 1897 there were 37 incorporated banks making returns to the Government, with 575 branches all over the Dominion.

Post-office savings banks under charge of the Government have been in operation in Canada since 1868; there are also Government savings banks, under the management of the Finance Department, in the Maritime Provinces, Manitoba, and British Columbia. In 1897 there were 779 offices of the former and 28 of the latter. In 1897 the post-office savings banks had 135,737 depositors and 32,380,829 dollars on deposit.

Internal Communications. Canada has a system of canal, river, and lake navigation over 2,700 miles in length, and vessels from the lake ports reach the Atlantic without breaking bulk. Up to 1897, 71,750,000 dollars had been spent on canals for construction alone. In 1896, 25,622 vessels, of 4,677,826 tons, passed through the Canadian canals, carrying 151,342 passengers and 3,413,674 tons of freight, chiefly grain, timber, and coal.

The Dominion of Canada had a network of railways of a total length of 16,687 miles completed at the end of June, 1897, being an increase of 300 miles over that of 1896. The number of miles in operation was 16,550. The Canadian Pacific Railway main line from Montreal to Vancouver is 2,906 miles in length. By means of this railway and a line of Pacific steamers subsidized by the Imperial and Dominion Governments, Montreal and Yokohama have been brought within 14 days of one another. There is a monthly steam service between Australia and British Columbia, for which the Dominion Government gives 25,000*l.* a year and the Australian 12,000*l.* a year.

The number of electric railways in Canada in 1897 was 35, with a mileage of 535; the number of passengers carried during the year was 83,811,306; the total paid up capital was 18,727,355 dollars, and the bonded debt, 9,894,452 dollars.

On June 30, 1897, there was 9,191 post offices in the Dominion. During the year ended on the foregoing date the number of letters sent through the post office was 123,830,000, of post cards 26,140,000, of newspapers, books, etc. 26,640,000, and of parcels 369,570. Newspapers sent from the office of publication are carried free. Their number in 1897 was estimated at upwards of 74,319,976. The letters and post cards posted amounted to 28.88 per head, and the other articles to 19.54 per head. Revenue, 4,311,243 dollars; expenditure, 4,897,783 dollars. A uniform rate of postage of three cents has been established over the whole Dominion. The number of money order offices in Canada in 1897 was 1,349 and of orders issued 1,162,209, their value having been 13,081,860 dollars.

There were 29,318 miles (2,786 being Government) of telegraph lines in Canada in 1897 and 70,761 miles of wire, with 2,572 offices, and the number of messages sent, as nearly as could be ascertained, 4,313,925. There were in 1894, 44,000 miles of telephone wire, and 33,500 sets of instruments; 72,500,000 messages were sent. The returns for 1897 do not vary greatly from those of 1894.

Area, Population, and Seats of Government of the Provinces.

PROVINCES.	Area, Square Miles.*	Population, 1891.	Seats of Government.
Alberta	100,000	25,278	Regina.
Assiniboia	90,340	30,374	Regina.
Athabaska	251,300	....	Regina.
British Columbia	383,300	98,173	Victoria.
Manitoba	73,956	†152,506	Winnipeg.
New Brunswick	28,200	321,270	Fredericton.
Nova Scotia	20,600	450,523	Halifax.
Ontario	222,000	2,114,475	Toronto.
Prince Edw'd Island	2,000	109,088	Charlottetown.
Quebec	347,350	1,488,586	Quebec.
Saskatchewan	114,000	11,146	Regina.
Mackenzie, Ungava, and Franklin	1,019,200	31,462	Regina.
Yukon	198,300	....	....
Keewatin	756,000	....	....
Great Lakes & Rivers	47,400	....	....
Total	3,653,946	4,823,875	

* Land and water included in area.
† 187,926 by census of 1896.

The following table shows the value of the leading imports and exports in 1897:—

Imports, 1897, for Home Consumption.	Dollars.	Exports of Canadian produce, 1897.	Dollars.
Wool, mfrs. of	7,125,748	Cheese	14,676,239
Iron, steel, and mfrs. of	10,613,630	Horned cattle	7,132,807
Coal and coke	9,276,534	Horses	1,710,922
Breadstuffs	1,136,263	Sheep	1,002,011
Cotton mfrs.	4,269,620	Eggs	978,479
Tea and coffee	4,034,208	Other animal products	13,744,794
Sugar of all kinds	8,560,790	Wood pulp	741,959
Cotton wool and waste	3,290,240	Wood and other mfrs. of	32,169,087
Silk and mfrs. of	1,988,305	Wheat and wheat flour	7,085,048
Provisions	655,316	Peas	2,352,891
Wool, raw	878,339	Apples	2,682,472
Wood and mfrs. of	861,728	Hay	999,238
Animals, living	397,902	Other agricultural products	4,862,997
Flax, hemp, jute, and mfrs. of	1,362,853	Codfish	2,706,827
Spirits and wines	1,379,436	Fish of other kinds	7,607,496
Coin and bullion	4,676,194	Coal	3,330,017
All other articles	50,786,915	Gold-b'r'g quartz & nuggets, etc.	2,804,101
		Other minerals	5,164,797
		Iron and steel and mfs.	522,988
		Leather and mfrs.	1,541,732
		Coin and bullion	327,298
		All other articles	9,815,638
		Foreign produce	13,990,415
Total	111,294,021	Total	137,950,253

ARGENTINE REPUBLIC.

The Constitution of the Argentine Republic, formerly known by the name of "Provincias Unidas del Rio de la Plata," bears date May 15, 1853, with modifications in 1860, when Buenos Ayres joined the confederacy. By its provisions, the executive power is left to a President, elected for six years by representatives of the fourteen provinces, equal to double the number of senators and deputies combined; while the legislative authority is vested in a National Congress, consisting of a Senate and a House of Deputies, the former numbering 30, two from the capital and from each province, elected by a special body of electors in the capital, and by the legislatures in the provinces; and the latter 133 members elected by the people. By the constitution as revised in 1898, there should be one deputy for every 33,000 inhabitants. A deputy must be 25 years of age, and have been a citizen for four years. The deputies are elected for four years, but one half of the House must retire every two years. Senators must be 30 years of age, have been citizens for six years, and have an annual income of 12,000 dollars. One third of the Senate is renewed every three years. The two chambers meet annually from May 1 to September 30. The members of both the Senate and the House of Deputies are paid for their services, each receiving 12,000 pesos per annum. A Vice-President, elected in the same manner and at the same time as the President, fills the office of Chairman of the Senate, but has otherwise no political power. The President is commander-in-chief of the troops, and appoints to all civil, military, and judicial offices, and has the right of presentation to bishoprics; he is responsible with the ministry for the acts of the executive; both President and Vice-President must be Roman Catholics, Argentine by birth, and cannot be re-elected.

The Ministry, appointed by and acting under the orders of the President, consists of eight Secretaries of State — namely, of the Interior, Foreign Affairs, Finance, War, Justice, Agriculture, Marine, and Public Works.

The President has a salary of 36,000 dollars, the Vice-President of 18,000 dollars, and each of the five ministers of 16,800 dollars per annum.

Local Government.— The Constitution, with certain small exceptions, is identical with that of the United States. Such matters as affect the Republic as a whole are under the superintendence of the Central Government. The governors of the various provinces are invested with very extensive powers, and in their constitutional functions are independent of the central executive. They are not appointed by the President of the Republic, but elected by the people of each province for a term of three years and four years. The provinces elect their own legislatures, and have complete control over their own affairs; they can contract loans (internal and external) under their sole and exclusive responsibility.

Religion and Instruction.— Although the Constitution recognizes the Roman Catholic religion as that of the State, all other creeds are tolerated. There are 1 archbishop and five suffragan bishops. For the instruction of the clergy there are 5 seminaries. In 1888 civil marriage was established in the Republic.

Primary education is free, secular, and compulsory for children from 6 to 14 years of age. The elementary schools are supported in the capital and each province by the taxes established in their Education Acts, aided by large subsidies from the general Government.

There are also 35 normal schools with 10,949 pupils. There are 3 universities, at Cordova, Buenos Ayres, and La Plata, comprising faculties of law, medicine, and engineering, with a total of 2,500 students; a school of mines (39 students), 2 colleges of agriculture, a naval and military school. There is a well-equipped national observatory at Cordova, and another at La Plata, museums at Buenos Ayres and La Plata, and a meteorological bureau.

Justice.— Justice is exercised by a Supreme Court of five judges and an attorney-general, which is also a court of appeal, and by a number of inferior and local courts, trial by jury being established by the Constitution for criminal cases. Each State has its own judicial system.

AUSTRIA-HUNGARY.

Austria and Hungary, or, as in international relations they are officially called, the Austro-Hungarian monarchy, consists of two States,— the Austrian Empire and the Hungarian Kingdom. The relation between the two States in its present form was fully regulated by the so-called Compromise of 1867. According to this agreement the two States are perfectly independent of each other, possessing each its own constitution, its legislative power, and its executive departments for most branches of State affairs. There is, however, a close political connection between them through the identity of the Sovereign and the community of certain departments of state affairs.

The common head of the monarchy is the Emperor (Kaiser) of Austria and King (Király) of Hungary. The crown is hereditary in the Habsburg-Lothringen dynasty, passing by right of primogeniture and lineal succession to males and (on failure of males) to females. The monarch must be a member of the Roman Catholic Church. He is styled "His Imperial and Royal Apostolic Majesty," being "Emperor of Austria, King of Bohemia, etc., and Apostolic King of Hungary."

Affairs common to the two States are: —(1) Foreign affairs; (2) military and naval affairs, but excluding legislation concerning the army; (3) finance relating to common affairs, but each State provides separately for the assessment, collection, and transmission of its contribution. The two States, moreover, form one commercial territory, having the same system of coinage and of weights and measures, a joint bank of issue, and the same commercial (as well as political) representation abroad, while the monopolies and taxes connected with industrial production (salt, tobacco, spirits, beer, sugar, and mineral oil) are the same in both. This commercial union, unlike the political connection, which has a permanent character, depends on a compromise renewable every ten years.

Legislative power relating to common affairs is exercised by the Parliaments of both States, but the voting of money to be applied to common purposes, and the control of the official action of the common ministries, belong to the so-called Delegations. Of these there are two, each consisting of 60 members, of whom 20 are chosen from each of the Upper Houses (the Austrian Herrenhaus and the Hungarian Förendiház), and 40 from each of the Lower Houses (the Austrian Abgeordnetenhaus and the Hungarian Képviselöhár). The members are appointed for one year. The Delegations are summoned annually by the Emperor, alternately at Vienna and Budapest. They deliberate independently of each other, their decisions being communicated reciprocally in writing; and if, after three such interchanges, they do not agree, then all the delegates (or an equal number of members from each Delegation) meet together, and, without discussion, settle the matter by vote. The three ministries or executive departments for common affairs are: —

1. The Common Ministry of Foreign Affairs and of the Imperial House.

2. The Common Ministry of War.

3. The Common Ministry of Finance.

To these departments must be added: —

The Common Court of Public Accounts.

The ministers are responsible for the discharge of their official functions to the Delegations.

Religion.—In Austria the relation of the State to the religious bodies is regulated by the statutes of December 21, 1867, and of May 25, 1868. In these the leading principle is religious liberty, the independence of the Church as regards the State, saving the rights of the sovereign arising from ecclesiastical dignity. Full liberty of faith and conscience is secured, and the enjoyment of civil and political rights is independent of religious profession. Every religious body, legally recognized, has the right of ordinary public worship, the management of its own affairs, and the undisturbed possession of its premises, endowments, and funds for the purposes of worship, instruction, or charity. Recognized religious bodies in Austria are: The Roman Catholic, Old Catholic, Greek-Oriental, Evangelical (Augsburg or Lutheran, and Helvetian or Reformed), the Evangelical Brotherhood, the Gregorian-Armenian, and the Jewish. The Minister for Ecclesiastical Affairs will grant legal recognition to any religious bodies if their doctrine, worship, constitution, and designation contain nothing illegal or immoral.

In Hungary there is perfect equality among all legally recognized religions. These are: The Roman and Greek Catholic, the Evangelical (Augsburg and Helvetian), the Greek-Oriental, the Gregorian-Armenian, the Unitarian, and the Jewish. Each has the independent administration of its own affairs.

Justice.—In Austria the ordinary judicial authorities are:—

(1) The Supreme Court of Justice and Court of Cassation (Oberste Gerichts-und Kassationshof) in Vienna. (2) The 9 higher provincial courts (Oberlandesgerichte). (3) The 71 provincial and district courts (Landes-und Kreisgerichte), and, in connection with these, the jury courts (Geschworenengerichte). (4) The 937 county courts (Bezirksgerichte). Of these the third and fourth groups are courts of first instance; the second group consists of courts of second instance. Courts of *first* instance act as courts of inquiry and have summary jurisdiction. Courts of second instance are courts of appeal from the lower courts, and have the supervision of the criminal courts in their jurisdiction. The jury courts try certain cases where severe penalties are involved, political offenses, and press offenses. The county courts exercise jurisdiction in cases of misdemeanor in the counties, and co-operate in preliminary proceedings regarding crime.

There are in all for Austria 71 provincial and 937 county or district courts.

There exist also special courts for commercial, revenue, military, and other matters.

In case of conflict between different authorities the Imperial Court (Reichsgerichte) in Vienna has power to decide.

In Hungary the ordinary judicial authorities are: —

The Royal Court (kir. kuria) in Budapest and the Supreme Court of Justice (Table of Septemvirs) in Zágráb (Agram), of the highest instance in all civil and criminal matters; 12 Royal Tables (királyi táblák) of second instance. As courts of first instance, 76 courts (törvényszékek) with collegiate judgeships; 456 county courts (járásbiróságok) with single judges; 15 jury courts (sajtóbiróságok) for press offenses, besides an army special court.

Instruction.—Public education in Hungary comprises the following grades: (1) Infant schools; (2) elementary schools; (3) middle or secondary schools, gymnasia and realschools (in Croatia and Slavonia, realgymnasia); (4) preparatory and training institutions for infant-school nurses and male and female teachers; (5) academies (high schools) of law; (6) institutions for religious education; (7) universities; (8) polytechnicum (technical high school). The schools for special subjects, such as agricultural, industrial, commercial, mining, and military schools, are for the greater part administered by the competent ministries, while the philanthropic and artistic schools are placed under the authority of the Ministry of Public Instruction.

Compulsory school attendance was established by law in 1868, for children of six to twelve years, and repetition courses for children of twelve to fifteen years; the industrial law of 1872 requires special courses for apprentices; and by the law of 1891, children from three to six years of age may be sent to infant schools, unless otherwise provided for.

Every parish or commune is bound to maintain an infant school.

The educational organization of Austria comprises: —

(1) Elementary schools; (2) gymnasia and realschulen; (3) universities and colleges; (4) technical high schools; and (5) schools for special subjects.

The erection of elementary schools is incumbent on the school districts. Compulsory attendance begins with the completion of the sixth year, and continues in Austria generally, till the completion of the fourteenth.

In Austria there are eight universities maintained by the State, each comprising four faculties, viz.: theology, law, medicine, philosophy.

Universities.	Professors, etc.	Students	Universities.	Professors, etc.	Students
			Cracow	153	1,201
			Lemberg	84	1,640
Vienna . .	444	5,796	Innsbruck	111	938
Prague, German	166	1,232	Czernowitz	40	369
Prague, Bohemian	168	2,470			
Graz . .	140	1,421	Total .	1,306	14,887

In addition to the universities there are in Austria 48 theological colleges, viz.: 44 Roman Catholic, 1 Greek Catholic, 1 Armenian Catholic, 1 Greek Oriental, and 1 Protestant, with a total of 2,068 students.

There are six Government technical high schools for various branches of engineering and technical chemistry, and a high school for agriculture in Vienna.

BELGIUM.

According to the Constitution of 1831 Belgium is "a constitutional, representative, and hereditary monarchy." The legislative power is vested in the King, the Senate, and the Chamber of Representatives. The royal succession is in the direct male line in the order of primogeniture. By marriage without the King's consent, however, the right of succession is forfeited, but may be restored by the King with the consent of the two Chambers. The King's person is declared sacred; and his ministers are held responsible for the acts of the Government. No act of the King can have effect unless countersigned by one of his ministers, who thus becomes responsible for it. The King convokes, prorogues, and dissolves the Chambers. In default of male heirs, the King may nominate his successor with the consent of the Chambers. If the successor be under eighteen years of age, which is declared to be the age of majority, the two Chambers meet together for the purpose of nominating a regent during the minority.

According to the law amending the constitution, promulgated 7th September, 1893, the Senate consists of members elected for eight years, partly directly, and partly indirectly. The number of Senators elected directly is proportioned to the population of each province, and is equal to half the number of members of the Chamber of Representatives. The constituent body is similar to that which elects deputies to the Chamber, except that the minimum age of electors is fixed at thirty years. In 1895–96 the number of electors was 1,186,000, disposing of 1,924,000 votes. Senators elected indirectly are chosen by the provincial councils, two for each province with less than 500,000 inhabitants; three for each with a population up to 1,000,000; and four for each with over 1,000,000. No one, during two years preceding the election, must have been a member of the council appointing him. All senators must be at least forty years of age, and those elected directly must pay not less than 1,200 francs in direct taxes, or own immovable property in Belgium yielding an income of 12,000 francs. In provinces, however, where the number eligible for the Senate would be less than one in 5,000 of population, the list is extended to this proportion by admission of the most highly taxed. Sons of the King, or failing these, Belgian princes of the reigning branch of the Royal Family are by right Senators at the age of eighteen, but have no voice in the deliberations till the age of twenty-five years.

The members of the Chamber of Representatives are elected directly. Their number is proportioned to the population, and cannot exceed one for every 40,000 inhabitants. They sit for four years, one half retiring every two years, except that after a dissolution a general election takes place. Every citizen over twenty-five years of age, domiciled for not less than one year in the same commune, and not legally disqualified, has a vote. Every citizen over thirty-five years of age, married or widower, with legitimate issue, and paying at least 5 francs a year in house tax, has a supplementary vote, as has also every citizen over twenty-five years of age owning immovable property to the value of 2,000 francs, or having a corresponding income from such property, or who for two years has derived at least 100 francs a year from Belgian funds either directly or through the Savings Bank. Two supplementary votes are given to citizens over twenty-five years of age who have received a diploma or certificate of higher instruction, or who fill or have filled offices or engaged in private professional practice, implying at least average higher instruction. No person has more than three votes; failure to vote is a misdemeanor, punishable by law. There were in 1896–97, 1,401,951 electors possessing, in all, 2,141,041 votes. Deputies must be not less than twenty-five years of age, and resident in Belgium. Each deputy has an annual indemnity of 4,000 francs (160*l.*), and a free pass over Government railways between his home and the place of Session.

The Senate and Chamber meet annually in the month of November, and must sit for at least forty days; but the King has the power of convoking them on extraordinary occasions, and of dissolving them either simultaneously or separately. In the latter case a new election must take place within forty days, and a meeting of the Chambers within two months. An adjournment cannot be made for a period exceeding one month without the consent of the Chambers. Money bills and bills relating to the contingent for the army originate in the Chamber of Representatives.

The Executive Government consists of eight departments, under the following Ministers:—

President of the Council.
Minister of Railways.
Minister of War.
Minister of Finance.
Minister of Foreign Affairs.
Minister of Justice.
Minister of Interior and Public Instruction.
Minister of Agriculture and Public Works.
Minister of Industry and Labor.

Besides the above responsible heads of departments, there are a number of "Ministres d'Etat," without portfolio, who form a Privy Council called together on special occasion by the sovereign. The acting ministers, as such, do not form part of the Privy Council.

Local Government.— The provinces and communes (2,607 in 1896) of Belgium have a large amount of autonomous government. The provincial and communal electors are the same as those who elect the senators directly. Communal electors must have been domiciled at least three years in the commune, and a supplementary vote is given to owners of real property yielding an income of at least 150 francs. No one has more than 4 votes. In communes with over 20,000 inhabitants there are councilors elected directly, by single vote, by citizens enrolled on the communal electoral lists, and possessing the qualifications requisite for electors to the Councils of Industry and Labor; half the councilors are appointed by the workingmen electors, and half by the electors who are industrial heads (chefs d' industrie). In communal elections vote by ballot is suppressed, except when there is merely a single mandate to be conferred. Candidates obtaining an absolute majority are declared elected; others have seats allocated in accordance with the system of "Proportional Representation." In the year 1896-97 there were 1,188,208 provincial and 1,124,276 communal electors. To be eligible to the Provincial or Communal Council, persons must be twenty-five years of age and domiciled in the province or commune. Half the Provincial Council is renewed every four years, and it meets fifteen days each year. There is a permanent deputation of six members elected, which is presided over by the Governor of the province. All provincial and communal interests, including local finances, are under the care of the Council, as far as they are not provided for in the general administration. The Communal Councils are elected for eight years, half being renewed every four years. In each commune there is a college composed of the burgomaster, president, and a certain number of aldermen, corresponding to the permanent deputation of the Provincial Council, and both are the organs of the central administration.

Religion.— The Roman Catholic religion is professed by nearly the entire population of Belgium. The Protestants number only 10,000, while the Jews number about 4,000. The State does not interfere in any way with the internal affairs of either Catholic or Protestant Churches. Full religious liberty is granted by the Constitution, and part of the income of the ministers of all denominations is paid from the national treasury.

Instruction.—There are four universities in the kingdom, three of them with four "facultés," or branches of study, and one Louvain, nursery of the clergy, with five; Ghent and Liège are State universities, Brussels and Louvain free.

Attached to the universities are various special schools of engineering, arts, manufactures, mining, etc.

Besides the above public schools there are many private or free schools—about 80 colleges, 65 middle-class schools for boys, 150 institutions for girls, besides many infant, primary, and adult schools, mostly under ecclesiastical care.

Justice.—Judges are appointed for life by the King from lists prepared by the Senate and by the Court. There is one Court of Cassation for the whole kingdom. There are three Courts of Appeal, and there are Assize Courts for criminal cases. The country is divided into 26 judicial arrondissements or districts, in each of which is a Court of first instance. In each canton there is a justice of the peace, a police court, and a judge of the peace; there are 216 such cantons. There are, besides, special military, commercial, and other tribunals. There is trial by jury in all criminal and political cases. The Gendarmerie (2,586) and the Garde Civique are utilized for the maintenance of internal order.

BRAZIL.

In 1807 the royal family of Portugal fled to Brazil; in 1815 the colony was declared "a kingdom"; and the Portuguese Court having returned to Europe in 1821, a National Congress assembled at Rio de Janeiro, and on May 13, 1822, Dom Pedro, eldest son of King João VI. of Portugal, was chosen "Perpetual Defender" of Brazil. He proclaimed the independence of the country on September 7, 1822, and was chosen "Constitutional Emperor and Perpetual Defender" on October 12 following. In 1831 he abdicated the crown in favor of his only son, Dom Pedro II., who reigned as Emperor until November 15, 1889, when by a revolution he was dethroned, and he and his family exiled, and Brazil declared a Republic under the title of the United States of Brazil.

General Deodoro Fonseca was the first President. On November 23, 1891, he resigned, and Vice-President Peixoto took his place. Dissatisfaction, occasioned principally by military interference in the States, led to a rising in Rio Grande do Sul, and to a naval revolt in the Bay of Rio de Janeiro. The rising in the South terminated in August, 1895, and the naval revolt was suppressed in March, 1894.

According to the constitution adopted by the National Congress in February, 1891, the Brazilian nation is constituted as the United States of Brazil Each of the old Provinces forms a State, administered at its own expense without interference from the Federal Government save for defense, for the maintenance of order, and for the execution of the Federal laws. Fiscal arrangements in such matters as import duties, stamps, rates of postage, and bank note circulation belong to the Union; but export duties are the property of the various States.

The legislative authority is exercised by the National Congress with the sanction of the President of the Republic. Congress consists of the Chamber of Deputies and the Senate. It meets annually on the 3d of May, without being convoked, unless another day be fixed by law, and sits four months, but may be prorogued or convoked extraordinarily. No member of Congress, after his election, can contract with the executive power or accept any commission or paid office, except such as are diplomatic or military or imposed by law. If, in ordinary circumstances, the acceptance of diplomatic or military office would cause the loss of the legislative services of a member, the permission of the Chamber is required. Nor can any member of Congress take part in the administration of any company which receives a subsidy from the Federal Government. Deputies and Senators are paid, and neither can be Ministers of State, and retain at the same time their seats in Congress. Deputies must have been Brazilian citizens for four years. Senators must be over thirty-five years of age and must have been citizens for six years.

The Chamber of Deputies consists of 212 members elected for three years by direct vote (providing for the representation of the minority), in a proportion not greater than one to every 70,000 of population as shown by a decennial census, but so that no State will have less than four representatives. It has the initiative in legislation relating to taxation.

Senators, 63 in number, are chosen by direct vote, three for each state, and for the Federal district, for nine years, and the Senate is renewed to the extent of one third every three years. The Vice-President of the Republic is President of the Senate.

The executive authority is exercised by the President of the Republic. He must be a native of Brazil, over thirty-five years of age. His term of office is four years, and he is not eligible for the succeeding term. The President and the Vice-President are elected by the people directly, by an absolute majority of votes. The election is held on the 1st of March in the last year of each presidential period in accordance with forms prescribed by law. No candidate must be related by blood or marriage, in the first or second degree, to the actual President or Vice-President, or to either who has ceased to be so within six months.

The President has the nomination and dismissal of ministers, supreme command of the army and navy, and, within certain limits, the power to declare war and make peace. He (with the consent of Congress) appoints the members of the Supreme Federal Tribunal and the diplomatic ministers. No minister can appear in Congress, but must communicate by letter, or in conference with commissions of the Chambers. Ministers are not responsible to Congress or the Tribunals for advice given to the President of the Republic.

The franchise extends to all citizens not under twenty-one years of age, duly enrolled, except beggars, "illiterates," soldiers actually serving, and members of monastic orders, etc., under vows of obedience.

There are six Secretaries of State at the head of the following Departments:—

1, Finance; 2, Justice, Interior and Public instructions; 3, War; 4, Marine; 5, Foreign Affairs; 6, Industry, Communications and Public Works.

In 1885 a bill was passed for the gradual extinction of slavery, and on May 13, 1888, an act was passed repealing all former acts on the subject, and abolishing slavery from the day of the promulgation of the law.

Local Government.—According to the new Constitution each State must be organized under the republican form of government, and must have its administrative, legislative, and judicial authorities distinct and independent. The governors and members of the legislatures must be elective; the magistrates must not be elective nor removable from office save by judicial sentence. The Federal executive cannot intervene directly in the local government of the States. In cases of obstinate infringement of the Federal Constitution by State authorities the only resource of the central power is an appeal to the Supreme Tribunal of Federal District. The Federal District is administered by a council elected by the citizens of the District, the municipal executive authority being exercised by a Prefect appointed for four years by the President of the Republic. There are in Brazil 892 municipalities and 1,886 parishes.

Religion.—The established religion under the Empire was the Roman Catholic, but under the Republic the connection between Church and State has been abolished, and absolute equality declared among all forms of religion. The Federal Government continues to provide for the salaries and maintenance of the existing functionaries of the Catholic Church. The population in 1890 contained 14,179,615 Catholics; 143,746 Protestants; 3,300 of other faiths; and 7,257 of no religious profession.

Brazil constitutes an ecclesiastical province, with a metropolitan archbishopric, the seat of which is at Bahia, 11 suffragan bishops, 12 vicars-general, and 2,000 curates. For the private instruction of the clergy there are 11 seminaries.

Instruction.—Public instruction is divided into three distinct forms or classes—namely, primary; secondary, or preparatory; and scientific, or superior. The higher education is controlled by the central Government. There are two schools of medicine, four of law, four military and one naval school, a school of mines, and a polytechnic. In 1890 these schools had, in all, 2,916 pupils. There are, besides, the Lyceum of Arts and Trades with 2,277 pupils, and five other special schools with 575 pupils. Connected with the observatory at Rio is a school for astronomy and engineering. The two establishments for secondary education, called jointly the *Gymnasio Nacional* (old Pedro II. college), confer a degree, and are controlled by Federal Government. The States Governments are allowed to found gymnasia with similar organization and privileges, and to a certain extent control this branch of instruction. All other secondary schools are private. Examinations are always official. Primary instruction in the Federal District is under the charge of the municipality, and in the States under the municipal and State authorities. According to the Constitution education is, at all stages, under lay management, and primary education is gratuitous. The central department complain that they can get no data from the States on public instruction. It seems that education is nowhere compulsory in Brazil. In 1889 there were, it was officially stated, 7,500 public and private primary schools, attended by 300,000 pupils in all. The number of illiterates is returned at 8,365,997, or 84 per cent. of the population.

Justice.—There is a supreme tribunal of Justice at Rio de Janeiro; and a court of appeal in the capital of each State. There are courts of first and second instance, both in civil and criminal cases. Judges are appointed for life. There are also municipal magistrates and justices of the peace, who are elected, and whose chief function is to settle cases by arbitration.

CHILE.

The Republic of Chile threw off allegiance to the Crown of Spain by the declaration of independence of September 18, 1810, finally freeing itself from the yoke of Spain in 1818. The Constitution voted by the representatives of the nation in 1833, with a few subsequent amendments, establishes three powers in the State—the legislative, the executive, and the judicial. The legislative power is vested in the National Congress, consisting of two assemblies, called the Senate and the Chamber of Deputies. The Senate is composed of members, elected for the term of six years, in the proportion of one Senator for every three Deputies; while the Chamber of Deputies, composed of members chosen for a period of three years, consists of one representative for every 30,000 of the population, or a fraction not less than 15,000; both bodies are chosen by the same electors—the Chamber directly by departments, and the Senate directly by provinces on the cumulative system of voting. Electors must be 21 years of age, and be able to read and write. In 1887 there were 134,119 registered electors, or 1 to 18 of the population. In the election of deputies in March, 1888, 89,977 citizens voted, or 67 per cent. of those who had the right to vote. Deputies must have an income of 100*l.* a year, and Senators 400*l.* The executive is exercised by the President of the Republic, elected for a term of five years, by indirect vote, the people nominating, by ballot, delegates who appoint the President. A retiring President is not re-eligible. In legislation the President has a modified veto; a bill returned to the Chambers with the President's objections may, by a two-thirds vote of the members present (a majority of the members being present), be sustained and become law. The day of a Presidential election is June 25 of the last of the five years of a Presidency, and the inauguration takes place on September 18 of the same year.

The salary of the President is fixed at 18,000 pesos, with 12,000 pesos for expenses.

The President is assisted in his executive

functions by a Council of State, and a Cabinet or Ministry, divided into seven departments, under six Ministers, viz.: Of the Interior; of Foreign Affairs; of Worship and Colonization; of Justice and Public Instruction; of Finance; of War and Marine; of Industry and Public Works. The Council of State consists of five members nominated by the President, and six members chosen by the Congress.

Local Government.— For the purposes of local government the Republic is divided into Provinces, presided over by *Intendents;* and the Provinces into Departments, with *Gobernadores* as chief officers. The Departments constitute one or more municipal districts each with a council or municipality of 9 members, inhabitants popularly elected for three years. The police of Santiago and of the capitals of departments is organized and regulated by the President of the Republic at the charge of the national treasury.

Religion.—The Roman Catholic religion is maintained by the State, but according to the Constitution all religions are respected and protected. There is one archbishop and three bishops. For 1898 the amount of subsidies to the clergy and for building and other purposes was 578,888 pesos. Civil marriage is the only form acknowledged by law.

Instruction.— Education is gratuitous and at the cost of the State, but is not compulsory. It is divided into superior or professional, medium or secondary, and primary or elementary instruction. Professional and secondary instruction is provided in the University and the National Institute of Santiago, and in the lyceums and colleges established in the capitals of provinces, and in some departments. In the University the branches included are law, physical and mathematical sciences, medicine, and fine arts. The number of students inscribed for the study of these branches in 1897 was 774. The number of students at the National Institute in 1897 was 1,278. There are 2 lyceums for girls in Santiago maintained by Government. There are, besides, provincial colleges, normal, agricultural, and other special schools. At the seats of the bishops there are seminaries under ecclesiastics where instruction is given similar to that in the Government colleges. There were, in 1897, 1,321 public primary schools, with 109,058 pupils, and an average attendance of 65,507, and 2,268 teachers. There were also 411 private schools, with an attendance of 18,052. The National Library contains over 86,000 volumes of printed books, and 24,048 manuscripts. Other educational institutions are the Pedagogic Institute, the National Conservatory of Music, the National Observatory, School of Arts and Trades, Institute for Deaf Mutes, and public museums. In 1897 the cost of higher instruction to the State was 2,000,000 pesos; the cost of maintaining the elementary schools was 1,920,200 pesos: and the total cost of instruction supplied by the State, including buildings, pensions, books, etc., in 1897, was 5,633,021 pesos.

Justice.— There are, in addition to a High Court of Justice in the capital, six Courts of Appeal, Courts of First Instance in the departmental capitals, and subordinate courts in the districts.

CHINA.

The laws of the Chinese Empire are laid down in the Ta-ts'ing-hwei-tien, or "Collected Regulations of the Ts'ing dynasty," which prescribe the government of the State to be based upon the government of the family.

The supreme direction of the Empire is vested in the Chün Chi Ch'u, the Privy Council, or Grand Council. The administration is under the supreme direction of the Nei-ko or Cabinet, comprising four members, two of Manchu and two of Chinese origin, besides two assistants from the Han-lin, or Great College, who have to see that nothing is done contrary to the civil and religious laws of the Empire, contained in the Ta-ts'ing-hwei-tien and in the sacred books of Confucius. These members are denominated "Ta-hsio-shih," or Ministers of State. Under their orders are the Ch'i-pu, or seven boards of government, each of which is presided over by a Manchu and a Chinese. These boards are: (1) the board of civil appointments, which takes cognizance of the conduct and administration of all civil officers; (2) the board of revenues, regulating all financial affairs; (3) the board of rites and ceremonies, which enforces the laws and customs to be observed by the people; (4) the military board; (5) the board of public works; (6) the high tribunal of criminal jurisdiction; and (7) the admiralty board at Tientsin, established in 1885.

Independent of the Government, and theoretically above the central administration, is the Tu-ch'a-yuen, or board of public censors. It consists of from 40 to 50 members, under two presidents, the one of Manchu and the other of Chinese birth. By the ancient custom of the Empire, all the members of this board are privileged to present any remonstrance to the sovereign. One censor must be present at the meetings of each of the Government boards.

The Tsungli Yamên, or Foreign Office, was created by a decree of January 19, 1861, and comprises among its members all those of the Council of State and six other officials of the highest rank. It controls not merely the matters with foreign nations, but also those institutions in which foreigners form part of the working staff, such as the Maritime Customs, and Peking University.

The present sovereign, reigning under the style of Kwangsii, is the ninth Emperor of China of the Manchu dynasty of Ts'ing, which overthrew the native dynasty of Ming, in the year 1644. There exists no law of hereditary succession to the throne, but it is left to each sovereign to appoint his successor from among the members of his family of a younger generation than his own. The late Emperor, dying suddenly in the eighteenth year of his age, did not designate a successor, and it was in consequence of arrangements directed by the Empress Dowager, widow of the Emperor Hien-Fêng, predecessor and father of T'ung-chi, in concert with Prince Ch'un, that the infant son of the latter was made the nominal occupant of the throne. Having become of age the young Emperor nominally assumed government in March, 1887. In February, 1889, he undertook the full control, but on September 22, 1898, an Imperial edict was issued announcing that the Emperor had resigned power to the Empress Dowager, who has since retained the direction of affairs.

Local Government.— Each of the 18 provinces is ruled by a Governor or Governor General, who is responsible to the Emperor for the entire administration, political, judicial, military, and fiscal. He is assisted by a council and various other officials, such as the Treasurer, the sub-Commissioner, and the Literary Chancellor. Each province is subdivided into departments ruled by prefects, and each department into districts, each with a district ruler. Two or more departments are sometimes united into a *tau*, the ruler of which is called a *tautai*. Each town and village has also its governing body, and among the various rulers there is regular gradation of rank, each being responsible to his immediate superior. Political office in the general administration of the Empire is less sought after than the position of viceroy or governor in the provinces, where the opportunities of acquiring wealth, not from official salaries but from gifts, etc., are abundant.

Religion.— Three religions are acknowledged by the Chinese as indigenous and adopted; viz., Confucianism, Buddhism, and Taoism.

The Emperor is considered the sole high priest of the Empire, and can alone, with his immediate representatives and ministers, perform the great religious ceremonies. No ecclesiastical hierarchy is maintained at the public expense, nor any priesthood attached to the Confucian religion. The Confucian is the State religion, if the respect paid to the memory of the great teacher can be called religion at all. But distinct and totally separate from the stated periodic observances of respect offered to the memory of Confucius as the Holy Man of old, and totally unconnected therewith, there is the distinct worship of Heaven (t'ien), in which the Emperor, as the "sole high priest," worships and sacrifices to "Heaven" every year at the time of the winter solstice, at the Altar of Heaven in Peking. With the exception of the practice of ancestral worship, which is everywhere observed throughout the Empire, and was fully commended by Confucius, Confucianism has little outward ceremonial. The study and contemplation and attempted performance of the moral precepts of the ancients constitute the duties of a Confucianist. Buddhism and Taoism present a very gorgeous and elaborate ritual in China, Taoism — originally a pure philosophy — having abjectly copied Buddhist ceremonial on the arrival of Buddhism 1,800 years ago. Large numbers of the Chinese in Middle and Southern China profess and practice all three religions. The bulk of the people, however, are Buddhists. There are probably about thirty million Mahometans, chiefly in the northeast and southwest. Roman Catholicism has long had a footing in China, and is estimated to have about 1,000,000 adherents, with 25 bishoprics besides those of Manchuria, Tibet, Mongolia, and Corea. Other Christian societies have stations in many parts of the country, the number of Protestant adherents being estimated at 50,000. Most of the aboriginal hill tribes are still nature worshipers, and ethnically are distinct from the prevailing Mongoloid population.

Instruction.— Education of a certain type is very general, but still there are vast masses of adult countrymen in China who can neither read nor write. There is a special literary class who alone know the literature of their country, to the study of which they devote their lives. There are boarding schools and day schools for boys and young men, the latter being held in the entrance halls of temples and in the spare chambers of guilds, and in all the important cities there are colleges for training candidates for degrees. Examinations, mainly confined to moral philosophy and literature, are held in the prefectorial cities of each province twice in three years for the lower degree necessary as a passport to the public service, but of the six or seven thousand candidates who come forward, not more than sixty can be admitted to the degree by the Literary Chancellor. For the higher degree, examinations are held in each provincial capital once in three years, and the successful candidates are subjected to a third and fourth examination, those who finally emerge being divided into four classes to wait for appointments to offices of different grades. There are, however, other means (*e. g.* military service) by which such appointments may be obtained. In 1887, for the first time, mathematics were admitted with the Chinese classics among the subjects of examination, and schools for the propagation of Western science and literature are now on the increase. The "Tung Wên Kwan," or College of Foreign Knowledge, at Peking, is a Government institution, where the English, French, German, Japanese, and Russian languages, and mathematics, chemistry, physiology, etc., are taught by European, Japanese, and American professors, while the Chinese education of the pupils is entrusted to Chinese teachers. There are, besides, numerous Catholic and Protestant mission schools and colleges at Shanghai and other ports, where the English language and lower branches of Western science are taught. The Chinese Government has of late years established naval and military colleges and torpedo schools in connection with the different arsenals at Tientsin, Nanking, Shanghai, and Foochow, in which foreign instructors are engaged to teach such young Chinese as intend to make their career in the army or navy of their country Western modes of warfare, besides Western languages and literature. Ten Chinese newspapers are published at Shanghai, and the success they have achieved has led to the establishment of others at some of the other treaty ports.

FRANCE.

Since the overthrow of Napoleon III., on September 4, 1870, France has been under a Republican form of government, confirmed on February 25, and June 16, 1875, by an organic law (*Constitution Wallon*), which has been partially modified in June, 1879, August, 1884, June, 1885, and July, 1889. It vests the legislative power in the Chamber of Deputies and the Senate, and the executive in the President of the Republic and the Ministry.

The President is elected for seven years, by a majority of votes, by the Senate and Chamber of Deputies united in a National Assembly, or Congress. He promulgates the laws voted by both Chambers, and ensures their execution. He selects a Ministry from the Chamber, appoints to all civil and military posts, has the right of individual pardon, and is responsible only in case of high treason. The President concludes treaties with foreign Powers, but cannot declare war without the previous assent of both Chambers. Every act of the President has to be countersigned by a Minister. With the consent of the Senate he can dissolve the Chamber of Deputies. In case of vacancy, the two Chambers united immediately elect a new President.

The Ministers or Secretaries of State, the number of whom varies, are usually, but not necessarily, members of the Senate or Chamber of Deputies. The President of the Council (Premier) chooses his colleagues in concert with the President of the Republic. Each Minister has the direction of one of the great administrative departments, and each is responsible to the Chambers for his acts, while the Ministry as a whole is responsible for the general policy of the Government.

The Ministry is constituted as follows: —

President of the Council and Minister of the Interior.

Minister of Finance.

Minister of Foreign Affairs.

Minister of War.
Minister of Marine.
Minister of Colonies.
Minister of Public Instruction and Worship.
Minister of Justice.
Minister of Commerce, Industry, and Posts and Telegraphs.
Minister of Agriculture.
Minister of Public Works.

The Chamber of Deputies is elected for four years, by universal suffrage, and each citizen 21 years old, not actually in military service, who can prove a six months' residence in any one town or commune, and not otherwise disqualified, has the right of vote. Deputies must be citizens and not under 25 years of age. The manner of election of Deputies has been modified several times since 1871. The *scrutin de liste*, under which each elector votes for as many Deputies as the entire department has to elect, was introduced in 1871. In 1876 it was replaced by the *scrutin d'arrondissement*, under which each department is divided into a number of *arrondissements*, each elector voting for one Deputy only; in 1885, there was a return to the *scrutin de liste*, and in 1889 the uninominal vote was reintroduced. In 1889 it was enacted that each candidate is bound to make, within the fortnight which precedes the elections, a declaration as to his being a candidate for a given constituency, and for one constituency only — all votes which eventually may be given for him in other constituencies being reckoned as void. Multiple elections and elections of persons previously condemned by the law courts are thus rendered impossible. The Chamber verifies the powers of its members. In each constituency the votes are cast up and the Deputy proclaimed elected by a commission of Councilors-General appointed by the Prefect of the department.

The Chamber is now composed of 584 Deputies; each *arrondissement* elects one Deputy, and if its population is in excess of 100,000, it is divided into two or more constituencies. There were 10,446,178 inscribed electors in 1893, and 7,427,354 voted.

The Senate is composed of 300 members, elected for nine years from citizens 40 years old, one third retiring every three years. The election of the Senators is indirect, and is made by an electoral body composed (1) of delegates chosen by the Municipal Council of each commune in proportion to the population; and (2) of the Senators, Deputies, Councilors-General, and District Councilors of the department. Besides the 225 Departmental Senators elected in this way, there were, according to the law of 1875, 75 Senators elected for life by the united two Chambers; but by the Senate Bill of 1884 it was enacted that vacancies arising among the Life Senatorships would be filled by the election of ordinary nine-years Senators, the department which should have the right to the vacant seat to be determined by lot. The Princes of deposed dynasties are precluded from sitting in either House.

The Senate and Chamber of Deputies assemble every year on the second Tuesday in January, unless a previous summons is made by the President of the Republic, and they must remain in session at least five months out of the twelve. The President is bound to convoke them if the demand is made by one half of the number of members composing each Chamber. The President can adjourn the Chambers, but the adjournment cannot exceed the term of a month, nor occur more than twice in the same session.

Bills may be presented either in the Chamber or Senate by the Government, or on the initiative of private members. In the first case they are remitted to the bureaux for examination; in the second, they are first submitted to a commission of parliamentary initiative. Financial laws must be first presented to and voted by the Chamber of Deputies.

The President and the Ministers may be impeached by the Chamber of high treason, in which case the Senate acts as a High Court of Justice. The same function is vested in the Senate for all other cases of high treason.

Senators and Deputies are paid 9,000 francs (£360) a year, and the Presidents of the two Chambers receive, in addition, 72,000 francs (£2,840) for the expense of entertainment. Members of both Chambers travel free on all railways by means of a small annual payment. The dotation of the President of the Republic is 600,000 francs, with a further allowance of 600,000 francs for his expenses.

France has, besides, a special institution under the name of *Conseil d'Etat*, which was introduced by Napoleon I., and has been maintained since. It is presided over by the Minister of Justice or (in his absence) by a vice-president, and is composed of Councilors, Masters of Requests (*Maîtres de Requêtes*), and Auditors, all appointed by the President of the Republic. Its duty is to give opinion upon such questions, chiefly those connected with administration, as may be submitted to it by the Government. It is judge in the last resort in administrative suits, and it prepares the rules for the public administration.

Local Government.—For administrative purposes France is divided into 86 departments, or 87 if the "territory of Belfort" (a remnant of the department of Haut-Rhin) be considered as a separate department. Since 1881 the three departments of Algeria are also treated.

for most purposes, as part of France proper. The department has representatives of all the Ministries, and is placed under a Prefect, nominated by Government, and having wide and undefined functions. He is assisted by a Prefectorial Council, an administrative body, whose advice he may take without being bound to follow it. The Prefect is a representative of the Executive, and, as such, supervises the execution of the laws, issues police regulations, supplies information on matters which concern the department, nominates subordinate officials, and has under his control all officials of the State. There is a sub-Prefect in every *arrondissement*, except capitals of departments and the department of the Seine.

The unit of local Government is the *commune*, the size and population of which vary very much. There are 36,170 communes, and new ones cannot be created otherwise than by law. Most of them (31,610) have less than 1,500 inhabitants, and 18,054 have even less than 500; while 117 communes only have more than 20,000 inhabitants. The local affairs of the commune are under a Municipal Council, composed of from 10 to 36 members, elected by universal suffrage, and by the *scrutin de liste* for 4 years by Frenchmen after 21 years and 6 months' residence; but each act of the Council must receive the approval of the Prefect, while many must be submitted to the Council General, or even to the President of the Republic, before becoming lawful. Even the commune's quota of direct taxation is settled by persons (*rêpartiteurs*) chosen by the Prefect from among the lists of candidates drawn up by the Municipal Council.

Each Municipal Council elects a Mayor, who is both the representative of the commune and the agent of the central government. He is the head of the local police and, with his assistants, acts under the orders of the Prefect.

In Paris the Municipal Council is composed of 80 members; each of the 20 *arrondissements* into which the city is subdivided has its own Mayor. The place of the Mayor of Paris is taken by the Prefect of the Seine, and, in part, by the Prefect of Police. Lyons has an elected Mayor, but the control of the police is vested in the Prefect of the department of the Rhone.

The next unit is the *canton* (2,899 in France), which is composed of an average of 12 communes, although some of the largest communes are, on the contrary, divided into several cantons. It is a seat of a justice of the peace, but is not an administrative unit.

The district, or *arrondissement* (362 in France), has an elected *conseil d'arrondisement*, with as many members as there are *cantons*, its chief function being to allot among the communes their respective parts in the direct taxes assigned to each *arrondissement* by the Council General. That body stands under the control of the sub-Prefect. A varying number of *arrondissements* form a department, which has its *conseil général* renewed by universal suffrage.

Religion.— All religions are equal by law, and any sect which numbers 100,000 adherents is entitled to a grant; but at present only the Roman Catholics, Protestants, and Jews have State allowances.

Instruction.— Public education in France is entirely under the supervision of the Government. The highest schools, or "facultés de l'Etat," are now often designated by the name of universities. There are 15 "facultés des lettres," one in each academy (except Chambéry) at Paris, Aix, Besançon, Bordeaux, Caen, Clermont, Dijon, Lille, Grenoble, Lyon, Montpellier, Nancy, Poitiers, Rennes, and Toulouse. At all of these, except Aix, are also "facultés des sciences," besides one at Marseilles (instead of Aix, belonging to the same academy). There are also 2 "facultés" of Protestant theology, 13 "facultés de droit," and 7 "facultés de médecine et pharmacie," 19 superior or preparatory schools of pharmacy, and 8 schools of law, science, or letters. In January, 1898, there were 137 students of Protestant theology; 9,371 of law; 7,426 of medicine; 3,544 of sciences; 3,404 of letters; and 4,661 at superior and preparatory schools of pharmacy, etc.; total, 28,543 students. To the support of the "facultés" the sum of 12,496,911 francs was set down in the budget of 1899. The Roman Catholic theological "facultés" were suppressed in 1885. Catholic "facultés" or "écoles libres" exist on certain conditions as private establishments. The "Collége de France," "Muséum d'histoire naturelle," "Ecole pratique des hautes études," "Ecole des chartes," etc., are public establishments for highest education. The "Ecole libre des Sciences politiques" is a private establishment.

There are many other public establishments for special training. For military and naval education: Ecole Supérieure de Guerre, Ecole Polytechnique, Ecole Speciale Militaire de St. Cyr, Ecole Supérieure de la Marine, Ecole Navale de Brest, etc.; for civil services and industry: Ecole des Mines, Ecole des Ponts et Chaussées, Ecole Centrale des Artes et Manufactures, Ecole Superieure des Hautes Etudes commerciales, Conservatoire des Artes et Metiers.

Elementary schools existed before the Revolution in the towns and in many of the rural parishes of France, but little was done for the advancement of education till near the first quarter of this century. In 1833 a law was passed requiring every commune to maintain at least one primary school, every town one higher primary school, and every department one primary normal school. A law of 1850 obliged every commune with a population of 800 (extended in 1867 to communes with a population of 500) to have a school for girls. Since 1878 elementary education has advanced rapidly; many schools have been built, the number of teachers and pupils has increased (until 1889), and the standard of education has been raised. In 1881 primary instruction was made free, and in 1882, obligatory for children from 6 to 13 years of age. In 1886 the system of education was reorganized, and it was ordained that all public schools should be under the charge of laymen. In 1892 there were only 50 communes which had no primary school, public or private.

Colonies and Dependencies.

	Year of Acquisition.	Area in Square Miles.	Population.
IN ASIA:			
India	1679	197	286,910
Annam	1884	81,000	6,000,006
Cambodia	1862	46,000	1,500,000
Cochin-China	1861	22,950	2,035,000
Tonking (with Laos)	1884–93	135,000	12,000,000
Total of Asia	....	285,147	21,821,910
IN AFRICA:			
Algeria	1830	184,474	4,430,000
Algerian Sahara	....	123,500	50,000
Tunis	1881	50,840	1,500,000
Sahara Region	....	1,684,000	2,500,000
Senegal	1637	115,800	2,000,000
Western Sudan	1880	250,190	4,900,000
Ivory Coast, etc	1843	64,420	650,000
Dahomey	1893	14,140	600,000
Congo	1884	496,920	8,950,000
Bagirmi	1895	65,650	1,000,000
Obock and Somali Coast	1864	8,640	30,000
Réunion	1649	970	171,720
Comoro Isles	1886	620	53,000
Mayotte	1843	143	8,700
Nossi-Bé	1841	113	7,800
Ste. Marie	1643	64	7,670
Madagascar	1896	227,750	3,500,000
Total of Africa	....	3,288,034	30,358,890
IN AMERICA:			
Guiana	1626	46,850	22,710
Guadeloupe and Dependencies	1634	688	167,100
Martinique	1635	380	187,690
St. Pierre and Miquelon	1635	93	6,250
Total of America	....	48,011	383,750
IN OCEANIA:			
New Caledonia and Dependencies	1854	7,630	51,000
Marquesas Islands	1841	480	4,450
Tahiti and Moorea	1880	455	11,800
Tubuaï and Raivavae	1881	80	880
Tuamotu and Gambier Islands	1881	390	5,250
Wallis Archipelago, etc	1887	100	5,000
Total of Oceania	....	9,135	78,380
Grand Total	....	3,630,327	52,642,930

Justice.—The Courts of First Instance in France are those of the Justices of Peace who try civil cases and act also as judges of Police Courts, where all petty offenses are disposed of. In criminal cases the Police Correctional Courts pronounce upon all graver cases of misdemeanour (*délits*), including cases involving imprisonment up to 5 years. They have no jury, and consist of 3 judges belonging to the civil tribunals. In all general cases, the preliminary inquiry is made in secrecy by an examining magistrate (*juge d'instruction*), who, acting under the public ministry (*Procureur*), may dismiss the case or send it for trial. The Court of Assizes is assisted by 12 jurors, who decide by simple majority on the fact with respect to crimes involving a severe penalty. The highest courts are the 26 Courts of Appeal, composed each of one President and 4 Councilors for all criminal cases which have been tried without a jury, and by one Court of Cassation which sits at Paris, and is composed of a first President, 3 Presidents of Sections, and 45 Councilors, for all criminal cases tried by jury.

For civil cases there is, under the Justice of Peace, in each *arrondissement*, a civil tribunal of first instance, then the Appeal Courts and Courts of Cassation. For commercial cases there are Tribunals of Commerce and Councils of experts (*prud'hommes*).

All Judges are nominated by the President of the Republic. They can be removed only by a decision of the Court of Cassation constituted as the *Conseil Supérieur* of the magistracy.

GERMAN EMPIRE.

The present German Empire is essentially different from the Holy Roman Empire which came to an end in 1806. But though Austria, the most important factor in the earlier Empire, is not a member of the present, a brief historical summary, including both, is for convenience inserted here. The imperial throne, after the extinction of the Carlovingian line, was filled by election, though with a tendency towards the hereditary principle of succession. At first the Emperor was chosen by the vote of all the Princes and Peers of the Reich; but the mode came to be changed in the fourteenth century, when a limited number of Princes, fixed at seven for a time, and afterwards enlarged to eight (nine from 1692 to 1777), assumed the privilege of disposing of the crown, and, their right being acknowledged, were called Electors. With the overthrow of the old Empire by the Emperor Napoleon, in 1806, the Electoral dignity virtually ceased, although the title of Elector was retained sixty years longer by the sovereigns of Hesse-Cassel, the last of them dethroned in 1866 by Prussia. The election of Wilhelm I., King of Prussia, as the German Emperor (1871) was by vote of the Reichstag of the North German Confederation, on the initiative of all the reigning Princes of Germany. The imperial dignity is hereditary in the House of Hohenzollern, and follows the law of primogeniture.

The Constitution of the Empire bears date April 16, 1871. By its terms, all the States of Germany "form an eternal union for the protection of the realm and the care of the welfare of the German people." The supreme direction of the military and political affairs of the Empire is vested in the King of Prussia, who, in this capacity, bears the title of Deutscher Kaiser. According to Art. 11 of the Constitution, "the Emperor represents the Empire internationally," and can declare war, if defensive, and make peace, as well as enter into treaties with other nations, and appoint and receive ambassadors. But when treaties relate to matters regulated by imperial legislation, and when war is not merely defensive, the Kaiser must have the consent of the Bundesrath, or Federal Council, in which body, together with the Reichstag, or Diet of the realm, are vested the legislative functions of the Empire. The Emperor has no veto on laws passed by these bodies. The Bundesrath represents the individual States of Germany, and the Reichstag the German nation. The 58 members of the Bundesrath are appointed by the Governments of the individual States for each session, while the members of the Reichstag, 397 in number (about one for every 131,604 inhabitants), are elected by universal suffrage and ballot for the term of five years. By the law of March 19, 1888, which came into force in 1890, the duration of the legislative period is five years.

Both the Bundesrath and the Reichstag meet in annual session, convoked by the Emperor. The Emperor has the right to prorogue and dissolve, after a vote by the Bundesrath, the Reichstag. Without consent of the Reichstag the prorogation may not exceed thirty days; while in case of dissolution new elections must take place within sixty days, and a new session must open within ninety days. All laws for the Empire must receive the votes of an absolute majority of the Bundesrath and the Reichstag. The Bundesrath is presided over by the Reichskanzler, or Chancellor of the Empire, and the President of the Reichstag is elected by the deputies.

The laws of the Empire, passed by the Bundesrath and the Reichstag, to take effect must be promulgated by the Emperor, and the promulgation, like all other official acts of the Emperor, requires the counter-signature of the Chancellor of the Empire. All the members of the Bundesrath have the right to be present at the deliberations of the Reichstag.

The following are the imperial authorities or Secretaries of State: they do not form a Ministry or Cabinet, but act independently of each other, under the general supervision of the Chancellor.

1. *Chancellor of the Empire.*
2. *Ministry for Foreign Affairs.*
3. *Imperial Home Office and "Representative of the Chancellor."*
4. *Imperial Admiralty.*
5. *Imperial Ministry of Justice.*
6. *Imperial Treasury.*

7. *Imperial Post Office.*
8. *Imperial Railways.*
9. *Imperial Exchequer.*
10. *Imperial Invalid Fund.*
11. *Imperial Bank.*
12. *Imperial Debt Commission.*

Acting under the direction of the Chancellor of the Empire, the Bundesrath represents also a supreme administrative and consultive board, and as such has twelve standing committees—namely, for army and fortifications; for naval matters; tariff, excise, and taxes; trade and commerce; railways, posts, and telegraphs; civil and criminal law; financial accounts; foreign affairs; for Alsace-Lorraine; for the Constitution; for the standing orders; and for railway tariffs. Each committee consists of representatives of at least four States of the Empire; but the foreign affairs committee includes only the representatives of Bavaria, Saxony, Würtemberg, and two other representatives to be elected every year.

Religion.—The Constitution provides for entire liberty of conscience and for complete social equality among all religious confessions. The relation between Church and State varies in different parts of the Empire. The order of the Jesuits is interdicted in all parts of Germany, and all convents and religious orders, except those engaged in nursing the sick and purely contemplative orders, have been suppressed. There are five Roman Catholic archbishops, and twenty bishoprics. The "Old Catholics" have a bishop at Bonn.

The various creeds were distributed as follows at the last religious census, 1895:—

Creed	Numbers	Per Cent. of Pop.
Evangelicals	1,440,240	69.2
Roman Catholics	621,474	29.9
Other Christians	7,451	0.36
Jews	11,887	0.57
Others	99	0.004

Instruction.—Education is general and compulsory throughout Germany. The laws of Prussia, which provide for the establishment of elementary schools (*Volksschulen*), supported from the local rates, in every town and village, and compel all parents to send their children to these or other schools, have been adopted, with slight modifications, in all the States of the Empire. The school age is from six to fourteen. The system of secondary education is also practically homogeneous. Above the elementary schools rank the middle schools of the towns, the *Bürgerschulen* and *Höhere Bürgerschulen*, which fit their pupils for business life. Children of the working classes may continue their education at the *Fortbildungs-Schulen* or continuation schools, which are open in the evening or other convenient time. The *Gymnasia* are the most fully developed classical schools, preparing pupils in a nine years' course for the universities and the learned professions. The *Progymnasia* differ from these only in not having the highest classes. In the *Realgymnasia*, Latin, but not Greek is taught, and what are usually termed "modern subjects" have more time devoted to them. *Realprogymnasia* have a similiar course, but have no class corresponding to the highest class in the preceding. In the *Oberrealschulen* and *Realschulen* Latin is wholly displaced in favor of modern languages. In 1897, 1,048 secondary schools (including 56 private schools), also 181 public *Lehrer-Seminare* and 32 public *Fachschulen*: total 1,261 institutions, possessed the right of granting certificates to pupils, entitling them to serve in the army as one-year volunteers. The teachers in German schools are required to hold a Government certificate, and to have undergone a year's probation. Higher schools for girls are called *Höhere Töchterschulen*. Besides these there are numerous *Gewerbeschulen* or technical schools, *Polytechnica*, normal schools, seminaries, and the universities.

There are 21 universities in the German Empire, besides the Lyceum Hosianum at Braunsberg (9 teachers and about forty students), which has only faculties of theology (Roman Catholic) and philosophy.

The following table gives the number of teachers for the summer half-year, 1898, and the number of students for the winter half-year, 1897-98.

Universities	Professors and Teachers	Students				
		Theology	Jurisprudence	Medicine	Philosophy	Total
Berlin	372	441	1,984	1,360	2,150	5,935
Bonn	147	304	409	264	694	1,671
Breslau	164	324	443	345	385	1,497
Erlangen	68	240	182	434	112	1,068
Freiburg	115	218	249	392	214	1,073
Giessen	72	58	236	224	156	674
Göttingen	123	137	336	236	445	1,154
Greifswald	91	209	167	293	87	756
Halle	144	411	346	265	584	1,606
Heidelberg	147	54	340	203	487	1,084
Jena	96	35	158	198	241	632
Kiel	102	61	125	263	131	580
Königsberg	113	67	211	235	171	684
Leipzig	208	348	1,032	724	1,173	3,277
Marburg	100	110	229	249	320	908
München	180	152	1,145	1,396	1,124	3,817
Münster	48	315	....	....	211	526
Rostock	49	30	119	106	196	451
Strassburg	137	82	335	329	320	1,066
Tübingen	98	409	441	255	121	1,226
Würzburg	101	146	249	742	288	1,425

In four universities, namely, Freiburg, München, Münster, and Würzburg, the faculties of theology are Roman Catholic; three are mixed, both Protestant and Roman Catholic—Bonn, Breslau, and Tübingen; and the remaining fourteen are Protestant.

Justice.—In terms of Judicature Acts in 1877 and 1879 a uniform system of law courts was adopted throughout the Empire not later than January 1, 1879, though with the exception of the Reichsgericht, all courts are directly subject to the Government of the special State in which they exercise jurisdiction, and not to the Imperial Government. The appointment of the judges is also a State and not an Imperial function. The Empire enjoys uniform codes of commercial and criminal law, and the civil code of August 18, 1896, will come into force on January 1, 1900.

The lowest courts of first instance are the *Amtsgerichte*, each with a single judge, competent to try petty civil and criminal cases. There was on January 1, 1897, 1,926 Amtsgerichte in the Empire, or one for every 27,144 inhabitants. The *Landgerichte* exercise a revising jurisdiction over the Amtsgerichte, and also a more extensive original jurisdiction in both civil and criminal cases, divorce cases, etc. In the criminal chamber five judges sit, and a majority of four votes is required for a conviction. Jury courts (*Schwurgerichte*) are also held periodically, in which three judges preside; the jury are twelve in number. There are 172 Landgerichte in the Empire, or one for every 303,953 of the population. The first court of second instance is the *Oberlandesgericht*. In its criminal senate, which also has an original jurisdiction in serious cases, the number of the judges is seven. There are twenty-eight such courts in the Empire. The total number of judges on the bench in all the courts above mentioned is 7,634. In Bavaria alone there is an *Oberste Landesgericht*, with eighteen judges, with a revising jurisdiction over the Bavarian Oberlandesgerichte. The supreme court is the *Reichsgericht*, which sits at Leipzig. The judges, eighty-four in number, are appointed by the Emperor on the advice of the Bundesrath. The court exercises an appellate jurisdiction over all inferior courts, and also an original jurisdiction in cases of treason. It has four criminal and six civil senates.

Foreign Dependencies.—Germany has declared her protection over various areas or spheres of influence in Africa, in China, and in the Western Pacific. The following is a list of the various foreign regions at present (1899) under the protection or influence of Germany, the estimates given being necessarily vague:—

	Date of Acquisition.	Method of Government.	Estimated Area, Sq. Miles.	Estimated Population.
IN AFRICA:—				
Togoland	1884	Imperial Commissioner	33,000	2,500,000
Kamerun	1884	Imperial Governor	191,130	3,500,000
German South-West Africa	1884–90	Imperial Commissioner	322,450	200,000
German East Africa	1885–90	Imperial Governor	384,180	4,000,000
Total African Possessions	1884–90		930,760	10,200,000
IN ASIA:—				
Kiauchau Bay	1897	Imperial Governor	120*	60,000*
IN THE PACIFIC:—				
Kaiser Wilhelm's Land	1885–86	New Guinea Company	70,000	110,000
Bismarck Archipelago	1885	New Guinea Company	20,000	188,000
Solomon Islands	1886	New Guinea Company	9,000	89,000
Marshall Islands, etc	1886	Imperial Commissioner	150	13,000
Total Pacific Possessions	1884–86		99,270	460,000
Total Foreign Dependencies	1884–97		1,030,030	10,660,000

* Exclusive of the Bay with an area of about 200 square miles, and the neutral zone with an area of about 2,500 square miles, and population of 1,200,000.

GREECE.

Greece, a province of the Turkish Empire since the commencement of the 16th century, gained its independence in the insurrection of 1821–29, and by the Protocol of London, of February 3, 1830, was declared a kingdom, under the protection of Great Britain, France, and Russia. Prince Leopold of Saxe-Coburg having declined the crown of Greece, on the ground that the boundaries proposed were insufficient, and especially excluded the island of Crete, it was offered to, and accepted by, Prince Otto of Bavaria, who ascended the throne January 25, 1833, being under the age of eighteen. He was expelled from the Kingdom, after a reign of 29 years, in October, 1862, which event was followed by the election, under the directing guidance of the three protecting Powers, of the present sovereign.

The King, according to Art. 49 of the Constitution of 1864, attains his majority upon completing his eighteenth year. Before he ascends the throne, he must take the oath to the Constitution in the presence of the ministers, the sacred synod, the deputies then in the metropolis, and the higher officials of the realm. Within two months at the most the King must convoke the Legislature. If the successor to the throne is either a minor or absent at the time of the King's decease, and no Regent has been appointed, the Legislative Chamber has to assemble of its own accord within ten days after the occurrence of that event. The constitutional royal authority in this case has to be exercised by the ministerial council, until the choice of a Regent, or the arrival of the successor to the throne. The present sovereign is allowed, by special exception, to adhere to the religion in which he was educated, the Protestant Lutheran faith, but his heirs and successors must be members of the Greek Orthodox Church.

The Constitution of Greece, adopted October 29, 1864, vests the whole legislative power in a single chamber, called the Boulé, consisting of 207 representatives, elected by manhood suffrage for the term of four years. Representatives must be at least 30 years of age, and electors 21. The elections take place by ballot, and each candidate must be put in nomination by the requisition of at least one thirtieth of the voters of an electoral district. At the election of 1881 there were 460,163 voters on the list, being 1 voter in every 4.3 of the population; the number who voted was 306,957, or 66 per cent. of the voters. The Boulé must meet annually for not less than three, nor more than six, months. No sitting is valid unless at least one half of the members of the Assembly are present, and no bill can pass into law without an absolute majority of members. Every measure, before being adopted, must be discussed and voted, article by article, thrice, and on three separate days. But the Legislative Assembly has no power to alter the Constitution itself; particular provisions may be reviewed after the lapse of ten years, with the exception of "fundamental principles." The Chamber of Deputies, unless specially convoked at an earlier date, for extraordinary occasions, must meet on November 1 (old style) of every year. The deputies are paid 2,000 old drachmai (equal to 1,800 new drachmai, or 72*l.*) each per session; for an extra session the allowance varies according to its length from 20*l.* to 72*l.*

The Ministry is as follows:—

President of the Council and Minister of Foreign Affairs.

Minister of Interior, Worship, and Instruction.

Minister of Marine.
Minister of War.
Minister of Finance.
Minister of Justice.

The Ministers of Finance and Justice are not members of the Cabinet.

Religion.—The great majority of the inhabitants of the Kingdom are adherents of the Greek Orthodox Church. Before the census of 1889 there were 1,902,800 belonging to the Greek Orthodox Church; 14,677 other Christians, mainly Roman Catholics; 5,792 Jews; and 24,165 Mohammedans. By the terms of the Constitution of 1864, the Greek Orthodox Church is declared the religion of the State, but complete toleration and liberty of worship is guaranteed to all other sects. Nominally, the Greek clergy owe allegiance to the Patriarch of Constantinople, though he now exercises no governing authority; he is elected by the votes of the bishops and optimates subject to the Sultan; his jurisdiction extends over Thrace and other countries, including Bosnia, as well as the greater part of Asia Minor. The real ecclesiastical authority, formerly exercised by him in Greece, was annulled by the resolutions of a National Synod, held at Nauplia in 1833, which vested the government of the Orthodox Church, within the limits of the Kingdom, in a permanent council, called the Holy Synod, consisting of the Metropolitan of Athens and four archbishops and bishops, who must during their year of office reside at the seat of the executive. The Orthodox Church has nine archbishops and eight bishops in Northern Greece; six archbishops and six bishops in the Peloponnesus; one archbishop and five bishops in the islands of the Greek Archipelago; and five archbishops and ten bishops in the Ionian Islands. There are 161 monasteries and nunneries, with 2,620 monks and 485 nuns.

Instruction.—All children between the ages of five and twelve years must attend school, but the law is not well enforced in country districts. Of the army recruits 30 per cent. are illiterate, and 15 per cent. can read only.

There are (1892) 2,745 primary schools, 295 secondary schools, and a university. The total number of teachers is 3,680, and of pupils, 139,385, of whom 22,100 are females. There are 2 agricultural schools in Greece with, together, 51 pupils. In 1895 an industrial and commercial school, with 40 teachers, was opened at Piræus to give instruction in the industries relating to wine, spirits, beer, soap, perfumes, dairy-keeping, cattle and silkworm rearing, and in the duties of commercial clerks. In 1895 the University of Athens had 2,987 students, of whom 967 studied medicine, 1,327 law, 516 philosophy, 51 theology, 124 chemistry. Of the total number 604 were from abroad, chiefly from Turkey.

ITALY.

The present Constitution of Italy is an expansion of the "Statuto fondamentale del Regno," granted on March 4, 1848, by King Charles Albert to his Sardinian subjects. According to this charter, the executive power of the State belongs exclusively to the Sovereign, and is exercised by him through responsible ministers; while the legislative authority rests conjointly in the King and Parliament, the latter consisting of two Chambers—an upper one, the Senato, and a lower one, called the "Camera de' Deputati." The Senate is composed of the princes of the royal house who are of age, and of an unlimited number of members, above forty years old, who are nominated by the King for life; a condition of the nomination being that the person should either fill a high office, or have acquired fame in science, literature, or any other pursuit tending to the benefit of the nation, or, finally, should pay taxes to the annual amount of 3,000 lire, or 120*l.* In 1897, there were 372 senators. By the electoral law of March 28, 1895, electors for deputies to the Lower House are all citizens over twenty-one years of age who can read and write and who possess one or other of the following qualifications: they must have reached a certain standard in elementary education; or must pay not less than 19.80 lire in direct (including provincial) taxation; or, if peasant farmers, must pay annually at least 500 lire of rent, or be managers, with a share in the profits, of farms on which direct (including provincial) taxes of not less than 80 lire are paid; or, being occupants of lodgings, shops, etc., in towns, pay an annual rent ranging from 150 lire in communes of 2,500 inhabitants to 400 lire in communes of 150,000 inhabitants. Non-commissioned officers and men in the army have no vote while under arms. Members of academies, professors, persons who have served their country under arms for two years, and numerous other classes are qualified to vote by their position. The number of deputies is 508, or 1 to every 57,000 of the population (census 1881). In 1896 the number of enrolled electors was 2,120,909, exclusive of the electors temporarily disfranchised on account of military service (39,029 in 1895). At the general election in March, 1897, the number of those who voted was 1,241,486, or 58.5 per cent. of those who had the right to vote. For electoral purposes the whole of the Kingdom is divided into 508 electoral colleges or districts, and these again into several sections. No deputy can be returned to Parliament unless he has obtained a number of votes greater than one sixth of the total number of inscribed electors, and than half the votes given. A deputy must be thirty years old, and have the requisites demanded by the electoral law. Incapable of being elected are all salaried Government officials, as well as all persons ordained for the priesthood and filling clerical charges, or receiving pay from the State. Officers in the army and navy, ministers, under-secretaries of State, and various other classes of functionaries high in office, may be elected, but their number must never be more than forty, not including the ministers and the under-secretaries of State. Neither senators nor deputies receive any salary or other indemnity, but are allowed to travel free throughout Italy by rail or steamer.

The duration of Parliament is five years; but the King has the power to dissolve the Lower House at any time, being bound only to order new elections, and convoke a new meeting within four months. It is incumbent upon the executive to call the Parliament together annually. Each of the Chambers has the right of introducing new bills, the same as the Government; but all money bills must originate in the House of Deputies. The ministers ha e the right to attend the debates of both the Upper and the Lower House; but they have no vote unless they are members. The sittings of both Chambers are public; and no sitting is valid unless an absolute majority of the members are present.

The executive power is exercised, under the King, by a ministry divided into 11 departments, as follows:

1. *President of the Council and Minister of Interior.*
2. *Minister of Foreign Affairs*
3. *Minister of the Treasury.*
4. *Minister of Finance.*
5. *Minister of Justice and of Ecclesiastical Affairs.*
6. *Minister of War.*
7. *Minister of Marine.*
8. *Minister of Commerce, Industry, and Agriculture.*
9. *Minister of Public Instruction.*
10. *Minister of Public Works.*
11. *Minister of Posts and Telegraphs.*

Local Government.—The two principal elective local administrative bodies are the communal councils and the provincial councils. According to the law of February 10, 1889, each commune has a communal council, a municipal council, and a syndic. Both the communal councils and the municipal councils vary according to population, the members of the latter being selected by the former from among themselves. The syndic is the head of the communal administration, and is a Government official; he is elected by the communal council from among its own members, by secret vote, in all the chief communes of provinces and districts, and in other communes having more than 10,000 inhabitants. In other communes the syndic is appointed by the King from among the communal councilors. Each province has a provincial council and a provincial commission, the members varying according to population. The council elects its president and other officials. The provincial commission is elected by the council from its own members. It conducts the business of the province when the latter is not sitting. Both communal and provincial councilors are elected for five years, one fifth being renewed every year. The communal council meets twice and the provincial once a year in ordinary session, though they may be convened for extraordinary purposes. All communal electors are eligible to the council except those having an official or pecuniary interest in the commune. Persons not resident in the province, or having no solid interest in it, or who do not pay taxes on movable property, as well as officials in any way interested in the province, are ineligible to the provincial councils. Electors must be Italian citizens, twenty-one years of age, and able to read and write, be on the Parliamentary electoral list, or pay a direct annual contribution to the commune, of any nature, or comply with other conditions of a very simple character.

Religion.—The Roman Catholic Church is, nominally, the ruling State religion of Italy; but many Acts of the Legislature, passed since the establishment of the Kingdom, and more especially since the suppression of the Supreme Pontiff's temporal government, have subordinated the power of the Church and clergy to the authority of the civil government, and secured freedom of worship to the adherents of all recognized religions. However, scarcely any other positive creed as yet exists but Roman Catholicism. At the census of 1881, of the total population about 62,000 were Protestants and 38,000 Jews. Of the Protestants 22,000 belonged to the Waldensian Church of Piedmont, about 10,000 to the other evangelical Italian Churches, and 30,000 to foreign Protestant bodies.

Under the Roman Pontiff, the Catholic episcopal hierarchy in Italy consists of 49 archbishoprics and 220 bishoprics besides the 6 cardinal bishoprics near Rome. Of these prelacies, 76 are immediately subject to the Apostolic See, 12 being archbishoprics. Thus there are altogether 37 metropolitan sees, the average number of suffragan sees to each metropolitan being about 4. Every archbishop or bishop is appointed by the Pope, on the advice of a council of Cardinals; but the royal *exequatur* is necessary for his installation. The number of parishes in 1881 was 20,465; of churches and chapels 55,263; of secular clergy, 76,560.

The immense wealth of the Italian clergy has greatly dwindled since the year 1850, when the Siccardi bill, abolishing external ecclesiastical jurisdiction and clerical privileges, passed the Sardinian Chambers. This law was extended, in 1861, over the whole Kingdom, and had the effect of rapidly diminishing the numbers as well as the incomes of the clergy.

In 1865 there were in Italy 2,382 religious houses, of which 1,506 were for men and 876 for women. The number of religious persons was 28,991, of whom 14,807 were men and 14,184 women. The mendicant orders numbered 8,229 persons, comprised in the above-mentioned total. A law for the entire suppression of all religious houses throughout the Kingdom was adopted by the Italian Parliament in 1866. This law provided a small pension to all religious persons who had taken regular vows before January 18, 1864. Several monasteries were temporarily set aside for such monks, friars, or nuns as might wish to continue their conventual life, the inmates, when come down to a certain number, to be drafted off to another house, and so again, until all finally died out. All collegiate chapters were likewise dissolved. The lands and goods of these suppressed bodies were appropriated by the State.

See and Church of Rome.—The "Statuto fondamentale del Regno" enacts, in its first article, that "the Catholic, Apostolic, and Roman religion is the sole religion of the State." By the Royal decree of October 9, 1870, which declared that "Rome and the Roman Provinces shall coustitute an integral part of the Kingdom of Italy," the Pope or Roman Pontiff was acknowledged supreme head of the Church, preserving his former rank and dignity as a sovereign prince. Furthermore, by a bill that became law May 13, 1871, there was guaranteed to His Holiness and his successors forever, besides possession of the Vatican and Lateran palaces and the villa of Castel Gandolfo, a yearly income of 3,225,000 lire or 129,000*l.*, which allowance (whose arrears would in 1899 amount to 93,525,000 lire, or 3,741,000*l.*) still remains unclaimed and unpaid.

Supreme Pontiff.—Leone XIII. (Gioacchino Pecci), born at Carpineto in the diocese of Anagni, March 2, 1810, son of Count Luigi Pecci; consecrated Archbishop of Damiata, 1843; Apostolic Nuncio to Belgium, 1843-46; Bishop of Perugia, 1846; proclaimed Cardinal, December 19, 1853; elected Supreme Pontiff, as successor of Pio IX., February 20, 1878; crowned, March 3 following. He is, therefore, now 88 years old, and has filled the Pontifical throne for 20 years.

The election of a Pope ordinarily is by *scrutiny.* Each Cardinal in conclave writes on a ticket his own name with that of the Cardinal whom he chooses. These tickets, folded and sealed, are laid in a chalice which stands on the altar of the conclave chapel; and each elector approaching the altar repeats a prescribed form of oath. Thereupon the tickets are taken from the chalice by scrutators appointed from the electing body; the tickets are compared with the number of Cardinals present, and when it is found that any Cardinal has two thirds of the votes in his favor he is declared elected. Should none have received the needful number of votes, another process is gone through, viz., *access*—so called because any Cardinal may accede to the choice of another by filling up another ticket made for that purpose. The present Pontiff, Leone XIII., was chosen almost unanimously. He is regarded as the 263d Pope (or thereabouts) from St. Peter.

The rise of the Roman Pontificate, as an avowed temporal sovereignty, dates from the year 755, when Pepin, King of the Franks, gave to Pope Stefano III. the Exarchate and Pentapolis (or Romagna), conquered from the Lombards, to which Charles the Great added part of Tuscany and Sabina; and three centuries later Countess

Matilda of Tuscany bequeathed to the Holy See her ample territories. Rome, however, with the Roman duchy, came practically under the Pope's civil dominion in the days of Gregorio the Great (590-604). In 1860 the whole Pontifical State comprised an area of about 16,000 square miles, with a population of 3,125,000 souls; thenceforth, until 1870, about 5,000 square miles and 692,000 souls.

The Bishop of Rome, or Pope, by Roman Catholics accounted Vicar of Jesus Christ upon earth, and, in that office, Successor of St. Peter, is the absolute and irresponsible ruler of the Roman Catholic Church, regarded as the whole Christian Church here below. His *ex cathedrâ* definitions on matters of faith or morals are held to be infallible, and against his judgments there is no appeal. Every baptized person is held to be spiritually subject to him, and his jurisdiction over such to be immediate. The Roman Pontiff has for advisers and coadjutors the Sacred College of Cardinals consisting, when complete, of seventy members, namely, six cardinal-bishops, fifty cardinal-priests, and fourteen cardinal-deacons, but hardly ever comprising the full number. In January 1899 the Sacred College consisted of six cardinal-bishops, forty-five cardinal-priests, and five cardinal-deacons.

The central administration of the Roman Catholic Church is carried on by a number of permanent committees called Sacred Congregations, composed of Cardinals, with Consultors and Officials. There are now twenty sacred Congregations, viz.: Inquisition or Holy Office, Consistorial, Apostolic Visitation, Bishops and Regulars, Council, Residence of Bishops, State of Regulars, Ecclesiastical Immunity, Propaganda, Propaganda for Eastern Rite, Index, Sacred Rites, Ceremonial, Regular Discipline, Indulgences and Sacred Relics Examination of Bishops, Fabric of St. Peter's, Lauretana, Extraordinary Ecclesiastical Affairs, Studies.

Instruction.—The State regulates public instruction, and maintains, either entirely or in conjunction with the communes and provinces, public schools of every grade. Every teacher in a public institution maintained by the State, or by any other public body, must have the qualifications required by law; and in all public institutions not belonging to the State, the same programme must be followed, and the same rules observed. No private person can keep a school without having obtained the authorization of the State.

Justice.—In Italy, justice in penal matters is administered in the first instance by the Pretori, by the penal Tribunals, and by the Courts of Assize; on appeal, by the penal Tribunals, and by the Courts of Appeal. The highest court is the Court of Cassation, which confines itself to inquiring whether the forms prescribed by law have been observed.

The Pretori have jurisdiction concerning all delicts (delitti) punishable by imprisonment not exceeding three months, or banishment not exceeding one year, or by fine not exceeding 1,000 lire and all misdemeanors (contravenzioni). The penal Tribunals have jurisdiction in the first instance in offenses (delitti) (excepting offenses for which the Code establishes a *minimum* of five years) punishable by imprisonment from ten months to ten years, or by fine exceeding 1,000 lire. The Courts of Assize, which in most cases have juries, have jurisdiction in all proceedings concerning serious offenses (delitti) punishable by imprisonment for life (ergastolo) or by imprisonment from ten to twenty-four years, or by minimum imprisonment exceeding five years. They have exclusive jurisdiction concerning offenses against the internal and external security of the State, and all press offenses. Appeal is allowed to the penal Tribunals from the sentences of the Pretori, and to the Courts of Appeal from those of the penal Tribunals. The Court of Cassation has power to annul, for illegality, sentences passed by the inferior Courts, and to decide questions of jurisdiction or competency.

Italy is divided, for the administration of justice, into twenty appeal court districts, each of which is subdivided into tribunal districts, 162 in all, and these again into mandamenti, each with its own magistracy (Pretura), 1,548 in all.

JAPAN.

The Japanese claim that their empire was founded by the first Emperor Jimmu 660 B. C., and that the dynasty founded by him still reigns. It was revived in the year 1868, when the now ruling (*de jure*) sovereign overthrew, after a short war, the power of the Shogun (the *de facto* sovereign), who had held the ruling power in successive families since the twelfth century; and in 1871 the feudal system (Hōken Seiji) was entirely suppressed. The sovereign bears the name of Kōtei, or Emperor; but the appellation by which he is generally known in foreign countries is the ancient title of Mikado, or "The Honorable Gate."

By the Imperial House Law of February 11, 1889, the succession to the throne has been definitely fixed upon the male descendants. In case of failure of direct descendants, the throne devolves upon the nearest Prince and his descendants.

The system of government of the Japanese Empire was that of an Absolute Monarchy. A Constitution was, however, promulgated on February 11, 1889.

By this Constitution the Emperor is the head of the Empire, combining in himself the rights of sovereignty, and exercising the whole of the executive powers with the advice and assistance of the Cabinet Ministers, who are responsible to him, and are appointed by himself. There is also a Privy Council, who deliberate upon important matters of State when they have been consulted by the Emperor. The Emperor can declare war, make peace, and conclude treaties. The Emperor exercises the legislative power with the consent of the Imperial Diet. It is the prerogative of the Emperor to give sanction to laws, to convoke the Imperial Diet, to open, close, and prorogue it, and to dissolve the House of Representatives. The Imperial Diet consists of two Houses, a House of Peers and a House of Representatives. Every law requires the consent of the Imperial Diet. Both Houses may respectively initiate projects of law, can make representations to the Government as to laws or upon any other subject, and may present addresses to the Emperor.

The House of Peers is composed of (1) male members of the Imperial family of the age of 20 and upwards; (2) princes and marquises of the age of 25 and upwards (11 princes and 28 marquises); (3) counts, viscounts, and barons of the age of 25 and upwards, and who have been elected by the members of their respective orders, never to exceed one fifth of each order (80 counts, 355 viscounts, 29 barons); (4) persons above the age of 30 years, who have been nominated members by the Emperor for meritorious services to the State or for erudition; (5) persons who shall have been elected in each Fu and Ken from among and by the 15 male inhabitants thereof, of above the age of 30 years, paying therein the highest amount of direct national taxes on land, industry, or trade, and have been nominated by the Emperor. The term of membership under (3) and (5) is seven years; under (1), (2), and (4) for life. The number of members under (4) and (5) not to exceed the number of other members. The entire membership of the House of Peers is to be about 300.

The members of the House of Representatives number 300, a fixed number being returned from each election district. The proportion of the number of members to the population is about one member to 128,000. The qualifications of electors are (1) male Japanese subjects of not less than full 25 years of age; (2) fixed permanent and actual residence in the Fu or Ken for not less than a year; (3) payment of direct national taxes to the amount of not less than 15 yen for one year in the Fu or Ken, and in case of income tax for three years.

The qualifications of persons eligible for election are generally the same as those of electors, except that they must be of not less than 30 years, and need not have fixed residence in the Fu or Ken. The term of membership is four years.

Disqualified for members of the House of Representatives are officials of the Imperial Household, judges, auditors, officials connected with the collection of taxes, police officials, officials of electoral districts within their own districts, military and naval officers, and priests or ministers of religion. The President and Vice-President of the House of Peers are nominated by the Emperor from among the members, and President and Vice-President of the House of Representatives are nominated by the Emperor from among three candidates elected by the House. The Presidents of both Houses receive an annual salary of 4,000 yen; Vice-Presidents, 2,000 yen; elected and nominated members of the House of Peers and members of the House of Representatives, 800 yen, besides traveling expenses. No one is allowed to decline these annual allowances.

The Imperial Diet has control over the finances and the administration of justice. Voting is by secret ballot, and the system is that of *scrutin de liste*. The Diet must be assembled once every year.

At the head of local administration in the provinces are the governors, one of them residing in each of the 46 districts (3 Fus and 43 Kens) into which Japan is divided. In 1879, city and prefectural assemblies were created, based on the principle of election; their power is confined to fixing the estimates of the local rates, subject to the confirmation of the governors, and finally of the Minister of the Interior. Eligible to the assembly are all male citizens 25 years of age, resident in the district at least three consecutive years, and paying land tax of more than ten yen annually. The franchise is conferred on all male citizens of 20 years residing in the district, and paying more than five yen land tax. Annually, or in every other year, governors are summoned to the Department of the Interior to deliberate upon matters of local administration. Each district is subdivided into cities (*ku*), and counties (*gun*), each with its chief magistrate (*chō*), who manages local affairs. The Island of Hokkaidô (Yezo) has a governor and a special organization.

To further carry out the principle of decentralization and self-government a system of local administration in *shi* (municipality), *cho* (town), and *son* (village) was established by Imperial Rescript, April 17, 1888, which came into effect April 1, 1889, and is to be applied gradually according to the circumstances and requirements of these localities.

Religion.—By the Constitution absolute freedom of religious belief and practice is secured, so long as it is not prejudicial to peace and order. The chief forms of religion are — (1) Shintoism, with 11 sects; (2) Buddhism, with 12 sects and 30 creeds. There is no State religion, and no State support. The principal Shinto temples are, however, maintained by State or local authorities. In 1895 — Shinto temples, 190,754; priests, 14,927; students, 1,939. Buddhist temples, 71,821; priests, 53,275; students, 9,286. There are also numerous Roman Catholics, adherents of the Greek Church, and Protestants.

Instruction. Elementary education is compulsory. The number of children of school age (6-14) on December 31, 1895, was 7,670,837. The following are the educational statistics for 1895:—

INSTITUTES.	Number.	Teaching Staff.	Students and Pupils.
Elementary schools	26,631	73,182	3,670,345
Lower middle schools	96	1,324	30,871
High schools	7	279	3,580
High girls' schools	15	186	1,266
Normal schools	49	743	7,734
Technical schools	97	1,078	14,806
Special schools	1,263	3,250	64,948
University schools	3	184	1,646
Kindergarten schools	220	482	17,481

The University consists of a University Hall, Colleges of Law, Science, Medicine, Literature, Engineering, and Agriculture. It is supported by Government. The bulk of the elementary and higher schools are also supported by Government and by local rates. One of the normal schools is for high school teachers.

In 1895 there were 25 libraries in Japan, with 441,034 volumes. In 1895, 26,792 books of various kinds, and 753 periodicals, monthly, weekly, daily, were published. Of the periodicals 409,429,528 copies were issued.

Justice.—A system of justice founded on modern jurisprudence has been established. Judges are irremovable, except by way of criminal or disciplinary punishment. There is a Court of Cassations at Tokio, which takes cognizance of civil and criminal appeals. There are seven courts of appeal for civil and criminal cases decided in the courts of first instance. There are 49 courts of first instance, one in each Fu or Ken, with branch courts in some Fus and Kens having unlimited original civil jurisdiction. As criminal courts they try and decide all lesser crimes, and also make preliminary examination of serious crimes. Justice of Peace Courts (301), established in principal towns and villages of every Fu and Ken, take cognizance of all petty offenses. Once in three months criminal courts are constituted in courts of appeal, and sometimes in courts of first instance, a president and four judges, to try serious crimes.

A few judges of high rank are directly appointed by the Emperor, and some are appointed by him on nomination by the Minister of Justice.

MEXICO.

The present Constitution of Mexico bears date February 5, 1857, with subsequent modifications down to May, 1896. By its terms Mexico is declared a federative republic, divided into States — 19 at the outset, but at present 27 in number, with 2 territories and the Federal District — each of which has a right to manage its own local affairs, while the whole are bound together in one body politic by fundamental and constitutional laws. The powers of the supreme Government are divided into three branches, the legislative, executive, and judicial. The legislative power is vested in a Congress consisting of a House of Representatives and a Senate, and the executive in a President. Representatives elected by the suffrage of all respectable male adults, at the rate of one member for 40,000 inhabitants, hold their places for two years. The qualifications requisite are, to be twenty-five years of age, and a resident in the State. The Senate consists of fifty-six members, two for each State, of at least thirty years of age, who are returned in the same manner as the deputies. The members of both Houses receive salaries of 3,000 dollars a year. The President is elected by electors popularly chosen in a general election, holds office for four years, and, according to an amendment of the Constitution in 1887, may be elected for consecutive terms. Failing the President through absence or otherwise, whether the disability be temporary or permanent, Congress has power to elect an acting-president who shall discharge the functions of President temporarily or, if necessary, to the end of the constitutional period. Congress has to meet annually from April 1 to May 30, and from September 16 to December 15, and a permanent committee of both Houses sits during the recesses.

The administration is carried on, under the direction of the President and a Council, by seven Secretaries of State, heads of the Departments of : — 1, Foreign Affairs ; 2, Interior ; 3, Justice and Public Instruction ; 4, Fomento, Colonization and Industry ; 5, Communications and Public Works ; 6, Financial and Public Credit ; 7, War and Marine.

Local Government.—Each separate State has its own internal constitution, government, and laws ; but inter-State customs duties are not permitted. Each has its governor and legislature popularly elected under rules similar to those of the Federation ; and the civil and criminal code in force in the Federal District prevails, with few exceptions (Vera Cruz and the State of Mexico), in the different States.

Religion, Instruction, and Justice. The prevailing religion is the Roman Catholic, but the Church is independent of the State, and there is toleration of all other religions. In 1889 there were 10,112 Roman Catholic churches and chapels, and 119 Protestant churches in the Republic. No ecclesiastical body can acquire landed property. On August 12, 1890, there were in the municipality of Mexico 320,143 Catholics and 2,623 Protestants.

In almost all the States education is free and compulsory, but the law has not been strictly enforced. In the municipality of Mexico there were in 1890, 15,268 persons who could read only, and 176,692 persons who could neither read nor write. Primary instruction is mostly at the expense of the states and municipalities, but the Federal Government makes frequent grants, and many schools are under the care of beneficent societies. Higher education is carried on in secondary schools and seminaries, and in colleges for professional instruction, including schools of law, medicine, engineering, mining, fine arts, agriculture, commerce, arts, and trades, music. In 1896 the number of schools supported by the States was 5,852, and by the municipalities, 3,218 ; the number of teachers in both was 13,352 ; there were 666,301 enrolled pupils, and an average attendance of 413,790. The cost of these schools for the year was 5,463,350 dollars. The private and clerical schools numbered 2,442, with 101,641 enrolled pupils, and an average attendance of 76,956. The total number of schools was thus 11,512, with 767,942 enrolled pupils, and an average attendance of 490,746. Of the average attendance, 300,272 were boys and 190,501 were girls. There are also one military and one naval college. The number attending the higher schools is stated at 21,000.

In 1896 there were in the Republic the National Library, with 159,000 volumes, and 102 other public libraries. There were in that year 17 museums for scientific and educational purposes, and 3 meteorological observatories. The number of newspapers published was 531, of which 7 were in English, 5 in Spanish and English, 2 in French, and 1 in German.

The judicial power, which is entirely distinct from and independent of the executive, consists of the Supreme Court, with 15 judges chosen for a period of six years, Circuit Courts, with 3 judges, and District Courts, with 32 judges.

The Ordinary, Civil, Criminal, and Correctional Courts are controlled by the Department of Justice and Public Instruction.

NETHERLANDS (THE).

The first Constitution of the Netherlands after its reconstruction as a kingdom was given in 1815, and was revised in 1848 and in 1887. According to this charter the Netherlands form a constitutional and hereditary monarchy. The royal succession is in the direct male line in the order of primogeniture ; in default of male heirs, the female line ascends the throne. In default of a legal heir, the successor to the throne is designated by the Sovereign and a joint meeting of both the Houses of Parliament (each containing twice the usual number of members), and by this assembly alone if the case occurs after the Sovereign's death. The age of majority of the Sovereign is eighteen years. During his minority the royal power is vested in a Regent — designated by law — and in some cases in the State Council.

The executive power of the State belongs exclusively to the Sovereign, while the whole legislative authority rests conjointly in the Sovereign and Parliament, the latter — called the States-General — consisting of two Chambers. The Upper or First Chamber is composed of 50 members, elected by the Provincial States from among the most highly assessed inhabitants of the eleven provinces, or from among some high and important functionaries, mentioned by law. Members of the First Chamber not residing in the Hague, where the Parliament meets, are allowed 10 guilders (16*s.* 8*d.*) a day during the session of the States-General. The Second Chamber of the States-General numbers 100 deputies, who are elected directly.

The Government and the Second Chamber only may introduce new bills; the functions of the Upper Chamber being restricted to approving or rejecting them, without the power of inserting amendments. The meetings of both Chambers are public, though each of them, by the decision of the majority, may form itself into a private committee. The ministers may attend at the meetings of both Chambers, but they have only a deliberative vote, unless they are members. Alterations in the Constitution can be made only by a bill declaring that there is reason for introducing those alterations, followed by a dissolution of the Chambers and a second confirmation by the new States-General by two thirds of the votes. Unless it is expressly declared, the laws concern only the realm in Europe, and not the colonies.

The executive authority, belonging to the Sovereign, is exercised by a responsible Council of Ministers. There are eight heads of departments in the Ministerial Council, namely:—

The Minister of Foreign Affairs and President of the Ministerial Council.

The Minister of the Interior.

The Minister of Finance.

The Minister of Justice.

The Minister of the Colonies.

The Minister of Marine.

The Minister of War.

The Minister of Public Works and Commerce.

Each of the above Ministers has an annual salary of 12,000 guilders, or 1,000*l*.

There is a State Council—"Raad van State"—of 14 members, appointed by the Sovereign, of which the Sovereign is president, and which is consulted on all legislative and a great number of executive matters.

Local Government.—The territory of the Netherlands is divided into 11 provinces and 1,123 communes. Each province has its own representative body, "the Provincial States." The members are elected for 6 years, directly from among the male Dutch inhabitants of the province who are 25 years of age, one half of the number being subject to re-election or renewal every three years. Except that they must be inhabitants of the province, the electors, as well as the mode of voting, are the same as for the Second Chamber. The number of members varies according to the population of the province, from 80 for Holland (South) to 35 for Drenthe. The Provincial States are entitled to make ordinances concerning the welfare of the province, and to raise taxes according to legal precepts. All provincial ordinances must be approved by the King. The Provincial States exercise a right of control over the municipalities. They also elect the members of the First Chamber of the States-General. They meet twice a year, as a rule in public. A permanent commission composed of six of their members, called the "Deputed States," is charged with the executive power in the province and the daily administration of its affairs. This committee has also to see the common law executed in the province. Both the Deputed as well as the Provincial States are presided over by a Commissioner of the Sovereign, who in the former assembly has a deciding vote, but in the latter named only a deliberative vote. He is the chief magistrate in the province. Only the members of the Deputed States receive an allowance.

The communes form each a Corporation with its own interests and rights, subject to the general law. In each commune is a Council, elected for six years directly, by the same voters as for the Provincial States, provided they inhabit the commune; one third of the Council retiring every two years. All the male Dutch inhabitants 23 years of age are eligible, the number of members varying from 7 to 41, according to the population. The Council has a right of making and enforcing bylaws concerning the communal welfare. The Council may raise taxes according to rules prescribed by common law; besides, each commune receives from the State Treasury an allowance proportioned to the total number of its inhabitants and to the share which its non-contributing inhabitants have failed to pay toward local taxes. All by-laws may be vetoed by the Sovereign. The Municipal Budget and the resolutions to alienate municipal property require the approbation of the Deputed States of the province. The Council meets in public as often as may be necessary, and is presided over by a Mayor, appointed by the Sovereign for six years. The executive power is vested in a college formed by the Mayor and 2, 3, or 4 Aldermen (wethouders) elected by and from the Council; this college is also charged with the execution of the common law. Municipal Police is under the authority of the Mayor; as a State functionary the Mayor supervises the actions of the Council; he may suspend their resolutions for 30 days, but is bound to inform the Deputed States of the province.

Religion.—According to the terms of the Constitution, entire liberty of conscience and complete social equality are granted to the members of all religious confessions. The royal family and the majority of the inhabitants belong to the Reformed Church. The salaries of several British Presbyterian ministers, settled in the Netherlands, and whose churches are incorporated with the Dutch Reformed Church, are paid out of the public funds. The State Budget contained fixed allowances for the different churches; for Protestant Churches, 1,379,852 guilders; for Roman Catholics, 578,035; and for Jews, 12,775.

Instruction.—Public instruction (primary) is given in all places where needed, but education is not compulsory nor necessarily free; religious convictions are respected.

From the beginning of this century elementary schools have been more or less under State regulation and inspection. In 1806, and more expressly in 1848, secular instruction was separated from religious or sectarian instruction. Elementary education is now regulated by the Primary Instruction Act, passed in 1857, supplemented by an Act of 1878, and again considerably altered by the Act of December 1889. By the last Act public instruction is diminished and a greater share in the education of the youths left to private instruction, which is now supported by the State. According to the regulations of the present Act the cost of public primary instruction is borne jointly by the State and the communes, the State contributing to the salaries of the teachers and being responsible for 25 per cent. to the costs of founding or purchasing schools. There are four universities—Leyden, Grongingen, Utrecht, and Amsterdam—attended by over 3,000 students; 1,278 private and higher schools; and 2,923 public elementary schools.

Justice.—Justice is administered by the High Court of the Netherlands (Court of Cassation), by 5 courts of justice (Courts of Appeal), by 23 district tribunals, and by 106 cantonal courts; trial by jury is unknown in Holland. All Judges are appointed for life by the King (the Judges of the High Court from a list prepared by the Second Chamber). They can be removed only by a decision of the High Court.

RUSSIA.

Constitution and Government.—The government of Russia is an absolute hereditary monarchy. The whole legislative, executive, and judicial power is united in the Emperor, whose will alone is law. There are, however, certain rules of government which the sovereigns of the present reigning house have acknowledged as binding. The chief of these is the law of succession to the throne, which, according to a decree of the Emperor Paul, of the year 1797, is to be that of regular descent, by the right of primogeniture, with preference of male over female heirs. This decree annulled a previous one, issued by Peter I., February 5, 1722, which ordered each sovereign to select his successor to the throne from among the members of the imperial family, irrespective of the claims of primogeniture. Another fundamental law of the realm proclaimed by Peter I. is that every sovereign of Russia, with his consort and children, must be a member of the orthodox Greek Church. The princes and princesses of the imperial house, according to a decree of Alexander I., must obtain the consent of the Emperor to any marriage they may contract; otherwise the issue of such union cannot inherit the throne. By an ancient law of Russia, the heir-apparent is held to be of age at the end of the sixteenth year, and the other members of the reigning family with the completed twentieth year.

The administration of the Empire is entrusted to four great boards, or councils, possessing separate functions. The first of these boards is the *Council of the State*, established in its present form by Alexander I., in the year 1810. It consists of a president — the Grand Duke Mikhail since 1882 — and an unlimited number of members appointed by the Emperor. In 1894 the Council consisted of 62 members, exclusive of the ministers, who have a seat *ex officio*, and six princes of the imperial house. The Council is divided into three departments, namely, of Legislation, of Civil and Church Administration, and of Finance. Each department has its own president, and a separate sphere of duties; but there are collective meetings of the three sections. The chief function of the Council of the Empire is that of examining into the projects of laws which are brought before it by the ministers, and of discussing the budget and all the expenditures to be made during the year. But the Council has no power of proposing alterations and modifications of the laws of the realm; it is, properly speaking, a consultative institution in matters of legislation. A special department is intrusted with the discussion of the requests addressed to the Emperor against the decisions of the Senate. The second of the great colleges or boards of government is the *Ruling Senate*, or "Pravitelstvuyuschiy Senat," established by Peter I. in the year 1711. The functions of the Senate are partly of a deliberative and partly of an executive character. To be valid a law must be promulgated by the Senate. It is also the high court of justice for the Empire. The Senate is divided into nine departments or sections, which all sit at St. Petersburg, two of them being Courts of Cassation. Each department is authorized to decide in the last resort upon certain descriptions of cases. The senators are mostly persons of high rank, or who fill high stations; but a lawyer of eminence presides over each department, who represents the Emperor, and without whose signature its decisions would have no force. In the *plenum*, or general meeting of several sections, the Minister of Justice takes the chair. Besides its superintendence over the courts of law, the Senate examines into the state of the general administration of the Empire, and has power to make remonstrances to the Emperor. A special department consisting of seven members is intrusted with judgments in political offenses, and another (six members) with disciplinary judgments against officials of the crown.

The third college, established by Peter I. in the year 1721, is the *Holy Synod*, and to it is committed the superintendence of the religious affairs of the Empire. It is composed of the three metropolitans (St. Petersburg, Moscow, and Kieff), the archbishops of Georgia (Caucasus), and of Poland (Kholm and Warsaw), and several bishops sitting in turn. All its decisions run in the Emperor's name, and have no force till approved by him. The President of the Holy Synod is the Metropolitan of Novgorod and St. Petersburg.

The fourth board of government is the *Committee of Ministers*. It consists of all the ministers, who are:—

1. *The Ministry of the Imperial House and Imperial Domains.*
2. *The Ministry of Foreign Affairs, Assistant Minister.*
3. *The Ministry of War.*
4. *The Ministry of the Navy.*
5. *The Ministry of the Interior.*
6. *The Ministry of Public Instruction.*
7. *The Ministry of Finance.*
8. *The Ministry of Justice.*
9. *The Ministry of Agriculture and State Domains.*
10. *The Ministry of Public Works and Railways.*
11 *The Department of General Control.*

12. ***The Procurator-General of the Holy Synod.***

Besides the Ministers, four Grand Dukes, and six functionaries, chiefly ex-ministers, form part of the Committee, of which Actual Privy Councilor *Durnovo* is President.

Minister and State Secretary for Finland.

Most of the above heads of departments have assistant ministers who supply their place on certain occasions. They all communicate directly with the sovereign.

The Emperor has two Private Cabinets, one of which is occupied with charitable affairs, and the other is devoted to public instruction of girls and to the administration of the institutions established by the late Empress Maria, mother of the Emperor Nicholas I. Besides, there is the Imperial Head-Quarters (Glavnaya Kvartira), and a Cabinet, which is entrusted also with the reception of petitions presented to the Emperor, formerly received by a special Court of Requests (abolished in 1884). According to a law of May 19, 1888, a special Imperial Cabinet having four sections (Administrative, Economical, Agricultural and Manufacturing, and Legislative) has been created, instead of the same departments in the Ministry of Imperial Household. According to the law of May 22, 1894, a special chief for the protection of the Imperial residences and trains has been appointed under the title of "General in Service at the Emperor' (*Dezhurnyi General*), General Aide-de-Camp *Tcherevin* holding this position.

Local Government.—The Empire is divided into general governments, or vice-royalties, governments, and districts. There are at present in European Russia (including Poland and Finland) 68 governments, with 635 districts (*uyezd*), 2 *otdyels*, and 1 *okrug*, also considered as separate governments. Some of them are united into general governments, which are now those of Finland, Poland, Wilna, Kieff, and Moscow. The Asiatic part of the Empire comprises 5 general governments: Caucasus, Turkestan, Stepnoye (of the Steppes), Irkutsh, and of the Amur, with 10 governments (*guberniya*), 17 territories (*oblasts*), and 3 districts (*okrug*, or *otdyel*: Zakataly, Chernomorsk, and Sakhalin). At the head of each general government is a governor-general, the representative of the Emperor, who as such has the supreme control and direction of all affairs, whether civil or military. In Siberia the governors-general are each assisted by a council, which has a deliberative voice. A civil governor assisted by a council of regency, to which all measures must be submitted, is established in each government, and a military governor in twenty frontier provinces. A vice-governor is appointed to fill the place of the civil governor when the latter is absent or unwell. There is also, in each government, a council of control under the presidency of a special officer, depending directly on the Department of Control. Each government is divided into from 8 to 15 districts, having each several administrative institutions. A few districts (*okrug* or *otdyel*) in Siberia, in the Caucasus, in Turkestan, and in the Transcaspian region are considered as independent governments. So also the townships (*gradonachalstvo*) of St. Petersburg, Odessa, Kertch, Sebastopol, and Taganrog; Cronstadt, Vladivostok, and Nikolaevsk are under separate military governors. In 1894, the Government of Warsaw has been increased by one district of Plock and one district of Lomja.

In European Russia the government of the parish, in so far as the lands of the peasantry are concerned, and part of the local administration, is entrusted to the people. For this purpose the whole country is divided into communes (107,676 in European Russia, exclusive of the three Baltic provinces), which elect an elder (Starosta), or executive of a commune, as also a tax-collector or superintendent of public stores. All these officers are elected at communal assemblies ("Mir"—which means both "the village" and "the world") by the peasants, and from among themselves. The communal assemblies are constituted by all the householders in the village, who discuss and decide all communal affairs. These communal assemblies are held as business requires. The communes are united into cantons, or "Voloste," each embracing a population of about 2,000 males (10,530 in European Russia). Each of the cantons is presided over also by an elder "Starshina," elected at the cantonal assemblies, which are composed of the delegates of the village communities in proportion of one man to every ten houses. The canton assemblies decide the same class of affairs as do the communal assemblies, but concerning each its respective canton. The peasants have thus special institutions of their own, which are submitted also to special colleges "for peasants' affairs," instituted in each government. In Poland the "Voloste" is replaced by the "Gmina," the assemblies of which are constituted of all landholders—nobility included, the clergy and the police excluded—who have each but one voice, whatever the area of land possessed. The "Gmina" has, however, less autonomy than the "Voloste," being subject directly to the "Chief of the District." In conjunction with the assemblies of the Voloste and Gmina are cantonal tribunals, consisting of from four to twelve judges elected at cantonal assemblies. Injuries and offenses of every kind, as well as disputes relating to property between the peasants, not involving more than a hundred roubles, come under the jurisdiction of these popular tribunals. Affairs of more importance, up to 300 roubles, are judged by Judges of Peace, elected in Central Russia, and nominated elsewhere; appeal against their judgments can be made to the "Syezd," or gathering of judges of the district, and further to the Senate. In 1889 an important change was made in the above organization. Justices of Peace have been replaced in twenty provinces of Central Russia by Chiefs of the district (*uyezdnyi nachalnik*), nominated by the administration from among candidates taken from the nobility, recommended by the nobility, and endowed with wide disciplinary powers against the peasants; in the cities, except St. Petersburg, Moscow, and Odessa, special "town magistrates" (*gorodskoi sudia*), nominated in the same way, are to take the place of the former Justices of Peace. As to the peasants' tribunals (*volostnoi sud*), they are placed in direct subjection to the "Chiefs of the Districts." The same measure has been extended in 1890 and 1891 over all the provinces endowed with provincial institutions (*zemstvos*).

Religion.—The established religion of the Empire is the Græco-Russian, officially called the Orthodox-Catholic Faith. It has its own independent synod, but maintains the relations of a sister Church with the four patriarchates of Constantinople, Jerusalem, Antioch, and Alexandria. The Holy Synod, the board of government of the Church, was established with the concurrence of the Russian clergy and the four Eastern patriarchs.

The Emperor is head of the Church; he appoints to every office in the Church, and is restricted only so far as to leave to the bishops and prelates the privilege of proposing candidates; and he transfers and dismisses persons from their offices in certain cases. But he has never claimed the right of deciding theological and dogmatic questions. Practically, the Procurator of the Holy Synod enjoys wide powers in Church matters.

The points in which the Græco-Russian Church differs from the Roman Catholic faith are, its denying the spiritual supremacy of the Pope, its not enforcing the celibacy of the clergy, and its authorizing all individuals to read and study the Scriptures in the vernacular tongue. With the exception of the restraints laid on the Jews, all religions may be freely professed in the Empire. The dissenters have been and are still, however, severely persecuted, though recently some liberty has been extended to those of the "United Church." It is estimated that there are more than 12,000,000 dissenters in Great Russia alone. The affairs of the Roman Catholic Church are entrusted to a Collegium, and those of the Lutheran Church to a Consistory, both settled at St. Petersburg. Roman Catholics are most numerous in the former Polish provinces, Lutherans in those of the Baltic, and Mohammedans in Eastern and Southern Russia, while the Jews are almost entirely settled in the towns and larger villages of the western and southwestern provinces.

Instruction.—Most of the schools in the Empire are under the Ministry of Public Instruction, and the Empire is divided into 11 educational districts (St. Petersburg, Moscow, Kazan, Orenburg, Kharkoff, Odessa, Kieff, Vilna, Warsaw, Dorpat, Caucasus, Turkestan, West Siberia, and East Siberia). However, many special schools are under separate Ministries. The total contribution for education from the various Ministries in 1894 was 39,336,096 roubles; of this, 7,294,473 roubles was for universities, 19,576,208 roubles for middle-class schools, and 7,403,612 roubles for primary schools.

Justice.—The organization of justice was totally reformed by the law of 1864; but the action of that law has not yet been extended to the governments of Olonets, Vologda, Astrakhan, Ufa, and Orenburg, and has been applied but in a modified form (in 1889) to the Baltic Provinces and the government of Arkhangelsk. In the above-named governments the Justice of Peace has been introduced, but the other tribunals remain in the old state. No juries are allowed in Poland and the Caucasus; the justices of peace are nominated by the Government in the provinces which have no *zemstvos.* In Poland there are judges of peace in the towns only, their functions in the villages being performed by Gmina courts, elected by the inhabitants of the Gmina. Siberia has maintained the tribunals of old; in the Steppe Provinces there are district judges, while courts of higher instance are represented by the Justice Department of the provincial administration.

There were in 1891, 2 appeal departments of the Senate, 10 high courts, 85 courts of first instance. There were besides—1,280 inquiry judges, and 1,345 notaries; 2,126 actual, and 3,652 honorary justices of peace. In the unreformed tribunals there were 604 judges, 129 public prosecutors, and 156 inquiry judges.

By a law, dated June 21, 1889, the functions of the juries were limited to some extent, especially as regards the crimes committed by the representatives of nobility in their elective functions.

By a law of April 6, 1891, reformed courts as well as chiefs of districts have been introduced in the provinces of the Kirghize Steppes. In Siberia, the reformed Courts and trial by jury were introduced in 1897, and in Turkestan in 1898.

SPAIN.

The present Constitution of Spain, drawn up by the Government and laid before a Cortes Constituventes, elected for its ratification, March 27, 1876, was proclaimed June 30, 1876. It consists of 89 articles or clauses. The first of them enacts that Spain shall be a constitutional monarchy, the executive resting in the King, and the power to make laws "in the Cortes with the King." The Cortes are composed of a Senate and Congress, equal in authority. There are three classes of senators —first, senators by their own right, or *Senadores de derecho propio;* secondly, 100 life senators nominated by the Crown—these two categories not to exceed 180; and thirdly, 180 senators, elected by the Corporations of State—that is, the communal and provincial states, the church, the universities, academies, etc.—and by the largest payers of contributions. Senators in their own right are the sons, if any, of the King and of the immediate heir to the throne, who have attained their majority; Grandees who are so in their own right and who can prove an annual *renta* of 60,000 pesetas, or 2,400*l.*; captain-generals of the army; admirals of the navy; the patriarch of the Indias and the archbishops; the presidents of the Council of State, of the Supreme Tribunal, of the Tribunal of Cuentas del Reino, and of the Supreme Council of War and of the Navy, after two years of office. The elective senators must be renewed by one half every five years, and by totality every time the Monarch dissolves that part of the Cortes. The Congress is formed by deputies "named in the electoral Juntas in the form the law determines," in the proportion of one to every 50,000 souls of the population. According to the law of June 26, 1890, the electoral qualification is held by all male Spaniards, 25 years of age, who enjoy full civil rights, and have been citizens of a municipality for at least two years. Members of Congress must be 25 years of age; they are re-eligible indefinitely, the elections being for 5 years. Deputies, to the number of 10, are admitted who, although not elected for any one district, have obtained a cumulative vote of more than 10,000 in several districts. Deputies to the number of 88 are elected by *scrutin de liste* in 26 large districts, in which minorities may be duly represented. There are in all 431 deputies. The deputies cannot take State office, pensions, and salaries; but the ministers are exempted from this law. Both Congress and Senate meet every year. The Monarch has the power of convoking them, suspending them, or dissolving them; but in the latter case a new Cortes must sit within three months. The Monarch appoints the president and vice-presidents of the Senate from members of the Senate only; the Congress elects its own officials. The Monarch and each of the legislative chambers can take the initiative in the laws. The Congress has the right of impeaching the ministers before the Senate.

The Constitution of June 30, 1876, further enacts that the Monarch is inviolable, but his ministers are responsible, and that all his decrees must be countersigned by one of them. The Cortes must approve his marriage before he can contract it, and the King cannot marry anyone excluded by law from the succession to the crown. Should the lines of the legitimate descendants of the late Alphonso XII. become extinct, the succession shall be in this order—first, to his sisters; next to his aunt and her legitimate descendants; and next to those of his uncles, the brothers of Fernando VII., "unless they have been excluded." If all the lines become extinct, "the nation will elect its Monarch."

The executive is vested, under the Monarch, in a Council of Ministers, as follows, March 4, 1899:—

President of the Council.
Minister of Foreign Affairs.

Minister of Justice.
Minister of Finance.
Minister of the Interior
Minister of War.
Minister of Marine.
Minister of Agriculture and Commerce and of Public Works.

The Ministry of the Colonies was abolished February 10, 1899.

Local Government.—The various provinces and communes of Spain are governed by the provincial and municipal laws. Every commune has its own elected Ayuntamiento, consisting of from five to thirty-nine Regidores, or Concejales, and presided over by the Alcalde, at whose side stand, in the larger towns, several Tenientes Alcaldes. The entire municipal government, with power of taxation, is vested in the Ayuntamientos. Half the members are elected every two years, and they appoint the Alcalde, the executive functionary, from their own body. In the larger towns he may be appointed by the King. Members cannot be re-elected until after two years. Each province of Spain has its own Parliament, the Diputacion Provincial, the members of which are elected by the constituencies. The Diputaciones Provinciales meet in annual session, and are permanently represented by the Commission Provincial, a committee elected every year. The Constitution of 1876 secures to the Diputaciones Provinciales and the Ayuntamientos the government and administration of the respective provinces and communes. Neither the national executive nor the Cortes have the right to interfere in the established municipal and provincial administration, except in the case of the action of the Diputaciones Provinciales and Ayuntamientos going beyond the locally limited sphere to the injury of general and permanent interests. In the Basque provinces self-government has been almost abolished since the last civil war, and they are ruled as the rest of Spain. Notwithstanding the provisions of the Constitution, pressure is too frequently brought to bear upon the local elections by the Central Government.

Religion.—The national Church of Spain is the Roman Catholic, and the whole population of the Kingdom adhere to that faith, except (in 1887) 6,654 Protestants, 402 Jews, 9,645 Rationalists, 510 of other religions, and 13,175 of religion not stated. There were in 1884 in Spain 32,435 priests in the 62 dioceses into which the country is divided; 1,684 monks resident in 161 monastic houses, and 14,592 nuns in 1,027 convents. The number of cathedrals was 65, of religious colleges 30, of churches 18,564, and of convents, religious houses, sanctuaries, and other buildings of a religious character 11,-202. According to Article 12 of the Constitution of 1876, a restricted liberty of worship is allowed to Protestants, but it has to be entirely in private, all public announcements of the same being strictly forbidden. The Constitution likewise enacts that "the nation binds itself to maintain the worship and ministers of the Roman Catholic religion." Resolutions of former legislative bodies not repealed in the Constitution of 1876, settled that the clergy of the Established Church are to be maintained by the State. On the other hand, by two decrees of the Cortes, passed July 23, 1835, and March 9, 1836, all conventual establishments were suppressed, and their property confiscated for the benefit of the nation. These decrees gave rise to a long dispute with the head of the Roman Catholic Church, which ended in the sovereign pontiff conceding the principle of the measure. By a concordat with Rome concluded in August, 1859, the Spanish government was authorized to sell the whole ecclesiastical property, except churches and parsonages, in return for an equal amount of untransferable public debt certificates bearing interest at the rate of 3 per cent.

Instruction.—The latest census returns show that a large proportion of the inhabitants are illiterate. In 1860 20.0 per cent. of the population could read and write; 4.6 per cent. could read only; and 75.3 per cent. could neither read nor write. In 1889, out of a population of 17,552,346 accounted for, 5,004,460 (3,317,855 males, and 1,686,615 females), or 28.5 per cent. could read and write; 608,005 (221,613 males, and 380,392 females), or 3.4 per cent. could read only; and 11,945,871 (5,067,098 males, and 6,878,773 females), or 68.1 per cent. could neither read nor write.

By a law of 1857 an elaborate system of primary education was ordained: education was to be compulsory, there was to be a primary school for every 500 inhabitants, and instruction was to be on a rigidly uniform plan. Compulsion has never been enforced, and, partly from political causes and partly from the wretched pay of most of the elementary teachers (10*l.* to 20*l.* per annum), education is very inefficient. In 1881, however, several improvements were introduced. Under the Minister of Public Works there is a Director-General of Public Instruction, with a council; there are ten educational districts, with the universities as centers, 49 inspectoral districts, and numerous local educational authorities. The public and primary schools are supported mainly by the municipalities, the total sum spent in each of the last three years on primary education, including a small contribution by Government, being about 1,000,000*l.* Most of the children are educated free.

TURKEY.

The present sovereign of Turkey is the thirty-fourth, in male descent, of the house of Othman, the founder of the empire, and the twenty-eighth Sultan since the conquest of Constantinople. By the law of succession obeyed in the reigning family, the crown is inherited according to seniority by the male descendants of Othman, sprung from the Imperial Harem. The Harem is considered a permanent State institution. All children born in the Harem, whether offspring of free women or of slaves, are legitimate and of equal lineage. The Sultan is succeeded by his eldest son, but only in case there are no uncles or cousins of greater age.

The fundamental laws of the empire are based on the precepts of the Koran. The will of the Sultan is absolute, in so far as it is not in opposition to the accepted truths of the Mahometan religion as laid down in the sacred book of the Prophet. Next to the Koran, the laws of the "Multeka," a code formed of the supposed sayings and opinions of Mahomet, and the sentences and decisions of his immediate successors, are binding upon the Sovereign as well as his subjects. Another code of laws, the "Cahon nameh," formed by Sultan Solyman the Magnificent, from a collection of "hatti-sheriffs," or decrees, issued by him and his predecessors, is held in general obedience, but merely as an emanation of human authority.

The legislative and executive authority is exercised, under the supreme direction of the Sultan, by two high dignitaries, the "Sadrazam," or Grand Vizier, the head of the temporal Government, and the "Sheïk-ul-Islam," the head of the Church. Both are appointed by the Sovereign, the latter with the nominal concurrence of the "Ulema," a body comprising the clergy and chief functionaries of the law, over which the "Sheïk-ul-Islam" presides, although he himself does not exercise priestly functions. Connected with the "Ulema" are the "Mufti," the interpreters of the Koran. The Ulema comprise all the great judges, theologians, and jurists, and the great teachers of literature and science, who may be summoned by the Mufti. The principal civic functionaries bear the titles of Effendi, Bey, or Pasha.

Forms of constitution, after the model of the West European States, were drawn up at various periods by successive Ottoman Governments, the first of them embodied in the "Hati-Huméyoun" of Sultan Abdul-Medjid, proclaimed February 18, 1856, and the most recent in a decree of Sultan Abdul-Hamid II., of November, 1876. But the carrying out of these projects of reform appears entirely impossible in the present condition of the Ottoman Empire.

The Grand Vizier, as head of the Government and representative of the Sovereign, is assisted by the Medjliss-i-Hass, or Privy Council, which corresponds to the British Cabinet. The Medjliss-i-Hass consists of the following members: 1, The Grand Vizier; 2, The Sheïk-ul-Islam; 3, The Minister of the Interior; 4, The Minister of War; 5, The Minister of Evkaf (Worship); 6, The Minister of Public Instruction; 7, The Minister of Public Works; 8, President of Council of State; 9, Minister of Foreign Affairs; 10, Minister of Finance; 11, Minister of Marine; 12, Minister of Justice; 13, Minister of Civil List.

The whole of the empire is divided into thirty Vilayets, or governments, and subdivided into Sanjaks, or provinces, Kazas, or districts, Nahiés, or subdistricts, and Kariés, or communities. A Vali, or governor general, who is held to represent the Sultan, and is assisted by a provincial council, is placed at the head of each Vilayet. The provinces, districts, etc., are subjected to inferior authorities (Mutesarifs, Caïmakams, Mudirs and Muktars) under the superintendence of the principal governor. The division of the country into Vilayets has been frequently modified of late for political reasons. For similar reasons six of the Sanjaks of the empire are governed by Mutesarifs appointed directly by the Sultan, and are known as Mutessarifats. All subjects, however humble their origin, are eligible to, and may fill, the highest offices in the State.

Under the capitulations foreigners residing in Turkey are under the laws of their respective countries, and are amenable for trial (in cases in which Turkish subjects are not concerned) to a tribunal presided over by their consul. Foreigners who own real property are amenable to the Ottoman civil courts in questions relative to their landed property. Cases between foreign and Turkish subjects are tried in the Ottoman courts, a dragoman of the foreign consulate being present to see that the trial be according to the law; the carrying out of the sentence, if against the foreigner, to be through his consulate. Cases between two foreign subjects of different nationalities are tried in the court of the defendant.

Religion and Education.—Mahometans form the vast majority of the population in Asiatic Turkey, but only one half of the population in European Turkey. Recognized by the Turkish Government are the adherents of seven non-Mahometan creeds—namely: 1, Latins, Franks, or Catholics, who use the Roman Liturgy, consisting of the descendants of the Genoese and Venetian settlers in the empire, and proselytes among Armenians; Bulgarians, and others; 2, Greeks; 3, Armenians; 4, Syrians and United Chaldeans; 5, Maronites, under a Patriarch at Kanobin in Mount Lebanon; 6, Protestants, consisting of converts chiefly among the Armenians; 7, Jews. These seven religious denominations are invested with the privilege of possessing their own ecclesiastical rule. The Bishops and Patriarchs of the Greeks and Armenians, and the "Chacham-Baschi," or high-rabbi of the Jews, possess, in consequence of those functions, considerable influence.

The Mahometan clergy are subordinate to the Sheïk-ul-Islam. Their offices are hereditary, and they can only be removed by Imperial iradé. A priesthood, however, in the strict sense of a separate class, to whom alone the right of officiating in religious services belongs, cannot be said to exist in Turkey.

The Koran and Multeka encourage public education and, as a consequence, public schools have been long established in most considerable Turkish towns; while "medresses," or colleges, with public libraries, are attached to the greater number of the principal mosques. But the instruction afforded by these establishments is rather limited.

The number of mosques in the Turkish Empire is 2,120, of which 379 are in Constantinople. The number of the clergy is 11,600. Connected with the mosques are 1,780 elementary schools, where education is supplied gratis. The private revenue of the Evkaf (church), previous to the war of 1878, was 30,200,000 piastres (250,000*l.*) per annum, but they have now been reduced to 20,000,000 piastres (166,000*l.*). The expenses are reckoned at 15,000,000 piastres (125,000*l.*). The stipend of the Sheïk-ul-Islam, 7,031,520 piastres (59,000*l.*), and those of the Naïbs and Muftis, 7,876,646 piastres (66,000*l.*), are paid by the State. The principal revenues of the Evkaf are derived from the sale of landed property which has been bequeathed it, and which is known under the name of Vacouf. Three fourths of the urban property of the empire is supposed to belong to the Vacouf. Purchasers of property of this description pay a nominal annual rent to the Evkaf; but should they die without direct heirs the property reverts to the Church.

SWEDEN AND NORWAY.

By the treaty of Kiel, January 14, 1814, Norway was ceded to the King of Sweden by the King of Denmark, but the Norwegian people did not recognize this cession, and declared themselves independent. A Constituent Assembly met at Eidsvold, and having adopted, on May 17, a Constitution, elected the Danish Prince, Christian Fredrik, King of Norway. The Swedish troops, however, entered Norway without serious resistance, and, the foreign Powers refusing to recognize the newly elected King, the Norwegians were obliged to conclude, August 14, the Convention of Moss, by which the independency of Norway in union with Sweden was solemnly proclaimed. An extraordinary *Storthing* was then convoked, which adopted the modifications in the Constitution made necessary by the union with

Sweden, and then elected King Carl XIII. King of Norway, November 4, 1814. The following year was promulgated a charter, the Riksakt, establishing new fundamental laws on the terms that the union of the two kingdoms be indissoluble and irrevocable, without prejudice, however, to the separate government, constitution, and code of laws of either Sweden or Norway.

The law of succession is the same in Sweden and Norway. In case of absolute vacancy of the throne, the two Diets assemble for the election of the future sovereign, and should they not be able to agree upon one person, an equal number of Swedish and Norwegian deputies have to meet at the city of Karlstad, in Sweden, for the appointment of the King, this nomination to be absolute. The common affairs are decided upon in a Council of State composed of Swedes and Norwegians. In case of minority of the King, the Council of State exercises the sovereign power until a regent or council of regency is appointed by the united action of the Diets of Sweden and Norway.

1. Sweden. — CENTRAL GOVERNMENT. The fundamental laws of the Kingdom of Sweden are: 1. The constitution or *Regerings-formen* of June 6, 1809. 2. The amended regulations for the formation of the Diet of June 22, 1866. 3. The law of royal succession of September 26, 1810. 4. The law on the liberty of the press of July 16, 1812. According to these statutes, the King must be a member of the Lutheran Church, and have sworn fealty to the laws of the land. His person is inviolable. He has the right to declare war and make peace, after consulting the Council of State. He nominates to all higher appointments, both military and civil; concludes foreign treaties, and has a right to preside in the Supreme Court of Justice. The princes of the blood royal, however, are excluded from all civil employments. The King possesses legislative power in matters of political administration, but in all other respects that power is exercised by the Diet in concert with the sovereign, and every new law must have the assent of the crown. The right of imposing taxes is, however, vested in the Diet. This Diet, or Parliament of the realm, consists of two Chambers, both elected by the people. The First Chamber consists of 150 members. The election of the members takes place by the *Landstings*, or provincial representations, 25 in number, and the municipal corporations of the towns, not already represented in the *Landstings*, Stockholm, Göteborg, Malmö, Norrköping, and Gefle. All members of the First Chamber must be above 35 years of age, and must have possessed for at least three years previous to the election either real property to the taxed value of 80,000 kronor, or 4,444*l.*, or an annual income of 4,000 kronor, or 223*l.* They are elected for the term of nine years, and obtain no payment for their services. The Second Chamber consists of 230 members, of whom 80 are elected by the towns and 150 by the rural districts. All natives of Sweden, aged 21, possessing real property to the taxed value of 1,000 kronor, or 56*l.*, or farming, for a period of not less than five years, landed property to the taxed value of 6,000 kronor, or 333*l.*, or paying income tax on an annual income of 800 kronor, or 45*l.*, are electors; and all natives, aged 25, possessing the same qualifications, may be elected members of the Second Chamber. The number of qualified electors to the Second Chamber in 1899 was 339,876, or 6.7 of the population; only 136,982, or 40.3 of the electors, actually voted. In the smaller towns and country districts the election may either be direct or indirect, according to the wish of the majority. The election is for the term of three years, and the members obtain salaries for their services, at the rate of 1,200 kronor, or 67*l.*, for each session of four months, or, in the case of an extra session 10 kronor (11*s.*) a day, besides traveling expenses. The salaries and traveling expenses of the deputies are paid out of the public purse. The members of both Chambers are elected by ballot, both in town and country.

Local Government.—The provincial administration is entrusted in Stockholm to a governor-general, and in each of the 24 governments to a prefect, who is nominated by the King. As executive officers of the prefects there are 118 bailles (*Kronfoglars*) and 520 sub-officers (*Länsmäns*). Each rural parish, and each town, forms a commune or municipality in which all who pay the local taxes are voters. The communal assembly or municipal council decides on all questions of administration, police and communal economy. Ecclesiastical affairs and questions relating to primary schools are dealt with by the parish assemblies, presided over by the pastor of the parish. Each government has a general council which regulates the internal affairs of the government. The council meets annually for a few days in September under a president appointed by the King from among its members. The members are elected by the towns and provincial districts. Towns having a population of 1-150th of the total population and towns already separated from the "*Landsthings*" are administered separately by their municipal councils; these towns are Stockholm, Göteborg, Malmö, Norrköping, and Gefle.

Religion.—The mass of the population adhere to the Lutheran Protestant Church, recognized as the State religion. There were 12 bishoprics, and 2,571 parishes in 1901. At the census of 1890, the number of Evangelical Lutherans was returned at 4,735,218, the Protestant Dissenters, Baptists, Methodists, and others numbering 44,378, including 23,307 unbaptized children. Of other creeds, there were 1,390 Roman Catholics, 46 Greek Catholics, 313 Irvingites, 3,402 Jews, and 234 Mormons. No civil disabilities attach to those not of the national religion. The clergy are chiefly supported from the parishes and the proceeds of the Church lands.

Instruction.— The Kingdom has two universities, at Upsala and Lund, the former frequented by 1,384 and the latter by 628 students in the spring of 1901. There are also a state faculty of medicine in Stockholm (250 students) and private philosophical faculties in

Stockholm and Göteborg. Education is well advanced in Sweden. In 1900 there were 79 public high schools, with 17,244 pupils; 29 people's high schools, 1,388 pupils; 13 normal schools for elementary school teachers, 1,299 pupils; 2 high and 6 elementary technical schools; 10 navigation schools, 709 pupils; 21 institutions and schools for deaf mutes and blind; besides medical schools, military schools, veterinary and other special schools. Public elementary instruction is gratuitous and compulsory, and children not attending schools under the supervision of the Government must furnish proofs of having been privately educated.

Justice.—The administration of justice is entirely independent of the Government. Two functionaries, the *Justitie-Kansler*, or Chancellor of Justice, and the *Justitie-Ombudsman*, or Attorney-General, exercise a control over the administration. The former, appointed by the King, acts also as a counsel for the Crown; while the latter, who is appointed by the Diet, has to extend a general supervision over all the courts of law. The Kingdom, which possesses one Supreme Court of Judicature, is divided into 3 high court districts and 208 district court divisions, of which 90 are urban districts and 118 country districts.

In town these district courts (or courts of first instance) are held by the burgomaster and his assessors; in the country by a judge and 12 jurors — peasant proprietors — the judge alone deciding, unless the jurors unanimously differ from him, when their decision prevails. In Sweden trial by jury only exists for affairs of the press.

Pauperism.—Each commune is bound to assist children under 15 years of age, if their circumstances require it, and all who from age or disease are unable to support themselves. In other cases the communal poor board decides what course to take. Each commune and each town (which may be divided) constitutes a poor district, and in each is a board of public assistance.

2. Norway.— CENTRAL GOVERNMENT. — The Constitution of Norway, called the *Grundloy*, bears date May 17, 1814, with several modifications passed at various times. It vests the legislative power of the realm in the *Storthing*, or Great Court, the representative of the sovereign people. The King, however, possesses the right of veto over laws passed by the *Storthing*, but only for a limited period. The royal veto may be exercised twice; but if the same bill pass three *Storthings* formed by separate and subsequent elections, it becomes the law of the land without the assent of the sovereign. The King has the command of the land and sea forces, and makes all appointments, but, except in a few cases, is not allowed to nominate any but Norwegians to public offices under the crown.

The *Storthing* assembles every year. New elections take place every three years. The meetings take place *suo jure*, and not by any writ from the King or the executive. They begin on the first week day after October 10 each year, and must receive the sanction of the King to sit longer than two months. Every Norwegian citizen of twenty-five years of age (provided that he resides and has resided for five years in the country) is entitled to elect, unless he is disqualified from a special cause, for instance, actual receiving of parish relief. Under the same conditions citizens thirty years of age, and having resided in Norway for ten years, are qualified to be elected. The mode of election is indirect. Every third year the people choose their deputies, one to fifty voters in towns where the election is administered by the magistrate, and one to a hundred in rural districts, where the election is presided over by the bailiff (*Lensmand*) or other member of the election committee. The deputies afterwards assemble and elect from among themselves, or from among the other qualified voters of the district, the *Storthing* representatives. Former members of the Council of State can be elected representatives of any district of the Kingdom without regard to their residence. No new election takes place for vacancies, which are filled by the persons already elected for that purpose, or, if not, who received the second largest number of votes. At the election in 1900 the number of electors was 440,174, or 19.73 per cent. of total population, while 238,617 votes, or 54.21 per cent. of the whole number, were recorded. The *Storthing* has 114 members — 38 from towns, 76 from rural districts.

Local Government.—The administrative division of the country is into twenty districts, each governed by a chief executive functionary (*Amtmand*), viz., the towns of Kristiania and Bergen, and 18 *Amts* (counties). There are 40 towns, 22 *Ladesteder* (ports), and 541 rural communes (*Herreder*), mostly parishes or sub-parishes (wards). The government of the *Herred* is vested in a body of representatives (from 12 to 48), and a council (*Formænd*), elected by and from among the representatives, who are four times the number of the *Formænd*. The representatives elect conjointly every third year from among the *Formænd* a chairman and a deputy chairman. All the chairmen of the rural communes of an *Amt* form with the *Amtmand* the *Amtsthing* (county Diet), which meets yearly to settle the budget of the *Amt*. The *Amtmand* is the chairman of the Diet. The towns and the ports form 60 communes, also governed by a council (5 to 21), and representatives (four times the size of the council); a chairman and a deputy chairman are yearly elected. The members of the local governing bodies are elected under the same conditions as the *Storthing*, with the exception that a limited suffrage was in 1901 accorded to women.

Religion and Instruction.—The evangelical Lutheran religion is the national Church and the only one endowed by the State. Its clergy are nominated by the King. All other Christian sects (except Jesuits), as well as the Jews, are tolerated, and free to exercise their religion within the limits prescribed by the law and public order. Ecclesiastically Norway is divided into 6 bishopricks, 83 *Provstier* (provostships, or archdeaconries), 482 *Præstegjeld* (clerical districts).

Education is compulsory, the school age being from six and a half in towns and seven in the country to fourteen.

Justice and Crime.—For civil justice Norway is divided into 109 districts, each with an inferior court. Of these 82 are rural courts, divided into 461 circuits. The other courts are in towns. There are three superior courts, having each one chief justice and two other justices, and one supreme court for the whole kingdom (*Höiesteret*), consisting of one president and at least 6 other justices. There is a court of mediation (*Forligelseskommission*) in each town and *Herred* (district) consisting of two men chosen by the electors, before which, as a rule, civil cases must first be brought.

According to the law of criminal procedure of July 1, 1887, all criminal cases (not military, or coming under the *Rigsret*—the court for impeachments) shall be tried either by jury (*Lagmandsret*), or *Meddomsret*.

DENMARK.

The present Constitution of Denmark is embodied in the charter of June 5, 1849, which was modified in some important respects in 1855 and 1863, but again restored, with various alterations, by a statute which obtained the royal sanction on July 28, 1866. According to this charter, the executive power is in the King and his responsible ministers, and the right of making and amending laws in the *Rigsdag* or Diet, acting in conjunction with the sovereign. The King must be a member of the Evangelical Lutheran Church, which is declared to be the religion of the State. The *Rigsdag* comprises the *Landsthing* and the *Folkething*, the former being a Senate or Upper House, and the latter a House of Commons. The *Landsthing* consists of 66 members. Of these 12 are nominated for life by the Crown, from among actual or former representatives of the Kingdom, and the rest are elected indirectly by the people for the terms of eight years. The choice of the latter 54 members of the Upper House is given to electoral bodies composed partly of the largest taxpayers in the country districts, partly of deputies of the largest taxpayers in the cities, and partly of deputies from the totality of citizens possessing the franchise. Eligible to the *Landsthing* is every citizen who has passed his twenty-fifth year and is a resident of the district. The *Folkething*, or Lower House of Parliament, consists of 114 members, returned in direct election, by universal suffrage, for the term of three years. According to the Constitution there should be one member for every 16,000 inhabitants. The franchise belongs to every male citizen who has reached his thirtieth year, who is not in the actual receipt of public charity or who, if he has at any former time been in receipt of it, has repaid the sums so received, who is not in private service without having his own household, and who has resided at least one year in the electoral circle on the lists of which his name is inscribed. Eligible for the *Folkething* are all men of good reputation past the age of twenty-five. Both the members of the *Landsthing* and of the *Folkething* receive payment for their services at the rate of 3 rixdalers (6s. 8d.) per day during the actual session, and are reimbursed for traveling expenses to and from the capital.

Religion.—The established religion of Denmark is the Lutheran, which was introduced as early as 1536, the Church revenue being at that time seized by the Crown, to be delivered up to the university and other religious and educational establishments. The affairs of the National Church are under the superintendence of seven bishops. The bishops have no political character. Complete religious toleration is extended to every sect, and no civil disabilities attach to Dissenters.

Instruction.—Elementary education has been widely diffused in Denmark since the beginning of this century, and in 1814 it was made compulsory. The school age is from 7 to 14. The public schools, maintained by communal rates, are free. Of elementary schools there are about 2,940 (28 in Copenhagen, 132 in other towns, and 2,780 in rural districts), with 307,633 pupils. For higher instruction there are: a veterinary and agricultural college at Copenhagen (founded 1892) with 37 professors and teachers and about 300 pupils in 1901; 21 agricultural or horticultural schools; 67 *folkehöjskoler* or popular high schools; 31 Latin schools (14 Government, 17 private); a college of pharmacy (founded 1892) with 7 teachers and 57 students; a Royal Academy of Arts (founded 1754) with 7 teachers and 200 pupils; a Polytechnic Institution (founded 1829) with 23 professors and teachers and about 450 students; 99 *realskoler* or technical and commercial schools. The *folkehöjskoler* are all private, but to them and the agricultural schools the State annually makes a grant of about 300,000 kroner. To 72 of the *realskoler* grants are made amounting annually to about 110,000 kroner, exclusive of the cost of apparatus, inspection, etc. The University of Copenhagen, founded in 1479, has five departments to all of which, except theology, women are admitted on equal terms with men. It has 85 professors and teachers and about 400 matriculated students.

Justice and Crime.—The lowest courts of justice in Denmark are those of the hundred or district magistrates (*herredsfogder* and *birkedommere*) and town judges (*byfogder*). From these courts an appeal lies to the superior court, or court of second instance, in Viborg with 9 judges, and in Copenhagen with 17 judges. The Copenhagen superior court, however, is identical with that of the civic magistrates. The supreme court (*Höjesteret*) or court of final appeal, with a chief justice, 12 puisne judges, and 11 special judges, sits in Copenhagen. Judges under 65 years of age can be removed only by judicial sentence.

SWITZERLAND.

On August 1, 1291, the men of Uri, Schwyz, and Lower Unterwalden, entered into a defensive League. In 1353 the League included eight cantons, and in 1513, thirteen. Various associated and protected territories were acquired, but no addition was made to the number of cantons forming the League till 1798. In that year, under the influence of France, the Helvetic Republic was formed, with a regular constitution. This failed to satisfy the cantons, and in 1803 Napoleon, in the Act of Mediation, gave a new constitution and increased the number of cantons to nineteen. In 1815, the perpetual neutrality of Switzerland and the inviolability of her territory were guaranteed by Austria, Great Britain, Portugal, Prussia, and Russia, and the Federal Pact, which had been drawn up at Zurich and which included three new cantons, was accepted by the Congress of Vienna. The Pact remained in force till 1848, when a new constitution, prepared without foreign interference, was accepted by general consent. This, in turn, was, on May 29, 1874, superseded by the constitution which is now in force.

The constitution of the Swiss Confederation may be revised either in the ordinary forms of Federal legislation, with compulsory *referendum*, or by direct popular vote, a majority both of the citizens voting and of the cantons being required, and the latter method may be adopted on the demand (called the *popular initiative*) of 50,000 citizens with the right to vote. The Federal Government is supreme in matters of peace, war, and treaties; it regulates the army, the postal and telegraph system, the coining of money, the issue and repayment of bank notes, and the weights and measures of the Republic. It provides for the revenue in general, and especially decides on the import and export duties in accordance with principles embodied in the constitution. It legislates in matters of civil capacity, copyright, bankruptcy, patents, sanitary police in dangerous epidemics, and it may create and subsidize, besides the Polytechnic School at Zurich, a Federal University and other higher educational institutions. There has also been intrusted to it the authority to decide concerning public works for the whole or great part of Switzerland, such as those relating to rivers, forests, and the construction of railways.

The supreme legislation and executive authority are vested in a parliament of two chambers, a *Ständerath*, or State Council, and a *Nationalrath*, or National Council. The first is composed of forty-four members, chosen and paid by the twenty-two cantons of the Confederation, two for each canton. The mode of their election and the term of membership depend entirely on the canton.

Local Government.—Each of the cantons and demi-cantons of Switzerland is *souverain*, so far as its independence and legislative powers are not restricted by the federal constitution; each has its local government, different in its organization in most instances, but all based on the principle of absolute sovereignty of the people. In a few of the smallest cantons, the people exercise their powers direct, without the intervention of any parliamentary machinery, all male citizens of full age assembling together in the open air, at stated periods, making laws and appointing their administrators. Such assemblies, known as the *Landsgemeinden*, exist in Appenzell, Glarus, Unterwald, and Uri. In all the larger cantons, there is a body chosen by universal suffrage, called *der Grosse Rath*, which exercises all the functions of the *Landsgemeinden*. In all the cantonal constitutions, however, except that of Freiburg and those of the cantons which have a *Landsgemeinde*, the *referendum* has a place. This principle is most fully developed in Zurich, where all laws and concordats, or agreements with other cantons, and the chief matters of finance, as well as all revision of the constitution, must be submitted to the popular vote. In many of the cantons, the *popular initiative* has also been introduced. The members of the cantonal councils, as well as most of the magistrates, are either honorary servants of their fellow citizens, or receive a merely nominal salary. In each canton there are districts (*Amtsbezirke*) consisting of a number of communes grouped together, each district having a Prefect (*Regierungstatthalter*) representing the canton. In the larger communes, for local affairs, there is an Assembly (legislative) and a Council (executive) with a president, maire or syndic, and not less than four other members. In the smaller communes there is a council only, with its proper officials.

Religion.—According to the Constitution of 1874 there is complete and absolute liberty of conscience and of creed. No one can incur any penalties whatsoever on account of his religious opinions. No one is bound to pay taxes specially appropriated to defraying the expenses of a creed to which he does not belong. No bishoprics can be created on Swiss territory without the approbation of the Confederation. The order of Jesuits and its affiliated societies cannot be received in any part of Switzerland; all functions clerical and scholastic are forbidden to its members, and the interdiction can be extended to any other religious orders whose action is dangerous to the State, or interferes with the peace of different creeds. The foundation of new convents or religious orders is forbidden.

The population of Switzerland is divided between Protestantism and Roman Catholicism, about 59 per cent. of the inhabitants adhering to the former, and 40 per cent. to the latter. According to the census of December 1, 1900, the number of Protestants amounted to 1,918,197, of Roman Catholics to 1,383,135, and of Jews to 12,551.

Instruction.—In the educational administration of Switzerland there is no centralization. Before the year 1848 most of the cantons had organized a system of primary schools, and since that year elementary education has steadily advanced. In 1874 it was made obligatory (the school age varying in the different cantons), and placed under the civil authority. In some cantons the cost falls almost entirely on the communes, in others it is divided between the canton and communes. In all the cantons primary instruction is free. In the north-eastern cantons, where the inhabitants are mostly Protestants, the proportion of the school-attending children to the whole population is as one to five; while in the half Protestant and half Roman Catholic cantons it is as one to seven; and in the entirely Roman Catholic cantons as one to nine. The compulsory law has hitherto not always been enforced in the Roman Catholic cantons, but is rigidly carried out in those where the Protestants form the majority of inhabitants. In every district there are primary schools, and secondary schools for youths of from twelve to fifteen. Of the contingent for military service in 1900, .18 per cent. could not read, and 62 per cent. could not write.

PANAMA.

The new republic of Panama extends about 460 miles from east to west and has an area of about 31,500 square miles — about one fourth less than the state of Ohio. The statistical bureau of the Department of Commerce at Washington estimates the population at about 300,000. It is chiefly the seacoast that is inhabited, most of the interior being dense jungle and unexplored. The city of Panama has about 25,000 people, and Colon, formerly known as Aspinwall, is a smaller place, with about 3,000. Colon dates from the building of the railroad, while Panama was founded a hundred years before the Pilgrims landed at Plymouth. The greatest drawback to the development of the isthmus has been the prevalence of fevers. American engineers, however, declare that with proper sanitary administration it could be made a favorite winter resort.

On November 3, 1903, dispatches to the daily papers informed the world that the inhabitants of the state of Panama were in revolt against the government of the United States of Colombia. On November 7, President Roosevelt, through Secretary Hay, recognized the Republic of Panama, and notified Colombia that she must not attempt to regain control of the isthmus. On the same day, the provisional government of the Republic of Panama, through the American consul, notified Secretary Hay that Philippe Bruneau-Varilla had been appointed its diplomatic agent in this country, and that a commission would leave Panama for Washington on November 10, to arrange for a treaty to govern the construction and operation of the canal. Singularly enough, M. Bruneau-Varilla holds a great deal of stock in the French Canal Company, of which concern he is also one of the engineers.

The promptness with which the United States and Europe showed a determination to prevent punitive action by Colombia caused many persons to assume that there had been concerted preparation. The theory has been both strongly supported and strongly contested. At any rate, a record in republic-making has been established, not only in speed but also in bloodlessness. Not a shot was fired, nor is there on record the wounding or killing of one man.

Only in Panama could such an undertaking have been carried through to success, and only under conditions actually existing in Colombia at the time. Necessary, also, was an incentive. The big canal gave that, because secession from the Federation meant the paying to Panama of many millions of dollars that would otherwise have gone into the Colombian treasury.

Cortez was the first to see that a canal across the isthmus was necessary, and he actually had a route surveyed. Then came Antonio Galvao, in 1550, who suggested digging a ditch along the identical route now proposed. In 1818, Spain decided that the work should be begun, but industrial progress was interfered with by a continuous insurrection inaugurated just then by Bolivar, the Liberator, who succeeded in organizing the United States of Colombia, which became the Republic of New Granada after his death. In 1840, Panama and Veragua seceded, but were quickly whipped back into the union. In 1843, the French government discussed the advisability of building the canal, but soon abandoned the idea. In 1846, when travel to the Pacific was increasing, the United States entered into a treaty with New Granada, wherein that government guaranteed that "The right of way or transit across the Isthmus of Panama, upon any mode of communication that now exists or may hereafter exist, shall be free and open to the government and citizens of the United States." In compensation, the United States, in the same treaty, guaranteed to maintain uninterrupted traffic between Panama and Colon, and to preserve "The rights of sovereignty and property which New Granada has and possesses over the said territory."

Then following the building of the trans-isthmian railway, which was completed in 1855. The next year Panama and Antioquia seceded, but were reincorporated in the Federation after a few years. In 1879, Ferdinand de Lesseps organized a large company for the construction of the canal and failed. In 1902, Congress passed a bill in which provision was made to purchase from the French company, for forty million dollars, its entire interest in the Panama Canal, and to pay Colombia ten millions for the right to build and control the canal, and an annual rental of two hundred and fifty thousand dollars for the territory traversed. The President was authorized to negotiate a treaty with Colombia, which he did, but, unfortunately, the Colombian senate adjourned on October 31, 1903, without ratifying it.

Italy and France have recognized the new republic of Panama, Germany has refused all invitations to interfere, and England is neutral.

In February, 1904, Panama was duly organized as an international state, and a treaty concluded with it by the United States, granting to the latter country the right to construct the Panama canal. In pursuance of this treaty, the President appointed a board of commissioners, made up for the most part of eminent civil and military engineers, to take charge of the construction of the canal. Work is expected to begin as soon as the appropriation becomes available, and after the title has been legally passed by the French company. Ten years is the time estimated for its completion.

International Copyright Protection. —By an act of Congress which went into effect on July 1, 1891, the United States Government removed the limitation of the privilege of copyright to citizens of the United States, thus making it possible for foreign authors to obtain protection in this country upon the same terms as native authors, except that they are required to pay a double fee. At the same time Congress stipulated that this copyright protection should apply only to a citizen of a foreign state or nation when such foreign state or nation permitted citizens of the United States to enjoy the benefits of copyright on substantially the same basis as its own subjects, or when such foreign state or nation should become a party to an international agreement providing for reciprocity in the granting of copyright. Under the operation of this amendment of the copyright law, therefore, the privileges of copyright in the United States have been extended, by presidential proclamation, to the authors of Belgium, Chili, Costa Rica, Denmark, France, Germany, Great Britain and her possessions (Australia, Canada, India, etc.), Italy, Mexico, Netherlands, Portugal, Spain, and Switzerland, and, as the result, the artists, composers, and authors of these nations are now entitled to receive copyright protection from the United States, and American authors and makers of works of art may demand the same privilege for their production under the laws of the other countries.

HEADS OF THE GOVERNMENTS OF THE WORLD.

DECEMBER 1, 1903.

Country.	Official Head.	Title.	Born.	Acceded.
Abyssinia	Menelik II	Emperor	1843	March 12, 1889
Afghanistan	Habibulla Khan	Ameer		Oct. 3, 1901
Annam	Thanh Thai	King	1879	Jan. 30, 1889
Argentine Republic	Julio A. Roca	President		Oct. 12, 1898
Austria-Hungary	Francis Joseph	Emperor	Aug. 18, 1830	Dec. 2, 1848
Baluchistan	Mir Mahmud	Khan		Aug., 1893
Belgium	Leopold II	King	April 9, 1835	Dec. 10, 1865
Bokhara	Seid Abdul Ahad	Ameer	1864	Nov. 12, 1885
Bolivia	Jose Manuel Pando	President		Oct. 24, 1899
Brazil	Francisco de P. Rodrigues Alves	President	July 7, 1848	Oct., 1902
Bulgaria	Ferdinand	Prince	Feb. 26, 1861	Aug. 11, 1887
Chile	Jerman Riesco	President	1851	Sept. 18, 1901
China	Kuang Hsu (Queen, his aunt, rules)	Emperor	Aug. 2, 1872	Jan. 12, 1875
Colombia	Jose M. Marroquin	Act. President		1900
Congo Free State	Leopold (King of the Belgians)	Sovereign	April 9, 1835	April 30, 1885
Costa Rica	Asuncion Esquivel	President		May 8, 1902
Cuba	Tomas Estrada Palma	President		May 20, 1902
Denmark	Christian IX	King	April 8, 1818	Nov. 15, 1863
Dominican Republic	Revolution in Progress	President		1903
Ecuador	General Leonidas Plaza	President		Aug. 31, 1891
Egypt	Abbas Pacha	Khedive	July 14, 1874	Jan. 7, 1892
France	Emile Loubet	President	Dec. 31, 1838	Feb. 18, 1899
Germany	William II	Emperor	Jan. 27, 1859	June 15, 1888
Prussia	William II	King		
Bavaria	Otto	King	April 27, 1848	June 13, 1886
Saxony	George	King	Aug. 8, 1832	June 19, 1902
Wurtemberg	William II	King	Feb. 25, 1848	Oct. 6, 1891
Baden	Frederick	Grand Duke	Sept. 9, 1826	Sept. 5, 1856
Hesse	Ernst Louis V	Grand Duke	Nov. 25, 1868	March 13, 1892
Lippe-Detmold	Alexander (a Regency)	Prince	Jan. 16, 1831	March 20, 1895
Anhalt	Frederick	Duke	April 29, 1831	May 22, 1871
Brunswick	Prince Albrecht	Regent	May 8, 1837	Oct. 21, 1885
Mecklenburg-Schwerin	Frederick Francis IV	Grand Duke	April 9, 1882	April 10, 1897
Mecklenburg-Strelitz	Frederick William	Grand Duke	Oct. 17, 1819	Sept. 6, 1860
Oldenburg	Frederick Augustus	Grand Duke	Nov. 16, 1852	June 13, 1900
Saxe-Altenburg	Ernest	Duke	Sept. 16, 1826	Aug. 3, 1853
Saxe-Coburg and Gotha	Leopold (Duke of Albany)	Duke	July 19, 1884	July 30, 1900
Saxe-Meiningen	George II	Duke	April 2, 1826	Sept. 20, 1866
Saxe-Weimar	William Ernest	Grand Duke	June 10, 1876	Jan. 5, 1901
Waldeck-Pyrmont	Frederick	Prince	Jan. 20, 1865	May 12, 1893
Great Britain and Ireland	Edward VII	King	Nov. 9, 1841	Jan. 22, 1901
Greece	George	King	Dec. 24, 1845	Oct. 31, 1863
Guatemala	Manuel Estrado Cabrera	President	Dec. 24, 1856	Sept. 25, 1898
Hayti	Nord Alexis	President		1902
Honduras	Manuel Bonilla	President	1849	Feb. 1, 1903
India, Empire of	Edward	Emperor	Nov. 9, 1841	Jan. 22, 1901
Italy	Victor Emmanuel III	King	Nov. 11, 1869	July 29, 1900
Japan	Mutsuhito	Mikado	Nov. 3, 1852	Feb. 13, 1867
Khiva	Seid Mahomed Rahim	Khan	1845	1865
Korea	Yi Hiung	Emperor	July 25, 1851	Jan., 1864
Liberia	George W. Gibson	President		Dec. 11, 1900
Luxembourg	Adolphus (Duke of Nassau)	Grand Duke	July 24, 1817	Nov. 23, 1890
Mexico	General Porfirio Diaz	President	Sept. 30, 1830	Dec. 1, 1884
Monaco	Albert	Prince	Nov. 13, 1848	Sept. 10, 1889
Montenegro	Nicholas	Prince	Oct. 7, 1841	Aug. 14, 1860
Morocco	Muley Abdul Azziz	Sultan	1878	June 11, 1894
Nepal	Surendra Bikram Shamsher Jang	Maharaja	Aug. 8, 1875	May 17, 1881
Netherlands	Wilhelmina	Queen	Aug. 31, 1880	Sept. 5, 1898
Nicaragua	General Jose S. Zelaya	President		1898
Oman	Seyyid Feysal bin Turkee	Sultan		June 4, 1888
Panama	Dr. Manuel Amador	President		1904
Paraguay	Manuel Diminguez	President		Nov. 25, 1902
Persia	Muzafer ed Din	Shah	Mar. 25, 1853	May 1, 1896
Peru	Julio Candamo	President		Sept. 8, 1903
Portugal	Carlos	King	Sept. 28, 1863	Oct. 19, 1889
Roumania	Charles	King	April 20, 1839	March 26, 1881
Russia	Nicholas II	Emperor	May 18, 1868	Nov. 2, 1894
Salvador	José Pedro Escalon	President	Mar. 24, 1857	March 1, 1903
Servia	Peter (Karageorgevitch)	King	1844	June 15, 1903
Siam	Khoulalongkorn	King	Sept. 21, 1853	Oct. 1, 1868
Spain	Alphonso XIII	King	May 17, 1886	May 17, 1886
Sweden and Norway	Oscar II	King	Jan. 21, 1829	Sept. 18, 1872
Switzerland	B. Comtesse	President		Jan. 1, 1904
Tunis	Hafiz Mehemet Pasha	Bey		July, 1900
Turkey	Abdul Hamid II	Sultan	Sept. 22, 1842	Aug. 31, 1876
United States of America	Theodore Roosevelt	President	Oct. 27, 1858	Sept. 14, 1901
Uruguay	Jose Batele y Ordonez	President		March 1, 1903
Venezuela	Cipriano Castro	President		Oct., 1899
Zanzibar	Seyyid Ali	Sultan	1856	1902

STATISTICS OF THE COUNTRIES OF THE WORLD.

Countries.	Populati'n.	Sq. Miles.	Capitals.
China	402,680,000	4,218,401	Peking
British Empire	381,037,874	11,335,806	London
Russian Empire	129.211,113	8,644,100	St. Petersburg
United States	76,000.000	3,602,990	Washington
United States and Colonies	85,000,000	3,756,380	Washington
Philippines	8,000,000	143,000	Manila
Porto Rico	900,000	3,600	San Juan
Hawaii	109,029	6,740	Honolulu
Sulus, Carolines, Guam	2,500	50	
France and Colonies	63,166,967	3,357,856	Paris
France	38,517,975	204,177	Paris
Colonies	21,448,064	2,923,679	
Algeria	3,870,000	260,000	Algiers
Senegal, etc	183,237	580,000	St. Louis
Tunis	1,500,000	45,000	Tunis
Cayenne	26,502	46,697	Cayenne
Cambodia	1,500,000	32,254	Saigon
Cochin-China	1,223,000	13,692	
Tonquin	12,000,000	60,000	Hanoi
New Caledonia	62,752	7,624	Noumea
Tahiti	12,800	462	
Sahara	1,100,000	1,550,000	
Madagascar	3,500,000	230,000	Antananarivo
German Empire	52,279,901	211,108	Berlin
Prussia	31,855,123	134,467	Berlin
Bavaria	5,589,382	29,291	Munich
Saxony	3,500,513	5,789	Dresden
Würtemberg	2,035,443	7,531	Stuttgart
Baden	1,656,817	5,803	Karlsruhe
Alsace-Lorraine	1,603,987	5,602	Strasburg
Hesse	956,170	2,965	Darmstadt
Mecklenburg-Schwerin	575,140	5,137	Schwerin
Hamburg	622,530	158	
Brunswick	372,580	1,425	Brunswick
Oldenburg	341,250	2,479	Oldenburg
Saxe-Weimar	313,668	1,387	Weimar
Anhalt	247,603	906	Dessau
Saxe-Meiningen	214,697	953	Meiningen
Saxe-Coburg-Gotha	198,717	760	Gotha
Bremen	180,443	99	
Saxe-Altenburg	161,129	511	Altenburg
Lippe	123,250	472	Detmold
Reuss (younger line)	112,118	319	Gera
Mecklenburg-Strelitz	98,371	1,131	Neu Strelitz
Schwarzburg-Rudolstadt	83,939	363	Rudolstadt
Schwarzburg-Sondershausen	73,623	333	Sondershausen
Lübeck	76,485	115	
Waldeck	56,565	433	Arolsen
Reuss (elder line)	53,787	122	Greiz
Schaumburg-Lippe	37,204	131	Buckeburg
German Africa	5,950,000	822,000	
Austria-Hungarian Empire	41,827,700	201,591	Vienna
Japan	41,089,940	147,669	Tokio
Netherlands	4,450,870	12,680	The Hague
Netherlands and Colonies	33,042,238	778,187	The Hague
Borneo	1,073.500	203,714	
Celebes	2,000,000	72,000	
Java	21,974,161	50,848	Batavia
Moluccas	353,000	42,420	Amboyna
New Guinea	200,000	150,755	
Sumatra	2,750,000	170,744	
Surinam	57,141	46,060	Paramaribo
Turkish Empire	33,559,787	1,652,533	Constantino'le
European Turkey	4,790,000	63,850	
Asiatic Turkey	16,133,900	729,170	
Tripoli	1,000,000	398.873	Tripoli
Bulgaria	3,154,375	37,860	Sofia
Egypt	9,700,000	400,000	Cairo
Italy	29,699,785	110,665	Rome
Italy and Colonies	34,970,785	425,765	Rome
Abyssinia	4,500,000	189,000	
Eritrea	660,000	56,100	
Somal Coast	210,000	70,000	
Spain	17,550,216	196,173	Madrid
Spanish Africa	437,000	203,767	
Spanish Islands	127,172	1,957	
Brazil	18,000,000	3,219,000	C. Rio Janeiro
Mexico	12,570,195	767,316	City of Mexico
Korea	10,519,000	85.000	Seoul
Congo State	8,000,000	802,000	
Persia	7,653,600	636,000	Teheran
Portugal	4,708,178	34,038	Lisbon
Portugal and Colonies	11,073,681	951,785	Lisbon
Portuguese Africa	5,416,000	841,025	
Portuguese Asia	847,503	7,923	
Sweden and Norway	6,785,898	297,321	
Sweden	4,784,981	172,876	Stockholm
Norway	2,000,917	124,445	Christiania
Morocco	6,500,000	314,000	Fez
Belgium	6,030,043	11,373	Brussels
Siam	5,700,000	280,550	Bangkok
Roumania	5,376,000	46,314	Bucharest
Argentine Republic	4 042,990	1,095,013	Buenos Ayres
Colombia	4,600,000	331,420	Bogota
Afghanistan	4,000,000	279,000	Cabul
Chile	3,500,000	256,860	Santiago
Peru	2,800,000	405,040	Lima
Switzerland	2,933,334	15,981	Berne
Bolivia	2,300,000	472,000	La Paz
Greece	2,433,806	24,977	Athens
Denmark	2,172,205	14,780	Copenhagen
Denmark and Colonies	2,288,193	101,403	Copenhagen
Iceland	72,445	39,756	Rejkjavik
Greenland	9,780	46,740	Godthaab
West Indies	33,763	118	
Venezuela	2,323,988	566,159	Caracas
Servia	2,096,043	18,757	Belgrade
Nepaul	2,000,000	56,800	Khatmandu
Cuba	1,600,000	41,655	Havana
Oman	1,600,000	81,000	Muscat
Guatemala	1,470,000	46,774	N. Guatemala
Ecuador	1,300,000	144,000	Quito
Liberia	1,050,000	14,000	Monrovia
Hayti	950,000	29,830	Port au Prince
Transvaal	800,000	110,193	Pretoria
Salvador	816,000	7,228	San Salvador
Uruguay	850,000	72,112	Montevideo
Khiva	700,000	22,320	Khiva
Paraguay	476,000	145,000	Asuncion
Honduras	450,000	42,658	Tegucigalpa
Nicaragua	400,000	51,660	Managua
Dominican Republic	350,000	20,596	San Domingo
Montenegro	245,380	3,486	Cettinje
Costa Rica	265,000	19,985	San Jose
Orange Free State	133,518	41,484	Bloemfontein

AUSTRALIAN FEDERATION.

Colonies.	Area in Sq. Miles.	Population.
New South Wales	310,700	1,346,000
Victoria	87,884	1,175,000
South Australia	903,690	367,000
Queensland	668,497	494,000
Western Australia	903,690	168,000
Tasmania	26,215	177,000
New Zealand	104,032	743,000
Fiji	7,423	125,402
British New Guinea	234,768	350,000
Total	3,246,729	4,945,402

DIVISION OF AFRICA

AMONG THE EUROPEAN POWERS.

	Area.	Population.
	Added by Conquest, 1900.	
	Transvaal.	
	119,139	1,091,156
	Orange River Colony.	
	48,326	207,503
BRITISH AFRICA: Basutoland, Bechuanaland Protectorate, Cape Colony, Central Africa, East Africa Protectorate, Uganda Protectorate, Zanzibar Protectorate, Mauritius, Natal, Niger Coast Protectorate, Territory of the Royal Niger Company, South Africa, West Africa, Zululand and Islands*..................	2,587,755	41,133,953
FRENCH AFRICA: Algeria, Senegal, French Soudan and the Niger, Gaboon and Guinea Coast, Congo Region, Somali Coast, Madagascar and Islands.........................	1,232,454	18,073,890
GERMAN AFRICA: Togoland, Cameroons, South West Africa, East Africa............	920,920	10,200,000
ITALIAN AFRICA: Eritrea, Somaliland..................	278,500	850,000
PORTUGUESE AFRICA: Angola, the Congo, Guinea, East Africa and Islands†............	735,304	4,431,970
SPANISH AFRICA: Rio de Oro, Adrar, Fernando Po and Islands........................	243,877	136,000
TURKISH AFRICA: Tripoli and the Mediterranean Coast, Egypt*........................	798,738	8,117,265
CONGO INDEPENDENT STATE. (Under the sovereignty of the King of the Belgians........	900,000	30,000,000
Total......................	7,697,548	113,243,070

Indebtedness and Finances of Nations.

COUNTRIES	NATIONAL DEBTS			Revenue	COMMERCE WITH THE UNITED STATES	
	Total	Interest Per Cent	Per Capita		Exports from United States to—	Imports into United States from—
Argentina................	$509,604,444	4½-6	$128.85	$63,339,188	$11,117,521	$9,455,634
Australasia..............	1,183,055,000	3 -5	263.90	167,335,000	28,163,722	5,262,962
Austria-Hungary	1,154,791,000	3 -4	25.80	73,659,000	6,843,980	10,042,401
Austria	642,194,000	3 -5	24.89	215,237,000	....	....
Hungary	904,941,000	3 -4	47.75	209,001,000	....	....
Belgium...................	504,459,540	2½-3	75.63	85,494,672	51,444,315	14,919,071
Bolivia...................	2,336,258	4 -5	1.16	3,431,000	120,033	22
Brazil....................	480,985,000	4 -5	33.56	90,152,000	11,516,681	64,914,507
British Colonies	265,541,000	3 -6	26.43	79,956,595	44,871,723	24,161,522
Canada	265,494,000	2½-5	50.59	51,020,000	105,789,214	42,482,163
Chile	113,240,000	4½-5	36.41	43,206,000	4,596,525	7,474,061
China	287,123,500	4½-7	.72	73,500,000	18,175,484	18,125,836
Colombia	15,809,000	3 -5	3.95	7,031,000	2,923,404	4,810,465
Costa Rica	13,124,000	3 -5	43.75	3,513,000	1,688,670	2,959,439
Cuba	....	....	....	....	27,007,024	46,663,511
Denmark	55,795,724	3	24.15	19,247,008	15,499,371	796,736
Ecuador	7,882,435	3½-5	6.21	3,564,000	1,590,055	1,577,486
Egypt	500,402,729	3 -4½	53.61	56,424,345	1,320,969	8,866,378
France	5,800,691,814	3 -3½	150.61	691,349,500	78,405,972	81,314,609
German Empire	557,626,622	3 -3½	9.96	471,002,000	184,678,723	99,969,851
German States	2,015,958,000	....	....	....	....	....
Greece	168,548,444	4 -5	69.25	13,650,533	286,236	1,447,303
Guatemala	20,826,507	4 -5	13.23	2,687,000	1,128,418	2,190,145
Honduras	89,376,920	4 -5	219.60	1,114,429	1,181,453	988,606
India, British	1,031,603,705	2½-4½	4.67	328,955,934	5,646,669	47,171,558
India, French	....	....	....	....	118,102	....
India, Dutch	....	....	....	....	1,652,604	32,308,633
Italy	2,583,983,780	3½-5	81.11	317,349,332	34,046,201	27,631,248
Japan.....................	206,799,994	4 -5	4.73	121,433,725	21,162,477	36,854,692
Mexico	168,771,428	3 -5	13.36	29,267,131	36,475,350	28,851,635
Netherlands	466,419,294	2½-3	90.74	58,323,000	83,721,501	17,273,111
Nicaragua	4,901,819	4 -6	9.80	1,459,950	1,482,194	2,035,636
Norway	53,211,132	3 -3½	25.08	21,457,420	....	....
Paraguay	19,972,000	3 -4½	30.45	844,000	8,487	1,740
Peru	20,321,784	4 -6	4.41	5,914,000	2,311,886	2,910,531
Philippine Islands	....	....	....	....	4,027,064	4,420,912
Portugal	670,221,374	3 -4½	143.82	56,363,000	4,544,088	3,641,452
Roumania	280,136,991	4 -5	47.37	28,001,000	31,037	101,042
Russia....................	3,167,320,000	3 -5	24.56	891,772,000	6,504,857	7,236,120
Servia	81,972,118	4 -5	33.43	15,144,548	369	3,156
Spain	1,727,994,620	4 -5	95.53	170,998,000	16,785,711	7,040,758
Sweden	85,154,320	3 -3½	16.71	39,043,000	11,520,574	4,369,984
Switzerland...............	15,919,219	3½	5.10	19,392,000	232,336	16,035,278
Turkey	726,511,195	3 -5	29.25	81,893,462	183,669	2,437,263
United Kingdom	3,060,926,304	2½-2¾	74.83	583,201,360	598,766,799	155,291,927
United States	969,457,241	2 -4	12.25	684,082,843	....	....
Uruguay	124,374,189	3½-5	148.06	16,608,000	1,480,820	1,974,977
Venezuela	37,725,814	4 -5	14.51	6,452,000	2,736,726	6,609,919
Total..................	....	....	$24.00	$5,902,879,975	$1,431,789,014	$852,624,280

RATES OF POSTAGE.

Letters.—Prepaid by stamps, 2 cents each ounce or fraction thereof to all parts of the United States and Canada; forwarded to another post office without charge on request of the person addressed; if not called for, returned to the writer free, if indorsed with that request. If the stamp is omitted the letter is forwarded to the Dead-Letter Office and returned to the writer. For registering letters the charge is 8 cents additional. Drop letters at letter-carrier offices, 2 cents per ounce or fraction thereof; at other offices, 1 cent per ounce or fraction thereof. On insufficiently prepaid matter mailed in Canada, 3 cents per ½ ounce or fraction thereof. Stamped postal cards, furnished only by government, 1 cent each; if anything except a printed address slip is pasted on a postal card, or anything but the address written on the face, letter postage is charged. Special delivery letters 10 cents additional. The Rural Delivery system is being extended in various parts of the country to the great accommodation of thousands.

Second-Class Matter.— Periodicals issued at regular intervals, at least four times a year, and having a regular list of subscribers, with supplement, sample copies, 1 cent a pound; periodicals, other than weekly, if delivered by letter carrier, 1 cent each; if over 2 ounces, 2 cents each. When sent by other than publishers, for 4 ounces or less, 1 cent.

Third-Class Matter (not exceeding four pounds).—Printed matter, books, proof-sheets, corrected or uncorrected, unsealed circulars, inclosed so as to admit of easy inspection without cutting cords or wrappers, 1 cent for each 2 ounces.

Fourth-Class Matter.— Not exceeding four pounds, embracing merchandise and samples, excluding liquids, poisons, greasy, inflammable or explosive articles, live animals, insects, etc., 1 cent an ounce. Postage to Canada and British North American states, 2 cents per ounce; must be prepaid; otherwise, 6 cents.

Postage Rates to Foreign Countries.— To the countries and colonies which, with the United States, comprise the Universal Postal Union, the rates of postage are as follows: Letters, per 15 grams (½ ounce), pre-payment optional, 5 cents; postal cards, each, 2 cents; newspapers and other printed matter, per 2 ounces, 1 cent. Commercial papers — First 10 ounces or fraction thereof, 5 cents; every additional 2 ounces, 1 cent. Samples of merchandise — First 4 ounces, 2 cents; every additional 2 ounces, 1 cent. Registration fee on letters or other articles, 10 cents. All correspondence other than letters must be prepaid at least partially.

Printed matter other than books received in the mails from abroad under the provisions of postal treaties or conventions is free from customs duty.

Postal Money Orders.— Not exceeding $2.50, 3 cents; over $2.50 to $5, 5 cents; over $5 to $10, 8 cents; over $10 to $20, 10 cents; over $20 to $30, 12 cents; over $30 to $40, 15 cents; over $40 to $50, 18 cents; over $50 to $60, 20 cents; over $60 to $75, 25 cents; over $75 to $100, 30 cents.

To Switzerland, Germany, Belgium, Portugal, Canada, Newfoundland, Italy, France, Algeria, New South Wales, Victoria, Tasmania, New Zealand, Jamaica: Fees, not exceeding $10, 15 cents. To Great Britain, Ireland, and adjacent islands: Fees, not exceeding $10, 25 cents. To British India: Fees, not exceeding $10, 35 cents.

THE NATIONAL BANK LAW.

In towns of a population of 3,000 or less the minimum capital allowed is $25,000. In towns of between 3,000 and 6,000 people the minimum capital allowed is $50,000; and in cities and towns having a population of 6,000 or more but not exceeding 50,000, the minimum capital must be $100,000; while in cities of over 50,000 people the bank must have a capital of at least $200,000. There is no limit to the amount of excess capital.

Every national bank must purchase and deliver to the Treasurer of the United States registered U. S. bonds to an amount not less than $50,000, except banks with a capital of $150,000, or less, the minimum amount of bonds required is one quarter of the capital.

The Government then issues and delivers to the bank circulating notes in denominations of $5, $10, $20, $50, $100, as desired, in total amount equal to the par value of the bonds deposited. A bank may deposit bonds and receive circulating notes to an amount equal to its capital.

Each bank is required to make a sworn statement of its condition to the Comptroller of the Currency at Washington at least five times a year, and to publish the same in a newspaper. Two examinations a year are made by capable men employed by the Government as national bank examiners, their visits being always without notice.

Requirement is made in the National bank act for the accumulation of a surplus by each bank from its earnings as an additional protection above its capital to the depositors. The depositors are further protected against loss by the liability of each stockholder to the payment of an amount equal to the par value of the stock held, in event of failure of the bank.

PARLIAMENTARY LAW CONDENSED.

Letters refer to Rules below.

Modifying or amending.	
8. To amend or to substitute, or to divide the question	K
To refer to committee.	
7. To commit (or recommit)	D
Deferring action.	
6. To postpone to a fixed time	C
4. To lay on the table	A E G
Suppressing or extending debate.	
5. For the previous question	A E M
To limit, or close, debate	A M
To extend limits of debate	A
Suppressing the question.	
Objection to consideration of question	A H M N
9. To postpone indefinitely	D E
4. To lay upon the table	A E G
To bring up a question the second time.	
To reconsider debatable question	D E F I
To reconsider undebatable question	A E F I
Concerning Orders, Rules, etc.	
3. For the orders of the day	A E H N
To make subject a special order.	M
To amend the rules	M
To suspend the rules	A E F M
To take up a question out of its proper order	A E
To take from the table	A E G
Questions touching priority of business	A
Questions of privilege.	
Asking leave to continue speaking after indecorum	A
Appeal from chair's decision touching indecorum	A E H L
Appeal from chair's decision generally	E H L
Question upon reading of papers	A E
Withdrawal of a motion	A E
Closing a meeting.	
2. To adjourn (in committees, to rise), or to take a recess, without limitation	A E F
1. To fix time to which to adjourn	B

Order of Precedence.— The motions above numbered 1 to 9 take precedence over all others in the order given, and any one of them, except to amend or substitute, is in order while a motion of a lower rank is pending.

RULE A. Undebatable, but remarks may be tacitly allowed.

RULE B. Undebatable if another question is before the assembly.

RULE C. Limited debate allowed on propriety of postponement only.

RULE D. Opens the main question to debate. Motions not so marked do not allow of reference to main question.

RULE E. Cannot be amended. Motion to adjourn can be amended when there is no other business before the house.

RULE F. Cannot be reconsidered.

RULE G. An affirmative vote cannot be reconsidered.

RULE H. In order when another has the floor.

RULE I. A motion to reconsider may be moved and entered when another has the floor, but the business then before the house may not be set aside. This motion can only be entertained when made by one who voted originally with the prevailing side. When called up it takes precedence of all others which may come up, excepting only motions relating to adjournment.

RULE K. A motion to amend an amendment cannot be amended.

RULE L. When an appeal from the chair's decision results in a tie vote, the chair is sustained.

RULE M. Requires a two-thirds vote unless special rules have been enacted.

RULE N. Does not require to be seconded.

General Rules.—No motion is open for discussion until it has been stated by the chair.

The maker of a motion cannot modify it or withdraw it after it has been stated by the chair, except by general consent.

Only one reconsideration of a question is permitted.

A motion to adjourn, to lay on the table, or to take from the table, cannot be renewed unless some other motion has been made in the interval.

On motion to strike out the words, "Shall the words stand part of the motion?" unless a majority sustains the words, they are struck out.

On motion for previous question, the form to be observed is, "Shall the main question be now put?" This, if carried, ends debate.

On an appeal from the chair's decision, "Shall the decision be sustained as the ruling of the house?" the chair is generally sustained.

On motion for orders of the day, "Will the house now proceed to the orders of the day?" This, if carried, supersedes intervening motions.

When an objection is raised to considering questions, "Shall the question be considered?" objections may be made by any member before debate has commenced, but not subsequently.

Draco's Laws.—Draco, an Athenian lawgiver and archon, was the author of the first written code of laws at Athens, which he is supposed to have published in the fourth year of the 39th Olympiad, 621 B. C. He was of distinguished birth, honored for his severe manners and his large experience in public affairs, and the people of Athens, a prey to anarchy, besought him to give them a code of laws. These, however, effected little change in the form of the state, but by being committed to writing put an end to the arbitrary administration of justice on the part of the archons, and resulted in the establishment of a court of appeals—that of the Ephetæ. The system which he proposed linked together civil and moral duties. He took the citizen at the moment of his birth, prescribed the manner in which he should be nourished and educated, and followed him with directions through the different epochs of life. His legislation had a beneficial and permanent effect upon the political development of Athens. The extraordinary severity of these laws, however, which punished the slightest theft, or even laziness, with death, no less than sacrilege, murder, and treason, caused them to be often neglected, and made them so hated that Solon was appointed to draw up a new code. Solon, though he softened their severity in some instances, retained that law which punished a murderer with death. Draco, at a later period, went to Ægina, where, after having introduced his laws, he is said to have been stifled in the theater by the garments thrown upon him as a mark of respect by the people. Extremely severe and sanguinary laws are still called *Draconic*, and in ancient Greece it was commonly said that Draco's laws "were written in blood."

Trial by Jury.—The form of trial by jury is generally conceded to be derived from the institutions of the Greeks and Romans. There was a custom in the ancient city of Athens whereby a certain number of freemen, selected by lot, heard and decided, under the direction of a presiding judge, every case to be tried at law, each case being heard and determined by a different set of men. A similar system was adopted in Rome; and as the Romans always introduced their laws and institutions into all their provinces, it is probable that their mode of judicial procedure was established among the Britains. Another form, called the trial by compurgation, was in use among the Saxons. In this, each party to a suit appeared, with certain of his friends, who swore with him to the truth of his case. As the number of the compurgators was usually six on each side, it is supposed by some that we have here the origin of the number of the modern jury. Witnesses were first brought in to aid the jury during the reign of Edward III., but it was not until the reign of Queen Anne that the law provided that those who had evidence to give could not serve as jurors. In Scotland the jury system was established at a very early date, but was soon after discontinued in civil cases. A jury in that country consists of fifteen, and a majority may render a verdict. The jury in civil cases was reintroduced in the time of George III. In Ireland the jury is substantially the same as in England; but the Repression-of-Crime bill, passed in 1882, provided for the trial of certain cases without juries. In France a jury is only allowed in cases of felony, where a majority of the jurors can render a verdict. In Germany, trial by jury in criminal cases was introduced early in the century. It was established in Prussia in 1819, and again by the Constitution of 1848; but in 1851 political offenses were withdrawn from its operation. The system was adopted by Austria in 1850, by Greece in 1834, and by Portugal in 1837. It has also been introduced in recent times into Italy, into Brazil, and finally into Russia, where the first trial by jury was held August 8, 1886. In each of these last-named countries a verdict can be rendered by the majority. The jury system has existed in Belgium since that country separated from Holland, and includes within its operations political offenses and those of the press. In Switzerland all crimes against the Confederation are tried by jury, and for other crimes each canton has its own machinery. The form of trial by jury was brought from England to America by the colonists, and is protected by mention in the Federal Constitution and in the Constitutions of most of the states. It is also in use in the South American republics. The origin of the institution as found in England is also ascribed by some to the establishment of Norman law there by William the Conqueror, as the Normans had a form of trial by jury much more like that of modern times than any legal usage of the Saxons.

Chinese Immigration Law.—According to the law passed by both houses of Congress and approved by the President in 1882, and amended in May, 1884, Chinese laborers are forbidden to come to the United States under penalty of being returned. The law further declares that any master of any vessel who shall knowingly land any Chinese laborer shall be deemed guilty of a misdemeanor, and for every Chinese brought shall be fined a sum not exceeding $500, and may also be imprisoned for one year. Chinese persons who are not laborers desiring to visit this country are obliged to bring with them from the Chinese Government (or any other Government of which they may at the time be subjects) certificates of identification, giving their names in full, description, statement of business, place of residence, etc., the certificates to be also indorsed by the American diplomatic representative in the country where issued, and the forgery or substitution of any name for the correct one in such certificates shall render the perpetrator thereof liable to a fine of $1,000 and an imprisonment of five years. A master of any vessel bringing into a United States port any such Chinese persons, not laborers, is required to give a list of them to the Collector of Customs of the port. Any master of a vessel who violates any of these provisions against admitting the Chinese forfeits his vessel to the Government, and any person aiding or abetting a Chinaman not lawfully entitled to visit this country to land here renders himself liable to a fine of $1,000 and one year's imprisonment. Further, any Chinese person found traveling in the United States without a proper certificate shall be removed to the country from whence he came at the cost of the United States, any person who may have been instrumental in bringing such Chinese to the United States being liable for all the expenses of his removal; and all peace officers of the several States and Territories are invested with the powers of a United States marshal for the purpose of carrying the law into effect. The only Chinese persons exempted from the action of this law are diplomatic officers traveling on the business of their Government, their retinue of servants, and Chinamen who arrived within ninety days after the passage of the act. The law also requires Chinese already established in the country to take out certificates, if they leave the United States, in order to prove their identity in the event of return.

Massachusetts Blue-Laws. — In regard to the so-called "blue-laws" of Massachusetts it is difficult to determine just where the line between fact and fancy is to be drawn. It is claimed that the founders of Connecticut borrowed most of their laws and judicial proceedings from Massachusetts. Many of these laws were enacted previous to 1640, and a number were the orders and sentences of the Massachusetts Court of Assistants and General Court. For instance, one order we find is as follows: "It is ordered, that all Rich. Clough's strong water shall presently be seazed upon, for his selling greate quantytie thereof to several men servants, which was the occasion of much disorder, drunkenes, and misdemeanor." Another record, in March, 1631, is to the effect that "Nich. Knopp is fyned 5£ for takeing upon him to cure the scurvey, by a water of noe worth nor value, which he solde att a very deare rate, to be imprisoned till hee pay his fine or give securitye for it, or else to be whipped; and shal be lyable to any man's action of whome he hath receved money for the said water." In September, 1634, a number of restrictions regarding the fashions of dress were enacted. One of them was as follows: "The court, takeing into consideration the greate, superflous, and unnecessary expenses occasioned by reason of some newe and immodest fashions, as also the ordinary weareing of silver, golde, and silke laces, girdles, hatbands, etc., hath therefore ordered that noe person, either man or woman, shall hereafter make or buy apparell, either woollen, silke or lynnen, with any lace on it, silver, golde, silke, or threed, under the penalty of forfecture of such cloathes." That there was restraint put upon the tongue is shown by the following, under date of September, 1636: "Robert Shorthose, for swearing by the bloud of God, was sentenced to have his tongue put into a cleft stick, and to stand so by the space of haulfe an houre." And here is one against cakes and buns: "It is ordered, also, that no person shall sell any cakes or buns, either in the markets or victualing houses, or elsewhere, upon paine of 10s. fine; provided that this order shall not extend to such cakes as shal be made for any buriall, or marriage, or such like spetiall occasion."

Prohibitory Laws. — The first actual prohibitory law was enacted in Maine in 1851. This was the famous Maine Liquor Law, and it is still in force in that State, and in 1884 its specifications were put in the form of a constitutional amendment, and adopted by a large popular majority. Vermont enacted a prohibitory law in 1852, its provisions, however, being much less stringent than those of the Maine law. It was strengthened by the passage in 1869 of a civil-damage act, which provided that damages might be collected from the liquor seller for injuries inflicted by his customers, while in a state of intoxication, upon themselves or others. A mild prohibitory law was also passed by New Hampshire in 1855, which has been strengthened by enactments since adopted. Damages are assessed on the liquor seller for the acts of drunkards in that state also, by an act passed in 1870. In Massachusetts the temperance excitement of 1852 resulted in the passage of a prohibitory law by the legislature, but the courts decided the law was unconstitutional, and in 1853 it was repealed. In 1855, the Know Nothing party being in power in the

Assembly, another prohibitory law was passed. This was on trial for several years before the courts, but at length its constitutionality was affirmed. In 1868 this law was repealed because of great popular dissatisfaction with its manner of working. A milder law was passed in 1869, but, being even more unsatisfactory, was abolished in 1875, and replaced by a license law, which still exists. In Rhode Island, as in Massachusetts, a law passed during the excited state of public feeling in 1852 was declared unconstitutional the following year. The law was then amended so as not to conflict with the constitution, and the question of its adoption being submitted to the people, it was approved by a small majority. In 1863, however, the law was repealed. In 1874 a similar law was passed, only to be abolished in the next year, when a license law prohibiting the sale of liquors to minors and drunkards, and also on Sundays, and providing for the collection of damages from the liquor dealer, was passed. An amendment was offered to the people in 1886, which was not adopted, but in the next year a stringent prohibitory law was passed. Connecticut passed a prohibitory law in 1854, but owing to some defect in the law, or to the indifference of the people, it could not be enforced, and became virtually a dead letter. About 1870, therefore, it was superseded by the present license law, which has the local option feature. This has given opportunity to a large number of towns and districts to positively forbid the sale of liquor in their localities, so that nearly half of the State is under practical prohibition. Michigan, in 1853, adopted a prohibitory law which was repealed almost immediately. A similar law, however, was adopted in 1855, which continued on the statute books for about twenty years. As it had become inoperative through popular indifference, it was replaced by a license law in 1875. This latter was strengthened in 1883 by the adoption of a damage clause. In 1885 New York passed a prohibitory law, which shared the fate of many similar enactments, being declared unconstitutional, and was repealed the following year. In 1861 efforts had been made to secure prohibition in the Revised Constitution, but the result was a failure. The extent of New Jersey's prohibition is a law passed in 1797, and still in force, forbidding the distribution or sale of liquors at a public auction. Pennsylvania once had a prohibitory statute on its books for a few months. It was adopted in 1855 and repealed in 1856. This law had been preceded by a "no-license act" which had been enacted by the Legislature in 1846, and had been pronounced unconstitutional by the Supreme Court. In 1872 a law was passed giving local option to the counties, and sixty-seven of them voted against licensing the traffic. In two years that law was repealed and a license law adopted, which is still in force. The prohibition issue was squarely before the people in the spring elections of this year (1889), and was defeated by a large popular majority. Delaware has tried prohibition twice. The first law was passed in 1847, only to be repealed in 1848. The second law was made in 1885; but it was in a few years displaced by a license law, which is still in existence. Three other States — Indiana, Illinois, and Iowa — adopted prohibitory laws in 1855. That of Indiana was declared void soon after, and has never been reënacted. The legislative enactment of Illinois was submitted to the people and rejected by them. Since then no effort has been made to make the State prohibitory, but a high license law was passed by the Legislature of 1882–'83. This law has been declared constitutional by the courts, and has been generally successful in its operation. The Iowa law has stood, with some modifications, and, where public opinion has supported it, has been generally executed. In 1882 a prohibitory clause was put into the Constitution by popular vote. This amendment has been declared void by the Supreme Court on account of certain technical errors in drawing it up. In 1884 a prohibitory law was passed. Ohio put a "no-license" clause in its constitution in 1851, and the sale of liquors has been virtually free throughout the State. Attempts have been made at several times to regulate the traffic by law, but all have failed. Two of the States adopted prohibitory laws while they were still under territorial organization — Minnesota in 1852 and Nebraska in 1855. In both cases the law was modified to make it fit public sentiment more nearly, and both States now have high license laws. Kansas adopted a modified prohibitory law in 1866. In 1880 the popular vote added an amendment to the Constitution prohibiting the manufacture and sale of intoxicating liquors in the State "except for medical, scientific, and mechanical purposes." In Georgia, ninety-five counties have suppressed the sale of liquor through the privilege of local option. Similar laws are made somewhat effective, also, in Texas, Arkansas, and Florida. Other States have laws forbidding the sale of liquor within a certain distance of a school, or to minors, to persons of notoriously intemperate habits, etc.

The Law of Subscriptions.— 1. Subscription is the placing of a signature under a written or printed engagement. By such an act a person contracts, in writing, to pay a sum of money for a specific purpose; as a subscription to a charitable institution, a subscription for a book, etc.

2. "The law on the subject of these subscription papers," says Parsons, "and of all voluntary promises of contribution, is substantially this: No such promises are binding unless something is paid for them, or unless some party for whose benefit they are made (and this party may be one or more of the subscribers), at the request, express or implied, of the promisor, and on the faith of the subscription, incurs actual expense or loss, or enters into valid contracts with other parties which will occasion expense or loss. As the objection to these promises, or the doubt about them, comes from the want of consideration, it may be removed by a seal to each name, or by one seal, which is declared in the instrument to be the seal of each."

3. A person subscribing for a book is bound to take it when delivered by the agent, provided it corresponds with the sample copy shown him when the subscription was given. The agent or publisher may recover at law the price of the book should the subscriber refuse to take it when presented to him.

4. There is no postal law regulating the transactions between publishers and subscribers. The ordinary rules of contract govern all relations between the parties concerned, and the post office has no part except to deliver the article, or return it when ordered to do so.

5. If the publisher of any paper or periodical sends his paper or magazine, the postmaster must deliver it, if the person to whom it is sent will take it. If he will not take it, the postmaster must notify the publisher.

6. If a person subscribes for a periodical for a given period, say one year, and the publisher sends it accordingly, the subscriber cannot terminate the contract by stopping his paper at any time during the year. But at the end of the year the subscriber may stop his paper even without paying the subscription due. He is under no legal obligation to take the paper another year. The fact that he has not paid for the expired year's subscription does not bind him to continue taking the paper. He can stop taking it at the end of the year and the publisher can sue for and collect his year's subscription only.

7. If at the end of the year the publisher continues to send his paper and the subscriber to receive it, the sending is the offer of another year's subscription at the same price, and the receiving of the paper is an acceptance. The implied contract from such action is a renewal of the subscription; and the publisher can send the paper for the renewed term of one year and collect the subscription price for that year as well as the preceding.

8. If the publisher advertises terms of subscription, all parties taking the paper under these conditions will be held according to the conditions.

RIGHTS AND OBLIGATIONS OF PARENTS AND CHILDREN.

In ancient domestic life the father ruled as absolute monarch over the family. So it is still in oriental countries. Christian civilization has greatly modified this and laws have been enacted that set forth the relation of parent and child, defining the duties and obligations of each.

Rights of Parents.—1. As long as a child is under age he is subject to the control of the parents, who have all reasonable authority to enforce obedience. As long as a child is properly treated by the parents no one has a right to interfere nor to take away and retain a child against their wishes.

2. *Adopting a Child.* When a child is adopted by another family its parents lose their claim upon it and the adopting persons take their place. A child cannot be adopted without the consent of its parents, but if consent is once given it cannot be revoked.

A child over fourteen must himself consent to the adoption. The Court has in all cases the right to consent to or refuse the adoption.

Application must therefore be made at the County Court and the Judge will consider it and pass upon it.

3. *Punishment.* Parents have a right to punish their minor children providing they are not guilty of cruelty. Brutality is severely punished by law as a crime. The punishment must be reasonable, leaving no bruises nor injuring the health of the child.

4. *Claims upon Earnings.* While the child is a minor parents have a right to all his earnings. They can claim them of his employer. Parents, however, may free the child and allow him to collect and use his own wages. When this is once made public the parents cannot thereafter collect the child's wages.

5. *A Runaway Child.* A child has no right to leave home without permission of the parents; if he does he can be brought back by force. Relations or others who would keep him can be forced by law to give him up unless it can be shown that the father is brutal in his treatment of the child or is not capable because of drunkenness or other causes to properly care for the child.

Obligations of Parents.—*Obligation to Support.* The law requires that parents shall support their minor children. A child having property of his own does not relieve the parents from supporting him. They can, however, by applying to the Court, get permission to use a part or all of the income from the child's property for his support. Beyond this the parents have no claim upon or control over the child's property.

Children's Rights and Obligations. — 1. A child can own property over which the parents have no control, except the use of the income of the same for the support of the child, as stated above.

2. Where it is shown that parents are unable to support themselves the child is under legal obligations to support and care for them, at least do what he can toward such support.

3. If a child commits a premeditated crime he is personally liable; parents cannot be held responsible for crimes committed by their minor children.

4. *Guardian.* A guardian may be appointed over an orphan child, or the child may choose his own guardian, who in a legal sense exercises all the authority of a parent.

LAW OF APPRENTICESHIP.

An apprentice is a minor, male or female, bound by due form of law to learn some art, trade, or business, and when so bound is under obligation to serve the master during the time of the apprenticeship.

The Contract should be signed by the apprentice and his father, or in case of death or incapacity of the latter, by the mother or legally constituted guardian. It is executed in duplicate, one copy going to the master, the other to the apprentice. The minor cannot be bound for a longer time than until he becomes of age. Without the consent of the parent or guardian, the contract would not be binding upon the minor.

Consent of Minor. The minor cannot be bound without his consent, which consent must be stated in the contract.

Duties of the Master. It is made the master's duty by the contract to teach the apprentice the trade or business which he himself follows, to provide him with suitable food, clothing, and shelter. He has no right to employ the apprentice in menial labors not connected with the trade or business which he undertook to teach him. If he corrects for misbehavior, the punishment must be moderate and reasonable.

Duties of the Apprentice. He is under obligation to serve his master faithfully and well; to obey all lawful commands; to guard his master's property and interests, and to faithfully endeavor to learn the business, and to perform what is required of him in the contract.

Termination of Apprenticeship. His time of service ends when he becomes of age, or in case his master dies, unless the contract includes the master's executors and administrators.

If the apprentice runs away, and enters the employment of another, the master is not bound to take him back, but is entitled to whatever he may earn, provided he can prove that the new employer was aware of the existence of the apprenticeship.

The apprentice cannot be compelled to leave the State, nor can he be assigned to anyone else.

BILLS OF LADING.

A bill of lading is a document delivered by a master or owner of a vessel, or the officer of a transportation company, and signed by such parties as an acknowledgment that the goods have been received for transportation.

The bill constitutes the contract between the shipper and the carrier. Three copies of the bill are made out, one is kept by the shipper, another by the party transporting the goods, and the third is sent to the person to whom the goods are directed.

Bills of Lading are transferable and assignable, and the assignee may sue for the recovery of the goods.

If the goods perish without fault of the master of a ship, the freight must be paid, otherwise the master or owner of a ship is liable for damages.

Railroad companies, as common carriers, are subject to the common State laws regulating such business; their bill of lading usually states as to how far they hold themselves responsible for the safe transportation of the goods.

WILLIAM SHAKESPEARE.

Book II.

Language and Literature.

Language and Literature.

LITERATURE,

In the general sense of the word, comprises the entire results of knowledge, and mental activity, expressed in writing; but in a narrower sense, it is used to denote the department of elegant letters, excluding works of abstract science and mere erudition. In this limited view it comprehends languages, particularly Greek and Latin, grammar, etymology, logic, rhetoric, poetry, history, criticism, bibliography, and a description of the attainments of the human mind in every sphere of research and invention. The history of literature represents the development and successive changes of civilization, so far as these are exhibited in written works, and embraces the history of the literature of special ages or countries, and of the separate branches of literature, as poetry, rhetoric, philology, and so forth.

LANGUAGES.

The classification of the different languages of the earth into a few great families is due to the science of comparative philology, and is of recent origin. Till the latter end of the last century the preference as to the antiquity of language was usually given to the Hebrew, but a striking improvement of linguistic study is dated from the discovery of the Sanskrit, the ancient language of the northern parts of Hindustan, in the latter part of the last century. A belief in an affinity in languages and a separation of them into certain great groups or families then arose.

The languages of the world are divided into four great branches; viz., the ARYAN, or Indo-European, the most important; the SEMITIC, the TURANIAN, and the DRAVIDIAN.

The TURANIAN family, called also the Tataric or Altaic, includes the numerous and widely different languages of the Manchoos, the Mongols, the Turks (in Asia and Europe), the Magyars (in Hungary), the Finns (in Russia), and a multitude of other tribes.

The DRAVIDIAN includes the Tamil and the dialects in Ceylon and the islands off Asia, etc.

The SEMITIC includes the Hebrew, Syriac, Arctic and Ethiopic, Basque (in the Pyrenees), etc.

The INDO-EUROPEAN, to which extensive family the English language belongs, is divided into six principal branches.

I. The *Indian* branch, represented by the Sanskrit, which has now ceased to be spoken, but is the mother of the Hindustani, Bengali, Mahratti, and the other numerous dialects of modern India.

II. The *Medo-Persic* branch, at the head of which is the Zend, in which the Zend-Avesta is composed, and the cuneiform inscriptions of Cyrus, Darius, and Xerxes. Next follow the Pehlevi, of the Sarsanian dynasty; the Parsee, in which the national poem of Ferdusi is written (A. D. 1000), and lastly the modern Persian.

III. The *Celtic* branch, divided into two dialects, the Gaelic and the Cymric; the former comprising the Irish or Erse, the Scottish Gaelic or Highland-Scotch, and the Manx of the Isle of Man; and the latter Welsh, the Cornish (now extinct) and the Armorican of Britanny.

IV. The *Græco-Latin* branch, comprising the two ancient classical languages, and the so-called Romanic languages, derived from the Latin, which are six in number; namely, the French, Italian, Spanish, Portuguese, Wallachian, and the Roumanish or Romanese spoken in the Grisons in Switzerland.

V. The *Teutonic* branch, which comprises all the different German and Scandinavian dialects.

VI. The *Slavonic* branch, divided into three principal classes: 1. The Lettic, comprising the Lithuanian, the Old Prussian (now extinct), and the Lettish, the language of Kurland and Livonia. 2. The Western Slavonic, comprising the Polish; the Bohemian or Tchechian, spoken in Bohemia; the Slovakian, spoken by the Slovaks in Hungary, and the Wendian, spoken in Lusatia. 3. The Eastern Slavonic, comprising the Old Slavonic, preserved in the translations of the Bible made by Cyrillus in the ninth century, and its derivate dialect, the Bulgarian; the Russian, Servian, Croatian, and Slovinian.

The *Teutonic* branch of the Indo-European family of languages is divided into two great branches, the German and Scandinavian.

The GERMAN is divisible into three principal dialects, the Mœso-Gothic, the Low German, and the High German, the two latter being so called because the Low German is spoken by the inhabitants of the low or flat country near the shores of the German Ocean, while the High German belongs to the higher country in the interior.

1. The MŒSO-GOTHIC, the most easterly of all the German dialects, has long ceased to be spoken, but is preserved in the translation of the gospels by Ulfilas.

2. The Low German comprised the following dialects: (1) *Anglo-Saxon*, which was cultivated with great success in England, and in which the second most ancient specimens of the Germanic language are preserved. (2) The *Old Saxon*, so called to distinguish it from the Anglo-Saxon in England, formerly spoken in Westphalia. (3) The *Frisian*, now confined to a small district in Holland. (4) The *Dutch*, the present language of Holland. (5) The *Flemish*, spoken in many parts of Belgium.

3. The High German comprises the Old High German, from the seventh to the eleventh century; the Middle High German, from the twelfth century to the Reformation, and the New High German, which since Luther's time has been the literary language of Germany.

The Scandinavian branch, of which the most ancient language is the Old Norse, the language of Norway, is represented by the Icelandic, which was carried into Iceland by the Norse colonists in the ninth century and which continues to be spoken on that island with little alteration. On the Continent the Old Norse is represented by the Swedish, Danish, and Norwegian, of which the last has now become a mere *patois*.

The following table exhibits the relationship of the different Teutonic languages:—

Teutonic
- I. German
  - 1. *Mœso-Gothic.*
  - 2. *Low German.*
    - (i) Anglo-Saxon. English.
    - (ii) Old Saxon.
    - (iii) Frisian.
    - (iv) Dutch.
    - (v) Flemish.
  - 3. *High German.*
    - (i) Old High German.
    - (ii) Middle High German.
    - (iii) New High German.
- II. Scandinavian
  - 1. *Old Scandinavian.*
    - (i) Icelandic.
    - (ii) Ferroic.
  - 2. *Modern Scandinavian.*
    - (i) Danish.
    - (ii) Swedish.
    - (iii) Norwegian.

The English Language is the descendant and representative of the Anglo-Saxon. It has lost very much of the inflection and very many of the words which belong to the parent language; and on the other hand it has borrowed words largely, to the extent even of half its vocabulary, from other languages, especially the French and the Latin. Yet all the inflections that remain in it, and most of its formative endings, the pronouns and particles, and in general the words which are in most frequent and familiar use, have come to it from the Anglo-Saxon. All the constituents of the English Language as it now exists are presented in a condensed form as follows:—

1st. Saxon and Danish words, of Teutonic and Gothic origin.
2d. British or Welsh, Cornish and Armoric, of Celtic origin.
3d. Norman, a mixture of French and Gothic.
4th. Latin.
5th. The French, chiefly Latin corrupted.
6th. Greek.
7th. A few words directly from the Italian, Spanish, German, and other Continental languages of Europe.
8th. A few foreign words introduced by commerce or by political and literary intercourse.

Capital Letters. — Begin with a capital:—

1. Every sentence and every line of poetry.

Examples.—Forget others' faults. How bright the day! What is fame? Custom forms us all.
"Time is the warp of life; oh! tell
The young, the fair, to weave it well."

2. All proper nouns, and titles of office, honor, and respect.

Examples.—Henry the Fowler, Emperor of Germany; Robert Roe, Esquire; His Honor the Mayor; Elizabeth Barrett Browning; the Red River; Union Square; the Superior Court of the City of New York.

3. All adjectives formed from proper names.

Examples.—African, Italian, Welsh, Ciceronian.

Also adjectives denoting a sect or religion.

Examples.—Methodist, Puritan, Catholic.

4. Common nouns, where personified in a direct and lively manner; not where sex is merely attributed to an inanimate object.

Examples.—Then *War* waves his ensanguined sword, and fair *Peace* flees sighing to some happier land. But, the *sun* pursues his fiery course; the *moon* sheds her silvery beams.

5. All appellations of the Deity. The personal pronouns *Thou* and *He* standing for His name are sometimes capitalized.

Examples.—The Almighty; the King of kings; the Eternal Essence; Jehovah; the Supreme Being; our Father.

In the standard editions of the Bible, the pronouns, when referring to God, are never capitalized, not even in forms of direct address to the Deity.

6. The first word of a complete quoted sentence not introduced by *that*, *if*, or any other conjunction.

Examples.—Thomson says, "Success makes villains honest." But, Thomson says that "success makes villains honest."

7. Every noun, adjective, and verb in the title of books and headings of chapters.

Examples.—Butler's "Treatise on the History of Ancient Philosophy"; Cousins' "Lectures on the True, the Beautiful, and the Good."

8. Words that denote the leading subjects of chapters, articles or paragraphs.

A word defined, for instance, may commence with a capital. Do not introduce capitals too freely under this rule. When in doubt use a small letter.

9. The pronoun *I* and the interjection *O*.

10. Words denoting great events, eras of history, noted written instruments, extraordinary physical phenomena and the like.

Examples.—The Creation; the Confusion of Languages; the Restoration; the Dark Ages; the Declaration of Independence; the Aurora Borealis.

11. Letters standing for words are generally written as capitals.

Examples.— A. D. for *Anno Domini*, the year of our Lord.

12. The months of the year, and the days of the week. The names of the seasons, however, should not generally be capitalized, although it is customary with some authors.

13. The words *North*, *South*, *East*, and *West*, and their compounds, as *Northwest*, when they signify a section of country. Also adjectives derived therefrom. This class of words should not be capitalized, however, when merely denoting direction.

Punctuation Points. — The Punctuation Points are as follows: —

Period	.	Paragraph	¶
Colon	:	Brace	{
Semicolon	;		
Comma	,	Acute Accent	´
Interrogation Point	?	Grave Accent	`
Exclamation Point	!	Circumflex Accent	^
Dash	—	Tilde, or Circumflex	~
Parentheses	( )	The Long, or Macron	¯
Brackets	[ ]	The Short, or Breve	˘
Hyphen	-	Diæresis	¨
Quotation Marks	" "	Cedilla	¸
Apostrophe	'	Asterisk	*
Ellipsis {	. . . .	Dagger, or Obelisk	†
	* * * *	Double Dagger	‡
Caret	∧	Section	§
Index	☞	Parallel	‖

Punctuation is the art of dividing composition by points or stops for the purpose of showing more clearly the sense and relation of the words, and of noting the different pauses and inflections required in reading.

The usage of to-day is not that of the past and will not be that of the future.

The following rules are the most important and are compiled from the best modern authorities: —

THE PERIOD must be placed after every declarative and imperative sentence and every abbreviated word.

Examples.— Obey your parents. Virtue is the only nobility. We write Jas. for James, N. Y. for New York, No. for number, George I. for George the First.

After all abbreviations.

Example.— Mdse.— Amt.— Ph. D.— LL. D.

After numbers written in the Roman notation.

Example.— XIX.— Psalm XC.

A nickname which is not really an abbreviation is not followed by a period.

Examples.— Dave Bidwell; Sam Slick.

A COLON is placed after a sentence which formally introduces a distinct quotation.

Example.— We are often reminded of this remark of Marshal Lannes: "Know, Colonel, that none but a poltroon would boast that he was never afraid."

The colon may be used to separate the great parts of a long complex sentence when the minor sentences therein are separated by the semicolon.

The colon is passing out of use, its place being taken by the dash, the semicolon, and the period.

A SEMICOLON is placed before *as*, *to wit*, *viz.*, *namely*, and *that is* when they introduce examples or illustrations.

Example.— Every solid has three dimensions; namely, length, breadth, and thickness.

Place a semicolon at the close of a sentence which by its terms promises another sentence.

Example.— "Tic-tac, tic-tac, go the wheels of thought; our will cannot stop them; they cannot stop themselves; sleep cannot still them; madness only makes them go faster; death alone can break into the case."

A semicolon may be used to separate short sentences which have but a slight connection with each other.

Example.— He was a poor boy; he had no showy accomplishments; he had no influential friends; but he was rich in youth, courage, and honesty of purpose.

COMMA.— Set off by the comma an explanatory modifier when it does not restrict the modified term.

Example.— The order, to fire, was given.

Set off by the comma a word or phrase that is independent.

Example.— To tell the truth, he was not at home.

Set off by the comma a phrase that is out of its natural order.

Example.— Shifting his burden, he hurried on.

Set off by the comma a particle used as an adjective.

Example.— The water, expanding, burst the pipe.

Set off by the comma connected words and phrases unless the conjunctions are all expressed.

Example.— "From the mountain, from the river, from the hill, and from the plain, we are sweeping to the rescue."

A comma is used before a direct quotation unless it is formally introduced. Greeley said, "The way to resume is to resume."

Set off by commas all parenthetical expressions and the following words when used as such; however, that is, indeed, of course, finally, again, first, second, also, therefore, yes, no, too, etc.

Example. — He is, indeed, worthy.

Use the comma *after* as, viz., to-wit, namely, and that is, when they introduce examples.

Example.—We will promote the man; that is, if he is worthy.

The parts of a complex sentence should be separated by a comma when the *auxiliary* precedes the *principal* sentence.

Example.— If the messenger calls, give him the letter.

Separate by the comma a phrase or sentence used as a subject and its verb.

Example.— "That all men are created equal, is a self-evident truth."

Words used in direct address should be separated by the comma.

Example.— "Stranger, I am Roderick Dhu."

THE INTERROGATION POINT must be placed after every interrogative sentence, member, and clause; also after the interjections *eh* and *hey* implying a question.

Example.—Has the air weight? Air has weight; do you not believe it? You thought it would rain, eh?

An interrogation inclosed in parentheses denotes doubt.

Example.—Your friend (?) told me this.

THE EXCLAMATION POINT should be placed after every exclamatory sentence, member, clause, and expression.

Examples.—How disgusting is vice! Life is short; how careful we should be to use it aright! For shame!

An exclamation point placed in parentheses denotes peculiar surprise.

A DASH is usually placed before the answer to a question when both are in the same paragraph.

Example.—Are you acquainted with the defendant?—I am.

A dash is often used in place of the parentheses.

Example.—With a firm step—for he was brave—he advanced.

Use the dash where there is an omission of such words as, *namely*, *that is*, *as*, introducing equivalent expressions and when letters or figures are omitted.

Example.—"Some wit has divided the world into two classes—the wise and the otherwise." General M —— was present.

Use the dash when there is a sudden transition.

Example.—We have learned the bitter lesson—let us bury the past.

PARENTHESES. Marks of Parenthesis are used to inclose words which explain, modify, or add to the main proposition, when so introduced as to break the connection between dependent parts and interfere with the harmonious flow.

Example.—The Saxons (for they descended from the ancient Sacæ) retained for centuries the energy and morality of their ancestors.

BRACKETS. Brackets are used principally in quoted passages, to inclose words improperly omitted or added by way of correction, observation, or explanation.

Example.—She is weary with [of] life.

In regard to the use of points before and after the brackets, and the punctuation of any sentence or clause within the brackets, the same rules apply that have been given in regard to the marks of parenthesis.

THE APOSTROPHE denotes the omission of a letter or letters, and the possessive case of nouns.

Examples.—'*Tis* for *it is*; *e'en* for *even*; *don't* for *do not*; *o'clock* for *on* [the] *clock*. So in the possessive: *hero's*, *Charles'*, *men's*, *heroes'*, *children's*.

Pronouns never take the apostrophe in the possessive case.

THE HYPHEN is used to connect the elements of a compound word, when each retains its own accent.

Example.—Castle-builder, father-in-law.

The hyphen is also used after a complete syllable at the end of a line, to connect the parts of a divided word; also to denote that the final vowel of a prefix does not form a diphthong with the first vowel of a primitive; but in this latter case a mark of diæresis is more appropriate.

Example.—Pre-engagement, re-establish [preëngagement, reëstablish.]

QUOTATION POINTS are used to inclose words quoted from an author or speaker, or represented in narrative as employed in dialogue.

Example.—"Remember now thy Creator in the days of thy youth."

When the substance merely is given, and not the exact words, quotation points are unnecessary.

Matter within quotation points is to be punctuated just as if it stood in any other position.

When quotation points are needed at the end of a sentence, they come after whatever other point is required there if this point applies to the quotation alone, but before this point if it applies to the whole sentence and not exclusively to the quotation.

Example.—Pilate asked, "What is truth?" Where now is the "man of destiny"?

When a quotation incloses within it another quotation, the external quotation has the double marks, and the one included has only the single marks.

Example.—It has been well said, "The command, 'Thou shalt not kill,' forbids many crimes besides that of murder."

If the inclosed or secondary quotation ends a sentence, three apostrophes will there come together, of which the first will belong to the inclosed quotation, and the other two to the original. When an inclosed quotation itself contains words or phrases that are quoted, those words or phrases have the double marks.

Example.—"French says, 'What a lesson the word "diligence" contains!'"

When the sentence becomes more involved than this, the additional marks of quotation would create confusion, and may therefore be omitted.

THE PARAGRAPH is used to indicate a new subject of remark. The sign is retained in the Holy Scripture but in ordinary composition is indicated to the eye by beginning a little to the right of the marginal line of the page.

ACCENT MARKS are used to denote the proper pronunciation of words. They are:—

The *Acute* [´], which marks the syllable which requires the principal stress in pronunciation; or to denote a rising inflection of the voice, or a close or short vowel.

The *Grave* [`] is used in opposition to the acute to distinguish an open or long vowel, or to denote the falling inflection of the voice.

The *Circumflex* [ˆ] generally denotes a broad sound or a combination of the acute and grave.

The *Breve* [˘] is used to denote either a close vowel or a syllable of short quantity.

The *Macron* [ˉ] is used to denote either an open vowel or a syllable of long quantity.

The *Diæresis* [¨] is placed over the latter of two vowels to show that they are to be pronounced in separate syllables, as *aërial.* In German this character is called the *Umlaut*, and denotes a modification of the sound of a vowel over which it is placed, peculiar to the Germanic languages.

The *Cedilla* [¸] is placed under the letter *c* to give it the sound of *s* before *a* or *o;* as in the words *façade, Alençon.*

The *Tilde* [˜] is placed over the letter *n* in Spanish words to give it the sound of *ny;* as, *señor, miñon.*

OTHER MARKS.—The *Ellipsis* or *Suppression* denotes the omission of some letters or words.

Examples.—K——g, for King; G * * * * m, for Graham; A . . . . s, for Adams; H—m—hr—y, for Humphrey.

The *Caret*, used only in writing, shows where to insert words or letters that have been accidentally omitted.

Example.—James said he ‸ be home to-night. (would)

The *Index* or *Hand* [☞] points out something remarkable, or what the reader should particularly observe.

The *Brace* [⏟] serves to unite a triplet, or to connect several terms to something to which they are all related.

Examples.—

Case { Nominative. Possessive. Objective.

Committee { W. Brown. H. Jones. R. Smith. M. Mills.

The *Section* [§] marks the smaller divisions of a book or chapter, and, with the help of numbers, serves to abridge references.

The *Paragraph* [¶] denotes the commencement of a new subject. The parts of discourse which are called paragraphs are in general sufficiently distinguished by beginning a new line and carrying the first word a little backwards.

Leaders [. . . . . .] are used in contents and indexes of books and similar matter to lead the eye to the end of the line for the completion of the sense.

Example.— Wharfage, ... $50.

Marks in Proof Reading.

¹a/ THOUGH severel differing opinions exist as to
the individual by wyom the art of printing was ²ɘ
first discovered; yet all authorities concur in
admitting Peter Schoeffer to be the person ³*Caps.*
who invented *cast metal types*, having learned
⁴ꝺ the art of of *cutting* the letters from the Gu-
⁵:/ tenbergs/ he is also supposed to have been
⁶# the first whoengraved on copper plates. The ⁷/-/
following testimony is preseved in the family, ⁸r/
⁹✓ by Jo. Fred. Faustus, of Ascheffenburg:
¹⁰□ 'Peter Schoeffer, of Gernsheim, perceiving ³*S. Caps*
¹¹✓ his master Fausts design, and being himself
¹²tr. desirous ardently to improve the art, found
out (by the good providence of God) the
method of cutting (*incidendi*) the characters ¹³*stet*
in a *matrix*, that the letters might easily be
⁵,/ singly *cast*/ instead of bieng *cut*. He pri- ¹²*tr.*
¹⁴ vately *cut matrices* for the whole alphabet: ¹⁵
Faust was so pleased with the contrivance,
that he promised Peter to give him his only ¹⁷*wf.*
¹⁶ daughter Christina in marriage, a promise ³*Ital.*
which he soon after performed.
¹⁹as/ But there were many difficulties at first ¹⁸*no ¶*
with these *letters,* as there had been before ³*Rom*
²⁰+ with wooden ones, the metal being too soft ³*Ital.*
to support the force of the im pression: but ²¹⁀
this defect was soon remedied, by mixing
a substance with the metal which sufficiently ¹²*tr.*
⁵⊙ hardened it/

and when he showed his master the letters cast from these matrices

THOUGH several differing opinions exist as to the individual by whom the art of printing was first discovered; yet all authorities concur in admitting PETER SCHOEFFER to be the person who invented *cast metal types*, having learned the art of *cutting* the letters from the Gutenbergs: he is also supposed to have been the first who engraved on copper-plates. The following testimony is preserved in the family, by Jo. Fred. Faustus, of Ascheffenburg:

'PETER SCHOEFFER, of Gernsheim, perceiving his master Faust's design, and being himself ardently desirous to improve the art, found out (by the good providence of God) the method of cutting (*incidendi*) the characters in a *matrix*, that the letters might easily be singly *cast*, instead of being *cut*. He privately *cut matrices* for the whole alphabet: and when he showed his master the letters cast from these matrices, Faust was so pleased with the contrivance, that he promised Peter to give him his only daughter *Christina* in marriage, a promise which he soon after performed. But there were as many difficulties at first with these letters, as there had been before with *wooden ones*, the metal being too soft to support the force of the impression: but this defect was soon remedied, by mixing the metal with a substance which sufficiently hardened it.'

A wrong letter in a word is noted by drawing a short perpendicular line through it, and making another short line in the margin, behind which the right letter is placed. (See No. 1.) In this manner whole words are corrected, by drawing a line across the wrong word and making the right one in the margin opposite.

A turned letter is noted by drawing a line through it, and writing the mark No. 2 in the margin.

If letters or words require to be altered from one character to another, a parallel line or lines must be made underneath the word or letter; viz., for capitals, three lines; small capitals, two lines; and italics, one line; and, in the margin opposite the line where the alteration occurs, caps, small caps, or ital. must be written. (See No. 3.)

When letters or words are set double, or are required to be taken out, a line is drawn through the superfluous word or letter, and the mark No. 4 placed opposite in the margin.

Where the punctuation requires to be altered, the correct point, marked in the margin, should be encircled.

When a space is omitted between two words or letters which should be separated, a caret must be made where the separation ought to be and the sign No. 6 placed opposite in the margin.

No. 7 describes the manner in which the hyphen and ellipsis line are marked.

When a letter has been omitted, a caret is put at the place of omission, and the letter marked as No. 8.

Where letters that should be joined are separated, or where a line is too widely spaced, the mark No. 9 must be placed under them, and the correction denoted by the marks in the margin.

Where a new paragraph is required, a quadrangle is drawn in the margin, and a caret placed at the beginning of the sentence. (See No. 10.)

No. 11 shows the way in which the apostrophe, inverted commas, the star, and other references, and superior letters and figures, are marked.

Where two words are transposed, a line is drawn over one word and below the other, and the mark No. 12 placed in the margin; but where several words require to be transposed, their right order is signified by a figure placed over each word, and the mark No. 12 in the margin.

Where words have been struck out, that have afterward been approved of, dots should be marked under them, and *stet* written in the margin.

Where a space sticks up between two words, a horizontal line is drawn under it, and the mark No. 14 placed opposite, in the margin.

Where several words have been left out, they are transcribed at the bottom of the page, and a line drawn from the place of omission to the written words (see No. 15); but if the omitted matter is too extensive to be copied at the foot of the page, *Out, see copy*, is written in the margin, and the missing lines are inclosed between brackets, and the word *Out* is inserted in the margin of the copy.

Where letters stand crooked, they are noted by a line (see No. 16); but where a page hangs, lines are drawn across the entire part affected.

When a smaller or larger letter, of a different font, is improperly introduced into the page, it is noted by the mark No. 17, which signifies wrong font.

If a paragraph is improperly made, a line is drawn from the broken-off matter to the next paragraph, and *No* ¶ written in the margin. (See No. 18.)

Where a word has been left out or is to be added, a caret must be made in the place where it should come in, and the word written in the margin. (See No. 19.)

Where a faulty letter appears, it is denoted by making a cross under it, and placing a similar mark in the margin (see No. 20); though some prefer to draw a perpendicular line through it, in the case of a wrong letter.

Where a word has been accidentally separated by a space, it is marked as in No. 21.

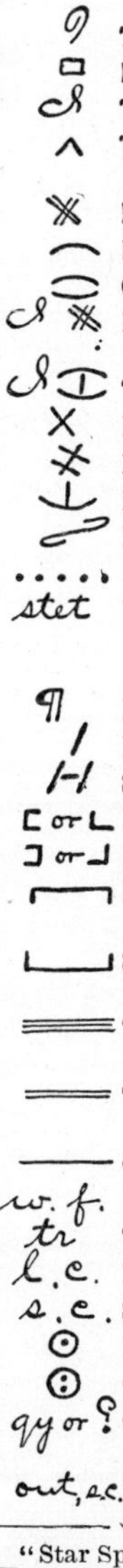

Turn letter.
Indent line one em quad.
Take out; expunge.
The caret shows where the letter or word is omitted.
Insert space.
Less space.
Close up entirely.
Remove type, and insert a space in place of what is removed.
Take out type and close up.
Bad type.
Push down space.
Plane down a letter.
No paragraph.
Placed under erased words, restores them.
Written in margin, restores a canceled word or words that have dots under them.
Begin a paragraph.
Letters stand crooked.
Should be a compound word.
Remove to left.
Remove to right.
Elevate a letter, word, or character that is sunk below the proper level.
Sink or depress a letter, word, or character raised above the proper level.
Three lines, beneath writing, denote capitals.
Two lines, beneath writing, denote small capitals.
One line, beneath writing, denotes italics.
Wrong font.
Transpose letters, words, or sentences.
Lower case, or small letters.
Small capitals.
Period.
Colon.
Calls attention to some doubtful word or sentence.
Words are omitted or wanting, see copy.

Famous Poems and Their Authors.

"Elegy Written in a Country Churchyard" is the master composition of Thomas Gray (1716-1771).

"The Minstrel" is the production of James Beattie (1735-1803).

"Rock of Ages" is from the pen of Augustus Montague Toplady (1740-1778).

"The Farmer's Boy" was written by Robert Bloomfield (1766-1823).

"The Burial of Sir John Moore" is the effort of Charles Wolfe (1791-1823).

"Woodman, Spare that Tree" is the work of George P. Morris (1802-1864).

"The Buccaneer" was composed by Richard Henry Dana (1789-1879).

"Star Spangled Banner" was written by Francis Scott Key (1790-1843).

"La Marseillaise" is the work of Rouget de L'Isle (1760-1836).

"Home, Sweet Home" is by John Howard Payne (1792-1852).

"From Greenland's Icy Mountains" is the composition of Reginald Heber (1783-1826).

"Battle Hymn of the Republic" was written by Julia Ward Howe (1819).

"Ben Bolt" is from the pen of Thomas Dunn English (1819).

"Rocked in the Cradle of the Deep" is by Emma C. Willard (1847-1870).

"Hail, Columbia" is the production of Joseph Hopkinson (1770-1842).

FAMILIAR ALLUSIONS.

Abderit. Democritus, the original laughing philosopher, was born in Abdera, a Thracian city. From him a scoffer or person given to continual laughing is called an Abderite.

Abraham's Bosom. The rest of the blessed dead.

Abyla and Calpe, the Pillars of Hercules, the exit from the Mediterranean.

Academics. Plato's disciples were so called from the Academy.

Academy. (Academe.) Plato founded his school in a gymnasium of this name near Athens, 368 B. C.

Academy, The French. A French scientific body limited to forty members.

Acadia. Formerly the name of Nova Scotia.

Adam's Apple. A part of the throat where, it is said, a piece of the forbidden fruit lodged.

Admirable Crichton, The. James Crichton, an accomplished Scotchman of the sixteenth century.

Admiral. The highest rank in the Navy.

Æneid. An epic poem by Virgil.

Ages. The five ages of the world according to Hesiod, are the Golden, the Silver, the Brazen, the Heroic. and the Iron.

Alabama. A Confederate privateer built in England. Sunk by the Kearsarge June 19, 1864.

Aladdin's Window, To Finish. Trying to complete another's work. Aladdin's palace was perfect except one window left for the Sultan to finish, but his treasure failed him.

Albany Regency. Name applied sixty years ago to some Democrats at Albany, N. Y.

Albino. A person with white skin and hair and red eyes. The Portuguese so called the white negroes.

Albion. England, so called from the chalky white cliffs.

Aldine Press. Founded by Aldus Manutius at Venice in 1496. Editions of the classics issued from this press were called the Aldine editions. This term is now applied to some elegant editions of English works.

Alexandrian Library. Was founded by Ptolemy Philadelphus. It contained 400,000 manuscripts, and was burned 47 B. C.

Alexandrine Age. 323-640, when Alexandria was the seat of the highest culture.

Alhambra. A magnificent palace and a fortress built by the Moors at Granada, in Spain.

All-Hallows. All Saints' day, November 1st.

Allah. Arabic name of God.

Almacks. Assembly room in London where the most exclusively aristocratic balls were given.

Almighty Dollar. A phrase first used by Irving in his Creole Village, and which has become quite common. The title of a play.

Alsatia. A quarter in London where criminals take refuge.

Alto-Relievo. Figures in marble or castings projecting one half or more from the tablet.

Ambrosia. Food of the Gods.

Anachronism. An error in computing time.

Anacreontics. Poems composed in the manner of Anacreon, a great poet noted for his exact imitation of nature.

Ancien Regime. The French Government previous to the revolution of 1798.

Angling, The Father of. Izaak Walton.

Annus Mirabilis. (Wonderful year.) A. D. 1666. Noted for the great fire in London, the Plague, and an English victory over the Dutch.

Antoninus, The Wall of. Was built by the Romans in A. D. 140 across Scotland between the Clyde and the Frith of Forth; an embankment of earth.

Apollo Belvedere. One of the most beautiful and perfect representations of the human form is the statue of Apollo in the Belvedere Gallery of the Vatican Palace at Rome.

Appian Way. The road from Rome to Capua. The oldest Roman road.

Apples of Sodom. Beautiful fruit, but full of ashes. Applied figuratively to the disappointment of sin.

Apple, Golden. Prize for beauty disputed before Paris, between Juno, Pallas, and Venus; awarded by him to Venus.

Arabesque. Decoration in Moorish style.

Arcadian. A shepherd; a Greek grazing country named Arcadia has furnished this word to the poets.

Argo. The ship in which Jason and his fifty-four companions sailed when going to Colchis for the Golden Fleece.

Argonauts. The adventurers on the Argo.

Argus-eyed. Crafty, watchful. Argus had a hundred eyes; the jealous Juno put him on detective duty over Io.

Armada, The Spanish. A fleet of 130 ships gathered by Philip II. of Spain for the invasion of England in 1588. Queen Elizabeth was busy preparing for resistance when the news came that a storm had completely wrecked the Armada.

Artesian Well. Boring in the earth until water is reached that will flow spontaneously. Their first use was in Artois, France.

Aryans. The stem of the Indo-European peoples.

Astor Library. Founded by John Jacob Astor in New York City.

Athens, The Modern. Boston.

Augustan Age. As the most flourishing period of the Roman literature was during the time of Augustus, that name is given to any age wherein literature is preeminent.

Auld Reekie. Edinburgh, Scotland.

Avalon. King Arthur's burial place, Glastonbury.

Ayrshire Poet, The. Burns. Born 1759, died 1796. His birthplace was near Ayr in Scotland.

Barnburners. A name given some years ago to radical Democrats, a leading man amongst whom was John Van Buren.

Babylonish Captivity. The seventy years' captivity of the Jews at Babylon, 608-538 B. C.

Baconian Philosophy. The inductive philosophy of Lord Bacon.

Balmoral Castle. A Scotch castle owned by Queen Victoria.

Bank of England. Founded 1694.

Bard of Avon. Shakespeare, so called from his home being Stratford-on-Avon.

Barmecide's Feast. A mockery, a delusion, and a sham. Barmecide asked a starving beggar to dinner, and seated him at a table of empty dishes.

Basilisk. A mythical serpent with power to kill by merely looking at its victim.

Basso Relievo. Figures in marble and castings that project but a little from the plane.

Bastile. French prison and fortress. People were incarcerated here by *lettre de cachet*, without notice or trial. Destroyed by a mob, 1789.

Battle of the Books. Satire by Dean Swift comparing ancient and modern literature.

Battle of the Kegs. A practical joke on the British General Loring. Detailed in a ballad of the Revolutionary War.

Battery, The. A park in New York City adjoining the river.

Beacon Street. The aristocratic residence street of Boston.

Beauty and the Beast. A fairy tale. Beauty lives with the Beast to save her father's life. By her love she disenchants the Beast, who proves to be a great Prince.

Bedlam. A mad-house.

Bee, The Attic. Plato; so called from his honeyed style.

Bee, The Busy. An example of communal industry.

Beelzebub. A Philistine deity.

Begging the Question. Assuming as true what you are to prove.

Belle France, La. Beautiful France.

Belgravia. Fashionable quarter of London.

Bell the Cat. In a convention of mice it was proposed to hang a bell on the cat's neck, to give warning of her coming. No one would serve on the committee.

Bell, The Passing. Rung formerly when persons were dying.

Beloved Disciple, The. St. John.

Bess, Good Queen. Queen Elizabeth.

Bibliotheque National. (National Library.) At Paris; contains over 1,000,000 books, 150,000 MSS.

Billingsgate. Coarse language. Such as is used at the fish market of Billingsgate in London; a fishwife's tongue being said to be remarkably expressive.

Black Death. A plague which desolated Europe, Asia, and Africa in the fourteenth century.

Black Friday. Gold panic Sept. 24, 1869. Immense fortunes lost and won same day. Investigation could never discover the true cause of it.

Black Hole of Calcutta. Dark prison cell wherein Surajah Dowlah shut up 146 British soldiers; only 23 lived till morning.

Black Prince, The. Edward, Prince of Wales, son of Edward III.

Black Republicans. The Republican party of U. S., so called when opposing the extension of slavery.

Blarney Stone. Its supposed virtue when kissed is to impart a smooth and oily tongue. Profusion of compliments is called Blarney. This stone is in Blarney Castle, near Cork, Ireland.

Bluebeard. A wife-killing tyrant, in a nursery story.

Blue Laws. Some severe New England statutes were so called.

Blue Stocking. A literary society at Venice in 1400, whose members wore blue stockings, is the origin of this name for a female pedant.

Bohemian. As opposed to Philistine, an artist or literary man living loosely by his wits.

Bois de Boulogne. A Parisian promenade.

Border, The. Frontier of England and Scotland.

Border Minstrel, The. Sir Walter Scott.

Border States. Maryland, Delaware, Virginia, Kentucky, Missouri.

Bourgeoisie. A class of the people of France mostly composed of traders and manufacturers.

Boulevard. A wide street in Paris, in the place of the ancient ramparts.

Bourse. Parisian stock exchange.

Bow Bells. A set of bells in the Church of St. Mary-le-Bow, London. One "born within sound of Bow Bells" is a Cockney.

Bowery, The. A New York thoroughfare.

Boycott. To refuse to have anything to do with a person. To let him severely alone. A trying ordeal passed through by Captain Boycott in Ireland in 1881. No one would sell to him, buy from him, work for him, or speak to him.

Brandy-Nose. Queen Anne of England.

Breeches Bible, The. An edition in which "aprons" in Gen. iii. 7 is rendered "breeches."

Bride of the Sea. Venice.

Bridge of Sighs. In Venice. Connects Doge's Palace and State Prison. Over this bridge the condemned passed when on their way to be executed.

British Museum. Library and museum in London.

Broadway. The principal business street of New York.

Brook Farm. A Socialistic community to carry out the idea of Fourierism; was founded at West Roxbury, Mass., 1841.

Brother Jonathan. America; an American. Some doubt as to its origin, but it is said to come from Gov. Jonathan Trumbull, of Connecticut, in speaking of whom Washington would say, "We must consult Brother Jonathan."

Buncombe. Clap-trap speeches, to cajole constituents, more than for immediate effect. Buncombe is in North Carolina. A North Carolina member said a fiery speech was not delivered to the House, but to Buncombe.

Bunker Hill Monument. An obelisk of granite marking the site of the battle of Bunker Hill, fought between the British and Americans, June 17, 1775.

Cachet, Lettres de. (Sealed letters.) Blank warrants with the seal of the French King already affixed for imprisoning or releasing any person in the Bastile.

Caledonia. Scotland.

Calumet. An Indian pipe. In old times a treaty of peace with the red men would be ratified by smoking the calumet.

Campagna. The plains around the city of Rome.

Carbonari. A secret political society organized in Italy, 1820.

Carmagnole. Song and dance in the French Revolution.

Cartesian Philosophy. From Descartes, "I think, therefore I exist."

Castle Garden. At New York City, the landing-place of emigrants.

Catacombs. Subterranean sepulchers. About three miles from Rome in the Appian Way a vast number of long underground passages about three feet wide and ten feet high. On each side in niches were deposited the bodies of the martyrs and early Christians. These niches were closed with tiles or slabs of marble having proper inscriptions on them. During the persecutions the Christians concealed themselves in these caves.

Cavalier Servente. The escort of a married woman.

Cecilia, St. A martyr; patroness of music.

Celestial Empire. China, whose first emperors were all divinities.

Central Park. The great park of New York City; contains 863 acres.

Champs de Mars. A field in Paris for military manœuvers.

Champs Elysees. A promenade in Paris.

Charter Oak. A tree in Hartford, Conn., in which the Colonial Charter was secreted in 1688. It was blown down in 1856.

Chauvinism. Patriotism of the blatant kind, from Chauvin, one of Scribe's characters.

Cheapside. A thoroughfare in London.

Chiltern Hundreds, To Accept the. A member of the English Parliament cannot resign, and cannot hold office during membership. If he wishes to leave, he can vacate his seat by accepting the office of Steward of the Chiltern Hundreds.

Chiltern Hundreds. A tract in Buckinghamshire and Oxfordshire, England, to which is attached the nominal office of steward under the crown.

Christ Church. The name of the largest college in the University of Oxford.

Cid, The. The Spanish hero, Don Roderigo Laynez, Count of Bivar.

Cincinnati, The. Society of American Revolutionary officers.

Citizen King, The. Louis Philippe of France.

Cockagne, Land of. An imaginary country of ease and pleasure; usually applied to London.

Colossus of Rhodes. A brass statue, one of the wonders of the world, which stood astride the entrance to the port of Rhodes.

Columbia. Poetical name of the United States.

Column of Vendome. A stone pillar in Paris erected by Napoleon, commemorating the successes of the French armies. It was thrown down by the Communists in 1871.

Confederate States. The eleven states which seceded in 1861, Alabama, Arkansas, Florida, Georgia, Louisiana, Mississippi, North Carolina, South Carolina, Tennessee, Texas, and Virginia.

Congressional Library. At Washington; it is the largest in the United States.

Consols. English public securities.

Copperheads. Northern sympathizers with the South in the Civil war.

Corncrackers, The. Kentuckians.

Corn Law Rhymer, The. Ebenezer Elliott.

Corso. The chief thoroughfare of Rome.

Crapaud Johnny. A Frenchman.

Credit Mobilier. An authorized stock company. The American Credit Mobilier formed for raising money for the Pacific Railroad raised a foul odor in 1873.

Crocodile Tears. Counterfeit sorrow. A fable says the crocodile weeps as it eats its victim.

Cumberland. A United States vessel sunk by the Confederate ram Merrimac in Hampton Roads, March 8, 1862.

Curfew Bell. At 8 o'clock, the ringing of the curfew bell in old times in England, all lights were extinguished, the fires raked up and covered, and the people of the Kingdom retired to bed. This rule, made by William the Conqueror, lasted for a long time, and even yet there is some sign of its observance in the nine o'clock bell rung in many parts of New England.

Damocles' Sword. Damocles, having commented upon the happiness which the tyrant Dionysius must enjoy, was invited by him to a feast where, whilst discussing the good things, he looked up and discovered a sword hanging by a single hair immediately over his head.

Darby and Joan. The loving couple.

Darwinian Theory. An explanation of the origin of species in animals, that they come from one or a few original forms, the present differences resulting from development and natural selection.

De Profundis. The 130th Psalm; part of the burial service.

Debatable Ground. Land on the western border of Scotland, disputed between England and Scotland.

Defender of the Faith. Henry VIII. received this title from Pope Leo X., and his successors have borne it ever since.

Directory, The French. By the Constitution of 1705 the executive power was vested in five Directors; it lasted only four years.

Dixie, The Land of. The Southern States.

Dizzy. The nickname of Benjamin Disraeli, Earl of Beaconsfield.

Doctors' Commons. The place where the Ecclesiastical Court sat in London.

Doctrinaire. A cant term in French politics, given

to the proposer of an impracticable compromise measure.

Doe, John. The fictitious plaintiff in ejectment suits, the defendant being Richard Roe.

Doomsday Book. Compiled by order of William the Conqueror. It contained a survey and an estimate of value of all the lands in England.

Donnybrook Fair. A once celebrated annual fair near Dublin.

Douay Bible, The. The English Bible authorized by the Roman Catholic Church; first published at Douay, France.

Downing Street. The official residence of the English Prime Minister since the time of Sir Robert Walpole is in Downing Street, London.

Drury Lane Theater. In London; was opened in 1688.

Dying Gladiator. An ancient statue in the Capitol at Rome.

Eastern States, The. Maine, New Hampshire, Vermont, Massachusetts, Rhode Island, and Connecticut.

Ecce Homo. A painting by Correggio representing the Saviour crowned with thorns.

Ecole Polytechnique. A Parisian school, the graduates of which are given places in the public service.

El Dorado. A fabulous region in South America, surpassing all other countries in the production of gems and precious metals. A name for any wealthy country.

Elephant, Seeing the. Seeing the world.

Elgin Marbles. A collection of Greek sculptures made by Lord Elgin. Now in the British Museum.

Escurial, The. A royal residence built by Philip II.; it is the largest structure in Spain, and one of the most splendid buildings in Europe. It is 22 miles from Madrid and contains a palace, a church, a monastery, free schools, and a mausoleum.

Eternal City, The. Rome.

Eureka. (I have found it.) Exclamation of Archimedes when he discovered the method of proving that the sum of the squares of the sides of a right-angled triangle equaled the square of the hypotenuse.

Evangelists, Symbols of the. Matthew has a scroll before him and holds a pen; Mark sits writing, with a winged lion by his side; Luke has a pen and a scroll, near him is an ox; John is a young man, behind whom is an eagle.

Exclusion, Bill of. A bill which passed the English House of Commons in 1679, proposing to exclude the Duke of York from the throne because he was a Roman Catholic.

Expounder of the Constitution, The. Daniel Webster.

Fabian Policy. Delaying; dilatory. From Quintus Fabius Maximus, the Roman General who successfully opposed Hannibal, the Carthaginian, by avoiding a battle and continually harassing him.

Fabius, The American. George Washington.

Fairmount Park. In Philadelphia, where the Centennial Exhibition of 1876 was held; contains nearly 3,000 acres.

Faineants, Les Rois. (Do-nothing Kings.) The last twelve Kings of the Merovingian Dynasty were so called. For about 100 years previous to 720, when Pepin dethroned Childeric III., they were mere puppets, and the supreme authority was exercised by the mayors of the palace.

Falernian. A celebrated ancient Italian wine grown at Falernum.

Faneuil Hall. In Boston, built 1742; called the "Cradle of Liberty," for there the Revolutionary patriots were wont to assemble.

Farmer George. George III. of England; so called from his love of agriculture.

Fata Morgana. A mirage in the Straits of Messina.

Father of his Country. George Washington.

Fathers of the Latin Church. St. Ambrose of Milan, St. Augustine, St. Bernard, St. Hilary, St. Jerome, Lactantius.

Faubourg St. Antoine. The part of Paris where the workingmen live.

Faubourg St. Germain. Aristocratic part of Paris.

Fenians. A society of Irishmen formed in the United States in 1865 to free Ireland.

Field of the Cloth of Gold. Plain in France where Francis I. and Henry VIII. met on a mutual visit. It is historical on account of the gorgeous display, both parties being most extravagant in their outfit

Fifth Avenue. A celebrated residence street in New York.

Fighting Joe. The American General Joseph Hooker.

First Gentleman in Europe. George IV. of England.

Five Points. A once notorious locality in New York.

Flagellants. Religious fanatics of the thirteenth century who went about naked and scourging themselves.

Fleet, The. A London prison taken down in 1845.

Flowery Kingdom, The. China.

Flying Dutchman. A specter ship cruising about the Cape of Good Hope. Forebodes trouble to whoever sees it.

Forte. Strong point.

Fort Sumter. In the harbor of Charleston, S. C. Here were heard the first sounds of the cannons' thunder in the late Civil War.

Fourierism. Charles Fourier, a French visionary, proposed a system of communism in which the world should be divided into "phalansteries" of four hundred families who were to live and work in common.

Freshman. A student in his first year at college.

Funk, Peter. A mock auction; a person employed to act as an apparent purchaser and bid up articles for sale.

Gadshill. Near Rochester, in Kent, England. Place where Falstaff met so many men in buckram. Charles Dickens' residence was at Gadshill.

Genre Painting. Represents ordinary domestic and rural scenes.

George, St., and the Dragon. St. George, the patron saint of England, is said to have slain in Libya a hideous dragon whose daily food was a virgin.

Gerrymander. The geographical apportionment of districts to give preponderance to one political party. Started in Massachusetts, and named from its Governor, Elbridge Gerry. Example, a shoestring district in Missouri.

Ghetto. The quarter in Rome to which the Jews were formerly restricted.

Ghibelline. One of a faction in Italy in the thirteenth century, which favored the German Emperors, in opposition to the Guelphs, adherents of the Pope.

Girondists; The Gironde. Moderate "Constitutional" Republican party in the French Revolution in 1798.

Glencoe. A pass in Argyleshire, Scotland. Here, February 13, 1691, were massacred thirty-eight of the McDonalds by one hundred and twenty soldiers under Capt. Campbell.

Gobelins. A tapestry and carpet manufactory at Paris, founded by Gobelin, a dyer, about 370 years ago.

Godiva, Lady. Wife of Leofric, Earl of Mercia, who offered to remit certain exactions to his tenants if she would ride naked through the streets of Coventry. She did so, all the people closing their doors and keeping within except one, "Peeping Tom," who was struck blind for peeping at her.

Golconda. The neighborhood of some rich diamond mines in India.

Gold Fever. 1849; peopled California.

Golden Age. A period of innocence and prosperity. Nearly always refers to some past age.

Golden Gate. The entrance to the harbor of San Francisco.

Golden Horn. The estuary of the Bosphorus, upon whose banks Constantinople is built.

Gordian Knot. A difficulty; an obstacle. Gordius, King of Phrygia, consecrated to Jupiter a wagon, the beam and yoke of which were tied together by such an intricate knot that no one could unravel it. An oracle having foretold that he who could untie this knot would be master of Asia, Alexander cut it asunder with his sword.

Gordon Riots, The. In 1780, in London, the bill passed by the House of Commons for the relief of the Roman Catholics caused so much ill feeling that Lord George Gordon, a fanatic, incited the mob to try to force its repeal. Dickens in his Barnaby Rudge gives a vivid description of these riots.

Gotham. A name sometimes applied to New York City.

Gotham, The Wise Men of. Noted for their folly. Gotham was an English village.

Great Commoner, The. William Pitt.

Great Duke, The. Wellington.

Great Eastern. The largest vessel ever launched. She was built to carry 1,000 passengers and 5,000 tons of cargo. Her chief work has been in the laying of ocean telegraph cables.

Great Pyramid, The. Is at Geezeh, Egypt. It is 481 feet high.

Greenbacks. United States Treasury notes. So named from their color.

Green Isle, The. Ireland. Sometimes also called the Emerald Isle.

Greenwood. A cemetery in Brooklyn, N. Y.

Gregorian Year. 1582; it being proved that the years were eleven minutes shorter than what they were counted at, Gregory XIII. took ten days of October out of that year and advanced the dates so as to correct the calendar. The reform has been accepted throughout Christendom, except in Russia. Example: George Washington, born February 11, O. S.

Gretna Green. A Scotch village famous for runaway matches.

Grub Street. In London; used to be noted for its literary denizens.

Guelphs. The adherents in the thirteenth century of the Papacy against the German Emperors. They were the constant opponents of the Ghibellines, and between them Italy was kept in turmoil.

Guildhall. The London town hall.

Gunpowder Plot, The. A plot to blow up the English Parliament in its House, November 5, 1605. A cellar underneath was stored with gunpowder intended to be touched off during the session by Guy Fawkes. The discovery was made in time to prevent mischief. To use a modern but inelegant phrase, the plot was considered by some people to be "a put up job."

Gyges' Ring. A ring which made the wearer invisible. Gyges, having found a man's corpse in a brazen horse that he discovered in a cave, took a ring from the finger of the dead that rendered him invisible. By using this ring he entered unseen the chamber of the King of Lydia and murdered him. He became King.

Habeas Corpus Act, The. Was passed in the time of Charles II. and provides that the body of any person restrained of his liberty must on proper application be brought before a judge and the reason of his confinement stated. The judge will then determine the amount of bail he shall furnish, or he will remand him to prison or allow him his freedom, as the case may require.

Halcyon Days. A period of happiness; days of peace and tranquillity. The halcyon, as the kingfisher was anciently called, was said to lay her eggs in nests on rocks near the sea during the calm weather about the winter solstice.

Handicap. Apportionment of the weights that must be carried in a race by different horses, considering their age and strength, to equalize their chances.

Hansard. Name of the firm which prints the debates of the British Parliament.

Hanse Towns. In the twelfth century some commercial cities in the north of Germany formed an association for the protection of commerce. To these other similar cities in Holland, England, France, Spain, and Italy acceded, and for centuries this confederacy commanded the respect and defied the power of kings.

Hanseatic League. The name of the confederation of Hanse towns. There were seventy-two cities in the league, and they held triennial conventions called Hansa. It has long since fallen to pieces. Four of its members, Lubeck, Hamburg, Bremen, and Frankfort, are called free cities, but are really part of the German Empire.

Hare, Mad as a March. The hare is wilder than usual in March.

Harpies. Three ravenous and filthy monsters, each having a woman's face and the body of a vulture. Their names were Aello, Ocypete, and Celeno. Juno sent them to plunder the table of Phineus.

Hari-Kari. (Happy dispatch.) Japanese official suicide.

Harvest Moon. The full moon at or nearest the fall equinox; rises for a number of days about sunset.

Heathen Chinee, The. A poem.

Heidelberg Castle. Ruins near Heidelberg, Germany.

Hegira. The date of Mohammed's flight from Mecca, July 16, 622. The epoch from which the Mohammedans compute their time.

High Church. The more conservative portion of the Episcopal Church.

High Seas, The. The sea beyond three miles from the coast.

History, The Father of. Herodotus, the Greek historian.

Hobson's Choice. Take what is offered or go without. Tobias Hobson, an English stable-keeper, made whatever customer came to hire a horse take the one nearest the door.

Holborn. A street in London by which criminals used to be carried out to execution at Tyburn.

Holy Alliance. Formed in 1816 by Austria, Prussia, and Russia.

Holy Family, The. The name of pictures representing in group the infant Jesus, St. Joseph, the Blessed Virgin, John the Baptist, Anna, and St. Elizabeth. The most celebrated are by Michael Angelo at Florence, by Raphael in London, and by Leonardo da Vinci in the Louvre.

Holy Land, The. Palestine.

Holy League, The. The alliance of Pope Julius II., France, Germany, Spain, and some of the Italian Republics in 1508, against Venice.

Honi soit qui mal y pense. (Shame to him who evil thinks.) Motto of the highest order of knighthood in Great Britain, that of the Garter, instituted by Edward III. At a ball, a garter of the Countess of Salisbury, having fallen off, was picked up by the King, who expressed himself in the above phrase and fastened it around his own knee. This incident led to the formation of the order.

Honors of War. Allowing a surrendered enemy to keep his arms.

Hotel de Ville. The city hall in French and Belgian cities.

Houris. Beautiful virgins of Paradise; promised by the Koran for the delight of the true believers.

Hundred Days, The. From March 20, 1815, when Napoleon escaped from Elba, to June 22, 1815, when he abdicated.

Iconoclast. (Image-breaker.) A radical reformer.

Iliad. A Greek epic poem by Homer, relating the story of the siege of Troy by the Greeks.

Independence, Declaration of. Issued July 4, 1776.

Independence Hall. In Philadelphia, Pa., where Congress met and adopted the Declaration of Independence.

Index Expurgatorius. A list of books forbidden to be read by the Roman Catholic Church.

Inns of Court. The four London law societies which have the sole right of admitting candidates to the Bar. They are Gray's Inn, Lincoln's Inn, the Inner Temple, and the Middle Temple.

Inquisition. A tribunal established in some countries to try heretics.

Irish Agitator, The. Daniel O'Connell.

Iron City, The. Pittsburg, Pa.

Iron Duke, The. The Duke of Wellington.

Iron Mask, The Man in the. A mysterious French state prisoner.

Jack Ketch. The hangman. The name of an English hangman.

Jack Robinson. Before you can say Jack Robinson; at once. Jack Robinson was noted for the shortness of his visits; the servant had scarcely time to repeat his name, before he would leave.

Jack, The Giant Killer. A nursery hero.

Jack, The American, or Union. The blue ground of the American flag with the stars but without the stripes.

Jacobins. A revolutionary club, 1789, in Paris, held its meetings in what had been the Jacobin Monastery. They were violent and extreme in the measures they proposed. Their name spread to all similar organizations and to individuals acting with them throughout France.

Jacobites. Adherents of James II. of England, and of the Stuarts, his descendants.

Jardin des Plantes. Botanical and zoölogical garden in Paris.

Jardin Mabille. Of world-wide notoriety. A Parisian resort where the can-can flourished. Suppressed in 1882.

Jericho, Gone to. Disappeared; ruined.

Jerusalem Delivered. An Italian epic poem by Torquato Tasso.

Jingo, Jingoism. Expression applied in England to those who wanted the English Government to assume an aggressive foreign policy, 1874-1880.

John Bull. England. Nickname for an Englishman.

John Chinaman. The Chinese in America.

Johnny Cakes. Made of Indian meal baked in the ashes.

Jubilee, Year of. Among the Jews the jubilee came every fiftieth year, which was the year after one week of weeks of years had passed (seven times seven). All slaves who were of Hebrew blood were freed, all debts were canceled, and all lands returned to original owners during the jubilee. In the Roman Catholic Church it is observed every twenty-fifth year.

Juggernaut. A Hindoo god who has a famous temple in India. There is an immense car in the service of this god, which, when moved about the country, causes the greatest excitement. The car resembles a large building, and its weight is very heavy. It is dragged along by the multitude, and their fanaticism is so great that crowds of devotees cast themselves under the wheels and are crushed to death, a fate which they believe insures paradise.

Julian Era, The. A method of reckoning time from 46 B.C., when Cæsar reformed the calendar.

Junius, Letters of. Some remarkable political letters written during the reign of George III. Their authorship is unknown.

Kansas, Bleeding. So called by Horace Greeley during the Free Soil controversy.

Kensington Gardens. A London Park near which Queen Victoria was born.

Kilkenny Cats, The. Disputing people; from the old verse:

There once were two cats in Kilkenny,
Who each thought there was one cat too many,
So they howled and they fit, and they scratched and they bit,
Until instead of two cats there wasn't any.

King can do no wrong, The. Meaning that the Ministers and not the King are responsible for mistakes of government.

King of Yvetot. The Seigneur of Yvetot was made king of his estate by the King of France as a recompense for the killing of his father. It was a kingdom of eight square miles.

King Cole. A legendary king of Britain, who affected tobacco and spirits.

King Cotton. A name given to the great Southern industry before the war.

King's Evil. The scrofula. So called from the belief that a king's touch would cure the disease.

King Log. A good-for-nothing ruler. The name comes from one of Esop's fables, wherein Jupiter puts a log to rule over the frogs.

King-Maker, The. Richard Nevill, the Earl of Warwick, who set up and deposed kings at his will during the Wars of the Roses, in the fifteenth century.

King Stork. A tyrant. The sequel to the Esop fable mentioned above. The frogs grew tired of King Log, whereupon King Stork was brought in at their request, who devoured the whole community.

Kit Kat Club, The. A London club founded in 1688. It had many eminent members.

Knickerbocker. A member of any old Dutch family in New York. Derived from Irving's immortal history.

Knight of Malta. A chivalric and monastic order founded during the Crusades, also called the Knights Hospitallers of St. John.

Know-Nothings. A political party in the United States, whose cardinal principle was opposition to foreign office-holders.

Koh-i-Noor. A Golconda diamond, the largest in the world, now one of the crown diamonds of England. Value, $625,000.

Koran, The. The Mohammedan Bible.

Kremlin, The. The Royal Russian residence in Moscow.

Labyrinth, The. A celebrated structure built by Minos, King of Crete, which consisted of a maze out of which no one who entered could find the way back.

Laconic. Curt. So called from the brief speech in fashion in old Laconia, afterwards called Sparta.

Lacrymal Christi. An Italian wine.

Lake School, The. A society of English poets consisting of Coleridge, Wordsworth, and Southey.

Land of Bondage, The. Egypt.

Land o' Cakes, The. Scotland.

Land of Nod, The. Sleep; Dreamland.

Land of Promise, The. Canaan, the goal of the Jewish wanderings in the wilderness.

Lang Syne. Long ago.

Langue d'Oc. Provence, a part of France so called from the dialect in use.

Langue d'Œil. All of France except Provence.

Laocoon, The. A celebrated statue in the Vatican representing Laocoon strangled by serpents.

Laodicean. A person lukewarm in religion.

Lares and Penates. The household gods.

Last Judgment, The. The theme of a number of frescoes of the Renaissance period in Italy.

Last Supper, The. Similar to the above. Leonardo da Vinci's best canvas is on this subject.

Lateran Palace, The. One of the Papal residences at Rome.

Laughing Philosopher, The. Democritus of Abdera, who believed that life was only to be laughed at.

Leaning Tower, The. A celebrated structure at Pisa, Italy, which leans fourteen feet out of the perpendicular; 180 feet high.

Learned Blacksmith, The. Elihu Burritt.

Leonine Verses. Verses which rhyme at the middle and the end.

Libby Prison. A Confederate jail for prisoners of war at Richmond, Va.

Lilliput. The pigmy land in Gulliver's travels.

Lingua Franca. A dialect of French, Italian, and Arabic spoken on the Mediterranean Sea.

Lion and Unicorn. The supporters of the British royal arms.

Lion of the North, The. Gustavus of Sweden, the great leader of the Protestant forces during the Thirty Years' War.

Lion's Share. The bigger portion in a division. So called from one of Esop's fables.

Little Corporal, The. Napoleon Bonaparte.

Little Giant, The. Stephen A. Douglas.

Lloyds. The originators of marine insurance.

Lombard Street. The financial street of London.

Lone Star State, The. Texas.

Long Parliament. The Parliament which sat for thirteen years at the beginning of the civil war in England. It sat from 1640 to 1653.

Lorelei. A malignant but beautiful water-sprite of the Rhine.

Lotus-Eaters, The. Homer in the Odyssey describes the effect of eating the lotus as making the eater forget his home.

Louvre, The. The art palace of Paris.

Low Church, The. A part of the Episcopal Church which is opposed to ceremonials.

Lusiad, The. The Portuguese epic poem, written by Camoens, describing Vasco da Gama's adventures.

Lynch Law. Mob law. The name comes from a Virginia farmer who instituted the first vigilance committee in America.

Mab, Queen. The queen of the fairies. So called from an Irish fairy princess named Medh, who flourished in the night of time.

Macadamize. Paving with broken stones. So called from the inventor, Sir John MacAdam.

Macaronic Verse. A verse made by mixing different languages.

Macchiavellism. Political trickery.

Madam Tussaud's Exhibition. A famous London wax-works show.

Mad Poet, The. Nathaniel Lee, an insane English dramatist.

Madman of Macedonia, The. Alexander the Great.

Madman of the North, The. Charles XII. of Sweden.

Madonna. The Blessed Virgin.

Maecenas. A noted patron of poets during the reign of Augustus of Rome.

Magna Charta. The charter making the corner stone of English liberty, extorted from King John Lack-Land.

Mahomet's Coffin. The body of Mahomet is said to hang in mid-air over Medina.

Maid of Orleans. Joan of Arc.

Maid of Saragossa. Augustina Zaragoza, the heroine of the siege of Saragossa in 1808–9.

Maiden Queen, The. Elizabeth of England.

Maine Law. A prohibitory law first adopted in Maine.

Malthusian Doctrine, The. The theory that the population of the world is growing faster than the food supply.

Mammoth Cave. A cave near the Green River, Kentucky, the largest cave in the world.

Man in the Moon. According to the legend the man who first broke the Sabbath.

Man of Destiny. Napoleon Bonaparte.

Man of Iron, The. Bismarck.

Man of Straw. An irresponsible person.

Mare's Nest. A matter which seems of importance but turns out to be nothing.

Marriage a la Mode. The title of six satirical pictures by Hogarth.

Marseillaise. The French national air, composed by Rouget de Lisle.

Martinet. A strict disciplinarian. So called from a French officer of the seventeenth century.

Mason and Dixon's Line. The north boundary of the Slave States, dividing Virginia and Maryland from Pennsylvania.

Mausoleum. The tomb of Mausolus, built by Queen Artemisia, one of the seven wonders of the world.

Mayfair. The west end of London.

Mercator's Projection (or Mercator's Chart) is so called after Gerard Mercator, a Flemish geographer of the sixteenth century, the first to give an unbroken view of the whole surface of the earth. In it all the meridians are straight lines *perpendicular* to the equator, and all the parallels *parallel* to the equator, the effect being to greatly exaggerate the polar regions.

Merry Andrew. A buffoon, from Andrew Borde, the whimsical physician of Henry VIII.

Merry Monarch, The. Charles II. of England.

Mesmerism takes its name from Mesmer, a German physician.

Mezzo Relievo. Carved or cast figures projecting from the tablet a little more than basso relievo, and something less than alto relievo, are called mezzo relievo.

Middle Ages, The. The period between the destruction of the Roman Empire and the revival of learning in Italy—476 to 1500.

Middle States, The. New York, Pennsylvania, New Jersey, and Delaware.

Minnesingers. (Love singers.) The German lyric poets of the twelfth and thirteenth centuries.

Miserere. The fifty-first psalm.

Mississippi Bubble, The. A hollow financial scheme.

Missouri Compromise, The. A measure that prohibited slavery north of 36° 30′ north latitude.

Mistress of the Seas. England.

Molly Maguires. A secret society in the United States. Many crimes were attributed to it, especially in Pennsylvania.

Monarch, Le Grand. Louis XIV. of France.

Monroe Doctrine. The United States is not to meddle in European affairs, nor to allow European Governments to meddle in the affairs of the American Continent.

Mont de Piete. A pawnbroker's shop.

Montmartre. A Parisian cemetery.

Monumental City, The. Baltimore, Md.

Morey Letter, The. A forged letter attributing to General Garfield anti-Chinese sentiments, 1880.

Morganatic Marriage. A marriage between a man of high rank and a woman of a lower one. She does not take her husband's title.

Mother of Presidents. Virginia; having produced seven Presidents of the United States.

Mother Carey's Chickens. Stormy Petrels.

Mother Goose. She lived near Boston, and was a nursery rhymer. She sang rhymes to her grandson, Thomas Fleet, who printed them in 1819.

Mount Vernon. The home of Washington, in Virginia.

Muscular Christianity. An expression of Charles Kingsley. "A sound mind in a sound body."

Music of the Spheres. Order, harmony. Plato taught that each planet had a siren whose song harmonized with the motion of our sphere and with that of the others.

Namby-Pamby. Childish. A term used for poor literary productions.

Nantes, Edict of. A decree issued at Nantes, France, in 1598, by Henry IV., granting toleration to the Protestant religion. Revoked by Louis XIV., October 22, 1685.

Nation of Shop-keepers. The name given to the English by Napoleon.

Natural Bridge, The. A natural arch over Cedar Creek near James River in Virginia. It is two hundred feet high.

Newgate. A London prison.

New World. The Americas.

Nibelungenlied. A German epic poem of the thirteenth century.

Nine Worthies, The. Joshua, David, Judas Maccabæus, Hector, Alexander, Julius Cæsar, Arthur, Charlemagne, and Godfrey of Bouillon.

Noctes Ambrosianæ. The title of a work by Professor Wilson (Christopher North).

Noel. Christmas day.

Non-Conformists. Dissenters from the Church of England.

Northern Giant, The. Russia.

Notre Dame. The Cathedral of Paris.

Odyssey. Homer's narrative poem of the adventures of Ulysses on his voyage from Troy to Ithaca.

Ogres. Giants who feed on human flesh.

Oi Polloi. The multitude.

Old Abe. Abraham Lincoln.

Old Bailey. A London criminal court.

Old Dominion, The. Virginia.

Old Guard, The. A favorite regiment of Napoleon Bonaparte. In the Chicago Convention, 1880, the friends of General Grant received this name.

Old Hickory. Gen. Andrew Jackson.

Old Probs. (Old Probabilities.) The United States Signal Service.

Old Public Functionary. President James Buchanan.

Old South, The. A famous church in Boston, Mass.

Orangeman. A Protestant Irishman. Member of an organization which cherishes the memory of William Prince of Orange.

Orange Peel. Sir Robert Peel.

Ordinance of 1787. An act fixing the government of the Northwest Territory of the United States.

Orlando Furioso. An Italian poem by Ariosto.

Ossian. The son of Fingal, a Scotch bard. Ossian's poems, published in 1760, were the work of James McPherson, a gifted Caledonian.

Ostend Manifesto. Issued by the United States Ministers to England, France, and Spain during Pierce's administration, declaring that Cuba must belong to the United States.

Ostracism. The Athenians expelled every public man against whom a sufficient number of votes were cast. The votes were written on oyster shells.

Palimpsest. A parchment having the original writing erased and new writing substituted.

Pall Mall. A street in London.

Palladium. Something that affords defense, protection, and safety. A statue of Pallas was the palladium of Troy.

Pantheon. A circular building in Rome erected in the time of Augustus. It is now a church, the Rotunda.

Paradise Lost. A poem by John Milton, treating of the fall of man.

Paradise Regained. Poem by Milton on the temptation and triumph of Jesus.

Paris of America, The. Cincinnati.

Parthenon. A temple of Minerva in Athens.

Partington, Mrs. The American Mrs. Malaprop. The creation of B. P. Shillaber.

Pasquinade. A lampoon or satirical writing. Political squibs used to be posted on an old statue that stood in Rome near the house of a sneering old cobbler named Pasquin.

Peeler. A policeman. Sir Robert Peel founded the Irish constabulary.

Peninsular War. The war between England and France in Spain and Portugal, 1808-1812.

People's William. William E. Gladstone.

Pere-la-Chaise. A cemetery near Paris.

Philippic. An invective. The orations of Demosthenes against Philip of Macedon originated this word.

Philistine. A word in use in the German universities for a person below caste.

Philosopher's Stone, The. A substance supposed to have the property of turning anything else into gold.

Phœnix. A mythical bird, without a mate, renews itself every five hundred years by being consumed in a fire of spices, whence it rises from the ashes and starts for a new flight.

Pied Piper of Hamelin, The. Not being paid for having drawn, by the sound of his pipe, the rats and mice out of Hamelin into the river, he piped the children of the town into Koppelberg hill, where 130 of them died.

Pigeon English. A mixture of English, Chinese, and Portuguese.

Plon-Plon. Prince Napoleon J. C. Bonaparte.

Plumed Knight, The. J. G. Blaine, American statesman.

Plymouth Rock. The rock at Plymouth, Mass., where the pilgrims landed in 1620.

Poet's Corner. A corner in Westminster Abbey where poets are buried. The poetical column in a newspaper.

Pons Asinorum. (The bridge of asses.) Fifth proposition, first book Euclid's Geometry.

Poor Richard. Benjamin Franklin.

Porkopolis. Cincinnati.

Prater, The. A promenade in Vienna, Austria.

Protestant Duke, The. The Duke of Monmouth, natural son of Charles II. of England.

Pyramids. A number of remarkable old structures in Egypt.

Quaker City, The. Philadelphia, Pa.

Quaker Poet, The. John G. Whittier.

Quartier Latin. A district of Paris inhabited principally by students.

Queen of the Antilles. The island of Cuba.

Ranz des Vaches. The air the Swiss mountaineers play on the Alpine horns when tending their cattle.

Railway King, The. George Hudson, an Englishman.

Rebellion, The Great. The war between Charles I. of England and Parliament.

Red Letter Day. A fortunate day. In old calendars a red letter was used to mark the saints' days.

Red Tape. Official routine.

Reign of Terror. The time during the French Revolution between the overthrow of the Girondists, May 31, 1793, and the fall of Robespierre, July 27, 1794.

Reynard the Fox. A romance of the fourteenth century.

Rialto, The. A bridge over the Grand Canal, Venice.

Rights, Declaration of. An instrument securing annual Parliaments, trial by jury, free elections, the right of petition, and denying to the crown the privilege of keeping a standing army or of levying taxes, was drawn up after the revolution of 1689, and accepted by William and Mary.

Roost, To Rule the. To take the leading part.

Robert the Devil. The first Duke of Normandy.

Robin Goodfellow. Puck, a celebrated fairy.

Roland for an Oliver, A. Tit for tat. Roland and Oliver, two peers of Charlemagne. So many romances were related of these knights that whenever one told an improbable story to match one that had been told before, it was called giving a Roland for an Oliver.

Rossius, The British. David Garrick.

Rough and Ready. Gen. Zachary Taylor.

Round Robin. A petition or remonstrance signed by the names in a circle, so as to conceal who signed it first.

Round Table, The. King Arthur's knights sat at a round table so that any distinction of rank was avoided.

Roundheads. The Puritans, who wore short hair.

Royal Martyr, The. Charles I. of England.

Royal Society, The. A society for the advancement of natural science, founded at London, 1645.

Rozinante. The horse of Don Quixote.

Rubicon, To Pass the. To take an irretrievable step. When Cæsar crossed the Rubicon he became an enemy of the Republic.

Rule Britannia. An English song.

Rump Parliament, The. A remnant of the Long Parliament broken up by Cromwell.

Rye House Plot. A conspiracy in 1683 to assassinate Charles II. and the Duke of York. Rye House was the name of the conspirators' place of meeting.

Sabbath Day's Journey. About one mile.

Sack, To Get the. To be discharged. The Sultan, when he wants to be rid of one of his harem, has her put into a sack and thrown into the Bosphorus.

Sadducees. A sect of the ancient Jews who denied the resurrection of the dead and the expectation of a future state.

Sagas. Scandinavian books containing the Northern legends.

Saint Bartholomew, Massacre of. Massacre of the French Huguenots in the reign of Charles IX., on St. Bartholomew's day, 1572.

Sailor King, The. William IV. of England.

Saint Cloud. A once famous French palace, destroyed in the Franco-Prussian war

Saint James, The Court of. The English court, so called from the Palace of St. James in London, formerly a royal residence.

St. Mark's. Cathedral of Venice, Italy.

Saint Paul's. The cathedral of London; designed by Sir Christopher Wren.

Saint Peter's. At Rome; is the most splendid church building in the world.

Saint Sophia. A mosque in Constantinople, Turkey.

Saint Stephens. A Gothic cathedral in Vienna, Austria.

Salt River. Oblivion. Gone up Salt River is generally taken to mean political defeat.

Sambo. Nickname for colored man.

Sanctum. One's private office.

Sandwich. A piece of meat between two pieces of bread.

Sang Azul. Of aristocratic descent.

Sanhedrim. The Jewish court of seventy elders.

Sans-Culottes. (Without trousers.) The French revolutionists.

Sans Souci. Palace of Frederick the Great, at Potsdam, near Berlin.

Santa Croce. A church in Florence, Italy; the burial place of Michael Angelo, Galileo, Machiavelli, and others.

Saturnalia. A festival in honor of Saturn observed annually by the Romans by giving way to the wildest disorders. Unrestrained license for all classes, even to the slaves, ruled the city for three days, December 17, 18, and 19.

Schoolmen. The mediæval theologians.

Scotland Yard. The headquarters of the London police.

Scourge of God, The. Attila, King of the Huns.

Scratch, Old. The Devil.

Scylla. (Avoiding Scylla he fell into Charybdis.) In trying to avoid one danger he fell into another. Scylla and Charybdis were the two dangers in the Straits of Messina, Italy.

Sea-girt Isle, The. Great Britain.

Secessia. The seceding Southern States.

Secular Games. Games held by the Romans once in a century.

Semiramis of the North. Catherine II., Empress of Russia.

September Massacres. The massacre of the French Royalist prisoners in Paris, September 2, 3, and 4, 1792. About 8,000 were killed.

Septuagint. A Greek version of the Old Testament prepared by seventy doctors.

Seven-hilled City, The. Rome.

Seven Wonders of the World. The pyramids of Egypt; the Temple of Diana at Ephesus; the hanging gardens of Babylon; the Colossus at Rhodes; the Mausoleum at Halicarnassus; the statue of Zeus by Phidias at Olympus; and the Pharos (or lighthouse) of Alexandria in Egypt.

Seven Years' War. The war of Frederick the Great against France, Austria, and Russia, 1756 to 1763.

Shamrock. The emblem of Ireland. St. Patrick made use of it to prove the doctrine of the Trinity.

Shibboleth. A countersign. The password of a secret society. When the Ephraimites, after being routed by Jephthah, tried to pass the Jordan, they were detected by not being able to pronounce properly the word Shibboleth.

Sick Man, The. The Ottoman Empire.

Sinews of War, The. Money.

Single-Speech Hamilton. An English statesman of the eighteenth century, W. G. Hamilton. He never made but one speech, but that one was most eloquent.

Six Hundred, Charge of the. At the battle of Balaklava, October 25, 1854, by a mistaken order, the British light cavalry, 670 strong, made a most gallant charge on the Russians.

Sleeping Beauty, The. A fairy tale.

Smell of the Lamp. A phrase first applied to the orations of Demosthenes, showing their careful and labored preparation. Demosthenes studied in a cave by lamplight.

Song of Roland. An old French poem recounting the deaths of Oliver and Roland at Roncesvalles.

Sorbonne, The. A university in Paris founded by Robert de Sorbonne in the thirteenth century.

Sortes Biblicæ. Fortune telling by consulting the Bible.

South Kensington Museum. A collection of works of art and manufactures in London.

South Sea Bubble, The. A company formed in 1710

in England to pay the national debt and to have in return a monopoly of the South Sea trade. This company lasted about ten years, and its failure was the ruin of thousands.

Spanish Main. The southwestern part of the Gulf of Mexico.

Sphinx. An emblem of silence and mystery. A monument near Cairo, Egypt; half woman, half lion.

Stabat Mater. A Latin hymn on the Crucifixion.

Stalwart. A member of the Republican party of the United States clinging to the principles and practices of the party. His opposite, a "Half-Breed," is a Republican unwilling to be controlled by the party leaders.

Star Chamber. A court of criminal jurisdiction in England having extensive powers. It existed from the time of Henry VIII. until that of Charles I.

"Stonewall" Jackson. Gen. Thomas J. Jackson, Confederate General.

Strasburg Cathedral. At Strasburg; Gothic; 468 feet high; has a wonderful clock.

Swedish Nightingale. Jenny Lind (Mme. Goldschmidt).

Tabooed. Prohibited. A Polynesian word meaning consecrated; used for what is out of date or in bad taste.

Tammany Hall. A section of the Democratic party in New York City, named from their place of meeting.

Tammany Ring, or the "Tweed Ring," or "the Ring." A set of New York City officials which absorbed large sums of the city money. Exposed in 1871.

Tammany, Saint. Patron saint of the Democratic party in New York. He was an Indian chief, whose name was really Timenund.

Tapis, On the. On the carpet; proposed for discussion. From the tapis or cloth on a council table.

Temple Bar. A stone house in London over which the heads of traitors used to be exposed. Torn down in 1878.

Termagant. A shrew. Termagant was, according to the Crusaders, the wife of Mahomet.

Terra Firma. Dry land.

Tertium Quid. A third somebody not to be named.

Theatre Francais. A theater in Paris.

Theleme, Abbey of. A creation of Rabelais in his Gargantua. Its motto was, "Do as you please."

Thirty Years' War, The. Between the Catholics and Protestants in Germany, 1618-1648.

Thistle. The national emblem of Scotland. One night when the Danes were attempting to surprise an encampment of the Scotch, one of them trod upon a thistle; the pain caused him to raise an alarm and the Scotch defeated them. Ever since the thistle has been the insignia of Scotland.

Thor. The god of war, son of Odin, the Scandinavian Myth.

Threadneedle Street, The Old Lady of. The Bank of England.

Three Estates of the Realm. The nobility, the clergy, and the commonalty; represented in the two houses of Parliament.

Thunderer, The. The London Times (newspaper).

Tick, On. On credit.

Tit for Tat. An equivalent; this for that.

Tom Thumb. Charles A. Stratton. Also a fairy tale.

Tory. The name of an English political party, opposite of Whig.

Tour, The Grand. From England, through France, Switzerland, Italy, Germany, and home.

Tower, The. The citadel of London.

Transfiguration, The. One of Raphael's most famous pictures, now in the Vatican.

Trimmer. One who takes a moderate course in politics.

Trinity Church. An Episcopal church on Broadway at the head of Wall street, New York. The richest church in America.

Triple Alliance, The. Alliance between Great Britain, Holland, and Sweden against France, 1668.

Troubadours. Provincial poets from the eleventh to the fourteenth century.

Trouveres. Northern French poets 1100 to 1400.

Trumpet, To Sound One's Own. To boast. The entrance of knights into a list was announced by the heralds with a flourish of trumpets.

Tuft-Hunter. A toady. At Oxford a nobleman was called a tuft because of the gold tuft on his college cap.

Tuileries. A French Royal palace burned by the Commune in 1871.

Tulip Mania. A European craze of the seventeenth century centering in Holland. Everybody was buying tulip bulbs, which ran up to enormous prices. Many fortunes were sunk in their acquisition.

Tune the Old Cow Died of. Words instead of alms. Old song: a man having nothing with which to feed his cow, sings to her of the grass which is to grow. The expression is also used for a worn-out, tiresome tune.

Tyburn. Once a London place of execution, now a wealthy and fashionable quarter called Tyburnia.

Uffizi. A building in Florence in which is a magnificent art collection.

Ultramontanes. In France, the more extreme adherents of the Pope.

Underground Railroad, The. Organization of the different means used for the escape of runaway slaves, about the middle of the present century.

Under the Rose. (Sub rosa.) Confidentially.

Unlicked Cub. An ill-bred boy. The bear cub was believed to be licked into shape by its dam.

Unter den Linden. A street in Berlin having four rows of lime trees.

Unwashed, The Great. The mob.

Up the Spout, or, more elegantly, "gone where the woodbine twineth," or "at my uncle's," means in pawn.

Upas Tree. An object that does harm and should be avoided. The upas tree is common in Java; its gum is poisonous, and fable states that the atmosphere about it is as deadly.

Upper Ten Thousand. The aristocracy; fashionable society.

Utilitarians. Those who believe that the fitness of anything to promote happiness is the right standard of morality.

Utopia. An ideal commonwealth. The imaginary island, scene of Sir Thomas More's romance of Utopia.

Valhalla. The palace of immortality, where the heroes slain in battle dwell. (From the Saga legends.)

Vampire. An extortioner. A fabulous bat said to suck the blood of persons during sleep.

Vatican. The palace of the Popes, Rome.

Vatican, Council of the. The Œcumenical Council, 1869, promulgated Papal infallibility.

Vedas, The. Revelations of Brahma in four sacred books.

Veni, Vidi, Vici. (I came, I saw, I conquered.) Phrase used by Julius Cæsar, announcing his victory at Zela.

Venus de Medici. A Greek statue at Florence.

Venus of Milo. A Greek statue found in the Island of Melos, 1820; it is now in the Louvre.

Verbum Sap. A word to the wise.

Veronica. A relic at St. Peter's, Rome.

Versailles. A palace at Versailles, ten miles from Paris.

Vespers, The Sicilian. The massacre of the French in Sicily, March 30, 1282. The sounding of the vesper bell was the signal.

Via Dolorosa. The sorrowful way of our Lord from the Mount of Olives to Golgotha.

Vinegar Bible, The. Has "vinegar" for "vineyard" in the head line of Luke xx., Oxford, 1617.

Virgin Queen, The. Queen Elizabeth of England.

Vitus Dance, St. A disease anciently supposed to be under control of St. Vitus.

Wabash Avenue. A street in Chicago.

Wall of China, The. A wall 1,200 miles long and 20 feet high, built as a protection against the Tartars.

Wall Street. The great financial street of New York.

Wallack's. A theater in New York.

Walton, An Izaak. An angler.

Wandering Jew, The. A legendary personage condemned to wander over the world until the day of judgment.

War of 1812. Between Great Britain and the United States, 1812-1815.

War of the Roses. The English civil wars in the fourteenth and fifteenth centuries, between the houses of York and Lancaster.

Ward, Artemus. C. F. Browne.

Washington Street. A street in Boston, Mass.

Wassail. (What hail!) A bowl of spiced ale used on New Year's day is the Wassail bowl.

Waters, The Father of. The Mississippi.

Ways and Means. An important committee of the House of Representatives; is charged with the duty of devising ways and means for the supply of the Government expenses.

Wedding. The first anniversary of a wedding is the *paper* wedding, the gifts being paper articles; the fifth, *wooden*; the tenth, *tin*; the fifteenth, *glass*, twenty-fifth, *silver*; fiftieth, *golden*; seventy-fifth, *diamond*.

Well of St. Keyne. A well in Cornwall. The first of a married couple to taste its waters will "wear the breeches."

Westminster Abbey. A church in London where many of the illustrious dead of England are buried.

Wetherell, Elizabeth. Pseudonym of Miss Susan Warner, author of The Wide, Wide World.

Whig. The name of a political party now extinct.

Whistle. (To pay too dearly for the whistle.) Dr Franklin's story. Cost greater than benefit.

White Feather, To Show the. A display of cowardice.

White House. The Presidential mansion at Washington.

Whiteboys. A secret society in Ireland, 1789.

Wild Huntsman, The. A spectral huntsman in the Black Forest. German legend.

Windmills, To Fight with. To oppose imaginary objects. Don Quixote.

Windsor Castle. A royal residence near London.

Wise Men of the East, The. The three Magi guided by a star to Bethlehem.

Witch of Endor, The. The soothsayer who foretold the death of Saul.

Witch-Hazel. A forked twig used for finding witches; in use still for finding water.

Wooden Horse. A ruse at the siege of Troy.

Woolsack, To Sit on the. To be Lord Chancellor of England.

Wyoming Massacre. The Valley of Wyoming was ravaged by Indians in 1778.

Xanthos. The prophetic horse of Achilles.

Xantippe. The scolding wife of Socrates.

Yahoo. A ruffian. The Yahoos in Gulliver's Travels are brutes shaped like men.

Yankee. A name given to all Americans. In America itself the name is only used for natives of New England.

Yarmouth Bloater. A red herring.

Yellow Jack. The yellow fever.

Young America. The growing generation.

Young Chevalier. Charles Edward Stuart, the second pretender to the throne of Great Britain. (1720–88.)

Young Germany. Heinrich Heine and his followers.

Yosemite Valley. In California. Also a picture by Bierstadt.

Yule. Christmas.

Yule-log. A large log of wood burnt on the hearth at Christmas.

Zend-Avesta, The. Persian Scriptures written in the Zend language.

Zollverein. An association between German States for the maintenance of uniform tariff rates.

THE LORD'S PRAYER.

Latin.—Pater noster, qui es in cœlis, sanctificetur nomen tuum. Adveniat regnum tuum. Fiat voluntas tua, sicut in cœlo, et in terra. Panem nostrum quotidianum da nobis hodie. Et remitte nobis debita nostra, sicut et nos remittimus debitoribus nostris. Et ne nos inducas in tentationem, sed libera nos a malo. Tibi enim est regnum, et potentia, et gloria, in sempiternum. Amen.

Italian.—Padre nostro, che sei ne' cieli, sia santificato i' tuo nome. Il tuo regno venga. La tua volontà sia fatta in terra come in cielo. Dacci oggi il nostro pane cotidiano. E rimettici i nostri debiti, come noi ancora gli rimettiamo a' nostri debitori. E non indurci in tentazione, ma liberaci dal maligno. Perciochè tuo è il regno, e la potenza, e la gloria, in sempiterno. Amen.

French.—Notre Pere qui es aux cieux, ton nom soit sanctifie. Ton règne vienne; ta volonté soit faite sur la terre, comme au ciel. Donne-nous aujourd'hui notre pain quotidien. Pardonne-nous nos péchés, comme aussi nous pardonnons à ceux qui nous ont offensés. Et ne nous abandonne point à la tentation, mais délivre nous du malin. Car à toi appartient le regne, la puissance, et la gloire, à jamais. Amen.

German.—Unser Vater in dem Himmel, dein Name werde geheiliget. Dein Reich komme. Dein Wille geschehe auf Erden wie im Himmel. Unser tägliches Brod gieb uns heute. Und vergieb uns unsere Schulden, wie wir unsern Schuldigern vergaben. Und führe uns nicht in Versuchung, sondern erlese uns von dem Uebel. Denn dein ist das Reich, und die Kraft, und die Herrlichkeit, in Ewigkeit. Amen.

GREAT MEN'S WORKS.

Shelley wrote "Queen Mab" at 18.
Mohammed began the Koran at 35.
Keats wrote his "Endymion" at 22.
Alexandre Dumas wrote plays at 22.
Disraeli wrote "Vivian Grey" at 21.
Heine published his first songs at 23.
Seneca wrote "De Beneficiis" after 50.
Swift wrote the "Tale of a Tub" at 37.
Richardson published "Pamela" at 51.
Racine wrote the "Andromache" at 28.
Paley wrote the "Horæ Paulinæ" at 47.
Coleridge published "Christabel" at 44.
Pliny finished the "German War" at 31.
Luther wrote his ninety-five theses at 34.
Poe wrote "The Raven" in his 36th year.
Confucius began his religious works at 30.
Butler wrote "Hudibras" after he was 60.
Shakespeare wrote his first play at about 24.
Sterne published "Tristram Shandy" at 46.
Owen Meredith published "Lucile" at 29.
Boileau wrote his first satirical poems at 24.
Corneille wrote "Melite," his first drama, at 21.
Calvin published his "Psychopannychia" at 25.
Spenser published the "Faerie Queene" at 38.
It is said that Horace wrote his first odes at 23.
Sheridan wrote his "School for Scandal" at 26.
Machiavelli completed "The Prince" at 45.
Sir Thomas More finished his "Utopia" at 73.
Livy is said to have finished his "Annals" at 50.
Goldsmith finished "The Deserted Village" at 42.
Josephus published his "Wars of the Jews" at 56.
Lamartine's poems appeared when the poet was 30.
Perseus is thought to have written his satires at 45.
Thackeray was 36 when "Vanity Fair" appeared.
Lord Bacon wrote the "Novum Organum" at 41.
Tacitus finished the first part of his history at 50.
David is said to have written his first psalm at 18.
Homer is said to have composed the Iliad after 60.
Bryant was 19 when made famous by "Thanatopsis."
Solomon is said to have collected the Proverbs at 56.
Baxter wrote the "Saint's Everlasting Rest" at 34.
Dante finished the "Divina Commedia" at about 51.
Von Ranke finished his "History of the Popes" at 39.
George Eliot was 39 when "Adam Bede" was printed.
Fichte wrote the famous "Wissenschaftslehre" at 32.
Robert Browning wrote "The Ring and the Book" at 57.
Samuel Johnson published "London" when he was 29.
The Bucolics of Virgil were written between 43 and 47.
Thomas à Kempis wrote the "Imitation of Christ" at 34.
Joseph Addison's first essays appeared when he was 29.
John Bunyan finished the "Pilgrim's Progress" at 50.
"The Robbers," by Schiller, made the author famous at 23.
Hannah More wrote "The Search After Happiness" at 28.
Martial is said to have written epigrams before he was 20.
Voltaire's first tragedy came out when the author was 22.
Adam Smith published "The Wealth of Nations" at 55.

THE WORLD'S BEST BOOKS.

Comprising more than one thousand titles based upon bibliographies **of the best authorities.** These books are all available in English or English translation.

List of publishers' abbreviations used and their explanation: —

Armstrong — A. C. Armstrong & Sons, New York.
Appleton — D. Appleton & Co., New York.
Amsterdam — The New Amsterdam Book Co., New York.
Benziger — Benziger Brothers, New York.
Coates — Henry T. Coates & Co., Philadelphia.
Crowell — T. Y. Crowell & Co., New York.
Caldwell — H. M. Caldwell Co., New York.
Clarendon Press — The Oxford University Press, New York.
Cassell — Cassell & Co., New York.
Century — The Century Co., New York.
Dutton — E. P. Dutton & Co., New York.
Doubleday — Doubleday & McClure Co., New York.
Dodd, Mead — Dodd, Mead & Co., New York.
Dana Estes — Dana Estes & Co., Boston.
Ginn — Ginn & Co., Boston.
Harpers — Harper & Brothers, New York.
Houghton — Houghton, Mifflin & Co., Boston.
Henry Holt — Henry Holt & Co., New York.
Lippincott — J. B. Lippincott Co., Philadelphia.
Little, Brown — Little, Brown & Co., Boston.
Longmans — Longmans, Green & Co., New York.
Lee & Shepard — Lee & Shepard, Boston.
Merriam — G. & C. Merriam, Springfield, Mass.
McKay — David McKay, Philadelphia.
Macmillan — The Macmillan Co., New York.
Page — L. C. Page & Co., Boston.
Putnams — G. P. Putnam's Sons, New York.
Routledge — Geo. Routledge & Sons, New York.
Rand-McNally — Rand, McNally & Co., Chicago.
Scribners — Chas. Scribner's Sons, New York.
Stokes — Frederick A. Stokes Co., New York.
Williams — Williams & Northgate, London.

Reference Books and Dictionaries.

Encyclopedia Britannica. 24v. Little, Brown
Johnson's Encyclopedia. 8v. Appleton
Webster's International Dictionary. 2v. Merriam
Indexed Atlas of the World. 2v. Rand-McNally
The Century Atlas of the World. Century
Spiers & Surrenne's French-English Dictionary. Appleton
Lewis, Latin Dictionary. Harpers
Roget, Thesaurus of English Words and Phrases. Longmans
Adler, German-English Dictionary. Appleton
Lewis, Harper's Book of Facts. Harpers
Peck, Dictionary of Classical Antiquities. 2v. Harpers
Liddell & Scott, Greek Lexicon. (Intermediate.) Harpers
Haydn, Dictionary of Dates. Putnams
Pfyfe, Seven Thousand Words Often Mispronounced. Putnams
Soule, Dictionary of Synonyms. Little, Brown
Wells, Things not Generally Known. Appleton
Brewer, Dictionary of Phrase and Fable. 2v. Cassell
Skeat, Etymological Dictionary. Clarendon Press
Mulhall, Dictionary of Statistics. Routledge
Brande, Dictionary of Science, Literature, and Art. 3 v. Longmans
Addis and Arnold, Catholic Dictionary. Benziger
Cheyne, Dictionary of the Bible. 4v. Macmillan
Thomas, Dictionary of Biography. Lippincott
Johnson, Dictionary of Geography. Longmans
Freeman, Historical Geography of Europe. Longmans
Kiepert, Ancient Geography. Macmillan

Language and Literature.

Earle, Introduction to English Grammar. Putnams
Sweet, New English Grammar. Macmillan
Brooke, History of Early English Literature. Macmillan
Trench, On the Study of Words. Macmillan
Hodgson, Errors in the Use of English. Appleton
Hill, The Principles of Rhetoric. Harpers
Tyler, History of American Literature. 4v. Putnams
Mason, Humorous Masterpieces from American Literature. 3 v. Putnams
Bain, Higher English Grammar, Henry Holt
Lounsbury, History of the English Language. Henry Holt
Earle, English Philology. Henry Holt
Saintsbury, A History of 19th Century Literature. Macmillan
Taine, History of English Literature. 4v. Henry Holt
Warren, History of the Novel. Henry Holt
Genung, The Practical Elements of Rhetoric. Ginn
Morley, English Writers. 11v. Cassell
Müller, The Science of Language. 2v. Scribners
Jevons, A History of Greek Literature. Scribners
Cruttwell, History of Roman Literature. Scribners
Scherer, History of German Literature. 2v. Clarendon Press
Saintsbury, History of French Literature. Clarendon Press
Brunetière, History of French Literature. Crowell
Lane, Latin Grammar. Harpers
Goodwin, Greek Grammar. Ginn
Whitney, German Grammar. Henry Holt
Matzke, Primer of French Pronunciation. Henry Holt
Dupuy, Great Masters of Russian Literature. Crowell
Aston, History of Japanese Literature. Appleton
Frazer, A Literary History of India. Scribners
Quackenbos, History of Ancient Literature. Harpers
Whitney, French Grammar. Henry Holt
Thomas, Practical German Grammar. Henry Holt

Education.

Davidson, Rousseau and Education. Scribners
Davidson, Aristotle and Ancient Educational Ideals. Scribners
Williams, History of Modern Education. Bardeen
De Garmo, Herbart and the Herbartians. Scribners
Hinsdale, Horace Mann and the Common Schools. Scribners
Ascham, The Schoolmaster. Lee & Shepard
Fitch, Thomas and Matthew Arnold. Scribners
West, Alcuin and the Rise of the Christian Schools. Scribners
Compayre, Abelard, and the Origin of Universities. Scribners
Hughes, Loyola and the Jesuits. Scribners
Bowen, Froebel and Education by Self-Activity. Scribners
Pinloche, Pestalozzi, and Elementary Education. Scribners
Comenius, The Great Didactic. Macmillan
Davidson, the Education of the Greek People. Appleton
Payne, Rousseau's Emile. Appleton
Laurie, Survey of pre-Christian Education. Longmans
Hill, The True Order of Studies. Putnams
Quick, Education Reformers. Appleton

Antiquities, Art, and Music.

Poynter, Art Handbooks. 9v. Scribners
Van Dyke, A History of Painting. Longmans
Hamlin, A History of Architecture. Longmans
Marquand, A History of Sculpture. Longmans
Jameson, Sacred and Legendary Art. 2v. Longmans
Evans, Animal Symbolism in Ecclesiastical Architecture. Henry Holt
Lavignac, Music and Musicians. Henry Holt
Taine, Lectures on Art. 2v. Henry Holt
Van Dyke, Modern French Masters. Century
Ruskin, Stones of Venice. 3v. Dana Estes
Ruskin, Modern Painters. 5v. Dana Estes
Von Lutzow, Art Treasures of Italy. 2v. Dana Estes
Fromentin, Old Masters of Belgium and Holland. Houghton
Von Reber, History of Ancient Art. Harpers
Von Reber, History of Medieval Art. Harpers
Didron, Christian Iconography. 2v. Macmillan
Chesneau, English School of Painting. Cassell
Kugler, The Italian School. 2v. Little, Brown
Parry, The Art of Music. Appleton
Fergusson, History of Architecture. 2v. Dodd, Mead
Lübke, Outlines of the History of Art. 2v. Dodd, Mead
Vasari, Lives of Painters, Sculptors, and Architects. Scribners

Becker, Charicles. Longmans
Becker, Gallus. Longmans
De La Sizeranne, English Contemporary Art. Stokes
Tolstoi, What is Art? Crowell

History and Biography.

Abbott, The Romance of Spanish History. Harpers
Abbott, A History of Greece. 4v. Putnams
Abbott, Heroes of the Nations. 23v. Putnams
Allen, Christian History in its Great Periods. 3v. Little, Brown
Allen, Outline of Christian History. Little, Brown
Adams and Cunningham. The Swiss Confederation. Macmillan
Boulger, History of China. 3v. W. H. Allen
Brugsch-Bey, The True Story of the Exodus. Lee & Shepard
Beha-ed-Din, Life of Saladin. Amsterdam
Boswell, Life of Johnson. 2v. Crowell
Brooks, William Ellery Channing. Little, Brown
Buckle, History of Civilization. 3v. Longmans
Bourinot, The Story of Canada. Putnams
Borgeaud, Amendments of Constitutions. Macmillan
Boutmy, The English Constitution. Macmillan
Bax, German Society at Close of Middle Ages. Macmillan
Bonomi, Nineveh and its Palaces. Macmillan
Bryce, The Holy Roman Empire. Macmillan
Bryce, The American Commonwealth. 2v. Macmillan
Burgess, The Middle Period. Scribners
Burgess, The Civil War and Reconstruction. 2v. Scribners
Besant and Palmer, Jerusalem. Scribners
Baird, History of the Huguenots. 2v. Scribners
Bourget, Antigone, and Other Portraits. Scribners
Curtius, The History of Greece. 5v. Scribners
Crawford, Ave Roma Immortalis. Macmillan
Channing, The United States of America. Macmillan
Church, The Beginning of the Middle Ages. Macmillan
Creasy, Fifteen Decisive Battles of the World. Harpers
Church, Oliver Cromwell—A History. Putnams
Creighton, History of the Papacy. 6v. Longmans
Creasy, History of the Ottoman Turks. Henry Holt
Coppée, Conquest of Spain by the Arab Moors. 2v. Little, Brown
Church, Life of St. Anselm. Macmillan
Coulanges, The Ancient City. Lee & Shepard
Carlyle, The French Revolution. 3v. Coates
Craddock, The Story of Old Fort Loudon. Macmillan
Clement, The Eternal City, Rome. 2v. Dana Estes
Carlyle, History of Frederick the II. 6v. Harpers
De Coubertin, Evolution of France. Crowell
Dobson, Four French Women. Dodd, Mead
Duruy, History of France. 2v. Crowell
Davis, Egyptian Book of the Dead. Putnams
Duruy, History of the Middle Ages. Henry Holt
Duruy, History of Modern Times. Henry Holt
Dicey, Studies in Constitutional Law. Macmillan
Davis, The Confederate Government. 2v. Appleton
Eckstein, Woman Under Monasticism. Macmillan
Emerton, Introduction to the Middle Ages. Ginn
Emerton, Medieval Europe. Ginn
Eusebius, Ecclesiastical History. Lippincott
Froude, Cæsar. Scribners
Froude, History of England. 12 v. Scribners
Fisher, Outlines of Universal History. American Book Co.
Fiske-Irving, Washington and his Country. Ginn
Freeman, The Norman Conquest. 6v. Clarendon Press
Fiske, The Discovery of America. 2v. Houghton, Mifflin
Fiske, The American Revolution. 2v. Houghton, Mifflin
Fiske, The Critical Period of American History. Houghton, Mifflin
Fisher, History of the Reformation. Scribners
Fyffe, History of Modern Europe. 3v. Cassell
Freeman, General Sketch of History. Henry Holt
Franklin, Autobiography of. Putnams
Frazer, The Story of British Rule in India. Putnams
Fowler, The City State of Greeks and Romans. Macmillan
Freeman, Comparative Politics. Macmillan
Freeman, History of Government in Greece and Italy. Macmillan
Freeman, William the Conqueror. Macmillan
Fisher, the Colonial Era. Scribners
Fisher, The Reformation. Scribners
Fisher, The Beginnings of Christianity. Scribners
Froude, The Spanish Story of the Armada. Scribners

Froissart, Chronicles. Macmillan
Gibbon, History of Rome. 7v. Macmillan
Guizot, History of Civilization. 2v. Appleton
Grote, History of Greece. 12v. Harpers
Green, History of the English People. 4v. Harpers
Gindely, History of the Thirty Years' War. 2v. Putnams
Griesinger, The Jesuits. 2v. Allen
Gardiner, History of the Great Civil War. 4v. Longmans
Gardiner, The Puritan Revolution. Longmans
Geiger. History of Persia. Clarendon Press
Gardiner, The Thirty Years' War. Longmans
Gower, Last Days of Marie Antoinette. Little, Brown
Griffis, The Mikado's Empire. Harpers
Hale, Lights of Two Centuries. American Book Co.
Hume, History of England. 6v. Harpers
Hallam and May, Constitutional History of England. 4v. Armstrong
Hildreth. The History of the United States. 6v. Harpers
Heilprin, A Chronological Table of Universal History. Appleton
Hodgkin, Charles the Great. Macmillan
Hodgkin, Italy and Her Invaders. 6v. Clarendon Press
Hodgkin, The Dynasty of Theodosius. Clarendon Press
Holden, The Mogul Emperors of Hindustan. Scribners
Hallam, History of Medieval Europe. 2v. Armstrong
Higginson, Tales of the Enchanted Isles. Macmillan
Irving, Columbus, His Life and Voyages. Putnams
Irving, History of Mahomet. Little, Brown
Johnston, American Orations. Putnams
Johnson, Chief Lives of the Poets. Henry Holt
James, Life of Richard Cœur de Lion. 2v. Macmillan
Jenks, History of the Australasian Colonies. Macmillan
Josephus, Histories and Miscellanies. 4v. Armstrong
Keary, The Dawn of History. Scribners
Keary, Norway and the Norwegians. Scribners
Keary, Primitive Belief among the Indo-Europeans. Scribners
Kossuth, Memories of My Exile. Appleton
Kinglake, The Invasion of Crimea. 6v. Harpers
Kingsford, History of Canada. 3v. Amsterdam
Kitchen, History of France. 3v. Clarendon Press
Keary, The Vikings of Western Christendom. Putnams
Lodge, Life of Washington. Houghton, Mifflin
Leland, The Gypsies. Houghton, Mifflin
Leroy-Beaulieu, The Empire Tsars and Russians. 3v. Putnams
Lecky, History of European Morals, 2v. Appleton
Lathrop, Spanish Vistas. Harpers
Lebon, The Story of Modern France. Putnams
Lancelotts, Queens of England and their Times. 2v. Appleton
Lyall, Warren Hastings. Macmillan
Lightfoot, Historical Essays. Macmillan
Lang, Helen of Troy. Scribners
Lenormont, The Beginnings of History. Scribners
Lodge, The Story of the Revolution. 2v. Scribners
Lanfrey, History of Napoleon. 4v. Macmillan
Mommsen, The History of Rome, 5v. Scribners
Michelet, The Life of Luther. Macmillan
Machiavelli, History of Florence. Macmillan
Mahaffy, Social Life in Greece. Macmillan
Moeller, History of the Christian Church. 2v. Macmillan
Montesquieu, Spirit of Laws. 2v. Macmillan
Morley, Life of Walpole. Macmillan
McMaster, History of the People of the United States. 6v. Appleton
Montesquieu, The Grandeur and Decadence of Rome. Appleton
Mueller, Political History of Recent Times. Harpers
Macaulay, History of England. 5v. Harpers
McCarthy, A History of Our Own Times. 3v. Harpers
Motley, History of the United Netherlands. 4v. Harpers
Motley, The Rise of the Dutch Republic. 3v. Harpers
Miller, The Story of the Balkan States. Putnams
Merivale, History of the Romans Under the Empire. 8v. Longmans
Muir, Life of Mohammed. Scribners
Mackenzie, The Nineteenth Century. Scribners
Michaud, History of the Crusades. 3v. Routledge
Menzel, History of Germany. 3v. Macmillan
Milman. The History of Latin Christianity. 4v. Armstrong
Maitland, The Dark Ages. Benziger
Napier, History of the Peninsular War. 3v. Routledge
Nadaillac, Prehistoric America. Putnams

Newman, The Arians of the 4th Century. Longmans
Nicolini, History of the Jesuits. Macmillan
Parton, Princes, Authors, and Statesmen of Our Time. Crowell
Prescott, Ferdinand and Isabella. 3v. McKay
Prescott, The Reign of Charles the V. 3v. Dana Estes
Prescott, The Reign of Philip the II. 3v. Dana Estes
Parkman, LaSalle and the Discovery of the Great West. Little, Brown
Parkman, The Old Regime in Canada. Little, Brown
Parkman, Montcalm and Wolfe. 2v. Little, Brown
Prescott, The Conquest of Mexico. 3v. McKay
Prescott, The Conquest of Peru. 2v. McKay
Probyn, Land Tenures in Various Countries. Cassell
Putnam, Tabular Views of Universal History. Putnams
Parkman, The Jesuits in North America. Little, Brown
Powell, Nullification and Secession in the U. S. Putnams
Plutarch, Lives (Dryden). 3v. Coates
Renan, History of the People of Israel. 5v. Little, Brown
Ranke, History of the Popes. 3v. Macmillan
Rawlinson, Ancient Monarchies. 5v. Dodd, Mead
Ranke, Universal History. Amsterdam
Rustor, The War for the Rhine Frontier. 3v. Blackwood
Rambaud, History of Russia. 2v. Dana Estes
Rawlinson, History of Phœnicia. Longmans
Ratzel, The History of Mankind. 3v. Macmillan
Roscoe, Life of Lorenzo de Medici. Macmillan
Rawlinson, Herodotus (Ed. by Grant.) 2v. Scribners
Rawlinson, The Origin of Nations. Scribners
Rawlinson, Egypt and Babylon. Scribners
Sabatier, Life of St. Francis of Assisi. Scribners
Stephens, History of the French Revolution. 3v. Scribners
Symonds, Short History of the Renaissance. Scribners
Symonds, Sketches and Studies in Italy and Greece. 3v. Scribners
Stockton, Buccaneers and Pirates of our Coasts. Macmillan
Suetonius, Lives of the Cæsars. Macmillan
Southey, Life of Nelson. Cassell
Schlegel, Lectures on the Philosophy of History. Macmillan
Stevens, Sources of the Constitution of the U. S. Macmillan
Southey, Life of Wesley. Macmillan
Smith, Cases from Roman Law. Macmillan
Schiller, The Revolt of the Netherlands. Harpers
Sismondi, A History of the Italian Republics. Harpers
Stepniak, Russian Peasantry. Harpers
Sainte-Beuve, Portraits of Celebrated Women, Little, Brown
Seebohm, English Village Community. Longmans
Seeley, The Expansion of England. Macmillan
Seeley, Life and Times of Stein. 3v. Macmillan
Samuelson, History of Bulgaria. Amsterdam
Stephens, History of Portugal. Putnams
Sloane, Life of Napoleon. 4v. Century Co.
Schoolcraft, Narrative of Exploration. Lippincott
Schoolcraft, the Myth of Hiawatha. Lippincott
Spence, Cloister Life in the Days of Cœur de Lion. Lippincott
Sybel, Founding of the German Empire, by William I. 7v. Crowell
Traill, History of Social Life in England. 6v. Putnams
Taine, The French Revolution. 3v. Henry Holt
Taine, The Ancient Regime. Henry Holt
Thiers, French Revolution. 4v. Appleton
Tacitus, The Annals and History. 2v. Macmillan
Thierry, History of the Norman Conquest. 2v. Macmillan
Thucydides, Athenian History (tr. Jowett). 2v. Scribners
Voltaire, Age of Louis the XIV. Scribners
Voltaire, History of Charles the XII. Houghton, Mifflin
Vambery, History of Hungary. Scribners
Wheeler, History of India. 4v. Amsterdam
Winsor, Narrative and Critical History of America. 8v. Houghton
Warner, Life of Capt. John Smith. Henry Holt
Wellhausen, Sketch of the History of Israel and Judah. Macmillan
Xenophon, Historical Works (tr. Watson). 3v. Macmillan

Religion, Theology and Mythology.

Arnold, Literature and Dogma. Scribners
Arnold, God and the Bible. Scribners
Addis and Arnold, Catholic Dictionary. Benziger
Alger, The Doctrine of a Future Life. Little, Brown
Athanasius, Against the Heathen. Scribners
Allen, Christian Institutions. Scribners
Brooks, Influence of Jesus. Dutton
Beecher, Evolution and Religion. Fords, Howard
Bulfinch, The Age of Fable. Lee and Shepard
Bulfinch, The Age of Chivalry. Lee and Shepard
Bulfinch, Legends of Charlemagne. Lee and Shepard
Bushnell, Vicarious Sacrifice. Scribners
Brooks, Essays and Addresses. Dutton
Butler, Analogy of Religion. Harpers
Brinton, Religions of Primitive Peoples. Putnams
Bushnell, Nature and the Supernatural. Scribners
Briggs, Introduction to the Study of Scripture. Scribners
Briggs, The Bible, the Church, and the Reason. Scribners
Bruce, Apologetics. Scribners
Brooke, Theology of the English Poets. Amsterdam
Collyer, Things New and Old. Dutton
Channing, Complete Works. 4v. Williams & Northgate
Curtin, Creation Myths of Primitive America. Little, Brown
Conway, The Sacred Anthology. Henry Holt
Chadwick, The Faith of Reason. Little, Brown
Chatterji, The Bhagavad-Gita. Houghton, Mifflin
Cuckson, Faith and Fellowship. Houghton, Mifflin
Cone, Gospel Criticisms and Historical Christianity. Putnams
Cone, The Gospel and Its Earliest Interpretations. Putnams
Clodd, The Childhood of Religions. Appleton
Calvin, Institutes of Christian Religion. 2v. Scribners
Cone, Life of St. Paul. Macmillan
Caird, Evolution of Religion. 2v. Macmillan
Cooke, Religion and Chemistry. Scribners
Cruttwell, Literary History of Early Christianity. 2v. Scribners
Dorner, System of Christian Ethics. Scribners
Dorner, System of Christian Doctrine. 4v. Scribners
Drummond, Philo Judaeus. 2v. Williams & Northgate
D'Alviella, Origin and Growth of the Conception of God. Scribners
Drummond, Via, Veritas, Vita. Scribners
Davids, Origin and Growth of Religion. Scribners
Driver, Literature of the Old Testament. Scribners
Elmendors, Elements of Moral Theology. (Aquinas.) Pott
Feuerbach, Essence of Christianity. Amsterdam
Figuier, The To-morrow of Death. Little, Brown
Figuier, Joys Beyond the Threshold. Little, Brown
Frothingham, The Religion of Humanity. Putnams
Fenelon, Spiritual Letters to Men and Women. 2v. Longmans
Freemantle, The World as the Subject of Redemption. Longmans
Fouard, St. Peter and the First Years of Christianity. Longmans
Farrar, Critical History of Free Thought. Appleton
Farrar, Life and Teachings of Christ. Doubleday & McClure
Fraser, Lyric Poetry from the Bible. 2v. Macmillan
Fiske, The Myths of Israel. Macmillan
Flint, Theism. Scribners
Guyau, The Non-Religion of the Future. Henry Holt
Gratry, Guide to the Knowledge of God. Little, Brown
Gordon, the Witness to Immortality. Houghton, Mifflin
Gould, The Meaning and the Method of Life. Putnams
Gore, Roman Catholic Claims. Longmans
Goulburn, Thoughts on Personal Religion. Appleton
Goulburn, Pursuit of Holiness. Appleton
Gladstone, The Impregnable Rock of Scripture. Scribners
Hatch, Greek Influence Upon the Christian Church. Scribners
Harris, Self Revelation of God. Scribners
Harnack, History of Dogma. 3v. Little, Brown
Hedge, Ways of the Spirit. Little, Brown
Hatch, Organization of the Early Christian Churches. Longmans
Hoole, The Apostolic Fathers. Longmans
Hessey, Sunday. Its Origin and History. Cassell
Hopkins, the Law of Love. Scribners
Julian, Dictionary of Hymnology. Scribners
King, Christianity and Humanity. Houghton, Mifflin
Kempis, Of the Imitation of Christ. Longmans
Knight, Aspects of Theism. Macmillan
Kuenen, National and Universal Religion. Scribners
Liddon, The Divinity of Jesus Christ. Rivington

Le Gallienne, The Religion of a Literary Man. Putnams
Lang, Modern Mythology. Longmans
Luckock, The History of Marriage. Longmans
Lang, The Making of Religion. Longmans
Legge, The Religions of China. Scribners
Manning, Sermons on Ecclesiastical Subjects. Benziger
Manning, Sin and Its Consequences. Benziger
Mansel, Limits of Religious Thought. Scribners
McCosh, Method of Divine Government. Macmillan
Müller, The Christian Doctrine of Sin. Scribners
Moxom, From Jerusalem to Nicæa. Little, Brown
Moxom, The Religion of Hope. Little, Brown
Mulford, The Republic of God. Houghton, Mifflin
Mill, Nature, The Utility of Religion, and Theism. Longmans
Maurice, The Conscience. Macmillan
Mills, God in His World. Harpers
McGiffert, The Apostolic Age. Scribners
Murray, Manual of Mythology. Scribners
Mackail, The Eversley Bible. 8v. Macmillan
Maurice, The Religions of the World. Macmillan
Müller, Origin and Growth of Religion. Scribners
Montefiore, Origin and Growth of Religion. Scribners
Noble Lectures (Harvard University). Houghton, Mifflin
Newman, A Grammar of Assent. Longmans
Newman, The Development of Christian Doctrine. Longmans
Neander, Life of Jesus in its Historical Connection. Macmillan
Oort and Hooykaas, The Bible for Learners. 3v. Little, Brown
Picard, Christianity or Agnosticism. Benziger
Parker, West Roxbury Sermons. Little, Brown
Proctor, History of the Book of Common Prayer. Macmillan
Paley, Evidences of Christianity. Scribners
Pfleiderer, Development of Theology. Macmillan
Philo. Works. 4v. Macmillan
Prideaux, Old and New Testament Connected. Harpers
Paine, The Age of Reason. Putnams
Percival, The Decrees and Canons of the Seven Councils. Scribners
Pfleiderer, Influences of Paul on Christianity. Scribners
Rickaby, Aquinas Ethicus. 2v. Benziger
Reuss, History of the New Testament Scripture. 2v. Houghton
Reville, The Devil, His Origin, Greatness and Decadence. Williams
Renan, The Apostles. Little, Brown
Renan, Anti-Christ. Little, Brown
Renan, Life of Jesus. Little, Brown
Ramsay, Regeneration. Putnams
Royce, The Conception of God. Macmillan
Ryle, The Canon of the Old Testament. Macmillan
Robertson, The Human Race and Other Sermons. Harpers
Ramsay, St. Paul, the Traveler and the Roman Citizen. Putnams
Renouf, Origin and Growth of Religion. Scribners
Renan, Hibbert Lectures, 1880. Scribners
Reville, Religions of Mexico and Peru. Scribners
Steenstra, The Being of God as Unity and Trinity. Houghton
Schaff, Creeds of Christendom. 3v. Harpers
Shedd, The Confessions of St. Augustine. Draper
Sanday, Inspiration. Longmans
Soderina, Socialism and Catholicism. Longmans
Smith, The Old Testament in the Jewish Church. Appleton
Smith, The Prophets of Israel. Harpers
Schaff, Revised Greek-English New Testament. Harpers
Stevens, Theology of the New Testament. Scribners
St. Augustine, Works. vols. 1 and 2. Scribners
Schurman, Belief in God. Scribners
Smith, The Bible and Islam. Scribners
Smyth, Dorner on the Future State. Scribners
Schleiermacher, On Religion. Scribners
Schopenhauer, Religion: a Dialogue. Scribners
Smith, Kinship and Marriage in Early Arabia. Macmillan
Sayce, Origin and Growth of Religion. Scribners
Smyth, Christian Ethics. Scribners
Toy, Judaism and Christianity. Little, Brown
Tyler, Bases of Religious Belief. Putnams
Van Dyke, The Reality of Religion. Scribners
Van Dyke, The Gospel for an Age of Doubt. Macmillan
Wilhelm and Scannell, Manual of Catholic Theology. 2v. Benziger
Wiseman, Doctrines of the Catholic Church. Benziger
Weizsacker, The Apostolic Age. 2v. Putnams
Wescott, History of the Canon of the New Testament. Macmillan
Wace, Christianity and Agnosticism. Appleton

Fiction and Description.

Auerbach, On the Heights. Caldwell
Auerbach, The Villa on the Rhine. 2v. Henry Holt
Anderson, The Improvisatore. Houghton, Mifflin
Blackmore, Lorna Doone. Crowell
Barrie, The Little Minister. Coates
Bulwer-Lytton, Last Days of Pompeii. Caldwell
Bulwer-Lytton, Last of the Barons. Caldwell
Bulwer-Lytton, Rienza. Caldwell
Bulwer-Lytton, Eugene Aram. Caldwell
Bulwer-Lytton, My Novel. Dana Estes
Bunyan, Pilgrim's Progress. Century
Boccaccio, The Decameron. 4v. Lippincott
Balzac, Père Goriot. Little, Brown
Balzac, Cæsar Birotteau. Little, Brown
Balzac, Cousin Bette. Little, Brown
Barham, Ingoldsby Legends. 2v. Coates
Bellamy, Looking Backward. Houghton, Mifflin
Bjornson, Novels (Anderson). 3v. Houghton, Mifflin
Bazin, The Italians of To-day. Henry Holt
Bremer, The Home; or Life in Sweden. Putnams
Beaconsfield, Endymion. Longmans
Beaconsfield, Lothair. Longmans
Beaconsfield, Vivian Grey. Longmans
Beaconsfield, Coningsby. Longmans
Balzac, Eugenie Grandt. Macmillan
Balzac, A Gondreville Mystery. Macmillan
Balzac, Ursule Mirouet. Macmillan
Balzac, The Country Doctor. Macmillan
Balzac, The Quest of the Absolute. Macmillan
Beckford, Vathek: An Eastern Romance. Scribners
Bronté, Jane Eyre. Crowell
Bourdillon, Aucassin and Nicolette. Macmillan
Burnaby, Khiva. Cassell
Cooper, Deerslayer. Rand, McNally
Cooper, Last of the Mohicans. Rand, McNally
Cooper, Pathfinder. Rand, McNally
Cooper, Pioneers. Rand, McNally
Cooper, The Prairie. Rand, McNally
Cooper, The Spy. Coates
Corelli, Thelma. Rand, McNally
Cervantes, Don Quixote. 2v. Crowell
Collins, The Woman in White. Harpers
Collins, The Moonstone. Harpers
Craddock, The Prophet of the Great Smoky Mountains. Houghton
Crane, Italian Popular Tales. Houghton
Caird, A Romance of the Moors. Henry Holt
Cox, Popular Romances of the Middle Ages. Henry Holt
Celiere, Startling Exploits of Dr. Quies. Harpers
Clifford, Mrs. Keith's Crime. Harpers
Coppée, Ten Tales. Harpers
Curtis, Prue and I. Harpers
Cable, Old Creole Days. Scribners
Crane, The Red Badge of Courage. Appleton
De Staël, Corinne. Crowell
Dickens, David Copperfield. Rand, McNally
Dickens, Tale of Two Cities. Rand, McNally
Dickens, Pickwick Papers. Rand, McNally
Dickens, Old Curiosity Shop. Coates
Dumas, Three Musketeers. Caldwell
Dumas, Twenty Years After. Caldwell
Dumas, Count of Monte Cristo. 2v. Caldwell
Doyle, Micah Clarke. Rand, McNally
Doyle, The White Company. Crowell
De Foe, Robinson Crusoe. Rand, McNally
Dumas, Vicomte De Bragelonne. Caldwell
Dumas, Louise de la Valliere. Caldwell
Dumas, The Man with the Iron Mask. Caldwell
Deland, John Ward, Preacher. Houghton, Mifflin
Daudet, The Apostate. Appleton
Daudet, Port Tarascon. Harpers
De Kay, The Vision of Nimrod. Appleton
De Kay, The Vision of Esther. Appleton
Doyle, The Refugees. Harpers
Du Maurier, Peter Ibbetson. Harpers
Du Maurier, Trilby. Harpers
Didier, Would Any Man? Williams & Wilkins
Daudet, Sappho; Parisian Manners. Macmillan
Daudet, Tartarin on the Alps. Macmillan
Daudet, The Nabob. 2v. Little, Brown
De Berville, The Chevalier. Scribners
Ebers, An Egyptian Princess. Caldwell

Ebers, Uarda. Caldwell
Eckstein, A Monk of the Aventine. Little, Brown
Eliot, Adam Bede. Rand, McNally
Eliot, Middlemarch. Rand, McNally
Eliot, Mill on the Floss. Rand, McNally
Eliot, Romola. Rand, McNally
Fothergill, The First Violin. Caldwell
Fielding, Tom Jones. Caldwell
Fawcett, The House at Highbridge. Houghton, Mifflin
Fawcett, Tinkling Cymbals. Houghton, Mifflin
Fenelon, Adventures of Telemachus. Houghton, Mifflin
Franzos, For the Right. Harpers
Fouque, Undine. Macmillan
Gaskell, Cranford. Putnams
Grün, The Last Night. Houghton, Mifflin
Gautier, A Winter in Russia. Henry Holt
Gautier, Constantinople. Henry Holt
Gautier, Chanson de Roland. Henry Holt
Green, That Affair Next Door. Putnams
Galdos, Dona Perfecta : a Story. Harpers
Goethe, Select Works. Vols. 5, 7, 8, 9. Macmillan
Goldsmith, The Vicar of Wakefield. Cassell
Hugo, Les Misérables. 2v. Caldwell
Hugo, Toilers of the Sea. Crowell
Hugo, Notre Dame de Paris. Crowell
Hardy, Far from the Madding Crowd. Rand, McNally
Hobbes, The School for Saints. Stokes
Hawthorne, House of the Seven Gables. Rand, McNally
Hawthorne, The Scarlet Letter. Rand, McNally
Halévy, Abbe Constantin. Rand, McNally
Holmes, Elsie Venner. Houghton, Mifflin
Howells, A Foregone Conclusion. Houghton, Mifflin
Howells, The Rise of Silas Lapham. Houghton, Mifflin
Howells, A Modern Instance. Houghton, Mifflin
Haggard, King Solomon's Mines. Cassell
Haggard, Cleopatra. Longmans
Haggard, She. Longmans
Heyse, The Children of the World. Henry Holt
Hope, The Prisoner of Zenda. Henry Holt
Hope, Rupert of Hentzau. Henry Holt
Howells, A Hazard of New Fortunes. 2v. Harpers
Howells, The Quality of Mercy. Harpers
Harland, Some Colonial Homesteads. Putnams
Harraden, Ships that Pass in the Night. Putnams
Hardy, Tess of the D'Urbervilles. Harpers
Hardy, The Woodlanders. Harpers
Hauff, The Caravan, the Sheik, etc. Macmillan
Heine, Travel Pictures (Storr). Macmillan
Hale, The Man Without a Country. Little, Brown
Harris, Evening Tales. Scribners
Holland, The Bay Path. Scribners
Holland, Arthur Bonnicastle. Scribners
Hughes, Tom Brown at Oxford. Rand, McNally
Hughes, Tom Brown's School Days. Rand, McNally
Irving, Alhambra. Rand, McNally
Irving, The Sketch Book. Rand, McNally
Irving, Tales of a Traveler. Crowell
Irving, Old Christmas. Macmillan
Ingraham, Prince of the House of David. Rand, McNally
James, The Portrait of a Lady. Houghton, Mifflin
James, Roderick Hudson. Houghton, Mifflin
Jackson, Ramona. Little, Brown
James, Daisy Miller. Harpers
Jokai, The Green Book. Harpers
Jokai, Eyes Like the Sea. Putnams
James, The Bostonians. Macmillan
Jokai, The Nameless Castle. Doubleday & McClure
Jacobs, History of Reynard the Fox. Macmillan
Kompert, Christian and Leah. Macmillan
Kipling, Light that Failed. Rand, McNally
Kipling, Soldiers Three. Rand, McNally
Kipling, Plain Tales from the Hills. Rand, McNally
Kingsley, Hypatia. Rand, McNally
Kingsley, Westward, Ho! Rand, McNally
King, The White Hills. Dana Estes
Kipling, The Day's Work. Doubleday & McClure
Kinglake, Eothen. Scribners
Le Sage, Gil Blas. Caldwell
Longfellow, Complete Prose Works. 2v. Houghton, Mifflin
Lyall, Hope the Hermit. Longmans
Lyall, Doreen ; the Story of a Singer. Longmans
La Farge, An Artist's Letters from Japan. Century
Lagerlof, The Story of Gösta Berling. Little, Brown
Lever, Charles O'Malley. Rand, McNally
La Quintana, The Cid Campeador. Longmans
Laboulaye, Abdallah. Scribners
Lang, Arabian Nights. Longmans

Meredith, The Egoist. Scribners
Maclaren, Beside the Bonnie Briar Bush. Dodd, Mead
Merimee, Carmen. Little, Brown
Meredith, Diana of the Crossways. Rand, McNally
Muloch, John Halifax, Gentleman. Rand, McNally
Muhlbach, Frederick the Great and his Court. Caldwell
Mitchell, Hugh Wynne, Free Quaker. Century
Mitchell, The Adventures of François. Century
Morris, The Story of the Glittering Plain. Little, Brown
Muloch, A Life for a Life. Harpers
Maartens, God's Fool. Appleton
Morier, Adventures of Hajji Baba of Ispahan. Macmillan
Manzoni, The Betrothed. Macmillan
Marco Polo, Travels. (Marsten.) Macmillan
Maundeville, The Marvellous Adventures of. Macmillan
Morell, Tales of the Genii. Macmillan
Mitford, Our Village. Macmillan
Mitchell, Reveries of a Bachelor. Scribners
Mitchell, Dream Life. Scribners
Morris, Old French Romances. Scribners
Oliphant, The Makers of Florence. Caldwell
Oliphant, The Makers of Venice. Caldwell
Pickering, Margot. Putnams
Porter, Scottish Chiefs. Appleton
Peacock, Maid Marion, and Crochet Castle. Macmillan
Peronne, The Veil of Liberty. Macmillan
Page, In Old Virginia. Scribners
Page, Red Rock. Scribners
Richardson, Clarissa Harlowe. Routledge
Rousseau, Confessions. 4v. Lippincott
Reade, It's Never too Late to Mend. Rand, McNally
Reade, The Cloister and the Hearth. Crowell
Roche, The Children of the Abbey. Rand, McNally
Rostand, Cyrano de Bergerac. Cassell
Rousselet, A Tale of the Indian Mutiny. Scribners
Reade, Put Yourself in his Place. Scribners
Sand, François the Waif. Little, Brown
Sand, The Devil's Pool. Little, Brown
Sand, Fadette. Little, Brown
Sand, The Master Mosaic Workers. Little, Brown
Sand, Consuelo. 2v. Caldwell
Sue, Mysteries of Paris. 2v. Caldwell
Sue, The Wandering Jew. 2v. Caldwell
Stowe, Uncle Tom's Cabin. Crowell
Scott, The Antiquary. Rand, McNally
Scott, Ivanhoe. Rand, McNally
Scott, Kenilworth. Rand, McNally
Scott, Heart of Midlothian. Rand, McNally
Scott, Fair Maid of Perth. Rand, McNally
Scott, Poems. Rand, McNally
Stevenson, Kidnapped. Rand, McNally
Stevenson, Master of Ballantrae. Rand, McNally
Stevenson, Treasure Island. Rand, McNally
Sand, Mauprat. Little, Brown
Sand, Nanon. Little, Brown
Schreiner, The Story of an African Farm. Little, Brown
Schreiner, Dreams. Little, Brown
Sterne, The Sentimental Journey. Longmans
Sterne, Tristram Shandy. Longmans
Sienkiewicz, Quo Vadis. Little, Brown
Sienkiewicz, With Fire and Sword. Little, Brown
Sienkiewicz, The Deluge. 2v Little, Brown
Santine, Picciola. Appleton
Saint-Pierre, Paul and Virginia. Appleton
Souvestre, An Attic Philosopher in Paris. Appleton
Strachey, Morte de Arthur. Macmillan
Smith, Greek Romances. Macmillan
Shorthouse, John Inglesant. Macmillan
Stepniak, King Stork and King Log. 2v. Scribners
Steel, Tales of the Punjab. Macmillan
Sheridan, The School for Scandal and the Rivals. Macmillan
Saintsbury, Marmontel's Moral Tales. Macmillan
Swan, Gesta Romanorum. Macmillan
Stevenson, The Black Arrow. Scribners
Stevenson, Dr. Jekyll and Mr. Hyde. Scribners
Stevenson, St. Ives. Scribners
Stimson, King Noanett. Scribners
Stimson, Guerndale. Scribners
Stockton, Rudder Grange. Scribners
Trollope, The Warden. Dodd, Mead
Trollope, Barchester Towers. 2v. Dodd, Mead
Trollope, Framley Parsonage. 2v. Dodd, Mead
Tolstoi, Anna Karenina. Crowell
Tolstoi, War and Peace. 2v. Crowell
Theuriet, Rustic Life in France. Crowell
Thackeray, Vanity Fair. Caldwell

Thackeray, Henry Esmond. Caldwell
Thackeray, The Newcomes. Caldwell
Thackeray, The Virginians. 2v. Dana Estes
Thackeray, Pendennis. Putnams
Turgenev, Rudin. Macmillan
Tugenev, Dream Tales. Macmillan
Valdes, The Marquis of Penalto. Crowell
Voltaire, Zadig et Micromegas. Routledge
Voltaire, Tales. Macmillan
Verne, Michael Strogoff. Scribners
Ware, Zenobia. Caldwell
Ware, Aurelian. Dana Estes
Weyman, The Castle Inn. Longmans
Weyman, Under the Red Robe. Longmans
Wallace, Ben Hur. Harpers
Ward, Robert Elsmere. Macmillan
Ward, Helbeck of Bannisdale. 2v. Macmillan
Zangwill, Dreamers of the Ghetto. Harpers
Zola, Paris. 2v. Macmillan
Zangwill, Children of the Ghetto. Macmillan
Zola, Rome. 2v. Macmillan

Classics, Poetry, and Drama.

Aldrich, Poetical Works. 2v. Houghton, Mifflin
Arnold, Poems. Crowell
Æschylus, Dramas (tr. Swanwick). Macmillan
Æschylus, Tragedies (tr. Buckley). Macmillan
Alger, The Poetry of the Orient. Little, Brown
Arnold, Collected Poems. 2v. Little, Brown
Ariosto, Orlando Furioso. 2v. Macmillan
Alfieri, Tragedies. 2v. Macmillan
Aristophanes, Comedies. Routledge
Aristotle, The Poetics. Macmillan
Arnold, The Light of Asia. Scribners
Bulwer-Lytton, Richelieu: a Drama. Dodd, Mead
Bryant, Complete Poetical Works. Stokes
Browning, Poetical and Dramatic Works. 6v. Houghton, Mifflin
Bryant, Homer's Iliad. Houghton, Mifflin
Bryant, Homer's Odyssey. Houghton, Mifflin
Browning, Mrs., Poetical Works. Crowell
Burns, Complete Works. Macmillan
Beaumont and Fletcher, Best Plays. 2v. Scribners
Cicero, the Academics (tr. Reid). Macmillan
Cicero, Nature of the Gods. Macmillan
Cicero, Officers, Old Age, etc. Macmillan
Cicero, Orations. 4v. Macmillan
Chaucer, Canterbury Tales (Pollard). 2v. Macmillan
Camoens, Luciad; or The Discovery of India. Macmillan
Coleridge, Poetical Works. Macmillan
Cowper, Poetical Works. Macmillan
Dryden, Poems. Crowell
Dryden, Works in Verse and Prose. 2v. Harpers
Doré, Dante's Inferno. Cassell
Doré, Dante's Purgatory and Paradise. Cassell
Doré, Milton's Paradise Lost. Cassell
De Vere, Select Poems. Macmillan
Dutt, Ancient Ballads and Legends of Hindustan. Scribners
Demosthenes, Orations. 5v. Macmillan
Firdusi, The Epic of Kings. Henry Holt
Goldsmith, Comedies. Stokes
Goethe, Faust (tr. Taylor). Houghton, Mifflin
Goldsmith and Gray, Poems. Houghton, Mifflin
Gladstone, Odes of Horace. Scribners
Holmes, Complete Poetical Works. Houghton, Mifflin
Homer, Iliad and Odyssey (tr. Pope). 2v. Crowell
Howells, Modern Italian Poets. Harpers
Hesiod, Callimachus, Theognis. Macmillan
Hugo, Dramatic Works. Macmillan
Hapgood, Epic Songs of Russia. Scribners
Holland, Bitter-Sweet. Scribners
Heine, Poems and Ballads. Scribners
Hood, Works in Prose and Verse. Scribners
Ibsen, Prose Dramas. vols. 1, 4, and 6. Scribners
Jackson, Complete Poems. Little, Brown
Juvenal, Thirteen Satires (Mayor). 2v. Macmillan
Keats, Poetical Works. Crowell
Khayyam, Rubaiyat. Page
Longfellow, Complete Poetical Works. Houghton
Longfellow, The Divina Commedia of Dante. 3v. Houghton.
Lowell, Poetical Works. Houghton
Lessing, Nathan the Wise. Henry Holt
Lessing, Dramatic Works. 3v. Macmillan
Lucan, The Pharsalia (Conway). Macmillan
Lucian, Dialogues of the Gods. Macmillan
Lanier, Poems. Scribners
Lettsom, The Fall of the Niebelungs. Scribners
Macdonald, Poems. Dutton
Milton, Complete Poetical Works. 2v. Crowell
Morris, Defence of Guenevere. Little, Brown
Morris, The Æneids of Virgil. Little, Brown
Morris, The Story of Sigurd the Volsung. Little, Brown
Molière, Dramatic Works. 3v. Macmillan
Milton, Areopagitica. Clarendon Press
Moore, Prose and Verse (Shepard). Scribners
Marlowe, Dramatic Works. Scribners
Norton, Dante's New Life. Houghton
Oman, The Great Indian Epics. Macmillan
Ossian, Poems (MacPherson). Macmillan
Ovid, Works. 3v. Macmillan
Poe, Complete Works. 6v. Armstrong
Pope, Complete Poetical Works. 2v. Crowell
Pliny, Letters (Melmoth). Macmillan
Petrarch, Sonnets, Triumphs, and Other Poems. Macmillan
Pindar, Works. Macmillan
Quintilian, Institutes of Oratory. 2v. Macmillan
Riley, Poetical and Dramatic Works. 4v. Scribners
Rosetti, Dante and His Circle. Little, Brown
Racine, Dramatic Works. 2v. Macmillan
Shakespeare, Complete Works. Houghton
Shelley, Complete Poetical Works. 2v. Crowell
Stedman, Victorian Poets. Scribners
Swinburne, Poems. Crowell
Sheridan, The Rivals, and School for Scandal. Macmillan
Schiller, Dramatic Works and Poems. 4v. Macmillan
Sophocles, Œdipus Tyrannus (Jebb). Macmillan
Sophocles, Antigone (Jebb). Macmillan
Sophocles, Electra (Jebb). Macmillan
Sallust, The Conspiracy of Catiline (Pollard). Macmillan
Sidney, Arcadia. Scribners
Tennyson, Complete Poetical Works. 2v. Crowell
Taylor, Poetical Works. Houghton
Tasso, Poetical Works. Macmillan
Tegner, Frithiof's Saga. Henry Holt
Thomson, The Seasons, and Castle of Indolence. Clarendon Press
Wordsworth, Complete Poetical Works. 2v. Crowell
Whittier, Poetical Works. Houghton

Essays and Criticisms.

Arnold, Essays and Criticism. Macmillan
Adler, Creed and Deed. Putnams
Bacon, Advancement of Learning. Clarendon Press
Bacon, The Essays. Longmans
Bacon, Novum Organum. Clarendon Press
Blackie, Four Phases of Morals. Scribners
Blackie, Natural History of Atheism. Scribners
Browne, Religio Medici. Scribners
Burton, Anatomy of Melancholy. Scribners
Burke, Works. Vol. 1. Macmillan
Choate, Addresses and Orations. Little, Brown
Channing, Self Culture. Crowell
Carlyle, Sartor Resartus. Stokes
Carlyle, Heroes and Hero Worship. Stokes
Carlyle, Past and Present. Routledge
Carlyle, Critical and Miscellaneous Essays. 2v. Houghton
Clarke, Self Culture. Houghton
Chesterfield, Worldly Wisdom (Hill). Clarendon Press
Coleridge, Age to Reflection. Macmillan
Coleridge, Table Talk. Macmillan
De Quincey, Complete Works. 6v. Houghton
Everett, Poetry, Comedy, and Duty. Houghton
Emerson, Works. Vols. 2, 3, 4, 6, 7, and 9. Houghton, Mifflin
Eliot, American Contributions to Civilization. Century
Epictetus, Discourses, Encheiridion, etc. 2v. Little, Brown
Fiske, The Unseen World and Other Essays. Houghton
Francke, Social Forces in German Literature. Henry Holt
Froude, Short Studies on Great Subjects. Scribners
Haweis, Music and Morals. Scribners
Hodgson, Time and Space. Putnams
Hazlitt, the Spirit of the Age. Putnams
Hamerton, The Intellectual Life. Little, Brown
Hamerton, Human Intercourse. Little, Brown
Hamerton, The Quest of Happiness. Little, Brown
Holmes, The Professor at the Breakfast Table. Houghton
Holmes, The Autocrat of the Breakfast Table. Houghton
Hunt, Men, Women and Books. Scribners

Hunt, Table Talk. Scribners
Higginson, Atlantic Essays. Putnams
Higginson, The Procession of the Flowers. Putnams
Higginson, Outdoor Papers. Putnams
Jessopp, Random Roamings in Time and Space. Putnams
Jessopp, Arcady: For Better, For Worse. Putnams
James, The Will to Believe. Putnams
Jerrold, The Barber's Chair. Scribners
King, Substance and Show. Houghton
Le Gallienne, If I Were God. Crowell
Lamb, Some Essays of Elia. Appleton
Longinus, On the Sublime. Macmillan
Luther, Table Talk. Macmillan
Mazzini, Essays. Macmillan
Massey, The Natural Genesis. Williams & Northgate
Macaulay, Complete Essays. 3v. Armstrong
Morris, Hopes and Fears for Art. Little, Brown
Pascal, Thoughts, Letters and Opuscules. Houghton
Pascal, Provincial Letters. Houghton
Phillips, Speeches, Lectures, and Letters. 2v. Lee & Shepard
Palmer, The Glory of the Imperfect. Crowell
Palmer, Self Cultivation in English. Crowell
Pater, Marius, the Epicurean. Macmillan
Smiles, Self Help. Harpers
Schiller, Essays. Macmillan
Smith, Selections. Putnams
Sainte-Beuve, English Portraits. Henry Holt
Selden, The Table Talk. Clarendon Press
Swift, Selections (Craik). 2v. Clarendon Press
Smith, Guess at the Riddle of Existence. Macmillan
Thoreau, Walden. Houghton
Taylor, Diversions of the Echo Club. Putnams
Van Dyke, Little Rivers; A Book of Essays. Scribners

Philosophy and Æsthetics.

Aquinas, On Universals (tr. Dering). Leamington
Alden, A Study of Death. Harpers
Abbott, Scientific Theism. Little, Brown
Allen, Evolution of the Idea of God. Henry Holt
Aristotle, Metaphysics (tr. McMahon). Macmillan
Aristotle, Nichomachian Ethics (tr. Peters). Scribners
Aristotle, Organon. 2v. Macmillan
Baldwin, Interpretations in Mental Development. Macmillan
Baldwin, Dictionary of Philosophy and Psychology. Macmillan
Berkeley, Philosophical Works. 3v. Macmillan
Boethius, Consolations of Philosophy. Macmillan
Bradley, Appearance and Reality. Macmillan
Bosanquet, A History of Æsthetics. Macmillan
Cobbe, An Essay on Intuitive Morals. Williams & Northgate
Clifford, Lectures and Essays. Macmillan
Clifford, Seeing and Thinking. Macmillan
Cousin, The True, the Beautiful, and the Good. Macmillan
Descartes, Method and Meditations. Scribners
Erdmann, History of Philosophy. 3v. Scribners
Everett, Ethics for Young People. Ginn
Fichte, Doctrine of Religion (tr. Smith). Amsterdam
Frothingham, Transcendentalism in New England. Putnams
Falckenberg, History of Modern Philosophy. Henry Holt
Fiske, Outlines of Cosmic Philosophy. 2v. Houghton
Fichte, Science of Knowledge (tr. Smith). Scribners
Fichte, Science of Rights. (tr Smith). Scribners
Gilman, Conduct as a Fine Art. Houghton
Green, Prolegomena to Ethics. Clarendon Press
Hyde, Practical Ethics. Henry Holt
Hyde, Practical Idealism. Macmillan
Hegel, Philosophy of Right (tr. Dyde). Macmillan
Hegel, Logic (tr. Wallace). 2v. Clarendon Press
Hegel, Philosophy of Mind (tr. Wallace). Clarendon Press
Hume, Treatise of Human Nature. Clarendon Press
Hume, Enquiry Concerning Human Understanding. Clarendon Press
Hegel, Philosophy of Religion. 3v. Scribners
James, Principles of Psychology. 2v. Henry Holt
Jevons, Studies in Deductive Logic. Macmillan
Jevons, The Principles of Science. Macmillan
Janet, Final Causes. Scribners
Janet, The Theory of Morals. Scribners
Kant, Principles of Politics. Amsterdam
Kant, Philosophy of Law. Scribners
Kant, Metaphysics of Ethics. Longmans
Kant, The Critique of Pure Reason, Macmillan
Kant, The Critique of Judgment (tr. Bernard). Macmillan
Kant, Prolegomena to Philosophy (tr. Bax). Macmillan
Lessing, Education of the Human Race. Amsterdam
Lotze, Microcosmos. 2v. Scribners
Leopardi, Essays and Dialogues. Amsterdam
Lewis, Biographical History of Philosophy. Appleton
Le Bon, The Crowd. Macmillan
Locke, An Essay Concerning Human Understanding. Clarendon Press
Lotze, Logic (tr. Bosanquet). 2v. Clarendon Press
Lotze, Metaphysics (tr. Bosanquet). 2v. Clarendon Press
Ladd, A Theory of Reality. Scribners
Ladd, Physiological Psychology. Scribners
Maudsley, Body and Will. Appleton
Mill, A System of Logic. Longmans
Mill, Utilitarianism. Longmans
Mackenzie, Introduction to Social Philosophy. Macmillan
Marshall, Pain, Pleasure, and Æsthetics. Macmillan
Mercier, The Nervous System and the Mind. Macmillan
Martineau, Types of Ethical Theory. Clarendon Press
Mivart, On Truth: a Systematic Inquiry. Benziger
Nordau, Degeneration. Appleton
Nash, Genesis of the Social Conscience. Macmillan
Nitti, Catholic Socialism. Macmillan
Powell, Our Heredity from God. Appleton
Preyer, Mental Development in the Child. Appleton
Paulsen, Introduction to Philosophy. Henry Holt
Paulsen, Ethics (tr. Thilly). Scribners
"Physicus," Theism. Amsterdam
Royce, The Spirit of Modern Philosophy. Houghton
Royce, The Religious Aspect of Philosophy. Houghton
Rosenkrantz, Philosophy of Education. Appleton
Royce, Studies of Good and Evil. Appleton
Rendall, Marcus Aurelius to Himself. Macmillan
Santayana, The Sense of Beauty. Scribners
Sidis, The Psychology of Suggestion. Appleton
Spencer, First Principles. Appleton
Spencer, Principles of Biology. 2v. Appleton
Spencer, Principles of Sociology. 3v. Appleton
Spencer, Principles of Ethics. 2v. Appleton
Spencer, Education. Appleton
Spencer, Philosophy of Style. Appleton
Stirling, The Secret of Hegel. Putnams
Spinoza, The Philosophy of. Henry Holt
Spinoza, Chief Works. 2v. Macmillan
Smith, Theory of the Moral Sentiments. Macmillan
Sigwart, Logic. 2v. Macmillan
Schopenhauer, The World as Will and Idea. 3v. Scribners
Schopenhauer, On Human Nature. Scribners
Taylor, Ancient Ideals. 2v. Putnams
Ueberweg, History of Philosophy. 2v. Scribners
Venn, The Logic of Chance. Macmillan
Voltaire, Philosophical Dictionary. 2v. Truelove
Von Hartman, The Philosophy of the Unconscious. 2v. Scribners
Wundt, Human and Animal Psychology. Macmillan
Wundt, The Facts of the Moral Life. Macmillan
Wundt, Ethical Systems. Macmillan
Windelbrand, History of Philosophy. Macmillan

Science and Travels.

Audubon, His Journals. 2v. Scribners
Allen, Physiological Æsthetics. Appleton
Amicis, Constantinople. Harpers
Amicis, Morocco: Its People and Places. Harpers
Agassiz, Geological Sketches. 2v. Houghton
Agassiz, Methods of Study in Natural History. Houghton
Argyle, Organic Evolution Cross Examined. Henry Holt
Bastian, The Brain as an Organ of Mind. Appleton
Barker, Physics. Henry Holt
Berdoe, Origin and Growth of the Healing Art. Amsterdam
Cajori, The History of Mathematics. Macmillan
Chrystal, Algebra. 2v. Macmillan
Carpenter, The Principles of Mental Physiology. Appleton
Clifford, The Common Sense of the Exact Sciences. Appleton
Clodd, Pioneers of Evolution. Appleton
Croll, Climate and Time. Appleton
Dana, Text Book of Mineralogy. Appleton
Donaldson, The Growth of Brain. Scribners
Darwin, Origin of Species. Appleton

Darwin, Descent of Man. Appleton
Darwin, A Naturalist's Voyage Around the World. Appleton
Ellis, Man and Woman. Scribners
Finck, Spain and Morocco. Scribners
Foster, Text Book of Physiology. 5v. Macmillan
Faraday, Chemistry of a Candle. Harpers
Friend, Flowers and Flower-lore. Amsterdam
Gummere, Germanic Origins. Scribners
Guyot, The Earth and Man. Scribners
Galton, Hereditary Genius. Appleton
Gray, Anatomy. Longmans
Huxley, Man's Place in Nature. Appleton
Holland, The Butterfly Book. Doubleday and McClure
Hertwig, Embryology of Man and Mammals. Macmillan
Hertwig, The Biological Problems of To-day. Macmillan
Humboldt, Cosmos. 5v. Macmillan
Haeckel, The History of Creation. 2v. Appleton
Haeckel, The Evolution of Man. 2v. Appleton
Huxley, Physiography. Macmillan
Huxley, Evolution and Ethics. Appleton
Huxley, Science and Christian Tradition. Appleton
Jordan, Footnotes to Evolution. Appleton
Jones, Logarithmic Tables. Macmillan
Kingsley, Natural History. 6v. Dana Estes
Kingsley, Health and Education. Appleton
Kingsley, Town Geology. Appleton
Kelvin, The Constitution of Matter. Macmillan
Lyell, Principles of Geology. 2v. Appleton
Lockyer, Dawn of Astronomy. Cassell
Le Conte, Evolution and Religious Thought. Appleton
Lubbock, Origin of Civilization. Appleton
Lubbock, The Beauties of Nature. Macmillan
Letourneau, Evolution of Marriage. Scribners
Manaceine, Sleep: a Study. Scribners
Mason, The Origins of Invention. Scribners
Mosso, Fear. Longmans
Muir, The Alchemical Essence and the Chemical Element. Longmans
Martin, The Human Body. Henry Holt
Maxwell, Electricity and Magnetism. 2v. Clarendon Press
Meyer, History of Chemistry. Macmillan
Maury, Physical Geography of the Sea. Amsterdam
Newton, Principia (tr. Main). Macmillan
Newcomb, Popular Astronomy. Harpers
Proctor, Other Worlds Than Ours. Appleton
Proctor, Light Science for Leisure Hours. Harpers
Packard, Textbook of Entomology. Macmillan
Quatrefages, The Natural History of Man. Appleton
Quatrefages, The Human Species. Appleton
Romanes, Animal Intelligence. Amsterdam
Reclus, The Earth. Harpers
Ribot, Heredity. Appleton
Ribot, Diseases of the Memory. Appleton
Roemer, Origins of the English People. Appleton
Romanes, Mental Evolution in Man. Appleton
Remsen, Inorganic Chemistry. Henry Holt
Stewart and Tait, The Unseen Universe. Macmillan
Scientific Series (International), Vols. 1, 2, 3, 4, 7, 16, 17, 21, 23, 31, 34, 36, 39, 40, 42, 44, 47, 50, 62, 65, 66, 67. Appleton
Thudicum, A Treatise on Wines. Macmillan
Tyndall, Forms of Water. Appleton
Tyndall, Heat as a Mode of Motion. Appleton
Tyndall, On Sound. Appleton
Tyndall, Fragments of Science. 2v. Appleton
Tyndall, Six Lectures on Light. Appleton
Tait, Dynamics. Macmillan
Tylor, Primitive Culture. 2v. Henry Holt
Verne, The Exploration of the World. 3v. Scribners
White, Natural History of Selbourne. 2v. Appleton
Wurtz, History of Chemical Theory. Macmillan
Weismann, Essays on Heredity. 2v. Clarendon Press
Winchell, Sketches of Creation. Harpers
Williams, Geological Biology. Henry Holt
White, The Warfare of Science. 2v. Appleton
Whewell, History of the Inductive Sciences. 2v. Appleton

Political Science, Economics, And Law.

Adams, The Science of Finance. Henry Holt
Ashley, English Economic History and Theory. 2v. Putnams
Aristotle, Politics (tr. Jowett). 2v. Clarendon Press
Burgess, Political Science and Constitutional Law. 2v. Ginn
Baldwin, Modern Political Institutions. Little, Brown
Bentham, Theory of Legislation. Amsterdam
Blackstone, Commentaries on English Law. 2v. Lippincott
Boehm, Capital and Interest. Macmillan
Buckalew, Proportional Representation. Phila
Bax, Ethics of Socialism. Scribners
Beaulieu, The Modern State. Scribners
Bagehot, Physics and Politics. Scribners
Bagehot, The English Constitution. Appleton
Bentham, Principles of Morals and Legislation. Clarendon Press
Bentham, A Fragment on Government. Clarendon Press
Bluntschli, The Theory of the State. Clarendon Press
Burke, Thoughts on the Present Discontents. Clarendon Press
Burke, Reflections on the French Revolution. Clarendon Press
Cairnes, Principles of Political Economy. Harpers
Curry, Constitutional Government in Spain. Harpers
Cossa, Taxation: its Principles and Methods. Putnams
Crane and Moses, Politics. Putnams
Coulanges, Origin of Property in Land. Scribners
Cossa, Introduction to Political Economy. Macmillan
Dawson, The Federalist. Scribners
De Tocqueville, Democracy in America. 2v. Century
Dicey, English Constitutional Law. Macmillan
De Laveleye, Primitive Property. Macmillan
Dunbar, History and Theory of Banking. Putnams
Dawson, The Unearned Increment. Scribners
De Laveleye, Elements of Political Economy. Putnams
De Laveleye, Luxury. Scribners
Ely, French and German Socialism. Harpers
Fiske, Civil Government in the United States. Houghton
Ford, Rise and Growth of American Politics. Macmillan
Goodnow, Comparative Administrative Law. 2v. Putnams
Gneist, History of the English Constitution. 2v. Putnams
George, The Science of Political Economy. Doubleday
George, Progress and Poverty. Doubleday
Giddings, Principles of Sociology. Macmillan
Gaius, Roman Law (tr. Poste). Clarendon Press
Holland, Elements of Jurisprudence. Clarendon Press
Holmes, The Common Law. Little, Brown
Hadley, Economics. Putnams
Hearn, The Aryan Household. Longmans
Hammond, Political Institutions of the Greeks. Macmillan
Hadley, Roman Law: Its History and System. Appleton
Hall, International Law. Clarendon Press
Hyslop, Democracy: A Study in Government. Scribners
Jenks, Law and Politics in the Middle Ages. Henry Holt
Johnston, History of American Politics. Henry Holt
Justinian, The Institutes (tr. Sandars). Longmans
Kent, Commentaries on American Law. 4v. Little, Brown
Knox, United States Notes. Scribners
Lavisse, Political History of Europe. Longmans
Lafargue, The Evolution of Property. Scribners
Letourneau, Property: Its Origin and Development. Scribners
Lieber, Civil Liberty and Self Government. Lippincott
Lincoln, Political Speeches and Writings. Dodd, Mead
Lieber, Political Ethics. 2v. Lippincott
Mulford, The Nation. Houghton
Mayne, Hindu Law and Usage. Stevens
Mill, The Subjugation of Women. Longmans
Mill, Principles of Political Economy. 2v. Appleton
Mill, Representative Government. Longmans
Mulhall, Industries and Wealth of Nations. Macmillan
Malthus, The Principle of Population. Scribners
Munro, The Constitution of Canada. Macmillan
Machiavelli, The Prince (tr. Thompson). Clarendon Press
More, Utopia. Clarendon Press
Maine, Ancient Law. Henry Holt
Maine, Early History of Institutions. Henry Holt
Maine, Popular Government. Henry Holt
Mackenzie, Introduction to Social Philosophy. Macmillan
Playfair, Subjects of Social Welfare. Cassell
Pollock and Maitland. History of English Law. 2v. Little, Brown

Paine, The Rights of Man. Putnams
Puchta, Science of Jurisprudence. Scribners
Pollock, Introduction to the Science of Politics. Macmillan
Plehn, An Introduction to Public Finance. Macmillan
Plato, The Republic (tr. Jowett). Clarendon Press
Plato, The Dialogues. 4v. Scribners
Rousseau, The Social Contract. Putnams
Richie, The Principles of State Interference. Scribners
Richie, Natural Rights. Macmillan
Rae, Contemporary Socialism. Scribners
Rannie, Outline of the English Constitution. Scribners
Stoddard, Abraham Lincoln. Fords
Shaw, Municipal Government in Great Britain. Century
Shaw, Municipal Government in Continental Europe. Century
Story, Equity Jurisprudence. Little, Brown
Samuelson, The History of Drink. Amsterdam
Story, The Conflict of Laws. Little, Brown
Story, Constitution of the United States. Harpers
Shaw-Lefevre, Agragrian Tenures. Cassell
Shearman, Natural Taxation. Doubleday
Smith, Wealth of Nations. 2v. Clarendon Press
Sohm, Institutes of Roman Law. Clarendon Press
Stubbs, Constitutional History of England. 3v. Clarendon Press
Stubbs, Select Charters. Clarendon Press
Simon, Government of M. Thiers. 2v. Scribners
Thwing, The Family. Little, Brown
Turner, The Germanic Constitution. Putnams
Von Holst, Constitutional History of the United States. Scribners
Ward, Dynamic Sociology. 2v. Appleton
Wells, Recent Economic Changes. Appleton
Wallace, Land Nationalization. Scribners
Wieser, Natural Value. Macmillan
Woolsey, Political Science. 2v. Scribners
Woolsey, International Law. Scribners
Woolsey, Communism and Socialism. Scribners
Walker, Political Economy. Henry Holt

Alphabets. The alphabets of different languages contain the following number of letters: English, 26; French, 23; Italian, 20; Spanish, 27; German, 26; Slavonic, 27; Russian, 41; Latin, 22; Greek, 24; Hebrew, 22; Arabic, 28; Persian, 32; Turkish, 33; Sanskrit, 50; Chinese, 214.

Early Literature. The first Greek writers were Homer and Hesiod, 1000 B. C., Tyrtæus and Archilochus, 700 B. C., and Alcæus, Sappho, and Anacreon, 600. The first Latin writers were Cluatua, Ennius, and Terentius, 200 B. C. The first British writers, Gildas, Nennius and Bede, 500 and 600 A. D. The first German writers, Eginhard, Wallafrid, and Rabanus, 800 A. D. The first French writers, Fort, Gregory, and Maralfe, 500 A. D. The first Spanish, Anian, Fulgentius, and Martin, 500 A. D. The first Polish, Yaraslof and Nestor in 1000 A. D. The first Italian, Gracian, Falcand and Campanus in 1100 A. D.

CHINESE LITERATURE.

The antiquity of Chinese literature is proportionate to that of the language, and its development has been greatly promoted by the early invention of the art of printing, which has been known in China for at least nine hundred years. The Chinese language presents a remarkable specimen of philological structure, which for ingenuity of arrangement and copiousness of expression, is not surpassed in any written literature. It belongs to that class of idioms which are called monosyllabic. Every word consists of only one syllable. The roots or original characters of the Chinese are only 214 in number, and it is supposed that a minute analysis would reduce them to a still smaller amount. Each of these characters represents one word, and each word an idea. Their various combinations form the whole language. Taken singly, they express the principal objects or ideas that are suggested in the common intercourse of life; and combined, according to obvious analogies, they are made to comprehend the entire field of thought. Thus the character, which originally represents the word "hand," is so modified and combined with others, as to denote every variety of manual labor and occupation. The Chinese characters are written from top to bottom, and from right to left. The lines are not horizontal, but perpendicular and parallel to each other. Much importance is attached by the Chinese to the graphic beauty of their written characters, which in picturesque effect, it must be owned, are superior to most forms of alphabetic symbols. The grammar of the language is very limited. The nouns and verbs cannot be inflected, and hence the relation of words to each other in a sentence can be understood only from the context, or marked by their position.

The Chinese literature is rich in works in every department of composition, both verse and prose. Their scholars are fond of discussions in moral philosophy, but they have also numerous books of history, geography, voyages, dramas, romances, tales, and fictions of all kinds. The labors of various European travelers and students have given us specimens of almost every description of Chinese literature. In legislation, we have a translation of the Penal Code of the Empire; in politics and morals, the sacred books of Confucius, and his successor Meng-Tsew; in philology and belles-lettres, a well-executed dictionary of the language; several translations and abstracts of history; and selections from the drama, criticism, and romance. Among the most successful explorers of the field of Chinese literature, we may mention Staunton, Davis, Morrison, Klaproth, and Remusat, who have followed up the earlier researches of the Jesuits at Pekin, and elucidated a subject which had been supposed to be inaccessible.

Chinese literature suffered a similar misfortune to that of the West in the destruction of the Alexandrian library; for their Emperor, Chee-whang-tee, ordered all writings to be destroyed, that everything might begin anew from his reign; consequently their books and records were recovered with great difficulty by succeeding emperors

GREEK LITERATURE.

The language which we call Greek was not the primitive language of Greece, for that country was originally inhabited by the Pelasgi, whose language had become extinct in the time of Herodotus. With regard to its origin, there is a diversity of opinion among the learned, although it evidently forms a branch of the extensive family of languages known by the name of the Indo-Germanic. It has existed as a spoken language for at least three thousand years, and, with the exception of the Arabic and the English, has been more widely diffused than any other tongue. Out of Greece, it was spoken in a great part of Asia Minor, of the South of Italy and Sicily, and in other regions which were settled by Grecian colonies. The Greek language is divided into four leading dialects, the Æolic, Ionic, Doric, and Attic, beside which there are several secondary dialects. The four principal dialects may, however, be reduced to two, the Hellenic-Doric, and the Ionic-Attic, the latter originally spoken in the northern part of Peloponnesus and Attica, the former in other parts of Greece. In each of these dialects, there are celebrated authors. To the Ionic dialect, belong in part the works of the oldest poets, Homer, Hesiod, Theognis; of some prose writers, especially Herodotus and Hippocrates; and the poems of Pindar, Theocritus, Bion, and Moschus. The Doric dialect was of the greatest antiquity. We have few remains of Doric prose, which consists chiefly of mathematical or philosophical writings. After Athens became the center of literary cultivation in Greece, the works of Æschylus, Sophocles, Euripides, Aristophanes, Thucydides, Xenophon, Plato, Isocrates, Demosthenes, and so forth, were regarded as standards of style, and made the Attic the common dialect of literature. Poetry, however, was not written in the Attic dialect. The peculiarities of Homer were imitated by all subsequent poets except the dramatists, and even they assumed the Doric to a certain degree in their choruses, for the sake of the solemnity of expression which belonged to the oldest liturgies of the Greeks. According to the general tradition, Cadmus the Phœnician was the first who introduced the alphabet into Greece. His alphabet consisted of but sixteen letters; four are said to have been invented by Palamedes in the Trojan war, and four more by Simonides of Ceos. It has been maintained, however, by some persons, that the art of writing was practiced by the Pelasgi before the time of Cadmus. On the other hand, many of the most sagacious critics place the origin of writing in Greece at a much later period.

The origin of Greek literature, or the intellectual cultivation of the Greeks, by written works, dates at a period of which we have few historical memorials. The first period of Grecian cultivation, which extends to eighty years after the Trojan war, is called the ante-Homeric period, and is destitute of any literary remains properly deserving the name. Of the poets previous to Homer, nothing satisfactory is known. The most ancient was Olen, who is mentioned by Pausanias. He was followed by Linus, Orpheus, Musæus, and others, but the poems which are circulated under their names cannot be regarded as their genuine productions. It was in the Greek colonies of Asia Minor that the first great impulse was given to the development of literature; and among them we find the earliest authentic specimens of Greek poetry and historical composition. Situated on the borders of a noble sea, enjoying a climate of delicious softness and purity, abounding in the most nutritious and tempting products of nature, whose fertility was not inferior to its beauty, these colonies possessed a character of refined voluptuousness which, if not favorable to the performance of great deeds, allured the dreamy spirit to poetical contemplations, and was manifested in noble creations of the fancy, which have not been surpassed in the progress of cultivation. Living near the scene of the Trojan war, the bards devoted their first poems to the celebration of Grecian heroism. With them commenced the second period of Greek literature, which we call the Epic age. Of these, Homer alone has survived. We have from him the two great poems, the Iliad and Odyssey, with several hymns and epigrams. He gave his name to the Homeridæ, an Ionian school of minstrels, who preserved the old Homeric and epic style, and who are probably the authors of much that has been ascribed to Homer himself.

Next to the Homeridæ, come the Cyclic poets, whose works embrace the whole circle of mythology and tradition, describing the origin of the gods and of the world, the adventures of the Heroic times, the Argonautic expedition, the labors of Hercules and Theseus, the principal events of the Theban and Trojan wars, and the fortunes of the Greeks after the fall of Troy. A transition between these historic poets and the later school of Ionian minstrelsy is formed by Hesiod, who conducted poetry back from Asia Minor into Greece. Of the sixteen works ascribed to him, we have the *Theogony*, the *Shield of Hercules*, and *Works and Days*, the last, an agricultural poem, interspersed with moral reflections and prudential maxims.

The third period commences with the growth of lyric poetry, of apologues and philosophy, with which history gained a new development and a higher degree of certainty. Lyric poetry sprung up on the decline of the Epic school, and was much cultivated from the beginning of the epoch of the Olympiads (776 B. C.) to the first Persian war. The poems of this period are considered among the most valuable productions of Grecian literature. Many of them resembled the epic, and contained the subjects of heroic song. They were sung by bands of youths and maidens, accompanied by instrumental music. Among the most celebrated of the lyric poets were Archilochus of Paros, the inventor of the Iambus; Tyrtæus, Terpander, and Alcman, whose martial strains enkindled the valor of the Spartans; Callimachus of Ephesus, inventor of the elegaic measure; Simonides and Anacreon of Ceos; the impassioned Sappho of Mitylene; Stesichorus, Hipponax, and Pindar. Many didactic poems, fables, and proverbs were written during this period, and served to prepare the way for prose composition.

The philosophy of this age was marked by its constant reference to practical affairs. Among its expounders we may consider the seven wise men of Greece, as they are called (Periander, or according to some, Epimenides of Crete, Pittacus, Thales, Solon, Bias, Chilo, and Cleobulus), of whom six acquired their fame, not by the teaching of speculative abstractions, but by their admirable wisdom in the affairs of life, and their skill in the offices of state. Their celebrated sayings are the maxims of experience, applied to the practical relations of life. But with the progress of intellectual culture, a taste for speculative inquiries was unfolded. This resulted in the establishment of the Ionic philosophy by Thales, the Italian, by Pythagoras, and the older and later Eleatic. With the development of these schools, we are brought to the scientific period of Greek literature. The Ionic school ascribed a material origin to the universe. Its principal followers were Pherecydes, Anaximander, Anaxamines, Anaxagoras, Diogenes of Apollonia, and Archilaus of Miletus. Of the Pythagorean school, which explained the organization of the world by number and measure, were Ocellus Lucanus, Timæus of Locris, Epicharmus, Theages, Archytas, Philolaus, and Eudoxus. To the older Eleatic school, which cherished a more sublime, but less intelligible conception of the origin of the world, assuming the fact of a pure necessary existence, belonged Xenophanes and Parmenides; to the later Eleatic, Melissus and Diagoras. Until about the commencement of the 90th Olympiad, the philosophers and their disciples were dispersed throughout the various Grecian cities. Athens subsequently became their chief residence, where the class of men called Sophists first rose into importance as public teachers. Of these, the most distinguished names that have been preserved to us are Gorgias of Leontium, Protagoras of Abdera, Hippias of Elis, Prodicus of Cos, Trasimæus, and Tisias. They were especially devoted to the subjects of politics and eloquence, but also made a study of the natural sciences, mathematics, the theory of the fine arts, and philosophy. Professing the art of logic as a trade, they were less earnest in the pursuit of truth than in the construction of plausible arguments. Their fallacious pretenses awakened the honest indignation of Socrates, who not only became their zealous antagonist, but gave a vigorous and original impulse to the progress of philosophy. This shrewd and subtle reasoner opened a new direction to philosophical research, turning it to the study of human nature and of the laws of psychology and ethics, instead of barren speculations and theories. Without leaving any written record of his genius, he is known at the present day by the affectionate and beautiful memorials which have been consecrated to his character in the productions of his disciples.

Among these, Plato was pre-eminent by the force and comprehensiveness of his reason, the marvelous keenness of his insight in the region of transcendental ideas, the vigor and acuteness of his logical faculties, and the winning sweetness and grace of expression, which lend a charm to his writings that has never been equaled in philosophical literature. The masterly conversations of Socrates, in which he expounded the principles of his philosophy in the streets and market place of Athens, are reproduced with admirable dramatic effect, in the glowing pages of his eloquent disciple.

The progress of history kept pace in Grecian cultivation with the development of philosophy. Among the oldest historical prose writers, are Cadmus, Dionysius, and Hecatæus of Miletus, Hellanicus of Mitylene, Pherecydes of Scyros. After them appears Herodotus, who has received the name of the Homer of history. He was followed by Thucydides, the grave, condensed, and philosophical historian of the Pelopennesian war. Strongly contrasted with his sternness and energy, is Xenophon, whose limpid narrative flows on with the charming facility of a graceful stream, presenting a delightful specimen of the tranquil beauty of Greek prose in its most simple form. These three historians distinguished the period from 450 to 400 B. C., during which time we have to notice the introduction of a new class of poetical creations.

The popular festivals which were celebrated after the vintage, with rude songs and dances, led to the gradual creation of the drama. A more artistic form was given to the wild choruses in honor of Bacchus; the recitation of fables by an intermediate speaker was introduced into the performances; and soon the games of the vintage festival were repeated on other occasions. The spirit of the drama was thus cherished, until the appearance of Æschylus, who may be deemed the author of the dramatic art in Greece. He divided the story into different portions, substituted the dialogue for recitation by a single person, and assigned the various parts to skillful actors. The three great tragic writers are Æschylus, Sophocles, and Euripides, while the most distinguished rank in comedy is held by Cratinus, Eupolis, Crates, and especially Aristophanes.

During this period we find several didactic and lyric poets, while the sister art of eloquence was illustrated by the names of Lysias, Demosthenes, Æschines, Antiphon, Gorgias, and Isocrates.

The succeeding period, which is usually called the Alexandrine, was characterized by the prevalence of a critical spirit; the luxuriant bloom of the earlier Greek literature had passed away; and the fresh creative impulses of genius were made to yield to the love of speculation and the influence of erudition. The glowing imaginative philosophy of Plato was succeeded by the more rigid system of Aristotle, who founded the Peripatetic school, and gave order and precision to the principles of reasoning. With the passion for subtle analysis, which was the characteristic of his mind, he drew a sharp line of distinction between logic and rhetoric, ethics and politics, physics and metaphysics, thus enlarging the boundaries of philosophy, and establishing a system which exercised an undisputed supremacy for ages. The dogmatic tendencies of Aristotle found their counterpart in the skeptical principles of which Pyrrho of Elis was the most distinguished advocate. The same principles prevailed to a certain extent in the Middle and New Academies founded by Arcesilaus and Carneades, while the Socratic philosophy was modified by the disciples of the Stoic school, established by Zeno, and of the Epicurean, which bears the name of its celebrated founder. At length the intellectual scepter, which had been so long wielded by the philosophers and poets of Greece, passed from Athens to Alexandria; the nation itself was absorbed in the progress of Roman conquest; Greek literature ceased to give birth to original productions; and its brilliant career became the subject of history.

HEBREW LITERATURE.

The literature of the ancient Hebrews, apart from its religious character and claims, presents a curious and important subject of investigation. It is the oldest literature of which any remains have come down to modern times. With a rich poetical coloring, a profound sentiment of humanity, and a lofty religious faith, it sustains a most intimate relation to the development of the intellect and the moral and political history of the race.

The Hebrew language is one of the oldest branches of the numerous family of languages which have received the name of Semitic, on account of the supposed descent of the nations by which they were spoken, from Shem, the son of Noah. These are the Chaldaic, the Aramaic, the Hebrew, the Syriac, the Arabic, the Phœnician, and the Ethiopian. The history of the language has been divided by many critics into four periods. I. From Abraham to Moses. II. From Moses to Solomon. III. From Solomon to Ezra. IV. From Ezra to the end of the age of the Maccabees, when it was gradually lost in the modern Aramaic and became a dead language. The differences, however, which can be traced in the language are so slight, that a sounder division would be into only two periods, the first extending from the time of Moses to the reign of Hezekiah, and the second from the reign of Hezekiah to its final extinction as a spoken language. The written characters or letters, which date from the time of Solomon, were the same as the Phœnician. During the Babylonish captivity, the Hebrews received from the Chaldees the square character in common use, and, in the time of Ezra, the old Hebrew manuscripts were copied in these characters. The punctuation of the language was not settled until after the seventh century of the Christian era. The accents, vowels, points, and divisions into words were also introduced at a later period.

The poetical and religious sentiment was the foundation of Hebrew literature. Lyric poetry received a rich development under David, to whom are ascribed several noble specimens of song and elegy. The fragments of didactic poetry which bear the name of Solomon are stamped with a character of practical wisdom, and often exhibit an energy of expression, which authorizes us to class them among the most extraordinary productions of ancient literature. After the division of the kingdom, the prophets became the great teachers of the people, and have left various collections of their writings, none of which have come down to us with completeness. Upon the return of the exiled people from the Babylonish captivity, the remains of Hebrew literature were collected by a college of learned men under the direction of Ezra, and from their labors we have received the books of the Old Testament in their present form.

ROMAN LITERATURE.

The language of the ancient Romans is usually called Latin, for, though Rome and Latium were originally separate communities, they always appear to have spoken the same language. The Latins, as far as we can decide on such a question at the present day, seemed to have formed a part of that great race which overspread both Greece and Italy under the name of Pelasgians. It is supposed that the Pelasgians who settled in Italy originally spoke the same language with the Pelasgians who settled in Greece. The Greek and Latin languages accordingly have many elements in common, though each has its own distinctive character.

The history of Roman literature may be divided into four periods: I. From the earliest times till Cicero. II. To the death of Augustus, A. D. 14. III. To the death of Trajan. IV. To the conquest of Rome by the Goths. During the first five hundred years of the Roman history, scarcely any attention was paid to literature. Its earliest attempts were translations and imitations of the Greek models. The Odyssey was translated into Latin by Livius Andronicus, a Greek captive of Tarentum, and the earliest writer of whom we have any account. His tragedies and comedies were taken entirely from the Greek. He was followed by Nævius, who wrote an historical poem on the first Punic war, by the two tragic writers Pacuvius and Attius, and by Ennius, B. C. 239, the first epic poet, and who may be regarded as the founder of Roman literature. Being a Greek by birth he introduced the study of his native language at Rome, and had among his pupils, Cato, Scipio Africanus, and other distinguished citizens of that day. At the same time, he taught the Romans the art of easy and graceful writing in their own language, and helped to inspire them with a love of literature by his refined taste and elegant cultivation. Contemporary with Ennius was Plautus, whose dramatic pieces, in imitation of the later comedies of the Greeks, were remarkable for their vivacity of expression and their genuine comic humor. He was followed by Cecilius and Terence, of whom the latter has left several admirable comedies, fully imbued with the Grecian spirit. The first prose writers were Quintus Fabius Pictor and Lucius Cincius Alimentus, who lived in the time of the second Punic war, and wrote a complete history of Rome. Their style was meager and insipid, aiming only at brevity, and entirely destitute of ornament or grace.

With the age of Augustus, in which some earlier writers are usually reckoned, a new spirit is exhibited in Roman literature. In didactic poetry, Lucretius surpassed his Grecian masters, by the force of thought, and the splendor of diction, which characterize his great philosophical poem on the origin of the universe. Catullus attempted various styles of poetry, in all of which he obtained eminent success. His lyric and elegiac poems, his epigrams and satires, are marked by singular versatility of feeling, frequent flashes of wit, and rare felicity of expression. Among the elegiac poets, of whose genius we still possess the remains, the highest distinction was gained by Tibullus, Propertius, and Ovid. The former of these poets was pronounced by Quintilian to be the greatest master of elegiac verse; Ovid possessed an uncommon fertility of invention and ease of versification; while Propertius tempers the voluptuous cast of his writings with a certain dignity of thought and vigorous mode of expression. The great lyric poet of the Augustan age is Horace, whose graceful and sportive fancy, combined with his remarkable power of delicate and effective satire, continues to make him a favorite with all who have the slightest tincture of classical learning.

The noblest production of this period, however, is the *Æneid* of Virgil, which with his elaborate poem on rural affairs, the Georgics, and his sweet and tender pastorals, or *Eclogues*, fairly entitles him to the position which has been given him by universal consent, of the most gifted epic and didactic poet in Roman literature.

The prose writings of the Latin authors, taken as a whole, betray a higher order of genius and cultivation than the works of the poets. In this department, the preëminence belongs to Cicero, whose various productions in eloquence, philosophy, and criticism are among the most valuable treasures of antiquity. In history, Cæsar, Sallust, and Livy are the most prominent names, who, each in his own peculiar style, have left models of historical composition which have been the admiration of every subsequent age. The literature of the Augustan period partook of the general character of the Roman people. Devoted to the realization of practical objects, with slight tendencies to the ideal aspect of things, and absorbed in the exciting game of politics and war, the Romans had little taste either for abstract speculation or for the loftiest flights of poetical fancy. Hence no new system of philosophy was produced in their literature; their best poets were essentially imitative; and of all branches of study, those connected with popular eloquence were held in the greatest esteem.

With the death of Augustus commenced the decline of Roman literature. Among the poets of this period are Phædrus, an ingenious fabulist, the satirists, Juvenal and Persius, whose works are more important for their illustrations of the manners of the age than for their poetical merit, and Lucan, who describes the wars of Cæsar and Pompey in an insipid historical epic. In prose, we have the somber but condensed and powerful histories of Tacitus, and the quaint and artificial treatises on ethics and philosophy by Seneca. Subsequent to the reign of Trajan, we meet with no writers who have any claim upon our attention, and the literature of Rome, after a brief interval of splendor, during the golden age between Cicero and Augustus, passes into unimportance and obscurity.

SANSKRIT LITERATURE.

Until the close of the last century, the Sanskrit literature was almost wholly unknown to the learned of Europe. The Roman Catholic missionaries in India had, to a certain extent, engaged in the study of the language at an earlier period, but it is only since the year 1790 that it has attracted the attention of eminent scholars. Among those who have given an impulse to the study of Sanskrit, and who have themselves pursued it with distinguished success, are Sir William Jones, Wilkins Forster, Colebrooke, Wilson, Haughton, Rosen, Chézy, Burnouf, A. W. Schlegel, Oldenberg, Max Müller, and Bopp. We are indebted to their labors for a knowledge of this rich and curious literature, which, on many accounts, may be considered as one of the most remarkable products in the history of intellectual culture.

The Sanskrit language is a branch of the Indo-Germanic family of languages, and is supposed to bear the greatest resemblance to the primitive type. In its construction, it is in the highest degree ingenious and elaborate, and the variety and beauty of its forms are well adapted to illustrate the laws of the formation of language. It is the sacred language of the Brahmans, and contains the Vedas, the oldest records of their religion. The last century before the Christian era was the period of its richest blossoming, although it extends back to a far more remote antiquity. It appears in its most ancient form in the Vedas, which date from the thirteenth century before Christ, and in that state exhibits many striking analogies with the Zend, the ancient language of Persia. These writings are the foundation of Sanskrit literature, and diffuse their influence through the whole course of its development.

The Vedas are divided into four classes, the first being in poetry, the second in prose, the third consisting of lyrical prayers, and the fourth of devotional pieces, intended to be used in sacrifices and other religious offices. Each Veda is composed of two parts, the prayers and the commandments. The Sanskrit possesses a variety of other works in sacred literature, which contain not only a copious exposition of religious doctrines, but numerous discussions of philosophical and scientific subjects, and an extensive collection of poetical legends.

The two oldest and most interesting epic poems are *The Ramayana*, describing the seventh great incarnation of Vishnu, and *The Mahabharata*, devoted to the wars of two rival lines descended from the ancient Indian monarch, Bharata. An episode from this work called *Bhagavat Gita* has been translated by Wilkins, Herder, Schlegel, and others, and has excited no small interest as an illustration of the early oriental philosophy.

A new character was given to Sanskrit poetry about one hundred years before the Christian era, by the introduction of themes connected with courts and princes. It lost the popular and national tendency which appears in the two great epics, alluded to above, and assumed a more artificial form. With a manifest improvement in the mere externals of style, the new poetry shows a degeneracy in point of thought, and an entire absence of original invention. In the principal works of this class we find labored descriptions of natural objects, and many curious artifices of composition, but they are destitute both of brilliancy of imagination and depth of reflection. The most fertile author of the new school is undoubtedly Kâlidâsa, who attempted almost every species of poetical composition, and whose epic, lyric, and dramatic productions must be allowed to possess considerable merit. His best descriptive poem, entitled *Meghaduta*, is a model of simplicity and elegance. It exhibits a highly ideal character, tracing out the spiritual significance of visible phenomena, and striving to penetrate into the hidden life of the universe. The drama called

Sakoontala or The Fatal Ring, by this author, has received the warmest commendation from modern critics. "All its scenes," says the genial Herder, "are connected by flowery bands, each grows out of the subject as naturally as a beautiful plant. A multitude of sublime as well as tender ideas are found in it, which we should look for in vain in a Greek drama." A valuable translation of this poem has been made by Sir William Jones.

The influence of religious speculation in India early gave birth to numerous philosophical writings. With the love of contemplation, to which the natives are so strongly inclined, and the progress of thought in opposition to the doctrines of the Vedas, a variety of philosophical systems was the natural consequence. The oldest of these is called the *Sankhya*. It teaches the duality of matter and spirit, which are essentially different in their nature, though found in such intimate union. The problem of life is the emancipation of the soul from the dominion of the senses, and the attainment of blessedness by the supremacy of the intellect. Another system of transcendental speculation is named the *Nyaya*. This is constructed from strict logical deductions, which it applies to the interpretation of nature, and arrives at a theory of materialism, the reverse of the Sankhya ideality. The Nyaya school has produced a multitude of writings. Opposed to each of these systems is the *Mimansa*, which maintains the doctrines of the Vedas in their original strictness, and strives to reconcile them with the suggestions of philosophy.

The Sanskrit literature, moreover, abounds in works on various other branches of learning. Its philological treatises, especially, are of great value. The Indian grammarians surpass those of any other ancient people. No less important are the Sanskrit works on rhetoric, criticism, music, astronomy, and jurisprudence. They well deserve the attention of the scholar, not only on account of their intrinsic character, but as precious memorials of the early development of the intellect, and significant illustrations of the history of the race.

ARABIC LITERATURE.

Literature, after its decay and final extinction in the Eastern and Western Roman Empires, revived first among the Arabic tribes in the East. Even before the era of Mahomet, there were renowned poets and story-tellers in Arabia. In the fifth century, during the great fairs of Mecca, poetical contests frequently took place, the victorious productions being lettered with gold and hung up in the Caaba. Among the most renowned poets of this period were Amralkeis, Tharafa, and Antar. Their works are distinguished by imaginative power, richness of illustration, and great skill in depicting the passions of love and revenge. With Mahomet commenced a memorable epoch in Arabic literature. Through the Koran, which was arranged from Mahomet's teachings, by Abubekr, the first caliph, the method of writing and the literary style of the nation were determined. The reigns of Haroun Al-Raschid and Al-Mamun in the seventh and eighth centuries were the most enlightened periods of the Arabic dominion, though for two centuries afterwards the nation produced many eminent geographers, philosophers, jurists, and historians. Under the government of Al-Mamun, excellent universities were established at Bagdad, Bussora, and Bokhara, and extensive libraries in Alexandria, Bagdad, and Cairo. The dynasty of the Abbassides in Bagdad emulated that of the Ommanides in Spain; during the tenth century the University of Cordova was almost the only refuge of literature in Europe. The labors of the Arabic scholars and travelers contributed greatly to the spread of geographical knowledge. Ibn Batuta, who in the thirteenth century visited Africa, India, China, and Russia, ranks with Marco Polo and Rubruquis.

In the twelfth century Abu'l Kasein wrote the history of the Arabs in Spain; Bohaeddin, a biography of Sultan Saladin; Ibn Arabschah described the exploits of Tamerlane, and Hadji Khalfa, in later times, has produced an encyclopedia of Arabic, Persian, and Turkish literature. The style of the Arabian historians is clear, concise, and unincumbered with imagery. The most renowned philosopher was Avicenna, who flourished in the eleventh century. Averrhoes, whose name is also familiar to scholars, was famous as an expounder of the system of Aristotle. In the departments of medicine, astronomy, geometry, and arithmetic, there are many Arabic works which exhibit great research and scientific knowledge.

The number and variety of the works produced by the Arabian poets is most remarkable, and their influence on the modern literature of Europe was greater than is generally suspected. In picturesque narration they have rarely been excelled, and the *Thousand and One Nights*, which first appeared in its collected form during the reign of Caliph Mansur, in the ninth century, has been naturalized in all modern languages. Only half of this, however, is Arabic, the remainder having been translated from the Sanskrit and Persian. The Arabian poets left many poetic chronicles, the most celebrated of which are: *The Deeds of Antar*, *The Deeds of the Warriors*, and *The Deeds of the Heroes*. Of late years several eminent French and German scholars have given their attention to the study of Arabic literature, the best works of which are now accessible through their translations.

PERSIAN LITERATURE.

The modern literature of Persia succeeded that of Arabia. After the conquests of the country by the caliphs, about the middle of the seventh century, the arts and sciences of the Arabs, together with the religion of Mahomet, were transplanted upon Persian soil, but the fruits of this new culture did not appear for several succeeding generations. The first Persian books, both of poetry and history, were written in the early part of the tenth century, and for several centuries there was no interruption in the list of renowned authors. Literature was encouraged and rewarded, whatever might be the political convulsions that affected the empire. Persian poetry consists for the most part of small lyrics, arranged in *divans*, or collections. There are also several voluminous historical, romantic, and allegorical poems, besides legends and narratives told in a mixture of prose and verse. The first Persian poet is Rudegi, who flourished about the year 952. Firdausi, the great epic poet of Persia, died in the year 1030, at the age of seventy. He wrote the *Shah Nameh, or King's Book*, describing the deeds of the Persian rulers, from the creation of the world to the downfall of the Sassanide dynasty in 632. He was thirty years in the composition of this work, which contains sixty thousand verses. The most celebrated portion is that recounting the adventures of the hero Rustem. Nisami, at the close of the twelfth century, wrote extensive romantic poems, the most remarkable of which were *Medjnoun and Leila*, and *Iskander-Nameh*, an epic on Alexander the Great. Chakani was a celebrated writer of odes in the thirteenth century. Saadi, one of the most celebrated Persian authors, was born in 1175, and lived till 1263. His poems are principally moral and didactic, but rich with the experience of a fruitful life, and written in a very simple and graceful style. His best works are the *Gulistan, or Garden of Roses*, and the *Bostan, or Garden of Trees*. Hafiz, the oriental poet of love, was born at Schiraz in the beginning of the fourteenth century, where he lived as a dervish in willing poverty, resisting the invitations of the caliphs to reside in Bagdad. In the year 1388 he had an interview with Tamerlane, by whom he was treated with much honor. His poems consisted of odes and elegies which have been collected into a *Divan*. His lyrics, devoted to the praise of love and wine, are full of fire and melody.

Djami, who died in 1492, was one of the most prolific of Persian writers. His life was spent at Herat, where, in the hall of the great mosque, he taught the people the precepts of virtue and religion. He left behind him forty works, theological, poetical, and mystical. Seven of his principal poems were united under the title of *The Seven Stars of the Bear*. His history of mysticism, entitled *The Breath of Man*, is his greatest prose work. Among the later Persian poems are the *Schehinscheh-Nameh*, a continuation of the *Book of Kings*, and the *George-Nameh*, an account of the conquest of India by the British. The Persian is the only Mahometan literature containing dramatic poetry. Its dramas strikingly resemble the old French mysteries. Of the collections of tales, legends, and fairy stories, the most celebrated are the *Anwari soheili, or Lights of the Canopy*, and the *Behari danisch, or Spring of Wisdom*. The historical works in the Persian language are very numerous and valuable. They embrace the history of the Mahometan races from Mongolia to Barbary. The principal works are the *Chronicles of Wassaf*, a history of the successors of Genghis Khan, which appeared in 1333; the *Marrow of the Chronicles*, by Khaswini, in 1370, and the *Rauset Essafa*, a great universal history, of which modern historians have made good use. It was written by Mirchond, about the year 1450. In the departments of ethics, rhetoric, theology, and medicine, the Persian scholars are only second to the Arabic. They also excelled in translation, and have reproduced, in Persian, nearly the entire literature of India.

ITALIAN LITERATURE.

The Italian language assumed a regular and finished character at the Court of Roger I., King of Sicily, in the twelfth century. Several poets arose, who, borrowing the forms of verse from the provençal troubadours, gave the people songs in their native language in place of the melodies of the Moors and Arabians. The Italian soon became the court language of Italy, and Malespina's History of Florence, which was written in the year 1280, is scarcely inferior in elegance and purity of style to any Italian prose works which have since been produced. The first genuine poet of Italy, however, was her greatest, and one of the greatest of all time. Dante commenced his great poem of the *Divina Commedia* in the year 1304, just before his exile from Florence, and completed it during his many years of wandering from one court of Italy to another. Out of the rude and imperfect materials within his reach, he constructed an epic which places his name beside that of him whom he humbly called his master, Virgil. Taking the religious faith of his time as the material, he conducts the reader through the sad and terrible circles of Hell, the twilight region of Purgatory, and the fair mount of Paradise, showing him all forms of torture and punishment for the vile, all varieties of supreme happiness for the pure and good. The poem takes a fierce and gloomy character from the wrongs and persecutions which the poet endured in his life. Dante died in 1321, at which time Petrarch, who was born in 1304, had commenced those studies which led to the restoration of classic literature to Italy. As an enthusiastic admirer of antiquity he imparted to his contemporaries that passion for the study of the Greek and Roman authors which preserved many of their masterpieces at a moment when they were about to be lost to the world. His songs and sonnets, most of which were inspired by his unfortunate love for Laura de Sade, gave him a worthy place after Dante in Italian literature. He died in 1374. Contemporary with Petrarch was the great master of Italian prose, Boccaccio, who was born in 1313. He early devoted his life to literature, and in 1341 assisted at the celebrated examination of Petrarch, previous to his coronation in the capitol. His principal work is the *Decameron*, a collection of one hundred tales, which, notwithstanding the impurities with which they are disfigured, are models of narration and exhibit the most varied powers of imagination and invention. Boccaccio is considered as the inventor of romances of love — a branch of literature which was wholly unknown to antiquity.

For a century following the death of Boccaccio, the literature of Italy shows no great name, though several scholars distinguished themselves by their attainments and the aid which they rendered to the cause of classic literature. The most noted of these were John of Ravenna; Leonardo Aretino, who wrote a history of Florence in Latin; Poggio Bracciolini, a most voluminous writer, who enjoyed the patronage of Cosmo de'Medici, at Florence; Francesco Fileflo and Lorenzo Valla, both men of great erudition, whose labors contributed to bring on a new era of Italian literature. Lorenzo de'Medici, called the Magnificent, towards the close of the fifteenth century, gave the first impulse to the cultivation of the Italian tongue, which had been lost sight of in the rage for imitating Latin poets. Besides being the author of many elegant songs and sonnets, his court was the home of all the authors of that period. Among these were Politiano, who wrote *Orfeo*, a fable formed on the myth of Orpheus, which was performed at the court of Mantua, in 1483; Luigi Pulci, the author of *Morgante Maggiore*, and Boiardo, author of the *Orlando Innamorato*. Both the last named poems are chivalrous romances, written in the *ottava rima*, and full of a quaint humor which before that time had only appeared in the prose of Boccaccio. But the master of the gay and sparkling poetic narrative was Ariosto, who was born in 1474, and first appeared as an author about the year 1500. Five years later he commenced his *Orlando Furioso*, which was not completed till 1516. This is a romantic poem in forty-six cantos, celebrating the adventures of Roland, the nephew of Charlemagne. It is one of the classics of Italy, and has been translated into all modern languages. After the death of Ariosto in 1533, no literary work of any prominence appeared until Torquato Tasso published his *Jerusalem Delivered* in 1581. Alamanni, Trissino and Bernardo Tasso flourished in the interval and produced labored poems, which are no longer read. The subject of Tasso's poem is the rescue of the Holy Sepulcher from the Moslems, by the Crusaders under Godfrey of Bouillon. The wrongs and persecutions heaped upon Tasso clouded his mind and shortened his days; he died in Rome in 1595, on the day before that appointed for his coronation. Three other Italian authors of the sixteenth century are worthy of mention: Cardinal Bembo, the most finished scholar of his day, and author of a history of Venice; Nicolo Machiavelli, whose name has become synonymous with all that is sinister and unscrupulous in politics, from his treatise entitled *The Prince*, for which, after his death, an anathema was pronounced against him; and Pietro Aretino, one of the most infamous and dissolute men of his time. Machiavelli wrote an admirable History of Florence, which is still a standard work.

In the half-century following the death of Tasso, there are but two poets who have attained any renown: Guarini, the author of *Pastor Fido*, and Tassoni, who wrote the *Secchia Rapita* (Rape of the Bucket). Filicaja, whose impassioned lyrics are still the revolutionary inspiration of Italy, belongs to the latter part of the seventeenth century; he died in 1707. After another long interval arose Frugoni, a lyric poet of some celebrity, who died in 1768, and Metastasio, the author of plays, operas, and ballets innumerable. He is remarkable for his wonderful command of the language, and the free and spirited movement of his dialogue. He died in Vienna in the year 1782. During this same period, Italian dramatic literature received a new accession in Goldoni, whose comedies are still the glory of the Italian stage. He had a rival in Count Gazzi, whose works, nevertheless, are far inferior to Goldoni's in humor and brilliancy. What Goldoni did for comedy, Alfieri accomplished for Italian tragedy. This author justly stands at the head of modern Italian literature. His tragedies, odes, and lyrics exhibit an eloquence and fervor of thought which are scarcely reached by any other author. His principal works are *Saul*, *Myrrha*, *Octavia*, *Brutus the Second*, and *Philip II.* Since the commencement of this century, Italy has not been barren of authors. Pindemonte, who has published several volumes of dramatic poetry; Ugo Foscolo, author of a poem called *The Sepulchres;* Manzoni, who wrote *I Promessi Sposi* (The Betrothed), a charming romance of life on the shores of Lake Como; Silvio Pellico, whose *Le Mie Prigione* is a narrative of his sufferings in the prison at Spielberg, and Niccolini, equally celebrated as a poet and prose writer. Mazzini, Triumvir of Rome during the brief period of the Republic, and Gioberti distinguished themselves as Italian authors, as did also Leopardi.

During the last half-century the rapid progress of political events in Italy seems to have absorbed the energies of the people, who have made little advance in literature. For the first time since the fall of the Roman empire the country has become a united kingdom, and in the national adjustment to the new conditions, and in the material and industrial development which has followed, the new literature has not yet, to any great extent, found voice. Yet this period of natural formation and consolidation, however, has not been without its poets, among whom a few may be here named. Aleardo Aleardi (d. 1882) is one of the finest poetical geniuses that Italy has produced within the last century, but his writings show the ill effects of a poet sacrificing his art to a political cause, and when the patriot has ceased to declaim, the poet ceases to sing. Prati (1815–1884), on the other hand, in his writings exemplifies the evil of a poet refusing to take part in the grand movement of his nation. He severs himself from all present interests and finds his subjects in sources which have no interest for his contemporaries. He has great metrical facility and his lyrics are highly praised. Carducci, like Aleardi, is a poet who has written on political subjects; he belongs to the class of closet democrats. His poems display a remarkable talent for the picturesque, forcible, and epigrammatic. The poems of Zanella are nearly all on scientific subjects connected with human feeling, and entitle him to a distinguished place among the refined poets of his country. A poet of greater promise than those already spoken of is Arnaboldi, who has the endowment requisite to become the first Italian poet of a new school, but who endangers his position by devoting his verse to utilitarian purposes.

The tendency of the younger poets is to realism and to representing its most materialistic features as beautiful. Against this current of the new poetry Alessandro Rizzi, Guerzoni, and others have uttered a strong protest in poetry and prose.

Among historians, Capponi is the author of a history of Florence; Zini has continued Farina's history of Italy; Bartoli, Settembrini, and De Sanctis have written histories of Italian literature; Villari is the author of able works on the life of Machiavelli and of Savonarola, and Berti has written the life of Giordano Bruno. In criticism philosophic, historical, and literary, Fiorentino, De Sanctis, Massarani, and Trezza are distinguished. Barili, Farina, Bersezio, and Giovagnoli are writers of fiction, and Cossa, Ferrari, and Giacosa are the authors of many dramatic works. The charming books of travel by De Amicis are extensively translated and very popular.

SPANISH LITERATURE.

The earliest essay in Spanish literature is the *Chronicle of the Cid*, which is supposed to have been written about the middle of the twelfth century. In form the poem is sufficiently barbarous, though the language is remarkably spirited and picturesque. It has been the fount of numberless songs and legends through the later centuries. It narrates the adventures of Ruy Diaz de Bivar, the Cid Campeador.

In the following century, Gonzales de Berceo, a monk, wrote nine voluminous poems on the lives of the saints. Alfonso X. of Castile, whose reign terminated in 1284, was the author of a poem entitled *The Philosopher's Stone*, besides several prose works. The first author of the fourteenth century was Prince Don John Manuel, who wrote a prose work entitled *Count Lucanor*, a collection of tales embodying lessons of policy and morality. He was followed by Pedro Lopez de Ayala and Mendoza, Marquis de Santillana; though the latter belongs properly to the next century. He produced a number of works, both prose and poetry, all of which were remarkable for the erudition they displayed. Some of his lighter poems are very graceful and melodious.

Under the reign of Charles V. Spanish literature first reached its full development. After the union of Arragon and Castile, and the transfer of the seat of the government to Madrid, the Castilian became the court language, and thus received a new polish and elegance. The first author of this period was Boscan, an imitator of Petrarch, in some respects, but a poet of much native fervor and passion. Garcilaso de la Vega, the friend of Boscan, surpasses him in the sweetness of his verses and in their susceptibility and imagination. He was a master of pastoral poetry, and his eclogues are considered models of that species of writing. His life was actively devoted to the profession of arms. He fought under the banner of Charles XI. in Tunis, Sicily, and Provence, and was finally killed while storming the walls of Nice. Don Diego de Mendoza, one of the most celebrated politicians and generals of that period, is generally awarded a place next to Garcilaso. He was a patron of classical literature, and the author of a history of the Moorish Revolt in the Alpuxarra, and a History of the War of Granada, but a man of cruel and tyrannical character. Montemayor, who flourished at the same time, attained much celebrity from his pastoral of Diana. These authors during the reign of Charles V. gave Spanish poetry its most graceful and correct form, and have since been regarded as models of classic purity. The great masters of Spanish literature, however, were reserved for the succeeding generation. Herrera and Ponce de Leon, lyrical poets, fill the interval between the age of Garcilaso de la Vega and Cervantes. Herrera is considered the first purely lyrical poet of Spain. Ponce de Leon, who was imprisoned five years by the Inquisition for having translated the Song of Solomon, was the author of several volumes of religious poetry.

Two of the brightest stars of Spanish literature, Cervantes and Lope de Vega, were contemporaries, and were followed in the next generation by the third, Calderon. Cervantes was born in 1549. He traveled throughout Italy, lost a hand at the battle of Lepanto, and was five years a slave in Barbary. He commenced his literary career by the writing of comedies and tragedies, the first of which, Galatea, was published in 1584. Thirty of his comedies have been entirely lost. His great work, *Don Quixote*, was published in 1605, and was immediately translated into all the languages of Europe. From this time until his death in 1616, he wrote many novels and comedies. The tragedy of *Numantia* and the comedy of *Life in Algiers* are the only two of his plays which have been preserved. To this same period belongs Don Alonzo de Ercilla, whose epic of *La Aracuana* was written during the hardships of a campaign against the Aracuanian Indians in Chile. Lope de Vega was born in 1562, and after a life of the most marvelous performances died in 1635. He was a prodigy of learning, imagination, and language. Out of eighteen hundred dramas which he wrote, one hundred were each produced in the space of a single day. His detached poems have been printed in twenty-seven volumes in quarto. Very few of his plays are now read or performed. The only remaining authors of eminence during this period are Quevedo, who wrote several moral and religious works and three volumes of lyrics, pastorals, and sonnets; Villegas, an Anacreonic poet; and the Jesuit Mariana, author of a History of Spain. The life of Calderon de la Barca, the illustrious head of the Spanish drama, extended from 1600 to 1687. His plays are of four kinds: sacred dramas, from Scriptural sources; historical dramas; classic dramas; and pictures of society and manners. The most celebrated are, *The Constant Prince*, *El Secreto a Voces* and *El Magico Prodigioso.* A number of small dramatists were contemporary with Calderon, but with his death Spanish literature declined, and has since produced few eminent names. Luyando, councilor of state, published two tragedies in 1750, and in 1758 appeared *The Life of Friar Gerund*, by Salazar — a work in the style of Don Quixote, but directed against the clergy instead of the chivalry. It abounds with wit and satire, and is perhaps the best Spanish prose work of the last century. Toward the close of the century Huerta achieved considerable reputation by his attempts to revive the Spanish drama. Tomas de Yriarte published in 1782 his Literary Fables, and a few years later Melendez appeared as the author of two volumes of idyls and pastorals. Both of these authors diplay considerable lyric genius.

The new life and health infused into literature in the age of Charles III. was checked by the French revolutionary wars in the reign of Charles IV., and afterwards by the restoration of civil despotism and the Inquisition, brought again into the country by the return of the Bourbon dynasty in 1814. Amidst the violence and confusion of the reign of Ferdinand VII. (1814–1833), elegant letters could hardly hope to find shelter or resting place. Nearly every poet and prose writer, known as such at the end of the reign of Charles IV., became involved in the fierce political changes of the time,—changes so varied and so opposite, that those who escaped from the consequences of one, were often, on that very account, sure to suffer in the next that followed. Indeed, the reign of Ferdinand VII. was an interregnum in all elegant culture, such as no modern nation has yet seen,—not even Spain herself during the War of the Succession. This state of things continued through the long civil war which arose soon after the death of that king, and indeed, it is not yet entirely abated. But despite the troubled condition of the country, even while Ferdinand was living, a movement was begun, the first traces of which are to be found among the emigrated Spaniards, who cheered with letters their exile in England and France, and whose subsequent progress, from the time when the death of their unfaithful monarch permitted them to return home, is distinctly perceptible in their own country.

The two principal writers of the first half of the century are the satirist Jose de Larra (d. 1837) and the poet Espronceda (d. 1842); both were brilliant writers, and both died young. Zorrilla (b. 1817) has great wealth of imagination, and Fernan Caballero is a gifted woman whose stories have been often translated. Antonio de Trueba is a writer of popular songs and short stories not without merit. Campoamor (b. 1817) and Bequer represent the poetry of twenty years ago. The short lyrics of the first named are remarkable for their delicacy and finesse. Bequer, who died at the age of thirty, left behind him poems which have already exercised a wide influence in his own country and in Spanish America; they tell a story of passionate love, despair, and death.

Perez Galdós, a writer of fiction, attacks the problem of modern life and thought, and represents with vivid and often bitter fidelity the conflicting interests and passions of Spanish life. Valera, a minister from Spain to the United States, is the author of the most famous Spanish novel of the day, *Pepita Jimenez*, a work of great artistic perfection, and his skill and grace are still more evident in his critical essays. Castelar gained a European celebrity as an orator and a political and miscellaneous writer, and was as well prëeminent in the field of diplomacy. The works of these authors, and of many others not named, show clearly that Spain is making vigorous efforts to bring herself socially and intellectually into line with the rest of Europe.

Of the Spanish colonies, Cuba has produced some writers of enduring renown. The most distinguished for poetic fame is Gertrude de Avelleneda; Heredia and Placido may also be mentioned. In Venezuela, Baralt is known as a historian, poet, and classical writer; Olmedo as a poet of Bolivia, and Caro a writer of the United States of Colombia.

PORTUGUESE LITERATURE.

Portugal first acquired its position as an independent kingdom after the battle of Ourigue, in 1139. The date of the origin of its literature is nearly coeval with that of the monarchy. Hermiguez and Moniz, two knights who flourished under Alfonso I., wrote the first ballads. King Dionysius, who reigned from 1279 to 1325, and his son Alfonso IV., were both renowned as poets; but few vestiges of their writings remain. It was not until the fifteenth century, however, that Portuguese literature attained any considerable merit. Macias, a Portuguese knight engaged in the wars with the Moors of Granada, was called El Enamorado, on account of the tender and glowing character of his amatory poems. The first distinguished poet of the country was Bernardin Ribeyro, who flourished under the reign of Emmanuel the Great, in the beginning of the sixteenth century. His most celebrated productions are his eclogues, the scenes of which are laid on the banks of the Tagus and the sea shores of Portugal. His lyrics of love, the origin of which is attributed to an unholy passion for the king's daughter, are wonderfully sweet and melodious. The first prose work in Portuguese worthy of note is a romance entitled *The Innocent Girl*, which appeared about this period. Saa de Miranda, who also attained celebrity as a Spanish author, was born in Coimbra in 1495, and wrote many sonnets, lyrics, and eclogues in his native tongue. He also wrote a series of poetical epistles, after the manner of Horace. Antonio Ferreira, who was born in 1528, followed the example of Miranda in his sonnets and eclogues, but surpassed him in entering the field of dramatic literature. His *Inez de Castro*, founded on the tragic story of that lady, displays much power and pathos in the delineation of the characters. The other poets of this generation were Andrade Caminha, Diego Bernardes, and Rodriguez de Castro, all of whom wrote lyrics, sonnets, and pastorals, few of which have survived them.

The sole star of Portuguese literature, who is now almost its only representative to other nations, was Luis de Camoëns, who was born in 1525. After studying at Coimbra, where he was coldly treated by Ferreira, he embraced the profession of arms, and lost an eye in the siege of Ceuta. Sailing for India in 1533, he reached Goa in safety, participated in an expedition against the king of Cochin-China, spent a winter in the islands of Ormuz, and afterwards, on account of a satire entitled Follies in India, directed against the Portuguese governor, was banished to Macao, on the coast of China. During his residence of five years in that place, he wrote his great epic of *The Lusiad*, devoted to celebrating the passage of the Cape of Good Hope by Vasco de Gama, and the triumph of Portuguese arms and commerce in the Orient. On his return to Portugal he was shipwrecked on the coast of Cambodia, and escaped by swimming, with *The Lusiad* in his hand, held above the waves. He died in great poverty in 1579. He left behind him many sonnets, songs, and pastorals, but most of them are penetrated with a vein of deep and settled melancholy. Among the successors of Camoëns, the most noted are Gil Vicente, a dramatic writer, who is supposed to have served as a model to Lope de Vega and Calderon; and Rodriguez Lobo, who was at one time considered a rival of Camoëns. He wrote the *Winter Nights*, a series of philosophical conversations, *Spring*, a romance, and numberless pastorals. Cortereal also described in a ponderous epic the adventures of Manuel de Sousa Sepulveda, a distinguished Portuguese.

The age of Camoëns also gave rise to a new branch of literature. John de Barros, born in 1496, is esteemed by his countrymen as the Livy of Portugal. He commenced his career by a romance entitled, *The Emperor Clarimond*, but after his return from service on the coast of Guinea, he devoted himself to the preparation of a grand historical work on the Portuguese empire. Only one-fourth of this, entitled *Portuguese Asia*, which was published in 1552, appeared. This is one of the most comprehensive, accurate, and interesting historical works of that age. Alfonso d'Albuquerque, one of the most distinguished contemporaries of Barros, wrote a series of *Commentaries*, and Couto and Castanheda undertook to complete the work which Barros had left unfinished. Bernardo de Brito, born in 1570, designed to give a universal history of Portugal, but, commencing with the Creation, he died by the time he reached the Christian Era. Osorio, Bishop of Sylvez, who died in 1580, wrote the History of King Emmanuel, describing the religious troubles of that time in a most liberal and enlightened spirit. Manuel de Faria, born in 1590, almost rivaled Lope de Vega in the amount of his works; his dissertations on the art of poetry are held in most value. He also wrote a history of Portugal and a commentary on Camoëns. After the subjugation of Portugal by Philip II. of Spain, the literature of the country declined, and presents no distinguished name for nearly a century following. The first author of the last century is the Count of Ericeyra, born in 1673. He was a general in the army, and a scholar of splendid attainments. His chief work was the *Henriqueïde*, an epic poem describing the adventures of Henry of Burgundy, the founder of the Portuguese monarchy. Towards the close of the last century, Antonio Garcao and the Countess de Vimieiro acquired some celebrity by their dramatic productions. The only Portuguese authors of note whom the present century has brought forth are Antonio da Cruz e Silva, who imitated Pope and other English poets, and J. A. da Cunha, an eminent mathematician and elegiac poet. The Portuguese colonies have produced a few writers, the most noted of whom are Vascencellos and Claudio Manuel da Costa.

FRENCH LITERATURE.

The literature of France was later in its development than that of the other nations of Southern Europe. It was necessary to wait the decline of the two romance-tongues of Normandy and Provence before the language could take a settled form, and a still further time elapsed before it was sufficiently matured for the purpose of the scholar and the author. During the thirteenth and fourteenth centuries the kingdom produced many romances, in which the influence of the literature of the Trouveres and Troubadours was manifest. Gilbert de Montreuil, Castellan de Coucy, and some others were noted for this species of composition; many sacred dramas and mysteries were written in the north of France, and about the middle of the fifteenth century, several romantic epics appeared. The only remarkable name of this early period is the renowned chronicler, Froissart, who was born in 1337, and in the course of his travels and sojourn at all the courts of Europe, was witness of many of the chivalrous events he describes in his "Chronicles of France, Spain, Italy, England, and Germany." Philip de Comines, who died in 1509, passed his life in the service of Louis IX., and left behind him the "Memoirs" of his time. The latter part of the fifteenth century produced many small writers of satires, odes, songs, etc., among whom Charles, Duke of Orleans, takes the first rank. The sacred mysteries, the first attempt at theatrical representation, gradually gave place to a rude form of drama and comedy, and a very successful comedy of French life appeared in 1475.

With the reign of Francis I. the study of the classics became popular in France, and from that time until the age of Louis XIV. the progress of French literature was rapid and uninterrupted. The sixteenth century produced a few great names. Scaliger and Casaubon were renowned for their scholastic acquirements; Clement Marot and Theodore Beza cultivated poetry under Francis I., whose sister, Margaret of Valois, published a collection of novels, called the Heptameron; Ronsard was the first French poet who showed strong original genius, and, with Regnier, gave the national poetry a freer and more characteristic tone. The drama was improved by Etienne Jodelle, who imitated the Greek tragedians; Claude de Seyssel wrote the History of Louis XII.; and Brantôme and Agrippa d'Aubigné left behind them many memoirs and historical essays. But the boast of the age is the names of Malherbe, Rabelais, and Montaigne. Malherbe, born in 1554, is considered the first French classic, in poetry; his language is most inflexibly pure and correct. Rabelais was born in 1483, and his romance of *Gargantua and Pantagruel* was first published in 1533. Notwithstanding its grossness it is one of the most lively, humorous, and brilliant books in the language. It satirizes the clerical and political characters of his time. Montaigne, whose life extended from 1533 to 1592, wrote three volumes of essays, on moral, political, and religious subjects, which on account of their elegant style no less than the treasures of thought they contain, have always held their place among French classics.

The seventeenth century is the glory of French literature. Under the auspices of Richelieu, Colbert, and Louis XIV. all departments of letters, science, and art reached a height unknown before. The French Academy was founded by Richelieu in 1635, and the language, at that time unrivaled in clearness, perspicacity, and flexibility, gradually became the polite tongue of Europe. Dramatic poetry, especially, founded on the principles of the Greek theater, attained a character it has never since reached. Corneille, born in 1606, was the father of the classic French drama. His first play, *The Cid*, belongs rather to the romantic drama, but through the influence of the Academy his later works, the most eminent of which are *Les Horaces*, *Cinna Polyeucte*, and *Mort de Pompée*, are strictly classical. His dramatic works amount to thirty-three. Racine, who was born in 1639, brought the classic drama to perfection. His language is the most elegant and melodious of all French dramatists, while he is inferior to none in his knowledge of nature and his command of the sentiments and passions. His plays, though constructed on the classic model, are not confined strictly to classic subjects. The most celebrated are *Andromaque*, *Bajazet*, *Mithridate*, *Phèdre*, *Esther*, and *Athalie*. After these two authors ranks Molière, the father and master of French comedy. His *Tartuffe* has a universal celebrity. He died in 1673. Crébillon, sometimes called the French Æschylus, was a writer of tragedies. Legrand, Regnard, and Scarron distinguished themselves as dramatists of secondary note. To this age belong Lo Sage, the author of *Gil Blas;* La Fontaine, the greatest fabulist since Æsop; and Boileau, the satirist and didactic poet, whose *Art Poétique* and *Lutrin* or "Battle of the Books" have been made classic. Mademoiselle de Scudery wrote many chivalrous romances, and Perrault's fairy tales soon became household words. The *Telémaque* of Fénelon was also produced during this period. This author, with Bourdaloue, Bossuet, and Massillon, were celebrated as theological writers and pulpit orators. Madame de Sevigné's letters are unsurpassed as specimens of graceful and spirited epistolary writing. As historians, Rollin is the most distinguished, but Mézeray, author of the national Chronicles, the Jesuit D'Orleans, author of Histories of Revolutions in England and Spain, and Bossuet's theological histories are worthy of notice.

During the eighteenth century, when the literature of Spain, Italy, and Portugal were on the decline, and England and Germany remained stationary, France still maintained her supremacy. In 1694 was born Voltaire, who in the course of his life made himself master of nearly every department of literature. His first play, *Œdipe,* was successfully performed in 1718, though his epic of the *Henriade*, written at the same time, was not published till 1729. Many of his succeeding plays were unsuccessful, and his satires and philosophical essays produced only banishment. His principal plays are *Zaïre*, *Alzire*, *Brutus*, *Oreste*, *Mahomet*, and *Tancrède*. After his return from Germany, he settled at Ferney on the Lake of Geneva, where for twenty years he devoted himself to literature. His principal works are *History of Charles XII. of Sweden; History of Russia under Peter The Great*, *Pyrrhonisme de l'Histoire*, *Droits de l'Homme* and the *Dictionnaire Philosophique*. Jean Jacques Rousseau, born in 1712, exercised scarcely less influence on French literature than Voltaire. His first work, a dissertation on Modern Music, appeared in Paris in 1743, about which time he wrote several comedies and tragedies and composed an opera. His romance entitled *Nouvelle Heloise*, was published in 1760, and his *Contrat Social* and *Emile* in 1762. His most remarkable work, the *Confessions*, was completed in 1770, and he died in 1778. As bold and independent as Voltaire in his philosophical views, he had nothing of his cynicism. His works, the style of which is absolutely fascinating, express a sincere sympathy with humanity. Montesquieu, whose *Spirit of Laws* is a standard work on jurisprudence, belongs to the first half of the eighteenth century. Among the historians contemporary with Voltaire, were Condorcet, author of a *History of Civilization*, and Barthélemy, who also wrote the *Voyage de Jeune Anacharsis*. La Bruyère, La Harpe, and Madame d'Epinay distinguished themselves by their didactic and epistolary writings. The most noted novelists were Marmontel, Bernardin de St. Pierre, author of *Paul and Virginia*, and Louvet. Marivaux attained distinction as a writer of comedies, and Beaumarchais as a dramatist and writer of operas. The well-known *Barber of Seville* is from his pen. France produced few lyric poets during the last century. Lebrun, Delille, and Joseph Chenier are the most worthy of mention, but the *Marseillaise* of Rouget de Lisle is the finest lyric of the century, if not of all French literature. Mirabeau, Barnave, Sièyes, and the leaders of the Revolution gave a new and splendid character to French oratory, toward the close of the century.

Chateaubriand, de Staël, and Béranger connect the age of Rousseau and Voltaire with the modern literature of France. Chateaubriand was born in 1769, and published his first work, the *Essay on Revolutions*, in London, in 1797, while in exile. His *Atala*, the subject of which was derived from his adventures among the Natchez tribe of Indians, on the Mississippi, appeared in 1801, and his *Génie du Christianisme* in 1802. He also published *Les Martyrs* in 1807, and an account of his travels in the East. He filled many diplomatic stations under the Bourbons, and was made peer of France. After his death, which took place in 1848, his autobiography was published, under the title of *Mémoires d'outre Tombe*. Madame de Staël, the daughter of M. Neckar, afterwards minister under Louis XVI., was born in 1766, and first appeared as an author in 1788, when she published a series of letters on the life and writings of Rousseau. During the French Revolution she remained in Switzerland and England, where she wrote several political pamphlets, dramas, and essays on life and literature. Her romance of *Corinne* was published in 1807, and her *De l'Allemagne*, which directed attention to the literature of Germany, in 1810. Her work entitled *Ten Years of Exile* was written in Sweden; she died in Paris in 1817. Béranger is the first song-writer of France. Many of his lyrics and ballads have become household words with the common people. Casimir Delavigne, who died in 1843, was among the first restorers of that lyric school which Lamartine, Victor Hugo, and Alfred de Musset have since carried to a high degree of perfection. The most renowned names in recent French Literature are, as poets, Alphonse de Lamartine, author of *Méditations Poétiques*, *Harmonies Poétiques* and *La Chute d'un Ange;* Victor Hugo, author of three volumes of lyrical romances and ballads; Alfred de Musset; Jean Reboul, a disciple of Lamartine; and Auguste Barbier, who mingles with his poems a vein of keen satire. Jasmin, a barber of Agen, has obtained much celebrity by his poems in the Gascon dialect. The new school of French romance has infected the modern literature of all countries. Balzac, who died in 1850, is unequaled as a painter of society and manners; Eugene Sue, whose *Mysteries of Paris* and *Wandering Jew* have been so widely read, delights in exciting subjects and the most intricate and improbable plots; Alexander Dumas, best known by his *Count of Monte Cristo*, and his romances of travel, is a master of picturesque narrative; Victor Hugo is best known as a novelist by his *Notre Dame de Paris*, a brilliant historical fiction, and *Les Misérables;* and Paul de Kock, as a lively though unscrupulous painter of Parisian life, enjoys a remarkable popularity.

The most striking and original writer of fiction is Madame Dudevant, better known as "George Sand," whose *Andre*, *Lettres d'un Voyageur*, and *Consuelo* have placed her in the first rank of French authors. It is somewhat remarkable that the excellence of this group of novelists has been maintained by a new generation of writers, Murger, About, Feuillet, Flaubert, Erckmann-Chatrian, Droz, Daudet, Cherbulliez, Gaboriau, Dumas, *fils*, Zola, Merimée, and others. As dramatists, Scribe, Leon Gozlan, Etienne Arago, Germain Delavigne, Sardou and Felix Pyat have distinguished themselves. The most prominent historical and political writers are Lamartine, Thiers, Michelet, Guizot, Louis Blanc, De Tocqueville and Thibaudeau; while Cousin and Comte are the founders of the new schools of philosophy. French oratory now occupies a higher position than ever before; its most illustrious names are Guizot, Thiers, Berryer, Lamartine, Odilon, Barrot, Victor Hugo, Lacordaire, Père Hyacinthe, and Coquerel. Renan is a prominent name in theological writing, and Montalembert a historian with strong religious tendencies. The great master of criticism is Sainte-Beuve (1804-1869), who possessed a rare combination of great and accurate learning, compass and profundity of thought, and, above all, sympathy in judgment. Henri Taine, whose works on English literature are among the best we have, Théophile Gautier, Arsène Houssaye, Jules Janin, Sarcy, and others, are distinguished in this branch of letters.

GERMAN LITERATURE.

The first period of German literature commenced with the reign of Charlemagne in the eighth century, and extended to the time of the Suabian emperors, at the close of the twelfth century. The first learned society was instituted by Alcuin, the greatest scholar of Charlemagne's time. In the succeeding period, Einhard, Rithard, and Lambert von Aschaffenburg distinguished themselves as historical and theological writers. About this time also originated those epic ballads and fragments which were afterwards collected under the title of the *Nibelungen-Lied*, or "Lay of the Nibelungen," and the "Song of Hildebrand." The Nibelungen-Lied, which has been called the German Iliad, received its present form about the year 1210. Its subject is the history of Siegfried, son of the King of the Netherlands, his marriage with Chriemhild, sister of Günther, King of the Burgundians, and the revenge of Brunhild, Queen of Ireland, who married Günther.

The second period terminates with the close of the fifteenth century. It includes the Minnesingers, or German Troubadours, who were the result of the intercourse of Germany with Italy and France, which made German scholars acquainted with the amatory literature of Provence. The most renowned Minnesingers were Wolfram von Eschenbach, who wrote *Percival;* Walter von der Vogelweide, the most graceful and popular of all, and Heinrich von Ofterdingen. Otto von Friesingen achieved renown for his histories, which were written in Latin.

The third period, dating from the commencement of the fifteenth century, at which time the German language was fully developed and subjected to rule, extends to the present time. It has been subdivided by German critics into three parts, viz.: 1, to the commencement of the Thirty Years' War; 2, to Klopstock and Lessing; 3, to our own day. The progress of the Reformation in the fifteenth century operated very favorably upon German literature. Melanchthon, Luther, Ulric von Hutten, and the other leaders of the movement were also distinguished scholars. The celebrated Paracelsus; the naturalist Gesner; the painter Albert Dürer, and the astronomers Kepler and Copernicus, flourished also in the fifteenth century. The most distinguished poet of this period was Hans Sachs, the shoemaker poet of Nuremberg. He was the master of a school or guild of poetry, which was then considered as an elegant profession. In the number of his works he rivals Lope de Vega, as he is said to have written 6048, 208 of which were comedies and tragedies. He died in 1576. Martin Opitz, who marks the commencement of a new era in German poetry, was born in 1597. He first established a true rhythm in poetry, by measuring the length of the syllables, instead of merely counting them as formerly. His principal poems are *Vesuvius*, *Judith*, and a number of lyrics. He was followed by Paul Flemming and Simon Dach, who wrote in the low German dialect. As prose writers of the seventeenth century, Puffendorf, a writer on jurisprudence and international law, Leibnitz, the distinguished philosopher, and the Brothers Baumgarten, are most prominent. There is no great name in German literature, however, from Opitz till the middle of the last century, when Gellert, Gessner, Klopstock, and Hagedorn were the inauguration of a new life. Under these authors, and others of less note, the language attained a richness of expression, a flexibility of style, and a harmony of modulation which it never possessed before. Gellert, born in 1715, is distinguished for his "Spiritual Songs and Odes," his letters, and his romance of *The Swedish Countess*, which is the first domestic novel written in the German language. Gessner is best known through his idylls, in which he followed the classic models. Hagedorn, who died in 1754, wrote many poems; he is supposed to have exercised considerable influence on Klopstock in his earlier years. As prose writers, Forster, Mendelssohn the philosopher, and Musäus, who made a collection of German legends and traditions, are worthy of note.

With Klopstock commenced the golden age of German literature, and the list of renowned names continues unbroken until the present time. Klopstock was born in 1724. In his odes and lyrical poems he struck out a new and bold path, casting aside the mechanical rules of the older schools of German poetry. His greatest work is the *Messias*, a sacred epic, which was commenced in 1745 and finished in 1771. Lessing, born in 1729, stands by the side of Klopstock as a poet, while he is also distinguished as a prose writer. He may be considered as the first successful German dramatist, his plays of *Emilia Galotti*, *Minna von Barnhelm*, *Nathan the Wise*, still keeping their place on the stage. As a critical writer on all the branches of the Fine Arts, he is also distinguished. Wieland follows next in the list of German classics. Born in 1733, he is the link between the age of Gellert and Klopstock, and that of Schiller and Goethe. He died in 1813. His principal works are *The New Amadis*, which illustrates the triumph of spiritual over physical beauty, the heroic epic of *Oberon*, a romance of the middle ages, the drama of *Alceste*, the *History of the Abderites*, a satirical romance, besides many letters, satires, and criticisms on literature and art. Herder, his contemporary, in addition to his fame as a poet, is celebrated for his philosophical and theological writings, and his *Spirit of Hebrew Poetry*. He died in 1803. At the commencement of the 19th century, Wieland, Herder, Goethe, and Schiller were gathered together at the court of Weimar — the most illustrious congregation of poets since Shakespeare, Spenser, Ben Jonson, and Fletcher met together in London. Goethe was born in 1749, and from his boyhood displayed a remarkable talent for literature, science, and art. His first romance, *The Sorrows of Werther*, produced a great sensation throughout all Europe. His tragedy of *Götz von Berlichingen*, written at the age of 22, established his fame as a poet. After his settlement at Weimar in 1774, his works followed each other rapidly. He produced the tragedies of *Iphigenia*, *Egmont*, *Tasso*, and *Clavigo*, the pastoral epic of *Hermann und Dorothea*, the philosophical romances of *Wilhelm Meister* and *Die Wahlverwandschaften*, the *West-Oestliche Divan*, a collection of poems founded in his studies of Oriental literature, and the first part of his greatest work, *Faust*. He also published narratives of travel in France and Italy, and *Wahrheit und Dichtung*, an autobiography of his life. His philosophic and scientific writings, especially his theory of color, are scarcely less celebrated than his literary works. He is equally a master in all departments of literature, and is generally acknowledged as the greatest author since Shakespeare. He died in 1832. Schiller, born in 1759, exercised scarcely less influence on German literature than Goethe. His tragedy of *The Robbers* produced nearly as great a revolution as *The Sorrows of Werther*. On account of this and other works he was obliged to fly from his native Würtemberg, and, after many vicissitudes, settled in Weimar, with his great colleagues. After a brief but intense and laborious life, he died in 1805. After *The Robbers*, he wrote the following dramatic works: *Fiesco*, *Cabal and Love*, *Don Carlos*, *The Maid of Orleans*, *Marie Stuart*, *William Tell*, *The Bride of Messina*, and *Wallenstein*. The last is the greatest drama in the German language. His lyrical poems are unsurpassed. His principal prose works are the *History of the Netherlands* and *History of the Thirty Years' War*. This period, so glorious for German literature, produced also the poets, Bürger, author of *Lenore* and *The Wild Huntsman;* Count Stolberg; Voss, author of *Luise;* Salis and Matthisson, elegiac poets; Tiedge, author of *Urania;* and the hero Korner, the Tyrtæus of the wars of 1812 and 1813. The department of prose was filled by many distinguished writers of philosophy, history, and romance. Kant, who lived from 1724 to 1804, is the father of modern German philosophy, and exercised a great influence on all his contemporaries. Schlegel, in the department of literary criticism, and Winckelmann, in that of art, are renowned names. Hegel and Fichte succeeded Kant as philosophers, and these in turn were followed by Ruge, Strauss, Feuerbach, Ulrici, Schopenhauer, and Von Hartmann; while Alexander von Humboldt became the leader of a new and splendid company of writers on cosmical science. The name of Tieck heads the school of modern German romance. He was born in 1773, and early attracted attention by his *Bluebeard* and *Puss in Boots*. In addition to a great number of plays, romances, and poems, he produced, in conjunction with Schlegel, a German translation of Shakespeare, which is the most remarkable work of its kind in all literature. Jean Paul Richter, the most original and peculiar of all German authors, was born in 1763 and died in 1825. His first work was a humorous and satirical production, entitled, *The Greenlandic Lawsuit*, followed by *Selections from the Devil's Papers*. His works are distinguished by a great knowledge of human nature, and a bewildering richness of imagination, and a style so quaint and involved as almost to form a separate dialect. His best works are *Titan*, *Hesperus*, *Die Unsichtbare Loge*, and *Flower, Fruit, and Thorn Pieces*. E. T. A. Hoffman is scarcely less original in his romances, which have a wild, fantastic, and supernatural character. Among other German authors, the brothers Grimm are celebrated for their *Kinder und Haus Mährchen*, the notorious Kotzebue for his plays, and Wolfgang Menzel for his *History of Germany* and *German Literature*.

Since the commencement of the 19th century Germany has been prolific of authors, but the limits of this sketch prohibit us from much more than the mere mention of their names. Baron de la Motte Fouque is known as the author of *Undine*, one of the most purely poetical creations of fiction, *Sintram*, and *Thiodolf, the Icelander*. Börne attained celebrity as a satirist, critic, and political writer. Uhland stands at the head of the modern generation of poets. His ballads, romances, and his epic of *Ludwig der Baier* are among the best German poems of the day. After him rank Ruckert, also renowned as an Oriental scholar; Hauff, a lyric poet, and author of the romance of *Lichtenstein;* Gustav Schwab, Justinus Kerner, author of the *Seeress of Prevorst;* Arndt, author of the *German Fatherland*, the national lyric; Anastasius Grün (Count Auersperg), author of the *Pfaff von Kahlenberg;* Nicholas Lenau, author of *Savonarola;* Ferdinand Freiligrath, a vigorous political poet; Heinrich Heine, author of many popular songs and ballads; Chamisso, who also wrote the romance of *Peter Schlemihl;* Gutzkow, distinguished as a dramatist; Halm, also a dramatist, and author of *Der Sohn der Wildniss;* and, as lyric poets, Herwegh, Geibel, and Beck. Among the distinguished prose writers are Schlosser, author of a Universal History; Neander, author of a History of the Church, and a Life of Christ; Prince Puckler-Muskau and the Countess Hahn-Hahn, critics and tourists; Zschokke (a Swiss), Auerbach and Freytag distinguished as novelists, and Feuerbach; Schelling as a philosopher; Strauss, author of a Life of Christ and head of the German "Rationalists"; Müller, as a historian, and Krummacher, a writer of fables and parables. As historians Rotteck, Niebuhr, and Ranke are among the most distinguished of the present century. One of the most popular prose writers is Adalbert Stifter, whose *Studien* are unsurpassed for exquisite purity and picturesqueness of style. In science the first place belongs to Humboldt's *Cosmos;* In chemistry Liebig is widely and popularly known; Du Bois-Raymond has made great researches in animal electricity, physics, and physiology; Virchow in biology; Helmholtz in physiological optics and sound; Haeckel has extended the theories and investigations of Darwin. Modern German literature is singularly rich in history, theology, and criticism.

SCANDINAVIAN LITERATURE.

Under this head we have grouped the literature of the three nations of Scandinavian origin,— Sweden, Norway, and Denmark. The old Scandinavian Eddas, or hymns of gods and heroes, may be traced back to the seventh or eighth century. The earlier Edda, which was collected and arranged by Samund in the year 1100, consists of legends of the gods, most of which were probably written in the eighth century. The latter Edda, collected by Snorre Sturleson in the first half of the thirteenth century, contains fragments of the songs of the Skalds who flourished in the ninth and tenth centuries, especially in the latter, when their genius reached its culmination in Norway and Iceland. Among the most renowned works of the Skalds were the *Eiriksmal*, the apotheosis of King Eric, who died in 952, and the *Hakonarmal*, describing the fall of Jarl Haco. A celebrated Skald was Egill Skalagrimsson, who wrote three epic poems, and two *drapas*, or elegiac poems. The power of the Skalds declined through the eleventh and twelfth centuries, and after the fourteenth, when the Christian element first began to appear in Icelandic poetry, wholly disappeared. Many sagas were written in prose, and the *Heimskringla* of Snorre Sturleson, who died in Iceland in 1238, contains the chronicles of Scandinavian history from its mythic period to the year 1177.

Previous to the establishment of the University of Upsala, in 1476, the only literature of Sweden was a few rhymed historic legends. The two centuries succeeding this period have left no great names, and few distinguished ones. Saxo-Grammaticus made a collection of legends in the fifteenth century; Olaus Magni wrote a history of the North in Latin; Messenius, who died in 1637, wrote comedies and a historical work entitled *Scandia Illustrata;* Axel Oxenstierna, the celebrated minister, was also a theologist and patron of literature; Olof Rudbeck, a distinguished scholar, published in 1675 his *Atlantica*, wherein, from the study of the old Sagas, he endeavored to show that Sweden was the Atlantis of the ancients. George Stjernhjelm, who died in 1672, was the author of a poem called *Hercules*, whence he is named the father of Swedish poetry. Swedenborg, the most striking character in Northern literature, was born in 1688. After several years of travel in England and on the continent, he established himself in Sweden, where he devoted his attention to science, and produced a number of works on natural philosophy, mineralogy, zoölogy, and other kindred subjects. The close of his life was entirely occupied with his religious studies, and the production of his *Arcana Cœlestia*, which contains his revelations of the future life, and his theory of the spiritual universe. These writings gave rise to a new religious sect, the members of which, in the United States, are supposed to number about 6,000. He professed to be visited by the Holy Spirit, and his works are considered by his disciples as equally inspired with those of the Apostles. He died in London in 1772. Dalin and Madame Nordenflycht were the first noted poets of the last century. They were succeeded by a multitude of lyric and didactic poets; but Swedish poetry did not attain a high character before the commencement of the present century. Among the authors most worthy of note are Lidner, Bellman, and Thorild. An important history of Sweden has been written by Professors Geijer, Fryxell, and Strinholm. The 19th century produced Atterbom and Dahlgren, poets of considerable celebrity, and Tegner, the first of Swedish poets, whose *Frithiof's Saga* has been translated into English, French, and German. Longfellow has translated his *Children of the Lord's Supper*. In the glow of his imagination, his fine artistic feeling, and his wonderful command of rhythm, Tegner ranks among the first of modern poets. He died in 1846. As writers of fiction, Count Sparre, author of *Adolf Findling*, Frederika Bremer, whose fame, as a painter of Swedish life, has extended over both hemispheres, and Madame Flygare-Carlen, author of the *Rose of Thistle Island*, have attained an honorable place. The most celebrated works of Miss Bremer are *The Neighbo:s*, *The Home*, and *Strife and Peace*.

There are few names in Danish literature before the last century. Ludwig von Holberg, born in 1685, was the first who achieved a permanent reputation as poet and historian. Towards the close of the last century Denmark produced many distinguished scholars and men of science. Rafn and Finn Magnusen rescued the old Icelandic sagas from oblivion, and established the fact of the discovery of New England by Bjorne in the tenth century; Petersen became renowned as a classical scholar and critic; Oersted is a well known name in science and philosophy; and Müller and Allen successfully labored in the department of history. Nearly all these authors first became known in the present century. At the head of Denmark's poets is Œhlenschlager, who died in 1850. His national tragedies, epics, and lyrics were written partly in German and partly in Danish. He is considered the originator of the artist-drama, of which his *Coreggio* is a masterpiece. Baggesen, who commenced his career in the last century, is one of the first Danish lyric poets. Heiberg devoted himself to vaudeville and the romantic drama, and Hauch to tragedy, in which he is justly distinguished. Hertz is known through his *King Rene's Daughters*, which has been successfully produced on the English stage. One of the most distinguished of modern Danish authors is Hans Christian Andersen, known alike as poet, novelist, and tourist. His romances of Danish life are the most characteristic of his works, though he is better known out of his native country by his *Improvisatore* and *The True Story of My Life*. Norway cannot be said to have had a literature distinct from the Danish until after its union with Sweden in 1814. The period from that time to the present has been one of great literary activity in all departments, and many distinguished names might be mentioned, among them that of Björnson whose tales have been extensively translated. Jonas Lie, who enjoys a wide popularity, Camilla Collett, and Magdalene Thoresen are also favorite writers. Wergeland and Welhaven were two distinguished poets of the first half of the century. Kielland is an able novelist of the realistic school, and Professor Boyesen is well known in the United States for his tales and poems in English. Henrik Ibsen is the most distinguished dramatic writer of Norway and belongs to the realistic school. Among other recent writers are Börjesson, whose *Eric XIV.* is a masterpiece of Swedish drama; Tekla Knös, a poetess whose claims have been sanctioned by the Academy; and Claude Gérard (*nom de plume*), very popular as a novelist.

RUSSIAN LITERATURE.

The first fragments of Russian literature belong to the tenth and eleventh centuries. They consist principally of rude songs and legends, the hero of which is Wladimir the Great, who first introduced Christianity into the country. Nestor, a monk in the monastery of Kiev, who died in the year 1116, left behind him a collection of annals, beginning with 852, which threw much light on the early history of Russia. After the empire was freed from the Mongolian rule by Ivan I. in 1478, the progress of literature and the arts were more rapid. The first printing press was established in Moscow in 1564, though the Academy in that city was not founded until a century later. Peter the Great devoted much attention to the Russian language and literature. At his command, the characters used in printing were greatly simplified and improved. The first Russian newspaper was printed in 1705, in this character.

From 1650 to 1750, Russia produced several authors, but principally among the clergy. and their works are dissertations on theology or lives of the saints. Tatitschev wrote a *History of Russia*, which still retains some value. The only poet of this period was Kantemir, son of the Hospodar of Moldavia, who entered the Russian service, devoted himself to study, and obtained much reputation from his satires. Towards the close of the last century, and especially during the reigns of Elizabeth and Catharine II., the establishment of universities and academies of science and art, contributed greatly to the development of the language and the encouragement of literature. The distinction between the old Slavic and modern Russian dialects is strongly exhibited in the works of Lomonosow, and the predominance of the latter was still further determined by Sumarakow, the first Russian dramatist, whose plays were performed on the stage. Cheraskow, who belongs to the last half of the eighteenth century, wrote a long epic poem on the Conquest of Kazan, and another on Wladimir the Great. He was considered the Homer of his time, but is now never read. Among his contemporary poets were Prince Dolgoruki, who wrote philosophic odes and epistles, and Count Chvostow, the author of some of the best lyric and didactic poetry in the language.

The first Russian poet whose name was known beyond the borders of the empire was Derzhavin, who was born at Kazan in 1743, and after filling important civil posts under the Empress Catharine, died in 1816. Many of his most inspired odes were addressed to his imperial patroness. His ode *To God* has been translated into nearly all languages, and a Chinese copy, printed in letters of gold, hangs upon the walls of the palace at Pekin. The prose writers of this period were Platon, Lewanda, and Schtscherbatow, who wrote a History of Russia. Under Alexander I., in the commencement of the present century, Russian literature made rapid advances. Karamsin, who stood at the head of Russian authors during this period, first freed the popular style from the fetters of the classic school, and developed the native resources of the language. Prince Alexander Schakowski wrote many comedies and comic operas, and Zukowski, following in the path of Karamsin, produced some vigorous and glowing poetry. Count Puschkin, one of the most celebrated Russian authors, was born in 1799. His first poem, published at the age of fourteen, attracted so much attention that he resolved to devote himself to literature. An *Ode to Freedom*, however, procured him banishment to the south of Russia, where his best poems were written. His works are *Russlan and Ljudmilla*, a romantic epic of the heroic age of Russia; the *Mountain Prisoner*, a story of life in the Caucasus; the *Fountains of Baktschissarai*, and *Boris Godunoff*, a dramatic poem. In his invention, the elegance of his diction, and the richness of his fancy, Puschkin excels all other Russian authors. He was killed in a duel in 1837. His contemporary, Baratynski, who stood nearest him in talent, died in 1844. Other poets of this period are Lermontow, Podolinski, and Baron Delwig. Russian romance is not yet fairly developed. The first names in this department are Bestuzew, who suffered banishment in Siberia and met death in the Caucasus, where his best work, *Amaleth-Beg*, was written, Bulgarin, author of *Demetrius and Mazeppa*, Count Tolstoi, and Turgenieff. The only histories written in Russia are histories of Russia. The best of these which have been produced by the present generation of authors are those of Ustrialow, Pogodin, Polewoi, and Michailowski-Danilewski.

POLISH LITERATURE.

The Polish language has received a more thorough development and boasts a richer literature than any other language of Slavic origin. It first reached a finished and regular form in the sixteenth century, though a fragment of a hymn to the Virgin remains, which was supposed to have been written by St. Adalbert, in the fifteenth century. The first bloom of Polish literature happened during the reigns of Sigismund I. and Augustus, from 1507 to 1572. Michael Rey, the father of Polish poetry, was a bold, spirited satirist. He died in 1586, and was followed by the brothers Kochanowski, Miaskowski, and Szymonowicz, who, for his Latin odes, was called the Latin Pindar. Bielski wrote the *Kronika*, a collection of Polish legends, and Gornicki, secretary to Sigismund, a *History of the Crown of Poland*. Orzechowski, one of the most distinguished orators of his day, wrote in the Latin language, the *Annales Poloniæ*.

After the commencement of the seventeenth century, Polish letters declined, and as the kingdom came under the ascendency of the Jesuits, a corresponding change came over the character of the literature. Kochowski, who died in 1700, was historiographer to King John Sobieski, and accompanied him against the Turks. Opalinski, the Woiwode of Posen, published in 1652 his *Satyres*, a lively and characteristic work, and a number of Jesuit historians undertook histories of the country, in which few of them were successful.

Through the influence of French authors, Polish literature made another advance, at the close of the first half of the last century. The first poet who served to concentrate the scattered elements of Polish poetry, was Krasicki, who was born in 1734, and in 1767 was made Bishop of Ermeland. He wrote a mock-heroic poem, *Myszeis* (The Mousead), an epic entitled *Woyna Chocimska* (The War of Chocim), and many fables in verse. The most prominent of the later poets are Godebski, Wezyk, author of romances and dramas, Felinski, author of *Barbara Radziwill*, and Gen. Kropinski, who wrote *Ludgarda*. Tropinski, who died in 1825, was the author of many admirable lyrics and idyls, and a tragedy called *Judyta*. Niemcewicz, his contemporary, wrote the *Historical Lives of Poland*, a History of the reign of Sigismund III., and a romance, *Johann v. Tenczyn*. The university of Wilna, which in 1815 was the seat of Polish learning, witnessed a revolution in the character of the literature. Several young authors, with Mickiewicz at their head, determined to free themselves from the classic spirit of the language, and imitate the later English and

German schools. From this time Polish fiction took a freer, bolder, and more varied form. Mickiewicz, born in 1798, published his first volume of poetry in 1822. Banished to the interior of Russia on account of political troubles, he wrote a series of sonnets which attracted the attention of Prince Galizin, under whose auspices his epic poem, *Konrad Wallenrod*, was published in 1828. His Polish epic of *Pan Tadeusz* first appeared in Paris in 1834. Among his contemporary authors the most noted are Odyniec, author of the drama of *Izora;* Korsac, a lyric and elegiac poet; Garczynski, who wrote many fiery battle-songs; and Czajkowski, a noted writer of Slavic romances. The later prose writers of Poland are the historical Lelewel, and Count Plater, and Henryk Sienkiewicz, author of *With Fire and Sword* and *Quo Vadis*, who is the first of Polish novelists, and second to none in this generation.

ENGLISH LITERATURE.

The English language, like other composite modern tongues, such as the French and Italian, passed through several phases before reaching its present form and character. During the prevalence of the Anglo-Saxon tongue, from the fifth century to the Norman conquest, England boasted several authors, whose names and works have in part descended to us. The venerable Bede, born in Northumberland in 672, is distinguished for his scholarship. He left an Ecclesiastical history of the Angles, which forms the basis of early English history. The monk Cædmon, who flourished in the seventh century, wrote a paraphrase of Genesis and some fragments which are supposed to have given Milton the first idea of *Paradise Lost*. The song of Beowulf, which belongs to the eighth century, is a spirited and stirring heroic. King Alfred's poems belong to the best specimens of Anglo-Saxon literature. The Norman conquest introduced the French language and the literature of the Trouvères, while the Anglo-Saxon was left to the peasants and thralls. Out of these elements, however, the English language was gradually formed, and under the reign of Edward III., in the fourteenth century, was made the language of the court. It then assumed a character which is intelligible to the educated English of the present day, and that period, therefore, may be considered as the first age of English literature.

The earliest English author is Chaucer, "the morning-star of English song," who was born in 1328, and produced his first poem, *The Court of Love*, in 1347. During his life he enjoyed the favor of Edward III., and his son, John of Gaunt. He filled various diplomatic stations, among others that of ambassador to Genoa. During his residence in Italy, he became familiar with the works of Dante, Boccaccio, and Petrarch, and is supposed to have visited the latter. He also wrote *Troilus and Cressida*, *The House of Fame* and *The Canterbury Tales*, his most famous work, an imitation, in poetry, of the Decameron. He died in 1400. The first prose works in the English language were translations of the gospels and of some of the classics. Wickliffe, the Reformer, who first made an English version of the Bible, was a contemporary of Chaucer. Sir Thomas Wyatt, and Henry Howard, Earl of Surrey, who flourished under the reign of Henry VIII., in the beginning of the sixteenth century, are the next English poets of note. They wrote principally songs and odes. Surrey was beheaded on charge of treason in 1547.

The reign of Elizabeth, at the close of the sixteenth century, was the golden age of English literature. Shakespeare, Spenser, Raleigh, Sidney, Ben Jonson, Beaumont, and Fletcher formed a constellation of poets and dramatists, such as no other age or country ever produced. Spenser, born in 1553, became early associated with Sir Philip Sidney, to whom, in 1579, he dedicated his first work, the *Shepherd's Calendar*, a pastoral. From 1586 to 1598, he was sheriff of the county of Cork, in Ireland, and resided at Kilcolman Castle, where his greatest work, *The Faery Queen*, was composed. This is an allegory in twelve books, written in stanza of his own invention (modeled, however, on the Italian *ottava rima*), and which now bears his name. He died in 1599. Sidney, who was born in 1554, is best known as the author of *Arcadia*, a pastoral romance, and the *Defence of Poetry*. He is the first writer who gave an elegant and correct form to English prose. Shakespeare, the greatest dramatic poet of any age, was born in 1564. He commenced his career by preparing for the stage the plays of some of his predecessors, and this fact has thrown some doubt about the authenticity of two or three of the plays included among his works. The order in which his own plays appeared has never been satisfactorily ascertained. The following, however, are known to have been written before 1598: *The Two Gentlemen of Verona; Love's Labor Lost; The Comedy of Errors; Midsummer Night's Dream; Romeo and Juliet; Merchant of Venice; Richard II.; Richard III.; Henry IV.;* and *King John*.

The Tempest, which appeared in 1611, is believed to be his last dramatic work. He also wrote the poems of *Venus and Adonis* and

The Rape of Lucrece, a lyric called *The Passionate Pilgrim*, and a great number of sonnets, some of which are the finest in the language. He died in 1616. Ben Jonson was born in 1574, and published his first dramatic work, the comedy of *Every Man in His Humor*, in 1596. In addition to other comedies, the best of which are *Volpone, the Fox*, and *The Alchemist*, he wrote many exquisite songs and madrigals. Sir Walter Raleigh is more distinguished as a gallant knight and daring adventurer than as an author, yet his lyrics and his *History of the World*, written during twelve years' imprisonment in the Tower, give him full claim to the latter title. He was born in 1552, and was beheaded by order of James I. in 1617. Beaumont and Fletcher, contemporaries and in some degree imitators of Shakespeare, deserve the next place after him among the dramatists of that period. Beaumont is supposed to have been the inventive genius of their plays, and Fletcher to have supplied the wit and fancy. The *Faithful Shepherdess* is the work of Fletcher alone. Many dramatists flourished during this and the succeeding generation, whose works are now but little read, but who would have attained eminence but for the greater lights with which they are eclipsed. The most noted of them are Marlowe, Marston, Chapman, Decker, Webster, Ford, and Massinger.

Between Shakespeare and Milton, the only name which appears in English literature is Cowley, the author of the *Davideis*, a forgotten epic. Milton was born in 1608, and in his early boyhood exhibited the genius which afterwards made him the first English poet and one of the great masters of English prose. His hymn on the *Nativity* was written in his twenty-first, and his mask of *Comus* in his twenty-third year. *L'Allegro, Il Penseroso*, and *Lycidas* soon afterward appeared. After his return from Italy, he devoted his attention to theology and politics. His treatise on *Marriage* was published in 1643, his *Areopagitica* in 1644, and his famous reply to Salmasius in 1651. In the following year he lost his sight, and was obliged to retire from public service. His *Paradise Lost* appeared in 1665, and was followed by *Paradise Regained* in 1671, and *Samson Agonistes*. He died in 1674. Dryden, who, born in 1631, was known as a poet during Milton's life, introduced a new school of poetry — the narrative and didactic. His first noted poem, the *Annus Mirabilis*, was produced in 1666, his satire of *Absalom and Achitophel* in 1681, and shortly afterwards his *Hind and Panther*, a religious satire. He also wrote several rhymed tragedies and an essay on *Dramatic Poesy*. Defoe, born in 1663, wrote the world-renowned narrative of *Robinson Crusoe*, which was first published in 1719. The seventeenth century was also an important epoch for English philosophical literature. Lord Bacon, born in 1561, published his *De dignitate et augmentis Scientarum* in 1605, and his celebrated *Novum Organum* in 1620. These, although written in Latin, are the most important philosophical works which have ever emanated from an English author. Hobbes, a writer on politics, jurisprudence, and moral philosophy, died in 1679. Locke, born in 1632, first published his *Essay on the Human Understanding* in 1690.

The commencement of the last century brings us to a group of authors of very different character. The influence of French literature began to be felt, and the characteristics of the English writers of this period are elegance and grace. This is properly the age of English prose, which was enriched successively by Addison, Horace Walpole, Swift, Sterne, Richardson, Smollett, Fielding, Hume, Gibbon, Chesterfield, and Robertson. The first poet who rose to eminence in the last century was Pope, who was born in 1688, and published his *Essay on Criticism* in 1711. His most celebrated poetical works are the *Rape of the Lock*, the *Essay on Man* and *The Dunciad*. Thomson, author of *The Seasons* and the *Castle of Indolence*, lived and died in the first half of the century. Gay, a contemporary poet, is distinguished for his Fables. Gray ranks as one of the finest lyric poets of England. The few odes he has left, and his *Elegy in a Country Churchyard*, belong to the classics of the language. Goldsmith was born in 1728 and died in 1774. His poems of *The Traveller* and *The Deserted Village*, and his romance of the *Vicar of Wakefield*, will live as long as his native tongue. Cowper closes the list of the poets of the last century. He died in 1800, after a life darkened by religious melancholy. His *Task*, *Table-Talk*, and ballad of *John Gilpin*, are his best poetical works. Returning to the prose writers, Addison is first in point of time, having been born in 1672. His best works are his essays, contributed to *The Spectator*, which he established in 1711, in conjunction with his friend Steele. His English has rarely been excelled for purity and elegance. Chesterfield, Lady Montague, and Horace Walpole are distinguished as epistolary writers. Dean Swift, born in 1667, was a politician and satirist, but is now best known by his *Tale of a Tub*, published in 1704, and *Gulliver's Travels*, in 1726. Sterne in his *Tristram Shandy* and *The Sentimental Journey*,

displayed a droll mingling of wit and pathos, in a style exceedingly lively and flexible. Richardson, one of the first English romance writers, was born in 1689. His principal novels, which are of immense length, are *Pamela*, *Clarissa Harlowe*, and *Sir Charles Grandison*. Smollett, his successor, published his *Roderick Random* in 1748, and *Humphrey Clinker*, his last work, in 1771. Hume, in addition to political and philosophical works, wrote the *History of England*, from the invasion of Cæsar to the rebellion of 1688, which was published in 1673-4. Smollett wrote four volumes in continuation of the history. Gibbon, born in 1737, completed, after twenty years' labor, his *History of the Decline and Fall of the Roman Empire*, which appeared from 1782 to 1788. Robertson, the contemporary of Gibbon, published his *History of Scotland* in 1759, and his *History of the Reign of Charles V.* in 1769. Dr. Johnson, whose *Rasselas*, *Lives of the Poets*, and contributions to *The Rambler* exercised such a salutary influence on the popular taste of his time, died in 1784. His *Dictionary of the English Language* was first published in 1755. Edmund Burke, one of the most finished and powerful of English orators, published, in 1756, his *Essay on the Sublime and Beautiful*, which is a model of philosophical writing. He died in 1797.

With the present century commenced a new era in English literature. The reign of the drama and the epic was over; the reign of romance, in both prose and poetry, and the expression of a higher and more subtle range of imagination now commenced. The language lost something, perhaps, of its classic polish and massive strength, but became more free and flowing, more varied in style, and richer in epithet. The authors in whom this change is first apparent are Coleridge and Wordsworth in poetry, and Scott in prose. Nearly coeval with the two former, but different in character, were Byron and Moore; the latter are the poets of passion, the former of imagination. Scott, in his Waverley novels, first developed the neglected wealth of English romance. Burns, although his best songs are in the Scottish dialect, stands at the head of all English song writers. Campbell, in the true lyric inspiration of his poems, is classed with Gray. Rogers and Southey can hardly be ranked among those poets who assisted in developing the later English literature. The former imitates the old models; the latter, more daring in his forms of verse and more splendid in his imagination, has never been able to touch the popular heart. Coleridge's prose works contain probably the most important contributions to English philosophical literature since the time of Bacon. The department of history has been amply filled by Scott, Alison, author of a *History of Europe*, Gillies and Grote, celebrated for their *Histories of Greece*, Napier in his *History of the Peninsular War*, Hallam in his *History of the Middle Ages*, and Macaulay in his *History of England*. Leigh Hunt wrote *The Rimini*. The field of historical romance opened by Sir Walter Scott has been successfully followed by Sir Edward Bulwer-Lytton and G. P. R. James.

As novelists of English life and society, under all its aspects, Dickens and Thackeray — and Miss Brontë, author of *Shirley* and *Jane Eyre* — stand preëminent. As essayists and critics, the names of Lords Jeffrey and Brougham, Sidney Smith, Macaulay, Professor Wilson, De Quincey, Carlyle, and Stevens surpass even the group who produced *The Tatler* and *The Spectator*. Carlyle, in his *Sartor Resartus*, *Past and Present*, and *Heroes and Hero Worship*, has made use of an idiom of his own — a broken, involved, Germanesque diction, which resembles that of no other English author. Some of the most prominent English poets of this period are Lord Byron, Shelley, Thomas Moore, Leigh Hunt, Rogers, Alfred Tennyson, Milnes, Barry Cornwall, Robert Browning, Elizabeth Barrett Browning, probably the most impassioned and imaginative of English female authors, Walter Savage Landor, Mary Howitt, R. H. Horne, author of *Orion*, Croly, Philip James Bailey, author of *Festus*, and T. N. Talfourd, author of the tragedy of *Ion*. Among later writers of poetry, Matthew Arnold has written some of the most refined verse of our generation, and among critics holds the first rank. Algernon Swinburne excels all living poets in his marvelous gift of rhythm and command over the resources of the language. Dante Rossetti had great lyrical power; Edwin Arnold has extraordinary popularity in the United States for his remarkable poem, *The Light of Asia*, and for other poems on Oriental subjects. Among other poets of the present generation whose writings are marked by excellences of various kinds are Lord Lytton ("Owen Meredith"), William Morris, Edmund Gosse, Austin Dobson, Andrew Lang, and Philip Marston. Among female writers, the poems of Jean Ingelow have a merited popularity; those of Adelaide Procter are pervaded by a beautiful spirit of faith and hope; while Christina Rossetti shows great originality and deep feeling. Chief in the field of fiction are the writings of "George Eliot," a woman of rare genius, whose works are among the greatest England has produced. Anthony Trollope has produced many works remarkable for their accurate pictures of English life and character. George Macdonald and Wilkie Collins are novelists of great merit, as are Mrs. Humphry Ward, Rudyard Kipling, and Richard Blackmore. Among others in popular favor are William Black, Mrs. Oliphant, Conan Doyle, and J. M. Barrie. Charles Darwin and Herbert Spencer have been the most distinguished authors identified with the scientific and philosophical aspects of evolution, and have had a wide influence on contemporary thought. Tyndall has done more than any other writer to popularize great scientific truths. Huxley stands foremost among physiologists and naturalists. Among numerous other writers distinguished in various branches of science, a few only can be here named. Walter Bagehot writes of Political Society; Alexander Bain on Mind and Body; Henry Maudsley on Brain and Mind; Norman Lockyer on Spectrum Analysis; and Sir John Lubbock on Natural History. The most distinguished historian of the times is James Anthony Froude, who shows great vigor of thought and power of description. The histories of John Richard Green and E. A. Freeman are valuable for their original research, and have wide celebrity. Max Müller has rendered important service to the sciences of Philology and Ethnology. Lecky is eminent for his *Rationalism in Europe* and *History of Morals*. Leslie Stephen, John Morley, and John Addington Symonds are distinguished in various departments of criticism and history. Thomas Hill Green and James Martineau are masters of Ethical Philosophy. John Stuart Mill holds a high place as a writer on Political Economy. All English works of any merit are now immediately reprinted in this country, and the English literature of the present century is as familiar to most Americans as their own.

AMERICAN LITERATURE.

The literature of the United States belongs almost exclusively to the last century. The language being that of England, and all the treasures of English literature the common inheritance of our countrymen, whatever American authors produce is necessarily measured by the English standard. The language comes to us finished and matured, while the means of intellectual cultivation—until a comparatively recent period—have been limited, and our abundant stores of legend and history are still too fresh to be available for the purpose of poetry and fiction. The present generation, however, has witnessed the growth of a national literature, which, if not peculiarly American in language, is at least so in style and the materials chosen.

The seventeenth century boasted two or three authors, but none we believe native to the soil. Mrs. Anne Bradstreet, wife of a governor of Massachusetts, published in 1640, a poem on the *Four Elements*, smoothly versified, but of little poetical merit. Cotton Mather, born in 1663, is almost the only prose writer worthy of note. His *Magnalia* contains some valuable historical matter. The last century produced some distinguished prose writers and some accomplished versifiers, though no poet in the true sense of the title. Franklin, born in 1706, was master of a singularly clear, compact, and vigorous style. Jonathan Edwards, who flourished during the last century, wrote a celebrated treatise on the *Will*, which is one of the first metaphysical works in the language. The Revolutionary struggle and the circumstances which preceded and succeeded it, produced a number of bold and brilliant writers and speakers, among whom were Jefferson, Hamilton, the Adamses, Richard Henry Lee, and Patrick Henry. The diplomatic correspondence of the Revolution has rarely been surpassed. Philip Freneau, who has been called the first American poet, wrote many patriotic songs, which were sung during the struggle, but none have retained their original vitality. Trumbull was the author of a Hudibrastic poem entitled *Mc-Fingal*, in which the Tories were held up to ridicule; the first part was published in 1775. Joel Barlow, who aspired to the rank of an epic poet, published, in 1787, his *Vision of Columbus*, which, in 1808, was expanded into the *Columbiad*, and printed in what was then a style of unusual magnificence.

Dana, Bryant, Washington Irving, Cooper, Paulding, and Everett, were all born towards the close of the last century. Dana may be considered as the first genuine poet the United States has produced. His *Buccaneer* is a picturesque and striking poem, founded on a legend of the pirates who formerly frequented the American coast. Irving's *Knickerbocker's History of New York* appeared in 1809, and instantly gave him a position as a writer of the purest style and of exquisite humor and fancy. A *Biography of Goldsmith*, to whom he has been compared, was published in 1849. Many of his works—among them *The Sketch Book*, *Bracebridge Hall*, *The Alhambra*, and the *Life of Columbus* — were first published in England, where he lived many years. Cooper's first essay in literature was a novel of society entitled *Precaution*, but he subsequently confined himself to the two fields in which he has earned his best fame—the forest and the ocean. His most successful novels are *The Spy*, *The Pioneers*, *The Deerslayer*, *The Pilot*, and *The Pathfinder*. Bryant first attracted notice by his poem of *Thanatopsis*, written in his nineteenth year. His first volume, *The Ages*, was published in 1825. William Ellery Channing's essays, criticisms, and moral, religious, and political writings won him much celebrity as a prose writer. William Wirt, author of *The British Spy*, a collection of letters written in a chaste and elegant style; Charles Brockden Brown, the earliest American novelist, author of *Wieland;* Richard Henry Wilde, author of a *Life of Tasso;* Chief Justice Marshall, who compiled a voluminous *Life of Washington;* Henry Wheaton, author of standard works on law and political economy; Judge Story, author of several celebrated legal works; Edgar Allan Poe, a most original and strongly marked character, who wrote the poem of *The Raven* and a number of weird and fantastic prose stories; Margaret Fuller, a woman of remarkable acquirements, who has left behind her much admirable descriptive and critical writing, are all entitled to distinguished mention.

The stories and poems of N. P. Willis, as well as his records of travels in Europe and the East, are unsurpassed in point of brilliancy. Hawthorne, author of *The Scarlet Letter*, *The House of Seven Gables*, and *The Marble Faun*, is remarkable for the delicacy of his psychological insight, his power of intense characterization, and for his mastery of the spiritual and the supernatural. His style is the pure colorless medium of his thought; the plain current of his language is always equable, full, and unvarying, whether in the company of playful children, among the ancestral associations of family or history, or in grappling with the mysteries and terrors of the supernatural world. Harriet Beecher Stowe, author of *Uncle Tom's Cabin*, and a crowd of other writers of various and high degrees of merit and reputation, followed in almost unbroken succession down to the present. Among these, as writers of fiction, may be mentioned William Ware, author of *Probus* and *Palmyra;* William Gilmore Simms, Oliver Wendell Holmes, author of the *Autocrat of the Breakfast Table;* George William Curtis, Donald G. Mitchell, William Dean Howells, Henry James, Helen Hunt Jackson, Frances Hodgson Burnett, Elizabeth Stuart Phelps, Louisa M. Alcott, F. Marion Crawford, George W. Cable, F. J. Stimson, Edward Everett Hale, Bret Harte, and Lew Wallace. Prominently devoted to poetry and criticism are Richard H. Dana, Emerson, Longfellow, Lowell, Whittier, Bayard Taylor, Walt Whitman, R. H. Stoddard, T. B. Aldrich, R. W. Gilder, Edgar Faucett, Joaquin Miller, James Whitcomb Rilev, John Hay, and Edmund Clarence Stedman.

To the historical school belong the names of Prescott, Motley, Parkman, Bancroft, Hildreth, Winsor, Fiske, and McMaster. The works of Prescott are among the finest models of historical composition, and they breathe freely the spirit of our liberal institutions. His *History of Ferdinand and Isabella*, of the *Conquest of Mexico*, and the *Conquest of Peru*, unite all the fascination of romantic fiction with the grave interests of authentic events. Motley's *History of the Rise of the Dutch Republic* is a work distinguished for its historical accuracy, philosophical breadth of treatment, and clearness and vigor of style. Bancroft has written the most accurate and philosophical account that has been given of the United States, which has been worthily supplemented by the volumes of McMaster. In Hildreth's *History of the United States*, rhetorical grace and effect give way to a plain narrative confined to facts gleaned with great care and conscientiousness. The writing of Winsor and Fiske has been confined to certain important epochs.

Of the statesmen of the present century who have contributed to our literature of oratory, the most eminent are Webster, Clay, and Calhoun. The speeches and forensic arguments of Webster are remarkable for clearness and impressiveness, and rise occasionally to grandeur. The speeches of Clay are distinguished by a sincerity and warmth which were characteristic of the man, who united the gentlest affections with the pride of the haughtiest manhood. His eloquence reached the heart of the whole nation. The style of John C. Calhoun was terse and condensed, and his eloquence, though sometimes impassioned, was always severe. He had great skill as a dialectician and remarkable power of analysis, and his works will have a permanent place in American literature. The writings and speeches of John Quincy Adams are distinguished by universality of knowledge and independence of judgment, and they are repositories of rich materials for the historian and political philosopher. Edward Everett, as an orator, had few equals, and his occasional addresses and orations have become permanent memorials of many important occasions of public interest. Of the numerous other orators, eminent as rhetoricians or debaters, a few only can be named; among them are Legaré, Randolph, Choate, Sumner, Phillips, Preston, Prentiss, Lincoln, and Robert G. Ingersoll.

Philosophy assumed its first distinctive character under the influence of the Transcendental School of New England. The first to plant the seeds of this philosophy was George Ripley, a philanthropist of high ideals. Theodore Parker owed his great power as a preacher to his faith in the Transcendental philosophy. The Absolute God, the Moral Law, and the Immortal Life he held to be the three cardinal attestations of the universal consciousness. The first place, however, belongs to Ralph Waldo Emerson, who lighted up its doctrines with the rays of ethical and poetical imagination. With many inconsistencies to be allowed for, he still remains the highest mind that the world of letters has produced in America. His essays are marvels of keen insight and profound wisdom. Other writers identified with the Transcendental movement are O. B. Frothingham, O. A. Brownson, James Freeman Clarke, Henry D. Thoreau, A. Bronson Alcott, C. P. Cranch, and Thomas Wentworth Higginson, the latter one of the most delightful prose writers of this generation. The most distinguished philosophical writer of the present day is Josiah Royce, a professor in Harvard University, with whom must be mentioned John Fiske, William James, Andrew D. White, Joseph Le Conte, and George T. Ladd.

The physical sciences, from an early period, have found able investigators in the United States, and the fields of theology, economy, and jurisprudence have furnished many honorable names. Among scientists those most prominent in chemistry and physics are Benjamin Franklin, Morse, Hare, Silliman, Henry, Edison, Remsen, and Rowland; in geology, Dana, Hitchcock, Hall, Hodge, Owen, Whitney, Le Conte; in botany, Torrey, Gray, Bessey, Coulter, and Campbell; in natural history, Holbrook, Audubon, Agassiz, Henry, and Jordan; in political economy, Henry C. Carey, Francis A. Walker, and Henry George; in psychology, William James and G. Stanley Hall.

French Academy, The, was created by Louis XIV. in 1635. Its original pursuits were eloquence and poetry. In 1648 it was extended to the fine arts; and in 1666, by Colbert, to the arts and sciences.

Runic Writing. The Scandinavians anciently employed an alphabet of letters formed principally of straight lines, which has been called Runic, from an Icelandic word, *runs*, meaning a furrow or line.

Volapük. — This so-called universal language was invented in 1879, by Johann Martin Schleyer, a Swabian pastor and latterly a teacher in Constance. Of the vocabulary, about one third is of English origin, while the Latin and Romance languages furnish a fourth. The grammar is simplified to the utmost. The most practical disciples limit their aims to making Volapük a convenience for commercial correspondence, a kind of extended international code.

Sanskrit is one of the Indo-European group of languages, intimately connected with the Persian, Greek, Latin, Teutonic, Slavonian, and Celtic languages. It is the classical language of the Hindus, and the parent of all the modern Aryan languages of India. It ceased to be a spoken language about the second century B. C. Sanskrit literature, which extends back to at least 1500 B. C., and is very voluminous, was introduced to the western world by Sir William Jones, who founded the Asiatic Society in Calcutta in 1784.

Languages of the World.— It has been estimated that there are over 3000 languages in the world. English is spoken by above 130,000,000 of the human race; German by 100,000,000; Russian by 70,000,000; French by 45,000,000; Spanish by 40,000,000; Italian by 30,000,000, and Portuguese by 13,000,000.

English is spoken by 4,000,000 Canadians; over 3,500,000 West Indians; 3,000,000 Australians; 1,000,000 East Indians; 38,000,000 in the British Isles, and 65,000,000 in America.

German is spoken by 2,000,000 in the United States and Canada; 2,000,000 in Switzerland; 40,000 Belgians; 46,000,000 in the German Empire, and 10,000,000 in the Austro-Hungarian Empire.

French is spoken by 2,250,000 Belgians; 1,000,000 in the United States and Canada; 1,000,000 in Algiers, India, and Africa; 600,000 Swiss; 600,000 in Hayti; 200,000 in Alsace–Lorraine, and 38,000,000 in France.

Troubadours were minstrels of southern France in the eleventh, twelfth, and thirteenth centuries. They were the first to discard Latin and use the native tongue in their compositions. Their poetry was either about love and gallantry, or war and chivalry. In northern France they were called Trouvères and the language employed was the Walloon.

Grub Street, London, is thus described in Dr. Johnson's Dictionary: "Originally the name of a street near Moorfields, in London, much inhabited by writers of small histories, dictionaries, and temporary poems, whence any production is called Grub Street." Andrew Marvell used the name in its appropriate sense, which later was freely used by Pope, Swift, and others.

Madrigal is a short lyric poem, generally on the subject of love, and characterized by some epigrammatic terseness or quaintness. It was written as a rule in iambic meter, and contained not less than six or more than thirteen lines, and ran chiefly upon three rhymes. The name is also applied to the music for a simple song sung in a rich, artistic style but without musical accompaniment.

Minnesingers, The, were love poets, contemporary in Germany with the House of Hohenstauffen. Though called love singers, some of their poems were national ballads, and some were extended romances. Walter of Vogelweide was by far the best of the lyrists; Heinrich of Veldig was the most naïve and ingenuous; Hartman the most classical; Wolfram the most sublime, and Gottfried the most licentious.

Iliad, The, is the tale of the siege of Troy, an epic poem in 24 books by Homer. Menelaus, King of Sparta, received as a guest, Paris, a son of Priam, King of Troy. Paris eloped with Helen, his host's wife, and Menelaus induced the Greeks to lay siege to Troy to avenge the perfidy. The siege lasted ten years, when Troy was taken and burned to the ground. Homer's poem is confined to the last year of the siege.

Lorelei, famed in song and story, is a rock which rises perpendicularly from the Rhine to the height of 427 feet, near St. Goar. It was formerly dangerous to boatmen, and has a celebrated echo. The name is best known from Heine's "Song of the Siren," who sits on the rock, combing her long tresses, and singing so ravishingly, that the boatmen, enchanted by the music of her voice, forget their duty, and are drawn upon the rock and perish.

Beauty and the Beast.—This venerable story, from Les Contes Marines, of Mme. Villeneuve (1740), is, perhaps, the most beautiful of all nursery tales. A young and lovely woman saved her father by putting herself in the power of a frightful but kind-hearted monster, whose respectful affection and melancholy overcame her aversion to his ugliness, and she consented to become his bride. Being thus freed from enchantment the monster assumed his proper form and became a young and handsome prince.

Æneid, The, Virgil's epic poem, is contained in twelve books. When Troy was taken by the Greeks and set on fire, Æneas, with his father, son, and wife, took flight, with the intention of going to Italy, the original birthplace of the family. The wife was lost, and the old man died on the way; but, after numerous perils by sea and land, Æneas and his son Ascanius reached Italy. Here Latinus, the reigning king, received the exiles hospitably, and promised his daughter Lavinia in marriage to Æneas; but she had been already betrothed by her mother to Prince Turnus, son of Valmus, king of Rutuli, and Turnus would not forego his claim. Latinus, in this dilemma, said the rivals must settle the dispute by an appeal to arms. Turnus being slain, Æneas married Lavinia, and ere long succeeded his father-in-law in the throne.

Gesta Romanorum, the deeds of the Romans, is the title of a collection of short stories and legends in the Latin tongue, widely spread during the Middle Ages, but of the authorship of which little is known save that it took its present form most likely in England, about the end of the thirteenth or the beginning of the fourteenth century. The stories are invariably moralized, and, indeed, this edifying purpose throughout is the sole unifying element of the collection. The title is only so far descriptive as the nucleus of the collection consists of stories from Roman history, or rather pieces from Roman writers, not necessarily of any greater historical value than that of Androcles and the Lion from Allus Gallius. Moralized, mystical, and religious tales, as well as other pieces, many of ultimate oriental origin, were afterwards added, and upon them edifying conclusions hung, bringing the whole up to about 180 chapters.

Bluebeard is the hero of the well-known nursery tale, and is so named from the color of his beard. The story is widely known in Western Europe, but the form in which it has become familiar is a free translation of that given by Perrault in 1697. In this story Bluebeard is a Signeur of great wealth, who marries the daughter of a neighbor in the country and a month after the wedding goes from home on a journey leaving his wife the keys of his castle, but forbidding her to enter one room. She cannot resist her curiosity, opens the door, to find the bodies of all Bluebeard's former wives, and at once sees the fate to which she herself is doomed. Bluebeard, on his return, discovers from a spot of blood upon the key which could not be cleaned off, that his wife has broken his command and tells her that she must die. She begs for a short respite to commend herself to God, sends her sister Anne to the top of the tower to seek for help, and finally is just on the point of having her head cut off, when her two brothers burst in and dispatch Bluebeard. There are many versions of the story, all agreeing in essential details. It is found in the German, French, Greek, Tuscan, Icelandic, Esthonian, Gaelic, and Basque folklore.

Sagas, The, belong to the Norse literature and are generally books in the form of a tale, like a Welch "mahinogi." "Edda" was the name of the Bible of the ancient Scandinavians. In the Edda there are numerous Sagas. As our Bible contains the history of the Jews, religious songs, moral proverbs, and religious stories, so the Edda contains the history of Norway, religious songs, a book of proverbs, and numerous stories. The original Edda was compiled and edited by Saemun Sigfusson, an Icelandic priest, in the eleventh century. It contains twenty-eight parts or books, all of which are in verse.

Two hundred years later, Snorro Sturlesson, of Iceland, abridged, re-arranged, and reduced the prose of the Edda, giving the various parts a kind of dramatic form like the Dialogues of Plato. It then became needful to distinguish between the two works; so the old poetical compilation is called the Elder or Rhythmical Edda, while the more modern work is called the Younger or Prose Edda, and sometimes the Snorro Edda. The Younger Edda is, however, partly original, containing the discourse of Bragi on the Origin of Poetry; here, too, we find the famous story called by the Germans "Nibelungen-Lied." Beside the Sagas contained in the Eddas there are a number of productions of various forms.

Miracle Plays, The, were founded on the historical parts of the Old and New Testaments and on the lives of the saints. They were performed at first in churches, and afterwards on platforms in the streets. Their design was to instruct the people in Bible history; but long before the Reformation, they had so far departed from their original character as to bring contempt upon the church and religion. The exhibition of a single play often occupied several days. The earliest recorded Miracle Play took place in England in the beginning of the twelfth century; but they soon became popular in France, Germany, Spain, and Italy.

In Germany these plays, with one exception, were suppressed in the year 1779. The villages of Oberammergau in the Bavarian Highlands, had, upon the cessation of a play, in 1633, vowed to perform the "Passion of Our Saviour" every tenth year out of gratitude, and also as a means of instruction to the people. The pleading of a deputation of Oberammergau peasants with Maximilian II. of Bavaria, saved their play from general condemnation. The play was remodeled and is perhaps the only Miracle Play that survives to the present day. The performance lasts for eight hours with an intermission of one hour at noon; and though occurring only once in a decade is repeated on several Sundays in succession during the season. The characters in the play number about 500. The personator of the Saviour seems to regard the performance of his part as an act of religious worship; and the other important actors are said to be selected for their holy life and to be consecrated to their work with prayer. Travelers from all parts of the world flock to Oberammergau during the time announced for its representation.

Cid Campeador, historically Roderigo Diaz, the noted Spanish warrior, is so intermingled with fable that it is almost impossible to get at the truth. His career is celebrated in the Spanish Epic, "Poem of the Cid." From this poem and other Spanish works Southey translated and compiled his "Chronicle of the Cid."

The Cid is supposed to have been born about the year 1026, and to have died at Valentia, 1099. He was such a terror to the Moors, and seemed so superior to all others, that he was called El Seid (Arabic for the Lord); and finally Cid Campeador (Lord Champion).

Rebecca, of Ivanhoe. Sir Walter Scott's model for this character was a young woman, Rebecca Gratz by name, of an honorable Jewish family of Philadelphia. She was born on the 4th of March, 1781, and in her younger days, and even beyond middle life, possessed singular beauty. She was noted for her benevolent and charitable life and for her devotion to the Jewish faith. One of the most intimate friends of her family was Washington Irving, who in the fall of 1817 first introduced the character to the notice of Scott during his visit to Abbotsford. During one of their many conversations, Irving spoke of his friend Rebecca Gratz of Philadelphia, described her wonderful beauty, and related the story of her firm adherence to her religious faith. Scott was deeply interested and conceived the plan of embodying a character like hers in one of his novels. Shortly after this he wrote Ivanhoe, and named his heroine Rebecca.

Romance of the Rose, the Iliad of France, is a poetical allegory begun by Guillaume de Loris in the latter part of the thirteenth century and continued by Jean de Munge in the fourteenth century. The poet dreams that Dame Idleness conducts him to the palace of pleasure, where he meets Love, whose attendant maidens are Sweet Looks, Courtesy, Youth, Joy, and Competence; by them he is conducted to a bed of roses. He has just singled out one rose when an arrow from Love's bow stretches him fainting on the ground and he is carried away. When he is revived he resolves to find his rose, and Welcome promises to aid him. Shyness, Fear, and Slander obstruct his way; Reason advises him to give up the quest; Pity and Kindness show him the object of his search; but Jealousy seizes Welcome and locks her in Fear Castle. Here the original poem ends. The sequel takes up the tale at this point, and is an extraordinary mixture of erudition and satire. The poem reached the height of its popularity in the sixteenth century.

A Curious Book.—A book belonging to the family of Prince De Ligne of France is said to be the most curious book in the world, because it is neither written nor printed. The letters of the text are cut out of each folio upon the finest vellum; and, being interleaved with blue paper, it is as easy to read as print. The labor bestowed upon it was excessive. Rudolph II. of Germany offered for it, in 1640, $60,000.

Koran, The, in the Arabic language signifies "The Reading." That Mohammed is the real author of the Koran there is no doubt; but the Mohammedans steadfastly deny it to be the work of their prophet, the orthodox among them believing it to be of divine origin. Mohammed left his revelations written upon palm leaves and skin, which were thrown promiscuously into a chest, bearing no dates but merely the places of revelation; some are marked Mecca and some Medina. Three years after the death of the prophet, in 635, Aby-Bekr collected and published these articles in the form of what is now called the Koran.

Goethe, the acknowledged prince of German literature, was born at Frankfort-on-the-Main, August 28, 1749, and died in Weimar on March 22, 1832. His greatest work is *Faust*, but it can never become popular, because its wisdom does not lie on the surface. When he had finished it, he said the work of his life was done. *Hermann and Dorothea* is as immortal as the *Vicar of Wakefield*. *The Sorrows of Werther* brought him equal fame. It is said that the Werther fever ran so high that in some countries booksellers were forbidden by law to sell it. Young women cried over it, and young men shot themselves with a copy of Werther in their hand.

Classic and Romantic Literature.—The term classic has, ever since the second century, been applied to writers of the highest rank. Latterly it has come to designate the best writers of ancient Greece and Rome. Romantic literature was the term first used in Germany, about the beginning of the present century, by a number of young poets and critics who wished to indicate that they sought the essence of art and poetry in the wonderful and fantastic.

Telemachus was written by François Fenelon, Archbishop of Cambrey. It is a French prose epic, in 24 books, and contains the adventures of Telemachus, the only son of Ulysses and Penelope, while in search of his father, who had been absent thirty years from his home. Telemachus is accompanied by the god of wisdom under the form of Mentor. There is perhaps no book in the French language which has been more read, and it is a class book in almost every European school.

Dante is called the father of Italian literature. Before his time the poets of northern Italy wrote in the Provençal language, which was the dialect spoken chiefly in southern France. But Dante wrote in Italian, and from his time the Italian became a real language.

His great work is the "Divine Comedy," an epic poem consisting of three parts, viz.: hell, purgatory, and paradise. This poem is an allegory conceived in the form of a vision, which was the most popular style of poetry in that age. As a poem, it is of the highest order, and ranks Dante with Homer and Milton.

Songs of the Gondoliers.—For more than two hundred years the gondoliers of Venice sang no other songs than strophes from Tasso's immortal epic, "Jerusalem Delivered." This poem commemorates the delivery of Jerusalem from the Saracens; and the hero of the poem is Godfrey de Bouillon, the first Christian king of Jerusalem. Tasso was born at Sorrento in 1544. He became melancholy, and was for seven years confined by the Duke Alfonso in an insane asylum. When released he went to Naples. Pope Clement VIII. invited him to Rome to receive the laurel crown of poet; but he died before the ceremony took place, April, 1595, and was buried on the day on which he was to have been crowned.

Writing, History of.—The very first origin of the art of writing has been a matter of speculation from the earliest times. The myths of antiquity ascribe it to Thoth, or to Cadmus, which only denotes their belief in its being brought from the East, or being, perhaps, primeval. The Talmud ascribes it to a special revelation. Unquestionably the first step toward writing was rude pictorial representations of objects, the next the application of a symbolic meaning to some of these pictures, and gradually all pictures became symbolic, and for convenience were abbreviated. Later they became conventional signs, and in time they were made to stand for the sounds of spoken language. The various systems of writing of the ancient world had probably at least three sources—the Egyptian, the Assyrian, and the Chinese systems—all of which were originally hieroglyphics, or made up of pictures. The Egyptians had four distinct styles of writing—the hieroglyphics, hieratic, enchorial, and Coptic. The hieroglyphic was probably in use before 4,000 B. C., and at first was made up entirely of pictures; but about 2,000 B. C. the hieratic form was introduced, in which the hieroglyphs were greatly simplified, and developed into purely linear forms. The enchorial form of writing was in use from 700 B. C. to A. D. 200, and was a still further simplification of the earlier forms, finally developing into the alphabetic form known as the Coptic. The cuneiform writing of the Assyrian empire disputes the honors of antiquity with the Egyptian early forms. This was probably hieroglyphic in its origin, but became modified by the different nations occupying the Assyrian empire until it assumed the form of the inscriptions as known to archæologists. The name of this writing is from a Latin word meaning a wedge, and it is so called because all the characters used are made up of different arrangements of a single pointed figure resembling a wedge in form. There were three classes of cuneiform characters used in the period of development of this form of writing; first, the Assyrian or Babylonian, which was very complicated, containing from six hundred to seven hundred symbols; the Scythian or Median, having about one hundred characters only; and the third, the Persian, which is purely alphabetic. The Chinese gives an example of a written language which was arrested in an early period of its development, before the alphabetic stage had been reached. The people of China still use a written character for a word, as they did thousands of years ago. The Egyptian is the most important of those early systems, as from it was probably derived the Phœnician alphabet, which became the parent of all the graphic systems of the modern world. The Egyptians never fully separated the hieroglyphic and phonetic symbols, but the Phœnicians adopted the latter only, and thus originated the first purely alphabetic plan of writing. The Phœnician alphabet was the parent of five principal branches of graphic forms, the most important of which is the Greek, which was the parent of the Roman alphabet, from which sprung the alphabets of all modern European nations, and those taken from them by the people who now inhabit the Western hemisphere.

Capital letters were first invented, and were in use for many centuries before the invention of small letters. The oldest manuscripts now in use, dating as far back as the third century, are written entirely in capitals, and without spacing between the words, or marks of punctuation. The small letters were first introduced about the seventh century.

Punctuation was unknown to the ancients. Aristophanes of Alexandria, about two and a half centuries before the Christian era, introduced some of the marks now used. But it was not until about the year 1500 A. D., that Aldus Manutius, a learned printer of Venice, reduced the art of punctuation to a system.

Surnames are so called from the early practice of writing them over the Christian names. In modern times they were first used in France, particularly in Normandy, where they can be traced to the latter part of the tenth century. They were introduced into England by the Normans after the conquest. The ancient Hebrews, Egyptians, Syrians, Persians, and others had but a single name which was generally significant of some feature connected with their birth. Thus, Rachel, dying, had called her child Benoni, "the son of my sorrow"; but Jacob gave him the name of Benjamin, "the son of my strength." These simple names, however, soon became so common to many owners, that they failed to convey individuality; and this led to the addition of other designations, now known to us as surnames. Only about a thousand surnames were taken up by the most noble families in France and in England about the time of Edward the Confessor. The lower nobility did not follow this example before the twelfth century and the citizens and husbandmen had no family names before the fourteenth century. English names have recruits among them from almost every race.

The three most numerous patronymics of Celtic origin now in use among the English are the O, the Mac, and the Ap. The Irish O originally meant grandson, the Scotch Mac and the Welch Ap meaning son.

The Jews were the last to adopt surnames, and it is only within the past hundred years that they were compelled by law to adopt them in England.

Sacred Books of the Hindus are of great antiquity. The oldest of their sacred books, the Vedas (knowledge or science), contain the revelation of Brahma, and were preserved by tradition until collected by Vyasa. The Vedas are three in number: first, the Rig-Veda containing hymns and mystic prayers; second, the Yajur-Veda containing the religious rites; third, the Sama-Veda, with prayers in the form of songs. The Vedas were written in Sanskrit and were first translated into English by Sir William Jones. The whole life of Ancient India is found in the Vedas, the Puranas, and the two great epics, called the Ramayana and the Mahabharata.

The Ramayana contains about 50,000 lines describing the youth of Rama who is an incarnation of their God Vishnu; his banishment and residence in central India. The Mahabharata of later date consists of about 220,000 lines and is divided into eighteen books. Five brothers, the descendants of Bharata are the heroes of the Mahabharata; and episodes in the lives of these heroes occupy three fourths of the poem. The Puranas relate largely to mythological legends. The gods Siva and Vishnu are the sole objects of worship in the Puranas.

Pilgrim's Progress, the chief work of John Bunyan, has gone through more editions and been translated into more languages, than any book, except the Bible. It is an allegory of a Christian's life from the time of his conversion to that of his death. The book was written during the author's incarceration in Bedford jail, where he passed twelve years of his life. He was born near Bedford, in England, in 1628, in 1655 became a Baptist minister and preached with great success until the restoration of Charles II., when an act against conventicles was passed, which put an end to his labors. His trial, conviction, and sentence followed. He was several times offered his liberty on the condition that he would give up preaching; but his answer was always, "If you let me out to-day, I will preach again to-morrow." He died in London, 1688.

Latin language first appears in literature as a written language as well as spoken, in the plain of Latium in the third century B. C. The conquering armies of Rome soon carried a knowledge of the Latin tongue to the utmost boundaries of the known world. Hence its presence is discernible in all European languages. Those languages which are the immediate offspring of the Latin, as the Italian, Spanish, Portuguese, and French, both Norman and Provençal, are called the Romance languages. Wallachian, the language of Roumania, in which Latin predominates, has not until lately been classified with the Latin language. Latin ceased to be a spoken language about 580 A. D.

Poet Laureate means "The Poet of the Laurel Wreath." It was the custom in early Greece to crown with a laurel wreath the successful poet in a contest; this custom was adopted by the Romans during the Empire. But the title of "Poet Laureate" originated in Germany during the twelfth century, when the ancient ceremony of crowning the poet par excellence was revived. The early history of the Laureateship in England is traditional. The story goes that Edward III., following the example of the coronation of Petrarch at Rome, conferred a similar honor upon Geoffrey Chaucer with the yearly pension of 100 marks and other perquisites. Although the Laureateship was generally recognized, it did not become an established office until 1619, with Ben Jonson.

Hungarian Literature is in the main confined to the Magyar language, which bears a resemblance to the Turkish. It is only of late years that this literature has assumed a popular character. The native language was excluded from public and official documents for eight centuries, but, notwithstanding this fact, the Hungarians possess to-day a literature, which, both in regard to quantity and quality, will sustain comparison with that of the most civilized of western nations. The Latin language was introduced about 1000 A. D. and became the tongue of both church and state until the close of the fifteenth century. The Hungarian language was revived in the sixteenth century and became the sole vehicle for sacred poetry. Translations of the Bible were multiplied, chronicles, histories, grammars, and dictionaries were published, and the period from 1702 to 1780 probably marks the Golden Age of literature in Hungary. But the native language suffered a severe reverse when the country came under the absolute dominion of Austria.

Renaissance, The, means simply a new birth or revival; but the word is always understood to mean a revival in learning. The period known as the Renaissance dates from the taking of Constantinople by the Turks (1453), but long before that epoch the love for classical literature had been reviving. This event, however, gave a decided impulse to the revival of learning in western Europe; the learned men of the Greek or eastern empire sought new homes in the Occident and established schools throughout Europe. The revival of learning, the invention of printing, the discovery of the new world, the decline of feudalism, the elevation of the middle classes, all contributed to bring about the Renaissance. It reached its climax about the beginning of the present century.

Theatrical Performances have been traced to the Grecian custom of celebrating every spring, in Athens, a festival in honor of Bacchus. Thespis originated the custom of introducing a single speaker to amuse the company with recitations. He also invented a movable car on which his performances were exhibited in various places. Theatrical performers are still called thespians. The car of Thespis was soon exchanged for a permanent stage in the Temple of Bacchus. Æschylus soon added a second speaker and a chorus, masks, scenery, etc., and is therefore called the "Father of Tragedy." At the festivals of Bacchus new plays were brought out yearly in competition. Æschylus won the prize every year until he was fifty-six years old, when he was defeated by Sophocles. Greek comedy derived its origin from the revels of the Comus (God of revelry) during the Bacchic festivals. Its great master was Aristophanes, 444 B. C.

FOREIGN WORDS AND PHRASES.

A bas.—Down with.
A capite ad calcem.—From head to foot.
A fin.—To the end.
A fortiori.—With stronger reason.
A l'abandon.—At random.
A la bonne heure.—Opportunely; in good time.
A la dérobée.—By stealth.
A la mode.—According to the fashion.
A main armée.—With force of arms.
A mensa et thoro.—From bed and board.
A posteriori.—From effect to cause; from the latter.
A priori.—From cause to effect; from the former.
A tempo giusto.—To sing or play in true time. (*Music.*)
A tempo rimo.—To restore the original movement. (*Music.*)
A vinculo matrimonii.—From the tie of marriage.
A votre santé.—To your health.
Ab extra.—From without.
Ab initio.—From the beginning.
Ab origine.—From the beginning.
Ab ovo.—From the beginning.
Ab urbe conditâ.—From the building of the city (Rome); abridged A. U. C.
Abit invidia.—All offense apart; let there be no malice.
Absit omen.—May it not prove ominous.
Absque hoc.—Without this or that.
Ac etiam.—And also.
Actum est de republica.—It is all over with the commonwealth.
Ad absurdum.—To show the absurdity.
Ad arbitrium.—At pleasure.
Ad astra per aspera.—To the stars through difficulties.
Ad captandum vulgus.—To catch the mob or the vulgar.
Ad eundem.—To the same point or degree.
Ad finem.—To the end.
Ad Græcas Calendas.—An indefinite postponement. (The Greeks had no calends.)
Ad hominem.—To the man (that is, to the interests or the passions of the man).
Ad infinitum.—Without end.
Ad inquirendum.—For inquiry.
Ad interim.—In the meanwhile.
Ad libitum.—At pleasure.
Ad litem.—For the action (at law).
Ad nauseam.—To a disgusting degree.
Ad referendum.—For further consideration.
Ad rem.—To the purpose.
Ad unguem.—To the nail; exactly; nicely.
Ad valorem.—According to the value.
Addendum.—An addition or appendix.
Adhuc sub judice lis est.—The affair is not yet decided.
Ægrescit medendo.—The remedy is worse than the disease.
Æquam servare mentem.—To preserve an equable mind.
Æquo animo.—With an equable mind.
Ære perennius.—More lasting than brass; enduring ever.
Affaire du cœur.—A love affair; an amour.
Afflatus.—Inspiration.
Agenda.—Things to be done.
Agitato.—A broken style of performance, to awaken surprise. (*Music.*)
Agnus Dei.—Lamb of God.
Aide-de-camp.—Assistant to a general.
Aide-toi, et le ciel t'aidera.—Help thyself, and Heaven will help thee.
Alere flammam.—To feed the flame.
Al fresco.—In the open air.
Alga.—A kind of seaweed.
Alguazil.—A Spanish constable.
Alias.—Otherwise; elsewhere.
Alibi.—Elsewhere; not present.
Alis volat propriis.—She flies with her own wings.
Aliunde.—From some other quarter or person.
Allegretto.—A movement quicker than *andante*, but not so quick as *allegro*. (*Music.*)
Allemande.—A kind of German dance.
Alma mater.—Benign mother (applied to a university).
Alter ego.—A second self.
Alto octavo.—An octavo higher.
Alto relievo.—High relief. (*Sculpture.*)
Alto ripieno.—The tenor of a great chorus.
Alto violino.—A small tenor violin.
Amende.—Compensation; apology.
Ami du peuple.—Friend of the people.
Amicus curiæ.—A friend of the court.
Amor patriæ.—Love of country.
Amour propre.—Self-love; vanity.
Ancien régime.—Former administration; ancient order of things.
Andante.—Moderately slow movement, between *largo* and *allegro*. (*Music.*)
Anglicè.—In English.
Anguis in herbâ.—A snake in the grass.
Animis opibusque parati.—Ever ready with our lives and property.
Animo et fide.—By (or with) courage and faith.
Animo facto.—Really and truly.
Animus furandi.—Felonious intent.
Anno Domini.—In the year of our Lord.
Anno lucis.—In the year of light.
Anno mundi.—In the year of the world.
Annus mirabilis.—Year of wonders.
Ante bellum.—Before the war.
Ante lucem.—Before light.
Ante meridiem.—Before noon.
Aperçu.—A brief sketch of any subject.
Appoggiatura.—A note in a smaller character than the regular notes of the piece. (*Music.*)
Apropos (Fr. *à propos*).—To the purpose.
Aqua vitæ.—Water of life; brandy.
Arbiter elegantiarum.—Master of ceremonies; an umpire in matters of taste.
Arcana imperii.—State secrets.
Arcanum.—A secret.
Argumentum ad crumenam.—An argument to the purse.
Argumentum ad fidem.—An appeal to faith.
Argumentum ad hominem.—An argument to the person.
Argumentum ad ignorantiam.—An argument founded on an adversary's ignorance of facts.
Argumentum ad judicium.—An appeal to the common sense of mankind.
Argumentum ad populum.—An appeal to the people.
Argumentum ad verecundiam.—An argument to modesty.
Argumentum baculinum.—Club law.
Arioso.—Light, airy.
Armiger.—One bearing arms; an esquire.
Arpeggio.—The notes of a chord played in rapid succession, and not simultaneously. (*Music.*)
Arrière-pensée.—Mental reservation.
Ars est celare artem.—True art is to conceal art.
Assumpsit.—It is assumed or taken for granted.
Astra castra, Numen lumen.—The stars my camp, the Deity my light.
At spes non fracta.—But hope is not broken.
Au fait.—Well instructed; master of it.
Au fond.—To the bottom, or main point.
Au pied de la lettre.—Literally.
Au pis aller.—At the worst.
Au revoir.—Farewell.
Audi alteram partem.—Hear the other side.
Aura popularis.—The gale of popular favor.
Auri sacra fames.—The accursed thirst for gold.
Autre droit.—Another's right.
Autrefois.—Another time.
Autre vie.—Another's life.
Aut vincere aut mori.—Victory or death.
Auto-da-fé, Auto-de-fe.—An act of faith; burning of heretics.
Auxilium ab alto.—Help from on high.
Avant-coureur.—A forerunner.
Ave, Maria.—Hail, Mary.

Badinage.—Light or playful discourse.
Bagatelle.—A trifle.
Bas bleu.—A bluestocking; a literary woman.
Basso-continuo.—Thorough bass.
Basso-relievo.—Figures in low relief.
Bateau.—A long light boat.
Beau-idéal.—A model of ideal perfection.
Beau monde.—The fashionable world.
Bel esprit.—A brilliant mind.
Bella-donna.—The deadly nightshade; fair lady.
Belles-lettres.—Polite literature.
Bellum internecinum.—A war of extermination.
Bellum lethale.—A deadly war.
Bene placito.—At pleasure. (*Music.*)
Benigno numine.—By the favor of Providence.

Ben trovato.—Well found; an ingenious solution.
Billet-doux.—A love letter.
Bis dat qui citò dat.—He gives twice who gives promptly.
Bis peccare in bello non licet.—To blunder twice is not allowed in war.
Bis vincit, qui se vincit in victoriâ.—He conquers a second time, who controls himself in victory.
Bizarre.—Odd; fantastic.
Blasé.—Surfeited.
Bon gré mal gré.—Willing or unwilling.
Bon jour.—Good-day; good-morning.
Bon mot.—A witty saying; a jest; a quibble.
Bon soir.—Good evening.
Bon ton.—High fashion; first-class society.
Bon vivant.—A high liver.
Bona fide.—In good faith.
Bon-bon.—A sweetmeat; confectionery.
Bonhomie.—Good-natured simplicity.
Bonis nocet quisquis pepercerit malis.—He hurts the good who spares the bad.
Bonne bouche.—A delicious morsel.
Bonus.—An extra payment for a service rendered or a thing received.
Boreas.—The north wind.
Boudoir.—A small private apartment.
Bourgeois.—A citizen of the trading class; a printing type.
Bourgeoisie.—The body of citizens.
Bravura.—A song of difficult execution.
Breveté.—Patented.
Brutum fulmen.—A harmless thunderbolt; unreasoning bluster.
Burletta.—A musical farce.

Cachet.—A seal.
Cacoethes.—A bad habit or custom.
Cacoethes carpendi.—A rage for finding fault.
Cacoethes loquendi.—An itch for speaking.
Cacoethes scribendi.—A passion for writing.
Cadenza.—The fall or modulation of the voice, in music.
Cœca est invidia.—Envy is blind.
Cœtera desunt.—The remainder is wanting.
Cœteris paribus.—Other things being equal.
Calibre.—Capacity or compass; mental power; a term in gunnery.
Camera obscura.—A dark chamber used by artists.
Campus Martius.—The field of Mars; a place of military exercise.
Canaille.—The rabble.
Candida Pax.—White-robed Peace.
Cantata.—A poem set to music.
Cantate Domino.—Sing to the Lord.
Cap-à-pie.—From head to foot.
Capias ad satisfaciendum.—You may take to satisfy.
Capriccio.—A fanciful irregular kind of musical composition.
Capriole.—A leap without advancing; capers.
Caput mortuum.—Dead head; the worthless remains.
Caret.—Is wanting or omitted.
Caret initio et fine.—It wants beginning and end.
Carpe diem.—Enjoy the present day.
Carte blanche.—Unconditional terms.
Casus belli.—An occasion for war.
Casus fœderis.—A case of conspiracy; the end of the league.
Catalogue raisonné.—A catalogue of books arranged according to their subjects.
Cause célèbre.—A remarkable trial in a court of justice.
Caveat actor.—Let the doer beware,
Caveat emptor.—Let the purchaser take heed or beware.
Cavendo tutus.—Safe through caution.
Ce n'est que le premier pas qui coûte.—It is only the first step which is difficult.
Cedant arma togæ.—Let military power yield to the civil.
Cede Deo.—Submit to Providence.
Certiorari.—To be made more certain.
Cessio bonorum.—Yielding up of goods.
C'est une autre chose.—That is quite a different thing.
Chacun à son goût.—Every one to his taste.
Chanson.—A song.
Chansonnette.—A little song.
Chapeau.—A hat.
Chapelle ardente.—The place where a dead person lies in state.
Chaperon.—An attendant on a lady, as a guide and protector.
Chargé d'affaires.—An ambassador of second rank.
Château.—A castle; a country mansion.
Chef-d'œuvre.—A masterpiece.
Chevalier d'industrie.—A knight of industry; one who lives by persevering fraud.
Chi tace confessa.—Silence is confession.
Chiaro-oscuro or *Chiaroscuro.*—Light and shadow in painting.
Chose qui plaît est à demi vendue.—A thing which pleases is already half sold.
Cicerone.—A guide or conductor.
Cicisbeo.—A dangler after a lady.
Ci-devant.—Formerly; former.
Circa.—About.
Citò maturum citò putridum.—Soon ripe, soon rotten.
Clarior e tenebris.—More bright from obscurity.
Clique.—A party; a gang.
Cognomen.—A surname.
Comme il faut.—As it should be.
Commune bonum.—A common good.
Communia propriè dicere.—To express common things with propriety.
Communibus annis.—One year with another.
Compos mentis.—Of sound mind.
Con amore.—With love or hearty inclination.
Concio ad clerum.—A discourse to the clergy.
Congé d'élire.—Permission to elect.
Connoisseur.—A skillful judge.
Consensus facet legem.—Consent makes the law.
Contour.—The outline of a figure.
Contra.—Against.
Contra bonos mores.—Against good manners.
Contretemps.—A mischance; disappointment.
Coram nobis.—Before us.
Coram non judice.—Before one who is not the proper judge.
Cornucopia.—The horn of plenty.
Corpus delicti.—The whole nature of the offense.
Corrigenda.—Corrections to be made.
Coryphœus.—A leader, or chief.
Cotillon.—A lively dance.
Couleur de rose.—Rose-color; an aspect of beauty and attractiveness.
Coup de grâce.—The finishing stroke.
Coup de main.—A bold and rapid enterprise.
Coup de pied.—A kick.
Coup de soleil.—A stroke of the sun.
Coup d'état.—A master stroke of state policy.
Coup d'œil.—Rapid view or glance.
Coûte qu'il coûte.—Cost what it may.
Credat Judœus.—A Jew may believe it.
Crescit amor nummi quantum ipsa pecunia crescit.—The love of money increases as rapidly as the money itself increases.
Crescit eundo.—It increases by going.
Crescite et multiplicamini.—Increase and multiply.
Crimen falsi.—Falsehood; perjury.
Crux criticorum.—The cross or puzzle of critics.
Cui bono?—To whose good?
Cui malo?—To whose harm?
Cul de sac.—The bottom of the bag; a difficulty; a street or lane that has no outlet.
Cum grano salis.—With a grain of salt; with some allowance.
Cum multis aliis.—With many others.
Cum privilegio.—With privilege.
Curia advisari vult.—The court wishes to be advised.
Curiosa felicitas.—A felicitous tact.
Currente calamo.—With a running pen; written off hand.
Custos rotulorum.—Keeper of the rolls.

Da capo.—Over again.
Damnant quod non intelligunt.—They condemn what they do not comprehend.
Data.—Things granted (sing. *datum*).
De bonis non.—Of the goods not yet administered on.
De die in diem.—From day to day.
De facto.—In fact; in reality.
De gustibus non est disputandum.—There is no disputing about tastes.
De jure.—By law or right.
De mortuis nil nisi bonum.—Say nothing but what is good of the dead.
De novo.—Anew.
De profundis.—Out of the depths.
De trop.—Out of place; not wanted.
Debito justitiæ.—By debt of justice.
Début.—Beginning of an enterprise; first appearance.
Deceptio visûs.—An illusion of the sight.
Dedimus potestatem.—We have given power.
Deficit.—A want or deficiency.
Dei gratiâ.—By the grace of God.

Déjeuner à la fourchette.— A breakfast or luncheon with meats.
Dele.— Blot out or erase.
Delenda est Carthago.— Carthage must be blotted out.
Delta (The Greek letter Δ).—A triangular tract of land toward the mouth of a river.
Dénouement.— An unraveling or winding up.
Deo adjuvante, non timendum.— God helping, nothing need be feared.
Deo favente.—With God's favor.
Deo gratias.— Thanks to God.
Deo juvante.— With God's help.
Deo non fortunâ.— From God, not fortune.
Deo volente or *D. V.*—God willing.
Dépôt.— A store; the recruiting reserve of regiments.
Dernier ressort.— The last resort.
Desideratum.— Something desired or wanted.
Desunt cœtera.—The other things are wanting.
Detinet.— He detains; he keeps.
Détour.— A circuitous march.
Detur digniori.— Let it be given to the more worthy.
Deus ex machinâ.— A god from the clouds; unexpected aid in an emergency.
Devastavit.— He wasted.
Devoir.— Duty.
Dexter.— The right hand.
Dictum.— A positive assertion (pl. *dicta*).
Dictum de dicto.— Report upon hearsay.
Dies faustus.— A lucky day.
Dies iræ.— Day of wrath.
Dies non.—A day on which judges do not sit.
Dieu et mon droit.—God and my right.
Dieu vous garde.—God protect you.
Dii majorum gentium.—The gods of the superior class; the twelve superior gods.
Dii penates.—Houshold gods.
Dilettanti.—Persons who devote themselves to science merely for amusement or relaxation (sing. *dilettante*).
Diluvium.—A deposit of superficial loam, sand, etc., caused by a deluge.
Dirigo.—I direct or guide.
Disjecta membra.—Scattered parts, limbs, or writings.
Distrait.—Absent in thought; absent-minded.
Distringas.—A writ for distraining.
Divide et impera.—Divide and govern.
Doce ut discas.—Teach, that you may learn.
Docendo dicimus.—We learn by teaching.
Dolce.—Soft and agreeable. (*Music.*)
Dolce far niente.—Sweet idleness.
Doli incapax.—Incapable of mischief.
Doloroso.—Soft and pathetic. (*Music.*)
Domicile (L. *domicilium*).—An abode.
Domine dirige nos.—O Lord, direct us.
Dominus vobiscum.—The Lord be with you.
Double entendre.—Double meaning (correctly written *double entente*).
Douceur.—A present or bribe; sweetness.
Draco.—A dragon; a constellation.
Dramatis personæ.—The characters in a play.
Duet (Ital. *duetto*).—A song for two performers.
Dulce est desipere in loco.—It is pleasant to jest or revel at the proper time.
Dulce et decorum est pro patriâ mori.—It is sweet and pleasant to die for one's country.
Dulia.—An inferior kind of worship.
Dum spiro spero.—Whilst I breathe, I hope.
Dum vivimus, vivamus.—While we live, let us live.
Duo.—Two; a two-part song.
Duodecimo.—A book having twelve leaves to a sheet.
Durante placito or *durante beneplacito.* — During pleasure.
Durante vitâ.—During life.
Dux fœmina facti.—A woman was the leader to the deed.

E pluribus unum.—One out of many; one composed of many; the motto of the United States.
Eau de vie.—Brandy; water of life.
Ecce homo.—Behold the man.
Ecce signum.—Behold the sign.
Eclaircissement.—The clearing up of an affair.
Eclat.—Splendor; applause.
Editio princeps.—The first edition.
Eheu!—Ah, alas!
Elan.—Buoyancy; dash.
Elegit.—He hath elected; a writ of execution.
Elève.—A pupil.
Elite.—The best part.
Embonpoint.—Roundness; good condition.
Emeritus.—One retired from active official duties.
Emeute.—Insurrection; uproar.
Empressement.—Eagerness; ardor.
En ami.—As a friend.
En avant!—Forward!
En flûte.—Carrying guns on the upper deck only.
En grande tenue.—In full dress.
En masse.—In a mass; in a body.
En passant.—By the way; in passing.
En rapport.—In communication.
En revanche.—In return.
En route.—On the way.
Enceinte.—Pregnant.
Enfans perdus.—Lost children; the forlorn hope.
Ennui.—Weariness; lassitude.
Ense petit placidam sub libertate quietem.—By his sword he seeks the calm repose of liberty.
Ensemble.—The whole taken together.
Entente cordiale.—The cordial understanding between two countries.
Entre nous.—Between ourselves.
Entrée.—Entrance.
Entremets.—Small and dainty dishes set between the principal ones at table.
Eo nomine.—By that name.
Equilibrium.—Equality of weight; even balance.
Ergo.—Therefore.
Eripuit cœlo fulmen, sceptrumque tyrannis. — He snatched the thunderbolt from heaven, and the scepter from tyrants.
Erratum.—A mistake or error (pl. *errata*).
Escrow.—A deed or writing left with another, to be delivered on the performance of something specified.
Espièglerie.—Waggish tricks.
Esprit de corps.—The animating spirit of a collective body.
Est modus in rebus.—There is a medium in all things.
Estoppel.—A stop, a preventive plea.
Esto perpetua.—May it last forever.
Et cœtera.—And the rest.
Eureka.—I have found it.
Ex.—Out of; late (as ex-consul).
Ex animo.—Heartily.
Ex cathedrâ.—From the chair; with high authority.
Ex concesso.—From what has been granted.
Ex curiâ.—Out of court.
Ex fumo dare lucem.—Out of smoke to bring light.
Ex nihilo nihil fit.—Nothing can come of nothing.
Ex officio.—By virtue of his office.
Ex parte.—On one side only (before a noun, *exparte*).
Ex pede Herculem.—We recognize a Hercules from the size of the foot; that is, we judge of the whole from the specimen.
Ex post facto.—After the deed is done.
Ex tempore.—Without premeditation.
Ex uno disce omnes.—From one learn all; from one judge of the whole.
Excelsior.—More elevated; onward.
Excerpta.—Extracts.
Exempli gratiâ.—As for example.
Exeunt omnes.—All retire.
Experimentum crucis.—A decisive experiment.
Experto credo.—Believe one who has experience.
Exposé.—An exposition; recital.

Faber suæ fortunæ.—The architect of his own fortune.
Facile primus, facile princeps.—By far the first or chiefest.
Facilis est descensus.—Descent is easy.
Facsimile.—Make it like; hence, an exact copy.
Factotum.—Do all; a man of all work.
Facta est lux.—There was light.
Fas est ab hoste doceri.—It is allowable to learn even from an enemy.
Fata obstant.—The fates oppose it.
Fauteuil.—An easy chair.
Faux pas.—A false step.
Felo de se.—A self-murderer.
Femme couverte.—A married woman.
Femme sole.—A woman unmarried.
Festina lente.—Hasten slowly; advance steadily rather than hurriedly.
Fête.—A feast or celebration.
Fête champêtre.—A rural feast.
Feu de joie.—A bonfire; a discharge of musketry on days of rejoicing.
Feuilleton.—A small leaf; a supplement to a newspaper; a pamphlet.
Fiat.—Let it be done.
Fiat justitia, ruat cœlum.—Let justice be done, though the heavens should fall.

Fiat lux.—Let there be light.
Fide, non armis.—By faith, not by arms.
Fide, sed cuivide.—Trust, but see whom.
Fides et justitia.—Fidelity and justice.
Fidus Achates.—Faithful Achates (that is, a true friend).
Fieri facias.—Cause it to be done (a kind of writ).
Filius nullius.—A son of nobody.
Fille-de-chambre.—A chambermaid.
Finale.—To close or end.
Finem respice.—Look to the end.
Finis.—The end.
Finis coronat opus.—The end crowns the work.
Flagrante bello.—While the war is raging.
Flagrante delicto.—In the commission of the crime.
Flâneur.—A lounger.
Flecti, non frangi.—To be bent, not to be broken.
Fleur-de-lis.—The flower of the lily (pl. *fleurs-de-lis*).
Forte.—In music, a direction to sing or play with force or spirit.
Fortes fortuna juvat.—Fortune assists the brave.
Fortissimo.—Very loud.
Fortiter in re.—Resolute in deed.
Fracas.—Bustle; a slight quarrel; more ado about the thing than it is worth.
Fruges consumere nati.—Born merely to consume the fruits of the earth.
Fugam fecit.—He has taken to flight.
Fuit Ilium.—Troy *has* been.
Functus officio.—Out of office.
Furore.—Excitement.

Gaieté de cœur.—Gayety of heart.
Gallicè.—In French.
Gardez bien.—Take good care.
Gardez la foi.—Keep the faith.
Gaucherie.—Awkwardness.
Gaudeamus igitur.—So let us be joyful.
Gendarme.—A military policeman.
Gendarmerie.—The body of the *gendarmes*.
Genius loci.—The genius of the place.
Genus irritabile vatum.—Irritable tribe of poets.
Gloria in excelsis.—Glory to God in the highest.
Gratis.—Free of cost.
Gratis dictum.—Mere assertion.
Gravamen.—The thing complained of.
Grisette.—Dressed in gray (a term applied to French shop girls, etc.).
Gusto.—Great relish.

Habeas corpus.—You are to have the body; a writ of right, by virtue of which every citizen can, when imprisoned, demand to be put on his trial.
Habitué.—A frequenter.
Hæc olim meminisse juvabit.—It will be pleasant hereafter to remember these things.
Haricot.—A kind of ragout; a kidney-bean.
Haud passibus æquis.—Not with equal steps. (Wrongly quoted: see *Non*, etc.)
Haut gout.—High flavor.
Hauteur.—Haughtiness.
Helluo librorum.—A bookworm.
Hic et ubique.—Here, there, and everywhere.
Hic jacet.—Here lies.
Hinc illæ lacrymæ.—Hence proceed these tears.
Hoc age.—Do this; attend to what you are doing.
Homme d'esprit.—A man of talent, or of wit.
Homo multarum literarum.—A man of much learning.
Honi soit qui mal y pense.—Evil be to him that evil thinks.
Honores mutant mores.—Honors change men's manners.
Hora fugit.—The hour or time flies.
Horresco referens.—I shudder to relate.
Hors de combat.—Disabled for fighting; vanquished.
Hortus siccus.—A collection of dried plants.
Hostis humani generis.—An enemy of the human race.
Hotel de ville.—A town hall.
Hôtel-Dieu.—The chief hospital in French cities.
Humanum est errare.—It is human to err.
Hunc tu caveto.—Beware of him.

Ibidem, contracted *ibid.* or *id.*—In the same place.
Ich dien.—I serve.
Id est.—That is; abridged *i. e.*
Id genus omne.—All of that sort.
Idem, contracted *id.*—The same. (*Id. ib.*, the same author; in the same place.)
Idoneus homo.—A fit man.
Ignoramus.—We are ignorant.
Ignorantia legis neminem excusat.—Ignorance of the law excuses no one.

Il a le diable au corps.—The devil is in him.
Imitatores, servum pecus.—Imitators, a servile herd.
Imperium in imperio.—One government existing within another.
Impransus.—One who has not dined.
Imprimatur.—Let it be printed.
Imprimis.—In the first place.
Impromptu.—A prompt remark without study.
In articulo mortis.—At the point of death.
In capite.—In the head.
In cœlo quies.—There is rest in heaven.
In commendam.—In trust.
In conspectu fori.—In the eye of the law; in the sight of the court.
In curiâ.—In the court.
In duplo.—Twice as much.
In equilibrio.—Equally balanced.
In esse.—In being.
In extenso.—At full length.
In extremis.—At the point of death.
In formâ pauperis.—As a pauper.
In foro conscientiæ.—Before the tribunal of conscience.
In hoc signo vinces.—In this sign thou shalt conquer.
In limine.—At the threshold.
In loco.—In the place.
In medias res.—Into the midst of things.
In memoriam.—To the memory of.
In perpetuum.—Forever.
In petto.—In reserve; in one's breast.
In posse.—In possible existence.
In posterum.—For the time to come.
In propriâ personâ.—In his own person.
In puris naturalibus.—Quite naked.
In re.—In the matter of.
In situ.—In its original situation.
In statu quo.—In the former state.
In te, Domine, speravi.—In thee, Lord, have I put my trust.
In terrorem.—By way of warning.
In totidem verbis.—In so many words.
In toto.—Altogether.
In transitu.—On the passage.
In utrumque paratus.—Prepared for either event.
In vacuo.—In empty space, or in a vacuum.
In vino veritas.—There is truth in wine.
Incognito.—Disguised, unknown.
Index expurgatorius.—A list of prohibited books.
Infra dignitatem.—Beneath one's dignity.
Innuendo.—Covert meaning; indirect hint.
Inops consilii.—Without counsel.
Insouciance.—Carelessness; indifference.
Instar omnium.—One will suffice for all; an example to others.
Inter alia.—Among other things.
Inter arma leges silent.—In the midst of arms the laws are silent.
Inter nos.—Between ourselves.
Inter se.—Among themselves.
Ipse dixit.—He himself said it; dogmatic assertion.
Ipsissima verba.—The very words.
Ipso facto.—By the fact itself; actually.
Ipso jure.—By the law itself.
Ira furor brevis est.—Anger is brief madness.
Ita lex scripta est.—Thus the law is written.
Item.—Also.

Jacta est alea.—The die is cast.
Jamais arrière.—Never behind.
Je ne sais quoi.—I know not what.
Jet d'eau.—A jet of water.
Jeu de mots.—Play upon words; a pun.
Jeu d'esprit.—A witticism.
Judicium Dei.—The judgment of God.
Juniores ad labores.—Young men for labors.
Jure divino.—By divine law.
Jure gentium.—By the law of nations.
Jure humano.—By human law.
Jus civile.—Civil law.
Jus gladii.—Right of the sword.
Juste milieu.—The golden mean; a just medium.
Justitiæ soror fides.—Faith is the sister of justice.

La critique est aisée, et l'art est difficile.—Criticism is easy, and art is difficult.
Labor ipse voluptas.—Labor itself is pleasure.
Labor omnia vincit.—Labor conquers all things.
Laissez-nous faire.—Let us alone.
Lapsus calami.—A slip of the pen; an error in writing.
Lapsus linguæ.—A slip of the tongue.
Lapsus memoriæ.—A slip of memory.

Lares et penates.—Household gods.
L'argent.—Money, or silver.
Laudator temporis acti.—A praiser of time past.
Laus Deo.—Praise to God.
Laus propria sordet.—Praise of one's own self defiles.
Le beau monde.—The fashionable world.
Le bon temps viendra.—The good time will come.
Le grand œuvre.—The great work; the philosopher's stone.
Le pas.—Precedence in place or rank.
Le savoir-faire.—The knowledge how to act; address.
Le tout ensemble.—All together.
Lege.—Read.
Leges legum.—The law of laws.
Lèse majesté.—High treason.
L'étoile du nord.—The north star.
Lettre de cachet.—A sealed letter; a royal warrant.
Levari facias.—That you cause to be levied; a writ of execution.
Levée.—A morning visit or reception.
Lex loci.—The law of the place.
Lex magna est, et prævalebit.—The law is great, and will prevail.
Lex non scripta.—The unwritten or common law.
Lex scripta.—Statute law.
Lex talionis.—The law of retaliation.
Lex terræ, lex patriæ.—The law of the land.
L'homme propose, et Dieu dispose.—Man proposes and God disposes.
Libretto.—A little book or pamphlet.
Licentia vatûm.—A poetical license.
Lingua Franca.—The mixed language spoken by Europeans in the East.
Liqueur.—A cordial.
Lis litem generat.—Strife begets strife.
Lis sub judice.—A case not yet decided.
Lite pendente.—During the trial.
Litera scripta manet.—The written letter remains.
Literati.—Men of letters or learning.
Loco citato.—In the place cited.
Loco parentis.—In the place of the parent.
Locum tenens.—One who holds a place for another.
Locus sigilli (L. S.).—The place of the seal.
Longo intervallo.—At a great distance.
Ludere cum sacris.—To trifle with sacred things.
Lusus naturæ.—A sport or freak of nature.

Macte virtute.—Proceed in virtue.
Mademoiselle.—A young unmarried lady.
Magna Charta.—The great charter of England.
Magna civitas, magna solitudo.—A great city is a great desert.
Magna est veritas, et prævalebit.—The truth is great, and will prevail.
Magni nominis umbra.—The shadow of a great name.
Magnum opus.—A great work.
Magnus Apollo.—Great Apollo; one of high authority.
Maison de ville.—The town house.
Maître d'hôtel.—An hotel keeper; a house steward.
Major-domo (Ital. *maior-domo*).—One who has the management of a household.
Malâ fide.—In bad faith; treacherously.
Mal à propos.—Out of time; unbecoming.
Malaria.—Noxious exhalations.
Malgré.—In spite of.
Malum in se.—Bad in itself.
Mandamus.—We command; a peremptory writ to compel obedience.
Manège.—A riding school.
Mania a potu.—Madness caused by drunkenness.
Manu forti.—With a strong hand.
Mardi gras.—Shrove Tuesday.
Mare clausum.—A closed sea; a bay.
Materfamilias.—The mother of a family.
Materia medica.—Substances used in the healing art.
Matinée.—A morning party.
Mauvais goût.—Bad taste.
Mauvais sujet.—A worthless fellow.
Mauvaise honte.—False modesty; bashfulness.
Maximum.—The greatest.
Maximus in minimis.—Very great in trifling things.
Me judice.—I being judge; in my own opinion.
Medio tutissimus ibis.—A medium course will be safest.
Meditatione fugæ.—In contemplation of flight.
Memento mori.—Remember death.
Memorabilia.—Things to be remembered.
Memoriter.—By rote.
Ménage.—Household.
Mens sana in corpore sano.—A sound mind in a sound body.
Mens sibi conscia recti.—A mind conscious of rectitude.
Mensa et thoro.—From bed and board.
Merum sal.—Pure salt; genuine Attic wit.
Meum et tuum.—Mine and thine.
Minimum.—The least.
Minutiæ.—Minute concerns; trifles.
Mirabile dictu.—Wonderful to be told.
Mirabilia.—Wonders.
Mittimus.—We send; a warrant for the commitment of an offender.
Modus operandi.—Manner of operation.
Montani semper liberi.—Mountaineers are always freemen.
Morceau.—A morsel.
More suo.—In his own way.
Mot du guet.—A watchword.
Multum in parvo.—Much in a small space.
Mutanda.—Things to be altered.
Mutatis mutandis.—The necessary changes being made.
Mutato nomine.—The name being changed.

Naïveté.—Ingenuousness; simplicity.
Ne cede malis.—Yield not to misfortune.
Ne exeat.—Let him not depart.
Ne plus ultra.—Nothing further; the uttermost point.
Ne quid nimis.—Not too much of anything; do nothing to excess.
Ne sutor ultra crepidam.—Let not the shoemaker go beyond his last.
Ne tentes, aut perfice.—Attempt not, or accomplish thoroughly.
Nec pluribus impar.—Not an unequal match for numbers.
Nec scire fas est omnia.—It is not permitted to know all things.
Necessitatis non habet legem.—Necessity has no law.
Née.—Born.
Nefasti dies.—Days upon which no public business was transacted; also, unlucky days.
Nemine contradicente.—No one contradicting.
Nemine dissentiente.—Without opposition or dissent.
Nemo me impune lacessit.—No one wounds me with impunity.
Nemo mortalium omnibus horis sapit.—No one is wise at all times.
Nemo repente fuit turpissimus.—No man ever became a villain at once.
Nemo solus sapit.—No one is wise alone.
Niaiserie.—Silliness.
Nihil debet.—He owes nothing; a plea denying a debt.
Nihil quod tetigit, non ornavit.—Whatever he touched he embellished.
Nil admirari.—To wonder at nothing.
Nil desperandum.—Never despair.
Nimium ne crede colori.—Trust not too much to looks.
N'importe.—It matters not.
Nisi Dominus frustra.—Unless the Lord be with us, all efforts are in vain.
Noblesse oblige.—Rank imposes obligation.
Nolens volens.—Willing or unwilling.
Noli me tangere.—Don't touch me.
Nolle prosequi.—Unwilling to proceed.
Nolo episcopari.—I am not willing to be made a bishop (an old former way of declining a bishopric).
Nom de guerre.—An assumed name.
Nom de plume.—A literary title.
Nomen et omen.—Name and omen; a name that is ominous.
Non compos mentis.—Not of sound mind.
Non deficiente crumenâ.—If the money does not fail.
Non est disputandum.—It is not to be disputed.
Non est inventus.—Not found.
Non libet.—It does not please me.
Non mi ricordo.—I don't remember.
Non nobis solum.—Not merely for ourselves.
Non obstante.—Notwithstanding.
Non omnis moriar.—I shall not wholly die.
Non passibus æquis.—Not with equal steps.
Non sequitur.—It does not follow; an unwarranted conclusion.
Non sibi, sed omnibus.—Not for itself, but for all.
Nonchalance.—Coolness; easy indifference.
Nonpareil.—Peerless; a small printing type.
Nosce te ipsum.—Know thyself.
Noscitur ex sociis.—He is known by his companions.
Nota bene.—Mark well.
Nous verrons.—We shall see.
Novus homo.—A new man.
Nudum pactum.—An invalid agreement.
Nulla crux, nulla corona.—No cross, no crown.

Nulla nuova, bona nuova.—The best news is no news.
Nullius filius.—The son of nobody.
Nunc aut nunquam.—Now or never.
O tempora! o mores!—Oh, the times! oh, the manners!
Obiit.—He (or she) died.
Obiter dictum.—A thing said by the way, or in passing.
Obsta principiis.—Resist the first beginnings.
Odi profanum.—I loathe the profane.
Odium theologicum.—The hatred of theologians.
Ohe! jam satis.—Oh, there is now enough.
Olla podrida.—An incongruous mixture.
Omne ignotum pro magnifico.—Whatever is unknown is thought to be magnificent.
Omnes.—All.
Omnia bona bonis.—All things are good with the good.
Omnia vincit amor.—Love conquers all things.
On-dit.—A rumor; a flying report.
Onus.—Burden.
Onus probandi.—The responsibility of producing proof.
Ope et consilio.—With assistance and counsel.
Ora et labora.—Pray and work.
Orator fit, poeta nascitur.—The orator is made by education, but a poet must be born.
Ore rotundo.—With full sounding voice.
Otium cum dignitate.—Dignified leisure.
Outré.—Preposterous; eccentric.
Oyer and Terminer.—A criminal court.

Pallida mors.—Pale death.
Par excellence.—By way of eminence.
Par nobile fratrum.—A noble pair of brothers; two just alike.
Pari passu.—With equal step; in the same degree.
Parole d'honneur.—Word of honor.
Pars pro toto.—Part for the whole.
Particeps criminis.—An accomplice.
Parturiunt montes, nascetur ridiculus mus.—The mountains are in labor; a ridiculous mouse will be brought forth.
Parva componere magnis.—To compare small things with great.
Parvenu.—A new comer; an upstart.
Pas.—A step; precedence.
Passe-partout.—A master key.
Passim.—In many places; everywhere.
Paterfamilias.—The father of a family.
Pater noster.—Our Father; the Lord's prayer.
Pater patriæ.—Father of his country.
Patois.—A provincial dialect.
Pax in bello.—Peace in war.
Peccavi.—I have sinned.
Penchant.—An inclination; a leaning toward.
Pendente lite.—While the suit is pending.
Penetralia.—Secret recesses.
Per aspera ad astra.—Through trials to glory.
Per capita.—By the head; equal division.
Per cent. or *per centum.*—By the hundred.
Per contra.—Contrariwise.
Per curiam.—By the court.
Per diem.—By the day.
Per fas et nefas.—Through right and wrong.
Per saltum.—With a leap; at once.
Per se.—By itself; alone.
Perdu.—Lost.
Père de famille.—The father of a family.
Petit.—Small; little.
Petitio principii.—A begging of the question.
Petit-maître.—A fop.
Peu à peu.—Gradually; a little by little.
Pinxit.—Painted it; placed after the artist's name on a picture.
Più.—More.
Plateau.—A plain; a flat surface.
Plebs.—Common people.
Pluries.—Very often; a third writ, after two writs have issued.
Poco.—A little.
Poeta nascitur, non fit.—A poet is born, not made.
Point d'appui.—Point of support; prop.
Poisson d'Avril.—April fool.
Populus vult decipi.—People like to be deceived.
Posse comitatûs.—The power of the county.
Postea.—Afterward; indorsement of the verdict upon the record.
Post mortem.—After death.
Postulata.—Things assumed.
Præcognita.—Things previously known.
Præmonitus præmunitus.—Forewarned, forearmed.
Preux chevalier.—A brave knight.
Primâ facie.—On the first view.
Primum mobile.—The primary motive, or moving power.
Primus inter pares.—Chief among equals.
Principia, non homines.—Principles, not men.
Principiis obsta.—Resist the first innovations.
Pro aris et focis.—For our altars and our hearths.
Pro bono publico.—For the public good.
Pro et con (for *contra*).—For and against.
Pro formâ.—For form's sake; according to form.
Pro hâc vice.—For this turn or occasion.
Pro loco et tempore.—For the place and time.
Pro patriâ.—For our country.
Pro ratâ.—In proportion.
Pro re natâ.—For a special emergency.
Pro tanto.—For so much.
Pro tempore.—For the time being.
Probatum est.—It has been tried and proved.
Procès-verbal.—A written statement.
Prochein ami.—The next friend.
Procul, O procul este, profani!—Far, far hence, O ye profane!
Pronunciamento.—A public declaration.
Propagandâ fide.—For extending the faith.
Protégé.—A person taken charge of, or patronized; a ward, etc.
Prudens futuri.—Thoughtful of the future.
Pugnis et calcibus.—With fists and heels; with all the might.
Punica fides.—Punic faith; treachery.

Quære.—Query; inquiry.
Quamdiu se bene gesserit.—So long as he shall conduct himself properly.
Quantum.—The due proportion.
Quantum libet.—As much as you please.
Quantum meruit.—As much as he deserved.
Quantum sufficit.—A sufficient quantity; enough.
Quare clausum fregit.—An action for damages to real estate.
Quare impedit.—Why he hinders.
Quasi dicas.—As if you should say.
Quelque chose.—A trifle.
Qui capit, ille facit.—He who takes it makes it.
Qui pense?—Who thinks?
Qui tam?—Who as well? The title given to a certain action at law.
Qui transtulit sustinet.—He who brought us hither still preserves us.
Qui va là?—Who goes there?
Qui vive?—Who goes there? hence, on the *qui-vive*, on the alert.
Quid-nunc?—What now? a newsmonger.
Quid pro quo.—One thing for another; "tit for tat."
Quid rides?—Why do you laugh?
Quis separabit?—Who shall separate us?
Quo animo?—With what intention?
Quo jure?—By what right?
Quo warranto?—By what warrant or authority?
Quoad hoc.—To this extent.
Quod avertat Deus!—Which may God avert!
Quod vide.—Which see.
Quodlibet.—A nice point; a subtlety.
Quondam.—Former.
Quorum.—Of whom; a term signifying a sufficient number for a certain business.
Quos Deus vult perdere, prius dementat.—Those whom God wishes to destroy, he first deprives of understanding.

Ragout.—A highly seasoned dish.
Rara avis.—A rare bird; a prodigy.
Re infectâ.—The business being unfinished.
Recte et suaviter.—Justly and mildly.
Rectus in curiâ.—Upright in the court; with clean hands.
Redolet lucernâ.—It smells of the lamp; it is a labored production.
Reductio ad absurdum.— A reducing a position to an absurdity.
Regina.—Queen.
Regium donum.—A royal donation (a grant from the British crown to the Irish Presbyterian clergy).
Regnant populi.—The people rule.
Rencontre.—An encounter.
Renaissance.—New birth; applied to the revival of the classic arts in the fifteenth and sixteenth centuries.
Requiescant in pace.—May they rest in peace.
Requiescat in pace.—May he rest in peace.
Rerum primordia.—The first elements of things.
Res angusta domi.—Narrow circumstances at home; poverty.

Res integra.—An entire matter.
Respice finem.—Look to the end.
Respublica.—The commonwealth.
Restaurateur.—A tavern keeper who provides dinners, etc.
Résumé.—An abstract or summary.
Resurgam.—I shall rise again.
Revenons à nos moutons.—Let us return to our subject.
Rex.—King.
Rouge.—Red coloring for the skin.
Rouge et noir.—Red and black (a kind of game).
Rus in urbe.—The country in town.
Ruse contre ruse.—Diamond cut diamond; trick for trick.
Ruse de guerre.—A stratagem of war.

Salle.—Hall.
Salus populi suprema lex est.—The welfare of the people is in the supreme law.
Salvo pudore.—Without offense to modesty.
Sanctum sanctorum.—Holy of Holies.
Sang-froid.—Coolness; self-possession.
Sans.—Without.
Sans cérémonie.—Without ceremony.
Sans peur et sans reproche.—Without fear and without reproach.
Sans souci.—Without care: free and easy.
Sans tâche.—Stainless.
Sans-culottes.—Without breeches; a term applied to the rabble of the French Revolution.
Sartor resartus.—The cobbler mended.
Satis, superque.—Enough, and more than enough.
Satis verborum.—Enough of words; you need say no more.
Sauve qui peut.—Save himself who can.
Savant.—A learned man.
Savior-faire.—Ability; skill.
Scandalum magnatum.—Scandal of the great.
Scienter.—Knowingly.
Scilicet.—That is to say; to wit.
Scire facias.—Cause it to be known.
Scripsit.—Wrote it.
Sculpsit.—Engraved it; placed after the engraver's name in prints.
Secundum artem.—According to rule.
Selon les règles.—According to rule.
Semper fidelis.—Always faithful.
Semper idem.—Always the same.
Semper paratus.—Always ready.
Senatûs consultum.—A decree of the senate.
Seriatim.—In order; successively.
Si quæris peninsulam amœnam circumspice.—If thou seekest a beautiful peninsula, behold it here.
Sic in originali.—So it stands in the original.
Sic itur ad astra.—Such is the way to immortality.
Sic passim.—So everywhere.
Sic semper tyrannis.—So be it ever to tyrants.
Sic transit gloria mundi.—Thus passes away the glory of the world.
Sicut ante.—As before.
Similia similibus curantur.—Like things are cured by like.
Simplex munditiis.—Of simple elegance.
Sine die.—Without naming a day.
Sine invidiâ.—Without envy.
Sine qua non.—An indispensable requisite.
Siste, viator.—Stop, traveler.
Sobriquet.—A nickname.
Soi-disant.—Self-styled; pretended.
Soirée.—An evening party.
Souvenir.—Remembrance; a keepsake.
Spartam nactus es, hanc exorna.—You have got something good; make the most of it you can.
Spectas et spectaberis.—You will see and be seen.
Spes mea Christus.—Christ is my hope.
Spolia opima.—The richest booty.
Stans pede in uno.—Standing on one foot.
Statu quo, or *in statu quo.*—In the same state.
Stet.—Let it stand.
Suaviter in modo, fortiter in re.—Gentle in manner, resolute in deed.
Sub judice.—Under consideration.
Sub rosâ.—Under the rose; privately.
Sub silentio.—In silence.
Subpœna.—Under a penalty; a summons to attend a court as a witness.
Succedaneum.—A substitute.
Sui generis.—Of its own kind; peculiar.
Summum bonum.—The chief good.
Supersedeas.—A writ to stay proceedings.
Super visum corporis.—Upon a view of the body.
Suppressio veri suggestio falsi.—A suppression of the truth is the suggestion of a falsehood.
Supra.—Above.
Suum cuique.—Let every one have his own.

Table d'hôte.—An ordinary at which the master of the hotel presides.
Tabula rasa.—A smooth or blank tablet.
Tædium vitæ.—Weariness of life.
Tale quale.—Such as it is.
Tant mieux.—So much the better.
Tant pis.—So much the worse.
Tapis.—The carpet.
Tartuffe.—A nickname for a hypocritical devotee, derived from the principal character in Molière's comedy so called.
Te judice.—You may judge.
Tempora mutantur, et nos mutamur in illis.—The times are changed, and we are changed with them.
Tempus edax rerum.—Time the devourer of all things.
Tempus fugit.—Time flies.
Tempus omnia revelat.—Time reveals all things.
Teres atque rotundus.—Smooth and round; polished and complete.
Terra firma.—Solid earth; a safe footing.
Terra incognita.—An unknown country.
Terre tenant.—A person in actual possession of the land.
Tertium quid.—A third something; a nondescript.
Tête-à-tête.—A conversation between two parties.
Tirade.—A tedious and bitter harangue.
Ton.—The fashion.
Torso.—The fragmentary trunk of a statue.
Tort.—A wrong; an injury.
Tot homines, quot sententiæ.—So many men, so many minds.
Totidem verbis.—In just so many words.
Toties quoties.—As often as.
Toto cœlo.—By the whole heavens; diametrically opposite.
Toto corde.—With the whole heart.
Toujours prêt.—Always ready.
Tour à tour.—By turns.
Tout bien ou rien.—The whole or nothing.
Tout ensemble.—The whole.
Tria juncta in uno.—Three united in one.
Tu quoque, Brute!—And thou too, Brutus!
Tuebor.—I will defend.
Tutto è buono che vien da Dio.—All is good which comes from God.
Tuum est.—It is your own.

Ubi jus incertum, ibi jus nullum.—Where the law is uncertain, there is no law.
Ubi libertas, ibi patria.—Where liberty dwells, there is my country.
Ubi supra.—Where above mentioned.
Ultima ratio regum.—The last argument of kings; military weapons; war.
Ultima Thule.—The utmost boundary or limit.
Ultimatum.—A final action or decision.
Un bel esprit.—A wit; a virtuoso.
Un sot à triple étage.—An egregious blockhead.
Unâ voce.—With one voice; unanimously.
Unique.—Singular; the only one of its kind.
Usque ad nauseam.—To disgust.
Usus loquendi.—Usage in speaking.
Ut infra.—As below.
Uti possidetis.—As you possess; state of present possession.
Utile dulci.—Utility with pleasure.

Vade-mecum.—Go with me; a constant companion.
Væ victis.—woe to the vanquished!
Vale.—Farewell.
Valet-de-chambre.—A servant who assists his master in dressing.
Variæ lectiones.—Various readings.
Veluti in speculum.—As in a mirror.
Venditioni exponas.—That you expose to sale; writ of execution.
Veni, vidi, vici.—I came, I saw, I conquered.
Venire.—To come; a writ to a sheriff directing him to summon jurors.
Venue.—The place from which the jury are drawn.
Verbatim et literatim.—Word for word and letter for letter.
Verbum sat sapienti.—A word is enough for a wise man.
Verdad es verde.—Truth is green.

Veritas vincit.—Truth conquers.
Versus.—Against; toward.
Vertu, Virtù.—Virtue; taste; art; skill.
Veto.—I forbid.
Vi et armis.—By force and arms.
Viâ.—By the way of.
Via media.—A middle course.
Vice.—In the room of.
Vice versâ.—The terms being exchanged; reversely.
Vide.—See.
Vide et crede.—See and believe.
Vide ut supra.—See as above.
Videlicet.—To wit, namely.
Videttes.—Sentinels on horseback.
Vignette.—A name given to slight engravings with which books, bank-notes, etc., are ornamented.
Vincit amor patriæ.—Love of country prevails.
Vinculum matrimonii.—The bond of marriage.
Virtuoso.—One skilled in matters of taste or art.
Virtute officii.—By virtue of office.
Vis inertiæ.—Inert power; the tendency of every body to remain at rest.
Vis medicatrix naturæ.—The healing tendency of nature.
Vis poetica.—Poetic genius.
Vis vitæ.—The vigor of life.
Vis-à-vis.—Face to face.
Vita brevis, ars longa.—Life is short, and art is long.
Vivâ voce.—By word of mouth; by the living voice.
Vivant rex et regina.—Long live the king and queen.
Vivat regina.—Long live the queen.
Vivat respublica.—Live the republic.
Vive la bagatelle.—Success to trifling.
Vive la reine.—Long live the queen.
Vive l'empereur.—Long live the emperor.
Vive le roi.—Long live the king.
Vive l'impératrice.—Long live the empress.
Vive, vale.—Farewell, and be happy.
Voilà tout.—That's all.
Voilà une autre chose.—That's quite a different matter.
Voir dire.—A preliminary examination to determine the competency of a witness.
Volens et potens.—Willing and able.
Volgo gran bestia.—The mob is a great beast.
Volere è potere.—To will is to do.
Volti subito.—Turn over quickly.
Vox, et præterea nihil.—A voice, and nothing more.
Vox populi, vox Dei.—The people's voice is God's voice.
Vox stellarum.—The voice of the stars; applied to almanacs.
Vulgo.—Vulgarly; commonly.
Vuelta.—Over, to next page, or (o).
Vulnus immedicabile.—An irreparable injury.
Vultus est index animi.—The countenance is the index of the mind.

Zonam solvere.—To loose the virgin zone.

ABBREVIATIONS IN GENERAL USE.

A.B. *Artium Baccalaureus*, Bachelor of Arts.
Abp. Archbishop.
Abr. Abridgment.
A.C. *Ante Christum*, before Christ; Arch-Chancellor.
Acad. Academy.
Acct. Account; Accent.
A.D. *Anno Domini*, in the year of our Lord.
A.D.C. Aide-de-camp.
Ad. Advertisement.
Adj. Adjective.
Adjt. Adjutant.
Adjt.-Gen. Adjutant-General.
Ad lib. *Ad libitum*, at pleasure.
Adm. Admiral; Admiralty.
Admr. Administrator.
Admx. Administratrix.
Adv. Adverb; Advent; Advertisement.
Æt. *Ætatis*, of age; aged.
Agr. Agriculture.
Agt. Agent.
Ala. Alabama.
A.M. *Anno mundi*, In the year of the world; *Artium Magister*, Master of Arts; *Ante meridiem*, Before noon, morning.
Ang. Sax. Anglo-Saxon.
Anon. Anonymous.
Ans. Answer.
A.R.A. Associate of the Royal Academy.
Arab. Arabic, or Arabia.
Ariz. Ter. Arizona Territory.
Ark. Arkansas.
Atty. Attorney.
Atty.-Gen. Attorney-General.
A.U.A. American Unitarian Association.
Aug. August.
B.A. Bachelor of Arts.
Bal. Balance.
Bart. or Bt. Baronet.
Bbl. Barrel.
B.C. Before Christ.
B.C.L. Bachelor of Civil Law.
B.D. Bachelor of Divinity.
B.E. Bachelor of the Elements.
B.M. Bachelor of Medicine.
B. Mus. Bachelor of Music.
Brig.-Gen. Brigadier-General.
Bro., Bros. Brother, Brothers
B.S. Bachelor of Science.
B.V. Blessed Virgin.
B.V.M. Blessed Virgin Mary.
C., Ch. or Chap. Chapter; Consul.
C. or Cent. A hundred, *Centum*.
Cal. California; Calends; Calendar.
Caps. Capitals.
Capt. Captain.
Capt.-Gen. Captain-General.
C.E. Civil Engineer; Canada East.
Cel. or Celt. Celtic.
C.H. Court-house.
Chap Chapter; Chaplain.
Chron. Chronicles.
Clk. Clerk.
C.M. Common Meter.
C.M.G. Companion of the Order of St. Michael and St. George.
Co. Company; County.
C.O.D. Cash (or collect) on delivery.
Col. Colonel; Colossians; Colorado.
Colo. Colorado.
Con. Against; In opposition; *Contra*.
Conn. or Ct. Connecticut.
Cor. Sec. Corresponding Secretary.
Cr. Creditor; Credit.
Ct., cts. Cent, Cents; Connecticut.
Cwt. Hundredweight.
d. Penny or Pence.
Dak. Ter. Dakota Territory.
D.C. District of Columbia.
D.C.L. Doctor of Civil Law.
D.D. Doctor of Divinity.
D.D.S. Doctor of Dental Surgery.
D.E. Dynamic Engineer.
Dec. December; Declaration.
Deft. or Dft. Defendant.
Del. Delaware; Delegate.
Dept. Department.
Deut. Deuteronomy.
Disc. Discount.
Dist.-Atty. District-Attorney.
D.M. Doctor of Music.
D.M.D. Doctor Dental Medicine.
Do. The Same, *Ditto*.
Dol., Dols., $. Dollars.
Doz. Dozen.
Dr. Debtor; Doctor.
Eccl. Ecclesiastes.
Ed. Editor; Edition.
e.g. For example, *Exempli gratia*.
Eng. England; English.
Ep. Epistle.
Eph. Ephesians; Ephraim.
Esq., Esqs. Esquire, Esquires.
et al. And others, *Et alii*.
etc. or &c. And other things; And so forth.
et. seq. And what follows, *Et sequentia*.
Ex. Example.
ex. g. For example, *Exempli gratia*.
Fahr. Fahrenheit.
F.A.M. Free and Accepted Masons.
F.A.S. Fellow of the Antiquarian Society.
fcap. or fcp. Foolscap.
Feb. February.
Fig. Figure; figurative.
Fla. Florida.
F.O.B. Free on Board.
F.R.A.S. Fellow of Royal Astr. Soc.
F.R.C.S.L. Fellow of the Royal College of Surgeons, London.
F.R.G.S. Fellow of the Royal Geographical Society.
Fri. Friday.
F.R.S. Fellow of the Royal Society.
F.R.S.E. Fellow of the Royal Society, Edinburgh.
F.S.A. Fellow of the Society of Arts.
Ga. Georgia.
Gal. Galations; Gallon.
Gen. Genesis; General.
Goth. Gothic.
Gov. Governor.
Gov.-Gen. Governor-General.
H.B.M. His or Her Britannic Majesty.
Heb. Hebrews.
Hhd. Hogshead.
H.R. House of Representatives.
H.R.H. His or Her Royal Highness.
Ia. Iowa.
Ib. or ibid. In the same place.
Id. The same, *Idem*.
Id. Ter. Idaho Territory.
i.e. That is, *Id est*.
I.H.S. Jesus the Saviour of men.
Ill. Illinois.
incog. Unknown, *Incognito*.
Ind. Indiana; Index; Indian.
Ind. Ter. Indian Territory.
Indef. Indefinite.
in loc. In the place; on the passage, *In loco*.
I.N.R.I. Jesus of Nazareth, King of the Jews.
Inst. Instant, of this month; Institute.

Io. Iowa.
I.O.F. Independent Order of Foresters.
I.O.O.F. Independent Order of Odd Fellows.
I.S.M. *Jesus Salvator mundi*, Jesus the Saviour of the world.
Ital. Italic; Italian.
Jan. January.
J.C.D. *Juris Civilis Doctor*, Doctor of Civil Law.
J.D. *Jurum Doctor*, Doctor of Laws.
J.P. Justice of the Peace.
Jr. or Jun. Junior.
J.U.D. or J.V.D. *Juris utriusque Doctor*, Doctor of both Laws (of the Canon and the Civil Law).
Jul. July; Julius.
Kas. Kansas.
K.B. King's Bench; Knight of the Bath.
K.C. King's Counsel; Knight of the Crescent, in Turkey.
K.C.B. Knight Commander of the Bath.
K.G. Knight of the Garter.
K.G.C. Knight of the Grand Cross.
K.G.C.B. Knight of the Grand Cross of the Bath.
Knt. Knight.
Ky. Kentucky.
Lev. Leviticus.
Lex. Lexicon.
L.I. Long Island.
Lib. *Liber*, book.
Lieut. Lieutenant.
LL.B. *Legum Baccalaureus*, Bachelor of Laws.
LL.D. *Legum Doctor*, Doctor of Laws.
loc. cit. *Loco citato*, in the place cited.
Lond. London.
L.S. *Locus sigilli*, Place of the seal.
Lt. Lieutenant.
M. *Meridies*, noon.
M. *Mille*, a thousand.
M. or Mons. *Monsieur*, Sir.
M.A. Master of Arts.
Maj. Major.
Maj.-Gen. Major-General.
Mar. March.
Mass. Massachusetts.
Math. Mathematics; Mathematician.
Matt. Matthew.
M.B. *Medicinæ Baccalaureus*, Bachelor of Medicine.
M.B. *Musicæ Baccalaureus*, Bachelor of Music.
M.C. Member of Congress.
Mch. March.
M.D. *Medicinæ Doctor*, Doctor of Medicine.
Md. Maryland.
Mdlle. or Mlle. *Mademoiselle.*
Mdse. Merchandise.
M.E. Methodist Episcopal; Military or Mechanical Engineer.
Me. Maine.
Mech. Mechanics, or Mechanical.
Med. Medicine.
Mem. Memorandum. *Memento*, remember.
Messrs. or MM. *Messieurs*, Gentlemen.
Mex. Mexico, or Mexican.
Mich. Michigan.
Minn. Minnesota.
Miss. Mississippi.
MM. Their Majesties; *Messieurs*, Gentlemen; Two thousand.
Mme. Madame.
M.M.S.S. *Massachusettensis Medicinæ Societatis Socius*, Fellow of the Massachusetts Medical Society.
Mo. Missouri; Month.
Mon. Monday.
Mons. *Monsieur*, Sir.
Mont. Ter. Montana Territory.
M.P. Member of Parliament; Metropolitan Police.
M.P.P. Member of Provincial Parliament.
Mr. Mister.
M.R.A.S. Member of the Royal Asiatic Society; Member of the Royal Academy of Science.
M.R.C.C. Member of the Royal College of Chemistry.
M.R.C.S. Member of the Royal College of Surgeons.
M.R.G.S. Member of the Royal Geographical Society.
M.R.I. Member of the Royal Institute.
Mrs. Mistress.
M.R.S.L. Member of the Royal Society of Literature.
M.S. *Memoriæ sacrum*, Sacred to the memory; Master of the Sciences.
MSS. Manuscripts.
Mus. B. Bachelor of Music.
Mus. D. Doctor of Music.
N. A. North America.
N.B. New Brunswick; North British; *Nota bene*, mark well, take notice.
N.C. North Carolina; New Church.
N.E. New England; Northeast.
Neb. Nebraska.
Nev. Nevada.
New Test. or N.T. New Testament.
N.F. Newfoundland.
N.H. New Hampshire; New Haven.
N.J. New Jersey.
N.Mex. New Mexico.
No. *Numero*, number.
Nol.pros. *Nolens prosequi*, I am unwilling to prosecute.
Non pros. *Non prosequitur*, He does not prosecute.
Non seq. *Non sequitur*, It does not follow.
Nov. November.
N.S. New Style (after 1752); Nova Scotia.
N.T. New Testament.
Num. Numbers; Numeral.
N.V.M. Nativity of the Virgin Mary.
N.Y. New York.
O. Ohio.
O.K. A slang phrase for "All correct."
Oct. October.
Old Test. or O.T. Old Testament.
Or. Oregon.
O.S. Old Style (before 1752).
O.S.F. Order of St. Francis.
O.T. Old Testament.
Oxon. *Oxoniensis, Oxonii*, of Oxford, at Oxford.
Oz. Ounce.
Pa. Pennsylvania.
Par. Paragraph.
Pd. Paid.
P.E. Protestant Episcopal.
Penn. Pennsylvania.
Per. or pr. By the.
Per cent. *Per centum*, by the hundred.
Phar. Pharmacy.
Ph.B. *Philosophiæ Baccalaureus*, Bachelor of Philosophy.
Ph.D. *Philosophiæ Doctor*, Doctor of Philosophy.
Pinx. *Pinxit*, He (or she) painted it.
Pl. or plur. Plural.
Plff. Plaintiff.
P.M. *Post meridiem*, Afternoon, Evening; Postmaster; Passed Midshipman; Paymaster.
P.O. Post office.
Pop. Population.
P.P.C. *Pour prendre conge*, to take leave.
Pp. or pp. Pages.
Pro tem. *Pro tempore*, for the time being.
Prov. Proverbs; Provost.
Prox. *Proximo*, next (month).
P.S. *Post scriptum*, Postscript.
P.S. Privy Seal.
Ps. Psalm or Psalms.
Pt. Part; Pint; Payment; Point; Port; Post-town.
Pub. Publisher; Publication; Published; Public.
Pwt. Pennyweight; Pennyweights.
Pxt. *Pinxit*, He (or she) painted it.
q.e.d. *Quod erat demonstrandum*, which was to be proved.
q.l. *Quantum libet*, as much as you please.
Q.M. Quartermaster.
Qr. Quarter.
q.s. *Quantum sufficit*, a sufficient quantity.
Qt. Quart.
Ques. Question.
q.v. *Quod vide*, which see; *quantum vis*, as much as you will.
R. *Recipe*, Take; *Regina*, Queen; *Rex*, King; River; Rod; Rood; Rises.
R.A. Royal Academy; Royal Academician; Royal Arch; Royal Arcanum; Royal Artillery.
Recd. Received.
Ref. Reference; Reform.
Rev. Reverend; Revelation (Book of); Review; Revenue; Revise.
R.I. Rhode Island.
R.M.S. Royal Mail Steamer.
R.N. Royal Navy.
Rom. Cath. Roman Catholic.
R.S.A. Royal Society of Antiquaries; Royal Scottish Academy.
R.S.D. Royal Society of Dublin.
R.S.E. Royal Society of Edinburgh.
R.S.L. Royal Society of London.
R.S.V.P. *Respondez s'il vous plait.* Answer if you please.
Rt. Hon. Right Honorable.
Rt. Rev. Right Reverend.
S.A. South America; South Africa; South Australia.
Sat. Saturday.
S.C. *Senatus consultum*, A decree of the Senate; South Carolina.
Sc. He (or she) engraved it.
sc. or scil. Namely.
Scot. Scotland.
Sculp. or sculp. He (or she) engraved it, *Sculpsit*.
S.D. Doctor of Science.
Sec. Secretary; Second; Section.
Sept. September; Septuagint.
Seq. Following, *Sequentia;* It follows, *Sequitur*.
Serg. Sergeant.
Serg. Maj. Sergeant Major.
S.J. Society of Jesus.
S.J.C. Supreme Judicial Court.
S.P. Without issue, *Sine prole.*
Sp. Spain.
Sq.ft. Square foot or square feet.
Sq. in. Square inch or inches.
Sq. m. Square mile or miles.
Sq. r. Square rood or roods.
Sq. yd. Square yard.
Sr. Sir or Senior; Sister.
SS. or ss. To wit, *Scilicet.*
St. Saint; Street; Strait.
Stat. Statute.
S.T.D. Doctor of Sacred Theology.
Ster. or Stg. Sterling.
S.T.P. Professor of Sacred Theology.
Subj. Subjective.
Subst. Substantive.
Supt. Superintendent.
Surg. Surgeon; Surgery.
Surg.-Gen. Surgeon-General.
Surv. Surveyor.
Surv.-Gen. Surveyor-General.
Syn. Synonym; Synonymous.

Tenn. Tennessee.
Ter. Territory.
Tex. Texas.
Th. or Thurs. Thursday.
Tr. Transpose; Translator; Translation.
Trans. Translator; Translation; Transactions.
Treas. Treasurer.
Tues. or Tu. Tuesday.
Typ. Typographer.
U.J.C. Doctor of both Laws (Civil and Canon).
U.K. United Kingdom.
ult. Last; of the last month, *Ultimo.*
Unit. Unitarian.
Univ. University.
U.S. United States.
U.S.A. United States Army.
U.S.A. United States of America.
U.S.M. United States Mail.
U.S.M. United States Marine.
U.S.M.A. United States Military Academy.
U.S.N. United States Navy.
U.S.N.A. United States Naval Academy.
Ut. Utah.
U.T. Utah Territory.
v. or vs. Against; In such a way; *Versus; Versiculo.*
Va. Virginia.
Vat. Vatican.
Ven. Venerable.
Ver. Verse; Version.
Vice-Pres. or V.P. Vice-President.
Visc. Viscount.
viz. or vi. To wit; Namely; That is to say; *Videlicet.*
Vo. Left hand page, *Verso.*
Vol. Volume.
V.R. Queen Victoria, *Victoria Regina.*
V.S. Veterinary Surgeon.
Vt. Vermont.
Vul. Vulgate (Latin version of the Bible).
Wash. Washington.
W.Ter. Washington Territory.
Wed. Wednesday.
Wisc. Wisconsin.
Wk. Week.
W.T. Wyoming Territory.
X. Ten or tenth.
Xmas or Xm. Christmas.
Xn or Xtian. Christian.
Yd. Yard.
Y.M.C.A. Young Men's Christian Association.
Y.M. Cath. A. Young Men's Catholic Association.
Yrs. Years; Yours.
&. And.
&c. And the rest; And so forth: *Et cœtera.*

CELEBRATED CHARACTERS IN THE LITERATURE OF THE WORLD.

The name of the character is given in black letter; the name of the author and of the work from which the character is taken, in italic.

Abdiel. *Paradise Lost, Milton.* The faithful angel who opposed Satan in his revolt.

Abigail. *The Bible.* A waiting maid.

Ablewhite, Godfrey. *Moonstone, Wilkie Collins.* A disreputable spy.

Abou Hassan. *Arabian Nights.* An Arab who was made to believe himself Caliph.

Absalom. 1. *The Bible.* The son of David, King of Israel. 2. *Absalom and Achitophel, Dryden.* A pseudonym for the Duke of Monmouth, an illegitimate son of King Charles II.

Absolute, Captain. *The Rivals, Sheridan.* The hero of the comedy, the gallant and fortunate lover.

Absolute, Sir Anthony. *The Rivals, Sheridan.* Father of Captain Absolute, a very irascible and absolute old gentleman.

Achitophel. *Absalom and Achitophel, Dryden.* The pseudonym for the Earl of Shaftesbury.

Acres, Bob. *The Rivals, Sheridan.* A cowardly boaster, the butt of the comedy.

Acrasia. *The Faery Queene, Spenser.* An old witch, the personification of intemperance.

Adam, Bell. *Reliques, Percy.* A celebrated archer.

Adams, Parson. *Joseph Andrews, Fielding.* An eccentric, good-natured clergyman.

Adriana. *Comedy of Errors, Shakespeare.* The wife of Antipholus.

Aguecheek, Sir Andrew. *Twelfth Night, Shakespeare.* A coward and a fool.

Aladdin. *Arabian Nights.* The owner of a magic lamp and ring, which gave the possessor every wish he made.

Allworthy, Squire. *Tom Jones, Fielding.* A good-natured old country gentleman.

Alp. *The Siege of Corinth, Byron.* A brave and devoted man.

Amadis de Gaul. *Amadis de Gaul.* The hero of a Portuguese chivalric romance, the authorship of which is unknown. It was translated into every language in Europe.

Amelia. *Amelia, Fielding.* A lovely woman, supposed to be drawn from Fielding's own wife.

Amine. *Arabian Nights.* A wicked sorceress, who changed her three sisters into hounds.

Amlet, Richard. *The Confederacy, Vanburgh.* A gambler.

Amri. *Absalom and Achitophel, Dryden.* Pseudonym for H. Finch.

Andrews, Joseph. *Joseph Andrews, Fielding.* A hero ridiculously upright and pure.

Anerley, Mary. *Mary Anerley, Blackmore.* A lovely and beautiful girl.

Apemantus. *Timon of Athens, Shakespeare.* A cynic.

Arden, Enoch. *Enoch Arden, Tennyson.* A sailor, supposed drowned, who returns home to find his wife married again.

Argante. *The Faery Queene, Spenser.* A giantess.

Ariel. *The Tempest, Shakespeare.* A spirit of the air, perhaps the daintiest creation of the myriad-minded poet.

Artful Dodger. *Oliver Twist, Dickens.* A young thief who understands his business.

Arthur, King. *Idyls of the King, Tennyson.* A legendary British King, who established an order of chivalry known as the Round Table, and about whom many popular legends are afloat in Wales and Western France.

Ashton, Lucy. *The Bride of Lammermoor, Scott.* A beautiful character, loved and lost by Ravenswood.

Atalanta. *Atalanta in Calydon, Swinburne.* One of Diana's maidens.

Autolycus. *Winter's Tale, Shakespeare.* An intellectual sneak thief.

Baba, Ali. *Arabian Nights.* The hero of the tale of the forty thieves, who breaks into the robbers' cave by means of the magical password "Sesame."

Baba, Cassim. *Arabian Nights.* Brother of the above, who forgets the password and is captured by the robbers.

Backbite, Sir Benjamin. *School for Scandal, Sheridan.* A scandal monger.

Bagstock, Joe. *Dombey and Son, Dickens.* A pompous fellow.

Bailey, Young. *Martin Chuzzlewit, Dickens.* A precocious youth.

Balderstone, Caleb. *Bride of Lammermoor, Scott.* The butler of Ravenswood.

Balthazar. 1. *Comedy of Errors, Shakespeare.* A merchant. 2. *Much Ado About Nothing, Shakespeare.* A servant.

Banquo. *Macbeth, Shakespeare.* A chieftain murdered by Macbeth; later in the same play, a ghost.

Bardell, Mrs. *Pickwick Papers, Dickens.* Mr. Pickwick's landlady, who sues him for breach of promise of marriage.

Bardolph. *Henry IV., Shakespeare.* A follower of Sir John Falstaff.

Barkis. *David Copperfield, Dickens.* A marrying man who eventually marries.

Bath, Major. *Amelia, Fielding.* A pompous officer.

Bayes. *The Rehearsal, Duke of Buckingham.* A pseudonym for Dryden.

Baynes, Charlotte. *Adventures of Philip, Thackeray.* The hero's sweetheart.

Bede, Adam. *Adam Bede, George Eliot.* An ideal workingman.

Belch, Sir Toby. *Twelth Night, Shakespeare.* Olivia's hard-drinking uncle.

Belford. *Clarissa Harlowe, Richardson.* The friend of Lovelace.

Belinda. *Rape of the Lock, Pope.* The heroine, whose hair is cut.

Bell, Laura. *Pendennis, Thackeray.* One of the sweetest heroines in English literature.

Bell, Peter. *Peter Bell, Wordsworth.* An extremely prosaic man.

Bellaston, Lady. *Tom Jones, Fielding.* One of Tom Jones' sweethearts.

Bellenden, Lady, *Old Mortality, Scott.* A Tory gentlewoman.

Belphœbe. *The Faery Queene. Spenser.* A pseudonym for Queen Elizabeth.

Belvidera. *Venice Preserved, Otway.* The heroine of the poem.

Benedick. *Much Ado About Nothing, Shakespeare.* A confirmed bachelor who was converted to matrimony by the lovely Beatrice. From this gentleman comes the name Benedick or Benedict applied to married men who were not going to marry.

Bennet, Mrs. *Amelia, Fielding.* An improper character.

Benvolio. *Romeo and Juliet, Shakespeare.* One of Romeo's friends.

Bertram. *All's Well that Ends Well, Shakespeare.* The hero of the play, who marries Helena.

Bianca. *Othello, Shakespeare.* Cassio's sweetheart.

Birch, Harvey. *The Spy, Cooper.* The chief character of the novel.

Bilfil. *Tom Jones, Fielding.* Allworthy's nephew, a talebearer.

Blember, Miss Cornelia. *Dombey and Son, Dickens.* A bluestocking governess.

Bobadil, Captain. *Every Man in His Humor, Jonson.* A boasting coward.

Bœuf, Front de. *Ivanhoe,* Scott. One of King John's followers. A ferocious scoundrel.

Boffin, Noddy. *Our Mutual Friend, Dickens.* The good-natured occupant of Boffin's Bower.

Bois Guilbert, Brian de. *Ivanhoe, Scott.* The master of the Knights Templars.

Boniface. *The Beaux Stratagem, Farquhar.* A landlord. Hence applied to landlords generally.

Booby, Lady. *Joseph Andrews, Fielding.* One of the minor characters.

Booth. *Amelia, Fielding.* The hero of the story.

Bottom, Nick. *A Midsummer Night's Dream, Shakespeare.* A ridiculous weaver with whom Titania, the queen of the fairies, is forced to fall in love by a charm.

Bounderby, Josiah. *Hard Times, Dickens.* A prosaic, matter-of-fact manufacturer.

Bowles, Tom. *Kenelm Chillingly, Bulwer.* A blacksmith.

Bowline, Tom. *Roderick Random, Smollett.* A sailor, whose name has been applied to mariners ever since.

Box and Cox. *Box and Cox, Morton.* The heroes of the farce.

Bradwardine, Baron. *Waverley, Scott.* The father of Rose Bradwardine.

Bramble, Matthew. *Humphrey Clinker, Smollett.* A walking epitome of dyspepsia.

Brangtons. *Evelina, Miss Burney.* Very vulgar people.

Brass, Sally and Sampson. *Old Curiosity Shop, Dickens.* A shystering lawyer and his sister.

Brick, Jefferson. *Martin Chuzzlewit, Dickens.* A ridiculous American editor.

Bridgenorth, Major Ralph. *Peveril of the Peak, Scott.* A prominent officer in the Puritan Army.

Bridget, Mrs. *Tristram Shandy, Sterne.* Tristram's nurse.

Brown, Tom. *Tom Brown's School Days* and *Tom Brown at Oxford, Thos. Hughes.* The hero of one of the best boys' books ever written in English.

Bucket, Inspector. *Bleak House, Dickens.* A detective.

Bumble. *Oliver Twist, Dickens.* A beadle.

Caius, Doctor. *Merry Wives of Windsor, Shakespeare.* Ann Page's Welsh lover.

Caliban. *The Tempest, Shakespeare.* Prospero's monstrous servant.

Candor, Mrs. *The Rivals, Sheridan.* A scandal monger.

Carker. *Dombey and Son, Dickens.* A scoundrelly clerk.

Cassio. *Othello, Shakespeare.* Othello's lieutenant.

Caudle, Mrs. *Curtain Lectures, Douglas Jerrold.* An artistic scold.

Caustic, Col. *The Lounger, Mackenzie.* A satirical gentleman.

Celia. *As You Like It, Shakespeare.* Rosalind's cousin.

Chadband. *Bleak House, Dickens.* A hypocrite.

Chamont. *The Orphans, Otway.* The hero of the play.

Chillingly, Kenelm. *Kenelm Chillingly, Bulwer.* The hero of the novel.

Christabel. *Christabel, Coleridge.* The heroine of the poem.

Christiana. *Pilgrim's Progress, Bunyan.* The wife of the hero Christian.

Chuzzlewit, Jonas and Martin. *Martin Chuzzlewit, Dickens.* The first a miser and murderer, the second the hero of Dickens' story.

Clare, Ada. *Bleak House, Dickens.* The wife of Carstone, and one of the most important characters in the story.

Clifford, Paul. *Paul Clifford, Bulwer.* A beautiful highwayman hero.

Clinker, Humphrey. *Humphrey Clinker, Smollett.* A philosophical young man who meets very singular adventures.

Cœlebs. *Cœlebs in Search of a Wife, Hannah More.* A gentleman who has very precise ideas on the subjects of matrimony and woman.

Coldstream, Sir Charles. *Used Up, Matthews.* A fatigued and weary man of the world.

Consuelo. *Consuelo, George Sand.* The heroine of the novel, a rather inflammable young lady.

Copper Captain, The. *Rule a Wife and Have a Wife, Beaumont and Fletcher.* A nickname applied to Perez, the boastful coward of the play.

Copperfield, David. *David Copperfield, Dickens.* The hero of the novel, supposed to be a picture of Dickens' own life and character.

Cordelia. *King Lear, Shakespeare.* The faithful daughter of the king in the play.

Corinne. *Corinne, Mme. de Staël.* The heroine of de Staël's greatest work.

Costigan, Captain. *Pendennis, Thackeray.* The father of Pendennis' first sweetheart, a hard drinking but amusing old man.

Coverley, Sir Roger de. *Spectator, Addison.* A model country gentleman of the olden time.

Crane, Ichabod. *Sleepy Hollow, Irving.* The schoolmaster in the sketch.

Crawley, Rawdon. *Vanity Fair, Thackeray.* The hero of "the novel without a hero." The husband of Becky Sharp.

Cressida. *Troilus and Cressida, Shakespeare.* The heroine of the play, in love with Troilus.

Crummles, Vincent. *Nicholas Nickleby, Dickens.* A theatrical head of a theatrical family.

Crusoe, Robinson. *Robinson Crusoe, De Foe.* The hero of the most remarkable novel ever written. It has been translated into every civilized language on the globe. The story relates Crusoe's adventures on a desert isle upon which he was cast by the sea, and is one of intense interest.

Cuttle, Captain. *Dombey and Son, Dickens.* A nautical character who indulges in a number of queer mannerisms.

Cymbeline. *Cymbeline, Shakespeare.* A heroic king of Britain.

Dalgarno, Lord. *The Fortunes of Nigel, Scott.* A Scottish nobleman of bad character.

Dalgetty, Dugald. *Waverley, Scott.* A famous and well drawn soldier of fortune, whose name has become proverbial.

Deans, Davie, Effie, and Jeanie. *Heart of Midlothian, Scott.* Famous characters in the story. Jeanie is the heroine.

Dedlock, Lady, and Sir Leicester. *Bleak House, Dickens.* Husband and wife, proud and unfortunate, but noble people.

Delamaine, Geoffrey. *Man and Wife, Collins.* A man of muscle.

Delphine. *Delphine, Mme. de Staël.* The heroine of the novel.

Deronda, Daniel. *Daniel Deronda, George Eliot.* The hero of the novel, one of the best character sketches which George Eliot has made.

Desdemona. *Othello, Shakespeare.* The unfortunate heroine of the play, wife of the Moor Othello.

Diddler, Jeremy. *Raising the Wind, Kinny.* The prototype of all modern deadbeats.

Dimmesdale, Rev. Arthur. *The Scarlet Letter, Hawthorne.* The seducer of Hester Prynne.

Dods, Meg. *St. Ronan's Well, Scott.* A landlady.

Dodson & Fogg. *Pickwick Papers, Dickens.* Mrs. Bardell's attorneys in her suit against Mr. Pickwick.

Dogberry. *Much Ado About Nothing, Shakespeare.* An absurd character who travesties justice.

Dombey, Florence, Mr. and Paul. *Dombey and Son, Dickens.* Characters in the novel.

Dominie, Sampson. *Guy Mannering, Scott.* An eccentric clergyman.

Don Quixote. *Don Quixote, Cervantes.* The hero of the novel. This has been described by eminent critics as the best work of fiction which the world has yet produced. It was written in Spanish by Miguel de Cervantes, as a protest against the ridiculous extravagances of what are known as Chivalric Romances. Don Quixote is the type upon which thousands of later novels have been founded. Crazed by the reading of knightly tales, he arms himself and goes out in search of adventures, on his steed Rozinante, and accompanied by his squire Sancho Panzo. These adventures are told so wittily, that the world has been laughing at them for centuries, and the book has never lost its fresh, boyish interest. The best English translation is Smollett's. Gustave Doré, the famous French artist, some years since completed a set of illustrations for Don Quixote, which have added greatly to its interest.

Dora. *David Copperfield, Dickens.* Copperfield's child-wife.

Dorimant. *The Man of Mode, Etherege.* A dandy.

Dorothea. *Middlemarch, George Eliot.* The heroine of the tale.

Dorrit, Edward, and "Little." *Little Dorrit, Dickens.* The father of the Marshalsea prison and his interesting daughter.

Drawcansir. *The Rehearsal, The Duke of Buckingham.* A bully.

Dulcinea del Toboso. *Don Quixote, Cervantes.* A country girl whom Don Quixote selects as his lady love.

Dundreary, Lord. *Our American Cousin, Taylor.* A typical and absurd English lord. The character was really created by the actor Sothern.

Edgar. *King Lear, Shakespeare.* The son of Gloucester.

Emilia. *Othello, Shakespeare.* Wife of Iago, the villain of the play.

Esmond, Beatrix, and Henry. *Henry Esmond, Thackeray.* Heroine and hero of the novel, which is of the time of the English Revolution.

Eugenia. *The Return of the Native, Hardy.* A beautiful and unfortunate girl.

Evangeline. *Evangeline, Longfellow.* Heroine of the poem; her wanderings are told in verse that will never die.

Evans, Sir Hugh. *The Merry Wives of Windsor, Shakespeare.* A Welsh clergyman.

Evelina. *Evelina, Miss Burney.* Heroine of the novel.

Eyre, Jane. *Jane Eyre, Brontë.* Heroine of the novel.

Fag. *The Rivals, Sheridan.* A servant.

Fagin. *Oliver Twist, Dickens.* The preceptor in the thieves' academy, where Oliver Twist is held a prisoner.

Faithful, Jacob. *Jacob Faithful, Marryat.* The hero of the novel.

Falkland. *The Rivals, Sheridan.* A jealous lover of Julia's, and friend to Captain Absolute.

Falstaff, Sir John. *Henry IV. and the Merry Wives of Windsor, Shakespeare.* This is Shakespeare's most comic character; Queen Elizabeth was so pleased with Sir John in Henry IV. that, at her request, Shakespeare composed The Merry Wives of Windsor, in order to give the fat knight a wider field for fun.

Fanny. *Under the Greenwood Tree, Hardy.* A pretty schoolmistress.

Fat Boy, The. *Pickwick Papers, Dickens.* One of the minor characters in the novel, given to sleep and pie.

Faust. *Faust, Goethe.* The hero of the great German tragedy, who sells his soul to the Devil, and gets in return youth, wealth, and an attendant devil, Mephistopheles. Goethe was to Germany what Shakespeare was to England.

Felton, Septimius. *Septimius Felton, Hawthorne.* The mystical hero of the novel.

Ferdinand. *The Tempest, Shakespeare.* Son of the king, falls in love with Prospero's daughter, Miranda.

Ferrers, Endymion. *Endymion, Benjamin Disraeli.* Hero of the novel.

Figaro. *The Marriage of Figaro, Beaumarchais.* An exceedingly comical and sharp-witted barber.

Firmin, Philip. *The Adventures of Philip, Thackeray.* The hero of the novel.

Florizel. *A Winter's Tale, Shakespeare.* The prince of Bohemia.

Fluellen. *Henry V., Shakespeare.* A pedantic but brave Welsh officer.

Foker, Harry. *Pendennis, Thackeray.* One of the minor characters.

Foppington, Lord. *The Relapse, Van Brugh.* An idiotic dandy.

Fosco, Count. *Woman in White, Collins.* A complicated scoundrel.

Frankenstein. *Frankenstein, Mrs. Shelley.* The dreadful result of the labors of a German student, who makes a man in the dissecting room out of corpses, and brings him to life by galvanism. The hideous hero of the novel has a series of most blood-curdling adventures.

Friar Tuck. *Reliques, Percy.* The jolly companion of Robin Hood, the outlaw of Sherwood Forest.

Friday. *Robinson Crusoe, De Foe.* Crusoe's savage servant.

Gadgrind, Jeremiah. *Hard Times, Dickens.* A tyrannical "practical" man.

Gamp, Sairy. *Martin Chuzzlewit, Dickens.* A comical and hard-drinking monthly nurse.

Gargantua. *Gargantua, Rabelais.* Hero of the tale.

Gaunt, Griffith. *Griffith Gaunt, Reade.* Hero of the novel.

Gay, Walter. *Dombey and Son, Dickens.* Marries Florence Dombey.

Gibbie, Goose. *Old Mortality, Scott.* A half-witted boy.

Gil Blas. *Gil Blas, Le Sage.* The hero of a very famous novel. His adventures are of the most surprising character, and are told in a most interesting manner.

Gilpin, John. *John Gilpin's Ride, Cowper.* The absurd hero of the poem.

Ginevra. *Ginevra, Rogers.* The heroine of the poem, accidentally locked in a trunk on her wedding day, and not found for years and years.

Gobbo, Launcelot. *The Merchant of Venice, Shakespeare.* A merry servant.

Goneril. *King Lear, Shakespeare.* The eldest daughter of the king, a traitor and an ingrate.

Gonzalo. *The Tempest, Shakespeare.* An old councilor.

Gosling, Giles. *Kenilworth, Scott.* A landlord.

Grandison, Sir Charles. *Sir Charles Grandison, Richardson.* Hero of the novel.

Gray, Vivian. *Vivian Gray, Disraeli.* Hero of the novel.

Grundy, Mrs. *Speed the Plow, Morton.* A old lady who represents worldly propriety and talebearing.

Gulliver, Lemuel. *Gulliver's Travels, Swift.* Hero of the romance.

Hamlet. *Hamlet, Shakespeare.* The melancholy Dane, hero of the play.

Harley. *The Man of Feeling, Mackenzie.* Hero of the novel.

Harlowe, Clarissa. *Clarissa Harlowe, Richardson.* Heroine of the novel.

Harris, Mrs. *Martin Chuzzlewit, Dickens.* A fictitious person invented by Sairy Gamp, for the purpose of enforcing her statements by quoting the opinions of Mrs. Harris upon the subject under discussion.

Headstone, Bradley. *Our Mutual Friend, Dickens.* A schoolmaster in love with Lizzie Hexam.

Heep, Uriah. *David Copperfield, Dickens.* A hypocrite and sneak.

Helena. *All's Well that Ends Well, Shakespeare.* Heroine of the play.

Hero. *Much Ado About Nothing, Shakespeare.* Daughter of Leonato.

Hexam, Lizzie. *Our Mutual Friend, Dickens.* Heroine of the novel.

Holofernes. *As You Like it, Shakespeare.* A schoolmaster and pedant.

Holt, Felix. *Felix Holt, George Eliot.* Hero of the novel.

Honeyman, Charles. *The Newcomes, Thackeray.* A fashionable preacher.

Honor, Mrs. *Tom Jones, Fielding.* Sophia Western's waiting woman.

Hopeful. *Pilgrim's Progress. Bunyan.* A pilgrim.

Horatio. *Hamlet, Shakespeare.* The friend of Hamlet.

Howe, Miss. *Clarissa Harlowe, Richardson.* Clarissa's friend.
Hudibras. *Hudibras, Butler.* Hero of the poem.
Hunter, Mr. and Mrs. Leo. *Pickwick Papers, Dickens.* Minor characters in the novel.

Iago. *Othello, Shakespeare.* The villain of the tragedy.
Imogen. *Cymbeline, Shakespeare.* Heroine of the play.
Isabella. *Measure for Measure, Shakespeare.* Heroine of the play.
Ivanhoe. *Ivanhoe, Scott.* Hero of the novel.

Jack, Col. *Col. Jack, DeFoe.* The criminal hero of the tale.
Jaffier. *Venice Preserved, Otway.* Hero of the poem.
Jaques. *As You Like It, Shakespeare.* The melancholy philosopher.
Jarndyce, John. *Bleak House, Dickens.* A benevolent old gentleman.
Javert. *Les Misérables, Hugo.* A detective.
Jessica. *Merchant of Venice, Shakespeare.* Shylock's daughter.
Jingle, Alfred. *Pickwick Papers, Dickens.* An amusing adventurer.

Kilmansegg, Miss. *The Golden Legend, Hood.* The golden-legged heroine of the poem.
Kitely. *Every Man in His Humor, Jonson.* A jealous husband.

Lady Bountiful. *The Beaux Stratagem, Farquhar.* A generous lady.
Laertes. *Hamlet, Shakespeare.* The son of Polonius, killed by his own sword.
Lalla Rookh. *Lalla Rookh, Moore.* Heroine of the poem, to whom Feramorz relates the stories told in the romance.
Languish, Lydia. *The Rivals, Sheridan.* Heroine of the play.
Lear, King. *King Lear, Shakespeare.* Hero of the play.
Leatherstocking, Natty. *Pathfinder, Deerslayer, and other novels, Cooper.* A huntsman and Indian fighter.
Legree. *Uncle Tom's Cabin, Stowe.* Slave master.
Leigh, Aurora. *Aurora Leigh, Browning.* Heroine of the romance.
Leila. *Giaour, Byron.* Heroine of the poem.
Lightwood, Mortimer. *Our Mutual Friend, Dickens.* Minor character in novel.
Lismahago, Capt. *Humphrey Clinker, Smollett.* A retired officer.
Little, Henry. *Put Yourself in His Place, Reade.* Hero of the novel.
Little Nell. *Old Curiosity Shop, Dickens.* Heroine of novel.
Locksley. *Ivanhoe, Scott.* One of Robin Hood's pseudonyms.
Long Tom Coffin. *Pilot, Cooper.* A boatman.
Lothair. *Lothair, Disraeli.* Hero of novel, supposed pseudonym for the Marquis of Bute.
Lothario. *The Fair Penitent, Rowe.* A rake.
Lovelace. *Clarissa Harlowe, Richardson.* A rake.
Lumpkin, Tony. *She Stoops to Conquer, Goldsmith.* A country squire.

Macbeth. *Macbeth, Shakespeare.* Hero of the play.
Macduff. *Macbeth, Shakespeare.* Rival of Macbeth.
MacIvor, Flora. *Rob Roy, Scott.* Heroine of novel.
Mackenzie, Mrs. *Newcomes, Thackeray.* A termagant widow.
Malagrother, Sir Mingo. *The Fortunes of Nigel, Scott.* An ill-natured courtier.
Malaprop, Mrs. *The Rivals, Sheridan.* A character famed for verbal blunders.
Malvolio. *Twelfth Night, Shakespeare.* Olivia's conceited steward.
Manfred. *Manfred, Byron.* Hero of the tragedy.
Mantalini. *Nicholas Nickleby, Dickens.* The absurd husband of the milliner in the story.
Marchioness, The. *Old Curiosity Shop, Dickens.* Mr. Dick Swiveller's remarkable little nurse.
Margaret. *Faust, Goethe.* The heroine of the tragedy.
Marlow, Young. *She Stoops to Conquer, Goldsmith.* Hero of the play.
Medora. *The Corsair, Byron.* Heroine of the poem.
Merdle, Mr. *Little Dorrit, Dickens.* A speculator.
Meister, Wilhelm. *Wilhelm Meister, Goethe.* Hero of the novel.
Mephistopheles. *Faust, Goethe.* The Devil.
Mercutio. *Romeo and Juliet, Shakespeare.* A wonderfully witty friend of Romeo's.
Micawber, Wilkins. *David Copperfield, Dickens.* A remarkable character, always waiting for something to turn up.
Miller, Daisy. *Daisy Miller, Henry James.* An alleged representative American girl.
Minna. *The Pirate, Scott.* One of the heroines of the novel.
Miranda. *The Tempest, Shakespeare.* Daughter of Prospero, beloved of Ferdinand; heroine of the play.
Monimia. *The Orphan, Otway.* Heroine of the poem.
Mouldy. *Henry IV., Shakespeare.* One of Falstaff's recruits.
Mucklewrath, Habakkuk. *Old Mortality, Scott.* A fanatical preacher.

Neuchatel, Adriana. *Endymion, Disraeli.* A wealthy young lady.
Newcome, Clive, Colonel, Ethel. *The Newcomes, Thackeray.* Characters in the best novel Thackeray has written.
Nickleby, Mrs. *Nicholas Nickleby, Dickens.* The exasperating mother of the hero, Nicholas.
Norna. *The Pirate, Scott.* An insane soothsayer.
Nydia. *Last Days of Pompeii, Bulwer.* A blind flower girl.

Obadiah. *Tristram Shandy, Sterne.* A servant.
Oberon. *Midsummer Night's Dream. Shakespeare.* The King of Fairyland.
Ochiltree, Edie. *The Antiquary, Scott.* A beggar of prominence.
Oldbuck, Jonathan. *The Antiquary, Scott.* Hero of the novel.
Old Mortality. *Old Mortality, Scott.* A gravestone cleaner.
Olifaunt, Nigel. *The Fortunes of Nigel, Scott.* Hero of the novel.
Ophelia. *Hamlet, Shakespeare.* Heroine of the tragedy.
Orville, Lord. *Evelina, Miss Burney.* Evelina's lover.
Othello. *Othello, Shakespeare.* Hero of the play, a Moor, husband of Desdemona.
O'Trigger, Sir Lucius. *The Rivals, Sheridan.* A fire-eating Irishman.
Overreach, Sir Giles. *A New Way to Pay Old Debts, Massinger.* A usurer.

Page, Anne and Mrs. *The Merry Wives of Windsor, Shakespeare.* Characters in the play.
Pamela. *Pamela, Richardson.* An intensely good young lady.
Pangloss. *The Heir-at-Law, Colman.* A pedantic teacher.
Pantagruel. *Pantagruel, Rabelais.* Hero of the sketch.
Partridge. *Tom Jones, Fielding.* The hero's trusty follower.
Pecksniff, Charity, Mercy, Mr. *Martin Chuzzlewit, Dickens.* Characters in the story.
Pendennis, Arthur, Helen, Major. *Pendennis, Thackeray.* Well drawn and forcible characters in the novel.
Perdita. *Winter's Tale, Shakespeare.* Florizel's sweetheart.
Petruchio. *The Taming of the Shrew, Shakespeare.* The hero, and husband of Katherine.
Pickle, Peregrine. *Peregrine Pickle, Smollett.* The wandering and immoral hero of the novel.
Pickwick, Samuel. *Pickwick Papers, Dickens.* Hero of the novel.
Pierre. *Venice Preserved, Otway.* A conspirator.
Pistol, Ancient. *Merry Wives of Windsor and Henry IV., Shakespeare.* Falstaff's most characteristic follower.
Pleydell, Paulus. *Guy Mannering, Scott.* A lawyer.
Poins, Ned. *Henry IV., Shakespeare.* A friend of Prince Hal.
Portia. *The Merchant of Venice, Shakespeare.* Heroine of the play.
Poundlint, Peter. *Old Mortality, Scott.* A preacher.
Primrose, Dr. *Vicar of Wakefield, Goldsmith.* The Vicar of Wakefield.
Primrose, Moses. Son of the preceding.

Prolius. *Two Gentlemen of Verona, Shakespeare.* One of the two gentlemen.

Proudfute. *Fair Maid of Perth, Scott.* A bonnet maker.

Prynne, Hester. *Scarlet Letter, Hawthorne.* Heroine of novel.

Pumblechook, Uncle. *Great Expectations, Dickens.* A bully and fraud.

Pynchon, Phœbe. *House of the Seven Gables. Hawthorne.* Heroine of the novel.

Quasimodo. *Our Lady of Notre Dame, Hugo.* A monster.

Quickly, Mrs. *Henry IV., Shakespeare.* The famed hostess of the Boar's Head Tavern, in Eastcheap.

Quilp. *Old Curiosity Shop, Dickens.* A vicious dwarf.

Quince, Peter. *Midsummer Night's Dream, Shakespeare.* Character in the interlude.

Random, Roderick. *Roderick Random, Smollett.* Hero of the novel.

Rashleigh. *Rob Roy, Scott.* The villain of the novel.

Rasselas. *Rasselas, Dr. Johnson.* Prince of Abyssinia, hero of the tale.

Rattler, Jack. *Roderick Random, Smollett.* A nautical character.

Ravenswood. *The Bride of Lammermoor, Scott.* Hero of the novel, lover of Lucy Ashton.

Rebecca. *Ivanhoe, Scott.* A lovely Jewess.

Redgauntlet. *Redgauntlet, Scott.* Hero of the novel.

Rob Roy. *Rob Roy, Scott.* A Scottish chief, hero of the novel.

Roderigo. *Othello, Shakespeare.* Iago's dupe.

Romeo. *Romeo and Juliet, Shakespeare.* The hero of the play, lover of Juliet.

Sabrina. *Comus, Milton.* River nymph.

Sacripant. *Orlando Furioso, Ariosto.* King of Circassia, in love with Angelica.

Saddletree, Bartoline. *Heart of Midlothian, Scott.* A learned peddler.

Sancho Panza. *Don Quixote, Cervantes.* Worthy squire of a worthy master; the right man in the right place.

Sandford, Harry. *Sandford and Merton, Day.* Hero of the story.

Sangrado, Doctor. *Gil Blas, Le Sage.* A confirmed phlebotomist.

Scheherezade, Queen. *Arabian Nights.* The Sultaness who tells the tales.

Scrub. *The Beaux Stratagem, Farquhar.* A facetious valet.

Sedley, Amelia. *Vanity Fair, Thackeray.* An amiable woman, but of no great decision.

Sedley, Joseph. *Vanity Fair, Thackeray.* A fat, bashful East Indian.

Selim. *Bride of Abydos, Byron.* The hero.

Shafton, Sir Piercie. *The Monastery, Scott.* A pedantic courtier.

Shandy, Tristram. *Tristram Shandy, Sterne.* Hero of the story.

Sharp, Rebecca. *Vanity Fair, Thackeray.* The designing heroine.

Shylock. *Merchant of Venice, Shakespeare.* A vindictive Jew.

Silvia. *Two Gentlemen of Verona, Shakespeare.* In love with Valentine.

Skimpole, Harold. *Bleak House, Dickens.* Always out of money.

Slipslop, Mrs. *Joseph Andrews, Fielding.* A waiting woman of doubtful character.

Slop, Doctor. *Tristram Shandy, Sterne.* An irascible physician.

Sly, Christopher. *Taming of the Shrew, Shakespeare.* A drunken tinker.

Slyme, Chevy. *Martin Chuzzlewit, Dickens.* A "gent short of funds."

Smyke. *Nicholas Nickleby, Dickens.* An ill-used, poor, half-witted pupil of Squeers.

Sneerwell, Lady. *School for Scandal, Sheridan.* A gossip and backbiter.

Snodgrass, Augustus. *Pickwick Papers, Dickens.* A poetical character.

Snow, Lucy. *Villette, Charlotte Brontë.* The heroine.

Sparkler, Edmond. *Little Dorrit, Dickens.* Man of fashion.

Squeers, Wackford. *Nicholas Nickleby, Dickens.* The brutal master of Dotheboys Hall.

Squeers, Master Wackford. *In same.* A spoiled child, the image of his father.

St. Leon. *St. Leon, William Godwin.* Hero of the tale, has the secret of perpetual youth, and the transmutation of metals.

Steerforth, James. *David Copperfield, Dickens.* Talented and profligate.

Steggs, Miss Carolina Wilhelmina Amelia. *Vicar of Wakefield, Goldsmith.* A pretender to gentility.

Stiggins, Elder. *Pickwick Papers, Dickens.* Affects pineapple rum and Mrs. Weller.

Strap, Hugh. *Roderick Random, Smollett.* Roderick's follower.

Surface, Sir Charles and Joseph. *School for Scandal, Sheridan.* The first a good-natured rake, the second a hypocrite.

Swiveller, Dick. *Old Curiosity Shop, Dickens.* A gay rattlepate and a good fellow.

Tamora. *Titus Andronicus, Shakespeare.* A Gothic queen.

Tapley, Mark. *Martin Chuzzlewit, Dickens.* Happiest when most miserable; jolly when he ought to cry.

Tappertit, Simon. *Barnaby Rudge, Dickens.* A ferocious little apprentice.

Tartuffe. *Tartuffe, Molière.* A hypocritical character.

Teazle, Lady. *School for Scandal, Sheridan.* The heroine.

Teazle, Sir Peter. *School for Scandal, Sheridan.* The old husband of Lady Teazle.

Thersites. *Iliad, Homer,* and *Troilus and Cressida, Shakespeare.* A foul-mouthed Greek.

Thwackum. *Tom Jones, Fielding.* A philosophical pedagogue.

Tillemina. *The Critic, Sheridan.* A maiden very much crossed in love.

Timon. *Timon of Athens, Shakespeare.* A misanthrope, hero of the play.

Tinto, Dick. *The Bride of Lammermoor* and *St. Ronan's Well, Scott.* An artist.

Titania. *Midsummer Night's Dream, Shakespeare.* The queen of fairies.

Titmouse, Tittlebat. *Ten Thousand a Year, Dr. Warren.* Astonished Parliament by an imitation of Chanticleer.

Tito. *Romola, George Eliot.* The handsome, but weak hero.

Todgers, Mrs. *Martin Chuzzlewit, Dickens.* The keeper of a commercial boarding house.

Toots. *Dombey and Son, Dickens.* A simple, eccentric fellow.

Topsy. *Uncle Tom's Cabin, Mrs. Stowe.* An ignorant young slave girl.

Touchstone. *As You Like It, Shakespeare.* A clown.

Touchwood, Peregrine. *St. Ronan's Well, Scott.* An irascible East Indian.

Tox, Miss. *Dombey and Son, Dickens.* A spinster, slightly curious.

Traddles, Tom. *David Copperfield, Dickens.* A barrister and friend of Copperfield.

Trapbois. *The Fortunes of Nigel, Scott.* A usurer.

Trim, Corporal, *Tristram Shandy, Sterne.* The follower of Uncle Toby.

Trinculo. *Tempest, Shakespeare.* A jester.

Triol, Marquis. *The Pirate, Scott.* A wealthy Zealander.

Trotwood, Betsy. *David Copperfield, Dickens.* The kindest of women, but with an aversion to trespassing donkeys.

Trulliber, Parson. *Joseph Andrews, Fielding.* An ignorant clergyman.

Trunnion, Commodore Hawser. *Peregrine Pickle, Smollett.* An odd nautical character.

Tulkinghorn, Mr. *Bleak House, Dickens.* A wily solicitor.

Tulliver, Maggie. *Mill on the Floss, George Eliot.* The heroine.

Tulliver, Tom. *Mill on the Floss, George Eliot.* The selfish, conceited brother of Maggie Tulliver.

Tupman, Tracy. *Pickwick Papers, Dickens.* An obese admirer of lovely women.

Turveydrop. *Bleak House, Dickens.* Dancing master and professor of deportment.

Tusher, Thomas. *Henry Esmond, Thackeray.* A sycophantic clergyman.

Twemlow, Mr. *Our Mutual Friend, Dickens.* A diner-out and friend of the Veneerings.

Twist, Oliver. *Oliver Twist, Dickens.* Hero of the novel.

Twysden, Talbott. *Philip, Thackeray.* A public officer.

Tybalt. *Romeo and Juliet, Shakespeare.* Nephew of Lady Capulet, slain by Romeo.

Ulrica. *Ivanhoe, Scott.* An old witch.

Una. *The Faery Queene, Spenser.* The personification of Truth.

Uncas. *The Last of the Mohican, Cooper.* A Mohican chief.

Uncle Toby. *Tristram Shandy, Sterne.* A noble veteran, the real hero of the story.

Uncle Tom. *Uncle Tom's Cabin, Stowe.* A pious and unfortunate slave, the hero of the novel. This book added more converts to the abolition party than any other factor. It is the most remarkable and effective American work printed.

Varden, Dolly. *Barnaby Rudge, Dickens.* The heroine of the story.

Vathek. *Vathek, Beckford.* The hero of Beckford's remarkable novel.

Vernon, Di. *Rob Roy, Scott.* The heroine of the novel.

Vholes. *Bleak House, Dickens.* A crafty lawyer.

Viola. *Twelfth Night, Shakespeare.* A sweet little lady in love with Orsino.

Virgilia. *Coriolanus, Shakespeare.* Wife of Coriolanus.

Virginia. *Paul and Virginia, St. Pierre.* Heroine of the novel.

Vivian. *Idyls of the King, Tennyson.* The mistress of Merlin, the Enchanter.

Wadman, Widow. *Tristram Shandy, Sterne.* The lady who seeks to decoy Uncle Toby into matrimony.

Wamba. *Ivanhoe, Scott.* A clown.

Wardle, Mr. *Pickwick Papers, Dickens.* A jolly country gentleman, friend of Mr. Pickwick.

Wegg, Silas. *Our Mutual Friend, Dickens.* The villain of the novel.

Weller, Tony and Samivel. *Pickwick Papers, Dickens.* Father and son; the latter, Mr. Pickwick's serving man, is undoubtedly the most original and most humorous creation of Dickens' exuberant fancy.

Werther. *Sorrows of Werther, Goethe.* Hero of the tale.

Western, Squire and Sophia. *Tom Jones, Fielding.* Father and daughter, the latter the heroine of the novel.

Whiskerandos, Don Ferolo. *The Critic, Sheridan.* The lover of Tilburina.

Wickfield, Agnes. *David Copperfield, Dickens.* Heroine of the novel.

Wild, Jonathan. *Jonathan Wild, Fielding.* A famous highwayman, and afterwards a noted thief-taker of London.

Wildair, Sir Harry. *The Constant Couple,* and *Sir Harry Wildair, Farquhar.* The hero of both plays.

Wilfer, Bella, Lavinia, Reginald, and Mrs. *Our Mutual Friend, Dickens.* One of the most entertaining family groups in English fiction. The first is the charming heroine of the novel. Lavinia is her abominable sister; Reginald, her angelic papa; while the somber background is made by the gloomy mamma, whose other name in the family is The Tragic Muse.

Wilfrid. *Rokeby, Scott.* Hero of the poem.

Williams, Caleb. *Caleb Williams, Godwin.* The hero of a very remarkable novel.

Wimble, Will. *Spectator, Addison.* Pseudonym for Thomas Morecraft.

Winkle, Rip Van. *Sketch Book, Irving.* The immortal sleeper of the Catskills.

Wishfort, Lady. *The Way of the World, Congreve.* Heroine of the play.

Worldly Wiseman, Mr. *Pilgrim's Progress, Bunyan.* One of Christian's difficulties.

Wray, Enoch. *The Village, Crabbe.* A noble old man.

Wren, Jenny. *Our Mutual Friend, Dickens.* The dolls' dressmaker.

Wronghead, Sir Francis. *The Provoked Husband, Vanburgh.* Hero of the play.

Yorick. *Tristram Shandy, Sterne.* A jester descended from the Yorick whose history is told by Hamlet.

Yseult. *Tristram and Yseult, Matthew Arnold.* A Cornish heroine of the olden time.

Zadoc. *Absalom and Achitophel, Dryden.* Pseudonym for Sancroft, Archbishop of Canterbury.

Zanoni. *Zanoni, Bulwer.* The mystical hero of the novel.

Zeluco. *Zeluco, Dr. J. Moore.* The prodigal hero of the novel.

Zobeide. *Arabian Nights.* The wife of the great Haroun al Raschid.

Zadig. *Zadig, Voltaire.* The Babylonian hero of the novel.

Zophiel. *Paradise Lost, Milton.* A swift-winged cherub.

Zuleika. *The Bride of Abydos, Byron.* Heroine of the poem.

LITERARY PSEUDONYMS.

A. L. O. E. (= *A Lady of England*)	Charlotte Maria Tucker.
Adeler, Max	Chas. Heber Clark.
Alexander, Mrs	Mrs. A. F. Hector.
Anstey, F.	F. Anstey Guthrie.
Atlas ("World")	Edmund Yates.
Bab	W. S. Gilbert.
Bede, Cuthbert	Rev. Edw. Bradley.
Bell, Acton	Anne Bronté.
Bell, Currer	Charlotte Bronté.
Bell, Ellis	Emily Jane Bronté.
Bibliophile, Jacob	Paul Lacroix.
Bickerstaff, Isaac	Dean Swift and Steele in *Tatler.*
Biglow, Hosea	J. Russell Lowell.
Billings, Josh	Henry W. Shaw.
Bon Gaultier	Sir Theodore Martin and W. E. Aytoun.
Boz	Chas. Dickens.
Breitmann, Hans	Chas. G. Leland.
Carmen, Sylva	Queen of Roumania.
Conway, Hugh	F. J. Fargus.
Cornwall, Barry	B. W. Procter.
Crayon, Geoffrey	Washington Irving.
Danbury Newsman	J. M. Bailey.
Elia	Charles Lamb.
Eliot, George	Mrs. Mary Ann Cross (*née* Evans).
Ettrick Shepherd	James Hogg.
Fern, Fanny	Mrs. Sara P. Parton.
Graduate of Oxford	John Ruskin.
Greenwood, Grace	Mrs. Lippincott.
Greville, Henry	Mme. Durand.
H. H.	Mrs. Helen Hunt Jackson.
Hamilton, Gail	Mary Abigail Dodge.
Harland, Marion	Mrs. M. V. Terhune (*née* Hawes).
Historicus	Sir W. Vernon Harcourt.
Jean Paul	J. P. F. Richter.
Kerr, Orpheus C.	R. H. Newell.
Knickerbocker, Diedrich	Washington Irving.
L. E. L.	Letitia E. Landon.
Lee, Vernon	Violet Paget.
Loti, Pierre	Julien Viaud.
Lyall, Edna	Ada Ellen Bayly.
Maitland, Thomas	R. Buchanan.
Malet, Lucas	Mrs. Harrison (*née* Kingsley).
Mathers, Helen	Mrs. Reeves (*née* Matthews).
Meredith, Owen	Earl of Lytton.
Miller, Joaquin	C. H. Miller.
Nasby, Petroleum V	D. R. Locke.
North, Christopher	Prof. John Wilson.
O'Dowd, Cornelius	Charles Lever.
Ogilvy, Gavin	J. M. Barrie.
Old Humphrey	G. Mogridge.
Omnium, Jacob	Matt. Jas. Higgins.
Opium Eater	T. De Quincey.
Optic, Oliver	Wm. T. Adams.
O'Rell, Max	Paul Blouet.
Ouida	Louise de la Rame.
Q	Douglas Jerrold. A. T. Quiller Couch.
Parley, Peter	Sam. G. Goodrich; W. Martin; G. Mogridge; W. Tegg; J. Bennett.
Phiz	Hablot K. Browne.
Pindar, Peter	John Wolcot.
Plymley, Peter	Sydney Smith.
Prout, Father	F. S. Mahony.
Quirinus	Dr. Döllinger.
Rob Roy	John Macgregor.

Sand, George................Mme. Dudevant (*née* Dupin).
Scriblerus, Martinus........Swift, Pope, and Arbuthnot.
Shirley......................John Skelton.
Slick, Sam...................T. C. Haliburton.
Stepniak.....................S. Kartcheffsky.
Stretton, Hesba..............Sarah Smith.
Syntax, Dr...................Wm. Combe.
Titcomb, Timothy.............J. G. Holland.
Titmarsh, Michael Angelo.....W. M. Thackeray.
Twain, Mark..................Samuel L. Clemens.
Tytler, Sarah................Miss H. Keddie.
Uncle Remus..................Joel Chandler Harris.
Urban, Sylvanus..............Editor of *The Gentleman's Magazine*.
Vacuus, Viator...............Thomas Hughes.
Voltaire.....................François Marie Arouet.
Ward, Artemus................Chas. F. Browne.
Warden, Florence.............Mrs. G. James.
Wetherell, Elizabeth.........Susan Warner.
Winter, John Strange.........Mrs. H. E. V. Stannard.
Zadkiel......................Capt. R. J. Morrison, R. N.

FIRST NEWSPAPERS.

In ancient Rome an official gazette, called *Acta Diurna*, was issued under the management and authority of the government, and posted up daily in some prominent place in the city.

In Venice a paper of public intelligence, called *Gazetta*, was published in 1620
In England the first *weekly* newspaper was published by Nathaniel Butler in 1622
In England the first *daily* newspaper in 1709
In France the first *weekly* newspaper was published in 1631
In France the first *daily* in 1777
In America, at Boston, a newspaper was published in 1690
In Ireland the first newspaper, called *Pue's Occurrences*, appeared in 1700
In Ireland the oldest Dublin newspaper, *The Freeman's Journal*, in 1755
In Germany the first newspaper was published in 1715
In Holland the first newspaper was published in 1732
In Turkey the first newspaper was published in 1795
In Australia the first newspaper was published in 1803

THE FORTY IMMORTALS OF THE FRENCH ACADEMY.

	Year Elected.	Name.	Born.	Predecessor.
1	1855	Ernest Wilfred Gabriel Baptiste Legouve	Paris, 1807	Ancelot
2	1862	Jacques Victor Albe, Duc de Broglie	Paris, 1821	Lacordaire Père
3	1870	Emile Ollivier	Marseilles, 1825	De Lamartine
4	1874	Alfred Jean François Mézières	Paris, 1826	St. Marc-Girardin
5	1876	Marie Louis Antoine Gaston Boissier	Nîmes, 1823	Patin
6	1877	Victorien Sardou	Paris, 1831	Autran
7	1878	Edmund Armand, Duc d' Audiffret Pasquier	Paris, 1823	Dupanloup (Bishop)
8	1880	Aimé Joseph Edmund Rousse	Paris, 1817	Jules Favre
9	1881	René François Armand, Sully-Prudhomme	Paris, 1839	Duvergier de Hauranne
10	1882	Adolphe Louis Albert Perraud	Lyons, 1828	Auguste Barbier
11	1884	François Edouard Joachin Coppée	Paris, 1842	De Laprade
12	1884	Ludovic Halévy	Paris, 1834	Comte d'Haussonville
13	1886	Vallery Clément Octave Gréard	Vire, 1828	Comte de Falloux
14	1886	Othénin P. de Cléron Comte d' Haussonville	Gurey, 1843	Caro
15	1888	Jules Arnaud Arsène Claretie	Limoges, 1840	Cuvillier-Fleury
16	1888	Eugène Marie Melchior, Vicomte de Vogué	Nice, 1848	Désiré Nisard
17	1890	Charles Louis de Saulses de Freycinet	Foix, 1828	Emile Augier
18	1891	Louis Marie Julien Viaud (Pierre Loti)	Rochefort, 1850	Octave Feuillet
19	1892	Ernest Lavisse	Nouvien, 1842	Jurien de la Gravière
20	1893	Vicomte Henri de Bornier	Lunel, 1825	Xavier Marmier
21	1893	Paul Louis Thureau-Dangin	Paris, 1837	Rousset
22	1893	Marie Ferdinand Brunetière	Toulon, 1849	Lemoinne
23	1894	Albert Sorel	Honfleur, 1842	Taine
24	1894	José Maria de Heredia	Santiago, Cuba, 1842	De Mazade
25	1894	Paul Bourget	Amiens, 1852	Maxime Du Camp
26	1894	Henri Houssaye	Paris, 1858	Leconte de Lisle
27	1895	Jules Lemaitre	Orleans, 1853	Jean Victor Duruy
28	1896	Jacques Anatole Thibault (Anatole France)	Paris, 1844	Comte de Lesseps
29	1896	Marquis Marie C. A. Costa de Beauregard	Nyotte, Savoy, 1839	Camille C. Doucet
30	1896	Gaston Bruno Paulin Paris	Avenay, 1839	Louis Pasteur
31	1896	Claude-Adhémar (André Theuriet)	Marly-le-Roi, 1833	Alexandre Dumas
32	1896	Louis Jules Albert Comte Vandal	Paris, 1861	Léon Say
33	1897	Albert Comte de Mun	Lumigny, 1841	Jules Simon
34	1897	Gabriel Hanotaux	Beaurevoir, 1853	Challemel-Lacour
35	1898	Claude Jean Baptiste Guillaume	Montbard, 1822	Duc d' Aumale
36	1899	Henri Leon Emile Lavedan	Orleans, 1859	Henri Meilhac
37	1899	Paul Deschanel	Brussels, 1856	Hervé
38	1900	Paul Hervieu	Neuilly, 1857	Pailleron
39	1900	Emile Faguet	La Roche, 1847	Cherbuliez
40	1900	Eugène Marcellin Berthelot	Paris, 1827	Bertrand

NIBELUNGEN LIED.

This famous historic poem, which is called the Iliad of Germany, was produced about 1210, and is divided into two parts, and thirty-two lieds or cantos. The first part ends with the death of Siegfried, and the second part with the death of Kriemhild.

Siegfried, the youngest of the kings of the Netherlands, went to Worms to crave the hand of Kriemhild in marriage. While he was staying with Günther, king of Burgundy (the lady's brother), he assisted him to obtain in marriage Brunhild, queen of Issland, who announced publicly that he only should be her husband who could beat her in hurling a spear, throwing a huge stone, and in leaping. Siegfried, who possessed a cloak of invisibility, aided Günther in these three contests, and Brunhild became his wife. In return for these services Günther gave Siegfried his sister Kriemhild in marriage. After a time the bride and bridegroom went to visit Günther, when the two ladies disputed about the relative merits of their respective husbands, and Kriemhild, to exalt Siegfried, boasted that Günther owed to him his victories and his wife. Brunhild, in great anger, now employed Hagan to murder Siegfried, and this he did by stabbing him in the back while he was drinking from a brook.

Thirteen years elapsed, and the widow married Etzel, king of the Huns. After a time she invited Brunhild and Hagan to a visit. Hagan, in this visit, killed Etzel's young son, and Kriemhild was like a fury. A battle ensued in which Günther and Hagan were made prisoners, and Kriemhild cut off both their heads with her own hand. Hildebrand, horrified at this act of blood, slew Kriemhild; and so the poem ends. Who was its author, or rather the man who cast it in its present form, is altogether unknown; the attribution of it to minnesingers of Kürenberg in Upper Austria now finds very little acceptance.

The Nibelungen Lied has been ascribed to Heinrich von Ofterdingen, a minnesinger; but it certainly existed before that epoch, if not as a complete whole, in separate lays, and all that Heinrich von Ofterdingen could have done was to collect the floating lays, connect them, and form them into a complete story.

The Völsunga Saga is the Icelandic version of the Nibelungen Lied. This saga has been translated into English by William Morris.

There is a continuation of the poem, called Nibelungen Klage, or Lament for the Nibelungs, a production much inferior to the Nibelungen Lied. In spite of the uncouth versification of this last, it exercises a strong fascination upon the reader, owing to the grandeur of its conception, its strong characterization, and tragic intensity.

THE MEANING OF CHRISTIAN NAMES.

CHRISTIAN NAMES OF MEN.

Aaron, *Hebrew*, a mountain, a loft.
Abel, *Hebrew*, vanity.
Abraham, *Hebrew*, the father of many.
Absalom, *Hebrew*, the father of peace.
Adam, *Hebrew*, red earth.
Adolphus, *Saxon*, happiness and help.
Adrian, *Latin*, one who helps.
Alan, *Celtic*, harmony; or *Slavonic*, a hound.
Albert, *Saxon*, all bright.
Alexander, *Greek*, a helper of men.
Alfred, *Saxon*, all peace.
Alonzo, form of Alphonso, *q. v.*
Alphonso, *German*, ready or willing.
Ambrose, *Greek*, immortal.
Amos, *Hebrew*, a burden.
Andrew, *Greek*, courageous.
Anthony, *Latin*, flourishing.
Archibald, *German*, a bold observer.
Arnold, *German*, a maintainer of honor.
Arthur, *British*, a strong man.
Augustus, Augustin, } *Latin*, venerable, grand.
Baldwin, *German*, a bold winner.
Bardulph, *German*, a famous helper.
Barnaby, *Hebrew*, a prophet's son.
Bartholomew, *Hebrew*, the son of him who made the waters to rise.
Beaumont, *French*, a pretty mount.
Bede, *Saxon*, prayer.
Benjamin, *Hebrew*, the son of a right hand.
Bennet, *Latin*, blessed.
Bernard, *German*, bear's heart.
Bertram, *German*, fair, illustrious.
Bertrand, *German*, bright raven.
Boniface, *Latin*, a well doer.
Brian, *French*, having a thundering voice.
Cadwallader, *British*, valiant in war.
Cæsar, *Latin*, adorned with hair.
Caleb, *Hebrew*, a dog.
Cecil, *Latin*, dim-sighted.
Charles, *German*, noble spirited.
Christopher, *Greek*, bearing Christ.
Clement, *Latin*, mild tempered.
Conrad, *German*, able counsel.
Constantine, *Latin*, resolute.
Cornelius, *Latin*, meaning uncertain.
Crispin, *Latin*, having curled locks.
Cuthbert, *Saxon*, known famously.
Dan, *Hebrew*, judgment.
Daniel, *Hebrew*, God is judge.
David, *Hebrew*, well-beloved.
Denis, *Greek*, belonging to the god of wine.
Douglas, *Gaelic*, dark gray.
Duncan, *Saxon*, brown chief.
Dunstan, *Saxon*, most high.
Edgar, *Saxon*, happy honor.
Edmund, *Saxon*, happy peace.
Edward, *Saxon*, happy keeper.
Edwin, *Saxon*, happy conqueror.
Egbert, *Saxon*, ever bright.
Elijah, *Hebrew*, God the Lord.
Elisha, *Hebrew*, the salvation of God.
Emmanuel, *Hebrew*, God with us.
Enoch, *Hebrew*, dedicated.
Ephraim, *Hebrew*, fruitful.
Erasmus, *Greek*, lovely, worthy to be loved.
Ernest, *Greek*, earnest, serious.
Esau, *Hebrew*, hairy.
Eugene, *Greek*, nobly descended.
Eustace, *Greek*, standing firm.
Evan or Ivan, *British*, the same as John.
Everard, *German*, well reported.
Ezekiel, *Hebrew*, the strength of God.
Felix, *Latin*, happy.
Ferdinand, *German*, pure peace.
Fergus, *Saxon*, manly strength.
Francis, *German*, free.
Frederic, *German*, rich peace.
Gabriel, *Hebrew*, the strength of God.
Geoffrey, *German*, joyful.
George, *Greek*, a husbandman.
Gerard, *Saxon*, strong with a spear.
Gideon, *Hebrew*, a breaker.
Gilbert, *Saxon*, bright as gold.
Giles, *Greek*, a little goat.
Godard, *German*, a godly disposition.
Godfrey, *German*, God's peace.
Godwin, *German*, victorious in God.
Griffith, *British*, having great faith.
Guy, *French*, a leader.
Hannibal, *Punic*, a gracious lord.
Harold, *Saxon*, a champion.
Hector, *Greek*, a stout defender.
Henry, *German*, a rich lord.
Herbert, *German*, a bright lord.

Hercules, *Greek*, the glory of Hera or Juno.
Hezekiah, *Hebrew*, cleaving to the Lord.
Horace, *Latin*, meaning uncertain.
Horatio, *Italian*, worthy to be beheld.
Howell, *British*, sound or whole.
Hubert, *German*, a bright color.
Hugh, *Dutch*, high, lofty.
Humphrey, *German*, domestic peace.
Ignatius, *Latin*, fiery.
Ingram, *German*, of angelic purity.
Isaac, *Hebrew*, laughter.
Jabez, *Hebrew*, one who causes pain.
Jacob, *Hebrew*, a supplanter.
James or Jacques, beguiling.
Joab, *Hebrew*, fatherhood.
Job, *Hebrew*, sorrowing.
Joel, *Hebrew*, acquiescing.
John, *Hebrew*, the grace of the Lord.
Jonah, *Hebrew*, a dove.
Jonathan, *Hebrew*, the gift of the Lord.
Joscelin, *German*, just.
Joseph, *Hebrew*, addition.
Joshua, *Hebrew*, a Savior.
Josiah or Josias, *Hebrew*, the fire of the Lord.
Julius, *Latin*, soft hair.
Lambert, *Saxon*, a fair lamb.
Lancelot, *Spanish*, a little lance.
Laurence, *Latin*, crowned with laurels.
Lazarus, *Hebrew*, destitute of help.
Leonard, *German*, like a lion.
Leopold, *German*, defending the people.
Lewis or Louis, *French*, the defender of the people.
Lionel, *Latin*, a little lion.
Llewellin, *British*, like a lion.
Llewellyn, *Celtic*, lightning.
Lucius, *Latin*, shining.
Luke, *Greek*, a wood or grove.
Manfred, *German*, great peace.
Mark, *Latin*, a hammer.
Martin, *Latin*, martial.
Matthew, *Hebrew*, a gift or present.
Maurice, *Latin*, sprung of a Moor.
Meredith, *British*, the roaring of the sea.
Michael, *Hebrew*, Who is like God?
Morgan, *British*, a mariner.
Moses, *Hebrew*, drawn out.
Nathaniel, *Hebrew*, the gift of God.
Neal, *French*, somewhat black.
Nicholas, *Greek*, victorious over the people.
Noel, *French*, belonging to one's nativity.
Norman, *French*, one born in Normandy.
Obadiah, *Hebrew*, the servant of the Lord.
Oliver, *Latin*, an olive.
Orlando, *Italian*, counsel for the land.
Orson, *Latin*, a bear.
Osmund, *Saxon*, house peace.
Oswald, *Saxon*, ruler of a house.
Owen, *British*, well descended.
Patrick, *Latin*, a nobleman.
Paul, *Latin*, small, little.
Paulinus, *Latin*, little Paul.
Percival, *French*, a place in France.
Percy, *English*, adaptation of "pierce eye."
Peregrine, *Latin*, outlandish.
Peter, *Greek*, a rock or stone.
Philip, *Greek*, a lover of horses.
Phineas, *Hebrew*, of bold countenance.
Ralph, contracted from Randolph, or Randal, or Ranulph, *Saxon*, pure help.
Raymond, *German*, quiet peace.
Reuben, *Hebrew*, the son of vision.
Reynold, *German*, a lover of purity.
Richard, *Saxon*, powerful.
Robert, *German*, famous in counsel.
Roderick, *German*, rich in fame.
Roger, *German*, strong counsel.
Roland or Rowland, *German*, counsel for the land.
Rollo, form of Roland, *q. v.*
Rufus, *Latin*, reddish.
Samson, *Hebrew*, a little son.
Samuel, *Hebrew*, heard by God.
Saul, *Hebrew*, desired.
Sebastian, *Greek*, to be reverenced.
Seth, *Hebrew*, appointed.
Silas, *Latin*, sylvan or living in the woods.
Simeon, *Hebrew*, hearing.
Simon, *Hebrew*, obedient.
Solomon, *Hebrew*, peaceable.
Stephen, *Greek*, a crown or garland.
Swithin, *Saxon*, very high.
Theobald, *Saxon*, bold over the people.
Theodore, *Greek*, the gift of God.
Theodosius, *Greek*, given of God.
Theophilus, *Greek*, a lover of God.
Thomas, *Hebrew*, a twin.
Timothy, *Greek*, a fearer of God.
Titus, *Greek*, meaning uncertain.
Toby, or Tobias, *Hebrew*, the goodness of the Lord.
Valentine, *Latin*, powerful.
Victor, *Latin*, conqueror.
Vincent, *Latin*, conquering.
Vivian, *Latin*, living.
Walter, *German*, a conqueror.
Walwin, *German*, a conqueror.
Wilfred, *Saxon*, bold and peaceful.
William, *German*, defending many.
Zaccheus, *Syriac*, innocent.
Zachary, *Hebrew*, remembering the Lord.
Zachariah, *Hebrew*, remembered of the Lord.
Zebedee, *Syriac*, having an inheritance.
Zedekiah, *Hebrew*, the justice of the Lord.

CHRISTIAN NAMES OF WOMEN.

Ada, *German*, same as Edith, *q. v.*
Adela, *German*, same as Adeline, *q. v.*
Adelaide, *German*, same as Adeline, *q. v.*
Adeline, *German*, a princess.
Agatha, *Greek*, good.
Agnes, *German*, chaste.
Alethea, *Greek*, the truth.
Althea, *Greek*, hunting.
Alice, Alicia, *German*, noble.
Alma, *Latin*, benignant.
Amabel, *Latin*, lovable.
Amy, Amelia, *French*, a beloved.
Angelina, *Greek*, lovely, angelic.
Anna, or Anne, *Hebrew*, gracious.
Arabella, *Latin*, a fair altar.
Aureola, *Latin*, like gold.
Aurora, *Latin*, morning brightness.
Barbara, *Latin*, foreign or strange.
Beatrice, Latin, making happy.
Bella, *Italian*, beautiful.
Benedicta, *Latin*, blessed.
Bernice, *Greek*, bringing victory.
Bertha, *Greek*, bright or famous.
Bessie, *short form* of Elizabeth, *q. v.*
Blanche, *French*, fair.
Bona, *Latin*, good.
Bridget, *Irish*, shining bright.
Camilla, *Latin*, attendant at a sacrifice.
Carlotta, *Italian*, same as Charlotte, *q. v.*
Caroline, *feminine of* Carolus, *the Latin of* Charles, noble spirited.
Cassandra, *Greek*, a reformer of men.
Catherine, *Greek*, pure or clean.
Cecilia, *Latin*, from Cecil.
Cecily, *a corruption of Cecilia, q. v.*
Charity, *Greek*, love, bounty.
Charlotte, *French*, all noble.
Chloe, *Greek*, a green herb.
Christiana, *Greek*, belonging to Christ.
Clara, *Latin*, clear or bright.
Clarissa, *Latin*, clear or bright.
Constance, *Latin*, constant.
Dagmar, *German*, joy of the Danes.
Deborah, *Hebrew*, a bee.
Diana, *Greek*, Jupiter's daughter.
Dorcas, *Greek*, a wild rose.
Dorothea or Dorothy, *Greek*, the gift of God.
Edith, *Saxon*, happiness.
Eleanor, *Saxon*, all fruitful.
Eliza, Elizabeth, *Hebrew*, the oath of God.
Ellen, *another form of* Helen, *q. v.*
Emily, *corrupted from* Amelia.
Emma, *German*, a nurse.
Esther, Hesther, *Hebrew*, secret.
Eudoia, *Greek*, prospering in the way.
Eudora, Greek, good gift.
Eudosia, *Greek*, good gift or well given.
Eugenia, *French*, well-born.
Eunice, *Greek*, fair victory.
Eva, or Eve, *Hebrew*, causing life.
Fanny, *diminutive of* Frances, *q. v.*
Fenella, *Greek*, bright to look on.
Flora, *Latin*, flowers.
Florence, *Latin*, blooming, flourishing.
Frances, *German*, free.
Gertrude, *German*, all truth.
Grace, *Latin*, favor.
Hagar, *Hebrew*, a stranger.
Hadassah, *Hebrew*, *form of* Esther, *q. v.*
Hannah, *Hebrew*, gracious.
Harriet, *German*, head of the house.
Helen, or Helena, *Greek*, alluring.
Henrietta, *fem. and dim. of* Henry, *q. v.*
Hephzibah, *Hebrew*, my delight is in her.
Hilda, *German*, warrior maiden.
Honora, *Latin*, honorable.
Huldah, *Hebrew*, a weasel.
Isabella, *Spanish*, fair Eliza.
Jane, or Jeanne, *fem. of* John, *q. v.*
Janet, Jeanette, little Jane.
Jemima, *Hebrew*, a dove.
Joan, *Hebrew*, *fem. of* John, *q. v.*
Joanna, or Johanna, *form of* Joan, *q. v.*
Joyce, *French*, pleasant.
Judith, *Hebrew*, praising.
Julia, Juliana, *feminine of* Julius, *q. v.*
Katherine, *form of* Catherine, *q. v.*
Keturah, *Hebrew*, incense.
Keziah, *Hebrew*, cassia.
Laura, *Latin*, a laurel.
Lavinia, *Latin*, of Latium.
Letitia, *Latin*, joy or gladness.
Lilian, Lily, *Latin*, a lily.
Lois, *Greek*, better.
Louisa, *German*, *fem. of* Louis, *q. v*
Lucretia, *Latin*, a chaste Roman lady.
Lucy, *Latin*, *feminine of* Lucius.
Lydia, *Greek*, descended from Lud.
Mabel, *Latin*, lovely or lovable.
Madeline, *form of* Magdalen, *q. v.*
Magdalen, *Syraic*, magnificent.
Margaret, *Greek*, a pearl.
Maria, Marie, *forms of* Mary, *q. v.*
Martha, *Hebrew*, bitterness.
Mary, *Hebrew*, bitter.
Matilda, *German*, a lady of honor

Maud, *German, dim. form of* Matilda, *q. v.*
May, *Latin*, month of May, or *dim. of* Mary, *q. v.*
Mercy, *English*, compassion.
Mildred, *Saxon*, speaking mild.
Minnie, *dim. of* Margaret, *q. v.*
Naomi, *Hebrew*, alluring.
Nest, *British, the same as* Agnes.
Nicola, *Greek, feminine of* Nicholas.
Olive, Olivia, *Latin*, an olive.
Olympia, *Greek*, heavenly.
Ophelia, *Greek*, a serpent.
Parnell, or Petronilla, little Peter.
Patience, *Latin*, bearing patiently.
Paulina, *Latin, feminine of* Paulinus.
Penelope, *Greek*, a weaver.
Persis, *Greek*, destroying.
Philadelphia, *Greek*, brotherly love.
Philippa, *Greek, feminine of* Philip.
Phœbe, *Greek*, the light of life.
Phyllis, *Greek*, a green bough.
Polly, *variation of* Molly, *dim. of* Mary, *q. v.*
Priscilla, *Latin*, somewhat old.
Prudence, *Latin*, discretion.
Psyche, *Greek*, the soul.
Rachel, *Hebrew*, a lamb.
Rebecca, *Hebrew*, fat or plump.
Rhoda, *Greek*, a rose.
Rosa, or Rose, *Latin*, a rose.
Rosalie, or Rosaline, *Latin*, little Rose.
Rosalind, *Latin*, beautiful as a rose.
Rosabella, *Italian*, a fair rose.
Rosamond, *Saxon*, Rose of peace.
Roxana, *Persian*, dawn of day.
Ruth, *Hebrew*, trembling, or beauty.
Sabina, *Latin*, sprung from the Sabines.
Salome, *Hebrew*, perfect.
Sapphira, *Greek*, like a sapphire stone.
Sarah, *Hebrew*, a princess.
Selina, *Greek*, the moon.
Sibylla, *Greek*, the counsel of God.
Sophia, *Greek*, wisdom.
Sophronia, *Greek*, of a sound mind.
Susan, Susanna, *Hebrew*, a lily.
Tabitha, *Syriac*, a roe.
Temperance, *Latin*, moderation.
Theodosia, *Greek*, given by God.
Tryphena, *Greek*, delicate.
Tryphosa, *Greek*, delicious.
Victoria, *Latin*, victory.
Vida, *Erse, feminine of* David.
Ursula, *Latin*, a she bear.
Walburga, *Saxon*, gracious.
Winifred, *Saxon*, winning peace.
Zenobia, *Greek*, life from Jupiter.

MISUSE OF WORDS.

A and An. A is used before all words beginning with consonants except those beginning with silent H, or when the word beginning with H is accented on some other syllable than the first. An is to be used before all vowel sounds, silent H, and when the words beginning with H are accented on some other syllable than the first.

Ability (for capacity). Capacity is the power of receiving and retaining knowledge with facility. Ability is the power of applying knowledge to practical purposes.

Abortive (for unsuccessful). A plan may be abortive, but an act cannot.

Acceptance (for acceptation). "No word is more vague in its general acceptance," should be "in its acceptation."

Accident (for wound). "Witch hazel cures accidents."

Accredit (for credit). Few, except very bad writers, employ it as a robust substitute for credit or believe.

Administer (for deal). "The blows were administered [dealt] by Policeman Johnson."

Admire (for desire). It is an error to follow this verb with an infinitive, as "I admire to see a man consistent." Doubly wrong, therefore, is the expression, "I should admire to go with you."

Aggravate (for irritate, worry, annoy). "There would be no danger in aggravating Violet by this expression of pity." Better "irritating."

Agriculturalist (for agriculturist). The first is never correct.

Ain't. The only legitimate contraction of I am not is I'm not.

Allow (for say, assert, express opinion). We may allow or admit that which we have disputed, but of which we have been convinced; or we may allow certain premises as the basis of argument; but we assert, not allow, our own opinions.

Allude (for say or mention). Allude (from *ludo, ludere*, to play) means to indicate jocosely, to hint at playfully; and so to hint at in a slight, passing manner. Allusion is the byplay of language.

Alone (for only). Alone means "quite by one's self," and is always an adjective, differing herein from only, which is both an adverb and an adjective. In some cases the words may be used indifferently, but as a rule there is a marked distinction between alone and only, as "I did it alone," quite by myself; "an only daughter;" "they differ on one point only."

Alternately (for by turns). This word should be used only in speaking of two objects or classes of objects. Whately rightly defines alternative as a choice between two objects.

Amateur (for novice). A professional actor who is new and unskilled in his art is a novice, and not an amateur. An amateur may be an artist of great experience and extraordinary skill.

Among (for between, when speaking of two). Gould says it should not be written amongst, but Worcester and Webster give both forms.

And. The commonest case in which it is violated is where and introduces a relative clause, no relative having occurred before, as "I have a book printed at Antwerp, and which was once possessed by Adam Smith." And for to is a frequent misuse. "Try to do it," not "try and do it."

Anyways (for anyway). This is a frequent misuse.

Anywheres (for anywhere). Belongs to the class of words frequently misused.

Apprehend (for comprehend). Apprehend denotes the laying hold of a thing mentally, so as to understand it clearly, at least in part. Comprehend denotes the embracing or understanding it in all its compass and extent. We may apprehend many truths which we do not comprehend.

As (for that). "I don't know as [that] I can go."

Assurance (for fire insurance). Webster and Worcester agree that this word is limited to life insurance.

At (for by). "I bought it at auction" is correct English, but "It is to be sold at auction" is American only.

At all. A needless expletive, as "I did not like the play at all."

Avocation (for vocation). Vocation is one's pursuit, employment, business; avocation refers to incidental or pleasure pursuits.

Acoustics takes a singular verb. Names of sciences, such as mathematics, economics, politics, physics, gymnastics, etc., are now regarded as singular in number.

Awful (for very or for ugly). "The crowd present was awfully boisterous."

Bad. "I feel bad," not "I feel badly."

Balance (for rest, remainder). Balance refers to the ledger account, and does not properly convey the same meaning as remainder.

Banquet (for dinner, supper). A banquet is a public, sumptuous feast.

Beau, a word used by the uneducated instead of escort.

Been to (for been). "Where have you been to?"

Between (for among). Between is only for two—by and twain. Carefully avoid such expressions as "Between every stitch."

Blame it on (for accuse). A common vulgarism.

Bountiful (for plentiful). Bountiful applies to persons, not to things, and has no reference to quantity.

Bourn (for place, instead of boundary). Frequently misused.

Bravery (for courage). Bravery is inborn, instinctive. Courage is the product of reason, calculation. Men who are simply brave are careless, while the courageous man is always cautious.

Bring (for fetch). Bring expresses motion toward, not away. A boy is properly told to take his books to school and to bring them home. A gardener may say to his helper, "Go and bring me yonder rake," but he might better say, "Fetch me yonder rake."

Bound (for determined). "He is bound to go West."

Bursted (for burst). "The pipes bursted during the cold weather."

But (for that or if). "I have no doubt but he will come to-night."

But that (for that). "I should not wonder but that was the case."

By (for upon). "By [upon] returning it to this office the finder will be rewarded."

Calculate (for expect). "I calculate [expect] to go to-morrow.

Can (for may). The boy says, "Can I go down street?" when he means "May I?" It is a question not of possibility but of permission.

Caption (for heading). Not sanctioned by good writers.

Casket (for coffin). A newspaper writer facetiously intimated that a man in a casket is not quite so dead as a man in a coffin.

Citizen (for person). A citizen is a person who has certain political rights. To say "Several citizens carried the victims of the accident into a shop," would be as absurd as to say, "several church members."

Come (for go). "I am coming to pay you a visit." Coming is right.

Commence to (for begin). Omit to. We begin to write. We commence writing.

Compulsion (for obligation). The former is a physical, the latter a moral, necessity.

Confess to (for confess). "I confess to a little curiosity on this subject." The natural rejoinder was, "Well, did the little curiosity absolve you?"

Construe (for construct). Writers construct; readers construe.

Consummate (for perform). "The marriage was consummated [performed] at Paris, last April."

Contemptible (for contemptuous). "To a gentleman who, at the close of a fierce dispute with Porson, exclaimed, 'My opinion of you is most comtemptible, sir,' he retorted, 'I never knew an opinion of yours that was not contemptible.'"

Continual (for continuous). A continuous action is one which is uninterrupted; continual is that which is constantly renewed and recurring, though it may be interrupted as frequently as it is renewed.

Continue on is often erroneously used for continue.

Corporeal, frequently misused for corporal, especially of punishment.

Cortege (for procession). A cortege is a procession, but every procession is not a cortege.

Credible (for credulous). "He is very credible [credulous]."

Creditable (for credible). "I am creditably [credibly] informed."

Dead and buried, dead and gone, and similar expressions are to be deprecated. Those who have died have usually been buried, and they are also gone.

Dearest. "A gentleman once began a letter to his bride, thus: 'My dearest Maria.' The wife replied: 'My dear John, I beg that you will mend either your morals or your grammar. You call me your "dearest Maria"; am I then to understand that you have other Marias?'"

Deduction (for induction). Induction is the mental process by which we ascend to the delivery of special truths; deduction is the process by which the law governing particulars is derived from a knowledge of the law governing the class to which particulars belong.

Demoralized (for scared). "The horse, in addition to losing all the hair on his tail, became considerably demoralized."

Departure. To take one's departure is a corruption of the accurate form, "to take one's leave."

Differ with, in opinion; differ from, in appearance.

Die with (for die of). A man dies of smallpox, not with smallpox.

Dock (for wharf or pier). A dock is an open place without a roof, into which anything is received, and where it is inclosed for safety. The shipping around a city lies at wharfs and piers, but goes into docks.

Done should be used only with has, had, or have; frequently misused for did.

Don't (for doesn't). Don't is the contraction for do not; doesn't the contraction for does not.

Doubt but (for doubt). "I have no doubt but that it is so."

Each and every (often followed by a plural verb). "When I consider how each of these professions are [is] crowded."

Emblem (for motto, sentiment). The figure is the emblem; not the accompanying motto.

Enthuse (for inspirit). This word is not sanctioned by good usage.

Epithet (as necessarily decrying). Is usually and erroneously applied to derogative adjectives.

Equally as well (for equally well). "He plays equally as well [equally well]."

Every once in a while is an absurd and meaningless expression.

Every (for entire or all). "Rendered them every assistance," is absurdly wrong. Every is separated, and can be applied only to a whole composed of many individuals. It is always singular in number.

Execute does not mean to put to death. The law is executed when the criminal is hanged or imprisoned.

Expect (for suppose). Expect refers only to that which is to come, and which, therefore, is looked for. We cannot expect backward.

Female (for woman). A vulgar misuse of English.

From out (for from). "From out the castle."

Farther, further. Farther properly signifies distance, further degree or quantity. "As he walked farther he saw they were further along with the work."

Future (for subsequent). "Her future life was virtuous and fortunate."

First two. Often written and spoken, two first.

Gent and pants. "Let these words go together, like the things they signify. The one always wears the other."

Gentleman, lady (for man, woman). The most important rule to observe is that where adjectives are used the nouns must be man, woman — not a polite gentleman, or a lovely lady; but a polite man, a lovely woman.

Girl (for daughter). A father, on being requested by a rich and vulgar fellow for permission to marry "one of his girls," gave this rather crushing reply: "Certainly. Which one would you prefer — the waitress or the cook?"

Graduated (for was graduated). Students do not graduate, but are graduated. "I graduated [was graduated] in 1876."

Great, big. Frequently used for large.

Gums (for overshoes). "Emily is outside, cleaning her gums upon the mat."

Get signifies possession obtained by exertion. "He has [not has got] red hair."

Had ought (for ought). "You had ought to have been with me."

Haven't no. Omit no. Do not use two words meaning no in the same sentence.

Healthy, healthful, wholesome. Healthy refers to living things. "The man is healthy." "The food is wholesome." "The surroundings are wholesome."

Is (for are). "Their general scope and tendency is [are] not remembered at all."

It is I (not me). It is he (not him). It is she (not her).

Jewelry (for particular jewels). Its use in the latter sense is always to be preferred. Think of Cornelia pointing to the Gracchi, "These are my jewelry."

Kids (for kid gloves). Colloquial and should not be used.

Last (for latest). "I have received your latest [not last] letter."

Lay (for lie). Remember that lay expresses transitive action, and lie means rest. We lay the book on the table and the book lies where we have placed it.

Learn (for teach). Learn means to acquire knowledge; teach, to impart it. This use of learn is found in respectable writers, but is now deemed improper, as well as inelegant.

Leave (without an object). "Anna Louise Carey will leave the stage," announces an exchange. "Thanks, Annie; we were afraid you would take the stage with you. So kind to leave it," rejoins the critic.

Leave (for let). "Leave [let] me be."

Let's (for let). "Well, farmer, let's you and I go by ourselves."

Liable. Frequently misused for likely.

Lit (for lighted). Much censured as an Americanism.

Look (followed by an adverb). "Miss Marlowe looked charmingly." Just as correct to say "Miss Marlowe looked gladly, or madly, or sadly, or delightedly."

Loan (for lend). The former word is a noun, the verbal form of which is to lend.

Mutual (for common). It should always convey a sense of reciprocity.

Nice is now applied to a sermon, to a jam-tart, to a young man, in short, to everything. The word should be used with extreme caution.

Nor (for than, after comparative). "Better nor fifty bushel."

Notion (for inclination). "I have a notion to go." Of course incorrect.

None is etymologically singular. "None but the brave deserves the fair," wrote Dryden.

Off of (for off). "A yard off of the cloth."

Over his signature (for under his signature). A letter is issued under or by the authority of the writer's signature.

Particle (for at all). As "not a particle," for "not at all."

Past two weeks. Better, the last two weeks.
Patron (for customer) is wrong.
Pile (for amount). "He owed me quite a pile."
Party (for person). Avoid it.
Posted (for informed). A colloquialism in the United States. Must be used with caution.
Previous (for previously). "Previous to my going."
Prolific (for frequent). "It was a prolific [frequent] source of annoyance."
Promise (for assure). "I promise [assure] you I was astonished."
Proof (for evidence). Proof is the result of evidence.
Quite is not to be used for nearly. Quite means wholly, completely, or thoroughly.
Raise (for bring up, educate). A peculiarity of the Southern states.
Real (for very). "Real [very] nice."
Reckon (for conjecture, conclude). Provincial and vulgar.
Restive (for restless). Restive signifies stubborn, unwilling to move, balky.
Remember (for recollect). We remember without effort. Recollect with some exertion.
Retire (for to go to bed). A vulgar but unfortunately very common euphemism.
Reverend (for the reverend). The article is absolutely required.
Right (for obligation). "The cars have as good a right to be stopped as the carriages."
Rise up (for rise). "He rose up and left the room."
Sabbath (for Sunday). Sunday is the name of the day, while Sabbath is the name of an institution.
Shall and Will. *Shall*, in an affirmative sentence, in the first person, and *will* in the second and third persons, merely announce future action. Thus, "I *shall* go to town to-morrow." "I *shall* wait for better weather." "We *shall* be glad to see you." "I *shall* soon be twenty." "We *shall* set out early, and *shall* try to arrive by noon." "You *will* be pleased." "You *will* soon be twenty." "You *will* find him honest." "He *will* go with us."

Shall, in an affirmative sentence, in the second and third person, announces the speaker's intention to control. Thus, "You *shall* hear me out." "You *shall* go, sick or well." "He *shall* be my heir." "They *shall* go, whether they want to go or not."

Will, in the first person, expresses a promise, announces the speaker's intention to control, proclaims a determination. Thus, "I *will* [I promise to] assist you." "I *will* [I am determined to] have my right." "We *will* [we promise to] come to you in the morning."

Shall, in an interrogative sentence, in the first and third person, consults the will or judgment of another; in the second person, it inquires concerning the intention or future action of another. Thus, "*Shall* I go with you?" "When *shall* we see you again?" "When *shall* I receive it?" "When *shall* I get well?" "When *shall* we get there?" "*Shall* he come with us?" "*Shall* you demand indemnity?" "*Shall* you go to town to-morrow?" "What *shall* you do about it?"

Will, in an interrogative sentence, in the second person, asks concerning the wish, and, in the third person, concerning the purpose or future action of others. Thus, "*Will* you have an apple?" "*Will* you go with me to my uncle's?" "*Will* he be of the party?" "*Will* they be willing to receive us?" "When *will* he be here?"

Will cannot be used interrogatively in the first person singular or plural. We cannot say, "*Will* I go?" "*Will* I help you?" "*Will* I be late?" "*Will* we get there in time?" "*Will* we see you again soon?"

Official courtesy, in order to avoid the semblance of compulsion, conveys its commands in the *you will* form instead of the strictly grammatical *you shall* form. It says, for example, "You will proceed to Key West, where you will find further instructions awaiting you."

A clever writer on the use of *shall* and *will* says that whatever concerns one's beliefs, hopes, fears, likes, or dislikes, cannot be expressed in conjunction with *I will.* Are there no exceptions to this rule? If I say, "I think I *shall* go to Philadelphia to-morrow," I convey the impression that my going depends upon circumstances beyond my control; but if I say, "I think I *will* go to Philadelphia to-morrow," I convey the impression that my going depends upon circumstances within my control — that my going or not depends on mere inclination. We certainly must say, "I fear that I *shall* lose it;" "I hope that I *shall* be well;" "I believe that I *shall* have the ague;" "I hope that I *shall* not be left alone;" "I fear that we *shall* have bad weather;" "I *shall* dislike the country;" "I *shall* like the performance." The writer referred to, asks, "How can one say, 'I *will* have the headache?'" I answer, very easily, as every young woman knows. Let us see: "Mary, you know you promised John to drive out with him to-morrow; how *shall* you get out of it?" "Oh, I *will* have the headache!" We request that people *will* do thus or so, and not that they *shall*. Thus, "It is requested that no one *will* leave the room."

Shall is rarely, if ever, used for *will;* it is *will* that is used for *shall*. Expressions like the following are common: "Where *will* you be next week?" "I *will* be at home." "We *will* have dinner at six o'clock." "How *will* you go about it?" "When *will* you begin?" "When *will* you set out?" "What *will* you do with it?" In all such expressions, when it is a question of mere future action on the part of the person speaking or spoken to, the auxiliary must be *shall* and not *will*.

Should and *would* follow the regimen of *shall* and *will*. *Would* is often used for *should; should* rarely for *would*. Correct speakers say, "I *should* go to town to-morrow if I had a horse." "I *should* not; I *should* wait for better weather." "We *should* be glad to see you." "We *should* have started earlier, if the weather had been clear." "I *should* like to go to town, and *would* go if I could." "I *would* assist you if I could." "I *should* have been ill if I had gone." "I *would* I were home again!" "I *should* go fishing to-day if I were home." "I *should* so like to go to Europe!" "I *should* prefer to see it first." "I *should* be delighted." "I *should* be glad to have you sup with me." "I knew that I *should* be ill." "I feared that I *should* lose it." "I hoped that I *should* see him." "I thought that I *should* have the ague." "I hoped that I *should* not be left alone." "I was afraid that we *should* have bad weather." "I knew I *should* dislike the country." "I *should* not like to do it, and *will* not [determination] unless compelled."

Shut to (for shut). "Shut the door to."
Somewheres (for somewhere). "The farmer had gone out somewheres."
Sparrowgrass, a corruption of asparagus.
Spoonsful (for spoonfuls). "Two spoonsful [spoonfuls] at bedtime."
Stopping (for staying). "At what hotel are you stopping?"
Such (for so). "Such an extravagant young man," for "So extravagant a young man."
Than (for when). "The admiral was hardly in the channel than [when] he was driven to sea by the storm."
Think for (for think). "You will find that he knows more than you think for."
Those sort of things. "I never approved of those [that] sort of things."
Those who (for they that). That and those, as demonstrative adjectives, refer backward, and are not therefore well suited for forward reference.
To (for at). "When I was to [at] home."
Try and (for try to). "I will try and [to] come to-morrow."
Unique (for beautiful). A thing is unique when it is the only one of its kind, whether it is good or bad, ugly or beautiful.
Vengeance (for revenge). Vengeance should never be ascribed save to God or to men acting as the executors of his righteous doom.
Vulgar (for immodest). The word vulgarity was formerly thought to mean indecent; now it simply means bad manners. Vulgar people are low, mean, coarse, plebeian, no matter where the wheel of fortune has placed them.
Warn't (for wasn't). Heard only as a vulgarism.
Was (for is, of general truths). "Truth is eternal." In the expression of general and necessary truths the present tense is to be preferred to the past tense.
Ways (for way). "He was a long ways [way] behind."
What (for that). "I don't know but what [that] I shall go."
Which (for that). "She would be all which [that] the emperor could desire."
Widow woman (for widow). Uselessly redundant.
You was (for you were). You takes the plural form of a verb.

DICTIONARY OF AUTHORS.

ABBREVIATIONS: Am., American; Br., British; Dan., Danish; Eng., English; fl., flourished; Fr., French; Ger., German; Gr., Greek; Ir., Irish; It., Italian; Nor., Norwegian; Port., Portuguese; Prus., Prussian; Rom., Roman; Russ., Russian; Scot., Scottish; Sp., Spanish; Sw., Swedish.

The numbers after each name indicate the years of birth and death.

Where the pronunciation is obvious, and follows regular English rules, no phonetic spelling is given, but in cases where doubt as to place of accent might arise, the accented syllable is marked. Where the pronunciation departs from regular English rules, as in many foreign names, the correct pronunciation is approximated by phonetic spelling, in parenthesis, following the name. In some instances, diacritical marks in accordance with the system used in Webster's Dictionary are employed to indicate the pronunciation more correctly.

Abbott, Jacob, 1803-79. Am. A prolific juvenile writer who published more than 200 volumes; among which are "The Rollo Books," the "Rainbow," and "Lucky Series," and a series of histories of America. He wrote in collaboration with his brother, John S. C. Abbott, a series of juvenile histories. His style is fascinating for the young and his books are still popular.

Abbott, John S. C., 1805-77. Am. historical and pedagogical writer, author of numerous popular works, all readable but of little critical value. Among his most noted books are "The French Revolution," "The History of Napoleon Bonaparte," "Napoleon at St. Helena," and "The History of the Civil War in America."

About *(a-boo′)*, **Edmond,** 1828-85. Fr. novelist and journalist, a brilliant, witty, but uneven writer, elected to the French Academy in 1885. His most popular stories are, "The King of the Mountains," "The Man with a Broken Ear," and "The Notary's Nose."

Ade, George, 1866- . . . . Am. journalist and author; born in Illinois, educated at Purdue University, began journalism in Chicago; first attracted notice by his "Stories of the Streets and Town," from which he constructed "Artie." His next books were "Pink Marsh," in dialect, and "Fables in Slang." Author of the librettos for "The Sultan of Sulu," and "Peggy from Paris," and of the rural comedy "The County Chairman."

Addison, Joseph, 1672-1719. Eng. poet and essayist; one of the great masters of English prose, unexcelled in natural dignity and propriety of style. His poems "The Letter" and "The Campaign," and also his "Tragedy of Cato," were exceedingly popular during his lifetime, but his most original and permanent production is the series of sketches in the *Spectator*, especially the portrayal of Sir Roger de Coverley, which is one of the most delightful character creations in English literature.

Ælfric *(ăl′frik)*, The Grammarian, about 930-1021. Old English writer, best known by his "Homilies," written in pure and vigorous English. He was given the title, Grammarian, on account of his Latin Grammar and "Colloquium," written in English for the use of the boys of England.

Æschylus *(es′ki-lus)*, 525-456 B.C., Gr. poet. With Sophocles and Euripides, whom he immediately preceded, considered the greatest of Athenian tragic poets; wrote a great number of plays of which seven tragedies now remain; of these the greatest is "Agamemnon," which rivals Sophocles' "King Œdipus" for first place among all Greek tragedies.

Aguilera *(ah-ge-lay′ra)*, **Ventura Ruiz,** 1820-81. Sp. lyric poet, called the Spanish Beranger. Among his most important works are the collections of poems entitled "Elegias," "Armonias y Cantares," "La Arcadia Moderna," and "Legenda de Noche Buena."

Ainsworth, William Harrison, 1805-82. Eng. novelist. His first novel was "Sir John Cheverton," published 1826, soon followed by "Rookwood," "Crichton," and "Jack Sheppard." He then devoted himself to magazine writing for a time. Among his later works are "Lancaster Witches," "The Star Chamber," "The Spanish Match," and "Merrie England." His works, which were very popular in England, are characterized by vividness of scene and directness of action, English scenery and the historical element being made prominent.

Aird, Thomas, 1802-76. Scot. poet. Educated at University of Edinburgh. His best known poem is the "Devil's Dream." While highly commended by Carlyle and other critics, his works, though of undoubted merit, have failed to win much popular praise.

Akenside, Mark, 1721-70. Eng. author; forerunner of the romantic poets. At age of twenty-three wrote the didactic poem "Pleasures of the Imagination," which gave him much celebrity, but his later poetry did not add to his reputation. Was educated in medicine, but an unsuccessful practitioner, though his medical treatises won for him distinction as a scholar.

Aksakoff *(ăk-sah′kof)*, **Ivan Sergeyevich,** 1823-86. Russian writer and journalist, Panslavist leader and best known poet of the cause.

Alamanni *(ah-la-man′ne)*, **Luigi,** 1495-1556. It. poet, born in Florence, but, like Dante, spent many years in exile. Conspired against Pope Clement, was detected, and fled to France, where he wrote most of his poems. His works embrace didactic poems, imitations of Virgil and the Iliad, translations, and vigorous satires.

Alarcon y Mendoza *(ah-lar-kon′ e men-do′tha)*, **Don Juan Ruiz de,** 1580-1639. Sp. dramatist, born in Mexico. Among his many dramas, the most important are, "Walls have Ears," and "The Weavers of Segovia." Ticknor says: "He is to be ranked with the very best Spanish dramatists during the best period of the national theater."

Alcæus *(al-see′-us)*, 620-580 B. C. Gr. lyric poet, contemporary of Sappho. Wrote many odes, hymns, and songs, of which only fragments remain; invented the stanza called Alcaic, which was later successfully imitated and established in the Latin language by Horace.

Alcman *(alk′man)*, Gr. poet; founder of Doric lyric poetry and forerunner of the bucolic poets, flourished about 670 B. C.

Alcott, Amos Bronson, 1799-1888. Am. educational reformer and philosopher of the Transcendental School. Established a school at Boston, 1828, which he taught according to his then novel methods, but soon discontinued on account of vehement opposition. He then lectured to spread his views, winning much attention. Failing in an attempt to found a community at Harvard, Mass., he went to Boston and soon to Concord, living the life of a peripatetic philosopher. He published "Orphic Sayings" in the *Dial*, the Transcendental organ; also a number of books, among which are "Concord Days," "Table Talk," and an essay on Ralph Waldo Emerson.

Alcott, Louisa May, 1832-88. Am. novelist and juvenile writer, daughter of A. Bronson Alcott; began as a teacher, was a volunteer army nurse during the Civil War; first attracted notice by "Little Women," 1869, her best and most popular production. The more noteworthy of her numerous juvenile stories are "An Old Fashioned Girl," "Little Men," and "Jo's Boys."

Alden, Mrs. Isabella McDonald, 1841- . . . . Am. author who writes under the pen-name "Pansy," author of much fiction, including the widely known "Pansy Books," a juvenile series of over sixty volumes.

Aldrich, Thomas Bailey, 1836- . . . . Am. poet and novelist, sometimes styled the "American Herrick," on account of his graceful verse. Editor of *Atlantic Monthly*, 1881-90, succeeding W. D. Howells. His published verse includes, "The Bells," "Cloth of Gold," "Flower and Thorn," "Pampinea," "Wyndham Towers." His best known novels are "Marjorie Daw," and "The Story of a Bad Boy," but his prose, like his verse, while finished, lacks constructive power.

Alfieri *(awl′fe-ay′re)* **Vittorio,** Count, 1749-1803. The most important Italian dramatic poet. His greatest works are his tragedies, "Virginia," "Agamenone," "Oreste," "Timoleone," "Maria Stuarda," and "Saul," his masterpiece, all classic in form and lofty in sentiment

His supreme aim was to unite "artistic truth with moral truth, beauty with morality."

Allibone, Samuel Austin, 1816-89. Am. author; most important works are his "Critical Dictionary of English Literature," "Poetical Quotations," and "Prose Quotations."

Almeida-Garrett (*al-may'e-da-gahr-ret'*), Viscount d', 1799-1854. Author and statesman, the greatest Portuguese poet of the nineteenth century. His most noteworthy poems are the epic "Camoens," the lyric epic, "Dona Branca," and his last poem "Fallen Leaves," which is unexcelled in emotional power in the Portuguese literature.

Almquist (*alm'kwist*), **Karl J. L.,** 1793-1866. Versatile Swedish writer but of unstable character; first made famous by romances in his "Book of the Thorn Rose." He wrote many lyrics, dramas, and novels, as well as many books on history, religion, and ethics, often contradictory in teaching. He is unexcelled in power of language, and his dramas show great tragic force.

Anacreon (*a-nak're-on*), 561-476 B. C. Gr. poet, one of the most highly esteemed lyricists of Greece; was exceedingly popular and great public honors were paid to him after his death. Of his many books of flowing verse only two complete poems remain.

Andersen (*ahn'der-sen*), **Hans Christian,** 1805-75. Celebrated Danish writer, the "Children's Poet." His parents were poor and he had but little education. At the age of fourteen he went to Copenhagen, worked hard and produced little, but at the end of ten years was able to publish his first book. In 1835 he began the first of the "Fairy Tales" which were to bring him world-wide fame. He wrote many novels, travels, and some poetry without much success; but in 1840, in his "Picture Books without Pictures," he revealed his genius for interpreting child nature and many books of stories followed, most of which have been translated into many languages and are the delight of children throughout the world.

Anderson, Rasmus Bjorn, 1846- . . . . Am. scholar and author. Educated at Luther College and University of Wisconsin. Professor of Scandinavian Languages in University of Wisconsin 1875-83. U. S. Minister to Denmark 1885-89. Among his books are "The Scandinavian Languages," "Viking Tales of the North," and translations of the works of Brandes and Bjornson.

Anna Comne'na, 1083-1148? Author of a valuable work on Byzantine history. Daughter of the Emperor Alexis I, educated at Constantinople; conspired against the succession of her brother to the throne; was imprisoned in a convent, where she wrote her history, the "Alexiad," a work of great merit.

Annunzio (*an-noon'tse-o*), **Gabrielle d',** 1864- . . . . Most widely known contemporary Italian writer. He published his first book of verse at fifteen; other promising volumes followed almost yearly; his first novel appeared in 1889, followed by several powerful stories which added greatly to his fame; among these are: "The Triumph of Death," "The Virgins of the Rocks," and "The Flame of Life." He has recently turned to the drama, producing plays modeled on classic Greek tragedy, the most popular ones, "La Gioconda" and "Francesca da Rimini."

Antimachus (*an-tim'a-kus*). Greek poet and critic, contemporary of Plato.

Apuleius (*ap-u-lee'yus*), **Lucius.** Roman satirist of the second century, whose reputation survives in his "Metamorphoses, or The Golden Ass," a satire on the vices of the age.

Ar'buthnot, John 1667-1735. Scot. author and physician, friend of Pope and Swift. His fame was established by his "History of John Bull," and "Martinus Scriblerus." The former is a satire on politics, the latter ridicules pedantry in all its forms.

Archilochus (*ar-kil'o-kus*), 714?-676 B.C. First of the Greek lyric poets. A native of the island of Paros. Ranked with Homer among the ancients. Is considered the inventor of the poetry of the passions. Bitter satire characterized his poems, of which only mere fragments remain.

Argyll (*ar-gīl'*), **George John Douglas Campbell,** eighth Duke of, 1823-1900. Eng. author and statesman, member of Gladstone's Cabinet. Best known as a writer by his masterly defense of theism entitled "The Reign of Law." All his works show great ability, among which are "Primeval Man," "Antiquities of Iona," "Organic Evolution," and a volume of poems, "The Burden of Belief."

Ariosto (*ar-yōs'to*), **Ludovico,** 1474-1533. Famous Italian poet, author of one of the world's greatest epic poems, "Orlando Furioso," based on the old chivalric romances.

Aristophanes (*ar-is-tof'a-nees*), 450-385 B.C. Gr. comic poet. Author of many comedies in verse, among them: "The Knights," "The Clouds," "The Wasps," "The Birds," "The Frogs." He was first among the brilliant comedy writers of his time, and in wit, humor, invention, and skill in using language has never been surpassed.

Arnold, Sir Edwin, 1832- . . . . English author, educated at Oxford. His most remarkable work is "The Light of Asia," a poetic exposition of Buddhism. He has also published "Pearls of the Faith," "The Light of the World," "The Tenth Muse," "East and West," and "The Voyage of Ithobal." He has popularized the philosophy of India. He excels in paraphrase and translation but lacks the originality of the great poets.

Arnold, Matthew, 1822-88. Eng. poet, essayist, and critic, son of Dr. Thomas Arnold of Rugby. While the volume of his verse is not large, in the opinion of many he will yet be ranked next to Tennyson and Browning among Victorian poets. His "Essays in Criticism" establish his place among great critics. His style is admirable and his thought of a high order.

Asbjornsen (*as-byern'sen*), **Peter Christen,** 1812-85. Nor. author and zoologist. Celebrated for his writings in folk lore, published in his "Norwegian Folk Tales" and "Norwegian Fairy Tales and Folk Legends."

Ascham (*as'kam*), **Roger,** 1515-68. English writer and classical scholar, educated at Cambridge. In 1545, in defense of the sport of archery, he wrote "Toxophilus," which ranks among the classics of pure English.

Aubigne (*o-bēn-yea'*), **Theodore Agrippa d',** 1550-1630. Fr. historian and militant poet. A classical scholar, Huguenot soldier, and one of the striking figures of the Reformation. His "Universal History" and other historical works are very valuable but extremely satirical. His greatest work is the group of poems called "The Tragedies" in which are unsurpassed descriptions of the horrors of religious warfare.

Auerbach (*ow'er-bok*), **Berthold,** 1812-82. Ger. novelist, of Jewish parentage; a founder of the German tendency novel of the present day; author of some forty volumes of fiction, much overweighted with philosophy. His reputation was established by his romance, "On the Heights." He excels in description but is weak in construction of plot.

Augier (*o-zhe-a'*), **Emile,** 1820-89. Fr. dramatist, author of a large number of successful plays. He is vigorous in style, possesses great moral earnestness, is a sincere student of nature, and will probably rank as the greatest French dramatist of his century.

Aurelius (*aw-reel'yus*), **Marcus,** 121-180. Roman emperor and noted Stoic philosopher. Author of a moral work entitled "Meditations," which is considered the finest product of Stoic philosophy.

Austen, Jane, 1775-1817. Eng. novelist. Her novels truthfully portray the everyday life of the middle class in her time, and show fine discrimination of character. "Sense and Sensibility," "Pride and Prejudice," "Emma," and "Mansfield Park" were published 1811-16; "Northanger Abbey" and "Persuasion" appeared after her death.

Austin, Alfred, 1835- . . . . Eng. poet, author of many volumes of verse, among which are "The Seasons," "Savonarola," "Songs of England," "A Tale of True Love." Although lacking the imagination of the greater poets, he has written graceful verse. Was made Poet-Laureate of England, 1896.

Aytoun (*a'toon*), **William E.,** 1843-65. Scot. poet. Established his reputation by his "Lays of the Scottish Cavalier." Following this were: "Fermilian," "Bothwell," and "Scottish Ballads"; his longer works are in the measure and manner of Walter Scott. His poems are marked by simplicity and rapidity of movement, while his prose tales contain a strong vein of humor which made them widely popular.

Bacheller, Irving, 1857- . . . . An American novelist, born in Pierpont, N. Y.; was graduated at St. Lawrence University in 1879 and became a reporter of the Brooklyn *Times*. Subsequently he established a newspaper syndicate. His novels are notable for originality, and for fresh and fascinating pen pictures of American life.

Bacon, Francis, 1561-1626, Viscount St. Albans. One of the most remarkable men of whom any age can boast; a reformer of philosophy, by founding it on the observation of nature, after it had consisted, for many centuries, of scholastic subtleties and barren dialecties. Born in London, his father being Sir Nicholas Bacon, lord keeper of the great seal. He contracted an advantageous marriage; was made solicitor-general and then attorney-general; in 1617 became lord keeper of the seals; in 1618 was made lord high chancellor and created Baron of Verulam, and in 1621, Viscount St. Albans. He might have lived in splendor without degrading his character by those acts which stained his reputation. He was accused before the House of Lords of having received money for grants of offices and privileges under the seal of state. He was unable to justify himself, and, desiring to avoid the mortification of a trial, confessed his crimes and threw himself on the mercy of the peers, beseeching them to limit his punishment to the loss of the high office which he had dishonored. The lords sentenced him to pay a fine of £40,000, and to be imprisoned in the Tower during the pleasure of the king. He was also declared forever incapable of place or employment, and forbidden to sit in Parliament or to appear within the verge of the court. He survived his fall only a few years. Efforts have been made to prove him the real author of the works of Shakespeare, and the controversy still goes on.

Bagehot, Walter, 1826-1877. An English writer on political economy and government.

Bain, Alexander, 1818-1877. Born at Aberdeen, professor of Logic, and twice Lord Rector in the university, where he was much esteemed by and exercised a great influence over his pupils; his chief works: "The Senses and the Intellect," "The Emotions and the Will," and "Mental and Moral Science."

Balzac, Honore de, 1799-1850. Native of Tours, France; one of the most brilliant as well as prolific novel writers of modern times; his productions are remarkable for their sense of reality; they show power of observation, warmth, and fertility of imagination, and subtle and profound delineation of human passion, his design in producing them being to make them form part of one great work, the "Human Comedy," the whole being a minute dissection of the different classes of society.

Bancroft, George, 1800-1891. An American statesman, diplomatist, and historian, born in Massachusetts; his chief work, "The History of the United States," issued finally in six volumes.

Barbauld, Anna Lætitia (*nee Aiken*), 1743-1825. A popular and accomplished English authoress; wrote "Hymns in Prose for Children," "Evenings at Home," in which she was assisted by a brother.

Barham, Richard Harris, 1788-1879. His literary name, Thomas Ingoldsby; born at Canterbury; minor canon of St. Paul's; friend of Sidney Smith; author of "Ingoldsby Legends," published originally as a series of papers in *Bentley's Miscellany.*

Barrie, James Matthew, 1860- . . . . A Scotch writer with a rich vein of humor and pathos; began his literary career as a contributor to journals; produced, among other works, "Auld Licht Idylls," "A Window in Thrums," and "Margaret Ogilvie," deemed by some likely to prove the most enduring thing he has yet written.

Baudelaire, Charles (*bo-de-lār′*), 1821-1867. French poet of the romantic school, born in Paris; distinguished among his contemporaries for his originality and his influence on others of his class; was a charming writer of prose as well as verse.

Beattie, James, 1735-1803. A Scottish poet and miscellaneous writer. In 1765 he published a poem, "The Judgment of Paris," and in 1770 his celebrated "Essay on Truth," for which the University of Oxford conferred on him the degree of LL.D.; and George III. honored him, when on a visit to London, with a private conference and a pension.

Beaumont, Francis, 1585-1615. English dramatic poet, contemporary of Shakespeare; bred for the bar, but devoted to literature; was a friend of Ben Jonson; in conjunction with his friend Fletcher, the composer of a number of plays, about the separate authorship of which there has been much discussion.

Bede or **Beda,** 672?-735. Surnamed "The Venerable," an English monk and ecclesiastical historian; spent his life devoted to quiet study and learning; his most important work, the "Ecclesiastical History" of England, written in Latin, and translated by Alfred the Great.

Bellamy, Edward, 1850-1898. An American writer, born in Chicopee Falls, Mass. He was educated in Germany; admitted to the bar; was on the staff of the *Evening Post* of New York in 1871-1872; and on his return from the Sandwich Islands in 1877, he founded the Springfield *News.* He is best known by his novel "Looking Backward," a socialistic work.

Beranger (*bā-ron-zhā′*), **Pierre Jean de,** 1780-1859. A celebrated French song-writer, the first of his countrymen who in that department rose to the high level of a true lyric poet; his first struggles with fortune were a failure; has been compared to Burns, but he lacked both the fire and the humor of the Scottish poet.

Berkeley, George, 1684-1753. Irish bishop, the interest in whom centers in his philosophic teaching, known as Idealism.

Besant, Sir Walter, 1838-1901. English man of letters, eminent chiefly as a novelist of a healthily realistic type; wrote a number of novels jointly with James Rice, and is the author of "French Humourists," as well as short stories.

Bjornson (*be-yörn′son*), **Bjornstjerne,** 1833- . . . . A Norwegian novelist, poet, and dramatist, born at Kvikne, Norway. He published his first story, "Synnove Solbakken," in 1857; "Arne" and "A Lively Fellow" established his reputation as a novelist.

Black, William, 1841-1898. A Scottish journalist and novelist, born in Glasgow, received his education at private schools. In 1874 he abandoned the career of journalism, which he had successfully pursued; visited the United States in 1876. His novels contain fine descriptions of scenery. They are very popular.

Bloomfield, Robert, 1766-1823. An English poet, by trade a shoemaker; author of "The Farmer's Boy," a highly popular production, translated into French and Italian; spent his last days in ill-health, struggling with poverty, which brought on dejection of mind.

Boccaccio (*bŏk-kaht′cho*), **Giovanni,** 1313-1375. Celebrated Italian novelist, author of the "Decameron." He was the friend of Petrarch, and was the first to bring copies of the Iliad and Odyssey from Greece to Naples.

Bo′denstedt, Friedrich Martin, 1819-1892. A German poet and miscellaneous writer.

Boileau, Nicolas, 1636-1711. A French poet, born at Paris.

Boswell, James, 1740-1795. A Scotch biographer; the son of Lord Auchinleck; born in Edinburgh. In 1791 appeared his "Life of Johnson," a work which he had been long preparing, and which at once gave readers the same delight that it has ever since inspired. By this time Boswell's health had greatly suffered from his too convivial habits, and he died in London, May 19, 1795.

Boucicault, Dion, 1822-1890. A dramatic writer, author of popular Irish pieces, as "The Colleen Bawn" and "The Shaughraun."

Bowles, William Lisle, 1762-1850. An English poet, born in Northamptonshire; his sonnets, by their "linking," as Professor Saintsbury has it, "of nature's aspect to human feeling," were much admired by Coleridge, and their appearance is believed to have inaugurated a new era in English poetry as developed in the Lake School.

Boyesen, Hjalmar Hjorth, 1848-1895. An American novelist, born at Frederiksvarn, Norway. After completing his university studies at Christiania, he came to the United States in 1869 and was editor of a Norwegian journal in Chicago. He returned to Europe in 1872 and studied Germanic Philology at Leipsic two years; then returning to this country, was Professor of German in Cornell University for six years, and of Germanic Languages and Literature in Columbia College till his death.

Braddon Miss (Mrs. John Maxwell), 1837- . . . . A popular novelist, born in London; authoress of "Lady Audley's Secret," "Aurora Floyd," and some 50 other novels; contributed largely to magazines.

Brandes, Georg, 1842- . . . . A Danish literary critic of Jewish family; born in Copenhagen, where he graduated at the University in 1864. Several books on æsthetic and philosophic subjects brought on him a charge of skepticism which was not removed by an epoch-making series of lectures, delivered before large audiences. In 1882 he returned to Copenhagen, his countrymen having guaranteed him an income of 4,000 crowns, with the one stipulation that he should deliver public lectures on literature.

Bremer, Fredrika, 1801-1865. A Swedish novelist, was born at Tuorla, Finland; was brought up at Arsta, about 20 miles from Stockholm. She varied her literary labor by long journeys in Italy, England, the United States, Greece, Palestine.

Bronte, Charlotte, 1816-1855. Born at Thornton, Yorkshire; removed with her father, at the age of four, to Haworth, a moorland parish in the same county, where she lived most of her days; spent two years at Brussels as a pupil-teacher; on her return, in conjunction with her sisters, prepared and published a volume of poems under the pseudonyms respectively of "Currer,

Ellis, and Acton Bell," which proved a failure. Nothing daunted, she set to novel writing and her success was instant; first "Jane Eyre," then "Shirley," and then "Villette," appeared, and her fame was established. In 1854 she married her father's curate, Mr. Nicholls, but her constitution gave way, and she died.

Browning, Elizabeth Barrett, 1809-1861. A distinguished English poetess, regarded by some as the greatest which England has ever produced; born in London. In 1846 she was married to Robert Browning; died at Florence, Italy.

Browning, Robert, 1812-1889. One of the greatest of the Victorian poets; born in Camberwell, England. His father, who was a clerk in a bank, had the boy educated in a school at Peckham, after which he attended lectures at University College. At the age of twenty he traveled on the Continent and resided for some time in Italy, where he made diligent study of its mediæval history. In 1846 he married Elizabeth Barrett, and settled with her in Florence, where they remained for nearly fifteen years. Recognition of his literary fame, which came slowly, was made in 1867, when he was elected an honorary fellow of Balliol, an M. A. of Oxford, and later, an LL.D. of Cambridge. He died in Venice and was buried in Westminster Abbey between Cowley and Chaucer.

Bryant, William Cullen, 1794-1878. Am. poet and journalist; born in Mass.; entered Williams College, read law, admitted to the bar in 1816; published "Thanatopsis" in 1816; became editor of the New York *Evening Post* in 1826.

Bryce, James, 1838- . . . . An Irish historian, born in Belfast. After graduating at Oxford in 1862, he studied at Heidelberg, and subsequently practiced law in London. From 1870 till 1893 he was Regius Professor of Civil Law in Oxford, and has had a distinguished political career.

Bulwer-Lytton, Edward, Lord Lytton, 1803-1873. An English novelist, playwright, and poet, born in London; was the son of Gen. Earle Bulwer and Elizabeth B. Lytton, heiress of Knebworth, to whose estates he succeeded in 1844, and assumed the surname of Lytton. In 1866 he was raised to the peerage as Baron Lytton. Altogether his works exceed 60 in number, and fill 110 volumes.

Bunyan, John, 1628-88. Eng. author; the son of a tinker, he followed that vocation and led for many years a wandering life; served in the Parliamentary army; joined the Anabaptists in 1654, and in 1655 became a Baptist minister; sentenced to transportation on a charge of promoting seditious assemblies, but sentence not enforced; was, however, imprisoned for more than twelve years, and during that time wrote his "Pilgrim's Progress."

Burdette, Robert Jones, 1844- . . . An American journalist and humorist, born in Greensboro, Pa. He served in the Union army during the Civil War. He is famous for humorous newspaper skits of rare variety, charm, and unrepetitious freshness. He was licensed as a Baptist clergyman in 1887.

Burger, Gottfried August, 1747-1794. A German poet, born in Molmerswende, Anhalt; died in Gottingen.

Burnett, Frances Hodgson, 1849- . . . An Anglo-American novelist, born in Manchester, England. Her family removed to Tennessee in 1865. She early wrote stories. In 1873 Miss Hodgson married Dr. Burnett, and, in 1875, settled in Washington. In 1898 she was granted a divorce from her husband, with the right to resume her maiden name.

Burton, Robert, 1576-1640. An English clergyman, born in Leicestershire; scholar of Christ Church, Oxford; lived chiefly in Oxford, spending his time there for some 50 years in study; author of "The Anatomy of Melancholy," which he wrote to alleviate his own depression of mind, a book which is a perfect mosaic of quotations on every conceivable topic, familiar and unfamiliar, from every manner of source.

Burns, Robert, 1759-1796. Scotland's national poet; born in a clay-built cottage less than two miles south of the town of Ayr, and not far from the river Doon. His father, William Burness (for so the name was originally spelled), the son of a Kincardineshire farmer, and a worthy and intelligent man, at the time of the poet's birth occupied a few acres of land, and acted as gardener and overseer for a neighboring gentleman. His mother, Agnes Brown, belonged to Ayrshire. He died at Dumfries, Scotland.

Burritt, Elihu (the Learned Blacksmith), 1810-79. Am. scholar, journalist, lecturer, and reformer; the son of a shoemaker, and apprenticed to a blacksmith, he devoted all of his spare time to study, and eventually mastered eighteen languages.

Byron, George Gordon Noel, Lord, 1788-1824. Eng. poet. In 1815 he married Anne Isabel Millbank, but separated from her and left England in 1816; in Italy he formed a *liaison* with the beautiful Countess Guiccioli; espousing the cause of the Greeks in their struggle for liberty, he left for Greece in 1823, and died the following year at Missolonghi from the effects of exposure while preparing for the siege of Lepanto.

Cable, George Washington, 1844- . . . . An American novelist; born in New Orleans, La.; received a common school education; entered the volunteer service of the Confederate army in 1863 and served till the close of the war, when he obtained employment in a mercantile house, and was on the editorial staff of the New Orleans *Picayune* from 1865-1879. His sketches of creole life in *Scribner's Monthly* proved so successful that in 1879 he turned his entire attention to literature. He has contributed numerous sketches to newspapers and magazines, and published various books.

Cædmon, fl. 670. An English poet, the fragment of a hymn by whom, preserved by Bede, is the oldest specimen of English poetry extant.

Caine, Thomas Henry Hall, 1853- . . . . An English novelist and dramatist; born in Runcorn, Cheshire, Eng. His novels, which are striking in their pictures of human motives and passions, are read throughout the world.

Calderon de la Barca, 1600-1681. The great Spanish dramatist, born at Madrid; entered the army, and served in Italy and Flanders, producing the while dramas which were received with great enthusiasm; took holy orders, and became a canon of Toledo, but to the last continued to write poems and plays; he was a dramatist of the first order, and has been ranked by the more competent critics among the foremost of the class in both ancient and modern times.

Camoens, 1524-1580. The poet of Portugal, born at Lisbon, studied at Coimbra; fell in passionate love with a lady of high rank in Lisbon, as she with him, but whom he was not allowed to marry; left Lisbon, joined the army, and fought against the Moors; volunteered service in India, arrived at Goa, and got into trouble with the Portuguese authorities; was banished to Macao, and consoled himself by writing his "Lusiad"; coming home he lost everything but his poem; died neglected and in poverty; the title of the poem is properly "The Lusiads," or the Lusitanians, *i. e,* the Portuguese, and is their national epic, called, not inaptly, the "Epos of Commerce"; it has been translated into most European languages, and into English alone no fewer than six times.

Campbell, Thomas, 1777-1844. A Scotch poet; born in Glasgow, died in Boulogne, and was interred at Poets' Corner, in Westminster Abbey, close to the tomb of Addison. Some of his poems have gained a permanent place in literature.

Carleton, Will, 1845- . . . . An American poet, born in Hudson, Mich. He is best known in literature by his ballads of home life, many of them having gained great popularity.

Carlyle, Thomas, 1795-1881. Author, born in Ecclefechan, Dumfriesshire, Scotland. He was the eldest son of James Carlyle, a mason, afterward a farmer, and was intended for the Church, with which object he was carefully educated. His first literary productions were short biographies and other articles for the "Edinburgh Encyclopædia." His career as an author may be said to have begun with the issue in monthly portions of his "Life of Schiller" in the *London Magazine* in 1823, this work being enlarged and published separately in 1825. The largest and most laborious work of his life was "The History of Friedrich II. of Prussia, called Frederick the Great," the last two volumes of which appeared in 1865, and after this time little came from his pen. While still in Scotland the sad news reached him that his wife had died suddenly in London. Toward the end of his life he was offered a government pension and a baronetcy, but declined both. Carlyle died in Chelsea.

Cary, Alice, 1820-1871. An American poetess, born near Cincinnati, O. In 1852 she, with her sister, Phœbe, removed to New York city, where they lived during the rest of their lives. She died in New York city.

Cary, Phœbe, 1824-1871. An American poetess and prose writer, sister of Alice; born in Cincinnati, O. She died in Newport, R. I.

Catull'us, Valerius, 86-57 B. C. A famous Roman poet, whose prænomen is stated by some to be Caius, by others Quintus.

Cervan'tes Saavedra, Miguel de, 1547-1616. Author of "Don Quixote," and one of the greatest writers of modern times; born in Alcala de Henares. He died in Madrid, where he had resided during the last years of his life. He was buried without any ceremony, and no tombstone marks the spot where he rests.

Channing, William Ellery, 1780-1842. An American preacher and writer; born in Newport, R. I.; studied at Harvard College. His early views are said to have been evangelical, but he soon became a decided Unitarian, and propagated the peculiarities of this theological system. His first appointment as a preacher was in 1803, when he obtained the charge of a congregation in Federal street, Boston. He died in Burlington, Vt.

Chateaubriand (*shah-to-bre-on'*), **Francois Auguste, Vicomte de,** 1768-1848. A French author and politician; born in St. Malo, Brittany. He lived to witness the terrible scenes in Paris in June, 1848. His memoirs of himself, on which he had been occupied for many years, appeared after his death, under the title of "Memoires d'outre Tombe."

Chaucer, Geoffrey, 1340-1400. "The father of English poetry;" born in London. He was the son of a vintner named John Chaucer. His most celebrated work, "The Canterbury Tales," was written at different periods between 1373 and 1400. It consists of a series of tales in verse, supposed to be told by a company of pilgrims at the shrine of St. Thomas (Becket) at Canterbury in 1386. In its pages we get such pictures of English life and English ways of thought in the fourteenth century as are found nowhere else. He died in London, and was buried in Westminster Abbey.

Chesterfield, Philip Dormer Stanhope, Earl of, 1694-1773. Statesman, orator, and man of letters; eldest son of the third earl, born in London; sat in the House of Commons from 1716 to 1726; was an opponent of Walpole; held office under the Pelhams; in 1748 retired, from deafness, or perhaps disgust, into private life; celebrated for his "Letters to his Son," models of elegance, though of questionable morality.

Churchill, Winston, 1871- . . . . An American author; born in St. Louis, Mo. He was graduated from the United States Naval Academy in 1894, and became an editor of the *Army and Navy Journal* the same year. He wrote "Richard Carvel."

Cicero, Marcus Tullius, 106 B. C.-43 B. C. A Roman orator; born in Arpinum. He was one of thel greatest orators the world has known, and a statesman and patriot of singularly pure conduct and motives. He was executed at the instance of the Triumvirate—Octavianus, Antony, and Lepidus.

Clarke, James Freeman, 1810-1888. An American Unitarian clergyman and author; born in Hanover, N. H.; settled in Boston, Mass., in 1841, and was pastor of the Church of the Disciples, which was organized especially for him, and of which he had charge till his death. From 1867 to 1871 he was Professor of Natural Religion. He died in Boston, Mass.

Clemens, Samuel Langhorne, 1835- . . . . Best known by his pen name of Mark Twain. An American humorist; born in Florida, Mo. Mr. Clemens made a lecturing tour of the world. His first book, "The Jumping Frog"; visited Europe, described in "Innocents Abroad"; married a lady of fortune; wrote largely in his peculiar, humorous vein, such as "Tramp Abroad"; produced a drama entitled "The Gilded Age," and compiled the "Memoirs of General Grant."

Clough, Arthur Hugh, 1819-1861. A lyric poet, born at Liverpool; son of a cotton merchant; educated at Rugby under Dr. Arnold, whom he held in the highest regard; was at Oxford, as a Fellow of Oriel, at the time of the Tractarian movement, which he arrayed himself against, and at length turned his back upon and tore himself away from by foreign travel; on his return he was appointed examiner in the Education Office; falling ill from overwork he went abroad again, and died at Florence.

Coleridge, Samuel Taylor, 1772-1834. English poet, philosopher, and critic; educated at Christ's Hospital; had Charles Lamb for schoolmate; at Cambridge devoted himself to classics; falling into debt, enlisted as a soldier, and was, after four months, bought off by his friends; gave himself up to a literary life; married, and took up house near Wordsworth, in Somersetshire, where he produced the "Ancient Mariner," "Christabel," and "Remorse"; preached occasionally in Unitarian pulpits; visited Germany and other parts of the continent; lectured in London in 1808; when there took to opium, broke off the habit in 1816, and went to stay with the Gillmans at Highgate as their guest, under whose roof, after four years' confinement to a sick-room, he died; among his works were "The Friend," his "Biographia Literaria," "Aids to Reflection," "Confessions of an Inquiring Spirit," "Literary Remains" and "Table Talk."

Collins, Wilkie, 1824-1889. English novelist, born in London; tried business, then law, and finally settled to literature; his novel "The Woman in White" was the first to take with the public, and was preceded and succeeded by others which have insured for him a high place among the writers of fiction.

Congreve, William, 1670-1729. English comic dramatist, born near Leeds; "The Old Bachelor" first brought him into repute; the production of "Love for Love" and the "Mourning Bride," a stilted tragedy, added immensely to his popularity, but his comedy "The Way of the World" being coldly received, he gave up writing plays, and only wrote a few verses afterwards.

Cooper, James Fenimore, 1789-1851. An American novelist, born in Burlington, New Jersey; having a passion for the sea, he entered the Navy as a midshipman in 1808, but in three years resigned his commission, married, and settled to literature; his novels achieved instant popularity; made him a great favorite with boys; showed him an expert in the narration of events, the description of scenes, as well as in the delineation of character. His well known "Leather Stocking" series of Indian tales have been translated into every European language.

Corel'li, Marie, 1864- . . . . An English authoress; born in Italy. In infancy she was adopted by Dr. Charles Mackay, the author. She was educated in London, and on beginning her literary career adopted as a pen name that which subseqently became her legal name. Among her works are "The Romance of Two Worlds" and "The Sorrows of Satan."

Corneille (*Kor-nale'*), **Pierre,** 1606-1684. The father of French tragedy, born at Rouen, was bred for the bar, but he neither took to the profession nor prospered in the practice of it, so gave it up for literature; threw himself at once into the drama; began by dramatizing an incident in his own life, and became the creator of the dramatic art in France. His first tragedies are "The Cid," which indeed is his masterpiece; "Horace," "Cinna," "Polyeucte," "Rodogune," and "Le Menteur."

Cowper, William, 1731-1800. An English poet; born in Berkhampstead; was the great-nephew of the Lord-Chancellor Cowper. In addition to translating Homer, he wrote "The Task," the best of all his poems; "Tirocinium;" and a host of smaller works. Died in Norfolk.

Crabbe, George, 1754-1832. An English poet; born in Aldborough, Suffolk, died in Trowbridge, Wilts.

Craik, Dinah Maria Mulock, 1826-1887. An English authoress; born in Stoke-upon-Trent in 1826. In 1865 she married George Lillie Craik, a partner in the publishing house of Macmillan and Company, and spent a period of quiet happiness and successful literary industry at her home in Kent, where she died.

Crawford, Francis Marion, 1854- . . . . An American novelist; born in Tuscany, Italy; son of Thomas Crawford. He was educated at Concord, N. H.; Trinity College, Cambridge; Karlsruhe, and Heidelberg. At Rome he devoted himself to the study of Sanskrit, and during 1879-1880 was engaged in press work at Allahabad, where he was admitted to the Catholic Church. Wrote the National Ode at the Centennial of the American Constitution, Sept. 17, 1887. His works, which are numerous, are chiefly novels.

Creasy, Sir Edward, 1812-1878. Chief-justice of Ceylon; author of "The Fifteen Decisive Battles of the World," "Rise and Progress of the British Constitution," etc.

Crockett, Samuel Rutherford, 1862- . . . . A Scotch novelist; born in Little Duchrae, Galloway. He was a tutor and university pupil-teacher at an early age; but a volume of verse, "Dulce Cor," and "The Stickit Minister," a volume of stories, showed literature to be his vocation.

Curtis, George William 1824-1892. An American author; born in Providence, R. I., February 24, 1824. He was an early abolitionist, and a leader in the Republican party from the first; for many years the editor of *Harper's Weekly*, and the writer of the "Editor's Easy Chair" in *Harper's Monthly*, besides the "Manners Upon the Road" series for *Harper's Bazar*. He was also a lecturer of great popularity. He died on Staten Island, N. Y.

Da Costa, Isaac, 1798-1860. A Dutch poet, born in Amsterdam, of Jewish parents; became a Christian, and after the death of Bilderdijk was chief poet of Holland.

Dahlgren, Fredrik August, 1816- . . . . A Swedish poet and dramatist; born in Nordmark, August 20, 1816. He has written many dialect songs and ballads. He has translated a great many dramas from foreign languages, and has written a history of the Swedish stage.

Dalin, Olof von, 1708-1763. A Swedish poet and historian; "father of modern Swedish literature;" born in Vinberga, in Holland.

Dana, Richard Henry, 1787-1879. An American poet and critic; editor of the *North American Review*, author of the "Dying Raven," "The Buccaneer," and other poems.

Dan'te (a contraction of Durante), **Alighieri,** 1265-1321. An Italian poet; born in Florence. He is famous as the author of the "Divina Commedia," containing awful word pictures of hell.

Daudet (*do-day*), **Alphonse,** 1840-1897. A noted French novelist of great versatility, born at Nimes, of poor parents; wrote poems and plays, and contributed to the *Figaro* and other journals; worked up into his novels characters and situations that had come under his own observation; has been likened to Dickens in his choice of subjects and style of treatment. Died suddenly.

Davis, Richard Harding, 1864- . . . . An American novelist and contributor to periodical literature; born in Philadelphia. He graduated at Lehigh University, and entered journalism in Philadelphia. He has, since 1891, been constantly engaged in story writing, and descriptive narrations of events, places, and people. In 1898 he was a war correspondent in Cuba and in 1900 he acted in the same capacity in South Africa.

Defoe, Daniel, 1661-1731. An English writer; born in London. In 1719 appeared the most popular of all his works," The Life and Surprising Adventures of Robinson Crusoe," the favorable reception of which was immediate and universal.

De Quincey, Thomas, 1788-1759. An English author; born in Manchester. He received a classical education at the grammar school of Bath, and entered the University of Oxford in 1803, where he remained till 1808. While there, he contracted the habit of eating opium, to which he remained a bounden slave for many years. The consequences were fearful, as he himself relates in his principal work, "The Confessions of an English Opium-Eater." He was a very prolific writer; but his works are mostly essays, and papers on historical, literary, and miscellaneous topics. He died in Lasswade, near Edinburgh.

Dibdin, Charles, 1745-1814. Musician, dramatist, and song-writer; born in Southampton; began life as an actor; invented a dramatic entertainment consisting of music, songs, and recitations, in which he was the sole performer, and of which he was for most part the author; wrote some 30 dramatic pieces, and it is said 1,400 songs; his celebrity is wholly due to his sea-songs. Was the author of "Tom Bowling."

Dickens, Charles, 1812-1870. Celebrated English novelist, born at Landport, Portsmouth; son of a navy clerk, latterly in great straits; was brought up amid hardships; was sent to a solicitor's office as a clerk, learned shorthand, and became a reporter, a post in which he learned much of what afterwards served him as an author; wrote sketches for the *Monthly Magazine* under the name of "Boz" in 1834, and the "Pickwick Papers" in 1836-37, which established his popularity; these were succeeded by "Oliver Twist," "Nicholas Nickleby," "Old Curiosity Shop," "A Tale of Two Cities," and many others. They were all written with an aim. He was a little man, with clear blue, intelligent eyes, a face of most extreme mobility, and a quiet shrewdness of expression.

Diderot, Denis, 1713-1784. A French philosopher, foremost of the "Encyclopædists."

Dobson, Austin, 1840- . . . . An English poet; born in Plymouth. Intended for a civil engineer, he accepted a place under the Board of Trade. His poems are inimitable in their artistic finish and grace of fancy.

Dodge, Mary Abigail, 1838-1896. An American journalist and author; born in Hamilton, Mass. For several years she was instructor in the high school at Hartford, Conn. From 1865 to 1867 she was one of the editors of *Our Young Folks*. Besides numerous contributions to current literature, she has written, under the pseudonym of "Gail Hamilton," a number of well known books.

Dodge, Mary Elizabeth Mapes, 1838- . . . . An American editor, author, and poet; born in New York city. Since 1873 she has been the editor of *St. Nicholas* (magazine), New York. Her best known work is "Hans Brinker, or the Silver Skates," which has gone through many editions and been translated into five foreign languages.

Doyle, Sir Arthur Conan, 1859- . . . . A British novelist; born in Edinburgh, Scotland. He was educated at the Roman Catholic college or school at Stonyhurst, Lancashire, and at the University of Edinburgh, where he graduated as Doctor of Medicine. After practicing for some years, chiefly at Southsea, the success of several of his books induced him to give up the profession for that of literature. He was knighted in 1902.

Dryden, John, 1631-1700. A celebrated English poet, "glorious John," born in Northamptonshire, of a good family of Puritan principles; educated at Westminster School and Cambridge; poet-laureate; prior to which and afterwards he produced a succession of plays for the stage, which won him great popularity, after which he turned his mind to political affairs and assumed the role of political satirist. On the accession of James II. he became a Roman Catholic, and wrote "The Hind and the Panther," which was really the most powerful thing of the kind in the language; at the Revolution he was deprived of his posts, but it was after that event he executed his translation of Virgil, and produced his celebrated odes and "Fables."

Dumas (*du-mah*), **Alexandre,** 1803-1870. The Elder; a French dramatist. He was the grandson of a French marquis, and a celebrated French romancist and San Domingo negress. The works which bear his name amount to some 1,200 volumes, including about 60 dramas; but the only claim he could lay to a great number of the productions issued under his name was that he either sketched the plot or revised them before going to press. He died near Dieppe.

Dumas, Alexandre, 1824-1895. The Younger; a French dramatist and romancist, son of the preceding; born and died in Paris.

Du Maurier (*du mo-re-ay'*), **George Louis Palmella Busson,** 1834-1896. Artist, caricaturist, and novelist; born in Paris, France. He studied in Paris and Antwerp, and going to London he began to draw on wood for *Once a Week*, the *Cornhill Magazine*, etc., and also exhibited at the Royal Academy. He subsequently joined the *Punch* staff, and become famous through his weekly drawings for that publication. He also illustrated a large number of books, including Thackeray's "Esmond and Ballads." In 1891 appeared his first novel. "Peter Ibbetsen," and in 1894 he issued "Trilby," a story which had great popularity both in book form and on the stage. He died in London.

Ebers (*ay'bers*), **Georg Moritz,** 1837-1898. A German Egyptologist and novelist; born in Berlin; was educated at Froebel's school, and studied law at Gottingen. He afterward devoted himself to the study of Egyptology at Berlin. His visit to Egypt resulted in the discovery of the celebrated hieratic medical "Papyrus Ebers." He died near Munich, Bavaria.

Edgeworth, Maria, 1767-1849. An English novelist; born at Hare Hatch, Berkshire.

Edwards, Amelia Blandford, 1831-1892. An English Egyptologist and writer; born in London; died in Weston-super-Mare, Somersetshire.

Eggleston, Edward, 1837-1902. An American author; born in Vevay, Ind. In fiction he achieved celebrity with stories of life in Southern Indiana in pioneer days, while as a historian he made a specialty of American subjects. Died at Jones Lock, Lake George, N. Y.

"Eliot, George," 1820-1880. The assumed literary name of Mary Ann, or, as she preferred to write the name in later years, Marian Evans, an English novelist. Her first literary undertaking was the continuation of a translation of Strauss's "Life of Jesus," commenced by her friend Mrs. Hennell, and completed by Miss Evans in 1846. In 1849 she went abroad, returning to England next year, and in 1851 she took up her abode as a boarder in the house of John Chapman, editor of the *Westminster Review*. It was not, however, till January, 1857, that she came prominently into public notice, when the first of a series of tales entitled "Scenes from Clerical Life" appeared in *Blackwood's Magazine*. These tales immediately arrested attention, and obtained the praise of the editor, who was informed that he was to know the author as George Eliot. John Blackwood was as ignorant of the author's identity for a considerable time as was all the world except George H. Lewes and one or two others. The "Scenes" came to an end in November, 1857, and in the February following the first chapters of "Adam Bede" were in the publisher's hands, the whole work being completed and sent in by October. The success which followed the publication of this powerful story of English rural life was unmistakable, and public curiosity was greatly excited as to the personality of the author. The credit of authorship was openly ascribed to several persons of varying note and was claimed by others of more or less modesty and honesty. The secret soon began to leak out. Months before her second novel, "The Mill on the Floss," was published, it was well known, among literary circles at least, that George Eliot was none other than Marian Evans, the Westminster reviewer. By this time was established that close association and literary fellowship with the talented philosophical writer, George H. Lewes, which terminated only with the death of the latter but a little more than two years before her own. In May, 1880, she married John Cross, but died rather suddenly at Chelsea.

Emerson, Ralph Waldo, 1803-1882. An American philosopher; born in Boston; he graduated at Harvard College in 1821, and was ordained minister of the Second Unitarian Church of Boston; but soon after formed peculiar views with regard to forms of worship, abandoned his profession and, retiring to the quiet village of Concord, devoted himself to the study of the nature of man and his relation to the universe. He was one of the most eminent modern philosophers of the Pantheistic school, and one of the most remarkable personifications of American genius. He died in Concord, Mass.

English, Thomas Dunn, 1819-1902. An American author; born in Philadelphia, Pa. Was a member of Congress in 1891-1895; author of "Ben Bolt," an exceedingly popular ballad, "Old Glory," etc.

Ennius, 239-169 B.C. An early Roman poet, the father of Roman epic poetry, born in Rudiæ, Calabria; promoted the study of Greek literature in Rome; of his poems, dramatic and epic, only a few fragments are extant.

Epicharmus, 540-430 B.C. A Greek philosopher and poet, in the island of Cos; studied philosophy under Pythagoras; conceived a taste for comedy; gave himself up to that branch of the drama, and received the name of the "Father of Comedy."

Epictetus, 60-120? A celebrated Stoic philosopher, originally a slave; lived and taught at Rome, but after the expulsion of the philosophers retired to Nicopolis in Epirus; was lame, and lived in poverty; his conversations were collected by Arrian, and his philosophy in a short manual under the Greek name of "Enchiridion of Epictetus."

Epinay (*day-pe-nay'*), **Madame d',** 1725-1783. A French writer, unhappily married in her youth; became notorious for her illicit intimacy with Rousseau and Grimm; her "Memoires et Correspondence" give a lively picture of her times.

Euripides, 480-406 B.C. A famous Greek tragic dramatist, born at Salamis, of wealthy parents; first trained as an athlete, and then devoted himself to painting, and eventually to poetry; of his plays the "Alcestes," "Bacchæ," "Iphigenia at Aulis," "Electra," and "Medea" may be mentioned; he won the tragic prize five times.

Evans, Augusta Jane (Mrs. Wilson), 1835- . . An American novelist; born in Columbus, Ga.

Fawcett, Edgar, 1847- . . . . An American author; born in New York city; was graduated at Columbia College in 1867; traveled in Europe and Italy; latterly resides in London.

Fenelon (*fay-neh-lon'*), **Francois de Salignac de la Mothe,** 1651-1715. A French prelate; born in the Chateau de Fenelon, province of Perigord, France; was educated at Plessis College, in Paris, and at the seminary of St. Sulpice, where he received holy orders in 1675. In 1694 he was created Archbishop of Cambray. A theological dispute with Bossuet, his former instructor, terminated in his condemnation by Pope Innocent XII., and his banishment to his diocese by Louis XIV. He was the author of numerous works on philosophy, theology, and belles-lettres. He died in Cambray, France.

Fessler, Ignaz Aurelius, 1756-1839. A Hungarian author. A Capuchin priest; his secret communication to Joseph II. in 1781 regarding the monasteries, brought about a radical reformation of them. Appointed Professor of Oriental Languages in the Vienna University, he had to leave the post and Austria for his atheistic and seditious tragedy "Sidney." He died in St. Petersburg, Russia.

Feuillet (*feeh-yay'*), **Octave,** 1821-1890. A French novelist. He was elected to the Academy in 1863. Beginning as a novelist of the discreetest sort, he ended in much the fashion of other French story-writers. He died in Paris.

Field, Eugene, 1850-1895. An American journalist; born in St. Louis, Mo.; by his poems and tales in the press he won a high reputation in the West, which before his death had become national. He died in Chicago.

Fielding, Henry, 1707-1754. An English novelist; born in Sharpham Park, Somersetshire, of the blood of the Hapsburgs. After ill success as playwright and lawyer he embarked upon a literary career, in which he won fame. He died in Lisbon.

Firdausi, or **Firdusi,** 935?-1020? A Persian poet. His true name was Abul Kasim Mansur. He is the greatest of Persian epic poets.

Fiske, John, 1842-1901. An American historian; born in Hartford, Conn.; was graduated at Harvard College in 1863, and in 1865 took his degree in law, but never practiced. He was for a while lecturer on philosophy at Harvard, and in 1872-1879 assistant librarian. He wrote "Outlines of Cosmic Philosophy," his principal work, in which he gives an exposition of the philosophy of natural evolution, and various other books, mostly dealing with American history. Died in Cambridge, Mass.

Fitzgerald, Edward, 1809-1883. An English poet; born in Bredfield House, near Suffolk, England. His father, John Purcell, assumed the name of Fitzgerald, which was his wife's family name. His writings are for the most part remodeled translations of poems in other languages; among them "The Rubaiyat of Omar Khayyam," a translation that won for Fitzgerald great celebrity, although at first published anonymously. He died in Merton, Norfolk, England.

Flaubert (*flo-bayr'*), **Gustav,** 1821-1880. A French novelist; born and died in Rouen, France.

Fletcher, John, 1570-1625. English dramatist, the son of a bishop of London; was left an orphan and in poverty; collaborated with Beaumont in the production of the plays published under their joint names: died of the plague.

Fontenelle (*day font-nel'*), **Bernard le Bovier de,** 1657-1757. A miscellaneous French writer, born at Rouen, a nephew of Corneille, whose life he wrote; became secretary and then president of the Academie des Sciences; died in his hundredth year; author of "Dialogues of the Dead," in imitation of Lucian, and "Conversations on the Plurality of Worlds."

Ford, Paul Leicester, 1865-1902. An American author; born in Brooklyn, N. Y. He was killed by his brother Malcolm, May 8, 1902. He wrote historical and biographical works as well as a number of novels.

Fox, John, 1516-1587. Martyrologist, born at Boston, Lincolnshire; his most famous work is his "Book of Martyrs," first published in Latin on the Continent, the noble English version appearing in 1563.

Frederic, Harold, 1856-1898. An American journalist and novelist; born in Utica, N. Y. He was for many years London correspondent of the New York *Times*. He died in London.

Freeman, Edward Augustus, 1823-1892. An English historian; born in Harborne, in Staffordshire. His first publication was a "History of Architecture," especially devoted to Gothic architecture. His architectural researches helped to turn his attention to history, but his earliest works were the product of his interest in contemporary questions. He was appointed Professor at Oxford, 1884. His contributions to the periodicals of his day were frequent and of great weight, and he was a fiery and unvarying champion of national freedom. He died in Alicante, in Spain.

Freytag (*fri-tahg*), **Gustav,** 1816-1895. A German author; born in Kreuzburg, Prussia. Among his works outside of the drama may be mentioned "Ancestors," a cycle of six stories portraying the German civilization from the beginning of historic times; and "Charlemagne." He died in Wiesbaden, Germany.

Froissart (*frois'ar*), **Jean,** 1337-1410? A French chronicler; born in Valenciennes, in Hainault. He began at twenty to write the history of the wars of the time, and made several journeys to examine the theater of the events he was about to relate. His chronicles form a work of permanent value, because of their accurate and impartial account of important events of the 14th century. They narrate events connected with France, England, Scotland, Spain, Brittany, etc. He is said to have died in poverty at Chimay.

Froude, James Anthony, 1813-1894. An English historian; born in Totness, Devonshire, England. In the beginning of the Tractarian controversy he was a close friend of Newman, and was a contributor to the "Lives of the English Saints." He took orders in the Anglican Church. He has written several standard historical works. He was the successor of Edward A. Freeman in the professorship of Modern History at Oxford.

Fuller, Sarah Margaret, Countess d'Ossoli, 1810-1850. Am. authoress.

Gaboriau (*ga-bo-re-o'*), **Emile,** 1835-1873. A French writer of detective stories. His early years were a succession of vicissitudes; the army, the law, and even the Church, were in turn the objects of his inconstant attentions till at last he wrote his way to fame and fortune in 1866. He died in Paris.

Garland, Hamlin, 1860- . . . . An American story writer; born in La Crosse, Wis.

Gaskell, Elizabeth Cleghorn, 1810-1865. An English author; born in Chelsea, London, England. She married in 1832 the Rev. William Gaskell, a Unitarian clergyman, then recently appointed minister of Cross Street Chapel, Manchester, and she died in Alton, Hampshire.

Gautier (*go-te-ay'*), **Theophile,** 1811-1872. A French poet and prose writer. He applied himself at first, but without much success, to painting; and then turned to literature. Merimee alone contests with him the palm as the prince of short-story writers. He was drawn early to feuilleton writing, and for more than thirty years contributed to the Paris newspapers criticisms on the theater and the salon. He died in Paris.

Gay, John, 1685-1732. An English poet; born near Barnstaple, Devonshire, England. He died in London.

Gellert, Christian Furchtegott, 1715-1769. A German poet; born in Saxony. After spending some years in teaching, he received a professorship at Leipsic, where he lectured on poetry, eloquence, and morals. Gellert came to occupy this position partly on account of his writings, but more on account of his personal character. He died in Leipsic.

Gibbon, Edward, 1737-1794. An English historian; born in Putney; studied at Westminster School, Magdalen College, Oxford, and Lausanne. In 1763 he went to Italy; and while sitting amid the ruins of the Capitol at Rome, he conceived the idea of writing the history of the decline and fall of that city. In the meantime he joined M. Deyvurdun, a Swiss scholar, in publishing a journal called "Literary Memoirs of Great Britain," which met with no success. In 1770 he began his celebrated history of the "Decline and Fall of the Roman Empire," He died in London.

Gifford, William, 1757-1826. An English man of letters; born in Ashburton, Devonshire; wrote a celebrated satire "The Baviad," and two years later "The Mæviad"; the work of translation, and the editing of Elizabethan poets occupied him till 1809, when he became the first editor of the *Quarterly Review*.

Gilbert, William Schwenck, 1836- . . . . Barrister, notable as a play writer and as the author of the librettos of a series of well known popular comic operas set to music by Sir Arthur Sullivan.

Gillies, John, 1747-1836. A Scotch historian; born in Brechin, Forfarshire; died in Clapham.

Goethe (*gur'teh*), **Johann Wolfgang von,** 1749-1832. Ger. poet and author, dramatist, scientist, and statesman; the greatest man, it is alleged, the world has seen since Shakespeare left it; born in Frankfort-on-the-Main; died in the small duchy of Weimar; was the son of an imperial chancellor and of Elizabeth Textor, daughter of the chief magistrate of the city, a woman of bright intelligence, who was only eighteen at the time of his birth. Spiritually and bodily he was the most perfectly formed, symmetrically proportioned, justly balanced, and completely cultivated man perhaps that ever lived, whose priceless value to the world lies in the harmony of his philosophy and life; to smaller people this union of the utmost scientific skepticism and the highest spiritual faith and worth in one person appears entirely and absolutely antagonistic, His life lies latent in his successive works, above all in "Goetz," in "Werter," in "Faust," and in "Meister." Of the last of the four works named, Carlyle, who has done more than anyone else yet to bring Goethe near us, once said, "There are some ten pages of that book that, if ambition had been my object, I would rather have written than all the literature of my time."

Goldsmith, Oliver, 1728-1774. English man of letters; born at Pallas or Pallasmore, Ireland, and celebrated in English literature as the author of the "Vicar of Wakefield"; produced poems, "The Traveller" and "The Deserted Village," besides comedies, such as "She Stoops to Conquer"; lived extravagantly, and died in debt; wrote histories of Greece and Rome, and "Animated Nature"; was a charming writer.

Goodrich, Samuel Griswold. 1793-1860. Pseudonym Peter Parley; an American author; born in Ridgefield, Conn. His "Peter Parley" books won great popularity, evidenced by the fact that the pen-name was attached to more than seventy spurious volumes. He died in New York city.

Gosse, Edmund, 1849- . . . . Poet, essayist, and critic; born in London; author of "History of Eighteenth Century Literature," a collection of lyrics, and a series of monographs, in particular, "Life of Gray."

Grant, Robert, 1852- . . . . An American author; born in Boston, Mass.; was graduated from Harvard in 1873 and the Harvard Law School in 1879. Since 1893 he has been a judge of probate and insolvency for Suffolk county, Mass.

Gray, Thomas, 1716-1771. English poet; born in Cornhill, London; produced in 1747 "Ode on a Distant Prospect of Eton College," and in 1750 his well known "Elegy written in a Country Churchyard"; these were followed by the "Pindaric Odes," the "Progress of Poesy," and "The Bard," which was finished in 1757; in 1760 he was presented by the Duke of Grafton with the professorship of Modern History in Cambridge, a sinecure office with £400 a year.

Green, John Richard, 1837-1883. Historian; born at Oxford; in 1874 he published his "Short History of the English People," which was speedily adopted in schools, and was accepted at large as one of the ablest summaries of the history of the country; the welcome with which this small work was received induced the author to essay a larger, which he accordingly by and by published in four volumes; this was followed by "The Making of England" and "The Conquest of England," the latter being published after his decease.

Green, Thomas Hill, 1838-1882. Philosopher; born in Yorkshire; studied at Balliol College, Oxford; was elected a Fellow and became eventually Whyte's professor of Moral Philosophy; his philosophy had a Kantian root, developed to a certain extent on the lines of Hegel; he was a great moral force in Oxford; his views on the purely spiritual nature and derivation of the Christian religion have, since his death, attracted attention, and are regarded with some anxiety by those whose faith requires a historical basis.

Grillparzer, Franz, 1791-1872. Popular Austrian dramatist; born at Vienna; studied law and then entered the civil service, in which he remained from 1813 to 1856; his first notable drama was the tragedy "Die Ahnfrau," the *motif* of which is an extreme fatalism; "Sappho," "Das goldene Vliess," and many others followed, all of which are marked by dramatic power and lyric grace; he stands in the front rank of Austrian poets.

Grimm, Jakob Ludwig, 1785-1863. A German philologist and literary historian. The labors of Grimm are of unrivaled importance in the broad field of German literary antiquities. The constant aim of his investigations was to trace the spiritual life of the German people as revealed in their laws, customs, faiths, and poetry. His "Deutsche Grammatik" is perhaps the greatest philological work of the age and may be said to have laid the foundation of the historical investigation of language. This work, as well as the great "Deutsches Worterbuch," commenced in 1852 in conjunction with his brother Wilhelm, he did not live to complete. He died in Berlin.

Grote, George, 1794-1871. An English historian. In 1832 he was elected a member of Parliament for the city of London, and his subsequent parliamentary career, until his retirement in 1841, was principally devoted to the advocacy of vote by ballot. In 1846 appeared the first two volumes of his "History of Greece." The remaining ten volumes followed in rapid succession, the final volume being published in 1856. The work terminates with the death of Alexander the Great.

Guizot (*gē-zō'*) **Francois Pierre Guillaume,** 1787-1874. A French historian. He was Minister of the Interior, Ambassador to Great Britain, and Minister of Foreign Affairs. After the fall of Louis Philippe, Guizot escaped and fled to England. Henceforth he practically retired from public life. Among his numerous works may be mentioned: "History of Civilization in France;" "General History of Civilization in Europe;" and "History of the English Revolution." He died in Val-Richer, France.

Haggard, Henry Rider, 1856- . . . . An English

novelist. He was a barrister by profession. At the age of nineteen he accompanied Sir H. Bulwer as secretary to Natal, and served on the staff of Theophilus Shepstone during his mission to the Transvaal. He wrote several very popular novels bearing on South Africa.

Hale, Edward Everett, 1822- . . . An American author and Unitarian clergyman; born in Boston, Mass. He was graduated at Harvard College and was called to the South Congregational (Unitarian) Church, Boston. During his ministerial career he was active in social, educational, and philanthropic enterprises; organized the Harry Wadsworth Club, which has numerous branches in the United States and Europe, and the Look-up Legion among American Sunday-schools; edited "Original Documents from the State Paper Office, London, and the British Museum, illustrating the History of Sir W. Raleigh's First American Colony and the Colony of Jamestown," and many historical works, pamphlets, and papers; contributed largely to the periodical press, and attained wide popularity as a lecturer. To the rising generation he is best known as a writer of charming fiction and history.

Halevy, Ludovic, 1834- . . . . A French dramatist; born in Paris, France. In 1861 he became secretary to the Corps Legislatif. He first made himself known as the writer of the librettos to Offenbach's burlesques (partly in collaboration with Meilhac). He wrote besides a large number of vaudevilles and comedies, and also some novels. Halevy was admitted to the Academy in 1886.

Hallam, Henry, 1777-1859. An English historian; born in Windsor, England. His "View of the State of Europe during the Middle Ages" was the first great result of his studies and researches. His masterly work on the "Constitutional History of England" was given to the world in 1827. The next great work of Hallam was his "Introduction to the Literature of Europe in the 15th, 16th, and 17th Centuries." He died in Penshurst, Kent, England.

Halleck, Fitz-Greene, 1790-1867. An American poet; born in Guilford, Conn. By his mother he was descended from John Eliot, "the apostle of the Indians." He became a clerk in a bank in New York in 1811, and in 1832 the private secretary of John Jacob Astor; in 1849 he retired, on an annuity of $200 left him by Astor, to his native town, where he spent the remainder of his days. From his boyhood Halleck wrote verses, and in 1819 he contributed, with Joseph Rodman Drake, a series of humorous satirical papers in verse to the New York *Evening Post*. In the same year he published his longest poem, "Fanny," a satire on the literature, fashions, and politics of the time. His complete "Poetical Writings" was published in 1869.

Hardy, Thomas, 1840- . . . . An English novelist; born in Dorset, England. He was brought up as an architect, and practiced some time at Dorchester, next prosecuted his studies in design at London, gaining professional distinction. His intention was now to become an art critic, but the experiment of a not wholly unsuccessful work of fiction shaped his destiny otherwise. He has written many popular books.

Harris, Joel Chandler, 1848- . . . . An American journalist and story writer; born in Eatonton, Ga. He had a thorough familiarity with the negro of the post-bellum period, and while editing an Atlanta paper, he produced for it the series of "Uncle Remus" sketches and songs which immediately made him known. In a more serious vein is his biography of the lamented Henry W. Grady, a work of genuine power.

Harte, Francis Bret, 1839-1902. An American novelist and poet; born in Albany, N. Y. He went to California in 1854, and figured as a coal dealer, a teacher, and a typesetter on the *Golden Era*, in which appeared some of his earliest literary efforts. He next became editor of the *Californian*, and in 1864 secretary of the United States Mint at San Francisco. In 1868 he became editor of the *Overland Monthly*, in which appeared, in 1869, the humorous poem of "The Heathen Chinee." In 1878 he became United States consul at Crefeld, whence he was transferred to Glasgow in 1880, and remained there till 1885. Among his best known works are "The Luck of Roaring Camp," and "The Outcasts of Poker Flat." During the last twenty-four years of his life Mr. Harte resided abroad. He died near Aldershot, England.

Hawkins, Anthony Hope, 1863- . . . . An English novelist; writing under the name "Anthony Hope"; born in London. He was admitted to the bar in 1887. Among his best known works are: "A Man of Mark" and "The Prisoner of Zenda."

Hawthorne, Julian, 1846- . . . . An American novelist and journalist, son of Nathaniel; born in Boston. On leaving Harvard University he studied civil engineering in Dresden, but took to authorship. His success was not rapid, but popular favor has been accorded to his novels. As a journalist he has traveled widely in prosecution of his work, and has written vivid descriptions of some famous trials.

Hawthorne, Nathaniel, 1804-1864. American novelist; born at Salem, Massachusetts; his early ambition was to be a literary man, and "Twice-told Tales" was the first production by which he won distinction, after the publication of which he spent some months at Brook Farm, leaving which he married and took up house at Concord; from 1848 to 1850 he held a State appointment, and in his leisure hours wrote his "Scarlet Letter," which appeared in the latter year, and established his fame as a master of literature; this was followed by "The House of the Seven Gables," "The Snow Image," "The Blithedale Romance," and by and by "The Marble Faun," and "Our Old Home."

Hay, John, 1838- . . . . An American statesman and writer; born in Salem, Ind. He was graduated from Brown University, and settled in Illinois as a lawyer, but went to Washington in 1861 as one of Lincoln's private secretaries, acting also as his aide-de-camp. He served under Generals Hunter and Gillmore with the rank of major and assistant adjutant-general. He was subsequently in the United States diplomatic service, stationed at Paris, Vienna, and Madrid. In 1897 he was made ambassador to England, and in 1898 Secretary of State. His literary reputation rests upon "Pike County Ballads"; "Castilian Days," a volume of travel; and "Life of Abraham Lincoln" (with J. G. Nicolay). As Secretary of State Mr. Hay has gained a standing equal to that of the most eminent men who have held that high office. In coolness, foresight, and statesmanlike appreciation of current and coming events he has no superior among living diplomats.

Hayne, Paul Hamilton, 1830-1886. An American poet; born in Charleston, S. C. At first a lawyer, he turned to journalism, and in 1855 his maiden volume of verse appeared. He served through the war, retired from the field in poverty, and wrote poetry. His productions mark him easily first among Southern poets. He died in Augusta, Ga.

Hazlitt, William, 1778-1830. An English critic; born in Maidstone, Kent, England. In 1805 he began his literary career with an essay, "On the Principles of Human Action." This was the germ of a long and successful career, during which he gave to the world "Lectures on the Literature of the Elizabethan Age"; "Lectures on the English Poets," etc.

Headley, Joel Tyler, 1813-1897. An American prose writer; born in Walton, N. Y. Graduating from Union College in 1846, he became assistant editor of the New York *Tribune*. His writings had great currency in their day, and contain much valuable information about early American history.

Heine, Heinrich, 1799-1856. A German poet and author; born of Jewish parents in Dusseldorf. He studied law at Bonn, Berlin, and Gottingen; took his degree at the last mentioned place, and in 1825 embraced Christianity. In 1830 he settled in Paris, supported himself by his literary labors, and dwelt there till his death. From 1837 to the overthrow of Louis Philippe in 1848 he enjoyed a pension of $960 from the French government. As a poet Heine is remarkable for the simplicity and pathos of many of his lyric pieces. During the later years of his life he suffered great agony from a spinal complaint which confined him almost constantly to bed.

Hemans, Felicia Dorothea, *nee* Browne, 1791-1835. Poetess, born in Liverpool; her marriage was an unhappy one, and after the birth of five children ended in permanent separation; she was the authoress of a number of works, the best of her productions being lyrics.

Herbert, George, 1593-1633. Poet, born in Montgomery Castle, Wales; failing in preferment at court, took holy orders and became rector of Bemerton, Wiltshire, a post he lived only two years to hold; was the author of a Christian poem entitled "The Temple"; held in high regard by people of the devout and reverently contemplative spirit of the author.

Herder, Johann Gottfried von, 1744-1803. A German author. From 1764 to 1769 he was an assistant teacher at the cathedral school of Riga, with which office that of a preacher was connected, and it was during this period that he published his "Fragments on German Literature." His greatest work is his "Ideas on the Philosophy of the History of Man."

Herod'otus, 484-408 B. C. The "Father of History," born at Halicarnassus, in Caria; traveled over Asia Minor, Egypt, and Syria as far as Babylon, and in his old age recorded with due fidelity the fruits of his observations and inquiries.

Herrick, Robert, 1591-1674. A Caroline poet, born in London, of good family; was incumbent of Dean Prior in Devonshire; author of the "Hesperides."

Hesiod, fl. 800 B. C. One of the earliest Greek poets; born in Ascra, Bœotia. His "Theogony," being an attempt to present a systematic view of the origin and powers of the gods, and of the order of nature, is of great importance for the history of the religion of the Greeks.

Higginson, Thomas Wentworth, 1823- . . . . An American author; born in Cambridge, Mass.; was graduated at Harvard College in 1841; served in the Civil War as captain in the 51st Massachusetts Volunteer Militia, colonel of the first South Carolina Union Volunteers, and colonel of the 33d United States Colored Infantry.

Hildreth, Richard, 1807-1865. An American historian; born in Deerfield, Mass. He first became known as a miscellaneous prose writer and political journalist. The "History of the United States" is his greatest work, covering the period from the discovery of America to the end of President Monroe's first administration. He went to Italy in 1861 as United States consul, and died in Florence.

Hogg, James, 1770-1835. A Scotch poet; born in Selkirkshire in 1770. After receiving a very scanty education he began to earn his bread by daily labor as a shepherd. His early rhymings brought him under the notice of Sir Walter Scott. The appearance of "The Queen's Wake" in 1813, with its charming ballad of Kilmeny, established Hogg's reputation as a poet.

Holberg, Ludwig, 1684-1754. A Danish poet. His works may be divided into four classes—poems, stage pieces, philosophical treatises, and historical works. His poems are chiefly of a satirical nature. He died in Copenhagen.

Holland, Josiah Gilbert, 1819-1881. An American author; born in Belchertown, Mass. He was graduated at the Berkshire Medical College, at Pittsfield, in 1844. He soon abandoned his profession, however, and became assistant editor of the Springfield *Republican*, of which he was part proprietor also from 1851 to 1866. In 1870, with Roswell Smith and the Scribners, he founded *Scribner's Monthly*, which he conducted successfully till his death.

Holmes, Oliver Wendell, 1809-1894. A celebrated American author, son of a Congregational minister; graduated in arts and medicine at Harvard; became professor of Anatomy and Physiology at Dartmouth College, but resigned and settled in Boston as a general practitioner. In 1847 he was elected to the chair of Anatomy in Harvard, a position he held till his resignation in 1882; a successful professor, it is as an essayist, novelist, and poet that he is remembered; the appearance of "The Autocrat of the Breakfast-Table," with its quaint humor, fresh thought, and charming egotism took literary America by storm; the "Professor" and the "Poet at the Breakfast-Table" followed in after years, and remain his most widely popular works; "Elsie Venner," a novel dealing with the problem of heredity, "The Guardian Angel," "Songs of Many Seasons," "Memoirs of Motley and of Emerson," are some of his many works, all of which have the impress of his bright, engaging personality.

Homer, fl. about 1000 B. C. The great epic poet of Greece, and the greatest of all time; author of the "Iliad" and the "Odyssey"; is said, when old and blind, to have wandered from city to city rehearsing his verses; it is only modern criticism that has called in question his existence, and has ventured to argue that the poems ascribed to him are a mere congeries of compositions of the early fabulous age of Greece, but the unity of the plan and the simplicity of the style of the poems go to condemn this theory.

Hood, Thomas, 1798-1845. An English poet and humorist; born in London. From 1829 to 1837 he conducted his "Comic Annual." At the same time his pen was employed on other subjects. It was during his last illness that he contributed to *Punch* "The Song of a Shirt," "The Bridge of Sighs," and "The Lay of a Laborer." Hood is unrivaled as a punster, and he possesses a singular power of combining the humorous with the pathetic.

Horace (Quintus Horatius Flaccus), 65-8 B. C. A Latin lyric poet, whom poverty drove to poetry. The talent which he had displayed procured him the friendship of two eminent poets, Virgil and Varius, and to them he was indebted for his first acquaintance with Mæcenas, a refined man of the world. Nine months after, Mæcenas received Horace into the circle of his intimate friends and after some years presented him with the Sabine estate which Horace so often mentions in his poems. It was sufficient to maintain him in ease and comfort during the remainder of his life.

Horne, Richard Henry (or Richard Hengist Horne, as he called himself after his return from Australia), 1803-1884. An English poet and miscellaneous author. He joined the Mexican navy and served through the war against Spain. On the conclusion of the war he was prostrated for a time by yellow fever, and after his recovery he traveled in the United States. In 1828 he began his literary career, writing tragedies, poems, etc.

Howells, William Dean, 1837- . . . . An American author; born in Martins Ferry, O. He learned the printers' trade with his father; was afterward assistant editor on the Ohio *State Journal*; published a life of Abraham Lincoln. From 1861 to 1865 he resided in Venice as United States consul, occupying his leisure in mastering Italian and French. Soon after his return appeared a series of papers under the title "Venetian Life" followed by a similar volume "Italian Journeys." After his return to the United States he was called to the editorial staff of the New York *Tribune*, and also became a regular contributor to the *Nation*. He was assistant editor of the *Atlantic Monthly* during the period 1866-1872, and editor-in-chief from 1872 till his resignation in 1881. From 1886-1892 he conducted the critical department of *Harper's Monthly* called "The Editor's Study."

Hughes, Thomas, 1823-1896. An English judge, author, and philanthropist; born in Uffington, Berkshire, where his grandfather was vicar. He represented Lambeth in the House of Commons from 1865 to 1868 as an advanced Liberal, and during the six years 1868–1874 he sat for Frome. He was deeply interested in the well-being of the working classes, and devoted much of his time to the support of the co-operative movement and other socialist schemes of a similar kind. As an author, Thomas Hughes is doubtless best known by his first work, "Tom Brown's School Days, by an Old Boy," published in 1856, which has gone through many editions and been translated into several languages. He died in Brighton.

Hugo, Vicomte Victor Marie, 1802-1885. A distinguished French poet, politician, and man of letters; born in Besancon, France. His father was a colonel in the French army. He received a classical education in a religious house, and, in 1822, brought out the first volume of his "Odes and Ballads." He reflected bitterly in subsequent works on the classical style of French dramatic literature. Shortly after the revolution of July, 1830, his "Marion de Lorme," which had been suppressed by the censorship under the Restoration, was performed with success. "The King Amuses Himself," was also performed at the Theatre Francais in January, 1832, but was indicted by the government the day after. Hugo, who published afterward a number of dramatic pieces of various merit, was, after much opposition, admitted into the Academy in 1841, and was created a peer of France by Louis Philippe. In 1849 he was chosen president of the Peace Congress of which he had been a leading member. On the coup d'etat of December 2, 1851, Hugo, then a member of the legislative assembly, was among those deputies who vainly attempted to assert the rights of the assembly and to propose the constitution. His conduct led to his proscription. He took refuge in the island of Jersey, and subsequently in that of Guernsey, having steadfastly refused to avail himself of the general amnesties issued in 1859 and in 1869. He wrote much after he had left France. His very trenchant satire, "Napoleon the Little," appeared at Brussels in 1852, and was rigorously suppressed in France, into which country it had been smuggled. On the fall of the empire in 1870 he returned to France, was elected to the National Assembly, but soon resigned and repaired to Brussels, whence he was expelled by the government on account of the violence of his political writings and his sympathy with the Communists. Returning to Paris, he was elected a senator for six years. He died in Paris and was buried in the Pantheon.

Hume, David, 1711-1776. Scotch historian and philosopher; born in Edinburgh, Scotland. In 1746 he became secretary to General St. Clair, whom he accompanied to the courts of Vienna and Turin. In 1752 appeared at Edinburgh his "Inquiry Concerning the Principles of Morals," which of all his writings is considered the best. In 1751 he published the first volume of his "History of England," which he did not complete till 1761. The work acquired considerable celebrity, and the author gained largely by its popularity, for, besides the profits it brought him, he obtained a pension through Lord Bute. He became under-secretary of state in 1767. He died in Edinburgh.

Hunt, James Henry Leigh, 1784-1859. An English poet and essayist. He was the personal friend of Byron, Shelley, Hazlitt, Lamb, and Coleridge. The "Story of Rimini" is his longest and perhaps his best known poem.

Ibsen, Henrik, 1828- . . . . A Norwegian novelist and dramatist; born in Skien, Norway. His youth was passed in extreme poverty. He made several unsuccessful literary attempts; in 1851, was appointed, by Ole Bull, director of the National Theater at Bergen. His attention was thus turned permanently to dramatic writing. In 1859 he became artistic director of the Norwegian Theater at Christiania. His plays are much admired for their discussion of social matters.

Ingelow, Jean, 1820-1897. An English poet and story writer. Her first published work appeared anonymously in 1850, but not till the publication of "Poems" in 1863 did Miss Ingelow become famous. This volume won the enthusiastic praise of critics and the instant approval of the public and has passed through many editions. She wrote a great many stories and novels. Miss Ingelow lived in London, engaged in benevolent and charitable works, and died in Kensington.

Irving, Washington, 1783-1859. An American author; born in New York, where his father had emigrated from Scotland before the Revolution. He was originally educated for the legal profession and in 1806 was called to the New York bar, but his tastes ere all in the direction of literature, in which field he made his first appearance by the publication, in 1802, of the "Letters of Jonathan Oldstyle," in the New York *Morning Chronicle;* in December 1809, appeared his celebrated "History of New York, by Diedrich Knickerbocker." During the war with Great Britain in 1812-1815 he edited the *Analectic Magazine* in Philadelphia, and acted also for a time as aide-de-camp and military secretary to the governor of the state of New York. In May, 1815, he embarked for England, where he commenced in 1818 the series of papers entitled "The Sketch-book," which were transmitted for publication to New York. Up to 1832 Mr. Irving continued to reside in Europe. During this period were composed some of his most famed literary works. In the spring of 1832 he returned t New York. In 1842 he became United States minister to Spain, and continued in this office till 1846, when he returned home. He died in "Sunnyside," N. Y.

Jackson, Helen Maria Fiske Hunt, 1831-1885. An American author; born in Amherst, Mass.; received an academic education; went with her husband to Colorado Springs, Colorado; became actively interested in the treatment of the Indians by the government, and strove to better their condition; was appointed a special commissioner to investigate the condition of the Mission Indians of California, in 1883, and studied the history of the early Spanish missions. She died in San Francisco, Cal.

James, George Payne Rainsford, 1801-1860. An English novelist; born in London, England. While still very young he manifested a considerable turn for literary composition, and produced, in 1822, a "Life of Edward the Black Prince." Some years afterward he composed his first novel. Its success determined him toward fiction, and a series of novels, above sixty in number, followed from his pen in rapid succession, besides several historical and other works. Latterly he accepted the office of British consul, first at Richmond, Va., and afterward at Venice, where he died.

James, Henry, 1843- . . . . An American writer; born in New York. He was educated in France and Switzerland and at Harvard Law School. Since 1869 he has made his home in England. He is a popular and prolific writer on various subjects.

Jerrold, Douglas, 1803-1857. An English humorist and dramatist. After being for a short time a midshipman, he was bound as an apprentice to a printer in London. He wrote about forty plays.

Jewett, Sarah Orne, 1849- . . . . An American writer; born in South Berwick, Me. She received an academic education.

Johnson, Samuel, 1709-1784. One of the most distinguished English writers; born in Lichfield, England, where his father, Michael Johnson, was a bookseller; he gained distinction as the editor of various important publications. Among many great works the most useful to mankind was his "Dictionary." In 1759 he wrote his celebrated romance of "Rasselas, Prince of Abyssinia," which fine production he composed in the evenings of one week in order to defray the funeral expenses of his aged mother. At length in 1762 the Bute administration granted him a pension of $1,500 per annum, which he accepted after a short struggle against the reception of a favor from the house of Hanover. The concluding portion of Johnson's life was saddened by the loss of many old friends and by declining health. In 1783 he was greatly alarmed by a paralytic stroke and his health never wholly recovered from the shock. His remains were interred in Westminster Abbey with great solemnity. His statue has been placed in St. Paul's.

Jokai (*yo'koi*), **Maurus,** 1825- . . . . A Hungarian novelist; born in Komora. He studied law, but never practiced. During the Hungarian struggle f 1848 he was an active patriot, but after the restoration of Austrian rule he was obliged to abstain from political writing and thereafter devoted himself to fiction. He wrote almost three hundred volumes, including novels, dramas, poems, etc. In January, 1894, all Hungary united in celebrating the 50th anniversary of his first book, "Working Days." He married Rosa Laborfalvi, the great Hungarian actress.

Jonson, Ben, 1573-1637. Dramatist, born at Westminster, posthumous son of a clergyman of Scottish descent; was in his youth first a bricklayer, fterwards a soldier in the Netherlands, whence he returned about 1592; marri d a shrew, and became connected with the stage; he was on of the m st learned men of his age; and for f rty years the foremost, except Shakespeare, in the dramatic and literary world; killing his challenger i a duel nearly cost him his life in 1598; he was branded on the left thumb, imprisoned, and his goods confiscated; in prison he turned Catholic, but twelve years later reverted to Protestantism; for nine years after Shakespeare's death he produced no dramas; in 1619 he received a degree, M.A., from Oxf rd; the laureateship and a small pension from the king; in the new reign he turned again to dramatic work with sadly diminished power; he died in poverty, but was buried in Westminster Abbey; he wrote at least sixteen plays, among them "Every Man in his Humour," in which Shakespeare acted, "The Poetaster," the tragedy of "Sejanus," "The Silent Woman," a farcical comedy, and his most elaborate and masterly work, "The Alchemist."

Juvenal (Decius Junius Juvenalis), 38-120. A Roman poet and satirist; born probably in Aquinum, Campania.

Kalida'sa, fl. 600? A great Indian dramatist and poet, was author of "The Lost Ring" and "The Hero and the Nymph," translated by Sir William Jones, much praised by Goethe and Max Muller.

Karamsin', Nikolai Mikhailovitch, 1766-1826. A Russian historian; his first work was "Letters of a Russian Traveller," in six volumes, which gained him a high reputation; it was followed by his "History of Russia," in twelve volumes, for the materials of which he had access to the most authentic documents as imperial historiographer, an office to which he was appointed in 1803, and the work is in the highest repute.

Keats, John, 1796-1821. An English poet; born in London, England. Leigh Hunt lent the kindly sanction of his name to the first poems Keats published in 1817. In the next year he published "Endymion," a poetical romance, and in 1820, his last and best work, "Lamia," and other poems. He died in Rome. Shelley lamented his poet friend in the beautiful and well known "Adonais."

Keble, John, 1792-1866. An English poet; born in Fairford, Gloucestershire, England. Of his great work, "The Christian Year," over 500,000 copies in all have been sold, and from its profits the author built one of the most beautiful parish churches in England.

Kerner, Andreas, 1786-1862. A lyric poet of the Swabian school, born in Wurtemberg; studied and wrote on animal magnetism and spiritualism.

Key, Francis Scott, 1780-1843. An American poet; born in Frederick co., Md. He was a lawyer by profession. Being detained on one of the British ships during the bombardment of Fort McHenry, Sept. 14, 1814, he composed the words of "The Star-Spangled Banner." He died in Baltimore, Md.

Kingsley, Charles, 1819-1875. Canon of Westminster and chaplain to the Queen, born at Holne Vicarage, near Dartmoor; studied at Cambridge; became rector of Eversley, in Hampshire, in 1844; was the author, in 1848, of a drama entitled "The Saint's Tragedy," with St. Elizabeth of Hungary for heroine, which was followed successively by "Alton Locke," and "Yeast," chiefly in a Socialistic interest; "Hypatia," a brilliant book in the interest of early Christianity in Alexandria, and "Westward Ho!" a narrative of the rivalry of England with Spain in the days of Elizabeth, and besides other works, including "Two Years Ago," "Water Babies," and "Hereward the Wake," he was the author of the popular ballads of "The Three Fishers," "The Starlings," and "The Sands of Dee." His writings had a great influence on his contemporaries, particularly on young men.

Kipling, Rudyard, 1865- . . . . An English author; born in Bombay. He was educated in England, and in 1882 went to India and joined the staff of the *Civil and Military Gazette*, Lahore, for which paper his earlier tales were written. He depicts Anglo-Indian and military life. He has gained well-earned recognition as one of the leading authors of the age.

Kleist, Heinrich von, 1777-1811. German dramatist and poet, born at Frankfort-on-the-Oder; entered the army, but afterwards devoted himself to literature; slow recognition and other trials preyed on his mind, and he shot himself near Potsdam.

Klopstock, Friedrich Gottlieb, 1724-1803. German poet, born at Quedlinburg; distinguished as the author of an epic poem entitled the "Messiah," which is his chief work, his treatment of which invested him with a certain sanctity, and the publication of which did much to quicken and elevate the literary life of Germany.

Kotzebue, August Friedrich Ferdinand von, 1761-1819. A German dramatist; born in Weimar. Of about 200 tragedies, comedies, dramas, and farces, many of them very popular at the time of their production, the best known now is "Misanthropy and Repentance" reproduced in Paris as late as 1862, and famous in the United States and England in Sheridan's adaptation entitled "The Stranger." During much of his life he was in Russian service; and was once banished to Siberia by the Emperor Paul. He was assassinated in Germany as a Russian Spy, by a student, in Mannheim.

La Fontaine, Jean de, 1621-1695. One of the classics of French literature; born in Chateau-Thierry, Champagne, France. The last thirty-five years of his life were spent in Paris. The twelve books of his "Fables" were published in equal parts in 1668 and 1678. It is through them that La Fontaine is universally known. He was admitted to the French Academy in 1684, conjointly with his friend Boileau; died in Paris.

La Harpe, Jean Francois de, 1739-1803. French litterateur and critic, born in Paris; wrote dramas and eloges, but his best known work is his "Cours de Litterature" in twelve volumes, of little account except for its criticism of French literature.

Lamartine, Alphonse de, 1792-1869. An eminent French historian, poet, orator, and statesman.

Lamb, Charles, 1775-1834. A brilliant English essayist. In 1796 and 1797 some short poems by him appeared along with others by Coleridge, and in 1798 he published a volume of poems in conjunction with his friend Charles Lloyd. It met with little success. On the other hand his tale of "Rosamund Gray" was well received. Under the name of "Elia" a series of his essays has been frequently republished in a collected form since 1823; latterly along with "Last Essays of Elia," first published in 1833. Here, in a style ever happy and original, and with humor of the rarest and most pungent description, he has carried the short essay to a point of excellence perhaps never before attained. He died in Edmonton, England.

Landor, Walter Savage, 1775-1864. An English poet; born in Warwick, England. He was educated at Rugby and Oxford. During the Peninsular War, raising a troop of cavalry at his own cost, he fought for the Spanish cause till the restoration of Ferdinand VII. After his marriage, in 1811, he took up his abode in Florence, where he resided for several years, and where many of his works were written. He afterward returned to England and remained there for some years, absorbed in literary occupations, but, his eccentric temper constantly involving him in difficulties and litigation, he went back to Italy. His principal poetical works are "Hellenics," "Poems and Inscriptions," "Dry Sticks," and "Last Fruit of an Old Tree." His most important prose work is the "Imaginary Conversations of Literary Men and Statesmen," which appeared in five volumes between 1824 and 1829. He died in Florence, Italy.

Lang, Andrew, 1844- . . . . A British author; born in Selkirk. He was educated at Edinburgh Academy, St. Andrew's University, and Balliol College, Oxford, where he took a distinguished position. A versatile writer, he published several volumes of ballads and other light verse; "Ballads and Lyrics of Old France," "Ballades in Blue China," "Custom and Myth," etc. He has written a number of prose books, and is a frequent contributor to periodical literature.

Lanier, Sidney, 1843-1881. American poet. The poems "Corn," one of his earliest pieces, and "Clover," "The Bee," "The Dove," etc., show insight into nature. His poetic works were collected and published after his death. He wrote also several works in prose, mostly pertaining to literary criticism and mediæval history; among the former are "The Science of English Verse"; "The English Novel and the Principles of its Development." He died in Lynn, N. C.

Larcom, Lucy, 1826-1893. An American poetess; born in Beverly Farms, Mass. In her youth she was a factory girl in Lowell, Mass., and was a contributor to the *Lowell Offering*, a magazine conducted by the workers in the cotton mills of that city; was a student for a time at Monticello Seminary, Godfrey, Ill.; afterward taught school; but the greater part of her life was devoted to literary work. In 1866–1874 she was editor of *Our Young Folks*. She wrote stories and four or five volumes of poetry. Died in Boston, Mass.

Lecky, William Edward Hartpole, 1838-1903. Historian; born near Dublin, Ireland. He was educated at Trinity College, where he graduated B.A. in 1859 and M.A. in 1863. Already in 1861 he had published anonymously, "The Leaders of Public Opinion in Ireland," four brilliant essays on Swift, Flood, Grattan, and O'Connell. Later works were his learned, luminous, and dispassionate "History of the Rise and Influence of the Spirit of Rationalism in Europe," "History of European Morals from Augustus to Charlemagne," and "History of England in the Eighteenth Century."

Le Sage, Alain Rene, 1668-1747. A French novelist and dramatist; born in Sarzeau, near Vannes; died in Boulogne-sur-Mer.

Lessing, Gotthold Ephraim, 1729-1781. A German author, and founder of modern German literature; born at Kamenz, Saxony, son of the pastor there; sent to study theology at Leipzig, studied hard; conceived a passion for the stage; wrote plays and did criticisms; wrote an essay on Pope; took English authors as his models, revolted against those of France; made it his aim to inaugurate or rather revive a purely German literature, and produced examples regarded as classics to this day; his principal dramas, all conceived on the soil, are "Miss Sara Sampson," "Minna von Barnhelm," "Emilia Galotti," and "Nathan der Weise," and his principal prose works are his "Fables," and "Laocoon," a critical work on art still in high repute.

Lever, Charles James, 1806-1872. A novelist, born at Dublin; was by profession a physician; author of numerous Irish stories written in a rollicking humor, "Harry Lorrequer" and "Charles O'Malley" among the chief; was a contributor to and for some time editor of *Dublin University Magazine;* held ultimately various consular appointments abroad, and after that wrote with success in a more sober style.

Lie, Jonas Laurits Idemil, 1833- . . . . A Norwegian novelist, son of a lawyer. His novels give admirable realistic pictures of life in Norway, especially of the fisher-folk of the west coast. His popularity is due to the delicate poetry that lights up his books, to the healthy tone of his writing, his fidelity to nature, and his genial humor.

Livy (Titus Livius Patavinus), 59 B.C.-18 A.D. A Roman historian of the Augustan age; born in Patavium (now Padua), Italy. After passing the early portion of his life in his native town, he appears to have gone to Rome during the reign of Augustus, where his literary talents soon obtained for him the favor and patronage of the emperor. Having spent the greater part of his life in the metropolis, he returned in old age to the town of his birth, and there died.

Longfellow, Henry Wadsworth, 1807-1882. An eminent American poet, born in Maine. He was graduated from Bowdoin College, and after studying on the continent became professor of modern languages in Harvard University. He wrote "Hyperion," a romance in prose, and a succession of poems as well as lyrics, among the former: "Evangeline," "The Golden Legend," "Hiawatha," and "Miles Standish."

Lossing, Benson John, 1813-1891. An American historian; born in Beekman, Dutchess county, N. Y. He was a voluminous writer, and equally at home in historical, biographical, and critical composition; but his most useful and enduring works were his great "Pictorial Field-Books" of the Revolution, the War of 1812, the Civil War, etc. He died near Dover Plains, N. Y.

Loti, Pierre, 1850- . . . . A French poet and novelist; real name Louis Marie Julien Viaud; born in Rochefort. He was a French naval officer. In 1892 he was elected a member of the French Academy. His works include many novels.

Lowell, James Russell, 1818-1891. American essayist, poet, and diplomatist; born in Cambridge, Mass.; graduated at Harvard in 1838; studied law, but, acquiring extensive scholarship, devoted himself to literature; succeeding Longfellow in the chair of Modern Languages and Literature in Harvard in 1855, he visited Europe to study, returned as United States minister to Spain in 1877, was transferred to England 1880-1885; of his prose work "My Study Windows" and "Among my Books" are essays on literary subjects; "Fireside Travels" contain reminiscences, and his last work was a "Life of Hawthorne." He died at Cambridge in the house of his birth.

Lucan (Marcus Annæus Lucanus), 39-65. A Latin poet; nephew of Seneca; born in Cordova, Spain. His uncle introduced him to the court of Nero, and for a time he was a favorite; but Nero envied his poetic talents and banished him from court. He died in Rome.

Lucian, 120?-200? A Greek author, distinguished for his ingenuity and wit; born in Samosata, Syria.

Lucilius, 149-103 B.C. A Roman poet, the creator of that form of poetic satire which was wielded so brilliantly by his successors, Horace, Persius, and Juvenal; born in Suessa Aurunca, Campania; died in Naples.

Lucretius, Titus Carus, 96?-58 B.C. One of the greatest Roman poets; born in Rome.

Lytton, Edward Robert, Earl of, 1831-1891. Statesman and novelist, under the *nom de plume* of Owen Meredith; entered the diplomatic service at an early age, became viceroy of India in 1876, and subsequently ambassador at Paris.

Lytton, George Edward Bulwer, Lord, 1803-1873. Statesman and novelist, born in London; entered Parliament at the age of twenty-six; began his parliamentary career as a Whig, but became a Conservative and ranked in that party for the greater part of his life; "Pelham," published in 1828, was his first novel, and this was followed by a long list of others of endless variety, all indicative of the conspicuous ability of the author, and to the last giving no sign of decay in power; he was the author of plays as well as novels.

Macaulay, Thomas Babington, 1800-1859. An English historian; born at Rothley Temple, Leicestershire, England. He composed a compendium of universal history before he was eight years old; went to school at Shelford and entered Cambridge in 1818. In 1826 he was called to the bar, but not succeeding in law practice he soon abandoned it. In 1825 he contributed to the *Edinburgh Review* an essay on Milton. Its effect was electrical, and its reception created such a blaze of popularity for its author that he at once took his place as one of the great literary characters of his time. By the failure of the firm of which his father was a member he was left without a fortune. At this juncture he was offered a seat in the Commons by Lord Lansdowne, entering in 1830 to represent what was then known as a "pocket borough." In 1834 he accepted a seat on the Supreme Council of India. Here he drafted a penal code which became the basis of the criminal code of India. In 1838 he returned to England, and was at once sent to Parliament from Edinburgh. In 1839 he became War-Secretary in Lord Melbourne's cabinet. In 1846 he was appointed Postmaster-General in Lord John Russell's cabinet, where he had time to devote himself to his "History of England," which he had now begun. He soon retired entirely to private life in order to prosecute this work, refusing a seat in the cabinet in 1852. In 1848 the first two volumes of the "History" appeared. No other historical work ever met with so favorable reception or circulated so rapidly. It was translated into ten European languages. In 1857 he was raised to the peerage as Baron Macaulay of Rothley. He died in Kensington, London.

MacDonald, George, 1824- . . . . A Scotch novelist and poet; born in Huntley, Aberdeenshire, Scotland; educated at King's College and University, Aberdeen, and at Independent College, Highbury, London. He was originally an Independent minister, but became a lay member of the Church of England. He lectured in the United States.

Mackay, Charles, 1814-1889. A Scotch journalist; born in Perth; was editor of the *Illustrated London News*, and lectured in the United States. While special correspondent of the London *Times* in New York during the Civil War (strongly favoring the Southern cause), he unearthed the Fenian conspiracy. He died in London.

McCarthy, Justin, 1830- . . . . An Irish historian; born in Cork, Ireland. He was a Home-Rule member of Parliament after 1879, and, after the fall of Parnell, chairman of the Irish Parliamentary party. He spent three years in the United States, traveling, lecturing, and engaged in literary work, being (among other things), connected editorially with the New York *Independent*. He revisited the United States in 1886.

McMaster, John Bach, 1852- . . . . An American historian; born in Brooklyn, N. Y. He was a civil engineer, 1873-1877; instructor in civil engineering in Princeton College, 1877-1883; Professor of American History in the University of Pennsylvania after 1883. He wrote "Benjamin Franklin as a Man of Letters," "History of the People of the United States," etc. He holds a high place among American historians.

Malherbe (*mahl-erb'*), **Francois de,** 1555-1628. A French lyric poet and miscellaneous writer of great industry, born at Caen; is, from his correct though affected style, regarded as one of the reformers of the French literature.

Malthus, Thomas Robert, 1766-1834. An English political economist; born in Albury, Surrey, England; died in Bath.

Marlowe, Christopher, 1564-1593. English dramatist and poet, precursor of Shakespeare; son of a shoemaker at Canterbury; besides a love poem entitled "Hero and Leander," he was the author of seven plays, "Tamburlaine," in two parts, "Dr. Faustus," "The Jew of Malta," "Edward the Second," "The Massacre of Paris," and "Dido." He dealt solely in tragedy, and was too devoid of humor to attempt comedy; his life was a short one.

Marryat, Frederick, 1792-1848. Novelist, born at Westminster; "Frank Mildmay," the first of his novels, proving a success, he resolved to devote the rest of his life to literature; his novels were numerous; "Peter Simple" and Midshipman Easy" are reckoned the best.

Martial (Marcus Valerius Martialis), 43-104. A Latin epigrammatist; born in Bilbilis, Spain. His poems are interesting for their allusions to the persons and manners of the times, but abound with indelicacies. He died in Spain.

Martineau, Harriet, 1802-1876. An English reformer, sister of James Martineau; born in Norwich, England. She visited the United States in 1834, aiding the abolitionists, and traveled in Palestine and the East in 1846. She labored under the remarkable disability of being all her life without the senses of taste and smell, and at sixteen became very deaf. She died in Ambleside, Westmoreland, England.

Martineau, James, 1805-1902. Rationalistic theologian, born in Norwich, brother of the preceding; began life as an engineer, took to theology, and became a Unitarian minister; was at first a follower of Bentham and then a disciple of Kant; at one time a materialist, he became a theist, and a most zealous advocate of theistic beliefs from the Unitarian standpoint; he was a thinker of great power, and did much both to elevate and liberate the philosophy of religion; his views are liberal as well as profound, and he is extensively known as the author of the "Endeavours after the Christian Life," "Hours of thought on Sacred Things," "Seat of Authority in Religion," etc.

Matthews, (James) Brander, 1852- . . . . An American author; born in New Orleans, La. He was graduated at Columbia College in 1871, and from Columbia Law School in 1873, being admitted to the bar the same year. He soon turned to literature. In fiction steadily gained in reputation, his short studies of New York city life in the realistic vein being among the very best of their kind. Since 1892 he has been Professor of Literature in Columbia University.

Maupassant, Guy de, 1850-1893. A clever French romancer, born at Fecamp; served in the Franco-German War, and afterwards gave himself to letters, producing novels, stories, lyrics and plays; he died insane.

Meredith, George, 1828- . . . , An English poet and novelist; born in Hampshire, England. He was educated in Germany; studied law, but essayed a literary career with a volume of poems in 1851. As a writer both of poetry and prose he has been eminently popular.

Merimee, Prosper, 1803-1870. A French author; born in Paris, France. He devoted himself to the study of the law, and passed advocate; but he attached himself to literature in his twenty-second year, under the nom de plume of Joseph Lestrange, and published what was professedly a translation from the Spanish, though really original. Other works followed in rapid succession. After the revolution of July, 1830, he was appointed secretary to the ministers of commerce and marine. Died in Cannes, France.

Mickiewicz, Adam, 1798-1855. A Polish poet, born in Lithuania, of a noble family; in 1834 published his great poem "Sir Thaddeus," and in 1840 was appointed to a professorship of Polish literature in Paris: died at Constantinople.

Mill, James, 1773-1836. Economist, born in Logie Pert, near Montrose; the son of a shoemaker; bred for the Church; wrote a "History of British India," "Elements of Political Economy," and an "Analysis of the Human Mind."

Mill, John Stuart, 1806-1873. Logician and economist, born in London, son of the preceding; was educated pedantically by his father; published "System of Logic" and "Political Economy"; entered Parliament in 1865, but lost his seat in 1868, on which he retired to Avignon, where he died; he wrote the books on "Liberty," on "Utilitarianism," on "Comte" and on "Sir William Hamilton's Philosophy" and left an "Autobiography."

Miller, Cincinnatus Heine, 1841- . . . . Better known as Joaquin Miller. An American poet; born in Wabash district, Ind.; his checkered life included the extremes of being a California gold miner, editor of an Oregon newspaper, an Oregon lawyer and judge, a social lion in London, journalist at Washington, D. C., etc. His "Collected Poems" appeared in 1882.

Milman, Henry Hart, 1791-1865. Dean of St. Paul's; ecclesiastical historian; born in London; edited Gibbon's "Decline and Fall," wrote "History of the Jews," "History of Christianity to the Abolition of Paganism Under the Empire," and "History of Latin Christianity," all learned works; was professor of poetry at Oxford.

Milton, John, 1608-1675. An English poet; born in London, Eng. His father, a notary, was a man of cultivated mind, and gave him a careful education, which was continued at St. Paul's School and the University of Cambridge. He entered the latter in 1624, and quitted it in 1631, without taking his degree of M.A. His first polemical work was a treatise "Of Reformation." On the establishment of the Protectorate, Milton became secretary to Cromwell, and remained so till the death of the latter in 1658. Several years before that time he had become totally blind, deliberately and heroically preferring, as he says, the loss of his sight to the desertion of his duty. The last short intervals of sight allotted him were devoted to the composition of the "Defense." In 1665, being in his 57th year, he completed "Paradise Lost." His second epic was written with great quickness, perhaps altogether during a retirement of several months which he made to Chalfont in Buckinghamshire, on the breaking out of the plague in London in 1665. He died in London.

Mitchell, Donald Grant, 1822- . . . . Pseudonym Ik Marvel, an American author; born in Norwich, Conn.; was graduated at Yale in 1841; traveled in Europe; studied law in New York; in 1850 he published "The Reveries of a Bachelor," and in 1851 his "Dream Life." In 1853 he became United States consul at Venice, and has since written many popular books.

Mitchell, Silas Weir, 1829- . . . . A distinguished American physician, poet, and novelist; born in Philadelphia, Pa.; studied at the University of Pennsylvania; was graduated at Jefferson Medical College; practiced in Philadelphia and become prominent as a physiologist, especially as a neurologist and toxicologist.

Mitford, Mary Russell, 1786-1855. Authoress, born at Alresford, Hants; lived with her father, an extravagant physician, at Lyme Regis and London; she published poems in 1810-11-12, but, forced to earn a living, took to dramatic work; "Julian," "The Foscari," and "Rienzi" were successful if ephemeral tragedies; her best work was "Our Village," sketches of homely English life written with much care.

Moliere, 1622-1673. The professional name of **Jean Baptiste Poquelin,** a French dramatist; born in Paris, France. He is called by Voltaire the Father of French Comedy, and alone among French comic writers is classical. His works, it is said, have been more frequently republished than those of any other French author.

Mommsen, Theodor, 1817-1903. A German historian; born in Garding, Schleswig. He was professor of ancient history at Berlin, 1868; member of the Prussian House of Delegates. His great work is "Roman History." He wrote besides, "Roman Chronology down to Cæsar" and "History of Roman Courage." His historical work incorporates the results of vast learning in widely severed fields. He died at Charlottenburg.

Montaigne, Michel de, 1533-1592. A sceptico-speculative thinker and moralist; born in the Chateau of Montaigne, Perigord; his fame rests on his "Essays," in which he records his observations of mankind.

Montagu, Lady Mary Wortley, 1689?-1762. An English authoress; the eldest daughter of Evelyn, Duke of Kingston; born in Thoresby, Nottinghamshire, England. In 1712 she married Edward Wortley Montagu, whom she accompanied in 1716 on his embassy to Constantinople, from which place she wrote "Letters" to Pope, Addison, and other eminent literati of the time, which are very interesting and contain many curious facts respecting the manners of the Turks. She also first introduced the practice of inoculation into her native country. Her collected works have been published in six volumes; and her "Letters" certainly place her at the head of female epistolary writers in Great Britain. She died in England.

Montesquieu, Charles de Secondat, Baron de, 1689-1755. A famous French writer; born in the castle of La Brede, near Bordeaux, France. In 1716 he became president of the Parliament of Bordeaux. The publication of the "Persian Letters" first made him famous as an author. His greatest work is the "Spirit of Laws," which occupied him twenty years; it was published in 1748, and secured to him a very high place among writers on political science. He died in Paris.

Montgomery, Robert, 1807-1855. Author of "The Omnipresence of Deity" and "Satan"; born at Bath, son of a clown; passed undistinguished through Oxford, and was minister of Percy Street Chapel, London; all his many works are forgotten save the above, which live in Macaulay's famous review.

Moore, Thomas, 1779-1852. An Irish poet; born in Dublin, Ireland. He married an actress, Bessy Dyke. Author of "Lalla Rookh." He died near Devizes, England.

More, Hannah, 1745-1833. English authoress, born near Bristol; wrote dramas; a novel entitled "Cœlebs in Search of a Wife," and a tract, "The Shepherd of Salisbury Plain."

More, Sir Thomas, 1478-1535. Chancellor of England; born in London; the author of "Utopia," an imaginary commonwealth; succeeded Wolsey as Chancellor, but resigned the seals of office because he could not sanction the king's action in the matter of the divorce, and was committed to the Tower for refusing to take the oath of supremacy, whence, after twelve months, he was brought to trial and sentenced to be beheaded; he ascended the scaffold, and laid his head on the block in the spirit of a philosopher; was one of the wisest and best of men.

Morley, John, 1838- . . . . Politician and man of letters, born in Blackburn; is an advanced Liberal in both capacities; besides essays and journalistic work, has written biographies, particularly on men associated with politics and social movements, such as Voltaire, Rousseau, and Diderot, as well as Burke, and is editor of "English Men of Letters."

Morris, George Pope, 1802-1864. An American journalist; born in Philadelphia, Pa.; died in New York city.

Morris, William, 1834-1896. Poet, art-worker, and socialist; born in Walthamstow, near London; son and heir of a wealthy merchant; studied at Oxford, where he became the lifelong bosom friend of Burne-Jones; of an artistic temperament, he devoted his working hours to decorative art, in particular designing wall papers; produced in 1858 "The Defence of Guenevere and other Poems," in 1867 "The Life and Death of Jason," and from 1868 to 1870 his masterpiece, "The Earthly Paradise." Among other works he translated the "Æneid" and the "Odyssey," and gave a splendid rendering of some of the Norse legends.

Motley, John Lothrop, 1814-1877. An American historian; born in Dorchester, Mass.; was educated at Harvard University and Gottingen, Germany; entered political life as a member of the Massachusetts House of Representatives. He published, after ten years' labor and a journey to Europe, his great "History of the Rise of the Dutch Republic," in 1856, a work which was further developed in the "History of the United Netherlands." He was minister from the United States to Austria, and to Great Britain. He died in Dorchester, England.

Moulton, Louise Chandler, 1835- . . . . An American poetess; born in Pomfret, Conn. She married William U. Moulton, a Boston publisher, and published children's stories, novels, essays, and poems.

Mulock, Dinah Maria (Mrs. Craik), 1820-1887. English novelist; born at Stoke-upon-Trent; authoress of "John Halifax, Gentleman," and other novels.

Murfree, Mary Noailles, 1850- . . . . Pseudonym, Charles Egbert Craddock; an American novelist; born in Murfreesboro, Tenn. Her subjects deal largely with Tennessee.

Murger (*moor-zhay*), **Henri,** 1822-1861. French novelist and poet; born at Paris; is chiefly distinguished as the author of "Scenes de la Vie de Boheme," from his own experiences, and instinct with pathos and humor, sadness his predominant tone; wrote lyrics as well as novels and stories.

Musset (*moosay'*), **Alfred de,** 1810-1857. The premier poet of modern French literature; born in Paris of good parentage; achieved his first signal success with the dramas "Andre del Sarto" and "Les Caprices de Marianne"; in the same year began his famous *liaison* with George Sand, involving him in the ill-fated expedition to Venice, whence he returned in the spring of 1834 shattered in health and disillusioned. "Confessions d'un Enfant du Siecle" appeared in 1836; his writings are chiefly remarkable for the intense sincerity of feeling which animates them, and which finds its highest expression in his four great lyrical pieces, "Les Nuits;" of his prose works, "Le Fils du Titien," "Mademoiselle Mimi Pinson," and the "Confessions" are his best.

Napier, Sir William, 1785-1860. Brother of the conqueror of Sinde; served all through the Peninsular War, and wrote, besides the "Conquest of Sinde," the "History of the Peninsular War," a celebrated work, written with matchless graphic power.

Nepos, Cornelius, fl. time of Augustus. Roman historian; born at Pavia; was a contemporary and friend of Cicero; was the author of several historical works no longer extant, and the one still extant ascribed to him, entitled "De Viris Illustribus," is believed to be an abridgment of an earlier work by him.

Niebuhr (*nee'boor*), **Barthold Georg,** 1776-1830. Distinguished historian; born at Copenhagen; on the establishment of the University of Berlin in 1810, gave in connection with it a course of lectures on Roman history, by which he established his reputation as a historian.

Nordau, Max Simon, 1849- . . . . A German author; born in Pest, Hungary; followed various avocations, studying and practicing medicine, traveling and writing for the press till 1880, when he went to Paris, and has since devoted himself to literature. He wrote a number of books, of which the best known, perhaps, in the United States is "Degeneration." He is a conspicuous figure in the Zionist movement.

Nye, Edgar Wilson, 1850-1896. An American humorist; born in Shirley, Me.; settled in Wyoming Territory; studied law, and was admitted to the bar in 1876. Afterward he removed to New York city, and became famous as a humorous lecturer and writer under the pseudonym of "Bill Nye." He died near Asheville, N. C.

Oehlenschlaeger (*er'len-shlay-ger*), **Adam Gottlieb,** 1777-1850. The greatest dramatic poet of the Scandinavian North; born in Vesterbro, near Copenhagen, Denmark. He commenced his career on the stage, but abandoned the profession for literature, and finally became professor of æsthetics in his native city. Among his greatest works is "The Death of Balder." Died in Vesterbro.

Ohnet (*o-nay'*), **Georges,** 1848- . . . . French novelist; born in Paris; author of a series of novels of social interest, entitled "Les Batailles de la Vie."

Oliphant, Mrs. Margaret (*nee* Wilson), 1828-1897. English authoress; began her literary career as a novelist; her first success was the "Chronicles of Carlingford"; she wrote on history, biography, and criticism, the "Makers of Florence," "Makers of Venice," "Makers of Modern Rome," lives of Dante, Cervantes, and Edward Irving.

Omar Khayyam (*omar' khi-yahm'*), . . . 1123. A Persian poet, astronomer. and mathematician; born in Nishapur in Khorasan. His scientific works, which were of high value in their day, have been eclipsed by his "Rubaiyat," a collection of about 500 epigrams in praise of wine, love, and pleasure, and at the same time depressingly pessimistic. He died in Nishapur.

O'Reilly, John Boyle, 1844-1890. An Irish-American poet; born in Dowth Castle, County Meath, Ireland. In 1863 he enlisted in the 10th Hussars, in Ireland, for the avowed purpose of spreading revolutionary doctrines among the soldiers. For this he was arrested, tried for treason, and sent for twenty years' penal servitude in Australia. The following year (1869) he escaped to America, going first to New York and afterward to Boston. In the latter city he found work on *The Pilot*, of which he subsequently became editor and principal owner. He died in Hull, Mass.

Ovid (Publius Ovidius Naso), 34 B.C.-18 A.D. Roman poet of Augustan age; born at Salmo; was the author, among other works, of the "Amores," "Fasti," and the "Metamorphoses"; the friend of Horace and Virgil, and the favorite of Augustus.

Page, Thomas Nelson, 1853- . . . . An American novelist; born in Oakland, Va. He was educated at Washington and Lee University, and practiced law at Richmond, Va. His books are widely read.

Paine, Robert Treat, Jr., 1773-1811. An American poet; born in Taunton, Mass. During the greater part of his career he was engaged in various literary pursuits, though he was at one time in business, and later practiced law for a brief period. He will be best remembered as the author of two songs, "Rise, Columbia," and "Adams and Liberty." He died in Boston.

Paine, Thomas, 1737-1809. An American political writer; born in England. At the outbreak of the Revolutionary War he, in 1774, emigrated to the United States; gave an impulse to the Revolution by his famous pamphlet called "Common Sense," in which he advocated the policy of separation and independence. He went to Paris in 1789. In September, 1792, he was elected a member of the French National Convention, acted with the Girondists, narrowly escaped death in the Reign of Terror, and brought out in 1795 his celebrated work entitled, "The Age of Reason." He returned to the United States in 1802; died in New York.

Parkman, Francis, 1823-1893. An American historian; born in Boston, Mass.; was graduated at Harvard in 1844; studied law for two years; then traveled in Europe; and returned to explore the Rocky mountains. The hardships he endured among the Dakota Indians seriously injured his health, yet in spite of this and defective sight Parkman worked his way to recognition as a historical writer on the period of rise and fall of the French dominion in America. He died in Boston, Mass.

Parton, James, 1822-1861. An American writer; born in Canterbury, England. He wrote many valuable biographies. He died in Newburyport, Mass.

Paulding, James Kirke, 1779-1860. An American author; born in Dutchess county, N. Y. He early showed a tendency to literature. In 1837 Van Buren appointed him Secretary of the Navy. Four years later he retired to a country residence at Hyde Park, N. Y., where he died.

Payne, John Howard, 1792-1852. An American dramatist; born in New York. At the age of sixteen he made his first appearance at the Park Theater. He also played in England and Ireland, a part of the time with Miss O'Neill. In 1851 was appointed United States consul to Tunis. He wrote, translated, and adapted over sixty plays, but is most famous as the author of "Home, Sweet Home," originally in the opera of "Clare." He died in Tunis.

Pemberton, Max, 1863- . . . . An English novelist; born in Birmingham, England. He was a contributor to *Vanity Fair*, and editor of *Chums*, a boys' paper, and in charge of *Cassell's Magazine*. He has published a number of stories of adventures.

Percival, James Gates, 1795-1856. American poet and geologist; born at Kensington, Conn.; he was for a few months professor of chemistry at West Point, but retired and gave himself to literature and geology; his scientific works are valuable; "Prometheus and Clio," appeared in 1822, "Dream of a Day," in 1843; he died at Hazel Green, Wisconsin.

Perrault (*pay-ro'*), **Charles,** 1628-1703. French man of letters; born in Paris; distinguished as the author of inimitable fairy tales, which have immortalized his name, as "Puss in Boots," "Cinderella," "Bluebeard," etc.

Persius, 34-62. Roman satirist; born in Etruria; wrote six short satires in the purity of a white-souled manhood, of much native vigor, though not equal to those of Horace and Juvenal, and that have commanded the regard of all scholars down to the present time.

Petrarch, Francesco, 1304-1374. Famous Italian lyric poet; born at Arezzo, in Tuscany; spent his youth in Avignon; intended for the profession of law, devoted his time to the study of Cicero and Virgil; met Laura a lady of surpassing beauty, in the church of St. Clare there in 1327, conceived a passion for her which she could not return, and wrote sonnets in praise of her, which immortalized both himself and her. His fame rests on his lyrics.

Pidgin, Charles Felton, 1844- . . . . An American statistician; born in Roxbury, Mass. He invented many machines for the mechanical tabulation of statistics, among them the electric adding and multiplying machine, addition register, and typewriter tabulator. He has written novels and musical compositions.

Pindar, 522-443 B.C. The great Greek lyric poet; born in or near Thebes, in Bœotia. Pindar excelled in all varieties of choral poetry, hymns to the gods, pæans, odes for processions, drinking songs, etc. But the only poems of his now extant are the "Epinikia," or triumphal odes, composed in celebration of victories at the great public games. Pindar attained the highest renown in his own age, and as a lyrical poet has no rival. When Thebes was destroyed by Alexander, the conqueror spared the house of Pindar.

Phædrus. A Latin fabulist; of the age of Augustus, born in Macedonia, and settled in Rome; originally a slave, was manumitted by Augustus; his fables, ninety-seven in number, were written in verse, and are mostly translations from Æsop.

Phelps, Elizabeth Stuart, 1844- . . . . American authoress; born at Andover; wrote "Gates Ajar" and other popular stories; advocate of social reform and the emancipation of women. See WARD.

Plautus, 227-184 B. C. A Latin comic poet, born in Umbria; he wrote about 130 comedies, but only twenty have survived, the plots mostly borrowed from Greek models; they were much esteemed by his contemporaries; they have supplied material for dramatic treatment in modern times.

Pliny (Caius Plinius Secundus), The Elder, 23-79. A distinguished Roman jurist and naturalist; perished in the eruption of Mount Vesuvius which overwhelmed Pompeii and Herculaneum. Pliny, the Younger (Caius Plinius Cæcilius Secundus), adopted son of the former, an eminent jurist and historian; born 61, died 122.

Plutarch, 50-120. Celebrated Greek biographer and moralist; born at Chæronea, in Bœotia; his fame rests on his "Parallel Lives" of forty-six distinguished Greeks and Romans, a series of portraitures true to the life, and a work one of the most valuable we possess on the illustrious men of antiquity.

Poe, Edgar Allan, 1809-1849. An American poet and story writer; born in Boston. Left an orphan early, he was adopted by John Allan, of Richmond, Va., and at the age of nineteen left this home and published his first volume of verse at Boston. He was a cadet at the United States Military Academy, 1830-1831; and subsequently embarked on a literary career. He was one of the most remarkable characters in literature, gifted with genius, but apparently without any genuine sense of moral obligation to friends and benefactors. His place among American poets, however, will always be high. Poe died in Baltimore, Md.

Polybius, 110-128 B. C. A Greek historian; born in Megalopolis, Greece. His great work is a general history of the affairs of Greece and Rome from 220 B. C. to 146 B. C. Five only of its forty books are now extant, with some fragments of the rest, but these are among the most important literary remains of antiquity. He wrote several other works, but they have perished.

Pope, Alexander, 1688-1744. An English poet; born in London, England. His education was a desultory one. In 1711 he published his poem the "Essay on Criticism," which was followed by "The Rape of the Lock," a polished and witty narative poem, founded on an incident of fashionable life. From 1713 to 1726 he was engaged on a poetical translation of Homer's works, the "Iliad" (completed in 1720) being wholly from his pen, the "Odyssey" only half.

Prentice, George Denison, 1802-1870. An American journalist; born in Preston, Conn.; became editor of the Louisville *Journal*, 1830, and held that post till his death, making the paper famous for satiric wit and exuberant fun. He died in Louisville, Ky.

Prescott, William H., 1796-1859. An eminent American historian; born at Salem, Massachusetts; son of a lawyer; turned to literature as a profession; growing blind, the result of an accident at college, he fortunately inherited means, employed assistants, and with great courage in 1826 began to study Spanish history. "Ferdinand and Isabella," appearing in 1838, established his reputation in both worlds; "The Conquest of Mexico" was published in 1843, and "The Conquest of Peru" in 1847; he died of apoplexy at Boston before completing the "History of Philip II."

Procter, Bryan Waller, 1787-1874. English lyrist, known by his pseudonym as Barry Cornwall; born in London; is chiefly memorable as the friend of all the eminent literary men of two generations, such as Wordsworth, Lamb, and Scott on the one hand, and Carlyle, Thackeray, and Tennyson on the other; he was no great poet.

Quintilian (Quintilianus Marcus Fabius), 42?-118? A Roman rhetorician; native of Spain. His great work is entitled "On Oratory as an Art," and was written after his retirement, but during the reign of Domitian. It is the most complete course of rhetoric handed down from ancient times, and is distinguished for its elegance of style, as well as for sound judgment, cultivated taste, and various knowledge.

Rabelais (*rah-be-lay'*), **Francois,** 1495-1553. A great French humorist; born at Chinon; the son of a poor apothecary; studied medicine, and for a time practiced it, particularly at Lyons; here he commenced the series of writings that have immortalized his name, his "Gargantua" and "Pantagruel" forming a succession of satires in a vein of riotous mirth on monks, priests, pedants, and all the incarnate solecisms of the time.

Racine, Jean, 1639-1698. An eminent French dramatic poet; born in La Ferte Milon, France. In 1688 appeared his "Andromaque," which placed him far above all his contemporaries except Corneille; and his fame was still further increased by the production of "Britannicus," "Berenice," and other tragedies. After a lapse of twelve years he wrote, by desire of Louis XIV. and Madame de Maintenon, the sacred dramas of "Esther" and "Athalie."

Ramsay, Allan, 1685-1758. A Scotch poet; born in Leadhills, Lanarkshire, Scotland. His fame reached its acme on the production of "The Gentle Shepherd," one of the finest dramatic pastorals ever penned. Ramsay died in Edinburgh.

Read, Opie, 1852- . . . . An American journalist; born in Nashville, Tenn. He established and edited for many years the *Arkansaw Traveler*. His studies of Arkansas life have been widely read.

Read, Thomas Buchanan, 1822-1872. An American portrait painter and poet; born in Chester county, Pa.; died in New York.

Reade, Charles, 1814-1884. An English novelist; born in Ipsden House, Oxfordshire, England. He was educated at Oxford. The books by which he first became known were his "Peg Woffington" and "Christie Johnstone." He died in London, England.

Regnard (*rehnar'*), **Jean Francois,** 1656-1709. A French comic dramatist; born in Paris. By common consent his rank in France is second to Moliere only. He died near Dourdan, France.

Regnier (*rayn-ye-ay'*), **Mathurin,** 1572-1613. French poet; born at Chartres; led when young a life of dissipation; ranks high as a poet, but is most distinguished in satire, which is instinct with verve and vigor.

Renan (*reh-non'*), **Joseph Ernest,** 1823-1892. A French writer; born in Treguier, France. In 1862 he was appointed professor of Hebrew, Chaldee, and Syriac in the College de France, but the skeptical views manifested in his "Life of Jesus," raised an outcry against him, and he was removed from his chair, to be restored again, however, in 1871. This work, the publication of which caused intense excitement throughout Europe, was the first part of a comprehensive work on the "History of the Origins of Christianity," written from the standpoint of one who disbelieves in the supernatural claims of Christianity. Renan's latest important work was the "History of the People of Israel till the Time of King David." Became a member of the French Academy 1877.

Richardson, Samuel, 1689-1761. Novelist; born in Derbyshire, the son of a joiner; was apprenticed to a printer in London, whose daughter he married; set up in the business for himself, and from his success in it became Master of the Stationers Company in 1754, and King's Printer in 1761; was fifty before he came out as a novelist; published his "Pamela" in 1740, his masterpiece "Clarissa," written in the form of letters, in 1748, and "Sir Charles Grandison" in 1153; they are all three novels of sentiment, are instinct with a spirit of moral purity, and are more praised than read.

Richter, Jean Paul Friedrich, 1763-1825. Usually called Jean Paul simply; the greatest of German humorists; born at Wunsiedel, near Baireuth, in Bavaria; the son of a poor German pastor; had a scanty education, but his fine faculties and unwearied diligence supplied every defect; his works are numerous, and the chief are novels, "Hesperus" and "Titan" being the longest and the best.

Riley, James Whitcomb, 1853- . . . . An American poet; born in Greenfield, Ind. His contributions to newspapers and magazines first attracted public attention about 1875. His writings soon became so popular that he devoted himself to literature and public readings of his work with great success. His poems are characterized by both humor and pathos and by their sympathy with the simplest phases of life. Those of the Hoosier type are especially popular.

Ridpath, John Clark, 1840-1900. An American educator; born in Putnam county, Ind.; held a professorship in Baker University, Kansas. In 1869 he became Professor of English Literature at Asbury University, Indiana, and was elected its vice-president in 1879. In 1874-1875 he published a "History of the United States," which he supplemented with another in 1877. In 1876 he issued a "School History," and in 1879 an "English Grammar." Desiring to devote his whole time to literature he resigned his university offices. He died in New York city.

Rogers, Samuel, 1763-1855. English poet; born in London; bred to banking, and all his life a banker—took to literature, produced a succession of poems: "The Pleasures of Memory" "Human Life" and "Italy," the chief.

Rollin, Charles, 1661-1741. A French historian; born in Paris. His best known work is the "Ancient History," often reprinted in France, England, and the United States. He died in Paris.

Ronsard (*de ron-sar'*), **Pierre de,** 1524-1585. A French poet; born in Vendomois, France. After a short diplomatic career, he devoted himself to literary studies and became the chief of the band of seven poets afterwards known as the "Pleiade." Ronsard's popularity and prosperity during his life were very great. Henry II., Francis II., and Charles IX. esteemed him, and the last bestowed several abbacies and priories on the poet. He died in Touraine.

Rossetti, Gabriele, 1783-1854. An Italian poet and critic. In 1826 he married Frances Mary Lavinia Polidori, daughter of a Tuscan father and English mother; soon afterward he was elected Professor of Italian in King's College, London. Died in London. His son, Gabriel Charles Dante Rossetti, 1828-1882, gained high reputation as poet and painter, and his daughter, Christina Georgina, born in 1830, also wrote poetry of a high order.

Rostand, Edmond, 1868- . . . . A French poet; born in Marseilles, France; his first play, "The Romanticists," was an instantaneous success and was followed by "Princess Lontaine"; "The Samaritan;" "Cyrano de Bergerac;" and "L'Aiglon." The last two were translated into English and played in the United States. Rostand's versification is of remarkable beauty. In 1901, he was elected one of the 40 "immortals" of the French Academy—the youngest candidate ever receiving that honor.

Rouget de Lisle (*roo-zhay' de leel*), 1760-1836. Officer of the Engineers; born at Lons-le-Saulnier; immortalized himself as the author of the "Marseillaise"; was thrown into prison by the extreme party at the Revolution, but was released on the fall of Robespierre; fell into straitened circumstances, but was pensioned by Louis Philippe.

Rousseau (*roo-so'*), **Jean Jacques,** 1712-1778. A Swiss-French philosopher; one of the most celebrated and influential writers of the 18th century; born in Geneva, Switzerland. Went to Paris, where he wrote a sort of novel, "Julia, or the New Heloise," which was published in 1760, being followed by "The Social Contract," a political work, and "Emile, or on Education," another story, in 1762. Persecution, exaggerated by his own morbid sensibility, forced Rousseau to flee to England, where he was welcomed by Hume, Boswell and others, in 1766. A malicious letter by Horace Walpole unluckily aroused his suspicions of his English friends, and in May, 1767, he returned to France. He lived in great poverty, supporting himself by copying music and publishing occasional works. His celebrated "Confessions" appeared at Geneva, in 1782. He died in Ermenonville, not without suspicion of suicide.

Royce, Josiah, 1855- . . . . An American educator and author; born in Grass Valley, Cal. He became Professor of the History of Philosophy in Harvard in 1892, and published: "A Primer of Logical Analysis;" "The Religious Aspect of Philosophy;" "The Conception of Immortality;" and many articles and lectures.

Ruckert, Friedrich, 1788-1866. A German poet; born in Schweinfurt, Bavaria. His most popular books are the collection of lyrics entitled "Springtime of Love," and the reflective poems gathered together as "The Wisdom of the Brahman."

Ruskin, John, 1819-1900. An English author; born in London; he was Slade Professor of Fine Arts at Oxford. In "Modern Painters" he advocated a complete revolution in the received conventions of art and art criticism. Ruskin was the first art critic to place criticism upon a scientific basis. In 1851 he appeared as a defender of pre-Raphaelitism. About 1860 he began to write as a political economist and social reformer; his chief works in this sphere being "Unto this Last," "Munera Pulveris," and "Fors Clavigera," a periodical series of letters to the working men and laborers of Great Britain. In this connection he founded, in 1871, the Guild of St. George; founded a linen industry at Keswick, and revived, in Langdale, hand loom weaving. After 1885 he lived at Brantwood, on Coniston Lake, where he died.

Sadi, or **Saadi,** 1184-1291. The most celebrated didactic poet of Persia; born in Shiraz, Persia. In his youth he visited Hindustan, Syria, Palestine, Abyssinia, and made several pilgrimages to Mecca and Medina. While in Syria he was taken by the Crusaders, and compelled to labor as a slave at the fortifications of Tripoli. After about 50 years of wandering he returned to his native city, delighting everybody with his poems and sage precepts.

Sainte-Beuve (*Sant-buve'*), **Charles Augustin,** 1804-1869. A French writer, and one of the greatest of modern critics; born in Boulogne, France. He studied medicine at Paris, but abandoned that science in favor of literature, his first work of importance being on the French literature of the 16th century. In 1840 he was appointed conservator of the Mazarin Library, and in 1845 admitted a member of the French Academy. In 1852 he was appointed Professor of Latin Poetry in the College of France; he also lectured for some years on French literature at the Ecole Normale Superieure. He wrote three volumes of poetry; died in Paris.

St. Pierre, Henri Bernardin de, 1737-1814. French novelist; born at Havre; an engineer by profession, was a disciple of Rousseau both sentimentally and speculatively; his chief work, "Paul and Virginia."

Sala, George Augustus Henry, 1828-1895. An English journalist; born in London, England. He acquired a large fortune in journalism, but was recklessly extravagant and finally became bankrupt. He died in Brighton, England.

Sallust, Caius Callustius Crispus, 86-35 B.C. A Roman historian. In 47 B.C., he was prætor-elect, and in the following year accompanied Cæsar to the African war, where he was left as governor of Numidia. He returned with immense wealth, and after Cæsar's death lived in luxurious retirement. Sallust wrote several historical works in a clear and concise style. He died in Rome.

Sand, George, 1804-1876. Best known name of Madame Armantine Lucile Aurore Dupin Dudevant, one of the greatest of French novelists; born in Paris. In 1822 she married Baron Dudevant, to whom she bore a son and a daughter; but in 1831 separated from him, and took up her residence in Paris. In conjunction with Jules Sandeau, a young lawyer, she wrote "Rose and White," which was published in 1831, with the pseudonym Jules Sand. The reception it met with afforded her an opportunity of publishing a novel solely by herself—"Indiana," under the name of George Sand, which she ever after retained. In 1836 she obtained a judicial separation from her husband, with the care of her children. In 1854 she published "Story of My Life," a psychological autobiography. Her published works consist of upward of sixty separate novels, a large number of plays, and numerous articles in literary journals. She died in Nohart.

Sappho, fl. B.C. 600. A renowned Greek lyric poet; born in the island of Lesbos. She wrote nine books of poems, but besides some small fragments of her poems we have in complete form only a "Hymn to Aphrodite" and an "Ode to a Beautiful Girl." In antiquity, as Homer was ever "The Poet" above all others, so Sappho was "The Poetess." She was also called "The Tenth Muse."

Sardou', Victorien, 1831- . . . . A French dramatist; born in Paris. He began play writing in early life, though intended originally for the medical profession. Among his plays are; "Cleopatra," "Thermidor," "Gismonda," "Madame Sans-Gene," "Pamela," etc. He was elected to the Academy in 1877.

Saxe, John Godfrey, 1816-1887. An American humorous poet; born in Highgate, Vt. His most popular verses include "Rhyme of the Rail" and "The Proud Miss McBride;" and many published works. He died in Albany, N. Y.

Scheffel, Joseph Victor von, 1826-1886. German poet, bred to law, but abandoned it for literature; his first and best work, "Der Trompeter von Sakkingen," a charming tale in verse of the Thirty Years' War, succeeded by "Gaudeamus," a collection of songs and ballads familiar to the German students all over the Fatherland.

Schiller, Johann Christoph Friedrich von, 1759-1805. A German poet; born in Marbach, Wurtemberg; in his twenty-second year, wrote the tragedy of "The Robbers," which at once raised him to the foremost rank among the dramatists of his country. In 1789 he was appointed to the chair of history in the University of Jena, and besides lecturing to crowded audiences he published his "History of the Thirty Years' War," and engaged in various literary enterprises which had great influence on the literature of Germany. Settled at Weimar, in order to direct the theater in conjunction with Goethe; and here at intervals he published the following works: "Wallenstein," "Mary Stuart," "Joan of Arc," and "William Tell." He died in Weimar, Germany.

Schreiner, Olive, 1863?- . . . . Authoress, daughter of a Lutheran clergyman at Cape Town; achieved a great success by "The Story of an African Farm" in 1883, which was followed in 1890 by "Dreams," also later "Dream Life and Real Life."

Scott, Sir Walter, 1771-1832. A British author; born in Edinburgh, Scotland. From the commencement of his literary career in 1796, when he published his translations of Burger's "Lenore" and "Wild Huntsman," to the year of his decease, he was constantly producing some literary work and reaped an abundant harvest. His romances are universally known. His patrimonial estate was considerable; and in 1800 he obtained the preferment of sheriff of Selkirkshire, with about £300($1,500) a year, and in 1806 he was appointed one of the principal clerks of the session in Scotland. In 1811 he built a mansion on the Tweed, to which he gave the name of Abbotsford. In 1825 the firm of Constable & Company, at Edinburgh, engaged Scott to compose a "Life of Bonaparte." It was in progress when these publishers became bankrupts, and Scott found himself involved on their behalf, and began, at the age of fifty-five, the task of redeeming a debt exceeding $500,000. His work, which appeared during the summer of 1827, in nine volumes, 8vo, realized the sum of $60,000, being at the rate of $165 a day for the time he had devoted to it. After the payment of $270,000, his creditors presented to him the library and manuscripts, curiosities, and plate which had once been his own. In 1831 he went to Italy for his health, returning the following year. He died in Abbotsford, and was buried in Dryburgh Abbey.

Seneca, Lucius Annæus, 5 ?-65. Roman statesman, moralist, and Stoic philosopher.

Shakespeare, William, 1564-1616. An English dramatist and poet; born in Stratford-on-Avon, Warwickshire, England. His birthplace, as pointed out by traditions, is the house in Henley street, Stratford, which belonged to his father. In his nineteenth year he married Anne Hathaway, daughter of a yeoman at the neighboring hamlet of Shottery, and eight years older than himself. He went to London about 1586, and lived there many years, leaving his wife and children at Stratford; he gained an honorable position as actor, playwriter, and shareholder in the theater of Blackfriars, and afterward in that of the Globe; enjoyed the favor and patronage of Queen Elizabeth, James I., and the Earl of Southampton, the warm friendship of Ben Jonson, and the highest respect and admiration of his associates, not only for his pre-eminence as a poet, but for his honesty, geniality, and worth as a man. Of his end we have no other account than the short statement in the diary of the Rev. John Ward, vicar of Stratford, that "Shakespeare, Drayton, and Ben Jonson had a merry meeting, and it seems drank too hard, for Shakespeare died of a fever then contracted." The first collected edition of Shakespeare's plays was the folio of 1623. His poems of "Venus and Adonis" and "The Rape of Lucrece" were published in 1593 and 1594 and were the only works which appeared with his name in his lifetime. Of the thirty-six plays (exclusive of "Pericles"), the dates of publication of only a few are known. "The Two Gentlemen of Verona," and "Love's Labors Lost," were among the earliest; and "Tempest," "Troilus and Cressida," "Henry VIII.," "Coriolanus," "Julius Cæsar," and "Antony and Cleopatra" among the latest. The "Midsummer Night's Dream," "Merchant of Venice," "Romeo and Juliet," "Richard II.," "Richard III.," "Henry IV.," and "King John," were all produced before 1598. A copy of "Hamlet" is extant, bearing the date 1602. "Twelfth Night" was produced in 1601; "King Lear" was printed in 1607; the "Tempest" was written in 1611. The second folio edition of the collected plays appeared in 1632, and two others subsequently. It is said that by 1830 not less than eighty-two editions had been published, without including separate plays, and poems, and commentaries. Since then the number has been enormously increased.

Shelley, Percy Bysshe, 1792-1821. An English poet; son of Sir Timothy Shelley; born in Horsham, England. At Oxford he published anonymously a scholastic thesis entitled "A Defense of Atheism." The authorship being known he was challenged, and, refusing either to acknowledge or deny it, was at once expelled. His first great poem, "Alastor, or the Spirit of Solitude," was followed by the "Revolt of Islam," a poem in the Spenserian stanza. In 1811 he eloped to Edinburgh with Harriet Westbrook, the daughter of a retired innkeeper. She was sixteen years of age, his own age being nineteen. The marriage turned out unhappily. In November, 1816, she committed suicide by drowning. Shelley was deeply affected by this event, but soon after married Mary Godwin; Shelley left England in March, 1818, and the whole short remainder of his life was passed in Italy. On July 8, 1821, he was sailing with a Mr. Williams in the Bay of Spezia, when both were drowned.

Sheridan, Richard Brinsley Butler, 1751-1816. Dramatist and politician; born in Dublin; scored his first success with "The Rivals"; "The School for Scandal" and "The Critic" set flowing the tide of prosperity; turning his attention next to politics he entered Parliament, and two years later became Under-Secretary for Foreign Affairs; his great speech impeaching Hastings placed him in the front rank of orators; he died in poverty, but was accorded a burial in Westminster Abbey.

Sidney, Sir Philip, 1554-1586. Poet and one of the most attractive figures at Elizabeth's court; born at Penshurst, Kent; the son of Sir Henry Sidney, lord-deputy of Ireland; sent as ambassador in 1576 to the court of Vienna; in 1583 he received a knighthood; he received his death wound at the battle of Zutphen, gallantly leading a troop of Netherlanders against the Spaniards: his fame as an author rests securely on his euphuistic prose romance "Arcadia," his critical treatise "The Defense of Poesy," and above all on his exquisite sonnet-series "Astrophel and Stella."

Sienkiewicz, (*se-en'ke-vix*) **Henry,** 1845- . . . . A Polish author; born in Lithuania. He is the author of the historical novel "Quo Vadis"; "With Fire and Sword," "Knights of the Cross," etc.

Sig'ourney, Lydia (Huntley), 1791-1865. An American author; born in Norwich, Conn. In her "Letters of Life," she enumerates forty-six distinct works wholly or partially from her pen, besides over 2,000 articles in prose and verse, contributed by her to nearly 300 periodicals. She died in Hartford, Conn.

Simms, William Gilmore, 1806-1870. A prolific American writer, born at Charleston, South Carolina; turned from law to literature; "Southern Passages and Pictures" contains characteristic examples of his poetry, and of his novels "The Yemassee," "The Partisan," and "Beauchampe" may be mentioned.

Smith, Sidney, 1771-1845. An English clergyman; born in Woodford, Essex, England. In 1804 he removed to London; about the same time married, and became renowned as one of the wittiest and most genial of men. In 1831, during the ministry of Earl Grey, he became one of the canons of St. Paul's. Died in London.

Smollett, Tobias George, 1721-1771. Novelist; born at Dalquhurn, Dumbartonshire, Scotland, of good family; bred to medicine, but drifted to literature; achieved his first success in "Roderick Random," which was followed by "Peregrine Pickle," "Count Fathom" and "Humphrey Clinker"; wrote a "History of England," and a political lampoon, "The Adventures of an Atom."

Snorri, Sturlason, 1178-1241. An Icelandic poet and historian; born in Hvami, in the Dala district of Iceland. Snorri was the last and one of the greatest of the Northern skalds. He wrote many panegyrics and heroic songs, and is believed to have been the author of part of the "Younger Edda." His principal work is the "Heimskringla" ("ring of the world"), a collection of sagas.

Soph'ocles, 495-406 B. C. A Greek tragic poet; born in the Attic demus or village of Colonus. He was fifteen when the battle of Salamis was fought, and for his remarkable beauty and skill in music he was chosen to lead the chorus which sang the pæan of victory. The number of plays attributed to him without question was 113. Seven only are extant, viz., "Antigone," "Electra," "Trachinian Women," "King Œdipus," "Ajax," "Philoctetes," and "Œdipus at Colonus." These exhibit his art in its maturity, and sustain the verdict of ancient and modern critics that Sophocles carried the Greek drama to its highest perfection.

Southey, Robert, 1774-1843. An English poet; born in Bristol, Ehgland. In 1801 he devoted himself to literature, and soon after took up his residence at Keswick, in Cumberland, where the remainder of his life was passed, he being thenceforth classed as one of the Lake poets. The latter years of his life were clouded by a mental imbecility which attended him to his death. His chief poems are: "Joan of Arc," "A Vision of Judgment," etc. Among his prose works are: "History of Brazil," "Life of Nelson." Among his translations was "The Chronicle of the Cid." He died near Keswick, England.

Spenser, Edmund, 1552-1599. Author of the "Faerie Queene," and one of England's greatest poets; details of his life are scanty and often hypothetical.

Spofford, Harriet Prescott, 1835- . . . . An American authoress; born in Calais, Me.; was graduated at the Pinkerton Academy in Derry, N. H., in 1852. In 1859 she published "In a Cellar" in the *Atlantic Monthly.* This story made her reputation, and thereafter she became a contributor to the chief periodicals of the country.

Stael *(deh stah-el')*, **Madame de,** 1766-1817. Distinguished French woman; born in Paris, daughter of Necker, and only child; a woman of eminent ability and an admirer of Rousseau; wrote "Letters" on his character and works; married a man ten years older than herself, the Baron de Stael-Holstein, the Swedish ambassador in Paris; her salon became the center of the literary and political activity of the time; the ambition of Napoleon exited her distrust, and forced her into opposition so expressed that in 1801 she was ordered to leave Paris; in 1802 she was left a widow, and soon after she went first to Weimar, where she met Goethe and Schiller, and then to Berlin; by and by she returned to France, but on the publication of her "Corinne,-- was ordered out of the country; after this appeared her great epoch-making work on Germany, "L-Allemagne,-- which was seized by the French censors; after this she quitted for good the soil of France and settled in Switzerland, at Coppet, where she died.

Stedman, Edmund Clarence, 1833- . . . . An American poet and banker; born in Hartford, Conn.; was a student at Yale, but did not graduate. He was a war correspondent of the New York *World* during the American Civil War. In 1884 he became a stock broker in New York city. The best known of his critical works are: "Victorian Poets," "Edgar Allan Poe,-- and "Poets of America." He edited, in collaboration with Ellen M. Hutchinson, "A Library of American Literature.--

Stephen, Leslie, 1832- . . . . Man of letters; born at Kensington; became editor of the *Cornhill* and of the "Dictionary of National Biography"; author of "Hours in a Library" and "History of English Thought in the Eighteenth Century."

Sterne, Laurence, 1713-1768. English humorist; born at Clonmel, Ireland; in 1759 appeared the first two volumes of "Tristram Shandy," and in 1767 the last two; in 1768 his "Sentimental Journey," and in the interim his "Sermons." Died in London of pulmonary consumption.

Stevenson, Robert Louis Balfour, 1850-1894. A British author; born in Edinburgh, Scotland; educated at the University of Edinburgh; studied law; in 1873 went abroad for his health; wrote for periodicals till 1878, when his first book appeared; visited California in 1879; spent the winter of 1887-1888 in the Adirondacks; cruised in the Pacific; bought a tract of land ("Vailima" or "Five Streams") in Samoa, where he made his home. He published a large number of works. Died in Vailima, near Apia, Samoa.

Stockton, Francis Richard, 1834-1902. An American author; born in Philadelphia, Pa.; became an engraver and draughtsman; joined the editorial staff of *Scribner's Monthly* and became assistant editor of *St. Nicholas*; attained an enviable reputation as a writer of highly entertaining short stories. He died in Washington, D. C.

Stowe, Harriet Elizabeth Beecher, 1811-1896. An American novelist, daughter of Lyman Beecher and sister of Henry Ward Beecher; born in Litchfield, Conn.; was married to Prof. Calvin Ellis Stowe; in 1864 she settled in Hartford, Conn., where she spent the remainder of her life. She published: "The Mayflower; or Sketches of Scenes and Characters among the Descendants of the Pilgrims," "Uncle Tom's Cabin'; or, Life Among the Lowly," and a large number of other works. Her best known work, "Uncle Tom's Cabin" (suggested by the life of Josiah Henson) has been translated into many languages, its sale exceeding that of any previous work of English fiction. She died in Hartford, Conn.

Sue, Marie Joseph Eugene, 1804-1857. A French novelist; born in Paris. His most famous works are: "The Mysteries of Paris," and "The Wandering Jew." In 1850 he was elected to the Constituent Assembly, aud sat as an advanced radical. After the coup d'etat by Napoleon III. in 1851 he left France and retired to Savoy. He died in Annecy, Savoy.

Swift, Jonathan, 1667-1745. The greatest of English satirists; born in Dublin, Ireland. He was the posthumous son of Jonathan Swift, an Englishman, steward of the Irish inns of court, and was educated at Kilkenny and at Trinity College, Dublin. In 1701 he took his doctor's degree, and in 1704 he published anonymously his famous "Tale of a Tub," to which was appended the "Battle of the Books." In 1708 appeared, among other things, an attact on astrology under the title of "Predictions for the Year 1708, by Isaac Bickerstaff, Esq.," and in 1709 a "Project for the Advance of Religion," dedicated to Lady Berkeley, the only work to which he ever put his name. His "Proposal for the Universal Use of Irish Manufactures" and his celebrated "Drapier's Letters," made him the idol of the Irish people. His famous "Gulliver's Travels" appeared in 1726. He died in Dublin, bequeathing the greatest part of his fortune to a hospital for lunatics and idiots.

Swinburne, Algernon Charles, 1837- . . . . An English poet and essayist, son of Admiral Charles Henry Swinburne; born in London, England. His first productions were "Queen Mother" and "Rosamund." They were followed by two tragedies: "Atalanta in Calydon," and "Chastelard," and by "Poems and Ballads," reprinted as Laus Veneris." He also wrote "A Study of Ben Johnson; "Astrophel, and other Poems;" "Studies in Prose and Poetry;' "The Tale of Balen, and "Rosamund, Queen of the Lombards."

Tacitus, Cornelius, 54?-117? Roman historian; born presumably at Rome. Of writings extant the chief are his "Life of Agricola,-- his "Germania," his "Histories" and his "Annals'-; his "Agricola" is admired as a model biography, while his "Histories' and "Annals" are distinguished for their conciseness, their vigor, and their pregancy of meaning.

Taine, Hippolyte Adolphe, 1828-1893. A French writer; born in Vouziers, Ardennes, France; was educated at the College Bourbon and the Ecole Normale. His "History of English Literature," one of the best and most philosophical works on the subject, appeared in 1864. He died in Paris.

Talfourd, Sir Thomas Noon, 1795-1854. Lawyer and dramatist; born at Doxey, near Stafford; was called to the bar in 1821, and practiced with notable success; was for some years a member of Parliament; author of four tragedies, of which "Ion -- is the best known.

Tasso, Torquato, 1544-1595. An Italian epic poet; born in Sorrento, Italy. Tasso wrote numerous poems, but his fame rests chiefly on his "Rime, or lyrical poems, his "Aminta,-- and his "Gierusalemme Liberata.-- His letters are also interesting.

Taylor, Bayard, 1825-1878. An American writer and traveler; born in Kennett Square, Chester county, Pa. He learned the trade of a printer; contributed to various magazines; made a journey through Europe on foot in 1844-1845; on his return published "Views Afoot in Europe,-- and in this way gained a position on the staff of the New York *Tribune.* He afterward traveled extensively. He resided in Germany for lengthened periods; was for some time United States secretary of legation at St. Petersburg, and latterly was United States minister to Germany. He died in Berlin.

Taylor, Jeremy, 1633-1667. "The modern Chrysostom;-- born in Cambridge, England. In 1638 he was appointed rector of Uppingham in Rutlandshire. In the civil war, Taylor took the royal side, and so lost all his preferments. For many years he lived in retirement in Wales, busily engaged in writing books. In 1658 he went, on the invitation of the Earl of Conway, to Ireland. Immediately after the Restoration he was made Bishop of Down and Connor, which see, as also that of Dromore, he held till his death at Lisburne.

Tegner, Esaias, 1782-1846. A popular Swedish poet; born at Kyrkerud; the son of a country parson. His poems, of which "Frithiof's Saga" is reckoned the finest, have the clearness and finish of classic models, but are charged with the fire and vigor of modern romanticism.

Tennyson, Alfred, Lord, 1809-1892. An English poet; born in Somersby, England. His literary career may be said to date from 1830, when he published a volume entitled "Poems, chiefly Lyrical." It was not received with any great favor by the public. Its success was sufficient to encourage the poet to prepare a second collection, which appeared in 1833, and contained such poems as "A Dream of Fair Women," "Œnone," and others. It was not till 1842 that he again appealed to the public with a selection of his poems in two volumes. His reputation was more than sustained by the works that immediately followed. He received the laureateship upon the death of Wordsworth. Thereafter hardly a year passed without his adding some gem to our language. In 1855 the University of Oxford conferred on Tennyson the honorary degree of D.C.L. Among his later compositions are the dramas, "Queen Mary," "Harold," "The Cup." Tennyson was raised to the peerage in 1884 as Baron Tennyson of Aldworth, Sussex, and Freshwater, Isle of Wight. He died in Aldworth, England, and was buried in Westminster Abbey.

Terence, 195-159 B.C. Roman comic poet; born at Carthage; brought thence as a slave; educated by his master, a Roman senator, and set free; composed plays, adaptations of others in Greek by Menander and Apollodorus; they depict Greek manners for Roman imitation in a pure and perfect Latin style, and with great dramatic skill.

Terhune, Mary Virginia (*Marion Harland*), 1831- . . . . An American authoress; born in Amelia county, Va.; early began to write for the press. Was for several years the editor of *Babyhood* and *The Home Maker;* conducted departments in *Wide Awake* and *St. Nicholas*, and served on the editorial staff of the Chicago *Daily News*.

Thackeray, William Makepeace, 1811-1863. An English novelist; born in Calcutta, India. Being well provided for, he chose the profession of an artist. He spent several years in France, Germany, and Italy, staying at Paris, Weimar, and Rome, but gradually became convinced that art was not his vocation, and, having lost his fortune, he resolved to turn his attention to literature. His first appearance in this sphere was as a journalist. In 1846-1848 his novel of "Vanity Fair" was published in monthly parts, with illustrations by himself; and long before its completion its author was unanimously placed in the first rank of British novelists. His next novel was the "History of Pendennis," completed in 1850. In 1851 he delivered a course of lectures in London on the "English Humorists of the Eighteenth Century," which was repeated in Scotland and America. In 1855-1856 he delivered a series of lectures in the United States—"The Four Georges"—and afterward in England and Scotland. In 1859 he became editor of the *Cornhill Magazine*, but he retired from that post in 1862. He died in Kensington Palace Gardens, London.

Thanet, Octave, (*Than-ay*) 1850- . . . . Pseudonym of Alice French, an American novelist; born in Andover, Mass.

Theocritus, flourished 280 B.C. A Greek poet; born at Syracuse. We have under his name thirty idyls or pastoral poems, of which, however, several are probably by other authors. Most of his idyls have a dramatic form and consist of the alternate responses of musical shepherds. His language is strong and harmonious.

Thompson, James Maurice, 1844-1901. An American author; born in Fairfield, Ind.; was state geologist of Indiana, 1885-1889; wrote nature studies. He published in book form: "Hoosier Mosaics," "The Witchery of Archery," "A Tallahassee Girl," "Alice of Old Vincennes," etc.

Thomson, James, 1700-1748. The author of the "Seasons"; born, the son of the parish minister, at Ednam, Roxburghshire; was educated and trained for the ministry at Edinburgh University; his poem "Winter" had immediate success, and raised up a host of friends and patrons; the "Masque of Alfred," with its popular song "Rule Britannia," and his greatest work, "The Castle of Indolence," were the outcome of his later years of leisure.

Thoreau, Henry David, 1817-1862. An American author; born in Concord, Mass. In 1845 he built for himself a hut in a wood near Walden pond, Concord, Mass. and there for two years lived the life of a hermit. After quitting his solitude, Thoreau pursued his father's calling of pencil maker at Concord. Besides contributing to the *Dial* and other periodicals, he published "A Week on the Concord and Merrimac Rivers," and "Walden, or Life in the Woods." After his death appeared "Excursions in Field and Forest," "The Maine Woods," "Cape Cod," and "A Yankee in Canada." Thoreau was a friend of Emerson, and imbibed much of his spirit and method of thought. He died in Concord.

Thucydides, 471?-400? B.C. Historian of the Peloponnesian War; born in Athens, of a wealthy family; served as naval commander in 424 in the Peloponnesian War, but from neglect of duty was banished; returned from exile twenty years after; his great achievement is his history, all derived from personal observation and oral communication, the materials of which were collected during the war, and the whole executed in a style to entitle it to rank among the noblest literary monuments of antiquity.

Tieck, Ludwig, 1773-1853. German poet; born in Berlin; was one of the founders of the Romantic school in Germany. Wrote novels and popular tales and dramas.

Timrod, Henry, 1827-1867. An American poet; born in Charleston, S. C.; died in Columbia, S. C.

Tocqueville, Alexis Clerel de, 1805-1861. French economist; born at Verneuil, of an old Norman family; bred to the bar, and especially distinguished as the author of two works in high repute, "La Democratie en Amerique" and "L'Ancien Regime et la Revolution"; died at Cannes, leaving much of his work unfinished.

Tolstoy, Count Lyof Alekseevich, 1828- . . . . A Russian novelist; born on the family estate of Yasnaya Polyana in the province of Tula, Russia. He served in the Crimean War, and afterward traveled extensively. In 1861 he took up permanent residence on his country estate. Among his earliest works are: "Detsvo" (Childhood), "Otrchestvo" (Boyhood), and "Iunost" (Youth); also "Cossacks," "Sevastopol" and a number of military sketches. "War and Peace" was published in 1865-1868; "Anna Karenina" in 1875-1878. His peculiar doctrines are promulgated in "My Confession," "In What My Faith Consists," etc.; many of them are forbidden in Russia. His later works are: "The Kreutzer Sonata"; "Death of Ivan Ilyitch," and "Master and Man." Nearly all have been translated into English and most other modern languages.

Tourgee, Albion Winegar, 1838- . . . . An American jurist and author; born in Williamsfield, O.; was graduated at Rochester University, N. Y., in 1862; admitted to the bar, 1864; served in the Civil War in the Union army, and was wounded on two occasions; at the close of the war commenced the practice of law at Greensboro, N.C., and at the southern loyalist convention at Philadelphia, 1866, drew up the report on the condition of the states lately in revolt. In 1868 he became judge of the Superior Court of North Carolina. Besides compiling "A Code of Civil Procedure for North Carolina," he wrote "A Fool's Errand"; "Bricks Without Straw," etc. In 1897 he was appointed United States consul at Bordeaux, France.

Trollope, Anthony, 1815-1882. An English novelist; born in London, England. He was educated at Harrow and Winchester; in 1834 became a clerk in the post office, and in 1841 was appointed clerk to a post office surveyor in Ireland. His Irish experiences gave him material for his first novels. His first success was "The Warden"; followed by "Barchester Towers," etc. He also published accounts of his travels. He died in London.

Trowbridge, John Townsend, 1827- . . . . An American author; born in Ogden, N. Y. He began his literary career in 1846 by writing for the magazines, and in 1850 became editor of *The Yankee Nation*, and co-editor with Lucy Larcom and Gail Hamilton, of *Our Young Folks*. Among his most popular works are: "Jack Hazard Stories," "Two Biddicut Boys," also several volumes of poems.

Tupper, Martin, 1810-1889. Author of "Proverbial Philosophy"; born in Marylebone; bred to the bar; wrote some forty works; the "Philosophy" had quite a phenomenal success.

Tur'genef, Ivan Sergyevich, 1818-1883. Russian novelist.

Tyrtæus, fl. 700 B. C. A lyric poet of ancient Greece, whose war songs greatly heartened the Spartans in their struggle with the Messenians.

Uhland, Johann Ludwig, 1787-1862. An eminent German poet.

Van Dyke, Henry Jackson, 1852- . . . . An American educator; born in Germantown, Pa.; was graduated at Princeton University in 1873, at the Princeton Theological Seminary in 1877, and at Berlin University in 1878; and soon afterward assumed the pastorate of the United Congregational Church in Newport, R. I. He was chosen pastor of the Brick Presbyterian Church in New York city in 1883 and continued in that charge till 1900, when he resigned to become Professor of English Literature in Princeton University. His publications include: "The Reality of Religion;" "The Poetry of Tennyson;" "The Ruling Passion," etc.

Vega, Lopez de la, 1562-1635. Known as Lope, Spanish dramatist; born in Madrid; began life as a soldier; served in the Armada; was secretary to the Duke of Alva; took orders and became an officer of the Inquisition; wrote a heroic pastoral entitled "Arcadia" at the instance of the duke, and the "Dragonica" over the death of Drake as the destroyer of the supremacy of Spain on the sea; was a man of fertile inventiveness, and is said to have written 2,000 plays, besides no end of verses, and was called by Cervantes a "Prodigy of Nature."

Verne, Jules, 1828-1905. A French novelist; born in Nantes, France. He studied law for some time, but afterward began writing short pieces for the stage. His more popular works are: "Twenty Thousand Leagues under the Sea," "From the Earth to the Moon," "Across Africa in a Balloon," "Michel Strogoff," "To the Center of the Earth," "Round the World in Eighty Days," "The Mysterious Island," etc. Most of his works have been translated into English and German.

Vigny (*deh veen-ye'*), **Alfred Comte de,** 1798-1864. French poet of the Romanticist school, born at Loches; produced a small volume of exquisitely finished poems between 1821 and 1829, and only one other, "Poemes Philosophiques," which was not published till after his death; wrote also romances and dramas, and translated into French "Othello" and "Merchant of Venice."

Virgil, 70-19 B. C. Great Latin poet; born near Mantua; author in succession of the "Eclogues," the Georgics," and the "Æneid"; studied at Cremona and Milan, and at sixteen was sent to Rome to study rhetoric and philosophy; lost property he had in Cremona during the civil war, but recommended himself to Pollio, the governor, who introduced him to Augustus, and he went to settle in Rome; here, in 37 B. C., he published his "Eclogues," a collection of ten pastorals, and gained the patronage of Mæcenas, under whose favor he was able to retire to a villa at Naples, where in seven years he, in 30 B. C., produced the "Georgics," in four books, on the art of husbandry, after which he devoted himself to his great work the "Æneid," or the story of Æneas of Troy, an epic in twelve books, connecting the hero with the foundation of Rome, and especially with the Julian family, and which was finished in 19 B. C.; on his deathbed he expressed a wish that it should be burned, and left instructions to that effect in his will; he was one of the purest minded poets perhaps that ever lived.

Voltaire, Francois Marie Arouet de, 1694-1778. Great French "persifleur"; born in Paris; son of a lawyer; began his literary career as a satirist and in the production of lampoons which cost him twice over imprisonment in the Bastille, on his release from which he left France in 1726 and went to England, where he stayed three years, and got acquainted with the free-thinking class there; on his return to Paris he engaged in some profitable commercial speculations and published his "Charles XII.," which he had written in England; retired to the chateau of Cirey, where he lived five years with Madame du Chatelet, engaged in study and diligent with his pen; after her death made his famous visit to Frederick the Great, with whom before three years were out he quarreled, and from whom he was glad to escape, making his headquarters eventually within the borders of France at Ferney; now and again visited Paris, where on his last visit he was received with such raptures of adulation that he was quite overcome, and had to be conveyed home to die, giving up the ghost exactly two months after. He was a man of superlative adroitness of faculty and more than any other the incarnation of the spirit of his time.

Wallace, Lewis (better known as Lew), 1827-1905. . An American military officer and author; born in Brookville, Ind.; was lieutenant in the Mexican War in 1846-1847; took a distinguished part in the Civil War in which he served in the campaigns in West Virginia and Kentucky; commanded a division at the capture of Fort Donelson; led the attack in the second day's fight in the battle of Shiloh; took part in the subsequent advance on Corinth; saved Cincinnati, O., from capture by Gen. E. Kirby Smith; and was president of the court appointed to investigate the conduct of General Buell; in 1864 he commanded the Middle Department and the Eighth Army Corps, and in the battle of Monocacy, prevented the capture of Washington and Baltimore by General Early. He was a member of the commission which tried the assassins of President Lincoln, and in the same year presided over the court which tried Captain Wirz, the commandant of the Andersonville prison. In 1866 he was sent to Mexico on a secret diplomatic mission to President Juarez; was appointed governor of New Mexico in 1880; and was United States Minister to Turkey in 1881-1885. When not engaged in public service he practiced law and devoted himself to literature. His publications include: "The Fair God;" "Ben Hur, a Tale of the Christ;" "The Prince of India;" "The Life of Gen. Benjamin Harrison," etc.

Walpole, Horace, Earl of Orford, 1717-1797. An English author; born in London. In 1741 he entered the House of Commons; in 1791 he succeeded his nephew in the peerage. He never took his seat in the House of Lords, and appears to have avoided using his title. The works of Horace Walpole are numerous; but his fame as a writer rests on his "Letters" and "Memoirs." The former are held to be unsurpassed in the English language. His romance "The Castle of Otranto" is also well known. He died in London.

Walton, Izaak, 1593-1683. An English author; known as the father of angling; born in Stafford, England. Walton's fame is mainly based on his "Compleat Angler; or the Contemplative Man's Companion," first published in 1653. Few more popular books exist, and the editions are consequently numerous. He died in Winchester, England.

Ward, Elizabeth Stuart Phelps, 1844- . . . . An American novelist and poet; born in Andover, Mass. In 1888 she married Herbert D. Ward, with whom she has sometimes collaborated. She is the author of many popular books. See PHELPS.

Ward, Mrs. Humphry (Mary Augusta Arnold), 1851- . . . . An English novelist; born in Hobart Town, Tasmania; is a niece of Matthew Arnold; translated Amiel's "Journal," a suggestive record, but is best known by her romance "Robert Elsmere."

Warner, Charles Dudley, 1829-1900. American editor and author; born in Plainfield, Mass.; was graduated from Hamilton College in 1851; he was the author of a large number of works, and editor of "A Library of the World's Best Literature"; died in Hartford, Conn.

Watts, Isaac, 1674-1748. An English hymnologist; born in Southampton, England. He wrote: "Hymns and Spiritual Songs," "Divine and Moral Songs for the Use of Children," "A Manual of Logic," several volumes of "Sermons," besides other works of less note. As a religious poet Watts has been always widely popular. He died in Theobaldo, Herts, England.

Watson, John ("Ian Maclaren.") 1850- . . . . Till 1893 Dr. Watson was known as a popular preacher and able minister, but in that year he acquired additional distinction and wider fame by writing a series of Scotch idylls for the *British Weekly*, under the title of "Beside the Bonnie Brier Bush"; they became widely popular in the United States and Great Britain. "The Days of Auld Lang Syne," a second series of idylls, published in 1895, also reached a large circulation. A novel from Dr. Watson's pen, "Kate Carnegie and Those Ministers," was published in 1896.

Watson, William, 1858- . . . . poet; born in Yorkshire; the first poem which procured him recognition was "Wordsworth's Grave"; among his later productions the most important is a volume entitled, "Odes and other Poems"; has also written an admirable volume of essays, "Excursions in Criticism."

Wesley, Charles, 1708-1788. An English hymnist; born in Epworth, England; younger brother of John Wesley; wrote numerous hymns, large collections from which have been frequently published. Two of his sons, Charles and Samuel, were celebrated for musical genius. He died in London.

Whately, Richard, 1787-1863. Archbishop of Dublin; born in London; is best known by his "Logic," for a time the standard work of the subject.

White, Richard Grant, 1822-1885. An American Shakespearean scholar; born in New York city. Among his published books are: "Memoirs of the Life of William Shakespeare, with an Essay towards the Expression of His Genius," etc., "Words and their Uses," "The Riverside Shakespeare," an annotated edition of Shakespeare, etc. He died in New York city.

Whitman, Walt, 1819-1892. An American poet; born in West Hills, Long Island, N. Y.; became editor of the Brooklyn *Eagle*. "Specimen Days and Collect" may be held to embrace the life work of Whitman as a writer. About the close of the war he received a subordinate clerkship under the government, and was summarily dismissed as the author of "an indecent book," though he fortunately obtained a similar post almost immediately. In 1874 he left Washington for Camden, N. J., where he lived till his death.

Whittier, John Greenleaf, 1807-1892. An American poet; born near Haverhill, Mass. The son of a poor farmer, who was also shoemaker, young Whittier obtained his education with that struggle which seems to foster genius, while the bodily frame, that so well served him till his decease, was developed and hardened by his healthy, outdoor life; was apprenticed to journalism; his poetry attracted the admiration of William Lloyd Garrison, who rode over from Newburyport to see Whittier when quite a lad, and became his lifelong friend. So it fell out that, if Garrison may be called the preacher or prophet, Whittier must be wreathed the poet laureate of abolition. Apart from this strenuous and heroic struggle there is nothing epoch making in Whittier's life, literary or personal. He died in Hampton Falls, N. H.

Wieland, Christoph Martin, 1733-1813. A German poet and novelist; born near Biberach, a small village in Swabia; son of a pastor of the pietist school; studied at Tubingen; became professor of philosophy at Erfurt, and settled in Weimar in 1772 as tutor of the two sons of the Duchess Amalia. His best work is an heroic poem entitled "Oberon."

Wiggin, Kate Douglas (*nee* Smith), 1857- . . . . An American authoress; born in Philadelphia, Pa. She went to California in 1876, where she studied the kindergarten system in Los Angeles; later, she taught a year in Santa Barbara College; then went to San Francisco, where she organized the first free kindergarten in the West. In 1880 she organized the California Kindergarten Training School. She has written many stories and books on and for the kindergarten.

Wilkins-Freeman, Mary Eleanor, 1862- . . . . An American authoress; born in Randolph, Mass. Her works, studies of New England country life, are: "The Love of Parson Lord," "Understudies," etc. She was married to Dr. Charles M. Freeman, January 1, 1902.

Willis, Nathaniel Parker, 1806-1867. An American author; born in Portland, Me.; established the *American Monthly Magazine*, which was merged in the New York *Mirror;* traveled in France, Italy, Greece, European Turkey, Asia Minor, and finally England. His numerous published writings include: "Pencilings by the Way," "Inklings of Adventure," etc. Died near Newburgh, N. Y.

Wilson, John, 1785-1854. The well known "Christopher North"; born in Paisley; son of a manufacturer, who left him a fortune of £50.000; lost his fortune and settled in Edinburgh; became editor of *Blackwood's Magazine*, and was in 1820 elected, over Sir William Hamilton, Professor of Moral Philosophy in Edinburgh University.

Winter, William, 1836- . . . . An American dramatic critic; born in Gloucester, Mass. He did journalistic work on the *Saturday Press*, *Vanity Fair*, the *Albion*, *Weekly Review*, and was dramatic critic for the New York *Tribune* from 1865.

Wood, Mrs. Henry (*nee* Price), 1820-1887. An English novelist; born in Worcestershire; her best novels, "The Channings" and "Mrs. Halliburton's Troubles," though her most popular, "East Lynne." She wrote some thirty, all popular, and deservedly so.

Woodworth, Samuel, 1785-1842. An American journalist; born in Scituate, Mass. He was one of the founders of the New York *Mirror;* edited the *Parthenon;* wrote a romantic history of the war, called "The Champions of Freedom," and several dramatic pieces. His famous poem is "The Old Oaken Bucket." He died in New York city.

Wordsworth, William, 1770-1850. An English poet; born in Cockermouth, Cumberland. He was the son of an attorney and in 1787 was sent to St. John's College, Cambridge. He crossed to France in November, 1791, and exhibited vehement sympathy with the revolution, remaining in France for nearly a year. After his return, disregarding all entreaties to enter on a professional career, he published his "Evening Walk and Descriptive Sketches." Two years afterward he received a legacy of $4,500 from Raisley Calvert. With this sum and the consecrated helpfulness of his sister Dorothy he contrived to keep house for eight years, while he gave himself to poetic effort as his high "office on earth." Coleridge induced the Wordsworths to go to Alfoxden, in his immediate neighborhood. Here the two poets held daily intercourse, and after a year they published "Lyrical Ballads" in literary co-partnership. After a winter spent in Germany, Wordsworth and his sister settled at Grasmere, where he proposed to write a great philosophical poem on man, nature, and society. Thenceforth his life was marked by few incidents. Died in Rydal Mount.

Xenophon, 430-357 B. C. A Greek historian and philosopher; Xenophon played an important part in the adventurous retreat known in history as the "Retreat of the Ten Thousand."

Yonge, Charlotte Mary, 1823- . . . . Popular novelist; born at Otterbourne, Hants; has written "Cameos of History of England," "Landmarks of History," etc.

Young, Edward, 1684-1765. An English poet; author of "Night Thoughts."

Zangwill, Israel, 1854- . . . . An English-Jewish novelist; born in London. He began life as a London teacher, and, while teaching, graduated at the London University; has written novels, essays, and poems; among his works, the "Bachelors' Club," "Old Maids' Club," "Children of the Ghetto," "Dreams of the Ghetto," "The Master," "Without Prejudice," etc.

Zola, Emile, 1840-1902. A French novelist; born in Paris, France; the son of an Italian engineer. After working for Paris publishers and writing for the press he attempted fiction with success. During 1897 and 1898 he took up with splendid courage the cause of Captain Dreyfus, whom he declared to have been illegally condemned, and was in consequence of his action prosecuted by order of the French government, and condemned to imprisonment. He escaped punishment by voluntary exile in England. Returning to Paris after the subsidence of the excitement caused by the Dreyfus case, he resumed his literary work; was accidentally killed by gas escaping from a coal fire.

Zschokke (*tshok′ke*), **Johann Heinrich,** 1771-1845. A German writer; born in Magdeburg; lived chiefly at Aarau, in Aargau, Switzerland, where he spent forty years of his life, and where he died; wrote histories, and a series of tales, but is best known by his "Stunden der Andacht" (*i. e.* hours of devotion).

NAPOLEON BONAPARTE.

Book III.

History and Biography.

History and Biography.

Chronological Eras.—The year 1899 corresponds to the year 7407-8 of the Byzantine era; to 5659-60 of the Jewish era, the year 5650 beginning at sunset on September 4; to 2652 since the foundation of Rome according to Varro; to 2675 of the Olympiads (the third year of the 669th Olympiad beginning July 1, 1899); to 2559 of the Japanese era, and to the 32d year of the Meiji; to 1316-17 of the Mohammedan era or the era of the Hegira, the year 1317 beginning on May 12, 1899. The 125th year of the Independence of the United States of America begins on July 4, 1900.

Date of Beginning of Epochs, Eras, and Periods.

NAME.		BEGAN.
Grecian Mundane Era	B. C.	5598, Sept. 1
Civil Era of Constantinople	"	5508, Sept. 1
Alexandrian Era	"	5502, Aug. 29
Ecclesiastical Era of Antioch	"	5492, Sept. 1
Julian Period	"	4713, Jan. 1
Mundane Era	"	4008, Oct. 1
Jewish Mundane Era	"	3761, Oct. 1
Era of Abraham	"	2015, Oct. 1
Era of the Olympiads	"	776, July 1
Roman Era (A. U. C.)	"	753, Apr. 24
Era of Nabonassar	"	747, Feb. 26
Metonic Cycle	"	432, July 15
Grecian or Syro-Macedonian Era	"	312, Sept. 1
Era of Maccabees	"	166, Nov. 24
Tyrian Era	"	125, Oct. 19
Sidonian Era	"	110, Oct. 1
Cæsarean Era of Antioch	"	48, Sept. 1
Julian Year	"	45, Jan. 1
Spanish Era	"	38, Jan. 1
Actian Era	"	30, Jan. 1
Augustan Era	"	27, Feb. 14
Vulgar Christian Era	A. D.	1, Jan. 1
Destruction of Jerusalem	"	69, Sept. 1
Era of Diocletian	"	284, Sept. 17
Era of Ascension	"	295, Nov. 12
Era of the Armenians	"	552, July 7
Mohammedan Era	"	622, July 16
Persian Era of Yezdegird	"	632, June 16

Divisions of Time.—The interval between two consecutive transits of a fixed star over any meridian or the interval during which the earth makes one absolute revolution on its axis is called a *Sidereal* Day, and is invariable, while the interval between two consecutive transits of the Sun over any meridian is called an *Apparent* Solar Day, and its length varies from day to day by reason of the variable motion of the earth in its orbit, and the inclination of this orbit to the equator, on which time is measured.

A *Mean* Solar Day is the average or mean of all the apparent solar days in a year. *Mean Solar Time* is that shown by a well-regulated clock or watch, while *Apparent Solar Time* is that shown by a well-constructed sundial; the difference between the two at any time is the *Equation of Time*, and may amount to 16 minutes and 21 seconds. The Astronomical Day begins at noon and the Civil Day at the preceding midnight. The Sidereal and Mean Solar Days are both invariable, but one day of the latter is equal to 1 day, 3 minutes, and 56.555 seconds of the former.

The interval during which the earth makes one absolute revolution round the Sun is called a *Sidereal Year*, and consists of 365 days, 6 hours, 9 minutes, and 9.6 seconds, which is invariable.

The Tropical Year is the interval between two consecutive returns of the Sun to the Vernal Equinox. If this were a fixed point, the Sidereal and Tropical Years would be identical; but in consequence of the disturbing influence of the moon and planets on the spheroidal figure of the earth, the Equinox has a slow, retrograde mean motion of 50.26 seconds annually, and the Sun returns to the Equinox sooner every year than he otherwise would by 20 minutes, 23.6 seconds; the Tropical Year, therefore, consists of 365 days, 5 hours, 48 minutes, and 46 seconds. The Tropical Year is not of uniform length; it is now slowly decreasing at the rate of .595 second per century, but this variation will not always continue.

Julius Cæsar, in B. C. 45, was the first to reform the calendar by ordering that every year whose date number is exactly divisible by 4 contain 366 days, and all other years 365 days. The intercalary day was introduced by counting the *sixth* day before the Kalends of March *twice;* hence the name bissextile, from bis, twice, and sex, six. He also changed the beginning of the year from first of March, to the first of January, and also changed the name of the fifth month (Quintilis) to July, after himself. The average length of the Julian year is therefore 365¼ days, which, however, is too long by 11 minutes and 14 seconds, and this would accumulate in 400 years to about three days. The Julian Calendar continued in use until A. D. 1582, when the date of the beginning of the seasons occurred 10 days later than in B. C. 45, when this mode of reckoning time was introduced.

The Gregorian Year was introduced by Pope Gregory XIII. with the view of keeping the Equinox to the same day of the month. It consists of 365 days, but every year exactly divisible by 4 and the centurial years which are exactly divisible by 400 contain 366 days; and if in addition to this arbitrary arrangement the centurial years exactly divisible by 4,000 contain 366 days, the error in the Gregorian system will amount to only one day in about 20 centuries. If, however, 31 leap years were intercalated in 128 years, instead of 32 as at present, the calendar would be practically exact, and the error would not amount to more than a day in 100,000 years. The length of the mean Gregorian Year may therefore be set down at 365 days, 5 hours, 49 minutes, 12 seconds. The Gregorian Calendar was introduced into England and her colonies in 1752, at which time the Equinox had retrograded 11 days since the Council of Nice in A. D. 325, when the festival of Easter was established and the Equinox occurred on March 21; hence September 3, 1752, was called September 14, and at the same time the commencement of the legal year was changed from March 25 to January 1, so that the year 1751 lost the months of January and February and the first 24 days of March. The difference between the Julian and Gregorian Calendars is now 12 days. Russia and the Greek Church still employ the Julian Calendar for civil and ecclesiastical purposes.

Standard Time.— Primarily, for the convenience of the railroads, a standard of time was established by mutual agreement in 1883, by which trains are run and local time regulated. According to this system, the United States, extending from 65° to 125° west longitude, is divided into four time sections, each of 15° of longitude, exactly equivalent to one hour, commencing with the 75th meridian. The first (eastern) section includes all territory between the Atlantic coast and an irregular line drawn from Detroit to Charleston, S. C., the latter being its most southern point. The second (central) section includes all the territory between the last named line and an irregular line from Bismarck, N. D., to the mouth of the Rio Grande. The third (mountain) section includes all territory between the last-named line and nearly the western borders of Idaho, Utah, and Arizona. The fourth (Pacific) section covers the rest of the country to the Pacific coast. Standard time is uniform inside each of these sections, and the time of each section differs from that next to it by exactly one hour. Thus at 12 noon in New York city (eastern time), the time at Chicago (central time) is 11 o'clock A. M.; at Denver (mountain time), 10 o'clock A. M., and at San Francisco (Pacific time), 9 o'clock A. M. Standard time is 16 minutes slower at Boston than true local time, 4 minutes slower at New York, 8 minutes faster at Washington, 19 minutes faster at Charleston, 28 minutes slower at Detroit, 18 minutes faster at Kansas City, 10 minutes slower at Chicago, one minute faster at St. Louis, 28 minutes faster at Salt Lake City, and 10 minutes faster at San Francisco.

Old English Holidays.—These holidays, with their names, had their origin in mediæval England when the State religion was that of the Church of Rome, and they are still observed generally or in some parts of England, Scotland, and Ireland.

JANUARY 6. TWELFTH DAY, or Twelfthtide, sometimes called Old Christmas Day, the same as Epiphany. The previous evening is Twelfth Night, with which many social rites have long been connected.

FEBRUARY 2. CANDLEMAS: Festival of the Purification of the Virgin. Consecration of the lighted candles to be used in the church during the year.

FEBRUARY 14. OLD CANDLEMAS: St. Valentine's Day.

MARCH 25. LADY DAY: Annunciation of the Virgin. April 6 is old Lady Day.

JUNE 24. MIDSUMMER DAY: Feast of the Nativity of John the Baptist. July 7 is old Midsummer Day.

JULY 15. ST. SWITHIN'S DAY. There was an old superstition that if rain fell on this day it would continue forty days.

AUGUST 1. LAMMAS DAY: Originally in England the festival of the wheat harvest. In the Church the festival of St. Peter's miraculous deliverance from prison. Old Lammas Day is August 13.

SEPTEMBER 29. MICHAELMAS: Feast of St. Michael, the Archangel. Old Michaelmas is October 11.

NOVEMBER 1. ALLHALLOWMAS: Allhallows or All Saints' Day. The previous evening is Allhalloween, observed by home gatherings and old-time festive rites.

NOVEMBER 2. ALL SOULS' DAY: Day of prayer for the souls of the dead.

NOVEMBER 11: MARTINMAS: Feast of St. Martin. Old Martinmas is November 23.

DECEMBER 28. CHILDERMAS: Holy Innocents Day.

Lady Day, Midsummer Day, Michaelmas, and Christmas are quarter (rent) days in England, and Whitsunday, Martinmas, Candlemas, and Lammas Day in Scotland.

Shrove Tuesday, the day before Ash Wednesday, and Maundy Thursday, the day before Good Friday, are observed by the Church. Mothering Sunday is Mid-Lent Sunday, in which the old rural custom obtains of visiting one's parents and making them presents.

Legal Holidays in the Various States. ALABAMA.—Jan. 1 (New Year's Day), Jan. 19 (R. E. Lee's Birthday), Shrove Tuesday, Feb. 22 (Washington's Birthday), Good Friday, June 3 (Jefferson Davis's Birthday), July 4, Thanksgiving, and Christmas.

ARIZONA.—Jan. 1, Feb. 22, May 30 (Memorial

Day), Arbor Day, July 4, Election Day, Thanksgiving, and Christmas.

ARKANSAS.—Arbor Day, Thanksgiving, July 4, and Christmas.

CALIFORNIA.—Jan. 1, Feb. 22, May 30, July 4, First Monday in September (Labor Day), Sept. 9 (Admission Day), Christmas, Thanksgiving, day of general election and every day appointed by the president or the governor.

COLORADO.—Labor Day (only statutory holiday, but other big holidays generally observed).

CONNECTICUT.—Jan. 1, Feb. 12 (Lincoln's Birthday), Feb. 22, May 30, July 4, Good Friday, Labor Day, Christmas, and Thanksgiving.

DELAWARE.—Jan. 1, Feb. 22, July 4, Arbor and Bird Days, Labor Day, Thanksgiving, and Christmas.

FLORIDA.—Jan. 1, Jan. 19, Feb. 22, April 26 (Confederate Memorial Day), June 3, July 4, Thanksgiving, and Christmas.

GEORGIA.—Jan. 19, April 26, June 3, July 4, Labor Day, and Christmas.

IDAHO.—Jan. 1, Feb. 22, Friday following May 1, July 4, Election Day, Christmas.

ILLINOIS.—Jan. 1, Feb. 12, Feb. 22, May 30, July 4, Labor Day, Thanksgiving, and Christmas.

INDIANA.—Jan. 1, Feb. 22, May 30, Thanksgiving, and Christmas.

IOWA.—Jan. 1, Feb. 22, May 30, Labor Day, Thanksgiving, and Christmas.

KANSAS.—Feb. 22, May 30, and Labor Day.

KENTUCKY.—Jan. 1, Feb. 22, July 4, Labor Day, Thanksgiving, and Christmas.

LOUISIANA.—Jan. 1, Jan. 8 (anniversary of the Battle of New Orleans), Feb. 22, Mardi-Gras (day before Ash Wednesday), Good Friday, June 3, July 4, Nov. 1 (All Saints' Day), Labor Day (fourth Saturday in November), Thanksgiving, and Christmas.

MAINE.—Jan. 1, Feb. 22, May 30, July 4, Fast Day, Thanksgiving, and Christmas.

MARYLAND.—Jan. 1, Feb. 22, Good Friday, May 30, July 4, Thanksgiving, and Christmas.

MASSACHUSETTS.—Feb. 22, April 19 (Patriots' Day, Anniversary Battle of Lexington), May 30, July 4, Labor Day, Thanksgiving, and Christmas.

MICHIGAN.—Jan. 1, Feb. 22, May 30, July 4, Labor Day, and Christmas.

MINNESOTA.—Jan. 1, Feb. 12, Feb. 22, Good Friday, May 30, July 4, Thanksgiving, and Christmas, Arbor and Bird Days (designated by the governor).

MISSISSIPPI.—Jan. 1, Feb. 22, July 4, Thanksgiving, and Christmas.

MISSOURI.—Jan. 1, Feb. 22, May 30, July 4, Labor Day, Thanksgiving, and Christmas.

NEBRASKA.—Jan. 1, Feb. 22, April 22 (Arbor Day), May 30, July 4, Thanksgiving, and Christmas.

NEVADA.—Jan. 1, Feb. 22, May 30, July 4, Oct. 31 (Admission Day), General Election Day, Thanksgiving, and Christmas.

NEW HAMPSHIRE.—Feb. 22, May 30, July 4, Labor Day, Fast Day, Thanksgiving, and Christmas.

NEW JERSEY.—Jan. 1, Feb. 12, Feb. 22, May 30, July 4, General Election Day, Thanksgiving, and Christmas.

NEW MEXICO.—Jan. 1, Feb. 22, May 30, Arbor Day (second Friday in March), Labor Day, Thanksgiving, Christmas, and Flag Day.

NEW YORK.—Jan. 1, Feb. 12, Feb. 22, May 30, July 4, Labor Day, Election Day, Thanksgiving, and Christmas.

NORTH CAROLINA.—Jan. 1, Jan. 19, Feb. 22, May 10 (Confederate Memorial Day), May 20 (Mecklenburg Declaration of Independence), July 4, October 12, Thanksgiving, and Christmas.

NORTH DAKOTA.—Jan. 1, Feb. 22, May 30, July 4, Election Day, Thanksgiving, and Christmas.

OHIO.—Jan. 1, Feb. 22, May 30, July 4, Thanksgiving, and Christmas.

OKLAHOMA.—Jan. 1, Feb. 22, Arbor Day, May 30, July 4, Labor Day, Thanksgiving, and Christmas.

OREGON.—Jan. 1, Feb. 22, May 30, July 4, Labor Day, Thanksgiving, and Christmas.

PENNSYLVANIA.—Jan. 1, Feb. 12, third Tuesday in February (local election), Feb. 22, Good Friday, May 30, July 4, Labor Day, November Election Day, Thanksgiving, and Christmas.

RHODE ISLAND.—Jan. 1, Feb. 22, second Friday in May, May 30, Labor Day, Election Day, Thanksgiving, and Christmas.

SOUTH CAROLINA.—Jan. 1, Feb. 22, May 10 (Confederate Memorial Day), July 4, Thanksgiving, and Christmas.

SOUTH DAKOTA.—Jan. 1, Feb. 22, May 30, July 4, Election Day, Thanksgiving, and Christmas.

TENNESSEE.—Jan. 1, Feb. 22, Good Friday, May 30, June 3, July 4, Labor Day, Election Day, and Thanksgiving.

TEXAS.—Jan. 1, Feb. 22, March 2 (Texas independence), April 21 (Battle of San Jacinto), July 4, Election Day, Thanksgiving, and Christmas.

UTAH.—Jan. 1, Feb. 22, Arbor Day, May 30, July 24 (Pioneers' Day), Labor Day, Thanksgiving, and Christmas.

VERMONT.—Jan. 1, Feb. 22, May 30, July 4, August 16 (Bennington Battle Day), Election Day, Thanksgiving, and Christmas.

VIRGINIA.—Jan. 1, Jan. 19, Feb. 22, July 4, Thanksgiving, and Christmas.

WASHINGTON.—Jan. 1, Feb. 12, Feb. 22, May 30, July 4, Election Day, Thanksgiving, and Christmas.

WEST VIRGINIA.—Jan. 1, Feb. 22, May 30, July 4, Labor Day, Election Day, Thanksgiving, and Christmas.

WISCONSIN.—Jan. 1, Feb. 22, May 30, July 4, Election Day, Thanksgiving, and Christmas.

WYOMING.—Jan. 1, Feb. 12, Feb. 22, May 30, Election Day, Thanksgiving, and Christmas.

SATURDAY HALF-HOLIDAYS.—After 12 o'clock noon. Legal holiday in Colorado and Louisiana (in cities and towns of 100,000 population and over), Delaware (Newcastle County only, in Wilmington throughout the year, and rest of county from June to September), District of Columbia, Maryland (Baltimore and Annapolis only), Michigan, Missouri (in cities of 100,000 or over), New Jersey, New York, Ohio (in cities of 50,000 or over), Pennsylvania, South Carolina (in Charleston County only), and Virginia.

There is no national holiday, not even the Fourth of July. Congress has at various times appointed special holidays. In the second session of the fifty-third Congress it passed an act making Labor Day a public holiday in the District of Columbia, and it has recognized the existence of certain days as holidays, for commercial purposes, but, with the exception named, there is no general statute on the subject. The proclamation of the President designating a day of Thanksgiving only makes it a legal holiday in those States which provide by law for it.

The Months and their Names.— January, the first month of the year, was among the Romans held sacred to Janus, from whom it derived its name, and was added to the calendar along with February by Numa in 713 B. C. It was not till the eighteenth century that January was universally adopted by European nations as the *first* month of the year, although the Roman's considered it as such as far back as 251 B. C.

February is the name given to the second month, in which were celebrated the Februa, or feasts to the manes of deceased persons.

March, the first month of the Roman year, and the third according to our present calendar, consists of 31 days. It was considered as the first month of the year in England until the change of style in 1752, and the legal year was reckoned from the 25th of March. Its last three days (old style) were once popularly supposed to have been *borrowed* by March from April, and are proverbially stormy.

To the fourth month of our year the Romans gave the name of *Aprilis*, derived from *aperire*, "to open," probably because it is the season when the buds begin to open. By the Anglo-Saxons it was called Eastermonth.

The name of the fifth month, May, is said to be derived from *Maia*, the mother of Mercury, to whom the Romans on the first day offered sacrifices. It was the third month of the Roman year.

June, the sixth month of the year in our calendar, but the fourth among the Romans, consisted originally of 26 days, to which four were added by Romulus, one taken away by Numa, and the month again lengthened to 30 days by Julius Cæsar.

The seventh month of the year in our calendar, and the fifth in the Roman calendar, was originally called Quintilis (the fifth). At first it contained 36 days, was reduced to 31, then to 30, but was restored to 31 days by Julius Cæsar, in honor of whom it was named July.

August, the eighth month of the year, was so named by the Emperor Augustus (B. C. 63 – A. D. 14), who commanded that his name should be given to the month. August was the sixth month of the Roman year and was previously called *Sextilis*.

September (Lat. *Septem*, seven) was the seventh month of the Roman calendar, but is the ninth according to our reckoning. The Anglo-Saxons called it *gerst-monath*, "barley-month."

October (Lat. *octo*, eight) was the eighth month of the so-called "year of Romulus," but became the tenth when (according to tradition) Numa changed the commencement of the year to January 1st, though it retained its original name.

November (Lat. *novem* nine) was among the Romans the ninth month of the year (the Ger. *Wind* month) at the time when the year consisted of ten months, and then contained 30 days. It subsequently was made to contain only 29, but Julius Cæsar gave it 31; and in the reign of Augustus the number was restored to 30, which number it has since retained.

December means the tenth month, and received that name from the Romans when the year began in March, and has retained its name since January and February were put at the beginning of the year.

The Origin of the Days of the Week.— The names of these are derived from Saxon idolatry. The Saxons had seven deities more particularly adored than the rest, namely: The Sun, the Moon, Tuisco, Woden, Thor, Friga, and Saeter.

Sunday being dedicated to the sun, was called by them Sunandaeg; his idol represented the bust of a man, with the face darting bright rays, holding a wheel before his breast, indicative of the circuit of the golden orb around our sphere.

Monday was dedicated to the moon, and was represented by a female on a pedestal, with a very singular dress and two long ears.

Tuesday was dedicated to Tuisco a German hero, sire of the Germans, Scythians, and Saxons. He was represented as a venerable old man, with a long, white beard, a scepter in his hand and the skin of a white bear thrown over his shoulders.

Wednesday was consecrated to Woden, or Odin, a supreme god of the northern nations, father of the gods and god of war. He was represented as a warrior in a bold martial attitude, clad in armor, holding in his right hand a broad, crooked sword and in his left a shield.

Thursday was consecrated to Thor, eldest son of Woden, who was the Roman Jupiter. He was believed to govern the air, preside over lightning and thunder, direct the wind, rain, and seasons. He was represented as sitting on a splendid throne, with a crown of gold adorned with twelve glittering stars, and a scepter in his right hand.

Friday was sacred to Friga — Hertha or Edith — the mother of the gods and wife of Woden. She was the goddess of love and pleasure and was portrayed as a female with a naked sword in her right hand and a bow in her left hand, implying that in extreme cases women should fight as well as men.

Saturday was named in honor of Saeter, who is the Roman Saturnus. He was represented on a pedestal, standing on the back of a prickly fish called a perch, his head bare, with a thin, meager face. In his left hand he held a wheel and in his right a pail of water with fruits and flowers. The sharp fins of the fish implied that the worshipers of Saeter should pass safely through every difficulty. The wheel was emblematic of their unity and freedom, and the pail of water implied that he could water the earth and make it more beautiful.

Anniversaries.

DATES OF HISTORICAL EVENTS CUSTOMARILY OR OCCASIONALLY OBSERVED.

Jan. 1. Emancipation Proclamation by Lincoln, 1863.
Jan. 8. Battle of New Orleans, 1815.
Jan. 17. Franklin born, 1706.
Jan. 17. Battle of the Cowpens, S. C., 1781.
Jan. 18. Daniel Webster born, 1782.
Jan. 19. Robert E. Lee born, 1807.
Jan. 27. German Emperor born, 1859.
Feb. 12. Abraham Lincoln born, 1809.
Feb. 15. Battle-ship Maine blown up, 1898.
Feb. 22. George Washington born, 1732.
Feb. 22-23. Battle of Buena Vista, 1847.
March 5. Boston Massacre, 1770.
March 15. Andrew Jackson born, 1767.
March 18. Grover Cleveland born, 1837
April 1. Bismarck born, 1815.
April 9. Lee surrendered at Appomattox, 1865.
April 12. Fort Sumter fired upon, 1861.
April 12. Henry Clay born, 1777.
April 13. Thomas Jefferson born, 1743.
April 14. Lincoln assassinated, 1865.
April 19. Primrose Day in England, Lord Beaconsfield died, 1881.
April 19. Battles of Lexington and Concord, 1775.
April 23. Shakespeare born, 1564.
April 27. General Grant born, 1822.
April 30. Washington was inaugurated first President, 1789.
May 1. Dewey destroyed the Spanish fleet at Manila, 1898.
May 13. First English settlement in America at Jamestown, 1607.
May 13. The Society of the Cincinnati was organized by officers of the Revolutionary Army, 1783.
May 17. Independence Day, Norway, 1814.
May 20. Mecklenburg, N. C., Dec. of Ind., 1775.
May 24. Queen Victoria born, 1819.
June 6. General Nathaniel Greene born, 1742.
June 15. King John granted Magna Charta at Runnymede, 1215.
June 17. Battle of Bunker Hill, 1775.
June 18. Battle of Waterloo, 1815.
June 28. Battle of Fort Moultrie, Charleston, S. C., 1776.
July 1. Dominion Day in Canada.
July 1-2. General assault on Santiago de Cuba, 1898.
July 1-3. Battle of Gettysburg, 1863.
July 3. Cervera's fleet was destroyed off Santiago, 1898.
July 4. Declaration of Independence, 1776.
July 14. The Bastille was destroyed, 1789.
July 16. Santiago surrendered, 1898.
July 21. Battle of Bull Run, 1861.
Aug. 13. Manila surrendered to the Americans, 1898.
Aug. 16. Battle of Bennington, Vt., 1777.
Sep. 1. Capitulation of Sedan, 1870.
Sep. 8. Battle of Eutaw Springs, S. C., 1781.
Sep. 10. Battle of Lake Erie, Perry's victory, 1813.
Sep. 11. Battle of Lake Champlain, McDonough's victory, 1814.
Sep. 13. Battle of Chapultepec, 1847.
Sep. 14. City of Mexico taken by the U. S. troops, 1847.
Sep. 17. Battle of Antietam, 1862.
Sep. 19-20. Battle of Chickamauga, 1863.
Sep. 20. Italians occupied Rome, 1870.
Oct. 7. Battle of King's Mountain, N. C., 1780.
Oct. 8-11. Great fire of Chicago, 1871.
Oct. 12. Columbus discovered America, 1492.
Oct. 17. Burgoyne surrendered at Saratoga, 1777.
Oct. 19. Cornwallis surrendered at Yorktown, 1781.
Nov. 5. Guy Fawkes Day in England. The Gunpowder Plot discovered, 1604.
Nov. 9. Great fire of Boston, 1872.
Nov. 10. Martin Luther born, 1483.
Nov. 25. British evacuated New York, 1783.
Dec. 2. Battle of Austerlitz, 1805.
Dec. 14. Washington died, 1799.
Dec. 16. Boston "Tea Party," 1773.
Dec. 16. The great fire in New York, 1835.
Dec. 22. Mayflower pilgrims landed at Plymouth Rock, 1620.
Dec. 25-26. Battle of Trenton, N. J., 1776.
Dec. 29. William Ewart Gladstone born, 1809.

The First Day of the Year.

Readers of Parish Registers and other ancient documents are sometimes puzzled by the dates, and especially by the apparent discrepancies in the time when the year commenced. It began:—

7th to 14th Centuries, at Christmas.
12th Century, by the Church, on March 25.
14th Century, by Civilians, same time.

In 1752 the New Style was introduced, and 1753 commenced on the 1st of January. Previous to this two dates were used, one for the civil year, and the other for the historical; the former commenced March 25, and the latter January 1; thus we find the same event with two dates, *e. g.*, Feb. 20, 1681–2. Another change was made in the calendar by the same Act, 24 Geo. II. c. 23; the day after September 2d was accounted the *fourteenth*, hence the difference between Old and New Michaelmas and other days.

General Councils.

		A. D.
Jerusalem	Against Judaizers	51
Arles	Against the Donatists	314
**Nice*	First Œcumenical Council	325
Constantinople	Arian	337
Rome	Athanasian	342
Sardis	Against Arius	347
**Constantinople*	Second Œcumenical	381
**Ephesus*	Third do	431
**Chalcedon*	Fourth do	451
**Constantinople*	Fifth do	553
**Constantinople*	Sixth do	681
Nice	Seventh do	787
Constantinople	Eighth do	870
Rome	First Lateran	1123
Rome	Second do	1139
Rome	Third do	1197
Rome	Fourth do	1215
Lyons	Emperor Frederick deposed	1243
Lyons	Temporary reunion of Greek and Latin Churches	1274
Vienne	Fifteenth Œcumenical	1312
Pisa	Popes elected and deposed	1409
Constance	Huss condemned to be burned	1414
Basle	Eighteenth Œcumenical	1431
Rome	Fifth Lateran	1512 to 1517
Trent	Nineteenth Œcumenical	1545 to 1563
Rome	Last Œcumenical	1870

* Only the six thus marked were indisputably General or Œcumenical. Some other councils, such as those summoned to Pavia and Siena, were designed to be Œcumenical, but led to no such result. The Greek Church recognizes seven.

A READY REFERENCE CALENDAR.

For ascertaining any Day of the Week for any given Time within Two Hundred Years from the introduction of the New Style, 1753 to 1952, inclusive.

YEARS 1753 TO 1952.

1753g	1781g	1800e	1828q	1856q	1884q	1900g	1928h
1754d	1782d	1801a	1829a	1857a	1885a	1901d	1929d
1755e	1783e	1802b	1830b	1858b	1886b	1902e	1930e
1756p	1784p	1803c	1831c	1859c	1887c	1903a	1931a
1757c	1785c	1804h	1832h	1860h	1888h	1904k	1932k
1758f	1786f	1805d	1833d	1861d	1889d	1905f	1933f
1759g	1787g	1806e	1834e	1862e	1890e	1906g	1934g
1760q	1788q	1807a	1835a	1863a	1891a	1907d	1935d
1761a	1789a	1808k	1836k	1864k	1892k	1908 l	1936 l
1762b	1790b	1809f	1837f	1865f	1893f	1909b	1937b
1763c	1791c	1810g	1838g	1866g	1894g	1910c	1938c
1764h	1792h	1811d	1839d	1867d	1895d	1911f	1939f
1765d	1793d	1812 l	1840 l	1868 l	1896 l	1912m	1940m
1766e	1794e	1813b	1841b	1869b	1897b	1913e	1941e
1767a	1795a	1814c	1842c	1870c	1898c	1914a	1942a
1768k	1796k	1815f	1843f	1871f	1899f	1915b	1943b
1769f	1797f	1816m	1844m	1872m		1916n	1944n
1770g	1798g	1817e	1845e	1873e		1917g	1945g
1771d	1799d	1818a	1846a	1874a		1918d	1946d
1772 l		1819b	1847b	1875b		1919e	1947e
1773b		1820n	1848n	1876n		1920p	1948p
1774c		1821g	1849g	1877g		1921c	1949c
1775f		1822d	1850d	1878d		1922f	1950f
1776m		1823e	1851e	1879e		1923g	1951g
1777e		1824p	1852p	1880p		1924q	1952q
1778a		1825c	1853c	1881c		1925a	
1779b		1826f	1854f	1882f		1926b	
1780n		1827g	1855g	1883g		1927c	

	Jan.	Feb.	Mar.	April.	May.	June.	July.	Aug.	Sept.	Oct.	Nov.	Dec.
a	4	7	7	3	5	1	3	6	2	4	7	2
b	5	1	1	4	6	2	4	7	3	5	1	3
c	6	2	2	5	7	3	5	1	4	6	2	4
d	2	5	5	1	3	6	1	4	7	2	5	7
e	3	6	6	2	4	7	2	5	1	3	6	1
f	7	3	3	6	1	4	6	2	5	7	3	5
g	1	4	4	7	2	5	7	3	6	1	4	6
h	7	3	4	7	2	5	7	3	6	1	4	6
k	5	1	2	5	7	3	5	1	4	6	2	4
l	3	6	7	3	5	1	3	6	2	4	7	2
m	1	4	5	1	3	6	1	4	7	2	5	7
n	6	2	3	6	1	4	6	2	5	7	3	5
p	4	7	1	4	6	2	4	7	3	5	1	3
q	2	5	6	2	4	7	2	5	1	3	6	1

TABLE OF DAYS.

1		2		3		4		5		6		7	
Monday	1	Tuesday	1	Wednesday	1	Thursday	1	Friday	1	Saturday	1	SUNDAY	1
Tuesday	2	Wednesday	2	Thursday	2	Friday	2	Saturday	2	SUNDAY	2	Monday	2
Wednesday	3	Thursday	3	Friday	3	Saturday	3	SUNDAY	3	Monday	3	Tuesday	3
Thursday	4	Friday	4	Saturday	4	SUNDAY	4	Monday	4	Tuesday	4	Wednesday	4
Friday	5	Saturday	5	SUNDAY	5	Monday	5	Tuesday	5	Wednesday	5	Thursday	5
Saturday	6	SUNDAY	6	Monday	6	Tuesday	6	Wednesday	6	Thursday	6	Friday	6
SUNDAY	7	Monday	7	Tuesday	7	Wednesday	7	Thursday	7	Friday	7	Saturday	7
Monday	8	Tuesday	8	Wednesday	8	Thursday	8	Friday	8	Saturday	8	SUNDAY	8
Tuesday	9	Wednesday	9	Thursday	9	Friday	9	Saturday	9	SUNDAY	9	Monday	9
Wednesday	10	Thursday	10	Friday	10	Saturday	10	SUNDAY	10	Monday	10	Tuesday	10
Thursday	11	Friday	11	Saturday	11	SUNDAY	11	Monday	11	Tuesday	11	Wednesday	11
Friday	12	Saturday	12	SUNDAY	12	Monday	12	Tuesday	12	Wednesday	12	Thursday	12
Saturday	13	SUNDAY	13	Monday	13	Tuesday	13	Wednesday	13	Thursday	13	Friday	13
SUNDAY	14	Monday	14	Tuesday	14	Wednesday	14	Thursday	14	Friday	14	Saturday	14
Monday	15	Tuesday	15	Wednesday	15	Thursday	15	Friday	15	Saturday	15	SUNDAY	15
Tuesday	16	Wednesday	16	Thursday	16	Friday	16	Saturday	16	SUNDAY	16	Monday	16
Wednesday	17	Thursday	17	Friday	17	Saturday	17	SUNDAY	17	Monday	17	Tuesday	17
Thursday	18	Friday	18	Saturday	18	SUNDAY	18	Monday	18	Tuesday	18	Wednesday	18
Friday	19	Saturday	19	SUNDAY	19	Monday	19	Tuesday	19	Wednesday	19	Thursday	19
Saturday	20	SUNDAY	20	Monday	20	Tuesday	20	Wednesday	20	Thursday	20	Friday	20
SUNDAY	21	Monday	21	Tuesday	21	Wednesday	21	Thursday	21	Friday	21	Saturday	21
Monday	22	Tuesday	22	Wednesday	22	Thursday	22	Friday	22	Saturday	22	SUNDAY	22
Tuesday	23	Wednesday	23	Thursday	23	Friday	23	Saturday	23	SUNDAY	23	Monday	23
Wednesday	24	Thursday	24	Friday	24	Saturday	24	SUNDAY	24	Monday	24	Tuesday	24
Thursday	25	Friday	25	Saturday	25	SUNDAY	25	Monday	25	Tuesday	25	Wednesday	25
Friday	26	Saturday	26	SUNDAY	26	Monday	26	Tuesday	26	Wednesday	26	Thursday	26
Saturday	27	SUNDAY	27	Monday	27	Tuesday	27	Wednesday	27	Thursday	27	Friday	27
SUNDAY	28	Monday	28	Tuesday	28	Wednesday	28	Thursday	28	Friday	28	Saturday	28
Monday	29	Tuesday	29	Wednesday	29	Thursday	29	Friday	29	Saturday	29	SUNDAY	29
Tuesday	30	Wednesday	30	Thursday	30	Friday	30	Saturday	30	SUNDAY	30	Monday	30
Wednesday	31	Thursday	31	Friday	31	Saturday	31	SUNDAY	31	Monday	31	Tuesday	31

NOTE—The letters in the list of "YEARS from 1753 to 1952" refer to the table headed with the MONTHS, the figures in which refer to the same figures at the head of the table of DAYS. For example: To know on what day July 4, 1900, will fall, look for 190[illegible] in the table of YEARS. The letter g is attached. Look for the same letter in the table of MONTHS, and in a parallel line under July is the figure 7, which directs to column 7 in the table of DAYS below, in which it will be seen that July 4 falls on Wednesday.

A DICTIONARY OF MYTHOLOGY.

A′bas. A son of Meganira. He was turned into a newt, or water-lizard, for deriding the ceremonies of the Sacrifice.

Absyr′tus. Brother of Medea.

Achelo′us. A son of Oceanus and Terra. He had the power of assuming all shapes, and in a conflict with Hercules he turned himself into a serpent, and then into a bull, but he was finally defeated, and he then turned himself into a river, which has since been called Achelous.

Ach′eron. One of the rivers of the infernal regions to which the spirits of the dead resorted, and waited there till Charon the ferryman took them over.

Achil′les. The most valiant of the Greek heroes in the Trojan War. He was the son of Peleus, king of Thessaly. His mother, Thetis, plunged him, when an infant, into the Stygian pool, which made him invulnerable wherever the waters had washed him; but the heel by which he was held was not wetted, and that part remained vulnerable. He was shot with an arrow in the heel by Paris, at the siege of Troy, and died of his wound.

Acida′lia. A name given to Venus, from a fountain in Bœotia.

A′cis. A Sicilian shepherd, loved by the nymph Galatea. One of the Cyclops who was jealous of him crushed him by hurling a rock on him. Galatea turned his blood into a river—the Acis at the foot of Mount Etna.

Actæ′on. The son of Aristæus, a famous huntsman. He intruded himself on Diana while she was bathing, and was changed by her into a deer, in which form he was hunted by his own dogs and torn in pieces.

Ado′nis. The beautiful attendant of Venus, who held her train. He was killed by a boar, and turned by Venus into an anemone.

Adrastæ′a. Another name of Nemesis, one of the goddesses of justice.

Adscripti′tii Dii. The gods of the second grade.

Æ′acus. One of the judges of hell, with Minos and Rhadamanthus.

Æcas′tor. An oath used only by women, referring to the Temple of Castor.

Æd′epol. An oath used by both men and women, referring to the Temple of Pollux.

Æge′on. A giant with fifty heads and one hundred hands, who was imprisoned by Jupiter under Mount Etna.

Æ′gis. The shield of Jupiter, so called because it was made of goat skin.

Æ′gle. The fairest of the Naiads.

Ael′lo. The name of one of the Harpies.

Æne′as. The son of Anchises and Venus. He was one of the few great captains who escaped the destruction of Troy. He behaved with great valor during the siege, encountering Diomed, and even Achilles himself. When the Grecians had set the city on fire Æneas took his aged father, Anchises, on his shoulders, while his son, Ascanius, and his wife, Creusa, clung to his garments. He saved them all from the flames. After wandering about during several years, encountering numerous difficulties, he at length arrived in Italy, where he was hospitably received by Latinus, king of the Latins. After the death of Latinus Æneas became king.

Æo′lus. The god of the winds. Jupiter was his reputed father, and his mother is said to have been a daughter of Hippotus.

Æscula′pius. The god of physic, was a son of Apollo. He was physician to the Argonauts in their famous expedition to Colchis.

Æ′son. Father of Jason, and was restored to youth by Medea.

Æ′ta. A king of Colchis, was father of Medea.

Agamem′non. The son of Plisthenes and brother of Menelaus. He was king of the Argives. His brother's wife was the famous Helen, daughter of Tyndarus, king of Sparta; and when she eloped with Paris, Agamemnon was appointed leader of the Greeks in their expedition against Troy.

Aganip′pides. A name of the Muses, derived from the fountain of Aganippe.

Agla′ia. One of the Three Graces.

Ag′ni. The Hindoo god of lightning.

A′jax. One of the bravest of the Greek warriors in the Trojan war. His father was Telamon, and his mother Eribœa. Some writers say that he was killed by Ulysses; others aver that he was slain by Paris; while others again assert that he went mad after being defeated by Ulysses, and killed himself. Another Ajax, son of Oileus, also took a prominent part in the Trojan War.

Alces′tis. Wife of Admetus, who, to save her husband's life, died in his stead, and was restored to life by Hercules.

Alci′des. One of the names of Hercules.

Alcme′na. The mother of Hercules, was daughter of Electrion, a king of Argos.

Alec′to. One of the Furies. She is depicted as having serpents instead of hair on her head, and was supposed to breed pestilence wherever she went.

Alec′tryon. A servant of Mars, who was changed by him into a cock because he did not warn his master of the rising of the sun.

Al′fadur. In Scandinavian Mythology the Supreme Being—Father of all.

Amal′thæ′a. The goat which nourished Jupiter.

Am′azons. A nation of women-soldiers who lived in Scythia. Hercules totally defeated them, and gave Hippolyte, their queen, to Theseus for a wife. The race seems to have been exterminated after this battle.

Ambarva′lia. Festivals in honor of Ceres, instituted by Roman husbandmen to purge their fields. At the spring festival the head of each family led an animal, usually a pig or ram, decked with oak boughs, round his grounds, and offered milk and new wine. After harvest there was another festival, at which Ceres was presented with the first fruits of the season.

Ambro′sia. Bacchanalian festivals.

Amphi′on. The son of Jupiter and Antiope. He was greatly skilled in music; and it it said that, at the sound of his lute, the stones arranged themselves so regularly as to make the walls of the city of Thebes.

Amphitri′te (or Salatia). The wife of Neptune, was a daughter of Oceanus and Terra. She was the mother of Triton, a sea god.

Amy′cus. King of Babrycia. He was a son of Neptune, and was killed by Pollux.

Ancæ′us. A son of Neptune, who left a cup of wine to hunt a wild boar, which killed him, and the wine was untasted. This was the origin of the proverb—"There's many a slip 'twixt cup and lip."

Ancil′ia. The twelve sacred shields. The first Ancile was supposed to have fallen from heaven in answer to the prayer of Numa Pompilius. It was kept with the greatest care, as it was prophesied that the fate of the Roman people would depend upon its preservation. An order of priesthood was established to take care of the Ancilia, and on 1st March each year the shields were carried in procession, and in the evening there was a great feast called Cœna Saliaris.

Androm′eda. The daughter of Cepheus, king of the Ethiopians, was wife of Perseus, by whom she was rescued when she was chained to a rock and was about to be devoured by a sea-monster.

Anem′one. Venus changed Adonis into this flower.

Angero′nia. Otherwise Volupia, was the goddess who had the power of dispelling anguish of mind.

Anna Peren′na. One of the rural divinities.

Antæ′us. A giant who was vanquished by Hercules. Each time that Hercules threw him the giant gained fresh strength from touching the earth, so Hercules lifted him off the ground and squeezed him to death.

An′teros. One of the two Cupids, sons of Venus.

Antic′lea. The mother of Ulysses.

Anti′ope. Was wife of Lycus, king of Thebes. Jupiter, disguised as a satyr, led her astray and corrupted her.

Anu′bis (or Herman′ubis). "A god half a dog, a dog half a man." Called *Barker* by Virgil and other poets.

Aon′ides. A name of the Muses, from the country Aonia.

Aph′rodi′te. A Greek name of Venus.

Apis. A name given to Jupiter by the inhabitants of the Lower Nile. Also the miraculous ox, worshiped in Egypt.

A′pis. King of Argivia. Afterwards called Serapis, the greatest god of the Egyptians.

Apol′lo. This famous god, sometime king of Arcadia, was the son of Jupiter and Latona. He was known by several names, but principally by the following: Sol (the sun); Cynthius, from the mountain called Cynthus in the Isle of Delos, and this same island being his native place obtained for him the name of Delius; Delphinius, from his occasionally assuming the shape of a dolphin. His name of Delphicus was derived from his connection with the splendid Temple at Delphi, where he uttered the famous oracles. Some writers record that this oracle became dumb when Jesus Christ was born. Other common names of Apollo were Didymæus, Nomius, Pæan, and Phœbus. The Greeks called him Agineus because the streets were under his guardianship, and he was called Pythius from having killed the serpent Python. Apollo is usually represented as a handsome young man without beard, crowned with laurel, and having in one hand a bow, and in the other a lyre. The favorite residence of Apollo was on Mount Parnassus, a mountain of Phocis, in Greece, where he presided over the Muses. Apollo was the accredited father of several children, but the two most renowned were Æsculapius and Phaeton.

Apothe′osis. The consecration of a god. The ceremony of deification.

Arach′ne. A Lydian princess, who challenged Minerva to a spinning contest, but Minerva struck her on the head with a spindle, and turned her into a spider.

Arca′dia. A delightful country in the center of Peloponnesus, a favorite place of the gods. Apollo was reputed to have been king of Arcadia.

Ar′cas. A son of Calisto, was turned into a he-bear; and afterwards into the constellation called Ursa Minor.

Areop′agi′tæ. The judges who sat at the Areopagus.

Areop′agus. The hill at Athens where Mars was tried for murder before twelve of the gods.

Arethu′sa. Was one of the nymphs of Diana. She fled from Alpheus, a river god, and was enabled to escape by being turned by Diana into a rivulet which ran underground. She was as virtuous as she was beautiful.

Ar′gonauts. This name was given to the fifty heroes who sailed to Colchis in the ship Argo under the command of Jason, to fetch the Golden Fleece.

Ar′gus. Was a god who had a hundred eyes which slept and watched by turns. He was charged by Juno to watch Io, but, being slain by Mercury, was changed by Juno into a peacock.

Ariad′ne. Daughter of Minos, king of Crete. After enabling Theseus to get out of the Labyrinth by means of a clew of thread, she fled with him to Naxos, where he ungratefully deserted her; but Bacchus wooed her and married her, and the crown of seven stars which he gave her was turned into a constellation.

Ari′on. Was a famous lyric poet of Methymna, in the island of Lesbos, where he gained great riches by his art.

Aristæ′us. Son of Apollo and Cyrene, was the god of trees; he also taught mankind the use of honey, and how to get oil from olives. He was a celebrated hunter. His most famous son was Actæon.

Arma′ta. One of the names of Venus, given to her by Spartan women.

Ar′temis. This was the Grecian name of Diana, and the festivals at Delphi were called Artemesia.

Arus′pices. Sacrificial priests.

Ascal′aphus. Was changed into an owl, the harbinger of misfortune, by Ceres, because he informed Pluto that Proserpine had partaken of food in the infernal regions, and thus prevented her return to earth.

Asca′nius. The son of Æneas.

Ascol′ia. Bacchanalian feasts, from a Greek word meaning a leather bottle. The bottles were used in the games to jump on.

Aso′pus. A son of Jupiter, who was killed by one of his father's thunderbolts.

Assabi′nus. The Ethiopian name of Jupiter.

Astar′te. One of the Eastern names of Venus.

Aste′ria. Daughter of Cæus, was carried away by Jupiter, who assumed the shape of an eagle.

Astre′a. Mother of Nemesis, was the goddess of justice; she returned to heaven when the earth became corrupt.

Atalan′ta. Daughter of Cæneus. The oracle told her that marriage would be fatal to her, but, being very beautiful, she had many suitors. She was a very swift runner, and, to get rid of her admirers, she promised to marry any one of them who should outstrip her in a race, but that all who were defeated should be slain. Hippomenes, however, with the aid of Venus, was successful. That goddess gave him three golden apples, one of which he dropped whenever Atalanta caught up to him in the race. She stopped to pick them up, and he was victorious and married her. They were both afterwards turned into lions by Cybele, for profaning her temple.

A′te. The goddess of revenge, also called the goddess of discord and all evil. She was banished from heaven by her father Jupiter,

Athe′na. A name obtained by Minerva as the tutelary goddess of Athens.

Atlas. King of Mauritania, now Morocco, in Africa. He was also a great astronomer. He is depicted with the globe on his back, his name signifying great toil or labor. For his inhospitality to Perseus that king changed him into the mountain which bears his name of Atlas. A chain of mountains in Africa is called after him, and so is the Atlantic Ocean.

At′reus. The type of fraternal hatred. His dislike of his brother Thyestes went to the extent of killing and roasting his nephews, and inviting their father to a feast, which Thyestes thought was a sign of reconciliation, but he was the victim of his brother's detestable cruelty.

At′ropos. One of the three sisters called *The Fates*, who held the shears ready to cut the thread of life.

A′tys. Son of Crœsus, was born dumb, but when in a fight he saw a soldier about to kill the king, he gained speech, and cried out, "Save the king!" and the string that held his tongue was broken.

A′tys. A youth beloved by Aurora, and was slain by her father, but, according to Ovid, was afterwards turned into a pine tree.

Aug′æas. A king of Elis, the owner of the stable which Hercules cleansed after three thousand oxen had been kept in it for thirty years. It was cleansed by turning the river Alpheus through it. Augæas promised to give Hercules a tenth part of his cattle for his trouble, but, for neglecting to keep his promise, Hercules shot him.

Au′gury. This was a means adopted by the Romans for forming a judgment of futurity by the flight of birds, and the officiating priest was called an augur.

Auro′ra. The goddess of the morning,

"Whose rosy fingers ope the gates of day."

She was daughter of Sol, the sun, and was the mother of the stars and winds.

Aus′ter. The south wind, a son of Jupiter.

Aver′nus. A poisonous lake, referred to by poets as being at the entrance of the infernal regions, but it was really a lake in Campania, Italy.

Averrun′cus Deus. A Roman god, who could divert people from evil doing.

Ba′al. A god of the Phœnicians.

Ba′al-Pe′or. A Moabitish god, associated with licentiousness and obscenity. The modern name is Belphegor.

Bac′chantes. The priestesses of Bacchus.

Bac′chus. The god of wine, and the son of Jupiter and Semele. He is said to have married Ariadne, daughter of Minos, king of Crete. after she was deserted by Theseus. The most distinguished of his children is Hymen, the god of marriage.

Ba′lios. A famous horse given by Neptune to Peleus as a wedding present, and afterwards given to Achilles.

Bassar′ides. The priestesses of Bacchus were sometimes so called.

Belisa′ma. A goddess of the Gauls. The name means the Queen of Heaven.

Beller′ophon. A hero who destroyed a monster called the Chimæra.

Bello′na. The goddess of war, and wife of Mars. The 24th March was called Bellona's day, when her votaries cut themselves with knives and drank the blood of the sacrifice.

Be′lus. The Chaldean name of the sun.

Berecyn′thia. A name of Cybele, from a mountain where she was worshiped.

Bi′formis. A name of Bacchus, because he was accounted both bearded and beardless.

Bo′na De′a. "The bountiful goddess," whose festival was celebrated by the Romans with much magnificence.

Bo′nus Even′tus. The god of good success, a rural divinity.

Bo′reas. The north wind, son of Astræus and Aurora.

Brah′ma. The great Indian deity, represented with four heads looking to the four quarters of the globe.

Bris′æus. A name of Bacchus, referring to the use of grapes and honey.

Bront′es. One of the Cyclops. He is the personification of a blacksmith.

Bubo′na. Goddess of herdsmen, one of the rural divinities.

Bud′dha. A pagan deity, the Vishnu of the Hindoos.

Byb′lis. A niece of Sol, mentioned by Ovid. She shed so many tears for unrequited love that she was turned into a fountain.

Cab′iri. The mysterious rites connected with the worship of these deities were so obscene that most writers refer to them as secrets which it was unlawful to reveal.

Cac′odæ′mon. Greek name of an evil spirit.

Ca′cus. A three-headed monster and robber.

Cad′mus. One of the earliest of the Greek demigods. He was the reputed inventor of letters, and his alphabet consisted of sixteen letters. It was Cadmus who slew the Bœotian dragon, and sowed its teeth in the ground, from each of which sprang up an armed man.

Cadu′ceus. The rod carried by Mercury. It has two winged serpents entwined round the top end. It was supposed to possess the power of producing sleep, and Milton refers to it in "Paradise Lost" as the "opiate rod."

Calis′to. An Arcadian nymph, who was turned into a she-bear by Jupiter. In that form she was hunted by her son Arcas, who would have killed her had not Jupiter turned him into a he-bear. The nymph and her son form the constellations known as the Great Bear and Little Bear.

Calli′ope. The Muse who presided over epic poetry and rhetoric. She is generally depicted using a stylus and wax tablets, the ancient writing materials.

Cal′pe. One of the pillars of Hercules.

Calyp′so. Queen of the island of Ogygia, on which Ulysses was wrecked, and where he was persuaded to remain seven years.

Ca′ma. The Indian god of love and marriage.

Camil′lus. A name of Mercury, from his office of minister to the gods.

Can′ache. The name of one of Actæon's hounds.

Cano′ba. The Indian Apollo.

Cano′pus. The Egyptian god of water, the conqueror of fire.

Cap′is or **Cap′ula.** A peculiar cup with ears, used in drinking the health of the deities.

Capitoli′nus. A name of Jupiter, from the Capitoline hill, on the top of which a temple was built and dedicated to him.

Caprip′edes. Pan, the Egipans, the Satyrs, and Fauns were so called from having goats' feet.

Cassan′dra. A daughter of Priam and Hecuba, who was granted by Apollo the power of seeing into futurity, but having offended that god he prevented people from believing her predictions.

Cassiope′ia. The Ethiopian qneen who set her beauty in comparison with that of the Nereides, who thereupon chained her to a rock and left her to be devoured by a sea-monster, but she was delivered by Perseus.

Casta′lia. One of the fountains in Mount Parnassus, sacred to the Muses.

Cas′tali′des. A name of the Muses, from the fountain Castalia or Castalius.

Cas′tor. Son of Jupiter and Leda, twin brother of Pollux, noted for his skill in horsemanship. He went with Jason in quest of the Golden Fleece.

Cau′ther. In Mohammedan mythology, the lake of paradise, whose waters are as sweet as honey, as cold as snow, and as clear as crystal; and any believer who tastes thereof is said to thirst no more.

Cel′eno. One of the Harpies, progenitor of Zephyrus, the west wind.

Cen′taur. A huntsman who had the fore part like a man, and the remainder of the body like a horse. The Centauri lived in Thessaly.

Ceph′alus. Married to Procris, whom he accidentally slew by shooting her, while she was secretly watching him, he thinking she was a wild beast. Cephalus was the type of constancy.

Cerau′nius. A Greek name of Jupiter, meaning The Fulminator, from his thunderbolts.

Cer′berus. Pluto's famous three-headed dog, which guarded the gate of the infernal regions, preventing the living from entering, and the inhabitants from going out.

Ce′res. Daughter of Saturn, the goddess of agriculture, and of the fruits of earth. She taught Triptolemus how to grow corn, and sent him to teach the inhabitants of the earth.

Ces′tus. The girdle of Venus, which excited irresistible affection.

Cha′os. Allegorically represented the confused mass of matter supposed to have existed before the creation of the world, and out of which the world was formed.

Char′on. The son of Nox and Erebus. He was the ferryman who conveyed the spirits of the dead, in a boat, over the rivers Acheron and Styx to the Elysian Fields. "Charon's toll" was a coin put into the hands of the dead with which to pay the grim ferryman.

Charyb′dis. A dangerous whirlpool on the coast of Sicily. Personified, it was supposed to have been a woman who plundered travelers, but was at last killed by Hercules. Scylla and Charybdis are generally spoken of together to represent alternative dangers.

Che′mos. The Moabitish god of war.

Chimæ′ra. A wild illusion, personified in the monster slain by Bellerophon. It had the head and breast of a lion, the body of a goat, and the tail of a serpent. It used to vomit fire.

Chi′ron. The centaur who taught Achilles hunting, music, and the use of medicinal herbs. Jupiter placed him amongst the stars, where he appears as Sagittarius the Archer.

Chlo′ris. The Greek name of Flora, the goddess of flowers.

Chou. An Egyptian god corresponding to the Roman Hercules.

Chro′nos. Time, the Grecian name of Saturn.

Cir′ce. The daughter of the sun. The knowledge of poisonous herbs enabled her to destroy her husband, the King of the Sarmatians, for which act she was banished. When Ulysses landed at Æcea, where she lived, she turned all his followers into swine.

Cisse′ta. The name of one of Actæon's hounds.

Cither′ides. A name of the Muses, from Mount Citheron.

Cli′o. One of the Muses, daughter of Jupiter and Mnemosyne. She presided over history.

Cloaci′na. The Roman goddess of sewers.

Clo′tho. One of the Fates. She was present at births, and held the distaff from which was spun the thread of life. See Atropos and Lachesis.

Clowns of Ly′cia, The. Changed into frogs by Latona, because they refused to allow her to drink at one of their streamlets.

Clu′aci′na. A name of Venus, given to her at the time of the reconciliation of the Romans and the Sabines, which was ratified near a statue of the goddess.

Cly′temnes′tra. Wife of Agamemnon, slew her husband and married Ægisthus. She attempted to kill her son Orestes, but he was delivered by his sister Electra, who sent him away to Strophius. He afterwards returned and slew both Clytemnestra and Ægisthus.

Clyt′ie. A nymph who got herself changed into a sunflower because her love of Apollo was unrequited. In the form of this flower she is still supposed to be turning towards Sol, a name of Apollo.

Cneph. In Egyptian mythology the creator of the universe.

Cocy′tus. The river of Lamentation. One of the five rivers of the infernal regions.

Cœ′culus. A violent robber, a son of Vulcan.

Cœ′lus. Also called Uranus (or Heaven), the most ancient of the gods.

Colli′na. One of the rural deities, the goddess of hills.

Co′mus. The god of revelry. He presided over entertainments and feasts.

Con′cord. The symbol of Concord was two right hands joined, and a pomegranate.

Concor′dia. The goddess of peace. One of the oldest Roman goddesses. She is represented as holding a horn of plenty in one hand, and in the other a sceptre, from which fruit is sprouting forth.

Consu′alia. Games sacred to Neptune.

Con′sus. A name given to Neptune as being the god of counsel.

Cophet′ua. A legendary king of Africa, who disliked women, but ultimately fell in love with a "beggar-maid," as mentioned in *Romeo and Juliet*.

Co′pia. The goddess of plenty.

Co′ran. One of Actæon's hounds was so named.

Coro′nis. A consort of Apollo and mother of Æsculapius. Another Coronis was daughter of a king of Phocis, and was changed by Athena into a crow.

Coryban′tes. Priests of Cybele. They obtained the name because they were in the habit of striking themselves in their dances.

Cory′don. A silly love-sick swain mentioned by Virgil.

Cory′thaix. A name given to Mars, meaning Shaker of the Helmet.

Cotyt′to. The Athenian goddess of immodesty.

Cu′pid. The god of love, the son of Jupiter and Venus. He is represented as a naked, winged boy, with a bow and arrows and a torch. When he grew up to be a man he married Psyche.

Cuvera. The Indian god of wealth, corresponding to the Greek Plutus.

Cy′bele. The mother of the gods, and hence called Magna Mater. She was wife of Saturn. She is sometimes referred to under the names of Ceres, Rhea, Ops, and Vesta.
Cy′clops or **Cy′clopes.** The gigantic, one-eyed workmen of Vulcan, who made Jove's thunderbolts. Hesiod gives their names as Arges, Brontes, and Steropes.
Cyg′nus. The bosom friend of Phaëton. He died of grief on the death of his friend, and was turned into a swan.
Cyl′laros. One of Castor's horses. The color is mentioned as being coal black, with white legs and tail.
Cyl′lo. The name of one of Actæon's hounds, which was lame.
Cyllop′otes. A name given to one of Actæon's hounds, which limped.
Cyn′osure. One of the nurses of Jupiter, turned by the god into a conspicuous constellation.
Cyparis′sus. A boy of whom Apollo was very fond; and when he died he was changed, at Apollo's intercession, into a cypress tree, the branches of which typify mourning.
Cy′pria. A name of Venus, because she was worshiped in the island of Cyprus.
Cyth′era. A name of Venus, from the island to which she was wafted in the shell.

Dacty′li. Priests of Cybele. They were given the name, because, like the fingers, they were ten in number.
Dæd′alus. A great architect and sculptor. He invented the wedge, the axe, the level, and the gimlet, and was the first to use sails. Dædalus also constructed the famous labyrinth for Minos, King of Crete.
Da′gon. A god of the Philistines, half man, half fish, like the mermaid, Milton describes him as "Upward man and downward fish."
Da′hak. The Persian devil.
Dai′tyas. In Hindoo mythology the devils or evil gods.
Dan′æ. A daughter of Acrisius and Eurydice. She had a son by Jupiter, who was drifted out to sea in a boat, but was saved by Polydectes and educated.
Dana′us. King of Argos. The father of fifty daughters, who, all but one, at the command of their father, slew their husbands directly after marriage. For this crime they were condemned to the task of forever trying to draw water with vessels without any bottoms.
Daph′ne. The goddess of the earth. Apollo courted her, but she fled from him, and was, at her own request, turned into a laurel tree.
Dar′danus. A son of Jupiter, who built the city of Dardania and by some writers was accounted the founder of Troy.
Deiani′ra. Daughter of Œneus, wife of Hercules. See Hercules.
De′lius. A name of Apollo, from the island in which he was born.
Del′phi. A town on Mount Parnassus, famous for its oracle, and for a temple of Apollo.
Del′phos. The place where the temple was built from which the oracle of Apollo was given.
De′marus. The Phœnician name of Jupiter.
De′mogor′gon. The tyrant genius of the soil or earth, the life and support of plants. He was depicted as an old man covered with moss, and was said to live underground. He is sometimes called the king of the elves and fays.
Deuca′lion. One of the demigods, son of Prometheus and Pyrrha. He and his wife, by making a ship, survived the deluge which Jupiter sent on the earth, circa 1503 B. C.
Dian′a. Goddess of hunting and of chastity. She was the sister of Apollo, and daughter of Jupiter and Latona. She was known among the Greeks as Diana or Phœbe, and was honored as a triform goddess, As a celestial divinity she was called Luna; as a terrestrial, Diana or Dictynna; and in the infernal regions, Hecate.
Dictyn′na. A Greek name of Diana as a terrestrial goddess.
Di′do. A daughter of Belus, King of Tyre. It was this princess who bought a piece of land in Africa as large as could be encompassed by a bullock's hide, and, when the purchase was completed, cut the hide into strips, and so secured a large tract of land. Here she built Carthage; and Virgil tells that when Æneas was shipwrecked on the neighboring coast, she received him with every kindness, and at last fell in love with him. But Æneas did not reciprocate her affections, and this so grieved her that she stabbed herself.
Di′es Pa′ter. Father of the Day, a name of Jupiter.
Dii Selec′ti. Composed the second class of gods. They were Cœlus, Saturn, Genius, Oreus, Sol, Bacchus, Terra, and Luna.
Din′dyme′ne. A name of Cybele, from a mountain where she was worshiped.
Diome′des. The cruel tyrant of Thrace, who fed his mares on the flesh of his guests, was overcome by Hercules, and was given to the same horses as food.
Dio′ne. A poetic name of Venus.
Diony′sia. Festivals in honor of Bacchus.
Diony′sus. A name of Bacchus, either from his father Jupiter (Dios), or from his nurses, the nymphs called Nysæ.
Dios′curi. Castor and Pollux, the sons of Jupiter.
Di′ræ. A name of the Furies.
Dis. A name of Pluto, god of hell, signifying riches.
Discor′dia. Sister of Nemesis, the Furies, and Death, was driven from heaven for having sown discord among the gods.
Dodo′na. A celebrated oracle of Jupiter.
Dodonæ′us. A name of Jupiter, from the city of Dodona.
Dola′bra. The knife used by the priests to cut up the sacrifices.
Door′ga. A Hindoo goddess.
Do′ris. Daughter of Oceanus, and sister of Nereus, two of the marine deities. From these two sisters sprang the several tribes of water nymphs.
Do′to. One of the Nereids or sea nymphs.
Dra′co. One of Actæon's hounds.
Dragon. Seven headed. See Geryon.
Dry′ads. Rural deities, the nymphs of the forests, to whom their votaries offered oil, milk, and honey.
Dweur′gar. Scandinavian god of the Echo—a pigmy.

E′acus. Son of Jupiter and Egina, one of the judges of the infernal regions, who was appointed to judge the Europeans.
Eb′lis. The Mohammedan evil genius.
Echid′na. A woman having a serpent's tail,
Echno′bas. One of Actæon's hounds.
Ech′o. A nymph who fell in love with Narcissus. But when he languished and died she pined away from grief and died also, preserving nothing but her voice, which repeats every sound that reaches her.
"Oft by Echo's tedious tales misled." OVID.
Egeon. A giant sea-god, who assisted the Titans against Jupiter.
Ege′ria. A nymph who is said to have suggested to Numa all his wise laws. She became his wife, and at his death was so disconsolate, and shed so many tears, that Diana changed her into a fountain.
E′gil. The Vulcan of northern mythology.
Egip′ans. Rural deities who inhabited the forests and mountains, the upper half of the body being like that of a man, and the lower half like that of a goat.
E′gis. The shield of Minerva, It obtained its name because it was covered with the skin of the goat Amalthæa, which nourished Jupiter.
Eleusin′ian Mysteries. Religious rites in honor of Ceres, performed at Eleusis in Attica.
Elys′ium or the **Elysian Fields.** The temporary abode of the just in the infernal regions.
Empyre′an, The. The fifth heaven, the seat of the heathen deity.
Endym′ion. A shepherd who acquired from Jupiter the faculty of being always young. One of the lovers of Diana.
Enyo. The Grecian name of Bellona, the goddess of war and cruelty.
E′os. The Grecian name of Aurora.
E′ous. One of the four horses which drew the chariot of Sol, the sun. The word is Greek, and means red.
Eph′ial′tes. A giant who lost his right eye in an encounter with Hercules, and the left eye was destroyed by Apollo.
Er′ato. One of the Muses, the patroness of light poetry; she presided over the triumphs and complaints of lovers, and is generally represented as crowned with roses and myrtle, and holding a lyre in her hand.
Er′ebus. Son of Chaos, one of the gods of Hades, sometimes alluded to as representing the infernal regions.
Erga′tis. A name given to Minerva. It means the work-woman, and was given to the goddess because she was credited with having invented spinning and weaving.
Eric′theus. Fourth King of Athens, the son of Vulcan.
Erin′nys. A Greek name of the Furies. It means Disturber of the Mind.

Erisich′thon. He was punished with perpetual hunger because he defiled the groves of Ceres and cut down one of the sacred oaks.
Er′os. The Greek god of love.
Eros′tratus. The rascal who burnt the temple of Diana at Ephesus, thereby hoping to make his name immortal.
Eryc′ina. A name of Venus, from Mount Eryx in Sicily.
Erythre′os. The Grecian name of one of the horses of Sol's chariot.
E′thon. One of the horses which drew the chariot of Sol—the sun. The word is Greek and signifies hot.
Et′na. A volcanic mountain, beneath which, according to Virgil, there is buried the giant Typhon, who breathes forth devouring flames.
Eu′dromos. The name of one of Actæon's hounds.
Eume′nides. A name of the Furies, meaning mild, and referring to the time when they were approved by Minerva.
Euphro′syne. One of the three Graces. See Graces.
Eu′rus. The east wind. A son of Æolus.
Eury′ale. One of the Gorgons, daughter of Phorcus and Ceto.
Euryd′ice. Wife of Orpheus, who was killed by a serpent on her wedding night.
Euryth′ion. A seven-headed dragon. See Geryon.
Eu′terpe. One of the Muses, the patroness of instrumental music. The word means agreeable.
Eu′vyhe. An expression meaning "Well done, son." Jupiter so frequently addressed his son Bacchus by those words that the phrase at last became one of his names.

Fame. A poetical deity, represented as having wings and blowing a trumpet. A temple was dedicated to her by the Romans.
Fates or **Parcæ.** The three daughters of Necessity. Their names were Clotho, who held the distaff; Lachesis, who turned the spindle; and Atropos, who cut the thread with the fatal shears.
Faun. A rural divinity, half man and half goat. They were very similar to the Satyrs. The Fauns attended the god Pan, and the Satyrs attended Bacchus.
Favo′nius. The wind favorable to vegetation, that is, Zephyr—the west wind.
Fe′bris (fever). One of the evil deities, worshiped that she might not do harm.
Feb′ruus. A name of Plato, from the part of the funeral rites which consisted of purifications.
Fero′nia. The Roman goddess of orchards; was patroness of enfranchised slaves. Some authors think Feronia is the same as Juno.
Fi′des. The goddess of faith and honesty, who had a temple in the Capitol of Rome.
Flath′in′nis. In Celtic mythology, Paradise.
Fleece, Golden. See Golden Fleece, Argonauts, and Jason.
Flo′ra. Goddess of flowers and gardens; was wife of Zephyrus. She enjoyed perpetual youth. Her Grecian name was Chloris.
Flora′lia. Licentious games instituted in honor of the goddess Flora.
Fortu′na. The goddess of fortune, who had a temple erected to her by Servius Tullius. She was supposed to be able to bestow riches or poverty on mankind, and was esteemed one of the most potent of the ancient goddesses.
Fraud. One of the evil deities; was represented as a goddess with a human face and a serpent's body, and in the end of her tail was a scorpion's sting. She lived in the river Cocytus, and nothing but her head was ever seen.
Frey. The Scandinavian god of fertility and peace. The patron god of Sweden and Iceland.
Frey′ja. The Scandinavian Venus. The goddess of love.
Fri′ga. The Saxon goddess of earthly enjoyments. The name Friday is derived from her. In Scandinavian mythology she is the goddess of marriage.
Fro. The Scandinavian god of tempests and winds.
Furies, The. The three daughters of Acheron and Nox. They were the punishers of evil doers. Their names were Tisiphone, Megæra, and Alecto, and were supposed to personify rage, slaughter, and envy.

Gabriel. In Jewish mythology, the prince of fire and thunder, and the angel of death to the favored people of God.
Galatæ′a. A sea nymph. Polyphemus, one of the Cyclops, loved her, but she disdained his attentions and became the lover of Acis, a Sicilian shepherd.
Gal′li. Priests of Cybele who used to cut their arms with knives when they sacrificed, and acted so like madmen that demented people got the name of Gallantes.
Gan′esa. The Indian Mercury. The god of wisdom and prudence.
Ganga. One of the three Indian river goddesses.
Gan′yme′de. A beautiful Phrygian youth, son of Tros, King of Troy. He succeeded Hebe in the office of cupbearer to Jupiter. He is generally represented sitting on the back of a flying eagle.
Gauta′ma. The chief deity of Burmah.
Genii. Domestic divinities. Every man was supposed to have two of these genii accompanying him; one brought him happiness, the other misery.
Gen′itor. A Lycian name of Jupiter.
Ge′ryon. A triple-bodied monster who lived at Gades, where his numerous flocks were guarded by Orthos, a two-headed dog, and by Eurythion, a seven-headed dragon. These guardians were destroyed by Hercules, and the cattle taken away.
Glau′cus. A fisherman who became a sea-god through eating a seaweed, which he thought invigorated the fishes and might strengthen him.
Glauko′pis. A name given to Minerva, because she had blue eyes.
Gno′mes. A name given by Plato to the invisible deities who were supposed to inhabit the earth.
Gnos′sis. A name given to Ariadne, from the city of Gnossus in Crete.
Golden Fleece, The. A ram's hide, sometimes described as white, and at other times as purple and golden. It was given to Phryxus, who carried it to Colchis, where King Æta entertained Phryxus, and the hide was hung up in the grove of Mars. Jason and forty-nine companions fetched back the golden fleece.
Gopy′a. Indian mythological nymphs.
Gor′gons, The. Three sisters, named Stheno, Euryale, and Medusa. They petrified every one they looked at. Instead of hair, their heads were covered with vipers. Perseus conquered them, and cut off the head of Medusa, which was placed on the shield of Minerva, and all who fixed their eyes thereon were turned into stone.
Graces, The. The attendants of Venus. Their names were Aglaia, so called from her beauty and goodness; Thalia, from her perpetual freshness; and Euphrosyne, from her cheerfulness. They are generally depicted as three cheerful maidens with hands joined, and either nude or only wearing transparent robes,—the idea being that kindnesses, as personified by the Graces, should be done with sincerity and candor, and without disguise. They were supposed to teach the duties of gratitude and friendship, and they promoted love and harmony among mankind.
Gradiv′us. A name given to Mars by the Romans. It meant the warrior who defended the city against all external enemies.
Gra′gus. The name by which Jupiter was worshiped in Lycia.
Grap′sios. A Lycian name of Jupiter.

Ha′da. The Babylonian Juno.
Hades. The Greek name of Pluto, the god of hell, the word signifying hidden, dark, and gloomy; the infernal regions; sometimes written. *Ades.*
Halcy′one. One of the Pleiades; was a daughter of Atlas and Pelione.
Halcy′ons. Sea birds, supposed to be the Greek kingfishers. They made their nests on the waves, and during the period of incubation the sea was always calm. Hence the modern term "Halcyon days."
Hamadry′ades. Wood-nymphs, who presided over trees.
Haroe′ris. The Egyptian god, whose eyes are the sun and moon.
Har′pies. Animals with the heads and breasts of women, the bodies of birds, and the claws of lions. Their names were Aello, Ocypete, and Celeno. They were loathsome creatures, living in filth and poisoning everything they came in contact with.
Harpi′kruti. The Egyptian name of the god Harpocrates.
Harpoc′rates. Son of Isis; was the god of silence and meditation. He is usually represented as a young man holding a finger of one hand to his lips, while in the other hand he holds a cornucopia.
Ha′zis. The Syrian war god.
He′be. The goddess of youth. She was cup-bearer to Jupiter and the gods, until she had an awkward fall at

a festival, and so displeased Jupiter that she was deprived of her office, and Ganymede was appointed in her stead.

Hec′ate. There were two goddesses known by this name, but the one generally referred to in modern literature is Hecate, or Proserpine, the name by which Diana was known in the infernal regions. In heaven her name was Luna, and her terrestrial name was Diana.

Hec′uba. The mother of Paris; was allotted to Ulysses after the destruction of Troy, and was afterwards changed into a hound.

Hel′ena. When a child was so beautiful that Theseus and Perithus stole her, but she was restored by Castor and Pollux. She became the wife of Menelaus, king of Sparta, but eloped with Paris, and thus caused the Trojan War. After the death of Paris she married Deiphobus, his brother, and then betrayed him to Menelaus. She was strangled by order of Polyxo, king of Rhodes.

He′liades. The daughters of Sol, and the sisters of Phaeton, at whose death they were so sad that they stood mourning till they became metamorphosed into poplar trees, and their tears were turned into amber.

Hel′icon. A mountain in Bœotia sacred to the Muses, from which place the fountain Hippocrene flowed.

Helico′nides. A name of the Muses, from Mount Helicon.

Heliop′olis. In Elysium; was the city of the sun.

He′lios. The Grecian sun-god, who went home every evening in a golden boat which had wings.

He′liotrope. Clytie was turned into this flower by Apollo.

Hel′le. Drowned in the sea, into which she fell from off the back of the golden ram, on which she and Phryxus were escaping from the oppression of their stepmother Ino. The episode gave the name of the Hellespont to the part of the sea where Helle was drowned, and it is now called the Dardanelles.

Hemph′ta. The Egyptian god Jupiter.

Hephæs′tos. The Greek Vulcan.

He′ro. The Greek name of Juno.

Her′cules. The son of Jupiter and Alcmena. The goddess Juno hated him from his birth, and sent two serpents to kill him, but though only eight months old he strangled the snakes. As he became older he was set by his master Eurystheus what were thought to be twelve impossible tasks, which have long been known as the "Twelve Labors of Hercules." They were: —

First, To slay the Nemean Lion.

Second, To destroy the Hydra which infested the marshes of Lerna.

Third, To bring to Eurystheus the Arcadian Stag with the golden horns and brazen hoofs.

Fourth, To bring to his master the Boar of Erymanthus.

Fifth, To cleanse the stable of King Augeas, in which three thousand oxen had been kept for thirty years, and which had never been cleaned out.

Sixth, To destroy the Stymphalides, terrible carnivorous birds.

Seventh, To capture the Bull that was desolating Crete.

Eighth, To capture the mares of Diomedes, which breathed fire from their nostrils, and ate human flesh.

Ninth, To procure the girdle of Hippolyta, queen of the Amazons.

Tenth, To bring to Eurystheus the flesh-eating oxen of Geryon, the monster king of Gades.

Eleventh, To bring away some of the golden apples from the garden of the Hesperides.

Twelfth, To bring up from Hades the three-headed dog, Cerberus.

All these tasks he successfully accomplished, and, besides, he assisted the gods in their wars with the giants.

Her′mæ. Statues of Hermes (Mercury), which were set up in Athens for boundaries, and as direction marks for travelers.

Hermathe′nae. Statues of Mercury and Minerva placed together.

Her′mes. A Greek name of the god Mercury.

Hermi′one. Daughter of Mars and Venus, who was turned into a serpent, and allowed to live in the Elysian fields. There was another Hermione, daughter of Menelaus; she was betrothed to Orestes, but was carried away by Pyrrhus, the son of Achilles.

He′ro. A priestess of Venus, with whom Leander was so enamored that he swam across the Hellespont every night to visit her, but at last was drowned, when Hero threw herself into the sea and was drowned also.

Hesper′ides. Three daughters of Hesperus, King of Italy. They kept in their garden the golden apples which Juno gave Jupiter on their wedding day.

Hes′perus. Brother of Atlas; was changed into the evening star.

Hes′tia. The Greek name of Vesta.

Hil′dur. The Scandanavian Mars.

Hippocam′pus. The name of Neptune's favorite horse.

Hippocre′nides. A name of the Muses, from the fountain of Hippocrene (the horse fountain), which was formed by a kick of the winged horse Pegasus.

Hippoly′te. Queen of the Amazons, daughter of Mars. Her father gave her a famous girdle, which Hercules was required to procure (see Hercules). She was conquered by Hercules, and given by him in marriage to Theseus.

Hippoly′tus. Son of Theseus and Hippolyte; he was killed by a fall from a chariot, but was raised to life again by Diana, or, as some say, by Æsculapius.

Hippo′na. A rural divinity, the goddess of horses.

Ho′rae. The daughters of Sol and Chronis.

Horten′sis. A name of Venus, because she looked after plants and flowers in gardens.

Ho′rus. A name of Sol, the Egyptian day god.

Hostil′ina. A rural divinity; goddess of growing corn.

Hyacin′thus. A boy greatly loved by Apollo, but he was accidentally slain by him with a quoit. Apollo caused to spring from his blood the flower Hyacinth.

Hy′ades. Seven daughters of Atlas and Æthra, who form a constellation which, when it rises with the sun, threatens rain.

Hy′dra. A famous monster serpent, which had many heads. It was slain by Hercules.

Hyge′ia. The goddess of health, a daughter of Æsculapius and Epione. She was represented as a young woman feeding a serpent, which is twined round her arm.

Hy′las. A beautiful boy beloved by Hercules. The nymphs were jealous of him, and spirited him away while he was drawing water for Hercules.

Hy′men. The Grecian god of marriage, either the son of Bacchus and Venus, or, as some say, of Apollo and one of the Muses. He was represented as a handsome youth, holding in his hand a burning torch.

Hype′rion. Son of Cœlus and Terra. The model of manly beauty, synonymous with Apollo. The personification of the sun.

Hypermnes′tra. One of the fifty daughters of Danaus, who were collectively called the Danaides. She was the one who refused to kill her husband on the wedding night.

Ib′lees. The Arabian Satan.

Ic′arus. Son of Dædalus, who, with his father, made himself wings with which to fly from Crete. They were fixed to the shoulders by wax. Icarus flew too near the sun, and the heat melting the wax, caused the wings to drop off, and he fell into the sea and was drowned.

Ichnoba′te. One of Actæon's hounds; it means tracker.

Idæ′a. A name of Cybele, from Mount Ida, where she was worshiped.

Idæ′an Mother. Cybele was sometimes so called.

Ida′lia. A name of Venus, from Mount Idalus.

Impera′tor. A name of Jupiter, given to him at Præneste.

I′nachus. One of the earliest of the demigods or heroes.

In′cubus. A Roman name of Pan, meaning The Nightmare.

Indig′etes. Deified mortals, gods of the fourth order. They were peculiar to some district.

In′dra. The Hindoo Jupiter; his wife was Indrant, who presides over the winds and thunder.

In′nus. A name of Pan, the same as Incubus.

I′no. Second wife of Athamas, King of Thebes, father of Phryxus and Helle. Ino had two children, who could not ascend the throne while Phryxus and Helle were alive, Ino therefore persecuted them to such a degree that they determined to escape. They did so on a ram, whose hide became the Golden Fleece (see Phryxus and Helle). Ino destroyed herself, and was changed by Neptune into a sea-goddess.

Ino′a. Festivals in memory of Ino.

Instrumental Music. See Euterpe.

I′o. A daughter of Inachus, and a priestess of Juno at Argus. Jupiter courted her, and was detected by Juno, when the god turned Io into a beautiful heifer. Juno demanded the beast of Jupiter, and set the hundred-eyed Argus to watch her. Jupiter persuaded Mercury to destroy Argus, and Io was set at liberty, and restored to human shape. Juno continued her persecutions, and Io had to wander from place to place till she came to Egypt, where she became wife of King Osiris, and won such good opinions from the Egyptians that after her death she was worshiped as the goddess Isis.

Iola′us. Son of Iphicles; assisted Hercules in conquering the Hydra, by burning with hot irons the place where the heads were cut off; and for his assistance he was restored to youth by Hebe. Lovers used to go to his monument at Phocis and ratify their vows of fidelity.

Io′thun. Celtic mythological monsters, or giants.

Iph′iclus. Twin brother of Hercules, and father of Iolaus.

Iphigeni′a. A daughter of Agamemnon. He made a vow to Diana, which involved the sacrifice of Iphigenia, but just at the critical moment she was carried to heaven, and a beautiful goat was found on the altar in her place.

I′ris. Daughter of Thaumas and Electra; was the attendant of Juno, and one of the messengers of the gods. Her duty was to cut the thread which detained expiring souls. She is the personification of the rainbow.

I′sis. Wife of Osiris.

I′tys. Killed by his mother Progne when six years old, and given to his father Tereus as food. The gods were so enraged at this that they turned Itys into a pheasant, Progne into a swallow, and Tereus into an owl.

Ixi′on. Son of Phlegyas, King of the Lapithæ. For attempting to produce thunder, Jupiter cast him into hell, and had him bound to a wheel, surrounded with serpents, which is forever turning over a river of fire.

Jan′i. A place in Rome where there were three statues of Janus, and it was a meeting place for usurers and creditors.

Ja′nitor. A title of Janus, from the gates before the doors of private houses being called Januæ.

Ja′nus. A king of Italy said to have been the son of Cœlus, others say of Apollo; he sheltered Saturn when he was driven from heaven by Jupiter. Janus presided over highways, gates, and locks, and is usually represented with two faces.

Jap′etus. Son of Cœlus and Terra, husband of Clymene. He was looked upon by the Greeks as the father of mankind. See Iapetos.

Ja′son. Son of Æson, king of Iolcos; he was brought up by the centaur Chiron. His uncle Æta sent him to fetch the Golden Fleece from Colchis (see Argonauts). He went in the ship Argo with forty-nine companions, the flower of Greek youth. With the help of Juno they got safe to Colchis, but the King Ætes promised to restore the Golden Fleece only on condition that the Argonauts performed certain services. Jason was to tame the wild fiery bulls, and to make them plow the field of Mars; to sow in the ground the teeth of a serpent, from which would spring armed men who would fight against him who plowed the field of Mars; to kill the fiery dragon which guarded the tree on which the Golden Fleece was hung. The fate of Jason and the rest of the Argonauts seemed certain; but Medea, the king's daughter, fell in love with Jason, and with the help of charms which she gave him he overcame all the difficulties which the king had put in his way. He took away the Golden Fleece and Medea also. The king sent his son Absyrtus to overtake the fugitives, but Medea killed him, and strewed his limbs in his father's path, so that he might be delayed in collecting them, and this enabled Jason and Medea to escape. After a time Jason got tired of Medea, and married Glauce, which cruelty Medea revenged by killing her children before their father's eyes. Jason was accidentally killed by a beam of the ship Argo falling on him.

Jocas′ta (otherwise Epicasta). Wife of Laius, King of Thebes, who in after life married her own son, Œdipus, not knowning who he was, and, on discovering the fatal mistake, hanged herself.

Jove. A very general name of Jupiter.

Judges in Hell, The. Rhadamanthus for Asiatics; Æacus for Europeans; Minos was the presiding judge. See Triptolemus.

Jugatin′us. One of the nuptial deities.

Ju′no. Daughter of Saturn and Ops, *alias* Cybele. She was married to Jupiter, and became queen of all the gods and goddesses, and mistress of heaven and earth. Juno was the mother of Mars, Vulcan, Hebe, and Lucina. She prompted the gods to conspire against Jupiter, but the attempt was frustrated, and Apollo and Neptune were banished from heaven by Jupiter. Juno is the goddess of marriage, and the protectress of married women; and she had special regard for virtuous women.

Jupiter. Son of Saturn and Cybele (or Ops); born on Mount Ida, in Crete, and nourished by the goat Amalthæa. When quite young Jupiter rescued his father from the Titans; and afterwards, with the help of Hercules, defeated the giants, the sons of earth, when they made war against heaven. Jupiter was worshiped with great solemnity under various names by most of the heathen nations. The Africans called him Ammon; the Babylonians, Belus; and the Egyptians, Osiris (see Jove). He was represented as a majestic personage seated on a throne, holding in his hands a scepter and a thunderbolt; at his feet stood a spread eagle.

Kali. A Hindoo goddess, after whom Calcutta is named.

Ka′loc. One of the chief of the Mexican gods.

Kam′a. The Hindoo god of love.

Keb′la. The point of the compass to which worshipers look during their invocations. Thus the Sol or Sun worshipers turn to the east, where the sun rises, and the Mohammedans turn towards Mecca.

Ke′derli. In Mohammedan mythology, is a god corresponding to the English St. George, and is still invoked by the Turks when they go to war.

Ki′un. The Egyptian Venus.

Kneph. An Egyptian god, having a ram's head and a man's body.

Krish′na. An Indian god, the revenger of wrongs; also called the Indian Apollo.

Kro′do. The Saxon Saturn.

Ku′ma′ra. The war god of the Hindoos.

Ku′vera. The Hindoo god of riches.

La′be. The Arabian Circe, who had unlimited power of metamorphosis.

Lach′esis. One of the three Fates or Parcæ. She spun the thread of life.

Lactura. One of the goddesses of growing corn.

La′don. The dragon which guarded the apples in the garden of the Hesperides. Also the name of one of Actæon's hounds. Also the river to which Syrinx fled when pursued by Pan, where she was changed into a reed, and where Pan made his first pipe.

Læ′laps. One of Diana's hunting dogs, which, while pursuing a wild boar, was petrified. Also the name of one of Actæon's hounds.

Laksh′mi. Hindoo goddess of wealth and pleasure. One of the wives of Vishnu.

Lam′ia. An evil deity amongst the Greeks and Romans, and the great dread of their children, whom she had the credit of constantly enticing away and destroying.

Lam′pos. One of Aurora's chariot horses, the other being Phaeton.

Laoc′o-on. One of the priests of Apollo, who was, with his two sons, crushed to death by serpents, because he opposed the admission of the wooden horse to Troy.

Laom′edon. Son of Ilus, a Trojan king. He was famous for having, with the assistance of Apollo and Neptune, built the walls of Troy.

Lap′is. The oath stone. The Romans used to swear by Jupiter Lapis.

Lap′ithus. Son of Apollo. His numerous children were called Lapithæ, and they are notorious for their fight with the centaurs at the nuptial feast of Perithus and Hippodamia.

La′res and **Pena′tes.** Sons of Mercury and Lara, or, as other mythologists say, of Jupiter and Lamida. They belonged to the lower order of Roman gods, and presided over homes and families.

Lato′na. Daughter of Cœus and Phœbus, mother of Apollo and Diana. Being admired so much by Jupiter, Juno was jealous, and Latona was the object of the goddess's constant persecution.

Laver′na. The goddess of thieves.

Le′da. The mother of Castor and Pollux, their father being Jupiter, in the shape of a swan. After her death she received the name of Nemesis.

Lem′ures. The specters of departed souls. Milton, in his "Ode to the Nativity," says—

"Lemures moan with midnight plaint."

They are sometimes referred to as the Manes of the dead.

Lerna. The lake near Argos where Hercules conquered the Hydra.

Le′the. One of the rivers of the infernal regions, of which the souls of the departed are obliged to drink to produce oblivion or forgetfulness of everything they did or knew while alive on the earth.

Leucoth′ea. The name of Ino after she was transformed into a sea nymph.

Leva'na. The deity who presided over newborn infants.
Liak'ura. Mount Parnassus.
Lib'issa. Queen of fays and fairies.
Libiti'na. The chief of the funeral deities.
Lige'a. A Greek siren or sea nymph.
Li'lith. A Jewish myth, who is a great enemy to newborn children. She was said to have been Adam's first wife, but, refusing to submit to him, was turned from Paradise and made a specter.
Li'na. The goddess of the art of weaving.
Lin'dor. A lover in the shape of a shepherd, like Corydon; a love-sick swain.
Lo'fen. The Scandinavian god who guards friendship.
Lof'ua. The Scandinavian goddess who reconciles lovers.
Loke. The Scandinavian Satan, the god of strife, the spirit of evil.
Lo'tis. A daughter of Neptune, who fled from Priapus, and only escaped from him by being transformed into a lotus plant.
Lu'cian. The impersonation of folly, changed into an ass.
Lu'cifer. The morning star.
Luci'na. The goddess who presides at the birth of children. She was a daughter of Jupiter and Juno.
Lud. In ancient British mythology the king of the Britons.
Lu'na. The name of Diana as a celestial divinity. See Diana and Hecate.
Lu'percus, or Pan. The Roman god of fertility; his festival day was 15th February, and the festivals were called Lupercalia.
Lycaon'ian Food. Execrable viands, such as were supplied to Jupiter by Lycaon. To test the divine knowledge of the god he served up human flesh, which Jove discovered, and punished Lycaon by turning him into a wolf.
Lycian Clowns. Turned into frogs by Latona or Ceres.
Lymni'ades. Nymphs who resided in marshes.
Lyn'ceus. One of the Argonauts. The personification of sharp-sightedness.
Lyre. This musical instrument is constantly associated with the doings of the ancient deities. Amphion built the walls of Thebes by the music of his lyre.

Mæn'ades. Priestesses of Bacchus.
Ma'ha'soor. The Hindoo god of evil.
Ma'ia. The mother of the Grecian Mercury.
Mam'mon. The money god.
Ma'nes. The souls of the departed. The god of funerals and tombs.
Mari'na. A name of Venus, meaning sea-foam, from her having been formed from the froth of the sea.
Mars. The god of war, the son of Jupiter and Juno. Venus was his favorite goddess, and amongst their children were Cupid, Anteros, and Harmonia. In the Trojan war Mars took the part of the Trojans, but was defeated by Diomede.
Mar'syas. The name of the piper who challenged Apollo to a musical contest, and, being defeated, was flayed to death by the god. He was the supposed inventor of the flute.
Ma'rut. The Hindoo god of tempestuous winds.
Matu'ra. One of the rural deities who protected the growing corn at time of ripening.
Max'imus. One of the appellations of Jupiter, being the greatest of the gods.
Mede'a. Wife of Jason, chief of the Argonauts.
Medu'sa. One of the Gorgons. Minerva changed her beautiful hair into serpents. She was conquered by Perseus, who cut off her head, and placed it on Minerva's shield. Every one who looked at the head was turned into stone.
Megæ'ra. One of the three Furies.
Mello'na. One of the rural divinities, the goddess of bees.
Melpom'ene. One of the Muses, the goddess of tragedy.
Men'des. An Egyptian god like Pan. He was worshiped in the form of a goat.
Menela'us. A Spartan king. The elopement of his wife Helen with Paris was the origin of the siege of Troy.
Me'nu. The Hindoo god of law.
Mer'cury. The son of Jupiter and Maia; was the messenger of the gods, and the conductor of the souls of the dead to Hades. He was the supposed inventor of weights and measures, and presided over orators and merchants.
Me'ru. The abode of the Hindoo god Vishnu. It is at the top of a mountain eighty thousand leagues high. The Olympus of the Indians.
Mi'das. A king of Phrygia, who begged of Bacchus the special gift that everything that he touched might be turned into gold. The request was granted, and as soon as he touched his food it also was turned to gold, and for fear of being starved he was compelled to ask the god to withdraw the power he had bestowed upon him. He was told to bathe in the river Pactolus. He did so, and the sands which he stood on were golden forever after. It was this same king who, being appointed to be judge in a musical contest between Apollo and Pan, gave the Satyr the palm; whereupon Apollo, to show his contempt, bestowed on him a pair of asses' ears. This gave rise to the term "Midas-eared," as a synonym for ill-judged, or indiscriminate.
Mi'lo. A celebrated Croton athlete, who is said to have felled an ox with his fist, and to have eaten the beast in one day.
Mimallo'nes. The "wild women" who accompanied Bacchus, so called because they mimicked his actions.
Mi'mir. In Scandinavian mythology the god of wisdom.
Miner'va. The goddess of wisdom, war, and the liberal arts; is said to have sprung from the head of Jupiter fully armed for battle. She was a great benefactress of mankind, and patroness of the fine arts. She was the tutelar deity of the city of Athens.
Mi'nos. The principal of the three judges of hell, before whom the spirits of the departed appeared and heard their doom.
Min'otaur. The monster, half man, half bull, which Theseus slew.
Mith'ra. A Persian divinity, the ruler of the universe, corresponding with the Roman Sol.
Mnemos'yne. Mother of the Muses and goddess of memory. Jupiter courted the goddess in the guise of a shepherd.
Moak'ibat. The recording angel of the Mohammedans.
Mo'loch. A god of the Phœnicians to whom human victims, principally children, were sacrificed. Moloch is figurative of the influence which impels us to sacrifice that which we ought to cherish most dearly.
Mo'mus. The god of sarcasm. The god who blamed Jove for not having made a window in man's breast, so that his thoughts could be seen. His bitter jests occasioned his being driven from heaven in disgrace.
Mone'ta. A name given to Juno by those writers who considered her the goddess of money.
Moon. The moon was, by the ancients, called *Hecate* before and after setting; *Astarte* when in crescent form; *Diana* when in full.
Mor'pheus. The god of sleep and dreams, the minister of Somnus.
Mors. Death, a daughter of Nox.
Mun'in. The Scandinavian god of memory, represented by the raven that was perched on Odin's shoulder.
Musca'rius. A name given to Jupiter because he kept off the flies from the sacrifices.
Mu'ses, The. Nine daughters of Jupiter and Mnemosyne. They presided over the arts and sciences, music and poetry. Their names were, Calliope, Clio, Erato, Thalia, Melpomene, Terpsichore, Euterpe, Polyhymnia, and Urania. They principally resided in Mount Parnassus, at Helicon.
My'thras. The Egyptian name of Apollo.

Nai'ads, The. Beautiful nymphs of human form who presided over springs, fountains, and wells. They resided in the meadows by the sides of rivers. Virgil mentions Ægle as being the fairest of them.
Nan'di. The Hindoo goddess of joy.
Nar'ae. The name of the infernal regions amongst the Hindoos.
Na'ra'yan. The mover of the waters. The Hindoo god of tides.
Narcis'sus. Son of Cephisus and the Naiad Liriope; a beautiful youth, who was so pleased with the reflection of himself which he saw in the placid water of a fountain that he could not help loving it, imagining that it must be some beautiful nymph. His fruitless endeavors to possess himself of the supposed nymph drove him to despair, and he killed himself. There sprang from his blood a flower, which was named after him, Narcissus.
Nas'trond. The Scandinavian place of eternal punishment, corresponding with Hades.
Na'tio. A Roman goddess who took care of young infants.

Nem′esis. The goddess of vengeance or justice, one of the infernal deities. Her mother was Nox. She was supposed to be constantly traveling about the earth in search of wickedness, which she punished with the greatest severity.

Nepha′lia. Grecian festivals in honor of Mnemosyne, the mother of the Muses.

Nep′tune. God of the sea, a son of Saturn and Cybele, and brother of Jupiter and Pluto. He quarreled with Jupiter because he did not consider that the dominion of the sea was equal to Jupiter's empire of heaven and earth; and he was banished from the celestial regions, after having conspired with Pluto to dethrone Jupiter.

Nere′ides, The. Aquatic nymphs. They were daughters of Nereus and Doris, and fifty in number. They are generally represented as beautiful girls riding on dolphins, and carrying tridents in the right hand.

Nere′us. A sea deity, husband of Doris. He had the gift of prophecy, and foretold fates; but he had also the power of assuming various shapes, which enabled him to escape from the importunities of those who were anxious to consult him.

Nes′sus. The name of the Centaur which was destroyed by Hercules for insulting Dejanira.

Nes′tor. A grandson of Neptune, his father being Neleus, and his mother Chloris. Homer makes him one of the greatest of the Greek heroes. He was present at the famous battle between the Lapithæ and the Centaurs, and took a leading part in the Trojan war.

Nid′hogg. In Scandinavian mythology the dragon who dwells in Nastrond.

Nif′lheim. The Scandinavian hell. It was supposed to consist of nine vast regions of ice beneath the North Pole, where darkness reigns eternally. See Nastrond.

Ni′obe. A daughter of Tantalus, and the personification of grief. By her husband Amphion she had seven sons and seven daughters. By the orders of Latona the father and sons were killed by Apollo, and the daughters (except Chloris) by Diana. Niobe, being overwhelmed with grief, escaped further trouble by being turned into a marble statue.

No′mius. A lawgiver; one of the names of Apollo. This title was also given to Mercury for the part he took in inventing beneficent laws.

Norns. Three Scandinavian goddesses, who wove the woof of human destiny.

Nox. The daughter of Chaos, and sister of Erebus and Mors. She personified night, and was the mother of Nemesis and the Fates.

Nun′dina. The goddess who took charge of children when they were nine days old — the day on which the Romans named their children.

Nuptia′lis. A title of Juno. When the goddess was invoked under this name, the gall of the victim was taken out and thrown behind the altar, signifying that there should be no gall (bitterness) or anger between married people.

Nu′riel. In Hebrew mythology the god of hailstorms.

Nycte′lius. A name given to Bacchus, because his festivals were celebrated by torchlight.

Nymphs. This was a general name for a class of inferior female deities who were attendants of the gods. Some of them presided over springs, fountains, wells, woods, and the sea.

Ny′sæ. The names of the nymphs by whom Bacchus was nursed.

Ny′sæus. A name of Bacchus, because he was worshiped at Nysa.

Ny′sus. A king of Megara who was invisible by virtue of a particular lock of hair. This lock his daughter Scylla cut off, and so betrayed her father to his enemies. She was changed into a lark, and the king into a hawk, and he still pursues his daughter, intending to punish her for her treachery.

Oan′nes. An eastern god, represented as a monster, half man, half fish. He was said to have taught men the use of letters in the daytime, and at night to have retired to the depth of the ocean.

Obam′bou. A devil of African mythology.

Ocean′ides. Sea nymphs, daughters of Oceanus and Tethys. Their numbers are variously estimated by different poets; some saying there were as many as three thousand, while others say there were as few as sixteen. The principal of them are mentioned under their respective names, as Amphitrite, Doris, Metis, etc.

Oce′anus. Son of Cœlus and Terra, and husband of Tethys. Several mythological rivers were called his sons, as Alpheus, Peneus, etc., and his daughters were called the Oceanides.

Ocrid′ion. A king of Rhodes, who was deified after his death.

Ocy′pete. One of the Harpies, who infected everything she touched. The word means swift of flight.

Ocy′roe. A daughter of Chiron, who had the gift of prophecy. She was metamorphosed into a mare.

O′din. In Scandinavian mythology the god of the universe, and reputed father of all the Scandinavian kings. His wife's name was Friga, and his two sons were Thor and Balder.

Œd′ipus. A son of Laius, King of Thebes, best known as the solver of the famous enigma propounded by the Sphinx.

Œno′ne. Wife of Paris, a nymph of Mount Ida, who had the gift of prophecy.

Ogyg′ia. An island, the abode of Calypso, in the Mediterranean Sea. It was so beautiful in sylvan scenery that even Mercury (who dwelt on Olympus) was charmed with the spot.

Ole′nus. A daughter of Vulcan, wife of Lethæa, a woman who thought herself more beautiful than the goddesses, and as a punishment she and her husband were turned into stone statues.

Olym′pius. A name of Jupiter, from Olympia, where the god had a splendid temple, which was considered to be one of the seven wonders of the world.

Olym′pus. The magnificent mountain on the coast of Thessaly, six thousand feet high, where the gods were supposed to reside. There were several other smaller mountains of the same name.

Oly′ras. A river near Thermopylæ, which, it is said, attempted to extinguish the funeral pile on which Hercules was consumed.

Omopha′gia. A Bacchanalian festival at which some uncooked meats were served.

Om′phale. The Queen of Lydia, to whom Hercules was sold as a bondsman for three years for the murder of Iphitus. Hercules fell in love with her, and led an effeminate life in her society, wearing female apparel, while Omphale wore the lion's skin.

Ona′rus. A priest of Bacchus, said to have married Ariadne after she had been abandoned by Theseus.

Onu′va. The Venus of the ancient Gauls.

Opa′lia. Roman festivals in honor of Ops, held on 14th of the calends of January.

Ops. Mother of the gods, a daugher of Cœlus and Terra. She was known by the several names of Bona Dea, Rhea, Cybele, Magna Mater, Proserpine, Tellus, and Thya; and occasionally she is spoken of as Juno and Minerva. She personified labor, and is represented as a comely matron, distributing gifts with her right hand, and holding in her left hand a loaf of bread. Her festival was the 14th day of the January calends.

Oræ′a. Certain sacrifices offered to the goddesses of the seasons to invoke fair weather for the ripening of the fruits of the earth.

Orbo′na. The goddess of orphans.

O′reads. Mountain nymphs, attendants on Diana.

Orgies. Drunken revels. The riotous feasts of Bacchus were so designated.

Ori′on. A famous handsome giant, who was blinded by Œnopion for a grievous wrong done to Merope, and he was expelled from Chios. The sound of the Cyclopes' hammers led him to the abode of Vulcan, who gave him a guide. He then consulted an oracle, and had his sight restored, as Longfellow says, by fixing

"His blank eyes upon the sun."

He was afterwards slain by Diana and placed amongst the stars, where his constellation is one of the most splendid.

Orithy′ia. A daughter of Erechtheus, whose lover, Boreas, carried her off while she was wandering by the river Ilissus. Her children were Zetes and Calais, two winged warriors who accompanied the Argonauts.

Or′muzd. In Persian mythology the creator of all things.

O′ros. The Egyptian Apollo.

Or′pheus. Son of Apollo and the muse Calliope. He was married to Eurydice; but she was stung by a serpent, and died. Orpheus went down to Hades to claim her, and played so sweetly with his lute that Pluto allowed Eurydice to return to the earth with Orpheus, but on condition that he did not look behind him until he had reached the terrestrial regions. Orpheus, however, in his anxiety to see if she were following him, looked round, and Eurydice disappeared from his sight, instantly and forever.

Osi′ris. The Egyptian god of the sun; he was worshiped under the form of an ox.

Os′sa. One of the mountains which the giants piled on the top of Olympus to enable them to ascend to heaven and attack the gods.

Pacto′lus. The river in Lydia where Midas washed himself by order of Bacchus, and the sands were turned to gold.

Pæ′an. A name given to Apollo, from *pæan*, the hymn which was sung in his honor after he had killed the serpent Python.

Palæ′mon, or Melicerta, a sea god, son of Athamas and Ino.

Pa′les. The goddess of shepherds and protectress of flocks; her festivals were called Palilia.

Palla′dium. A famous statue of the goddess Pallas (Minerva). She is sitting with a spear in her right hand, and in her left a distaff and spindle. Various accounts are given of the origin of it. Some writers say it fell from the skies. It was supposed that the preservation of the statue would be the preservation of Troy; and during the Trojan War the Greeks were greatly encouraged when they became the possessors of it.

Pal′las, or Minerva. The name was given to Minerva when she destroyed a famous giant named Pallas.

Pan. The Arcadian god of shepherds, huntsmen, and country folk, and chief of the inferior deities; usually considered to have been the son of Mercury and Penelope.

Pando′ra. According to Hesiod, the first mortal female. Vulcan made her of clay, and gave her life. Venus gave her beauty; and the art of captivating was bestowed upon her by the Graces. She was taught singing by Apollo, and Mercury taught her oratory. Jupiter gave her a box, the famous "Pandora's Box," which she was told to give to her husband, Epimetheus, brother of Prometheus. As soon as he opened it there issued from it numberless diseases and evils which were soon spread all over the world, and from that moment they have afflicted the human race. It is said that Hope alone remained in the box.

Panthe′on. The temple of all the gods, built by Agrippa at Rome, in the reign of Augustus.

Pap′remis. The Egyptian Mars.

Par′cæ, The. Goddesses who presided over the destiny of human beings. They were also called the Fates, and were three in number, Atropos, Clotho, and Lachesis.

Paris. Son of Priam, king of Troy, and his mother was Hecuba. It had been predicted that he would be the cause of the destruction of Troy, and his father therefore ordered him to be strangled as soon as he was born; but the slave who had been intrusted with this mission took the child to Mount Ida, and left it there. Some shepherds, however, found the infant and took care of him. He lived among them till he had grown to man's estate, and he then married Œnone, a nymph of Ida. At the famous nuptial feast of Peleus and Thetis, Discordia, who had not been invited, attended secretly; and when all were assembled, she threw amongst the goddesses a golden apple, on which was inscribed, "Let the fairest take it." This occasioned a great contention, for each thought herself the fairest. Ultimately, the contestants were reduced to three, Juno, Pallas (Minerva), and Venus; but Jove himself could not make these three agree, and it was decided that Paris should be the umpire. He was sent for, and each of the goddesses courted his favor by offering all sorts of bribes. Juno offered him power, Pallas wisdom, and Venus promised him the most beautiful woman in the world. Paris gave the golden apple to Venus. Soon after this episode Priam owned Paris as his son, and sent him to Greece to fetch Helen, who was renowned as being the most beautiful woman in the world. She was the wife of Menelaus, king of Sparta; but during his absence Paris carried Helen away to Troy, and this gave rise to the celebrated war between the Greeks and the Trojans, which ended in the destruction of Troy. Paris was among the 676,000 Trojans who fell during or after the siege.

Parnas′sides. A name common to the Muses, from Mount Parnassus.

Parnas′sus. The mountain of the Muses in Phocis, and sacred to Apollo and Bacchus. Anyone who slept on this moutain became a poet. It was named after one of the sons of Bacchus.

Par′thenon. The temple of Minerva (or Pallas), at Athens. It was destroyed by the Persians, and rebuilt by Pericles.

Par′thenos. A name of Juno, and also of Minerva.

Pasiph′æ. The reputed mother of the Minotaur killed by Theseus. She was said to be the daughter of Sol and Perseis, and her husband was Minos, king of Crete.

Pasith′ea. Sometimes there are *four* Graces spoken of; when this is so, the name of the fourth is Pasithea.

Pa′van. Hindoo god of the winds.

Peg′asus. The famous winged horse which was said to have sprung from the blood of Medusa when her head was cut off by Perseus. His abode was on Mount Helicon, where, by striking the ground with his hoof, he caused water to spring forth, which formed the fountain afterwards called Hippocrene.

Pe′leus. A king of Thessaly, who married Thetis, one of the Nereids.

Pe′lias. A son of Neptune and Tyro. He usurped the throne of Cretheus, which Jason was persuaded to relinquish to take the command of the Argonautic expedition. On the return of Jason, Medea, the sorceress, undertook to restore Pelias to youth, but required that the body should first be cut up and put in a caldron of boiling water. When this had been done, Medea refused to fulfill her promise.

Pe′lias. The name of the spear of Achilles, which was so large that none could wield it but the hero himself.

Pe′lion. A well-wooded mountain, famous for the wars between the giants and the gods, and as the abode of the Centaurs, who were expelled by the Lapithæ.

Pe′lops. Son of Tantalus, king of Phrygia. His father killed him, and served him up to be eaten at a feast given to the gods, who, when they found out what the father of Pelops had done, restored the son to life, and he afterwards became the husband of Hippodamia.

Pena′tes. Roman domestic gods.

Perseph′one. The Greek name of Proserpine.

Per′seus. A son of Jupiter and Danæ, the daughter of Acrisius. His first famous exploit was against the Gorgon, Medusa. He was assisted in this enterprise by Pluto, who lent him a helmet which would make him invisible. Pallas lent him her shield, and Mercury supplied him with wings. He made a speedy conquest of the Gorgons, and cut off Medusa's head, with which he flew through the air, and from the blood sprang the winged horse Pegasus. As he flew along he saw Andromeda chained to the rock, and a sea-monster ready to devour her. He killed the monster, and married Andromeda. When he got back, he showed the Gorgon's head to King Polydectes, and the monarch was immediately turned into stone.

Pha′eton. A son of Sol, or, according to most mythologists, of Phœbus and Clymene. Anxious to display his skill in horsemanship, he was allowed to drive the chariot of the sun for one day. The horses soon found out the incapacity of the charioteer, became unmanageable, and overturned the chariot. There was such great fear of injury to heaven and earth, that Jove, to stop the destruction, killed Phaeton with a thunderbolt.

Pha′on. A boatman, who received from Venus a box of ointment, with which, when he anointed himself, he grew so beautiful that Sappho became enamored of him; but when the ointment had all been used Phaon returned to his former condition, and Sappho, in despair, drowned herself.

Philocte′tes. Son of Pœas, and one of the companions of Jason on his Argonautic expedition. He was present at the death of Hercules, and received from him the poisoned arrows which had been dipped in the blood of the Hydra. These arrows, an oracle declared, were necessary to be used in the destruction of Troy, and Philoctetes was persuaded by Ulysses to go to assist at the siege. He appears to have used the weapons with great dexterity and with wonderful effect, for Paris was among the heroes whom he killed.

Philome′la. A daughter of Pandion, king of Athens, who was transformed into a nightingale.

Phleg′ethon. A river of fire in the infernal regions. It was the picture of desolation, for nothing could grow on its parched and withered banks.

Phle′gon (earth loving). One of the four chariot horses of Sol.

Phle′gyas. Son of Mars and father of Ixion and Coronis. For his impiety in desecrating and plundering the temple of Apollo at Delphi, he was sent to Hades, and there was made to sit with a huge stone suspended over his head, ready to be dropped on him at any moment.

Phœ′bus. A name of Apollo, signifying light and life.

Phor′cus. A son of Neptune, father of the Gorgons.

Picum′nus. A rural divinity, who presided over the manuring of lands, called also Sterentius.

Pi′cus. A son of Saturn, father of Faunus; was turned into a woodpecker by Circe, whose love he had not requited.

Pier′ides. A name of the Muses, derived from Pieria, a fountain near Mount Olympus, where they were supposed to have been born. Also, the daughters of Pierus, a king of Macedonia, who settled in Bœotia. They challenged the Muses to sing, and were changed into magpies.

Pilum'nus. A rural divinity, who presided over the corn while it was being ground.

Pirith'ous. A son of Ixion and great friend of Theseus, king of Athens.

Pi'tho. The goddess of Persuasion, daughter of Mercury and Venus. She is sometimes referred to under the name of Suada.

Plei'ades, The. Seven daughters of Atlas and Pleione. Their names were Electra, Alcyone, Celæno, Maia, Sterope, Taygete, and Merope.

Plu'to. King of the infernal regions. He was a son of Saturn and Ops, and husband of Proserpine, daughter of Ceres. He is sometimes referred to under the name Dis, and he personifies hell. His principal attendant was the three-headed dog Cerberus, and about his throne were the Eumenides, the Harpies, and the Furies.

Plu'tus. The god of riches; was son of Jason and Ceres. He is described as being blind and lame; blind because he so often injudiciously bestows his riches, and lame because fortunes come so slowly.

Plu'vius. A name of Jupiter, because he had the rain in his control.

Podalir'ius. A famous surgeon, a son of Æsculapius, who was very serviceable among the soldiers in the Trojan war.

Pol'lear. Son of Siva, the Hindoo god of wisdom.

Pol'lux. Twin brother of Castor. Their father was Jupiter and their mother Leda. He and his brother form the constellation Gemini. His Greek name was Polydeuces.

Polybo'tes. One of the giants who made war against Jupiter.

Polydec'tes. Turned into stone when Perseus showed him Medusa's head.

Polyhym'nia. Daughter of Jupiter and Mnemosyne. One of the Muses, who presided over singing and rhetoric.

Polyphe'mus. One of the most celebrated of the Cyclopes, a son of Neptune. He captured Ulysses and twelve of his companions, and it is said that six of them were eaten. The rest escaped by the ingenuity of Ulysses, who destroyed the Cyclop's one eye with a firebrand.

Polyx'ena. Daughter of Priam, king of Troy. It was by her treachery that Achilles was shot in the heel.

Pomo'na. The Roman goddess of fruits and gardens.

Portu'nus (Palæmon). Son of Ino; was god of harbors.

Posei'don. A name of Neptune.

Prac'riti. The Hindoo goddess of nature.

Pri'am. The last king of Troy.

Pria'pus. The guardian of gardens and god of natural reproduction; was son of Venus and Bacchus.

Pris'ca. Another name of Vesta.

Pro'cris. Daughter of the king of Athens.

Prome'theus. Son of Japetes and father of Deucalion. He presumed to make clay men, and animate them with fire which he had stolen from heaven. This so displeased Jupiter that he sent him a box full of evils, which Prometheus refused; but his brother Epimetheus, not so cautious, opened it, and the evils spread over all the earth. Jupiter then punished Prometheus by commanding Mercury to bind him to Mount Caucasus, where a vulture daily preyed upon his liver, which grew in the night as much as it had been reduced in the day, so that the punishment was a prolonged torture. Hercules at last killed the vulture and set Prometheus free.

Pros'erpine. A daughter of Jupiter and Ceres. Pluto carried her off to the infernal regions and made her his wife. She was known by the names of "the Queen of Hell," Hecate, Juno Inferna, and Libitina.

Pro'teus. A marine deity, who could foretell events and convert himself at will into all sorts of shapes.

Psy'che. The wife of Cupid. The name is Greek, signifying the soul or spirit.

Pygma'lion. A famous sculptor, who had resolved to remain unmarried, but he made such a beautiful statue of a goddess that he begged Venus to give it life. His request being granted, Pygmalion married the animated statue.

Pylo'tis. A Greek name of Minerva.

Pyr'acmon. One of the chiefs of the Cyclopes.

Py'rois (luminous). One of the four chariot horses of Sol.

Py'thia. The priestess of Apollo at Delphi, who delivered the answers of the oracle. Also the name of the games celebrated in honor of Apollo's victory over the Python.

Py'thon. A famous serpent killed by Apollo.

Quadratus. A surname given to Mercury, because some of r's statues were four-sided.

Quad'rifrons. Janus was sometimes depicted with four faces instead of the usual two, and he was then called Janus Quadrifrons.

Qui'es. The Roman goddess of rest; she had a temple just outside the Collini gate of Rome.

Quiri'nus. A name given to Mars during war time; and Virgil refers to Jupiter under the same name.

Ra'ma. A Hindoo god, who was the terrestrial representative of Vishnu.

Rem'bha. The Hindoo goddess of pleasure.

Rhadaman'thus. A son of Jupiter and Europa; was the judge of the Asiatics in the infernal regions.

Rhamnu'sia. A name of Nemesis, from Rhamnus, a town in Attica, where she had a temple in which was her statue, made of one stone ten cubits high.

Rhe'a. The Greek name of Cybele.

Rim'mon. A Phrygian god of whom Milton says—

" . . . Rimmon, whose delightful seat
Was fair Damascus, on the fertile banks
Of Abana and Pharpar, lucid streams."

Rom'ulus. The traditional founder of Rome. He was a son of Mars and Ilia, and twin prother of Remus. The infants were thrown into the Tiber, but were miraculously saved and suckled by a she-wolf till they were found by Faustulus, a shepherd, who brought them up. Remus was killed in a quarrel with his brother, and Romulus became the famous emperor.

Rumi'a Dea. The Roman goddess of babes in arms.

Runci'a. The goddess of weeding or cleansing the ground.

Sa'ga. The Scandinavian goddess of history.

Sal'amanders. The genii who, according to Plato, lived in fire.

Sal'ii. The priests of Mars who had charge of the sacred shields.

Salmo'neus. A king of Elis who, for trying to imitate Jupiter's splendors, was sent by the god straight to the infernal regions.

Sa'lus. The Roman god of health.

Sappho. A celebrated poetess, a native of Lesbos, who flourished B. C. 610. Her only connection with the goddesses of the time is that the Greeks called her "the tenth Muse."

Sat'urn. King of the Universe; was father of Jupiter, Neptune, and Pluto. These gods quarreled among themselves as to the division of their father's kingdom, which ended in Jupiter having heaven and earth, Neptune the sea, and Pluto the infernal regions.

Saturna'lia. Festivals held in honor of Saturn about the 16th or 18th of December. Principally famous for the riotous disorder which generally attended them.

Satur'nius. A name given to Jupiter, Neptune, and Pluto, as sons of Saturn.

Satyavra'ta. The Hindoo god of law. The same as Menu.

Sat'yrs. The attendants of Silenus, who were similar in most respects to the fauns who attended Pan.

Scyl'la. A beautiful nymph who excited the jealousy of Neptune's wife, Amphitrite, and was changed by the goddess into a frightful sea monster, which had six fearfully ugly heads and necks, and who, rising unexpectedly from the deep, used to take off as many as six sailors from a vessel, and carry them to the bottom of the sea. An alternative danger with Charybdis.

Scyl'la. A daughter of Nysus, who was changed into a lark for cutting off a charmed lock of her father's hair.

Seges'ta. A rural divinity who protected corn during harvest time.

Sem. The Egyptian Hercules.

Sem'ele. The mother of Bacchus, who was born in a miraculous manner after Jupiter had visited her, at her special request, in all his terrible splendor. She was deified after her death and named Thyone.

Semi-Dei. The demi-gods.

Semo'nes. Roman gods of a class between the "immortal" and the "mortal," such as the Satyrs and Fauns.

Septe'rion. A festival held in honor of Apollo, at which the victory of that god over the Python was grandly represented.

Sera'pis. The Egyptian Jupiter, and generally considered to be the same as Osiris.

Serpent. The Greeks and Romans considered the serpent as symbolical of guardian spirits, and as such were often engraved on their altars.

Sesha, or Ananta. The Egyptian Pluto.

Sile'nus. A Bacchanalian demi-god, the chief of the Satyrs. He is generally represented as a fat, drunken old man, riding on an ass, and crowned with flowers.

Si′rens, The. Sea nymphs, who by their music allured mariners to destruction. To avoid the snare when nearing their abode, Ulysses had the ears of his companions stopped with wax, and had himself tied to the mast of his ship. They thus sailed past in safety; but the Sirens, thinking that their charms had lost their powers, drowned themselves.

Sis′yphus. Son of Æolus and Enaretta. He was condemned to roll a stone to the top of a hill in the infernal regions, and, as it rolled down again when he reached the summit, his punishment was perpetual.

Si′va. In Hindoo mythology the "changer of form."

Sleip′ner. The eight-legged horse of Odin, the chief of the Scandinavian gods.

Sol. The sun. The worship of the god Sol is the oldest on record, and though he is sometimes referred to as being the same as the god Apollo, there is no doubt he was worshiped by the Egyptians, Persians, and other nations long before the Apollo of the Greeks was heard of.

Som′nus. The god of sleep, son of Nox (Night). He was one of the infernal deities, and resided in a gloomy cave, void of light and air.

Sos′pita. A name of Juno, as the safeguard of women.

So′ter. A Greek name of Jupiter, meaning deliverer.

Sphinx, The. A monster having the head and breasts of a woman, the body of a dog, the tail of a serpent, the wings of a bird, the paws of a lion, and a human voice. She lived in the country near Thebes, and proposed to every passer-by the following enigma: "What animal is that which walks on four legs in the morning, two at noon, and three in the evening?" Œdipus solved the riddle thus: "Man is the animal; for when an infant he crawls on his hands and feet, in the noontide of life he walks erect, and as the evening of his existence sets in he supports himself with a stick." When the sphinx found her riddle solved she destroyed herself.

Steren′tius. The Roman god who invented the art of manuring lands.

Ster′opes. One of the Cyclopes.

Stymphali′des. The carnivorous birds destroyed in the sixth labor of Hercules.

Styx. A noted river of hell, which was held in such high esteem by the gods that they always swore, "By the Styx," and such an oath was never violated.

Sua′da. The goddess of Persuasion.

Surade′vi. The Hindoo goddess of wine.

Su′ry′a. The Hindoo god corresponding to the Roman Sol, the sun.

Sylphs. Genii who, according to Plato, lived in the air.

Sylves′ter. The name of Mars when he was invoked to protect cultivated land from the ravages of war.

Syr′inx. The name of the nymph who, to escape from the importunities of Pan, was by Diana changed into reeds, out of which he made his celebrated pipes, and named them "The Syrinx."

Tac′ita. The goddess of Silence.

Tan′talus. Father of Niobe and Pelops, who, as a punishment for serving up his son Pelops as meat at a feast given to the gods, was placed in a pool of water in the infernal regions; but the waters receded from him whenever he attempted to quench his burning thirst. Hence the word tantalizing.

Tar′tarus. An inner region of hell, to which the gods sent the exceptionally depraved.

Telchi′nes. Priests of Cybele, who were famous magicians.

Tel′lus. A name of Cybele, wife of Saturn.

Temple. An edifice erected to the honor of a god or goddess, in which the sacrifices were offered.

Tenth Muse. Sappho was so called.

Ter′eus. A son of Mars. He married Progne, daughter of the king of Athens, but became enamored of her sister Philomela, who, however, resented his attentions, which so enraged him that he cut out her tongue. When Progne heard of her husband's unfaithfulness she took a terrible revenge (see Itys). Progne was turned into a swallow, Philomela into a nightingale, Itys into a pheasant, and Tereus into a hoopoo, a kind of vulture,—some say an owl.

Tergemi′na. A name of Diana, alluding to her triform divinity as a goddess of heaven, earth, and hell.

Tĕr′minus. The Roman god of boundaries.

Terpsich′ore. One of the nine Muses; she presided over dancing.

Terra. The earth; one of the most ancient of the Grecian goddesses.

Thales′tris. A queen of the Amazons.

Thali′a. One of the nine Muses; she presided over festivals and comedy.

Thali′a. One of the Graces.

Tham′yris. A skillful singer, who presumed to challenge the Muses to sing, upon condition that if he did not sing best they might inflict any penalty they pleased. He was, of course, defeated, and the Muses made him blind.

The′ia. A daughter of Cœlus and Terra; wife of Hyperion.

The′mis. A daughter of Cœlus and Terra, and wife of Jupiter; was the Roman goddess of laws, ceremonies, and oracles.

The′seus. One of the most famous of the Greek heroes. He was a son of Ægeus, king of Athens.

The′tis. A sea goddess, daughter of Nereus and Doris. Her husband was Peleus, king of Thessaly, and she was the mother of the famous Achilles, whom she rendered all but invulnerable by dipping him into the river Styx. See Achilles.

Thor. The Scandinavian war god (son of Odin), who had rule over the Aerial regions, and, like Jupiter, hurled thunder against his foes.

Thor's Belt. A girdle which doubles his strength whenever the war god puts it on.

Thoth. The Mercury of the Egyptians.

Thya′des. Priestesses of Bacchus, who ran wild in the hills, wearing tiger skins and carrying torches.

Thyr′sus. A kind of javelin.

Time (or Saturn). The husband of Virtue and father of Truth.

Tisiph′one. One of the Furies.

Ti′tan. Elder brother of Saturn, who made war against him, and was ultimately vanquished by Jupiter.

Ti′tans. The supporters of Titan in his war against Saturn and Jupiter.

Titho′nus. The husband of Aurora. At the request of his wife the gods granted him immortality, but she forgot at the same time to ask that he should be granted perpetual youth. The consequence was that Tithonus grew old and decrepit, while Aurora remained as fresh as the morning. The gods, however, changed him into a grasshopper, which is supposed to moult as it gets old, and grows young again.

Tit′yus. A son of Jupiter. A giant who was thrown into the innermost hell for insulting Diana. He, like Prometheus, has a vulture constantly feeding on his ever-growing liver.

Triptol′emus. A son of Oceanus and Terra. He was a great favorite of the goddess Ceres, who cured him of a dangerous illness when he was young, and afterwards taught him agriculture.

Triteri′ca. Bacchanalian festivals.

Tri′tons. Sons of Triton, a son of Neptune and Amphitrite. They were the trumpeters of the sea gods, and were depicted as a sort of mermen—the upper half of the body being like a man, and the lower half like a dolphin.

Tropho′nius. One of Jupiter's most famous oracles.

Troy. The classic poets say that the walls of this famous city were built by the magic sound of Apollo's lyre.

Truth. A daughter of Time, because Truth is discovered in the course of Time. Democritus says that Truth lies hidden at the bottom of a well.

Tutel′ina. A rural divinity—the goddess of granaries.

Ty′phon. A monster with a hundred heads who made war against the gods, but was crushed by Jove's thunderbolts, and imprisoned under Mount Etna.

Ty′phon. In Egyptian mythology the god who tried to undo all the good work effected by Osiris.

Ul′ler. The Scandinavian god who presided over archery and duels.

Ulys′ses. A noted king of Ithaca, whose exploits in connection with the Trojan war, and his adventures on his return therefrom, are the subject of Homer's Odyssey. His wife's name was Penelope, and he was so much endeared to her that he feigned madness to get himself excused from going to the Trojan war; but his artifice was discovered, and he was compelled to go. He was of great help to the Grecians, and forced Achilles from his retreat and obtained the charmed arrows of Hercules from Philoctetes, and used them against the Trojans. He enabled Paris to shoot one of them at the heel of Achilles, and so kill that charmed warrior. During his wanderings on his homeward voyage he was taken prisoner by the Cyclopes, and escaped, after blinding Polyphemus, their chief. At Æolia he obtained all the winds of heaven, and put them in bags; but his companions, thinking that the bags contained treasure which they could rob him of when they got to Ithaca, cut them and let out the winds, and the ships were immediately blown black to Æolia. After Circe had turned his companions into swine on an island where he and they were shipwrecked, he compelled the goddess to restore them to their human shape again. As he passed the islands of the Sirens he escaped their allurements by stopping the ears of his companions with wax, and fastening himself to the mast of his ship. His wife Penelope was a pattern of constancy; for, though Ulysses was reported to be dead, she would not marry anyone else, and had the satisfaction of having her husband return after an absence of about twenty years.

Un′dine. A water nymph, or sylph.

Unx′ia. A name of Juno, relating to her protection of newly-married people.

Ura′nia. A daughter of Jupiter and Mnemosyne—one of the Muses, who presided over astronomy.

Ura′nus. The Greek name of Cœlus; his descendants are sometimes called Uranids.

Ur′gus. A name of Pluto, signifying the Impeller.

Ut′gord Lo′ki. In Scandinavian mythology the king of the giants.

Valhal′la. The Scandinavian temple of immortality, inhabited by the souls of heroes slain in battle.

Va′li. The Scandinavian god of archery.

Vallo′nia. The goddess of valleys.

Varu′na. The Hindoo Neptune—generally represented as a white man riding on a sea horse, carrying a club in one hand and a rope in the other.

Vejo′vis. "Little Jupiter"—a name given to Jupiter when he appeared without his thunder.

Ve′nus. The goddess of beauty, and mother of love. She is said to have sprung from the foam of the sea, and was immediately carried to the abode of the gods on Olympus, where they were all charmed with her extreme beauty. Vulcan married her, but she permitted the attention of others of the gods, and notably of Mars, their offspring being Hermione, Cupid, and Anteros. After this she left Olympus and fell in love with Adonis, a beautiful youth, who was killed when hunting a wild boar. Venus indirectly caused the Trojan war, for, when the goddess of discord had thrown among the goddesses the golden apple inscribed "To the fairest," Paris adjudged the apple to Venus, and she inspired him with love for Helen, wife of Menelaus, King of Sparta. Paris carried off Helen to Troy, and the Greeks pursued and besieged the city (see Helen, Paris, and Troy). Venus is mentioned by the classic poets under the names of Aphrodite, Cypria, Urania, Astarte, Paphia, Cythera, and the laughter-loving goddess. Her favorite residence was at Cyprus. Incense alone was usually offered on her altars, but if there was a victim it was a white goat. Her attendants were Cupids and the Graces.

Verti′cor′dia. A Roman name of Venus, signifying the power of love to change the hard hearted. The corresponding Greek name was Epistrophia.

Vertum′nus. God of spring, or, as some mythologists say, of the seasons; the husband of Pomona, the goddess of orchards.

Ves′ta. Daughter of Saturn and Cybele; was the goddess of fire. She had under her special care and protection a famous statue of Minerva, before which the Vestal Virgins kept a fire or lamp constantly burning.

Ves′tal Vir′gins. The priestesses of Vesta, whose chief duty was to see that the sacred fire in the temple of Vesta was not extinguished. They were always selected from the best families, and were under a solemn vow of chastity, and compelled to live perfectly pure lives.

Via′lis. A name of Mercury, because he presided over the making of roads.

Vic′tory. A goddess, the daughter of Styx and Acheron, generally represented as flying in the air holding out a wreath of laurel. See Nicephorus.

Vi′dor. A Scandinavian god, who could walk on the water and in the air. The god of silence (corresponding with the classic Harpocrates).

Vir′tue. A goddess worshiped by most of the ancients under various names. The way to the temple of honor was through the temple of virtue.

Vish′nu. The Preserver, a principal Hindoo god.

Vul′can. The god of fire; was the son of Jupiter and Juno. He offended Jupiter, and was by him thrown out of heaven; he was nine days falling, and at last dropped into Lemnos with such violence that he broke his leg, and was lame forever after. Vulcan was married to Venus. He is supposed to have formed Pandora out of clay. His servants were the Cyclopes. He was the patron deity of blacksmiths.

Vulca′nia. Roman festivals in honor of Vulcan, at which the victims were thrown into the fire and burned to death.

Wo′den. The Anglo-Saxon form of the Scandinavian god Odin; Wednesday is called after him.

Xan′thus. The name of the wonderful horse of Achilles.

Ya′ma. The Hindoo devil, generally represented as a terrible monster of a green color, with flaming eyes.

Ygdra′sil. The famous ash tree of Scandinavian mythology, under which the gods held daily council.

Y′mir. The Scandinavian god corresponding to Chaos of the classics.

Zeph′yr. The god of flowers, a son of Æolus and Aurora; the west wind.

Ze′tes. With his brother Calais, drove the Harpies from Thrace.

Ze′thus. Twin brother of Amphion.

Zeus. The Greek name of Jupiter.

THE HALL OF FAME.

March 5, 1900, the Council of New York University accepted a gift of $100,000 from a donor whose name was withheld, for the erection and completion on University Heights, New York city, of a building to be called "The Hall of Fame for Great Americans." A structure was accordingly built in the form of a semi-circle, 506 feet long, 15 feet wide, and 170 feet high, connecting the University Hall of Philosophy with the Hall of Languages. Within the colonnade 150 panels, each 2 by 8 feet, are to be placed, to bear the names of Americans deemed the greatest in their respective fields.

Under the rules adopted only persons born on what is now United States territory and who shall have been dead ten or more years are eligible to be chosen, and they must be selected from fifteen classes of citizens, to wit: Authors and editors, business men, educators, inventors, missionaries and explorers, philanthropists and reformers, preachers and theologians, scientists, engineers and architects, lawyers and judges, musicians, painters and sculptors, physicians and surgeons, rulers and statesmen, soldiers and sailors, distinguished men and women outside the above classes. Fifty names were to be inscribed on the tablets at the beginning, and five additional names every fifth year thereafter, until the year 2000, when the 150 inscriptions will be completed. Should there be a failure to select the entire fifty names at the beginning, the vacancies shall be filled in a following year.

The rules prescribed that the Council should invite nominations from the public. Every nomination seconded by a member of the University Senate should be submitted to an electorate of one hundred eminent citizens selected by the Council, each of whom must vote for fifty of the candidates.

In October, 1900, the University Senate received the ballots of the judges. Of the one hundred judges selected, ninety-seven voted. The number of names which had been submitted to them was 252. Of these each judge returned a vote for fifty. The rule required that no candidate receiving less than fifty-one votes could be accepted. The returns showed that but twenty-nine candidates received the required number and were chosen. These were as follows: George Washington, Abraham Lincoln, Daniel Webster, Benjamin Franklin, Ulysses S. Grant, John Marshall, Thomas Jefferson, Ralph Waldo Emerson, Henry W. Longfellow, Robert Fulton, Washington Irving, Jonathan Edwards, Samuel F. B. Morse, David G. Farragut, Henry Clay, Nathaniel Hawthorne, George Peabody, Robert E. Lee, Peter Cooper, Eli Whitney, John J. Audubon, Horace Mann, Henry Ward Beecher, James Kent, Joseph Story, John Adams, William E. Channing, Gilbert Stuart, Asa Gray.

OUTLINES OF HISTORY.

Chronological and Historical Tabulations Designed for Ready Reference.

Prehistoric Ages.—Sir J. Lubbock distinguishes four prehistoric ages, as follows: 1. The Paleolithic or Early Stone Age. 2. The Neolithic or Polished Stone Age. 3. The Bronze Age. 4. The Iron Age. In the Stone Age man knew nothing of pottery or agriculture and had no domestic animals except the dog. In the Bronze Age arms and cutting instruments were made of bronze. In the Iron Age bronze was superseded by iron.

B.C.	FROM THE DELUGE TO THE TIME OF CYRUS			
2350	**The Deluge.** 2200 (*circa*). Hia dynasty founded in China. 1996. Birth of Abraham. 1921. Call of Abraham. 1896. Isaac born. 1837. Jacob and Esau born. 1822. Egyptian alphabet invented. 1729. Joseph sold into Egypt. 1706. Jacob removes into Egypt. 1700. Rameses, King of Egypt. 1618. Sesostris, King of Egypt. 1582. Beginning of the chronology of the Arundelian marbles, brought to England A.D. 1627. 1574. Moses born. 1571. Aaron born. 1491. **The Exodus. The Law given from Sinai.** 1451. Moses and Aaron die. 1451. Joshua leads the Israelites into Canaan.			
	The Hebrews	**Egypt**	**Assyria**	**Greece, etc.**
		The Pharaohs.		
1300	45. Gideon conquers the Midianites.		73. Rise of the Assyrian Empire. Semiramis.	63. Jason and the Argonauts.
1200	88. Jephthah. 56. Eli. 36. Samson slays the Philistines. 20. Samuel.		50. Nebuchadnezzar I. 30. Tiglath Pileser.	94. The Trojan War. 84. Capture of Troy. Chow dynasty founded in China.
1100	95. Saul, King. 55. David, King. 42. The Ark removed to Jerusalem. 23. Revolt of Absalom. 15. Solomon, King. 12. The Temple begun.			69. Codrus dies for his people. 68. Archons chosen.
1000	90. Queen of Sheba visits Solomon. 75. Solomon dies. Revolt of the ten tribes—two Kingdoms formed: **Judah**: Rehoboam, King. 58. Abijah. 55. Asa. 4. Jehoshaphat. **Israel**: Jeroboam, King. 54. Nadab. 26. Samaria built. 18. Ahab and Jezebel.	78. Shishak. 71. Invades Judea and plunders the Temple.	900. Erection of the Northwest Palace of Nimroud.	
900	**Judah**: 89. Jehoram. 88. The Philistines plunder Jerusalem. 78. Joash. **Israel**: 97. Elijah translated. 92. Syrians besiege Samaria. 84. Jehu. 40. Jehoash defeats King Benhadad of Syria.		75. Sardanapalus. 70. The Assyrians conquer Phœnicia.	Homer. 84. Legislation of Lycurgus at Sparta. 78. Carthage founded by Dido.
800				

B.C.	Judah	Israel	Assyria	Egypt	Greece, Rome
700	Joel, prophet. 59. Jotham. 42. Ahaz pays tribute to Tiglath Pileser. 41. Pekah, King of Israel, besieges Jerusalem; 120,000 of his men are slain in one day. 26. Hezekiah. Isaiah. Nahum. 10 Sennacherib's army destroyed.	Jonah. 47. Assyrians invade Israel. 30. Hosea pays tribute. 21. The ten tribes carried into captivity. 9. Esarhadon, King of	47. Nabonassar. 41. Tiglath Pileser. 28. Shalmaneser. 23. Invades Phœnicia. 17. Sennacherib.	11. Sennacherib's invasion.	76. Commencement of Olympiads—first authentic date in Greek history. 53. Rome founded by Romulus. 50. Sabine war in Rome.
		Babylonia			
600	97. Manasseh. 42. Amon. 41. Josiah. Jeremiah. Habakkuk. 6. Jerusalem taken by Nebuchadnezzar.	6. Nebuchadnezzar the Great defeats Necho of Egypt, invades Judea and takes Jerusalem.		11. Necho II. loses 200,000 men trying to cut canal to Red Sea. 6. Nebuchadnezzar defeats Necho.	24. Code of Draco, Athens. 16. Tarquin the Elder, King of Rome.
	98. Jehoiachin. 96. Zedekiah. 88. Jerusalem destroyed.	89. Nebuchadnezzar invades Phœnicia. 79. Takes Tyre. Destroys Nineveh.		94. Apries, King. 79-72. Conquered and devasted by Nebuchadnezzar. Amasis. Psammenit. 25. Conquest by Cambyses, son of Cyrus.	94. Solon gives laws at Athens. 78. Servius Tullius, Rome. 34. Tarquin the Proud.
	Ezekiel. Jews carried captive to Babylon. 55. Belshazzar. 38. Cyrus, the Mede, captures Babylon and establishes the Persian Empire. 36. Cyrus ends captivity of the Jews. 29. Death of Cyrus.				

FROM CYRUS TO ALEXANDER

B.C.	Persia	Greece	Macedonia	Rome
500	21. Darius I. Zechariah, prophet. Haggai. 15. Dedication of second temple at Jerusalem. 8-6. Conquest of Thrace, Pæonia, and Macedonia.	10. The Pisistratidæ expelled from Athens. Republic. 4. Sardis burned by the Greeks.	8. Subdued by Darius of Persia.	10. The Tarquins vanquished. Republic. Consuls. 1. Dictators.
400	94. Darius invades Greece. 90. Defeated at Marathon. 81. Xerxes invades Greece. 79. Returns defeated. 67. Ezra returns to Jerusalem. 65. Artaxerxes I. 60. Egypt revolts. 56. Esther. 55. Jerusalem rebuilt by Nehemiah. 1. Battle of Cunaxa; Cyrus the Younger slain.	90. Miltiades defeats the Persians at Marathon. 80. Leonidas at Thermopylæ. Themistocles at Salamis. Xerxes destroys Athens. 80-50. Anaxagoras teaches philosophy. 79. Battles of Mycale and Platæa; Persians retreat. 44. Pericles supreme. 43. The Parthenon built by Phidias. 31. Peloponnesian war. 29. Death of Pericles. Socrates. 14. Battle of Syracuse. 13. Athenians invade Sicily.		93. Tribunes chosen. 91. Coriolanus conquered. 89. Besieges Rome. 88. Retires at his mother's suit. 58. Cincinnatus Dictator. 51. First decemvirate. 49. Virginius kills his daughter to save her honor. 40. Famine in Rome.

B.C.	Persia	Greece	Macedonia	Rome
	Artaxerxes Mnemon.	95. Corinthian war.	98. Amyntas.	
	94. Persians and Athenians in battle of Cnidus.			90. Rome burnt by the Gauls.
		80. Olinthian war.		76. Civil war between patricians and plebeians.
		78. Theban war—Epaminondas, Theban general.	58. Philip II.	69. Tribunes abolished.
			38. Athenians and Thebans defeated at Chæronea.	40. Samnian war begins.
	36. Darius III. (Codomanus).	39. War with Macedon.	36. Murder of Philip. Accession of Alexander the Great.	37. War with Latins.
		35. Greeks conquered by Alexander the Great. Thebes destroyed.	34. Battle of the Granicus.	35. Surrender of Latium.
	34. Persia invaded and conquered by Alexander the Great of Macedon.	33. Battle of Issus.		
		33. Capture of Damascus. Siege of Tyre.		
	32. Alexander captures Tyre and conquers Egypt. Alexandria founded.			32. Treaty with Alexander.
	31. Battle of Arbela—subjugation of Persia.			
	30. Darius assassinated.			
	28. Alexander invades India.			
	24. Alexander dies at Babylon.			

FROM ALEXANDER TO AUGUSTUS

B.C.	Egypt	Syria	Greece	Macedonia	Rome
	22. Ptolemy I. 1. Battle of Issus. Final division of Alexander's dominions.	23. Seleucus I.			21. Romans defeated by Pontius.
300					
	Ptolemy Lagus. 84. Ptolemy Philadelphus.	83. Antiochus I.	99. Athens taken by Demetrius. 97. Republic re-established.	98. Philip IV.	81. War with Pyrrhus, King of Epirus. 80. Pyrrhus invades Italy. 74. Pyrrhus defeated at Beneventum.
			87. Birth of Archimedes (d. 212). 91. Achæan league. 79. Irruption of the Gauls.	88. Lysimachus, King of Thrace, subjects Macedonia.	65. Rome supreme over all Italy. 64. First Punic war.
	46. Ptolemy Evergetes.	46. Seleucus I.	51. Achæan league renewed.		56. Defeat of Carthaginians. 55. Regulus capt'd by Carthaginians
	Egyptians conquer Syria.				41. Catullus defeats Carthaginians. 18. Second Punic war. Hannibal defeats Romans at Ticinus.
			26. Reforms of Cleomenes.		
	21. Ptolemy Philopater.	23. Antiochus the Great.			17. Hannibal passes the Apennines.
				20. Philip V.	16. Battle of Cannæ. 11-5. First Macedonian war.
				11. War with Rome	7. Carthaginians defeated at Metaurus. 3. Scipio carries war into Africa.
200	4. Ptolemy Epiphane.				2. Hannibal defeated.

B.C.	Egypt	Judea	Syria	Greece	Macedonia	Rome
	80. Ptolemy Philometer.	Egyptians driven out by Antiochus.	98. Independent.	91. Sparta joins the league.	99. Second war with Rome.	99. Second war with Macedonia.
				88. Laws of Lycurgus abolished by Philopœmen.	78. Perseus.	
			75. Antiochus IV. 70. Plunders Jerusalem.		72. Third war with Rome. 68. Battle of Pydna.	72. Third war with Macedonia.
		65. Antiochus defeated by Judas.			Macedonia made a Roman province.	
				46. Corinth taken by Mummius.		49. Third Punic war. 46. Carthage destroyed.
	45. Ptolemy Physcon.	35. John Hyrcanus.				34. First Servile war. 33. Conquest of Spain.
			30. Antiochus VII.			
	17. Ptolemy Lathyrus.	6. Aristobulus. 5. Alexander Jannæus.	23. Antiochus VIII. 12. Antiochus IX.			2. Second Servile War
100						
				90-88. The Social war in Italy.		
	Ptolemy Alexander.	78. Alexandra, Queen.		88. War with Pontus. Civil war—Marius and Sulla.		
		70. Hyrcanus II.	69. Antiochus XIII.	73-72. Victories of Lucullus.		
	65. Berenice.	67. Aristobulus II. 63. Jerusalem taken by the Romans.	64. Pompey makes Syria a Roman province.	63. Second conspiracy of Catiline—Cicero's orations. 60. First triumvirate: Pompey, Julius Cæsar, Crassus.		
			55. Cæsar invades Britain. Crassus killed by the Parthians.			
	48. Murder of Pompey.	51. Gaul subjugated. 49. Civil war between Cæsar and Pompey. Cæsar dictator. 48. Battle of Pharsalia.				
	45. Cleopatra.	45. War in Spain. Pompeians defeated at Munda. Cæsar dictator for life.				
		44. Cæsar assassinated. Antony master of Rome. Corinth and Carthage rebuilt.				
	30. Death of Antony and Cleopatra. Egypt subdued by Rome.	43. Second triumvirate—Octavius, Antony, Lepidus. Cicero put to death. Ovid born. 42. Battle of Philippi. Death of Brutus and Cassius. Triumvirs masters of the Roman world.				
		40. Herod made King of the Jews. 32. War between Octavius and Antony.				

31. Battle of Actium.
Establishment of the **Roman Empire.**
27. Cæsar Octavius, Emperor, under the title of Augustus.
17-7. Temple of Jerusalem rebuilt by Herod.
12. Drusus invades Germany.
4. **The Advent of Christ** (according to Usher).

B.C.

FROM AUGUSTUS TO CHARLEMAGNE

A.D.	
	4-6. Tiberius in Germany. 9. Varus and his legions destroyed by the Germans under **Hermann.** 29. **The Crucifixion of Jesus Christ.** (Some authorities give A.D. 33 as the date.) 37. Caligula. 41. Claudius. 54. Nero. 61. Insurrection of the Britons under Boadicea. 64. Rome burned. Christians persecuted. 70. Jerusalem destroyed by Titus. 79. Pompeii and Herculaneum destroyed by eruption of Vesuvius.
100	17. Hadrian. 30. Birth of Galen. 63. Persecution of Christians. 96. Severus captures Byzantium.
200	2. Persecution of Christians. 9. Severus invades Caledonia. 31. Persian war. 36. Persecution of Christians renewed. 52-67. Dreadful pestilence. 63. The Franks invade Gaul.
300	3. Diocletian persecutes Christians. 6. Constantine the Great. 11. Edict to stop persecutions. 23. Constantine sole emperor. 25. Council of Nice. 26. Arian controversy. 64. Valentinian and Valens joint emperors. Final division of the empire.

A.D.	The Western Empire	The Eastern Empire
300	93. Honorius, Emperor. 94. Theodosius master of the whole Roman world. 95. Death of Theodosius.	76. Valens allows the Huns to settle in Thrace. 78. Constantinople threatened by the Goths. 95. Arcadius, Emperor of the East. The Huns invade the Eastern provinces.
400	400. The Goths, under Alaric, overrun Italy. 9. Romans driven from Spain. 10. Alaric sacks Rome. 11. Roman legions recalled from Britain. 40. Leo I. (the Great) Bishop of Rome. 49. Landing of Anglo-Saxons in Britain. 52. Attila invades Italy. 53. Death of Attila. 55. Genseric sacks Rome. 57. Hengist founds the kingdom of Kent. 72. The Visigoths conquer Spain. 76. Odoacer, King of Italy. End of Western Empire. 86. The Franks in Gaul. 89. The Ostrogoths in Italy.	8. Theodosius II. 28. Nestor, Patriarch of Constantinople. 29. Vandals, under Genseric, invade Africa. 33. Attila, King of the Huns. 39. The Vandals surprise Carthage. 47. Attila ravages the empire and exacts tribute. 50. Marcian. 65. Great fire at Constantinople.
500	7. Kingdom of the **Franks** founded by Clovis. 39. Belisarius in Italy. 52. Ostrogoths expelled from Italy. 96. The Lombards overrun Italy.	2. The empire ravaged by the Persians. 29. The Justinian code published. 81. The Slavonians in Thrace.
600	28. Dagobert, King of France. 56. Clovis II., King of France. 62. Lombards defeat Constans II. in Italy. 78. Cadwallader, last King of the Britons. 97. Anefesto, Doge of Venice.	12. **Mahomet** spreads his doctrines. 14. Persians ravage Syria and Palestine. 22. The Hegira. 40. The Saracens invade Egypt. 73. Siege of Constantinople. 97. Saracens conquer Northern Africa.
700	11. Saracens invade Spain. 14. Charles Martel, Duke of France. 32. **Battle of Tours.** Saracens defeated by the Franks under Charles Martel. 52. Pepin the Short, King of France. 68. Succeeded by his sons, Charlemagne and Carloman. 72–85. Charlemagne conquers the Saxons. 74. Charlemagne conquers the Lombards. 87. The Danes in England. 91–96. Charlemagne establishes the margravate of Austria.	20. The Saracens defeated at Constantinople. 30. Iconoclasts burn and destroy works of art.
800	800. **Charlemagne** crowned Emperor of the West by Pope Leo III.	Haroun al Raschid, Caliph of Arabia.

FROM CHARLEMAGNE TO NAPOLEON

A.D.	England	France	Germany	Eastern Empire
800 900	**The Anglo-Saxons** 28. Egbert, King. 71. Alfred the Great.	41. Charles the Bald. 61. Pillaged by Northmen.	**House of France** 14. Louis the Debonnaire separates Germany from France.	11. Bulgarians defeat the Greek Emperor.
1000	24. Athelstane. 37. Defeats Danes, Scots, etc. 79. Edward the Martyr assassinated.	12. Robert, Duke of Normandy. **Capetian Dynasty** 88. Hugh Capet, King. 96. Robert II. Paris made capital.	**House of Saxony** 18. Henry I. (the Fowler). 34. Conquers Huns, Danes, Vandals, Bohemians. 62. Otho I. crowned Emperor by Pope. 83. Otho III.	69. John Zimisces.
1100	Ethelred. 16. Edmund. **The Danes** 17. Canute sole ruler. 34. Canute II. 42. **Saxons** restored. Edward the Confessor. 66. Battle of Hastings. **The Normans** William I. (the Conqueror). 87. William II.	31. Henry I. 60. Philip I. 87. War with England.	**House of Bavaria** 2. Henry II. (Saint). **House of Franconia** 22. Conrad II. 39. Henry III. 56. Henry IV. 73. War with Saracens. 77. Henry goes to Canossa and submits to Pope.	54. Schism of Greek Church. 81. Alexius Comnenus. 96. Suspicious reception of Crusaders.
1200	Henry I. 35. Stephen. **The Plantagenets** 54. Henry II. 71. Invasion of Ireland. 89. Richard Cœur de Lion. 99. John Lackland.	8. Louis the Fat. 37. Louis VII. 80. Philip II.	6. Henry V. 38. Conrad III. 52. Frederick I. Barbarossa. 54. Invades Italy. 62. Destroys Milan. 67. Italian League.	43. Manuel Comnenus. 47. Treachery to German Crusaders.
1300	15. **Magna Charta** signed. 16. Henry III. 62. War of the Barons. 65. Barons defeated. 72 Edward I. 82. Conquest of Wales. 97. Sir William Wallace in Scotland.	14. Philip Augustus. Battle of Bouvines. 26. Louis IX. 48. Louis IX leads seventh crusade. 70. Dies before Tunis. Philip III.	9. Otto IV. 18. Frederick II. 41. Hanseatic League formed. **House of Hapsburg** 73. Rudolph I. 92. Adolph. 98. Albert I.	4. Baldwin I. 6. Peter de Courtenay. 19. Robert de Courtenay. 28. Baldwin II. 61. Michael Paleologus.
1400	7. Edward II. 14. Battle of Bannockburn. 27. Edward III. 46. Battle of Cressy. 56. Battle of Poictiers. 77. Richard III. **House of Lancaster** 99. Henry IV.	1. Philip IV. quarrels with the Pope. 14. Louis X. **House of Valois** 28. Philip VI. 50. John II. 64. Charles V. 80. Charles VI.	7. Swiss revolt. William Tell. 15. Battle of Morgarten. Swiss independence. **House of Luxemburg** 49. Charles IV. 78. Wenceslaus.	28. Andronic III. 41. John Paleologus. 60. The Turks in Adrianople. 91. Manuel Paleologus.
	13. Henry V. War with France. 15. Battle of Agincourt. 22. Henry VI. 53. War of the Roses. **House of York** 61. Edward IV. 83. Edward V. **House of Tudor** 85. Henry VII.	22. Charles VII. 29. Joan of Arc raises siege of Orleans. 51. English expelled. 61. Louis XI. 83. Charles VIII. **Valois-Orleans** 98. Louis XII.	10. Sigismund. 15. John Huss burned. **House of Austria** 38. Albert II. 40. Frederick III. 93. Maximilian I.	25. John Paleologus II. 48. Constantine Paleologus. 53. Amurath captures Constantinople. **Turkey** 56. Turks defeated at Belgrade.

FROM CHARLEMAGNE TO NAPOLEON

A.D.	Spain	Italy	Russia	Scandinavia	Contemporary
800 900	73. Kingdom of Navarre founded by Sancho Inigo.	42. Invasion by the Saracens.	2. Ruric, the Norman, establishes first regular government at Novgorod.	800-1000. Viking Period. Norwegians colonize Iceland.	9. Haroun al Raschid, Caliph of Arabia, dies.
1000		90. Genoa becomes rich and powerful.	4. Oleg invades Greek empire. 88. Vladimir the Great embraces Christianity.	Eric. 93. Olaf, first Christian King of Sweden.	
1100	26. Sancho II. King of Castile. 31. Ramirez I. King of Aragon. 91. Moors seize Saracen possessions. 95. Henry of Besançon takes Portugal from Saracens.	16-17. Saracens expelled by the Normans. 73-85. Gregory VII. establishes universal sovereignty of Papacy.		2. Massacre of Danes by Ethelred of Eng. 3. Avenged by Svenn, King of Denmark. 13. Svenn conquers England. 80. Inge the Elder King of Sweden.	1. The Northmen discover America. 65. Turks take Jerusalem. 96. First Crusade. 98. Crusaders take Antioch. 99. Crusaders take Jerusalem.
1200	Exploits of the Cid Ruy Diaz. 1094-1144. Dynasty of the Almoravides at Cordova 44. Alphonso of Leon defeats the Moors in several battles.	20. Rise of Lombard cities. 25. The glory of Venice. 54. Barbarossa. 61. Wars of the Guelphs and Ghibellines. 76. Barbarossa defeated at Legnano. 83. Peace of Constance.		55. Eric Edwardson.	4. Crusaders take Acre. 46. Second Crusade. 72. Saladin's conquest in Asia. 87. Third Crusade. 94. Fourth Crusade.
1300	33-48. Ferdinand III. takes Cordova, Toledo, etc., from the Moors. 38. Moors found Granada. 74. Crown of Navarre passes to France.	36-50. Wars of Frederick II. 77. The Visconti at Milan. 82. The Sicilian Vespers. French expelled from Sicily.	23. Irruption of Tartars. 42. Tartars establish empire of Kaptschak.	44. Danes invade Russia; defeated by Alexander Newski. 79. Magnus. 90. Birger.	1200. Fifth Crusade. 17. Sixth Crusade. 18. Genghis Khan, the Mogul, conquers Asia. 68. Eighth and last Crusade. 99. Osman I., Turkish empire.
1400	27. King of Granada brings 200,000 Moors from Africa. 40. Alphonso XI. of Castile defeats Moors at Tarifa.	8. Pope Clement V. removes to Avignon. 39. First Doge of Genoa appointed 47. Rienzi frees Rome. 51. Death of Rienzi	80. War with Tartars. 83. Moscow burned 95. Invasion by Tamerlane.	89. Margaret offered the Swedish Crown. 97. Union of Calmar: Sweden, Norway and Denmark. Eric King.	11. Knights Templars suppressed. 96. Battle of Nicopolis. Christians defeated.
	74. Ferdinand II. of Aragon marries Isabella of Leon and Castile. 80-84. Inquisition established. 92-98. Jews persecuted. 92. Ferdinand takes Granada.	95. Charles VII. conquers Naples 96. Charles loses Naples. 99. Louis XII., aided by Venice, conquers Milan, but does not hold it long.	62. Ivan the Great founds present monarchy. 79. Great Tartar invasion. 91. Tartars defeated.	14. War with Schleswig. 34. Revolt of peasantry. 39. Eric dethroned 70. Sten Sture.	7. Battle of Angora Tamerlane captures Bajazet 22. Amurath II. consolidates Ottoman Empire 42. Hungarians defeat Turks at Vasag. 92. Columbus discovers America. 97. Cabot discovers Newfoundland.

A. D.	England	France	Germany	America
1500	9. Henry VIII. 13. Battle of Flodden. 15. Wolsey. 20. Field of the Cloth of Gold. 36. Anne Boleyn beheaded. 47. Edward VI. 53. Mary. 54. Marries Philip of Spain. 58. Elizabeth. 87. Mary of Scots beheaded. 88. Spanish Armada.	13. English Invasion. 15. Francis I. 25. Battle of Pavia. 47. Henry II. 59. Francis II. 60. Huguenot War. 72. Massacre of St. Bartholomew. 74. Henry III. **House of Bourbon** 89. Henry IV. of Navarre.	17. Protestant Reformation — Luther. 19. Charles V. 21. Diet of Worms. 30. Augsburg Confession. 36. Death of John of Leyden. 56. Charles V. abdicates. Ferdinand I. 64. Maximilian II. 76. Rudolph II.	12. Florida discovered by Ponce De Leon. 13. Balboa discovers the Pacific Ocean. 21. Cortez conquers Mexico. 44. De Soto discovers the Mississippi. 85. First American settlement founded by Walter Raleigh.
1600	**House of Stuart** 3. James I. 25. Charles I. 49. **Commonwealth** Oliver Cromwell. 60. Stuarts restored. Charles II. 66. Great London fire. 79. Habeas Corpus Act. 85. James II. 88. William and Mary. 90. Battle of the Boyne.	10. Louis XIII. 24. Richelieu. 27. Siege of Rochelle. 43. Louis XIV. 48. Wars of the Fronde. 72. Holland invaded. 85. Edict of Nantes revoked. 89. War with England. 97. Peace of Ryswick.	12. Mathias. 18. Thirty Years' War. 19. Ferdinand II. 20. Battle of Prague. 30. Gustavus Adolphus of Sweden invades Germany. 32. Battle of Lutzen. Death of Gustavus Adolphus. 34. Death of Wallenstein. 37. Ferdinand III. 48. Treaty of Westphalia closes war and establishes religious toleration. 59. Leopold I. 99. Peace of Carlowitz.	7. Jamestown settlement. 14. New Amsterdam settled. 20. Puritans land at Plymouth Rock. 80. William Penn.
1700	2. Anne. **House of Hanover** 14. George I. 27. George II. 39. War with Spain. 46. Stuart troubles in Scotland. Battle of Culloden. 56. War with France. 60. George III. 75. War with American Colonies. 97. Nelson destroys French fleet near Alexandria.	4. Defeated by Marlborough at Blenheim. 13. Peace of Utrecht. 15. Louis XV. 16. Speculation era. George Law. 45. Battle of Fontenoy. 46. Victories of Marshal Saxe. 48. Peace of Aix-la-Chapelle. 74. Louis XVI. 78. Aids America. 87. Assembly of Notables. 88. States General. 89. Revolution. 93. Reign of Terror. Louis beheaded. **Republic** 99. Napoleon, First Consul.	5. Joseph I. 11. Charles VI. 42. Charles VII. War of Austrian succession. **House of Lorraine** 45. Francis I. (husband of Maria Theresa). 56-63. Seven Years' War. 65. Joseph II. 90. Leopold II. 92. Francis I. Battle of Valmy.	33. Oglethorpe founds Savannah. 59. Quebec captured by the English. 63. Peace of Paris. France cedes Canada to England. 75. Battle of Lexington 76. Declaration of Independence. 89. George Washington, President. 97. John Adams, President.
1800	1. Union with Ireland. 3. War with France. 5. Napoleon defeated at Trafalgar. 8. Peninsular War. 12. War with U. S. 14. Peace with U. S. 15. Battle of Waterloo.	4. Napoleon, Emperor. 5. Battle of Austerlitz. 6. Jena. 9. Wagram. 12. Russian campaign. 12. War with all Europe. 14. Allies enter France. Napoleon sent to Elba. **Restoration** Louis XVIII., King. 15. Napoleon returns. Battle of Waterloo. Napoleon sent to St. Helena.	4. Francis renounces title Emperor of the Romans and assumes that of Emperor of **Austria** 5. Napoleon establishes Kingdoms of Würtemberg and Bavaria. 6. Dissolution of German Empire. Confederation of the Rhine formed. 7. Kingdom of Westphalia. 8. Serfdom abolished in Prussia. 13. War of Liberation (against Napoleon). 13. Battle of Leipzig. 14. Prussians occupy Paris. 14-15. Congress of Vienna. German Confederation formed.	1. Thomas Jefferson, President. 4-6. Lewis and Clarke explore the Upper Missouri. 9. James Madison, President. 15. Battle of New Orleans.

A. D.	Spain	Italy	Russia	Scandinavia	Contemporary
1500	1500-22. Mohammedans expelled. 12. Ferdinand conquers Navarre. 16. Accession House of Austria Charles I., King of Spain. 19. Charles becomes Emperor of Germany as Charles V. 57. War with France. 61. Turks defeated at Lepanto. 80. Portugal conquered. 88. Armada defeated.	9. Venice stripped of Italian possessions. 13-22. Pope Leo X.	33. Ivan IV. 53. Trade with England begun. 54. Siberia discovered. 98. The race of Ruric, which governed Russia for 700 years, becomes extinct.	20. Christian II. 21. Sweden breaks loose from Union of Calmar. Gustavus Vasa. 59. Frederick II. of Denmark. 60. Eric XIV. King of Sweden. War between Denmark and Sweden. 70. Peace of Stettin. 93. Augsburg Confession accepted at Upsala.	35. Order of Jesuits founded. 72. Holland, under William of Orange, rebels against Philip's tyranny. 81. Holland a republic. 82. Reformation of calendar.
1600	1600-10. 300,000 Moors banished. 40. Portugal independent.	27-31. War of Mantuan succession. 93. Battle of Marsaglia. French defeat Duke of Savoy.	6. Demetrius the impostor. 10. Interregnum. 13. Michael Fedorovitz, Czar, establishes the house of Romanoff. 45. Alexis. 54. Victories in Poland. 81. The Cossacks subdued. 82. Ivan and Peter the Great. 89. Peter sole ruler.	1600. Charles IX. 11. Gustavus Adolphus. Axel Oxenstjerna. 17. Russia cedes Finland to Sweden. 30. Gustavus defeats Tilly. 32. Gustavus Adolphus killed at battle of Lutzen. Christina. 54. Charles X. 97. Charles XII.	35. Tulip mania. 52. Van Tromp sweeps the Channel. 69. Turks take Candia. 83. Sobieski, King of Poland, defeats the Turks at Vienna. 99. Peace of Carlowitz.
1700	Philip V. (Bourbon). 2. War of Succession. 4. English capture Gibraltar. 13. Siege of Barcelona. 35. Charles conquers Naples. 59. Charles III. 96. War with England. 97. Battle of Cape St. Vincent.	6. Battle of Turin. 13. Peace of Utrecht. Italy divided 96-97. Bonaparte's first victories in Italy. 98. Pius VI. deposed by Bonaparte.	1700. War with Sweden. 3. St. Petersburg founded. 9. Peter defeats the Swedes at Pultowa. 11. War with Turkey. 25. Catharine I. 30. Peter II. deposed. 41. Elizabeth. 62. Catharine the Great. 69-84. Conquest of the Crimea. 95. Partition of Poland completed. 96. War with Persia.	1700. Swedes defeat Russians at Narva. 9. Pultowa. Peter sends 14,000 Swedish prisoners to colonize Siberia.	40. Maria Theresa, Queen of Hungary.
1800	5. Battle of Trafalgar. 8. French take Madrid. Charles IV. abdicates. Joseph Bonaparte, King. 12. Battle of Salamanca. 13. Wellington occupies Madrid. 14. Ferdinand VII. restored.	2. Italian Republic, Bonaparte president. 5. Napoleon crowned King of Italy. 14. Fall of Napoleon. Kingdom overthrown. 15. Lombardo-Venetian Kingdom established by Austria.	1. Alexander I. 5. Russia joins coalition against France. 7. Treaty of Tilsit. Peace with France. 12. Napoleon invades Russia. Burning of Moscow. 15. Alexander organizes the "Holy Alliance."	9. Finland ceded to Russia. 14. Union of Sweden and Norway.	3. Humboldt traverses Mexico. 5. Mungo Park murdered in Africa. 15. Treaty of Vienna.

FROM NAPOLEON TO THE PRESENT TIME

A. D.	England	France	Prussia	Austria	America
1800	20. George IV. 24. Death of Lord Byron.	24. Charles X.	18. Zollverein formed. 19. Death of Marshal Blucher.		17. James Monroe, President.
1825	26. Great commercial crisis. 29. Catholic relief bill. 30. William IV. 37. Victoria. Hanover separated from Great Britain. 39. War with China. 40. Penny postage. 46. Repeal of the Corn Laws. 48. Chartist riots. 49. Cholera.	27. War with Algiers. 30. Louis Philippe. Conquest of Algiers. 31. Hereditary peerage abolished. 48. Revolution. Republic proclaimed. Outbreak of Red Republicans Louis Napoleon President.	34. Zollverein includes most of the German States. 40. Frederick William IV. 48. Revolution. 50. New Constitution.	25. Hungarian Diet meets. 36. Ferdinand I. 48. Insurrection at Vienna. Hungarian war. Francis Joseph. 49. Hungarian revolution put down.	25. John Quincy Adams, President. 29. Andrew Jackson, President. 33. Martin Van Buren, President. 41. Wm. H. Harrison, President. John Tyler, President. 45. James K. Polk, President. 49. Zachary Taylor, President.
1850	51. First "Great Exhibition." 54. Crimean War. 56. War with China. War with Persia. 57. Indian mutiny. Great commercial crisis. 58. Jewish disabilities removed. 67. War with Abyssinia. Fenian trouble 69. Disestablishment of Irish Church. 73. Ashantee war.	51. **Coup d'etat.** Louis Napoleon re-elected. 52. Empire re-established by popular vote and the President declared Emperor as Napoleon III. 59. War with Austria. Magenta and Solferino. 70. War with Prussia. Battle of Sedan. Napoleon surrenders. 71. The Commune. Republic. Thiers, President. 73. MacMahon, President.	53. Plot to overthrow government at Berlin. 61. William I. 62. Bismarck appointed premier. 64. War with Denmark. 66. War with Austria. Battle of Sadowa. Hanover annexed. 70. War with France. William made Emperor of **Germany**	56. Amnesty to Hungarians. 59. War w. France and Sardinia. Solferino. Death of Prince Metternich. 61. Disaffection in Hungary. 63. Insurrection in Poland. 64. War with Denmark. 66. Defeat at Sadowa. Austria withdraws from German confederation. 67. New constitution. 73. International Exhibition. Vienna.	53. Franklin Pierce, President. 57. James Buchanan, President 58. Atlantic cable. 61. Abraham Lincoln, President. Civil war. 65. Andrew Johnson, President. 69. Ulysses S. Grant, President.
1875	76. Queen proclaimed Empress of India. 78. Great commercial depression. War in Afghanistan. 79. Zulu war. 80. Famine in Ireland. Land League. 82. War in Egypt. 88. Irish Home Rule discussion. 93. Gladstone's Home Rule bill. 98. Gladstone died	79. Jules Grevy, President. 87. Sadi-Carnot, President. 89. Boulanger excitement. 94. Sadi-Carnot assassinated. Casimir-Perier, President. 95. Casimir-Perier resigns. Felix Faure, President 99. President Faure assassinated. M. Loubet, President. Dreyfus case re-opened.	78. Attempt to assassinate the Emperor. 80. Trouble with Socialists. 82. Imperial rescript. 88. Accession and death of Frederick III. William II. 89. Mining strikes. 96. Trouble with England over Transvaal. 98. Death of Prince Bismarck.	78. Occupation of Herzegovina and Bosnia. 79. Count Andrassy resigns. 80. Agreement with Germany on Eastern question. 93. Attempt to assassinate the Emperor. 98. Empress assassinated at Geneva.	77. R. B. Hayes, President. 81. Garfield, President. 81. Arthur, President. 85. Cleveland, President. 89. Harrison, President. 93. Cleveland, President. 97. McKinley, President. 98. War with Spain. 99. Acquisition of Cuba, Porto Rico and Philippines.
1900	01. Death of Queen Victoria. Boer war. 02. Edward, King. British-Japanese alliance. Boer war ended. 03. Irish Land bill.	01. Diplomatic relations with Turkey severed.	01. Prussia celebrates its bi-centenary.		01. Pan-American Exposition. Civil gov't in Philippines. 02. Palma, President of Cuba.

FROM NAPOLEON TO THE PRESENT TIME

A.D.	Spain	Italy	Russia	Scandinavia	Contemporary
1800	17. Slave trade abolished. 20. Revolution. 23. French invest Cadiz. Revolution crushed.			18. Charles XIV. (Bernadotte).	18. Sir John Ross explores Baffin's Bay.
1825	28. French evacuate Cadiz. 29. Cadiz made a free port. 30. Salique law abolished. 33. Isabella II. Christina, Regent. 34. Carlist War. 39. Don Carlos defeated. 41. Espartero, Regent. 43. Driven out. Queen 13 years old declared of age. 47. Espartero restored.	37. Charles Albert of Sardinia promulgates new code. 48-49. Sardinia defeated by Austria. 49. Victor Emanuel II. Roman Republic. Overthrown.	25. Death of Alexander. Nicholas, Czar. 26. War with Persia. 28. War with Turkey. 30. Polish War of Independence. 31. Russians take Warsaw. 32. Poland made integral part of Russian empire.	44. Oscar I., King of Sweden. 48. War between Denmark and Germany.	27. Greece independent. 29-32. James Ross discovers magnetic pole. 31. Belgium independent. 45. Franklin's exp. to North Pole. 47. Liberia founded.
1850	56. Insurrection. O'Donnell, dictator. 59. War with Morocco. 60. Moors defeated. 66. Prim insurrection. 68. Successful revolution led by Prim and Serano 70. Crown accepted by Amadeus. 72-76. Carlist war. 73. Abdicates. Republic. Alfonso XII.	55. Sardinia joins alliance against Russia. 59. War with Austria. 60. Garibaldi invades Naples. Sardinian army defeats Papal troops. Sicily and Naples annexed to Sardinia. 61. Victor Emanuel, King of Italy 66. War with Germany. 70. Rome annexed.	54. War with Turkey, France, and England. Siege of Sebastopol. Balaklava. Inkerman. 55. Alexander II. 56. Amnesty. Treaty of Paris 61. Polish insurrection. 63. Serfs freed.	59. Charles XV. 64. Christian IX of Denmark renounces claim to Schleswig and Holstein. 72. Oscar II., King of Sweden and Norway.	58. Livingstone's Zambezi expedition. (Africa.) 71-7. Stanley in Africa.
1875 **1900**	79. Death of Queen Mercedes. 80. Slavery abolished in Cuba. 90. Castillo, premier. 93. War with Moors. 95. Republican uprisings. 95-97. Cuban revolt 97. Revolt in the Philippines. 98. War with United States. 99. Canova's death 01. Martial law proclaimed in Madrid. 02. Alfonso crowned King of Spain.	78. Death of Victor Emmanuel. Humbert, King. Death of Pius IX. Leo XIII. Pope. 80. Republican agitation. 96. Defeated in Abyssinia. 00. Assassination of King Humbert. Victor Emmanuel III., King. 03. Death of Leo XIII. Pius X., Pope.	76. Conquest of Khiva. 77. War with Turkey. Russians take Plevna and Osman Pasha. 78. Occupy Adrianople. Treaty of Berlin. 81. Alexander II. assassinated. Alexander III. 94. Nicholas II. 96. Coronation of Nicholas II. 98. Lease of Port Arthur from China. 99. Czar's universal peace proposal. 01. Tolstoi excommunicated. 04. War with Japan. 05. Fall of Port Arthur.	98. Norwegian Arctic expedition on the "Fram."	78. Montenegro independent. Servia free state. Roumania ind. 81. Thessaly ceded to Greece. 81-5. Greely's North Pole exp. 85. Congo Free State constituted 87-9. Stanley penetrates to Lake Albert Nyanza. 90. Heligoland transferred to Germany. 94. War between China and Japan. 95. Armenian massacres. 96. X ray discovery 97. Turko-Grecian War. 00. Boxer outbreak in China. 01. Queen of Holland wedded.

A.D.	HISTORY OF AMERICA
	985. The Icelandic discovery.—Leif Erikson and the Northmen.
1400	92. Columbus discovers the island of Guanahani, of the Bahamas, which he names San Salvador, Oct. 12. He discovers Cuba, Oct. 28; Hayti, Dec. 6. 97. Cabot discovers Labrador. 99. Amerigo Vespucci's voyage.
1500	1. Negro slaves imported into Hispaniola. 6. Death of Columbus. 13. Balboa discovers the Pacific Ocean. 21. Cortez conquers Mexico. 28. Narvaez visits Florida. 34. Cartier explores the St. Lawrence. 41. De Soto conquers Louisiana. 44. De Soto discovers the Mississippi. 64. The Huguenots in Florida. 65. St. Augustine, in Florida, founded by the Spaniards. 85. First settlement, at Roanoke Island, founded by Walter Raleigh, a failure.

The Colonies

A.D.			
1600	1607. Settlement at Jamestown.	**Virginia**	20. Dutch vessel, with first negro slaves, enters James River.
	9. Hendrik Hudson discovers the Hudson River.	**New York**	14. New Amsterdam (now New York City), settled by the Dutch.
	20. The Puritans land at Plymouth Rock.	**Massachusetts**	30. Boston founded.
	27. Settlement by Swedes and Finns at Cape Henlopen.	**Delaware**	38. Peter Minuit at Christina.
	34. Maryland granted to Lord Baltimore.	**Maryland**	34. Settlement by English Catholics at St. Mary's.
	35. Settlement by English at Windsor, Hartford, and Wethersfield.	**Connecticut**	
	36. Settlements by English, under Roger Williams, at Providence.	**Rhode Island**	
	64. Elizabethtown settled.	**New Jersey**	(First settlement by Dutch, at Bergen, 1620.)
	65. Clarendon Colony settlement.	**North Carolina**	
	70. First settlement, English, Ashley River.	**South Carolina**	80. Charleston founded.
	82. First settlement in Pennsylvania by English under William Penn.	**Pennsylvania**	86. Odious administration of Sir Edmond Andros. 89. King William's War.
1700	33. English settlement, under Oglethorpe, at Savannah.	**Georgia**	2. Queen Anne's War.
	41. New Hampshire separated from Massachusetts.	**New Hampshire**	(First settlement in New Hampshire, Eng., Little Harbor, 1623.) 44. King George's War.

54. French and Indian War. Kentucky settled by Daniel Boone.
55. Braddock's defeat. 58. Fort Du Quesne taken by Washington.
63. France cedes Canada to England.
65. Colonial Congress at New York resists the stamp act. 66. Stamp act repealed.
67. Tax on tea. 68. General Gage sent to Boston.
70. Boston Massacre. Repeal of the duties on tea. 73. Destruction of tea in Boston harbor.
74. First Continental Congress meets in Philadelphia, Sept. 5. Issues declaration of rights, Nov. 4.
75. **Revolutionary War** begins with battle of Lexington. Battle of Bunker Hill.
76. **Declaration of Independence.**
77. Lafayette joins the Americans. Federal government adopted by Congress and recognized by **France.** Battle of Princeton. Battle of Brandywine. Burgoyne surrenders at Saratoga.
78. Battle of Monmouth.
81. Battle of Cowpens. Cornwallis surrenders at Yorktown.
83. Treaty of peace. 86. Cotton introduced into Georgia.
87. The Constitution adopted.
88. The Constitution of the **UNITED STATES** ratified by eleven States.

A.D.	United States	Canada	Spanish America
1789	**GEORGE WASHINGTON,** President. John Adams, Vice-President. 90. Indian war in Ohio. 91. **Vermont** admitted. 92. **Kentucky** admitted. 94. Whisky insurrection. 96. **Tennessee** admitted.	91. Canada is given a constitution and divided into two provinces. 94. Toronto capital of Upper Canada.	
1797	**JOHN ADAMS,** President. Thomas Jefferson, Vice-President. 99. Capital removed from Philadelphia to Washington.		
1801	**THOMAS JEFFERSON,** President. Aaron Burr, Vice-President. 3. **Ohio** admitted. 3. Louisiana purchase. War with Tripoli. 4. Burr-Hamilton duel. 5. George Clinton, Vice-President. 7. Trial of Aaron Burr.	3. Slavery abolished.	3. Hayti republic. 8. King of Portugal goes to Brazil.
1809	**JAMES MADISON,** President. George Clinton, Vice-President. 11. Battle of Tippecanoe. 12. **Louisiana** admitted. **War with England.** Canada invaded. Mackinaw surrenders. 13. Commander Perry captures English fleet. Elbridge Gerry, Vice-President. Battle of the Thames. 14. Battle of Lundy's Lane. English capture Washington and burn public buildings. Bombardment of Fort McHenry. 15. **Battle of New Orleans.** 16. **Indiana** admitted.	12. British capture Detroit. 13. Americans capture Toronto and Fort George. Death of Tecumseh. 16. Sir John Sherbroke, Governor of Lower Canada.	9. War of Independence in Buenos Ayres. 11. Dr. Francia dictator of Peru. Venezuela independent. 11-24. Simon Bolivar's struggles for liberty. 15. Brazil made a kingdom. 16. Buenos Ayres independent.
1817	**JAMES MONROE,** President. Daniel Tompkins, Vice-President. **Mississippi** admitted. 18. **Illinois** admitted. Seminole war in Florida. 19. **Alabama** admitted. Purchase of Florida. 20. Missouri Compromise. **Maine** admitted. 21. **Missouri** admitted. 22. South American republics acknowledged. 23. Monroe doctrine declared. 24. Visit of Lafayette.	18. Duke of Richmond, Governor of Lower Canada. 17-25. Political agitation in Upper Canada. Robert Gourlay. 22. Antagonism between French and English in Lower Canada. 24. Welland Canal incorporated.	17. Chile independent. 21. Central America independent. 22. Brazil independent. Dom Pedro, Emperor. Iturbide, Emperor of Mexico. 24. Simon Bolivar dictator of Peru. 25. Bolivia independ't.

A.D.	United States	Canada	Spanish America
1825	**JOHN QUINCY ADAMS**, President. John C. Calhoun, Vice-President. 28. Protective tariff bill passed.	25. Agitation in Upper Canada over alien bill. 26. Mob destroys Mackenzie's printing office.	28. Uruguay independent.
1829	**ANDREW JACKSON**, President. John C. Calhoun, Vice-President. 32. United States Bank bill vetoed. Black Hawk war. 33. Martin Van Buren, Vice-President. Public funds withdrawn from United States Bank. 35. Seminole war. 36. **Arkansas** admitted.	29. Agitation for responsible government in Upper Canada. 30. Lord Aylmer Governor of Lower Canada. 32. Imperial duties surrendered to assembly. 35. Pupinean party demand total separation from Great Britain.	29. Formation of United States of Colombia. 31. Dom Pedro abdicates. His six-year-old son, Dom Pedro II., Emperor of Brazil. 32. The Texans revolt. 33. Defeat of the Mexicans.
1837	**MARTIN VAN BUREN**, President. Richard M. Johnson, Vice-President. **Michigan** admitted. Financial crisis. Banks suspend specie payment. Business failures and general distress. 40. Northeastern boundary line disputes.	37-38. Insurrection. 38. End of rebellion in Upper Canada. 39. Union of Upper and Lower C. Lord Sydenham, Governor. 40. Responsible government established.	
1841	**WILLIAM H. HARRISON**, President. John Tyler, Vice-President. Harrison dies April 4. **JOHN TYLER**, President. Veto of bank bill. 43. Dorr rebellion in Rhode Island. 44. Texas applies for annexation.	44. Government removed to Montreal.	
1845	**JAMES K. POLK**, President. George M. Dalias, Vice-President. **Texas** annexed. **Florida** admitted. **War with Mexico.** 46. **Iowa** admitted. 48. Acquisition of New Mexico and California. **Wisconsin** admitted.	45. Great fire at Quebec 47. Lord Elgin, Governor. Agitation over rebellion losses bill.	45. Venezuela independent. War bet. Mexico and U. S. 46. Battles of Palo Alto and Resaca de la Palma. 47. Buena Vista, Cerro Gordo, Contreras. City of Mexico captured.
1849	**ZACHARY TAYLOR**, President. Millard Fillmore, Vice-President. 50. **MILLARD FILLMORE**, President. **California** admitted. Fugitive slave law passed.	49. Annexation to U. S. advocated. Riots in Montreal. 50. Reciprocity with U. S. urged.	50. Lopez' attempt on Cuba. 51. Lopez garroted.
1853	**FRANKLIN PIERCE**, President. William Rufus King, Vice-President. 55. Kansas-Nebraska bill. Commotion in Kansas.	52. Government removed to Quebec. 55. Sir Edmund W. Head, Governor.	53. Santa Ana, dictator of Mexico. 56. Walker's expedition to Nicaragua.
1857	**JAMES BUCHANAN**, President. John C. Breckinridge, Vice-President. Dred Scott decision. Mormon Insurrection. Financial distress. 57. **Oregon** admitted. 58. **Minnesota** admitted. 59. John Brown's insurrection. 60. **South Carolina secedes.** 61. **Kansas** admitted.		58. Juarez, President of Mexico. 60. Walker invades Honduras.

A.D.	The United States	The Confederate States	Canada	Spanish America
1861	**ABRAHAM LINCOLN,** President. Hannibal Hamlin, Vice-President. Attack on Fort Sumter. Harper's Ferry and Norfolk seized.	61. Mississippi, Florida Alabama, Georgia, Louisiana and Texas secede. Jefferson Davis elected President. Arkansas, North Carolina, and Tennessee secede. Virginia secedes. Battles of Bull Run, Wilson's Creek.	61. Lord Monck, Governor.	
	62. Battle of Antietam.	62. Ft. Donelson captured. Battles of Pea Ridge, Shiloh, Bull Run, Wilson's Creek.		62. France at War with Mexico.
	63. Proclamation of Emancipation. **West Virginia** admitted. Battle of **Gettysburg.**	63. Chancellorsville. Siege of Vicksburg.		63. The French enter City of Mexico. Archduke Maximilian of Austria invited to become Emperor.
	64. The Kearsarge sinks the Alabama.	64. Battle of the Wilderness. Siege of Petersburg Sherman's march to the sea.		64. He accepts.
	65. Andrew Johnson, Vice-President. Surrender of Gen. Lee, April 9. Lincoln assassinated April 14. **ANDREW JOHNSON,** Pres. The war ended. Amnesty issued by the President.	65. Battle of Five Forks Petersburg and Richmond captured. Surrender of Gens. Lee, Johnston, Morgan, Taylor and Kirby Smith.	65. Great Fire at Quebec	65. Paraguay at war with Uruguay, Brazil, Argentine Republic. Chile and Spain at war.
			66. Reciprocity treaty with U. S. Fenian invasion.	66. Juarists in Mexico have great success.
	67. **Nebraska** admitted. Alaska purchased. Southern States organized as military districts. 68. Impeachment, trial, and acquittal of President Johnson.		67. Canada, New Brunswick and Nova Scotia form the Dominion of Canada.	67. Maximilian surrenders and is shot.
1869	**ULYSSES S. GRANT,** President. Schuyler Colfax, Vice-President. Pacific Railroad completed. 70. Fifteenth amendment ratified. 71. Great fire at Chicago. Tweed ring exposed. Geneva award. 72. Great fire at Boston. Political disabilities of Southern people removed. Modoc war. 73. Henry Wilson, Vice-President. The Virginius troubles with Spain. Financial panic. 75. Passage of act for specie resumption in 1879. **Colorado** admitted. 76. Centennial Exposition, Philadelphia. Custer massacre.		71. British Columbia becomes part of the Dominion. 72. Prince Edward Island joins the Dominion. Lord Dufferin, Governor-General.	69. Cuban revolt.
1877	**RUTHERFORD B. HAYES,** President. William A. Wheeler, Vice-President. Railroad riots. 78. Yellow fever epidemic along Lower Mississippi. 79. Resumption of specie payment.		77. Great Fire at St. John, N. B. 78. Marquis of Lorne appointed Viceroy.	79. War between Chile and Peru.

A.D.	The United States	Canada	Spanish America
1881	**JAMES A. GARFIELD,** President. Chester A. Arthur, Vice-President. President Garfield shot by Guiteau. **CHESTER A. ARTHUR,** President. Treaty with China. 83. Opening of Brooklyn Bridge. Apaches captured by General Crook. General strike of telegraph operators.	84. Dynamite explosions in Parliament buildings, Quebec.	
1885	**GROVER CLEVELAND,** President. Thomas A. Hendricks, Vice-President. 86. Labor agitations. Anarchist riot at Chicago. 88. Lord Sackville, British Minister, dismissed.	85. Rebellion of Louis Riel. Riel captured and hanged. 88. Lord Stanley, Governor-General. Fisheries treaty rejected by U. S.	
1889	**BENJAMIN HARRISON,** President. Levi P. Morton, Vice-President. **North Dakota, South Dakota, Washington,** and **Montana** admitted to the Union. Opening of Oklahoma. Johnstown flood. Pan-American Congress. 90. **Idaho** and **Wyoming** admitted. Reciprocity treaty with South American republics. McKinley tariff law goes into effect. Sioux war. Death of Sitting Bull. Eleventh census—population, 62,622,250. 92. Birth of the People's party at Omaha.	89. Great Fire at Quebec 90. Reciprocity defeated in House of Commons. Toronto University burned.	89. Civil war in Hayti. Dom Pedro of Brazil deposed. 91. Balmaceda, President of Chile, deposed. Commits suicide.
1893	**GROVER CLEVELAND,** President. Adlai E. Stevenson, Vice-President. Sandwich Islands ask to be annexed. World's Columbian Exposition at Chicago. Great financial depression. Cleveland calls special session of Congress to repeal Sherman bill. Congress of Religions, Chicago. 94. Great coal strike. Great railroad strike. 95. Free Silver movement. Venezuela boundary dispute with Great Britain. 96. **Utah** admitted to the Union.	93. The Earl of Aberdeen, Governor-Gen.	93. Revolution in Brazil. Revolution in Argentine. 95. War for Independence in Cuba. 96. Maceo assassinated.
1897	**WILLIAM McKINLEY,** President. Arbitration Treaty with Great Britain signed; rejected by the Senate. Greater New York charter granted. 98. Annexation of Hawaii. Battle-ship Maine blown up. Spanish-American war. Acquisition of Cuba, Porto Rico, and the Philippines by treaty. Commercial treaty with France. 99. Philippine war. Many Trusts formed.	98. Earl of Minto Governor-General. Meeting of the U. S. and Canadian High Commission.	General Weyler recalled from Cuba. Attempted assassination of President Moraes of Brazil. 98. United States intervenes in behalf of Cuba. Cuba under the U. S. protectorate. Campos Salles elected Pres. of Brazil. U. S. of Central America formed.
1900	Troubles with China. 01. President McKinley shot, Sept. 6. **THEODORE ROOSEVELT,** President. Civil government in Philippines. Cuban independence. 02. Great coal strike. 03. Panama Canal Treaty signed. 04. W. H. Taft, secretary of war.	00. Parliamentary elections carried by Liberals. 02. Canadian-Australian cable completed.	00. President Sandemente of Colombia resigned. 01. War between Venezuela and Colombia. 02. Revolution in Venezuela; trouble with Great Britain and Germany.
1905	05. **THEODORE ROOSEVELT,** President, inaugurated March 4.		

CALENDAR OF AMERICAN BATTLES.

Naval engagements are indicated by *italics*; * means that it was a drawn battle; † means a general estimate.

JANUARY.

Year.	Name of Battle.	Opponent.	Victor.	Casualties. United States. Killed.	Casualties. United States. Wounded.	Casualties. Opponents. Killed.	Casualties. Opponents. Wounded.
1815	New Orleans....	English......	*	11	23	20	30†
1863	*Galveston*	Confederates	Conf...	17	20†	26	117
1863	Murfreesboro (continued)	Confederates	U.S....	....	....	....	....
1863	Murfreesboro (ended)	Confederates	U.S....	1,533	7,245	1,384	6 892
1777	Princeton	English......	U.S....	31	64	49	151
1862	Huntersville, Va.	Confederates	*	1	3	2	4
1781	*Pilgrim–Mary*	English......	U.S....	4	16	13	22
1813	*Ultor-boats*	English......	U.S....	0	2	1	7
1813	*Fox-Lapwing*	English......	U.S....	1	3	14	8
1862	Middle Creek	Confederates	U.S....	3	8	11	32
1815	New Orleans	English......	U.S....	4	13	700	1,400
1847	*San Gabriel*	Mexican.....	U.S....	2	9	70	150
1863	Springfield	Confederates	U.S....	14	145	23	164
1779	*Protector–Admiral Duff*	English......	U.S....	1	3	140	3
1863	Arkansas Post (continued)	Confederates	U.S....	6	25	10†	30†
1863	Hartsville	Confederates	U.S....	7	69	18	74
1865	Scottsboro	Confederates	U.S....	1	8	14	32
1863	*Hatteras–Alabama*	Confederates	Conf...	2	6	0	1
1863	Arkansas Post (ended)	Confederates	U.S....	129	831	60	78
1865	Beverly, W. Va.	Confederates	Conf...	5	20	3	6
1848	San Blas	Mexican.....	U.S....	0	2	3	8
1865	*Fort Fisher* (continued)	Confederates	U.S....	....	....	....	....
1813	*Comet–frigate*	Portuguese..	U.S....	1	3	10	14
1863	Carney's Bridge	Confederates	U.S....	7	27	14	36
1865	*Fort Fisher* (continued)	Confederates	U.S....	....	....	....	....
1865	Red Hill	Confederates	U.S....	7	27	14	36
1815	*President–Endymion*	English......	Eng....	24	56	11	14
1865	*Fort Fisher* (ended)	Confederates	U.S....	184	749	150	249
1864	Gen. Sturgis	Confederates	U.S....	8	32	16	49
1781	Cowpens	English......	U.S....	12	60	120	199
1813	Frenchtown	English......	U.S....	12	55	30†	50†
1862	Mill Spring (Logan Cross Roads)	Confederates	U.S....	39	207	192	132
1864	Sturgis' Raid (January 16–28)	Confederates	U.S....	6	17	30	62
1863	*Sabine Pass*	Confederates	Conf...	1	3	0	2
1814	Emucfau	Indians......	U.S....	20	75	220†	0
1813	Frenchtown No. 2	English......	Eng....	357	64	150	155
1813	Stony Creek	Indians......	Ind....	400	0	0	0
1814	Enotachopco	Indians......	U.S....	40	60	200†	0
1813	*Dolphin–squadron*	English......	U.S....	3	8	6	9
1813	*Union–Iris*	English......	Eng....	1	3	0	2
1814	Camp Defiance	Indians......	U.S....	17	132	37	0
1815	*Surprise–Star*	English......	U.S....	0	0	1	1
1814	*Alligator*	English......	U.S....	2	2	8	14†
1863	Bear River	Indians......	U.S....	12	49	224	8
1862	Kelly's Stores	Confederates	*	24	80	22	28
1864	*Underwriter*	Confederates	Conf...	9	20	6	32
1863	*Off Charleston*	Confederates	Conf...	23	24	0	0

FEBRUARY.

Year.	Name of Battle.	Opponent.	Victor.	Casualties. United States. Killed.	Casualties. United States. Wounded.	Casualties. Opponents. Killed.	Casualties. Opponents. Wounded.
1864	Bachelor's Creek	Confederates	Conf...	24	77	13	22
1800	*Constellation–Vengeance*	French......	U.S....	14	25	50	110
1864	Patterson Creek	Confederates	Conf...	0	3†	4	5†
1863	Dover, Col. Harding	Confederates	U.S....	16	60	150	400
1863	Mingo Swamp	Confederates	U.S....	0	0	8	20
1865	Sakelhatchie	Confederates	U.S....	18	70	20	80
1863	Batesville	Confederates	U.S....	2	4	5†	7†
1865	Dabney's Mills (continued)	Confederates	U.S....	....	....	....	....
1862	*Fort Henry*	Confederates	U.S....	17	27	5	11
1865	Dabney's Mills (continued)	Confederates	U.S....	....	....	....	....
1832	*Qualla Battoo*	Malays.......	U.S....	2	11	120†	200†
1865	Dabney's Mills (ended)	Confederates	U.S....	232	1,062	249	751
1862	Roanoke Island	Confederates	U.S....	47	198	25	30
1865	Williston Station	Confederates	U.S....	2	3	3	6
1799	*Constellation–Insurgent*	French......	U.S....	2	3	29	41
1862	*Elizabeth City*	Confederates	U.S....	2	2	4	10
1863	Old River	Confederates	U.S....	5	7	4	7
1865	Aikens	Confederates	U.S....	6†	9†	31	160
1864	Rock House	Confederates	U.S....	3	5	15	23†
1862	Blooming Gap	Confederates	U.S....	0	2	13	26
1776	Moore's Creek	English......	U.S....	0	3	13	22
1813	*Lottery–boats*	English......	Eng....	8	10	2	4
1862	Fort Donelson	Confederates	U.S....	560	746	466	1,534
1804	*Philadelphia (frigate)*	Tripolitans..	U.S....	0	1	100†	0
1847	*San José*	Mexican.....	U.S....	3	8	13	30†
1781	*Holker–Hypocrite*	English......	U.S....	3	1	4	7

FEBRUARY—*Continued.*

Day.	Year.	NAME OF BATTLE.	Opponent.	Victor.	CASUALTIES. United States. Killed.	United States. Wounded.	Opponents. Killed.	Opponents. Wounded
17	1813	*Highflyer-Poictiers*	English	Eng	1	3	0	0
18	1815	*George Little-Granicus*	English	Eng	2	6	0	1
19	1862	*Winton, N. C.*	Confederates	*	0	0	1	4
20	1815	*Constitution-Cyane and Levant*	English	U.S	4	10	35	42
20	1864	Olustee	Confederates	Conf	193	1,175	150	350
20	1865	Town Creek	Confederates	U.S	5†	8†	8†	18†
21	1865	Cumberland, Md	Confederates	U.S	1	3	2	8
22	1812	*Hazard-Caledonia*	English	U.S	0	7	2	11
22	1847	Buena Vista (continued)	Mexican	U.S	....	....	....	....
22	1864	Tunnel Hill	Confederates	U.S	150†	200†	80†	180
23	1813	*Cora-boats*	English	Eng	1	3	1	2
23	1847	Buena Vista (ended)	Mexican	U.S	267	456	568	1,241
24	1813	*Hornet-Peacock*	English	U.S	1	4	5	33
24	1863	*Indianola*	Confederates	Conf	1	1	2	5
25	1815	*Chasseur-St. Lawrence*	English	U.S	5	8	15	23
26	1863	Falmouth	Confederates	Conf	5†	8†	6	8
27	1847	Chihuahua	Mexican	U.S	3	5	33	67
28	1863	Van Buren, Ark	Confederates	U.S	0	3	2	5
29	1812	*Courier-Andromache*	English	Eng	0	3	0	1

MARCH.

Day.	Year.	Name of Battle.	Opponent.	Victor.	U.S. Killed.	U.S. Wounded.	Opp. Killed.	Opp. Wounded
1	1813	*Canonnier-Warspite*	English	Eng	1	3	0	1
2	1815	*America-Elizabeth*	English	U.S	0	0	2	13
3	1863	*Fort McAllister*	Confederates	Conf	0	1	0	1
4	1863	Thompson's Station (continued)	Confederates	Conf	....	....	....	....
5	1863	Spring Hill	Confederates	Conf	8	14	1	4
5	1863	Thompson's Station (ended)	Confederates	Conf	99	301	152	453
6	1862	Pea Ridge (continued)	Confederates	U.S	....	....	....	....
7	1778	*Randolph-Yarmouth*	English	Eng	311	0	5	12
7	1862	Pea Ridge (continued)	Confederates	U.S	....	....	....	....
8	1862	*Merrimac in Hampton Roads*	Confederates	Conf	250	301	8	11
8	1862	Pea Ridge (ended)	Confederates	U.S	203	972	1,040	3,638
8	1865	Wilcox's Bridge (continued)	Confederates	Conf	....	....	....	....
9	1862	*Monitor-Merrimac*	Confederates	U.S	0	1	0	2
9	1865	Wilcox's Bridge (continued)	Confederates	Conf	....	....	....	....
10	1865	Wilcox's Bridge (ended)	Confederates	Conf	80	421	132	643
11	1863	*Fort Pemberton* (continued)	Confederates	Conf	....	....	....	....
12	1863	*Fort Pemberton* (continued)	Confederates	Conf	....	....	....	....
12	1864	*Fort De Russey*	Confederates	U.S	18	29	14	33
13	1863	*Port Hudson*	Confederates	U.S	8	7	0	0
13	1863	*Fort Pemberton* (continued)	Confederates	Conf	....	....	....	....
14	1862	*New Berne*	Confederates	U.S	102	432	50	152
14	1863	*Fort Pemberton* (continued)	Confederates	Conf	....	....	....	....
15	1781	Guilford Court-House	English	Eng	123	314	231	318
16	1779	*Hazard-Active*	English	U.S	3	5	13	20
16	1863	*Fort Pemberton* (ended)	Confederates	Conf	7	19	3†	8†
16	1865	Averysboro	Confederates	U.S	77	477	86	632
17	1813	*Antelope-Zephyr*	English	Eng	1	3	0	2
18	1865	Bentonville (continued)	Confederates	U.S	....	....	....	....
18	1865	Bentonville (ended)	Confederates	U.S	191	1,108	267	1,381
19	1776	*Industry-brig*	English	Eng	0	3	2	6
20	1863	Vaught's Hill	Confederates	U.S	23	33	63	241
21	1864	Henderson's Hill	Confederates	U.S	1	3	5	18
22	1865	Wilson's Raid (to April 24)	Confederates	U.S	99	598	352	1,231
23	1815	*Hornet-Penguin*	English	U.S	1	11	10	28
23	1862	Kernstown	Confederates	U.S	103	441	80	342
24	1847	Vera Cruz	Mexican	U.S	11	56	981	2,000†
25	1865	Fort Stedman	Confederates	U.S	68	337	134	698
26	1865	Spanish Fort (to April 8)	Confederates	U.S	99	695	152	401
27	1814	Horseshoe Bend	Indians	U.S	26	106	557	0
28	1814	*Essex-Phœbe and Cherub*	English	Eng	58	66	5	10
29	1779	*Tyrannicide-Revenge*	English	U.S	0	8	11	22
29	1813	*Revenge-Narcissus*	English	Eng	0	3	0	1
30	1814	La Colle Mill	English	Eng	8	66	11	47
30	1863	Somerset	Confederates	U.S	11	38	24	73
31	1865	Boydton and White Oak Road	Confederates	U.S	177	1,134	236	998

APRIL.

Day.	Year.	Name of Battle.	Opponent.	Victor.	U.S. Killed.	U.S. Wounded.	Opp. Killed.	Opp. Wounded
1	1865	Five Forks	Confederates	U.S	124	706	450	750
2	1865	Forts Greggs and Alexander	Confederates	U.S	198	304	249	353
2	1865	Selma	Confederates	U.S	153	347	198	409
2	1865	Petersburg	Confederates	U.S	298	2,565	341	3,092
3	1780	*Boats-Black Snake*	English	U.S	0	2	3	5
4	1864	Col. Gooding	Confederates	U.S	8	26	18	39
5	1779	*Hibernia-brig of war*	English	*	1	3	3	9
6	1865	Sailor's Creek	Confederates	U.S	166	1,014	268	2,032
6	1862	Pittsburgh Landing (continued)	Confederates	U.S	....	..	....	....
7	1776	*Glasgow*	English	Eng	10	14	1	3

APRIL—*Continued.*

Day.	Year.	Name of Battle.	Opponent.	Victor.	Casualties. United States. Killed.	United States. Wounded.	Opponents. Killed.	Opponents. Wounded.
7	1862	Island No. 10	Confederates	U.S.	19	32	1	3
7	1862	Pittsburg Landing (ended)	Confederates	U.S.	1,735	7,882	1,128	8,012
7	1863	*Ironclads at Charleston*	Confederates	*	3	18	0	3
7	1864	Red River	Confederates	U.S.	23	39	45	88
8	1782	*Hyder Ally-Gen. Monk*	English	U.S.	4	11	20	33
8	1864	Sabine Cross Roads	Confederates	Conf.	199	893	486	1,024
8	1864	Pleasant Hill (continued)	Confederates	U.S.	....	....	....	....
9	1777	*Trumbull-transports*	English	U.S.	7	8	9	14
9	1864	Pleasant Hill (ended)	Confederates	U.S.	99	688	348	1,654
9	1865	Appomattox	Confederates	U.S.	203	297	189	386
9	1865	Fort Blakely	Confederates	U.S.	113	516	242	874
10	1863	Franklin	Confederates	U.S.	17	20	79	163
10	1863	Prairie d'Anne	Confederates	U.S.	8	15	18	36
11	1863	Fort Pulaski	Confederates	Conf.	1	3	1	7
12	1864	Fort Pillow	Confederates	Conf.	348	52	19	61
12	1864	Lexington, Red River	Confederates	U.S.	0	0	164	341
13	1813	*Canonnier-Medusa*	English	Eng.	1	3	0	4
14	1779	*Hunter-armed ship*	English	*	0	4	3	6
14	1780	Monk's Corner	English	Eng.	26	73	3	6
15	1813	*Diligent-squadron*	English	Eng.	1	3	0	1
16	1863	*Vicksburg*	Confederates	U.S.	0	3	7	18
16	1865	Columbus, Ala	Confederates	U.S.	10	14	30	50
17	1776	*Lexington-Edward*	English	U.S.	2	2	5†	8†
17	1864	Fort Wessels	Confederates	Conf.	20	31	29	42
18	1814	*York-Lord Somers*	English	*	0	0	6	12
18	1847	*Tuspan*	Mexican	U.S.	3	11	25	34
18	1847	Cerro Gordo	Mexican	U.S.	63	368	100†	500†
18	1863	Fayetteville	Confederates	U.S.	4	26	17	36
19	1775	Lexington	English	Eng.	7	9	0	0
19	1864	*Southfield-Albemarle*	Confederates	Conf.	2	12	0	0
20	1862	South Mills or Camden	Confederates	U.S.	15	98	12	67
20	1863	McMinnville	Confederates	U.S.	0	0	4	8
20	1864	Plymouth	Confederates	Conf.	41	59	125	174
21	1775	Concord and retreat	English	Eng.	49	34	74	199
22	1847	Perote	Mexican	U.S.	0	3	0	4
23	1862	*New Orleans*	Confederates	U.S.	37	147	12	40
23	1864	Cane River	Confederates	U.S.	98	152	108	164
24	1778	*Ranger-Drake*	English	U.S.	2	6	18	24
25	1781	Hobkirk's Hill	English	Eng.	52	141	38	104
25	1862	*Fort Macon*	Confederates	U.S.	0	3	7	18
25	1864	Mark's Mills	Confederates	Conf.	98	142	126	394
26	1863	Cape Girardeau	Confederates	U.S.	6	18	22	43
26	1864	Red River	Confederates	U.S.	17	31	28	61
27	1805	Derne	Turkish	U.S.	6	8	10†	20†
27	1813	York	English	U.S.	66	203	100†	302
28	1863	Streight's Raid (to May 3)	Confederates	U.S.	12	69	0	0
29	1814	*Peacock-Epervier*	English	U.S.	0	2	8	15
29	1862	Bridgeport, Ala	Confederates	U.S.	3	8	31	42
29	1863	Grand Gulf	Confederates	Conf.	19	57	8	16
30	1814	*Saucy Jack-Pelham*	English	U.S.	2	9	4	11
30	1863	Chancellorsville (continued)	Confederates	Conf.	....	....	....	....
30	1864	Jenkins Ferry	Confederates	U.S.	222	978	842	1,458

MAY.

Day.	Year.	Name of Battle.	Opponent.	Victor.	U.S. Killed.	U.S. Wounded.	Opponents Killed.	Opponents Wounded.
1	1863	Port Gibson	Confederates	U.S.	130	718	144	832
1	1863	Chancellorsville (continued)	Confederates	Conf.	....	....	....	....
1	1898	*Manila*	Spanish	U.S.	0	7	318	298
2	1863	Chancellorsville (continued)	Confederates	Conf.	....	....	....	....
3	1863	Siege of Suffolk, N. C. (ended)	Confederates	U.S.	15	94	898	1,202
3	1863	Chancellorsville (continued)	Confederates	Conf.	....	....	....	....
4	1863	Chancellorsville (ended)	Confederates	Conf.	1,512	9,518	1,718	10,563
5	1813	Fort Meigs	English	U.S.	64	124	30†	60†
5	1813	Rapids of Miami	English	U.S.	80	101	15	45
5	1862	Williamsburg	Confederates	U.S.	456	1,400	351	1,403
5	1864	Dunn's Bayou	Confederates	Conf.	38	64	4	18
5	1864	*Albemarle*	Confederates	U.S.	4	25	0	0
5	1864	Wilderness (continued)	Confederates	U.S.	....	....	....	....
6	1814	Oswego	English	U.S.	6	38	70	165
6	1864	Wilderness (continued)	Confederates	U.S.	....	....	....	....
7	1779	*Providence-Diligent*	English	U.S.	4	10	8	19
7	1862	West Point	Confederates	U.S.	84	110	3	15†
7	1864	Wilderness (ended)	Confederates	U.S.	2,309	12,188	1,956	10,444
8	1846	Palo Alto	Mexican	U.S.	4	42	102	127
8	1862	McDowell's	Confederates	Conf.	80	176	71	390
8	1864	Spottsylvania (continued)	Confederates	U.S.	....	....	....	....
9	1847	Resaca de la Palma	Mexican	U.S.	39	83	160	228
9	1864	Spottsylvania (continued)	Confederates	U.S.	....	....	....	....
9	1864	Swift Creek (continued)	Confederates	Conf.	....	....	....	....

MAY—*Continued.*

Day.	Year.	Name of Battle.	Opponent.	Victor.	Casualties.			
					United States.		Opponents.	
					Killed.	Wounded.	Killed.	Wounde
9	1864	Cloyd's Mountain and New River Bridge	Confederates	U.S....	126	585	248	652
10	1775	Ticonderoga	English......	U.S....	....	....	....	....
10	1862	*Fort Pillow*	Confederates	U.S....	0	4	2	1
10	1864	Swift Creek (ended)	Confederates	Conf..	90	401	124	376
11	1864	Spottsylvania (ended)	Confederates	U.S...	3,288	19,278	3,342	20,187
11	1777	*Hancock-Fox*	English......	U.S....	3	5	14	18
12	1780	Siege of Charleston (ended)	English......	Eng....	92	142	76	189
12	1863	Raymond	Confederates	U.S....	69	341	103	720
13	1864	Resaca	Confederates	U.S....	598	2,147	861	1,949
14	1863	Jackson	Confederates	U.S....	37	228	64	392
15	1780	Waxhaws	English......	Eng....	250	130	5	14
15	1847	Puebla	Mexican.....	U.S....	18	62	83	142
15	1862	Drewry's Bluff	Confederates	Conf...	422	2,380	514	1,086
15	1864	New Market, Pa	Confederates	Conf...	120	563	96	306
16	1811	*President-Little Belt*	English......	U.S....	0	0	11	21
16	1863	Champion Hills	Confederates	U.S....	426	1,842	486	1,954
16	1864	Marksville	Confederates	U.S....	9	18	32	64
17	1863	Black River	Confederates	U.S....	29	242	40	186
18	1864	Spottsylvania (continued)	Confederates	U.S....	2,031	7,956	1,752	7,248
19	1863	Vicksburg (continued May 22)	Confederates	Conf...	....	....	....	....
19	1864	Yellow Bayou	Confederates	U.S....	42	108	74	158
20	1863	Fort Blunt	Confederates	U.S....	12	38	25	37
21	1863	Gum Swamp	Confederates	U.S....	3	8	4	16
22	1863	Vicksburg (continued to May 25)	Confederates	Conf...	....	....	....	....
23	1862	Front Royal	Confederates	Conf...	32	122	0	13
23	1862	Lewisburg	Confederates	U.S....	11	52	49	76
24	1862	New Bridge	Confederates	U.S....	3	5	4	15
25	1862	Winchester	Confederates	Conf...	38	154	68	329
25	1863	Vicksburg (ended)	Confederates	U.S....	1,848	2,378	1,420	2,151
26	1864	Bermuda Hundreds (continued)	Confederates	U.S....	....	....	....	....
26	1864	North Anna (continued)	Confederates	U.S....	....	....	....	....
27	1813	Fort George	English......	U.S....	39	121	108	163
27	1862	Hanover Court-House	Confederates	U.S....	53	344	198	732
27	1863	Port Hudson	Confederates	Conf...	293	1,549	110	173
27	1864	Bermuda Hundreds (continued)	Confederates	U.S....	....	....	....	....
27	1864	North Anna (ended)	Confederates	U.S....	223	1,460	304	1,513
28	1781	*Alliance-squadron*	English......	U.S....	5	20	11	30
28	1864	Bermuda Hundreds (continued)	Confederates	U.S....	....	....	....	....
29	1813	*Sackett's Harbor*	English......	U.S....	21	84	29	101
29	1864	Bermuda Hundreds (continued)	Confederates	U.S....	....	....	....	....
30	1814	Sandy Creek	English......	U.S....	1	3	13	28
30	1864	Bermuda Hundreds (ended)	Confederates	U.S....	201	998	864	2,136
31	1862	Seven Pines, or Fair Oaks	Confederates	*	891	3,627	1,987	2,233

JUNE.

1	1813	*Chesapeake-Shannon*	English......	Eng....	47	99	24	59
2	1780	*Trumbull-Watt*	English......	*	19	20	39	52
2	1864	Cold Harbor (continued)	Confederates	Conf...	....	....	....	....
3	1776	*Boats-tender to Nautilus*	English......	U.S....	1	3	4	18
3	1776	*Lady Washington-barges*	English......	U.S....	0	2	3	11
3	1864	Cold Harbor (ended)	Confederates	Conf...	1,905	10,570	364	1,336
4	1780	*Gen. Pickering-Achilles*	English......	U.S....	1	3	8	12
4	1782	*Charming Sally-Revenge*	English......	U.S....	1	4	3	6
5	1862	Harrisonburg	Confederates	U.S....	15	32	20	50
5	1864	Columbia, Ark	Confederates	U.S....	19	73	22	81
5	1864	Piedmont	Confederates	U.S....	130	650	633	2,337
6	1813	Stony Creek	English......	Eng....	17	38	20†	30
6	1862	*Memphis*	Confederates	U.S....	10	4	20†	30†
7	1863	Milliken's Bend	Confederates	U.S....	154	223	148	294
8	1862	Cross Keys	Confederates	*	125	498	29	302
9	1862	Port Republic	Confederates	Conf...	67	361	104	796
9	1863	Beverly Ford	Confederates	Conf...	156	289	253	354
10	1864	Brice's Cross-Roads, Miss	Confederates	Conf...	223	394	124	582
10	1864	Kellar's Bridge	Confederates	U.S....	13	54	0	0
11	1864	Trevilian Station (continued)	Confederates	U.S....	....	....	....	....
11	1898	*Camp McCalla* (continued)	Spanish......	U.S....	....	....	....	....
12	1863	Middletown	Confederates	U.S....	1	4	18	32
12	1864	Trevilian Station (ended)	Confederates	U.S....	85	490	124	582
12	1898	*Camp McCalla* (continued)	Spanish......	U.S....	....	....	....	....
13	1776	*Tyrannicide-Dispatch*	English......	U.S....	1	2	2	5
13	1898	*Camp McCalla* (continued)	Spanish......	U.S....	....	....	....	....
14	1863	Port Hudson	Confederates	*	250	680	188	364
14	1863	Winchester (continued)	Confederates	Conf...	....	....	....	....
14	1898	*Camp McCalla* (ended)	Spanish......	U.S....	6	11	60†	140†
15	1847	*Near Tabasco*	Mexican.....	U.S....	0	7	20†	30†
15	1863	Winchester (ended)	Confederates	Conf...	203	397	50	81
16	1862	Secessionville	Confederates	Conf...	137	438	63	141
17	1775	Bunker Hill	English......	Eng....	145	304	359	695
17	1776	*Defense-transports*	English......	U.S....	0	9	18	30†

JUNE — *Continued.*

Day.	Year.	Name of Battle.	Opponent.	Victor.	Casualties. United States. Killed.	Casualties. United States. Wounded.	Casualties. Opponents. Killed.	Casualties. Opponents. Wounded.
17	1815	*Guerriere-Mashouda*	Algerine	U.S.	3	11	12	18
17	1863	St. Charles	Confederates	U.S.	136	20	6	8
17	1863	*Weehawken-Atlanta*	Confederates	U.S.	0	0	0	8
17	1864	Lynchburg (continued)	Confederates	Conf.	....	....	....	....
18	1864	Lynchburg (ended)	Confederates	Conf.	99	503	47	157
18	1781	Ninety-six	English	Eng.	48	107	24	61
19	1864	*Kearsarge-Alabama*	Confederates	U.S.	1	2	9	21
19	1864	Petersburg (from June 15)	Confederates	*	1,298	7,474	984	6,721
20	1864	Petersburg (continued to June 30)	Confederates	U.S.	....	....	....	....
21	1863	Upperville	Confederates	U.S.	30	70	50	100
22	1813	*Craney Island*	English	U.S.	0	0	75†	125†
22	1898	*Santiago forts bombarded*	Spanish	*	1	11	(?)	(?)
23	1812	*President-Belvidere*	English	U.S.	3	19	2	22
23	1864	Weldon Railroad	Confederates	U.S.	604	2,494	156	344
24	1813	Beaver Dam	English	Eng.	25	50†	30†	34
24	1898	Las Guasimas	Spanish	U.S.	16	50	28	124
25	1862	Oak Grove, near Richmond	Confederates	U.S.	51	401	60	300
25	1876	Big Horn	Indians	Ind	261	0	81	126
26	1862	Mechanicsville	Confederates	U.S.	149	224	156	236
27	1861	*Mathias Point*	Confederates	Conf.	1	4	0	0
27	1862	Gaines Mill	Confederates	Conf.	3,000	4,500	2,000	4,000
27	1863	Shelbyville	Confederates	U.S.	143	361	164	344
27	1864	White River	Confederates	U.S.	52	148	162	341
28	1776	Fort Moultrie	English	U.S.	11	26	68	437
28	1778	Monmouth	English	U.S.	72	160	294	170
28	1779	Stone Ferry	English	Eng.	51	99	31	63
28	1814	*Wasp-Reindeer*	English	U.S.	11	15	25	42
28	1862	*Farragut at Vicksburg*	Confederates	U.S.	15	30	0	0
28	1863	Donaldsonville	Confederates	U.S.	1	3	85	114
29	1862	White Oak Swamp	Confederates	U.S.	34	42	65	86
30	1815	*Peacock-Nautilus*	English	U.S.	0	0	6	8
30	1847	Tamultay	Mexican	U.S.	6	53	42	103
30	1864	Petersburg (ended)	Confederates	U.S.	112	506	801	1,417
30	1864	Wilson's Raid (June 22–30)	Confederates	U.S.	76	265	48	252

JULY.

Day.	Year.	Name of Battle.	Opponent.	Victor.	U.S. Killed.	U.S. Wounded.	Opp. Killed.	Opp. Wounded.
1	1862	Malvern Hill	Confederates	U.S.	2,860	3,500	3,023	4,077
1	1863	Gettysburg (continued)	Confederates	U.S.	....	....	....	....
1	1863	Cabin Creek	Confederates	U.S.	8	15	42	108
1	1898	El Caney	Spanish	U.S.	88	356	120	400
1	1898	San Juan (continued)	Spanish	U.S.	....	....	....	....
2	1863	Gettysburg (continued)	Confederates	U.S.	....	....	....	....
2	1898	Aguadores (including July 1)	Spanish	U.S.	0	12	10	30
2	1898	San Juan (continued)	Spanish	U.S.	....	....	....	....
3	1778	Wyoming, or Fort Forty	English	Eng.	225	0	2	8
3	1863	Gettysburg (ended)	Confederates	U.S.	2,834	13,709	4,000	14,000
3	1898	San Juan (ended)	Spanish	U.S.	151	1,007	204	1,340
3	1898	*Spanish squadron destroyed off Santiago*	Spanish	U.S.	1	1	342	461
4	1863	Helena	Confederates	U.S.	98	152	205	504
4	1863	Tibb's Bend	Confederates	U.S.	6	23	280	687
4	1863	Vicksburg (ended)	Confederates	U.S.	545	3,688	25	20
5	1814	Chippewa	English	U.S.	60	244	199	328
5	1862	Lebanon	Confederates	Conf.	4	8	3	4
6	1776	*Sachem-privateer*	English	U.S.	1	3	2	6
6	1781	Jamestown Island	English	Eng.	37	81	21	49
6	1864	Chattahoochee (continued)	Confederates	U.S.	....	....	....	....
7	1777	Castletown	English	Eng.	211	583	35	141
7	1862	Cache Swamp	Confederates	U.S.	8	45	110	150
7	1864	Legareville	Confederates	Conf.	36	61	12	25
8	1864	Chattahoochee (continued)	Confederates	U.S.	....	....	....	....
9	1780	*Hazard-Duff*	English	U.S.	2	4	31	64
9	1864	Monocacy	Confederates	Conf.	90	579	78	322
10	1864	Chattahoochee (ended)	Confederates	U.S.	80	450	201	402
10	1898	Santiago (continued)	Spanish	U.S.	....	....	....	....
11	1812	*Decatur-Commerce*	English	U.S.	0	0	4	7
11	1898	Santiago (continued)	Spanish	U.S.	....	....	....	....
12	1863	Jackson	Confederates	U.S.	88	765	71	504
12	1863	Near Donaldsonville	Confederates	Conf.	151	349	88	126
12	1898	Santiago (ended)	Spanish	U.S.	2	13	0	0
13	1862	Murfreesboro	Confederates	U.S.	33	62	47	103
13	1863	Falling Waters	Confederates	U.S.	25	80	125	354
14	1813	*Asp, attack on the*	English	Eng.	4	6	10	21
15	1862	*Arkansas*	Confederates	U.S.	18	50	10	15
15	1863	Shepardstown	Confederates	*	22	78	34	66
15	1864	Tupelo, Harrisonburg, and Old Town Creek	Confederates	U.S.	85	563	184	516
16	1779	Stony Point	English	U.S.	20	70	63	31
16	1863	*Wyoming-Japanese batteries*	Japanese	U.S.	6	4	100	200
16	1863	James Island	Confederates	U.S.	24	76	48	152

JULY—*Continued.*

Day.	Year.	Name of Battle.	Opponent.	Victor.	Casualties. United States. Killed.	Casualties. United States. Wounded.	Casualties. Opponents. Killed.	Casualties. Opponents. Wounded.
17	1863	Honey Springs	Confederates	U.S.	17	60	153	378
18	1863	Wytheville	Confederates	Conf.	21	62	3	8
18	1863	Fort Wagner	Confederates	Conf.	624	876	26	74
19	1863	Near Pomeroy	Confederates	U.S.	2	8	12	41
20	1864	Peach Tree Creek	Confederates	U.S.	301	1,411	880	3,916
21	1861	Bull Run	Confederates	Conf.	481	1,011	362	1,390
22	1812	*Highflyer-Caledonia*	English	U.S.	0	7	3	9
22	1864	Atlanta, Hood's first sortie	Confederates	U.S.	499	2,142	1,162	7,337
23	1864	Martinsburg (continued)	Confederates	U.S.	....	....	....	....
24	1863	Manassas Gap	Confederates	U.S.	30	59	41	79
24	1864	Martinsburg (ended)	Confederates	U.S.	342	836	26	152
25	1779	*Jason-privateer*	English	U.S.	1	3	3	6
25	1814	Niagara (Lundy's Lane)	English	U.S.	171	572	201	559
26	1863	New Lisbon	Confederates	U.S.	1	12	22	43
26	1864	Big Creek	Confederates	U.S.	18	32	48	102
27	1864	Fort Smith	Confederates	Conf.	10	15	12	19
28	1864	Ezra Chapel	Confederates	U.S.	99	601	864	3,778
29	1863	Stony Lake	Indians	U.S.	12	42	32	98
30	1779	*Holker-brig*	English	U.S.	6	16	6	20
31	1812	*Julia-Gloucester*	English	U.S.	0	0	0	3
31	1864	Petersburg (from July 1, exclusive of losses at the Crater and Deep Bottom)	Confederates	U.S.	419	2,076	799	4,023

AUGUST.

Day.	Year.	Name of Battle.	Opponent.	Victor.	U.S. Killed.	U.S. Wounded.	Opponents Killed.	Opponents Wounded.
1	1801	*Enterprise-Tripoli*	Tripolitan	U.S.	0	0	20	30
1	1812	*Yankee-Royal Bounty*	English	U.S.	0	2	2	7
1	1863	Culpepper Court-House	Confederates	*	16	98	22	104
2	1813	Fort Stephenson	English	U.S.	1	7	50	101
3	1804	*Attack on Tripoli*	Tripolitan	*	1	13	60	70
3	1812	*Atlas-Planter and Pursuit*	English	U.S.	2	5	2	4
3	1814	Comoeta Creek	English	U.S.	2	8	10	20
4	1812	Brownstown	English	Eng.	17	30	0	0
4	1862	Malvern No. 2	Confederates	U.S.	6	8	10	18
5	1813	*Decatur-Dominica*	English	U.S.	4	16	18	45
5	1862	Baton Rouge	Confederates	U.S.	99	203	125	234
5	1864	*Farragut in Mobile*	Confederates	U.S.	145	170	12	20
6	1777	Fort Schuyler	English	Eng.	120	268	86	204
6	1862	Kirksville	Confederates	U.S.	28	60	180	498
7	1781	*Trumbull-Iris*	English	Eng.	5	11	0	3
7	1804	*Attack on Tripoli*	Tripolitan	*	22	6	50†	80†
8	1862	Cedar Mountain (continued)	Confederates	Conf.	....	....	....	....
9	1812	Maguaga	English	U.S.	18	58	50	75
9	1862	Cedar Mountain (ended)	Confederates	Conf.	450	660	223	1,060
10	1861	Wilson Creek	Confederates	U.S.	223	721	331	764
11	1814	Stonington	English	U.S.	1	5	21	55
12	1776	*Andrea Doria-Racehorse*	English	U.S.	4	8	6	3
12	1898	*Manzanillo*	Spanish	U.S.	0	0	10†	(?)
13	1812	*Essex-Alert*	English	U.S.	0	0	0	3
13	1863	Pineville	Confederates	U.S.	3	18	28	92
13	1898	Manila	Spanish	U.S.	8	40	....	....
14	1813	*Argus-Pelican*	English	Eng.	6	17	2	5
15	1814	Fort Erie	English	U.S.	17	56	222	309
16	1777	Bennington	English	U.S.	30	41	59	81
16	1780	Camden	English	Eng.	94	281	80	245
17	1862	London, Ky	Confederates	Conf.	12	18	3	8
18	1779	Paulus Hook	English	U.S.	2	3	5	12
18	1864	Strawberry Plains, etc	Confederates	U.S.	401	1,754	338	762
18	1864	Six-Mile House (continued)	Confederates	U.S.	....	....	....	....
19	1780	Catawba Fords	English	Eng.	162	281	2	21
19	1812	*Constitution-Guerriere*	English	U.S.	7	7	15	63
19	1847	Contreras	Mexican	U.S.	20	40	700	2,200
19	1864	Six-Mile House (continued)	Confederates	U.S.	....	....	....	....
20	1779	*Mars-Active*	English	U.S.	0	3	2	7
20	1847	Churubusco	Mexican	U.S.	131	876	1,000†	3,000†
20	1864	Six-Mile House (continued)	Confederates	U.S.	....	....	....	....
21	1863	Lawrence	Confederates	Conf.	140	22	3	14
21	1864	Six-Mile House (ended)	Confederates	U.S.	212	1,155	862	3,138
22	1814	*Diomede-Upton*	English	U.S.	0	0	1	2
23	1864	Duvall's Bluff	Confederates	Conf.	13	42	6	33
24	1814	Bladensburg	English	Eng.	30	42	183	297
25	1864	Ream's Station	Confederates	*	127	546	289	1,211
26	1863	White Sulphur Springs	Confederates	Conf.	63	144	42	75
27	1776	Long Island	English	Eng.	62	188	61	257
27	1862	Manassas Junction	Confederates	Conf.	14	28	11	16
27	1863	Bayou Metea	Confederates	U.S.	2	8	11	31
28	1861	*Fort Hatteras*	Confederates	U.S.	0	0	4	25
29	1779	Newtown	Indians	U.S.	8	22	12	34
29	1862	**Bull Run No. 2 (continued)**	Confederates	Conf.	....	....	....	....
30	1814	Moorfields	English	U.S.	0	3	13	20
30	1862	**Bull Run No. 2 (ended)**	Confederates	Conf.	798	4,023	1,090	6,154

AUGUST—*Continued.*

Day.	Year.	Name of Battle.	Opponent.	Victor.	Casualties. United States. Killed.	Casualties. United States. Wounded.	Casualties. Opponents. Killed.	Casualties. Opponents. Wounded.
30	1862	Richmond, Ky.	Confederates	Conf...	199	689	153	248
31	1864	Petersburg (August 1 to August 31)	Confederates	U.S....	87	484	101	605
31	1864	Jonesboro, Ga. (continued)	Confederates	U.S....	....	....	....	....

SEPTEMBER.

Day.	Year.	Name of Battle.	Opponent.	Victor.	U.S. Killed.	U.S. Wounded.	Opp. Killed.	Opp. Wounded.
1	1814	*Wasp-Avon*	Confederates	U.S....	2	1	10	32
1	1864	Jonesboro (ended)	Confederates	U.S....	0	1,149	498	1,502
2	1812	*Dolphin-two ships*	Confederates	U.S....	4	7	3	8
3	1777	*Raleigh-Druid*	English	U.S....	1	2	6	26
3	1863	Whitestone Hill	Indians	U.S....	8	23	194	42
4	1804	*Intrepid*	Tripolitan	Trip ...	13	0	20	30
5	1812	Fort Harrison	Indians	U.S....	2	2	8	20
5	1813	*Enterprise-Boxer*	English	U.S....	2	10	4	17
6	1781	*Congress-Savage*	English	U.S....	11	19	25	31
6	1781	New London	English	Eng....	88	34	86	142
7	1813	*Gen. Armstrong-Queen*	English	U.S....	0	1	10	19
8	1781	Eutaw Springs	English	U.S....	130	349	85	402
8	1862	*Boat attack on Charleston*	Confederates	Conf...	23	57	0	2
8	1863	*Sabine Pass*	Confederates	Conf...	17	19	0	0
9	1847	Del Rey	Mexican	U.S....	8	31	46	89
10	1813	*Lake Erie*	English	U.S....	27	96	41	94
10	1863	Little Rock	Confederates	U.S....	22	59	31	45
11	1777	Brandywine	English	Eng....	289	568	98	398
11	1814	Plattsburg	English	U.S....	37	62	50	98
11	1814	*Lake Champlain*	English	U.S....	52	58	84	110
12	1861	Lexington, Mo	Confederates	*	42	108	33	65
13	1814	Near Baltimore	English	Eng....	24	139	80	301
13	1847	Chapultepec	Mexican	U.S....	116	671	1,000†	2,000†
13	1863	Harper's Ferry	Confederates	Conf...	80	120	0	0
14	1862	South Mountain	Confederates	U.S....	312	1,234	224	860
14	1862	Crampton Gap	Confederates	U.S....	115	418	98	342
14	1862	Mumfordsville	Confederates	Conf...	15	22	29	31
15	1814	Fort Bowyer	English	U.S....	4	5	32	40
16	1776	Harlem Plains	English	*	7	8	2	20
16	1812	*Rossie-Princess Amelia*	English	U.S....	0	8	3	0
16	1862	Antietam (continued)	Confederates	U.S....	....	....	....	....
17	1814	Fort Erie (sortie)	English	U.S....	79	216	110	250
17	1862	Antietam (ended)	Confederates	U.S....	2,010	9,416	1,812	9,399
18	1778	*Vengeance-Harriet*	English	U.S....	1	3	3	8
18	1863	Chickamauga (continued)	Confederates	Conf...	....	....	....	....
19	1777	Stillwater	English	U.S....	98	252	161	328
19	1862	Iuka	Confederates	U.S....	144	598	385	692
19	1863	Chickamauga (continued)	Confederates	Conf...	....	....	....	....
19	1864	Opequan	Confederates	U.S....	653	3,719	1,632	3,868
20	1777	*Lexington-Alert*	English	Eng....	3	10	2	3
20	1863	Chickamauga (ended)	Confederates	Conf...	1,644	9,262	6,000	10,000
21	1777	Gen. Wayne	English	Eng....	94	162	2	5
22	1862	Wood Lake	Indians	U.S....	8	24	84	138
23	1779	*Bonhomme Richard-Serapis*	English	U.S....	49	67	49	68
23	1864	Athens, Ala	Confederates	U.S....	0	0	12	18
24	1846	Monterey	Mexican	U.S....	142	364	200†	450†
25	1812	*Globe-Sir Simon Clark*	English	U.S....	2	1	4	4
26	1814	*Gen. Armstrong-British boats*	English	U.S....	2	7	137	107
27	1864	Fort Davidson	Confederates	Conf...	47	154	245	756
28	1812	*Nonesuch-privateer*	English	U.S....	3	8	7	16
28	1813	*Lake Ontario*	English	U.S....	10	17	12	20
28	1864	New Market Heights (continued)	Confederates	U.S....	....	....	....	....
29	1864	New Market Heights (continued)	Confederates	U.S....	....	....	....	....
30	1863	Major Montgomery	Confederates	Conf...	14	40	0	2
30	1864	New Market Heights (ended)	Confederates	U.S....	398	2,031	399	1,601
30	1864	Preble's Farm (continued)	Confederates	U.S....	....	....	....	....

OCTOBER.

Day.	Year.	Name of Battle.	Opponent.	Victor.	U.S. Killed.	U.S. Wounded.	Opp. Killed.	Opp. Wounded.
1	1864	Preble's Farm (ended)	Confederates	U.S....	141	788	214	686
1	1864	Harrison	Confederates	U.S....	8	24	16	46
2	1863	Anderson's Cross-Roads	Confederates	U.S....	8	16	32	41
3	1814	*Saucy Jack-troop ship*	English	U.S....	8	15	3	2
3	1862	Corinth (continued)	Confederates	U.S....	...	....	....	....
4	1777	Germantown	English	Eng....	189	542	98	402
4	1812	Ogdensburg	English	U.S....	0	0	3	6
4	1862	Corinth (ended)	Confederates	U.S....	315	1,812	1,423	5,692
4	1863	Baxter's Springs	Confederates	Conf...	80	21	12	32
5	1813	Moravian towns	English	U.S....	7	22	80	101
5	1864	Allatoona	Confederates	U.S....	142	352	338	704
6	1777	Forts Montgomery and Clinton	English	Eng....	84	166	62	141
6	1782	*Wasp-packet*	English	U.S....	3	10	4	17
7	1777	Saratoga	English	U.S....	32	61	98	156
7	1780	King's Mountain	English	U.S....	28	60	168	284
7	1812	*Caledonia and Detroit-boats*	English	U.S....	1	4	5	10

OCTOBER—*Continued.*

Day.	Year.	Name of Battle.	Opponent.	Victor.	Casualties. United States. Killed.	Casualties. United States. Wounded.	Casualties. Opponents. Killed.	Casualties. Opponents. Wounded.
7	1863	Farmington	Confederates	U.S	8	16	22	37
8	1780	*Saratoga–Molly*	English	U.S	2	4	6	10
8	1862	Perryville	Confederates	U.S	916	2,943	980	1,520
8	1779	Savannah	English	Eng	98	136	20	35
9	1779	Assault on Savannah	English	Eng	68	173	18	37
9	1814	*Prince de Neuchatel–Endymion*	English	U.S	7	23	33	37
10	1863	Blue Springs	Confederates	U.S	33	62	48	94
11	1776	*Lake Champlain*	English	Eng	30	50	15	26
12	1800	*Boston–Berceau*	French	U.S	4	11	4	17
12	1863	Arrow Rock (continued)	Confederates	Conf	....	....	....	....
13	1812	Queenstown	English	Eng	90	160	50	101
13	1863	Arrow Rock (ended)	Confederates	U.S	45	162	84	205
14	1863	Bristow Station	Confederates	*	50	150	150	250
15	1779	*Vengeance–Defiance*	English	U.S	3	5	4	11
16	1776	*Ranger–privateer*	English	U.S	3	11	16	24
17	1862	Fort Ridgeley	Indians	U.S	1	6	44	108
18	1812	*Wasp–Frolic*	English	U.S	5	5	15	47
19	1781	Yorktown (ended)	English	U.S	8	16	199	353
19	1814	Cook's Mills	English	U.S	11	54	20	60
19	1863	Buckland's Mills	Confederates	Conf	8	23	4	31
19	1864	Cedar Creek	Confederates	U.S	588	3,516	961	3,239
20	1863	Philadelphia, Tenn	Confederates	Conf	26	73	34	62
21	1861	Ball's Bluff	Confederates	Conf	223	226	58	242
22	1777	Red Bank	English	U.S	11	21	142	258
22	1862	Pocotaligo (continued)	Confederates	Conf	....	....	....	....
23	1862	Pocotaligo (ended)	Confederates	Conf	84	152	14	102
24	1864	Big Blue (continued)	Confederates	U.S	....	....	....	....
25	1776	White Plains	English	*	24	66	89	144
25	1812	*United States–Macedonian*	English	U.S	5	7	36	68
25	1863	Pine Bluff	Confederates	U.S	17	40	39	111
25	1864	Big Blue (ended)	Confederates	U.S	41	62	78	135
26	1846	*Tabasco*	Mexican	U.S	0	0	4	10
27	1863	Wauhatchie (continued)	Confederates	U.S	....	....	....	....
27	1864	*Albemarle*	Confederates	U.S	2	0	0	0
27	1864	Hatcher's Run	Confederates	*	56	1,047	247	763
27	1864	Fair Oaks (continued)	Confederates	*	....	....	....	....
28	1863	Wauhatchie (continued)	Confederates	U.S	....	....	....	....
28	1864	Fair Oaks (ended)	Confederates	*	120	783	150	301
29	1863	Wauhatchie (ended)	Confederates	U.S	76	339	153	208
30	1864	Petersburg (September 1–October 30)	Confederates	U.S	170	822	240	761
31	1799	*Norfolk–Picaroons*	Picaroons	U.S	0	0	65	70

NOVEMBER.

Day.	Year.	Name of Battle.	Opponent.	Victor.	U.S. Killed.	U.S. Wounded.	Opp. Killed.	Opp. Wounded.
1	1779	*Jason–Perseus*	English	Eng	18	12	7	9
2	1813	*Governor Tompkins–Mary Ann*	English	U.S	0	0	1	4
3	1813	Talluschatches	Indians	U.S	5	41	186	0
3	1863	Near Opelousas	Confederates	*	26	124	58	298
4	1812	*Marengo–Leonidas*	English	U.S	0	0	0	1
5	1812	*Paul Jones–Hassan*	English	U.S	0	1	1	1
6	1861	Belmont (continued)	Confederates	Conf	....	....	....	....
6	1863	Droop Mountain	Confederates	U.S	41	79	82	158
6	1863	Rogersville	Confederates	Conf	5	12	3	24
6	1863	Campbell Station	Confederates	Conf	112	186	136	214
7	1811	Tippecanoe	Indians	U.S	37	151	120	180
7	1861	*Port Royal*	Confederates	U.S	8	23	11	48
7	1861	Belmont (ended)	Confederates	U.S	90	173	231	682
7	1863	Rappahannock Station	Confederates	U.S	149	250	80	160
8	1813	*Globe–packets*	English	U.S	8	18	9	18
9	1813	Talladega	Indians	U.S	15	86	299	0
10	1813	*Saucy Jack–Sherbroke*	English	U.S	0	3	2	5
11	1813	Chrysler's Fields	English	*	102	237	22	147
12	1813	*Tom–Townsend*	English	U.S	0	2	8	13
13	1776	*Alfred–transports*	English	U.S	0	2	3	10
14	1813	*Wile Renard–ship*	English	U.S	6	40	82	0
15	1779	*Impertinent–Harlem*	English	U.S	0	1	8	3
16	1776	*Industry–brig*	English	*	2	6	3	8
16	1776	Mount Washington	English	Eng	48	101	252	448
17	1847	Guaymas	Mexican	U.S	0	0	12	18
17	1863	Knoxville	Confederates	*	24	72	18	64
18	1813	Hillabee towns	Indians	U.S	0	0	61	0
19	1847	Urias	Mexican	U.S	0	0	8	12
20	1780	Ennoree Ford	English	U.S	3	4	92	102
20	1856	*Canton Forts* (continued)	Chinese	U.S	....	....	....	....
21	1847	San José	Mexican	U.S	0	3	8	20
21	1856	*Canton Forts* (continued)	Chinese	U.S	....	....	....	....
22	1776	*Lee–ship*	English	*	1	3	2	8
22	1856	*Canton Forts* (ended)	Chinese	U.S	12	28	400	540
23	1863	Chattanooga, including Orchard Knob, Lookout Mountain, and Missionary Ridge (continued)	Confederates	U.S	....	....	....	....

NOVEMBER—*Continued.*

Day.	Year.	Name of Battle.	Opponent.	Victor.	Casualties.			
					United States.		Opponents.	
					Killed.	Wounded.	Killed.	Wounded.
24	1863	Chattanooga, etc. (continued)	Confederates	U.S....	....	....	....	....
25	1863	Chattanooga, etc. (ended)	Confederates	U.S....	757	4,529	850	2,150
26	1863	Operations at Mine Run (continued)	Confederates	U.S....	....	....	....	....
27	1863	Operations at Mine Run (continued)	Confederates	U.S....	....	....	....	....
28	1812	Niagara batteries	English......	U.S....	8	12	14	30
28	1863	Mine Run (ended)	Confederates	U.S....	99	398	121	432
29	1813	Autosse	Indians......	U.S....	11	54	204	0
29	1863	Knoxville	Confederates	U.S....	24	68	259	432
30	1864	Franklin, Tenn.	Confederates	U.S....	189	1,033	1,141	5,113
30	1864	Honey Hill, S. C.	Confederates	Conf...	66	645	18	114

DECEMBER.

Day.	Year.	Name of Battle.	Opponent.	Victor.	U.S. Killed.	U.S. Wounded.	Opponents Killed.	Opponents Wounded.
1	1782	*Commerce-brig and schooners*	English......	*	1	2	14	24
2	1777	*Massachusetts-Lawnsdale*	English......	U.S....	3	5	6	13
3	1815	*Kemp-merchantmen (armed)*	English......	U.S....	1	4	3	8
4	1781	*Prosperity-privateer*	English......	U.S....	3	8	4	9
5	1863	Coffeeville	Confederates	Conf...	38	62	21	32
6	1812	*Montgomery-armed ship*	English......	U.S....	4	13	6	21
6	1864	Deveraux's Neck (continued)	Confederates	*	....	....	....	....
7	1777	Chestnut Hill	English......	*	14	36	42	64
7	1862	Prairie Grove	Confederates	U.S....	167	798	164	817
7	1862	Hartsville	Confederates	Conf...	48	102	35	115
8	1864	Deveraux's Neck (continued)	Confederates	*	....	....	....	....
9	1862	Col. Matthews	Confederates	U S....	18	22	32	68
9	1864	Deveraux's Neck (ended)	Confederates	*	39	390	112	228
10	1812	*Saratoga-Morgiana*	English......	U.S....	3	7	2	5
11	1862	Fredericksburg (continued)	Confederates	Conf...	....	....	....	....
12	1862	Fredericksburg (continued)	Confederates	Conf...	....	....	....	....
13	1862	Fredericksburg (ended)	Confederates	Conf...	1,152	9,101	505	4,061
14	1814	*Lake Borgne*	English......	Eng....	6	35	17	77
14	1862	Kinston	Confederates	U.S....	90	478	71	268
15	1775	Great Bridge	English......	U.S....	0	0	24	81
15	1864	Nashville (continued)	Confederates	U.S....	....	....	....	....
16	1864	Nashville (ended)	Confederates	U.S....	399	1,741	584	3,021
17	1812	Massasinewa	Indians......	U.S....	11	26	39	0
18	1862	Foster's expedition (ended)	Confederates	U.S....	90	478	201	538
19	1776	*Rover-Africa*	English......	U.S....	0	3	23	0
20	1862	Holly Springs	Confederates	Conf...	3	4	2	21
21	1779	*Sally-transports*	English......	*	5	12	6	11
22	1778	*Saratoga-Chance*	English......	U.S....	4	9	5	13
23	1813	Econochaca	Indians......	U.S....	1	6	30	0
23	1814	Near New Orleans	English......	Eng....	24	113	99	230
24	1864	*Fort Fisher* (continued)	Confederates	Conf...	....	....	....	....
25	1776	Trenton	English......	U.S....	2	4	17	78
25	1864	*Fort Fisher* (continued)	Confederates	Conf...	20	63	3	55
26	1781	*St. James-ship (armed)*	English......	*	1	4	3	8
27	1862	Vicksburg assault (continued)	Confederates	Conf...	....	....	....	....
28	1814	Near New Orleans	English......	U.S....	7	8	120	149
28	1862	Vicksburg assault (ended)	Confederates	Conf...	724	990	63	134
29	1778	Savannah	English......	Eng....	28	69	7	19
29	1812	*Constitution-Java*	English......	U.S....	9	25	60	101
30	1862	Murfreesboro (continued)	Confederates	U.S....	....	....	....	....
31	1775	Quebec	English......	Eng....	18	42	1	8
31	1862	Parker's Cross-Roads	Confederates	U.S....	23	139	48	152
31	1862	Murfreesboro (continued)	Confederates	U.S....	....	....	....	....

THE RULERS OF FRANCE FROM THE REVOLUTION OF 1792.

The First Republic.

The National Convention first sat..........Sept. 21, 1792
The Directory nominated..................Nov. 1, 1795

The Consulate.

Bonaparte, Cambacérès, and Lebrun.......Dec. 24, 1799
Bonaparte, Consul for ten years............May 6, 1802
Bonaparte, Consul for life ....Aug. 2, 1802

The Empire.

Napoleon I. decreed Emperor..............May 18, 1804
Napoleon II. (never reigned) ....died July 22, 1832

The Restoration.

Louis XVIII. re-entered Paris ....May 3, 1814
Charles X. (dep. July 30, 1830, d. Nov. 6, 1836) 1824

The House of Orleans.

Louis Philippe, King of the French........ 1830
(Abdicated Feb. 24, 1848, died Aug. 26, 1850.)

The Second Republic.

Provisional Government formed...........Feb. 22, 1848
Louis Napoleon elected President...........Dec. 19, 1848

The Second Empire.

Napoleon III. elected Emperor.............Nov. 22, 1852
(Deposed Sept. 4, 1870, died Jan. 9, 1873.)

The Third Republic.

Committee of Public Defense..............Sept. 4, 1870
L. A. Thiers elected President.............Aug. 31, 1871
Marshal MacMahon elected President......May 24, 1873
Jules Grévy elected President ....Jan. 30, 1879
Marie F. S. Carnot elected President.......Dec. 3, 1887
(Assassinated at Lyons, June 24, 1894.)
Jean Casimir Perier elected President......June 27, 1894
Felix François Faure elected President....Jan. 17, 1895
(Assassinated, in Paris, Feb. 16, 1899.)
M. Emile Loubet elected President.........Feb. 18, 1899

A TABLE OF THE KINGS AND QUEENS OF ENGLAND.

NAME.	SAXONS AND DANES.	Accession.	Died.	Age.	Reigned.
Egbert	First King of all England	827	839	..	12
Ethelwulf	Son of Egbert	837	858	..	21
{ Ethelbald	Son of Ethelwulf	858 }	860	..	2
{ Ethelbert	Second son of Ethelwulf	858 }	866	..	8
Ethelred	Third son of Ethelwulf	866	871	..	5
Alfred	Fourth son of Ethelwulf	871	901	52	30
Edward the Elder	Son of Alfred	901	925	46	24
Athelstan	Eldest son of Edward	925	940	..	15
Edmund	Brother of Athelstan	940	946	23	6
Edred	Brother of Edmund	946	955	..	9
Edwy	Son of Edmund	955	958	20	3
Edgar	Second son of Edmund	958	975	31	17
Edward the Martyr	Son of Edgar	975	979	17	4
Ethelred II	Half-brother of Edward	979	1016	..	37
Edmund Ironside	Eldest son of Ethelred	1016	1016	28	1
Canute	By conquest and election	1017	1035	40	18
Harold I	Son of Canute	1035	1040	..	5
Hardicanute	Another son of Canute	1040	1042	..	2
Edward the Confessor	Son of Ethelred II	1042	1066	64	24
Harold II	Brother-in-law of Edward	1066	1066	..	0
	THE HOUSE OF NORMANDY.				
William I	Obtained the Crown by conquest	1066	1087	60	21
William II	Third son of William I	1087	1100	43	13
Henry I	Youngest son of William I	1100	1135	67	35
Stephen	Third son of Stephen, Count of Blois	1135	1154	49	19
	THE HOUSE OF PLANTAGENET.				
Henry II	Son of Geoffrey Plantagenet	1154	1189	56	35
Richard I	Eldest surviving son of Henry II	1189	1199	42	10
John	Sixth and youngest son of Henry II	1199	1216	51	17
Henry III	Eldest son of John	1216	1272	65	56
Edward I	Eldest son of Henry III	1272	1307	67	35
Edward II	Eldest surviving son of Edward I	1307	1327	43	20
Edward III	Eldest son of Edward II	1327	1377	65	50
Richard II	Son of the Black Prince, eldest son of Edward III.	1377	Dep. 1399	33	22
	THE HOUSE OF LANCASTER.				
Henry IV	Son of John of Gaunt, fourth son of Edward III.	1399	1413	46	14
Henry V	Eldest son of Henry IV	1413	1422	34	9
Henry VI	Only son of Henry V. (died 1471)	1422	Dep. 1461	49	39
	THE HOUSE OF YORK.				
Edward IV	His grandfather was Richard, son of Edmund, fifth son of Edward III.; and his grandmother, Anne, was great-granddaughter of Lionel, third son of Edward III	1461	1483	41	22
Edward V	Eldest son of Edward IV	1483	1483	12	0
Richard III	Younger brother of Edward IV	1483	1485	33	2
	THE HOUSE OF TUDOR.				
Henry VII	Son of Edmund, eldest son of Owen Tudor, by Katharine, widow of Henry V.; his mother, Margaret Beaufort, was great-granddaughter of John of Gaunt	1485	1509	52	24
Henry VIII	Only surviving son of Henry VII	1509	1547	55	38
Edward VI	Son of Henry VIII., by Jane Seymour	1547	1553	16	6
Mary I	Daughter of Henry VIII., by Katherine of Aragon	1553	1558	42	5
Elizabeth	Daughter of Henry VIII., by Anne Boleyn	1558	1603	69	45
	THE HOUSE OF STUART.				
James I	Son of Mary Queen of Scots, granddaughter of James IV. and Margaret, daughter of Henry VII.	1603	1625	58	22
Charles I	Only surviving son of James I	1625	1649	48	24
Commonwealth {	Commonwealth declared May 19	1649	....	..	
	Oliver Cromwell, Lord Protector	1653	1658	59	”
	Richard Cromwell, Lord Protector	1658	Res. 1659	..	”
	THE HOUSE OF STUART—RESTORED.				
Charles II	Eldest son of Charles I	1660	1685	54	25
James II	Second son of Charles I. (died Sept. 16, 1701)	1685	Dep. 1688	68	3
	(Interregnum, Dec. 11, 1688—Feb. 13, 1689.)		Dec. 1701	..	..
William III and {	Son of William, Prince of Orange, by Mary, daughter of Charles I. }	1689	{ 1702	51	13
Mary II {	Eldest daughter of James II }		{ 1694	32	5
Anne	Second daughter of James II	1702	1714	49	12
	THE HOUSE OF HANOVER.				
George I	Son of Elector of Hanover, by Sophia, daughter of Elizabeth, daughter of James I	1714	1727	67	13
George II	Only son of George I	1727	1760	77	33
George III	Grandson of George II	1760	1820	82	60
George IV	Eldest son of George III	1820	1830	68	10
William IV	Third son of George III	1830	1837	72	7
Victoria	Daughter of Edward, fourth son of George III	1837	1901	81	64
Edward VII	Son of Victoria	1901	——	—	——

DICTIONARY OF BIOGRAPHY.

ABBREVIATIONS: Am., American; Br., British; Dan., Danish; Eng., English; fl., flourished; Fr., French; Ger., German; Gr., Greek; Ir., Irish; It., Italian; Nor., Norwegian; Port., Portuguese; Prus., Prussian; Rom., Roman; Russ., Russian; Scot., Scottish; Sp., Spanish; Sw., Swedish.

The numbers after each name indicate the years of birth and death.

An interrogation mark denotes that the date is doubtful. After the names of the popes, the first date indicates the time of accession unless otherwise stated.

Where the pronunciation is obvious, and follows regular English rules, no phonetic spelling is given, but in cases where doubt as to place of accent might arise, the accented syllable is marked. Where the pronunciation departs from regular English rules, as in many foreign names, the correct pronunciation is approximated by phonetic spelling, in parentheses following the name. In some instances, diacritical marks in accordance with the system used in Webster's Dictionary are employed to indicate the pronunciation more exactly.

See, also, the "Dictionary of Authors" for biographical information concerning those whose most noted achievements have been distinctly in the line of literary productions.

Abbas I *(ab-bas')*, The Great, 1557-1628. Shah of Persia. Wrested throne from his father at age of 18; defeated the Uzbeks at Herat, 1597; overthrew Turks and Tartars at Sultanieh, 1618; captured Bagdad, 1623; noted for magnificent court and important reforms.

Abbas-Mirza *(ab-bas' meer'za)*, 1783-1833. A Persian prince; led Persian army in the unsuccessful wars of 1813 and 1826 against Russia when Persia lost her territories in the Caucasus and Armenia.

Abbassides *(ab-bass'i-dees)*, The. Caliphs of Bagdad. The most celebrated dynasty of Saracen rulers, flourished at Bagdad and Damascus 749-1258.

Abbate *(ab-bah'te)*, 1512-71. Ital. painter and fresco artist, follower of Raphael and Correggio.

Abbe, Cleveland, 1838- . . . . Am. astronomer; meteorologist to U. S. weather bureau; initiated adoption of present standard time; author of several publications on meteorology.

Abbey, E. A., 1852- . . . . Am. figure painter and illustrator, ranking among the strongest colorists and most intellectual painters of America. His important work, "The Search for the Holy Grail," decorates a room in the Boston Public Library.

Abbot, C. C., 1843-. . . . Am. naturalist, archæologist, author of numerous books on outdoor observation, among which are, "A Naturalist's Rambles," "In Nature's Realm."

Abbott, Lyman, 1835-. . . Am. clergyman and editor, son of Jacob A. Abbott. Succeeded Henry Ward Beecher at Plymouth Church, editor of the *Outlook*.

Abd-el-Kader *(abd'-el-kaw'-der)*, 1807-83. Emir of Algeria, soldier and patriot.

Abelard *(Eng. pron. ab'e-lard)*, **Pierre,** 1079-1142. Fr. philosopher, theologian, and teacher, the boldest thinker of his time; celebrated for his romantic love of Heloise, his pupil, noted for her beauty and attainments. Their mutual constancy under most painful circumstances of separation as shown by their correspondence still preserved, has made the loves of Heloise and Abelard immortal.

Abercrombie, John, 1780-1844. Eminent Scotch physician, author of philosophical works.

Abercromby, James, 1706-81. British general in America, unsuccessful military career, ended with his repulse at Ticonderoga, 1758.

Abercromby, Sir Ralph, 1734-1801. Distinguished British general, successful in Flanders, 1795, West Indies, 1796, operated with great credit in Holland, 1799, defeated French in battle of Alexandria, 1801, where he was mortally wounded.

Abernethy, John, 1764-1831. Eminent Eng. surgeon, pupil of Hunter, author of important medical works.

Abraham. Born about 2000 B. C., died at age of 175. Hebrew prince and patriarch. The Father of the Hebrews.

Abruzzi *(a-broot'se)*, Prince **Luigi Amadeo,** Duke of the, 1873-. . . . Ital. traveler and Arctic explorer; his expedition of 1899-1900 attained the northernmost latitude yet reached, 86° 33'.

Abt *(abpt)*, **Franz,** 1819-85. German song writer and musical conductor; a prolific composer; published about 600 books of music. His songs are remarkable for simplicity and clearness of melody.

Abu-bekr *(ah-boo-beck''r)*, 570-634. The first caliph. The father of Ayeshah, wife of Mohammed; upon the death of Mohammed, 632, he was made the caliph or successor of the Prophet.

Abu-bekr, Mohammed, 1100-85. Famous Ar. physician, poet, philosopher and mathematician; born in Andalusia, died in Morocco.

Abujaafar *(jaw'-far)*, called El Sadik, "The Righteous," 699-765. A caliph, author of works on alchemy, augury and omens, and most prominent Arabian representative of the so-called art of prophesying from cabalistic tablets.

Abulfazl *(ah-bool-faz'l)*, Sixteenth Century. Vizier and historiographer of Akbar, the great Mongol emperor.

Abulfeda *(a-bool-fay'da)*, 1273-1331. Moslem prince and historian, patron of literature and science, author of "An Abridgment of the History of the Human Race" from the creation to 1328.

Achard *(ahk'-art)*, **Franz Karl,** 1753-1821. Ger. chemist, founder of beet sugar industry.

Adams, Charles Francis, 1807-86. Am. diplomat and statesman, arbitrator for the United States at Geneva in 1871 in the case of the Alabama Claims against England; son of John Quincy Adams.

Adams, John, 1735-1826. First vice-president and second president of the United States; minister for the colonies in Holland; one of the negotiators of treaty of peace with Great Britain, 1782; defeated for the presidency by Jefferson, 1800, he retired to private life.

Adams, John Quincy, 1767-1848. Son of John Adams; sixth president of the United States, defeated by Jackson, 1828; elected to the House in 1830, his oratory gained for him the title of "Old Man Eloquent"; member of the House until 1848, in which year, while in his seat at the Capitol, he received a stroke of paralysis which caused his death.

Adams, Samuel, 1722-1803. Governor of Massachusetts, one of the popular leaders of the Revolution; signer of the Declaration of Independence.

Adanson *(ä'dong'song')*, **Michel,** 1727-1806. Fr. naturalist and physicist, one of the first to recognize electrical nature of lightning. Most important work was in botany.

Adler, Felix, 1851-. . . . Ger.-Am. educator and reformer, graduated at Columbia University, 1870, studied at Berlin and Heidelberg, Professor of Hebrew at Cornell University, 1874, and in 1876 founded "Society of Ethical Culture." His principal literary works are "Creed and Deed" and "The Education of Children."

Adrian I., pope from 772-795; II., 867-72; III., 884-5; IV., 1154-9; V., 1276, dies same year; VI., 1521-3.

Æschines *(esk'-i-nees)*, 389-314 B. C. A Gr. orator, rival of Demosthenes; overthrown by the latter's famous speech "On the Crown," and went into exile 330 B. C.

Æsop *(ees'-op)*, 619?-564? B. C. Gr. writer of fables said to have been a slave but liberated by his master on account of his talents. There is so much obscurity and conflict concerning his life and writings, that many doubt that he ever existed. Whatever the facts may be, his name soon became attached to the beast fables which are the common property of the Indo-European peoples,

Affre *(affr')*, **Denis Auguste,** 1793-1848. Archbishop of Paris, killed while trying to conciliate the insurgents during the insurrection of 1848.

Agardh (*ah'gard*), **Karl Adolph**, 1785-1859. Swedish botanist. His work on Algæ, "Systema Algarum" is an important contribution to botanical knowledge.

Agassiz (*ăg'a-see*), **Alexander**, 1835- . . . Am. naturalist and capitalist, only son of Louis. Graduated at Harvard, 1855. With his knowledge of geology and engineering he developed the Calumet and Hecla copper mines, south of Lake Superior, bringing him great wealth, which he has devoted to zoological research, donating over one million dollars to endowment of the Harvard Museum of Comparative Zoology; author of several zoological works, mostly on deep sea animals.

Agassiz, Louis, 1807-73. Distinguished Swiss-Am. naturalist, born in Switzerland; educated at German Universities; studied under Cuvier at Paris; professor of natural history, Neufchatel, 1832-46; lectured at Boston, 1846, which led to his appointment to the professorship of natural history Harvard, 1848, still held by him at his death. Pre-eminently a teacher of great force, clearness, and enthusiasm; whose lectures, everywhere in demand, were the inspiration of a new era in American biological research. Founded the Museum of Comparative Zoology, Cambridge, 1858. Author of important zoological works.

Agric'ola (*a-gric'o-la*), **Cnæus Julius**, 37-92. Roman general; was the first to effect complete conquest of Britain, to circumnavigate the island, and to establish some degree of civilization.

Agrip'pa, Marcus Vipsanius, 63-12 B. C. Roman general and statesman, commanded fleet of Octavianus in battle of Actium.

Aguinaldo (*ah-ge-nawl'do*), **Emilio**, 1870-. . . Leader of Filipino insurrections against Spain and the United States. Educated at Dominican College in Manila. Became prominent in the uprising of 1896, went into exile at Hong Kong on condition of a large payment from Spain. Returned in 1898, ostensibly to aid the United States against Spain, but after battle of Manila, organized widespread insurrection, which he managed with great ability. Established a provisional government and in 1899 made an unsuccessful attack on U. S. forces at Manila; continued unsuccessful warfare until captured by Gen. Fred Funston, March 23, 1901.

Akbar (*ăk'ber*), 1542-1605. Emperor of Hindustan, the greatest of modern Asiatic rulers.

Akers, Benj. P., 1825-66. Am. sculptor. It is said that the character of Kenyon in Hawthorne's "Marble Faun" is drawn after Akers. Among his noted works are "Una and the Lion," "Milton," "The Dead Pearl Diver" and "Isaiah."

Aladdin, fl., 1375. Son of Osman and organizer of the Janissaries.

Alaric (*ăl'a-ric*), 350?-410. The greatest chief of the Visigoths. Invaded Italy, captured Rome 410.

Albani (*al-bah'nee*), **Francesco**, 1578-1660. Ital. painter of the Caracci school, follower of Guido Reni, sometimes styled the Anacreon of painting.

Albati'ni, 850-929. Famous Arab astronomer; computed the length of the year to within two minutes.

Albert or Albert Francis, Prince of Saxe-Coburg-Gotha, 1819-61, Consort of Queen Victoria.

Albert, Count of Bollstadt, 1193-1280. Ger. philosopher, styled Albertus Magnus. Noted for his learning and efforts to spread the doctrines of Aristotle.

Albert (*Fr. pron. ăl-băr'*), **Eugene F. C. d'**, 1864- . . . Pianist and composer. Pupil of Liszt. Ranks among the most eminent pianists of the world.

Albert, Joseph, 1824-86. Ger. photographer; inventor of the "Albertype" process.

Albo'ni, Marietta, 1823-94. It. contralto. Next to Malibran the great contralto of the 19th century.

Albuquerque (*al-boo-ker'-ke*), **Alfonso**, The Great. Viceroy of the Portuguese Indies. Conquered Malacca, Ceylon, and the Sunda Isles, and established the Portuguese power in the East Indies.

Alcibiades (*al-si-bi'-a-dees*), 450-404 B. C. Athenian politician and general, educated by his uncle, Pericles; a brilliant and successful soldier, banished from Athens, but recalled after defeating his enemies, again exiled, and finally put to death by order of the thirty tyrants of Athens.

Alcmæon (*alk-mee'-on*). Gr. physician and naturalist, sixth century B. C.; the first to practice dissection.

Alcuin (*ăl'-kwin*), 735-804. The greatest scholar of the 8th century; adviser and confidant of Charlemagne. Founded schools and wrote many learned works.

Aldrovandi (*al-dro-van'-de*), **Ulysse**, 1522-1605. It. naturalist, professor of botany at Bologna; published many volumes on birds, and other animals.

Alexander, the Great, 356-323 B. C King of Macedon; taught by Aristotle; ascended the throne of Macedon 336, destroyed Thebes and was chosen commander of the Greeks against Persia; invaded Asia Minor in 334, defeating Darius on the banks of the Granicus: in 333 he almost annihilated the Persian army at the battle of Issus; cut the Gordian knot and caused the Ammonian oracle to declare him the son of Jupiter Ammon; captured Tyre in 332, and, having invaded Egypt, founded Alexandria; in 331 he defeated Darius at Arbela; elated by his success, he claimed the homage due to a god, stabbing his foster-brother Clitus for refusal to pay such homage: invaded India in 327, advancing as far as the Hyphasis: his death is said to have been caused by excessive drinking.

Alexander Nevski (*nef'-ski*), 1220-63. Russ. hero and saint; won a great victory over the Swedes on the Neva, whence his surname Nevski. Peter the Great built a magnificent convent on the battle field and founded a knightly order in his honor.

Alfred, the Great, 849-901. King of Wessex, England, 871-901; a wise ruler, zealous scholar, and patron of learning; called the founder of the Anglo-Saxon race.

Allen, Ethan, 1737-89. Am. soldier, famous for his capture of Fort Ticonderoga, 1775, where he forced the commander to surrender "in the name of the Almighty God and Continental Congress."

Allston, Washington, 1779-1843. Eminent Am. painter, sometimes called the "American Titian."

Alma Tadema (*awl'ma taw-dă'ma*), **Lourenz**, 1836- . . . . Dutch painter, born in Holland, studied at Antwerp under Leys, but has lived in London since 1870. His art is devoted mostly to depicting life and manners of the Greeks and Romans.

Altdorfer (*awlt'dor-fer*), **Albrecht**, 1480-1538. Bavarian painter and engraver. Celebrated pictures are: "The Victory of Alexander at Arbela," and "Adoration of the Shepherds."

Alva, Fernando Alvarez, Duke of, 1508-83. Sp. general, commander in the Netherlands, where he left a record of cruelty unequaled in modern times.

Alvarado (*al-va-rah'do*), **Pedro de**, ... -1541. Sp. adventurer (companion of Cortez) and conqueror of Guatemala.

Alvarez (*awl-var'eth*), **Jose**, 1768-1827. Sp. sculptor, son of a stone mason; student at Granada and Paris, and later lived at Rome, where he associated with Canova and Thorwaldsen. His group "Saragossa" at Madrid assures his permanent fame.

Amari (*a-mah're*), **Michele**, 1806-89. It. historian. His masterpiece is "The War of the Sicilian Vespers."

Ambrose, Saint, 340-397. Bishop of Milan. One of the most celebrated of the ancient Fathers of the Church.

Ames, Fisher, 1758-1808. Am. orator and statesman.

Ames, Oakes, 1804-73. Am. manufacturer and legislator; builder of the Union Pacific Railroad.

Amherst, Jeffrey, Baron, 1717-97. Br. general in America, commanded at siege of Louisburg, 1757, replaced Abercrombie and successfully led expedition against Ticonderoga and Crown Point, 1759. Field Marshal of England, 1796.

Ampere (*ong-payr'*), **Andre Marie**, 1775-1836. Distinguished Fr. physicist.

Anaxag'oras, 500-428 B. C. Gr. philosopher, the last great representative of the Ionian school. He turned philosophy from thought about things to a consideration of Thought itself.

Anaximan'der, 610-546 B. C. Gr. mathematician and philosopher; introduced the sundial into Greece and is said to have invented maps.

Andrassy (*on'drah-she*), **Gyula**, Count, 1823-90. Hungarian statesman.

Andre, John, 1751-80. Eng. spy, hanged for connection with the Arnold treason.

Andrews, Elisha Benjamin, 1844- . . . . Am. educator and author. Graduated Brown University 1870, President Brown University 1889-98, Superintendent of schools Chicago 1898-1900, President University of Nebraska 1900- . . . . Author of many text books and also published "Wealth and Moral Law," "An Honest Dollar" and "History of the U. S."

Andros, Sir Edmund, 1637-1714. Br. colonial governor of New England, 1687 and of Virginia, 1692.

Angel'ico, Fra, 1387-1455. A gifted Italian painter who passed his life in a convent. His paintings of religious subjects are of a high order, and show great beauty and skill.

Anne, 1664-1714. Queen of Great Britain and Ireland, last of the Stuarts.

Anthony, Susan B., 1820- . . . . Am. reformer; was first active in anti-slavery and total abstinence movements, but since the Civil War has devoted herself entirely to the woman suffrage movement; published an extensive "History of Woman Suffrage," 1881-87.

Antipater (*an-tip'a-ter*), 400-319 B.C. Distinguished Gr. general under Philip of Macedon and Alexander the Great.

Antisthenes (*an-tis'the-nees*) of Athens; b. about 440 B.C. The founder of the Cynic School of Greek philosophy.

Antoinette (*ong-twah-net'*) **Marie,** 1755-93. Queen of Louis XVI. of France; guillotined during the French Revolution.

Anto'nius, Marcus (*Mark Antony*), 83-30 B.C. Rom. general and statesman, who with Octavianus defeated Brutus and Cassius at Philippi; after uniting with Cleopatra in Egypt was overthrown by Octavianus in naval battle of Actium.

Antony, Saint, of Thebes, 251-356. Egyptian founder of monachism, and perhaps most popular saint in the Catholic church.

Apelles (*a-pel'lees*) 4th century B.C. The most celebrated painter of ancient times, probably a native of Asia Minor; studied at Ephesus; became the friend of Alexander the Great, who sat to no other painter.

Aquinas (*a-kwi'nas*) **Thomas,** Saint (The Angelic Doctor), 1224-74. Theologian, teacher, and writer; educated at Naples, member of the Order of St. Dominic; the greatest of the schoolmen of the Middle Ages. His teachings are the basis of Roman Catholic theology and philosophy.

Arago (*ar-a-go'*) **Dominique Francis,** 1786-1853. Celebrated Fr. astronomer and physicist; made many important discoveries in electro-magnetism.

Aram, Eugene. 1704-59, Eng. scholar; executed for the murder of one Daniel Clark, whom he is said to have killed to procure means for prosecuting his studies; chief character in one of Bulwer's novels.

Archimedes (*ar-ki-mee'dees*), 287-212 B.C. Greek geometrician; the greatest mathematician of antiquity; born in Sicily, studied at Alexandria, was killed at the fall of Syracuse. Among his works still extant are important treatises on plane and solid geometry, arithmetic, and mechanics. Invented the spiral pump called "Archimedes' Screw."

Arditi (*ar-dee'tee*) **Luigi,** 1822- . . . . It. composer and musical conductor; conducted opera many seasons in New York and London; was Patti's favorite conductor; wrote famous waltz songs sung by Patti and other prima donnas, and composed the operas "The Spy," "The Brigands," and "The Corsair."

Argyle (*ar-gīl'*) **Archibald Campbell,** eighth earl, 1598-1661. Scot. Covenanter; defeated by Montrose; executed for treason.

Aristides (*ar-is-ti'dees*) called the Just, 550-467 B.C. Gr. general and statesman; commanded at the great battles of Marathon, Salamis, and Platæa. Was chief archon of Athens and leading rival of Themistocles.

Aristippus (*ar-ist-tip'pus*) Gr. philosopher born in Africa about 435 B. C.; pupil but only partially a follower of Socrates; founded the Cyrenaic or Hedonistic school of philosophy, which declares that pleasure is the supreme good.

Aristotle (*ar'is-totl*), The Stagirite, 384-22 B.C. Gr. philosopher; pupil of Plato; instructor of Alexander the Great. Founded analytic philosophy. Left a vast number of writings, bearing upon almost every important field of knowledge. The extent of his researches was enormous, and his influence on human thought has continued to the present day. He was the first to develop a definite method of reasoning. His analysis and clear distinction of ideas have had an incalculable influence in advancing scientific inquiry.

Ar'ius, 256-336. Patriarch of Alexandria, and the father of Arianism.

Arkwright, Sir Richard 1732-92. Eng. manufacturer, originated the modern factory, invented the spinning jenny and one of the first to use steam power.

Armin'ius (Hermann), 16 B.C.-21. A.D. Ger. hero; defeated the Romans 9 A.D., near the Lippe.

Arnaud (*ar-no'*) **Henri,** 1641-1721. Historian, pastor, and leader of the Waldenses (Vaudois).

Arnold, Benedict 1740-1801. Am. general and traitor; his plot to deliver West Point into the hands of the British was followed by the capture of Major Andre, and he himself barely escaped; he became a colonel in the British army.

Arnold of Brescia (*bresh'a*). It. clerical reformer, executed by Frederick I.

Arnold, Thomas 1795-1842. English educator and historian; the famous master of Rugby.

Arnold von Winkelried (*ar'nold-fun-vin'kle-reet*) . . . . -1380. Swiss patriot who broke the Austrian phalanx at the battle of Sempach by throwing himself against the points of their spears.

Artedi (*ar-tay'de*) **Peter,** 1705-35. Swedish naturalist; friend of Linnæus; author of an important work on fishes.

Artemisia (*ar-te-mizh'i-a*), 350 B. C. Queen of Caria; erected a magnificent monument to her husband Mausoleus, whence the word mausoleum.

Artevelde (*ar-te-vel'deh*), **Jacob van,** 1290-1345. A popular leader of the Flemings, captain general of Ghent.

Artevelde, Philip van, son of Jacob, 1340-1382. Leader of the Flemings, defeated and slain in battle against Charles VI. at Roosebeke.

Arthur, Chester Alan, 1831-86. Twenty-first president of the United States; born at St. Albans, Vermont; read law, was admitted to the bar, and began practice in New York city; 1860, quartermaster general on the staff of Governor Morgan; 1871, collector of the port of New York, but superseded, 1878, by General Merritt; 1880, nominated for vice-president by the Republicans and elected; succeeded to the presidency on the death of Garfield.

Arundel (*ar'un-del*), **Thomas Howard,** Earl of, 1592-1646. English art collector widely known for his collection called the "Arundel Marbles."

Ashburton, Alexander Baring, Baron 1774-1848. English financier and statesman; negotiated the "Ashburton Treaty" with the United States; head of the great Baring banking house.

Asbury, Francis, 1745-1816. First Methodist bishop ordained in the United States; father of Methodism in America.

Aspa'sia of Miletus, ... -432? B.C. Mistress of Pericles, the Athenian law not permitting a citizen to marry a foreigner; Socrates called himself one of her disciples.

Astor, John Jacob, 1763-1848. Am. merchant, native of Germany; settled in New York city and entered the fur trade, establishing trading posts in the northwest as far as the Pacific, and founding Astoria in 1811; he made extensive investment in real estate, and when he died he left property amounting to thirty millions.

Athana'sius, Saint, 293-373. Bishop of Alexandria, founder of Greek orthodoxy; most noted theologian of the fourth century.

Atkinson, Edward, 1827- . . . . Am. economist, has published many books on banking, railways, money, the tariff, and other economic subjects.

Attila, (*at'ti-la*) . . . . -453. King of the Huns, called the "Scourge of God," conquered and devastated a large part of the Roman Empire.

Auber (*o-bār'*), **Daniel F. E.,** 1782-1871. Famous Fr. composer, founder of grand opera; best known work the opera "Fra Diavolo."

Augereau (*ozh-ro'*), **Pierre Francois Charles,** Duke of Castiglione. Distinguished general, one of Napoleon's marshals and a peer of France.

Au'dubon, John James, 1780-1851. Am. ornithologist; spent many years in studying and illustrating from life the birds of America.

Au'gustine, Saint 354-430. Latin father of the Church and founder of Roman Catholic theology.

Augus'tus Cæ'sar, 63 B. C.-14 A. D. First emperor of Rome.

Averrhoes (*a-ver'ro-ez*), 1126-98. Famous Arabic philosopher and jurist, born at Cordova; commentator of Aristotle.

Avicen'na, 980-1037. Great Arabic physician and philosopher, author of a system of medicine, and of treatise on metaphysics.

Avogadro (*a-vo-gah'dro*), **Amadeo,** 1776-1856. Italian physicist; author of scientific treatises; celebrated for first formulating a fundamental principle of chemistry known as Avogadro's rule.

Babbage, Charles, 1792-1871. An English mathematician and inventor of a calculating machine; born near Teignmouth, England. Died in London.

Baber, 1483-1530. The founder of the Mogul empire in Hindustan, a descendant of Tamerlane; thrice invaded India, and became at length master of it in 1526; left memoirs; his dynasty lasted for three centuries.

Bach, Johann Sebastian, (*bäk*), 1685-1750. Celebrated Germany musician, born at Eisenach, Upper Saxony, entered the choir of Saint Michael's, Luneberg, as a soprano singer. In 1703 he became court musician at Weimar; the following year organist at Arnstadt, and in 1708 court organist at Weimar. In 1717 he was made Director of Concerts, and six years afterward Director of Music and Cantor to St. Thomas' School, Leipsic, an appointment which he held to his death. With the exception of Handel, Bach had no rival as an organist.

Backhuy'sen, Ludolph, 1631-1709. A Dutch painter, famous for his sea-pieces and skill in depicting sea-waves; was an etcher as well as painter.

Bacon, Roger, 1214-1294. A Franciscan monk; born at Ilchester, Somerset; a fearless truth seeker of great scientific attainments; accused of magic, convicted and condemned to imprisonment, from which he was released only to die; suggested several scientific inventions, such as the telescope, the air-pump, the diving-bell, the camera obscura, and gunpowder, and wrote some eighty treatises.

Baedeker, Karl, 1801-1859. A German publisher; originator of a celebrated series of guidebooks for travelers.

Baffin, William, 1584?-1622. An English navigator and discoverer. In 1615 he took service as pilot of the *Discovery* in search of a northwest passage, and made a careful examination of Hudson Strait. His recorded latitudes and notes of the tides are in remarkable agreement with those of a later date. In the following year, with Captain Bylot, he discovered, charted, and named Smith Sound, and several others, and explored the large inlet now associated with his name. His last voyages, 1616-1621, were to the East. At the siege of Ormuz, which the English were helping the Shah of Persia to recover from the Portuguese, he was killed.

Bailey, Liberty Hyde, 1858- . . . . An American horticulturist and editor; born in South Haven, Mich.

Bailly, Jean Sylvain, 1736-1793. A French astronomer and statesman; born in Paris. The Revolution drew him into public life. As mayor of Paris his moderation and impartial enforcement of the law failed to commend themselves to the people, and his forcible suppression of mob violence, July 17, 1791, aroused a storm which led to his resignation. He was condemned by the Revolutionary Tribunal, and executed.

Baird, Spencer Fullerton, 1823-1887. A distinguished American naturalist; born at Reading, Pa. His writings cover nearly every branch of natural history. He died at Wood's Holl, Mass.

Bajazet (*baj-a-zet'*), or **Bayazeed I.,** 1347-1402. An Ottoman sultan. He was the first of his family who assumed the title of sultan. After defeating Hungarians, Germans, and French at Nicopoli, on the Danube, September 28, 1396, Bajazet is said to have boasted that he would feed his horse on the altar of St. Peter at Rome. His progress, however, was arrested by a violent attack of the gout. Bajazet was preparing for an attack on Constantinople, when he was interrupted by the approach of Timur the Great, by whom he was defeated at Angora. He was taken captive, and died about nine months afterward, at Antioch in Pisidia.

Baker, Edward Dickerson, 1811-1861. An American soldier and politician; born in London, England; came to the United States in youth; was sent to Congress in 1844. He served under General Scott in the war with Mexico and was elected United States Senator from Oregon in 1860. He entered the Federal army at the outbreak of the Civil War, and was killed at the battle of Ball's Bluff.

Baker, Sir Samuel White, 1821-1893. A distinguished English traveler; born in London. Discovered lake Albert Nyanza, 1864. On his return home he was received with great honor and was knighted. In 1869 he returned to Africa as head of an expedition sent by the Khedive of Egypt to suppress the slave trade and to annex and open up to trade a large part of the newly explored country, being raised to the dignity of pasha. In 1879 he explored the island of Cyprus, and subsequently he traveled in Asia and America.

Balbo'a, Vasco Nunez de, 1475-1517. A Castilian noble; established a settlement at Darien; discovered the Pacific; took possession of territory in the name of Spain; put to death by a new governor, from jealousy of the glory he had acquired and the consequent influence in the state.

Baldwin I., 1058-1118. King of Jerusalem; succeeded his brother Godfrey de Bouillon; made himself master of most of the towns on the coast of Syria; contracted a disease in Egypt; returned to Jerusalem, and was buried on Mount Calvary.

Baldwin, James Mark, 1861- . . . . An American psychologist, born in Columbia, S. C.; educated at Princeton College, Leipsic, Berlin, and Tubingen Universities.

Balfe, Michael William, 1808-1870. Composer; born in Dublin; in 1826 he wrote the music for a ballet, "La Perouse," performed at Milan; and in 1827 he sang in the Italian Opera at Paris with great applause, his voice being a pure, rich baritone. In 1833 he returned to England, and in 1846 was appointed conductor of the London Italian Opera; author of "Bohemian Girl." He died at Rowley Abbey, his estate in Hertfordshire.

Balfour, Arthur James, 1848- . . . . A British statesman; born in Scotland; entered Parliament in 1874; was private secretary to his uncle, the Marquis of Salisbury, in 1878-1880, and accompanied him to the Berlin Congress; was member of Parliament for Hertford in 1879, and for the East Division of Manchester in 1885; president of the Local Government Board in 1885; Secretary for Scotland in 1886, with a seat in the Cabinet; Lord Rector of St. Andrew's University in 1886; Secretary for Ireland in 1887-1891; member of the Gold and Silver Commission in 1887-1888; Lord Rector of Glasgow University in 1890; Chancellor of Edinburgh University in 1891; First Lord of the Treasury in 1891-1892; became the leader of the Conservative opposition in the House of Commons in 1892. In 1895 he again became First Lord of the Treasury and leader of the House. He was an effective speaker. As Chief Secretary for Ireland, he was successful. He passed the Crimes Act and Law Act, secured a free grant for railways, made a tour of investigation and created the Congested Districts Board. On the resignation of Lord Salisbury, Mr. Balfour became prime minister, July 12, 1902.

Baliol (*ba'le-ol*), **John de,** 1249-1314. Son of the following; laid claim to the Scottish crown on the death of the Maid of Norway in 1290; was supported by Edward I., and did homage to him for his kingdom, but rebelled, and was forced publicly to resign the crown; died in 1314 in Normandy, after spending some three years in the Tower.

Baliol, Sir John de, ... -1269. Of Norman descent; a guardian to the heir to the Scottish crown on the death of Alexander III.; founder of Baliol College, Oxford.

Ballou, Hosea, 1796-1861. An American Universalist clergyman, journalist, and historian, born at Halifax, Vt.; was the first president of Tufts College, and was very successful as editor of the *Universalist Magazine.* He died at Somerville, Mass.

Balmace'da, Jose Manuel, 1840-1891. A Chilian statesman; early distinguished as a political orator; advocated in Congress separation of Church and State; as Premier, in 1884, introduced civil marriage; elected President in 1886. A conflict with the Congressional Party, provoked by his alleged cruelties and official dishonesty, and advocacy of the claim of Senor Vicuna as his legally elected successor, resulted in Balmaceda's overthrow and suicide.

Banks, Sir Joseph, 1744-1820. A zealous naturalist, particularly in Botany; a collector, in lands far and wide, of specimens in natural history; left his collection and a valuable library and herbarium to the British Museum.

Banks, Nathaniel Prentiss, 1816-1894. An American legislator and soldier; born in Waltham, Mass. At first a factory worker, he studied law, and became successively a member of the State and National Legislatures. He was Speaker of Congress in 1856 and in 1858, and in 1859 he was elected governor of his native state. On the outbreak of the Civil War, he took a command in the army, at first on the Potomac, then at New Orleans, and finally on the Red river. Relieved of his command in 1864, he re-entered Congress.

Banquo, ... -1066. A famous Scottish thane. In conjunction with Macbeth, cousin of Duncan, the king, he obtained a victory over the Danes, who had landed on the Scottish coast. Macbeth, shortly afterward, violently dethroned Duncan, and caused him to be secretly assassinated. Banquo, though not an accomplice, was a witness of the crime; and, being subsequently regarded by Macbeth with fear and suspicion, the latter invited him and his son to supper, and hired assassins to attack them on their return home during the darkness of night. Banquo was slain, but the youth made his escape. Shakespeare has interwoven this occurrence with the theme of his tragedy of "Macbeth."

Barbarossa (*i. e.,* Red-beard), **Horuk,** 1473-1518. A native of Mitylene; turned corsair; became sovereign of Algiers by the murder of Selim the emir, who had adopted him as an ally against Spain; was defeated twice by the Spanish general Gomarez and slain.

Barberini. A celebrated Florentine family, which,

since the pontificate of Maffeo Barberini (Urban VIII., 1623 to 1644), has occupied a distinguished place among the nobility of Rome.

Barclay de Tolly, Michael, 1761-1818. A Russian general and field marshal, of Scottish descent, and of the same family as Robert Barclay the Quaker; distinguished in successive Russian wars; made commander-in-chief; commanded the Russians at Dresden and Leipsic, and led them into France in 1815; he was afterwards Minister of War at St. Petersburg, and elevated to the rank of prince.

Baring, Sir Francis, 1740-1810. Founder of the great banking firm of Baring Brothers & Co.; amassed property, value of it said to have been nearly seven millions.

Bar′macides. Flourished ninth century; a Persian family celebrated for their magnificence, and that in the end met with the cruelest fate. Yahya, one of them, eminent for ability and virtue, was chosen by the world-famous Haroun-al-Raschid on his accession to the caliphate to be his vizier; and his four sons rose along with him to such influence in the government as to excite the jealousy of the caliph so much that he had the whole family invited to a banquet, and every man, woman, and child of them massacred at midnight in cold blood.

Barnard, Edward Emerson, 1857- . . . . An American astronomer; born in Nashville, Tenn.; was astronomer in Lick Observatory, California, in 1887-1895, and then became Professor of Astronomy in Chicago University and Director of the Yerkes Observatory. His principal discoveries are the fifth satellite of Jupiter in 1892, and sixteen comets. He has made photographs of the Milky Way, the comets, nebulæ, etc.

Barnato, Barney, 1845?-1897. A South African speculator. His real name is believed to have been Bernard Isaac. He was born in London, England, of Hebrew parents. He began business there as a dealer in diamonds, and in five years earned enough to buy shares in the Kimberly diamond mines. He established a partnership with Cecil Rhodes, and when, in 1886, gold was discovered, secured possession of the greater part of the region. He committed suicide by jumping from the deck of the steamer *Scot* bound from Cape Town to Southampton.

Barnes, Albert, 1798-1870. An American Presbyterian minister; born in Rome, N. Y.; he was best known by his "Notes" on the New Testament (of which over one million volumes are said to have been circulated), Isaiah, Job, Psalms, etc. He died at Philadelphia.

Barneveldt (*bar′-neh-velt*), **Johann van Olden,** 1547-1619. Grand Pensionary of Holland, of a distinguished family; studied law at the Hague, and practiced as an advocate there; fought for the independence of his country against Spain; concluded a truce with Spain, in spite of the Stadtholder Maurice, whose ambition for supreme power he courageously opposed; being an Arminian, took sides against the Gomarist or Calvinist party, to which Maurice belonged; was arrested, tried, and condemned to death as a traitor and heretic, and died on the scaffold at seventy-one years of age, with sanction, too, of the Synod of Dort.

Barras, Paul Francois Jean Nicolas, Comte de, 1755-1829. A French Jacobin; born in Provence. July 14, 1789, he took part in the attack upon the Bastille, and August 10, 1792, upon the Tuileries. In 1792 he was elected a member of the National Convention, and voted for the unconditional death of Louis XVI. In February, 1795, he was elected president of the convention, and, in that capacity, declared Paris in a state of siege, when the assembly was attacked by the populace. Afterward, when the convention was assailed, Bonaparte, by Barras' advice, was appointed to command the artillery; and that general decisively repressed the royalist movement. For his services, Barras was now named one of the Directory, and took a prominent part in the changes which that body underwent until Napoleon's coup d'etat, which effectually overthrew the power of Barras and his colleagues.

Barrett, Lawrence, 1838-1891. An American actor; born in Patterson N. J.; he supported Mr. Burton, Charlotte Cushman, Edwin Booth, and other eminent actors. He served as a captain in the 28th Massachusetts Infantry in the early part of the Civil War. Later he was engaged by Mr. Booth to play Othello to his Iago. After this he became an associate manager of the Varieties Theater, in New Orleans, where for the first time he played the parts of Richelieu, Hamlet, and Shylock. He gained steadily in distinction both as manager and actor. He died in New York city.

Barry, Elizabeth, 1658-1713. An English actress, was said to be the daughter of Colonel Barry, a prominent royalist in the civil war. She was known as "the great Mrs. Barry," and is said to have created over 100 roles. She died in London.

Barthol′di, Frederic Auguste, 1834- . . . . A French sculptor; born in Colmar, Alsace; principal works: the "Lion of Belfort"; statue of Lafayette, in Union Square, New York; bronze group of Lafayette and Washington, in Paris; and the colossal figure in New York harbor, "Liberty Enlightening the World."

Bartolomme′o, Fra, 1469-1517. A celebrated Florentine painter of sacred subjects; born at Florence; "St. Mark" and "St. Sebastian" among his best productions.

Barton, Clara, 1830- . . . . An American philanthropist; born in Oxford, Mass. On the outbreak of the Civil War became a volunteer nurse in the army hospitals and on the battlefield. On the breaking out of the Franco-Prussian War, in 1870, she aided the Grand Duchess of Baden in preparing military hospitals, assisted the Red Cross Society, and at the request of the authorities, superintended the distribution of work to the poor of Strasburg, in 1871, after the siege, and in 1872 did a like work in Paris. At the close of the war, she was decorated with the Golden Cross of Baden and the Iron Cross of Germany. On the organization of the American Red Cross Society in 1881, she was made its president. In 1889 she had charge of movements in behalf of sufferers from the floods at Johnstown, Pa.; in 1892 distributed relief to the Russian famine sufferers; in 1896 personally directed relief measures at the scenes of the Armenian massacres; in 1898 took relief to the Cuban reconcentrados, and performed field work during the war with Spain; and in 1900 undertook to direct the relief of sufferers at Galveston, but broke down physically. In 1903 she undertook the reorganization of the Red Cross Society in the United States.

Bartram, John, 1699-1777. An American botanist, born in Chester county, Pa.; died at Kingsessing, near Philadelphia, Pa.

Barye (*Ba-ree′*), **Antoine Louis,** 1795-1875. A French sculptor, born in Paris.

Bascom, John, 1827- . . . . An American educator and philosophical writer, born at Geneva, N. Y. He was President of the University of Wisconsin in 1874-1887, and in 1900 was Professor of Political Science in Williams College.

Bashkirtseff, Marie, 1860-1884 A precocious Russian young lady of good family, but of delicate constitution, who traveled a good deal with her mother, noted her impressions, and left a journal of her life, which created, when published after her death, an immense sensation from the confessions it contains.

Bastian, Adolf, 1826- . . . . A German traveler and ethnologist. He has traveled very extensively and his numerous writings throw light on almost every subject connected with ethnology or anthropology, as well as psychology, linguistics, non-Christian religions, geography, etc.

Bastien-Lepage, Jules, 1848-1884. A French painter, born at Damvilliers. He died at the height of his fame.

Bates, Edward, 1793-1869. An American lawyer; born in Belmont, Va. He was Attorney-General of the United States in Lincoln's first administration; and had been a candidate for the presidential nomination in 1860. He died in St. Louis, Mo.

Bayard, or more properly **Bayart, Pierre du Terrail, Chevalier de,** 1476-1524. Called the "knight without fear and without reproach"; born in the castle of Bayard, near Grenoble; was one of the most spotless characters of the Middle Ages.

Bayle, Pierre, 1647-1706. Born at Carlat, France; first Protestant, then Catholic, then skeptic; Professor of Philosophy at Padua, then at Rotterdam, and finally retired to the Boompjes in the latter city; known chiefly as the author of the famous "Dictionnaire Historique et Critique."

Bazaine, Francois Achille, 1811-1888. A French military officer; born in Versailles. He served in Algeria, in Spain against the Carlists, in the Crimean War, and joined the Mexican expedition as general of division, in 1862, and in 1864 was made a marshal of France. He commanded the Third Army Corps in the Franco-Prussian War, when he capitulated at Metz, after a seven weeks' siege, with an army of one hundred and seventy-five thousand men. For this act he was tried by court-martial in 1871, found guilty of treason, and condemned to death. This sentence was commuted to twenty years' seclusion in the Isle St. Marguerite, from which he escaped and retired to Spain. He died in Madrid.

Beaconsfield, Benjamin Disraeli, Earl of, 1804-1881. An English statesman and author; born in London. In 1868, he reached the summit of his ambition, becoming premier on the resignation of Lord Derby, but being in a minority after the general election he had to give up office the following December. In 1874 he again became prime minister with a strong Conservative majority, and he remained in power for six years. This period was marked by his elevation to the peerage. In the spring of 1880 Parliament was rather suddenly dissolved, and the new Parliament showing an overwhelming Liberal majority, he resigned office, though he still retained the leadership of his party. Not long after this he published "Endymion."

Beauharnais (*bo-ar-nay′*), **Eugene de,** 1781-1824. Son of Josephine, wife of Napoleon I.; adopted by the latter; served with distinction in the Napoleonic wars. Beauharnais was wounded at Acre; contributed to the victory of Marengo; was created Prince of the Empire in 1805, and Viceroy of Italy. He served in the campaign of 1809, defeated the Austrians at Raab, and distinguished himself at Wagram. His military talents were particularly evinced in the retreat from Moscow, and in the following campaigns of 1813-1814. To Beauharnais may be mainly ascribed the victory of Lutzen.

Beauharnais, Hortense Eugenie, 1783-1837. Sister of the preceding, ex-queen of Holland; wife of Louis Bonaparte, an ill-starred union; mother of Napoleon III.

Beauregard, Pierre Gustave Toutant, 1818-1893. An American military officer; born in St. Martin's parish, La. He distinguished himself in the Mexican War, where he won the brevet of major; was appointed commander of the Confederate forces at Charleston, S. C., and there opened the hostilities of the Civil War by bombarding Fort Sumter. He attempted to aid General Joseph E. Johnston in opposing General Sherman, but surrendered with the former to the latter. After the war he became president of the New Orleans, Jackson, and Mississippi Railroad Company, Adjutant-General of the State, and a manager of the Louisiana State Lottery. In 1866 the chief command of the Rumanian army was tendered him, and in 1869 that of the army of the Khedive of Egypt, both of which he declined. He died in New Orleans.

Becket, Thomas a, 1119-1170. Archbishop of Canterbury; born in London of Norman parentage; entered the Church; was made Lord Chancellor; had a large and splendid retinue, but, on becoming Archbishop, cast all pomp aside and became an ascetic, and devoted himself to the vigorous discharge of the duties of his high office; King Henry II. grew restive under his assumption of authority, and got rid of him by the hands of four knights who, to please the king, shed his blood on the steps of the altar of Canterbury Cathedral, for which outrage the king did penance four years afterwards at his tomb.

Becquerel (*bek-rel′*), **Antoine Cesar,** 1785-1878. A French physician and member of the Institute; born in Chatillon-sur-Loing. In early life he served in the French army in Spain as an officer of engineers. He invented a new psychometer in 1866. He died in Paris. His son, Alexandre Edmond, also an eminent physicist, was born in Paris, 1820. Besides his conjoint labors with his father, he made important researches on the nature of light and its chemical effects, on phosphorescence, on the conductivity and magnetic properties of many substances. He died in Paris, 1891.

Bedford, John, Duke of, 1389-1435. Brother of Henry V.; protector of the kingdom and regent of France during the minority of Henry VI., whom, on the death of the French king, he proclaimed King of France. The enthusiasm created by Joan of Arc turned the tide against him and hastened his death. Previous to this, however, he prevailed over the dauphin, and burned Joan at the stake.

Beecher, Henry Ward, 1813-1887. An American clergyman; born in Litchfield, Conn.; was graduated from Amherst in 1834; studied in Lane Theological Seminary, near Cincinnati, Ohio; and began ministerial duty as pastor of a church in Lawrenceburg, Ind., removing to Indianapolis in 1839. From 1847 until his death he was pastor of Plymouth Congregational Church in Brooklyn. He was one of the founders of the *Independent* and of the *Christian Union* (now the *Outlook*). He was also a prominent anti-slavery orator, as well as a famous lecturer. He died in Brooklyn, N. Y.

Beethoven (*bay′to-ven*), **Ludwig von,** 1770-1827. One of the greatest musical composers; born in Bonn, of Dutch extraction; the author of symphonies and sonatas that are known over all the world; showed early a most precocious genius for music, commenced his education at five as a musician; trained at length under the tuition of the most illustrious of his predecessors, Bach and Handel; revealed the most wonderful musical talent; quitted Bonn and settled in Vienna; attracted the attention of Mozart; at the age of forty was attacked with deafness that became total and lasted for life; continued to compose all the same, to the admiration of thousands; during his last days was a prey to melancholy; during a thunderstorm he died.

Behring or Bering, Vitus, 1680-1741. A Danish explorer; born in Jutland; entered the service of Russia while still young; became a captain-commander in 1722, and was sent by the Empress Catharine in charge of an expedition (planned by Peter the Great before his death), the object of which was to determine if Asia and America were united. Crossing Siberia he sailed from the river of Kamchatka in July, 1728, and reached lat. 67° 18′ N., having passed through the strait, since called after him, without knowing it. Discovering that the land trended greatly to the west he concluded that the continents were not united, and returned; without, however, seeing America. In another voyage, in 1741, he touched upon the American coast, in lat. 58° 21′ N., and gave name to Mount St. Elias. In returning his ship was cast upon an island, since named after him, an outlier of the Aleutian group, and here he and many of his crew perished.

Belisa′rius, 505-565. A general under the Emperor Justinian, born in Illyria; defeated the Persians, the Vandals, and the Ostrogoths; was falsely accused of conspiracy, but acquitted and restored to his dignities by the emperor.

Bell, Alexander Graham, 1847- . . . . Inventor of the telephone; was born in Edinburgh. He was educated at Edinburgh and in Germany, and settled in Canada in 1870. In 1872 he came to the United States and introduced for the education of deaf mutes the system of visible speech contrived by his father. He became Professor of Vocal Physiology in Boston University, and at the Philadelphia Exhibition, in 1876, exhibited his telephone, designed and partly constructed some years before. He was also the inventor of the photophone in 1880, of the graphophone in 1887, and of kindred instruments.

Bell, John, 1797-1869. An American statesman, born near Nashville, Tenn. Member of Congress from 1827 to 1841; Speaker in 1834, and Secretary of War in 1841. He sat in the United States Senate from 1847 to 1859, and in 1860 was nominated for the Presidency by the "Constitutional Union" Party. He afterwards took no active share in politics, and died at Cumberland Ironworks.

Belli′ni, Gentile, 1421-1508. The son of Jacopo Bellini; was distinguished as a portrait painter; decorated along with his brother the council chamber of the ducal palace; his finest picture was the "Preaching of St. Mark."

Belli′ni, Giovanni, 1426-1516. Brother of the preceding; produced a great many works; the subjects religious, all nobly treated; had Giorgione and Titian for pupils; among his best works, "The Circumcision," "Feast of the Gods," "Blood of the Redeemer."

Bellows, Henry Whitney, 1814-1882. An American Unitarian clergyman and writer; born at Walpole, N. H.; was chief founder and long an editor of the *Christian Inquirer;* chief originator of the United States Sanitary Commission, and its president during the Civil War. He was an effective preacher and public speaker. He died in New York.

Bendire, Charles Emil, 1836- . . . . A German-American military officer and ornithologist; born in Darmstadt, Germany; came to the United States in 1852, and entered the army in 1854. He served through the Civil War. After the war he was transferred to the West. During his stay in the West he applied himself to the study of ornithology, and collected a vast amount of material in various branches of natural history. In 1870 he began to collect the eggs of North American birds, which finally numbered more than eight thousand specimens, and this collection he presented to the United States National Museum. He is the author of "The Life Histories of North American Birds, with Special Reference to their Breeding Habits and Eggs."

Benedict, Saint, 480-543. The founder of the Order of the Benedictine Monks; was born at Nursia, in the Dukedom of Spoleto, in Italy.

Benjamin, Judah Philip, 1811-1884. An American lawyer; born in St. Croix, West Indies; was of English parentage and of Jewish faith. Admitted to the bar in New Orleans; elected to the United States Senate in 1852 and 1858. At the beginning of the Civil War, he resigned from the Senate and declared his adhesion to the State of Louisiana. In 1861 he accepted the office of Attorney-General in the Cabinet of Jefferson Davis, and afterward became successively Confederate Secretary of

War and Secretary of State. After the war he went to London, England, where he was admitted to the bar in 1866. He gained a successful practice, and in 1872 was formally presented with a silk gown. He wrote a "Treatise on the Law of Sale of Personal Property." He died in Paris.

Benjamin, Park, 1809-1864. An American journalist, poet, and lecturer; born at Demerara, British Guiana. He studied law originally. His poems, of a high order of merit, have never been collected. He died in New York.

Bennett, James Gordon, 1795-1872. An American journalist; born at Keith, Scotland; trained for the Catholic priesthood; emigrated, a poor lad of nineteen, to America; got employment in a printing office in Boston as proof reader; started the New York *Herald* in 1835 at a low price as both proprietor and editor, an enterprise which brought him great wealth and success.

Bentham, Jeremy, 1748-1832. An English jurist; born in London. He was called to the bar, but did not practice, and, having private means, devoted himself to the reform of civil and criminal legislation. He died in London, leaving his body for dissection.

Benton, Thomas Hart, 1782-1858. An American statesman; born near Hillsboro, N. C.; settled in Tennessee, where he studied law, and was elected to the Legislature. In 1812 he raised a regiment of volunteers, and also served on General Jackson's staff. After the war, he started a newspaper in St. Louis, by which he became involved in several duels. On the admission of Missouri as a state, he was chosen United States Senator in 1820, and, in this post, during thirty years' continuous service, took a leading part in public affairs. He died in Washington.

Bergerac (*berzh-rak*), **Savinien Cyrano de,** 1619-1655. A French author; born in Paris; distinguished for his courage in the field, and for the number of his duels, more than a thousand, most of them fought on account of his monstrously large nose. His writings are often crude, but full of invention, vigor, and wit. He was made the hero of a drama bearing his name, written by Edmond Rostand, the French playwright.

Berkeley, George, 1684-1753. Irish Protestant prelate and metaphysician; founded the philosophy of idealism.

Berlichingen (*ber'lik-ing-en*), **Goetz von,** 1480-1562. Surnamed "The Iron Hand"; a brave but turbulent noble of Germany, the story of whose life was dramatized by Goethe.

Berlioz (*ber-le-oze'*), **Hector,** 1803-1869. A French composer; born in La Cote St. Andre. He forsook medicine to study music at the Paris Conservatoire, where he gained the first prize in 1830 with his cantata, "Sardanapale." He died in Paris.

Bernadotte, Jean Baptiste Jules, 1764-1844. A French general, afterward raised to the Swedish throne. In 1798 he married Mademoiselle Clary, sister-in-law of Joseph Bonaparte. The following year he became for a short time Minister of War, and on the establishment of the Empire was raised to the dignity of Marshal of France, and the title of Prince of Ponte-Corvo. On the death of the Prince of Holstein-Augustenburg, the heir apparency to the Swedish crown was offered to the Prince of Ponte-Corvo, who accepted with the consent of the Emperor, went to Sweden, abjured Catholicism, and took the title of Prince Charles John. In the maintenance of the interests of Sweden, a serious rupture occurred between him and Bonaparte, followed by his accession, in 1812, to the coalition of sovereigns against Napoleon. At the battle of Leipsic, he contributed effectually to the victory of the allies. At the close of the war became King of Sweden on the death of Charles XIII., in 1818, under the title of Charles XIV. During his reign agriculture and commerce made great advances, and many important public works were completed. He was succeeded by his son Oscar.

Bernard, Claude, 1813-1878. A distinguished French physiologist; born at St. Julien; discovered that the function of the pancreas is the digestion of ingested fats, that of the liver the transformation into sugar of certain elements in the blood, and that there are nervous centers in the body which act independently of the great cerebro-spinal center.

Bernard, Saint., 1091-1174. Abbot of Clairvaux; born at Fontaines, in Burgundy; pronounced one of the grandest figures in the church militant; founded in 1115 a monastery at Clairvaux, in Champagne; drew around him disciples who rose to eminence as soldiers of the cross; prepared the statutes for the Knights-Templar; defeated Abelard in public debate and procured his condemnation; founded 160 monasteries; awoke Europe to a second crusade.

Bernhardt, Rosine Sarah, 1844- . . . . A French actress; born in Paris. At an early age her Jewish parents placed her in a convent at Versailles. When fourteen years old she left the convent, and entered the Paris Conservatoire, and there studied tragedy and comedy. Her first great success was as Marie de Neuberg, in Victor Hugo's "Ruy Blas." Becoming very popular by her representations, notably in "Andromaque" and "La Sphinx," she was soon recognized as the foremost actress in French tragedy. Made successful appearances in the United States, and visited Switzerland, Holland, South America, Italy, Algeria, Australia, etc. In 1899 she appeared in a new rendering of "Hamlet" in Paris, and scored a most flattering triumph. She has also done considerable work in painting, sculpture, and literature.

Bernini (*ber-nee'nee*), **Giovanni Lorenzo,** 1598-1680. An Italian painter, sculptor, and architect, born at Naples; produced his "Apollo and Daphne" at eighteen, his masterpiece; designed the colonnade of St. Peter's.

Bernouil'li, James, John, Daniel. Swiss mathematicians, born at Basel, though of Dutch origin. John, 1667-1748, is the most celebrated; was professor first at St. Petersburg and then at Basel; discovered the exponential calculus and the method of integrating rational fractions, as well as the line of swiftest descent.

Berthelot (*bert-lo'*), **Pierre Eugene Marcellin,** 1827- . . . . A French chemist, born in Paris; in 1878 he became president of the committee on explosives which introduced smokeless powder. His labors also led to the discovery of dyes extracted from coal tar.

Berthier (*ber-te-ay'*), **Alexander,** 1753-1815. Prince of Neufchatel and Wagram, Marshal, Vice-Constable of France, etc.; born in Versailles; killed himself.

Berthollet (*ber-to-lay'*), **Count,** 1744-1822. A famous chemist, native of Savoy, to whom we owe the discovery of the bleaching properties of chlorine, the employment of carbon in purifying water, etc., and many improvements in the manufactures.

Berze'lius, Johan Jakob, Baron, 1779-1848. A celebrated Swedish chemist, one of the creators of modern chemistry; instituted the chemical notation by symbols based on the notion of equivalents; discovered silenium, and shared with Davy the honor of propounding the electro-chemical theory; he ranks next to Linnæus as a man of science in Sweden.

Bessemer, Sir Henry, 1813-1898. An English inventor; born in Charlton, Hertfordshire; began modeling and designing patterns when eighteen years old; chose engineering as a profession, and, after long and costly experiments, announced in 1856 his discovery of a means of rapidly and cheaply converting pig iron into steel, by blowing a blast of air through the iron when in a state of fusion. For this discovery the Institution of Civil Engineers awarded him the Gold Telford Medal, and several foreign governments honored him with valuable tokens. In the United States appreciation of his great discovery took the form of creating industrial cities and towns under his name. He was elected President of the Iron and Steel Institute of Great Britain in 1871; knighted by the Queen in 1879, and received the freedom of the city of London in 1880. He died in London.

Bessey, Charles E., 1845- . . . . An American botanist; born in Wilton, O.; educated at Harvard University; Professor of Botany in the Iowa Agricultural College in 1870-1884; Professor of Botany in the University of Nebraska since 1884. He was also President of the Society for the Promotion of Agricultural Science in 1883-1885; President of the Nebraska Academy of Sciences in 1891; Acting Chancellor of the University of Nebraska in 1888-1891; Fellow of the American Association for the Advancement of Science.

Bewick, Thomas, 1753-1828. A distinguished wood-engraver; born in Northumberland; apprenticed to the trade in Newcastle; showed his art first in woodcuts for his "History of Quadrupeds," the success of which led to the publication of his "History of British Birds," in which he established his reputation both as a naturalist, in the truest sense, and as an artist.

Bichat (*be'shah'*), **Marie Francois Xavier,** 1771-1802. French physiologist; the greatest physician of modern times and founder of general anatomy.

Biddle, John, 1615-1662. Father of the modern Unitarians, born in Wotton-under-Edge, in Gloucestershire, England; was educated at Oxford. He was repeatedly imprisoned for his anti-Trinitarian views. To save his life, Cromwell banished him to St. Mary's Castle, Sicily, and assigned him 100 crowns annually. Here he remained three years, until the Protector liberated him in

1658. He then continued to preach his opinions till the death of Cromwell, and also after the restoration, when he was committed to jail in 1662, and died a few months after.

Biela, Wilhelm, Baron von, 1782-1856. An Austrian army officer, born in Roslau, Prussia; known from his discovery of the comet bearing his name. He died in Venice.

Bierstadt, Albert, 1830-1902. An American painter; born near Duesseldorf, Germany; removed with his parents to Salem, Mass., in 1831; began to paint in oils in 1851, and in 1853 returned to Duesseldorf to study his art, spending a winter in Rome, traveling in Italy and Switzerland, and returning to the United States in 1857. In 1861 he finished his painting "Laramie Peak" and in 1863 "View of the Rocky Mountains — Lander's Peak." These at once gave him a high reputation. He died in New York city.

Bigelow, Jacob, 1787-1879. An American physician; born in Sudbury, Mass.; graduated at Harvard College, and began medical practice in Boston in 1810. He early became known as a botanist, and a number of plants were named for him by Sir J. E. Smith. He died in Boston.

Bigelow, Poultney, 1855- . . . . An American author; born in New York; graduated at Yale University and at the Columbia Law School, and was admitted to the bar. In 1875-1876 he took a journey around the world in a sailing ship, which was wrecked on the coast of Japan. He traveled in China, Africa, the West Indies, and Demerara. He has made canoe voyages on the principal waters of Europe, and was the first person to take a canoe through the Iron Gates of the Danube.

Binney, Horace, 1780-1875. An American lawyer; born in Philadelphia; was graduated at Harvard, and for many years was at the head of the Pennsylvania bar. He had a number of distinguished cases in his career, the most noted one being the defense of the city of Philadelphia against the executors of Stephen Girard. He was also a director in the United States Bank. He wrote many valuable papers, and was the author of "The Leaders of the Old Bar of Philadelphia," and "The Privilege of the Writ of Habeas Corpus Under the Constitution." He died in Philadelphia.

Biot (*be-o'*), **Jean Baptiste,** 1774-1862. An eminent French mathematician, astronomer, and physicist; born at Paris; Professor of Physics in the College of France; took part in measuring an arc of the meridian along with Arago; made observations on the polarization of light, and contributed numerous memoirs to scientific journals; wrote works on astronomy.

Bishop, Sir Henry Rowley, 1786-1855. An English composer, born in London; composer and director of music in Covent Garden Theater for fourteen years; produced sixty pieces, of which "Guy Mannering," "The Miller and His Men," are still in favor; was for a brief space Professor of Music in Edinburgh University, and eventually held a similar chair in Oxford.

Bismarck-Schoenhausen, Eduard Leopold, Prince von, 1815-1898. Born at Schoenhausen; woke up into civil life by the events of 1848; took a bold stand against revolutionary ideas and measures; conceived the idea of freeing the several states of Germany from foreign control, and welding them into one under the crown of Prussia. Summoned in 1862 by King William to be his political adviser; his influence was at first distrusted, but the annexation of Sleswig-Holstein by force of arms in 1863 raised him into general favor. His next feat, the humiliation of Austria at Koeniggraetz in 1866, and the consequent erection of a German Confederation, with Prussia at its head, made him the idol of the nation. His treatment of Napoleon III. provoked the latter into a declaration of war, and to an advance on the part of the French against Berlin. To the surprise of nearly all Europe, the Germans proved to be a nation of soldiers, marshaled as army never was before, and beat the French ignominiously back from the Rhine. Count Bismarck had the satisfaction of seeing the power of France, that still threatened, as well as that of Austria, helpless at his feet; the German empire restored under a Hohenzollern king, and himself installed as chancellor of the monarch he had served so well. Nothing he did after this—though he reformed the coinage, codified the law, established protection, increased the army, and repressed Socialism—equaled this great feat, and for this a grateful nation must ever honor his name.

Bizet (*be-zay'*), **Georges,** 1838-1875. An operatic composer; born at Paris; his greatest work, "Carmen"; died of heart disease shortly after its appearance.

Black, Jeremiah Sullivan, 1810-1883. An American lawyer; born in Glades, Pa. In 1857 he was appointed Attorney-General of the United States by President Buchanan, and in 1860-1861 was United States Secretary of State. On the accession of President Lincoln he retired from public life. He died in York, Pa.

Blackie, John Stuart, 1809-1895. A Scottish author; born in Glasgow; died in Edinburgh.

Blackstone, Sir William, 1723-1780. An English jurist; born in London. In 1743 he was elected fellow of All Souls' College, Oxford, and in 1746 was called to the bar; but, having attended the Westminster law courts for seven years without success, he retired to Oxford. Here he gave lectures on law, which suggested to Mr. Viner the idea of founding a professorship at Oxford for the study of the common law; and Blackstone was, in 1758, chosen the first Vinerian Professor. In 1765 he published the first volume of his famous "Commentaries on the Laws of England."

Blackwood, William, 1776-1834. A Scotch publisher; born at Edinburgh. He started as a bookseller in 1804, and soon became also a publisher. After his death the business, which had developed into a large publishing concern, was carried on by his sons, and the magazine he founded is still a leading periodical.

Blaine, James Gillespie, 1830-1893. An American statesman; born in West Brownsville, Pa. In 1854 he removed to Augusta, Me., and engaged in journalism. He was one of the founders of the Republican party. In 1862 he was elected to the House of Representatives of the National Congress. He became Speaker of the House in 1869, and held that office for six years; was a member of the Senate from 1876 to 1881; was twice Secretary of State. He was defeated for the presidency in 1884 by Grover Cleveland. Besides his numerous speeches and writings on the public questions of his day, his best known work is his "Twenty Years of Congress," a historical production of great and permanent value. He died in Washington, D. C.

Blair, Hugh, 1718-1800. A Scotch clergyman and educational writer; born in Edinburgh; was noted for the eloquence of his sermons, and also for "Lectures on Rhetoric," which attained great popularity.

Bland, Richard P., 1835-1899. An American legislator; born near Hartford, Ky.; practiced law in Missouri, California, and Nevada, and was engaged for some time in mining. He was a member of Congress in 1873-1895, and from 1897 till his death. In 1896 he was a conspicuous candidate for the presidential nomination in the Democratic National Convention. Mr. Bland was best known as the leader of the Free Silver movement in the Lower House of Congress and the author of the Bland Silver Bill. He died in Lebanon, Mo.

Blashfield, Edwin Howland, 1848- . . . . An American artist; born in New York city; studied in Paris under Leon Bonnat; and began exhibiting in the Paris Salon in 1874. He returned to the United States in 1881, and has since distinguished himself by the execution of large decorative works.

Blavatsky, Helene Petrovna, 1831-1891. A noted theosophist; born in Yekaterinoslav, Russia; founded the Theosophical Society in New York in 1875. She died in London.

Blouet (*bloo-ay'*), **Paul** (Max O'Rell) 1848-1903. A French lecturer and author; born in Brittany, France. During his early life he was an officer of cavalry in the French army, but in 1873 went to England and became a teacher. After the publication of his first book, "John Bull and His Island," he abandoned teaching and devoted himself to literature. He made several lecturing tours of the United States. Died in Paris.

Blucher (*bloo'ker*), 1742-1819. Prussian field-marshal, familiarly named "Marshal Forwards"; born at Rostock; served first in the Swedish army, then in the Prussian; distinguished as a leader of cavalry, and met with varying fortune; at the age of seventy commanded the center of the Allied Army in 1813; distinguished himself at Lutzen and Leipsic; pursued the French across the Rhine; pressed forward to Paris at the time of Napoleon's abdication; defeated by Napoleon at Ligny, June 16, 1815; arrived on the field of Waterloo just as the French were preparing to make their last charge, and contributed to decide the fate of the day.

Blumenbach, Johann Friedrich, 1752-1840. A German naturalist; born in Gotha. He advocated the doctrine of the unity of the human species, which he divided into five varieties,—Caucasian, Mongolian, Negro, American, and Malay. He died in Gottingen.

Boabdil (*bo-ab-deel'*), ... -1536? The last Moorish King of Granada; dethroned his father, Abu-l-Hasan, in 1481, and two years later was defeated and taken prisoner by the Castilians near Lucena. He was set free on condition of paying tribute, and returned to Granada to struggle with his father and with his heroic uncle, Ez-Zaghal, for the throne. Going to Africa, he there flung away his life in battle.

Bodley, Sir Thomas, 1544-1612. The founder of the Bodleian Library at Oxford; was born at Exeter. Died in London.

Boerhaave (*bore'hav*), **Hermann,** 1668-1738. A celebrated Dutch physician, one of the most influential medical authorities living in the eighteenth century; born in Voorhout, near Leyden.

Boe'thius, Anicius Manlius Severinus, 470?-524? A Roman statesman and philosopher, called "the last of the classic writers"; Theodoric, King of the Ostrogoths, then master of Italy, loaded him with marks of favor and esteem, and raised him to the first offices in the empire. Later, however, he was accused of a treasonable correspondence with the court of Constantinople. He was arrested, imprisoned, and executed.

Bogardus, James, 1800-1874. An American inventor; born in Catskill, N. Y.; early showed the bent of his mind by improvements in the construction of eight-day clocks, and by the invention of a delicate engraving machine. The dry gas meter is his invention; invented a pyrometer, a deep sea sounding machine, and a dynamo-meter; died in New York.

Boleyn, or **Bullen** (*bool'en*) **Anne,** 1507-1536. Second wife of Henry VIII. and mother of Elizabeth; after a three years' residence at the French Court became maid of honor to Queen Catherine; attracted the admiration of Henry; was married to him, and became queen; charged with adultery and conspiracy, was found guilty and beheaded.

Bolingbroke, Henry St. John, Viscount, 1678-1751. An English statesman and political writer; born in Battersea, near London. He died in Battersea.

Bolivar, Simon, 1783-1830. A South American military officer and statesman (named El Libertador, from his having rescued Central South America from the Spanish yoke); born in Caracas. At Venezuela he entered upon his military career as a colonel in the service of the newly founded republic. At length, in 1821, the Independent troops were successful in the battle of Carabobo, where the Royalists lost upward of 6,000 men, and which decided the cause against Spain. On August 20 of the same year a republican constitution was adopted, and decreed to continue, as then defined, till 1834. Bolivar was chosen President, and he turned his attention to the internal administration of the country. In 1823 he assisted the Peruvians to obtain their independence, and was declared their liberator, and invested with supreme authority. On February 10, 1825, however, he convoked a congress, and resigned his dictatorship. He now visited the upper provinces of Peru, which, calling a convention at Chuquisaca, gave the name of Bolivia to their country, in honor of their liberator, and appointed him Perpetual Protector, and to draw up a constitution. On May 25, 1826, he presented his Bolivian code to the Congress of Bolivia, which was afterward adopted, with some dissatisfaction, however, although it was also subsequently adopted by the Congress of Lima, where, under its provisions, he himself was elected President for life. He now set out for Colombia, where disaffection and party strife were at their height. His conduct here was misconstrued, and he was supposed to be assuming the powers of a dictator. In 1829 new disturbances arose, and, in 1830, a convention was called for the purpose of framing a new constitution for Colombia. The proceedings were begun by Bolivar, who once more tendered his resignation, his last act in relation to public affairs. He died at San Pedro, near Carthagena.

Bonaparte, Charles Louis Napoleon (Napoleon III.), 1808-1873. Son of Louis Bonaparte; emperor of the French; as claimant to the throne of France, attempted in 1836 to take Strasburg, but was banished; imprisoned in Ham, 1840, for an attempted insurrection at Boulogne, but escaped to England, 1846; returning to France after revolution of 1848, he was elected President, gained support of the army, and, abolishing popular representation by the *coup d'etat* of 1851, was declared Emperor; in 1853 he married Eugenie, Countess de Teba. Having surrendered at Sedan, after the decisive battle of the Franco-German War, he was deposed and retired to Chiselhurst, in England.

Bonaparte, Joseph, 1768-1844. Eldest brother of Napoleon; born at Corte, in Corsica. After the coronation of Napoleon was made commander-in-chief of the army of Naples; in 1805, ruler of the Two Sicilies, and in 1806, King of Naples. In 1808 Joseph Bonaparte was summarily transferred by his brother to the throne of Spain, and Murat took his place as King of Naples. After the defeat of the French at Vittoria in 1813, he returned to his estate at Morfountaine, in France. After Waterloo Joseph sailed to the United States, became an American citizen, and lived for some years at Bordentown, N. J. In 1832 he returned to Europe, and died at Florence.

Bonaparte, Louis, 1778-1846. Third brother of Napoleon. After rising from one honor to another, he was made King of Holland in 1806; he resigned in favor of his son in 1810; returned to Paris in 1814, where he was coldly received by the Emperor.

Bonaparte, Napoleon (Napoleon I.), 1769-1821. Emperor of the French and greatest of modern generals; born at Ajaccio, Corsica. Attended military school, 1779 to 1784. Entered army as sub-lieutenant in 1785, and in 1792 had risen to the rank of captain of artillery. In 1793 he submitted a plan for the reduction of Toulon, held by the English and Spaniards, and was intrusted with its execution. His success won for him a commission as brigadier-general. In the spring of 1795, on the remodeling of the army, he was suspended and placed upon half-pay, the reason given by the authorities being that he was too young to command the artillery of an army. In the fall, on the breaking out of an insurrection led by the National Guard, the convention recalled Napoleon, who gained a brilliant victory after a brief but bloody engagement. This virtually made him commander-in-chief of the army of the interior. In 1796 he was appointed to the command-in-chief of the army of Italy, and in the same year he married Josephine de Beauharnais. In his very first campaign Napoleon appeared a consummate general. In a few weeks he gained four victories, conquered Lombardy and captured Mantua, almost annihilating three Austrian armies. He then turned his arms against the Pope, compelling him to pay 30,000,000 lire and surrender many valuable works of art. After defeating another Austrian army sent to Italy, Napoleon concluded a treaty securing his success. In 1798 he was given command of a powerful expedition into Egypt, the intention being to strike at the power of Great Britain, and gained decisive victories over the Mamelukes and Turkish auxiliaries. Returning to France he overthrew the Directory and was elected first consul. In 1800 he gained the great victory of Marengo. Made peace with England, 1802, granted general amnesty, established public order, re-established the Catholic faith, and produced his Civil Code. Napoleon became emperor in 1804, and engaged in war with England, Russia, Sweden, and Prussia. Divorced from Josephine in 1809, he married Maria Louise, daughter of the emperor of Austria, in 1810. In 1812 occurred the ill-fated Russian campaign, Napoleon's loss being estimated at 450,000 men. Beaten at Leipsic, 1813, he made a disastrous retreat. In 1814 the allies entered Paris, compelled Napoleon to abdicate, and sent him to Elba, granting him the sovereignty of that island, with a yearly pension of 6,000,000 francs. Returning again to France, he was enthusiastically received and raised an army of about 125,000, but was completely defeated at Waterloo, 1815. He abdicated again, and, unable to carry out his intention of embarking for America, surrendered to the captain of a British man-of-war. Carried to the island of St. Helena, he died there in 1821.

Bonar, Horatius, 1808-1889. A celebrated Scotch hymnist; born in Edinburgh; wrote "Hymns of Faith and Hope," many of which have been taken into the hymnals of most of the Protestant churches. He also wrote more than twenty volumes on theological and religious subjects.

Bonaventura Saint, 1221-1274. An Italian friar of the Order of St. Francis; born in Tuscany. He died from sheer ascetic exhaustion.

Bonheur (*bo-nur'*), **Rosa** (or Rosalie), 1822-1899. Fr. painter of animals, born at Bordeaux; brought up in poverty from ill-fortune; taught by her father; exhibited when she was nineteen; her best known works are the "Horse Fair" and the "Hay Harvest in Auvergne."

Boniface, Winifred, Saint. Apostle of Germany, 680-755.?

Bonner, Edmund (Bloody Bonner), 1490?-1569. Bishop of London, noted for persecution of Protestants.

Bonnivard (*bo-ne-var'*), **Francois de,** 1496-1570. Hero of Byron's "Prisoner of Chillon."

Boone, Daniel, 1735-1820? American pioneer; born in Pennsylvania, but removed in boyhood to North Carolina; he visited Kentucky, hitherto unexplored, and signalized himself by his many daring exploits against the Indians.

Booth, Edwin Thomas, 1833-1893. An American

actor; born near Belair, Md.; the fourth son of Junius Brutus Booth. When sixteen years of age, he made his first appearance on the stage, in the part of Tressel, his father acting as Richard III. He visited England (1861-1862), and in 1864 produced "Hamlet" at New York for 100 nights consecutively. In 1869 he opened a splendid theater in New York, whose building cost over $1,000,000, but which involved him in pecuniary ruin. He revisited California in 1876, and in the spring of 1877 was able to settle with his creditors, having earned during the season over $600,000. Booth visited Great Britain and Germany in 1880-1882, and was everywhere received with enthusiasm.

Booth, John Wilkes, 1838-1865. An American actor; born in Harford county, Md.; another son of Junius Brutus Booth. He sided with the Confederates in the Civil War, and to avenge the defeat of their cause he formed a conspiracy against the life of President Lincoln. He mortally wounded the President, while the latter was attending a performance in Ford's Theater, in Washington, on April 14, 1865; broke his leg in escaping from the building; and concealed himself in Virginia till the 26th, when, on being discovered, and refusing to surrender, he was shot.

Booth, Junius Brutus, 1796-1852. An Anglo-American tragedian; born in the parish of St. Pancras, London. He received a classical education, but early manifested a predilection for the stage, and when seventeen years of age appeared in some unimportant parts. Subsequently he played Richard III. at Covent Garden, a part in which he suddenly became famous. In 1821 he came to the United States, where for the ensuing thirty years he followed his profession with much success. He died suddenly on board a Mississippi river steamer.

Booth, William, 1829- . . . . Founder and General of the Salvation Army; was born at Nottingham, England, educated there, and, from 1850 to 1861, acted as minister of the Methodist New Connection. From the first he was zealous in holding evangelistic services, but the new departure which led to the creation of the Salvation Army on military lines began in 1865 with mission work among the lower classes in the East End of London. Since 1878 Booth's movement has been known as the Salvation Army, of which he has continued to be the mainspring and the controlling power, directing its movements at home and abroad from his headquarters in London.

Borchgrevink, Carsten Egebert, 1864- . . . . A Norwegian explorer and lecturer; born in Christiania, his mother being English and his father a Scandinavian. He went to sea at an early age, but returned to go to college. In 1898 he went to Australia, joined the Survey Department, and scaled Mount Lindsay. In 1894-1895 he was in Antarctic waters, a region fully explored by him in 1897, when he attempted to reach the South Pole, without success. In 1899 (Feb. 17) he had, however, reached Robertston Bay. Returning to London in 1900 he reported having reached lat. 78.50 S., long. 195.50 E., the farthest point south ever reached by man.

Borghese (*bor-gay′say*), **Princess Marie Pauline,** 1780-1825. The beautiful sister of Napoleon; born in Ajaccio; died in Florence; she left many legacies, and a donation, the interest of which was to enable two young men of Ajaccio to study medicine and surgery. The rest of her property she left to her brothers, the Count of St. Leu and the Prince of Montfort. The whole property amounted to 2,000,000 francs.

Borgia (*bor′ja*), **Cesare** 1478-1507, the natural son of Pope Alexander VI., and of a Roman lady named Vanozza. He was raised to the rank of Cardinal in 1492, but afterward divested himself of the office, and was made Duc de Valentinois by Louis XII. At the head of a body of mercenaries, carried on a series of petty wars, made himself master of the Romagna, attempted Bologna and Florence, and had seized Urbino when Alexander VI. died, 1503. Borgia was arrested and carried to Spain. He at length made his escape to his brother-in-law, the King of Navarre, and was killed before the castle of Viana. He was charged with the murder of his elder brother, of the husband of his sister Lucretia, and the stiletto or secret poisoning was freely used against those who stood in his way. With all his crimes he was a patron of art and literature.

Borgia, Lucretia, 1480-1523. Daughter of Pope Alexander VI., and sister of Cesare Borgia. She was accused of almost every species of crime; but several modern writers maintain that the charges against her are false or much exaggerated. She patronized art and literature.

Borromeo, Carlo, Saint, 1538-1584. Italian cardinal.

Bossuet, Jacques Benigne, 1627-1704. Fr. prelate and controversialist, and considered the greatest of Christian orators; first advocate of papal infallibility.

Botha, Louis, 1864?- . . . . A Boer commander; born in Greytown, Natal, about 1864. He began life as a farmer, and, as a young man, had a share in the establishment of the Transvaal Republic. Later he fought in the Kaffir campaign. He was elected to the Volksraad at Pretoria. Upon the outbreak of the Boer War with England in 1899, he was given a subordinate command, and, upon the death of General Joubert, in March, 1900, he became commander of the Boer forces. He demonstrated great capacity by his victories at Spion Kop and Colenso.

Bottger, or **Bottiger, Johann Friedrich,** 1682-1719. A German alchemist, the inventor of the celebrated Meissen porcelain; born in Schleiz. He found refuge in Saxony, where the Elector erected a laboratory for him, and forced him to turn his attention to the manufacture of porcelain, resulting in the invention associated with his name. He died in Dresden.

Botticelli (*bot-te-chel′lee*), **Sandro,** or **Alessandro,** 1447-1515. A celebrated painter of the Florentine school; began as a goldsmith's apprentice; a pupil of Fra Lippo Lippi; the best known examples of his art are on religious subjects, though he was no less fascinated with classical-mythological conceptions; is distinguished for his attention to details and for delicacy, particularly in the drawing of flowers.

Bougainville (*boo-gan′vel*), **Louis Antoine de,** 1729-1811. A French navigator; born in Paris; voyaged around the world, which occupied him two years and a half; his "Travels" had a remarkably stimulating effect on the imaginations of the "philosophes," as described by him in "Un Voyage autour du Monde."

Bouguereau (*boog-ro′*), **Adolphe,** 1825- . . . . A distinguished French painter; born at Rochelle; his subjects both classical and religious, as well as portraits.

Boulanger (*boo-lan′-je*), **Georges Ernest Jean Marie,** 1837-1891. A French soldier; born in Rennes. After a successful career in Algeria and in the East he became Minister of War. In the ministerial crisis of 1887 he lost his portfolio, and was appointed to the command of the 13th Army Corps, but was retired March 28, 1888. In January, 1889, he was elected Deputy to the National Assembly by 81,000 majority, in consequence of which the Floquet ministry resigned. In August, 1889, he was charged with embezzlement, treason, and conspiracy, and found guilty by the Senate; the elections in the twelve cantons were annulled, and he was sentenced to deportation. He died in Brussels.

Bourdaloue (*boor-da-loo′*), **Louis,** 1632-1704. A Jesuit and one of the greatest preachers France ever produced. The extreme popularity of his sermons induced his superiors to call him to Paris, and he became the favorite preacher of Louis XIV.

Bourne, Hugh, 1772-1852, founder of the sect of Primitive Methodists; born in Staffordshire, England. In the course of his life he visited Scotland, Ireland, Canada, and the United States, where his ministrations were attended with great success.

Bowditch, Nathaniel, 1773-1838. American mathematician; born at Salem, Massachusetts; a practical scientist; published "Practical Navigation," translated the "Mecanique Celeste" of Laplace, accompanied with an elaborate commentary.

Boyle, The Hon. Robert, 1626-1691. A distinguished natural philosopher; devoted his life and contributed greatly to science, especially chemistry, as well as pneumatics; was one of the originators of the "Royal Society"; refused the presidentship of the Royal Society, and declined a peerage.

Bozza′ris (*bot′zah-ris*), **Marcos,** 1790-1823. Patriotic leader in Greek war for independence.

Braddock, Edward, 1695?-1755. A British soldier; born in Perthshire, Scotland; was appointed major-general in 1754. Nine months later he sailed as commander against the French in America; leaving the baggage behind, he pushed forward with a chosen force to invest Fort Duquesne, on the present site of Pittsburg, Pa.; was attacked by a party of about 900 French and Indians. No less than 63 out of 86 officers, and 914 out of 1,373 men engaged, were either killed or wounded. The French loss was trifling. Braddock was carried from the field, and died at Great Meadows.

Bradford, William, 1588-1657. An American colonial governor and author; born in Austerfield, Yorkshire, England. He was one of the signers of the celebrated compact on the Mayflower; and, in 1621, on the death of the first governor, John Carver, was elected to the same office, which he continued to fill (with the exception of a brief period when he declined re-election) until his death. His administration was remarkably efficient and successful, especially in dealing with the Indians. He died in Plymouth, Mass.

Bragg, Braxton, 1817-1876. An American military officer; born in Warren Co., N. C.; served with distinction under General Taylor in the Mexican War; at the outbreak of the Civil War, he became a Brigadier-General in the Confederate army. On Johnston's death he was appointed to his command, with the full rank of General, and succeeded General Beauregard as commander of the Department, in July of the same year. The last command he resigned in December, 1863. After the war he was chief engineer of the State of Alabama, and superintended the improvements in Mobile Bay. He died in Galveston, Tex.

Brahe (*brah*), **Tycho,** 1546-1601. A Swedish astronomer, of noble birth; spent his life in the study of the stars; discovered a new star in Cassiopeia.

Brahms, Johannes, 1833- . . . . A distinguished composer; born at Hamburg; settled in Vienna; the appearance of compositions of his an event in the musical world; approaches Beethoven as no other does.

Breckinridge, John Cabell, 1821-1875. Vice-President of the United States; born near Lexington, Ky. He sat in Congress in 1851-1855, and in 1856 was elected Vice-President with James Buchanan as President. In 1860 he was the pro-slavery candidate for the presidency, but was defeated by Abraham Lincoln. United States Senator from March to December, 1861.

Brewer, David Josiah, 1837- . . . . An American jurist; born in Smyrna, Asia Minor; graduated at Yale College; he studied law in the office of his uncle, David Dudley Field, and was admitted to the bar in New York city in 1858. Removing to Kansas, he became prominent in his profession. He was judge of the Supreme Court of Kansas, 1870-1881, and was appointed United States Judge for the eighth circuit in 1884. He rendered a memorable decision on the Kansas Prohibition Law, affirming the right of liquor manufacturers to compensation, for which he was severely criticised by the Prohibitionists. President Harrison elevated him to the Supreme Court of the United States in 1889. He was made a member of the Venezuelan Commission by President Cleveland in 1896, and was chosen its chairman.

Brewster, Sir David, 1781-1868. An eminent Scottish natural philosopher; born at Jedburgh; specially distinguished for his discoveries in light, his studies in optics, and for his optical inventions, such as the kaleidoscope and the stereoscope; wrote a Life of Newton, as well as Lives of Euler, Kepler, and others of the class; Principal of the United Colleges of St. Andrews, and afterwards of Edinburgh.

Brian (surnamed **Boroimhe**), 926-1014. King of Ireland; continued for many years to rule his dominions with vigor and prosperity. Having, however, disputed with Maelmora, the King of Leinster, Maelmora revolted, and, inviting Danes to his assistance, brought on the battle of Clontarf, in which King Brian fell, after gaining a glorious victory over the united forces of the invaders and revolted natives.

Bridget, Saint, 453-523. An Irish saint; born at Dundalk; takes rank in Ireland with St. Patrick and St. Columba. Also the name of a Swedish saint in the fourteenth century; founded a new order and seventy-two monasteries of the order.

Bridgman, Laura, 1829-1889. An American blind mute; born in Hanover, N. H. At two years of age both sight and hearing were entirely destroyed by fever. In 1839 Dr. Howe, of Boston, undertook her care and education at the deaf and dumb school. The first attempt was to give her a knowledge of arbitary signs, by which she could interchange thoughts with others. Then she learned to read embossed letters by touch; next, embossed words were attached to different articles, and she learned to associate each word with its corresponding object. Her touch grew in accuracy as its power increased; she learned to know people almost instantly by the touch alone. In a year or two more she was able to receive lessons in geography, algebra, and history. She learned to write a fair, legible, square hand, and to read with great dexterity, and at last even to think deeply, and to reason with good sense and discrimination.

Bright, John, 1811-1889. An English statesman; born in Lancashire. When the Anti-Corn Law League was formed in 1839 he was one of its leading members, and, with Mr. Cobden, engaged in an extensive free trade agitation throughout the kingdom. He is credited with having exercised a greater influence upon the conduct of public affairs in England and abroad than perhaps any other man. He was the greatest English orator of modern times.

Brockhaus, Friedrich Arnold, 1772-1823. A German publisher; born at Dortmund; a man of scholarly parts; began business in Amsterdam, but settled in Leipsic; publisher of the famous "Conversations Lexikon," and a great many other important works.

Brooks, Phillips, 1835-1893. An American clergyman of the Episcopal Church; born in Boston. He was an impressive pulpit orator, had great spiritual force, and published many volumes of sermons and lectures. He died in Boston.

Brougham (*broo-am*), **Henry Peter, Lord Brougham and Vaux,** 1788-1868. A British statesman, orator, and author; born in Edinburgh. In 1802 he helped to found the *Edinburgh Review*. The article on Byron's "Hours of Idleness," provoked the poet to write his "English Bards and Scotch Reviewers." In 1810 Brougham entered Parliament, where his remarkable eloquence gave him at once a commanding place. He was counsel for Queen Caroline in George IV.'s suit against her, winning a decisive victory, which raised him to the height of fame and popularity. He became Lord Chancellor in 1830, and was at the same time created a baron. He died in Cannes, France.

Brown, John, 1800-1859. An American opponent of slavery; born in Torrington, Conn. He early conceived a hatred for slavery, and, having removed to Osawatomie, Kan., in 1855, he took an active part against the pro-slavery party. In the summer of 1859 he rented a farmhouse about six miles from Harper's Ferry, and organized a plot to liberate the slaves of Virginia. On October 16, he, with the aid of about twenty friends, surprised and captured the arsenal at Harper's Ferry, but was wounded and taken prisoner by the Virginia militia next day, and was tried and executed at Charlestown.

Brown, Robert, 1773-1858. A Scotch botanist; born in Montrose. In 1800 he was appointed naturalist to Flinders' surveying expedition to Australia. He returned with nearly four thousand species of plants. He died in London.

Brown-Sequard, Edouard, 1818- . . . . A Franco-American physiologist and physician; was born in Mauritius, his father being a sea captain from Philadelphia, who married on the island a lady named Sequard. The son studied in Paris, and graduated M.D. in 1846. He devoted himself mainly to physiological research, and received numerous prizes, French and British, for the results of valuable experiments on blood, muscular irritability, animal heat, and the spinal cord.

Bruce, Robert, 1274-1329. The heroic king of Scotland, who totally defeated the English under Edward II. at Bannockburn.

Brummel′, George Bryan, 1778-1840. The sometime famous Beau Brummel; born in London. On his father's death, inheriting a fortune of about $150,000, he began his career as a man of fashion, and became the intimate associate of the Prince of Wales (afterward George IV.). He it was who inaugurated the reign of dandyism, and for a period of twenty years exercised almost despotic sway over English society in the matter of dress. His fortune being soon swallowed up, he maintained his position in society by his success at play, and the indescribable charm of his manner and conversation. After a rupture with the prince, his influence gradually declined; and oppressed by debt, and the falling off of former friends, he retired to Calais, and afterward to Caen, where he was appointed British consul, and where he died.

Bruno, Saint, 1030-1101. Born at Cologne; retired to a lonely spot near Grenoble with six others, where they lived in cells apart, and they met only on Sundays; founder of the Carthusian Order of Monks, the first house of which was established in the desert of Chartreuse.

Brutus, Lucius Junius. Flourished 500 B.C.; Roman patriot.

Brutus, Marcus Junius. 80-36 B.C.; one of Cæsar's assassins.

Bryan, William Jennings, 1860- . . . . An American political leader; born in Salem, Ill. He was graduated at Illinois College in 1881, preparing subsequently for the bar at Union College, Chicago. In 1887 he removed to Lincoln, Neb., and was elected to Congress in 1890, and again in 1892. Four years later he was nominated for the presidency of the United States by the Democratic National Convention at Chicago. He advocated the free and unlimited coinage of silver by the United States at a ratio of 16 to 1, regardless of the action of the other nations. The presidential campaign resulted in his defeat. During the war with Spain, he became colonel of a regiment of volunteers, stationed in Florida. In 1900, he again appeared as Democratic candidate for the presidency upon a platform of free silver, opposition to trusts, and anti-imperialism, and was again defeated by William McKinley. Colonel Bryan continues to retain large influence in his party.

Buchanan, James, 1791-1868. Fifteenth president of the United States; born in Pennsylvania; admitted to the bar, 1812; member of Congress, 1821-31; minister to Russia, 1832-4; United States Senator, 1834-5; secretary of state, 1845-9; minister to England, 1853-6; signed Ostend Manifesto, 1854; president, 1857-61; in his last message, President Buchanan censured the Northern people for the imminent disruption of the Union, holding that neither the executive nor Congress had power to coerce a state.

Buckland, Francis Trevelyan, 1826-1880. An English naturalist; born in Oxford; he founded the journal, *Land and Water*, of which he was editor. He was an authority on fish culture, and as such was consulted by foreign governments. He was a resolute opponent of Darwinism.

Buckle, Henry Thomas, 1822-1862. An English historian; born in Kent. His chief work, a philosophic "History of Civilization," of which only two volumes were completed. He died, while traveling, at Damascus.

Buddha (or **Boodha**), **Gautama,** 624-523 B.C. Hindoo reformer; founder of Buddhism.

Buell, Don Carlos, 1818-1898. An American military officer; born near Lowell, O. He was graduated at West Point, and served in the Mexican War. When the Civil War broke out he was Adjutant-General of the regular army, and was made a Brigadier-General of Volunteers and attached to the Army of the Potomac. In November, 1861, he succeeded General W. T. Sherman in command of the Department of the Ohio. He died near Rockport, Ky.

Buffon, George Louis Leclerc, Count de, 1707-1788. One of the most celebrated naturalists; born in Montbard, Burgundy; his appointment, as superintendent of the Royal Garden (now the Jardin des Plantes), in 1739, gave his mind a decided turn toward that science in which he immortalized himself. The most perfect part of his work is the "History of Quadrupeds"; the weakest, the "History of Minerals," in which his imperfect acquaintance with chemistry and his inclination to hypothesis led him into many errors. His last days were disturbed by a painful disease, which did not, however, prevent the prosecution of his great plan. He died in Paris.

Bull, Ole Bornemann, 1810-1880. A Norwegian violinist; born in Bergen. He secured great triumphs both throughout Europe and in the United States by his wonderful playing. He lost all his money in a scheme to found a colony of his countrymen in Pennsylvania, and had to take again to his violin to repair his broken fortunes. He afterward settled in Cambridge, Mass., and had also a summer residence in his native city, where he died.

Buelow, Friedrich Wilhelm, Baron von, 1755-1816. A Prussian general; served his country in the war with revolutionary France; defeated the French under the Empire in several engagements, and contributed to the victory at Waterloo.

Bunsen, Christian Karl Josias, Chevalier, 1791-1860. A distinguished German statesman and philosopher; born in Korbach; died in Bonn.

Bunsen, Robert Wilhelm Eberhard, 1811-1899. A German chemist; born in Gottingen; among his many discoveries and inventions are the production of magnesium in quantities, magnesium light, spectrum analysis, and the electric pile and the burner which bear his name. He died in Heidelberg.

Burke, Edmund, 1730-1797. Irish orator, statesman, and writer; prominent as the ablest member of the Commons to oppose the ministry's American policy; impeached Warren Hastings in 1788.

Burgoyne, John, 1723-1792. English general, and distinguished as the last sent out to subdue the revolt in the American colonies, and after a victory or two, being obliged to capitulate to General Gates at Saratoga, fell into disfavor; devoted his leisure to poetry and the drama.

Burne-Jones, Sir Edward, 1831-1898. Artist; born at Birmingham, of Welsh descent; he was one of the foremost, if not the foremost, of the artists of his day; imbued with ideas that were specially capable of art-treatment.

Burnside, Ambrose Everett, 1824-1881. American general.

Burr, Aaron, 1756-1836. American statesman and lawyer. In 1800 Burr and Jefferson were the Democratic candidates for president and vice-president; receiving the same number of votes, the House gave the higher office to Jefferson. Burr's course in endeavoring to supplant Jefferson cost him the regard of his party. Unsuccessful as candidate for governor of New York in 1804, Burr attributed his defeat to Alexander Hamilton, whom he killed in a duel. After the expiration of his term as vice-president, Burr was tried for treason, charged with the subversion of federal authority, and with raising an expedition for the conquest of Mexico, but acquitted.

Bushnell, Horace, 1802-1876. An American clergyman and noted writer on religion, morality, and other topics; born near Litchfield, Conn.; died in Hartford.

Butler, Benjamin Franklin, 1818-1893. American politician, lawyer, and general; born in New Hampshire; military governor of New Orleans in 1862, ruling with vigor and efficiency and preserving the city from the yellow fever; went to Congress as a Republican in 1866, and was re-elected for several terms; elected governor of Massachusetts in 1882 by the Democrats, but defeated for the same office a year later.

Butler, Joseph, 1692-1752. An eminent English divine; born at Wantage; became preacher at the Rolls, where he delivered his celebrated "Sermons"; made dean of St. Paul's, and finally bishop of Durham; his great work, "The Analogy of Religion, Natural and Revealed, to the Constitution and Course of Nature."

Cabet (*ca-bay'*), **Etienne,** 1788-1856. A French communist; born in Dijon, and educated for the bar, but turned his attention to literature and politics. Cabet sent a French colony to the Red river in Texas, but the colonists who went out in 1848 found Texas anything but a Utopia. Their ill fortune did not deter Cabet from embarking at the head of a second band of colonists. On his arrival he learned that the Mormons had just been expelled from Nauvoo, Ill., and that their city was left deserted. The Icarians established themselves there in 1850. Cabet's efforts, however, were not successful. He was finally obliged to leave Nauvoo and retire to St. Louis, where he died.

Cabot, John, ... -1498? A Venetian pilot; born at Genoa; settled in Bristol; entered the service of Henry VII., and discovered part of the mainland of North America, at Labrador, about 1497.

Cabot, Sebastian, 1474-1557. Son of the preceding; born either in Venice or Bristol; accompanied his father to North America; was the first to notice the variation of the magnetic needle, and to open up to England trade with Russia.

Cabrera, 1810-1877. A Spanish general; born at Tortosa, Catalonia; a zealous supporter of the claims of Don Carlos; died in England; he was an unscrupulous adversary.

Cade, Jack, ... 1450. The leader of a popular insurrection in the reign of Henry VI. of England. He collected 20,000 followers, chiefly Kentish men, who in June, 1450, flocked to his standard, that they might claim redress for the grievances so widely felt. Cade defeated a detachment of the royal forces at Seven Oaks, and obtained possession of London, the king having retired to Kenilworth; but, Cade having put Lord Say to death, and laid aside the appearance of moderation which he had at first assumed, the citizens rose, gave his followers battle, dispersed them, and put Cade to death.

Cæsar, Caius Julius, 100-44 B. C. The greatest of Roman generals. Elected consul 60 B. C.; formed a secret alliance with Pompey and Crassus known as the first triumvirate. It is said that during his Gallic wars a million of men were slain, eight hundred cities and towns captured, and three hundred tribes subdued. Pompey having become his enemy through jealousy, Cæsar crossed the Rubicon 49 B. C., and in a short time became master of Italy; having conquered all his enemies, and subdued Spain and Africa, he was made perpetual dictator, and received from the senate the title of Imperator. Although beloved by the masses, the patricians feared and hated him, and the result of a conspiracy of Cassius, Brutus, and others was his assassination.

Cagliari (*kal'ya-ree*), **Paul,** 1528-1588. Also known under the name of Paul Veronese, a painter of Verona; his portraits are spirited and noble, and his coloring splendid. He died in Venice.

Cagliostro (*kal-yos'tro*), **Alessandro, Count of,** (real name Giuseppe Balsamo), 1743-1795. A celebrated charlatan; born in Palermo, Italy. The discovery of the philosopher's stone, the preparation of a precious elixir vitæ, etc., were the pretenses by means of which he extracted considerable sums from credulous people. He died in the summer of 1795 in the Castle of St. Leo, in the States of the Church.

Calhoun, John Caldwell, 1783-1850. Am. statesman; born in South Carolina; elected to Congress, 1810; Secretary of War, 1817; Vice-President, 1825-32, resigning to enter the Senate; Secretary of State, 1844; returned to the Senate, 1845; Calhoun was an avowed champion of slavery and states' rights.

Caligula, Caius Cæsar, 12-41. Emperor of Rome; cruel and sensual; built a temple to himself; assassinated.

Calixtus, George, 1586-1656. A Lutheran theologian of an eminently tolerant type; born at Sleswick; accused of heresy, or rather apostasy, for the liberal spirit in which he had learned to treat both Catholics and Calvinists, and for considering the Apostles' Creed a broad enough basis for Christian union and communion.

Callim'achus, fl. 400 B. C. Greek architect, inventor of the Corinthian order.

Calvert, George, Lord Baltimore, 1580?-1632. An English colonist, born in Yorkshire; was for some time Secretary of State to James I.; raised to the Irish peerage, his title being from Baltimore, a fishing village of Cork. He had previously obtained a grant of land in Newfoundland, but, as this colony was much exposed to the attacks of the French, he left it, and obtained another patent for Maryland. He died before the charter was completed.

Calvin, John, 1509-1564. Fr. theologian; established Presbyterian form of church government; the fundamental principle of his theology is that of predestination to eternal happiness or misery by the absolute decree of God.

Cambaceres (*kon-bah-say-res'*), **Jean Jacques de,** 1753-1824. A French senator; born in Montpellier; drew up a "Plan of a Civil Code," which became the basis of the "Napoleonic Code." On the abdication of Napoleon, in 1814, Cambaceres withdrew into private life, but on the return of the emperor from Elba, he was promoted to the office of Minister of Justice. He died in Paris.

Cambronne (*kon-bron'*), **Pierre Jacques Etienne de,** 1770-1842. French general; born at Nantes; served under the Republic and the Empire; accompanied Napoleon to Elba in 1814; commanded a division of the Old Guard at Waterloo; fought to the last; though surrounded by the enemy and summoned to surrender, refused, and was taken prisoner; is credited with the saying, *La Garde meurt, et ne se rend pas*, "The Guard dies, but does not surrender."

Cameron, James Donald, 1883- . . . . An American capitalist and politician; born in Middletown, Pa.; was graduated at Princeton College in 1852. In 1876 President Grant appointed him Secretary of War, and in 1877 he succeeded his father as United States Senator from Pennsylvania, retiring from the Senate in 1897.

Cameron, Simon, 1799-1889. An American statesman; born in Maytown, Lancaster county, Pa. From 1845 to 1849 he was United States Senator from Pennsylvania, and in 1856 was again elected United States Senator. In 1861 he was appointed Secretary of War by President Lincoln. In January, 1862, he resigned from the cabinet, and was appointed minister to Russia. In November of the same year he resigned, and lived in retirement till 1866, when he was again elected to the United States Senate. In 1877 he retired from the Senate in favor of his son, James Donald Cameron. Died in Maytown, Pa.

Campbell, Alexander, 1788-1866. Irish founder of the denomination of "Christians," or "Disciples of Christ."

Camphausen, Wilhelm, 1818-1885. A German painter; born in Duesseldorf. He was specially famous for battle pieces.

Canby, Edward Richard Sprigg, 1817-1873. American army officer; born in Kentucky; served in the Mexican War; commanded the United States troops in New York city during the draft riots of 1863; succeeded General Banks in the command of the army in Louisiana, 1864; became Brigadier-General, 1866. He was treacherously shot by an Indian while negotiating for the removal of the Modocs from Northern California.

Candolle (*kon-doll'*), **Augustin Pyrame de,** 1778-1841. An eminent botanist; born at Geneva, of Huguenot descent; studied in Paris; attracted the attention of Cuvier and Lamarck, whom he assisted in their researches; his great contribution to botanical science is connected with the classification of plants.

Canning, George, 1770-1827. A distinguished British statesman and orator; born in London; studied for the bar; entered Parliament as a protege of Pitt, whom he strenuously supported; on the death of Pitt became Minister of Foreign Affairs; under Portland distinguished himself by defeating the schemes of Napoleon; on the death of Liverpool was made Prime Minister, and after a period of unpopularity became popular by adopting, to the disgust of his old colleagues, a liberal policy.

Canova, Antonio, 1757-1822. A great Italian sculptor; born in Venetia; his first great work, which established his fame, was the group of "Theseus and the Minotaur," which was by-and-by succeeded by his "Cupid and Psyche," distinguished by a tenderness and grace quite peculiar to him, and erelong by "Perseus with the Head of Medusa," perhaps the triumph of his art; his works were numerous, and brought him a large fortune.

Canute, or **Cnut,** . . . . -1036. King of England and Denmark; succeeded his father, and confirmed the Danish power in England. He died at Shaftesbury, leaving Norway to his eldest son, Sweyn; to the second, Harold, England; to the third, Hardicanute, Denmark.

Capet (*kay-pay'*), **Hugues,** 928?-996? Founder of the Capetian (third) dynasty of French monarchs. He was Count of Paris, and usurped the throne on the death of Louis V., the last of the Carlovingian line. The Capets gave one hundred and eighteen sovereigns to Europe; thirty-six kings to France, and a smaller number to Spain, Portugal, Naples and Sicily, Hungary and Navarre; also three emperors to Constantinople, and dukes to Brittany, Burgundy, Lorraine, and Parma.

Cardan, Jerome, 1501-1576. Italian physician and mathematician; born at Pavia; was far-famed as a physician; studied and wrote on all manner of known subjects, made discoveries in algebra, believed in astrology, left a candid account of himself entitled "De Vita Propria"; was the author of "Cardan's Formula," a formula for the solution of cubic equations; he is said to have starved himself to death so as to fulfill a prophecy he had made as to the term of his life.

Carey, Henry Charles, 1793-1879. An American economist; born in Philadelphia; trained in his father's publishing house, he accumulated a competence from the business and retired to devote himself to study. The "Essay on the Rate of Wages" and "The Principles of Political Economy" won him an authoritative international position. He died in Philadelphia.

Carnegie, Andrew, 1835- . . . . Ironmaster; born in Dunfermline, Scotland; son of a weaver; made a large fortune by his iron and steel works at Pittsburg, and has liberally endowed institutions and libraries, both in America and his native country. Author of "Triumphant Democracy," "The Empire of Business," etc.

Carnot, (*kar-no'*), **Marie Francois,** 1837-1894. French civil engineer and statesman; born at Limoges. Finance Minister in 1879 and 1887; became President in 1887; was assassinated at Lyons by an anarchist in 1894.

Carroll, Charles, 1737-1832. The last surviving signer of the Declaration of American Independence; born in Annapolis, Md. He studied at Paris, became a member of the Inner Temple at London; returned to his native country in 1764; was elected to Congress in 1775, and, along with the other members, signed the Declaration. In 1804, he withdrew to private life at Carrollton, his patrimonial estate. He died in Baltimore.

Carson, Christopher, 1809-1868. Commonly called Kit; an American trapper and scout; born in Kentucky. He served under General Fremont in his Rocky Mountain expeditions, and fought in the Mexican and Civil Wars, attaining the rank of brevet brigadier-general. He died at Fort Lynn, Col.

Cartier (*kar-te-ay'*), **Jacques,** 1494-1554. A French navigator; born at St. Malo; made three voyages to North America in quest of a northwest passage, at the instance of Francis I.; took possession of Canada in the name of France, by planting the French flag on the soil.

Cartwright, Edmund, 1743-1823. An English inventor; born in Marnham. In 1785 he brought his invention, the first power loom, into action. He died in Hastings.

Cartwright, Peter, 1785-1872. An American clergyman; born in Virginia. In 1823 removed to Illinois, where he labored for nearly half a century. He also sat in the State Legislature there, and in 1846 was defeated by Abraham Lincoln in an election for Congressman. He died near Pleasant Plains, Ill.

Carver John, 1575?-1621. A "Pilgrim Father," the first governor of the Plymouth colony; born in England. He joined the Leyden colony of English exiles about 1608, and assisted in securing a charter from the Virginia Company and in selecting and equipping the *Mayflower*. He was elected governor after the *Mayflower* reached Provincetown, and established by a treaty peaceful relations with the Indians.

Casaubon, Isaac, 1559-1614. An eminent classical scholar and commentator; born in Geneva; Professor of Greek at Geneva and Montpellier, and afterwards of belles-lettres at Paris, invited thither by Henry IV., who pensioned him.

Casimir-Perier, 1847- . . . . President of the French Republic; born in Paris; a man of moderate views and firm character; was premier in 1893; succeeded Carnot in 1894; resigned 1895, because, owing to misrepresentation, the office had become irksome to him.

Castlereagh, Robert Stewart, Viscount, 1769-1822. Second marquis of Londonderry; British statesman; prominent in suppressing the Irish rebellion of 1798; committed suicide.

Castro, Joan de, 1500-1548. Portuguese general and navigator.

Catherine, Saint, 1347-1380. Italian nun at Siena; mediator between the rival popes in the great schism.

Catherine I., 1682-1727. Empress of Russia; succeeded to the throne on death of her husband, Peter the Great.

Catherine, II., the Great, 1729-1796. Empress of Russia; born at Stettin; daughter of Prince of Anhalt-Zerbst; "a most clever, clear-eyed, stout-hearted woman;" became the wife of Peter III., a scandalous mortal, who was dethroned and then murdered, leaving her empress; ruled well for the country, and, though her character was immoral and her reign despotic and often cruel, her efforts at reform, the patronage she accorded to literature, science, and philosophy, and her diplomatic successes, entitle her to a high rank among the sovereigns of Russia; she reigned from 1763 to 1796, and it was during the course of her reign, and under the sanction of it, that Europe witnessed the three partitions of Poland.

Catherine of Aragon, 1486-1536. Queen of Henry VIII. of England; divorced.

Catherine de Medici, 1510-1589. Queen of Henry II. of France; opponent of the Huguenots.

Catiline, Lucius Sergius, 108?-62 B.C. Roman conspirator.

Cato, Marcus Portius (the Elder), 234-149 B. C. Roman statesman and author.

Cato, Marcus Portius (the Younger), 95-46 B. C. Opponent of Cæsar: famed for purity and nobility; committed suicide.

Cavaignac (*kah-van'yak*), **Louis Eugene,** 1802-1857. A French officer; he was appointed Governor-General of Algeria by the provisional government of the republic, 1848, and the same year he was recalled and made dictator of France; in the same year he was municipal rival of Louis Napoleon for the presidency.

Cavalier (*kah-val-yay'*), **Jean,** 1679-1740. Leader of the Camisards; born at Ribaute; haughtily received by Louis XIV., passed over to England; served against France, and died governor of Jersey.

Cavendish, Henry, 1731-1810. Natural philosopher and chemist; born at Nice, of the Devonshire family; the first to analyze the air of the atmosphere, determine the mean density of the earth, discover the composition of water, and ascertain the properties of hydrogen.

Cavour (*kah-voor'*), **Camillo, Count di,** 1810-1861. A distinguished Italian statesman. He contributed largely to the unification of Italy, and, as Prime Minister from 1852 to his death, framed and had adopted laws guaranteeing liberty of the press, religious toleration, and free commerce.

Caxton, William, 1422-1491. An English printer and scholar; his "Recuyell (collection) of the Histories of Troy," translated by him from the French, appears to have been printed in 1474, most probably at Bruges in Belgium. It was the first book in English reproduced by typography. He set up a printing-office in Westminster, 1477; and on November 18 of that year issued "The Dictes and Sayings of the Philosophers," folio, a work ever memorable as the first book printed in England.

Cecilia, Saint. Fl. second century; Roman martyr; patroness of music.

Cenci (*chen'chee*), **Beatrice,** 1576-1599. "The beautiful parricide;" daughter of Count Francisco Cenci, a notorious Italian libertine; she became the victim of her father's lust, and vainly imploring the protection of Pope Clement VIII., she, with other members of the family, was charged with a conspiracy to assassinate her father, and despite their protestations of innocence all were executed. Guido Reni's beautiful portrait of Beatrice in the Barberini Gallery, Rome, is familiar to all visitors.

Cesno'la, Luiga Palma di, 1832- . . . . An American archæologist; born in Piedmont, Italy. He served in the Italian War with Austria and came to the United States in 1860, serving in the Civil War. He was United States Consul at Cyprus, where he made extensive archæological discoveries. In 1878 he became a trustee and director of the Metropolitan Museum of Art, in New York city.

Chaillu (*sha-yu*), **Paul B. du,** 1835-1903. An American of French descent, celebrated for his travels in Central Africa: he was the first to positively verify the existence of the gorilla.

Chalmers, Thomas, 1780-1847. A noted Scotch divine; born in Fife, in 1780. He may be regarded as the founder of the Free Church of Scotland. He died in Morningside.

Chamberlain, Joseph, 1836- . . . . An English statesman; born in London; was mayor of Birmingham from 1873 to 1876, and chairman of the Birmingham school board from 1874 to 1876. After unsuccessfully contesting Sheffield against Mr. Roebuck in 1874, he was returned for Birmingham without opposition in June, 1876. He soon made his mark in Parliament; he came to be regarded as the leader of the extreme Radical party and of the Liberal-Unionists when the Duke of Devonshire went to the Upper House. Lord Salisbury sent him to Washington as commissioner on the Canadian fishery dispute, and in 1895 he was made Colonial minister in the Unionist Cabinet. As such he had to face the troubles in South Africa, and to cherish closer fellow-feeling with the Colonies. He carried the Australian Federation measure in Parliament, and later had to face opposition from within the Liberal Party. After the Boer war he visited South Africa and made himself personally acquainted with the situation there. His recent advocacy of "fair trade," or a modified protective tariff caused great disturbance in the ministry and its supporters, and in September, 1903, Mr. Chamberlain resigned as a member of the Cabinet.

Champlain, Samuel de, 1570-1635. A French navigator; born at Brouage, in Saintonge; was founder of Quebec, and French governor of Canada; wrote an account of his voyages.

Champollion (*shon-pol-yon'*), **Jean Francois,** 1790-1832. A celebrated French Egyptologist; early gave himself to the study of Coptic and Egyptian antiquities; was the first to decipher the hieroglyphics of ancient Egypt, a great discovery; conducted a scientific expedition to Egypt in 1828, and returned in 1830 with the fruits of his researches; a chair of Egyptology was in consequence instituted in the College of France, and he was installed as the first professor; his writings on the science, of which he laid the foundation, are numerous.

Charlemagne (*sharl'mane*), 742-804. Son and successor to Pepin le Bref, and grandson to Charles Martel; King of France. He conquered a large part of Spain and Italy, and all of Germany to the Bohemian borders, being crowned Emperor of the West by the Pope in 800. He was the most enlightened as well as the most energetic European sovereign of the century.

Charles. The name of numerous European emperors, kings, and lesser potentates, Germany having had four kings and three emperors bearing this name; Sweden fifteen kings, the present ruler being the fifteenth; Spain four, France ten, Naples four, Navarre three, England two, Sardinia two, and Hungary two kings. The name was also borne by Dukes of Baden, Lorraine, Savoy, and Burgundy.

Charles II. (the Bald—Charles II. of France), 823-877. Emperor of Germany; invaded Italy and was crowned emperor. **Charles III.** (the Fat), 832?-888. **Charles IV.,** 1316-1378. Emperor of Germany and king of Bohemia. **Charles V.,** 1500-1558. Emperor of Germany; king of Spain as Charles I.; in 1521, summoned the Diet of Worms to check the progress of Luther's doctrines; in 1527, warring with Francis I. of France and Pope Clement VII., Rome was sacked and the pope made prisoner; convened the Diet of Augsburg to suppress the Reformation, but, the Protestants having united, liberal terms were granted them; in 1535, defeated Barbarossa and captured Tunis, liberating thousands of Christian slaves; defeated in 1552 by the Protestant forces under Maurice of Saxony, he signed the treaty of Passau, establishing the Protestant church on a firm basis; three years later he retired to the monastery of St. Yuste.

Charles I. (Charles Stuart), 1600-1649. King of England; beheaded, after attempting to subdue his rebellious subjects. **Charles II.** 1660-1685, witty, but careless and voluptuous; the habeas corpus act was passed during his reign.

Charles XII., 1682-1718. King of Sweden, ascended the throne in 1697; a league being formed against him by Russia, Denmark, and Poland in 1700, he besieged

Copenhagen, forced Denmark to make peace, and beat the Russians; he then invaded Poland, compelling King Augustus to resign; invading Russia, he was badly defeated at Pultowa; he fled to Turkey, but soon returned; marching into Norway, he was killed at the siege of Frederickshall.

Charles Martel, 694?-741. The illegitimate son of the Duke of Austrasia, who by his bravery and wisdom became Duke of the Franks. His son, Pepin le Bref, was made King of France, and was the founder of the illustrious Carlovingian line of kings, the name being taken from Charles Martel.

Chase, Salmon Portland, 1808-1873. American statesman and jurist.

Chatham, William Pitt, Earl of ("the Great Commoner"), 1708-1778, English statesman and orator; opposed taxation of American colonies.

Cherubini, Luigi Zenobio Salvatore, 1760-1842. Founder of the French Conservatory and instructor of hundreds of eminent musicians; born in Florence; in the interval from 1780 to 1788, he composed eleven Italian operas, including "Iphigenia in Aulide," the most successful of the series. He died in Paris.

Chevreul, Michel Eugene, 1786-1899. A French chemist. He wrote various works on chemistry, dyeing, etc.

Chippendale, Thomas. Flourished eighteenth century. An English cabinetmaker; went to London from Worcestershire before 1750. The style of furniture named from him was less heavy and severe than that of his successors, and was rather elaborate, delicate, and baroque, with classical tendencies.

Chitty, Joseph, 1776-1813. An English lawyer and legal writer. He achieved eminence as a barrister in London, but his celebrity rests mainly upon his legal works. He died in London.

Choate, Rufus, 1799-1858. A distinguished American lawyer and statesman. He served with distinction in the lower house of Congress, and from the death of Daniel Webster was recognized as the ablest and most eloquent advocate of the country.

Chopin (*sho'-peen*), **Frederick,** 1810-1849. An eminent musical composer and pianist; born in Poland; died in Paris.

Chouteau (*sho-to'*), **Auguste,** 1739-1829. An American pioneer; born in New Orleans, La. He was from his early youth a fur trader, and with his brother Pierre founded the city of St. Louis in 1764. He died in St. Louis.

Chouteau, Pierre, 1749-1849. An American pioneer; born in New Orleans. With his brother Auguste he set out in 1763, joining a government expedition. He stopped in the heart of an unsettled country and founded, with his brother, the city of St. Louis. He died in St. Louis.

Christina, 1628-1689. Queen of Sweden; daughter and only child of Gustavus Adolphus; received a masculine education, and was trained in manly exercises; governed the country well, and filled her court with learned men; her royal duties becoming irksome to her, she declared her cousin her successor, resigned the throne, and turned Catholic; her cousin dying, she claimed back her crown, but her subjects would not now have her; retired to Rome, where she spent twenty years of her life engaged in scientific and artistic studies, and died.

Chrysostom, John, Saint ("Golden-mouthed"), 344?-407. A celebrated Greek father of the church; born in Antioch; died at Comana, in Pontus.

Cid (*sid*). Flourished eleventh century. A chief; applied to Ruy or Roderigo Diaz, Count of Bivar (El Cid Campeador); a champion of Christian and Spanish royalty against the Moors.

Cimabu'e, 1240-1302. A Florentine painter and founder of the Florentine school, which ranked among its members such artists as Michael Angelo, Raphael, and Leonardo da Vinci; was the first to leave the stiff traditional Byzantine forms of art and copy from nature and the living model, though it was only with the advent of his great disciple, Giotto, that art found beauty in reality; his "Madonna," in the Church of Santa Maria, has been long regarded as a marvel of art, and of all the "Mater Dolorosas" of Christianity, Ruskin does not hesitate to pronounce his at Assisi the noblest.

Cincinnatus, Lucius Quintus, 520-438 B.C. Roman patriot and dictator; elected consul while cultivating a farm, having lost his property; conquered the Æqui; twice chosen dictator, and at the expiration of each term of office, he returned to the plow.

Cinq-Mars (*sank-mar'*), **Henri, Marquis de,** 1620-1642. A French courtier, a favorite of Louis XIII.; a man of handsome figure and fascinating manners; died on the scaffold for conspiring with his friend De Thou against Richelieu.

Clarke, Adam, 1762-1832. An English theologian; celebrated for his "Commentary on the Bible."

Claude, Jean, 1619-1687. A French Protestant controversial divine; a powerful antagonist of Bossuet and other Catholic writers.

Claude Lorrain, 1600-1682. A great landscape painter; born in Lorraine, of poor parents; went to Rome; became servant and color-grinder to Tassi, who instructed him in his art; by assiduous study of nature in all her aspects attained to fame; was eminent in his treatment of aerial perspective, and an artist whom it was Turner's ambition to rival.

Claudius I., Tiberius Drusus, 10 B.C.-54 A.D. Surnamed **Germanicus;** brother of Tiberius; emperor of Rome from 41 to 54; born at Lyons; raised by soldiers to the imperial throne, a post which he filled with honor to himself and benefit to the state. Agrippina had him poisoned to make way for her son Nero.

Clay, Henry, 1777-1852. American statesman and orator; "The Great Pacificator;" born in Virginia; removed to Kentucky, 1797; practiced law; elected to Kentucky legislature in 1804, and two years later chosen to fill a short term in the United States Senate; re-elected to the Senate, 1809, and to the House of Representatives, 1811, of which body he was made speaker; re-elected speaker, 1813; signed treaty of Ghent, 1815; re-elected speaker four times; in 1824, he was one of four candidates for the presidency; when the election devolved on the House, his influence decided the contest in favor of Jackson; a bloodless duel between Clay and Randolph, in 1826, was the result of charges against Clay growing out of this election; re-elected to the Senate in 1831 for six years; in 1832, defeated for the presidency as the candidate of the anti-Jackson party; again elected to the Senate, 1836, but resigned, 1842; Whig candidate for the presidency in 1844; re-elected senator, 1848. To Clay is due the credit for the "Missouri Compromise," believed to have postponed for ten years the Civil War.

Clemens, Alexandrinus. Flourished second and third century. One of the Greek fathers of the church; had Origen for pupil; brought up in Greek philosophy; converted in manhood to Christianity; his "Stromata," or "Miscellanies," contain facts and quotations found nowhere else.

Cleopatra (*kle-o-pay'tra*), 69-30 B.C. Daughter of Ptolemy Auletus, and Queen of Egypt, notorious for her beauty and licentiousness. She captivated Julius Cæsar when but seventeen, and bore him a son. After his death she persuaded Marc Antony to repudiate his wife Octavia, and bore him several children. After the defeat of Antony at Actium, she despaired of making terms with Augustus, and put an end to her life by permitting an asp to bite her.

Cleveland, Grover, 1837- . . . . An American statesman; twice president of the United States; born in Caldwell, Essex county, N. J.; son of a Presbyterian clergyman. He settled in Buffalo and studied law, and in 1863 became assistant district attorney of Erie county, N. Y. After becoming in succession sheriff and mayor of Buffalo, he was chosen governor of New York in 1882. In 1884 he received the Democratic nomination for the presidency, and was elected, defeating James G. Blaine. He was renominated in June, 1888, but was defeated by Benjamin Harrison, November 6 following. After a successful law practice of four years he was again nominated by the Democratic National Convention of 1892, and elected by very large majorities. Some of the measures of his administration were: The settlement of the Venezuelan boundary question with Great Britain; the consolidating of post offices in large centers so as to increase the scope of the civil service rules; and most notably the conclusion in January, 1897, of a general arbitration treaty with Great Britain, which, however, was rejected by the Senate. He married Frances Folsom in June, 1886.

Clinton, De Witt, 1769-1828. An American lawyer and statesman; born in Little Britain, N. Y. Was United States Senator from New York; candidate for president; was the chief originator of the Erie canal; died in Albany, N. Y.

Clinton, Sir Henry, 1738?-1795. A British general; was sent in 1775, with the rank of Major-General, to America, where he distinguished himself in the battle of Bunker Hill. He defeated the Americans at Long Island, but had to evacuate Philadelphia to General Washington. In 1782 he returned to England. He died in Gibraltar.

Clive, Robert, Lord, 1725-1774. An English general who rose from ensign through his gallantry and talents to the viceroyalty of India. He distinguished himself by winning several victories from the French in 1751, and in 1757 routed Suraj-ad-Dowlah with an army of fifty thousand, at the head of an English force of only three thousand. Toward the close of his life he became insane.

Clootz, Anacharsis, 1755-1794. Baron Jean Baptiste de Clootz; a French Revolutionary; born at Cleves; was one of the founders of the worship of Reason, and styled himself the "Orator of the human race"; was guillotined under protest in the name of the human race.

Clovis. The name of three kings of France. **Clovis I.,** son and successor of Childeric I.; king of the Franks; born 467; died 511; he was the real founder of the French monarchy; driving the Romans from Gallia, and defeating the Alemanni, he married the Christian princess Clotilda, of the house of Burgundy, and soon after embraced Christianity with three thousand of his subjects. On his death his kingdom was divided among his four sons. **Clovis III.,** born 657; reigned as a child five years, under the tutelage of Pepin d'Heristal, mayor of the palace; died 695.

Cobb, Howell, 1815-1868. An American statesman; born in Georgia. He represented Georgia in the lower house of Congress, and was elected Speaker in 1849; was Governor of his state, and Secretary of the Treasury under President Buchanan; resigned when Georgia seceded; was president of the Confederate Congress and a Brigadier-General in the Confederate army.

Cobden, Richard, 1804-1865. A great English political economist and the Apostle of Free Trade; born near Midhurst, Sussex; on the formation of the Corn Law League in 1838, gave himself heart and soul to the abolition of the Corn Laws; became member of Parliament; on the conversion of Sir Robert Peel to Free Trade principles saw these laws abolished in 1846; for his services in this cause he received the homage of his country as well as of Continental nations, but refused all civic honors.

Coddington, William, 1601-1678. The founder of the colony of Rhode Island; born in England; removed in 1638 to Aquidneck, or Rhode Island, where he founded a colony to be governed "by the laws of the Lord Jesus Christ." It was soon found necessary to abandon this vague scheme; in 1640 he himself was chosen governor, and again in 1674 and 1675.

Coke, Sir Edward, 1551-1634. A great English jurist and author of law books.

Colbert (*kohl'bair*), **Jean Baptiste, Marquis de Seignelay,** 1619-1683. A French peasant, who became Superintendent of Finance, Minister of Marine, on recommendation of Mazzarin. **Colbert, Jean Baptiste, 2d,** his son, 1651-1690, succeeded him as Minister of Marine, and raised the French navy to its greatest efficiency.

Colburn, Warren, 1793-1833. A distinguished American mathematician; born in Massachusetts. His "First Lessons in Intellectual Arithmetic" was immensely popular in America and England.

Cole, Thomas, 1801-1848. An American landscape painter; born in Lancashire, England. He painted "The Voyage of Life," showing childhood, youth, manhood, and old age. Very popular and well known through engravings. He died in Catskill, N. Y.

Colfax, Schuyler, 1823-1885. An American statesman; grandson of Gen. Wm. Colfax, commander of Washington's Life Guards; born in New York city. Removing to Indiana, he was elected to the lower house of Congress, became Speaker in 1863, and was elected Vice-President on the ticket with General Grant, 1868.

Coligny (*ko-le'ne*), **Gaspard de,** 1517-1572. French admiral; born at Chatillon; a leader of the Huguenots; on St. Bartholomew's Eve he fell the first victim to the conspiracy.

Collier, Jeremy, 1650-1726. An English divine; refused to take oath at the Revolution; was imprisoned for advocating the rights of the Stuarts; wrote with effect against "The Profaneness and Immorality of the Stage," as well as an "Ecclesiastical History of Great Britain," and a translation of the "Meditations of Marcus Aurelius."

Collyer, Robert, 1823- . . . . An American clergyman; born in Keighley, Yorkshire, England. He came to the United States in 1849, being then a Wesleyan preacher and a blacksmith, but became a Unitarian and preached some years in Chicago, where he founded Unity Church in 1860. He was made pastor of the Church of the Messiah, New York city, in September, 1879, and pastor emeritus in 1896.

Colt, Samuel, 1814-1862. An American inventor; born in Hartford, Conn. He perfected a revolver and patented it in 1835. Its great success led to the erection by him at Hartford of one of the most extensive weapon factories in the world. He died in Hartford.

Columba, Saint, 521-597. A native of Ireland. About 563 he landed in the island of Hy, now called Iona, and founded his church; traversed the whole of Northern Scotland, preaching the Christian faith and founding monasteries; the Columban Church was in some points of doctrine and ceremonial opposed to that of Rome, to which it owed no allegiance. He died in Iona.

Columbus, Christopher (It.: Cristoforo Colombo; Sp.: Cristoval Colon), 1436-1506. Genoese navigator; became a sailor at fourteen; studied mathematics at the University of Pavia; removed to Lisbon at the age of thirty; was employed in several expeditions to the west coast of Africa; meditated reaching India by a western route, and unsuccessfully solicited the aid of John II. of Portugal; but finally Ferdinand and Isabella of Spain furnished him two small vessels, and another was added by the efforts of friends; with one hundred and twenty men he set sail from Palos, August 3, 1492, and discovered the island of San Salvador, October 12 of same year; supposing that he had reached India, he called the natives Indians; after visiting Cuba and Hayti, he returned to Spain, where he was received triumphantly; in 1493 he again sailed across the Atlantic, this time with seventeen ships, and discovered Jamaica and Porto Rico; in 1498 he made his third voyage, with six vessels, discovering the mainland at the mouth of the Orinoco; in 1499, complaints having been made to the court of the conduct of Columbus at Hispaniola, he was carried to Spain in chains by Francisco de Bobadilla; Columbus's last voyage to America was made in 1502, to Honduras; he died neglected.

Comenius, John Amos, 1592-1670. A Moravian educational reformer; his two most famous books are his "Janua Linguarum" and his "Orbis Sensualium Pictus."

Comte (*komt*), **Isidore Auguste Marie Francois Xavier,** 1798-1857. A French philosopher; born in Montpellier. He invented a religion which consists in referring the whole harmony of existence to, and concentrating its essence in, one great Being, whom he termed Humanity. He died in Paris.

Conde (*kon'da*). The name of a French family, the younger branch of the Bourbons, who took their name from the town of Conde, Department of Nord. The greatest of these was Louis, Prince of Conde, born in 1621, who defeated William of Orange, afterward William the Third, of England, at Senef in 1674, and died in 1686.

Condillac (*kon-de-yak'*), **Etienne Bonnot,** 1715-1780. A French philosopher; born at Grenoble; commenced as a disciple of Locke, but went further; he lived as a recluse, and had Rousseau and Diderot for intimate friends.

Condorcet (*kon-dor-say'*), **Marquis de,** 1743-1794. A French mathematician and philosopher; his works are voluminous, and the best known is his "Exquisse du Progres de l'Esprit Humain"; he was not an original thinker, but a clear expositor.

Confucius, or **Kong-Foo-Tse,** 551-478 B. C. Chinese philosopher; the son of a soldier, he was raised to the rank of mandarin at nineteen; commenced public teaching at twenty-two; became, in 499 B. C., minister of crime, and soon after retired from public life, devoting his time to study, travel, and the dissemination of his doctrines. The philosophy of Confucius relates to the present life only; he placed great importance upon the outward forms of politeness, being the first to enunciate, in substance, the golden rule; his influence has been enormous, his teachings affecting two thirds of humanity for twenty-three centuries.

Conger, Edwin Hurd, 1843- . . . . An American diplomatist; born in Knox county, Illinois. He was elected to Congress in 1884 and twice re-elected, as a Republican. In 1890 he was appointed Minister to Brazil, serving four years. In 1897 he was again appointed to that post and, in the following year, was transferred to China. He was at his post throughout the Chinese crisis of 1900, in Pekin, being imprisoned with his family and the entire diplomatic corps in the British legation compound from June 20 to August 15. He narrowly escaped slaughter at the hands of the Boxers.

Conkling, Roscoe, 1829-1888. An American legislator; born in Albany, N. Y.; sat in Congress as a Republican, and was elected to the United States Senate. He became an influential member of his party; in 1876 he received ninety-three votes for the presidential nomination, and in 1880, by his support of Grant and his personal opposition to Blaine, divided the Republicans into two sections. In 1881 he and his colleague, Thomas C. Platt, suddenly resigned from the Senate. Conkling afterward practiced law in New York city.

Constable, John, 1776-1837. An eminent landscape painter; born in Suffolk, England; his works were more generously appreciated in France than in his own country, where they had to stand comparison with those of Turner; enormous prices have been given of late for his best pictures; some of his best works adorn the walls of the National Gallery.

Constant, Benjamin, 1845- . . . . A highly popular French painter of the Realistic school; born at Paris; his first picture was "Hamlet and the King"; afterwards he took chiefly to Oriental subjects, which afforded the best scope for his talent; occupies a high place in the modern French school.

Constant de Rebecque, Henry Benjamin de, 1760-1830. A French politician, of liberal constitutional principles; born at Lausanne, of Huguenot parents; was expelled from France in 1802, along with Mme. de Stael, for denouncing the military ascendency of Napoleon; translated Schiller's "Wallenstein"; he was a supporter of Louis Philippe, and a rationalist in religion, and declared himself opposed to the supernatural element in all religions.

Constantine I. (the Great), 272-337. Emperor of Rome; embraced Christianity, and transferred his court from Rome to Byzantium, thenceforth called Constantinople.

Cook, Joseph, 1838-1901. An American lecturer and author; born in Ticonderoga, N. Y. In 1873 he began a series of "Monday Lectures" in Boston, which, endeavoring to harmonize science and religion, and discussing social and political questions, became very popular; and in 1880 he began an extended lecturing tour around the world.

Cooper, Peter, manufacturer and philanthropist; born in New York city, Feb. 12, 1791; apprenticed to a carriage maker; engaged in furniture manufacture; mover in laying the Atlantic cable; took great interest in education; founded Cooper Institute; died April 4, 1883.

Cope, Edward Drinker, 1840-1897. An American naturalist and comparative anatomist; born in Philadelphia. He received the Bigsby gold medal of the Geological Society of London in 1879, in recognition of his services in the field of vertebrate palæontology.

Copernicus (Kopernik), Nicholas, 1473-1543. German astronomer; father of modern astronomy; disproved the Ptolemaic theory; in his great work, "The Revolution of the Celestial Orbs," the first copy of which was handed to him on the day of his death, he demonstrated that the sun is the center of the system.

Copley, John Singleton, 1737-1815. American portrait and historical painter; born in Boston; painted Washington's portrait at the age of eighteen; went to England in 1776; painted portraits of the king and the queen; began the historical works on which his fame chiefly rests, perhaps the most widely known of which is the "Death of Chatham," now in the National Gallery, London.

Coquelin (*kok-lan'*), **Benoit Constant,** 1841- . . . . A French actor; born in Boulogne; made his debut at the Theatre Francais, Dec. 7, 1860. For over a quarter of a century he played there with unbroken success. He appeared in 1887 in London, in 1888 in South America and the United States.

Corday (*kor-day'*) **d'Armans, Charlotte,** 1768-1793. Granddaughter of the dramatist Corneille; born in Normandy, France; stung to patriotic desperation by the atrocities of Marat, she obtained access to his house by a pretense, and while in the act of handing him a false list of suspects she stabbed him to the heart. She was guillotined, preserving her fortitude to the last.

Cornelius, Peter von, 1783-1867. A German painter; born in Duesseldorf. He studied the great masters, especially Raphael. In 1811 he went to Rome, where, in conjunction with Overbeck, Veit, and other associates, he may be said to have founded a new school of German art, and revived fresco-painting in imitation of Michael Angelo and Raphael. In 1841 he was invited to Berlin by Frederick William IV., who intrusted him with the painting of the royal mausoleum or Campo Santo. He died in Berlin.

Cornell, Ezra, 1807-1874. An American philanthropist; born in Westchester Landing, N. Y. He accumulated a large fortune and is best known as the founder of Cornell University. He began life as a mechanic and miller at Ithaca, N. Y., and subsequently became a contractor for the erection of telegraph lines. He died in Ithaca.

Cornwallis, Lord, 1738-1805. An English general and statesman; saw service in the Seven Years' and the American wars; besieged in the latter at Yorktown, was obliged to capitulate; became Governor-General of India, and forced Tippoo Sahib to submit to humiliating terms; as Lord-Lieutenant of Ireland crushed the rebellion of 1798; re-appointed Governor-General of India; died there.

Corot (*ko-ro'*), **Jean Baptiste Camille,** 1796-1875. French painter.

Correg'gio, Antonio Allegri da, 1494-1534. Italian painter; known as "the divine"; his work excels in harmony, grace, and sweetness of color and form,

Cortez, Hernando, 1485-1547. Spanish conqueror of Mexico.

Corwin, Thomas, 1794-1865. An American statesman and orator; born in Bourbon county, Ky. He was successively a member of Congress, governor of Ohio, United States Senator, Secretary of the Treasury, member of Congress, and United States Minister to Mexico. He died in Washington, D. C.

Cotta, Johann Friedrich Baron von, 1764-1832. A German bookseller. He was the publisher for many great writers in Germany, including Goethe, Schiller, the Humboldts, and others.

Coues, Elliott, 1842-1899. An American naturalist; born in Portsmouth, N. H. He was connected with the Smithsonian Institution, and was author of "Key to North American Birds," etc.

Cousin, (*coo-zan'*), **Victor,** 1792-1867. A French philosopher; born in Paris; founder of an eclectic school; had a considerable following; retired from public life in 1848, and died at Cannes; he left a number of philosophic works behind him, the best known among us being "Discourses on the True, the Beautiful, and the Good."

Coverdale, Miles, 1467-1568. An English prelate, and one of the earliest reformers. He published the first entire English Bible, 1535.

Cowper, William, 1731-1800. A popular English poet; born at Great Berkhampstead, Hertford, of noble lineage; his greatest poem, "The Task."

Cox, Kenyon, 1856- . . . . An American painter; born in Warren, O.; he studied in Paris under Duran and Gerome, settling in New York in 1883 as a portrait and figure artist. He did two decorations in the Library of Congress, and similar works elsewhere.

Cox, Palmer, 1840- . . . . An American artist and writer for young people; born in Granby, Quebec. Since 1875 his home has been in New York. He is best known as the originator of the "Brownies," a series of funny pictures and verse for children.

Cox, Samuel Sullivan, 1824-1889. An American statesman and author; born in Zanesville, O.; he served in Congress, and became minister to Turkey; he died in New York; a statue was erected to his memory in New York city by the letter carriers, whose interests he had advocated in Congress.

Cranmer, Thomas, 1489-1556. Archbishop of Canterbury; born in Nottinghamshire; recommended himself to Henry VIII. by favoring his divorce, writing in defense of it, and, pleading for it before the Pope; a zealous promoter of the Reformation. By Henry's will he was appointed one of the council of regency to Edward VI. On the accession of Mary, he was committed to the Tower, along with Latimer and Ridley. He suffered martyrdom as his fellow-reformers had done, opposite Baliol College, Oxford.

Crawford, Thomas, 1814-1857. An American sculptor; born in New York; died in London. Among his works are the bronze statue of Beethoven in Boston Music Hall, an equestrian statue of General Washington at the Capitol, Richmond, Va., and a number of marble and bronze pieces in the Capitol, Washington, D. C.

Crichton (*kri'-ton*), **James,** 1560-1582. An accomplished Scotchman; assassinated at Mantua. He was surnamed Admirable, from his great natural gifts and accomplishments.

Crittenden, John Jordan, 1787-1863. An American legislator; born in Woodford county, Ky.; he was elected to the United States Senate. He resigned but subsequently was re-elected twice. In 1848 he became governor of Kentucky. Through his influence the state remained loyal to the Union in the Civil War. He died near Frankfort, Ky.

Crockett, David, 1786-1836. An American pioneer, hunter, politician, and humorist; born in Limestone, Tenn. He was member of Congress from Tennessee; served in the Texan War; and was one of the eccentric characters of the Southwest; he was killed at Fort Alamo, San Antonio, Texas.

Crœsus (*kre'-sus*), 590-548 B.C. The last king of Lydia; famed for his immense riches; assassinated by order of Cambyses, King of Persia, son of Cyrus, by whom Crœsus was defeated and captured.

Cromwell, Oliver, 1599-1659. English general and leader of the political and religious revolution in England; entered the Parliamentary army, in 1642, as captain of cavalry; rapidly promoted, and led left wing at Marston Moor, 1644; commanded right wing at Naseby, 1645, and became leader of the Independents; transferred the custody of the king from Parliament to the army, 1647; won the battle of Preston, 1648; signed the death warrant of Charles I., 1649; made commander-in-chief, 1650, and defeated the Scotch at Dunbar and Charles at Worcester; dissolved Parliament in 1653, and was, in 1654, proclaimed by the army Lord Protector of the Commonwealth.

Cronje (*kron'ya*), **Piet,** 1835- . . . . A Boer military commander; born near Pretoria in 1835; he has been prominent in all the history of the South African Republic. Bred to farm life, he entered politics, refused office under British annexation, commanded a brigade in the war of 1880-1881, became a member of the Transvaal executive government, and captured Sir John Willoughby and his force after the Jameson raid of 1896. During the war with England in 1899-1900, Cronje rose to the military leadership of the Boers, and held out heroically with an inferior force till forced to surrender to Lord Roberts at Klip River, near Paardeberg, Orange Free State. He was exiled to St. Helena in May, 1900, being released at the end of the war.

Crookes, Sir William, 1832- . . . . An English physicist and chemist; born in London; he invented the radiometer and the otheoscope, and announced his discovery of the fourth or ultra-gaseous state of matter; he is recognized as an expert on sanitary matters.

Crosby, Howard, 1826-1891. An American clergyman and scholar; born in New York city. In 1863 he was made pastor of the Fourth Avenue Presbyterian Church in New York city; was in 1873 a delegate to the first Presbyterian General Council, held in Edinburgh. Dr. Crosby was one of the founders and president of the Society for the Prevention of Crime.

Cruden, Alexander, 1701-1770. A Scotch writer; born in Aberdeen. His "Concordance to the Old and New Testaments" is the familiar authority on the subject. He died in London.

Cruikshank, George, 1792-1878. An English pictorial satirist; born in London; his illustrations for Hone's political squibs and pamphlets, and especially those dealing with the Queen Caroline trial, attracted much attention; he illustrated a number of Dickens's works. In his late years he devoted himself to oil-painting.

Cumberland, William Augustus, Duke of, 1721-1765. Second son of George II.; was defeated at Fontenoy by the French in 1745; defeated the Pretender next year at Culloden; earned the title of "The Butcher" by his cruelties afterwards; was beaten in all his battles except this one.

Cunard, Sir Samuel, 1787-1865. Founder of an English steamship line; born in Halifax, Nova Scotia, where his father, a Philadelphia merchant, had settled. Becoming early a successful merchant and ship owner, he went to England in 1838, joined with George Burns, Glasgow, and David M'Iver, Liverpool, in founding the British and North American Royal Mail Steam Packet Company, and obtained a contract from the British government for the mail service between Liverpool and Halifax, Boston, and Quebec. The first passage was that of the *Britannia* in 1840. From its small but successful beginning, Cunard's undertaking soon developed into one of the vastest of private commercial concerns. He died in London.

Cushing, Caleb, 1800-1879. An American jurist, statesman, and diplomatist; born in Salisbury, Mass. He was United States commissioner to China; Attorney-General; counsel before the Geneva Arbitration Tribunal; minister to Spain. He died in Newburyport, Mass.

Cushman, Charlotte Saunders, 1816-1876. An American actress; born in Boston; appeared first in opera in 1834, and as "Lady Macbeth" in 1835. In 1844 she accompanied Macready on a tour throughout the Northern states and afterward appeared in London. Miss Cushman retired from the stage in 1875, and died in Boston.

Custer, George Armstrong, 1839-1876. American soldier; born in New Rumley, O.; served with distinction during the Civil War. He afterward had various cavalry commands in the West, and several times defeated hostile Indians. With a force of 1,100 men, he attacked a body of Sioux, afterward found to number some 9,000, encamped on the Little Big Horn, in Montana, and he and his entire command were destroyed.

Cuvier, Georges C. L. F., Baron, 1769-1832. French naturalist; the greatest of zoologists and founder of comparative anatomy.

Cyrus, surnamed the **Great,** or the **Elder,** 560-529 B. C. Founder of the Persian empire; began his conquests by overthrowing his grandfather Astyages, king of the Medes; subdued Crœsus, king of Lydia; laid siege to Babylon and took it, and finished by being master of all western Asia.

Cyrus, surnamed the **Younger,** . . . . -401 B.C. Second son of Darius II.; conspired against his brother Artaxerxes Mnemon, was sentenced to death, pardoned, and restored to his satrapy in Asia Minor; conspired anew, raised a large army, including Greek mercenaries, marched against his brother, and was slain at Cunaxa, of which last enterprise and its fate an account is given in the "Anabasis" of Xenophon.

Czerny (*zair'ne*), **Carl,** 1791-1857. An Austrian pianist and musical composer; born in Vienna. Among his pupils were Liszt, Thalberg, and other distinguished musicians.

Daguerre (*da-gair'*), **Louis Jacques Mande,** 1789-1851. French artist; inventor of the daguerreotype.

Dahlgren, John Adolphe, 1809-1870. An American naval officer; born in Philadelphia, Pa.; rose through the grades to the rank of rear-admiral. He rendered efficient service in suppressing blockade-running during the Civil War. He invented the Dahlgren gun; died in Washington, D. C.

Dallas, George Mifflin, 1792-1864. Born in Pennsylvania; elected to the U. S. Senate, 1831; Attorney-General of Pennsylvania, 1835; appointed minister to Russia, 1837, and in 1844 elected Vice-President of the U. S. Sent as minister to Great Britain, 1856.

Dalton, John Call, 1825-1889. An American physiologist; born in Chelmsford, Mass. He was successively Professor of Physiology at the University of Buffalo, at the Vermont Medical School, at the Long Island College Hospital, and at the New York College of Physicians and Surgeons. He served as an army surgeon throughout the Civil War. Died in New York city.

Dana, Charles Anderson, 1819-1897. American journalist; born in Hinsdale, N. H. In 1847 he became managing editor of New York *Tribune* with which he remained until 1861. From 1862 to 1865 he was in the service of the United States government, during the last two years as Assistant Secretary of War under President Lincoln. In 1867 Mr. Dana, with several associates, purchased the New York *Sun*, which achieved great success under his editorship.

Dana, James Dwight, 1813-1895. An American scientist; born in Utica, N. Y. His researches into geology made him famous. He died in New Haven.

Dan'dolo, Enrico, 1105-1205. Doge of Venice, to which high office he was chosen when in his eighty-seventh year. He carried on the war with the Pisans and undertook, with the Crusaders, in 1203, the siege of Constantinople, at which he greatly distinguished himself. He was created despot of Rumania.

Danton (*don'-ton*), **George Jacques,** 1759-1794. A French revolutionist. He played a very important part during the first years of the French Revolution. Robespierre hated him, and succeeded in bringing about his downfall. Condemned to death as an accomplice in a conspiracy for the restoration of monarchy.

Darius I. (surnamed **Hystaspis**), ... -485. King of Persia. He was wise and successful in his civil policy, but was defeated in an invasion of Scythia, and also at Marathon, Greece. **Darius II.** (Nothus), a natural son of Artaxerxes Longimanus; deposed the usurper Sogdianus, and became king of Persia, 424 B.C.; died 405. **Darius III.,** called Codomannus, the last of the ancient Persian kings, succeeded Arses 336 B.C. Defeated by Alexander the Great at Issus and Arbela. Darius was assassinated by Bessus, one of his satraps, while escaping from the battlefield. Statira, daughter of Darius, became one of the wives of Alexander.

Darley, Felix Octavius Carr, 1822-1888. An American artist; born in Philadelphia. His illustrations of literary masterpieces gave pleasure to thousands, and made him famous. He died in Claymont, Del.

Darling, Grace, 1815-1842. A young maiden, daughter of the lighthouse keeper of one of the Farne Islands, who with her father, amid great peril, saved the lives of nine people from the wreck of the *Forfarshire*, on September 7, 1838.

Darnley, Henry Stuart, Lord, 1545-1567. A Scottish noble, of the royal blood of England and Scotland; became the second husband of Mary, Queen of Scots, 1565. His open profligacy alienated her affections, and it is generally believed she connived at his assassination, which was planned and carried out by the Earl of Bothwell.

Darwin, Charles Robert, 1809-1882. English naturalist; originator of the theory of evolution; in his "Origin of Species by Means of Natural Selection," published 1859, he propounds the theory that all forms of life have been produced by a series of gradual changes in natural descent; in his "Descent of Man," he infers that "man is descended from a hairy quadruped furnished with a tail and pointed ears, probably arboreal in its habits."

Darwin, Erasmus, 1731-1802. English physician and poet.

David, King of Israel, eleventh century, B.C. Born in Bethlehem; slew Goliath with a stone and a sling; was anointed by Samuel; succeeded Saul as king; conquered the Philistines; set up his throne in Jerusalem, and reigned thirty-three years; suffered much from his sons, and was succeeded by Solomon.

David, Felicien, 1810-1876. A French composer; born at Vaucluse; author, among other compositions, of "The Desert," a production which achieved an instant and complete triumph.

David, Jacques Louis, 1748-1825. Founder of the modern French school of painting; born in Paris. In the Revolution he was a violent Jacobin and wholly devoted to Robespierre. Several of the scenes of the Revolution supplied subjects for his brush. He was appointed first painter to Napoleon about 1804; and after the second restoration of Louis XVIII. he was included in the decree which banished all regicides from France, when he retired to Brussels, where he died.

David, Pierre Jean, 1789-1856. A French sculptor; born in Angers (hence commonly called David d'Angers). He executed a great number of medallions, busts, and statues of celebrated persons of all countries, among whom we may mention Washington and Lafayette. He died in Paris.

Davies, Charles, 1798-1876. An American mathematician; born in Washington, Conn. He was educated at the United States Military Academy and was appointed Professor of Mathematics there in 1828. He held the same post subsequently at Columbia College and in the University of New York. He died in Fishkill Landing, N. Y.

Davis, David, 1815-1886. An American jurist; born in Cecil county, Md.; he was appointed an Associate Justice of the Supreme Court of the United States. He resigned in 1877 to enter the United States Senate, of which he became president *pro tem.* in 1881, and retired in 1883. He died in Bloomington, Ill.

Davis, Jefferson, 1808-1889. American statesman and president of the Confederacy; born in Kentucky; graduate of West Point; served in Black Hawk and Mexican wars; elected to United States Senate from Mississippi, 1847; Secretary of War, 1853-1857; re-elected Senator, 1857; inaugurated provisional president of the Confederate States, 1861, and elected for six years, 1862; imprisoned in Fortress Monroe for two years after the fall of Richmond.

Davitt, Michael, 1846- . . . . Founder of the Irish Land League; born near Straid, County Mayo, Ireland; supplied with funds from the United States, he began an anti-landlord crusade in Ireland, which culminated in the foundation of the Irish Land League. Davitt was henceforward in frequent collision with the government, and from February, 1881, to May, 1882, was imprisoned in Portland. Mr. Davitt was elected to the British Parliament in 1892 and 1895.

Davout, (*day-voo'*) **Louis Nicholas,** 1770-1823. A Marshal of France. He studied with Napoleon at Brienne, and accompanied Napoleon in his Italian campaigns and in his expedition to Egypt. In 1804 he was made a marshal of the empire. The victories of Ulm and Austerlitz were mainly due to him. After the battle of Waterloo he lived in retirement till 1819, when he took his seat in the Chamber of Peers. He died in Paris.

Davy, Sir Humphry, 1778-1829. English chemist, inventor of the safety lamp.

Decatur, Stephen, 1779-1820. American naval commander; defeated the Algerines; killed in a duel.

De Haas, Maurice Frederick Hendrick, 1832-1895. An American marine painter; born in Rotterdam; in 1857 he was made artist to the Dutch navy, and in 1859 he went to New York, where he lived till his death. His best known American work is "Farragut Passing the Forts."

De Kalb, John, Baron, 1732-1780. German general; accompanied Lafayette to America, and served under Washington; killed at battle of Camden.

Delacroix (*d'lah-krwaw'*), **Eugene,** 1799-1863. A French painter, chief of the Romantic school; born near Paris. In 1857 he was chosen by the Institute to fill the place of Delaroche. He was an artist of great versatility.

Delaroche (*d'lah-rosh'*), **Hippolyte** (familiarly styled Paul), 1797-1856. A French painter; born in Paris His signal merits consist in correct drawing, brilliant and harmonious color, and great distinctness and perspicuity in treatment, rendering the story of his pictures at once intelligible. He died in Paris.

Delaware, or Delawarr, Thomas West, ... 1618. An American colonial governor; born in England. He succeeded his father as third Lord Delaware in 1602 and some years later was appointed governor of Virginia.

Del Sarto, Andrea Vanucchi, 1486-1531. Florentine painter.

Democritus, 460-361 B. C. "The laughing philosopher of Greece."

De Morgan, Augustus, 1806-1871. An eminent English mathematician; born in Madura, South India; wrote treatises on almost every department of mathematics, on arithmetic, algebra, trigonometry, differential and integral calculus, the last pronounced to be "the most complete treatise on the subject ever produced in England."

Demosthenes, 385?-332 B. C. Athenian orator; conquered an impediment in his speech, and by perseverance and determination became the greatest of orators; opposed Philip of Macedon, against whom he delivered his "Philippics"; condemned to death by Antipater he committed suicide by poison.

Denis (*den-ee'*), **Saint,** fl. 3d century. The first bishop of Paris; martyred about 272 in the Valerian persecution. St. Denis is the tutelary saint of France.

Derby, Edward Geoffrey Smith-Stanley, 14th Earl of, 1799-1869. A distinguished orator, statesman and publicist, the head of the ancient house of Stanley, descended from the blood-royal of England and Scotland. He was for years the Parliamentary leader of the Conservatives. Succeeded Earl Russell as Prime Minister, 1852.

Descartes (*day-kahrt'*), **Rene,** 1596-1650. French philosopher and mathematician; represented the revolt against scholasticism, re-examining all questions and discarding the authority of great names; "I think, therefore I am."

Desmoulins (*day-moo-lahn'*), **Benoit Camille,** 1762-1794. A French revolutionist. In 1793 he gave his vote for the death of the king. Having become closely connected with Danton and the party of opposition to Robespierre, and inveighing against the reign of blood and terror, he was arrested on the order of the latter, tried and executed.

De Soto, Hernando, 1500-1542. A Spanish explorer; served under Pizarro in Peru, and afterward commanded an expedition which landed on the Florida coast, and from there marched inland, discovering the Mississippi river, on the banks of which he died of fever.

Dessalines (*day-sa-leen'*), **Jean Jacques,** 1730?-1806. The first emperor of Hayti, an African negro; assassinated by Christopher and Petion; was the favorite officer and succeeded Toussaint l'Ouverture in the bloody Dominican insurrection, proclaiming himself emperor in 1804.

De Wet, Christian, 1860?- . . . . A Boer military officer; born in Dewetsdorf, Orange Free State (now Orange River State); was bred a farmer and made a small fortune; became a member of the Volksraad. Though practically without military experience, he served ably in the Boer-British War of 1899-1900, attaining the rank of general and outwitting the pursuit of Kitchener and Roberts in the summer of 1900, and of the former in the early part of 1901. His stand at Sanna's Post was highly praised by military experts.

Dewey, George, 1837- . . . . An American naval officer; born in Montpelier, Vt.; was appointed a cadet at Annapolis, in the class which graduated in 1858; when the Civil War broke out was commissioned a lieutenant and assigned to the *Mississippi* His first serious taste of war was when the West Gulf squadron, early in 1862, forced a passage up the Mississippi river ahead of Farragut. In 1896 he was promoted to Commodore, and at the beginning of 1898 was given command of the Asiatic squadron; with his squadron he left Mirs bay, China, April 27, 1898, with orders to "capture or destroy the Spanish squadron," which was then supposed to be in Manila bay, under command of Admiral Montojo. The squadron entered the channel of Manila at 11.30 p. m., Saturday, April 30, and early on Sunday morning, May 1, sank, burned, or captured all the ships of the Spanish squadron in the bay, silenced and destroyed three land batteries, obtained complete control of the bay, so that he could take the city, the chief port of the Philippine Islands, at any time, and all without losing a single man, and having only nine slightly wounded. In recognition of this achievement, Commodore Dewey received the thanks of Congress, which awarded to him a magnificent sword, and medals to his men. As a further recognition of his achievement, Commodore Dewey was (May 7, 1898) promoted to be a Rear-Admiral, and subsequently (March 3, 1899) was made Admiral of the Navy under an act of Congress, approved March 2, 1899, restoring that rank for the especial purpose of enabling the country to adequately honor the hero of Manila bay. In 1901 he was president of the Schley Court of Inquiry, and in 1902 was appointed commander-in-chief of the united squadrons and fleets mobilized for extraordinary maneuvers.

De Witt, Jan, 1625-1672. A Dutch statesman; born at Dort; like his father, Jacob De Witt, before him, was a declared enemy of the House of Orange, and opposed the Stadtholdership, and for a time he carried the country along with him, but during a war with England his influence declined, the Orange party prevailed, and elected the young Prince of Orange, William III., Stadtholder. He and his brother Cornelius were murdered at last by the populace.

Diaz (*dee-az*), **Porfirio,** 1830- . . . . A Mexican statesman; born in Oaxaca; received a classical education at the Oaxaca Institute, and had begun studying law when the war with the United States broke out; served through that struggle in the National Guard, and on the conclusion of peace made a study of military science. On Santa Ana's accession to the dictatorship, he left the army and practiced law; but returned and bore a conspicuous part in the revolution of 1854; took the field to oppose the French troops and was taken prisoner, but made his escape; harassed Maximilian's troops till forced to surrender a second time at Oaxaca in 1865; besieged and captured Puebla in 1867, and immediately marched on Mexico city, which surrendered to him June 21. In 1872 and 1876 he led revolutions against the government, and after three severe battles occupied the capital in the latter year. In 1877 he was elected president to fill the unexpired term of the fugitive president, Lerdo. According to the "plan of Tuxtepec," which he had proclaimed, he was ineligible to succeed himself. His secretary, General Gonzales, was elected president, and General Diaz was appointed Chief Justice of the Supreme Court, and elected Governor of Oaxaca. In 1884 he was re-elected President; in 1886 his partisans secured the abolition of the law prohibiting a second consecutive presidential term, and he was thereafter continuously re-elected, his sixth term expiring Nov. 30, 1904. His government of Mexico has been an era of marvelous progress and pacification, and he is justly regarded as one of the greatest living Americans.

Diderot (*dee-dro'*), **Denis,** 1712-1784. French philosopher and novelist; chief editor of "The Encyclopædia," and librarian of Catherine of Russia.

Diemen, Anton Van, 1593-1645. A Dutch administrator; having gone to India, he speedily rose to the highest dignities; and was at length made Governor-General. Abel Tasman, whom he sent with a vessel to the South Seas in 1642, gave the name of Van Diemen's Land to the island now called Tasmania.

Diocletian (Caius Valerius Aurelius Diocletianus), 245?-313. A Roman general; proclaimed emperor by the imperial guard after the assassination of Numerianus, 284; divided the empire with Maximian, and governed Asia and Egypt. In 303, he signed an edict against the Christians.

Diogenes (*di-oj'e-neez*), 421-325 B.C. A distinguished cynic; born in Sinope, Asia Minor; died at Corinth. He spent most of his life in Athens, where he lived upon alms, and taught his philosophy from a tub.

Dioscor'ides. Flourished first century; a Greek physician; born in Cilicia; left a treatise in five books on materia medica, a work of great research, and long the standard authority on the subject.

Doel'linger, 1799-1890. A Catholic theologian; born in Bamberg, Bavaria; head of the old Catholic party in Germany; wrote extensively on theological and ecclesiastical topics; lived to a great age, and was much honored to the last.

Domenichino (*do-main-e-kee'no*), 1581-1641. A distinguished Italian painter; his true name was Donnico Zampieri. His "Communion of St. Jerome," in the Vatican, is considered among the finest works of the Masters.

Dom'inic, Saint, 1170-1221. The founder of the order of the Dominicans; born in Old Castile; died in Bologna; was canonized in 1234 by Pope Gregory IX. St. Dominic is usually considered the founder of the Inquisition, but this claim is denied, on the ground that two Cistercian monks were appointed inquisitors in 1198.

Domitian (*do-mish'yan*), 35?-96. Roman emperor; the last of the twelve Cæsars; his vanity was wounded by the non-success of his arms, and his vengeful spirit showed itself in a wholesale murder of the citizens; many conspiracies were formed against his life, and he was at length murdered by an assassin, abetted by his wife.

Donatello (properly, Donato di Betto Bardi), 1383-1466. One of the revivers of the art of sculpture in Italy; born and died in Florence.

Donizetti (*do-nid-zet'te*), **Gaetano,** 1798-1848. An eminent Italian musical composer.

Dore (*do-ray'*), **Paul Gustave,** 1833-1883. A French draughtsman and painter; born in Strasburg; he distinguished himself greatly as an illustrator of books; his illustrations of the Bible, and Milton's "Paradise Lost," are of high excellence; in later years Dore also won fame as a sculptor.

Doria (*do're-a*), **Andrea,** 1468-1560. A distinguished Genoese; he belonged to a family which gave his native city several doges and admirals, and was the ablest naval commander of the age, commanding both the French and German fleets.

Dorr, Thomas Wilson, 1805-1854. Born in Providence, R. I.; the leader of Dorr's Rebellion. He died in Providence.

Dow or **Douw, Gerard,** 1613-1675. A distinguished Dutch genre painter; born at Leyden; a pupil of Rembrandt; his works, which are very numerous, are the fruit of a devoted study of nature, and are remarkable for their delicacy and perfection of finish.

Douglas (*dug'las*). A Scotch baronial house of ancient and brilliant fame, descended from Sir James, the bosom friend of King Robert Bruce. They were long known as the "King Makers of Scotland." Archibald, Fifth Earl of Angus, surnamed "The Great," led 10,000 of his clan to the field of Flodden, 1544, and was killed with five of his sons.

Douglas, Stephen Arnold, 1813-1861. An American statesman; born in Vermont. He represented Illinois in both branches of the United States Congress, defeating Abraham Lincoln in a memorable contest for the Senate, 1859. Defeated for the regular Democratic nomination for the presidency, 1860, he was nominated by a convention of seceding Democrats, and received nearly as many popular votes as his successful competitor, Mr. Lincoln.

Douglass, Frederick, 1817-1895. An American lecturer and journalist; the son of a negro slave; born in Tuckahoe, Md. He taught himself to read and write, and was employed by the Anti-Slavery Society as one of their lecturers. In 1845 he published his autobiography, and afterwards made a successful lecturing tour in England. In 1871 he was appointed secretary of the commission to Santo Domingo; in 1872, presidential elector; and in 1877 marshal for the District of Columbia. He was commissioner of deeds for that district, 1881-1886; and United States minister to Haiti in 1890. He died in Washington, D. C.

Dow, Neal, 1804-1897. An American temperance reformer; born in Portland, Me. He was the author of the bill which prohibited the manufacture and sale of intoxicating liquors in the state of Maine, widely known as the "Maine Law." During the Civil War he was colonel of a Maine regiment and a brigadier-general of volunteers.

Dozy, Reinhart, 1820-1883. A Dutch Orientalist and historian; born in Leyden.

Draco (*dray'ko*). Flourished seventh century B.C. Was the first lawgiver of Athens. His code was published 623 B.C. The laws were severe, and popularly said to have been written in blood.

Drake, Sir Francis, 1540-1595. An English naval hero; first English circumnavigator of the globe.

Drake, Friedrich, 1805-1882. A German sculptor; born at Pyrmont; executed numerous statues and busts, among others busts of Oken, Ranke, Bismarck, and Moltke; his chief works are the "Eight Provinces of Prussia," represented by large allegorical figures, and the "Warrior crowned by Victory."

Draper, John William, 1811-1882. A chemist, scientist, and man of letters; born at Liverpool; settled in the United States; wrote on chemistry, physiology, and physics generally, as well as works of a historical character, such as the "History of Intellectual Development of Europe," and the "History of the Conflict between Science and Religion," an able book.

Dreyfus (*dri'fus*), **Alfred,** 1859- . . . . A French military officer; born in Alsace. In 1889 he became a captain. He was arrested in 1894 charged with selling military secrets to Germany and Italy. He was convicted, and on January 5, 1895, publicly degraded from his rank in the presence of five thousand troops. His sentence included life imprisonment on the Isle du Diable, off the coast of French Guiana, where he was rigidly confined till 1899, when the French Senate voted for revision of the Dreyfus case. He was accordingly brought back to France, re-tried by court martial and again convicted. The French government granted him a pardon almost immediately. He published "Five Years of My Life."

Dreyse (*dri'zeh*), **Johann Nikolaus von,** 1787-1867. A German inventor; born in Sommerda, near Erfurt, in Prussia. In 1827 he invented a muzzle-loading, and in 1836 a breech-loading, needle-gun, which was adopted in the Prussian army in 1840. In 1864 Dreyse was ennobled.

Drouet (*dru-ay'*), **Jean Baptiste,** 1763-1824. Notable king-taker, a violent Jacobin and member of the Council of the Five Hundred; was postmaster at St. Menehould when Louis XVI., attempting flight, passed through the place, and by whisper of surmise had the progress of Louis and his party arrested at Varennes, June 21, 1791, for which service he received honorable mention and due reward in money; was taken captive by the Austrians at last; perched on a rock one hundred feet high, descended one night by means of a paper kite he had constructed, but was found at the foot helpless with leg broken.

Du Chaillu (*du sha-yu'*), **Paul Belloni,** 1835-1903. A French-American explorer and writer; born in Paris. His travels in Africa, in which he discovered the gorilla and the pigmies, are detailed in "A Journey to Ashango Land" and "My Apingi Kingdom." "The Land of the Midnight Sun" deals with Norway. "The Viking Age" is a more ambitious work, intended to recreate the old Norse civilization. He also wrote many books for the young. See CHAILLU.

Duguay-Trouin (*doo-gay-troo-ahn'*), **Rene,** 1673-1742. A distinguished French admiral. He defeated the Dutch and English, and captured Rio de Janeiro in 1711.

Duguesclin (*du-gah-klan'*), **Bertrand,** 1314-1380. Constable of France, and among the ablest military commanders of the age. He twice drove the English out of nearly every point they occupied in France, although defeated and captured by Edward the Black Prince.

Duncan I. Flourished eleventh century. King of Scotland, son of Beatrix, daughter of Malcolm II., murdered by Macbeth, Thane of Cawdor.

Dunois (*doo'nwaw*), **Jean de** (Bastard of Orleans), 1402-1468. French national hero; natural son of the Duke of Orleans; defeated the English at Montargis in 1427, and assisted at the siege of Orleans in 1429; expelled the English from Normandy and Guienne, and was created Count d'Orleans.

Duns Scotus, John, 1265-1308. A learned Scotch theologian. He became professor at Oxford and Paris, and founded the school of Scotists, opposed to the Thomists, followers of St. Thomas Aquinas.

Dunstan, Saint, 900?-988. An English monk who was made Archbishop of Canterbury, and obtained great political influence, which he subsequently lost.

Dupont', Samuel Francis, 1803-1865. An American naval officer; born in Bergen Point, N. J. During the Mexican War he saw much active and gallant service on the California coast. He was promoted to Rear-Admiral in August, 1862. He greatly contributed to the organization of the naval school at Annapolis. He died in Philadelphia.

Dupleix (*doo-play'*), **Joseph,** 1697-1873. A French merchant, who rose to be governor of the French settlements in India, and received the dignity of marquis; jealousy at home, however, led to his recall, and he was left to end his days in neglect and poverty.

Duquesne (*doo-kain'*), **Abraham, Marquis,** 1610-1688. A French admiral. He successively defeated the Spaniards, Dutch, and Danes, winning a signal victory over the celebrated Dutch admiral, De Ruyter, near Catania, 1676, the latter losing his life in the battle.

Durer (*doo'rair*), **Albrecht,** 1471-1528. A German engraver and painter. He is considered the inventor of etching.

Duse (*doo'sa*), **Eleanora,** 1861- . . . . An Italian actress; born in Vigevano. She has played in all the principal countries of Europe and visited the United States. She has been twice married and divorced.

Dvorak (*dvor'zhahk*), **Antonin,** 1841- . . . . A Bohemian composer; born near Muehlhausen. Attention was first called to him by what remains his best work, a "Stabat Mater," the most modern and one of the finest settings of this hymn. He came to the United States in 1892, and became director of the National Academy of Music in New York city.

Dwight, Timothy, 1752-1817. An American theologian; grandson of Jonathan Edwards, and much esteemed in his day both as a preacher and a writer; his "Theology Explained and Defended," in five volumes, was very popular at one time, and was frequently reprinted.

Eads, James Buchanan, 1820-1887. An American engineer; born in Lawrenceburg, Ind. He early designed some useful boats for raising sunken steamers, and in 1861, when called to advise the National government, constructed within one hundred days eight ironclad steamers for use on the Mississippi and its tributaries. He afterward built a number of other ironclads and mortar-boats, which were of considerable service to the North. His steel bridge across the Mississippi at St. Louis, with its central arch embracing a clear span of 520 feet, ranks deservedly among the notable bridges of the world; his works for improving the South Pass of the Mississippi delta were successfully completed in 1875-1879; and his great plan for deepening the river as far as the mouth of the Ohio by means of jetties has been demonstrated to be entirely practicable. In 1884 he received the Albert medal of the Society of Arts, being the first American citizen to whom this honor had been awarded.

Early, Jubal Anderson, 1816-1894. An American military officer; born in Franklin county, Va.; served in the Florida and Mexican wars. During most of the years 1838-1861, he practiced law in his native state. On the outbreak of the Civil War he entered the Confederate service as a colonel. In 1864, after some successes, he was defeated by Sheridan in several battles; and, Custer having also routed him at Waynesboro, in March, 1865, he was relieved of his command a few days later. He subsequently returned to the practice of law.

Eastlake, Sir Charles Locke, 1793-1865. An English artist, and critic and historian of art; born in Plymouth. He died in Pisa, Italy.

Eck'hart, Meister, ... -1327. A German philosopher and divine, profoundly speculative and mystical; entered the Dominican order, and rapidly attained to a high position in the Church.

Eck, John, properly **Maier,** 1486-1543. A German theologian, of Swabian birth; a violent antagonist of Luther and Luther's doctrines; in his zeal went to Rome, and procured a papal bull against both; undertook at the Augsburg Diet to controvert Luther's doctrine from the Fathers, but not from the Scriptures; was present at the conferences of Worms and Regensburg.

Edison, Thomas Alva, 1847- . . . . American inventor; born in Milan, O. His first invention to be patented was a commercial stock indicator, and the proceeds of this invention, which at once came into wide use, enabled him to establish a laboratory at Newark, N. J., afterward removed to Menlo Park, and then to its present location at West Orange, N. J. From this beginning he became known to all the world as one of the greatest inventors of the nineteenth century. More than three hundred patents have been issued on his inventions; among his more important inventions may be named the phonograph, a telephone for long distance transmission, a system of duplex telegraphy (which he subsequently developed into quadruplex and sextuplex transmission), the carbon telephone transmitter, the microtasimeter, the aerophone, megaphone, the incandescent electric lamp, the kinetoscope, and a storage battery for street railway cars and automobiles. In 1878 he was made Chevalier of the Legion of Honor by the French government, a commander of the Legion in 1889, and was the recipient of the insignia of a grand officer of the Crown of Italy bestowed the same year by King Humbert.

Edward I. (Longshanks), 1239-1307. King of England; conquered Wales and Scotland. **Edward II.,** 1284-1327. Defeated by Bruce at Bannockburn; dethroned by the queen and her favorite, Roger de Mortimer, 1326; murdered the following year. **Edward III.,** 1312-1377. Son of Edward II.; proclaimed king in 1327; executed Mortimer, and imprisoned the queen-mother; carried on war with France and won the great victory of Crecy. **Edward IV.,** 1441-1483. **Edward V.,** 1470-1483. Ascended the throne at the age of thirteen, assassinated two months later. **Edward VI.,** 1537-1553.

Edward, Prince of Wales (the Black Prince), 1330-1376. Son of Edward III.; participated in invasion of France commanding the main body of the English at Crecy; won the battle of Poictiers.

Edwards, Jonathan, 1703-1758. A celebrated divine; born at East Windsor, Conn.; was elected to the presidency of Princeton College; wrote an acute and original work, "The Freedom of the Will," a masterpiece of cogent reasoning; has been called the "Spinoza of Calvinism."

Edwin, ... -633. King of Northumbria in the sixth century; through the influence of his wife Ethelburga, Christianity was introduced into England by St. Augustine; founded Edinburgh.

Eg'mont, Lamoral, Count of, 1522-1568. Born in Hainault; became attached to the court of Charles V., by whom, for distinguished military and diplomatic services, he was appointed governor of Flanders; fell into disfavor for espousing the cause of the Protestants of the Netherlands, and was beheaded in Brussels by the Duke of Alva.

Eiffel (*i'fel*), **Gustave,** 1832- . . . . A French engineer; born in Dijon, and in 1858 was intrusted with the construction of the large iron bridge over the Garonne at Bordeaux, and was one of the first to introduce caissons worked with compressed air. In the huge framework erected for Bartholdi's "Statue of Liberty" may be seen the germ of the idea which afterward assumed the form of the colossal iron structure on the Champ-de-Mars in Paris, with which his name is identified.

Eldon, John Scott, Earl of, 1751-1838. An English jurist, lord chancellor for many years; born in Newcastle. In 1821 he was created an earl by George IV. He died in London; as a lawyer he was a master of English jurisprudence; as a politician he was opposed to reform.

Eliot, Charles William, 1834- . . . . Educator; born in Boston, Mass.; was graduated in the Harvard class of 1853. The following year he was appointed assistant professor of mathematics, and gave himself to the study of chemistry; in 1858 was made assistant professor of chemistry and mathematics and in 1861 professor of chemistry in the Lawrence Scientific School of the college. Two years later he went to Europe for study of chemistry and to investigate the educational institutions of that continent, and while at Vienna was chosen in 1865 professor of analytical chemistry to Massachusetts Institute of Technology, which post he filled for a period of four years and again went to Europe and spent fourteen months in further investigation, mainly in France. Dr. Thomas Hill having resigned the presidency of Harvard College Mr. Eliot was in 1869 chosen to that office, which he has since filled. During his administration many notable changes in the government of the college have occurred, its scope has been broadened and a great increase in the number of its professors and students is seen, while its wealth by gifts and benefactions has greatly increased, so that now it successfully competes with the great European universities in its curriculum. Mr. Eliot was given the honors of LL.D. by Williams and Princeton colleges in 1869 and by Yale in 1870, and is an honored member of many scientific and literary bodies, and has written and, in connection with Professor F. H. Storer, published two excellent manuals on chemistry, besides other notable productions; he is recognized as among the chief educators of his time.

Eliot, John, 1604-1690. The apostle of the Indians; born in Hertfordshire; entered the Church of England, but seceded and emigrated to New England; became celebrated for his successful evangelistic expeditions among the Indians during his lifelong occupancy of the pastorate at Roxbury.

Elizabeth, 1533-1603. Queen of England; the daughter of Henry VIII. and of Anne Boleyn; born in Greenwich. Upon the death of Mary, November 17, 1558, ascended the throne; she restored, or may be said to have established, the Protestant religion; assisted projects for English colonization of America; repulsed the Spanish Armada; encouraged literature, and made England respected abroad. Personally she had serious faults, and her execution of Mary, Queen of Scots, is a blot on her name, but her reign was an oasis of glory compared with the rule of the sovereigns who immediately preceded her, and those who followed her up to William and Mary.

Elizabeth, 1709-1762. Empress of Russia; daughter of Peter the Great and Catherine I.; assisted Maria Theresa in the War of the Austrian Succession; opposed Frederick the Great in the Seven Years' War; indolent and licentious, she left the affairs of the state mainly in the hands of favorites.

Elizabeth, Saint, 1307-1331. A very pious, but also a very fanciful young women; daughter of Andreas II., King of Hungary; her husband, a Thuringian landgraf, going to the Crusade, "where he died straightway," Carlyle guesses, "partly the fruit of the life she led him; lodging beggars, sometimes in her very bed; continually breaking his night's rest for prayer and devotional exercises of undue length, 'weeping one moment, then smiling in joy the next;' meandering about, capricious, melodious, weak, at the will of devout whim mainly; went to live at Marburg after her husband's death."

Ellenborough, Edward Law, Earl of, 1790-1871. An English Conservative statesman; entered Parliament in 1813; held office under the Duke of Wellington and Sir Robert Peel; appointed Governor-General of India; subsequently First Lord of the Admiralty and Indian Minister under Lord Derby.

Elliot, Daniel Giraud, 1835- . . . . An American zoologist; born in New York; traveled in Europe, Africa, and parts of Asia in 1856-1878; subsequently in Canada, Alaska, South America, and the greater part of the United States. He afterward became curator of zoology in the Field Columbian Museum.

Ellsworth, Oliver, 1745-1807. An American jurist; born in Windsor, Conn.; sent as delegate from Connecticut to the first Continental Congress; made judge of the Connecticut Superior Court in 1784. He was a member of the convention that framed the Federal Constitution, and influential in organizing Congress and the judiciary. In 1796 he was appointed Chief Justice, and in 1799 made member of a diplomatic commission to France, with Patrick Henry and William R. Davie. On account of ill health he sent home his resignation as Chief Justice, but in 1807 was reappointed.

Elzevir (*el'ze-veer, or el'ze-vir*). Of or belonging to the Elzevir family. Elzevir editions of the classics, etc., published by the Elzevir family at Amsterdam and Leyden, from about 1595 to 1680, highly prized for accuracy and elegance. A peculiar cut of type.

Emmanuel (The Great), 1469-1521. King of Portugal.

Emmet, Robert, 1780-1803. Irish patriot and orator; became a leader of the "United Irishmen," and was implicated in the killing of Lord Kilwarden, Chief Justice of Ireland, and others; although defending himself with great eloquence, he was sentenced to death and paid the penalty of his complicity.

Emmet, Thomas Addis, 1764-1827. Brother of Robert Emmet; a leader of the "United Irishmen," and imprisoned from 1798 till 1801; removed to America in 1804, and was in 1812 elected Attorney General of New York.

Encke (*en'ke*), **Johann Franz,** 1791-1865. A German astronomer; born in Hamburg. During the War of Liberation he served as artillerist in the German army; after the peace he became assistant in the Observatory of Seeberg, near Gotha; here he calculated the orbit of the comet observed by Mechain, Miss Herschel, and Pons, predicted its return, and detected a gradual acceleration of movement ascribed by him to the presence of a resisting medium. The comet is now known as Encke's comet. The fame of his works, "The Distance of the Sun," and "The Transit of Venus of 1769," led to his appointment as director of the Berlin Observatory, a position which he held till his death.

Endlicher, Stephen Ladislaus, 1804-1849. An Austrian botanist; born in Presburg; in 1840 was appointed Professor of Botany in the University of Vienna, and director of the botanic garden; he took part on the popular side in the German revolution of 1848.

Endicott, John 1589-1665. A colonial governor of Massachusetts; born in Dorchester, England. He landed as manager of the plantation of Naumkeag (Salem) in 1628. Giving place in 1630 to John Winthrop, he headed a sanguinary expedition against the Indians in 1636; was deputy-governor in 1641-1644, 1650, and 1654, and governor in 1644, 1649, 1650-1653 and 1655-1665. Endicott was an austere Puritan, choleric, benevolent, and brave. He died in Boston.

Enghien (*on-gan'*), **Louis de Bourbon, Duc d',** 1772-1804. An ill-fated French Royalist; born at Chantilly; joined the Royalists and took part in the Rhine campaign against the republicans; was suspected of being concerned in a Bourbon plot to assassinate the Emperor Napoleon; was seized, brought to Vincennes, and, after an inconclusive and illegal trial, shot by Napoleon's orders.

Epicurus, 340?-270 B.C. Greek philosopher; founder of the Epicurean school.

Erasmus, Desiderius, 1466-1536. Dutch scholar and printer of the first Greek New Testament.

Erastus, Thomas, 1524-1583. German physician and writer.

Eratosthenes, 276-196? B.C. German geometer; considered the founder of the science of astronomy.

Eric the Red, flourished 1000. Scandinavian navigator; discovered Greenland.

Ericsson, John, 1803-1889. Swedish engineer and inventor; constructed the first *Monitor*, with revolving turrets for guns, which destroyed the Confederate iron clad *Merrimac*.

Erigena (*e-rij'e-na*), **Joannes Scotus,** 810?-875? An Irish theologian. His writings, denounced by the Roman Catholic Church, are among the most profound of the Middle Ages.

Erskine, Henry, 1746-1817. A famous Scotch lawyer; born at Edinburgh; called to the bar and became lord advocate; a Whig in politics; brought about useful legal reforms; noted as a brilliant wit and orator.

Erskine, Thomas, 1750-1823. A Scotch baron; born in Edinburgh; became a noted forensic orator and jurist, attaining most of his renown as a pleader in support of the accusations of corruption made against Lord Sandwich. He was a member of the House of Commons in 1790-1806. About the latter date he was created Baron Erskine of Restormel, on becoming lord chancellor. He died near Edinburgh.

Escobar', Mendoza Antonio, 1589-1669. A Spanish Jesuit and casuist; born at Valladolid; a preacher and voluminous writer.

Esparte'ro, Joachim Baldomero, Duke of Vittoria, 1783-1879. A Spanish general and statesman. He refused the crown on the abdication of Isabella, 1870.

Espy, James Pollard, 1785-1860. A meteorologist; born in Pennsylvania; did notable work in investigating the causes of storms, and in 1841 published "The Philosophy of Storms"; was appointed to the Washington Observatory, where he carried on experiments in the cooling of gases and atmospheric expansion.

Essex, Robert Devereux, Earl of, 1567-1601. A favorite of Queen Elizabeth; born at Netherwood, Hereford; served in the Netherlands; won the capricious fancy of Elizabeth; lost favor by marrying clandestinely the widow of Sir Philip Sidney, but was restored, and led a life of varying fortune, filling various important offices, till his final quarrel with the Queen and execution.

Estaing (*aiz'-tahn*), **Comte d',** 1729-1794. A French admiral; "one of the bravest of men"; fought against the English in the Indies and in America; winced as a Royalist at the outbreak of the French Revolution; his loyalty to royalty outweighed, it was thought, his loyalty to his country, and he was guillotined.

Esterha'zy de Galantha. The name of a powerful and famous Hungarian family holding the rank of Princes of the Empire since the seventeenth century. Their estates include upwards of four thousand villages, sixty market towns, many castles and lordships, but they are heavily mortgaged. Among the more prominent members of the family are; **Paul IV.,** Prince Esterhazy, 1635-1713, a general and literary savant. His grandson, **Nicholas Joseph,** 1714-1790. A great patron of arts and music; founder of the school in which Haydn and Pleyel, among others, were formed. **Nicholas,** Prince Esterhazy, 1765-1883. Distinguished as a field marshal and foreign ambassador. **Prince Paul Anthony,** 1786-1866. A distinguished and able diplomatist; was successively Austrian ambassador at Dresden, Rome, and Britain.

Ethelbert, 552-616. A king of Kent, in whose reign Christianity was introduced by Saint Augustine and a band of missionaries in 597; drew up the first Saxon law code.

Ethelred II., 968-1016. The Unready; a worthless king of Saxon England; married Emma, daughter of Richard, Duke of Normandy, a step which led in the end to the claim which issued in the Norman Conquest.

Euclid, fl. 300 B.C. A celebrated Greek mathematician, who collected all the fundamental principles of pure mathematics, which had been delivered down by Thales, Pythagoras, Eudoxus, and other mathematicians before him, which he digested into regularity and order, with many others of his own, on which account he is said to have been the first who reduced arithmetic and geometry into the form of a science. He taught mathematics in Alexandria.

Eugene (*oo-zhain'*), **Francois, Prince of Savoy,** 1663-1736. A renowned general; born at Paris; he renounced his native land, and entered the service of the Austrian Emperor Leopold; first gained distinction against the Turks, whose power in Hungary he crushed in the great victory of Pieterwardein (1697); co-operated with Marlborough in the war of the Spanish Succession, and shared the glories of his great victories, and again opposed the French in the cause of Poland.

Eugenie (*oo-zhay'-nee*), (**Eugenie Maria de Guzman,**) 1826- . . . . Daughter of Conde de Montijo, and wife of Napoleon III.; born in Granada, Spain; crowned empress of the French, 1853; appointed regent while her husband was with the army, 1870; fled to England after the loss of the battle of Sedan.

Euler, Leonard, 1707-1783. A distinguished mathematician; born in Basel; in 1741 he accepted an invitation from Frederick the Great to become Professor of Mathematics in the Berlin Academy, but in 1766 went to St. Petersburg, where he died, in the office of director of the mathematical class of the academy; he applied the analytic method to mechanics and greatly improved the integral and differential calculus.

Euse'bius Pamphili, 266-340? A distinguished early Christian writer; born in Palestine; bishop of Cæsarea in 313; headed the moderate Arians at the Council of Nice, who shrank from disputing about a subject so sacred as the nature of the Trinity; wrote a history of the world to 328 A.D.; his "Ecclesiastical History" is the first record of the Christian Church up to 324.

Eustachio (*ay-oos-tah'ke-o*), **Bartolommeo,** 1500?-1574? An Italian physician and anatomist; he devoted himself to medical science and in particular to anatomy, which he much enriched by his researches. Among his discoveries were the Eustachian tube and the Eustachian valve of the heart.

Evans, Oliver, 1755-1819. An American inventor; born in Newport, Del.; in 1777 he invented a machine for making card teeth. Among his other inventions are the automatic flour mill; the high pressure steam engine; a steam dredge, and the boiler known as the "Cornish boiler." He died in New York.

Evarts, William Maxwell, 1818-1901. An American lawyer; born in Boston, Mass.; was the principal counsel for President Johnson in his impeachment trial; Attorney General of the United States; in 1877 principal counsel for the Republican party before the Electoral Commission on the Hayes-Tilden election returns; in 1877-1881 United States Secretary of State; and in 1885-1891 United States Senator from New York. He also represented the United States in the Alabama claims case, and was the principal counsel for Henry Ward Beecher in his defense against the charges preferred by Theodore Tilton. He died in New York.

Everett, Edward, 1794-1865. An American statesman; born in Dorchester, Mass. After traveling for some years in Germany and England he returned to America in 1819 to occupy the chair of Greek Literature at Harvard; became successively member of Congress, governor of Massachusetts, and Minister Plenipotentiary to England; in 1845 he was appointed President of Harvard College, and in 1852 Secretary of State; shortly after he retired to private life; a graceful and powerful orator, he was chosen to deliver the oration at Gettysburg, when his noble periods were entirely eclipsed by Lincoln's simple, immortal words. He died in Boston.

Ewald (*ay-vald*), **Georg Heinrich August von,** 1803-1875. A German Orientalist and Biblical critic; born in Gottingen; in 1827 he became extraordinary, in 1831 ordinary, Professor of Theology, and in 1835 Professor of Oriental Languages; in 1837 he lost his chair at Goettingen on account of his protest against the king's abrogation of the liberal constitution, became Professor of Theology at Tuebingen, but in 1848 returned to his old chair at Gottingen. He died in Gottingen.

Ewell, Richard Stoddard, 1817-1872. Military officer; born in Georgetown, D. C.; served during the Mexican War with Scott from Vera Cruz to the City of Mexico, and was promoted captain for gallantry and meritorious conduct at Contreras and Churubusco. At the outbreak of the Civil War he resigned his commission in the National Army and joined the Confederates; he took part in the Maryland campaign and in the battles of Bull Run, Gettysburg, and the Wilderness, and attained the rank of Lieutenant-General. After the war he retired to private life; he died in Springfield, Tenn.

Ewing, Thomas, 1789-1871. An American jurist and statesman; born in Virginia; he was a member of the United States Senate, Secretary of the Treasury, and first Secretary of the Interior.

Exmouth, Edward Pellew, Viscount, 1757-1833. An English admiral. Noted for his expedition to Algiers, 1816, when in a bombardment of four hours he destroyed the Algerian ships, silenced their forts, shelled the palace, and compelled the Dey's submission and the release of 1,200 European prisoners.

Eyck (*ike*), **Jan Van** (John of Bruges), 1390-1440. One of the greatest of Flemish painters. His brother Hubert, 1366-1426, was also a noted artist. The brothers have been pronounced the originators of oil painting.

Ezekiel, born about 570 B.C. In Scripture one of the greater Hebrew prophets; son of the priest Bezi, who, with Jehoiakim, king of Judah, was carried captive to Mesapotamia. The date of his death is unknown. The book of Ezekiel contains his prophecies.

Ezra, fl. fifth century B.C. In Scripture a Jewish priest, who led the second expedition of his people home from the Babylonian exile, 458 B.C. A tomb said to be his is still shown on the Tigris, some twenty miles above its junction with the Euphrates. The book of Ezra relates the events connected with the second return, that of Nehemiah (formerly first book of Ezra), the incidents of the first return, twenty-one years before.

Fab'ius Maximus, Quintus (Cunctator), 203 B.C. Roman consul and general; inaugurated the "Fabian" policy, carrying on only a defensive war against Hannibal.

Faed, John, 1820- . . . . A Scottish artist; born at Barley Mill, Kirkcudbright; his paintings are chiefly of humble Scottish life, the "Cotter's Saturday Night" among others.

Faed, Thomas, 1826- . . . . Brother of the preceding, born at Barley Mill; distinguished himself in his art studies at Edinburgh; went to London, where his pictures of Scottish life won him a foremost place among those of his contemporaries.

Fahrenheit (*far'en-hite*), **Gabriel Daniel**, 1690-1740. A distinguished German philosopher. He invented the thermometer known by his name.

Fairfax, Thomas, Lord, 1611-1671. An English general who commanded the Parliamentary army at the outbreak of the civil war, 1642; and again in 1645. **Thomas Lord Fairfax**, 1691-1782, his grandson, spent part of his life in Virginia, and was the friend and patron of General Washington.

Faliero, or **Falieri, Marino**, 1274?-1355. A Venetian noble; succeeded Andrew Dandolo as Doge of Venice, in 1354. When he succeeded to the office of doge, he was eighty years of age, and had a young and beautiful wife. He had enemies among the dominant nobility of Venice; and to avenge himself on them he entered into a conspiracy with the plebeians to overturn the government and massacre the patricians. On the night before it was to be carried into effect, the plot was discovered, and Faliero was beheaded.

Fallopius, Gabriello, 1523-1562. Anatomist, born at Modena; Professor of Anatomy at Pisa and at Padua; the Fallopian tubes which connect the ovaries with the uterus, first accurately described by him, are called after his name, as also the duct which transmits the facial nerve after it leaves the auditory nerve.

Faneuil (*fan'el* or *fun'el*), **Peter**, 1700-1743. An American merchant; born in New Rochelle, N. Y.; settled in Boston, Mass., where he became a successful merchant. In 1740 he offered to build a market house at his personal expense as a gift to the town, which he completed two years later. He died in Boston.

Faraday, Michael, 1791-1867. English chemist and natural philosopher; founder of science of magneto-electricity.

Farragut, David Glascoe, 1801-1870. American admiral; passed the New Orleans forts and captured New Orleans in 1862.

Farrar, Frederick William, 1831-1903. An English clergyman, dean of Canterbury; born in Bombay, India; sixteen years master at Harrow; canon and archdeacon of Westminster, and chaplain to the queen. Of his religious and theological writings the most notable are: "The Witness of History to Christ," "The Life of Christ," "Life and Works of St. Paul," "The Early Days of Christianity," and "Eternal Hope," a work which has been severely criticised on account of its lax doctrine regarding the question of everlasting punishment.

Faust (*foust*), or **Fust, Johann**, ... -1466. One of the three artists to whom the invention of printing has been ascribed; was the son of a goldsmith at Mentz, Germany. The other two were Gutenburg and Schaffer.

Fawkes, Faux, or **Vaux, Guy**, 1570-1606. An English conspirator; born in York, England; he enlisted in the Spanish army in the Netherlands, and returned to England in 1604, after agreeing to assist in the Gunpowder Plot; after collecting the necessary combustibles, Fawkes worked his way into the coal cellar under the House of Lords, and after storing it with gunpowder, etc., was appointed to the dangerous duty of firing the mine. The government having had timely information of the detestable plot, the House of Lords and its cellar were searched, and Fawkes found secreted amid some casks of gunpowder, Nov. 5, 1605; he was at once arrested, soon after tried, and suffered death at Westminster with several of the other conspirators.

Ferdinand V., 1452-1516. Founded the Spanish monarchy.

Fergusson, James, 1808-1886. A Scotch writer; born in Ayr, Scotland; his monumental achievement, which constitutes him perhaps the greatest of writers on the subject, is "History of Architecture in all Countries." He died in London.

Ferry (*fay-ree'*), **Jules Francois Camille**, 1832-1893. A French statesman; he was minister to Athens in 1872-1873, and in 1879 became minister of Public Instruction and began an agitation against the Jesuits. Their expulsion was effected, and brought about the dissolution of the ministry in September, 1880; became premier, with a policy of colonial expansion, involving a war in Madagascar and the invasion of Tonquin. He died in Paris.

Feuerbach (*foy'er-bok*), **Paul Johann Anselm von**, 1775-1833. A German penalogist; born in Hainichen, near Jena; died in Frankfort-on-the-Main.

Fichte (*fik'-ta*), **Johann Gottlieb**, 1762-1814. A German philosopher; he was appointed Professor of Philosophy in the University of Jena in 1794, and the following year published his "Doctrine of Science," a fundamental departure from Kant. He died in Berlin.

Field, Cyrus West, 1819-1894. Born at Stockbridge, Mass.; founded the Atlantic Telegraph Company in 1856; on the successful laying of the 1866 cable, since which time communication between the Old and New worlds has never been interrupted, he was awarded a gold medal and the thanks of the nation.

Field, David Dudley, 1805-1894. An eminent American jurist; born in Haddam, Conn.; brought about judiciary reforms, and drew up, under Government directions, political, civil, and penal codes; interested himself in the international law, and labored to bring about an international agreement whereby disputes might be settled by arbitration and war done away with.

Field, Stephen Johnson, 1816-1899. An American jurist; born in Haddam, Conn.; brother of Cyrus West and David Dudley Field; studied law and was admitted to the bar; removed to San Francisco in 1849; became a justice of the Supreme Court of California in 1857; was appointed its chief justice in 1859; and in 1863 was appointed an associate justice of the United States Supreme Court, which office he resigned in April, 1897; he died in Washington, D. C.

Fildes, S. Luke, 1844- . . . . An English artist; born in Lancashire; contributed to various magazines and illustrated books, notably Dickens's "Edwin Drood"; his most noted pictures are "Applicants for a Casual Ward," "The Widower," and "The Doctor."

Fillmore, Millard, 1800-1874. American statesman; thirteenth president of the United States; born in New York; learned fullers' trade; read law and acquired lucrative practice in Buffalo; elected to Congress, 1832, and continued a member till 1842; elected vice-president, 1848; became president on the death of Taylor, 1850; approved the Fugitive Slave Law and the compromise measures of Henry Clay, and made Daniel Webster Secretary of State.

Fischer, Kuno, 1824- . . . . A German historian of philosophy; he was interdicted from teaching philosophy at Heidelberg in 1853; but, after filling professorships in Berlin and Jena, he had the satisfaction of being called to the chair of philosophy at Heidelberg in 1872.

Fish, Hamilton, 1808-1893. An American diplomatist; born in New York city; he was elected a congressman in 1842, and governor in 1848. In 1851 he was elected to the United States Senate, where he opposed the repeal of the Missouri Compromise and joined the Republican party on its foundation. He was Secretary of State under Grant from 1869 to 1877, signing, as one of the commissioners, the Washington Treaty of 1871, and carrying through the settlement of the "Alabama" question.

Fisher, George Park, 1847- . . . . An American author and educator; born in Wrentham, Mass.; studied theology at the Yale Divinity School; at Andover, and in Germany, was Professor of Divinity from 1854-1861, and subsequently of Ecclesiastical History at Yale. Author of many theological and historical works.

Fitch, John, 1743-1798. An American inventor; born in Connecticut; in 1785 he brought out a model steamboat with side wheels, and in 1788 and in 1790 constructed larger vessels, one of the latter being for some time employed as a passenger boat; some of his plans are said to have fallen into Robert Fulton's hands and given him the idea of his steamship; disheartened by the ill-success of a trip to France he committed suicide at Bardstown, Kentucky.

Fitzgerald, Edward, Lord, 1763-1798. A noble Irishman, son of the Duke of Leinster. He was an enthusiastic patriot, and joined the society of United Irishmen, and was leader in the "rising" of 1798. Arrested on a charge of treason, he died while awaiting trial.

Flaminius, Caius, ... -217 B.C. Roman general and consul.

Flaminius, Titus Quintius, 230-174 B.C. Roman general and consul.

Flamma'rion, Camille, 1842- . . . . A French astronomer, writer on descriptive astronomy, and "astronomical novelist"; born in Montigny-le-Roi, Haute Marne, France.

Flandrin, (*flon-dran'*), **Jean Hippolite,** 1809-1864. A French painter; born in Lyons, France. Among his chief works are the fine series of frescoes in the churches of St. Germain-des-Pres and St. Vincent de Paul, Paris, which are reckoned among the masterpieces of modern painting. He died in Rome, Italy.

Flaxman, John, 1755-1826. An English sculptor and draughtsman; born in York, England. The monuments to Nelson, Howe, and Reynclds in St. Paul's are by his hand. One of his finest productions is the "Shield of Achilles." He died in London.

Flint, Austin, 1812-1886. An American physician; born in Petersham, Mass.; he was the author of numerous text-books, clinical reports, and medical papers. He died in New York city.

Flotow, Frederick Ferdinand Adolphus von, 1812-1883. German composer of operas; his best known work is "Martha."

Flourens (*floo-ron'*), **Marie Jean Pierre,** 1794-1867. A French physiologist; in 1840 he was elected member of the French Academy; in 1846 was made a peer of France and in 1855 professor in the College of France. He was promoted grand officer of the Legion of Honor, and made member of the municipal Council of Paris in 1864. He died in Montgeron, near Paris.

Fluegel, Johann Gottfried, 1788-1855. A German lexicographer. He spent many years in the United States in business, diplomatic, and official occupations. He died in Leipsic.

Foley, John Henry, 1818-1874. An Irish sculptor; born in Dublin. The most popular of his works is a statue of Seldon placed in the new palace of Westminster, considered his masterpiece. He died in Hampstead, near London, England.

Fonta'na, Domenico, 1543-1607. An Italian architect. Under Pope Sixtus V. he erected the Egyptian Obelisk in front of St. Peter's, Rome, 1586, and later built the Lateran and Quirinal palaces, and the Vatican Library.

Foote, Andrew Hull, 1806-1863. An American naval officer; born in New Haven, Conn. In command of the China station in 1856, when the Chinese and English were at war, he exerted himself to protect American property, and was fired upon by the Celestials. His demand for an apology was refused and he stormed and captured four Chinese forts. In 1861 he commanded the expedition against Forts Henry and Donelson on the Tennessee and Cumberland rivers, and directed the attack on Island Number 10. In 1862 he was promoted rear-admiral, and in 1863 was ordered to take command of the South Atlantic Squadron, but died in New York while preparing to join his flag-ship.

Forney, John Weiss, 1817-1881. An American journalist; born in Lancaster, Pa.; clerk of the National House of Representatives from 1851 to 1855, and secretary of the United States Senate from 1861 to 1868. He was connected with several papers in Philadelphia and Washington. He died in Philadelphia, Pa.

Forrest, Edwin, 1806-1872. An American actor; born in Philadelphia, Pa. He played with remarkable success in Europe and the United States; in 1871 retired from the stage. He died in Philadelphia.

Foster, John Watson, 1836- . . . . An American diplomatist; born in Pike county, Ind.; was graduated at the Indiana State University in 1855; studied law, and was admitted to the bar in Evansville, Ind. After the Civil War, during which he served with distinction, he was editor of the Evansville *Daily Journal* and postmaster of that city; minister to Mexico from 1873-1880, to Russia in 1880-1881, and to Spain from 1883-1885; was special commissioner to negotiate reciprocity treaties with Spain, Germany, Brazil, and the West Indies, in 1891; United States Secretary of State in 1892-1893. Subsequently he was agent before the Bering Sea Arbitration Tribunal at Paris; participated in the peace negotiations with Japan, and in 1898 served as a member of the Anglo-American Commission.

Foster, Stephen Collins, 1826-1864. An American song writer; born in Pittsburg, Pa. He composed the music and wrote the words of over 125 popular songs and melodies. Died in New York city.

Fouche (*foo-shay'*), **Joseph, Duke of Otranto,** 1763-1820. Born at Nantes; voted for the death of Louis XVI.; advised Napoleon to abdicate in 1814 and again after Waterloo; served under Louis XVIII. for a time but was obliged at length to quit France for good; died at Trieste.

Fouquier-Tinville (*foo-ke-ai'tang-veel'*), **Antoine Quentin,** 1747-1795. A bloodthirsty French Jacobin; was public accuser before Robespierre's Revolutionary Tribunal, and gloated over the death of thousands of innocent victims; sentenced to the same fate, he exhibited the most abject cowardice.

Fourier (*foo're-ai*), **Francois Marie Charles,** 1772-1837. A French social economist. At first in trade, then in the army. After seeing a cargo of rice thrown into the sea to raise its price he was led to attempt a reform abolishing the competitive system, by means of associated production and life in "phalansteries." He died in Paris.

Fourier, Jean Baptiste Joseph, Baron, 1768-1830. A French mathematician. He was an active Jacobin during the French Revolution. His later energies were divorced from politics and given up to science. He died in Paris.

Fowler, Orson Squire, 1809-1887. An American phrenologist; born in Cohocton, Steuben county, N. Y.; was graduated at Amherst College in 1834, and opened a phrenological office in New York in 1835. He died near Sharon Station, Conn.

Fox, Charles James, 1749-1806. English orator and statesman; entered Parliament in 1768 as a Tory, but joined the opposition in 1773, and became leader of the Whigs, opposing the policy of Pitt.

Fox, George, 1624-1690. Born in Leicestershire, Eng.; founder of the society of Friends, or Quakers.

Fra Diavolo, 1760-1806. Chief of a band of Italian brigands; born in Calabria; leader in sundry Italian insurrections; was hanged at Naples for treachery, in spite of remonstrances from England; gave name to an opera by Auber, but only the name.

Francesca da Rimini. A beautiful Italian lady of the 13th century, whose pathetic love story finds a place in Dante's "Inferno"; she was betrothed by her father, the Lord of Ravenna, to Giovanni of Rimini, but her affections were engaged by Paolo, his brother; the lovers were found together by Giovanni and murdered by him.

Francia, Jose Gaspar Rodriguez, 1757-1840. Dictator of Paraguay; born in Asuncion; began his public career as a barrister. In 1811, soon after the revolution in the Spanish possessions of South America became general, was appointed secretary to the independent junta of Paraguay; in 1813, he was appointed consul of the republic, with Yegros for his colleague. In 1817 unlimited despotic authority was conferred upon him, which he exercised during the remainder of his life. He died in Asuncion.

Francis I., 1494-1547. King of France; born in Cognac, France; succeeded to the throne in 1515, on the death of Louis XII., who died without male issue. He died at the Chateau de Rambouillet, and was succeeded by his son, Henry II.

Francis II., 1543-1560. King of France; the eldest son of Henry II. and his queen Catherine de Medici, born in Fontainebleau. He succeeded his father in July, 1559, having in the preceding year married Mary Stuart, daughter of James V. of Scotland.

Francis de Borgia, Saint, 1510-1572. Duke of Gandia and viceroy of Catalonia; joined the Society of Jesus and became general of the order.

Francis de Paula, Saint, 1416-1507. Italian Franciscan monk; founded the order Fratres Minimi.

Francis de Sales, Saint, 1567-1622. Bishop of Geneva; born of a noble Savoyard family, in the chateau of Sales, near Geneva. In 1610 he founded the Order of the Visitation, of which the first directress was his friend, Madame de Chantal; was canonized by Pope Alexander VII. in 1665.

Francis, Saint, or **Francis of Assisi,** 1182-1226. Founder of the Order of Franciscan friars; born in

Assisi. His proper name was Giovanni Bernardone, but he afterward received the name of Franciscus. He died in Assisi; was canonized by Pope Gregory IX. in 1228.

Francis, Philip, Sir, 1740-1818. An Irish-English statesman, the best accredited of the candidates for authorship of the "Junius" letters; born in Dublin.

Franklin, Benjamin, 1706-1790. American statesman and philosopher; born in Boston; son of a tallow chandler; youngest of a family of seventeen children; learned the trade of a printer and studied diligently; removed to Philadelphia, where he established the *Pennsylvania Gazette;* began the publication of *Poor Richard's Almanac* in 1735; discovered the identity of lightning and electricity in 1752, by means of a kite; Franklin occupied many positions of public trust and was the recipient of many honors.

Franklin, Sir John, 1786-1847. English Arctic explorer.

Franz, Robert, 1815-1892. A German musician; born in Halle, Prussia. He was famous for his songs, which were of a peculiar lyric beauty. His first published composition appeared in 1843. The latter years of his life were spent in editing the works of Bach, Handel, *et als.*

Fraunhofer (*frown'hof-er*), **Joseph von,** 1787-1826. A German optician; born in Bavaria; his name is associated with many discoveries in optical science as well as inventions and improvements in the optician's art; but he is chiefly remembered for his discovery of the dark lines in the solar spectrum, since called after him the Fraunhofer lines.

Frederick I. (Barbarossa), 1121-1190. Emperor of Germany; crowned by Pope Adrian IV.; reduced Milan in 1158, but was defeated by the Lombards near Legnano; joined the third crusade in 1189 with one hundred and fifty thousand men, and defeated the Turks at Iconium; died in the Holy Land. **Frederick II.,** 1194-1250. Opposed by the Guelphs and the pope in his project to unite Italy and Germany in one empire; began a crusade against the Moslems in 1227, but turned back, and was excommunicated by Pope Gregory IX.; resumed the crusade in 1228, captured Jerusalem, and made peace with the pope; defeated the Guelphs at Cortenuova, 1237, and renewed war with the pope.

Frederick William (the Great Elector), 1620-1668. Elector of Brandenburg; founder of the Prussian monarchy.

Frederick I., 1657-1713. First king of Prussia. **Frederick II.** (Frederick the Great), 1712-1788. Subjected to inhuman treatment in youth by his father, he gave but little promise of his future greatness; ascended the Prussian throne in 1740, and invaded Silesia, which was ceded to him by Maria Theresa in 1742; an alliance having been formed against him by Austria, Russia, and France, he began the Seven Years' War in 1756 by invading Saxony; gained a great victory at Prague in 1757; but was defeated at Kolin soon afterward; in the same year he defeated a French army twice as large as his own at Rossbach, and won a brilliant and decisive victory over the Austrians at Leuthen; in 1759 he was defeated at Kunnersdorf, and Berlin was captured by the allies, but in 1760 he gained the victories of Liegnitz and Torgau, and peace was made in 1763, Prussian Poland being added to Frederick's dominions. Frederick was a voluminous writer, and a friend of Voltaire, who spent several years at his court.

Frelinghuysen, Frederick Theodore, 1817-1885. An American statesman; born in Millstone, N. J.; became an eminent lawyer; United States Senator in 1868-1877, and Secretary of State under President Arthur in 1881-1885. He died in Newark, N. J.

Fremont, John Charles, 1830-1890. An American politician, explorer, and general; Republican candidate for the presidency, 1856.

French, Daniel Chester, 1850- . . . . An American sculptor; born in Exeter, N. H.; was educated in Boston and in Florence, Italy; had studios in Boston and Concord, N. H., and in New York city.

Fresnel (*fray-nail'*), **Augustin Jean,** 1788-1827. A French physicist; born in Broglie, France; the discoverer of the polarization of light; made important researches respecting the wave theory of light. The result of his great discovery is shown in the system of lens lighting apparatus, which has changed the mode of lighthouse illumination over the whole world. He died near Paris.

Frobisher, Martin, Sir, 1518-1594. An English naval officer and navigator: the first who sought a northwest passage in North America.

Froebel (*fray'bel*), **Friedrich,** 1782-1852. A German educator; he was for some time associated with Pestalozzi, but evolved a theory of education of his own. To explain it he wrote "The Education of Man," a work of deep and original thought; he opened the first kindergarten or children's garden at Blankenburg, Thuringia, in 1840; he died in Marienthal.

Fry, Mrs. Elizabeth, 1780-1845. English philanthropist; born at Norwich; third daughter of John Gurney, the Quaker banker; devoted her life to prison reform and the reform of criminals, as well as other benevolent enterprises.

Fulton, Robert, 1765-1815. American engineer and inventor; born in Pennsylvania; after spending some years in London as an artist, he turned his attention to civil engineering and inland navigation; went to Paris, there he invented a submarine torpedo; returned to New York, 1801, and, with the assistance of Robert Livingston, discovered steam navigation; in 1806 he built the steamer *Clermont,* which made regular trips between Albany and New York at a speed of five miles an hour; although he spent a large amount of money on his invention, the patent did not prove of pecuniary value to him.

Fuseli (*fu'ze-li*), **John H.,** 1742-1825. Swiss historical painter.

Gadsden, Christopher, 1724-1805. An American patriot; born in Charleston, S. C.; was a member of the first Colonial Congress, which convened in New York in October, 1765; was also a member of the first Continental Congress, which assembled in Philadelphia in 1774. He joined the American army as colonel at the beginning of the Revolution; was promoted brigadier-general.

Gadsden, James, 1788-1858. An American diplomatist; born in Charleston, S. C.; served with distinction in the War of 1812; and afterward took part in the campaign against the Seminole Indians. He was appointed minister to Mexico in 1853, and negotiated the Gadsden Purchase which fixed a new boundary between Mexico and the United States. He died in Charleston, S. C.

Gage, Thomas, 1721-1787. A British general; he fought with the British troops in America in 1755, 1758, and 1760; was commander-in-chief in North America in 1775, and returned to England the same year; he was promoted general in 1782. The battles of Lexington and Bunker Hill took place during his generalship.

Gagern (*gaw-gern*), **Heinrich Wilhelm August, Baron of,** 1799-1880. A German statesman; born in Bayreuth, Bavaria; in 1821 entered political life under the government of Grand-ducal Hesse; in 1850 he served as major in the Schleswig-Holstein War; in 1852 he removed to Heidelberg; he died in Darmstadt.

Gainsborough (*gainz'bro*), **Thomas,** 1727-1878. An eminent English landscape painter.

Galba, Servius Sulpicius, 3 B.C.-69 A.D. Roman emperor, successor of Nero; after his election he soon made himself unpopular by cruelty and avarice, and was slain in the forum.

Galen, 131-205? Greek physician, medical writer and philosopher, living at Rome; his works remained authority until the fifteenth century.

Galilei (*gah-le-lai'e*), **Galileo** (Galileo), 1564-1642. Italian astronomer; discovered, about 1584, the isochronism of the vibrations of a pendulum, and the law by which the velocity of falling bodies is accelerated; adopted in astronomy the system of Copernicus; constructed his wonderful telescope, 1609; through it he discovered the satellites of Jupiter, and was enabled to explore the surface of the moon and view the phases of Venus; he also ascertained that the "Milky Way" was composed of myriads of stars; in 1632 he produced his "Dialogues on the Ptolemaic and Copernican Systems," but was compelled by the Inquisition to abjure the theory of the motion of the earth; he was detained in prison for several years, but it does not appear that he was severely treated, as he was allowed to pursue his studies until prevented by blindness.

Galit'zin, Gallitzin, Galyzin, or **Golyzin.** One of the most powerful and distinguished Russian families, whose members have been equally prominent in war and diplomacy from the sixteenth century downward. **Prince Dimitri Alexeievitch,** 1738-1803. A Russian diplomat and statesman; was ambassador to the court of France in 1763, and to The Hague in 1773. He was in correspondence with Voltaire and other literary men of his day and was the author of several works relating to geology. He died in Brunswick, Germany. **Dimitri Augustine,** 1770-1841. Son of the foregoing; born in The Hague; became a Roman Catholic in his seventeenth year, and was ordained a priest in the United States by Bishop Carroll of Baltimore in 1795; he declined to return to Russia on his father's death, and as a Catholic priest was adjudged to have lost his right of inheritance. He wrote various controversial works. He died in Loretta, Pa.

Gall, Franz Joseph, 1758-1828. Founder of phrenology; born in Tiefenbronn, Baden, Germany. He studied medicine at Strasburg and Vienna and settled in the latter city in 1785 as a physician. With Spurzheim, who became his associate in 1804, he quitted Vienna in 1805, and began a lecturing tour through Germany, Holland, Sweden, and Switzerland. He reached the height of his fame when in 1807 he settled as a physician in Paris till his death.

Galland (*gal-lon′*), **Antoine,** 1646-1715. French Orientalist; professor of Arabic in the College of France; was the first to translate the "Arabian Nights" into any European tongue.

Gallatin, Albert, 1761-1849. American statesman; born in Geneva, Switzerland; in 1793 he was elected to the United States Senate from Pennsylvania, but was declared ineligible. From 1795 to 1801 he served in the House of Representatives, and from 1801 to 1813 he was Secretary of the Treasury, in which post he showed himself one of the first financiers of his day. From 1815 to 1823 he was minister at Paris, and in 1826 he was sent to London as ambassador extraordinary. On his return in 1827 he settled in New York, and devoted much of his time to literature.

Galle (*gawl′eh*), **Johann Gottfried,** 1812- . . . . A German astronomer; born in Pabsthaus, Prussia; studied natural sciences and mathematics. He was the first to observe the planet Neptune.

Galton, Francis, 1822- . . . . An English scientist. Having traveled in North Africa, he explored in 1850 lands hitherto unknown in South Africa, publishing his experiences in his "Narrative of an Explorer in Tropical South Africa." Later he specially devoted himself to the problem of heredity.

Galva′ni, Luigi, 1737-1798. An Italian anatomist; born in Bologna, Italy. He studied theology and subsequently medicine at the university there, and was elected professor of anatomy. Galvani owes the wide celebrity attached to his name to his discoveries in animal electricity. He died in Bologna.

Gama, Vasco de, 1460-1524. A Portuguese navigator; he was the first to double the Cape of Good Hope, 1497.

Gambetta, Leon, 1838-1884. A French lawyer and statesman; escaped from Paris, 1870, in a balloon, and continued to direct the war with Germany from Bordeaux.

Gambier, James, Lord, 1756-1833. British admiral; born in the Bahamas; was made rear-admiral, and in 1799 vice-admiral; for his gallant conduct as commander of the English fleet at the bombardment of Copenhagen he was made a baron; on the accession of William IV. he was made admiral of the fleet.

Garcia (*gar-thee′ah*), **Calixto,** 1836-1898. A Cuban patriot; born in Holguin, Cuba, and took up the profession of law. In 1868 he organized the revolution which has since been called the "Ten Years' War"; was appointed a brigadier-general and subsequently commander-in-chief of the Cuban army. In 1896 he led a successful filibustering expedition to Cuba. Later, while planning a second expedition, he was arrested by United States government officers, gave bail, which he forfeited, and again landed in Cuba. When Santiago was taken by the Americans in 1898 he withdrew from the Cuban army. Subsequently, however, he accepted the new conditions. He died in Washington, D. C.

Garcia, Manuel, 1775-1832. A noted singer and composer; born at Seville; he spent his closing years in Paris as a teacher of singing, his voice being greatly impaired by age as well as fatigue; his eldest daughter was the celebrated Madame Malibran.

Garfield, James Abram, 1831-1881. Twentieth president of the United States; born in Ohio; worked on a farm in boyhood, and learned the trade of a carpenter; afterward became driver and helmsman of a canal-boat; graduated at Williams College in 1856; appointed Professor of Latin and Greek at Hiram College, Ohio, and chosen president of that institution in 1858; married Miss Lucretia Randolph, and occasionally acted as a Campbellite minister; elected to the State Senate, 1859, and in 1861 was chosen colonel of an Ohio regiment; promoted to the rank of brigadier-general; elected to Congress, 1862, and remained in that body until 1880, when he was made senator; nominated for the presidency by the Republican party in 1880, and elected; shot by Charles J. Guiteau, in Washington, July 2, 1881, and died on September 19 of same year.

Garibal′di, Giuseppe, Gen., 1807-1881. A distinguished Italian patriot; born at Nice; died at Caprera. He was an exile for several years, residing in New York city and vicinity.

Garland, Augustus Hill, 1832-1899. An American lawyer; born near Covington, Tenn. He opposed secession as a policy, but was afterward elected to the Confederate Senate, which office he held till the close of the war; in 1874 was elected Governor under the new constitution of Arkansas. In 1885 he became Attorney-General in the cabinet of President Cleveland. He died in Washington, D. C.

Garrick, David, 1710-1779. A distinguished English tragedian; born at Hereford.

Garrison, William Lloyd, 1804-1879. An eminent American journalist and anti-slavery agitator; born in Massachusetts.

Gassen′di, or **Gassend, Pierre,** 1592-1655. A French philosopher and mathematician. Kepler and Galileo were numbered among his friends. His "Astronomical Institute" is a clear and connected representation of the state of the science in his own day; in his "Lives of Tycho Brahe, Copernicus, Regiomontanus, *et als.*," he gives not only a masterly account of the lives of these men, but likewise a complete history of astronomy down to his own time. He died in Paris.

Gates, Horatio, 1728-1806. American Revolutionary general; born in England; captured Burgoyne's army at Saratoga.

Gatling, Richard Jordan, 1818-1903. An American inventor; born in Hertford county, N. C. In 1861 he conceived the idea of the revolving battery gun which bears his name. In 1865 he improved his invention, and in the year following, after satisfactory trial, it was adopted into the United States service. It was used by the Canadian government in putting down the half-breed rebellion. It has also been adopted by several European governments.

Gauss (*gowss*), **Karl Friedrich,** 1777-1855. A distinguished German mathematician; born at Brunswick.

Gavar′ni, Paul, 1801-1866. The *nom de plume* of Sulpice Guillaume Chevalier, caricaturist, born in Paris; most of his best work appeared in *Le Charivari*, but some of his bitterest and most earnest pictures, the fruit of a visit to London, appeared in *L'Illustration;* he also illustrated Balzac's novels, and Sue's "Wandering Jew."

Gavazzi (*ga-vat′see*), **Alessandro,** 1809-1889. An Italian anti-papal agitator; born at Bologna; one of the most energetic supporters of Pius IX. in his liberal policy; he afterwards withdrew his allegiance, joined the Revolution of 1848, and ultimately fled to England on the occupation of Rome by the French.

Gay-Lussac (*gay-lu-sak′*), **Louis Joseph,** 1778-1850. French chemist and physicist; employed himself in chemical and physical research, in connection with which he made two balloon ascents; became Professor of Chemistry at the Paris Polytechnic School; was elected to a similar chair at the Jardin des Plantes; created a peer of France; became chief assayer to the Mint; his name is associated with many notable discoveries in chemistry and physics, *e. g* the law of volumes, isolation of cyanogen, etc.

Gegenbaur (*gay′gen-bower*), **Karl,** 1821- . . . . A German anatomist. In 1855 he was called to a medical professorship at Jena, but from 1858 to 1873 he taught principally anatomy. He removed to Heidelberg in 1873. His fame rests on his "Outline of Comparative Anatomy."

Geikie (*gee′-ke*), **Sir Archibald,** 1835- . . . . A Scottish geologist; born in Edinburgh, Scotland; was Murchison Professor of Geology in Edinburgh University; and director-general to the survey of the United Kingdom, being at the same time placed at the head of the Museum of Practical Geology, London.

Genghis Khan (*jain′gis kan*), 1163-1227. Mogul conqueror; subdued China and Persia.

Gen′seric, 406?-477. King of the Vandals; invaded Africa 429; defeated the Romans in numerous battles; captured Carthage, 439; captured and sacked Rome, 455; defeated the navy of the Emperor Marjorian, 457.

Gentz, Friedrich von, 1764-1832. A German politician and writer; born in Breslau, Prussia; died near Vienna.

Genung, John Franklin, 1850- . . . . An American educator; born in Willseyville, N. Y.; was graduated in Union College in 1870 and at the Rochester Theological Seminary in 1875; became Professor of Rhetoric in Amherst College; has written a number of excellent text-books.

Geoffroy (*jef′frey*), **St. Hilaire, Etienne,** 1772-1544.

A French naturalist; as a member of the Egyptian expedition in 1798 he founded the Institute of Cairo; in 1807 he was made a member of the Institute, and in 1809 Professor of Zoology at the Faculty of Sciences. He devoted himself especially to the philosophy of natural history; he died in Paris.

George I. (Lewis), 1660-1727. King of Great Britain. **George II.** (Augustus), 1683-1760. Defeated the French at Dettingen in 1743; Charles Edward Stuart was defeated at Culloden, 1746, by the Duke of Cumberland, and the latter part of the reign of George II. was marked by victories over the French in Canada, in India, and on the ocean. **George III.** (William Frederick), 1738-1820. Arbitrary and ignorant and through his obstinacy lost the American colonies; became insane in 1810. **George IV.** (Augustus Frederick), 1762-1830. "The first gentleman of Europe"; led a dissipated life and incurred an immense debt; married, in 1786, Mrs. Fitzherbert; she being a Roman Catholic, the marriage was illegal; his father refusing to pay his debts unless he contracted a regular marriage, he was induced, 1795, to marry his cousin, whom he regarded with great dislike, a separation being the result; became regent, 1811; took little interest in public affairs; one year before his death an act was passed relieving Roman Catholics from political disabilities.

George, Saint. Flourished third century; bishop of Alexandria; patron saint of England; to him is attributed the destruction of a terrible dragon.

George, Henry, 1839-1898. American author and economist, and advocate of the single tax.

Gerard (*zhay-rar'*), **Etienne Maurice, Comte**, 1773-1855. Marshal of France; at Austerlitz he won his brigade, and subsequently fought at Jena, Erfurt, and Wagram; he joined Napoleon after his flight from Elba, and was wounded at Wavre; on the downfall of the emperor he quitted France, but returned in 1817; he was War Minister under Louis Philippe.

Gerard, Francois Pascal Simon, Baron, 1770-1837. Painter; born at Rome, of French and Italian parentage; in 1795 his "Blind Belisarius" brought him to the front, while subsequent work as a portrait painter raised him above all his contemporaries; his masterpiece, "Entry of Henri IV. into Paris," brought him a barony at the hands of Louis XVIII.; his historical paintings, characterized by minute accuracy of detail, include "Napoleon in his Coronation Robes" and "Battle of Austerlitz."

Gerhardt, Karl Friedrich, 1816-1856. Chemist; born at Strasburg; made experiments along with Cahours on essential oils, which bore fruit in an important treatise; he received the chair of Chemistry at Montpellier, but returned to Paris four years later; there he matured and published his theories of types, homologous series, etc., which have greatly influenced the science of chemistry.

Gerome (*zhay-rome'*), **Jean Leon**, 1824-1904. Celebrated French painter; born at Vesoul; he studied at Paris under Paul Delaroche, with whom he subsequently traveled in Italy; among his most famous pictures, all characterized by vivid coloring and strong dramatic effect, are "The Age of Augustus and the Birth of Christ," "Roman Gladiators in the Amphitheatre," and "Cleopatra and Cæsar."

Gerry, Elbridge, 1744-1812. American Revolutionary statesman; signer of the Declaration of Independence; Governor of Massachusetts, 1810; Vice-President, 1812.

Gese'nius, 1785-1842. An eminent German Hebraist and Biblical scholar; his labors form an epoch in the study of the Hebrew Scriptures; was thirty years professor of the language in Halle; produced a Hebrew grammar and lexicon.

Ges'ner, Konrad von, 1516-1565. A Swiss naturalist; born in Zurich, Switzerland. He collected more than 500 plants undescribed by the ancients, and appears to have been the first who made the great step toward a scientific classification of distinguishing genera by the fructification. He died in Zurich, Switzerland.

Ghiberti (*ge-bair'te*), **Lorenzo**, 1378-1455. Italian sculptor and designer; born at Florence; his most famous achievement, which immortalized his name, was the execution of two doorways, with bas-relief designs, in the baptistery at Florence; he spent fifty years at this work, and so noble were the designs and so perfect the execution that Michael Angelo declared them fit to be the gates of Paradise.

Gibbons, James, 1834- . . . . An American clergyman; born in Baltimore, Md.; first appointed assistant in St. Patrick's Cathedral, Baltimore; later he became the private secretary of Archbishop Spalding, and chancellor of the diocese. In 1868 he was made vicar-apostolic of North Carolina, with the rank of bishop; and in 1877 became Archbishop of Baltimore. He was elevated to the cardinalate in 1886, being the second Roman Catholic in the United States to receive that promotion. He went to Rome in the summer of 1903, and took part in the election of Pius X. as successor to Leo XIII.

Gibson, John, 1790-1866. Sculptor; born at Gyffin, near Conway, Wales; he took to carving in wood and stone, and supported by Roscoe became a pupil of Canova and afterwards of Thorwaldsen in Rome; his best works are "Theseus and the Robber," "Amazon thrown from her horse," statues of George Stephenson, Peel, and Queen Victoria.

Giddings, Joshua Reed, 1795-1864. An American statesman; born in Athens, Pa.; elected a member of Congress in 1838, where he was prominent as an opponent of slavery. In 1861 he was appointed Consul-General to British North America. He died in Montreal.

Gifford, Robert Swain, 1840- . . . . An American artist; born in Naushon Island, Mass.; studied with Albert Van Baest in Rotterdam, Holland; traveled through California and Oregon in 1869, and in Europe and North America in 1870-1871.

Gifford, Sanford Robinson, 1823-1880. An American artist; born in Greenfield, N. Y.; died in New York city.

Gilbert, Sir John, 1817-1897. English artist; was for long an illustrator of books, among the number an edition of Shakespeare; he was a Chevalier of the Legion of Honor.

Giotto (*jot'-to*), 1276-1336. A great Italian painter; born at a village near Florence; was a shepherd's boy, and at ten years of age, while tending his flock and drawing pictures of them, was discovered by Cimabue, who took him home and made a pupil of him. Ruskin says of him: "His special character among the great painters of Italy was that he was practical person; what others dreamed of he did, he could work in mosaic, could work in marble, and paint; could build . . . built the Campanile of the Duomo, because he was then the best master of sculpture, painting, and architecture in Florence, and supposed in such business to be without a superior in the world."

Girard, Stephen, 1750-1831. An American philanthropist; born in France; died in Philadelphia; he made a large fortune as a merchant in Philadelphia, and at his death left $2,000,000 to found a college for orphan boys, to be conducted on strictly secular principles. The building is one of the finest in the country.

Giulio Romano (*joo'le-o ro-mah'no*), (properly Giulio Pippi de' Giannuzzi,) 1492-1546. An Italian artist; born in Rome; assisted Raphael in the execution of several of his finest works.

Gladstone, William Ewart, 1809-1898. A British statesman; born in Liverpool; his political career began in 1833, and up to the time of his death he held a prominent, and often leading, place in public affairs. He brought about the gradual enfranchisement of the common people of England, and he almost succeeded in gaining home rule for Ireland. He was lacking in foresight as he showed in his public assertion that the United States could not subdue the Confederacy, but he always meant well, and his mistakes were never of the heart. He died at Hawarden Castle.

Gluck (*glook*), **Christoph Willibald**, 1714-1787. A German composer; he conjoined with himself in his labors the poet Ranieri di Calzabigi, and his opera, "Helena and Paris," was received with tumults of applause. In 1774 he went to Paris, and presented there successively several masterpieces. He died in Vienna.

Godfrey (*god'-fre*) **of Bouillon** (*boo-yon'*), 1058-1100. The principal chief of the first Crusade. He captured Jerusalem, 1098.

Godiva (*go-de'va*). Flourished 11th century. The wife of Leofric, Earl of Mercia and Lord of Coventry in the reign of Edward the Confessor. Tradition says that, in 1040, she rode on her palfrey naked through the town of Coventry on her husband's promise that if she would do so he would relieve the inhabitants of certain exactions which bore heavily on them. She had first proclaimed that no one should leave his house before noon, that all windows and other apertures in the houses should be closed, and that no one should even look out till noon was past. Only one person, "Peeping Tom," the story says, attempted to look out, and he was immediately struck blind.

Godkin, Edwin Laurence, 1831-1901. An American journalist and essayist; born in Moyne, Ireland; he graduated from Queen's College, and came to the United States in early manhood. After 1865 he was prominent in journalism, and especially as editor of the *Evening Post*; he had a trenchant and even a bitter style, and provoked vigorous antagonism.

Go'mez, Maximo, 1838- . . . . A Cuban military officer; born in Bani, San Domingo. In 1868 he joined the Cuban insurrection known as the Ten Years' War. He aided in the capture of Jugnani, Bayamo, Tunas, and Holguin, and was a leading actor in many other successful engagements; was promoted major-general and later succeeded General Agramonte as commander-in-chief. At the beginning of the war of 1895-1898 he again took up arms with the Cubans and fought with marked distinction till the Americans occupied Cuba.

Gomez, Sebastiano, 1616-1690. Spanish painter; a slave of Murillo, who liberated him and took him into his studio.

Gonsal'vo, or **Gonzalo of Cordova, Hernandez de Aguilar,** 1453-1515. A Spanish general, called "The Great Captain"; born near Cordova, Spain. He first distinguished himself in the great war of Ferdinand and Isabella with the Moors, which ended with the conquest of Granada in 1492. When Louis XII. renewed the invasion of Italy, Gonsalvo took command there, expelled the French, established the Spanish rule, and was named viceroy of Naples. Through the jealousy of Ferdinand, and the calumnies of the courtiers, he was deprived of his office in 1507, when he retired to Granada.

Gonzalez, Manuel, 1833-1893. A Mexican military officer; fought with distinction in the war against the French and Maximilian. He participated with Diaz in various revolts; was his secretary of war in 1877-1880, and succeeded him as president in 1880. After his retirement he was governor of Guanajuato. He died in Mexico city.

Goodyear, Charles, 1800-1860. An American inventor; born in New Haven, Conn. He failed as an iron manufacturer in 1830, but in 1834 turned his attention to india-rubber, the manufactured products of which had hitherto proved failures because of their liability to soften in the heat of summer. Amid poverty and ridicule, sometimes in prison for debt, he patiently pursued the experiments which, after he had obtained a fresh idea from his assistant Hayward's use of sulphur, ended, in 1844, in the issue of his patent for vulcanized rubber. This process he afterward perfected, discovering new uses to which his product could be applied, till it required sixty patents to secure his inventions. He died in New York city.

Gordon, Charles George (called "Chinese Gordon" and "Gordon Pasha"), 1833-1885. An English soldier; born in Woolwich, England. From 1874 to 1879 he was governor of the Sudan under the khedive. In 1882 he was sent to withdraw the garrisons shut up in the Sudan by the insurgent Mahdi. He was shut up in Khartum by the rebels, and gallantly held that town for a whole year. A British expeditionary force under Lord Wolseley was dispatched for his relief; an advance corps of which sighted Khartum January 24, 1885, to find that the town had been treacherously betrayed into the hands of the Mahdi two days before, and Gordon had been murdered.

Gortchakoff (*gor-cha-kof'*), **Prince Alexander Michaelovitch,** 1798-1883. A Russian statesman; born in St. Petersburg. As Russian minister of Foreign Affairs he declined to associate himself with France and Great Britain in their unfriendly attitude toward the United States. He was appointed chancellor in July, 1863. From this time till the ascendency of Bismarck he was the most powerful minister in Europe. After his retirement he left Russia for Baden-Baden, where he died.

Gough, John Ballantine, 1817-1886. A temperance orator; born in Kent, England; bred a bookbinder; early a victim to intemperance; took the pledge in 1842, and became an eloquent and powerful advocate of the temperance cause both in England and America.

Goujon (*goo-zhon'*), **Jean,** 1515-? A French sculptor and architect; born in Paris; he was the author of what is considered the masterpiece of French sculpture, the "Huntress Diana," now in the Louvre collection.

Gould, Jay, 1836-1892. An American financier; born in Roxbury, N. Y.; was brought up on his father's farm; attended Hobart College a short time, acquired a taste for mathematics and surveying; made surveys of Ulster, Albany, and Delaware counties, and began his railroad career directly after the panic of 1857; invested in bonds of the Rutland and Washington Railroad, and became president, treasurer, and superintendent of the road; removed to New York, opened a broker's office, and began dealing in Erie stocks and bonds; invested heavily in the various Pacific railroads, secured control of a number of important lines, built branches, and effected combinations which resulted in the establishment of what is known as the "Gould System"; he died in New York city, leaving property valued at $72,000,000.

Gounod (*goo-no'*), **Charles Francois,** 1818-1893. A French composer; born in Paris; in 1859 he produced "Faust," his chief work, which at once attained European popularity, and raised its composer to the foremost rank of contemporary musicians; from 1870 to 1875 he resided in England; he died in St. Cloud, France.

Gracchus, Caius Sempronius, 159-126 B.C. Roman statesman.

Gracchus, Tiberius Sempronius, 168?-133? B.C. Brother of the preceding. Roman statesman.

Graham, John, Viscount Dundee (Claverhouse), 1650?-1689. Scottish officer; noted for merciless severity toward the Covenanters.

Grant, Ulysses Simpson, 1822-1885. Eighteenth president of the United States; born in Ohio; graduated at West Point, 1843; served in Mexico; became a captain in 1853; resigned in 1854, and after passing some time at St. Louis removed to Galena, Ill., in 1859, and engaged in business; in 1861 he was made aide-de-camp to the governor of Illinois, but soon after was chosen colonel of the Twenty-first Illinois Volunteers, and in July of same year was made brigadier-general; made commander-in-chief of the Union armies in March, 1864; elected to the presidency in 1868, and again in 1872, and after the expiration of his second term he traveled extensively in Europe and Asia.

Grattan, Henry, 1746-1820. Irish orator and statesman.

Gray, Asa, 1810-1888. An American botanist; born in Paris, Oneida county, N. Y. In 1842 he became Fisher Professor of Natural History at Harvard. In 1873 he retired from the chair, but still retained charge of the great herbarium he had presented to the university in 1864, and in 1874 he succeeded Agassiz as a regent of the Smithsonian Institution. He ranked among the leading botanists of his age, and became an influential supporter of the Darwinian theories of evolution. He died in Cambridge, Mass.

Greeley, Horace, 1811-1872. American journalist; born in New Hampshire; learned the printers' trade and worked as a journeyman printer in New York for one year; founded the New York *Tribune*, 1841; a stanch Whig and Republican, he favored Fremont for the presidency in 1856, and Lincoln in 1860; accepted the Democratic nomination in 1872, but was defeated by Grant.

Greene, Nathaniel, General, 1742-1786. An American patriot; born in Rhode Island. He ranked next to General Washington in the Revolutionary struggle.

Greenough (*green'oh*), **Horatio,** 1805-1852. An American sculptor; born in Boston, Mass. He studied for two years at Harvard, and from 1825 spent the greater part of his life in Italy. His principal work was the colossal statue of Washington in front of the National Capitol. He died in Somerville, Mass.

Gregory VII., Hildebrand, 1020?-1085. Son of a carpenter; born in Soano, Tuscany; he was the friend and counselor of Leo IX. and the four succeeding popes, and on the death of Alexander II. was elected to succeed him in 1073. He obtained confirmation in his election from the Emperor Henry IV., and immediately applied himself zealously to reform simony and the licentiousness of the clergy. In his view, however, marriage, no less than concubinage, was a sin in them. He menaced the Emperor and the King of France, the latter without effect. In 1074 he assembled a council, by which it was forbidden the prelates to receive investiture of a layman, and this was the first step in the quarrel with the Emperor, which lasted so many years. Henry, disregarding the papal authority, was summoned to Rome; but he held a diet at Worms and pronounced the deposition of the Pope. To this Gregory replied by procuring the deposition of the Emperor and the election of another, Rudolph of Suabia. Henry now promised submission, and in the early winter of 1077 went with his wife and child to Italy. The Pope was at the castle of Canossa, and there, after keeping the penitent Emperor of Germany three days waiting at the gate, he received him and gave him absolution. The terms imposed on him were intolerable, and he soon broke them, made war on Rudolph, and defeated him, set up a rival pope in Guibert, Archbishop of Ravenna, with the title of Clement III., and after several unsuccessful attempts entered Rome in 1084, had himself crowned emperor by his own pope, and besieged Gregory in San Angelo. Gregory was delivered by Guiscard, and retiring to Salerno died there.

Gregory XIII., Buoncompagno, 1502-1585. A native of Bologna, and succeeded Pope Pius V. in 1572. He was deeply versed in the canon and civil law and had distinguished himself at the Council of Trent. He ornamented Rome with many fine buildings and fountains; but his pontificate is chiefly memorable for the reformation of the calendar which took place under his auspices and bore his name.

Gregory, Saint, 257?-332. Surnamed Illuminator; the founder of the Armenian Church; born in Valarshabad, Armenia. From 302 to 331 he was Patriarch of the Armenian Church, but having resigned the patriarchate in favor of his second son Aristaces, Gregory in 331 retired to a cave at the foot of Mount Sebuh in Upper Armenia, where he died.

Gregory Nazianzen, Saint, 326-389. Bishop of Constantinople; born near Nazianzus, Cappadocia. He excelled all his contemporaries in pulpit eloquence. Many of his works are extant, and consist of orations, letters, and poems.

Gregory of Tours, 540?-594. A Frankish historian; born in Arverna (now Clermont), Auvergne, France. He belonged to one of the most distinguished Roman families of Gaul. His fame rests on his "History, or Annals," the chief authority for the history of Gaul in the sixth century. He died in Tours, France.

Gresham, Walter Quinton, 1832-1895. An American jurist; born near Lanesville, Harrison county Ind.; served in the Civil War, rising to brigader-general of volunteers; at its close resumed the practice of law, and in 1869 was appointed by President Grant United States District Judge for Indiana; in 1883 was appointed Postmaster-General by President Arthur; in 1884 became Secretary of the Treasury, and later was appointed one of the judges of the United States Circuit Court. He died in Washington, D. C.

Grevy (*gray′ve*), **Francois Paul Jules,** 1813-1891. A French statesman. Grevy was chosen president of the National Assembly which met in 1871. In 1876, 1877, and 1879 he again represented the Jura in the French Parliament, and in the latter year he was chosen president of the republic by an enormous majority. In 1886 he was re-elected, but on account of a scandal in which his son-in-law was implicated was forced to resign.

Grey, Lady Jane, 1537-1554. The ill-fated "nine days' queen"; born at Bradgate, Leicestershire; was the daughter of the Duke of Suffolk and the great-granddaughter of Henry VII.; her talents were of a rare order, and sedulously cultivated; she attained to great proficiency in Greek, Latin, and also in modern languages, while she was skilled in all the accomplishments of womanhood; a plot entered into by Suffolk and the Duke of Northumberland, whose son Lady Jane had been forced to espouse at fifteen, brought about her proclamation as Queen in 1553; the attempted usurpation was crushed in ten days, and four months later Lady Jane and her husband were executed.

Grotius (*gro′shus*), **Hugo (De Groot),** 1583-1645. A distinguished Dutch jurist and author. His "International Law" is still authority.

Grouchy (*groo-she′*), **Emmanuel, Marquis de,** 1766-1847. A French marshal. He refused to march his corps from Wavre to the assistance of Napoleon I. at Waterloo, without orders, and has been charged with treachery.

Guatemozin (*gwah-te-mo′zin*), ... -1522. Successor of Montezuma, emperor of Mexico, and the last prince of the Aztec dynasty; was cruelly tortured by order of Cortez, and afterwards put to death.

Guelf, or **Guelph.** The name of a family which in the eleventh century was transplanted from Italy to Germany, where it became the ruling race of several countries. The family still continues in the two lines of Brunswick, the royal in England and the ducal in Germany.

Guido Reni, 1575-1642. Italian painter of the school of Bologna; best known by his masterpiece "Aurora and the Hours" at Rome, painted on a ceiling, and his unfinished "Nativity" at Naples.

Gustavus I. (Gustavus Vasa), 1496-1559. King of Sweden. **Gustavus II.** (Gustavus Adolphus), 1594-1632. Defeated the Polish and Russian armies invading Sweden; became the head of the Protestant league in Germany and defeated Tilly at Leipsic in 1631, and on the banks of the Lech in 1632; at the great battle of Luetzen, Wallenstein now commanding the imperial army, Gustavus was killed; his troops nevertheless gained a complete victory. **Gustavus III.,** 1746-1792. Assassinated. **Gustavus IV.,** 1778-1837. Ascended the throne in 1792, but was deposed in 1809.

Gutenberg, Johann (Gansfleisch), 1400-1468. German inventor of movable type and the printing press; first books printed about 1457; died in poverty.

Hachette (*ah-shet′*), **Jeanne,** 1454- . . . . A French heroine, born in Beauvais, who took part in the defense of her native town when besieged in 1472 by Charles the Bold.

Hackett, James Henry, 1800-1871. An American actor; born in New York city. He was particularly successful in impersonating Yankees and Westerners, but was best known by his Falstaff, which he played first about 1832. He wrote "Notes and Comments on Shakespeare." Died in Jamaica, N. Y.

Hadley, Arthur Twining, 1856- . . . . An American educator; born in New Haven, Conn.; was graduated at Yale College in 1876; studied at the University of Berlin; was Professor of Political Science at Yale University from 1886-1899 and was then elected its president; has written authoritatively on a number of economic themes.

Hadrian, 76-138. Roman emperor; born in Rome; distinguished himself under Trajan, his kinsman; was governor of Syria, and was proclaimed emperor by the army on Trajan's death in 117 A.D.; visited Gaul in 120, whence he passed over to Britain, where he built the great wall from the Tyne to the Solway; he was a Greek scholar, and had a knowledge of Greek literature, encouraged industry, literature, and the arts, as well as reformed the laws.

Haeckel (*hay′kel*), **Ernest Heinrich,** 1834- . . . . A distinguished German naturalist; born in Potsdam, Prussia; he became Professor of Zoology at the University of Jena, in 1865; his purely scientific works have been translated into many languages.

Hah′nemann, Samuel Christian Friedrich, 1755-1843. A distinguished German physician and chemist, originator of the homœopathic system of medical practice; died in Paris.

Hale, John Parker, 1806-1873. An American statesman; born in Rochester, N. H.; elected to Congress, in 1842, as a Democrat; his name was afterward removed from the party ticket because he refused to support the annexation of Texas; in 1847 Hale was elected to the United States Senate, where he served for sixteen years; he was minister to Spain from 1865 to 1869, and died in Dover, N. H.

Hale, Sir Matthew, 1609-1676. Lord Chief Justice of England; born in Alderley, Gloucestershire, England; after the restoration he was made Chief-Baron of the Court of Exchequer, and eleven years later was transferred to the Chief-Justiceship of the Court of King's Bench; he resigned his office in February, 1676, and died in Alderley on Christmas day of that year.

Halevy (*hah-lay-ve′*), **Jacques Francois Elias,** 1799-1862. A French operatic composer; born at Paris; became a professor at the Conservatoire; wrote a large number of operas, of which "La Juive" and "L'Eclair" were the best.

Hall, Marshall, 1790-1857. An English physician and physiologist; specialist in nervous diseases. His name is also associated with a well known method of restoring suspended respiration. He died in Brighton, England.

Halleck, Henry Wager, 1815-1873. An American general; distinguished himself on the side of the North in the Civil War, and was promoted to be commander-in-chief; was author of "Elements of Military Art and Science."

Haller, Albert von, 1708-1777. A celebrated anatomist, physiologist, botanist, physician, and poet; born at Bern; professor of Medicine at Goettingen; was a voluminous author and writer.

Hals, Franz, 1580?-1666. The Elder; a Dutch portrait and genre painter; born probably in Antwerp; he is usually regarded as the founder of the Dutch school of genre painting. He died in Haarlem, Netherlands. His brother, **Dirk Hals** (before 1600-1656), a pupil of Abraham Bloemaert, was also an excellent genre painter. Several of Franz's sons were artists, the most celebrated being **Franz Hals,** the Younger, who flourished from about 1637 to 1669.

Hamilton, Alexander, 1757-1804. American orator, statesman, financier, and general; born in the West Indies; secretary and aide-de-camp to Washington in Revolutionary War; chosen to the Continental Congress, 1782, but resigned in order to practice law; leading member of the convention of 1787; Secretary of the Treasury, 1789-1795; became recognized leader of the Federal party. Hamilton died from a wound received in a duel with Aaron Burr, and his death was deeply deplored.

Hamilton, Sir William, 1788-1856. Scotch metaphysician.

Hamilton, Sir William Rowan, 1805-1865. An English mathematician and astronomer; born in Dublin,

Ireland. His fame is chiefly founded on his invention of the calculus of quarternions, a new method in the higher mathematics.

Hamlin, Hannibal, 1809-1891. An American statesman; born in Paris, Me.; was elected to the United States Senate in 1848 to fill an unexpired term; re-elected in 1851 and again in 1857; resigned in 1861, after being elected Vice-President on the ticket with Abraham Lincoln; was again a United States Senator from 1869-1881, and then accepted the post of minister to Spain. He died in Bangor, Me.

Hammond, William Alexander, 1828-1900. An American surgeon; born in Annapolis, Md.; joined the United States army in 1849 as assistant surgeon; became surgeon-general in April, 1862; was found guilty of misdemeanor by court-martial and discharged from the army in 1864; practiced in New York till 1878, when the proceedings of the court-martial were reviewed and he was restored to his former rank in the army and retired. He died in Washington, D. C.

Hampden, John, 1594-1643. An English patriot and Parliamentary leader; killed at Chalgrove Hill. He was a champion of popular rights against the oppressive measures of Charles I., and suffered prosecution and imprisonment.

Hampton, Wade, 1818-1902. An American military officer; born in Charleston, S. C. At the outbreak of the Civil War he was believed to be one of the richest of Southern planters, and owned the greatest number of slaves. He entered the Confederate army; was promoted major-general and appointed commander-in-chief of the Confederate cavalry in Northern Virginia; was promoted lieutenant-general in 1865. He greatly distinguished himself in several important actions: was elected governor of South Carolina; held a seat in the United States Senate from 1878-1890, and was appointed Commissioner of Railroads in 1893.

Hancock, John, 1737-1793. American statesman; president of the Continental Congress.

Hancock, Winfield Scott, 1824-1886. American general; second in command at Gettysburg; Democratic candidate for president in 1880.

Handel, George Frederick, 1684-1759. German composer; settled in England in 1712; "The Messiah," the greatest of oratorios, was produced, 1741; Handel was stricken with blindness, 1751, but continued to conduct his oratorios; buried in Westminster Abbey.

Hannibal, 247-183 B.C. Carthaginian general; considered the greatest general of the world; sworn by his father, Hamilcar Barca, to eternal enmity toward Rome; became commander of the Carthaginian forces, 221 B.C.; subdued several powerful Spanish tribes, and in 219 captured Saguntum; crossed the Alps, 218; defeated the Romans near the Ticinus and on the banks of the Trebia; routed Flaminius at Lake Thrasymene, 217; almost destroyed a superior Roman army near Cannæ, 216; captured Capua; recalled to Carthage to repel a Roman invasion under Scipio Africanus, he was defeated at Zama in 202; banished from Carthage about 194, through the emnity of the aristocracy; finally ended his life by taking poison, to escape falling into the hands of the Romans.

Harcourt, Sir William Vernon, 1827- . . . . English statesman; in 1873 he became Solicitor-General, and received a knighthood; he was a vigorous opponent of the Disraeli government, and on the return of the Liberals to power in 1880 became Home Secretary; under Mr. Gladstone in 1886, and again in 1892, he held the office of Chancellor of the Exchequer; became leader of the Opposition in the House of Commons on Mr. Gladstone's retirement.

Harley, Robert, Earl of Oxford, 1661-1724. A celebrated English politician; entered Parliament shortly after the Revolution (1688) as a Whig, but after a period of vacillation threw in his lot with Tories and in 1701 became Speaker of the House; he became Chancellor of the Exchequer and head of the government; was created Earl of Oxford and Lord High Treasurer; was impeached for intriguing with the Jacobites and sent to the Tower; two years later he was released, and the remainder of his life was spent in the pursuit of letters and in the building up of his famous collection of MSS., now deposited in the British Museum.

Harold. The name of two of England's early kings. **Harold I.,** . . . . -1040. Surnamed Harefoot, because of his fleetness; was second son of Canute the Great, and succeeded to the throne, 1037. **Harold II.,** 1021?-1066. Son of Godwin, Earl of Kent; was proclaimed king, 1066, as successor of Edward the Confessor; he defeated an invasion of Norsemen the same year, but was himself defeated and overthrown by William, Duke of Normandy, a few days later.

Haroun-al-Raschid (*hah-roon' al rash'id*), 766?-809. The most eminent of the Abbassides caliphs.

Harrison, Benjamin, 1833-1901. President of the United States; born at North Bend, Ohio; proved himself a brave and efficient commander during the Civil War; engaging actively in politics, he in 1880 became a United States Senator; as the nominee of the Protectionist or Republican party he won the presidency against Cleveland, but at the election of 1892 the positions were reversed; in 1893 he became a professor in Stanford University, Cal.

Harrison, William Henry, Gen., 1773-1841. Ninth president of the United States; born in Virginia; died one month after the inauguration. He was the hero of the Indian battle of Tippecanoe, in Indiana, 1811, and also defeated a British force on the Thames, Canada, 1813; afterward elected to the United States Senate, and sent as minister to Colombia, 1828-1829.

Hartley, David, 1705-1757. An English philosopher and physician; wrote "Observations on Man, his Fame, his Duty, and his Expectations"; ascribed sensation to vibration in the nerves, and applied the doctrine of the association of ideas to mental phenomena.

Hartmann, Edward von, 1842- . . . . A German philosopher; born at Berlin; established his fame by a work entitled the "Philosophy of the Unconscious"; founder of a new school of philosophy, which professes to be a synthesis of that of Hegel and that of Schopenhauer, and to aim at the reconciliation of philosophic results with scientific.

Harvard, John, 1607-1638. An American clergyman; born in England; he was graduated at Emmanuel College, Cambridge, England, and came to the United States in 1637; he was made a citizen of Massachusetts and given a tract of land in Charlestown, where he began preaching as a Congregational minister, and in his will bequeathed $3,750 and 320 volumes from his library for the establishment of a college. A granite monument was erected over his remains in Charlestown in 1828, and a memorial statue on the Delta at Harvard University was unveiled in 1884.

Harvey, William, 1478-1657. English physician and anatomist, and the greatest of physiologists; discovered the circulation of the blood.

Hasdrubal, ... -207 B. C. Punic general; brother of Hannibal; defeated the Scipios; slain at the Metaurus.

Hastings, Warren, 1732-1818. British general and statesman; president of the Council of Bengal, and governor- general of India; defeated Hyder Ali, king of Mysore; after perpetrating great outrages in order to replenish the treasury, he resigned in 1775 and returned to England; impeached soon afterward, and opposed in his trial by Burke, Sheridan, and Fox, but acquitted.

Haussman (*ose'mahn*), **George Eugene, Baron,** 1809-1891. Celebrated French Prefect of the Seine, who carried through extensive architectural improvements in Paris, which transformed it into one of the handsomest cities of Europe; ennobled by Napoleon III.

Havelock, Sir Henry, 1795-1869. An English general. In 1857, upon the breaking out of the Sepoy mutiny, he made a forced march from Allahabad to Cawnpur, but reached the latter city too late to prevent the massacre which occurred there; continued his march toward Lucknow, then beleaguered by a formidable force of mutineers. After victoriously fighting a number of battles with the enemy he accomplished the relief of its exhausted garrison. For this service he received general rank, was created a baronet, and decorated with the cross of the Bath.

Hawke, Edward, Lord, 1715-1781. An English admiral; born in London; defeated a French fleet off Finisterre and captured six ships of the line in 1759; defeated Admiral Conflans off Belleisle; was made a peer in 1776.

Hawkins, Sir John, 1530-1595. An English navigator and admiral; born at Plymouth; was rear admiral of the fleet sent against the Armada and contributed to its defeat; has the unenviable distinction of having been the first Englishman to traffic in slaves, which he carried off from Africa and imported into the West Indies.

Haydn, Joseph, 1732-1809. German musical composer; his masterpiece, the oratorio of "The Creation," was produced in 1798.

Haydon, Benjamin Robert, 1786-1848. English painter.

Hayes, Isaac Israel, 1832-1881. American Arctic explorer.

Hayes, Rutherford Birchard, 1822-1893. Nineteenth president of the United States; born in Connecticut; admitted to the bar, 1845; brigadier-general in Civil War; in Congress, 1865-1868; governor of Ohio, 1868-1876; Republican candidate for the presidency, 1876; inaugurated president, 1877, the electoral commission to determine the result of the election of 1876 having decided, by a vote of eight to seven, that Hayes had received 185 electoral votes as against 184 for Samuel J. Tilden, the Democratic candidate.

Hayne, Robert Young, 1791-1840. American orator and statesman; opponent of Webster in discussing the Constitution; governor of South Carolina.

Hearst, William Randolph, 1865- . . . . Son of the late Senator George F. Hearst and of Phebe Hearst; born in San Francisco. He has been a successful journalist from early life, and owns Hearst's *Chicago American*, the New York *American* and *Journal*, and San Francisco *Examiner;* all newspapers of great influence and circulation. Prominently mentioned in 1904, especially by the labor element, as Democratic candidate for president of the United States.

Hebert (*a-bair′*), **Jacques Rene,** 1756-1794. Commonly called Pere Duchesne as editor of a journal of that name, a violent revolutionary organ; took part in the September massacres; brutally insulted the queen at her trial, to the disgust of Robespierre; was arrested by his colleagues, whom he dared to oppose, and guillotined.

Hegel (*hay′-gel*), **Georg Wilhelm Friedrich,** 1770-1831. German philosopher; the greatest of all; born in Stuttgart; first announced himself in 1807 by his work, "Phenomenology of the Spirit"; became rector of the Academy at Nuremberg, where in 1812-1816 he composed his "Logic"; was in 1816 appointed professor of Philosophy at Heidelberg, whence he was removed to Berlin in 1818, where, his philosophy being now matured, he began to apply it with intense earnestness to every subject of human interest; he was the last of a line of thinkers beginning with Kant, with whom, however, he affiliated directly. His system may be grouped under three heads, the "Science of Logic," the "Philosophy of Nature," and the "Philosophy of Spirit."

Heilprin, Michael, 1823-1888. An American scholar; born in Poland; came to the United States in 1856, and contributed to various literary journals. He published "The Historical Poetry of the Ancient Hebrews." He died in Summit, N. J.

Hein′sius, Anthony, 1641-1720. A noted Dutch statesman; born at Delft; became Grand Pensionary of Holland; was the intimate friend and correspondent of William III. of England, who left the guidance of Dutch affairs largely in his hands.

Hel′ler, Stephen, 1814-1888. A distinguished pianist and composer; born at Pesth; in 1838 he settled in Paris, and gave himself to teaching and composition; he ranks beside Chopin as a master of technique.

Helm′holtz, Hermann Ludwig Ferdinand von, 1821-1894. A German physicist; born in Potsdam; his work has been chiefly in acoustics and optics; he was ennobled by the German emperor in 1883.

Hel′mont, Jan Baptista van, 1577-1644. A celebrated German chemist, the father of chemistry; born at Brussels; his early years were divided between the study of medicine and the practice of a religious mysticism; mixed up a good deal of mysticism and alchemy with his scientific discoveries, and made a special study of gases; he was the first to prove the indestructibility of matter; he invented the word gas, first used the melting-point of ice and the boiling-point of water as limits of a thermometric scale.

Heloise (*ay-lo-eze′*), 1101-1164. Niece of Canon Fulbert; born at Paris; celebrated for her amour with Abelard; became prioress of the convent of Argenteuil and abbess of the Paraclete, where she founded a new convent and lived a pious life.

Helst, Bartholomæus van der, 1613-1670. One of the greatest of the Dutch portrait painters; born at Haarlem, but spent his life in Amsterdam; his "Muster of the Burgher Guard" was considered by Sir Joshua Reynolds to be "the first picture of portraits in the world."

Helvetius (*hel-ve′shus*), **Claude Adrien,** 1715-1771. A French philosopher; born in Paris, of Swiss origin; author of a book entitled "De l'Esprit," which was condemned by the Parliament of Paris for views advocated in it that were considered derogatory to the dignity of man, and which exposed him to much bitter hostility, especially at the hands of the priests; man he reduced to a mere animal, made self-love the only motive of his actions, and the satisfaction of our sensuous desires the principle of morals, notwithstanding which he was a man of estimable character and of kindly disposition.

Hendricks, Thomas Andrews, 1819-1886. American statesman.

Hengist, ... -488. Jutish chief; founded kingdom of Kent.

Hennepin, Louis, 1640-1702? French Catholic missionary and explorer of the Mississippi.

Henry I. (Beauclerc), 1068-1135. King of England; defeated his brother Robert and usurped the throne.

Henry II., 1133-1189. First of the Plantagenets; issued constitutions of Clarendon, which were, however, repealed about ten years later; conquered Ireland; during his reign Thomas a Becket was killed.

Henry VI., 1421-1471. His reign was made memorable by the War of the Roses.

Henry VII., 1456-1509. Founded the Tudor dynasty.

Henry VIII., 1491-1547. Defeated the French at Guinegaste and the Scotch at Flodden, 1513; made Thomas Wolsey prime minister; applied unsuccessfully to the pope for a divorce from Catherine of Aragon, his wife; favored the Reformation; deposed Wolsey and elevated Thomas Cranmer; had himself declared head of the church; married Anne Boleyn after the convocations of York and Canterbury had declared his marriage with Catherine invalid; declared the English church independent of the papal see and abolished the monasteries; had Anne Boleyn executed in 1536, and married Jane Seymour the day after the execution; excommunicated by the pope, 1538; his third wife having died in 1537, he married Anne of Cleves in 1540; was divorced from her the same year and married Catherine Howard, who was executed on a charge of adultery in 1542; married Catherine Parr in 1543, she surviving him.

Henry, Joseph, 1797-1878. An American physicist; born in Washington, D. C.; discovered how to produce the electro-magnet, about 1827, and afterward greatly improved it. He built the first electro-magnetic telegraph, about a mile long, in 1830; designed the first electro-magnetic engine in 1831; was connected with the Smithsonian Institution from 1846-1878; was twice offered the presidency of Princeton College. He died in Washington, D. C.

Henry, Patrick, 1736-1799. American patriot and orator; member of the Continental Congress; governor of Virginia.

Heraclitus, fl. fifth century, B.C. A Greek philosopher; born at Ephesus; was the first to note how everything throughout the universe is in constant flux, and nothing permanent but in transition from being to nothing and from nothing to being.

Herbart, Johann Friedrich, 1776-1841. German philosopher; born at Oldenburg; Kant's successor at Koenigsberg, professor also at Gottingen; founded his philosophy like Kant on the criticism of subjective experience, but arrived at different results, and it arrayed itself against the whole post-Kantian philosophy of Germany.

Herkimer, Nicholas, 1715-1777. An American military officer; born in New York of German parents. He joined the patriots of the Revolutionary War, and was a powerful element in his own state in determining the success of the Revolution. His most noteworthy feat was the relief of Fort Schuyler when invested by Colonel St. Leger after the battle of Ticonderoga. He died in Danube, N. Y.

Herod the Great, 72-4 B.C. King of the Jews by favor of the Romans; made away with all his rivals, caused his own children to be strangled on suspicion of their conspiring against him, and died a painful death.

Herod Antipas. Son of the preceding; tetrarch of Galilee; beheaded John the Baptist; Christ was remitted to him by Pilate for examination; died in exile at Lyons.

Herrera (*er-ray′rah*), **Francisco de,** 1576-1656. A distinguished Spanish painter, founder of the Seville school; born at Seville; his finest paintings include "The Last Judgment" and a "Holy family," both in churches at Seville; others are in the Louvre, Paris; they exhibit boldness of execution with faultless technique.

Herschel, Sir John, 1790-1871. Astronomer, only son of Sir William; prosecuted with great diligence and success the same researches as his father; spent four years at the Cape of Good Hope, and added much to our knowledge of the stars and meteorology.

Herschel, Lucretia, 1750-1848. Sister of the succeeding; was his assistant, and made important observations of her own, which were published; retired after her brother's death to Hanover, where she died.

Herschel, Sir William, 1738-1822. A distinguished

astronomer; born at Hanover, Germany; went to England at the end of the Seven Years' War, and had sundry appointments as an organist; gave his leisure time to the study of astronomy and survey of the heavens; discovered the planet Uranus in 1781, which he called *Georgium sidus* in honor of George III.; discovered also the two innermost belts of Saturn, as well as drew up a catalogue of 5000 heavenly bodies or clusters of them.

Hertz, Henrik, 1798-1870. Danish poet; born in Copenhagen of Jewish parents; his best known work is "King Rene's Daughter," which has been translated into English for the fourth time; he is considered one of the greatest of modern Danish lyrists and dramatists.

Hezekiah. A king of Judah; reigned from 725 to 697 B.C.; distinguished for his zeal in the celebration of the worship of Jehovah and for his weakness in making a parade of his wealth; reigned in the golden age of Hebrew prophecy, Isaiah and Micah being his contemporaries.

Hicks, Elias, 1748-1830. An American preacher of the Quaker connection, who adopted Unitarian views and caused a split in the body.

Hill, Sir Rowland, 1795-1879. The author of the penny-postage system; born in Kidderminster, England; he was also the originator of the money-order system, and of post office savings banks; he died in Hampstead, near London.

Hippoc′rates, 460?-377? B.C. The greatest physician of ancient times, usually designated the "Father of Medicine"; born in the Island of Cos; among his authentic writings are: "Prognosis," "Aphorisms," "On Epidemics," "On Diet in Acute Diseases," "On Air, Water, and Place," "On Wounds of the Head"; he was distinguished for his remarkable skill in diagnosis, and his accurate and vivid description of morbid symptoms; he died in Larissa, Thessaly.

Hitchcock, Edward, 1793-1864. An American geologist; born in Deerfield, Mass.; he was made president of Amherst College in 1845, but resigned in 1854, continuing his professorship there till his death. Amherst College owes to him the founding of its Museum of Natural History, and his writings were among the earliest to call attention in the United States to the study of geology; his "Religion of Geology and its Connected Sciences" marks a distinct epoch in scientific study in this country; he died in Amherst, Mass.

Hob′bema, Meindert, 1638-1709. A famous Dutch landscape painter; born at Amsterdam; his fine, subdued pictures of woodland life and scenery are ranked among the masterpieces of Dutch landscape painting.

Hobbes (*hobs*), **Thomas,** 1588-1679. An English philosopher, psychologist, and moralist, born at Malmesbury; translated Thucydides. wrote a number of works, "De Cive" among others, and the "Leviathan," all more or less leading up to the doctrine that the absolute sovereign power in all matters of right and wrong is vested in the state as the achieved fact of the emancipation of the race from savagery.

Hoe, Richard March, 1812-1886. An American inventor; born in New York city. In 1846 he perfected a rotary printing press which was called "Hoe's lightning press." Subsequently he invented the Hoe web-perfecting press. These were especially adapted to newspaper printing, and made a revolution in that art. He died in Florence, Italy.

Hofer, Andreas, 1767-1810. A Tyrolese patriot; born in St. Leonard, in the valley of Passeyr. When the Tyrol, long a part of the Austrian dominions, was given by the treaty of Presburg to the King of Bavaria, then the ally of Napoleon, the Tyrolese revolted, and Andreas Hofer became their leader. Within a week from the outbreak of the insurrection, early in April, 1809, the Bavarian forces were everywhere defeated and the Tyrol freed. Three French armies then invaded the province, and after temporary success on their part, Hofer won the victory of Innspruck, and again freed his country. A second French invasion ended in defeat, and the people were a third time freed. For a few weeks Hofer was, virtually, sovereign of his country; but on the renewed invasion of French and Bavarians, he was betrayed to his enemies, condemned by a court-martial at Mantua, and shot.

Hogarth, William, 1697-1764. A truly great and original painter of life and manners; born in London, England; in 1720 commenced painting portraits, and making designs and bookplates for the booksellers; his "Rake's Progress" and similar works attracted universal attention.

Holbach (*G., hole′bok, F., ole-bahk′*), **Baron von,** 1723-1789. A French philosopher; born in Heidelsheim, in the Palatinate, of wealthy parents; lived in Paris, kept a good table, and entertained all the "Encyclopedie" notabilities at his board; wrote "Systeme de la Nature"; was a materialist in philosophy and an atheist in religion, but a kind hearted man.

Holbein (*hol′bine*), **Hans,** 1497-1554. A German painter; born at Augsburg; attracted the attention of Erasmus, who took a great interest in him, and persuaded him to go to England, and introduced him to Sir Thomas More, who in turn introduced him to Henry VIII.; here under Henry's patronage he remained, executing numerous portraits of his courtiers, till his death of the plague; his "Last Supper" and "Dance of Death" are well known.

Holden, Sir Isaac, 1807-1897. Scotch inventor; discovered the principle of the lucifer match; became established near Paris, where he carried out elaborate experiments, which resulted in improvements in wool-combing machinery that brought him fame and fortune; in 1859 he transferred his works to the vicinity of Bradford; entered Parliament, and was created a baronet.

Holley, Alexander Lyman, 1832- . . . . An American metallurgist; born in Lakeville, Conn. About 1863 he went to England and purchased for Corning, Winslow & Company the Bessemer patents for the manufacture of steel. The first Bessemer works were built by him in Troy, N. Y., in 1865, and the second plant in Harrisburg, Pa., in 1867. He was lecturer on the manufacture of iron and steel at Columbia University from 1879-1882.

Hopkins, Johns, 1795-1873. An American philanthropist; born in Anne Arundel county, Md. In 1873 he gave property worth $4,500,000 to found a free hospital; he presented Baltimore with a public park, and he also gave over $3,000,000 to found the Johns Hopkins University in Baltimore.

Hopkinson, Francis, 1737-1791. An American political writer; born in Philadelphia. His humorous ballad, "The Battle of the Kegs," was widely known. He was one of the signers of the Declaration of Independence.

Houdon (*oo-don′*), **Jean Antoine,** 1740-1828. A French sculptor; born in Versailles; after studying in Italy, he returned to Paris, and executed the busts of Voltaire, Rousseau, Moliere, Franklin, Buffon, Catherine II., *et als.* He was invited to the United States and carved the statue of Washington now at the Virginia State Capitol in Richmond, which is considered the most authentic likeness of "the father of our country." Died in Paris.

Houston, Sam, 1793-1863. American general and statesman; governor of Tennessee, 1827-1829; passed a number of years with the Cherokee Indians; commander-in-chief of the Texan forces in revolt against Mexico, and defeated and captured Santa Ana in 1836; elected president of Texas same year, and re-elected 1841; elected senator from Texas after its admission to the Union, in 1845, and governor in 1859.

Howard, John, 1726-1790. An English philanthropist. When about nineteen years of age, on the death of his father he was left an independent fortune. Devoted his time to the investigation of the means of correcting abuses in the management of prisons; visited most of the English county jails and houses of correction, and laid the result of his inquiries before the House of Commons. In 1789 he published an "Account of the Principal Lazarettos in Europe." In the same year he made a final journey through Germany and Russia. He died of fever in Cherson in South Russia.

Howe, Elias, 1819-1867. An American inventor; born in Spencer, Mass. He patented the first sewing machine.

Hudson, Hendrik, 1580-1611? An English navigator; discovered the river in New York state which bears his name, while in the service of the Dutch East India Company, 1609; in 1611 discovered Hudson's bay.

Humboldt, Friedrich Heinrich Alexander, Baron von, 1769-1859. A distinguished German traveler, scientist, and author.

Humboldt, Karl Wilhelm, Baron von, 1767-1835. Brother of the preceding; was an eminent statesman and philologist, styled "the creator of comparative philology."

Huss (*hoos*), **Johann,** 1373-1415. A distinguished religious reformer; born in Bohemia; burned at the stake by order of the Council of Constance. His followers, called Hussites, inaugurated a war for religious freedom, 1418, and continued with such success that the Emperor Sigismund granted them acceptable terms and peace was restored.

Huxley, Thomas Henry, 1825-1895. Eminent English scientist; born at Ealing, Middlesex; was professor of Natural History in the Royal School of Mines; distinguished by his studies and discoveries in different sections of the animal kingdom; was a zealous advocate of evolution, in particular the views of Darwin; he was a man of eminent literary ability as well as scientific, and of the greatest in that regard among scientific men.

Hypatia, fl. fifth century. A far-famed lady teacher of Greek philosophy in Alexandria, distinguished for her beauty and purity of life, who, one day in 415, on her return home from her lecture room, was massacred in the streets of the city, at the instance of both Jews and Christians, as a propagator of paganism.

Iberville (*e-bayr-veel'*), **Pierre le Moyne, Sieur d',** 1661-1706. A French-Canadian naval and military commander; born in Montreal. In 1699, by order of the French government he built Fort Biloxi at the head of Biloxi bay, the first post on the Mississippi river. He afterward established other posts in the same region and was preparing to attack the coast of North Carolina when he died in Havana, Cuba.

Ibrahim (*ib-rah-heem'*) **Pasha,** 1789-1848. A viceroy of Egypt; born in Cavella, Albania; Ibrahim crossed the Egyptian border with an army in 1831, took Acre by storm, and quickly made himself master of the whole of Syria; the interference of the great powers eventually compelled him to relinquish all his Syrian conquests, and to return to Egypt; in 1848 he went to Constantinople, and was installed by the Porte as viceroy of Egypt; he died in Cairo.

Ignatius, Saint (surnamed Theophorus), 32?-107. Bishop of Antioch; martyred in Rome; his writings are still held in high esteem.

Ingersoll, Robert Green, 1833-1899. An American lawyer; born in Dresden, N. Y.; was admitted to the bar in 1854; soon became distinguished in the courts and in Democratic politics as an orator; recruited the 11th Illinois Cavalry in 1862, and entered the army as its colonel. On Nov. 28, 1862, while trying with a force of 600 men to intercept a Confederate raiding body, he was captured by a force of 10,000 men, but was soon paroled and given command of a camp in St. Louis. He soon afterward resigned. After the war he became a Republican; was made attorney general of Illinois in 1866; was a delegate to the Republican National Convention in 1876 and there nominated for president, James G. Blaine, whom he termed "the plumed knight." He was prominent in politics for several years, and had he not given strong expression to his views as an agnostic he would doubtless have been honored with high offices. He settled in New York city in 1882 and practiced law there till his death; he died in Dobbs Ferry, N. Y.

Ingres (*angr*), **Jean Dominique Auguste,** 1781-1867. A French historical painter; born in Montauban. Ingres occupies a middle place between the classical and romantic schools, and is chiefly remarkable for correct design, ideal composition, and sober painting.

Inman, Henry, 1801-1846. An eminent American artist; born in New York; died while at work on a large order from Congress for the historical embellishment of the Capitol.

Inness, George, 1825-1894. An American painter; born in Newburg, N. Y.; resided in Italy from 1871-1875. His pictures are noted for the accuracy with which they represent the American climate and the aspects of American scenery.

Innocent I. (Saint), ... -417. Pope, ruling 402-417; during his reign Rome was sacked by Alaric.

Innocent III. (Lotharius), 1161-1216. Chosen pope, 1198; put France under the ban, 1190, because Philip Augustus repudiated his wife; promoted the Fourth Crusade, the result of which was the capture of Constantinople; deposed Otho, emperor of Germany, transferring the crown to Frederick of Sicily; subjected John of England to the Papal see, compelling him to pay an annual tribute; crushed the Albigenses in 1214, and died two years later.

Irenæus, Saint, fl. second century. One of the fathers of the church; was Bishop of Lyons, and suffered martyrdom about 202; wrote against the Gnostics in a work in Greek, of which all but a few fragments in Latin is lost.

Irving, Sir Henry, 1838- . . . . An English actor; born in Keinton, England. His family name was Brodribb, which was changed to Irving by royal patent. His roles include Mephistopheles, Hamlet, Coriolanus, King Lear, and a repertory that has been presented not only in England, but in the United States, Australia, and France. He was knighted in 1895.

Isabella I. (the Catholic), 1451-1504. Queen of Castile; wife of Ferdinand of Aragon; patroness of Columbus.

Isabelle of France, 1292-1358. Queen of England wife of Edward II., whom her adherents deposed, and with whose assassination she is charged; her son, Edward III., ascended the throne and ordered her arrest, and she died after twenty years' incarceration.

Isaiah, 750?-700? B.C. One of the great Hebrew prophets, the son of one Amoz; was a citizen of Jerusalem, evidently of some standing; like Amos, he foresaw the judgment that was coming on the nation for its unfaithfulness, but felt assured that God would not altogether forsake his people, and that "a remnant," God's elect among them, would be saved.

Iturbide (*e-toor-be'day*), **Augustine de,** 1783-1824 A Mexican general; emancipated Mexico from the yoke of Spain; seized the crown and was proclaimed emperor in 1822; was obliged to abdicate next year and leave the country, but returning, was immediately arrested and shot.

Ivan III. (*e-vahn'*) (surnamed The Threatening), . . . -1505. Sought to free Russia from the yoke of the Tartars who had held it tributary for two centuries; gained victories over the Tartars and the Poles, and was the first to receive at Moscow ambassadors from other powers of Europe; reigned from 1462 to 1505.

Ivan IV. (surnamed The Terrible), 1530-1584. Grandson of the preceding; assumed the sovereignty at fourteen, had himself crowned in 1545, and took the title of Czar; his first great ambition was to destroy the Tartar power, which he did at Kasan and Astrakhan, receiving homage thereafter from almost all the Tartar chiefs; on the death of his wife in 1563 he lost all self-restraint, and by the ferocity of his wars provoked hostility, which the pope, who had been appealed to, interposed to appease; in a fit of passion he killed his eldest son, whom he loved, remorse for which embittered his last days and hastened his end.

Jackson, Andrew, 1767-1845. Seventh president of the United States; born in South Carolina; son of an Irishman; received but little education; served against the British in 1781; began the practice of law at Nashville, 1788; Congress, 1796; United States Senate, 1797; judge Tennessee Supreme Court, 1798-1804; fought several duels, killing Charles Dickinson in 1806; defeated the Creek Indians, 1814, and was commissioned brigadier-general; defeated the British at New Orleans, 1815; successfully carried on war against the Seminoles, 1817-1818; Senate, 1823; and nominated for the presidency, the opposing candidates being Clay, J. Q. Adams, and W. H. Crawford; Jackson had the highest number of votes, but not a majority, and Adams was elected by the House of Representatives; Jackson was elected to the presidency, however, in 1828; he was the first president to remove public officers on account of their politics; re-elected in 1832; in that year, the convention of South Carolina having declared the tariff laws of 1828 null and void, Jackson issued a proclamation declaring his intention to check by force of arms all movements tending to disunion.

Jackson, Thomas Jonathan (Stonewall), 1824-1863. Confederate general; native of Virginia; defeated General Banks at Cedar Mountain, and captured Harper's Ferry with 10,000 prisoners, 1862; killed by a company of his own men, mistaking him and his staff for Federal cavalry.

Jacobi (*yah-ko'be*), **Friedrich Heinrich,** 1743-1817. A German philosopher and poet; born in Duesseldorf. His expositions are distinguished by acuteness, and adorned by so remarkable a grace that his disciples have named him the modern Plato.

Jacquard (*zhah-kahr'*), **Joseph Marie,** 1752-1834. A French inventor; born in Lyons. After a long period of hardship he made his name famous by the invention of his new loom, which was publicly exhibited in 1801.

James I. of England and **VI.** of Scotland, 1566-1625; born in Edinburgh Castle; was the only child of Mary Queen of Scots, by her cousin Henry Stuart, Lord Darnley. In the following year, Mary being forced to resign the crown, he was solemnly crowned at Stirling and from that time all public acts ran in his name. In 1603 James having succeeded to the crown of England on the death of Queen Elizabeth proceeded amid the acclamations of his new subjects to London. Urged by national feelings for the Protestant cause he was induced to declare war against Spain and the Emperor, and troops were sent over to Holland to act in conjunction with Prince Maurice. The defeat of this enterprise hastened the king's death.

Jameson, Leander Starr, 1853- . . . . A British administrator; born in Edinburgh; he was educated at

London University. Having become associated with Rhodes in the development of South Africa, he was appointed administrator of Rhodesia in 1891, and held the position with distinction till the raid on the Transvaal in 1895, when he was defeated at Krugersdorp. Became premier of Cape Colony in 1904.

Janauschek (*yah'no-shek*), **Francesca Romana Magdalena,** 1830-1904. . . A Polish actress; born in Prague, Bohemia; in 1852 she was married to Capt. Frederick Pillot, of the German navy; she made her first tour in America in 1867-1869, and at once secured favorable notice; returning to Germany she studied English, and in 1873 made her second visit to the United States, when she played in English the most exacting Shakespearean roles; she retired from the stage in 1898.

Janse'nius, Cornelius, 1585-1638. A Flemish theologian; he founded the body of sectaries in the Roman Catholic Church known as Jansenists; he was made Bishop of Ypres.

Jay, John, 1745-1829. American statesman, born in New York; took a part in the struggle for independence second only to Washington's; represented his country subsequently in Madrid and London; was first chief-justice of the United States.

Jefferson, Joseph, 1829-1905. . . An American comedian; born in Philadelphia, Pa. Jefferson was on the stage from his very infancy, appearing as Cora's child in "Pizarro" when only three years of age; in 1865 he visited London, and at the Adelphi Theater played for the first time his world famous part of Rip Van Winkle, Sept. 4, 1865. With this character his name is identified, and though he has shown himself an admirable comedian in many characters, to the English speaking world he is always Rip Van Winkle.

Jefferson, Thomas, 1743-1826. American statesman; third president of the United States; born in Virginia; admitted to the bar, 1767; elected to Virginia House of Burgesses, 1769; Continental Congress, 1775; drafted the Declaration of Independence; governor of Virginia, 1779-1781; minister plenipotentiary, 1784, to negotiate treaties with European powers; minister at Paris, 1785-1789; secretary of state, 1789-1793; elected vice-president, 1796, and president in 1800, holding that office from 1801 to 1809.

Jeffrey, Francis, 1773-1850. A British critic and essayist; born in Edinburgh. After graduating at the universities of Glasgow and Oxford, Jeffrey, in 1794, was admitted to the Scottish bar. From 1816 till he ceased to practice Jeffrey was the acknowledged leader of the Scottish bar.

Jeffreys, or **Jefferies, George, Lord,** 1640?-1689. An English jurist; born in Acton, England. In 1683 he was appointed chief justice of the King's Bench, and, in 1685, lord chancellor. His cruelties on the western circuit toward the deluded followers of the Duke of Monmouth were excessive; yet they gave great satisfaction to James II., who, with a grim pleasantry, called this "Jeffreys' Campaign." He died a prisoner in the Tower of London.

Jenner, Edward, 1749-1823. An English physician; born in Berkeley, Gloucestershire. After many years devoted to the consideration of, and experiments made with, vaccine lymph as a specific for smallpox, Jenner was for the first time, in 1796, enabled to satisfy many medical men of the valid properties of this new agent as a preventive of the disease known as smallpox.

Jerome, or **Hieronymus,** 331-420. One of the fathers of the church; born at Stridon, on the frontiers of Dacia.

Jerome of Prague, 1360?-1416. A Bohemian reformer; was in faith and sufferings the companion of the famous John Huss; was burned at the stake, and his ashes thrown into the Rhine.

Jervis, Sir John, 1734-1823. An English admiral; born in Staffordshire; rose to be Rear-Admiral of the White in 1790; he defeated the Spanish fleet of twenty-seven ships with one of fifteen ships off St. Vincent in 1797, in consequence of which he was raised to the peerage as Earl St. Vincent; was buried in St. Paul's, London.

Joan of Arc (Jeanne d' Arc), 1411?-1431. French heroine ("the Maid of Orleans"); born in Lorraine of an humble peasant family; believing herself commissioned by heaven to liberate France, and convincing Charles VII. of her divine authority, she was given command of a considerable force, and by the victories she gained enabled Charles to be crowned at Rheims; although she wished to return home and resume her former humble life, she was induced to retain her command in the army; she was captured in 1430 by the Burgundians, delivered to the English, and burned at the stake after a mock trial.

John (surnamed Lackland), 1166-1216. King of England; born in Oxford; was the youngest son of Henry II. by Eleanor of Guienne. He gave up his kingdom to the pope, receiving it again as a vassal. He rendered himself the object of such universal contempt and hatred that his nobles combined to limit his power and establish their privileges; thus was obtained that basis of English constitutional freedom known as "Magna Charta," which not only protected the nobles against the crown, but secured important privileges to every class of freemen. Died in Newark.

John III. (**John Sobieski**), 1624?-1696. King of Poland; was youngest son of James Sobieski, governor of Cracow, and educated at Paris. In 1665 he was made grand marshal and general of the Polish armies. He retook several cities from the rebellious Cossacks. In 1673 he gained the memorable battle of Choczim, near the Dniester, in which the Turks lost 28,000 men. On the death of Michael in the following year he was elected King of Poland, and shortly afterward compelled the Turks to sue for peace. He died in Warsaw.

John of Austria, or **Don John,** 1547-1578. A Spanish soldier; the natural son of the Emperor Charles V.; born in Ratisbon, Bavaria. He was brought up in such ignorance of his birth that, till summoned by Philip II., his brother, to Spain, and there acknowledged as the emperor's son, he had been in total darkness as to who his parents were. His first triumph was a victory over the Turkish galleys in the Gulf of Lepanto, in which the Ottomans lost 30,000 men; he next invaded Tunis, and in 1576 was sent by Philip as governor of the Low Countries; here, in a succession of splendid victories, he so reduced his antagonists that the country must soon have submitted and returned to its allegiance, had he not been suddenly carried off by poison, near Namur, Belgium.

John of Gaunt, Duke of Lancaster, 1340-1399. Third son of Edward III.; born in Ghent. He was a noted character in English history. He died in London, England.

Johnson, Andrew, 1808-1875. American statesman; seventeenth president of the United States; born in North Carolina; learned the trade of a tailor in Tennessee; in Congress, 1843-1853; governor, 1853-1857; senator, 1857; military governor, 1862; elected vice-president, 1864, and succeeded to the presidency on the death of Lincoln, 1865; became involved in a bitter quarrel with the leaders of the Republican party, and was impeached in 1868, but acquitted, although thirty-five senators voted for conviction to only nineteen against, a two-thirds majority being necessary; he was subsequently elected to the Senate from Tennessee as a Democrat.

Johnson, Eastman, 1824- . . . . An American painter, born in Lovell, Me.; went to Duesseldorf, where he studied two years, and afterward resided for four years at The Hague. He returned to New York in 1856. His favorite subjects are the American rustic and negro, and glimpses of domestic life.

Johnson, Reverdy, 1796-1876. An American lawyer and statesman; born in Annapolis, Md.; in 1845 was chosen United States senator, and in 1849 was appointed, by President Taylor, attorney-general. In 1868, he was appointed United States minister to the Court of St. James, where he negotiated a treaty for the settlement of the *Alabama* claims, which the United States rejected. He died in Annapolis.

Johnston, Albert Sidney, 1803-1862. An American military officer; born in Mason county, Ky.; resigned his commission in the United States army in 1834, and enlisted in the army of Texas, of which he became commander-in-chief; made secretary of war of the Republic of Texas in 1838. He used all his influence in bringing about the annexation of Texas to the United States, and served in the Mexican War with marked distinction. When the Civil War broke out he was in command of the Department of the Pacific, but promptly resigned; was made a general in the Confederate army and assigned to the command of the Department of Kentucky. He was killed at Pittsburg Landing.

Johnston, Joseph Eggleston, 1807-1891. An American military officer; born in Cherry Grove, Va.; greatly distinguished himself in the Florida and Mexican wars; made major-general of Virginia volunteers and later full general in the Confederate service; took an active part in the first battle of Bull Run, where he personally led a charge with the colors of the Fourth Alabama Regiment in his hands; took command of Bragg's army at Dalton, Ga.; was succeeded in this command by General Hood;

after the war he engaged in business; was member of Congress in 1876-1878, and United States commissioner of railways in 1885-1889; he died in Washington, D. C.

Jones, Inigo, 1573-1652. Architect; born in London; studied in Italy, and, returning to England, obtained the patronage of James I., and became chief architect in the country; the Royal Chapel at Whitehall is reckoned his masterpiece; Heriot's Hospital, Edinburgh, is from his design; his style follows Palladio of Venice.

Jones, John Paul, 1747-1792. A naval adventurer, whose real name was John Paul; born in Kirkcudbright, Scotland; took to the sea, engaged in the slave trade, settled in Virginia, threw in his lot with the colonists and against the mother country, and offered his services as a sea captain; in 1778 he infested the British coast, and made a descent on the shores of his native country; his sympathies were with the French in their struggles for liberty, and he fought in their service as well; he died in Paris, where he languished in poverty, but the National Assembly granted him a "ceremonial funeral," attended by a deputation.

Jones, Sir William, 1746-1794. English Orientalist; born in London; early devoted to Eastern languages and literature, he published numerous translations and other works, concluding with "Sakuntala" and "The Laws of Manu"; he founded the Asiatic Society at Calcutta, where he died.

Jordaens (*yor'dahnz*), **Jakob,** 1615-1678. A Dutch painter and engraver; born at Antwerp; was a friend of Rubens, and ranks next him among the Flemings.

Jordan, David Starr, 1851- . . . . An American educator; born in Gainesville, N.Y.; he studied at Cornell and Harvard; after holding important professorships he served as president of the University of Indiana from 1885 to 1891; in the latter year he was made president of Leland Stanford Jr. University; served on a number of important government commissions, especially in connection with the fisheries; he wrote "Care and Culture of Men," and many other educational and scientific books.

Joseph I., 1676-1711. Emperor of Germany. **Joseph II.,** 1741-1790. Abolished feudal serfdom.

Josephine, 1763-1814. Empress of the French; wife of Napoleon Bonaparte.

Josephus, Flavius, 37?-95? Jewish historian.

Joshua, A Jewish military leader, born of the tribe of Ephraim, the minister and successor of Moses, under whose leadership the Jews obtained a footing in the Land of Canaan.

Joubert, Petrus Jacobus, 1834-1900. A Boer military officer; born in Cango, Cape Colony; was elected to the Transvaal Volksraad in 1863; acting president of the republic in 1874; appointed a member of the triumvirate of 1880 to conduct war against Great Britain. On February 27, 1881, he surprised the British encampment with a small force and won a decided victory, which soon resulted in terms of peace. He was acting president of the republic again in 1883-1884, trained the Boer army in the tactics which proved so successful against the vastly superior British army sent against the Transvaal and Orange Free State in 1898. He died in Pretoria.

Jouffroy d'Arbans, (*zhoo-frwah' dar-bon*), **Claude, Marquis de,** 1751-1832. Claimed by the French as the inventor of steam navigation; in 1783 made a small paddle-wheel steamboat sail up the Rhone at Lyons — the connection between piston and paddle-wheel axle being rack-and-pinion. Compelled to emigrate by the Revolution, he failed, on account of financial ruin, to float a company till after Fulton had made his successful experiments on the Seine in 1803.

Juarez (*hoo-ah'reth*), **Benito Pablo,** 1806-1872. President of Mexico; born in Oaxaca, of Indian extraction; was twice elected to the presidency, in 1861 and 1867.

Judson Adoniram, 1788-1850. An American missionary; born in Malden, Mass.; in February, 1812, he sailed with his wife for Asia. During the voyage he was converted from the Congregational faith to that of the Baptist church. In 1814, when the Baptists of the United States organized a missionary union he was taken under its care. He settled in Burma; mastered the language, and labored there for nearly forty years. He died at sea.

Justin (surnamed the Martyr), 103?-165? An early Christian apologist; born in Sichem, Samaria; studied philosophy in the Stoic and Platonic schools, and was converted to Christianity, was the author of two "Apologies for the Christians," rather than for Christianity or its dogmas, and a "Dialogue with Trypho the Jew"; suffered martyrdom.

Justinian I. (**Flavius Anicius Justinianus**), 483?-565. A Byzantine emperor; born in Tauresium, Dardania, Illyricum. The glory of his reign is the famous Justinian Code.

Kane, Elisha Kent, 1820-1857. An American explorer; born in Philadelphia; accompanied, in 1850, the first Grinnell expedition to the Arctic seas, and commanded the second in 1853, after three years returning with many discoveries; he wrote accounts of both expeditions.

Kant (*kahnt*), **Immanuel,** 1724-1804. German philosopher; born in Koenigsberg, Prussia. His three great works were: "Critique of Pure Reason," which attempts to define the nature of those of our ideas which lie outside of experience, and to establish the basis of valid knowledge; "Critique of the Practical Reason," which bases the ideas of God, freedom, and immortality on the ethical consciousness alone, denying that we have any right to hold them otherwise; and "Critique of the Power of Judgment." He died in Koenigsberg.

Kean, Edmund, 1787-1833. Distinguished English tragedian; born in London; his first success was Shylock in the "Merchant of Venice," in 1814, and the representation of it was followed by equally famous representations of Richard III., Othello, and Sir Giles Overreach; he led a very dissipated life, and under the effect of it his constitution gave way; he broke down one evening beside his son as Iago, as he was playing the part of Othello; was carried off the stage, and never appeared on the boards again.

Kearney, Philip, 1815-1862. An American military officer; born in New York city. After entering the Ecole Polytechnique, Paris, and serving as a volunteer in the ranks of the Chasseurs d'Afrique in an Algerine campaign, Kearney returned to the United States in 1840; served throughout the Mexican campaign, and was brevetted major for his distinguished gallantry at Contreras and Churubusco. On the outbreak of the Civil War in 1861, Kearney was appointed brigadier-general of volunteers, and exhibited his dashing courage in all the battles of the Chickahominy campaign. In 1862 he was commissioned major-general of volunteers, and was killed while making a personal reconnoissance within the Confederate lines at Chantilly.

Kellermann, Francois Christophe; 1735-1820. A marshal of France; born in Strasburg gained great distinction in the Seven Years' War; on the breaking out of the Revolution, he was given the command of the army of the North, and in 1792 gained the splendid victory of Valmy over the Prussians, and was, in 1795, intrusted with the command of the armies of Italy and the Alps; Napoleon superseded Kellermann.

Kemble, Charles, 1775-1854. English actor; born at Brecon; appeared first at Sheffield as Orlando, in 1792, and two years later went to London, where he continued playing till 1840, when he was appointed examiner of plays.

Kemble, Frances Anne, 1809-1893. Daughter of Charles; born in London; made her *debut* in 1829, and proved a queen of tragedy; in 1832 came to America, where, in 1834, she married a planter, from whom she was divorced in 1848; resuming her maiden name, Fanny Kemble, she gave Shakespearean readings for twenty years.

Kemble, John Philip, 1757-1823. English actor; born at Prescott, Lancashire; appeared first at Wolverhampton in 1776; after touring in Yorkshire and Ireland he went to London in 1783, playing Hamlet at Drury Lane; became manager of that theater in 1788; in 1802 transferred himself to Covent Garden; he retired in 1817, and lived at Lausanne, Switzerland, till his death.

Kem'pis, Thomas a, 1380-1471. A German mystic; born in Kempen (whence his name, "Thomas from Kempen"), near Cologne; his true name was Hamerken; he was author of the "Imitation of Christ," one of the most famous of books.

Kent, James, 1763-1847. An American jurist; born in Philippi, N. Y.; author of the famous "Commentaries on American Law," which holds in this country a position similar to that occupied by Blackstone's "Commentaries" in Great Britain; he was chief-justice and chancellor of the state of New York.

Kepler, John, 1571-1630. Illustrious German astronomer; born in Wurtemberg; studied at Tuebingen, chiefly mathematics and astronomy; joined Tycho Brahe at Prague as assistant; removed to Lintz; lived in a *camera obscura* tent, doing ingenious things, photographing the heavens, "inventing toys, writing almanacs . . . busy discovering the system of the world—grandest conquest ever made, or to be made," adds Carlyle, "by the sons of Adam"; he was long occupied in studying the "'motions of the star' Mars, with calculations repeated seventy times, and with the discovery of the planetary laws of the Universe"; these last are called from his discovery of them Kepler's Laws. Poverty pursued Kepler all his days, and he died of fever at Ratisbon.

Kidd, William, ... -1701. An American pirate; born probably in Greenock, Scotland. A ship of thirty guns was fitted out by a private company in London, was given to Kidd, who was to seize pirates. In January, 1697, he reached Madagascar, but ere long reports reached England that Captain Kidd was playing the game of pirate himself. After a two years' cruise he returned to the West Indies and later went to Boston. He was arrested and sent to England, where he was tried for piracy and murder. Of the latter charge he was found guilty, and hanged.

Kilpatrick, Hugh Judson, 1836-1881. An American military officer; born in Deckerton, N. J.; served through the Civil War with credit; was minister to Chile from 1865 to 1870, and reappointed in 1881. He died in Valparaiso.

King, Rufus, 1755-1827. An American statesman; born in Scarboro, Me.; elected to the United States Senate three times and was appointed twice as minister to England. He was the Federalist candidate for the vice-presidency in 1804 and 1808. He died in Jamaica, Long Island.

King, Thomas Starr, 1824-1864. An American clergyman; born in New York city. During the Civil War he was the chief factor in raising the large sums of money which enabled the United States Sanitary Commission to carry on its work. He was a brilliant preacher and writer.

King, William Rufus, 1786-1853. An American statesman; born in Sampson county, N. C. He was United States senator from that state; minister to France; presiding officer in the United States Senate. In 1852 he was elected vice-president of the United States; died near Cahawba, Ala.

Kitchener, Horatio Herbert, Viscount and Baron Kitchener of Khartum, 1850- . . . . A British military officer. From 1888 till 1892 he was adjutant-general and second in command of the Egyptian army, and in 1892 he became Sirdar. He commanded the Anglo-Egyptian force which recovered Dongola for Egypt in 1896. Soon after he led another expeditionary force up the Nile valley. He was appointed governor-general and commander-in-chief of the Egyptian Sudan in 1899, but he resigned this post to accompany Lord Roberts to South Africa as chief of his staff in the war with the Boers. When Lord Roberts left South Africa toward the end of 1900 Lord Kitchener succeeded him as commander-in-chief. On the termination of the war in 1902, Lord Kitchener was created a viscount by King Edward and voted a grant of $250,000 by Parliament.

Kleber (*klay-bare'*), **Jean Baptiste,** 1753-1800. French general; born at Strasburg; accompanied Bonaparte to Egypt, and was left by him in command, where, after a bold attempt to regain lost ground, and while in the act of concluding a treaty with the Turks, he was assassinated by an Arab fanatic.

Knox, Henry, 1750-1806. An American military officer; born in Boston. For his signal service at Yorktown he was made major-general. In 1785 he was appointed by Congress secretary of war. He resigned from the cabinet in 1795, retiring to private life. He died in Thomaston, Me.

Knox, John, 1505-1572. A Scotch religious reformer; born in Giffordsgate, near Haddington, Scotland. A pioneer of Puritanism; prisoner of war, for nineteen months confined in the French galleys; friend of Calvin and Beza; a preacher of sermons that moved their hearers to demolish convents; with a price on his head, yet never faltering; arrested for treason, an armed "congregation" at his heels; burned in effigy, for years a dictator — he spent his life forwarding the Reformation in Scotland. His great work distinguished in Scottish prose was his "History of the Reformation of Religion within the Realm of Scotland." He died in Edinburgh.

Koscius'ko, Thaddeus, 1746?-1817. Polish patriot and general; commanded the Polish insurgent army; bravely defended Warsaw, but was defeated.

Kossuth (*kosh'oot*), **Louis,** 1802-1894. Hungarian patriot, orator, and statesman; leading spirit in the insurrection of 1848-1849.

Krapot'kin, Peter Alexievich, Prince, 1842- . . . A Russian scientist; born in Moscow. He was in the Russian army for a time, and made extensive journeys in Siberia and Manchuria. Charged with anarchist affiliations, he was imprisoned two years in Russia; escaped, founded the anarchist paper *La Revolte* in Geneva, and after being expelled from Switzerland in 1881, commenced a crusade against the Russian government in the English and French press; is the author of various works on nihilistic subjects.

Krueger (*kree'her*), **Stephanus Johannes Paulus,** 1825-1904. . . A Boer statesman; born near Colesberg, Cape Colony; in 1882 he was elected president of the Transvaal for the first time; in 1883 he was re-elected for five years, and in 1888, after a contest with General Joubert, he was again chosen president, being re-elected in 1893 and 1898; on the breaking out of dissensions between the Uitlanders and the Boers in 1896, and the raid of Dr. Jameson in aid of the former, vigorous measures were adopted by President Krueger, resulting in the capture of Jameson and his 700 men and the suppression of the rebellion; in 1899 his policy led to war with England; the Boer reverses led to his departure for Europe, where he established himself in Holland.

Krupp, Alfred, 1812-1887. A German metal founder and steel gun manufacturer; born in Essen, Prussia; discovered the method of casting steel in very large masses. His world-wide fame was made by the production of the enormous steel siege guns with which the Germans did such terrible execution when they invested Paris. Krupp made his first cannon in 1846.

Kublai Khan (*koo-blee kan'*). Flourished thirteenth century; the founder of the twentieth Chinese dynasty, that of the Mongols or Yen; he was the grandson of Genghis Khan; he reigned, at first, only in Mongolia and the countries conquered by Genghis Khan; but he invaded China in 1267; captured the Chinese emperor in 1279, and thus overthrew the Song dynasty, which had ruled for 319 years; he extended his conquests over Tibet, Pegu, Cochin China, and formed the greatest empire known in history, embracing the whole of Asia and part of Europe, from the Dnieper to Japan. He patronized letters, and encouraged agriculture, industry, and commerce; Marco Polo passed seventeen years at his court.

Kyrle (*kurl*), **John,** 1637-1724. Philanthropist; born in Gloucestershire; was distinguished for his benefactions; has given name to a society founded, among other things, for the betterment of the homes of the people.

Labouchere (*lah-boo-sher'*), **Henry,** 1831- . . . . An English journalist and politician; born in London; was in the diplomatic service in the United States; established the London *Truth*.

Lacepede (*lah-say-pade'*), **Bernard de la Ville, Count de,** 1756-1825. A French naturalist; professor of Natural History in the Jardin des Plantes and in the university; senator in 1799; minister of state in 1809; peer of France in 1814. Besides continuing Buffon's "Natural History" at Buffon's own request, he wrote "Natural History of Fishes," etc. He died of smallpox in Epinay, near St. Denis.

Lacordaire (*la-kor-dare'*), **Jean Baptiste Henri Dominique,** 1802-1861. One of the greatest of modern pulpit orators; born in Recey-sur-Ource, Cote-d'Or, France. He distinguished himself greatly as a preacher, and was offered the post of vicar-general by the Bishop of New York. The Revolution of 1830 alone prevented him from leaving for the United States. In 1860 he was elected to the Academie Francaise, in succession to De Tocqueville. Of his numerous works his "Lettres a un jeune Homme sur la Vie Chretienne," have been much admired.

Lactan'tius, Lucius Cœlius Firmianus, 290-325? The most eloquent and learned of the Christian fathers; born in Africa.

La Fayette, Marie Jean Paul Roch Yves Gilbert Motier, Marquis de, 1757-1834. French general and patriot; came to America in 1777 to aid the Americans in their struggle for independence, and was commissioned major-general; fought at Brandywine, where he was wounded, and in numerous other engagements; visited France and obtained supplies and munitions, returning 1779; commanded the advance guard at Yorktown, 1781; returned again to France; chosen commandant of the French National Guard, 1789; visited America, 1824, and was enthusiastically received; took a prominent part in the revolution of 1830.

Laennec (*la-nek'*), **Rene Theodore Hyacinthe,** 1781-1826. A distinguished French physician. In 1816 he became chief physician to the Hospital Necker, where he soon after made the discovery of "mediate" auscultation, *i. e.*, of the use of the stethoscope. In 1819 he published his "Treatise on Mediate Auscultation," which has undoubtedly produced a greater effect, in so far as the advance of diagnosis is concerned, than any other single book.

Lagrange, Joseph Louis, Comte, 1736-1813. Famous mathematician; born at Turin of French parentage; appointed director of Berlin Academy in 1766, he pursued his researches there for twenty-one years; in 1787 he removed to Paris, where he received a pension of 6000 francs from the Court, and remained till his death.

Lamar, Lucius Quintus Cincinnatus, 1825-1893. An American jurist; born in Jasper county, Ga. He entered the Confederate army and achieved distinction; after the downfall of the rebellion was Professor of Political Economy and Law Professor in the University of Mississippi, and afterward served in both Houses of Congress; in 1885 was appointed Secretary of the Interior, and in 1887 became an Associate Justice of the United States Supreme Court. He died in Macon, Ga.

Lamarck, Jean Baptiste Pierre Antoine de Monet, Chevalier de, 1744-1829. A French naturalist; born in Bazantin, Picardy, France. His great and excellent work, the "History of Invertebrate Animals," will ever entitle him to take his place in the very first rank of zoologists. As a conchologist his name stands preeminent, and the Lamarckian arrangement of shells is still that of the present day. In his latter days he became blind and comparatively poor. He died in Paris.

Landseer, Sir Edwin, 1802-1883. An English painter; born in London, England. He began to draw animals when a mere child; exhibited regularly at the Academy and the British Institution; took the very highest rank among animal painters, and, though he was blamed for introducing too human a sentiment and expression into some of his animals, the humor and pathos of animal nature has had no finer exponent.

Lannes (*lahn*), **Jean, Duc de Montebello,** 1769-1809. Marshal of France; was much esteemed by Napoleon, whom he zealously supported; went with him to Egypt, was with him at Marengo, distinguished himself at Austerlitz and in Spain, and fell mortally wounded at Essling.

Laplace (*lah-plahs'*), **Pierre Simon, Marquis de,** 1749-1827. A celebrated French mathematician; becoming member of the Academie des Sciences in 1785, he attained a position among mathematicians and astronomers almost equal to Newton's; his "Three Laws" demonstrated the stability of the solar system; he published many treatises on lunar and planetary problems, electricity, magnetism, and a nebular hypothesis; his "Mecanique Celeste" is unrivaled in that class of work.

Larousse (*lah-russ'*), **Pierre,** 1817-1875. A celebrated French grammarian and lexicographer; best known by his "Grand Dictionnaire Universel du xixme Siecle."

La Salle (*lah sal'*), **Robert Cavelier, Sieur de,** 1643-1687. A French explorer; born in Rouen, France. Settling in Canada at the age of twenty-three, he began his travels with an attempt to reach China by descending the Ohio river, which he supposed to empty into the Pacific. Formed the project of descending the Mississippi to the sea. After many and severe hardships this long voyage was concluded, and the arms of France set up at the mouth of the great river on April 9, 1682. Two years later an expedition was fitted out to establish a permanent French settlement on the Gulf, which should secure France's claims to the Mississippi valley. But La Salle's bad fortune pursued him; he mistook Matagorda bay for a mouth of the Mississippi, landed there and then spent two years in unsuccessful journeys to discover the great river, while his colonists and soldiers gradually dwindled away. His harshness of manner, more than his want of success, embittered his followers, and he was assassinated by some of them.

Lat'imer, Hugh, 1472-1555. An English reformer and martyr; made Bishop of Worcester 1535; burned at the stake with Bishop Ridley.

Latrielle (*lah-tree-el'*), **Pierre Andre,** 1762-1833. French naturalist; one of the founders of the science of entomology; succeeded Lamarck as professor of Natural History in the Jardin des Plantes; wrote several works on entomology.

Latour (*lah-tur'*), **d' Auvergne, Theophile Malo Corret de,** 1743-1800. French officer; called, by Napoleon, "The First Grenadier of France."

Laud, William, 1573-1645. An English prelate; Archbishop of Canterbury in the reign of Charles I.; born in Reading, Berkshire, England. His endeavors to introduce the liturgy into Scotland created him numerous enemies; therefore, he was impeached by the Commons, and sent to the Tower. After lying there three years he was declared guilty of treason, and the archbishop was accordingly beheaded on Tower Hill. He was in the seventy-second year of his age and met his fate with great fortitude.

Laurens, Henry, 1724-1792. An American statesman; born in South Carolina; he was sent on a mission to The Hague, 1780, and en route was captured by the English and kept a prisoner in the Tower of London for fourteen months.

Laurens, John, 1756-1782. An American military officer; son of the preceding; born in South Carolina; joined the American Continental Army in 1777, becoming aid-de-camp and secretary to Washington. Laurens so highly distinguished himself in the battles of Germantown and Monmouth, and in other operations of the War of Independence, as to earn for himself the title of the "Bayard of the Revolution"; he was killed in action at the Combahee river, S. C.

Lau'rier, Sir Wilfred, 1841- . . . . A Canadian statesman; born in St. Lin, Quebec; in 1874 he was elected to the Federal Assembly, and his high personal character, his undoubted loyalty and attachment to the connection of the colony with Great Britain, together with his great oratorical powers, soon gave him high rank in the Liberal party; on the retirement of Mr. Blake in 1891 he was chosen as leader of the Liberal party, and at the general election of 1896 he led his followers to a notable victory, becoming premier of the Dominion; this office he has filled with signal ability.

Lavater (*lah-vah-tair'*), **Johann Caspar,** 1741-1801. Swiss physiognomist.

Lavoisier (*lah-vwaw-zeay'*), **Antoine Laurent,** 1743-1794; French chemist; founder of modern chemistry; guillotined by French revolutionary tribunal.

Law, John, 1671-1729. Scotch financier in France; promoted the "South Sea Bubble."

Lawrence, Abbott, 1792-1855. An American diplomatist; born in Groton, Mass.; was a commissioner in 1842 to settle the Northeastern Boundary question, and arranged a basis for settlement with Lord Ashburton which was satisfactory to both the United States and England; was minister to Great Britain, 1849-1852; founded the Lawrence Scientific School of Harvard University, to which he gave $100,000. He died in Boston, Mass.

Lawrence, James, 1781-1813. American naval hero; as commander of the *Chesapeake*, he engaged the British frigate *Shannon* off Boston and was killed in the action; his last words were: "Don't give up the ship."

Lawton, Henry Ware, 1843-1899. An American military officer; born in Manhattan, O. He was conspicuous as an Indian fighter. At the beginning of the American-Spanish war Lawton was a lieutenant-colonel, and was made a major-general of volunteers, July 8, 1898. He was in command of the 2d Division of the 5th Army Corps before Santiago, and was in the thick of the fighting preceding the capture of San Juan hill, and will go down in history as the "hero of El Caney." At the close of the war with Spain General Lawton was transferred to the Philippines, where he began active operations against the insurgents; captured Santa Cruza, a Filipino stronghold, April 10, 1899, and San Isidro, May 15; was placed in command of Manila, June 1; while on the firing lines at San Mateo, he was killed by insurgent sharpshooters.

Layard, Sir Austin Henry, 1817-1894. An English archæologist; born in Paris, France. He is best known by his books: "Nineveh and its Remains," and "Discoveries in the Ruins of Nineveh and Babylon." He died in London, England.

Le Brun, Charles, 1619-1690. A celebrated French painter; born in Paris; studied in Rome, settled in Paris; he exercised for about forty years a great influence on the art of the period; he decorated Versailles and the Louvre.

Le Brun, Marie, 1755-1842. A French painter; born in Paris, France.

Le Conte, Joseph, 1823-1901. An American scientist; born in Liberty county, Ga.; studied natural history under Agassiz. He subsequently held several professorships, and after 1869 occupied the chair of geology and natural history in the University of California. He died in the Yosemite Valley, California.

Ledru-Rollin, Alexandre Auguste, 1807-1874. A French agitator; born near Paris, France; died in Fontenay.

Ledyard, John, 1751-1789. An American traveler; born in Groton, Conn. He was a companion of Captain Cook in his third voyage round the world He planned a journey through Northern Europe and Asia in the early part of 1788, but reached no farther than Irkuska, Russia, where he was arrested on suspicion of being a spy, and was compelled to abandon his enterprise. In June of the same year he started on a voyage of exploration to Central Africa, under direction of the African Association, which was cut short by his death, in Cairo, Egypt.

Lee, Ann, 1736-1784. Founder of the Society of Shakers in America; born in Manchester, England. She was poor and uneducated, and in 1758 joined the Shakers, a sect allied in their belief to the Friends, but who were peculiar in their form of worship. She believed herself inspired, and was imprisoned in 1770 for preaching the new doctrine of celibacy. In 1774 she emigrated to America and founded the Society of Shakers. She was greatly revered by her followers, and by them was called "Mother Ann." She died in Watervliet, N. Y.

Lee, Fitzhugh, 1835- . . . . An American military officer; born in Clermont, Fairfax county, Va.; entered the Confederate army, rising through its grades to that of major-general. He was governor of Virginia from 1886 to 1890. Appointed consul-general at Havana in 1893 he served there till 1898, and was at the head of affairs in Cuba during the period immediately preceding the outbreak of the war with Spain. During the ensuing war with Spain he was a major-general of volunteers, serving in Cuba, and becoming at the close of hostilities military governor of Havana. In 1900 he was made commander of the Department of the Missouri.

Lee, Henry, 1756-1818. An American soldier; born in Leesylvania, Va.; on the outbreak of the Revolutionary War joined Washington's army; he speedily won distinction for his dash and daring, being styled "Light-horse Harry Lee." He led the army of 15,000 men that put down the "whisky insurrection" in Pennsylvania in 1794. Statesman; governor of Virginia.

Lee, Robert Edward, 1807-1870. American general; commander-in-chief of the Cenfederate army; son of Henry Lee; born in Virginia; graduate of West Point; chief engineer of General Scott's army in Mexico; Confederate brigadier-general, 1861 and appointed to the chief command, 1865; surrendered at Appomattox, April 9, 1865; subsequently chosen president of Washington College, at Lexington, Va., where he died; he was a man of devout religious faith, a high sense of duty, and great courage and ability as a soldier.

Leech, John, 1817-1864. An English artist and humorist; born in London, England; he died suddenly in London.

Leibnitz (*libe'nits*), or more correctly **Leibniz, Gottfried Wilhelm Freiherr von,** 1646-1716. One of the most celebrated scholars and philosophers that Germany has ever produced; born in Leipsic; early directed his attention to mathematics, and attained great eminence in this science. Authorities seem generally agreed that he discovered the differential calculus independent of any knowledge of Newton's method of fluxions, so that each of these great men in reality attained the same result for himself.

Leicester (*les'ter*), **Robert Dudley, Earl of,** 1532?-1588. An English noble and favorite of Queen Elizabeth; in 1588, on the threatened invasion of the Spanish Armada, Leicester was appointed lieutenant-general of the kingdom.

Leighton (*lay'ton*), **Sir Frederick,** 1830-1896. An English artist; born in Scarborough, England; died in London.

Lely, Sir Peter, 1617-1680. An Anglo-Dutch painter; born in Soest, Westphalia; died in London, England.

Leonidas. Flourished fifth century B. C.; king of Sparta from 491 to 480 B.C.; opposed Xerxes, the Persian, who threatened Greece with a large army, and kept him at bay at the Pass of Thermopylæ with 300 Spartans and 5,000 auxiliaries till he was betrayed by Ephialtes, when he and his 300 threw themselves valiantly on the large host, and perished fighting to the last man.

Leopold II., 1835- . . . . King of the Belgians. He early manifested an interest in Africa, and in 1885 he became sovereign of the Kongo Free State. During his reign there has been an extension of the suffrage and a spread of advanced ideas in Belgium; he is very wealthy, and is regarded as one of the best business men in Europe.

Leo XIII. (Gioacchino Pecci), 1810-1903. Pope; born in Carpineto, Italy. Was elected pope in 1878, on the death of Pius IX.; he died at Rome after a short illness, due to old age; he was noted for his personal good qualities, and his abilities as a statesman, and sought to bring the Roman Church into line with modern progress.

Lesseps (*les'eps*), **Ferdinand, Vicomte de,** 1805-1894. A French diplomat and engineer; born in Versailles; in 1854, on the invitation of Said Pasha, he visited Egypt to study the problem of canalizing the Isthmus of Suez; the results of his studies were stated in a memoir, "Piercing the Isthmus of Suez." He was made chief director of the works in 1856. The canal was opened to traffic August 15, 1869. His attempt to pierce the Isthmus of Panama resulted in failure and a great political scandal.

Leutze Emanuel, 1816-1868. An American artist; born in Gmund, Wurtemberg; was brought to the United States in infancy. He died in Washington, D. C.

Leverrier (*lay-vair-re-ai'*), **Urban Jean Joseph,** 1811-1877. French astronomer distinguished in chemistry before he devoted himself to astronomy; rose to eminence in the latter science by a paper on the variations in the orbits of the planets; discovered Neptune.

Lewes, George Henry, 1817-1878. An English critic and man of letters; born in London; Lewes was married unhappily and had children when his connection with George Eliot began in July, 1854; it ended only with his death at their house in Regent's Park.

Lewis, Meriwether, 1774-1809. An American explorer; born in Virginia. Lewis, in company with Clarke, explored the then unknown region in which the Missouri rises, and traced the Columbia to its mouth.

Lick, James, 1796-1876. An American philanthropist; born in Fredericksburg, Pa. In 1847 he emigrated to California, taking with him $30,000, which he invested in real estate in San Francisco, and its rapid advance in value made him wealthy. In 1874 he placed his entire property in the hands of trustees, to be devoted to public and charitable purposes. The total amount thus given was $1,765,000, of which $700,000 was for Lick Observatory, to be connected with the University of California; $150,000 for free public baths in San Francisco, and $540,000 for an institution to be called the California School of Mechanical Arts. He died in San Francisco, Cal.

Liddon, Henry Parry, 1829-1890. Canon of St. Paul's, London; eminent both as a scholar and a preacher; author of an eloquent course of lectures, the Bampton, "On the Divinity of Jesus Christ"; belonged to the Liberal section of the High-Church party.

Liebig (*lee'big*), **Justus, Baron von,** 1803-1873. A German chemist; born in Darmstadt; no other chemist of great rank has so sedulously striven to make the science a tender to practical utilities.

Li Hung Chang, 1823-1901. A Chinese statesman and diplomatist; born in Ho Fei, province of Anhwei, China; he was a friend to foreigners and to Western civilization and culture; in 1896 he made a tour of the world, traveling overland, and was everywhere received with eclat as a highly distinguished guest; he acted a prominent part in adjusting the relations of China with foreign powers after the suppressing of the uprisings of 1900-1901; he died in Peking, China.

Liliuokalani, 1838- . . . . Queen of Hawaii; she was a sister of King Kalakaua, whom she succeeded as queen. She married John O. Dominis, an American, who became governor of Oahu; he died in 1891 and in the same year she ascended the throne; in 1893 she was deposed, the islanders adopting a republican form of government; she used every effort to regain her supremacy and endeavored to secure assistance from the United States, visiting Washington in 1896 for that purpose, but was unsuccessful in interesting the government in her behalf; on the annexation of Hawaii to the United States, in 1898, she returned to the island.

Lincoln, Abraham, 1809-1865. Sixteenth president of the United States; "with malice toward none, with charity to all;" born in Kentucky; removed to Indiana when eight years old; captain in the Black Hawk War, 1832; elected to the Illinois legislature, 1834; admitted to the bar 1836, and removed to Springfield, Ill.; elected to Congress in 1846; Republican candidate for United States senator in 1854, his opponent being Stephen A. Douglas; nominated for the presidency and elected, 1860; re-elected, 1864, but assassinated April 14, 1865, by John Wilkes Booth; his death was universally deplored, for his wise administration of affairs during the Civil War had won for him the regard of both factions of the bloody controversy.

Lincoln, Benjamin, 1733-1810. An American military officer; born in Hingham, Mass.; appointed by Washington to the command of the central division at the siege of Yorktown. On the surrender of Cornwallis he was deputed to receive the submission of the captured troops. In 1781 he was chosen by Congress secretary of war, and served in that office for three years; in 1789 was commissioner to treat with the Creek Indians; and in 1793 again, to make peace with the Western tribes. He was the author of various papers, historical, agricultural, etc. He died in Hingham, Mass.

Lind, Jenny, 1821-1882. A distinguished vocalist. She retired from the stage on her marriage to Otto Goldschmidt, 1851, and resided in London.

Linne (*lin-neh'*), **Karl von,** 1707-1775. Commonly called Linnæus; the greatest botanist of his age; born in Rashult, Sweden; died in Upsala.

Lippi, Fra Filippo, 1412-1469. Commonly known as Lippo Lippi; a Florentine painter; born in Florence; died in Spoleto, Italy.

Lister, Sir Joseph, 1827- . . . . An English surgeon. In addition to important observations on the coagulation of the blood, the early stages of inflammation, and other matters, his great work is known as the antiseptic system of surgery. Lister was awarded many foreign honors, and received the medal of the Royal Society in 1880, the prize of the Academy of Paris in 1881. He was made baronet in 1883 and a peer in 1897.

Liszt (*list*), **Franz,** 1811-1886. An eminent Hungarian pianist and musician; he entered a convent in 1865.

Littleton, or **Lyttleton, Sir Thomas,** 1402-1481. An English jurist; born in Frankley, Worcestershire, England. Littleton's reputation rests on his work on "Tenures," which was originally written in Norman-French, or rather law French. It treats of the English law relating to rights over land, and was the first scientific attempt to classify the subject. He died in Frankley.

Littre (*lee'tr*), **Maximilien Paul Emile,** 1801-1881. A French philologist; born in Paris. He was one of the greatest linguists and scientists of the century, best known for his celebrated "Dictionary of the French Language." In addition to his labors as a philologist he contributed to various scientific and philosophical journals, was active in politics, translated the works of Hippocrates, which admitted him to the Academy of Inscriptions, and Pliny's "Natural History," and wrote a "History of the French Language," etc. In 1871 he was elected to the French Academy. He died in Paris.

Livermore, Mary Ashton (Rice), 1821- . . . An American reformer and lecturer; born in Boston, Mass.; conspicuous in her efforts to promote the woman suffrage and temperance movements. Among her popular lectures are: "What Shall We Do with Our Daughters?" "Women of the War," "The Moral Heroism of the Temperance Reform."

Livingston, Edward, 1764-1836. An eminent American statesman and jurist; born in New York.

Livingston, Robert, 1746-1813. An American statesman; born in New York. He was one of the committee to prepare the Declaration of Independence; was appointed secretary of foreign affairs in 1780; and throughout the War of the Revolution signalized himself by his zeal and efficiency in the cause; in 1801 was appointed by Jefferson minister plenipotentiary to France.

Livingstone, David, 1815-1873. A distinguished Scotch explorer; died at Itaca, Africa.

Lloyd, Henry Demarest, 1847-1903. An American writer on economics; born in New York. His chief work is the notable book "Wealth Against Commonwealth." He died at his home in Winnetka, Ill.

Locke, John, 1632-1704. English philosopher; founded the sensational school of philosophy, claiming that all knowledge comes through the senses.

Lodge, Henry Cabot, 1850- . . . . American statesman and author; born in Boston, Mass.; was editor of the *North American Review* in 1873-1876, and lecturer on History at Harvard College in 1876-1879; he then entered political life, and in 1893 was elected United States senator from Massachusetts and re-elected in 1899; he is the author of a "Life of Daniel Webster," and of lives of Alexander Hamilton and George Washington; also of "Boston" in the series of "Historic Towns"; of a "Short History of the English Colonies in America," etc.

Logan, John Alexander, 1826-1886. An American soldier and statesman; born in Jackson county, Ill.; rose to the rank of major-general in the civil war, being distinguished throughout the struggle for valor and patriotism; elected United States senator from Illinois; nominated for the vice-presidency on the ticket headed by James G. Blaine, 1884, but was defeated; he died in Washington, D.C.

Longstreet, James, 1821-1904. An American military officer; born in Edgefield district, S. C.; he served with distinction in the Mexican war; after the battle of Fredericksburg, General Longstreet was given the command of a corps, with the rank of lieutenant-general; the gallantry and skillful generalship he displayed on all occasions caused him to be regarded as one of the leading generals in the Confederate army; was made minister to Turkey, and United States marshal for the District of Georgia; in 1897 he was appointed United States commissioner of Pacific railroads.

Loubet (*loo-bay'*) **Emile,** 1838- . . . . President of the French Republic; born in Marsanne, Drome, France; in 1876 he was elected to a seat in the Chamber of Deputies; was re-elected in 1877, and again in 1881, but in 1885 he moved up to the senate; was minister of public works in the short-lived Tirard Cabinet on the refusal of M. de Freycinet to reassume the presidency of the cabinet, was intrusted by President Sadi-Carnot with the task of organizing the ministry with the larger part of its former constituents, himself assuming the portfolio of the Interior and the presidency of the cabinet. M. Loubet was elected president of the senate in 1896, to which position he was re-elected in January, 1898; he succeeded Felix Faure as president, Feb. 18, 1899.

Louis I. (le Debonnair), 778-840. Emperor of the West and King of France; divided the empire among his sons. **Louis VI.** (the Fat), 1078?-1137. King of France. **Louis IX.** (Saint), 1215-1270. Led a large army againt the Saracens in 1248; defeated and taken prisoner in Egypt, but effected his ransom; led another crusade in 1270, but died the same year near Tunis; a wise ruler, and noted for many virtues.

Louis XIV., 1636-1715. The "Grand Monarque," eldest son of **Louis XIII.;** was only nine when his father died, and the government was in the hands of his mother, Anne of Austria, and Cardinal Mazarin, her minister; under the regency the glory of France was maintained in the field, but her internal peace was disturbed by the insubordination of the parliament and the troubles of the Fronde; by a compact on the part of Mazarin with Spain, before he died, Louis was married to the Infanta Maria Theresa in 1659, and in 1660 he announced his intention to rule the kingdom alone, which he did for fifty-four years with a decision and energy no one gave him credit for, in fulfillment of his famous protestation *L'etat, c'est moi*, choosing Colbert to control finance, Louvois to reorganize the army, and Vauban to fortify the frontier towns; he sought to be as absolute in his foreign relations as in his internal administration, and hence the long succession of wars which, while they brought glory to France, ended in exhausting her; at home he suffered no one in religious matters to think otherwise than himself; he revoked the Edict of Nantes, sanctioned the dragonnades in the Cevennes, and to extirpate heresy encouraged every form of cruelty; yet when we look at the men who adorned it, the reign of Louis XIV. was one of the most illustrious in letters and the arts in the history of France: Corneille, Racine, and Moliere, eminent in the drama; La Fontaine and Boileau in poetry; Bossuet in oratory; Bruyere and Rochefoucauld in morals; Pascal in philosophy; Saint-Simon and Retz in history, and Poussin, Lorraine, Lebrun, Perault, *et als.*, in art.

Louis XV., 1710-1774. King of France; born in Versailles, France; was crowned in 1722, and declared of age the following year. The beginning of his reign was rendered disastrous by the Mississippi scheme of John Law, which ruined thousands of people. In his foreign wars he was at first successful, but was ultimately defeated both by Prussia and England, and his reign witnessed the loss of the French possessions in North America. His personal conduct was unspeakably immoral, the French people groaned under the exactions made necessary by his lavish and licentious expenditures, and he himself is said to have foreseen the upheaval that followed in the next reign, without seeking to prevent it. He died in Versailles, France.

Louis XVI., 1754-1793. The grandson of the preceding and his successor; had in 1770 married Marie Antoinette, the youngest daughter of Maria Theresa of Austria, and a woman young, beautiful, and accomplished, in high esteem for the purity of her character; his accession was hailed with enthusiasm, and he set himself to restore the ruined finances of the country by taking into his counsel those who could best advise him in her straitened state, but these one and all found the problem an impossible one, owing to the unwillingness of the nobility to sacrifice any of their privileges for the public good; this led to the summoning of the States-General in 1789, and the outbreak of the Revolution by the fall of the Bastille in July of that year; in the midst of this Louis, well-intentioned but without strength of character, was submissive to the wishes of his court and the queen, lost his popularity by his hesitating conduct, the secret support he gave to the Emigrants, his attempt at flight, and by his negotiations with foreign enemies, and subjected himself to persecution at the hands of the nation; he was therefore suspended from his functions, shut up in the Temple, arraigned before the convention, and condemned to death as "guilty of conspiracy against the liberty of the nation and a crime against the general safety of the State"; he was accordingly guillotined on the 21st of January.

Louis Philippe, 1773-1850. King of the French from 1830 till 1848; born in Paris. In 1793, during the Revolution, he fled to Austria and Switzerland and supported himself by teaching; after three years in the United States he went to London, in 1800; on the fall of Napoleon repaired to Paris and recovered his estates; he gained popularity with the *bourgeoisie*, and when the revolution of July, 1830, overthrew Charles X. he succeeded to the throne as the elected sovereign of the people; under the "citizen king" France prospered; but his government gradually became reactionary and violent; he used his great wealth in giving bribes, tampered with trial by jury and the freedom of the press, and so raised against him both the old aristocracy and the working classes; political agitation culminated in the revolution of February, 1848; he was forced to abdicate and escaped with his queen to England, where he died.

Louisa, 1776-1810. Queen of Prussia; born in Hanover. Her father, Duke Karl of Mecklenburg-Strelitz, was then commandant. She was married to the Crown-prince of Prussia, afterward Frederick William III., December 24, 1793, and was the mother of Frederick William IV. and William III., afterward emperor. After her husband's accession to the throne she became exceedingly popular, her great beauty being united with dignity and grace of manners, and with much gentleness of character and active benevolence. She died in Strelitz.

Louvois (*loo-vwah'*), **Francois Michel le Tellier, Marquis de,** 1641-1691. The war-minister of Louis XIV.; born in Paris, France. Louvois took a leading part in the persecution of the Protestants through the dragonnades after the revocation of the Edict of Nantes.

Loyola, Ignatius de (Saint Ignatius), 1491-1566. Spanish founder of the Society of Jesus, or Jesuits; entered the army at an early age; crippled by a wound in 1520, he turned his attention to religion; made a pilgrimage to Jerusalem in 1523, and subsequently studied at the University of Paris, where he met Francis Xavier and James Lainez, in conjunction with whom, in 1543, he formed the society which has since become so celebrated.

Luini, or **Luvino, Bernardino,** 1470?-1531? The best painter of the Milan school; is supposed to have been born in the village of Luino near Lake Maggiore; but it is only known for certain that his works were mostly executed between 1520 and 1530.

Luther, Martin, 1483-1546. Leader of the Protestant Reformation; born at Eisleben, Germany, the son of a miner; educated at the University of Erfurt, and in 1505 entered the Augustine convent at that place; ordained a priest, 1507; became professor of philosophy at Wittenberg, 1508; visited Rome, 1510; denounced the sale of indulgences, 1517, and became involved in numerous controversies; cited to appear before Leo X., he refused to comply; burned the papal bull containing an order to destroy certain of his works, and denied the authority of the pope; excommunicated; enjoyed the support of the elector of Saxony; attended the Diet of Worms, convened for his trial, in 1521; laid aside his monastic dress in 1524, and married Catherine von Bora, an ex-nun, in 1525; enjoyed, during the latter part of his life, the greatest distinction from the princes of Germany. Luther completed, in 1522, his translation of the New Testament, and in 1534 that of the Old Testament; the central point of his theology is justification by faith.

Luxembourg (*look-som-boor'*), **Francois Henri de Montmorenci,** 1628-1695. One of the greatest of French generals; he successively defeated the Spanish in the Low Countries, the combined forces of Austria, Holland, and Spain, and the English.

Lycurgus. Flourished ninth century, B.C. The lawgiver of Sparta; traveled over Crete, Ionia, and Egypt, and on his return, finding his country in complete anarchy, made a new division of property, and remodeled the whole constitution, military and civil; next he bound the citizens by oath not to change his laws till he came back, and then left Sparta to be no more seen; his memory was honored as that of a god with a temple and yearly sacrifices.

Lyell, Sir Charles, 1797-1875. A British geologist; born in Kinnordy, Forfarshire, Scotland; resolved to devote his time and fortune to geological research; for this purpose he visited the United States and the continent of Europe; in his "Antiquity of Man" he summarized the evidence in favor of the theory that the race of man was much older than was currently believed; he died in London, England.

Macadam, John Loudon, 1756-1836. A Sootch engineer; inventor of the system of road making known as "macadamizing"; born in Ayr, Scotland; he went to New York in 1770, entered his uncle's counting house, became a successful merchant, and on his return to Scotland in 1783 bought the estate of Sauchrie, Ayrshire; he began in 1810 to make experiments in the construction of roads, which became a passion with him, and in gaining experience he traveled 30,000 miles, and spent $25,000; in 1816 he was appointed surveyor to the Bristol Turnpike Trust, and remade the roads there cheaply and well; his methods formed the subject of a select committee of the House of Commons in 1819; he was voted $50,000 and appointed surveyor-general of metropolitan roads in 1827; he declined knighthood; he died in Moffat, Dumfriesshire.

Macbeth, ... -1056. A thane of the north of Scotland who, by assassination of King Duncan, became king; reigned seventeen years, but his right was disputed by Malcolm, Duncan's son, and he was defeated by him and fell at Lumphanan.

McClellan, George Brinton, 1826-1885. American general; born in Philadelphia; served in the Mexican war. Became commander of the armies of the United States, 1861; defeated in Peninsular campaign, was superseded but recalled to command and defeated Lee at Antietam; soon relieved of command; was defeated for the presidency, 1864; retired to private life.

McClernand, John Alexander, 1812-1900. An American lawyer and soldier; born in Breckenridge county, Ky.; member of Congress, 1843-1851; joined the Union forces and was made a brigadier-general of volunteers, and later promoted major-general. He died in Springfield, Ill.

McCook, Alexander McDowell, 1831-1903. An American military officer; born in Columbiana county, O.; was made brigadier-general of volunteers in September, 1861, major-general in 1862, and was brevetted brigadier-general, U. S. A., in 1865. He was promoted brigadier-general, U. S. A., in 1890, major-general in 1894, and was retired April 22, 1895. He represented the United States at the coronation of the Czar of Russia in 1896.

McCormick, Cyrus Hall, 1809-1884. An American inventor; born in Walnut Grove, W. Va, The reaping machine invented by him won him many gold medals and distinctions. He established the Presbyterian Theological Seminary of the Northwest in Chicago, 1859. He died in Chicago, Ill.

McCosh, James, 1811-1894. A Scotch-American theologian; born in Carskeoch, Ayrshire, Scotland. In 1868, at the solicitation of the faculty and trustees of Princeton College, N. J., he came to the United States and became president of that institution. Under his guidance and the influence of his name Princeton advanced to a higher place than ever before among the universities of the United States. He resigned the presidency of Princeton in 1888. He died in Princeton, N. J.

Macdonald, 1765-1840. Marshal of France; born at Sancerre, of Scotch descent; entered the army at the time of the Revolution as a lieutenant, and rapidly rose in rank; served with distinction under Napoleon, especially at Wagram, when he was made Duke of Taranto; supported the Bourbons on their restoration.

Maceo, Antonio, 1843-1896. A Cuban patriot; born in Santiago de Cuba. In 1890 he was formally banished from Cuban soil by the Spanish government, but at the outbreak of the war of 1895-1898 he returned to Cuba and took command of 7,000 insurgents in his native province, and was thereafter engaged in various battles and skirmishes with the Spanish armies. Early in December, 1896, while attempting to penetrate the Spanish lines with a skirmishing troop, he was killed.

Machiavelli (*mak-ke-ah-vail'le*), **Niccolo,** 1469-1530. Statesman and historian; born in Florence, Italy; was secretary of the Florentine Republic from 1498 to 1512, and during that time conducted its diplomatic affairs with a skill which led to his being sent on a number of foreign embassies; he was opposed to the restoration of the Medici family, and on the return of it to power was subjected to imprisonment and torture as a conspirator, but was at last set at liberty; he spent the remainder of his life chiefly in literary labors, producing among other works a treatise on government, entitled "The Prince," the principles of which have established for him a notoriety wide as the civilized world.

McKinley, William, 1843-1901. Twenty-fifth president of the United States; born in Ohio. He enlisted as a private in the Twenty-third Ohio Volunteer Infantry, when but eighteen years of age. Passed rapidly to captain and was brevetted major when only twenty-two years of age for gallantry on the field of battle. Later he studied law, was admitted to the bar in 1867, elected member of Congress, 1876-1891. He was elected governor of Ohio in 1891 and re-elected in 1893. Elected president in 1896 by 603,854 popular plurality; re-elected in 1900 by 849,455. As president he proved unusually able and enjoyed in a remarkable degree the confidence of the people. Shot by Leon Czolgosz at Buffalo, September 6, 1901, and died September 14.

Macma′hon, Marie Edme Patrice Maurice de, Duke of Magenta, 1808-1893. A marshal of France; born in Sully, near Autun, France. Entering the army, he saw much active service in Algeria, and in the Italian campaign of 1859, winning a marshal's baton and the dignity of Duke of Magenta for the decisive part he took in the battle of that name. In 1873 he was elected president of the republic for a period of seven years. He resigned on January 30, 1879, and afterward lived in retirement; died in Paris.

Macpherson, James Birdseye, 1828-1864. An American military officer; born in Sandusky, O.; entered service in the Civil War, and was chief engineer on the staff of General Grant in 1862; was distinguished for brilliant services at Champion Hill and at Vicksburg, and was commander of the Army of the Tennessee when he was killed at Atlanta, Ga.

Macready, William Charles, 1793-1873. An English tragedian; born in London, England; in 1826 he made his first visit to America, and in 1828 played in Paris, with great success in both countries; he did much to reform the stage and cultivate the public taste for Shakespearean drama; revisited the United States in 1849; returned to England; gave a series of farewell performances, and finally retired from the stage in 1851; he died in Cheltenham, England.

Madison, James, 1751-1836. American statesman and fourth president of the United States; born at Port Conway, Virginia; devoted himself to politics in 1776; he took part in framing the Virginia constitution, and subsequently secured religious liberty in the state; with Jay and Hamilton he collaborated to establish the federation of the states and to frame the Federal Constitution; the "three fifths" rule, which won the adhesion of the slave-holding states, was his suggestion; elected to the first Congress, he attached himself to Jefferson's party, and was secretary of state during Jefferson's presidency, 1801-1809; he succeeded his former leader and held office for two terms, during which the war of 1812-1814 with England was waged; his public life closed with his term of office, 1817.

Maecenas (*mi-se′nas*), **Caius Cilnius,** 70?-8 B.C. A man whose name is imperishably associated with the Augustan literature of Rome; his great glory was the happy influence that he exercised over the emperor as a patron of learning, and his own munificence and taste in the same direction.

Magel′lan, the incorrect but generally received name of **Magalhaens, Ferdinand,** 1480?-1521. A celebrated Portuguese navigator; born in Saboroso, Portugal; in 1520 he discovered and passed the straits which have since been called by his name, and was the first to circumnavigate the world; he was slain in a skirmish with the natives on Mactan, one of the Philippine Islands.

Magruder, John Bankhead, 1810-1871. An American military officer; born in Winchester county, Va.; served in the Mexican War; at the outbreak of the Civil War entered the Confederate army; afterward served under the Emperor Maximilian, of Mexico, and died in Houston, Tex.

Mahmud′, 979?-1030. Sultan of Ghazna, the founder of the Mohammedan empire in India; born in Ghazna, Afghanistan. His father, Sabaktagin, governor of Ghazna, owed a nominal allegiance to Persia, but was really independent. On his death Mahmud put aside his elder brother; formed an alliance against the Persian monarch, overthrew his kingdom and laid the foundation of an extensive empire in Central Asia. He then turned his attention to India, and in a series of twelve invasions secured a great amount of treasure and vastly extended his power. He was a patron of literature, and brought many men of learning about his court. He died in Ghazna.

Maimonides (*my-mon′a-dees*), **Moses,** 1135-1204. A Jewish philosopher; born in Cordova, Spain. He harmonized Judaism and philosophy. Driven with his family from Spain, he resided in Fez; then traveled by way of Palestine to Cairo, becoming there chief rabbi and the caliph's physician. His chief work, written in Hebrew, is "Mishneh Torah," a masterly exposition of the whole of the Jewish law as contained in the Pentateuch and the voluminous Talmudic literature. He died in Cairo, Egypt.

Maintenon (*mahnt′non*), **Francoise d'Aubigne, Marchioness de,** 1635-1719. Born in Niort, France. She was first the mistress, and later the second wife, of King Louis XIV. of France.

Maitland, William, 1525-1573. Scottish politician and reformer; played a prominent part in the various movements of his time, but gained the confidence of no party; he adhered to the party of Moray as against the extreme measures of Knox, and proved a highly astute ambassador at the English Court; he connived at Rizzio's murder, but regained Mary's favor, and when she fled to England he acted in her interest; died in Leith prison.

Malcolm. The name of various Scottish rulers. **Malcolm III.,** surnamed Canmore (Great Head), 1024?-1093. After the murder of his father, Duncan, by Macbeth, he sought aid from Siward of Northumbria; his cause was also espoused by Edward the Confessor. On the defeat and death of Macbeth he was crowned at Scone in 1058. In 1068 he granted asylum to Edgar Atheling, his mother, and two sisters (one of whom, Margaret, he married in 1070), with a number of Saxon exiles. His reign, which was mostly taken up with wars with England, had nevertheless an important bearing on the civilization and consolidation of Scotland.

Malesherbes (*mahl′zahrb*), **Lamoignon de,** 1721-1794. French statesman; born in Paris; a good and upright man; was twice called to be one of Louis XVI.'s advisers; defended Louis at his trial; was guillotined.

Malibran, Marie Felicita (*nee* Garcia), 1808-1836. French vocalist and actress; made her debut in London in 1825, and soon her reputation extended over Europe. She married M. Malibran, a French merchant, who soon became bankrupt; she then returned to the stage, and was received with great enthusiasm in France, England, Germany, and Italy. Her first marriage having been dissolved, she married M. Beriot, a famous violinist, in 1836. She was one of the greatest of operatic singers. Died in Manchester, England.

Malpighi (*mal-pe′gee*), **Marcello,** 1628-1694. Italian anatomist and professor of medicine; noted for his discovery of the corpuscles of the kidney and the spleen, named after him.

Malthus, Thomas Robert, 1766-1834. An English clergyman and political economist. He held that population increased faster than the necessaries of life, and opposed early marriages.

Mandeville, Sir John, fl. fourteenth century. An English traveler; he was the author of a popular book of travels of that country.

Manfred, 1231-1266. King of the two Sicilies; had to struggle for his birthright with three popes, Innocent IV., Alexander IV., and Urban IV.; the last excommunicated him, and bestowed his dominions on Charles of Anjou.

Mann, Horace, 1796-1859. An American educator; born in Franklin, Mass. He was member of Congress from Massachusetts, 1848-1853; president of Antioch College, 1852-1859. He died in Yellow Springs, O.

Manning, Henry Edward, 1808-1892. An English clergyman and writer; born in Totteridge, Hertfordshire. Originally a clergyman of the Church of England, he became a Roman Catholic priest in 1851; Archbishop of Westminster in 1865; cardinal in 1875; founded the Roman Catholic University in Kensington in 1874. He died in Westminster.

Mansard. The name of two French architects, born in Paris — **Francois,** 1598-1666, who constructed the Bank of France, and **Jules Hardoun,** 1645-1708, his grandnephew, architect of the dome of the Invalides and of the palace and chapel of Versailles.

Mansfield, William Murray, Earl of, 1705-1793. A Scotch jurist; in 1754 he was attorney-general, and in 1756 he was appointed chief-justice of the King's Bench, and made Baron Mansfield; in 1776 he was advanced to the dignity of earl; he frequently refused high office, notably that of chancellor; in 1788 he resigned his office of chief-justice, and the remainder of his life was spent in retirement; he died in London, England.

Mantegna (*man-tane′yah*), **Andrea,** 1431-1506. An Italian painter; born in Padua, Italy; Mantegna excelled in perspective, which was then a rare merit; he introduced the art of engraving on copper into Upper Italy.

Manteuffel (*man'toi-fel*), **Edwin Hans Karl Freiherr von,** 1809-1885. A Prussian soldier; born in Dresden; he entered the war of 1870 as commander of the First Corps, but was soon promoted to the command of the Army of the North, which fought successfully at Amiens and other places. When peace was proclaimed he was placed at the head of the army of occupation in France, and in 1879 was appointed imperial viceroy of the newly organized provinces, Alsace-Lorraine; he died in Carlsbad, Bohemia.

Marat (*mah-rah'*), **Jean Paul,** 1744-1793. A French revolutionist; born in Baudry, Neufchatel, Switzerland; president of the Jacobin Club; the fall of the Girondists was a triumph for him and his friends, but it led quickly to his own end; it was at this time that Charlotte Corday resolved to rid the world of him, and he was stabbed by her in Paris.

Marcel'lus, M. Claudius, ... -208 B.C. A Roman general and member of one of the most eminent plebeian families; in his first consulship (222 B.C.) he defeated the Insubrian Gauls; in the second Punic war Marcellus took command after the disaster of Cannæ, and put a check on the victorious Hannibal at Nola, in Campania (216 B.C.). Again consul in 214 B.C., he gave a fresh impulse to the war in Sicily; in his fifth consulship, 208 B.C., he fell in a skirmish against Hannibal.

Marco'ni, William, 1874- . . . . An Anglo-Italian electrician; born in Griffone, near Bologna, Italy. His mother was an Englishwoman. He began experimenting in wireless telegraphy in 1895. His first English exhibition was given in 1896, and was private. After that public interest was aroused and experiments were tried with varying degrees of success. He visited the United States to induce the government to buy the right to use his system, but did not succeed, as what was regarded as a superior system had been perfected by the Signal Service. Various European navies, however, adopted it.

Marcy, William L., 1786-1857. A distinguished American statesman; born in Massachusetts. His mature life was spent in New York, of which state he was governor three times; was also secretary of war in President Polk's cabinet, 1845, and secretary of state in President Pierce's cabinet, 1853-1857.

Margaret (Semiramis of the North), 1353-1412. Queen of Norway, Sweden, and Denmark.

Margaret of Anjou, 1429-1482. Queen of Henry VI. of England.

Margaret of Angouleme, 1492-1549. Queen of Navarre and authoress.

Margaret of Austria, 1480-1530. Regent of the Netherlands.

Margaret of Valois, 1553-1615. Queen of France.

Maria de' Medici, 1573-1642. Queen of France.

Maria Louisa, 1791-1847. Empress of the French.

Maria Theresa, 1717-1780. Queen of Hungary and Bohemia, Archduchess of Austria, and Empress of Germany; daughter of the Emperor Charles VI.; born in Vienna. In 1736 she married Duke Francis Stephen of Lorraine, who in 1737 became Grand Duke of Tuscany. The day after her father's death, in 1740, she ascended the throne of Hungary, Bohemia, and Austria, and declared her husband joint ruler. Assailed by powerful foes she maintained long and costly wars in successful defense of her dominions. She died in Vienna.

Marie Antoinette (*mah-re' on-twah-net'*), 1755-1793. Queen of France; born in Vienna, Austria. She was the daughter of the Emperor Francis I. and the celebrated Maria Theresa. She left Vienna for Versailles in 1770, when only fifteen years of age, to give her hand to the young Duke of Berri, afterward Louis XVI. of France. When her husband ascended the throne in 1774, she gained the affections of the people by repeated acts of generosity. It was the queen who advised the flight of the royal family from Paris in June, 1791, which ended in their capture and return. At length came the fatal 10th of August, 1792. Prepared for the worst, the queen exerted all her power to induce the king to meet death sword in hand; but he thought resistance was in vain, and was led with his consort before the Legislative Assembly, where she heard his deposition announced, and then accompanied him to the prison of the Temple. There, deprived of every semblance of royalty, and bereft of every comfort, she displayed the magnanimity of a heroine and the patient endurance of a martyr. In January, 1793, she had a parting interview with her husband, on whom sentence of death had been passed by the Convention. In August following she was removed to the Conciergerie, and in October she was brought before the revolutionary tribunal, and finally perished under the guillotine.

Marion, Francis, 1732-1795. An American military officer; born near Georgetown, S. C. At the outbreak of the Revolutionary War, in 1775, he was elected to Congress, but afterward obtained various commands in the Continental army. He died in Pond Bluff, S. C.

Marius, Caius, 157-86 B.C. Roman general and consul.

Marlborough, John Churchill, Duke of, 1650-1722. English commander; commanded the English forces in the Netherlands, 1689; commanded in Ireland, 1690; accused of treason, deposed, and confined in the Tower, 1692; reinstated, 1696; commanded the allied armies in Holland, 1702; won the battle of Blenheim, 1704; Ramilles, 1706; Oudenarde, 1708; Malplaquet, 1709.

Marmont, 1774-1852. Duke of Ragusa and marshal of France; served under Napoleon, and distinguished himself on many a battlefield; received the title of Duke for his successful defense of Ragusa against the Russians; was present at Wagram, Luetzen, Bautzen, and Dresden, but came to terms with the allies after the taking of Paris, which led to Napoleon's abdication in 1814; obliged to flee on Napoleon's return, he came back to France and gave his support to the Bourbons.

Marochet'ti, Baron, 1805-1867. Italian sculptor; born in Turin; after working in Paris, went to England in 1848, and executed several public statues, one of Queen Victoria among others.

Marquette (*mar-ket'*), **James,** 1637-1675. A French missionary and explorer; born in Laon, France. He became a Jesuit priest in 1666 and went to Canada as a missionary; in 1673-1674 he made an extensive missionary journey through the Lake Superior and Green bay region, traveling, exploring, and preaching; was one of the early voyagers down the Mississippi river, of which he wrote an interesting account; he died near Marquette river, Mich.

Marshall, John, 1755-1835. An American jurist; born in Germantown, Va.; was an officer in the Colonial army from 1775 to 1779, where he won distinction, especially on courts-martial, in which he acted frequently as judge-advocate; he went as an envoy to France in 1798, but was superseded on account of his Federalistic views; in 1799 he entered Congress, and in 1800 was appointed secretary of war, and a little later secretary of state; in 1801 he was nominated chief justice of the United States by President John Adams, and confirmed unanimously by the Senate; this office he held thirty-four years, during which his decisions on constitutional questions established precedents in the interpretation of the Constitution that have been accepted ever since; he died in Philadelphia.

Marshman, Joshua, 1768-1837. An English missionary; born in Westbury Leigh, England; was sent in 1799 by the Baptist Missionary Society to Serampore, where he had Carey, Ward, and others as fellow laborers; translated a great portion of the Bible into Chinese; he died in Serampore, India. His son, John Clark Marshman, founded the first English weekly newspaper in India.

Martel', Charles, Duke of Austrasia (the Hammer), 694-741. Conquered the Saracens in the great battle of Tours, or Poictiers, 732. *See* CHARLES MARTEL.

Marx, Karl, 1818-1883. German socialist; born at Treves, of Jewish descent; was at first a student of philosophy and a disciple of Hegel, but soon abandoned philosophy for social economy; early adopted socialistic opinions, for his zeal in which he was driven from Germany, France, and finally Belgium, to settle in London, where he spent the last thirty years of his life; founded the "International," and wrote a work, "Das Kapital," which has become the text-book of Socialism.

Mary I. (Bloody Mary), 1516-1558. Queen of England; married Philip II, of Spain; persecuted the Protestants.

Mary Stuart, 1542-1587. Queen of Scots; daughter of James V. and Mary of Guise; educated in France, where she was married to the Dauphin in 1558, who the following year ascended the French throne as Francis II., but died childless 1560; invited to the throne of Scotland, and married her cousin, Lord Darnley; suppressed, 1565, a revolt of the Protestants instigated by Queen Elizabeth; joined, 1566, a league to extirpate heresy, and, wearying of the arrogance and dissoluteness of Lord Darnley, bestowed her confidence on David Rizzio, an Italian musician, whose murder was instigated the same year by Mary's jealous husband; Lord Darnley was killed in 1567, and Queen Mary married the Earl of Bothwell the same year; public sentiment in Scotland against her became so intense that she was compelled to fly to England, where she was finally beheaded on an unproved charge of conspiracy.

Masaniello (*mah-sa-ne-el'lo*), 1623-1647. The commonly received name of Tommaso Aniello, a fisherman of Naples; born in Amalfi; he headed the populace in their revolt against the Spanish viceroy in 1647, when only twenty-four years of age. His career lasted but nine days, in which time he had 150,000 men under his orders, and was elevated to sovereign authority. He was murdered by four assassins at Naples. He has since been venerated as the liberator of his country.

Mascagni (*mas-kan'yee*), **Pietro,** 1863- . . . . An Italian composer; born in Leghorn, Tuscany. He produced a one-act opera, "Cavalleria Rusticana," in competition for a prize.

Maspero', Gaston Camille Charles, 1846- . . . . A French Egyptologist; born of Italian parents, in Paris, France. As an explorer he excavated or opened the pyramids of the kings belonging to the fifth and sixth dynasties, and the burial fields of Sakkara and Dashur, and discovered new sepulchral sites of great value at Deir el-Bahari, near the entrance to the Valley of the Tombs of the Kings, at Eckmin, 130 miles south of Thebes, and at other places.

Mas'sasoit, 1580?-1660. Indian chief; born in Massachusetts; in March, 1621, three months after the landing of the Pilgrims, he sent a warrier named Samoset to Plymouth, who shouted in English, which he had learned from Penobscot fishermen, "Welcome, Englishmen!" Later Massasoit visited the Pilgrims in person and arranged a treaty of friendship. This is the oldest diplomatic act recorded in the history of New England, and was faithfully kept for fifty-four years.

Mather, Cotton, 1663-1728. An American divine; born in Boston; notorious for his belief in witchcraft, and for the persecution he provoked against those charged with it by his zeal in spreading the delusion.

Mathew, Theobald, 1790-1856. An Irish reformer; born in Thomastown Castle, near Cashel, Ireland; was ordained in the Franciscan order. On April 10, 1838, he signed a total abstinence pledge and began a temperance crusade. He traveled over all parts of Great Britain and Ireland, and in the United States. The immediate results of his preaching were a marked decrease in crime and intoxication. Thousands of Father Mathew Total Abstinence Societies have been organized throughout the world in his honor. Died in Queenstown.

Maupertuis', Pierre Louis Moreau de, 1698-1759. French mathematician and astronomer; born at St. Malo; went to Lapland to measure a degree of longitude, to ascertain the figure of the earth; wrote a book "On the Figure of the Earth."

Maurice of Nassau, 1567-1625. Prince of Orange; one of the most famous generals of modern times; son of William the Silent, on whose assassination he was elected Stadtholder, and became by his prowess the liberator of the United Provinces from the yoke of Spain; his name is stained by his treatment of Barneveldt, who saw and opposed his selfish designs.

Maxim, Hiram S., 1840- . . . . American inventor; born at Tangerville, Me.; showed early a decided mechanical talent, and is best known in connection with the invention of the gun named after him; among his other inventions are the smokeless powder, the incandescent lamp carbons, and search-lights.

Maximil'ian (Ferdinand Maximilian Joseph), 1832-1867. Archduke of Austria and emperor of Mexico; executed by the Mexicans.

Mazarin (*maz-a-ran'*), **Jules,** 1602-1661. An Italian ecclesiastic; born in Pescina, Italy; he became a cardinal, and succeeded the great Richelieu as prime minister of France. He was very niggardly and avaricious, and had acquired in various ways, fair and foul, an immense fortune, amounting to $60,000,000, which he offered to the king, Louis XIV., shortly before he died. He died in Vincennes, France.

Mazep'pa, Ivan, 1644-1709. Hetman of the Cossacks; born in Podolia; became page to John Casimir, king of Poland; he won the confidence of Peter the Great, who made him a prince under his suzerainty, but in an evil hour he allied himself with Charles XII. of Sweden, and lost his principality; fled to Bender on the defeat of the Swedish king at Pultowa in 1709.

Mazzini (*mat-ze'nee*), **Giuseppe,** 1805-1872. An Italian patriot; born in Genoa; joined the Carbonari; was arrested by the authorities of Piedmont on the charge of conspiring against the government, but after being imprisoned for six months, was released for lack of evidence. Founded the famous secret revolutionary society "Young Italy." At the outbreak of the revolution of 1848 he became a member of the triumvirate in the republic of Rome, but was exiled at the restoration of the papal power. In 1870 he engaged in an insurrection at Palermo and was captured, but afterward released at the general amnesty after the occupation of Rome. He died in Pisa, Italy.

Meade, George Gordon, 1816-1872. An American general; born at Cadiz, Spain; died in Pennsylvania. He commanded the Federal forces at the important battle of Gettysburg, Penn., and was second in command to General Grant in the Richmond campaign.

Medici (*med'e-che*). A noble Florentine family, founded by Giovanni de' Medici in the fourteenth century, and became extinct in the male line, 1737. Several of its members were distinguished as soldiers, others as statesmen and patrons of the arts.

Medici, Alessandro de', 1510-1537. First duke of Florence; assassinated.

Medici, Cosimo de' (the Great), 1519-1574. First grand duke of Tuscany.

Medici, Lorenzo de' (the Magnificent), 1448-1492. Prince of Florence; scholar and patron of literature and art.

Meissonier (*may-so-ne-a'*), **Jean Louis Ernest,** 1814-1891. A French painter; born in Lyons, France. All his works were painted with Flemish care and finish but were thoroughly original in their treatment. His pictures, though of small size, sold for large sums. He died in Paris.

Melanch'thon, Philip, (real name P. Schwarzerdt), 1497-1550. An eminent German theologian and reformer; he was the contemporary, friend, and successor of Luther as the head of the German Reformation.

Mencius or **Meng-tze,** 372-289 B.C. A celebrated Chinese sage; a disciple, some say a grandson, of Confucius; his teachings are collected in a book entitled the "Book of Meng-tze," which is full of practical instruction.

Men'delssohn-Barthol'dy, Felix, 1809-1847. Celebrated German composer; born in Hamburg; his compositions consist of symphonies, operas, oratorios, and church music; his oratorios of "St. Paul" and "Elijah" are enduring monuments of his genius.

Men'delssohn, Moses, 1729-1786. A German philosopher, born at Dessau, of Jewish descent; was author of "Phædon, a Discourse on the Immortality of the Soul," and did a great deal in his day to do away with the prejudices of the Jews and the prejudices against them.

Men'elek, or **Menelik, II.,** 1842- . . . . King or Negus of Abyssinia; son of Hailo Menelek, King of Shoa; succeeded Johannes II. in 1889, and was crowned in 1890; he is of Negro blood with a strain of Jew, Arab, and Galla, and claims descent from Solomon and the Queen of Sheba; at the battle of Adowa, in the spring of 1896, his troops inflicted an overwhelming defeat on the Italian army, thus securing the independence of his territories.

Menzel, Adolph, 1815- . . . . German painter; born at Breslau; professor at Berlin; best known for his historical pictures and drawings.

Mer'genthaler, Ottmar, 1854-1899. An American inventor; born in Wuertemberg, Germany; came to the United States in 1872 and received a government position in Washington to care for the mechanism of bells, clocks, and signal service apparatus, became connected with a mechanical engineering firm in Baltimore, Md., in 1876; subsequently, while still engaged with that company, he began experiments which resulted in the invention of the type setting machine bearing his name; he died in Baltimore, Md.

Mesmer, Friedrich Anton. 1733-1815. A German physician; born near Constance; was the founder of animal magnetism, called mesmerism after him, his experiments in connection with which created a great sensation, particularly in Paris, until the quackery of it was discovered by scientific investigation.

Met'ternich, Clemens Wenzel Nepomuk Lothar von, 1775-1859. Austrian statesman.

Meyerbeer, Giacomo (Jakob Meyer-Beer), 1791-1864. German musical composer.

Michael Angelo (Michelangelo Buonarroti), 1475-1564. Italian painter, sculptor, architect, and poet; "the Dante of the arts;" patronized by Lorenzo the Magnificent; invited to Rome by Pope Julius II., where he designed the church of St. Peter; became architect of that magnificent structure in 1546, and devoted the rest of his life almost exclusively to its completion.

Mifflin, Thomas, 1744-1800. An American statesman and general; born in Pennsylvania. He was a member of the Continental Congress, and governor of his native state nine years.

Mill, John Stuart, 1806-1873. An English philosopher and political economist; born in London, England. From 1835 to 1840 he was editor and part proprietor of the *London and Westminster Review*, in which many of his own articles appeared. His "System of Logic, Ratiocinative and Inductive," appeared in 1843 and was followed by a long list of standard works. His "Autobiography" was published after his death, which occurred in Avignon, France.

Millais, Sir John Everett, 1829-1896. An English painter; born in Southampton, England. In portraiture he held the foremost rank, and painted a number of the most distinguished men of his day. Many of the works of Millais are well known by engravings. He died in London.

Miller, Hugh, 1802-1856. Scotch journalist and geologist, self-taught; born in Cromarty, of sailor ancestry; began life as a stone mason; editor of the *Witness* newspaper from 1839 till his death; wrote the "Old Red Sandstone," "Footprints of the Creator," and the "Testimony of the Rocks," besides being the author of an account of his life, "My Schools and Schoolmasters"; died by his own hand at Portobello.

Millet (*mil-lay′*), **Jean Francois,** 1814-1874. A French painter. In 1849 he settled among the peasants of Barbizon, on the edge of Fontainebleau forest, and devoted himself to transferring their simple everyday life to his canvases, which he did with great truth of sentiment and subdued poetic charm. Of his paintings may be mentioned "The Angelus," which was sold by auction in Paris, in 1889, for about $115,000. He died in Barbizon, France.

Milti′ades. Flourished 500 B.C. An Athenian general, famous for his decisive defeat of the Persians at Marathon, 490 B.C.

Milton, John, 1608-1674. Poet of the Puritans; educated at Cambridge; passed several years in travel; advocated the popular party, opposing prelacy and the established church; wrote many political and controversial works in prose; was appointed in 1648 Latin secretary of the Council of State; in 1654 he had become entirely blind; his "Paradise Lost" was completed in 1655, and sold for £10, half of which was not to be paid until the sale of 1,300 copies.

Minie, Claud Etienne, 1814-1879. A French military officer; born in Paris, France. He devoted his principal thought to the perfecting of firearms, and in 1849 invented the Minie rifle. In 1858 the Khedive of Egypt appointed him director of a small arms factory and musketry school in Cairo.

Mirabeau (*mee-rah-bo′*), **Honore Gabriel de Riquetti, Comte de,** 1749-1791. French orator and statesman; entered the army in 1776; exiled and imprisoned for debt; separating from his wife, he eloped with a young woman in 1776, for which offense he was condemned to death; escaped, however, with four years' imprisonment; led a wandering life for several years, engaging in numerous intrigues; sent to Berlin on a secret mission in 1786, and elected to the States-General in 1789, and later to the National Assembly, of which he became president in 1791.

Mitchel, Ormsby Macknight, 1810-1862. American general and astronomer.

Mitchell, John, 1869- . . . . An American labor executive; born in Braidwood, Ill.; received a common school education; later studied law; worked in coal mines in 1882; joined the Knights of Labor in 1885, and went West, where he worked in coal mines till 1890; became secretary-treasurer of the sub-district of the United Mine Workers of America in 1895; president of the United Mine Workers of America in 1898; and was vice-president of the American Federation of Labor in 1898 and 1900. President Mitchell had personal charge of the great strike in the anthracite coal mines in the summer and autumn of 1902.

Mithrida′tes the Great, 135 ?-63 B.C. King of Pontus, who overran all Asia Minor, but was defeated by Pompey, and committed suicide; reigned from 120 to 63 B.C.

Mivart, St. George, 1827-1901. French naturalist; a Roman Catholic professor at Louvain, distinguished for his opposition to Darwinianism.

Modjeska, Helena, 1844- . . . . A Polish actress; born in Cracow, Poland. She began to act in a traveling company in 1861. Four years later she made a great name at Cracow; she settled with her second husband, near Los Angeles, Cal., to try farming; but the enterprise not succeeding, she returned to the stage, and won a complete triumph at San Francisco in 1877.

Mohammed (or **Mahomet**), 569-632. Conquerer and prophet, and founder of the Moslem religion, which threatened to subdue the Christian world; pretended, at the age of forty, to have received a revelation from Allah, and thenceforth devoted himself to the propagation of his new religion; previous to this time he had been an idolater; his new faith, which included the unity of God, was rejected at Mecca, where a conspiracy was formed against him, but was warmly embraced in Medina, to which place the prophet fled in 622; from this flight, called the Hegira, the Mussulmans compute their time; after this event, Mohammed propagated the faith of Islam by the sword, gaining numerous victories, and spreading his religion over a large portion of Western Asia.

Moltke (*molt′ka*), **Count von** (surnamed the Silent), 1800-1891. Great German field marshal; born in Mecklenburg-Schwerin, of an old family; was pre-eminent as a military strategist, planned and conducted the Prussian campaign against Austria in 1866, and the German campaign against France in 1870-1872; was in the service of Denmark before he entered the Prussian service.

Monk, George, Duke of Albemarle, 1608-1670. English general; restored the monarchy.

Monmouth, James Scott, Duke of, 1649?-1685. Natural son of Charles II.; rebelled, but was defeated and executed.

Monroe, James, 1758-1831. Fifth president of the United States; born in Virginia; captain in the Revolutionary War; studied law under Jefferson; in Congress, 1783; opposed the Constitution; governor of Virginia, 1799; envoy extraordinary to France, 1802; re-elected governor, 1811; appointed secretary of state same year by Madison; elected president, 1816, and re-elected 1820.

Montalembert (*mon-tal-aim-bair′*), **Comte de,** 1810-1870. A French politician; born in London; son of a French emigrant; spent his life in advocating the cause of a free unfettered system of national education; wrote the "Monks of the West," his chief work.

Montcalm de St. Veran, Louis Joseph, Marquis de, 1712-1759. A French general; killed simultaneously with his gallant antagonist, General Wolfe, on Quebec Heights.

Montefio′re, Sir Moses, 1784-1885. A philanthropic Jewish banker; born in Leghorn; a friend to the emancipation not only of the oppressed among his own race, but of the slaves in all lands; lived to a great age.

Montezu′ma II., 1466-1520. The last of the Mexican emperors; submitted to Cortez when he landed; died of a wound he received as he pleaded with his subjects to submit to the conquerer, aggravated by grief over the failure of his efforts in bringing about a reconciliation.

Mont′fort, Simon de, 1208-1265. A leader of the English barons in rebellion against Henry III.; De Montfort, when in almost absolute power, was the first to summon representatives of the boroughs to Parliament and thereby originated the House of Commons. Killed in the battle of Evesham.

Montgolfier (*mon-golf-e-ay′*), **Joseph Michel,** 1740-1810, and **Jacques Etienne,** 1745-1799. Joint inventors of the balloon; were born in Vidalon-les-Annonay, in the department of Ardeche, in France. Their first balloon, inflated with rarefied atmospheric air, ascended from Annonay in 1782, and the invention soon brought them fame and honors. Joseph was also the inventor of the water-ram.

Montgomery, Richard, 1737-1775. An American military officer; born in Swords, Ireland; was with Wolfe at the taking of Quebec in 1759. On his return to England he resigned his commission and emigrated to America. On the breaking out of the Revolutionary War, the command of the Continental forces in the northern department was bestowed on him. He reduced Fort Cherokee and took Montreal. He fell in an attempt on Quebec, being struck by a ball from the only gun fired by the enemy.

Montrose, James Graham, Marquis of, 1613-1650. A Scotch noble, and a distinguished royalist leader under Charles I.; born in Edinburgh, Scotland. He took a very active part on the side of the king, was created a marquis, and in a few months gained the battles of Perth, Aberdeen, and Inverlochy. In 1645 his fortune changed, and he was obliged to leave the kingdom; in 1648 he landed in Orkney with a few followers, but was soon overpowered, conveyed to Edinburgh, and there decapitated and quartered.

Moody, Dwight Lyman, 1837-1899. An American evangelist; born in Northfield, Mass.; received a common school education; united with the Mount Vernon Congregational Church in Boston in 1850; settled in

Chicago, Ill., in 1856, and there built up a mission Sunday school with more than 1,000 pupils. He subsequently built a church in Chicago, which was destroyed in the great fire in 1871, but was afterward rebuilt under the name of the Chicago Tabernacle. In 1873 he began, with Ira D. Sankey, the evangelistic work which soon made him famous. He met with unparalleled success both in the United States and Great Britain. In 1879 he founded a school for poor girls at Northfield, Mass., which later grew into the celebrated Northfield and Mount Hermon Institutions. It is said that during his ministry Mr. Moody addressed over 50,000,000 people. He died in Northfield, Mass.

Moore, Sir John, 1761-1809. A British military officer; born in Glasgow, Scotland; he served at Minorca, in the American war; as brigadier-general in the West Indies, 1795; in Ireland during the rebellion of 1798; in Holland in 1799, and in Egypt in 1801. Moore was then regarded as the greatest living British general, and in 1805 he was knighted. In 1808 he was appointed commander-in-chief of the British army in Portugal to operate against Napoleon. He advanced to Salamanca in spite of the gravest difficulties, but was finally compelled to retreat to Corunna, a distance of 200 miles, in face of a superior force. The absence of a fleet to receive his army forced him to a battle against Marshal Soult, in which Moore fell, mortally wounded, in the hour of victory.

More, Sir Thomas, 1480-1535. English statesman and philosopher; educated at Oxford; entered Parliament, 1504; produced "History of Richard III.," 1513; "Utopia," 1516; became a great favorite of Henry VIII., who made him lord chancellor in 1530; being an ardent Catholic, he refused to sanction the divorce of Queen Catherine, and resigned his office in 1532; imprisoned in 1534 for declining to take an oath acknowledging the validity of the king's marriage to Anne Boleyn, and executed the following year for denying the king's supremacy as head of the church.

Morgan, John Pierpont, 1837- . . . . An American capitalist; born in Hartford, Conn.; was educated at the University of Gottingen, Germany. He returned to the United States in 1857, and became connected with the banking firm of Duncan, Sherman & Co. In 1871 he was made a partner of the firm of Drexel, Morgan & Co., which afterward became J. Pierpont Morgan & Co. He became widely known as an organizer of large railroad and industrial interests. Mr. Morgan has been a large donor to charitable and educational institutions.

Morris, Gouverneur, 1752-1816. An American statesman; born in Morrisania, N. Y. He was member of the Continental Congress; of the committee that drafted the Constitution; minister to France, 1792-1794; United States senator from New York, 1800-1803. He died in Morrisania.

Morris, Robert, 1734-1806. An American financier, and a signer of the Declaration of Independence; born in Lancashire, England. Coming to America at an early age, he embarked in mercantile business in Philadelphia, and rapidly acquired wealth. On the outbreak of the Revolution, he took a prominent part in upholding the national cause. In 1775, he was elected to Congress, and in 1781 appointed superintendent of finance. He died in Philadelphia, Pa.

Morse, Samuel Finley Breese, 1791-1872. American inventor of the magnetic telegraph; graduate of Yale College; studied painting in England, returning to America in 1832; constructed small recording electric telegraph in 1835; finally obtained aid from Congress in 1843, and constructed a line between Washington and Baltimore in 1844.

Morton, James Douglas, Earl of, 1530-1581. Regent of Scotland; joined the Reforming party; was made Chancellor; took part in the murder of Rizzio, and was privy to the plot against Darnley; joined the confederacy of the nobles against Mary, fought against her at Langside, and became regent in 1572; became unpopular; was charged with being accessory to Darnley's murder, and beheaded.

Moses, 1568?-1448? B.C. In Scripture the Hebrew lawgiver and leader of the Israelites from Egypt; born in Egypt; died on Mount Pisgah, at the age of 120 years.

Mott, Lucretia, 1793-1880. An American reformer; born in Nantucket, Mass. In 1818 she joined the Friends. In 1833 she assisted in the formation of the American Anti-Slavery Society, and in 1840 went to London as its delegate to the World's Anti-Slavery Convention. She was one of the four promoters of the Woman's Rights Convention in the United States, and was an active exponent of the cause of equal suffrage. She died in Philadelphia, Pa.

Moultrie, William, 1731-1805. An American military officer; born in South Carolina. In 1776 he was designated to construct a fort, which afterward received his name, on Sullivan's Island; was promoted a major-general by Congress; in 1785 he was elected governor of South Carolina, and again in 1794, after which he retired to private life. He died in Charleston, S. C.

Mozart (*mo-zart'; Ger., mo'tzart*), **Johann Chrysostomus Wolfgang Amadeus,** 1756-1791. German composer; composed short pieces at the age of six, and at seven gave concerts in Paris and London; distinguished for the universality of his genius; he gave artistic form to opera.

Muehlenberg, Henry Melchior, 1711-1787. Founder of the German Lutheran church in America.

Muehlenberg, John Peter Gabriel, 1746-1807. American general.

Mueller, Friedrich Max, 1823-1900. A German philologist; born in Dessau, Germany; son of Wilhelm Mueller, the German poet. He was the author of "A History of Ancient Sanskrit Literature," "On the Origin and Growth of Religion as Illustrated by the Religions of India," etc. He died in Oxford, England.

Muenchhau'sen, Baron von, 1720-1797. A cavalry officer in the service of Hanover, famed for the extravagant stories he used to relate of his adventures and exploits, which, with exaggerations, were collected by one Raspe, and published in 1785 under Muenchhausen's name.

Munkac'sy, Michael, 1846-1900. A Hungarian painter, whose real surname was Lieb; born in Munkacs, Hungary. In 1872 he settled in Paris. He visited New York in 1886. Except a few portraits, his works are nearly all genre pictures. He died in Bonn, Germany.

Muril'lo, 1618-1682. A celebrated Spanish painter; born at Seville; his subjects were drawn partly from low life and partly from religious or scripture themes, such as the Immaculate Conception and the Assumption of the Virgin, as well as "Moses Smiting the Rock," the "Miracle of the Loaves and Fishes," etc.; died from a fall from a scaffold while painting an altar-piece at Cadiz.

Murray, James Stuart, Earl of, 1533-1570. A natural son of King James V. of Scotland; he was chief minister of his half sister, Mary Queen of Scots, and became regent on her deposition; was assassinated.

Na'dir Shah, 1688-1747. A Turkish chief; given command of the Persian army, 1729; he defeated the Turks, and in 1736 usurped the Persian throne. Overrunning Afghanistan and capturing Delhi, 1738-1739, he massacred 120,000 of the inhabitants of that city; was assassinated.

Nansen, Fridjof, 1861- . . . . A Norwegian scientist and explorer; born in Great Froen, near Christiania, Norway. In 1893, with a crew of eleven men, he set sail from Christiania for the polar regions, and reached a point about 225 miles from the Pole; he was appointed professor of Zoology in the University of Christiania.

Napier, Sir Charles, 1782-1853. English general; born at Westminster; served in the Peninsular War; was in 1841 made commander-in-chief of the Bombay army; defeated the Sikhs at Meeanee in 1848 in a brilliant engagement; became governor of Sinde. Having returned to England, he died at Portsmouth.

Napier, John, 1550-1617. A Scotch mathematician, the inventor of logarithms; born in Merchiston, near Edinburgh, Scotland; traveled on the Continent, and ultimately settled down at the family seats of Merchiston, near Edinburgh, and Gartness, in Stirlingshire, as a recluse student, where he died.

Napier, Robert, Lord, 1810-1890. An English military officer; born in Ceylon; was made commander-in-chief of the British army sent out to Abyssinia for the rescue of the English captives held there by its semi-barbarous ruler, King Theodore; raised to the peerage as Lord Napier of Magdala, and also made a Knight Grand Cross of the Star of India; in 1869, he was appointed commander-in-chief of the British Indian army; and governor of Gibraltar in 1876; he died in London, England.

Nash, John, 1752-1835. English architect; born in London; was the architect of Buckingham Palace and the Pavilion at Brighton.

Nash, Richard, 1674-1761. Known as "Beau Nash"; born at Swansea, Wales; installed himself as master of the ceremonies at Bath, and ruler of the assemblies of fashion in that resort; died in poverty but was honored with a public funeral.

Nast, Thomas, 1840-1902. An American artist; born in Landau, Bavaria; he is best known for his political cartoons, which were of great influence in the various political campaigns, and were effective in the exposure of the "Tweed ring"; in 1902 he was appointed United States consul at Guayaquil, where he died of yellow fever.

Nebuchadnez'zar, 626?-562 B.C. King of Babylon; captured Jerusalem in 606 and carried away many captives, including the prophet Daniel; afterward took Tyre, and reduced Egypt.

Necker, Jacques, 1732-1804. An eminent French financier and statesman; born in Switzerland; he was father of the celebrated Madame de Stael.

Nelson, Horatio, Viscount, 1758-1805. The greatest of Britain's admirals; entered the navy at thirteen; post captain, 1779; rear admiral, 1797, his promotion having been earned by his share in the victory of St. Vincent; lost his right arm in an unsuccessful attack on Teneriffe; won the battle of the Nile in 1798, for which he was raised to the peerage as Baron Nelson of the Nile; became separated from his wife, owing to his infatuation with Lady Hamilton, which lasted until his death; created a viscount for the victory of the Baltic, where, being second in command, he disobeyed the orders directing him to retreat; fell at Trafalgar, where his fleet gained a decisive victory over the French and Spanish; his last words, "Thank God, I have done my duty."

Nes'selrode, Count von, 1780-1862. Celebrated Russian diplomatist; born at Lisbon; represented Russia at a succession of congresses, played a prominent part at them, and directed the foreign policy of the empire under Alexander I. and Nicholas I., from 1816 to 1856.

Neuville', Alphonse de, 1836-1885. French painter of battle scenes; born at St. Omer; he was an illustrator of books, among others Guizot's "Histoire de France."

Newman, John Henry, Cardinal, 1801-1890. English theologian; recognized leader of the High Church party until 1845, when he became a Catholic; appointed rector of Catholic University at Dublin, 1854, and made a cardinal by Pope Leo XIII. in 1879.

Newton, Sir Isaac, 1642-1727. English philosopher; the son of a farmer; graduated at Cambridge, 1665, about which time he invented the "method of fluxions," and discovered the laws of gravitation; discovered, 1668, that light is not homogeneous, but consists of rays of different refrangibility.

Ney, Michel, Duke of Elchingen and Prince of the Moskwa, 1769-1815. French marshal; the son of a cooper; entered the army at eighteen as a private, and was gradually promoted; Napoleon called him "the bravest of the brave," and his titles were conferred upon him for his services at Elchingen, in 1805, and his victory at the battle of Borodino; commanded the rear guard in the retreat from Moscow; defeated by Bernadotte at Dennewitz, 1813; submitted to Louis XVIII. upon the abdication of Napoleon, against whom he was sent with an army in 1815, but united his army with that of his old commander; had five horses shot under him at Waterloo, where he fought with his usual valor; was captured soon after, and shot on a charge of treason.

Nicholas I., 1796-1855. Emperor of Russia; third son of the Emperor Paul I.; born near St. Petersburg, Russia. He ascended the throne in 1825. He made war with Persia, 1827-1828; joined in the treaty of London, which secured the independence of Greece; and made one of the allied powers who destroyed the Turkish fleet at Navarino in 1827. This affair led to war between Russia and Turkey, in which the latter was defeated. Early in 1852 began the Russian effort to take over the holy places and assume the protectorate of the Christians in Palestine. This led to the Crimean war, before the close of which Nicholas died from lung disease in St. Petersburg.

Nicholas II., 1868- . . . . Emperor of Russia; son of Alexander III.; born in St. Petersburg, Russia. His mother was the Princess Dagmar, a daughter of the king of Denmark. During the famine of 1891 he was, at his own request, made president of the Committee of Succor, and worked hard in the organization of relief. As czarevitch he held several military commands in his own country—in the famous Preobrajensky regiment among others—and in England he had conferred on him in 1893 the Order of the Garter. He succeeded to the throne November 1, 1894. He married the Princess Alix of Hesse-Darmstadt November 26, 1894. His coronation took place with impressive and elaborate ceremonial at Moscow in May, 1896. Nicholas II. originated The Hague Peace Conference, and is understood to be strongly opposed to war.

Nicot (*ne-ko'*), **Jean,** 1530-1600. French diplomatist; born in Nimes, France; was French ambassador at Lisbon; introduced into France the tobacco plant, having obtained its seeds from a Dutchman, who obtained them from Florida; it was called after him Nicotiana. Died in Paris, France.

Nightingale, Florence, 1820- . . . . An English philanthropist; born in Florence, Italy. During the Crimean War she promptly volunteered to organize a select band of nurses at Scutari. The offer was accepted by the British War Office, and within a week Miss Nightingale was on her way to the East, where she rendered invaluable service. She was consulted during the American Civil War and the Franco-German War. She published "Notes on Hospitals," "Notes on Nursing," "Notes on Lying-in Institutions."

Nobel, Alfred Bernhard, 1833-1896. A Swedish chemist and physicist; born in Stockholm, Sweden. In 1863 took out a patent for the manufacture of an explosive composed of nitroglycerin and ordinary blasting powder, and in 1864 a second patent. In 1867 he invented dynamite; in 1876 gelatinous nitroglycerin; in 1889 ballistite, which led the way to the invention of smokeless powder. Invented also artificial gutta-percha; manufactured cannon, and, with his brother, Louis, developed the petroleum deposits at Baku, in the Caucasus. He lived for a long time in Paris, but had a villa and laboratory at San Remo, Italy, where he died. Nobel left his fortune of $9,200,000 to found a prize fund, the annual interest of which was to be divided into five equal parts (each amounting to about $40,000, the sum available), to be distributed every year to the persons who, during the year, had done best in (1) physical science; (2) chemistry; (3) physiology or medicine; (4) idealistic literature; and (5) the advancement of universal peace.

North, Frederick, Eighth Lord North and Second Earl of Guilford, 1732-1792. An English statesman; became a lord of the treasury in 1759; chancellor of the exchequer and leader of the House of Commons in 1767; and prime minister in 1770. He was largely responsible for the measures that brought about the loss of the American colonies.

Noyes, George Rapall, 1798-1868. An American Biblical scholar; born in Newburyport, Mass. In 1840 he was made professor of Hebrew and Oriental Languages and Dexter lecturer on Biblical Literature at Harvard. Besides many reviews and sermons, he published new translations, with notes, of several books of the Old Testament. He died in Cambridge, Mass.

Oates, Titus, 1650-1705. Fabricator of a popish plot for the overthrow of the Protestant faith in England, the allegation of which brought to the block several innocent men; rewarded at first with a pension and safe lodgment in Westminster Hall, was afterwards convicted of perjury, flogged, and imprisoned for life, but at the revolution was set at liberty and granted a pension.

Oberlin, Jean Friedrich, 1740-1826. A benevolent Protestant pastor; born at Strasburg; labored all his life at Ban de la Roche, a wild mountain district of Alsace, and devoted himself with untiring zeal to the spiritual and material welfare of the people.

Occam or **Oakham, William of,** 1280-1347. An English scholastic philosopher; born at Oakham, Surrey; surnamed *Doctor Invincibilis;* studied under Duns Scotus and became his rival, and a reviver of Nominalism in opposition to him, by his insistance on which he undermined the whole structure of scholastic dogmatism.

O'Connell, Daniel, 1775-1847. Irish patriot and orator; advocated Catholic emancipation, but opposed resort to arms; elected to Parliament, 1828, but not allowed to take his seat until 1829, when the bill for Catholic emancipation was passed; gave up his law practice and gave his entire attention to public duties; began advocating the repeal of the union in 1840; was convicted in 1844 on a charge of treason, but sentence was reversed by the House of Lords.

Octavia, 70?-11 B.C. The sister of Augustus; a woman distinguished for her beauty and her virtue; was married first to Marcellus, and on his death to Mark Antony, who forsook her for Cleopatra.

Odoa'cer, 434?-493. The first barbarian king of Italy; son of one of Attila's officers; was assassinated.

Œcolampadius (*ek-o-lam-pa'di-us*), **Joannes,** 1482-1531. One of the leaders of the Reformation; born at Weinsberg, in Wuertemberg; became preacher at Basel; assisted Erasmus in his edition of the New Testament; entered a convent at Augsburg; came under Luther's influence and adopted the reformed doctrine.

Oersted (*air'sted*), **Hans Christian,** 1777-1851. Danish natural philosopher; founder of the science of electro-magnetism.

Of'fenbach, Jacques, 1819-1880. A musical composer;

born at Cologne, of Jewish parents; creator of the *opera bouffe;* was the author of "La Belle Helene," "Orphee aux Enfers," "La Grande Duchesse," "Madam Favart," etc.

Oglesby, Richard James, 1824-1899. An American lawyer; born in Oldham county, Ky.; promoted major-general in the Civil War; he was three times governor of Illinois, being first elected in 1864, re-elected in 1872, and again in 1885; he was elected United States senator in 1873 and served six years; died in Elkhart, Ill.

Oglethorpe, James Edward, 1696-1785. An English military officer and philanthropist; born in London, England; it was through his efforts that a colony was formed of insolvent debtors and persecuted Protestants, whom he brought to the United States and settled in Georgia, in 1733; he remained in the United States till 1743, when he returned to England; he died in Cranham Hall, Essex, England.

O'Higgins, Bernardo, 1778-1842. A Chilean general and statesman; son of Ambrosio O'Higgins; born in Chillan; was a prominent leader of the Chilean patriots in 1810, and in 1813 was made commander of the army; in the conflict with Spain in 1814 the combined forces of O'Higgins and Carrera were defeated at Rancagua and they fled across the Andes; O'Higgins joined San Martin in the invasion of Chile and a few days after their victory at Chacabuco (Feb. 12, 1817) he was made supreme dictator of Chile; the rule of O'Higgins was an excellent one; he was forced to resign by a revolution and retired to Peru, where he died.

Ol′iphant, Laurence, 1829-1888. Religious enthusiast and mystic; born in Perthshire; spent his boyhood in Ceylon; he married one Alice l'Estrange, an alliance which grew into one of the most intimate character; with her he went to Palestine, pitched his tent under the shadow of Mount Carmel, and wrote two mystical books under her inspiration.

Olmsted, Frederick Law, 1822-1903. An American landscape architect; born in Hartford, Conn. In co-operation with Calvert Vaux he prepared the general design for Central Park in New York. He was also consulted regarding the park systems of Boston, Chicago, Buffalo, and other cities, besides the United States Capitol grounds and terrace.

Omar Pasha, 1806?-1871. A Turkish general; born in Plaski, Turkey. On the invasion of the Danubian Principalities by the Russians in 1853, he collected an army of 60,000 men, and, crossing the Danube in presence of the enemy, intrenched himself at Kalafat, where he successfully withstood the Russians; February 9, 1855, he embarked for the Crimea, and repulsed with great loss 40,000 Russians who attacked him at Eupatoria. In September, 1861, he was charged to pacify Bosnia and Herzegovina, which were in insurrection. This being accomplished he attacked the Montenegrins, captured Cettinje, and overran the country in 1862.

Orange, William, Prince of (the Silent), 1553-1584. Founder of the Dutch republic; leader of the insurrection which broke out when it was attempted to introduce the Inquisition into the Netherlands; assassinated.

Orella′na, Francisco de, 1490-1549. A Spanish explorer; born in Truxillo, Spain; accompanied Pizarro to Peru in 1531. Ambitious of adventure, he set out to explore the continent of South America east from Peru; passed down a branch of the Amazon into that vast river, and thence to the sea; thus being the first European navigator of the Amazon. His accounts of the marvelous country he had crossed induced Charles V. to authorize him to settle colonies there, and he returned for that purpose in 1549, but died soon after his arrival.

Orfila (*or-fe′lah*), **Mateo Jose Bonaventura,** 1787-1853. A French physician of Spanish parentage, and the founder of the science of toxicology; born in Mahon, Minorca. His "Treatise on Legal Medicine" is the greatest work on medical jurisprudence extant.

Origen, 186?-253. Greek theologian and preacher; endeavored to harmonize the teachings of Christ and Plato.

Orleans, Louis Philippe Joseph, Duc d', 1747-1793. Took the popular side on the assembling of the States-General, renounced his titles, and assumed the name of *Egalite* (Equality); voted for the death of his cousin, Louis XVI.; condemned by the revolutionary tribunal and executed; his son, Louis Philippe, afterward became king of the French.

Or′loff. The name of two brothers, Russians: **Gregory,** 1734-1783, the favorite of Catherine II., and **Alexis,** 1737-1809, a man remarkable for his stature and strength, who murdered Peter III. and was banished by Paul I.

Orsi′ni, Felice, 1819-1858. Italian conspirator; with three others attempted the life of Louis Napoleon; was defended by Jules Favre, but condemned to death and guillotined.

Oscar I., Joseph Francois Bernadotte, 1799-1859. King of Sweden and Norway; son of Bernadotte (Charles XIV.); born in Paris France; he acceded to the throne in 1844; he took little part in foreign politics; he resigned in favor of his eldest son in 1857.

Oscar II., 1829- . . . . King of Sweden and Norway. He is grandson of Napoleon I.'s famous general, Marshal Bernadotte, the first king of the new independent kingdom of Norway. He ascended the throne in 1872, in succession to his brother, Charles XV. He married, in 1857, the Princess Sophia of Nassau, by whom he had four sons.

Osceo′la, 1813?-1838. A chief of the Seminole Indians; born in Florida. In 1835, while on a visit to Fort King, his wife was claimed as a slave, as being the daughter of a fugitive slave woman, and carried off as such. Osceola resolved upon vengeance, and some months afterward, finding General Thompson outside of the fort, killed him and six other whites in his company; he was seized and kept in confinement at Fort Moultrie till his death.

Othman or **Osman I.** (surnamed the Conqueror), 1259-1326. The founder of the empire of the Ottoman Turks; born in Bithynia.

Otho (*o′toe*), 32-69. Roman emperor; had been a companion of Nero; was created emperor by the Pretorian Guards in succession to Galba, but being defeated by the German legionaries, stabbed himself to death after a reign of three months.

Otis, James, 1725-1783. An American statesman; born in West Barnstable, Mass. Through his efforts the Stamp Act Congress was assembled in 1765. He was the author of a number of political essays and orations. He died in Andover, Mass. He had a leading part in animating the American people to a defense of their liberties.

Ot′terbein, Philip William, 1726-1813. Founder of the Church of the United Brethren in Christ; born at Dillenburg, Nassau, Germany; came as missionary to America in 1752; was a powerful preacher, and started a great revival in 1766. He was reluctant to separate formally from the German Reformed Church, but took that step in 1800, when along with Rev. Martin Boehm, a Mennonite, and long his associate in revival work, he was ordained bishop of the new society.

Oudinot (*oo-de-no′*), **Duke of Reggio,** 1767-1847. Marshal of France; born at Bar-le-Duc; led the retreat from Moscow, and was wounded; joined the Royalists after the fall of Napoleon, and died governor of the Hotel des Invalides.

Owen, Sir Richard, 1804-1892. Celebrated English naturalist and comparative anatomist; born in Lancaster.

Ox′enstiern, Axel, Count, 1583-1654. Swedish statesman; favorite minister of Gustavus Adolphus; supported him through the Thirty Years' War, though he disapproved of his engaging in it, and managed the affairs of the state with great ability after his death.

Packard, Alpheus Spring, 1839- . . . . An American naturalist; born in Brunswick, Me. He is best known as an entomologist; his classification of insects, proposed in 1863, has been generally accepted.

Paderew′ski, Ignace Jan, 1860- . . . . A celebrated pianist; born at Podolia, in Russian Poland; made his debut in 1887 with instant success; his first appearance created quite a furore in Paris and London; has several times visited the United States.

Pagani′ni, Nicolo, 1784-1840. A phenomenal Italian violinist; he was extremely profligate.

Paine, Robert Treat, 1731-1814. An American jurist; signer of the Declaration of Independence; born in Boston, Mass.; was a delegate to provincial and continental congresses, and held offices of attorney-general of Massachusetts and judge of the Supreme Court; was an able judge. He died in Boston.

Pakenham, Sir Edward Michael, 1778-1815. An English military officer; born in Ireland; he commanded the British expedition against New Orleans in 1814; he led the British bravely in the battle of New Orleans, January 8, 1815, and was killed while urging on his men.

Palestri′na, Giovanni Pierluigi da, 1524-1594. Celebrated composer of sacred music; surnamed the Prince of Music; born at Palestrina; produced a number of masses which at once raised him to the foremost rank among composers; was the author of a well known *Stabat Mater*.

Paley, William, 1743-1805. Born at Peterborough

England; held various church preferments, and died archdeacon of Carlisle; was a clear writer and cogent reasoner on common sense lines; author of "Horæ Paulinæ," "Evidences of Christianity," and "Natural Theology," as well as "Moral and Political Philosophy."

Palfrey, John Gorham, 1796-1881. An American clergyman and author; born in Boston; was pastor of Brattle Street Unitarian Church, Boston; professor in Harvard; secretary of state of Massachusetts; and member of the Anti-Slavery Congress at Paris, 1867; his enduring work is "The History of New England"; died in Cambridge, Mass.

Palissy (*pah-le-se'*), **Bernard,** 1508?-1589. A French potter and chemist; born in Agen; his pottery has become celebrated, and few things are more prized by the connoisseur than the famous "Palissy ware"; being a Protestant, he was arrested by the Leaguers toward the end of the reign of Henri III., and died in the Bastille.

Palla'dio, Andrea, 1518-1580. An Italian architect; born at Vicenza, of poor parents; was precursor of the modern Italian style of architecture; his works, which are masterpieces of the Renaissance, consist principally of palaces and churches.

Pallas, Peter Simon, 1741-1811. A German traveler and naturalist; born in Berlin; professor of Natural History in St. Petersburg; explored Siberia, and contributed to the geographical knowledge of the Russian empire.

Palma, Tomas Estrada, 1835- . . . . A Cuban statesman and soldier, called the "Franklin of Cuba"; born in Bayamo, Santiago de Cuba. On December 31, 1901, he was elected first president of the new Cuban republic, according to the constitution adopted by the Cuban national convention. His administration has been conservative and successful.

Palmer, John McAuley, 1817-1900. An American lawyer; born in Eagle Creek, Scott county, Ky.; served with distinction in the Civil War, retiring in 1866 with the rank of major-general; United States senator in 1890. In 1896 he was the candidate of the Gold Democrats for president of the United States. He died in Springfield, Ill.

Palmerston, Henry John Temple, Viscount, 1784-1865. English statesman; born, of an Irish family, at Broadlands, Hants; succeeded to his father's title, an Irish peerage, in 1802, and entered Parliament in 1807 as member for Newport, Isle of Wight; in 1852 joined Lord Aberdeen's coalition ministry, and on its fall became himself prime minister in 1855; he prosecuted the Crimean war and the Chinese war of 1857, and suppressed the Great Mutiny in India; he was prime minister when he died.

Pao'li, Pasquale de, 1726-1807. A Corsican patriot; sought to achieve the independence of his country, but was defeated by the Genoese, aided by France, in 1769; took refuge in England; returned to Corsica and became lieutenant-general under the French republic; raised a fresh insurrection, had George III. proclaimed king, but failed to receive the viceroyalty, and returned to England, where he died a disappointed man.

Pap'in, Denis, 1647-1712. French physicist; born at Blois; made a special study of the expansive power of steam and its motive power, invented a steam-digester with a safety-valve, since called after him.

Pap'penheim, Count von, 1594-1632. Imperial general; born in Bavaria; played a prominent part in the Thirty Years' War; was mortally wounded at Luetzen.

Paracel'sus, 1493-1541. A Swiss physician, alchemist, and mystic, whose real name was Theophrastus Bombastus; born at Einsiedeln, in Schwyz.

Pare (*pa-ray'*), **Ambroise,** 1517-1590. Great French surgeon; born at Laval; was from the improved methods he introduced in the treatment of surgical cases entitled to be called, as he has been, the father of modern surgery. His writings exercised a beneficent influence on the treatment of surgical cases in all lands.

Pare'pa-Rosa, Madame (Euphrosyne Parepa de Boyesku), 1836-1874. A British operatic singer; born in Edinburgh; first appeared in England in 1857 and in the United States in 1866. Her voice was a soprano of great power and compass and she was greatly admired in oratorio singing; she died in London.

Park, Mungo, 1771-1805. A distinguished Scottish African explorer; perished while on his second expedition in the African wilds.

Parker, Alton Brooks, 1852- . . . . Chief judge of the Court of Appeals of New York; born in Cortland, N. Y.; educated in the public schools, in Cortland Academy and Cortland Normal School; was admitted to the bar, and practiced at Kingston; was surrogate (the New York term for judge of probate) of Ulster county, 1877 to 1885; delegate to Democratic National Convention, 1884, when Grover Cleveland was nominated for president; in 1885 was offered the office of first assistant postmaster-general; was chosen chairman of the Democratic State Executive Committee in that year, and was also elected, the same year, justice of the Supreme Court; member of the Court of Appeals, Second Division, 1889 to 1893; member of the General Term, Appellate Division, 1893-1897; chief judge since 1898.

Parker, Theodore, 1810-1860. An American theologian; born in Lexington, Mass.; he was chosen, in 1837, minister of a Unitarian congregation at West Roxbury; visited Europe in 1843; the prejudice against him led to his quitting West Roxbury, and settling at Boston in 1846, as minister of the Twenty-eighth Congregational Society; he distinguished himself as the fearless opponent of the Fugitive Slave Law and sheltered slaves in his own house; early in 1859 he was compelled to relinquish his duties and seek health in France and Italy; he died in Florence.

Parker, Matthew, 1504-1575. Archbishop of Canterbury; born in Norwich; in 1544 he was appointed master of Corpus Christi College, Cambridge, and elected vice-chancellor of that University the following year; when Queen Mary succeeded to the throne Parker was deprived of his offices, and remained in concealment till the accession of Elizabeth in 1558; by royal command he was summoned to Lambeth, and appointed archbishop of Canterbury.

Parnell, Charles Stewart, 1846-1891. An Irish statesman: born at his father's estate of Avondale, Wicklow county, Ireland. His mother was the daughter of Admiral Stewart of the United States navy. Became member of Parliament in 1875; organized the "active" Home Rule Party, and developed its obstruction tactics; he died in Brighton, England.

Parrhasius (*par-ray'she-us*), flourished 400 B.C. A gifted painter of ancient Greece; born at Ephesus; went to Athens and became the rival of Zeuxis; he was the contemporary of Socrates.

Parry, Sir William Edward, 1790-1855. Celebrated Arctic explorer; born at Bath; visited the Arctic Seas under Ross in 1818; conducted a second expedition himself in 1819-1820; a third in 1821-1823; a fourth in 1824-1826, with unequal success, and a fifth in 1827 in quest of the North Pole.

Pas'cal, Blaise, 1623-1662. Illustrious French thinker and writer; born at Clermont, in Auvergne; was distinguished at once as a mathematician, a physicist, and a philosopher; an accident which befell him turned his thoughts to religious subjects, and in 1654 he retired to the convent of Port Royal where he spent as an ascetic the rest of his days, and wrote his celebrated "Provincial Letters" in defense of the Jansenists against the Jesuits, and his no less famous "Pensees," which were published after his death.

Pas'ta, Judith, 1798-1865. A famous Italian operatic singer; born near Milan, of Jewish birth; her celebrity lasted from 1822 to 1835, after which she retired into private life; she had a voice of great compass.

Pasteur (*pas-ter'*), **Louis,** 1822-1895. A French chemist and physicist; born in Dole, Jura; was especially successful in proving the part played by microbes in fermentation and decomposition, in introducing a successful treatment of diseases in silkworms and cattle, and achieved great success in his efforts to check hydrophobia by means of inoculation. He died in Paris.

Patrick, Saint, flourished fifth century. The apostle and patron saint of Ireland; his birthplace uncertain; his mission, which extended over great part of Ireland, was eminently successful. Various miracles are ascribed to him, and among the number the extirpation from the soil of all venomous reptiles.

Pat'ti, Adelina Maria Clorinda, 1843- . . . . A popular operatic singer of Italian extraction; born in Madrid, Spain. Her debut in London took place in 1861, and she was ever afterward looked upon as one of the first singers of the day. Her residence is Craig y Nos Castle, Wales.

Pattison, Mark, 1813-1889. A distinguished English scholar; born at Hornby, Yorkshire; became rector of Lincoln College, Oxford; his chief literary work, a "Life of Isaac Casaubon."

Paul, Saint (originally called Saul), flourished first century. The great Apostle of the Gentiles; born at Tarsus, in Cilicia; by birth a Jew and a Roman citizen. He did more for the extension, if not the exposition, of the Christian faith at its first promulgation than any of the Apostles, and perhaps all of them together, and it is questionable if but for him it would have become, as it has become, the professed religion of the most civilized section of the world.

Pausanias, ... -477 B.C. A famous Spartan general; the grandson of Leonidas, who, as a commander-in-chief of the Greeks, overthrew the Persian army under Mardonius at Platæa in 479.

Peabody, George, 1795-1869. Philanthropist; born at Danvers, now Peabody, Mass.; made a large fortune as a dry goods merchant in Baltimore and as a stockbroker in London; gave away for benevolent purposes in his lifetime a million and a half of money; died in London.

Peale, Charles Wilson, 1741-1827. American writer and artist; born in Maryland; he attained distinction as a portrait painter and naturalist; died in Philadelphia.

Peale, Rembrandt, 1778-1860. An American artist; born in Bucks county, Pa.; when seventeen years old, executed a portrait of Washington, from whom he had three sittings; it was purchased by Congress; he died in Philadelphia, Pa.

Peary, Robert Edwin, 1856- . . . . An arctic explorer and civil engineer in the United States navy; born in Cresson, Pa.; he made a number of voyages to the arctic regions, returning from the last in 1902; reached lat. 83° 50′ N.

Peel, Sir Robert (Orange Peel), 1788-1850. English statesman; repealed the corn laws.

Penn, William, 1644-1718. An eminent member of the Society of Friends, who received a grant of Pennsylvania from the English Crown in payment of a debt owing his father, and led the colony which founded Philadelphia; born and died in England.

Pepin (The Short), 714?-768. A king of the Franks; the first of the Carlovingian kings. He assisted Pope Stephen III. against the Lombards; defeated the Saxons, Bavarians, and other German nations, and united Aquitaine to his crown. After a reign of sixteen years, he died in St. Denis. His son Charlemagne succeeded him as king of the Franks.

Pepys, Samuel, 1632-1703. An English author; secretary to the admiralty in the reigns of Charles II. and James II.; born in Brampton, Huntingdonshire; his title to fame rests upon his "Diary" (1659-1669), which is a most entertaining work, revealing the writer's own character very plainly, giving an excellent picture of contemporary life, and of great value for the history of the court of Charles II.

Pericles, 495?-429 B.C. Athenian orator, statesman, and general; became the leader of the democratic party and the first man in Athens; erected many noble public works, including the Parthenon; his age is called "the golden age of Athens."

Perry, Oliver Hazard, 1785-1819. An American naval officer; born in South Kingston, R. I.; famous for his defeat of a British force on Lake Erie in 1813; died of yellow fever in Trinidad, and was buried at Newport, R. I.

Perugino (*pay-roo-je′no*), **Pietro,** 1446-1524. An Italian painter; born in Leitta Della Pieve. His real name was Pietro Vanucci. He was employed for ten years in the Sistine Chapel and the Stanze of the Vatican, and on his return to Perugia opened a school, and had Raphael among his pupils. His best work is the "Pieta," in the Pitti Palace.

Pestalozzi (*pes-ta-lote′se*), **Johann Heinrich,** 1746-1827. A Swiss philanthropist and educational reformer; devoted his time and substance to training children whom he collected in large numbers in his own house, and this good work he carried on for over twenty years. Later he opened a school in the Castle of Yverdun (canton Vaud), which the government had placed at his disposal. His novel "Lienhardt und Gertrud" exerted a powerful moral influence, while his educational treatises have laid the foundation for the more rational system of elementary instruction which now obtains in America and Europe.

Peter, ... -64? The Greek surname of an apostle of Jesus. Peter's real name was Simon, his father's Jonas, his brother's Andrew. Peter was of an impulsive temperament, generous, but too forward in speech, and rash in action. After the Ascension, he was for a time the most prominent of the apostles. Tradition makes him die as a martyr at Rome, crucified with his head downward. Roman Catholics claim him as the first bishop of Rome, and consider that the authority delegated him by Jesus appertains also to his successors, the popes of Rome.

Peter I. (the Great), 1672-1725. Czar of Russia and founder of the Russian monarchy; organized an army and entered it as a private; studied practical seamanship, and formed a navy; traveled *incognito* in Western Europe; worked as a ship carpenter in Holland; founded schools and effected a number of reforms; defeated Charles XII. of Sweden, at Pultowa, 1709; founded St. Petersburg; his second wife, Catherine, was a prisoner of war, of obscure parentage; the crown prince, Alexis, opposing the czar's policy, was forced to renounce the succession, and is said to have been poisoned by his father.

Peter the Hermit, 1050?-1115. Preacher of the First Crusade.

Phidias, 490-432 B.C. The greatest of Greek sculptors, and architect of the Parthenon; he was never excelled in expressing the ideal majesty of the human form, and his Zeus, at Olympia, is counted among the wonders of the world.

Philip II., 382-336 B.C. King of Macedonia; father of Alexander the Great.

Philip II. (Augustus), 1165-1223. King of France; annexed Normandy, Anjou, and Lorraine; won the battle of Bouvines.

Philip IV. (the Fair), 1268-1314. Reduced the power of the feudal nobles; imprisoned Pope Boniface III. and caused him to remove his seat to Avignon; suppressed the order of Knights Templars. **Philip VI.** (of Valois), 1293-1350.

Philip II., 1527-1598. King of Spain; son of Charles V.; provoked insurrection in the Netherlands by his attempt to introduce the Spanish Inquisition; married, on the death of Mary Tudor, his second wife, Isabella of France, the betrothed of his son, Don Carlos; equipped the "Invincible Armada" for the conquest of England.

Philip, ... -1676. Sachem of the Wampanoag tribe of Indians; was the second son of Massasoit, who for nearly forty years had been the first and staunchest ally of the Pilgrim settlers of Plymouth, and had obtained English names for his two sons; in 1661 Philip succeeded his brother, and formally renewed the treaties of his father, which he kept for some years; during the progress of King Philip's War this sachem was slain and his head cut off.

Phillips, Wendell, 1811-1884. Slavery abolitionist and emancipationist generally; born at Boston, Mass., and bred to the bar; was Garrison's aid-de-camp in the cause, and chief after his death.

Phips, or **Phipps, Sir William,** 1651-1694. Governor of Massachusetts; born in Pemmaquid (Bristol), Me.; in 1687 recovered from a wrecked Spanish ship off the Bahamas bullion plate and treasure valued at $1,500-000; this gained him a knighthood and the appointment of sheriff of New England; in 1690 he captured Port Royal (now Annapolis) in Nova Scotia, but failed in the following year in a naval attack on Quebec; in 1692, through the influence of Increase Mather, he was appointed governor of Massachusetts.

Phocion (*fo′she-on*), 402-317 B.C. A distinguished Athenian general and statesman; opposed to the democracy of Athens, led on by Demosthenes in the frantic ambition of coping with Philip of Macedon and his son Alexander, and pleaded for a pacific arrangement with them; but having opposed war with Antipater, the successor of the latter, he was accused of treason, and condemned to drink hemlock.

Piccolomini (*pik-ko-lo′me-nee*), **Ottavio,** 1599-1656. Austrian general; conspirator against Wallenstein; gained great distinction in the Thirty Years' War; led Spanish army in Flanders.

Pickering, Timothy, 1745-1829. An American statesman; born in Salem, Mass. He participated in the battle of Lexington; in 1776 joined the Continental army, in command of 700 men; was soon appointed adjutant-general by Washington; in 1780 was selected for the post of quartermaster of the army; he was secretary of state under Presidents Washington and Adams, but was dismissed during the "X. Y. Z." papers dispute in 1800. He retired from politics for a time, but was elected to the United States Senate in 1804, and from that time continued active in politics. He died in Salem.

Pierce, Franklin, 1804-1869. An American statesman; fourteenth president of the United States; born in Hillsboro, N. H. In 1833 he entered Congress, serving four years, and in 1837 was elected to the United States Senate. In 1846 he enlisted for the Mexican War; was appointed brigadier in the volunteer army, and led his brigade in the battles of Contreras and Churubusco. In 1852 he was nominated for the presidency, and elected over General Scott. During his administration the Missouri Compromise was repealed; a reciprocity treaty for trade with the British American colonies was made; a treaty with Japan was established, and the Mexican boundary disputes settled. After his term expired, failing of a renomination, he traveled abroad for three years, and, returning, lived thereafter in retirement at Concord, where he died.

Pierrepont (*peer′pont*), **Edwards,** 1817-1892. An American diplomatist; born in North Haven, Conn.; he was elected a judge of the Superior Court of New York in 1857; in 1875 he became attorney-general of the United States in Grant's administration, and in the following year was appointed United States minister to Great Britain. He tried many famous cases during his professional career, and was noted as an orator. He died in New York city.

Pilate, Pontius, ... -37? A Roman ruler, who became governor of Judæa, 26 A.D.; he commanded in that country ten years; the Jews brought Jesus Christ before Pilate, who, perceiving that envy and malice occasioned their charges, would have scourged the prisoner and dismissed him, but, being threatened with the wrath of Cæsar, Pilate delivered Jesus, whom he pronounced innocent, to be crucified.

Pinckney, Charles Cotesworth, 1746-1825. An American statesman; born in Charleston, S. C.; he was Washington's aid-de-camp at the battles of Brandywine and Germantown; member of the convention that framed the Constitution of the United States; declined the secretaryship of war in 1794, and of state in 1795; in 1796 he was sent as minister to France; in 1800, 1804 and 1808 he was an unsuccessful Federalist candidate for the presidency.

Pitman, Benn, 1822- . . . . An American phonographer; born in Trowbridge, England; brother of Sir Isaac Pitman, the inventor of phonography; came to the United States in 1853, and founded the Phonographic Institute in Cincinnati; invented the electro-process of relief engraving in 1856; was military recorder of state trials during the Civil War.

Pitman, Sir Isaac, 1813-1897. An English stenographer; born in Trowbridge, England; he was the inventor of the phonetic system of shorthand writing and published his first treatise on the subject entitled "Stenographic Soundhand" in 1837; he was the head of the Phonetic Institute at Bath, and was identified with the spelling reform.

Pitt, William, 1759-1806. An English statesman and orator; son of the earl of Chatham; born in Hayes, England; was elected to Parliament in 1780; head of the great coalition against Bonaparte; in 1783 he became prime minister; was active in the negotiations of peace with the United States, and was instrumental in the passage of many important measures; he died in Putney, England.

Pius IX. (Giovanni Maria Mastai Ferretti), 1792-1878. Chosen to the pontificate, 1846; during his incumbency the dogmas of the immaculate conception and of papal infallibility were promulgated, temporal power overthrown, 1870, and the papal states annexed to Italy.

Pizarro, Francisco, 1496-1541. Spanish conqueror of Peru.

Plato, 428-347 B.C. Greek philosopher; disciple of Socrates; held that the human soul has always existed, and that an idea is an eternal thought of the divine mind; Emerson says, "Plato is philosophy, and philosophy is Plato."

Pliny (the Elder), 23-79. Roman naturalist; perished at an eruption of Vesuvius.

Pliny (the Younger), 62?-116. Roman orator and author.

Plotinus, 205-270. Greek Neo-Platonic philosopher.

Pocahontas, 1595?-1617. Daughter of Powhatan; saved the life of Captain John Smith, an English explorer; was converted to Christianity, and married an Englishman named Rolfe.

Polk, James Knox, 1795-1849. American statesman; eleventh president of the United States; born in North Carolina; removed to Tennessee; admitted to the bar; Congress, 1825; speaker for two terms; governor of Tennessee, 1839-1841; elected president on the Democratic ticket, holding that office from 1845-1849.

Polk, Leonidas, 1806-1864. Episcopal bishop and Confederate general; prominent at Shiloh and Stone River.

Polo, Marco, 1252-1323. A distinguished Italian traveler and writer; the first European to penetrate China.

Polycarp, Saint, 80?-169? Bishop of Smyrna; martyr.

Pombal, Sebastiao Joze de Carvalho, Marquis de, 1699-1782. An eminent Portuguese statesman; as prime minister he abolished the Inquisition, expelled the Jesuits and gave liberal encouragement to commerce and manufactures.

Pompey (the Great), 106-48 B.C. Roman general and triumvir; conquered Suetonius and Mithridates; became leader of the aristocracy and opponent of Cæsar; defeated at Pharsalia.

Ponce de Leon, Juan, 1460-1521. Spanish discoverer of Florida.

Poniatowski (*po-ne-ah-tov′ske*), **Joseph, Prince,** 1763-1813. A Polish general; born in Warsaw, Poland. On the defeat of Kosciusko, Poniatowski sought refuge in Vienna, till the French entered Warsaw in 1806, when he was appointed to the command of the Polish army which was to co-operate with the French against Russia. Napoleon estimated his services so highly, that shortly before the battle of Leipsic he created him a marshal of France.

Pontiac, 1712?-1769. Chief of the Ottawas; formed coalition of Indians against the whites, and attempted to capture Detroit.

Porter, David Dixon, 1813-1891. An American admiral; born in Pennsylvania. He commanded the flotilla, 1862, which reduced Forts Jackson and Saint Philip, on the Mississippi below New Orleans.

Powers, Hiram, 1805-1873. An American sculptor; born in Woodstock, Vt. In 1835 he went to Washington; two years later he was enabled to go to Italy to study his art, and he resided in Florence till his death. There he produced his statue of "Eve," which excited the admiration of Thorwaldsen, and in 1843 the still more popular "Greek Slave," of which six copies in marble, with cast copies innumerable, were produced. Among the other works the chief were "Proserpine," "Il Penseroso," "California," "America," and busts of Washington for the state of Louisiana, of Calhoun for South Carolina, and Daniel Webster for Boston, as well as those of John Q. Adams, Andrew Jackson, Marshall, Van Buren, and other distinguished Americans. He died in Florence, Italy.

Powhatan′, 1550?-1618. An Indian chief; was the father of Pocahontas, who is celebrated in the colonial history of Virginia as the rescuer of John Smith.

Praxit′eles, 360?-280 B.C. A celebrated Greek sculptor; executed several fine statues in bronze and marble of Bacchus, a satyr, Venus, and Apollo. An ancient copy of one of his works, the "Apollo Sauroctonos," is the only example extant. He excelled by the grace, tenderness, and finish of his works. He was esteemed as second to Phidias only.

Priestley, Joseph, 1733-1804. A Socinian divine; born near Leeds; wrote in defense of Socinianism, and in defense of Christianity; gave himself to physical research, particularly pneumatic chemistry; is claimed as the discoveror of oxygen; sympathized with the French Revolution; was mobbed, and had to flee to America, where he died.

Prim, Juan, 1814-1870. A Spanish general; distinguished as a statesman; rose to be minister of war, but aspiring to dictatorship, was shot by an assassin.

Ptolemy (*tol′e-mee*) **(Claudius Ptolemæus),** flourished second century. Ancient astronomer and geographer; born in Egypt; was the author of the system of astronomy called after him; left behind him two writings bearing one on astronomy and one on geography.

Puf′fendorf, Samuel, Baron von, 1632-1694. Eminent German jurist; born at Chemnitz, Saxony; wrote several works on jurisprudence, one of which, under the ban of Austria, was burned there by the hangman, but his "De Jure Naturæ et Gentium" is the one on which his fame rests.

Pulas′ki, Casimir, Count, 1747-1779. A Polish patriot. He won distinction in the revolution against Russia and afterward came to America, 1777, when he was appointed brigadier-general; killed at the siege of Savannah.

Purcell, Henry, 1658-1695. Eminent English musician; born at Westminster; excelled in all forms of musical composition; was the author of anthems, cantatas, glees, etc., which attained great popularity.

Pusey, Edward Bouverie, 1800-1882. An English theological writer; a leader of the Anglo-Catholic party in the Established Church; born near Oxford. He published "The Holy Eucharist a Comfort to the Penitent," a sermon which resulted in his suspension for three years; two sermons on "The Entire Absolution of the Penitent," equally revolutionary. Of his larger works the most important are "The Doctrine of the Real Presence," and "The Real Presence of the Body and Blood of Christ the Doctrine of the English Church."

Putnam, Israel, 1718-1790. American Revolutionary general; conspicuous at the battle of Bunker Hill.

Pyle, Howard, 1853- . . . . An American illustrator and author; born in Wilmington, Del.; an illustrator for periodicals, and has become popular also as a writer, chiefly of juvenile literature. His works include "Buccaneers and Marooners of America," etc.

Pym, John, 1584-1643. English republican statesman and orator.

Pyrrho, 376-288 B.C. Greek skeptic and philosopher.

Pyr'rhus, 318?-272 B.C. King of Epirus and one of the greatest of ancient generals; defeated the Romans and conquered Macedonia.

Pythag'oras, 600? 510? B.C. First Greek philosopher; taught the doctrine of transmigration of souls; basis of his philosophy, number and harmony; soul distinct from body.

Quatrefages (*kahtr-fahzh'*) **de Breau,** 1810-1892. French naturalist and anthropologist; was professor at the Natural History Museum in Paris; devoted himself chiefly to anthropology.

Quatremere (*kahtr-mair'*), **Etienne Marc,** 1782-1857. French Orientalist; born in Paris; was professor at the College of France; was distinguished for his knowledge of Arabic and Persian, as well as for his works on Egypt.

Quay, Matthew Stanley, 1833-1904. . . An American legislator; born in Dillsburg, Pa.; entered the Union army in 1861 and won distinction; was promoted lieutenant-colonel and assistant commissary general; received a congressional medal of honor for exceptional service; elected United States senator in 1887, and again in 1901.

Quesnay (*kay-nay'*), **Francois,** 1694-1774. A French physician and economist; born near Paris, France; he was the founder of the school of economists called Physiocrats, and very influential on Adam Smith and all modern political economy.

Quincy, Josiah, 1744-1775. An American lawyer, orator and essayist; born in Massachusetts; his son **Josiah,** 1772-1864, was also distinguished as an orator; while a member of Congress he opposed the admission of Louisiana, also the War of 1812 with Great Britain.

Quitman, John Anthony, 1799-1858. An American military officer; born in Rhinebeck, New York; in 1846, he was appointed brigadier-general of the United States army in the war with Mexico, distinguishing himself at Monterey, Vera Cruz, and Cerro Gordo, after which latter engagement he was brevetted major-general, and was voted a sword by Congress for gallantry; he participated in the attack on Chapultepec, and was foremost in the assault on the city of Mexico, which city he governed till order was established.

Rachel, Eliza, 1821-1858. A great French tragedienne; born in Switzerland, of Jewish parents; made her debut in Paris in 1838, and soon became famous as the interpreter of the principal characters in the masterpieces of Racine and Corneille, her crowning triumph being the representation, in 1843, of Phedre in the tragedy of Racine.

Radcliffe, John, 1650-1714. Physician; born at Wakefield; studied at Oxford; commenced practice in London; by his art and professional skill rose to eminence; left £40,000 to found a public library in the University of Oxford.

Radet'zky, Johann, Count von, 1766-1858. Austrian field marshal; born in Bohemia; entered the Austrian army in 1784; distinguished himself in the war with Turkey in 1788-1789 and in all the wars of Austria with France; checked the revolution in Lombardy in 1848; defeated and almost annihilated the Piedmontese army under Charles Albert in 1849, and compelled Venice to capitulate in the same year, after which he was appointed governor of Lombardy.

Rae, John, 1813-1893. Arctic voyager; born in Orkney; studied medicine in Edinburgh; first visited the Arctic regions as a surgeon; was engaged in three expeditions to these regions, of which he published reports.

Raeburn, Sir Henry, 1756-1823. Portrait painter; born at Stockbridge, near Edinburgh; went to Italy; was introduced to Reynolds by the way, and after two years' absence settled in Edinburgh, and became famous as one of the greatest painters of the day; the portraits he painted included likenesses of all the distinguished Scotchmen of the period, at the head of them Sir Walter Scott.

Raleigh, Sir Walter, 1552-1618. English courtier, statesman, navigator, and author; a favorite of Queen Elizabeth; executed by James I.

Rameau (*ra-mo'*), **Jean Philippe,** 1683-1764. French composer; born at Dijon; wrote on harmony, and, settling in Paris, composed operas, his first "Hippolyte et Aricie," and his best "Castor et Pollux."

Ram'eses. The name of several ancient kings of Egypt, of which the most famous are **Rameses II.,** who erected a number of monuments in token of his greatness, and at whose court Moses was brought up; and **Rameses III.,** the first king of the twentieth dynasty under whose successors the power of Egypt fell into decay.

Ramus, Peter, or **Pierre de la Ramee,** 1515-1572. A French philosopher and humanist; son of poor parents; became a servant in the College of Navarre; devoted his leisure to study, and became a great scholar; was interdicted from teaching philosophy, but the judgment was reversed by Henry II., and he was made a royal professor; was massacred on the eve of St. Bartholomew.

Randolph, John, 1773-1833. A noted eccentric American politician; born at Cawsons, Va.; entered Congress in 1799, and held a commanding position there as leader of the Democratic party; was a witty, sarcastic speaker; sat in the Senate from 1825 to 1827, and in 1830 was minister to Russia; liberated and provided for his slaves.

Ranke (*rank'ee*), **Leopold von,** 1795-1886. A German historian; born in Wiehe, between Gotha and Halle. The works, "A History of the Roman and German People from 1494 to 1535," and "A Criticism on Modern Historians," procured him a call to Berlin as professor of History, in 1825. Among his later works are "The Princes and Peoples of Southern Europe in the 16th and 17th Centuries," and "The Roman Popes in the 16th and 17th Centuries," one of his great masterpieces of historical writing. He began his "Universal History" when he was an old man of eighty-two.

Raphael, Raffaello Sanzio, or **Santi d' Urbino,** 1483-1520. The greatest of modern painters; born in Urbino, Italy. He received his earliest instructions from his father, Giovanni Santi, after whose death, in 1494, he became the pupil of Perugino. In 1504 he visited Florence, and lived there till 1508, when he was called to Rome by Pope Julius II., and employed to paint the chambers of the Vatican. Raphael spent the rest of his short life at Rome. In the numerous works, frescoes, and oil paintings of this unrivaled master, three styles are distinctly recognizable. The first is the "Peruginesque," the second "Florentine," and the third style "Roman," and is peculiarly Raphael's own — that which constitutes him the greatest of painters. Its supreme excellence is the equable development of all the essential qualities of art, composition, expression, design, coloring. Among Raphael's oil paintings are the "St. Cecilia," at Bologna; the famous "Madonna di San Sisto," now in the Dresden gallery; the "Spasimo di Sicilia," now at Madrid; and the "Transfiguration," his last work. His drawings are very numerous, and are to be found in most of the public and private museums of America and Europe. Raphael, who had occupied himself with architecture as well as painting, was charged, on the death of his friend Bramante, in 1514, with the direction of the building of St. Peter's. Raphael died in Rome from the effects of a cold, and after an illness of a fortnight, on his thirty-seventh birthday.

Rauch, Christian, 1777-1857. Eminent Prussian sculptor; born in Waldeck; patronized by royalty; studied at Rome under Thorwaldsen and Canova; resided chiefly in Berlin; executed statues of Bluecher, Duerer, Goethe, Schiller, and others, as well as busts; his masterpiece is a colossal monument in Berlin of Frederick the Great.

Rawlins, John Aaron, 1831-1869. An American military officer; born in Galena, Ill.; adjutant-general of General Grant in September, 1861, and served as such in the campaigns of 1862 and 1863; in March, 1865, was appointed chief of General Grant's staff, with the rank of brigadier-general in the United States Army. He became secretary of war in March, 1869. He died in Washington, D. C.

Ray, or **Wray, John,** 1628-1705. An English naturalist; born in Black Notley, Essex, England. Ray's zoological works are considered by Cuvier as the foundation of modern zoology. He died in Black Notley.

Raymond, Henry Jarvis, 1820-1869. An American journalist; born in Lima, N. Y.; was graduated at the University of Vermont in 1840; in 1841 he became managing editor of the New York *Tribune*. In 1864, was chosen as representative from New York to the thirty-ninth Congress. He died in New York.

Read, Nathan, 1759-1849. An American inventor; claimed to have been the first to use steam engines for propelling boats and carriages; born in Worcester county, Mass. He converted the condensing engine of Watt into a complete working, portable, high-pressure engine, twelve years before the high-pressure engine was known. In 1790 he petitioned Congress for a patent for land carriages to be driven by steam. It created so much amusement that he withdrew it. He built in 1789, a small steamboat, substantially identical with Fulton's of 1807. It is alleged that his combinations amounted to the inland steamers now in use. Died in Belfast, Me.

Reaumur (*ray-ow'mur*), **Rene**, 1683-1757. French scientist; born in La Rochelle; is best known as the inventor of the thermometer that bears his name.

Recamier (*ray-kahm-e-ay'*), **Jeanne Francoise Julie Adelaide Bernard**, 1777-1849. French lady noted for her beauty and accomplishments.

Reclus (*ray-klu'*), **Elisee**, 1830- . . . . A celebrated French geographer; from his extreme democratic opinions left France in 1851, lived much in exile, and spent much time in travel; wrote "Geographie Universelle," his greatest work.

Red Jacket, 1760-1830. Seneca Indian chief.

Reed, Thomas Brackett, 1839-1902. An American statesman; born in Portland, Me.; member of the Maine Legislature, 1868-1869, and of the Senate, 1870; state attorney-general, 1870-1872; member of Congress, 1877-1899; and speaker of fifty-first, fifty-fourth, and fifty-fifth Congresses. In 1896 Mr Reed was a prominent candidate for the Republican presidential nomination. He resigned from Congress in 1899, and resumed the practice of law in New York city. He died of uræmia at Washington, D. C.

Regnault (*reh-no'*), **Henri**, 1843-1871. French painter; born in Paris; son of following; a genius of great power and promise, of which several remarkable works by him are proof; volunteered in the Franco-German War, and fell at Buzenval.

Regnault, Henri Victor, 1810-1878. A noted French physicist; born at Aix-la-Chapelle; important discoveries in organic chemistry won him election to the Academy of Sciences in 1840; lectured in the College de France and the Ecole Polytechnique; became director of the imperial porcelain manufactory of Sevres; did notable work in physics and chemistry, and was awarded medals by the Royal Society of London.

Reg'ulus, flourished third century, B.C. A Roman of the Romans, was twice consul, in 267 and 256 B.C.; defeated the Carthaginians, both by sea and land, but was at last taken prisoner and subjected to excruciating tortures.

Reich'enbach, Karl, Baron von, 1788-1869. Expert in the industrial arts, particularly in chemical manufacture; he was a zealous student of animal magnetism, but is best known from his theories concerning od.

Reinhart, Charles Stanley, 1844-1866. An American artist; born in Pittsburg, Pa.; he exhibited in Paris, Munich, and New York city, and was a member of numerous art associations; he died in Philadelphia, Pa.

Rembrandt van Ryn, Paul, 1607-1669. Dutch painter; chief of the Dutch school; the greatest master of colors, and unrivaled as an etcher.

Remenyi (*ray-mane'yeh*), **Edouard**, 1830-1898. An Hungarian violinist; born in Heves, Hungary; in 1854 he visited London, where he was appointed solo violinist to Queen Victoria; in 1860 returned to Hungary, where he attained great distinction; in 1878 he came to the United States, where he spent much of his time and gave many concerts; died in San Francisco, Cal.

Remington, Frederick, 1861- . . . . An American artist and author; born in Canton, N. Y.; he is one of the most conspicuous of American artists in "black and white."

Remsen, Ira, 1846- . . . . An American chemist; born in New York city; was professor of Chemistry at Williams College, 1872-1876; founded the *American Chemical Journal* in 1879. He is a member of many scientific organizations and societies, and the author of numerous text-books, including "The Principles of Theoretical Chemistry," "Inorganic Chemistry," "Chemical Experiments," etc.; became professor of Chemistry at Johns Hopkins University in 1876, and succeeded Dr. Daniel Coit Gilman as president there in 1901.

Remusat (*ray-moo-sah'*), **Charles, Comte de**, 1797-1875. French politician and man of letters; born in Paris; drew up a protest against the ordinances of Polignac, which precipitated the Revolution of July; was minister of the Interior under Thiers; was exiled after the *coup d'etat*, and gave himself mainly to philosophical studies thereafter.

Resz'ke, Edouard de, 1855- . . . . A Polish opera singer; born in Warsaw, Poland; a brother of Jean de Reszke. He made his first appearance in Paris, in 1876, taking rank as a leading star with a voice of remarkable range and power. He has made several visits to the United States, filling the chief roles in grand opera.

Reszke, Jean de, 1852- . . . . A Polish opera singer; born in Warsaw, Poland. His debut was made in Venice in 1874, under the name of De Reschi, as a baritone. In 1876 and in 1883 he sang at the Theatre Francais, Paris; and in the latter year, his voice changed to a tenor of remarkable scope. He has made several tours in America.

Reuter (*roi'ter*), **Paul Julius, Baron**, 1821-1899. A German-English news agent, at one time well known from the familiar newspaper heading, *Reuter's Telegram*; born in Cassel. In 1851 he transferred his headquarters to London. As telegraphs extended throughout the world he multiplied the ramifications of his system till it embraced the remotest regions. He even maintained couriers where the telegraphs did not reach—*e. g.*, between Peking and Kiachta.

Revere, Paul, 1735-1818. American engraver and Revolutionary patriot; carried the news of Gage's impending attack to Concord.

Reynolds, John Fulton, 1820-1863. An American military officer; born in Lancaster, Pa.; served in the Mexican War; was appointed commandant at West Point in 1859; served in the Civil War in active service; in 1863 was promoted major-general of volunteers. His corps was the vanguard at Gettysburg, where he was killed.

Reynolds, Sir Joshua, 1723-1792. The chief of English portrait painters; born near Plymouth; visited Italy and the great centers of art there, when he lost his hearing, and settled in London in 1752, where he began to paint portraits, and had as the subjects of his art the most distinguished people, "filled England with the ghosts of her noble squires and dames."

Rhodes, Cecil John, 1853-1902. A South African statesman; born in Hertfordshire, England. Was sent for his health to Natal, where his brother was a planter. He subsequently went to the Kimberley diamond diggings; there he soon became conspicuous and amassed a fortune. He went back to England, and entered at Oriel College, Oxford, and, though his residence was cut short by ill-health, he ultimately took his degree. He entered the Cape House of Assembly as member for Barkly. In 1890 he became prime minister of Cape Colony. He died in Cape Town, South Africa. In his will Mr. Rhodes left about $10,000,000 to found a number of three-year scholarships tenable at Oxford, England. The income for each scholarship was $1,500 a year, and two were offered to each state and territory in the American Union.

Ribe'ra, Jusepe, 1588-1656. A Spanish painter; born near Valencia; indulged in a realism of a gruesome type; had Salvator Rosa and Giordano for pupils.

Ricardo, David, 1772-1823. English political economist; born in London, of Jewish parentage; realized a large fortune as a member of the Stock Exchange.

Richard I. (Cœur de Lion), 1157-1199. King of England; led a large army into Palestine; conquered Acre and defeated Saladin. **Richard II.**, 1366-1400. **Richard III.**, 1452-1485. Last of the Plantagenets.

Richelieu (*reesh'le-oo*), **Armand Jean Duplessis, Cardinal de**, 1585-1642. Born in Paris, of a noble family; was minister of Louis XIII., and one of the greatest statesmen France ever had; from his installation as prime minister in 1624 he set himself to the achievement of a threefold purpose, and rested not till he accomplished it—the ruin of the Protestants as a political party, the curtailment of the power of the nobles, and the humiliation of the House of Austria in the councils of Europe; his administration was signalized by reforms in finance, in the army, and in legislation; he was a patron of letters, and the founder of the French Academy.

Rienzi (*re-en'ze*), **Cola di**, 1313-1354. Roman tribune; born at Rome, of humble origin; incited his fellow citizens to rise against the tyranny to which they were subjected at the hands of the nobles; but his own rule became intolerable, and he was assassinated just seven years after the commencement of his political career.

Risto'ri, Adelaide, 1821- . . . . Distinguished Italian tragedienne; her career on the stage was a continuous triumph; the role in which she specially shone was that of Lady Macbeth.

Rit'tenhouse, David, 1732-1796. An American astronomer; born near Philadelphia, Pa.; originally a clock and mathematical instrument maker; he became master of the United States mint, and succeeded Franklin as president of the American Philosophical Society;

he was the first to use spider lines in the focus of a transit instrument; he died in Philadelphia, Pa.

Robert II., 1316-1390. King of Scotland from 1371-1390; son of Walter Stewart and Marjory, only daughter of Robert Bruce; succeeded David II., and became the founder of the Stuart dynasty.

Robertson, Frederick William, 1816-1853. Distinguished preacher; born in London; entered the Church in 1840; was curate first at Winchester, next at Cheltenham, and finally settled in Brighton; is known far and wide by his printed sermons, for his insight into, and his earnestness in behalf of, Christian truth.

Robespierre (*ro-baiz-pe-ayr'*), **Maximilien Marie Isidore**, 1758-1794. A notorious French revolutionist; died on the guillotine, to which he had assigned thousands of innocent men and women as president of the "Committee of Public Safety," in association with Couthon and Saint-Just.

Robin Hood. The hero of a group of old English ballads; represented as an outlaw and a robber, but of a gallant and generous nature, whose familiar haunts are the forests of Sherwood and Barnsdale, where he fleets the time carelessly in the merry greenwood. He is ever genial and good-natured, religious, respectful to the Virgin and to all women for her sake, with a kind of gracious and noble dignity in his bearing. There is no evidence worth anything that Robin Hood was ever more than a mere creation of the popular imagination.

Rochambeau (*ro-shon-bo'*), **Jean Baptiste Donatien de Vimeur de, Count**, 1725-1807. French marshal; general in America in 1781.

Rockefeller, John Davidson, 1839- . . . . An American capitalist; born in Richford, Tioga county, N. Y. He engaged in business when he was nineteen and soon showed ability in detail and discretion in management. When discoveries of petroleum roused speculative interest in 1860, he owned a refinery in Cleveland, Ohio. He was quick to perceive that his opportunities were at hand. His business developed and enlarged with amazing rapidity. In 1870 he became president of the Standard Oil Company, a monopolistic corporation, and through which he accumulated immense wealth. He has made large donations to educational institutions, notably to the University of Chicago, to which he has given several millions of dollars. He has also made large contributions to religious and charitable purposes. He is believed to be the richest man in America.

Rodgers, John, 1771-1838. An American commodore; born in Maryland. He won distinction in operations against France, Tripoli, and England. **Rodgers, John**, 1809-1882. Son of the preceding, also a naval officer; born in Maryland; served with credit during the Civil War, and was appointed rear-admiral, 1870.

Roebling, John Augustus, 1806-1869. An American engineer; born in Muhlhausen, Prussia; came to the United States in 1831, and settled in Pittsburg, Pa. His greatest work was the bridge over the East river, connecting New York and Brooklyn. He died while the construction was in progress, in Brooklyn, and the bridge was completed by his son.

Roland, Manon Jeanne Philippon, Madame, 1754-1793. Wife of Jean Marie, and herself the spirit of the Girondin party; born in Paris; she became the wife of Roland in 1779, and as her love for him was founded on his antique virtues and his philosophic spirit, she has been called "The Heloise of the eighteenth century." She became the sharer in all his studies, aided him in editing his works, and during his two ministries acted as his secretary and entered into all the intrigues of his party without debasing herself by their meanness. After the flight of her husband, Madame Roland was arrested by order of the Paris Commune under the dictation of Marat and Robespierre, and consigned to the Abbaye prison, from which, on October 31, she was removed to a more wretched abode in the Conciergerie, until her execution.

Rollo, 860-932. A Norwegian, who became the chief of a band of Norse pirates who one day sailed up the Seine to Rouen and took it, and so ravaged the country that Charles the Simple was glad to come to terms with them by surrendering to them part of Neustria, which thereafter bore from them the name of Normandy; after this Rollo embraced Christianity, was baptized by the Bishop of Rouen, and was the first Duke of Normandy.

Ro'manoff, Romanov, or **Romanow.** The surname of the dynasty of Russia founded by **Michael Feodorovitch**, ... -1645, son of the Metropolitan of Rostov; elected Czar 1613; the direct line became extinct, 1732, the empress Elizabeth being succeeded by her nephew, Peter III., founder of the Romanoff-Oldenburg or Romanoff-Holstein-Gottorp dynasty.

Rom'ulus. The traditionary founder of Rome, twin brother of Remus, sons of Rhea Sylvia, by the god Mars; mother and children being cast into the Tiber, the boys were rescued and nurtured by a she wolf; Remus was killed in a dispute over the building of the wall; the city was peopled by outlaws, who obtained wives by the "Rape of the Sabines"; Romulus was a bold and successful warrior, and was translated to heaven and made a god under the name of Quirinus.

Rosa, Salvator, 1615-1673. Italian painter; born near Naples; a man of versatile ability; his paintings of landscape were of a somber character, and generally representative of wild and savage scenes; he lived chiefly in Rome, but took part in the insurrection of Masaniello at Naples in 1647.

Roosevelt, Theodore, 1858- . . . . An American statesman, and twenty-sixth president of the United States; born in New York city; was graduated at Harvard University in 1880 and began the study of law; the next year he was elected to the Assembly from the twenty-first district of New York, serving in the Legislatures of 1883, 1884, and 1885; Republican canditate for mayor against Abram S. Hewitt, United Democracy, and Henry George, United Labor, in 1886; Mr. Hewitt was elected by about 22,000 plurality. Appointed a Republican member of the United States Civil Service Commission by President Cleveland in his first administration; called by President McKinley, April 6, 1897, to be assistant secretary of the navy; when war was declared against Spain Mr. Roosevelt refused to remain in the quiet government office; for years he had spent his summers on a Dakota ranch, and learned to know cowboys as strong, sincere men, on whom the nation could rely; from these the famous cavalry troop known as the "Rough Riders" was largely recruited; for bravery in the battle of Las Guasimas Roosevelt was promoted colonel and in the three days of fighting before Santiago, and especially in the magnificent charge up San Jaun hill, he acted with conspicuous gallantry; on the return of the Rough Riders from Cuba, Roosevelt was the popular idol of the country, and despite considerable opposition from professional politicians was nominated for governor of New York on the Republican ticket, Sept. 27, 1898; he was elected by a plurality of 18,000, Nov. 4; in the Republican National Convention held in Philadelphia in the summer of 1900 Roosevelt was enthusiastically nominated for vice-president on the Republican ticket headed by William McKinley; he was elected Nov. 4, and was formally installed March 4, 1901; on the death of President McKinley in Buffalo, N. Y., Sept 14, 1901, Roosevelt took the oath of office as his successor, and became the twenty-sixth president of the United States; he wrote "Winning of the West," "Life of Gouverneur Morris," "Life of Thomas Hart Benton," "Naval War of 1812," "History of New York," "Amercan Ideals and Other Essays," "The Wilderness Hunter," "Hunting Trips of a Ranchman," "Ranch Life and the Hunting Trail," "The Rough Riders," "Life of Cromwell," "The Strenuous Life," etc.

Ross, Sir John, 1777-1856. Arctic explorer; born in Wigtownshire; made three voyages, the first in 1811 under Parry; the second in 1829, which he commanded; and a third in 1850, in an unsuccessful search for Franklin, publishing on his return from them accounts of the first two, in both of which he made important discoveries.

Rossi'ni, Gioacchino, 1792-1868. Celebrated Italian composer of operatic music; born at Pesaro; his operas were numerous, of a high order, and received with unbounded applause, beginning with "Tancred," followed by "Barber of Seville," "La Gazza Ladra," "Semiramis," "William Tell," etc.; he composed a "Stabat Mater," and a "Mass" which was given at his grave.

Rothschild, Mayer Anselm, 1743-1812. Jewish banker at Frankfort, Germany; founder of the house of Rothschild.

Rubens, Peter Paul, 1577-1640. The greatest of the Flemish painters; born at Siegen, in Westphalia; went with his widowed mother in 1587 to Antwerp, where he sedulously cultivated the painter's art, and early revealed his masterly gift of coloring; went to Italy, and for a number of years was in the service of the Duke of Mantua, who encouraged him in his art, and employed him on a diplomatic mission to Philip II. of Spain; executed at Madrid some of his finest portraits; returned to Antwerp in 1609; completed in 1614 his masterpiece, "The Descent from the Cross," in Antwerp Cathedral; with the aid of assistants he painted the series of twenty-one pictures, now in the Louvre, illustrating the principal events in the life of Maria de' Medici during 1628-1629; diplomatic missions engaged him at the Spanish and

English courts, where his superabundant energy enabled him to execute many paintings for Charles I.

Ru′binstein, Anton Gregor, 1829-1894. A Polish musician; born near Jassy, Rumania; in 1848 settled in St. Petersburg as teacher of music, where he succeeded in getting a musical conservatory founded, and became its director. In 1872 he came to the United States and had an enthusiastic reception. He ended his concert tours in 1886. As a pianist he held the highest rank, being usually reckoned the greatest since Liszt. He ceased playing in public some time before his death, which occurred in Peterhof, Russia.

Rudolf I., 1218-1291. Of the House of Hapsburg; founder of the Austrian dynasty; greatly increased his father's domain by marriage, inheritance, and conquest, becoming the most powerful prince in southern Germany; acquired a remarkable ascendency among the German princes, and was elevated to the imperial throne in 1273, and by friendly concessions to the pope, Gregory IX., terminated the long struggle between the church and the empire; shattered the opposition of Ottocar, king of Bohemia, and brought peace and order to Germany.

Rumford, Benjamin Thompson, Count, 1753-1814. An American scientist; born in Woburn, Mass. Being a Tory in sympathy, he lived in London during the American Revolution. After serving England for a time, he entered the service of the Elector of Bavaria; rose to the position of minister of war, and was finally created a count of the Holy Roman Empire. He spent the last years of his life at Auteuil, busily engaged in scientific researches. Died in Auteuil, near Paris.

Rupert of Bavaria, Prince, 1619-1682. An English military officer; born in Prague, Bohemia; was made admiral of the English royal fleet. After the Restoration he was appointed lord-high-admiral and served with Monk against the Dutch. As one of the founders and the first governor of the Hudson Bay Company, his name was given to Rupertsland. He died in London, and was buried in Westminster Abbey.

Rush, Benjamin, 1745-1813. An American physician; born in Philadelphia; in 1769 was made professor of Chemistry in the Philadelphia Medical College. Elected a member of the Continental Congress, he signed the Declaration of Independence. In April, 1777, he was appointed surgeon-general, and in July physician-general, of the Continental army. He was a founder of the Philadelphia dispensary, the first in the United States. In 1799 Rush was appointed treasurer of the United States mint, which post he held till his death. He was called "the Sydenham of America," and his medical works brought him honors from several European sovereigns. He died in Philadelphia.

Ruysdael (*rois′dayhl*), **Jacob,** 1628-1682. A famous Dutch landscape painter; born and died at Haarlem; few particulars of his life are known; his best pictures, to be seen in the galleries of Dresden, Berlin, Paris, etc., display a fine poetic spirit.

Ruyter (*roi′ter*), **Michael de,** 1607-1675. A famous Dutch admiral; born of poor parents at Flushing; was ennobled in 1660 by the king of Denmark for services rendered in the Dano-Swedish war; for two years fought against Turkish pirates in the Mediterranean; commanded the Dutch fleet in the second war against England, and in 1667 struck terror into London by appearing and burning the shipping in the Thames; held his own against England and France in the war of 1672; co-operated with Spain against France; was routed and mortally wounded off the coast of Sicily; a man of sterling worth.

Sagas′ta, Praxedes Mateo, 1827-1903. A Spanish statesman; born in Torrecilla. He had a place in Prim's cabinet; supported Amadeus; held office under Serrano; and under the new monarchy became leader of the Liberals, being premier 1897-1899, thus conducting public affairs during the trying period of the Spanish-American War.

Saint Arnaud (*ar-no′*), **Jacques Leroy de,** 1796-1854. A noted French marshal; born at Bordeaux; entered actively into the plans of Louis Napoleon to overthrow the Republic; commanded the French forces at the outbreak of the Crimean War, and took part in the battle of the Alma, but died a few days later.

St. Clair, Arthur, 1734-1818. An American military officer; born in Thurso, Scotland. He was at Louisburg in 1758 and Quebec in 1759; engaged in the battles of Trenton and Princeton; was in command in 1777 at Ticonderoga; was at the battle of Yorktown; president of Congress in 1787; governor of Northwest Territory in 1789-1802. The expeditionary force against the Miami Indians, numbering 1,400, commanded by him, was cut to pieces near Miami village in 1791. He resigned his command in 1792, and died near Greensburg, Pa.

Saint Gau′dens, Augustus, 1848- . . . . An American sculptor; born in Dublin, Ireland; came to the United States in infancy. In 1871, while in Rome, he produced his first figure, "Hiawatha," but returned to the United States in 1872. He designed the Medal of Award of the Columbian Exposition, and a number of presentation medals authorized by Congress.

Saint-Just, Antoine Louis Leon Florelle de, 1767-1794. A French revolutionist; became the right hand of Robespierre, and was one of the most energetic and resolute members of the Mountain party. He fell with Robespierre, and perished on the same scaffold with him.

Saint Saens (*san son′*), **Charles Camille,** 1835- . . . . A French musician; born in Paris; for nineteen years organist of the Madeleine; composer of a number of operas indifferently successful, and of much orchestral and chamber music of a masterly kind; is held to be one of the greatest pianists and organists.

Saint-Simon (*san se′mawn*), **Claude Henri, Comte de,** 1750-1825. A versatile French philanthropist, political economist, philosopher and author. He served in the American army in the Revolution; returning to France he spent a fortune in endeavoring to establish an ideal society; he was also the founder of the philosophical sect of which Thierry, Comte, and Chevalier were the principal apostles.

Saladin (*sal′ah-deen*), (**Malek Nasir Youssouf**), 1137-1193. An eminent Saracen sultan; became vizier, 1168, and sovereign of Egypt, 1173. He captured Jerusalem but was defeated and besieged in Acre, by Richard Cœur de Lion and Philip Augustus of France, 1189, surrendering under a three years' truce, 1191, retaining Jerusalem. He was of a chivalric and noble character.

Salisbury (*sawls′bury*), **Robert Arthur Talbot Gascoyne Cecil, third Marquis of,** 1830-1903. An English statesman; born in Hatfield, Herts, England. As Lord Robert Cecil he entered Parliament in 1853; in 1866 he was appointed secretary of state for India. In 1865 he became Lord Cranborne and heir to the marquisate. He retired from the ministry, but on the death of his father in 1868 and his elevation to the House of Lords he returned to his old party associations. He resumed the secretaryship for India in 1874. In 1878 he accompanied Disraeli to the congress at Berlin, and on the death of that statesman became the recognized leader of the Conservative party. He became premier on the fall of the Gladstone government in 1885. Gladstone succeeded again to the power in the end of the same year, but in the June following Salisbury again became the premier and foreign secretary. In 1892 the majority in Parliament being in favor of a Home Rule bill for Ireland, Salisbury retired from office. In 1895 he was recalled.

Sal′omon, Johann Peter, 1745-1815. A German violinist and composer; born at Bonn; went to London, and is remembered for the great stimulus he gave to musical culture; composed songs, glees, violin pieces, etc.; buried in Westminster Abbey.

Salvini (*sal-vee′nee*), **Tommaso,** 1830- . . . . An Italian tragedian; born in Milan. In 1849 he fought with distinction in the revolutionary war. He scored successes in Brussels and Madrid; visited the United States in 1874 and England 1875, but after another visit to the United States in 1881, and to Great Britain in 1884, he retired from the stage to enjoy a life of leisure in his villa near Florence.

Sankey, Ira David, 1840- . . . . An American evangelist; born in Edinburgh, Pa. Was associated with the evangelist, the late Dwight L. Moody, for some years, attracting and holding the attention of great audiences by singing hymns composed by himself.

Santa Ana, or **Santa Anna, Antonio Lopez de,** 1795-1876. A Mexican president; born in Talaha, Mexico. He took a prominent part in the expulsion of the Spaniards from Mexico, and proclaimed the Mexican Republic in 1822. He was president in 1846 and commanded in the war with the United States, 1846-1848. After General Scott's occupation of the city of Mexico, in September, 1847, he resigned and left the country, but was president in 1853-1855. He died in the city of Mexico.

Santos-Dumont, 1874? . . . . A French aeronaut; born in Brazil, South America. In 1900 he made several partly successful attempts to fly with his dirigible balloon; but it was not till 1901 that he succeeded in perfectly controlling his machine in the face of a strong wind. In September, 1901, he won the Deutsch prize of $20,000 for the navigation of a flying machine under certain conditions. In January, 1902, he made several successful flights near Monte Carlo.

Sardanap′alus. Flourished 900? B.C. The last king of Assyria; led a luxurious, effeminate life, but, surprised when at his ease by a large army of invaders he suddenly developed into a hero, till hard pressed at length and shut up in Ninevah, and after two years' defense finding resistance hopeless, he reared a funeral pile, and, setting fire to it, threw himself upon it and perished in the flames.

Sartain, John, 1808-1897. An American artist; born in London, England; came to the United States in 1830, and was one of the first to introduce mezzotint engraving. He was the author of a large number of engravings for book illustration, and engraved many historical paintings; designed the monument to Washington and Lafayette in Monument Cemetery, Philadelphia, and published interesting personal reminiscences. He died in Philadelphia, Pa.

Saul. Flourished eleventh century, B.C. A Benjamite, the son of Kish, who fell in with Samuel, as he was on the way in search of his father's asses that had gone astray, and from his stature and stately bearing was anointed by him to be first king of Israel; he distinguished himself in the field against the enemies of his people, but fell at the hands of the Philistines after a reign of forty years, and after several insane attempts on the life of David, who had been elected to succeed him.

Savonaro′la, Girolamo, 1452-1497. A distinguished Italian orator and religious reformer; martyred.

Saxe, Hermann Maurice, Count de, 1690-1750. A distinguished marshal of France; son of Augustus (The Strong); Elector of Saxony and King of Poland; he gained the great victories of Fontenoy and Laufeld, in Flanders.

Say, Jean Baptiste Leon, 1826-1896. A French statesman and economist; born in Paris; became minister of finance in the government of M. Thiers; was appointed ambassador to London in 1880, and soon afterward was elected president of the Senate. Among his works are: "Finances of France," "State Socialism," "Democratic Solution of the Tariff Question," and "Turgot." He edited "The Dictionary of Finance" and "The New Dictionary of Political Economy."

Scan′derbeg (Prince or Bey Alexander), 1403-1468. The patriot chief of Albania, and the great hero of Albanian independence, who in the fifteenth century renounced Islamism for Christianity, and by his military prowess and skill freed Albania from the Turkish yoke; throughout his lifetime maintained its independence, crushing again and again the Turkish armies; was known among the Christians as George Castriot.

Schaff, Philip, 1819-1893. A theologian; born in Switzerland; studied in Germany; came, recommended by high names, to the United States, and became a professor, first in Pennsylvania, and finally in New York.

Scheele, Carl Wilhelm, 1742-1786. Swedish chemist; born in Pomerania; was an apothecary at Upsala and Koeping; during his residence at the latter made numerous important discoveries, and published many chemical papers, his chief work "Experiments on Air and Fire."

Schef′fer, Ary, 1795-1858. An eminent French painter. His works belong to the sentimental class, and are considered by some critics as wanting in color and power.

Schel′ling, Friedrich Wilhelm Joseph von, 1775-1854. One of the most eminent of German metaphysical philosophers, ranking with Kant, Hegel, and Fichte.

Schleiermacher (*shli′er-mahk-er*), **Friedrich Ernest Daniel,** 1768-1834. Great German theologian; born at Breslau; brought up among the Moravians, his mind revolted against the narrow orthodoxy of their creed, though the religious feeling he inherited never left him. He elaborated one of the most influential systems of religious philosophy.

Schoolcraft, Henry Rowe, 1793-1864. An American author, noted as an Indian authority; born in Albany county, New York; thirty years of his life he spent among the Indians, and through him many laws were enacted for their protection; among his numerous publications are: "Travels in the Central Portions of the Mississippi Valley," "The Indian and his Wigwam," etc.; he died in Washington, D.C.

Scho′penhauer, Arthur, 1788-1860. A German philosopher; born in Dantzic; the principal work of Schopenhauer is entitled "The World as Will and Idea"; he published several other works of philosophy, of which the most important is: "The Two Sound Problems of Ethics"; he died in Frankfort-on-the-Main.

Schu′bert, Franz Peter, 1797-1828. An Austrian composer; born in Vienna, Austria. The number and variety of his compositions is extraordinary; the most admired are his songs, and among them "The Erl King" and "Ave Maria" are perhaps the best known; but he wrote also operas, sonatas, symphonies, overtures, cantatas, six masses, etc. Schubert spent almost his whole life at Vienna.

Schumann, Robert, 1810-1856. A German musical composer; born in Zwickau, Saxony. In the year following his marriage he published nearly 150 songs, many on Heine's words; he then commenced his great series of orchestral works, his symphony in B flat being first performed at the close of 1841; under stress of work, however, his reason failed him, and after an attempt to drown himself in 1854 he was confined in a lunatic asylum, where he died.

Schurz, Carl, 1829- . . . . An American statesman; born in Sibhar, near Cologne, Prussia. About 1852 he came to the United States, and settled in Madison, Wis. In 1861 he was appointed minister to Spain, but when the Civil War broke out resigned that he might return and join the Union army. In 1869 was elected United States senator from Missouri. He was secretary of the interior under President Hayes from 1877 to 1881. He afterward wrote several books, among them a "Life of Henry Clay."

Schuyler (*sky′ler*), **Philip,** 1733-1804. An American military officer; born in Albany, N. Y. He was Federalist United States senator from New York, 1789-1791, and was again elected a senator, in place of Aaron Burr, in 1797. He died in Albany.

Schwartz, Berthold, 1300-1369. A German monk (Franciscan), who invented gunpowder.

Schwarz′enberg, Karl Philipp, Prince von, 1771-1820. An Austrian general. He negotiated the marriage of Napoleon I. and the Austrian princess, and commanded the allies at the victory of Leipsic.

Schwat′ka, Frederick, 1849-1892. An American Arctic explorer; born in Galena, Ill. In 1886 he commanded the New York *Times* Alaskan expedition, and did much to encourage the settlement of that territory; published "Along Alaska's Great River," "The Children of the Cold," etc. He died in Portland, Ore.

Schwei′nitz, Lewis Davis von, 1780-1824. An American botanist; born in Bethlehem, Pa. His original researches resulted in an addition of over 1,400 new species to the catalogue of American flora. He bequeathed his large and valuable collection of plants to the Academy of Natural Science of Philadelphia.

Scipio (*sip′e-o*) **Africanus Major, Publius Cornelius,** 235-184? B.C. Roman general; invaded Africa and defeated Hannibal.

Scipio Æmilianus Africanus Minor, Publius Cornelius, 185?-29 B.C. Roman general; destroyed Carthage.

Scott, Winfield, 1786-1866. An American general; born in Virginia. He was commander-in-chief of the U. S. Army from 1841 till 1861, and in 1852 was an unsuccessful candidate for the presidency.

Sebastian, Saint. A Roman soldier at Narbonne, and martyred under Diocletian when it was discovered he was a Christian; is depicted in art bound naked to a tree and pierced with arrows, and sometimes with arrows in his hand offering them to Heaven on his knees, he having been first shot with arrows and then beaten to death.

Seelye, Julius Hawley, 1824-1895. An American educator; born in Bethel, Conn. He was president of Amherst College, 1876-1890, and inaugurated the "Amherst system" of self-government, which was productive of good results. He died in Amherst, Mass.

Selkirk, Alexander, 1676-1723. A Scotch adventurer; born in Largo, Scotland; made several voyages to the South Sea, in one of which, having quarreled with his commander, he was put ashore on the island of Juan Fernandez, with a few necessaries, a fowling-piece, gunpowder, and shot. Here he lived alone during four years and four months, and was then rescued by Captain Woods Rogers. During the time of his remaining on the island he had nearly forgotten his native language. He returned to England in 1711, and is said to have given his papers to Defoe, who took from them his story of "Robinson Crusoe."

Semir′amis. Flourished 1250 B.C. Assyrian queen; built Babylon and greatly increased her dominions; invaded India, but was defeated.

Semmes (*sems*), **Raphael,** 1810-1877. An American naval officer; born in Maryland. He resigned his commission at the outbreak of the Civil War, and became the most daring and successful commander in the Confederate service. His vessel, the *Alabama*, was sunk by the United States steamer *Kearsarge*, Captain Winslow, off Cherbourg, France, June 19, 1864, but Semmes and most of his crew escaped on the British yacht *Deerhound*.

Seneca, L. Annæus, ... -65. Philosopher; born at Cordova, and brought to Rome when a child; practiced as a pleader at the bar, studied philosophy, and became the tutor of Nero; acquired great riches; was charged with conspiracy by Nero as a pretext, it is believed, to procure his wealth, and ordered to kill himself, which he did by opening his veins till he bled to death; he was of the Stoic school in philosophy, and wrote a number of treatises bearing chiefly on morals.

Sennach′erib. A King of Assyria, whose reign extended from 702 to 681 B.C., and was distinguished by the projection and execution of extensive public works; he endeavored to extend his conquests westward, but was baffled in Judea by the miraculous destruction of his army.

Serve′tus, Michael, 1509-1553. Spanish theologian; martyred through the intolerance of Calvin.

Sesos′tris, flourished 1400?-1250? B.C. The most celebrated of the early kings of Egypt; he, on succeeding to the throne, became ambitious of military fame, and marched at the head of a numerous army to make the conquest of the world; he marched through Asia, and penetrated farther into the East than the conqueror of Darius; he also invaded Europe; in his old age, he, having grown infirm and blind, destroyed himself. Sesostris, so called by the Greeks, is identical with Rameses II., one of the most famous of the Pharaohs.

Seve′rus, Lucius Septimius, 146-211. Roman emperor; born in Leptis Magna, in Africa; was in command at Pannonia, and elected emperor on the murder of Partinax; subdued a rebellion in Britain, and secured South Britain against invasions from the north by a wall; died at York, England.

Seward, William Henry, 1811-1872. A distinguished American statesman; born in New York; he was governor of his native state, a member of the United States Senate, and secretary of state in President Lincoln's cabinet.

Seymour, Horatio, 1811-1886. American statesman; Democratic nominee for the presidency in 1868.

Shaftesbury, Anthony Ashley Cooper, third Earl of, 1671-1713. English philanthropist, author, and freethinker.

Shaler, Nathaniel Southgate, 1841- . . . . An American geologist; born near Newport, Ky.; he served two years as an artillery officer in the Union army during the Civil War; professor of Geology and dean of Lawrence Scientific School; he has written a number of popular scientific works.

Shays, Daniel, 1740-1825. An American captain in the Revolution; born in Massachusetts; died in New York; he became notorious as leader of an abortive rebellion against the state laws of Massachusetts, 1786.

Sheridan, Philip Henry, 1831-1888. American general; victorious at Winchester, Cedar Creek, and Five Forks; made lieutenant-general, 1869, and promoted to the chief command on retirement of General Sherman, 1883.

Sherman, John, 1823-1900. An American statesman; born in Lancaster, Ohio. Member of Congress, 1855-1861. He took a prominent part in the proceedings of the House; was on the Committee of Inquiry sent to Kansas, and joined the movement for the formation of the Republican party. In 1861-1877 he was in the Senate; was secretary of the treasury, 1877-1881, and superintended the resumption of specie payment in 1879, after a suspension of seventeen years; re-elected to the Senate in 1881 and continued to hold that office till 1897, when he was appointed secretary of state by President McKinley; resigned that office, however, in 1898, on account of failing health. He died in Washington, D. C.

Sherman, Roger, 1721-1793. An eminent American statesman; born in Massachusetts.

Sherman, William Tecumseh, 1820-1891. A distinguished American general; born in Lancaster, Ohio; distinguished himself at the battles of Bull Run and Shiloh; received promotion, and as second in command to Grant rendered valuable service in reducing Vicksburg and Memphis; captured the stronghold of Atlanta, and after a famous march seaward with 65,000 men took Savannah, which he followed up with a series of victories in the Carolinas, receiving, on 26th April, 1865, the surrender of General Johnston, which brought the war to a close; was created general and commander-in-chief of the army in 1869, a position he held till 1883.

Sickles, Daniel Edgar, 1825- . . . . Major-general U. S. A., retired; born in New York. Was in the state senate, 1856-1857, and in the latter year was elected to Congress, and re-elected in 1859. His bravery in the Civil War was recognized by promotion to major-general. He lost a leg at Gettysburg. He was placed on the retired list of the army, with the rank of major-general, and was United States minister to Spain 1869-1873. He has since been president of the New York State Board of Civil Service Commissioners, commissioner of Emigration, sheriff of New York, and member of Congress.

Siddons, Sarah, 1755-1831. The most distinguished of English tragediennes. She belonged to the Kemble family, noted as actors.

Sidney or **Sydney, Algernon,** 1622-1683. A noted politician and soldier of extreme republican views; went from Ireland to England in 1642, joined the Parliamentarians, rose to a colonelcy and command of a regiment in 1645; entered Parliament, and, although appointed one of the commissioners to try Charles I., absented himself from the proceedings, but afterwards approved of the execution; withdrew from politics during Cromwell's Protectorate; intrigued with Louis XIV. against Charles II., assisted William Penn in drawing up the republican constitution of Pennsylvania, was on trumped-up evidence tried for complicity in the Rye House Plot and summarily sentenced to death.

Siemens (*see′menz*), **Sir Charles William,** 1823-1883. A German engineer; born in Hanover. The great works of Siemens Brothers at Charlton, West Woolwich, for the manufacture of submarine electric telegraph cables, were established in 1858; and the great steel works at Landore, Swansea, in 1868. He labored mainly in two distinct fields, the applications of heat and the applications of electricity, and won a great reputation in both. He was knighted, April 1883, in recognition of his services, which had been previously recognized by numerous scientific societies, and by the Universities of Oxford, Glasgow, Dublin, and Wuerzburg. He died in London.

Sieyes (*se-ay-yais′*), **Abbe,** 1748-1836. A conspicuous figure all through the French Revolution, the Consulate, and the Empire; represented Paris in the States-General; sat in the center in the Legislative Assembly; renounced the Christian religion in favor of the goddess of Reason; projected a constitution which was rejected; supported Napoleon; fled to Belgium on the return of the Bourbons, and returned to France in 1830, by which time he was politically defunct.

Sigel (*see′gel*), **Franz,** 1824-1902. An American military officer; born in Sinsheim, Baden. He came to the United States in 1852, and when the Civil War broke out, organized a regiment and went to the front, where he served with unusual distinction, being promoted major-general.

Silliman Benjamin, 1816-1885. An American chemist; born in New Haven, Conn.; he was made professor of Chemistry in the School of Applied Chemistry; delivered the first series of lectures on agricultural chemistry ever given in the United States; was one of the original members of the National Academy of Sciences in 1863. He died in New Haven, Conn.

Simon (*se-mon′*), **Jules Francois,** 1814-1896. A French statesman; born in Lorient, Morbihan, Brittany; was a disciple of Victor Cousin, and succeeded him in the chair of philosophy at the Sorbonne; in 1863 he was elected to the Corps Legislatif, where he served till the fall of the empire, when he was placed with Thiers and Gambetta at the head of the provisional government, whose affairs he administered during the siege; from the conclusion of peace in 1871 till the fall of Thiers he was prominent in the Assembly at Bordeaux and at Versailles, and in 1875 was elected a life senator; he died in Paris, France.

Sismon′di, Jean Charles Leonard Simonde de, 1773-1842. Celebrated Swiss historian; born at Geneva; the works which have established his reputation are his great histories of "The Italian Republics in the Middle Ages," "European Literature," and "A History of the French."

Sko′beleff, Michael, 1841-1882. A Russian general; distinguished himself by his bravery in the Russo-Turkish War of 1877-1878; was a leader in the Panslavist movement; died suddenly.

Slidell, John, 1793?-1871. An American statesman; born in New York city; elected to Congress in 1843; made minister to Mexico in 1845, and was in the United States Senate in 1853-1861; in September, 1861, he was appointed a Confederate commissioner to France, where he succeeded in negotiating a large loan and in securing the ship *Stonewall* for the Confederate government; after the war he settled in London, England, where he died.

Slocum, Henry Warner, 1827-1894. An American military officer; born in Delphi, Onondaga county, N. Y. When the Civil War broke out he was commissioned a colonel of volunteers in the Union army; was placed in command of a corps on the left wing of General Sherman's army, and took part in the great "march to the sea," leading the left wing of the army from Atlanta to Savannah; he was elected to Congress in 1869 and served till 1873; he died in Brooklyn, N. Y.

Smeaton, John, 1724-1792. An English civil engineer; born in Austhorpe, near Leeds, England. In 1751 he invented a machine for measuring a ship's way at sea, and also a new form of compass. In 1755 he was intrusted with the rebuilding of the Eddystone lighthouse. It stood till 1882, when it was replaced by a new structure. He also perfected Newcomen's steam engine.

Smith, Adam, 1723-1790. Political economist; born in Kirkcaldy, Fife; in 1776 he produced his "Inquiry into the Nature and Causes of the Wealth of Nations," a work to which he devoted ten years of his life, and which has rendered his name world-famous; in 1778 he settled in Edinburgh as commissioner of customs for Scotland, and in 1787 was elected lord rector of Glasgow University.

Smith, Goldwin, 1823- . . . . English man of letters; born in Berks; came to America as professor of English History in Cornell University; in 1871 settled in Canada, and believes that Canada will be annexed to the United States; has written a number of books and pamphlets, one on the "Relations between England and America" and another on "The Political Destiny of Canada"; he is an ultra-Liberal.

Smith, John, Captain, 1579-1631. English explorer; founder of Virginia.

Smith, Joseph, 1805-1844. Founder of the Mormon church.

Smith, William, 1769-1839. The "father of English geology"; born in Churchill, Oxfordshire, England; died in Northampton, England.

Smithson, James, 1754?-1829. An English philanthropist; natural son of Hugh Percy, third Duke of Northumberland; was graduated at Oxford, and elected a member of the Royal Society. In 1835 his property, amounting to $508,318, came into the possession of the United States government, having been bequeathed by him "for the purpose of founding an institution at Washington, D. C., to be called the Smithsonian Institution for the increase and diffusion of knowledge among men." He died in Genoa, Italy.

Soci'nus, Faustus, 1530-1601. A theologian; born in Italy; was much persecuted for his opinions; in Cracow, where he dwelt for a time, he was dragged from a sick-bed half naked along the street, had his house robbed and his papers burned.

Socrates, 469-399 B.C. Athenian philosopher; pronounced by the Delphic oracle the wisest of men; he lived all his days in Athens, and gathered about him as his pupils all the ingenuous youth of the city; he wrote no book, propounded no system, and founded no school, but was ever abroad in the thoroughfares in all weather talking to whoso would listen, and instilling into all and sundry a love of justice and truth; he was charged with not believing in the state religion, with introducing new gods, and corrupting the youth, convicted by a majority of his judges and condemned to die.

Solomon, 1035-975 B.C. In Scripture, the third king of Israel; youngest son of David, and the most celebrated of the Hebrew royal line. He is the reputed author of the book of Ecclesiastes, Song of Solomon, Proverbs, and part of the Psalms.

Solon, flourished sixth century B.C. The first Athenian constitutional lawgiver, and one of the Seven Wise Men of Greece.

Solyman (Suleiman). The name of three Turkish Sultans, the most noted being **Solyman** (the Magnificent), 1496-1566. Succeeded his father, Selim I., 1520. He overran nearly the whole of central Europe, Arabia, and Persia, but was repulsed at the siege of Malta, 1565.

Sothern, Edward Askew, 1826-1881. Comedian; born in Liverpool; made his mark in Tom Taylor's "Our American Cousin," in which he appeared thousands of times in America and England; scored a great success also as David Garrick.

Soult (*soolt*), **Nicolas Jean de Dieu,** 1769-1851. Duke of Dalmatia and marshal of France; gallant conduct in Swiss and Italian campaigns under Massena won him rapid promotion, and in 1804 he was created a marshal; served with the emperor in Germany, and led the deciding charge at Austerlitz; at the head of the French army in Spain he outmaneuvered the English in 1808, conquered Portugal, and opposed to Wellington a skill and tenacity not less than his own; turned Royalist after the abdication of Napoleon, but on his return from Elba rallied to the emperor's standard, and fought at Waterloo; became active in the public service, and was honored as ambassador in England in 1838; retired in 1845, with the honorary title of "Marshal-General of France."

Soulouque (*soo-look'*), **Faustin,** 1785-1867. A negro slave; born in Hayti; died in France. He was manumitted when a child, joined the army, rose to be general, was elected president and declared himself emperor, under the title of Faustin I., 1849. He proved a brutal tyrant, and was driven from his throne and the island, 1859.

Sou'sa, John Philip, 1854- . . . . An American musician; born in Washington, D. C. He was band leader of the United States Marine Corps, 1880-1892, and in the latter year organized the famous Sousa Band, which gave concerts in England, France, Germany, and all over the United States. He composed numerous songs, waltzes, operas, and orchestral suites, but was best known from his marches, which were republished throughout Europe.

Sparks, Jared, 1789-1866. An American historian; born in Willington, Conn.; he was professor of Ancient and Modern History at Harvard, 1839-1849; president of the college, 1849-1863; and the author of a large number of sermons, biographical and historical works, theological papers, etc., most notably "The Library of American Biography," and "Correspondence of the American Revolution"; he died in Cambridge, Mass.

Spar'tacus. Leader of the revolt of the slaves at Rome, which broke out about 73 B.C.; was a Thracian by birth; a man of powerful physique; in succession a shepherd, a soldier, and a captain of banditti; was slain in one of his predatory expeditions.

Speke, John Hanning, 1827-1864. An English African explorer; he discovered lake N'yanza, 1858, and claimed to have traversed the Nile to its source, 1862.

Spencer, Herbert, 1820-1904. An English philosopher; born at Derby; about the year 1859 he projected his scheme of philosophy, based on the principle of evolution in its relation to life, mind, society, and morals; this large scheme has been only partially fulfilled.

Spinoza (*spe-no'zah*), **Benedict,** 1632-1677. Great modern philosopher; born in Amsterdam; left Amsterdam and finally settled at The Hague, where, absorbed in philosophic study, he lived in seclusion, earning a livelihood by polishing optical glasses, which his friends disposed of for him; his days were short; he suffered from ill health, and died of consumption. His great work, his "Ethica," was published a year after his death.

Spofford, Ainsworth Rand, 1825- . . . . An American librarian; born in Gilmanton, N. H. Was librarian of the Congressional Library 1864-1897, when he became chief assistant. Published "The American Almanac," for several years, and, with others, edited "Library of Choice Literature," "Library of Wit and Humor," etc.

Spohr, Ludwig, 1784-1859. Musical composer and violinist; born in Brunswick, Germany; produced both operas and oratorios, "Faust" among the former, the "Last Judgment" and the "Fall of Babylon" among the latter.

Spurgeon, Charles Haddon, 1834-1892. An English preacher; born in Kelvedon, England. His followers built for him his well known "Tabernacle" in Newington Butts, opened in 1861. Spurgeon preached in the Tabernacle every Sunday to thousands of hearers. His sermons were published weekly from 1854, and yearly volumes were issued from 1856. They had an enormous circulation, many of them being translated into various languages. He died in Mentone, France.

Spurzheim (*spoorts'hime*), **Johann Gaspar,** 1776-1832. Phrenologist; born in Treves; in 1832 he proceeded to America on a lecture tour, but had hardly started on his mission when he died at Boston; he wrote numerous works bearing on phrenology, education, etc.

Standish, Miles, 1584-1656. Captain of Plymouth colony.

Stanford, Leland, 1824-1893. American lawyer and philanthropist; born in Watervliet, Albany county, N. Y.; in 1852 he went to California, where he engaged in mining, but in 1856 removed to San Francisco and there engaged in business, laying the foundation of a fortune estimated at more than $50,000,000; he was elected president of the Central Pacific railroad in 1861; was governor of California, 1861-1863; and in 1885 was elected to the United States Senate. In memory of a deceased son,

Leland Stanford, Jr., he gave $20,000,000 for the founding of Leland Stanford University at Palo Alto, Cal.; he died in Palo Alto.

Stanford, Jane Lathrop, 1825-1905. . . An American philanthropist; born in Albany, N. Y.; the widow of Leland Stanford, the founder of the Leland Stanford, Jr., University; she built and endowed the Children's Hospital in Albany, N. Y., at a cost of $200,000; gave $160,000 to the kindergartens in San Francisco, Cal., and after the death of her husband in 1893 devoted herself to the development and support of the Leland Stanford University; in 1901 she supplemented her gifts to the university by turning over to its trustees stocks valued at $18,000,000; her residence in San Francisco, valued at $400,000, for a museum and art gallery, and 1,000,000 acres of land worth $12,000,000; these gifts swelled the endowment of the university to more than $45,000,000, making it the most richly endowed educational institution in the world.

Stanley, Arthur Penrhyn, 1815-1881. Widely known as Dean Stanley; born at Alderley, in Cheshire, England; held a professorship of Ecclesiastical History in Oxford for a time, and published lectures on the Eastern Church, the Jewish Church, the Athanasian Creed, and the Church of Scotland; accompanied the Prince of Wales to the East in 1862, and became dean of Westminster next year in succession to Trench; wrote "Historical Monuments of Westminster Abbey" and "Christian Institutions."

Stanley, Henry Morton, 1840-1904. . . African explorer; born in Denbigh, Wales, his parental name being Rowlands, he having assumed the name of Stanley after that of his adopted father, Mr. Stanley, New Orleans; served in the Confederate army; became a newspaper foreign correspondent to the New York *Herald* at length; was summoned to go and "find Livingstone"; after many an impediment found Livingstone on 10th November, 1871, and after staying with him, and accompanying him in explorations, returned to England; published "Congo and its Free State," "In Darkest Africa," etc.; elected to the British Parliament, 1895.

Stanton, Edwin McMasters, 1814-1869. An American statesman; born in Steubenville, Ohio; appointed attorney-general of the United States; succeeded Simon Cameron as secretary of war and held that office for six years. On December 20, 1869, he was nominated by President Grant as an associate justice of the Supreme Court of the United States, but died before taking his seat.

Stanton, Elizabeth Cady, 1815-1902. An American reformer; born in Johnstown, N. Y.; called the first Woman's Rights Convention in Seneca Falls, N. Y., in 1848, and was an unsuccessful candidate for Congress in 1868. She was the author of "The History of Woman Suffrage," and other works.

Stark, John, 1728-1822. An American military officer; born in Londonderry, N. H.; joined the troops under Major Rogers in the war against the French and Indians in 1754; rendered efficient service at Ticonderoga in 1758, and was actively employed in the subsequent campaign. In 1775, after the battle of Lexington, he received a colonel's commission, and recruited a regiment which formed the left of the American line at Bunker Hill. For his victory at Bennington he was promoted brigadier-general. He died in Manchester, N. H.

Stein, Heinrich Friedrich Karl von, Baron, 1757-1831. Prussian statesman.

Stephen, Saint. Stoned 36?; first Christian martyr.

Stephens, Alexander Hamilton, 1812-1883. American statesman and writer; the "Nestor of the Confederacy"; born in Georgia; admitted to the bar, 1835; Congress, 1843; opposed the secession of his state; vice-president of the Confederate States; elected to the United States Senate from Georgia, but not permitted to take his seat; member of the House of Representatives, however, from 1874 until his death.

Stephenson, George, 1781-1848. English engineer; inventor of the locomotive engine.

Stephenson, Robert, 1803-1859. Son of George Stephenson; English engineer; inventor of tubular bridge.

Steuben, Frederic William Augustus, Baron, 1730-1794. An American military officer; born in Magdeburg, Prussia. He came to America in 1777, and having received the appointment of inspector-general, with the rank of major-general, he proved of efficient service to the American army. He spent his whole fortune in clothing his men and gave his last dollar to the soldiers. Congress made tardy reparation, and in 1790 voted him an annuity of $2,500 and a township of land in the state of New York, both of which he divided with his fellow officers. He died on his estate near Utica, N. Y.

Stevens, Thaddeus, 1792-1868. An American statesman; born in Danville, Vt. In 1848 and also in 1850 he was elected to Congress from Pennsylvania, and again in 1858, retaining his seat till his death.

Stewart, Alexander Turney, 1803-1876. An American merchant; born near Belfast, Ireland; came to the United States in 1823 and engaged in teaching. In 1825 he began, in New York city, a dry goods business which gradually expanded into one of the largest mercantile concerns in the world. He died in New York.

Stewart, Dugald, 1753-1858. Scottish philosopher; born in Edinburgh; he wrote "Elements of the Philosophy of the Human Mind," "Philosophical essays," etc.

Stone, Lucy (Mrs. Blackwell), 1818-1893. An American reformer; born in West Brookfield, Mass. She was graduated at Oberlin College in 1847. She published a protest, "Taxation Without Representation." In 1869 she helped organize the American Woman's Suffrage Association. Her lectures on woman suffrage made her known throughout the country. She died in Boston.

Story, Joseph, 1779-1845. An American jurist; born in Marblehead, Mass. In 1811 he was appointed an associate justice of the United States Supreme Court, and held the office till his death. He wrote extensively on jurisprudence. He died in Cambridge, Mass.

Story, William Wetmore, 1819-1895. Poet and sculptor; son of preceding. He died in Vallombrosa, near Florence, Italy.

Strabo, 63? B.C.-24? A.D. A noted geographer; born in Amasea, Pontus; his geography in seventeen books has been preserved entire with the exception of the seventh book, of which there is only an epitome; the first two books are introductory, the next ten treat of Europe, the four following of Asia, and the last of Africa.

Stradivar'i, Antonio (Stradivarius), 1649?-1737. An Italian violin maker; born in Cremona, Italy; it was he who settled the typical pattern of the Cremona violin, and his instruments, for tone and finish, have never yet been excelled; he died in Cremona.

Strauss, Johann, 1825-1899. An Austrian musician; born in Vienna; after composing dance music for many years, he undertook an operetta, "Indigo," which was produced in 1871, and met with instantaneous success; subsequently he produced "The Forty Thieves"; "Cagliostro," "The Gypsy Baron," etc., and numerous waltzes, the best known being "The Beautiful Blue Danube"; he died in Vienna.

Stuart, Gilbert Charles, 1755-1828. An American painter; born in Narragansett, R. I.; in 1775 he made his way to London, where he led for two years a Bohemian life; upon his talent being recognized, he became a fashionable portrait painter; in 1792 he returned to the United States, and painted portraits of Washington, Jefferson, Madison, John Adams, and many of the distinguished men of the period; he died in Boston.

Sulla or Sylla, Lucius Cornelius, 138-78 B.C. Roman statesman and general.

Sumner, Charles, 1811-1874. American statesman and abolitionist; born in Boston; was brought into public notice by his fourth of July oration, 1845, on "The True Grandeur of Nations," an eloquent condemnation of war; was one of the founders of the Free Soil Party, and in 1851 was elected to the United States Senate, a position he held until the close of his life.

Swedenborg, Emanuel, 1688-1772. Swedish theosophist; in his theosophy the central point is the correspondence of the natural and the supernatural. He was founder of the sect known as the Swedenborgians or the Church of New Jerusalem.

Tait, Archibald Campbell, 1811-1882. Archbishop of Canterbury; born in Edinburgh, Scotland. In 1842 he was appointed successor to Dr. Arnold as head master of Rugby; in 1849 became Dean of Carlisle, and in 1856 Bishop of London, as successor to Blomfield. In 1868 he was made primate of all England by Mr. Disraeli. The Lambeth Conference of 1878 took place under his auspices.

Talleyrand (*tah-le-ron'*) **de Perigord, Charles Maurice, Prince of Benevento,** 1754-1838. French statesman and diplomatist; born in Paris; was educated for the Church; made bishop of Autun; was excommunicated by the pope, resigned his bishopric, and embarked on a statesman's career. In 1796 was appointed minister of foreign affairs; supported Bonaparte in his ambitious schemes, and on the latter becoming emperor, was made grand chamberlain and Duke of Benevento, while he retained the portfolio of foreign affairs; in a fit of irritation Napoleon one day discharged him, and he refused to accept office again when twice over recalled; he attached himself to the Bourbons on their return, and, becoming foreign minister to Louis XVIII., was made a peer, and sent ambassador to the Congress of Vienna; retired from public life shortly before his death.

Talmage, Thomas De Witt, 1832-1902. An American clergyman; born in Bound Brook, N. J. He was pastor of the Central Presbyterian Church in Brooklyn, N. Y., in 1869-1894, and afterward became pastor of the First Presbyterian Church in Washington, D. C. He was for many years the editor of the *Christian Herald*, and was the author of "Crumbs Swept Up," "Woman: Her Powers and Privileges," "From Manger to Throne," "Every-Day Religion," etc. He died in Washington, D. C.

Talma, Francois Joseph, 1763-1826. A famous French tragedian; born in Paris; during the Revolution he was the foremost actor at the Theatre de la Republique, and subsequently enjoyed the favor of Napoleon; his noble carriage and matchless elocution enabled him to play with great dignity such characters as Othello, Nero, Orestes, Leicester, etc.

Tam′erlane or **Timur,** 1336-1405. A great Asiatic conqueror; born at Hesh, near Samarcand; the son of a Mongol chief, raised himself by military conquest to the throne of Samarcand; built up an empire that at the time of his death extended from the Ganges to the Grecian Archipelago; died while leading an expedition against China.

Tan′cred, 1078-1112. A famous crusader; hero of Tasso's great poem; for great deeds done in the First Crusade he was rewarded with the principality of Tiberius; stands as the type of "a very gentle, perfect knight"; died at Antioch of a wound received in battle.

Taney (*taw′ni*), **Roger Brooke,** 1777-1864. An American statesman; born in Calvert county, Maryland; succeeded John M. Berrien as attorney general of the United States; was appointed secretary of the treasury under President Jackson, but was forced to resign; was nominated chief-justice of the United States and confirmed by the United States Senate March 15, 1836; while in this office he rendered decisions on many important cases, notably those of Dred Scott, and Sherman M. Booth, both bearing on the Fugitive Slave Law; he died in Washington, D. C.

Tarquinius, Lucius Priscus, ... -576 B.C. The fifth king of Rome, and first of the Tarquins; crowned 614 B.C.; **Tarquinius Lucius Superbus,** his grandson, married two sisters, daughters of Servius Tullius, whom he assassinated at the instigation of his later wife, 534 B.C.; **Tarquinius Sextus,** his son, the notorious hero of the rape of Lucretia, was the last of the race, and with his expulsion, 510 B.C., Rome became a republic.

Taylor, Bayard, 1825-1878. A noted American writer and traveler; born at Kennett Square, Pa.; for a number of years contributed, as travel correspondent, to the *Tribune*, visiting in this capacity Egypt, the greater part of Asia, Central Africa, Russia, Iceland, etc.; during 1862-1863 acted as secretary of the legation at St. Petersburg, and in 1878 was appointed ambassador at Berlin; his literary reputation rests mainly on his poetic works: "Poems of the Orient," "Rhymes of Travel," etc., and an admirable translation of Goethe's "Faust."

Taylor, Zachary, 1784-1850. American general and statesman; twelfth president of the United States; born in Virginia; entered the army in 1808; served in Seminole and Black Hawk wars; major-general in Mexican War, and won the battles of Resaca de la Palma and Buena Vista; elected president by the Whigs in 1848.

Tecumseh, 1770-1813. Chief of the Shawnee Indians; defeated by Harrison at Tippecanoe; killed in the battle of the Thames.

Tell, Wilhelm, flourished 1305; legendary Swiss hero; said to have been drowned in the Schaechen, in attempting to save the life of a friend.

Temple, Sir William, 1628-1699. An English statesman; born in London. In conjunction with DeWitt he concluded the treaty between England, Holland, and Sweden. Latterly lived in epicurean ease, in the enjoyment of his garden, and in the pursuit of letters at his villa at Sheen, and, after 1686, at Moor Park, in Surrey, where he had Swift for secretary.

Teniers, David (The Elder), 1582-1649. An eminent Dutch painter. **Teniers, David** (the Younger), 1610-1690. Son of the preceding; he excelled his father. Both were pupils of Rubens.

Terry, Ellen Alice, 1848- . . . . An English actress; born in Coventry, England, and made her first appearance on the stage during Charles Kean's Shakespearean revivals in 1858. In 1864 she married and left the stage, but reappeared again in October, 1867. She accompanied Henry Irving on his numerous American tours, playing with unprecedented success all over the United States.

Tertullian, Quintus Septimius Florens, 150-230. One of the Latin fathers; born at Carthage; was converted to Christianity; became presbyter of Carthage, and embraced Montanist views; wrote numerous works, apologetical, polemical, doctrinal, and practical, the last of an ascetic tendency.

Tet′zel, John, 1455-1519. A Dominican monk; born at Leipsic; was employed in the sale of indulgences to all who subscribed to the fund for building St. Peter's at Rome; in opposition to him and his doings Luther published his celebrated theses in 1517.

Thalberg (*tahl′burg*), **Sigismund,** 1812-1871. A celebrated pianist; born at Geneva; took rank as one of the most brilliant pianists of the age.

Tha′les, flourished seventh century B.C. Philosopher of Greece, and one of her seven sages; was a philosopher of the physical school, and the father of philosophy in general.

Themis′tocles, 520-453 B.C. Celebrated Athenian general and statesman; rose to political power on the ostracism of Aristides, his rival; commanded at Salamis and routed the fleet of Xerxes.

Theodo′ra, 508-548. The famous consort of the Byzantine emperor, Justinian I.; she became Justinian's truest counselor, bore a chief share in the work of government, and saved the throne by her high courage at the crisis of the Nika riots. She lavished her bounty on the poor, and especially on the unfortunate of her own sex.

Theod′oric (the Great), 455?-526. A king of the Goths, who, after the fall of the Western Empire, ruled as king of Italy, 493-526.

Theodo′sius. The name of three emperors, **Theodosius I. (Flavius),** 346?-395. Surnamed "The Great"; born in Spain; reigned 378-395. With the close of his reign the disintegration of the Roman Empire set in. He was the author of the bloody massacre of Thessalonica, for which Ambrose, the fearless archbishop of Milan, compelled him to do penance. **Theodosius II.,** 401-450. His grandson; succeeded his father Arcadius as emperor of the East. **Theodosius III. (Adramyttenus),** 654-716. Succeeded Anastasius II. as emperor of the East; crowned 715.

Theophras′tus, ... -286 B.C. A peripatetic philosopher; born in Lesbos; pupil, heir, and successor of Aristotle, and the great interpreter and expounder of his philosophy.

Theresa, Saint, 1515-1582. A Spanish Carmelite nun; eminent for learning and piety; founder of a reformed society of barefooted members of that order; canonized by Pope Gregory XV.

Thierry (*te-ay-ree′*), **Amedee Simon Dominique,** 1797-1876. A distinguished French historian; his brother, **Jacques Nicolas Augustin,** 1795-1856, was even more eminent as an author.

Thiers (*te-air′*), **Louis Adolphe,** 1797-1877. An eminent French statesman and historian. He was the first president of the Republic, elected 1871, resigned 1873, and succeeded by Marshal MacMahon.

Thomas, George Henry, 1816-1870. American Federal general; won the battles of Chickamauga and Nashville.

Thomson, Sir William, Lord Kelvin, 1824- . . . Great British physicist; born at Belfast; professor of Natural Philosophy in Glasgow in 1846; it is in the departments of heat and electricity he has accomplished his greatest achievements; he has invented a number of ingenious and delicate scientific instruments, and written extensively on mathematical and physical subjects.

Thor′waldsen, Bertel, 1770-1844. An eminent Danish sculptor; born near Copenhagen, the son of a poor Icelander; studied in Rome, where Canova encouraged him, and a fine statue of Jason established his reputation; executed a colossal group of "Christ and the Twelve Apostles," "St. John Preaching in the Wilderness," and other religious subjects, besides statues of Copernicus and Galileo, and the celebrated reliefs, "Night" and "Morning"; bequeathed to his country his large fortune and nearly 300 of his works, now in the Thorwaldsen Museum, Copenhagen.

Thurman, Allen Granbery, 1813-1895. An American jurist; born in Lynchburg, Va.; elected to Congress in 1844; chosen judge of the Supreme Court of Ohio in 1851, and was elected United States senator in 1869 and 1874, where he became leader of the Democratic side; vice-president of the United States, 1889-1893. Popularly known as "The Old Roman." He died in Columbus, Ohio.

Tiberius, ... -37 A D. Second Roman emperor; born at Rome; his reign was distinguished by acts of cruelty; given up to debauchery, he was suffocated in a fainting fit by the captain of the Prætorian Guards, and succeeded by Caligula; it was during his reign Christ was crucified.

Tilden, Samuel Jones, 1814-1886. American statesman; born at New Lebanon, N. Y.; Mr. Tilden became leader of the Democratic party in New York state in 1868, and in that capacity strenuously opposed the corrupt administration of the Tweed faction; in 1874 he was elected governor of New York, and during his term of office broke up the notorious "canal ring"; in 1876 he was nominated for the presidency by the National Democratic Convention; died in "Greystone," his country seat, near Yonkers, N. Y.

Tilly, Johann Tzerklas von, Count, 1559-1632. German general in Thirty Years' War; fell at the battle of the Lech.

Tintoret'to, Giacomo Robusti, Il, 1512-1594. Italian painter; born at Venice; save for a few lessons under Titian he seems to have been self-taught; took for his models Titian and Michael Angelo, and came specially to excel in grandeur of conception and in strong chiaroscuro effects; among his most notable pictures are "Belshazzar's Feast," "The Last Supper," "The Crucifixion," "The Last Judgment," "The Resurrection," etc.

Tisch'endorf, Constantin von, 1815-1874. Biblical scholar; born in Saxony; spent his life in textual criticism; his great work "Critical Edition of the New Testament."

Titian (*tish'yan*), **Vecellio,** 1477-1576. Great Italian painter; born at Capo del Cadore; the prince of colorists, and head of the Venetian school; he was a master of his art from the very first, and his fame led to employment in all directions over Italy, Germany, and Spain; his works were numerous, and rich in variety; he ranks with Michael Angelo and Raphael as the head of the Italian renaissance.

Titus, Flavius Sabinus Vespasianus, flourished first century A.D. A Roman general and emperor; before he ascended the throne he captured and destroyed Jerusalem, 70.

Tod'leben, Eduard Ivanovitch, 1818-1884. A noted Russian general of German descent; greatly distinguished himself by his defensive operations at Sebastopol during its siege by the French and English in the Crimean War, and subsequently by the reduction of Plevna, his greatest achievement, which brought to a close the war with Turkey in 1877; subsequently became commander-in-chief in Bulgaria.

Tome, Jacob, 1810-1898. An American philanthropist; born in Manheim township, York county, Pa.; went to Port Deposit, Md., in 1833. In 1884 he presented to Dickinson College a valuable building for scientific uses. His largest gift was for the foundation of the Jacob Tome Institute, at Port Deposit, $1,600,000, a sum that was increased by his will to more than $3,500,000. He died in Port Deposit, Md.

Tompkins, Daniel D., 1774-1825. An American statesman; born in Fox Meadows, Westchester county, N. Y.; member of Congress, 1804-1807, when he resigned to become judge of the Supreme Court of New York; governor, 1807-1817, and vice-president of the United States, 1817-1825. He died on Staten Island, N. Y.

Toombs, Robert, 1810-1885. An American statesman; born in Wilkes county, Georgia; was a Whig member of Congress from Georgia, 1845-1853, and a United States senator, 1853-1861. He was expelled from the Senate in 1861, and in the same year was elected to the Confederate Congress and also became Confederate secretary of state. He resigned to become a brigadier-general in the Confederate army. He died in Washington, Ga.

Torquema'da, Tomas de, 1420-1498. Spanish Dominican monk; inquisitor-general.

Torricelli (*tor-ri-chel'li*), **Evangelista,** 1608-1647. Italian physicist; he invented the barometer.

Tour'ville, Anne Hilarion de Cotentin, Comte de, 1642-1701. A distinguished French admiral and marshal.

Toussaint L'Ouverture (*too-sahn' loo-ver-toor'*), 1743-1803. A negro general and president of Hayti; in the insurrection and massacre of the whites, 1791, he was the leader, and was afterward elected president for life. Treacherously arrested by General Leclerc, 1802, while negotiations were in progress, he was carried to France and held a state prisoner till his death.

Trajan, Marcus Ulpius, 56-117. Roman emperor; born in Spain; ruled the empire with wisdom and vigor, set right the finances, upheld an impartial justice, and set on foot various schemes of improvement; suppressed the Christians as politically dangerous, but with no fanatic extravagance; is said to have erected the famous Trajan Column, which still stands in Rome.

Trev'ithick, Richard, 1771-1833. An English inventor; born in Illogan, Cornwall. He perfected a high-pressure steam engine, and began to experiment in the construction of locomotive engines. Passengers were first conveyed by steam by means of his road locomotive in 1801, and he soon after successfully worked a tram-road locomotive. His ideas were afterward taken up and developed by Stephenson. He was the first to recognize the value of iron in ship building, and the application of steam to agriculture. He died in Dartford, Kent.

Trumbull, John, 1756-1843. An American artist; born in Lebanon, Conn.; served in the Revolutionary War on the staffs of Generals Washington and Gates; became a pupil of Benjamin West; in 1786 he produced his first historical picture, "The Battle of Bunker Hill"; in 1817 he was employed by Congress to paint four pictures for the rotunda of the Capitol at Washington. He died in New York city.

Trumbull, Jonathan, 1710-1785. An American patriot; born in Lebanon, Conn.; took a very prominent part in forwarding the Revolutionary War; Washington placed great reliance on him, and frequently consulted him; to this habit, and his phrase, often repeated when in doubt, "Let us hear what Brother Jonathan says," has been traced the name which stands for a personification of the United States.

Truxtun, Thomas, 1755-1822. An American naval officer; born in Long Island, N. Y.; he was made a lieutenant in the navy and assigned to the *Congress*; in all of his engagements with the enemy he was uniformly victorious; placed in command of the *Constellation*, and was ordered to protect American commerce in the West Indies; in February, 1799, he fought a severe battle with the powerful French ship *L'Insurgente*, and captured her after killing twenty-nine of her crew and wounding forty-four; in January, 1800, he defeated the French Frigate *La Vengeance*; in 1802 he was assigned to command a fleet to participate in the war with Tripoli, and went to Norfolk to join the *Chesapeake*; about the same time he requested the appointment of a captain for his flagship; his letter was taken to mean his resignation, which was accepted against his wishes; he died in Philadelphia, Pa.

Turenne (*too-ren'*), **Henri de la Tour d'Auvergne, Vicomte de,** 1611-1675. The greatest military commander of his age; grandson of William the Silent, Prince of Orange; born at Sedan, France; accidentally killed by a shot while reconnoitering an intended battlefield. In the civil wars of France, he fought first on the Protestant side and afterward on the Catholic.

Turner, Joseph Mallord William, 1775-1851. English landscape painter.

Tyler, John, 1790-1862. Tenth president of the United States; born in Virginia; practiced law; in Congress, 1816-1821; governor of Virginia, 1825; senator, 1827; sympathized with the nullifiers and opposed Jackson; resigned, 1836; elected vice-president on Whig ticket, 1840; succeeded Harrison in 1841.

Tyndall, John, 1820-1893. An English physicist; born in Leighlin Bridge, near Carlow, Ireland. In 1872 he lectured in the United States; the profits of which he devoted to a fund "in aid of students who devote themselves to original research." He died in Haslemere, Surrey, England.

Ulloa, Antonio, Don, 1716-1795. A distinguished Spanish statesman, mathematician, and author. He was appointed governor of Louisiana, 1741.

Ul'philas, or **Ulfilas,** 313-383. The apostle of the Goths; translated the Scriptures into Gothic.

Unger, Johann Friedrich, 1750-1813. German printer and engraver.

Urban. The name borne by eight popes. **Urban II.,** 1088-1097. Urged the First Crusade, 1095. **Urban VI.,** 1378-1389. Clement VIII. was elected at the same time, and held sway at Avignon, originating the "western schism" which divided the church for nearly half a century.

Ursula, Saint. A traditionary virgin martyr; reputed daughter of a British prince, who, with eleven thousand other virgins, suffered cruel martyrdom at Cologne in the third or fourth century.

Urquhart, David, 1805-1877. Scotch writer and politician.

Ussher, James, 1580-1656. Irish prelate and scholar.

Valens, Flavius, 328-378. Emperor of the East from 364 to 378; nominated by his brother Valentinian I. emperor of the West; was harassed all his reign by the Goths.

Valette′, Jean Parisot de la, 1494-1565. Grand-master of the order of St. John; famous for his military exploits and for his defense of Malta against the Turks in 1565.

Vallan′digham, Clement Laird, 1820-1871. An American politician; born in New Lisbon, Ohio; was a member of Congress, 1858-1863, and during the Civil War was a strong friend of the Southern Confederacy. He was arrested in May, 1863, by United States troops, on a charge of uttering disloyal sentiments; was tried by court-martial, and sentenced to confinement till the end of the war. This was afterward commuted to banishment to the Confederate lines. He died in Lebanon, Ohio.

Van Buren, Martin, 1782-1862. Eighth president of the United States; enrolled at the bar in New York in 1803, and elected to the state senate; state attorney-general, 1815; leader of the "Albany Regency"; United States senator, 1821; governor, 1828; secretary of state, 1829-1831; vice-president, 1833-1837; president, 1837-1841.

Vancouver, George, 1758-1798. English navigator.

Vanderbilt, Cornelius, 1794-1877. American capitalist.

Vandyke, or **Van Dyck, Sir Anthony**, 1599-1641. Flemish painter; resided in England for several years before his death, where he became the most popular artist of his time.

Vane, Sir Henry, 1612-1662. English republican statesman.

Van Rensselaer, Stephen (the Patroon), 1764-1839. American statesman and landholder.

Varus, Publius Quintilius. Flourished 7 A.D. Roman general; defeated by Arminius.

Vauban (*vo′ban*), **Sebastien le Prestre, Seigneur de**, 1633-1707. Marshal of France, and the greatest military engineer of that country; entered the army, where he rose to the highest military rank by his merit and services. He was made governor of the citadel of Lille in 1688, commissioner-general of fortifications in 1677, and marshal of France in 1703. He died at Paris. As an engineer he carried the art of fortification to a degree of perfection unknown before his time. He strengthened and improved above 300 citadels, erected thirty-three new ones, and directed fifty-three sieges.

Veit (*vite*), **Philipp**, 1793-1877. Painter of the Romanticist school; born at Berlin; his best known work is a fresco, "Christianity bringing the Fine Arts to Germany."

Velas′quez, Diego de Silva, 1599-1660. Greatest of Spanish painters; born at Seville, of Portuguese family; portrait painting was his forte, one of his earliest being a portrait of Olivarez, succeeded by one of Philip IV. of Spain, considered the most perfect extant. Specimens of his work are found in different countries, but the best are in Madrid, Spain; they include sacred subjects, genre, landscape, and animal paintings, as well as portraits.

Velde, Willem van der (the elder), 1610-1693. Dutch marine painter.

Velde, Willem van der (the Younger), 1633-1707. Dutch marine painter.

Verboeckhoven (*ver-book′ho-ven*) **Eugene Joseph**, 1799-1881. Belgian painter.

Ver′di Giuseppe, 1813-1898. Italian composer; born at Roncole, Parma; his musical talent was slow of recognition, but the appearance of his "Lombardi" and "Ernani" established his repute, which was confirmed by "Rigoletto," "Il Trovatore" and "La Traviata."

Verestchagin (*va-res-tchah′gin*), **Vassili**, 1842-1904. Russian painter; realistic to an extreme degree, and anti-conventional; confined himself largely to martial subjects; perished with the sinking battleship *Petropavlovsk* at the siege of Port Arthur.

Vernet (*ver-nay′*), **Claude Joseph**, 1714-1789. A distinguished French marine painter. His son, **Antoine Charles Horace**, 1758-1836. was eminent as a painter of battle scenes. **Horace**, 1789-1863, son of the latter, exceeded his father in the painting of battle scenes, and ranks as the first artist of his age.

Veronese (*va-ro-na′se*), **Paolo**, 1528-1588. Painter of the Venetian school; born at Verona; painted his "Temptation of St. Anthony" for Mantua Cathedral, and settled in Venice in 1555, where he soon earned distinction and formed one of a trio along with Titian and Tintoretto; the subjects he treated were mostly scriptural, the most celebrated being the "Marriage Feast at Cana of Galilee."

Vesa′lius, Andreas, 1514-1564. An eminent anatomist and surgeon; born at Brussels.

Vespa′sian (Titus Flavius Vespasianus), 9-79. Roman emperor from 70 to 79, and tenth of the twelve Cæsars; born in the Sabine territory, of humble parentage; rose by his valor to high rank in the army and in favor with it, till at length he was elected by it to the throne.

Vespucci (*ves-poot′chee*), **Amerigo** (*ah-ma-ree′go*), 1451-1512. Navigator; born at Florence, Italy; made two voyages to America in 1499 and in 1501, and from him the two continents derived their name, owing, it is said, to his first visit being misdated in an account he left, which made it appear that he had preceded Columbus.

Victor Emmanuel I., 1759-1824. Brother of Charles Emmanuel IV., King of Sardinia, who abdicated in his favor; crowned 1802; abdicated in favor of his brother, Charles Felix, 1821. **Victor Emmanuel II.**, 1820-1878. Succeeded his father, Charles Albert, 1849, and became king of Italy, 1861.

Victoria, Alexandrina, 1819-1901. Queen of Great Britain and Ireland, and Empress of India; daughter of Edward, Duke of Kent, fourth son of George III.; succeeded her uncle, William IV., 1837; married Albert of Saxe-Coburg-Gotha, 1840, who died 1861. Victoria assumed the title Empress of India, 1876, by act of Parliament.

Vincent de Paul, Saint, 1576-1660. An eminent French philanthropist and reformer; canonized by Pope Clement XII., 1737; he organized the Congregation of Missions and founded the order of Sisters of Charity.

Vinci (*vin′che*), **Leonardo da**, 1452-1519. Florentine painter.

Vla′dimir (the Great), 949-1015. Grand Duke and first Christian ruler of Russia.

Vol′ta, Alessandro, Comte, 1745-1827. An eminent Italian chemist and natural philosopher; inventor of the Voltaic pile.

Wade, Benjamin Franklin, 1800-1879. An American statesman; born in Massachusetts. He represented Ohio in the United States Senate for many years.

Wagner, Wilhelm Richard, 1813-1883. Great musical composer; born at Leipsic; his principal works were "Rienzi," "The Flying Dutchman," "Tannhauser," "Lohengrin," "Tristan and Isolde," "The Mastersingers of Nurnberg," and the "Ring of the Nibelungen," the composition of which occupied twenty-five years; this last was performed in 1876 at Bayreuth, in presence of the emperor of Germany and the principal musical artists of the world; "Parsifal" was his last work.

Waite, Morrison Remick, 1816-1888. An American jurist; born in Lyme, Conn.; in 1871 was appointed one of the attorneys to represent the United States before the tribunal of arbitration at Geneva; nominated by President Grant to be chief-justice of the United States Supreme Court in 1874, and was unanimously confirmed by the Senate; died in Washington, D. C.

Waldemar I. (the Great), 1131-1181. King of Denmark. He conquered southern Norway and Wendish Germany. **Waldemar II.**, 1203-1241. Second son of the former; succeeded his brother Canute VI. **Waldemar III.**, ... -1375. Crowned 1340.

Walker, William, 1824-1860. A noted filibuster; born in Tennessee; captured and shot at Truxillo, Central America.

Wallace, Alfred Russell, 1823- . . . . An English naturalist; born in Usk, Monmouthshire, England; spent many years in traveling, especially in South America and the Asiatic islands. His observation of animal life early led him on the track of natural selection, and before Darwin gave his famous work to the world he had published "Speculations on the Origin of Species." He wrote many scientific and popular books and papers.

Wallace, Sir William, 1270?-1305. Scotch general and patriot; defeated by Edward I. of England; betrayed and executed.

Wallenstein, Albrecht Wenzel Eusebius von, Count, 1583-1634. Austrian general; hero of one of Schiller's dramas; entered the imperial army at the beginning of the Thirty Years' War; raised an army at his own expense in 1625, invading Denmark; banished from court by Emperor Ferdinand, but recalled on the death of Marshal Tilly; defeated by Gustavus Adolphus at Luetzen in 1632, but gained several victories in Silesia; again lost the emperor's favor, being charged with aspirations to the throne of Bohemia, was deprived of his command and assassinated.

Walpole, Sir Robert, Earl of Orford, 1676-1745. An English statesman; born in Houghton, England. He was secretary at war and leader in the House of Commons in 1708; paymaster of the forces in 1714 and 1720, and first lord of the treasury and chancellor of the exchequer in 1715, and again in 1721, and prime minister from 1715-1717 and from 1721-1742. During his long administration the Hanoverian succession, to which he was zealously attached, became firmly established. He died in Houghton, England.

Warburton, William, 1698-1779. An English divine; born at Newark; was bishop of Gloucester; was author of the famous "Divine Legation of Moses," characterized by Gibbon as a "monument of the vigor and weakness of the human mind"; a singular friendship subsisted between the author and Pope.

Ward, Henry Augustus, 1834- . . . . An American naturalist; born in Rochester, N. Y.; was professor of Natural Sciences in Rochester University, 1860-1865; and manager of gold mines in Montana and South Carolina, 1866-1869. In 1870 he began to travel in various countries, making large and valuable cabinets of mineralogy and geology, which he distributed among the universities and colleges of the United States.

Warren, Joseph, 1741-1775. American physician; Revolutionary general and patriot; fell at Bunker Hill.

Warwick, Richard Neville, Earl of (the king maker), 1420?-1471. English warrior; set up and deposed Edward IV.

Washington, Booker Taliaferro, 1859?- . . . . An American educator; born a slave in Hale's Ford, Va. After the Civil War he removed to West Virginia, where he worked in the mines, attending school in the winter. In 1875 he was graduated with honors at the Hampton Institute, Va.; was a teacher there till in 1881, when he was elected by the state authorities of Alabama principal of the Tuskegee Normal and Industrial Institute, which he organized and built up. He received the degree of A. M. from Howard University in 1896, and dined with President Roosevelt in 1902.

Washington, George, 1732-1799. Commander-in-chief in the American Revolution, and first president of the United States; "the father of his country;" born in Virginia; aid-de-camp to Braddock in the Indian campaign of 1755; married Martha Custis, 1759; chosen to Congress, 1774; appointed commander-in-chief of the colonial army in 1775; his first important operation in that capacity was to drive the English out of Boston, but, the British rallying, he was defeated at Brandywine and Germantown in 1777; next year, in alliance with the French, he drove the British out of Philadelphia, and in 1781 compelled Cornwallis to capitulate in an attack he made on Yorktown, and on the evacuation of New York by the British the independence of America was achieved, upon which he resigned the command; in 1789 he was elected to the presidency of the Republic, and in 1793 was re-elected, at the end of which term he retired into private life after paying a dignified farewell.

Watt, James, 1736-1819. Scotch engineer and inventor; improved and completed the steam engine; also credited with the discovery of the composition of water.

Watteau (*wat-toe'*), **Antoine,** 1684-1721. A distinguished French painter.

Watts, George Frederick, 1817- . . . . Eminent English painter; born in London; is distinguished as a painter at once of historical subjects, ideal subjects, and portraits; did one of the frescoes in the Poets' Hall of the Houses of Parliament and the cartoon of "Caractacus led in Triumph through the Streets of Rome"; has, as a "poet-painter," by his "Love and Death," "Hope," and "Orpheus and Eurydice," achieved a world-wide fame; he was twice offered a baronetcy, but on both occasions he declined.

Wayland, Francis, 1796-1865. An eminent American divine and author; of the Baptist denomination; born in New York.

Wayne, Anthony, 1745-1796. An eminent American general; born in Pennsylvania. He was the hero of the assault and capture of Stony Point, 1779, and at the close of the Revolution led successful campaigns against the Southern and Western Indians.

Weber, Karl Maria Friedrich Ernst von, Baron, 1786-1826. German musical composer.

Webster, Daniel, 1782-1852. American lawyer, orator, and statesman; "the expounder of the Constitution;" born in New Hampshire; in Congress, 1812-1816, 1822-1828; in Senate, 1828-1841; secretary of state; re-entered Senate in 1844; again became secretary of state in 1850; nominated for the presidency in 1834, but defeated; candidate for the Whig nomination in 1848, but defeated by Taylor, whom he supported; Webster's reply to Hayne, of South Carolina, is considered the greatest speech ever made in Congress.

Webster, Noah, 1758-1843. Lexicographer; born at Hartford, Conn.; bred to law; tried journalism; devoted twenty years to his "Dictionary of the English language."

Wedgwood, Josiah, 1730-1793. Celebrated English potter; born at Burslem; in 1759 started a pottery on artistic lines in his native place; had the good fortune to enlist Flaxman as a designer, and so a ware known by his name became famous for both its substantial and artistic excellence; he was a man of varied culture and of princely generosity, having by his art amassed a large fortune.

Weed, Thurlow, 1797-1882. An American journalist; born in Cairo, N.Y.; served as a private in the War of 1812; in 1830 he founded the Albany *Evening Journal*, an anti-Jackson, Whig, or Republican paper, which became the organ of the party, and which he controlled for thirty-five years; supported Lincoln and the Civil War, and went for him on a mission to Europe, 1861-1862; he died in New York city.

Weismann (*vyse'mahn*), **August,** 1834- . . . . German biologist; born at Frankfort-on-the-Main; it is with the discussions on the question of heredity that his name is most intimately associated.

Wellington, Arthur Wellesley, first Duke of, 1769-1852. Greatest of British generals; gained great distinction in India, in the war against the Mahrattas; major-general, 1802; Parliament, 1805; secretary for Ireland, 1807; defeated the Danes at Kioge, and was given command of an army sent to Spain against the French, 1808; triumphantly entered Madrid, 1812; defeated Jourdan and Soult, 1813; invaded France and gained numerous victories; defeated Napoleon at Waterloo, 1815; was afterward prime minister and minister of foreign affairs.

Wenceslaus, or **Wenzel,** 1361-1419. Emperor of Germany and king of Bohemia.

Werner, Abraham Gottlob, 1750-1817. An eminent German scientist and author.

Wesley, John, 1703-1791. A distinguished English divine and founder of the sect known as Wesleyans or Methodists. **Charles Wesley,** 1708-1788. Brother of the above; also a clergyman and poet; was associated with John in his religious labors.

West, Benjamin, 1738-1820. An American painter; born in Springfield, Pa., of Quaker parents. He went to Rome, Italy, in 1760, and proceeded to England in 1763, where he made his permanent residence. His "Death of General Wolfe" was among the first of his productions that attracted public notice. He died in London.

Westmacott, Sir Richard, 1775-1856. Sculptor; born in London; studied at Rome under Canova; he executed statues of Pitt, Addison, and others, and a number of monuments in Westminster Abbey and St. Paul's; his latest work was the sculptured pediment of the British Museum.

Wharton, Francis, 1820-1889. An American jurist; born in Philadelphia, Pa.; held the chair of international law in the Boston Law School. In 1885 he was appointed solicitor for the State Department. Under a resolution of Congress, 1888, he was made editor of the Revolutionary diplomatic correspondence of the United States. He wrote extensively on legal and theological subjects. Died in Washington, D. C.

Wheatstone, Charles, 1802-1878. A distinguished English scientist. He was the inventor of several important electrical appliances, and introduced the electric telegraph into England.

Whistler, James Abbott McNeill, 1834-1903. An American painter; born in Lowell, Mass.; studied for a time at the United States Military Academy; went to Paris, and afterward settled in London. The finest of his oil pictures are "The Artist's Mother—an Arrangement in Black and Gray," the "Portrait of Thomas Carlyle," and the "Portrait of Miss Alexander—Harmony in Gray and Green." Whistler's art in original and individual.

Whitefield, George, 1714-1770. Founder of Calvinistic Methodism; born at Gloucester, England; died at Newburyport, Mass.

Whitney, Eli, 1765-1825. A distinguished American inventor; born in Massachusetts; died in Connecticut. He invented the cotton gin and important improvements in firearms.

Whitney, William Dwight, 1827-1894. American philologist; born in Massachusetts; studied at Yale College, where he became professor of Sanskrit, in which he was a proficient, and to the study of which he largely contributed; has done much for the science of language.

Wiertz (*veerts*), **Antoine,** 1806-1865. A Belgian painter; born at Dinant; did a great variety of pictures on a variety of subjects, some of them on a large scale, and all in evidence of a high ideal of his profession, and an original genius for art.

Wilberforce, William, 1759-1833. English philanthropist and statesman; secured the abolition of the slave trade.

Wilder, Burt Green, 1841- . . . . An American educator; born in Boston, Mass.; served in the Union army as medical cadet, assistant surgeon, and surgeon of the 55th Massachusetts Infantry, 1862-1865; he became professor of Neurology, Vertebrate Zoology, and Physiology at Cornell University in 1867.

Willard, Frances Elizabeth, 1839-1898. An American temperance reformer; born in Churchville, near Rochester, N. Y.; after some years spent in teaching she became professor of Æsthetics in the Northwestern University, and was made president of the Woman's College in February, 1871; she began her active temperance work in 1874, and was made secretary of the National Woman's Christian Temperance Union; in 1879 she was made president of that organization and held the office till her death; she was chosen as president of the World's Christian Temperance Union in 1888, and in 1892 visited England as the guest of Lady Henry Somerset, the well known temperance worker; she was an orator of great eloquence, humor, and power; her executive ability and genius for organization were wonderful and her work for temperance and social purity will live in the history of her country; died in New York city.

William I. (the Conquerer), 1027-1087. King of England; duke of Normandy; conquered England.

William III. (William Henry of Nassau, Prince of Orange), 1650-1702. King of England; born in The Hague, Holland; his coronation as King of England took place in 1689; the year following William went to Ireland, where he defeated James at the battle of the Boyne; in 1691 he headed the confederate army in the Netherlands; took Namur in 1692, and in 1697 was acknowledged King of England by the treaty of Ryswick; on the death of Mary in 1694, the Parliament confirmed to him the royal title; his death was owing to a fall from his horse.

William I., 1797-1888. Emperor of Germany and king of Prussia. Born in Berlin. In 1849, as commander-in-chief of the Prussian army, he acted against the revolutionary Badeners; and in 1858, William was appointed regent. This position he occupied till Frederick William's death, in 1861, when he succeeded to the throne. In 1866, war was declared by Prussia against her old ally, Austria, and after a short campaign, Austria was compelled to make a humiliating peace. By this war Prussia obtained supremacy in Germany. In July, 1870, the Emperor Napoleon III., taking umbrage at Prussian interference with the succession to the vacant Spanish throne, or prompted by other motives, rashly declared war against Prussia, a power long prepared for such a contingency. On this, William, forming an alliance with the South German states, crossed the Rhine, and in a short campaign defeated the French, took Napoleon and his principal commanders prisoners, and received the capitulation of Paris, in February, 1871. His success in the war with France led to an offer from the German states of the imperial crown of Germany, which he accepted. He was crowned Emperor of Germany at Versailles, Jan. 18, 1871.

William II., 1859- . . . . German emperor and king of Prussia; ascended the throne June 15, 1888, upon the death of his father, Frederick III. of Prussia, and Frederick I. of Germany. Although of warlike tastes, his reign has been peaceful. He has maintained the German army at a high grade of efficiency, and has energetically promoted the construction of a powerful navy. He supports with vigor the imperial dignity, and causes any unfavorable reflection or innuendo regarding the ruling house to be punished with severity. He is a man of much learning and considerable ability, usually distant, but at times most gracious in his demeanor. His rule, on the whole, has been beneficial to Germany and to the world.

Williams, Roger, 1599-1683. English Puritan minister; founder of Rhode Island colony; born in Wales.

Wilmot, David, 1814-1868. An American statesman; author, 1846, of the "Wilmot Proviso," a bill declaring that slavery should not be permitted to exist in any territory acquired from Mexico. The bill passed the House, but failed in the Senate. He represented his state, Pennsylvania, in both houses of Congress.

Wilson, Henry, 1812-1876. An American statesman; born in New Hampshire. He represented Massachusetts in both Houses of the Federal Congress, and was elected vice-president on the ticket with General Grant, 1872.

Winchell, Alexander, 1824-1891. An American geologist; born in Dutchess county, New York. He lectured extensively, and wrote a number of fascinating books on scientific subjects. He died in Ann Arbor, Mich., while a professor in the University of Michigan.

Winthrop, John, 1588-1649. First governor of Massachusetts; born in Groton, England. He came with the first colonists to Salem in 1630 as their governor, and remained in that office, with the exception of six or seven years, till his death. He left a journal of the proceedings of the colony, which has been published, and is a valuable contribution to the early history of Massachusetts. He died in Boston.

Wirt, William, 1772-1834. An American lawyer; born in Bladensburg, Md.; in 1806, settled in Richmond, Va., where he became a prominent lawyer; he distinguished himself at the trial of Aaron Burr in 1807, as one of the counsel for the prosecution; he was appointed United States attorney-general in 1817, holding the latter office till 1829, through three administrations; he was nominated for president in 1832 by the Anti-Masonic party and received the electoral vote of Vermont; he died in Washington, D. C.

Wit'tekind, ... -807. Leader of the Saxon struggle against Charlemagne; annihilated the Frankish army in 783; in retaliation Charlemagne executed 4,500 Saxons he had taken prisoners; this roused the entire Saxon people to arms, and led to a drawn battle at Detmold, upon which Wittekind accepted baptism, and was promoted to a dukedom by the Frankish king.

Wolf, Friedrich August, 1759-1824. Great classical scholar; born near Nordhausen; professor of Philology at Halle; became world famous for his theory of the Homeric poems.

Wolfe, James, 1727-1759. Major-general; born in Kent, England; Pitt appointed him to a command in Canada; here he distinguished himself first at the siege of Louisburg, and then by the capture of Quebec, where he fell at the moment of victory.

Wolff, Johann Christian von, 1679-1754. German philosopher and mathematician; born at Breslau; he was a disciple of Leibnitz, and the father of the philosophy that prevailed in Germany before the time of Kant; his merits as a philosopher were threefold; he claimed for philosophy the entire field of knowledge, he paid special attention to method in philosophical speculation, and he first taught philosophy to express itself in German, or made German the philosophical language.

Wollaston, William Hyde, 1766-1828. A distinguished English chemist and natural philosopher.

Wolsey, Thomas, Cardinal, 1471-1530. An English prelate; born in Ipswich, England. When Henry VIII. became king, Wolsey was successively appointed Canon of Windsor, Dean of York, Bishop of Lincoln, Archbishop of York, and his nomination as cardinal in 1515 and pope's legate in 1518 completed his ecclesiastical dignities. In 1515 he was also appointed lord-chancellor of the kingdom. Part of his immense revenues he expended in display, and part more laudably for the advancement of learning. Wolsey lost the royal favor when he failed to obtain from Pope Clement a decision granting the king's divorce from Catherine of Aragon. He was banished from court, stripped of his dignities, and sentenced to imprisonment. Finally he was arrested at Cawood Castle on a charge of high treason, and on his way to London as a prisoner died in Leicester Abbey.

Worcester, Edward Somerset, Marquis of, 1601?-1667. One of the earliest inventors of a steam engine. He was engaged in the service of Charles I. during the civil war, and was imprisoned in the Tower from 1652-1655. He afterward spent his time in retirement, and in 1653 published a book entitled "Scantlings of One Hundred Inventions," in which he first gave a description of the uses and effects of his steam engine.

Worcester, Joseph Emerson, 1784-1865. An eminent American lexicographer; author of the popular Dictionary bearing his name; born in New Hampshire.

Wrangel, Frederick, 1784-1877. Prussian field marshal; born at Stettin; served with distinction in various campaigns, and commanded in the Danish War of 1864, and was present in the Austro-Prussian War of 1866, though without command.

Wren, Sir Christopher, 1632-1723. The greatest of English architects; born in East Knoyle, Wiltshire, England. He had been appointed by Charles II. to restore old St. Paul's, but after the great fire in 1666 it became necessary to rebuild the cathedral. It was begun in 1675, and the architect saw the last stone laid by his son thirty-five years afterward. Among the other notable buildings which Wren designed are: the modern part of the palace at Hampton Court, the library of Trinity

College, Cambridge, the hospitals of Chelsea and Greenwich, the churches of St. Stephen's, Walbrook; St. Mary-le-bow, Cheapside; St. Michael, Cornhill; St. Bride, Fleet street; as also the campanile of Christ Church, Oxford, and Marlborough House, Pall Mall. From 1685 to 1700 represented various boroughs in Parliament. He died in Hampton Court.

Wu Ting-Fang, 1842- . . . . A Chinese diplomatist; born in Hsin-hui, district of Kwangtung, China; studied Chinese literature and classics together with English in Canton, and took a law course in England, 1874-1877. On his return to China he directed the construction of the first railroad in his native land; was the first secretary of the Chinese commission to negotiate with Japan in 1895, and was afterward a plenipotentiary to ratify the treaty. He was appointed envoy extraordinary and minister plenipotentiary to the United States, Peru, and Spain in May, 1897. While residing in Washington he became very popular. In 1900 the degree of LL.D. was conferred on him by the University of Pennsylvania.

Wycliffe or **Wickliffe, John,** 1324-1384. An English reformer; founder of the Lollards, and translator of the Scriptures into English.

Xantip'pe. The wife of Socrates; notorious for bad temper, but credited by her husband with many domestic virtues.

Xavier (*zav'e-er*), **Francis, Saint,** 1506-1552. Spanish Jesuit missionary to India and Japan. He was canonized in 1622.

Xenoph'anes. Flourished sixth century B.C. A Greek writer and philosopher; born in Colophon. Exiled from his Ionian home, he established himself at Elea in Southern Italy.

Xerxes (*zerk'sees*), ... -465 B.C. King of Persia, 485-465 B.C. He invaded Greece, 480, with an immense army, but was finally forced to fly with a few personal attendants, his army being destroyed at Platæa and his fleet at Mycale on the same day, 479.

Ximenes (*he-may'neth*) **de Cisneros, Francisco,** 1436-1517. Spanish cardinal and statesman; born in Castile; in 1495 became archbishop of Toledo, but not till he was sixty years of age; in ten years after this he became regent of Spain, and conducted the affairs of the kingdom with consummate ability.

Yale, Elihu, 1648-1721. An Anglo-American philanthropist; born in Boston, Mass. He went to England while very young, and was there educated, never returning to America. About 1678 he went to the East Indies as a trader, and acquired great wealth. From 1687 to 1692 he was governor at Fort St. George, Madras. He gave to the Saybrook Collegiate School books and money valued at $4,000, a gift which resulted in the connection of his name with the college after its removal to New Haven. He died in London, and was buried at Wrexham, a town in North Wales.

Young, Brigham, 1801-1877. An American Mormon; born in Whitingham, Vt. He died in Salt Lake City.

Zaleu'cus. Flourished seventh century, B.C. Greek legislator and reformer; first to make a written code of laws.

Zamojski, John Sarius, 1541-1605. Polish general, statesman, and scholar.

Zedeki'ah. Flourished sixth century, B.C. The last king of Judah; placed on the throne 598 B.C., by Nebuchadnezzar, Jehoiachin, his nephew and predecessor, being carried captive to Babylon; Zedekiah, having rebelled, was taken prisoner to Babylon, 586, B.C., and put to death.

Ze'no. Flourished 500 B.C. Greek philosopher of the Eleatic school; was the founder of the dialectic so successfully adopted by Socrates, which argues for a particular truth by demonstration of the absurdity that would follow from its denial, a process of argument known as the *reductio ad absurdum.*

Zeno. Flourished third century, B.C. Greek philosopher; the founder of Stoic philosophy; born at Citium, in Cyprus; went to Athens, and after posing as a cynic at length opened a school of his own in the Stoa, where he taught to extreme old age.

Zeno'bia. Flourished third century, A.D. A Queen of Palmyra, who succeeded to the throne as regent for her sons on the murder of her husband Odenathus, 266 A.D. According to Zosimus she died on her way to Rome.

Zin'zendorf, Nikolaus Ludwig von, Count, 1700-1760. A German count; born in Dresden; established a religious community on his estate at Herrnhut, in Saxony, consisting chiefly of a body of Moravian brethren, who had been driven out of Bohemia and Moravia on account of their religious opinions, and were called Herrnhuters, of which he became one of the leaders and chief apostles.

Ziska, John, 1360-1424. A distinguished Hussite leader, who won distinction in war against the Teutonic knights, Turks, French, and Imperialists, defeating the latter in thirteen pitched battles.

Zoroaster (*zo'ro-as-ter*), **Zarathush'tra,** or **Zer'-dusht.** The founder or reformer of the Parsee religion; though certainly a historical personage, nothing whatever is known except that his family name was Spitama, that he was born in Bactria, and that he could not have flourished later than 800 B.C.

Zurbaran (*thur-ba-ran'*), **Francesco,** 1598-1662. A distinguished Spanish painter.

Zwin'gle, Ulrich (Zuinglius), 1484-1531. A distinguished Swiss reformer; killed at the battle of Cappel.

DERIVATIONS AND FICTITIOUS NAMES OF STATES AND TERRITORIES.

ALABAMA (Ala.).—The name is of Indian origin, signifying "Here we rest."

ARIZONA (Ariz.).—An Indian word, meaning "Sand hills."

ARKANSAS (ARK.).—French and Indian words, signifying "Bow of Smoky Waters." The fictitious name of the state is "Bear State," from the number of these animals formerly found there.

CALIFORNIA (Cal.).—From Spanish words, meaning "Hot furnace." The fictitious name is "The Golden State."

COLORADO (Colo.).—Spanish word, meaning "Colored."

CONNECTICUT (Conn.).—An Indian name, signifying "The long river." The nicknames are "Freestone State," "Nutmeg State," and "Land of Steady Habits."

DAKOTA (Dak.).—Indian word meaning "allied."

DELAWARE (Del.).—Named in honor of Lord De La War. It is called "The Diamond State," from its small size and its intrinsic worth; also "Blue Hen State."

FLORIDA (Fla.).—From the Spanish, meaning "flowery"; so called from the abundance of flowers, and the day (Easter Sunday) upon which it was discovered. From its shape it is sometimes called "The Peninsular State."

GEORGIA (Ga.).—Named in honor of King George II. of England. The nickname is the "Empire State of the South."

ILLINOIS (Ill.).—An Indian word, signifying "Tribe of men." The sobriquet is "Prairie State"; also "Sucker State."

INDIANA (Ind.).—So called from the Indians. The original meaning of the word India is "country of the river." The nickname is "The Hoosier State."

IOWA (Ia.).—An Indian word meaning "The Sleepy Ones." The fictitious name is "The Hawkeye State."

KANSAS (Kan.).—Indian word, signifying "Smoky Water." The sobriquets are "Garden of the West" and "Jayhawker State."

KENTUCKY (Ky.).—Indian name signifying "The Dark and Bloody Ground." The nickname is "The Corn-Cracker State."

LOUISIANA (La.).—Named in honor of King Louis XIV. of France. "The Creole State."

MAINE (Me.).—So called from Maine in France. "The Pine Tree State."

MARYLAND (Md.).—Named in honor of Queen Henrietta Maria of England.

MASSACHUSETTS (Mass.).—An Indian name, signifying "Blue Hills." The fanciful name is "The Bay State."

MICHIGAN (Mich.).—Indian word, meaning "The Lake Country." It is nicknamed "The Lake State"; also "The Wolverine State."

MINNESOTA (Minn.).—From Indian words meaning "Cloudy Water." It is called "The Gopher State."

MISSISSIPPI (Miss.).—Indian word for "Father of Waters." It is nicknamed "The Bayou State."

MISSOURI (Mo.).—Indian word, meaning "Muddy Water."

MONTANA (Mont.).—From the Spanish, meaning "Mountain Land."

NEBRASKA (Neb.).—An Indian word, meaning "Shallow River."

NEVADA (Nev.).—Spanish word, signifying "Snow-clad." The fictitious name is "The Sage Hen State."

NEW HAMPSHIRE (N. H.).—Named from Hampshire county, Eng. The sobriquet is "The Granite State."

NEW JERSEY (N. J.).—Named for the Isle of Jersey. The sobriquet is "The Jersey Blue."

NEW MEXICO (N. M.).—Spanish. Named from the country of Mexico, meaning "The Place of Aztec, God of War."

NEW YORK (N. Y.).—Named in honor of the Duke of York and Albany. It is called "The Excelsior State" and "The Empire State."

NORTH CAROLINA (N. C.)—Named, with South Carolina, in honor of Charles II. of England. "The Old North State," "The Tar State," and "The Turpentine State."

OHIO.—An Indian word, signifying "Beautiful." Called "The Buckeye State."

OKLAHOMA (Okl.).—Signifies in Cherokee "Home of the Red Man."

OREGON (Ore.).—Signifies "River of the West."

PENNSYLVANIA (Pa.).—"Penn's Woodland" is the signification. The sobriquet is "The Keystone State."

RHODE ISLAND (R. I.).—Named from the Isle of Rhodes, in the Mediterranean. Rhodes signifies a "rose." It is nicknamed "Little Rhody."

SOUTH CAROLINA (S. C.).—Named in the same manner as North Carolina, which see. The sobriquet is "The Palmetto State."

TENNESSEE (Tenn.)—Derived from Indian words signifying "River of the Big Bend." It is nicknamed "The Big Bend State."

TEXAS (Tex.).—Spanish; said to signify "Friends." It is nicknamed "The Lone Star State."

UTAH.—Named from the Utes, or Utah Indians.

VERMONT (Vt.).—From the French, signifying "Green Mountain." It is called the "Green Mountain State."

VIRGINIA (Va.).—Named for Elizabeth, Queen of England—the "Virgin Queen." It is nicknamed "The Mother of States," also "The Old Dominion."

WASHINGTON (W.).—Named for President Washington.

WEST VIRGINIA (W. Va.).—It is nicknamed the "Panhandle State."

WISCONSIN (Wis.).—Named from its principal river, and that from the French, meaning "flowing westward." The fictitious name is "The Badger State."

WYOMING (Wyo.).—An Indian term, meaning "large plains."

THE SPANISH AMERICAN WAR.

War began Thursday, April 21, 1898, 7.00 A. M.

Peace Protocol signed Friday, August 12, 1898, 4.23 P. M.

Treaty of Peace signed December 10, 1898.

CHRONOLOGICAL RECORD.

January 1-12. The North Atlantic Squadron assembled in the neighborhood of Dry Tortugas, Gulf of Mexico.

January 15-20. Hostile demonstrations at Havana by Spanish volunteers against Americans caused the Governor-General to place a guard around the United States Consulate.

January 25. The battle-ship Maine arrived at Havana on a friendly visit.

February 8. A letter by Minister De Lome, in which he wrote disparagingly of President McKinley, was published. On learning of the exposure the Minister requested his government to accept his resignation.

February 9. The United States Senate discussed intervention in Cuba.

February 14. Resolutions requesting the President to transmit information relative to the situation in Cuba were adopted by Congress.

February 14. Señor Luis Polo y Bernabe was appointed Spanish Minister to the United States to succeed Señor De Lome.

February 15. The battle-ship Maine was blown up in the harbor of Havana by a floating mine; 260 American lives were destroyed.

February 16. Spain officially expressed regret for the Maine "incident."

February 17. A naval court of inquiry into the cause of the destruction of the Maine was appointed by the United States Government.

February 18-25. The Spanish cruiser Vizcaya visited New York harbor. On the last date she sailed for Havana.

February 20. The Court of Inquiry began its session in Havana.

February 22. The cruiser Montgomery proceeded to Havana.

March 5. Spain asked for the recall of Consul-General Lee, which was promptly refused by the United States Government.

March 7. A bill appropriating $50,000,000 for the national defense was introduced in the House of Representatives. It passed the House March 8 and the Senate March 9, and was signed by the President.

March 11. The War Department began the mobilization of the army.

March 12. The battle-ship Oregon sailed from San Francisco to join the Atlantic squadron.

March 12. Armistice was offered by Spain to the Cuban insurgents.

March 14. The Spanish fleet sailed from Cadiz for the Canary Islands.

March 14. Senator Proctor's report on Spanish atrocities in Cuba was published.

March 19. The Maine Court of Inquiry completed its labors. Its report was delivered to the President March 25, and transmitted by him to Congress March 28.

March 25. Commodore Schley took command of the Flying Squadron in Hampton Roads.

March 30. The President requested permission of Spain to relieve the reconcentrados, which was granted.

April 2. The Spanish fleet arrived at the Cape de Verde Islands.

April 4. The pope appealed to Spain in the interests of peace.

April 5. United States consuls in Cuba were recalled.

April 7. The diplomatic representatives of the great powers of Europe waited on the President with a plea for peace.

April 9. Consul-General Lee with many Americans departed from Havana.

April 11. The President sent a message to Congress outlining the situation, declaring that intervention was necessary, advising against the recognition of the Cuban Government, and requesting Congress to take action.

April 19. Congress adopted resolutions declaring Cuba independent and directing the President to use the forces of the United States to put an end to Spanish authority in Cuba.

April 20. The president signed the resolutions of Congress. An ultimatum to Spain was cabled to Minister Woodford.

April 20. The Spanish Cortes met and received a warlike message from the Queen-Regent.

April 21. The Spanish Government sent Minister Woodford his passports, thus beginning the war.

April 21. Congress passed an act for increasing the military establishment.

April 21. Great Britain notified Spain that coal was contraband of war.

April 22. Proclamation to the neutral powers announcing war was issued by the President.

April 22. Admiral Sampson's fleet sailed from Key West. The blockade of Cuban ports began.

April 22. The gunboat Nashville captured the Spanish ship Buena Ventura, the first prize of the war.

April 23. The President issued a call for 125,000 volunteers.

April 24. Great Britain issued a proclamation of neutrality and was followed subsequently by the other powers, except Germany.

April 24. Spain formally declared that war existed with the United States.

April 25. Congress passed an act declaring that war had existed since April 21.

April 25. Commodore Dewey's fleet sailed from Hong Kong for the Philippines.

April 26. Congress passed an act for the increase of the regular army.

April 27. Batteries at Matanzas were bombarded.

April 30. Admiral Cervera's fleet left the Cape de Verde Islands for the West Indies.

May 1. Commodore Dewey destroyed the Spanish fleet at Manila. American loss, six men slightly wounded.

May 5-7. Riots in Spain.

May 11. Commodore Dewey was made a rear-admiral.

May 11. Attack on Cienfuegos and Cardenas. Ensign Bagley and four men on the torpedo-boat Winslow were killed.

May 11. Admiral Cervera's fleet appeared off Martinique.

May 12. Admiral Sampson bombarded San Juan de Porto Rico.

May 13. The Flying Squadron left Hampton Roads for Eastern Cuba, via Key West.

May 18. A new Spanish Ministry under Señor Sagasta came into office.

May 19. Admiral Cervera's fleet arrived in the harbor of Santiago de Cuba.

May 22. The cruiser Charleston sailed from San Francisco for Manila.

May 24. The battle-ship Oregon reached Jupiter Inlet, Florida.

May 25. The President issued a second call for volunteers, the number being 75,000.

May 25. The first Manila expedition from San Francisco started.

May 30. Admiral Sampson's fleet arrived at Santiago from Porto Rico.

May 31. Forts at the entrance of Santiago Harbor were bombarded.

June 3. Lieutenant Hobson sank the Merrimac in the entrance to Santiago Harbor.

June 4. Captain Gridley, of the Olympia, died at Kobe, Japan.

June 6. Spanish cruiser Reina Mercedes was sunk by American navy at Santiago.

June 10. War Revenue bill was finally passed by Congress. It was signed by the President, June 13.

June 11. Marines landed at Guantanamo, and skirmished with the Spaniards the following day.

June 12-14. General Shafter's army of invasion, 16,000 strong, embarked at Key West for Santiago.

June 14-15. There was fighting between marines and Spaniards at Guantanamo Bay and a bombardment of the fort at Caimanera by warships.

June 15. Admiral Camara's fleet sailed from Cadiz for the Suez Canal.

June 20-22. General Shafter's army landed at Daiquiri; one killed, four wounded.

June 21. The Ladrone Islands were captured.

June 22. The auxiliary cruiser, St. Paul, repulsed a Spanish torpedo-boat attack off San Juan, Porto Rico.

June 24. Juragua was captured. The Spaniards were defeated at Las Guasimas. Capron and Fish were killed.

June 26. Admiral Camara's fleet reached Port Said.

June 28. General Merritt departed for Manila.

July 1-2. The Spanish earthworks at El Caney and San Juan, Santiago, were carried by assault, with heavy loss, in which the Rough Riders and the Seventy-first New York participated.

July 3. Admiral Cervera's fleet, attempting to escape from Santiago, was destroyed by the American war vessels.

July 3. The surrender of Santiago was demanded.

July 6. Hobson and his comrades were exchanged.

July 8. Admiral Dewey's vessels took possession of Isla Grande in Subig Bay, near Manila, and the German gunboat Irene, which had been interfering, withdrew.

July 8. Admiral Camara started to return through the Suez Canal to Spain. He reached Cadiz, July 29.

July 10. Bombardment of Santiago was resumed.

July 11. General Miles arrived at American headquarters in Cuba.

July 13. Admiral Cervera and captured Spanish prisoners arrived at Portsmouth, N. H.

July 17. Santiago surrendered.

July 20. General Leonard Wood was appointed Military Governor of Santiago.

July 21. Last naval engagement on the coast of Cuba. Four United States warships entered the harbor of Nipe, and after a furious bombardment took possession of that port.

July 25. United States Army under General Miles landed at Guanica, Porto Rico. The town surrendered, and Ponce followed, July 28.

July 26. The Spanish government, through French Ambassador Cambon, asked for terms of peace.

July 29. General Merritt landed at Cavité, Manila Harbor.

July 30. The President, through the French Ambassador, stated the American terms.

July 31. The Americans repulsed the Spaniards, with loss on both sides, at Malate, near Manila.

August 7. The Rough Riders left Santiago for Montauk Point, L. I.

August 9. General Ernst defeated a Spanish force at Coamo, Porto Rico.

August 9. Spain formally accepted the President's terms of peace.

August 12. The peace protocol was signed and an armistice was proclaimed. The blockade of Cuba was raised.

August 13. Manila surrendered to the American forces after a short land fight and bombardment by the fleet.

August 20. Imposing naval demonstration in the harbor of New York. The battleships Iowa, Indiana, Massachusetts, Oregon, and Texas, and cruisers New York and Brooklyn, amid a great popular ovation, steamed up the Hudson river to Grant's Tomb and saluted.

August 30. General Merritt sailed from Manila for Paris to attend the Peace Conference.

September 9. United States Peace Commissioners were appointed. They sailed for France, September 17.

September 10. The United States Cuban Evacuation Commissioners arrived at Havana.

September 13. Admiral Cervera and other Spanish naval officers sailed for Spain.

September 18. Spanish Peace Commissioners were announced.

September 20. The evacuation of Porto Rico by the Spaniards began.

September 24. A commission appointed by the President to investigate the conduct of the War Department, began its sessions at Washington.

October 1. The conferences of the Peace Commissioners began in Paris.

October 12. The battleships Oregon and Iowa sailed from New York for Manila.

October 18. Peace Jubilee celebration at Chicago.

October 18. The American army and navy took formal possession of the island of Porto Rico at San Juan.

October 24. Time limit for the evacuation of Cuba by the Spaniards was extended to January 1, 1899.

October 27. After a long and earnest contention the Spanish Peace Commissioners accepted the American ultimatum not to assume the Spanish Cuban debt.

October 31. The United States Peace Commissioners presented the demand of the United States for the Philippines.

November 1. The captured cruiser Infanta Maria Teresa was abandoned in a gale off San Salvador.

November 7. The Cuban Assembly was organized at Santa Cruz del Sur. Domingo Mendez Capote was elected president.

December 10. The Treaty of Peace was signed at Paris at 8.45 o'clock P. M.

Casualties in the Navy During the War.—Lost on the Maine preceding the war, 2 officers and 257 men. Manila, May 1, 7 wounded. Cienfuegos, May 11, 1 killed, 11 wounded. Cardenas, May 11, 5 killed, 3 wounded. San Juan, May 12, 1 killed, 7 wounded. Guantanamo, June 11-20, 6 killed, 16 wounded. Santiago, June 22, 1 killed, 9 wounded. Santiago, July 3, 1 killed, 1 wounded. On the Yankee, June 13, 1 wounded. On the the Eagle, July 12, 1 wounded. On the Bancroft, July 2, 1 killed. On the Amphitrite, August 7, 1 killed. Total for the war, 19 killed and 48 wounded, exclusive of the loss on the Maine. In addition to the above, 1 man died of disease, and 6 were invalided. Only 18 were killed in battle. The average strength of the navy and marine corps together was 26,102 for the 114 days of hostilities. The total deaths from disease were 56, while 29 died from injuries received in battle.

Casualties in the Army During the War.—Losses of Santiago Campaign—Killed: Officers, 23; men, 237. Wounded: Officers, 99; men, 1,332.

Losses of Porto Rico Campaign—Killed: Officers, 0; men, 3. Wounded: Officers, 4; men, 36.

Losses of Manila Campaign—Killed: Officers, 0; men, 17. Wounded: Officers 10; men, 96.

Total losses from all causes up to October 1, 1898 — Killed: Officers, 33; men, 257. Wounded: Officers, 4; men, 61. Died of disease: Officers, 80; men, 2,485. Total of 107 officers and 2,803 men; or a percentage of 159-1,000, being an aggregate of 2,910 out of a total of 274,717 officers and men, the total of the war.

Died in Camps in the United States and Cuba, and at Sea.—Camp Thomas, 245; Camp Cuba Libre, 246; Tampa, Fla., 56; Cuba (of disease only), 427; at sea, 87; Camp Wikoff, 257; Manila, 63; Porto Rico, 137; Camp Wheeler, 35; Camp Hamilton, 29; Camp Alger, 107; Camp Meade, 64; Camp Merritt, 139; Camp Poland, 23; Camp Shipp, 12; other camps, 378.

Arms Captured at Santiago.—Mauser rifles, 16,902; Argent rifles, 872; Remington rifles, 6,118; Mauser carbines, 833; Argent carbines, 84; Remington carbines, 330; revolvers, 75. Rifled cannon—Bronze, 30; cast iron, 10; steel, 8; smooth bore and obsolete, 44; mortars, 5. Projectiles — 3,551 solid shot, 437 shrapnel, 2,577 shells. Small-arm ammunition — Mauser, 1,471,200 rounds; Argent, 1,500,000 rounds; others, 1,680,000 rounds.

Spanish Vessels Captured or Destroyed by the Navy.— By Admiral Sampson's Squadron, July 3 — Cristobal Colon, Vizcaya, Maria Teresa, Admiral Oquendo, all armored cruisers; torpedo-boat destroyers Furor and Pluton.

Destroyed July 18 — Gunboats Maria Ponton, Delgado Perado, José Garcia, Cuba, and Espanola, all burned at Manzanillo; transport Gloria sunk.

By Admiral Dewey's Squadron, May 1 and subsequently — Cruisers Reina Cristina, Castilla, Ulloa, Isla de Cuba, General Lozo; gunboats Duero, Correo, Velasco, Mindano, and one transport on May 1. Subsequently captured — Torpedo boat Barcelow; gunboats Callao, Leyte, Manila, and Mindanao.

Vessels captured in Cuban waters all gunboats of about 300 tons, — Hernan Cortez, Pizarro, Vasco Nuñez, Diego Valasquez, Alerta, Ardilla, Tradera, Flecha, Ligera, Satellite,

Margarit, Vigia. General Blanco, Intrepida, and Cauto. The Alvarado was captured at Santiago. The Sandoval was sunk in Guantanamo Harbor, but was raised by Commander McCalla.

DECISIVE BATTLES OF HISTORY.

ACTIUM, B. C. 31. The combined fleets of Antony and Cleopatra defeated by Octavius, and imperialism established in the person of Octavius.

PHILIPPI, B. C. 42. Brutus and Cassius defeated by Octavius and Antony. The fate of the Republic decided.

METAURUS, B. C. 207. The Carthaginians under Hasdrubul were defeated by the Romans under Caius and Marcus Livius.

ARBELA, B. C. 331. The Persians defeated by the Macedonians and Greeks under Alexander the Great. End of the Persian empire.

SYRACUSE, B. C. 414. The Athenians defeated by the Syracusans and their allies, the Spartans, under Gylippus.

MARATHON, B. C. 490. The Athenians under Miltiades defeated the Persians under Datis. Free government preserved.

WINFELD-LIPPE, A. D. 9. Teutonic independence established by the defeat of the Roman legions under Varus at the hands of the Germans under Arminius (Hermann.)

CHALONS, A. D. 451. The Huns under Attila, called the "Scourge of God," defeated by the confederate armies of Romans and Visigoths.

TOURS, A. D. 732. The Saracens defeated by Charles Martel and Christendom rescued from Islam.

HASTINGS, A. D. 1066. Harold, commanding the English army, defeated by William the Conqueror, and a new régime established in England by the Normans.

SIEGE OF ORLEANS, A. D. 1429. The English defeated by the French under Joan of Arc.

DEFEAT OF THE SPANISH ARMADA, A. D. 1588. England saved from Spanish invasion.

LUTZEN, A. D. 1632. Decided the religious liberties of Germany. Gustavus Adolphus killed.

BLENHEIM, A. D. 1704. The French and Bavarians under Marshal Tallard defeated by the English and their allies under Marlborough.

PULTOWA, A. D. 1709. Charles XII. of Sweden defeated by the Russians under Peter the Great.

SARATOGA, A. D. 1777. Critical battle of the American War of Independence. The English defeated by the Americans under General Gates.

VALMY, A. D. 1792. An invading army of Prussians, Austrians, and Hessians under the Duke of Brunswick, defeated by the French under Kellermann. The first success of the Republic against foreigners.

TRAFALGAR. On the 21st of October, **A. D. 1805, the great naval battle of Trafalgar** was fought. The English defeated the French and destroyed Napoleon's hopes to successfully invade England.

WATERLOO, A. D. 1815. The French under Napoleon defeated by the allied armies of Russia, Austria, Prussia, and England under Wellington.

SIEGE OF SEBASTOPOL, A. D. 1854-5. The Russians succumbed to the beleaguering armies of England, France, and Turkey, and the result was delay in the expansion of the Russian Empire.

GETTYSBURG, July, A. D. 1863. The deciding battle of the war for the Union. The Confederates under General Lee defeated by the Union forces under Meade.

SEDAN, A. D. 1870. The decisive battle of the Franco-German war.

RECENT DESPERATE WARS.

Indian Mutiny. General disaffection from a variety of real or supposed grievances had been for a long time smoldering amongst the Sepoys, who were the flower of the British East India Company's forces, but when a report spread that cartridges smeared with cow and pork fat were to be used by the native soldiers, open mutiny, attended with great cruelty, broke out. The war, which may be said to have commenced in March, 1857, raged until June, 1858. It was marked by a succession of romantic, pathetic, and heroic incidents — the siege of Delhi, the massacre of Cawnpore, the relief and capture of Lucknow — but was suppressed in the latter year, when the East India Company ceased to exist, and the government of India was assumed by the British crown. A cruel vengeance was taken on the mutineers, hundreds of whom were strung together and blown to pieces at the mouths of cannon.

The Abyssinian War arose out of the imprisonment of Consul Capt. C. Cameron, Rev. H. Stern, a missionary, and others by King Theodore, in consequence of a supposed slight by the British government, 1864. Mr. Rassam was sent on a mission to Abyssinia for their release. On the refusal of the king to surrender the prisoners, an English army, some 12,000 strong, under Sir Robert (afterwards Lord) Napier, defeated the Abyssinian forces at Arogee, April 10, 1868, and three days later stormed the fortress of Magdala. In consequence of this King Theodore comıitted suicide. The prisoners were released, nd the war terminated.

American Civil War. This began April 3, 1861, with the capture of Fort Sumter, Charleston, by the Confederate forces. The North prepared for the contest with energy, nd blockaded the Southern ports. Throughout the war the Confederates chiefly acted upon the defensive, the Federals or Northern orces, being the attacking party, and possessing the advantage of superior forces, money, nd war material. The principal generals of he South were Lee, "Stonewall" Jackson, Hood, Albert Sidney Johnston, Longstreet, Bragg, Beauregard, Stuart, Joseph E. Johnson; and of the North, Grant, Sherman, Sheridan, McClellan, Thomas, Rosecrans, Pope, Butler, Halleck, Baker, Burnside, Frémont, Meade, Banks, and McDowell. In the campaign of 1861 the advantage was chiefly on the ide of the Confederates, who were victorious t Bull Run (Manassas, Va.) and Ball's Bluff, Va. (October 21), but suffered a reverse at Springfield, Mo. (Aug. 10), and lost Fort Hatteras, N. C., captured by Butler (August 29). During 1862 the Confederates were successful t Bull Run (August 20) and in Virginia (June) at Fredericksburg, Va. (Dec. 10-15), but sustained severe defeats at Mill Springs, Ky. (January 19), Pea Ridge, Ark. (March 6-8), Winchester, Va. (March 23), Williamsburgh, Va. Great battles were fought at Shiloh, Tenn. (April 7), Fair Oaks, Va. (May 31, June 1), on the Chickahominy (June 25-July 1) and Antietam Creek, Md. (September 17), in none of which either party could claim a victory; but the battle of Antietam Creek obliged Lee to abandon his invasion of the North. During this year the naval operations of the Federals were generally successful, Admiral Farragut running past the forts of the Mississippi and seizing New Orleans (May). The memorable conflict between the "Merrimac" (Confederate) and the Federal "Monitor" resulted (March 9) in the repulse of the former, the "Merrimac" being burned by the Confederates on the capture of their arsenal at Norfolk, Va. (May 11). The war during 1863 was decidedly in favor of the Federal forces, although the Confederates, under "Stonewall" Jackson, defeated Hooker at Chancellorsville (May 2-4), Jackson subsequently dying from his wounds (May 10), and Lee invaded Maryland and Pennsylvania. At Gettysburg, Pa. (July 1-3), Lee was defeated, and retreated into Virginia, while at Chattanooga, Tenn. (Nov. 24, 25), the Confederates, under Bragg, sustained a severe repulse. Grant made a successful campaign in Tennessee, gaining several battles and capturing Vicksburg, Miss., which, after a gallant defense, surrendered (July 4). In August, the siege of Charleston began, and Fort Sumter was destroyed (August 21, 22), but the city was not taken until 1865 (February 18). With the appointment of Grant as commander-in-chief, in the early part of 1864 (March 3), and his vigorous reorganization of the army, the power of the North was greatly strengthened. Taking the command of the army of the Potomac, Grant opposed the Confederates under Lee, while Sherman operated against Joseph E. Johnston. In the Virginian campaign, after two days' severe fighting (May 3-6) at the Wilderness, the result was indecisive, and Grant's attempt to cut off Lee's army from Richmond was unsuccessful. At Atlanta, Ga., Sherman, in three battles (July 20, 22, 28), defeated the Confederates under Hood. In the Shenandoah valley the Federals were victorious in several engagements (August), and under Sheridan at Winchester (September 9), and Cedar Creek (October 19). In November General Sherman marched through Georgia to Savannah, which was entered December 21, while at Nashville, Tenn., the Confederates under Hood were defeated (December 14-16) by the Federals under Thomas. Among the incidents of this year were the sinking (June 19) by the Federal corvette "Kearsarge" of the Confederate steamer "Alabama," commanded by Captain Semmes, which had caused great devastation among the Federal shipping, and the destruction (August 5), by Admiral Farragut, of the Confederate flotilla at Mobile. The war closed in 1865 by the defeat of Lee at Five Forks, Va. (March 31-April 2), by Sheridan, who again defeated Lee at Sailor's Creek (April 6). Lee subsequently surrendered (April 9) his army to Grant, who had occupied Richmond, the capital of the Confederate States (April 2) on its evacuation by the Southern forces. The other Confederate armies soon afterwards surrendered. An amnesty, with certain limitations, was proclaimed (May 29) by President Andrew Johnson (1865-69), who, as vice-president, succeeded Abraham Lincoln, assassinated in Ford's Theater, Washington, by J. Wilkes Booth (April 14), Lincoln having but newly entered on his second term of office.

Russo-Turkish Wars. Of the many wars between the Muscovite and Mohammedan powers, we cite the two latest: (1) The first arose from a demand on the part of Nicholas, the Czar of Russia, of a protectorate over the Greek Christians in Turkey. The Sultan refused the demand, and appealed to his allies. Russia declared war against Turkey, November 1, 1853. England and France declared war against Russia, March 27, 28,

1854. Sardinia joined the allies, January 26, 1855. Among the great battles of this war were Alma (September 20, 1854), Balaklava (October 25, 1854), during which occurred the memorable "Charge of the Six Hundred." Inkerman (November 5, 1854), Tchernaya (August 16, 1855), in all of which the Russians were defeated. The great event of the war was the siege of Sebastopol (commenced October 17, 1854), which fell September 8, 1855. The war which is usually termed the Crimean war, was ended by the treaty of peace concluded at Paris, March 30, 1856. One of the articles of this treaty was that the Christians of Turkey, without any preference to Russia, should have the protection of all the Powers concerned in the treaty. (2) The second war arose (1877-8) from substantially the same cause as the war of 1853-6, viz., the desire of Russia to protect the Greek Christians of Turkey. By a protocol of March 31, 1877, the Great Powers agreed to see the promised reforms of Turkey carried out. This protocol was repudiated by Turkey, and war was declared by Russia against Turkey, April 24. Among the more prominent events of this war were General Gourko's march through the Balkans (July 13), his defeat by Suleiman Pasha at Eski Sagra (July 30), and Suleiman Pasha's desperate, but fruitless, attempt to gain the Schipka Pass, held by General Gourko; the fall of Kars (November 18), and of Plevna (December 10), and Suleiman Pasha's defeat by Skobeloff and Radetsky at Senova (January 9, 1878), the battle which virtually ended the war. Treaty of San Stefano (March 3), modified by treaty of Berlin (July 13), by which Bulgaria was created an automatic and tributary principality, Servia and Roumania were declared independent, and Bosnia and Herzegovina were ordered to be occupied and administered by Austria.

Zulu War (1879). Cetewayo, king of Zululand, became embroiled with the British, on the annexation by the latter of the Transvaal and the British, under Lord Chelmsford, crossed the Tugela, and entered Zululand (January 12). They suffered a terrible reverse at Isandhlwana (January 22), with a loss of eight hundred men, and, in spite of the heroic defense of Rorke's Drift (January 22), had to retreat. Eventually reinforcements arrived, and the Zulus were defeated at Ginghilono (April 2), and Ulundi (July 4). Cetewayo was captured (August 28), and a dispatch from Sir Garnet Wolseley (September 3) announced the end of the war. Cetewayo died (February 8, 1884), the New Republic was formed by a party of Transvaal Boers (1886-87), and the annexation of the remainder of Zululand as a British possession wa[s] proclaimed (June 21, 1887). Trouble subsequently arose, and several Zulu chiefs wer[e] convicted of high treason and sentenced t[o] various terms of imprisonment (1888-9). Towards the end of 1891, the resolution of th[e] colonial authorities to impose Zibebu as chie[f] upon the northern tribes, was protested agains[t] by Miss Colenso as likely to lead to furthe[r] troubles in Zululand.

Franco-German War. The frictio[n] between France and Prussia, arising from th[e] proposed cession of Luxembourg, became accentuated by the demand of France that th[e] Crown of Spain, offered (1870) to Prince Leopold of Hohenzollern, should not be accepted by that Prince. On the refusal of Prussia t[o] accede to this request, war was declared by France (July 19, 1870). The Prussian forces, about 640,000 strong, in which were associated the states of the North and South German Confederation, were divided into four armies, the first, that of the North, commanded by General Vogel von Falkenstein; the second, that of the Center, commanded by General Steinmetz; the third, that of the Right, under Prince Frederick Charles, and the fourth, that of the Left, led by the Crown Prince, the King (William) of Prussia being commander-in-chief, with General Von Moltke as head of the staff. The whole army was in the highest state of preparation and efficiency.

The French army, about 300,000 strong, on the other hand, badly organized and practically unprepared for the contest, was formed into six army corps, respectively commanded by Generals Frossard, De Failly, Bazaine, MacMahon, Ladniérault and Marshal Canrobert. The Emperor, nominally commander-in-chief, had as his second in command, General Le Bœuf, to whom, later, Marshal Bazaine succeeded. The war resulted in an almost unbroken series of successes for the Germans. After victories at Woerth and Forbach (both on August 6), the Germans invested the fortress of Strasburg (August 10—capitulated September 28), and sat down before Metz, which capitulated (October 27), after the battles of Longueville (August 14), Mars La Tour (August 16), Gravelotte or Rézonville (August 18), and unsuccessful attempts at a sortie by Marshal Bazaine (August 26 and October 6). At Sedan the French under Marshal MacMahon were hopelessly beaten (September 1), and the Emperor surrendered to the Prussian king (September 2), and was deported as prisoner to Wilhelmshöhe (Cassel). At Paris (September 4) the deposition of the Imperial dynasty was declared, and the establishment of a *Republic* proclaimed by M. Gambetta and other members of the Left in the Legislative Assembly. A government of defense was proclaimed, with General Trochu as President, M. Gambetta as Minister of the Interior, M. Jules Favre (Foreign), General Le Flo (War). The Empress Eugénie fled from Paris (September 4), and settled at Chiselhurst. Negotiations for peace between M. Favre and Count Bismarck ended in failure (September 24), and a proclamation from the Government at Tours was issued calling upon the people "to fight to the bitter end."

The siege of Paris was commenced by the Germans (September 15), and five days later the troops at Versailles surrendered, and the Crown Prince of Prussia occupied the place. A *levée en masse* of all under twenty-five years of age was ordered by the Government (September 23), and all Frenchmen between twenty and twenty-five years were prohibited (September 26) leaving France, those between twenty-one and forty years being organized as a national *garde mobile*. M. Gambetta, escaping by means of a balloon from the beleaguered city (October 7), was appointed by the government at Tours, Minister of War.

An attempt on the part of the Red Republicans at Paris, headed by Blanqui, Lédru-Rollin, and others to establish a Commune in that city, was successfully defeated (October 14). The news of the capitulation of Metz caused riots at Paris (October 31). As the result of a *plébiscite* to confirm the powers of the Government of Defense, the votes recorded were 557,976 for, 62,638 against. The successes of the German arms continued, the army of the Loire was defeated by the Grand Duke of Mecklenburg (November 17), the fortresses of Verdun (November 8) and Thionville (November 27) capitulated. The army of the Loire under General Chanzy was again attacked and defeated at Beaugency (December 8). After various battles, the army of the Loire, fighting and retreating, was defeated by Prince Frederick Charles at Le Mans (January 11, 1871), and near Vosges (January 15, 16).

The army under General de Paladines, intrenched at Orleans, suffered defeat by Prince Frederick Charles (December 4), and Orleans surrendered, Rouen being two days later occupied by General Manteuffel, who engaged the army of the North under General Faidherbe at Pointe à Noyelles (December 23), and at Bapaume (January 2, 3, 1871), the French retreating in each case. General Bourbaki was also defeated by the German general Von Werder, near Belfort (January 15-17), and General Von Goeben gained a victory over the French under Faidherbe at St. Quentin (January 19). After gallant but unsuccessful sorties from Paris by Generals Trochu and Ducrot (November 20 and January 21), the city, which had been bombarded, capitulated (January 28). Following the fall of Paris, General Bourbaki's army was defeated (January 30-February 1) by the Germans under General Manteuffel, and driven across the frontier into Switzerland. The fortress of Belfort capitulated (February 16) with military honors after a long defense. An armistice took place preparatory to negotiations for peace. On the resignation of M. Gambetta a National Assembly was elected (February 8) of which M. Grévy was chosen president, M. Thiers becoming head of the executive power. The French Government was recognized by the chief European powers (February 18), and (February 26) preliminaries of peace were signed by MM. Thiers and Favre and fifteen delegates of the National Assembly on the part of France, and Count Bismarck on the part of Germany. By this France was to cede certain parts of Lorraine, including Metz and Thionville and Alsace, excluding Belfort. In addition, five milliards of francs ($1,000,000,000) were to be paid as war indemnity to Germany; certain departments to be occupied by German troops until this was fully discharged. The treaty, signed February 26, was accepted by the National Assembly sitting at Bordeaux (March 1), by 546 votes to 107, at the same time unanimously confirming the fall of the Empire. The Germans, after occupying Paris for forty-eight hours (March 1-3), withdrew from Versailles (March 12). A Peace Conference met at Brussels (March 28), and at Frankfort a definite treaty of peace was signed (May 10), and ratified by the French Assembly (May 21). The last installment of the indemnity was paid September 5, 1873, and the last of the German troops quitted French soil (September 16). The Red Republicans under the lead of Blanqui, Gustav Flourens, and Felix Pyat rose in revolt (March 18, 1871) against the Government, held Paris and established the Commune, which was not suppressed until the insurgents had committed many outrages and destroyed much property, after holding possession of Paris until May 28, when the troops under Marshal MacMahon captured the city; some eight hundred troops were killed, the Communist forces losing fifty thousand. One fourth of Paris was destroyed, the loss to property being estimated at $160,000,000. Great numbers of the Communists were subsequently tried, some executed, and the remainder transported. Since this period France has enjoyed a respite from martial dissensions, though the temper of the people is a continual menace to stability of rule.

Philippine War.—The Philippine Islands, an archipelago in the Pacific Ocean, southeast of Asia, separated by the China sea from China and the Indo-Chinese peninsula, became a possession of the United States in 1899, in accordance with terms of the treaty of Paris of that year, arranging peace between the governments of the United States and Spain. These islands, said to exceed 1,400 in number, had been under Spanish dominion for centuries, since their discovery by Magellan in 1521. The Bay of Manila, upon which is located the city of the same name, the capital of the islands, was the scene of the first engagement in the Spanish-American War, the American squadron on the Asiatic station, under command of Commodore Dewey (now Admiral), attacking and destroying the Spanish squadron, commanded by Admiral Montijo in the morning of May 1, 1898. At the close of the war the islands were ceded to the United States, as agreed on in the peace negotiations, in consideration of the payment to Spain of the sum of $20,000,000. The natives of the islands, known as Filipinos, had been for some time in rebellion against Spain when the war began, their principal grievance being against the religious orders, which, it was alleged, used their power with the Spanish authorities to extort money and gain absolute power over the natives of the islands. Having signed a compact with the Philippine authorities, accepting promises of reform and a large sum of money, twenty of the leaders of the revolution surrendered and took up their abode in Hong Kong. The insurrection, however, continued, and when Admiral Dewey destroyed the Spanish fleet, a large number of armed Tagalogs surrounded Manila. Aguinaldo and his chieftains in Hong Kong, taking advantage of the presence of the American squadron, were eager to return to the islands as friendly allies of the Americans. Consul-General Wildman, of Hong Kong, and Consul-General Pratt, of Singapore, were visited by the insurgent chieftains and it was arranged with Admiral Dewey to permit Aguinaldo and the chieftains to return to the Philippines aboard the American ships. Dewey was without land support, the American force not having arrived, and it was deemed expedient to establish friendly relations with the Filipino army laying siege to the blockaded port. Under promise that Aguinaldo would place his forces under command of the American admiral and generals, Consul-General Wildman placed the insurgent leader and his suite aboard an American vessel one week after the naval battle of Manila harbor. The insurgents were permitted to try to land arms and soon had a formidable force in the field, taking some seven thousand Spanish prisoners and occupying most of the territory outside of Manila, establishing a dictatorial government and assuming a national independence. When the terms of peace with Spain were made known to the Philippine people and American sovereignty was declared over the archipelago, Aguinaldo and the Filipino leaders demanded the recognition of the Filipino Republic, the repulsion of the friars, and asked for American naval protection. For months the tension between the American forces under Generals Green, Merritt, and Otis and the Filipino army had grown until the smoldering hostility culminated in the outbreak of February 4, 1899. Aguinaldo proclaimed war against the United States, and a battle occurred with terrible loss to the Filipinos, their main forces being driven back several miles from Manila.

The principal events of the struggle which followed, ending with the pacification of the islands and the substitution of civil for military control, were frequently sharp and decisive, though more often must be characterized as mere gunning expeditions.

The war had become a desultory contest, with guerrillas in the less accessible parts of the islands, in 1901. The Federal party, organized among the Filipinos late in 1900 to favor American rule, petitioned Congress in January to authorize the President to establish civil government in the Philippines. Aguinaldo was captured on March 23, and took the oath of allegiance on April 2. Municipal civil government was established at Manila, May 3. On June 21 President McKinley promulgated an order establishing civil government in the islands and appointed Judge William H. Taft Governor. The civil government was inaugurated at Manila with imposing ceremonies on July 4. On the same date Major-General MacArthur turned over the military authority to his successor, Major-General Chaffee. In his annual report to the War Department, dated July 4, 1901. General MacArthur stated that between May 5, 1900, and June 30, 1901, there were 1,026 meetings between American troops and insurgents, with the following casualties: Americans killed, 245; wounded, 490; captured, 118, missing, 20. Insurgents killed, 2,854; wounded, 1,193; captured, 6,572; surrendered, 23,095.

The pacification of the Philippines was declared complete during the summer of 1902, and President Roosevelt formally declared the restoration of peace, issuing at the same time, on July 4, a proclamation extending general amnesty to the insurgents.

The Boer War.— It was on October 11, 1899, that the ultimatum presented to Great Britain by the government at Pretoria expired, and, as no satisfactory answer was received within the limit of time set, the order for the movement of the Boer forces was given. In this letter of ultimatum State Secretary Reitz had enumerated the grievances of the South African Republic against Her Majesty's Government, and had concluded by exacting the following conditions as the only ones under which a continuance of peace would be possible:—

The Ultimatum.—(*a*) That all points of mutual differences shall be regulated by the friendly course of arbitration or by whatever amicable way may be agreed upon by this Government with Her Majesty's Government.

(*b*) That the troops on the borders of this Republic shall be instantly withdrawn.

(*c*) That all reinforcements of troops which have arrived in South Africa since June 1, 1899, shall be removed from South Africa within a reasonable time to be agreed upon with this Government, and with the mutual assurance and guarantee on the part of this Government that no attack upon or hostilities against any portion of the possessions of the British Government shall be made by the Republic during further negotiations within the period of time to be subsequently agreed upon between the governments, and this Government will, on compliance therewith, be prepared to withdraw the armed burghers of this Republic from the borders.

(*d*) That Her Majesty's troops which are now on the high seas shall not be landed in any portion of South Africa.

Great Britain's failure to accept these conditions left no alternative but the immediate declaration of war, and on October 10, 1899, the proclamation of martial law in both the South African Republic and the Orange Free State was issued. Hostilities began on the 11th, when the Boer forces invaded Natal, and the chief events of the war which followed were:—

The Diary of The War.

1899.

Oct. 12. Great Britain replies to Boer ultimatum. Mr. Conyngham Greene leaves Pretoria. Mafeking isolated.
13. Mafeking armored train disaster. First reconnoissance from Ladysmith.
14. Newcastle abandoned.
18. Action near Acton Homes. Militia called out.
20. Battle of Glencoe.
21. Battle of Elandslaagte.
23. Sortie from Mafeking. Death of General Symons.
24. Boers defeated by General White at Rietfontein, near Ladysmith.
27. Sorties from Mafeking and Ladysmith.
30. Battle of Farquhar's Farm. Surrender at Nicholson's Nek.

Oct. 31. General Sir Redvers Buller arrives at Cape Town.

Nov. 1. Fighting near Colenso. Boers invade Cape Colony.
2. Ladysmith besieged.
3. Colenso evacuated. Proclamation of martial law in Northern Cape Colony.
5. Boers destroy the bridges over the Orange River.
6. Bombardment of Ladysmith commences.
14. Burghersdorp occupied by the Boers.
23. Victory of Belmont.
25. Battle of Enslin.
28. Battle of Modder River.

Dec. 10. General Gatacre's reverse at Stormberg. Disaster at Magersfontein. Death of Gen. Wauchope.
15. General Sir Redvers Buller repulsed on the Tugela.
16. Lord Roberts appointed Commander-in-Chief in South Africa, with Lord Kitchener as Chief of Staff.

1900.

Jan. 2. Colonel Pilcher defeats Boers at Sunnyside
6. Attack on Ladysmith repulsed.
23. Spion Kop captured.
25. Spion Kop abandoned.

Feb. 5. General Sir Redvers Buller crosses the Tugela.
7. Lord Roberts and Lord Kitchener leave Cape Town for Modder River.
11. Lord Roberts commences the Kimberley relief movement.
15. Magersfontein and Spytfontein evacuated. Boers capture a British convoy. Relief of Kimberley.
20. Lord Roberts defeats Boers at Paardeberg.
22. Severe fighting at Grobler's Kloof.
27. General Cronje surrenders to Lord Roberts. General Sir Redvers Buller captures Pieters Hill.
28. Relief of Ladysmith.

March 5. General Gatacre occupies Stormberg.
7. Lord Roberts defeats Boers at Poplar Grove.
10. Lord Roberts defeats Boers at Driefontein.
13. Lord Roberts occupies Bloemfontein.
27. Death of General Joubert.
31. Koorn Spruit disaster.

May 17–18. Relief of Mafeking.
28. Orange Free State annexed.
30. Mr. Kruger leaves Pretoria.

June 5. Occupation of Pretoria.
12. Lord Roberts defeats General Botha at Diamond Hill.

July 4. Lord Roberts and General Buller meet at Vlakfontein.
11. Surrender of Scots Greys and Lincolns at Uitval's Nek.

Oct. 25. Formal annexation of the Transvaal.

Nov. 6. Defeat of De Wet at Bothaville.
23. Dewetsdorp garrison captured by De Wet.
29. Lord Kitchener becomes Commander-in-Chief in South Africa.

Dec. 11. Lord Roberts sails from Cape Town for England.
13. General De la Rey defeats General Clements at Nooitgedacht. Mishap at Zastron.
16. Boer raid into Cape Colony.
29. Surrender of Liverpools at Helvetia.

1901.

Jan. 3. Action with General Botha at Lindley.
18. Defeat of General De la Rey near Ventersburg.

Feb. 28. Lord Kitchener confers with General Botha.

March 16. General Botha breaks off negotiations.

May 29. General De la Rey defeated by General Dixon at Vlakfontein.

July 20. Death of Mrs. Kruger at Pretoria.

Aug. 6. Lord Kitchener's Boer leader banishment proclamation.

Sept. 17. Major Gough's force surrenders near Utrecht.

Oct. 8. Martial law proclaimed throughout Cape Colony.
9. Commandant Scheepers's commando defeated by Colonel Atherton and Major Kavanagh.
11. Commandant Lotter sentenced to death and executed.
12. Commandant Scheepers captured.
16. Boers reach Saldanha Bay.

Oct. 23. General Sir Redvers Buller relieved of his command.
Dec. 10. General Bruce Hamilton defeats Boers at Trichardsfontein.
16. Commandant Kritzinger captured.
25. Yeomanry rushed by Boers at Tweefontein under De Wet.

1902.
Jan. 8. General Elliott engages General De Wet near Heilbron.
17. Commandant Scheepers executed.
26. Commandant Ben Viljoen captured.
30. Colonel Price defeats Commandants Wessels and Besters at Klaarfontein.
Feb. 3. Colonel Byng defeats Commandant De Wet near Reitz.
5. Major Leader defeats Boers near Klerksdorp.
10. Attack on convoy near Fraserburg.
16. Engagement with Commandant De Wet at Tronmel.
18. Scots Greys cut off near Heidelberg.
23. Engagement of Colonel Byng's outposts; New Zealanders' heavy loss.
26. Convoy captured by Boers near Klerksdorp.
27. Great Boer drive, Harrismith line; 600 killed or captured.
March 7. Lord Methuen's force and five guns captured by General De la Rey. Lord Methuen wounded.
13. Lord Methuen released and sent to Klerksdorp.
18. General Emmett and Commandant Celliers captured.
23. Mr. Schalk Burger, Mr. Reitz, and Commandants Lucas Meyer and Krogh arrive at Pretoria as peace delegates.
31. General Kitchener defeats General De la Rey near the Hart River.
April 7. Commandant Kritzinger acquitted.
10. Boer leaders in conference at Klerksdorp.
12. Boer peace delegates arrive at Pretoria.
18. Peace delegates leave Pretoria to consult the commandoes.
30. Capture of Commandant Maurice Botha near Frankfort.
May 7. Ookiep relieved.
8. Armored train derailed near Pretoria.
15. Peace delegates confer at Vereeniging.
18. Boer delegates conclude conference at Vereeniging and go to Pretoria.

The Terms of Peace.— On May 31, 1902, the terms of peace were signed at Pretoria. They were as follows: —

(1) The burgher forces in the field will forthwith lay down their arms, hand over all guns, army rifles, and munitions of war in their possession or under their control, and desist from any further resistance to the authority of His Majesty King Edward VII., whom they recognize as their lawful sovereign.

(2) All burghers in the field outside the limits of the Transvaal and Orange River Colony and all prisoners of war at present outside South Africa will, on duly acclaiming their acceptance of the position as subjects of His Majesty the King, be brought back to their homes as soon as transport can be provided and their means of subsistence assured.

(3) Burghers so surrendering or so returning will not be deprived of their personal liberty or their property.

(4) No proceedings, civil or criminal, will be taken against any of the burghers surrendering or so returning for any acts in connection with the prosecution of the war. The benefit of this clause will not extend to certain acts contrary to the usages of war.

(5) The Dutch language will be taught in schools when the parents of the children desire, and will be allowed in the courts of law when necessary.

(6) Possession of rifles will be allowed in the Transvaal and Orange River Colony to persons requiring them for their protection, on obtaining licenses according to law.

(7) The military administration of the two colonies will at the earliest possible date be succeeded by civil government, and as soon as circumstances admit, representative institutions leading up to self-government will be introduced. The question of granting the franchise to rebels will not be decided until after the introduction of self-government.

(8) No special tax will be imposed on landed property in the Transvaal or Orange River Colony to pay the expenses of the war.

(9) As soon as circumstances permit, a commission, on which the local inhabitants will be represented, will be appointed in each district in the Transvaal and Orange River Colony for the purposes of restoration of the people to their homes and supplying those who, owing to war losses, are unable to provide themselves with food, shelter, and the necessary amount of seed, stock, implements, etc., indispensable to the resumption of their normal occupation.

(10) For this purpose the commissioners will be placed by His Majesty's Government in the possession of £3,000,000.

In addition to the above named grant of £3,000,000 His Majesty's Government will be prepared to make advances on loan for the same purpose, free of interest for two years, and afterward to be repayable over a period of years at 3 per cent. interest. No foreigner or rebel will be entitled to share in the benefits of this clause.

CIVIL LISTS OF EUROPEAN SOVEREIGNS.

Austria-Hungary, Emperor of, $3,875,000.
Bavaria, King of, $1,412,000.
Belgium, King of, $660,000.
Denmark, King of, $227,775; and Crown Prince, $33,330.
Greece, King of, $260,000, including $20,000 a year each from Great Britain, France, and Russia.
Italy, King of, $2,858,000, of which $180,000 for family.
Netherlands, King of, $250,000, also a large revenue from domains, and $62,500 for royal family, courts, and palaces.
Norway and Sweden, King of, $575,525.
Portugal, King of, $634,440.
Prussia, King of, $3,852,770; also a vast amount of private property, castles, forests, and estates.
Russia, Czar of, has private estates of more than 1,000,000 square miles of cultivated land and forests, besides gold and other mines in Siberia. The annual income has been estimated at about $12,000,000.
Spain, King of, $1,400,000, besides $600,000 for family.
Würtemberg, King of, $449,050.

PRESIDENTS OF THE UNITED STATES.

No.	Presidents.	Born.		Parents.		Term of Office.	
		Date.	Birthplace.	Father.	Mother.	From	To
1	Washington.	Feb. $\frac{11}{22}$, 1732	Bridges Creek, Va....	Augustine....	Mary Ball...........	Apr. 30, 1789	Mar. 4, 1797
2	Adams, John	Oct. $\frac{19}{30}$, 1735	Braintree, Mass.......	John..........	Susanna Boylston.....	Mar. 4, 1797	Mar. 4, 1801
3	Jefferson....	Apr. $\frac{2}{13}$, 1743	Shadwell, Va..........	Peter.........	Jane Randolph........	Mar. 4, 1801	Mar. 4, 1809
4	Madison.....	Mar. $\frac{5}{16}$, 1751	Port Conway, Va......	James.........	Nellie Conway........	Mar. 4, 1809	Mar. 4, 1817
5	Monroe......	Apr. 28, 1758	Westmoreland Co., Va.	Spence.......	Elizabeth Jones.......	Mar. 4, 1817	Mar. 4, 1825
6	Adams, J. Q.	July 11, 1767	Quincy, Mass..........	John..........	Abigail Smith..........	Mar. 4, 1825	Mar. 4, 1829
7	Jackson.....	Mar. 15, 1767	Mecklenburg Co., N.C.	Andrew......	Elizabeth Hutchinson	Mar. 4, 1829	Mar. 4, 1837
8	Van Buren..	Dec. 5, 1782	Kinderhook, N. Y....	Abraham.....	Mary Hoes...........	Mar. 4, 1837	Mar. 4, 1841
9	Harrison, W.	Feb. 9, 1773	Berkeley, Va.........	Benjamin....	Elizabeth Bassett.....	Mar. 4, 1841	Apr. 4, 1841
10	Tyler........	Mar. 29, 1790	Charles City Co., Va.	John..........	Mary Armistead......	Apr. 6, 1841	Mar. 4, 1845
11	Polk.........	Nov. 2, 1795	Mecklenburg Co., N.C.	Samuel.......	Jane Knox...........	Mar. 4, 1845	Mar. 4, 1849
12	Taylor.......	Nov. 24, 1784	Orange Co., Va.......	Richard......	Sarah Strother.......	Mar. 4, 1849	July 10, 1850
13	Fillmore.....	Jan. 7, 1800	Summer Hill, N. Y....	Nathaniel....	Phebe Millard........	July 10, 1850	Mar. 4, 1853
14	Pierce.......	Nov. 23, 1804	Hillsborough, N. H...	Benjamin....	Anna Kendrick.......	Mar. 4, 1853	Mar. 4, 1857
15	Buchanan...	Apr. 23, 1791	Stony Batter, Pa......	James.........	Elizabeth Speer.......	Mar. 4, 1857	Mar. 4, 1861
16	Lincoln......	Feb. 12, 1809	Nolin Creek, Ky.......	Thomas.......	Nancy Hanks.........	Mar. 4, 1861	Apr. 15, 1865
17	Johnson.....	Dec. 29, 1808	Raleigh, N. C.........	Jacob.........	Mary McDonnough...	Apr. 15, 1865	Mar. 4, 1869
18	Grant........	Apr. 27, 1822	Point Pleasant, Ohio..	Jesse Root....	Harriet Simpson......	Mar. 4, 1869	Mar. 4, 1877
19	Hayes........	Oct. 4, 1822	Delaware, Ohio.......	Rutherford...	Sophia Birchard......	Mar. 4, 1877	Mar. 4, 1881
20	Garfield......	Nov. 19, 1831	Orange, Ohio..........	Abram........	Eliza Ballou..........	Mar. 4, 1881	Sep. 19, 1881
21	Arthur.......	Oct. 5, 1830	Fairfield, Vt..........	William.......	Malvina Stone........	Sep. 20, 1881	Mar. 4, 1885
22	Cleveland....	Mar. 18, 1837	Caldwell, N. J........	Rich'd Falley.	Anne Neale...........	Mar. 4, 1885	Mar. 4, 1889
23	Harrison, B..	Aug. 20, 1833	North Bend, Ohio.....	John Scott...	Elizabeth F. Irwin....	Mar. 4, 1889	Mar. 4, 1893
24	**Cleveland....**	**Mar. 18, 1837**	**Caldwell, N. J.........**	**Richard F....**	**Anne Neale............**	**Mar. 4, 1893**	**Mar. 4, 1897**
25	McKinley ...	Jan. 29, 1843	Niles, Ohio...........	William......	Nancy C. Allison.....	Mar. 4, 1897	Sep. 14, 1901
26	Roosevelt ...	Oct. 27, 1858	New York City, N. Y..	Theodore	Martha Bullock.......	Sep. 14, 1901	

Biographical Statistics.

	Age.*	Died.			Age.†	Where Buried.
		When.	Where.	Cause.		
Washington..	57	Dec. 14, 1799	Mt. Vernon, Va.........	Acute laryngitis..........	67	Mt. Vernon, Va.
Adams, John.	61	July 4, 1826	Quincy, Mass..............	Natural decline...........	90	Unitarian Church, Quincy, Mass.
Jefferson.....	57	July 4, 1826	Monticello, Va...........	Chronic diarrhœa.........	83	Monticello, Albemarle Co., Va.
Madison......	57	June 28, 1836	Montpelier, Va...........	Natural decline...........	85	Montpelier, Hanover Co., Va.
Monroe.......	58	July 4, 1831	New York City, N. Y....	Natural decline...........	73	Originally 2d Ave. Cemetery, N. Y., transferred, 1858, to Hollywood Cemetery, Richmond, Va.
Adams, J. Q..	57	Feb. 23, 1848	Halls of Congress, Washington, D. C...........	Paralysis..................	80	Unitarian Church, Quincy, Mass.
Jackson.......	61	June 8, 1845	Hermitage, near Nashville, Tenn............	Dropsy	78	Hermitage, near Nashville, Tenn.
Van Buren...	54	July 24, 1862	Kinderhook, N. Y.......	Asthma.....................	79	Village Cemetery, Kinderhook, N. Y.
Harrison.....	68	Apr. 4, 1841	White House, Washington, D. C..........	Pleurisy fever.............	68	North Bend, Ohio.
Tyler.........	51	Jan. 17, 1862	Ballard House, Richmond, Va.............	Bilious attacks, with bronchitis....................	71	Hollywood, Richmond, Va.
Polk..........	49	June 15, 1849	Nashville, Tenn.........	Chronic diarrhœa.........	53	Nashville, Tenn.
Taylor........	64	July 9, 1850	White House, Washington, D. C.............	Cholera morbus and typhoid fever.............	65	Near Louisville, Ky. (Springfield).
Fillmore......	50	Mar. 9, 1874	Buffalo, N. Y...........	Paralysis..................	74	Forest Lawn, Buffalo, N. Y.
Pierce........	48	Oct. 8, 1869	Concord, N. H...........	Dropsy and inflammation of the stomach...........	64	Minot Cemetery, Concord, N. H.
Buchanan....	65	June 1, 1868	Lancaster, Pa...........	Rheumatic gout	77	Woodward Hill Cemetery, Wheatland, Pa.
Lincoln.......	52	Apr. 15, 1865	Washington, D. C.......	Assassinated by Booth....	56	Oak Ridge Cemetery, Springfield, Ill.
Johnson......	56	July 31, 1875	Greeneville, Tenn.......	Paralysis..................	66	Greeneville, Tenn.
Grant	46	July 23, 1885	Mt. McGregor, N. Y.....	Cancer of the tongue.....	63	Riverside, New York City.
Hayes	54	Jan. 17, 1893	Fremont, Ohio...........	Neuralgia of the heart...	71	Fremont, Ohio.
Garfield......	49	Sep. 19, 1881	Elberon, Long Branch, N. J..................	Assassinated by Guiteau..	49	Lake View Cemetery, Cleveland, Ohio.
Arthur.......	50	Nov. 18, 1886	New York, N. Y.........	Bright's disease, culminating in paralysis and apoplexy............	56	Rural Cemetery, Albany, N.Y.
Cleveland....	47					
Harrison.....	55	Mar. 13, 1901	Indianapolis, Ind.......	Pneumonia	67	Crown Hill Cemetery, Indianapolis, Ind.
McKinley....	53	Sep. 14, 1901	Buffalo, N. Y...........	Assassination............	57	Cemetery, Canton, Ohio.

*** Upon accession to office.** **† At death.**

Biographical Statistics (*Continued*).

	Educational Advantages.	Profession.	Early Vocation.	Ancestry.	Father's Business.	Religious Connection.*
Washington	Common school	Planter	Surveyor	English	Planter	Episcopalian.
Adams	Harvard College, 1755	Lawyer	Teacher	English	Farmer	Unitarian.
Jefferson	College William and Mary, 1762	Lawyer	Lawyer	Welsh	Planter	Liberal.
Madison	Princeton College, 1771	Lawyer	Lawyer	English	Planter	Episcopalian.
Monroe	Entered College William and Mary	Politician	Lawyer	Scotch	Planter	Episcopalian.
Adams, J. Q.	Harvard College, 1787	Lawyer	Lawyer	English	Lawyer	Unitarian.
Jackson	Self-taught	Lawyer	Lawyer	Scotch-Irish	Farmer	Presbyterian.
Van Buren	Academy	Lawyer	Lawyer	Dutch	Farmer	Dutch Reformed.
Harrison, W.	Entered Hampden-Sydney College	Army	Medicine	English	Statesman	Episcopalian.
Tyler	College William and Mary, 1806	Lawyer	Lawyer	English	Jurist	Episcopalian.
Polk	University of North Carolina	Lawyer	Lawyer	Scotch-Irish	Farmer	Presbyterian.
Taylor	Common school	Army	Soldier	English	Planter	Episcopalian.
Fillmore	Public school	Lawyer	Tailor	English	Farmer	Episcopalian.
Pierce	Bowdoin College, 1824	Lawyer	Lawyer	English	Farmer	Episcopalian.
Buchanan	Dickinson College, 1809	Lawyer	Lawyer	Scotch-Irish	Merchant	Presbyterian.
Lincoln	Self-taught	Lawyer	Farmer	English	Farmer	Liberal.
Johnson	Self-taught	Politician	Tailor	English	Sexton	Liberal.
Grant	West Point Military Academy, 1843	Army	Tanner	Scotch	Tanner	Methodist.
Hayes	Kenyon College, O., 1842	Lawyer	Lawyer	Scotch	Merchant	Methodist.
Garfield	Williams College, 1856	Lawyer	Teacher	English	Farmer	Disciples.
Arthur	Union College, 1848	Lawyer	Teacher	Scotch-Irish	Clergyman	Episcopalian.
Cleveland	Common school	Lawyer	Teacher	English	Clergyman	Presbyterian.
Harrison, B.	Miami University, O., 1851	Lawyer	Lawyer	English	Farmer	Presbyterian.
McKinley	Entered Allegheny College	Lawyer	Lawyer	Scotch-Irish	Iron Mfr.	Methodist.
Roosevelt	Harvard	Public Official	Publicist	Dutch	Merchant	Dutch Reformed.

* Adams married a minister's daughter, and was inclined to Unitarianism. Jefferson was not a believer, at least while he was Chief Magistrate. Madison's early connections were Presbyterian. Monroe is said to have favored the Episcopal Church. John Quincy Adams was like his father. Jackson was a Presbyterian and died in the communion of that church. Van Buren was brought up in the Reformed Dutch Church, but afterward inclined to the Episcopal Church. Harrison leaned toward the Methodist Church, and Tyler was an Episcopalian. Polk was baptized by a Methodist preacher after his term of office expired. Taylor was inclined to the Episcopal communion. Fillmore attended the Unitarian Church, and Franklin Pierce was a member, but not a communicant, of a Congregationalist Church at Concord. Buchanan was a Presbyterian, as was also Benjamin Harrison. General Grant attended the Methodist Church, and President Garfield the Church of the Disciples. President McKinley was a member of the Methodist Church. Roosevelt attends the Dutch Reformed Church.

Biographical Statistics (*Continued*).

	Married.			Children.		Wife.	
	Date.	To Whom.	Where.	Boys.	Girls.	Birthplace.	Date.
Washington	Jan. 17, 1759	Mrs. Martha Custis	Williamsburg, Va.	0	0	New Kent Co., Va.	May, 1732
Adams, John	Oct. 25, 1764	Abigail Smith	Weymouth, Mass.	3	2	Weymouth, Mass.	Nov. 11/22, 1744
Jefferson	Jan. 1, 1772	Mrs. Martha Skelton	The Forest, Va.	0	6	Charles C. Co., Va.	Oct. 8/19, 1748
Madison	Oct. 1794	Mrs. Dorothy Todd	Harewood, Va.	0	0	North Carolina	May 20, 1772
Monroe	Feb. 23, 1786	Eliza Kortwright	New York, N. Y.	0	2	New York, N. Y.	1768
Adams, J. Q.	July 26, 1797	Louisa C. Johnson	London, Eng.	3	1	London, Eng.	Feb. 11, 1775
Jackson	Jan. 1791	Mrs. Rachel Robards	Natchez, Miss.	3	0	....	1767
Van Buren	Feb. 1807	Hannah Hoes (Goes)	Kinderhook, N. Y.	4	0	Kinderhook, N. Y.	Mar. 8, 1783
Harrison	Nov. 22, 1795	Anna Symmes	North Bend, Ohio	6	4	Morristown, N. J.	July 25, 1775
Tyler	Mar. 29, 1813	Letitia Christian	Cedar Grove, Va.	3	4	Cedar Grove, Va.	Nov. 12, 1790
	June 26, 1844	Julia Gardiner	New York City, N. Y.	4	2	East Hampton, N. Y.	1820
Polk	Jan. 1, 1824	Sarah Childress	Murfreesboro, Tenn.	0	0	Murfreesboro, Tenn.	Sept. 4, 1803
Taylor	1810	Margaret Smith	Near Louisville, Ky.	1	3	Calvert Co., Md.	1790
Fillmore	Feb. 5, 1826	Abigail Power	Moravia, N. Y.	1	1	Stillwater, N. Y.	Mar. 13, 1798
	Feb. 18, 1858	Mrs. Caroline McIntosh	Albany, N. Y.	0	0	....	Oct. 21, 1813
Pierce	Nov. 19, 1834	Jane Means Appleton	Amherst, N. H.	3	0	Hampton, N. H.	Mar. 12, 1806
Buchanan	....	Unmarried	....	...	...	....	Unmarried.
Lincoln	Nov. 4, 1842	Mary Todd	Lexington, Ky.	4	0	Lexington, Ky.	Dec. 12, 1818
Johnson	May 17, 1827	Eliza McCardle	Greenville, Tenn.	3	2	Leesburg, Tenn.	Oct. 4, 1810
Grant	Aug. 22, 1848	Julia Dent	St. Louis, Mo.	3	1	St. Louis, Mo.	Jan. 26, 1826
Hayes	Dec. 30, 1852	Lucy Ware Webb	Cincinnati, Ohio	7	1	Chillicothe, Ohio	Aug. 28, 1831
Garfield	Nov. 11, 1858	Lucretia Rudolph	Hiram, Ohio	4	1	Hiram, Ohio	Apr. 19, 1832
Arthur	Oct. 29, 1859	Ellen Lewis Herndon	New York, N. Y.	1	1	Culpeper C. H., Va.	Aug. 30, 1837
Cleveland	June 2, 1886	Frances Folsom	Washington, D. C.	1	3	Buffalo, N. Y.	July 21, 1864
Harrison	Oct. 20, 1853	Caroline Lavinia Scott	Oxford, Ohio	1	1	Oxford, Ohio	Oct. 1, 1832
McKinley	Jan. 25, 1871	Ida Saxton	Canton, Ohio	0	2	Canton, Ohio	June 8, 1847
Roosevelt	1883 and 1886	Alice Lee & Edith Carow	....	4	2	....	....

VICE-PRESIDENTS OF THE UNITED STATES.

	Name.	Birthplace.	Year.	Paternal Ancestry.	Residence.	Qualified.	Politics.	Place of Death.	Year.	Age at Death.
1	John Adams.........	Quincy, Mass.........	1735	English......	Mass.	1789	Fed..	Quincy, Mass.........	1826	90
2	Thomas Jefferson....	Shadwell, Va...........	1743	Welsh........	Va...	1797	Rep..	Monticello, Va.........	1826	83
3	Aaron Burr.........	Newark, N. J..........	1756	English......	N. Y.	1801	Rep..	Staten Island, N. Y...	1836	80
4	George Clinton.......	Ulster Co., N. Y.......	1739	English......	N. Y.	1805	Rep..	Washington, D. C....	1812	73
5	Elbridge Gerry.......	Marblehead, Mass.....	1744	English......	Mass.	1813	Rep..	Washington, D. C.....	1814	70
6	Daniel D. Tompkins..	Scarsdale, N. Y........	1774	English......	N. Y.	1817	Rep..	Staten Island, N. Y...	1825	51
7	John C. Calhoun.....	Abbeville, S. C........	1782	Scotch-Irish.	S. C..	1825	Rep..	Washington, D. C.....	1850	68
8	Martin Van Buren...	Kinderhook, N. Y.....	1782	Dutch........	N. Y.	1833	Dem.	Kinderhook, N. Y.....	1862	79
9	Richard M. Johnson.	Louisville, Ky..........	1780	English......	Ky...	1837	Dem.	Frankfort, Ky..........	1850	70
10	John Tyler...........	Greenway, Va..........	1790	English......	Va...	1841	Dem.	Richmond, Va.........	1862	72
11	George M. Dallas.....	Philadelphia, Pa......	1792	English......	Pa...	1845	Dem.	Philadelphia, Pa......	1864	72
12	Millard Fillmore.....	Summerhill, N. Y......	1800	English......	N. Y.	1849	Whig	Buffalo, N. Y...........	1874	74
13	William R. King.....	Sampson Co., N. C....	1786	English......	Ala..	1853	Dem.	Dallas Co., Ala........	1853	67
14	John C. Breckinridge	Lexington, Ky.........	1821	Scotch.......	Ky...	1857	Dem.	Lexington, Ky..........	1875	54
15	Hannibal Hamlin....	Paris, Me..............	1809	English......	Me...	1861	Rep..	Bangor, Me.............	1891	81
16	Andrew Johnson.....	Raleigh, N. C..........	1808	English......	Tenn.	1865	Rep..	Carter Co., Tenn......	1875	66
17	Schuyler Colfax......	New York city, N. Y...	1823	English......	Ind..	1869	Rep..	Mankato, Minn.........	1885	62
18	Henry Wilson.........	Farmington, N. H.....	1812	English......	Mass.	1873	Rep..	Washington, D. C.....	1875	63
19	William A. Wheeler..	Malone, N. Y...........	1819	English......	N. Y.	1877	Rep..	Malone, N. Y...........	1887	68
20	Chester A. Arthur....	Fairfield, Vt...........	1830	Scotch-Irish.	N. Y.	1881	Rep..	New York city, N. Y..	1886	56
21	Thos. A. Hendricks..	Muskingum Co., Ohio.	1819	Scotch-Irish.	Ind..	1885	Dem.	Indianapolis, Ind.....	1885	66
22	Levi P. Morton......	Shoreham, Vt..........	1824	Scotch.......	N. Y.	1889	Rep..	....	....	..
23	Adlai E. Stevenson...	Christian Co., Ky.....	1835	Scotch-Irish.	Ill....	1893	Dem.	....	....	..
24	Garret A. Hobart	Long Branch, N. J....	1844	English	N. J..	1897	Rep..	Paterson, N. J.........	1899	55
25	Theodore Roosevelt ..	New York city, N.Y...	1858	Dutch	N. Y.	1901	Rep..	....	....	..

SPEAKERS OF THE U. S. HOUSE OF REPRESENTATIVES.

Congress.	Years.	Name.	State.	Born.	Died.
1	1789-91	F. A. Muhlenburg...	Pa....	1750	1801
2	1791-93	Jonathan Trumbull.	Ct.....	1740	1809
3	1793-95	F. A. Muhlenburg...	Pa....	1750	1801
4, 5	1795-99	Jonathan Dayton ...	N. J...	1760	1824
6	1799-1801	Theo. Sedgwick.....	Mass..	1746	1813
7-9	1801-07	Nathaniel Macon....	N. C..	1757	1837
10, 11	1807-11	Joseph B. Varnum..	Mass..	1750	1821
12, 13	1811-14	Henry Clay..........	Ky....	1777	1852
13	1814-15	Langdon Cheves....	S. C...	1776	1857
14-16	1815-20	Henry Clay..........	Ky....	1777	1852
16	1820-21	John W. Taylor......	N. Y..	1784	1854
17	1821-23	Philip P. Barbour...	Va....	1783	1841
18	1823-25	Henry Clay..........	Ky....	1777	1852
19	1825-27	John W. Taylor......	N. Y..	1784	1854
20-23	1827-34	Andrew Stevenson..	Va....	1784	1857
23	1834-35	John Bell............	Tenn..	1797	1869
24, 25	1835-39	James K. Polk.......	Tenn..	1795	1849
26	1839-41	R. M. T. Hunter.....	Va....	1809	1887
27	1841-43	John White..........	Ky....	1805	1845
28	1843-45	John W. Jones......	Va....	1805	1848
29	1845-47	John W. Davis......	Ind...	1799	1850
30	1847-49	Robert C. Winthrop.	Mass..	1809	1894
31	1849-51	Howell Cobb	Ga....	1815	1868
32, 33	1851-55	Linn Boyd...........	Ky....	1800	1859
34	1855-57	Nathaniel P. Banks.	Mass..	1816	1894
35	1857-59	James L. Orr........	S. C...	1822	1873
36	1859-61	Wm. Pennington....	N. J...	1796	1862
37	1861-63	Galusha A. Grow....	Pa....	1823	....
38-40	1863-69	Schuyler Colfax.....	Ind...	1823	1885
41-43	1869-75	James G. Blaine......	Me....	1830	1893
44	1875-76	Michael C. Kerr.....	Ind...	1827	1876
44-46	1876-81	Samuel J. Randall..	Pa....	1828	1890
47	1881-83	John W. Keifer.....	Ohio..	1836	....
48-50	1883-89	John G. Carlisle.....	Ky....	1835	....
51	1889-91	Thomas B. Reed......	Me.....	1839	1903
52, 53	1891-95	Charles F. Crisp	Ga....	1845	1896
54, 55	1895-99	Thomas B. Reed....	Me....	1839	1903
56, 57	1899-03	David B. Henderson	Ia.....	1840	....
58	1903-	Joseph G. Cannon...	Ill.....	1836	....

PRESIDENTIAL CABINET OFFICERS.

SECRETARIES OF STATE.

Presidents.	Cabinet Officers.	Residence.	Date of Appointment.
Washington.	Thomas Jefferson.......	Va.....	1789
"	Edmund Randolph	"	1794
"	Timothy Pickering	Mass...	1795
Adams.......	" "	" ..	1797
"	John Marshall	Va.....	1800
Jefferson....	James Madison..........	" ..	1801
Madison.....	Robert Smith	Md.....	1809
"	James Monroe	Va.....	1811
Monroe......	John Quincy Adams....	Mass...	1817
J. Q. Adams.	Henry Clay..............	Ky.....	1825
Jackson.....	Martin Van Buren......	N. Y...	1829
"	Edward Livingston.....	La.	1831
"	Louis McLane...........	Del.....	1833
"	John Forsyth	Ga	1834
Van Buren...	" "	"	1837
Harrison	Daniel Webster..........	Mass...	1841
Tyler	" "	"	1841
"	Hugh S. Legaré.........	S. C....	1843
"	Abel P. Upshur	Va.....	1843
"	John C. Calhoun........	S. C....	1844
Polk........	James Buchanan........	Pa......	1845
Taylor.......	John M. Clayton.........	Del.....	1849
Fillmore.....	Daniel Webster..........	Mass...	1850
"	Edward Everett..........	" ...	1852
Pierce......	William L. Marcy,......	N. Y...	1853
Buchanan...	Lewis Cass..............	Mich...	1857
" ...	Jeremiah S. Black......	Pa.....	1860
Lincoln.....	William H. Seward......	N. Y...	1861
Johnson. ...	" " "	" ...	1865
Grant.......	Elihu B. Washburne....	Ill......	1869
"	Hamilton Fish...........	N. Y...	1869
Hayes	William M. Evarts......	" ...	1877
Garfield.....	James G. Blaine........	Me.....	1881
Arthur	F. T. Frelinghuysen	N. J....	1881
Cleveland ...	Thomas F. Bayard......	Del.....	1885
Harrison	James G. Blaine	Me.....	1889
"	John W. Foster..........	Ind.....	1892
Cleveland ...	Walter Q. Gresham.....	Ill......	1893
" ...	Richard Olney..........	Mass...	1895
McKinley....	John Sherman	Ohio...	1897
"	William R. Day.........	Ohio...	1897
"	John Hay	Ohio...	1898

Presidential Cabinet Officers—*Continued.*

SECRETARIES OF THE TREASURY.

Presidents.	Cabinet Officers.	Residence.	Date of Appointment.	Presidents.	Cabinet Officers.	Residence.	Date of Appointment.
Washington.	Alexander Hamilton	N. Y.	1789	Fillmore	Thomas Corwin	Ohio	1850
“	Oliver Wolcott	Ct	1795	Pierce	James Guthrie	Ky	1853
Adams	“	“	1797	Buchanan	Howell Cobb	Ga	1857
“	Samuel Dexter	Mass	1801	“	Philip F. Thomas	Md	1860
Jefferson	“	“	1801	“	John A. Dix	N. Y.	1861
“	Albert Gallatin	Pa	1801	Lincoln	Salmon P. Chase	Ohio	1861
Madison	“	“	1809	“	William P. Fessenden	Me	1864
“	George W. Campbell	Tenn	1814	“	Hugh McCulloch	Ind	1865
“	Alexander J. Dallas	Pa	1814	Johnson	“	“	1865
“	William H. Crawford	Ga	1816	Grant	George S. Boutwell	Mass	1869
Monroe	“	“	1817	“	William A. Richardson	“	1873
J. Q. Adams.	Richard Rush	Pa	1825	“	Benjamin H. Bristow	Ky	1874
Jackson	Samuel D. Ingham	“	1829	“	Lot M. Morrill	Me	1876
“	Louis McLane	Del	1831	Hayes	John Sherman	Ohio	1877
“	William J. Duane	Pa	1833	Garfield	William Windom	Minn	1881
“	Roger B. Taney	Md	1833	Arthur	Charles J. Folger	N. Y.	1881
“	Levi Woodbury	N. H	1834	“	Walter Q. Gresham	Ind	1884
Van Buren	“	“	1837	“	Hugh McCulloch	“	1884
Harrison	Thomas Ewing	Ohio	1841	Cleveland	Daniel Manning	N. Y.	1885
Tyler	“	“	1841	“	Charles S. Fairchild		1887
“	Walter Forward	Pa	1841	Harrison	William Windom	Minn	1889
“	John C. Spencer	N. Y.	1843	“	Charles Foster	Ohio	1891
“	George M. Bibb	Ky	1844	Cleveland	John G. Carlisle	Ky	1893
Polk	Robert J. Walker	Miss	1845	McKinley	Lyman J. Gage	Ill	1897
Taylor	William M. Meredith	Pa	1849	Roosevelt	Leslie M. Shaw	Iowa	1902

SECRETARIES OF WAR.

Presidents.	Cabinet Officers.	Residence.	Date of Appointment.	Presidents.	Cabinet Officers.	Residence.	Date of Appointment.
Washington	Henry Knox	Mass	1789	Taylor	George W. Crawford	Ga	1849
“	Timothy Pickering	“	1795	“	Edward Bates	Mo	1850
“	James McHenry	Md	1796	Fillmore	Charles M. Conrad	La	1850
Adams	“	“	1797	Pierce	Jefferson Davis	Miss	1853
“	John Marshall	Va	1800	Buchanan	John B. Floyd	Va	1857
“	Samuel Dexter	Mass	1800	“	Joseph Holt	Ky	1861
“	Roger Griswold	Ct	1801	Lincoln	Simon Cameron	Pa	1861
Jefferson	Henry Dearborn	Mass	1801	“	Edwin M. Stanton	Ohio	1862
Madison	William Eustis	“	1809	Johnson	“	“	1865
“	John Armstrong	N. Y.	1813	“	U. S. Grant (*ad. in.*)	Ill	1867
“	James Monroe	Va	1814	“	Lor. Thomas (*ad. in.*)	....	1868
“	William H. Crawford	Ga	1815	“	John M. Schofield	N. Y.	1868
Monroe	Isaac Shelby	Ky	1817	Grant	John A. Rawlins	Ill	1869
“	Geo. Graham (*ad. in.*)	Va	1817	“	William T. Sherman	Ohio	1869
“	John C. Calhoun	S. C	1817	“	William W. Belknap	Ia	1869
J. Q. Adams	James Barbour	Va	1825	“	Alphonso Taft	Ohio	1876
“	Peter B. Porter	N. Y.	1828	“	James Don Cameron	Pa	1876
Jackson	John H. Eaton	Tenn	1829	Hayes	George W. McCrary	Ia	1877
“	Lewis Cass	Ohio	1831	“	Alexander Ramsey	Minn	1879
“	Benjamin F. Butler	N. Y.	1837	Garfield	Robert T. Lincoln	Ill	1881
Van Buren	Joel R. Poinsett	S. C	1837	Arthur	“	“	1881
Harrison	John Bell	Tenn	1841	Cleveland	William C. Endicott	Mass	1885
Tyler	“	“	1841	Harrison	Redfield Proctor	Vt	1889
“	John McLean	Ohio	1841	“	Stephen B. Elkins	W. Va.	1891
“	John C. Spencer	N. Y.	1841	Cleveland	Daniel S. Lamont	N. Y.	1893
“	James M. Porter	Pa	1843	McKinley	Russell A. Alger	Mich	1897
“	William Wilkins	“	1844	“	Elihu Root	N. Y.	1899
Polk	William L. Marcy	N. Y.	1845	Roosevelt	W. H. Taft	Ohio	1904

SECRETARIES OF THE NAVY.

Presidents.	Cabinet Officers.	Residence.	Date of Appointment.	Presidents.	Cabinet Officers.	Residence.	Date of Appointment.
Adams	George Cabot	Mass	1798	Tyler	Thomas W. Gilmer	Va	1844
“	Benjamin Stoddert	Md	1798	“	John Y. Mason	“	1844
Jefferson	“	“	1801	Polk	George Bancroft	Mass	1845
“	Robert Smith	“	1801	“	John Y. Mason	Va	1846
“	Jacob Crowninshield	Mass	1805	Taylor	William B. Preston	“	1849
Madison	Paul Hamilton	S. C	1809	Fillmore	William A. Graham	N. C	1850
“	William Jones	Pa	1813	“	John P. Kennedy	Md	1852
“	B. W. Crowninshield	Mass	1814	Pierce	James C. Dobbin	N. C	1853
Monroe	“	“	1817	Buchanan	Isaac Toucey	Ct	1857
“	Smith Thompson	N. Y.	1818	Lincoln	Gideon Welles	“	1861
“	Samuel L. Southard	N. J	1823	Johnson	“	“	1865
J. Q. Adams	“	“	1825	Grant	Adolph E. Borie	Pa	1869
Jackson	John Branch	N. C	1829	“	George M. Robeson	N. J	1869
“	Levi Woodbury	N. H	1831	Hayes	Richard W. Thompson	Ind	1877
“	Mahlon Dickerson	N. J	1834	“	Nathan Goff, Jr.	W. Va.	1881
Van Buren	“	“	1837	Garfield	William H. Hunt	La	1881
“	James K. Paulding	N. Y.	1838	Arthur	William E. Chandler	N. H	1882
Harrison	George E. Badger	N. C	1841	Cleveland	William C. Whitney	N. Y.	1885
Tyler	“	“	1841	Harrison	Benjamin F. Tracy	“	1889
“	Abel P. Upshur	Va	1841	Cleveland	Hilary A. Herbert	Ala	1893
“	David Henshaw	Mass	1843	McKinley	John D. Long	Mass	1897
				Roosevelt	Wm. H. Moody	Mass	1902

Presidential Cabinet Officers.—*Continued.*

POSTMASTERS-GENERAL.*

Presidents.	Cabinet Officers.	Residence.	Date of Appointment.	Presidents.	Cabinet Officers.	Residence.	Date of Appointment.
Washington	Samuel Osgood	Mass	1789	Buchanan	Joseph Holt	Ky	1859
"	Timothy Pickering	"	1791	"	Horatio King	Me	1861
"	Joseph Habersham	Ga	1795	Lincoln	Montgomery Blair	Md	1861
Adams	"	"	1797	"	William Dennison	Ohio	1864
Jefferson	"	"	1801	Johnson	"	"	1865
"	Gideon Granger	Ct	1801	"	Alexander W. Randall	Wis	1866
Madison	"	"	1809	Grant	John A. J. Cresswell	Md	1869
"	Return J. Meigs, Jr.	Ohio	1814	"	James W. Marshall	Va	1874
Monroe	"	"	1817	"	Marshall Jewell	Ct	1874
"	John McLean	"	1823	"	James N. Tyner	Ind	1876
J. Q. Adams	"	"	1825	Hayes	David McK. Key	Tenn	1877
Jackson	William T. Barry	Ky	1829	"	Horace Maynard	"	1880
"	Amos Kendall	"	1835	Garfield	Thomas L. James	N. Y.	1881
Van Buren	"	"	1837	Arthur	Timothy O. Howe	Wis	1881
"	John M. Niles	Ct	1840	"	Walter Q. Gresham	Ind	1883
Harrison	Francis Granger	N. Y.	1841	"	Frank Hatton	Iowa	1884
Tyler	"	"	1841	Cleveland	William F. Vilas	Wis	1885
"	Charles A. Wickliffe	Ky	1841	"	Don M. Dickinson	Mich	1888
Polk	Cave Johnson	Tenn	1845	Harrison	John Wanamaker	Pa	1889
Taylor	Jacob Collamer	Vt	1849	Cleveland	Wilson S. Bissell	N. Y.	1893
Fillmore	Nathan K. Hall	N. Y.	1850	"	William L. Wilson	W. Va.	1895
"	Samuel D. Hubbard	Ct	1852	McKinley	James A. Gary	Md	1897
Pierce	James Campbell	Pa	1853	"	Charles Emory Smith	Pa	1898
Buchanan	Aaron V. Brown	Tenn	1857	Roosevelt	Henry C. Payne	Wis	1901

SECRETARIES OF THE INTERIOR.

Taylor	Thomas Ewing	Ohio	1849	Grant	Columbus Delano	Ohio	1870
Fillmore	James A. Pearce	Md	1850	"	Zachariah Chandler	Mich	1875
"	Thos. M. T. McKernon	Pa	1850	Hayes	Carl Schurz	Mo	1877
"	Alexander H. H. Stuart	Va	1850	Garfield	Samuel J. Kirkwood	Iowa	1881
Pierce	Robert McClelland	Mich	1853	Arthur	Henry M. Teller	Colo	1882
Buchanan	Jacob Thompson	Miss	1857	Cleveland	Lucius Q. C. Lamar	Miss	1885
Lincoln	Caleb B. Smith	Ind	1861	"	William F. Vilas	Wis	1888
"	John P. Usher	"	1863	Harrison	John W. Noble	Mo	1889
Johnson	"	"	1865	Cleveland	Hoke Smith	Ga	1893
"	James Harlan	Iowa	1865	"	David R. Francis	Mo	1896
"	Orville H. Browning	Ill	1866	McKinley	Cornelius N. Bliss	N. Y.	1897
Grant	Jacob D. Cox	Ohio	1869	"	Ethan A. Hitchcock	Mo	1899

SECRETARIES OF AGRICULTURE.

Cleveland	Norman J Colman	Mo	1889	Cleveland	J. Sterling Morton	Neb	1893
Harrison	Jeremiah M. Rusk	Wis	1889	McKinley	James Wilson	Iowa	1897

ATTORNEYS-GENERAL.

Washington.	Edmund Randolph	Va	1789	Polk	Isaac Toucey	Ct	1848
"	William Bradford	Pa	1794	Taylor	Reverdy Johnson	Md	1849
"	Charles Lee	Va	1795	Fillmore	John J. Crittenden	Ky	1850
Adams	"	"	1797	Pierce	Caleb Cushing	Mass	1853
"	Theophilus Parsons	Mass	1801	Buchanan	Jeremiah S. Black	Pa	1857
Jefferson	Levi Lincoln	"	1801	"	Edwin M. Stanton	Ohio	1860
"	Robert Smith	Md	1805	Lincoln	Edward Bates	Mo	1861
"	John Breckinridge	Ky	1805	"	Titian J. Coffey (*ad. in.*)	Pa	1863
"	Cæsar A. Rodney	Del	1807	"	James Speed	Ky	1864
Madison	"	"	1809	Johnson	"	"	1865
"	William Pinkney	Md	1811	"	Henry Stanbery	Ohio	1866
"	Richard Rush	Pa	1814	"	William M. Evarts	N. Y.	1868
Monroe	"	"	1817	Grant	Ebenezer R. Hoar	Mass	1869
"	William Wirt	Va	1817	"	Amos T. Ackerman	Ga	1870
J. Q. Adams.	"	"	1825	"	George H. Williams	Ore	1871
Jackson	John McP. Berrien	Ga	1829	"	Edwards Pierrepont	N. Y.	1875
"	Roger B. Taney	Md	1831	"	Alphonso Taft	Ohio	1876
"	Benjamin F. Butler	N. Y.	1833	Hayes	Charles Devens	Mass	1877
Van Buren	"	"	1837	Garfield	Wayne MacVeagh	Pa	1881
"	Felix Grundy	Tenn	1838	Arthur	Benjamin H. Brewster		1881
"	Henry D. Gilpin	Pa	1840	Cleveland	Augustus H. Garland	Ark	1885
Harrison	John J. Crittenden	Ky	1841	Harrison	William H. H. Miller	Ind	1889
Tyler	"	"	1841	Cleveland	Richard Olney	Mass	1893
"	Hugh S. Legare	S. C.	1841	"	Judson Harmon	Ohio	1895
"	John Nelson	Md	1843	McKinley	Joseph McKenna	Cal	1897
Polk	John Y. Mason	Va	1845	"	John W. Griggs	N. J	1897
"	Nathan Clifford	Me	1846	"	Philander C. Knox	Pa.	1901

SECRETARY OF COMMERCE AND LABOR.

Roosevelt	George B. Cortelyou	N. Y.	1903

JUSTICES OF THE UNITED STATES SUPREME COURT.

(Names of the Chief Justices in Italics.)

Name.	Service.		Born.	Died.	Name.	Service.		Born.	Died.
	Term.	Yrs				Term.	Yrs		
John Jay, N. Y	1789–1795	6	1745	1829	Samuel Nelson, N. Y.	1845–1872	27	1792	1873
John Rutledge, S. C.	1789–1791	2	1739	1800	Levi Woodbury, N. H.	1845–1851	6	1789	1851
William Cushing, Mass.	1789–1810	21	1733	1810	Robert C. Grier, Pa.	1846–1870	23	1794	1870
James Wilson, Pa.	1789–1798	9	1742	1798	Benjamin R. Curtis, Mass.	1851–1857	6	1809	1874
John Blair, Va	1789–1796	7	1732	1800	John A. Campbell, Ala.	1853–1861	8	1811	1889
Robert H. Harrison, Md.	1789–1790	1	1745	1790	Nathan Clifford, Me.	1858–1881	23	1803	1881
James Iredell, N. C.	1790–1799	9	1751	1799	Noah H. Swayne, Ohio	1861–1881	20	1804	1884
Thomas Johnson, Md.	1791–1793	2	1732	1819	Samuel F. Miller, Iowa	1862–1890	28	1816	1890
William Paterson, N. J.	1793–1806	13	1745	1806	David Davis, Ill.	1862–1877	15	1815	1885
John Rutledge, S. C.	1795–1795	..	1739	1800	Stephen J. Field, Cal.	1863–1897	34	1816	....
Samuel Chase, Md.	1796–1811	15	1741	1811	*Salmon P. Chase*, Ohio	1864–1873	9	1808	1873
Oliver Ellsworth, Ct.	1796–1800	4	1745	1807	William Strong, Pa.	1870–1880	10	1808	1895
Bushrod Washington, Va.	1798–1829	31	1762	1829	Joseph P. Bradley, N. J.	1870–1892	22	1813	1892
Alfred Moore, N. C.	1799–1804	5	1755	1810	Ward Hunt, N. Y.	1872–1882	10	1811	1886
John Marshall, Va.	1801–1835	34	1755	1835	*Morrison R. Waite*, Ohio	1874–1888	14	1816	1888
William Johnson, S. C.	1804–1834	30	1771	1834	John M. Harlan, Ky.	1877–....	..	1833	....
Brock. Livingstone, N. Y.	1806–1823	17	1757	1823	William B. Woods, Ga.	1880–1887	7	1824	1887
Thomas Todd, Ky.	1807–1826	19	1765	1826	Stanley Matthews, Ohio	1881–1889	8	1824	1889
Joseph Story, Mass.	1811–1845	34	1779	1845	Horace Gray, Mass.	1881–....	..	1828	....
Gabriel Duval, Md.	1811–1836	25	1752	1844	Samuel Blatchford, N. Y.	1882–1893	11	1820	1893
Smith Thompson, N. Y.	1823–1843	20	1767	1843	Lucius Q. C. Lamar, Miss.	1888–1893	5	1825	1893
Robert Trimble, Ky.	1826–1828	2	1777	1828	*Melville W. Fuller*, Ill.	1888–....	..	1833	....
John McLean, Ohio	1829–1861	32	1785	1861	David J. Brewer, Kan.	1889–....	..	1837	....
Henry Baldwin, Pa.	1830–1844	14	1779	1844	Henry B. Brown, Mich.	1890–....	..	1836	....
James M. Wayne, Ga.	1835–1867	32	1790	1867	George Shiras, Jr., Pa.	1892–....	..	1832	....
Roger B. Taney, Md.	1836–1864	28	1777	1864	Howell E. Jackson, Tenn.	1893–1895	2	1832	1895
Philip P. Barbour, Va.	1836–1841	5	1783	1841	Edward D. White, La.	1893–....	..	1845	....
John Catron, Tenn.	1837–1865	28	1786	1865	Rufus W. Peckham, N. Y.	1895–....	..	1837	....
John McKinley, Ala.	1837–1852	15	1780	1852	Joseph McKenna, Cal.	1897–....	..	1843	....
Peter V. Daniel, Va.	1841–1860	19	1785	1860	Oliver W. Holmes, Mass.	1902–....	..	1841	....
					William R. Day, Ohio	1903–....	..	1849	....

SOME FAMOUS NAVAL BATTLES.

From the naval battle of Salamis to the great sea fight at Manila is a "far cry," B. C. 480 to A. D. 1898, more than 2,000 years. Salamis was the first great recorded battle of the world. Salamis drove the Persians from Greek soil; Manila drives Spain from Asiatic waters. The loss of life at Salamis has been variously estimated at from 5,000 to 50,000; at Manila from 400 to 2,000. Triremes were at Salamis, and shield and sword and brute numbers; at Manila the hell of monster guns and ironclads, the scream of shell, and the carnage of high explosives. Salamis was fought in the youth of nations; Manila in the dawn of the greatness of the American people, the night of Spain. One notable parallel to Manila is found in the battle of the Nile, fought August 1, 1798—Lord Nelson and the English fleet against Admiral Brueys and the French fleet. Nine French line-of-battle ships were taken, two burned, and two escaped. The French L'Orient, with Brueys and 1,000 men on board, blew up, and only seventy or eighty escaped. Nelson's cry for this engagement was: "Victory or Westminster Abbey!" Other famous sea contests of the world are:

Winchelsea—English defeat 40 Spanish vessels and capture 36, August 29, 1350.

Harfleur—English capture or destroy 500 French vessels, August 15, 1416.

Gibraltar Bay—Dutch defeat the Spanish, April 25, 1607.

Dover Strait—Dutch destroy the English fleet, November 29, 1652.

Portsmouth—English defeat the Dutch and destroy 11 men-of-war and 36 merchantmen, February 18, 1653.

North Foreland—100 English and Dutch men-of-war engaged; 11 Dutch taken and 6 sunk, June 2, 1683.

Coast of Holland—English sink 30 Dutch men-of-war, July 31, 1653.

Santa Cruz—Spanish fleet burned by the English, April 20, 1627.

Harwich—Dutch lose 18 ships to the English, June 3, 1605.

Thames—Dutch lose to English 24 men-of-war, 4 admirals killed, and 4,000 seamen, July 25, 1666.

Messina—Spanish fleet, 29 vessels, destroyed by English, July 11, 1718.

Gibraltar—English defeated combined fleets of Spain and France, September 13, 1782.

Trafalgar—Nelson sunk 10 French and Spanish vessels after fighting with 27 ships, 33 of the combined fleet; Nelson killed, October 21, 1805.

Navarino—The fleets of England, France, and Russia destroy 30 Turkish men-of-war, October 20, 1827.

Most notable of American naval battles preceding Manila are the following:

Coast of Scotland—Paul Jones captures the Serapis and Scarborough, 70 guns, September 23, 1779.

Off St. Kitts—The Constellation, 26 guns, captures the French L'Insurgent, 40 guns, February 9, 1799.

Coast of United States—Constitution, 44 guns, sinks the Guerriere, 38 guns, in 30 minutes, August 19, 1812.

Madeira—United States, 44 guns, captures the Macedonian, 40 guns, October 25, 1812.

Brazil—Constitution captures the Java, Dec. 29, 1812.

Demerara River—Hornet captures the Peacock, February 24, 1813.

Lake Erie—Perry, with 54 guns, defeats English fleet with 63 guns, September 10, 1813.

Lake Champlain—McDonough, with 86 guns, defeats English fleet with 96 guns, September 11, 1814.

Manila Bay—Rear Admiral Dewey, with six ships: the Olympia (flagship), Boston, Baltimore, Petrel, Raleigh, and Concord, destroyed Spain's Asiatic Squadron, 13 vessels, under Admiral Montejo: Isla de Cuba, Isla de Luzon, Castilla, Don Antonio de Ulloa, Don Juan de Austria, Reina Cristina, Callao, El Cano, El Correo, General Lezo, Hercules, Marques del Duero, Rapido; also the navy yard and nine batteries. American loss, eight wounded and about $5,000 damage to ships. Spanish loss, about 1,200 killed or wounded and some $6,000,000 in vessels destroyed or captured. May 1, 1898.

Santiago de Cuba—Cervera's squadron of six vessels: the Vizcaya, Almirante Oquendo, Maria Teresa, Cristobal Colon, Furor, and Pluton, made a bold dash to escape from the harbor, and was destroyed by Sampson's fleet: The Oregon, Iowa, Indiana, Texas, Brooklyn, Gloucester, and Vixen. American loss: 1 killed, 2 wounded. Spanish loss: 360 killed, 165 wounded, 1,650 taken prisoners. July 3, 1898.

At Santiago de Cuba the armies and navies were both engaged. Army losses: United States, 272 killed, 1,000 wounded; Spain, 2,000 killed, 1,500 wounded, 1,650 taken prisoners. Total army and navy losses: United States, 274 killed, 1,002 wounded. Spain, 2,360 killed, 1,665 wounded, 3,300 taken prisoners.

In all her naval conflicts with England, France, Spain, and the Tripoli pirates, the United States has never sustained what would be considered a crushing defeat. She has lost individual vessels, but only after the most desperate resistance, giving proof of the saying that "Americans do not fight to save their skins."

DICTIONARY OF HISTORY.

Abbeys and Monasteries robbed of their plate and jewels by William the Conqueror, 1069; entirely dissolved by Henry the VIII., 1540. This ruler suppressed in England and Wales 643 monasteries, 90 colleges, 2374 churches and chapels, and 110 hospitals; and had the abbots of Reading, Glastonbury, and St. John's, Colchester, hanged and quartered for refusing to surrender their abbeys, and denying his supremacy.

Aberdeen, University of, founded 1477; King's College founded 1500; Marechal College founded 1593; the town of Aberdeen and its vicinity was visited by a destructive inundation August 8, 1829.

Aboukir, in Egypt, surrendered to the English forces March 18, 1801.

Abydos is a town of Asia Minor, situated on the Hellespont. Tradition places here the story of Hero and Leander; history tells that this was where Xerxes led his vast army over the Hellespont on a bridge of boats; and Byron here swam the Hellespont, and rendered it ever famous by his "Bride of Abydos."

Acre, taken by Richard I. and other Crusaders July 12, 1191, after a siege of two years and the loss of 300,000 men; attacked by the French under Bonaparte, who, failing in the twelfth assault, retired with great loss of men, May 21, 1799.

Actium, in Epirus, naval battle of, which rendered Augustus master of the Roman Empire, September 2, 31 B. C.

Adrianople, taken by the Ottomans, 1360; taken from the Turks by the Russians, 1829.

Agincourt, Battle of, between the French and English, gained by Henry V., October 25, 1415; 10,000 of the French killed and 14,000 taken prisoners, the English losing only 40. In the French army were four times as many men as in the English.

Aix-la-Chapelle, taken by the French, 1793; and again, September 21, 1794; Congress at, September 29, 1818.

Albans, St., the first battle between the Houses of York and Lancaster, in which the former was victorious, May 22, 1455; another battle was fought, February 2, 1461, between the Yorkists, under the Earl of Warwick, and the Lancastrians, under Queen Margaret; the latter were the victors.

Alderton Moor, Yorkshire, Battle of, where the Royalists routed the Parliamentarians, June 29, 1643.

Alessandria, Italy, taken by the French, 1798; surrendered to the Austrians and Russians, July 24, 1799.

Alexandria, Egypt, built by Alexander in 17 days, the walls whereof were six miles in circuit, B. C. 333; taken by Cæsar, B. C. 46; by Dioclesian, 296 A. D.; by the Persians, 615 A. D.; by the Saracens, 640 A. D; by the French, 1798. Battle of, between the French and English, in which the former were defeated, but the English general, Abercromby, was killed, 1801.

Alhambra, The, is a palace and fortress of the Moors, founded about 1253, by Mohammed I. Celebrated as the palace of the kings of Granada. Its two courts, that of the Myrtles and that of the Lions, are beautiful examples of Arabian art in Spain. The Alhambra was surrendered to the Christians by the Moors about 1491.

Albinos, called also Leucoethiopes, or white negroes, and by the Dutch and Germans *Kakerlaken*, were at one time considered a distinct race, but closer observation has shown that the same phenomenon occurs in individuals of all races, and that the peculiar white appearance rises from an irregularity of the skin. The iris of the eye is red in the Albino. Albinoism occurs also in other mammalia, birds, and insects.

Alabama, first settlement was made by the French, at Mobile, in 1711. The commerce of the state is considerable, and its manufacturing interests are increasing rapidly; chiefly cotton and cotton goods, yarn, thread, iron, leather, and lumber. Its mining interests are being rapidly developed; but the principal industry is agriculture, cotton and corn being the leading productions. Various cereals, sugar cane, rice, and tobacco are also produced.

Alaska was purchased by the United States from Russia in 1867, for $7,200,000 in gold, and was formally taken possession of October 9th of the same year by General Rousseau on behalf of the United States, at New Archangel, on the Island of Sitka. With the islands, it comprises 580,107 square miles, or nearly one sixth of the entire area of the United States previous to this purchase. The land abounds in fur-bearing animals; the seas yield fur-bearing seals and others, and fish in immense quantities. Among other important resources of the Territory are lumber and minerals of all kinds. The southwestern part is covered for thousands of miles with dense forests of yellow cedar, white spruce, and balsam fir. Among the valuable minerals, coal has been found at different places along the coast: petroleum, lead, iron, and graphite at various points; copper, marble, and sulphur in great abundance; also gold and silver and valuable stones, such as amethysts, garnets, agates, and carnelians. The climate of the Territory is very severe in the inland districts, but mild along the coast. At Fort Yukon the thermometer sinks as low as seventy degrees below zero in the winter; the summers are short and hot, the winters long and cold. In Southern Alaska the winter climate is the average winter climate of Kentucky, and the summer climate about that of Minnesota. The capital of Alaska is Sitka, and the Territory is governed by a Governor and other necessary officers appointed by the authorities at Washington. Alaska is divided into three judicial districts with headquarters at Juneau, Eagle City, and St. Nicholas. These courts appoint commissioners who act throughout the territory. With the developments following the great gold discoveries, Congress, in 1898, extended the Homestead Laws to Alaska.

Alexandrian Library, consisting of 400,000 manuscripts, destroyed by fire B. C. 47. The second library, consisting of 700,000 volumes, was destroyed by the Saracens, under Caliph Omar, at whose command they for six months burned books instead of wood, for the purpose of heating water for their baths, 640 A. D.

Algiers, formerly the country called Numidia, as united under Massinissa and Jugurtha. It became a Roman province 44 B.C.; afterwards it was independent, till the inhabitants invited Barbarossa the pirate to assist them against the Spaniards, who, however, seized it, 1516. Sometime afterward it became the property of the Turks; reduced by Admiral Blake, 1655: bombarded by the French, 1761; bombarded by the British fleet, and the Christian captives set free August 27, 1816. The French army, under the command of General Bourmont, landed in the Bay of Sidi Ferach, June 14, 1830; the city was taken July 5th; and the whole of the territory of Algiers was subsequently reduced, and became a province of France.

Altars, instituted by Pope Sixtus I., 117 A. D.; first Christian altar erected in Britain, 634; first consecrated by Pope Sylvester, 1334.

Amazons, The, made an irruption into Attica about 1209 B. C.; a queen of, visited Alexander the Great and cohabited with him, in the hopes of having issue, but died soon after her return home, 330 B. C.

America, first discovered by Columbus, 1492; South America, completely, by Americus Vespucius, a Florentine, and North America by John Cabot, a Venetian, 1497; thirteen colonies declared themselves independent of the British crown, July 4, 1776, and recognized as such by England, 1783. South American independence was established and recognized by the United States and England, who sent consuls to the new state, 1824. American Congress, first met at Philadelphia September 5, 1775; removed to Washington, 1801.

Amerigo Vespucci was a naval astronomer, from whom America accidentally received its name. He was born at Florence, March 9, 1451, and was at the head of a large Florentine firm in Seville in 1496. He fitted out Columbus' third fleet, and in 1499 himself sailed for the New World with Ojeda, and explored the coast of Venezuela. The accident which fastened his name on two continents may be traced to an inaccurate account of his travels published at St. Dié in Lorraine in 1507, in which he is represented to have reached the mainland in 1497 — which would have been before either Cabot or Columbus — and in which the suggestion is made that he should give his name to the world he had discovered.

Anglesey, the Mona of the Romans, reduced by Julius Agricola, 76 A. D.; by the English, 1295.

Anjou, Battle of, where the Duke of Clarence and 1,500 English were slain, 1421.

Anglo-Saxons, first landed in Britain 449.

Anointing, first used at the coronation of Alfred, 872.

Antioch, in Syria, built by Seleucus after the battle of Ipsus, B. C. 300; 100,000 of its inhabitants killed by the Jews in one day, B. C. 145.

Antonio, Battle of, in Mexico, between the Royalists and Independents, August 18, 1813; the latter were defeated.

Appian Way, aqueducts, etc., constructed at Rome, B. C. 311.

Arkansas (Bear State)—First settlement, by the French, at Arkansas Post, 1685. Admitted to the Union in 1836. Ranks fifth in cotton, ninth in mules, twenty-second in miles of railway, twenty-fifth in population and in square miles, thirty-first in wealth. The mineral resources of the State are very large, and receiving much attention. Stock raising is extensive. Agriculture is the chief industry; corn, cotton, and wheat being the leading productions. Oats, tobacco, sweet potatoes, and fine fruits are also produced to a considerable extent.

Arbela, Battle of, when Alexander conquered Persia, B. C. 331.

Arcadians, Colony of, conducted by Evander into Italy, B. C. 1243.

Areopagus, The famous senate of, established at Athens in the reign of Cecrops, B. C. 1509.

Argentria, in Alsace, Battle of, where the German tribe, the Alemanni, were defeated by the Romans, with a loss of 35,000 out of 40,000 men, May, 378 A. D.

Arizona was first explored by the Spaniards in 1526, and missions were established in this region before 1600. It ranks fifth in silver, eighth in sheep, ninth in gold. Mining and cattle raising are the chief industries.

Armada, The Spanish, consisting of 130 ships, with 50,000 men, arrived in the English channel July, 1588, but was dispersed by a storm.

Arms, Coats of, became hereditary in families in the latter end of the twelfth century. They took their rise from the knights painting their banners with different figures, to distinguish them in the Crusades. The arms of England and France were first quartered by Edward the III., 1358; the French arms discontinued by the English kings, January 1, 1801.

Army, first standing one in modern times, established by Charles VII. of France, 1445; introduced into England by Charles I., 1638; declared illegal, together with the Royal Guards, 1679.

Ascalon, Judea, Battle of, where Richard I. defeated Saladin's army of three hundred thousand men, 1191.

Assyria, Kingdom of, began under Ninus, called Assur, B. C. 2084; lasted about one thousand two hundred and sixty-fours years, ending with Sardanapalus.

Athens, founded by Cecrops, B. C. 1571; kingdom ended in Codrus, 1070; governed by annual archons, 684; city taken by Xerxes, 480; by the Romans, 87; by the Venetians, A. D. 1204; by the Turks, 1687; by the Greeks, 1826.

Austerlitz, Battle of, December 2, 1805.

Austria, anciently the Belgic Gaul of the Romans, taken from Hungary and annexed to Germany, when it received its present name, 1040; erected into a duchy, 1156; made an empire, August 11, 1804; Francis II., emperor of, made a formal resignation of the high office of Emperor of Germany, August 7, 1806. Austria and Russia united against France, August, 1805. The Austrian army, under Mack, surrendered at Ulm to Napoleon, October 20, 1805.

Avignon, taken from the Pope by the French, 1769; restored, 1773; declared to belong to France by the National Assembly, 1791; and confirmed by the congress of allied sovereigns, 1815.

Aztecs The, were the early inhabitants of Mexico, who became highly civilized, and adopted a monarchical form of government in 1352. Their most celebrated king was Montezuma-Illumicamina, who erected several magnificent buildings, the remains of which are still to be seen. They believed in a Supreme Being, whom they never represented by sculpture or painting, as they believed him to be invisible. The Aztecs were conquered by the Spaniards under Cortez, 1521.

Babylon, founded by Nimrod, the grandson of Ham, B. C. 2640; city walled, 1243; taken by Cyrus, 588: by Darius, 511. According to Herodotus, the ancient city of Babylon stood on a broad plain, and was an exact square, 120 stadia (equal to fourteen miles) each way, so that the entire circuit of the city was 480 stadia. It was surrounded by a broad and deep moat, full of water, behind which rose a wall 50 royal cubits (equal to 93⅓ feet) in width, and 200 in height. On the top, along the edges of the wall, were constructed buildings of a single chamber, facing one another, leaving between them room for a four-horse chariot to turn. In the circuit of the walls were a hundred gates, all of brass, with brazen lintels, and side-posts. Subsequent writers reduce the circuit of the city to 360 stadia, and the height of the wall to from 60 to 70 feet. The other walls ran along the banks of the Euphrates, and the quays with which it was lined, each contained twenty-five gates, which answered to the number of the streets they led into. The most remarkable edifice in the city was the Temple of Bel, a pyramid of 8 square stadia, the basement stage being over 200 yards each way. On the summit were a golden image of Bel, 40 feet high, two other statues of gold, a golden table 40 feet long and 15 broad, and many other colossal objects of the same precious metal. At the base was a second shrine, with a table and images, and altars. A similar temple stood at Borsippa, the suburb of Babylon; and it is believed that the ancient Babel of the Bible was also at Borsippa, a little below the later Babylon. The city came prominently into notice about 747 B. C., but its great importance dates from the fall of Nineveh, when Nabopolassar made it the capital of the Chaldean empire, and began the series of fortifications and public works, completed by his son, Nebuchadnezzar. It was several times dismantled, and, when Alexander the Great took possession of it, was a comparative ruin. Much of the material from which it was built was used by his successors to build Seleucia. That city, in its turn, fell into decay, and from its material several other cities were built, among them Bagdad. Since 1847 it has been established beyond reasonable doubt that the village Hilleh is located on the site of ancient Babylon.

Baltimore, Battle of, in which 9,000 British, under General Ross were repulsed by the Americans, and General Ross killed, September 12, 1814.

Bannockburn, Battle of, between 30,000 Scotch and 200,000 English, when the latter were routed with a loss of 50,000 slain, and 30,000 prisoners, June 25, 1314.

Barbers, the profession first brought to Rome from Sicily, B. C. 299; barbers and surgeons in London made one company, 1540; separated, 1744. They formerly exhibited a head or poll at their doors, and the barber's pole now used by them is a burlesque imitation of it.

Barcelona, said to be built by Hamilcar, the Carthaginian general, who subdued Spain; reduced by Louis XIV. of France, 1714.

Baron, Title of, first used in England, 1388. The barons attended Parliament in complete armor, in the reign of Henry III.

Baronets, English, first created, 1611; Scotch, 1625; thirteen new ones created, December 9, 1827.

Bastille, at Paris, taken, and the governor killed, July 14, 1789.

Bastille, this famous French stronghold was originally built by Charles V., as a chateau, in 1369. The high wall around it was subsequently erected by Philippe-Auguste. Louis XI. first used it as a state prison, and it was eventually demolished by the people during the Revolution, July 14, 1789. The "Man in the Iron Mask" was imprisoned there, and died in 1703.

Battle of Lake Erie, between the British squadron, commanded by Captain Barclay, and the United States, commanded by Captain Perry, in which the whole British force was captured, September 10, 1813.

Belgium, incorporated with the French republic, September 30, 1794; incorporated with Holland by the Congress of Vienna, 1815; declared itself independent, October 4, 1830, and has since chosen a king as its ruler.

Belgrade, Battle of, between the Germans and Turks, when the latter were beaten and lost 40,000 men, 1456; the city taken by the Turks, 1690; battle of, between the Hungarians under Prince Eugene, and the Turks, when the latter were defeated, July 16, 1717.

Bermuda Islands, discovered 1609; settled 1612; settlements destroyed by a hurricane, October 11, 1780.

Bedouins, The, are that class of Arabs who lead a nomadic life. Living in the desert of Arabia, they have evolved characteristics as robbers and herdsmen intimately connected with their mode of life. Keen of physical sense, with active imagination, yet destitute of solid knowledge, the Bedouin unites independence and love of liberty, with a violent passion, an infamous love of plunder, and an entire disregard of the rights of property. They are professedly Mohammedan. Bigamy is rare; polygamy scarcely known.

Bible Societies, first commenced under the auspices of Granville Sharp, March 7, 1804; the pope issued a bull against them, March 20, 1807.

Bithynia, a kingdom of Asia, conquered by Crœsus, king of Lydia, B. C. 560; by Alexander, 332. From its ruins rose the Ottoman Turks, who made Prusa their capital before they possessed Constantinople, 1327.

Blenheim, Battle of, between the English and French, when the latter were defeated, with a loss of 27,000 killed and 13,000 prisoners; while the total loss of the English amounted to no more than 13,000 in killed, wounded, and prisoners, August 3, 1704.

Boadicea, queen of Iceni, at the head of the Britons, attacked the Romans, burned London, and massacred 70,000 of its inhabitants; but being shortly afterward captured by Suetonius, poisoned herself, 65 A. D.

Boulogne, France, besieged and taken by Henry VIII., 1544; sold to France for 400,000 crowns, 1550; Sir Sidney Smith failed in an attack on the flotilla there, November, 1806.

Boyne, battle of, between King William and King James, when the latter was defeated, July 1, 1690.

Brazil, discovered by the Portuguese, 1500, who settled there 1549; diamond mines discovered 1730; the royal family arrives at, 1807; revolution took place, 1821; its independence declared and the prince regent declared emperor, 1822; the king of Portugal ratified the treaty and took the title of emperor of, 1825; war with Buenos Ayres, 1826; death of the dowager princess of, at Lisbon, August 8, 1829; revolution and expulsion of the emperor, Dom Pedro, and the appointment of a regency in the name of his son, 1830; became a republic, 1889.

Brochs are prehistoric structures in Scotland resembling low, circular, roofless towers, with walls of great thickness of unhewn stones, and inclosed by a narrow passage, chiefly in Orkney, Shetland, etc. The brochs of Mousa is a typical and the best preserved example.

Buenos Ayres, founded 1535 by Pedro de Mendoza; rebuilt 1580; taken from the Spaniards by Sir Home Popham, June 21, 1806; retaken after an attack of three days, August 12; British attack on, under Lieutenant General Whitelock, in which the British were repulsed, July 6, 1807; declaration of independence published, July 19, 1816.

Bulgarians, defeated by Basilius, Emperor of the East, who made 15,000 of them prisoners and caused their eyes to be put out, except one in a hundred, whom he left one eye, that they might serve as leaders to the rest, 1014.

Byzantium, built by a colony of Athenians, B. C. 670. The seat of empire removed thither from Rome, A. D. 300, and its name changed to Constantinople.

California, first settled by the Spaniards, 1769, at San Diego. Ranks first in barley, grape culture, gold, and quicksilver; second in wool; third in hops; fifth in wheat and salt; seventh in silk goods; eighth in soap and silver; and ninth in wealth. Mining, manufacturing, stock raising, and agriculture form the principal industries of the state. Commerce is extensive with China, Japan, the East Indies, and Australia, and with other states and territories. No state in the Union has developed so rapidly.

Caledonia is the name given by the Romans to that part of Scotland lying between the Forth and the Clyde; so called from the tribe of Caledonii. The name disappears in the fourth century, and the people of Scotland began to be called Picts (to the east) and Scots (to the west). In more modern times Caledonia is a poetical name for Scotland.

Canada, discovered, 1499; settled by the French, 1534; Quebec built by Samuel Champlain, 1608; conquered by the English, 1759; ceded to them, 1763.

Canary Islands, discovered by a Norman, 1405; conquered by the Spaniards, 1491.

Candia, the ancient Crete, once subject to Greece, sold to the Venetians till taken by the Turks after 22 years' siege, 1669.

Canna, Battle of, where 40,000 Romans were killed by the Carthaginians, B. C. 216.

Carthage, founded by the Tyrians, B. C. 1259; built by Queen Dido, about 869; destroyed, B. C. 704.

Catalonia, Kingdom of, conquered by the Goths, 414; by the Saracens, 714; taken by the Moors, 800; united to Spain, 1492.

Central America. Under the name of Central America are included the republics of Guatemala, Honduras, San Salvador, Nicaragua, Costa Rica, and the territory known as British Honduras. In 1502 Columbus discovered the eastern shore of Central America, and shortly afterward the Spaniards took possession of it, retaining it until 1820, when it rebelled, and many of the states which then composed it were annexed by Mexico. Three years afterwards was formed the Central American Confederation, but in 1839 Nicaragua withdrew, as did also Costa Rica in 1840, and Guatemala in 1847. In 1872 Guatemala, Costa Rica, San Salvador, and Honduras became united, forming the Central American Union, the object of the union being the maintenance of peace in the several states and of the republican form of government.

The representatives of the Greater Republic of Central America, which was formed by the treaty of Amapala, concluded June 20, 1895, on August 27, 1898, adopted a federal constitution, in which the name was changed to "the United States of Central America." It was composed of the states of Honduras, Nicaragua, and Salvador. The Republics of Costa Rica and Guatemala did not enter into this union.

November 30, 1898, the Federal Organizers formally declared the union dissolved, the three States resuming respectively absolute sovereignty. The collapse was due to the failure of the troops of Honduras, acting in behalf of the Federal Organizers, to suppress an outbreak in Salvador against the proposed federation, and to force Salvador into the union.

The Central American coalition lasted nominally just one month. The new régime was ushered in by elaborate celebrations at Amapala on November 1. Under the proposed form of government, the administration was to pass into the control of a representative from each of the three republics — Dr. Salvador Callego, of Salvador; Señor Miguel Agnelugarte, of Honduras, and Dr. Manuel Corrolel Matus, of Nicaragua. These were to continue in power until March 14, 1899, when they were to elect a president of the United States of Central America, to hold office four years. It was understood that the three States had virtually agreed upon Señor J. Rosa Pacose, of Salvador, for the Executive chair. In the meantime the presidents of the three republics were to assume the grade of governors.

From the outset the Salvadorians opposed the coalition, as the expense of maintaining the federal government would have fallen chiefly upon them. General Regalado headed an insurrection, whose avowed purpose was to defeat the plans of the Federal Organizers. President Zelaya, of Nicaragua, declined to allow the Nicaraguan troops to suppress the outbreak, and the task was assigned to the armies of Honduras. The latter entered Salvador, but were compelled to retire unsuccessful. Thus, unable to bring Salvador into the union, the promoters of the coalition scheme had no alternative but to abandon it.

Chartists, The, were a body of the English people who, on the passage of the Reform Bill (1832) demanded the People's Charter, the points of which were: (1) Universal suffrage; (2) vote by ballot; (3) annual parliaments; (4) payment of members; (5) abolition of property qualification; (6) equal electoral districts. Great demonstrations and damage done in 1838-9. After demonstration and presentation of petition, April 10, 1848, the movement subsided, although the government had meanwhile dealt severely with some of the leaders.

Chaldeans, The, or Akkadians, are a non-Semitic race, who came originally from the mountain country of Elam, and were formerly the dominant people of Babylonia. One of the four great cities of Shinar was Accad. The Babylonians were indebted to the Sumero-Akkadians for their cuneiform writing, religion, and mythology.

Champ de Mars, The, or "Field of March," was a grand general assembly of Frank warriors, held from time to time in Gaul, from the fifth century till the time of Charles le Chauve (877), when all trace of them disappears. The objects of these conventions were twofold: (1) That of military reviews, in which the freemen came to pay homage to their chief and bring their annual gifts; and (2) consultative deliberations upon what expeditions should be made, what should be done for the defense of the nation, and what laws should be passed for the better government of the State. From 755 these assemblies were held in May. Napoleon I. announced a gathering to be held in the great plain called the Champ de Mars of Paris, on May 26; but it was not held till June 1, 1815. The object was to proclaim *L'Acte additionel aux constitutions de l'Empire.*

Charing Cross was originally a London suburb, where was erected the last of the crosses in memory of Eleanor, queen of Edward I. The cross was destroyed in 1647, but a new one was placed on the spot in 1865.

Chillon is a celebrated castle of Switzerland, at the eastern end of the Lake of Geneva. It stands on an isolated rock, and long served as a state prison. Here for six years (1530-36) Bonnivard endured the captivity immortalized by Byron's "Prisoner of Chillon" (1821).

China, Monarchy of, commenced B. C. 2367; but its history does not extend above the Greek Olympiads. Fohi is by many writers supposed to be the founder of the Empire, and its first sovereign, B. C. 2247. The country conquered by the eastern Tartars, when the emperor and his family killed themselves, A. D. 1644. First voyage to China from the United States made from New York, February 22, 1784.

Cimbri, The, were the ancient inhabitants of Jutland, of disputed nationality. They made serious incursions into Italy, but were utterly routed by the Romans, 101 B. C., and were afterwards merged in the Saxons.

Colorado (Centennial state). First settlement, by Americans, near Denver, about 1850. Organized as a territory, 1861. Ranks first in silver, fourth in gold, eighth in square miles, seventeenth in miles of railway, thirty-fifth in population and wealth. About one third of the state is good agricultural land and easy of irrigation, bringing forth bountiful harvests of all the cereals. As a grazing and dairy country it is unsurpassed, its nutritious grasses having peculiar advantages for herding. Its chief production is mining; in its yield of gold and silver, it is the leading state of the Union.

Commune, The, is the unit or lowest division in the administration of France, corresponding in the rural districts to our township, and in towns to a municipality. The rising of the Commune at Paris in 1871, and which should not be confounded with communism, was a revolutionary assertion of the autonomy of Paris, that is, of the right of self-government through its commune or municipality. The theory of the rising was that every commune should have a real autonomy, the central government being merely a federation of communes. The movement was based on discontent at Paris, where the people found themselves in possession of arms after the siege by the Germans. The rising began on the 18th of March, 1871, and was only suppressed ten weeks later, after long, bloody fighting between the forces of the Commune and a large army of the central government; 6,500 Communists having fallen during 20-30th of May, and 38,578 having been taken prisoners.

Covent Garden, originally the garden of the Abbot of Westminster, is a spacious square in London, celebrated for a great market held within it of fruit, vegetables, and flowers. The square was formed about 1631, and is famous from its connection with the modern history of London.

Confederation of the Rhine, The, formed July 12, 1806, was a federation of the Germanic States, formed by Napoleon Bonaparte, whose disastrous Russian campaign (1812) caused the dissolution of the confederation, the Germanic Confederation taking its place.

Connecticut, first settled by the English at Windsor 1633. Ranks first in clocks; third in silk goods; fourth in cotton goods; eighth in tobacco; fourteenth in wealth. Manufactures cotton, woolen, and worsted goods, hardware, jewelry, plated ware, leather goods. Agriculture and manufacture are carried on to a considerable extent. Several extensive granite and freestone quarries are successfully worked as are also mines of lead, copper, and iron. Many of the towns have an extensive coasting trade, and foreign commerce with the West Indies.

Comedy, the first acted at Athens on a stage, B. C. 562; those of Terence first acted, B. C. 154; the first regular one performed in England, 1551.

Constantinople, founded by Argives, B. C. 658; besieged and destroyed, 193; received its present name from Constantine the Great, who removed there the seat of the Eastern Empire, 324; suffered greatly by fire, pestilence, famine, and an earthquake, that overturned its walls and towers, 446; had first an emperor, 1268; taken from the Greeks by Mahomet II., who slew the emperor and 60,000 inhabitants—this put an end to the eastern empire, which began with the reign of Arcadus, 395, and continued 1055 years; the embassadors of England and France arrived at, June 20, 1829.

Convention, for forming the constitution of the United States, met at Philadelphia, May 25, 1787, and reported the same to the States for adoption, September 17, of the same year.

Cook, Captain, sailed July 30, 1768, to go round the world; returned August, 1771; again to explore the southern hemisphere, July 13, 1772; returned July 29, 1775. Killed by savages on a voyage to the Sandwich Islands, 1879; ship returned, 1780.

Copenhagen burned, 77 streets destroyed, 1723; Sir Hyde Parker and Lord Nelson passed the sound, and, after destroying the fleet, made peace with the Danes, April 2, 1801; garrison of, capitulated to the British troops after a severe bombardment of three days, September 6, 1807.

Cordova, the first Roman colony in Spain, settled by Marcellus; the residence of the Moorish princess, 759; kingdom of, destroyed, 1014.

Corsica, dependent on Genoa until 1730; became free, 1733; elected Theodore king, 1736; ceded to France by Genoa, 1779; sold to Germany, 1781; the Corsicans acknowledged George III. as their king, 1794; the island evacuated by the English, November, 1796.

Crusades, or Holy Wars, between the Christians and Mohammedans, which, in the end, cost the lives of two hundred million men. The first, in 1095, was under Peter the Hermit and Godfrey de Bouillon; the second, in 1146, under Emperor Conrad III. and Louis VII. of France; the third, in 1188, by Frederick Barbarossa, joined in 1190 by Philip II. of France and Richard I. of England; the fourth, in 1204, under Baldwin, Count of Flanders; the fifth, in 1228, under Frederick II.; the sixth, in 1248, under Louis IX. of France against Egypt; the seventh, in 1270, also by Louis IX., against Tunis, where Louis lost his life.

Curfew Bell was established in England in 1068, which, to prevent fires, obliged people to put out their fire and candles at eight in the evening, when the bells rang; abolished in 1100.

Danes, their first descent upon England was at Portland, 787; their second in Northumberland, 794, when they were repelled and perished by shipwreck. Successive invasions took place up to the year 998; defeated the English at Ipswich, 1010; took Canterbury and put nine out of ten of the inhabitants to death, 1011; settled in Scotland, 1020; expelled the English, 1041; landed again at Sandwich, 1047, and carried off great plunder to Flanders; joined the Northumbrians, burned York, and slew 3,000 Normans, 1069; invaded England again, but, bribed by William II., quitted it, 1140.

Dakotas, The, first settled by Americans at Pembina. Admitted into the Union as two states, North and South Dakota, 1889. Ranks third in gold, ninth in silver, thirty-ninth in population.

Delaware, first settlement made by Swedes at Cape Henlopen, 1658. The principal industries are agricultural pursuits and mining. Fruit grows in great abundance. Considerable manufacturing is done in the northern part of the state.

Delft, one of the most ancient towns of South Holland, is situated on the Schie, eight miles northwest of Rotterdam by rail, and is intersected by numerous canals. Delft was noted from the sixteenth to the eighteenth century for its Delft ware, but has now entirely lost its high reputation for this manufacture.

Decemvirs, The, were men who drew up a code of Roman laws, and who, in 451 B. C., had the whole government of Rome in their hands. They were successful in their administration till the incident of Appius Claudius and Virginia led to the appointment of consuls.

Delphi was an ancient northern Greek town, celebrated for the oracles pronounced by the Pythian priestess in the temple of Apollo. The oracle was known as early as 900 B. C., and the temple became the repository of immense treasures. It was plundered by the Phocians and Nero, the latter taking away three hundred costly statues in 67 A. D.

Denmark, the ancient kingdom of the Goths; its first king reigned 714; embraced Christianity, 940; united with the Crown of Norway, 1412, and with Sweden, 1497; separated from Sweden in 1528; crown made hereditary and absolute, 1660; Copenhagen bombarded by the English, 1807; commercial treaty between Denmark and England, 1824.

Diana, Temple of, at Ephesus, burned by the Amazons, about 1182; again by Erostratus, in order to perpetuate his name, B. C. 356; again by the Goths, in their third invasion, about 256.

Dionysius, Usurpation of, B. C. 409; besieged Rhegium, 388, and took it after eleven months; began the first Punic war, 384; expelled from Syracuse by Dion, 357.

Doomsday Book, The, or "Domesday Book" (1085-1086), was a statistical survey of that part of England which was under the sway of William the Conqueror. So called, probably, because it was of authority in all dooms, *i. e.*, judgments in disputed questions which afterwards arose on matters contained therein. It was anciently known as the "Liber de Wintonia" (Book of Winchester), because at one time it was preserved in the royal treasury of that city, under three locks and keys. It was printed and published in 1783, in two folio volumes. In 1816 two supplementary volumes were published.

Dublin, city, wall built about 838; stormed by Dermond, 1171; its first charter granted, 1173; castle built, 1220; its University founded, 1591; Parliament House begun, 1729; finished, 1739; insurrection in and murder of Lord Kilwarden, July 23, 1803.

Duke, Title of, first given in England to Edward, son of Edward III., March 17, 1336; quite extinct, 1572, but has since been renewed in many instances.

Egypt, The kingdom of, began under Misraim, the son of Ham, the second son of Noah, B. C. 2188, and lasted 1,663 years; conquered by Cambyses, 525; revolted from the Persians, assisted by the Athenians, 463; taken by Alexander, 332; reduced to a province, 31; conquered by the Turks, A. D. 1517; invaded by the French under Bonaparte, 1798, who, by the aid of the British, were eventually expelled, 1800. Egypt, since the year 1807, has been under the dominion of the Mohammedans.

England, originally inhabited by the Britons, a branch of the ancient Gauls or Celtæ; the western part in the time of the Romans was inhabited by the Belgæ; the northern part by the Brigantes; South Wales by the Silures, and Norfolk and Suffolk by the Iceni. Invaded by Julius Cæsar, B. C. 54; subdued by Claudius, 44, and completely so by Agricola, in 85 A. D. The Romans kept possession of it until 410. Conquered by the Saxons, 455, who were invited over by the ancient inhabitants, and who divided it into seven kingdoms, called the Heptarchy. Ravished by the Picts and Scots, 448. Erected into a kingdom by Egbert, by a union of all the kingdoms of the Heptarchy, 827. Conquered by the Danes, 877; recovered by Alfred, 880. Divided into counties and hundreds, 886; invaded by the Scots, who were defeated by Athelstan, 921; by the Welsh, 984; by Sweyn, king of Denmark, 1003; again by Sweyn and almost subdued by him, 1013; by the Irish, 1069; by Malcolm, king of Scotland, 1071, and again 1091; again, 1093, when Malcolm and his son were killed at Alnwick; by Robert, Duke of Normandy, 1101; by David of Scotland, 1136; by the Scots again, in 1183; by Henry, Duke of Richmond, 1485; England declared war against Spain, January 4, 1762; the famous dynasty of the Plantagenets commenced with the reign of Henry of Anjou. The Magna Charta was adopted during John's reign, in 1215. The reign of Elizabeth was signalized by the defeat of the Spanish Armada, 1588. James VI., of Scotland, was the first ruler of Great Britain.

Epirus, Kingdom of, first known in history by the great warlike achievements of Pyrrhus, about B. C. 950; a second Pyrrhus was renowned for his wars against the Romans, B. C. 280; became a republic, 240, but was subdued by the Romans, B. C. 167. It was finally conquered by Mahomet II., 1466, and became part of the Ottoman Empire.

Falk Laws, The, 1873, were so called from Dr. Falk, who insisted on the compulsory education of the clergy of Prussia. The laws are four in number: (1) The first was directed against the abuse of ecclesiastical discipline for political purposes, such as "boycotting," excommunication, and anathemas; (2) the next regulated the effect of secession from the Church on the obligation to meet certain taxes; (3) the third law was directed at the evasions by Roman Catholics of state education incumbent on all Germans; and (4) abolished the legality of papal tribunals, recognizing the judgments of the German ecclesiastical courts as the only authority on Church matters. In 1874 these four laws were supplemented by others, to insure more perfect obedience. Dr. Adalbert Falk was appointed by Prince Bismarck "Minister of Public Worship," January 22, 1872. In 1872 Prince Bismarck carried through the Prussian Houses a bill to transfer the control of primary education from the Church to the State authorities.

Famous Retreat, The, of the ten thousand, occurred B. C. 401-399. It was conducted by Xenophon, the historian, who had joined the expedition of Cyrus. In the battle of Cunaxa, Cyrus lost his life, and the Greeks were left without a leader. Xenophon volunteered to lead them back to Greece, and has left a historical narrative of this famous retreat, called "Xenophon's Anabasis."

Feudal Law, introduced 1070. This consisted in dividing the kingdoms into baronies, giving them to certain persons and requiring those persons to furnish the king with money and a stated number of soldiers.

First French Revolution.—Its chief leaders: Comte de Mirabeau, 1789-1791; Danton, from the death of Mirabeau to 1793; Robespierre, from June, 1793, to July 27, 1794. Next to these three were St. Just, Couthon, Marat, Carrier, Hébert, Santerre, Camille Desmoulins, Roland and his wife, Brissot, Barnave, Sieyès, Barras, Tallien, etc. Its great days: 1789, June 17, the *Tiers Etat* constituted itself into the "National Assembly"; June 20, the day of the *Jeu de Paume*, when the Assembly took an oath not to separate till it had given France a constitution; July 14, Storming of the Bastile; October 5, 6, the king and National Assembly transferred from Versailles to Paris. This closed the ancient *régime* of the court. 1791, June 20, 21, flight and capture of the king, queen, and royal family. 1792, June 20, attack on the Tuileries by Santerre; August 10, attack on the Tuileries and downfall of the monarchy; September 2, 3, 4, massacre of the state prisoners. 1793, January 21, Louis XVI. guillotined; May 31, commencement of the Reign of Terror; June 2, the Girondists proscribed; October 16, Marie Antoinette guillotined; October 31, the Girondists guillotined. 1794, April 5, downfall of Danton; July 27, downfall of Robespierre.

Florida (Peninsular State).—First settlement by the Spaniards, at St. Augustine, 1565. Admitted to the Union, 1845. Ranks third in sugar and molasses; sixth in rice; tenth in cotton; twenty-first in square miles; twenty-seventh in miles of railway; thirty-fourth in population; thirty-sixth in wealth. The inhabitants confine themselves to agriculture. The chief products are cotton, sugar cane, rice, corn, and sweet potatoes, and tropical fruits of great variety. There is considerable trade also in lumber.

France, the country of the ancient Gauls; a colony of the Belgæ from Germany were permitted to settle in it B. C. 200; conquered by the Romans, B. C. 25; by the Goths, Vandals, Alans, Suevi, and Burgundi, who divided it amongst them, from 400 to 486. The Franks, from whom the French are derived, occupied part of Brabant, one hundred and thirty years before the reign of Clovis; it is the only state in Europe that can boast a perpetual succession from the conquerors of the western empire. Its first king was Pharamond, who began to reign in 418; Clovis was the first Christian king, 481; the Assemblies, called the States-General, first met, 1302, and continued to 1614; the English crown lost all its possessions in France between 1341 and 1359. The Revolution in France began 1789; the nobility and all religious orders suppressed, 1790; Louis XVI. beheaded, January 21, 1793; his queen, Marie Antoinette, beheaded, October 16, 1793; Bonaparte made first consul, 1799; Louis XVIII. made his second entry into Paris, July 8, 1815; Louis was succeeded in 1824, by his brother, Charles X., who was expelled, with his family, in July, 1830, and the Duke of Orleans raised to the throne under the title of Louis Philippe, king of the French. In 1830 war was commenced with Algeria, which country, as a consequence, was ceded to France. In 1848, the Bourbons were again driven out, and a republic established, with Napoleon III. as president. In December, 1851, Napoleon seized the absolute power, set aside the constitution, and shortly afterward was crowned emperor. A war with Prussia was precipitated in 1870, at the conclusion of which the present republic was established.

Franks, The, arose from a confederacy of the inhabitants of the Lower Rhine and Weser about 240.

Freemasons, The society of, are said to have taken rise from a set of foreigners who called themselves freemasons, whose secrets were kept intact; they are said to have introduced the art of building with stone into England about 670; another version has it that the institution is as early as the building of Solomon's Temple. The first lodge opened in America was at Boston, July 30, 1733.

Friedland, The great battle of, between the Russians and French, in which the former were completely overthrown, with the loss of 80 pieces of cannon, and 17,000 men killed, May 4, 1807.

Games, Olympic, first celebrated in Elis by the Idæi Dactyli, B. C. 1453; instituted by Pelops, 1307; celebrated by Hercules, 1222; restored at Elis by Iphitus, Lycurgus, and Cleosthenes, 884: Isthmian, instituted at Corinth by King Sisyphus, B. C. 1326; restored, 584; Pythian, first celebrated by Adrastus, king of Argos, B. C. 1263; instituted at Delphi, in Greece, 591; Capitoline, instituted by Domitian, A. D. 86; Secular, celebrated at Rome, A. D. 88.

Genoa, Republic, founded B. C. 63; the present one, A. D. 950; the first Duke of, chosen 1337; republic restored to its liberties by Doria, 1528; bank failed, 1750; the city in 1799, then in possession of the French, was taken by the united forces of Austria and England, and in 1815 was united to the Sardinian monarchy.

Georgia (Empire State of South). First settlement, by the English, Savannah, 1733. Ranks second in rice and sweet potatoes; third in cotton and molasses; fourth in sugar; seventh in mules; tenth in hogs; thirteenth in population; fifteenth in miles of railway; nineteenth in square miles; twenty-fifth in wealth. The leading industry is agriculture, the products being corn, rice, cotton, and sweet potatoes, and manufacturing, in which it leads all other Southern States, having fine facilities. Gold, iron, marble, and slate abound.

Germany, from Germann or warlike man, being anciently divided into several independent states, was insignificant in history until B. C. 25, when the people withstood the power of the Romans, and expelled them in 290; Charlemagne became master of the whole, 802. The Emperor of Germany assumed the title of Emperor of Austria, August 11, 1804. In 1521, at the Diet of Worms, Luther made his famous defense; religious dissensions occupied the country for a long period after the retirement of Charles V., in 1556, and in 1618, the Thirty Years' War broke out; Germany secured her religious freedom by the Peace of Westphalia, in 1648. The foundation of the Prussian monarchy was laid in 1675. Numerous wars took place during the eighteenth century, and constant mutations occurred in the map of Germany. Under the famous Fredericks, the Kingdom of Prussia developed into a first-class power. German unification began under William I.; the war with Prussia was declared on July 19, 1870, and resulted in the complete unification of Germany; the king of Prussia, by this treaty, was proclaimed Emperor of Germany.

Ghent, Belgium, stands on 26 islands, connected with each other by 80 bridges. The city of Venice is built on 80 islands, connected by nearly 400 bridges. In Venice canals serve for streets, and gondolas for carriages.

Gibraltar, taken by Sir George Rooke, July 24, 1704; besieged by the Spaniards, February 24, 1727; again, May, 1731; besieged again by the Spaniards, from 1780 to September 13, 1782, when their floating battery was burned with red hot balls from the garrison commanded by General Elliott. Gibraltar came into the possession of the English in 1704.

Girondins, The, in English "The Girondists," were the pure republican party in the National Assembly and National Convention of the first French Revolution. So called because it consisted mainly of the deputies of the Gironde. This party was distinguished for its oratory, and for a time dominated the assembly; but, horrified at the September massacres, they condemned the Reign of Terror, and tried to bring in more moderate measures. This drew upon them the hatred of the demagogues, and on May 31, 1793, some twenty-nine of the Girondists were arrested at the instigation of Robespierre, and on October 31 twenty of them were guillotined, among whom were Brissot, Gensonné, Vergniaud, Ducos, and Sillery. Valazé stabbed himself while he stood in the dock.

Gordian Knot, the knot of the thong in the wagon of Gordius, who was elected king of Phrygia from driving a wagon, and which he afterwards deposited in the temple of Jupiter. Whoever loosed this knot, the ends of which were not discoverable, the Oracle declared should be emperor of Persia. Alexander the Great cut away the knot till he found the ends, and thus interpretated the Oracle, B. C. 330.

Goths, The, who inhabited all the countries from the Baltic to the Euxine seas, first mentioned as invading the Romans, 250; waged war with them, 366; from which time may be derived the fall of the Roman Empire. The whole nation, a million in number, through fear of the Huns, removed to the waste land in Thrace, 376; rebelled against the Romans, 377, and were quelled; afterwards attacked by Valens, the Roman army was cut to pieces, and the emperor killed. The Goths capitulated with and submitted to the Romans, October 3, 382. Embraced Christianity, 400; pillaged Rome and massacred the inhabitants, 410; slew 300,000 inhabitants of Milan, 539.

Granada, Kingdom of, conquered by the Moors, 715; in 1235 it became the capital of a new kingdom, and attained to almost matchless splendor; the last Moorish prince was Abou-Abdillah, who was conquered by the Castilians, 1492.

Grecian Monarchy, commenced by Alexander the Great's victory over Darius, the last Persian monarch, B. C. 328; empire began under Nicephorus, 1811, ended, 1453.

Greece, The early history of, is surrounded with legend and myth. The heroic age of Greece is a fragment of the poetic imagination. Hellen was claimed by the Greeks as their common ancestor, the popular belief being that from his sons, Dorus and Æolus, and his grandsons, Ion and Æchæus, sprang the four different branches of the nation—the Dorians, the Æolians, the Ionians, and the Æchæns. From first to last, Greece was divided into numerous independent states. Authentic history begins 776 B. C., when the first Olympiad was held. In B. C. 431, began the Peloponnesian war. Greece passed under Macedonian rule about 344 B. C.; in B. C. 214 occurred the first collision between the Greeks and the Romans; from the fifth to the eighth centuries Slavic and other foreign people appeared in Greece, but were finally expelled; in the eleventh century the Normans plundered and ravaged the cities of Thebes, Athens, and Corinth. In 1203, the Latin princes appeared in the Crusades, conquered Constantinople, and divided Greece among them, which divisions were swept away by the Turks in 1453. In 1687 the Christian league besieged and took Athens, and the Moslem rule was again established; the Ottoman yoke was completely thrown off in 1821, and was accomplished by what is known as the modern revolution. Moslem rule was again attempted in 1822, but the allied powers of Europe decided to create Greece an independent kingdom; in 1866 a revolution in Crete strained the relations of Greece and Turkey; a renewed outbreak in 1896 led to a war with Turkey, which resulted in favor of Turkey, but did not imperil the independence of Greece.

Gretna Green is a village in Dumfriesshire, Scotland, and the place where, for nearly a century, runaway couples were made man and wife. These irregular marriages were discountenanced by law in the year 1856.

Guelphs and Ghibellines.—At the great battle of Weinsberg, in Suabia, A. D. 1140, the Emperor Conrad of Hohenstaufen, and Welf, uncle of Henry the Lion, Duke of Saxony, rallied their followers by the respective war cries, "Hie Waiblingen!" "Hie Welf!" As the chief theater of the conflict of these parties was Italy, the original names took the Italian form of Ghibellini and Guelfi, and under these names they became two great parties, whose conflicts may almost be said to make up the history of Italy and Germany from the eleventh till the fourteenth century. The Ghibellini may, in general, be described as the supporters of the imperial authority in Italy, the Guelphs as the opponents of the emperors and adherents of the popes. Five great crises in the strife of the Guelphs and Ghibelline parties are commonly noted by historians: Under Henry IV., in 1055; under Henry the Proud, in 1127; under Henry the Lion, in 1140; under Frederick Barbarossa, in 1159; and in the pontificate of the great champion of Church temporal power, Innocent III. The cities of northern Italy were divided between the two parties—Florence, Bologna, Milan, and other cities, as a general rule, taking the side of the Guelphs; while Pisa, Verona, and Arezzo were Ghibelline. In general, it may be said that the nobles of the more northern provinces of Italy inclined to the Ghibelline side, while those of the central and southern provinces were Guelph. After the downfall of the preponderance of the German emperors in Italy, the contest ceased to be a strife of principles and degenerated into a mere struggle of rival factions. From the fourteenth century the Guelphs or Ghibellines are seldom heard of as actually existing parties; but in the sense already explained, the conflict of principles which they represented is found in every period of political history.

Gypsy Tribes.—Gypsies, a term applied to a mysterious, vagabond race, scattered over the whole of Europe, and parts of Asia, Africa, and America. Whence they originally came, is not definitely known, but India seems to have been the cradle of the tribe. They are called Bohemians, in France; Zingari, in Italy. For centuries past they have drifted about over Europe, in small bands, having no permanent homes; living by begging, fortune telling, and various tricks. The first notice of them, which occurs in European literature, is embodied in a free paraphrase, in German, of the Book of Genesis, written by an Austrian monk, about 1122. On August 17, 1427, a band of them, coming from Bohemia, made their appearance before Paris, which, however, they were not allowed to enter, but were lodged at La Chapelle Saint Denis. Other hordes succeeded these in the following years, spreading in rapid succession over all parts of Germany, over Spain, England, Russia, Scandinavia, and, indeed, over the remotest parts of Europe. The account which they most frequently gave of themselves was, that they originally came from "Little Egypt," that the king of Hungary had compelled about 4,000 of them to be baptized, had slain the remainder, and had condemned the baptized to seven years' wandering. In France, Germany, Scotland, and other countries, the most stringent laws were formerly enforced against them, and they were slain by thousands. The jargon spoken by the Gypsies is styled Romany, and contains many Sanscrit words and corrupted Hebraisms.

Hanseatic League, The, was a trades-union to protect merchandise from pirates and the pillage of nobles. It began with the three towns of Hamburg, Bremen, and Lübeck, but ultimately contained eighty-five trading towns. The league was divided into four colleges, viz., Lübeck, Cologne, Brunswick, and Dantzig. Of these, Lübeck was the chief, and presided in all the conferences.

Hebrew Race, The, is distributed over the Eastern continent as follows: In Europe there are 5,400,000; in France, 63,000; Germany, 562,000, of which Alsace-Lorraine contains 39,000; Austro-Hungary, 1,544,000; Italy, 40,000; Netherlands, 82,000; Roumania, 265,000; Russia, 2,552,000; Turkey, 105,000, and in other countries 35,000, Belgium containing the smallest number, only 3,000. In Asia there are 319,000; Asiatic Turkey, 47,000, in Palestine there being 25,000; Asiatic Russia, 47,000; Persia, 18,000; Middle Asia, 14,000; India, 19,000, and China, 1,000. Africa contains 350,000; Egypt, 8,000; Tunis, 55,000; Algiers, 35,000; Morocco, 60,000; Tripoli, 6,000, and Abyssinia, 200,000. The entire number of Hebrews in the world is nearly 6,300,000.

Heptarchy, The Saxon, consisting of the kingdoms of Kent, the South Saxons, the West Saxons, the East Saxons, Northumberland, the East Angles, and Mercier, commenced in the sixth century, and continued till 800, when Egbert reigned alone. The Saxons, notwithstanding this division of the kingdom, were subject to one monarch, who was called King of Britain; the monarchy was not then hereditary, but that person succeeded who had the greatest power.

Herculaneum, first suffered by an earthquake, February 5, 63 A. D.; totally overwhelmed, with Pompeii, by an eruption of Mt. Vesuvius, November 1, 79 A. D.

Hittites, The, were one of the most important tribes in the south of Canaan. They are mentioned in Gen. x. as the descendants of Heth, a son of Canaan. In the age of Abraham the Hittites inhabited Hebron and its neighborhood (Gen. xxiii.). The primitive seat of the Hittites was probably the Taurus mountains of Asia Minor, from whence, as indicated by the cuneiform records of Tel-el-Amarna, in the latter part of the eighteenth Egyptian dynasty, they invaded Syria, and later, in the reign of Rameses II., were settled at Kadesh, ultimately spreading to the south of Palestine. In race the Hittites were probably Turanian, and in their language allied to the Alarodian family. The peculiar hieroglyphic writings found on Hittite monuments in Syria, Asia Minor, etc., are beginning to be deciphered. In common with the Hyksos, the deity of the Hittites was Seti, the Egyptian Typhon, and the local goddess of Kadesh Anata, the Canaanitish goddess of war.

Hivites, The, were a Canaanitish people, specially associated with the Amorities, dwelling in the time of Joshua (Josh. ix.) near the center of Palestine, and near Mount Hermon and Mount Lebanon, the latter being regarded as the country of the Amorites in the Egyptian texts, and Tel-el-Amarna tablets. The Hivites are first mentioned in Scripture in Gen. x.: 17; they were subjected to tribute by Solomon, after whose reign their name no longer appears.

Holland, in the fourteenth century, after being ruled for four centuries as a province of France or Germany, came under the rule of the Duke of Burgundy. Several wars, growing out of an attempt to extend the power of the inquisition, occurred between Holland and Spain, the last ending in 1648, when the Netherlands achieved their independence; was overrun by the French, January, 1785; secret expedition against, commenced by the Duke of York, August, 1799; British troops evacuated, November, 1799; Louis Bonaparte proclaimed king of, June 11, 1806; decree for annexing it to France, July 9, 1810; the French expelled, 1813.

Holy Alliance, The, was a league formed by the Emperors Alexander I. of Russia, Francis of Austria, and King Frederick William III. of Prussia, after the second abdication of Napoleon. The main principles of the alliance were: 1. That the different Governments of Europe belonged to one family of nations. 2. That all the different creeds of Christendom were to be accorded full and equal rights in the alliance. 3. That the Christian religion was to be regarded as the moral principle governing in the international conduct and comity of the states. 4. That the Christian religion was to regulate the whole system of public law. 5. That the allied sovereigns were to give one another united aid in all cases when required. A special article of the treaty also provided that no member of the Bonaparte family should ever sit upon a European throne. Alexander of Russia drew up the agreement and gave it a name. It was signed by the three monarchs, September 26, 1815, but it was not wholly made public until February 2, 1816. All the Governments of Europe, except Rome, which had not been invited, probably through fear that the Pope would claim the first place in its councils, and thus revive the old difficulty of the supremacy of the Church over Christian Governments, and England, which had declined, became members of the alliance. The alliance accomplished but little, and after Alexander's death, in 1825, the compact lost authority, and the French Revolution of 1830 caused a wide breach between the parties to it. The formation of the Prussian Diet, in 1847, the European uprising in 1848, the re-establishment of the Napoleon dynasty in 1850, and finally the war of Russia against England, France, and Turkey in 1854, brought about the complete dissolution of the alliance.

Hottentots, The, are an African native race, occupying the country north from the Cape Colony to Mossamedes, stretching westward to the Atlantic, and bounded on the east by the Kalahari desert. Formerly a numerous nation, the Hottentots have been greatly diminished by the oppression of the Boers, and the race is now nearly extinct. The Hottentots include the Griquas, Bushmen, Korannas, Namaquas, and Damaras.

Huguenots, Protestants first called so in France, from a German word signifying "allied by oath," 1560; massacre of them at Paris, August 24, 1572.

Hungary, the Pannonia of the ancients, was subject to the Romans, B. C. 11; conquered by the Huns under Attila, when the kingdom began, A. D. 433; annexed to Germany under Charlemagne, but became independent, 920; the Turks contended with the Germans for it from 1540 to 1739, when by the treaty of Belgrade, it was ceded to the latter; in 1848 occurred the Hungarian revolution, led by Kossuth, and which ended in the independence of Hungary, July 8, 1867; the dual monarchy between Austria and Hungary was established in 1867.

Huns, savage inhabitants of part of Siberia; their kingdom was founded B. C. 230; kingdom taken and divided A. D. 48; embraced Christianity, 416; conquered Scythia and Germany, about 432; the kingdom destroyed soon after the death of Attila, 453.

Idaho.—Ranks sixth in gold, seventh in silver, twelfth in square miles, forty-third in miles of railway, forty-fifth in population. Population, 1890, 84,385. First settlement, by Americans, 1842. Organized as a Territory, 1863. Admitted to the Union in 1890.

Independents, The, or Puritans, in the reign of Charles I. were called "Roundheads." The royalists were nicknamed "The Cavaliers." The former wore their hair short, and dressed with great simplicity; the latter wore their hair flowing over their shoulders, and dressed showily and expensively. The two came into collision about the expulsion of the bishops from the House of Lords. The Roundheads insisted on their expulsion, and the severance of the clergy from all secular and state offices. It was in this brawl that the two parties gave each other the nicknames of Roundheads and Cavaliers.

Indian Territory was originally set apart as a reservation for peaceful tribes. Organized in 1834, but not under the same forms of government as the other territories. The lands are held in common by the Indians, each being allowed to cultivate as much as desired, and whites can hold land only by marrying an Indian. Grazing and agriculture are the leading industries. Oklahoma was opened up to white settlers in 1889, and organized as a territory in the following year, its capital being fixed at Guthrie.

Indian War, King Philip's, commenced in New England and ended by his death, August 12, 1767.

Indiana, first settlement by the French at Vincennes, 1730. Ranks second in wheat, fourth in corn, hogs, and agricultural implements, sixth in coal, and population; seventh in horses, oxen, and other cattle, malt and distilled liquors, and wealth; ninth in hay and milch cows. The inhabitants are largely engaged in agriculture. Large quantities of corn, wheat, oats, pork, and beef are exported. Its mining and manufacturing interests are constantly increasing.

Indies, East, first discovered by the Romans; Alexander marched into, B. C. 328; discovered by the Portuguese, A. D. 1487; conquered in 1500, and settled by them in 1506; the first settlement was Goa; the East India Company, established 1600.

Illinois, first settlement made by the French at Kaskaskia, 1682. Illinois is in the front rank as an agricultural state, surpassing all others in the production of wheat and corn, and second to none in the extent of stock raising. It ranks fourth in population, and next to Missouri in manufacturing, and the sixth in the Union; its fruit and orchard products are very large. The state abounds in mineral production, coal, lead, and salt being the chief. Its great rivers and lakes present natural facilities for an extensive commerce. The railroads of the state are greater in the number of miles within the state than any other.

Iowa, first settlement made by the French Canadians at Burlington, 1788. Agriculture and mining are the leading pursuits. The state takes a leading position in the production of wheat, corn, and cattle. The manufactures are important and show great progress annually. It ranks first in hogs, second in milch cows, oxen, and other cattle, corn, hay, and oats; third in horses, fifth in barley, sixth in potatoes and rye, seventh in coal and wheat.

Ireland, was originally occupied by the Celts; in 432 Christianity was introduced by St. Patrick; from the eighth to the twelfth centuries perpetual warfare existed between the petty kings and their chiefs; conquered in 1174 by Henry II. of England, and apportioned among his Anglo-Norman followers; Parliamentary union with Great Britain took place in 1800; Catholic Emancipation Act passed, 1829; Fenian riots, 1867.

Iron Crown of Lombardy, The, is not an iron crown, but a magnificent gold diadem, containing a narrow iron band about three-eighths of an inch broad and one-tenth of an inch in thickness, This band was made out of a nail given to Constantine by his mother, and said to be one of the nails used in the crucifixion. The outer circlet of the crown is of beaten gold, set with large rubies, emeralds, and sapphires, and the iron band is within this circlet. The first Lombard king crowned with it was Agilulph, at Milan, in 591. Charlemagne was crowned with it in 774; Friedrich III., in 1452; Karl V., in 1530; and Napoleon I., May 23, 1805, crowned himself with it as "King of Italy" in Milan Cathedral. It was given up to Victor Emmanuel on the conclusion of peace with Austria, in 1866. The motto on the crown is, "God has given it me; beware who touches it."

Israel, kingdom divided, B. C. 979; ended, and the ten tribes carried captive by Shalmanezar, king of Syria, 720.

Issus, Battle of, between Darius and Alexander, in which the former lost 100,000 men, B. C. 333.

Italy, the successor of ancient Rome, suffered considerable political change by the aggressions of Napoleon I. In 1801 Savoy and Piedmont were united to France, the Duchy of Milan, formed the Cis-Alpine republic, to which, in 1805, the Duchy of Venice was added, forming together the kingdom of Italy, and Genoa was incorporated with France; Naples was seized, the Pope was deposed, and all Italy, except Sardinia and Sicily, were subjected to France. In 1814, the states were restored to their former rulers, except the Duchies of Milan and Venice, which were given to Austria, and formed the Lombardo-Venetian kingdom. In 1848 the great revolution was inaugurated, originating from a simultaneous insurrection in Lombardy and Venice. March 14, 1861, Victor Emmanuel was declared king of Italy, under whom the kingdom was strengthened and consolidated. He was succeeded by Humbert, the present ruler, in 1878.

Jacobins were the members of a political club which exercised a great influence during the French Revolution. It was originally called the *Club Breton*, and was formed at Versailles, when the States-General assembled there in 1789.

Jacobites (from the Latin *Jacobus*, "James"), was the name given after the Revolution of 1688 to the adherents of the exiled Stuarts — James II. (1633-1701), and his son and two grandsons, James Francis Edward, the Chevalier de St. George (1688-1766), Charles Edward (1720-88), and Henry Benedict, Cardinal York (1725-1807). Those adherents were recruited from the Catholics, the Nonjurors, the High Churchmen, and Tories generally, discontented and place-seeking Whigs, the Episcopalians and Highlanders of Scotland, and the great body of the Irish people.

Jamaica, discovered by Columbus, 1494; settled by the Spaniards, 1509; taken from the Spaniards by Admiral Penn, May 7, 1655.

Japan, Empire of, founded by Jimmu, 660 B. C.; first discovered by the Portuguese, 1549; Buddhism was introduced into Japan in the sixth century; in 1549 St. Francis Xavier introduced Christianity; in 1615 the priests were exiled, and all foreigners expelled from the island; in 1637, massacre of the Christians began; commercial treaty between the United States and Japan ratified in 1854.

Jerusalem, Temple of, built B. C. 1094; city taken by Nebuchadnezzar after a siege of eighteen months, 587; the second temple finished under Darius, B. C. 515; destroyed by Titus, A. D. 70; pillaged by the Persians, and 90,000 inhabitants killed, 613; taken by the Saracens, 637; taken by Godfrey of Boulogne, who was elected king of it, July 5, 1100; conquered by Saladin, 1187; now subject to the Turks.

Jugurthine War, begun B. C. 111, and continued five years.

Juries, first instituted, 970; trial of civil causes by in Scotland enacted, 1815.

Justice of the Peace, first appointed, 1076.

Justinian Code, first published, 529.

Kansas (Garden of the West). Settled by Americans. Admitted to the Union, 1861. Ranks fifth in cattle, corn, and rye, seventh in hay and miles of railway, ninth in hogs, horses, wheat, and coal, fourteenth in square miles, twenty-first in population, twenty-fourth in wealth. Agriculture and stock raising form the chief pursuits of the inhabitants. Every variety of cereal and farm products is raised in great quantities. Nearly 2,000,000 acres are mineral lands. Three fourths of the state is suited for agriculture.

Kentucky, first settled at Boonesboro, 1775, by the English. Agriculture is the main pursuit. Wheat, corn, hemp, flax, and tobacco are leading productions. Fruits of an excellent quality abound. Horses and cattle are reared in great numbers. Thousands of swine fatten in the woods. Mining is carried on to a large extent. Kentucky produces nearly one half the tobacco raised in the United States.

Knights Templars, a religious order instituted 1119; flourished in England during the reign of Henry II.; all of them arrested in France in one day; they were charged with great crime and great riches; 59 of them were burned alive at Paris, October 13, 1307; their order destroyed by Philip of France, 1311.

La Belle Alliance is the name of a farm some thirteen miles from Brussels; ever memorable for being the position occupied by the center of the French infantry in the battle of Waterloo (June 18, 1815). Napoleon himself was in the vicinity of this farm, but Wellington was at Mont St. Jean, two miles further north. Between these two spots was La Haye Sainte, where were posted the French tirailleurs. The Prussians call the battle of Waterloo the "Battle of la Belle Alliance," and the French call it the "Battle of Mont Saint Jean."

Liberia, First settlement of, on the west coast of Africa, made in 1820, under the patronage of the American Colonization Society.

Ligny, Battle of, Prussians under Blucher, totally defeated by the French, June 16, 1815.

Lincoln's Inn, London, the palace of the Bishop of Chichester, about 1226; converted into an inn of court about 1310.

Louisiana (Creole state). First settlement, by the French, at Iberville, 1699. Admitted to the Union, 1812. Ranks first in sugar and molasses; third in rice; ninth in salt; twenty-second in population; twenty-seventh in wealth; twenty-eighth in square miles; twenty-ninth in miles of railway. Holding, as it does, the outlet to the Mississippi Valley, the state is able to control both the foreign and domestic trade of this large and rich section, hence commerce is large and important. The manufacturing interests are comparatively small, except in sugars and molasses. Agriculture is the chief pursuit. This state is the only part of our country producing sugar in large quantities. Cotton is largely cultivated, Louisiana ranking fourth in its production. The rice crop is also large. Indian corn and other cereals are also produced to a considerable extent. The tropical fruits are abundant.

Lombardy, kingdom of, began 573; made numerous conquests till 1771, when Desiderius, their last king, was taken by Charlemagne and territories annexed to the German empire.

London, formerly called Augusta, founded by the Romans, 49; walled and a palace built, 368; city repaired by Alfred, 885; burned to the ground, about 912; nearly destroyed by fire, 1077, and again in 1110; the chief magistrate in the time of William I. was called port-reeve; Richard I. ordained two bailiffs, but King John changed them to a mayor; obtained their first free charter for electing their own magistrates, 1208; gates of the city taken down, 1760; the common council ordered to wear blue silk gowns at court, September 16, 1761; practice discontinued, 1775; London bridge built about 1098. The largest and richest city in the world.

Louisburg, taken by the French, July 27, 1758.

Lycurgus, established his laws at Lacedæmon, B. C. 884; his institutions renounced by the Spartans, 188.

Mahrattas, The, are a native Indian race which founded an empire in Central and Western India, 1674. After 1795, Scindia, Holkar, and Berar became independent; the confederacy of Mahratta states came to an end in 1818, and all the chiefs became dependants of the British Crown.

Massachusetts, first settled by the English at Plymouth in 1620. Ranks first in cotton, woolen, and worsted goods, cod and mackerel fishing; second in commerce; third in manufactories, printing, and publishing; fourth in silk goods; fifth in soap and in wealth, sixth in iron and steel; ninth in agricultural implements. Its manufactured articles include leather and morocco, flour and meal, lumber and furniture, refined molasses and sugar, machinery, ship-building, animal and vegetable oils. Manufacturing and commerce chiefly engage the attention of its inhabitants. The middle and western parts are fertile. Farms are highly cultivated.

Madagascar, first seen by the Portuguese, 1506; attempts at colonization were made by the English and French from 1644 to 1773. The island is at present under a native ruler, though tributary to France.

Madeira Islands, discovered by the Portuguese, 1419.

Madrid, built B. C. 936; occupies the site of the ancient Mantua-Carpepanorum, called Majoritium in the Middle Ages. Its importance commenced in 1563, when it was made the capital of Spain by Philip II. It was held by the French from 1808 to 1812, and here Napoleon placed his brother Joseph on the throne of Spain.

Marriage, first institution of, by ceremony, ascribed to Cecrops, king of Athens, B. C. 1556; celebration in churches first ordained by Pope Innocent III. about 1200, before which the only ceremony was that of a man leading his bride home to his house; marriage in Lent forbidden by the Church, 364; forbidden to priests, 1015; publication of bans instituted about 1210.

Maryland, first settled by the English, 1634, at St. Mary's. The chief industries are agriculture and manufacturing. Corn, wheat, and tobacco are the leading agricultural products. Coal is mined extensively. Among other commercial products are flour and meal, smelted copper, refined sugar and molasses, cotton goods, lumber and furniture, malt and distilled liquors, tobacco and cigars, oysters, fish, and vegetables, leather goods, clothing, printing and publishing. The foreign commerce of the state is carried on chiefly through the city of Baltimore, which has all the advantages of a seaport. The chief exports are tobacco, flour, canned fruits, and oysters.

Maine (Pine Tree State).—Settled by French at Bristol, 1625; admitted to the Union, 1820. Ranks fifth in buckwheat and copper; eighth in hops and potatoes; eleventh in hay; twenty-first in wealth; twenty-seventh in population; thirty-third in miles of railway; thirty-sixth in square miles. Industries: Extensive lumber and ship-building trade, fisheries, cotton, woolens, tanned and curried leather, boots and shoes, lime, etc. The agricultural portion of the state lies in the valley of St. John, and between the Penobscot and Kennebec rivers.

Magna Charta, The, was the great charter or document, founded mainly upon earlier Saxon charters, which the English barons compelled King John to sign at Runnymede (June 15, 1215). The most important provisions are: (1) No scutage or aid shall be raised, except in the case of the king's captivity, the knighting of his eldest son, or the marriage of his eldest daughter, except by the general council of the kingdom; (2) no freeman shall be imprisoned or disseised, outlawed, or proceeded against other than by the legal judgment of his peer, or by the law of the land; (3) that right or justice shall not be sold, delayed, or denied to any; (4) that the civil court shall be stationary, and not follow the king's person. Other provisions were directed against the abuse of the power of the king as lord paramount, the tyranny of the forest laws, and grievances connected with feudal tenure. The Charter of Forests was granted at the same time. Both documents have been confirmed by Act of Parliament thirty-two times.

Manitoba was first settled by the French in 1731, and English traders first made their appearance in 1767. It is a wheat-growing country, and furs are also a leading product. All kinds of garden vegetables, as well as oats, barley, Indian corn, hops, flax, hemp, potatoes, and other root crops are easily raised. The grassy savannas of the Red River afford abundant pasturage. The climate is very severe in winter, but occasionally hot in summer. Winnipeg is the capital.

Massacres at Alexandria of many thousand citizens by order of Antoninus, 213; of Thessalonica, when upwards of 7,000 persons were put to the sword by order of Theodosius, 390; of 35,000 persons at Constantinople, 532; of the Jews, 1189; of the Huguenots at Paris, by order of Charles IX., when 70,000 where destroyed, June 12, 1418; of the Swedish nobility at a feast, by order of Christian II., 1520; at Paris, when the king led the way and nearly 10,000 Protestants were slain, 1572; of the Christians in Croatia by the Turks, when 65,000 were slain, 1592; of the English factory by the Dutch at Amboyna, 1623, in order to dispossess them of the Spice Islands; of the Irish at the Island of Magee, when 40,000 English Protestants were killed, 1641; of the whites in San Domingo by the negroes, 1803 and 1804; of the Greeks at Scio, 1823.

Memnon, the Egyptian, invented letters, B. C. 1822.

Mexico, first conquered by Spain, 1521, by Cortez; a revolution, fomented by the clergy, took place in 1810; a constitution was proclaimed in 1812, and in May, 1822, Don Augustin Iturbide was elected emperor of Mexico; he abdicated in 1823; became a federal republic in 1824; in 1863, a French army invaded Mexico and occupied the capital. Under the patronage of Napoleon the III., Maximilian of Austria became emperor of Mexico from 1864 till 1867, when he was shot and a republic reproclaimed.

Minnesota (Gopher State).—First settlement, by Americans, Red River, 1812. Admitted to the Union, 1858. Ranks fourth in wheat and barley; eighth in oats and hay; twelfth in miles of railway; thirteenth in square miles; seventeenth in wealth; twenty-sixth in population. The leading industries are: 1. Agriculture; the staple productions being corn, wheat, and oats, while other cereals are largely raised. 2. Lumbering; great quantities of lumber are sawed in this state, and immense rafts of logs are floated down the Mississippi, to be sawed in other states. 3. Manufacturing; the principal articles being sawed lumber and flour.

Missouri (Pennsylvania of the West).—First settlement, by the French, at St. Genevieve, 1764. Admitted to the Union, 1821. Ranks first in mules; third in oxen, hogs, corn, and copper; fifth in population; sixth in iron ore, wool, milch cows, and horses; seventh in oats; eighth in wealth, wheat, and tobacco; ninth in sheep and potatoes; tenth in miles of railway; sixteenth in square miles. Agriculture is the leading occupation. Mining is extensively carried on in the section south of St. Louis. The iron resources of the state exceed those of any other. The manufacturing interests are large and increasing. The chief agricultural products are great crops of corn, wheat, rye, tobacco, hemp, and grapes.

Mississippi.—First settlement made by the French at Natchez, 1716. This state ranks second in cotton; fifth in rice; fifth in mules and molasses; seventh in sugar. It is almost exclusively an agricultural state. Great quantities of rice, corn, sugar, and sweet potatoes are produced. Many tropical fruits grow in abundance. The labor is largely performed by negroes. Horses, mules, swine, and cattle, are extensively raised.

Microscopes.—First used in Germany, 1621; with two glasses, invented by Drebbel, 1624; solar, invented by Lieberkuk, 1470.

Milan, anciently Liguria, the seat of the Roman empire, 303; conquered by the Goths in the fifth century, who were dispossessed by the Lombards, 572; subdued by the Emperor Charlemagne, 800; the French expelled about 1525; taken by the Imperialists, 1706; recovered by France and Spain, 1743; restored to Austria, 1748; in

1805 the French made it the capital of the kingdom of Italy; retaken by Austria in 1814; in 1859 was incorporated with Lombardy in the kingdom of Italy.

Minstrels, originally piers appointed by the Lords of Manor to divert their copyholders whilst at work; owed their origin to the gleemen or harpers of the Saxons; continued until about 1500; female harpers not uncommon in Britain, 680.

Mint.—First established in London as a privileged place, 1066; for the coinage of money, 1813; mint of the United States first established at Philadelphia, April 2, 1792; coinage of gold commenced July 31, 1795.

Michigan (Wolverine State).—First settled by the French, at Detroit, 1650. Admitted to the Union, 1837. Ranks first in copper, lumber, and salt; second in iron ore; third in buckwheat and wool; fifth in hops and potatoes; sixth in wheat, barley, and wealth; seventh in agricultural implements; ninth in oats, population, and miles of railway, and twentieth in square miles. Agriculture, mining, lumbering, manufacturing, and commerce command the attention of the inhabitants. Large crops of wheat, corn, oats, and potatoes are produced, as also great quantities of wool, butter, and cheese. Fruit raising is extensively followed, the value of the orchard products exceeds that of New Jersey or California. The copper mines of the state are the richest known, and are extensively worked. The production of sawed lumber is greater than that of any other state. The value of manufacturing exceeds $100,000,000. The fisheries form one of the secondary, yet important sources of wealth, large quantities being taken for home use and export.

Montana ranks fourth in silver, and square miles; fifth in gold; fifteenth in cattle; thirty-sixth in miles of railway, and forty-fourth in population. The population of Montana, according to census of 1880, was 39,159, but in 1884 the total vote cast for delegate to Congress was 26,969, and in 1886, 32,262. In 1890, the population numbered 132,159. First settlement, by Americans, 1852. Organized as a territory, 1864. Admitted to the Union in 1889.

Mogul Empire.—First conquered by Jenghis Kahn, a Tartar prince, who died 1226; Timur Bek became great mogul by conquest, 1399; the dynasty continued in his family until the conquest of Tamerlane in the fifteenth century; Kouli Khan, the famous Sophi of Persia, considerably diminished the power of the mogul, and since that event many of the nabobs have made themselves independent; the last sovereign, Shah Allum, died in 1806, a pensioner of England.

Monkery began in Egypt and Persia; tolerably well established about 330; in Egypt alone there were 96,000 monks. St. Anthony, the first example of a monastic life, 305, established the first monastery on Mt. Colzim, near the Red Sea. Athanasius introduced monastic life into Rome, 341.

Mount Vernon, memorable as the residence and the burial place of George Washington, is on the right bank of the Potomac, in Virginia, fifteen miles below Washington. In 1856 the mansion and surrounding property were saved from the auctioneer's hammer, and secured as a national possession.

Moors, driven out of Spain, after they had continued there 900 years, 1620, for attempting to free themselves from the Inquisition; they were in number about 900,000.

Morocco, Empire of, anciently Mauritania, first known, 1008; possessed by the Romans, B. C. 25; about 1116 Abdallah, the leader of a sect of Mohammedans, founded the dynasty of Almahides, which ended in the last sovereign's total defeat in Spain, 1212; Morocco was afterwards seized by the King of Fez, but the descendants of Mahomet, about 1550, subdued and united the three kingdoms, and formed what is called the Empire of Morocco. The present sovereign of Morocco belongs to the ninth dynasty, founded in 1648.

Moscow, burned, 30,000 houses destroyed, in 1739; entered by the French, September 14, 1812, and burned by the Russians, in consequence of which the French retreated with great loss.

Museum, The British, established 1753; large additions made to the building and the library of George III. given to the institution by George IV., 1827.

Nantes, Edict of, passed by Henry IV., by which Protestants enjoyed toleration in France, 1598, revoked by Louis XIV., 1685; in consequence of which 50,000 French Protestants emigrated to England; they engaged largely in the manufacture of silk; some introduced the art of making crystal glasses for watches and pictures.

Naples, anciently Capua and Campania, kingdom of, begar 1020; given by the pope to the Comte D'Anjou, 1266; Alphonsus of Arragon united Sicily to it, and the kings have since been called king of the Two Sicilies, 1442; taken from the French and annexed to Spain, 1504; order of the Crescent founded, 1464; taken by the French, January 24, 1799; Joseph Bonaparte was made king of Naples in 1805, but replaced by Murat in 1808; the Austrians took possession in 1814; in 1861 the last king of Naples was expelled by Garibaldi, and the two Sicilies were merged in the kingdom of Italy.

Nebraska.—First settlement made by Americans. Beef, cattle, and other livestock are raised in great numbers upon the grazing sections. Corn, wheat, and other cereals, and fruit growing are carried on extensively and with great success. The cheap and fertile lands offer great inducements for settlement to immigrants.

New Hampshire (Granite State).—First settlement by the English at Little Harbor, 1623. Ranks third in manufacture of cotton goods; fifteenth in potatoes; twenty-second in wealth; thirty-first in population; thirty-seventh in miles of railway; forty-first in square miles. Largely engaged in manufacturing; the abundant water power affords great advantages. Agriculture, pasturage, and drainage occupy a large number.

New Mexico.—First settled by the Spaniards at Santa Fe, 1537; organized as a territory, 1850. Ranks eighth in silver; eleventh in gold; nineteenth in sheep, and twenty-second in cattle. Chief industries, mining and cattle raising.

Nevada.—First settled, by Americans, in 1850. Ranks second in gold; fourth in silver, and thirty-seventh in wealth. The leading industry is mining. The mines of the state yield over three fifths of all the silver produced in the United States. Stock raising is also largely followed, owing to the large amount of good pasture land.

Netherlands were placed under the sovereignty of the house of Orange and became a kingdom, 1815; in 1816, the Prince of Orange was elevated to the rank of King of the Netherlands, with increased territories, extending over the present kingdom of Belgium; Belgium was then erected into a kingdom, and the present limits of the kingdom of the Netherlands were defined in 1833.

New England, First settlement of, made at Plymouth, November 10, 1620; states united, 1643.

Newfoundland, discovered by Cabot about 1500; began to be settled by the English, 1520; in 1713 it was declared by the treaty of Utrecht to belong wholly to Great Britain.

New Jersey (Jersey Blue).—First settlement by the Dutch at Bergen, 1620. Ranks first in fertilizing marl, zinc, and silk goods; fourth in iron ore; fifth in iron and steel; sixth in buckwheat, manufactories, and soap; seventh in rye, twelfth in wealth; nineteenth in population; twenty-sixth in miles of railway; forty-third in square miles. Manufactures: Molasses and sugar refining, flour, machinery, leather and leather goods, hats, caps, and clothing, woolen and cotton goods, bleaching and dyeing, glass. Industries: The commerce of the state is small, its manufactures large and various. Its shad and oyster fisheries are extensive. Mining is also a leading industry. But its chief industry is agriculture and market gardening, the state being one immense garden, the mildness of its climate being such that small fruits are very productive, and, being adjacent to the markets of New York and Philadelphia, farmers and fruit raisers find large profits from their labor.

New Orleans.—First laid out by the French, 1720; battle of, January 8, 1815.

New Zealand, in the South Seas, first discovered by Abel J. Tasman, 1642; visited by Pope Marcus, 336; formally taken possession of as a British colony in 1840.

New York (Empire State).—First settlement by the Dutch at New York (New Amsterdam), 1614. Ranks first in value of manufactories, population, soap, printing, and publishing, hops, hay, potatoes, buckwheat, milch cows, and wealth; second in salt, silk goods, malt and distilled liquors, and barley; third in agricultural implements, iron ore, iron and steel, oats and rye; fourth in wool and miles of railway; twenty-seventh in square miles. In population, wealth, and commerce, New York is the first in the Union. The commerce extends to all parts of the world. Manufacturing is large, and constantly increasing. Agriculture is one of the chief pursuits, wheat and corn being the staple productions. The development of the salt springs of the interior is also one of the industries of the state. Its magnificent system of canals and railroads has done much to increase its domestic trade.

North Carolina (Old North State).—First settlers, English, Cowan river, 1650. Ranks first in tar and turpentine; second in copper; third in peanuts and tobacco; fourth in rice; ninth in cotton; fifteenth in population; twentieth in miles of railway; twenty-third in wealth; twenty-sixth in square miles. Agriculture is the leading industry, the chief articles being corn, wheat, tobacco, sweet potatoes, oats, rice, and cotton. Vast forests furnish three times as much pitch, tar, and resin as all the other states together. There are valuable gold mines, and iron, copper, and coal abound.

Normandy, erected into a dukedom, 876; ceded to France by Henry III., May 20, 1259; taken by the English in 1419, and retained until 1425; finally joined to France under Charles VII.

Norway, the ancient Scandinavia, including Sweden, united with Denmark, 998; in 1319 Norway and Sweden, for a short time, became united under Magnus V.; in 1397 Norway, Sweden, and Denmark were again united, which union remained in force until 1523, when Sweden emancipated herself; Norway was annexed to Sweden, November 4, 1814, by the treaty of Kiel.

Notaries Public, originally appointed by the Fathers of the Christian Church to collect the acts and memoirs of martyrs in the first century; since changed into commercial offices.

Nova Scotia, charter granted, 1621; afterwards in the possession of the French, but ceded to England, 1713; peopled by England, 1749.

Nova Zembla, discovered by Capt. Hugh Willoughby, 1553; has no permanent inhabitants.

Oath, swearing on the Gospels, first used, 528; first administered in judicial proceedings by the Saxons about 600.

Ohio was first settled by the English, at Marietta, in 1788. Ranks first in agricultural implements and wool; second in petroleum, iron, and steel; third in population, wheat, sheep, coal, malt, and distilled liquors; fourth in printing and publishing, salt, soap, and wealth; fifth in milch cows, hogs, horses, hay, tobacco, iron ore, and miles of railway. The agricultural interest is very large. Great crops of wheat, corn, oats, barley, hay, potatoes, garden and orchard products are raised; also flax, tobacco, and grapes. Coal and iron mining are extensively carried on in the eastern and southern parts, and large numbers of live stock are sent to the eastern markets. Its commerce by lake, river, canal, and railroad transportation, is very large.

Olympiads, games instituted at Olympia by Pelops, in honor of Jupiter, B. C. 1307; they were revived by the Greeks about 400 years after the destruction of Troy, and continued until the reign of Theodosius the Great, when a new code of reckoning began; the first Olympiads began July 23, 776, Corœbus being then the Olympic victor; the last ended about 440 B. C.

Ontario is the most important province of Canada. Principal products are grain, fruit, lumber, petroleum, copper, and iron. The population of Ontario is one third of the whole Dominion. Toronto, the capital, is the manufacturing and educational center. The population of the province is largely of British descent.

Oregon was first settled by the Americans in 1811. Agriculture, stock raising, and lumbering are the chief pursuits; wheat being the staple article of the former, while most of the cereals of the middle states flourish. Cutting timber from the immense pine forests of the state gives employment to great numbers of inhabitants.

Orange, Title of, first in the Nassau family by the marriage of Claude de Chalons, the Prince of Orange's sister, with the Count of Nassau, 1530; the Prince of Orange was applied to by England for assistance, 1688; landed at Torbay, in England, with an army, November 5, 1688; took on him the government at the invitation of the Lords; declared king of England, February 13, 1689.

Organs.—First introduced into churches by Pope Vitallian I., 683; into the western churches, 826.

Ostrogoths, their kingdom began in Italy, 476; ended 554.

Ottoman, or Turkish Empire, founded by Othman I., in 1299, in Asia Minor, and soon extended into Europe. With the capture of Constantinople, in 1453, it suc-[illegible]ed to the Byzantine Empire.

[illegible]anism, finally overthrown in the Roman Empire [illegible] reign of Theodosius between 388 and 395.

[illegible]tines.—Seven thousand families of these poor [illegible]tants were driven by the French from their habitations on the banks of the Rhine, and came to England; a brief was granted to collect alms for them. Five hundred families went under the protection of the government to Ireland and the rest were sent to New York and Hudson's Bay; they finally went to Pennsylvania, where they settled, 1709.

Pandects, a system of laws accidentally discovered at Amalfi, Italy, 1137.

Pantheon, The, at Rome, built by Agrippa B. C. 25.

Paris, made the capital of France, 510; consumed by fire, 588; barricaded to oppose the entry of the Duke of Guise, 1588; again 1688, in opposition to the regency; first parliament held, 1302; general confederation in the Champ de Mars, July 14, 1790; an armed mob forced the Tuileries and insulted the king of France, June 20, 1792; Tuileries again attacked and Swiss Guard massacred by the Populists, August 10, 1792; royal family imprisoned in the temple, August 14; massacre of the state prisoners, September 2-5, 1792; Lord Malmesbury negotiated for peace, October 28, 1796; Napoleon arrived at midnight, December 18, 1812; allied sovereigns entered, March 31, 1814; Louis XVIII. entered May 3, 1814; Napoleon returned to, from Elba, March 21, 1815; left it to meet the allied forces, May 2, 1815; capitulated to the allies, July 3, 1815; treaties of general peace signed, November 20, 1815.

Pauls, St., London, built by Ethelbert, King of Kent, on the foundation of an old temple of Diana, 596; burned, 964; rebuilt and consecrated, 1240; it was 150 years building; again burned down, it was rebuilt, 1631; first stone of the present building laid, 1675; finished, 1710, at an expense of about $5,000,000.

Persecution, by the Jews, the first in 33; second, 44; first general of the Christians under Nero, 64; second under Domitian, 93; third under Trajan, 107; fourth under Marcus Aurelius, 164; fifth under Severus, 202; sixth under Maximinus, 235; seventh under Decius, 250; eighth under Valerian, 257; ninth under Aurelian, 272; tenth under Diocletian, 302; eleventh by the Arians under Constantius, 337; twelfth under Julian the Apostate, 361; Luther's followers persecuted in Franconia, 1525. The Protestants persecuted in England, 1556; in France, 1723.

Persian Empire, began under Cyrus after his conquest of Media, B. C. 536; ended in the conquest of Darius, about 330; a new empire called the Parthian was founded upon its ruins by the Persians under Arbaces, B. C. 250, but took its original name under Artaxerxes, 229; the Saracens, however, A. D. 651, put an end to that empire and Persia became a prey to the Tartars, and the province of Hindustan, until the emperor Kouli Kahn raised it to a powerful kingdom; emperor assassinated by his relatives, 1747.

Pennsylvania (Keystone State).—First settlement, English, Philadelphia, 1682. Ranks first in rye, iron and steel, petroleum, and coal; second in wealth, population, manufactories, buckwheat, potatoes, printing, and publishing; third in miles of railway, milch cows, hay, soap; fourth in oats and tobacco; fifth in silk goods, wool, malt and distilled liquors; sixth in salt, copper, and agricultural implements; eighth in horses and sheep; thirtieth in square miles. Pennsylvania ranks next to New York in wealth, population, and manufactures. Industries: The people are largely engaged in agriculture, mining, and manufactures; wheat, corn, orchard fruits, potatoes, butter, and wool, are the chief products. The farms are generally large and well conducted. The manufactures are very extensive, and comprise a great variety of articles; iron, cotton, and woolen goods being the leading articles. In the production of coal and iron Pennsylvania surpasses all other states.

Pharsalia, Battle of, where Pompey was defeated by Cæsar, B. C. 47.

Philippi, Battle of, which terminated in the Roman Republic, B. C. 41.

Phœnicians, by order of Pharaoh Necho, sailed from the Red Sea, round Africa, and returned by the Mediterranean, B. C. 607.

Picts.—First mentioned in history, 284; kingdom of, began in Scotland, 823; extirpated by the Scots, 840; Pict's wall between England and Scotland built, 123.

Plague.—Almost the whole world visited by one, B. C. 767; in Rome, which carried off 10,000 persons in a day, 78 A. D.; in England, that carried off 34,000, 772; in Scotland, wherein 40,000 died, 954; in England, 1247; again, 1347; in Germany, which cut off 90,000 people, 1348; in Paris and England, when 57,000 died in England, 1362; again in England, 30,000 killed in London, 1407; at Constantinople, when 200,000 persons died, 1611; at Lyons, where 60,000 died, 1632; again at London, where 68,000 were destroyed, 1665; at Marseilles, fatal to 18,000 persons, 1720; at Bassora, in Persia, when 80,000 persons died, 1773.

Poet Laureate.—The first mention of one is in the reign of Edward IV., though the present office under this title is derived from the "King's Versifier," of whom we hear in 1251.

Poictiers, Battle of, between the French and English, in which the former were defeated, September 19, 1356.

Poland, made a duchy, 694; kingdom of began, under Boleslaus, 999; Red Russia added to it, 1059; Pomerania united with it, 1465; embraced Christianity, 965; seized and divided between Russia, Prussia, and Austria, 1773; annexed to Russia, 1815; revolution commenced at Warsaw, November 29, 1830.

Pope, Title of, formerly given to all bishops; but Boniface III., 606, influenced the emperor Phocas to confine it to the Bishops of Rome; Hygenus was the first Bishop of Rome that took the title, 138; pope's supremacy over the Christian church, first established by Boniface III., 607; John XIX., a layman made pope, 1024; first pope that kept an army was Leo IX., 1054; pope Gregory obliged Henry IV., emperor of Germany, to stand three days, in the depth of winter, barefooted, at his castle gate, to implore his pardon, 1077; the pope's authority first introduced into England, 1079; abrogated by Parliament, 1534: the word pope struck out of all English books, 1541.

Portugal, formerly called Lusitania, with the rest of Spain, subject to the Moors, 713; held by the Moors until the end of the eleventh century; Portuguese monarchy established, 1139; first conquest abroad made in 1415, upon the discovery of the Island of Madeira; in 1500 Brazil was discovered by Cabral, which was followed by the establishment of a colony; taken by the Spaniards, 1580; revolted from Spain, and the Duke of Braganza sat on the throne under Philip IV. of Spain, and the III. of Portugal, 1640; in the latter year, the Duke of Braganza expelled the Spaniards, and ascended the throne under the title of John IV.; invaded by France in 1807, when the royal family went to Brazil; from 1827 to 1833 the throne was usurped by Don Miguel. The erection of Brazil into an independent empire in 1826, robbed Portugal of her richest possession.

Post, method of carrying letters invented by the University of Paris about 1470; general post office, established in England, 1643.

Potatoes.—First introduced into England from America by Sir Francis Drake, 1586; introduced into Ireland, 1610.

Protestants, Name of, began from the Diet of Spires, when several of the German states protested against a decree of the Diet to support the doctrine of the Church of Rome, April 19, 1530.

Prussia, anciently possessed by the Venedi, B. C. 320; the Venedi were conquered by Borussi who inhabited the Riphæan Mountains; whence the country was called Borussia or Prussia, which was subdued by the Mercian knights, sent by the Emperor Frederick II., 1215; revolted to Jagello, King of Poland, 1219; the grand master of the Teutonic order conquered the Poles and kept possession till 1700, when he was made a king.

Public Houses, power of licensing them, first granted to Sir Giles Montesson and Sir Francis Michel, 1621.

Punic Wars, First, began B. C. 264, lasted twenty-three years; second, began 218, and ended 200; third, began 150.

Quakers, founded by George Fox, 1646; sixty transported from England to America by order of Council, 1664; their affirmation adopted by Act of Parliament for an oath, 1696.

Quebec, a province of Canada, was originally settled by the French, and the present population is largely composed of descendants of the Voyagers. The capital, Quebec, is the oldest city in the Dominion. Its fortifications were at one time considered next to Gibraltar, the strongest in the world. Nevertheless, the fortress was captured by General Wolfe; taken by the English, December 13, 1758; unsuccessful attack on, by the Americans, under General Montgomery, December 31, 1775. The metropolis, Montreal, is noted for its churches. Ship building is the chief manufacturing industry. There are also manufactures of iron castings, machinery, cutlery, nails, leather, musical instruments, boots and shoes, paper, India rubber goods, tobacco and steel. The staple of export is timber. Quebec was first visited by Jacques Cartier in 1535. It then consisted of an Indian village called Stadacona. In July, 1608 Champlain founded the city, giving it its present name.

Reformation, The, first set on foot by John Wycliffe, 1370; began in England by Henry VIII. casting off the pope's supremacy and introducing the Protestant religion, 1534; completed by Edward VI., 1547.

Revolution, in Great Britain, took place through the Prince of Orange taking possession of the throne, November 5, 1688; in France, began 1789; in the United States, July 4, 1776; in Sweden, in 1772; second French revolution, July, 1830.

Rhodes.—An island of the Turks, peopled from Crete, B. C. 916; the republic completed, 480; the city built, 432; taken by the Saracens and the Colossus sold, 652; taken from the Turks, 1308; retaken by them from the Knights of Jerusalem, 1523; almost destroyed by an inundation, B. C. 314; Hipparchus began his astronomical observations here, 167.

Rhode Island.—First settlement made by the English at Providence, 1636. Ranks second in cotton, flax, and linen goods; twentieth in wealth. The state is largely engaged in manufacturing. It has considerable commerce. Farming is carried on to some extent; the chief productions are grain, fruit, butter, and cheese.

Romans.—First engaged in naval affairs and defeated the Carthaginians, B. C. 260; first crossed the Po, pursuing the Gauls, who had entered Italy, 223; defeated by Hannibal at Cannæ, 216; commenced the auxiliary war against Philip in Epirus, which was continued at intervals, 216; subdued Spain and Sparta, 194; defeated Antiochus at Thermopylæ, 194; made war against the Achæans, 147; destroyed Carthage, 146; 80,000 defeated on the banks of the Rhone by the Cimbri and Teutones, 105; Cyrene left them by Ptolemy Apion, 97; first invaded England, B. C. 54; quitted Britain, 426.

Rome, built by Romulus, B. C. 753; republican government established, 509; first alliance between Rome and Carthage, 508; burned by the Gauls, 390; first coining of silver, 269; first divorce known, 235; surgery introduced, 219; gold first coined, 206; Asiatic luxury first introduced by the army, from the spoils of Antiochus, 190; first library created with books obtained from Macedonia, 168; philosophers and rhetoricians banished, 161; sumptuary law, limiting the expenses of eating and drinking, 110; set on fire by Nero, A. D. 64; Capitol and Pantheon destroyed by fire, 80.

Russia, anciently Sarmatia, was inhabited by the Scythians; came into renown in 864, when the natives attempted to take Constantinople. The foundation of the Russian empire was laid by the Rus or Varangians, a body of Scandinavians led by Rurick, at Novgorod, about 862; in the twelfth, thirteenth, and fourteenth centuries, Russia was tributary to the Mongols; the country was consolidated and extended under Ivan the Great, and Ivan the Terrible, 1462-1584. Peter the Great was the most distinguished ruler of Russia, 1672-1725. Important events of more recent times were: The dismemberment of Poland, of which the greater part became Russian; the wars of Napoleon and the burning of Moscow, 1812; the Crimean war, 1853-55; the vast increase in area by war and treaty of the Asiatic provinces, 1858-73; the abolition of serfdom, 1851; the sale of Alaska to the United States, 1867; the Turko-Russian war, 1877-78.

Rubicon, The, is a river of Italy, flowing into the Adriatic, which formed the boundary between Cisalpine Gaul and Italy proper. The passage of this river by Julius Cæsar was necessarily the signal for civil war, the issue of which could not be foreseen, as Roman generals were forbidden to cross this river at the head of an army.

Rye House Plot, a plot to assassinate Charles II. at a place called Rye House on his way to Newmarket, was prevented by the king's house at Newmarket accidentally taking fire, which hastened his departure eight days before the plot was to take place; discovered June 12, 1683.

Sacred War, first, concerning the temple of Delphi, B. C. 448; second war, on Delphi being attacked by the Phocians, 356; war finished by Philip taking all the cities of the Phocians, 348.

St. Helena, first taken possession of by the Englis[h] 1600; taken by the Dutch, 1673; retaken by the En[glish] the same year; celebrated as the place of exile of [Napo]leon Bonaparte, 1815, where he died May 5, 1821

Saints, tutelar, St. George of England, St. A[ndrew of] Scotland, St. Patrick of Ireland, St. David of W[ales, St.] Dennis of France, St. James of Spain.

Saracens, conquered by Spain, 713; 70,00[0]

battle by Ramirus, king of Spain, 844; empire of, ended by the taking of Bagdad by the Tartars, 1258.

Sardinia, conquered by the Spaniards, 1303, in whose possession it continued until 1708, when it was taken by an English fleet and given to the Duke of Savoy, with the title of king.

Savoy.—Part of Gallia, Narbonensis, submitted to the Romans, B. C. 118; the Alemanni seized it in 395; the Franks, 496; it shared the revolutions of Switzerland till 1040, when Conrad, Emperor of Germany, gave it to Hubert with the title of earl; erected into a duchy, 1417.

Sabines, The, were an important tribe of ancient Italy, allied to the Latins, Samnites, etc. Famous in Roman history as the people whose daughters were treacherously seized by the Romans at the Consualia or games in honor of the god Consus. A treaty of peace was concluded with the Sabines, 750 B. C. After frequent wars, the Sabines were finally defeated, 449 B. C., by M. Horatius, and were incorporated with Rome in the third century B. C.

Salic Law, The, was the code of the Salian Franks, introduced into France (Gaul) by the Franks. It contained four hundred articles, chiefly concerning debt, theft, murder, and battery, the penalty in every case being a fine. The most famous article of the code is Title lxii. 6, according to which only males could succeed to the Salic land or *lod, i. e.* to the lands given for military service. In 1316, at the death of Louis le Hutin, the law was extended to the crown, and continued to be observed to the end of the monarchy.

San Marino, in Italy, on the coast of the Adriatic Sea, is the oldest republic in the world. It is, next to Monaco, the smallest state in Europe. The exact date of the establishment of this republic is not known, but according to tradition it was in the fourth century, by Marinus, a Dalmatian hermit, and has ever since remained independent. It is mountainous and contains four or five villages. The word "liberty" is inscribed on its Capitol.

St. James's Palace is a large, inelegant brick structure, fronting towards Pall Mall. Originally a hospital dedicated to St. James, it was reconstructed and made a manor by Henry VIII., who also annexed to it a park. Here Queen Mary died, 1558; Charles I. slept here the night before his execution; and here Charles II., the Old Pretender, and George IV. were born. When Whitehall was burned, in 1697, St. James became the regular London residence of the British sovereigns, and it continued to be so till Queen Victoria's time. The Court of St. James is a frequent designation of the British Court. St. James Park lies southward from the Palace, and extends over fifty-eight acres.

Saxons, The ancient, were pirates, and inhabited three small islands at the month of the Elbe, and some part of the shores of the Baltic; were invited to England, A. D. 449, by the Britons.

Scotland, anciently Caledonia. History began, B. C. 328, when Fergus I. was sent over by the people of Ireland; accepted the Christian faith about 203; united under one monarchy by Kenneth II. and called Scotland, 838; divided into baronies, 1032; invaded by the King of Norway, near Loch Lomond, 1263; on the death of Alexander III. was disputed by twelve candidates, who submitted their claims to the arbitration of Edward I. of England, 1285, which gave him an opportunity to conquer it; recovered by the Scots, 1314; first General Assembly of the church held, December 20, 1560; United with England under the reign of James VI. of Scotland and James I. of England.

Sealing of Writings.—First introduced into England, 1085.

Sicily.—First colonized from Italy, B. C. 1294; usurped by Agathocles, 317; Servile war began and continued three years, 135.

Slave Trade, Abolition of, in England proposed in Parliament, 1789; abolished, 1807; abolished by France, Spain, and Holland, 1817; treaty concluded between Great Britain and Brazil for the abolition of, 1826. The importation of slaves into the United States prohibited after January 1, 1808; emancipation proclamation issued, 1863.

Smyrna, built by the people of Cumæ, B. C. 1050; destroyed by an earthquake, 1040 A. D., and again, 1688; the chief commercial emporium of West Asia.

South Carolina (Palmetto State).—First settlers, English, Ashley river, 1670. Ranks first in phosphates and rice; fifth in cotton; twentieth in population; twenty-eighth in miles of railway; thirtieth in wealth; thirty-seventh in square miles. Agriculture is the principal industry, the state producing a larger amount of rice than any other state. "Sea Island Cotton" is of the finest quality, and superior to all other, and is raised on several islands along the coast of this state, and Georgia. Corn, oats, wheat, sweet potatoes, and tobacco, are extensively raised. The export of rice and cotton is large. But few manufactures are as yet established in the state, though considerable attention is being given to them.

Spain.—First civilized by the Phœnicians; conquered by the Romans, B. C. 206; the Goths and Vandals overturned the Roman power, 409, and continued in possession of the country till it was conquered by the Moors in 712; the Moors kept possession till the small kingdoms were swallowed up in Castile and Aragon; kingdom founded by the union of the two crowns of Castile and Aragon, 1504; the king and princes of the House of Bourbon ceded their claims to the throne of Spain in 1808; Joseph Bonaparte became king in the same year; Ferdinand's rule was shortly afterwards re-established, but was marked by serious insurrections; he was succeeded by his daughter Isabella II., who was forced to abdicate in 1868; in 1876 a constitution was proclaimed, providing that the government shall be a constitutional monarchy. War was declared against Spain by the United States in April, 1898.

Sparta, built by Lacedæmon, B. C. 1490; kingdom of commenced under Euristhenes and Procles, B. C. 1102; ephori established at, 760.

Straits of Babelmandeb, The, the passage from the Persian Gulf into the Red Sea, are called the Gate of Tears by the Arabs. The channel is only about twenty miles wide, is rocky and very dangerous for passage in rough weather. It received its melancholy name from the number of shipwrecks that occurred there.

Surnames, first used among the nobility, 1200; many of the most common were taken by the Flemings who were naturalized in England about 1435.

Sweden, anciently Scandinavia, kingdom of, began 481; united to the crown of Denmark and Norway from 1394 to 1525, when Gustavus Vasa expelled the Danes; Christianity introduced there 829; no nobility before 1500; popery abolished and the crown declared hereditary, 1544; the house of Vasa ascended the throne in 1523, and gave to Sweden the great Gustavus Adolphus; it was succeeded by the House of Deux-Ponts, which furnished the famous Charles XII.; in 1810 Marshal Bernadotte of France was chosen Crown Prince and ascended the throne as Charles John XIV. in 1818; the union with Norway took place in 1814.

Switzerland, inhabited formerly by the Helvetii, who were subdued by Cæsar B. C. 57; became part of the kingdom of Burgundy, 888; the confederation was founded January 1, 1308; in 1803 Napoleon I. organized a new confederation composed of 19 cantons; this confederation was modified in 1815, the number of cantons being increased to 22; a new constitution was adopted in 1848.

Tarpeian Rock, The, was so called from Tarpeia, daughter of Spurius Tarpeius, governor of the citadel on the Saturnian Hill of Rome. The story is that the Sabines bargained with the Roman maid to open the gates to them for the "ornaments on their arms." As they passed through the gates, they threw on her their shields saying, "These are the ornaments we bear on our arms." She was crushed to death, and buried on the Tarpeian Hill. Ever after, traitors were put to death by being hurled headlong from the hilltop.

Tarquin.—The last king of Rome, expelled B. C. 509.

Tartary.—The first ruler was Genghis Khan, 1206, whose descendants held the empire until 1582, when the Mongols revolted to the Manchew Tartars in China; the Eluths became a separate state about 1400.

Taxes.—Originated from those levied by Solon at Athens, B. C. 540; the first paid in money in England were in 1067.

Tea.—First brought into Europe by the Dutch East India Company, early in the seventeenth century; a quantity of it was brought from Holland by Lord Arlington and Lord Ossory, 1666; from this time it became universal; taxed in North America, 1770, Americans refused to receive it with the duty on, and threw a cargo of it into the sea at Boston, 1773.

Texas (Lone Star State).—First settlement by the Spaniards, at San Antonio, 1692. Admitted to the Union, 1845. Ranks first in cattle and cotton and square miles; second in sugar, sheep, mules, and horses; sixth in miles of railway; seventh in milch cows; eighth in rice and hogs; eleventh in population; nineteenth in wealth. Stock raising is the leading industry, Texas ranking first in this production. Agriculture extensively engages the attention of its inhabitants; corn, wheat, and the other cereals are raised in the northern part; sweet potatoes, sugar cane, tobacco, and tropical fruits in the southern part. Its commerce consists of exports of cotton, hides, and live stock. The state has vast resources that have not, as yet, been fully developed; an abundance of most valuable timber, large deposits of coal, iron, and salt, and other useful minerals.

Teutones, The, were a German tribe, mentioned by Roman writers as inhabiting the northwest part of Germany north of the Elbe. In conjunction with the Cimbri, they invaded Gaul, 103 B. C., destroying three Roman armies, and then proceeded to invade Italy; but the Teutones were defeated and almost annihilated by Marius at Aquæ Sextiæ, 102 B. C., and the Cimbri at Campus Raudius, near Verullæ, 101 B. C.

Tennessee, settled at Fort Loudon, 1757, by the English. Agriculture is the most important industry, the staples being wheat, cotton, corn, hemp, and tobacco. In the production of tobacco, the state ranks third. The iron and coal interests are growing rapidly, and will prove one of the richest resources. The marbles of the state are esteemed for their color and variety. Immense numbers of swine and mules are raised in the state. The manufacturing industries are better developed than in any of the southern central states. A large internal commerce is carried on by means of the rivers and railroads of the state.

Theater, that of Bacchus at Athens, first ever erected, built by Philos, B. C. 420; the ruins still exist; plays were opposed by the Puritans, 1633, and suspended till 1660, when Charles II. licensed two companies; till this time boys performed women's parts; Sir William Davenant introduced operas, 1684.

Thebes, founded 1571 B. C.; citadel built by Cadmus, 1493; flourished as a republic, 820; destroyed by Alexander, with the slaughter of 120,000 persons, when he left only the house of Pindar, the poet, standing, 335; rebuilt by Cassander, B. C. 315.

Thermopylæ, defended by Leonidas B. C. 480, during the invasion of Xerxes; Romans defeated Antiochus at, 191.

Thrace, a considerable part of ancient Greece annexed to Macedon by Philip and Alexander about 355; conquered by the Romans, 168; Byzantium was its capital, on the ruins of which Constantinople was built; taken by the Turks, 1453.

Tilts and Tournaments, instituted by Henry I. of Germany, 919; forbidden by the Council of Rheims, 1131; in fashion in England in the eleventh and twelfth centuries; abolished in France 1560, Henry II. having been killed in one.

Tithes, first given by Moses to the tribe of Levi, B. C. 1490; established in France under Charlemagne; established by law by the Lateran Council, 1215.

Tobacco Plant, found by the Spaniards in the peninsula of Yucatan, 1220; introduced into France by Nicot, 1560; first brought into England by Ralph Lane, 1583.

Toulouse, France, founded about B. C. 615: a dreadful tribunal established there to extirpate heretics, 1229; dissolved 1242; the troubadours or rhetoricians of, had their origin about 1150, and consisted of a fraternity of poets whose art was extended throughout Europe and gave rise to the Italian and Spanish poetry.

Trojan War commenced B. C. 1193. The kingdom of Troy began by Scamander, from Crete, B. C. 1546; city built, B. C. 1255; burned, B. C. 1184, when an end was put to the kingdom.

Tunis and Tripoli, formerly the republic of Carthage. Carthage stood nearly where Tunis now stands. The former was besieged by Louis IX. of France, 1270; it remained under African kings till taken by Barbarossa under Solyman the Magnificent; Barbarossa was expelled by Charles V. but the country was recovered by the Turks under Selim II., since which it has been tributary to the Grand Seignior; it has long been a dependency of Turkey.

Turkish Empire, founded about 998; at the end of the thirteenth century, Othman established the present empire in Asia Minor; in the fourteenth century they invaded Europe and in 1453 took Constantinople; the capture of Constantinople was followed by other important conquests, among which were Greece and Arabia; the glory of the empire culminated in the reign of Solyman the Magnificent, 1520-1566; after his death began the decline of the Ottoman empire; Austria expelled them from Hungary, Russia deprived them of the provinces between the mouths of the Danube and the Caucasus in Europe, and those forming western Trans-Caucasia in Asia; the Greeks formed an independent state; Algiers was wrested from them by the French; the power of the Porte has nearly vanished from the provinces of Asia Minor, Arabia, and Egypt, and finally the Russo-Turkish war of 1877-78 has deprived the Porte of much of the territory in Europe.

Tuileries, The, is the name of a garden and palace in Paris, built on the site of an ancient *fabrique de tuiles.* It was composed of three great pavilions, called *the pavillon de Marsan* (north), the *pavillon de Flôre* (south), and the *pavillon de l'Horloge* (center). It was joined to the Louvre by Napoleon III. (1851-6). The land was bought by François I. in 1564, and the original palace was made for Catherine de Medicis after the design of Philibert Delorme.

Tuscany, the ancient seat of the Etruscans, belonged to Germany till 1240.

Tyre, a city of great antiquity, suffered destruction at an early period; rebuilt under Nimus; taken by Nebuchadnezzar after a siege of thirteen years; it became subject to the Romans, B. C. 64.

Utah was first settled by Americans at Salt Lake City, 1847. Organized as a territory, 1850: admitted as a state, 1896. Ranks third in silver; tenth in gold; fifteenth in coal.

Varangians, The, were the Norse vikings, who, in the ninth century laid the foundations of the Russian Empire. Many of them entered the service of the Byzantine emperors, and in the days of the Comneni the Varangians regularly formed the imperial bodyguard at Constantinople. The Varangians at Constantinople were largely recruited by Anglo-Saxons and Danes from England after the Norman Conquest.

"Vaticanus Mons" is a hill at Rome, chiefly noted for its magnificent palace of the popes, the Vatican, with its superb gardens, its museums, celebrated library, and basilica of St. Peter. The palace was constructed in 498, but has often been enlarged.

Valencia, conquered by the Moors under Abdallah Ciz, and lost by them, 1094; relinquished to the Moors again by the king of Castile; soon after taken again by James I. of Aragon, 1238, and with Aragon united with Spain, 1492; capitulated to the French January 9, 1812.

Vandals, The, inhabited Germany and embraced Christianity, 400; began their kingdom in Spain, 411; invaded and conquered the Roman territories in Africa under Genseric, 430; sacked and pillaged Rome, 455.

Vermont (Green Mountain State).—First settled by the English, Fort Dummer, 1764. Ranks fourth in copper; seventh in hops and buckwheat; twenty-sixth in wealth; thirty-second in population; fortieth in square miles; forty-first in miles of railway. The state is noted for its rich quarries of marble, soapstone, and slate, which are worked at several points. It is also noted as a good grazing country. The dairy products are extensive and valuable. Stock raising is carried on to a considerable extent.

Vendome Column, The, in Paris was erected by Napoleon I. 1806, in the Place Vendôme, to commemorate his successful campaign in Germany; pulled down by the Communists 1871, but restored by the National Assembly, 1874. It is one hundred and thirty-two feet high, with a statue of Napoleon I. at the top.

Venice.—Originally inhabitated by the Veneti; conquered by the Gauls and made a kingdom about B. C. 356; conquered for the Romans by Marcellus, 221. The islands on which the city now stands began to be inhabited by Italians about 421; its university founded, 1592.

Vesuvius, eruptions of, A. D. 79, 203, 272; ejected flames that were seen at Constantinople; obscured the sun at noonday, and ravaged all Campania; was in an active state of eruption upward of 35 times, between the years 472 and the present.

Vienna, the capital of Austria-Hungary, was originally Vindobona of Upper Pannonia; afterwards capital of the east provinces of the empire of Charlemagne; besieged by the Turks in 1529, and again in 1683; the French took it in 1806 and in 1809; the Congress of Vienna, which fixed for a time the limits of the countries of Europe, was held here November, 1814, to June, 1815.

Vikings, The, were the piratical Northmen who infested the coasts of the British Islands and of France in the eighth, ninth, and tenth centuries. This word is quite unconnected with "king," being derived from the Scandinavian *vik,* "a bay" (the same which appears in the names Lerwick, Berwick, etc.), and this class of marauders were so called because their ships put off from the bays and fiords.

Visigoths, The, or Western Goths, were the descendants of that branch of the Gothic race established by Aurelian in Dacia (270). The descendants of the other branch of the race, which remained in Southern Russia, were called Ostrogoths (Eastern Goths). On the death of Theodosius, the Visigoths, under Alaric, overran Greece (396) and Italy (400). After Alaric's death (410) they established a kingdom at Toulouse (418) which eventually comprised the whole of Gaul south of the Loire and west of the Rhone, as well as Provence and the greater part of Spain. With the defeat (and death) of Alaric II. by Clovis, on the field of Vouglé (or Vouillé or Voclad) near Poitiers (507), the kingdom of Toulouse came to an end, and the Visigoths abandoned to the conqueror all their territories north of the Pyrenees, with the exception of a small tract of country in Gaul, including the cities of Carcassone, Narbonne, and Nîmes.

Virginia, first settled at Jamestown by the English, 1607. Ranks first in peanuts; second in tobacco; eighth in salt and iron ore; sixteenth in wealth. Agriculture is the leading industry; tobacco, wheat, corn, and potatoes being the great staples. The mineral resources are vast; the mountains containing rich deposits of coal and iron, valuable marble, slate, and stone quarries with important salt springs.

Wales.—The first king was Edwawl, 690; it was conquered and divided by William I., 1091; Griffith, the last king, died 1137; the sovereign from that time forward was the prince; completely conquered and annexed to the crown of England, 1283.

Walloons, The, are the inhabitants of the southeastern division of Belgium, their country comprising the provinces of Hainault, Namur, Liége, and Luxemburg, with part of Brabant. The Walloons are Romanized Gauls, lineal representatives of the ancient Belgæ, distinguished from their Flemish (Teutonic) neighbors by their Romance language, their stronger physique, and their darker complexion. The Walloon language, however, a strongly marked dialect of Northern France (the Langue d'Oil), is now merely a provincial *patois*, French being the written standard and official language of the whole kingdom.

Warsaw, after two days' hard fighting, capitulated and was taken possession of by the Russians, September 7, 1831.

Washington ranks eighth in gold, seventeenth in square miles, forty-first in population, forty-second in miles of railway. Population, according to territorial census in 1885, 127,292; United States Census, 1890, 349,390. First settlement, by Americans, at Astoria, 1811. Organized as a territory, 1853. Admitted to the Union, 1889.

Wat Tyler's insurrection occurred November 5, 1380, a peasant's revolt, immediately due to the imposition of a poll-tax on all persons above fifteen. Almost the whole of the peasantry of the southern and eastern counties of England rose in arms, murdering and plundering, under the leadership of Wat Tyler, said to have been a soldier in the French wars. On June 12, 1381, they gathered on Blackheath. On June 14, Richard II., then a lad of fifteen, met the Essex contingent at Mile End, and, promising the abolition of villenage, induced them to return home. On June 15, he met the Kentish men at Smithfield, and in the parley Wat Tyler was killed by William Walworth, mayor of London, and others. The peasants were about to avenge his death, when Richard, with great presence of mind, rode forward alone, and induced them to follow him to Islington, when, a body of troops coming to the king's aid, and Richard being profuse of promises, they dispersed.

Waterloo, Battle of, in which Napoleon with 69,000 men attacked a combined army of 89,000 English, Dutch, Belgian, and Hanoverian troops; a dreadful slaughter continued until four o'clock, when two Prussian corps of 30,000 and 40,000, under Bulow and Blucher, successively arrived, and, turning his right wing, the whole army fled in confusion at half past nine o'clock, June 18, 1815.

West Virginia.—The first settlers were English, Wheeling, 1774. Agriculture is the leading industry, and the principal staples are tobacco, wheat, and corn. The mountain pastures are well adapted to stock raising. Its mineral resources are rich deposits of coal, iron, and numerous oil wells, and salt springs.

Westminster Abbey, built by Sebert, king of Essex, on the spot where the Temple of Apollo had once stood; its monastery, consecrated by Edward the Confessor, 1065; rebuilt and consecrated, 1269; turned into a collegiate church, 1560.

Wills are of a very high antiquity; Solon introduced them at Athens; there are many regulations respecting wills in the Koran; the Roman had this power; so had the native Mexican, so that it prevailed at least in three parts of the globe; lands were devisable by will before the conquest; privilege of making wills granted by Henry I. in 1100.

Wisconsin (Badger State).—First settlement, by the French, Green Bay, 1660. Admitted to the Union, 1848. Ranks second in hops, third in barley and potatoes, fourth in rye and buckwheat, fifth in oats and agricultural implements, seventh in iron, steel, and wool, eighth in hay and milch cows, ninth in copper, tenth in wealth, eleventh in miles of railway, sixteenth in population, and twenty-third in square miles. The chief industry is agriculture, with large crops of corn, wheat, oats, barley, hay, potatoes, and hops, as the staple productions. Live stock is largely raised. In the production of wool and cheese it is among the leading states. The manufacturing interests are large and increasing. The great pine forests in abundance, and the most valuable timber, lead, iron, zinc, and marble mines are extensively worked. Lakes Michigan and Superior, and the Mississippi, afford great natural highways for commerce.

Witchcraft.—Six hundred condemned as wizards, and most of them burned in France, 1609; Grandier, parish priest of Loudan, burned on the supposition of having bewitched a whole convent of nuns, 1634; nine old women were burned at Kalish, in Poland, charged with having bewitched and rendered unfruitful the lands belonging to a gentleman in that palatinate; the last punished in England for witchcraft, was October 29, 1808.

Wyoming.—Ranks ninth in square miles, twelfth in cattle, fourteenth in gold, sixteenth in coal, forty-fourth in miles of railway, forty-sixth in population. First settlement, by Americans, 1867. Organized as a territory, 1868. Admitted to the Union in 1890.

HISTORIC TREATIES.

843. Contract of Verdun. This treaty concluded the war between Lothar, Louis the German, and Charles the Bald, over their respective shares of the imperial dominions on the death of their father, Louis the Pious.

911. Treaty of St.-Clair-sur-Epte: concluded the war between the invading Norsemen under Rollo and the French king, Charles the Simple.

1122. Concordat of Worms: an agreement between the emperor and the pope, closing the long strife known as the war of investitures.

1183. Treaty of Constance: between the emperor, Frederick Barbarossa, and the Lombard cities.

1360. Peace of Bretigny: a treaty that interrupted the Hundred Years' war between France and England.

1397. Union of Calmar: the treaty by which Denmark, Sweden, and Norway were united under Queen Margaret of Denmark.

1420. Treaty of Troyes: interrupted the Hundred Years' war on terms most favorable to England.

1435. Treaty of Arras: a compact between Burgundy and France.

1466. Treaty of Thorn: settled the terms of the Polish conquest of West Prussia.

1482. Treaty of Arras: settled the dispute between Louis XI. of France, and Maximilian of Austria.

1493. Bull of Pope Alexander VI.: arranged the conflicting claims of Spain and Portugal to newly discovered lands.

1508. League of Cambray: a union formed by Louis XII. of France and the Emperor Maximilian, which the pope and others were invited to join.

1526. Treaty of Madrid: formed between Charles V. of Germany and Francis I. of France.

1529. Treaty of Cambray: between Francis I. and Charles V.

1544. Treaty of Crespy: concluded the fourth and last war between Francis I. and Charles V.

1579. Union of Utrecht: laid the foundations of the Dutch Republic.

1648. Peace of Westphalia: concluded the Thirty Years' War.

1659. Peace of the Pyrenees: closed the long war between France and Spain.

1660. Treaty of Copenhagen: between Denmark and Sweden.
1667. Treaty of Breda: between England and Holland.
1668. Triple Alliance: between England, Holland, and Sweden to defend Spain against Louis XIV.
1668. Treaty of Aix-la-Chapelle: between France and Spain.
1668. Treaty of Lisbon: between Spain and Portugal through the mediation of England.
1678. Peace of Nymwegen: ended the Dutch war.
1697. Peace of Ryswick: closed the war between France under Louis XIV. and the principal states of Europe — called the War of the Palatinate.
1699. Peace of Carlowitz: between Turkey on the one hand and the Emperor of Germany, the King of Poland, and the republic of Venice on the other.
1713-14. Treaties of Utrecht, Rastadt, and Baden: concluded between the states taking part in the war of the Spanish succession.
1717. Triple Alliance: between Great Britain, France, and Holland.
1718-19. Quadruple Alliance: between Great Britain, France, Holland, and the emperor against the aggressions of Spain.
1718. Peace of Passarowitz: between the sultan and emperor.
1721. Peace of Nystadt: between Sweden and Russia.
1738. Treaty of Vienna: between France and Germany.
1742. Peace of Breslau: between Frederick II. of Prussia and Maria Theresa of Austria.
1748. Peace of Aix-la-Chapelle: between Great Britain, France, and Holland; Austria, Spain, Sardinia, Genoa, and Modena being accessories.
1761. The Family Compact: between the Bourbon rulers of France and Spain.
1763. Peace of Paris: terminated the Seven Years' war, known in United States history as the French and Indian war.
1772. First Partition of Poland: executed by Russia, Austria, and Prussia.
1774. Peace of Kutchuk-Kainardji: between Russia and Turkey.
1783. Treaty of Paris: in which Great Britain acknowledged the independence of the North American colonies.
1783. Treaty of Versailles: between Great Britain, France, and Spain.
1792. First Coalition against France: involved all the powers except Sweden, Switzerland, Denmark, Tuscany, Venice, and Genoa.
1795. Peace of Basel: between France and Prussia.
1795. Jay Treaty: between the United States and Great Britain.
1797. Treaty of Tolentino: between the French republic and the pope.
1797. Treaty of Campo Formio: between Napoleon and the emperor of Germany.
1798. Second Coalition against France: initiated by Russia; afterward comprised England, Austria, Naples, Portugal, and Turkey.
1802. Peace of Amiens: between Great Britain on the one hand, and France, Spain, and the Batavian republic on the other.
1803. Treaty between France and the United States: touching the purchase of Louisiana.
1805. Peace of Pressburg: between Austria and France.
1807. Treaties of Tilsit: concluded between France, Prussia, and Russia.
1809. Treaty of Schönbrunn: between France and Austria.
1814. First Peace of Paris: between France and the principal European powers; after the defeat of Napoleon at Leipzig.
1814. Treaty of Ghent: between the United States and Great Britain.
1815. Congress of Vienna: attended by the principal European powers.
1815. Second Peace of Paris: between France and the allies after the defeat of Napoleon at Waterloo.
1815. Holy Alliance: formed at Paris between the monarchs of Russia, Austria, and Prussia.
1818. Congress of Aix-la-Chapelle: participated in by Great Britain, Russia, Prussia, and France.
1827. Treaty of London: between Great Britain, Russia, and France, to put an end to the war between Turkey and Greece.
1829. Treaty of Adrianople: between Russia and Turkey.
1840. Quadruple Treaty of London: between Great Britain, Austria, Prussia, and Russia on the one hand and Turkey on the other, touching Mehemet Ali of Egypt.
1842. Treaty of Nanking: concluded the so-called opium war between Great Britain and China.
1842. Ashburton Treaty: signed at Washington to define the northeastern boundary between the United States and British North America.
1848. Treaty of Guadalupe Hidalgo: between the United States and Mexico.
1854. Treaty between the United States and Japan: negotiated by Commodore Perry.
1856. Treaty of Paris: after the Crimean war.
1858. Treaties of Tientsin: between China and each of the four nations, Great Britain, France, Russia, and United States.
1859. Peace of Zurich; settled the dispute between France and Sardinia on the one hand and Austria on the other.
1864. Peace of Vienna: concluded the war between Austria, Prussia, and Denmark, growing out of the Schleswig-Holstein question.
1865. Convention of Gastein: a compact between Prussia and Austria.
1866. Peace of Prague: concluded the war between Prussia and Austria.
1871. Treaty of Frankfort: between France and Germany.
1871. Treaty of Washington: to adjust the Alabama claims.
1878. Treaty of San Stefano supplemented by the Congress of Berlin: closed the Russo-Turkish war.
1879. Triple Alliance: between Austria, Germany, and Italy.
1895. Treaty of Shimonoseki: concluded the war between China and Japan.
1898. Treaty of Paris: concluded the Spanish-American war.

THOMAS A. EDISON.

Book IV.

Science, Invention, Discovery.

Science, Invention, Discovery.

Alcoholic Drinks. — The number of alcoholic drinks is surprisingly large and varied. The following are the principal: Agua ardiente, made in Mexico, from the fermented juice of agave; arrack, made in India from the juice of the palm and from rice; araka, made in Tartary, from fermented mare's milk; araki, made in Egypt from dates; brandy, made in nearly all wine countries from wine and from fruits; Geneva or Holland gin, made in Holland from malted barley or rye, rectified on juniper berries; gin made in England from malted barley, rye, or potatoes, and rectified with turpentine; goldwasser, made at Dantzic from various kinds of corn and rectified with spices; kirchwasser, made in Switzerland from the Mahaleb cherry; lau, made in Siam from rice; maraschino, made in Dalmatia from the Macarska cherry; Mahwah arrack, made in India from the flowers of the madhuca tree; rum, made in the West Indies and South America from cane sugar and molasses; rakia, made in Dalmatia from the husks of grapes, mixed with aromatics; rossolio, made at Dantzic from a compound of brandy with certain plants; slatkai-trava, made at Kamtschatka from a sweet grass; show-choo, made in China from the lees of rice wine; trosta, made in the Rhenish provinces from the husks of grapes fermented with barley and rye; tuba, made in the Philippine Islands from palm wine; vino mescal, made in Mexico by distilling the fermented juice of the agave; whisky, made in Scotland, Ireland, and United States from raw and malted grain, and south of France from sloes.

Air.— The gaseous envelope of the earth. Our planet has two coverings: one the water, which is distributed as lakes and seas, filling up the deep cavities of the solid surface, tending to produce a more level superficies; the second covering is the air or atmosphere, which rests upon the top of the water and the dry land, enveloping the highest mountains, and rising upwards to an altitude somewhat above forty-five miles; it is a true, aeriform ocean surrounding our earth and has upon its upper surface waves and tides, and, throughout its mass, currents flowing in constant and variable directions, precisely as those of the ocean comport themselves; it is held down to the surface of the earth by attraction, and rotates with the planet; its density varies with its actual height at the place of observation, of which the barometric pressure is the evidence. This pressure diminishes as the elevation above the sea increases, owing to the upper portions of the atmosphere pressing upon and condensing the lower strata, so much so, that one half the actual weight of the atmosphere is comprised within the space of the lower five miles of its total height, the remaining forty miles in height containing the other half. The air is highly compressible and elastic, and its volume diminished inversely as the pressure increases. This accounts for the facility of setting it in motion and its velocity. Like fluids, it presses equally in every direction, and when it comes in contact with a more expanded and therefore lighter portion of air, it pushes it up and occupies its place, producing currents of air and winds when it flows in streams, and sounds when it is thrown into vibrations or undulations. The air is warmed solely by the earth, and not by the transmitted rays of the sun,— hence warm air exists within the tropics, and diminishes towards the poles, and insensibly decreases every three hundred and fifty feet of elevation.

Acoustics. — The doctrine of the different sounds of vibrating strings, and the communication of sounds to the ear by the vibration of the atmosphere, was probably first explained by Pythagoras, about 500 B. C. Mentioned by Aristotle, 330 B. C. The speaking trumpet is said to have been used by Alexander the Great, 335 B. C. The discoveries of Galileo were made about 1600 A. D. The velocity of sound was investigated by Newton before 1700. Galileo's theorem of the harmonic curves was demonstrated by Dr. Brook Taylor, in 1714; and further perfected by D'Alembert, Euler, Bernoulli, and LaGrange, at various periods of the eighteenth century.

Algebra. — Where Algebra was first used, and by whom, is not precisely known. Diophantus first wrote upon it, probably about 170 A. D.; he is said to be the inventor. Brought into Spain by the Saracens, about 900; and into Italy by Leonardo of Pisa, in 1202. The first writer who used algebraical signs was Stifelius of Nuremberg, in 1544. The introduction of symbols for quantities was by Francis Vieta, in 1590, when algebra came into general use. The binomial theorem of Newton, the basis of the doctrine of fluxions, and the new analysis, 1668. Descartes applied algebra to geometry about 1637.

Almanacs.—The Egyptians computed time by instruments. Log calendars were anciently in use. The word almanac is of Saxon origin. Michael Nostradamus, the astrologer, wrote an almanac in the style of Merlin, 1556. The first published is said to have been by Martin Hykus, at Buda in 1470. The first almanac in England was printed at Oxford, in 1673.

Anatomy.— The human body was studied by Aristotle about 350 B. C., and its structure was made part of the philosophical investigations of Plato and Xenophon; it became a branch of medical education, under Hippocrates about 420 B. C. Erasistratus and Herophilus first dissected the human form, and may be regarded as the fathers of anatomy; it is said that they practiced upon the bodies of living criminals about 300 and 293 B. C. Galen, who died 193 A. D., was a great anatomist. In England the schools were long supplied with bodies unlawfully exhumed from graves; and until 1832 the bodies of executed murderers were ordered for dissection. Pope Boniface VIII. forbade the dissection of dead bodies, 1297. The first anatomical plates, designed by Titian, were employed by Vesalius, about 1538. The discoveries of Harvey were made in 1616. The anatomy of plants was discovered in 1680.

Angling.— The origin of this art is involved in obscurity; allusion was made to it by the Greeks and Romans, and in the most ancient books of the Bible, as *Amos*. It came into general repute in England about the period of the reformation. Winkin de Worde's *Treatyse of Fysshinge*, the first book printed on angling, appeared in 1496. Isaac Walton's book was printed in 1653.

Arithmetic.— Where first invented is not known, at least with certainty. It was brought from Egypt into Greece by Thales, about 600 B. C. The oldest treatise upon arithmetic is by Euclid, about 300 B. C. The sexagesimal arithmetic of Ptolemy was used A. D. 130. Diophantus of Alexandria was the author of thirteen books of arithmetical questions (of which six are extant) in 156. Notation by nine digits and zero, known at least as early as the sixth century in Hindostan — introduced from thence into Arabia, about 900, into Spain 1050, into England 1253. Arithmetic of decimals invented 1482. First work printed in England on arithmetic was by Tonstall, bishop of Durham, 1522. The theory of decimal fractions was perfected by Lord Napier in 1617.

Assaying.— The assaying of silver and gold is affected by a process called cupellation. Cupels are small flat crucibles made by pressing bone ash moistened with water, into circular steel molds, and they are dried by exposure to the air. The principle upon which the operation depends is, that all metals with which gold and silver are usually alloyed, are convertible into oxides by exposure to atmospheric air at a high temperature, whereas the precious metals remain unacted upon.

To assay silver by cupellation the silver is flattened and wrapped up in an envelope of lead. A muffle or oven is heated in an assay furnace and the two metals put into it. The metals melt and the lead becomes converted into an oxide, which as well as any baser metals before combined with the silver is absorbed by the substance of the cupel until at length the silver is left absolutely pure.

The assaying of gold is performed, to a certain extent in a similar way, and if the gold were alloyed only with copper, the process would be as simple as that of silver assaying. Usually, however, gold contains silver, and this cannot be got rid of by cupellation, the parting process is, therefore, had recourse to; this consists in dissolving the silver by dilute nitric acid, which leaves the gold perfectly pure.

Iron ores are assayed by separating the oxygen from the iron, by the greater affinity of charcoal for that element at high temperatures. The ore, some charcoal, and an alkaline flux are heated in a crucible; and the result is that all the impurities in the ore are made to leave the iron so that the latter is presented in a purely metallic form.

Copper ores usually contain sulphur, and in order to assay them a flux is prepared of fluor spar, borax, slacked lime, argol, and niter.

Automobile.— This name covers all forms of self-propelling vehicles for use on country roads or city streets, whether driven by steam produced by the combustion of fuel, stored steam, compressed air, oil or gasoline engines, or by electric motors taking current from accumulators. Automobiles are not of recent origin, as many generally suppose, but date back to the early days of the steam engine, to the time of Sir Isaac Newton, who, in 1680, proposed a form of steam carriage which embodied the essential features of a steam automobile. In 1790 Nathan Read patented and constructed a model steam carriage. But the first actual experiments were made in 1769, by a French army officer, Nicholas Cugnot, who built a three wheel carriage. In America, Oliver Evans, as early as 1786, suggested a form of road wagon to be propelled by steam. In 1803 Richard Trevithick built a full sized carriage which was exhibited in London, having driven itself 90 miles *en route* from Camborne, where it was constructed. David Gurney built and operated a steam carriage in 1827, in which he made frequent and long journeys, covering as much as 85 miles in 10 hours. He was excelled by Walter Hancock who established several stage lines. Since 1895 the construction of automobiles has been carried on with great energy, and many improvements have been made. So far the most satisfactory results have been obtained with the steam, oil, and electric carriages. In tire construction the pneumatic tire occupies the first place in public favor, although solid rubber tires are largely employed. The highest speed is obtained by use of light oils, preferably gasoline; steam motors are most successfully used with heavy trucks and vans; the electric motor has given the best satisfaction when employed on vehicles for city cab and carriage work and short radius runs.

Æolian Harp was the invention, it is believed, of Athanasius Kircher, who lived in the seventeenth century, and it is so called from Æolus, the god or ruler of the winds. It is a simple musical instrument, the sounds of which are produced by the vibrations of strings moved by wind. It may be composed of a rectangular box made of thin boards, five or six inches deep and about the same width, and of a length sufficient to extend across the window it is to be set at, so that the breeze coming in can sweep over it. At the top of each end of the box a strip of wood is glued, about a half-inch in height; the strings are then stretched lengthwise across the top of the box, and may be tuned in unison by means of pegs constructed to control their tension, as in the case of a violin. The sounds produced by the rising and falling wind, in passing over the strings, are of a drowsy and lulling character, and have been beautifully described by the poet Thomson as supplying the most suitable kind of music for the *Castle of Indolence*.

Aerial Navigation.— Pilatre des Rosiers made the first balloon ascension at Paris, November 21, 1783. His balloon was inflated with heated air. December 1, 1783, an ascension was made by M. Charles, a professor of Natural Philosophy, at Paris, and at about the same time successful ascensions were also made by Messrs. Rittenhouse and Hopkins, of Philadelphia, hydrogen gas being used in these instances for inflating purposes. The valve at the top of the balloon, and the hoop attached to the balloon with netting, by which is suspended the car, are the inventions of M. Charles. In 1785 a successful passage of the English Channel was made by M. Blanchard, the first professional aeronaut, and an American traveler named Dr. Jeffries. The use of ropes for the purpose of steadying balloons was first adopted by M. Gay-Lussac, in 1803. From 1852 to 1884 French, German, and American aeronauts labored with degrees of success to improve the method of construction and to invent a means for the propulsion of balloons, and in the latter year Captains Renard and Krebs produced an air ship which was considered the crowning effort in this line of invention. This ship was a cigar-shaped balloon, carrying a platform, on which the steering and propelling apparatus was placed. The balloon was made of strong silk and covered with a light netting of cords. It was 197 feet long and 39 feet in diameter. To the netting was suspended the platform, 131 feet long and 10 feet broad, on the front of which was fixed the propeller, a screw of light, wooden framework and air-tight cloth. The rudder was at the rear of the platform. The propeller was driven by electricity, generated by a dynamo, which was in turn driven by stored electricity. The first ascension of this ship fully satisfied the most sanguine expectations of its builders. It was driven seven miles and back in the space of forty minutes, and obeyed fully every movement of the rudder. During the siege of Paris, in the Franco-German war of 1870-71, ballooning was extensively used by the besieged for communication with the outer world, and also by the besiegers for military purposes, and since that date military ballooning has become an important subject of study and experiment by soldiers.

American Clocks and Watches.— The first attempt to manufacture watches or clocks on a large scale in America was made by Eli Terry, a Connecticut Yankee, who invented wooden wheels for clocks in 1792. In 1837 Chauncey Jerome, of Massachusetts, first applied machinery to the making of metal-wheeled clocks, and as a result drove the wooden-wheeled clocks out of the market. The manufacture of watches by machinery, which has since become such an important business, was begun at Roxbury, Mass., in 1850, and was continued there untii 1854, when the works were removed to Waltham.

Archimedes, Principle of. — Archimedes, the most celebrated of ancient mathematicians, was born at Syracuse about 287 B. C. He is said to have been a kinsman of King Hiero, though he does not seem to have held any public office, but devoted himself entirely to science. He is the only one of the ancients who contributed anything satisfactory on the theory of mechanics and on hydrostatics. He first established the truth that a body plunged in a fluid loses exactly as much of its weight as is equal to the weight of the fluid displaced by it. This is one of the most important principles in the science of hydrostatics, and is called by his name. It was by this law that he determined how much alloy the goldsmith, whom Hiero had commissioned to make a crown of pure gold, had fraudulently mixed with the metal. The solution of the problem had suggested itself to him as he was entering the bath, and he is reported to have been so overjoyed as to hasten home without waiting to dress, exclaiming, "I have found it! I have found it!" Among the numerous inventions ascribed to Archimedes is that of the endless screw, and the cochlea, or water-screw, in which the water is made in a manner to ascend by its own gravity.

Atlantic Cables.—In July, 1866, the first permanent Atlantic cable was laid from Valentia Bay, Ireland, to Trinity Bay, N. F., and in September of the same year a cable which had been lost in 1865 was recovered and its laying completed, thus giving two lines between the two points. These lines were known as the Anglo-American Cable, and were managed by a company of the same name. The French Atlantic Telegraph Company was formed in 1868, and it laid a line from Brest, France, to Roxbury, Mass., the following year. In the summer of 1873 the fourth Atlantic telegraph cable was laid from Valentia, Ireland, to Heart's Content, Trinity Bay, N. F., and the Brazilian telegraph cable was laid from Rio de Janeiro, Brazil, to a bay on the coast of Portugal a few months later. The Direct United States Cable Company was formed, and laid a line from Ballenskillings Bay, Ireland, to Rye, N. H., via Nova Scotia, in 1874. The same year a sixth line across the Atlantic was laid from Ireland to Newfoundland, and in 1880 another French line was laid from Brest to St. Pierre, an island in the Gulf of St. Lawrence. In 1884-'85, the companies owning all these lines having previously formed a combination to keep up rates, a competing company was formed by James Gordon Bennett and Mr. Mackay, who laid two lines from Ireland to Nova Scotia, and also a connecting line from Ireland to France. The difficulty with these submarine cables at first was to send through them a current of sufficient power to record the message. The method adopted is as follows: Two keys, which when depressed transmit respectively positive and negative currents, are employed at the sending station, in connection with the battery. The current of the battery does not pass directly into the cable, but into a condenser, which passes it into the submarine line. This greatly increases the force of the current used, and serves to cut off interfering earth-currents. The receiving-instrument first employed was a reflecting galvanometer. Upon the magnet of this instrument is carried a small curved mirror. About two feet in front of it is placed a lamp behind a frame in which is a vertical slit, while above it is a screen. The light from this lamp, passing through the slit, falls on the surface of the mirror, which throws it back upon the screen. The flash of light, moving from right to left with the motion of the needle, indicates the message sent. This method, however, has been of late years almost entirely superseded by an invention called the syphon galvanometer. In this the movements of the needle are recorded by means of ink spurted from a fine glass syphon-tube. This tube is attached to a coil suspended between two fixed magnets, which swing to right or left as the pulsations of the needle pass through it. The possibility of laying an electric cable in the Atlantic from Europe was suggested by Professor Morse as far back as 1843, but it was not until 1854 that Mr. Cyrus W. Field discussed the means of practically realizing the idea, and it is to his energy that the successful completion of this great work is due.

Aurora Borealis.—Since the discovery of electricity, and especially electro-magnetism, all speculation on the nature of the aurora has taken in that force as a principal element, and modern experiments have been especially turned to securing proof of the electric nature of the auroral display. The theory advanced by M. De La Rive, a Genoese scientist, and which is generally accepted, is, that the aurora is caused by the recomposition of the positive and negative electricity, always to be found in the upper and lower strata of air respectively. Miniature auroras have been produced by electricity by M. De La Rive, and also by a M. Lenstrom. In M. Lenstrom's experiments, which were made in Finland in 1882, the peak of a mountain was surrounded with a coil of copper wire, pointed at intervals with tin nibs. This wire was charged with electricity, and a yellow light was produced on the tin points, in which the spectroscope analysis revealed the greenish yellow ray that characterizes the aurora borealis. The aurora was supposed to be of supernatural origin by the ancients.

Armor.—The warlike Europeans at first despised any other defense than the shield. Skins and padded hides were first used; and brass and iron armor, in plates or scales, followed. The first body armor of the Britons were skins of wild beasts, exchanged, after the Roman conquest, for the well tanned leathern cuirass. This latter continued until the Anglo-Saxon era. Hengist is said to have had scale armor, A. D. 449. The heavy cavalry were covered with a coat of mail, 1216. Armor became exceedingly splendid about 1350. The armor of plate commenced, 1407. The armor of Henry VII. consisted of a cuirass of steel, in the form of a pair of stays, about 1500. Armor ceased to reach below the knees in the time of Charles I., 1625.

Artillery.— The first piece was a small one, contrived by Schwartz, a German cordelier, soon after the invention of gunpowder in 1330. Artillery was used, it is said, by the Moors at Algeciras in Spain, in the siege of 1341; it was used, according to historians, at the battle of Cressy, in 1346, when Edward III. had four pieces of cannon, which gained him the battle. Artillery was used at the siege of Calais, 1347. The Venetians first employed artillery against the Genoese at sea, 1377. Cast in England, together with mortars for bombshells, by Flemish artists in Sussex, 1543. Made of brass, 1635. From this time forward the improvement in field artillery has been rapid and important.

Astronomy.— The earliest accounts we have of this science are those of Babylon, about 2234 B. C. The study of astronomy was much advanced in Chaldea under Nabonassur; it was known to the Chinese about 1100 B. C.; some say many centuries before. Lunar eclipses were observed at Babylon with exceeding accuracy, 720 B. C. Spherical form of the earth, and the true cause of lunar eclipses, taught by Thales, 640 B. C. Further discoveries by Pythagoras, who taught the doctrine of celestial motions, and believed in the plurality of habitable worlds, 500 B. C. Hipparchus began his observations at Rhodes, 167 B. C., began his new cycle of the moon in 143, and made great advances in the science, 140 B. C. The procession of the equinoxes confirmed, and the places and distances of the planets discovered, by Ptolemy, A. D. 130. After the elapse of nearly seven centuries, during which time astronomy was neglected, it was resumed by the Arabs about 800; and was afterwards brought into Europe by the Moors of Barbary and Spain, but not sooner than 1201, when they also introduced geography. True laws of the planetary motions discovered by Kepler 1619; the discoveries of Galileo were made about 1631. Newton's Principia published and the system as now taught incontrovertibly established, A. D. 1687; *Mecanique Celeste*, published by La Place, 1796.

Ax-Wedge.— These instruments, with the lever, and various others of a coarse construction and still in common use, are said to have been invented by Dædalus, an artificer of Athens, to whom also is ascribed the invention of masts and sails for ships, 1240 B. C. Many tools are represented on the Egyptian monuments.

Beer, Origin of.—The Germans, Gauls, and Bretons manufactured beer from barley and wheat as far back as there are any written records regarding them. Tacitus tells us that beer was a common beverage of the Germans when he wrote, in the first century. We learn from Pliny that "The people of Spain, in particular, brew this liquor so well that it will keep a long time." He describes it as made from corn and water. The earliest of Greek writers speak of wine made from barley, and of the art of making it as derived from the Egyptians. It is believed that Archilochus, the Parian poet, who lived about 700 B. C., referred to beer drinking when he depicted the follies and vicious indulgences of his time. In the ancient writings of China reference is made to a fermented drink called "sam-shoo," made from rice. When it was first invented is unknown, but it was probably long before the Christian Era.

Blood, Circulation of.— The true theory regarding the circulation of blood was discovered by the celebrated English physiologist, William Harvey, about 1616. He received his diploma as Doctor of Medicine from the University of Padua in 1602, and in 1615 was made Lecturer at the College of Physicians in London, an appointment which he held for forty years. It is generally supposed that he expounded his views regarding blood circulation in his first course of lectures. He died at London June 3, 1657.

Bonnet.— The English bonnet, which was superseded in the early part of the sixteenth century by the hat, was made of cloth, silk, or velvet, less or more ornamented, according to the taste or means of the wearer. In Scotland, however, bonnets were universally worn for a century or two later, and they still are, to a certain extent, a national characteristic. The bonnet worn by the Lowland Scottish peasantry was of a broad, round, and flat shape, overshadowing the face and neck, and of a dark-blue color, excepting a red tuft like a cherry on the top. It was made of thick milled woolen, and with reasonable care would last a man his whole life. From having been worn, till comparatively late times, by small rural proprietors — such as owners of a cottage and an acre or two of land — it gave to these local notabilities the distinctive appellation of Bonnet Lairds. The bonnets worn by the Highlanders were made of the same fabric, but rise to a point in front and are without any rim. From time immemorial these various kinds of Scots bonnets have been manufactured at Stewarton, a small town in Ayrshire. Formerly the Stewarton bonnet makers formed a corporation, which, like other old guilds, was governed by regulations conceived in a narrow and often amusingly absurd spirit; one of the rules of of the fraternity, however, can be spoken of only with commendation, for it enforced a certain weight of material in each bonnet, as well as durability in the color.

Botanic Gardens.— In 1309 A. D., the first approach to a botanic garden was made in the garden of Matthæus Salvaticus, at Salerno, botanic science, however, being merely subservient to medicine; and it was not until 1533 that the first true botanic garden was formed. This was made for Gaspar de Gabrieli, a wealthy Tuscan noble at Padua, and was followed by similar gardens at Pisa, Florence, Bologna, and Rome, the first public garden being that at Pisa. In 1545 a public garden was established at Padua by decree of the Republic of Venice. In 1580 the Elector of Saxony established a public botanic garden at Leipzig, which was soon followed by others. There was no botanic garden in France till Louis XIII. established the *Jardin des Plantes* at Paris, which was completed in 1634. The first public botanic garden was established in England at Oxford by the Earl of Danby, although numerous private gardens had existed in England for the greater part of a century. The botanic garden at Edinburgh, the first in Scotland, was founded about 1680. The botanic garden at Kew occupies a high place among British national institutions, and possesses one of the richest collections of plants in the world. The gardens connected with the imperial palace at Schönbrunn, in Austria, and that of Berlin, are the greatest in Germany. The *Jardin des Plantes* in Paris undoubtedly may be regarded as holding the first place on the continent of Europe, both with reference to the strictly scientific study of botany and to the care bestowed upon the introduction and diffusion of useful or beautiful plants from all parts of the world. In the United States the botanic gardens of New York and Philadelphia are the most worthy of notice.

Brain.— The latest classification of races, according to Bastian and other experts, shows weight of brain, in ounces, as follows: Scotch, 50.0; Germans, 49.6; English, 49.5; French, 47.9; Zulus, 47.5; Chinese, 47.2; Pawnees, 47.1; Italians, 46.9; Hindoo, 45.1; Gypsy, 44.8; Bushmen, 44.6; Esquimaux, 43.9. Compared with size of body, the brain of the Esquimau is as heavy as the Scotchman's.

The measurement of that part of the skull which holds the brain is stated in cubic inches thus: Anglo-Saxon, 105; German, 105; Negro, 96; Ancient Egyptian, 93; Hottentot, 58; Australian native, 58.

In all races the male brain is about 10 per cent. heavier than the female. The highest class of apes has only 16 oz. of brain.

A man's brain, it is estimated, consists of 300,000,000 nerve cells, of which over 3,000 are disintegrated and destroyed every minute. Every one, therefore, has a new brain once in sixty days. But excessive labor, or the lack of sleep, prevents the repair of the tissues, and the brain gradually wastes away. Diversity of occupation, by calling upon different portions of the mind or body, successively affords, in some measure, the requisite repose to each. But in this age of overwork there is no safety except in that perfect rest which is the only natural restorative of exhausted power. It has been noticed by observant physicians in their European travels that the German people, who, as a rule, have no ambition and no hope to rise above their inherited station, are peculiarly free from nervous diseases; but in America, where the struggle for advancement is sharp and incessant, and there is nothing that will stop an American but death, the period of life is usually shortened five, ten, or twenty years by the effects of nervous exhaustion.

After the age of 50 the brain loses an ounce every ten years. Cuvier's weighed 65, Byron's 79, and Cromwell's 90 ounces, but the last was diseased. Post-mortem examinations in France give an average of 55 to 60 ounces for the brains of the worst class of criminals.

Beds.—The ancients slept on skins. Beds were afterwards of loose rushes, heather, or straw. The Romans are said to have been the first to use feathers. An air-cushion is said to have been used by Heliogabalus, 218-222; air beds were in use in the sixteenth century. Feather beds were used in England in the reign of Henry VIII. The bedsteads of the Egyptians and later Greeks, like modern couches, became common among the Roman upper classes.

Bells were used among the Jews, Greeks, and Romans. The responses of the Dodonean oracle were in part conveyed by bells. The monument of Porsenna was decorated with pinnacles, each surmounted by bells. Said to have been introduced by Paulinus, bishop of Nole, in Campagna, about 400; and first known in France in 550. The army of Clothaire II., king of France, was frightened from the siege of Sens by the ringing of the bells of St. Stephen's church.

Bells were used in churches by order of Pope John IX., about 900, as a defense, by ringing them, against thunder and lightning. Bells are mythically said to have been cast by Turketul, Abbot of England, about 941. His successor improved the invention, and caused the first tunable set to be put up at Croyland Abbey, 960. In most Catholic states, bells are baptized as we do ships, but with religious solemnity.

Billiards.—Invented by the French, by whom, and by the Germans, Dutch, and Italians, they were brought into general vogue throughout Europe. The French ascribe their invention to Henrique Devigne, an artist, in the reign of Charles IX., about 1571. Slate billiard tables were introduced in England in 1827.

Boots, said to have been the invention of the Carians, were mentioned by Homer, 907 B. C., and frequently by the Roman historians. A variety of forms may be seen in Fairholt's "Costume in England." An instrument of torture "termed the boot" was used in Scotland upon the Covenanters about 1666.

Botany.—Aristotle is considered the founder of the philosophy of botany. The *Historia Plantarum* of Theophrastus was written about 320 B. C. Authors on botany are numerous from the earlier ages of the world to the close of the fifteenth century, when the science became better understood. The study was advanced by Fuchsius, Bock, Bauhin, Cæsalpinus, and others, between 1535 and 1600. The system and arrangement of Linnæus, the first botanist of modern times, made known about 1750; Jussieu's system, in 1758. At the time of the death of Linnæus, A. D. 1778, the species of plants actually described amounted in number to 11,800. The number of species of all denominations now recorded cannot fall short of 100,000.

Bottles in ancient times were made of leather. The art of making glass bottles and drinking-glasses was known to the Romans at least before 79 A. D.; for these articles and other vessels have been found in the ruins of Pompeii. Bottles were made in England about 1558.

Bread.— Ching-Noung, the successor of Fohi, is reputed to have been the first who taught men (the Chinese) the art of husbandry, and the method of making bread from wheat, and wine from rice, 1998 B. C. Baking of bread was known in the patriarchal ages; it became a profession at Rome, 170 B. C. During the siege of Paris by Henry IV., owing to the famine which then raged, bread, which had been sold whilst any remained for a crown a pound, was at last made from the bones of the charnel-house of the Holy Innocents, A. D. 1594. In the time of James I. the usual bread of the poor was made of barley; in Iceland codfish beaten to powder is made into bread; potato bread is used in Ireland. Bread was made with yeast by the English bakers in 1634. In 1856 and 1857, Dauglish patented a mode of making "aerated bread" in which carbonic acid gas is combined with water and mixed with the flour, and which is said to possess the advantages of cleanliness, rapidity, and uniformity.

Bricks were used in Babylon, Egypt, Greece, and Rome; in England by the Romans about 44. Made under the direction of Alfred the Great, about 886. The size regulated by order of Charles I., 1625. Brick machines were invented by Messrs. Cook and Cunningham in 1839; by Messrs. Dixon and Corbett in 1861.

Butter.— It was late before the Greeks had any notion of butter, and by the early Romans it was used as a medicine only, never as food. The Christians of Egypt burned butter in their lamps instead of oil, in the third century. In Africa vegetable butter is made from the fruit of the shea tree, and is of richer taste, at Kebba, than any butter made from cow's milk.

Calico Printing.— The art of calico printing was introduced into Europe about the seventeenth century, although it is believed to have been known in India and Egypt as early as the first or second centuries. In this early period the printing was done by means of blocks on which the designs to be transferred to the cloth had been engraved in relief. These were dipped into dye-stuff, and then pressed upon the material by hand. Later, presses for this block-printing were invented, and the use of several was introduced so engraved as to fill up each other's vacancies, and thus several colors were put into the pattern. About 1770 copper-plate printing was invented in England. By this method the design was cut into plates, the color filled into the sunken parts of the engraving, and the cloths were printed by being pressed upon it. This invention finally led to the introduction of cylinder-printing, the method now in use. The cylinders are of copper, and the design is engraved upon their surface. A separate cylinder is required for each color or shade of color to be used in printing the cloth, and in fine and intricate designs as many as twenty cylinders are sometimes used. These are set in a strong frame against the face of a large central drum made of iron and covered with woolen cloth in several folds, between which and the cylinders the calico is printed as it passes. The color is spread upon the cylinders, as they revolve, by contact with another roller, which dips into a trough containing the coloring-matter properly thickened. This roller is made of an absorbent, elastic material, similar to the roller used in inking a printing press. Each cylinder thus receives its proper color, and imparts it, in revolving, to the calico pressed between its face and that of the fixed drum. A sharp blade of metal pressing against the copper cylinder removes all superfluous color from its surface, so that only the design cut in the metal is imprinted in clear outline upon the cloth. The employment of a number of rollers to make one design is attended with much difficulty, as in passing under them the cloth is in much danger of being displaced and the regularity of the print destroyed. As the cloth leaves the printing-machine it is drawn over rollers through a hot-air chamber, by which it is thoroughly dried, and the colors become fully set.

Candles.— It was not until the fourteenth century that candles having any resemblance to those now in use were manufactured. Previous to that time our English ancestors soaked splints of wood in fat or oil to obtain their light. The candles used by the Greeks and Romans were rude torches made by dipping strips of papyrus or rushes into pitch and then coating them with wax. These candles were also in use in Europe during the middle ages, and were very large and heavy. A dipped candle made from tallow was introduced in England in the fourteenth century, and wax-candles were also made at the same time. These latter were very costly, and were considered great luxuries. In 1484 a company for the manufacture of wax candles was incorporated in London. Mold candles are said to be the invention of the Sieur Le Brez, of Paris.

Casting Plate-Glass.— The whole operation of casting a plate of glass occupies but a very short time. The casting-tables, the most important pieces of apparatus in plate-glass works, are 19 feet long, 14 feet wide, and 7 inches thick. Each is provided with an iron roller 30 inches in diameter and 15 feet long. Strips of iron on each side of the table afford a bearing for the rollers and determine the thickness of the plate of glass to be cast. The rough plate is commonly 9-16ths of an inch in thickness. After polishing, it is reduced to 6-16ths or 7-16ths. The casting-tables are mounted on wheels, and run on a track that reaches every furnace and annealing-oven in the building. The table having been wheeled as near as possible to the melting-furnace, the pot of molten glass is lifted by means of a crane and its contents quickly poured on the table. The heavy iron roller is then passed from end to end, spreading the glass into a layer of uniform thickness. The cold metal of the table cools the glass rapidly. As soon as possible the door of the annealing-oven is opened and the plate of glass introduced. The floor of the oven is on the same level as the casting-table so the transfer can be conveniently and quickly made. When, after several days, the glass is taken out of the oven, its surface is found to be decidedly rough and uneven. A small quantity is used in this condition for skylights and other purposes where strength is required without transparency. It is known as rough-plate. The greater part of the glass, however, is ground, smoothed, and polished before it leaves the establishment. Few industries offer such fine scenic displays as the pouring of the molten glass.

Celluloid is made from the cellulose contained in cotton cloth or raw cotton. The cotton is treated to a weak solution of nitric acid. This has the effect of making a pulp of cotton very much like paper pulp. After the acid has acted the pulp is treated to a copious water-bath that in a large measure washes out the acid. Then it goes through a partial drying process, and a large quantity of camphor-gum is mixed with it, and it is rolled into sheets ready for the drying-room, where it is dried on hot cylinders, the same as paper is dried. It can be softened by steam, but hardens again when it is dry. Celluloid, when ready for market, burns as readily as ordinary sealing-wax.

Chess, Origin of.— Although the origin of chess is enshrouded in considerable mystery, there is but little doubt that its birthplace was in India, and that it is an offspring of a game called Chaturanga, which is mentioned in Oriental literature as in use fully 2,000 years before the Christian era. From India chess spread into Persia, and thence into Arabia, and ultimately the Arabs took it to Spain and the rest of Western Europe. The game was in all probability invented for the purpose of illustrating the art of war. The Arab legend upon this point is that it was devised for the instruction of a young despot by his father, a learned Brahman, to teach him that a king, notwithstanding his power, was dependent for safety upon his subjects. The Greek historians credit the invention of the game to Palamedes, who, they claim, devised it to beguile the tedium of the siege of Troy during the Trojan war.

Common Names of Chemical Substances.

Aqua Fortis,	Nitric Acid.
Aqua Regia,	Nitro-Muriatic Acid.
Blue Vitriol,	Sulphate of Copper.
Cream of Tartar,	Bitartrate Potassium.
Calomel,	Chloride of Mercury.
Chalk,	Carbonate Calcium.
Salt of Tartar,	Carbonate of Potassium.
Caustic Potassa,	Hydrate Potassium.
Chloroform,	Chloride of Gormyle.
Common Salt,	Chloride of Sodium.
Copperas, or Green Vitriol,	Sulphate of Iron.
Corrosive Sublimate,	Bi-Chloride of Mercury.
Diamond,	Pure Carbon.
Dry Alum.	Sulphate Aluminium and Potassium.
Epsom Salts,	Sulphate of Magnesia.
Ethiops Mineral,	Black Sulphide of Mercury.
Galena,	Sulphide of Lead.

Glauber's-Salt,	Sulphate of Sodium.
Glucose,	Grape Sugar.
Iron Pyrites,	Bi-Sulphide Iron.
Jeweler's Putty,	Oxide of Tin.
King's Yellow,	Sulphide of Arsenic.
Laughing Gas,	Protoxide of Nitrogen.
Lime,	Oxide of Calcium.
Lunar Caustic,	Nitrate of Silver.
Muriate of Lime,	Chloride of Calcium.
Niter or Saltpeter,	Nitrate of Potash.
Oil of Vitriol,	Sulphuric Acid.
Potash,	Oxide of Potassium.
Realgar,	Sulphide of Arsenic.
Red Lead,	Oxide of Lead.
Rust of Iron,	Oxide of Iron.
Sal-ammoniac,	Muriate of Ammonia.
Slacked Lime,	Hydrate Calcium.
Soda,	Oxide of Sodium.
Spirits of Hartshorn,	Ammonia.
Spirit of Salt,	Hydro-Chloric, or Muriatic Acid.
Stucco, or Plaster of Paris,	Sulphate of Lime.
Sugar of Lead,	Acetate of Lead.
Verdigris,	Basic Acetate of Copper.
Vermilion,	Sulphide of Mercury.
Vinegar,	Acetic Acid (diluted).
Volatile Alkali,	Ammonia.
Water,	Oxide of Hydrogen.
White Precipitate,	Ammoniated Mercury.
White Vitriol,	Sulphate of Zinc.

Chemistry was introduced into Spain by the Moors about 1150. The Egyptians and Chinese claim an earlier acquaintance with chemistry. The first chemists were alchemists; but chemistry was not a science until the seventeenth century, during which it was promoted by Bacon, Hooke, Mayow, and Boyle. In the early part of the eighteenth century, Dr. Stephen Hales laid the foundation of pneumatic chemistry, and his contemporary, Boerhaave, combined the study of chemistry with medicine. These were succeeded by Bergman, Stahl, Black, and others. In 1772, Priestley published his researches on air, having discovered the gases, oxygen, ammonia, etc., and thus commenced a new chemical era. The nineteenth century opened with the brilliant discoveries of Davy, Dalton, Faraday, Thompson, and Silliman. Organic chemistry has been very greatly advanced by Berzelius, Liebig, Dumas, Laurent, Hoffmann, Cahours, Frankland, and others, since 1830.

Climate.— *Climate* is the state of the atmosphere in regard to temperature, winds, moisture, and salubrity.

The climate of a place as regards temperature depends upon: —

Latitude.— The general law is that the amount of heat is greatest at the equator, and diminishes toward the poles. There are three reasons for this: 1. The sun's rays fall perpendicularly upon the earth at the equator, and more and more obliquely as we go toward the poles. 2. The area covered by a given amount of heating power from the sun is smaller at the equator. 3. Where the sun's rays fall perpendicularly they pass through a less amount of atmosphere, and the absorption of heat is less.

Altitude.— The decrease in temperature is about 3 deg. F. for every 1,000 feet of elevation. As the air receives most of its heat by radiation and reflection from the earth, and as the higher we go the less dense the air, the less heat is absorbed either from the earth or from the direct rays of the sun.

Prevailing Winds.— Winds blowing from the tropical regions carry the heat with them, and, conversely, winds from the polar regions lower the temperature. Whichever wind prevails throughout the year in a given place will consequently modify the temperature of that place.

Length of Day.— During the day the earth receives from the sun more heat than it radiates into space; while during the night it radiates more than it receives. Hence a succession of long days and short nights results in an accumulation of heat, raising the average temperature and producing summer; while long nights and short days result in a temperature below the average, producing winter. The heating power of the sun is greater in summer, because at that season it is shining more directly upon that part of the earth, and conversely in winter. In the tropical regions the inequality of day and night is very little, but increases toward the poles. The temperature in the tropics is therefore more uniform. The length of day makes up for the lessened intensity of the sun's rays; hence a place in high latitude may have at times higher temperature than a place within the tropics.

Ocean Currents.— The warm waters of the tropical regions being brought toward the polar regions bring the heat with them, radiating it into space, and it is absorbed by the atmosphere.

Mountain Ranges.— A mountain range will make a country near it warmer or colder, according as it shields it from a cold or warm wind.

The Distribution of Land and Water.— Land heats or cools rapidly, absorbing or emitting but little heat. Water heats or cools slowly, absorbing or emitting large quantities of heat. Hence the land is subject to great and sudden changes of temperature; the water to small and gradual changes. Places situated near the sea have, therefore, a more equable climate.

Character of Soil.— Dry, sandy soil heats and cools more rapidly than wet and marshy lands; hence the latter will have a more uniform temperature.

Slope of Land.— Land which slopes so that the sun's rays will strike it nearer vertically will receive more heat. The south side of a hill is warmer in winter than the north side.

In regard to *winds* the climate of a place depends upon: —

Temperature.— As winds are but masses of air set in motion by the unequal heating, the winds of any given place depend primarily upon the temperature, though not necessarily upon the temperature of that place. As the air is heated in the tropical parts of the earth by the sun, it rises, and colder air flows in from the polar regions to take its place; hence the primary currents, which are modified in various ways by other causes.

Rotation of the Earth.— The winds are turned out of their course by the rotation of the earth in the same manner as the ocean currents.

Land and Water.— The land becomes warmer during the day than the sea, and, the air rising, a cooler air flows in from the sea. At night the land parts with its heat more rapidly than the water and becomes cooler; then the wind sets the other way. Hence we have the land and sea breezes.

Elevation of the Land.— Mountains, as has already been stated, shelter places from winds. Some of the great plains are subject to almost constant winds.

In regard to *moisture*, the climate of a place depends upon: —

Prevailing Wind.— If a wind blows from large bodies of water in a warm region it will be laden with moisture which will be likely to be precipitated on reaching a colder country.

Mountains.— The contact of a moisture-laden wind with the cold sides of mountains will cause a precipitation of its moisture, and the regions beyond the mountains will not receive it.

Forests, by shading the earth, keep its surface cool, and this tends to condense the moisture.

Cultivation of the Soil, causing it to absorb moisture from the atmosphere, and by capillary attraction in dry weather bring up moisture from below to the surface.

Temperature.— Increased heat causes greater evaporation, and hence more moisture in the atmosphere. More rain falls within the tropics than in the temperate or polar regions.

Land and Water.— More rain falls on the coasts of a country than in the interior, because the winds are more moist. More rain falls in the northern hemisphere than in the southern, because there is a greater diversity of land and water, the evaporation coming mainly from the ocean, and the condensation from the diversified land surface.

Isothermal lines are lines connecting places that have the same mean temperature.

There is a line or limit of elevation, above which the surface is covered with perpetual snow; this is called the *snow-line*.

Coaches.— Covered carriages appear to have been used by the old Romans. In the year 1588, Duke Julius of Brunswick published an act against riding in coaches. Philip II. of Pomerania-Stettin published a similar document in 1608. Coaches appear to have been used in France very early. An ordinance of Philip the Fair, issued in 1294, for suppressing luxury, forbids citizens' wives to ride in coaches. Coaches were first used in England in 1565, the first being that made for the Earl of Rutland. In 1601 an act was passed to prevent men riding in coaches, on the score of its effeminacy. Coaches began to be common in 1605, and were petitioned against by the saddlers and other. Hackney coaches introduced in 1634. In 1661, a stage coach was two days going from London to Oxford, and the "flying coach" was thirteen hours, even in summer weather, when the roads were at their best.

Coffins.— Athenian heroes were buried in coffins of the cedar tree, owing to its aromatic and incorruptible qualities. Coffins of marble and stone were used by the Romans. Alexander is said to have been buried in one of gold; and glass coffins have been found in England. The earliest record of wooden coffins among the English speaking people is that of the burial of King Arthur in an entire trunk of oak, hollowed, A. D. 542. The patent coffins were invented in 1796.

Coin.— Silver was first coined by Phidon, King of Argos, 869 B. C. In Rome, silver money was first coined 269 B. C. Gold and silver coins first used in the East. Coin first used in Britain 25 B. C., and in Scotland not until 248 years later. In 1101, round coins were first used in England. Silver halfpence and farthings were coined in the reign of John, and pence were the largest current coins. Gold was first coined in England in 1087; in Bohemia, in 1301. In 1531, groats and half-groats were the largest silver coin in England. Gold was first coined in Venice in 1346. Shillings were first coined in England in 1068. Crowns and half-crowns were first coined in 1551. Henry III. introduced copper money into France in 1580. Copper money introduced into England by James I. in 1620. The process of milling coin introduced in 1662. The mint of the United States of America was established in 1793.

Comets.— It has been lately suggested that there is a great degree of affinity between comets and meteors — in fact, that a comet is merely an aggregation of meteors. Comets have been supposed to be bodies of burning gas. Their mass is very great, and their brilliant tails are many millions of miles in extent. In their orbits, they differ greatly from the planets. While the latter are direct in their wanderings, comets are most irregular and eccentric. When first seen, the comet resembles a faint spot of light upon the background of the sky. As it comes nearer, the brightness increases and the tail begins to show.

The term comet signifies a hairy body. A comet consists usually of three parts: the nucleus, a bright point in the center of the head; the coma (hair), the cloud-like mass surrounding the nucleus; and the tail, a luminous train extending generally in a direction from the sun.

It is not understood whether comets shine by their own or by reflected light. If their nuclei consist of white-hot matter, a passage through such a furnace would be anything but desirable.

The discovery of the elliptical orbit of comets is due to Halley. He discovered a comet in 1682 which he demonstrated to be a return of the comet described by Kepler in 1607; that it had appeared in 1531, and that it was the comet that had appeared still earlier by the same period of seventy-five years, in 1457, and that had caused such consternation among the Christians, who regarded it as a sign,—Constantinople having just fallen and all Europe being threatened by the Turks. Halley also predicted the return of the comet in 1757. It reached its perihelion in 1759. Its last appearance was in 1835. It will be looked for in 1911.

Encke's, Biela's, and the comets of 1843 and 1858 are comparatively recent. Others came in 1861, 1874, 1883. In 1881, two comets appeared. Some comets of antiquity were very remarkable, and are reputed to have equaled the sun in magnitude. One tail is usually supposed to be the distinguishing mark of a comet, but in 1774 one appeared with six tails, arranged something like a fan. Sometimes the tail is separated from the head. Some comets appear at regular intervals, and their approach can be determined with accuracy. Of course we only see those which are attracted by the sun, or those which revolve in the solar system. There must be thousands of other comets which we never see at all.

Compass, The.—The directive power of the magnet seems to have been unknown in Europe until late in the twelfth century. It appears, however, on very good authority, that it was known in China and throughout the east generally at a very remote date. The Chinese annals assign its discovery to the year 2634 B. C., when, they say, an instrument for indicating the south was constructed by the Emperor Hon-ang-ti. At first, they would appear to have used it exclusively for guidance in traveling by land. The earliest date at which we hear of their using it at sea is somewhere about A. D. 300. According to one account, a knowledge of the compass was brought to Europe by Marco Polo on his return from Cathay. It was long contended that the compass as a nautical instrument was first invented by Flavio Gioja, a native of Amalfi, about the year 1362, and that the section of the Kingdom of Naples where he was born has a compass for its arms. For this there is no authority whatever, as the compass was well known as a nautical instrument before his time. The phenomena of the magnetic needle which perplex scientists most are that in every place it is subject to variations. By observation at Paris it was found that in 1681 the needle varied 2 degrees 30 minutes to the west; in 1865, 18 degrees 44 minutes to the west. At London, between 1580 and 1692, the needle varied from 10 degrees 15 minutes east to 6 degrees west. In Dakota the average variation is 12 degrees 30 minutes east, in Minnesota 11 degrees east, while in Montana it is 20 degrees east. In a work on Government Surveys it is stated that "the needle does not point due north except in a few localities, and at no place does it continue to point with a given angular distance from the north for any stated length of time. It changes secularly, annually, diurnally and hourly, and is, further, subject to fluctuations reducible to no method of tabulation." In the vicinity of iron or magnetic sands, the needle is deflected toward the material attracting it.

Compressed-Air Engines.—The arrangements of atmospheric engines is largely identical with that of non-condensing steam-engines, and they are used very generally both in the United States and Europe in the construction of tunnels, their great advantage being that in place of escaping heat and steam, which would seriously vitiate the close air in the shaft, the working of the engine gives out pure cold air, serving also the purpose of ventilation. An engine worked by compressed air, however, can never be a prime motor in itself, since the air which propels it must be compressed by another power—either steam, electricity, falling water, or animal force. There are several ways of applying this compressed air. One is to fill with it a large, strong cylinder or reservoir, and use it to work a piston in the same way that steam is used. Another is to conduct the air from the prime motor in tubes to several smaller engines. In the construction of the Mont Cenis Tunnel the hydraulic power of a cataract near the entrance of a tunnel was used as a prime motor to compress air in reservoirs, whence it was conducted by flexible tubes to work the rock-boring machines. When this boring is done by percussion of steel drills, the atmospheric pressure moves a piston connected with them. When the boring is performed by rotation, as is the case with the diamond drill, the atmospheric engine is either a rotary or reciprocating one. Compressed air is also used with steam as a motor. Air when compressed greatly becomes very hot, and if it is then forced through hot water it becomes saturated with steam, and this steam and air are found to have enormous expansive power. This motive-power has been very successfully applied to the propulsion of street cars. In the working of electric-light machinery compressed air is used to a considerable extent.

Copernican System, The, is that which represents the sun to be at rest in the center of the universe, and the earth and planets to move round it as a center. It got its name from Copernicus, who (although some vague general notion of the system seems to be due to Pythagoras) first distinctly drew the attention of philosophers to it, and devoted his life to its demonstration. For the rest, the glory of developing on the lines he broadly laid down, belongs to Kepler, Galileo, and others, and to Newton, who finally marked out the form of modern theoretical astronomy. Many who reverence the name of Copernicus in connection with this system, would be surprised to find, on perusing his work, how much of error, unsound reasoning, and happy conjecture combined to secure for him in all time the association of the system with his name; yet, with all its faults, that work marks one of the greatest steps ever taken in science.

Corsets.—An article of dress somewhat resembling the corsets now worn by women was used in Germany and France as early as the thirteenth century, and it found its way into England in the latter half of the fourteenth century. It contained rods and plates of whalebone and steel, and was designed, we are told, to conceal the defects and exaggerate the beauties of the figure. This stiff arrangement was discarded at the time of the French Revolution owing to the Greek costume having been brought into vogue, and its place was taken by a smoothly fitting under waist.

Cotton, a vegetable wool, is the product of a shrub indigenous to the tropical regions of India and America. Indian cotton cloth is mentioned by Herodotus, was known in Arabia in the time of Mahomet 627, and was brought into Europe by his followers. It does not appear to have been in use among the Chinese till the thirteenth century; to them we are indebted for the cotton fabric termed *nankeen.* Cotton was the material of the principal articles of clothing among the American Indians, when visited by Columbus. It was grown and manufactured in Spain in the tenth century; and in the fourteenth century was introduced into Italy. Indian muslins, chintzes, and cottons were so largely imported into England in the seventeenth century, that an act of parliament followed prohibiting their introduction. Cotton became the staple commodity of England in the present century. First cotton factory in America established at East Bridgewater, Mass., 1787. First power looms in the United States, 1813. The method of spinning cotton was formerly by hand; but about 1767 Mr. Hargraves, of Lancashire invented the spinning jenny with eight spindles; he also erected the first carding machine with cylinders. Sir Richard Arkwright obtained a patent for a new invention of machinery in 1769; and another patent for an engine in 1775. Crompton invented the mule, a further and wonderful improvement in the manufacture of cotton in 1779, and various other improvements have been since made. In 1793, Eli Whitney, an American, invented the cotton gin, a machine by which cotton wool is separated from the pod and cleaned with great ease and expedition.

Cremation.—The reduction of the human body to ashes by fire was a very early and widespread usage of antiquity. The early Aryans, as opposed to the non-Aryan aborigines of India, Greeks, Romans, Sclavs, Celts, and Germans, burned their dead; therefore cremation may be regarded as the universal custom of the Indo-European races. The graves of North Europe throughout the "bronze age" contain only jars of ashes. The advocates of disposing of the dead by cremation are at the present time numerous, their principal arguments in favor of it being of a sanitary nature. According to the method which is most favored by modern cremationists, the body is placed in an oblong brick or iron-cased chamber, underneath which is a furnace. The air of the chamber is raised to a very high temperature before the body is put in, and a stream of heated hydro-carbon from a gasometer is then admitted, which on contact with intensely-heated air within immediately bursts into flame. The chamber is, of course, so constructed as neither to admit draughts of air from without nor to permit the escape of gas from within. The noxious gases which are evolved in the beginning of the combustion process are passed through a flue into a second furnace, where they are entirely consumed. By this process a body weighing 144 pounds can be reduced in about fifty minutes to not more than four pounds of lime-dust. In the cremation of each body about 200 pounds of fuel is used.

Crockery.—The materials used in the manufacture of crockery are kaolin, pipe-clay, quartz or flint, and feldspar — the kaolin and quartz to give hardness, and the pipe-clay and feldspar to yield a flux sufficient to bind the masses firmly together. The materials are ground into a fine powder and then mixed with water in a machine called a "blunger," which is a box containing paddles worked very rapidly. When the matter has been thoroughly mixed it is drawn off and forced by a hydraulic pump through a series of sieves and then worked up in what is called a pug-mill, after which it is cut by a fine wire into rectangular blocks. These blocks are then molded into the shape of the article desired, some by the use of a lathe, and some by simply shaping them with the hands. The pieces are thus partially dried, turned on a lathe with a sharp tool to give them a uniform surface, dried slowly in a drying room, then baked in an oven. In baking the ware is kept at a white heat for thirty-six hours. The pieces are then glazed by being dipped in a mixture of ground feldspar, ground flint, sal soda, plastic clay, and boracic acid, the whole pulverized and mixed with a small proportion of white lead and a little cobalt blue. This glaze is mixed with water, the articles are dipped in it one by one, receiving a deposit like a thin paste on the surface, which, when placed in the oven again, fuses and flows over it, making a coating of glassy smoothness. Fine, white china or porcelain is of course made of finer material than crockery, but the process of manufacture is similar.

Cryolite is a snow-white mineral, partially transparent, of a vitreous luster and of brittle texture. It is so named from its fusibility in the flame of a candle. It is a compound of sodium, fluorine, and aluminum, and is used for the preparation of the metal aluminum. It occurs in veins in gneiss with pyrites and galena, and has been found in western Greenland and at Miyask in the Ural Mountains. It is extensively employed in the United States in the manufacture of white porcelain glass, and also in the preparation of caustic soda.

Daguerreotype.— The name given to a process invented by M. Daguerre of Paris in 1839, by which perfect facsimiles of objects are transferred upon thin copper plates, plated with silver. The images are produced by the action of light upon the iodine through the focus of the camera obscura. An apparatus somewhat kindred in design was in contemplation about the same time by M. Niepce, and about five years previously by Henry Fox Talbot of London; the original idea, however, is traceable as far back as the days of Roger Bacon. So important a discovery in the fine arts was the daguerreotype deemed by the French government, that it awarded to its inventor a life pension of 6,000 francs.

Damascus Steel.— The skill of the Damascenes in the manufacture of steel became famous in Europe at the time of the Crusades, but the secrets of their process have never been revealed. A Russian mining engineer, General Anosoff, by analysis and examination, however, succeeded in making steel that could scarcely be distinguished from it in appearance. The essential point of his process was melting the iron in crucibles with graphite and a small quantity of dolomite; but the details of working these materials with success were of course known only by himself, and the quality of the steel produced by the works since his death has very much deteriorated. An imitation of Damascus steel is also made in America and is often known by that name, though its proper appellation is damask steel, so called from the peculiar damask figures on its surface.

Damask Linens and Silks. — They were first manufactured at Damascus, and hence the name; have been imitated by the Dutch and Flemish. The manufacture was introduced into England by artisans who fled from the persecutions of Alva, 1571-3.

Day and Night.—The earth has two constant motions: (1) its daily motion, or rotation on its axis (its shorter diameter), from west to east; (2) its yearly motion, or movement in a nearly circular path (called its orbit) around the sun. The length of time the earth is turning on its axis is called a day. Every part of the earth's surface being successively carried into light and shade, the daily rotation causes the phenomena of day and night. The length of time the earth is in passing around the sun is called a year. It turns on its own axis in the same time about $365\frac{1}{4}$ times, hence there are $365\frac{1}{4}$ days in a year. As the earth revolves from west to east, the sun will appear to travel from east to west. At the equator the days and nights are always twelve hours long; the farther a point lies from the equator, the longer are its longest day and its longest night. At the poles the year is made up of but one day and one night, each lasting six months. All places in about $66\frac{1}{2}$ degrees of latitude, north or south, have one day in the year twenty-four hours long, and one night of an equal length.

Dew.— For any assigned temperature of the atmosphere there is a certain quantity of aqueous vapor which it is capable of holding in suspension at a given pressure. Conversely, for any assigned quantity of aqueous vapor held in suspension in the atmosphere there is a minimum temperature at which it can remain so suspended. This minimum temperature is called the dew point. During the daytime, especially if there has been sunshine, a good deal of aqueous vapor is taken into suspension in the atmosphere. If the temperature in the evening now falls below the dew point, which after a hot and calm day generally takes place about sunset, the vapor which can be no longer held in suspension is deposited on the surface of the earth, sometimes to be seen visibly falling in a fine mist. Another form of the phenomenon of dew is as follows: The surface of the earth, and all things on it, and especially the smooth surfaces of vegetable productions, are constantly parting with their heat by radiation. If the sky is covered with clouds, the radiation sent back from the clouds nearly supplies an equivalent for the heat thus parted with; but if the sky be clear, no equivalent is supplied, and the surface of the earth and things growing on it become colder than the atmosphere. If the night also be calm, the small portion of air contiguous to any of the surfaces will become cooled below the dew point, aud its moisture deposited on the surface in the form of dew. If the chilled temperature be below 32 degrees Fahrenheit, the dew becomes frozen, and is called *hoar-frost*. The above two phenomena, though both expressed in our language by the word "dew"—which perhaps helps to lead to a confusion of ideas on the subject—are not necessarily expressed by the same word. For instance, in French, the first phenomenon—the falling evening dew—is expressed by the word *serein;* while the latter—the dew seen in the morning gathered in drops on the leaves of plants or other cool surfaces—is expressed by the word *rosée*. Similar to *rosée* is the moisture which condenses on the outside surface of pitchers or glasses of ice-water. The air in immediate contact is cooled below the dew point and deposits the suspended moisture.

Dictionary.—A standard dictionary of the Chinese language, containing about 40,000 characters, most of them hieroglyphics, or rude representations somewhat like our signs of the zodiac, was perfected by Pa-out-she, who lived about 1100 B. C. Cyclopedias were compiled in the fifteenth and sixteenth centuries. The first dictionary of celebrity, perhaps the first, is by Ambrose Calepini, a Venetian friar; it is in Latin; he wrote another in eight languages, about A. D. 1500. Chambers's Cyclopedia, the first dictionary of the circle of the arts and sciences, was published in 1728. The English dictionary by Samuel Johnson appeared in 1755. Noah Webster's great American dictionary of the English language in two volumes was published at New Haven in 1828. Worcester's dictionary appeared in 1860. Harper's Latin Dictionary (founded upon Andrews's translation of Freund's Latin-German lexicon), adopted as the standard authority in English and American universities, was published in 1879.

Discovery of Gold in California.—On January 19, 1848, John W. Marshall was building a mill for himself and Sutter on the south fork of the American River, fifty-four miles east of Sutter's Fort. This mill, it was expected, would supply the ranches and settlements with pine lumber. On this particular morning Marshall picked up from the bed-rock of the race of the mill a small piece of yellow metal which weighed about seventeen grains. It was malleable, heavier than silver, and in all respects resembled gold. Marshall showed the piece in the afternoon to those who were working at the mill. The result of the discussion which ensued was the rejection of the gold theory. Marshall, however, was not satisfied, and afterward tested it with nitric acid, and found it was actually gold. He discovered pieces like it in all the surrounding gulches wherever he dug for it. The news of the discovery soon spread, and in April reports of the find were published.

Diving Bells.—The principle of the diving bell is extremely simple, and can be seen by pressing any hollow vessel mouth downward into water. Although some species of diving bell was probably used in the time of Aristotle—for it is recorded that divers took with them a vessel which enabled them to remain under water—and in mediæval times, it was not until about 1715 that any practical method of supplying the bell with air while under water was discovered. About that year this want was met by a Doctor Halley. He used two water-tight barrels, each supplied with a hose, also attached to the diving bell, and these, attached to heavy weights, were dropped on each side of the bell, and the diver could, therefore, remain under water as long as the air supplied by the barrels was fit to breathe. The diver's cap, which was made of metal and fitted with a tube for conveying air to it from the bell, so that the wearer could leave the bell and walk around the bottom of the sea, was soon after devised by the same inventor. In 1779, the air pump, which forced down air from above, was applied to diving bells by an engineer named Smeaton. The most practical bell in use at present is a sort of submarine boat, called the Nautilus, with double sides, between which water is forced to cause the boat to descend and air to cause it to rise.

Dyeing is attributed to the Tyrians, about 1500 B. C. The English are said to have sent fine goods to be dyed in Holland till the art was brought to them, probably in 1608. A statute against abuses in dyeing passed in 1783. The art has been greatly improved by chemical research. Among the most prominent names connected with the art of dyeing is that of Dr. Stenhouse, who in 1848 invented a number of beautiful dyes,— mauve, magenta, red, green, black.

Dynamite.— As generally manufactured, dynamite consists of infusorial earth, porcelain earth, coal-dust, siliceous ashes or the like, saturated with about three times its weight of nitro-glycerine, a compound which is produced by the action of a mixture of strong nitric and sulphuric acids on glycerine at low temperatures, though the proportions vary with different makers. According to its elements, it is to the eye a grayish-brown, reddish, or blackish powder, damp and greasy to the touch, and without smell. Its explosive power is about eight times greater than that of gunpowder. The manufacture of dynamite is attended with great danger, owing to the proneness of nitro-glycerine to explosion even at the slightest shock. The explosive force of the latter substance, which has the appearance of common oil, is about ten times greater than that of gunpowder.

Dynamite Gun.— The nitro-gelatine or dynamite gun, known as the "Zalinski gun," was the invention of Lieutenant Zalinski and Captain Bartlett of the United States army. It is a long tube made of wrought iron, lined with seamless brass tubing one eighth of an inch thick. The projectile used is shaped like a huge rocket, five or six feet in length. The stick of the rocket has a wooden or metal base large enough to fill the bore of the gun, and against this base the pressure of the air (the propelling force being compressed air) — 1,000 pounds to the square inch — is exerted. The head of the rocket contains from fifty to sixty pounds — or more — of nitro-gelatine, a new explosive made of nitro-glycerine and gun-cotton. The projectile, being shot from the gun, is exploded, after reaching its mark, by electricity. A small battery is fixed in the head of each shot, and the discharge is effected by concussion if the shot strikes, or by action of water on a sensitized surface if the shot lights in the sea. It is thought that a submarine explosion within 100 feet of a ship will be disastrous in eight cases out of ten. The gun is from 40 to 75 feet in length, and of caliber from 6 to 10 inches. The mechanical arrangement for compressing the air in the gun and discharging the piece is said to be taken from an invention of B. T. Babbitt, patented in 1878.

Earth's Surface, The.— The earth's surface covers an area of about 197,000,000 square miles, of which only about one fourth is land.

Lowlands are tracts, either level or diversified by hill and vale, not elevated more than 1,000 feet above sea-level. *Deserts* are extensive tracts destitute of water, and, consequently, of vegetation and animal life.

Silvas are forest plains. Plains that produce grass, but not trees, are known in North America as *prairies;* in South America as *llanos* and *pampas;* in Asia and Southeastern Europe as *steppes.*

The desert of Sahara, as far as known, consists partly of table lands and partly of low plains. It is interspersed with *oases*, or fertile spots, which are generally lower than the surrounding country; some of these are of considerable extent and well populated.

A *mountain* is an elevation of land exceeding 2,000 feet in height. A *hill* is less than 2,000 feet in height.

A *mountain chain* is a long, elevated ridge, or several mountains extending in a line.

Mountains are of great use to man. They attract the clouds, condense their moisture, and store up in reservoirs the water received from them, sending it forth again in streams, from thousands of springs, to fertilize the soil. They increase the surface of the earth, giving variety to its vegetable productions. They protect the adjacent countries from cold and piercing winds, and thus exert a favorable influence on their climate.

An *avalanche* is a large mass of snow, ice, and earth, sliding or rolling down a mountain. A water shed is the mountain chain or ridge of land which separates one basin from another, and from which the rivers flow.

A *mountain pass* is an elevated road crossing a mountain chain through a natural opening or depression.

Glaciers are immense masses of ice formed by the accumulated snows upon the mountain tops. They fill in vast valleys, and have an onward motion throughout like a liquid or semi-liquid body. Their course down the slopes is very slow, but, like rivers, they flow faster in the middle than at the bottom and sides. The lower extremities are constantly melting, forming torrents and mountain streams, while the upper parts are fed by the snows. Rocks of immense size are torn off and carried down by glaciers. They occur in the greatest numbers in the Alps. When a glacier reaches the ocean large fragments are broken off and float away as *icebergs.*

Earthquakes.— The phenomena connected with earthquakes have been variously described. Many writers refer to appearances in the heavens, or changes in the atmosphere, which to them seem to have some connection with the catastrophes they narrate. They tell of irregularities in the seasons preceding or following the shock; of sudden gusts of wind, interrupted by sudden calms; of violent rains at unusual seasons or in countries where such phenomena are almost unknown; of a reddening of the sun's disk; of a haziness in the air, often continued for months; and similar phenomena. But these are so irregular in their appearance, and have been so seldom observed associated with more than a single earthquake, that in the absence of any decided reason to the contrary there seems good ground for believing they have no real connection with the earthquake. The general opinion of investigators is that these agitations proceed from within outward, and are not of atmospheric or other external origin. True, Professor Alexis Perry, of Dijon, France, thought he discovered relations between the ages of the moon and these occurrences which seemed to sustain the theory of Zantedeschi that the liquid nucleus of the earth responds to the moon's attraction in tides, somewhat as the coast does; but the theory that the earth has a liquid nucleus covered with only a thin, solid crust is losing adherents continually. All theorists are agreed, as to the connection between volcanoes and earthquakes, that they are produced by the same subterraneous agency. Mr. Mallet, in an elaborate report on the subject presented to the British Association, proposed an ingenious theory. He assumes that volcanoes and the centers of earthquake disturbances are near the sea or other large supplies of water; and he says that when an eruption of igneous matter takes place beneath the sea-bottom the first action must be to open up large fissures in its rocky material, or to lift and remove its incoherent portions, such as sand, mud, gravel, etc. The water, on meeting the heated surface, assumes the spheroidal state. While in this condition the intestine motion may be great, but little steam is generated; but no sooner have the surfaces cooled than the water comes into close contact with them, and a vast volume of steam is evolved explosively and blown off into the deep and cold water of the sea, where it is condensed, and thus a blow of the most tremendous sort is given at the volcanic focus, and, being transferred outwardly in all directions, is transmitted as the earthquake shock. Whatever their origin, whether of one cause or various causes, the prevailing opinion still is that the vibrations of every earthquake can be traced to a focus within the earth, and that this lies directly beneath the point of greatest disturbance on the earth's surface. There are creditable records of between 6,000 and 7,000 earthquakes, between 1606 B. C. and A. D. 1842. In the great Lisbon earthquake no less than 60,000 perished, while in that of Calabria, in the end of the last century, 40,000 were destroyed. It is estimated that at least 13,000,000 of the human race have perished in this way.

Electric Light, The, was first invented by Sir Humphry Davy, in the early part of this century, who produced the arc light with a battery of 2,000 cells. It was not in practical use, however, until 1844, when improvements in its manner of construction were made by a Frenchman named Foucault, and it was used to illuminate the Place de la Concord, in Paris. In 1855, Jules Duboscq's electric lamp—thus far the most perfect of the kind—was shown at the Paris Exposition; but, though improvements were made in the invention during the twenty years following, little was accomplished toward practical electric lighting until the invention of Jablochkoff's candle. Paul Jablochkoff was a Russian, who resigned his position under the government in 1875 to devote his time wholly to scientific study. It was his intention to visit the Centennial Exposition in America, but he was induced to remain in Paris, where, in 1876, he produced the electric candle, whose discovery made a great sensation. The light given by this candle was soft and steady, and a great many of them speedily came into use in Europe. In the last fifteen years great progress has been made, and there are now many different styles and forms, but in their essential features they nearly all come under two general classes — the arc light and the incandescent light. The arc light is, in principle, the same as that invented by Davy, the improvements consisting in different devices for regulating and maintaining at a constant distance the tips, and in different preparations for the substance of these tips, which are generally of carbon. The light is produced as follows: Two tips connected with the opposite poles of a strong battery are brought near to each other. The electricity, overcoming the resistance of the air, jumps from one tip to the other, and in so doing generates such an intense heat that the particles on the end of the one tip are volatilized and carried to the other in a condition of white heat, forming an arc of light of intense brilliancy. Thus one tip is slowly consumed and the other somewhat increased, and hence the necessity of regulators for the tips, whence these lights are sometimes called regulated lamps. The Brush patent is the arc light best known and most used in America. In lights of the incandescent class a lighter current is used, and the luminous substance is not consumed, being inclosed in a sealed glass bulb from which the air has been exhausted. It consists of a loop of a thin fiber of some infusible substance (carbon has been found the best), inclosed in a vacuum, as just stated. The ends of this fiber are carried through the neck of the bulb and connected with the opposite poles of the battery; then the current, in passing through such a small conductor, has to overcome a high resistance, and in so doing generates a heat sufficient to maintain the entire loop at a steady temperature of white heat. The principal forms of the incandescent light are those of Edison, Swan, Maxim, and Siemens. It is perhaps worthy of note that the great impetus given to electric lighting by the work of Thomas Edison has been not so much in improving the lamp as in cheapening the process of generating the electricity and inventing a ready mode of dividing the light. Hitherto the two principal barriers in the way of applying the electric light to public use had been the expense attendant upon the production of the electric force and the difficulty of using it simultaneously at a large number of illuminating points.

Electricity.— As far back as 321 B. C., the ancient philosopher Theophrastus mentions the power of amber to attract straws and dry leaves. Pliny, in 70 A. D., writes concerning the same phenomenon, and it is from the Greek name of "amber," pronounced "electron," that we call this phenomenon "electricity." Dr. Gilbert, of Colchester, may be considered the founder of the *science* of electricity, for it was he that carefully repeated the observations of the ancients, and experimented in various ways and published these experiments in a book during the period between 1540 and 1603. Sir William Watson (1715 to 1807) distinctly announced the theory of *positive* and *negative* electricity, which was afterwards elaborated by Dr. Benjamin Franklin. Dr. Franklin also established the fact that the lightning was an electrical spark, similar to that made by an electric machine or Leyden jar. In 1790, Galvani discovered that the contact of metals produced muscular contraction in the legs of a dead frog, and in 1800, Volta discovered the art of generating electricity by contact of metals with damp cloths. From these we obtained the galvanic battery and the voltaic pile.

It remained with Prof. H. C. Oersted, of Copenhagen, however, to bring foward the most important fact, viz.: the magnetic action of the electrical current. This was in 1820. As soon as the discovery reached France, the eminent French philosopher Ampère set to work to develop the important consequences it involved. Faraday in 1820, discovered electric-magnetic rotation. From this time up, experimentists and theorists were busy searching for ways and means by which the electrical energy could be utilized as a mechanical power, and to-day the galvanic battery and electric dynamo are rapidly ousting steam, and in a thousand ways doing its work with less noise, expense, and better results.

As to the question of the real nature of electricity, recent experiments and further knowledge of its properties rather open fresh avenues to new hypotheses than point to the truth of any one special theory. Some identify electricity with energy, some with matter, and some with the subtle all-pervading "ether." At all events it has been computed that in every single cubic foot of ether there are locked up 10,000 foot-tons of energy! The latest researches give well-founded hopes that this inconceivably vast storehouse of power will one day be accessible to man. And herein lies the splendid possibility of a new and mighty successor to the decreasing energy of our coal-fields, with the speedy extinction of which alarmists threaten us. By creating in a room a powerful electrostatic field alternating very rapidly, Professor Nicola Tesla brought it to such a state that illuminating appliances could be placed anywhere, and kept lighted without being electrically connected with anything! He suspended two sheets of metal, each connected with a terminal of the electric coil, between which an exhausted tube, carried anywhither, remained always luminous. A true flame can now therefore be produced without chemical aid — a flame yielding light and heat without the consumption of material or any chemical process! Further, these and similar experiments on electric radiation, which now advances so brilliantly to the forefront, by Tesla and Crookes, etc., point to the bewildering possibility of telegraphy without wires, without cables, without posts. There is considerable evidence to show that, could the electric ether-waves be obtained sufficiently short, the rays would fall within the limits of visibility, and thus place the final crown of proof on the magnificent experiments of Hertz and others, who would make light an electric phenomenon.

As regards the effect on the human body of alternating currents of very high frequency (which at best have a very doubtful reputation) it has been found that, as the rapidity of the alternation increases, they become, not more but less dangerous. In fact, Tatum has shown that their fatal effects are nearly inversely proportionate to their frequency. Thus, with currents alternating about 5,000 per second, the current needed to become fatal is about ten times greater than at the ordinary low frequency of about 120 per second. With still higher frequencies used by Tesla (up to 20,000 per second) the currents are incomparably less dangerous than at low frequencies; but still altogether harmless.

Electricity, Storage of.—The storage of electricity is the conversion of electricity into chemical energy under such circumstances that it may be readily converted back into electricity. The secondary batteries, which are used for storing purposes, are termed "accumulators." The first battery of this kind was made by Ritter about 1840, and it consisted of a series of disks of a single metal, alternated with cloth or card moistened in a liquid by which the metal would not be affected chemically. In 1859 Mr. Gaston Plante made a secondary battery, for which he used plates of lead instead of plates of platinum. Passing a current through these, lead oxide was deposited, and after the charging-current was removed the lead and lead-oxide were found to yield a very slight current. To increase this, Plante devised the plan of first charging the plates, then discharging, then charging again with the battery-current reversed, and so on, until, by repeated oxidations and subsequent reductions of the oxidized material, very porous plates were made. These, by their porosity, exposed a large surface to the oxidizing action of the current, so that a small porous plate took up as much electricity as one of large superficial area. Plante found that by connecting a number of cells together, and, after charging them, arranging them in series — that is, the positive plate of one connecting with the negative plate of another, and so on — he could store for use quite powerful currents of electricity. In 1880 another electrician, M. Camille Faure, devised the plan of coating Plante's lead-plates with red-lead, and then incasing them in flannel. The advantage of the red-lead is that it is very quickly made porous, and therefore the process of repeated charging of the plates, known as the "forming" process, was reduced from weeks to days, and even to hours. This discovery, by reducing the time and expense of making the secondary battery, gave it a commercial value that it never had before, and it was hailed as a great advantage. Since that time a number of patents have been obtained for storage-batteries, and they now exist in different forms, but generally modeled on the inventions of Plante and Faure. The efforts of inventors have been mainly directed toward reducing the weight of the cells and to devising new ways of holding red-lead on the plates. This last-named substance, becoming porous, drops off readily, and for this reason the incasements of flannel, etc., were first devised. In some of the storage-batteries a plate or frame of cast lead is used, with receptacles, cells, etc., which are filled with the red-lead.

Electroplating. — The first to gild the baser metals by means of the galvanic current was Brugnatelli, in 1803; but the first to make the process a success was the chemist De la Rive, and it has since been greatly improved by later inventions. The process depends upon the peculiar power which the electric current possesses of separating certain compound bodies into their constituent parts. For instance, if a current from a galvanic battery is passed by means of platinum electrodes through water to which sulphuric acid has been added, this chemical separation, which is called electrolysis, will take place, the water being resolved into its constituent gases, oxygen and hydrogen. Now, if some sulphate of copper be thrown into the liquid, electrolysis will still go on, with a double result: the water will be separated into its elements, and the hydrogen, by its stronger affinity, will form a new compound with the sulphur in the sulphate, setting the copper free; and the liberated copper, being electro-positive in character, will be deposited on the platinum electrode, which is negative. On this general principle the process of electroplating or electrotyping depends, and its art consists in applying the metals thus released from their solutions to artistic and useful purposes. To carry on electroplating on a large scale oblong vats are used, which hold 200 gallons of solution. Silver plates connected with a powerful galvanic battery are placed at intervals in the vats; they form the positive electrodes and correspond in extent of surface with the articles to be coated, and face them on both sides. These articles act as the negative electrodes, and are suspended by copper wire from brass rods laid lengthwise over the vats and connected with the battery. The articles are prepared for plating by being first boiled in a solution of potash to free them from all grease; they are then quickly dipped in red nitrous-acid to remove any oxide that may have formed on the surface, and after this are well washed in water to remove every trace of the acid; they are then dipped into a solution of mercury and then washed in water again. The effect of this latter operation is to make the film of silver adhere more readily.

The articles are then weighed and suspended in the solution, and are left there until a sufficient amount of silver has been deposited upon them. This amount is tested by weight. If the additional weight is not gained within the expected time the article is put in the solution again. When finally taken out, the articles are rubbed with brushes of fine wire and cleaned with fine sand; they are then polished on revolving brushes with rotten-stone, then with chamois-leather and rouge. The process of electro-gilding is essentially the same, with the exception that gold is substituted for silver.

Embalming.— The ancient Egyptians believed that their souls, after many thousand years, would come to re-inhabit their bodies, in case these latter were preserved entire. Hence arose their practice of embalming the dead. The Egyptian manner of preserving the dead has been the admiration and wonder of modern times. They render the body not only incorruptible, but it retains its full proportion of size, symmetry of feature, and personal likeness. They called the embalmed bodies mummies, some of which, buried 3,000 years ago, are perfect to this day. The art of such embalming is now lost. When Nicodemus came with Joseph of Arimathea to pay the last duties to our Saviour after his crucifixion, he brought a mixture of myrrh and aloes to embalm his body. Carbolic acid was successfully employed by Professor Seely in America, in 1868. The modern method of embalming generally consists of an injection of camphorated spirits of wine into the arteries and veins, though many other chemical substances are successfully used.

Embroidery.—Its invention is generally ascribed to the Phrygians; but the Sidonians excelled in it, and it is mentioned by Homer and other ancient authors, in the year 1491 B. C. The latter were particularly skilled in decorative species of needlework. The first embroidery machine is said to have been invented by John Duncas, of Glasgow, in 1804. Heilman's embroidery machine was patented by Kochlin. An ancient existing specimen of beautiful embroidery is the Bayeux tapestry, worked by Matilda, the queen of William the First of England. It is nineteen inches wide, 214 feet long, and is divided into compartments showing the events from the visit of Harold to the Norman court to his death at Hastings. It was reproduced by autotype process, with notes, in 1875.

Emery is found, upon analysis, to be composed of alumina, oxide of iron, and silica, with a little lime. It is a dull, opaque substance, sometimes of a grayish black, sometimes of a bluish color, and it is prepared for use by crushing the lumps in a stamp mill, and then passing the powder through sieves of different degrees of fineness. For the most delicate uses of opticians the powder is graded by the process known to chemists as elutriation. Emery was for a long time brought from the island of Naxos in the Grecian Archipelago. The Greek government granted a monopoly of its trade to an English merchant. In 1847, Dr. J. Lawrence Smith, an American explorer in the employ of the Turkish government, found deposits of the mineral at various points in Asia Minor, and the monopoly was destroyed and the price lowered. Deposits of emery have since been found in Bohemia, in the Ural Mountains, in Australia, and in North Carolina, Georgia, and Montana. The supply from these deposits is too small, however, to compete with that which is brought from Turkey and Naxos.

Engraving.— The engraving of gems is a branch of art of the highest antiquity. The earliest writers make mention of engraved seals and seal rings, and there still exist many antique engravings equal to later productions of similar artists. Engraving from plates and wood is chiefly of modern invention, having its origin about the middle of the fifteenth century. Engraving on glass was perfected to an art by Boudier of Paris, 1799. The art of engraving, especially in photographic processes, has made great progress in the United States during the past quarter century. Prints from engraved copper plates made their appearance about 1450, and were first produced in Germany. Masso is considered to have been the first Italian engraver, about 1440. Etchings on copper by means of aqua fortis is reputed to have been discovered by Francis Mazzuoli, about 1532. Etching was later practiced by Albert Durer, and most especially by Rembrandt. Its revival began about 1860. Mezzotints are said to have been discovered by Colonel Von Siegen, who engraved the portrait of Princess Amelia of Hesse in mezzotint, in 1643; it was improved by Prince Rupert in 1648; and by Sir Christopher Wren, about 1662. The mode of engraving on soft steel, which after it has been hardened will multiply copper plates and fine impressions, indefinitely, was introduced into England by Messrs. Perkins & Heath of Philadelphia, in 1819.

Entomology, the science of insects, is based upon the arrangements of Linnæus, A. D. 1739. The Entomological Society of London was instituted in 1833. A national entomological exhibition at the Westminster aquarium was opened March, 1878. Numerous chairs of entomology have been established in colleges and universities in the United States and Europe within a recent period.

Etching, Art of.—About the middle of the fifteenth century Tomaso Finiguerra, a Florentine, introduced the art of etching. In Germany, Italy, and France its value met with prompt recognition, but it was not carried to a state of perfection till later times. It was at first regarded as an industrial art, but it soon grew to have a higher value, reproducing in graceful freedom and precision of touch the very feeling of the artist. The first step in etching is to cover the plate with a composition of wax, asphaltum, gum-mastic, resin, etc., dissolved by heat. An outline of the design, made on paper in pencil or red chalk, is then "transferred" to the surface of this composition by being passed through a press. The subject is then drawn on the ground with the etching point, which cuts through it and exposes the copper. Etching-points or needles resemble large sewing needles shortened and fixed into handles four or five inches long. Some are made oval, to produce broader lines. A rim of wax being put around the plate, acid is poured on, and corrodes the copper not protected by the ground. If the acid is found not to have acted sufficiently, it may be applied again to the whole design, or only to portions of it, by stopping up with a mixture of lamp-black and Venice turpentine, applied with a camel's-hair pencil, what has been sufficiently *bitten-in*. When a series of parallel lines are wanted, as in backgrounds, etc., an ingenious machine called a ruler is employed, the accuracy of whose operation is exceedingly perfect. This is made to act on the etching-ground by a point or diamond connected with the apparatus, and the tracings are bit in with *aqua fortis* in the ordinary way. The art of etching was popularized by Sandro Botticelli, who embellished an edition of "Dante" with etching illustrations about the end of the fifteenth century. The great German etchers of that time were Shoengauer, Bechellin, and Wohlgemuth, and the Italian representatives were Bacio Baldini, Pollajuoli, and Montegna. In the succeeding century Goltzius and others reproduced the works of the old masters, through etching, with wonderful mobility. Toward the latter end of the seventeenth century the art was carried to a high degree of perfection by Le Bas and by the Spanish school. Then, for a time, the art declined, its place being taken by steel engraving, which in turn gave way to the chromo, and that to the lithograph. The revival of the art in England is largely due to Philip Gilbert Hamerton. At that time Seymour Haden was the leading etcher in England, as was Count de Gravesande in France. Whistler, the eccentric American, is now one of the leading lights in the art in England, and Hamilton Hamilton is probably the most popular etcher in America. Among the greatest of modern etchers are Salonne, Couteau, Waltner, Rajon, De Baines, and Koepping.

Ether was known to the earliest chemists. Nitric ether was first discovered by Kunkel, in 1681; and muriatic ether, from the chloride of tin, by Courtanvaux in 1759. Acetic ether was discovered by Count Lauraguais, same year; and hydriodic ether was first prepared by Gay-Lussac. The phosphoric was obtained by M. Boullay. Ether is said to have been first applied to the purpose of causing insensibility to pain by Dr. Horace Wells of Connecticut, in 1846. The discovery that by inhaling ether the patient is rendered unconscious of pain, is due to Dr. Charles T. Jackson, of Boston; but to Dr. Morton of the same place, probably belongs the credit of first demonstrating, by actual experiment, the use of ether in dentistry and surgery. The practice was first copied in Europe by Dr. Robertson, of Edinburgh, and Dr. Booth, of London, in 1846.

Ethnology is the science which treats of the division of man into races, with their origin, relations, and characteristics. Naturalists divide mankind, according to certain physical characteristics, into varieties, or races. Authorities differ greatly in this classification. Cuvier made three races; Pritchard, seven; Agassiz, eight, and Pickering, eleven; but the classification most commonly accepted is that into five races, as made by Blumenbach, as follows: The Caucasian, European, or white race; the Mongolian, Asiatic, or yellow race; the Ethiopian, African, or black race; the American Indian, or red race; the Malay, or brown race. The first three are much more clearly marked, and are considered by Guyot as primary races; the others, being modifications of these three, he designates as secondary races. Because of the blending of types, it is difficult to make a classification, hence the difference among authorities. The points on which the classification is based are mainly the size and proportions of the body, the shape of head and the features, the hair and beard, and the color of the skin.

The Caucausian race is characterized by tall stature, oval head and face, high forehead, regular features, abundance and softness of hair and beard, and usually fair skin, but in some it is tawny or swarthy, as in the Hindoos, Arabs, and others. This race stands at the head in intelligence and civilization. It is represented by the principal inhabitants of Europe and their descendants in America, and by the inhabitants of India, Arabia, and of Western Asia and Northern Africa.

The Germanic nations are descendants of the numerous tribes of the ancient German stock that destroyed the Roman empire and erected different states upon its ruins.

The Romanic nations occupy Southern Europe, and are so called because their languages are mostly derived from the Latin spoken by the ancient Romans. They are mixed nations, descended partly from the ancient Pelasgians and partly from other branches of Aryan stock.

The Italians derive their origin from the Romans, German Longobards, and Normans, with a slight intermixture of the Arabic stock.

The Spanish and Portuguese have sprung from a mixture of Celts, Romans, Germans, and Arabs.

The Mongolian race are distinguished by short stature, round head, wide face, high cheek bones, obliquely set eyes, coarse, straight hair, scarcely any beard, and yellowish color of the skin. They are distributed over the whole of Eastern Asia, except in India, and include the Esquimaux of the northern part of North America.

The Ethiopian race are characterized by medium stature, generally ungainly form, low and retreating forehead, head full back of the ears, flat, broad nose, projecting jaws, thick lips, short, curly hair, and skin generally black or dark. They occupy all of Africa, except the northern part, and many of their descendants are found in America.

The American race resemble the Mongolian, but the head is not so round, the face less wide and flat, the eyes horizontal, the hair black and straight, and beard scanty and the skin a reddish or copper color. They occupy North and South America, except on the Arctic shores.

The Malay race resemble also the Mongolian, but have thicker lips, horizontal eyes, hair less straight, generally full beards, and color usually brown. They occupy the Malay peninsula and the islands of the Pacific and Indian Oceans.

Evolution Theory, The.—Ancient writers occasionally seemed to have a glimmering knowledge of the fact of progress in nature, but as a theory "evolution" belongs to the enlightenment of the nineteenth century. In the latter part of the seventeenth century Leibnitz expressed the opinion that the earth was once in a fluid condition, and about the middle of the eighteenth century Kant definitely propounded the nebular hypothesis, which was enlarged as a theory by the Herschels. About 1750 the transmutation of species among animals was suggested by Buffon, and other writers followed out the idea. The eccentric Lord Monboddo was the first to suggest the possible descent of man from the ape, about 1774. The evolution theory declares the universe as it now exists to be the result of a long series of changes, which were so far related to each other as to form a series of growths analogous to the evolving parts of a growing organism. Herbert Spencer defines evolution as a progress from the homogeneous to the heterogeneous; from general to special; from the simple to the complex elements of life; and it is believed that this process can be traced in the formation of worlds in space, in the multiplication of types and species among animals and plants, in the origin and changes of language and literature and the arts, and also in all the changes of human institutions and society. Asserting the general fact of progress in nature, the evolution theory shows that the method of this progress has been (1) by the multiplications of organs and functions; (2) according to a definite unity of plan, although with (3) the intervention of transitional forms, and (4) with modifications dependent upon surrounding conditions. The two great apostles of the evolution theory were Charles Darwin and Herbert Spencer. The latter began his first great work, the "First Principles of Philosophy," showing the application of evolution in the facts of life, in 1852. In 1859 appeared Darwin's "Origin of Species." The hypothesis of the latter was that different species originated in spontaneous variation, and the survival of the fittest through natural selection and the struggle for existence. This theory was further elaborated and applied by Spencer, Darwin, Huxley, and other writers in Europe and America; and though, to-day, by no means all the ideas upheld by these early advocates of the theory are still accepted, still evolution as a principle is now acknowledged by nearly all scientists. It is taken to be an established fact in nature — a valid induction from man's knowledge of natural order.

Facts as to Sound.— In air, sound travels from 1,130 to 1,140 feet per second. In water, it passes at the rate of 4,700 feet per second. A bell sounded under water may be heard under water at 1,200 feet distance. Sounds are distinct at twice the distance on water that they are on land. On Table Mountain, a mile above Cape Town, every noise in it, and even words, may be heard distinctly. Dr. Jamieson says that in calm weather he heard every word of a sermon at the distance of two miles. The sound of a tuning fork may be distinctly heard at a distance of 200 yards, by connecting the stem by pack threads with the ear.

Fire is said to have been first produced by striking flints together. The poets supposed that fire was stolen from heaven by Prometheus. Heraclitus, about 596 B. C., maintained that the world was created from fire, and deemed it to be an omnipotent God; he taught this theory about 506 B. C. Zoroaster, king of Bactria, was the founder of the sect of the Magi, or worshipers of fire, still numerous in the countries of the East, 2115 B. C. In the Scriptures, God is said often to have appeared in fire, or was encompassed by it,— as in the burning bush at Mt. Horeb. The wrath of God is described as a consuming fire, and the angels, as his ministers, are compared to it.

Fire Engines, to force water, existed in very ancient times. The first of the kind now in use, but of a vastly inferior character, was invented by two Dutchmen, each named Jan Van der Heide, at Amsterdam, in 1518. In 1657, an improved engine was introduced at Nuremberg by John Hantsch. Fire engines were first known at Paris in 1699. The first volunteer fire company in America was the Union of Philadelphia, about 1736.

Freezing, Fusing, and Boiling Points.

SUBSTANCES.	Reaumur	Centigrade.	Fahrenheit.
FREEZING—			
Bromine freezes at....	—16°	—20°	—4°
Oil Anise............	8	10	50
" Olive............	8	10	50
" Rose............	12	15	60
Quicksilver............	—31.5	—39.4	—39
Water............	—1	0	32
FUSING—			
Bismuth metal fuses at	200	264	507
Cadmium............	248.8	315	592
Copper............	874.6	1093	2000
Gold............	961	1200	2200
Iodine............	92	115	239
Iron............	1230	1538	2800
Lead............	255.5	325	617
Potassium............	46	58	136
Phosphorus............	34	41	111
Silver............	816.8	1021	1870
" Nitrate............	159	198	389
Sodium............	72	90	194
Steel............	1452	1856	3300
Sulphur............	72	90	194
Tin............	173	230	446
Zinc............	328	410	770
BOILING—			
Alcohol boils at.......	63	78	173
Bromine............	50	53	145
Ether............	28	35	95
" Nitrous............	11	14	57
Iodine............	140	175	347
Olive Oil............	252	315	600
Quicksilver............	280	350	662
Water............	80	100	212

First Railroads.— The first railroad ever built for general traffic was the Stockton and Darlington in England, which was thirty-five miles long, constructed in 1825 by Edward Pease and George Stephenson. In the same year a railroad was projected in America by Gridley Bryant, but it was not constructed until the following year, when Bryant secured the assistance of Col. T. H. Perkins in the enterprise. This road was four miles long, and was used for carrying granite from the quarries in Quincy, Mass., to the site of the Bunker Hill Monument. In 1827 the Mauch Chunk Railway, a coal road, thirteen miles long, was built, and February 27 of the same year the Maryland Legislature granted a charter to the Baltimore and Ohio road. The first locomotive which proved of practical value was invented by George Stephenson, the celebrated English engineer, and was used on the Stockton and Darlington Railway. In 1829 a railway line was built between Liverpool and Manchester, of which Stephenson was the principal engineer, and for this road he constructed the engine known as the Rocket, which accomplished the till then undreamed-of speed of thirty-five miles an hour. The first locomotive built in America was used on the Baltimore and Ohio Railroad.

Flies Walking on the Ceiling.— For a long time it was supposed that the ability of the fly to walk on the ceiling was owing to each of his feet being a miniature air-pump. This, however, was proved to be fallacious, and then a theory was propounded that it was by means of a viscous substance exuded from the hairs on its feet. Some eight years or so ago this theory was thoroughly investigated by Dr. Rombouts, who demonstrated that it was only partly sound; for, though the hairs with which the foot-cushion is covered do certainly exude an oily liquid, the liquid is not sticky, and does not harden when dry. Dr. Rombouts proved by his experiments that the true theory of the walking of flies on smooth substances is that they hang on by the help of capillary adhesion — the molecular attraction between solid and liquid bodies. By a series of nice calculations, such as weighing hairs and measuring their diameters, and sticking the cut end of hair in oil or water to make it adhere when touched to glass, this scientist proved that capillary attraction would uphold a fly were it four ninths as heavy again as it is at present. It is true that the foot-hairs are very minute, but as each fly is said to be furnished with 10,000 to 12,000 of these, we need not be surprised at what they can do. Reasoning from this theory, we would conclude that flies find it difficult to mount a glass slightly dampened, because of the repulsion between the watery surface and the oily liquid exuding from the feet; and they are likewise impeded by a slight coating of dust, because the interspaces between the hairs are filled with dust, and observation seems to show this to be the case. When we see a fly making his toilet, he is not, as we might suppose, cleaning his body, but his feet, so that they may the more readily adhere.

Forks were in use in Europe in the thirteenth and fourteenth centuries, though this is disputed as being too early. In Moryson's "itinerary" it is said that at Venice each person was served (besides his knife and spoon) with a fork to hold the meat while he cuts it, for there they deem it ill manners that one should touch it with his hand. Thomas Coryate, an Englishman, describes with much solemnity, the manner of using forks in Italy, and adds, "I myself have thought it good to imitate the Italian fashion since I came home to England," 1608. Two pronged forks were made at Sheffield soon after. Three pronged forks are more recent. Silver forks, previously only used by the highest classes, came into general use in England about 1814.

Galvanized Iron is merely ordinary iron which has been dipped in molten zinc and retains a surface coating of the zinc when removed. It has come to be of great importance and usefulness, as by this simple process any article may be made to combine the strength and cheapness of iron, and yet be entirely free from rust, as the zinc is unaffected by air or water, oxidizing only at a high temperature.

Gasoline is simply air which has been impregnated with very volatile hydro-carbons. Previous to 1836 it was made by passing air over benzol made from coal tar, but between that year and 1858 numerous machines were patented for its manufacture. The cost of benzol was at first a great obstacle in the manufacture of gasoline, but the discovery of petroleum rendered it possible to make air gas at twenty-five cents per gallon, the former price, when benzol was used, having been $1.50. The machines used for making this gas include a "generator," a large vessel more or less complicated in construction, in which a quantity of liquid petroleum or naphtha is exposed in shallow trays for evaporation. A current of air is introduced, which mingles with the distilled vapor and forms air gas. This is a dangerous substance, as it bursts into flame with a sharp explosion upon contact with fire. If the generator, however, is placed at some distance from the point where the gasoline is to be used, conveying it thither in air-tight pipes, the danger is removed. Gasoline is extensively used for the lighting of hotels, factories, and private residences in small towns or rural districts.

Geography.— The first correct record we have of geographical knowledge is from Homer. He describes the shield of Achilles as representing the earth surrounded by the sea, and also the countries of Greece, islands of the archipelago, and the site of Troy. The priests taught that the temple of Apollo at Delphos was the center of the world. Anaximander of Miletus was the inventor of geographical maps, about 568 B. C. Hipparchus attempted to reduce geography to a mathematical basis, about 135 B. C. Strabo, the Greek geographer, lived 71-14 B. C. Ptolemy flourished about 139 A. D. The science was brought to Europe by the Moors of Barbary and Spain about 1240. Maps and charts were introduced into England by Bartholomew Columbus to illustrate his brother's theory respecting a western continent, 1489. Geography is now divided into mathematical, physical, and political, and its study has been greatly promoted during the present century by expeditions at the expense of various governments and societies. There are in the world about sixty-five geographical societies.

Geologic Ages, The. — There are seven great geologic ages, or divisions of time, known as the Azoic, the Silurian, the Devonian, the Carboniferous, the Reptilian, the Mammalian, and the Age of Man. Our knowledge of the plants and animals of the ages preceding the creation of man is derived from their remains dug out of the earth, and called fossils.

The Azoic Age is the era, as its name implies, when there was no life, either vegetable or animal, on the globe. The crystalline minerals and all the igneous rocks date back to this age, and hence they are destitute of fossils.

During the Silurian Age, the second in antiquity, there was no terrestrial life; but mollusks — animals with soft, fleshy bodies, without any internal skeleton, like the oyster and the snail — abounded in the waters. The oldest sandstone and limestone belong to this period. Its plant fossils are sea weeds.

The Devonian Age was the age of fishes, remarkable for their thick, bony scales. The sea also teemed with shells, corals, and sea weed; while the land, though yet limited in extent, began to be covered with vegetation. Insects, the earliest of terrestrial animals, now first appeared.

The Carboniferous Age, or age of coal, is fourth. From colossal tree ferns, leaves, and branches, deposited in successive centuries, were formed, by gradual decomposition under water, those vast coal beds on which the industrial pursuits of the present day so largely depend. The animals of this age consisted mainly of insects of various kinds; and inferior tribes of reptiles.

The Reptilian Age was marked by the great number, variety, and size of its reptiles, the appearance and habits of which are known from the remains, found buried in the rocks of this period. The rocks of this age are the freestones, extensively used for building, sandstone formations, intersected with ridges of trap of igneous origin, limestone and gypsum, laminated and plastic clays, and chalk beds, containing layers of flint.

The Mammalian Age was the sixth. The reptiles now dwindled in size and diminished in number, being succeeded by quadrupeds, some of which were much larger than any modern species. The deinotherium, mastodon, megatherium and fossil elephant were among the gigantic animals of this era, while the plants resembled those of the present time, palms, oaks, maples, magnolias, etc., being found in the forests.

The Age of Man is the last of the seven geologic ages. The huge monsters that gave the preceding period its peculiar character became extinct, and were replaced by smaller animals — those we see around. Man was created, and invested with dominion over the earth. This is the "era of the finished world — the era, also, of man's progress and preparation for another and a higher life."

Geometry.— Its origin is ascribed to the Egyptians; the annual inundations of the Nile having given rise to it by carrying away the landmarks, and the boundaries of farms. Thales introduced geometry into Greece, about 600 B. C. The doctrine of curves originally attracted the attention of geometricians from the conic sections, which were introduced by Plato about 390 B. C. Euclid's elements were compiled about 280 B. C. Geometry was taught in Europe in the thirteenth century. Books on the subject of geometry and astronomy were destroyed in England in 1552, being regarded as infected with magic. The science was greatly improved and augmented by Sir Isaac Newton and LaPlace.

Geysers are intermittent, spouting, hot springs, and have a temperature at the boiling point. They are found in Iceland, New Zealand, and in the "National Park" at the head waters of the Yellowstone River in the Rocky Mountains.

The most celebrated is the Great Geyser of Iceland. It consists of an immense well, or funnel, 10 feet wide at its mouth, and about 70 feet deep, surmounted at the surface with a basin 65 feet in diameter and 7 feet deep, formed by the deposit of mineral matter from the water. At intervals it sends up a column of water and steam to the height of 100 feet. More remarkable even than the geysers of Iceland are some that are found in the "National Park." One, the Giantess, throws water to the height of 200 feet. Grasshoppers and other insects, and pieces of wood which fall into the waters, soon become incrusted with quartz, which is held in solution by the water, thus permanently petrifying them.

Glacial Period is a term used in geology to designate the period when the greater part of the northern hemisphere was enveloped in one great ice-sheet. This period belongs to the post-tertiary or later formations, in the geological succession, and is important in its relations to the general question of the earth's history, and especially to the appearance of man upon the earth. Geologists are generally agreed that long before the advent of man, parts of the northern hemisphere were elevated several thousand feet higher than they are at present, causing the cold of the Arctic zone to extend far southward into present temperate regions, and that a vast glacier rising in the vicinity of Hudson Bay covered the American continent north of the fortieth parallel. The loose soil which covers so large a part of the surface of the northern continent to a depth varying from thirty to one hundred feet, over which lie the vegetable deposits of later ages, is considered by geologists the effects of glaciers that in the quaternary or latest geological age slowly moved southward across the country. Upon examination it is found that the erratic bowlders scattered over the western prairies and other northern regions are unlike the native rocks of the same regions, being entirely foreign to the localities where they now appear. Sometimes the nativity of the rock is traced hundreds of miles north of where it now rests, showing that some powerful agency has carried it southward. Again, if the native rock be uncovered and closely examined, it will be observed to be polished and grooved with parallel marks, running north and south, as if chiseled out by some coarse and heavy instrument. These marks are attributed to sharp, hard rocks projecting through the lower surfaces of the glaciers. That glaciers do produce such markings is proved by examination of the rocks which the moving ice-fields of Switzerland and other glacial regions have worn and are marking to-day; also, the general appearance of the loose, unstratified, heterogeneous deposit is similar to that of the moraines that the modern glaciers leave as they slowly melt away. In New York and other Eastern states, the rocks are scratched from a northwesterly direction, in Ohio from a northerly direction, showing in each state the direction of the origin of the glacier. Scotland, Ireland, and the major portion of England, were enveloped in this great ice-sheet, and Scandinavia was invested with a sheet of ice which filled up the Baltic and extended into Northern Germany. The Glacial Period, or Ice Age, as it is also called, is estimated to have begun upward of 200,000 years ago, and lasted for 160,000 years.

Glass.—The Egyptians are said to have been taught the art of making glass by Hermes. Pliny says the discovery of glass took place in Syria. Glass houses were erected in Tyre, where glass was a staple manufacture for many ages. This article is mentioned among the Romans in the time of Tiberius; and it is known from the ruins of Pompeii, that windows were formed of glass before A. D. 79. Italy had the first glass windows, next France, whence they came to England. Used for windows in private houses in the reign of Henry II. of England, 1177, but imported. The manufacture was established in England at Crutched-Friars in 1557. It was improved, 1635, and was brought to great perfection in the reign of William the Third. Plate glass for coach windows, mirrors, etc., was made at Lambeth by Venetian artists, 1673. The manufacture was improved by the French, who made very large plates; and further improvements have been made in Lancashire, England, and the United States.

Glass, Discovery of.—There is comparatively little known in regard to the invention of glass. Some of the oldest specimens are Egyptian, and are traced to about 1500 years before Christ (by some, 2300 B. C.). Transparent glass is believed to have been first used about 750 years before the Christian era. The credit of the invention was given to the Phœnicians by the ancient writers. The story of the Phœnician merchants who rested their cooking-pots on blocks of natron (subcarbonate of soda), and found glass produced by the union, under heat, of the alkali and the sand on the shore, is a familiar one. The world no doubt owes the art of glass-making to the Egyptians. It was introduced into Rome in the time of Cicero, and among the Romans attained a high degree of perfection. Some of the most beautiful specimens of glass ever manufactured were made in Rome before the Christian era; as, for instance, the exquisite Portland vase in the British Museum. During the middle ages the Venetians were the most famous makers of fine glassware, and after them the Bohemians. Though the art of making glass and blowing it into all kinds of shapes was known so early, this material does not seem to have been used for windows until about A.D. 300.

Glucose, termed also grape sugar, starch sugar, and diabetic sugar, is a natural organic compound, consisting of carbon, hydrogen, and oxygen. It is found to some extent in the animal kingdom and very largely in the vegetable kingdom, being a constituent of the juice of almost all sweet fruits and vegetables. The name "diabetic" is due to its large occurrence in the urinary secretion and other fluids of the body in the disease called diabetes. It is manufactured in large quantities from starch and is used in the manufacture of beer and a coarse kind of alcohol. It is in taste much the same as ordinary sugar, but less sweet. It has a peculiar effect upon a ray of polarized light, passing through it; and there are two varieties comprising fruit sugar, one of which turns the plane of polarization to the right, and is called dextro-glucose, and the other turning the plane of polarization to the left, and called lævo-glucose, or dextrose and lævulose respectively.

Grain.—The origin of its cultivation is attributed to Ceres, who, having taught the art to the Egyptians, was deified by them, 2409 B. C. Corn, or grain, provided a common article of food from the earliest ages of the world. The first importation of corn into England of which we have any knowledge was in 1347, though it was introduced into Britain in the sixth century.

Graphite.—The name is derived from the Greek *graphein*, to write. It is also commonly but incorrectly called black lead and plumbago. It contains no lead, but is an allotropic form of carbon, and therefore identical in composition with charcoal and diamonds. It occurs as a mineral, both massive and disseminated through the rock, generally in granite, gneiss, mica schist, and crystallized limestone. It is also a product in the destructive distillation of coal, and can be artificially obtained by other methods in the laboratory. It is lighter than water, and this property is made use of in separating it from the rock in which it is found. The ore is pulverized and then thrown into large, shallow tanks; the particles of rock sink, while the particles of graphite float and are taken from the surface free from the rock, and are formed into solid blocks by great pressure. The mine at Burrowdale, in Cumberland, England, has been known since the time of Queen Elizabeth and probably furnished the first lead pencils ever made, but became exhausted many years ago. Large deposits of graphite have been found in the northeastern part of Siberia, and in Germany, France, Austria, and in several portions of the United States. Its most important use is in the manufacture of lead pencils. But, as it is infusible and a good conductor of electricity, it has found other important applications, as for crucibles and the linings of small furnaces, and in the process of electrotyping. It is unctuous to the touch and has a high metallic luster, and is used also in polishing and lubricating compounds, but for this latter purpose has been found too hard to be satisfactory.

Graphophone.— This instrument is, in its essential features, identical with Edison's phonograph. [See *Phonograph.*] The graphophone now in experimental use is the invention of Mr. Sumner Tainter, aided by Professor Bell. In a correct nomenclature the phonograph would represent a machine for making a record of speech, the record made would be termed a phonogram, and the graphophone would be a machine for reproducing speech from the phonogram. The words are all derived from the same two Greek roots, which mean "write" and "speak."

Gravitation, as a supposed innate power, was noticed by the Greeks, and also by Seneca, who speaks of the moon attracting the waters, about 38 A. D. Kepler investigated the subject about 1615; and Hooke devised a system of gravitation about 1674. The principles of gravity were demonstrated by Galileo, at Florence, about 1633; but the great law on this subject, laid down by Newton in his Principia, in 1687, is said to have been proved by him, in 1670. His attention was directed to the subject by the fall of an apple from a tree, in 1666. In 1867, M. Chasles laid before the Paris Academy of Sciences some letters alleged to have been written by Newton to Pascal and others tending to show that to Pascal was due the theory of gravitation. The authenticity of these letters was denied and their forgery afterward shown.

Guillotine, the instrument of decapitation was introduced during the French Revolution by the Convention, and named after its supposed inventor, Joseph Ignace Guillotin, a physician, who, however, was only the person who first proposed its adoption. It was erected and first employed to execute a highwayman on the Place de Grève, Paris, 25th April, 1792. It is composed of two upright posts, grooved on the inside, and connected at the top by a cross-beam. In these grooves a sharp iron blade, having its edge cut obliquely, descends by its own weight on the neck of the victim, who is bound to a board laid below.

Gun-Barrels. — The finest musket-barrels are made of iron which contains a portion of steel, or undergoes some steeling process. Laminated, twisted, or Damascus steel is used in the manufacture of the best barrels. Scraps of saws, steel pens, files, springs, and steel tools are collected from various workshops, for the material of laminated steel. These are cut in small and nearly equal pieces, cleansed and polished by revolving in a cylinder, fused into a semi-fluid state, and gathered into a "bloom" or mass. This bloom is forged with a three-ton hammer, and hardened and solidified with a tilt-hammer. It is then rolled into rods, each rod is cut into pieces six inches long, and these pieces are welded together. The rolling, cutting, and welding process is then repeated several times, and thus finally the metal is brought into a very hard, tough, fibrous, and uniform state. Twisted steel for barrels is made by taking thin plates of iron and steel, laying them alternately one on another in a pile, welding them by heat and hammering, and twisting them by very powerful mechanical agency until there are twelve or fourteen complete turns to an inch. The length becomes reduced one half and the thickness doubled by this twisting. Barrels made of Damascus steel are manufactured of steel which has undergone a still further series of welding and twisting operations. Some barrels are made of a mixture of old files with old horseshoe nails; these are called stub Damascus barrels. The files are heated, cooled in water, broken with hammers, and pounded in a mortar into small fragments. Three parts of these fragments are mixed with five of stub and the mixture is fused, forged, rolled, and twisted. An inferior kind of Damascus twist is made by interlaying scraps of sheet iron with charcoal and producing an appearance of twist, but without the proper qualities. Inferior kinds of barrel-iron are known as "threepenny-skelp" and "twopenny skelp"; but the worst of all is "sham-dam skelp." The finest barrels are all twisted in form. The skelps, or lengths of prepared steel, are twisted into a close spiral a few inches long; several of these spirals are welded end to end, and the fissures are closed up by heating and hammering. The rough barrel, with a core or mandrel temporarily thrust in it, is placed in a groove and hammered cold until the metal becomes very dense, close, strong, and elastic. The interior is then bored truly cylindrical by a nicely adjusted rotating cutting tool. If, on close inspection, the interior is found to be straight and regular, the exterior is then ground on a rapidly revolving stone and finally turned in a lathe. The skelps for the commoner barrels are heated, laid in a semi-cylindrical groove, hammered until they assume the form of that groove, placed two and two together, and heated and hammered until one barrel is made from two halves. These are browned externally with some kind of chemical stain. The finest barrels are rubbed externally with fine files and polished with steel burnishers.

Gunpowder, Discovery of.— It is generally conceded that gunpowder was used by the Chinese as an explosive in prehistoric times. When they first discovered or applied its power as a propellent is less easily determined. There is an account of a bamboo tube being used, from which the "impetuous dart" was hurled a distance of 100 feet; this was at a very early period, but it is difficult to say precisely when. It is alleged, however, that in the century before the Christian era a cannon was employed bearing the inscription, "I hurl death to the traitor and extermination to the rebel." It has also been asserted that India has equal claims with China to the first acquaintance with gunpowder. The ancient Sanskrit writings appear to point very plainly to the operation of some primitive sort of cannon, when, in recording the wars of the Egyptian Hercules in India, it is stated that the sages remained unconcerned spectators of the attack on their stronghold till an assault was attempted, when they repulsed it with whirlwinds and thunders, hurling destruction on the invaders; and a Greek historian of Alexander's campaign testified that the Hindoos had the means of discharging flames and missiles on their enemies from a distance. According to Meyer, the preparation of gunpowder was described by Julius Africanus, A. D. 215. In 1073 King Solomon of Hungary bombarded Belgrade with cannon, and in 1085 the ships of Tunis, in the naval battle near Toledo, were said to shoot "fiery thunder." All of which would go to prove that the custom of ascribing the discovery of gunpowder to Bertholdus Schwartz in 1330, or even to Roger Bacon in 1267, is open to considerable objection, although these men probably introduced it in European warfare.

Gutta-Percha.— The name "gutta-percha" is Malayan, *gutta* signifying the concrete juice of a plant, and *percha* the name of the particular tree from which it is obtained. It is the dried milky juice of the tree which is found in the peninsula of Malacca and the Malayan Archipelago. Its use was first discovered by Europeans about 1843. It is imported in blocks and lumps of five to ten pounds weight in various forms, chiefly like large cakes, or rounded into gourd-like lumps. It has a cork-like appearance when cut, and a peculiar cheese-like odor. Before it can be used it has to undergo some preparation. This consists in slicing the lumps into thin shavings, which are placed in a *deviling* or tearing machine revolving in a trough of hot water. This reduces the shavings to exceedingly small pieces, which, by the agitation of the tearing teeth, are washed free from many impurities, especially fragments of the bark of the tree, which, if not separated, would interfere with the compactness of its texture. The small fragments, when sufficiently cleansed, are kneaded into masses, which are rolled several times between heated cylinders, which press out any air or water and render the mass uniform in texture. It is then rolled between heated steel rollers into sheets of various thicknesses for use, or is formed into rods, pipes for water or speaking tubes, and an endless number of other articles. The great value of gutta-percha arises from the ease with which it can be worked, and its being so complete a non-conductor of electricity. It softens in warm water, and can be molded into any form in that state, as, when soft, it is not sticky, and turns well out of molds.

Hats and Caps.— A covering for the head was early adopted by the inhabitants of northern climes, and was usually a hood made of fur; but it was not until the Phrygians had conquered Asia Minor that the people of warmer latitudes wore any head-covering. The Phrygians were the first to adopt the fashion, and they did it in order to distinguish themselves from the conquered race with whom they lived. Their head-dress was a small, close-fitting cap, which was also soon adopted by the Roman free citizens. In 1404 a Swiss manufacturer of Paris invented the first hat.

Hearse.— The word "hearse," or *herse*, is of French origin, and means a harrow or frame for setting candles in, and was originally applied to a bar or framework with upright spikes for the reception of candles; and it was used at the ceremonies of the Church and at funeral services. In the fifteenth and sixteenth centuries hearses of great splendor came into use, and were erected in the churches over the bodies of distinguished personages. The framework was of iron or brass, sometimes of beautiful workmanship, square, octagonal, etc., in plan, with pillars at the angles, and arched framework above forming a canopy. The whole was hung over with rich cloths and embroidery, and lighted up with hundreds of wax candles and decorated with wax images. From this the transition to the modern hearse can easily be traced. In Roman Catholic churches of the present day the hearse still exists as a triangle with spikes on which candles are placed.

Heliography.— The idea of first conveying signals by means of mirrors, which is the meaning of heliography, is said to have been employed by Alexander the Great, 333 B. C. The heliostat, an instrument invented by a Hollander early in the eighteenth century, and the heliograph, invented by Mr. Mance in 1875 have both been used by the British army in their Eastern campaigns. The instruments differ somewhat in construction, but the result arrived at is the same in both. Signals are produced by causing a reflected ray of the sun to appear and disappear alternately at a distant point, the intervals of appearance and obscuration being carried in length so as to produce the combination of long and short signals, known as the Morse alphabet. The reflecting body is a glass mirror which varies in size according to the distance to which it is desired to signal. A five inch mirror has given, when atmospheric conditions were favorable, distinct signals at a distance of sixty miles. The heliograph has also been found of great service in defining distant points for large surveys, and was used for verifying the arc of the meridian by the astronomers at the Cape of Good Hope.

Horse Power of Steam Engines.— The unit of nominal power for steam engines, or the usual estimate of dynamical effect per minute of a horse, called by engineers a "horse power," is thirty-three thousand pounds at a velocity of one foot per minute, or, the effect of a load of two hundred pounds raised by a horse for eight hours a day, at the rate of two and a half miles per hour, or 150 pounds at the rate of 220 feet per minute.

RULE.— Multiply the area of the piston in square inches by the average force of the steam in pounds and by the velocity of the piston in feet per minute; divide the product by thirty-three thousand, and seven tenths of the quotient equals the effective power.

Human Family, The.— The three primary divisions of man, as indicated by Latham, are the Indo-European, the Mongolian, and the African.

I. THE INDO-EUROPEAN OR CAUCASIC race originally extended from India across Europe, and, increasing ever in civilization and intellectual power from age to age, has become the dominant one in the world, extending its influence to every part of the earth, supplanting many inferior races, and repeopling wide areas, as in America and Australia.

The Caucasic race comprises two principal branches — the Aryan and the Semitic. A third branch, according to M. de Quatrefages, includes the Caucasians proper, Euscarians (Basques), and others.

Most of the inhabitants of Europe belong to the Aryan Family; they are arranged in the following groups: —

1. The Keltic, in the N. W., comprising the Welsh, Gaels, Erse, Manx, and Armoricans.

2. The Italic, chiefly in the S. W. and S., comprising the Italian and other Romance nations — French, Spanish, Portuguese, Roumanesch, and Roumanians.

3. The Thraco-Hellenic, in the S. E., Greeks, and Albanians.

4. The Teutonic, in the N. N. W. and center, comprising the Germans, Scandinavians, Danes, Icelanders, Dutch, Flemings. English.

5. The Lithuanian, S. E. of the Baltic.

6. The Slavonic, in the E., comprising the Russians, Poles, Tsekhs, Serbs, Croats, Bulgarians, etc.

The Indo-European or Caucasic race in Asia comprises the Hindoos, Baluchis, Afghans, Iranians (Persia), Galchas (Zarafshan), and the Semitic tribes of Armenia, Syria, Arabia, etc.

II. THE MONGOLIAN is divisible into three branches, according to geographical position, which again form numerous smaller families.

1. The Asiatic, comprising the Mongolians of the Chinese Empire, India, and Indo-China; the Kalmucks, adjoining the Turks, who extend from Southern Europe far into Central Asia; the Magyars of Hungary; the Yakuts and Samoeids (or Samoyedes) of Siberia; with the Lapps, Finns, and various tribes of East Europe.

2. The Oceanic Mongolians are composed of two classes. 1. The black-skinned found in New Guinea, Australia, Tasmania, and the islands between New Zealand, and New Caledonia. II. The yellow, olive, or brown race, occupying New Zealand, the Malay Peninsula, Sumatra, Borneo, Java, Moluccas, Philippines, Madagascar, etc.

3. The American Mongolians comprise a large number of tribes, the chief of which in North America are — the Athabaskans, Algonkins, Sioux, Paducas, and Mexicans. In South America, the Quichuas, Chilians, and Patagonians extend along the west coast. The Caribs, Maypures, Brazilians, Moxos, and Chiquitos occupy the north, east, and center of the continent. The Eskimos form a connecting link between the Asiatic and American branches of this family.

III. THE AFRICAN, forming the third great division of the human race, is exhibited in its purest form by the natives of Western Africa. The Negroes occupy the whole central portion of the country from Cape Verde on the west to Khartoom on the east, and south to the Congo. South of the Negroes are the Bantus (including the Kafirs), inhabiting the greater part of Africa between the 4th parallel of N. lat. and the Cape. In the S. W. are the Hottentots. Certain dwarfish tribes are found in different parts of the continent, as the Bushmen of the Kalahari Desert, the Obongo of Ogowe basin and others. The Fulas and Nubas occupy parts of the Soudan; the former, in the N. W., extend from the Senegal and Niger towards Lake Tchad; the latter are found in Nubia, Kordofan, Darfur, etc. The Gallas, Copts, Somali, of the Sahara, Egypt, and East Africa; the Abyssinians; and the Berbers, Kabyles, Tuareks and other tribes of North Africa, belong to the Hamitic race, which is closely allied to the Semitic race. The latter is represented by the Arabs of the N. coast, and of the Arabian Peninsula, and by the Tigres and other tribes of Abyssinia.

Hypnotism is a method for the alleged cure of disease, by the concentrated action of the mind upon the body while in a state of trance, induced by causing the patient to fix his eyes and concentrate his mind upon a disc of bright metal held at a distance of about twelve inches above the level of the eyes. The first effort to investigate hypnotism in a scientific manner was made by James Braid, of Manchester (1846), from which circumstance hypnotism is sometimes called Braidism. The power to hypnotize is possessed only by persons of peculiar mental organization. While in the hypnotized condition, which renders them insensible to pain, patients may be operated upon for surgical or medical purposes, the patient being entirely subject to the will of the hypnotizer. Hypnotism can, however, only be considered as of quasi medical utility, though investigation is being made with the view to placing it on a sound scientific basis.

Igneous Rocks are those which have been produced from materials fused by heat. They differ from the sedimentary rocks in their origin, structure, and position. They invariably come from below upward, breaking through the older rocks, and are generally ejected in a melted state from volcanic vents, or from fissures opened to some seat of fires within or below the earth's crust. The materials of sedimentary strata are fragments of pre-existing rocks worn by the action of water either into a fine mud or into rounded particles of greater or less size; whereas igneous rocks exhibit either a vitreous structure, as when they have been quickly cooled, or a granular structure composed of more or less minute crystals, according to the rate of cooling, or a vesicular structure when they have been expanded by the contained gases, or by being brought into contact with water. In position, also, they may be distinguished from the sedimentary rocks, very seldom occurring regularly stratified with parallel upper and under surfaces, but generally local, thinning out into wedge-shaped beds, or having that irregular stratification which may be seen in modern lava. They are also found as upright walls and columns, of which the famous Giant's Causeway and Fingal's Cave are notable examples. Igneous rocks when filling a narrow fissure in an older stratum, and also when speading beyond the fissure and forming an extensive superstratum, are called a dike. The rocks above mentioned are dikes, as are also the Palisades on the Hudson, Salisbury Crags near Edinburgh, many rocks around Lake Superior, over the western slope of the Rocky Mountains, and numerous other localities. The outflow in some cases has been very large, the lava floods of Oregon, Nevada, and northern California being estimated to comprise a total area of not less than 200,000 square miles, with a maximum thickness of 3,500 feet, the average being probably 2,000 feet. The most common rocks of dikes are dolerite (often called trap) and peridotite; both sometimes called basalt when not granular in texture.

Ignis-Fatuus.—A number of theories have been advanced in explanation of the luminous appearance which is frequently seen in marshy places, church yards, and stagnant pools, and which is known as ignis-fatuus. Of these it is only necessary to mention two. The first is that the ignis-fatuus is due to phosphureted hydrogen gas, which possesses the power of spontaneous ignition on coming in contact with dry atmospheric air; the gas would be generated by the decomposition of animal matter present in a marshy soil. The motion of the ignis-fatuus (it floats in the air at about two feet from the ground, is sometimes fixed, and sometimes travels with great rapidity) is accounted for by the flame being communicated along the line of a stream of gas. The second is that it is due to the combustion of light carbureted hydrogen gas arising from the decomposition of vegetable matter; but, though this supposition satisfactorily accounts for many appearances connected with the ignis-fatuus, the gas itself is not spontaneously combustible, and an additional supposition requires to be made to account for its ignition. The ignis-fatuus generally appears a little after sunset as a pale, bluish-colored flame, varying in size and shape; sometimes it shines steadily till morning, at other times disappears and reappears within about half-hourly intervals. In general it recedes on being approached, and *vice versa*, though several successful attempts have been made to light a piece of paper by it. In former times, under the names of *Will-o'-the-Wisp*, *Jack-o'-Lantern*, *Spunkie*, etc., it was an object of superstition among the inhabitants of the districts where it appears, and was believed to be due to the agency of evil spirits attempting to lure the traveler to his destruction; and unfortunately there are many instances on record of travelers mistaking the ignis-fatuus for a lamp, and being thus decoyed into marshy places, where they perished. The ignis-fatuus is not a common phenomenon, but it is not unfrequently seen in the north of Germany, the swampy and moorland districts in the south and northwest of England, and in the lowlands of Scotland.

Important Origins.—*Air Balloons*, invented by Gusmac, a Jesuit, in 1729. Revived in France by M. Montgolfier, in 1783.

Air Guns, invented by Guhr, of Nuremberg, in 1656.

Arquebus, introduced about 1520, and remained in use until after 1567, when the matchlock supplanted it. In 1630 the flint lock was invented, and the musket was introduced.

Banking.—The first bank in Europe was the Bank of Venice, 1171. The Bank of England was established in 1694, the Bank of North America, 1781.

Barometers, invented in 1626; wheel barometers in 1668, phosphoric in 1675, pendent in 1695, and marine in 1700.

Battering Ram, invented 441 B. C.

Bayonets, invented at Bayonne, in 1670. First used in England in 1693. At first these had wooden handles fitting into the guns, but in 1699 the socket bayonet was introduced.

Bellows.—Strabo informs us that the invention of bellows is due to the Scythian philosopher, Anacharsis, who lived in the time of Solon.

Bombs, invented at Venlo, in 1588, and used first in the service of France, in 1634.

Bridges. The first bridge of stone in England was that built at Bow, near Stratford, in 1087.

Bullets of stone used in 1514. Iron bullets first mentioned in 1550.

Camera Obscura, invented by Baptista Porta, in 1515.

Chain Shot, invented by DeWitt, Dutch Admiral, in 1666.

Chimneys, first introduced in England, in 1200, but at first only in the kitchen or large hall.

China, made at Dresden, in Saxony, in 1706; at Chelsea (England) in 1752; by Mr. Wedgwood in 1762.

Chronograph, A, is an instrument noting time within the fraction of a second. By the electrical chronograph used by astronomers, the transit of a star can be recorded to within one hundredth of a second.

Chronometer, The, is an instrument for measuring time, now generally applied only to those watches specially made for determining longitude at sea. A chronometer which gained a prize of $100,000, offered by the British Board of Longitude for a timepiece to ascertain longitude within thirty miles, was made in 1761, by John Harrison of Foulby, near Pontefract.

Clepsydra, The, is an instrument to measure time by the trickling or escape of water. In Babylonia, India, and Egypt, the clepsydra was used from before the dawn of history, especially in astronomical observations.

Clocks are of ancient date, one having been made by Pacificus, archdeacon of Verona, in the ninth century. Clocks with wheels were used in monasteries about the twelfth century, and were made to strike the hour. Pendulum said to have been first applied by Harris, 1641; dead-beat pendulum invented 1700, and the compensating pendulum, 1715.

Coal Mines, discovered in the neighborhood of Newcastle about 1234. Coals were first used in London in the reign of Edward I., when the smoke was supposed to corrupt the air to such an extent that he forbade the use of them by a proclamation, 1273; first brought from Newcastle to London, 1381.

Coffee introduced into Arabia Felix, 1454; became known at Constantinople and coffee houses opened, 1554; brought to Marseilles, 1644; the art of roasting and making it introduced at London by a Greek servant, and house opened in Georgeyard, Lombard street, 1652.

Cosmos is a term used to denote the order and harmony of the universe. Originally used by Homer to denote "order," it was applied by Heraclitus and Anaxagoras to the divine order and arrangement of nature; by Plato to celestial and terrestrial order. It was further applied to the habitable world and the world generally as an orderly system.

Delf (*or Delft*) earthenware invented at Firenze in 1450.

Envelopes for letters are mentioned by Swift, 1726. Stamped adhesive envelopes came into general use shortly after the establishment of the penny postal system in 1840. Machinery for their manufacture was patented in 1844; many improvements have since been made.

Express.—The first American express was opened between New York and Boston, in 1821, by W. F. Harnden.

Figures, in arithmetic, introduced into Europe by the Saracens from Arabia, 991; till then, letters were used.

Flag.—The American flag was first used by Washington at Cambridge, January 1, 1776.

Guns, invented by Swartz, a German, about 1378; brought into use by the Venetians, 1382; great ones first used at the battle of Crecy,

1346; first used in England at the Siege of Berwick, 1405; first cast in England, 1554.

Handkerchiefs were first manufactured at Paisley, in Scotland, in 1743.

Homœopathy was introduced into the United States in 1825.

Horseshoes.— Although the ancients protected the hoofs of their horses with some covering, horseshoes, of the kind now known, were not in general use until the ninth century.

Hydrometer.— The oldest mention of this instrument belongs to the fifth century, but its invention has been attributed to Archimedes.

Lace.— The knitting of lace is a German invention, first known about the middle of the sixteenth century.

Life-Boats, invented by Greathead, who received a premium from Parliament in May, 1802.

Lightning-Rods were first used by Benjamin Franklin about 1752.

Linen, first made in England by Flemish weavers, 1253; staining of linen first known in England, 1579; linen trade in Ireland, began by Lord Wentworth, 1634; British Linen Company erected, 1746.

Lithography, discovered, 1808; introduced into England, 1817; into the United States, 1828.

Magnifying-Glasses, first made in England by Roger Bacon, 1260.

Marble Paper.—A German invention belonging to the seventeenth century.

Microscopes, first used in Germany in 1621. Improved by Torricelli in 1624.

Organs, first introduced into churches by Pope Vitalian I., 683; into the western churches, 826.

Parchment, invented by King Attalus, of Pergamus, 887 B. C.

Paving with Stones, first introduced at Paris in 1186.

Post Office, first established between Vienna and Brussels in 1516. Posts established regularly between London and all the principal towns throughout England in 1635. Postage stamps were introduced in England in 1840; in the United States in 1847.

Ribbon Looms.— It has been asserted that these looms were first known to the Swiss, but others claim their invention for a German in the town of Dantzic in the sixteenth century.

Ruling Machines, invented by a Dutchman in London in 1792.

Sewing Machine, first patented in England, in 1755. The first complete machine was constructed by an American, Elias Howe, in 1846.

Sextant, invented by Tycho Brahe, at Augsburg, in 1550.

Silk, Raw, first made by people of China, called Sers, B. C. 150; first introduced from India, 374; a pound at this time was worth a pound of gold; manufacture of, introduced into Europe from India by some monks, 551; first worn in dress, 1455; first silk manufactured in France, 1521.

Sleeping Cars were first used in 1858. Pullman's patent dates from 1864.

Speaking Trumpets, invented by Kircher, a Jesuit, in 1652.

Stirrups, according to a statement made by the Emperor Mauritius, were first used in the sixth century. Hippocrates and Galen speak of a disease which, in their time, was occasioned by long and frequent riding, because the legs hung down without any support.

Sun-dials, invented 558 B. C. The first in Rome, 308 B. C., was that erected by Papirius Cursor, when time was divided into hours.

Tanning Leather, a new and more expeditious method than that previously in use was invented in 1795.

Tapestry, invented by Sir Francis Train, 1255; the first manufactured in England, 1620.

Tin Mines, first discovered in Germany, 1240; till then those in England were the only ones in Europe.

Ventilators, first introduced by the Rev. Dr. Hales in 1740.

Violins of the modern kind invented about 1477. Introduced into England by Charles II.

Wall Papers, first used in Spain and Holland in 1555. Flock or velvet wall papers were first used in 1620.

Watches, supposed to have been invented by Peter Hale at Nuremberg, 1490; though Robert, king of Scotland, had one about 1310; first used in the astronomical observations by Purbach, 1500; spring watches invented by Hooke, 1658. Repeaters invented, 1676.

Water Mills for grinding corn are said to have been invented by Belisarius when Rome was besieged by the Goths in 555. Pliny, however, mentions wheels turned by water.

Weathercocks.—The earliest mention of a weathercock is that made by Vitruvius, concerning that on the tower built at Athens by Andronicus Cyrrhestes.

Weights and Measures, invented by Phidon, Tyrant of Argos, B. C. 864; fixed in England, A. D. 1257; equalized, 1825; weights originally taken from grain of wheat, the lowest of which is called a grain.

Windows of some kind were glazed as early as the third century; the fashion was introduced into England about 680, but did not become general until 1180.

Wine, the art of making, brought from India by Bacchus; none produced in France in the time of the Romans; sold by apothecaries as a cordial, 1300; licenses for vending it, established 1661.

Woolen Cloth.— Although the making of woolen cloth is one of the most ancient of arts, its manufacture was not known in France until 1646, when it was made at Sedan. It was first made in England in 1331, but was not dyed or dressed until 1667.

Indian Summer.— Scientists differ regarding the cause of this phenomenon, which is peculiar to North America and certain parts of Central Europe. A change in the condition of the upper strata of the atmosphere, confining the radiating heat-rays in the lower strata, is generally held to be the true explanation. A theory to account for the smoky appearance, which appears plausible, is that it is due to the decay or slow chemical combustion of leaves, grass, and other vegetable matter under the action of frost and sun. It was to forest and prairie fires kindled by the Indians that the early settlers attributed the smoky appearance of the season. Hence the name "Indian Summer."

Infusoria are minute animalcules, some large enough to be barely visible to the naked eye (1-100 inch), but most of them altogether microscopic and almost exceeding the power of the glass to detect. They belong to the lowest order of animal life, have neither vessels nor nerves, and are made up of a uniform tissue called by Huxley *protoplasm*. The body has some well-defined form, of which the varieties are very great in different species. Many in the higher orders are furnished with hairs, the motion of which carries them with great rapidity through the fluid in which they live, and by means of which, also, currents are created in the fluid to bring food to the mouth. Some infusoria have a few slender filaments instead of hairs, which they agitate with an undulatory movement. Others move by contractions and extensions of their bodies. Some have stiff, bristle-like organs, which they use as feet for crawling on the surfaces of other bodies, and some have hooks, by which they attach themselves to foreign bodies. The food of the infusoria consists of organic particles of various kinds, and the different species have been remarked to show a preference, like those of higher animals, for particular kinds of food. The numbers of the infusoria are prodigious. They are found in all parts of the world, both in fresh and salt water, and in stagnant pools; but they are most usually developed in infusions of decayed animal and vegetable substances.

Iron, Discovery of.—The actual discovery of iron was probably made so early in the history of the human race that it cannot now be accurately placed. The Bible ascribes the discovery of working iron to Tubal-Cain. The Egyptians ascribe it to one of their early mythological kings, Hephæstus, who has been identified by students with the Hephæstus of Greek and the Vulcan of Roman mythology. The Egyptians and the Assyrians made iron at a very early period of their history. In ancient tombs and ruins but recently unearthed, many implements of iron are found, cooking utensils, and weapons of various kinds. The Chalybes, a Scythian tribe living south and east of the Black Sea, who attained great skill in iron working, are accredited by ancient writers with being the first to use coal in their furnaces, the inventors of steel or hardened iron, and the discoverers of magnetic iron. The books of Moses mention the use of iron some eleven centuries before the Christian era, and the Arundelian marbles fix a date for it before 1370 B. C.

Jacquard Loom.— The Jacquard apparatus, for the purpose of pattern weaving, was invented by M. Joseph Marie Jacquard, a native of Lyons, France, in 1801. Being necessitated to carry on the weaving business of his father, for which he had a distaste, he endeavored to improve the existing machinery, and the Jacquard loom was the result. He enabled, by his invention, an ordinary workman to produce, with comparative ease, the most beautiful patterns in a style which had only previously been accomplished by skilled labor. The reception of his great invention by the public, however, was most discouraging, for although rewarded with a small pension by Napoleon, the silk weavers offered such violent opposition to its introduction that on one occasion he narrowly escaped with his life. The machine was destroyed by the weavers on the public square of Lyons. The merit of the invention, however, was too great to admit of its being long suppressed, and when its value was once fairly recognized it effected a complete revolution in the art of weaving, especially in the finer kinds of figured silk fabrics.

Jelly Fishes consist of a jelly-like mass, containing a cavity which generally has a mouth from which extend tentacles, varying in length from thirty to one hundred feet. From the center, tubes pass to connect with other tubes around the circumference. Their food is smaller marine animals, which they catch with thread-like lassos attached to their tentacles. Agassiz divided jelly fishes, or *medusæ*, into three orders: *Beroid medusæ*, *medusæ* proper, and *hydroidæ*. Of the beroids the most curious are the pleurobrachia, found off the northeast coast of America. The medusæ proper, known as the "sun fisn, when large is one of the most beautiful of the jelly fishes. The Gulf of Mexico furnishes the finest hydroids.

Lace-Making.— The application of machinery to lace making has cheapened lace that would otherwise always have remained expensive, and has consequently deprived a large number of the inhabitants of towns in France and elsewhere of a lucrative source of income. The great centers of the manufacture of real lace, as hand-made lace is called to distinguish it from machine-made or imitation lace, are Belgium, France, and England. In the former country there are at least 900 lace schools, and over 150,000 women find employment in this trade. Brussels lace, which is of very fine thread and intricate design, has a world-wide reputation. Mechlin lace, a fine and transparent web, is made at Mechlin, Antwerp, Lierre, and Turnbrout. Valenciennes is largely made in Flanders, but is extinct in its native city, from which it derived its name. The towns of Ypres, Bruges, Courtrai, Menin, Ghent, and Alost produced this lace in large quantities and fine quality. Before the introduction of machinery the number of lace-makers in France was estimated to be at least 250,000, but this number has been greatly reduced within the last few years. The celebrated Point d'Alençon lace, which is made entirely by hand with a small needle, in small pieces, which are afterward united by invisible seams, is made chiefly at Bayeux. Another favorite lace, the Chantilly, which was formerly made almost altogether at Chantilly, is now made at Bayeux and Caen. Lille lace, which though simple in design is fine and beautiful, is the production of the town of Lille. The lace of Bailleul is strong and cheap, and extensively used for trimming. In the district of Auvergne, of which the town of Le Puy is the center, over 100,000 women are employed in lace-making, and nearly every kind of lace is made. The industry is considered more extensive and more ancient in this district than in any other portion of France. In England the counties of Buckingham, Devon, and Bedford are the centers of lace-making. The most widely known of the English lace is Honiton, so called from the town of this name in Devonshire The manufacture of hand-made laces was an important industry in Nottingham some years ago, but it has been almost entirely destroyed by the introduction of machinery. Lace is made to a limited extent in Limerick, Ireland; also in Scotland, and in fact in nearly every country in Europe. The imitation or machine-made lace is manufactured in Caen, France; in Nottingham, England; and also in the United States.

Lamps are mentioned in all the early ages; they were in use in Egypt, Greece, and Rome. The earthen lamp which Epictetus, the philosopher, had in his study, sold, after his death, for 3,000 drachmas. Lamps with horn sides are said to be the invention of Alfred. London streets were first lighted with oil lamps in 1681, and with gas lamps in 1814. A lamp constructed to produce neither smoke nor smell was patented, in 1784, by a Frenchman, and was brought into general use in England early in the present century. On the principle of Argand are founded the lamps invented by Carcel, about 1803, and since 1825 the moderator lamps of Levavasseur, Hadrot, and Neuburger. The domestic lamp is now of elegant manufacture and many artistic designs.

Latitude.—First determined by Hipparchus, of Nice, about 170 B. C. It is the extent of the earth, or of the heavens, reckoned from the equator to either pole. Maupertuis, in 1737, measured a degree of latitude, and made it 69.493; Swanberg, in 1803, made it 69.292. At the equator, in 1744, four astronomers made it 68.732; and Lambton made it 68.743; Mudge, in England, made it 69.148; Cassini, in France, made it 69.12, and Biot, 68.769; while a recent measure, in Spain, makes it 68.63—less than at the equator, and contradicts all others, proving the earth to be a prolate spheroid, which was the opinion of Cassini, Bernouilli, Euler, and others, while it has more generally been regarded as an oblate spheroid.

Life Insurance, Origin of.— The rise of life insurance may be traced to several sources. The doctrine of probabilities developed by Pascal and Huyghens as to games of chance was applied to life contingencies by the great Dutch statesman Jan De Witt in 1671, but it was not till some time after that it was applied to life insurance. In 1696 there was a hint at modern life insurance in a London organization, and this was followed by another association two years after. The operators of these two seem to have passed away without giving to their successors any clear account of their plan of operations. In 1706 the Amicable Society for a Perpetual Assurance Office was founded in London, and this is considered the first actual life insurance company established. Its plan was mutual—that is, each member, without reference to age, paid a fixed admission fee and a fixed annual payment per share on from one to three shares; at the end of the year a portion of the fund was divided among the heirs of deceased members in proportion to the shares held by each. In after years the limitations as to age, occupation, and health were added.

Liquid Air.— Popular attention has been attracted to this subject recently in America by the experiments of Mr. Charles E. Tripler, although the liquefaction of gases is by no means new. It was first accomplished by Northmore in 1806, who succeeded in obtaining liquid chlorine by pressure. Faraday followed. Two factors are necessary to liquefy a gas, pressure and cold. Every gas, so far as now known, will liquefy under a given pressure, provided it is cooled to a certain temperature known as its "critical temperature." In 1877 two French experimenters, Pictet, Cailletet, working separately, and along different lines, succeeded in liquefying oxygen. This was followed in 1883 by successful experiments by two Russian physicists, Wrobleski and Olszewski. Among other surprising results they succeeded in freezing alcohol. It was not until 1890 that liquid air and oxygen were produced in any quantity. This was first done by Prof. Dewar, of the Royal Institution, London. About this time Mr. Tripler, of New York, developed a form of apparatus which may be said to be a practical machine. The capacity of his plant was soon found inadequate. The process claimed by this physicist is also claimed by Mr. Thompson in England, and Dr. Carl Linde of Munich, Germany.

The effects of the intense cold which can be produced by evaporating liquid air, oxygen, or hydrogen are almost beyond comprehension; practically all plastic or soft materials when immersed in it become hard and brittle, leather being an exception; some metals become brittle, and can be broken or crumbled; alcohol may be frozen, and air and oxygen themselves solidify if placed in liquid hydrogen. The possibilities of liquid air are many. It can be used for refrigeration; motor vehicles and launches can be operated by it; surgeons can use it in operations, and for ventilating and cooling rooms it is invaluable.

Magnet. — The iron ore which possesses the property of attraction was given the name of magnet by the Greeks, because it was first found in Magnesia in Asia Minor, or according to another account because it was first discovered by a shepherd named Magnes, who had iron tips on his shoes, and while walking over some rocks found that his feet stuck to them in a mysterious way. The ore is now called magnetite, and is an oxide of iron containing about seventy-three per cent. of iron when pure. It is a very valuable ore, and supplies a large amount of the finest iron and steel of commerce. Large deposits occur in Norway and Sweden, Finland and the Ural; in the Adirondack region in northern New York; in northern New Jersey; in eastern Pennsylvania, the most noted locality being Cornwall, Lebanon County, where the mines have been worked for over a hundred years; in North Carolina, California, and Oregon, and several places in Canada. It is also found in the form of sand in some places in North America, India, and New Zealand. One of the largest occurrences of magnetic sand is on the south shore of Long Island, near Quogue, where a furnace was built and an attempt made to work it; but the enterprise proved unsuccessful and was abandoned.

Mariner's Compass.— The Chinese ascribed the invention of the compass to their Emperor Hong-Ti, who they say was a grandson of Noah; some of their historians refer the invention of it to a later date, 1115 B. C. The honor of its discovery, however, though much disputed, is generally given to Flavio Gioja, a native of Amalfi, an ancient commercial city of Naples, A. D. 1302. The compass is also said to have been known to the Swedes in the time of King Jarl Birger, 1250. The variation of the needle was first discovered by Columbus in his voyage of discovery, 1492. The compass box and hanging compass, used by navigators, were invented by William Barlowe, an English divine and natural philosopher, in 1608. The measuring compass was invented by Jost Bing, of Hesse, in 1602. The dipping needle was invented by Robert Norman, a compass maker of Ratcliffe, England, in 1580.

Matches, Invention of.— Previous to 1829 the matches in use consisted of a slender stick with a pointed end, which had been dipped in sulphur; and they were lighted by touching them to a spark struck into tinder by flint and steel. In that year, however, what was known as the "Instantaneous Light-Box" was invented. It consisted of a small tin box containing a bottle, in which was placed some sulphuric acid, with sufficient fibrous asbestos to soak it up and prevent its spilling out of the bottle, and a supply of properly prepared matches. These consisted of small splints of wood about two inches long, one end of which was coated with a chemical mixture prepared by mixing chlorate of potash, powdered loaf-sugar and powdered gum arabic, the whole colored with a little vermilion, and made into a thin paste with water. The splints were readily inflamed by dipping the prepared ends into the sulphuric acid. These were succeeded by the lucifer, or loco-foco match, which was ignited by friction; and that, in turn by the Congreve, which was similar to the sulphur matches now in use; and this, shortly afterward, by the present parlor match.

Maxim Self-Acting Gun was invented

by Hiram S. Maxim of England. The peculiar features of this gun are: Every round after the first is fired by the recoil of the previous explosion; the cartridges are picked out of the cartridge belt, one end of which is placed in the gun mechanism on one side by the automatic action of the gun, and the belt and cartridge shells are ejected after firing; every recoil of the gun brings the next cartridge into position, forces it into the barrel, cocks the hammer, pulls the trigger, extracts the empty shell, and ejects it from the gun — all these processes going on with such marvelous rapidity that six hundred rounds are fired in a minute. The gun can be turned in any direction by means of a crank, and the rate of discharge is regulated by a controlling chamber, ingeniously contrived so that the gun may be fired rapidly or slowly, as desired. At the moment of firing, the recoil drives the barrel back about three quarters of an inch, and it is this recoil which directs the mechanism of the gun and makes its discharges continuous.

Medicine appears to have been first practiced by the Egyptian priests. Pythagoras endeavored to explain the philosophy of disease and the action of medicine about 529 B. C. Hippocrates, the Father of Medicine, flourished about 422 B. C., and Galen, born A. D. 131, was the oracle of medical science. About 980, Avicenna, an Arab, wrote a system of medicine. The art was brought into Europe from the East, about A. D. 1150. In the early stages of the practice, the preparation of simples was principally confined to ecclesiastics in Europe generally, until the close of the fifteenth century. The dogmatic age of medicine lasted until the Reformation, when it was attacked by Paracelsus (1493-1541) and Vasalius (1514-64). Since 1800 medical practice has been completely transformed by physiological and chemical research. The practice of medicine is now one of the highest sciences, and in most countries is in the hands of learned and distinguished men; various statutes have been enacted to discourage pretenders to the healing art.

Meerschaum is a mineral existing in many parts of the world. In Europe, it is found chiefly at Hrubschitz in Moravia, and at Sebastopol and Kaffa in the Crimea; and in Asia it is found abundantly just below the soil in the alluvial beds at Kittisch and Bursa in Natolia; and in the rocks of Eske-Hissar, in the same district, it is mined so extensively as to give employment to nearly a thousand men. Meerschaum, from its having been found on the seashore in some places, in peculiarly rounded snow white lumps, was ignorantly imagined to be petrified froth of the sea, which is the meaning of its German name. It is composed of silica, magnesia, and water. When first dug from the earth it is quite soft and soap-like to the touch, and as it lathers with water and removes grease, it is employed by the Turks as a substitute for soap in washing. After being molded into pipes, these are boiled in oil or wax and baked until hard.

Mesmerism was first brought into notice by Frederick Anton Mesmer, a German physician, in 1766, when he published a thesis on "The Influence of the Planets on the Human Body," claiming that the heavenly bodies diffused through the universe a subtle fluid which acts on the nervous system of animated beings; and he further stated that he regarded the new force, which, he said, could be exerted by one living organism upon another, as a means of alleviating or curing disease. In 1778 he left Vienna for Paris, where he gained numerous proselytes and much money. His discovery was fostered by Dr. D'Elson, physician to the king's brother, and in 1784 the French government ordered the medical faculty of Paris to investigate Mesmer's theory. A committee was appointed, who subsequently reported that "The violent effects which are observed in the public practice of magnetism are due to the manipulations, to the excitement of the imagination which leads us to repeat anything which produces an impression upon the senses." One year later, 1785, Mesmer's popularity had so far declined that he left Paris and retired to Switzerland, where he spent the balance of his life. Mesmerism excited some attention again in 1848, when Miss Harriet Martineau and others announced their belief in it.

Meteors.— Meteors are small, erratic bodies rushing through the planetary system, and, getting hot in the process, appear in the atmosphere surrounding our earth as "shooting stars." Some of these falling bodies have reached the earth, and such are called "aërolites" or "meteorites." Numbers, of course, are burned up before they reach us, and who can tell what destruction such a catastrophe may represent, or whether it be or be not an inhabited world which has thus been plunged to destruction by fire? They are of a metallic or stony nature. On certain nights in August and November it has been calculated that these meteors will appear. They fall from certain constellations, after which they are named; as Leonides, from Leo, in the November displays.

The star showers sometimes present the appearance of a beautiful display of rockets. Millions of them rush round the sun, and when, as occasionally happens, our earth comes near them, we have a grand display of celestial fireworks.

It is estimated that the average number of meteors that traverse the atmosphere daily, and which are large enough to be visible to the eye on a dark, clear night, is 7,500,000; and if to these the telescopic meteors be added, the number will be increased to 400,000,000. In the space traversed by the earth there are, on the average, in each volume the size of our globe (including its atmosphere), as many as 13,000 small bodies, each one capable of furnishing a shooting star visible under favorable circumstances to the naked eye.

Metric System, The, originated in France about 1790. In 1799, on the invitation of the Government, an international convention, at which were present representatives from France, Holland, Denmark, Sweden, Switzerland, Spain, Savoy, and the Roman Republics, assembled at Paris to settle, from the results of the great Meridian Survey, the exact length of the "definitive meter." As a result of the investigations of this learned body, the Metric System was based upon the length of the fourth part of a terrestrial meridian. The ten-millionth part of this arc was chosen as the unit of measures of length, and called Meter. The cube of the tenth part of the meter was adopted as the unit of capacity, and denominated Liter. The weight of a liter of distilled water at its greatest density was called Kilogramme, of which the thousandth part, or Gramme, was adopted as the unit of weight. The multiples of these, proceeding in decimal progression, are distinguished by the employment of the prefixes *deca*, *hecto*, *kilo*, and *myria* (ten, hundred, thousand, ten thousand) from the Greek, and the subdivisions by *deci*, *centi*, and *milli* (tenth, hundredth, thousandth) from the Latin.

Measures of Length (Unit, Meter).

EQUAL TO	*Inches.*	*Feet.*	*Yards.*	*Fathoms.*	*Miles.*
Millimeter	0.03937	0.003281	0.0010936	0.0005468	0.0000006
Centimeter	0.39371	0.032809	0.0109363	0.0054682	0.0000062
Decimeter	3.93708	0.328098	0.1093633	0.0546816	0.0000621
METER	39.37079	3.280988	1.0936331	0.5468165	0.0006214
Decameter	393.70790	32.809892	10.9363306	5.4681653	0.0062138
Hectometer	3,937.07900	328.089917	109.3633056	54.6816528	0.0621381
Kilometer	39,370.79000	3,280.899167	1,093.6330556	546.8165278	0.6213824
Myriameter	394,707.90000	32,808.991667	10,936.3305556	5,468.1652778	6.2138242

Cubic Measures, or Measures of Capacity (Unit, Liter).

EQUAL TO	*Cubic Inches.*	*Cubic Feet.*	*Pints.*	*Gallons.*	*Bushels.*
Milliliter, or cubic centimeter	0.06103	0.000035	0.00176	0.0002201	0.0000275
Centiliter, 10 cubic centimeters	0.61027	0.000353	0.01761	0.0022010	0.0002751
Deciliter, 100 cubic centimeters	6.10271	0.003532	0.17608	0.0220097	0.0027512
LITER, or cubic Decimeter,	61.02705	0.035317	1.76077	0.2200967	0.0275121
Decaliter, or Centistere	610.27052	0.353166	17.60773	2.2009668	0.2751208
Hectoliter, or Decistere	6,102.70515	3.531658	176.07734	22.0096677	2.7512085
Kiloliter, or Stere, or cubic meter,	61,027.05152	35.316581	1,760.77341	220.0966767	27.5120846
Myrialiter, or Decastere	610,270.51519	353.165807	17,607.73414	2,200.9667675	275.1208459

Measures of Weight (Unit, Gramme).

EQUAL TO	*Grains.*	*Troy Oz.*	*Avoirdupois Lbs.*	*Cwt. of* 112 *Lbs.*	*Tons.*
Milligramme	0.01543	0.000032	0.0000022	0.0000000	0.0000000
Centigramme	0.15432	0.000322	0.0000220	0.0000002	0.0000000
Decigramme	1.54323	0.003215	0.0002205	0.0000020	0.0000001
GRAMME	15 43235	0.032151	0.0022046	0 0000197	0.0000010
Decagramme	154.32349	0.321507	0.0220462	0.0001968	0.0000098
Hectogramme	1,543.23488	3.215073	0.2204621	0.0019684	0.0000984
Kilogramme	15,432.34880	32.150727	2.2046213	0.0196841	0.0009842
Myriagramme	154,323.48800	321.507267	22.0462129	0.1968412	0.0098421

Square Measures, or Measures of Surface (Unit, Are).

EQUAL TO	*Sq. Feet.*	*Sq. Yards.*	*Sq. Perches.*	*Sq. Roods.*	*Sq. Acres.*
Centare, or square meter	10.794299	1.196033	0.0395383	0.0009885	0.0002471
ARE, or 100 square meters	1,076.429934	119.603326	3.9538290	0.0988457	0.0247111
Hectare, or 10,000 square meters	107,642.993419	11,960.332602	395.3828959	9.8845724	2.4711434

Microphone, The, is the black carbon button used in telephones, and is an instrument for magnifying sound. The most sensitive substance, so far as yet discovered, to have the peculiar power, when placed in the electric current, of magnifying sound, is willow charcoal plunged, when at white heat, into mercury. A piece of such charcoal an inch long, placed vertically between two blocks of carbon, hollowed to receive its ends, wires connecting the blocks with an electric battery, and the ordinary receiving instrument of a telephone, constitute one of the simplest forms of a microphone. The invention of the microphone is claimed by Professor Hughes of England, and Thomas Edison, the American inventor.

Microscope, Invention of the.— It is generally believed that the first compound microscope was made in 1590 by a Hollander named Zacharias Jansen. Pocket microscopes were first made in London in 1740 by Benjamin Martin. The discovery of the magnifying power of the simple lens was undoubtedly made long before the Christian era, as it is known that the Greeks used magnifiers of glass which they called "reading-glasses," and rude lenses of crystal have been found in Egyptian ruins.

Mirage.— Mirage (sometimes called *Fata Morgana*) is the appearance in the air of the image of some distant object, seen either in connection with the object itself, above or below the latter, or suspended in the air, the object being invisible. It is a very curious but sufficiently common phenomena, and in the Asiatic and African plains it is frequently observed. When the weather is calm and the ground hot, the Egyptian landscape appears like a lake, and the houses look like islands in the midst of a widely-spreading expanse of water. This causes the mirage, which is the result of evaporation, while the different temperatures of the air strata cause an unequal reflection and refraction of light, which give rise to the mirage. Travelers are frequently deceived, but the camels will not quicken their usual pace until they scent water.

The Fata Morgana and the inverted images of ships seen at sea are not uncommon on European coasts. Between Sicily and Italy this phenomenon is seen in the Sea of Reggio with fine effect. Palaces, towers, fertile plains, with cattle grazing on them, are seen, with many other terrestial objects, upon the sea — the palaces of the Fairy Morgana. The inverted images of ships are frequently perceived, and many most extraordinary but perfectly authentic tales have been related concerning the reflection and refraction of persons and objects in the sky and on land, when no human beings nor any of the actual objects were within the range of vision.

Mirrors.— In ancient times mirrors were made of metal; those of the Jewish women of brass; mirrors of silver were introduced by Praxiteles, 328 B. C. Mirrors or looking-glasses were made at Venice, A. D. 1300; and in England, at Lambeth, near London, in 1673. The French excelled in their manufacture of them in the last century. Various methods of coating glass by a solution of silver, thus avoiding the use of mercury, so injurious to the health of the workman, have been made known, by M. Petitjean, in 1851; by M. Cimeg, in 1861, and by Liebig and others.

Mother-of-Pearl.—The shells of many molluscous animals display a brilliant pearly and iridescent luster, resulting from the peculiar manner in which the layers of calcareous matter of which they are composed have been successively formed. Such shells, even when small in size, form bright and, especially to the untutored eye, attractive ornaments, and as such are used for necklaces and similar purposes. When the shells are of sufficient size to cut and shape for purposes of utility, they become articles of some commercial importance under the name of Mother-of-Pearl. This term, though applicable to all pearly shells, is in commerce principally applied to the shells of the bi-valve pearl mussel, which is the principal source of the commercial product.

The largest and steadiest consumption of mother-of-pearl is in the button trade, and much is also consumed by cutlers for handles of fruit and dessert knives and forks, pocket-knives, and other forms of cutlery. It is also used in the inlaying of Japanese and Chinese lacquers, European lacquered papier-maché work, trays, toys, and as an ornamental inlay generally. In an innumerable variety of small and fancy articles, mother-of-pearl is also employed, its use being limited only by the moderate dimensions and thickness of material obtained, and its rather brittle nature.

The carving of pilgrim shells, and the elaboration of crucifixes and ornamental work in mother-of-pearl is a distinctive industry of the monks and other inhabitants of Bethlehem. Among the South Sea Islands the shell is largely fashioned into fishing hooks, a purpose for which its brilliant, conspicuous appearance seems to render it suitable without the addition of any bait or other lure.

Music.— Lucretius ascribes its invention to the whistling of the winds in hollow reeds. Franckinus, to the various sounds produced by the hammers of Tubal-Cain; Pontique and others to the singing of birds; and Zarlino to the sound of water. It is however agreed that music was first reduced to rules by Jubal, 1800 B. C. The flute and harmony or concord in music was invented by Hyagnis, 1506. Vocal choruses of men are first mentioned 56 B. C. The first six musical notes are said to have been invented by Guy Aretino, a Benedictine monk of Arezzo, about 1025. The notes of present use were perfected in 1338. Musical pitch was settled in France in 1859. Pythagoras maintained that the motion of the twelve spheres must produce delightful sounds inaudible to mortal ears, which he called the music of the spheres. Saint Cecilia, a Roman lady, is said to have excelled so eminently in music, that an angel was enticed from the celestial regions by the fascinating charms of her melody; this hyperbolical tradition has been deemed sufficient authority to make her the patroness of music. She died in the third century.

Nails.—It is only since 1810 that machinery has been employed to any extent in the manufacture of nails. Previous to that date, they were made by hand by forging on an anvil, and great numbers of men were employed in the industry, there having been as many as 60,000 nailers in the neighborhood of Birmingham alone. It appears that as early as 1606 a patent was obtained for cutting nail rods by water power, by Sir Davis Bulmer. An improvement on this was patented in 1618, and a new invention in 1790, which last was the first nail machine in actual use; it was patented by Thomas Clifford, and used in French's factory at Wimburn, Staffordshire, in 1792. Toward the close of the last century many patents were obtained in the United States for new machines and improvements on old ones. Many of the first inventors spent large sums of money on their machines, and it has been estimated that it cost fully $1,000,000 to bring them to the perfection attained in 1810, when a machine made 100 nails a minute. The machine invented by Jesse Reed of Massachusetts, about 1800, is the one which first came into general use, and this, with some improvements, is the one most largely used to-day. In 1810, Joseph C. Dyer of Boston, then a merchant in London, took out patents in England for the nail machinery invented in Massachusetts. It was at once widely introduced, and large manufacturing establishments were soon founded. Some factories at Birmingham are now capable of making over 40,000,000 nails a week. The term penny, used to indicate the size of nails, is supposed to be a corruption of pound; thus a fourpenny nail was one such that 1,000 of them weighed four pounds; a tenpenny, such that 1,000 weighed ten pounds. Originally, the "hundred," when applied to nails, meant sixscore, or 120; consequently the thousand was 1,200. In France, the greater part of the nails used in carpentry-work are made of soft iron wire, pointed with the hammer, and the head is formed by pinching them in a toothed vise.

Nebular Hypothesis.—The Nebular Hypothesis assumes that the solar system was once an enormous mass of gaseous substance. Rapid rotation arising in this gaseous mass, it took the form of a disc, and at last inertia (popularly but erroneously called centrifugal force), overcoming cohesion, whole rings and fragments flew off from this disc, and by gravitation contracted into spheroid masses. As, in the original mass, the velocity of the outer circle of each body thrown off is greater than the inner circle, this causes each spheroid to revolve on its own axis. This process goes on, and the central mass continues to cool and shrink until we have at last a central body with a number of smaller spheroidal bodies revolving around it in orbits; the smaller, the nearer they are to the central orb. Certain points are assumed in this hypothesis to explain the distribution of matter in our solar system. It is assumed that in throwing off great masses from the central disc, immense quantities of minute particles were also thrown, which continue to revolve, in the same plane with the large mass around the central body. By slow degrees these minute atoms, by the law of gravitation, were aggregated into the mass nearest to them. These subordinate aggregations would form with most difficulty nearest the large central mass, because of the superior attractive force of the latter, wherefore the interior planets — Mercury, Venus, the Earth, and Mars — are smaller than the two great orbs in the zone beyond them. These two enormous planets, Jupiter and Saturn, occupy the space where conditions are most favorable to subordinate aggregations; but beyond them the gravity of aggregating material becomes reduced, and so the planets found in the outer zone, Uranus and Neptune, are smaller than the planets of the middle zone. This hypothesis was first suggested by Sir William Herschel, and was adopted and developed by Laplace.

Needles.— The making of Spanish needles was first taught in England by Elias Crowse, a German, about the eighth year of Queen Elizabeth, and in Queen Mary's time there was a negro who made fine Spanish needles in Cheapside, London. At his death the secret of fabrication was lost, and not recovered again till 1566. The family of Greenings, ancestors of Lord Dorchester, established a needle factory in Bucks a little later. German and Hungarian steel is of best repute for needles. The manufacture was greatly improved at White Chapel, London; Redditch, in Gloucestershire; and Hathersage, in Derbyshire. An exhibition of ancient needles and needlework was formed at South Kensington museum in 1873.

Nickel was first obtained as a metal in Germany about 1751; but the ore had been previously known to miners, who called it *kupfernickel*, or Old Nick's copper, for the reason that, though it looked like copper ore, no copper could be obtained from it. Nickel, when pure, is silvery white, and does not oxidize or tarnish in the air. It is found in many parts of the world, but the principal mines are in Russia, Sweden, Germany, Austria, England, and Scotland, and in the states of Pennsylvania and Connecticut in America. Its chief use is for plating other metals, but it is also used in alloys.

Oceans, Depths of.— The average depth of all the oceans is from 2,000 to 3,000 fathoms. Soundings have been made in the Atlantic Ocean, ninety miles off the island of St. Thomas, in the West Indies, which showed a depth of 23,250 feet, or about four and one-half miles. In 1872-'74, the ship Challenger made a voyage around the world for the purpose of taking deep-sea soundings, and the result showed that the greatest depth in the Pacific Ocean was between four and one-half and five miles, while that of the Atlantic was probably as given above.

Ocean Steam Navigation.— The first ocean steam navigation in the world was by the steamboat Phœnix, built by Colonel John Stevens, and navigated from Hoboken, N. J., to Philadelphia in 1808 by Robert L. Stevens. In 1819, the Savannah, an American vessel of 380 tons burden, built at Corlear's Hook, N. Y., made the first steam voyage across the Atlantic. The steamer went from New York to Savannah, Ga., and thence to England. From England she proceeded to St. Petersburg, Russia, where an effort was made to dispose of her to the czar. The sale not being consummated, she returned to New York, and was afterwards converted into a sailing vessel.

Ohm's Law is so named from its discoverer, Georg Simon Ohm, a German physicist, born 1787, died 1854. He devoted himself particularly to the investigation of the laws governing galvanic currents, and by a combination of mathematical and experimental investigation, carried on for many years, he at length discovered and established the law which forms the basis of the mathematical theory of electricity. His discoveries were first announced in scientific journals in 1825-'26. This fundamental theorem, known as Ohm's Law, may be briefly stated as follows: The strength of a galvanic current is equal to the electro-motive force divided by the resistance. The term ohm is now used to designate the standard measure or unit of galvanic resistance, and is equal to the resistance of a cylindrical wire of pure copper one twentieth of an inch in diameter and 250 feet long.

Oleomargarine.— The belief which is prevalent among the masses that the ingredients which constitute oleomargarine are unclean is fallacious, as will be seen by the following description: Clean beef fat and a proportionate quantity of salt are by process of machinery and heat transformed into what is called white stearine and butter oil, otherwise the oil which has been pressed from the fat. This oil is then churned in the proportion of about 442 pounds of butter oil, 120 pounds of milk, 37½ pounds of cream-made butter, and 1¾ ounces of bicarbonate of soda. To this some coloring matter is added, and the mixture churned for some fifty minutes, giving as a result a smooth mass resembling an emulsion of cream. This is put into ice-cream freezers and kept constantly agitated until it solidifies. It is then worked over with revolving butter-workers to get the necessary amount of salt well into it, and is then packed in firkins or made into molds. Science shows that chemically, pure oleomargarine butter differs but slightly from pure cream butter. By analysis the constituents of cream butter are: Water 11.968, butter solids 88.032. Those of oleomargarine are: Water 11.203, butter solids 88.797. The process of making oleomargarine was invented by M. Hippolyte Niege, a French chemist, about 1872; but later experiments, made by Doctor Mott of New York, added to the commercial value of the original process. The name is derived from two words — oleine and margarine. Oleine is the thin, oily part of fats, and margarine is a peculiar, pearl-like substance, extracted from some vegetable oils, and also from some animal fats, the name being of Latin origin, from margarita, a pearl.

Painting.— An art, according to Plato, of the highest antiquity in Egypt. Osymandyas caused his exploits to be represented in painting, 2100 B. C. Pausias, of Sicyon, was the inventor of the encaustic, a method of burning the colors into wood or ivory, 335 B. C. The ancients considered Sicyon the nursery of painters. Antiphiles, an Egyptian, is said to have been the inventor of the grotesque, 332 B. C. The art was introduced at Rome from Etruria, by Quintus Fabius, who on that account was styled Pictor. The first excellent pictures were brought from Corinth by Mummius, 146 B. C. After the death of Augustus not a single painter of eminence appeared for several ages; Ludius, who was very celebrated, is supposed to have been the last, about A. D. 14. Painting on canvas seems to have been known at Rome in A. D. 66. Bede, the Saxon historian, who died in 735, knew something of the art. It revived about the end of the thirteenth century and to Giovanni Cimabue of Florence is awarded the honor of its restoration. It was at once encouraged and generously patronized in Italy. John Van-Eyck, of Bruges, and his brother Hubert, are regarded as the founders of the Flemish school of painting in oil, 1415. Paulo Uccello was the first to study perspective. The earliest mention of the art in England is A. D. 1523, about which time Henry the Eighth patronized Hulbein, and invited Titian to his court. Wilkins invented a process of using oil with mineral colors for frescoes in 1853. The first practicing ^rtist of celebrity in the United

States was John Watson, who commenced painting portraits in New Jersey, 1715. Benjamin West was the first native American artist; born in Chester County, Pennsylvania, 1708. John Singleton Copley, born in Boston, 1738, began his first important work in 1760. Other noted American painters, belonging to the early period, were Charles W. Peale, Gilbert Charles Stuart, John Trumbull, William Dunlap, and E. G. Malbone. Latterly American artists have been greatly influenced by the French schools.

Paper Hangings.—The invention of hangings of paper to take the place of other more costly hangings, has been attributed to a manufacturer of paper hangings named Breitkopf, of Leipsic. That kind known as velvet paper is said to have been invented by Jerome Lanyer, an Englishman, who received a patent for it in 1634, although the invention has also been claimed for François, a Frenchman, who is asserted to have introduced it at Rouen, in 1620.

Paper, History of.—It is generally conceded that the Egyptians were the first manufactures of paper, which they made from papyrus, a species of reed. In former times this plant grew in abundance on the banks of the Nile, but it is now said to have disappeared from Egypt. It was called by the Egyptians "papu"; by the Greeks "papyrus"; our word paper is a later derivative. Herodotus named it "byblus," whence came the Greek "biblion" (book) and our word Bible. The ancient Mexicans used a kind of paper prepared from the maguey plant that grows on tablelands and closely resembles the Egyptian papyrus. This paper took ink and color well, as is attested by specimens which have been preserved. The credit of being first to form from fiber the web which constitutes modern paper belongs to the Chinese, and the art was known to them as early as the commencement of the Christian era. In the seventh century the Arabians learned the art of making it from cotton from the Chinese, and the first manufactory was established at Samarcand, about A. D. 706. From thence it was taken into Spain, where under the Moors paper was made, it is thought, of hemp and flax as well as cotton. Just when linen rags were first used in the composition of paper is uncertain; but the best evidence is offered by the Arabian physician Abdollatiph, who writes, in an account of his visit to Egypt in the year 1200, "that the cloth found in the catacombs and used to envelop mummies was made into garments or sold to the scribes to make paper for shopkeepers"; and as there is no doubt that these mummy cloths were linen, it proves the use of this material to be of considerable antiquity. Of the use of linen rags in Europe, the earliest proof is the celebrated document found by Ichwandner in the monastery of Goss, in Upper Styria, which purports to be a mandate of Frederick II., Emperor of the Romans, and is dated 1242. It is written on paper which has been proved to have been made of linen. The practice of making a distinctive watermark on paper was also of very early date, as manuscripts as old as the thirteenth century bear it. There is, however, no really satisfactory information respecting the exact time or place of the introduction of paper making into Europe. By some it is supposed that Spain was the first to receive the art, and that thence it spread to France and Holland, and subsequently to England; but it is quite certain that England was a long time behind the other countries. As proof of this we find that the first patent for paper making was taken out in 1665, by one Charles Hildeyerd, but it was for "the way and art of making blew paper used by sugar-bakers and others." Ten years later, 1675, a patent was taken out by Eustace Barneby for "the art and skill of making all sorts of white paper for the use of writing and printing, being a new manufacture, and never practiced in any way in any of our kingdome or dominions." Paper is now made out of cotton and linen rags, waste paper, straw, esparto grass, wood, cane, jute, and manilla.

Papier-Mache has been in use for more than a century in Europe, and it is thought probable that it was first suggested by some of the beautiful productions of Sinde and other parts of India, where it is employed in making boxes, trays, etc., as well as in China. Its first application, as far as is known, was to the manufacture of snuff boxes by a German named Martin in 1740, who learned it of a Frenchman named Lefevre. The cheaper articles of papier-maché are made of paper reduced to a pulp with water and glue, and pressed in oiled molds. Better articles are produced by pasting together sheets of paper, and when a proper degree of thickness is attained it is pressed into the shape desired. When moist, this substance may be made to take any form, and when dry may be planed into any shape. A brilliant surface can be had by polishing with rotten stone and oil. Papier-maché is much used to make architectural ornaments, both for exterior and interior decorations. The sheets of paper, placed in layers with glue, are pressed into metal molds for some hours; then they are removed, and a composition of paper pulp, mixed quite thin with resin and glue, is poured in, and the paper impressions are again put in and subjected to powerful pressure. This causes the composition to adhere to the molded articles, and gives them the rough surface that is desired. Papier-maché can be made waterproof by adding to the pulp sulphate of iron or some of the silicates, and fireproof by mixing with clay and borax, phosphate of soda, or any alkali.

Parchment. — The ordinary writing-parchment is made from the skins of the sheep and she-goat; the finer kind, known as *vellum*, is made from those of very young calves, kids, and lambs. The thick, common kinds of parchment, which are used for drums, tambourines, battledoors, etc., are made from the skins of old he-goats and she-goats and in northern Europe from wolves; and a peculiar kind which is used for tablets, is made from asses' skins. Parchment, as a writing material, was known at least as early as 500 B. C. Herodotus speaks of books written upon skins in his time. Pliny, without good grounds, places the invention as late as 196 B.C., stating that it was made at Pergamos (hence the name *Pergamena*, corrupted into English parchment). Possibly the Pergamian invention was an improvement in the preparation of skins, which had certainly been used centuries before. The manufacture rose to great importance in Rome about a century before Christ, and soon became the chief writing material; and its use spread all over Europe, and retained its pre-eminence until the invention of paper from rags.

Pearl Fisheries.— The cause of the pearl is the introduction of a grain of sand or other foreign substance into the shell of the pearl oyster. This causes an irritation of the delicate tissues of the oyster, which immediately deposits the pearly matter around it for protection. Advantage of this fact has been taken to put substances within the shells of young oysters to induce the formation of pearls, and the Chinese by this method force a species of fresh-water mussels to produce the jewel. The most important pearl fisheries of the world are those of Ceylon and Coromandel, in the Indian Sea, whence pearls have been obtained since the earliest times of history. The divers are natives, trained to the pursuit, who are accustomed to descend to the depth of six or eight fathoms some forty times a day, and remain under water from a minute to a minute and a half. The fishing season begins in March or April and lasts but one month. A single shell may contain from eight to twenty pearls, varying in size from that of a small pea to about three times that size. The coasts of Java, Sumatra, Japan, and also Colombia and other points on the shores of South America have yielded large quantities of pearls; but they are usually smaller than the Oriental pearls.

Percussion Caps, Composition of.— The explosive which is used in the making of percussion caps is a fulminate of mercury, made by first dissolving 100 parts mercury in 1,000 parts of nitric acid — or 740 parts by measure. When the solution is heated to 130 degrees Fahrenheit it should be slowly poured through a glass funnel tube into 830 parts alcohol, sp. gr. .830 — or 1,000 parts by measure. After effervescence, filtering, washing, and drying, the explosive is dropped into the copper cap.

Perfumery.— Directions are given for making the holy incense in Exodus, chapter 30, 1490 B. C. The Scriptures abound with instances of the use of incense and perfumes. Philip Augustus of France granted a charter to the master perfumers in 1190. Perfumes became fashionable in England in the reign of Elizabeth. No such trade as a perfumer was known in Scotland in 1763. A stamp tax was laid on various articles of perfumery in England, and the vender was obliged to take out a license, in 1786. In 1860 there were about forty manufacturing perfumers in London; in Paris about eighty.

Petrified Bodies.— Petrifaction is simply the substitution of the organic substance by the inorganic, atom by atom. As a molecule of wood or bone decays, a molecule of stone takes its place. This can only occur when the air, or earth, or water surrounding the organic substance holds in solution some readily precipitated mineral. In the case of a woody substance, or of bone, while decomposition goes on there yet remains a framework whose interstices are gradually filled by the mineral substance; but in the case of flesh no such framework exists. The very rapid decay of flesh also makes it impossible for the very slow process of petrifaction to have any effect upon it. The stories of petrified bodies found in graveyards, that float periodically through the press, are usually made up of "whole cloth," as the saying is, though it is true that bodies of both men and animals have been found incrusted with silicious substance so as to resemble petrifactions. These, however, when veritable finds, are fleshless skeletons, the soft parts of the body having decayed while the slow process of incrustation was going on. It may be noted here that but one true human bone petrifaction has ever been found, and that is the "Fossil Man of Mentone," discovered in 1873-74. The majority of fossils, be it remembered, are of great age, antedating the existence of man on the earth. In places where the silicious deposits have been rapid, as in limestone caverns, human bones, fossilized, have been discovered. Two human skeletons were found in an apparent state of complete petrifaction on the Island of Guadaloupe early in the present century. One of these was placed in the British Museum, and the other in the museum at Paris. But examination showed that in these the bony structure still remained, though it was completely incased in the calcareous deposits. In excavating in the cavern of Mentone, in France, on the coast of the Mediterranean, some fifteen years ago, M. Rivière, a noted French scientist, found a number of human bones and a complete skeleton in a true fossil condition, which were complete evidence of the existence of men upon the earth at a period of very great antiquity.

Phonograph.—The phonograph is a machine for recording and then transmitting sounds, speech, music, etc. It is the invention of Thomas A. Edison, the most noted electrician of this age. The phonograph was accidentally discovered. Mr. Edison was at work on an apparatus for recording a telegraphic message, by having an armature (with a needle fastened in one end) of the sounder make indentations on a piece of tin foil wrapped around a cylinder. The message would thus be punctured or indented on this tin foil, then, by substituting another needle — blunt — for the sharp one and turning the cylinder, the armature would be vibrated as the needle entered into and passed out of the indentations. While experimenting, he turned the cylinder very rapidly, and instead of a succession of "clicks," a musical sound was produced. He seized the idea, and the Edison phonograph is the result.

The perfected phonograph of to-day consists of a cylinder of wax, or other plastic material, which is revolved either by hand, foot power, or an electric motor. This cylinder, called the phonogram, is used for recording the sound. This is done by a diaphragm — such as is used in a telephone — into the center of which is fastened a sharp needle, which rests upon and just touches the phonogram. When the words are spoken the diaphragm vibrates, moving this needle up and down, and a series of indentations are made in a spiral line on the phonogram, which is turning around about eighty-five times a minute. To make the phonograph speak, or repeat the words, another diaphragm, similar to the first or recorder, but having a blunt instead of a sharp needle, is placed at the starting point and the phonogram made to revolve; of course, as the needle passes over the indentations it vibrates the diaphragm and the words are reproduced, as in a telephone.

The phonograph faithfully reproduces music, whistling, singing, speech, or any sounds, and the phonograms can be packed into a mailing tube and sent all over the world to be used as often as desired.

Phosphorescence is the property which some bodies possess of being luminous in the dark without the emission of sensible heat. There are five kinds distinguished by physicists, and designated as follows: Spontaneous phosphorescence; phosphorescence from the effects of heat; from mechanical action; from the action of electricity; by insolation or exposure to the light of the sun. The first is by far the most common and familiar phenomenon, being exhibited by certain living organisms both in the vegetable and animal kingdoms. There are flowers of a bright red or yellow color which have been observed to emit light flashes in the dark, and other plants which give out a faint, continuous light, caused probably by the oxidation of some hydro-carbon which they secrete. The best known examples, however, are those seen in animals, as the glow-worm or firefly, and the myriads of minute animalcula which cause the magnificent displays of phosphorescence that are often seen at sea by night, especially in the tropics, and in temperate zones during the summer. Various causes have been assigned for this animal phosphorescence, and they doubtless vary with different animals. In the glow-worm and firefly it is thought to be produced by an act of the will. M. Jousset discovered the liquid which exudes from the crushed eggs of the glow-worm to be phosphorescent, and to remain so until dried up. In the marine animalcula, it is believed that a subtle luminous matter is thrown off as a secretion supplied by glands having this special function; and some naturalists assert that it contains epithelial cells in a state of fatty degeneration, the decomposing fat being the cause of the phosphorescence. That phosphorescence seen in decaying fish and other animal matter, and in wood (called "fox-fire"), is due to a species of slow combustion by which vibrations are excited capable of emitting luminous rays. The other kinds of phosphorescence are, for the most part, seen only in scientific experiments, except the last, which is now receiving some application in articles of everyday use, as match boxes, clock-faces, etc.; they are covered with a preparation possessing this property, and remain luminous, and therefore easily visible in the dark. Certain compounds have been discovered which exhibit the property in a high degree, as Canton's phosphorus, Bolognese phosphorus, etc. It is probably due to the absorption of the energy of the vibrations falling upon them, which is afterward radiated from them again. It is probable that all bodies possess the quality in a greater or less degree; but with the great majority the duration of the phenomenon is very short — rarely more than a small fraction of a second. The phenomenon has no connection with ordinary phosphorus, but the name is thence derived from the similar light emitted by phosphorus in the dark, which is due to the slow combustion of this element, which oxidizes at a very low temperature.

Photography.— The action of light on chloride of silver was known as early as the sixteenth century. The phenomenon was studied by Scheele (1777), Senebier (1790), Ritter and Wollaston (1801). From the results of these investigations, experiments were made by Thomas Wedgwood and Humphry Davy, which were published, 1802. Wedgwood may be regarded as the first photographer. His paper was entitled "An Account of a method of copying paintings upon glass, and of making profiles by the agency of light upon nitrate of silver." Further discoveries were made by Niepce in 1814, and by Sir J. Herschel in 1819. Daquewe commenced his experiments in 1824; and in 1826 joined Niepce, and worked with him till the death of the latter in 1833. In 1839, Henry Fox Talbot first published his mode of multiplying photographic impressions, by producing a negative photograph (*i. e.*, with the lights and shades reversed), from which any number of positive copies may be obtained. His patent is dated February, 1841. From this time improvements have been made with great rapidity.

Celestial photography began with Professor Bond, the astronomer, of Cambridge, Mass., in 1851. It was greatly improved by Dr. Draper in 1859 to 1881, and by others more recently.

Photogravure.— The earliest attempt at photographic engraving dates back to 1827, which was six years previous to the introduction of the daguerreotype process, and was the invention of M. Nicephore Niepce of Paris, who first discovered that thin plates of bitumen were curiously affected by light. He therefore coated metal plates with a thin layer of bitumen of the kind called Jew's pitch, and placed them in a *camera obscura*, so arranged that he could insure their exposure to the same image for several hours. The plate was then submitted to the action of oil of spike, which readily dissolved those portions not acted upon by the light, but exerted little action upon the remainder. The metal exposed by the solution of the bitumen was then acted upon by acid, which produced a complete etching plate, the picture part being protected by its bituminous varnish from the action of the acid. The art, which can now be performed by several different methods, is also known by the names of photo-zincography and process-engraving. In ordinary zincography the picture is laid, by the help of transfer paper, on a zinc plate; the parts to be protected are then covered with a varnish that will resist acid, and the whole is then dipped in a bath of dilute nitrous acid. This is repeated until the *biting-in* is sufficient, when the plate is dried and the ink taken off with benzine. In another process brass plates are used, which are covered with white wax, the design being drawn with an etching point upon the wax. The plate is then submitted to a powerful acid, which acts upon the parts of the metal exposed by the lines, but does not affect the wax. In photo-zincography the drawing is photographed to the right size, and an ordinary negative on glass is taken. This is then laid on a sensitized zinc plate, on which the picture is printed by the action of light. The zinc is coated with bitumen, and after the picture is printed, so much of the bitumen as has not become insoluble by the action of light is removed by a wash of turpentine. In another process — the photographic etching process — the negative is printed on a sensitized carbon paper, which is then laid on a polished zinc plate, and, being wet, all the carbon paper that does not hold the lines of the drawing is readily removed. The plate is then *bitten-in* in an acid bath. In what is called the Ives process a negative is applied to a gelatine plate, sensitized with bichromate of potash. This plate is then put into water, and all the parts not touched by the negative will swell. A cast is then taken of this in plaster of paris, which serves to form a base for electrotypes. The lines of engraving can also be reproduced by photography, and a late process produces successfully intaglio plates. Photo-engraving has enormously cheapened the reproduction of pictures, but it does not give plates that print with the clearness and distinctness of those taken from wood engravings.

Physics has been described as a science of unbounded extent, and as reaching from an atom to God himself. It is made to embrace the entire doctrine of the bodies and existences of the Universe: their phenomena, causes, and effects. Lockwood would include God, angels, and spirits under this term. The origin of physics is referred to the Brahmans, magi, and Hebrew and Egyptian priests. From these it was passed to the Greek sages, particularly Thales, who first professed the study of nature in Greece, about 595 B. C. Pythagoras endeavored to explain the philosophy of disease and the action of medicine, about 529 B. C. From him, together with Plato and the Peripatetic Schools, it descended into Italy and the rest of Europe.

Pianoforte.—Invented by Schröter of Dresden, in 1717; he presented a model of his invention to the court of Saxony. Some time after, Silberman, a musical-instrument maker, began to manufacture pianofortes with considerable success. The invention has also been ascribed to Cristofalli, an Italian instrument maker of Florence, and Marius, a Frenchman, early in the eighteenth century. The square pianoforte was first made by Friederici, an organ builder of Saxony, about 1759. Pianofortes were made in London by M. Zumpie, a German, 1766, and have been since greatly improved by Clementi, Broadwood, Collard, Kirkman, Erard, Pleyel, Chickering, Steinway, and others. Upright pianos, first made in the United States, were suggested by Isaac Hawkins, in 1800, and Thomas Loud, in 1802.

Pins are first mentioned in the statutes of England, A. D. 1483. Brass pins were brought from France in 1540, and were first used in England it is said by Catherine Howard, queen of Henry VIII. Before the invention of pins both sexes used ribbons, loop holes, laces with points and tags, clasps, hooks and eyes, and skewers of brass, silver, and gold. Pins were made in England in 1543. They were first manufactured by machinery in 1824, under a patent of Lemuel Wellman Wright of the United States.

Playing-Cards.—The invention of playing-cards has been variously attributed to India, China, Arabia, and Egypt. There seems to be but little doubt that they originated in Asia, and were introduced into Europe by the Saracens about the close of the thirteenth century. There is historical mention of the game of cards in Germany in 1275, in Italy in 1299, but not in France until 1393. An active trade in cards sprung up in Germany as early as the fifteenth century, where they were manufactured for other portions of Europe. One hundred years later we find the manufacture of cards a flourishing business in England, and under Edward IV. their importation was forbidden, thus protecting the home industry. Owing to their supposed immoral influences they were at times prohibited by various European governments. The marks upon the suits of cards are believed to have been chosen to represent symbolically the different classes of society. Thus, the hearts stood for the clergy, clubs for the soldiery, spades for the serfs, and diamonds for the merchants. In the early French cards the kings were pictures of David, Alexander, Cæsar, and Charlemagne, representing the monarchies of the Jews, Greeks, Romans, and French; the queens were Argine, Esther, Judith, and Pallas. The number of the cards, the ace, and the knave, were probably based on similar ideas. The suits of the earliest German cards were designated by hearts, bells, leaves, and acorns. Italian cards had swords, batons, cups, and money. The court cards at first were the king, chevalier, and knave. The queen was first substituted for the chevalier by the Italians. The English cards in the seventeenth century were embellished with heraldic designs, the king of clubs bearing the coat-of-arms of the Pope of Rome, and those of hearts, diamonds, and spades being adorned respectively with the armorial device of the kings of England, Spain, and France. The club of modern cards derived its form from the trefoil, a French design. A pack of Hindustani cards in the possession of the Royal Asiatic Society of England is supposed to be fully 1,000 years old. It consists of eight suits of divers colors. The kings are mounted on elephants; the viziers, or second honors, upon horses, tigers, and bulls; and some of the common cards have such curious marks as a pineapple in a shallow cup, and a something like a parasol without a handle, and with two broken ribs sticking through the top.

Post Offices, Origin of.—The name post office originated in the posts placed at intervals along the roads of the Roman Empire, where carriers were kept in readiness to bear dispatches and intelligence; but the posts of ancient times were never used for the conveyance of private correspondence. The first letter post seems to have been established in the Hanse towns in the early part of the thirteenth century. A line of letter posts followed, connecting Austria with Lombardy, in the reign of the Emperor Maximilian, which are said to have been organized by the princes of Thurn and Taxis; and the representatives of the same house established another line of posts from Vienna to Brussels, connecting the most distant parts of the dominions of Charles V. In England, in early times, both public and private letters were sent by messengers, who, in the reign of Henry III. wore the royal livery. They had to supply themselves with horses until the reign of Edward I., when posts were established where horses were to be had for hire. Camden mentions the office of "Master of the Postes" as existing in 1581, but the duties of that officer were probably connected exclusively with the supply of post horses. A foreign post for the conveyance of letters between London and the Continent seems to have been established by foreign merchants in the fifteenth century; and certain disputes which arose between the Flemings and Italians regarding the right of appointing a postmaster, which were referred to the privy council, led to the institution of a "Chief Postmaster of England," who should have charge both of the English and the foreign posts. Thomas Randolph was the first Chief Postmaster of England, appointed in 1581. In 1635 a mail was established to run weekly between London and Edinburgh, and soon eight other lines were instituted. Far back in the twelfth century the University of Paris, whose students gathered from all the civilized nations, employed foot runners to carry letters for its members to all parts of Europe. But not until 1524 was permission granted to the Royal French posts to carry other letters than those for the Government and the nobility. In the United States, Massachusetts was the first colony to provide by legislation for a postal system. This was done in 1639, and Virginia followed in 1657. In 1762 a monthly post was instituted between Boston and New York. In the beginning, letters arriving in this country from beyond the seas were delivered on board the ship. Letters not called for were left by the captain at a coffee house near the wharf, where they were spread on a table or shelf, awaiting call. These coffee houses gradually grew into common use for letters between cities and the interior, until regular posts were instituted. The establishment of a general post office department was one of the first acts of the Continental Congress, and Benjamin Franklin was appointed as the first Portmaster-General.

Postage Stamps, First.— Postage stamps, in the form of stamped envelopes, were first used by M. de Velayer, who owned a private post in the city of Paris in the reign of Louis XIV. Over a century later, in 1758, M. de Chamouset, also the proprietor of a post, issued printed postage slips to be attached to letters. In Spain, in 1716, and in Italy also, stamped covers for mail matter were tried; but it was not until 1840 that stamps, as we know them now, were put in use. This was in England, the Government adopting the system devised by Rowland Hill. Brazil was the first country to take up the new invention. Russia adopted the postage stamp next, in 1845; then Switzerland, in 1846; and March 3, 1847, the Congress of the United States authorized the issue of postage stamps. These were at first a five-cent stamp and a ten-cent stamp. The reduction of rates in 1851 gave a new set of stamps, valued at one, three, and twelve cents respectively. Other stamps of different values were added from time to time to meet the exigencies of postal arrangements, reduction of postage to foreign countries, etc. Before 1845, the postal rate on letters in the United States varied from six cents for carrying a distance of thirty miles to twenty-five cents for over four hundred miles. By the reduction of that year the postage was made five cents for three hundred miles or less, and ten cents for any distance above that. In 1851 the rate was fixed at three cents for every half ounce for three thousand miles, and six cents for any greater distance within the United States. In 1883 the postage was reduced to two cents for half an ounce for letters sent less than three thousand miles, and in 1885 to two cents an ounce.

Potatoes.— The potato was used as a food in America long before the advent of Europeans, and was probably indigenous from Chili to Mexico. It was taken from Peru to Spain, and thence into the Netherlands, Burgundy, and other parts of Europe early in the sixteenth century. In 1563 or 1565 it was carried from Virginia to Ireland by Sir John Hawkins, and Sir Francis Drake introduced it into England in 1585. Its importance as a vegetable was not recognized, however, until the time of Sir Walter Raleigh, who cultivated it on a considerable scale on his estates in the County of Cork, Ireland. Through the exertions of Raleigh it was developed in quality and popularized as food to such an extent in Ireland that its cultivation spread into England, where it became known as the "Irish potato." The potato mentioned by early English writers before the seventeenth century was the same as the Spanish batatas, or sweet potato.

Printing Crockery.—Common crockery, when it is in the state called biscuit ware— that is, when it has been whitened by baking but has not been glazed—is figured upon or decorated by applying to its surface a design freshly printed upon paper. The ware absorbs the enamel ink, and the paper is removed by water. It is then fired in seggars, or a muffle, to fix the color, dipped in glaze, and then again fired, which converts the glaze into a perfectly transparent glassy covering all over the surface of the pottery. Porcelain decoration has long held a righ rank as a fine art; and the exquisite skill shown in some of the finest works of the continental manufacturers, and also in those of Great Britain, has fairly entitled it to that rank. The colors employed are all colored glasses ground to impalpable powder, and mixed with borax, or some other fluxing material; for use they are generally made liquid with oil of spike, and they are laid on with hair pencils in the same way as oil colors. The whole process is exactly the same as in painting or staining glass, the glaze on the biscuit porcelain being true glass, and the enamel colors being exactly the same as those used by the glass decorator. Peculiar and beautiful metallic lusters are produced upon pottery by precipitated platinum and other metals. The manufacture of pottery is carried on with great activity at Trenton, N. J., Philadelphia, Liverpool (in Ohio), and other places in the United States.

Printing in America.—Printing was introduced into America at Mexico by the Viceroy Mendoza in 1536. The first book printed was the *Escala espiritual de San Juan Climaco*, of which no copy is known to exist; but the oldest American book now extant is the *Manual de Adultos*, dated 1540, of which only the last four leaves are to be found in the library of the Cathedral of Toledo. The name of the earliest printer is a matter of question.

Cambridge, Massachusetts, is entitled to the distinction of having the first printing press in North America, which was under the charge of Stephen Daye. For this press the colony was mainly indebted to the Rev. Jesse Glover, a nonconformist minister possessed of a considerable estate, who had left England to settle among his friends in Massachusetts. Some gentlemen of Amsterdam also "gave towards furnishing of a printing press with letters, forty-nine pounds and something more." This was about 1638. The first book issued was the *Bay Psalm Book*, in 1640.

The first book issued in the Middle Colonies was an almanac, printed by William Bradford in 1685, near Philadelphia. Bradford was brought out from England in 1684 by William Penn. As the government of Pennsylvania became very restrictive in regard to the press, Bradford in 1693 removed to New York, and was appointed printer to that colony, where he established, in 1725, the *New York Gazette*, the first newspaper published there. He died May 23, 1752, after an active and useful life of eighty-nine years.

The first newspaper in America was the *Boston News Letter*, which was first issued by John Campbell on Monday, April 24, 1704; it was regularly published for nearly seventy-two years. The second was the *Boston Gazette*, begun December 21, 1719. The third was the *American Weekly Mercury*, issued in Philadelphia, by Andrew Bradford, on December 22, 1719. James Franklin, an elder brother of Benjamin, established the *New England Courant*, August 17, 1721.

The oldest living paper of the United States is the *New Hampshire Gazette*, published at Portsmouth, New Hampshire, and founded in the year 1756.

The *North American and United States Gazette* leads the existing daily press of this country in point of antiquity. It is the successor of the *Pennsylvania Packet* (begun in 1771 and becoming a daily paper in 1784), and is still the chief commercial journal of Philadelphia.

The first paper mill in America was established near Germantown, Pa., in 1690, by William Rittenhouse.

Ptolemaic System, The.—Ptolemy of Alexandria (A. D. 130-150) was the founder of a theory called the Ptolemaic system, based largely upon the materials gathered by previous astronomers, such as Hipparchus, already mentioned, and Eratosthenes, who computed the size of the earth by means even now considered the best—the measurement of an arc of the meridian. The advocates of the Ptolemaic theory assumed that every planet revolves in a circle, and that the earth is the fixed center around which the sun and the heavenly bodies move. They conceived that a bar, or something equivalent, is connected at one end with the earth; that at some part of this bar the sun is attached; while between that and the earth, Venus is fastened, not to the bar directly, but to a sort of crank; and farther on, Mercury is hitched on in the same way. They did not fully understand the nature of these bars—whether they were real or only imaginary—but they did comprehend their action, as they thought; and so they supposed the bar revolved, carrying the sun and planets along in a large circle about the earth; while all the short cranks kept flying around, thus sweeping each planet through a smaller circle.

The movements of the planets were to the ancients extremely complex. Venus, for instance, was sometimes seen as "evening star" in the west; and then again as "morning star" in the east. Sometimes she seemed to be moving in the same direction as the sun, then, going apparently behind the sun, she appeared to pass on again in a course directly opposite. At one time she would recede from the sun more and more slowly and coyly, until she would appear to be entirely stationary; then she would retrace her steps, and seem to meet the sun. All these facts were attempted to be accounted for by an incongruous system of "cycles and epicycles."

The system of Ptolemy passed current for 1400 years, and during this time astrology was ranked as one of the most important branches of knowledge. Star diviners were held in the greatest estimation, and the issue of any important undertaking, or the fortune of an individual, was foretold by means of horoscopes representing the position of the stars and planets. The system of the astrologers was very complicated, and contained regular rules to guide the interpretation, so intricate that years of study were required for their mastery. Venus foretold love; Mars, war; the Pleiades, storms at sea. Not only the ignorant were the dupes of this system, Lord Bacon believing in it most firmly.

Pulley.— The pulley, together with the vise, and other mechanical instruments, is said to have been invented by Archytas of Tarentum, a disciple of Pythagoras, about 516 B. C. Ctesibius of Alexandria, architect and mechanic, is said to have invented the pump, with other hydraulic instruments, about 224 B. C., although the invention was ascribed to Danaus, 1485 B. C. They were in general use in England, A. D. 1425. The air pump was invented by Otto Guericke in 1654, and was improved by Boyle in 1657.

Rainbow.— A rainbow can only be seen when the spectator stands between it and the sun; its center must always be directly opposite the sun, moving with the sun's motion, falling if the sun is rising, and rising if the sun is declining. A rainbow occurs when the sun or moon, not too far above the horizon, throws its beams upon a sheet of falling rain-drops on the opposite side of the heavens. Thus, a ray of light from the sun strikes a rain-drop obliquely; part of it is reflected at the surface of the drop; the rest, passing into the drop, is refracted; on the other side of the drop part of the ray passes through, and the rest is again reflected; on passing from the drop on the same side that it entered, a second refraction occurs. These successive reflections and refractions separate the ray of white light into its component colored rays, and as the angles of incidence and emergence vary for each color, the eye of a spectator perceives them as distinct bands. Now, every drop in the sheet of falling water which has equal obliquity to the spectator's eye will send to it rays of the same color. But the only drops which can fulfill these conditions of like obliquity of reflected rays are those which define the base of a cone whose apex is the eye, and the center of whose base is in a right line passing through the sun and the eye of the spectator. At or near sunset, when the sun and the observer are in the same horizontal plane, the bow will be seen to form a complete semicircle; when the sun is higher in the sky, a smaller arch is seen; the entire circle could only be visible to a spectator on the top of a very high and narrow mountain peak, which would elevate his plane much above that of the sun's rays without cutting off their light. A complete circle may also be sometimes seen in the rainbow formed by the sunlight on the spray arising from cataracts. The lunar rainbow, which is a comparatively rare but very beautiful phenŏmenon, differs from the solar simply in the source and intensity of the light by which it is produced; and, as in all cases of feeble light, the distinction of the colors is very difficult. In fact, except under the most favorable circumstances, the lunar rainbows rarely show colors at all, giving a pale, ghostly gleam of apparently white or yellow light.

Reaper, First in the United States. — In 1803 a reaping machine was patented by Richard French and John J. Hawkins, but it did not prove successful. Prior to 1832 there were granted eight patents for machines for cutting grain. No inventor, however, succeeded in producing machines that possessed sufficient practical merit to be used otherwise than experimentally until we come to Bell, Hussey, and McCormick, whose machines have since become so well known. At the meeting of the British Association at Dundee, September, 1867, the Reverend Patrick Bell stated that he invented his reaping machine in 1826. McCormick's American machine was patented in 1834, and, with improvements added in 1845 and 1847, received a medal at the World's Fair in London, 1851. In 1833, Obed Hussey, then of Cincinnati, Ohio, patented a machine to which he applied saw-toothed cutters and guards. This machine was at once put into practical operation, and gave general satisfaction. Hussey, in 1847, patented the open-topped slotted finger. The practical use of self-rakers, in this country, dates from the invention of W. H. Seymour of New York, in 1851. He arranged a quadrant-shaped platform directly behind the cutters, a reel to gather the grain, and a rake moving over the platform in the arc of a circle depositing the sheaves on the ground. In 1856, Owen Dorsey of Maryland combined the reel and rake, and his improvement has been extensively used here and abroad, with some modifications, one of which was by Johnston in 1865, who arranged it so that the size of the sheaves, or gavels, as they are called, could be regulated at the will of the driver. The names of Haines, Ketchum, Manny, and Wood are prominent among inventors of improvements in mowers and harvesters.

Saddles.— Pliny informs us that one Pelethronus was the first to introduce a piece of leather fastened to the back of a horse for the accommodation of its rider. For a long time these cloths and pieces of leather were regarded as unmanly, and were consequently treated by soldiers with great scorn. The old German races despised the Roman cavalry for riding on such effeminate contrivances. Saddles of the kind now used appear to have been in use in 385. Side-saddles were first used in 1380. Previous to their introduction women always rode astride.

Salt, Sources of.— At one time nearly the whole of the salt used as food and for industrial purposes was obtained from sea-water, and in many countries where the climate is dry and warm and there is a convenient seaboard, large quantities are still so obtained. In Portugal more than 250,000 tons are annually produced, and about the same quantity is obtained on the Atlantic and Mediterranean coasts of France. Spain has salt-works in the Balearic Islands, the Bay of Cadiz, and elsewhere, which turn out annually 300,000 tons; and even the small Adriatic seaboard of Austria produces every year from 70,000 to 100,000 tons. The peninsula and islands of Italy yield about 165,000 tons, and there are still a few establishments in England and Scotland; but in these latter countries the industry has been almost entirely driven out by the rock-salt works. The salt obtained from this source is called "sea" or "bay" salt. The works are generally called salt gardens — *salina* (Spanish) — *salz garten*, in Austria. They consist of a series of large, shallow evaporating reservoirs. The sea water is admitted, and flows slowly from one to another, all the while evaporating under the heat of the sun, until finally the dry salt remains in crystalline crusts on the salting-tables in the final basins. These reservoirs vary from ten to sixteen inches in depth, the sediment and many of the impurities being deposited in the earlier and deeper basins in the first stages of evaporation. Between the temperatures of 25 and 26 degrees (Baumé) pure salt is deposited, equal to about twenty-five per cent. of the whole. This is kept pure by conducting the brine to separate salting-tables at this temperature, and, after it reaches 26 degrees, carrying it on to other basins, where a second quality, equal to about sixty per cent. of the whole, is formed. After the brine reaches 28.5 degrees it is led into still other basins, where the remainder of the salt is deposited. The salt is raked up and sold just as it is formed, with the slight purification resulting from a few months' exposure to the weather, which is customary. The evaporating surface of these shallow basins covers, in many establishments, hundreds of acres. Those at Berre, on the Mediterranean, have an area of 815 acres. Sea-salt has been obtained in this way in many of the seaboard States of the United States, but not to any extent. The other great source of common salt is the vast mineral deposits. Salt also occurs as a mineral in an almost pure state, and associated with the rocks of almost every geologic period. Many of the deposits are of vast extent, and are another great commercial source of this substance. This mineral deposit is called rock-salt, and is evidently the result of the evaporation of great shallow bodies of salt-water in remote ages, as is proved by its generally stratified nature, with beds of clay intervening, and the occurrence of marine shells and fossils in the surrounding rock formation. Large mines are worked in England and all the European countries, and in many places throughout the world. The most famous of all is the mine at Williczka, nine miles from Cracow, in Galicia, which has been worked continuously for upward of six hundred years. It is stopped-out in longitudinal and transverse galleries, with frequent large vaulted chambers supported by massive pillars. These extend on four different levels, and have a total length of 30 miles, the mine being 1 mile 1,279 yards long by 830 yards wide and 284 yards deep. The lower levels contain streets and houses, constituting a complete village; and many of the miners, of whom there are 800 to 1,000, rarely come above ground. The salt is sold just as it is dug out of the mine, and 55,067 tons are annually extracted. The total extent of this deposit is 500 by 200 miles, with an average depth of 1,200 feet. Salt is also obtained in many localities from mineral deposits by means of salt-wells. In some cases the water occurs naturally in the salt strata, and the saturated brine is reached by deep borings (sometimes 1,500 feet); in other cases water is introduced into the borings and then pumped out again, two concentric tubes being employed. After the brine is secured it is evaporated by artificial heat in large iron vats. The salt-wells in Onondaga County, New York, near Syracuse and Salina, are a large and important industry. Michigan has the largest output next to New York, and many other States produce it to some extent: but the home supply is not equal to the demand, and there is a large annual importation into the United States.

Saw.— Invented by Dædalus. Talus, it is said, having found the jaw bone of a snake, employed it to cut through a piece of wood, and then formed an instrument of iron like it. Sawmills were erected in Madeira in 1420; at Breslau in 1427. Norway had the first sawmill in 1530. The attempts to introduce sawmills in England were violently opposed, and one erected by a Dutchman in 1663 was forced to be abandoned. Sawmills were erected near London about 1770, and thenceforward became general.

Screw Propeller, The.—In 1802 Dr. Shorter, an English mechanician, produced motion by the agency of a screw; but his discovery was of no value at the time, as the steam engine had not then been applied to navigation. In 1832, Mr. B. Woodcroft patented a screw propeller with an increasing pitch; and four years later Mr. F. P. Smith patented a screw making two whole turns, which he reduced in 1839 to one whole turn. In 1837 he and Captain Ericsson brought the matter practically forward on the Thames, where a small screw steamer, forty-five feet long, eight feet broad, and of twenty-seven inches draught, towed a vessel of six hundred and thirty tons against the tide at four and one half knots an hour. This experiment was followed by a number of others, some undertaken under the direction of the British Admiralty, which clearly established the practicability of the screw, and its advantages for ships of war became incontestable. From the entire submergence of the propeller, and the consequent lowness of its engines in the ship, the chances of injury from an enemy's shot were reduced almost to nothing. The screw propeller is of the same construction as the common screw, but with the narrow thread exaggerated into a broad, thin plate, and the cylinder diminished to a mere spindle. If a screw of this form were turned round in an unyielding substance, as wood, it would for each turn advance as much as the center of the blade (or thread) had moved along the spindle in forming the screw, *i. e.*, the distance. If, on the other hand, the screw itself were prevented from moving longitudinally, and the piece of wood *not* fixed, the latter would be compelled to advance along the screw the same distance. When the screw is fixed beneath a ship and made to revolve in the water, the case lies between the two just supposed — the screw moves forward, and with it the ship, and the water in which it has been working moves backward. The backward motion should only be small proportionately, and the ratio between it and the sum of the backward motion of the water and the forward motion of the ship is called the slip. Screws have been formed with two, three, four, and six blades, or arms; but the form most commonly used is two blades for ships of war, and three or four blades in the merchant service.

Ship Building.—This art is attributed to the Egyptians, as the first inventors; the first ship (probably galley) being brought from Egypt to Greece by Danaus, in 1485 B. C. The first double-decked ship was built by the Tyrians, 786 B. C. The first double-decked one built in England was by order of Henry VII., 1509. It was called the Great Harry and cost 14,000 pounds. Portholes and other improvements were invented by Descharges, a French builder at Brest, in the reign of Louis XII., about 1500. Ship building was first treated as a science by Hoste, 1696. Iron is now greatly used in ship building. For beautiful models and fast sailing, the shipping of the United States (especially the packet ships and steamers sailing from New York) is not surpassed, and probably not equaled, by that of any other nation in the world.

Signals, Wind and Weather.— A red flag with a black center indicates that a storm of marked violence is expected. A yellow flag with a white center indicates that the winds expected will not be of extreme severity. A red pennant indicates easterly winds — that is, from northeast to south, inclusive, and that, generally, the storm center is approaching. If shown above the red flag, winds from the northeast are more probable; if below, winds from the southeast may be expected. A white pennant indicates westerly winds — that is, from north to southwest, inclusive, and that, generally, the storm center has passed. If shown above the red flag, winds from northwest will probably prevail; if below, winds from southwest. A white flag indicates fair weather. A blue flag indicates rain or snow. A black triangular flag refers to temperature; when placed above the white or blue flag it indicates warmer weather; and when placed below them, colder weather. A white flag with black square in center indicates the approach of a sudden and decided fall in temperature, and is usually ordered at least twenty-four hours in advance of a cold wave. When displayed on poles, the signals are arranged to read downward; when displayed from horizontal supports, a small streamer is attached to indicate the point from which the signals are to be read.

Silkworm.— It is the general belief that the great importance of the silkworm was first discovered by Se-ling, the wife of the Chinese Emperior Hoangti, who reigned about 2637 B. C., and that she also invented and taught the art of silk-spinning and weaving. The worms are exceedingly tender, and liable to perish from the slightest changes of temperature and dampness. They feed upon the leaves of various trees and bushes, but experiments go to show that the best silk is produced when the worm is fed upon mulberry leaves. The great centers of this industry are China, Japan, India, and Southern Europe, and they have been successfully raised in California, Ohio, Kansas, East Tennessee, Northern Georgia, Kentucky, and in some parts of New Jersey.

Soap is a salt, a compound of fatty acid with an alkali, soda, or potash. The Hebrew borith, translated soap, is merely a general term for cleaning substances. Pliny declares soap to be an invention of the Gauls, though he preferred the German to the Gallic soap. In remote periods clothes were cleansed by being rubbed or stamped upon in water. Homer tells us that Nausicaa and her attendants washed clothes by treading upon them with their feet in pits of water. The Roman's used fuller's earth. Savon, the French word for soap, is ascribed to its having been manufactured at Savona, near Genoa. The manufacture of soap began in London in 1524, before which time it was supplied by Bristol at one penny per pound.

Soaps, Natural.— From time immemorial the Egyptian soaproot and the Spanish soaproot have been employed for washing in Southern Europe and Egypt, and are, to some extent, exported for use in cleansing fine articles. In the West Indies and South America, a pulpy fruit, which grows on a tree known as the soap-tree, is said to have such cleansing properties that it will clean as much linen as sixty times its weight of manufactured soap. There is also a tree in Peru, *Quillaja Saponaria*, whose bark, in infusion, yields a soapy liquid much valued for washing woolens, and is largely imported to England and other countries for this purpose. The juice of the soapwort, or, as it is commonly called in the United States and Great Britain, the "Bouncing Bet," strongly possesses the saponaceous qualities. In California the roots of the *Phelangium Pomaridianum*, which grows there abundantly, are much used for washing. This plant has a strong odor of brown soap in its leaves and stems, as well as the roots. The South Sea Islands and the islands of the Caribbean Sea also produce plants which are used as soap substitutes.

Solar System, The.— So named from *sol* (Latin), the sun, consists of the sun in the center, numerous planets, and an unknown number of bodies named comets. The word planet is from the Greek *planao*, to wander, because the few such bodies known to the ancients were chiefly remarkable in their eyes on account of their constantly shifting their places with reference to the other luminaries of the sky. Comets are so named from *coma* (Latin), a head of hair, because they seem to consist of a bright spot, with a long brush streaming behind.

Some of the planets have other planets moving round them as centers — the moon, for instance, round the earth. These are called secondary planets, moons, or satellites; while those that move round the sun are called primary planets. The primary planets consist — 1st, of eight larger planets, including the Earth; their names, in the order of their nearness to the sun, are — Mercury, Venus, the Earth, Mars, Jupiter, Saturn, Herschel or Uranus, and Neptune. 2d. A group of small planets or planetoids, called also asteroids, considerable in number. The discovery of a new asteroid by Professor Borelli, places the entire number of planets in the solar system at one hundred and eighteen, against six known in 1781, when Sir W. Herschel discovered Uranus.

The planets move round the sun on nearly one level or plane, corresponding with the center of his body, and in one direction, from west to east. The secondary planets, in like manner, move in planes round the centers of their primaries, and in the same direction, from west to east. These are denominated revolutionary motions; and it is to be observed that they are double in the case of the satellites, which have at once a revolution round the primary, and a revolution, in company with the primary, round the sun. The path described by a planet in its revolution is called its orbit.

Each planet, secondary as well as primary, and the sun also, has a motion in its own body, like that of a bobbin upon a spindle. An imaginary line, forming, as it were, the spindle of the sun or planet, is denominated the axis, and the two extremities of the axis are called the poles. The axes of the sun and planets are all nearly at a right angle with the plane of the revolutionary movements. The motion on the axis is called the rotary motion, from *rota*, the Latin for a wheel. The sun, the primary planets, and the satellites, with the doubtful exception of two attending on Uranus, move on their axes in the same direction as the revolutionary movements, from west to east.

NAME.	Mean Distance From Earth in Millions of Miles.	Mean Distance From Sun, Millions of Miles.	Sidereal Period, Days.	Orbit Velocity, Miles per Second.	Mean Diameter, Miles.
Sun.....	92.9	....	....	....	866,400
Mercury	56.9	36.0	87.969	23 to 35	3,030
Venus...	25.7	67.2	224.701	21.9	7,700
Earth...	....	92.9	365.256	18.5	7,918
Mars....	48.6	141.5	686.950	15.0	4,230
Jupiter.	390.4	483.3	4,332.58	8.1	86,500
Saturn..	793.2	886.0	10,759.22	6.0	71,000
Uranus..	1,689.0	1,781.9	30,686.82	4.2	31,900
Neptune	2,698.8	2,791.6	60,181.11	3.4	31,800

The number of asteroids discovered up to present dates is 330. A number of these small planets have not been observed since their discovery, and are practically lost. Consequently it is now sometimes a matter of doubt, until the elements have been computed, if the supposed new planet is really new, or only an old one rediscovered.

It is supposed that *a* Centauri, one of the brightest stars of the Southern Hemisphere, is the nearest of the fixed stars to the earth. The researches on its parallax by Henderson and Maclear gave it for its distance from the earth, in round numbers, 20,000,000,000,000 of miles. At the inconceivably rapid rate at which light is propagated through space, it would require three years and three months to reach the earth from this star.

Some Interesting Dates.— FRUITS, FLOWERS, ETC.— The cherry dates back to A. D. 100; the lily, 800; jasmine, 1500; mulberry, 1520; mignonette, 1528; the plum, 1530; geranium, 1534; gooseberry, 1540; melons, 1540; hyssop, 1548; pomegranate, 1548; lemon, 1554; peach, 1562; carnation, 1567; pink, 1567; lavender, 1568; pineapple, 1568; quince, 1573; tulip, 1578; oleander, 1600; Virginia creeper, 1629; black walnut, 1629; hickory nut, 1640; nectarine, 1652; honeysuckle, 1656; sassafras, 1663; hawthorn, 1683; passion flower, 1692; raspberry, 1696; foxglove, 1696; currant, 1705; snowdrop, 1756; chrysanthemum, 1790; dahlia, 1803; camellia, 1811; petunia, 1823; verbena, 1827; fuchsia, 1835.

FOODS AND COOKERY.— Forks first used, 1220; sugar in Europe, 1250; first English cook book, 1498; cabbages, 1510; turkeys, 1523; guinea fowl, 1540; potatoes, 1565; cauliflower, 1603; tea, 1610; cattle imported to America, 1611; coffee, 1616; bread made with yeast, 1634; rice, 1690; celery, 1704; ice cream, 1760; United States fish culture, 1804; Liebig's extract, 1847; condensed milk, 1849; food adulteration act, 1854; aërated bread, 1856; cooking schools, 1873.

FUEL AND LIGHT.— Wood fuel, prehistoric; charcoal, B. C. 1800; oil lamps, B. C. 1000; wax candles, B. C. 200; peat, B. C. 60; rush lights, A. D. 1300; coal gas, 1739; Davy's safety lamp, 1802; sperm candles, 1811; paraffine, 1825; petroleum, 1859; natural gas, 1870; water gas, 1873; electric heating, 1876; incandescent electric light, 1878.

THE WORLD'S CLOTHING.— Spinning and weaving and dyeing are prehistoric. The *peplon*, or long cloak, was worn in Greece, B. C. 600; Tyrian purple dye used, B. C. 600-300; Roman toga worn, B. C. 250-A. D. 100; breeches worn by the Scythians, B. C. 550; kilts and trews worn by the Celts, B. C. 100; figured weaving in Italy, A. D. 100-1000; Dutch and Flemish weaving, A. D. 1100; silk weaving at Palermo, A. D. 1146; linen cloth made in England, 1253; English wool trade flourished from A. D. 1337; Brabant looms brought to England, 1340; linen shirts in common use, 1560; silkworms brought to France, 1600; felt in common use, 1610; fly shuttles, 1738; calico printing, 1764; spinning jenny, 1767; carding machine, 1770; mule, 1779; power loom, 1785; cotton gin, 1791; shoddy, 1813; sewing machine, 1841; silkworm disease, 1854; rubber coats, 1875; electric looms, 1889.

Specific Gravity of Substances.— A gallon of water or wine weighs 10 lbs., and this is taken as the basis of the following table:—

LIQUIDS.		TIMBER.		METALS.	
Water	100	Cork	24	Zinc	719
Sea Water	103	Poplar	38	Cast iron	721
Dead Sea	124	Fir	55	Tin	729
Alcohol	84	Cedar	61	Bar iron	779
Olive oil	92	Pear	66	Steel	783
Turpentine	99	Walnut	67	Brass	840
Wine	100	Cherry	72	Copper	895
Urine	101	Maple	75	Silver	1,051
Cider	102	Ash	84	Lead	1,135
Beer	102	Apple	79	Mercury	1,357
Woman's milk	102	Beech	85	Gold	1,926
Cow's milk	103	Mahogany	106	Platina	2,150
Goat's milk	104	Oak	117		
Porter	104	Ebony	133		
PRECIOUS STONES.					
Emerald	277.5	Diamond	353.0	Garnet	406.3
Crystal	265.3	Topaz	401.1	Ruby	428.3
SUNDRIES.					
Indigo	77	Peat	133	Porcelain	226
Ice	92	Opium	134	Stone	252
Gunpowder	93	Honey	145	Marble	270
Butter	94	Ivory	183	Granite	278
Clay	120	Brick	200	Chalk	279
Coal	130	Sulphur	203	Glass	289

SELECTED WEIGHTS.

	Lbs. per Cub. Ft.		Lbs. per Cub. Ft.		Lbs. per Cub. Ft.
Cork	15	Oak	70	Iron	470
Cedar	36	Clay	72	Copper	520
Beech	51	Coal	80	Silver	630
Butter	56	Brick	120	Lead	712
Water	62	Stone	150	Gold	1,203
Mahogany	66	Granite	166		
Coke	70	Glass	172		

Spectacles and Reading Glasses were unknown to the ancients. They are generally supposed to have been invented in the thirteenth century by Alexander de Spina, a monk of Florence in Italy, about A. D. 1285. According to Dr. Plott they were invented by Roger Bacon, about 1280. Manni attributes them to Salvino, who died in 1317.

Spinning Wheel.— The invention of the art of spinning was ascribed by the ancients to Minerva, the Goddess of Wisdom. It is said that Arcas, the King of Arcadia, taught his subjects the art about 1500 B. C. The use of the spindle and distaff, however, was known in Egypt even earlier than this, as is shown by pictures upon Egyptian monuments. The distaff was a simple stick, around which the fiber was coiled, and was held in the left hand. The spindle was a species of top, which was set in motion by a twirl of the hand and by combining its rotary motion with a gradual movement away from the spinner. The size of the fiber was equalized by passing it between the finger and thumb of the right hand until the motion of the spindle was exhausted, when the thread was wound around it, and the process was repeated. The improvement upon this method by placing the spindle in a frame, and making it revolve by mechanical action of the hand or foot in connection with a wheel and treadle, constituted the spinning wheel, which, though probably in use long before, cannot be traced farther back than A. D. 1530. The spinning jenny, a machine of eight spindles, was first invented in 1767, and subsequent to that time many improvements in spinning by machinery have been made.

Sponges and Sponge Fishing.— Sponges belong to the very lowest order of animal life, and are attached like plants to rocks, or similar substances. Those fit for use are found generally in the seas of warm climates. They consist of a framework, which is sometimes of an elastic fibrous substance, and sometimes is made up of an aggregation of hard, siliceous spicules. A sponge, when fixed to a rock, increases in size by a regular process of growth. To free them from the jelly-like animal matter which they contain when first brought, they are buried for some days in the sand, and are then soaked and washed. In the Turkish sponge fisheries the sponge is obtained by diving, and the diver guides himself beneath the water with a stone, to which a cord from the boat is attached. The best sponges are obtained from eight to ten fathoms below the surface of the water. In the Greek sponge fisheries of the Morea, and on the Bahama Islands, a pronged fork at the end of a long pole is used to detach the sponges from the rocks below. Two species are found in the Levant, another on the Bahamas, and still another on the coasts of Florida and Mexico.

Spontaneous Combustion may be defined as the ignition of inflammable bodies without the application of flame, or without obvious cause of increase of temperature, and arises from the well-understood liability of certain bodies to undergo chemical changes which develop sufficient heat to set them on fire. Recently expressed fixed oils are particularly disposed to oxidize when exposed to light and air. They then absorb oxygen, and give out carbonic acid and hydrogen. If the process goes on rapidly, as it usually does when the oil is diffused through light inflammable substances, as cotton, tow, the waste used in lubricating machinery, oatmeal, etc., the heat may be sufficient to set them on fire. Bituminous coal lying in large heaps is liable to be ignited by the heat evolved in the decomposition of the sulphuret of iron which it commonly contains. The rapid absorption of water by quicklime is also attended with development of heat sufficient to ignite combustible bodies in contact with the lime. Strong nitric acid will act on straw, hay, and such bodies, so as to render them spontaneously combustible.

Stars, The.— The idea at which astronomers have arrived respecting the stars, is, that they are all of them suns, resembling our own, but diminished to the appearance of mere specks of light by the great distance at which they are placed. As a necessary consequence to this supposition, it may be presumed that they are centers of light and heat to systems of revolving planets, each of which may be further presumed to be the theater of forms of beings bearing some analogy to those which exist upon earth.

The stars seen by the naked eye on a clear night are about two thousand in number. This, allowing a like number for the half of the sky not seen, gives about four thousand, in all, of visible stars. These are of different degrees of brilliancy, probably in the main in proportion to their respective distances from our system, but also, perhaps, in some measure in proportion to their respective actual sizes. Astronomers class the stars under different magnitudes, not with regard to apparent size, for none of them present a measurable disc, but with a regard to the various quantities of light flowing round them; thus, there are stars of the first magnitude, the second magnitude, and so on. Only six or seven varieties of magnitude are within our natural vision; but with the telescope vast numbers of more distant stars are brought into view; and the magnitudes are now extended by astronomers to at least sixteen.

Steam Engines.— The application of steam as a moving power is claimed by various nations, but the first extensive employment of it, and most of the improvements made upon the steam engine, the world indisputably owes to the English and the Americans. It would appear that as early as 1543 a Spanish captain named Blasco de Garay showed in the harbor of Barcelona a steamboat of his own invention. It is most likely that Blasco's engine was on the principle of the Æolipile of Hero, invented 130 B. C., in which steam produces rotatory motion by issuing from orifices as water does in Barker's mill. The preacher Mathesius, in his sermon to miners in Nuremberg in 1562, prays for a man who "raises water from fire and air," showing the early application of steam power in Germany. An Italian engineer, G. Branca, invented in 1629 a sort of steam windmill, the steam being generated in a boiler, which was directed by a spout against the flat vanes of a wheel, which was thus set in motion. In England, among the first notices we have of the idea of employing steam as a propelling force is one contained in a small volume, published in 1647, entitled "The Art of Gunnery," by Nat. Nye, mathematician, in which he purposes to "charge a piece of ordnance without gunpowder" by putting in water instead of powder, ramming down an air-tight plug of wood and then the shot, and applying a fire to the breech "till it burst out suddenly." But the first successful effort was that of the Marquis of Worcester. In his "Century of Inventions," the manuscript of which dates from 1655, he describes a steam apparatus by which he raised a column of water to the height of forty feet. This, under the name of "Fire Waterwork," appears actually to have been at work at Vauxhall in 1656. The first patent for the application of steam power to various kinds of machines was taken out in 1698 by Captain Savery. In 1699 he exhibited before the Royal Society a working model of his invention. His engines were the first used to any extent in industrial operations. In all the attempts at pumping engines hitherto made, including Savery's, the steam acted directly upon the water to be moved, without any intervening part. To Dr. Papin, a celebrated Frenchman, is due the idea of the piston. It was first used by him in a model constructed in 1690. The next great step in advance was made in 1705, in the "atmospheric engine," conjointly invented by Newcomen, Cawley, and Savery. This machine held its own for nearly seventy years, and was very largely applied to mines. The next essential improvements on the steam engine were those of Watt, which began a new era in the history of steam-power. His first and most important improvement was the separate condenser, patented in 1769. He had observed that the jet of cold water thrown into the cylinder to condense the steam necessarily reduced the temperature of the cylinder so much that a great deal of the steam flowing in at each upward stroke of the piston was condensed before the cylinder got back the heat abstracted from it by the spurt of cold water used for condensing the steam in the cylinder. The loss of steam arising from this was so great that only about one fourth of what was admitted into the cylinder was actually available as motive power. This difficulty was overcome by Watt's invention. The principal improvements that have been made since Watt's time have been either in matters relating to the boiler, in details of construction consequent upon our increased facilities, improved machinery, and greater knowledge of the strength of materials, in the enlarged application of his principle of expansive working, or in the application of the steam engine to the propulsion of carriages and vessels.

Steel, Manufacture of.—Steel, which is a compound of iron and carbon, was used by the Egyptians, Assyrians, and Greeks. The oldest method of making it is the pot-steel process, which consists at first in melting wrought iron with carbon in clay crucibles, and this process is still used to some extent. The direct process of making steel by immersing malleable iron in a bath of cast-iron was first invented in 1722 by Reaumur. Improvements in this manufacture were made in the early part of this century by Mushat and Lucas, and the eminent metallurgist, Heath, first successfully melted the ingredients of cast steel on the open hearth of the reverberatory furnace about 1839. He patented his process in 1845, but it was not regarded as successful until practical conditions were furnished for it by the invention of the Siemens regenerative gas-furnace in 1862. By the Bessemer process, which was first patented in 1855, and which is now the most generally used, twenty tons of crude iron have been converted into cast steel in twenty-three minutes. Sir Henry Bessemer has received in royalty on this process some $10,000,000. The manufacture of steel has been carried to the highest perfection in the United States, and the output of American steel works is about 600,000 tons yearly.

Steel Pens, Invention of.— During the last century many efforts were made to improve the quill pen, the great defect of which was its speedy injury from use, and the consequent trouble of frequent mending. These efforts were chiefly directed to fitting small metal, or even ruby, points to the nib of the quill pen; but the delicacy of fitting was so great that but very little success attended the experiments. At the beginning of this century pens began to be made wholly of metal. They consisted of a barrel of very thin steel, and were cut and slit so as to resemble the quill pen as closely as possible. They were, however, very indifferent, and, being dear, they made but little way. Their chief fault was hardness, which produced a disagreeable scratching on the paper. In 1820 Joseph Gillott perfected the present form of steel pens and began their manufacture at Birmingham, England. The first gross of steel pens ever sold at wholesale were sold for $36, in 1820, at Birmingham. In 1830 the price was $2; in 1832, $1.50; in 1860, 12 cents; while an article as good as those manufactured in 1820 was sold at 4 cents. The annual production of steel pens in Birmingham alone ranges from 8,000,000 to 15,000,000 gross.

Stenography.— The art of writing in shorthand is said to have been practiced by the ancients. It is said to have followed from the hieroglyphics of the Egyptians. It is also attributed to the poet Ennius, to Tyro, and still more to Seneca. The Ars Scribendi Characteris, written about 1412, is the oldest system extant. Dr. Timothy Bright's "Characterie, or the art of short, swift, and secret writing," published in 1588, is the first English work on shorthand. Peter Bales, the famous penman, wrote on stenography in 1590. There are now numerous systems of it, many of them of easy acquirement and great simplicity. Byrom's system was invented, 1767; Guerney's, 1710; Mason's, 1750; Taylor's, 1786; Mavor's, 1789; Pitman's (phonographic), 1837.

Stereotyping.— The *papier-maché* process, which is the most general, was first used in France in 1848. It is extremely simple. The types being set, corrected, made into pages, and fixed in a frame, are laid upon the stone or table used, face upward, and a little fine oil is brushed over them to prevent the *papier-maché* from adhering to the face of the types. This *papier-maché*, which is used for making the matrix or mold, is formed by pasting upon a sheet of tough brown paper, several sheets of tissue paper, and a sheet of soft, absorbent white paper. It is made in sheets, and usually, to make a matrix of the desired thickness, several sheets are used. It is kept moist for use, and is lightly covered with pulverized French chalk when laid upon the face of the types. Then it is beaten with a stiff brush to force the soft paper into all the interstices of the types. Other sheets of prepared paper are added to secure the desired thickness, and the whole is then covered with a woolen blanket and put into a press, the bed of which is moderately heated, and the press is screwed down. The heat soon dries the matrix, which, when taken out of the press, is a stiff card, showing a perfect reversed impression of the types. A mold of metal is then taken from the matrix, in which the exact face of the types are reproduced for printing. When the plate is to be run on a rotary press, it is cast in a box which is curved inside, so that the form of the plate will fit the cylinder of the press. By this method an entire large plate can be made in a quarter of an hour, or even less time. For fine book work the matrices are made of plaster of paris, which is a much slower and more costly way, but produces a finer and cleaner plate when finished. This process was invented about 1731.

Suez Canal, The, is the most important shipping enterprise known to history. It enables two ships to do the work of three in trading between Europe and the East. From London to Bombay, by way of the Cape, is 10,595 miles; by the canal, 6,330. It cost £17,000,000, was begun in 1856, and finished in 1869. Its length is ninety-two miles, depth, twenty-six feet; the tolls average £800 per vessel, or eight shillings per ton of net tonnage. The estimated saving to commerce is £5,000,000 a year. In 1889, 3,425 vessels went through, the mean time of passing being twenty-seven hours. Electric lights are now used to enable ships to pass at night as readily as in the daytime.

Sugar is supposed to have been known to the ancient Jews. Found in the East Indies by Nearchus, admiral of Alexander the Great, 325 B. C. An oriental nation in alliance with Pompey used the juice of the cane as a common beverage. It was prescribed as a medicine by Galen, second century. Brought into Europe from Asia, A. D. 625; in large quantities, 1150. Its cultivation was attempted in Italy, but not succeeding the Portuguese and Spaniards carried it to America about 1510. Sugar cane first grown in the territory now constituting the United States, 1751. First American sugar mill built near New Orleans, 1758. Sugar refining was made known to Europeans by a Venetian, 1503; and was first practiced in England in 1659. The invaluable vacuum pan was invented by Howard, 1812, and Dr. Scoffern's processes were patented in 1848-50.

Sugar manufactured from sorghum was first successfully reported in 1888. The sap of the rock or sugar maple, a tree growing in the United States and Canada, yields a local supply of sugar, which also, in some measure, finds its way into commerce.

Telegraph, The. — The word is Greek, meaning "to write from a distance." The Greeks never thought of doing such a thing. Like most scientific designations, it is a made-up word out of that wonderful tongue. Before Morse's time it had come to mean the giving of any information from afar. The ideas of speech, quick delivery, are involved. If time is not the essential, we may go or send. Indians use columns of smoke. We use signals and the heliograph. Vessels at sea have long used visual telegraphic signals. But as soon as it was known that electricity could be sent long distances over wires, human genius began to devise means for using it for sending messages. Many of these devices were tried and failed. Some of them seem now to us absurd, because they were attempted before even the battery was invented, when the current was obtained by friction. In 1832 an American, Morse, while on a voyage home from Europe in a sailing vessel, began to think of making what we now know as a telegraph. After more than eight years of waiting, Congress made an appropriation for building a line between Baltimore and Washington. The story of this first line is curious, almost absurd, showing how little the inventor knew when he began it, and how much was learned during its construction. Morse had an assistant named Alfred Vail, who is the author of most of the features of the telegraph which have proved useful, as we now know it.

In principle, and even in practice, the telegraph is one of the simplest of electrical appliances. Any two operators can communicate with each other over a great distance with two parts only; a battery and a wire, for the wonderful alphabet of Vail, the dots and dashes, can be read in any language, and by sight, hearing, tasting, or feeling. Something to produce a current, and a wire to carry it, are all that are absolutely necessary. There is usually only one wire. There would be two, but the earth acts in place of the return wire, and the connection is simply made at the battery, along the wire, and into the ground. The only machine, so to speak, that is necessary in practice is the small electro-magnet which one hears pulling down the armature to it every time a connection is made by the operator at the other end of the circuit who is sending a message, and spelling out the words of it with the click and pause sound which would be the dot and dash of the old roll of paper indented by a pointed stylus, now discarded. This electro-magnet and its action with an interrupted current has been briefly explained. The key with which the message is spelled out is a lever with a button at the end, which, when pressed down, makes a contact and completes the circuit over the wire and the windings of the electro-magnet, and, when released, breaks it again.

Telephone, The.— This wonderful advance in electrical science was made practical in 1875, and is the invention of Prof. A. G. Bell, Chicago. There were simultaneous inventions by Gray, Edison, and others. In reality, the telephone is simple in construction, but it is difficult to explain in words. The human voice, recognizable in articulate words, is apparently carried for miles on a wire. Yet it is well to understand in the beginning that such is not the case. The listener does not hear any person talk. All that goes over the wire is thousands of varying impulses of electricity. The entire secret lies in electrical induction.

It has been shown that electricity produces magnetism. Following it has been shown that this process can be reversed, and that magnetism produces electricity. This last fact was made use of in the original Bell telephone. The Blake transmitter is now used, slightly modifying the action, but not altering the principle of the instrument, and an endeavor to explain this will be made. It has been shown that an approach to, or a receding from, a wire carrying a current, produces an induced current. Then it was shown that if one of the pieces were a magnet, and there was a rapid approach and receding by a piece of soft iron, an induced current would also be produced.

Now there is in the transmitting instrument of a telephone a bar magnet, and on one end of this is wound several layers of fine insulated wire. The ends of this wire run off and become a part of the circuit between two telephones. No current passes over this circuit ordinarily, but one can be induced if a piece of iron is made to move quickly, to tremble, near the bar. This is accomplished by placing crosswise to the end of the bar magnet the thin black disc of sheet-iron against which, so to speak, one talks when using the telephone. The voice impinging upon this, causes it to tremble; to approach to and recede from the magnet, not vaguely and without rule, but precisely in proportion to the *tone* of the voice. Every time one of these very small movements of the disc occurs a small impulse is sent from the magnet out over the circuit whose coil incloses it.

At the other end of the circuit there is a precisely similar arrangement of bar magnet and coil and disc, inclosed in that trumpet-shaped receiving instrument which is held to the ear. The magnetism in this last magnet is increased with each impulse in precise proportion to the power of the impulse, and this disc of the receiving instrument is drawn toward its magnet and released again in unison with the movements of the disc in the transmitter, which movements, as stated, are great or small, or slow or fast, in accordance with the tones of the voice of the speaker.

It follows that the mechanical rattle of a disc of sheet-iron held close to the ear produces sounds that vary in pitch and intensity precisely as those do which are produced by the impinging of the human voice upon the other disc, a mile or more away. The movement of the transmitting disc controls those of the receiving disc through the medium of varying impulses of electricity sent to the magnet of the latter by the magnet of the former. The movements of the former are controlled by the human voice. It follows that the movements of the latter are also controlled by the same voice. It is the reversal of a process. If a disc is moved by the voice in a certain way, the moving of a disc *in the same way* by some other means will imitate the voice. So far as volume is concerned the imitation is microscopic. But it can be heard, and answers all purposes. It is doubtful if, among all the productions of human genius, there will ever be anything nearer the miraculous than the almost universally used telephone.

Telescopes.— This invention is noticed by Leonard Digges, about 1571. Roger Bacon, A. D. 1250, described telescopes and microscopes exactly, and yet neither was made till one Metius, at Alkmaar, and Jansen, of Middleburg, made them about the same time; the latter from an accidental discovery made by his children, 1590–1609. Galileo imitated their invention by its description, and made three in succession, one of which magnified a thousand times. With these he discovered Jupiter's moons, and the phases of Venus. Telescopes became very popular, and were improved by Zucchi, Huygens, Gregory, and Newton; and finally by Martin, Hall, Dolland, and Herschel. Achromatic telescopes were made by Hall about 1723. Many excellent and powerful telescopes have since been constructed.

Terms in Electricity.— The technical terms used in regard to electricity refer to units of various nature. Thus the unit of capacity is one farad; the unit of activity, one watt; the unit of work, one joule; the unit of quantity, one coulomb; the unit of current, one ampere; the unit of resistance, one ohm; the unit of magnetic field, one gauss; the unit of pressure, one volt; the unit of force, one dyne. The names are mostly derived from the names of men that have been famous in the field of electrical research. Thus Michael Faraday, James Watt, and James P. Joule, famous English discoverers, give their names to the first three units mentioned; Charles A. Coulomb and Andre M. Ampère, French inventors, to the two units following; G. S. Ohm and Carl F. Gauss, Germans, name two more units; and the volt is named from the Italian discoverer, Volta. The dyne is derived from the root word of dynamo, itself meaning force.

Thermometer, The.— The thermometer is an instrument for measuring the heat or temperature of bodies by the regular expansion of mercury or alcohol in a graduated glass tube. Halley proposed the substitution of mercury for alcohol in 1697. The thermometers usually employed are Fahrenheit's, the Centigrade, and Reaumur's, the first invented in 1726, and the two others soon afterwards.

The following table is interesting as a comparison of the three thermometers: —

	Reaumur.	Centigrade.	Fahrenheit.
Freezing point	0	0	32
Vine cultivation	8	10	50
Cotton cultivation	16	20	68
Hatching eggs	32	40	104
	40	50	122
	48	60	140
	56	70	158
	64	80	176
	72	90	194
Water boils	80	100	212

Ice melts at 32°; temperature of globe, 50°; blood heat, 98°; alcohol boils, 174°; water boils, 212°; lead melts, 594°; heat of common fire, 1,140°; brass melts, 2,233°; iron melts, 3,479°.

Thunder is caused by the sudden reentrance of the air into a vacuum which is supposed to be caused by the lightning in its passage through the atmosphere. The electricity exerts a powerful repulsive force upon the particles of air along the path of its discharge, thus making a momentary vacuum. Into this void the surrounding air rushes with a violence proportioned to the intensity of the electricity, and is thus thrown into vibrations, which are the source of the sound.

Tides, The.— The ebb and flow of tidal waters depend upon the moon to a great extent Twice every day we have the tides, twelve hours apart, and the flow and ebb are merely examples of the attraction of gravitation which is exercised on all bodies, whether liquid or solid. The tides may be compared to a great wave, which, raised by the moon's attraction, follows her in her course round the earth. The sun also aids in this effect, but as the moon is so much nearer the earth her influence is far greater. The tides are highest at the equator and lowest at the poles, because the tropics are more exposed to the lunar attraction.

Tobacco.— The name tobacco is thought by some to have been taken from Tobacco, a province of Yucatan; by others from Tobago, an island in the Caribbean Sea; and by still others from Tobasco, in the Gulf of Florida. The plant, although it is asserted that the Chinese have used it from earliest times, was not introduced into Europe until after the discovery of America by Columbus. He first found it in use on the Island of San Domingo in the West Indies. The Indian, among all the tribes from Peru to Upper Canada, smoked it in pipes. The seed of the plant was first introduced in Europe by Gonzalo Hernandez de Oviedo, who took it to Spain and cultivated it for ornamental purposes; but its narcotic qualities were shortly afterward discovered and the practice of smoking it soon became general, and its manufacture into snuff followed in course of time. It was introduced in Italy and France in 1560, and was brought into the latter country by Jean Nicot, the French Embassador to Portugal, in whose honor it received its botanical name *Nicotiana*, whence the name nicotine. The plant was introduced into England by Sir Walter Raleigh. It was along in the seventeenth century before it was known to be used in Asia, but the Oriental nations at the present time are probably the greatest smokers in the world.

Type-Setting Machines. — The first type-setting machine appears to have been invented by William Church of Connecticut about 1820. This, after the lapse of twenty years, was followed by a number of others, scarcely a year passing without one or more being made the subject of a patent. In 1857 a machine was invented by Robert Hattersley which is capable of setting from 4,000 to 6,000 types in an hour — about three men's work. This machine, which occupies a space of about two or three feet, has a horizontal stage on which is placed a partitioned tray, containing the rows of type running from back to front, each row being, of course, all the same letter. Descending vertically along the front of this tray is a series of as many wires with pistons as there are rows of types, and these pistons are depressed by the keys acting by bell cranks, and then return to their positions by means of India rubber bands or springs. A propeller kept in a state of tension by an India rubber string is placed in the rear of each row of types, and draws them forward to the piston. When the girl working the machine presses down, say, an *e* key, it depresses the *e* piston, which pulls down with it an *e* type, and drops it into a tube or channel, which conveys it to what represents the composing-stick, and so on with every letter, figure, comma, or space. Another successful machine is the Mitchell type-setter. The compositor has a key-board, each key of which strikes out a type from a brass slide placed on an incline. The type travels along an endless band to a spot where it is turned on end and pushed forward by a notched wheel. The apparatus comprises numerous bands, the lengths and velocities of which so vary as to enable the types at different distances from the wheel to reach it in the order in which the keys are struck. The words are built up in rows thirty inches long, and "justified," as is the case with the Hattersley machine, by hand.

Typewriters.— Perhaps the earliest form of a typewriter is a rude machine invented in England in 1714, without any practical fruits. M. Foucault sent to the Paris Exposition of 1855, a writing machine for the blind, but the first of what are now popularly known as typewriters, was patented in 1868 by C. L. Sholes, of Wisconsin. This has been improved, until now it is possible to attain a speed of seventy-five to eighty words a minute in writing with this machine, which is fast enough for reporting speeches. The principal advantages gained are rapidity of execution and legibility. A typewriter can write with both hands and several fingers in instant succession, every letter being made with a single light touch, instead of requiring from three to seven distinct strokes and dots, as in ordinary script.

Umbrellas are by no means a modern invention. They are found sculptured on the monuments of Egypt, and on the ruins of Nineveh, and their use in China and India is also very ancient. In Greece they had a part in certain religious ceremonies; and there is no doubt, from the paintings on ancient Greek vases, that umbrellas very much like those in use at the present time were known many years before the Christian era. They were also used among the Romans, but only by women. The umbrella also seems to have been a part of an insignia of royalty, as is still the case in parts of Asia and Africa. An English dictionary, published in 1708, defines an umbrella as "a screen commonly used by women to keep off rain." Jonas Hanway is said to have been the first man to have carried an umbrella through the streets of London in rainy weather, about 1750, and he was hooted and jeered at by boys for his fears of a wetting. It is not known, however, when their use began in England, as representations of such articles are found in very ancient manuscripts. Umbrellas were introduced in America in the latter part of the eighteenth century, but their use at first was confined almost exclusively to women, as it was considered very effeminate to carry one.

Undulatory Theory of Light.— For a long while there were two rival theories to account for the nature of light and optical phenomena, and it is only of late years that the observations and experiments of scientists have fully established the undulatory theory and disproved the corpuscular theory. The former maintains that light is a transference of energy to the eye; the latter, that it is a transference of matter. The undulatory theory assumes the entire universe and all matter to be pervaded with a highly elastic imponderable fluid, which is called ether. Light, then, consists in the propagation of energy by a wave motion through this fluid — a process exactly analogous to the transmission of sound in air and of waves in water. This theory explains the nature of radiant heat also and its relation to light, considering it is an undulatory motion, in this same ether, of similar character but different degree. The now discarded corpuscular theory, which was supported by no less a man than Sir Isaac Newton, assumed that an infinite number of minute material particles emanated from a luminous body, and, impinging on the eye, gave the sensation of light. Huygens has the credit of having propounded, developed, and illustrated the undulatory theory. His propositions and conclusions were finally and fully substantiated by the successive experiments and demonstrations of Young, Fizeau, and Foucault. The velocity of light, or the rate at which this wave motion is communicated through the ether, is 186,000 miles a second.

Vaccination, as a preventive of smallpox, was discovered by Dr. Edward Jenner, an English physician. His attention was directed to the subject upon casually hearing that persons engaged in milking cows frequently had the cowpox, a mild disorder of the eruptive kind appearing on the udder of the animal, and communicated in a similar form to the hands, and that the belief was common among the agricultural classes that whoever had taken the disease was secure against the infection of smallpox. After frequent experiments he ascertained that only one form of the eruption on the cow's udder possessed this property, a number of these experiments being made upon his son, a boy six years old. He labored against opposition for many years before the value of his discovery was acknowledged by the medical profession. There are several places in the United States where a business is made of supplying the market with "vaccine points" — small quills, with a coating of the cow virus on the ends. The name is derived from *vacca*, meaning a cow.

Vacuum. — This word means, literally, empty space, or space wholly devoid of matter. In this sense, the results of modern scientific investigation tend to prove that a vacuum cannot exist, as all space is pervaded by the imponderable elastic fluid called ether, whose existence must be allowed to explain the transmission of light and heat from distant luminous bodies. (See Undulatory Theory of Light.) In common language, a vacuum (more or less perfect) is said to be produced when ordinary ponderable matter, as air, has been removed from the interior of a closed vessel. Until the beginning of the present century the most perfect vacuum that could be obtained was what is called the Torricellian vacuum — *i. e.*, the space above the mercury in a carefully filled barometer tube. Such a vacuum is, however, almost useless for experimental purposes; and, besides, it contains mercurial vapor. By modern scientific methods and appliances a vacuum may be obtained in which there is left less than 1-135,000 of the original volume of air. An ordinary air-pump in good working order will remove all but about 1-120 of the air in the receiver. The old phrase that "Nature abhors a vacuum," was used to account for various phenomena in the past — among them the rise of water in pumps. Most of these are now well understood, the simple natural laws governing them. Water, for instance, rises in a tube, when the air is exhausted above it, owing to the pressure of the atmosphere on the open surface of the liquid in which the end of the tube is immersed. This pressure or weight of the atmosphere is equal to the weight of a column of water about thirty-two feet high, and, accordingly, will raise the water to this height.

Velocity.—The average velocity of various bodies is here given: —

	Per hour.			Per sec.	
A man walks	3	miles,	or	4	feet.
A horse trots	7	"	or	10	"
A horse runs	20	"	or	29	"
Steamboats move	18	"	or	26	"
Sailing vessels move	10	"	or	14	"
Slow rivers flow	3	"	or	4	"
Rapid rivers flow	7	"	or	10	"
A moderate wind blows	7	"	or	10	"
A storm moves	36	"	or	52	"
A hurricane moves	80	"	or	117	"
A rifle ball moves	963	"	or	1,466	"
Sound moves	743	"	or	1,142	"
Light moves	192,000	miles per second.			
Electricity moves	288,000	" " "			

Violin.— The origin of the violin can be traced back to a stringed instrument called the ravanastron, invented, it is believed, in 5000 B. C., by Ravana, King of Ceylon. The crwth, which was in use in Wales long before the sixth century, and to which the Anglo-Saxons gave the name of fythel, whence our fiddle, was a similar instrument. The violin of modern form was not made until the fifteenth or sixteenth centuries, and its earliest maker was Gaspard di Salo, of Lombardy; and the Italian school of violin-making was probably founded by him at Brescia. These Brescian instruments — that is to say, those made by Giovanni Paolo Magini, still hold a place among the best ever made. It was not long, however, after the establishment of the Brescian school when the makers of Cremona began to produce instruments which have been objects of wonder and admiration from their time to the present. The three greatest Cremonese makers were Nicholas Amati, Joseph Guarneri del Gesu and Antonius Stradivarius. To those who at the present time willingly pay hundreds and even thousands of dollars for a violin made by one of these great makers, it may be of interest to know that they all were simple, hard-working artisans, who sold their works of genius for a few florins.

Volcanoes.— A volcano is a mountain, or opening in the earth's crust, through which issue fire, smoke, ashes, lava, steam, etc. Volcanoes may be distinguished as extinct and active. Extinct volcanoes are such as are now at rest, but were subject to eruptions in former ages, as is shown by their form and structure, and the presence of craters. Active volcanoes are such as are either in a constant state of eruption, or have eruptions from time to time, with intervals of rest.

Volcanoes throw out an enormous amount of material. Whole islands and portions of continents have been formed by volcanic action. Iceland is an example of a volcanic island.

The lava, when it first issues from a volcano, is somewhat like melted iron running from a furnace, but soon cools on the surface and forms a black, porous crust. Sometimes the streams are so thick that the interior remains hot for twenty years.

A terrific eruption of Mt. Vesuvius, A. D. 79, destroyed the flourishing cities of Pompeii, Herculaneum, and Stabiæ, and covered them with ashes and cinders to the depth of fifteen feet.

About sixty eruptions of Mt. Etna are recorded. In 1669, a stream of lava from this mountain overflowed the ramparts of Catania, sixty feet in height, and destroyed a portion of the city. In 1832, several craters opened in the sides of the mountain, and a stream of lava eighteen miles long, one mile broad, and thirty feet deep, poured over the adjacent fields.

In 1835, the terrible eruption of Conseguina occurred. It lasted three days, the sun being obscured over half of Central America, 40,000 square miles covered with dust, ashes, and lava.

In 1902 a violent eruption of Mt. Pelée took place, killing over 2,000 people.

Water Gas.— Much of the illuminating gas now used is made by the comparatively new process in which the main volume of the gas, consisting of hydrogen, is taken out of water. In the original coal gas process the illuminating agent is obtained directly from the distillation of soft or bituminous coal; and impurities being removed by washing it with water and then passing it through lime, the gas is ready for burning. The new process is, in outline, as follows: Steam is passed through retorts filled with anthracite coal raised to a white heat by an air blast. In its passage it is decomposed, and the gas issuing from the pipes at the top consists of a mixture of hydrogen and carbon dioxide. This serves as the carrier for the true illuminating agents, which are a comparatively small percentage of the entire volume, and these are combined by mingling with naphtha vapor. This mixture has now about the same composition as the ordinary coal gas, but must be fixed — that is, made a stable compound — by subjecting it to the effect of heat and cold. This is accomplished by conducting it through two series of pipes, surrounded in one case by cold, running water, and in the other by steam. It is then purified in the same way as mentioned above. By passing it through a water tower loosely filled with something, as charcoal, down through which water trickles as the gaseous mixture ascends, the ammonia is dissolved out; then, by passing it through thin layers of lime, the other main impurity, sulphureted hydrogen, is removed. It is then ready for distribution through the city. Its illuminating power is about the same as, or somewhat greater than, that of coal gas. The water process produces the gas at a much lower cost; but in the other process there are a number of by-products derived from the distillation of the coal — *e. g.*, coke, coal tar, and also aqua ammonia, which is present in greater quantities in the coal gas — which are sold, and thus make the entire cost of manufacture about the same in each case.

Weaving.— The art of weaving appears to have been practiced in China from the earliest antiquity — more than a thousand years before it was known in Europe or Asia. Poets assign the art to the spider. Women originally spun, wove, and dyed; and the origin of these arts is ascribed, by ancient nations, to different women as women's art. The Egyptians ascribed the art to Isis, the Greeks to Minerva, and the Peruvians to the wife of Manco Capac. In most Eastern countries, the employment of weaving is still performed by the women. The Saviour's vest, or coat, had not any seam, being woven from the top throughout, in one whole piece. In 1331, two weavers from Brabrant settled at York, England, where they manufactured woolen. Flemish dyers, cloth drapers, linen makers, silk throwsters, etc., settled at Canterbury, Norwich, Colchester, Southampton, and other places, on account of the Duke of Alva's persecution, 1567, and carried on the occupation of weaving.

Whisky.—The process of distilling liquors from grain is thought to have been first discovered in India, and introduced into Europe by the Moors about 1150. Its use in Ireland dates back to about the same time, but it was not introduced into England until the close of the century. When first made, whisky was used as a medicine; and directions for making usquebaugh, or aqua vitæ, are contained in the "Red Book of Ossory," a volume compiled in the fourteenth century, in which it is described as a panacea for all diseases. The name whisky was at first given by the Scotch Highlanders to the liquor which they distilled from barley only, and had not, until later times, its present more general application. Usquebaugh was a Celtic name for the liquor, from which the word whisky is no doubt derived.

Wire.— The invention of drawing wire is ascribed to Rodolph of Nuremberg, about 1410. Mills for this purpose were set up at Nuremberg in 1563. The first wire mill in England was erected at Mortlake in 1663. The astonishing ductility, which is one of the distinguishing qualities of gold, is no way more conspicuous than in gilt wire. A cylinder of forty-eight ounces of silver, covered with a coat of gold weighing only one ounce, is usually drawn into a wire, two yards of which weigh only one grain; so that ninety-eight yards of the wire weigh no more than forty-nine grains, and one single grain of gold covers the whole ninety-eight yards. Eight grains of gold, covering a cylinder of silver are commonly drawn into a wire 13,000 feet long; yet so perfectly does it cover the silver that even a microscope does not discover any appearance of the silver underneath.

X or Röntgen Rays are a newly discovered form of energy that is radiated from a highly exhausted discharge tube, and developed by an electrical discharge. The rays are so called for their discoverer, Prof. W. C. Röntgen of Würtzburg, who gave them the name "X rays" because he was ignorant of their precise nature, the letter "X" being the usual algebraic symbol for an unknown quantity. The Röntgen rays resemble ordinary light in being propagated in straight lines, in being capable of reflection, in causing phosphorescence, and in affecting a sensitized plate. They differ from it in being invisible, in not being capable of refraction or polarization, and in being able to traverse many substances that are opaque to ordinary light. The phenomena caused by the passage of electricity through exhausted tubes have long attracted attention. It was noticed by Faraday in 1837, and by Plucker, in 1858, who was the first to cause apparatus to be made whereby a practically permanent vacuum could be maintained in a glass bulb. The physicist Crookes improved the tube and made many experiments with "cathode rays." The discovery of Röntgen was announced in 1896 as a new form of radiation. The discovery was accidental, and was made by observing that a highly flourescent substance with which he was experimenting gave out light whenever a neighboring Crookes tube was excited, though this tube was covered with an opaque cloth. The phenomena differed from cathode rays, and it was found that when the human hand was interposed between the tube and a photographic plate, the new rays caused a marked shadow picture of the skeleton to appear on the plate. Nothing but a shadow picture was possible owing to the fact that the rays are capable of but slight reflection. Extraordinary and widespread interest was at once aroused, but the purely scientific interest was for the time being overshadowed in the public mind by the sensational announcement that a means of "seeing through" the human body had been devised. Notwithstanding these exaggerations, experimenters in all countries verified Prof Röntgen's own claims.

The shadow pictures are used for a great variety of purposes, such as locating foreign bodies, examining fractures and malformations of bones, in dental surgery, and in detecting adulterations. The rays have also been utilized in France for the study of fossils.

Zodiac, The, is the name given by the ancients to an imaginary band extending around the celestial sphere, having as its mesial line the ecliptic or apparent path of the sun. The signs of the zodiac embrace the twelve important constellations which, owing to the motions of the earth, appear to revolve through the heavens within a belt extending nine degrees on each side of the sun's apparent annual path, and within or near which all the planets revolve. Since the sun appears successively in each of these constellations during the year, the zodiac was divided into twelve equal parts, corresponding to the months. These signs and their subdivisions were used in measuring time, and as a basis of astronomical and astrological calculations and predictions. Astronomers now, for convenience, use these signs, giving to each constellation an extent of thirty degrees, although the constellations vary in size. These signs are Aries, representing the ram; Taurus, the bull; Gemini, the twins; Cancer, the crab; Leo, the lion; Virgo, the virgin; Libra, the balance; Scorpio, the scorpion; Sagittarius, the archer; Capricornus, the goat; Aquarius, the water-bearer, and Pisces, the fishes. On the 20th of March the sun enters Aries, and at midnight

Virgo, the opposite constellation, will be overhead. During the month of April the sun will pass into Taurus, and at midnight Libra will be overhead. The early astronomers were astrologers, and claimed to be able to predict the future careers of individuals and nations by observing the positions and movements of the planets and the condition of the weather at the most important periods of men's lives. A man born when the sun was in the constellation Scorpio was believed to be naturally bent toward excessive indulgence of the animal passions; one born when the sun was in Aries was destined to be a great scholar or ruler; one born when the sun was in Pisces was predestined to grovel or be a servant, and so on. The porticoes of the temples of Denderah and Esne, in Egypt, have representations of the zodiacal constellations which are of great antiquity and have formed a fruitful theme of discussion; but the truth seems to be that nothing is as yet known respecting these ancient representations, for the manner in which the investigations have been mixed up with the Biblical question of the antiquity of man has prevented any truly scientific research. The Greeks would seem to have borrowed their constellations from the Egyptians and Babylonians, and this is corroborated to some extent by occasional remarks of Greek writers as to the positions of various constellations at certain times, which positions are inconsistent with the supposition of the observer being in Greece. The zodiacal figures of the Hindus, ancient Persians, Chinese, and Japanese have such a remarkable resemblance to those of the Egyptians that there can be little doubt as to their common origin.

Zoölogy is that science which treats of animals, their structure, habits, and classification.

There are four principal divisions of animals, based on distinct types of structure, and including all the denizens of the earth, the water, and the air. Following are the divisions of the animal kingdom, beginning with the lowest:—

SUB-KINGDOMS OR DIVISIONS.	CLASSES OF SUB-DIVISIONS.
I. PROTOZOA—First-living things, or lowest form of animal life.	1. Amœba, sponges, protei, etc. They have no mouth, and no distinct members, but are capable of making many changes in their form.
II. RADIATA—Radiates, that is, such as are shaped like a star or flower, and have their organs arranged uniformly around a common center.	1. Coral animals, sea-anemones, etc. 2. Jelly-fishes, sea-nettles. 3. Star-fishes, sea-urchins.
III. MOLLUSCA—Mollusks, that is, soft-bodied, without joints, and without vertebræ, but usually protected by a shell.	1. Bryozoa, that is, moss animals; as sea-mats, white sea-weeds, etc. 2. Brachiopods, that is, with arm-feet, or spiral appendages; as the lingulæ, spirifers, etc. 3. Ascidians, that is, pouch-like; as salpæ, etc. 4. Acephals, that is, headless; as oysters, etc. 5. Cephalates, that is, with heads; as snails, etc. 6. Cephalopods, that is, with heads and feet, or, more strictly, tentacles.
IV. ARTICULATA—Articulates, that is, animals having the body and members jointed, but without an internal skeleton.	1. Worms, as earthworms, leeches, etc. 2. Crustaceans, as crabs, lobsters, etc. 3. Centipedes, etc. 4. Spiders, etc. 5. Beetles, butterflies, etc.
V. VERTEBRATA—Vertebrates, that is, animals that have a backbone, and an articulated or jointed skeleton, and a great nervous cord, the spinal marrow, inclosed in a bony sheath.	1. Fishes. 2. Reptiles, that is, creeping things, as turtles, frogs, snakes, lizards, etc. 3. Birds, that is, "every winged fowl." 4. Mammalia, that is, animals with teats.

The last class, Mammalia, is further subdivided into fourteen orders, of which the most distinctive, still ascending from the lower to the higher, are four, namely:—

1. Cetacea, that is, of the whale tribe.
2. Quadrupeds, that is, four-footed animals generally.
3. Quadrumana, that is, four-handed; as the gorilla, chimpanzee, ape, and monkey.
4. Bimana, that is, two-handed; of which the only representative is man.

Bicycle (from the Latin *bis*, twice, and the Greek, *kuklos*, a wheel).—A two-wheeled machine, much used of late years for the purpose of human locomotion. The first bicycle was introduced into England from France about the year 1815, and was known as the *hobby-horse;* it was propelled by the feet of the rider being pushed against the ground. The improved bicycle at present in use was also a French invention, but the principle has been greatly developed by British and American manufacturers. *Tricycles*, or three-wheeled machines, are also largely used.

Many thousands of these machines are now constructed in America and Europe annually. With the possible exception of skating, bicycling is the quickest means of locomotion that man possesses. A fair bicyclist can outstrip a horse in a day, whilst an expert can do so in an hour.

Aerial Navigation or Aeronautics is the art of navigating the air. Within the past few years, and ever since the beginning of the twentieth century, air navigation has made notable progress toward practical results. Santos Dumont and others have shown that the flight of their machines can be directed even against contrary currents of air, and this is a most important advance. It still remains, however, for a dirigible machine to make long flights, and to be able to carry loads that would prove it commercially useful. The feat of flying has often been attempted; even among the ancients it was tried, and, we are informed, succeeded to some slight extent.

The most notable modern experiments with a view to attaining this end have been conducted by Hiram Maxim, of England, and Prof. Samuel P. Langley, of Washington, D. C.; the former constructing his machine on the plane system, and the latter designing his somewhat in the form of a fish. The flying machine proper is heavier than air, depending on the motions of mechanically propelled wings for its support. But the more usual and hitherto most successful type is the manageable balloon. In such a one Santos Dumont, in September, 1901, succeeded in winning the prize of $20,000 offered to the aeronaut who should first (under given conditions) circle the Eiffel tower, in Paris. An experiment with Professor Langley's machine at Washington, October, 1903, proved an utter failure.

Radium.—A recently discovered element with marvelous properties. By the light emitted from it photographs can be taken as with the Roentgen rays, and the photographs show the bones in the hand, or the coins in a pocket-book.

The astonishing feature of radium is that in spite of its enormous activity, which is in the form of minute corpuscles thrown off at the speed of 120,000 miles a second, it does not appreciably diminish in substance. This suggests the possibility that, at last, the long-sought agent which will give light without heat, or combustion, has been found. The discoverers say, however, that radium is extremely rare. It takes enormous quantities of pitch-blende to yield a minute quantity of radium. At present, a piece of radium a seventieth part of a grain in weight costs two dollars; so that a pound, if it could be had, would be worth nearly a million dollars.

Osteopathy.—A system of healing. In spite of the apparent etymology of the name, the system does not confine itself to the treatment of bone diseases, but claims to be a general system founded on the principle that "all bodily disorders are the result of mechanical obstruction to the free circulation of vital fluids and forces." No medicine whatever is used and no surgery employed, except in cases where the latter is needed exclusively.

Antitoxin.—An antidote to diseases produced by bacteria, which is obtained by inoculating a horse or other animal with the specific poison of the disease, increasing the strength of the material until the horse gains immunity from the disease. The serum of the horse's blood is then employed to inoculate persons attacked with the disease experimented on. This treatment has hitherto been used principally in diphtheria, and with marked success.

The establishment of the principles and the introduction of this treatment are due especially to Behring of Germany and Roux of Paris. The underlying principle of the treatment is based on the fact that, if a susceptible animal is inoculated first with small and then with increasing doses of the toxin produced by the bacillus, the blood of the animal is found to contain a substance called antitoxin, which has the power of neutralizing or rendering harmless the toxin. In order to obtain large quantities of the healing serum a horse is generally selected for the process of immunization. By proper methods very powerful antitoxins can be obtained. Dr. William H. Welch, of the Johns Hopkins University, in 1895, in an analysis of over 7,000 cases of diphtheria treated by antitoxin found that the fatality was reduced by this treatment by over 50 per cent of the previous death-rates; he concluded that the antitoxin serum is a specific curative agent for diphtheria, surpassing in its efficacy all other known methods of treatment for this disease. Since his report, this conclusion has been confirmed and even more favorable results have been obtained.

Phrenology (from the Greek *phrēn*, mind, and *logos*, a discourse).—The name given to a science which professes to found a philosophy of the mind upon the physiology of the brain, and upon the form of the brain and the comparative size of its parts as indicated by the shape of the skull. The first propounder of the science was Franz Joseph Gall, who was afterwards joined by Johann Gaspar Spurzheim. In 1810-12 they published jointly in Paris a work entitled *The Anatomy and Physiology of the Nervous System, and of the Brain in Particular*, in which the principles of the science were unfolded. The first English treatise on the subject was that of George Combe. That there is some connection between the brain and the mind is indisputable, and many of the theories of Gall and Spurzheim seem to be sustained to some extent by observation.

THE HOME OF WASHINGTON.

Book V.

Domestic Economy, Hygiene, Dietetics.

Domestic Economy, Hygiene, Dietetics.

AIR.

The common air is a fluid composed mainly of two gases, in certain proportions; namely, oxygen as twenty and nitrogen as eighty parts in a hundred, with a very minute addition of carbonic acid gas. Such is air in its pure and right state, and such is the state in which we require it for respiration. When it is loaded with any admixture of a different kind, or its natural proportions are in any way deranged, it cannot be breathed without producing injurious results. We also require what is apt to appear a large quantity of this element of healthy existence. The lungs of a healthy full-grown man will inhale the bulk of twenty cubic inches at every inspiration, and he will use no less than fifty-seven hogsheads in twenty-four hours.

Now, there are various circumstances which tend to surround us at times with vitiated air, and which must accordingly be guarded against. That first calling for attention is the miasma or noxious quality imparted to the air in certain districts by stagnant water and decaying vegetable matter. It is now generally acknowledged that this noxious quality is in reality a subtle poison, which acts on the human system through the medium of the lungs, producing fevers and other epidemics.

Putrid matter of all kinds is another conspicuous source of noxious effluvia. The filth collected in ill-regulated towns, ill-managed drains, collections of decaying animal substances placed too near or within private dwellings, are notable for their effects in vitiating the atmosphere, and generating disease in those exposed to them. In this case, also, it is a poison diffused abroad through the air which acts so injuriously on the human frame.

The human subject tends to vitiate the atmosphere for itself, by the effect which it produces on the air which it breathes. Our breath, when we draw it in, consists of the ingredients formerly mentioned; but it is in a very different state when we part with it. On passing into our lungs the oxygen, forming the lesser ingredient, enters into combination with the carbon of the venous blood (or blood which has already performed its round through the body); in this process about two fifths of the oxygen is abstracted and sent into the blood, only the remaining three fifths being expired, along with the nitrogen nearly as it was before. In place of the oxygen consumed, there is expired an equal volume of carbonic acid gas, such gas being a result of the process of combination just alluded to. Now, carbonic acid gas, in a larger proportion than that in which it is found in the atmosphere, is noxious. The volume of it expired by the lungs, if free to mingle with the air at large, will do no harm; but, if breathed out into a close room, it will render the air unfit for being again breathed. Suppose an individual to be shut up in an air-tight box: each breath he emits throws a certain quantity of carbonic acid gas into the air filling the box; the air is thus vitiated, and every successive inspiration is composed of worse and worse materials, till at length the oxygen is so much exhausted that it is insufficient for the support of life. He would then be sensible of a great difficulty in breathing, and in a little time longer he would die.

Most rooms in which human beings live are not strictly close. The chimney and the chinks of the doors and windows generally allow of a communication to a certain extent with the outer air, so that it rarely happens that great immediate inconvenience is experienced in ordinary apartments from want of fresh air. But it is at the same time quite certain that, in all ordinary apartments where human beings are assembled, the air unavoidably becomes considerably vitiated, for in such a situation there cannot be a sufficiently ready or copious supply of oxygen to make up for that which has been consumed, and the carbonic acid gas will be constantly accumulating. This is particularly the case in bedrooms, and in theaters, churches, and schools.

Perhaps it is in bedrooms that most harm is done. These are generally smaller than other rooms, and they are usually kept closed during the whole night. The result of sleeping in such a room is very injurious. A common fire, from the draught which it produces, is very serviceable in ventilating rooms, but it is at best a defective means of doing so. The draught which it creates generally sweeps along near the floor between the door and the fire, leaving all above the level of the chimney-piece unpurified. Yet scarcely any other arrangement is anywhere made for the purpose of changing the air in ordinary rooms.

FOOD.

A food is a substance which, when introduced into the body, supplies material which renews some structure or maintains some vital process; and it is distinguished from a medicine in that the latter modifies some vital action, but does not supply the material which sustains such action. It is essential to the idea of a food that it support or increase vital actions; whilst medicines usually may lessen, increase, or otherwise modify some of them. "Foods are derived," says Dr. Edward Smith, "from all the great divisions of nature and natural products, as earth, water, and air, solids, liquids, and gases; and from substances which are living and organic, or inanimate and inorganic. The popular notion of food as a solid substance derived from animals and vegetables, whilst comprehensive is too exclusive, since the water which we drink, the air which we breathe, and certain minerals found in the substance of the earth, are, adopting the definition given, of no less importance as foods. It is, however, of great interest to note how frequently all these are combined in one food, and how closely united are substances which seem to be widely separated. Thus water and minerals are found in both flesh and vegetables, whilst one or both of the components parts of the air, viz., oxygen and nitrogen, are distributed through every kind of food which is alone capable of sustaining life. Hence, not only may we add food to food to supply the waste of the body, but we may within certain limits substitute one for another as our appetites or wants demand. . . . Further, there seems to be an indissoluble bond existing between all the sources of food. There are the same classes of elements in flesh as in flour, and the same in animals as in vegetables.

"The vegetable draws water and minerals from the soil, whilst it absorbs and incorporates the air in its own growth, and is then eaten to sustain the life of animals, so that animals gain the substances which vegetables first acquired. But in completing the circle the vegetable receives from the animal the air (carbonic acid) which was thrown out in respiration, and lives and grows upon it; and at length the animal itself in whole or in part, and the refuse which it daily throws off, become the food of the vegetable. Even the very bones of an animal are by the aid of nature or man made to increase the growth of vegetables and really to enter into their structure; and being again eaten, animals may be said to eat their own bones, and live on their own flesh." It will be seen from this that animal and vegetable foods contain precisely the same elements though in different combinations. At the same time they differ sufficiently to make a due proportion of each necessary to perfect nutrition. One sterling point of difference is, that nitrogen constitutes a much larger percentage of animal bodies than of vegetables. Nitrogen is one of the most important elements of food; only such substances as contain it can efficiently produce flesh or repair wasted tissue. So important is this distinction, in fact, that one of the divisions of food most generally recognized by physiologists is into nitrogenous and non-nitrogenous, or, as Liebig termed them, the flesh-forming and the heat-producing. Both kinds are essential to the maintenance of life, and it is because vegetables as a whole are deficient in nitrogen that the highest degree of bodily vigor cannot be kept up by them alone.

It is understood that the structures of the body are in a state of continual change, so that atoms which are present at one hour may be gone the next, and when gone the structures will be so far wasted, unless the process of waste be accompanied by renewal. But the renewing substance must be of the same nature as that wasted, so that bone shall be renewed by the constituent elements of bone, and flesh by those of flesh. This is the duty assigned to food,— to supply to each part of the body the very same kind of material that it lost by waste. As foods must have the same composition as the body, or supply some such other materials as can be transformed into the substances of the body, it is desirable to gain a general idea of what these substances are. The following is a summary of the principal materials of which the body is composed: —

Flesh, in its fresh state, contains water, fat, fibrin, albumen, besides compounds of lime, phosphorus, soda, potash, magnesia, silica, and iron, and certain extractives, whose nature is unknown. Blood has a composition similar in elements to that of flesh.

Bone is composed of cartilage, fat, and salts of lime, magnesia, soda, and potash, combined with phosphoric and other acids.

Cartilage consists of chondrin, from which gelatine is formed, with salts of soda, potash, lime, phosphorus, magnesia, sulphur, and iron.

The brain is composed of water, albumen, fat (so-called), phosphoric acid, osmazome, and salts.

The liver consists of water, fat, and albumen, with phosphoric and other acids, in conjunction with soda, lime, potash, and iron.

The lungs are formed of a substance called connective tissue, from which gelatine is formed by prolonged boiling, albumen, a substance analogous to casein, various fatty and organic acids, with salts of soda and iron, and water.

Bile consists of water, fat, resin, sugar, fatty and organic acids, cholesterin, and salts of potash, soda, and iron.

Hence, it is requisite that the body should be provided with salts of potash, soda, lime, magnesia, sulphur, iron, and manganese, as well as sulphuric, hydrochloric, phosphoric, and fluoric acids and water; also, nearly all the fat which it consumes daily, and probably all the nitrogenous substances which it requires and which are closely allied in composition, as albumen, fibrin, etc. "So great an array of mysterious substances," says Dr. Smith, "might well prevent us from feeding ourselves or others if the selection of food depended solely upon our knowledge or judgment; but it is not so, for, independently of the aid derived from our appetites, there is the great advantage of having foods which contain a proportion of nearly all these elements; and combinations of foods have been effected by experience which protect even the most ignorant from evil consequences. Thus flesh, or the muscular tissue of animals, contains precisely the elements which are required in our flesh-formers, and, only limited by quantity, our heat-generators also; and life may be maintained for very lengthy periods upon animal food and water. Seeing, moreover, that the source of flesh in animals which are used as food, is of vegetable origin, it follows that vegetables should contain the same elements as flesh, and it is a fact of great interest that in vegetables we have food elements closely analogous to those contained in the flesh of animals. Thus, in addition to water and salts, common to both, there is vegetable chondrin, vegetable albumen, vegetable fibrin, and vegetable casein, all having a composition almost identical with animal albumen, fibrin, chondrin and casein." The articles containing most of the three articles needed generally in the body are as follows: for fat and heat-making — butter, lard, sugar and molasses; for flesh or muscle-forming — lean meat, cheese, peas, beans, and lean fishes; for brain and nerves — shell fish, lean meats, pease, beans, and very active birds and fishes, who live chiefly on food in which phosphorus abounds. In a meat diet, the fat supplies the carbon for keeping up the heat of the body, and the lean furnishes nutriment for the muscles, brain, and nerves. Green vegetables, fruits, and berries furnish additional supplies of the acids, the salts, and water needed.

Kinds of Food.— The simplest and most powerful agent in determining the character of our food is climate. In cold countries the requirements of man are very different from those felt in the tropics, and from the Esquimaux, who, according to Dr. Kane, will drink ten or twelve gallons of train oil in a day, to the Peruvians and other tropical nations for whom the banana suffices for nearly all seasons of the year, there are various gradations in which the constituents of the diet bear a very direct relation to the prevailing temperature. In cold regions man requires such food as not only supplies him with nutriment, but also with heat; as oil, butter, fat, sugar, and other substances in which carbonaceous elements predominate. In warm countries, on the contrary, it is one of the most essential conditions of good health, that his food should be as little heating as possible. In our own climate this law holds good as between summer and winter; in the latter season, plenty of lean meat, butter, potatoes, eggs, sugar, and similar food are necessary to keep the animal machine in working order, while in summer the diet should consist chiefly of those substances of which nitrogenous or flesh-forming elements compose the largest part. There is probably no other cause so fruitful in producing the dyspepsia and similar diseases of which Americans, as a nation, are in a peculiar degree the victims as the neglect to harmonize the food with the changing seasons.

The next most important question in determining the character of our food is that of its digestibility; and it must be borne in mind that the nutritive value and the digestibility of food have no necessary relation to each other. A food may have a very high nutritive value and yet be so indigestible as to be practically useless, and on the other hand it may be very easily digested and worth little or nothing for nutrition. No general rules as to the digestibility of different foods can be laid down, because it depends very largely upon individual habits and conditions. Persons who have a strong constitution, and take sufficient exercise, may eat almost anything with apparent impunity; but young children who are forming their constitutions, and persons who are delicate, and who take but little exercise, are very dependent for health upon a proper selection of food. As a general thing, when the body requires a given kind of diet, specially demanded by brain, lungs, or muscles, the appetite will crave that food until the necessary amount is secured. If the food in which the needed aliment abounds be not supplied, other food will be taken in larger quantities than needed until that amount is gained; for all kinds of food have supplies for every part of the body, though in different proportions. Thus, for example, if the muscles are worked a great deal, food in which nitrogen abounds is required, and the appetite will remain unappeased until the requisite amount of nitrogen is secured. Should food be taken which has not the requisite quantity, the consequence will be that the vital powers will be needlessly taxed to throw off the excess. There are other kinds of food which are not only nourishing but stimulating, so that they quicken the functions of the organs on which they operate; the condiments used in cookery, such as pepper, mustard, and spices, are of this nature. There are certain states of the system in which these stimulants may be beneficial and even necessary; but persons in perfect health, and especially young children, never receive any benefit from such food, and just in proportion as condiments operate to quicken the action of the internal organs, they tend to wear down their powers. The same observation applies to the use of wines and other spirituous and malt liquors. Under certain conditions where the vital powers are low, they are a highly important addition to ordinary food; but when used habitually, their temporary stimulation is gained at the expense of permanently weakening the digestive organs which finally refuse to perform their work without some such external aid. It follows from the above that the requirements of food in each case may in a normal condition of things be left to the individual taste, to be selected and prepared as is indicated by experience to be most appropriate.

Nutritiousness of Food.—The following table from authentic sources shows the ascertained percentage of nutriment in the common articles of table consumption:—

Kind of Food.	Preparation.	Per cent. of Nutriment.	Time of Digestion. H.	M.
Almonds	raw	66	—	—
Apples	raw	10	1	30
Apricots	raw	26	—	—
Barley	boiled	92	2	00
Beans, dry	boiled	87	2	30
Beef	roast	26	3	30
Blood	...	22	—	—
Bread	baked	80	3	30
Cabbage	boiled	7	4	30
Carrots	boiled	10	3	15
Cherries	raw	25	2	00
Chickens	fricasseed	27	2	45
Codfish	boiled	21	2	00
Cucumbers	raw	2	—	—
Eggs	whipped	13	1	30
Flour, bolted	in bread	21	—	—
Flour, unbolted	in bread	35	—	—
Gooseberries	raw	19	2	00
Grapes	raw	27	2	30
Haddock	boiled	18	2	30
Melons	raw	3	2	00
Milk	raw	7	2	15
Mutton	roast	30	3	15
Oatmeal	baked	74	3	30
Oils	raw	96	3	30
Pease, dry	boiled	93	2	30
Peaches	raw	20	2	00
Pears	raw	10	3	30
Plums	raw	29	2	30
Pork	roast	21	5	15
Potatoes	boiled	13	2	30
Rice	boiled	88	1	00
Rye flour	baked	79	3	30
Sole	fried	21	3	00
Soup, barley	boiled	20	1	30
Strawberries	raw	12	2	00
Turnips	boiled	4	3	30
Veal	fried	25	4	30
Venison	broiled	22	1	30
Wheat bread	baked	95	3	30

Digestibility of Food.—In Order of Time. The following table of the digestibility of the most common articles of food, prepared from standard authorities, is approximately correct, and is of very general practical interest:—

Quality.	Preparation.	Time of Digestion. H.	M.
Cole slaw	....	1	00
Rice	boiled	1	00
Pig's feet, soused	boiled	1	00
Tripe, soused	boiled	1	00
Eggs, whipped	raw	1	30
Trout, salmon, fresh	boiled	1	30
Trout, salmon, fresh	fried	1	30
Soup, barley	boiled	1	30
Apples, sweet, mellow	raw	1	30
Venison steak	broiled	1	35
Brains, animal	boiled	1	45
Sago	boiled	1	45
Tapioca	boiled	2	00
Barley	boiled	2	00
Milk	boiled	2	00
Liver, beef's, fresh	broiled	2	00
Eggs, fresh	raw	2	00
Codfish, cured, dry	boiled	2	00
Apples, sour, mellow	raw	2	00
Cabbage, with vinegar	raw	2	00
Milk	raw	2	15
Eggs, fresh	roasted	2	15
Turkey, wild	roasted	2	18
Turkey, domestic	boiled	2	25
Gelatine	boiled	2	25
Turkey, domestic	roasted	2	30
Goose, wild	roasted	2	30
Pig, sucking	roasted	2	30
Lamb, fresh	broiled	2	30
Hash, meat and vegetables	warmed	2	30
Beans, pod	boiled	2	30
Cake, sponge	baked	2	30
Parsnips	boiled	2	30
Potatoes, Irish	roasted	2	30
Cabbage, head	raw	2	30
Spinal marrow, animal	boiled	2	40
Chicken, full grown	fricasseed	2	45
Custard	baked	2	45
Beef, with salt only	boiled	2	45
Apples, sour, hard	raw	2	50
Oysters, fresh	raw	2	55
Eggs, fresh	soft boiled	3	00
Bass, striped, fresh	broiled	3	00
Beef, fresh, lean, rare	roasted	3	00
Pork, recently salted	stewed	3	00
Mutton, fresh	broiled	3	00
Soup	boiled	3	00
Chicken soup	boiled	3	00
Aponeurosis	boiled	3	00
Dumpling, apple	boiled	3	00
Cake, corn	baked	3	00
Oysters, fresh	roasted	3	15
Pork steak	broiled	3	15
Mutton, fresh	roasted	3	15
Bread, corn	baked	3	15
Carrot, orange	boiled	3	15
Sausage, fresh	broiled	3	30
Flounder, fresh	fried	3	30
Catfish, fresh	fried	3	30
Oysters, fresh	stewed	3	30
Butter	melted	3	30
Cheese, old, strong	raw	3	30
Soup, mutton	boiled	3	30
Oyster soup	boiled	3	30
Bread, wheat, fresh	baked	3	30
Turnips, flat	boiled	3	30
Potatoes, Irish	boiled	3	30
Eggs, fresh	hard boiled	3	30
Green corn and beans	boiled	3	45
Beets	boiled	3	45
Salmon, salted	boiled	4	00
Beef	fried	4	00
Veal, fresh	broiled	4	00

Composition of Various Articles of Food.— In 100 parts.

Kind of Food.	Water.	Albumen, etc.	Carbohydrates. Starch.	Carbohydrates. Sugar.	Fat.	Salts.
Arrowroot	18		82.0			
Bacon, dried	15	8.8			73.3	2.9
Bacon, green	24	7.1			66.8	2.1
Barley meal	15	6.3	69.4	4.9	2.4	2.0
Beans	11.75	24.3			2.5	3.3
Beef, fat	51	14.8			29.8	4.4
Beef, lean	72	19.3			3.6	5.1
Beer and porter	91	0.1		8.7		0.2
Biscuit	8	15.6			1.3	
Bread	37	8.1	47.4	3.6	1	1.7
Butter and fat	15				83.0	2.0
Buttermilk	88	4.1		6.4	0.7	0.8
Cabbage	91	2.0			0.5	0.7
Carrots	83	1.3	8.4	6.1	0.2	1.0
Cheese	36.8	33.5			24.3	5.4
Cheese, cheddar	38	28.4			31.1	4.5
Cheese, skim	44	44.8			6.3	4.9
Corn meal	14	11.1	64.7	0.4	8.1	1.7
Cream	66	2.7		2.8	26.7	1.8
Eels	75	9.9			13.8	1.3
Egg, entire	74	14.0			10.5	1.5
Egg, white of	78	20.4				1.6
Egg, yolk	52	16.0			30.7	1.3
Fish, white	78	18.1			2.9	1.0
Liver, ox	74	18.9			4.1	3.0
Meat, cooked, roasted	54	27.6			15.45	3.0
Milk, human	88	3.4	4.6		3.49	.21
Milk, new	86	4.1	4.9	5.2	3.9	0.8
Milk, skimmed	88	4.0	5	5.4	1.8	0.8
Mutton, fat	53	12.4			31.1	3.5
Mutton, lean	72	18.3			4.9	4.8
Oatmeal	15	12.6	58.4	5.4	5.6	3.0
Parsnips	82	1.1	9.6	5.8	0.5	1.0
Pease	15	23.0	55.4	2.0	2.1	2.5
Pork, fat	39	9.8			48.9	2.3
Potatoes	75	2.1	18.8	3.2	0.2	0.7
Poultry	74	21.0			3.8	1.2
Rice	13	6.3	79.1	0.4	0.7	0.5
Rye meal	15	8.0	69.5	3.7	2.0	1.8
Salmon	77	16.1			5.5	1.4
Sugar	5			95.0		
Treacle	23			77.0		
Tripe	68	13.2			16.	2.4
Turnips	91	1.2	5.1	2.1		0.6
Veal	63	16 5			15.8	4.7
Wheat flour	15	10.8	66.3	4.2	2.0	1.7

Quantity of Food.— With regard to the quantity of food to be taken, this also depends upon individual conditions and cannot be formed into a general rule. Where hunger is felt it may safely be assumed that when the hunger has been fully appeased sufficient food has entered the stomach. Such are the circumstances of civilized life, however, that in most cases hunger is a very rare sensation; and food is prepared and eaten more to gratify the palate than because nature demands it. On this point each individual is and must be a law unto himself, and we can only point out the consequences of eating a larger quantity than is needed. When too great a supply of food is put into the stomach, the gastric juice only dissolves that portion of it which the wants of the system demand; most of the remainder is ejected in an unprepared state, the absorbents take portions of it into the circulatory system, and all the various bodily functions dependent on the blood are thus gradually and imperceptibly injured. Very often, indeed, intemperance in eating produces immediate results, such as colic, headache, indigestion, and vertigo; but the more common result is the gradual undermining of all parts of the human frame, shortening life by thus weakening the constitution.

As to the hours of meals these are of no importance provided they are regular and come at regular intervals. This interval should never be less than five hours, as the stomach requires at least three hours to digest its supply of food, and not less than two hours should be allowed it for rest and recuperation.

Eating between meals is a most injurious practice, the source in children, especially, of endless stomachic disorders. It may be well to give children under ten years of age one more meal during the day than the three which adults in this country usually allow themselves; but these, as we have said above, should be at regular times and with stated intervals between them.

After taking a full meal, it is very important to health that no great bodily or mental exertion be made till the labor of digestion is over. Muscular exertion draws the blood to the muscles, and brain work draws it to the head; and in consequence of this the stomach loses the supply which is necessary to it when performing its office, the adequate supply of gastric juice is not afforded, and indigestion is the result. The heaviness which is felt after a full meal is a sure indication of the need of quiet; when the meal is moderate, the process of digestion will be sufficiently advanced in an hour, or an hour and a half, to justify the resumption of bodily or mental labor.

The Diet of Brain Workers.— It has long been one of the pet theories of popular physiology, that fish and other substances composed largely of phosphorus, are the most appropriate diet for brain workers; but it is now conceded that the best food for the brain is that which best nourishes the whole body with special reference to the nervous system, viz.: fat and lean meat, eggs, milk, and the cereals. Discussing this point in a recent treatise, Dr. George M. Beard says: "The diet of brain workers should be of a large variety, delicately served, abundantly nutritious, of which fresh meat, lean and fat, should be a prominent constituent. In vacations, or whenever it is desired to rest the brain, fish may, to a certain extent, take the place of meat. We should select those articles that are most agreeable to our individual tastes, and, so far as possible, we should take our meals amid pleasant social surroundings. In great crises that call for unusual exertion, we should rest the stomach, that for the time the brain may work the harder; but the deficiency of nutrition ought always to be supplied in the first interval of repose."

CHEMICAL COMPOSITION OF THE HUMAN BODY.

The human body is composed of the following elements, all of which are found also in the food provided by nature, or in air or water, and all must be supplied, day by day, or some bad results are sure to follow:—

	LB.	OZ.	GR.
Oxygen, a gas, in quantity sufficient to occupy a space equal to 750 cubic feet,	111	0	0
Hydrogen, a gas, in quantity sufficient to occupy 3000 feet, which with oxygen, constitutes water, the weight of the two indicating nearly the necessary amount of water........................	14	0	0
Carbon, constituting fat, and used also for fuel to create animal heat..........	21	0	0
Nitrogen, which constitutes the basis of the muscles, and solid tissues, and which is supplied by that part of the food which we shall denominate Nitrates..................................	3	8	0
Phosphorus, the physical source of vitality, and the most important of the mineral elements, will represent the whole class which we shall denominate the Phosphates..........................	1	12	190
Calcium, the metallic base of lime, which is the base of the bones...............	2	0	0
Fluorine, found combined in small quantities in bones..........................	0	2	0
Chlorine, constituting, with sodium, common salt, found in the blood..........	0	2	47
Sodium, the base of all the salts of soda..	0	2	116
Iron, which is supposed to give color to the blood..............................	0	0	100
Potassium, the base of all the salts of potash....................................	0	0	290
Magnesium, the base of magnesia, and magnesian salts	0	0	12
Silicon, the base of silex, which is found in the hair, teeth, and nails............	0	0	2

The elements of a man weighing 154 lbs.

Classification of Food.— Food may be divided into three classes. That class which supplies the lungs with fuel, and thus furnishes heat to the system, and supplies fat or adipose substance, etc., we shall call Carbonates, carbon being the principal element; that which supplies the waste of muscles, we shall call Nitrates, nitrogen being the principal element; and that which supplies the bones, and the brain, and the nerves, and gives vital power, both muscular and mental, we shall call the Phosphates, phosphorus being the principal element. These last might be subdivided into the fixed and the soluble phosphates,—the fixed being a combination principally with lime to form the bones, and the soluble being combinations with potash and soda, to work the brain and nerves; but our analyses as yet are too imperfect to allow a subdivision, and as all the mineral elements are more or less combined with each other, and all reside together in articles of food, we shall include all mineral elements under the term Phosphates.

The waste, and consequently the supply, of these three classes of elements is very different, four times as much carbonaceous food being required as nitrogenous, and of the phosphates not more than two per cent. of the carbonates. Altogether, the waste of these principles will average in a man of moderate size, with moderate heat, more than one pound in a day, varying very much according to the amount of exercise and the temperature in which he lives. These elements must all be supplied in vegetable or animal food, not one being allowed to become a part of the system unless it has been first organized with other elements of food, in some vegetable, or in water, or the atmosphere; but being appropriated by some animal, remain organized and adapted to the human system, so that animal and vegetable food contain the same elements in the same proportion and nearly the same chemical combinations, and are equally adapted to supply all necessary elements.

In Animal Food,	The Carbonates are furnished in	Fat.
	The Nitrates in	Albumen, Fibrin, and Casein.
In Vegetable Food,	The Carbonates are furnished in	Sugar, Starch, and a little Fat.
	The Nitrates in	Gluten, Albumen, and Casein.

The Phosphates in both animal and vegetable food are found inseparably connected with the nitrates, none being found in any of the carbonates, and generally in the proportion of from two to three per cent. of all the principles in vegetable, and from three to five in animal food.

The Carbonates of both animal and vegetable food are chemically alike — fat, sugar, and starch, all being composed of carbon, oxygen, and hydrogen, and in about the same chemical combinations and proportions.

The Nitrates, also albumen, gluten, fibrin, and casein, are alike in chemical combinations and elements, being composed of nitrogen, oxygen, and hydrogen, and a little carbon not digestible. These simple bodies are not, however, capable of being assimilated and converted into tissue; they must be previously combined, primarily by the vegetable kingdom

Analysis of Articles of Food in their Natural State.

Articles.	Nitrates.	Carbonates.	Phosphates.	Water.
Wheat	15.0	69.8	1.6	14.0
Barley	17.0	69.5	3.5	14.0
Oats	17.0	66.4	3.0	13.6
Northern corn, or maize	12.0	73.0	1.0	14.0
Southern corn	35.0	45.0	4.0	14.0
Tuscarora corn	5.0	80.0	1.0	14.0
Buckwheat	8.6	75.4	1.8	14.2
Rye	13.8	71.5	1.7	13.0
Beans	24.0	57.7	3.5	14.8
Pease	23.4	60.0	2.5	14.1
Lentils	26.6	58.5	1.5	14.0
Rice	6.5	79.5	0.5	13.5
Potatoes	1.4	22.5	0.9	75.2
Sweet potatoes	1.5	26.5	2.9	67.5
Parsnips	1.2	7.0	1.0	82.0
Turnips	1.1	4.0	0.5	90.5
Carrots	0.6	6.6	1.0	87.5
Cabbage	4.0	5.0	1.0	90.0
Cauliflower	6.4	3.6	1.0	90.0
Cucumbers	1.5	1.0	0.5	97.0
Apples	5.0	10.0	1.0	84.0
Milk of cow	5.0	8.0	1.0	86.0
Human milk	3.0	7.0	0.5	89.5
Veal	16.0	16.5	4.5	62.5
Beef	15.0	30.0	5.0	50.0
Lamb	11.0	35.0	3.5	50.5
Mutton	12.5	40.0	3.5	44.0
Pork	10.0	50.0	1.5	38.5
Chicken	20.0	35.0	4.5	73.0
Codfish	14.0	very little	5 or 6	79.0
Haddock	13.0	very little	5 or 6	82.0
Sole	15.0	very little	5 or 6	79.0
Plaice	14.0	very little	5 or 6	80.0
Flounder	15.0	some fat	3 or 4	78.0
Turbot	14.0	very little	5 or 6	79.0
Trout	17.0	very little	5 or 6	75.0
Whiting	15.0	very little	5 or 6	78.0
Smelt	17.0	very little	5 or 6	75.0
Salmon	20.0	some fat	6 or 7	74.0
Eels	17.0	some fat	3 or 4	75.0
Herring	18.0	some fat	4 or 5	75.0
Halibut	18.0	some fat	3 or 4	74.0
Oyster	10.0	very little	2 or 3	87.0
Clam	12.0	very little	2 or 3	....
Lobster	14.0	very little	5 or 6	79.0
Eggs, white of	15.5	none	4.5	80.0
Eggs, yolks of	17.5	28¾	5.5	54.0
Butter	....	all carbonates	....	....

CLEANLINESS.

To keep the body in a cleanly condition is the third important requisite for health. This becomes necessary in consequence of a very important process which is constantly going on near and upon the surface of the body.

The process in question is that of perspiration. The matter here concerned is a watery secretion produced by glands near the surface of the body, and sent up through the skin by channels imperceptibly minute and wonderfully numerous. From one to two pounds of this secretion is believed to exude through these channels, or pores, in the course of twenty-four hours, being, in fact, the chief form taken by what is called the waste of the system, the remainder passing off by the bowels, kidneys, and lungs. To promote the egress of this fluid is of great consequence to health; for, when it is suppressed, disease is apt to fall upon some of the other organs concerned in the discharge of waste.

One of the most notable checks which perspiration experiences is that produced by a current of cold air upon the skin, in which case the pores instantly contract and close, and the individual is seized with some ailment either in one or the other of the organs of waste, whichever is in him the weakest, or in the internal lining of some part of the body, all of which is sympathetic with the condition of the skin. A result of the nature of that last described is usually recognized as a cold or catarrh. We are not at present called on particularly to notice such effects of checked perspiration, but others of a less immediately hurtful or dangerous nature.

The fluid alluded to is composed, besides water, of certain salts and animal matters, which, being solid, do not pass away in vapor, as does the watery part of the compound, but rest on the surface where they have been discharged. There, if not removed by some artificial means, they form a layer of hard stuff, and unavoidably impede the egress of the current perspiration. By cleanliness is merely meant the taking proper means to prevent this or any other matter accumulating on the surface, to the production of certain hurtful consequences.

Ablution or washing is the best means of attaining this end; and accordingly it is well for us to wash or bathe the body very frequently. Many leave by far the greater part of their bodies unwashed, except, perhaps, on rare occasions, thinking it enough if the parts exposed to common view be in decent trim. If the object of cleaning were solely to preserve fair appearances, this might be sufficient; but the great end, it must be clearly seen, is to keep the skin in a fit state for its peculiar and very important functions. Frequent change of the clothing next to the skin is of course a great aid to cleanliness, and may partly be esteemed as a substitute for bathing, seeing that the clothes absorb much of the impurities, and, when changed, may be said to carry these off. But still this will not serve the end nearly so well as frequent ablution of the whole person. Anyone will be convinced of this, who goes into a bath, and uses the flesh-brush in cleansing his body. The quantity of scurf and impurity which he will then remove, from even a body which has changes of linen once a day, will surprise him.

EXERCISE.

Bodily exercise is absolutely essential to the maintenance of good health. The human body may be regarded as a complex machine, the various parts of which are so beautifully adapted to each other, that, if one be disturbed, all must suffer. The bones and muscles are the portions of the frame on which motion most depends. There are four hundred muscles in the body, each of which has certain functions to perform that cannot be disturbed without danger to the whole, and it is a wise provision of nature that the more these muscles are exercised the stronger do they become; hence it is that laborers are stronger and more muscular than persons whose lives are passed in easy or sedentary occupations. Besides strengthening the limbs, muscular exercise has a most beneficial influence on respiration and the circulation of the blood. Says a distinguished medical writer: "Exercise tells by inciting both heart and lungs to increased action and energy, and this, done in a pure air, is great gain to the purification of the blood; but exercise does much more, for not only are the lungs, with their large capacity for air, great purifiers, but the skin is little less effective towards the same end. All know the palpable effect of exercise upon the skin; but many are not aware that the sensible perspiration is but an increase of an insensible perspiration which is unceasingly poured out from myriads of little pores — the mouths of the sweat glands and the oil glands of the skin. The ordinary insensible perspiration is continually freeing us from a mass of impurity which cannot be retained in our system without injury. Convert the insensible perspiration into sensible, by exercise, and produce moderate sweating, and if the clothing be rational, you will give off to the winds the cause of many a headache and gloomy thoughts. Now this increased skin secretion must come from somewhere; and so it does, for the increased exertion causes increased wear and tear of system; every step works up tissue; and muscles, blood vessels, nerves, are all used quicker than when there is no action. Off go these used-up matters, probably the worst first, through lungs and skin, as fast as they can, and the man begins to feel this waste, for from all sides there are telegraphs to the stomach for supplies, and he finds himself getting excessively hungry, the dinner hour very welcome, and the formerly capricious stomach ready for anything; and so new supplies go in to supply the place of the old used-up works, and the physical man is greatly renovated — taken to pieces, as it were, and built up again.

1. In order that exercise may be truly advantageous, the parts must be in a state of sufficient health to endure the exertion. In no case must exercise be carried beyond what the parts are capable of bearing with ease; otherwise a loss of energy, instead of a gain, will be the consequence.

2. Exercise to be efficacious, even in a healthy subject, must be excited, sustained, and directed by that nervous stimulus which gives the muscles the principal part of their strength, and contributes so much to the nutrition of parts in a state of activity.

3. The waste occasioned by exercise must be duly replaced by food; as, if there be any deficiency in that important requisite, the blood will soon cease to give that invigoration to the parts upon which increased health and strength depend.

Kinds of Bodily Exercise.— Exercise is usually considered as of two kinds — active and passive. The active consists in walking, running, leaping, riding, fencing, rowing, skating, swimming, dancing, and various exercises, such as those with the poles, ropes, etc., prescribed in gymnastic institutions. The passive consists in carriage-riding, sailing, friction, swinging, etc.

Walking is perhaps the readiest mode of tak-

ing exercise, and the one most extensively resorted to. If it brought the upper part of the body as thoroughly into exertion as the lower, it would be perfect, for it is gentle and safe with nearly all except the much debilitated. To render it the more effectual in the upper part of the body it were well to walk at all times, when convenient, singly and allow the arms and trunk free play. It is best to walk with a companion, or for some definite object, as the flow of nervous energy will be by these means promoted, and the exercise be rendered, as has been already explained, the more serviceable.

Very long or rapid walks should not be attempted by individuals of sedentary habits, nor by weakly persons. Their frames are totally unprepared for such violent exertion.

Running as an Exercise.— Among the means which nature has bestowed on animals in general for the preservation and enjoyment of life, running is the most important. Since, then, it is pointed out to us by nature, it must be in a high degree innocent. It is very singular that we should apparently do all we can —which, fortunately, is not much —to make our children unlearn the art of running. Our earliest physical treatment of them seems calculated to destroy their aptitude for it; in a little time, it is too often the case that the city boy scarcely dares look as if he wished to run, we prohibit it so strongly as vulgar, and when he is more grown up gentility steps in and prohibits it altogether. Medical prejudices and our own convenience contribute likewise their share, and never allow our children, boys and girls, to acquire an art innocent of itself and necessary to all. It is possible that a person may get injury from running, but the fault is not in the exercise, but in the person who runs without having had proper training and practice.

Running should only be practiced in cool weather; as, for instance, in the late fall, winter, and early spring months.

The clothing should be light, the head bare, and the neck uncovered. As soon as the exercise is finished, warm clothing should be put on and gentle exercise continued for some time. It is not necessary to have a race course. The teacher of a school may take his pupils into the fields and find suitable ground for them. Then his pupils may exercise their bodies in other ways, acquire strength, agility, health, and the capacity of continued exertion; the will is brought into play vigorously, which is a great aid in the battle of life.

Care must be taken not to overdo, and thus, perhaps for life, weaken or injure the heart. The race, at first, should be short and frequently repeated, rather than long, and full speed should not be attempted for some time.

Running is well adapted to young and middle aged persons, but not to those who are fat. Sedentary persons may find great benefit in it after the day's work is ended. If they live in cities, a quiet spot in the park may be selected, and short trials adapted to the strength entered into. Invalids may do the same thing, only they must be more careful than the robust never to over-exert themselves.

Girls may run as well as boys, and, while they cannot go so fast, they can race much more gracefully and beautifully. Indeed, there can be few more attractive sights than that of a race between beautiful girls from ten to twelve years of age. After maturity, the change in the formation of the bones of the pelvis in girls renders running less easy and graceful. In ancient Greece girls were trained to run races as well as boys, and to their superb physical culture was in great part due the grandeur and beauty of Greek life during the years of their ascendency. The modern style of dress for young women is also entirely unsuited to running.

Fencing is of all active exercises that which is the most commendable, inasmuch as it throws open the chest, and at the same time calls into action the muscles both of the upper and lower extremities. Add to this that it improves very much the carriage of the body; for which reason it may be reckoned a branch of polite education.

Dancing is exhilarating and healthful, and seems to be almost the only active exercise which the despotic laws of fashion permit young ladies to enjoy.

Rope Jumping. — As the cool weather approaches the jumping rope may be more and more in the hands of girls. Properly used it is not an objectionable plaything. But children cannot be too frequently cautioned against jumping against time or competing to see who can jump the greatest number of times without stopping.

Repose a Condition Demanded by Exercise.— Exercise demands occasional periods of repose, and, in particular, that a certain part of every twenty-four hours be spent in sleep. After having been engaged in daily occupations for fourteen or sixteen hours, a general feeling of fatigue and weakness is induced; the motions of the body become difficult, the senses confused, the power of volition or will suspended, and the rest of the mental faculties, becoming more and more inactive, sink at length into a state of unconsciousness. The sense of sight first ceases to act by the closing of the eyelids; then the senses of taste and smell become dormant; and then those of hearing and touch. The muscles, also, dispose themselves with a certain reference to ease of position, those of the limbs having grown indolent before those that support the head, and those that support the head before those of the trunk. In proportion as these phenomena proceed, the respiration becomes slower and more deep, the circulation diminishes in impetus, the blood proceeds in great quantity toward the head, and all the functions of the internal organs become retarded. In this state, shut out as it were from the external world, the mind still retains its wonted activity, deprived, however, of the guidance of judgment and the power of distinct recollection; in consequence of which, it does not perceive the monstrous incongruities of the imagery which sweeps before it, and takes but faint cognizance of the time which elapses.

It may be laid down as an axiom, that the more uninterrupted sleep is, the more refreshing and salutary will be its effects; for during this period, the body undoubtedly acquires an accession of nervous energy, which restlessness, however induced, must disturb; and therefore the state of the body before going to sleep, the kind of bed, and the manner of clothing, require especial attention. As the functions of the body are performed more slowly during our sleeping than our waking hours, a full meal or supper, taken immediately before going to bed, imposes a load on the stomach which it is not in a condition to digest, and the unpleasant consequence of oppressive and harassing dreams is almost certain to ensue. When the sleeper lies on his back, the heart pressing, while pulsating, on the lungs, gives rise to a sense of intolerable oppression on the chest, which seems to bear down upon the whole body, so that in this painful state not a muscle will obey the impulse of the will, and every effort to move appears to be altogether unavailing. This constitutes incubus or nightmare; and it may be observed, that, as acidity on the stomach, or indigestion, gives rise to such dreams, so all dreams of this disturbed character are converse indications of indigestion; for which reason the great physiologist Haller considered dreaming to be a symptom of disease.

The kind of bed on which we repose requires attention. Some are advocates for soft, others for hard, beds; hence some accustom themselves to feather beds, others to mattresses. The only difference between a soft and a hard bed is this — that the weight of the body in a soft bed presses on a larger surface than on a hard bed, and thereby a greater degree of comfort is enjoyed. Parents err in fancying that a very hard bed contributes to harden the constitution of their children; for which reason they lay them down on mattresses, or beds with boarded bottoms. A bed for young children cannot be too soft, provided the child does not sink into it in such a manner that the surrounding parts of the bed bend over and cover the body. The too great hardness of beds, says Dr. Darwin, frequently proves injurious to the shape of infants, by causing them to rest on too few parts at a time; it also causes their sleep to be uneasy and unrefreshing. Whatever be the time chosen for sleep, it is evident that no person can with impunity convert day into night. Eight o'clock for children, and eleven for adults, may be recommended as good hours for retiring to rest. It is well known that children require more sleep than adults; and more sleep is requisite in winter than in summer. The average duration of sleep which may be recommended for adults is eight hours; but much depends upon habit, and many persons require only six. It is scarcely necessary to observe that, on rising in the morning, the strictest attention should be paid to washing the face, neck, and hands; the mouth and teeth should also be well cleansed. The most simple powder for the teeth is finely brayed charcoal, a little of which will clear away all impurities, and preserve the teeth. On leaving the bedroom, the windows should be opened, and the clothes of the bed turned down, in order that the exhalations of the body during sleep may be dissipated. If, instead of this, the bed be made immediately after we have risen, these exhalations are again folded up with the clothes — a practice which is not consonant either with cleanliness or health.

Overworking the Undeveloped Brain. — "Overwork," properly so-called, can only occur when the organ upon which the stress of the labor falls is as yet immature, and, therefore, in process of development. When an organ has reached the maturity of its growth it can only work up to the level of its capacity or faculty for work! Fatigue may produce exhaustion, but that exhaustion will come soon enough to save the organ. Repeated "efforts" may, under abnormal conditions, follow each other too rapidly to allow of recuperation in the intervals of actual exertion, and as the starting point will, in each successive instance, be lower than the previous state, there may be a gradual abasement; but even this process should not seriously injure a healthy and well developed organ. In short, a great deal of nonsense has been said and written about the "overwork" of mature brains, and there are grounds for believing that an excuse has been sought for idleness, or indulgence in a valetudinarian habit, in the popular outcry on this subject which awhile ago attracted much attention. Nevertheless there can be no room to question the extreme peril of "overwork" to growing children and youths with undeveloped brains.

The excessive use of an immature organ arrests its development by diverting the energy which should be appropriated to its growth, and consuming it in work. What happens to horses which are allowed to run races too early happens to boys and girls who are overworked at school. The competitive system as applied to youths has produced a most ruinous effect on the mental constitution which this generation has to hand down to the next, and particularly the next but one ensuing. School work should be purely and exclusively directed to development. "Cramming" the young for examination purposes is like compelling an infant in arms to sit up before the muscles of its back are strong enough to support it in the upright position, or to sustain the weight of its body on its legs by standing while as yet the limbs are unable to bear the burden imposed on them.

A crooked spine or weak or contorted legs is the inevitable penalty of such folly. Another blunder is committed when one of the organs of the body — to wit, the brain — is worked at the expense of other parts of the organism, in face of the fact that the measure of general health is proportioned to the integrity of development, and the functional activity of the body as a whole in the harmony of its component systems. No one organ can be developed at the expense of the rest without a corresponding weakening of the whole.

Mental Exercise.— The same rules and regulations by which exercise may be serviceable to the physical system, hold good respecting the mental faculties. These, as is generally allowed, however immaterial in one sense, are connected organically with the brain — a portion of the animal system nourished by the same blood, and regulated by the same vital laws, as the muscles, bones, and nerves. As, by disuse, muscle becomes emaciated, bone softens, blood vessels are obliterated, and nerves lose their natural structure, so, by disuse, does the brain fall out of its proper state, and create misery to its possessor; and as, by over-exertion, the waste of the animal system exceeds the supply, and debility and unsoundness are produced, so, by over-exertion, are the functions of the brain liable to be deranged and destroyed. The processes are physiologically the same, and the effects bear an exact relation to each other. As with the bodily powers, the mental are to be increased in magnitude and energy by a degree of exercise measured with a just regard to their ordinary health and native or habitual energies. Corresponding, moreover, to the influence which the mind has in giving the nervous stimulus so useful in bodily exercise, is the dependence of the mind upon the body for supplies of healthy nutriment; and, in like manner with the bodily functions, each mental faculty is only to be strengthened by the exercise of itself in particular.

It ought to be universally known, that the uses of our intellectual nature are not to be properly realized without a just regard to the laws of that perishable frame with which it is connected; that, in cultivating the mind, we must neither overtask nor undertask the body, neither push it to too great a speed, nor leave it neglected; and that, notwithstanding this intimate connection and mutual dependence, the highest merits on the part of the mind will not compensate for muscles mistreated, or soothe a nervous system which severe study has tortured into insanity. To come to detail, it ought to be impressed on all, that to spend more than a moderate number of hours in mental exercise diminishes insensibly the powers of future application, and tends to abbreviate life; that no mental exercise should be attempted immediately after meals, as the processes of thought and of digestion cannot be safely prosecuted together; and that, without a due share of exercise to the whole of the mental faculties, there can be no soundness in any, while the whole corporeal system will give way beneath a severe pressure upon any one in particular. These are truths completely established with physiologists, and upon which it is undeniable that a great portion of human happiness depends.

THE HUMAN PULSE.

The phenomenon known as the arterial pulse or arterial pulsation is due to the distention of the arteries consequent upon the intermittent injection of blood into their trunks, and the subsequent contraction which results from the elasticity of their walls. It is perceptible to the touch in all excepting very minute arteries, and, in exposed positions, is visible to the eye. The pulse is usually examined at the radial artery at the wrist, the advantages of that position being that the artery is very superficial, and that it is easily compressed against the bone. It is usual and convenient, though not quite accurate, to include under the term the conditions observed between the beats, as well as those produced by them.

The condition of the pulse depends mainly on two factors, each of which may vary independently of the other: First, the contraction of the heart, which propels the stream of blood along the artery; and, second, the resistance in the small arteries and capillaries, which controls the rate at which it leaves the artery. The first determines the frequency and rhythm of the pulse and the force of the beats; but the tension of the artery between them and their apparent duration depends mainly upon the peripheral resistance. "Feeling the pulse," therefore, gives important information besides the rate of the heart's action, and implies much more than the mere counting of pulsations. Dr. Broadbent says: "A complete account of the pulse should specify (1) the frequency—*i. e.*, the number of beats per minute, with a note of any irregularity or intermission or instability of the rhythm; (2) the size of the vessel; (3) the degree of distention of the artery between the beats; (4) the character of the pulsation—whether its access is sudden or gradual, its duration short or long, its subsidence abrupt or slow, note being taken of dicrotism, when present; (5) the force or strength of both the constant and variable pressure within the artery, as measured by its compressibility; (6) the state of the arterial walls."

The frequency of the pulse varies with age, from 130 to 140 per minute at birth to 70 to 75 in adult males, and with sex, being six or eight beats more in adult females. In some individuals it deviates considerably from this standard, and may even be habitually below forty or above ninety without any signs of disease. It is increased by exertion or excitement, by food or stimulants, diminished in a lying posture or during sleep. In disease (acute hydrocephalus, for example), the pulse may reach 150 or even 200 beats; or, on the other hand (as in apoplexy and in certain organic affections of the heart, it may be as slow as between 30 and 20.

The normal regular rhythm of the pulse may be interfered with either by the occasional dropping of a beat (intermission), or by variations in the force of successive beats, and in the length of the intervals separating them (irregularity). These varieties often occur in the same person, but they may exist independently of each other. Irregularity of the pulse is natural to some persons; in others it is the mere result of debility; but it may be caused by the most serious disorders, as by disease of the brain, or by organic disease of the heart.

The other qualities of the pulse are much more difficult to recognize though of no less importance. The degree of tension or resistance to compression by the fingers varies greatly: in a soft or "low tension" pulse the artery may be almost imperceptible between the beats; in a hard or "high tension" pulse it may be almost incompressible. An unduly soft pulse is usually an indication of debility; an unduly hard one is most often characteristic of disease of the kidneys and gout. But the tension, like the frequency of the pulse, undergoes considerable variations in health from temporary causes, and may in certain individuals be habitually above or below the average without actual disease.

The force of the beats is a measure of the vigor and efficiency of the heart's action. A strong pulse is correctly regarded as a sign of a vigorous state of the system; it may, however, arise from hypertrophy of the left ventricle of the heart, and remain as a persistent symptom even when the general powers are failing. As strength of the pulse usually indicates vigor, so weakness of the pulse indicates debility. Various expressive adjectives have been attached to special conditions of the pulse, into the consideration of which our space will not permit us to enter. Thus, we read of the jerking pulse, the hobbling pulse, the corded pulse, the wiry pulse, the thrilling pulse, the rebounding pulse, etc. The full significance of changes of the pulse in disease can only be appreciated by considering them in connection with the other signs and symptoms of the case.

Average frequency at different ages in health.

AGES:	BEATS PER MINUTE:
In the fœtus in utero	between 150 and 140
Newborn infants	between 140 and 120
During the first year	from 130 down to 115
During the second year	from 150 down to 100
During the third year	from 105 down to 95
From 7th to 14th year	from 90 down to 80
From 14th to 21st year	from 85 down to 75
From 21st to 60th year	from 75 down to 70
In old age	between 75 and 70

Co-Relation of Pulse and Temperature.— As a general rule the co-relation of pulse and temperature may be stated as follows, namely:—

An increase of temperature of one degree above 98° F. corresponds with an increase of ten beats of the pulse per minute, as in the following table:—

Temperature of	98°	corresponds with a pulse of	60
"	99°	" " " " "	70
"	100°	" " " " "	80
"	101°	" " " " "	90
"	102°	" " " " "	100
"	103°	" " " " "	110
"	104°	" " " " "	120
"	105°	" " " " "	130
"	106°	" " " " "	140

Thermometry.— In children the temperature is normally one or two degrees higher than in adults.

The temperature is normally one degree higher under the tongue than in the axilla. It is highest upon awakening in the morning; lowest at midnight.

A rise of one degree in temperature usually marks an increase of the pulse from six to ten beats a minute.

Continued temperature above 98.50° indicates prostration and illness; 101° to 105°, severe fever; 105° to 108°, danger; 108° to 109°, impending death.

A temperature of 105° or 106° on the first day of illness, is *prima facie* evidence of ephemeral fever; it is not typhoid or typhus, but probably malarious.

Though the typical evidences of pneumonia are present, if the thermometer fails to reach 101.70°, it may be concluded no soft infiltration of lungs is present.

High temperature after the eruption of measles has faded, indicates complications. An evening typhoid temperature of 103.5° indicates a mild course of fever; 105° in the evening or 104° in the morning, in the third week, indicates danger. A temperature of 104° and upwards, in pneumonia, indicates a severe attack. A temperature of 104° is always alarming in acute rheumatism; look for cardiac complications. In jaundice a rise of temperature is unfavorable. A rise of temperature in a puerperal female indicates the approach of pelvic inflammation. An increase of temperature in tuberculosis shows an advance of the disease, or rise of complications.

Daily fluctuations of temperature are associated with malarial fever, typhus, typhoid, exanthemata, rheumatism, pyæmia, pneumonia, and acute tuberculosis. An even temperature from morning until evening is favorable. A high temperature from evening until morning is unfavorable. A falling temperature from evening until morning is favorable. A rising temperature from evening until morning is dangerous. The temperature of the body must be normal before convalescence begins.

Respiration.

Two months to two years	35 per minute
Two to six years	23 " "
Six to twelve years	20 " "
Twelve to fifteen years	18 " "
Fifteen to twenty-one years	16 to 18 " "

Respiration and pulsation in the adult female is usually a trifle faster than in the male, especially during pregnancy.

ALE.

This a liquor manufactured from malt, which is usually produced from the parched grain of germinating barley by a process of great antiquity called brewing. It can, however, be made from the dried germinating grain of wheat and other cereals; any substance containing sugar being capable of yielding a wort or solution which may be fermented or converted into ale or beer. In several of the English pale ales the proportion of alcohol is as high as 10 per cent., and the average is from 5 to 7 per cent. So that a pint of good ale contains the same amount of alcohol as a bot- of claret. These ales, with those of Scotland, are largely imported, and are generally much superior to the American product. Burton ale, so called from the place where it is made, is one of the strongest and most intoxicating. It is of a somewhat thick, glutinous consistence, and sweetish to the taste; a small quantity of it produces intoxication in those who are not accustomed to it. The best English ales are Bass and Allsopp's. Scotch ale, especially the Edinburgh brands, has a pale flavor, extremely vinous and very like some of the light French wines. It is mild in its effect, pale in color, and the taste of the hops does not predominate as in the India pale ale (manufactured especially for the Indian market) and Allsopp's. Scotch ales are also said to be less liable to adulteration than the English. American ales are very light, as compared with many foreign products, but they contain alcohol sufficient to intoxicate, even when taken in small quantities, by those not accustomed to alcoholic stimulants. Often, too, ingredients are used which are injurious to the system, in addition to the poison of the alcohol.

BATH.

The skin of the human being is not merely an outward covering for the body, but an organ the proper performance of whose work is of vital importance to good health. Its seven million pores are not a useless part of the animal economy, but form the sluices through which the system throws off a portion of its waste and deleterious matter; this matter is removed in the form of an imperceptible watery vapor, mixed with a few saline and gaseous substances, and the quantity capable of being gotten rid of in this way, in the space of twenty-four hours, amounts in round numbers to twenty ounces. The retention of this, by reason of the inability of the skin to perform its functions, is of course productive of great injury to the system, throwing more than their due share of work on the other secretive organs. The only method of keeping the skin clear and in proper working order is bathing with sufficient frequency. Bathing not only removes the matter which the skin has already discharged, but stimulates its activity, and increases its efficiency. The temperature of the water is a highly important circumstance, and medical writers usually classify baths, as cold, warm, and hot.

Cold Bath.— The cold bath is taken in water which is cold as compared with the normal heat of the body, or at a temperature of 33° to 65°. The effect of such a bath on a person in good health is, on first plunging in, a sensation of extreme cold (the duration of which depends on the temperature of the water and the condition of the bather), and is followed by a reaction which brings on a sensation of warmth and a feeling of lightness and vigor. By degrees, if the body continue to be immersed, the bather again begins to feel cold, chilliness, accompanied by shivering, comes on, the pulse grows feebler and slower, and the whole body becomes languid and powerless. The time to leave the bath is during the period of warmth, before the second chilliness begins; and immediately on stepping out the bather should rub himself dry with a coarse towel, and continue rubbing till the skin is in a glow. The ultimate effect of the cold bath has been differently described by different physicians, and some are strongly opposed to its use at all; but, where it agrees, it is tonic and bracing, it improves the digestion, stimulates the skin, and renders the circulation more active and vigorous. It also hardens the system and causes it to be much less sensitive to changes of temperature, being on this account an excellent protection against taking cold on exposure. Its beneficial effect depends much on the strength of the reaction; if, therefore, on coming out of the cold bath, the person feels dull and chilly, or complains of headache, or a sensation of tightness across the chest, the cold bath disagrees, and should be discontinued or modified.

But many persons experiencing these symptoms seem to need just the sort of stimulus the cold bath gives. This they can get by applying cold water with a wash rag to a square foot or two of the skin at a time, rubbing the space into a glow with a towel, and repeating the process until the whole body has been bathed. The writer knows instances where this method has cured people too sensitive to cold.

The diseases for which cold baths are valuable as a remedy are morbid irritability and sensibility, accompanied by general debility; also for asthma, in the intervals between the paroxysms, when the system is in other respects in a proper condition for it. When there is a tendency to colds and rheumatism, the cold bath is an excellent preventive; for this purpose it should be used continuously throughout the year. It is improper in the case of those who have a tendency to consumption, or who are constitutionally liable to bowel complaints; and it should never be ventured on by anyone suffering from chronic inflammation of the mucous membranes of the bronchia and intestinal canal. The best time for taking a cold bath is in the early morning just after rising. But persons of feeble circulation in whom reaction does not readily follow, had better not take a cold bath before their breakfast is digested.

Warm Bath. — This includes all baths ranging in temperature from 66° to 95°. Its effect is very different from that of the cold bath. There is no shock, but the temperature is grateful to the bather; the blood circulates more rapidly, and a gentle glow pervades the body; the skin absorbs water, is softened, and throws off the scales of decomposed matter which may have accumulated on it; pain is allayed, and nervous irritation is soothed. The warm bath is especially grateful and beneficial after excessive muscular exertion, or after the fatigue and excitement of traveling. It refreshes and tranquilizes the system; but, on the other hand, it has none of the tonic influence of the cold bath, and its frequent use tends to relax and debilitate, while rendering the system more sensible to changes of temperature. The best temperature for the bath of a healthy person is what is called tepid, and it is also the most agreeable. A distinctly warm bath taken just before going to bed will probably cure any tendency to wakefulness, especially if the wakefulness come from overuse of the brain. No bath whatever should be taken while digestion is going on — say in less than two hours after a meal.

Hot Bath.— This has a temperature ranging from 98° (blood-heat) to 112°. It is a very powerful stimulant, and should never be used by persons in a good state of health. Even in cases of disease, it should only be taken under a physician's advice. As the object is to stimulate the vital actions, the bather should never remain long enough in the bath to produce exhaustion,— the average time is from ten to fifteen minutes. The best way to obtain the full beneficial effect of the hot bath is to commence with tepid water and gradually increase the temperature. The hot bath is chiefly used where it is desirable to produce abundant perspiration, when it should be followed by rolling the patient in blankets.

Shower Bath.— When cold water is used, the effect of this bath is similar to that of the ordinary cold bath, but the shock from the shower bath is greater than that from simple immersion, especially if the quantity of water be large, the temperature low, and the fall considerable. Its effects are also more speedy, and extend more to the internal organs than those of the common bath. When the result is beneficial the glow is felt almost immediately, consequently, when recourse is had to it, the bather should withdraw immediately after the shock; if its use is prolonged it quickly lowers, and at last destroys the sensibility, and is then highly injurious. For delicate persons, the tepid shower bath is preferable; and salt added to the water is an improvement. When used for hygienic purposes the best time to take the shower bath is immediately after rising in the morning. Vigorous rubbing and overexertion should be guarded against immediately following the bath.

SMALL POINTS ON TABLE ETIQUETTE.

Delicacy of manner at table stamps both man and woman, for one can, at a glance, discern whether a person has been trained to eat well — *i. e.*, to hold the knife and fork properly, to eat without the slightest sound of the lips, to drink quietly, to use the napkin rightly, to make no noise with any of the implements of the table, and last, but not least, to eat slowly and masticate the food thoroughly. All these points should be most carefully taught to children, and then they will always feel at their ease at the grandest tables in the land. There is no position where the innate refinement of a person is more fully exhibited than at the table, and nowhere that those who have not been trained in table etiquette feel more keenly their deficiencies. The knife should never be used to carry food to the mouth, but only to cut it up into small mouthfuls; then place it upon the plate at one side, and take the fork in the right hand, and eat all the food with it. When both have been used finally, they should be laid diagonally across the plate, with both handles toward the right hand; this is understood by well-trained waiters to be the signal for removing them, together with the plate.

Be careful to keep the mouth shut closely while masticating the food. It is the opening of the lips which causes the smacking which seems very disgusting. Chew your food well, but do it silently, and be careful to take small mouthfuls. The knife can be used to cut the meat finely, as large pieces of meat are not healthful, and appear very indelicate. At many tables, two, three, or more knives and forks are placed on the table, the knives at the right hand of the plate, the forks at the left, — a knife and a fork for each course, so that there need be no replacing of them after the breakfast and dinner is served. The smaller ones, which are for game, dessert, or for hot cakes at breakfast, can be tucked under the edges of the plate, and the large ones, for the meat and vegetables, are placed outside of them. Be very careful not to clatter your knives and forks upon your plates, but use them without noise. When passing the plate for a second helping, lay them together at one side of the plate, with handles to the right. When you are helped to anything, do not wait until the rest of the company are provided, it is not considered good breeding. Soup is always served for the first course, and it should be eaten with dessert spoons, and taken from the sides, not the tips of them, without any sound of the lips, and not sucked into the mouth audibly from the ends of the spoon. Bread should not be broken into soup or gravy. Never ask to be helped to soup a second time. The hostess may ask you to take a second plate, but you will politely decline. Fish chowder, which is served in soup plates, is said to be an exception which proves this rule, and when eating of that it is correct to take a second plateful if desired.

Another generally neglected obligation is that of spreading butter on one's bread as it lies on one's plate, or but slightly lifted at one end of the plate; it is very frequently buttered in the air, bitten in gouges, and still held in the face and eyes of the table with the marks of the teeth on it. This certainly is not altogether pleasant, and it is better to cut it, a bit at a time, after buttering it, and put piece by piece in the mouth with one's finger and thumb. Never help yourself to butter, or any other food with your own knife or fork. It is not considered good taste to mix food on the same plate. Salt must be left on the side of the plate, and never on the tablecloth.

Let us mention a few things concerning the eating of which there is sometimes doubt. A cream cake and anything of similar nature should be eaten with knife and fork, never bitten. Asparagus — which should be always served on bread or toast so as to absorb superfluous moisture — may be taken from the finger and thumb; if it is fit to be set before you, the whole of it may be eaten. Pastry should be broken and eaten with a fork, never cut with a knife. Raw oysters should be eaten with a fork, also fish. Pease and beans, as we all know, require the fork only; however, food that cannot be held with a fork should be eaten with a spoon. Potatoes, if mashed, should be mashed with the fork. Green corn should be eaten from the cob; but it must be held with a single hand.

Celery, cresses, olives, radishes, and relishes

of that kind are, of course, to be eaten with the fingers; the salt should be laid upon one's plate, not upon the cloth. Fish is to be eaten with the fork, without the assistance of the knife; a bit of bread in the left hand sometimes helps one to master a refractory morsel. Fresh fruits should be eaten with a silver-bladed knife, especially pears, apples, etc.

Berries, of course, are to be eaten with a spoon. In England they are served with their hulls on, and three or four are considered an ample quantity. But then, in England they are many times the size of ours; there they take the big berry by the stem, dip into powdered sugar, and eat it as we do the turnip radish. It is not proper to drink with a spoon in the cup; nor should one, by the way, ever quite drain a cup or glass.

Don't, when you drink, elevate your glass as if you were going to stand it inverted on your nose. Bring the glass perpendicularly to the lips, and then lift it to a slight angle. Do this easily.

Drink sparingly while eating. It is far better for the digestion not to drink tea or coffee until the meal is finished. Drink gently, and do not pour it down your throat like water turned out of a pitcher.

When seating yourself at the table, unfold your napkin and lay it across your lap in such a manner that it will not slide off upon the floor; a gentleman should place it across his right knee. Do not tuck it into your neck, like a child's bib. For an old person, however, it is well to attach the napkin to a napkin hook and slip it into the vest or dress button-holes, to protect the garments, or sew a broad tape at two places on the napkin, and pass it over the head. When the soup is eaten, wipe the mouth carefully with the napkin, and use it to wipe the hands after meals. Finger bowls are not a general institution, and yet they seem to be quite as needful as the napkin, for the fingers are also liable to become a little soiled in eating. They can be had quite cheaply, and should be half filled with water, and placed upon the side table or butler's tray, with the dessert, bread and cheese, etc. They are passed to each person half filled with water, placed on a parti-colored napkin with a dessert plate underneath, when the dessert is placed upon the table. A leaf or two of sweet verbena, an orange flower, or a small slice of lemon, is usually put into each bowl to rub upon the fingers. The slice of lemon is most commonly used. The finger tips are slightly dipped into the bowl, the lemon juice is squeezed upon them, and then they are dried softly upon the napkin. At dinner parties and luncheons they are indispensable.

Spoons are sometimes used with firm puddings, but forks are the better style. A spoon should never be turned over in the mouth.

Ladies have frequently an affected way of holding the knife half-way down its length, as if it were too big for their little hands; but this is as awkward a way as it is weak; the knife should be grasped freely by the handle only, the forefinger being the only one to touch the blade, and that only along the back of the blade at its root, and no further down.

At the conclusion of a course, where they have been used, knife and fork should be laid side by side across the middle of the plate — never crossed; the old custom of crossing them was in obedience to an ancient religious formula. The servant should offer everything at the left of the guest, that the guest may be at liberty to use the right hand. If one has been given a napkin ring, it is necessary to fold one's napkin and use the ring; otherwise the napkin should be left unfolded.

Never, if possible, cough or sneeze at the table. If you feel the paroxysm coming on, leave the room. It may be worth while to know that a sneeze may be stifled by placing the finger firmly upon the upper lip.

POSOLOGICAL TABLE.

Medicines, with doses for adults. For patients over 20 years of age, the full dose; from 14 to 20 years, $\frac{2}{3}$ of full dose; 7 to 14 years, $\frac{1}{2}$ dose; 4 to 7 years, $\frac{1}{3}$ dose; 3 years, $\frac{1}{6}$ dose; 2 years, $\frac{1}{8}$ dose; 1 year, $\frac{1}{12}$ dose.

MEDICINE.	DOSE.
Arsenic, Fowler's Solution of	2 to 10 drops
Aconite, Extract of	$\frac{1}{8}$ to $\frac{1}{2}$ grain
Aconite, Tincture of	1 to 5 drops
Aloes, Purified	1 to 5 grains
Aloes, Pills of	1 to 4 pills
Aloes, Pills of Asafœtida and	1 to 4 pills
Asafœtida, Mixture of	$\frac{1}{2}$ to 2 tablespoonfuls
Asafœtida, Tincture of	$\frac{1}{2}$ to 2 tablespoonfuls
Asafœtida, Pills of	1 to 4 pills
Atropia, Sulphate of	$\frac{1}{200}$ to $\frac{1}{60}$ of a grain
Belladonna, Extract of	$\frac{1}{4}$ to 1 grain
Belladonna, Fluid Extract of	1 to 5 drops
Belladonna, Tincture of	5 to 30 drops
Bismuth, Subnitrate of	10 to 30 grains
Bromide of Ammonia	5 to 20 grains
Bromide of Potassium	5 to 20 grains
Bromide of Sodium	5 to 20 grains
Buchu, Fluid Extract of	10 to 60 drops
Calibar Bean, Extract of	$\frac{1}{2}$ to 1 grain
Calomel	$\frac{1}{6}$ to 10 grains
Camphor, Spirits of	5 to 15 drops
Camphor Water	1 to 4 teaspoonfuls
Capsicum, Tincture of	10 to 20 drops
Castor Oil	$\frac{1}{4}$ to 2 tablespoonfuls
Chloral, Hydrate of	5 to 30 grains
Cinchona, Sulphate of	5 to 30 grains
Cinchona, Compound Tincture of	1 to 4 teaspoonfuls
Cod Liver Oil	$\frac{1}{2}$ to 1 tablespoonful
Copper, Sulphate of	$\frac{1}{8}$ to $\frac{1}{2}$ grain
Corrosive Sublimate	$\frac{1}{60}$ to $\frac{1}{10}$ grain
Cream of Tartar	5 to 60 grains
Croton Oil	1 to 2 drops
Digitalis, Extract of	$\frac{1}{2}$ to 2 grains
Digitalis, Tincture of	5 to 60 drops
Dover's Powder	5 to 10 grains
Epsom Salts	$\frac{1}{2}$ to 2 tablespoonfuls
Ergot, Fluid Extract of	$\frac{1}{2}$ to 2 teaspoonfuls

MEDICINE.	DOSE.
Gelsemium, Fluid Extract of	5 to 10 drops
Gentian, Extract of	1 to 5 grains
Hydrochloric Acid, dilute	1 to 5 drops
Hyoscyamus, Fluid Extract of	5 to 20 drops
Hyoscyamus, Tincture of	½ to 2 teaspoonfuls
Iodine, Compound Tincture of	2 to 5 drops
Iodide of Potassium	5 to 30 grains
Ipecacuanha, Fluid Extract of	2 to 30 drops
Ipecacuanha, Syrup of	1 to 4 teaspoonfuls
Ipecacuanha, Troches of Morphine and	1 to 10 troches
Iron, Reduced	1 to 2 grains
Iron, Pyrophosphate of	2 to 5 grains
Iron, Tincture of the Chloride of	5 to 30 drops
Lactic Acid	15 to 30 drops
Laudanum	15 to 40 drops
Lead, Sugar of	½ to 5 grains
May Apple, Resin of	⅛ to ¼ grain
May Apple, Extract of	3 to 8 grains
Muriatic Acid, dilute	5 to 10 drops
Morphine	⅛ to ⅓ grains
Magnesia, Sulphate of	½ to 2 tablespoonfuls
Mustard, Ground	1 to 2 teaspoonfuls
Nitre, Sweet Spirits of	½ to 1 teaspoonful
Nitro-Muriatic Acid, dilute	2 to 10 drops
Nux Vomica, Tincture of	10 to 25 drops
Opium, Extract of	½ to 2 grains
Opium, Tincture of	15 to 40 drops
Opium, Camphorated Tincture of	¼ to 2 tablespoonfuls
Paregoric	¼ to 2 tablespoonfuls
Potassium, Bicarbonate of	5 to 20 grains
Potassium, Bitartrate of	5 to 60 grains
Potassium, Bromide of	5 to 20 grains
Potassium, Chlorate of	5 to 20 grains
Potassium, Iodide of	5 to 30 grains
Potassium, Liquor of	2 to 20 drops
Pepsin	5 to 10 grains
Quassia, Tincture of	5 to 60 drops
Quinine	2 to 10 grains
Salicin	5 to 20 grains
Senna, Confection of	1 to 2 teaspoonfuls
Senna, Fluid Extract of	1 tablespoonful
Soda, Bicarbonate of	5 to 30 grains
Soda, Salicylate of	10 to 30 grains
Squill, Syrup of	½ to 1 teaspoonful
Strychnia, Sulphate of	$\frac{1}{20}$ to $\frac{1}{12}$ of a grain
Turpentine, Spirits or Oil of	5 to 10 drops
Valerian, Tincture of	½ to 2 teaspoonfuls
Veratrum Viride, Tincture of	1 to 4 drops
Zinc, Oxide of	½ to 5 grains

DISINFECTANTS AND HOW TO USE THEM.

The National Board of Health of the United States of America, consisting of a number of our leading physicians and chemical experts, of which Professor C. F. Chandler of New York was chairman, have issued the following instructions for disinfection, intended especially for the guidance of physicians and nurses in the yellow fever districts, but which are equally applicable in other classes of contagious diseases. In submitting this report the chairman says: —

It has been the aim of the committee to prepare concise directions for disinfection, so simple and clear that they may be easily followed by any person of intelligence.

In the selection of disinfecting agents the aim has been: 1st, to secure agents which can be relied upon to accomplish the work; 2d, which can be procured in a state of comparative purity in every village in the United States; 3d, so cheap that they may be used in adequate quantities.

It is extremely important that the people should be instructed with regard to disinfection. They must be taught that no reliance can be placed upon disinfectants simply because they smell of chlorine or carbolic acid, or possess the color of permanganate, and that, in general, proprietary disinfectants with high-sounding names are practically worthless, as they either have no value whatever, or, if value, cost many times as much as they are worth, and cannot be used in sufficient quantity.

Explanations.— Disinfection is the destruction of the poisons of infectious and contagious diseases.

Deodorizers, or substances which destroy smells, are not necessarily disinfectants, and disinfectants do not necessarily have odor.

Disinfection cannot compensate for want of cleanliness or ventilation.

I.— DISINFECTANTS TO BE EMPLOYED.

1. Roll sulphur (brimstone) for fumigation.

2. Sulphate of iron (copperas) dissolved in water in the proportion of one and a half pounds to the gallon; for soil, sewers, etc.

3. Sulphate of zinc and common salt, dissolved together in water in the proportion of four ounces sulphate and two ounces salt to the gallon; for clothing, bed linen, etc.

NOTE.— Carbolic acid is not included in the above list for the following reasons: It is very difficult to determine the quality of the commercial article, and the purchaser can never be certain of securing it of proper strength; it is expensive, when of good quality, and experience has shown that it must be employed in comparatively large quantities to be of any use; it is liable by its strong odor to give a false sense of security.

II.— HOW TO USE DISINFECTANTS.

1. *In the Sick Room.*— The most available agents are fresh air and cleanliness. The clothing, towels, bed linen, etc., should at once, on removal from the patient, be placed in a pail or tub of the zinc solution, boiling hot if possible, before removal from the room.

All discharges should either be received in vessels containing copperas solution, or, when this is impracticable, should be immediately covered with copperas solution. All vessels used about the patient should be cleansed with the same solution.

Unnecessary furniture—especially that which is stuffed — carpets and hangings, when possible, should be removed from the room at the outset; otherwise, they should remain for subsequent fumigation and treatment.

2. *Fumigation* with sulphur is the only practicable method for disinfecting the house.

For this purpose the rooms to be disinfected must be vacated. Heavy clothing, blankets, bedding, and other articles which cannot be treated with zinc solution, should be opened and exposed during fumigation, as directed below. Close the rooms as tightly as possible, place the sulphur in iron pans supported upon bricks, set it on fire by hot coals, or with the aid of a spoonful of alcohol, and allow the room to remain closed for twenty-four hours. For a room about ten feet square, at least two pounds of sulphur should be used; for larger rooms, proportionally increased quantities.

3. *Premises.*— Cellars, yards, stables, gutters, privies, cesspools, water-closets, drains, sewers, etc., should be frequently and liberally treated with copperas solution. The copperas solution is easily prepared by hanging a basket containing about sixty pounds of copperas in a barrel of water.

4. *Body and Bed Clothing, etc.*—It is best to burn all articles which have been in contact with persons sick with contagious or infectious diseases. Articles too valuable to be destroyed should be treated as follows: —

a. Cotton, linen, flannels, blankets, etc., should be treated with the boiling hot zinc solution, introducing piece by piece, securing thorough wetting, and boiling for at least half an hour.

b. Heavy woolen clothing, silks, furs, stuffed beds covers, beds, and other articles which cannot be treated with the zinc solution, should be hung in the room during fumigation, pockets being turned inside out, and the whole garment thoroughly exposed. Afterward they should be hung in the open air, beaten, and shaken. Pillows, beds, stuffed mattresses, upholstered furniture, etc., should be cut open, the contents spread out and thoroughly fumigated. Carpets are best fumigated on the floor, but should afterward be removed to the open air and thoroughly beaten.

SLEEPLESSNESS.

Nothing lowers the vital forces more than sleeplessness, which may generally be traced to one of four causations: (1) mental worry; (2) a disordered stomach; (3) excessive muscular exertion; (4) functional or organic disease. Loss of sleep is, when rightly understood, one of Nature's premonitory warnings that some of her physical laws have been violated. When we are troubled with sleeplessness, it becomes requisite to discover the primary cause, and then to adopt suitable means for its removal. When insomnia, or sleeplessness, arises from mental worry, it is indeed most difficult to remove. The best and perhaps the only effectual plan under such circumstances to reach the root of the disorder is a spare diet, combined with plenty of outdoor exercise, thus to draw the blood from the brain; for it is as impossible for the brain to continue active without a due circulation of blood as it is for an engine to move without steam.

When suffering from mental distress, a hot soap bath before retiring to rest is an invaluable agent for obtaining sleep, as by its means a more equable blood pressure becomes established, promoting a decrease of the heart's action and relaxation of the blood vessels. Many a sleepless night owes its origin to the body's temperature being unequal. In mental worry, the head is often hot and the feet cold, the blood being driven to the brain. The whole body should be well washed over with carbolic soap and sponged with very hot water. The blood then becomes diverted from the brain, owing to an adequate diffusion of circulation. Tea and coffee should not be taken of an evening when persons suffer from insomnia, as they directly induce sleeplessness, being nervine stimulants. A sharp walk of about twenty minutes is also very serviceable before going to bed.

Sleeplessness is sometimes engendered by a disordered stomach. Whenever this organ is overloaded, its powers are disordered, and wakefulness or a restless night is its usual accompaniment. Dr. C. J. B. Williams, F.R.S., remarks that no food should be taken at least within one hour of bedtime. It cannot be too generally realized that the presence of undigested food in the stomach is one of the most prevailing causes of sleeplessness.

Persons suffering from either functional or organic disease are peculiarly liable to sleeplessness. When inability to sleep persistently occurs, and cannot be traced to any perverted mode of life or nutrition, there is good reason for surmising that some latent malady gives rise to a condition so truly distressing. Under these circumstances, instead of making bad worse, by swallowing deadly sleeping drugs, a scientific physician should be without delay consulted. Functional disorders of the stomach, liver, and heart, are often the primary source of otherwise unaccountable wakefulness.

Recently the dangerous and lamentable habit of promiscuously taking sleeping draughts has unfortunately become very prevalent, entailing misery and ill health to a terrible degree. Most persons addicted to this destructive practice erroneously think that it is better to take a sleeping draught than lie awake. A greater mistake could hardly exist. All opiates more or less occasion mischief, and even the state of stupefaction they induce utterly fails to bring about that revitalization resulting from natural sleep. The physiological effect of hypnotics, or sleeping draughts, upon the system is briefly as follows: (1) They paralyze the nerve centers and disorder the stomach, rendering it unfit for its duties; witness the sickness and loss of appetite consequent upon a debauch. Chloral, chloroform, opium, etc., act upon the system much in the same way as inebriation. (2) One and all anæsthetics introduced into the body have life-destroying properties in a low degree — proved by an overdose being fatal. (3) The condition they produce is not sleep, but a counterfeit state of unconsciousness. (4) They directly poison the blood, consequent upon its carbonization, resulting from their action. While speaking of sedatives, we cannot omit drawing special attention to chloral. This powerful drug is popularly supposed to give a quiet night's rest, without any of the after effects (headache, etc.) produced by various preparations of morphia. Now chloral is what is termed cumulative in its action, which implies that even the same dose, persisted in for a certain length of time, may cause death. Of all hypnotics, chloral is by far the most deadly, and should never, under any circumstances, be taken except under medical supervision.

To epitomize what has already been said regarding sleeplessness: its rational cure should be arrived at in each individual case by seeking out the cause, and then removing the morbid action, of which it is but a natural sequence.

Lastly, sleeplessness, under no circumstances, should be neglected, as it acts disastrously both on the mental and physical forces.

DRUGS.

In purchasing drugs, whether in the raw state or in the form of extracts, tinctures, etc., it is very important to obtain them from a reputable chemist, who will take care that the article is genuine and properly labeled. The adulteration of drugs is carried on to an enormous extent, and, as commonly sold by irresponsible parties, the strength is seldom above one half of what it ought to be. Besides this, there is the danger of substituting a cheap drug for a dear one. Drugs are, most of them, soon spoiled by keeping, and in all cases they should be preserved in well-stoppered bottles — with the exception of Epsom salts, niter, soda, and some few others, which will keep without injury for an indefinite time. All vegetable medicines lose their virtues in the course of a few months, if not carefully closed from the air; and even in bottles, they seldom keep good for a year. It is desirable, therefore, to purchase them in small quantities at a time, and to renew them at intervals of twelve months. Most drugs simply lose their strength with time; but laudanum, on the contrary, becomes stronger, especially if it be left uncorked; the spirit evaporates, leaving almost pure opium. This must be guarded against, as the most fatal results might occur from giving a dose much greater (in point of strength) than was intended.

A few drugs requiring extended notice are given under separate titles in this work.

The additional ones given below are least liable to abuse, in family use. Each is introduced in alphabetical order, with its properties and effects given under the respective heads — (*a*) *Physical properties;* (*b*) *Therapeutical effects;* (*c*) *Use;* and (*d*) *Dose and mode of administration.* Extracts, tinctures, and all such compounds as will bear keeping, and are likely to be useful in a family, are better when bought of a good druggist than as made at home. They are therefore given without direction to manufacture. It should be borne in mind, however, that drugs of any kind should be used very sparingly except by direction of a physician.

Acid, Acetic. Vinegar distilled from wood, and purified.

(*a*) *Physical properties.* Limpid, colorless, volatile; odor, pungent and fragrant; taste, acid.

(*b*) *Therapeutical effects.* Stimulant, escharotic, but, when diluted with water, cooling.

(*c*) *Used* in lotions for cooling purposes diluted with water, also in ringworm and removing warts.

(*d*) *Dose.* It is not given internally, except in combination with other medicines.

Acid, Acetic (*diluted*). Diluted acetic acid, prepared from the acid just described.

(*a*) *Physical properties.* A clear acid fluid.

(*b*) *Therapeutical effects.* Astringent, diaphoretic, cooling, and antiseptic. It is useful in making the acetate of lead more soluble. Externally, it is stimulant in its full strength, or, when mixed with water, cooling.

(*c*) *Used* in fevers internally; or as a gargle with capsicum; or as an inhalation in sore throat. A useful lotion when mixed with spirit and water, in bruises, sprains, and burns.

(*d*) *Dose.* Half a drachm to one drachm.

Acid, Benzoic.

(*a*) *Physical properties.* White and shining crystals, with flakes of a fragrant aromatic odor, and acid taste. Sparingly soluble in water, but is easily dissolved in alcohol. When heated, is completely evaporated, with an agreeable and peculiar odor; but if the temperature is raised too high, it takes fire, and burns with a yellow flame.

(*b*) *Therapeutical effects.* Stimulant and expectorant.

(*c*) *Used* in chronic bronchitis.

(*d*) *Dose.* Five grains to half a drachm twice a day.

Acid, Carbolic (*pure and impure*). A powerful antiseptic substance, obtained from coal tar oil.

(*a*) *Physical properties.* The *pure* anhydrous acid is in long, colorless, prismatic crystals, turning a pale pink on keeping. It rapidly deliquesces in moist air. The *impure* is a more or less brown liquid. Both strongly resemble tar in smell.

(*b*) *Therapeutical effects.* Strongly antiseptic, antifermentative, and caustic.

(*c*) The pure acid is applied on cotton for allaying tenderness and pain in decayed teeth. Being a caustic, it should be carefully kept from touching anything but the tooth; when properly used, it is the best application for toothache arising from this cause, and is indeed a specific.

Dose. About a grain of the acid is enough for toothache. One drachm of carbolic acid to a pint of water is strong enough for disinfectant purposes.

Acid, Citric, prepared from the juice of lemons.

(*a*) *Physical properties.* Sharp acid taste, white semi-transparent crystals of a rhomboidal shape. Decomposed by heat; soluble in twice their weight of cold, and half their weight of boiling water.

(*b*) *Therapeutical effects.* Refrigerant.

(*c*) *Used* in febrile and inflammatory complaints; dissolved in water as a substitute for lemon juice, and added to soda to form the common effervescing draught.

(*d*) *Dose.* 10 grains to 1 scruple; 15 grains of the acid neutralize 20 grains of bicarbonate of soda, to form the effervescing draught.

Acid, Gallic, prepared from galls.

(*a*) *Physical properties.* A powder of nearly colorless semi-crystalline appearance; dissipated by heat; dissolves in water and spirit.

(*c*) *Used* in discharges of blood and diarrhœa, and in other mucous discharges. Also in hemorrhoids.

(*d*) *Dose.* 2 to 5 grains. As an injection half a drachm dissolved in one ounce of water; an ointment, 20 grains are mixed with an ounce of lard, with the addition of 30 or 40 grains of powdered opium.

Acid, Hydrochloric (*diluted*). Hydrochloric acid, mixed with three times its bulk of water.

(*a*) *Physical properties.* Taste, intensely acrid and caustic; smell, acrid and suffocating; the acid is colorless when pure, but usually is of a straw color, with the presence of peroxide of iron, or nitrous acid.

(*b*) *Therapeutical effects.* Tonic, antiseptic, and partially diuretic, by promoting all the secretions.

(*c*) *Used*, when combined with diluted nitric acid, in affections of the liver; also with bitters, to prevent the generation of worms; in gargles for sore throat.

(*d*) *Dose.* 20 minims to 40.

Acid, Sulphuric (*diluted*). Sulphuric acid mixed with about eleven times its bulk of water.

(*a*) *Physical properties.* Strong acid taste, inodorous, colorless, and transparent. Specific gravity, 1.103.

(*b*) *Therapeutical effects.* Tonic, astringent, and antiseptic.

(*c*) *Used* in dyspepsia, also to check sweatings, salivation, and diarrhœa; likewise as a gargle.

(*d*) *Dose.* 10 minims to 30, diluted largely (2 drachms to 8 ounces) as a gargle, with honey, sage, etc.

Acid, Tartaric.

(*a*) *Physical properties.* Colorless imperfect crystals, inodorous, very acid, soluble, largely in water.

(*b*) *Therapeutical effects.* Refrigerant, antiseptic, diuretic, and slightly aperient.

(*c*) *Used* in fevers, etc., with some soda or potassium, as an effervescing draught, instead of citric acid; the proportions being the same.

Æther, Sulphuric.

(*c*) *Physical properties.* A limpid, volatile, inflammable fluid, without color, produces great cold by evaporation; taste, peculiar, but hot and pungent; sparingly soluble in water, readily so in alcohol.

(*b*) *Therapeutical effects.* A diffusible stimulant, afterwards narcotic and antispasmodic; externally cooling; when inhaled producing anæsthesia.

(*c*) *Used* in hysteria, faintings, asthma, and other spasmodic complaints.

(*d*) *Dose.* 20 minims to 60, in water.

Aloes, Barbadoes.— The inspissated juice, of the cut leaf of the *Aloe spicata*, imported from the Cape of Good Hope and West Indies.

(*a*) *Physical properties.* Of a dark brown color, and shining resinous surface, with a strong disagreeable odor, and very bitter taste; very difficult to powder, and soluble in diluted alcohol.

(*b*) *Therapeutical effects.* A stimulating purgative, producing its chief effects on the lower bowels. Apt to produce and aggravate hemorrhoids.

(*c*) *Used* in dyspepsia and in head affections; also as a common purgative.

(*d*) *Dose.* One fourth of a grain to 5 grains, well powdered, or dissolved in hot water.

Alum.

(*a*) *Physical properties.* A semi-transparent, rough, irregular mass of saline matter. Taste, acid-astringent. Soluble in 18 parts of water at 60 degrees, and in a little more than an equal weight of water at 212 degrees.

(*b*) *Therapeutical effects.* Astringent and styptic.

(*c*) *Used* internally in hemorrhages; externally in ophthalmia, or as a gargle.

(*d*) *Dose.* 10 grains to 20. As gargle—1 drachm to a pint of water.

Ammonia, Liquor of. Ammonia condensed in water.

(*a*) *Physical Properties.* A stimulating solution. Blisters the skin.

(*b*) *Therapeutical effects.* Stimulating, diaphoretic, anti-acid, when given internally. Externally, irritant and eschorotic.

(*c*) *Used*, when largely diluted, in faintings, asphyxia, hysteria, spasms, acidities of the stomach; and, externally, as an irritant of the skin.

(*d*) *Dose.* The aromatic spirits of ammonia is the usual form for internal use. Dose from 15 to 40 minims.

Ammonia, Sesqui-Carbonate of. Ammonia united with carbonic acid.

(*a*) *Physical properties.* A mass of irregular crystals, somewhat resembling white sugar, but more transparent and striated. Smell, pungent; taste, sharp and alkaline; soluble in four times its weight of cold water; becomes opaque and friable on exposure to the air.

(*b*) *Therapeutical effects.* Stimulating, antispasmodic, diaphoretic, and anti-acid.

(*c*) *Used* in dyspepsia, hysteria, and all diseases requiring a rapidly acting diffusible stimulant. Externally, to the nostrils in syncope.

(*d*) *Dose.* 2 grains to 5, in pills or dissolved in any fluid.

Antimony, Potassio-Tartrate of. Tartar emetic.

(*a*) *Physical properties.* A colorless, transparent, inodorous, crystallized salt, with a slightly metallic taste. Soluble in fifteen times its weight of cold water, and twice its weight of boiling water; insoluble in pure alcohol, but soluble in proof spirit or wine. The aqueous solution becomes decomposed by keeping.

(*b*) *Therapeutical effects.* Emetic in large doses; diaphoretic in small ones; expectorant, slightly aperient and alterative; externally applied, produces a crop of pustules.

(*c*) *Used* to evacuate the stomach, to slow the circulation, and to produce profuse perspiration. Externally applied in the form of an ointment, to produce counter-irritation.

(*d*) *Dose.* As an emetic, 1 grain to 4 grains in solution; in pneumonia, 1-2 a grain to 3 grains, often repeated; as an expectorant, or diaphoretic, 1-8 of a grain to 1-2 a grain.

Asafœtida, Gum.

(*a*) *Physical properties.* A mass of irregular pieces, varying in color from red or reddish-brown to white; odor resembling garlic, but more fetid; taste, bitter and slightly acrid; difficult to powder, unless rubbed with carbonate of ammonia. Forms a milky mixture with water.

(*b*) *Therapeutical effects.* Antispasmodic, expectorant, anthelmintic.

(*c*) *Used* in hysteria, flatulence, colic, etc.

(*d*) *Dose.* 5 to 10 grains.

Bismuth, Trisnitrate of. The metal bismuth united with nitric acid.

(*a*) *Physical properties.* A white, tasteless, inodorous powder, very slightly soluble in water.

(*b*) *Therapeutical effects.* Antispasmodic, stomachic, and tonic.

(*c*) *Used* much in dyspepsia, attended with pain of the stomach, and water brash, and diarrhœa.

(*d*) *Dose.* 5 to 10 grains.

Borax. Biborate of soda.

(*a*) *Physical properties.* Sweetish, shining, efflorescent crystals, soluble in twelve parts of cold and two parts of boiling water.

(*b*) *Therapeutical effects.* Absorbent, cooling, and alterative.

(*c*) *Used* in intestinal irritation of infants. Externally applied to thrush, and to cutaneous diseases.

(*d*) *Dose.* 5 grains to 30. Externally applied, dissolved in eight times its weight of honey, or mucilage, or, better, in pure water.

Calomel. *See* MERCURY.

Camphor. A peculiar substance, obtained by distillation from the wood of the *Laurus camphor*.

(*a*) *Physical properties.* In large, white semi-transparent cakes, with a strong peculiarly fragrant and aromatic odor; taste, bitter and acrid; insoluble in water; soluble in alcohol, ether, acetic acid, and the fixed oils.

(*b*) *Therapeutical effects.* Stimulant, diaphoretic, sedative; externally, soothing.

(*c*) *Used* in hysteria, asthma, chorea, and generally in spasmodic diseases. Externally, in muscular pains, bruises, etc.

(*d*) *Dose.* 3 grains to 5, in pills. When dissolved in water as camphor mixture, the quantity is scarcely appreciable.

Cantharides, Plaster of. Blistering plaster. Sometimes prepared in the form of a tissue paper, imbued with the active principle.

(*a*) *Physical properties.* The plaster is a firm preparation requiring the warmth of the hand to enable it to be spread upon leather or calico. It soon spoils by keeping; and if more than a month old should, after spreading, be dusted over with powdered cantharides.

(*b*) *Therapeutical effects.* To raise the cuticle from the cutis, producing at the same time a large secretion of serous fluid. The time varies from 3 hours to 12, or even more. In babies the blister should always be carefully watched after 3 hours, as it often rises rapidly and would be liable to produce severe ulceration of the skin. Blistering may be promoted by applying a poultice after the removal of the cantharides.

Capsicum.

(*a*) *Physical Properties.* Berries of a red color, and an extremely pungent odor and taste, which is yielded to alcohol, ether, vinegar, and water.

(*b*) *Therapeutical effects.* Stimulant, stomachic, and rubefacient.

(*c*) *Used* in dyspepsia, flatulence; externally, as an ingredient in gargles for relaxed sore throat.

(*d*) *Dose.* 3 grains to 5 grains, in pills; 2 drachms to 8 ounces form the strength for using as a gargle diluted largely with water.

Castor Oil, obtained from *Ricinus communis.*

(*a*) *Physical properties.* A pale yellow-colored, transparent and viscid oil, with a faint odor and nauseous taste.

(*b*) *Therapeutical effects.* Mildly aperient.

(*c*) *Used* in colic and in those cases of constipation which will not bear drastic purgatives; also for mixing with gruel for the ordinary enema.

(*d*) *Dose.* A teaspoonful to one or two tablespoonfuls; an ounce is the proper quantity for mixing with gruel to make an enema.

Cerate. A species of ointment made rather hard with wax.

(*a*) **Simple Cerate.** Add 20 ounces of melted wax to a pint of olive oil, and mix while warm, stirring till cold.

(*b*) **Cerate of Spermaceti.** Melt together eight ounces of white wax and ten of spermaceti; then add a pint of olive oil, and stir together till they cool.

(*c*) **Cerate of Acetate of Lead.** Melt four ounces of white wax in eight fluid ounces of olive oil; then gradually add four drachms of powdered acetate of lead, previously rubbed with two fluid ounces of olive oil, and stir with a spatula till they unite.

(*d*) **Cerate of Resin.** Mix together 15 ounces each of resin and wax, and melt them over a slow fire; then add a pint of olive oil, and press the cerate, while hot, through a linen cloth.

Chalk, prepared. Friable carbonate of lime, rubbed into a fine powder and washed.

(*a*) *Physical properties.* An inodorous, insipid, white, friable powder, heavy, and insoluble in water.

(*b*) *Therapeutical effects.* Anti-acid, astringent, and absorbent.

(*c*) *Used* in acidities of the stomach and bowels, and to correct the irritation which is established in diarrhœa. Externally as a mild application of sores and burns.

(*d*) *Dose.* 10 to 15 grains.

Chamomile Flowers.

(*a*) *Physical properties.*

The flowers are small, with a strong, fragrant odor, and bitter aromatic taste, and some slight degree of warmth. Water and alcohol both absorb the virtues of this plant.

(*b*) *Therapeutical effects.* Tonic, stomachic, and carminative. The warm infusion, when weak, is emetic. Externally soothing.

(*c*) *Used* in dyspepsia, hysteria, flatulence, and also to work off emetics.

(*d*) *Dose* of the powder. 30 to 40 grains twice a day. The infusion—a half ounce to a pint of water—is usually preferred.

Chloride of Zinc. A combination of Zinc with chlorine.

(*a*) *Physical properties.* In solid piece, snow-white, inodorous, having a strongly styptic and metallic taste.

(*b*) Powerfully caustic, destroying the vitality of the part with which it is in contact, and causing very severe pain. In solution it is used as a disinfectant, appearing to act more energetically than chlorinated soda or lime, with a less disagreeable odor of chlorine.

(*c*) *Used* as a caustic in cancer and fungoid disease. In solution, it is applied to cutaneous diseases, and to mucous membranes, but requires great caution in its use. As a disinfectant, it must be largely diluted. (*See* DISINFECTANTS.)

Cincona Bark (*yellow*).

(*a*) *Physical properties.* Larger, thicker, and less rolled than the pale bark. Externally of a brownish yellow, and internally of a cinnamon brown. The fracture is fibrous; taste bitter, and less aromatic than the pale, with scarcely any degree of astringency.

(*b*) *Therapeutical effects.* Astringent, tonic, antiseptic, and febrifuge.

(*c*) *Used* in typhoid fevers, and in all low states of the system, being in such cases superior to quinine.

(*d*) *Dose.* 10 grains to 50, in wine or wine and water.

Cinnamon, Bark, oil, and water, used as a warm and cordial spice to prevent the griping of purgatives, etc.

Cod-Liver Oil, Prepared from the liver of the codfish.

(*a*) *Physical properties.* An oil of three different colors: pale yellow, pale brown, and dark brown. The pale brown appears to possess the highest virtues.

(*b*) *Therapeutical effects.* Nutritive and acting also on the general system.

(*c*) *Used* largely in consumption and chronic bronchitis to diminish the secretion from the lungs, and arrest, to some extent, the waste incident to these diseases; in nervous affections as a nerve-food, and in some skin diseases; also in other exhausting diseases.

(*d*) *Dose.* One drachm carried up to 4 in any convenient vehicle, as infusion of cloves.

Colocynth. The peeled fruit of the bitter cucumber.

(*a*) *Physical properties.* A white, soft, porous, medullary substance, investing the seeds with an intensely bitter, acrid, and nauseous taste.

(*b*) *Therapeutical effects.* Powerfully aperient.

(*c*) *Used,* with warm cordial spices, as an ordinary aperient. (*See* EXTRACTS.)

(*d*) *Dose.* 5 to 10 grains.

Conium (Hemlock). The leaves of *Conium maculatum*, an indigenous plant.

(*a*) *Physical properties.* Has a heavy narcotic smell, with a bitter, nauseous, and herbaceous taste; color, dull green; powers soon destroyed by light. Should be gathered just as the plant comes into flower, and dried in the sun, or in a stove.

(*b*) *Therapeutical effects.* Sedative, narcotic — in some cases alterative, and even tonic.

(*c*) *Used* in scirrhous and cancerous affections externally, and internally for neuralgia and pulmonary complaints; also in scrofulous complaints of children, especially in ophthalmia — in all cases requiring great caution; externally as a poultice, made by scalding the fresh leaves.

(*d*) *Dose.* 2 to 3 or 4 grains.

Copaiba Balsam.

(*a*) *Physical properties.* A liquid of a transparent yellowish color, and peculiar smell and taste, which is pungent, acrid, and nauseous; when fresh, of the consistency of linseed oil, gradually becoming thicker by exposure to the air, till at last it is as solid as resin; soluble in ether and alcohol.

(*b*) *Therapeutical effects.* Stimulant, diuretic, purgative in large doses; allays irritation of the mucous membranes, and especially those of the urinary passages.

(*c*) *Used* in chronic bronchitis, spasmodic asthma, whooping-cough, and in chronic inflammation of the bladder, etc.

(*d*) *Dose.* 10 minims to 30 in emulsion, or in the gelatine capsules in which it is sold.

Creosote. A peculiar liquid prepared from pyroxylic oil.

(*a*) *Physical properties.* An oily, colorless, transparent fluid, with a disagreeable smell, resembling somewhat the odor of badly-smoked meat.

(*b*) *Therapeutical effects.* Tonic, stomachic, diaphoretic, antiseptic, and styptic.

(*c*) *Used* internally in phthisis; also in troublesome vomiting, from any cause not readily understood, as seasickness.

Decoction of Cinchona.

(*a*) Boil 10 drachms of bruised yellow cinchona in a pint of water for ten minutes, in a closed vessel, then strain.

(*b*) *Therapeutical effects.* Antiseptic, astringent, tonic, febrifuge.

(*c*) *Used* in fever, malignant sore throat, dyspepsia.

(*d*) *Dose.* 1½ to 3 ounces twice or thrice a day.

Decoction of Dandelion.

(*a*) Boil 4 ounces of bruised dandelion in 1½ pints of distilled water to a pint, and strain.

(*b*) *Therapeutical effects.* Diuretic, slightly aperient, and specially acting on the liver.

(*c*) *Used* in torpid conditions of the liver, jaundice, habitual constipation, etc.

(*d*) *Dose.* 2 or 3 ounces twice or thrice a day.

Decoction of Iceland Moss.

(*a*) Boil 5 drachms of Iceland moss in a pint and a half of water down to a pint, and strain.

(*b*) *Therapeutical effects.* Tonic, emollient, slightly astringent.

(*c*) *Used* in consumption and dysentery.

(*d*) *Dose.* 1 to 2 ounces.

Decoction of Logwood,

(*a*) Boil 10 drachms of sliced logwood in 1½ pints of water to a pint, and strain.

(*b*) *Therapeutical effects.* Astringent and tonic.

(*c*) *Used* in diarrhœa and dysentery.

(*d*) *Dose.* 1 ounce to 2 ounces after each action of the bowels.

Decoction of Poppyheads.

(*a*) Boil five ounces of bruised poppyheads in 3 pints of water for a quarter of an hour, and strain.

(*b*) *Therapeutical effects.* Anodyne and soothing.

(*c*) *Used* as a fomentation in painful swellings and inflammation.

Decoction of Sarsaparilla (*simple*).

(*a*) Boil four ounces of sarsaparilla in 4 pints of water to 2 pints, and strain.

(*b*) *Therapeutical effects.* Alterative, diaphoretic, and tonic.

(*c*) *Used* in cutaneous diseases, chronic rheumatism, and scrofula.

(*d*) *Dose.* 2 ounces, twice or thrice a day.

Decoction of Sarsaparilla (*compound*).

(*a*) Mix 4 pints of boiling decoction of sarsaparilla, 10 drachms of sliced sassafras, 10 drachms of guaiacum-wood shavings, 10 drachms of bruised stick-liquorice, and 3 drachms of mezereon bark; boil for a quarter of an hour, and strain.

(*b*) (*c*) (*d*) *Therapeutical effects.* The same as the last, but warmer, and therefore better suited to weak stomachs.

Dill Water. Prepared from Dill seeds by distillation.

(*a*) *Physical properties.* An aromatic odor, with a pungent agreeable taste.

(*b*) *Therapeutical effects.* Carminative and stimulative.

(*c*) *Used* in the flatulence and gripings of children.

(*d*) *Dose.* ½ drachm to 1½ ounce.

Extract of Gentian.

(*a*) Made from the gentian root.

(*b*) *Therapeutical effects.* Tonic and stomachic.

(*c*) *Used* in dyspepsia.

(*d*) *Dose.* 5 to 20 grains.

Extract of Henbane. Prepared from the leaves of *Hyoscyamus niger*.

(*a*) *Physical properties.* An extract of a dingy olive color, and a peculiar disagreeable smell; taste, bitterish and saline.

(*b*) *Therapeutical effects.* Narcotic, anodyne, and antispasmodic.

(*c*) *Used* instead of opium, in irritability of the nervous system, or mucous surfaces, or in combination with purgatives to prevent their griping, as it does not cause constipation.

(*d*) *Dose.* 5 to 8 grains.

Extract of Hop.

(*a*) *Physical properties.* A dark-colored bitter extract, without much smell.

(*b*) *Therapeutical effects.* Tonic and sedative.

(*c*) *Used* in chronic dyspepsia and loss of sleep.

(*d*) *Dose.* 10 to 15 grains.

Extract of Sarsaparilla (*liquid*). Prepared from sarsaparilla, and used for the same purposes as the decoction. It is sold both as a simple and compound extract.

(*a*) *Dose.* 30 drops to 1 drachm two or three times a day in water.

Gamboge. A gum resin, of a purgative nature, but too powerful for domestic use.

Horseradish (the fresh root).

(*a*) *Physical properties.* Pungent odor, biting, acrid taste; communicates its active principles partially to water, but completely to alcohol.

(*b*) *Therapeutical effects.* Stimulant, diuretic, sudorific, emetic.

(*c*) *Used* in paralytic affections and chronic rheumatism.

(*d*) *Dose.* 1 to 2 drachms, cut into small pieces, or made into an infusion.

Infusion of Chamomile.

Chamomile tea.

(*a*) Macerate 5 drachms of chamomile flowers in a pint of boiling distilled water for ten minutes, in a closed vessel, and strain.

(*b*) *Therapeutical effects.* Tonic, stomachic; emetic, when warm. Externally soothing.

(*c*) *Used* in dyspepsia, and to assist the operation of emetics.

(*d*) *Dose.* 1 to 2 ounces. For emetic purposes, a weaker infusion is used in large quantities.

Infusion of Cloves.

(*a*) Macerate 3 drachms of bruised cloves in a pint of boiling water, in a covered vessel, and strain.

(*b*) *Therapeutical effects.* Stimulant, stomachic, slightly tonic.

(*c*) *Used* as a vehicle for more active tonics, especially cod-liver oil.

(*d*) *Dose.* 1 ounce to 2 or 3.

Infusion of Gentian (*compound*).

(*a*) Macerate 2 drachms of sliced gentian, 2 drachms of dried orange-peel, and 4 drachms of lemon peel in a pint of boiling water for an hour, in a covered vessel, and strain.

(*b*) *Therapeutical effects.* Stomachic and tonic.

(*c*) *Used* in dyspepsia and general debility.

(*d*) *Dose.* 1½ to 2 ounces two or three times a day.

Infusion of Linseed (*compound*).

Linseed tea.

(*a*) Macerate 6 drachms of bruised linseed and 10 drachms of sliced fresh liquorice in a pint of boiling water, for four hours, near the fire, in a covered vessel, and strain.

(*b*) *Therapeutical effects.* Soothing, especially to the mucous passages.

(*c*) *Used* in chronic bronchitis and strangury.

(*d*) *Dose, ad libitum.*

Infusion of Orange-peel (*compound*).

(*a*) Macerate half an ounce of dried orange-peel, two drachms of lemon-peel, one drachm of cloves bruised, in a pint of boiling water, for a quarter of an hour, in a covered vessel, and strain.

(*b*) *Therapeutical effects.* Stimulant, stomachic, and tonic.

(*c*) *Used* in dyspepsia, and as a vehicle for other remedies.

(*d*) *Dose.* 1 ounce to 2 or 3, at short intervals.

Infusion of Quassia.

(*a*) Macerate 10 scruples of quassia sliced, in a pint of boiling water for two hours, in a covered vessel.

(*b*) *Therapeutical effects.* Tonic and stomachic.

(*c*) *Used* in dyspepsia.

(*d*) *Dose.* 1½ to 2 ounces.

Infusion of Rhubarb.

(*a*) Macerate 3 drachms of sliced rhubarb root in a pint of boiling water for two hours, in a covered vessel, and strain.

(*b*) *Therapeutical effects.* Stomachic, tonic, and aperient.

(*c*) *Used* in dyspepsia accompanied with constipation, especially in combination with gentian.

(*d*) *Dose.* ½ half ounce to 1½ ounce.

Infusion of Roses (*compound*).

(*a*) Put three drachms of the dried red rose leaves into a pint of boiling water, then add a fluid drachm and a half of diluted sulphuric acid. Macerate for two hours, and strain the liquor; lastly, add 6 drachms of sugar.

(*b*) *Therapeutical effects.* Astringent, refrigerant, and antiseptic.

(*c*) *Used* as a drink in fevers; also as a vehicle for sulphate of magnesia, quinine, etc.

(*d*) *Dose.* 1½ to 2 ounces.

Infusion of Senna (*compound*).

Senna tea.

(*a*) Macerate 15 drachms of senna leaves, and four scruples of bruised ginger in a pint of boiling water for an hour in a closed vessel, and strain.

(*b*) *Therapeutical effects.* Aperient.

(*c*) *Used* as a vehicle for more active purgatives, which it assists; or by itself as a mild purgative.

(*d*) *Dose.* 1 to 3 ounces.

Ipecacuanha, the root.

(*a*) *Physical properties.* In pieces of three or four inches in length, with a resinous fracture; an acrid, aromatic somewhat bitter taste, slightly nauseous; peculiar odor; yields its active principle to water, spirit, and wine.

(*b*) *Therapeutical effects.* Emetic, diaphoretic, expectorant, and acting peculiarly on the liver.

(*c*) *Used* as an emetic; also as an expectorant in bronchitis, asthma, etc., as a nauseate in pneumonia, diarrhœa, dysentery; as a diaphoretic in various diseases, and in torpid liver, to promote its proper secretions.

(*d*) *Dose.* As an emetic, 15 to 30 grains; as a nauseate, 2 to 4 grains; as a diaphoretic, 1 grain, with a small dose of opium; as an expectorant or for torpid liver, ½ to 1 grain.

Jalap, the Root.

(*a*) *Physical properties.* Thin, transverse slices, or round masses; solid, hard, and heavy; dark gray color, striated appearance; sickly smell; taste sweetish but nauseous.

(*b*) *Therapeutical effects.* Actively aperient.

(*c*) *Used* in obstinate constipation, worms, dropsy; requires a carminative to prevent griping and nausea.

(*d*) *Dose.* 10 grains to 30.

Laudanum. (*See* Opium.)

Liniment of Ammonia.

(*a*) To 1 fluid ounce of the solution of ammonia add 2 fluid ounces of olive oil and shake together.

(*b*) *Therapeutical effects.* Stimulant and rubefacient.

(*c*) *Used* in sore throat externally, also in chronic rheumatism, with friction.

Liniment of Camphor.

(*a*) Dissolve 1 ounce of camphor in 4 fluid ounces of olive oil.

(*b*) *Therapeutical effects.* Stimulant.

(*c*) *Used* in chronic rheumatism, with friction.

Liniment of Camphor (*Compound*).

(*a*) Dissolve 2½ ounces of camphor and 1 drachm of oil of lavender in 17 fluid ounces of rectified spirits of wine; then add 3 fluid ounces of the strong solution of ammonia, and shake well together.

(*b*) *Therapeutical effects.* Stimulant.

(*c*) *Used* with friction in the same way as the simple liniment, but it is more powerful.

Liniment of Turpentine.

(*a*) Shake well together 2 ounces of soft soap and an ounce of camphor, with 16 fluid ounces of the spirit of turpentine, until mixed.

(*b*) *Therapeutical effects.* Stimulant.

(*c*) *Used* in paralytic affections and chronic rheumatism; also to burns and scalds.

Liquor of Acetate of Lead. Sold by the druggists.

(*a*) *Therapeutical effects.* Sedative and astringent when applied externally.

(*b*) *Used* as a lotion to inflamed surfaces when largely diluted with water. Goulard water is prepared from it by adding a fluid drachm and a half of it and 2 fluid drachms of proof spirit to a pint of distilled water.

Magnesia, Carbonate of.

(*a*) *Physical properties.* A solid, white, tasteless, inodorous powder, insoluble in water.

(*b*) *Therapeutical effects.* Anti-acid and purgative.

(*c*) *Used* in dyspepsia with costiveness, in the constipation of children and delicate grown persons (*d*) *Dose.* ½ drachm to 1 drachm or 2.

Magnesia, Sulphate of. Epsom salts.

(*a*) *Physical properties.* Small, pointed crystals of a transparent, colorless appearance; inodorous, with a disagreeable bitter taste; dissolves readily in water.

(*b*) *Therapeutical effects.* Purgative.

(*c*) *Used* as a cooling laxative, washing the bowels out, but not searching them.

(*d*) *Dose.* 1 drachm to 1 ounce.

Marsh Mallows.

(*a*) *Physical properties.* A root; long cylindrical; grayish without, white within; inodorous; taste sweetish.

(*b*) *Therapeutical effects.* Soothing.

(*c*) *Used* to make a soothing drink in irritation of the mucous membranes, or as a fomentation; boiling the leaves and roots to form it.

Mercury, Ammonia-chloride of. White precipitate.

(*a*) *Physical properties.* A white, inodorous powder; insipid, insoluble in water and alcohol.

(*b*) *Therapeutical effects.* Used externally only; it is detergent.

(*c*) *Used* for cutaneous diseases and for destroying lice, etc., in its powdered condition.

Mercury, Mild Chloride of. Calomel.

(*a*) *Physical properties.* A white, semi-transparent crystalline mass, inodorous, insipid, and insoluble. Usually sold as a heavy white powder.

(*b*) *Therapeutical effects.* Alterative, purgative, and producing absorption.

(*c*) *Used* in chronic diseases of the liver and general torpidity of the stomach and bowels; in dropsy, in combination with other medicines. A most dangerous medicine when employed by those who are not aware of its powerful effects.

(*d*) *Dose.* 1 grain twice a day as an alterative, 4 to 5 grains as an aperient, combined with, or followed by, some mild vegetable purgative.

Mercury, Nitric Oxide of. Red precipitate.

(*a*) *Physical properties.* A powder of a brilliant red color, insoluble in water.

(*b*) *Therapeutical effects.* Stimulant, external.

(*c*) *Used* in old ulcers and to heal indolent sores of all kinds when made into an ointment with lard. (See Ointments.)

Mint-water. Prepared from peppermint or spearmint. These are sold in the shops.

(*a*) *Therapeutical effects.* Both are carminative and slightly stimulating. Spearmint water is also diuretic.

(*b*) *Used* as a vehicle for other remedies.

Mixture of Chalk.

(*a*) Rub ½ ounce of prepared chalk and 3 drachms of sugar with a fluid ounce and a half of mixture of acacia and 8 fluid ounces of cinnamon water.

(*b*) *Therapeutical effects.* Anti-acid, absorbent, and astringent when given in diarrhœa.

(*c*) *Used* in diarrhœa.

(*d*) *Dose.* A tablespoonful every two hours.

Mixture of Iron (*compound*).

(*a*) Rub 2 drachms of powdered myrrh and 1 drachm of carbonate of potassium with a fluid ounce of spirit of nutmeg; to these, while rubbing, add 18 fluid ounces of rose-water, 2 drachms of sugar, and 2½ scruples of powdered sulphate of iron. Put the mixture in a well-stoppered bottle.

(*b*) *Therapeutical effects.* Stomachic, astringent, tonic, emmenagogue.

(*c*) *Used* in chlorotic girls, and in all the defective secretions of young females.

(*d*) *Dose.* 1 to 1½ ounce.

Ointment of Creosote.

(*a*) Rub half a fluid drachm of creosote with an ounce of lard, until they are incorporated.

(*b*) *Therapeutical effects.* Stimulant.

(*c*) *Used* in scald head, etc.

Ointment of Galls (*compound*).

(*a*) Mix 6 drachms of finely powdered galls, 6 ounces of lard, and 1½ drachm of powdered opium.

(*b*) Astringent and anodyne.

(*c*) *Used* for hemorrhoids; but one quarter of the quantity of gallic acid answers much better.

Ointment of Green Iodide of Mercury.

(*a*) Mix from 30 grains to 1 drachm of green iodide of mercury with 1 ounce of lard.

(*b*) *Used* in scald head, for which it is very efficacious.

Ointment of Nitric Oxide of Mercury.

(*a*) Rub 1 ounce of finely powdered nitric oxide of mercury with 10 ounces of wax, and 6 ounces of lard.

(*b*) *Therapeutical effects.* Stimulant.

(*c*) *Used* in indolent ulcers.

Ointment of Zinc.

(*a*) Mix 1 drachm of oxide of zinc with 6 drachms of lard.

(*b*) *Used* as a cooling, astringent, and drying ointment.

Olive Oil.

(*a*) *Physical properties.* A transparent fixed oil, of a yellowish color; inodorous and without much taste.

(*b*) *Therapeutical effects.* Soothing, and slightly aperient.

(*c*) *Used* in bronchial irritation; also as a vehicle for other medicines in the form of liniment.

(*d*) *Dose.* 1 to 2 drachms.

Peruvian Balsam.

(*a*) *Physical properties.* Of the consistence of honey; color, brown; agreeable smell, and hot, acrid taste.

(*b*) *Therapeutical effects.* Stimulant, expectorant; externally applied to indolent ulcers.

(*c*) *Used* in catarrh and chronic rheumatism.

(*d*) *Dose.* 15 minims to half a drachm.

Pill of Mercury. Blue pill.

(*a*) The metal partially oxidated, and mixed with confection of roses.

(*b*) *Therapeutical effects.* Alterative and purgative, especially on the liver.

(*c*) *Used* in dyspepsia, torpidity of the liver, and constipation.

(*d*) *Dose.* 1 to 5 or 6 grains.

Pill of Rhubarb (*compound*).

(*a*) Made up of rhubarb, aloes, and myrrh.

(*b*) *Therapeutical effects.* Laxative.

(*c*) *Used* in dyspepsia and constipation.

(*d*) *Dose.* Two at bedtime.

Pitch, Burgundy. The impure resin of the Norway spruce fir.

(*a*) *Physical properties.* A tenacious mass, of fragrant odor, semi-transparent, and unctuous.

(*b*) *Therapeutical effects.* Stimulant and rubefacient.

(*c*) *Used* externally in the form of a plaster in bronchitis, whooping cough, etc.

Poultice of Charcoal.

(*a*) Macerate for a short time before the fire 2 ounces of bread in 2 fluid ounces of boiling water; then mix and gradually stir in 10 drachms of linseed meal; with these mix 2 drachms of powdered charcoal, and sprinkle a drachm on the surface.

(*b*) Antiseptic and digestive.

(*c*) *Used* in gangrene.

Poultice of Hemlock.

(*a*) Make a poultice of linseed meal; then add 1 ounce of extract of hemlock previously softened with water, or 4 ounces of the fresh leaves scalded and bruised.

(*b*) *Therapeutical effects.* Anodyne and discutient.

(*c*) *Used* in glandular swellings and cancerous sores.

Poultice of Linseed.

(*a*) Put into a basin enough meal to form a poultice, making a hole in its center; then pour upon it boiling water to fill that hole, and stir rapidly with a kitchen knife. This will generally be sufficient to make the poultice of the proper consistency. It is always better to add enough water at first, as it is not so smooth if added piecemeal.

(*b*) *Therapeutical effects.* Stimulant, and yet soothing.

(*c*) *Used* for abscesses and ulcers when inflamed.

Poultice of Mustard.

(*a*) Make either a bread or a linseed-meal poultice, then sprinkle over it enough flour of mustard to conceal its surface, and wet it with a little boiling water. Some people add hot vinegar to wet it with.

(*b*) *Therapeutical effects.* Stimulant, and often inclined to blister the skin.

(*c*) *Used* as a rapid counter-irritant.

Poultice of Yeast.

(*a*) Mix 5 ounces of yeast with an equal quantity of water, at 100 degrees; with these stir up a pound of flour, so as to make a poultice; place it by the fire till it swells, and use.

(*b*) Stimulant, emollient.

(*c*) *Used* for indolent abscesses and sores.

Powder of Ipecacuanha (*compound*). Dover's powder.

(*a*) *Physical properties.* Compound of opium, ipecacuanha, and sulphate of potassium.

(*b*) *Therapeutical effects.* Diaphoretic, anodyne, and narcotic.

(*c*) *Used* to produce perspiration in rheumatism and dysentery, etc.

(*d*) *Dose.* 5 to 10 grains.

Quinine, Sulphate of.

(*a*) *Physical properties.* Colorless, inodorous, lustrous, bitter efflorescent crystals, totally soluble in water previously acidulated with sulphuric acid.

(*b*) *Therapeutical effects.* Stomachic, stimulant, febrifuge, and tonic.

(*c*) *Used* in general debility, neuralgia, and after fever.

(*d*) *Dose.* 1 to 3 grains.

Rhubarb.—The root, whole and powdered.

(*a*) *Physical properties.* The root is in firm, flattish, irregular pieces, occasionally pierced with large holes; color, bright yellow, externally; odor, peculiar and aromatic; taste, bitter, astringent, and somewhat nauseous; imparts its virtue to water and alcohol. The powder is of a reddish yellow.

(*b*) *Therapeutical effects.* Purgative and stomachic; acting on the small bowels.

(*c*) *Used* as a mild purgative in the constipation of children and adults.

(*d*) *Dose.* 10 to 30 grains.

Saffron.

(*a*) A coloring matter obtained from the *Crocus sativus.*

Senna.— The leaves.

(*a*) *Physical properties.* Leaves of a pale green color; leaflets broad, lanceolate; the two sides unequal; odor faint, somewhat like green tea; taste, nauseous and bitter. Yields its properties to spirit and water.

(*b*) *Therapeutical effects.* Cathartic.

(*c*) *Used* in constipation, and to lower the system. Made into the infusion.

(*d*) *Dose.* 5 grains to 25, rubbed down with ginger and sugar.

Soda, Bicarbonate of.

(*a*) *Physical properties.* A heavy white powder, without smell, and tasting slightly soapy. Entirely soluble in water.

(*b*) *Therapeutical effects.* Anti-acid.

(*c*) *Used* in the manufacture of effervescing draughts, and for acidities of the stomach.

(*d*) *Dose.* 5 to 30 grains.

Soda, Sulphate of.— Glauber's salts.

(*a*) *Physical properties.* Crystals, of an exceedingly bitter taste, and without smell. Soluble in water.

(*b*) *Therapeutical effects.* Purgative and diuretic.

(*c*) *Used* in costiveness.

(*d*) *Dose.* ½ to 1 ounce.

Spirit of Ammonia (*aromatic*).

(*a*) *Physical properties.* A compound, containing carbonate of ammonia and aromatics, with spirit; and possessing an aromatic, warm, and alkaline taste. Miscible with water, which it renders milky.

(*b*) *Therapeutical effects.* Stimulant and cordial.

(*c*) *Used* as the ordinary diffusible stimulus in faintings and hysteria; also added to senna to prevent griping.

(*d*) *Dose.* 30 to 60 drops.

Spirit of Ammonia (*fetid*).

(*a*) *Physical properties.* The same as the above, with the addition of asafœtida.

(*b*) *Therapeutical effects.* Stimulant and antispasmodic.

(*c*) *Used* in hysterical fits.

(*d*) *Dose.* 30 to 60 drops.

Spirit of Horse-radish (*compound*).

(*a*) Mix 20 ounces of sliced horse-radish, 20 ounces of dried orange peel, 5 drachms of bruised nutmegs, and a gallon of rectified spirit with 10 pints of water; then distill to a gallon, with a slow fire.

(*b*) *Therapeutical effects.* Stimulant, diaphoretic and diuretic.

(*c*) *Used* internally in dyspepsia, and in paralysis, externally rubbed into the skin.

(*d*) *Dose.* 1 to 2 drachms.

Spirit of Nitric Ether. Sweet spirits of niter.

(*a*) *Physical properties.* A colorless, transparent, volatile, inflammable fluid, of an ethereal odor.

(*b*) *Therapeutical effects.* Cooling, diuretic, and diaphoretic; also slightly antispasmodic.

(*c*) *Used* in febrile diseases, dropsy, and spasm.

(*d*) *Dose.* 20 to 60 minims, largely diluted.

Squill.— The sea onion.

(*a*) A root of a pear shape, covered with several thin dry tissues, under which are oval, flaky, red or white scales; odor, pungent; taste, acrid and bitter. Imparts its virtue to vinegar, spirits, and water.

(*b*) *Therapeutical effects.* Expectorant, emetic, diuretic.

(*c*) *Used* in chronic bronchitis and asthma.

(*d*) *Dose.* 2 to 6 grains. Syrup of squills, dose, 1 to 1½ drachms.

Syrup of Iodide of Iron is used in order to preserve the iodide of iron from injury.

(*b*) *Therapeutical effects.* Alterative, and affording the effects of iron and iodine.

(*c*) *Used* in scrofulous diseases, and in cachectic states of the system.

(*d*) *Dose.* 20 to 40 minims.

Turpentine, Spirit of.

(*a*) *Physical properties.* A limpid, colorless fluid, of a strong odor and hot taste, exceedingly inflammable.

(*b*) *Therapeutical effects.* Stimulant, diuretic, carthartic, and destructive to worms.

(*c*) *Used* in hemorrhages, lumbago, etc., and to destroy worms; also externally as a rubefacient.

(*d*) *Dose.* 10 drops to 30 internally, or 2 to 4 drachms mixed with castor oil as a vermifuge; but it should not be given internally without the sanction of a physician.

Tincture of Camphor (*compound.*) Paregoric elixir.

(*a*) A tincture containing camphor, opium, anise, and benzoic acid.

(*b*) *Used* in coughs.

(*c*) *Dose.* 1 drachm.

Tincture of Ginger.

Dose. 1 drachm.

Tincture of Iodine. (*See* Iodine.)

Dose. 5 to 15 minims.

Tincture of Myrrh.

Dose. 30 to 60 minims. Useful as a wash for the teeth. Rarely used internally.

Tincture of Opium. Laudanum.

Dose. 6 to 20 minims.

Tincture of Quinine.

Dose. Teaspoonful.

Tincture of Rhubarb (*compound*). A very warm, useful preparation.

Dose. 2 to 4 drachms.

Tincture of Valerian (*compound*).

Dose. 30 to 60 minims, in dyspepsia and hysteria.

Tolu, Balsam of.

(*a*) *Physical properties.* Of considerable consistence: reddish brown in color; odor, very pungent; taste, warm, and sweetish.

(*b*) *Therapeutical effects.* A stimulant expectorant.

(c) *Used* in chronic coughs, and also in wounds and ulcers.

(d) *Dose.* 10 grains.

Valerian.

(a) *Physical properties.* Several long, slender, dusky-brown fibers, issuing from one head; strong, fetid odor; warm, bitterish, subacid taste.

(b) *Therapeutical effects.* Antispasmodic, tonic.

(c) *Used* in hysteria.

(d) *Dose.* 1 drachm.

Wine of Iron.

(a) Digest for 30 days 2 ounces of tartarated iron in a pint of sherry.

(b) *Therapeutical effects.* Stomachic and tonic.

(c) *Used* the same as other steel medicines.

(d) *Dose.* Two tablespoonfuls.

Wine of Opium.

(a) Prepared with opium and spices.

(b) *Therapeutical effects.* Stimulant, afterwards anodyne.

(c) *Used* chiefly as an application to the eyes.

(d) *Dose.* 10 to 20 minims.

Wine of Potassio-tartrate of Antimony. Antimonial wine.

(a) Dissolve 2 scruples of potassio-tartrate of Antimony in a pint of sherry.

(b) *Therapeutical effects.* Emetic and diaphoretic.

(c) *Used* in inflammatory diseases.

(d) *Dose.* 15 to 60 minims.

Zinc, Chloride of. A powerful drug, but scarcely adapted to domestic use, except as a disinfectant, for which it is sold in solution. (*See* DISINFECTANTS.)

Zinc, Sulphate of. White vitriol.

(a) *Physical properties.* Transparent crystals.

(b) *Therapeutical effects.* Tonic, astringent, and emetic.

(c) *Used* as a wash or as an emetic.

(d) *Dose.* As an emetic, 10 to 30 grains; tonic, 2 grains.

CARE OF THE EYES.

A writer on the care of the eyes, in an English paper, says: "All are anxious to preserve the eyesight, but few know how effectually to do so, and many never think of the matter till failing sight warns them that it is absolutely necessary. By the latter," adds the same writer, "the following suggestions will be read with interest: —

"The sight in most persons begins to fail from forty to fifty years of age, as is evidenced by an instinctive preference for large print; a seat near the window for reading is selected; there is an effort to place the paper at a convenient distance from the eye, or to turn it so as to get a particular reflection of the light; next the finger begins to be placed under the line read, and there is a winking of the eye as if to clear it, or a looking away at some distant object to rest it; or the fingers are pressed over the closed lids in the direction of the nose, to remove the tears caused by straining.

"Favor the failing sight as much as possible. Looking into a bright fire, especially a coal fire, is very injurious to the eyes. Looking at molten iron will soon destroy the sight; reading in the twilight is injurious to the eyes, as they are obliged to make great exertion. Reading or sewing with a side light injures the eyes, as both eyes should be exposed to an equal degree of light. The reason is, the sympathy between the eyes is so great that if the pupil of one is dilated by being kept partially in the shade, the one that is most exposed cannot contract itself sufficiently for protection, and will ultimately be injured. Those who wish to preserve their sight should observe the following rules and preserve their general health by correct habits: —

"1. By sitting in such a position as will allow the light to fall obliquely over the shoulder upon the page or sewing.

"2. By not using the eyes for such purposes by any artificial light.

"3. By avoiding the special use of the eyes in the morning before breakfast.

"4. By resting them for a half minute or so while reading or sewing, or looking at small objects; and by looking at things at a distance or up to the sky; relief is immediately felt by so doing.

"5. Never pick any collected matter from the eyelashes or corners of the eyes with the finger nails; rather moisten it with the saliva and rub it away with the ball of the finger.

"6. Frequently pass the ball of the finger over the closed eyelids toward the nose; this carries off an excess of water into the nose itself by means of the little canal which leads into the nostril from each inner corner of the eye, this canal having a tendency to close up in consequence of the slight inflammation which attends weakness of eyes.

"7. Keep the feet always dry and warm, so as to draw any excess of blood from the other end of the body.

"8. Use eyeglasses at first, carried in the vest pocket attached to a guard, for they are instantly adjusted to the eye with very little trouble, whereas, if common spectacles are used, such a process is required to get them ready that to save trouble the eyes are often strained to answer a purpose."

ANTIDOTES FOR POISONS.

The following list gives some of the more common poisons and the remedies most likely to be on hand in case of need:—

Acids.— These cause great heat and sensation of burning pain from the mouth down to the stomach. The remedies are: Magnesia, soda, pearl ash, or soap dissolved in water, every two minutes; then use the stomach pump or an emetic.

Alkali.—Drink freely of water with vinegar or lemon juice in it, made very strong of the sour.

Ammonia.— Remedy is lemon juice or vinegar.

Arsenic Remedies.— Give prompt emetic of mustard and salt, a tablespoonful of each, in a coffeecup of warm water; then follow with sweet oil, butter made warm, or milk. Also may use the white of an egg in half a cupful of milk or lime water. Chalk and water is good, and the preparation of iron, ten drops in water every half hour; hydrated magnesia.

Alcohol.— First cleanse out the stomach by an emetic, then dash cold water on the head, and give ammonia (spirits of hartshorn).

Laudanum, Morphine, Opium.— First give a strong emetic of mustard and water, then very strong coffee and acid drinks; dash cold water on the head, then keep in motion.

Belladonna.— Give an emetic of mustard, salt and water; then drink plenty of vinegar and water or lemonade.

Corrosive Sublimate, Saltpetre, Blue Vitriol, Bedbug Poison.— Give white of egg, freshly mixed with water, in large quantities; or give wheat flour and water, or soap and water freely, or salt and water, or large draughts of milk.

Lead.— White lead and sugar of lead. Give an emetic, then follow with cathartics, such as castor oil, and Epsom salts especially.

Nux Vomica. — First emetics and then brandy.

Oxalic Acid (frequently taken for Epsom salts).—First give soap and water, or chalk or magnesia and water. Give every two minutes.

White Vitriol.— Give plenty of milk and water.

Nitrate of Silver (lunar caustic). — Give a strong solution of common salt and water, and then an emetic.

Verdigris.— Give plenty of white of egg and water.

MEDICAL DICTIONARY.

Abatement. Decrease of fever.
Abdomen. The belly.
Abnormal. Unnatural, irregular.
Abscess. A collection of purulent matter.
Absorption, absorptive. Taking up or soaking up.
Acephalous. Without a head.
Acid. Sour; a substance which neutralizes alkalies.
Adhesive strips, adhesive plaster. Cloth or other material coated on one side with sticking composition.
Afterbirth. A body attached to the womb and by a cord to the child, supplying blood and nourishment before birth.
Albumen, albuminous. One of the elements of the body that hardens with heat. The white of an egg.
Aliment, alimentary. Food. The alimentary canal begins with the mouth and ends with the rectum.
Alkali. Caustic; a substance which neutralizes acids.
Alterative. Altering or purifying the blood.
Alternating. One medicine following another after an interval.
Altruism. Regard for another.
Alveoli. The bony sockets to the teeth.
Alvine. Pertaining to the intestines.
Anæmia. Deficiency in blood. The want of red corpuscles gives the pallid appearance to the skin.
Anæsthesia. Deprived of sensation.
Anaphrodisiac. An agent to blunt sexual appetite.
Anastomosis. Communication between blood vessels.
Anatomy. A description of the organs of the body.
Anodyne. Relieving pain.
Antacid. Neutralizing acid.
Antibilious. A term applied to active cathartics.
Antidote. Medicines counteracting poisons and rendering them inert.
Anti-malarial. Preventing an attack of malaria.
Antiperiodic. Breaking up periodicity or appearance at regular intervals.
Antiperistaltic. Forcing the contents of the bowels backward into the stomach.
Antiseptic. Destroying poison.
Antispasmodic. Stopping spasms.
Antrum. A cavity in the superior maxillary bone, connected with the nose.
Anus. The lower opening of the bowel.
Aorta. A large artery arising from the heart.
Aperient. A gentle laxative or purge.
Aphonia. Loss of voice.
Aphthous. Affected with aphthæ; a curd-like covered sore.
Areola, areolar. The connecting tissue between fibers and vessels. Pertaining to areolæ.
Artery. A blood vessel which (with one exception) carries the red blood.
Asphyxia. Suspended animation.
Aspirator. A pumping apparatus with a long, fine, sharp-pointed tube for removing fluids from internal parts.
Assimilation. The act of transforming the food into various parts of the body.
Asthenic. Debilitated.
Atrophy, atrophied. Wasting away. Withered.
Auscultation. Discovering chest diseases by listening.
Axillary. Arising from a depression between the stem and leaf-stock.

Bandage. A long piece of cloth, of variable width, used for binding.
Benumb. To deprive of sensibility.
Bicuspid teeth. The fourth and fifth teeth from the center of the lips.
Bile, bilious. A fluid secreted by the liver. Pertaining to bile; a peculiar temperament.
Blastema. A germ.
Bloodletting. Opening a vein in the arm to let out blood.
Bolus. A large pill or anything of its size.
Bougie. A flexible instrument for dilating the urethra.
Bronchial tubes. Vessels carrying air to the lungs. Bronchi.
Bronchus, bronchi. The lower air-passage.
Buccal walls. Inner surface of the cheeks.

Cacoplasm. Bad or low form of organization.
Cæcum. A part of the intestines emptying into the colon; the blind gut.
Calcareous. Of the nature of lime.
Calculus, calculous. A stony formation. Pertaining to calculus.
Capillary. Blood vessels, hair-like in size.
Capsule. A covering or case.
Carbon. One of the elementary bodies or metalloids.
Cardiac. Pertaining to the heart.

Carnivora. Flesh-eating animals.
Cartilage, cartilaginous. A white, elastic solid part of the body. Gristle. Gristly.
Caseous. Like cheese.
Castration. Removing the testicles.
Catamenial. Relating to the monthly flow.
Cathartics. Agents that produce evacuation of the bowels.
Catheter. A tube with an eyelet near its end, used for conveying fluids.
Caustics. Corrosive or burning substances.
Celibate. A bachelor.
Cell. The smallest particle of living matter. The body and all of its parts are made up of cells.
Cellular tissue. The tissue uniting all parts of the body.
Cerebellum. The small or lower brain.
Cerebrum. The great or upper brain.
Cerumen, ceruminous. Ear-wax. Waxy.
Cholesterine. A crystallizable substance formed in the bile.
Chronic. Long standing, seated.
Chyle. The milky fluid formed from digested food, and which is emptied directly into the blood vessels.
Chyme. Digested food.
Cicatrix, cicatrices. The scar from a wound. Scars.
Circulation. The flow of blood from the heart to the extremities and back again.
Circumcision. The act of cutting off the foreskin or prepuce of males.
Clonic. Rigid, with occasional relaxation of the muscles.
Coagulate. To harden, as the white of an egg, by boiling.
Coitus. Sexual connection.
Collapse. Complete prostration or inaction.
Colliquative. Exhaustive.
Coma. Comatose, profound sleep.
Conception. Being with child in the womb.
Congenital. Dating from birth.
Congestion. The flow of blood to a part. Stagnant circulation.
Conjunctiva. The membrane covering the ball of the eye and inner surface of the eyelids.
Contagion. Communication of disease from one to another by touch, food, drink, or the atmosphere.
Continence. Abstinence from sexual congress.
Convalesce, convalescence. To recover health and strength. Period of recovery.
Convulsions. Spasms.
Cornea. The tough transparent membrane in the front of the eyeball.
Corpuscle. A minute body. A particle.
Corroborant. A remedy which gives strength; tonic.
Corrosive. Burning.
Cortical. The bark or external portion.
Costiveness. Irregular and delayed motion of the bowels. Constipation.
Counter-irritation. Irritating one part to relieve irritation in another.
Cramps. Sudden and painful contractions of muscles.
Cranial. Belonging to the skull.
Crisis. The period of change ; it may be to worse or to better.
Cul-de-sac. A pouch.
Cupping. Drawing blood by lancing, and the application of a heated cup.

Decussate. To cross each other.
Defecation. Evacuation of the bowels.
Dejections. Matter voided from the bowel.
Delirium. Mental aberration.
Deltoid muscle. A muscle passing over the shoulder and terminating at the center and outer part of the upper arm.
Depurative. Purifying. Removing impurities.
Dextrine. A substance obtained from starch.
Diagnosis. Discovery of a disease by its symptoms; discriminating between a disease and others with which it may be confounded.
Diaphoretic. Inducing perspiration; sweating.
Diaphragm. The muscle separating the chest and its contents from the abdomen and its contents.
Diastaltic. Reflex action induced by the spinal marrow.
Diathesis. Tendency of the constitution to a particular disease.
Diathetic. Relating to predisposition to disease.
Dietic, dietetic. Relating to the food and drink.
Digestion. Conversion of the food into form suitable for nourishment and into refuse or excrement.
Disinfectant. Purifying or cleansing from infection.
Diuretic. Increasing by secretion the quantity of urine.
Dram. One-eighth of an ounce, or a teaspoonful of fluid.
Drastic. Very powerful cathartic action.
Duc. Canal.
Duodenum. The first part of the intestines.
Dysmenorrhœa. Painful menstruation.
Dyspnœa. Difficult breathing.

Economy. The parts constituting the body or the laws governing them.
Effete. Worn out; useless.
Effusion. Escape of a fluid.
Elimination. Ejection by stimulating the secreting organs.
Eliminatives. Agents which expel substances from the body, as by the skin, kidneys, etc.
Emaciation. Loss of flesh.
Embryo. The animal in its earliest existence in the uterus.
Emesis. Vomiting.
Emission. A discharge.
Emulsion. A pharmacal compound of oil and water.
Emunctory. Any organ of the body acting as the outlet of effete and worn-out matter.
Enciente. Pregnant.
Encephalon. The head ; all within the head.
Encysted. Covered with a membrane or sac.
Endosmosis. Fluids passing through membranes into structures.
Enema. Liquid injections into the bowel.
Enervation. Weakness.
Enteric. Intestinal.
Entozoa. Worms.
Epidemic. A disease attacking many individuals in a locality at the same time.
Epithelial. Relating to the thin covering to the eyes, lips, mouth, intestines, and the like.
Erosion. Corrosion ; eating away.
Erosis. Amatory passion.
Eructations. Wind or gases raised from the stomach with some noise.
Essence, essential. The active principle of plants. A diluted oil.
Eustachian tube. A canal about two inches in length connecting the ear and back of the mouth (pharynx).
Exacerbation. Increase in fever.
Exanthematous. Attended with fever and skin eruptions.
Excito-motory. Reflex nervous action.
Excito-nutrient. Affecting nutrition by reflex nervous action.
Excito-secretory. Affecting secretion by reflex nervous action.
Excrement, excrementitious. Matter ejected from the bowel.
Excretion, excretive. The faculty of selecting and discharging from the system fluids, as in sweating and in urine, useless matter as in feces, and impurities by either.
Exhaling. Breathing out; throwing off vapor.
Expectorant. Remedies which loosen phlegm in the air-passages, and hence facilitate its discharge and relieve oppressed breathing.
Expectorate. To discharge mucosities by coughing and spitting.
Expiration. Exhaling air by the lungs.
Extravasate. To escape from the containing vessel and permeate the surrounding textures.
Exudation. Escaping or discharging through pores.

Farinaceous. Containing farina or flour.
Fascicles. Little bundles of fibers.
Fauces. The back of the mouth and upper part of the throat.
Feces, fecal. That part of the food remaining after digestion and which is ejected at intervals from the bowels.
Feculent. Foul.
Fermentation. Chemical action and combination by which new substances are formed.
Fiber, fibrous. The hard, elastic, organic particle which, aggregated, forms muscle and other tissues.
Fibrine. An organic substance, fluid, coagulable, found in the blood, lymph, etc.

Filaments. A thready fiber.
Flagellation. Flapping the body with the corner of a wet towel or the snap of a whip.
Flatulence. Wind in the stomach and bowels.
Fœtus, fœtal. The young of any animal during uterine existence. Pertaining to the unborn.
Follicle. A little depression throwing off moisture to keep the contiguous part soft and supple.
Foreskin. The prolonged skin of the penis, which covers the glans or head.
Fumigation. Disinfection by gas, smoke, or vapor.
Function. The normal or healthy action of an organ.
Fundament. The seat; anus.
Fungus. Parasitical plant.

Ganglion. Masses of nerves resembling brain.
Ganglionic. Composed of ganglia.
Gangrene. Mortification; local death.
Gastric juice. The digestive fluid secreted by the stomach.
Generative. Productive.
Genetic. Pertaining to the genital organs.
Genitals. The generative organs.
Germ theory. The theory of the propagation of disease by germs floating in the atmosphere.
Gestation. The period of carrying the young in the womb.
Glands, Glandular. Organs of the body, each possessing vital properties peculiar to itself, as secretion of tears, milk, saliva, urine, excretion, etc.
Glans. The conical end of the penis, covered by the foreskin.
Gluten. The ingredient in flour (farinæ) which gives it adhesiveness.
Grain. One sixtieth of a drachm.
Graminivora. Grain-eating animals.
Granular. Consisting of little grains.
Granules. Little grains.
Griping. The pains of colic.
Gullet. The canal for food leading from the throat to the stomach.
Gynæcology. That part of the science of medicine devoted to the diseases of women.

Hectic. Debilitated; exhausted.
Hereditary. Transmitted from parent to child.
Hibernate, hibernation. A partial suspension of animation. Animals that sleep through the winter hibernate.
Histogenetic. Tissue-forming.
Hydragogues. Medicines producing copious, watery, alvine discharges.
Hydrocarbons. Starch, sugar, and oils.
Hydrogen. A light, inflammable gas, forming, by chemical combination, water and animal and vegetable matter.
Hygiene, hygienic. The science of the preservation of health.
Hymen. A fold of membrane at the outer orifice of the vagina, found sometimes, but not always, in virgins.
Hypertrophy. Increased nutrition and consequent growth.
Hypnotic. Producing sleep.
Hypochondriasis. Belief in the possession of an imaginary disease.
Hypodermic. Under the skin.
Hypodermic syringe. An instrument for injecting liquid remedies under the skin.

Ileum. The convoluted portion of the intestines.
Impotence. Loss of sexual power; inability to copulate.
Indications. The symptoms or conditions needing medication.
Infection, infecting. The communication of disease by touch, food, drink, or the breath.
Infecundity. Unfruitfulness.
Infiltrate. To penetrate the pores of a part.
Inflammation. A condition attended with heat, pain, redness, and swelling.
Injection. Passing a liquid into a cavity of the body, through and by means of a syringe.
Innocuous. Harmless.
Inoculation. Taking a disease by contact with an abraded surface.
Insolation. Sunstroke.
Insomnia. Inability to sleep.
Inspiration. Inhaling air by the lungs.
Inspissated. Thickened by evaporation.
Instinct. An inborn principle directing to health and self-preservation.
Intercostal. Between the ribs.
Intestine, intestinal. The canal from the stomach to the anus; the bowels. Relating to the intestines.
Invermination. Infested with worms.
Iris. The colored membrane seen in the eyeball; it is blue in blue eyes, gray in gray eyes, etc.
Irritation. Local excitement, or excess of vital action.

Kidneys. Two organs, one on each side of the spine, internally and above the small of the back, which secrete the urine from the blood.

Lachrymal gland. Organ for forming tears.
Lachrymation. Weeping.
Lacteal. Milky. Vessels containing chyle.
Larynx. The Adam's apple of the neck; the upper part of the windpipe which contains the organs of voice.
Lancinating. A deep and sudden pain, compared to the stab of a lance.
Leeching. Removing blood by the application of a leech.
Lesion. A diseased change.
Leucocytes. White corpuscles of the blood.
Leucorrhœa. Whites.
Liquor sanguinis. The fluid part of the blood, holding in solution fibrine, albumen, etc.
Liver. The great assimilating gland of the body. It is situated below the diaphragm or midriff, and above the stomach, bowels, and kidney, and extends from the base of the chest to the spine, and from side to side.
Lobe. A rounded, projecting part.
Loins. The small of the back, between the ribs and pelvis.
Lungs. Two organs situated in the chest, one on each side, with the heart between; the organs of respiration.
Lymph, lymphatic. The fluid secretion of the lymphatic glands, which is emptied into the circulation.

Mackintosh. Cloth covered with waterproof material.
Malaria. Poisoning emanations in the air, producing disease.
Mammary gland. The female breast.
Mastication. Chewing the food.
Masterbation. Personal excitement of the sexual organs.
Median line. An imaginary line dividing the body into the right and left side.
Medulla oblongata. An organ, marrow-like, lying at the base of the skull.
Medullary. Pertaining to the marrow.
Membrane, membranous. A thin, web-like structure covering parts and organs, and lining cavities.
Meninges. Coverings of the brain and spinal cord.
Mensis, menses. The monthly uterine flow during the middle age of women.
Menstrual. Pertaining to the monthly flow.
Mesentery. The folds of the peritoneum which hold the intestines in place.
Metamorphosis. Transformation.
Metastasis. Change in the seat of a disease.
Miasm, miasmatic. The germs of disease floating in the air, which produce infection.
Microscope. An instrument for magnifying minute objects.
Micturate. To evacuate the bladder.
Molar teeth. The sixth, seventh, and eighth teeth from the center of the lips.
Molecule. A little portion of any body.
Morbid. Diseased.
Motor. Moving.
Mucilages. The gummy principle of plants.
Mucoid. Like mucus.
Mucus, mucous. A viscid fluid, which in health keeps the membranes in their proper condition.
Myopic. Near-sighted.

Narcotic. A stupefying remedy; in large doses destroying life.
Nausea. Sickness at the stomach; ineffectual effort to vomit.
Navel. The round scar at the center of the abdomen, marking the place of attachment of the cord previous to and at birth.
Neuralgia. Nerve-pain.
Neurine. The substance of which the brain is composed.

Nitrogen, nitrogenous. The gas constituting four fifths of the volume of the atmosphere.
Noxious. Poisonous; harmful.
Nucleus, nuclei. The germinal point in a cell; kernel.
Nutrition. Increasing in growth, or supplying the materials for growth.

Obcordate. Half egg-shape and half heart-shape.
Obesity. Excessively fat.
Œsophagus. The food-passage from the throat to the stomach.
Œstruation. Periodical sexual desire; heat.
Oleaginous. Oily.
Ophthalmoscope. An instrument for examining the interior of the eye by concentrated and reflected light.
Cptic nerve. The nerve conveying visual impressions from the eye to the brain.
Osmosis. Attraction of fluids for each other through moist membranes and their motion.
Occicles. Little bones.
Ounce. One sixteenth of a pound; in fluids, eight drachms or teaspoonfuls.
Oxygen. The gas constituting one fifth the volume of the atmosphere. It supports combustion.

Pad. A folded cloth used as a support.
Palate. Roof of the mouth.
Palatine arch. The arch in the rear of the mouth, formed by the palate bone.
Palsy. Loss of sensation or motion, or both; paralysis.
Pancreas, pancreatic juice. A large gland in the abdomen, beneath and behind the stomach. Its secretion.
Papillæ. Little raised points upon the surface; they can be seen upon the tongue.
Papulose, papular. With dry pimples.
Paralysis. To lose the power of motion in a part, or sensation, or both.
Parasites. Animals or plants that subsist upon others.
Parenchyma. The texture of organs like the liver, kidneys, etc.
Parotid gland. A gland at the angle of the lower jaw which secretes saliva and discharges it by a short tube upon the cheek near an upper molar (back) tooth.
Paroxysm. The period of more aggravated symptoms, following an interval of comparative freedom.
Parturition. Childbirth.
Pathology. That department of medical science whose object is the knowledge of disease.
Pelvis. The bony structure at the termination of the spine, enveloping and protecting the lower intestines, bladder, genitals, etc.
Pentandria Monogynia. A name given to a class of plants having five stamens and one style.
Percussion. Striking with the finger-tips to discover by the resonance the condition of internal parts.
Perineum. The part between the genitals and the anus or tip of the spine.
Periodicity. Occurring at regular periods, as a chill every other day, etc.
Periosteum. The tough membrane covering all bones.
Peristaltic. The peculiar motion of the intestines which propels its contents forward, somewhat like the crawling of a worm.
Peritoneum. The membrane lining the abdominal walls and covering the intestines.
Petaloid. Resembling a leaf-stock.
Petals. The colored leaves of a flower.
Pharmacist, pharmaceutist. One who manufactures drugs.
Pharmacy. The manufacture of drugs.
Pharynx. The posterior portion of the cavity of the mouth, behind the palate, above the windpipe and gullet. The breath and food pass through it.
Phosphorus, phosphates. A substance familiar to us in matches. It is a constituent of the brain and nerves.
Phrenic nerve. The respiratory nerve. It arises in the neck, passes through it and the chest, and is mainly distributed to the diaphragm.
Physiology. The functions of the organs of the body; the phenomena of life.
Pile-compressor. An instrument supporting the rectum and anus.
Placenta. A fleshy body attached to the womb and by a cord to the child, supplying blood and nourishment before birth.
Plasma. The fluid portion of the blood holding in solution fibrine, albumen, etc.
Plastic. Formative.
Plethora. Abounding in blood; full-blooded.
Pleura. A wetted membrane lining the walls of the chest and covering the outer surface of the lung. There are two.
Plexus. A network of blood-vessels or nerves.
Pneumogastric nerve. The great nerve distributed to the chest and stomach.
Polypus. A kind of tumor.
Post-mortem. After death.
Prepuce. The prolonged skin of the penis which covers the glans or head.
Probang. A whalebone rod with a sponge on one end.
Probe. A wire for examining wounds, canals, etc.
Prophylactic. Preventive.
Prostate gland. A gland at the upper portion of the urethra surrounding it and touching the bladder.
Psoas muscle. The great muscle which draws the thigh up to the abdomen.
Puberty. That period of life, about the age of 13, when the procreative organs most rapidly develop; hair grows about them and upon the face of the male, the breasts of the female enlarge, and, in fact, the period of youth has passed and that of manhood or womanhood arrived.
Pubic bone. A bone in the lower abdomen immediately under that part of the surface covered with hair.
Pulse. The beating or throbbing of arteries produced by afflux of blood from heart.
Pupil. The circular opening in the colored part of the eye (iris).
Purgative. A medicine causing free alvine discharges.
Pus. Matter discharged from inflamed tissue.
Pustules. Mattery pimples.

Receptaculum chyli. A hollow organ for holding chyle.
Rectum, rectal. That portion of the bowels nearest the outlet.
Recuperate. To regain health and strength.
Regurgitate. To flow backward.
Remission. Decrease in fever.
Renal. Pertaining to the kidney.
Respiration. Breathing.
Retching. Ineffectual effort to vomit.
Retina. The lining of the eye.
Revulsive. Agents which create diseased action on the surface to relieve internal disorder.
Roborant. Strengthening; tonic.
R, recipe. Take the articles following.

Saccharine. Of the nature of sugar.
Saliva. One of the digestive fluids which is mixed with the food during mastication.
Sanitarium. A remedial institute.
Schneiderian membrane. The lining of the nasal cavity.
Scrofulous. Of the nature of scrofula.
Scrotum. The skin covering the testicles.
Sebaceous. A name given to the oil-glands of the skin.
Secernent. Secreting.
Secrete, secretion. Drawing out fluids from the blood; each gland absorbs material peculiar to itself.
Sedatives. Remedies which control or depress excessive vital action.
Self-pollution. Personal excitement of the sexual organs.
Semen. The fecundating fluid of the male which is secreted by the testicles.
Seminal. Pertaining to semen or sperm.
Sensorium. The center of sensations.
Sepals. The leaves of the envelope of a flower.
Serum, serous. The watery portion of animal fluids.
Sigmoid flexure. A bend in the intestines just above the rectum.
Sinapism. An irritating plaster.
Sound. A solid rod, catheter shape.
Spasms. Violent and involuntary muscular movements.
Specific disease. Syphilitic diseases; private diseases.
Speculum. An instrument for dilating the orifice to internal canals or cavities.
Spermatic. Pertaining to sperm or the organs of generation.

Spermatic cord. A cord consisting of blood-vessels, nerves, and the canal of the sperm, which supports the testicle.
Spermatozoa. The formative agents in generation found in the semen of the male.
Sphincter. A round muscle closing an outlet.
Spicula. A splinter of bone.
Spleen. A spongy organ situated deep in the upper abdomen, between the kidney and stomach.
Sputa. Expectorated matter.
Squamous. Scaly.
Stercoraceous. Excrementitious.
Sternutatives. Remedies which provoke sneezing.
Stethoscope. An instrument for exploring the chest.
Sthenic. Possessing excessive strength.
Stun. Unconsciousness produced by a blow or fall.
Stupor. Diminished sensibility or exercise of the intellectual faculties.
Styptic. Arresting hemorrhage; astringent.
Sublingual gland. A salivary gland under the tongue.
Sudoriferous. A name given to the sweat glands of the skin.
Suppository. A semi-solid medicine deposited in the rectum.
Suppurate. To discharge matter or pus.
Suspensory bandage. A bandage for supporting the scrotum.
Sympathetic nerves. The nervous system of the automatic functions.
Symptom. A sign of disease.
Syncope. Fainting.

Tampon. A plug made of lint or cotton.
Tapping. Drawing off fluids in cavities by puncturing the surface.
Tenesmus. Violent contractions.
Testes. The male organs contained in the scrotum.
Testicles. Testes.
Tetanus. Permanent contraction of muscles.
Therapeutics. The department of medical science concerned in the treatment of disease.
Thoracic. Pertaining to the chest.
Thyroid glands. Throat glands.
Tissues. The anatomical elements cf organs.
Tonics. Remedies which improve the health and strength.
Tonsil. A gland at the side of the throat near the soft palate.
Toxic. Poisonous.
Trachea. That part of the windpipe between the larynx or vocal organs and the bronchial tubes.
Traumatic. Pertaining to a wound.
Tubercle. Concretions of degenerated matter.
Tubule. A little tube or canal.
Tympanitic. Having a drum-like sound from the accumulation of air.
Tympanum. The drum of the ear.

Ulcer, ulceration. A chronic sore situated in the soft parts. A diseased action resulting in ulcer.
Umbilicus. The navel.
Uræmic. Pertaining to urine.
Urea. A constituent of urine.
Ureters. The canals, two in number, carrying the urine from the kidneys to the bladder.
Urethra. The canal or pipe leading from the bladder for the conveyance of urine from the body.
Uric acid. A constituent of urine ; in excess it forms combinations, producing calculus or stone.
Urine. The secretion of the kidneys which collects in the bladder and is discharged through the urethra.
Uterus. An organ situated between the bladder and rectum and above the vagina, which holds the fœtus during gestation.
Uvula. A fleshy organ hanging from the center of the soft palate.

Vaccine. Pertaining to smallpox.
Vagina. The canal, five or six inches in length, leading to the uterus or womb.
Varicose. Pertaining to a dilated vein.
Vascular. Full of blood-vessels.
Vaso-motor. Affecting vessels by reflex nervous action.
Vein. A blood-vessel which, with one exception, carries the blue or venous blood.
Ventricle. A chamber in the heart.
Vertigo. Dizziness.
Vesicle. A bladder-like sac.
Vesicular. Full of little vessels.
Vicarious. In place of another; a function performed through other than the natural channels.
Virus. The poison transmitting infectious disease.
Viscus, viscera. An organ of the body. Organs.
Vitality. The vital principle.
Void. To evacuate.
Vomiting. Emptying the stomach upward.

Water-brash. A profuse flow of saliva.
Womb. An organ situated between the bladder and rectum and above the vagina, which holds the fœtus during gestation.

Zoon, Zoa. Animal. Animals.
Zymotic. Epidemic and contagious.

THE BANK OF ENGLAND

Book VI.

Finance, Industry, Transportation.

Finance, Industry, Transportation.

EARLY FORMS OF CURRENCY.

Skins of wild animals cured constitute one of the earliest forms of currency known, and while employed in the most ancient times, are not yet disused in some portions of the world. Such a medium seems appropriate among those who subsist by the chase, as all primeval peoples must in some degree, and it is not, therefore, surprising to find that in the transactions of the Hudson Bay Fur Company with the Indians, the unit of value by which the price of other articles was reckoned was the beaver skin.

Pastoral people employ similarly the skins of tame animals, originally delivering the entire skin, a cumbrous process deficient in convenience and economy, but finally employing a small disc cut from the leather as a representative of its value. Live stock is also widely employed, as it has been from the days of Abraham, and though a rude, it is still a substantially uniform, denominator of value. The Greeks stamped the image of an ox on a piece of leather, and the image had thence the current value of the animal represented. In the East, the camel, the ass, and the sheep have been, ever since they were subdued to the uses of mankind, employed to reckon possessions or determine the amount of tribute or marriage portions. In Lapland and some portions of Sweden and Norway, the amount of wealth possessed by a person is denominated in reindeer. Among the Tartars the number of mares similarly determines the opulence of their possessors. Among the Esquimaux it is customary to speak of one another as worth so many dogs.

Slaves have been employed to determine ratios of value since the state of bondage was first established among men. In New Guinea the slave is still the unit by which the value of other possessions is recorded, as he used to be among the Portuguese traders of the Gold Coast. The Portuguese also found small mats called libongoes, valued at about one and one half pence each, employed as currency on the African coast, and bunches of red feathers serve by their comparative stability to mark the fluctuations of yams and breech-clouts in some of the tropical islands of the Pacific. Some tribes of North American Indians found wampum as useful in their rather limited mercantile transactions as the merchant of South street or Burling slip finds greenbacks or bills of exchange.

Cowry shells are still extensively used in East India, Siam, and among some of the islands of the Indian Archipelago. Among the Fijians whales' teeth pass readily from hand to hand, effecting all necessary interchanges, the red teeth being taken at about twenty times the value of the white ones.

Ornaments of all kinds have in all times constituted measures of value. In Egypt, Phœnicia, Etruria, and many other ancient countries, as well as in Ireland and Northumbria, rings have been found which were designed to serve the double purpose of ornament and currency, and the same dual function may be ascribed to the anklets, armlets, and earrings which are worn throughout British India, Persia, Egypt, and Abyssinia. The Goths and Celts fashioned their rings of thick golden wire wound in spirals, from which various lengths could be broken to accommodate the varying needs of traffic. Gold chains have been similarly employed. In many countries golden beads are yet hoarded, worn, and circulated, fulfilling thus the triple functions of money, inasmuch as they constitute at once a store of value, a standard of value, and an instrument of exchange. Amber was used as currency by the savage races of the Baltic in the period of the Roman dominion, as it still is in some of the regions of the East. The Egyptian scarabee carved on sard or nephrite or other precious stones, circulated freely throughout the Mediterranean coasts and islands probably before the first Phœnician coin was impressed; and engraved gems and precious stones were employed to transfer wealth as well from one country to another as from hand to hand until a comparatively recent period. In Africa ivory tusks pass to and fro in the processes of trade, rudely defining the ratio of value of other articles. Among the Tartars, bricks of tea, or cubes of that herb pressed into a solid form, pass from hand to hand as freely as beaver skins do at the trading posts of Hudson Bay or the Saskatchewan. Among the Malayans the only currency entirely equal to the requirements of trade consists of rough hardware, such as hoes, shovels, and the like. Pieces of cotton cloth of a fixed length, called Guinea cloth, for a long period constituted the unit of value in Senegal, Abyssinia, Mexico, Peru, Siberia, and some of the islands of the Pacific Ocean. In Sumatra, cubes of beeswax of a fixed weight; in Scotland handmade nails; in Switzerland, eggs; in Newfoundland, dried codfish; in Virginia, tobacco; in Yucatan, cacao nuts; in the Greek Islands and the Levant, olive oil; in the regions of the Upper Nile, salt, have all, at one time or another, served the purposes of commercial interchange. In agricultural countries it is not strange that corn should have early been adopted as a measure of value. The leases of the great school foundations of Britain, Cambridge, Oxford, and Eton, with probably many others, were "corn leases," that is, specifying that the rental should consist of so many quarters of corn. In Norway, corn is deposited in banks and lent and borrowed on time or call loans, as money is with us. In Central America and Mexico, maize was long employed to serve the uses of currency.

In New England, in the early colonial days, leaden bullets were employed to indicate value, and that metal is still coined and circulated in Burmah. Pewter has often been coined, and in many countries, though not to the same extent as tin. In fact, tin coins are not only of immense antiquity, but their impress has been sanctioned by government authority down to a recent period. The Phœnician mariners freighted their galleys with the tin of Britain before Carthage was founded, and coins of the same oiled the wheels of commerce in the marts of Tyre and Sidon before Solomon built the temple at Jerusalem. In England, as late as the period of William and Mary, tin half-pence and farthings were struck, though they failed to become a permanent part of the circulation. In numismatical collections, series of tin coins stamped with the effigy and legend of several of the Roman emperors are abundant. In Java as well as Mexico, tin coins were once current, and the metal, measured by weight, is still a sort of legal tender in the Straits of Malacca.

METALLIC COINS.

In all civilized countries, gold, silver, and copper have always constituted the main elements of coinage and the most familiar forms of currency. The ratio of value between the first two has probably varied less during the last 2,500 years than that between any other known substances. Copper has fluctuated more, but its function has always been subsidiary and limited to small transactions. In the hierarchy of the metals used as coins, gold may represent the king, silver the lord, and copper the slave. The latter is now practically emancipated, bronze and nickel taking its place. Indium, osmium, and palladium have been proposed as substitutes for gold, and aluminum and manganese for silver, but without any practical result thus far. Platinum, which is mainly found in the Ural Mountains, has been coined to some extent by the Russian government; but, although a beautiful and valuable metal, possessing many of the qualities to render it acceptable as coin, its employment as money has been found to be impracticable.

Great numbers of alloys have been employed in coinage, and indeed it may be said that almost the entire system of metallic currency throughout the world is composed of alloys. The Tuscan sequin, the purest coin known in history, contained 999 parts of gold in 1,000. The six ducat piece of Naples was next in purity, having only an alloy of 4, while old Byzantine coins called bezants contained an alloy of 14 parts in 1000. Pure gold and silver, however, are soft metals, and untempered by others are subject to serious loss by abrasion. They are, therefore, rendered more useful by the admixture of a small portion of copper which, in the English system, in the case of gold, may be expressed decimally by 916.66, and of silver 925 parts in 1,000. Nickel is usually alloyed with three parts of copper, and it is noteworthy that its adoption as a subsidiary coinage in Germany, coincident with the demonetization of silver, caused it to advance rapidly in price, while the latter was as rapidly declining. The old Roman *as* was made of the mixed metal called *æs*, a compound of copper and tin, and in quality and value not unlike bronze. Brass was also extensively used from the time of Hiram of Tyre to that of the Emperor Otho. The old Kings of Northumbria coined a small money called stycas out of a natural alloy, composed of copper, zinc, gold, silver, lead, and tin, which the metallurgists of that rude northern coast had not enough chemical skill to separate.

Lycurgus established an iron coinage for Lacedæmon, not only making the coins of such weight and bulk as to forbid their export, but depriving them of their metallic value by causing them while heated to be plunged into vinegar, thereby destroying their malleability.

While these coins were the largest of which historic mention is made, the Portuguese rei, too small to be actually coined, is doubtless the smallest unit of value in the money systems of the world. It is only about the nineteenth part of an English penny, and is considerably smaller than the Chinese cash, which, of actual coins, is perhaps of the lowest value known. In Sweden, during the last century, huge squares of copper, weighing between three and four pounds, with a stamp in each corner and one in the center, were issued as coin, and curious specimens of them may still be seen in numismatical collections. These, with the Maundy money, a small portion of which is still annually struck at the British Mint, and distributed by Her Majesty in alms, probably represent the extremest variation of dimensions known among modern systems of coinage, the smallest piece of the Maundy money being a silver penny.

The Chinese probably illustrate in the most extreme manner the length to which loose views concerning currency can be carried. The history of their currency presents that mingling of the grotesque with the tragic which most of their actions have when viewed through Western eyes. Coined money was known among them as early as the eleventh century before Christ, but their inability to comprehend the principles upon which a currency should be based has led them into all sorts of extravagances, which have been attended by disorder, famine, and bloodshed. Coins came at last to be made so thin that one thousand of them piled together were only three inches high ; then gold and silver were abandoned, and copper, tin, shells, skins, stones, and paper were given a fixed value and used until, by abuse, all the advantages to be derived from the use of money were lost, and there was nothing left for the people to do but to go back to barter, and this they did more than once. They cannot be said now to have a coinage ; 2900 years ago they made round coins with a square hole in the middle, and they have since made no advance beyond that. The well-known cash is a cast brass coin of that description, and although it is valued at about one mill and a half of United States money, and has to be strung in lots of one thousand to be computed with any ease, it is the sole measure of value and legal tender of the country. Spanish, Mexican, and the new trade dollars of the United States are employed in China ; they pass because they are necessary for larger operations, and because faith in their standard value has become established ; but they are current simply as stamped ingots, with their weight and fineness indicated.

The coined money of Great Britain is the most elegantly executed, and among the purest in the world. The greater part of the continental coinage is poorly executed and basely alloyed. In Holland, and most of the German states, the coins legally current as silver money are apparently one third brass, and resemble the counterfeit shillings and sixpences of a former period in England. In France and Belgium, the new gold and silver coins are handsome, and so likewise are the large gold and silver pieces of Prussia. The coins and medals executed by direction of Napoleon in France are in a high style of art.

The Latin Monetary Union was established in December, 1865, for the purpose of maintaining the double standard of metallic currency, or keeping silver at a constant ratio with gold. The combination was formed by a union of France, Italy, Belgium, and Switzerland.

The possible depreciation of silver was foreseen, and some of its fluctuations had been experienced, but it was thought that, by a close union of silver-using powers rating silver at a common value, its price could be made permanent. At first the combination proceeded boldly. It threw open the mints of the Union to bullion owners, declaring that it would coin silver at the ratio to gold that it had established of fifteen and one half to one, and proclaimed that the coins thus issued should have in the markets both a legal tender efficiency and an intrinsic efficiency in exchange exactly represented by that proportion.

The plan worked well until the year 1873, when Germany demonetized silver. But in the meantime it was sought to give the double standard a broader foundation by bringing other nations into the combination. For this purpose, at the invitation of the French government, forty-five representatives of twenty-three countries met at Paris, in 1867. The proposed double standard was examined and discussed from every point of view by men skilled in financial science, and was at last rejected by a vote of forty-three to two. In 1870, there was a second gathering of the same kind, which, by a smaller majority, arrived at the same conclusion. Meantime silver had begun to accumulate, and depreciation to foreshadow itself more clearly. The demonetization of the metal by Germany gave the first sharp alarm. The Union was immediately forced to limit the coinage for 1874 to $24,000,000. This was increased to $30,000,000 in 1875, but again reduced in 1876 to $24,000,000, and in 1877, to $11,600,000. In the meantime, also, France, Belgium, and Switzerland stopped the coinage of five-franc pieces, thus reducing what silver they had to a large subsidiary currency. Later signs of the dissolution of the Union with the defeat of its objects were supplied by the failure of the monetary conference at Paris, and by the withdrawal of Switzerland from the Union.

GREAT BRITAIN, COINED MONEY OF.

In Great Britain, money of the current and standard coinage is frequently signified by the term sterling, as "one pound sterling," etc. With respect to the origin of the word sterling there are three opinions. The first is that it is derived from Stirling Castle, and that Edward I., having penetrated so far into Scotland, caused a coin to be struck there, which he called Stirling. The second opinion derives it from the figure of a bird called starling, which appears about the cross in the ancient arms of England. The third most probably assigns its true origin, by deducing it from Esterling; for in the time of Henry III., it is called Moneta Esterlingorum, the money of the Esterlings or people of the East, who came hither to refine the silver of which it was made, and hence it was valued more than any other coin, on account of the purity of its substance. The denomination of the weights and their parts is of the Saxon or Esterling tongue, as pound, shilling, penny, and farthing, which are so called in their language to the present day. The term sterling is now disused in England in all ordinary transactions, but is still used in Scotland to distinguish sums from the ancient money of the country, as referred to in old deeds and notices of pecuniary transactions. The old Scots' money, previous to the Union of 1707, was in pounds, shillings, and pence, but these were only a twelfth of the value of sterling money of the same denomination; thus a pound Scots was only twenty pence sterling. The word sterling is also in use in the colonies, to distinguish the legal standard of Great Britain from the currency money in these places.

It is customary to estimate the purity of gold by an imaginary standard of 24 carats. If in a piece of gold weighing 24 carats there be 1-24th of alloy, then the piece is one below the standard. What is called jewelers' gold is seldom purer than 20 fine to 4 of alloy — the alloy being usually silver, but sometimes copper, which gives a deeper red tinge to the metal. Perfectly pure gold is never seen either in trinkets or coins, for it is too ductile, and for that and other reasons requires a certain quantity of alloy. Sovereigns, and other modern English gold coins, contain one twelfth of alloy, but this twelfth is not reckoned as gold in point of value. At present the gold coin of Great Britain is issued at very nearly its precise market value as bullion. A pound weight of gold of 22 carats fineness produces coins to the amount of 46 pounds, 14 shillings, and 6 pence, which is about the price at which bullion sells for in the market. Thus the gold of that country is coined free of expense. In coining silver, the government is allowed by the Act of 56, George III., a profit or seigniorage of about 6 per cent.; the pound weight of silver, which should produce 62 shillings, being coined into 66 shillings. The silver coins being therefore of a little less real value than the sums they represent, they are not liable to be melted down by silversmiths for the manufacture of articles in their trade.

AMERICAN COINAGE, EARLY.

The earliest coinage that can be called American, in the sense of Anglo-American, was ordered by the original Virginia Company only five years after the founding of Jamestown. The coin was minted at Somers Island, now known as the Bermudas. For a long while the standard currency of Virginia was tobacco, as in many of the early settlements of the Northwest it was beaver skins, and other pelts reckoned as worth such a fraction of a beaver skin or so many beaver skins. In 1645 the Assembly of the Virginia Colony, after a preamble reciting that "It had maturely weighed and considered how advantageous a quoine would be to this colony, and the great wants and miseries which do daily happen unto it by the sole dependency upon tobacco," provided for the issue of copper coins of the denomination of twopence, threepence, sixpence, and ninepence; but this law was never carried into effect, so that the first colonial coinage of America was that struck off by Massachusetts under the order of the General Court of that colony, passed May 27, 1652, creating a "mint house" at Boston, and providing for the mintage of "twelvepence, sixpence, and threepence pieces, which shall be for forme flatt, and stamped on the one side with N. E., and on the other side with xiid., vid., and iiid., according to the value of each pence." In 1662 from this same mint appeared the famous "pine tree shillings," which were twopenny pieces, having a pine tree on one side. This mint was maintained for thirty-four years. In the reign of William and Mary copper coins were struck in England for New England and Carolina. Lord Baltimore had silver shillings, sixpences, and fourpences made in England to supply the demand of his province in Maryland. Vermont and Connecticut established mints in 1785 for the issue of copper coin. New Jersey followed a year later. But Congress had the establishment of a mint for the confederated States under advisement, and in this same year agreed upon a plan submitted by Thomas Jefferson, and the act went into operation on a small scale in 1787. After the ratification of the Constitution of the United States in 1789 all the state mints were closed, as the Constitution specifically places the sole power of coining money in the Federal Government.

The gold pieces are: —

1. The double eagle, or $20 piece. Coinage of the double eagle was authorized by the Act of March 3, 1849. Its weight is 516 grains. Its fineness is 900. (This technical form of expression means that 900 parts in 1,000 are pure metal, the other 100 parts are alloy.) The amount of coinage of the double

eagle is far greater than that of all the other gold pieces of the country.

2. The eagle, or $10 piece. Its coinage was authorized by the Act of April 2, 1792. The weight was first established by law at 270 grains, but was changed forty-two years afterward, by the Act of June 28, 1834, to 258 grains, where it has remained ever since. Its fineness was in the beginning made 916⅔, but was changed by the Act of June 28, 1834, the same act that lowered its weight, to 899.225. Two years and a half subsequently its fineness was increased — less than one part in a thousand — to 900. Its weight and fineness have remained thus fixed to the present day.

3. The half eagle, or $5 piece. This elegant coin has undergone the same vicissitudes as the eagle. Its coinage was authorized by the same Act of April 2, 1792. Its weight was 135 grains, and its fineness 916½. By the Act of June 28, 1834, its weight was reduced to 129 grains, and its fineness to 899.225. By the Act of January 16, 1857, its fineness was slightly raised to the uniform standard of 900. Its weight and fineness have thus remained to our time.

4. The quarter eagle, or $2.50 piece. This fine coin belongs to the same family with the eagle and half eagle. Its coinage was authorized, its weight and fineness correspondingly altered, by the same acts. The statute of 1792 made its weight 67.5 grains and its fineness 916½. Its weight was reduced to 64.5 grains and its fineness to 800.225 by the Act of 1834. The Act of 1837 raised its fineness to 900.

5. The dollar. This pretty little gold piece was created by the Act of March 3, 1849, the same act that authorized the coinage of the double eagle. It has remained unchanged. Its weight is 25.8 grains and its fineness 900.

6. Three-dollar piece. An Act of February 21, 1853, established this irregular coin. Its weight, 77.4 grains, and its fineness 900, are of the normal standard, and have not been changed by subsequent acts.

In gold coin the alloy was at first a compound of silver and copper. It was forbidden by statute that the alloy should be more than half silver. It is now nearly all copper, owing to advances in the art of assaying and improved methods in coinage.

There are four coining mints, located at Philadelphia, Pa.; San Francisco, Cal.; Carson City, Nev.; and New Orleans, La., the last one being put in operation on January 20, 1879. The largest proportion of assaying and refining is done at New York city; Helena, Montana; Boisé City, Idaho; and Denver, Colorado.

The Philadelphia Mint is capable of turning out about $1,500,000 in coined money a month; the San Francisco Mint, $1,000,000; the Carson City Mint, $500,000; and the New Orleans Mint about 500,000 pieces of various denominations. Under the law of February 28, 1878, which required that between 2,000,000 and 4,000,000 of the new ("Bland") dollars should be turned out by the mints every month, the coining facilities of the government were severely tested to produce this particular silver coin, and maintain the usual supply of gold and subsidiary coins. Silver is sent from the assay offices to the mints pure, or 999 fine, which is about as pure as silver can be. It is sent in large bars, and, when received at the mint, is melted and alloyed with copper. Coin silver is 900 fine.

The first silver coins were struck in 1794 (authorized in 1792), at the Philadelphia Mint, and consisted of 1,758 dollars, and 10,600 half dollars, and a few half dimes (5 cents), more for curiosities than use. In the succeeding year the issue was 203,033 dollars, 323,038 half dollars, no quarters, no dimes, and 86,416 half dimes. In 1796 the mint coined only 72,920 dollars, and 3,918 half dollars, with 2,948 quarters. In 1797 the number of dollars issued was 2,776, and the mint records state that there were no half dollars and only 252 quarters. Dollars only were coined in 1798. In 1796 the head of Liberty was changed, and a new head, inferior in point of comeliness, substituted. This also had flowing locks, but these were bound by a broad fillet, and hence the name "fillet dollars." In 1798 there were no halves nor quarters, and there were none in 1799, nor again in 1800. But in the following year the half dollars were commenced again, being of the fillet series, with the heraldic eagle on the reverse.

1804 is the *annus mirabilis* of the American silver coins. According to the records, 19,570 dollars were issued, 156,519 halves, and 6,738 quarters. There are but two dollars of 1804 known to exist, and these are said to have been struck surreptitiously from the original die at the Philadelphia mint in 1827. The value of these two to numismaticians is enormous; as high as $1,000 has been refused for one of them.

The first dollar pieces (1792) contained 416 grains of silver of 892.7 fineness, and this proportion was maintained until 1873, when the quantity of silver was reduced to 412.5 grains, and the fineness increased to 900. The fifty-cent pieces, from 1792 to 1837, contained 208 grains, 892.7 fineness, and the twenty-five cent pieces a proportionate amount; and both were subjected to a reduction in number of grains and increase in fineness in 1873. The ten-cent pieces contained 41.6 grains, of standard fineness, and now bear 38.58 grains under the new standard of fineness. From 1851 to 1853, the five-cent pieces were composed of 12.375 grains, 750 fine, and from 1853 to 1873, when their coinage was abolished, 11.52 grains, 900 fine. The old copper cents, authorized in 1792, contained 264 grains; the next year the amount was reduced to 208, and three years later to 168. As a purely copper token this coin was abolished shortly after the last reduction in the number of grains. The two-cent piece of April, 1864, contained 96 grains of copper, zinc, and tin, and was discontinued in 1873. The half-cent pieces were established in 1792, containing 132 grains; this amount was reduced in 1793 to 104, and in 1796 to 84. None are coined now. An act of March, 1875, authorized the coinage of a silver twenty-cent piece, containing 77.16 grains, 900 fine. This coin being but a trifle smaller than the twenty-five cent piece, led to such a general confusion of the two, that in 1878 its coinage was stopped. But few are now found in circulation. The one-cent piece of present use was authorized in 1857, and consisted of 72 grains of copper and nickel, and in 1864 this composition was changed to 48 grains of copper, zinc, and tin. Finally, the five and three cent nickel pieces were authorized in 1866 and 1865 respectively; the latter has a comparatively small circulation.

The amount of standard silver dollars coined from February 28, 1878, to October 31, 1882, was $128,329,880, of which $93,006,382 remained in the Treasury, and $35,323,498 was placed in circulation. Of the $30,007,175 coined in the thirteen months preceding October 31, 1882, $2,950,072 went into circulation, and $27,057,103 remained in the Treasury.

The total value of the minor coin in the Treasury on September 1, 1882, was $504,515.29. The supply of five-cent nickel coins in the Treasury, which three years previous reached the sum of $1,184,252.95, had been exhausted, and their coinage was resumed by the mint. None of these coins are supplied by the Treasury, but the one-cent and five-cent pieces are furnished in multiples of $20 by the mint, which bears the expense of their transportation.

BANKS.

The term bank, in reference to commerce, signifies a place of deposit of money, and is derived from the Italian *banco*, a seat or bench, because the early custodians and dealers in money in Italy were accustomed to sit on benches in the market places of the principal towns. During the middle ages, in which commerce was but little developed, there could be no field open for banking as a business; but on the revival of business in the twelfth century, and when the cities of Italy engrossed nearly all the trade of Europe, the necessity arose again for the employment of bankers. The successful manufacturing efforts of the Florentines brought them into commercial dealings with different countries in Europe, and thence arose the establishment of banks as private concerns. The earliest public bank established in modern Europe was that of Venice, which was founded in 1157. About the year 1350, the cloth merchants of Barcelona, then a wealthy body, added the business of banking to their other commercial pursuits; being authorized so to do by an ordinance of the King of Aragon, which contained the important stipulation that they should be restricted from acting as bankers until they should have given sufficient security for the liquidation of their engagements. In 1401 a bank was opened by the functionaries of the city, which was both a bank of deposit and of circulation, the first of the kind ever established in Europe.

The Bank of Genoa was planned and partially organized in 1345, but was not brought into operation until 1407, when the numerous loans which the Republic had contracted with its citizens were consolidated, and formed the nominal capital stock of the bank. As security for its capital in the hands of the Republic, this bank, which was given the name of the Chamber of St. George, received in pledge the Island of Corsica, and several other dependencies of Genoa. Since 1800, when the French, besieged in Genoa, appropriated its treasure to the payment of their troops, the bank has had little other than a nominal existence.

The banks of note next established, of which records remain, were opened in Holland and in Hamburg. The most celebrated of these was the Bank of Amsterdam, established in 1609, simply as a bank of deposit, under the guaranty of the city. The credit given in the bank for foreign coin and the worn coin of the country was called bank money, to distinguish it from current money of the place; and as the regulations directed that all bills drawn upon or negotiated at Amsterdam, of the value of 600 guilders and upwards, must be paid in bank-money, every merchant was obliged to keep an account with the bank, in order to make his ordinary payments. The Bank of Hamburg was established in 1619, on the model of that of Amsterdam originally. Deposits are received only in bullion, and a charge is made for their safe keeping. It advances money on jewels up to three fourths of their value. The city is responsible for all deposits, which may be sold at auction if they remain eighteen months without payment of charges. If the value is not claimed within three years, the property in the deposits is lost, and passes to the poor fund of the city.

Next in point of date among these establishments is the Bank of England, which was opened in 1694. It was originally chartered for ten years, and the charter has since been prolonged, by various renewals, till August 1, 1879, and, from that date, subject to a year's notice. The Bank of England is, and always has been, the government bank, transacting for it all the banking business of the nation, receiving the produce of the taxes, loans, etc., and paying the interest of the public debt, the drafts of the Treasury, and other public departments, transferring stock, etc. For this service the bank receives, exclusive of the use of the balances of the public money in its hands, about £95,000 a year.

Down to 1797 the bank always had paid its notes on demand. But in 1796 and the early part of 1797, owing to rumors of a French invasion, there was a run made on the bank, and it was feared that a suspension was inevitable. In February, 1797, Mr. Pitt, apprehensive that he might not be able to obtain sufficient specie for foreign payments, in consequence of the low state of the bank reserve, procured the issue of an order in council, requiring the bank to suspend specie payments. The suspension lasted till 1819, and is known to writers on finance as "the period of the bank restriction." The bank's notes, however, continued to circulate, and a committee of the House of Commons reported soon after the suspension that the bank was not merely possessed of the most ample funds to meet all its engagements, but that it had a surplus stock, after the deduction of all demands, of no less than £15,513,000.

The Bank of England is the custodian of the reserves of the several London banks and private bankers. These deposited reserves are, for the most part, loaned out by the bank. Then, again, the reserves of the country banks, and of the Scotch and Irish bankers as well, are deposited with the great English banks, which, in their turn, keep their reserves at the Bank of England. Therefore the reserve in the banking department of the Bank of England is the banking reserve not only of the Bank of England but of all London, and not only of all London, but of all England, Ireland, and Scotland. The credit system of Great Britain depends upon the security of the Bank of England.

The Bank of Vienna, established in 1703 as a bank of deposit and circulation, became a bank of issue in 1793. This institution now does comparatively little commercial business, being recognized as a means of the government for managing the public debt and finances.

The Banks of Berlin and Breslau were founded in 1765 under the direct authority of the government. They are banks of deposit and issue, and also discount bills of exchange. In some important particulars the banking system of Germany resembles that of the United States, the Imperial Bank and its branches in nearly every town corresponding to the American chain of National Banks. The Imperial Bank enjoys an enormous monopoly of immunities and powers.

Russian Banks. During the reign of the Empress Catharine, three different banks were established in St. Petersburg: the Loan Bank, the Assignation Bank; and the Loan Bank for the nobility and towns. The first, opened in 1772, made advances upon deposits of bullion and jewels, and allowed interest upon all sums remaining for one year and over. At present the operations of this bank are carried on for the benefit of the Foundling Hospital in St. Petersburg. The Assignation Bank was opened in St. Petersburg in 1768, and in Moscow in 1770. It issues paper money, and is really an imperial institution. The Loan Bank, for the nobility and towns, advances money on real security, discounts commercial paper, and carries on an insurance business. In 1797 the Aid Bank was established for the purpose of advancing money to relieve estates from mortgages, and to provide for their improvement. There is also the Commercial Bank of Russia, whose capital is declared to be sacred by the government, and free from all taxes, attachments, and calls from the State. It has numerous branches throughout the empire, receives deposits of coin and bullion, discounts paper, and makes advances upon merchandise of domestic production.

The Bank of Stockholm was founded in 1688, when its direction was assumed by the Assembly of the States of the Kingdom of Sweden, and it became a bank of deposit, discount, and circulation. Since 1766, when the affairs of the bank fell to a very low state, and the Assembly assisted it with a large loan, a committee, composed of members of each of the three States, nobles, clergy, and burghers, is appointed triennially to inspect its condition, securities, and prospects.

The Bank of France, originally formed in 1800, was placed on a solid basis in 1806, when its capital was raised to 90,000,000 francs. The bank is now the only authorized source of paper money in France. Its charter and exclusive privileges have been conferred, varied, or continued by different governments and under various laws; the year 1897 was the time fixed at which the terms made with the bank by the public might be ended. The bank has branches scattered throughout all the departments. Besides discounting, the Bank of France advances upon deposits of stock and pledges of a miscellaneous kind. It also undertakes the safe custody of valuables. A council of twenty-one members conducts the direction of affairs, viz.: a governor and two sub-governors, who are to be nominees of the head of the government; fifteen directors and three censors, nominated by the shareholders.

UNITED STATES BANKS.

The first United States bank was established by Act of Congress, approved July 25, 1791. It was organized at Philadelphia, with a capital of $10,000,000, divided into 25,000 shares of $400 each. The act prescribed that any person, copartnership, or body politic might subscribe for any number of shares not exceeding 1,000 — only the United States could subscribe for more than this number of shares; that with the exception of the United States the subscriptions should be payable one fourth in gold and silver, and the remaining three fourths in certain six per cent. bonds of the United States; that the subscribers should be incorporated under the name of "The President, Directors, and Company of the Bank of the United States," and the organization should continue until March 4, 1811; that the bank could hold property of all kinds, inclusive of its capital, to the amount of $15,000,000; that twenty-five directors should be chosen, who in turn should choose from their number a President; that as soon as $400,000 in gold and silver was received on subscription, the bank could organize, after giving a notice of its intention. The general effect of this institution was very salutary. The credit of the United States became firmly established. The bank notes stood at par with gold and silver. The large deposits made the money available for the use of the Treasury, and the State bank currency, which had flooded the country with no prospects of redemption, was greatly reduced. But with all its recognized advantages, the act to recharter was defeated in 1811 by the casting vote of the Vice-President, George Clinton. Its loss, however, was immediately felt in the sudden and rapid increase of the currency of the State banks. To ward off an impending crisis, a second bank was established by an act approved by President Madison, April 10, 1816, at Philadelphia. A capital of $35,000,000 was required, which was to be equally divided into 350,000 shares, of which the United States took 70,000. The charter extended to March 3, 1836. The bank was prohibited from lending, on account of the United States, more than $500,000, or to any prince or foreign power any sum whatever, without the sanction of law first obtained; and it was also prohibited from issuing bills of less denomination than $5. In time, to facilitate business, branch offices were established in every state. In December, 1829, however, the bank met strenuous opposition in the message of President Jackson, who argued, as did Jefferson when the first bank was started, against the constitutionality of its charter; and when Congress, in 1832, passed a bill to recharter the institution he imposed his veto, and soon after removed from the bank the United States deposits. The bank corporation, however, continued to exist until 1836, when the charter terminated.

Savings Banks. — These are banks for receiving and taking charge of small sums, the savings of industry, and were instituted for the benefit of workmen and others, who were able to spare a little from their earnings. It is believed that Quaker thrift in Philadelphia, Pa., led to the inception of the idea, and that the first savings bank in the world was founded in that city in 1816. As the scheme grew in popularity throughout the United States, guardians of minor children, administrators of estates of deceased persons, and other holders of trust funds, found the savings banks very serviceable as places of deposit for money that had to be laid away for a specified period of time. Hence, the exigencies of business transactions forced an innovation upon the original plan. In the United States this use of savings banks is still maintained; but during the past fifteen years safe deposit and trust companies have been numerously established for the special purpose of holding funds, both in trust and in legal dispute, besides securities of all kinds, jewelry, diamonds, and articles of like value. Thus a guardian, an administrator, or a society will invest money in Government, State, or City bonds, or, if permitted by the terms of trust, in real estate, or stock of various corporations, and place the bond, certificate of stock, or other acknowledgment of the indebtedness, with a safe deposit or trust company for safe keeping. The savings banks are allowed by law to invest their money in first-class securities only, so as to prevent their officers from using the fund in the irregular pursuit of "wild-cat" speculation.

VALUE FOREIGN COINS IN UNITED STATES MONEY.

COUNTRY.	Standard.	Monetary Unit.	Value in U. S. Gold Dollar.	COINS.
Argentine Rep...	Gold & Sil.	Peso..................	$0.96,5	Gold: argentine ($4.82,4) and ½ argentine. Silver: peso and divisions.
Austria-Hungary	Gold.......	Crown..............	.20,3	Gold: former system—4 florins ($1.92,9), 8 florins ($3.85 8), ducat ($2.28,7), and 4 ducats ($9.14,9). Silver: 1 and 2 florins. Gold: present system—20 crowns ($4.05,2) and 10 crowns ($2.02,6).
Belgium..........	Gold & Sil.	Franc................	.19,3	Gold: 10 and 20 francs. Silver: 5 francs.
Bolivia...........	Silver......	Boliviano............	.43,6	Silver: boliviano and divisions.
Brazil............	Gold.......	Milreis..............	.54,6	Gold: 5, 10, and 20 milreis. Silver: ½, 1, and 2 milreis.
Canada..........	Gold.......	Dollar...............	1.00	
Central America.	Silver......	Peso*................	.43,6	Silver: peso and divisions.
Chile.............	Gold.......	Peso.................	.36,5	Gold: escudo ($1.82,5), doubloon ($3.65), and condor ($7.30). Silver: peso and divisions.
China............	Silver......	Tael... Shanghai..	.64,5	
		Haikwan..	.71,8	
		Tientsin...	.68,4	
		Chefoo....	.67,5	
Colombia.........	Silver......	Peso.................	.43,6	Gold: condor ($9.64,7) and double-condor. Silver: peso.
Costa Rica.......	Gold.......	Colon................	.46,5	Gold: 2, 5, 10, and 20 colons ($9.30,7). Silver: 5, 10, 25, and 50 centimos.
Cuba.............	Gold & Sil.	Peso.................	.92,6	Gold: doubloon ($5.01,7). Silver: peso.
Denmark.........	Gold.......	Crown...............	.26,8	Gold: 10 and 20 crowns.
Ecuador.........	Silver......	Sucre................	.43,6	Gold: condor ($9.64,7) and double-condor. Silver sucre and divisions.
Egypt............	Gold.......	Pound (100 piasters).	4.94,3	Gold: pound (100 piasters), 5, 10, 20, and 50 piasters. Silver: 1, 2, 5, 10, and 20 piasters.
Finland..........	Gold.......	Mark................	.19,3	Gold: 20 marks ($3.85,9), 10 marks ($1.93).
France..........	Gold & Sil.	Franc................	.19,3	Gold: 5, 10, 20, 50, and 100 francs. Silver: 5 francs.
Germany.........	Gold.......	Mark................	.23,8	Gold: 5, 10, and 20 marks.
Great Britain....	Gold.......	Pound sterling......	4.86,6½	Gold: sovereign (pound sterling) and ½ sovereign.
Greece...........	Gold & Sil.	Drachma............	.19,3	Gold: 5, 10, 20, 50, and 100 drachmas. Silver: 5 drachmas.
Hayti.............	Gold & Sil.	Gourde..............	.96,5	Silver: gourde.
India.............	Silver......	Rupee...............	.20,7	Gold: mohur ($7.10,5). Silver: rupee and divisions.
Italy.............	Gold & Sil.	Lira.................	.19,3	Gold: 5, 10, 20, 50, and 100 lire. Silver: 5 lire.
Japan............	Gold.......	Yen..................	.49,8	Gold: 1, 2, 5, 10, and 20 yen. Silver: 10, 20, and 50 sen.
Liberia...........	Gold.......	Dollar...............	1.00	
Mexico...........	Silver......	Dollar...............	.47,4	Gold: dollar ($0.98,3), 2½, 5, 10, and 20 dollars. Silver: dollar (or peso) and divisions.
Netherlands......	Gold & Sil.	Florin................	.40,2	Gold: 10 florins. Silver: ½, 1, and 2½ florins.
Newfoundland...	Gold.......	Dollar...............	1.01,4	Gold: 2 dollars ($2.02,7).
Norway...........	Gold.......	Crown...............	.26,8	Gold: 10 and 20 crowns.
Peru..............	Silver......	Sol..................	.43,6	Silver: sol and divisions.
Portugal.........	Gold.......	Milreis..............	1.08	Gold: 1, 2, 5, and 10 milreis.
Russia...........	Gold.......	Ruble...............	.51,5	Gold: imperial ($7.71,8) and ½ imperial ($3.86). Crown and ½ crown. Silver: ¼, ½, and 1 ruble.
Spain.............	Gold & Sil.	Peseta..............	.19,3	Gold: 25 pesetas. Silver: 5 pesetas.
Sweden...........	Gold.......	Crown...............	.26,8	Gold: 10 and 20 crowns.
Switzerland......	Gold & Sil.	Franc................	.19,3	Gold: 5, 10, 20, 50, and 100 francs. Silver: 5 francs.
Turkey...........	Gold.......	Piaster..............	.04,4	Gold: 25, 50, 100, 250, and 500 piasters.
Uruguay..........	Gold.......	Peso.................	1.03,4	Gold: peso. Silver: peso and divisions.
Venezuela........	Gold & Sil.	Bolivar..............	.19,3	Gold: 5, 10, 20, 50, and 100 bolivars. Silver: 5 bolivars.

* Not including Costa Rica. † Value of the rupee to be determined by consular certificate.

Coinage at United States Mints.

The total coinage to June 30, 1902, was $3,227,630,701.97, being an increase in two years of $231,067,469.70.
Total coinage of the mints since their organization, 1792 (Philadelphia):—

DENOMINATIONS.		DENOMINATIONS.		DENOMINATIONS.	
GOLD.		Dollars (Lafayette souv.)	$50,026.00	MINOR.	
Double eagles..........	$1,628,668,640.00	Half dollars............	154,045,493.00	5 cent pieces, nickel..	$20,876,352.70
Eagles..................	365,098,470.00	Half dollars (Columbian souvenir)...........	2,501,052.50	3 cent pieces, nickel..	941,349.48
Half eagles............	283,820,325.00	Quarter dollars.........	71,270,994.75	2 cent pieces, bronze.	912,020.00
Three dollar pieces.....	1,619,376.00	Quarter dollars (Columbian souvenir)....	10,005.75	1 cent pieces, copper.	1,562,887.44
Quarter eagles.........	29,428,252.50	Twenty cent pieces.....	271,000.00	1 cent pieces, nickel..	2,007,720.00
Dollars.................	19,499,337.00	Dimes...................	41,047,121.90	1 cent pieces, bronze.	11,603,018.24
Total gold...........	$2,328,134,400.50	Half dimes............	4 880,219.40	½ cent pieces, copper,	39,926.11
SILVER.		Three cent pieces........	1,282,087.20	Total minor......	$37,943,273.97
Dollars................	*$550,229,103.00	Total silver.........	$861,553,027.50	Total coinage....	$3,227,630,701.97
Trade dollars..........	35,965,924.00				

* Silver-dollar coinage under acts of April 2, 1792, $8,031,238; February 28, 1878, $378,166,793; July 14, 1890, $158 952,600; March 3, 1891, $5,078,472; total, $550,229,103.

Approximate Amount of Money in the World.

Countries.	Population.	Stock of Gold.	Stock of Silver.			Uncovered Paper.	Per Capita.			
			Full Tender.	Limited Tender.	Total.		Gold.	Silver.	Paper.	Total.
United States.....	78,400,000	$1,174,600,000	$573,500,000	$91,500,000	$660,000,000	$437,800,000	$14.98	$8.48	$5.58	$29.04
Austria-Hungary..	47,100,000	257,000,000	....	80,000,000	80,000,000	39,900,000	5.45	1.70	.85	8.00
Belgium...........	6,700,000	19,700,000	20,000,000	3,300,000	23,300,000	98,600,000	2.94	3.48	14.71	21.13
British Empire:										
Australasia.....	5,500,000	128,600,000	....	6,100,000	6,100,000	....	23.38	1.11	....	24.49
Canada..........	5,500,500	20,000,000	....	5,000,000	5,000,000	56,900,000	3.64	.91	10.34	14.89
Cape Colony.....	2,300,000	3,750,000	....	1,000,000	1,000,000	....	16.30	.43	....	16.73
Great Britain....	41,600,000	528,000,000	....	116,800,000	116,800,000	116,200,000	12.69	2.81	2.79	18.29
India............	295,000,000	49,200,000	485,300,000	....	485,300,000	32,400,000	.17	1.64	.11	1.92
S. African Rep..	1,100,000	29,200,000	....	1 200,000	1,200,000	....	26.54	1.09	....	27.63
Bulgaria	3,700,000	1,400,000	2,000,000	1,200,000	3,200,000	2,500,000	.38	.86	.67	1.91
Cuba	1,600,000	2,000,000	....	1,500,000	1,500,000	....	1.25	.93	....	2.18
Denmark..........	2,600,000	15,500,000	....	5,900,000	5,900,000	7,500,000	5.96	2.27	2.88	11 11
Egypt.............	9,800,000	30,000,000	....	6,400,000	6,400,000	....	3.06	.65	....	3.71
Finland	2,700,000	4,100,000	....	600,000	600,000	7,300,000	1.52	2.70	.22	4.44
France.............	39,000,000	903,500,000	373,500,000	46,300,000	419,800,000	134,500,000	23.17	10.76	3.45	37.38
Germany..........	56,400,000	762,800,000	73,000,000	134,500,000	207,500,000	153,400,000	13.52	3.68	2.72	19.92
Greece	2,400,000	400,000	500,000	1,000,000	1,500,000	29,800,000	.17	.62	12.42	13.21
Hayti..............	1,000,000	1,300,000	1,000,000	1,500,000	2,500,000	3,300,000	1.30	2.50	3.30	7 10
Italy...............	32,500,000	101,500.000	16,000,000	22,400,000	38,400,000	174,800,000	3.12	1 18	5.38	9.68
Japan..............	46,500,000	43,400,000	....	29,500,000	29,500,000	71,100,000	.93	.63	1.53	3.09
Netherlands.......	5,100,000	38,500,000	52,200,000	3,800,000	56,000,000	39,600,000	7.55	10.98	7.76	29.29
Norway	2,200,000	8,200,000	....	3,100,000	3,100,000	6,000,000	7.86	1.40	2.73	11.99
Portugal	5,400,000	8,600,000	....	34,100,000	34,100,000	74,100,000	1.59	6.32	13.72	21.63
Roumania.........	6,000,000	9,500,000	....	800,000	800,000	18,300,000	1.58	.13	3.05	4.76
Russia.............	130,800,000	714,600,000	....	103,200,000	103,200,000	....	5.46	.79	....	6.25
Servia	2,500,000	1,400,000	....	1,700,000	1,700,000	3,700,000	.56	.68	1.48	2.72
South Am. States..	39,600,000	76,900,000	4,000,000	14,700,000	18,700,000	1,115,100,000	1.94	.47	28.16	30.57
Spain..............	17,800,000	79,100,000	....	173,700,000	173,700,000	165,300,000	4.44	9.76	9.28	23.48
Sweden............	5,100,000	17,500,000	....	7,000,000	7,000,000	27,600,000	3.43	1.37	5.41	10 21
Switzerland.......	3,300,000	27,500,000	....	10,700,000	10,700,000	18,600,000	8.33	3.24	5.64	17.21
Turkey	24,200,000	50,000,000	30,000,000	10,000,000	40,000,000	....	2.06	1.65	....	3.71
Central Am. States	4,000,000	2,000,000	7,000,000	....	7,000,000	30,200,000	.50	1.75	7.55	9.80
China..............	330,100,000	....	750,000,000	....	750,000,000	....	....	2.24	....	2 24
Mexico............	13,500,000	8,600,000	106,000,000	....	106,000,000	54,000,000	.63	7.85	4.00	12.48
Siam...............	6,300,000	22,300,000	193,000,000	....	193,000,000	2,600,000	3.54	30.63	.41	34.58
Straits Settlem'ts.	5,100,000	....	240,000,000	2,000,000	242,000,000	....	....	47.45	....	47.45
Total.........	1,282,400,000	$5,174,400,000	$2,927,000,000	$920,500,000	$3,847,500,000	$2,921,100,000	$4.03	$3.00	$2.28	$9.31

World's Annual Production of Gold and Silver.

Countries.	Gold.		Silver.	
	Oz., fine.	Value.	Oz., fine.	Coining Value.
United States..............................	3,805,500	$78,666,700	55,214,000	$71,387,800
Mexico....................................	497,527	10,284,800	57,656,549	74,545,900
Canada....................................	1,167,216	24,128,500	5,242,697	6,778,400
Africa.....................................	489,704	9,089,500	....	....
Australasia...............................	3,719,080	76,880,200	18,775,816	24,275,800
Russia.....................................	1,165,412	22,850,900	156,993	203,000
Austria-Hungary	103,363	2,136,700	1,996,706	2,581,600
Germany..................................	2,893	59,800	5,521,648	7,139,100
Norway....................................	....	....	165,902	214,500
Sweden....................................	2,017	41,700	53,986	69,800
Italy..	1,704	35,200	751,335	971,400
Spain.......................................	418	8,600	3,185,316	4,118,400
Greece.....................................	....	....	1,154,046	1,492,100
Turkey.....................................	1,185	24,500	429,180	554,900
France.....................................	....	....	452,151	584,600
Great Britain.............................	13,360	276,200	221,673	286,600
Argentine.................................	1,451	30,000	45,166	58,400
Bolivia.....................................	5,786	119,600	10,254,260	13,258,000
Chile..	51,626	1,067,200	10,395,333	13,440,400
Colombia..................................	135,513	2,801,300	1,881,649	2,432,800
Brazil	134,260	2,775,400	....	....
Venezuela.................................	15,538	321,200	....	....
Guiana (British).........................	85,701	1,771,600	....	....
Guiana (Dutch)...........................	19,621	405,600	....	....
Guiana (French)..........................	96,750	2,000,000	....	....
Peru..	64,300	1,329,200	5,600,848	7,241,500
Central America.........................	30,974	640 300	879,666	1.137,400
Japan	58,127	1,201,600	1,729,603	2,236,300
China.......................................	439,801	9,091,500	....	....
Korea	217,687	4,500,000	....	....
India (British)............................	454,527	9,395,900	....	....
East Indies (British).....................	41,685	861,700	....	....

SAVINGS BANK DEPOSITS.

STATES AND TERRITORIES.	Number of Depositors.	Amount of Deposits.	Average to Each Depositor.	STATES AND TERRITORIES.	Number of Depositors.	Amount of Deposits.	Average to Each Depositor.
Maine	193,005	$72,082,694	$373.47	South Carolina	23,164	$5,785,792	$249.78
New Hampshire	147,928	60,249,862	407.29	Florida	877	225,395	257.01
Vermont	128,529	41,987,497	326.68	Louisiana	10,518	3,284,892	312.31
Massachusetts	1,593,640	560,705,752	351.84	Texas	2,980	584,424	196.12
Rhode Island	138,366	71,900,541	519.64	Tennessee	19,823	3,519,333	177.54
Connecticut	425,588	193,248,909	454.07	Ohio	103,405	48,180,438	465.94
New York	2,229,661	1,051,689,186	471.68	Indiana	24,362	7,288,506	299.17
New Jersey	227,130	69,866,709	307.60	Illinois	277,879	100,072,804	360.13
Pennsylvania	396,877	120,441,275	303.47	Wisconsin	3,908	719,009	183.98
Delaware	4,187	1,265,586	302 26	Minnesota	63,293	15,526,701	245.31
Maryland	186,293	64,367,767	345.52	Iowa	238,421	85,703,614	359.46
Dist. of Columbia	10,845	1,309,555	120.75	California	256,467	180,438,675	703.55
West Virginia	4,687	680,372	155.16				
North Carolina	12,201	2,451,838	200.95	United States	6,755,623	$2,769,839,546	$412.53

No returns for 1902 from the following States and returns for previous years are given: Alabama, 1893-94 depositors, 2,500; amount, $102,347. New Mexico, depositors, 217; amount of deposits, $37,951. Washington 1894-95, depositors, 5,512; amount of deposits, $1,148,104. Oregon, depositors, 1,631; amount of deposits, $972,298. Georgia, depositors, 5,384; amount, $288,010. Utah, depositors, 6,522; amount, $2,252,124.

Approximate Value of the Product of Gold and Silver in the United States in 1899.

STATES AND TERRITORIES.	Gold Value.	Silver Coining Value.	Total Value.	STATES AND TERRITORIES.	Gold Value.	Silver Coining Value.	Total Value.
Alabama	$4,300	$129	$4,429	New Mexico	$584,100	$650,731	$1,234,831
Alaska	5,459,500	181,140	5,640,640	North Carolina	34,500	388	34,888
Arizona	2,566,100	2,040,630	4,606,730	Oregon	1,429,500	173,641	1,603,141
California	15,197,800	1,065,762	16,263,562	South Carolina	160,100	517	160,617
Colorado	25,982,800	29,301,527	55,284,327	South Dakota	6,469,500	188,251	6,657,751
Georgia	113,000	517	113,517	Texas	6,900	672,323	679,223
Idaho	1,889,000	4,980,105	6,869,105	Utah	3,450,800	9,171,135	12,621,935
Maine	3,600	646	4,246	Vermont	100	....	100
Maryland	800	129	929	Virginia	7,100	129	7,229
Michigan	100	145,843	145,943	Washington	685,400	330,990	1,016,390
Missouri	100	129	229	Wyoming	29,200	517	29,717
Montana	4,760,100	20,810,990	25,571,090				
Nevada	2,219,000	1,090,457	3,309,457	Total	$71,053,400	$70,806,626	$141,860,026

Wild-cat Banks.— The fraudulent institutions known as wild-cat banks were started principally in the West and South after the closing up of the United States Bank and the transfer of its deposits to State banks in 1832. The scarcity of capital in these regions made it comparatively easy to put in circulation anything that purported to be money. Hence, anyone with a very limited capital — or, in fact, without any capital at all — could open a bank, issue $10,000 or more in small notes, and pass them over in easy loans to land speculators, who, in their turn, paid them out in country villages and among farmers, where the standing of the bank of issue would necessarily be unknown. Hundreds of these banks were started, and immense amounts of so-called money were loaned to build cities in the wilderness, and to contractors anxious to build railroads without material, tools, or means of paying wages. In some cases the real place of issue was, for instance, New Orleans or Buffalo, while the bills purported to be issued and payable in, say, Georgia or Illinois. This method of doing business lasted four years, when the panic of 1837, one of the most painful and prolonged crises in the financial history of the United States, overtook the country. Fortunately this led to the adoption in nearly all the States of such banking laws as rendered similar schemes impossible in the future. These institutions were called wild-cat banks, owing to their utter lawlessness and because their victims were "most awfully clawed."

Trade Dollars.— Previous to the coinage of this dollar, which was brought into existence through the demand on the Pacific coast for a coin to be used in commercial relations, particularly with China and Japan, the old silver dollar of $371\frac{1}{4}$ grains was the only one known. The new dollar contained 420 grains, and eventually was extensively circulated all over the Union, but was retired after the Forty-fourth Congress enacted that it was not a legal tender.

Clearing House.— The clearing house is

an institution founded not merely upon the idea of saving time and trouble in the use of the precious metals, but also of circulating notes. The Clearing House of London, which was the first of the kind, originated among the bankers of that city, whose transactions in the checks, bills, and drafts drawn upon each other became so large as to call for the daily, and even hourly, use of vast sums in bank-notes by all of them. Appreciating how readily the debts and credits respectively due or held by them might be set off, one against the other, they formed the clearing house, where, up to four o'clock each day, all drafts, bills, etc., upon each individual member were taken. This system of the London Clearing House has, however, been much extended and improved. Clearing houses exist in New York, Philadelphia, Boston, Chicago, and other cities in the United States. A description of the system in use in Philadelphia will, in the main, answer for all. The clearings are made each morning at 8.30, just before which hour a messenger and a clerk from each bank are at the clearing house. The clerks take their seats at a series of desks arranged in the form of a half oval. The messenger brings with him from his bank a sealed package for each other bank, containing all checks or drafts on such banks. The name of the bank sending, and that of the bank to which it is sent, is printed on each package, and the amount sent is written thereon. The messengers take their places near the desks of their respective banks, and they have with them tabular statements of the amount sent to each bank, and the aggregate. These are exhibited to the respective clerks and noted by them on the blank forms. At 8.30 o'clock precisely, the manager calls to order and gives the word, when all the messengers move forward from left to right of the clerks, handing in to those clerks the packages addressed to their respective banks, and taking receipts for them on their statements. The several clerks then pass around a memorandum of the debts, credits, and balances, each of his respective bank. When these memoranda have made the circuit, each clerk has on his statement the debts, credits, and balances, whether debtor or creditor, of each bank. If these debits and credits, or debtor or creditor balances, are found to balance, the clerks now leave the clearing house. If not, they remain until the error or errors are discovered. The balances due by the several banks are paid into the clearing house that day by 11.30 o'clock A. M., and are receivable by the creditor bank by 12.30 P. M. Each bank is obliged daily to furnish to the clearing house a statement of its condition at the end of the business on that day, and tables are daily furnished to the several banks of all the banks in the clearing house.

Freedman's Bank was established in March, 1865, as a charitable enterprise, to encourage frugality and thrift among the newly-liberated slaves. The institution was started at first in Washington, but afterward branch banks to the number of thirty-four were located in different parts of the Union. The bank was not intended to be a money-making concern, either for bankers or for depositors, but as a place of deposit for the savings of negroes, which savings were to be invested in the stocks, bonds, Treasury notes, and other securities of the United States. During the existence of the bank, nine years, it handled no less than $56,000,000 of deposits, the negroes being led to believe that the safety of the institution was guaranteed by the Government, which was untrue. The institution was managed by a number of trustees of unsavory financial reputation, and, as a consequence, at the expiration of nine years it suspended payment. At the investigation which was made by a committee appointed by Congress a most scandalous condition of affairs was discovered. The regulations of the charter had been completely ignored, and the funds had been dissipated by loans made upon inadequate securities. By law the investments of the bank were confined to Government securities alone. Unimproved real estate, unsalable stocks and personal notes, were among the assets of the bank. Deficits and embezzlements at the branch banks also produced many losses. The unsecured debts owed to the depositors amounted to $2,900,000, and the assets yielded about $1,700,000. For some years three bank commissioners were employed, at a salary of $3,000 each, to wind up the affairs of the institution. After $475,-000 had been expended in this "winding-up" process the affairs of the bank were all turned over to the Comptroller of the Currency. Dividends have been paid at various times; but many small depositors, through ignorance and despair, forfeited their dividends by not calling for them. In all, 77,000 dividends, amounting to $112,000, were thus forfeited.

Revenues of the Government, year ending June 30, 1903 :—

From customs,	$284,479,582.00
From internal revenue,	230,810,124.00
From sales of public lands,	11,024,744.00
From other miscellaneous sources,	34,082,224.00
Total receipts,	$560,396,674.00

Expenditures for the same period :—

For the civil establishment,	$124,944,290.00
For the military establishment,	118,619,520.00
For the naval establishment,	82,618,034.00

For Indian service,	$12,935,168.00
For pensions,	138,425,646.00
For interest on public debt,	28,556,385.00
Total expenditures,	$506,099,007.00
Showing a surplus of,	$54,297,667.00

DIVISION OF LABOR.

The Statistical Yearbook for the German Empire, for 1903, gives the following figures with reference to the occupation of the population of different countries:—

COUNTRY.	Agriculture. Per cent.	Industries. Per cent.	Commerce. Per cent.	Other Pursuits. Per cent.
German Empire.	37.5	37.4	10.6	14.5
Austria	38	37	11	14
Hungary	64	22	6	8
Italy	57	28	4	11
Switzerland	37	41	11	11
France	44	34	9	13
England, Wales.	10	57	11	22
Scotland	14	58	10	18
Ireland	44	31	5	20
Great Britain	15	54	10	21
United States	36	24	16	24

With reference to the percentage of females employed, the United States stands first, with only 14.3 per cent., the Netherlands and Sweden coming next. In Germany the percentage of females employed to the total self-supporting population is 25, while in England it comes up to 27. In Italy the percentage is 40 and in Austria 47.

Trades Unions.—In one form or another, combinations have always existed since the employed and employing classes became distinguishable from each other. Trades unions, organized for purposes such as those which contemporary unions contend for, have existed for more than three centuries. So early as 1548 a statute of Edward VI. is directed, among other culprits, against certain "artificers, handicraftsmen, and laborers," who had "sworn mutual oaths" to do only certain kinds of work, to regulate how much work should be done in a day, and what hours and times they should work. The usual penalties of fines, pillory, and loss of ears were to follow a breach of its enactments. Add the regulation of wages and the employment of union or non-union men to the objects enumerated in this statute, and we have in effect the trades unions of the present day. Many fruitless acts were afterward passed to prevent combinations for raising wages; but since that time the trades unions have increased in numbers and membership, until they include nearly all the laboring classes of England and America. The advocates of the unions insist that they are the only means by which workmen can defend themselves against the aggressions of employers. It is argued that the individual laborer has no chance of resisting the capitalist on equal terms; that starvation treads too closely on his heels to permit his successfully opposing a reduction of his wages, no matter how arbitrary or unjust. It is urged that associations of employers are practically universal, and that their object is mainly to secure for themselves the largest possible share of the profits which are the product of capital and labor united. What has probably been the greatest result of the trades union idea is the passage of laws looking to the welfare of the workingman. There is scarcely a state in the Union that has not statutes providing for the hours of labor, the sanitary conditions of workshops, the liability of employers, the age limit for the employment of children. The public is beginning to understand that better conditions for workmen mean better communities, more schools, and more intelligence. Organization of labor has undoubtedly had an effect in maintaining wages.

Mississippi Scheme.—The gigantic commercial scheme commonly known by this name was projected in France by the celebrated financier John Law of Edinburgh in 1717, and collapsed in 1720. Its primary object was to develop the resources of the Province of Louisiana and the country bordering on the Mississippi, a tract at that time believed to abound in the precious metals. The company was incorporated in August, 1717, under the title of the "Company of the West," and started with a capital of 200,000 shares of 500 livres each. They obtained the exclusive privilege of trading to the Mississippi, farming the taxes and coining money. The prospectus was so inviting that shares were eagerly bought; and when, in 1719, the company obtained the monopoly of trading to the East Indies, China, and the South Seas, and all the possessions of the French East India Company, the brilliant vision opened up to the public gaze was irresistible. The "Company of the Indies," as it was now called, created 50,000 additional shares; but a rage for speculation had seized all classes, and there were at least 300,000 applicants for the new shares, which consequently rose to an enormous premium. Law, as director general, promised an annual dividend of 200 livres per share, which, as the shares were paid for in the depreciated *billets d'ctat*, amounted to an annual return of 120 per cent. The public enthusiasm now rose to absolute frenzy, and Law's house and the street in front of it were daily crowded by applicants of both sexes and of all ranks, who were content to wait for hours — nay, for days together — in order to obtain an interview with the modern Plutus. While confidence lasted a factitious impulse was given to trade in

Paris, the value of manufactures was increased fourfold, and the demand far exceeded the supply. The population is said to have been increased by hundreds of thousands, many of whom were glad to take shelter in garrets, kitchens, and stables. But the Regent had meanwhile caused the paper circulation of the National Bank to be increased as the Mississippi scheme stock rose in value, and many wary speculators, foreseeing a crisis, had secretly converted their paper and shares into gold, which they transmitted to England or Belgium for safety. The increasing scarcity of gold and silver becoming felt, a general run was made on the bank. The Mississippi stock now fell considerably, and despite all efforts it continued to fall steadily and rapidly. In 1720 the National Bank and the Company of the Indies were amalgamated; but, though this gave an upward turn to the share market, it failed to put the public credit on a sound basis. The crisis came at last. In July, 1720, the bank stopped payment, and Law was compelled to flee the country. The French Government was nearly overthrown, and widespread financial distress and bankruptcy were occasioned.

Credit Mobilier.— The Credit Mobilier of America was a joint stock company organized in 1863 for the purpose of facilitating the construction of public works. In 1867 another company, which had undertaken to build the Union Pacific Railroad, purchased the charter of the Credit Mobilier, and the capital was increased to $3,750,000. In 1872 a lawsuit in Pennsylvania developed the startling fact that much of the Credit Mobilier was owned by members of Congress. A suspicion that those members had voted corruptly in the legislation affecting the Pacific Railway at once seized the public mind, and led to a Congressional investigation, in the course of which many scandalous transactions were brought to light, and the reputation of many public servants suffered greatly. The investigation showed that some of the members of Congress who had this stock in their possession had never paid for it; in other words, that their votes had probably been obtained by giving them stock. In other cases it was shown that persons whose integrity could not be questioned had been reported as stockholders, for the purpose of influencing others to subscribe or to regard the project favorably. The report of the committee exonerated many whose names had been used without authority in connection with the scheme. Owing to the profitableness of the work in which the company was engaged, the stock rose rapidly in value previous to the investigation, and enormous dividends were paid to the shareholders.

Boycott and Boycotting.— The origin of the term "Boycotting" was as follows: A Captain Boycott was the agent of a land owner in Ireland. His policy proved to be distasteful and offensive to the tenants, and such was their feeling in the matter that they asked the landlord to remove him. This was refused, and in retaliation the tenants and their friends refused to work for or under Boycott. They would not harvest his crops, and they made an agreement among themselves that none of them or theirs should assist or work for him in the harvest. His crops were endangered, when relief arrived in the person of certain Ulster men, who, under the protection of troops, harvested the crops of Boycott. The defensive league of the tenantry was much more powerful and effective than might be supposed from the single instance of the combination referred to above. The ramifications of their compact were very numerous and extensive. For example, if anyone had dealings with Boycott or those who represented him, then no one was to have any dealings with that person. If a man worked for Boycott he was looked upon by his old friends and neighbors as a stranger — no one would sell to or buy of him, no one was to know him. The effect of this agreement when carried to this extent was just what its authors proposed, and "Boycotting" has become a very forcible phrase.

Debt, Imprisonment for.—During late years the laws of most countries bearing upon imprisonment for debt have been greatly modified. In England the old harsh laws concerning debtors, which made the issuance of 101,000 writs for debt in one year, 1825, possible, were abolished in 1838; and in 1869, by the passage of the "Debtors' Act," still more lenient regulations were adopted. Imprisonment is still possible there, in certain cases, as when it is believed a debtor intends leaving the country, or when a debtor refuses, when he is able, to settle a claim decided against him by the courts, or when there is palpable evidence of premeditated fraud. The imprisonment cannot continue, however, longer than a specified time— usually one year. Imprisonment for debt was abolished in France by a decree of March 9, 1793, was re-enacted several years later, was again abolished in 1848, and was again re-established the same year. Since that time, however, the law has been greatly modified, and now imprisonment is permitted for a limited period only, and certain classes are exempted from the law; as, for instance, those under twenty years or over seventy years of age, ecclesiastics, and women not engaged in commerce. In France, as in most all continental countries, the entire cession of the property of the debtor to his creditors will procure immunity from personal process, even though it may not cover the amount owed. New York was the first state in the United States to abolish imprisonment for debt. This was done in 1831, and the example was shortly followed by the other states; and though there is great difference in the insolvent laws of the several states, they all permit debtors their freedom, except in cases wherein dishonesty or peculation render the debtor also amenable to the Penal Code. Both in Greece and in Rome, in ancient times, the creditor had a claim to the person of the debtor. In Rome, thirty days after judgment was pronounced against the debtor, he was given into the hands of his creditor, who kept him sixty days in chains, exposing him on three market-days, and proclaiming his debt. If no one stepped in to release him, the debtor, at the end of that time, might be sold for a slave or put to death. If there were several creditors, the letter of the law permitted them to cut their debtor in pieces, sharing him in proportion to their claims. The common practice, however, was to treat him as a slave, and make him work out the debt. The children in his power, in accordance with the constitution of society at Rome, followed his condition.

Wealth of Principal Nations

Argen. Rep	$2,545,000,000	Holland	$4,900,000,000
Australia	6,836,000,000	Italy	14,815,000,000
Austria	19,275,000,000	Mexico	3,190,000,000
Belgium	5,035,000,000	Norway	1,215,000,000
Canada	4,900,000,000	Portugal	2,040,000,000
Denmark	2,020,000,000	Russia	25,445,000,000
France	42,990,000,000	Spain	12,580,000,000
Germany	32,185,000,000	Sweden	3,185,000,000
United Km.	47,000,000,000	Switzerland	2,470,000,000
Greece	1,500,000,000	U. States	64,120,000,000

American Mine, Oldest.— The first recorded account of the discovery of coal in the United States is contained in Hennepin's narrative of his explorations in the West, between 1673 and 1680, when he saw the coal outcrop in the bluffs of the Illinois river, not far from Ottawa and La Salle. In New Mexico and Arizona, there are silver mines which were operated by the Toltecs and Aztecs years before the Spanish invasion. So there are copper mines in the Lake Superior region in which the tools and mining marks of ancient miners of prehistoric times were found by the pioneers of the present American mining companies. Where the first colonists of Virginia got the ship load of "fool's gold" which they sent back to England, to the great disgust of the London Company, is not certainly known; but it is known that at the same time, in 1608, they shipped a quantity of iron from Jamestown, which yielded seventeen tons of metal —the first pig-iron ever made from American ore. In North and South Carolina, and Georgia, there are diggings, now overgrown with forests, which are supposed to have been excavated by the followers of De Soto and his immediate successors between 1539 and 1600. The oldest mining enterprise of the United States, still active, is generally conceded to be the mine La Motte, in the lead district of Eastern Missouri, which was opened about 1720 under Renault, of Law's notorious Mississippi Company. It was named after La Motte, the mineralogist of the expedition, and has been worked at intervals ever since it was opened.

Liverpool Docks.— The docks, at Liverpool, England, extend on the city side of the river Mersey 6¼ miles, and have a water area of 333½ acres, and a lineal quayage of 22 miles. The great landing stage at Liverpool is the finest structure of the kind in the world. It was originally built in 1857, and was greatly enlarged in 1874, but shortly after its completion, July 28, 1874, it accidentally caught fire and was entirely consumed. It was again built in the most substantial manner. Its length is 2,063 feet, and its breadth is 80 feet. It is supported on floating pontoons, which rise and fall with the tide, and is connected with the quay by seven bridges, beside a floating bridge 550 feet in length for heavy traffic. The great system of docks at Liverpool was commenced by the corporation in 1709, and was for a century under the control of the City Council, but since 1856 their management has been in the hands of a board. The amount of capital invested in these docks is £10,000,000, of which £7,000,000 is in Liverpool proper, and the revenue derived from them is over £1,250,000 annually. They are constructed as water-tight inclosures, with flood gates, which are opened during the flowing and closed during the ebbing of the tide, so that vessels within can be kept afloat and at the same level while being loaded and unloaded

Communism and Socialism.—Communism is the doctrine that society should be reorganized on the basis of abolishing individual ownership of property and control of wages, and most of the now generally admitted rights of individuals in their private and domestic relations, and substituting therefor community ownership and control of every person and everything. Attempts to realize Communism have been made in both England and France, but in all cases resulted in disaster to the communities. The communistic leader in England was Robert Owen, who made two attempts to carry out his views in that country. Fourier and St. Simon, French Communists, made similar efforts in France, but the results were not more fortunate. A community of St. Simonians established a college or corporation at Menilmontant, with a "supreme father" at their head. The leaders were brought to trial by Louis Philippe on a charge of undermining morality and religion. They were subjected to imprisonment, and not having public feeling with them, they were unable to bear up against contumely thus thrown on them. Socialism is a sort of limited Communism. It would not entirely abolish individual rights of all, but would make such rights subordinate to the common good, and in a manner limit them to it.

Locomotives, Weight and Cost.— The average weight of the locomotive engines now on the standard gauge roads is from twenty-five to thirty-five tons. As locomotives are now built, anything above thirty-five tons would be considered heavy, although there have been locomotives built weighing one hundred and twenty-five tons. The cost of a locomotive for the standard gauge roads is about $10,500. It is usually computed by railroad men that in weight and cost the locomotives on the narrow gauge roads are from one third to one half less than those of the standard gauge lines.

Fur Trade, American.— The Northwest Fur Company, a British organization, practically controlled the fur industry along the great lakes and westward at the beginning of this century. A rival company, composed of American and French, and called the Mackinaw Fur Company, was formed about that time; but the importance of the American fur trade is undoubtedly due to the commercial genius of John Jacob Astor. In 1783 Mr. Astor landed in America with a few hundred dollars' worth of musical instruments, which he immediately exchanged for furs. This action was brought about through a conversation with a furrier during the voyage, who impressed upon the young emigrant the great profit to be gained in the fur traffic. From that time until 1809 he made repeated visits to the scattered settlements of western New York and Canada for the purchase of furs, and did much business with the Northwest Fur Company. All direct trade between the United States and Canada was then forbidden by laws of the British Government; hence furs purchased in the latter had first to be taken to London before they could be brought to New York. These restrictions on trade with Canada were removed by treaty in 1794. In 1809 the American Fur Company, an organization with $1,000,000 capital, was granted a charter by the New York Legislature, and it was generally understood that the capital for this enterprise was furnished by Mr. Astor — in fact that he was the company. In 1811 Mr. Astor, in connection with certain parties formerly connected with the Northwest Fur Company, purchased the Mackinaw Fur Company and merged it, with the American Fur Company, in another organization known as the Southwest Fur Company. Four years later, 1815, Mr. Astor bought all the shares of this company and pushed the American Fur Company to the front again, and in the same year succeeded in having a bill passed through Congress excluding all foreigners from taking any part in the fur trade of the United States — thus securing at one stroke a monopoly of the business. From that time he accumulated enormous wealth.

Gold Exports.— When this country buys abroad more than it sells abroad it must pay the difference, which is called the balance of trade, in sterling exchange. The par value of sterling exchange is $4.867, that is, a pound sterling is worth $4.867 in United States gold. The price or demand of sterling exchange varies according to the supply and demand of bills drawn against London. If we have made heavy shipments to London, or if Europe has been a heavy buyer of our securities, there is plenty of sterling exchange in the market, and it can be bought below its par value. When we have made heavy imports from Europe, or when Europe has been a heavy seller of our securities, or when American travelers have spent a large amount of money in Europe, the supply of sterling exchange is limited and its price rises. If the price of sterling bills is as high as $4.88\frac{7}{8}$ it is just as cheap to ship gold bars to London and pay the expenses of the shipment as it is to buy the exchange. If sterling exchange is $4.89\frac{1}{4}$ gold coin can be shipped without loss. If rates go higher, as, for instance, to $4.90, gold coin or bars can be shipped at a good profit and exchange sold against them. When the rate of sterling exchange falls to $4.83\frac{1}{2}$ gold can be imported from London without loss, and if it goes lower it can be imported with a profit.

The South Sea Bubble.— The "South Sea Bubble," as it is generally called, was a financial scheme which occupied the attention of prominent politicians, communities, and even nations in the early part of the eighteenth century. Briefly, the facts are: In 1711, Robert Hartley, Earl of Oxford, then Lord Treasurer, proposed to fund a floating debt of about £10,000,000, sterling, the interest, about $600,000, to be secured by rendering permanent the duties upon wines, tobacco, wrought silks, etc. Purchasers of this fund were to become also shareholders in the "South Sea

Company," a corporation to have the monopoly of the trade with Spanish South America, a part of the capital stock of which was to be the new fund. But Spain, after the treaty of Utrecht, refused to open her commerce to England, and the privileges of the "South Sea Company" became worthless. There were many men of wealth who were stockholders, and the company continued to flourish, while the ill success of its trading operations was concealed. Even the Spanish war of 1718 did not shake the popular confidence. Then in April, 1720, Parliament, by large majorities in both houses, accepted the company's plan for paying the national debt, and after that a frenzy of speculation seized the nation, and the stock rose to £300 a share, and by August had reached £1,000 a share. Then Sir John Blunt, one of the leaders, sold out, others followed, and the stock began to fall. By the close of September the company stopped payment, and thousands were beggared. An investigation ordered by Parliament disclosed much fraud and corruption, and many prominent persons were implicated, some of the directors were imprisoned, and all of them were fined to an aggregate amount of £2,000,000 for the benefit of the stockholders. A great part of the valid assets was distributed among them, yielding a dividend of about 33 per cent.

Trusts. — A "Trust," in its broad sense, is a combination of individuals or corporations for controlling the price of a commodity. It seeks to do this by restricting production or by "cornering" the market, and strives to accomplish its end without incurring the penalties of the law. This endeavor to keep within the law has given rise to many forms of "trust" agreements. The simplest is a mere naked contract between manufacturers or dealers that each shall carry on his business in his own way, but that none shall sell below an agreed minimum price. Examples of this are agreements between the coal producers of Pennsylvania and the trades union agreements. Another simple form of combination is an agreement that all shall carry on their business independently, but that profits shall all be turned into a common fund and divided in a definitely agreed on ratio, no matter what the profits of each individual may actually have been. Of such a nature are railroad pools. Another kind occurs when a corporation leases the works, or contracts to take all the products of other corporations, or enters into partnership with them. In all of these cases, however, there is a danger of overstepping the bounds of legality. Courts in all parts of the country have repeatedly refused to enforce such contracts if deemed to be injurious to the public, and some authorities have declared them criminal, if dangerous to the common good. This has led to the invention of a subtile and elusive form which we may call the "Trust" proper. In this, the stock of all the stockholders of all the corporations comprising it is placed in the hands of a few men as trustees, thus securing to a dozen or so persons the absolute control of stock representing many millions of dollars and possibly thousands of owners. The Standard Oil Trust and the Sugar Trust illustrate this form, the Standard Oil being probably the pioneer in this line, and now one of the most powerful moneyed institutions in the world. Whether this "Trust" will stand the attacks of its enemies or, in its turn, will be decided to be illegal, it is too soon to judge. In a recent case the New York Supreme Court has declared it illegal and the charters of its constituent corporations liable to forfeiture. As has been said, a "Trust" is not a corporation, nor subject to the restrictions placed by law on incorporated companies.

Strikes, Statistics.— The plan of settling labor difficulties by strikes is a very old one. The first strike in the United States occurred in New York city in 1803, when a number of sailors struck for an advance of wages. According to "Bradstreet's Commercial Reports" there were 697 strikes in 1888, involving 211,841 employees — a decline from 1887 of 23 per cent. in the number of strikes and of 38 per cent. in strikers. Against 1886 the decrease in number of strikers is 52 per cent. Higher wages or fewer hours were the cause of strikes by 68 per cent. of the strikers in 1888, against 62 per cent. in 1887. Trades union questions were behind the strike of 17 per cent. of the men involved in 1888, against 22 per cent. of the year before. About 45 per cent. of striking was in Pennsylvania in 1888, against 32 per cent. in 1887. Only 38 per cent. of the strikes in 1888 resulted in favor of the employees.

During the past few years almost every phase of labor has been organized and strikes have greatly multiplied. Many recent strikes have been national in their effects.

May 12, 1902, began the great coal strike in Pennsylvania, the most disastrous and far-reaching in effect on record. The strike lasted five months involving 147,000 men with a loss in wages of thirty to forty million dollars. Millions of people were affected by the shortage of coal, increasing their fuel bills from 50 to 150 per cent.

Watering Stock.—The credit of having originated the process of watering the stock of railroad companies belongs unquestionably to the late Commodore Vanderbilt. The plan of operation is simple, and consists only in estimating the stock of the road at a figure greatly above its real value. For instance, when Commodore Vanderbilt secured control of the New York Central as well as the Hudson River Railroad in 1868, the combined stock of the two roads was only about $36,000,000. Early in the following year he declared a tremendous dividend of new stock to the stockholders, and raised the estimated value of the two roads to $90,000,000. This action of Vanderbilt was for the purpose of evading a law of the State of New York which provided that when the dividends of any railroad corporation should reach 10 per cent. the state could declare how the surplus above the 10 per cent. should be applied. This provision, it is plain, was rendered nugatory by Vanderbilt's scheme, as, if a railroad can at any time declare stock dividends with no reference whatever to the costs of construction and repair, a dividend of 10 per cent. may never be declared, though the road may be actually earning 30 or 40 per cent. upon its actual cost.

India Rubber.— This is mostly obtained from the Seringueros of the Amazon, who sell it for about 12 cents a pound to the merchants of Para, but its value on reaching England or the United States is over 50 cents a pound. The number of tons imported into Great Britain and the United States has been as follows:—

	1860.	1870.	1880.	1887.
United States............	1,610	4,316	7,529	12,900
Great Britain............	2,150	7,606	8,479	11,800

The best rubber forests in Brazil will ultimately be exhausted, owing to the reckless mode followed by the Seringueros or tappers. The ordinary product of a tapper's work is from 10 to 16 pounds daily. There are 120 india rubber manufacturers in the United States, employing 15,000 operatives, who produce 280,000 tons of goods, valued at $260,000,000, per annum.

How the Price of Southern Confederate Money Dropped.— When the first issue of the Confederate money was scattered among the people, it commanded a slight premium. It then scaled down as follows: June, 1861, 90c.; December 1, 1861, 8 c.; December 15, 1861, 75c.; February 1, 1 6 , 60c.; February 1, 1863, 20c.; June, 1863, 8c.; January, 1864, 2c.; November, 1864, 4½c.; January, 1865, 2½c.; April 1, 1865, 1½c. After that date, it took from $800 to $1,000 in Confederate money to buy a one-dollar greenback.

Facts about Gold and Silver. — A ton of gold or silver contains 29,166.66 ounces.

A ton of gold is worth $602,875; silver, $37,704.84.

The United States money standard for gold and silver is 900 parts pure metal and 100 parts of alloy in 1,000 parts of coin.

The value of an ounce of pure gold is $20.67; 23.22 grains of pure gold equals $1.

The term carat when used to distinguish fineness of gold means one twenty-fourth; pure gold is 24-carat gold.

A cubic foot of gold weighs 1,203 pounds, and is worth about $361,808.

In round numbers the weight of $1,000,000 in standard gold coin is 1¾ tons (3,685 lbs.); standard coin, 26¾ tons; subsidiary silver coin, 25 tons; minor coin, 5-cent nickel, 100 tons.

Glossary of Mining and Milling Terms.

Battery— Generally applied to a set of five stamps. *Bullion*— Ingots of gold or silver ready for the mint. *Bumping-table*— A concentrating table with a jolting motion. *Cage*— A mine elevator. *Chute*— A body of ore, usually elongated, extending downward within a vein; a slide for ore or waste rock. *Cobbing*— Breaking ore for sorting. *Concentrator*— Machine for removing waste matter from mineral. *Copper plates*— Plates of copper coated with quicksilver, upon which the gold is caught as the ore flows from the stamps. *Cord*— A cord weighs about eight tons. *Country-rock*— The rock on each side of a vein. *Crevice*— A fissure, split, or crack; the vein is called "the crevice." *Cribbing*— The timbers used to confine wall rock. *Cross-cut*— A level driven across the course of a vein. *Deposit*— Ore bodies not confined to a lode. *Drift*— A tunnel; a horizontal passage underground. *Dump*— A place of deposit for ore or refuse. *Feeder*— A small vein joining a larger one. *Fissure-vein*— A crack or cleft in the earth's crust filled with mineral matter. *Float*— Loose ore or rock detached from the original formation. *Flume*— A pipe or trough to convey water. *Foot-wall*— Layer of rock beneath the vein. *Free milling*— Ores containing mineral that will separate from the gangue by simple methods. *Hanging-wall*— The layer, or rock, or wall, over a lode. *Ladderway*— That part of mine shaft containing the ladders. *Lagging*— Timbers over and upon the sides of a drift. *Ledge or Lead*— Mineral ores or gangue within fissure veins. *Mill-run*— A test of the value of a given quantity of ore. *Ores*— Compound of metals with oxygen, sulphur, arsenic, etc. *Paystreak*— The richest streak in the vein. *Pocket*— A rich spot in the vein or deposit. *Refractory*— Resisting the action of heat and chemical re-agents. *Shaft*— A well-like passage into a mine. *Sluices*— Troughs in which ore is washed. *Smelting*— Reduction of ores in furnaces. *Spur*— A branch of a vein. *Stamps*— Weights for crushing ores. *Stope*— The part of a vein above or below the drift from which the ore has been removed. *Stoping*— Excavating the ore from the roof or floor of a drift. *Stratum*— A bed or layer. *Stulls*— A framework to support the rubbish when stoping. *Sump*— A well at the bottom of a shaft to collect water. *Tailings*— The refuse left after washing ores containing metals not saved in the first treatment. *Tunnel*— A level driven across a vein. *Whim*— A machine used for raising ore or refuse. *Winze*— An interior shaft sunk from one level to another.

Harvest Months of the World.— JANUARY.— The greater part of Chile, portions of the Argentine Republic, Australia, and New Guinea.

FEBRUARY to MARCH.— The East Indies.

APRIL.— Mexico, Egypt, Persia, and Syria.

MAY.— Japan, China, Northern Asia Minor, Tunis, Algiers, Morocco, and Texas.

JUNE.— California, Spain, Portugal, Italy, Sicily, Greece, and some of the southern departments of France.

JULY. — The larger part of France, Austria, Southern Russia, and the larger part of the United States of America.

AUGUST.— Germany, England, Belgium, Netherlands, part of Russia, Denmark, part of Canada, and the Northeastern States of America.

SEPTEMBER.— Scotland, the larger part of Canada, Sweden, Norway, and the north midlands of Russia.

OCTOBER.— The northern parts of Russia and the northern parts of the Scandinavian peninsula.

Wine Production of the World.— The average production of wine in the principal vine-growing countries of the world is as follows: France, 765,175,972 imperial gallons; Algeria, 722,000,000 imperial gallons; Italy, 605,000,000 imperial gallons; Spain, 484,000,000 imperial gallons; Austria-Hungary, 187,000,000 imperial gallons; Portugal 88,000,000 imperial gallons; Germany, 81,290,000 imperial gallons; Russia, 77,000,000 imperial gallons; Cyprus, 35,200,000 imperial gallons; Switzerland, 28,600,000 imperial gallons; Greece, 28,600,000 imperial gallons; United States, 18,000,000 imperial gallons; Turkey, 22,000,000 imperial gallons; Cape of Good Hope, 15,400,000 imperial gallons; Roumania, 15,400,000 imperial gallons; Servia, 11,000,000 imperial gallons; Australia, 1,933,800 imperial gallons; total, 2,485,599,772 imperial gallons.

CENTRAL AND SOUTH AMERICAN TRADE.

IMPORTS AND EXPORTS.

COUNTRIES.	Imports.	Exports.	COUNTRIES.	Imports.	Exports.
Argentine Republic	$113,485,069	$154,600,412	Hayti	$3,943,786	$12,747,930
Bolivia	13,444,114	35,657,690	Honduras	1,409,788	2,656,661
Brazil	122,000,000	137,000,000	Mexico	65,083,451	148,656,339
Chile	128,538,142	167,674,635	Nicaragua	2,487,952	2,838,557
Colombia	11,346,028	19,735,734	Paraguay	20,977,419	21,382,895
Costa Rica	6,084,898	6,321,196	Peru	18,734,949	30,725,911
Dominican Republic	3,233,178	6,005,864	Salvador	6,000,000	9,142,690
Ecuador	13,431,179	15,419,222	Uruguay	23,977,606	29,388,187
Guatemala	3,880,668	15,377,460	Venezuela	8,159,624	14,378,115

Population According to Latest Estimates.

Argentine Republic (official)	4,000,000	Honduras (estimate)	420,000
Bolivia (estimate)	2,500,000	Mexico (official)	12,570,195
Brazil (official)	18,000,000	Nicaragua (estimate)	420,000
Chile (official)	3,500,000	Paraguay (estimate)	500,000
Colombia (estimate)	4,600,000	Peru (estimate)	3,000,000
Costa Rica (official)	285,003	Salvador (official)	800,500
Ecuador (estimate)	1,300,000	Santo Domingo (estimate)	600,005
Guatemala (official, 1890)	1,470,000	Uruguay (official)	818,843
Hayti (estimate)	1,211,625	Venezuela (official)	2,444,816

TELEGRAPH RATES TO FOREIGN COUNTRIES.

These rates are from New York city. The address and signature are included in the chargeable matter, and the length of words is limited to fifteen letters. When a word is composed of more than fifteen letters, every additional fifteen or the fraction of fifteen letters will be counted as a word.

	Per Word.		Per Word.		Per Word.		Per Word.
Algeria	$0.32	Demerara	$1.49	Matanzas	$0.44	Santo Domingo	$1.32
Alexandria (Egypt)	.56	Denmark	.35	Melbourne, Vic	1.43	Scotland	.25
Antigua	.86	Ecuador	1.25	Mexico City..$1.75. 10 words		Servia	.36
Argentine Republic	1.00	England	.25	Nassau, Bahamas	.35	Sicily	.32
Austria	.34	France	.25	Natal (South Africa)	1.52	Siam	1.19
Barbadoes	.96	Germany	.25	Netherlands	.32	Singapore	1.35
Belgium	.30	Gibraltar	.43	New South Wales	1.45	Spain	.40
Bermuda	.42	Greece	.38	New Zealand	1.52	St. Thomas	1.01
Bolivia	1.25	Guatemala	.55	Norway	.35	Sweden	.39
Brazil	1.35	Havana	.40	Orange Free State	1.52	Switzerland	.30
Bulgaria	.38	Hayti	1.55	Panama	.97	Sydney, N. S. W	1.45
Burmah	1.27	Hungary	.34	Paraguay	1.00	Tangier	.45
Callao (Peru)	1.25	India	1.23	Penang	1.35	Tasmania	1.58
Cairo (Egypt)	.61	Ireland	.25	Peru	1.25	Transvaal	1.52
Cape Colony (S. Africa)	1.52	Italy	.32	Porto Rico	1.17	Trinidad	1.03
Ceylon	1.25	Jamaica	.48	Portugal	.39	Turkey (Europe)	.37
Chile	1.25	Japan	1.76	Queensland	1.50	Turkey (Asia)	.47
China	1.60	Java	1.47	Roumania	.36	Uruguay	1.00
Cochin China	1.35	Korea (Seoul)	1.96	Russia (Europe)	.43	Venezuela	1.70
Colon	.97	Malta	.36	Russia (Asia, West)	.50	Vera Cruz....$1.75, 10 words	
Cypress	.56	Martinique	1.32	Russia (Asia, East)	.56	Victoria (Aus.)	1.43

APPROXIMATE ANNUAL EXPORT TRADE OF THE UNITED STATES.

Articles.	Quantities.	Values.
Domestic Merchandise.		
Agricultural Implements	......	$16,286,740
Animals	......	44,871,684
Books, Maps, Engravings, and other Printed Matter	......	3,997,977
Brass, and Manufactures of	......	1,930,810
Breadstuffs: Corn....bush.	26,636,552	16,185,673
" Wheat. bush.	154,856,102	112,875,222
" Wheat Flour..bbls.	17,759,203	65,661,974
Carriages, Cars, and other Vehicles and parts of	......	9,872,516
Chemicals, Drugs, Dyes, and Medicines	......	13,288,218
Clocks and Watches	......	2,144,490
Coal: Anthracite......tons.	1,570,490	7,117,809
" Bituminous.....tons.	5,400,694	13,647,652
Copper Ore.........tons.	25,076	2,601,697
" Manufactures of	......	41,218,373
Cotton, Unmanufactured.lbs.	3,500,778,763	290,651,819
" Manufactures of	......	32,108,362
Earthen, Stone, and China Ware	......	600,798
Fertilizers	......	6,256,035
Fibers, Vegetable, and Textile Grasses, Manufac'es of	......	4,575,219
Fish	......	6,563,199
Fruits, Apples, Green or Ripe bbls.	459,719	1,628,886
Fruits and Nuts, all other	......	7,090,458
Furs and Fur Skins	......	5,030,204
Glass and Glassware	......	1,960,106
Glucose or Grape Sugar	......	2,319,286
Gunpowder and other Explosives	......	2,062,381
Hay	......	2,580,622
Hops.........lbs.	10,715,151	1,550,657
India Rubber Manufactures.	......	4,032,100
Instruments for Scientific Purposes	......	5,389,476
Iron and Steel, Manufactures of	......	98,552,562
Leather, and Manufac'es of.	......	29,798,323
Domestic Merchandise.		
Malt Liquors	......	$1,290,062
Marble, Stone, and Mfr'es of	......	1,761,696
Musical Instruments	......	3,694,143
Naval Stores	......	11,733,562
Oil Cake, Oil Cake Meal..lbs.	1,648,093,619	19,943,198
Oils: Animal..........gals.	2,121,661	910,697
" Mineral, Crude...gals.	133,536,800	6,084,818
" Mineral, Refined or Manufactured	......	66,218,004
" Vegetable	......	15,308,633
Paints, Pigments, and Colors	......	2,096,379
Paper, and Manufactures of.	......	7,312,030
Paraffine, Paraffine Wax.lbs.	173,583,203	8,858,844
Provisions: Beef Prod's..lbs.	451,987,178	40,719,626
" Hog Prod's..lbs.	1,337,315,909	127,651,341
" Oleomar'ne..lbs.	144,267,342	12,856,490
" Other Meat Pro's	......	11,529,151
" Dairy Products.	......	7,104,770
Seeds: Clover...........lbs.	7,256,573	594,733
" All other	......	7,433,091
Soap	......	1,630,938
Spirits, Distilled..proof gals.	2,956,889	3,011,894
Starch	28,183,967	656,705
Sugar, Molasses, and Syrup gals.	17,777,253	2,465,031
Sugar, Refined..........lbs.	7,213,050	292,715
Tobacco, Unmanufac'd..lbs.	301,007,475	27,103,996
" Manufactures of	......	5,668.853
Vegetables	......	2,546,287
Wood, and Manufactures of.	......	47,779,848
Wool, and Manufactures of.	......	1,525,826
All other Articles	......	55,247,142
Total Exports, Dom. Mdse.	......	$1,355,481,861
Exports, Foreign Mdse	......	26,237,540
Specie: Gold { Domestic	......	$46,761,438
Specie: Gold { Foreign	......	1,807,512
" Silver { Domestic	......	45,971,249
" Silver { Foreign	......	3,761,141
Total Ex., Dom. and For'gn	......	$1,480,020,741

APPROXIMATE ANNUAL IMPORTS.

Articles.	Quantities.	Values.
Merchandise.		
Sugar....................lbs.	3,031,915,875	$55,061,097
Hides and Skins, other than Fur..............lbs.	326,124,103	58,006,618
Chemicals, Drugs, Dyes, and Medicines	......	57,723,622
Coffee..................lbs.	1,091,004,252	70,982,155
Silk, Unmanufactured	......	42,635,351
Cotton, Manufactures of	......	44,460,126
Fibers, Vegetable, Manufactures of	......	39,036,364
India Rubber and Gutta-Percha, Crude..........lbs.	67,790,069	25,652,977
Silk, Manufactures of	......	32,640,242
Fibers, Vegetable, Unmanufactured	......	31,545,962
Wood, and Manufactures of.	......	24,445,599
Iron and Steel, and Mfr'es of	......	27,180,247
Wool, Unmanufactured..lbs.	166,576,966	17,711,788
Fruits, including Nuts	......	21,480,525
Tin, in Bars, Blocks, or Pigs. lbs	79,352,356	19,461,850
Jewelry and Precious Stones	......	25,990,570
Wool, Manufactures of	......	17,384,463
Tobacco....................lbs.	29,428,837	15,211,671
Tobacco, Manufactures of	......	2,494,822
Leather, and Manufac'es of.	......	11,317,785
Copper, and Mfr'es of (not ore)	......	10,968,948
Furs, and Manufactures of	......	15,623,601
Tea.......................lbs.	75,579,125	9,390,128
Earthen, Stone, and China Ware	......	9,680,156
Cotton, Unmanufactured.lbs.	98,715,680	11,712,170
Wines	......	8,921,138
Oils	......	9,300,198
Cocoa, Crude, and Shells of. lbs.	51,379,396	6,656,504
Merchandise.		
Glass and Glassware	......	$6,205,052
Animals	......	4,624,531
Coal, Bituminous.......tons.	1,941,422	5,310,450
Feathers, Flowers, etc	......	5,110,923
Paper, and Manufactures of.	......	4,223,125
Spirits, Distilled	......	4,445,154
Books, Maps, Engravings, etc.	......	4,133,215
Spices	......	3,685,242
Paper Stock, Crude	......	2,770,255
Cement.....................lbs.	423,844,160	1,478,452
Lead.......................lbs.	206,750,967	4,632,770
Toys	......	4,023,670
Vegetables	......	7,039,835
Hats, Bonnets, and Materials for	......	3,050,478
Hair, and Manufactures of	......	2,055,536
Art Works	......	3,516,536
Rice.......................lbs.	157,658,894	2,926,921
Provisions (Meat and Dairy Products)	......	3,510,696
Bristles...................lbs.	2,013,109	2,047,331
Cork Wood, and Manufactures of	......	2,464,934
Clocks and Watches, and Parts of	......	2,460,324
Malt Liquors............gals.	3,751,511	1,880,348
Fertilizers	......	2,426,758
All other Articles	......	96,621,735
Total Merchandise	......	$903,320,948
Specie: Gold	......	$52,021,254
" Silver	......	28,232,254
Total Imports	......	$983,574,456

VALUE OF IMPORTS AND EXPORTS OF MERCHANDISE.

Year Ending June 30.	Exports.		Total Exports.	Imports.	Total Exports and Imports.	Excess of Exports.	Excess of Imports.
	Domestic.	Foreign.					
1875	$499,284,100	$14,158,611	$513,442,711	$533,005,436	$1,046,448,147	....	$19,562,725
1876	525,582,247	14,802,424	540,384,671	460,741,190	1,001,125,861	$ 79,643,481	....
1877	589,670,224	12,804,996	602,475,220	451,323,126	1,053,798,346	151,152,094	....
1878	680,709,268	14,156,498	694,865,766	437,051,532	1,131,917,298	257,814,234	....
1879	698,340,790	12,098,651	710,439,441	445,777,775	1,156,217,216	264,661,666	....
1880	823,946,353	11,692,305	835,638,658	667,954,746	1,503,593,404	167,683,912	....
1881	883,925,947	18,451,399	902,377,346	642,664,628	1,545,041,974	259,712,718	....
1882	733,239,732	17,302,525	750,542,257	724,639,574	1,475,181,831	25,902,683	....
1883	804,223,632	19,615,770	823,839,402	723,180,914	1,547,020,316	100,658,488	....
1884	724,964,852	15,548,757	740,513,609	667,697,693	1,408,211,302	72,815,916	....
1885	726,682,946	15,506,809	742,189,755	577,527,329	1,319,717,084	164,662,426	....
1886	665,964,529	13,560,301	679,524,830	635,436,136	1,314,960,966	44,088,694	....
1887	703,022,923	13,160,288	716,183,211	692,319,768	1,408,502,979	23,863,443	....
1888	683,862,104	12,092,403	695,954,507	723,957,114	1,419,911,621	....	28,002,607
1889	730,282,609	12,118,766	742,401,375	745,131,652	1,487,533,027	....	2,730,277
1890	845,293,828	12,534,856	857,828,684	789,310,409	1,647,139,093	68,518,275	....
1891	872,270,283	12,210,527	884,480,810	844,916,196	1,729,397,006	39,564,614	....
1892	1,015,732,011	14,546,137	1,030,278,148	827,402,462	1,857,680,610	202,875,686	....
1893	831,030,785	16,634,409	847,665,194	866,400,922	1,714,066,116	....	18,735,728
1894	869,204,937	22,935,635	892,140,572	654,994,622	1,547,135,194	237,145,950	....
1895	793,392,599	14,145,566	807,538,165	731,969,965	1,539,508,130	75,568,200	....
1896	863,200,487	19,406,451	882,606,938	779,724,674	1,662,331,612	102,882,264	....
1897	1,032,007,603	18,985,953	1,050,993,556	764,730,412	1,815,723,968	286,263,144	....
1898	1,210,291,913	21,190,417	1,231,482,330	616,050,654	.......:	615,431,676	....
1899	1,203,931,222	23,092,080	1,227,023,302	697,148,489	1,924,171,791	529,874,813	....
1900	1,370,763,571	23,719,511	1,394,483,082	849,941,184	2,244,424,266	544,541,890	....
1901	1,460,462,806	27,302,185	1,487,764,991	823,172,165	2,310,937,156	664,592,826	....
1902	1,355,481,861	26,237,540	1,381,719,401	903,320,948	2,285,040,349	478,398,453	....
1903	1,392,231,302	27,910,377	1,420,141,679	1,025,719,237	2,445,860,916	394,422,442	....

BONDED DEBTS AND ASSESSED VALUATION OF STATES.

States and Territories.	Real Valuation.	Personal Valuation.	Total Valuation Assessed.	Bonded Debts.	Tax Rate Per $1,000 1895	Tax Rate Per $1,000 1902
Alabama	....	....	$284,622,937	$9,357,600	....	....
Arizona	....	....	68,000,000	2,787,347	....	....
Arkansas	$127,062,903	$62,936,142	189,999,045	1,271,000	$5.00	$5.75
California	942,353,309	238,227,393	1,228,292,457	2,281,500	4.93	4.98
Colorado	....	....	465,000,000	2,300,900	4.00	4.50
Connecticut	....	....	694,200,162	1,720,827	....	....
Delaware	....	....	76,000,000	769,750	....	....
Dist. of Columbia	182,525,608	15,962,805	198,488,413	14,284,650	15.00	15.00
Florida	79,688,902	16,998,052	96,686,954	1,032,500	3.25	5.00
Georgia	243,468,385	161,323,752	456,347,034	7,631,500	4.61	5.44
Idaho	....	....	51,440,758	546,500	8.75	4.75
Illinois	....	....	999,231,829	18,500	....	....
Indiana	....	....	1,360,445,139	3,887,615	1.00	.90
Iowa	405,541,075	152,921,513	558,462,588	10,937	....	2.90
Kansas	....	....	363,156,045	582,000	3.80	5.60
Kentucky	499,400,657	177,655,718	667,056,375	1,171,394	....	5.00
Louisiana	....	....	301,215,222	10,877,800	....	....
Maine	268,434,909	68,264,740	336,609,649	2,453,000	2.50	2.90
Maryland	....	....	643,812,408	2,662,344	1.78	1.70
Massachusetts	2,370,550,196	1,611,236,303	3,981,876,499	13,674,173	....	....
Michigan	1,046,453,013	310,997,015	1,317,450,028	416,800	2.73	1.20
Minnesota	....	....	585,083,328	2,009,000	....	....
Mississippi	131,315,281	63,236,476	222,847,525	2,887,026	5.00	6.00
Missouri	....	....	1,004,469,071	5,680,839	5.75	3.00
Montana	75,039,256	73,373,706	153,412,962	860,000	....	2.50
Nebraska	....	....	174,439,095	None.	8.00	7.22
Nevada	19,299,526	9,091,726	28,391,252	265,210	....	8.00
New Hampshire	....	....	282,517,963	1,781,323	....	....
New Jersey	....	....	918,418,741	None.	....	....
New Mexico	....	....	36,547,439	1,152,100	....	17.29
New York	5,168,645,989	585,783,522	5,754,429,511	10,075,660	3.24	1.20
North Carolina	167,368,632	139,229,083	306,597,715	6,287,350	4.13	4.30
North Dakota	73,574,494	43,629,991	117,204,485	1,006,393	4.50	4.50
Ohio	1,377,253,183	591,026,817	1,968,280,000	451,665	....	2.89
Oregon	....	....	141,398,523	1,238	....	6.32
Pennsylvania	2,766,829,685	761,755,893	3,528,585,578	7,815,299	....	....
Rhode Island	320,318,384	87,086,388	407,404,772	3,278,000	....	1.80
South Carolina	103,258,440	86,074,669	189,333,109	6,846,082	5,25	5.00
South Dakota	....	....	173,206,733	588,300	....	3.20
Tennessee	293,359,783	51,737,072	345,096,855	16,625,666	7.00	6.73
Texas	699,872,560	282,315,305	982,187,865	717,200	3.35	3.46
Utah	....	....	112,580,296	900,000	....	8.00
Vermont	119,783,775	59,231,217	179,014,992	333,965	2.50	1.75
Virginia	316,563,279	107,279,401	423,842,680	24,363,795	4.00	4.00
West Virginia	149,898,172	78,510,553	228,408,725	None.	....	3.50
Washington	188,816,290	71,363,814	260,180,104	1,345,000	....	7.60
Wisconsin	1,186,349,139	249,934,861	1,436,284,000	2,251,000	1.40	1.57
Wyoming	....	....	39,581,216	300,000	....	6.50

ANNUAL WHEAT CROP OF THE WORLD, IN BUSHELS.

COUNTRIES.	Bushels.	COUNTRIES.	Bushels.	COUNTRIES.	Bushels.
United States	756,269,573	Italy	133,045,279	Egypt	10,035,725
Canada	87,555,891	Spain	123,296,049	Algeria	22,281,545
Argentina	74,751,525	France	307,388,463	Australasia	57,323,526
Chile	9,462,134	Germany	91,815,989	Mexico	3,233,292
Austria	44,026,823	Belgium	13,117,344	Other countries	37,645,913
Hungary	132,966,433	Great Britain	56,205,837		
Roumania	73,142,703	Portugal	10,035,725	The world	2,820,333,614
Turkey	61,648,024	Russia	427,780.477		
Bulgaria	38,709,225	British India	248,593,946		

Estimate made by the Russian Ministry of Finance.

The rye crop of principal countries, in bushels: United States, 23,996,000; Germany, 336,624,000; Austria-Hungary, 107,500,000; Russia in Europe, 903,931,000; France, 63,546,000; Japan, 35,000,000; the world, 1,601,826,000. The barley crop of the world, in bushels, was 919,224,000; corn crop, 2,735,090; oats crop, 3,095,497,000.

ANIMAL, VEGETABLE, AND MINERAL PRODUCTIONS.

With the Names of the Countries Producing Them.

Agates—Africa and several parts of Europe, but chiefly Iceland, Saxony, and Tuscany.

Alabaster—Spain, Italy, England, America.

Alcanet (root)—Imported from the Levant, or the neighborhood of Montpellier in France.

Alligator—North America, South America, and the northern parts of Africa.

Almonds—Spain, France, Italy, the Levant, Arabia, Asia, Africa. Indigenous to Greece.

Aloes—America, the West Indies. The medicinal Aloes are indigenous to India, Africa, and Italy.

Amber—In mines in Prussia, near the seacoast; on the shores of Sicily and the Adriatic; on the southern shores of the Baltic and eastern shores of England; Mexico.

Amethyst—Sweden, Bohemia, Saxony, and other parts of Europe; Siberia, India (Ceylon), Mexico, Brazil.

Anchovy—The Mediterranean (chiefly off Gorgona), off the coast of Spain, France, and Italy; and occasionally off those of England.

Anise Seeds—Egypt, to which they are indigenous; Syria and other Eastern countries; Spain, Malta, America.

Ant-Bear—South America (Brazil, Guiana), East Indies, and Cape of Good Hope.

Antelope—Europe, Asia, Africa, Arabia.

Apes—Asia (the East Indies), and Africa.

Armadillo—Mexico, South America.

Arnotto—South America, East Indies, West Indies.

Arrack (a spirituous liquor)—Batavia, from rice; Goa, from the juice of the cocoa tree.

Arrowroot—East Indies, South America, West Indies.

Arsenic—Great Britain, Saxony, Bohemia, Hungary, Mexico.

Asafœtida (a kind of gum)—Persia.

Asbestos (an incombustible kind of earth)—The Ural and some other European mountains; Swedish Lapland, Candia, China, North America.

Asphaltum (a friable kind of bitumen)—The Dead Sea, many parts of Europe and America, the Island of Trinidad.

Baboons—Asia (Borneo and the Philippine Islands), and the hot parts of Africa.

Bamboo Cane—The East Indies, China, West Indies and America.

Banana—Egypt and the West Indies, and other tropical countries.

Barilla (an alkaline salt, used in making glass)—Spain and other parts of Europe, South America, West Indies.

Bear—The northern parts of Europe, Asia, Arabia. Egypt, Barbary, Japan, Ceylon, North America, Peru.

Beaver—The north part of Europe, Asia, and America.

Bergamot (a perfume)—Bergamo, in Italy.

Beryl (a gem)—Siberia, Dauria, on the frontiers of China, Saxony, south of France, North America, Brazil.

Betel (a shrub, whose leaf is chewed)—The East Indies.

Bird of Paradise—The islands of Papua and Droo.

Bison—Poland, Lithuania and North America.

Black Bear—India, Africa, America, Kamchatka.

Black Eagle—Abyssinia.

Black Fox—The north of Europe, Siberia, North America.

Black Swan—Botany Bay.

Boa Constrictor—Africa, South America, India.

Box Wood—Spain, Turkey, America.

Brandy—France, (chiefly in Cognac and Nantes); also in England, Spain, and the United States, but of inferior quality.

Brazil-Wood—Brazil (Pernambuco) and other parts of America; the East Indies.

Bread-Fruit—Otaheite and other South Sea Islands.

Buffalo—Asia, Africa, America.

Burgundy Wine—France.

Calabash Tree—The East Indies, America, West Indies.

Camel—Tartary, Siberia, Thibet, China.

Camelopard—Africa, Senaar, Abyssinia, Ethiopia, and the neighborhood of the Cape of Good Hope.

Camphor (a vegetable product)—China, Japan, and the East India Islands, Borneo, and Ceylon.

Canary Birds—Africa, the Canary Islands, Italy, and Greece.

Cantharides (a kind of beetle used in making blisters)—Spain, Italy, and south of France.

Cape Madeira Wine—The Cape of Good Hope.

Capers (the buds of a plant)—The south of France, Italy, and the Levant.

Capsicum (a pepper plant)—East Indies, Mexico, South America, West Indies.

Caraway Seeds—England, America.

Cardamom Seeds—East Indies (Malabar).

Carmine (a color prepared from cochineal)—East Indies, Mexico, South America.

Cassada (an edible root)—South America and the West Indies.

Cassia (an aromatic bark)—China, East Indies, South America, West Indies.

Castor Oil (from the seeds of a species of palm)—The East Indies, South America, West Indies.

Cat's-Eye (a kind of gem)—Ceylon, Siberia, America.

Catechu (a vegetable extract)—East Indies, Bombay, Bengal.

Caviare (a food made from the roes of sturgeon)—Russia.

Cedar—Syria, chiefly about Mt. Libanus; America.

Cayenne Pepper—East Indies, South America, West Indies.

Chameleon—Egypt and Barbary, India, Mexico, Guiana.

Chamois Goat—The Alps and Pyrenees.

Champagne Wine—France, United States.

Chestnut—Italy, France, Spain, Portugal, America.

Chigger (a species of flea that breeds under the skin)—South America.

Chinchilla (fur)—Chile.

Chocolate (Cacao)—Mexico, South America. West Indies.

Cinnabar (a red paint)—The palatinate of Germany, Bohemia, Almaden in Spain, and India.

Cinnamon—The East Indies, chiefly Ceylon; South America (Guiana).

Citron—Europe (Italy), Asia, West Indies.

Civet (an animal perfume)—Africa (coast of Guinea), India, Brazil.

Claret Wine — The neighborhood of Garonne on the western coast of France; United States.

Cloves — The Molucca Islands (chiefly Amboyna); the isles of France and Bourbon; South America (Cayenne).

Cochineal (an insect used in dyeing and painting)— The East Indies, Mexico, South America.

Cockatoo — East Indies, and the islands of the Indian Ocean; Banda, Ceram, the Philippines, and Sunda Isles.

Cocoanut — The East Indies, Arabia, Africa, South America, West Indies.

Cockroach (a kind of beetle)— Asia, America, West Indies.

Coffee — Arabia (Mocha), East Indies, West Indies, South America.

Condor (a bird of prey) — South America.

Constantia Wine — Constantia Farm, at the Cape of Good Hope.

Copal (a kind of resin) — Africa (Guinea), and America.

Copper — Anglesea and Cornwall, Sweden, Norway, Iceland, the Faroe Islands, and various parts of the continent of Europe, China, and Japan; Southern Africa, United States, Peru, and Chili.

Coral (a marine animal production) — The Mediterranean (about Sicily, Majorca, and Minorca), the Red Sea; off the coasts of Africa and America; in the South Seas.

Coriander Seed — South of Europe; England and America.

Cork — Portugal, Spain, and other parts in the south of Europe; Sicily (on Mt. Etna), the shores of the Mediterranean, South America.

Cornelian — The East Indies, Arabia, Egypt, various parts of Europe, several of the British shores, America.

Cotton — The Levant, Egypt, the East Indies, South America, United States, West Indies. The finest now produced is the Sea Island Cotton of Georgia, South Carolina, and Florida.

Crocodile — Africa (the rivers Nile and Senegal, and all the rivers of Guinea); India (the Ganges).

Crystal (a kind of gem)— Madagascar, South America (Brazil, Guiana), North America, Norway, the Alps, Scotland.

Currants — The islands of the Grecian Archipelago, England, and the United States.

Cypress — The east of Europe, the Levant, Asia, America.

Dates — Egypt, the African coast of the Mediterranean, Arabia, the East Indies, Persia, Spain, and Italy.

Diamonds —The East Indies (Golconda, Raolconda, Borneo), Mexico, Brazil, South Africa.

Dolphin — The Atlantic and Pacific seas.

Dragon's-Blood (a kind of resin)— Japan, Cochin-China, Java, and other parts of the East.

Dromedary— The deserts of Arabia and other parts of Asia, and of Africa.

Ebony — The East Indies (chiefly Ceylon), and West Indies.

Eider Down (from the Eider Duck) — The north of Europe (chiefly Iceland), Asia, America.

Elephant —Africa and the East Indies. The most esteemed are those of Ceylon.

Elk or Moose Deer — North America, some parts of Europe and Asia, as far south as Japan.

Emerald — Egypt and Ethiopia, Russia, the confines of Persia, Mexico, Peru.

Emery (mineral used in polishing steel) — The Levant, Naxos, and other Grecian Islands, Germany, Guernsey, Spain, Italy, United States.

Ermine (a species of ferret) — Norway, Lapland, Finland, North America, Siberia, China.

Fan Palm — The south of Europe, the East Indies (Malabar and Ceylon), Japan, Cochin China.

Figs —Italy, the Levant, Turkey, the Grecian Islands, Portugal, Spain, and south of France.

Fire-fly— America, India, Japan.

Fitchet (a species of weasel)—India, New South Wales.

Flamingo — Africa, South America, West Indies.

Flax — Every quarter of the globe.

Flying-fish—Inhabits the European, Red, and American seas, but is found chiefly between the tropics.

Flying squirrel—North America.

Frankincense (a kind of gum) — Arabia.

French Plums — Chiefly from Bordeaux.

Frontignac wine — Languedoc, France.

Fuller's Earth — Sweden, Saxony, Portugal, England; the finest and most plentiful found at Warden, near Woburn.

Galls (a vegetable excrescence)— Asia Minor, and Syria, the best from Aleppo.

Gamboge (a resinous gum) — Tonquin, the East Indies.

Garnet — Bohemia, and other parts of Europe, Madagascar, Ethiopia, India, Syria.

Gazelle — India, Persia, Egypt, Ethiopia.

Gentian (a kind of bitter root)— The Alps, and other mountainous parts of the continent of Europe.

Gin — Originally Schiedam, a village near Rotterdam in Holland, and hence sometimes called Holland Gin. Common gin, a deleterious mixture, made in great quantities in England and the United States.

Ginger (an aromatic root) — The East Indies, West Indies, Abyssinia, coasts of Guinea.

Gold — Asia (Arabia), India, Java, Sumatra, Peru, China, Japan, Siberia, Africa, Mexico, Brazil, Chile, United States.

Golden Eagle —Europe, Siberia, Abyssinia.

Golden Pheasant — China.

Gourd — America, south of Europe.

Grapes — France, Portugal, America, in great perfection; not so in England and other less genial climates.

Guava (a fruit) — The West Indies.

Guaiacum (the resin of the Lignum Vitæ tree)—South America and West Indies.

Guinea Fowl — Africa.

Gum Arabic — Egypt, Barbary, Turkey, Persian Gulf.

Gypsum (or Plaster of Paris) —America, Spain, Italy, England.

Heliotrope (or blood-stone) — Siberia, Persia, Bukharia.

Hemp — Russia and other parts of Europe (the best from Riga), America, the East Indies, and some parts of England.

Hickory Nut — North America.

Hippopotamus — All the lakes and a number of rivers of Africa.

Hock Wine — Hockstedt in Suabia.

Humming Bird — South America (Guiana), West Indies, and United States.

Hyena (a species of wild dog) — India, Persia, Africa.

Ichneumon (a species of weasel)— Egypt, Barbary, the south of Asia, and the Indian Islands.

Incense (a resinous perfume) — America.

India Rubber (the inspissated resinous juice of a tree) — Guiana, and other parts of South America.

Indigo (a deep blue vegetable dye) — East Indies, Africa, America, West Indies.

Ipecacuanha (a kind of root used chiefly as an emetic) —South America (Brazil), and the West Indies.

Iron — Sweden, Norway, Russia, England, Scotland, North America, Africa.

Isinglass (fish glue)— Russia.

Ivory — Asia (Achem and Ceylon), Africa (Guinea and the Cape of Good Hope).

Jackal (a species of wild dog) — Africa and the warm parts of Asia.

Jalap (a purgative root) — Chiefly from Xalapa in Mexico.

Jasper — Egypt, Siberia, Spain, Sicily, Hungary, Bohemia, Saxony, Silesia, Mexico.

Jet — Great Britain, Germany, France, and Spain.

Juniper Berries (from which Holland gin is distilled) — Sweden, Holland, Germany, the south of Europe, Asia, America.

Kangaroo — Australasia.

Lac (a vegetable substance prepared by an insect) — The East Indies, Bengal.

Llama (a species of camel)—Peru and Chile.

Lantern Fly — Surinam, and other parts of South America.

Lapis Lazuli (a kind of siliceous earth) — Siberia, China, Tartary, America, and various parts of Europe.

Lemons — Portugal, Spain, France, Italy, the Levant, Arabia, Jamaica, Mexico, and Florida.

Leopard — Senegal, Guinea, and other parts of Africa.

Lignum Vitæ — West Indies, chiefly Jamaica.

Limes — America, West Indies.

Lion—Africa, India, Persia, Japan.
Lodestone—Denmark, Sweden, Norway, Lapland.
Locust—Inhabits Tartary, and migrates in great swarms into various parts of Europe, Africa, and America.
Logwood—Honduras and the West Indies.
Lory (a beautiful species of parrot)—The Molucca Islands, Java, and New Guinea.
Lotus (a species of water lily)—The hot parts of Africa, East Indies, America.
Lynx (a species of cat)—The north of Europe, Asia, and America.

Macaroni—Italy, Sicily, Germany.
Mace—Banda Isle and other East Indies.
Madder (a root used in dyeing)—The south of Europe, Holland, and England.
Madeira Wine—The Island of Madeira.
Mahogany—Jamaica (the best), Cuba, Hayti, the Bahama Islands, Honduras, Panama, South America.
Maize or Indian Corn—America.
Malmsey Wine—Malvesia, one of the Grecian Islands.
Manganese (a species of calcareous earth)—Sweden, Germany, France, England.
Mangrove—Asia, Africa, and South America, between the tropics.
Manna (a vegetable product)—The south of Europe, particularly Sicily and Calabria.
Maple Sugar—Europe and North America.
Marble—Spain, France, Italy, Sweden, Norway, the Island of Paros, England, Scotland, America. The Statuary Marble is from Paros and Carrara.
Melons—Asia, South of Europe, Egypt, Arabia, America, West Indies.
Mica (a kind of argillaceous earth)—Siberia, Bengal, Malabar, Russia, Finland, Sweden, Saxony.
Millet Seed—The south of Europe, Africa, East Indies, and America.
Mocho Stone—East Indies, Iceland, the palatinate of the Rhine and other parts of Europe.
Monkeys—South America and the hottest regions of Asia and Africa.
Molasses—West Indies, United States (Louisiana).
Morocco Leather—The Levant, Barbary, Spain, France, Flanders, England, and America.
Mosquito (a species of gnat)—The hot parts of Europe, Asia, Africa, and America.
Mother of Pearl (the lining of the pearl mussel's shell)—The Red Sea, East Indies, America.
Mulberry—Italy (black), China, (white), United States (white and red), East Indies, Japan, Siberia, Russia.
Muscatel Wine—Languedoc in France.
Musk (an animal odoriferous substance)—Siberia, Persia, Thibet, Tonquin, Cochin China.
Musk Ox—North America.
Myrrh (a gum resin)—The coast of the Red Sea.

Naphtha (a highly inflammable fluid bitumen)—Baku, on the shore of the Caspian Sea, Persia, Media, Tartary, China, Italy, Peru.
Natron (soda)—Denmark, Hungary, Switzerland, Egypt, China, Bengal, Persia, Syria, South America.
Nautilus Argonauta—The Mediterranean, African, and Indian Seas.
Nitre (a neutral salt, the chief ingredient in gunpowder)—Spain, France, Naples, Egypt, East Indies, America.
Nutmegs—The East Indies, South America.

Olives—Portugal, Spain, France, Italy, Northern Africa, Mexico.
Onyx—East Indies, Siberia, Bohemia, Saxony, Portugal, Mexico.
Opium (a concreted juice, obtained from a species of poppy)—Arabia, Persia, and other warm regions of Asia, especially the East Indies.
Opossum—America.
Orang-outang—Africa.
Oranges—Spain, Majorca, Portugal, Italy, Genoa, Nice, the Azores, America, West Indies. Oranges for wine from Seville in Spain.
Orpiment (yellow arsenic)—Hungary, Georgia, Turkey, the Levant, England.
Orris Root—Italy and other parts of the south of Europe.
Ostrich—The torrid regions of Asia and Africa, South America.
Ottar, or Attar, of Roses—Arabia, Persia, Turkey, East Indies.
Ounce—The torrid parts of Africa and Asia.

Palm Oil Tree—South America.
Panther—Africa and the hot parts of Asia.
Papyrus (a plant which formed the paper of the early times)—Egypt, Abyssinia, Ethiopia, Syria, Sicily, Madagascar.
Parrots—Africa, East Indies, South America, West Indies.
Pearl (a gem produced by a species of oyster or mussel)—Arabia, Persia, the East Indies, America.
Pearl Ashes—America.
Pelican—South America, all the warm latitudes of the old and new continents, the lakes of Judea and Egypt, and the rivers Nile and Strymon.
Penguin—The South Islands, Europe, America.
Pepper—The East Indies, America, West Indies, Cape of Good Hope.
Peruvian Bark—South America (Peru and Quito).
Petroleum—The East Indies, Persia, Media, Siberia, France, England, Germany, Spain, Italy, and the United States.
Pimento—The West Indies, particularly Jamaica.
Pineapple—Mexico, South America, the hot parts of Africa, India, the West Indies.
Pitch—United States, Sweden, Norway.
Plantain (a fruit)—Africa, South America, West Indies.
Platina—South America (near Quito, Santa Fé, and Choco).
Plumbago—England, and several countries on the continent of Europe, America.
Pomegranate—Spain, Italy, Africa, West Indies.
Porcupine—Spain, Italy, India, Persia, South Tartary, Africa, America.
Porphyry—Egypt, Italy, Germany, and other parts of the continent.
Potash—Russia and America.
Prunes—France (chiefly from the neighborhood of Marseilles).
Ptarmigan (white grouse)—The mountainous parts of Europe and Siberia.
Pomace Stone—The neighborhood of Vesuvius and other volcanoes.
Pumpkin—Germany and America.

Quagga (a quadruped of the horse species)—South America.
Quassia (the root, bark, and wood, of a tree)—South America, and the West Indies.
Quicksilver—Ionia, Hungary, Spain, Italy, East Indies, South America.

Raccoon (a species of badger)—North America, Jamaica.
Raisins—Spain and Turkey, Asia Minor, California.
Rattan Cane—The East India Islands.
Red Port Wine—Oporto in Portugal.
Reindeer—Lapland, British America, Greenland.
Resin (the residuum from the distillation of the oil of turpentine)—Sweden and Norway, United States.
Rhenish Wine—The banks of the Rhine.
Rhinoceros—Africa, East Indies (Bengal, Java, Sumatra, Ceylon).
Rhubarb—Asiatic Turkey, Russia, China, Persia, Tartary, East Indies, and America.
Rice—Asia (the East Indies and China), Egypt, north of Africa, America (the best from Carolina), Spain, Italy, Turkey.
Rock Salt—England, Italy, Poland, America.
Rosewood—Jamaica, the Canary Islands.
Ruby—The East Indies, Peru, Brazil.
Rum—Jamaica, and other West India Islands.

Sable (a species of ferret)—Siberia, Kamchatka, and the northern parts of Europe and America.
Saffron (the flower of a plant)—Egypt, Europe, America.
Sago (a fecula obtained from the pith of a species of palm)—Africa, Malabar, and the East Indian Islands.
Sal Ammoniac—India, Persia, Isle of Bourbon, Egypt, the neighborhood of Ætna, Vesuvius, Hecla, and other volcanoes, the Lapiri Islands.
Sandal Wood—The East Indies, and Sandwich Islands.
Sapphire—Brazil, East Indies, Persia, Bohemia, France.
Sardonyx—Iceland, the Faroe Islands, Bohemia, Saxony, Ceylon.
Sarsaparilla (root of a plant)—North America.

Sassafras (the root, bark, and wood of a tree)—North America.

Scorpion — Africa, India, Persia, America.

Seal — The north of Europe, Greenland, and the Arctic Sea, the lower parts of South America, in both oceans.

Senna (the leaves of a plant) — Arabia, Persia, and Upper Egypt.

Shaddock (a species of citron) — East Indies, West Indies.

Shagreen (a grained leather prepared from the skin of a species of shark) — Constantinople, Tripoli, Algiers, and some parts of Poland.

Sherry Wine — Xeres in Spain.

Silk — Spain, the south of France, Italy, the Levant, Persia, China, East Indies, and United States.

Silver — Africa, Mexico, Peru, United States, Spain, Germany, Siberia, Sweden, Norway, and England.

Silver Bear — The confines of Russia.

Soy (a liquid condiment prepared from a kind of pulse) — China and Japan.

Spermaceti — The produce of the Cachalot, a whale, inhabiting the European seas, the coasts of America, and Davis Straits.

Sponge (a marine animal production) — The Archipelago, the Mediterranean and Indian Seas.

Spoonbill—South America, Mexico, Jamaica.

Stork—Abyssinia, Arabia, Asia.

Sturgeon — European and American seas and rivers.

Sugar — East India Islands, China, West Indies, Louisiana.

Sulphur — Italy, Sicily, Naples, Spain, Norway, Siberia.

Sumach (a plant used in dyeing and tanning)—Spain, Portugal, the Levant, and United States.

Swordfish — The Mediterranean, Atlantic and East Indian Seas.

Tamarinds — Arabia, the East Indies, America, West Indies.

Tapir (an animal of the class mammalia)—South America.

Tar — Russia, Sweden, Norway, France, Switzerland, America.

Tarantula Spider—South of Europe, Barbary, East and West Indies.

Tea—China, Japan, India.

Teak Wood—East Indies, (Malabar, Pegu).

Tiger—East Indies, China, Japan, Africa.

Tin—England, the Scilly Islands, Bohemia, Saxony, Silesia, Banca, Molucca, Chile, Mexico.

Timber—Norway, Prussia, Russia, America.

Tobacco — United States, Peru, the West Indies, Asiatic Turkey, China, Philippine Islands.

Tokay Wine—Hungary.

Tolu Balsam (a fragrant concreted juice) — South America.

Topaz — Africa, East Indies, Siberia, Russia, Bohemia, Saxony, Mexico, Brazil.

Tortoise — Africa, Sardinia, America, and West Indies.

Treacle (a gross fluid, obtained in the manufacture of sugar) — The West Indies and Louisiana.

Turpentine (the resinous product of different species of pine, from which an essential oil is distilled) — North America, Russia, Norway, France, Switzerland, the Pyrenees, and Germany.

Turquoise (a mineral of a pale sky blue color) — Persia, Mount Caucasus, Egypt, Arabia, Hungary, France.

Vampire Bat — East Indian Islands, South America, Guinea, Madagascar, New Holland, New Hebrides, Friendly Islands, New Caledonia.

Vanilla (a plant whose aromatic pods are used in the manufacture of chocolate) — South America, West Indies.

Vulture — Egypt, Abyssinia, Arabia, Syria, Persia, South America, West Indies.

Walrus — The coast of Spitzbergen, Nova Zembla, Hudson's Bay, Gulf of St. Lawrence, and the Icy Sea.

Whale — Greenland, Davis Straits, the Arctic and Antarctic Seas.

Whisky (a spirit drawn from barley, rye, corn) — United States, Scotland, and Ireland.

White Bear — Tartary.

Wolf — Europe, Asia, Africa, America.

Yams (the edible roots of a creeping plant) — America, West Indies, East Indies, Africa.

Zebra (a species of horse)— The plains of Southern Africa.

Zinc— Germany, United States, and South America.

RAILWAY MILEAGE IN THE UNITED STATES.

BY STATES AND TERRITORIES.

State or Territory.	Mileage on June 30, 1902.			State or Territory.	Mileage on June 30, 1902.		
	Official.	Unofficial.	Total Mileage.		Official.	Unofficial.	Total Mileage.
Alabama	4,384.51	42.45	4,426.96	New Jersey	2,271.60	......	2,271.60
Alaska (see footnote)	......	......	......	New Mexico	2,017.86	......	2,017.86
Arizona	1,620.52	......	1,620.52	New York	8,185.21	3.50	8,188.71
Arkansas	3,505.48	73.07	3,578.55	North Carolina	3,885.01	10.50	3,895.51
California	5,956.70	22.40	5,979.10	North Dakota	2,950.78	......	2,950.78
Colorado	4,791.00	......	4,971.00	Ohio	8,959.94	13.00	8,972.94
Connecticut	1,026.12	......	1,026.12	Oklahoma	1,455.52	......	1,455.52
Delaware	335.81	......	335.81	Oregon	1,685.40	......	1,685.40
District of Columbia	31.75	......	31.75	Pennsylvania	10,544.91	36.56	10,581.47
Florida	33,22.00	80.21	3,402.21	Rhode Island	211.89	......	211.89
Georgia	6,006.91	15.50	6,022.41	South Carolina	3,041.03	33.00	3,074.03
Idaho	1,446.63	......	1,446.63	South Dakota	2,992.10	......	2,992.10
Illinois	11,291.43	8.00	11,299.43	Tennessee	3,298.43	20.42	3,318.85
Indiana	6,756.70	......	6,756.70	Texas	10,740.80	20.60	10,761.40
Indian Territory	1,793.05	......	1,793.05	Utah	1,557.30	7.25	1,564.55
Iowa	9,493.79	......	9,493.79	Vermont	1,054.42	......	1,054.42
Kansas	8,777.75	......	8,777.75	Virginia	3,756.41	75.80	3,832.21
Kentucky	3,123.49	20.12	3,143.61	Washington	3,092.87	64.92	3,157.79
Louisiana	3,221.63	64.16	3,285.79	West Virginia	2,475.74	98.10	2,573.84
Maine	1,932.59	......	1,932.59	Wisconsin	6,827.87	6.00	6,833.87
Maryland	1,414.47	......	1,414.47	Wyoming	1,238.92	......	1,238.92
Massachusetts	2,117.02	......	2,117.02				
Michigan	8,352.27	63.46	8,415.73	Grand total in U. S. 1902	201,672.83	799.02	*202,471.85
Minnesota	7,347.24	20.00	7,367.24	Grand total in U. S. 1901	196,075.07	1,162.37	197,237.44
Mississippi	3,136.96	......	3,136.96	Grand total in U. S. 1900	192,940.67	405.11	193,345.78
Missouri	7,086.15	......	7,086.15	Grand total in U. S. 1899	188,277.49	1,017.17	189,294.66
Montana	3,214.63	......	3,214.63	Grand total in U. S. 1898	185,370.77	1,025.55	186,396.32
Nebraska	5,742.94	......	5,742.94	Grand total in U. S. 1897	182,919.82	1,508.65	184,428.47
Nevada	951.49	......	951.49	Grand total in U. S. 1896	181,153.77	1,622.86	182,776.63
New Hampshire	1,248.09	......	1,248.09	Grand total in U. S. 1895	179,175.51	1,481.96	180,657.47

* Excludes 20.40 miles in Alaska.

RAILROAD TRAFFIC OF THE WORLD.

Countries.	Miles of Railroad.	Cost of Roads and Equipments.	Passengers Carried.	Tons of Freight Carried.	Receipts.	Expenditures.
Europe	176,174	$18,335,000,000	2,460,000,000	1,043,000,000	$1,640,000,000	$945,000,000
America	249,906	14,570,000,000	610 000,000	820,000,000	1,305,000,000	910,000,000
Africa	12,501	515,000,000	24,000,000	7,000,000	46,500,000	23,500,000
Asia	37,469	1,375,000,000	226,000,000	38,000,000	110,000,000	55,000,000
Australia	14,922	725,000,000	60,000,000	12,000,000	53,500,000	31,500,000
Total	490,962	$35,520,000,000	3,380,000,000	1,920,000,000	$3,155,000,000	$1,865,000,000

This table of statistics of the railroads of the world is by Mulhall, and represents the business of the year 1897.

Railroad Mileage by Countries.

The following by *Archiv fur Eisenbahnwesen* represents the world's railway mileage.

Countries.	Miles.
All of Germany	31,933
Austria-Hungary (including Bosnia, etc.)	22,917
Great Britain and Ireland	21,864
France	26,611
Russia (including Finland)	29,892
Italy	9,810
Belgium	3,943
Netherlands (including Luxembourg)	1,994
Switzerland	2,351
Spain	8,300
Portugal	1,476
Denmark	1,865
Norway	1,286
Sweden	7,034
Servia	359
Roumania	1,925
Greece	605
European Turkey, Bulgaria, and Roumelia	1,952
Malta, Jersey, Man	68
Total, Europe	176,174
United States	197,887
British North America	17,831
Newfoundland	641
Mexico	9,055
Central America	718
Total, North America	221,549
United States of Colombia	400
Cuba	1,134
Venezuela	634
San Domingo	117
Brazil	9,195
Argentina	10,171
Paraguay	157
Uraguay	1,144
Chile	2,850
Peru	1,036
Bolivia	621
Ecuador	186
British Guiana	55
Jamaica, Barbadoes, Trinidad, Martinique, Porto Rico, Salvador	657
Total, S. America & W. Indies	28,357
British India	23,758
Ceylon	297
Asia Minor and Syria	1,715
Russia (Transcaspian District)	1,658
Siberia	3,852
Persia	34
Dutch India	1,301
Japan	3,661
Portuguese India	51
Malay Archipelago	273
China	401
Korea	26
Siam	203
Cochin China, Pondicherry, Malacca, and Tonquin	238
Total, Asia	37,469
Egypt	2,087
Algiers and Tunis	2,642
British South and Cent. Africa	2,937
Natal	737
Rhodesia	1,203
Orange River Colony	597
Mauritius, Reunion, Congo, Senegal, and other States	2,298
Total, Africa	12,501
Australasia	14,922

RECAPITULATION.

Europe	176,174
North America	221,549
South America	28,357
Asia	37,469
Africa	12,501
Australasia	14,922
Total	490,962

INSURANCE.

A Stock Insurance Company is one whose capital is owned by stockholders, they alone sharing the profits, and they alone being liable for losses. The business of such a company, and also of a mixed company, is managed by directors chosen by the stockholders. Policy holders, unless at the same time stockholders, have no voice in the management of the company's business or in the election of its officers.

A Mutual Insurance Company is one in which the profits and losses are shared among the policy holders (the insured).

Mixed Companies are a combination of the foregoing. In a mixed company all profits above a certain fixed dividend are usually divided among the policy holders.

Some mutual and mixed companies issue what are called *non-participating policies*. The holders of these do not share in the profits or losses.

Fire Insurance.— Policies for fire insurance are generally issued for periods of one to five years. Ordinarily, in case of loss by fire, the insured will be paid the extent of his loss up to the amount of insurance, unless the insurance company prefer to replace or repair the damaged property, which privilege is usually reserved. If the policy contains the "average clause" the payment will cover only such portion of the loss as the amount of insurance bears to the value of the property insured.

A Floating Policy is one which covers property stored in several buildings or places. The name is applied more particularly to policies which cover goods whose location may be changed in process of manufacture, or in the ordinary course of business. The "average clause" is a usual condition of policies of this class.

Short Rates are rates for a term less than a year. If an insurance policy is terminated at the request of the policy holder, the company retains the customary "short rates" for the time the policy has been in force, as shown by the following table :—

Policy for 1 year.	Policy for 2 years.	Policy for 3 years.	Policy for 4 years.	Policy for 5 years.	Charge this proportion of whole Premium.
1 mo.	2 mo.	3 mo.	4 mo.	5 mo.	20 per cent.
2 "	4 "	6 "	8 "	10 "	30 "
3 "	6 "	9 "	12 "	15 "	40 "
4 "	8 "	12 "	16 "	20 "	50 "
5 "	10 "	15 "	20 "	25 "	60 "
6 "	12 "	18 "	24 "	30 "	70 "
7 "	14 "	21 "	28 "	35 "	75 "
8 "	16 "	24 "	32 "	40 "	80 "
9 "	18 "	27 "	36 "	45 "	85 "
10 "	20 "	30 "	40 "	50 "	90 "
11 "	22 "	33 "	44 "	55 "	95 "

When a policy is terminated at the option of the company, a ratable portion of the premium is refunded for the unexpired term.

Life Insurance.—In ordinary life policies a certain premium is to be paid every year until the death of the insured, when the policy becomes payable to the beneficiary. There are other kind of policies, however, and these are described below :—

Limited Payment Life Policy.— Conditions: Premiums to be paid annually for a certain fixed number of years, or until the death of the insured, should that occur prior to the expiration of this period. Policy payable at death of the insured. Advantages: Payments on this kind of policy may all be made while the insured is best able to make them, and if he live to an old age, the policy will not be a continual burden, but will rather be a source of income, as the yearly dividends may be taken out in cash or added to the amount of insurance.

Term Life Policy.— In this method of insurance, the insurance company agrees to pay to the beneficiaries a certain sum on the death of the insured, should that event occur within a fixed term.

Endowment Policy.— A combination of a Term Policy and a Pure Endowment. These policies are issued for endowment periods of 10, 15, 20, 25, 30, or 35 years, and may be paid up by a single payment, by an annual premium during the endowment period, or by five or ten annual payments. Conditions: 1. Insurance during a stipulated period, payable at the death of the insured, should that event happen within said period. 2. An endowment of the same amount as the policy, payable to the insured, if still living at the end of the period fixed. Advantages: Limited term of payments; insurance during the time when the death of the insured would cause most embarrassment to his family; provision for old age, as the amount of the policy will be paid to the insured if still living, at a time when advanced age may make it of great benefit.

Annuity Policies are secured by a single cash payment and insure the holder the yearly payment of a certain sum of money during life.

Joint Life Policy.— An agreement to pay a certain sum on the death of any one of two or more persons thus insured.

Non-forfeiting Policies do not become void for non-payment of premiums. In some companies all limited-payment life policies, and all endowment policies, after premiums for three (or two) years have been paid, and the original policy is surrendered within a certain time, provide for paid-up assurance for as many parts of the original amount assured as there shall have been complete annual premiums received in cash by the company. Some companies voluntarily apply all credited dividends to the continuance of the insurance. Others apply the legal reserve to the purchase of term insurance at regular rates.

Special Forms.—The Reserve Endowment, Tontine Investment, and other special policies guarantee to the holder a definite surrender value at the termination of certain periods. The surrender value of a policy is the amount in cash which the company will pay the holder of a policy on its surrender — the legal reserve less a certain per cent. for expenses.

The Reserve of life insurance policies is the present value of the amount to be paid at death, less the present value of all the net premiums to be paid in the future.

The Reserve Fund of a life insurance company is that sum in hand which, invested at a given rate of interest, together with future premiums on existing policies, should be sufficient to meet all obligations as they become due. It is the sum of the separate reserves of the several policies outstanding.

Marine and Transit Insurance.—Insurance of vessels and their cargoes against the perils of navigation is termed *Marine Insurance.*

Inland and Transit Insurance refer to insurance of merchandise while being transported from place to place either by rail or water routes, or both.

Insurance Certificates, showing that certain property has been insured and stating the amount of the insurance and the name of the party abroad who is authorized to make the settlement, are issued by marine companies. They are negotiable and are usually sent to the consignee of the merchandise to make the loss payable at the port of destination.

The adjustment of marine policies in case of loss is on the same principle as the adjustment of fire policies containing the "average clause."

Open Policies are those upon which additional insurance may be entered at different times.

PUBLIC DEBT OF THE UNITED STATES.

STATEMENT TO JANUARY 1, 1903.

INTEREST-BEARING DEBT.

Consols of 1930, 2 per cent	$445,940,750.00
Loan of 1908-1918, 3 per cent	97,515,660.00
Funded loan of 1907, 4 per cent	233,178,450.00
Refunding certificates, 4 per cent	31,370.00
Loan of 1925, 4 per cent	119,318,950.00
Loan of 1904, 5 per cent	19,385,050.00
Aggregate of interest-bearing debt	$915,370,230.00

DEBT ON WHICH INTEREST HAS CEASED SINCE MATURITY.

Aggregate debt on which interest has ceased since maturity	$1,256,820.26

DEBT BEARING NO INTEREST.

United States notes	$346,681,016.00
Old demand notes	53,847.50
National bank notes:	
Redemption account	44,695,092.50
Fractional currency	6,872,593.63
Aggregate of debt bearing no interest	$398,302,549.63

CERTIFICATES AND NOTES ISSUED ON DEPOSITS OF COIN AND LEGAL-TENDER NOTES AND PURCHASES OF SILVER BULLION.

Gold certificates	$367,078,569.00
Silver certificates	467,442,000.00
Treasury notes of 1890	25,796,000.00
Aggregate of certificates and Treasury notes, offset by cash in the Treasury	$860,316,569.00

CLASSIFICATION OF DEBT.

Interest-bearing debt	$915,370,230.00
Debt on which interest has ceased since maturity	1,256,820.26
Debt bearing no interest	398,302,549.63
Aggregate of interest and non-interest bearing debt	$1,314,929,599.89
Certificates and Treasury notes offset by an equal amount of cash in the Treasury	860,316,569.00
Aggregate of debt, including certificates and Treasury notes	$2,175,246,168.89

CASH IN THE TREASURY.

Gold certificates	$367,078,569.00	
Silver certificates	467,442,000.00	
Treasury notes of 1890	25,796,000.00	
		$860,316,569.00
National bank 5 per cent. fund	$14,664,321.09	
Outstanding checks and drafts	9,027,091.49	
Disbursing officers' balances	56,203,466.94	
Post-Office Department account	3,821,445.66	
Miscellaneous items	2,240,970.82	
		85,957,306.00
Reserve fund	$150,000,000.00	
Available cash balance	206,421,878.30	
		356,421,878.30
Aggregate		$1,302,695,753.30
Cash balance in the Treasury exclusive of reserve and trust funds		$206,421,878.30

Wages and Cost of Living.

From the report of the Secretary of State on the state of labor in Europe, derived from facts reported by the United States Consuls corrected to 1892, the following tables are gleaned :—

COMPARATIVE RATES OF WEEKLY WAGES PAID IN EUROPE AND IN THE UNITED STATES.

	France.	Germany.	Italy.	Great Britain.	U. S.	
					New York.	Chicago.
	$	$	$	$	$	$
Bakers	5.55	3.50	3.90	6.50– 6.60	5– 8	8– 12
Blacksmiths	5.45	3.55	3.94	7.04– 8.12	10–14	9– 12
Bookbinders	4.85	3.82	3.90	.50– 7.83	12–18	9– 20
Bricklayers	4.00	3.60	3.45	7.58– 9.03	12–15	9– 10½
Cabinetmakers	6.00	3.97	3.95	7.70– 8.48	9–13	7– 15
Carpenters & Joiners	5.42	4.00	4.18	7.33– 8.25	9–12	7½–12
Farm Laborers	3.15	2.87	3.50	3.40– 4.25	......	....
Laborers, Porters, etc	....	2.92	2.60	4.50– 5.00	6– 9	5½– 9
Painters	4.90	3.92	4.60	7.25– 8.16	10–16	6– 12
Plasterers	....	3.80	4.35	7.68–10.13	10–15	9– 15
Plumbers	5.50	3.60	3.90	7.13– 8.46	12 18	12– 20
Printers	4.70	4.80	3.90	7.52– 7.75	8–18	12– 18
Shoemakers	4.75	3.12	4.32	7.35	12–18	9– 18
Tailors	5.10	3.58	4.30	5.00– 7.30	10–18	6– 18
Tinsmiths	4.40	3.65	3.60	6.00– 7.30	10–14	9– 12

Night Signals on Ocean Steamship Lines.

American—Red light, roman candle throwing six red balls.
Anchor—Red and white lights alternately (lanterns).
Allan—Three blue lights displayed in form of triangle.
Cunard—Blue light and two roman candles, each throwing six blue balls.
French—Blue light forward, white light amidships, red light aft simultaneously.
Guion—Blue lights, forward, aft, and on bridge simultaneously.
Hamburg—Two red, white, blue Coston lights at stern of vessel in succession.
Inman—Blue light forward and aft, and red light on bridge simultaneously.
Monarch—Green, white, green Coston light.
National—Blue light forward and aft, and red light on bridge forming a triangle.
North German Lloyd—Two blue, red Coston lights, one forward and one aft simultaneously.
Red Star—Red light forward, amidships, and aft, together.
State—Blue, red Coston lights.
White Star—Two green lights simultaneously.

Designating Marks of Ocean Steamship Lines.

LINES. FUNNEL MARKS.

American—Lower two thirds red, with white keystone, black top.
Anchor—Black.
Allan—Red, with white ring under black top.
Cunard—Red, with black top.
French—Red, with black top.
Guion—Lower two thirds black, a red band and black top.
Hamburg—Black.
Inman—Lower two thirds black, white band and black top.
Monarch—French-gray and black top.
National—White, with black top.
North German Lloyd—Black.
Red Star—Cream color, with black top with red star.
Royal Netherlands—Black, with band having green border.
State—Lower two thirds buff, red band under black top.
White Star—Cream, black top.

PRODUCTION OF COAL.

AREA OF THE WORLD'S COAL FIELDS, IN SQUARE MILES.

China and Japan, 200,000; United States, 194,000; India, 35,000; Russia, 27,000; Great Britain 9,000; Germany, 3,600; France, 1,800; Belgium, Spain, and other countries, 1,400. Total, 471,800.

The coal fields of China, Japan, Great Britain, Germany, Russia, and India contain apparently 303,000,000,000 tons, which is enough for 450 years at present rate of consumption. If to the above be added the coal fields in the United States, Canada, and other countries, the supply will be found ample for 1,000 years. Improved machinery has greatly increased the yield per miner, and thus produced a fall in price to the advantage of all industries.

The production of the principal countries in 1899 in metric tons (2,204.6 lbs.) was: United States, 228,717,579; United Kingdom, 223,616,279; Germany, 135,844,419; Austria-Hungary, 38,738,372; France, 32,862,712; Belgium, 22,072,068; Russia (*e*), 12,800,000; Japan, 6,721,798; Australasia (*e*), 6,700,000; India, 5,016,055; Canada, 4,142,242; Spain, 2,600,279; Mexico, 409,125; Sweden, 239,344; Italy, 388,534; all other countries (*e*), 2,500,000; total, partly estimated, 723,617,836. (*e*) Estimated.

ANNUAL COAL PRODUCTION IN THE UNITED STATES.

States.	Tons.	Value at Mine. Total.	Value at Mine. Per Ton.
Bituminous.			
Alabama	9,099,052	$10,000,892	$1.64
Arkansas	1,816,136	2,068,613	1.14
California	151,079	394,106	2.61
Colorado	5,635,435	6,248,151	1.11
Georgia	354,825	426,685	1.20
Illinois	27,331,552	28,163,937	1.03
Indiana	6,918,225	7,016,143	1.01
Indian Territory	2,421,781	3,915,268	1.62
Iowa	5,617,499	7,822,605	1.39
Kansas	4,900,528	5,991,599	1.22
Kentucky	5,469,986	5,213,076	.95
Maryland	5,113,127	5,046,491	.99
Michigan	1,241,241	1,753,064	1.24
Missouri	3,802,088	4,707,164	1.24
Montana	1,396,081	2,009,316	1.44
Nebraska	‖	‖	‖
New Mexico	1,384,257	1,540,357	1.42
North Carolina	¶	¶	¶
North Dakota	166,601	214,151	1.29
Ohio	20,943,807	20,928,158	1.00
Oregon	69,011	173,646	2.52
Pennsylvania	82,305,945	81,397,586	.99
Tennessee	3,633,200	$4,067,389	$1.12
Texas	1,107,953	1,907,024	1.72
Utah	1,322,614	1,666,082	1.26
Virginia	2,725,873	2,353,989	.96
Washington	2,578,217	4,271,076	1.66
West Virginia	24,068,402	20,848,184	.87
Wyoming	4,485,374	6,060,462	1.33
Total bituminous. Sh. tons	225,759,980	$236,305,214	$1.05
Total bituminous. Met. tons	204,808,110	......	1.15
Anthracite.			
Colorado	64,580	$193,740	$3.00
New Mexico	2,289	6,295	2.75
Pennsylvania	67,471,667	112,504,020	1.67
Total anthracite Sh. tons	67,538,536	$112,704,055	$1.67
Total anthracite Met. tons	61,270,558	......	1.86
Grand total coal Sh. tons	293,298,516	$349,009,269	$1.19
Grand total coal Met. tons	266,078,668	......	1.31

‖ Included in California. ¶ Included in Georgia.

PRODUCTION COPPER, TIN, ZINC

World's annual production of copper in tons: United States, 268,787; Spain and Portugal, 54,872; Chile, 25,700; Japan, 27,840; Germany, 20,410; Mexico, 22,050; Australasia, 23,000; South Africa, 6,490; other countries, 32,345; total, 486,084 tons.

Annual copper production of the United States in pounds: Arizona, 115,403,846; California, 29,639,987; Colorado, 7,826,949; Michigan, 144,227,340; Montana, 254,460,713; Utah, 18,504,726; Eastern and Southern States, 6,918,122; all others, 12,536,850; copper in sulphate (*a*), 11,313,962.

Production of tin in the world, in tons: England, 4,100; Straits Settlements, 46,070; Australasia, 3,178; Banka, Billiton, and Singkep, 17,640; Bolivia, 6,937; India and China, 877; United States, none; total, 78,802.

Production of zinc in the world, in tons: Austria, 6,836; Belgium, Holland, and the Rhine district of Germany, 189,301; Upper Silesia, 102,316; France, 38,000; Spain, 6,200; United Kingdom, 30,307; Russia, 5,969; United States, 111,794; total, 490,973.

THE FLEET OF TRANSATLANTIC PASSENGER STEAMERS.

Steamships.	Built. Year.	Built. Place.	Builders.	Tonnage. Net.	Tonnage. Gross.	Horse Power. Indicated.	Horse Power. Registered.	Commander.	Dimensions in Feet. Length.	Breadth.	Depth.
New York and Glasgow, Pier foot West 21st St.			ALLAN-STATE LINE. (Office, 53 Broadway.)					State Line Established 1872.			
State of Nebraska	1880	Glasgow	Lond. & Gl'gow Co., Ld.	2580	4000	......	650	Brown	385	43	32
Mongolian	1891	Glasgow	Lond. & Gl'gow Co., Ld.	3080	4838	......	....	Braes	400	45	33.6
Numidian	1891	Glasgow	Lond. & Gl'gow Co., Ld.	3080	4838	......	....	....	400	45	33.6
Laurentian	1872	Glasgow	Lond. & Gl'gow Co., Ld.	....	4522	......	....	....	400	42.5	35.3
New York and Southampton, Pier foot Fulton St., N. R.			AMERICAN LINE. (Office, 6 Bowling Green.)					Established 1892.			
St. Louis	1894	Philadelphia	Wm. Cramp & Sons	5894	11629	20000	....	Randle	535.8	63	42
St. Paul	1894	Philadelphia	Wm. Cramp & Sons	5874	11629	20000	....	Jamison	535.8	63	42
Paris	1889	Glasgow	J. & G. Thomson	6289	10795	20000	2000	Watkins	580	63.3	42
New York	1888	Glasgow	J. & G. Thomson	6318	10803	20000	2000	Passow	580	63.3	42
New York and Glasgow, Pier foot West 24th St.			ANCHOR LINE. (Office, 7 Bowling Green.)					Established 1852.			
City of Rome	1881	Barrow	Barrow S. B. Co.	3453	8144	......	1500	Young	561	53	37
Anchoria	1874	Barrow	Barrow S. B. Co.	2713	4168	......	617	John Wilson	408	40	34
Bolivia	1873	Port Glasgow	R. Duncan & Co.	2626	4050	......	1120	Craig	400	40	25
Circassia	1878	Barrow	Barrow S. B. Co.	2770	4272	......	600	....	400	42	25
Ethiopia	1873	Glasgow	A. Stephen & Son	2604	4005	......	720	Wadsworth	402	42	25
Furnessia	1880	Barrow	Barrow S. B. Co.	2613	5495	......	600	Harris	445	45	35

The Fleet of Transatlantic Passenger Steamers—*Continued.*

Steamships.	Built. Year.	Built. Place.	Builders.	Tonnage. Net.	Tonnage. Gross.	Horse Power. Indicated.	Horse Power. Registered.	Commander.	Dimensions in Feet. Length.	Dimensions in Feet. Breadth.	Dimensions in Feet. Depth.
New York, Queenstown, and Liverpool, Pier foot Clarkson St.			CUNARD LINE. (Office, 4 Bowling Green.)					Established 1840.			
Campania	1892	Fairfield	Fairfield Co.	5000	12950	30000	*	Walker	620	65.3	43
Lucania	1892	Fairfield	Fairfield Co.	5000	12950	30000	*	H. McKay	620	65.3	43
Etruria	1885	Fairfield	John Elder & Co.	3257	7718	14500	2500	Ferguson	501.6	57.2	38.2
Umbria	1884	Fairfield	John Elder & Co.	3245	7718	14500	2500	Dutton	501.6	57.2	38.2
Aurania	1883	Glasgow	J. & G. Thomson	4029	7268	8500	1560	A. McKay	470	57.2	37.2
Servia	1881	Glasgow	J. & G. Thomson	3971	7391	10000	1000	Watt	515	52.1	37
New York and Havre, Pier foot Morton St.			FRENCH LINE. (Office, 3 Bowling Green.)					Established 1860.			
La Touraine	1890	St. Nazaire	Cie Gle Transatlantique.	....	9778	12000	....	Santelli	536	55	38
La Gascogne	1886	Toulon	Soc. des Forges, etc	4158	7416	9000	....	Simon	508	52	38
La Champagne	1886	St. Nazaire	Cie Gle Transatlantique.	3906	7110	9000	....	Poirot	508	51	38
La Bretagne	1886	St. Nazaire	Cie Gle Transatlantique.	3889	7010	9000	....	Rupé	508	51	38
La Normandie	1882	Barrow, Eng.		3475	6112	6500	....	Fajolle	459	50	34
New York, Cherbourg, Southampton, Boulogne, and Hamburg, Pier foot 1st St., Hoboken.			HAMBURG-AMERICAN LINE. (Office, 37 Broadway.)					Established 1847.			
Fürst Bismarck	1890	Stettin	Vulcan S. B. Co	....	10000	16400	2800	Albers	520	58	40
Augusta Victoria	1889	Stettin	Vulcan S. B. Co	....	10000	13500	2500	Kaempff	520	56	38
Pennsylvania	1897	Belfast	Harland & Wolff	....	12500	6000	....	Spliedt	560	62	42
Pretoria	1897	Hamburg	Blohm & Voss	....	12500	6000	....	Kopff	560	62	42
Palatia	1894	Stettin	Vulcan S. B. Co	....	8000	5500	....	Karlowa	460	52	32
Patria	1894	Stettin	Vulcan S. B. Co	....	8000	5500	....	Bauer	460	52	32
Phœnicia	1894	Hamburg	Blohm & Voss	....	8000	5500	....	Leithauser	460	52	32
Armenia	1896	Newcastle	Palmers	....	7000	3000	....	Magin	400	50	30
Arcadia	1896	Belfast	Harland & Wolff	....	7000	3000	....	Martens	400	49	30
Arabia	1896	Belfast	Harland & Wolff	....	7000	3000	....	Pietsch	400	49	30
Asturia	1896	Newcastle	Palmers	....	7000	3000	....	Kuhn	390	53	29
Andalusia	1896	Newcastle	Palmers	....	7000	3000	....	Schroeder	400	50	30
Adria	1896	Newcastle	Palmers	....	7000	3000	....	Reuter	400	50	30
Ambria	1896	Flensburg	Flensburg S. B. Co	....	5043	5000	....	Froehlich	404	32	25
Alesia	1896	Flensburg	Flensburg S. B. Co	....	5060	5000	....	Krech	404	32	25
Aragonia	1896	Flensburg	Flensburg S. B. Co	....	5250	5000	....	H. Schmidt	404	32	25
Graf Waldersee	1897	Hamburg	Blohm & Voss	....	13000	6000	....		565	62	42
Patricia	1897	Stettin	Vulcan S. B. Co	....	13000	6000	....		565	62	42
Bulgaria	1898	Hamburg	Blohm & Voss	....	10236	4000	....		501	62	34½
Brasilia	1898	Belfast	Harland & Wolff	....	10221	4000	....		501	62	34½
Deutschland†	..	Stettin	Vulcan S. B. Co	....	16000	33000	....		685	66	42
New York, Boulogne, Amsterdam, and Rotterdam, Piers foot 5th and 6th Sts., Hoboken.			HOLLAND-AMERICA LINE. NETHERLANDS-AMERICAN LINE. (Office, 39 Broadway.)					Established 1874.			
Rotterdam	1897	Belfast	Harland & Wolff	5000	8000	5000	....	Van der Zee	485	53	34
Spaarndam	1881	Belfast	Harland & Wolff	3123	4539	3500	....	Stenger	430	42	31
Maasdam	1872	Belfast	Harland & Wolff	2702	3984	3500	....	Ald. Potjer	420	41	31
Werkendam	1881	Belfast	Harland & Wolff	2654	3657	2500	....	Bruinsma	410	39	29
Amsterdam	1879	Belfast	Harland & Wolff	2681	3627	2500	....	W. Bakker	411	39	29
Edam	1878	Belfast	Harland & Wolff	2361	3329	2100	....	S. de Vries	390	38	29
Statendam	1898	Belfast	Harland & Wolff	7000	10500	5500	....	Bonjer	525	60	42
New York, Southampton, and Bremen, Pier 2d St., Hoboken.			NORTH GERMAN LLOYD. (Office, 2 Bowling Green.)					Established 1857.			
Kaiser Wilhelm Der Grosse	1897	Stettin	Vulcan Shipbuilding Co.	....	13800	27000	....	Englehart	649	66	43
Kaiser Friedrich	1898	Danzig	Schichau Shipbuild'g Co.	....	12800	25000	....	Stormer	600	64	41
Kaiserin Maria Th.	1898	Stettin	Vulcan Shipbuilding Co.	3769	7800	17000	....	Meier	546	52	37
Lahn	1887	Fairfield	Fairfield E. & S. B. Co.	2879	5581	8800	....	Pohle	464	49	37
Saale	1886	Glasgow	Elder & Co.	2779	5381	7500	....	Blanke	455	48	36
Trave	1886	Glasgow	Elder & Co.	2779	5831	7500	....	Christoffers	455	48	36
Friedrich d. Grosse	1896	Stettin	Vulcan Shipbuilding Co.	....	10500	7000	....	Eichel	546	60	35
Königin Luise	1896	Stettin	Vulcan Shipbuilding Co.	....	10500	7000	....	v. Schuckm'nn	544	60	35
Barbarossa	1896	Hamburg	Blohm & Voss	....	10500	7000	....	Richter	546	60	35
Bremen	1896	Danzig	Schichau Shipbuild'g Co.	....	10500	8000	....	Reimkasten	544	60	35
H. H. Meier	1892	Newcastle	Mitchell, Armstrong Co.	....	5306	3800	....	Steencken	481	48	29
New York and Genoa, Pier foot 2d St., Hoboken.			NORTH GERMAN LLOYD. (Office, 2 Bowling Green.)					Established 1892.			
Kaiser Wilhelm II	1888	Stettin	Vulcan Shipbuilding Co.	4776	6990	6500	....	Hogemann	465	52	27
Aller	1886	Glasgow	Elder & Co.	2779	5381	7500	....	Nierich	455	48	36
Ems	1884	Glasgow	Elder & Co.	2893	5192	7000	....	Harrassowitz	445	47	35
New York and Antwerp, Pier foot Fulton St., N. R.			RED STAR LINE. (Office, 6 Bowling Green.)					Established 1873.			
Friesland	1889	Glasgow	J. & G. Thomson	5023	6824	......	800	Nickels	455	51	38
Westernland	1883	Birkenhead	Laird Bros	4320	5994	......	700	Mills	455	47	35
Noordland	1883	Birkenhead	Laird Bros	4019	5398	......	500	Loesewitz	419	47	35
Southwark	1893	Dumbarton	W. Denny & Bros	5642	8607	......	1237	Bence	494	57	37
Kensington	1894	Glasgow	J. & G. Thomson	5645	8669	......	1237	Bond	494	75	37

* 26,500 registered. † Building.

The Fleet of Transatlantic Passenger Steamers—*Continued.*

Steamships.	Built.		Builders.	Tonnage.		Horse Power.		Commander.	Dimensions in Feet.		
	Year.	Place.		Net.	Gross.	Indicated.	Registered.		Length.	Breadth.	Depth.
New York, Christiania, Copenhagen, and Stettin, Pier foot 4th St., Hoboken.			SCANDINAVIAN-AMERICAN LINE. (Office, 28 State St.)					Established 1879.			
Hekla	1884	Greenock	Scott & Co	....	3258	2150	....	Thomsen	333	41	29
Island	1882	Copenhagen	Burmeister & Wain	....	2844	2000	....	Skjödt	324	39	29
Norge	1881	Glasgow	Stephens & Son	....	3359	1600	....	Knudsen	340	41	32
Thingvalla	1874	Copenhagen	Burmeister & Wain	....	2524	1000	....	Laub	301	37	21
New York, Queenstown, and Liverpool, Pier foot West 10th St.			WHITE STAR LINE. (Office, 9 Broadway.)					Established 1870.			
Teutonic	1889	Belfast	Harland & Wolff	4269	9984	16000	1875	Cameron	565	57	39
Majestic	1889	Belfast	Harland & Wolff	4269	9965	16000	1875	E. J. Smith	565	57	39
Britannic	1874	Belfast	Harland & Wolff	3152	5004	4590	890	Haddock	455	45	33
Germanic	1874	Belfast	Harland & Wolff	2989	5065	4500	765	McKinstry	455	45	33
Cymric	1898	Belfast	Harland & Wolff	8000	12340	6700	1197	Lindsay	585	64	38
Oceanic	1899	Belfast	Harland & Wolff	7930	17000	.....	....	....	685	68	44
New York and Hull, Wilson Pier, Brooklyn Borough.			WILSON LINE. (Office, 29 Broadway.)					Established 1840.			
Buffalo	1885	Newcastle	Palmers	2909	4431	.....	600	Malet	385	46	28
Ohio	1880	Dumbarton	A. McMill & Sons	2557	3967	.....	450	Akester	360	43	25
Colorado	1887	Hull	Earles	2787	4220	.....	600	Whitton	370	45	28
Martello	1884	Hull	Earles	2424	3709	.....	550	Potter	370	43	28
Francisco	1891	Newcastle	R. Stephenson & Co., Ld.	2971	4604	.....	600	Jenkins	370	47	28
Hindoo	1889	Newcastle	R. Stephenson & Co., Ld.	2407	3720	.....	500	Wing	368	43	28
Idaho	1897	Wallsend	Swan & Hunter	4000	6000	.....	....	....	470	50	42
Chicago	1898	W. Hartlepool	Furness, Withy & Co	4384	7000	.....	....	....	490	52¼	34½

FASTEST ATLANTIC OCEAN PASSAGES.

Route.	Steamer.	Line.	Date.	D.	H.	M.
Queenstown to New York	Lucania	Cunard	Oct. 21-26, 1894	5	7	23
New York to Southampton	Kaiser Wilhelm der Grosse	North German Lloyd	Nov. 23-29, 1897	5	17	8
Cherbourg to New York	Deutschland	Hamburg-American	Aug. 23-29, 1901	5	12	5
Havre to New York	La Savoie	French	Aug. 31-Sept. 6, 1901	6	11	..
New York to Cherbourg	Kaiser Wilhelm der Grosse	No. German Lloyd	Jan. 4-10, 1900	5	16	..
New York to Plymouth	Deutschland	Hamburg-American	Sept. 5-10, 1900	5	7	38

TRANSATLANTIC PASSENGER STEAMERS ADDED 1900-1901.

Steamships.	Built.		Builders.	Tonnage.		Horse Power.		Commander.	Dimensions in Feet.		
	Year.	Place.		Net.	Gross.	Indicated.	Registered.		Length.	Breadth.	Depth.
			AMERICAN LINE.								
Philadelphia	1901	Belfast	Harland & Wolff	6289	10787	20000	2000	Mills	560	63.3	42
Haverford	1901	Glasgow	John Brown & Co.	7493	11635	....	....	Neilsen	530	59	36
			ANCHOR LINE.								
Columbia	1901	Glasgow	D. & W. Henderson	....	8900	....	....	......	503	56	..
			ATLANTIC TRANSPORT LINE.								
Minneapolis	1900	Belfast	Harland & Wolff	8651	13401	1224	....	Layland	600.7	65.5	39.7
Minnehaha	1900	Belfast	Harland & Wolff	8647	13403	1227	....	Robinson	600.7	65.5	44
			FRENCH LINE.								
La Savoie	1900	St. Nazaire	Cie Gle Transatlantique.	....	15000	22000	....	Poirot	580	60	40
			HAMBURG-AMERICAN LINE.								
Deutschland	1900	Stettin	Vulcan S. B. Co.	....	16000	37500	....	Albers	686½	67½	44
Moltke	1901	Hamburg	Blohm & Voss	....	12000	8000	....	Dempwolf	550	62	42
Blücher	1901	Hamburg	Blohm & Voss	....	12000	8000	....	......	550	62	42
			WHITE STAR LINE.								
Celtic	1901	Belfast	Harland & Wolff	13449	20904	13000	2295	Lindsay	700	75	49
			NORTH-GERMAN LLOYD LINE.								
Grosser Kurfürst	1900	Dantzig	F. Schichau	....	12200	8000	....	Reimkasten	581½	62	39
Main	1900	Hamburg	Blohm & Voss	....	10200	5000	....	......	520	58	40
Kronprinz-Wilh'm	1901	Stettin	Vulcan S. B. Co.	....	15000	33000	....	Störmer	663	66	43
			RED STAR LINE.								
Vaderland	1900	Glasgow	John Brown & Co.	7490	11899	....	1627	Albrecht	580	60	42
Zeeland	1901	Glasgow	John Brown & Co.	7511	11905	....	1627	Roberts	580	60	42
			WILSON LINE.								
Consuelo	1900	Wallsend	Swan & Hunter	3970	6030	....	....	Watson	462	52	31
Toronto	1900	Hartlepool	Wm. Gray & Co.	3949	6035	....	....	Jones	455	52	31

THE SUBMARINE CABLES OF THE WORLD.

[From report issued by the International Bureau of Telegraph Administrations.]

The following table sets forth the entire system of submarine cables of the world, including those along the shores and in the bays, gulfs, and estuaries of rivers, but excepting those in lakes and the interior water-courses of continents. The list includes all cables operated by private companies, and in addition thereto under the name of each nation is given the list of cables operated by the government of that nation.

Companies.	Number of Cables.	Length of Cables in Nautical Miles.
Anglo-American Telegraph Co.:		
Transatlantic System — Valentia (Ireland) to Heart's Content (Newfoundland)	4	7,510
Minon, near Brest (France), to St. Pierre-Miquelon	1	2,718
Communication on American coasts	9	1,964
European Communication	1	101
Total	15	12,293
Commercial Cable Co.:		
Transatlantic System—Waterville (Ireland) to Canso (Nova Scotia)	3	6,893
Canso, N. S., to New York	1	826
Canso, N. S., to Rockport, Mass	1	511
Communication in Europe	2	839
Total	7	9,069
Direct United States Cable Co.:		
Ballinskellig's Bay (Ireland) to Halifax (Nova Scotia)	1	2,564
Halifax, N. S., to Rye Beach, N. H	1	535
Total	2	3,099
Western Union Telegraph Co.:		
Transatlantic System — Sennen Cove, near Penzance, England, to Dover Bay, near Canso, N. S.	2	5,107
Dover Bay, N. S., to New York	2	1,776
Gulf of Mexico System	8	459
Total	12	7,342
Compagnie Française du Télégraphe de Paris à New York:		
Brest (France) to St. Pierre-Miq	1	2,282
St. Pierre to Cape Cod, Mass	1	828
Other branch lines	2	422
Total	4	3,532
Compagnie Française des Câbles Télégraphiques:		
Brest (France) to Cape Cod, Mass	1	3,250
African Direct Telegraph Co	8	2,938
Black Sea Telegraph Co	1	337
Brazilian Submarine Telegraph Co.:		
Carcavellos, near Lisbon (Portugal), to Madeira, to St. Vincent (Cape Verde Island), to Pernambuco (Brazil)	6	7,375
Central and South American Telegraph Co	15	7,500
Compagnie Allemande des Câbles Télégraphiques	1	1,114
Compania Telegrafico-Telefonica dèl Plata	1	28
Compania Telegrafico del Rio de la Plata	1	28
Cuba Submarine Telegraph Co	4	1,048
Direct Spanish Telegraph Co	4	710
Direct West India Cable Co.:		
Bermuda-Turk's Island, and Turk's Island-Tamarique	2	*
Eastern and South African Telegraph Co	13	8,832
Eastern Extension Australasia and China Telegraph Co	27	17,359
Eastern Telegraph Co.:		
Anglo-Spanish-Portuguese System	12	4,185
System West of Malta	17	4,603
Italo-Greek System	2	253
Austro-Greek System	1	503
Greek System	12	699
Turko-Greek System	4	578
Turkish System	15	842
Egypto-European System	4	2,530
Egyptian System	1	155
Egypto-Indian System	13	11,805
Total	81	26,153
Europe and Azores Telegraph Co	2	1,053
Great Northern Telegraph Co.:		
Cables in Europe and Asia	24	6,982
Halifax and Bermuda Cable Co	1	850
Indo-European Telegraph Co	2	14
India Rubber, Gutta Percha, and Telegraph Works Co	3	145
Mexican Telegraph Co	3	1,527
River Plate Telegraph Co	1	32
Société Française des Télégraphes Sous-Marins	19	4,720
South American Cable Co	2	2,048
United States and Hayti Telegraph and Cable Co	1	1,389
West African Telegraph Co	11	2,977
West Coast of America Telegraph Co	8	1,964
Western and Brazilian Telegraph Co	16	6,154
West India & Panama Telegraph Co	22	4,557
Total	318	146,419

* Official figures not announced when this list was revised.

Cables Owned by Nations.

Austria	41	214
Belgium	2	55
Denmark	73	235
France	54	5,035
Germany	58	2,225
Great Britain and Ireland	135	1,989
Greece	47	55
Holland	24	62
Italy	39	1,061
Norway	325	324
Portugal	4	115
Russia	9	231
Spain	15	1,744
Sweden	14	96
Switzerland	2	10
Turkey	23	344
Argentine Republic and Brazil	49	119
Australia and New Zealand	31	345
Bahama Islands	1	213
British America	1	200
British India (Indo-European Telegraph Department)	111	1,919
China	2	113
Cochin China and Tonquin	2	774
Japan	70	1,508
Macao	1	2
Nouvelle Calédonie	1	1
Netherlands Indies	7	891
Senegal, Africa — Dakar to Gorée Island	1	3
Total	1,142	19,880

OCCUPATIONS IN THE UNITED STATES.

NUMBER OF PERSONS ENGAGED IN PRINCIPAL SPECIFIED OCCUPATIONS.

OCCUPATIONS.	Males.	Females.
All occupations	18,820,950	3,914,711
Agriculture, fisheries, mining	8,333,692	679,509
Agricultural laborers	2,556,930	447,085
Dairymen and dairywomen	16,072	1,734
Farmers, planters, overseers	5,055,130	226,427
Fishermen and oystermen	59,887	263
Gardeners, florists	70,186	2,415
Lumbermen and raftsmen	65,829	28
Miners (coal)	208,330	219
Miners (others)	140,906	133
Quarrymen	37,628	30
Stock raisers, herders, drovers	70,047	687
Wood choppers	33,665	32
Professional service	632,641	311,682
Actors	5,779	3,949
Architects	8,048	22
Artists and teachers of art	11,676	10,810
Authors and scientific persons	3,989	2,725
Clergymen	87,060	1,235
Dentists	17,161	337
Designers and inventors	9,086	306
Engineers (civil, mechanical, electrical, and mining)	43,115	127
Journalists	20,961	888
Lawyers	89,422	208
Musicians, teachers of music	27,636	34,519
Officials (government)	74,789	4,875
Physicians and surgeons	100,248	4,555
Professors in colleges	4,697	735
Teachers	96,581	245,230
Theatrical managers, showmen, etc	17,421	634
Domestic and personal service	2,692,820	1,667,686
Barbers and hairdressers	82,151	2,825
Bartenders	55,660	147
Boarding and lodging house keepers	11,756	32,593
Engineers and firemen (not locomotive)	139,718	47
Hotel-keepers	38,825	5,315
Janitors	18,776	2,780
Laborers	1,858,504	54,813
Launderers and laundresses	31,816	216,627
Nurses and midwives	6,688	51,402
Saloon keepers	69,137	2,275
Servants	237,523	1,205,876
Soldiers, sailors, and marines	126,744	....
Trade and transportation	3,097,653	228,309
Agents (claim, commission, real estate, insurance, etc.)	169,704	4,875
Bankers and brokers (money and stocks)	29,516	504
Bookkeepers and accountants	131,602	27,772
Clerks and copyists	492,852	64,048
Commercial travelers	58,089	612
Foremen and overseers	35,117	983
Hackmen, teamsters, etc	368,265	237
Hostlers	54,005	24
Hucksters and peddlers	56,824	2,259
Livery-stable keepers	26,719	48
Locomotive engineers and firemen	79,459	4
Merchants (retail)	638,609	25,451
Merchants (wholesale), importers	27,334	198
Messengers and office boys	48,446	2,909
Newspaper carriers, newsboys	5,216	72
Officials of companies	39,719	237
Porters and helpers	24,002	325
Sailors	55,875	29
Salesmen and saleswomen	205,931	58,449
Steam railroad employees	381,312	1,438
Stenographers, typewriters	12,148	21,185
Street railway employees	37,423	12

OCCUPATIONS.	Males.	Females
Telegraph and telephone operators	43,740	8,474
Telegraph and electric light employees	10,465	669
Undertakers	9,817	83
Manufacturing and mechanical industries	4,064,144	1,027,525
Bakers	57,908	2,273
Blacksmiths	205,256	59
Bleachers, dyers, scourers	12,495	1,697
Bookbinders	12,289	11,498
Boot and shoe makers	179,838	33,609
Brewers and maltsters	20,277	72
Brick and tile makers	60,007	194
Broom and brush makers	8,944	1,173
Builders and contractors	45,976	10
Butchers	105,313	129
Butter and cheese makers	10,941	499
Cabinetmakers	35,891	35
Carpenters and joiners	611,226	191
Carpet-makers	11,545	10,745
Carriage and wagon makers	34,294	278
Clock and watch makers	20,543	4,760
Compositors	23,702	6,286
Confectioners	17,562	5,606
Coopers	47,435	54
Cotton mill operatives	80,144	92,914
Distillers and rectifiers	3,340	9
Door, sash, and blind makers	5,034	28
Dressmakers	828	288,155
Engravers	8,016	303
Glass workers	32,660	1,722
Glove makers	2,760	3,663
Gold and silver workers	16,890	3,335
Gunsmiths, locksmiths, and bell hangers	9,065	89
Harness and saddle makers and repairers	42,612	856
Hat and cap makers	17,336	6,694
Hosiery and knitting mill operatives	8,706	20,513
Iron and steel workers	142,087	2,449
Leather curriers and tanners	39,032	313
Machinists	176,937	139
Manufacturers and officials	101,216	2,049
Marble and stone cutters	61,006	63
Masons (brick and stone)	158,874	42
Meat and fruit packers and canners	4,604	1,398
Mill and factory operatives	51,561	41,850
Millers (flour and grist)	52,745	99
Milliners	406	60,058
Molders	66,241	47
Painters, glaziers, varnishers	218,622	1,246
Paper-hangers	12,313	54
Paper mill operatives	18,869	8,955
Photographers	17,834	2,195
Piano and organ makers	14,360	357
Plasterers	38,912	23
Plumbers and gas and steam fitters	56,555	42
Potters	12,943	2,020
Printers and pressmen	80,899	5,565
Publishers of books and newspapers	6,207	219
Rubber factory operatives	9,886	6,463
Saw and planing mill employees	133,216	302
Seamstresses	3,988	145,716
Ship and boat builders	22,929	3
Silk mill operatives	14,192	20,622
Steam boiler makers	21,272	6
Tailors and tailoresses	121,586	63,611
Tinners and tinware makers	54,427	947
Tobacco factory operatives	83,601	27,821
Wire Workers	11,255	1,093
Wood Workers	63,529	3,696
Woolen mill operatives	47,636	36,435

THE WORLD'S PRODUCTION OF WOOL

Of the world's wool production 2,118,884,704 pounds are of classes one and two, washed and unwashed, and 581,000,000 pounds of class three of the American tariff classification.

Countries.	Pounds.
North America:	
United States†	302,502,328
British Provinces	12,000,000
Mexico	5,000,000
Total	319,502,328
Central America and West Indies	5,000,000
South America:	
Argentina	370,000,000
Brazil	1,500,000
Chile	7,500,000
Uruguay	96,000,000
Venezuela	15,000,000
All other South America	20,000,000
Total	510,000,000
Europe:	
Great Britain and Ireland*	141,146,376
France	103,610,000
Spain	102,600,000
Portugal	13,410,000
Germany	49,590,000
Italy*	21,451,000
Austria-Hungary	64.300,000
Russia, inc. Poland	361,100,000
Sweden and Norway	8,200,000
Turkey and Balkan Peninsula	67,500,000
All other Europe	14,000,000
Total	946,907,376
Asia:	
Russia	60,000,000
Central Asia	46,000,000
Asia—*Continued:*	
British India	85,000,000
Asiatic Turkey	33,000,000
China	35,000,000
All other Asia	15,000,000
Total	274,000,000
Africa:	
Algeria and Tunis	30,425,000
Cape Colony, Natal, Orange Free State	100,000,000
Egypt	3,000,000
All other Africa	1,000,000
Total	134 425,000
Australasia	510,000,000
Oceanica	50,000
Grand total	2,699,884,704

*** Fleece washed. Great Britain and Ireland, product of 1900. † Washed and unwashed.**

RAILROAD SPEED.

NOTABLE FAST RUNS OF PASSENGER TRAINS FOR LONG DISTANCES.

Date.	Railroad.	Terminals.	Distance, Miles.	Inclusive. Time. H. M.	Inclusive. Miles per Hour.	Stops. Number.
May, 1848.	Great Western (England)	London—Didcot	53.25	0.47	68	..
July, 1885.	West Shore	East Buffalo—Frankfort	201.7	4.00	50.4	..
Aug., 1888.	L. & N. W., and Caledonian	London—Edinburgh	400	7.38	52.4	3
Sept., 1891.	New York Central & H. R.	New York—East Buffalo	436.32	7.19.5	59.56	3
Mar., 1892.	New York Central & H. R.*	Oneida—DeWitt	21.37	0.17⅔	72.69	0
Nov., 1892.	New York Central & H. R.*	Syracuse—Utica	51.67	0.46	67 38	0
Nov., 1892.	New York Central & H. R.*	Chittenango—Schenectady	116.16	1.50	63.38	0
May, 1893.	New York Central & H. R.*	Syracuse—Rochester	80.38	1.11	68.45	0
May, 1893.	New York Central & L. S.	New York—Chicago	964	19.57	48.20	10
Aug., 1894.	Plant System, Atlantic Coast Line	Jacksonville—Richmond	661.5	12.51	51.48	26
Aug., 1894.	Plant System, A. C. L., Pa. R. R.	Jacksonville—Washington	760.9	15.49	49 37	34
April, 1835.	Pennsylvania	Camden—Atlantic City	58.3	0.45¾	76.50	0
April, 1895.	Delaware, Lackawanna & Hudson	Binghamton—East Buffalo	197	3.05	60.64§	2
Aug., 1895.	London & Northwestern	London—Aberdeen	540	8 32	63 28‡	3
Sept., 1895.	New York Central & H. R.	New York—Buffalo	436.50	6.47	64.33‡	2
Sept., 1895.	N. Y. Central "World Flyer"	Albany—Syracuse	148	2.10	68.3	0
Oct., 1895.	Lake Shore & Michigan Southern	Chicago—Buffalo	510	8.1	65.7¶	5
Oct., 1895.	Long Island	Long Island City—Amagansett	104	1.46	58 9	2
Mar., 1896.	Phila., Wilmington & Baltimore	Baltimore—Gray's Ferry	92.5	1.28	63	1
Feb., 1897.	Chicago, Burlington & Quincy	Chicago—Denver	1,025	18.52	58.74	20
Mar., 1897.	Central R. R. of New Jersey	Jersey City—Washington	231	4.8	60	(*a*)
April, 1897.	Lehigh Valley, Black Diamond Ex.	Alpine, N.Y.—Geneva Junction, N.Y.	43.96	0.33	80	0
May, 1897.	Chicago, Burlington & Quincy	Mendota—Chicago	79	.76	60	2†
July, 1897.	New York Central & H. R.*	Syracuse—Buffalo	149	2.23	62.5	1
Aug., 1897.	Union Pacific	North Platte—Omaha	291	4.39	63.49	..
Feb., 1898.	A., T. & S. F., "Santa Fe Route"	La Junta, Col.—Dodge City, Kansas	204.4	3.44	56.7§	..
May, 1898.	Chicago & Alton	Willow Spring—Springfield	168.1	2.46	60.7	..
July, 1898.	Lehigh Valley, Black Diamond Ex.	Sayre—Buffalo	177	2.59	59.32	2
Oct., 1899.	Burlington Route	Mendota—Clyde	74.3	0.65	68.58	..
May, 1900.	Burlington Route	Burlington—Chicago	205.8	3.08½	65.5§	..
Dec., 1900.	Burlington & Mo. River	Ravenna—Seneca	130	2.5	66	(*b*)
Mar., 1901.	Sav., Fla. & Wes. (Plant System)	Fleming—Jacksonville	149	2.10	68.8	1

* By "Empire State Express." † Six minutes. ‡ Including stops. § Excluding stops. ¶ Exclusive of stops, or 63.61 miles per hour including stops. Made the trip from Chicago to New York, 952 miles, in 17 hours, 45 minutes, 23 seconds (or 54.20 miles per hour, including 10 stops). (*a*) Including "slow-ups" for taking water, changing engines, etc. (*b*) A delay of 7 minutes at Anselmo should be deducted from running time.

In making a comparison between English and American trains, certain conditions must be taken into consideration. In the former instance the average weight of the train making the record between London and Aberdeen in August, 1895, was between 105 and 120 tons. The "Empire State Express" in the record of September, 1895—New York to Buffalo—was similar in make-up to the train that made the English record, but weighed 250 tons, a vast difference and necessarily an important factor in speed. London to Paris—On a special run over the L. C. & D. Ry. to Paris, 287¼ miles (via Calais), for the Grand Prix, running time 6 hours, 30 minutes, 12 seconds, or from 57.5 to 60.1 miles per hour.

AVERAGE SPEED, INCLUDING STOPS, OF FOREIGN EXPRESS TRAINS PER HOUR IN MILES.

England, 51.75; Germany, 51.25; France, 49.88; Belgium, 45.04; Holland, 44.73; Italy, 42.34; Austria-Hungary, 41.75.

Fastest Recorded Runs for Short Distances.

Date.	Railroad.	Terminals.	Distance, Miles.	Time, M. S.	Miles per Hour.
July, 1890......	Philadelphia & Reading............	Skillmans—Belle Meade......	4.1	2 30	98.4
Aug., 1891......	Philadelphia & Reading............	Somerton—	1	0 39.8	90.5
Nov., 1892......	Central of New Jersey..............	Fanwood—Westfield, N. J....	1	0 37	97.3
May, 1893......	N. Y. Central & Hudson River.....	Grimesville—	1	0 35	102.8
May, 1893......	N. Y. Central & Hudson River.....	Crittenden — "Empire State Express"...................	1	0 32	112.5
Aug., 1895......	Pennsylvania	Landover—Anacosta..........	5.1	3 00	102
Aug., 1898......	Wabash	Boody—Blue Mound..........	6	4 7	87.46
Jan., 1899......	Burlington Route..................	Siding—Arion................	2.4	1 20	130
Mar., 1901......	Plant System........................	Fleming—Jacksonvilie.......	5	2 30	120

DISTRIBUTION OF HOG PRODUCTS EXPORTED FROM THE UNITED STATES.

Countries. 1898-99.	Bacon. Pounds.	Hams. Pounds.	Pork. Pounds.	Total Meats. Pounds.	Lard. Pounds.	Aggregate, 1898-99.	Aggregate, 1897-98.	Aggregate, 1896-97.
United Kingdom....	395,474,204	177,702,854	90,686,214	663,863,272	204,645,770	868,599,042	899,520,708	731,256,560
France..............	12,366,110	1,145,490	212,936	13,724,536	32,312,597	46,037,133	24,973,722	23,362,350
Germany.............	36,151,678	9,813,118	15,515,225	61,480,021	229,230,175	290,710,196	306,950,114	197,917,382
Belgium.............	29,519.843	14,984.833	9,586,676	54,091,352	37,307,555	91,398,907	102,421,995	69,408,128
Netherlands..........	10,014.623	4,265.556	10,011,680	24,291,859	74,865,099	99,156,958	96,331,133	76,541,487
Denmark......... ...	1,843,326	691.562	874,175	3,409,063	10,536,795	13,945,858	12,211,972	5,437,494
Sweden and Norway.	28,363,412	463,206	5,124,728	33,951,346	13,157,399	47,108,745	11,781,097	11,912,596
Spain................	147,006	1,500	24,588	173,094	5,100	178,194	34.552	128,008
Italy..................	12,435,593	187,966	383,973	13,007,532	7,483,483	20,491,015	8,719,038	2,510,936
Cuba	11,353,301	6,229,486	752,766	18,335,553	27,291,504	45,627,057	34,676,437	40,534,401
Hayti..................	516	117,395	6,727,685	6,845,596	1,532,484	18,378,080	10,922,596	14,474,343
Porto Rico...........	1,138,421	127,234	3,332,800	4,598,455	4,741,704	9,340,159	8,264,637	9,530,145
British West Indies..	358,427	984,977	8,777,720	10,121,124	2,473,287	12,594,411	12,772,738	11,788,213
Mexico..............	184,482	277,623	10,518	472,623	2,270,339	3,742,962	3,924,008	7,562,331
Brazil	6,040,051	32,412	117,900	6,190,363	17,839,650	24,030,013	23,285,009	29,463,167
Colombia............	27,325	194,327	171,474	393,126	1,766,263	2,159,389	2,386,385	3,253,714
Venezuela...........	30,667	450,093	20,000	500,760	5,536,080	6,036,840	7,260,904	7,258,636
British Guiana	10,551	193,330	3,407,400	3,611,281	420,578	4,031,859	3,771,077	3,409,058
Peru	5,740	27,157	12,800	45,697	422,963	468,660	525,539	430,164
Quebec, Ontario, etc.*	9,729,041	5,635,192	12,232,093	27,596,326	6,568,568	34,164,894	42,785,483	23,702,153
Nova Scotia, etc.....	25,354	173,283	1,914,954	2,113,591	189,101	2,302,692	1,770,306	4,080,295
Newfoundland, etc..	50,318	124,784	3,847,407	4,022,509	263,190	4,285,699	3,277,416	3,710,432
All other.............	7,381,491	2,023,372	4,761,852	14,166,715	29,400,167	43,566,882	41,429,276	23,059,317
Year, to June 30....	562,651,480	225,846,750	178,507,564	967,005,794	711,259,851	1,678,265,645	1,659,996,202	1,300,731,310
Value	$41,557,067	$20,774,084	$10,639,727	$72,970,878	$42,208,465	$115,179,343	$110,801,151	$82,580,867

* Includes Manitoba, Northwest Territories, and British Columbia.

The tables of statistics of hog products were compiled by the Cincinnati *Price Current.*

The Department of Agriculture reported the following farm animals in the United States on January 1, 1900: Horses, 13,537,534, value, $603,969,442; mules, 2,086,127, value, $111,717,092; milch cows, 16,292,360, value, $514,812,106; oxen and other cattle, 27,610,054, value, $689,486,260; sheep, 41,883,065, value, $122,665,916. Total value farm animals, $2,212,756,578.

PRODUCTION OF TOBACCO.

STATEMENT OF PRODUCTION IN THE UNITED STATES FROM THE LAST REPORT OF THE SECRETARY OF AGRICULTURE.

States.	Acres.	Pounds.	Value.	States.	Acres.	Pounds.	Value.
Arkansas...............	1,932	1,195,908	$131,550	North Carolina..........	63,510	42,043,620	$3,783,926
Connecticut.............	6,731	10,176,908	1,628,305	Ohio........................	37,493	32,468,938	1,753,323
Illinois	2,980	1,790,980	132,533	Pennsylvania.............	21,341	26,228,089	2,360,528
Indiana..................	5,369	3,841,952	199,782	Tennessee	39,300	26,724,000	2,405,160
Kentucky................	236,927	183,618,425	10,099,013	Virginia..................	54,592	35,593,984	2,135,639
Maryland................	11,822	7,010,380	420,623	West Virginia............	3,737	2,634,585	263,459
Massachusetts...........	2,323	3,449,655	314,966	Wisconsin.................	18,066	14,669,592	792,158
Missouri.................	11,581	8,296,749	755,004				
New York	5,530	6,934,620	554,770	Total.....................	523,103	406,678.385	$27,760,739

Careful estimate by the Department of Agriculture: Area, 595,000 acres; product, 403,004,000 pounds; value, $24,258,000; yield per acre, 678 pounds. This is the last year that an estimate has been made by the Department.

The number of cigarettes manufactured in the United States in 1890-91 was, according to the Internal Revenue returns, 2,877,799,440. The value of domestic leaf tobacco exported from the United States, year ending June 30, 1895, was $25,622,776; value of leaf tobacco imported same period, $14,745,720.

The product of tobacco in Europe is nearly equal in quantity to the average production of the United States. Neumann-Spallart has usually made it about 500,000,000 pounds. Austria-Hungary produces about one third of it, Russia one tenth, Germany nearly as much, France about 35,000,000 pounds, and the other countries a small quantity. Europe can easily produce all the tobacco required, but two reasons are prominent for importation of tobacco from this country. It is very cheap, and it is very desirable for mixing with and fortifying European leaf.

TEA AND COFFEE.

Tea.—The production of tea in 1888, by countries, according to Mulhall, was, in pounds: China, 290,000,000; India, 90,000,000; Japan, 40,000,000; Ceylon, 19,000,000; Paraguay, 10,000,000; Java, 7,000,000.

The consumption of tea is estimated by the same authority as follows, in pounds: Great Britain and Ireland, 184,500,000; United States, 80,000,000; Russia, 37,000,000; Canada, 22,000,000; Australia, 20,000,000; various other countries, 106,500,000.

The importation of tea into the United States in the fiscal year of 1896 was 93,998.372 pounds, valued at $12,704,440.

Coffee.— The total production of coffee in the world in 1889 was 1,249,000,000 pounds, of which Brazil produced 812,000,000, other parts of America, 253,000,000, East Indies and Africa, 184,000,000.

The consumption by countries, according to Mulhall, is in tons: United States, 215,000; Germany, 105,000; Brazil, etc., 78,000; France, 65,000; Netherlands, 40,000; Austria, 36,000; Belgium, 25,000; Scandinavia, 25,000; Italy, 14,000; Great Britain, 15,000; Russia, 8,000; Spain and Portugal, 5,000. The importation of coffee into the United States in 1896 was 580,597,915 pounds, valued at $84,793,124.

In 1897 the consumption of coffee in the United States was 636,340,000 pounds, or 9.95 pounds to each individual. In all Europe it was 610,300,000 pounds.

The English are the greatest tea drinkers among western nations, the Americans the greatest coffee drinkers.

CANALS.

A Ship Channel, connecting the waters of the Great Lakes between Chicago, Duluth, and Buffalo, giving channel 300 feet wide, 20 to 21 feet depth, is under construction by engineers of the United States Army.

The Harlem River Ship Canal, connecting the Hudson River and Long Island Sound, by way of Spuyten Duyvil Creek and Harlem River, was opened for traffic on June 17, 1895, and cost about $2,700,000.

New York Canals.— The whole number of tons of freight carried upon the state canals during the season of 1896 was 3,714,894, of which the Erie Canal carried 2,742,438; Champlain, 802,510; Oswego, 57,245; Black River, 57,953; Cayuga and Seneca, 54,739. The tonnage was 214,580 tons in excess of that of 1895. The increase of tonnage on wheat over 1895 was 128,507 tons; on rye, 77,050 tons; on barley, 29,691 tons; on oats, 103,434 tons; and on apples, 21,666 tons.

Suez Canal.— The Suez Canal is ninety-two miles long and cost $102,750,000. One thousand four hundred and fifty-eight ships, of 4,045,238 tons net, passed through the Suez Canal during the first six months of 1897, yielding $7,437,975 in dues. As to the nationality of the vessels, the British were 908, German 161, French 101, Dutch 106, Austro-Hungarian 37, Italian 39, Norwegian 28, Turkish 4, Spanish 27, Russian 19, Egyptian 3, Japanese 18, American 1, Chinese 2, Danish 2, Mexican 1.

Manchester Canal.— A statement of the traffic for the year 1896 shows a total tonnage of 1,509,658 — 944,558 of which were imported and 565,100 were exported. In 1895 the total was 1,087,443 tons, of which 592,581 tons were imported and 494,862 tons exported. The chief articles of import in 1896 were as follows, in tons: Timber, 179,859; paper and paper making materials, 95,478; dyewoods, 18,948; pig iron, 56,129; manufactured iron, 22,980; iron ores and pyrites, 44,427; American cotton, 44,409; Egyptian cotton, 22,419; grain, 75,265; flour, meal, etc., 31,968; food stuffs (not described), 14,334; fruit (dried), 5,091; fruit (green), 27,137; sugar, 23,131; tea, 2,267; oil in barrels (chiefly from New York), 17,449 tons.

Baltic Canal.— Also known as the "North Sea and Baltic" and "Kiel" Canal. During the year ending June 30, 1896, 16,834 vessels of 1,505,983 tons passed through from one sea to the other, the receipts and expenditures amounting to about $200,000. The canal is, of course, a waterway of great strategical importance for the Imperial fleets. It permits the German naval forces to concentrate themselves either in one sea or the other in a very few hours.

Panama Canal.— The canal has been reorganized under the corporate name of Compagnie Nouvelle du Canal de Panama (the New Panama Canal Company). The new company has not any governmental character, but is organized under the general laws of France by the representatives of financial institutions of alleged unquestioned strength and powerful influence, with a capital stock of 65,000,000 francs, and is not inviting any outside financial aid, but has conducted with its own resources the great undertaking, and demonstrating the success of the practical questions involved before public aid is again invited. The work of constructing and rebuilding the canal has been carried on, and a large force of men has been engaged upon the work during the past two years, under the direction of eminent engineers. At present the chief work is being done on the cutting of the Culebra Hill.

It is anticipated that the canal will be completed. It is thought that $20,000,000 more may finish the work. The distance between the two oceans is 45 miles. Of this twelve miles on the Atlantic coast and three miles upon the Pacific coast are approaching completion.

Nicaragua Canal was projected to connect the Atlantic and Pacific oceans, using the waters of Lake Nicaragua. Total distance from ocean to ocean, 169.4 miles; depth of canal, 30 feet; least width at bottom, 100 feet; time transit from ocean to ocean, 28 hours; length of Lake Nicaragua, 110 miles; average width, 40 miles; surface area, about 2,600 square miles; area of watershed of lake, about 8,000 square miles.

From New York to San Francisco by water, around Cape Horn, the distance at present is 15,660 miles; by the Nicaragua Canal the distance between the same points will be 4,907 miles, a saving of 10,753 miles. The distance in statute miles from New York to the Pacific Ocean by the principal land and water routes is as follows: By water to Cape Horn, 7,897; by Southern Pacific Railroad, 3,709; by Canadian Pacific Railroad, 3,619; by Central Pacific Railroad, 3,269; by Northern Pacific Railroad, 3,237; by Nicaragua Canal, 2,519. Estimated cost of construction of Nicaragua Canal by the Nicaragua Canal Commission was $133,472,893.

DICTIONARY OF LAW AND BUSINESS TERMS.

Abandonment. The relinquishing to the underwriters, under an insurance, of all the property saved from a wreck, in order to entitle the insured to claim for a total loss.

Abate. To break down, destroy, or remove; as, for instance, to abate (remove or put an end to) a nuisance.

Abduction. The unlawful taking or detention of a woman (having property in possession or expectancy), against her will, with the intention of procuring her marriage or defilement. Also the unlawful taking of an unmarried girl under the age of sixteen years, out of the possession and against the will of the father, or other person having the lawful care of her, although done without force or corrupt motives. The former is a felony, and the latter a misdemeanor.

Abettor. A person who encourages or excites another to commit an offense punishable by law.

Abeyance. The fee simple of lands is in abeyance when there is no person in being in whom it can vest, so that it is in a state of expectancy or waiting until a proper person shall appear, or the right thereto is determined. The same applies to dignities or offices.

Abortion. The offense of procuring the miscarriage of a woman quick with child.

Abstract of Title. An epitome of the deeds and documents constituting the evidence of title to an estate.

Above Par. Stock which sell for more than their face value are said to be above par.

Acceptance. The act by which a person on whom a bill of exchange is drawn, undertakes to pay it at maturity. The bill of exchange itself is sometimes called, in common parlance, an acceptance.

Accessory. A person concerned in a felonious offense, although not the actual perpetrator, nor present at its performance. He may be accessory either before or after the fact.

Accommodation Bill. A bill of exchange accepted without value, for the purpose of raising money thereon by discount.

Action. The method of demanding the enforcement of a legal right, and procuring redress for a civil injury in the courts of common law.

Accept. To acknowledge by signature; to accept a draft is to acknowledge the obligation to pay it when due.

Acceptance "supra-protest" or for honor. An acceptance by some third party after protest for non-acceptance by the drawee, with the view of saving the honor of the drawer or of some particular indorser.

Acceptor. The party who accepts a draft so as to bind himself to pay the sum specified in it.

Acknowledge. To admit; to certify by signature to the genuineness of a deed or mortgage; to give information of the arrival of a letter or remittance.

Accrued. Interest or increase due and unpaid.

Account. A statement; an arrangement of debits and credits in relation to any person or thing; a record of business transactions.

Account Sales. A statement of the product arising from the sale of goods received by a merchant from another party, and sold for his benefit, together with the costs and charges incurred in making such sale.

Accountant. One who is skilled in accounts.

Actuary. A clerk of certain courts and insurance offices; one skilled in annuities; an acting officer.

Administrator. He that has the goods of a person dying without a will committed to his care, for the purpose of legal distribution. The nearest of kin is entitled to administration.

Ad Valorem. Stamp duties, the amount of which is regulated according to the value of the property, etc., are so termed.

Adjust. To put in order; to bring to a satisfactory state, so that parties can agree in the result.

Advance. Additional price, stocks above par.

Advances. Sums of money paid by a merchant upon goods lodged in his hands for sale at a future time. This term also covers money loaned by bankers on bills of lading.

Adventure. Property ventured in a voyage; a speculation.

Advice. Counsel given, usually in regard to the purchase and sale of goods.

Adulteration. Mixing a spurious with a genuine article.

Affidavit. A written statement upon oath. It must be sworn before a person authorized to administer oaths; who that is, depends upon what the affidavit relates to. The same officer is not usually empowered to administer oaths in all the courts.

Affinity. Relation by marriage between the husband or wife and the blood relations of either; but not between the husband and wife themselves.

Affirmation. A solemn declaration in lieu of an oath.

Agent. A person appointed to do an act for another. The act when performed is, in law, the act of the principal; the maxim being "*qui facit per alium facit per se.*"

Alibi. Elsewhere. A defense by which it is proved that the accused was not at the place where the offense was committed at the time of its commission.

Alien. One born in a foreign country out of the allegiance of the head or laws thereof.

Alimony. An allowance made by a husband to his wife when living apart from her.

Allocatur. The certificate by which a taxing master certifies the amount at which he has taxed a bill of costs.

Allonge. A slip of paper attached to a note, draft.

or other negotiable paper, to receive indorsements when the back of the paper will hold no more.

Allowance. Abatement, a deduction made for various reasons.

Amount. The sum total; the aggregate. Gross amount is the total without deduction. Net amount is the total less deduction.

Ambassador. An envoy of the highest rank sent to a foreign government.

Ancestor. The law distinguishes between ancestor and predecessor; the former is applied to individuals, the latter to corporations.

Ancient Demesne. A tenure of lands partaking of the properties both of copyhold and freehold.

Annuity. A periodical payment of money, amounting to a fixed sum in each year, the moneys so paid being either a gift or in consideration of a gross sum received.

Anticipate. To take beforehand, or pay before due.

Antedate. To date beforehand.

Appeal. The removal of a cause from an inferior into a superior court, for the purpose of impeaching the judgment of the inferior court.

Appearance to Action. The first formal step by a defendant in an action of suit. It is a notice that he intends to defend.

Appellant. The person appealing to a superior from the decision of an inferior court.

Appraiser. A person who values personal chattels.

Appropriation. The appropriation of a payment means the applying of it to the discharge of a particular debt, where the creditor to whom it is made has more than one debt due from the same debtor.

Appraisement. The act of setting a value upon goods or other property.

Appurtenance. That which appertains or belongs to something else.

Arbitration. An extrajudicial method of settling matters in difference by referring them to the arbitrament or determination of persons appointed by the disputants, and termed arbitrators.

Arraignment. A term of criminal procedure. A prisoner, after having had the indictment read over him, is commanded to state whether or not he is guilty. This proceeding is termed the arraignment.

Arrest. A legal seizure, capture, or taking of a man's person which is effected by corporeal touching, or something equivalent thereto. In civil cases a man can only be arrested under legal process. The officer cannot break open a man's outer door for the purpose of arresting him; nor can arrest on a civil process be effected on a Sunday, except after an escape.

Arrest of Judgment. Where the court stays a judgment, after a verdict on some question of law.

Arson. Felonious house burning.

Articles of Peace. A complaint against a person to compel him to find sureties to keep the peace.

Arbitraging. Operating in the same stock or product in two different markets to make a profit out of the difference in price or "spread" between them, as, for instance, buying wheat in St. Paul, and selling it in Chicago.

Arrear. That which is behind in payment.

Assault and Battery. An attempt or offer, with force and violence, to do a corporal hurt to another is an assault; an injury actually done to the person of another in an angry, revengeful, or insolent manner, be it ever so small, is a battery.

Assets. Property, whether real or personal, in the hands of an executor, etc., for the purpose of satisfying debts.

Assignee. A person to whom any real or personal property is transferred by the act of law, as an executor, an assignee of a bankrupt, etc., or by the act of party, as a purchaser of a lease.

Assignment. A transfer of any kind of property from one person to another.

Assumpsit. A verbal or parol promise expressed or implied, springing out of a simple contract. The law always implies a promise to do that which a party is legally bound to perform. An action of assumpsit or promise is the remedy for breach of a parol as distinguished from a written contract.

Assurance. The securing the payment of a sum of money or other benefit on the happening of a certain event, as, for instance, the death of a person. This is the term now usually applied to life contingencies, as contradistinguished from fires, losses at sea, etc., as to which the term insurance is still used.

Assessment. A call upon the holders of stock or policies to pay into the treasury a certain sum in order to pay off debts or effect a reorganization.

Assign. To transfer or make over to another, the right one has in any object, as in an estate, especially in trust for the security of creditors.

Assay. To determine the amount of a particular metal in an ore or metallic compound.

Assess. To tax, or value for the purpose of taxing.

Assignor. One who makes a transfer to another.

Association. A company of persons united for a particular purpose.

Assume. To take on one's self or become liable for the debts of another.

Attachment. A process of the courts of law and equity for compelling, by arrest, the performance of an act, which a party is already in contempt for not performing. Also an ancient remedy open to creditors in London, and some other cities, to attach the money or goods of their debtor in the hands of a third party within the city.

Attorney. A person appointed by another by letter or power of attorney to do anything for him in his absence.

Attorney-at-Law. An officer of the superior courts of law, legally authorized to transact the business of other persons—termed his clients—in those courts.

Attach. To take by legal authority.

Attest. To call to witness or give official testimony required in solemn instruments.

Auditor. A person authorized to examine and adjust accounts.

Average. A contribution to a general loss. When, for the safety of a ship in distress, any destruction of property is incurred, all persons having goods on board contribute ratably to the loss; this is called average.

Award. The judgment or decision of an arbitrator.

Backing a Warrant. The indorsing by a justice of the peace of the county where a warrant (which has been granted by the justice of the peace of another county) is about to be executed, and is a necessary act to be done before a person can be apprehended in a county different to that in which the warrant was issued.

Bail. The sureties for the reappearance of a person released from custody.

Bail-bond. A document under seal, by which a person becomes bail.

Bailee. An individual intrusted with the custody of goods; for instance, a carrier.

Bailiff. There are various kinds of bailiffs; the most common being those appointed by the sheriff, commonly called sheriff's officer.

Bailment. A delivery of a thing in trust for some special object or purpose.

Bailor. The person who makes a bailment, or delivers goods to a bailee.

Banker. A person who holds the money of another, and disposes of it as the other from time to time directs.

Bank Note. A promise by a banker to pay a specified sum to the holder.

Barristers. A body of men qualified by admission in one of the Inns of Court, to plead as advocates; such admission is termed, being "called to the bar."

Battel. A trial by combat, formerly allowed by the law, by which the innocence or guilt of a party was decided.

Balance. The arithmetical difference between the two sides of an account; the sum necessary to make the two sides of an account equal in amount, spoken of as a debit or credit balance; (verb) to bring into a state of equality; to settle by paying what remains due on an account.

Balance of Trade. The difference in value between our exports and our imports.

Bank. An establishment for the custody and issue of money; the office in which the transactions of a banking association are conducted.

Bankable. Receivable as cash by a bank, such as checks, express orders, money orders, etc.

Bank Bill. The note of a bank payable on demand, and used as currency; a bank note.

Bank Book. The book kept by a depositor, in which the receiving teller writes the separate deposits, and the bookkeeper of the bank enters the paid checks.

Bank Clearing. The aggregate amount of the checks and drafts exchanged between banks (members of clearing house association). In large cities less than ten per cent. of the commercial business is done with currency. While the clearings do not represent the sum total of the counter transactions of banks for any given time, they form a good basis for calculation as to the comparative volume of trade from week to week. They really indicate the growth or shrinkage of trade.

Bequest. A testamentary disposition of personal estate.

Bear. A stock exchange phrase used to designate a man who, having sold more stock than he possesses, endeavors to depress its value, that he may buy at a low rate, and so make good his deficiency.

Bigamy. The criminal offense of a married man or woman pretending to marry again, his wife or her husband (as the case may be) being still alive.

Bill. The term applied to an intended statute when passing through Congress, prior to its becoming law.

Bill of Exceptions. A mode of appealing from the decision of a judge on a point of law.

Bill of Exchange. A written order for payment of money by one person (called the drawer), upon another (termed the drawee). When the drawee has undertaken to pay the bill, which he does by writing his name across it, he is termed the acceptor. Bills of exchange are negotiable, *i. e.*, they confer on the holder the right of suing upon it, which he could not do in the case of a mere ordinary contract, for the want of that privity which the law in ordinary cases requires between the parties to a contract. The law as to bills of exchange is governed by the Law Merchant. (See Law Merchant.)

Bill of Lading. A memorandum or receipt signed by the master of a ship, acknowledging the shipment of goods, which are usually made deliverable to the consignee by post. By indorsing the bill of lading the property in the goods is passed to the indorsee, and so from hand to hand. The bill of lading, properly indorsed, forms, in fact, the title to the goods, and without the production of which the captain would not deliver the goods.

Bill of Sale. An assignment of goods and chattels, by writing; generally, but not necessarily, under hand and seal.

Bill of Lading. A negotiable receipt for goods delivered to a transportation company for carriage.

Bill of Parcels. A written statement given by the seller to the buyer, containing particulars of the goods bought and their prices.

Bills Discounted. Promissory notes, acceptances, or bills of exchange discounted for the accommodation of an indorser by bankers.

Bills Payable. Promissory notes or drafts held by a merchant against others for future payment.

Bills Receivable. Promissory notes or drafts due to a merchant by others.

Bill of Rights. A bill permitting an importer to examine his goods at the custom house.

Block. A number of shares, say 5,000 or 10,000, massed together and sold or bought in a lump.

Bona Fide. With good faith.

Bond. A written obligation, under seal. If for the payment of a sum of money upon or after the death of a person, it is then termed a post-obit bond. The person making a bond is called the obligor, and he to whom it is given, the obligee.

Borough. A town having now, or having formerly had, corporate rights.

Bottomry. The borrowing of money by the master on the bottom or hull of a ship; to be paid with interest, if the ship return in safety, but otherwise to be lost or forfeited.

Board of Trade. A voluntary association of business men for the regulation and advancement of commercial interests.

Bond. An instrument under seal, by which the maker binds himself, and usually his heirs, executors, and administrators, to do or not to do a specified act. A certificate of ownership of a specified portion of a capital debt due by a government, a city, a railroad, or other corporation, to individual holders, and usually bearing a fixed rate of interest.

Bonded Goods. Imported goods left in a bonded warehouse until the duties are paid.

Bonded Warehouse. A government warehouse in which bonded goods are stored until the duties thereon are paid.

Bonus. A premium on a loan; something extra or in addition.

Boom. A rush of business. A quick inflation of values.

Breach of Covenant. The doing of an act which a party has covenanted not to do, or neglecting to do that which he has covenanted to perform.

Breach of the Peace. An act by which the public repose is disturbed, and the safety of the community more or less endangered.

Breach of Promise. The doing, or abstaining from doing, something, contrary to an understanding or contract.

Breach of Trust. A neglect of duty by a trustee, or person standing in a fiduciary relation, in violation of his trust.

Bribery. The giving or receiving any reward for corrupt purposes.

Brief. An abridgment of a client's case, for the instruction of counsel on trial or hearing in court.

Broker. An agent employed to buy or sell goods; a sort of middleman between vendor and purchaser. He is not, like a factor, intrusted with the possession of the articles he vends.

Brokerage. The commission paid to a broker.

Brand. A trade-mark; a particular kind of goods.

Break. A quick, small decline.

Burglary. The offense of entering a dwelling-house, in the night, with the intent to commit felony.

Bursar. The treasurer of a college. In Scotland it is nearly synonymous with sizar in the English universities.

Bucket Shop. A place where bets are made on quotations of prices, established on legitimate Exchanges, and Boards of Trade. Pretended trading. Illegal in most States.

Bulge. A quick, small advance.

Bull. A person whose interest is to secure higher prices; a buyer for an advance.

Bulling. Raising the price of stocks, etc.

BUSINESS CHARACTERS.

@	At.	,,	Ditto, the same.
a/c	Account.	X	By, as 9 X 12.
%	Per cent.	1^1,	One and one fourth.
#	Number.	1^2,	One and one half.
$	Dollars.	1^3,	One and three fourths.
¢	Cents.	+	Addition.
√	Check mark.	—	Subtraction.
d.	Pence.	X	Multiplication.
£	Pound sterling.	÷	Division.
s.	Shillings.	=	Equal to.

Buyer Three. A Wall street expression signifying that the buyer has three days in which to pay for his purchase.

Bullion. Uncoined gold or silver, including gold dust, ingots, and bars.

By-Law. A private law made by those duly authorized by charter, custom, or prescription; but such by-law must be consonant to the public laws and statutes, and for the common benefit.

By-Bidder. One who bids at an auction in behalf of the owner for the purpose of running up the price of articles.

Canon Law. A collection of ecclesiastical constitutions, definitions, and rules, derived from the ancient councils, the writings of the fathers, ordinances of popes, etc. At the Reformation it was enacted that a review should be had of the Canon Law; but that, until such review, the existing law should continue in force, except as far as the same should be repugnant to the law of the land or the Royal Prerogatives — this still remains the state of the law, such review never having been made. The canons of 1603 having been made by the clergy, and confirmed by the king, James I., alone, but not by Parliament, do not bind the laity.

Capias. A writ authorizing the arrest of a defendant in a suit. It is issued, either after judgment, or when it is satisfactorily shown that the defendant is about to leave the realm before trial.

Capias ad Satisfaciendum, or CA-SA. The writ of capias when issued after judgment; so termed, because the defendant is taken to satisfy the plaintiff's demands.

Carrier. A person whose business it is to carry goods for the proper delivery and safety of which he is legally responsible.

Caveat. A proceeding to prevent an act being done, such as the granting of administration, without notice to the party entering the caveat.

Caveat Emptor. Let the purchaser beware. It signifies that a vendor is not bound to answer for the goodness of his wares, unless he expressly warrants them.

Call. A privilege to buy at a certain time for an agreed price, called the "call price," which is always a little above market price.

Call Loans. Money loaned subject to the call or demand of lender. It must be returned the day it is called for before the close of banking hours.

Capital. Money or other property invested in business.

Cashier. The clerk who has charge of the cash; the second executive officer in a bank.

Carat. Weight showing the degree of fineness of gold.

Cargo. A ship's lading or freight.

Carte Blanche. Signature of an individual or individuals on blank paper with space above to write a note; full power.

Certiorari. A writ for the removal of a cause from an inferior to a superior court. This writ always lies, unless where expressly taken away by statute, and herein it differs from an appeal, which can never be had unless expressly given.

Certificate. A written voucher attesting a fact.

Certified Check. A check to which the cashier of a bank certifies in writing as to the genuineness of the signature of the drawer, and that he has funds on deposit sufficient to meet it, the bank reserving the amount certified and regarding it as having been already paid, and therefore unavailable for other use.

Challenge. An exception taken by a prisoner against one or more jurors, who, when challenged, are set aside, if the challenge be allowed, and new ones put in their places.

Chancellor. An officer of the highest dignity and authority in various departments.

Chancery. The highest court of judicature next to the Parliament, and of very ancient institution. The Court of Chancery is called a Court of Equity, because it was instituted for the purpose of proceeding by the rules of equity and conscience, and of moderating the rigor of the common law; equity being the correction of that wherein the law, by reason of its universality, is deficient. Yet the Court of Chancery is not intended to act in opposition to, but in assistance of, the common law, supplying its deficiencies, not contradicting its rules; no judgment of law being reversible by a decree in Chancery.

Charter. A royal grant or privilege, granted to corporations, companies, etc.

Charter-Party. An instrument between merchants and owners or masters of ships, containing the particulars of the contract for the hire of the ship. It is in fact a mercantile lease of the ship.

Chattels. There are two kinds, chattels real and chattels personal; the former are leasehold property, and the latter personal goods or chattels, as furniture or money.

Chose. A thing. Chose-en-action is a thing of which a man has not the possession, and which he can only claim by action, as, for instance, a debt owing to him by another.

Chattel Mortgage. A mortgage of personal property.

Check. An order upon a bank, or banker, to pay on demand to the person named in the check, or to his order, the sum of money specified in the body of the check in writing.

Choses in Possession. Things of which one has the possession.

Citation. The first step in an ecclesiastical cause, analogous to the writ of summons in an action.

Civil Law. The Roman law is comprised in the institutes, code, and digest of the Emperor Justinian.

Cipher Code. An arrangement of words to stand for phrases, numbers, or quotations, so that telegrams may be thus sent in a private and condensed form.

Client. Anciently, a Roman citizen, taken under the protection of some great man, who was styled his patron. The term is now applied to a party who employs a solicitor or counsel in any legal proceeding.

Clear. To exchange checks and bills, and to settle balances as is done in a clearing house.

Clearing House. An organization for the settlement of balances between members Usually applied to banks.

Clearing House Certificates. Certificates issued by a clearing house against collateral approved by the loan committee, and used in the settlement of the daily balances between its members.

Clearance. Certificate from the custom authorities permitting a vessel to leave port.

Clearing. Act of leaving port.

Clique. A combination of persons "to run a deal" or manipulate a market. Usually applied to stocks, grain, and provisions.

Closed Policy. A policy in which the amount insured is definitely stated.

Codicil. A supplement to a will.

Commission. The warrant, or letters patent, authorizing any inquiry judicial or otherwise; as the commission of the judges, the commission of the peace, etc.

Commitment. The sending a person who has been guilty of any crime, to prison, by warrant or order.

Committee. Persons to whom the consideration of any matter is referred; as a Committee of the House of Congress.

Common (Rights of). These are of four sorts: viz., pasture, piscary, estovers, and turbary. Common of pasture is the right of feeding one's cattle on the land of another; piscary, that of fishing in waters belonging to another; estovers, the right of taking wood from another's estate, for household use and implements in husbandry; and turbary, the right of digging turf upon another's ground.

Common Law. The law of England is composed of Acts of Parliament or statutes, and the custom of the realm, the latter consisting of those rules or maxims which have obtained by common consent an immemorial usage. The former are designated the *lex scripta*, or statute law; the latter the *lex non scripta*, or common law. This term is also applied to the superior courts of Westminster, which are called Courts of Common Law, as distinguished from the Court of Chancery, which is the Court of Equity.

Complainant. One who complains of the act of another in a court of justice, more commonly called plaintiff.

Compounding Offenses. Entering into an agreement not to prosecute an offender, for any consideration received or to be received, constitutes a crime, for which the offender may be indicted.

Compounding with Creditors. An agreement by which creditors take a portion of their claims in discharge of the whole.

Conditions of Sale The terms upon which a vendor undertakes to sell to a purchaser.

Confirmation. A deed by which a voidable estate in land is made perfect.

Conjugal Rights. Those rights of husband and wife which spring out of their relationship.

Consanguinity. Relationship by blood, in contradistinction to affinity, which is a relationship by marriage.

Conservator. A standing arbitrator, appointed to compose and adjust differences that may rise between parties, etc.

Consideration. The price or motive of a contract, without which a simple contract is void. In technical language, it may be defined as "some detriment to the plaintiff sustained for the sake or at the instance of the defendant, or some benefit to the defendant moving from the plaintiff."

Consignee. A person to whom goods are delivered either as purchaser, or more generally for sale on commission.

Consignor. The person by whose act or direction goods are delivered to the consignee.

Consignment. The act of making over, or delivering, goods to another.

Conspiracy. A combination of two or more persons to carry into effect an unlawful purpose.

Consul. An officer appointed by government to reside abroad and watch over the interests of our countrymen who may happen to reside in or be passing through the place where the consul is located.

Contempt. A disobedience to the rules, orders, or process of a court, which has power to punish such offense, which it does by imprisonment.

Contract. A covenant or agreement between two or more persons with a lawful consideration.

Contribution. Where one surety or joint contractor has been obliged to satisfy the whole demand, he may obtain contribution from his fellow surety or contractor.

Contributory. One liable to contribute to the liquidation of the liabilities of a joint stock company, under the Winding-up Acts.

Conveyance. A deed which passes or conveys land from one person to another.

Conveyancers. Persons who devote themselves to the preparation of formal documents concerning property.

Convict. He that is found guilty of an offense by the verdict of a jury.

Coroner. An officer whose duty it is to inquire into the cause by which any person came to a sudden or violent death, which must be done, before him and the jury assembled for the purpose, upon view of the body.

Costs. The expenses incurred in the prosecution or defense of legal proceedings, of which there are two kinds, those between party and party, and those between attorney and client.

Count. In common law pleadings, is a section of a declaration.

County Court. Local courts established throughout the country.

Covenant. An agreement under seal.

Coverture. The state of a married woman as being under the protection and influence of her husband or baron. She is called a feme covert.

Coalers. Coal roads. A term usually applied on stock exchanges to describe the Reading, Lackawanna, Delaware and Hudson, and Jersey Central Railroads.

Cocket. A custom house warrant to show that goods have been entered.

Collaterals. Stocks, bonds, notes, or other value, given in pledge as security when money is borrowed.

Collateral Security. Security for the payment of money or the performance of covenants in addition to a principal promise or bond, e. g., a warehouse receipt or a paid-up insurance policy given as security for the payment of a promissory note would be collateral.

Combine. A word expressing the same meaning as "trust" and supposed not to be quite so distasteful to the opponents of monopolies.

Commercial Paper. Negotiable paper, such as drafts, bills of exchange, etc., given in the due course of business.

Common Stock. The ordinary shares in a corporation.

Compromise. An agreement embracing mutual concessions.

Concern. The business itself considered as a person independent of its ownership.

Consign. To send goods or property to an agent or broker. The sender of the goods is a consignor; the receiver is a consignee, and the goods or things sent are a consignment.

Consols. A contraction of "consolidated." It represents the consolidation of Great Britain's bonded debt, and is the leading English funded government security.

Contango. (London Stock Exchange.) A rate paid for carrying shares over until next settlement day. When a broker desires to "continue shares" or to postpone the day of payment or delivery, the premium paid is called in the seller's case "backwardation" and, in the buyer's case, "contango."

Conversion. Bonds are frequently issued with a provision whereby they can at any moment be exchanged for equivalent stock. Such securities are called "convertible," and the act of substitution is called "conversion."

Corner. An artificial scarcity created by holding property off the market for the extortion of abnormally high prices. Where the purchases of any party or parties exceed the amount of contract grain in regular warehouses on the last delivery day of the month for which such purchases have been made, the grain so bought is said to be cornered.

Corporation. A corporate body authorized by law to act as a single individual.

Coupon Bonds. Bonds payable to bearer without any registration of the owner's name anywhere. The interest in these bonds is evidenced by coupons which, when they become due, are cut off the original bond and collected.

Cover. The buying in of grain or stocks to fill short contracts is called "covering."

Covering Shorts. Buying in property to fill contracts (usually for future delivery) previously made.

Coasting. A sailing near land, or trade carried on between ports in the same country.

C. O. D. Collect on delivery. Goods sent by express marked in this way must be accompanied by the bill for them. This bill is collected and receipted by the messenger of the express company, before delivering the goods.

Commerce. Interchange of values or commodities.

Common Carrier. One who makes it a business to transport goods: railroad companies are common carriers.

Compact. An agreement by which the parties are firmly bound together.

Company. An association of persons for a common enterprise.

Contraband. Prohibited; illegal.

Condition Precedent. A condition which must be carried out before the obligation is performed.

Copartnership. Joint concern in business.

Correspondence. An interchange of letters, or intercourse.

Counterfeit. A forgery; spurious bank bills.

Countersign. To sign, as secretary or subordinate officer, a writing which has been signed by the superior.

Coupon. An interest certificate attached to a bond; when paid, it is cut off.

Cross-Examination. The interrogation of a witness by or on behalf of the party against whom the evidence is given.

Credentials. Testimonials; that which gives credit or authority.

Custom. A law, not written, established by long use, and the consent of our ancestors; if it be universal, it is common law; if particular, it is then properly custom.

Customs. Duties levied on commodities exported and imported.

Curb. Prices made by private transactions not in trading hours are called curb markets.

Curbstone Market. A hanger-on of Board of Trade or Stock Exchanges, who does business on the sidewalk. An irregular speculator, with the street for his place of business, and for his office his hat.

Currency. Money in current use.

Custom House. A government place where imported goods are entered and duties collected.

Damages. The amount of money awarded by a jury, to be paid by a defendant to a plaintiff, as a compensation for the injury of which the latter complains.

Days of Grace. Usually three days allowed for the payment of a note after maturity.

Debenture Bonds. Concentration of floating capitalization into convenient bonded form. Originally, notes in the form of bonds.

Debenture. A written instrument of the nature of a bond or bill for a certain sum of money.

De Bonis Non. When an administrator dies, the right does not descend to his own representative, but a fresh grant of administration must be obtained of the goods remaining unadministered, and which is called an administration de bonis non.

Declaration. In an action at law, signifies the plaintiff's statement of his cause of action.

Declaration of Trust. A written or verbal expression or statement, by which a person acknowledges himself to be a trustee for another. If relating to lands, it must be in writing.

Deed. A writing sealed and delivered by the parties to it.

De Facto. A thing actually done or existing.

Default (judgment by). If a defendant omits to appear or plead to an action, within the time allowed, the plaintiff can sign judgment by default.

Defaulter. A person who neglects to perform an act required to be done.

Defeasance. A collateral deed made at the same time with some other deed, and containing certain conditions which may defeat or render null and void the provisions of such other deed.

Defendant. The party against whom an action or suit is brought.

Demesne. Lands which formerly the lord kept in his own hands, being next to his mansion.

Demise. A word used in conveyances of estates for terms of years.

Demurrage. A compensation or allowance for detaining a ship beyond the usual or specified time.

Demurrer. A mode of raising a point of law, upon the facts stated in the pleadings, assuming them to be true.

Deposition. The testimony of a witness taken down in writing and signed by him.

Devise. The giving away of lands or other real estate by will.

Debtor. A party who owes a debt; one who owes another money, goods, or services.

Delivery Day. The first trading day of the month is usually called delivery day, but, as all transactions are at the option of the seller, he may select and deliver the grain on any day of the month for which it has been sold.

Deposit. To place funds in a bank; a sum deposited at a certain time; the amount on deposit at any given time.

Defalcation. A deduction, abatement, or diminution, as in a promissory note.

Debt. What one owes to another.

Delivery. To pass money or goods to another; a giving.

Demand. An asking by authority; a claim by right.

Depository. One to whom something is intrusted; a guardian.

Deputy. One appointed to act for another; a representative.

Disability. A legal incapacity to do an act.

Disclaimer. A renunciation by an executor or trustee of the office imposed upon him, also a mode of defense in equity, etc.

Discovert. A term applied to a widow or unmarried woman.

Disfranchise. To take away from certain places or persons any privilege, freedom, or liberty.

Disseisin. A wrongful invasion of the possession of another, and turning him out from the occupation of his lands, either by force or surprise.

Distress. The distraining or taking the effects of a tenant, in order to satisfy the rent due to his landlord.

Dishonor. To refuse to accept a draft, or to pay a note of acceptance.

Direct Evidence. Evidence which applies directly to the fact to be proved.

Discount. In mercantile transactions, a discount means a deduction of a certain amount from the face of a bill for cash. In banking, a discount means the deduction of a certain amount from the face value of a note or bill, as a payment for allowing the holder of the note the immediate use of the money; the rate of discount varies.

Dividend. A portion allotted to stockholders in dividing the profits.

Domicile. The domicile of a person is where he has his permanent home. There are three sorts of domiciles — by birth, by choice, and by operation of law.

Dower. A widow is entitled, at the death of her husband, to a life interest in a third part of the estates of inheritance of which her husband was seised, and did not dispose of by deed or will.

Domiciliated. A negotiable instrument payable in a different place from that in which it is drawn is domiciliated where payable.

Donee. One to whom a gift is made or a bequest is given.

Donor. One who gives or bestows.

Dormant. Not acting; a partner who takes no share in the active business of the concern, but shares in the gains or losses.

Drop. In stocks or grain it is equivalent to a "break" except that it may be due to wholly natural causes.

Draft. A bill of exchange used for domestic purposes.

Drawback. Duty refunded on exported goods.

Drawee. One on whom a draft is drawn; the payor.

Drawer. One who draws a bill or draft.

Duress. Anything done under compulsion and through unavoidable necessity.

Dun. To press urgently the payment of a debt.

Duty. A government tax paid on goods imported or exported.

Duplicate. A copy or transcript of anything.

Easement. A convenience which one has in or over the lands of another, as a way or a water course.

Earnest. A pledge, like money deposited, affords good grounds for reliance.

Effects. Goods or property of any kind.

Ejectment. An action at law to recover the possession of lands.

Elegit. A writ of execution under which all the debtor's lands may be seized or extended, and held by the judgment creditor until his judgment is satisfied.

Embezzlement. The act of appropriating that which is received in trust for another, which is a criminal offense.

Embargo. Prohibition of vessels from sailing.

Embarrassment. Financial distress; on the verge of bankruptcy.

Embassy. A public message or commission; the person by whom it is sent.

Emporium. A commercial center.

Enfeoff (To). The act of conveying an estate of freehold by deed of feoffment.

Enfranchisement. The admittance of a person into a society or body politic. Enfranchisement of copyholds is a conversion of copyholds into freehold tenure.

Engrossing. A style of writing, not now generally used, for deeds, but still used for the probates of wills.

Enrollment. The registering of deeds as required by certain statutes; as, for instance, deeds conveying lands to charitable uses.

Entail. That inheritance whereof a man is seized to him and the heirs of his body. Tail-general is where lands and tenements are given to one, and the heirs of his body generally. Tenant in Tail-special is where the gift is restrained to certain heirs of the donee's body, as male or female.

Entry. A record of a business transaction; depositing of a ship's papers at custom house to procure license to land goods.

Endorse. To write one's name on the back of a check, note, or draft.

Equitable Mortgage. The most familiar instance is the deposit (either with or without a memorandum, although it is better to have one) of the title deeds of an estate by way of security, which constitutes an equitable mortgage without the execution of any formal mortgage deed.

Equity of Redemption. The right which equity gives to a mortgager of redeeming his estate after the appointed time for payment has passed, and which right can only be barred by a foreclosure.

Equity. In law, qualifying or correcting the law in extreme cases.

Error. A writ of error is a commission to judges of a superior court, by which they are authorized to examine the record upon which a judgment was given in an inferior court, and to affirm, reverse, or vary the same, according to law.

Errors Excepted. A phrase inserted as a proviso, that the person who renders a statement may have the power of correcting any mistake that he may have committed.

Escheat. Is where lands, for want of heirs, or from forfeiture, escheat or fall back to the sovereign or lord of the fee as the original grantor.

Estate. The interest which a person has in lands, or other property.

Estoppel. Where a man is precluded in law from alleging or denying a fact in consequence of his own previous act, allegation, or denial to the contrary.

Estreat. Where a recognizance becomes forfeited by any of its conditions being broken, it is estreated; that is, extracted from the record, and sent up to the Exchequer, whence a process will issue to recover the penalty.

Evidence. Proof, either written or unwritten, of the facts in issue in any legal proceeding.

Excise. A tax or impost charge by government on certain commodities.

Execution. The act of putting the sentence of the law into force.

Executor. One appointed by a person's last will to administer his personal estate.

Exhibits. Documents, etc., produced in evidence, and marked for the purpose of identification.

Ex Officio. Anything done by virtue of an office. An information filed by the attorney-general, by virtue of his office, is called an Ex Officio-Information.

Ex Parte. A statement is called ex parte where only one of the parties gives an account of a transaction, in which two or more are concerned.

Ex Post Facto. An ex post facto law is a law made purposely to restrain or punish an offense already committed.

Extrajudicial. Any act done by a judge beyond his authority, or any opinion expressed by him not strictly pertinent to the matter in issue before him.

Exhaust Price. The point at which one's margins will be exhausted. If trades are not re-margined they are likely to be closed out by the broker at the exhaust price, if it is reached by the market.

Exchange. Act of bartering; a bill drawn for money; a place where merchants meet; a difference between the value of money in two places, or the premium and discount arising from the purchase and sale of funds.

Executory. Yet to be performed.

Exports. Goods or produce carried abroad in commerce.

Express. A special messenger; a regular conveyance for packages, etc.

Factor. An agent intrusted with the possession of goods for sale belonging to his principal. A broker, on the other hand, has not the custody of the goods of his principal.

Faculty. A privilege or dispensation granted by an ecclesiastical court in certain cases.

False Pretenses. The criminal offense of obtaining any chattel, money, or valuable security by means of a false pretense; it is punishable by transportation, fine, or imprisonment.

Face. The amount expressed on a note or draft.

Failure. Act of becoming insolvent.

Facsimile. An exact copy.

Fancy Stocks. Term applied to stocks subject to sudden fluctuation in price.

Favor. A note or draft is said to be in favor of the payee.

Fee Simple. That estate or interest in lands which a person holds to him and his heirs forever. During his life he possesses over it a perfectly free and unrestrained power of disposition, and on his death, without having alienated it by deed or will, it descends to his heirs, both lineal and collateral, male and female, according to an established order of descent.

Felony. Formerly defined as comprising "all capital crimes below treason." It may now more accurately be defined as comprising all crimes occasioning a forfeiture of lands or goods or both.

Feme Covert. A married woman.

Feme Sole. An unmarried woman.

Feoffment. A mode of conveyance of lands in fee, accompanied by certain solemnities. It is rarely, if ever, now used.

Fiat. An order or warrant for a thing to be done or executed.

Fieri Facias. A writ of execution, by which the sheriff is commanded to levy the debt and damages of the goods and chattels of the defendant.

Finding. A finder of goods may appropriate them to his own use if he really believes when he takes them that the owner cannot be found; but if a jury should say that the finder appropriated the goods, not having (or that he could reasonably be supposed not to have had) such belief at the time of appropriation, it amounts to a theft, and can be punished criminally.

Finding a Bill. The grand jury either find or ignore the bills against prisoners; if they find a true bill, the case goes into court, and is tried.

Fire Policy. An instrument by which an insurance company guarantees to a person, who has insured his property, the payment of a sum of money, if it is injured or destroyed by fire.

Fixtures. This term is generally used to denote those personal chattels which, though annexed to the freehold of demised premises, a tenant is nevertheless entitled to remove. They consist of trade fixtures, and of those put up for the ornament or convenience of the premises.

Finance. Revenue; income; pertaining to money.

Financier. An officer of finance; one having charge of the revenue.

Firm. A partnership, trading house, or its name.

Fiscal. Pertaining to a treasury or revenue.

Flat. A term signifying that stocks are sold without reference to accumulated interest; low in price; dull as to sales.

Flotsam. Goods which float after being thrown overboard at sea or in case of shipwreck. The goods thus cast away are called jetsam or jettison, if they sink and remain under water.

Foreclosure. The barring the equity of redemption on mortgages.

Foreign Bill of Exchange. A bill drawn by a person abroad, and accepted in the United States, or vice versa.

Forfeiting Recognizances. When a person who has entered into recognizances fails to comply with their conditions, the same are forfeited or estreated.

Forfeiture. A punishment consequent upon the commission of certain criminal offenses or illegal acts.

Forgery. The crime of counterfeiting a signature, seal, or mark; or the fraudulent alteration of a writing to the prejudice of another.

Foreclose. To cut off the power of redemption under a mortgage.

Forestall. To buy goods before they reach the market.

Folio. Page of a book, usually the two opposite pages.

F. O. B. Free on board; the bill or invoice with F. O. B. includes the transporting to the shipping port and all the shipping expenses.

Foreign Exchange. Drafts drawn on the financial centers of Europe; for instance, London, Berlin, or Paris. Drafts on London are called Sterling Exchange, as they are drawn in pounds sterling.

Franchise. A royal privilege to which a subject is entitled — as a fair, a market, a free warren, a park.

Fraud. A dishonest and illegal artifice, by which undue advantage is taken of another, or by which the interests of that other are unjustly prejudiced. Fraud strikes at the root of every transaction, and vitiates every contract, whether by record, deed, or otherwise.

Freehold. Land held in fee simple, fee tail, or at least for life.

Freight. The remuneration due to the owner of a ship for the conveyance of goods or merchandise, on which he has a lien for the freight.

Franc. A French silver coin, value about twenty cents.

Frank. A free letter.

Free Trade. The policy of conducting international commerce without duties.

Fractional Orders. Orders for less than 5,000 bushels of grain or 100 shares of stock are called fractional orders, as the above amounts represent the units of speculation. Fractional orders are entirely regular, both on the Chicago Board of Trade and the Stock Exchanges. Orders are executed in 1,000 bushel lots of wheat, but not in corn or oats. Neither is there any market for small quantities of provisions or cotton.

Frozen Out. Said of deals or trades closed out compulsorily because of inability to further protect contracts with re-margins.

Funded Debt. The public debt of this country, consisting of an immense sum which, from time to time, has been lent to government by individuals, and which they or their assigns receive interest for, out of the taxes.

Future Estates. Estates not in possession, but in expectancy, as a remainder.

Funds. Stock or capital, a sum of money.

Funded. Put into a permanent loan on which an annual interest is paid.

Futures. Buyers of cash grain protect themselves against possible loss by selling an agreed amount for future delivery in some general market, usually Chicago. Such contracts are called futures because they do not terminate until some designated month in the future. These transactions pass from hand to hand and may be turned over hundreds and thousands of times in an active market before maturity, and this is called dealing in futures. Nearly all speculative operations are in futures.

Garnishee. The party in whose hands money, due to a defendant, is attached.

Gain. Profit; benefit; increase in wealth.

Gauging. Measuring the contents of casks, etc.

Gist. The main point of a case; the turning point.

Gift. A voluntary conveyance or gift of lands or goods. If of the former, it is liable to be defeated in the lifetime of the grantor, by his conveying the same lands to a purchaser, for a valuable consideration, even though with notice of the prior gift.

Gold and Silver Certificates. Certificates issued by the United States government, circulating as money, on the security of gold deposited with the government for that purpose, or of silver coin belonging to itself.

Gross Weight. Weight of goods including case, bag, etc.

Grace, Days of. The name given to the days of indulgence allowed to the acceptor of a bill of exchange after it becomes due. The number of such days varies in different countries. In some, as in France, they are abolished altogether. In England, three days are allowed, so that a bill at a month drawn on the first of one month, will become due on the fourth of the next.

Grand Jury. The jury to whom all bills of indictment are referred in the first instance. It is the duty of this jury to interrogate the witnesses for the prosecution, and ascertain whether or not a prima facie case is made out against the prisoner; if so, they find a true bill, and he takes his trial; if not, they ignore the bill, and he is discharged.

Grant. A mode of conveyance, formerly applicable only to incorporeal hereditaments, reversions, etc.; but its significance has been extended by a recent statute, and it is now the instrument most usually employed in the conveyance of land.

Granger Roads. Western railroads. This term was originally applied in Wall street to the Chicago and Northwestern, and the Chicago, Milwaukee, and St. Paul roads, but is now employed on Stock Exchanges to designate those railroads which handle principally farm produce.

Gross. Whole; entire; total; specifically without deduction, as for damage or waste material; without allowance of tare, opposed to net, as gross sum or amount, gross profits, income or weight.

Guaranty. An engagement to be responsible for the debts or duties of a third person.

Guarantor. A warrantor.

Guaranteed Stock. Stocks of leased or subsidiary company guaranteed by the principal company.

Habeas Corpus. A writ of right for those who are grieved by illegal imprisonment. The Habeas Corpus Act is next in importance to Magna Charta, for, so long as this statute remains, no subject of England can long be detained in prison, except under legal process.

Habendum. One of the formal parts of a deed: its office is to limit or define the estate granted. It is so called because it begins with the words "to have."

Harbor. A place of rest or safety for ships; a port for loading and unloading.

Heir. The legal representative of his ancestor, with respect to the real property of such ancestor. He takes all the real property not otherwise disposed of by the ancestor in his lifetime or by his will.

Heir Apparent. Is one whose right of inheritance is certain, and which nothing can defeat, provided he outlives his ancestor; as the eldest son or issue. Heir presumptive is one who would inherit, provided his ancestor were to die at that particular time, but whose right of inheritance might be defeated by some nearer heir being afterwards born; as a brother or nephew, whose presumptive succession may be destroyed by the birth of a child.

Heirlooms. Such personal chattels as go to the heir along with the inheritance, and not to the executor of the deceased.

Hereditaments. All things which may be inherited, that is, which would descend to the heir, if not disposed of by deed or will. Hereditaments are of two kinds, corporeal and incorporeal.

Hedge. The operation called hedging by speculators is practically the same as straddling, though the terms are not synonymous. Traders hedge to avert a loss and straddle for a profit.

High Seas. Waters of the ocean outside of the jurisdiction of any country.

Homicide. The crime of killing any human being; of which there are three kinds — justifiable, excusable, and felonious.

Honor. To accept and pay when due.

Hue and Cry. The old common law process of pursuing felons "with horn and voice." Also, the name of a paper now circulated amongst the police containing the names and description of felons.

Hypothecate. A term used for pawning a ship and goods, or either, for necessaries, which a master of a ship may do when in distress at sea.

Ignore. When the grand jury reject a bill of indictment, they are said to ignore it, from the Latin word ignoramus.

Illegal Condition. A condition annexed to anything which is illegal, immoral, impossible, or otherwise contrary to law.

Immoral Contracts. Contracts infringing the rules of morality which, for reasons of public policy, are void at law.

Impaneling. Writing in a parchment schedule the names of the jury by the sheriff.

Import. To bring from another country.

Importer. One who brings goods from abroad.

Impost. Duty on goods paid by the importer.

Incorporeal Hereditaments. Hereditaments of a non-tangible nature, and consisting of rights or benefits issuing out of corporal or tangible things,—as a rent, an advowson, etc.

Incumbent. The present possessor of an ecclesiastical benefice.

Incumbrance. A charge or lien upon property, as a mortgage.

Indemnity. A written instrument whereby one undertakes to free another from responsibility.

Indenture. A deed or writing, formerly cut or indented; now the name usually given to deeds, although indenting is no longer essential.

Indictment. A written accusation of one or more persons, of a crime or misdemeanor, preferred to, and presented on oath, by a grand jury.

Indorsement. Anything written on the back of a deed or other instrument; such as a bill of exchange.

Infant. Every person is by the law styled an infant till he has attained the age of twenty-one years.

Inheritance. An estate in lands or tenements to a man and his heirs.

Injunction. A prohibitory writ granted by the Court of Chancery forbidding certain acts to be done under pain of contempt. It may be granted in urgent cases ex parte, but notice is sometimes required to be given.

Inquest. A meeting of jurors, who are summoned to take into consideration certain matters, which may appear in evidence before them, and to bring in their verdict accordingly.

Inquiry (writ of). A writ directed to the sheriff, commanding him to summon a jury and assess the damages in an action; as, for instance, when the defendant has suffered judgment by default.

Insolvency. The state of a person who is unable to pay his debts.

Insurance. A security or indemnification against the risk of loss from the happening of certain events. The usual kinds are fire and marine.

Interpleader. When two or more persons claim the same thing of a third, the latter may call upon them to interplead, *i. e.*, to try the right to it between themselves; he, the third person, retaining possession of the thing in the meantime, as a kind of stakeholder.

Interrogatories. Written questions to which the parties interrogated are to give written answers on oath.

Intestate. A person dying without a will, or, having made a will, without appointing an executor thereof.

Innuendo. That part of the declaration, in actions of libel and slander, which explains the meaning, or points the application, of the libelous or slanderous matter complained of.

In Re. In the matter of.

Installment. Part of a sum of money paid or to be paid from time to time.

Interest. The use of money; premium paid for the use of money.

Investment. The laying out of money in the purchase of property.

Inventory. A list of goods.

Invoice. A list of goods bought or sold, or consigned.

In Sight. Said of stocks of grain, cotton, coffee, or other merchandise, available for immediate use. Grain stored in private warehouses, or held by producers, is not usually included in the supply "in sight."

Inspection. Grain received at Chicago is inspected and graded by sworn inspectors under rules established by the Board of Railroad and Warehouse Commissioners, appointed by the state of Illinois. From this inspection, if not satisfactory, an appeal may be taken to the Inspection Committee of the Board of Trade. In other states similar laws exist.

I. O. U. A written acknowledgment of a debt. This instrument is regarded in a court of law as evidence of an account stated. It is not a promissory note and does not require a stamp.

Issue. The disputed point or question to which the parties in an action have, by pleading, narrowed their several allegations, and are hence said to join issue. If it be an issue of fact, it is tried by a jury, if of law, by the court. Issue is also the legal term for children or remoter descendants.

Jettison. A voluntary throwing of goods overboard at sea in a storm to lighten the ship.

Joinder in Action. The coupling or joining two parties in one suit or action.

Joint Tenants. Persons who hold lands, etc., jointly by one title. On the death of one the survivor takes the whole.

Jointure. A settlement of lands or tenements on a woman, to take effect after her husband's death in lieu of dower.

Journal. A book used to classify and arrange business transactions.

Judgment. The sentence of the law pronounced by the court upon the matter contained in the record.

Jury. A certain number of men sworn to deliver a verdict upon such evidence of facts as shall be delivered to them, touching the matter in question.

Judgment Note. A note in the usual form, with the addition of the power to confess judgment if not paid.

Jurisdiction. The authority by which judicial officers take cognizance of and decide causes.

Landlord. A proprietor of lands occupied by another, which latter party is termed the tenant.

Lapse. A forfeiture of the right of presentation to a church by the neglect of the patron to present. The word is also applied where a testamentary gift falls by the death of its object in the lifetime of the testator.

Larceny. The wrongful and unlawful taking and carrying away by one person of the personal goods of another, with the felonious intention of converting them to his own use.

Law. This word signifies generally an inflexible rule of action. The law of England is composed of written laws or statutes, and unwritten laws, or the customs of the realm. The latter is also termed the common law.

Law of Nations. A system of rules or principles deduced from the law of nature, and intended for the regulation of the mutual intercourse of nations.

Leading Question. A question put or framed in such a form as to suggest the answer sought to be obtained. Such a question is not allowed to be put to a witness, except on cross-examination.

Lease. A conveyance or demise of lands of tenements for life, or years, or at will, but always for a less term than the party conveying has in the premises.

Lease and Release. The form of conveyance, until recently commonly used for conveying land; but a lease, commonly called a lease for a year, is no longer necessary; the release alone being now as effectual as a lease and release were formerly.

Leasehold. Lands held on lease, which (however long the term) are considered as chattels real, and go to the next of kin, and not to the heir, on the death of the owner intestate.

Legacy. A gift or bequest of money, goods, or other personal property by will. The person to whom it is given is styled the legatee; and, if the gift is of the residue, after payment of debts and legacies, he is then styled the residuary legatee.

Lessor and Lessee. The person who grants a lease is called the lessor, the party to whom it is granted, the lessee, and the person to whom either of them assigns, the assignee.

Letters of Administration. The instrument granted by the Probate Court under which administrators derive their title to administer the goods and chattels of an estate.

Letters (or Power) of Attorney. A writing, under seal, empowering another person to do any act instead of the person granting the letter. It may be either general or special; the attorney represents his principal in the matters prescribed by the letter until it be revoked.

Letters of License. An instrument whereby creditors grant to their debtor time for the payment of his debts, and bind themselves not to molest him until that time has expired.

Levy. The seizing of goods or chattels by a sheriff under an execution is called a levy.

Ledger. Book of accounts.

Letters of Credit. A letter authorizing the holder to receive money on account of the writer.

Legal Debts. Debts that are recoverable in a court of common law.

Legal Tender. That which the law authorizes to be tendered in payment of debts. Strictly speaking, it is the exact amount of the debt in current funds. It is not a legal tender to demand change.

Letter of Advice. A letter of information concerning a shipment of goods or of the drawing of a draft.

Libel. A malicious defamation, expressed either in printing or writing, or by signs, pictures, etc., tending either to blacken the memory of one who is dead, or the reputation of one who is alive, and thereby exposing him to public hatred, contempt, or ridicule.

Lien. A qualified right which a person has in or to a thing in his possession, arising from a claim upon the owner. Liens are of two kinds, particular or general.

Limited Liability. The limitation of the liability of shareholders in a company to the amount unpaid upon their shares, introduced by recent Acts, and applicable to all companies registered thereunder; such companies are bound to use the word "Limited" in their title after the word "Company."

Lineal Descent. That which goes from father to son, from son to grandson, and so on.

Liquidated Damages. Damages, the amount of which is fixed or ascertained.

Liability. Debt or claim against a person.

License. Legal permission to sell goods or to do certain things.

Liquidate. To pay off, as debts; to settle or adjust accounts.

Lighterage. A charge for conveying goods to or from a vessel in a harbor.

Limit. A set figure, at which one's trade is to be made or closed.

Liquidation. When employed by speculators, this term signifies the selling out of property previously bought or contracted for. The expression "liquidation by longs," is in contradistinction to "covering by shorts." In a market where both processes are extensively carried on, it is called "evening up."

Loan. To deliver to another for temporary use; the thing lent.

Long. One who has property bought in anticipation of a rise in price. Hence, for a trader to be "long" of stocks or grain presupposes him to be a "bull." Also used adjectively.

Long Market. A market that is overbought, the volume of open contracts to buy property for future delivery being in dangerous excess of the probable demand.

Lunatic. One who has had understanding, but, by grief, disease, or other accident, has lost the use of his reason generally, though he may have lucid intervals.

Magna Charta. The great charter of English liberties granted by, or rather extorted from, King John, at Runnymede, between Windsor and Staines, on the 15th of June, 1215, and afterwards confirmed by Henry III.

Maihem or **Mayhem.** The violently depriving another of the use of such of his members as may render him less able, in fighting, either to defend himself or to annoy his adversary.

Malice Prepense. Malice aforethought; *i. e.*, deliberate, predetermined malice.

Mandamus. A writ commanding the completion or restitution of some right, or the performance of a duty.

Manor. A territorial domain, held partly by the lord and partly by his tenants; it must have continued from time immemorial, and have annexed to it a Court Baron, with at least two suitors.

Manslaughter. The unlawful killing of another, but without malice.

Manumission. The making a bondman free.

Marque and Reprisal (Letters of). Commissions granted to individuals to fit out privateers in time of war; not used in the late war, and abandoned by all the great powers at the Congress of Paris, 1856.

Master of the Rolls. An assistant of the Lord Chancellor, who hears and decides the cases assigned to him, at his own court in the Rolls Yard. He holds his office by patent for life.

Maturity. Bills, or notes, when due, are said to be at their maturity.

Maxims in Law. Certain proverbial axioms, which form part of the general custom or common law of the land. As, "No man is bound to criminate himself." "Conditions against law are void." "It is fraud to conceal fraud," etc., etc.

Malfeasance. An act which one has no right to do.

Mandatory. One to whom business is intrusted or charge given.

Manifest. A list of articles comprising a vessel's cargo.

Manufacture. The process of converting raw material into articles of use and sale.

Margin. A sum of money deposited with a broker, in stock transactions, to protect him against loss by the depreciation of stocks held by him for another party. Also the difference between the value of securities deposited as collateral and the amount loaned upon them.

Marine. Relating to the sea.

Maritime Law. Law relating to harbors, ships, and seamen.

Mart. A place of public sale; a market.

Maximum. The highest figure.

Merger. The sinking of a smaller estate into a greater, whereby the former is utterly extinguished and destroyed. It takes place when two estates meet together, without any intermediate estate between them, to both of which estates the same individual is entitled in one and the same right—as where a tenant for life afterwards acquires the fee simple.

Mesne-Process. Commonly used to describe the first process in an action, as where a party used to be arrested on mesne-process, as distinguished from an arrest on a final judgment.

Mercantile Law. Law relating to business transactions.

Mercantile Agency. A concern which procures information relating to the financial standing and credit of merchants for the use of others, to whom said merchant may apply for credit.

Misdemeanor. An indictable offense, which, though criminal, does not amount to felony.

Misprision. A neglect, oversight, or contempt; as, for example, misprision of treason is a negligence in not revealing treason.

Minimum. The lowest figure.

Mint. The place where money is coined.

Misfeasance. Doing in an improper manner, by which another receives an injury.

Mitigation. Lessening the amount of a judgment, penalty, or punishment.

Moot Point. An obscure point of law not definitely settled; and therefore open for discussion.

Mortgage. A conveyance of lands by way of security, for the repayment of a sum of money borrowed, or owing.

Mortmain. Lands held by corporations are said to be held in mortmain.

Motion. An occasional application to the court, to obtain some rule or order in the progress of a cause.

Money. Current coin and circulating medium.

Money Broker. A broker who deals in money or exchanges.

Monopoly. The sole power of vending goods.

Mortgagee. The person to whom the conveyance is made.

Mortgagor. One who makes the mortgage.

Municipal Law. That which pertains solely to the citizens of a particular state, city, or province.

Muniments. Deeds, evidences, and writings in general.

Murder. Unlawfully killing any person, with malice aforethought, either express or implied by law.

Mutiny Act. An Act annually passed to punish mutiny and desertion, and for the better regulation of the army.

Naturalization. The making a foreigner a lawful subject of the state.

Negotiable Instruments. Those instruments which confer on the holders the legal right to sue for the money or property thereby secured, and which by delivery pass such money or property from man to man — as bills of exchange, bills of lading.

Next Friend. The party in whose name an infant or feme-covert brings an action or suit.

Negotiable. That may be transferred by indorsement and delivery, or by delivery alone.

Negotiate. To transact business or treat with another respecting trade or treaty.

Net. Clear of all charges and deductions.

Net Proceeds. The sum left after deducting commission or discount, etc.

Negotiable Paper. Notes, drafts, or other written obligations, which may be bought and sold.

Net Cash. A term applied to a bill of goods to be paid without any allowance or discount, and without reference to time, but by common custom understood to be thirty days, unless otherwise specified.

Nisi Prius. A term applied to those courts in which civil causes are tried before a judge and jury.

Nolle Prosequi. An acknowledgment by the plaintiff that he will not further prosecute his suit, as to the whole or a part of the cause of action.

Non Assumpsit. He has not promised. A plea by which a defendant denies his liability in an action of assumpsit.

Non Pros. When the plaintiff neglects to take any step within the prescribed time, the defendant may move for a judgment against him, which is called judgment of non pros.

Nonsuit. A renunciation of a suit by a plaintiff, after which he may still commence another action for the same cause, which he could not do if a verdict goes against him.

Notary Public. A person whose business it is to note and protest bills of exchange, and who also attests deeds and writings, to make them authentic in another country.

Non Feasance. The non-performance of an act that should be done.

Note. An obligation without a seal; a written promise to pay.

Nominal. Existing in name only.

Nuisance. Anything which unlawfully annoys or does damage to another. Nuisances may be either public or private.

Nuncupative Will. An oral will before a sufficient number of witnesses, and afterwards reduced to writing — now abolished, except as to soldiers and sailors.

Nunc Pro Tunc. Literally, now for then; and is often so used in legal proceedings.

Oath. An appeal to God as a witness of the truth of what is affirmed or denied in evidence, in the presence of a judge, magistrate, or other officer authorized to administer oaths.

Obligation. That which legally binds a party to perform a duty.

Official Assignees. Officers of the Court of Bankruptcy, one of whom is allotted to each bankrupt's estate. He acts with the assignees appointed by the creditors in the administration of the estate; but his especial duty is to keep the assets of the estate, and receive and pay all money on account of it.

Onus Probandi. The burden of proof. It is a legal principle that the issue in an action must be proved by the party who states an affirmative; not by the party who states a negative. The burden of proof, therefore, is on the former party.

On Call. When money is loaned "on call," it is understood that it must be returned the day it is called for, before the close of banking hours, and without previous notice.

Open Policy. A policy upon which amounts yet to be ascertained and insured, may be entered at different times.

Option. Property bought or sold at the call or demand of the buyer or seller as may be specified; a conditional contract.

Ostensible Partner. A person whose name appears to the world as a partner in a firm. Although such a person may not have any interest in the partnership, he is liable for its debts and engagements.

Outlawry. The act or process by which a person is excluded from, or deprived of, the benefit of the laws, attended with a forfeiture of his goods to the Crown.

Outlawed. Term applied to a debt or note which has run beyond the time when its payment can be enforced by law.

Overt Act. An open act, capable of being manifested by legal proof.

Overdraw. To issue a check for more than the concern's deposit.

Overdue. Remaining unpaid after maturity.

Overissue. An issuing as of stock, beyond or in excess of the capital stock.

Oversold. The reverse of overbought.

Owe. To be indebted to, or bound to pay.

Oyer and Terminer. A commission directed to the judges and others, by virtue whereof they have power to hear and determine treasons, felonies, etc.

O Yes. A corruption of the French oyez, hear ye! The term is used by a public crier to enjoin silence and attention.

Panel. A schedule or slip of parchment, containing the names of such jurors as have been returned by the sheriff to serve on trials.

Paraphernalia. Things to which a wife is entitled over and above her dower, consisting of wearing apparel and ornaments suitable to her rank and station in life. The husband may (with the exception of his wife's wearing apparel) dispose of them in his lifetime, but not by will. On his death they belong to the wife absolutely.

Parol. Word of mouth, verbal.

Particeps Criminis. A participator in the crime.

Partition. The dividing of lands held by joint tenant, coparceners, or tenants in common, into two distinct portions.

Pawn. A delivery of goods and chattels, to be retained until a debt is discharged.

Par. Equal value; when market value equals face value.

Partnership. Company; union of two or more in business.

Pawnbroker. One who lends money on a pledge or deposit of goods.

Payee. The party to whom payment is to be made.

Payor. One who pays or is bound to pay.

Paper Profits. Profits on contracts not yet closed, and consequently not yet in hand.

Par of Exchange. Equivalent value of the currency of a country in that of another.

Partial Payment. Part payment of a debt.

Partner. An associate in business.

Passing a Dividend. When the directors of a corporation vote against declaring a dividend it is said to be "passed." This is nearly always the cause of great weakness in the stock.

Penance. An ecclesiastical punishment, varied according to the nature of the offense, in which the penitent is supposed to make satisfaction to the Church for the scandal he has given by his evil example.

Perjury. The offense committed by a person who, having been sworn to tell the truth in a matter pending in a court of justice, willfully and deliberately takes a false oath.

Perpetuity. A rule that land cannot be limited beyond a life or lives in being and twenty-one years afterwards, and the period of gestation, if it actually exists, is commonly called the rule against perpetuities.

Personal Estate, or **Personalty.** Movable things, whether alive or dead, as distinguished from land, or immovables, which are termed real estate.

Petitioning Creditor. A creditor who petitions the Court of Bankruptcy to make his debtor a bankrupt.

Pin Money. An allowance set apart by the husband for the personal expenses of a wife, *i. e.*, for her dress and pocket money.

Pit Traders. Brokers who are in the pit daily trading for their own account.

Plaintiff. The complainant in an action or suit.

Plea. The defendant's answer to the plaintiff's declaration.

Pleader. A lawyer, who draws the pleadings in actions.

Pleadings. The mutual allegations or statements which are made by the plaintiff and defendant in an action.

Pledge. A pawn; a deposit as security.

Posse Comitatus. The power of the county. This includes the aid and attendance of all men, except ecclesiastics and inferior persons, above the age of fifteen, within the county; which force may be used in cases of riot or rebellion, or where any resistance is made to the execution of justice.

Postea. The verdict of the jury drawn up in due form, and entered on the back of the record.

Pound Breach. The indictable offense of breaking open a pound for the purpose of taking cattle therefrom.

Policy of Insurance. Contract between the insurer and the insured.

Portage. The price of carrying; cost paid by the captain for running his vessel.

Point. On stock exchanges "a point" is understood to mean one dollar a share. A decline in Missouri Pacific from twenty-five to twenty-two would be a decline of three points.

Pool. The stock and money contributed by a syndicate to control the price of a given surety or commodity. Also refers to the individuals composing the pool.

Post Date. To date after the real day.

Pre-emption. The right of first buying.

Prescription. A title acquired by use and time, and allowed by law.

Presentment. The notice taken by a grand jury or inquest of any offense, etc., from their own knowledge or observation.

Primogeniture. The right of the eldest son to inherit his ancestor's estate, to the exclusion of the younger son, where the ancestor has died intestate.

Privilege. An exemption from the general rules of law. It is of two kinds—real, attaching to any place, or personal, attaching to persons, as ambassadors, etc.

Probate. The copy of a will made out on parchment with a certificate of its having been proved.

Process. A general term applied to formal judicial proceedings.

Prohibition. A writ issuing out of the superior courts directing the judge of an inferior court not to proceed further in a suit.

Promissory Note. A written promise by which one person engages or promises to pay a certain sum of money to another.

Pro Rata. In proportion.

Protest. On bills of exchange. A protest means the solemn declaration of a public notary of the dishonor of a bill.

Proviso. A condition inserted in a deed, on the performance whereof the validity of the deed frequently depends.

Premises. Things previously mentioned; houses, lands, etc.

Premium. The sum paid for insurance; the excess of value above par.

Price. Value set or demanded; current value.

Price Current. A table of the current price of merchandise, stocks, bills of exchange, etc.

Prima Facie. On the first view of the matter.

Primage. A charge imposed in addition to the freight.

Principal. An employer; the head of a commercial house; the sum loaned, upon which interest is paid.

Preferred Stock. Shares of a corporation having preference over ordinary shares, but not over bonded or mortgaged indebtedness. Preferred stock is usually issued for borrowed capital. Earnings, if any are left after paying interest on the bonded debt, go next to pay a dividend on the preferred stock, and only what then remains is applied to the common stock.

Privileges. "Puts" and "Calls." A "put" is the privilege or option, which a person purchases, of "putting," *i. e.*, delivering, property or contracts for property to the seller of such privilege, at a named price within a stipulated time—one or more days, weeks, or months. "Puts" are good (from the buyer's standpoint) when the market declines below the "put" price within the time covered by the privilege contract. The buyer can then buy the property at the cheaper figure and "put" it to the person who sold him the risk, his profit being the difference between the "put" price and the quotation at which the property is bought with which to make the delivery. A "call" is the reverse of a "put," the purchaser of a "call" acquiring the right to "call" upon the seller of the privilege for property, or contracts for property, at a named price within a stipulated time. "Calls" are good when the market advances above the call price, and the buyer of such privilege is enabled to sell at a profit the property "called" from the seller of the privilege. The seller of privileges occupies, in a sense, the position of an insurance or guaranty company. He sells market risks as an insurance company sells fire, life, or accident risks. Trading in privileges is illegal in some states, notably in Illinois. Prices paid for privileges are usually $1.00 per thousand bushels for a single day, $1.25 for a week or ten days, and from $2.50 to $7.50 for a month or during the life of a distant option.

Promoters' Shares. Those issued by corporations in payment of the services of promoters in the organization of companies.

Pyramiding. Enlarging one's operations by the use of profits which one has made. For instance, if one buys 5,000 bushels and the market advances 2 cents, he sells, realizes $100 profit, and with this in addition to his additional margin he buys 10,000 bushels of wheat, which he closes on a further advance and makes a still larger investment. On steadily advancing markets with moderate reactions this plan makes large profits, but must not be followed too far and liberal margins should be kept.

Quarantine. Signifies 40 days. It is applied to the period which persons coming from infected countries are obliged to wait on board ship before they are allowed to land. But in law it more strictly applies to the similar period during which a widow, entitled to dower, is permitted to remain in her husband's capital mansion after his death, whilst she awaits the assignment of her dower.

Quash. To annul or cancel.

Quasi Contract. An implied contract.

Quid Pro Quo. Giving one thing for another, being the mutual consideration in contracts.

Quo Warranto. An ancient writ still in use, directed against any person or corporation, who usurps any office, franchise, or liberty, calling upon them to show by what authority they support their claim.

Quotations. A statement of the prices of articles of merchandise, given for the information of correspondents.

Rape. The carnal knowledge of a female who is above the age of ten years, against her will; or of a girl under the age of ten years, although with her permission. The age of consent varies.

Rate. The proportion or standard.

Real Estate or Realty. The term applied to land, in contradistinction to personalty.

Recital. The formal statement of some matter of fact in any deed or writing. It usually commences with the formal word "Whereas."

Recognizance. An obligation of record which a man enters into, with condition to do some particular act; as, to appear at the assizes, to keep the peace, to pay a debt, or the like.

Record. An authentic testimony, in writing, contained in rolls of parchment, and preserved in a court of record.

Re-Entry, proviso for. A stipulation in a lease that, on non-payment of rent or non-performance of the covenants, the leasor may re-enter.

Registrars. Officers having custody of a Registry, such as the registrars of births, marriages, and deaths.

Rejoinder. The answer of a defendant in an action to the plaintiff's replication.

Release. A form of conveyance. Also, an acquittance under seal of a debt or other obligation.

Remainder. A vested or contingent estate or interest in land, limited to take effect and come into possession on the determination of a prior estate created at the same time.

Rent. The annual return made by the tenant to his landlord, which may be either money, labor, or provisions.

Replevin. An action to try the validity of a distress. The things distrained are re-delivered to the tenant on security or pledges given by him to try the right.

Reprieve. A suspension of the execution of sentence of death on a criminal.

Rescue. A resistance against lawful authority, as, for instance, the violently taking away a man who is under legal arrest.

Residuary Devisee. The person to whom a testator devises the remainder of his lands, not otherwise disposed of.

Residuary Legatee. A legatee to whom is bequeathed the residue or remainder of a testator's personal estate, after payment of all legacies, claims, and demands.

Residue or Residuary Estate. The portion of a testator's estate not specifically disposed of.

Retainer. A fee given to counsel to secure his services. It may be either general or special. The former secures the services of the counsel to the party giving it in all matters; the latter only in one cause or matter. The fee in the former cause is five guineas, in the latter one guinea.

Return of a Writ. The certificate of the sheriff made to the court of what he has done towards the execution of any writ directed to him.

Reversal. The making a judgment void, in consequence of some error in the same.

Reversion. The residue of an estate left in the grantor, and returning to him or his heirs, after the grant is determined.

Receipt. A writing acknowledging the taking of money or goods.

Refund. To repay or pay back.

Resources. Pecuniary means; effects; property.

Respondential Bond. A pledge of a cargo at sea.

Retail. To sell in small quantities.

Revenue. Tax; income; rents; customs and duties.

Revocation. The recall of power or authority conferred, as the revocation of an agency.

Receiver's Certificates. Those issued by a receiver for the purpose of raising money for a company in the jurisdiction of a court. When approved by the court and issued, they are a first lien upon the net earnings and property of the company.

Registered Bonds. That class of Government Bonds which are payable to the order of some individual or corporation, whose name is registered as the owner thereof in the government offices at Washington. Such bonds, if stolen or lost, cannot be realized upon.

Remittance. Value, as bills or money transmitted to another.

Renewal of a Note. Extending the time of its payment by giving a new note in exchange for it.

Rule. An order made by the court at the instance of one of the parties in an action. It may either be a rule absolute, or merely a rule nisi, or to show cause.

Rules of Court. The rules framed by the judges for regulating the practice of the different courts of law.

Salvage. An allowance made for saving ships or goods from enemies, or wreck, or loss at sea.

Scire Facias. A judicial writ founded on matter of record, and used for various purposes, as, for instance, to enforce against a shareholder a judgment against a Joint Stock Company, which it is unable to satisfy.

Scrivener. One intrusted with other men's moneys to put out for them, and for which he charges a commission, or bonus.

Scrip. Dividends issued by a stock company payable in stock. Scrip dividends are simply an increase of the capital of the company, as the stock issued to meet them is added to the capital, and in its turn is entitled to future dividends.

Scalper. One who trades in options continually, and, by reading the temper of the market at the moment, tries to get a profit out of the minor fluctuations; also applied to irregular railroad ticket brokers. The term is coming into general use in other lines.

Scalping. Buying and selling on small fluctuations of the market. Taking a small profit or a small loss.

Seizin. Possession of a freehold estate. Seizin in deed is when actual possession is obtained. Seizin in law is a right to lands of which actual possession has not been obtained.

Separate Estate. Real or personal property settled upon a married woman, and which she may dispose of as if she were a single woman.

Sequestration. Used in several cases; but most frequently as signifying an execution for debt against a beneficed clergyman, in which case the debt is satisfied out of the tithes and other profits of the benefice. In Scotland a sequestration is nearly equivalent to our term "bankruptcy."

Set-off. A mode of defense, whereby a defendant sets up a demand of his own to counterbalance the plaintiff's claim either wholly or in part.

Seaworthy. Fit for a voyage; in a proper condition to venture at sea.

Secondarily. Applied to the indorser of a note or the drawer of a bill, signifying that he is only conditionally liable, or liable if the maker and drawee fail.

Seigniorage. The difference between the commercial value of bullion in coin and the face value of the coin itself.

Shipment. Goods; act of shipping.

Short Market. A market that is oversold; the volume of open contracts to deliver property being in dangerous excess of available supply.

Short Selling. The process of selling property for future delivery in the expectation of being able to obtain the property cheaper before the maturity of contract, or of being able to close out the contract at a profit without the actual delivery of the property.

Simony. The corrupt presentation of anyone to an ecclesiastical benefice, for money, gift, or reward.

Simple Contract. An agreement entered into verbally or by writing not under seal.

Sight. The time of presenting a bill to the drawee.

Signature. The peculiar style in which a person signs his name.

Sinking Fund. A fund created by a government or corporation for the extinction of its indebtedness, by the gradual purchase of its outstanding obligations, and the application of the interest saved on these obligations thus redeemed to further purchases.

Silent Partner. One who invests his capital in a business house, but whose name does not appear in the firm. His liability is limited to the extent of his contribution, except in cases where he fails to make the proper publication of his connection with the concern.

Silver Certificates. Those issued against standard silver dollars deposited in the treasury, in denominations of $1, $2, $5, and $10, and higher denominations. Not legal tender but receivable for public dues.

Slander. The malicious defamation of a man by word of mouth, analogous to libel, which is slander by writing.

Solicitor. One who solicits; a lawyer or advocate in a court of chancery.

Solvency. Ability to pay all debts.

Special Pleading. When the pleadings in an action are not in the ordinary form, but are of a more complex character, they are termed special pleadings.

Specific Performance. A remedy in equity, to compel the performance of a contract according to its terms, instead of proceeding at law to recover damages merely.

Specialty. A writing sealed and delivered, containing some agreement.

Speculation. Buying commodities not needed for use, or selling commodities not owned, with the hope of making profits by fluctuations in the values of these commodities. A speculator buys wheat because he hopes to sell it at a better price, but not because he needs it for use. He sells sugar stock because he believes he can buy it at a cheaper price later, and make the difference.

Statutes. The written laws of the kingdom are of two kinds, public or private; the former applies to all statutes which affect the public generally, and of which the judges take cognizance without being specially pleaded. The latter relates to the private rights of individual bodies, as, for instance, the various acts for the management of railway and other companies are private acts.

Stoppage in Transitu. Goods sold on credit to a person, since becoming insolvent or bankrupt, may be seized by the vendor at any time before their actual and complete delivery to the vendee. This seizure is called stoppage in transitu; it is often a nice and difficult question to determine when the transit has ended and the purchaser's possession begun.

Stipend. Settled pay for services; daily, monthly, or annual salary.

Stipulation. An agreement or contract.

Stocks. Shares in joint stock companies, and notes on the government.

Stock Broker or Jobber. One who speculates in stocks.

Statute of Limitations. An assigned period within which legal action must be commenced to enforce payment.

Statement. Usually a list of property, or resources and liabilities.

Statistics. A collection of facts respecting any particular thing.

Sterling Exchange. A bill of exchange drawn on London. This is the most general current exchange, and is good for the payment of debts anywhere. Our shippers of cotton, grain, flour, and merchandise receive bills of lading with draft attached, which they sell to foreign exchange houses here, who issue their bankers' bills against these commercial bills.

Stock. Certificates issued by a corporation certifying that the person in whose name they are written and stand registered on the corporation books is entitled to share in the company's profits, to vote, etc.

Stock, Assessable. That is liable to assessment.

Stock, Cumulative. One on which a corporation agrees to pay past due dividends before declaring a dividend on stocks coming after it in the distribution of net earnings.

Stock Exchange. An incorporated body of brokers, who buy and sell stocks, bonds, and other values.

Stock, Non-Assessable. Stock carrying with it no liabilities.

Subornation of Perjury. The offense of procuring another to take a false oath.

Subpœna. A writ used for the purpose of compelling witnesses to attend and give evidence.

Sufferance. A tenant at, is a person who acquired the possession of lands by right, and holds over after his right is determined.

Suit. Proceedings in equity are usually termed suits, as distinguished from the proceedings at common law, which are termed actions.

Summons, Writ of. The process used for the commencement of all action in the courts of law.

Supersedeas. A command to stay some ordinary proceedings at law, on good cause shown.

Sue. To prosecute in law.

Surety. Security against loss; a person bound for the faithful performance of a contract by another.

Suspend. To stop payment temporarily.

Syndicate. A number of capitalists who unite to dispose of a loan, or to conduct a great financial enterprise.

Tacit. That which is understood; implied.

Tare. An allowance for weight of box, case, bag, cask, etc., containing merchandise.

Tariff. A list of prices; duties on imports and exports.

Tax. A rate or sum of money imposed on persons or property for public use.

Tenancy. The holding of property under tenure.

Tenant. One who holds lands of another as a tenant for life, for years, in tail, etc.; it is a word extensively used in legal phraseology.

Tender. A legal tender is an unconditional offer to pay a debt, which, if refused, may be afterwards pleaded in bar to an action.

Tenement. Property held by a tenant; it comprises lands, houses, and every species of real property which may be holden.

Tenure. The system of holding lands in subordination to some superiors.

Testamentary Guardian. A person appointed by a father in his will to be the guardian of his child.

Testator or **Testatrix.** The maker of a will.

Teste. The clause at the bottom of a writ beginning with the word "witness," is so called.

Tenants in Common. Persons holding lands and tenements by several and distinct titles, and not by a joint title.

Title. The evidence of the right which a person has to the possession of property.

Time Draft. A draft maturing at a future specified time.

Tonnage. Weight of a ship's load; capacity of a vessel. Also a duty on ships estimated per ton.

Traverse. A plea which denies the truth of some part of the plaintiff's declaration in an action.

Treasure Trove. Any money, etc., found hidden under the earth the owner thereof being unknown.

Trespass. Any wrong or damage which is done by one man to another, whether it relates to his person or property, but it usually signifies a wrongful entry on another's premises.

Trial. The formal method of examining and adjudicating upon a question of fact in a court of law.

Trover. The form of action used to try a disputed question of property in goods or chattels, in which the plaintiff can only recover their estimated value, and not the goods or chattels themselves.

True Bill. The words indorsed upon an indictment by a grand jury, when satisfied that the charge against the offender is made out.

Trust. A trust exists where a party, called the cestui que trust, has a right in equity to the beneficial enjoyment of property, the legal ownership of which is vested in another, who is hence called a trustee.

Transact. To perform any act of business; to manage.

Transfer. To convey; to sell or alienate title.

Treasury. A place where public money is kept.

Trustee. One to whom some special trust is assigned.

Trade. A company of persons engaged in the same occupation; business of buying and selling.

Trade Discount. A deduction of a certain rate per cent. from the face of a bill made by wholesale houses and others in trade.

Trade-Mark. A distinguishing mark used by a manufacturer on his goods or labels.

Trunk Lines. Through lines of railroad from the Atlantic seaboard to Chicago or more western points.

Trust. A combination of manufacturers or dealers for the purpose of limiting production and advancing prices for their own benefit.

Umpire. A third person chosen to decide a matter in dispute left to arbitration, in case the arbitrators should not agree.

Under-Lease. A lease granted by one who is himself only a lessee of the premises under-let.

Under-Lessee. The person to whom an under-lease is granted.

Unliquidated Damages. Damages not fixed or ascertained, and which require therefore to be estimated by a jury.

Uncurrent. Not passing in common payment, as pounds, shillings, and pence in the United States.

Underwriter. An insurer; so called because he underwrites his name to the conditions of the policy.

Use. A right to the beneficial enjoyment of land nominally vested in another.

Usury. The extortion of unlawful gain; the taking more for the use of money than is allowed by law; but the usury laws in this country are now abolished, any rate of interest therefore may now be lawfully taken.

Usage of Trade. Custom, or the frequent repetition of the same act in business transactions.

Usance. A fixed time on bills of exchange; business habit generally acted upon from force of custom.

Value Received. The words usually, but unnecessarily, appearing in bills of exchange and promissory notes.

Valid. Of binding force; strong; effectual.

Value. The rate of worth or amount or price of a commodity.

Venditioni Exponas. A writ directed to the sheriff, commanding him to sell goods which he has taken possession of under a writ of *fieri facias*, and which remain in his hands unsold.

Vendor and Vendee. A vendor is the person who sells, and a vendee the person who buys, anything.

Venue. The county at which an action at law is intended to be tried.

Verdict. A verdict is the unanimous judgment or opinion of the jury on the issue of fact submitted to them.

Vend. To sell; to transfer for a pecuniary consideration.

Versus. Against.

Viva Voce. By word of mouth.

Voluntary Conveyance, or Settlement. A conveyance or settlement without any valuable consideration.

Voucher. A receipt or discharge.

Void. Having no binding force or effect.

Voidable. That which has some force or effect, but which, in consequence of some inherent quality, may be annulled or avoided.

Waifs. Stolen goods which the thief has thrown away or left behind him.

Ward. An infant under the guidance and protection of a guardian.

Warrant. An authority or precept from a justice, commanding the apprehension of an offender, or a search to be made for stolen goods.

Warrant of Attorney. An authority given by anyone to an attorney at law, to appear and plead for him; or to suffer judgment to pass against him, by confessing the action.

Warranty. As applied to goods and chattels, may be either expressed or implied; the implied warranty only extends to the title of the vendor. If that proves deficient, the purchaser may demand satisfaction from the seller.

Watercourse, Right of. A right to an uninterrupted flow of water.

Way, Right of. The right of going over another man's ground.

Wages. Compensation for services.

Waiver. The relinquishment or refusal to accept of a right.

Wares. Goods; merchandise; commodities.

Wash Trades. Pretended trading. Trades made on an open market by parties between whom there is a tacit or private understanding that they shall be void. Done with a view to influence prices and considered a reprehensible practice.

Watered Stock. An increase in capitalization without a corresponding increase in assets.

Wharfinger. The owner or keeper of a wharf.

Will. A will is the legal written declaration of a man's intentions of what he wills to be performed after his death with reference to the disposition of his property. It must be in writing, signed by the testator, and attested by two witnesses, who must not only be present and see the testator sign, but must themselves subscribe the will as witnesses in the presence of the testator and of each other. Without these formalities the will is invalid. A codicil is a kind of addendum or supplement to a will. Its execution and attestation must be attended with the same formalities as the will itself.

ST. PETER'S, ROME.

Book VII.

Religion, Education, Fine Arts.

Religion, Education, Fine Arts.

European Cathedrals. — Among the most noted and magnificent cathedrals in Europe are St. Peter's, in Rome; the cathedral of Cologne, and that of Milan; St. Mark's, in Venice; Westminster and Salisbury, in England; Rouen and Notre Dame, in France; Seville and Strasburg, in Spain and Germany, respectively. St. Paul's, in London, though architecturally much inferior to the others, is yet so noted as to deserve a brief description. It is built in the form of a cross, 514 feet long and 287 feet wide. The cost of the whole building, which is of Portland stone, was nearly $4,000,000, being the proceeds of a tax on the coal brought into the port of London during its erection. The edifice was built under the direction of Sir Christopher Wren, was thirty-five years in course of erection, and was commenced and finished under the same bishop, the same architect, and the same mason. The great bell of this cathedral is only tolled on the occasion of a death in the royal family. St. Peter's, at Rome, was commenced about the year 1503 by Julius II. under the direction of Bramante, but the present form of the basilica is due almost entirely to Michael Angelo. The interior is 613 feet in length, the height of the nave 152 1-2 feet; the length of the transepts is 446 1-2 feet; the interior diameter of the dome is 139 feet, the exterior 195 1-2 feet. The colonnades around the piazza inclose a space 787 feet in diameter, and are connected with the façade by two galleries 296 feet in length. The façade is 379 feet long, and 148 1-2 feet high, and contains five doors, which admit to the grand entrance, which occupies the whole width of the church, 468 feet long, 66 feet high, and 50 feet wide. The height from the pavement to the top of the cross is 476 feet. The Cologne cathedral is one of the noblest specimens of Gothic architecture in Europe. It is said to have had its origin in an erection by Archbishop Hildebold, during the reign of Charlemagne, in 814. Frederic the Red-bearded bestowed upon it, in 1162, the bones of the three holy kings, which he took from Milan, and this gift contributed greatly to the increase of its importance. The bones are retained as precious relics to this day, but the old structure was burned in 1248. According to some accounts the present cathedral was begun in the same year, but others fix the date of its commencement in 1270-'75. To whom the design of this noble building is to be ascribed is uncertain. The work was carried on, sometimes more actively, sometimes more slowly, till the era of the Reformation, when it was suspended; and during the subsequent centuries not only was nothing done to advance it, but what had been already executed, was not kept in repair. In the beginning of the present century, however, attention was directed to its unrivaled beauties, and the necessary funds to repair and complete it according to the original designs were raised. The body of the church measures 500 feet in length, and 230 feet in breadth; the towers are above 500 feet high. Since 1823 $4,500,000 have been expended on the building; the total cost of the whole is estimated at $10,000,000. The cathedral at Milan is also of Gothic architecture, but the façade is marred by classic doors and windows, and the altars within are in the same style. The edifice is nearly 500 feet long, and 250 feet wide through the transepts, and the height of the nave is about 150 feet. The central spire is more than 350 feet high. The throng of statues (some 4,500 in all) and the many pinnacles are marked features of the exterior.

The celebrated church of St. Sophia, at Constantinople, was originally built by the Emperor Constantine in 325-326, and is so called as being dedicated, not, as commonly supposed, to a saint of that name, but to *Hagia Sophia* (Holy Wisdom); that is, to the Eternal Wisdom of God, or the Logos, the second person of the Trinity. The church was twice destroyed and rebuilt, the present edifice having been built by the Emperor Justinian about 532. It may be described as a square of 241 feet, forming interiorly a Greek cross, and surrounded in the interior by a woman's choir or gallery, supported by magnificent pillars, for the most part borrowed from ancient buildings. In the center rises a dome, which is supported by two great semi-domes, the whole presenting a series of unexampled beauty. The height of the dome is 175 feet. The building is approached by a double porch, which is about 100 feet in depth. The whole of the interior was richly decorated with sculptured marble and mosaics. The building occupied seven years in its erection, and the history of the work and of the details of its material and construction is full of marvels. Ten thousand workmen are said to have been employed upon it. The materials were supplied from every part of the empire, and comprised remains of almost every celebrated temple of the ancient paganism. The sedilia of the priests and those of the patriarchs were of silver gilt. The dome of the tabernacle was of pure gold, and was surmounted by a gold cross weighing 75 pounds and incrusted with precious stones. All the sacred vessels and other apparatus were of gold. The altar cloths were embroidered with gold and pearls; and the altar itself was composed of a mass of molten gold, into which were thrown pearls, sapphires, diamonds, onyxes, and every other object which could raise its costliness to the highest imaginable degree. The total cost of the structure is stated by the ancient authorities at 320,000 pounds. Some regard this as pounds-weight of silver, others as of gold. If the latter, which is most generally adopted, the cost reaches the enormous sum of $65,000,000. On the capture of Constantinople by the Turks in 1453 St. Sophia was appropriated as a mosque, and has since been put to that use.

Easter.— The festival of the Resurrection of Christ probably derives its Teutonic name from the festival of the goddess Ostara — in Anglo-Saxon, Eastre — which the Saxons of old were wont to celebrate about the same season at which the Christian festival of Easter occurs. In the second century a dispute arose as to the proper time for celebrating Easter between the Eastern and Western Churches. The great mass of Eastern Christians celebrated Easter on the 14th day of the first month or moon, considering it to be equivalent to the Jewish Passover, when Christ was crucified. The Western Christians celebrated it on the Sunday after the 14th, holding that it was the commemoration of the Resurrection of Jesus. The Council of Nice, A. D. 325, decided in favor of the Western usage. At the time of the introduction of the Gregorian Calendar it was debated whether Easter should continue a movable feast or whether a fixed Sunday after the 21st of March should not be adopted. In deference to the ancient custom, the ecclesiastical authorities decided to adhere to the method of determining the day by the moon. It must be understood, however, that it is not the actual moon in the heavens, nor even the mean moon of the astronomers, that regulates the time of Easter, but an altogether imaginary moon, whose periods are so contrived that the new (calendar) moon always follows the real new moon — sometimes by two, or even three days. The effect of this is that the 14th of the calendar moon — which had from the time of Moses been considered full moon for ecclesiastical purposes — falls generally on the 15th or 16th of the real moon, and thus after the real full moon, which is generally on the 14th or 15th day. With this explanation, then, of what is meant by "full moon" viz., that it is the 14th day of the calendar moon, the rule is that Easter day is always the first Sunday after the Paschal full moon, i. e., the full moon which happens upon or next after the 21st of March; and if the full moon happens on a Sunday, Easter day is the Sunday after.

Apostles, Deaths of.— It is generally believed that only one of Christ's Apostles, John, escaped martyrdom. Matthew is supposed to have been slain with a sword in Ethiopia. James, son of Zebedee, was beheaded at Jerusalem. James, the brother of our Lord, was thrown from a pinnacle of the Temple and then beaten to death with a fuller's club. Philip was hanged up against a pillar at Hieropolis, a city of Phrygia. Bartholomew was flayed alive at Albanapolis, in Armenia. Andrew suffered martyrdom on a cross at Patræ, in Achaia. Thomas was run through the body with a lance at Coromandel, in the East Indies. Thaddeus was shot to death with arrows. Simon Zelotes was crucified in Persia. Peter was crucified, head downward it is said, during the Neronian persecution. Matthias was first stoned and then beheaded, and Paul was beheaded at Rome by the tyrant Nero. Judas Iscariot, after the betrayal of our Lord, hung himself.

Bible, English Translations of.— Between the eighth and tenth centuries portions of the Bible were translated into Anglo-Saxon by Aldhelin, Egbert, Bede, and others. In 1290 an English version of the Psalms was made. Wycliffe's version of the New Testament was finished in 1380, and a little later he completed the Old. The seven penitential Psalms were apparently printed in 1505. Before 1526 William Tyndale had completed an English translation of the New Testament. In the beginning of that year they were secretly conveyed to England from the Continent, where the translation had been made, where they were bought up and burned. The excellence of his translation is evidenced by the fact that in our present version a very large portion of the New Testament is taken *verbatim* from Tyndale's translation. In 1535 the first English version of the whole Bible was published by Miles Coverdale, a friend of Tyndale's, and was dedicated to Henry VIII. Between that year and 1557 several versions of the Bible were printed, but they were in the greater part revisions of Tyndale's previous work. The Geneva Bible, or, as best known, the Breeches Bible, appeared in 1557. It was translated by several English divines who had fled to Geneva to escape from the persecutions of Bloody Mary, and received the name of Breeches Bible on account of the rendering of Genesis iii, 7: "Then the eyes of both of them were opened, and they knew that they were naked, and they sewed fig-tree leaves together and made themselves *breeches.*" The Bishops' Bible was published in London in 1568. The text of this was compared with the original by eight bishops and seven other scholars of reputation, who appended their initials to their respective tasks. In 1582 appeared, at Rheims, in France, an English version of the New Testament, prepared by several Roman Catholic exiles, and in 1609-'10 a similar version of the Old Testament at Douay. They form the standard English Scriptures of the Roman Catholics, being generally known as the Douay Bible. In July, 1604, King James appointed fifty-four scholars to prepare a new version of the Bible. Only forty-seven accepted the appointment, and the result of their labors was the publication in 1610 of the version known as "King James's Bible," which has been in common use from that time to this, slightly modified by the revision prepared by the most learned English and American scholars a few years ago.

Benefit of Clergy.—Until the reign of Henry VI. all members of the clerical order were almost totally exempted from the jurisdiction and authority of the secular magistrate in respect of crimes and offenses. This was called "Benefit of the Clergy." If a priest or "clerk" happened to be imprisoned by the secular arm on a criminal charge, he was, on the demand of the bishop, instantly delivered up without any further inquisition — not to be let loose upon the community, it is true, but to be detained by the ordinary till he had either purged himself from the offense, or, having failed to do so, had been degraded. In the reign mentioned this was so far altered that the prisoner had first to be arraigned, but could arrest judgment by plea, declining the jurisdiction either before or after conviction. At first the test of admission to this singular privilege was the clerical dress and tonsure; but in course of time all who could read — a mark of great learning in those days — whether of the clergy or laity, were allowed the privilege. A layman, however, could only claim it once, and upon doing so was burned on the hand and discharged. He was then tried by the bishop, and usually acquitted, even though he had been previously convicted either by his country or his own confession. By this acquittal the offender was restored to his liberty, his credit, and his property — in short, in the eye of the law he became a new and innocent person. The test of reading was applied as follows: On conviction, the felon demanded his clergy, whereupon a book (commonly a Psalter) was put into his hand, which he was required to read, when the judge demanded of the bishop's commissary, *Legit ut clericus?* If the answer was simply *legit*, the prisoner was burned on the hand and discharged; but if it was *non legit*, he suffered the punishment due to his offense. During the reign of Queen Anne the benefit of clergy was extended to all persons convicted of clergyable offenses, whether they could read or not, but it was discretionary with the judge whether a fine or imprisonment was inflicted. The benefit of clergy was totally abolished during the reign of George IV.

Catacombs.— Those in Paris were originally quarries which had existed under the city from the earliest time. In 1774 the Council of State issued a decree for clearing the Cemetery of the Innocents, and for removing its contents, as well as those of other graveyards, into these quarries. These quarries — or catacombs, as they were called — were consecrated with great solemnity on April 7, 1786, and the work of removal from the cemeteries was immediately begun. The bones were brought at night in funeral cars, covered with a pall, and followed by priests chanting the service of the dead. At first the bones were heaped up without any kind of order except that those from each cemetery were kept separate; but in 1810, a regular system of arranging them was commenced, and the skulls and bones were built up along the wall. From the main entrance to the catacombs, which is near the Barriers d'Enfer, a flight of ninety steps descends, at whose foot galleries are seen branching in various directions. Some yards distant is a vestibule of octagonal form, which opens into a long gallery lined with bones from floor to roof. The arm, leg, and thigh bones are in front, closely and regularly piled, and their uniformity is relieved by three rows of skulls at equal distances. This gallery conducts to several rooms resembling chapels, lined with bones, variously arranged. One is called the "Tomb of the Revolution," another the "Tomb of Victims" — the latter containing the relics of those who perished in the early period of the Revolution and in the "massacre of September." It is estimated that the remains of fully 3,000,000 human beings lie in this receptacle. Owing to the unsafe condition of the roof, admission to the catacombs has been forbidden for years. Of the other catacombs in existence, the most celebrated are those on the Via Appia, at a short distance from Rome, where, it is believed, the early Christians were in the habit of retiring in order to celebrate their new worship in times of persecution. These catacombs consist of long, narrow galleries, usually about eight feet high and five feet wide, which twist and turn in all directions, very much resembling mines, and at irregular intervals into wide and lofty vaulted chambers. The graves, where are buried many of the saints and martyrs of the primitive church, were constructed by hollowing out a portion of the rock at the side of the gallery large enough to contain the body. The catacombs at Naples, cut into the Capo di Monte, resemble those at Rome, and evidently were used for the same purpose, being in many parts literally covered with Christian symbols. In one cf the large vaulted chambers there are paintings which have retained a freshness which is wonderful. Similar catacombs have been found at Palermo and Syracuse, and in Greece, Asia Minor, Syria, Persia, Egypt, and in Peru and other parts of South America.

Apocrypha, The.—In the earliest churches the word Apocrypha was applied with very different significations to a variety of writings; sometimes it was given those whose authorship and original form were unknown; sometimes to writings containing a hidden meaning; sometimes to those whose public use was not thought advisable. In this last signification it has been customary, since the time of Jerome, to apply the term to a number of writings which the Septuagint had circulated among the Christians, and which were sometimes considered as an appendage to the Old Testament, and sometimes as a portion of it. At the Council of Laodicea, 360 A. D., the Greek Church rejected all books except those in the present Protestant canon. In 474 Pope Gelasius convened a council of seventy bishops, which confirmed the opinion of Pope Innocent I., recognizing the Apocryphal books as sacred, and rejecting some of the doubtful books of the New Testament. The Council of Trent, 1545-'63, finally settled the question for the Roman Catholic Church, accepting the Apocrypha as a part of the sacred canon. The Protestant churches reject their use in public worship. It was customary at one time to bind up the Apocrypha between the authorized versions of the Old and New Testaments, though this has now ceased, and, as a consequence, this curious, interesting, and instructive part of Jewish literature is now known only to scholars.

Inquisition, The, was a tribunal in the Roman Catholic Church for the discovery, repression, and punishment of heresy, unbelief, and other offenses against religion. From the very first establishment of Christianity as the religion of the Roman empire, laws more or less severe existed, as in most of the ancient religions, for the repression and punishment of dissent from the national creed, and the Emperors Theodosius and Justinian appointed officials called "inquisitors," whose special duty it was to discover and to prosecute before the civil tribunals offenders of this class. For several centuries cases of heresy were tried before the ordinary courts, but in course of time the examination of those accused of this crime was handed over to the bishops. Special machinery for the trial and punishment of heretics was first devised in the eleventh and twelfth centuries against the various sects who had separated from the Church, and who became known under the general term of Albigenses. Heresy was then regarded as a crime against the state as well as the Church, and the civil, no less than the ecclesiastical, authorities were arrayed against those sects. The murder of a papal legate in 1205 gave a pretext for declaring against the Albigenses a war in which thousands perished, and in 1299 the Council of Toulouse decreed the "Inquisition" for their extermination. The searching out of heretics was first given to the bishops of the Church, but the Pope (Gregory IX.), fearing that these would not be active enough, transferred their work to the Dominican friars. A guild was also formed called the "Militia of Jesus Christ," whose object was to aid inquisitors in their work. The Church found the heretics, examined, and sentenced them, and then called in the civil authority to put its sentence into execution. The inquisitorial courts at first only held occasional sessions, but after 1248 they sat permanently. A person, if suspected of heresy or denounced as guilty, was liable to be arrested and detained in prison, only to be brought to trial when it might seem fit to his judges. The proceedings were conducted secretly. He was not confronted with his accusers, nor were their names, even, made known to him. The evidence of an accomplice was admissible, and the accused himself was liable to be put to torture, in order to extort a confession of guilt. The punishments to which, if found guilty, he was liable, were death by fire, as exemplified in the terrible auto-da-fé, or on the scaffold, imprisonment in the galleys for life or for a limited period, forfeiture of property, civil infamy, and in minor cases retraction and public penance.

Inquisition, Spanish.—The Inquisition was introduced in Spain in 1232, by Pope Gregory's appointment of the Dominicans of Aragon as inquisitors, and it ultimately came to be viewed by the people with most abject terror. At first it passed no sentence more severe than the confiscation of property, but toward the close of the fifteenth century, the zeal of Mendoza, the archbishop of Seville, gave a new impulse to the institution. At that time there was a real or pretended alarm lest the Jews and Moors in Spain should unite against the Christians. Bishop Mendoza proposed to King Ferdinand, in 1477, that an inquisition should be established in Castile, with the primary object of searching out the Jews who had relapsed into Judaism after having professed Christianity, or who simply feigned conversion. The Inquisitorial Court of Seville was established in September, 1480, in the person of two Dominican friars. Torquemada, another Dominican, appointed in 1483, was Grand Inquisitor for fifteen years. Under him three new tribunals of the Holy Office were erected at Cordova, Jaen, and Villa Real; afterwards a fifth was added to Toledo. These Tribunals were always popular with the lower orders and the clergy in Spain, but terrible in the eyes of the nobles and the rich middle class, who believed that they were often used by the Government as engines of political repression in order to diminish their influence. Ranke calls the Spanish Inquisition "a royal tribunal furnished with spiritual weapons." In 1492 an edict was issued for the banishment of all Jews refusing to embrace Christianity from Spain, chiefly on account of their alleged incorrigible obstinacy in persisting in the attempt to convert Christians to their own faith and instruct them in their rites. About a hundred thousand accordingly went into banishment.

The history of the Spanish Inquisition was written by Llorente, who was secretary to the tribunal of Madrid from 1790 to 1792. Although he is supposed to have possessed great opportunities for obtaining exact information, his estimate of the persons condemned to death is now considered very much exaggerated. The figures of Llorente include not only those condemned for heresy, but besides persons charged with many other crimes, such as polygamy, seduction, unnatural crime, smuggling, witchcraft, sorcery, imposture, etc., civil offenses within the jurisdiction of the Inquisition and punishable with death.

The celebrated *Autos-da-Fe* (Acts of the confession of the faith), says Möhler, "were as a rule bloodless. But few inquisitional processes terminated with the death of the accused." The *Auto*, speaking generally, was a form of reconciling culprits to the Church. Nevertheless the severities practiced by the tribunals were such that Rome frequently interfered. By the beginning of the seventeenth century, the Inquisition, having largely obliterated heresy in Spain, became more lenient; its efforts were then principally directed against heretical books, and occasionally decreed an execution. The jurisdiction of the Inquisition had been greatly restricted when Joseph Bonaparte abolished it in December, 1808. It was restored by Ferdinand VII. in 1814, but was again abolished by the Constitution of the Cortes in 1820. After the second restoration a tribunal was re-established at Valencia in 1826. It was finally abolished, however, in 1834, and in 1835 all its property was confiscated for the public debt.

Celibacy in the Roman Catholic Church.— Previous to the close of the fourth century there was no law nor uniformity of opinion regarding the celibacy of the Romish priests. About this time, however, Pope Siricius forbade priests to marry, and those who had married previous to ordination were commanded to put away their wives. Children born to a clergyman after ordination were declared by the Emperor Justinian to be illegitimate and incapable of inheritance. This doctrine was opposed by the Eastern Church, and in 692 it was condemned as heretical by the Council of Constantinople, and the marriage of priests has, therefore, always been sanctioned by the Orthodox Greek Church. Notwithstanding the action taken by the Romish Church, it was several centuries before celibacy was firmly established, and this was not accomplished until Pope Gregory VII., in the face of violent opposition in all countries, deposed all married priests and excommunicated all laymen who upheld them in the exercise of their spiritual functions. This decree was carried out with the utmost rigor, and brought about the result which the Church had been aiming at for centuries, and which still continues to be the canonical law.

Indulgences. — Originally, indulgences meant a release from the temporal penalties which remained due after the sin itself had been remitted by confession and absolution, and were granted during the first centuries of the Christian churches, not only by the pope, but by all bishops, to infirm persons or to those penitents who showed extraordinary contrition. An indulgence cannot be granted for unforgiven sin. It is not the remission of sin nor of the eternal punishment due to mortal sin, still less is it a permission to commit sin in the future. Before an indulgence can be gained, sin must have been previously remitted by repentance. Thus, instead of being an encouragement to sin, it is a strong motive to repentance. Many indulgences have been abrogated, or declared apocryphal by the Roman Catholic Church. The Council of Trent prohibited the "disreputable gains" made at some places at the expense of those who desired to obtain indulgences. The same council prescribes that all indulgences must be granted "gratis."

Cambridge, University of, is situated at the town of Cambridge, forty-eight miles northeast of London. The first regular society of students was that of Peter-House, founded in 1257. The history of the University, however, may be said to date from the opening of the twelfth century, but until the year mentioned there were no public halls or hostels, each student living in his own hired lodging. About 1257 the students began to live together in hostels, under the rule of a principal. These hostels were named after the saints to whom they were dedicated, the churches which they adjoined, or the persons who formerly built or possessed them. In the year 1280 there were as many as thirty-four, and some of them contained from twenty to forty masters of arts, and a proportionate number of younger students. These hostels were the beginning of what may be called the college system, which distinguishes the sister universities of Oxford and Cambridge from those of Edinburgh, London, and the Continent. All the royal and religious foundations, with one exception, which now constitute the University were endowed between the latter part of the thirteenth and the close of the sixteenth century. The governing body of the university is the senate; but, before being submitted to it, all university laws must be approved by the council, a body elected by the resident members of the senate. After the chancellor and high steward, the chief executive power is vested in the vice-chancellor, who is elected annually from the heads of colleges. There are three terms in this university — the Michaelmas, or October term; the Lent term, and the Easter term. To take an ordinary B.A. degree, a student must reside nine terms. The M.A. degree follows, without examination, about four years after. There are four classes of students — Fellow Commoners and Noblemen, Pensioners, Sizars and Subsizars, and the more distinguished, who are elected Scholars on the foundation of this college. The pensioners are the great body of students, are not on the foundation, and pay for their own commons, viz., dinners in halls, etc., and for their rooms. The sizars are poorer students, selected, however, by examination, who receive free commons and certain money payments, and are admitted at lower charges than the pensioners, but wear the same dress and are no longer subject to the performance of menial offices, as they once were. The scholars are elected, by examination, from the pensioners and sizars. They are on the foundation of the college, from which they receive certain emoluments. The fellows are subsequently elected from the scholars and the students who have distinguished themselves in the Tripos examinations. The University has forty professors, in addition to readers, demonstrators, and assistants. The tutor of the college is understood to be *in loco parentis* to his pupils, the dean has the oversight of "religion and morals," and instruction is given by college lecturers. The great prizes at the University are the Fellowships, of which there are about four hundred. The following is a list of the colleges and their founders: St. Peter's College or Peter-House, founded by Hugh de Balsham, Bishop of Ely, 1257; Clare College, founded under the name of University Hall by Richard Baden in 1326, was burned in 1338, and rebuilt and endowed by Elizabeth, Countess of Clare; Pembroke College, founded by the Countess of Pembroke, 1347; Gonville and Caius College, founded by Edward Gonville in 1348; Trinity Hall, founded by William Bateman, Bishop of Norwich, 1350; Corpus Christi or Benedict College, founded by the guilds of Corpus Christi and the Blessed Virgin, 1351; King's College, founded by Henry VI., 1441; Queens' College, founded by Margaret of Anjou, wife of Henry VI., 1446; St. Catherine's College or Hall, founded by Robert Wodelarke, provost of King's College, 1473; Jesus College, founded by John Alcock, Bishop of Ely, 1496; Christ College, founded by the Countess of Richmond, 1505; St. John's College, founded by the Countess of Richmond, 1511; Magdalene College, founded by Thomas, Baron Audley, of Walden, 1519; Trinity College, founded by Henry VIII., 1546; Emmanuel College, founded by Sir Walter Mildmay, 1584; Sidney Sussex College, founded by Lady Frances Sidney, 1598; Downing College, founded by Sir George Downing, 1800.

Oxford University is one of the two greatest seats of learning in Great Britain. It is situated at Oxford, fifty-two miles from London, and comprises twenty colleges and six halls — the latter for the residence of students. The colleges, their founders, and the dates thereof, are as follows: University College, founded by William of Durham, 1249; Balliol, by John Balliol and Devorgilla, his wife, between 1263 and 1268; Merton, by Walter de Merton, Bishop of Rochester, at Malden, in 1264, and removed to Oxford before 1274; Exeter, by Walter de Stapleton, Bishop of Exeter, 1314; Oriel, by Edward II., 1326; Queen's, by Robert Eglesfield, chaplain to Philippa, queen of Edward III., 1340; New, by William of Wykeham, Bishop of Winchester, 1386; Lincoln, by Richard Fleming, Bishop of Lincoln, 1427; All Souls', by Henry

Chichele, Archbishop of Canterbury, 1437; Magdalen, by William of Waynflete, Lord Chancellor, 1456; Brasenose, by William Smith, Bishop of Lincoln, 1509; Corpus Christi, by Richard Fox, Bishop of Winchester, 1516; Christ Church, by Henry VIII., 1546-'47; Trinity, by Sir Thomas Pope, 1554; St. John's, by Sir Thomas White, 1555; Jesus, by Queen Elizabeth, 1571; Wadham, by Nicholas Wadham, 1613; Pembroke, by James I., at the expense of Thomas Tisdale and Richard Wrightwick, 1620; Worcester, by Sir Thomas Cookes, 1714; Keble as a memorial to the Rev. John Keble, by public subscription, in 1870.

Adam and Eve.— To the Scriptural account of the creation and fall of Adam and Eve, the later Jewish writers in the Talmud have made many additions. According to them, the stature of Adam, when first created, reached to the heavens, while the splendor of his countenance surpassed that of the sun. The very angels stood in awe of him, and all creatures hastened to worship him. Then the Lord, in order to show the angels his power, caused a sleep to fall upon Adam, and removed a portion of every limb. He thus lost his vast stature, but remained perfect and complete. His first wife was Lilith, the mother of demons; but she fled from him, and afterward Eve was created for him. At the marriage of Adam and Eve angels were present, some playing on musical instruments, others serving up delicious viands, while the sun, moon, and stars danced together. The happiness of the human pair excited envy among the angels, and the seraph Sammael tempted them, and succeeded in leading them to their fall from innocence. According to the Koran, all the angels paid homage to Adam excepting Eblis, who, on account of his refusal, was expelled from Paradise. To gratify his revenge, Eblis seduced Adam and Eve, and they were separated. Adam was penitent, and lived in a tent on the site of the Temple of Mecca, where he was instructed in the divine commandments by the Archangel Gabriel. After two hundred years of separation, he again found Eve on Mount Arafat.

Celebrated Paintings.— It is generally agreed by art critics that Michael Angelo and Raphael stand at the head of the line of master painters. Conspicuous among the great paintings of the former are "The Last Judgment," "The Conversion of St. Paul," and "The Crucifixion of St. Peter"; and among those of the latter, "The Dispute Concerning the Sacrament," the "Madonna di Foligno," and the "Madonna del Pisce, or Virgin of the Fish." "The Last Judgment" is a large fresco-painting, sixty feet high by thirty feet wide, occupying the wall opposite the entrance of the Sistine Chapel, in the Vatican Palace at Rome. Over three hundred figures are represented in "the most violent attitudes and most admired disorder." "The Conversion of St. Paul" is another large fresco-painting in the Vatican. "The Crucifixion of Peter," also in the Vatican, is one of the last from the hands of Angelo. "The Dispute Concerning the Sacrament" is a fresco, representing, above, a convocation of the saints around the Almighty, the Saviour, and the Virgin, enveloped in heavenly glory, while beneath the ceremony of the Consecration of the Sacrament is depicted. This is found in the Camera della Segnatura of the Vatican. "The Madonna di Foligno," in the Vatican gallery, derives its name from the city of Foligno, which is represented in the background. The "Madonna del Pisce," now in the gallery at Madrid, Spain, represents the Virgin and Child enthroned, with St. Jerome on one side, and on the other an archangel with the young Tobit, who carries a fish, from which circumstance the name is derived. "The Madonna di San Sisto" is considered by many critics the best of Raphael's works. It is located in the gallery of Dresden, Germany, and represents the Madonna standing upon the clouds surrounded with glory, holding in her arms the eternal son. Saint Sixtus and Saint Barbara kneel at the sides. It was originally painted on wood, but has been transferred to canvas. The painting of "The Last Supper," by Leonardo da Vinci, is recognized as one of the masterpieces. It was originally painted, by order of the Duke of Milan, on the walls of the refectory in the Dominican convent of the Madonna della Grazie. Rubens' paintings of the "Descent from the Cross" and "Elevation of the Cross," at Antwerp, rank high as masterpieces. The "Adoration of the Trinity," by Albert Durer, at Vienna, and his two pictures containing life-size figures of Peter and John, Mark and Paul, presented to the Council of Nuremberg, Germany, are also very famous. The two pictures of Mary Magdalen are also among the most famous in the world — "La Bussendi Magdalina," by Corregio, now in the Dresden Gallery, and one by Guido Reni.

Venus, Statues of.— The Roman goddess of love and beauty, subsequently identified with the Greek Aphrodite, was a favorite subject of ancient sculptors. The most famous specimen still existing is the Venus de Medici, executed by Cleomenes, the Athenian, about 200 B. C., and generally admitted to be the finest relic of ancient art. It was dug up in several pieces, either at the villa of Hadrian, near Tivoli, or at the Portico of Octavia, in Rome, in the seventeenth century. After remaining for some time in the Medici Palace in Rome (whence its name) it was carried to Florence by Cosmo III., about 1680, where it is now preserved in the Uffizi Gallery. From the exquisite grace and symmetry of the figure it has become a sort of standard of excellence for the female form. The beautiful Venus de Milo is so called because it was found on the Island of Milo, or Melos, in the Grecian Archipelago. It is now in the Louvre, at Paris. Of modern statues, that by Canova is the most famous.

Buddhism.—The religion known as Buddhism is one of the oldest existing religions, and traces its origin back to Siddhartha or Buddha, a Hindoo prince. In Hindustan, the land of its birth, it has now little hold, except among the Nepaulese and some other northern tribes, but it bears full sway in Ceylon and over the whole eastern peninsula. It divides the adherence of the Chinese with the system of Confucius. It prevails also in Japan and north of the Himalayas. It is the religion of Thibet, and of the Mongolian population of Central Asia. Its adherents are estimated at 340,000,000. According to the Buddhist belief, when a man dies he is immediately born again, or appears in a new shape; and that shape may, according to his merit or demerit, be any of the innumerable orders of being composing the Buddhist universe, from a clod to a divinity. If his demerit would not be sufficiently punished by a degraded earthly existence — in the form, for instance, of a woman or a slave, of a persecuted or a disgusting animal, of a plant, or even of a piece of inorganic matter — he will be born in some one of the one hundred and thirty-six Buddhist hells situated in the interior of the earth. These places of punishment have a regular gradation in the intensity of the suffering and in the length of time the sufferers live, the least term of life being 10,000,000 years, the longest term being almost beyond the powers of even Indian notation to express. A meritorious life, on the other hand, secures the next birth either in an exalted and happy position on earth or as a blessed spirit, or even divinity, in one of the many heavens in which the least duration of life is about 10,000,000,000 years. But however long the life, whether of misery or bliss, it has an end, and at its close the individual must be born again, and may again be either happy or miserable. The Buddha himself is said to have gone through every conceivable form of existence on the earth, in the air and in the water, in hell and in heaven, and to have filled every condition in human life; and a great part of the Buddhist legendary literature is taken up in narrating his exploits when he lived as an elephant, as a bird, as a stag, and so on. A second Buddhist doctrine is embodied in the "Four Sublime Verities." The first asserts that pain exists; the second that the cause of pain is desire or attachment; the third that pain can be ended by *Nirvana;* and the fourth shows the way that leads to Nirvana, from simple faith to complete regeneration. Theoretically this religion has no priests, nor clergy, nor public religious rites. Every man is his own priest and confessor, and the monks are ascetics only for their own advancement in holy living; but in fact Buddhist countries swarm with priests or religious teachers, so reputed. The central object in a Buddhist temple, corresponding to the altar in a Roman Catholic church, is an image of the Buddha, or a dagoba or shrine containing his relics. Here flowers, fruit, and incense are daily offered, and processions are made, with singing of hymns. Of the relics of the Buddha, the most famous are the teeth, that are preserved with intense veneration in various places. The quantities of flowers used as offerings are prodigious. A royal devotee in Ceylon, in the fifteenth century, offered on one occasion 6,480,320 flowers at the shrine of the tooth, and at one temple it was provided that there should be offered "every day 100,000 flowers, and each day a different flower."

Eden, Garden of.— The question of the locality of the Garden of Eden, or of the exact sense in which the Mosaic narrative is to be understood, is involved in inexplicable mystery. Josephus and several of the Fathers conceived that Eden was a term denoting the entire region between the Ganges and the Nile. Calvin, Huet, Bochart, and Wells have, with slight differences of detail, concluded in favor of Kornah, in Babylonia, not far from the Persian Gulf; while Armenia, near the sources of the Tigris and Euphrates, and the region near Damascus, have been selected by other celebrated scholars. The modern German school of Biblical critics, convinced that the Hebrew account is traditional, and, in its present form, of very late composition, and impressed, beside, with the vast antiquity of the far East, have, almost without exception, sought the cradle of the human race in Bactria or Cashmere, or the region lying to the north of it, a part of which is to this day called Audyana, the Garden. The Mohammedans, it may also be mentioned, believe Eden to have been in one of the seven heavens — some say the moon — and that the expulsion from Paradise consisted in Adam being cast down upon the earth after the fall. The endeavor to positively identify the river system of Eden with anything known at present is useless. There is no river on the face of the globe of which the Euphrates and Tigris (Hiddekel) are separate "heads," as they are said to be in the second chapter of Genesis; for, although the Euphrates and Tigris *now* unite for a short space on their way to the Persian Gulf, yet until the time of Alexander the Great they kept entirely distinct courses, and therefore it has been assumed that the Deluge completely altered the physical character of the region denoted by the term Eden. This was Luther's notion, to which, however, it has been objected that the narrative in Genesis is so worded as to convey the idea that the countries and rivers spoken of were existing in the time of the historian. Besides, the science of geology has thrown so much doubt on the universality of a deluge so late as the period assigned to Noah that it is hazardous to argue on the hypothesis of any extensive physical changes having taken place since the first appearance of man on the planet — at least if that be dated only some six thousand years back. In all the theories which have been advanced regarding the location of Eden two things have not been explained by anyone; these are the statement that the four rivers flow from one river, and the river Pison "compasseth the whole land of Havilah." Until these are solved the location of the Garden of Eden will continue to remain a mystery.

Diet of Worms was an assembly convoked by Emperor Charles V., for the purpose of considering state affairs, and principally the course to be pursued toward the Reformation and Martin Luther. It was composed of the princes and other leading representatives of the several states of the German Empire. Luther appeared before this august body, and his defense of himself and his followers against the charge of heresy was dignified and eloquent, and compelled the admiration of the assembly and many of his former foes. He was allowed to leave the city under escort, and at the instigation of his friend, the Elector of Saxony, who feared that he might be assassinated if he continued in active life, he was taken to the Castle of Wartburg, where he remained, virtually a prisoner, for about one year. When his adherents had become numerous enough and strong enough for him to advocate his principles without fear of molestation, he was restored to liberty.

Confucianism is termed a religion, but it ought rather to be regarded as a system of social and political life, built upon a slight foundation of philosophy. It contains no trace of a personal God. There are, indeed, a number of allusions to a certain heavenly agency or power — Shang-te — whose outward emblem is Tien, or the visible firmament; but this Shang-te, in the opinion of the most enlightened Chinese scholars, is nothing more than a verbal personification of "the ever-present Law and Order and Intelligence which seem to breathe amid the wonderful activities of physical creation, in the measured circuit of the seasons, in the alternation of light and darkness, in the ebb and flow of tides, and in the harmonious and majestic revolutions of the heavenly bodies." Confucius lived about 550 B. C. He strove to direct the attention of men to the duties of social and political life, and Confucianism is epitomized in the following words of the great teacher: "I teach you nothing but what you might learn yourselves, viz., the observance of the three fundamental laws of relation between sovereign and subject, father and child, husband and wife, and the five capital virtues — universal charity, impartial justice, conformity to ceremonies and established usages, rectitude of heart and mind, and pure sincerity." Confucianism appeals to "practical" men. It lauds the present world; rather doubts, than otherwise, the existence of a future one; and calls upon all to cultivate such virtues as are seemly in citizens — industry, modesty, sobriety, gravity, decorum, and thoughtfulness.

Millennium. — The idea of the millennium, literally a thousand years' time, originated proximately in the Messianic expectation of the Jews; but more remotely, it has been conjectured, in the Zoroastrian doctrine of the final triumph of Ormuzd over Ahriman, and was connected by the Christians with the second coming of Christ. The notion of a golden age, preserved by the converts from heathenism to Christianity, as well as the oppression and persecution to which they were long subjected by the state authorities, were naturally calculated to develop and strengthen such hopes. The chief basis of the millennium idea in Judaism, as well as in Christianity, however, is the ardent hope for a visible Divine rule upon earth, and the identification of the Church with that of which it is merely a symbol. In the Mosaic account of creation we find the primitive ground for making the victorious era of the Church last a thousand years. By a strictly literal interpretation of the 4th verse of the 90th Psalm it was supposed that a day of God was arithmetically equal to a thousand years; hence the six days of creation were understood to indicate that the earth would pass through 6,000 years of labor and suffering, to be followed by a seventh day — that is, 1,000 years of rest and happiness. In the book of Revelation this view is presented. Still, the rabbinical traditions differ widely among themselves as to the duration of the happy period During the civil and religious wars in France and England the belief in millennianism was prominent. The Fifth-monarchy men of Cromwell's time were millenarians of the most exaggerated and dangerous sort, and marked by extreme arrogance Their peculiar tenet was that the millennium *had* come and *they* were the saints who were to inherit the earth. Great eagerness and not a little ingenuity have been exhibited by many persons in fixing a date for the commencement of the millennium. The celebrated theologian Johann Albrecht Bengel asserted, from a study of the prophecies, that the millennium would begin in 1836. This date was long popular. Swedenborg held that the last judgment took place in 1757, and that the new Church, or "Church of the New Jerusalem," as his followers designate themselves — in other words, the millennium era — then began. In America considerable agitation was excited by the preaching of one William Miller, who fixed the second advent of Christ about 1843. Of late years the most noted millenarian was Dr. John Cummings of England, who originally placed the end of the present dispensation in 1866 or 1867; but as the time drew near without any millennial symptoms, he was understood to have modified his views considerably, and came to the belief that the beginning of the millennium will not differ so much, after all, from the years immediately preceding it as people commonly suppose.

Ecole Polytechnique, a celebrated military academy of France, established in 1794 through the instrumentality of M. Lamblardie, director of the *Ponts et Chaussées*. The academy was first called the *Ecole Centrale des Travaux Publics;* but in the following year, 1795, the name was changed to *Ecole Polytechnique*, and numerous alterations were made in its organization. It was dissolved in 1816, again in 1830, and again in 1832, on account of the impetuous way in which the scholars mixed themselves up with the political disturbances of those years; but it was reestablished on each occasion, after the restoration of tranquillity. Candidates are admitted by competitive examination, which takes place yearly. To be eligible as a candidate the youth must be French, and must be more than sixteen and less than twenty years of age before the first of January following; but soldiers are admissible up to twenty-five, provided they can give proof of service in the regular army. The course of instruction lasts for two years, when graduates have the privilege of choosing, from the various public services supplied from this school, the particular branch they wish to enter. The school was last reorganized by a decree of the 15th of April, 1873.

Benedictines, as the order of monks were called who followed the rule of St. Benedict, are regarded as the main agents in the spread of Christianity, civilization, and learning in the west. At one time the order is said to have had as many as 37,000 monasteries, and counted among their branches the great Order of Clugny, founded about 910; the still greater Order of the Cistercians, founded in the following century; the congregations of Monte Casino in 1408, of St. Vanne in 1600, and of St. Maur on the Loire in 1627. All the Benedictine houses in France were affiliated to this last congregation. Among the monks of St. Maur were many noted scholars, and the services they rendered to literature it would be difficult to overestimate. At the Revolution in 1792 the Benedictines were suppressed in France and their splendid conventual buildings were destroyed, but the order was revived later. Most of the richest abbeys and all the cathedral priories (excepting Carlisle) in England belonged to the Benedictines, and they had numerous monasteries in Scotland. The Benedictines gained great distinction in both Italy and Germany — in the former as literati, jurists, and physicians, and in the latter as promoters of education and as the founders of mediæval scholasticism. As early as 1354 this order could boast of having numbered among its followers 24 popes, 200 cardinals, 7,000 archbishops, 15,000 bishops, 1,560 canonized saints, and 5,000 holy persons judged worthy of canonization, besides 20 empresses, 47 kings, above 50 queens, 20 sons of emperors, 48 sons of kings, 100 princesses, and an immense number of the nobility. In the fifteenth century the order had 15,107 monasteries, of which only 5,000 were left after the Reformation, and there are now not more than 800. They were commonly styled the "Black Monks" from their dress, a long black gown with a cowl or hood of the same, and a scapulary. The rule of St. Benedict was much less severe than that which the eastern ascetics followed. Besides implicit obedience to their superiors, the Benedictines were to shun laughter, to hold no private property, to live sparely, to exercise hospitality, and, above all, to be industrious.

ARCHITECTURE.

Architecture, or the art of planning and raising edifices, appears to have been among the earliest inventions. The first habitations of men were such as nature afforded, with but little labor on the part of the occupant, and sufficient to supply his simple wants — grottoes, huts, and tents. In early times, the country of Judea, which is mountainous and rocky, offered cavernous retreats to the inhabitants, who accordingly used them instead of artificial places of shelter. From various passages in scripture, it appears that these caves were often of great extent, for, in the sides of the mountain of Engedi, David and six hundred men concealed themselves. In the course of time, art was employed to fashion the rude cavernous retreats, and to excavate blocks by which rude buildings were compiled in more convenient situations. The progress of architecture, however, from its first dawn, differed in almost every different locality. Whatever rude structure the climate and materials of any country obliged its early inhabitants to adopt for their temporary shelter, the same structure, with all its prominent features, was afterward kept up by their refined and opulent posterity.

From the cause now mentioned the Egyptian style of building had its origin in the cavern and mound; the Chinese architecture, with its pavilion roofs and pointed minaret, is molded from the Tartar tent; the Grecian is derived from the wooden cabin; and the Gothic from the bower of trees. It is evident that necessity as much as choice or chance led to the adoption of the different kinds of edifices.

After mankind had learned to build houses, they commenced the erection of temples to their gods, and these they made still more splendid than private dwellings. Thus architecture became a fine art, which was first displayed on the temples, afterward on the habitations of princes and public buildings, and at last became a universal want in society.

Traces of these eras of advancement in the art of erecting buildings are found in various quarters of the globe, especially in Eastern countries, where the remains of edifices are discovered of which fable and poetry can alone give any account. The most remarkable of these vestiges of a primitive architecture are certain pieces of masonry in the island of Sicily, as well as in some other places, called the works of the Cyclops, an ancient and fabulous race of giants, mentioned by Homer in his Odyssey. By whom these walls were actually erected is unknown.

Of the progressive steps from comparative rudeness to elegance of design, history affords no certain account, and we are often left to gather facts from merely casual notices. The most ancient nations known to us among whom architecture had made some progress where the Babylonians, whose most celebrated buildings were the temple of Belus, the palace and the hanging gardens of Semiramis; the Assyrians, whose capital, Nineveh, was rich in splendid buildings; the Phœnicians, whose cities, Sidon, Tyre, Aradus, and Sarepta, were adorned with equal magnificence; the Israelites, whose temple was considered as a wonder of architecture; the Syrians and the Philistines. No architectural monument of these nations has, however, been transmitted to us; but we find subterraneous temples of the Hindoos, hewn out of the solid rock, upon the islands Elephanta and Salsette, and in the mountains of Elora. These temples may be reckoned among the most stupendous ever executed by man. The circuit of the excavations is about six miles. The temples are 100 feet high, 145 feet long, and 62 feet wide. They contain thousands of figures, appearing, from the style of their sculpture, to be of ancient Hindoo origin. Everything about them, in fact, indicates the most persevering industry in executing one of the boldest plans.

Egyptian Architecture. — All the architectural remains of ancient times sink into insignificance when compared with those of Egypt. The obelisks, pyramids, temples, palaces, and other structures of this country, are on the grandest scale, and such as could only have been perfected by a people considerably advanced in refinement. The elementary features of Egyptian architecture were chiefly as follows: 1. Their walls were of great thickness, and sloping on the outside. This feature is supposed to have been derived from the mud walls, mounds, and caverns of their ancestors. 2. The roofs and covered ways were flat, or without pediments, and composed of blocks of stone, reaching from one wall or column to another. The principle of the arch, although known to the Egyptians, was seldom if ever employed. 3. Their columns were numerous, close, short, and very large, being sometimes ten or twelve feet in diameter. They were generally without bases, and had a great variety of capitals, from a simple square block, ornamented with hieroglyphics, or faces, to an elaborate composition of palm leaves, not unlike the Corinthian capital. 4. They used a sort of concave entablature or cornice, composed of vertical flutings or leaves, and a winged globe in the center. 5. Pyramids, well known for their prodigious size, and obelisks, composed of a single stone, often exceeding seventy feet in height, are structures peculiarly Egyptian. 6. Statues of enormous size, sphinxes carved in stone, and sculptures in outline of fabulous deities and animals, with innumerable hieroglyphics, are the decorative objects which belong to this style of architecture.

The main character of Egyptian architecture is that of great strength with irregularity of taste. This is observable in the pillars of the temples, the parts on which the greatest share of skill has been lavished. The temple of Karnak is an example.

In these columns we may notice that sturdiness is the prevailing characteristic. The design has been the support of a great weight, and that without any particular regard to proportion or elegance, either as a whole or in parts. When assembled in rows or groups, the columns had an imposing effect, because, from their height and thickness, they filled the eye and induced the idea of placid and easy endurance.

Grecian Architecture.—From Egypt, the architectural art spread to Greece, where it passed from the gigantic to the chaste and elegant. The period in which it flourished in the greatest perfection was that of Pericles, about 440 before Christ, when some of the finest temples at Athens were erected. After this, it declined with other arts, and was carried to Rome, where, however, it never attained the same high character.

Aided doubtless by the examples of Egyptian art, the Greeks gradually improved the style of architecture, and originated those distinctions which are now called the "Orders of Architecture." By this phrase is understood certain modes of proportioning and decorating the column and its entablature. They were in use during the best days of Greece and Rome, for a period of six or seven centuries. They were lost sight of in the dark ages, and again revived by the Italians at the time of the restoration of letters. The Greeks had three orders, called the Doric, Ionic, and Corinthian. These were adopted and modified by the Romans, who also added two others called the Tuscan and Composite.

The Doric Order.—This is the earliest of the Greek orders, and we see in it a noble simplicity on which subsequent orders were founded. The shaft of the Doric column had no base, ornamental or otherwise, but rose directly from the smooth pavement or stylobate. It had twenty flutings, which were superficial, and separated by angular edges. The perpendicular outline was nearly straight. The Doric capital was plain, being formed of a few annulets or rings, a large echinus, and a flat stone at top called the abacus. The architrave was plain; the frieze was intersected by oblong projections called triglyphs, divided into three parts by vertical furrows, and ornamented beneath by guttæ, or drops. The spaces between the triglyphs were called metopes and commonly contained sculptures. To have a just idea of the Doric, therefore, we must go back to the pure Grecian era. The finest examples are those of the temple of Theseus and the Parthenon at Athens. The Parthenon, which is now a complete ruin, has formed a model in modern architecture. It was built by the architect Ictinus, during the administration of Pericles, and its decorative sculptures are supposed to have been executed under direction of Phidias. The platform or stylobate consists of three steps, the uppermost of which is 227 feet in length and 101 in breadth. The number of columns is eight in the portico of each front, and seventeen in each flank, besides which there is an inner row of six columns, at each end of the cell.

The Ionic Order.—In this order the shaft begins to lengthen, and to possess a degree of ornament, but still preserving a great degree of simplicity of outline. In the best examples, as in the Parthenon, the column was eight or nine diameters in height. It had a base often composed of a torus, a scotia, and a second torus, with intervening fillets. This is called the Attic base. Others were used in different parts of Greece. The capital of this order consisted of two parallel double scrolls, called volutes, occupying opposite sides, and supporting an abacus, which was nearly square, but molded at its edges. These volutes have been considered as copied from ringlets of hair, or perhaps from the horns of Jupiter Ammon. The Ionic entablature consisted of an architrave and frieze, which were continuous or unbroken, and a cornice of various successive moldings, at the lower part of which was often a row of dentils, or square teeth. The examples at Athens of the Ionic order were the temple of Erectheus, and the temple on the Ilissus, both now destroyed. Modern imitations are common in public edifices.

The Corinthian Order.—This was the lightest and most highly decorated of the Grecian orders. The base of the column resembled that of the Ionic, but was more complicated. The shaft was often ten diameters in height, and was fluted like the Ionic. The capital was shaped like an inverted bell, and covered on the outside with two rows of leaves of the plant acanthus, above which were eight pairs of small volutes. Its abacus was molded and concave on its sides, and truncated at the corners, with a flower on the center of each side. The entablature of the Corinthian order resembled that of the Ionic, but was more complicated and ornamented, and had, under the cornice, a row of large oblong projections, bearing a leaf or scroll on their under side, and called modillions. No vestiges of this order are now found in the remains of Corinth, and the most legitimate example at Athens is in the choragic monument of Lysicrates. The Corinthian order was much employed in the subsequent structures of Rome and its colonies. The finest Roman example of this order is that of three columns in the Campo Vaccina, at Rome, which are commonly considered as the remains of the temple of Jupiter Stator.

Caryatides.— The Greeks sometimes departed so far from the strict use of the orders as to introduce statues, in the place of columns, to support the entablature. Statues of slaves, heroes, and gods appear to have been employed occasionally for this purpose. The principal specimen of this kind of architecture which remains is in a portico called Pandroseum, attached to the temple of Erectheus at Athens, in which statues of Carian females, called Caryatides, are substituted for columns.

Roman Architecture.— Roman architecture possessed no originality of any value; it was founded on copies of the Greek models, and these were modified to suit circumstances and tastes. The number of orders was augmented by the addition of the Tuscan and Composite.

Tuscan Order.— This order is not unlike the Doric, and is chaste and elegant. The shaft had a simple base, ornamented with one torus, and an astragal below the capital. The proportions were seven diameters in height. Its entablature, somewhat like the Ionic, consisted of plain running surfaces.

The Composite Order.— Of this there were various kinds, differing less or more either in the ornaments of the column or in the entablature. The simplest of this hybrid order was that which combines parts and proportions of the Doric, the Ionic, and the Tuscan.

The temples of the Romans sometimes resembled those of the Greeks, but often differed from them. The Pantheon, which is the most perfectly preserved temple of the Augustan age, is a circular building, lighted only from an aperture in the dome, and having a Corinthian portico in front. The amphitheater differed from the theater, in being a completely circular or rather elliptical building, filled on all sides with ascending seats for spectators, and leaving only the central space, called the arena, for the combatants and public shows. The Coliseum is a stupendous structure of this kind. The aqueducts were stone canals, supported on massive arcades, and conveying large streams of water for the supply of cities. The triumphal arches were commonly solid oblong structures ornamented with sculptures, and open with lofty arches for passengers below. The edifice of this kind most entire in the present day is the triumphal arch of Constantine, at Rome.

The basilica of the Romans was a hall of justice, used also as an exchange or place of meeting for merchants. It was lined on the inside with colonnades of two stories, or with two tiers of columns, one over the other. The earliest Christian churches at Rome were sometimes called basilicæ, from their possessing an internal colonnade. The monumental pillars were towers in the shape of a column on a pedestal, bearing a statue on the summit, which was approached by a spiral staircase within. Sometimes, however, the column was solid. The thermæ, or baths, were vast structures, in which multitudes of people could bathe at once. They were supplied with warm and cold water and fitted up with numerous rooms for purposes of exercise and recreation.

Italian Architecture.— After the dismemberment of the Roman empire, the arts degenerated so far that a custom became prevalent of erecting new buildings with the fragments of old ones, which were dilapidated and torn down for the purpose. This gave rise to an irregular style of building, which continued to be imitated, especially in Italy, during the dark ages. It consisted of Grecian and Roman details, combined under new forms, and piled up into structures wholly unlike the unique originals. Hence the names Græco-Gothic and Romanesque architecture have been given to it. After this came the Italian style, which was professedly a revival of the classic styles of Greece and Rome, but adapted to new manners and wants — a kind of transition from ancient to modern times. Its great master was Andrea Palladio, a Venetian (born 1518, died 1580).

There are considerable variety and beauty in the foliate and other enrichments of an architectural character in many structures in Italy, but very little ornament enters into the columnar composition of Italian architecture. Friezes, instead of being sculptured, are swollen; the shafts of columns are very seldom fluted, and their capitals are generally poor in the extreme; moldings are indeed sometimes carved, but not often; rustic masonry, ill-formed festoons, and gouty balustrades for the most part supply the place of chaste and classic ornaments.

The Chinese Style.— The ancient Tartars and wandering shepherds of Asia appear to have lived from time immemorial in tents, a kind of habitation adapted to their erratic life. The Chinese have made the tent the elementary feature of their architecture; and of their style anyone may form an idea by inspecting the figures which are depicted upon common china ware. Chinese roofs are concave on the upper side, as if made of canvas instead of wood. A Chinese portico is not unlike the awnings spread over shop windows in summer time. The veranda, sometimes copied in dwelling houses, is a structure of this sort. The Chinese towers and pagodas have concave roofs, like awnings, projecting over their several stories. Such structures are built with wood or brick; stone is seldom employed.

The Saracenic, Moorish, and Byzantine Styles.— The Arabs, or Saracens, as they are more usually called, and the Moors, introduced into Spain certain forms of architecture which differed considerably from the Grecian in appearance, though founded on its remains in Asia and Africa.

The chief peculiarity of this architecture was the form of the arch; the Saracens are understood to have made it of greater depth than width, thus constituting more than half a circle or ellipse, and therefore unphilosophical and comparatively insecure; while the Moorish style was principally distinguished by arches in the form of a horseshoe or a crescent.

We associate with these styles another, which arose at Constantinople, called the Byzantine, likewise formed on the remains of Grecian art, and partaking of a slightly Eastern character. It became known in Western Europe along with the Lombard, another degenerate Grecian style, about the ninth and tenth centuries.

Saxon Style.— This style commenced at the establishment of Christianity among the Saxons in the sixth century, and is called Saxon from its having prevailed during the reigns of the Saxon and Norman kings in England.

Gothic or Pointed Style.— The term Gothic is a modern error, which, being now impossible to correct, is suffered to remain as the generally distinguishing appellation of the kind of architecture possessing pointed arches. This style originated in Germany about the middle of the thirteenth century, and was zealously pursued as the leading fashion for ecclesiastical structures all over Europe. Executed by a class of skilled artisans, who wandered from country to country, the finest specimens of the pointed style are the cathedrals of Strasburg, Cologne, and Antwerp, and the splendid abbeys of Melrose and Westminster.

In this fanciful and picturesque style of architecture, the slender columns, always united in groups, rise to a lofty height, resembling the giants of the grove, in whose dark shade the ancient Teuton used to build his altar. In the obscure depth of the dome, the mind is awakened to solemn devotional feelings.

When the circular arch totally disappeared in 1220, the early English style commenced. The windows of this style were at first very narrow in comparison with their height; they were called lancet shaped, and were considered very elegant; two or three were frequently seen together, connected by dripstones. In a short time, however, the windows became wider, and divisions and ornaments were introduced. Sometimes the same window was divided into several lights, and frequently finished at the top by a light in the form of a lozenge, circle, trefoil, or other ornament.

About the year 1300, the architecture became more ornamental, and from this circumstance received the name of the decorated English style, which is considered the most beautiful for ecclesiastical buildings.

The transition from the decorated to the florid, or perpendicular, style was very gradual. Ornament after ornament was added, till simplicity disappeared beneath the extravagant additions; and about the year 1380 the architecture became so overloaded and profuse that it obtained the title of florid, which by some persons is called the perpendicular, because the lines of division run in upright or perpendicular lines from top to bottom, which is not the case in any other style.

Norman, Tudor, and Modern Gothic. — Throughout England may be seen many aged castles, some still in a state of good preservation, but the greater number in ruins, and occupying, with their picturesque remains, the summit of a rising ground or rocky precipice. These castles are of a style which prevailed during the feudal ages in Europe, and was brought to England by the Normans, who erected them as fastnesses, into which they might retire and oppress the country at pleasure.

The feudal castles in England, like those on the Rhine, consisted for the most part of a single strong tower, or keep, the walls of which were from six to ten feet thick, and the windows only holes of one or two feet square, placed at irregular intervals. The several floors were built on arches, and the roof was flat or battlemented, with notches in the parapet, from which the inhabitants or retainers of the chieftain might defend themselves with instruments of war. The accommodations for living were generally mean, and what would now be called uncomfortable. Around or in front of the main tower there was usually a courtyard, protected by a high wall, and the arched entrance was carefully secured by a falling gate or portcullis. Outside, there was in many cases a regular wet ditch or fosse. Castles of greater magnitude consisted of two or more towers and inner buildings, including a chapel and offices for domestics, and stables for horses and other animals. Some of them were on a great scale, and possessed considerable grandeur of design.

As society advanced and civil tranquillity was established, these military strengths gradually assumed a character of greater elegance and less the appearance of defense. The wet ditch disappeared, and was superseded by a lawn or shrubbery. Instead of the drawbridge and portcullis, there was a regular approach and gate of ordinary construction. The windows became larger, and were fitted with glass frames, and stone was abandoned for the greater comfort of wooden floors. Instead, also, of a bare region around, in which no foe might lurk, gardens were established, and a long avenue of trees led to the front of the modernized mansion. In some instances the pepper-box turrets at the upper corners of the building remained. Of the class of structures that sprang up in this period of transition, which we may refer in England to the fifteenth and sixteenth and in Scotland to the seventeeth centuries, there are several highly interesting remains. These edifices of the nobility and gentry were no longer called castles; they took the name of halls, and as such had attained so great a pitch of magnificence in the reigns of Henry VIII. and Elizabeth, as to have subsequently given a name to a new style — the Tudor or Elizabethan. Latterly, and with no very distinct reference to any particular period, this remarkable fashion of building has been pretty generally called the old English style of architecture. One of the best existing specimens of the Tudor era of architecture is Haddon Hall, in Derbyshire, the property of the Duke of Rutland.

Modern British Architecture.— During the sixteenth century, an extraordinary effort was made in Italy to restore the purity of Grecian architecture; and in this attempt Palladio was followed by the not less eminent Michael Angelo Buonaroti, who, at an advanced age, in 1546, undertook the continuation of the building of St. Peter's at Rome, a work on which the greatest splendors of the Italian style are lavished. Into England, this revived taste for the Grecian was introduced at the beginning of the seventeenth century by Inigo Jones, to whose contemptuous observations on the German or pointed style the term Gothic has been traced; and after his decease, the Grecian, or more properly the Italianized Grecian, was perpetuated on a scale still more extensive by Sir Christopher Wren. The edifices erected by this great master are characterized by the finest taste, and his spires in particular are models of elegance. The greatest work of Wren was St. Paul's Cathedral in London, in which the Italian is seen in all its glory.

The eighteenth century was an era of decline in architectural taste. Every other style merged in that of a spiritless and often mean Græco-Italian, out of which the architects of the nineteenth century have apparently had a difficulty to emerge. Latterly, there has been a revival in England of a purer kind of Grecian, and also, as we have already said, of old English, and the Gothic or pointed style, and in most instances with good effect. It is only to be lamented that, by the manner in which state patronage is distributed in this branch of the fine arts, some of the largest and most expensive structures — Buckingham Palace and the National Gallery, for example — have been erected on the poorest conceptions of the Grecian style, and with a general effect far from pleasing. In Paris there now exist some modern structures after correct Grecian models, which cannot be too highly praised; we would, in particular, instance the building called the Madeleine, the Bourse, and the interior of the church of St. Genevieve, which are exceedingly worthy of being visited by young and aspiring architects from Britain. Of the superb buildings springing up on all sides of this vast continent, it is unnecessary to speak. While those already in existence, notably in Washington, are admirable copies of the great Greek and Roman periods, the so-called Queen Anne is now the especial craze.

For palatial and other secular edifices in England, the Renaissance for the most part was in favor in the earlier part of this century. The attempt of Stuart and others in favor of Greek art had but little influence upon architecture, while the effort of Scott and others, especially Ruskin, to bias the public mind in the direction of the Gothic has succeeded far beyond all efforts of the same kind in other countries. In churches and educational institutions, it found especial favor, and, in 1836, it was decided that the legislative halls of the Empire should be rebuilt in this style, according to the plans of Sir Charles Barry. These contemplated a Gothic, rich but not ornate, with square supporting towers at certain points, flanked, like the walls, with massive buttresses. The New Palace of Westminster, as it is called, covers eight acres and contains upwards of five hundred apartments clustered around eleven open quadrangles or courts. The edifice is of gray limestone, and is not only one of the noblest structures of this century, but a most successful attempt to secularize this truly northern style of architecture.

Architecture in the United States. — During the Colonial period of the United States there was neither time nor opportunity for the practice of the fine arts. When the Revolution was over, however, Congress in spite of heavy debt proceeded to lay out a National Capital and erect national buildings. These latter were the first to receive serious architectural treatment, and until recently were, together with the state capitols, in what may be called a classic style, because they had porticoes with columns and other features of the ancient orders.

The Capitol at Washington, the inception of which belongs to the last century, is unquestionably the grandest pile in that city, and probably the most monumental of United States buildings. Notwithstanding its conventionally classic style it is an edifice of which a great nation may be proud, majestic both within and without, and gaining in effect from its position on a commanding site. The corner stone of the Capitol was laid in 1793. It is of the Renaissance, and consists of two stories rising from a lofty rustic basement. The ground plan is a central pavilion with north and south wings. The principal façade is on the east side, where a portico of Corinthian columns thirty feet in height fronts the pavilion, while pilasters of the same order are continued along the wings. The eight middle columns project so as to admit of another inner row, and these sixteen columns support a noble pediment adorned with a bas-relief. The subject is allegorical, Liberty attended by Hope and Justice, and is said to have been designed by John Quincy Adams. The approach to this imposing portico is by a flight of broad marble steps. The central portion of the edifice is, for the most part, occupied by a circular apartment, measuring about one hundred feet in diameter and height, and known as the Rotunda. It is ornamented with paintings and bas-reliefs illustrative of our national history. The paintings are separated from one another by gilded pilasters, which rise to the dome forming the roof. The dome compares well with those that are famous in the world, and, taken as a whole, the Capitol is more stately than the Houses of Parliament, and is open to as little criticism as the buildings of its class in other lands.

Treasury and Patent Office. — Among the older government buildings may be cited the United States Treasury, a structure with four fronts. The building commonly known as the Patent Office, which has recently been subjected to considerable alteration, is also a four fronted building with a portico in the center of each of its sides, the principal consisting of two rows of eight columns. As Grecian structures these monumental piles are not unworthy, but the incongruity between their appearance and their purpose is manifest.

Pension Bureau.— The newer government structures at Washington have followed neither the Grecian nor the vernacular Palladian. The Pension Bureau is a large and severely symmetrical structure in the style of Bramante, having three stories of rectangular windows, a bold cornice and an attic in the center. The decorations are of terra cotta.

The Congressional Library is of the Italian Renaissance order of architecture; it has three stories with a dome; and is in area 470 by 340 feet, covering nearly three and one half acres of ground, with four inner courts. The building is surmounted on all sides by a carved balustrade. The dome is finished in black copper with panels gilded with a thick coating of gold leaf. The cresting of the dome above the lantern terminates in a gilded finial representing the torch of Science ever burning. The general plan of the structure consists of a great central rotunda, from which radiate book stacks and which is inclosed in a parallelogram of galleries and pavilions. The building material employed for the exterior walls is white granite from New Hampshire, and for the inner courts Maryland granite and white enameled bricks. The interior is rich in choice marbles from Europe, Africa, and America. The entrance to the building is by massive stairways of the central pavilion, and through bronze doors to the central stair hall. This magnificent apartment is pronounced to be unsurpassed by any other entrance hall in the world. It is lined throughout with fine Italian marble highly polished. On the sides rise lofty rounded columns, with elaborate carved capitals of Corinthian design; while the arches are adorned with marble rosettes, palm leaves, and foliated designs of exquisite finish and delicacy. The newel posts of the stairway are enriched by beautiful festoons of leaves and flowers, and are surmounted by two bronze lamp bearers. The staircases are ornamented with miniature marble figures by Martiny, carved in relief, representing in emblematic sculpture the various arts and sciences. This beautiful and spacious entrance hall has been described as a "vision in polished stone," and taken in connection with the grand corridors and rich decorations may be pronounced the finest marble interior in America.

The Bureau of Printing and Engraving is in

red and brown brick, round arched, and without the orders, and may, perhaps, be called Romanesque. Other specimens of Washington architecture worthy of mention are the new Corcoran Art Gallery, the Smithsonian Institution, and the War, State, and Navy building.

Besides the buildings of the Greek style erected in Washington, others, not only by the government but by banking corporations, commercial houses, etc., have been erected in various parts of the country. The two best of these are probably the Sub-Treasury building at New York and Girard College at Philadelphia. Both are of white marble, and the latter modeled, as to the exterior, after the Parthenon,— that is so far as possible, while employing a different order of architecture. It is considered the Greek building par excellence of America, as the Madeleine is of France, and is a Corinthian peristyle resting upon a Grecian stylobate. Its monolithic colonnade is quite imposing, but as a whole it fails to excite in the beholder much of that emotion which is awakened by the Grecian edifice. Cold and unimpressive, it seems rather like some rare exotic — a thing to be gazed and wondered at rather than enjoyed. This is no doubt attributable in part to its position, for while the Greek temple always crowned some lofty height, or some jutting spur, this edifice is built in the middle of a broad, flat plain, without any relief from the blue sky or jagged mountain side.

Several of the state capitols illustrate pleasing styles of architecture. The state house at Newport is a perfectly symmetrical brick and stone structure, commenced in 1738. It has rectangular windows with quoins, a balcony over the entrance, above the balcony a broken pediment, and over this a truncated gable. Over all rises a low octagonal turret. The old state house at Boston is of the same period; it is a very plain structure, with a wide entrance and curious end gables. Independence Hall and the White House belong to the same period.

The State Capitol at Albany, as originally designed, was an immense rectangular Renaissance block, in which an order was given to each story, much after the style practiced at Venice by Sansovino and San Micheli, and was crowned by a domical tower of grand proportions. The design was improved by Richardson, and the upper portions of the edifice were completed according to it. There is great beauty in the newer portion, but it cannot be said that there is congruity. The towers are Romanesque, while the cornice of the order below is changed to Gothic. Parts of the interior, as the Hall of Assembly, the work of Eidlitz, are Gothic of the most beautiful kind — vaulted mediæval halls enshrined in a classical exterior.

The Capitol at Hartford, Connecticut, although it has a dome like many other capitols, is far from being an ordinary structure, and may be reckoned one of the finest public buildings in the United States. The style is Gothic, and the regular façade is broken into a center, curtains, and wings. The center has two low towers in every way subordinate to the tall tambour and dome which rise behind them. This cupola crown tower is decidedly Gothic in the sentiment of its details.

The City Hall, Philadelphia, is among the largest of modern buildings, slightly exceeding the Capitol at Washington in area. Seldom has a better opportunity been afforded for architectonic display than is given by its position at the junction of two of the principal streets of the city. It occupies what was once Penn Square and thus stands free all around. This immense structure is conceived in the style of the Louvre at Paris with central and angle pavilions, the whole surmounted by a mansard roof of great height. Each front is a symmetrical whole, and, with the exception of the slight difference in length, the fronts are alike. The central feature is a gigantic tower which rises upward of 537 feet above the pavement. This tower was designed to be the loftiest in the world, but in this respect has already been surpassed by the Washington Monument at the National Capital. The magnificence of this edifice consists in its imposing dimensions, the rich array of marble and polished granite, and the beautiful sculpture which adorns its façades and entrance halls.

In our largest cities we find many church edifices both completed and in process of erection which are worthy of attention for their architecture as well as the solidity and beauty of material employed. Most of these are of the Gothic style.

Trinity Church in New York, completed in 1846, was the first stone edifice after the Gothic, in America. It is most nearly allied to the early English, and the architect deserves the gratitude of all lovers of the beautiful, for giving his countrymen so elegant and chaste a model.

Grace Church in the same city, built of granite, is of a more ornate style and presents nearly all the peculiar features of the Gothic, although in small dimensions.

St. Patrick's Cathedral, fronting on Central Park, affords us the best specimen of the Gothic as it prevailed in Europe in the fourteenth century. The style is commonly known as the Decorated or Geometric Gothic. Trinity Church,

Boston, a Romanesque or Byzantine structure, is the work of Richardson. The original design was improved in 1886, and, as now completed, furnishes perhaps the noblest church edifice in the United States.

The Cathedral of St. John the Divine, New York, which gives promise of great architectural beauty, is in the modified Romanesque style of architecture.

The Temple Emmanuel in New York city has a most ornate and symmetrical exterior, with two towers and an arcade in the center, and although the effect is pretty and fanciful rather than grand, it ranks among the finest of the religious edifices of that city. The Rodef Shalom synagogue, Philadelphia, has an effective façade, and is Gothic in sentiment notwithstanding its Moorish forms. The Synagogue Emmanuel in San Francisco is peculiar among synagogues from the fact that the windows are filled with Gothic tracery and its walls and towers set with Gothicized buttresses.

Memorial Hall of Harvard University is built of brick banded in the Lombard style with buff tiles bearing geometric designs in blue. The central tower rises above the Memorial Hall while smaller towers, all of the English Gothic, flank its walls.

The Art Museum at Cincinnati, in the Romanesque style, has two ranges of rectangular twin windows, and the plain walls of the uppermost story are unrelieved save by blind arches. The central hall is the most striking feature of the interior. The walls are of local blue limestone, with cornices and arches of Missouri granite; the roof is of red Akron pantiles. The eastern wing has a fine polygonal apse with nine pairs of windows and a tall tower on the line of the entrance front.

The Museum of Fine Arts at Boston, commenced in 1871, is one of the first buildings in the United States upon which terra cotta—made in England from the architect's drawing—has been extensively used. This structure may be called Italian Gothic; upon the ground floor it has arched openings in groups separated by buttresses, while above these large panels, some of them filled with sculptures, mask the picture gallery. The entrance is through a pair of arches.

The Masonic Temple of Philadelphia is a very imposing and massive building. It dominated Penn Square until the City Hall arose beside it. It is built of gray granite, and the exterior is round arched and may be called Romanesque, but does not strictly conform to the Norman phase of that style.

Harvard College, time honored in this country, though it would be young in the old world, marks in its various structures all the phases through which American architecture has passed. Its finest buildings are undoubtedly its most modern ones. These are the Memorial Hall, the Gymnasium, the Law School and Seaver Hall, the last three of which are the work of Richardson.

The University of Pennsylvania comprises a group of Gothic structures built of green serpentine, with dressings of Ohio stone. There is little ornament, but the grouping is effective and the general effect satisfactory. Recent buildings have been added of a very pleasing style and admirably express their purpose.

Stone Hall, Wellesley College, is a fine structure and what may be called Free Classic, but in its stepped gables and in the lines of its central pavilion approaches Flemish Renaissance. The entrance is well accentuated, contrasting admirably with the curtain-walls which intervene between it and the tower-like blocks which mark the intersection of the center with its wings.

The Art School at Yale is a species of Gothic, but is of heavy outline, and its tower is without sufficient prominence. Most of the newer Yale buildings are in this style, including the Peabody Museum, which is perhaps the best.

Princeton has a good Gothic dormitory, and the Lecture Hall of the theological seminary, with its groups of cusped windows, is effective. The buildings of the Chicago University and Leland Stanford, Jr., University exhibit unique and pleasing styles.

Some of the best specimens of architecture in America, in addition to those already noticed, are the City Hall of San Francisco, Allegheny Court House of Pittsburg, the Boston Public Library, Ridgway Library of Philadelphia, the Libraries at Burlington, Vt., and Woburn, Massachusetts, the Metropolitan Opera House, New York city, the Casino of the same city, Memorial Hall in Fairmount Park, Ponce de Leon Hotel at St. Augustine, Auditorium Theater, Chicago, the Century and Metropolitan Clubs, New York, the Carnegie Library at Pittsburg, the Pennsylvania Railroad Station at Philadelphia, South Terminal Station, Boston, and the National Academy of Design, New York city; though many more might be mentioned of varying degrees of merit.

Alexandrian Codex is an important manuscript of the Sacred Scriptures written in Greek. It is written on parchment, in finely-formed uncial letters, and is without accents, marks of aspiration, or spaces between the words. Its probable date is the latter half of the sixth century. With the exception of a few gaps, it contains the whole Bible in Greek, along with the Epistles of Clemens

Romanus. This celebrated manuscript, which is now in the British Museum, belonged, as early as 1098, to the library of the Patriarch of Alexandria. In 1628 it was sent as a present to Charles I. of England, by Cyrillus Lucaris, Patriarch of Constantinople, who declared that he got it from Egypt; and that it was written there appears from internal and external evidence.

Alexandrian Library contained in the time of Cleopatra about 700,000 volumes or rolls, and was founded at the suggestion of Demetrius Phalereus, a fugitive from Athens in the reign of Ptolemy Soter. The greater portion of this remarkable collection was destroyed during the Alexandrine war. This loss, however, was repaired by Mark Antony, who presented to Cleopatra the library taken at the siege of Pergamos. From this time until about the year 391 A. D., the library increased in size and reputation, and contained treasures of learning in all known tongues. At the burning of the Temple of Jupiter Serapis by the Christians under Theodosius the Great, about that year a portion of the library was destroyed, and when the Arabs, under Caliph Omar, took the city in 640 A. D., the destruction of the remainder was completed.

Egyptian Labyrinth was situated at Crocodilopolis, near Lake Mœris, in the vicinity of the present pyramid of Biakhmu. It was built of polished stone, with many chambers and passages, said to be vaulted, having a peristyle court with 3,000 chambers, half of which were under the earth and the others above ground, which formed another story. The upper chambers were decorated with reliefs; the lower were plain, and contained, according to tradition, the bodies of the twelve founders of the building and the mummies of the sacred crocodiles, conferring on the building the character of a mausoleum, probably conjoined with a temple — that of Sebak, the crocodile god. The Labyrinth stood in the midst of a great square. Part was constructed of Parian marble and of Syenitic granite; it had a staircase of ninety steps, and columns of porphyry, and the opening of the doors echoed like the reverberation of thunder. There is great difference of opinion among authors as to the name of the king under whom this remarkable work was constructed and the purpose for which it was intended, and it is probable that it was not built in a single reign. According to some ancient authorities it was supposed to have been inhabited by the Dodicarchy, or twelve kings, who conjointly ruled Egypt before Psammetichus I.; while others claim it to have been the place of assembly of the governors of nomes, or districts — twelve in number, according to Herodotus; sixteen, according to Pliny; and twenty-seven, according to Strabo. The Labyrinth was extant in the time of Pliny, A. D. 78, and was then, according to that author, 3,600 years old. The ruins of the foundations or lower chambers have been found at the modern village of Howara, in Fayoom. The next labyrinth in renown to the Egyptian was the Labyrinth of Crete, supposed to have been built by Dædalus for the Cretan monarch, Minos, in which the Minotaur was confined by his orders. The third of the labyrinths of antiquity was the Samian, constructed by Theodorus and artists of his school, in the age of Polycrates, 540 B. C., supposed to be a work of nature embellished by art, having 150 columns erected by a clever mechanical contrivance. Other inferior labyrinths existed at Nauplia, at Sipontum in Italy, at Val d'Ispica in Sicily, and elsewhere.

Councils of Nice.— The first Council of Nice was held in the Emperor Constantine's palace, June 19, A. D. 325, and was attended by 318 bishops of the Catholic Church, and resulted in the adoption of the Nicene Creed, expounding the faith of the Church. August 17, A. D., 786, the second Council of Nice was convened by order of the Empress Irene and her son Constantine, at which there were 376 bishops present. This council was held for the purpose of establishing the use of images in the churches, which had been interdicted by the Emperor Leo and his son Constantine, but was dissolved owing to the tumults raised by the party in opposition. It was reconvened September 24, A. D. 787, when the use of images was restored.

Islam, or, as it is called, Eslam, is the proper name of the Mohammedan religion. The word is Arabic, and means "Submission to God," or, according to some authorities, "Salvation." Islam, it is held, was once the religion of all men; and every child, it is believed, is born in Islam, or the true faith, and would continue in it till the end were it not for the wickedness of its parents, "who misguide it early and lead it astray to Magism, Judaism, or Christianity." Whether wickedness and idolatry came into the world after the murder of Abel, or at the time of Noah, or only after Amru Ibn Lohai, one of the first and greatest idolaters of Arabia, are moot-points among Moslem theologians.

Albigenses.— About the beginning of the thirteenth century various sects of heretics abounded in the south of France, and to these was applied the name Albigenses. The name arose from the circumstance that the district of Albigeois in Languedoc — now in the department of Tarn, of which Albi is the capital—was the first point against which the crusade of Pope Innocent III., 1209, was directed. The immediate pretense of the crusade was the murder of the papal legate and inquisitor, Peter of Castelnau, who had been commissioned to extirpate heresy in the dominions of Count Raymond VI. of Toulouse; but its real object was to deprive the count of his lands, as he had become an object of hatred from his toleration of the heretics. It was in vain that he had submitted to the most humiliating penance and flagellation from the hands of the legate, Milo, and had purchased the papal absolution by great sacrifices. The expedition took by storm Beziers, the capital of Raymond's nephew Roger, and massacred 20,000 of the inhabitants, Catholics as well as heretics. Simon, Count of Montfort, who conducted the crusade under the legates, proceeded in the same relentless way with other places in the territories of Raymond and his allies. The conquered lands were given to Simon de Montfort, and by him were eventually ceded to Louis VIII. Raymond VI. and Raymond VII. disputed the possession of the land by the king, and after thousands had perished on both sides, a peace was concluded in 1229, at which Raymond VII. purchased relief from the ban of the church by immense sums of money, gave up Narbonne and several lordships to Louis IX., and had to make his son-in-law, the brother of Louis, heir of his other possessions. The heretics were handed over to the proselyting zeal of the Order of Dominicans and the bloody tribunals of the Inquisition, and both used their utmost power to bring the recusant Albigenses to the stake. From the middle of the thirteenth century the name of the Albigenses gradually disappears.

Juggernaut.— The temple in the town of Juggernaut, one of the chief places of pilgrimage in India, contains an idol of the Hindoo god, called *Jaggernaut* or *Juggernaut*, a corruption of the Sanskrit word *Jagannatha*, *i. e.*, lord of the world. The legend regarding the building of the town, the erection of the temple, and the formation of the idol is as follows: A king, desirous of founding a city, sent a learned Brahmin to pitch upon a proper spot. The Brahmin, after a long search, arrived upon the banks of the sea, and there saw a crow diving into the water, and, having washed its body, making obeisance to the sea. Understanding the language of birds, he learned from the crow that if he remained there a short time he would comprehend the wonders of this land. The king, apprised of this occurrence, built on the spot where the crow had appeared a large city and a place of worship. The Rajah one night heard in a dream a voice saying: "On a certain day cast thine eyes on the seashore, when there will arise out of the water a piece of wood 52 inches long and 1½ cubits broad; this is the true form of the Deity; take it up and keep it hidden in thine house seven days; and in whatever shape it shall then appear, place it in the temple and worship it." It happened just as the Rajah had dreamed, and the image, called by him Jagannatha, became the object of worship of all ranks of people, and performed many miracles. The car-festival, when Jagannatha is dragged in his car on a yearly visit to his country quarters, is currently believed to be the occasion of numerous cases of self-immolation, the frantic devotees committing suicide by throwing themselves before the wheels of the heavy car. This has been proved, however, upon good authority, to be untrue.

Children's Crusade.— In the summer of 1212 two immense armies of children were gathered at Cologne, in Germany, and at Vendome, in France, summoned thither by two boy prophets, Stephen of Cloys (France) and Nicholas of Cologne (Germany), both about twelve years of age. These boy prophets believed or pretended to believe, that they were inspired by heaven, and the crusade which they preached was not a crusade of blood against the Saracens, but a crusade of prayer. The children were to march to the sea, which would open, as it once did for the Israelites, to permit them to pass over into Palestine dry shod. There they were to convert the leaders of Islam and baptize the heathen. The excitement aroused by this preaching spread so among the children that within short intervals of each other two unarmed hosts of German children, drawn from all classes, and nearly all under twelve years of age, left Cologne to march over the sea to the Holy Land. The first was led by the famous Nicholas, and the second by a boy whose name is not known. Their combined numbers are believed to have been 40,000. At about the same time an army of French children to the number of about 30,000 left Vendome under Stephen. The mortality among the German children in their passage across the Alps was frightful. Nearly 30,000 succumbed to exposure, fatigue, and hunger. Of the French army, 10,000 died before it reached Marseilles. The army under Nicholas was broken up at Genoa when it was found that the sea did not open to let them pass, and some of the children were returned to their homes by the humane Genoese; but others pressed on to Pisa and obtained passage by ship to the Holy Land. A part of the children under the unknown leader were shipped to Palestine from Brindisi, and about 5,000 of the French children were shipped from Marseilles, and all who survived the voyages were sold as slaves to the Turks. Of the 70,000 children who joined this crusade, it is probable that less than 20,000 were ever heard of afterward by their parents.

Latter-day Saints, commonly called "Mormons," constitute a religious sect officially styled "The Church of Jesus Christ of Latter-day Saints." The church was organized at Fayette, N. Y., April 6, 1830, through the instrumentality of Joseph Smith, the son of a Vermont farmer. Joseph Smith announced that in 1820, when he was fifteen years old, he received in answer to prayer a visitation of heavenly personages; and that in 1827 an angel delivered to him an ancient record engraved on plates of gold. This record Joseph Smith translated by Divine aid, and the modern version appeared in print in 1830 as the Book of Mormon. The book purports to be a history of the ancient inhabitants of the western continent; and it is regarded by the Latter-day Saints as a volume of sacred writ of equal authority with the Jewish and Christian Scriptures, but not superseding or supplanting them. Persecution assailed the youthful prophet and the church from the first. In 1831 the people established themselves at Kirtland, Ohio, where they erected a temple which is still standing. Branches of the church had already been organized in many of the states, when in 1838, owing to continued and increasing persecution, a general westerly migration was inaugurated. Most of the people located in Illinois, where in 1839 they began the erection of a town, first called Commerce but later known as Nauvoo. Here, with untiring zeal they built another temple, costlier and more imposing than the first. Persecution followed the church and culminated in the assassination of Joseph and his brother Hyrum, the latter being patriarch of the church. This tragedy occurred June 7, 1844, as the result of a mobocratic attack on the jail at Carthage, Ill., where the two were confined awaiting trial on some minor charge. Brigham Young then became the head of the church, and in 1846 the exodus from Nauvoo began. The people fled westward and settled in the valley of the Great Salt Lake, then a part of the Mexican domain. The pioneers of the colonizing hosts entered the valley July 24, 1847. With marvelous energy, amid unmeasured hardships and sacrifices, these zealous religionists transformed the desert into a garden of beauty, and every year witnessed the uninterrupted growth of the church. The commonwealth thus founded in the heart of the American Desert has scarcely suffered a temporary check in its progress and growth to the present time. The practice of plural marriage led to much persecution. This practice was never general and has now been formally discontinued. It has been confused in the minds of many with "Celestial marriage," which differs from the ordinary marriage ceremony only in being a covenant between husband and wife for "time and all eternity" instead of a contract for this mortal probation alone. A summary of the doctrinal features of "Mormonism," as given over the signature of the founder, and as still professed by the church, is as follows:—

ARTICLES OF FAITH.

Of the Church of Jesus Christ of Latter-day Saints.

1. We believe in God, the Eternal Father, and in His Son, Jesus Christ, and in the Holy Ghost.

2. We believe that men will be punished for their own sins, and not for Adam's transgression.

3. We believe that through the atonement of Christ, all mankind may be saved, by obedience to the laws and ordinances of the Gospel.

4. We believe that the first principles and ordinances of the Gospel are: First, faith in the Lord Jesus Christ; second, repentance; third, baptism by immersion for the remission of sins; fourth, laying on of hands for the gift of the Holy Ghost.

5. We believe that a man must be called of God, by "prophecy, and by the laying on of hands," by those who are in authority, to preach the gospel and administer in the ordinances thereof.

6. We believe in the same organization that existed in the primitive church, namely, Apostles, Prophets, Pastors, Teachers, Evangelists, etc.

7. We believe in the gift of tongues, prophecy, revelation, visions, healing, interpretation of tongues, etc.

8. We believe the Bible to be the word of God, as far as it is translated correctly; we also believe the Book of Mormon to be the word of God.

9. We believe all that God has revealed, all that He does now reveal, and we believe that He will yet reveal many great and important things pertaining to the kingdom of God.

10. We believe in the literal gathering of Israel and in the restoration of the ten tribes. That Zion will be built upon this continent. That Christ will reign personally upon the earth, and that the earth will be renewed and receive its paradisical glory.

11. We claim the privilege of worshiping Almighty God according to the dictates of our conscience, and allow all men the same privilege, let them worship how, where, or what they may.

12. We believe in being subject to kings, presidents, rulers, and magistrates, in obeying, honoring, and sustaining the law.

13. We believe in being honest, true, chaste, benevolent, virtuous, and in doing good to ALL MEN; indeed we may say that we follow the admonition of Paul, "We believe all things, we hope all things," we have endured many things, and hope to be able to endure all things. If there is anything virtuous, lovely, or of good report or praiseworthy, we seek after these things. —Joseph Smith.

Ark of the Covenant.—Previous to the destruction of the Temple of Solomon by the Babylonians the Ark of the Covenant was contained therein, but what became of it after that time is unknown. It is believed by some to have been taken away or destroyed by

Nebuchadnezzar, while certain of the Jews believe that it was concealed from the spoilers, and account it among the hidden things which will be revealed by the Messiah. That the old Ark was not contained in the second Temple all Jewish writers agree; and the absence of the Ark is one of the important particulars in which this Temple was held to be inferior to that of Solomon. It is held by some writers, however, that the Jews could not properly carry on their worship without an Ark, hence that a new one must have been made and placed in the Temple if the original Ark was not recovered. The silence of Ezra, Nehemiah, the Maccabees, and Josephus, who repeatedly mention all the other sacred utensils but never name the Ark, would, nevertheless, seem conclusive on this subject.

Mount Ararat. — The mountains of Ararat, referred to in the Scriptures, overlook the plain of Araxes in Armenia, and are divided into two peaks, Great Ararat and Little Ararat. The summit of the former is 17,323 feet above the level of the sea, and of the latter 13,000 feet. It is believed that the resting place of the Ark was upon some lower portion of this range rather than upon the peaks, and in support of this view is the fact that at an elevation of 6,000 or 7,000 feet the climate is temperate, the harvests are quick to mature and abundant; while the peaks, for more than 3,000 feet below their summits, are continuously covered with ice and snow.

Obelisks.— The word is from the Greek, and signifies a prismatic monument of stone or other material terminating in a pyramidal or pointed top. They are found principally in Egypt, and date back to the most remote periods of antiquity. They were placed before the gateways of the principal temples, and correspond in Egyptian art to the columns of the Romans and stelæ of the Greeks, and appear to have been erected to record the honors or triumphs of the monarchs. They are also called "monoliths," being cut out of a single piece of stone, and have four faces, broader at the base than at the top, the width at the base being one tenth the height of the shaft to the beginning of the pyramidion, or cap, which is also one tenth of the same height. The sides are generally sculptured with one vertical line of deeply cut hieroglyphs and representations. Some of them were originally capped with bronze or gold. Their height varied from a few inches to upward of one hundred feet, the tallest known being that of Karnuk, which rises to 105 feet 7 inches. A number of them were removed to Rome by Augustus and later emperors, and they were afterwards transported to various cities of Italy and France and used to adorn squares and public parks. Among the most notable of these relics of ancient art are the two known as Cleopatra's Needles, which, from the inscriptions on them, appear to have been set up at the entrance of the Temple of the Sun, in Heliopolis, Egypt, by Thothmes III., about 1831 B. C. Two centuries after their erection the stones were nearly covered with carvings, setting out the greatness and achievements of Rameses II. Twenty-three years before the Christian era they were moved from Heliopolis to Alexandria by Augustus Cæsar and set up in the Cæsarium, a palace which now stands, a mere mass of ruins, near the station of the railroad to Cairo. In 1819 the Egyptian Government presented one of them to England, but it was not taken to London until 1878. The other was transported to New York in 1880, it having been presented to the United States, and was raised on its pedestal in Central Park, New York, January 22, 1881. The material of these, and indeed of most of the obelisks, is granite brought from Syene, near the first cataract of the Nile. They were cut at the quarry, and floated into and down the Nile during one of the annual overflows.

Lake School.— Toward the close of the last century the poets Wordsworth, Coleridge, and Southey took up their residence in the Lake district of Cumberland and Westmoreland, in England, for the purpose, as they said, of seeking the sources of poetical inspiration in the simplicity of nature, rather than in the works of their predecessors and the fashions of the time. On this account they were given the name of the Lake School by the *Edinburgh Review*

Kissing the Book.— The custom of swearing on the Bible comes from the ancient Jews, who at first touched their phylacteries — small cases containing strips of parchment inscribed with texts from the Old Testament — in taking oaths, and later laid their hands upon the Book of the Law; and the various customs of taking oaths in different countries have all a similar origin. The early Anglo-Saxons regarded stones as sacred to their gods, therefore laid their hands on a pillar of stone. In mediæval times it was customary to touch a relic, and this was regarded as giving the oath more sacredness than when sworn upon the missal, or prayer book. Another custom of the same times was swearing by churches. A certain number were mentioned, and the attestor was obliged to go to each one, take the ring of the church door in his hand, and repeat his oath. The custom of kissing the cross to attest an oath has been observed in Russia from very early times, and has extended into other countries. According to the laws of the Order of the Garter in the time of Henry VIII., Knights Templars were required in taking oath to touch the book and kiss the cross. Since the Reformation the taking of oaths by kissing the Bible has not been permitted in Scotland. In other portions of Great Britain it is the common method.

French Renaissance.—"Renaissance" is the name given to the style of art, especially architecture, in Europe which succeeded the Gothic and preceded the rigid copyism of the classic revival in the first half of the present century. It is also used to denote the time during which this style of art prevailed, and also to include the development of the European races in other lines as well as art. The name signifies the "new birth." The date of the beginning of this period coincides with that of the fall of the Byzantine Empire, and the latter was no doubt the cause of the former; for when the Turks took possession of Constantinople all the memorials, paintings, books, etc., that could be removed from the destroying hand of the invaders were hastily conveyed to Italy. These inspired just admiration among the Italian people, and aroused not only a desire to emulate the construction of such worthy works, but also an interest in ancient works and models. In 1494 Charles VIII., King of France, made a warlike expedition into Italy, and on his return brought some Italian workmen to supervise the construction of the royal buildings. This was the first introduction of the renaissance into France. Communication between France and Italy was also stimulated by this expedition, and the growth of Italian ideas among the French was steady, though slow. In the reign of Louis XII., 1498-1515, the work was further stimulated by the founding of a school of architecture under an artist from Verona. But it was under Francis I., 1515-'47, that the new growth was most stimulated and aided. This prince was possessed both of learning and intellectual power. He had a sincere love for literature, science, and art, and a keen appreciation of the beautiful in these departments. He invited a number of Italian artists to his court. Among the most famous of these were Leonardo da Vinci and Benvenuto Cellini. These and others introduced Italian details in their designs, which native architects applied to old forms, with which they were familiar; so that the French renaissance was similar to that of Italy, but different from it in many important respects. All lines of art felt the renaissance spirit; and not merely architecture, painting, and sculpture, but also music, poetry, and literature were stimulated. The minor plastic and decorative arts, engraving, working in wood and metals, pottery, tapestry, etc., were cultivated with eagerness and skill. The study of the classics also received a new impulse, and this era had, in France, some of the greatest scholars of the times. Historical writers usually consider the renaissance period as one of the most important influences in hastening the growth of individuality and the work of the Reformation, and in ushering in the progress that has marked the modern history of the world. In Germany, Russia, and every country in Europe, the renaissance prevailed in a manner similar to that above described.

Lollards, or Lollhards, acquired their name from their practice of singing dirges at funerals — the Low German word *lullen*, or lollen, signifying to sing softly or slowly. The Lollards were a semi-monastic society formed in Antwerp about the year 1300, the members of which devoted themselves to the care of the sick and the dead. They were also called, from their frugal life and the poverty of their appearance, *Matemans;* also, from their patron saint, *Brethren of St. Alexius;* and on account of their dwelling in cells, *Fratres Cellitæ.* In the frequent pestilences of that period, the Lollards were useful and everywhere welcome, and the order spread through the Netherlands and Germany. Owing to the fact that they were persecuted and reproached with heresy by the clergy and begging-friars, their name was afterward very commonly given to different classes of religionists; and in England it became a designation of the followers of Wycliffe.

French Academy, The, had its origin in a literary coterie which held meetings in Paris during the time of Louis XIV., and its purpose and unity were given to it by Cardinal Richelieu. His object was to have a fixed standard of grammar and rhetoric given to the language, believing that this would tend to the unification and peace of France. The duties which were imposed upon the members of the Academy were "to purify and fix the national tongue, to throw light upon its obscurities, to maintain its character and principles, and at their private meetings to keep this object in view. Their discussions were to turn on grammar, rhetoric, and poetry; their critical observations on the beauties and defects of classical French authors, in order to prepare editions of their works, and to compose a new dictionary of the French language." The original Academy was swept away in 1793, and the present Academy preserves but little of its original character of a mere coterie of grammarians. This present Academy came into existence with the restoraion of the Bourbons. It meets at the Palace Mazarin, Paris. Its chief officer is its secretary, who has a life tenure of his position. He receives a salary of 12,000 francs a year, the society being allowed by the Government 85,000 francs a year for the payment of its officers and the care of its library. The Academy is always to consist of forty members, all vacancies being filled by the votes of those already composing the body. To belong to it is regarded as a high honor, the members being spoken of as "the forty immortals."

Majolica Ware was first manufactured in the island of Majolica, and from thence the art was taken to Italy, where, during the fourteenth and fifteenth centuries, it was carried on to a considerable extent. A factory for manufacturing this ware was established in Fayence, France, in the latter century, and the name faience was substituted for that of majolica. About 1530, plates and other ware were manufactured in Italy, decorated with subjects derived from the compositions of Raphael and Marc Antonio, and painted in gay and brilliant colors. The establishment was abandoned in 1574, but pieces of majolica continued to be fabricated in various cities of Italy till the eighteenth century. During the decadence of the art of making enameled pottery in Italy, it flourished greatly in France at the famous Palissy pottery works at Paris and the factories at Nevers and Rouen, where it was manufactured till the end of the seventeenth century.

The Boxers are a Chinese secret society, partly religious and partly patriotic. The Chinese name of the society is Yi-Ho-Chuan, meaning in English, "righteousness, harmony, and 'fists'"; the derived name "boxers" has evidently been applied because of the athletic aspect the society first assumed. It was first organized in groups which began gymnastic exercises in the Chinese villages, and drilling as a military organization was quickly developed, with broadswords for arms. On account of the swords the boxers have also been known as the "Big Knives." They first made themselves felt in Shan-Tung province, where the Germans secured the lease of Kiao-Chou bay, and large railroad and mineral rights. Each band, it is said, is governed by a "demonized" leader, who, by the selection of an epileptic patient, or, by the aid of hypnotism, causes a medium to display wild and unnatural symptoms, or to utter wild and strange speech, this serving as a basis for the claim of the society to spiritual power. Every boxer is assured of immunity from death or physical injury. The assault upon Christianity by the Boxers was particularly directed against native converts, but later developed into a general anti-foreign crusade. Though revolutionary in their methods they profess fealty to the reigning dynasty, and devotion to the ancient religion, while attacking the foreign influences which they believe to be undermining the ancient institutions and nationality of China.

Libraries, Foreign.— First among the libraries of Great Britain, and second to few, if any, on the continent, is that of the British Museum. It contains about 1,300,000 printed volumes, besides rare and extensive collections of manuscripts, maps, prints, and drawings. Next in rank is the Bodleyan or Bodleian Library at Oxford, which contains 300,000 volumes in addition to 20,000 to 30,000 in manuscript. The third and fourth places are occupied by the Public or University Library of Cambridge, and the Library of the Faculty of Advocates at Edinburgh, which are nearly on a par as regards extent and value, containing not less than 265,000 volumes each. The Library of Trinity College, Dublin, with about 192,000 volumes, is the largest and most valuable in Ireland. These five libraries have long been, and still are, entitled by statute to a free copy of every book published in the empire. The great National Library of France — *La Bibliothèque du Roi*, as it used to be called, *La Bibliothèque Nationale*, as it is called at present — is one of the largest and most valuable collections of books and manuscripts in the world. The number of printed volumes contained in it is estimated at nearly 2,500,000, and of manuscripts at about 150,000. Among libraries of the second class in Paris, the Arsenal Library with 300,000 volumes, the Library of Ste. Genevieve with 200,000, and the Mazarine Library with 160,000, are the chief. In Italy the Library of the Vatican at Rome stands pre-eminent. The number of printed volumes is only about 200,000, but the manuscript collection is the finest in the world. The Casanata Library, also at Rome, is said to contain 120,000 volumes; the Ambrosian Library at Milan, 140,000 volumes; the Magliabechi Library at Florence, 200,000 volumes; the Royal Library at Naples, 200,000 volumes; the Library of St. Mark's at Venice, 120,000 volumes and 10,000 manuscripts. The Laurentian Library at Florence consists almost entirely of manuscripts. The principal libraries of Spain are the Biblioteca Nacional at Madrid, numbering nearly 430,000 volumes, and the Library of the Escorial, which contains numerous manuscript volumes, treasures of Arabic literature. The Imperial Library at Vienna is a noble collection of not fewer than 400,000 volumes, of which 15,000 are of the class called *incunabula*, or books printed before the year 1500. The Royal Library at Munich contains 900,000 volumes, including 13,000 *incunabula*, and 22,000 manuscripts. The Royal Library at Dresden is a collection of 500,000 volumes, among which are included some of the scarcest specimens of early printing, among others the Mainz Psalter of 1457, the first book printed with a date. The Royal Library of Berlin contains about 700,000 volumes of printed books, and 15,000 volumes of manuscripts. Of the other libraries in Germany, that of the University of Göttingen contains upward of 500,000 volumes, the Ducal Library of Wolfenbuttel about 270,000 volumes, and the University Library at Strasburg over 513,000 books and manuscripts. In Holland, the principal library is the Royal Library at the Hague, containing about 200,000 printed volumes. The Royal Library at Copenhagen contains nearly 550,000 volumes. The largest library in Sweden is that of the University of Upsala, consisting of nearly 200,000 volumes. One of its chief treasures is the famous manuscript of the Gothic Gospels of Ulfilas, commonly known as the *Codex Argenteus*. The number of volumes in the Imperial Library of St. Petersburg, Russia, is estimated to be at least 900,000, in addition to 35,000 manuscripts.

Church of England.—This important Christian body is that portion of the universal church of Christ having, for its ministers, bishops, priests, and deacons, and being legally and historically continuous with the church of the most ancient times—a "true apostolic church, teaching and maintaining the doctrine of the apostles." In mediæval Acts of Parliament it was called by the same name as at present, and was distinguished from the church of Rome, which latter was usually described as the court (*curia*) of Rome. From 1066 to 1356 there was a constant struggle between the civil and ecclesiastical powers. Then came Wycliffe's translation of the Bible into English and his continued war against some of the leading doctrines of the Romish Church, which led to the formation of a new sect called Lollards (*See* LOLLARDS), holding views similar to those of the present Church. Despite persecutions, the new doctrines spread and had many adherents. The Reformation is ordinarily assigned to the reign of Henry VIII., the two most important acts being passed in 1532 and 1534; but the main feature of these acts was the declaration of the independence of the Church in England and the supremacy of the king over that Church. They had cast off the bondage of Rome, but in doctrine the churches were still in accord; and it was not until thirty years afterward — 1563, in the reign of Queen Elizabeth — that the Thirty-Nine Articles of Faith were finally reviewed and adopted, and the Protestant Church of England finally and fully established. In 1801, by the "Act of Union," the Episcopal churches in England and Ireland were united; but the latter church was disestablished and disendowed in 1869. The Episcopal Church in Scotland is not, politically speaking, in union with that of England; but an Act of Parliament, passed in 1864, has taken away many restrictions imposed on Scottish Episcopalians after the battle of Culloden, and clergy ordained by Scotch bishops may now, under some slight restrictions, be presented to benefices in England.

Christian Association, Young Men's. — Associations of young men for Christian work have existed in Great Britain and Ireland, for upward of two centuries, and also in Germany and Switzerland. In 1710 it is recorded that Cotton Mather addressed kindred societies in New England, which were known as "Young Men Associated." In 1849, the societies which had been established in Germany took a wider scope, and from these associations grew the German associations of the present day. The English Young Men's Christian Association commenced in a meeting of clerks organized by George Williams in a mercantile establishment in London in 1844. The example of the British metropolis was speedily followed by the various cities of Great Britain founding associations, and in December, 1851, America caught the enthusiasm of the movement, and formed an association in Montreal, modeled after the one in London. Then Boston undertook the formation of one for itself, and their growth and influence since that time have been simply wonderful. They now flourish in every Protestant Christian country; and in almost every place where a colony of Christians are gathered, these associations are to be found.

Blind, Education of The.—The main end to be sought in the education of the blind is to fit them to compete in as many ways as possible with the more fortunate who can see, and take them out of their despondency and give them a worthy object to accomplish in life. The first institution for the blind was founded in Memmingen by Weef VI. in 1178, the second in Paris by Louis IX. in 1260, and the first for the employment of the adult blind in Edinburgh by Dr. Johnston in 1793. The work in a school for the blind is about equal to the ordinary high school course. Pupils are classified as in other schools; but persons who become blind at the age of twenty, for instance, must begin with the alphabet, as little children do. Writing is taught by tracing with a pencil letters sunk into a stiff card. This manner of writing can be read by seeing persons only. The point systems — Braille's and Waite's — are generally used by blind persons to communicate with each other. In the Illinois Institution for the Blind the use of the typewriter is being taught, and it is said that some excellent work has already been done by the pupils. In the study of music the notes are read to the pupil, who writes them down in the Braille or Waite systems, and then studies them at the instrument until they are memorized. In most schools books in raised print are used. The first book of this character was printed in Paris in 1784 by M. Valentine Haüy.

Gnostic, a word sometimes confounded with *agnostic*, and employed in a loose and general way to designate a freethinker. Correctly speaking, gnosticism is the term applied to various forms of philosophical speculation which sprang up in the early history of the Church. They were generally regarded as heretical, but the term itself means simply *knowledge*, and does not contain any idea of antagonism to Judaism or Christianity. There were three main schools, or centers, of gnostic speculation: the Syrian of Antioch; the Alexandrian of Egypt, and that of Asia Minor, represented by Marcion of Pontus. Gnosticism represents the first efforts to construct a philosophical system of faith, and the main questions with which it concerned itself were the same which in all ages have agitated inquiry and baffled speculation — the origin of life and origin of evil, how life sprang from an infinite source, how a world so imperfect as this could proceed from a supremely perfect God. All of the schools agreed in the existence of an infinitely Supreme Being, their differences arising in their various speculations to account for the passage from the higher spiritual world to this lower material one. In the Alexandrian thought, evil is but degenerated good. The Syrian school assumed the existence of two living, active, independent principles, good and evil. The former system embraced Judaism as a divine institution, although inferior and defective in its manifestation of the divine character; the latter rejected it as being wholly the work of the Spirit of Darkness. The anti-Judaical spirit was developed to the extreme in Marcion and his followers. The gnostics accepted Christ, but in different and modified lights. According to the Alexandrian school, he is a higher Divine Being, proceeding from the Spiritual Kingdom for the redemption of this lower material kingdom; but however superior, he is yet allied to the lower angels and the Demiurgos, who is an inferior manifestation of Deity partaking of the Divine nature, the intermediary between the Infinite Spirit and the material world, and the immediate creator and governor of this world. The Syrian school, on the other hand, regarded Christ as a being totally distinct from the Demiurgos, who was in their system not the representative and organ of the Supreme Spirit, but a rival Spirit of Darkness; and hence, in coming into this lower world, he was invading the realms of the powers of darkness, in order to seek out and rescue any higher spiritual natures who were living here under the power of the Evil One. Gnosticism has been well termed an extraordinary conglomeration of Monotheism, Pantheism, Spiritualism, and Materialism. It was vague, confused, and irrational for the most part, and yet its influence in the world was not altogether bad. It compelled Christian teachers to face the great problems of which it attempted the solution in so many fantastic forms. It expanded the horizon of controversy within as without the Church, and made the early fathers feel that it was by the weapons of reason and not of authority that they must win the triumph of Catholic Christianity. It may be said to have laid the foundations of Christian science; and Antioch and Alexandria, the centers of half-pagan and half-Christian speculation, became the first centers of rational Christian theology. The several schools began to decline after the middle of the third century. Their doctrines were revived several times by certain sects in the middle ages, but have had no considerable body of adherents since the thirteenth century.

Hades. — The word "hades" is from the Greek. Its etymology is somewhat doubtful, but it is generally believed to have come from the verb *eidein*, meaning to see, and the negative particle *a*. Hence it may mean what is out of sight, the invisible, or, where nothing can be seen, the place of darkness. In Homer the name is applied to Pluto, the lord of the lower regions, perhaps because he was the deity who had the power of making mortals invisible. The Greeks, however, gave up the latter application of the word, and when the Greek Scriptures were written the word was always used to designate the place of departed spirits. It was the common receptacle of departed spirits, the good as well as the bad, and was divided into two parts — the one an Elysium of bliss for the good, the other a Tartarus of punishment and grief for the wicked, and its locality was supposed to be underground in the mud regions of the earth. In the very early stages of Grecian history no complete theory of punishments or rewards in hades had found its way into the popular creed. The prevalent belief was merely that the souls of the departed — with the exception of a few who had personally offended against the gods — were occupied in the lower world in the unreal or shadowy performance of the same actions that had employed them when in the region of day. The poets and dramatists introduced the accessories of tribunals, trials of the dead, a paradise for the good, and place of torture for the bad. The modes of punishment imagined were ingenious, such as that of Ixion, who was bound to an ever-revolving wheel; that of Sisyphus, who was set to roll a huge stone up a steep hill, a toil never ending and still beginning, for as soon as it reached the summit it rolled back again to the plain; or that of Tantalus, who was placed up to his chin in the water, but was unable to quench his thirst, as the water constantly slipped away from him as he raised it to his lips. Over his head also hung a branch loaded with fruit, but, as he stretched forth his hand to grasp it, it sprang from him toward the clouds. It is plain that these punishments had their origin in the imagination of poets rather than of priests or religious teachers.

Illiteracy of Various Nations.— In Russia, Servia, Roumania, and Bulgaria over 80 per cent. of the population are illiterate, Spain 63 per cent., Italy 48 per cent., Hungary 43 per cent., Austria 39 per cent., Ireland 21 per cent., France and Belgium 15 per cent., Holland 10 per cent., United States (whites) 8 per cent., Scotland 7 per cent., Switzerland 2.5 per cent., some parts of Germany 1 per cent. In Sweden, Denmark, and Bavaria, Wurtemberg and Saxony, only rarely a person cannot write.

Hanging Gardens of Babylon.—The Hanging Gardens of Babylon, so celebrated among the Greeks, contained a square of four plethra — that is, 400 feet on every side — and were carried up aloft into the air in the manner of several large terraces, one above another, till the height equaled that of the walls of the city. The ascent was from terrace to terrace by stairs ten feet wide. The whole pile was sustained by vast arches, raised upon other arches, one upon another, and strengthened by a wall, surrounding it on every side, of twenty-two feet thickness. On the top of the arches were first laid large flat stones, sixteen feet long and four broad; over these was a layer of reeds, mixed with a quantity of bitumen, upon which were two rows of bricks, closely cemented together with plaster. The whole was covered with thick sheets of lead, upon which lay the mold of the garden; and all this flooring was contrived to keep the moisture of the mold from running away through the arches. The mold, or earth, laid thereon was so deep that the greatest trees might take root in it; and with such the terraces were covered, as well as with all other plants and flowers that were proper for a garden of pleasure. In the upper terrace there was an engine or kind of pump by which water was drawn up out of the river, and from thence the whole garden was watered. In the spaces between the several arches, upon which the whole structure rested, were large amd magnificent apartments that were very light, and had the advantage of an exceedingly beautiful prospect.

Pan, the chief Grecian god of pastures, forests, and flocks. He was, according to the most common belief, a son of Hermes by a daughter of Dryops, or by Penelope, the wife of Ulysses; while other accounts make Penelope the mother, but Ulysses himself the father — though the paternity of the god is also ascribed to the numerous wooers of Penelope in common. The original seat of his worship was the wild, hilly, and wooded solitudes of Arcadia, whence it gradually spread over the rest of Greece, but was not introduced into Athens until after the battle of Marathon. He is represented as having horns, a goat's beard, a crooked nose, pointed ears, a tail, and goat's feet. He had a terrible voice, which, bursting abruptly on the ear of the traveler in solitary places, inspired him with a sudden fear (whence the word panic). He is also represented as fond of music and of dancing with the forest nymphs, and as the inventor of the syrinx or shepherd's flute, also called Pan's pipe. The fir tree was sacred to him, and he had sanctuaries and temples in various parts of Arcadia, at Troezene, at Sicyon, at Athens, etc. When, after the establishment of Christianity, the heathen deities were degraded by the Church into fallen angels, the characteristics of Pan — the horns, the goat's beard, the pointed ears, the crooked nose, the tail, and the goat's feet — were transferred to the devil himself, and thus the "Auld Hornie" of popular superstition is simply Pan in disguise.

Æsthetics is a term invented about the middle of the last century by Baumgarten, a Professor of Philosophy in the University of Frankfort-on-the-Oder, to denote the science of the Beautiful, particularly of art, as the most perfect manifestation of the Beautiful. Notwithstanding the fact that the Beautiful was a favorite subject of contemplation among the ancients, Baumgarten is held to be the first who considered the subject from the true scientific point of view, and therefore entitled to be called the founder of the philosophy of art. All sensuous apprehension, not in one form or manifestation only, but in every possible form or manifestation, was included in his view of the subject, and this conception he expressed by the word Æsthetics, from the Greek *aisthanomai*, I feel—indicating not absolute or objective knowledge of things, but such as is conditioned subjectively by the play of our sensibilities. Beauty was, with Baumgarten, the result of the highest and purest æsthetic perception, to the realization of which the finer portion of our nature aspires; and to trace which, through the whole sphere of art, was the work of æsthetic philosophy.

COMPULSORY SCHOOL LAWS.

United States.—Thirty one States and two Territories have passed compulsory school laws defining the ages to which the law shall apply, the annual term of school attendance, and the penalty imposed upon parents or guardians for violation of the law.

These requirements are summarized in the following table:—

Compulsory Education Requirements in the United States.

STATE.	AGE.	ANNUAL PERIOD.	PENALTY ON PARENTS OR GUARDIANS.
Maine	8–15	16 weeks (2 terms of 8 weeks each, if practicable).	Fine, $25 (maximum).
New Hampshire	6–16	12 weeks	Each offense, $10 (maximum).
Vermont	8–15	20 weeks	Fine, $10 to $50.
Massachusetts	8–14 or 15	30 weeks	Each offense, forfeit not exceeding $20.
Rhode Island	7–15	12 weeks; 6 consecutive	Each offense, fine $20 (maximum).
Connecticut	*a* 8–14 or 15	8 to 13 years of age, 24 weeks; 13 to 14, 12 weeks.	For each week's neglect, fine $5 (maximum).
New York	*a* 8–14	8 to 12 years of age and unemployed youths 14 to 16, full term; for children 12 to 14, at least 80 days consecutive.	First offense, fine $5 (maximum); each subsequent offense, $50 (maximum) or imprisonment 30 days.
New Jersey	*b* 7–12	20 weeks; 8 consecutive	Each offense, $10 to $25, or imprisonment 1 to 3 months.
Pennsylvania	*a* 8–13	70 per cent. of the entire term.	First offense, $2 (maximum); each subsequent offense, $5 (maximum).
District of Columbia	*c* 6–15	12 weeks; 6 consecutive	Fine, $20 (maximum).
West Virginia	8–14	16 weeks	Fine, not exceeding $5.
Kentucky	7–14	8 consecutive weeks	Fine, $5 to $20 (first offense); $10 to $50 each subsequent offense.
Ohio	*a* 8–14	20 weeks, city district; 16 weeks, village and township districts.	Fine, $5 to $20.
Illinois	7–14	16 weeks; 8 consecutive	Fine, $3 to $20.
Indiana	8–14	12 consecutive weeks	$10 to $50; also, if court so orders, imprisonment 2 to 90 days.
Iowa	7–14	16 consecutive weeks	Fine of not less than $3 nor more than $20 for each offense.
Michigan	*d* 8–14	16 weeks; 6 consecutive	First offense, $5 to $10; each subsequent offense, $10 (minimum).
Wisconsin	7–13	12 weeks	Fine, $3 to $20.
Minnesota	8–16	12 weeks; 6 consecutive	First offense, $10 to $25; each subsequent offense, $25 to $50.
North Dakota	8–14	Full term	First offense, $5 to $20; each subsequent offense, $10 to $50.
South Dakota	8–14	....do	Fine, $10 to $20.
Nebraska	8–14	12 weeks	Each offense, $10 to $50.
Kansas	8–14	12 weeks; 6 consecutive	First offense, fine $5 to $10; each subsequent offense, $10 to $20.
Montana	8–14	....do	Each offense, $5 to $20, or 30 days' imprisonment.
Wyoming	*e* 6–21	12 weeks	Each offense, $25 (maximum).
Colorado	8–14	12 weeks; 8 consecutive	Each offense, $5 to $25.
New Mexico	8–16	12 weeks	Fine, $1 to $25, or imprisonment for not more than 10 days.
Utah	8–14	16 weeks; 10 consecutive	First offense, $10 (maximum); each subsequent offense, $30.
Nevada	*c* 8–14	16 weeks; 8 consecutive	First offense, $50 to $100; each subsequent offense, $100 to $200.
Idaho	8–14	....do	First, $5 to $20; subsequent offenses, $10 to $50.
Washington	8–15	12 weeks	Fine, $10 to $25.
Oregon	8–14	12 weeks; 8 consecutive	First offense, $5 to $25; subsequent offense, $25 to $50.
California	8–14	Two thirds of school term; 12 weeks consecutive.	First offense, $20; each subsequent offense, $20 to $50.

a To 16 if unemployed in labor.
b The law applies to youths 12 to 16 years of age if discharged from employment in order to receive instruction.
c Law not enforced.
d In cities, 7 to 16.
e Penalty imposed only for children 7 to 16.

Compulsory Education in Foreign Countries.

COUNTRY.	AGE.	ATTENDANCE REQUIRED.	PENALTY.
Austria	6-14	Until scholar has acquired prescribed subjects, religion and reading, writing and arithmetic.	Fine, $3.50 (maximum), or imprisonment up to 2 days.
Bavaria	*a* 6-14	....Do	Fine, $11 (maximum), or 8 days' imprisonment.
Belgium	....	No compulsory law	
France	6-13	For 4 absences of half a day in a month the parent is summoned before local school committee.	First and second offenses, warning; subsequent fine, $3 (maximum) and imprisonment 5 days.
England	5-13	Full school term unless by special arrangement.	Determined by local by-laws.
Scotland	5-13	....Do	Fine, $5, or imprisonment 14 days.
Holland	....	No compulsory law	
Hungary	*b* 6-12	8 months, country; 10 months, town.	Fine, from 35 cents to $1.50.
Italy	6-9	No fixed rule	Each offense, 10 cents to $2.
Norway	(*c*)	12 weeks per annum	Fines.
Prussia	6-14	8 years, or until elementary education is completed.	Each offense, 70 cents (maximum), or imprisonment up to three days.
Saxony	*d* 7-15	Same as Austria	Fine, $1.50 to $7.00, or imprisonment from 1 day to 6 weeks.
Sweden	7-14	34½ weeks	
Berne	6-15	Five sixths of possible attendances.	Fines and imprisonment.
Geneva	6-15	4 days a week, 6 hours a day..	Do.
Neufchatel	7-16	After 13 years of age, 10 hours a week.	Fine, 38 cents (minimum), or imprisonment 30 days (maximum).
Tessin (Switzerland)..	6-14	28 hours a week for 6 to 9 months.	Each offense 2 to 3 cents, and 4 hours' imprisonment.
Vaud (Switzerland)...	7-16	33 hours a week	
Grisons (Switzerland).	7-15	....	Fines or imprisonment.
Zurich	6-16	Every day; penalties for 10 absences.	Warnings; subsequently fines, 60 cents to $3.
Wurtemberg	6-14	Every school day	Fine or imprisonment.
British Columbia	7-12	....	Do.
Cape Colony	....	No compulsory law	
New Zealand	7-13	One half the period during which the school is open.	Fine, $10 (maximum).
Nova Scotia	7-12	80 days a year	Fine, $2.
Ontario	7-13	100 days a year	$1 per month for each of the children not attending a school.
Prince Edward Island	8-13	13 weeks a year	Fine.
Quebec	....	No compulsory law	
Queensland	6-12	60 days in each half year, but law not yet enforced.	Fine, $5 to $25, or imprisonment 7 to 30 days.
South Australia	7-13	35 school days per quarter....	Fine, $1.25 to $5.
Tasmania	7-13	3 days a week	

a 13 to 16 in secular Sunday Schools.
b 12 to 15 continuation.
c From 8 until confirmation; in town from 7 until confirmation.
d Special dispensation after 7 years' attendance and 1 year's prolongation for ignorance.

Halacha is the term for the Jewish oral law, and is supposed to be, like the written law contained in the Bible, of divine origin. It embraces the whole field of juridico-political, religious, and practical life down to its most minute and insignificant details. It began to be written down when the sufferings to which the Jews were almost uninterruptedly subjected from the first exile downward had made many portions of it already very uncertain and fluctuating, and threatened finally to obliterate it altogether from memory. The first collection of laws was instituted by Hillel, Akiba, and Gamaliel; but the final reduction of the general code, Mishna, is due to Jehudah Hanassi, A. D. 220. The Halacha was further developed in subsequent centuries by the Saboraim, Geonim, and the authorities of each generation.

Oneida Community is a society of Perfectionists, or Bible Communists, founded by John Humphrey Noyes, who was born at Brattleborough, Vt., in 1811. He was originally a lawyer, then studied theology at Andover and Yale, and became a Congregational minister, but soon lost his license to preach on account of the views which he adopted. The Community is situated on Oneida Creek, in Lenox township, Madison County, N. Y., where it owns a fine estate, several mills and manufactories, and is said to be in a prosperous condition. The cardinal principles of the Community are four in number: reconciliation to God, salvation from sin, recognition of the brotherhood and equality of man and woman, and the community of labor and its fruits. The last named principle embraces a scheme by which all the male and all the female members of the Community are held in a sense to be married to each other. This has led to the charge being made against them of being "free-lovers"; but, says one writer, "The system, as regulated by the 'principle of sympathy' and controlled by that free public opinion which constitutes the supreme government of the society, is far from being amenable to the reproach of immorality in any sense of the word." The Community reject all rules of conduct except those which each believer formulates for himself, subject to the free criticism of his associates. They hold that the Mosaic law and ordinances were abrogated by the second coming of Christ, which they place at A. D. 70, and at which time the reign of sin was concluded; and true believers have since been free to follow the indications of the Holy Spirit in all things, nothing being good or bad in itself. While all the males and females are united by a "complex marriage," their intercourse — which, in theory, is unfettered by any law — is, in practice, subject to a good deal of regulation. Like everything else, it is subject to the opinion of the society, and certain principles have been so steadily applied to it that they have gained the force of laws. First, there is the principle of the ascending fellowship. There should be contrast, the Perfectionists say, between those who become united in love. That there should be differences of temperament and of complexion has, they say, been well ascertained by physiologists. They hold that there should be a difference in age also, so that the young and passionate may be united to those who have, by experience, gained self-control. In virtue of this principle, the younger women fall to the older men, and the younger men to the older women. A second principle is that there should be no exclusive attachment between individuals; a third, that persons should not be obliged to receive the attentions of those whom they do not like; and, lastly, it is held indispensable that connections should be formed through the agency of a third party; because, without this, the question of their propriety might be open to criticism, and also because this affords the lady an easy opportunity of declining.

Pagodas are in most instances pyramidal-shaped temples consisting of various layers of stones piled one upon another in successive recession, and covered all over with the richest ornamentation. They are among the most remarkable monuments of Hindoo architecture. The pilasters and columns, which take a prominent rank in the ornamental portion of these temples, show the greatest variety of forms; some pagodas are also overlaid with strips of copper, having the appearance of gold. Though the word pagoda is used to designate but the temple, it is in reality an aggregate of various monuments, which in their totality constitute the holy place sacred to the god. Sanctuaries, porches, colonnades, gateways, walls, tanks, etc., are generally combined for this purpose according to a plan which is more or less uniform. Several series of walls form an inclosure; between them are alleys, habitations for the priests, etc.; and the interior is occupied by the temple itself, with buildings for the pilgrims, tanks, porticoes, and open colonnades. The walls have, at their openings, large pyramidal gateways higher than themselves, and so constructed that the gateway of the outer wall is always higher than that of the succeeding inner wall. These gateways are pyramidal buildings of the most elaborate workmanship, and consist of several, sometimes as many as fifteen, stories. The pagoda of Chalambron, in Tanjore, is one of the most celebrated and most sacred of these monuments in India. The buildings of which this pagoda is composed cover an oblong square 360 feet long and 210 wide. The pagodas of Juggernaut on the north end of the coast of Coromandel are three in number, and are surrounded by a wall of black stone, whence they are called by Europeans the Black Pagodas. The height of the principal one is said to be 344 feet; according to some, however, it does not exceed 120-123 feet. The term pagoda is also applied, but not correctly, to those Chinese buildings of a tower form, as the Porcelain Tower of Nanking. These buildings differ materially from the Hindoo pagodas, not only as regards their style and exterior appearance, but inasmuch as they are buildings intended for other than religious purposes. The word pagoda is, according to some, a corruption of the Sanskrit word *bhâgavata*, from *bhagavat*, sacred; but according to others, a corruption of *put-gada*, from the Persian *put*, idol, and *gada*, house.

Hampshire Shakers.— This community of Shakers settled in the New Forest, near Lymington, Hampshire, England, in 1872 or 1873, and consisted of eighty-three persons. Their leader, a Mrs. Girling, wife of an Ipswich builder, declared herself to be the woman of the twelfth chapter of Revelations, who was "clothed with the sun, and the moon under her feet." These Girlingites, or Bible Christians, as they called themselves, believed that the earth and the fullness thereof belonged to the elect, and that they were the elect. They professed to take the literal scriptures for their guide in all things, yet were so little inclined to earn their bread by the sweat of their brow that they got into debt, mortgaged the cottages which had been secured for them by a Miss Wood, a convert, and finally lost their property in 1878, when, as a community, they passed out of existence.

Pantheon of Rome, a famous temple of circular form, built by M. Agrippa, son-in-law of Augustus, in his third consulship, about 27 B. C. The edifice was called the Pantheon, not, as is commonly supposed, from its having been sacred to all the gods, but from its majestic dome, which represented, as it were, the "*all-divine*" firmament. It was dedicated to Jupiter Ultor. Beside the statue of this god, however, there were in six other niches as many colossal statues of other deities, among which were those of Mars and Venus, the founders of the Julian line, and that of Julius Cæsar. The Pantheon is by far the largest structure of ancient times, the external diameter being 188 feet, and the height to the summit of the upper cornice 102 feet, exclusive of the flat dome or calotte, which makes the entire height about 148 feet. It has a portico, in the style of the Corinthian architecture, 110 feet in length and 44 feet in depth, made up of 16 granite columns, with marble capitals and bases, placed in three rows, each column being 5 feet in diameter and 46½ feet high. These columns supported a pediment with a roof of bronze. The Pantheon stands near the ancient Campus Martius, and, after the lapse of 1900 years, is still the best preserved of the old Roman buildings. It was given to Boniface IV. by the Emperor Phocas in 609, and was dedicated as a Christian church to the Virgin and the Holy Martyrs, a quantity of whose relics was placed under the great altar. In 830, Gregory IV. dedicated it to all the saints. It is now known as the Church of Santa Maria Rotunda. This consecration of the edifice, however, seems to have afforded it no defense against the subsequent spoliations, both of emperors and popes. The plates of gilded bronze that covered the roof, the bronze bassi-relievi of the pediment, and the silver that adorned the interior of the dome, were carried off by Constans II., A. D. 655, who destined them for his imperial palace at Constantinople; but, being murdered at Syracuse when on his return with them, they were taken by their next proprietors to Alexandria. Urban VIII. carried off all that was left to purloin — the bronze beams of the portico, which amounted in weight to more than 45,000,000 pounds. During eight centuries it has suffered from the dilapidations of time and the cupidity of barbarians. The seven steps which elevated it above the level of ancient Rome are buried beneath the modern pavement. Its rotunda of brick is blackened and decayed; the marble statues, the bassi-relievi, the brazen columns, have disappeared; its ornaments have vanished, its granite columns have lost their luster, and its marble capitals their purity. Yet, under every disadvantage, it is still pre-eminently beautiful. No eye can rest on the noble simplicity of the matchless portico without admiration. Its beauty is of that sort which, while the fabric stands, time has no power to destroy.

Oracles dated from the highest antiquity, and flourished in the most remote ages. The word signifies the response delivered by a deity or supernatural being to a worshiper or inquirer, and also the place where the response was delivered. These responses were supposed to be given by a certain divine afflatus, either through means of mankind, as in the orgasms of the Pythia, and the dreams of the worshiper in the temples; or by its effect on certain objects, as the tinkling of the caldrons at Dodona, the rustling of the sacred oak, the murmuring of the streams; or by the action of sacred animals, as exemplified in the Apis or sacred bull of Memphis, and the feeding of holy chickens of the Romans. These responses, however, had always to be interpreted to the inquirer by the priesthood. It is probable that all the Egyptian temples were oracular, although only a few are mentioned by Herodotus, as the oracles of Latona in the city of Buto; those of Hercules, Mars, Thebes, and Meroe. Oracles were also used by the Hebrews. The Grecian oracles enjoyed the highest reputation for truthfulness, and the most renowned of all was the Delphic Oracle. Sacrifices were offered by the inquirers, who walked with laurel crowns on their heads, and delivered sealed questions; the response was deemed infallible, and was usually dictated by justice, sound sense, and reason, till the growing political importance of the shrine rendered the guardians of it fearful to offend, when they framed answers in ambiguous terms, or allowed the influence of gold and presents to corrupt the inspirations. There were numerous other oracles in Greece and in Asia Minor, and written ones existed of the prophecies of celebrated seers. Those of the Sibyls or prophetic women enjoyed great popularity.

Holy Grail.— The Holy Grail was one of the leading themes of mediæval romance, fabled to have been the cup or chalice used by Christ in the Last Supper, and in which he changed the wine into blood. This chalice, preserved by Joseph of Arimathea, had also received the blood which flowed from the side of Christ on the cross. This is what the apocryphal gospel of Nicodemus says, but no early mention is made of it by either profane or ecclesiastical writers. In the twelfth century it reappears as the central subject of the prophecies of Merlin and the object of the adventurous quest of the Knights of the Round Table. It was also mixed up, by romance, with the struggles in Spain between Moors and Christians, and with the foundation of the Order of Templars in Palestine.

Peter the Hermit was the apostle of the first crusade, and was born in the diocese of Amiens, France, about the middle of the eleventh century. After engaging in several pursuits he became a hermit, and in 1093 undertook a pilgrimage to Jerusalem, where the oppression he witnessed and experienced determined him to arouse the people of Christendom to undertake a war for the liberation of the holy sepulcher. The first host of crusaders was led by Peter in person, and was unsuccessful. He was associated with the expedition under Godfrey of Bouillon. While the crusaders were besieged in Antioch, he deserted, but was captured and brought back. On the conquest of Jerusalem he preached a sermon to the crusaders on the Mount of Olives. After this he returned to Europe and founded the Abbey of Neufmoustier, near Huy, where he died in 1115.

UNIVERSITIES AND COLLEGES OF THE UNITED STATES.

Organized.	Colleges.	Location.	Denominational Control.	President or Chairman of Faculty.	Instructors.*	Students.*	Volumes in Library.	Productive Funds—Amount of.
1873	Add-Ran Christ. Un.†	Waco, Tex.	Christian	E. C. Snow, A.M. (Act. Pres.)	16	225	4,000	$10,000
1896	Adelphi College†	Brooklyn, N. Y	Non-Sect	C. H. Levermore, Ph.D	25	166	8,500	....
1859	Adrian College†	Adrian, Mich	Meth. Prot.	T. H. Lewis, D.D	15	164	4,000	66,307
1872	Alabama Poly. Inst.†	Auburn, Ala	Non-Sect	W.LeRoy Broun, M.A. LL.D.	32	412	15,579	252,500
1861	Albion College†	Albion, Mich	Meth. Epis.	Samuel Dickie, LL.D	25	490	15,000	255,000
1836	Alfred University†	Alfred, N. Y.	Non-Sect	Rev. Boothe C. Davis, Ph.D.	25	240	13,700	293,000
1815	Allegheny College†	Meadville, Pa.	Meth. Epis.	William H. Crawford, D.D.	18	323	15,000	225,000
1886	Alma College†	Alma, Mich	Presbyter'n	Rev. A. F. Bruske, M.S., D.D.	23	259	17,500	225,000
1893	Am. Un. of Harriman†	Harriman, Tenn.	Non-Sect	J. F. Spence, A.M., LL.D.	30	350	2,500	....
1891	American Univ.†(*b*)	Washington, D. C.	Meth. Epis.	John F. Hurst, D.D., LL.D.	..	..	8,000	....
1821	Amherst College	Amherst, Mass	Non-Sect	George Harris, D.D., LL.D.	36	410	75,000	1,700,000
1872	Amity College† (*q*)	College Springs, Ia	Non-Sect	Rev. J. C. Calhoun, A.B., A.M.	11	146	4,000	....
1807	Andover Theol. Sem.	Andover, Mass	Congregat'l.	Chas. O. Day, D.D	8	12	52,000	800,000
1853	Antioch College†	Yellow Springs, O.	Non-Sect	William A. Bell, M.A., LL.D.	12	118	7,000	101,000
1872	Arkansas College†	Batesville, Ark	Presbyter'n	Eugene R. Long, Ph.D	10	124	4,200	....
1893	Armour Inst. Tech'y†.	Chicago, Ill. (*q*)	Non-Sect	V. C. Alderson (Act. Pres.)	38	1,000	15,000	2,500,000
1842	Asheville College‡	Asheville, N. C	Non-Sect	Archibald A. Jones	17	200	2,500	None
1869	Atlanta University†	Atlanta, Ga	Non-Sect	Horace Bumstead, D.D.	15	300	11,000	44,000
1820	Auburn Theol. Sem'y.	Auburn, N. Y.	Presbyter'n	Rev. G. B. Stewart, D.D	8	56	27,140	625,000
1869	Augsburg Seminary	Minneapolis, Minn	Lutheran	Georg Sverdrup	8	170	2,000	None
1860	Augustana College†	Rock Island, Ill.	Lutheran	Gustav Andreen, Ph.D.	33	619	18,000	60,000
1858	Baker University†	Baldwin, Kan.	Meth. Epis.	Lemuel H. Murlin, A.M	32	715	10,000	20,000
1846	Baldwin University†	Berea, O.	Meth. Epis.	Rev. R. M. Freshwater, D.D.	22	372	7,000	85,362
1889	Barnard College‡(*d*)	Manh'n Boro, N.Y.	Non-Sect	Laura D. Gill, A.B. (Dean)	50	400	1,500	....
1863	Bates College†	Lewiston, Me.	Free Bapt.	George C. Chase, D.D., LL.D.	23	330	25,000	366,000
1845	Baylor University†	Waco, Tex.	Baptist	Oscar H. Cooper, LL.D.	47	936	11,000	12,600
1880	Bellevue College†	Bellevue, Neb.	Presbyter'n	Rev. D. R. Kerr, Ph.D., D.D.	20	125	4,000	24,000
1847	Beloit College†	Beloit, Wis.	Non-Sect	G. L. Collie, Ph.D. (Act. Pres.)	28	355	30,000	856,000
1855	Berea College†	Berea, Ky.	Non-Sect	Wm. G. Frost, Ph.D., D.D.	33	825	18,500	450,000
1881	Bethany College† (*q*)	Lindsborg, Kan.	Lutheran	Rev. C. Swensson, Ph.D	30	700	5,000	....
1854	Bethel College	Russellville, Ky.	Baptist	Rev. E. S. Alderman, D.D.	7	104	6,000	125,000
1867	Biddle University§	Charlotte, N. C.	Presbyter'n	Rev. D. J. Sanders, D.D	14	234	13,000	....
1869	Boston University†	Boston, Mass.	Meth. Epis.	W. F. Warren, D.D., LL.D.	144	1,350	......	752,000
1794	Bowdoin College	Brunswick, Me.	Congregat'l.	Wm. De Witt Hyde, D.D.	40	360	70,000	788,000
1877	Brigham Young Col.†	Logan, Utah	Latter Day	James H. Linford, B.S., B.D.	28	510	2,700	100,000
1764	Brown University†	Providence, R. I.	Non-Sect	W. H. P. Faunce, A.M., D.D.	75	899	115,000	1,874,297
1880	Bryn Mawr College‡	Bryn Mawr, Pa.	Non-Sect	M. Carey Thomas, LL.D	44	417	36,123	100,000
1872	Buchtel College†	Akron, O.	Univ'rsalist.	Rev. A. B. Church, A.M., B.A.	18	245	6,000	....
1846	Bucknell University†.	Lewisburg, Pa.	Baptist	John H. Harris, LL.D.	32	530	22,000	430,000
1848	Burritt College†	Spencer, Tenn.	Christian	W. N. Billingsley, A. M.	13	252	4,350	....
1850	Butler College†	Indianapolis, Ind.	Non-Sect	Scot Butler, A.M., LL.D	25	396	7,000	300,000
1870	Canisius College (*b*).	Buffalo, N. Y.	R. Catholic.	Rev. Aloysius Pfeil, S. J.	38	380	24,000	....
1866	Carleton College†	Northfield, Minn.	Congregat'l.	W. H. Sallman, D.D	21	366	15,400	200,000
1851	Carson & Newman C.†	Jeff. City, Tenn.	Baptist	J. T. Henderson, A.M.	14	331	4,000	50,000
1870	Carthage College†	Carthage, Ill	Lutheran	Rev. Fred. L. Sigmund, A.M.	14	175	5,000	50,000
1880	Case Sc. Appl. Science	Cleveland, O	Non-Sect	Cady Staley, Ph.D., LL.D.	24	350	2,000	....
1851	Catawba College† (*q*)	Newton, N. C.	Reformed	C. H. Mebane, A.B	10	162	2,500	....
1887	Catholic Univ. Am. (*f*)	Washington, D. C.	R. Catholic.	Rt. Rev. T. J. Conaty, S.T.D.	27	150	35,000	890,000
1894	Cedarville College†	Cedarville, O	Ref. Presb.	Rev. D. McKinney, D.D.	11	95	1,200	20,000
1855	Central College†	Fayette, Mo	Meth. Ep. S.	T. B. Smith, A.M. (Act. Pres)	11	271	6,500	60,000
1855	Central Penn'a Coll.†	New Berlin, Pa.	Evangelical.	Rev. A. E. Gobble, A.M., D.D.	10	100	5,330	69,300
1853	Central University†	Pella, Iowa	Baptist	L. A. Garrison, B. A.	13	235	5,000	44,000
1874	Central University	Danville, Ky	Presbyterian	*See note "h" on page* 532	112	1,280	18,000	550,000
1864	Central Wesleyan Col.†	Warrenton, Mo.	Meth. Epis.	Geo. B. Addicks, D.D., A.M.	14	235	6,500	....
1891	Charles City College†	Charles City, Iowa	Meth. Epis.	J. F. Hirsch, M.A.	9	246	1,500	25,000

Universities and Colleges of the United States.—*Continued.*

Organized.	Colleges.	Location.	Denominational Control.	President or Chairman of Faculty.	Instructors.*	Students.*	Volumes in Library.	Productive Funds—Amount of.
1875	Charleston College....	Charleston, S. C...	Non.Sect....	Harrison Randolph, LL.D..	7	58	14,511	$299,000
1851	Christian Univ.† (*q*)...	Canton, Mo........	Disciples....	D. R. Dungan, A.M.........	20	280	1,000	....
1869	Claflin University†§...	Orangeburg, S. C..	Meth. Epis..	L. M. Dunton, A.M., D.D...	30	750	6,000	5,000
1869	Clark University†.....	Atlanta, Ga........	Meth. Epis..	Chas.M.Melden, Ph.D.,D.D.	21	550	1,000	None
1887	Clark University†.....	Worcester, Mass..	Non-Sect....	G. Stanley Hall,Ph.D.,LL.D.	..	..	20,000	....
1889	Clemson Agri. College	Clemson Col., S. C.	Non-Sect....	Henry S. Hartzog, LL.D.....	40	510	5.500	....
1881	Coe College†...........	Cedar Rapids, Ia..	Presbyterian	Rev. S. B. McCormick, D.D.	18	326	3,500	61,000
1818	Colby College†........	Waterville, Me....	Baptist......	Rev. Chas. L. White, A.M..	14	180	37,000	417,507
1819	Colgate University....	Hamilton, N. Y....	Baptist......	Geo. E. Merrill, D. D., LL. D.	32	360	30,000	1,500,000
1847	College City of N. Y..	Manh'n Boro. N.Y.	Non-Sect....	Alex. Stewart Webb,LL.D...	80	2,126	34.386	....
1874	Colorado College†.....	Colorado Sp's, Col.	Non-Sect....	W. F. Slocum, LL.D., D.D..	34	515	25.000	356,000
1754	Columbia Univ. (*d*)....	Manh'n Boro, N.Y.	Non-Sect....	N. M. Butler,LL.D.(Act.Pr.)	384	4,036	311,000	13,361,977
1821	Columbian Univ. (*e*)...	Washington, D. C.	Non-Sect....	Charles W. Needham, LL.D,	164	1,415	20,000	256,075
1839	Concordia College....	Fort Wayne, Ind..	Lutheran ...	Jos. Schmidt, A.M..........	8	162	4,600	....
1890	Converse College‡.....	Spartanburg, S.C..	Non-Sect....	Benj. Wilson, B. A., M. A..	31	426	5,400	320,000
1853	Cornell College†.......	Mt. Vernon, Iowa.	Meth. Epis..	Wm. F. King, D.D., LL.D..	35	716	20,000	188,813
1868	Cornell University†...	Ithaca, N. Y.......	Non-Sect....	J. G. Schurman, LL.D......	366	2,980	250,000	6,891,627
1889	Cotner University†....	Bethany, Neb......	Christian....	W. P. Aylsworth, LL.D.....	39	237	2,000	....
1878	Creighton University.	Omaha, Neb........	R. Catholic..	Rev. M. P. Dowling, S. J...	58	380	11,500	200,000
1842	Cumberland Univ.†....	Lebanon, Tenn....	Cumb. Pres..	N,Green, LL.D.(Ch. Fac.)...	23	237	6,000	105,000
1885	Dakota University†...	Mitchell, S. Dak...	Meth. Epis..	Rev.W.I.Graham, D.D.,A.M	13	368	3,000	....
1769	Dartmouth College (*q*)	Hanover, N. H....	Non-Sect....	Wm. J. Tucker, D.D., LL.D.	68	768	93,000	2,500,000
1837	Davidson College......	Davidson, N. C....	Presbyterian	Henry L. Smith, A. B.,A.M.	13	175	15,000	125,000
1850	Defiance College†......	Defiance, O.........	Christian....	J. R. H. Latchaw,A.M.,D.D.	10	150	1 000	20,000
1833	Delaware College......	Newark, Del.......	Non-Sect....	Geo. A. Harter, M. A.,Ph.D.	19	110	12,000	83,000
1831	Denison University†..	Granville, O.......	Baptist......	Rev. Emory W. Hunt, D.D.	34	484	21,000	650,000
1864	Denver University†...	Univ. Park, Col....	Meth. Epis..	H. A. Buchtel, D.D., LL.D..	114	878	12,000	214,000
1837	De Pauw Univ.† (*q*)....	Greencastle, Ind..	Meth. Epis..	Rev. H. A. Gobin, D.D......	28	635	12,983	....
1865	Des Moines College†..	Des Moines, Iowa.	Baptist......	Geo. D. Adams, A. M., D.D.	15	181	6,000	....
1783	Dickinson College†....	Carlisle, Pa........	Meth. Epis..	Geo. E. Reed, S. T. D.,LL.D.	29	490	35,000	350,000
1872	Doane College†........	Crete, Neb.........	Congregat'l..	David B. Perry, A. M., D.D.	10	169	8,300	152,405
1891	Drake University†....	Des Moines, Iowa.	Christian....	Wm. B. Craig, D.D., LL.D..	90	1,764	7,000	150,000
1866	Drew Theol. Sem.......	Madison, N. J.....	Meth. Epis..	Henry A. Buttz, D.D.,LL.D.	7	185	69,000	400,000
1873	Drury College†........	Springfield, Mo....	Non-Sect....	Homer T. Fuller,Ph.D.,D.D.	21	350	25,000	235,000
1847	Earlham College†......	Richmond, Ind....	Or. Friends..	Joseph J. Mills, A.M.,LL.D.	14	298	31,000	204,000
1855	Elmira College‡ (*q*)....	Elmira, N. Y.......	Presbyterian	Rev. A. C. MacKenzie. D.D.	20	200	8,000	....
1890	Elon College†..........	Elon College, N. C.	Christian....	Rev.W.W.Staley, A.M.,D.D.	10	150	2,500	....
1838	Emory & Henry Col...	Emory, Va.........	Meth. Ep. S.	R.G. Waterhouse, M.A.,D.D.	9	112	11,000	20,000
1836	Emory College	Oxford, Ga.........	Meth. Ep. S.	C. E. Dowman, A.M., D.D...	14	279	20,000	145,431
1883	Emporia College†......	Emporia, Kan.....	Presbyterian	Rev. J. C. Miller, A.M.,D.D.	12	140	5,000	....
1855	Eureka College†.......	Eureka, Ill.........	Disciples....	R. E. Hieronymus, A.M.....	16	225	6,500	40,000
1867	Ewing College†........	Ewing, Ill..........	Baptist......	J. A. Leavitt,F.R.,D.D.,G.S.	12	215	5,500	16,000
1895	Fairmount College†...	Wichita, Kan......	Congregat'l..	N. J. Morrison, D.D., LL.D.	21	233	21.000	100,000
1888	Fargo College†........	Fargo, N. Dak.....	Congregat'l..	Rev.J.H.Morley,A.M.,LL.D.	12	163	3,935	....
1886	Findlay College†.......	Findlay, O.........	Ch. of God..	Rev. C. Manchester, D.D...	15	285	1,300	49,571
1866	Fisk University† (*c*)...	Nashville, Tenn ...	Congregat'l..	Rev. Jas. G. Merrill, D.D....	30	502	7,142	48,600
1881	Fort Worth Univ.†....	Fort Worth, Tex..	Meth. Epis..	Rev. O. L. Fisher,A.M.,D.D.	51	869	3,000	....
1834	Franklin College†.....	Franklin, Ind......	Baptist......	Rev. W. T. Stott, D.D.,A.M.	11	178	13,000	214,000
1825	Franklin College†.....	New Athens, O....	Non-Sect....	R. Barclay Spicer..........	10	80	500	None
1787	Franklin & Marshall..	Lancaster, Pa......	Ref. in U. S.	Rev. J. S. Stahr, Ph.D.,D.D.	26	403	35,702	345,000
1854	Furman University†..	Greenville, S. C....	Baptist......	A. P. Montague, LL.D......	13	243	....	65,000
1844	Gale College† (*q*)......	Galesville, Wis....	Presbyterian	Wm. D. Thomas,D.D.,Ph.D.	10	120	10,000	....
1817	General Theol. Sem....	Manh'n Boro, N.Y.	Prot. Epis...	E. A. Hoffman, D.D. (Dean)	14	144	30,281	2,150,415
1848	Geneva College†.......	Beaver Falls, Pa..	Ref. Presb...	W. P. Johnston,A.M., D.D..	15	215	4,500	127,000
1829	Georgetown Col.† (*q*)..	Georgetown, Ky..	Baptist......	A. Yager, Ph.D. (Act. Pres.)	19	360	12,000	....
1889	Georgetown Univ.....	Washington, D. C.	R. Catholic..	Rev.Jerome Daugherty,S.J	108	725	85,600	47,000
1848	Girard College	Philadelphia, Pa..	Non-Sect....	A.H.Fetterolf, Ph.D., LL.D.	67	1,693	16,174	15,987,593
1872	Granbury College†....	Granbury, Tex....	Meth. Ep. S.	H. A. Scomp, Ph.D.,LL.D..	9	174	1,000	....
1867	Grant University†.....	Ch't'n'ga, Tenn.††.	Meth. Epis..	Rev.John H.Race,A.M.,D D	72	821	6.000	10,800
1838	Greensboro College‡..	Greensboro, N. C..	Meth. Ep. S.	Dred Peacock, A. B., A. M.	14	165	7,000	None
1794	Gr'nville & Tusc. Col.†	Tusculum, Tenn...	Presbyterian	Rev. Jere. Moore, D.D......	(*q*) 7	(*q*)106	8,200	....
1891	Greer College†........	Hoopeston, Ill.....	Non-Sect....	J. M. Clary, A. B., LL. B....	8	230	400	40,000
1876	Grove City College†...	Grove City, Pa....	Non-Sect....	Rev. I. C. Ketler,Ph.D.,D.D.	18	662	5,000	....
1837	Guilford College†......	Guilford Col., N.C.	Friends......	Lewis L. Hobbs, A. B., A.M.	10	200	6,000	53,000
1862	Gustav. Adolphus C†..	St. Peter, Minn....	Lutheran....	M. Wahlstrom, A.M., Ph.D.	21	351	10,000	10,400
1812	Hamilton College......	Clinton, N. Y......	Non-Sect....	M. W. Stryker, D.D., LL.D.	20	183	41,000	505,000
1854	Hamline Univ.†.......	St. Paul, Minn. (*x*)	Meth. Epis..	Rev. G. H. Bridgman, D.D..	67	448	6,500	100,000
1776	Hampden-Sidney Col..	Hamp.-Sidney, Va.	Non-Sect....	Richard McIlwaine, D.D...	9	109	15,000	150,000
1868	Hampton Inst.† (*j*)....	Hampton, Va......	Non-Sect....	Rev. H. B. Frissell, D.D....	80	1,061	11,000	927.000
1828	Hanover College†......	Hanover, Ind......	Presbyterian	D. W. Fisher, D.D., LL.D...	13	175	15,000	200,000
1834	Hartford Theol. Sem.†	Hartford, Ct......	Congregat'l..	Rev. C. D. Hartranft, D.D..	(*q*)17	(*q*) 75	74,000	....
1636	Harvard University...	Cambridge, Mass..	Non-Sect....	Charles Wm. Eliot, LL.D...	483	5,124	576,900	13,119,538
1830	Haverford College. ..	Haverford, Pa.....	Friends......	Isaac Sharpless,Sc.D., LL.D	19	125	38,500	1,000,000
1850	Heidelberg Univ.†....	Tiffin, O...........	Ref. in U. S.	F. A. Sonnedecker, A.M....	22	374	20,000	125,000
1884	Hendrix College......	Conway, Ark......	Meth. Ep. S.	Rev. A. C. Millar, A.M......	10	151	6,500	30,000
1892	Henry College†........	Campbell, Tex.(*k*)	Non-Sect....	T. H. Bridges...............	19	350	800	18,000
1857	Highland University†	Highland, Kan....	Presbyterian	Amos A. Davis, A.B., A.M..	7	55	1,500	40,000
1855	Hillsdale College......	Hillsdale, Mich....	Free Baptist	C. H. Gurney,A.M.(Act.P't).	14	341	9,861	170,323

Universities and Colleges of the United States.—*Continued.*

Organized.	Colleges.	Location.	Denominational Control.	President or Chairman of Faculty.	Instructors.*	Students.*	Volumes in Library.	Productive Funds—Amount of.
1850	Hiram College†	Hiram, O	Disciples	E. B. Wakefield, A.M.	25	450	10,000	....
1849	Hiwassee College†	Hiwassee, Tenn	Non-Sect	Rev. J. E. Lowry, A.M.	6	135	6,000	....
1822	Hobart College	Geneva, N. Y.	Prot. Epis.	Rev. Robt. E. Jones, S.T.D.	15	94	38,688	$449,731
1843	Holy Cross College	Worcester, Mass.	R. Catholic	Rev. Jos. F. Hanselman, S.J	26	370	....	....
1866	Hope College†	Holland, Mich.	Ref. in Am.	Gerrit J. Kollen, A.M., LL.D.	14	170	15,000	240.000
1841	Howard College†	East Lake, Ala.	Baptist	F. M. Roof, A.M.	10	150	6,000	1,500
1867	Howard University†	Washington, D. C.	Non-Sect	J. E. Rankin, D.D., LL.D.	55	910	20,000	....
1890	Howard Payne Coll.†	Brownwood, Tex.	Baptist	J. H. Grove, M.S.D., A.M.	8	214	2,000	....
1829	Illinois College	Jacksonville, Ill.	Non-Sect	C. W. Barnes, M.A., B.D.	15	125	14,000	....
1850	Ill. Wesleyan Univ.†	Bloomington, Ill.	Meth. Epis.	Edgar M. Smith, M.A, D.D.	34	1,421	10,000	100.000
1820	Indiana University†	Bloomington, Ind.	Non-Sect	Joseph Swain, LL.D.	70	1,137	39,000	600,000
1848	Iowa College†	Grinnell, Iowa	Congregat'l.	Daniel F. Bradley, D.D.	30	442	27,916	360,000
1868	Iowa State College†	Ames, Iowa	Non-Sect	A. B. Storms, D.D.	69	1,160	14,000	682,833
1844	Iowa Wesleyan Univ.†	Mt. Pleasant, Iowa	Meth. Epis.	J. W. Hancher, A.M., S.T.D.	24	428	7,200	58,255
1894	Jacob Tome Inst.†	Port Deposit, Md.	Non-Sect	A. W. Harris, A.M. (Director)	39	550	8,000	....
1883	John B. Stetson Un.	De Land, Fla.	Baptist	John F. Forbes, A.M., Ph.D.	38	369	12,000	208,000
1876	Johns Hopkins U. (*a*)	Baltimore, Md.	Non-Sect	Ira Remsen, LL.D.	143	651	100,000	2,500,000
1855	Kalamazoo College†	Kalamazoo, Mich.	Baptist	A. G. Slocum, LL.D.	14	217	7,116	208,802
1886	Kansas Wesleyan U.†	Salina, Kan.	Meth. Epis.	M. E. Phillips, D.D. (Chan.)	26	618	3,000	None
1858	Kentucky Univ.†	Lexington, Ky (*y*)	Christian	B. A. Jenkins, A.M., B.D.	61	1,108	18,500	....
1866	Ky. Wesleyan Col.†	Winchester, Ky.	Meth. Ep. S.	Rev. John L Weber, Litt.D.	12	150	6,500	45,000
1825	Kenyon College	Gambier, O.	Prot. Epis.	Rev. W. F. Peirce, M.A., LHD.	25	215	25,000	375,000
1892	Keuka College†	Keuka Park, N. Y.	Free Bapt.	Rev. Geo. H. Ball, A.M., D.D.	16	160	3,000	200,000
1837	Knox College†	Galesburg, Ill.	Non-Sect	Thomas McClelland, D.D.	26	665	9,000	250,000
1832	Lafayette College	Easton, Pa.	Presbyterian	E. D. Warfield, LL.D.	29	426	21,200	446,828
1858	La Grange College†	La Grange, Mo.	Baptist	Jere. T. Muir, LL.D., A.M.	12	160	7,000	....
1857	Lake Forest Univ.†	Lake Forest, Ill. (*p*)	Presbyterian	Richard D. Harlan, A.M.	55	373	17,000	695,000
1829	Lane Theol. Seminary	Cincinnati, O.	Presbyterian	....	6	20	19,000	322,837
1863	La Salle College	Philadelphia, Pa.	R. Catholic	Brother Wolfred	18	193	9,500	None
1847	Lawrence Univ.†	Appleton, Wis.	Int'denom'l.	Samuel Plantz, Ph.D., D.D.	26	451	18,410	239,000
1866	Lebanon Valley Col.†	Annville, Pa.	U. Brethren.	Rev. H. U. Roop, A.M., Ph.D.	25	433	10,000	40,000
1866	Lehigh University	S. Bethlehem, Pa.	Non-Sect	Thomas M. Drown, LL.D.	44	542	100,000	....
1891	Leland Stanford, Jr.†	Palo Alto, Cal.	Non-Sect	David Starr Jordan, LL.D.	115	1,378	75,000	16,000,000
1870	Leland University†§	New Orleans, La.	Non-Sect	R. W. Perkins, M.A., Ph.D.	29	748	2,000	....
1856	Lenox College†	Hopkinton, Iowa.	Presbyterian	Andrew G. Wilson, A.M.	12	165	4,500	....
1875	Liberty College†	Glasgow, Ky.	Baptist	Rev. J. H. Burnett, A.M.	11	233	1,000	None
1893	Lima College†	Lima, O.	Lutheran	Rev. S. P. Long, A.M.	9	286	1,000	....
1865	Lincoln College†	Lincoln, Ill.	Cumb. Pres.	J. L. Goodknight, A.M., D.D	14	174	3,000	115,000
1882	Livingstone College†§	Salisbury, N. C.	Afric. Meth.	Wm. H. Goler, D.D.	15	350	2,500	121,000
1851	Lombard College†	Galesburg, Ill.	Universalist.	Charles E. Nash, A.M., D.D.	20	215	7,000	175,000
1884	Macalester College†	St. Paul, Minn.	Presbyterian	James Wallace, Ph.D.	14	168	7,500	....
1853	Manhattan College	Manh'n Boro, N.Y.	R. Catholic	Rev. Bro. Charles, F.S.C.	38	561	10,290	None
1835	Marietta College†	Marietta, O.	Non-Sect	Alfred T. Perry, A.M., D.D.	21	300	60,000	260,000
1819	Maryville College†	Maryville, Tenn.	Presbyterian	Samuel F. Wilson, D.D.	15	378	12,000	250,000
1863	Mass. Agric. College†	Amherst, Mass.	Non-Sect	Henry H. Goodell, LL.D.	21	185	22,150	365,075
1865	Mass. Inst. Techn'lgy†	Boston, Mass.	Non-Sect	Henry S. Pritchett, LL.D.	139	1,430	53,851	1,784,234
1830	McCormick Th. Sem.	Chicago, Ill.	Presbyterian	J. R. Stevenson, D.D. (Chm.)	10	105	21,000	540,000
1828	McKendree College†	Lebanon, Ill.	Meth. Epis.	McK. H. Chamberlin, LL.D.	15	206	8,000	42,728
1858	McMinnville College†	McMinnville, Ore.	Baptist	H. L. Boardman, A.M.	7	120	3,000	40,000
1837	Mercer University	Macon, Ga.	Baptist	P. D. Pollock, A.M., LL.D.	15	260	15,000	207,000
1824	Miami University†	Oxford, O.	Non-Sect	Rev. David S. Tappan, D.D.	15	144	18,000	43,000
1857	Mich. Agric. College†	Lansing, Mich.	Non-Sect	J. L. Snyder, M.A., Ph. D.	60	662	22,000	97,621
1800	Middlebury College†	Middlebury, Vt.	Non-Sect	Ezra Brainerd, D.D., LL.D.	11	116	24,895	380,000
1887	Midland College†	Atchison, Kan.	Lutheran	Rev. Jacob A. Clutz, D.D.	14	153	5,000	26,097
1882	Milligan College†	Milligan, Tenn.	Christian	Josephus Hopwood, A.M.	10	208	2,000	....
1871	Mills College‡	Seminary Park, Cal	Non-Sect	Mrs. C. T. Mills, Litt. D.	28	190	6,000	....
1892	Millsaps College	Jackson, Miss.	Meth. Epis.	Wm. B. Murrah, D.D., LL.D	12	230	3,000	110,000
1867	Milton College†	Milton, Wis.	7th Day Bap.	W. C. Whitford, A.M., D.D.	12	141	6,342	83,244
1878	Mississippi A.& M.C.†	Starkville, Miss.	Non-Sect	J. C. Hardy, A.M., LL.B.	35	550	9,000	....
1826	Mississippi College	Clinton, Miss.	Baptist	Rev. W. T. Lowrey, D.D., A.M	9	288	3,000	40,000
1889	Missouri Valley Col.†	Marshall, Mo.	Cumb. Pres.	William H. Black, D.D.	13	221	7,000	135,000
1856	Monmouth College†	Monmouth, Ill.	United Pres.	John H. McMillan, Litt. D.	18	303	15,000	185,000
1853	Moore's Hill College†	Moore's Hill, Ind.	Meth. Epis.	Chas. W. Lewis, D.D.	10	174	5,000	20,000
1890	Morningside College†	Sioux City, Iowa.	Methodist	W. S. Lewis, D.D., A.M.	25	440	4,000	....
1880	Morris Brown College†	Atlanta, Ga.	Methodist	Rev. J. M. Henderson, A.M.	18	512	1,500	....
1887	Mount Angel College	Mount Angel, Ore.	R. Catholic	F. Dominic, O.S.B.	24	135	4,000	....
1837	Mt. Holyoke College‡	S. Hadley, Mass.	Non-Sect	Mary E. Woolley, M.A. Litt.D	46	612	21,000	568,000
1808	Mt. St. Mary's College	Emmitsburg, Md.	R. Catholic	Very Rev. W. L. O'Hara, A.M.	35	215	25,000	None
1846	Mt. Union College†	Alliance, O.	Meth. Epis.	Albert B. Riker, D.D., A.M.	23	532	6,191	75,000
1867	Muhlenberg College	Allentown, Pa.	Lutheran	Rev. Theo. L. Seip, D.D.	12	151	10,800	161,000
1837	Muskingum College†	New Concord, O.	United Pres.	Rev. Jesse Johnson, D.D.	13	215	3,650	37,000
1887	Neb. Wesleyan Univ.†	University Pl., Neb.	Meth. Epis.	D. W. C. Huntington, D.D.	41	600	5,000	10,000
1886	Nevada State Univ.†	Reno, Nev.	Non-Sect	Joseph E. Stubbs, D.D., LL.D	24	392	8,300	....
1858	Newberry College†	Newberry, S. C.	Lutheran	Geo. B. Cromer, LL.D.	8	165	9,000	36,000
1874	New Orleans Univ.†	New Orleans, La.	Meth. Epis.	Frederic H. Knight, A.B.	28	613	5,000	25,000
1825	Newton Theol. Inst.	Newton C'tre, Mass.	Baptist	Rev. Nathan E. Wood, D.D.	8	60	24,000	850,000
1831	New York Univ. (*w*)	New York City (*w*)	Non-Sect	H. M. MacCracken, DD., LLD	186	1,824	60,000	994,470
1856	Niagara University	Niagara Falls, N.Y.	R. Catholic	Very Rev. W. F. Likly, C.M.	20	200	12,000	None

Universities and Colleges of the United States.—*Continued.*

Organized.	Colleges.	Location.	Denominational Control.	President or Chairman of Faculty.	Instructors.*	Students.*	Volumes in Library.	Productive Funds—Amount of.
1889	Nor.C.Ag.& Mh.Arts..	West Raleigh,N.C.	Non-Sect	Geo. T. Winston, LL.D....	27	330	3,900	....
1852	North Carolina Col....	Mt.Pleasant, N.C..	Lutheran....	Rev. W. A. Lutz, A.M.......	6	102	4,500	$15,000
1861	Northern Ill. Col.†...	Fulton, Ill.........	Non-Sect	J. E. Bittinger, A.M........	10	120	2,500	900
1861	Northwestern Col.†...	Naperville, Ill.	Evangelical..	H.J.Kiekhoefer,A.M.,Ph.D.	22	360	5,690	104,000
1851	Northwestern Univ.†..	Evanston, Ill......	Meth. Epis..	E. J. James, Ph.D..........	244	3,600	45,764	2,950,000
1865	Northwestern Univ.†..	Watertown, Wis..	Lutheran....	A. F. Ernst, Ph.D..........	9	165	4,523	....
1861	Norwegian Luth. Col..	Decorah, Iowa....	Lutheran....	Rev. Laur. Larsen	10	185	10,248	10,588
....	Notre Dame Univ.....	See "University of	Notre Dame.	"				....
1833	Oberlin College†......	Oberlin, O.........	Non-Sect	Henry C. King, D.D	84	1,357	62,400	1,066,787
1877	Ogden College	BowlingGreen,Ky.	Non-Sect	Wm. A. Obenchain, A.M....	5	80	3,600	130,000
1872	Ohio State Univ.†......	Columbus, O.......	Non-Sect	W.O.Thompson, D.D.,LL.D.	130	1,465	36,000	538,031
1804	Ohio University†......	Athens, O..........	Non-Sect	Alston Ellis, Ph.D., LL.D ..	26	405	16,000	37,500
1844	Ohio Wesleyan Univ.†	Delaware, O........	Meth. Epis..	James W. Bashford, D.D. ..	115	1,358	37,000	736,000
1870	Oregon Agric. Col.†...	Corvallis, Ore......	Non-Sect	Thos. M. Gatch, M.A., Ph.D	28	502	2,900	131,556
1865	Ottawa University†...	Ottawa, Kan........	Baptist.......	J.D.S. Riggs, Ph.D., L.H.D.	23	603	4,000	85,000
1847	Otterbein Univ.†......	Westerville, O.....	U. Brethren.	George Scott,Litt.D., Ph.D.	30	316	10,000	70,000
1886	Ouachita College†.....	Arkadelphia, Ark.	Baptist.......	John W. Conger, A.B.,A.M.	26	486	4,000	None
1849	Oxford College‡ (*q*)....	Oxford, O.	Non-Sect	John H. Thomas, D.D......	19	150	3,000	....
1891	Pacific College†........	Newberg, Ore.	Friends	Edwin McGrew, B.S., M.S..	8	150	600	....
1854	Pacific University†....	Forest Grove, Ore.	Congregat'l..	Wm. N. Ferrin, A.M.(Dean)	14	211	10,800	196,566
1875	Park College†..........	Parkville, Mo.......	Presbyterian	L. M. McAfee (Act. Pres.)..	21	355	12,000	200,000
1875	Parsons College†......	Fairfield, Iowa....	Presbyterian	Rev. F. W. Hinitt, Ph.D. ...	18	277	5,000	160,000
1874	Peabody Nor. Col.†....	Nashville, Tenn...	Non-Sect	James D. Porter, LL.D.....	35	607	15,000	....
1873	Penn College†.........	Oskaloosa, Iowa...	Friends	A. Rosenberger, A.B., LL.D	15	383	4,000	80,000
1870	Pennsylvania College‡	Pittsburg, Pa......	Presbyterian	Rev. C. Martin, A.M., D.D..	25	254	....	....
1832	Pennsylvania College†	Gettysburg, Pa.....	Lutheran....	H.W.McKnight, D.D.,LL.D	16	276	24,000	210,000
1862	Penna. Military Col...	Chester, Pa........	Non-Sect	Col. Chas. E. Hyatt, C.E. ..	14	133	1,600	....
1859	Penna. State College†.	State College, Pa..	Non-Sect	Geo. W. Atherton, LL.D....	46	456	17,800	517,000
1877	Philander Smith Col.†	Little Rock, Ark..	Meth. Epis..	Rev. James M. Cox, D.D....	14	467	1,500	None
1881	Pike College†	Bowling Green,Mo	Non-Sect	Chas. R. Wakeland, B.S....	10	126	600	....
1854	Polytechnic Institute	Brooklyn, N. Y...	Non-Sect	Henry S. Snow, A.B.,LL.D.	50	700	12,000	....
1888	Pomona College†......	Claremont, Cal....	Congregat'l..	George F. Gates, LL.D.	17	212	4,600	117,000
1887	Pratt Institute†......	Brooklyn, N. Y...	Non-Sect	Charles M. Pratt............	128	3,121	74,979	....
1880	Presbyterian Col.S.C.†	Clinton, S. C.......	Presbyterian	Almon E.Spencer,B.A.,M.A.	6	65	1,900	None
1812	Princeton Theol. Sem..	Princeton,N.J......	Presbyterian	W. M. Paxton, D.D., LL.D..	11	132	70,000	1,367,747
1746	Princeton University	Princeton,N.J......	Non-Sect	F. L. Patton, D.D., LL.D....	102	1,340	171,256	....
1868	Pritchett College†	Glasgow, Mo.......	Non-Sect	C. S. Hemenway,A.B.,Ph.D	9	90	750	77,000
1871	Proseminar College..	Elmhurst, Ill......	Evangelical..	Rev. D. Irion................	7	108	3,930	4,000
1874	Purdue University†..	Lafayette, Ind.....	Non-Sect	W. E. Stone, A.M., Ph.D....	79	1,056	11,020	340,000
1852	Racine College.........	Racine, Wis........	Prot. Epis...	Henry D. Robinson, M.A....	7	115	11,000	....
1879	Radcliffe College‡....	Cambridge,Mass..	Non-Sect	Prof. Le Baron R. Briggs...	112	435	17 000	300,000
1830	Randolph-Macon Col.	Ashland, Va.......	Meth. Ep. S..	W. G. Starr, A.M., D.D.....	13	132	10,000	155,355
1893	Randolph-Macon Col.‡	Lynchburg, Va....	Methodist...	Wm. W. Smith, A.M., LL.D.	23	276	4,000	109,000
1824	Rensselaer Poly. Inst.	Troy, N. Y.........	Non-Sect	Palmer C. Ricketts, C E....	21	240	6,500	....
1832	Richmond College†..	Richmond, Va......	Baptist.......	F. W. Boatwright, M.A......	15	216	14,000	275,000
1876	Rio Grande College† .	Rio Grande, O	Free Bap.....	Rev. J. M. Davis, D.D......	6	135	3,200	71,000
1851	Ripon College†.........	Ripon, Wis........	Non-Sect	R. C. Hughes, A.M., D.D...	21	175	8,000	209,104
1853	Roanoke College......	Salem, Va..........	Lutheran....	J. D. Dreher, A.M., Ph.D...	10	195	22,000	65,000
1856	Rock Hill College....	Ellicott City, Md..	R. Catholic ..	Rev. Bro. Abraham.........	22	150	8,000	None
1863	Roger Williams U. †§	Nashville, Tenn..	Baptist.......	Rev. P. B. Guernsey, A.M..	14	250	5,000	None
1885	Rollins College†......	Winter Park, Fla..	Non-Sect	Rev. G. M.Ward,D.D.,LL.B.	21	179	3,000	....
1874	Rose Poly. Inst.	Terre Haute, Ind..	Non-Sect	C. Leo Mees, Ph.D..........	21	165	10,000	....
1766	Rutgers College	N.Brunswick, N.J.	Non-Sect	Austin Scott, Ph.D., LL.D..	29	222	42,656	....
1871	San Fran. Theol. Sem.	San Anselmo, Cal.	Presbyterian	Rev. Thos. F. Day, D.D.....	7	20	16,000	240,821
1866	Scio College†	Scio, O............	Meth. Epis..	....	21	341	2,000	None
1870	Scotia Seminary‡§....	Concord, N. C.....	Presbyterian	Rev. D. J. Satterfield, D.D..	17	287	2,000	5,300
1856	Seton Hall College....	South Orange,N.J.	R. Catholic..	Rev.John A.Stafford, S.T.L.	22	150	40,000	....
1865	Shaw University†§....	Raleigh, N. C......	Baptist.......	Charles F. Meserve, LL.D...	28	578	1,500	32,000
1835	Shurtleff College† (*q*)..	Upper Alton, Ill...	Baptist.......	Rev.Stanley A.McKay, D.D.	15	183	8,500	136,828
1867	Simpson College†....	Indianola, Iowa..	Meth. Epis..	Charles E. Shelton, A.M....	32	629	3,050	55.798
1875	Smith College‡........	N'hampton, Mass.	Non-Sect	L. Clark Seelye, D.D., LL.D.	83	1,043	7,000	868,366
1801	South Carolina Col.†..	Columbia, S. C.....	Non-Sect	F. C. Woodward, Litt.D....	16	227	33,000	None
1859	S'th'n Bap. Theo. Sem.	Louisville, Ky.....	Baptist.......	E. Y. Mullins, D.D., LL.D..	8	250	25,000	500,000
1856	Southern University†	Greensboro', Ala..	Meth. Ep. S..	Rev. S. M. Hosmer, D.D....	11	162	7,000	40,000
1845	Southwe'n Bap. U.†..	Jackson, Tenn.....	Baptist	G. M. Savage, A.M., LL.D..	23	376	....	80,000
1875	Southwe'n Pres. Univ.	Clarksville, Tenn..	Presbyterian	George Summey, D.D........	11	85	8,500	276,000
1873	Southwestern Univ.†	Georgetown, Tex.	Meth. Ep. S..	Robert S. Hyer, A. M.......	23	483	3,500	....
1885	Southwest Kansas C.†	Winfield, Kan. ...	Meth. Epis..	Fred. C. Demorest, D.D....	14	270	2,449	....
1836	Spring Hill College..	Mobile, Ala.......	R. Catholic..	Rev. Wm. J. Tyrrell, S.J....	20	154	25,000	None
1865	State College of Ky.†..	Lexington, Ky......	Non-Sect	J. K. Patterson,Ph.D.,LL.D.	38	620	4,000	100,000
1847	State Univ. of Iowa†.	Iowa City, Iowa...	Non-Sect	George E. MacLean, LL.D..	130	1,542	58,000	235,000
1879	State Univ. of Ky.†§(*q*)	Louisville, Ky....	Baptist.......	Rev. Chas. L. Purce, D.D...	11	200	500	....
1870	Stevens Inst. of Tech.	Hoboken, N. J.....	Non-Sect	Henry Morton, Ph.D., LL.D.	22	270	10,000	550,000
1889	St. Anselm's College..	Manchester, N. H.	R. Catholic..	Rt. Rev. Abbot Hilary, D.D.	26	104	2,400	None
1858	St. Benedict's College	Atchison, Kan.....	R. Catholic..	Rt. Rev. I. Wolf, D.D........	27	135	15,000	....
1847	St. Francis Xavier C.	Manh'n Boro, N. Y	R. Catholic..	Rev. D. W. Hearn, S. J......	17	710	50,000	....
1848	St. Charles College....	Ellicott City, Md..	R. Catholic..	Rev.C.B.Schrantz,S.S.,A.M.	31	240	15,000	....
1789	St. John's College....	Annapolis, Md.....	Non-Sect	Thomas Fell, Ph.D., LL.D..	13	155	8,000	30,000

Universities and Colleges of the United States.—*Continued.*

Organized.	Colleges.	Location.	Denominational Control.	President or Chairman of Faculty.	Instructors.*	Students.*	Volumes in Library.	Productive Funds—Amount of.
1865	St. John's College....	Washington, D. C.	R. Catholic..	Rev. Bro. Abdas, F.S.C.....	10	147	4,000	....
1841	St. John's College....	Fordham, N. Y. C.	R. Catholic..	Rev. Geo. A. Pettit, S.J.....	39	335	39,500	None
1857	St. John's University	Collegeville, Minn.	R. Catholic..	Rt. Rev. Peter Engel, Ph.D.	37	243	16,000	None
1858	St. Lawrence Univ.†..	Canton, N. Y.....	Universalist.	Rev. Almon Gunnison, D.D.	16	150	13,000	500,000
1829	St. Louis University..	St. Louis, Mo. ...	R. Catholic..	Rev. W. B. Rogers, S.J......	34	435	41,000	50,000
1869	St. Mary's College....	St. Mary's, Kan...	R. Catholic..	Rev. James McCabe, S.J....	30	330	10,500	None
1821	St. Mary's College....	St. Mary's, Ky....	R. Catholic..	Rev. David Fennessy, C.R..	10	110	4,000	None
1874	St. Olaf College†.....	Northfield, Minn..	Lutheran....	Rev. John N. Kildahl......	17	306	3,400	....
1860	St. Stephen's College	Annandale, N. Y.	Prot. Epis...	Rev. Lawrence T. Cole, Ph.D.	9	50	17,000	....
1842	St. Thomas College..	Villanova, Pa.....	R. Catholic..	L. A. Delurey, O.S.A., A.M.	26	205	7,500	....
1865	St. Vincent's College..	Los Angeles, Cal..	R. Catholic..	Rev. J. S. Glass, C.M., D.D.	15	133	3,500	....
1869	Swarthmore College†	Swarthmore, Pa..	Friends	Wm. W. Birdsall, A.M.......	28	206	21,000	425,000
1871	Syracuse University†	Syracuse, N. Y...	Meth. Epis..	Rev. J. R. Day, LL.D. (Chan.)	201	2,451	80,000	1,399,506
1857	Tabor College†........	Tabor, Iowa......	Congregat'l..	J. Gordon, D.D...............	13	141	12,000	155,000
1867	Talladega College† (*c*)	Talladega, Ala....	Congregat'l..	G. W. Andrews (Act. Pres.).	25	586	6,000	137,500
1883	Tarkio College†	Tarkio, Mo........	Un. Presb....	Rev. J. A. Thompson, D.D..	17	399	1,219	98,271
1893	Taylor University†....	Upland, Ind.......	Meth. Epis..	Rev. T. C. Reade, A.M., D.D.	17	565	10,000	15,000
1887	Teachers' College†¶..	Manh'n Boro, N.Y.	Non-Sect....	Jas. E. Russell, Ph.D. (Dean)	93	623	16,697	8,866
1870	Thiel College† (*q*)......	Greenville, Pa.....	Lutheran....	Theophilus B. Roth, D.D....	10	137	8,000	....
1891	Throop Poly. Inst.†..	Pasadena, Cal.....	Non-Sect....	Walter A. Edwards, A.M...	24	216	1,900	24,379
1824	Trinity College........	Hartford, Ct.......	Prot. Epis...	Geo. W. Smith, D.D., LL.D.	25	141	43,000	850,000
1900	Trinity College‡......	Washington, D. C.	R. Catholic..	Sister Lidwina, S.N.D......	12	47	3,500	....
1853	Trinity College†......	Durham, N. C.....	Meth. Ep. S..	John C. Kilgo, D.D., A.M...	22	167	15,000	333,750
1869	Trinity University†..	Tehuacana, Tex...	Cumb. Pres..	Jesse Anderson, A.M........	11	145	1,500	32,000
1855	Tufts College†........	Tufts Coll., Mass..	Universalist.	Elmer Hewitt Capen, D.D.	125	900	43,000	1,300,000
1834	Tulane University† (*n*)	New Orleans, La..	Non-Sect....	Edwin A. Alderman, LL.D..	80	1,145	25,000	1,231,000
1881	Tuskegee Institute†§..	Tuskegee, Ala....	Non-Sect....	Booker T. Washington, A.M.	88	1,253	12,000	252,971
1859	Union Christian Col.†	Merom, Ind........	Christian....	Rev. L. J. Aldrich, A.M., D.D.	15	238	3,680	80,000
1886	Union College†........	Barbourville, Ky..	Meth. Epis..	James P. Faulkner, A.M....	8	184	1,200	4,840
1891	Union College†........	College View, Neb.	Advent. ...	L. A. Hoopes	23	286	3,000	....
1795	Union College........	Schenectady, N. Y.	Non-Sect....	Rev. A. V. V. Raymond, D.D.	20	192	36,139	554,199
1836	Union Theol. Sem.†..	Manh'n Boro, N.Y.	Presbyterian	Rev. Chas. Cuthbert Hall...	18	125	75,000	....
1831	Univ. of Alabama†....	Tuscaloosa, Ala. ‡‡	Non-Sect....	Wm S. Wyman, LL.D......	46	413	25,000	300,000
1891	Univ. of Arizona†....	Tucson, Ariz......	Non-Sect....	F. Y. Adams (Act. Pres.)....	18	225	16,000	....
1872	Univ. of Arkansas† ..	Fay'teville, Ark. (*g*)	Non-Sect....	J. L. Buchanan, A.M., LL.D.	36	642	8,239	130,000
1868	Univ. of California†..	Berkeley, Cal.	Non-Sect....	Benj. Ide Wheeler, LL.D..	230	2,932	90,000	3,035,027
1891	Univ. of Chicago†	Chicago, Ill.	Non-Sect (*t*).	Wm. R. Harper, Ph.D., D.D	296	3,520	300,000	7,372,559
1819	Univ. of Cincinnati†.	Cincinnati, O.....	Non-Sect....	Howard Ayers, LL.D.......	150	1,287	150,000	3,357,308
1877	Univ. of Colorado†....	Boulder, Col.......	Non-Sect....	Jas. H. Baker, M.A., LL.D..	92	900	23,000	....
....	Univ. of Denver†	See "Denver	University"					
1801	Univ. of Georgia......	Athens, Ga........	Non-Sect....	Walter B. Hill, LL.D.	131	1,994	30,000	382,500
1889	Univ. of Idaho†	Moscow, Idaho....	Non-Sect....	James A. MacLean, Ph D...	21	329	7,200	....
1868	Univ. of Illinois†	Urbana, Ill. (*r*)....	Non-Sect....	Andrew S. Draper, LL.D...	334	3,000	53,792	561,895
1866	Univ. of Kansas†.....	Lawrence, Kan. ..	Non-Sect....	W. C. Spangler (Act. Chan.)	80	1,150	35,800	140,000
1865	Univ. of Maine†	Orono, Me.........	Non-Sect....	G. E. Fellows, LL.D........	60	554	27,000	218,300
1837	Univ. of Michigan† ..	Ann Arbor, Mich..	Non-Sect....	James B. Angell, LL.D.	233	3,800	155,524	545,946
1868	Univ. of Minnesota† ..	Minneapolis, Minn	Non-Sect....	Cyrus Northrop, LL.D......	250	3,550	84,000	1,307,219
1848	Univ. of Mississippi†.	Near Oxford, Miss	Non-Sect....	Robert B. Fulton, LL.D....	21	260	18,000	696,000
1840	Univ. of Missouri†....	Columbia, Mo. (*u*)	Non-Sect....	Richard Henry Jesse, LL.D	109	1,021	40,000	1,235,849
1895	Univ. of Montana†...	Missoula, Mont. ..	Non-Sect....	Oscar J. Craig, A.M., Ph.D.	13	235	6,300	....
1785	Univ. of Nashville† (*q*).	Nashville, Tenn...	Non-Sect....	W. H. Payne, LL.D., Ph.D..	67	1,370	15,000	100,000
1869	Univ. of Nebraska† ..	Lincoln, Neb.	Non-Sect....	E. Benj. Andrews, LL.D. ..	220	2,256	51,000	....
1892	Univ. of N. Mexico† (*q*)	Albuquerque, N.M	Non-Sect....	C. L. Herrick, Ph.D..........	10	105	5,000	....
....	Univ. of New York....	See "New York	University"					
1795	Univ. of N. Carolina†.	Chapel Hill, N. C.	Non-Sect....	Francis P. Venable, Ph.D..	45	546	33,000	127,000
1883	Univ. of N. Dakota† ..	Grand Forks, N.Dk	Non-Sect....	Webster Merrifield, M.A....	25	375	7,000	None
1842	Univ. of Notre Dame.	Notre Dame, Ind..	R. Catholic..	Rev. A. Morrissey, C.S.C....	65	800	55,000	None
1892	Univ. of Okla.† (*q*)	Norman, Okla.....	Non-Sect....	David R. Boyd, A.M........	21	272	7,000	....
1880	Univ. of Omaha† (*q*) ..	Omaha, Neb.......	Presbyterian	David R. Kerr, D.D., Ph.D.	80	325	4,000	160,000
1872	Univ. of Oregon†	Eugene, Ore.......	Non-Sect....	Frank Strong, A.M., Ph.D..	62	456	15,000	200,000
1852	Univ. of the Pacific†..	San José, Cal.	Meth. Epis..	Eli McClish, D.D..........	12	247	5,000	16,000
1740	Univ. of Pennsyl'nia†.	Philadelphia, Pa...	Non-Sect....	C. C. Harrison, LL.D. (Prov.)	268	2,475	200,000	3,384,705
1850	Univ. of Rochester† ..	Rochester, N. Y...	Baptist......	Rush Rhees, D.D., LL.D....	19	263	37,202	760,741
1880	Univ. of S. Cal.† (*q*)...	Los Angeles, Cal..	Meth. Epis..	Geo. F. Bonard, A.M., D.D.	12	150	4,500	None
1882	Univ. of S. Dakota† ..	Vermilion, S.Dak.	Non Sect....	Garrett Droppers............	28	425	7,000	None
1868	Univ. of the South....	Sewanee, Tenn....	Prot. Epis...	B. L. Wiggins, M.A., LL.D.	62	518	43,789	204,430
1794	Univ. of Tennessee† (*c*)	Knoxville, Tenn...	Non-Sect....	C. W. Dabney, Ph.D., LL.D.	85	721	17,100	425,000
1883	Univ. of Texas†	Austin, Tex. (*s*)....	Non-Sect....	Wm. L. Prather, LL.D......	97	1,121	35,000	170,750
1850	Univ. of Utah†........	Salt Lake City, U.	Non-Sect....	J. T. Kingsbury, Ph.D., D.Sc.	28	643	20,000	244,000
1791	Univ. of Vermont†....	Burlington, Vt. ..	Non-Sect....	Mat. H. Buckham, D.D.....	62	560	62,300	420,000
1825	Univ. of Virginia	Charlottesville, Va	Non-Sect....	Edwin A. Alderman, LL.D.	55	600	48,000	378,850
1862	Univ. of Washington†	Seattle, Wash.....	Non-Sect....	F. P. Graves, Ph.D., LL.D..	53	614	13,000	None
1848	Univ. of Wisconsin†..	Madison, Wis.....	Non-Sect....	Charles K. Adams, LL.D...	171	2,619	70,000	500,000
1869	Univ. of Wooster†	Wooster, O........	Presbyterian	Rev. Louis E. Holden, D.D.	26	800	22,000	250,000
1887	Univ. of Wyoming† ..	Laramie, Wyo.....	Non-Sect....	Rev. Elmer E. Smiley, D.D.	16	177	11,000	None
1857	Upper Iowa Univ.†....	Fayette, Iowa.....	Meth. Epis..	Rev. Guy P. Benton, A.M...	26	391	7,000	100,000
1869	Ursinus College†......	Collegeville, Pa...	German Ref.	Rev. H. T. Spangler, D.D...	26	189	9,000	185,000
1802	**U. S. Military Acad...**	West Point, N. Y.	Non-Sect....	Col. A. L. Mills, U.S.A. Supt..	71	464	45,000	....

Universities and Colleges of the United States.—*Continued.*

Organized.	Colleges.	Location.	Denominational Control.	President or Chairman of Faculty.	Instructors.*	Students.*	Volumes in Library.	Productive Funds—Amount of.
1845	U. S. Naval Academy.	Annapolis, Md....	Non-Sect....	Com. R. Wainwright, U.S.N.	69	333	42,000	....
1888	Utah Agri. College† ..	Logan, Utah.....	Non-Sect....	Wm. J. Kerr, B.S., D.Sc....	35	381	8,000	$15,592
1872	Vanderbilt Univ.†	Nashville, Tenn...	Meth. Ep. S.	J. H. Kirkland, LL.D., Ph.D.	100	754	30,000	1,300,000
1861	Vassar College‡	Poughkeepsie, N.Y	Non-Sect....	James M. Taylor, D.D., LL.D.	72	798	35,000	972,026
1806	Vincennes Univ.†	Vincennes, Ind....	Non-Sect....	James E. Manchester, D.Sc.	10	175	5,500	....
1839	Virginia Mil. Inst.....	Lexington, Va. ...	Non-Sect....	Gen. Scott Shipp, LL.D.....	19	250	11,741	20,000
1871	Virginia Poly. Inst. ..	Blacksburg, Va. ..	Non-Sect....	J. M. McBryde, Ph.D., LL.D.	35	442	3,000	None
1831	Wabash College	Crawf'rdsville, Ind	Non-Sect....	Rev. Wm. P. Kane, D.D....	15	200	37,000	....
1833	Wake Forest College..	Wake Forest, N.C.	Baptist......	C. E. Taylor, D.D., LL.D....	16	307	15,000	210,000
1867	Walden University† ..	Nashville, Tenn...	Meth. Epis..	Jay B. Hamilton, D.D.......	32	578	....	....
1865	Washburn College† ...	Topeka, Kan.	Congregat'l.	....	23	294	8,000	80,000
1892	Washington Ag. Col...	Pullman, Wash. ..	Non-Sect....	Enoch A. Bryan, A.M.......	45	628	8,000	....
1802	Wash. & Jefferson Col.	Washington, Pa...	Presbyterian	Rev. Jas. D. Moffat, D.D....	23	360	16,000	322,000
1749	Wash. & Lee Univ. ..	Lexington, Va. ...	Non-Sect....	Geo. H. Denny, M.A., Ph.D.	22	222	40,000	634,000
1783	Washington College† .	Chestertown, Md.	Non-Sect....	C. W. Reid, Ph.D., A M.....	9	110	2,500	20,000
1795	Washington College† .	Wash'n Col., Tenn.	Presbyterian	Rev. Jas. T. Cooter, M.A....	8	135	3,000	5,000
1853	Washington Univ.† ..	St. Louis, Mo.	Non-Sect....	W. S. Chaplin, LL.D........	190	2,086	7,500	4,609,678
1851	Waynesburg College†.	Waynesburg, Pa...	Cumb. Pres..	A. E. Turner, A.M..........	18	391	3,000	40,000
1870	Wellesley College‡....	Wellesley, Mass...	Non-Sect....	Caroline Hazard, M.A., Litt.D	80	821	52,400	599,296
1868	Wells College‡	Aurora, N. Y......	Non-Sect....	J. W. Freley, M.S. (Act. Pres.)	22	126	8,500	200,000
1831	Wesleyan Univ.†......	Middletown, Ct. ..	Meth. Epis..	B. P. Raymond, D.D., LL.D.	36	350	59,000	1,405,615
1856	Western College†§	Toledo, Iowa......	U. Brethren.	L. Bookwalter, A.M., D.D..	14	340	3,000	....
1867	West. Maryland Col.†.	Westminster, Md.	Meth. Prot..	Rev. T. H. Lewis, D.D., A.M.	22	250	6,000	....
1826	West. Reserve Univ. (o)	Cleveland, O.	Non-Sect....	Charles F. Thwing, D.D....	175	800	40,000	1,300,000
1787	West. Univ. of Penn.†	Pittsburg, Pa. (m).	Non-Sect....	S.B. McCormick, D.D. (Chan.)	115	869	20,000	595,668
1865	Westfield College†	Westfield, Ill.	U. Brethren.	William S. Reese, D.D......	9	192	3,000	....
1853	Westminster College..	Fulton, Mo.	Presbyterian	John H. MacCracken, Ph.D.	11	98	6,000	209,000
1852	Westminster Col.†	N. Wilmington, Pa.	United Pres.	Rev. R. G. Ferguson, D.D..	13	292	5,500	90,000
1867	W. Virginia Univ.† (q).	Morgant'n, W. Va.	Non-Sect....	....	57	885	15,200	114,369
1860	Wheaton College†	Wheaton, Ill.	Congregat'l.	Charles A. Blanchard, D.D..	18	240	3,000	61,000
1859	Whitman College†....	Walla Walla, Wn.	Congregat'l.	Rev. S. B. L. Penrose, A.B..	19	300	9,000	190,000
1856	Wilberforce Univ.†§..	Wilberforce, O....	Meth. Epis..	Joshua H. Jones, A.M., D.D.	22	360	10,000	28,000
1873	Wiley University†§...	Marshall, Tex.	Meth. Epis..	Rev. M. W. Dogan, A.M....	15	439	4,200	....
1844	Willamette Univ.†....	Salem, Ore.	Meth. Epis .	Willis C. Hawley, A.M......	49	447	4,817	40,000
1693	William & Mary Col...	Williamsburg, Va.	Non-Sect....	Lyon G. Tyler, M.A., LL.D..	16	184	10,000	132,327
1849	William Jewell Col....	Liberty, Mo.......	Baptist......	John P. Greene, D.D., LL.D.	23	352	12,000	200,000
1793	Williams College......	Williamst'n, Mass.	Non-Sect....	....	34	393	47,000	1,664,887
1870	Wilmington College†..	Wilmington, O....	Friends	James B. Unthank, M.Sc....	11	143	4,000	40,000
1870	Wilson College‡ (q)...	Chambersburg, Pa	Presbyterian	Rev. S. A. Martin, D.D.....	30	298	7,000	250,000
1845	Wittenberg College†..	Springfield, O.....	Lutheran....	J. M. Ruthrauff, D.D........	20	456	12,000	200,000
1854	Wofford College†.....	Spartanburg, S. C.	Meth. Ep. S.	James H. Carlisle, LL.D....	10	257	10.000	63,000
1888	Woman's College‡ (q).	Baltimore, Md....	Meth. Epis..	J. F. Goucher, D.D., LL.D..	30	319	7,600	187,000
1865	Worcester Poly. In. (q)	Worcester, Mass..	Non-Sect....	T.C. Mendenhall, Ph.D. LL.D	32	275	7,000	615,000
1701	Yale University (v)...	New Haven, Conn.	Non-Sect....	Arthur T. Hadley, LL.D....	280	2,680	315,000	6,000,000
1881	Yankton College†.....	Yankton, S. Dak..	Congregat'l..	Rev. Henry K. Warren, M.A	16	284	7,000	114,590
1890	York College†.........	York, Neb.........	U. Brethren.	Wm. E. Schell, A.M.........	11	342	1,000	....

* All departments.
† Co-education of the sexes.
‡ Education of women only.
§ For the education of colored students.
¶ Teachers College is now part of Columbia University.
‡‡ Medical Department at Mobile, Ala.
†† At Athens, Tenn., also.
(*a*) Co-education in Medical Department.
(*b*) Not yet organized for instruction. Is intended solely for post-graduate work.
(*c*) No restriction as to color.
(*d*) Certain courses are open to women in Columbia University, with use of library, who are students of Barnard or Teachers College.
(*e*) Co-education in the literary departments.
(*f*) Confined strictly to post-graduate work. The national university of the church.
(*g*) Academic and Technical Departments at Fayetteville; Law and Medical Departments at Little Rock; Normal School (for negroes), Pine Bluff, Ark.
(*h*) W. C. Roberts, D.D., LL.D., President, and L. H. Blanton, D.D., LL.D., Vice-President; consolidated with Centre College.
(*i*) Presbyterian in sympathy.
(*j*) For Indians and colored youth, both sexes.
(*k*) Also at Lancaster, Tex.
(*m*) Located in Pittsburg and Allegheny.
(*n*) Separate department for women in the H. Sophie Newcomb Memorial College.
(*o*) For both sexes, except that Adelbert College Annex is for women only.
(*p*) Dental and Law Schools at Chicago.
(*q*) Report at close of 1900.
(*r*) Schools of Pharmacy and Medicine at Chicago.
(*s*) Medical Department at Galveston.
(*t*) President and two-thirds Trustees must be Baptists.
(*u*) School of Mines at Rolla, Mo.
(*v*) Women admitted to graduate school and Departments of Fine Arts and Music.
(*w*) Co-education in law, pedagogy, graduate, and commerce. The University proper is at University Heights, Bronx Borough, New York; Law School at Washington Square, New York.
(*x*) College of Liberal Arts at St. Paul, Minn.; College of Physicians and Surgeons at Minneapolis.
(*y*) Medical Department located in Louisville.

Foreign Universities.

Date of foundation.	Locality.	Number of students.	Date of foundation.	Locality.	Number of students.
1200	Paris, France	11,090	1821	Montreal, Canada	1,082
1809	Berlin, Prussia, Germany	9,629	1743	Erlangen, Bavaria, Germany	1,075
1365	Vienna, Austria	7,026	....	Urbana	1,075
1508	Madrid, Spain	6,143	1343	Pisa, Italy	1,066
1224	Naples, Italy	5,108	....	Rome, Italy (University Pont.)	1,033
1755	Moscow, Russia	4,461	1572	Nancy, France	1,013
1465	Budapest, Hungary	4,407	1812	Genoa, Italy	1,010
1472	Munich, Bavaria, Germany	3,814	1673	Innsbruck, Tyrol, Austria	1,009
1819	St. Petersburg, Russia	3,392	1743	Santiago (Chile)	1,000
1200	Oxford, England	3,365	1431	Poitiers, France	957
1837	Athens, Greece	3,258	1527	Marburg, Prussia, Germany	908
1409	Leipzig, Saxony, Germany	3,126	1444	Catania, Sicily	902
1851	Manchester, England (about)	3,000	1559	Geneva, Switzerland	862
1257	Cambridge, England	2,929	1804	Kasan, Russia	837
1583	Edinburgh, Scotland	2,850	1575	Leyden, Holland	816
1348	Prague, Austria (Bohemian)	2,815	1832	Zürich, Switzerland	814
1588	Kijew, Kieff, Russia	2,565	1456	Greifswald, Prussia, Germany	813
1412	Turin, Italy	2,434	1494	Aberdeen, Scotland	789
1875	Lyons, France	2,198	1558	Jena, Thuringia, Germany	758
1472	Bordeaux, France	2,160	1834	Berne, Switzerland	755
1640	Helsingfors, Finland, Russia	2,015	1409	Aix-en-Provence, France	748
1478	Copenhagen, Denmark	2,000	1636	Utrecht, Holland	732
1451	Glasgow, Scotland	1,924	1665	Kiel, Prussia, Germany	727
1303	Rome, Italy (Royal University)	1,914	1437	Caen, France	726
1450	Barcelona, Spain	1,887	1772	Klausenburg, Hungary	726
1233	Toulouse, France	1,808	1209	Valencia, Spain	726
1586	Graz, Styria, Austria	1,761	1544	Königsberg, Prussia, Germany	683
1818	Bonn, Prussia, Germany	1,726	1816	Ghent, Belgium	676
1864	Bucharest, Roumania	1,680	1853	Melbourne, Victoria, Australia	668
1426	Louvain, Belgium	1,669	1607	Giessen, Hessia, Germany	667
1502	Halle, Prussia, Germany	1,645	1666	Lund, Sweden	665
1119	Bologna, Italy	1,629	1722	Dijon, France	634
1868	Tokyo, Japan	1,620	....	Kingston	601
1222	Padua, Italy	1,616	1349	Florence, Italy	595
1804	Charkow, Russia	1,576	1865	Odessa, Russia	581
1477	Upsala, Sweden	1,499	1838	Messina, Italy	553
1808	Rennes, France	1,477	1339	Grenoble, France	540
1402	Würzburg, Bavaria, Germany	1,467	1537	Lausanne, Switzerland	538
1288	Coimbra, Portugal	1,429	1422	Parma, Italy	524
1506	Breslau, Prussia, Germany	1,424	1419	Rostock, Mecklenburg, Germany	514
...	Prague (German)	1,424	1460	Basel, Switzerland	510
1784	Lemberg, Galicia, Austria	1,398	1874	Agram, Croatia, Hungary	484
1827	Toronto, Canada	1,353	....	Belgrade	465
1361	Pavia, Italy	1,345	1850	Sydney, Australia	454
1779	Palermo, Sicily, Italy	1,343	1614	Groningen, Holland	452
1181	Montpellier, France	1,342	1860	Jassy, Roumania	422
1834	Brussels, Belgium	1,316	1683	Modena, Italy	412
1364	Krakow, Galicia, Austria	1,313	1832	Durham, England (about)	400
1477	Tübingen, Würtemberg, Germany	1,289	1875	Czernowitz, Bukowina, Austria	390
1808	Lille, France	1,283	1540	Macerata, Italy	358
1817	Liege, Belgium	1,267	....	Freiburg, Switzerland	348
1243	Salamanca, Spain	1,247	1872	Adelaide, Australia	320
1632	Dorpat, Russia	1,233	1266	Perugia, Italy	298
....	Havana, Cuba	1,226	1777	Siena, Italy	257
1632	Amsterdam, Holland	1,218	....	Toronto (Victoria University)	250
1811	Christiania, Norway	1,150	1596	Cagliari, Italy	237
1737	Göttingen, Prussia, Germany	1,149	1411	St. Andrew's, Scotland	222
1605	Manila, Philippine Islands	1,144	1727	Camerino, Italy	207
1457	Freiburg, Baden, Germany	1,143	1808	Clermont, France	206
1591	Dublin, Ireland	1,128	1422	Besançon, France	169
1386	Heidelberg, Baden, Germany	1,115	1556	Sassari, Italy	166
1567	Strassburg, Alsace, Germany	1,098	....	Amsterdam (free university)	109
....	Manchester, England (Owens College)	1,092	....	Ferrara	99
1816	Warsaw, Poland, Russia	1,088	1671	Urbino, Italy	93

Humanities are those branches of education or study which are included in what are called polite or elegant learning, as languages, grammar, philosophy, and poetry, with that pertaining to what is called polite literature, including the ancient classics. The name implies that the study of these branches, in opposition to the physical sciences, which especially develop the intellectual faculties, has a tendency to humanize man, to cultivate particularly those faculties which distinguish him as man in all his relations, social and moral; that is, which make him a truly cultured man.

Animal Worship.— Among primitive peoples, all animals are supposed to be endowed with souls which in many cases have formerly animated human beings. Hence a likeness is often recognized between an animal and some deceased friend, and the animal is addressed as the person would have been, and honored with a kind of worship. Many tribes call themselves by the name of, and even derive their pedigree from, some animal. Its cries become the omens of the tribe; and thus originate the divination and augury of more civilized nations. In the modern world the most civilized people among whom animal-worship vigorously survives lie within the range of Brahmanism. Here the sacred cow is not merely to be spared; she is as a deity worshiped and bowed to daily by the pious Hindoo. Siva is incarnate in Hanuman, the monkey god. The divine king of birds, Garuda, is Vishnu's vehicle, and the forms of fish and boar and tortoise assumed in the avatar legends of Vishnu. Perhaps no worship has prevailed more widely than that of the serpent. It had its place in Egypt and among the Hebrews; in Greece and Rome; among the Celts and Scandinavians in Europe; in Persia and India; in China and Thibet; in Mexico and Peru; in Africa, where it still flourishes as the state religion in Dahomey; in Java and Ceylon; among the Fijians and elsewhere in Oceanica; and even within the limits of Christianity we find the sect of the Ophites, who continued or renewed snake-worship, blended curiously with purer rites.

Pyramids. — The weight of authority among modern Egyptologists inclines to the view that the Pyramids were a new and bold architectural type, invented in its entirety between the fifth and twelfth dynasties, in Middle Egypt, and not the development from earlier forms of tomb-mounds. "Pyramid," in its strict geometrical sense, denotes a building having a polygonal base, and plain triangular sides which meet in an apex. There are various forms of ancient tomb-mounds of earth and stone and stepped structures, as the *mastaba* in Egypt, and early temples and mausolea in Mexico and Assyria, and there are also some inferior imitations of later date; but the true pyramidal construction is seen only in Egypt, and comprises about seventy structures on the banks of the Nile, none of which are later than the twelfth dynasty (about 2000 B. C.). They are all built upon a square base, with the four sides facing the four cardinal points of the compass, and in the earlier forms are composed of horizontal layers of rough-hewn blocks with a small amount of mortar — degenerating in the buildings of the sixth and succeeding dynasties to a cellular system of retaining walls filled with loose chips, and finally, in the twelfth dynasty, to a mass of mud bricks. But there was, in all cases, on the outside, a casing of fine stone, beautifully polished and jointed, the inner chambers having a similar finish. These casing stones were not a mere veneer or film, but were massive blocks, usually greater in thickness than in height. Inside of each pyramid, always low down, and usually beneath the level of the ground, was built a sepulchral chamber, and this was reached by a downward passage from the north side. This passage had a lesser chamber in its course, and was blocked once or oftener with a massive stone portcullis. The interior was probably in every case accessible to the priests for the purpose of making offerings, the passageway being closed by a stone door turning on a horizontal pivot, the location of which was known to them. The chambers were always roofed by great sloping cantalevers of stone projecting from the north and south sides, on which they rested without pressing on each other along the central ridge, so that there was no thrust, nor indeed any force to disturb the buildings; and now, after a lapse of four thousand years, in spite of the brutal treatment of enemies and the greed of later builders (who have removed almost all of the casing stones), they still stand as colossal monuments of the work of man. Owing to the loss of the casing stones, their present appearance presents a series of huge, rough steps, and their height has been considerably diminished by the encroachment of the sand of the desert around their bases. Many archæologists believe these vast piles, especially the great Pyramid of Cheops at Gizeh, to have been constructed under divine inspiration, and to embody in the living rock great astronomical facts and mathematical principles, and memorials of a system of weights and measures for universal use. It is also maintained that Masonic emblems and symbols have been found within them. Whatever the builders embodied in the details of their construction, their immediate object and use was undoubtedly to serve as royal mausolea. As for these theories, future investigations will probably develop or explode them; but that there is great mathematical knowledge and wonderful accuracy of measurement displayed in them is well established. In the great Pyramid at Gizeh, the four sides have a mean error of only six tenths of an inch, and twelve seconds in angle from a perfect square. This pyramid is the largest of all, and by far the most remarkable in its construction. It is somewhat different from the others in its internal arrangement, having the subterranean chamber, which is but half finished, and having also an upward passage leading to two large upper chambers, highly finished with great slabs of polished red granite. Probably both of these chambers contained originally a polished sarcophagus of the same Syenitic granite; and the larger one — the "King's" — although in the very heart of this huge pile, is perfectly ventilated by two air passages about nine inches square, which run to the north and south faces of the Pyramid. It was built by Cheops or Khufu of the fifth dynasty, and its construction is thought to have employed 100,000 men for thirty years or more — probably half a century. The masonry consisted originally of 89,028,000 cubic feet, and still amounts to 82,111,000. The height is at present 450 feet (originally 479), and the length of the sides 746 feet (originally 764). The King's Chamber is 19 feet 1 inch in height, and in area 34 feet 3 inches by 17 feet 1 inch; the Queen's Chamber is 20 feet 3 inches in height, and in area 17 feet by 18 feet 9 inches. It is now generally agreed that there were no inscriptions on the external surface of any of the pyramids, the casing-stones bearing a smooth polish. The mechanical means employed by the builders have been partly ascertained. The hard stones, granite, diorite, and basalt, were, in all fine work, sawn into shape by bronze saws set with jewels (either corundum or diamonds); hollows were made (as in sarcophagi) by tubular drilling with tools like our modern diamond rock-drills, and small articles were turned in lathes fitted with mechanical tool rests and jewel pointed tools. The questions of the transport and management of such huge stones, weighing oftentimes more than thirty tons apiece, remain still to be answered.

Septuagint. — The most ancient Greek translation of the Old Testament that has come down to us, and the one commonly in use at the time of Christ, was the Septuagint. Its origin is shrouded in deep obscurity. There are a number of myths concerning it, but the principal one is that it was made during the reign of Ptolemy Philadelphus, 284-247 B. C. This king, it is stated, anxious to embody in a collection of laws of all nations, on which he was engaged, also those of the Jews, invited 72 men of learning and eminence from Palestine, who performed the task of translation in 72 days. The facts upon which this legend, now rejected as a piece of history, rests, cannot well be ascertained. It seems clear, however, that Ptolemy, aided by his librarian, Demetrius Phalereus, did cause a Greek version of the Pentateuch to be executed, probably during the time of his being co-regent of Ptolemy Lagi; but the translators were not Palestinian but Egyptian Jews. This is evidenced from the state of the text from which the translation must have been made, and from the intimate acquaintance with Egyptian manners and customs which it evinces. The Septuagint was held in the very highest repute among the Alexandrine Jews, while the Palestinians looked upon it as a dangerous innovation, and even instituted the day of its completion as a day of mourning. Gradually, however, it also found its way into Palestine. It was read and interpreted in the synagogues for some centuries after Christ, until the increasing knowledge of the original, fostered by the many academies and schools, and the frequent disputations with the early Christians, brought other and more faithful and literal translations.

Holy Coat, a garment which is alleged to be the seamless coat of our Saviour, and to have been discovered in the fourth century by the Empress Helena on her visit to Palestine. It was deposited by her at Treves, where it is preserved in the cathedral of that city with the greatest reverence. The Treves relics were concealed from the Normans in the ninth century in crypts; but the Holy Coat was rediscovered in 1196, and then solemnly exhibited to the public gaze, which did not take place again till 1512, when Leo X. appointed it to be exhibited every seven years. In 1810 the exhibition was attended by 227,000 people, and in 1844 by still greater multitudes. The exhibition of the Holy Coat in this latter year led to the secession of the German Catholics from the Church of Rome.

Portland Vase.— The celebrated Portland Vase, which is one of the most valued relics of antiquity in the British Museum, was made, it is believed, to hold the ashes of the Roman Emperor Alexander Servius, and was discovered during the sixteenth century in a rich sarcophagus on Monte del Grano, where it had been for about thirteen hundred years. It is an urn, ten inches high. The groundwork is of blue glass, enameled with white glass cut in cameo, to represent the wedding of Thetis and Peleus. It was placed in the museum by the Duke of Portland in 1810, and in 1845 was maliciously broken by a man named Lloyd. The pieces, however, were collected and cemented together, but the vase has not been on exhibition since that date. It was at one time known as the Barberina Vase, and was owned by Sir William Hamilton, who found it in the Barberina Palace, and purchased it in 1770. In time it passed into the possession of the Duchess of Portland, and was disposed of as related.

Shakers is the popular name given to a religious sect who call themselves the "United Society of Believers in Christ's Second Appearing." They were founded in England about the year 1770 by an Englishwoman named Ann Lee, in whose person they believed that Christ has appeared a second time. Shortly before the outbreak of the Revolutionary War a small band of them, with Ann Lee at their head, emigrated to America, and penetrated far into the wilderness to Niskenna, and there founded the settlement, which still exists at Watervliet, N. Y. In the spring of 1780, when they had been three years and a half at Niskenna, a religious revival took place at Albany, and spread through the surrounding districts; and from Hancock and New Lebanon a deputation was sent to Niskenna, to see what light its inhabitants enjoyed as to the way of salvation. The deputation consisted of Joseph Meacham and Lucy Wright, subsequently the heads of the Shaker Society. These persons became believers in Ann Lee, and through their agency other converts were won, and a Shaker Society established at New Lebanon. Toward the close of 1780, the Revolutionary War being then in progress, notoriety was given to Ann Lee through an incident seemingly unfavorable. On suspicion of being a British spy she was imprisoned for some time at Poughkeepsie, and before she obtained her liberty, in December, 1780, all the colonies had heard of the "female Christ," and in the following year she started on a missionary tour through New England and the adjacent colonies, and made not a few converts. She died in 1784, and was succeeded in the headship of the society by Joseph Meacham and Lucy Wright. Her death was a surprise to many of her followers, who believed that she was to live with them forever. Their doctrine has been, to some extent, developed as well as systematized since the death of "Mother Ann." They believe that the Kingdom of Heaven has come; that Christ has come upon earth a second time in the form of "Mother Ann," and that the personal rule of God has been restored. Then they hold that the old law has been abolished and a new dispensation begun; that Adam's sin has been atoned; that man has been made free of all errors except his own; that the curse has been taken away from labor; that the earth and all that is on it will be redeemed. Believers, on going "into union," die to the world and enter upon a new life, which is not a mere change of life but a new order of being. For them there is neither death nor marriage; what seems death is only a change of form, a transfiguration, which does not hide them from the purified eyes of the saints; and in union, as in Heaven, there is no marrying nor giving in marriage. They believe that the earth, now freed from the curse of Adam, is Heaven; they look for no resurrection besides that involved in living with them in "resurrection order." The believer, upon entering into union, leaves behind all his earthly relationships and interests, just as if he had been severed from them by death. And since to be in union is heaven, the Shakers hold that no attempt should be made by them to draw men into union. They believe that they live in daily communion with the spirits of the departed believers. The Shaker settlements are composed of from two to eight "families," or households. A large house, divided through the middle by wide walls, and capable of accommodating from 30 to 150 inmates, is erected by each family, the male members occupying one end and the female the other. Their meals are taken in a common room, and in silence. They possess an average of seven acres of land to the member, and are very industrious. The settlements are at New Lebanon and Watervliet, N. Y.; Hancock, Tyringham, Harvard, and Shirley, Mass.; Enfield, Conn.; Canterbury and Enfield, N. H.; Alfred and Gloucester, Me.; Union Village, White Water, and North Union, Ohio; and at Pleasant Hill and South Union, Ky., and number, in all, 2,400 members.

Roman Baths, The, were among the most magnificent and extensive architectural ornaments of the city in the time of the Empire. They were erected by different emperors for the use of the populace, and the vast ruins still existing testify to their great size and the unparalleled luxury of their arrangements. In these great *thermæ*, as they were called, the primitive object of bathing was largely lost sight of, and they became favorite places of general resort for pleasure. The most famous were those erected by the Emperors Titus, Caracalla, and Diocletian. Caracalla's baths were 1,500 feet long by 1,250 feet broad, and the swimming bath or *natatorium* in those of Diocletian was 200 feet long by 100 feet wide; and it is calculated that in this entire establishment 18,000 people could bathe at one time. There were separate structures for the exclusive use of women, and in some cases separate apartments in the same building, but these were generally inferior to those for the men. They were built entirely of stone and polished marble, and all the apartments were beautifully ornamented with mosaic, and profusely adorned with painting, stuccowork, and statuary. The public baths of Pompeii were uncovered in 1824 and the complete internal arrangement disclosed, which is probably similar to, though on a smaller scale than, those in Rome. The process of bathing was this: After undressing in the *apodyterium*, or "room for undressing," the bather was rubbed and anointed with some of the fragrant oils and ointments used by the ancients, and then proceeded to a spacious apartment devoted to exercises of various kinds, among which games at ball held a prominent place. After exercise, he went into the *caldarium*, either merely to sweat or to take the hot bath; and during this part of the process the body was scraped with *strigiles* (small curved instruments usually made of bronze). Being now dried with cloths, and slightly anointed all over with perfumed oils, he resumed his dress, and then passed a short time, successively, in the *tepidarium* and the *frigidarium*, or temperate and cold rooms, which softened the transition from the great heat of the *caldarium* into the open air. The artificial bath has been used from the most ancient times of which we have any record. It is mentioned in Homer, the vessel for bathing being described as of polished marble and the warm baths referred to as effeminate. Public baths were common in Greece during the historic period, and they were in use at Rome from early times; but during the Republic they continued small, dark, and inconvenient, and it was not until the time of the Empire that they reached their great size and splendor.

Russia, Religion of.—The Established Church of Russia, to which the great majority of the inhabitants belong, is identical in doctrine with, and is a branch of, the Greek Church. The liturgy used is the same as that originally used by the Church at Constantinople, but it is read, not in Greek, but in the Sclavonic tongue. Previous to the time of Alexander II., dissent in all its forms was not only discouraged but often rigorously repressed and it has only been during very late years that general toleration has been permitted. The Roman Catholic Church has been the object of especial severity in the past, particularly during the reign of the Czar Nicholas. Under the laws of Alexander II., all Catholics and Protestants enjoy civil rights with members of the Established Church, and are equally admissible to the highest offices of the empire. Christianity was introduced into Russia in the ninth century.

Taj Mahal was built by the Shah Jihan of India as a mausoleum for the remains of his wife Nourmahal, and is situated at Agra. It is of white marble, 100 feet in diameter and 200 feet in height, built in the form of an irregular octagon, and rising from a marble terrace, under which is a second terrace of red sandstone. At the corners of the marble terrace are lofty minarets, and in the center of the main building rises a dome, flanked by cupolas of similar form. Every part, even the basement, the dome, and the upper galleries of the minarets, is inlaid with ornamental designs in marble of different colors, principally of pale brown and bluish violet. Here and there, also, the exterior and interior are decorated with mosaics of precious stones. The whole Koran is said to be written in mosaics of precious stones on the interior walls. In the construction of this magnificent building, which, as Bayard Taylor says, alone repays a visit to India, 20,000 men were employed twenty years. Although the labor cost nothing, over $20,000,000 were expended in its construction. The doors are of solid silver, and an enormous diamond was placed upon the tomb itself.

SUNDAY-SCHOOL STATISTICS OF ALL COUNTRIES.

The following statistics of Sunday schools were reported at the World's Third Sunday-School Convention, held in London July 11 to 16, 1898, and are the latest extant:

Countries.	Sunday Schools.	Teachers.	Scholars.
EUROPE:			
England and Wales	43,632	613,036	6,843,072
Scotland	6,338	63,939	713,360
Ireland	3,620	27,980	319,316
Belgium	83	403	4,616
Austria	208	533	7,340
Denmark	819	4,275	71,371
Finland	7,611	12,928	165,140
France	1,475	3,876	61,200
Germany	7,131	39,872	814,175
Greece	4	7	180
Italy	336	1,482	15,787
Netherlands	1,900	4,962	168,110
Norway	749	3,311	65,311
Portugal	18	70	1,419
Russia	83	785	15,679
Spain	48	220	4,275
Sweden	5,360	18,144	252,247
Switzerland	1,762	7,490	122,567
European Turkey	30	170	1,420
ASIA:			
India, including Ceylon	5,578	13,937	247,472
Persia	107	440	4,876

Countries.	Sunday Schools.	Teachers.	Scholars.
ASIA—Continued.			
Siam	16	64	809
China	105	1,053	5,264
Japan	150	390	7,019
Central Turkey	516	2,450	25,833
AFRICA	4,246	8,455	161,394
NORTH AMERICA:			
United States	132,697	1,394,630	10,893,523
Canada	8,986	75,064	582,070
Newfoundl'nd and Labrador	375	2,363	23,856
West Indies	2,306	10,769	111,335
Central America and Mexico	550	1,300	15,000
SOUTH AMERICA	350	3,000	150,000
OCEANICA:			
Australasia	7,458	54,670	595,031
Fiji Islands	1,474	2,700	42,909
Hawaiian Islands	230	1,413	15,840
Other Islands	210	800	10,000
The World	246,658	2,378,921	22,540,392

The total number of teachers and scholars in the world, according to this report, was 24,919,313.

The table does not include the schools of the Roman Catholic and Non-Evangelical Protestant churches. The number of scholars in Roman Catholic Sunday schools in the United States is estimated by clerics at 900,000.

The World's 4th Sunday-School Convention held in Jerusalem April, 1904.

RELIGIOUS STATISTICS.

NUMBERS IN THE WORLD ACCORDING TO CREED.

The following estimates, by M. Fournier de Flaix, are the latest that have been made by a competent authority.

Creeds.	No. of Followers.	Creeds.	No. of Followers.
1 Christianity	477,080,158	5 Buddhism	147,900,000
2 Worship of Ancestors and Confucianism	256,000,000	6 Taoism	43,000,000
3 Hindooism	190,000,000	7 Shintoism	14,000,000
4 Mohammedanism	176,834,372	8 Judaism	7,186,000
		9 Polytheism	117,681,669

CHRISTIANITY.

Churches.	Total Followers.	Churches.	Total Followers.
Catholic Church	230,866,533	Armenian Church	1,690,000
Protestant Churches	143,237,625	Nestorians	80,000
Orthodox Greek Church	98,016,000	Jacobites	70,000
Church of Abyssinia	3,000,000		
Coptic Church	120,000	Total	477,080,158

DISTRIBUTION OF SEMITIC ARYAN RACES.

Geographical Divisions.	Christianity.			Mohammedanism.	Judaism.
	Catholic Church.	Protestant Churches.	Orthodox Churches.		
Europe	160,165,000	80,812,000	89,196,000	6,629,000	6,456,000
America	58,393,882	57,294,014	....	....	*130,000
Oceanica	6,574,481	2,724,781	....	24,699,787	....
Africa	2,655,920	1,744,080	....	36,000,000	400,000
Asia	3,007,250	662,750	8,820,000	109,535,585	200,000
Total Followers	230,866,533	143,237,625	98,016,000	176,834,372	7,186,000

RELIGIOUS DIVISIONS OF EUROPE.

Countries.	Catholic Church.	Protestant Churches.	Orthodox Churches.	Jews.	Mohammedans.	Unclassified.
Russia	9,600,000	3,400,000	73,310,000	3,400,000	3,000,000	290,000
Germany	17,100,000	29,478,000	....	590,000	....	32,000
Austria-Hungary	31,100,000	3,900,000	3,100,000	1,700,000	....	100,000
France	35,387,000	580,000	....	49,000	....	84,000
United Kingdom	6,500,000	30,100,000	....	100,000	....	500,000
Italy	29,850,000	62,000	....	38,000	....	50,000
Spain	16,850,000	29,000	....	5,000	....	....
Belgium	5,880,000	15,000	....	3,000	....	2,000
Roumania	100,000	15,000	4,800,000	400,000	30,000	55,000
Ottoman Empire	320,000	11,000	1,700,000	60,000	2,708,000	70,000
Netherlands	1,545,000	2,756,000	....	83,000	....	16,000
Portugal	4,300,000	....	....	....	....	1,000
Sweden	1,000	4,698,000	....	2,000	....	1,000
Switzerland	1,172,000	1,710,000	....	8,000	....	10,000
Denmark	3,000	2,089,000	....	4,000	....	4,000
Greece	10,000	10,000	1,930,000	5,000	45,000	....
Servia	6,000	1,000	1,973,000	5,000	15,000	....
Bulgaria	29,000	....	1,393,000	....	571,000	....
Norway	1,000	1,958,000	....	....	....	1,000
Roumelia	30,000	....	700,000	4,000	240,000	2,000
Montenegro	5,000	....	290,000	....	....	1,000
Luxembourg	200,000	....	....	....	....	....
Malta	160,000	....	....	....	....	....
Gibraltar	16,000	....	....	....	....	....
Total Followers	160,165,000	80,812,000	89,196,00	6,456,000	6,629,000	1,219,000

The distinction between followers and actual communicants should be observed.

ENGLISH-SPEAKING RELIGIOUS COMMUNITIES OF THE WORLD.

Episcopalians	29,200,000	Lutherans, etc	2,800,000
Methodists of all descriptions	18,650,000	Unitarians	2,600,000
Roman Catholics	15,500,000	Minor religious sects	5,500,000
Presbyterians of all descriptions	12,250,000	Of no particular religion	17,000,000
Baptists of all descriptions	9,230,000		
Congregationalists	6,150,000	English-speaking population	124,130,000
Free Thinkers	5,250,000		

A very large number—more than 18,000,000—of Hindoos, Mohammedans, Buddhists, and others in the East also speak and read English.

The estimates in the last table are from Whitaker's (London) Almanack, 1895.

The *Encyclopedia Britannica*, last edition, makes a rough estimate of numbers of Protestants in the world speaking all civilized languages, and places the Lutherans at the head, with over 42,000,000 members (mostly in Germany and Scandinavia), and the Anglican Church second, with about 20,000,000 members.

* United States census of 1890.

RELIGIOUS DENOMINATIONS IN THE UNITED STATES.

The following figures were compiled by *The Independent* for 1901, aggregating 28,000,000. The increase for 1902 is 90,630, or a total membership of 28,090,630. The membership of the various denominations has varied but slightly.

Denominations.	Ministers.	Churches.	Communicants.
Adventists:			
Evangelical	34	30	1,147
Advent Christian	883	580	25,816
Seventh-Day	372	1,470	55,316
Church of God	19	29	647
Life and Advent Union	60	33	3,000
Church of God in Jesus Christ	94	95	2,872
Armenians	15	21	8,500
Baptists:			
Regular, North	7.415	9,374	973,820
Regular, South	12,058	18,963	1,608,413
Regular, Colored	14,351	15,654	1,864,600
Six Principle	14	18	937
Seventh-Day	119	115	8,991
Freewill	1.619	1,486	85,109
Original Freewill	118	167	11,864
General	450	550	28,000
Separate	113	103	6,479
United	25	204	13,209
Church of Christ	80	152	8,254
Primitive	2.040	3,222	121,347
Old Two Seed in the Spirit Predestinarian	300	473	12,851
Brethren (River):			
Brethren in Christ	152	78	4,000
Old Order, or Yorker	7	8	214
United Zion's Children	20	25	525
Brethren (Plymouth):			
Brethren (I.)	....	109	2,289
Brethren (II.)	....	88	2,419
Brethren (III.)	....	86	1,235
Brethren (IV.)	....	31	718
Catholics:			
Roman Catholics	11,636	12,062	8,610,226
Polish Branch	19	18	15,000
Old Catholics	6	5	10,000
Reformed Catholics	6	6	1,500
Catholic Apostolic	95	10	1,394
Chinese Temples	....	47	....
Christadelphians	....	63	1,277
Christians	1,248	1,520	112,835
Christian Catholic (Dowie)	55	50	40,000
Christian Missionary Ass'n	10	13	754
Christian Scientists	12,000	600	1,000,000
Christian Union	183	294	18,214
Church of God (Winnebrennerian)	460	580	38,000
Church Triumphant (Schweinfurth)	....	12	384
Church of the New Jerusalem*	143	173	7,679

Denominations.	Ministers.	Churches.	Communicants.
Communistic Societies:			
Shakers	....	15	1,728
Amana	....	7	1,600
Harmony	....	1	250
Separatists	....	1	200
Altruists	....	1	25
Church Triumphant (Koreshan Ecclesia)	....	5	205
Adonai Shomo	....	1	20
New Icaria	....	1	21
Congregationalists	5,614	5,604	629,874
Disciples of Christ	6,528	10,528	1,149,982
Dunkards:			
German Baptists (Conservatives)	2,612	850	95,000
German Baptists (Old Order)	150	100	3,500
German Baptists (Progressive)	231	173	12,787
Seventh-Day Baptists (German)	5	6	194
Episcopalians:			
Protestant Episcopal	4,961	6,686	716,431
Reformed Episcopal	103	104	9,743
Evangelical Bodies:			
Evangelical Association	1,052	1,806	118,865
United Evangelical Church	478	985	60,993
Friends:			
Friends (Orthodox)	1,279	820	91,868
Friends (Hicksite)	115	201	21,992
Friends (Wilburite)	38	52	4,329
Friends (Primitive)	11	9	232
Friends of the Temple	4	4	340
German Evangelical Protestants	44	52	36,156
German Evangelical Synod	909	1,129	203,574
Greek Church:			
Greek Orthodox	4	4	20,000
Russian Orthodox	41	58	45,000
Jews	201	570	1,058,135
Latter-Day Saints†:			
Church of Jesus Christ of Latter-Day Saints	1,700	796	300,000
Reorganized Church of Jesus Christ of Latter-Day Saints‡	2,200	600	45,500
Lutherans (General Bodies):			
General Synod	1,226	1,568	194,442
United Synod in the South	215	390	38,639
General Council	1,156	2,019	370,409
Synodical Conference	2,029	2,650	581,029
(Independent Synods):			
United Norwegian	354	1,083	126,872
Joint Synod of Ohio	457	604	77,362
Buffalo	25	39	4,600
Hauge's, Norwegian	97	205	11,483
Texas	11	14	1,700
German of Iowa	402	824	74,058

Religious Denominations in the United States—*Continued.*

Denominations.	Ministers.	Churches.	Communicants.
Lutherans—*Continued:*			
Norwegian Lutheran	272	725	67,208
Michigan	56	86	7,860
Danish in America	47	66	10,000
Icelandic	8	26	3,350
Immanuel	45	50	6,118
Suomai, Finnish	11	50	5,925
Norwegian Free	125	375	37,500
Danish United	84	151	8,506
Independent Congregations	85	200	25,000
Waldenstromians	140	150	20,000
Mennonites:			
Mennonite	418	288	22,443
Bruederhoef	9	5	352
Amish	365	124	13,051
Old Amish	71	22	2,038
Apostolic	2	2	209
Reformed	43	34	1,680
General Conference	138	79	10,395
Church of God in Christ	18	18	471
Old (Wisler)	17	15	610
Bundes Conference	41	16	3,050
Defenseless	20	11	1,176
Brethren in Christ	45	82	2,953
Methodists:			
Methodist Episcopal	17,521	26,021	2,716,437
Union American M. E	63	61	2,675
African Methodist Episcopal	5,659	5,775	673,504
African Union Methodist Protestant	80	70	2,000
African Methodist Episcopal Zion	3,155	2,906	536,271
Methodist Protestant	1,647	2,400	181,316
Wesleyan Methodist	587	506	17,201
Methodist Episcopal, South	6,041	14,244	1,457,864
Congregational Methodist	210	240	20,000
Congregational Methodist (Colored)	5	5	319
New Congregational Methodist	20	17	1,059
Zion Union Apostolic	30	27	2,346
Colored Methodist	2,187	1,300	199.206
Primitive Methodist	65	92	6.470
Free Methodist	944	1,123	28,588
Independent Methodist	8	14	2,569
Evangelist Missionary	87	13	4,600
Moravians	118	111	14,817
Presbyterians:			
Presbyterian in U. S. of A. (North)	7,335	7,469	973,433
Cumberland Presbyterian	1,734	2,957	180,192
Cumberland Presbyterian (Colored)	400	150	39,000
Welsh Calvinistic	105	185	12,000
United Presbyterian	918	911	115,901
Presbyterian in U. S. of A. (South)	1,461	2,959	225,890
Associate Church of North America	12	31	1,053
Associate Reform Synod of the South	104	131	11,344
Reform Presbyterian in the U. S. (Synod)	124	113	9,790
Reform Presbyterian in N. A. (General Synod)	33	36	5,000
Reform Presbyterian (Covenanted)	1	1	40
Reform Presbyterian in U. S. and Canada	1	1	608
Reformed:			
Reformed in America (Dutch)	698	619	107,594
Reformed in U. S. (German)	1,082	1,660	243,545
Christian Reformed	96	145	18,096
Salvation Army	2,689	753	40,000
Schwenkfeldians	3	4	306
Social Brethren	17	20	913
Society for Ethical Culture	....	4	1,064
Spiritualists	....	334	45,030
Theosophical Society	....	40	695
United Brethren:			
United Brethren in Christ	1,897	4,229	243,841
United Brethren (Old Constitution)	670	817	226,643
Unitarians	550	459	71,000
Universalists	735	764	48.426
Volunteers of America	500	200	....
Independent Congregations	54	156	14,126

* Swedenborgians. † Mormons. ‡ Seceding Mormons.

The aggregate of about 28,000,000 represents actual church membership, and includes all Catholics, but not all persons affiliated by family ties to Protestant bodies. The larger of the Protestant bodies may claim twice the number of their communicants as nominal adherents.

Scriptural Measures of Capacity.—The measures of capacity referred to in the Scriptures, with their English equivalents, are as follows: The Chomer or Homer in King James's translation was 75,625 gals. liquid, and 32,125 pecks dry. The Ephah or Bath was 7 gals. 4 pts., 15 ins. sol. The Seah=1-3 of Ephah, 2 gals. 4 pts., 3 ins. sol. The Hin=1-6 of Ephah, 1 gal., 2 pts., 1 in. sol. The Omer=1-10 of Ephah, 5 pts., 0.5 in. sol. The Cab=1-18 of Ephah, 3 pts., 10 ins. sol. The Log=7 1-72 of Ephah, $\frac{1}{2}$ pt., 10 ins. sol. The Metretes of Syria (John ii, 6)=Cong. Rom. 7$\frac{1}{8}$ pts. The Cotyla Eastern=1-

100 of Ephah, ½ pt., 3 ins. sol. This Cotyla contains just 10 ozs. avoirdupois of rain water; Omer, 100; Ephah, 1,000; Chomer or Homer, 10,000.

Scriptural Measures of Length.— The measures of length used in the Scriptures, with their English equivalents, are as follows: The great Cubit was 21.888 ins.=1.824 ft., and the less 18 ins. A span, the longer=½ a cubit=10.944 ins.=.912 ft. A span, the less =1-3 of a cubit=7.296 ins.=.608 ft. A hand's breadth=1-6 of a cubit=3.684 ins.= .304 ft. A finger's breadth=1-24 of a cubit =.912 ins.=.076 ft. A fathom=4 cubits= 7.296 ft. Ezekiel's Reed=6 cubits=10.944 feet. The mile=4,000 cubits=7,296 ft. The Stadium, 1-10 of their mile=400 cubits= 729.6 ft. The Parasang, 3 of their miles= 12,000 cubits, or 4 English miles and 580 ft. 33.164 miles was a day's journey — some say 24 miles; and 3,500 ft. a Sabbath day's journey; some authorities say 3,648 ft.

Theosophy.— The name "theosophy" is from the Greek word *theosophia*, divine wisdom. The object of theosophical study is professedly to understand the nature of divine things. It differs from both philosophy and theology in that all reasoning processes are excluded as imperfect, and claims to derive its knowledge from direct communication with God. It does not accept the truths of recorded revelation as immutable, but as subject to modification by later direct and personal revelations. It is really but another name for mysticism, although the latter name implies much more; and the direct and immediate knowledge or intuition of God to which the Mystics laid claim was, in fact, the foundation of that intimate union with God, and consequent abstraction from outer things, which they make the basis of their moral and ascetical system. The theosophic system dates from a very high antiquity. Since the Christian era we may class among theosophists such sects as Neoplatonists, the Hesychasts of the Greek Church, and in later times the disciples of Paracelsus, Thalhauser, Böhme, and Swedenborg.

Bayeux Tapestry, The, is a web of canvas or linen cloth upon which is embroidered, in woolen threads of various colors, a representation of the invasion and conquest of England by the Normans. The canvas is 214 feet long by 20 inches broad, and is preserved in the public library at Bayeux. Tradition asserts that it is the work of Matilda, wife of William the Conqueror, and it is believed that if she did not actually stitch the whole of it with her own hands, she at least took part in it, and directed the execution of it by her maids, and afterwards presented it to the Cathedral of Bayeux as a token of her appreciation of the effective assistance which its bishop, Odo, rendered her husband at the battle of Hastings. Some antiquarians contend that it was not the work of Queen Matilda (the wife of the Conqueror), who died in 1083, but of the Empress Matilda (the daughter of Henry I.), who died in 1167. The tapestry contains, beside the figures of 505 quadrupeds, birds, sphinxes, etc., the figures of 623 men, 202 horses, 55 dogs, 37 buildings, 41 ships and boats, and 49 trees — in all, 1,512 figures. It is divided into 72 distinct compartments, each representing one particular historical occurrence, and bearing an explanatory Latin inscription. A tree is usually chosen to divide the principal events from each other. This pictorial history — for so it may be called — gives an exact and minute portraiture of the manners and customs of the times; and it has been remarked that the arms and habits of the Normans are identical with those of the Danes as they appear in the earlier formative periods of the English people.

Amen is a Hebrew word signifying "Yes," "Truly." In Jewish synagogues the amen is pronounced by the congregation at the conclusion of the benediction. Among the early Christians the prayer offered by the presbyter was concluded by the word amen, uttered by the congregation. Justin Martyr is the earliest of the fathers who alludes to the use of the response. According to Tertullian, none but the faithful were permitted to join in the response. A somewhat noisy and irreverent practice prevailed in the celebration of the Lord's Supper until the sixth century, after which it was discontinued. "Upon the reception both of the bread and of the wine, each person uttered a loud 'amen,' and at the close of the consecration by the priest, all joined in shouting a loud 'amen.'" The same custom was observed at baptism, when the sponsors and witnesses responded vehemently. In the Greek Church the amen was pronounced after the name of each person of the Trinity; and at the close of the baptismal formula the people responded. At the conclusion of prayer it signifies (according to the English Church Catechism) *so be it;* after the repetition of the creed, *so it is.*

Shintuism is the prevailing religion of Japan. Its characteristics are the absence of an ethical and doctrinal code, of idol worship, of priestcraft, and of any teachings concerning a future state. It requires pre-eminently purity of heart and general temperance. The principal divinity is the sun-goddess Amaterasu, whose descendant and vice-regent on earth is the Mikado, who is therefore worshiped as a demigod. Their temples are singularly devoid of ecclesiastical paraphernalia. A metal mirror generally stands on the altar as a symbol of purity. The spirit of the enshrined deity is supposed to be in a case, which is exposed to view only on the day of the deity's annual festival. The worship consists merely in washing the face in a font, striking a bell, throwing a few cash into the money box, and praying silently for a few seconds. In addition to the chief deity, there are a legion of canonized heroes and benefactors who are worshiped. Many Japanese temples are magnificent specimens of architecture in wood, and are remarkable for their vast tent-like roofs and their exquisite wood-carving.

Arundel Marbles are a collection of ancient sculptures consisting of 37 statues, 128 busts, and 250 inscribed stones, which were found on the island of Paros about 1610. They were collected by Mr. W. Pefty, purchased by Lord Arundel, and given by his grandson, Henry Howard — afterward Duke of Norfolk — to the University of Oxford in 1667. These sculptures contain inscriptions in the Greek tongue. In their perfect state they evidently contained a chronological table of the principal events of Grecian history from the time of Cecrops, 1582 B. C., to the archonship of Diognetus, 264 B. C. The chronicle of the last ninety years of this period, however, is lost, and the portion still extant is much corroded and defaced.

Babel, Tower of.— The distinction of being a remnant of the Tower of Babel has been claimed for three different masses, but the majority of opinions are in favor of the Birs Nimrud in Babylonia, the ruins of this temple appearing to more nearly correspond with the conceived notion of that structure. It is of an oblong form, the total circumference being 762 yards. At the eastern side it is cloven by a deep furrow, and it is not more than 50 or 60 feet high; but on the western side it rises in a conical figure to the elevation of 198 feet; and on its summit is a solid pile of brick 37 feet high by 28 in breadth, diminishing in thickness to the top, which is broken and irregular, and rent by a large fissure extending through a third of its height. The fire-burnt bricks of which it is built have inscriptions on them; and so excellent is the cement, which appears to be lime-mortar, that it is nearly impossible to extract a whole brick. The other parts of the summit of the hill are occupied by immense fragments of brickwork of no determinate figure, tumbled together, and converted into solid, vitrified masses, as if they had undergone the action of the fiercest fire or had been blown up with gunpowder. These ruins stand on a prodigious mound, the whole of which is itself in ruins, channeled by the weather, and strewed with fragments of black stone, sandstone, and marble. Taken in connection with the ancient tradition that the Tower of Babel was rent and overthrown by fire from heaven, this is a curious circumstance.

Sunday.— The name of the first day of the week is derived from the Saxon *Sunnan daeg*, or day of the sun; in the Roman calendar, *dies Solis*. We have no definite information as to when the observance of the first day of the week was substituted by the Christians for that of the seventh day, the ancient Jewish Sabbath. It undoubtedly arose among the earliest practices of the Christian Church, and was regarded as the fittest day to be held as sacred, because, in the words of one of the Fathers, "It is the first day in which God changed darkness and matter, and made the world; and on the same day, also, Jesus Christ, our Saviour, rose from the dead." Various additional reasons, taken from the Old Testament, were advanced by others of the early Fathers in support of the observance of this day. The first law, either ecclesiastical or civil, by which the sabbatical observance of Sunday is known to have been ordained, is an edict of Constantine, A. D. 321, forbidding all work but necessary husbandry on the "venerable Sunday." In the Theodosian Code it is enjoined that "on the Sunday, rightfully designated by our ancestors as the Lord's Day, all lawsuits and public business shall cease." Since the ninth century, Sunday has been a thoroughly established institution of the Christian Church as a day of rest and religious exercises, and one exempt from any occupations of a purely secular character, except such as were absolutely necessary.

Peri.— According to the mythical lore of the East, a Peri is a being begotten by fallen spirits, which spends its life in all imaginary delights; it is immortal, but is forever excluded from the joys of Paradise. They take an intermediate place between angels and demons, and are either male or female; when the latter, they are of surpassing beauty. One of the finest compliments to be paid to a Persian lady is to speak of her as Perizadeh (born of a Peri; Greek, *Parisatis*). They belong to the great family of genii, or jin, a belief in whom is enjoined in the Koran, and for whose conversion, as well as for that of man, Mohammed was sent.

Peter-Pence, the name given to a tribute offered to the Roman pontiff in reverence to the memory of St. Peter, whose successor the pope is believed by Roman Catholics to be. The first idea of an annual tribute appears to have come from England. It is ascribed by some to Ina (A. D. 721), King of the West Saxons, who went as a pilgrim to Rome, and there founded a *hospice* for Anglo-Saxon pilgrims, to be maintained by an annual contribution from England; by others, to Offa and Ethelwulf, at least in the sense of their having extended it to the entire Saxon territory. The tribute consisted in the payment of a silver penny by every family possessing land or cattle of the yearly value of thirty pence, and it was collected during the five weeks between St. Peter's and St. Paul's day, and August 1. Since the total annexation of the Papal states to the kingdom of Italy the tribute has been largely increased in France, Belgium, England, and Ireland.

Public Schools.—The origin of the public school system of America dates back to the time of the settlement of Massachusetts and Connecticut. In the very beginning of their history these colonists made provision for the establishment of schools in every town, and parents were required to send their children to them or educate them otherwise. At first these schools were not entirely free; that is, those who could pay were required to do so; but the evil of separating the children into paupers and rate-payers in time became apparent, and shortly after the colonies became states the school taxes were increased and the schools were made free. The example of these colonists was quickly followed by other New England colonies; but in other sections of the country schools were either private or parochial for many years, except in cases where a free school was established and supported by private beneficence. When the vast territories west of the Allegheny mountains came into the possession of the United States, every sixteenth section in each Congressional township was set aside by the government as a nucleus of a public school fund; later, this was increased to two sections for the benefit of the newer states. The Southern states were the last to embrace the free school system in its entirety, having done so only since the close of the civil war. Maine, Vermont, Massachusetts, Connecticut, New Hampshire, New York, New Jersey, Kansas, Nevada, Wisconsin, Ohio, Michigan, California, Arizona, Wyoming, and Washington Territory have compulsory educational laws. The average age up to which school attendance is required is, in the United States, fourteen and one half years, which is older than that in any other country.

Colossus of Memnon.—The celebrated vocal statue of Memnon, on the plain of Thebes, was originally sixty feet high, and is of a coarse, hard gritstone or breccia. The peculiar characteristic of this statue was its giving out at various times a sound resembling the breaking of a harp string or a metallic ring. Considerable difference of opinion has prevailed as to the reason of this sound, which has been heard in modern times, it being ascribed to the artifice of the priests, who struck the sonorous stone of which the statue is composed, the passage of light draughts of air through the cracks, or the sudden expansion of aqueous particles under the influence of the sun's rays. This remarkable quality of the statue is first mentioned by Strabo, who visited it in company with Ælius Gallus, about 18 B. C.; and upwards of 100 inscriptions of Greek and Roman visitors, incised upon its legs, record the visits of ancient travelers to witness the phenomenon, from the ninth year of Nero, A. D. 63, to the reign of the Emperor Severus, when it became silent.

Colossus of Rhodes.—The gigantic Colossus of Rhodes was a statue of Apollo, so placed as to bestride the entrance to the harbor. It is said to have been commenced by Chares of Lindus, a famous pupil of Lysippus, and was completed by Laches. It was formed of metal which was cast in separate pieces, a process which lasted for twelve years, and was finished in 280 B. C. The Colossus was over 100 feet high, and its thumb was so large that a man could not clasp it with his arms. It cost 300 talents, and sixty years after its erection it was thrown down by an earthquake. When, after lying on the ground for centuries, it was removed, the metal that composed it loaded 900 camels. The Colossus of Rhodes ranks as one of the Seven Wonders of the World.

Sanhedrim, as the supreme national tribunal of the Jews was called, was established at the time of the Maccabees, and was the court before which Christ was tried for high treason against the Roman Emperor. It was presided over by the Nasi (Prince), at whose side was the Ab-Beth-Din (Father of the Tribunal). Its members, of which there were seventy-one, belonged to the different classes of society; there were priests, elders—that is, men of age and experience—scribes, or doctors of law, and others exalted by eminent learning, which was the sole condition for admission. The limits of its jurisdiction are not clearly known, but it is believed that the supreme decision over life or death was exclusively in its hands. The regulation of the sacred times and seasons was vested in it. It fixed the beginnings of the new moons; intercalated the years when necessary; watched over the purity of the priestly families by carefully examining the pedigrees of those priests born out of Palestine, so that none born from a suspicious or ill-famed mother should be admitted to the sacred service. The mode of procedure was extremely complicated; and such was the caution of the court, especially in matters of life and death, that capital punishment was pronounced in the rarest instances only. The Nasi had the supreme direction of the court, and convoked it when necessary. He sat at the head, and at his right hand was the seat of the Ab-Beth-Din; the rest of the seventy-one took their places, according to their dignity, in front of them, in the form of a semicircle, so that they could be seen by both the chief officers. The meeting place of the court was, on ordinary occasions, in a hall at the southeast corner of the Temple, but on extraordinary occasions it met in the house of the high priest. It met daily, with the exception of Sabbaths and feast days. After the destruction of the Temple and Jerusalem, the Sanhedrim, after many emigrations, was finally established at Babylon.

Host.— In conformity with the doctrines of the Roman Catholic Church, the consecrated bread of Eucharist is called the Host. In the Latin Church it is a thin circular disk of unleavened bread, made of the finest flour, and generally bearing some emblematic device. In the Greek and other Oriental churches, as well as in the various Protestant communities, the Eucharist is celebrated in leavened bread, only differing from ordinary bread in being of finer quality.

Schoolmen and Scholastics are the terms applied to the class of learned theologians and philosophers who flourished in Europe, mainly in France and England, during the middle ages. They were largely given to hair-splitting logic and endless argumentations and speculations on points of the most unimportant and often silly nature. Still, in their number were included men of great learning and ability, as Duns Scotus, Thomas Aquinas, and Albertus Magnus, with whom this system of philosophical theological scholasticism culminated in the fourteenth century. Johannes Erigena Scotus was not strictly a scholastic; he lived in the ninth century, in the preparatory period of scholasticism.

Colosseum, The.— The Flavian amphitheater at Rome, known as the Colosseum, was begun by the Emperor Vespasian, and was finished by the Emperor Titus, A. D. 80. It covers about five acres of ground, and contained seats for 87,000 persons and standing room for 15,000 more. It was in the form of an oval, the longer diameter being 612 feet and the shorter diameter 515 feet, and the height of the walls from 160 to 180 feet. The arena where the gladiators fought and the deadly conflicts with wild beasts took place was 281 by 178 feet. The exterior consists of three rows of columns, Doric, Ionic, and Corinthian, and above, a row of Corinthian pilasters. Between the columns there are arches which form open galleries throughout the whole building, and between each alternate pilaster of the upper tier there is a window. There were four tiers or stories of seats, corresponding to the four external stories. The first of these is supposed to have contained twenty-four rows of seats, and the second sixteen. These were separated by a lofty wall from the third story, which is supposed to have contained the populace. Statues, sculptures, figures of chariots, metal shields, and other embellishments adorned the niches and salient points. On the occasion of the dedication of the Colosseum by Titus, 5,000 wild beasts were slain in the arena, the games having lasted for nearly 100 days. There were means by which, when the combats were ended, the immense arena could be filled with water for the exhibition of sea-fights. During the various persecutions of the early Christians many of these were thrown to the wild beasts in this amphitheater. One of the first of these was St. Ignatius, who was torn to pieces by lions. In the sixth century, when Christianity gained the ascendancy, the Church put an end to the use of the Colosseum. It still stood entire in the eighth century, but subsequently large quantities of the marble was used in the construction of public and private buildings. It was consecrated as a monument to the martyrs who had suffered within its walls by Pope Benedict XIV., who erected crosses and oratorios within it, and so put an end to the process of destruction.

Parsees, the followers of the ancient Persian religion as reformed by Zerdusht, or Zoroaster, as he is commonly called. According to Zerdusht there are two intellects, as there are two lives — one mental and one bodily; and, again, there must be distinguished an earthly and a future life. There are two abodes for the departed — Heaven and Hell. Between the two there is the Bridge of the Gatherer, or Judge, which the souls of the pious alone can pass. There will be a general resurrection, which is to precede the last judgment, to foretell which Sosiosh, the son of Zerdusht, spiritually begotten, will be sent by Ahuramazdao. The world, which by that time will be utterly steeped in wretchedness, darkness, and sin, will then be renewed. Death, the arch fiend of Creation, will be slain, and life will be everlasting and holy. The Parsees do not eat anything cooked by a person of another religion. Marriages can only be contracted with persons of their own caste and creed. Their dead are not buried, but exposed on an iron grating in the Dokhma, or Tower of Silence, to the fowls of the air, to the dew and to the sun, until the flesh has disappeared, and the bleaching bones fall through into a pit beneath, from which they are afterward removed to a subterranean cavern. The temples and altars must forever be fed with the holy fire, brought down, according to tradition, from heaven, and the sullying of whose flame is punishable with death. The priests themselves approach it only with a half-mask over their faces, lest their breath should defile it, and never touch it with their hands, but with holy instruments. The fires are of five kinds; but, however great the awe felt by Parsees with respect to fire and light, they never consider these as anything but emblems of Divinity. There are also five kinds of "sacrifice," which term, however, is rather to be understood in the sense of a sacred action.

Koran, the sacred book of the Mohammedan religion. According to that belief a copy of it, in a book bound in white silk, jewels, and gold, was brought down to the lowest heaven by the angel Gabriel, in the blissful and mysterious night of Al-Khadr, in the month of Ramadan. Portions of it were, during a space of twenty-three years, communicated to Mohammed, both at Mecca and Medina, either by Gabriel in human shape, "with the sound of bells," or through inspirations from the Holy Ghost "in the Prophet's breast," or by God himself, "veiled and unveiled, in waking or in the dreams of night." Mohammed dictated his inspirations to a scribe, not, indeed, in broken verses, but in finished chapters, and from this copy the followers of the Prophet procured other copies. The chief doctrine laid down in the Koran is the unity of God and the existence of one true religion with changeable ceremonies. When mankind turned from it at different times, God sent prophets to lead them back to truth; Moses, Christ, and Mohammed being the most distinguished. Both punishments for the sinner and rewards for the pious are depicted with great diffuseness, and exemplified chiefly by stories taken from the Bible, the Apocryphal writings, and the Midrash. Special laws and directions, admonitions to moral and divine virtues, more particularly to a complete and unconditional resignation to God's will, legends principally relating to the patriarchs, and almost without exception borrowed from the Jewish writings, form the bulk of the book, which throughout bears the most palpable traces of Jewish influence. The outward reverence in which the Koran is held throughout Mohammedanism is exceedingly great. It is never held below the girdle, never touched without previous purification; and an injunction to that effect is generally found on the cover. It is consulted on weighty matters; sentences from it are inscribed on banners, doors, etc. Great lavishness is also displayed upon the material and the binding of the sacred volume. The copies for the wealthy are sometimes written in gold, and the covers blaze with gold and precious stones. Nothing, also, is more hateful in the eyes of a Moslem than to see the book in the hands of an unbeliever.

Palace of the Cæsars.— The palace of Augustus, built upon the site of the houses of Cicero and Catiline, was the beginning of the magnificent pile of buildings known as the Palace of the Cæsars, and each succeeding Emperor altered and improved it. Tiberius enlarged it, and Caligula brought it down to the verge of the Forum, connecting it with the Temple of Castor and Pollux, which he converted into a vestibule for the imperial abode. Nero added to it his "Golden House," which extended from the Palatine to the Cælian Hill, and even reached as far as the Esquiline. This latter portion was afterward used by Titus for his famous baths. The ruins of the palace extend over the three hills of Rome, and cover an area of 1,500 feet in length and 1,300 feet in width. The Golden House, as can be imagined from its name, was a building of extraordinary magnificence. It was surrounded by a triple portico a mile in length, and supported by a thousand columns; and within this lay an immense lake, whose banks were bordered by great buildings, each representing a little city, about which lay green pastures and groves, where sported "all animals, both tame and wild." The ceilings of the banqueting rooms were fretted into ivory coffers made to turn, that flowers might be showered down upon the guests, and also furnished with pipes for discharging perfumes. The principal banqueting room was round, and by a perpetual motion, day and night, was made to revolve after the manner of the universe. The interior walls of the palace were covered with gold and precious stones, and adorned with the finest paintings that the world afforded. In the vestibule stood a statue of Nero, 120 feet in height.

Chinese Burial Customs.—Immediately upon the decease of a person in China a priest is called, whose prayers are supposed to free the departed spirit from the necessity of going to hell, and to secure his admittance to Paradise. The body is arrayed in the most splendid garments that the family can afford. In one hand is placed a fan, and in the other a prayer written on a piece of paper, which is a letter of recommendation to open the gates of Heaven. The coffin is a very solid, substantial case. The corpse when put in it, is laid in a bed of lime or cotton, or covered with quicklime, and the edges of the lid are closed with mortar in the groove, so that no smell escapes. The nature of the site for burial is regarded as having an important influence on the prosperity of the living, the people fearing ill luck, disease, and accident if the dead are not satisfied with the site of their graves. The selection of propitious sites is made by geomancers, a class of quacks who pretend to supernatural wisdom. When the day of burial arrives, which is — if a satisfactory place for the tomb has been found — the nearest lucky day to the third seventh day after death, the friends assemble at the house. An offering of cooked provisions is laid out near the coffin. This is intended to occupy the attention of the spirit of the dead, which is supposed to linger near the body, or any other vagrant spirits that may be hovering around, and keep them from doing any mischief or harm to the living. All mourners are dressed entirely in white, and they assemble about the coffin and in turn prostrate themselves before it, a band of music playing meanwhile. The procession is then formed, the coffin going first, borne on an unwieldy bier carried by sixty-four men, or even more. A man goes before the procession and scatters paper money, to buy the good will of any stray, tricky spirits that may be prowling about. Immediately after the coffin, in a separate sedan, is borne the ancestral tablet of the deceased with the offering of food. Different figures, banners, and tablets are also carried, according to the means and rank of the family. When the grave is reached the coffin is let down, and lime is abundantly mixed with the earth thrown in upon it. Crackers are then fired, libations are poured out, prayers are recited, and finally paper molds of houses, clothes, horses, money, and everything that the dead man can possibly want in the land of shadows, are burned. The origin of this latter custom is unquestionably the idea that everything that had been enjoyed or used in this life would be desired in the other. The ancient custom was to burn a man's household belongings, to kill upon his grave his favorite horse, hound, or bird, and sometimes his chosen servant, that their shadows might go with him into the life beyond. After the funeral the elaborate dishes that have been borne to the grave are carried back, and the mourners feast upon them. Bodies are in some instances kept in or about the house for many years, and incense is burned before them morning and evening.

Delphi, Temple at.— The edifice known to have existed at Delphi, Greece, at the beginning of the historic period, is said to have been the work of two architects named Trophonius and Agamedes. In 548 B. C., this temple having been destroyed, the Amphictyons undertook to build another for the sum of three hundred talents, of which the Delphians were to pay one fourth, and the remainder was to be contributed by other cities of Greece. The temple is said to have been of the Doric order without, and the Ionic within. The front was built of Parian marble, and the sculptured decorations were rich and beautiful. The arches above the entrances were adorned with representations of legends of mythology, and similar adornments were carved on the panels of the walls. Images and statues in brass and marble enriched the interior, and the golden shields taken at Marathon, and also in battles with the Gauls, adorned the architraves. The attempts of the Persians, in 480 B. C., and of the Gauls, in 279 B. C., to rob the temple, were both, it was said, prevented by the miraculous interference of Apollo, and the sacred character of the place long protected it from other would-be plunderers. It was, however, eventually plundered by Sulla, and again by Nero, who silenced the oracle. It was restored by Hadrian, and then despoiled of many of its most beautiful works of art by Constantine the Great, and finally destroyed in the latter part of the fourth century.

Sinai.— The exact position of Sinai, the mount on which God gave to Moses the Ten Commandments and the other laws by which the Israelites were bound, is a matter of some dispute, but it is probably to be found in the mountains occupying the greater part of the Arabian peninsula, lying between the Gulf of Suez and Akabah. This mountain mass is divisible into three groups — a northwestern, reaching, in Mount Serbel, an elevation of 6,340 feet; an eastern and central, attaining in Jebel Katherin a height of 8,160 feet, and a southeastern, whose highest peak, Um Shaumer, is the culminating point of the whole Sinaitic range. Serbal, with its five peaks, looks the most magnificent mountain in the peninsula and is identified with Sinai by the early Church Fathers, Eusebius, Jerome, Cosmas, etc.; but the requirements of the Hebrew narrative are not met by it, and even as early as the time of Justinian, the opinion that the Serbal was the Sinai of Moses had been abandoned, and to a ridge of the second or eastern range that honor had been transferred, the northern summit of which is termed Horeb; and the southern, Jebul-Musa, or Mount of Moses, continues to be regarded by a majority of scholars as the true Sinai. The famous monastery of Mount Sinai stands at the eastern base of Jebul-Musa, in solitary peace. There were numerous other convents, chapels, and hermitages around the mountain in earlier times.

Jesuits, Society of, was founded by Ignatius of Loyola, assisted by Peter Le Fevre, a Savoyard; James Lainez, Francis Xavier, Nicholas Bobadilla, Spaniards, and a Portuguese named Rodriguez, in the year 1534. The society, when first conceived, had for its object a pilgrimage to the Holy Land and the conversion of the infidels. This purpose, however, was abandoned owing to the warfare existing at that time between the Turks and the Western powers, and Loyola and his associates turned their attention to an organization designed to labor zealously in resisting the spread of the Reformation. In 1539 the rule of the proposed order—"To the greater glory of God"—and the vow by which they bound themselves to go as missionaries to any country which the Pope might indicate was submitted to Paul III., and Loyola was made the first general of the order. The Society of Jesuits is one of the most celebrated religious orders of the Roman Catholic Church, and its history has been closely identified at times with that of several of the leading countries of Europe. By reason of legislative influences the Jesuits were obliged to suspend operations in France, Italy, Spain, and several other countries. Notwithstanding that many good Roman Catholics are not in sympathy with the Jesuit order, yet it can be said that in their pioneer missionary operations they undoubtedly accomplished a great deal of good.

Mosaics.—The origin of the art of producing artistic designs by setting small square pieces of stone or glass of different colors, so as to give the effect of painting, is obscure, but it was much practiced by the Romans, especially for ornamental pavements, specimens of which are almost always found wherever the remains of an old Roman villa are discovered. Under the Byzantine empire it was also much used for the ornamentation of churches, in which it formed a large portion of the wall decoration. Christian mosaics admit, says one writer, of two general divisions, the later Roman and the Byzantine styles, the material in use being, in general, cubes of colored glass, inlaid, in the Roman school, on a ground of blue and white, although in the latter the tesseræ are frequently irregular in size and the workmanship coarse. The former style flourished in Italy chiefly in the fifth and sixth centuries, the most splendid specimens being found in the churches of Rome and Ravenna. The Florentine mosaic dates from the time of the Medici, and is made entirely of precious or semi-precious stones, such as amethyst, agate, jasper, onyx, and others, cut and inlaid in forms or thin veneers best suited to produce the effects desired. The objects represented are most frequently birds, flowers, fruits, vases, sometimes buildings, and, more rarely, portraits and landscapes. In reference to the present Roman mosaics, it may be said that the smalti or small cubes of colored glass which compose the pictures are stuck into the cementing paste, or mastic, in the same manner as were the colored glass, stone, and marble sectilia and tesseræ of the ancients. Within quite recent years mosaics of surpassing beauty, both in design and material, have been produced by Russian artists in the Imperial Glass Manufactory of Russia.

Trajan's Column, a celebrated column at Rome, which was reared A. D. 114, by the Roman Senate and people, in honor of the Emperor Trajan. It is considered not only the greatest work of its architect, Apollodorus, but one of the noblest structures of its kind ever erected. The pedestal is covered with bas-reliefs of warlike instruments, shields, and helmets; and a very remarkable series of bas-reliefs, forming a spiral around the shaft, exhibits a continuous history of the military achievements of Trajan. These are in excellent preservation, and, independently of their beauty as works of art, they are invaluable as records of ancient costumes. A spiral staircase in the interior of the column leads to its summit. The height of the entire column is 132 feet. It stands erect in all its ancient beauty amid the ruins of Trajan's Forum. The summit was originally crowned by a colossal statue of the emperor, which has been incongruously replaced by one of St. Peter.

Vulgate, The, the Latin translation of the Bible, which is the received version in the Roman Catholic Church. The original Vulgate was completed in A. D. 405 by Jerome, and between that date and 1546, when it was first declared the authorized version of the Roman Church, it underwent several revisions which completely changed the character of the work. In the latter year the Tridentine Council decreed the preparation of an authentic edition, and the task was undertaken by the Papal Chair; but it was not until 1590 that Sixtus V. produced the work. This, however, turned out to be so utterly incorrect and faulty throughout that the copies were speedily suppressed, and another edition, which appeared in 1592, was prepared under Clement VIII., to which, in the next year (1593), that other edition succeeded, which has since remained the normal edition of the Church of Rome, and has been reprinted, unchanged, ever since.

The Smithsonian Institution is situated in Washington, D. C., and was organized by act of Congress in August, 1846, to carry into effect the provisions of the will of James Smithson. That celebrated English physician bequeathed to his nephew £120,000, the whole of his property, which, in the event of the death of the latter without heirs, was to revert to the United States, to found at Washington an establishment for "the increase and diffusion of knowledge among men," and which was to be named the Smithsonian Institution. The conditions on which the bequest was to take effect in the United States occurred in 1835 by the death of the nephew without issue, and the Hon. Richard Rush was sent to London to prosecute the claim. On September 1, 1838, he deposited in the United States Mint $515,169, being the proceeds of the estate. The Institute is governed by regents appointed by the federal government, and contains a museum, library, cabinets of natural history, and lecture rooms. It receives copies of all copyrighted books, and exchanges with other countries, and its museum is enriched with the gatherings of national exploring expeditions. A portion of its funds is devoted to scientific researches and the publication of works too expensive for private enterprise. There are departments of astronomy, ethnology, meteorology, and terrestrial magnetism. The courses of public lectures by eminent scientific men are among the attractions of the capital.

REQUIREMENTS FOR THE PRACTICE OF LAW.

Qualifications as to citizenship, personal character, education, and professional attainments required by the several states, from those who are admitted to the practice of law.

From reports to the United States Bureau of Education.

Alabama. Actual, *bona fide* citizenship. High moral character as testified to by a member of the profession. Education judged from examination. If the study period is passed in a law office, then the judges of the supreme court must make written examination, except in the case of those graduating from Alabama University.

Arkansas. Must be a citizen of the state and of good moral character. The liberal education feature is left to court which examines. The circuit and supreme courts are the only bodies authorized to grant license to practice law. Applicant must stand satisfactory examination in open court, by the supreme court, and by a committee of three lawyers appointed by circuit court when applicant is examined by that court.

Arizona. A declaration of citizenship and proof of good moral character are required, but there is no distinction between liberal and professional education. The only thing necessary for admission to practice here, if not armed either with a diploma or license from another jurisdiction, is to stand the examination in open court, and by that show such familiarity with the law as will satisfy the court that the applicant is qualified to take care of a practice.

California. A declaration of citizenship and certificate from two attorneys of court to which applicant has applied for admission that he possesses the character and attainments that entitle him to admission. Examination in open court after filing certificate from two attorneys.

Colorado. Must declare intention to become a citizen three months before applying; must have certificate of good moral character; but no special attention paid to liberal education feature. If not a member of the bar of another state, must pass an examination before supreme court or a committee appointed by it in each judicial district.

Connecticut. Must be a citizen of the United States, 21 years old, and be of good moral character, and must have graduated from a college or secondary school or have been admitted to a college or preparatory school, or passed an examination before committee, for which last he must pay a fee of $5.00. Must have studied law after arriving at the age of 18 for two years, if a college or law school graduate; otherwise, for three years in a law school or under competent professional instruction in the office of a practicing attorney or with the judge of the superior court or both, of which period one year, at least, must be spent in this state. Applicants shall be required to pass a satisfactory examination, before a standing committee of fifteen, upon the law of pleading, practice, and evidence, constitutional law, the law of real and personal property, contracts, torts, equity, criminal law, wills, and administration, corporations, partnership, negotiable paper, agency, bailments, domestic relations, and such additional subjects as committee shall deem advisable.

Delaware. Must be a resident of the state and of "fair" character, and must have a general knowledge of English and American history, mathematics, English grammar, and Latin. A legal course in a law office is not necessary. All applicants for admission except practicing lawyers of other states are required to study three years under direction of a lawyer or a judge of the state. Examination is made by a committee of the bar.

Florida. Must satisfy judge that he is 21 years of age, and of good moral character. Shall be examined by the judge to whom application is made or a committee of two appointed by judge.

Georgia. Must be a citizen of the circuit wherein he makes application and of good moral character, as shown by a certificate of two attorneys known to court. Must undergo examination before committee appointed by court on common law, pleading, and evidence, equity, and equity pleading and practice, Code of Georgia, United States and State Constitutions, and the rules of court. Diplomas of certain law schools in Georgia will obviate necessity of examining candidate.

Idaho. Must be a citizen of the United States; nothing required in the way of liberal education. He must have a knowledge of the law; it is immaterial how he gets it. A committee appointed by court ascertains fitness.

Illinois. Must make affidavit that he is of age, a citizen of the state, and a certified transcript from a court of record in this state showing that he is a man of good moral character. Nothing required as to liberal education. Every applicant to practice law, except those who apply for admission upon a license granted in another state, or upon a diploma issued by a law school in the state, shall present to one of the appellate courts proof that he has studied law three years, the same studies prescribed by the regularly established law schools in the state, or a course equivalent thereto, naming the books studied, under the direction and supervision of one or more licensed lawyers or firms of lawyers, and that the applicant has submitted to satisfactory examinations by such lawyer or lawyers at convenient intervals during such period of study, covering progressively the entire course studied, such proof to consist of the affidavit of the applicant and also of the certificate or certificates of the lawyer. Examination is held in open court.

Indiana. Every person of good moral character, being a voter, shall be entitled to admission to practice law in all courts of justice. (Constitution, Art. VII., sec. 21.) From the letter of the attorney-general, Honorable William A. Ketchum: The words, "being a voter" has been held by the courts to have no limitation in excluding those who are not voters, and women are admitted to practice. The only substantial requirement is that the applicant shall be of good moral character, and at times this may not be very rigidly insisted upon. It seems to be the theory that it is not very important who is admitted to practice law, as after he has been admitted to practice if he does not know enough to justify his admission, he will not get any practice anyhow.

Iowa. Must be a citizen (of the state) and of good moral character. There is no provision regarding a liberal education, but the want of it is considered in determining the applicant's qualifications. Must pursue a regular course in the study of law for at least two years in the office of a practicing attorney of this state, or a course of two years of thirty-six weeks each in some reputable law school in the United States. Examination is conducted by three members of the bar, one of whom must be attorney-general. The written questions are prepared by the supreme court; the oral examination is conducted in open court.

Kansas. Any person being a citizen of the United States, who has read law for two years, the last of which must be in the office of a regularly practicing attorney, who shall certify as to the good character and domicil of the applicant, after passing a satisfactory examination before any district court of the state, and taking the prescribed oath, shall be admitted to practice. Graduates of the School of Law of the University of Kansas are admitted to practice in the district and inferior courts without further examination.

Louisiana. Must be citizen of state; present certificate of good moral character. Must present certificate that two years have been spent in study of law. The court will not be satisfied with the qualifications of a candidate in point of legal learning unless it shall appear that he is well read in the following course of studies at least: Constitution (Story), Law of Nations (Vattel or Wheaton), History of the Civil Law in Louisiana, Louisiana Civil Code, Code of Practice, General Statutes, Institutes of Justinian, Domat's Civil Law, Pothier on Obligations, Blackstone's Commentaries (fourth book), Kent's Commentaries, Mercantile Law (Smith), Insurance (Wood), Negotiable Paper (Story, or Parsons and Daniel), Evidence (Greenleaf, Starkie or Phillips), Crimes (Russell), criminal procedure (Bishop), and the Jurisprudence of Louisiana.

Maine. Nothing in the way of citizenship or liberal education, but character must be satisfactory to justice presiding at time of examination. Must have studied law two years in a lawyer's office or law school, and must be vouched for by the member of bar with whom the student has read. The examining committee is composed of three members of the bar in each county.

Maryland. Must have been a citizen two years (of state), and be of good moral character. No liberal education required by law. Must have been a student of law for the two years immediately preceding his application, and must be examined by court, if not a graduate of a law school in state. The court selects the examining committee.

Massachusetts. Must be a citizen of the state, or have declared his intention to become such, and must be of good moral character. Undoubtedly, applicant's command of English, as shown in examination papers, is of weight. Must pass a thorough examination.

Michigan. Must be a resident in the state, a citizen of the United States, and of good moral character (affidavit of at least two members of the bar of the state in good standing). The board of examiners will regard applicants who have received bachelors' degrees from any reputable college or university as having *prima facie* the requisite general educational qualifications for admission to the bar. So also as to graduates of Michigan normal or high schools, or other reputable institutions of similar character. Recent first grade teachers' certificate will also be accepted. Otherwise applicant must pass examination, especially in arithmetic, grammar, elementary algebra, general American and English history, civil government, composition and rhetoric, and English literature. If the professional examination papers of a college or other graduate show deficiencies in education, the writer will be subject to examination. Graduates from law department of Michigan University or Detroit College of Law, both having a three years' course, are admitted to bar on their diploma. Others must have studied law for three years previous to applying for admission, which shall be conditioned on the applicant's answering correctly seventy per cent. of the questions asked him in a written and oral examination.

Minnesota. Applicant must present his affidavit that he is of age and is a citizen of the United States, or has declared his intention to become such. Also affidavits from two practicing attorneys that he is a person of good moral character. Board shall examine applicants in such branches of general education as it may deem expedient. Must be examined by state board of examiners in law of real property, conveyances and trusts, equity jurisprudence, pleading and practice, common law, statute law, code pleading and practice, constitutional law, international law, criminal law, contracts, sales, bailments and negotiable instruments, landlord and tenant, insurance, partnership, agency, suretyship, frauds, damages and liens, torts, domestic relations, executors, administrators, and wills. Attorneys of five years' standing from any other state or territory of the United States or District of Columbia may, in the discretion of the board, be admitted without examination.

Missouri. Must be an actual resident and of good character. No particular qualification as to liberal education. Graduates of the St. Louis, Kansas City, and Columbia law schools are exempted from examination. Others are required to pass an examination in open court.

Montana. Must be a resident of the United States, or have made a *bona fide* declaration of his intention to become such, and that he is of age; must have testimonials of good moral character, and have studied law for two years, as certified to by two reputable counselors at law. The examination is conducted in open court.

Nebraska. Must be a resident, of age, of good repute, and have studied law for two years. Must at least have a good common school education, which is judged from his composition and spelling at examination. Graduates of the College of Law of the University of Nebraska shall be admitted, as far as professional learning is concerned, without examination. Others are examined by court.

Nevada. Resident of the state and of good moral character. A general education only required. Familiarity with the various branches and general practice of the law required, and to this end study in law office is desirable, although not required. The examination is by court or committee.

New Jersey. Must take the oath of allegiance, be of age, and of good moral character. Must have served a clerkship of four years with some practicing attorney of the state unless he is a graduate of some college or university in the United States, when his clerkship may be acquitted in three years. During the clerkship he must not have been engaged in any other business incompatible with the full and fair *bona fide* service of his clerkship. No person shall be recommended for license as a counselor at law in this state, unless he first submit himself to examination and give satisfactory evidence of his knowledge of the principles and doctrines of the law, and of his abilities as a pleader, nor shall any be admitted to such examination until he shall have practiced as an attorney for three years at least. The examination for attorneys and counselors shall be both written and oral. The examining committee is composed of six counselors, two going out each year.

New Mexico. Must be a citizen of the United States or have declared intention to become such, of good moral character, and *bona fide* resident of New Mexico. Must undergo an examination in open court.

New York. Must be a citizen and present certificate of good moral character. Liberal education is required. For college graduates two years' study of law is required (for others, three years) either in law school or in office. There is a state board of law examiners.

North Carolina. One year residence in the state required, as also a certificate of good moral character, signed by two members of the bar. All must undergo an examination and must have read law in a law office or in a law school for twelve months at least. Supreme court conducts examination.

North Dakota. Must be a resident, of good moral character. All are examined, but applicants must have read law in an office or studied in some reputable law school for two years (thirty-six weeks of session being taken as a year). Supreme court examines applicants.

Ohio. Must be a citizen of the United States or have declared intention, have resided one year in state, and be a person of good moral character. Nothing in the way of liberal education. All must pass an examination, to which those only are admitted who have studied law three years either in an office or in a law school. Supreme court appoints a committee of nine members to examine applicants.

Oklahoma. Must possess a good moral character. Must have acquired the requisite learning. This fact is ascertained through examination by the court. Applicant is examined in open court by committee.

Pennsylvania. He must be a citizen of the United States and of a good moral character as certified to by two persons. He must have a good English education and a knowledge of the elements of Latin as evidenced by examination. In most counties the rules of court require a two or three years' course of study (prior to final examination, by a committee) in the office of a member of the local bar and require at least one year's actual work in an office, even for students of regular law schools.

South Carolina. Citizenship required. Must be of age and of a good moral character. Graduates at the law school of the State University are admitted without examination; others must undergo the examination upon the course of study prescribed by supreme court.

South Dakota. Must be a resident of the state, of age, and of good moral character. All are required to pass an examination in open court.

Tennessee. Must be of age and of good moral character. No other requirement. The professional attainments of the applicant are ascertained by any two judges.

Texas. Six months' residence in the state required. Applicant must be of age, and have a good reputation. Graduates from the University of Texas are admitted without examination. Others are examined by a committee on Blackstone's Commentaries, Kent's Commentaries, Stephens on Pleading, Story's Equity Pleading, first volume of Greenleaf, Story on Notes, Story on Partnership, Story's Equity Jurisprudence, or books of like character. He is expected to have some knowledge of the Constitution and statutes of Texas and the practice of her courts.

Utah. Citizen of United States or one having declared intention to become a citizen. Must be of age and of good moral character. All applicants are strictly examined in open court.

Vermont. Must have resided in Vermont six months, be of age, and of good moral character. All are examined in open court by a committee of the bar; but applicant must have studied three years in the office of a practicing attorney, though not more than two of these years may be spent in attendance at a law school chartered by any state of the United States.

Virginia. Must have resided in state six months, be of age, and a person of honest demeanor. It appears that all are subject to examination by the supreme court of appeals on common law, equity, commercial law, and practice, and the Code of Virginia, but the diploma of a law school duly incorporated by one of the United States "is considered."

Washington. Must be a citizen of the United States, have resided in state one year, have a good moral character, and be 21 years of age. The supreme court, by two of its judges, satisfies itself that the applicant has sufficient general learning, but an attorney of the state must certify that applicant has studied law for two years previous to his application and that he believes him to be a person of sufficient legal knowledge and ability to discharge the duties of an attorney and counselor at law.

West Virginia. Must be a citizen, one year a resident of the county, and have a good moral character. All applicants are now (1897) examined by the law faculty of the University of West Virginia for the supreme court.

Wisconsin. Must be a resident of the state and be of good moral character. Graduates of the law department of the University of Wisconsin are admitted on their diplomas; others are examined by state board of examiners, if they have studied law at least two years prior to the examination.

Wyoming. Must be a citizen, of age, of good moral character, and learned in the law, all of which must be passed upon by the standing committee on admission of each court. An examination is made into the private character and unprofessional literary attainments of applicant.

CHRISTIAN SCIENCE.

The following are the claims of Christian Science, as stated by Mrs. Laura Lathrop, C. S. D., New York:—

The revelation of Christian Science came to Rev. Mary Baker G. Eddy in the year 1866, and its truth and power were immediately demonstrated by signs following. For thirty-two years sinners have been reclaimed, depraved appetites for opium and intoxicating drinks have been destroyed, the sick have been healed of every disease, including insanity; the blind have received their sight, the deaf their hearing, shortened limbs have been elongated, crooked spines have been straightened, and law after law of the human mind has been broken. The one great text-book of this science is "Science and Health," with key to the Scriptures, by Mary Baker G. Eddy, supplemented by another book by the same author called "Miscellaneous Writings." "Science and Health" is now in its one hundred and sixtieth edition, and the demand for it is increasing daily. The Christian Science Publishing House is at 95 Falmouth street, Boston, Mass., and here are published, besides the two books above mentioned, other works by the same author, also *The Christian Science Monthly Journal*, *The Christian Science Weekly*, and the "Christian Science Bible Lessons." In the October *Journal* for 1898 there were mentioned 1,916 practitioners, 289 regularly organized churches, 113 services where no church has as yet been organized, and 81 institutes. One hundred and twenty of these practitioners are in Greater New York, and sixty-seven in Manhattan Borough. There are six regularly organized churches of this denomination in New York city, three of which own church buildings. A beautiful building is now being erected at the corner of Central Park West and Sixty-eighth street by the Second Church of Christ Scientist, New York city.

Flourishing churches have been organized in London, England; Paris, France; Dresden and Hanover, Germany, and in Canada, Brazil, and Scotland. Many handsome church edifices have been built in different cities, and many others are in process of erection. The mother church is located in Boston, Mass., and those all over the country are its branches. Their services are uniform, consisting of two meetings on Sunday and one on Wednesday evening. No sermons are preached by a personal pastor, but a sermon made up of selections from the Bible and "Science and Health," with key to the Scriptures, is read by two readers, called the first and second readers. This church is emphatically a healing church, and many cases of restoration to health have been testified to during the past few years, brought about by attendance on one of these meetings.

Christian Science is demonstrable Christianity. Through the spiritual understanding of the teachings of Christ Jesus, its followers are enabled to obey his command to "heal the sick" and do the works he and his disciples did. The omnipotence, omnipresence, and omniscience of God are proved to be true. Christian Science is not mind cure, as that is popularly understood, because it recognizes but one mind, God. It is not faith cure, because it does not perform its wonderful works through blind faith in a personal God, but through the understanding of man's relation to God. It is not mesmerism nor hypnotism, because it denies absolutely the power of the human mind and human will, and claims no will but God's. Through recognizing the one mind and man as the reflection of that mind, it forever establishes the brotherhood of man. It is the perfect salvation from sin, disease, and death Christ Jesus came to bring. In "Rudimental Divine Science," Mrs. Eddy defines Christian Science "as the law of God, the law of good, interpreting and demonstrating the principle and rule of eternal harmony."

REQUIREMENTS FOR PRACTICE OF MEDICINE.

Qualifications as to citizenship, personal character, education, and professional attainments required by the several states from those who are licensed to practice medicine. From reports to the United States Bureau of Education.

California. No qualifications are specified except that the individual must be a graduate of a "recognized" college; that is, one recognized by the Association of American Medical Colleges.

Colorado. Diploma of recognized reputable school, or ten years' practice of medicine as a business. Anatomy, chemistry, physiology, pathology, surgery, practice of medicine, and obstetrics and diseases of women.

Connecticut. He may be a common drunkard, a notorious libertine, or a criminal abortionist as far as the letter of the law disqualifies him. Anatomy, physiology, medical chemistry, obstetrics, surgery, pathology, diagnosis, therapeutics, practice and materia medica. Examination and diploma necessary.

Delaware. Must furnish proof of good moral character and good common school education. Must have studied medicine at least four years, including three regular courses of lectures in different years in some legally incorporated college or colleges, prior to his having received a diploma.

Florida. Diploma of a college recognized (by the American Medical Association); but any holder of a diploma of a medical college may demand an examination, which all must pass.

Georgia. Three courses in a regular medical college and successful passage of examination before board.

Idaho. Citizen of United States or has declared intention of becoming such, and evidence of good moral character. But said board may also refuse a license for unprofessional conduct, etc. The words "unprofessional conduct, etc.." is declared to mean—First. The procuring or aiding or abetting in procuring a criminal abortion. Second. The employment of what are popularly known as "cappers" or "steerers" in procuring practice. Third. The obtaining a fee on the assurance that a manifestly incurable disease can be permanently cured. Fourth. The willful betrayal of a professional secret to the detriment of a patient. Fifth. All advertisements of medical business in which untruthful and improbable statements are made. Sixth. All advertisements of any medicine or means whereby the monthly periods of women can be regulated or the menses can be re-established if repressed. Seventh. Conviction of any offense involving moral turpitude. Eighth. Habitual intemperance in the use of ardent spirits, narcotics, or stimulants. Diploma of a reputable medical college and an examination.

Illinois. Good moral character. A diploma or certification of graduation from a high school or evidence of having passed the matriculation examination to a recognized literary or scientific college, or a certificate of successful examination by the faculty of any reputable university or college, or by the state superintendent of public instruction in the following branches: English grammar, arithmetic, elementary physics, United States history, geography, Latin (equivalent to one year in a high school). One year is allowed in which to cure defects in Latin, but the student must be provided with a certificate of proficiency in this branch of learning from the designated authorities before he can be accepted as a second course student.—(Medical Practice Act.) Diplomas of colleges recognized by the state board of health as being in "good standing." Diplomas from conditional colleges are recognized, but must be supplemented by an examination in medicine, surgery, gynecology, and obstetrics, a percentage of 80 being required. Graduates of colleges in the United States that are not recognized by the board are required to pass an examination in all the branches of medicine. Graduates of Canadian colleges and foreign colleges and universities are required to supplement their diplomas with an examination in practice, surgery, gynecology, and obstetrics, unless they present evidence of their right to practice medicine and surgery in the province and country in which the college is located from which they receive their diplomas.

Indiana. Must reside within the state and possess a good moral character, attested by two freeholders under oath. After July 1, 1899, no medical college will be recognized as in good standing which does not require the entrance qualifications prescribed by the Association of American Medical Colleges as a prerequisite for matriculation. (Same as Illinois.) Since 1899, July 1, no diploma will be recognized if given by a college possessing an inadequate equipment for teaching medicine, which has not clinical and hospital facilities, and which does not have an active and competent faculty, embracing the departments of anatomy, physiology, chemistry, materia medica, therapeutics, medicine, surgery, obstetrics, histology, pathology, bacteriology, ophthalmology, otology, gynecology, laryngology, dermatology, hygiene, and state medicine, and which does not enjoin attendance upon 80 per cent. of four regular courses of instruction of not less than twenty-six weeks each in four different years, and which does not exact an average grade of 75 per cent. on an examination as a condition of graduation.

Iowa. Certificate refused to one who is incompetent, convicted of felony, grossly immoral, or is an habitual drunkard. Good character must be certified to by two physicians of the state. Literary qualifications same as those of Illinois. Diploma of recognized medical college teaching in a four or more years' course anatomy, physiology and hygiene, chemistry, materia medica and therapeutics, theory and practice of medicine, pathology and pathological anatomy, surgery, obstetrics and gynecology, bacteriology and microscopy, and medical jurisprudence. Each course shall continue for twenty-six weeks.

Kansas. Good moral character is required. A diploma of a recognized medical school. Registration.

Louisiana. A good moral character, average education, as shown by technical examination before board. Must have diploma from medical college in good repute, having three courses of six months each in different years. An examination before the board on all the branches of medicine.

Maine. Certificate of good moral character, only so far as the board may take it upon itself to decide. All must pass an examination on anatomy, physiology, pathology, materia medica, therapeutics, surgery, the principles and practice of medicine, obstetrics, or such branches thereof as the board may deem necessary that the applicant should possess.

Maryland. Testimonials to moral character. The candidate should at least possess a high school education. Must be a graduate of some reputable medical school having a three years' course, but an effort is being made to extend the course to four years. Non-graduates of a college of medicine are examined in practice, surgery, anatomy, materia medica, therapeutics, physiology, chemistry, jurisprudence, obstetrics, gynecology, hygiene, and pathology.

Massachusetts. Good moral character and twenty-one years old. All applicants are required to pass a satisfactory examination in surgery, physiology, pathology, obstetrics, and practice of medicine. College diplomas not a factor in testing an applicant's qualifications for practice.

Michigan. Every graduate of any legally authorized medical college in the state, or in any one of the United States, or in any other country, shall be deemed qualified to practice medicine and surgery in all its departments after having registered.

Minnesota. Good moral character. Evidence of ignorance in ordinary spelling and writing count against a candidate, at option of examiner. The applicant for license must present evidence of having attended upon three separate courses of medical study at a college having not less than six months' duration each. Study with physician not necessary. [Other] applicants are required to pass an examination in anatomy, physiology, histology, pathology, chemistry, medical jurisprudence, preventive medicine, obstetrics, practice, surgery, diseases of women and children, materia medica, eye and ear diseases, toxicology.

Missouri. The law prescribes no qualifications; but in regard to personal character and citizenship the board has made a rule, which has not been questioned, according to which an applicant must present two letters of recommendation from physicians as to his moral and professional character, and he must be a resident of the state unless he makes affidavit that he resides in a county of another state, which county lies upon the border of Missouri. Under a recent decision of the supreme court it is necessary only to be the possessor of a diploma from a legally chartered medical school in good standing to be admitted to registration. The good standing of the school to be determined, like the reputation of an individual, by testimony. The court decided that the law did not authorize the board to set up a standard.

Montana. None; but board may refuse to grant license on moral grounds. Applicants must possess a diploma from a reputable school of medicine, whose professors and teachers are graduates of a school of that kind, and which requires attendance upon four courses of lectures of at least six months each.

Nebraska. Diploma of a recognized medical college and an examination.

Nevada. A medical education and a diploma from some regularly chartered medical school, said school to have a bona fide existence at the time when said diploma was granted.

New Hampshire. Good moral character and twenty-one years of age. Must have graduated from a registered college or satisfactorily completed a full course in a registered academy or high school, or had a preliminary education considered and accepted by the regent (state superintendent of education) as fully equivalent. Our state pays now (1899) no attention to medical college diplomas except from Dartmouth. Since 1893 Dartmouth graduates have been obliged to stand examination. Applicant must have studied medicine not less than four full school years of at least nine months each, including four satisfactory courses of at least six months each, in four different calendar years, in a medical college registered as maintaining at the time a satisfactory standard. The regent shall accept as the equivalent for any part of these requirements or those concerning a literary education, evidence of five or more years of reputable practice provided that such substitution be specified in the license, or has either received the degree of bachelor or doctor of medicine from some registered medical school, or a diploma or license conferring full right to practice medicine in some foreign country. (Recent law.)

New Jersey. Nothing as to citizenship, but at least two physicians, one of New Jersey, must vouch for personal character. Candidates must be graduates from an accredited literary or scientific college, or have completed satisfactorily not less than a three years' course in an accredited high school or academy, or have received a preparatory education covering the following branches, viz., orthography, arithmetic, English grammar and composition, geography, history of the United States, algebra, and physics, or what this board of examiners may consider their equivalent. Candidates must have received a diploma conferring the degree of doctor of medicine from some legally incorporated medical college (which in the opinion of the board was in good standing at the time of issuing said diploma) in the United States or a diploma or license conferring the full right to practice all the branches of medicine and surgery in some foreign country, and have also studied medicine four years, including three courses of lectures in different years in some legally incorporated American or foreign medical college or colleges prior to the granting of said diploma or foreign license; provided, however, that two courses of medical lectures, both of which shall be either begun or completed within the same calendar year, shall not be considered as satisfying the above requirements. All examinations shall be written in the English language and the questions shall be, except in materia medica and therapeutics, such as can be answered in common by all schools of practice.

New Mexico. Two certificates well accredited as to personal character and professional standing. Our board disproves of medical schools doing their own examination of candidates for matriculation. It requires that each candidate for admission to a medical school shall furnish as a minimum a high school certificate — preferably a college degree. No study with a physician required. As to professional study our board has not specified at length its requirements except as to time (four years), and terms of lectures [courses] (four) and conditions for matriculation. [A diploma of a legally chartered medical institution in good standing will admit to practice — law.]

New York. Certificate of good moral character from not fewer than two physicians in good standing; also evidence that applicant has the general education required preliminary to receiving the degree of bachelor or doctor of medicine in this state (medical student certificate), or graduation from a registered college, or satisfactory completion of a full course in a registered academy or high school, or had a preliminary education considered and accepted by the regents of the University of the State of New York as equivalent to such high school course. Evidence that applicant has studied medicine not less than four full years of at least nine months each, including satisfactory courses of at least six months each, in four different calendar years in a medical school registered as maintaining at the time a satisfactory standard. The applicant for license to practice medicine in New York state [not a graduate] must pass examinations in anatomy, physiology, hygiene, chemistry, surgery, obstetrics, pathology, and diagnosis, therapeutics, practice, and materia medica.

North Carolina. Certificate of good moral character from some one known to the board. Education decided by character of papers handed in on examination. No attention paid to diplomas. Satisfactory examination in all branches of medicine. No study with physician required. Examinations are comprehensive but are liberal; 80 per cent. is necessary to pass however.

Ohio. Good moral character from two registered physicians of the state. All medical colleges of the United States requiring a minimum of three years of study of medicine and two courses of lectures for graduation prior to 1886, and possessing proper facilities for teaching and a faculty embracing the chairs of anatomy, physiology, chemistry, materia medica, therapeutics, medicine, surgery, and obstetrics, shall be recognized as in good standing, and diplomas issued by the same and properly verified shall entitle the holders thereof to register as graduates in medicine. For the ten years ending in February, 1896, all medical colleges exacting the foregoing requirements and possessing facilities and a faculty as specified above shall, by virtue of such facts, be recognized as in good standing to and including the year 1892, but that no medical college shall be recognized as in good standing which has not since 1892 possessed the foregoing facilities and faculty, and in addition has not exacted an entrance qualification and attendance upon three regular courses of lectures as a condition of graduation. On and after July 1, 1899, no medical college will be recognized as in good standing which does not require the entrance qualification prescribed by the Association of American Medical

Colleges as a prerequisite for matriculation, which does not possess an adequate equipment for teaching medicine, which has not clinical and hospital facilities based upon a minimum municipal population of 50,000, and which does not have an active faculty embracing the departments of anatomy, physiology, chemistry, materia medica and therapeutics, medicine, surgery, obstetrics, histology, pathology, bacteriology, ophthalmology and otology, gynecology, laryngology, hygiene, and state medicine, and which does not enjoin attendance upon 80 per cent. of four regular courses of instruction of not less than twenty-six weeks each, in four different years, and which does not exact an average grade of 75 per cent. on an examination as a condition of graduation, providing that the rule relative to population as a basis for clinical and hospital facilities shall not apply to institutions under state control and which by virtue of such control receives gratuitously patients from all parts of the state in which such colleges are located.

Oklahoma. Certificate of good moral character, and that holder is not an habitual drunkard. None, if a graduate from a medical college in good standing; if not a graduate, applicant must have been a practicing physician for five years, and pass an examination before the board on the several branches of medicine.

Oregon. Good moral character required. No attention paid to college diplomas. All must stand an examination before state medical board on anatomy, physiology, etc.

Pennsylvania. Applicant must be twenty-one years of age, of good moral character and have a high school education or its equivalent. Four years study of medicine in some legally incorporated medical college of the United States or a diploma or license conferring the full right to practice all the branches of medicine and surgery in some foreign country. Others must stand an examination before the Board.

Rhode Island. Citizenship is a new question, and has never occurred to us before, but will now receive attention. Personal character has not been required. It is difficult to establish [true] character of applicant, but we do not issue certificate until applicant has been in practice for three months in this state, and if he turn out an advertising, charlatanic person we refuse to grant certificate. A high school or academic education is required of all colleges in "good standing." Examination on eleven branches of medicine required. Applicant [for examination] must have obtained diploma from a school having a four years' course in medicine during the year of graduation. One year at a veterinary or dental school will not pass for a year of study in medicine. School must have a course of twenty-six weeks, teach all main and supplementary branches. Study with physician not required, nor is it accepted as a part of the four years. Diplomas of schools located in cities of fewer than fifty thousand people not accepted.

South Carolina. None but graduates of a medical school entitled to an examination; and the state board examines on all the branches of medicine.

South Dakota. Good moral character, and must not be an habitual drunkard. Anyone who is a graduate of a lawful medical college, who has attended three full courses of medical lectures of six months each. No two full courses to be taken within the same year.

Tennessee. Must be a bona fide resident of the state, and located at some designated place. We have no law allowing us to examine into personal character. Applicant must have a fair education, of which the board may be the judge. Law pays no attention to diplomas, but requires all applicants to stand an examination on anatomy, physiology, etc.

Texas. Must have an education equal to that given in a high school. A diploma from any college or university is held by the higher courts as equal to a certificate from one of the district examining boards.

Utah. No special requirements other than a diploma from a reputable medical college; and passing an examination in all the branches of medicine and surgery.

Vermont. Diploma from a reputable and recognized school and passing examination before a state board of examiners on anatomy, physiology, surgery, chemistry, materia medica, practice, obstetrics, and pathology.

Washington. Board has large powers of discretion as to estimating moral character. The state medical examining board does not regard a diploma [of a school] of any state as sufficient to entitle holder of same to practice in this state, but will consider such diploma in connection with the examination of the holder of the same for a license. All applicants are examined in nervous diseases, obstetric diseases of women and children, anatomy, practice, histology, surgery, physiology, medical jurisprudence, materia medica, chemistry, diseases of the eye and ear, preventive medicine.

West Virginia. Good moral character and English education. Diplomas are not recognized. All must pass examination by state board.

Wisconsin. Must not have been convicted of crime in course of professional business. All are examined save those who possess a diploma from a medical college having three or more courses of lectures of six months each, and after the year 1904 at least four courses of not less than six months each, no two courses to be taken during the same year.

Wyoming. None. No person shall be allowed to practice medicine, surgery, or obstetrics who has not received a medical education and a diploma from some regularly chartered medical school, said school to have a bona fide existence at the time when said diploma was granted.

Windsor Castle is situated on the right bank of the Thames, twenty-three miles west of London, near the town of Windsor. The royal residence and the buildings connected with it cover twelve acres of ground, and stand in the midst of a park known as "Little Park," which is four miles in circumference, and is connected by a long avenue of trees, south of the castle, with the "Great Park," which is eighteen miles in circuit. The castle was founded by William the Conqueror. The original plans were enlarged upon and completed by Henry I., and the castle was first used as a royal residence about 1110. The history of the existing edifice, however, begins in the reign of Henry III., but it was not until the time of Edward III. that all its portions were completed. The buildings may be said to be grouped in three portions—the middle ward containing the Round Tower, which was built by Edward III., in the eighteenth year of his reign, to receive the Round Table of the Knights of the newly formed Order of the Garter; the lower ward, on the west, containing St. George's chapel, which was begun by Henry III., completed by Edward III., rebuilt by Henry VII., and added to by Cardinal Wolsey, and the houses of the military knights, cloisters, etc.; and the upper ward, on the east, containing the sovereign's private apartments. Some additions were made to the buildings by Henry VIII., and Queen Elizabeth formed the terraces and built the gate now called by her name. The Star building was erected by Charles II. In 1824-'28, the castle was repaired and enlarged; but little alteration has since been made. The park and forest immediately adjoining contain many historical trees — such as Elizabeth's Oak; Shakespeare's Oak; the Long Walk, made in the reign of Charles II.; and Queen Anne's Ride of Elms, three miles long. Herne's Oak, rendered so famous by Shakespeare, was blown down in September, 1863, and a stone and a young tree now mark the spot. The oldest planted timber in England — that of the reign of Elizabeth — is also in Windsor Park; and there are many oaks of which it is well established the age must be one thousand years. In the royal vaults connected with St. George's chapel a number of kings and queens are buried.

Vedas and Puranas, as the great body of the sacred literature of the Hindoos is called, are written in poetry in the most ancient form of the Sanskrit language. The Vedas, which were believed to be inspired, treat of the thirty-three gods of the heavens, of the air, and of the earth; of the creation of all things, of the relation of the gods to each other, and the relations and duties of men to each other and to the gods; of surgery, medicine, music, dancing, war, architecture, mechanical arts, astronomy, astrology, grammar, poetry, etc. The Puranas are eighteen in number, and are regarded with great reverence as the production of holy men. They treat of law, theology, including histories of their gods, logic, and metaphysics in general, but are filled in the main with superstitions and silly and disgusting narratives.

Unitarians.— The Unitarians of the present day, like almost all Christian sects, must be divided into two classes — a conservative and a progressive class — or, as they are often called, an old and new school. The former adopt the old rule of the sufficiency of Scripture, though with such qualifications as the scientific criticism of the Bible has rendered indispensable. The most conservative Unitarian, for example, would not contend for the literal truth of the first chapter of Genesis, nor for the doctrine of verbal inspiration in any shape. "The Bible is *not*, but it *contains*, the Word of God," is the form which best expresses their position on this subject. They generally hold the simple humanity of Christ, and even reject the supernatural birth, thinking the part of the gospels which record that event to be less authentic than the parts referring to the ministry, the death, and resurrection of Christ. What, however, chiefly distinguishes the Unitarians of this school from those of the new or progressive school is the place which they give to the miracles as supernatural sanctions of the truth of Christianity. Denying that man has any immediate knowledge of the intuition of spiritual things, they regard Christianity as a system of moral and religious truth external to man's nature, and requiring, in proof of its divine origin, certain evidences beyond its inherent credibility and adaptation to human wants. This evidence they find in the miracles, which they accept as well-attested facts, on the same ground on which all historical facts are accepted. The Unitarians of the progressive school, so far from regarding man as entirely dependent upon his reasoning powers for his knowledge of religion, rather look upon him as standing in a living relationship with the one infinite source of all truth, and as having within his own nature the germs of the highest religious faith. To this view of Christianity the miracles are not felt to be essential as proofs. Generally speaking, the Unitarians of this school are disposed to regard with favor the freest criticism of the Bible. Unitarians of all shades of opinion are agreed in rejecting the entire orthodox scheme — including the doctrines of the Trinity, the vicarious atonement, the deity of Christ, original sin, and everlasting punishment — as both unscriptural and irrational. They celebrate the Lord's Supper in their churches, not as a sacrament, but as a service commemorative of Christ's death and expressive of spiritual communion with him.

St. Nicholas and Christmas.— The origin of the idea that presents are presented at Christmas time by St. Nicholas, or Santa Claus, probably originated from the following circumstance: St. Nicholas is said to have been Bishop of Myra, and to have died in the year 326. He was noted for his fondness for children, and became their patron saint, and the young were universally taught to revere him. He is said to have supplied three destitute widows with marriage portions by secretly leaving money at their windows, and as this occurred just before Christmas, he thus became the purveyor of the gifts of the season to all children in Flanders and Holland, who hung up their shoes and stockings in the confidence that Knecht Clobes, as they called him, would put in a prize for good conduct. Formerly, and still, in some parts of Germany, the practice is made of all the parents in a small village sending the presents to some one person, who, in high buskins, a white robe, a mask, and an enormous flax wig, goes from house to house on Christmas eve, and, being received with great pomp and reverence by the parents, calls for the children and bestows the intended gifts upon them, after first severely questioning the father and mother as to the character and conduct of the child. As this custom became less frequent, the custom of children hanging up their stockings was substituted; and, as the purveyor no longer visited the houses, it was necessary to explain it by telling the children that he came into the house at night, coming down the chimney and leaving their presents and departing. The custom of decking the houses and churches at Christmas with evergreens is derived from ancient Druidical practices. It was an old belief that sylvan spirits flock to the evergreens and remain unnipped by frost until a milder season, and it was probably on account of the good omen attached to the evergreen that Christmas trees came into use.

Valentinians, a Gnostic sect or school [*see* GNOSTIC] founded by Valentinus, who went from Alexandria to Rome about A. D. 140. The distinguishing feature of his system lies, in the first place, in his recognizing heathenism as a preparatory stage of Christianity, and then his dividing the higher spiritual world into fifteen pairs of æons, each consisting of a male and a female. The first pair, or syzygy, is made up of Bythos, or God in himself, and Ennoia, or God as existing in his own thoughts. From these emanated, next, Nous (Intelligence) and Aletheia (Truth), and so on. As the last æon, Sophia, transgressed the bounds that had been laid down by the æon Heros, and a part of her being became lost in Chaos, there was formed a crude being called Achanroth, which, through the Demiurgos that emanated from it, created the corporeal world. Heros now imparted to the souls of men (for all the bodies composing the corporeal world are possessed of souls) a pneumatic, or spiritual, element; but this only attained to full activity when Christ, a collective emanation from all the æons, appeared as a Saviour and united himself with the man Jesus. In the end, all that is pneumatic, and even the originally psychic, or soul element, in as far as it has assimilated itself to the psychic, will return into the Pleroma.

Universalists.—The distinctive peculiarity of the Universalist faith consists in the belief that "evil" will ultimately be eradicated from the world, and that all erring creatures will be brought back to God through the irresistible efficacy of Christ's divine love. They argue that when an infinite, wise, holy, and benevolent God resolved to create man, it could only be with a view to his everlasting good; that if he did allow him to be tempted and to fall, it must have been because he foresaw that through sorrow and suffering man could rise to higher degrees of perfection; that, therefore, all punishment is of necessity designed as a remedial agent, and not intended to satisfy God's indignation as a sovereign at the disobedience of his subjects; that no other view of the subject is compatible with the scriptural, and especially the New Testament, representation of God as a "Father," or with the oft-repeated declaration (in various terms) that Jesus Christ was a propitiation for the sins of the whole world. Universalism, as a mode of belief, is of very ancient origin, and its modern adherents, beside urging its congruity with the divine plan of redemption as revealed in Scripture, point to the earliest Christian writings, *e. g.*, the Sibylline oracles of Rome, and cite passages in favor of the doctrine from many of the Church fathers. Universalism was preached in the United States as early as 1741, but the first separate Universalist church was not established until 1780, when the Rev. John Murray started one at Gloucester, Mass. Since his time an important body has sprung up which contains many able, learned, and pious divines.

Roman Catholic Church, the name generally given to that very numerous body of Christians who acknowledge the Pope, or Bishop of Rome, as head of their church. This name also signifies that the Roman Catholic Church is "Roman in its center and Catholic in its circumference" Its foundation began in the first century. St. Peter is said to have been the first Bishop of Rome, and tradition says that he was martyred there. The mighty importance of the city of Rome naturally gave its bishop a great position, but the fact that it became for a while the arbiter and ruler of all Christendom is the most remarkable fact in the history of Christianity. The controversy between Rome and Protestantism involves two main questions: In the first place, Protestants deny the authority of a pope over them at all; and, secondly, a large portion of the doctrine of the Roman Catholic Church is rejected, as being a corruption of Apostolic Christianity. The Roman church recognize seven sacraments, viz.: Baptism, Confirmation, the Holy Eucharist, Penance, Extreme Unction, Holy Orders, Matrimony. One of the chief characteristics of this religion is that of invoking help of the Virgin and Saints. With regard to all matters relating to faith, Roman Catholics draw a sharp line between what is of doctrine and what of discipline. Doctrine is what was taught by Christ and his apostles; discipline, the different rules laid down by the various councils of the church, and liable to change at any time. There are various religious orders, both for men and women, who are obliged to take the three vows of poverty, chastity, and obedience. Their work consists in superintending charitable institutions, such as asylums, orphanages, and hospitals, and some of the orders have large schools attached to them. The number of Roman Catholics all over the world is about two hundred and twenty million. The growth of the Roman church in the United States in recent years has been rapid, owing to immigration. The church has over eight million adherents in this country. Since the Vatican Council of 1870, when Pius IX. put forth the doctrine of the infallibility of the pope, the utterances of the pontiff have been taken as the groundwork of the faith and practice of the church. His pronouncements are regarded as infallible when he defines a doctrine regarding faith and morals to be held by the whole church. The work of the church in the world is directed immediately by the bishops, who receive their jurisdiction from the pope. The power inherent in the Episcopal character and order is received from God directly and immediately. When established in a diocese by the pope, the bishop, by virtue of his title, receives the power of governing and of taking cognizance of all spiritual causes which regard his flock, whether laymen or ecclesiastics, with the exception of what is specially reserved to the head of the church, and he possesses and exercises these prerogatives under the jurisdiction of and in dependence on the pope.

The Reformation, term universally applied by Protestants denoting change from Roman Catholic to the Protestant religion, which was originated in Germany by Luther, A.D.1517, but had been begun in England by Wycliffe, and was afterwards completed by Henry VIII., who assumed the title of "Head of the Church."

Luther's conflict with the Church of Rome began when he boldly attacked the doctrine of indulgences. The proclamation of indulgences was not new in Germany, nor was opposition to it on the part of the people and of both civil and ecclesiastical authorities new. The struggle was precipitated, however, when Albert of Brandenburg appointed John Tetzel, of Leipsic, a learned and eloquent Dominican, to preach the indulgences among the people. New opposition at once broke out, and Luther took the lead. He drew up his objections in the shape of ninety-five propositions, which he fastened to the door of the Castle church at Wittenberg, on All Saints' Eve (Oct. 31, 1517). In these he attacked the abuse, not the doctrine, of indulgences, pronouncing anathema on whosoever spoke against the truth of papal indulgences. Nevertheless the propositions contained the germs of his future heresy and gave rise to the movement known as the Protestant Reformation. He at once gained a number of adherents, among them men of influence both in church and state. A vigorous and oftentimes exceedingly discourteous controversy followed which led to Luther's being summoned to Rome to defend himself. At the request of the Elector Frederick, the Diet of Augsburg was substituted for Rome as the place of the trial, and Cardinal Cajetan, papal legate, was appointed to represent the pope at the Diet. Luther claimed that he had said naught against the Scriptures, the doctrine of the church, the decrees of popes, or reason. In short, made a complete retraction, and fled from Augsburg angry at heart. In 1520 he launched out pamphlet after pamphlet assailing in virulent terms the whole office and dignity of the papacy, setting out that the Bible was the only source of faith. These doctrines caught the hearts of the multitudes. Luther appealed strongly to the spirit of nationality and aggrandizement. He addressed the emperor, the nobles, and the people. He urged the emperor to overthrow the power of the pope, confiscate the wealth of the church, abolish feasts and holidays and masses for the dead. On June 15, 1520, the pope issued a bull specifically condemning Luther's teachings, and excommunicating him if he refused to retract within sixty days. Luther appealed from the authority of the pope to a general council, and publicly burned the pope's bull at Wittenberg, consigning the pope himself to "fire eternal." The Diet of Worms placed him under the ban of the empire as a heretic, but the circumstances of the time and the opposition of the German States rendered the edict ineffective. From these beginnings the Reformation spread throughout the German Empire and thence to various other countries.

Christianity is based upon a new and specific revelation in the person of Jesus Christ. Its aim is to restore to mankind the lost fellowship with God in an eternal kingdom, set up here on earth, and called the Church, to be brought to its full and perfect consummation in the world to come. The foundation of a Christian's faith and practice is ultimate, and, in truth, the only appeal must be to the facts, the doctrines, and the precepts of the Scriptures, especially those of the New Testament. The history of Christianity, then, is the record of the facts pertaining to the nature and growth of the Kingdom of God upon earth, in their external and internal relations. This history falls into three main divisions: Ancient, Mediæval, and Modern. The Ancient history of Christianity is the narrative of the supremacy won by the church over Greek culture and the Roman Empire. It closes and the Mediæval history begins, with the epoch of the Carlovingian dynasty. The Mediæval comprises the victories of the church over the Celtic, Teutonic, Slavonian, and Scandinavian tribes in the center and north of Europe, the conflicts and rupture of the eastern and western branches of the church, and the contest between the imperial and papal powers for supremacy. This period closes with the Reformation. The Modern history recites the struggles between Catholicism and Protestantism, between Christianity and philosophy, and the growth of Protestant civilization.

The history of the world presents no phenomenon so striking as the rise and early progress of Christianity. Originating in a country not remarkable for any political, commercial, or literary influence, emanating from One who occupied an humble sphere in the community amidst which he appeared, and announced in the first instance by men of mean extraction, of no literary culture, and not endowed with any surpassing gifts of intellect,—it nevertheless spread so rapidly that in an incredibly short time it had been diffused throughout the whole civilized world, and in the fourth century of its existence became recognized as the established religion of the Roman Empire. When it is remembered that this result was achieved not only without the aid of any worldly influence, but in the face of the keenest opposition on the part of all the learning, wealth, and power of the most enlightened and mightiest nations, the conclusion is strongly forced upon us that a power beyond that of man was concerned in its success, and that its early and unexampled triumphs afford an incontestible proof of its inherent truth and its divine origin. The continual and steady growth of Christianity, its vigorous life in spite of various seasons of unavoidable ebb, and notwithstanding the presence of many forms of corruption, and its continual rejuvenescence, are no ordinary proof of its supreme fitness for the position in the world which it claims to occupy.

Harvard University, the oldest school in America, was founded in 1636, six years after the first settlement of Boston. The Commonwealth of Massachusetts, through its General Court, in that year made a grant of 400 pounds "to advance learning and perpetuate it to posterity," and in the following year appointed twelve of the principal men in the colony "to take order for a college at Newtown." Two years afterward the Rev. John Harvard, a Non-Conformist clergyman of Charlestown, who the year before had graduated at Emmanuel College, Cambridge University, England, gave by his will the sum of 779 pounds, and 300 books, more than half of his estate. Nine students entered the first class. All of these distinguished themselves in after life, one of them, Sir George Downing, achieving the unenviable distinction of serving both the Commonwealth and the king in the English Revolution. John Harvard's bequest was followed by other gifts, such as a font of letters, books, silver spoons, cooking utensils, garden tools, and others, varying in value from 3 shillings to £200. The first gift of real estate was two and one half acres of land given by the town of Cambridge, thereby changing the nominal location from Newtown to Cambridge. The General Court, in lieu of the money it had promised, granted to Harvard College the right of ferry between Charlestown and Boston. In 1642, the board of overseers, consisting of the governor and deputy governor of the colony, the magistrates then in jurisdiction, the president of the college, and the teaching elders, was constituted. In 1643 the present seal of the University and its motto, "Christo et Ecclesiæ," was adopted. The college charter was granted in 1650, and the college corporation created. In 1653 Rev. Henry Dunster, the first president, fell under suspicion of favoring the Anti-pædo Baptists and as a consequence was indicted by the grand jury for disturbing the ordinance of infant baptism in the Cambridge church. He was tried, convicted, and besides being compelled to resign, and being laid under bonds for good behavior, was sentenced to receive an admonition once a year. Previous to this, Nathaniel Eaton, the first person in charge of the institution, was dismissed for beating his usher. The presidents in succession, with their terms of office, have been as follows: Henry Dunster, 1640-1654; Charles Chauncy, 1654-1672; Leonard Hoar, 1672-1675; Urian Oakes, acting president, 1675-1679; president, 1679-1681; John Rogers, 1682-1684; Increase Mather, acting president, 1685-1686; rector, 1686-1692; president, 1692-1701; Charles Morton, vice-president, 1697-1698; Samuel Willard, vice-president, 1700-1707; John Leverett, 1707-1724; Benjamin Wadsworth, 1725-1737; Edward Holyoke, 1737-1769; Samuel Locke, 1770-1773; Samuel Langdon, 1774-1780; Joseph Willard, 1781-1804; Samuel Webber, 1806-1810; John Thornton Kirkland, 1810-1828; Josiah Quincy, 1829-1845; Edward Everett, 1846-1849; Jared Sparks, 1849-1853; James Walker, 1853-1860; Cornelius Conway Felton, 1860-1862; Thomas Hill, 1862-1868; Charles William Eliot, 1869 to the present time.

During the term of the second president, a hall, costing £350, was erected, for the purpose of giving instruction to Indians, but one Indian only applied for admittance and was graduated by the college. Before this, a single building had served all the purposes of the college. All the college halls that were erected after this during the seventeenth century were subsequently razed or destroyed, so that the oldest building now standing on the Harvard yard is Massachusetts Hall, erected in 1720. Harvard College, from that time on, prospered, and now has property and endowment aggregating almost fifteen million dollars. The University is divided into the following departments, with sepaı ate faculties or board of administration: Harvard College, Lawrence Scientific School, Graduate School, Divinity School, Law School, Medical School, Dental School, School of Veterinary Medicine, Bussey Institution (a school of agriculture), Arnold Arboretum, University Library, Museum of Comparative Zoölogy, University Museum, Botanic Garden, Herbarium, Astronomical Observatory, Peabody Museum of American Archeology and Ethnology. Radcliffe College, formerly known as the Harvard Annex for women, though intimately connected with the University, is still a separate institution. The degrees granted by the University are: Bachelor of arts, of agricultural science, of divinity, of laws, of science, master of arts, and doctor of philosophy, science, laws, medicine, veterinary medicine, and dentistry. Since the foundation of Harvard College, nearly twenty thousand students, in all, have been graduated, of whom some eleven thousand are alive.

Yale University was founded in 1701 by the Revs. John Pierrepont, Andrew, and Russel, of Branford and Milford, three graduates of Harvard, assisted by Cotton and Increase Mather, Eleazor Kimberly, John Eliot, and the judges of the General Court then in session at New Haven. The first gift to the projected school consisted of books from the libraries of each of the three founders, and of 637 acres of wild land given by Major James Fitch, who also agreed to furnish, without cost, the glass and nails for the college house. The trustees first placed the school at Saybrook, provided for a baccalaureate course of three years, with three further years for the master's degree, and fixed the price of tuition at thirty shillings for undergraduates and ten shillings for graduates. The first degree was given to Nathaniel Chauncy, who passed all examinations, after mere private study. In 1717 the college was removed to the town of New Haven, which had offered £2,000 and eight acres, but, owing to the division between the trustees concerning the best site, some of the students went to Saybrook, others to East Guilford, others to Wethersfield and Hartford, and others again to New Haven, according to their preferences and those of their tutors. As a consequence, two commencements were held in 1717, one at Wethersfield and one at New Haven. The controversy was ended by the gift of Elihu Yale, the former governor of Madras, whose official conduct and rapid acquisition of wealth had led to his recall to England. Cotton Mather wrote to him for help, promising the adoption of his name by the new college, and Governor Yale accordingly sent to New Haven three bales of goods, a portrait of George I., the royal coat of arms, and a box of books. In 1721 Elihu Yale died, leaving £500 to the school that bore his name; but for certain reasons the will could not be probated, and the money was lost to the college. In 1722, Rector Cutler and several of the tutors changed their faith from the Congregational church to the Episcopal church, which led to their enforced resignation. As a consequence there ensued an interregnum of three years, during which the college was without rector or proper instruction. At the end of this period the charter was amended. In 1729 the college received valuable gifts from Bishop Berkeley, the philosopher, and in 1752 Benjamin Franklin added a collection of books. By a new charter of 1744, the Collegiate School became Yale College. During the War of the Revolution, the college was twice suspended. When Washington came to New Haven the students formed a company, and, with Noah Webster as their cornet, gave Washington the first military escort in New England. Commencements were not resumed until 1781. Professional schools were added during the presidency of Day. Advanced instruction for graduates was begun in 1847. The first degrees in philosophy were given three years later. The Sheffield Scientific School was organized in 1859. The Art School, succeeding the Trumbull Art Gallery, was erected in 1864, with the Peabody Museum and Conservatory of Music following shortly afterward.

The rectors and presidents — all clergymen, the first six of whom were Harvard graduates, all the rest graduating from Yale — have been: Abraham Pierson, 1701-1707; Samuel Andrew, 1707-1719; Timothy Cutler, 1719-1722; Samuel Andres, 1724-1725; Elisha Williams, 1725-1739; Thomas Clapp, 1739-1766; Naphtali Daggett, 1766-1777; Ezra Styles, 1777-1795; Timothy Dwight, 1795-1817; Jeremiah Day, 1817-1846; Theodore D. Woolsey, 1846-1871; Noah Porter, 1871-1886; Timothy Dwight, 1886-1899; Arthur T. Hadley, LL.D., 1899-. The University comprises four departments, each under a distinct faculty, to wit: Philosophy and art, theology, medicine, and law. The first embraces the academical department of Yale College, with the Sheffield Scientific School, Graduate School, and the School of Fine Arts and Music, each with its own organization and corps of instructors. The library, Peabody Museum, and observatory have independent organizations. The degrees are: B.A., B.S., M.A., B.D., LL.B., Ph.B., C.E., M.E., M.D., Ph.D., LL.D., D.C.L. with further degrees in fine arts and music. In all departments, nearly seventeen thousand alumni have been graduated, of whom more than ten thousand are living.

Princeton University.— The first charter was granted in 1746, and the second, making the trustees a self-perpetuating body, in 1748. The college was opened at Elizabethtown, near New York, with Rev. Jonathan Dickinson as president, and was removed to Newark, and soon afterward, in 1753, to Princeton. During the next two years Nassau Hall was erected. Though this hall has twice been damaged by fires, in 1802 and 1855, it still stands. The presidents have been: Jonathan Dickinson, 1747; Aaron Burr, 1748-1757; Jonathan Edwards, 1757-1758; Samuel Davies, 1759-1761; Samuel Finley, 1761-1766; John Witherspoon, 1768-1794; Samuel Stanhope Smith, 1795-1812; Ashbel Green, 1812-1822; James Carnahan, 1823-1854; John MacLean, 1854-1868; James McCosh, 1868-1888; Francis Landey Patton, S.T.D., LL.D., 1888, to the present. The Green School of Science was added in 1873, and a department of engineering in 1875. The sesqui centennial of the college was celebrated in 1896, which marked a material increase of the endowment; the trustees transformed the college into a university, changing its name from the College of New Jersey to Princeton University. The degrees conferred are: A.B., A.M., Ph.D., L.H.D., Litt.D., and LL.D.

University of Pennsylvania.—Through the efforts of Benjamin Franklin a fund was raised in 1749 to change Penn's Charity School, begun in 1720, into an academy. It was opened in 1751, and four years later received a college charter. The first commencement was held in 1757. The school languished for several years so that Provost Smith had to be sent to England to raise funds. He there met the commissioner of King's College, now Columbia University, and they both agreed to share the proceeds of their joint efforts, some six thousand pounds. After his return Provost Smith sided with the "War Party," and was cast into prison for publishing an alleged libelous pamphlet against the Assembly. While in jail he continued to give lectures to his classes, but in 1759 was compelled to flee to England, where he was received with great honor, and made a doctor by Oxford University. He returned after a peaceful settlement of his differences with the Assembly with twenty thousand pounds funds for the college. In 1791 the college was amalgamated with the new school, which was the first to be called a university in this country. The Medical School dates from 1765. A German school was added in 1785, and a law school in 1790. The college continued as an old fashioned classical college until 1868, when the elective system was introduced. In 1872 the Department of Arts was reorganized, and the Department of Science, known as the Towne Scientific School, was established. In 1877 a department of music, and in 1878 one of dentistry were added. The provosts and presidents have been: Benjamin Franklin, 1749-1756; Richard Peters, 1756-1764; James Hamilton, 1764; John Penn, 1764-1771; James Hamilton, 1771-1773; Richard Penn, 1773-1774; John Penn, 1774-1779; Benjamin Franklin, 1789-1790; William White, 1790-1791; John Ewing, 1791-1802; John McDowell, 1802-1810; Dr. Andrews, 1810-1813; Frederick Beaseley, 1813-1828; William H. DeLancey, 1828-1833; John Ludlow, 1833-1853; Henry Vethake, 1853-1860; Daniel R. Goodwin, 1860-1868; Charles J. Stille, 1868-1880; Charles C. Harrison, LL.D., the present incumbent.

The University buildings, twenty-two in number, are situated on forty-eight acres of ground in West Philadelphia. The General Library, containing more than 150,000 volumes and 50,000 pamphlets, contains a number of private collections. The most notable of these are the Colwell collection, one of the most complete finance libraries in the world, and the Bechstein Library containing 15,000 books on German philology and literature. The Museum of Archæology and Paleontology contains collections of American, Asiatic, and Egyptian antiquities of great value. Its Babylonia collection is declared to rank equal with those of the British Museum and the Louvre. Houston Hall, a clubhouse for students, was finished in 1896, and has proved a valuable aid to college discipline. The usual academic and technical degrees are conferred.

Cornell University was incorporated by the Legislature of the State of New York, April 27, 1865, and opened October 7, 1868. The existence of the University is due to the combined bounty of the United States, the state of New York, and Ezra Cornell. Ezra Cornell's wish was to found an institution where any person could find instruction in any study; while the state stipulated that the college should be strictly non-sectarian, and that it should annually receive from each Assembly district of the state, one student free of charge. The first gift of Ezra Cornell was $500,000 with 200 acres of land. The first college buildings were built by the students; women were admitted, and a large dormitory known as Sage College was erected for them in 1872. There are no other dormitory buildings on the campus proper, the situation of which, on a plateau between two waterfalls, overlooking Cayuga Lake, and the settled valley at its head, is unique. In 1890, after a long lawsuit, the large property left to the University by Mrs. Jennie McGraw Fiske, was withheld from it by a ruling of the supreme court of the United States. To make up for this, Henry W. Sage, a previous benefactor of Cornell, gave $560,000 for the cost and endowment of the new University Library. In addition to this the University has received other large benefactions. The presidents have been: Andrew D. White, 1865-1885; Charles K. Adams, 1885-1890; Jacob Gould Schurman, 1890 to the present.

Columbia University. King's College, as Columbia University was formerly called, was founded in 1754, under royal charter. The college was established on a grant of land known as the King's Farm, the property of Trinity Church overlooking the Hudson river. It was then declared by travelers to have the finest site of any college in the world. In 1857 it was removed to a block between 49th and 50th streets, New York city, overlooking the East river. From the beginning this location was regarded as temporary. The present site on Morningside Heights, between 116th and 120th streets, was the field of the battle of Harlem. It overlooks the Hudson river on one side, and north New York on the other, and is once more declared to be one of the finest sites in the world. The original charter made the college non-sectarian. The first class was graduated in 1760 with eight students. During the Revolutionary war instruction had to be suspended, the president of the college, a royalist, having been forced to flee to England. Names and terms of the presidents are as follows: Samuel Johnson, 1754-1763; Myles Cooper, 1763-1775; Benjamin Moore, 1775-1776; William Samuel Johnson, 1787-1800; Charles H. Wharton, 1801; Benjamin Moore, 1801-1811; William Harris, 1811-1829; William Alexander Duer, 1829-1842; Nathaniel F. Moore, 1842-1849; Charles King, 1849-1864; Frederick A. P. Barnard, 1864-1889; Seth Low, LL.D., 1890-.

A medical faculty was established in King's College in 1767 and consisted at first of six professors. In 1860 the College of Physicians and Surgeons became the medical department of Columbia University. Instruction in law was given in 1793. The School of Mines, now the School of Applied Science, through the efforts of Thomas Eggleston, was founded in 1863. In 1880 a School of Political Science was opened. Barnard College, where instruction is given to women, was founded in 1889. The School of Philosophy was established in 1890, and that of Pure Science in 1892. The degrees conferred in the various schools are, B.A., B.S., LL.B., M.D., M.A., Ph.D., L.H.D., and LL.D.

Catholic University of America was founded in 1884 after a gift by Miss Caldwell of $300,000 to the American Episcopate. From 1889 to 1895 its educational activity was confined to the School of Divinity. In 1895, after the pope had expressed a hope that the University might be able to adapt its work to modern educational needs in a wider sense, schools of philosophy and the social sciences were opened, with departments of philosophy, letters, mathematics, physics, chemistry, biology, technology, sociology, economics, political science, and law. During the last few years twelve chairs for the teaching of the arts and sciences have been endowed by individuals. The University is governed by seventeen directors and a chancellor, who is at present Cardinal Gibbons of Baltimore. With the directors, who are for the most part prominent members of the Catholic clergy, are associated by virtue of their office all the Catholic archbishops in the country. The School of Divinity grants baccalaureate, licentiate, and the doctor's degrees; the School of Philosophy confers degrees in letters and philosophy; the School of Social Science, degrees of B.A. and M.A.; the Law School, degrees of LL.B., LL.M., D.C.L., J.C.D., J.U.D., and LL.D.; while in the Institute of Technology, degrees in civil, electrical, and mechanical engineering, with corresponding master's degrees are conferred. The present rector is Very Reverend Thos. J. Conaty, D.D., J.C.D.

University of California was instituted by a law which received the approval of the governor, March 23, 1868. Instruction was begun in Oakland in the autumn of 1869. The commencement exercises of 1873 were held at Berkeley, July 16, when the University was formally transferred to its permanent home. Instruction began at Berkeley in the autumn of 1873. The new constitution of 1879 made the existing organization of the University perpetual. The College of California, which had been organized several years before the University, transferred its property and students upon terms which were mutually agreed upon, and closed its work of instruction in 1869. It had been incorporated in 1855, and through its agency a part of the Oakland property of the University, and the Berkeley site now owned and occupied by the latter, were secured; a domain of about two hundred and fifty acres, situated on the slope of the Contra Costa hills, about five miles from Oakland, facing the Golden Gate. The undergraduate colleges were the only ones actually included in the original organization. The professional colleges in San Francisco have been added from time to time. The Lick Observatory was formally transferred to the University in June, 1888. The Mark Hopkins Institute of Art, in 1893. The University comprises the following departments: College of Letters, College of Social Sciences, College of Natural Sciences, College of Agriculture, College of Mechanics, College of Mining, College of Civil Engineering, College of Chemistry, Lick Astronomical Department, Mark Hopkins Institute of Art, Hastings College of Law, Medical Department, Post Graduate Medical Department, College of Dentistry, and California College of Pharmacy. The curricula of the various departments lead to degrees of B.A., B.L., B.S., M.A., C.E., D.D.S., D.V.S., LL.B., M.S., M.E., M.D., Ph.G., Ph.B., and Ph.D. The president is Benjamin Ide Wheeler, Ph.D., LL.D.

University of Chicago. The first University of Chicago was founded in 1857, by the Baptist Society of Chicago, and was presided over for many years by the Rev. Dr. Burroughs. In 1886 its doors were closed, owing to lack of funds. Its successor, the present University of Chicago, was founded by John D. Rockefeller, who subscribed $600,000 of its original endowment fund of one million dollars, to which he afterward added three and a half million dollars in bonds. The original site, valued at $125,000, was given by Marshall Field, who also gave $100,000 in money. More than one million dollars for new schools and buildings have since been donated or bequeathed to the University. A president for the University, William R. Harper, Ph.D., LL.D., was elected in the spring of 1891. Work on the new buildings began in the autumn of the same year. On October 1, 1892, the new school opened its doors to some six hundred students. Cobb Lecture Hall and two dormitories for graduates were the only buildings then ready for use. Since that time fifteen of the projected forty-two buildings have been erected, while the number of students has risen to over two thousand. The University includes five divisions: the university proper; the university extension; the university libraries, laboratories, and museums; the university press; the university affiliations. The university proper includes: the Graduate School of Arts and Literature, the Ogden School of Science, the Divinity School, the School of Law, School of Medicine, the School of Technology, the School of Fine Arts, and the School of Music; the colleges of arts, literature, and science.

Leland Stanford, Jr., University was founded in 1884, by Leland Stanford and Jane Lathrop Stanford, who determined to found a university for both sexes, and with all colleges, schools, seminaries, institutes, museums, and collections appropriate thereto. In the following year the Legislature of California passed an authorizing act, and in 1885 the grant was made. The corner stone was laid in 1887, at Palo Alto, some three miles from the sea, near the Monte Diable Mountain, thirty-three miles from San Francisco. David Starr Jordan, the present president, was installed in 1891. The suit for fifteen million dollars or the original endowment, between the University and the Federal Government, was decided in the University's favor, in 1895. An additional endowment was made by deed of Jane Lathrop Stanford, amounting to more than ten million dollars, in 1899. In the same year the number of women to be admitted to the University in any one year was restricted to five hundred. The University is governed by twenty-four trustees chosen for life. The various courses of instruction lead to the degrees: B.A., B.S., and C.E., while the degrees M.A., M.E., and Ph.D. are conferred after resident post graduate work. No honorary degrees are conferred.

University of Virginia was the first State University established in this country. Thomas Jefferson, after great opposition from all other Virginia colleges, founded the University in 1819. It was then united with Central College, and, after full acceptance of Jefferson's original plans, opened its doors to students in 1825. The University buildings were finished by Italian sculptors, whom Jefferson had imported. Dr. Thomas Cooper, the first professor of the new university, by reason of his heterodox views, was forced to resign immediately after his election, to Jefferson's great chagrin. The founder thereupon turned to Europe for new material, calling no less than four professors from England. In 1824 the new school was visited by George Ticknor of Harvard College, who is believed to have there assimilated the reforms in regard to discipline and elective study, which were afterward introduced by him at Harvard. Two years later, Thomas Jefferson died, after having had sole charge of the University for one year as its first rector. He was buried on the roadside of the highway leading from his house to the University, and his grave is marked by a monument, erected by Congress, bearing the inscription: "Here was buried Thomas Jefferson, author of the declaration of American independence, of the statute of Virginia for religious freedom, and father of the University of Virginia. Born April 2, 1743, o. s. Died July 4, 1826."

After Jefferson's death, the University became heavily indebted, until the state legislature freed its annual appropriation from all incumbrances. A medical school was added in 1827, which has since been enlarged by schools of medical jurisprudence, of surgery, and anatomy. In 1851 the Law School was created, followed in 1856, by the two schools of language and of history, the last of which was endowed with $50,000 by W. W. Corcoran. A school of technology was added in 1867, followed in 1870 by the establishment of a school of agriculture, on Samuel Miller's endowment of $100,000. An astronomical observatory was given by Leander J. McCormick in 1882. Connected with it was Professor Sylvester, the famous mathematician. During the war, instruction in the University was suspended. In October, 1895, the Rotunda and Annex built by Jefferson were destroyed by fire, including many books and works of art. Since that time sufficient funds have been raised among the alumni to restore these buildings, and to erect a public hall, physical and chemical laboratories, costing in all, $250,000. The Rotunda, henceforth, is to be used for library purposes only.

Westminster Palace was erected in 1840 on the site of the old houses of Parliament, which were destroyed by fire in 1834. It is 900 feet long by 300 feet wide, is built of limestone from the Yorkshire quarries, and cost about $8,000,000. The palace contains the House of Lords and the House of Commons, which are separated by an octagonal hall with a diameter of 70 feet. The House of Lords is 100 feet long, 45 feet wide, and 45 feet high. The room is profusely decorated, and in niches between the windows are statues of barons who signed the Magna Charta — eighteen in number. The gorgeous gilt and canopied throne which is occupied by the Queen when she opens Parliament is in this room, as is also the wool-sack — a large, square bag of wool covered with red cloth — of the Chancellor of Great Britain. The House of Commons is not as handsome as the House of Lords in the matter of decorations, and is not so long, but is the same height and width. The palace also contains a number of other rooms, among which are the Queen's robing room, the guard room, the libraries, committee rooms etc. In the center of the edifice, above what is known as the Octagon Hall, is a tower 300 feet high. At the southwest corner is the Victoria tower, 346 feet high. At the northwest corner is the clock tower, which is surmounted by a belfry spire 320 feet high. In this tower is a clock with four faces, each 30 feet in diameter, and the hours are struck on a bell called "Big Ben," which weighs nine tons. At the southwestern extremity of the building is the state entrance of the Queen, which communicates directly with what are known as the royal apartments. The entrance to the Octagon Hall is by a passage known as Saint Stephen's Hall, which communicates also with Westminster Hall, a much older building, on the north.

West Point Academy.— Each Congressional District and Territory, also the District of Columbia, is entitled to have one cadet at the United States Military Academy at West Point, the cadet to be named by the representative in Congress. There are also ten appointments at large, specially conferred by the President of the United States. The number of students is thus limited to 344. The course of instruction, which is quite thorough, requires four years, and is largely mathematical and professional. The discipline is very strict — even more so than in the army — and the enforcement of penalties for offenses is inflexible rather than severe. Academic duties begin September 1st and continue until June 1st. From the middle of June to the end of August cadets live in camps, engaged only in military duties, and receiving practical military instruction. Cadets are allowed but one leave of absence during the four years' course, and this is granted at the expiration of the second year. The pay of a cadet is $540 a year. Upon graduation, cadets are commissioned as second lieutenants in the United States Army.

Music.— The cradle of music was Egypt. The Hebrews took with them to Palestine the songs they had learned there, and many of the hymns of the early Christian Church were necessarily old Temple melodies. Ambrose, Archbishop of Milan (374), and after him Pope Gregory the Great (590), were the fathers of music in the Western Church. Harmonies were introduced in the ninth century; the present musical notation was invented by Guido Aretino (*d.* 1055); counterpoint was perfected by the Belgian Josquin Despres (*d.* 1521), and the Italian Palestrina (1555); and Italian opera was founded in 1600. The influence of the Italian school spread all over Europe; but in the sixteenth century England had a national school of her own, comprising such names as Tallis, Farrant, and Orlando Gibbons. Among the great composers of the seventeenth century were Monteverde in Italy, Lully in France, and Purcell in England. In the eighteenth century music made enormous advances, especially in Germany. Church music attained to its highest development under Bach, the oratorio under Handel (1685-1759), the opera under Mozart and Gluck, and orchestral music under Haydn and Beethoven (1770-1827). The nineteenth century has been illustrated by such names as Mendelssohn, Weber, Meyerbeer, Auber, Schubert, Spohr, Schumann, Chopin, Rossini, Bellini, Verdi; and in England, Sterndale, Bennett, and Macfarren. Of the later German school the chief exponents have been Wagner (1813-'83) and Liszt (*d.* 1886). Other leading composers are Gounod, in France; Boito, in Italy; Rubinstein and Brahms, in Germany; Dvořák, in Bohemia; Grieg, in Scandinavia, and Sullivan, Mackenzie, Stanford, and Cowen, in England.

The Name of God in Forty-Eight Languages.

Hebrew	Eleah, Jehovah	French	Dieu	Slav	Buch
Chaldaic	Eiliah	Spanish	Dios	Polish	Bog
Assyrian	Eleah	Portuguese	Deos	Polacca	Bung
Syrian and Turkish	Alah	Old German	Diet	Lapp	Jubinal
Malay	Alla	Provincial	Diou	Finnish	Jumala
Arabic	Allah	Low Breton	Done	Runic	As
Languages of the Magi	Orsi	Italian	Dio	Zemblian	Fetiza
Old Egyptian	Teut	Irish	Dia	Pannonian	Istu
Armenian	Teuti	Olotu tongue	Deu	Hindoostanee	Rain
Modern Egyptian	Teun	German and Swiss	Gott	Coromandel	Brahma
Greek	Theos	Flemish	God	Tartar	Magatai
Cretan	Thios	Dutch	God	Persian	Sire
Ædian and Dorian	Ilos	English	God	Chinese	Prussa
Latin	Deus	Teutonic	Goth	Japanese	Goezer
Low Latin	Diex	Danish and Swedish	Gud	Madagascar	Zannar
Celtic Gaelic	Diu	Norwegian	Gud	Peruvian	Puchecammae

The Salvation Army. The Salvation Army is a missionary organization set on foot in England by William Booth, who was called the "General" of the Army. The plan of operation is for a company to march about cities, towns, and villages, singing popular sacred songs and speaking between whiles for about five minutes. The Army has also a large number of religious periodicals and small books. Mr. Booth was a minister of the Methodist New Connexion, which he left in 1861 to begin "revivalistic services" in a tent in Whitechapel. In 1865 his little band of followers called themselves "The East London Christian Revival Society," afterwards changed to "The Christian Mission." In 1869 the Mission made expeditions to provincial towns. Lastly, in 1873, the name was changed to "The Salvation Army." Its literary organ, called *The Christian Mission*, first appeared monthly in 1874. In 1879 it was called *The Salvationist* and in the same year its title was changed into *The War Cry*. Its flag now flies in thirty-four countries or colonies, where, under the leadership of 11,149 men and women, whose lives are entirely given up to the work, 49,800 religious meetings are held every week. The Army has 27 weekly newspapers and 15 magazines, with a total annual circulation of 49,015,044. It has accumulated $4,015,085 worth of property, pays rentals amounting to $1,100,000 per annum for its meeting places, and has a total income from all sources of $3,750,000. The Army literature is issued in 15 languages and services are held in 29 languages. The number of local officers, bandsmen, and office employees is 23,540. The United States branch was established in 1880. There are now in this country 536 corps and outposts and 1,487 officers, and 15,000 adherents. The value of the property held by the United States wing of the Army is $175,000.

United States Naval Academy at Annapolis.— There are allowed at the Academy one naval cadet for each member or delegate of the United States House of Representatives, one for the District of Columbia, and ten at large. The appointment of cadets at large, and for the District of Columbia, is made by the President. The Secretary of the Navy, as soon after March 5 in each year as possible, must notify in writing each member and delegate of the House of Representatives of any vacancy that may exist in his district. The nomination of a candidate to fill the vacancy is made on the recommendation of the member or delegate, by the Secretary. Candidates must be actual residents of the districts from which they are nominated.

The course of naval cadets is six years, the last two of which are spent at sea. Candidates, at the time of their examination for admission, must not be under fifteen nor over twenty years of age, and physically sound, well formed, and of robust condition. They enter the Academy immediately after passing the prescribed examinations, and are required to sign articles binding themselves to serve in the United States Navy eight years (including the time of probation at the Naval Academy), unless sooner discharged. The pay of a naval cadet is five hundred dollars a year, beginning at the date of admission.

Appointments to fill all vacancies that occur during a year in the lower grades of the Line and Engineer Corps of the Navy and of the

Marine Corps are made from the naval cadets, graduates of the year, at the conclusion of their six years' course, in the order of merit as determined by the Academic Board of the Naval Academy. At least ten appointments from such graduates are made each year. Surplus graduates who do not receive such appointments are given a certificate of graduation, an honorable discharge, and one year's sea pay.

The Academy was founded in 1845, by the Hon. George Bancroft, Secretary of the Navy in the administration of President Polk. It was formally opened October 10th of that year, with Commander Franklin Buchanan as superintendent. During the civil war it was removed from Annapolis, Md., to Newport, R. I., but was returned to the former place in 1865. It is under the direct supervision of the Navy Department.

Royal Academy.

President—Sir Edward John Poynter. *Keeper*—E. Crofts. *Treasurer*—J. C. Horsley. *Secretary*—Frederick A. Eaton. *Registrar*—C. McLean.

ROYAL ACADEMICIANS.

1898 Abbey, Edwin Austin.
1898 Aitchison, George.
1879 Alma-Tadema, Lawrence.
1879 Armstead, Henry Haugh.
1896 Boughton, George Henry.
1891 Brock, Thomas.
1867 Cooper, Thomas Sidney.
1896 Crofts, Ernest.
1877 Davis, Henry Wm. Banks.
1891 Dicksee, Frank.
1887 Fildes, S. Luke.
1895 Ford, Edward Onslow.
1893 Gilbert, Alfred M. V. O.
1863 Goodall, Frederick.
1891 Gow, Andrew Carrick.
1881 Graham, Peter.
1898 Gregory, Edward John.
1890 Herkomer, Hubert,
1860 Hook, James Clarke.
1896 Jackson, Thomas Graham.
1898 Leader, Benj. Williams.
1876 Leslie, George Dunlop.
1898 Lucas, John Seymour.
1893 MacWhirter, John.
1877 Orchardson, Wm. Quilter.
1881 Ouless, Walter William.
1880 Pearson, John Lou'bor'ugh.
1876 Poynter, Sir Edward John.
1894 Prinsep, Valentine C.
1895 Richmond, Sir William Blake, K. C. B.
1881 Rivière, Briton.
1869 Sant, James.
1897 Sargent, John Singer.
1877 Shaw, Richard Norman.
1887 Stone, Marcus.
1888 Thornycroft, Wm. Hamo.
1885 Waterhouse, Alfred.
1895 Waterhouse, John William.
1870 Wells, Henry Tanworth.
1893 Woods, Henry.
1878 Yeames, Wm. Frederick.

Honorary Retired Academicians—1853, William Powell Frith; 1857, Frederick R. Pickersgill; 1864, Thomas Faed; 1867, George F. Watts; 1864, John Calcott Horsley.

ASSOCIATES.

Bates, Harry (sculptor).
Blomfield, Sir Arthur William.
Bodley, George Frederick.
Bramley, Frank
Brett, John.
Clausen, George.
Crowe, Eyre.
Forbes, Stanhope A.
Frampton, George James.
Hacker, Arthur.
Henry, Charles N.
Hunter, Colin.
La Thangue, Henry H.
Macbeth, Robert Walker.
Morris, Philip Richard.
Murray, David.
North, John W.
Parsons, Alfred.
Shannon, James J.
Smythe, Lionel P.
Solomon, J. Solomon.
Storey, George Adolphus.
Swan, John MacAllan.
Waterlow, Ernest Albert.
Wyllie, W. L.

Honorary Retired Associates—Henry Le Jeune, Erskine Nicol, Frederic Stacpoole.

Presidents of the Royal Academy—1768, Sir Joshua Reynolds; 1792, Benjamin West; 1805, James Wyatt; 1806, Benjamin West; 1820, Sir Thomas Lawrence; 1830, Sir Martin A. Shee; 1850, Sir Charles Eastlake; 1866, Sir Edwin Landseer, elected, declined, Sir Francis Grant; 1878, Sir Frederic Leighton (Lord Leighton); 1896, Sir John Everett Millais, Bart; 1896, Sir Edward John Poynter.

The Seven Bibles of the World are the Koran of the Mohammedans, the Eddas of the Scandinavians, the Try Pitikes of the Buddhists, the Five Kings of the Chinese, the Three Vedas of the Hindoos, the Zendavesta, and the Scriptures of the Christians. The Koran is the most recent of these seven Bibles, and not older than the seventh century of our era. It is a compound of quotations from the Old and New Testaments, the Talmud, and the Gospel of St. Barnabas. The Eddas of the Scandinavians were first published in the fourteenth century. The Pitikes of the Buddhists contain sublime morals and pure aspirations, and their author lived and died in the sixth century before Christ. There is nothing of excellence in these sacred books not found in the Bible. The sacred writings of the Chinese are called the Five Kings, king meaning web of cloth, or the warp that keeps the threads in their place. They contain the best sayings of the best sages on the ethico-political duties of life. These sayings cannot be traced to a period higher than the eleventh century before Christ. The Three Vedas are the most ancient books of the Hindoos, and it is the opinion of Max Müller, Wilson, Johnson, and Whitney that they are not older than the eleventh century before Christ. The Zendavesta of the Persians is the grandest of all the sacred books, next to our Bible. Zoroaster, whose sayings it contains, was born in the twelfth century before Christ. Moses lived and wrote his Pentateuch in the fifteenth century before Christ, and therefore has a clear margin of three hundred years older than the most ancient of the sacred writings.

Nationality of the Popes.—The various nations of Europe are represented in the list of Popes as follows: English, 1; Dutch, 1; Swiss, 1; Portuguese, 1; African, 2; Austrian, 2; Spanish, 5; German, 6; Syrian, 8;

Greek, 14; French, 15; Italian, 197. Eleven Popes reigned over 20 years; 69, from 10 to 20; 57, from 5 to 10; and the reign of 116 was less than 5 years. The reign of Pius IX. was the longest of all, the only one exceeding 25 years. Pope Leo XIII. is the 258th Pontiff. The full number of the sacred college is 70, namely: cardinal bishops, 6; cardinal priests, 50; cardinal deacons, 14. At present there are 62 cardinals. The Roman Catholic hierarchy throughout the world, according to official returns published at Rome in 1884, consisted of 11 patriarchs, and 1,153 archbishops and bishops. Including 12 coadjutor or auxiliary bishops, the number of Roman Catholic archbishops and bishops now holding office in the British Empire is 134. The numbers of the clergy are approximate only.

William and Mary College was established at Williamsburg, Va., in 1693, and next to Harvard College is the oldest institution of learning in America. At its endowment it was placed under the patronage of the King and Queen of Great Britain. The trustees of the Hon. R. Doyle, the English philosopher, who left his personal estate for "charitable and pious uses," presented a great part of it to this college for the education of Indians. During the Revolutionary war the college lost most of its possessions, and its buildings were used by the French troops as a hospital. Among the noted men who were graduated from William and Mary, were Presidents Jefferson, Madison, and Monroe, Chief Justice Marshall, and General Scott.

Sculpture, the art of giving form and expression, by means of the chisel and other implements, to masses of stone or other hard substances, so as to represent figures of every description, animate and inanimate. It is generally thought that sculpture had its origin from idolatry, as it was found necessary to place before the people the images of their gods to enliven the fervor of their devotion. But to form conclusions concerning the rise and progress of the arts and sciences, without the aid of historical evidence, by analogies which are sometimes accidental, and often fanciful, is a mode of reasoning which, at best, must ever be liable to suspicion. In whatever country the earliest attempts were made, the Egyptians were the first who adopted a certain style of art. Their works were gloomy and grave, but still they were full of deep sentiment, and connected, as would appear by the hieroglyphics which covered them, with poetry and history, and by the mummies, with the belief of immortality. Interesting as the subject would doubtless prove, it is far beyond our limited means to trace the progress of this beautiful art through all its stages in the classic days of Greece, till its decline in Rome, where, though all the treasures of the Grecian sculptors had been carried to deck the Roman capital, the art never became naturalized. During the long and gloomy interval of barbarism that succeeded the downfall of Imperial Rome, sculpture, with the sister arts, lay dormant and forgotten. At length, however, through the genius of Michael Angelo Buonarroti, and the skill and perseverance of some of his distinguished successors, seconded by the patronage of the illustrious house of Medici, the treasures of antiquity were collected, and modern art nobly tried to rival the grace and sublimity which existed in the ancient models. Though till within the last century it could hardly be said that a British school of sculpture existed, yet the talent that has been successfully called into action has produced many works of sterling merit. The names of Flaxman, Chantrey, Baily, and Westmacott, are alone sufficient to redeem the national character in this department of art. In the United States, the productions of Greenough, Powers, and other distinguished artists, have been received with admiration by the most fastidious connoisseurs. The very essence of sculpture is correctness; and when to correct and perfect form is added the ornament of grace, dignity of character, and appropriate expression, as in the Apollo, the Venus, the Laocoön, the Moses of Michael Angelo, and many others, this art may be said to have accomplished its purpose.

SCHOOLS OF ART.

Certain modes of drawing and painting, followed by pupils of a great master, have led to the foundation of well defined "schools" of painters, since the revival of the Art among the Byzantine and Tuscan painters of the thirteenth and fourteenth centuries, which diverged into the Florentine and Genoese schools (Cimabue and Giotto taking the head of the former), and the schools of Umbria and Bologna. The fifteenth century was the great period of artistic development, whence we may trace modern excellence, commencing with the Florentine School, at the head of which were Fiesole and Masaccio. This school diverged into the different styles, consisting of — 1. Such as studied exact natural truth, and whose first exponent was Ghirlandajo; 2. Such as combined therewith a species of poetic treatment, as Fra Filippo Lippi, Sandro Botticelli, and Benozzo Gozzoli; 3. Such as adopted a sculpturesque treatment of the figure, as seen in works of Andrea del Castagno, Antonio Pollajuolo, and Andrea Veroccio. During the first half of the sixteenth century, this school was adorned by the genius of Leonardo da Vinci and Michael Angelo.

The Roman School (into which that Bologna Romagna merged) is the most important for its solid and legitimate effect; a result which may be attributed to the purity of study and delicacy of feeling engendered by its great head, Raffaelle Sanzio d'Urbino, followed out by Giulio Romano, Mazzolina di Ferrara, Zucchero, Baroccio, Carlo Maratti, and others.

The Venetian School gloried in its color, and the magic pencil of Titian gave it a position for which Giorgione and Sebastian del Piozbino had but prepared it. The pupils and successors of him who "dipped his pencil in the rainbow," viz. Bonifazio, Bordone, Tintoretto, Paul Veronese, Bassano, Garofalo, and others, followed in his footsteps, and gave this school a European renown.

The Lombard School, also known as that of the Eclectics, was established by the Caracci, the principles of which have been explained by Agostino in a sonnet of his own composing, which may be thus translated: "Adopt the design of the Romans, with the color of the Lombard school, adding the motion and shade of that of Venice. Join the just symmetry of Raphael with the power of Michael Angelo, the purity of Correggio, the truth of Titian, the decorum and solidity of Tebaldi, the learned invention of Primaticcio, and a little of Parmigiano's grace." To this school belong Correggio and Parmigiano, and such were the painters from whom the Caracci were induced to select the qualities of the Eclectic style; "for Agostino and Annibal were, at the commencement of their career, unacquainted with the works of the originators of the beauties which they professed to imitate. Before opening their celebrated school, however, they visited Parma and Venice, and became familiar with the works of Correggio and Titian; but it was only mediately, through the works of the masters above mentioned, that they could demonstrate their principles to their scholars. The St. Cecilia of Raphael was not, and could not have been, taken as a standard of that great master. Lodovico is the real founder of the Bolognese school; he was the guide and instructor of his cousins, who were some years his juniors." Their style of proceeding in "making up" a painter according to their own recipe above given, has been severely commented upon by Fuseli in the eleventh lecture. Certainly with the age of the Macchinisti began the decadence of that great and pure Art revived again by the genius of Raphael; and a meretricious and untrue style, in which the dictum of the school took the place of the teachings of nature, and led to the adoption of individual whims, which, following so rapidly one upon another, caused the school to sink from Guido Reni, and Guercino, to Giordano. Nicolas Poussin endeavored to prop its fall by a reversion to the purer principles of classic Art; but neither his genius, nor that of the men who had ranked themselves as opposers of the school under the name of Naturalisti, could prevent the decay of Italian Art. "This decline resulted with many painters from a light and pleasing but superficial invention, accompanied by a corresponding skillful but decorative treatment; in others, it proceeded from a close but spiritless adherence to a set of obsolete rules, which destroyed the peculiarity of individuals as well as of schools. With few exceptions, sound technical science, as the basis of manipulation in painting, was lost."

The German School may be said to have originated with the versatile genius of Albert Durer, and was followed by Lucas van Leyden, Holbein, Netscher, Mengs and others. It was remarkable for a strict adherence to nature, and for much power of drawing, qualifications which still remain the chief characteristics of its modern disciples, under Cornelius, Kaulbach, and Overbeck.

The Flemish School combines with German after the middle of the sixteenth century. Its early history begins with the Van Eycks, who have given to the world a school of their own in Roger of Bruges, Hans Hemling, Jan Mabuse, and Quentin Matsys. Its great glories center in Rubens and Vandyke; their works are remarkable for brilliance of color, exactness of drawing, and great command of chiaro-oscuro; but Rubens wants grace, and in founding his style on nature, relying on his power of exhibiting her as he saw her, he frequently lacks dignity. Teniers excelled in arrangement and harmony, though he very frequently lost his proper position in the lowness of his subjects. Steinwick, Spranger, Snyders, Neeffs, and others, may be particularized as among the remarkable men of a school which may be considered as the legitimate descendant of the Venetian school of colorists.

The Dutch School is even lower in refinement; but the great genius displayed by its principal painter, Rembrandt, elevated it into importance. His marvelous power over light and shade was what the world had never before seen, and it has died with him who first exhibited it. It was too much the fault of this school to select the vulgarest scenes of life for the employment of the pencil; thus we find great power of drawing, coloring, and a perfect mastery of the mechanism of Art, combined with high artistic feeling, devoted to some unworthy subject, which no genius can redeem, and which but excites a feeling of regret to see talent so misdirected. Ostade, Gerard Dow, the two Breughels, Karel du Jardin, Pieter Laer (called Bamboccio), Jan Lingelbach, Nicolas Maas, Gabriel Metzu, Frans van Mieris, Eglon van der Neer, Gaspar Netscher, Cornelius Poelemburg, Paul Potter, Godfried Schalken, Pieter van Slingeland, Jan Steen, Gerard Terburg, and Philip Wouverman may be named as the principal exponents of the power of this school. Of the landscape and marine painters of the same period, the following were the principal: Ludolph Bakhuyzen, Nicolas Berghem, Jan and Andries Both, Albert Cuyp, Simon van der Does, Jan van Goyen, Aart van der Neer, Jacob Ruisdael, Mindert Hobbema, Herman Swanevelde, Adam Pynacker, Adrian, and the two Williams Vandervelde, and Antony Waterloo. Of architectural painters: G. Hoekgeest, Jan van der Heyden, Pieter Neefs, Hendrik van Vliet, and Hendrik van Steenwyck. Of painters of birds, still life, fruit, flowers, etc., the following: Jan Davidsz de Heem, Melchior de Hondekoeter, Jan van Huysum, Rachel Ruisch, Jan Weenix, Jan Wynants, Adrian van Utrecht, and Willem Kalf.

The Spanish School, while it possesses great power, has for its characteristics a certain gloom and wildness belonging to the national mind. This peculiar school of painting appears to have been one of the more recently established of the modern schools of Europe; in its prevailing characteristics, it exhibits a close connection with some of the schools of Italy, especially those of Venice and Naples, though its earlier development seems to have been due to the immigration of Flemish artists into Spain. The principal works undertaken in Spain date from the time of Philip II.; they were chiefly executed by Italians, and the principal Spanish painters studied in Italy. Titian spent a few years in Spain in the reign of Charles V.; but the works he executed were oil pictures, and chiefly easel pieces, which, though guides in coloring to the Spanish painters, were less the models of the great masters of Spain than those executed in Philip's time. The painters of Spain have been classified into three principal schools, but these divisions are as much local as characteristic; they are those of Valencia, Madrid, and Seville. The following are the principal masters of these several schools, with the names of the places where they chiefly resided, and worked, arranged chronologically, from the sixteenth century, inclusive; Of the sixteenth: Antonio del Rincon, Toledo; Alonso Berruguete, Castile and Toledo; Luis de Vargas, Seville; Alonso Sanchez Coello, Madrid; Luis de Morales, el Divino, Badajoz; Dominico Theotocopuli, el Greco, Toledo; Vicente Joanes, Valencia; Miguel Barrosa, Escorial and Toledo; and Alonso Vazquez, Seville. Of the seventeenth century: Pablo de Cespedes, Cordova and Seville; Juan de las Roelas, Seville; Francisco de Ribalta, Valencia; Juan del Castillo, Seville; Francisco Pacheco, Seville; Alonso Cano, Andalusia and Madrid; Antonia de Pereda, Madrid; Diego Velasquez, Madrid; Juan de Pereja, Madrid; Francisco Zurbaran, Seville and Madrid; Francisco Rizi, Madrid; Claudio Coello, Madrid and Zaragoza; Juan de Valdes Leal, Madrid; Antonio Palomino y Velasco (the Spanish Vasari), Cordova; Bartolome Esteban Murillo, Seville; and Francisco de Herrera, el Mozo (the Young), Madrid and Seville. This list comprises all the great painters of Spain; there were no very distinguished Spanish masters in the eighteenth century. The following are the most distinguished of those above mentioned: Antonio del Rincon, Luis de Vargas, Morales, Joanes, Cespedes, Roelas, Ribalta, Pacheco, Alonso Cano, Velasquez, Zurbaran, and Murillo.

The French School of painting was, until the latter part of the eighteenth century, in all respects a branch of the schools of Italy. The earliest mature development dates from the reign of Francis I., who employed many distinguished Italian artists in France; and what is termed the French school arose from the examples left by these Italians at Fontainebleau. The masters who engrafted the Italian principles of art among the French were Il Rosso, Primaticcio, and Niccolo dell'Abate. The earliest French painters of distinction, and the only two who cannot be said to belong to this Italianized school of the sixteenth century, were Jean Cousin and François Clouet, called Jeannet, who belonged to what is termed the Gothic school, and painted in the manner of the Italian quattro-centisti. The three greatest names in French art are Claude Lorraine, Nicolas Poussin, and Anthony Watteau. Le Brun, Le Sueur, Dufresnoy, Jouvenet, and others, can but be considered as the people of a transition period, whose works picture the taste of an age, rather than the exposition of true art. It was with J. L. David that a new era commenced in art, which may possibly have been generated by the revived classicalities of a revolutionary mania which convulsed France. The Greek ideal of a monumental kind was adopted by him for historic painting, and has been happily characterized as "a morbid imitation of the antique." He was followed in his stiff insipidities by Gros, Girodet, and Guerin; but nature again appealed to the world in the work of Guerin's celebrated pupil, Gericault, whose "Wreck of the Medusa" appalled by its truth to nature and power in art. Leopold Robert followed in the same track, and produced some remarkable and life-like scenes. Paul Delaroche, took up his wondrous pencil, to delineate history with the power of a genius and the truthfulness of a historian, and nature again appeared on the walls of the French exhibition rooms. No painters excel the modern French school in history; but in landscape they are inferior to those of England and Belgium.

The English School is the youngest of the cycle of Arts; but its youthful vigor has given it a wondrous position in a comparatively short time. The first great native genius, who neither copied in a school nor followed its rules, — who struck out his own path, in which he has hitherto been alone, and whose thoughts, subjects, and sympathies were all essentially English, — was William Hogarth. "Hogarth," says Walpole, "had no model to follow and improve upon. He created his art, and used colors instead of language. His place is between the Italians, whom we consider as epic poets and tragedians, and the Flemish painters, who are as writers of farce and editors of burlesque nature." Hogarth's was the period of the revival of painting in England in every department of the art; the hitherto brightest names in the annals of English painting were his contemporaries — Sir Joshua Reynolds, Gainsborough, Wilson, West, Romney, Cotes, Cosway, Barry, and Mortimer; to whom may be added the foreigners — De Loutherbourg, Zoffany, Cipriani, Moser, and Fuseli, all domiciliated in England. Toward the end of the century, the most conspicuous masters in the department of history were — Opie, Northcote, Westall, Copley, Harlow, Hilton, and others; in portrait — Sir T. Lawrence, Hoppner, Jackson, and Raeburn; in genre — Wilkie, Bird, Smirke, and Newton; and in landscape — Constable, Callcott, and Collins.

The American School has been more or less influenced by the French, and has not yet attained to the distinction of independent characteristics. The most noted names are: Malbone (1777-1807), Copley (1738-1815), C. W. Peale (1741-1827), Gilbert C. Stuart (1756-1828), J. Trumbull (1756-1843), W. Allston (1779-1843), Thomas Cole (1801-48), Rembrandt Peale (1778-1860), W. M. Hunt (1824-79), W. Page (1811-85), D. Huntingdon (1816), S. R. Gifford (1823-80), Eastman Johnson (1824), Elihu Vedder (1836), Bierstadt (1830).

Russian art, dormant since the Byzantine period, has during the last forty years produced Swedomsky Verestchagin (1842), and Kramskoë.

Scandinavian art has been represented in modern times by Uhde, and Edelfeldt.

Pyramids.— The great pyramid of Gizeh is the largest structure of any kind ever erected by the hand of man. Its original dimensions at the base were 764 feet square, and its perpendicular height in the highest point is 488 feet; it covers four acres, one rood and twenty-two perches of ground, and has been estimated by an eminent English architect to have cost not less than £30,000,000, which in United States currency would be about $145,200,000. Internal evidences prove that the great pyramid was begun about the year 2170 B. C., about the time of the birth of Abraham. It is estimated that about 5,000,000 tons of hewn stones were used in its construction.

Sphinx.— The word sphinx is from the Greek and means the strangler, and was applied to a fabled creature of the Egyptians, which had the body of a lion, the head of a man or an animal, and two wings attached to its sides. In the Egyptian hieroglyphs the sphinx symbolized wisdom and power united. It has been supposed that the fact that the overflow of the Nile occurred when the sun was in the constellations Leo and Virgo gave the idea of the combinations of form in the sphinx, but this idea seems quite unfounded. In Egypt the reigning monarch was usually represented in the form of a sphinx. The most remarkable sphinx is that near the pyramids at Gizeh. It is sculptured from the rock, masonry having been added in several places to complete the form. It is 172½ feet long by 53 feet high, but only the head of this remarkable sculpture can now be seen, the rest of the form having been concealed by the heaped up sands of the desert.

Obelisks.— The oldest of all the obelisks is the beautiful one of rosy granite which stands alone among the green fields upon the banks of the Nile, not far from Cairo. It is the gravestone of a great ancient city which has vanished and left only this relic behind. The city was the Bethshemesh of the Scriptures, the famous On, which is memorable to all Bible readers as the residence of the priest of Potipherah, whose daughter, Asenath, Joseph married. The Greeks called it Heliopolis.

Cleopatra's Needle.— The two obelisks known as Cleopatra's Needles were set up at the entrance of the Temple of the Sun, in Heliopolis, Egypt, by Thothmes III., about 1831 B. C. We have no means of knowing when they were built, or by whom, except from the inscriptions on them, which indicate the above time. The material of which they were cut is granite, brought from Syene, near the first cataract of the Nile. Two centuries after their erection Rameses II. had the stones nearly covered with carving setting out his own greatness and achievements. Twenty-three years before Christ, Augustus Cæsar moved the obelisks from Heliopolis to Alexandria and set them up in the Cæsarium, a palace, which now stands, a mere mass of ruins, near the station of the railroad to Cairo. In 1819 one of these obelisks was presented by the Egyptian government to England, but, as no one knew how to move them, it was not taken to London until 1878. Subsequently the other obelisk was presented to the United States.

Parthenon, a celebrated temple at Athens, on the summit of the Acropolis, and sacred to Minerva. The Parthenon in beauty and grandeur surpassed all other buildings of the kind, and was constructed entirely of Pentelic marble. It was built during the splendid era of Pericles, and the expense of its erection was estimated at 6,000 talents. It contained innumerable statues raised upon marble pedestals, and other works of art. The colossal statue of Minerva, which was in the eastern end of the temple, was thirty-nine feet high, and was composed of ivory and gold, the value of the latter being forty-four talents, or about $465,000. The temple was reduced to ruins in 1687. A part of the matchless friezes, statues, etc., of the Parthenon now form the most valuable and interesting portion of the British Museum, they having been taken from the temple by Lord Elgin in 1800, and by him sold to the British Government.

German Philosophers.— Leibnitz, the founder of modern German philosophy, was a marvelous specimen of precocious genius, his first philosophical treatise being written at the age of seventeen. His system of philosophy supposed the mind and body to be two distinct machines, acting independently of but in harmony with each other. He also held to the theory of "monads"— that is, the indestructible entities of matter and of mind — claiming the Deity to be the prime monad, and asserted that all ideas were innate. He lived from 1646 to 1716. The great opponent of Leibnitz was Christian Wolf, who founded all his philosophy on logical propositions, and set aside those very doctrines on which Leibnitz grounded all his reasoning. After these two philosophers had passed away there was a term of quiescence in German philosophy, broken by the teachings of Emanuel Kant, the philosopher of "Pure Reason," and the father of modern philosophical criticism. The central point of his system lies in the proposition that before we can know anything concerning objects we must understand how we perceive objects, and what degree of knowledge perception can give us. Fichte was a disciple of Kant, but went beyond his master in transforming all knowledge into pure idealism. Schelling was the next writer to gain a general influence. He was at first simply an expounder of Fichte, but gradually developed a philosophy of his own, founded on the theory that the true sources of knowledge are not experience or reflection, but intellectual intuition. Hegel, who succeeded Schelling as the leader in German philosophy, was a more vigorous and logical thinker. The foundation of his system is that the union of assertion and negation, the harmonizing of every proposition with its contradictory, is the source of all knowledge. The Hegelian system has been modified largely by the speculations of Schleiermacher, Schubert, and others, but it still remains the most powerful school of German philosophy. The principal opposing system is that of Schopenhauer, whose fundamental doctrine is that the only essential reality in the universe is *will*, all phenomena being but manifestations of the single original will.

Classification of Mankind.— In regard to religion, mankind may be divided into two general classes: *Monotheistic*, those who worship one god, and *polytheistic*, those who worship more than one god, also called pagans, or heathen. Of the first class we have: (1) the *Christian*, which recognizes the Bible as the revealed word of God, and Jesus Christ as the Son of God; (2) the *Jewish*, which recognizes the Old Testament as the word of God, but does not acknowledge Christ; (3) the *Mohammedan*, or the religion of *Islam*, whose two articles of faith are, "There is no god but God, and Mohammed is the prophet of God."

Of the second class there are: (1) *Brahminism*, or *Hindooism*, the religion of the people of India, a very ancient religion which has many good moral doctrines, but strange ideas of a future state; (2) *Buddhism*, an offshoot of Brahminism, now practiced by the people of China and Japan, founded by Sakya-Muni, who adopted the title of Buddha (the enlightened), a religion which has been more enthusiastic in making converts than any other, except Christianity, and has many good moral precepts, but is practically atheistic; (3) *Fetichism*, a very low form of superstition, which consists in the worship of material objects, either living or dead, as animals or idols of wood or stone.

In regard to general culture and intelligence, mankind may be divided into: (1) *Savages*, those who are scarcely elevated above the brutes, live in tribes, and subsist by hunting and fishing; (2) *Barbarians*, those who have possessions, as flocks and herds, and practice agriculture to some extent, yet have made no progress in arts and sciences; (3) *Half-civilized*, those who have made some progress in the arts, have towns and cities, but depend chiefly upon agriculture; (4) *Civilized*, those who have made considerable progress in science and art, engage in commerce, and have a written language; (5) *Enlightened*, those who stand at the head of the scale, have a division of labor, systems of education, and have made the greatest progress in science, art, and in morality.

The Jewish Religion.—In their religious observances modern Jews adhere to the rules of the Mosaic dispensation. Their service consists chiefly in reading the law in their synagogues, together with a variety of prayers. They abstain from the meats prohibited by the Levitical law, and they continue to observe the ceremonies of the Passover, as nearly as possible. They offer prayers for the dead, because they believe that the souls of the wicked go to a place of temporary punishment, where they remain under trial a year, and they think that very few will be condemned to suffer eternally. We give a summary of the confession of faith, in which all orthodox Jews must live and die. It is made up of thirteen articles, and was drawn up in the eleventh century by a celebrated rabbi named Maimonides. These articles declare in substance: (1) That there is one God, creator of all things, who may exist without any part of the universe, but without whom nothing can maintain existence; (2) that God is uncompounded and indivisible, but different from all other unities; (3) that God is an immaterial being, without any admixture of corporeal substance; (4) that God is eternal, but everything else had a beginning in time; (5) that God alone ought to be worshiped, without mediators or intercessors; (6) that there have been inspired prophets, and may be more; (7) that Moses was the grandest prophet that ever appeared; (8) that the law of Moses was, in every syllable, dictated by the Almighty, not only in its written letter, but in traditionary exposition; (9) that this law is immutable, neither to be added to nor diminished; (10) that God knows all our actions and governs them as He will; (11) that the observance of the law is rewarded and its violation punished in this world, but in a greater degree in the next; (12) that a Messiah is yet to appear, the time of whose coming may not be prescribed or foretold; and (13) that God will raise the dead at the last day and pass judgment upon all.

Quakers.—The Society of Friends or Quakers was founded in 1646, by George Fox, a shoemaker of Drayton, in Leicestershire. They believe in the main fundamental principles of what is called "Orthodox Christianity," but they express their religious creed in the very words of the New Testament Scripture, and each member has the liberty of interpreting the words. Their main specialty is the belief of "The Light of Christ in man," and hence they entertain a broader view of the Spirit's influence than other Christians. In morals, propriety of conduct, good order, and philanthropy, the Quakers are a pattern society.

The Peabody Education Fund.—In 1867 and 1869 George Peabody established a fund of $3,500,000 to be devoted to education in the Southern states of the Union. Unfortunately, $1,380,000 of this amount was in Mississippi and Florida bonds, which those states have repudiated. The fund was placed in the charge and control of fifteen trustees, of which the Hon. Robert C. Winthrop of Massachusetts was the chairman. Mr. Peabody died in London in 1869. The trustees hold meetings annually, usually in New York. They fill vacancies caused by death or resignation. The present trustees are: Chief Justice Fuller, who is president of the board; Hon. Joseph H. Choate, first vice-president; D. C. Gilman, LL.D., president of the Carnegie Institution, second vice-president; Hon. Jabez L. M. Curry, LL.D., general agent; Hon. Seth Low, mayor of New York; J. Pierpont Morgan, of New York; President Theodore Roosevelt, of New York; Samuel A. Green, Hon. Richard Olney and Hon. George F. Hoar, of Massachusetts; William Wirt Henry, of Virginia; ex-Mayor William A. Courtenay, of South Carolina; James D. Porter, of Tennessee; Henderson M. Somerville, of New York; George Peabody Wetmore, of Rhode Island; Charles E. Fenner, of Louisiana, and Hon. Hoke Smith, of Georgia. Dr. Curry is general agent of the fund, with headquarters at Washington, D. C., and has charge of the distribution of the fund in the several Southern States. In its earlier history the chief aim of the fund was to encourage and secure the establishment of public school systems for the free education of all children. That having been accomplished, the income of the fund is now used for the training of teachers through normal schools and teachers' institutes. At its session in October, 1896, the board declared it to be inexpedient to close the Trust in February, 1897, the power to do which was left to its discretion. In the thirty years since the organization of the trust, over $2,500,509 have been spent, as the income of the sum left by Mr. Peabody. Mr. J. Pierpont Morgan is the treasurer.

The John F. Slater Fund.— In 1882 Mr. John F. Slater, of Connecticut, placed in the hands of trustees the sum of $1,000,000, for the purpose of "uplifting the lately emancipated population of the Southern states and their posterity." For this patriotic and munificent gift the thanks of Congress were voted, and a medal was presented. Neither principal nor income is expended for land or buildings. Education in industries and the preparation of teachers are promoted in institutions believed to be on a permanent basis. The board consists of D. C. Gilman, of Johns Hopkins University, as president; Chief Justice Fuller, as vice-president; Morris K. Jesup, as treasurer; J. L. M. Curry, as secretary and general manager, and Bishops Potter and Galloway, and Messrs. William E. Dodge, William A. Slater, John A. Stewart, Alexander E. Orr, ex-Governor Northen, and Wm. L. Wilson. The fund is a potential agency in working out the problem of the education of the negro, and over half a million dollars has already been expended. Schools established by states, denominations, and individuals are helped by annual donations. Among the most prominent are the Hampton Normal and Industrial, the Spelman, the Tuskegee, and schools at Orangeburg, S. C., Tougaloo, Miss., Marshall, Tex., the Meharry Medical College at Nashville, Tenn., etc.

National Academy of Design.

COUNCIL, 1898–1899.

President, Thomas W. Wood; *Vice-President*, James M. Hart; *Corresponding Secretary*, H. W. Watrous; *Recording Secretary*, George H. Smillie; *Treasurer*, James D. Smillie; J. Carroll Beckwith, C. D. Weldon, J. C. Nicoll, F. S. Church, Frederick Dielman, H. Bolton Jones; *Clerk of Academy*, H. G. Grannis.

NATIONAL ACADEMICIANS.

Elected.	
1862.	Beard, William H., 51 West 10th St.
1894.	Beckwith, J. Carroll, 58 West 57th St.
1860.	Bierstadt, Albert, 1271 Broadway.
1888.	Blashfield, Edwin H., 58 West 57th St.
1859.	Blauvelt, Charles F., Annapolis, Md.
1893	Blum, Robert, 90 Grove St.
1871.	Boughton, George H., London, Eng.
1872.	Brandt, Carl L., Hastings-on-Hudson, N. Y.
1863.	Brevoort, J. R., 52 East 23d St.
1881.	Bridgman, Frederick A., Paris, France.
1875.	Bristol, John B., 52 East 23d St.
1863.	Brown, J. G., 51 West 10th St.
1873.	Butler, George B., Century Club.
1875.	Calverley, Charles, 107 East 27th St.
1890.	Chase, William M., 234 East 15th St.
1849.	Church, Frederic E., Hudson, N. Y.
1885.	Church, F. S., 1512 Broadway.
1898.	Clinedinst, B. West, 110 Fifth Ave.
1862.	Colman, Samuel, Newport, R. I.
1851.	Cropsey, J. F., Hastings-on-Hudson, N. Y.
1863.	Dana, W. P. W., Paris, France.
1888.	Dewing, Thos. W., 911 Seventh Ave.
1883.	Dielman, Frederick, 1512 Broadway.
1849.	Flagg, Jared B., 37 West 22d St.
1882.	Gaul, Gilbert, 170th St., near Tenth Ave.
1878.	Gifford, R. Swain, 152 West 57th St.
1867.	Griswold, C. C., 139 West 55th St.
1865.	Guy, Seymour Joseph, 51 West 10th St.
1868.	Hall, George Henry, Rome, Italy.
1889.	Hamilton, Hamilton, Baldwin's, L. I.
1859.	Hart, James M., 11 East 14th St.
1891.	Hartley, J. S., 145 West 55th St.
1861.	Hazeltine, W. Stanley, Boston, Mass.
1863.	Hennessy, W. J., London, Eng.
1869.	Henry, E. L., Century Club.
1865.	Homer, Winslow, Scarboro, Me.
1897.	Howe, Wm. H., Bronxville, N. Y.
1882.	Howland, Alfred C., 52 East 23d St.
1840.	Huntington, Daniel, 49 East 20th St.
1861.	Johnson, David, 69 West 131st St.
1860.	Johnson, Eastman, 65 West 55th St.
1851.	Jones, Alfred, 86 Trinity Place.
1894.	Jones, Francis C., 253 West 42d St.
1883.	Jones, H. Bolton, 253 West 42d St.
1869.	Lafarge, John, 51 West 10th St.
1897.	Lippincott, Wm. H., 286 West 84th St.
1890.	Low, Will H., 42 West 15th St.
1876.	Magrath, William, 11 East 14th St.
1875.	Martin, Homer D., Century Club.
1885.	Maynard, Geo. W., 156 East 36th St.
1875.	Miller, Charles H., 108 West 23d St.
1885.	Millet, F. D., Broadway, Eng.
1895.	Moeller, Louis, Mount Vernon, N. Y.
1884.	Moran, Thomas, 37 West 22d St.
1891.	Mowbray, H. Siddons, 66 West 11th St.
1887.	Murphy, J. Francis, 222 West 23d St.
1870.	Nehlig, Victor, Paris, France.
1885.	Nicoll, J. C., 51 West 10th St.
1897.	Palmer, Walter L., 5 Lafayette St., Albany, N. Y.
1884.	Parton, Arthur, 52 West 23d St.
1869.	Perry, E. Wood, 51 West 10th St.
1880.	Porter, Benj. C., 3 North Washington Sq.
1851.	Richards, T. Addison, National Academy.
1878.	Robbins, Horace Wolcott, 56 East 57th St.
1863.	Rogers, John, New Canaan, Ct.
1897.	Sargent, John S., 33 Tite St., London, Eng.
1875.	Sellstedt, L. G., Buffalo, N. Y.
1861.	Shattuck, Aaron D., Granby, Ct.
1888.	Shirlaw, Walter, 3 North Washington Sq
1890.	Shurtleff, R. M., 44 West 22d St.
1882.	Smillie, George H., 51 East 59th St.
1876.	Smillie, James D., 156 East 36th St.
1861.	Sonntag, William L., 120 East 22d St.
1889.	St. Gaudens, Augustus, 148 West 36th St.
1858.	Tait, Arthur F., 82 Waring Place, Yonkers, N. Y.
1880.	Tiffany, Louis C., 335 Fourth Ave.
1891.	Tryon, D. W., 226 West 59th St.
1886.	Turner, C. Y., 35 West 14th St.
1883.	Van Elten, Kruseman, 51 West 10th St.
1865.	Vedder, Elihu, Rome, Italy.
1891.	Vinton, Frederic P., Boston, Mass.
1891.	Walker, Horatio, 51 West 10th St.
1883.	Ward, Edgar M., 51 West 10th St.
1863.	Ward, J. Q. A., 119 West 52d St.
1895.	Watrous, Harry W., 58 West 57th St.
1886.	Weir, J. Alden, 146 West 55th St.
1866.	Weir, John F., New Haven, Ct.
1861.	Whittredge, Worthington, Summit, N. J.
1898.	Wiles, Irving R., 106 West 55th St.
1873.	Wilmarth, Lemuel E., 352 Adelphi St., Brooklyn, N. Y.
1871.	Wood, Thomas Waterman, 51 West 10th St.
1880.	Yewell, George H., 51 West 10th St.

The addresses of members of the Academy given in the list refer to the city of New York when not otherwise specified. The National Academy was founded in 1826.

University Extension has for its object the provision of "the means of higher education for persons of all classes, and of both sexes engaged in the regular occupations of life." This movement commenced with the University of Cambridge in 1872, and was subsequently taken up by Oxford University, the London Society for the extension of University Teaching, Dublin University, Owens College, Manchester, the Scottish Universities, the University of Sydney, New South Wales, and the Chautauqua Home Reading Club in the United States. In 1890 Cambridge, Oxford, and the London Society had two hundred and twenty-seven centers, seventy-nine lecturers, and 40,336 students attending lectures. The lecture study system was organized in the United States at the University of Pennsylvania. Other institutions, notably the University of Chicago and the University of Wisconsin, have engaged in the work, and many centers for lectures and study in history, science, art, and literature have been formed.

Columbian University, Washington, D. C., originated with the Rev. Luther Rice, who, in 1819, with a number of associates, paid $7,000 for a tract of land adjoining the city of Washington, with the understanding that it should be held for higher educational purposes. John Quincy Adams, John C. Calhoun, thirty-two members of Congress, and leading citizens of Washington, were among the contributors to this fund. A charter was procured from Congress in February, 1821, during the presidency of James Monroe, "erecting the Columbian College in the District of Columbia." The construction of a college building had been commenced in 1820, and it was completed in 1822, at a cost of $35,000. Dr. Stoughton, a native of England, and an eminent pulpit orator, was the first president of the institution. Agents were sent to Europe, and among the contributors to the founding of the college were several Englishmen prominent in politics and literature, including the chancellor of the exchequer and Sir James Mackintosh, the historian.

The first commencement of the college was held December 15, 1824, and was attended by the President of the United States and members of both Houses of Congress and General Lafayette; a formal address of welcome being made to General Lafayette by the president of the college. Upon the conclusion of the exercises, General Lafayette and his suite, Secretary John Quincy Adams, Secretary John C. Calhoun, Henry Clay, and other distinguished citizens dined with the faculty and board of trustees at the house of President Stoughton.

Dr. Stoughton resigned the presidency in 1827, after a rather stormy period, during which the college was at times greatly embarrassed for money, and in 1828 Rev. Steven Chapin, D.D., was chosen his successor. The presidents since that time have been: Rev. Joel S. Bacon, D.D., elected 1843; Rev. Joseph G. Binney, D.D., elected 1855; Rev. George W. Samson, D.D., elected 1859; James C. Welling, LL.D., elected 1871; Benaiah L. Whitman, M.A., D.D., LL.D., elected 1895; Charles W. Needham, LL.D.

In 1873, Congress passed an act providing that the corporation "shall hereafter be known and called by the name of the Columbian University." In 1879 it was decided to remove all departments of the University into the heart of Washington, and in 1884 the present university buildings, at the corner of 15th and H streets, were occupied by the academic, law, and scientific schools of the University.

John Quincy Adams was among the earliest friends of the college to lend aid during its periods of financial need. He loaned it $18,000, a part of which debt he remitted. From 1835 to 1861 John Withers of Virginia made frequent gifts to cancel debts, to repair buildings, and for general purposes, amounting in the aggregate to nearly $70,000. In 1865 William W. Corcoran presented the college with a building for its Medical School, valued at $30,000. His subsequent gifts have reached about $150,000, in grateful memory of which was established, in 1884, the Corcoran Scientific School.

The University comprises the following divisions: The Columbian College, the Corcoran Scientific School, the School of Graduate Studies, the Law School, the School of Jurisprudence and Diplomacy, the Medical School, the Dental School, the Graduate Veterinary School, and the Summer School.

In 1898, as an organic part of the University, there was established a School of Comparative Jurisprudence and Diplomacy, the first of that character in the United States. Such a school had been a long cherished hope of the University authorities, and owed its germinal conception to a former president of the University, James Clarke Welling, LL.D. The design of the school is to afford a training in the subjects of higher legal knowledge, comparative government, applied economics, and the history, science, and practice of diplomacy. Two courses are now given, leading respectively to the degrees Doctor of Civil Law (D. C. L.) and Master of Diplomacy (M. Dip.), depending upon the emphasis awarded to jurisprudence or diplomatic studies. The lecturers, together with their assignment of subjects, are as follows:—

Charles W. Needham, LL.D., *President; Transportation and Interstate Commerce Law.*

Henry St. George Tucker, LL.D., *Dean; International Private Law.*

Hon. John M. Harlan, LL.D., *Comparative Constitutional Law.*

Hon. David J. Brewer, LL.D., *International Public Law.*

Hon. John W. Foster, LL.D., *American Diplomacy and Treaties.*

Hon. David Jayne Hill, LL.D., *European Diplomacy and Treaties.*

Hon. William Wirt Howe, LL.D., *Ancient, Roman, Mediæval Law; Modern Civil Law.*

Hon. Hannis Taylor, LL.D., *Constitutional and Common Law of England.*

Hon. Martin A. Knapp, LL.D., *Interstate Commerce Law.*

Hon. Carroll D. Wright, LL.D., *Social Economics and Statistics.*

Charles C. Swisher, PH.D., L.H.D., *Comparative Politics and Political Geography.*

Hon. Lyman J. Gage, LL.D., *Public Finance.*

John F. Crowell, PH.D., L.H.D., *International Trade.*

Hon. Edward H. Strobel, M.A., LL.B., *Jurisprudence of France and Spain.*

N. W. Hoyles, K.C., LL.D., *Jurisprudence of Canada.*

Special lectures are provided upon the Jurisprudence of England, France, Germany, Austria-Hungary, and Italy, who are authorities in their respective subjects.

Greek Church, The, in its widest sense, comprehends all Christians following the Greek or Greco-Slavonic rite, who receive the first seven General Councils, but reject the authority of the Roman pontiff and the later councils of the Western church. The Greek Church calls itself "The Holy Orthodox Catholic and Apostolic Church," and includes three distinct branches—the church in the Ottoman empire, subject directly to the Patriarch of Constantinople; the church in the kingdom of Greece; the Russo-Greek Church in the dominions of the czar.

The proper history of the Greek Church, as a separate body, dates from the commencement of the Greek schism, or, rather, from the commencement of the efforts on the part of the Church of Constantinople to establish for itself a distinct jurisdiction and an independent headship in the eastern division of the empire. The ecclesiastical preëminence of Constantinople followed upon the political distinction to which it rose as the seat of the imperial residence and the center of the imperial government. Originally Byzantium (called Constantinople after 330 A. D.) was but a simple episcopal see, but the rank rose with the fortunes of the city; and before the close of the fourth century a canon of the first council of Constantinople, held in 381, assures to it, on the ground that Constantinople is the "new Rome," the precedence of honor next after the ancient Rome. The present total number of adherents of the Greek Church is about 90,000,000.

College de France, founded by Francis I., 1530, is now a very important educational institution, giving instruction over a very wide field of literature, history, and science. It is independent of the University of France, directly under the Minister of Public Instruction, and is supported by the government. As in the Sorbonne, the lectures are gratuitous, and for the most part are designed to attract auditors older than ordinary university students. The College comprises two faculties, one literary, one scientific; each has about twenty professors. Among the professors are some of the most distinguished scholars and scientists in France. The subjects mainly covered are political economy, Assyrian and Egyptian archæology, Arabic, Slavonic literature, French literature, physiology, anatomy, and embryology.

Escurial, The, is a famous monastery of New Castile, Spain, in the province of Madrid. This solitary pile of granite has been called the eighth wonder of the world, and at the time of its erection surpassed every building of the kind in size and magnificence. It owes its origin, it is said, to an inspired vow made by Philip II. during the battle of St. Quentin. On that occasion he implored the aid of St. Lorenzo, on whose day the battle was fought; and vowed that should victory be granted to him he would dedicate a monastery to the saint. The Escurial was begun in 1563 and finished in 1584, and was intended to serve as a palace, mausoleum, and monastery. It has a splendid chapel, with three naves. The Pantheon, or royal tomb, is a magnificently decorated octagonal chamber, in the eight sides of which are numerous black marble sarcophagi. Something of the immensity of the Escurial may be conceived when it is stated that it has 14,000 doors, and 11,000 windows, and its cost was 6,000,000 ducats, or nearly $14,000,000. Its library, previous to the sack of the Escurial by the French in 1808, contained 30,000 printed and 4,300 manuscript volumes, mainly treasures of Arabic literature. In 1872 the Escurial was struck by lightning and partially destroyed.

Jewish Temple, The, at Jerusalem, was erected by Solomon, and, from the descriptions which have come down to us, probably equaled in magnificence and dimensions any similar building in the ancient world. The influence of the Assyrian and Egyptian styles of architecture was probably exhibited in its construction, and at no time did the Jews possess a style which might be called their own. It was consecrated 1004 B. C.; pillaged by Shishak, 971; restored by Joash, 856; polluted by Ahaz, 740; again restored by Hezekiah, 726; pillaged and burned by Nebuchednezzar, 588-587; rebuilt, 536, at the period of the return from captivity; pillaged by Antiochus, 168; rebuilt by Herod, 18; and finally destroyed by Titus, A. D. 70. Its supposed site is now covered by the Mosque of Omar.

GLOSSARY OF ART AND MUSICAL TERMS.

Accompaniment. A secondary part added to the principal for the improvement of the general effect.

Acanthus. A plant, the ornamental foliage of which is largely employed for architectural decoration, especially on the Corinthian capital. There are two principal species, *acanthus mollis* and *acanthus spinosa*, the latter somewhat resembling a thistle.

Acropolis. A fortified city, or the fortified part of a city, on the summit of a hill.

Adagio. A slow movement.

Ad Libitum. Implies that the time of the movement is left to the discretion of the performer.

Allegretto. With cheerful quickness.

Amphiprostyle. A Greek temple, having two open porticos in front and rear projecting beyond the side walls.

Amphitheater. A building for gladiatorial and other shows, generally elliptical in form.

Amphora. A wide earthenware jar with two handles.

Andante. Somewhat sedate; slowly.

Animato, Animaso, or **Con Animata.** Animated; with spirit.

Angels. In mediæval art divided into nine degrees: Seraphim, Domination, Princedom, Cherubim, Virtues, Archangels, Thrones, Powers, Angels. The Cupid-like angels were only introduced in the time of the Renascence.

Antae. Rectangular pilasters forming the ends of the walls of the cella of a Greek temple, and supporting the extremities of the architrave. A temple of this form was called a temple " in antis."

Annulus, Annulet. Rings of moldings above the lower part of the echinus of Doric capitls.

Antefixa. Terra cotta ornaments placed above the cornice and on the ridge of the roof of Greek temples.

Apse. The extremity of a church, generally semicircular in form and surmounted by a semi-dome.

Aquatint. A process of engraving by acid laid on in even washes with a brush, upon a broken surface formed by a crackled film of resin on the copper.

Arabesque. An ornament composed of stems, foliage, leafage of plants, scrolls, and fantastic animals. Not, as its name implies, an Arab invention but found in Greek and Roman architecture.

Arcade. A series of arches.

Arch. A curved structure, generally a segment or segments of the circle. Semicircular arches were used by the Romans; horseshoe arches by the Byzantines and Moors; pointed arches formed of two intersecting segments of circles by the Gothic builders.

Archaic. The early period of art when forms were stiff, conventional, and symbolic.

Architrave. The horizontal part of a structure resting immediately on the capital of column or pilaster.

Assai. Very; used as an adverb with another word.

Astragal. A small semicircular molding at the top of a column beneath the capital, also used to divide the architrave horizontally into parts. Named, from its supposed resemblance to a row of knucklebones.

A Temp. In regular time.

Atlantes. Human male figures, employed instead of columns to support the architrave.

Atrium. A covered court in a Roman house, with an opening in the center (compluvium) and roof sloping inwards.

Baldachino. A canopy over seats and other places of honor.

Barrel Vault. A vault of cylindrical form.

Baroque. Rococo.

Base. The lower division of a column on which the shaft is placed; absent in the Doric order.

Basilica. A rectangular hall divided by rows of columns into three naves, and used by the Romans as a court of justice. Adopted as the typical form of early Christian churches.

Bas Relief. (Basso relievo.) Figures sculptured on panel projecting less than half their proportions from the surface.

Bastion. A projecting polygonal buttress on a fortification.

Battlement. A parapet of a fortification, consisting of alternate raised portions and spaces, the latter called crenels or embrasures.

Bay. A portion of a structure marked off by the division of the vaulting, the arches, or the buttresses.

Beat. An indication of a certain duration of time.

Ben. Implying well, as *ben marcato*.

Body Color. In water-color painting, color made opaque by intermixture with white.

Boss. An architectural ornament of ceilings, placed generally where the ribs of the vault meet.

Buttress. A piece of wall built at right angles to the wall of a building to strengthen the structure, either immediately against the wall or connected by an arch called a flying buttress.

Byzantine. The style of architecture and painting in use at Constantinople from the sixth to the twelfth century

Calando. A gradual diminution in speed and tone.

Caduceus. A wand of laurel or olive on which two snakes are intertwined; the emblem of Hermes.

Capital. The, usually ornamented, member which crowns the top of a column or pillar, and by the form of which the different orders are characterized.

Caryatides. Female figure, employed instead of columns to support the architrave.

Cella. The internal part inclosed by the walls of a Greek temple.

Chromatic. Proceeding or formed by semi-tones.

Chevron. A zigzag molding used in Romanesque architecture.

Chevet. A form of apse inclosed by an arcade with a series of chapels round it, common in Romanesque and Gothic churches in France.

Chiaro-oscuro. The distribution of light and shade.

Cinquefoil. An ornamental foliation, consisting of five projecting cusps.

Clerestory. The row of windows forming the third or upper division of the nave wall of a church, rising above the roof of the outer portion of the structure.

Cloister. A quadrangular covered walk, forming a portion of a monastic building.

Clustered Column. A pier formed by a number of shafts clustered together, either united, or separate.

Con. With; as *Con expressione*.

Column. A column consists of three principal parts: base, shaft, and capital.

Composite. The last of the five Roman architectural orders, formed by the combination of the Ionic volute with the foliage capital of the Corinthian.

Corinthian. The third order in the Roman classification, of Greek origin. Shaft slender and smooth; capital richly decorated with acanthus leaf ornaments.

Cornice. The horizontal molded projection terminating a building.

Corona. A molding forming part of a conical, with lower part grooved to form a dripstone.

Crescendo. A gradual increase in tone.

Crypt. A subterranean chapel beneath a church.

Cupola. A concave roof.

Cusp. Pointed foliations in architectural tracery.

Cyma. An undulated molding, formed of a concave and convex arc. When the upper arc is convex it is called cyma reversa; when the upper is hollow, it is called cyma recta.

Da. By.

Dales, or **Dal.** In a soft, quiet manner.

Damascened. Metal ornamented by inlaying another metal.

Delicato. With delicacy.

Decorated. The second of the pointed or Gothic styles of architecture in England

Dentils. Ornaments in the form of small cubes or teeth.
Diaper. A mode of decoration by a repeated pattern.
Doloroso. In a melancholy, sad style.
Doric. The oldest and simplest of the Greek orders of architecture.
Dormer. A gable window in the sloping side of a roof.
Dry-Point. Direct engraving upon copper with the etching needle.

Echinus. The ovolo molding of a capital.
Elevation. The vertical plan of a building.
Entablature. The horizontal superstructure which lies upon the columns in classic architecture.
Entasis. The swelling of the shaft of a column.
Epinaos. The portico situated at the back of a temple.
Espressivo, or **Con Espressione.** With expression.
Etching. Engraving by the action of acid on a copperplate covered with a wax ground on which lines have been scratched by the etching needle.

Facade. The face or front of a building.
Fan Tracery. Elaborate carved work spread over an arched surface.
Fine. The end.
Fillet. A plain band used in architecture to separate ornaments and moldings.
Finial. An ornament of carved work representing foliage on a pinnacle or spire.
Flamboyant. The style of French architecture peculiar to the fifteenth century, contemporary with perpendicular in England.
Flutes. Small semicircular grooves or channels cut in the shafts of columns or pilasters.
Forte, or **For.** Strong, loud.
Fresco. Painting executed on a freshly laid ground of stucco.
Fret. An angular, interlaced architectural ornament.
Frieze. (1) The middle division of an entablature which lies between the architrave and cornice. (2) Any horizontal sculptured band.
Furioso. With great animation.

Gable. The triangular end of a house from the eaves to the top.
Genre. Scenes from domestic life.
Giusto. In perfect time.
Grave. The slowest time or movement.
Grisaille. A style of painting in gray by which solid bodies are represented as if in relief.
Groin. The angular curve formed at the intersections of a vaulted roof.
Gusto, Con Gusto. With style; taste.
Gymnasium. A large building used by the Greeks in which gymnastics were taught and practiced.

Helix. A small volute like the tendril of a vine placed under the Corinthian abacus.
Hypostyle. A roof supported by columns.

Il. The.
Impetuoso. Impetuously.
Impasto. The thickness of the body of pigment laid on to a painting.
In. In; as in tempo.
Intrado, or **Introduzione.** An introduction to a piece of music.
Intaglio. A stone in which the design is sunk beneath the surface, and gives impression of a bas relief.
Ionic. The second order in Greek architecture. Distinguished by the voluted ornaments of its capital.

Jamb. The side of any opening in a wall.

Keystone. The top stone of an arch.
Klaft. A royal Egyptian headdress forming a kind of hood and terminating in two flaps, which form over the breast.

Largo. A slow and solemn degree of time.
Lancet. A pointed arch, obtuse at the point, resembling a surgeon's lancet.
Lantern. A small turret above the roof of a building having windows all round it.
Legato. In a smooth, even manner.
Leggiando. Lightly.
Lintel. The stone or beam placed across the top of a door or window.
Loggia. The gallery or corridor of a palace.
Lotus. A water lily. In Egypt and India held sacred.

Marcato. In a marked manner.
Mansard. A roof with two sets of rafters of which the upper part is less steep than the lower. Named after a French architect.
Marquetry. Inlaid work of ornamental woods and stones of various colors.
Mausoleum. (1) The tomb of Mausolus, king of Caria. (2) Any tomb of imposing size and magnificence.
Meme. The same.
Mezzo. In a medium degree; as *mezzo forte.*
Medallion. A circular or oval tablet on the face of a building.
Metope. A kind of panel between the triglyphs in the Doric frieze.
Mezzo Relievo. Sculpture in relief in which half of the figure projects.
Mezzo Tinto. A method of engraving by smoothing away the lights from a ground mechanically roughened.
Moderato. Moderately.
Molto. Very; as *molto forte.*
Movimento. Movement; time.
Monolith. An object formed of a single block of stone.
Mosaic. An imitation of painting by joining together minute pieces of hard substances of different colors.
Mullion. The slender pieces which separate a window into compartments.
Mutule. An architectural ornament of the Doric order, consisting of a square block placed at equal intervals in a Doric cornice.

Naos. The interior apartment of a Greek temple.
Nave. The middle part or body of a church from the choir to principal entrance between the aisles.
Nimbus. A halo or circular disk around the head of sacred personages. After the eighth century, living persons were in Italy distinguished by a square nimbus, which sometimes assumes the form of a scroll partly unrolled. The heads of statues of gods and of Roman emperors were decorated with a crown of rays. The same is found in the Oriental representation of Buddha.

Obbligato. An essential portion of a composition.
Ogee. An arch described with four centers so as to be concave in lower and convex in upper part.
Ogive. A pointed arch.
Order, An, in architecture consists of two parts: the one, vertical, consisting of a column and its base and capital; the other, a horizontal entablature, consisting of architrave, frieze, and cornice. The word is only used when the order is one of the five whose dimensions and details were fixed and defined by Palladio and other architects of the sixteenth century; these are the Doric, Ionic, Corinthian, Tuscan (supposed to be a simpler form of Doric), and Composite (a Roman modification of Corinthian).
Oriel. A projecting angular window, generally triangular or pentagonal in shape.
Ottava, or **8va.** An octave.
Ovolo. A convex molding much used in classical architecture.

Pagoda. A religious building of the Hindoos.
Palaestra. A place for wrestling, formerly part of the gymnasium.
Pedale, or **Ped.** Signifies that performer must press down pedal.
Pen. A little.
Pediment. A triangular crowning of a portico usually supported by a row of columns.
Pendentive. The part of a vault between two arches supporting a dome.
Peripteral. A name given to a temple which had a portico of six columns on each front and a detached colonnade of 11 on each side of the cella.
Peristyle. A building, the interior of which is surrounded with columns.
Perspective. The art of representing on a flat surface the appearance of objects from one given point of view.
Piano, or **P.** Soft.
Pianissimo, or **PP.** Very soft.
Pier. Perpendicular supports from which arches spring.
Pilaster. Square pillar on a wall partly imbedded in it, less than one fourth of its thickness projecting.

Pinnacle. A small spire.
Piscina. A stone basin usually placed in a niche in the wall of the chancel at which the priest might wash his hands.
Plus. More.
Plinth. The lower projecting base of a column.
Poco a Poco. Gradually; by a regular gradation.
Pomposo. Pompously.
Precipitato. Very quickly; hurriedly.
Premiere. First; as *première fois*; first time.
Presto. Very quick.
Primo. First, as *violino primo*, first violin.
Pronaos. The portico situated in front of a temple.
Propylaea. Gateway or entrance to an Egyptian temple.

Quasi. In the manner of; like.
Quieto. With repose, quietly.
Quatrefoil. An ornament in pointed architecture, consisting of four foils.

Rapido. Rapidly.
Rinforzando. Rinf. or Rf., with increase.
Ritenente, Ritenato. Decreasing in speed.
Rococo. A style of decoration distinguished by a superfluity of confused and discordant detail.
Romanesque. The debased style of architecture and ornament adopted in the later Roman empire, and the styles founded upon it.
Rose Window. A large, circular window divided into compartments by curved mullions.
Rubble. Rough stones and broken bricks, used to fill up between walls.
Rustication. Hewn stone masonry, the joints of which are rendered conspicuous by grooves or channels.

Sarcophagus. A stone coffin.
Scumbling. The process of going over a painting with a brush, nearly dry, to soften and blend the tints.
Segno. Sign, as *al segno*, go back to sign.
Sempre. Always, as *sempre piano*.
Serioso. Seriously.
Shaft. The body of a column.
Solo, Sola. Alone. A composition rendered by one person.
Sostenuto or **Sost.** Prolonged, sustained.
Spirito. With spirit.
Sphinx. A human head on a lion's body, typifying the union of intellectual and physical power. An Egyptian emblem, signifying the religious mystery.
Staccato. Each note to be distinctly marked.
Stesso. The same.
Stylobate. The common base of a row of columns.
Syncopation. Connecting the last note of a bar with the first note of the following, thus forming one prolonged note with a duration equal to the two.
Syncopate. In a syncopated style.

Tanto or **Ton.** Not so much.
Tardo. Slowly.
Taenia. A band which separates the Doric frieze from the architrave.
Tempo Comodo. Conveniently.
Tempera. Painting with pigments mixed with chalk or clay, and diluted with size.
Theme. A subject.
Thalamus. The nuptial chamber in a Rome house.
Torso. The trunk of the statue of a human figure.
Tranquillo. Tranquilly.
Tremendi. With terrific expression.
Tremando, Tremolo. The rapid striking of a note so as to produce a tremulous effect.
Trille, or **Trillo.** A trill or shake.
Trio. A composition for three performers.
Triplet. A group of three notes equal in duration of time to two notes of the same value.
Tracery. Geometrical ornament.
Transept. A transverse nave, passing in front of the choir, and crossing the longitudinal nave of a church.
Transom. The horizontal cross bar in a window.
Trefoil. An ornament of three foils.
Triforium. The second or middle story of the nave wall of a Gothic church, consisting of a gallery over the ceiling of the side aisle and below its roof.
Triglyph. An ornament, consisting of three flutings or upright groupings, separating the metopes in a Doric frieze.
Triptych. A form of pictures in three panels.
Tympanum. The triangular space between the horizontal and sloping cornices. The name is also given to the space included between the lintel of a door and the arch over it.

Un. A, as *un poco*, a little.

Vault. An arched ceiling or roof of stone.
Veloce. Rapidly.
Velocissimo. With great rapidity.
Vigoroso. With vigor.
Vivace. Vivamented; briskly.
Volti Subito. Turn over quickly.
Volute. A spiral scroll.
Voussoirs. The wedge-shaped stones used in constructing an arch.

Zoophorus, Zophorus. (Lit. bearing animals.) A continuous frieze, decorated with figures of animals, conventional and real.

University of Michigan.—This university was established by a legislative act of 1821, repealing a previous act of 1817, by which a "university or catholepistemiad" had been created by the *ipse dixit* of Judge C. B. Woodward. The university was not organized until March of 1837, when the regents obtained a loan of $100,000 from the state, and erected five buildings at Ann Arbor. In the fall of the same year instruction was begun with a faculty of two, and an entering class of six. Until 1853 the school remained in a state of partial development, owing to incessant interference from the legislature and internal dissensions among the faculty. In 1852 a new board of regents was constituted, with a president to whom independence of action was guaranteed. Dr. Henry P. Tappan was elected and continued in office until 1863, when he was summarily removed. This action was protested against by the faculty as well as by the students and alumni, and was twice made a subject of censure by subsequent boards of regents. During Dr. Tappan's presidency the university more than quadrupled in numbers, and made itself recognized as a school of liberal learning on both sides of the Atlantic. Since that time the presidents have been: E. O. Haven, 1863-1869; Henry S. Frieze, 1869-1871; and James B. Angell, from 1871 until the present time.

The university is a part of the public educational system of the state. The governing body is a board of eight regents, elected by popular vote for eight years. The university comprises the department of literature, science, and arts, including the graduate and summer school, the department of engineering, of medicine and surgery, of law, the school of pharmacy, the homeopathic medical college, and that of dental surgery.

The various courses lead respectively to the degrees, B.A., B.Sc., Ph.B., Litt.B., the corresponding Master's degrees and doctorates, as well as the usual professional degrees.

LIBRARY OF CONGRESS, WASHINGTON, D. C.

Book VIII.

Miscellaneous Facts and Figures.

Miscellaneous Facts and Figures.

Signers of the Declaration of Independence.

Name.	Order.*	Colony.	Occupation.	Born.	Birthplace.	Died.	Age.†
Adams, John	6	Massachusetts Bay	Lawyer	Oct. 19, 1735	Braintree, Mass.	July 4, 1826	92
Adams, Samuel	2	Massachusetts Bay	Merchant	Sep. 22, 1722	Boston, Mass.	Oct. 3, 1803	81
Bartlett, Josiah	9	New Hampshire	Physician	Nov., 1729	Amesbury, Mass.	May 19, 1795	67
Braxton, Carter	51	Virginia	Planter	Sep. 10, 1736	Newington, Va.	Oct. 10, 1797	62
Carroll, Charles	31	Maryland	Lawyer	Sep. 20, 1737	Annapolis, Md.	Nov. 14, 1832	96
Chase, Samuel	44	Maryland	Lawyer	Apr. 17, 1741	Somerset Co., Md.	June 19, 1811	71
Clark, Abraham	14	New Jersey	Lawyer	Feb. 15, 1726	Elizabethtown, N. J.	Sep., 1794	69
Clymer, George	38	Pennsylvania	Merchant	Jan. 24, 1739	Philadelphia, Pa.	Jan. 23, 1813	75
Ellery, William	22	R. I. and Prov. Plan.	Lawyer	Dec. 22, 1727	Newport, R. I.	Feb. 15, 1820	93
Floyd, William	5	New York	Farmer	Dec. 17, 1734	Setauket, N. Y.	Aug. 1, 1821	87
Franklin, Benjamin	46	Pennsylvania	Printer	Jan. 17, 1706	Boston, Mass.	Apr. 17, 1790	85
Gerry, Elbridge	8	Massachusetts Bay	Merchant	July 17, 1744	Marblehead, Mass.	Nov. 23, 1814	71
Gwinnett, Button	40	Georgia	Merchant	1732	England	May 27, 1777	45
Hancock, John	1	Massachusetts Bay	Merchant	Jan. 12, 1737	Braintree, Mass.	Oct. 8, 1793	57
Hall, Lyman	47	Georgia	Physician	1731	Conn.	1784	53
Harrison, Benj	54	Virginia	Farmer	1740	Berkeley, Va.	April, 1791	51
Hart, John	13	New Jersey	Farmer	1715	Hopewell, N. J.	1780	65
Hewes, Joseph	35	North Carolina	Lawyer	1730	Kingston, N. J.	Nov. 10, 1779	49
Heyward, Jr., Thos	56	South Carolina	Lawyer	1746	St. Luke's, S. C.	March, 1809	63
Hooper, Wm.	23	North Carolina	Lawyer	June 17, 1742	Boston, Mass.	Oct., 1790	49
Hopkins, Steph	12	R. I. and Prov. Plan.	Farmer	Mar. 7, 1707	Scituate, Mass.	July 13, 1785	79
Hopkinson, Francis	29	New Jersey	Lawyer	1737	Philadelphia, Pa.	May 9, 1791	54
Huntington, Sam'l	11	Connecticut	Lawyer	July 3, 1732	Windham, Conn.	Jan. 5, 1796	64
Jefferson, Thos	32	Virginia	Lawyer	Apr. 13, 1743	Shadwell, Va.	July 4, 1826	83
Lee, Richard Henry	48	Virginia	Soldier	Jan. 20, 1732	Stratford, Va.	June 19, 1794	63
Lee, Francis Lightfoot	55	Virginia	Farmer	Oct. 14, 1734	Stratford, Va.	April, 1797	63
Lewis, Francis	7	New York	Merchant	March, 1713	Llandaff, Wales	Dec. 30, 1803	91
Livingston, Philip	3	New York	Merchant	Jan. 15, 1716	Albany, N. Y.	June 12, 1778	63
Lynch, Jr., Thos	43	South Carolina	Lawyer	Aug. 5, 1749	Pr. George's Co., S. C.	1779	30
M'Kean, Thos	39	Delaware	Lawyer	Mar. 19, 1734	New London, Pa.	June 24, 1817	84
Middleton, Arthur	50	South Carolina	Lawyer	1743	Middleton Pl., S. C.	Jan. 1, 1788	44
Morris, Lewis	15	New York	Farmer	1726	Morrisania, N. Y.	Jan. 22, 1798	72
Morris, Robert	24	Pennsylvania	Merchant	Jan. 20, 1734	Lancashire, Eng.	May 8, 1806	73
Morton, John	16	Pennsylvania	Surveyor	1724	Ridley, Pa.	April, 1777	53
Nelson, Jr., Thos	49	Virginia	Statesman	Dec. 26, 1738	York, Va.	Jan. 4, 1789	51
Paca, William	28	Maryland	Lawyer	Oct. 31, 1740	Wye Hall, Md.	1799	59
Paine, Robert Treat	4	Massachusetts Bay	Lawyer	1731	Boston, Mass.	May 11, 1814	84
Penn, John	18	North Carolina	Lawyer	May 17, 1741	Caroline Co., Va.	Sep., 1788	48
Read, George	41	Delaware	Lawyer	1734	Cecil Co., Md.	1798	64
Rodney, Cæsar	52	Delaware	General	1730	Dover, Del.	1783	53
Ross, George	37	Pennsylvania	Lawyer	1730	Newcastle, Del.	July, 1779	49
Rush, Benjamin	46	Pennsylvania	Physician	Dec. 24, 1745	Berberry, Pa.	Apr. 19, 1813	68
Rutledge, Edward	34	South Carolina	Lawyer	Nov., 1749	Charleston, S. C.	Jan. 23, 1800	51
Sherman, Roger	19	Connecticut	Shoemaker	Apr. 19, 1721	Newton, Mass.	July 23, 1793	73
Smith, James	36	Pennsylvania	Lawyer	1710	Ireland	July 11, 1806	96
Stockton, Richard	10	New Jersey	Lawyer	Oct. 1, 1730	Princeton, N. J.	Feb. 28, 1781	51
Stone, Thomas	30	Maryland	Lawyer	1742	Pointoin Manor, Md.	Oct. 5, 1787	45
Taylor, Geo	33	Pennsylvania	Physician	1716	Ireland	Feb. 23, 1781	65
Thornton, Matthew	17	New Hampshire	Physician	1714	Ireland	June 24, 1803	89
Walton, George	53	Georgia	Lawyer	1740	Frederick Co., Va.	Feb. 2, 1804	64
Whipple, William	20	Connecticut	Sailor	1730	Kittery, Me.	Nov. 28, 1785	55
Williams, William	26	Connecticut	Statesman	Apr. 8, 1731	Lebanon, Conn.	Aug. 2, 1811	81
Wilson, James	42	Pennsylvania	Lawyer	1742	St. Andrews, Scot.	Aug. 28, 1798	56
Witherspoon, John	21	New Jersey	Minister	Feb. 5, 1722	Yester, Scot.	Nov. 15, 1794	73
Wolcott, Oliver	25	Connecticut	Physician	Nov. 26, 1726	Windsor, Conn.	Dec. 1, 1797	72
Wythe, George	45	Virginia	Lawyer	1726	Elizabeth Co., Va.	June 8, 1806	80

* Order in which they signed. † Age at death.

Position of the Center of Population.

Years.	North Latitude.	West Longitude.	Approximate Location by Important Towns.	Westward Movement During Preceding Decade.
1790	39° 16.5′	76° 11.2′	23 miles east of Baltimore, Md	
1800	39 16.1	75 56.5	18 miles west of Baltimore, Md	41 miles.
1810	39 11.5	77 37.2	40 miles northwest by west of Washington, D. C.	36 "
1820	39 5.7	78 33 0	16 miles north of Woodstock, Va	50 "
1830	38 57.9	79 16.9	19 miles west-southwest of Moorefield, W. Va	39 "
1840	39 2.0	80 18.0	16 miles south of Clarksburg, W. Va	55 "
1850	38 59.0	81 19 0	23 miles southeast of Parkersburg, W. Va	55 "
1860	39 0.4	82 48.8	20 miles south of Chillicothe, Ohio	81 "
1870	39 12.0	83 35.7	48 miles east by north of Cincinnati, Ohio	42 "
1880	39 4.1	84 39.7	8 miles west by south of Cincinnati, Ohio	58 "
1890	39 11.9	85 32.9	20 miles east of Columbus, Ind	48 "
1900	39 9.5	85 48.9	6 miles southeast of Columbus, Ind	14 "

THE ARMY DURING THE CIVIL WAR.

The following table shows the dates of the President's proclamations for men, the number of men called for, and the number secured.

Date of President's Proclamation.	Number Called for.	Period of Service.	Number Obtained.
April 15, 1861	75,000	3 months	93,326
May 3, 1861	82,748	3 years	714,231
July 22 and 25, 1861	500,000		
May and June, 1862		3 months	15,007
July 2, 1862	300,000	3 years	431,958
August 4, 1862	300,000	9 months	87,588
June 15, 1863	100,000	6 months	16,361
October 17, 1863	300,000	2 years	374,807
February 1, 1864	200,000		
March 14, 1864	200,000	3 years	284,021
April 23, 1864	85,000	100 days	83,652
July 18, 1864	500,000	1, 2, 3 years	384,882
December 19, 1864	300,000	1, 2, 3 years	204,568
Total	2,942,748		2,690,401

NUMBER OF MEN IN THE UNION ARMY FURNISHED BY EACH STATE AND TERRITORY, FROM APRIL 15, 1861, TO CLOSE OF WAR.

States and Territories.	Number of Men Furnished.	Aggregate Reduced to a Three Years' Standing.
Alabama	2,556	1,611
Arkansas	8,289	7,836
California	15,725	15,725
Colorado	4,903	3,697
Connecticut	55,864	50,623
Delaware	12,284	10,322
Florida	1,290	1,290
Georgia	....	....
Illinois	259,092	214,133
Indiana	196,363	153,576
Iowa	76,242	68,630
Kansas	20,149	18,706
Kentucky	75,760	70,832
Louisiana	5,224	4,654
Maine	70,107	56,776
Maryland	46,638	41,275
Massachusetts	146,730	124,104
Michigan	87,364	80,111
Minnesota	24,020	19,693
Mississippi	545	545
Missouri	109,111	86,530
Nebraska	3,157	2,175
Nevada	1,080	1,080
New Hampshire	33,937	30,849
New Jersey	76,814	57,908
New York	448,850	392,270
North Carolina	3,156	3,156
Ohio	313,180	240,514
Oregon	1,810	1,773
Pennsylvania	337,936	265,517
Rhode Island	23,236	17,866
South Carolina	....	....
Tennessee	31,092	26,394
Texas	1,965	1,632
Vermont	33,288	29,068
Virginia	....	....
West Virginia	32,068	27,714
Wisconsin	91,327	79,260
Dakota	206	206
District of Columbia	16,534	1,506
Indian Territory	3,530	3,530
Montana	....	....
New Mexico	6,561	4,432
Utah	....	....
Washington	964	964
U. S. Army	....	....
U. S. Volunteers	....	....
U. S. Colored Troops	93,441	91,789
Total	2,778,304	2,326,168

The number of casualties in the volunteer and regular armies of the United States, during the war of 1861-'65, according to a statement prepared by the Adjutant-General's office, was as follows: Killed in battle, 67,058; died of wounds, 43,012; died of disease, 199,720; other causes, such as accidents, murder, Confederate prisons, etc., 40,154; total died, 349,944; total deserted, 199,105. Number of soldiers in the Confederate service who died of wounds or disease (partial statement), 133,821. Deserted (partial statement), 104,428. Number of United States troops captured during the war, 212,608; Confederate troops captured, 476,169. Number of United States troops paroled on the field, 16,431; Confederate troops paroled on the field, 248,599. Number of United States troops who died while prisoners, 30,156; Confederate troops who died while prisoners, 30,152.

The Strength of the Federal Army.

Date.	On Duty.	Absent.	Total.
January 1, 1861	14,663	1,704	16,367
July 1, 1861	183,588	3,163	186,751
January 1, 1862	527,204	48,714	575,917
January 1, 1863	698,802	219,389	918,181
January 1, 1864	611,250	249,487	860,737
January 1, 1865	620,924	338.536	959,460
May 1, 1865	797,807	202,709	1,000,516

The Union losses at Bull Run (first Manassas), July 21, 1861, were: Killed, 470, wounded, 1,071; captured and missing, 1,793; aggregate, 3,334.

The Confederate losses in particular engagements were as follows: Bull Run (first Manassas), July 21, 1861, killed, 387; wounded, 1,582; captured and missing, 13; aggregate, 1,982. Fort Donelson, Tenn., February 14-16, 1862, killed, 466; wounded, 1,534; captured and missing, 13,829; aggregate, 15,829. Shiloh, Tenn., April 6-7, 1862, killed, 1,723; wounded, 8,012; captured and missing, 959; aggregate, 10,694. Seven Days' Battle, Virginia, June 25-July 1, 1862, killed, 3,478; wounded, 16,261; captured and missing, 875; aggregate, 20,614. Second Manassas, August 21-September 2, 1862, killed, 1,481; wounded and missing, 7,627; captured and missing, 89; aggregate, 9,197. Antietam campaign, September 12-20, 1862, killed, 1,886; wounded, 9,348; captured and missing, 1,367; aggregate, 12,601. Fredericksburg, December 13, 1862, killed, 596; wounded, 4,068; captured and missing, 651; aggregate, 5,315. Stone River, Tenn., December 31, 1862, killed, 1,294; wounded, 7,945; captured and missing, 1,027; aggregate, 10,266. Chancellorsville, May 1-4, 1863, killed, 1,665; wounded, 9,081; captured and missing, 2,018; aggregate, 12,764. Gettysburg, July 1-3, 1863, killed, 2,592; wounded, 12,706; captured and missing, 5,150; aggregate, 20,448. Chickamauga, September 19-20, 1863; killed, 2,268; wounded, 13,613; captured and missing, 1,090; aggregate, 16,971.

"Gettysburg was the greatest battle of the war; Antietam the bloodiest. The largest army was assembled by the Confederates at the seven days' fight; by the Unionists at the Wilderness."

THE GREAT BATTLES OF THE CIVIL WAR.

As to the loss in the Union armies, the greatest battles in the war were:—

DATE.	BATTLE.	Killed.	Wounded.*	Missing.	Aggregate.
July 1-3, 1863	Gettysburg	3,070	14,497	5,434	23,001
May 8-18, 1864	Spottsylvania	2,725	13,413	2,258	18,396
May 5-7, 1864	Wilderness	2,246	12,037	3,383	17,666
September 17, 1862	Antietam †	2,108	9,549	753	12,410
May 1-3, 1863	Chancellorsville	1,606	9,762	5,919	17,287
September 19, 20, 1863	Chickamauga	1,656	9,749	4,774	16,179
June 1-4, 1864	Cold Harbor	1,844	9,077	1,816	12,737
December 11-14, 1862	Fredericksburg	1,284	9,600	1,769	12,653
August 28-30, 1862	Manassas‡	1,747	8,452	4,263	14,462
April 6-7, 1862	Shiloh	1,754	8,408	2,885	13,047
December 31, 1862	Stone River§	1,730	7,802	3,717	13,249
June 15-19, 1864	Petersburg (assault)	1,688	8,513	1,185	11,386

* Wounded in these and the following returns includes mortally wounded.
† Not including South Mountain or Crampton's Gap.
‡ Including Chantilly, Rappahannock, Bristol Station, and Bull Run Bridge.
§ Including Knob Gap and losses on January 1 and 2, 1863.

Secession and Readmission of Confederate States.

	Seceded.	Readmitted.
South Carolina	Dec. 20, 1860	June 11, 1868
Mississippi	Jan. 9, 1861	Feb. 3, 1870
Alabama	Jan. 11, 1861	June 11, 1868
Florida	Jan. 11, 1861	June 11, 1868
Georgia	Jan. 19, 1861	April 20, 1870
Louisiana	Jan, 26, 1861	June 11, 1868
Texas	Feb. 1, 1861	Mar. 15, 1870
Virginia	April 16, 1861	Jan. 15, 1870
Arkansas	May 6, 1861	June 20, 1868
North Carolina	May 21, 1861	June 11, 1868
Tennessee	June 24, 1861	July, 1866

The whole number of men obtained by draft was 168,649. The whole number of colored troops obtained was 186,097. The greatest number in active service in the army at any one time was 797,807.

The Diplomatic Service.—The diplomatic service of the United States, all of which is in charge of the Secretary of State, consists of Envoys Extraordinary and Ministers Plenipotentiary, Ministers Resident, Charges d'Affaires, Consuls-General, Consuls and Commercial Agents.

The highest class of ministers are those sent to France, Germany, Great Britain, and Russia; they are paid $17,500 per year. The second class ($12,000 a year) are sent to Austria, Hungary, Brazil, China, Italy, Japan, Mexico, and Spain. The third class ($10,000 a year) go to Chile, Peru, and the Central American States. Ministers Resident receive $7,500 (with the exception of the one in Bolivia, $5,000, and the one in Liberia, $4,000), and are in the Argentine Republic, Belgium, Colombia, Hawaiian Islands, Hayti, the Netherlands, Sweden and Norway, Turkey and Venezuela. Charges d'Affaires have $5,000 a year, and are in Denmark, Portugal, Switzerland, Uruguay, and Paraguay. There are five Consuls-General in British dominions, at Calcutta, Melbourne, London, Halifax, and Montreal; two in Germany, at Berlin and Frankfort; two in Turkey, at Cairo and Constantinople; and one each in Paris, Vienna, Rome, St. Petersburg, Bucharest, Bangkok, Shanghai, Kanagawa, and Mexico. Their salaries range from $2,000 to $6,000. There are the following ranks of consulates: Five at $6,000 a year; two at $5,000; one at $4,500; six at $4,000; eight at $3,500; twenty-one at $3,000; sixteen at $2,500; thirty-seven at $2,000; forty-seven at $1,500; and twenty at $1,000. All consuls receiving a fixed salary pay into the treasury all fees received by virtue of their office. But there are many consuls and agents whose only compensation comes from fees. Such officers are usually allowed to go into business.

Mason and Dixon's Line.— A name given to the southern boundary line of the free state of Pennsylvania which formerly separated it from the slave states of Maryland and Virginia. It was run — with the exception of about twenty-two miles — by Charles Mason and Jeremiah Dixon, two English mathematicians and surveyors, between Nov. 15, 1763, and Dec. 26, 1767. During the excited debate in Congress, in 1820, on the question of excluding slavery from Missouri, the eccentric John Randolph of Roanoke made great use of this phrase, which was caught up and re-echoed by every newspaper in the land, and thus gained a celebrity which it still retains.

Famous Giants and Dwarfs.— The most noted giants of ancient and modern times are as follows: —

Name.	Place.	Height, Feet.	Period.
Goliath	Palestine	11.0	B. C. 1063.
Galbara	Rome	9.9	Claudius Cæsar.
John Middleton	England	9.3	A. D. 1578.
Frederick's Swede	Sweden	8.4	....
Cujanus	Finland	7.9	....
Gilly	Tyrol	8.1	....
Patrick Cotter	Cork	8.7	1806.
Chang Gow	Pekin	7.8	1880.

Many of the great men of history have been rather small in stature. Napoleon was only about 5 ft. 4 in., while Grant was 5 ft. 7 in. One of the greatest of American statesmen, Alexander H. Stephens, never excelled 115 pounds in weight, and in his old age his weight was less than 100 pounds.

The more notable human mites are named below: —

Name.	Height, Inches.	Date of Birth.	Place of Birth.
Count Borowlaski	39	1739	Warsaw.
Tom Thumb (Chas. S. Stratton)	31	1837	New York.
Mrs. Tom Thumb	32	1842	New York.
Che-Mah	25	1838	China.
Lucia Zarate	20	1863	Mexico.
General Mite	21	1864	New York.

Summer Heat in Various Countries. — The following figures show the extreme summer heat in the various countries of the world: Bengal and the African desert, 150° Fahrenheit; Senegal and Guadaloupe, 130°; Persia, 125°; Calcutta and Central America, 120°; Afghanistan and the Arabian desert, 110°; Cape of Good Hope and Utah, 105°; Greece, 104°; Arabia, 103; Montreal, 103°; New York, 102°; Spain, India, China, Jamaica, 100°; Sierra Leone, 94°; France, Denmark, St. Petersburg, Shanghai, the Burman Empire, Buenos Ayres, and the Sandwich Islands, 90°; Great Britain, Siam, and Peru, 85°; Portugal, Pekin, and Natal, 80°; Siberia, 77°; Australia and Scotland, 75°; Italy, Venezuela, and Madeira, 73°; Prussia and New Zealand, 70°; Switzerland and Hungary, 66°; Bavaria, Sweden, Tasmania, and Moscow, 65°; Patagonia and the Falkland Isles, 55°; Iceland, 45°; Nova Zembla, 34°.

Curious Misnomers.— Arabic figures were not invented by the Arabs, but the early scholars of India.

Cleopatra's needles were not erected by that queen, neither do they commemorate any event in her history. They were set up by Rameses the Great.

The Jerusalem artichoke has no connection whatever with the holy city of the Jews. It is a species of sunflower, and gets its name from girasole, one of the scientific names of that genus of plants.

The word "pen" means a feather, and is from the Latin penna, a wing. Surely the expression "a steel pen" could be improved upon.

Galvanized iron is not galvanized at all, but is coated with zinc by being plunged into a bath of that metal and muriatic acid.

Pompey's pillar at Alexandria was neither erected by Pompey nor to his memory.

Common salt is not a salt and has long since been excluded from the class of bodies denominated "salts."

Rice paper is not made from either rice or straw, but from a pithy plant called tungtsua, found in China, Corea, and Japan.

Brazil grass neither comes from nor grows in Brazil. It is strips from a species of Cuban palm.

Rare United States Coins and their Value.— The rarest of the Half-cents are as follows: 1793 valued at $1: 1796 valued at $10; 1831, 1836, 1840 to 1849, and 1852, valued at $4.

The rarest of the Cents are as follows: 1793 with wreath is valued at $2.50; 1793 with chain valued at $3.50; 1793 with liberty cap, valued at $4; 1799 valued at $25; 1804 valued at $200; 1809 valued at $1.

The rarest of the Silver Dollars are as follows: 1794 valued at $35; 1798, with small eagle, valued at $2; 1799, with five stars facing, valued at $2; 1804 valued at $800; 1836 valued at $5; 1838 valued at $25; 1839 valued at $15; 1851 valued at $20; 1852 valued at $25; 1854 valued at $6; 1855 valued at $5; 1856 valued at $2; 1858 valued at $20.

The rarest of the Silver Half Dollars are as follows: 1794 valued at $5; 1796 valued at $40; 1797 valued at $30; 1801 valued at $2; 1802 valued at $2; 1815 valued at $4; 1836 reeded, valued at $3; 1838 Orleans, valued at $5; 1852 valued at $3; 1853, no arrows, valued at $15.

The rarest of the Silver Quarter Dollars are as follows: 1796 valued at $3; 1804 valued at $3; 1823 valued at $50; 1853, no arrows, valued at $4.

The rarest of the Silver Twenty-cent pieces

are as follows: 1874 proof, valued at $10; 1877 proof, valued at $2; 1878 proof, valued at $2.

The rarest of the Silver Dimes, or Ten-cent pieces, are as follows: 1796 valued at $3; 1797, 16 stars, valued at $4; 1797, 13 stars, valued at $4.50; 1798 valued at $2; 1800 valued at $4; 1801 to 1804, each valued at $3; 1804 valued at $5; 1805 to 1811, each valued at 50 cents; 1811 valued at 75 cents; 1822 valued at $3; 1846 valued at $1.

The rarest of the Silver Half-Dimes, or Five-cent pieces, are as follows: 1794 valued at $3; 1795 valued at 75 cents; 1796 and 1797 valued at $2 each; 1800 valued at 75 cents; 1801 valued at $1.50; 1802 valued at $50; 1803 valued at $1.50; 1805 valued at $3; 1846 valued at $1.

The rarest of the Silver Three-cent pieces are as follows: 1851 to 1855 valued at 15 cents each; 1855 valued at 25 cents; 1856 to 1862 valued at 15 cents each; 1863 to 1873 valued at 50 cents each.

Feminine Height and Weight.— It is often asked how heavy a woman ought to be in proportion to her height. A very young girl may becomingly be thinner than a matron, but the following table gives a fair indication of proper proportions: —

	Pounds.		Pounds.
Five ft. in height, about	100	Five ft. seven in., about	150
Five ft. one inch "	106	Five ft. eight in. "	155
Five ft. two inches "	113	Five ft. nine in. "	163
Five ft. three in. "	119	Five ft. ten inches "	169
Five ft. four in. "	130	Five ft. eleven in. "	176
Five ft. five inches "	138	Six feet "	180
Five ft. six inches "	144	Six feet one inch "	186

Great Financial Panics.— The most remarkable crises since the beginning of the present century have been as follows: 1814, England, two hundred and forty banks suspended; 1825, Manchester, failures two millions; 1831, Calcutta, failures fifteen millions; 1837, United States, "Wild-cat" crisis, all banks closed; 1839, Bank of England saved by Bank of France; severe also in France, where ninety-three companies failed for six millions; 1844, England, state loans to merchants, Bank of England reformed; 1847, England, failures twenty millions, discount thirteen per cent.; 1857, United States, 7,200 houses failed for one hundred and eleven millions; 1866, London, Overend-Gurney crisis, failures exceeded one hundred millions; 1869, Black Friday in New York (Wall street), September 24.

Yankee-Doodle.— The air known as "Yankee-Doodle" was originally "Nankee-Doodle," and is as old as the time of Cromwell. It was known in New England before the Revolution, and is said to have been played by the English troops in derisive allusion to the then popular nickname of the New Englanders; and afterwards the New Englanders, saying that the British troops had been made to dance to "Yankee-Doodle," adopted the air.

Yankee, Origin of the Name.— The theories which have been advanced as to the origin of this name are numerous. According to Thierny it was a corruption of Jankin, a diminutive of John, which was a nickname given by the Dutch colonists of New York to their neighbors in the Connecticut settlements. In a history of the American war, written by Dr. William Gordon, and published in 1789, was another theory. Dr. Gordon said that it was a cant word in Cambridge, Mass., as early as 1713, used to denote especial excellence — as a Yankee good horse, Yankee good cider, etc. He supposed that it was originally a byword in the college, and, being taken by the students into parts of the country, gradually obtained general currency in New England, and at length came to be taken up in other parts of the country, and applied to New Englanders as a term of slight reproach. Aubury, an English writer, says that it is derived from a Cherokee word — *eankke* — which signifies coward and slave. This epithet was bestowed on the inhabitants of New England by the Virginians for not assisting them in a war with the Cherokees. The most probable theory, however, is that advanced by Mr. Heckewelder, that the Indians, in endeavoring to pronounce the word English, or Anglais, made it Yengees, or Yangees, and this originated the term.

The World's Fairs.

Where Held.	Year.	Area Covered. (Acres.)	Exhibitors.	Visitors.	Days Open.	Receipts.
London	1851	21	13,937	6,039,195	141	$1,780,000
Paris	1855	24½	20,839	5,162,330	200	644,100
London	1862	23½	28,653	6,211,103	171	1,614,260
Paris	1867	37	50,226	8,805,969	217	2,103,675
Vienna	1873	40	50,000	6,740,500	186	1,032,385
Philadelphia	1876	60	30,864	10,164,489	159	3,813,724
Paris	1878	60	40,366	16,032,725	194	2,531,650
Sydney	1879	26	9,345	1,117,536	210	200,000
Melbourne	1880	....	....	1,330,279	210	....
Fisheries Exhibition, London	1883	9	3,000	2,703,051	147	585,000
Health Exhibition, London	1884	....	....	4,153,390	151	892,545
Inventions Exhibition, London	1885	....	....	3,760,581	163	750,000
Colonial and Indian, London	1886	13	....	5,550,745	164	1,025,000
Glasgow	1888	....	....	5,748,379	161	566,330
Paris	1889	75½	55,000	28,149,353	185	8,300,000
Chicago	1893	633	....	27,539,521	184	14,000,000
Paris	1900	549	75,531	50,000,000	212	....
Buffalo	1901	Notable on account of its display of electrical power and contrivances.				
St. Louis	1904	The largest in extent of exhibits, buildings, and general equipment in history.				

The Average Velocities of Various Bodies.— A man walks 3 miles per hour or 4 feet per second. A horse trots 7 miles per hour or 10 feet per second. A horse runs 20 miles per hour or 29 feet per second. Steamboat runs 20 miles per hour or 26 feet per second. Sailing vessel runs 10 miles per hour or 14 feet per second. Rapid rivers flow 3 miles per hour or 4 feet per second. A moderate wind blows 7 miles per hour or 10 feet per second. A storm moves 36 miles per hour or 52 feet per second. A hurricane moves 80 miles per hour or 117 feet per second. A rifle ball moves 1,000 miles per hour or 1,466 feet per second. Sound, 743 miles per hour or 1,142 feet per second. Light, 192,000 miles per second. Electricity, 288,000 miles per second.

Table of the Principal Alloys.—A combination of copper and tin makes bath metal.

A combination of copper and zinc makes bell metal.

A combination of tin and copper makes bronze metal.

A combination of tin, antimony, copper, and bismuth makes britannia metal.

A combination of tin and copper makes cannon metal.

A combination of copper and zinc makes Dutch gold.

A combination of copper, nickel, and zinc, with sometimes a little iron and tin, makes German silver.

A combination of gold and copper makes standard gold.

A combination of gold, copper, and silver makes old standard gold.

A combination of tin and copper makes gun metal.

A combination of copper and zinc makes mosaic gold.

A combination of tin and lead makes pewter.

A combination of lead and a little arsenic makes sheet metal.

A combination of silver and copper makes standard silver.

A combination of tin and lead makes solder.

A combination of lead and antimony makes type metal.

A combination of copper and arsenic makes white copper.

How to Mix Printing Inks and Paints in the Preparation of Tints. — The first named color always predominates.

Mixing dark green and purple makes bottle green.

Mixing white and medium yellow makes buff tint.

Mixing red, black, and blue makes dark brown.

Mixing bronze, blue, lemon yellow, and black makes dark green.

Mixing, white, medium yellow, and black makes drab tint.

Mixing white, lake, and lemon yellow makes flesh tint.

Mixing lemon yellow and bronze blue makes grass green.

Mixing white and black makes gray tint.

Mixing white and purple makes lavender tint.

Mixing red, black, and medium yellow makes maroon.

Mixing lake and purple makes magenta.

Mixing medium yellow and purple makes olive green.

Mixing medium yellow and red makes orange.

Mixing white, ultramarine blue, and black makes pearl tint.

Mixing white and lake makes pink.

Mixing ultramarine blue and lake makes purple.

Mixing orange, lake, and purple makes russet.

Mixing medium yellow, red, and white makes sienna.

Mixing white and ultramarine blue makes sky blue.

Mixing ultramarine blue, black, and white makes slate.

Mixing vermilion and black makes Turkey red.

Mixing white, yellow, red, and black makes umber.

Durability of Different Woods.— Experiments have been lately made by driving sticks, made of different woods, each two feet long and one and one half inches square, into the ground, only one half an inch projecting outward. It was found that in five years all those made of oak, elm, ash, fir, soft mahogany, and nearly every variety of pine, were totally rotten. Larch, hard pine, and teak wood were decayed on the outside only, while acacia, with the exception of being also slightly attacked on the exterior, was otherwise sound. Hard mahogany and cedar of Lebanon were in tolerably good condition; but only Virginia cedar was found as good as when put in the ground. This is of some importance to builders, showing what woods should be avoided, and what others used by preference in underground work.

The durability of wood when kept dry is very great, as beams still exist which are known to be nearly 1,100 years old. Piles driven by the Romans prior to the Christian era have been examined of late, and found to be perfectly sound after an immersion of nearly 2,000 years.

The wood of some tools will last longer than the metals, as in spades, hoes, and plows. In other tools the wood is first gone, as in wagons, wheelbarrows, and machines. Such wood should be painted or oiled; the paint not only looks well, but preserves the wood; petroleum oil is as good as any other.

Hard wood stumps decay in five or six years; spruce stumps decay in about the same time; hemlock stumps in eight to nine years; cedar, eight to nine years; pine stumps, never.

Cedar, oak, yellow pine, and chestnut are the most durable woods in dry places.

Timber intended for posts is rendered almost proof against rot by thorough seasoning, charring, and immersion in hot coal tar.

Time in Which Money Doubles.

Per Cent.	Simple Interest.	Comp. Interest.	Per Cent.	Simple Interest.	Comp. Interest.
2	50 years	35 years	5	20 years	14 yrs 75 da
2½	40 years	28 yrs 26 da	6	16 yrs 8 mo	11 yrs 327 da
3	33 yrs 4 mo	23 yrs 164 da	7	14 yrs 104 da	10 yrs 89 da
3½	28 yrs 208 da	20 yrs 54 da	8	12½ years	9 yrs 2 days
4	25 years	17 yrs 246 da	9	11 yrs 40 da	8 yrs 16 da
4½	22 yrs 81 da	15 yrs 273 da	10	10 years	7 yrs 100 da

"A Dollar Saved, a Dollar Earned." —The way to accumulate money is to save small sums with regularity. A small sum saved daily for fifty years will grow at the following rate:—

Daily Savings.	Result.	Daily Savings.	Result.
One cent	$950	Sixty cents	$57,024
Ten cents	9,504	Seventy cents	66,528
Twenty cents	19,006	Eighty cents	76,032
Thirty cents	28,512	Ninety cents	85,537
Forty cents	38,015	One dollar	95,208
Fifty cents	47,520		

Pecuniary Value of Metals.— Few people have any idea of the value of precious metals other than gold, silver, and copper, which are commonly supposed to be the most precious of all. There are many metals more valuable and infinitely rarer. The following table gives the names and prices of all the known metals of pecuniary worth:—

	Price, Av. Pound		Price, Av. Pound
Gallium	$68,600.00	Tellurium	$490.00
Vanadium	10 780.00	Chromium	490.00
Rubidium	9,800.00	Gold	300.00
Thorium	8,330.00	Molybdenum	245.00
Glucinium	5,800.00	Platinum	144.00
Calcium	4,900.00	Thallium	122.50
Lanthanum	4,900.00	Iridium	112.00
Lithium	4,900.00	Tungsten	36.00
Indium	4,410.00	Potassium	28.00
Tantalum	4,410.00	Selenium	18.80
Yttrium	4,410.00	Cobalt	8.00
Didymium	4,410.00	Magnesium	4.50
Strontium	4,200.00	Bismuth	2.75
Arium	3,675.00	Sodium	2.50
Erbium	3,675.00	Cadmium	1.30
Ruthenium	2,695.00	Manganese	1.10
Niobium	2,450.00	Arsenic	.40
Rhodium	2,450.00	Aluminium	.34
Barium	1,960.00	Tin	.25
Titanium	1,102.00	Copper	.25
Zirconium	1,040.00	Antimony	.16
Osmium	1,040.00	Zinc	.11
Uranium	980.00	Lead	.08
Palladium	560.00		

VALUE OF METALS AS CONDUCTORS.

	Heat.	Electricity.		Heat.	Electricity.
Gold	100	94	Iron	37	16
Platinum	98	16	Zinc	36	29
Silver	97	74	Tin	30	15
Copper	90	100	Lead	18	8

TENACITY OF METALS.

A wire, 0.84 of a line in diameter, will sustain weights as follows:—

Lead	28 lbs.	Silver	187 lbs.
Tin	35 "	Platinum	274 "
Zinc	119 "	Copper	302 "
Gold	150 "	Iron	549 "

FLUID DENSITY OF METALS.

Zinc	6.48	Copper	8.22
Iron	6.88	Silver	9.51
Tin	7.03	Lead	10.37

Mode of Execution in Every Country.

Country.	Mode.	Publicity.
Austria	Gallows	Public.
Bavaria	Guillotine	Private.
Belgium	Guillotine	Public.
Brunswick	Ax	Private.
China	Sword or cord	Public.
Denmark	Guillotine	Public.
Ecuador	Musket	Public.
France	Guillotine	Public.
Great Britain	Gallows	Private.
Hanover	Guillotine	Private.
Italy	Sword or gallows*	Public.
Netherlands	Gallows	Public.
Oldenberg	Musket	Public.
Portugal	Gallows	Public.
Prussia	Sword	Private.
Russia	Musket, gallows, or sword	Public.
Saxony	Guillotine	Private.
Spain	Garrote	Public.
Switzerland—		
Fifteen cantons	Sword	Public.
Two cantons	Guillotine	Public.
Two cantons	Guillotine	Private.
United States (other than N. Y., Ohio and Massachusetts)	Gallows	Mostly Private.
N.Y., Ohio, and Mass	**Electricity**	**Private.**

* Capital punishment abolished in 1876.

Great Fires and Conflagrations.— London, September 2-6, 1666.— Eighty-nine churches, many public buildings, and 13,200 houses destroyed; 400 streets laid waste, 200,000 persons homeless. The ruins covered 436 acres.

New York, Dec. 16, 1835.— 600 buildings; loss, $20,000,000. Sep. 6, 1839.—$10,000,000 worth of property.

Pittsburg, April 10, 1845.— 1,000 buildings; loss, $6,000,000.

Philadelphia, July 9, 1850.— 350 buildings; loss, $1,500,000; 25 persons killed; 9 drowned; 120 wounded.

St. Louis, May 4, 1851.— Large portion of the city burned; loss, $15,000,000.

San Francisco, May 3-5, 1851.—2,500 buildings; loss, $3,500,000; many lives lost. June 22, 1851.— 500 buildings; loss, $3,000,000.

Santiago (Spain), Dec. 8, 1863.— A fire in the church of the Campania, beginning amid combustible ornaments; 2,000 persons killed, mostly women.

Charleston, S. C., Feb. 17, 1865.— Almost

totally destroyed, with large quantities of naval and military stores.

Richmond, Va., April 2 and 3, 1865.—In great part destroyed by fire at time of Confederate evacuation.

Portland, Me., July 4, 1866.— Almost entirely destroyed; loss, $15,000,000.

Chicago, Oct. 8 and 9, 1871.—Three and one half square miles laid waste; 17,450 buildings destroyed; 200 persons killed; 98,500 made homeless. July 14, 1874.— Another great fire; loss, $4,000,000.

Great forest fires in Michigan and Wisconsin, Oct. 8–14, 1871.— 2,000 lives lost.

Boston, Nov. 9–11, 1872.— 800 buildings; loss, $73,000,000; 15 killed.

Fall River, Mass., Sept. 19, 1874.— Great factory fires; 60 persons killed.

St. John, N. B., June 20, 1877.— Loss, $12,500,000.

Brooklyn Theater **burned, Dec. 5, 1876.— 300 lives lost.**

Seattle and Spokane, Wash., 1889.—About $10,000,000 each.

Jacksonville, Fla., May 3, 1901.—Property loss $10,000,000.

Iroquois Theater, Chicago, Dec. 30, 1903.— Entailed a loss of 639 lives.

Baltimore, Md., Feb. 7 and 8, 1904.—More than 75 city blocks destroyed, covering 140 acres; financial loss, $85,000,000.

Rochester, N. Y., Feb. 26, 1904.—Fire in business center; loss, $2,700,000.

Toronto, Canada, April 19, 1904.—Destruction of business district causes losses of $12,000,000.

Great Floods and Inundations.—An inundation in Cheshire, England, A. D. 353. —3,000 persons perished.

Glasgow, A. D. 758.—More than 400 families drowned.

Flanders, 1108.—Inundated by the sea, and the town and harbor of Ostend completely submerged.

Dort, April 17, 1421.—72 villages submerged; 100,000 people drowned.

Overflow of the Severn, A. D. 1483, lasting ten days.—Men, women, and children carried away in their beds, and the waters covered the tops of many mountains.

General inundation in Holland, A. D. 1530.—By failure of dikes; 400,000 said to have been drowned.

At Catalonia, A. D. 1617.—50,000 drowned.

Johnstown, Pa., May 31, 1889.—By the bursting of a huge reservoir on the mountains the town was almost entirely destroyed, and about 6,000 persons perished. The water in its passage to Johnstown descended about 250 feet, with a velocity of nearly fifty miles an hour, and as it swept through the valley it cut trees away as though they were stalks of mullein.

Galveston, Tex., Sept. 8, 1900.—Greatest in the history of the country. Six thousand or more lives lost and $30,000,000 worth of property destroyed. The strong wind from the sea drove the great waves with such tremendous force that almost everything was swept before it. The effect of this terrific water storm was felt for miles into the interior.

The Great Waterfalls.— According to a recent calculation, the highest waterfalls in the world are the Yosemite Falls, California, 1,500 feet. **Krimbs Falls have a total height of 1,148 feet.** The three falls next in height are found in Scandinavia — the Verme Fuss, in Romsdal, 984 feet; the Vettis Foss, on the Sogne Fiord, 853 feet; the Rjuken Foss, in Thelemarken, 804 feet. With a decrease in height of 213 feet, the three Velino Falls, 591 feet, near Zerni (the birthplace of Tacitus), follow next in order, and they are succeeded by the three Tessa Falls, in the Val Formazza, 541 feet. The Gastein Falls, in the Gastein Valley, 469 feet, rank between the Skjaggedal Foss, in the Hardanger Fiord, 424 feet, and the Boring Foss, in the same fiord. If the width of the falls is taken into consideration, the most imposing are those of the Victoria Falls of the Zambesi, which are 391 feet high, with a width of 3,200 feet. A long way behind these falls come the Niagara Falls, 177 feet high and 1,968 feet wide.

Weight of Eggs.—The following table of the weight of eggs per pound of various breeds of fowls and the number of eggs laid in a year is approximately fair, though it may vary under exceptionally adverse or favorable conditions:—

Varieties.	Eggs per pound.	No. Eggs per year.
Light Brahmas	7	130
Dark Brahmas	8	130
Partridge Cochins	7	130
Black, White, Buff Cochins	7	120
Plymouth Rocks	8	150
Houdans	8	155
La Fleche	7	135
Creve Cœurs	8	145
Black Spanish	8	155
Leghorns	8	160
Hamburgs	9	150
Dominiques	8	135
Games	9	140
Bantams	16	90

Life Insurance.

Countries.	Insurance in Force.	Year's Premiums.	Year's Losses.	Countries.	Insurance in Force.	Year's Premiums.	Year's Losses.
United States	$14,125,548,072	$339,280,913	$165,718,804	Austria	$370,621,530	$14,613,420	$4,098,025
Great Britain	3,290,521,720	126,458,455	78,496,735	Scandinavia	128,213,755	4,365,360	1,147,995
Germany	1,320,163,685	50,313,925	16,767,830	Russia	47,925,979	1,757,681	584,707
France	695,231,550	40,351,080	10,647,060	Switzerland	70,390,250	3,025,100	1,170,225

Wars of the United States.

STATEMENT OF THE NUMBER OF UNITED STATES TROOPS ENGAGED.

Wars.	From —	To —	Regulars.	Militia and Volunteers.	Total.*
War of the Revolution	April 19, 1775	April 11, 1783	130,711	164,080	309,781
Northwestern Indian Wars	Sept. 19, 1790	Aug. 3, 1795	....	....	8,983
War with France	July 9, 1798	Sept. 30, 1800	....	....	†4,593
War with Tripoli	June 10, 1801	June 4, 1805	....	....	†3,330
Creek Indian War	July 27, 1813	Aug. 9, 1814	600	13,181	13,781
War of 1812 with Great Britain	June 18, 1812	Feb. 17, 1815	85,000	471,622	576,622
Seminole Indian War	Nov. 20, 1817	Oct. 21, 1818	1,000	6,911	7,911
Black Hawk Indian War	April 21, 1831	Sept. 31, 1832	1,339	5,126	6,465
Cherokee disturbance or removal	1836	1837	....	9,494	9,494
Creek Indian War or disturbance	May 5, 1836	Sept. 30, 1837	935	12,483	13,418
Florida Indian War	Dec. 23, 1835	Aug. 14, 1843	11,169	29,953	41,122
Aroostook disturbance	1836	1839	....	1,500	1,500
War with Mexico	April 24, 1846	July 4, 1848	30,954	73,776	112,230
Apache, Navajo, and Utah War	1849	1855	1,500	1,061	2,561
Seminole Indian War	1856	1858	....	3,687	3,687
Civil War ‡	**1861**	1865	....	....	2,772,408
Spanish-American War	April 21, 1898	Aug. 12, 1898	....	....	§274,717

* Including all branches of the service. † Naval forces engaged. ‡ The number of troops on the Confederate side was about 600,000. § Troops actually engaged about 60,000.

Percentage of Alcohol in Various Liquors.

Scotch Whisky	54.53	Currant Wine	20.50
Irish Whisky	53.9	Port	22.90
Rum	53.68	Madeira	22.27
Gin	51.6	Teneriffe	19.79
Brandy	53.39	Sherry	19.17
Burgundy	14.57	Claret	15.1
Cape Muscat	18.25	Elder	8.79
Champagne (still)	13.80	Ale	6.87
Champagne (sp'rkl'ng)	12.61	Porter	4.02
Cider	5.2 to 9.8	Malaga	17.26
Constantia	19.75	Rhenish	12.8
Gooseberry Wine	11.48	Small Beer	1.28

Quantity of Seeds Required per Acre.

Wheat	1½ to 2	bu.	Beets	3	lbs.
Rye	1½	"	Carrots	2	"
Oats	3	"	Ruta-baga	¾	"
Barley	2	"	Millet	½	bu.
Peas	2 to 3	"	Clover, white	4	qts.
White beans	1½	"	Clover, red	8	"
Buckwheat	½	"	Timothy	6	"
Corn, bro'dc'st	4	"	Orchard grass	2	bu.
Corn, in drills	2 to 3	"	Red top	1 to 2	pks.
Corn, in hills	4 to 8	qts.	Blue grass	2	bu.
Broom corn	½	bu.	Mix'd lawn gr.	1 to 2	"
Potatoes	10 to 15	"	Tobacco	2	oz.

Wood for Fuel.—In regard to the relative values of woods as heat producers, different woods vary some by different methods of experimenting. The most accurate would be their value as steam producers. The following test was made from a fire tubular horizontal boiler:—

Shellbark Hickory	100	Hard Maple	59
Pignut Hickory	95	White Elm	58
White Oak	84	Red Cedar	56
White Ash	77	Wild Cherry	55
Dogwood	75	Yellow Pine	54
Scrub Oak	73	Chestnut	52
White Hazel	72	Yellow Poplar	51
Apple Tree	70	Butternut	43
Red Oak	67	White Birch	43
White Beech	65	White Pine	30
Yellow Oak	60		

These figures are from air-dried wood. No accurate result could be obtained from green wood, as it is not in a proper condition, and would vary considerably from any figures that might be made.

Common Sizes of Flat Papers.

Name.	Size.	Name.	Size.
Flat Letter	10 x 16	Medium	18 x 23
Small Cap	13 x 16	Double Small Cap	16 x 26
Flat Cap	14 x 17	Royal	19 x 24
Demy	16 x 21	Double Cap	17 x 28
Folio	17 x 22		

Sizes of Newspapers.

Term.		Size.
Five-column	Folio	20 x 26 inches
Six-column	Folio	22 x 31 inches
Six-column	Folio, extra margin	22 x 32 inches
Seven-column	Folio	24 x 35 inches
Seven-column	Folio, extra margin	24 x 36 inches
Eight-column	Folio	26 x 40 inches
Nine-column	Folio	28 x 44 inches
Four-column	Quarto	22 x 31 inches
Five-column	Quarto	26 x 40 inches
Six-column	Quarto	30 x 44 inches
Seven-column	Quarto	35 x 48 inches

The Language of Flowers.

SINGLE FLOWERS.

Arbor Vitæ — Unchanging friendship.

Camellia, White — Loveliness.

Candytuft — Indifference.

Carnation, White — Disdain.

China Aster — Variety.

Clover, Four-Leaf — Be mine.

Clover, White — Think of me.

Clover, Red — Industry.

Columbine — Folly.

Daisy — Innocence.

Daisy, Colored — Beauty.

Dead Leaves — Sadness.

Deadly Nightshade — Falsehood.

Fern — Fascination.

Forget-me-not.

Fuchsia, Scarlet — Taste.

Geranium, Horseshoe — Stupidity.

Geranium, Scarlet — Consolation.

Geranium, Rose — Preference.

Golden-rod — Be cautious.

Heliotrope — Devotion.

Hyacinth, White — Loveliness.

Hyacinth, Purple — Sorrow.
Ivy — Friendship.
Lily, Day — Coquetry.
Lily, White — Sweetness.
Lily, Yellow — Gayety.
Lily, Water — Purity of heart; elegance.
Lily of the Valley — Unconscious sweetness.
Mignonette — Your qualities surpass your charms.
Monkshead — Danger is near.
Myrtle — Love.
Oak — Hospitality.
Orange Blossoms — Chastity.
Pansy — Thoughts.
Passion Flower — Faith.
Primrose — Inconstancy.
Rose — Love.
Rose, Damask — Beauty ever new.
Rose, Yellow — Jealousy.
Rose, White — I am worthy of you.
Rosebud, Moss — Confession of love.
Smilax — Constancy.
Straw — Agreement.
Straw, Broken — Broken agreement.
Sweet Pea — Depart.
Tuberose — Dangerous pleasures.
Thistle — Sternness.
Verbena — Pray for me.
White Jasmine — Amiability.
Witch Hazel — A spell.

IN COMBINATIONS.

Moss Rosebud, Myrtle.	A confession of love.
Mignonette, Colored Daisy.	Your qualities surpass your charms of beauty.
Lily of the Valley, Ferns.	Your unconscious sweet- ness has fascinated me.
Yellow Rose, Broken Straw, Ivy.	Your jealousy has broken our friendship.
Scarlet Geranium, Passion Flower, Purple Hyacinth, Arbor Vitæ.	I trust you will find con- solation, through faith, in your sorrow; be assured of my unchang- ing friendship.
Columbine, Day Lily, Broken Straw, Witch Hazel, Colored Daisy.	Your folly and coquetry have broken the spell of your beauty.
White Pink, Canary Grass, Laurel.	Your talent and perseverance will win you glory
Golden-rod, Monkshead, Sweet Pea, Forget-me-not.	Be cautious; danger is near; I depart soon; forget me not.

Weights and Measures.

MEASURES OF LENGTH.

	In.	*Ft.*	*Ys.*	*Pls.*	*Ch.*	*Fs.*
A Palm	3					
A Hand	4					
Foot	12					
Yard	36	3				
Rod, pole, or perch	198	16½	5½			
Chain	792	66	22	4		
Furlong	7,920	660	220	40	10	
Mile	63,360	5,280	1,760	320	80	8

PARTICULAR MEASURES OF LENGTH.

12 lines 1 inch.
3 inches 1 palm.
4 inches 1 hand.
A cubit 18 inches.
A pace, military, 2 feet 6 inches.
A pace, geometrical, 5 feet.
A fathom 6 feet.
A cable's length 240 yards.
A degree 69⅛ miles = 60 nautical knots or geographical miles.
A league 3 miles.

SQUARE OR SURFACE MEASURE.

	In.	*Ft.*	*Yds.*	*Pls.*	*Ch.*	*R.*
Square foot	144	1				
Square yard	1,296	9	1			
Rod, pole, or perch.	39,204	272¼	30¼	1		
Square chain	627,264	4,356	484	16	1	
Rood	1,568,160	10,890	1,210	40	2½	1
Acre	6,272,640	43,560	4,840	160	10	4

A square mile contains 640 acres, 2,560 roods, 6.400 chains, 102,400 rods, poles, or perches, or 3,097,600 square yards.

APOTHECARIES' WEIGHTS AND MEASURES BY WHICH MEDICINES ARE COMPOUNDED.

20 Grains	=1 Scruple ℈	= 20 grs.
3 Scruples	=1 Drachm ʒ	= 60 "
8 Drachms	=1 Ounce ℥	= 480 "
12 Ounces	=1 Pound ℔	=5750 "

Drugs are purchased by Avoirdupois Weight.

FLUID MEASURE.

		Marked.
60 Minims ♏	=1 Fluid Drachm	f ʒ
8 Drachms	=1 Ounce	f ℥
20 Ounces	=1 Pint	O
8 Pints	=1 Gallon	gal.

PARTICULAR WEIGHTS.

A Stone, Horseman's weight	= 14 lbs.
A Firkin of Butter	= 56 "
A Firkin of Soft Soap	= 64 "
A Barrel of Raisins	= 112 "
A Barrel (or pack) of Soft Soap	= 256 "
A Fodder of Lead, London and Hull	= 19½ cwt.
" " Derby	= 22½ "
" " Newcastle	= 21½ "

A Sack — Potatoes, 168 lbs.; Coals, 224 lbs.; Flour, 280 lbs.

MEASURE OF TIME.

60 Seconds	= 1 Minute.
60 Minutes	= 1 Hour.
24 Hours	= 1 Day.
7 Days	= 1 Week.
28 Days	= 1 Lunar Month.
28, 29, 30, or 31 Days	= 1 Calendar Month.
12 Calendar Months	= 1 Year.
365 Days	= 1 Common Year.
366 Days	= 1 Leap Year.

ANGULAR MEASURE.

60 Seconds.	= 1 Minute.
60 Minutes	= 1 Degree.
30 Degrees	= 1 Sign.
90 Degrees	= 1 Quadrant.
4 Quadrants, or 360°	= 1 Circumference, or Great Circle.

CUBIC OR SOLID MEASURE.

1728 Cubic Inches	= 1 Cubic Foot.
27 Cubic Feet	= 1 Cubic Yard.
40 Do. of Rough, or 50 Do. of Hewn Timber	= 1 Ton or Load.
42 Cubic Feet of Timber	= 1 Shipping Ton.
108 Cubic Feet	= 1 Stack of Wood.
128 Cubic Feet	= 1 Cord of Wood
40 Cubic Feet	= 1 Ton Shipping.

LIQUID MEASURES.

	Gals.	Qts.	Pts.
Four Gills, one Pint	...	...	1
Quart	...	1	2
Gallon	1	4	8
Firkin or Quarter Barrel	9	36	72
Kilderkin or Half Barrel	18	72	144
Barrel	36	144	288
Hogshead of Ale (1½ barrel)	54	216	432
Puncheon	72	288	576
Butt of Ale (3 barrels)	108	432	864

Practically, the only measures in use are gallons and quarts, the others are merely nominal; *e. g.*, the hogshead of 54 gallons, *old measure*, contains but 52 gallons, 1 quart, 1 pint, and 3.55 gills imperial measure, and of wine six nominal quart bottles go to the gallon. Of imported wines the following are the usual measurements: —

Pipe of Port or Masdeu	= 115	Gallons.
" Teneriffe	= 109	"
" Marsala	= 93	"
" Madeira and Cape	= 92	"
Butt of Lisbon and Bucellas	= 117	"
" Sherry and Tent	= 108	"
Aum of Hock and Rhenish	= 30	"
Hogshead of Claret	= 46	"

DRY OR CORN MEASURE.

4 Quarts	= 1 Gallon.
2 Gallons	= 1 Peck.
4 Pecks	= 1 Bushel.
3 Bushels (four of corn)	= 1 Sack.
12 Sacks	= 1 Chaldron.
8 Bushels, or two sacks	= 1 Quarter.
5 Quarters	= 1 Load.

MEASURES OF WEIGHT.—*Avoirdupois.*

27⅓ Grains	= 1 Drachm	= 27⅓ Grains.
16 Drachms	= 1 Ounce	= 437½ Grains.
16 Ounces	= 1 Pound	= 7000 Grains.
8 Pounds	= 1 Stone of Butcher's Meat.	
14 Pounds	= 1 Ordinary Stone.	
28 Pounds	= 1 Quarter (qr.).	
4 Quarters	= 1 Hundredweight (cwt.).	
20 Cwt.	= 1 Ton.	

This weight is used in almost all commercial transactions, and common dealings.

TROY WEIGHT.

3⅛ Grains	= 1 Carat.
24 Grains	= 1 Pennyweight.
20 Pennyweights	= 1 Ounce....480 grs.
12 Ounces	= 1 Pound....5760 "

HAY AND STRAW.

Truss of Straw, 36 lb.
Truss of Old Hay, 56 lb.
Truss of New Hay, 60 lb.
Load, 36 Trusses = Straw, 11 cwt. 2 qrs. 8 lb.; Old Hay, 18 cwt.; New Hay, 19 cwt. 1 qr. 4 lb.

WOOL.

		Cwt.	Qr.	Lb.
7 Pounds	= 1 Clove	0	0	7
2 Cloves	= 1 Stone	0	0	14
2 Stones	= 1 Tod	0	1	0
6½ Tods	= 1 Wey	1	2	14
12 Sacks	= 1 Last	39	0	0

Boxes of Different Measure.— A box 24 inches long by 16 inches wide, and 28 inches deep, will contain a barrel (3 bushels).

A box 24 inches long by 16 inches wide, and 14 inches deep, will contain half a barrel.

A box 16 inches square, and 8 2-5 inches deep, will contain one bushel.

A box 16 inches by 8 2-5 inches wide, and 8 inches deep, will contain half a bushel.

A box 8 inches by 8 2-5 inches square, and 8 inches deep, will contain one peck.

A box 8 inches by 8 inches square, and 4 1-5 inches deep, will contain one gallon.

A box 7 inches by 4 inches square, and 4 4-5 inches deep, will contain half a gallon.

A box 4 inches by 4 inches square, and 4 1-5 inches deep, will contain one quart.

In purchasing anthracite coal, 20 bushels are generally allowed for a ton.

The Longest Tunnels.— The Mount St. Gothard Tunnel, Italy, is 48,840 feet long, or nearly 10 miles long, and the longest in the world.

Mount Cenis Tunnel, Italy, is 39,840 feet long, or about seven and one-half miles long.

Hoosac Tunnel, Mass., is 25,080 feet long, or about 4¾ miles.

The Nochistongo Tunnel, is 21,659 feet long, or about four miles.

The Sutro Tunnel is 21,120 feet long, or four miles.

Thames and Medway, Eng., is 11,880 feet long, or about two miles.

Variations in Time.

Washington, D. C.,	12.00 m.	Madrid, Spain,	4.53 p. m.
Athens, Greece,	6.43 p. m.	Mecca, Arabia,	7.49 p. m.
Auckland, New Zealand,	4.51 a. m.	Mexico, Mexico,	10.27 a. m.
Augusta, Me.,	12.29 p. m.	New Orleans, La.,	11.08 a. m.
Austin, Texas,	10.37 a. m.	New York, N. Y.,	12.12 p. m.
Batavia, Java,	12.15 a. m.	Olympia, Washington,	8.57 a. m.
Bombay, India,	10.00 p. m.	Omaha, Neb.,	10.44 a. m.
Boston, Mass.,	12.24 p. m.	Paris, France,	5.42 p. m.
Berlin, Germany,	6.01 p. m.	Pekin, China,	12.54 a. m.
Calcutta, India,	11.01 p. m.	Philadelphia, Pa.,	12.13 p. m.
Canton, China,	12.41 a. m.	Pittsburg, Pa.,	11.48 a. m.
Charleston, S. C.,	11.49 a. m.	Rio Janeiro, Bra.,	2.16 p. m.
Chicago, Ill.,	11.18 a. m.	Rome, Italy,	5.58 p. m.
Constantinople, Turkey,	7.04 p. m.	St. Louis, Mo.,	11.07 a. m.
Copenhagen, Denmark,	5.58 p. m.	St. Petersburg, Russia,	7.09 p. m.
Denver, Col.,	10.07 a. m.	Salt Lake City, Utah,	9.40 a. m.
Dublin, Ireland,	4.43 p. m.	San Francisco, Cal.,	8.58 a. m.
Gibraltar, Spain,	4.51 p. m.	Tallahassee, Fla.,	11.30 a. m.
Glasgow, Scot.,	4.51 p. m.	Toronto, Can.,	11.51 a. m.
Halifax, N. S.,	12.54 p. m.	Valparaiso, Chile,	12.21 p. m.
Harrisburg, Pa.,	12.01 p. m.	Yeddo, Japan,	2.27 a. m.
Lima, Peru,	12.00 m.		
London, Eng.,	5.07 p. m.		

Alcoholic Liquors.—A table of the comparative consumption of alcoholic liquors was compiled by the London *Times* recently, with some interesting results. The average yearly consumption per head is given in liters (a liter is a little less than a quart): —

	Spirits. Liters.	Wine. Liters.	Beer. Liters.
Canada	3.08	0.29	8.51
Norway	3.90	1.00	15.30
United States	4.79	2.64	31.30
Great Britain and Ireland	5.37	2.09	143.92
Austria-Hungary	5.76	22.40	28.42
France	7.28	119.20	21.10
Russia	8.08	Unknown.	4.65
Sweden	8.14	0.36	11.00
German Zollverein	8.60	6.00	65.00
Belgium	9.20	3.70	169.20
Switzerland	15.30	55.00	37.50
Netherlands	9.87	2.57	27.00
Denmark	18.90	1.00	33.33

Belgium, it seems, contains the greatest number of beer drinkers, with Great Britain second in this list, and Germany, contrary to common opinion, only third. France drinks the most wine, and Switzerland comes next, while the amount accredited to the United States, though comparatively small, yet exceeds that of Great Britain. Canada is the most moderate drinker of all.

Cost of the British Royal Family.— The annuities paid by the British people to the royal family for its support are as follows: The Queen, $1,925,000; Prince of Wales, $200,000; Princess of Wales, $50,000; Dowager Empress Frederick of Germany, $40,000; Duke of Edinburgh, $50,000; Princess Christian, $30,000; Princess Louise, $30,000; Duke of Connaught, $125,000; Princess Beatrice, $30,000; Duke of Cambridge (the Queen's cousin), $60,000; Duchess of Albany, $30,000; Duchess of Mecklenburg-Strelitz (the Queen's cousin), $15,000; children of the Prince of Wales, $180,000. Total, $2,765,000. The Queen also receives the revenues of the Duchy of Lancaster. During recent years these have amounted to about $250,000 per annum. When the royal children marry, dowries are usually provided for them. The last of the Queen's children to marry, Princess Beatrice, received $150,000 as dowry from the British people by Parliamentary grant. The Duchess of Teck, the Queen's cousin, who died in 1897, enjoyed an annuity of $25,000.

Library of Congress.— The new building for the Library of Congress was provided for by an act of Congress, approved April 15, 1886. The library was opened to the public in the new building in November, eleven years later. The actual cost of the building was $6,032,124.54, or $213,443.40 less than the limit fixed by law. The book shelving is 231,680 running feet, or about 44 miles, which will accommodate 2,000,000 volumes. When completely filled, the library, without encroaching on pavilions, reading rooms, or exhibition halls, will accommodate 4,500,000 volumes, occupying a little less than 100 miles of shelving. The library embraces 800,000 printed books, in which is included the law library of 100,000 volumes. There are also 240,000 pamphlets, 25,000 original manuscripts, 60,000 graphic arts, 210,000 pieces of music, 45,000 bound volumes of newspapers and periodicals. There is also a pavilion for the blind, open daily, with a special library of books in raised letters.

Most Notable Bridges.—Brooklyn bridge was commenced, under the direction of W. A. Roebling, in 1870, and completed in about thirteen years. It is 3,475 feet long and 135 feet high. The cost of building was nearly $15,000,000.

The cantalever bridge, over the Niagara, is built almost entirely of steel. Its length is 910 feet; the total weight is 3,000 tons, and the cost was $900,000.

The Niagara suspension bridge was built by Roebling, in 1852-55, at a cost of $400,000. It is 245 feet above water, 821 feet long, and the strength is estimated at 1,200 tons.

The bridge at Havre de Grace, over the Susquehanna, is 3,271 feet long, and is divided into twelve wooden spans, resting on granite piers.

The Britannia bridge crosses the Menai strait, Wales, at an elevation of 103 feet above high water. It is of wrought iron, 1,511 feet long, and was finished in 1850. Cost, $3,008,000.

The new London bridge is constructed of granite, from the designs of L. Rennier. It was commenced in 1824, and completed in about seven years, at a cost of $7,291,000.

The old London bridge was the first stone bridge. It was commenced in 1176, and completed in 1209. Its founder, Peter of Colechurch, was buried in the crypt of the chapel erected on the center pier.

Coalbrookdale bridge, England, is the first cast iron bridge. It was built over the Severn in 1779.

The bridge at Burton, over the Trent, was formerly the longest bridge in England, being 1,545 feet. It is now partly removed. Built in the twelfth century.

The Rialto, at Venice, is said to have been built from the designs of Michael Angelo. It is a single marble arch, 98 1-2 feet long, and was completed in 1591.

The Bridge of Sighs, at Venice, over which condemned prisoners were transported from the hall of judgment to the place of execution, was built in 1589.

The Bridge of the Holy Trinity, at Florence, was built in 1569. It is 322 feet long, constructed of white marble, and stands unrivaled as a work of art.

The covered bridge at Pavia, over the Ticino, was built in the fourteenth century. The roof is held by 100 granite columns.

The St. Louis bridge, over the Mississippi, is 1,524 feet long, exclusive of approaches. There are three arched spans of cast steel, the center arch being 520 feet, with a rise of 47 1-2 feet; and the side spans 502 feet each, with a rise of 46 feet. The width on top, between rails, is 50 feet. The piers rest on the bedrock of the river, 136 feet below high water mark. Captain James B. Eads was the engineer.

Rush street bridge, Chicago, Ill., erected in 1884, at a cost of $132,000, is the largest general traffic drawbridge in the world. Its roadway will accommodate four teams abreast, and its footways are seven feet wide.

The Victoria bridge, Montreal, one of the most famous in the world, is nearly two miles in length.

The Cleveland (O.) viaduct is 3,211 feet in length, 64 feet wide, 42 feet of which is roadway; the drawbridge is 332 feet in length, 46 feet wide, and is 68 feet above ordinary stage of water.

Politics of the Presidents.— The subjoined table will be found interesting, as a reference, to many of our readers. Of course the name of Washington heading the list does not mean that he was the candidate of any party or faction, but is placed there to complete the roll: —

NAME.	INAUGURATION.	POLITICS.
George Washington,	April 30, 1789,	Unanimous.
John Adams,	March 4, 1797,	Federal.
Thomas Jefferson,	March 4, 1801,	Democrat.
James Madison,	March 4, 1809,	Democrat.
James Monroe,	March 4, 1817,	Democrat.
John Quincy Adams,	March 4, 1825,	Federal.
Andrew Jackson,	March 4, 1829,	Democrat.
Martin Van Buren,	March 4, 1837,	Democrat.
Wm. Henry Harrison,	March 4, 1841,	Whig.
John Tyler,	April 6, 1841,	Whig.
James K. Polk,	March 4, 1845,	Democrat.
Zachary Taylor,	March 5, 1849,	Whig.
Millard Fillmore,	July 9, 1850,	Whig.
Franklin Pierce,	March 4, 1853,	Democrat.
James Buchanan,	March 4, 1857,	Democrat.
Abraham Lincoln,	March 4, 1861,	Republican.
Andrew Johnson,	April 16, 1865,	Republican.
U. S. Grant,	March 4, 1869,	Republican.
R. B. Hayes,	March 5, 1877,	Republican.
James A. Garfield,	March 4, 1881,	Republican.
Chester A. Arthur,	Sept. 20, 1881,	Republican.
Grover Cleveland,	March 4, 1885,	Democrat.
Benj. Harrison,	March 4, 1889,	Republican.
Grover Cleveland,	March 4, 1893,	Democrat.
William McKinley,	March 4, 1896,	Republican.
Theodore Roosevelt,	Sept. 14, 1901,	Republican.

The President's Salary.— Most people believe that the $50,000 a year which the president gets as his salary is the sum total. This is a mistake. $36,064 is given him, in addition to his salary of $50,000, to pay the salaries of his subordinates and clerks. His private secretary is paid $3,250, his assistant private secretary, $2,250; his stenographer, $1,800; five messengers, each, $1,200; a steward, $1,800; two doorkeepers, each, $1,200; four other clerks, at good salaries; one telegraph operator, two ushers, $1,200 and $1,400; a night usher, $1,200; a watchman, $900; and a man who takes care of the fires, who receives $864 a year. In addition to this, there is given him $8,000 for incidental expenses, such as stationery, carpets, and the care of the presidential stables. And under another heading there is given him nearly $40,000 more. Of this, $12,500 is for repairs and refurnishing the White House; $2,500 is for fuel; $4,000 is for the greenhouse, $15,000 is for gas, matches, and the stable. The White House, all told, costs the country, in connection with the president, considerably over $125,000 a year.

Insanity.— It is estimated that the number of insane persons in the United States is 168,900; in Germany, 108,100; in France, 93,900; in England, 81,600; in Russia, 80,000; Italy, 44,100; Austria, 35,000; Ireland, 19,500; Scandinavia, 18,100; Spain and Portugal, 13,000; Scotland, 11,600; Belgium and Holland, 10,400; Canada, 7,300; Australia, 4,900; Switzerland, 3,100.

Causes of Insanity.— Hereditary, 24 per cent.; drink, 14 per cent.; business, 12 per cent.; loss of friends, 11 per cent.; sickness, 10 per cent.; various, 29 per cent.

The above result is the medium average arrived at on comparing the returns for the United States, England, France, and Denmark.

Height of noted cathedrals, monuments, buildings, etc.: —

	FEET.
Eiffel Tower, Paris	990
Washington Monument	555
Pyramid, Cheops, Egypt	543
Cathedral, Cologne	511
" Antwerp	476
" Strasburg	474
Tower, Utrecht	464
Steeple, St. Stephen's, Vienna	460
Pyramid, Khafras, Egypt	456
St. Martin's Church, Bavaria	456
Chimney, Port Dundas, Glasgow	454
St. Peter's, Rome	448
Notre Dame, Amiens	422
Salisbury Spire, England	406
Cathedral, Florence	380
" Cremona	372
" Freiburg	367
St. Paul's, London	365
Cathedral, Seville	360
Pyramid, Sakkarah, Egypt	356
Cathedral, Milan	355
Notre Dame, Munich	348
Invalides, Paris	347
Parliament House, London	340
Cathedral, Magdeburg	337
St. Patrick's, New York	328
St. Mark's, Venice	328
Cathedral, Bologna	321
" Norwich, England	309
"World" Building, New York	309
Statue of Liberty, New York	305
Cathedral, Chichester, England	300
" Lincoln, England	300
Capitol, Washington	300
St. James' Cathedral, Toronto	316
Trinity Church, New York	283
Cathedral, Mexico	280
" Montreal	280
Brooklyn Bridge	278
Campanile Tower, Florence	276
Masonic Temple, Chicago	265
Column, Delhi	260
Cathedral, Dantzic	250
Porcelain Tower, Nankin	248
Custom House, St. Louis	240
Canterbury Tower, England	235
Notre Dame, Paris	232
Chicago Board of Trade	230
St. Patrick's, Dublin	226
Cathedral, Glasgow	225
Bunker Hill Monument	220
Notre Dame, Montreal	220
Cathedral, Lima	220
" Reims	220
" Garden City, L. I.	219
Sts. Peter and Paul, Philadelphia	210
Washington Monument, Baltimore	210
Vendome Monument, Paris	153

Largest Cities of the Earth.

POPULATION ACCORDING TO THE LATEST OFFICIAL CENSUSES.

Cities.	Census Year.	Population.
London	1901	4,536,063
New York	1900	3,437,202
Paris	1896	2,536,834
Berlin	1900	1,884,151
Chicago	1900	1,698,575
Vienna	1901	1,635,647
Canton	est.	1,600,000
Tokio, Japan	1898	1,440,121
Philadelphia	1900	1,293,697
St. Petersburg *	1897	1,267,023
Constantinople	est.	1,125,000
Calcutta	1901	1,121,664
Peking	est.	1,000,000
Moscow	1897	988,614
Osaka	1898	821,235
Bombay	1901	770,843
Glasgow	1901	760,423
Hamburg	1900	705,738
Liverpool	1901	685,276
Buenos Ayres	1895	663,854
Warsaw	1897	638,209
St. Louis	1900	575,238
Brussels*	1899	570,844
Cairo, Egypt	1897	570,062
Boston	1900	560,892
Naples	1899	544,057
Manchester, England	1901	543,969
Amsterdam	1899	523,557
Rio de Janeiro	1890	522,651
Birmingham, England	1901	522,182
Rome	1899	512,423
Madrid	1897	512,150
Barcelona	1897	509,589
Madras	1901	509,397
Baltimore	1900	508,957
Buda-Pesth	1891	505,763
Munich	1900	499,959
Milan	1899	492,162
Melbourne	1891	490,900
Lyons	1896	466,028
Leipzig	1900	455,089
Haidarabad*	1901	446,291
Marseilles	1896	442,239
Leeds	1901	428,953
Breslau	1900	422,738
Odessa	1897	405,041
Mexico City	1900	402,000
Dresden	1900	395,349
Sydney	1891	383,390
Cleveland	1900	381,768
Sheffield	1901	380,717
Shanghai	est.	380,000
Dublin *	1901	373,179
Cologne	1900	372,229
Turin	1899	359,295
Kioto	1898	353,139
Buffalo	1900	352,387
Belfast	1901	348,965
San Francisco	1900	342,782
Bristol, England	1901	328,842
Cincinnati	1900	325,902
Pittsburg	1900	321,626
Santiago, Chile	1895	320,628
Rotterdam	1899	319,866
Alexandria	1897	319,766
Edinburgh	1901	316,479
Lodz	1897	315,209
Copenhagen	1890	312,859
Stockholm	1899	302,462
Lisbon	1890	301,206
Palermo	1899	292,799
Frankfort-on-Main	1900	288,489
New Orleans	1900	287,104
Detroit	1900	285,704
Milwaukee	1900	285,315

Cities.	Census Year.	Population.
Bucharest	1899	282,071
Antwerp	1899	282,018
Bradford	1901	279,809
Washington	1900	278,718
West Ham, England	1901	267,308
Montreal	1901	266,826
Montevideo	est.	266,000
Lucknow	1901	263,951
Nuremberg	1900	261,022
Bordeaux	1896	256,906
Riga	1897	256,197
Bangkok	est.	250,000
Teheran	est.	250,000
Kiev	1897	247,432
Newark	1900	246,070
Manila	1901	244,732
Nagoya	1898	244,145
Hull	1901	240,618
Nottingham	1901	239,753
Genoa	1899	237,486
Havana	1899	235,981
Hanover	1900	235,666
Rangoon	1901	232,326
Magdeburg	1900	229,663
Kristiania	1900	225,686
Hong Kong	1891	221,441
Salford	1901	220,956
Lille	1896	216,276
Florence	1899	216,051
Kobe, Japan	1898	215,780
Newcastle	1901	214,803
Dusseldorf	1900	213,767
Leicester	1901	211,574
Stettin	1900	210,680
Delhi	1901	208,385
Toronto	1901	207,971
Chemnitz	1900	206,584
Jersey City	1900	206,433
The Hague	1899	205,328
Valencia	1897	204,768
Louisville	1900	204,737
Benares	1901	203,095
Minneapolis	1900	202,718
Smyrna	est.	201,000
Seoul, Korea	est.	201,000
Cawnpore	1901	197,000
Yokohama	1898	193,762
Charlottenburg, Prussia	1900	189,290
Portsmouth, England	1901	189,160
Agra	1901	188,300
Konigsberg	1900	187,897
Prague	1891	184,109
Mandelay	1901	182,498
Tabriz	1881	180,000
Stuttgart	1900	176,318
Allahabad	1901	175,748
Providence	1900	175,597
Kharkov	1897	174,846
Bahia	1890	174,412
Liege	1899	171,031
Indianapolis	1900	169,164
Bolton	1901	168,205
Cardiff	1901	164,420
Kansas City, Mo	1900	163,752
Bremen	1900	163,418
St. Paul	1900	163,065
Ghent	1899	163,030
Rochester	1900	162,608
Amritsar	1901	162,548
Altona, Germany	1900	161,507
Dundee	1901	160,871
Vilna	1897	159,568
Jaipur	1901	159,550
Bangalore	1901	159,030

Cities.	Census Year.	Population.
Bologna	1899	158,975
Trieste	1891	158,344
Howrah	1901	157,847
Venice	1899	157,785
Elberfeld	1900	156,937
Halle-on-Salle	1900	156,611
Messina	1899	156,552
Tunis	est.	153,000
Strasburg	1900	150,268
Zurich	1900	150,239
Toulouse	1896	149,963
Adelaide *	1899	148,644
Ahmadabad	1891	148,412
Sunderland	1901	146,565
Seville	1897	146,205
Bagdad	est.	145,000
Aberdeen	1901	143,722
Valparaiso	1900	143,022
Dortmund	1900	142,418
Barmen	1900	141,947
Dantzig	1900	140,539
Damascus	est.	140,500
Manheim	1900	140,384
Fez, Morocco	est.	140,000
Oporto	1890	138,860
Oldham, England	1901	137,238
Saratov	1897	137,109
St. Etienne	1896	136,030
Aachen	1900	135,235
Patna	1901	135,172
Catania	1899	134,680
Croydon, England	1901	133,875
Denver	1900	133,859
Toledo	1900	131,822
Kazan	1897	131,508
Allegheny	1900	129,896
Lemberg	1891	128,419
Brunswick	1900	128,177
Colombo, Ceylon	1891	127,836
Blackburn	1901	127,527
Aleppo	est.	127,150
Goteborg	1899	126,849
Malaga	1897	125,579
Columbus	1900	125,560
Roubaix	1896	124,661
Nagpur	1901	124,599
Nantes	1896	123,902
Brighton	1901	123,478
Srinagar	1901	122,536
Heroshima	1898	122,306
Yekaterinoslav	1897	121,216
Lahore	1901	120,058
Bogota	1886	120,000
Rostov-on-Don	1897	119,889
Havre	1896	119,470
Essen, Germany	1900	118,863
Beirut	est.	118,800
Worcester	1900	118,421
Surat	1901	118,364
Bareilly	1901	117,433
Posen	1900	117,014
Meerut	1901	116,642
Karachi	1901	115,407
Willesden	1901	114,815
Rhondda	1901	113,735
Gratz	1891	113,540
Rouen	1896	113,219
Astrakhan	1897	113,001
Preston	1901	112,982
Basle	1900	112,842
Norwich	1901	111,728
Pernambuco	1890	111,556
Athens	1896	111,486
Poona *	1901	111,385
Birkenhead	1901	110,926

* With suburbs.

NOTE.—The population of Chinese cities other than Canton, Peking, and Shanghai is omitted, because reports respecting it are utterly untrustworthy. There are forty or more Chinese cities whose inhabitants are numbered by rumor at from 200,000 to 1,000,000 each, but no official censuses have ever been taken; and, setting aside consideration of the Oriental tendency to exaggeration, there is reason to believe that the estimates of population in many instances covered districts of country bearing the same names as the cities, instead of definite municipalities.

The American Indian.

From the report of the United States Bureau of Indian Affairs.

Arizona	40,189	Kansas	1,211	New York	5,334	Utah	2,115
California	11,431	Michigan	7,557	North Carolina	1,436	Washington	9,827
Colorado	995	Minnesota	8,952	North Dakota	8,276	Wisconsin	10,726
Florida	575	Montana	10,076	Oklahoma	13,926	Wyoming	1,642
Idaho	3,557	Nebraska	3,854	Oregon	4,063	Miscellaneous	849
Indian Ter	86,265	Nevada	8,321	South Dakota	19,212		
Iowa	385	New Mexico	9,480	Texas	290	Total	270,544

Of the above 98,199 wore citizen's dress and 32,846 wore a mixture of Indian and civilized clothing. Those who could read numbered 46,044 and 57,975 could carry on an ordinary conversation in English. The Indian population increased about 30,000 between 1890 and 1900.

INDIAN POPULATION IN DETAIL.

The total Indian population of the United States, exclusive of Alaska, but including 32,567 counted in the general census, being the taxed or taxable Indians, numbers 249,273. The following table gives the division of the Indians in detail: —

Indians on reservations or at school, under control of the Indian office (not taxed or taxable)	133,382
Indians incidentally under the Indian office, and self-supporting: —	
The five civilized tribes, Indians and colored—Cherokees, 29,599; Chickasaws, 7,182; Choctaws, 14,397; Creeks, 14,632; Seminoles, 2,561; total, 68,371. Total Indians, 52,065; total colored Indian citizens and claimants, 14,224; grand total	66,289
Pueblos of New Mexico	8,278
Six Nations, Saint Regis, and other Indians of New York	5,304
Eastern Cherokees of North Carolina	2,885
Indians taxed or taxable, and self-sustaining citizens, counted in the general census (98 per cent. not on reservations)	32,567
Indians under control of the War Department, prisoners of war (Apaches at Mount Vernon Barracks)	384
Indians in State or Territorial prisons	184
Total	249,273

"Uncle Sam."— The practice of calling the United States Government "Uncle Sam" is believed to have originated in the following manner: During the Revolutionary war a man named Samuel Wilson was a beef inspector at Troy, N. Y., and was very popular with the men in his employ, who always called him Uncle Sam. After the inspection of the beef, it was shipped by him to a contractor named Elbert Anderson, and was always marked "E. A. U. S." A joking workman, being asked what those letters were the abbreviations of, replied that he did not know, unless they were for Elbert Anderson and "Uncle Sam." The joke was kept up and spread, until it became common to refer to all packages marked "U. S." as belonging to "Uncle Sam."

Expectation of Life.

Age	Expectation in years.	Age.	Expectation in years.	Age.	Expectation in years.	Age.	Expectation in years.	Age.	Expectation in years.
0	28.15	20	34.22	40	26.04	60	15.45	80	5.85
1	36.78	21	33.84	41	25.61	61	14.86	81	5.50
2	38.74	22	33.46	42	25.19	62	14.26	82	5.16
3	40.01	23	33.08	43	24.77	63	13.66	83	4.87
4	40.73	24	32.70	44	24.35	64	13.05	84	4.66
5	40.88	25	32.33	45	23.92	65	12.43	85	4.57
6	40.69	26	31.93	46	23.37	66	11.96	86	4.21
7	40.47	27	31.50	47	22.83	67	11.48	87	3.90
8	40.14	28	31.08	48	22.27	68	11.01	88	3.67
9	39.72	29	30.66	49	21.72	69	10.50	89	3.56
10	39.23	30	30.25	50	21.17	70	10.06	90	3.43
11	38.64	31	29.83	51	20.61	71	9.60	91	3.32
12	38.02	32	29.43	52	20.05	72	9.14	92	3.12
13	37.41	33	29.02	53	19.49	73	8.69	93	2.40
14	36.79	34	28.62	54	18.92	74	8.25	94	1.98
15	36.17	35	28.22	55	18.35	75	7.83	95	1.62
16	35.76	36	27.78	56	17.78	76	7.40		
17	35.37	37	27.34	57	17.20	77	6.99		
18	34.98	38	26.91	58	16.63	78	6.59		
19	34.59	39	26.47	59	16.04	79	6.21		

Rubicon, the ancient name of a small stream—thought to be the modern Fiumicino—which formed the boundary between Italy and Cisalpine Gaul. It is celebrated from Cæsar's having hesitated about crossing it with his army, and initiating civil war, in the year 49 B. C. When he came to the river he paused upon the brink, but finally, saying, "The die is cast!" he spurred on his horse, and dashed into the water. Hence, "To pass the Rubicon" has become a proverbial phrase, to denote the taking of the first step in a momentous undertaking, from which one cannot or will not recede.

Illegitimacy.— The percentage of illegitimate births for various countries, as stated by Mulhall, is as follows: Austria, 12.9; Denmark, 11.2; Sweden, 10.2; Scotland, 8.9; Norway, 8.05; Germany, 8.04; France, 7.02; Belgium, 7.0; United States, 7.0; Italy, 6.8; Spain and Portugal, 5.5; Canada, 5.0; Switzerland, 4.6; Holland, 3.5; Russia, 3.1; Ireland, 2.3; Greece, 1.6.

Positivism.— The system of philosophy known as positivism, taught by Auguste Comte (1799-1857), discarding the possibility of knowing the beginning and the end of anything, concerns itself only with what lies between. It accepts neither atheism, theism, nor pantheism. It may be divided into two parts: The historic conception and the co-ordination of the sciences. The former is this: That the human mind passes through three stages, viz., the theological, the metaphysical, and the positive. In all subjects capable of experiment it passes from metaphysics to experimental verification or exact science. In regard to the co-ordination of the sciences the basis is mathematics; then follow astronomy, physics, chemistry, biology, and sociology. Take the last: The science of society is impossible without the science of life. The science of life is impossible without chemistry. Chemistry presupposes physics, physics astronomy, and astronomy mathematics.

Executive Civil List.

Department, Bureau, Office, or Commission.	Number.
Executive Office	21
Civil Service Commission	62
State Department	122
Treasury Department	15,163
War Department	14,967
Department of Justice	704
Post Office Department	8,465
Navy Department	1,252
Positions registered under Navy Department regulations	5,063
Interior Department	9,713
Pension Examining Surgeons	4,120
Department of Agriculture	2,241
Department of Labor	95
Commission of Fish and Fisheries	183
Interstate Commerce Commission	142
Smithsonian Institution	292
Library of Congress	39
Superintendent State, War, and Navy Building	25
Total Departmental Service	62,669
General Statement.	
Departmental Service	62,669
Post Office Service	104,811
Government Printing Office	2,852
Custom House Service	5,103
Internal Revenue Service	3,282
Total Executive Civil List, United States	178,717

The Defective Classes.—*The Insane.*—The total number of insane in the United States on June 1, 1890 (census of the United States), was 106,485—whites, 99,719; negroes, 6,535; Chinese, Japanese, and civilized Indians, 231. The number of insane males was 53,473, and of insane females 53,012. The total number of insane reported in 1880 was 91,959. The number of insane in each 100,000 of the population in 1890 was 387.0 for the foreign whites, 140.5 for the native whites, and 88.6 for the colored. In 1880 the corresponding figures were 398.8, 161.9, and 91.2.

The proportion of insanity was much greater among the whites than among the negroes, and very much greater among the foreign born than among the native born.

The number of insane in asylums in 1890 was 74,028—whites, 69,729; negroes, 4,299. The number of insane in asylums in each 1,000 of insane was: whites, 699; negroes, 658.

The number of insane admitted to public institutions from 1881 to 1889, inclusive, was 190,458. The number admitted to private institutions in the same period, 13,833.

Reports from thirty states to the Committee on States of the National Conference of Charities and Correction showed 102,000 insane persons in 1896. At this rate the whole United States would have 145,000 insane.

The Feeble Minded.—The total number of feeble minded in the United States on June 1, 1890, was 95,609—whites, 84,997; negroes, 10,574; males, 52,962; females, 42,647; native born whites, 75,910; foreign born whites, 9,087.

The Deaf and Dumb. The total number of deaf mutes in the United States on June 1, 1890, was 40,592—whites, 37,447; negroes, 3,115; others, 30; males, 22,429; females, 18,163; native born whites, 33,278; foreign born whites, 4,169.

The number of persons so deaf as to be unable to hear loud conversation on June 1, 1890, was 121,178, of whom 80,611 were able to speak. The latter were 49,278 males, 31,338 females, 77,308 whites, 3,308 negroes.

The Blind.—The total number of blind in the United States on June 1, 1890, was 50,568—whites, 43,351; negroes, 7,060; others, 157; males, 28,080; females, 22,488; native born whites, 34,205; foreign born whites, 9,146. The number of blind in one eye only was 93,988.

The number of insane persons in England in 1889, according to Mulhall, was 84,345, or 2,907 per million population; in Scotland, 11,954, or 2,890 per million. The number of insane in Germany in 1884 was 108,100; France, 93,900; Russia, 80,000; Austria, 44,500.

Holidays.*—The legal holidays in the United States are as follows:—

New Year's Day, January 1. In all states and territories, except Arkansas, Delaware, Georgia, Kentucky, Maine, Massachusetts, New Hampshire, North Carolina, South Carolina, and Rhode Island.

Anniversary of the Battle of New Orleans, January 8. In Louisiana.

Lincoln's Birthday, February 12. In Louisiana.

Washington's Birthday, February 22. In all states and territories except Alabama, Arkansas, Florida, Illinois, Iowa, Indiana, Kansas, Maine, Missouri, North Carolina, Ohio, Texas, Oregon, and Tennessee.

Shrove Tuesday, March 1. In Louisiana, and cities of Mobile, Montgomery, and Selma, Ala.

Anniversary of Texan Independence, March 2. In Texas.

Firemen's Anniversary, March 4. In Louisiana.

Good Friday, April 15. In Florida, Louisiana, Minnesota, and Pennsylvania.

Memorial Day, April 26. In Georgia.

*For later and revised list of holidays by states see page 229.

Battle of San Jacinto, April 21. In Texas.

Decoration Day, May 30. In Colorado, Maine, Vermont, Connecticut, Michigan, New Hampshire, New Jersey, Rhode Island, New York, Pennsylvania, and District of Columbia.

Fourth of July. In all states and territories.

General Election Day, generally on Tuesday after first Monday in November. In California, Maine, Missouri, New Jersey, New York, Oregon, South Carolina, and Wisconsin.

Thanksgiving Day, usually last Thursday in November, and Fast days whenever appointed by the president are legal holidays in all states and territories.

Christmas Day. In all the states and territories.

Labor Day, first Monday in September. All states.

Weight and Specific Gravities of Liquids.

Liquids at 32° Fahr.	Weight of one cubic foot.	Weight of one gallon.	Specific gravity.
	Pounds.	Pounds.	Water=1.
Mercury	848.7	136.0	13.596
Bromine	185.1	29.7	2.966
Sulphuric acid, max. concentration	114.9	18.4	1.84
Nitrous acid	96.8	15.5	1.55
Chloroform	95.5	15.3	1.53
Water of the Dead Sea	77.4	12.4	1.24
Nitric acid, of commerce	76.2	12.2	1.22
Acetic acid, maximum concentration	67.4	10.8	1.08
Milk	64.3	10.3	1.03
Sea water, ordinary	64.05	10.3	1.026
Pure water (distld.) at 39° 1 F.	62.425	10.0	1.000
Wine of Bordeaux	62.1	9.9	0.994
Wine of Burgundy	61.9	9.9	0.991
Linseed oil	58.7	9.4	0.94
Poppy oil	58.1	9.3	0.93
Rape seed oil	57.4	9.2	0.92
Whale oil	57.4	9.2	0.92
Olive oil	57.1	9.15	0.915
Turpentine oil	54.3	8.7	0.87
Potato oil	51.2	8.2	0 82
Petroleum	54.9	8.8	0.88
Naphtha	53.1	8.5	0.85
Ether, nitric	69.3	11.1	1.11
Ether, sulphurous	67.4	10.8	1.08
Ether, nitrous	55.6	8.9	0.89
Ether, acetic	55.6	8.9	0.89
Ether, hydrochloric	54.3	8.7	0.87
Ether, sulphuric	44.9	7.2	0.72
Alcohol, proof spirit	57.4	9.2	0.92
Alcohol, pure	49.3	7.9	0.79
Benzine	53.1	8.5	0.85
Wood spirit	49.9	8.0	0.80

The World's Seven Wonders. — The seven wonders of the world are: The Pyramids, the Colossus of Rhodes, Diana's Temple at Ephesus, the Pharos of Alexandria, the Hanging Gardens at Babylon, the Statue of the Olympian Jove, and the Mausoleum by Artemisia at Halicarnassus. The Pyramids are numerous, and space forbids anything like even a list of them. The great piles were constructed of blocks of red or syenitic granite, and of a hard calcareous stone. These blocks were of extraordinary dimensions, and their transportation to the sites of the pyramids and their adjustment in their places, indicate a surprising degree of mechanical skill. The Great Pyramid covers an area of between twelve and thirteen acres. The masonry consisted originally of 89,028,000 cubic feet, and still amounts to about 82,111,000 feet. The present vertical height is 450 feet, against 479 feet originally, and the present length of the sides is 746 feet, against 764 feet originally. The total weight of the stone is estimated at 6,316,000,000 tons. The city of Rhodes was besieged by Demetrius Poliorcetes, King of Macedon, but, aided by Ptolomy Soter, King of Egypt, the enemy were repulsed. To express their gratitude to their allies and to their tutelary deity, they erected a brazen statue to Apollo. It was 105 feet high, and hollow, with a winding staircase that ascended to the head. After standing fifty-six years, it was overthrown by an earthquake, 224 years before Christ, and lay nine centuries on the ground, and then was sold to a Jew by the Saracens, who had captured Rhodes, about the middle of the seventh century. It is said to have required nine hundred camels to remove the metal, and from this statement it has been calculated its weight was 720,000 pounds. The Temple of Diana, at Ephesus, was built at the common charge of all the Asiatic States. The chief architect was Chersiphon, and Pliny says that 220 years were employed in completing the temple, whose riches were immense. It was 425 feet long, 225 broad, and was supported by 125 columns of Parian marble (sixty feet high, each weighing 150 tons), furnished by as many kings. It was set on fire on the night of Alexander's birth by an obscure person named Erostratus, who confessed on the rack that the sole motive which prompted him was the desire to transmit his name to future ages. The temple was again built, and once more burned by the Goths in their naval invasion, A. D. 256. The colossal statue of Jupiter in the temple of Olympia, at Elis, was by Phidias. It was in gold and ivory, and sat enthroned in the temple for 800 years, and was finally destroyed by fire about A. D. 475. From the best information, it is believed that the Mausoleum at Halicarnassus was a rectangular building surrounded by an Ionic portico of thirty-six columns, and surmounted by a pyramid, rising in twenty-four steps, upon the summit of which was a colossal marble quadriga with a statue of Mausolus. The magnificent structure was erected by Artemisia, who was the sister, wife, and successor of Mausolus.

The Blarney Stone.— Blarney is a village in Ireland, in the County of Cork, about five miles from the far famed city of that name. It is chiefly celebrated as giving the name to a peculiar kind of eloquence which is said to be characteristic of the light-hearted natives of the Emerald Isle. The old castle at Blarney contains the identical stone, the kissing of which is believed to give the person peculiar skill in speech. It is one of those superstitions which can be traced back until the mind of man runneth not to the contrary.

The Coal Area of the World.— The coal area of the world is distributed as follows: —

	Sq. Miles.		Sq. Miles.
United States	192,000	Germany	1,800
British America	18,000	Belgium	518
Great Britain	12,000	Rest of Europe	100,000
Spain	4,000	China	2,000
France	2,000	Japan	5,000

Salaries Paid to Heads of Governments.— Various governments pay their chiefs as follows: The United States, $50,000 a year; Persia, $30,000,000; Russia, $10,000,000; Siam, $10,000,000; Spain, $3,900,000; Italy, $3,000,000; Great Britain, $3,000,000; Morocco, $2,500,000; Japan, $2,300,000; Egypt, $1,575,000; Germany, $1,000,000; Saxony, $700,000; Portugal, Sweden, and Brazil, each $600,000; France, $200,000; Hayti, $240,000; Switzerland, $3,000.

Train Management.—STANDARD CODE.—A train while running must display two green flags by day and two green lights by night, one on each side of the rear of the train.

After sunset, or when obscured by fog or other cause, must display headlight in front, and two red lights in rear.

Two green flags by day and two green lights by night, displayed in the places provided for that purpose on the front of an engine, denote that the train is followed by another train running on the same schedule, and entitled to the same time-table rights as the train carrying the signals.

Two white flags by day or two white lights by night, carried in the same manner, denote that the train is an extra.

A blue flag by day and a blue light by night, placed on the end of a car, denotes that car inspectors are at work under or about the car or train, and that it must not be coupled to or moved until the blue signal is removed.

Colored Flag or Lantern Signals — Torpedoes. STANDARD CODE.— Red signifies danger.

Green signifies caution, go slowly.

White signifies safety.

Green and white signifies stop at flag stations for passengers or freight.

One cap or torpedo on rail means stop immediately.

Two caps or torpedoes on rail means reduce speed immediately, and look out for danger signal.

Telescopes.— The largest refracting telescope in the world was presented by Charles T. Yerkes to the University of Chicago, in 1893. It has a lens 40 inches in diameter. The column and head of cast iron rise to a height of 43 feet, and weigh 50 tons. The tube is of steel, 64 feet long, and 52 inches in diameter at the center, tapering towards the ends. Its weight is 6 tons. The total weight of the telescope is 75 tons. Cost $250,000. The lens of the telescope at Lick Observatory is 36 inches in diameter. The largest reflector is that of Lord Ross in England, 72 inches.

Divorces in Different Countries.— In Australia divorces have never been sanctioned.

Divorces are scarcely ever known to occur in modern Greece.

In Hindostan either party, for a slight cause, may leave the other party and marry.

In the olden times the Jews had a discretionary power of divorcing their wives.

Divorces are scarcely allowed in Thibet, unless with the consent of both parties. Remarriage is forbidden.

In Cochin China the parties desiring divorce break a pair of chopsticks in the presence of witnesses, and the thing is done.

Two kinds of divorces are granted in Circassia. By the first, the parties can immediately marry again; by the second, not for a year.

Among some tribes of American Indians the sticks given witnesses of the marriage are broken as a sign of divorce.

If the wife of a Turkoman asks his permission to go out, and he says "Go," without adding, "Come back again," they are divorced.

In Siberia, if a man is dissatisfied with the most trifling acts of his wife, he tears a cap or veil from her face, and that constitutes a divorce.

In Siam the first wife may be divorced, but not sold as the others may be. She may claim the first child. The others belong to the husband.

Among the Moors, if the wife does not become the mother of a boy, she may be divorced with the consent of the tribe, and can marry again.

In the Arctic regions a man who wants a divorce leaves home in anger, and does not return for several days. The wife takes the hint, and departs.

In China divorces are allowed in all cases of

criminality, mutual dislike, jealousy, incompatibility of temperament, or too much loquacity on the part of the wife.

Among the Tartars, if the wife is ill-treated, she complains to the magistrate, who, attended by the principal people, accompanies her to the house and pronounces a divorce.

Books were originally made of boards, or the inner bark of trees; afterwards of skins and parchment. Papyrus, an indigenous plant, was adopted in Egypt. Books with leaves of vellum were invented by Attalus king of Pergamus, about 198 B. C., at which time books were in volumes or rolls. The MSS. in Herculaneum consists of papyrus rolled and charred and matted together by the fire, and are about nine inches long, and one, two, or three inches in diameter, each being a separate treatise. The first printed books were printed on one side only, the leaves being pasted back to back.

Title pages to printed books in England were not introduced until shortly before 1490; they were used by Wynkyn de Worde, but not by Caxton in the fifteenth century.

The prices of ancient books were enormous. Jerome (who died 420 A. D.) states that he had ruined himself by buying a copy of the works of Origen. A large estate was given by Alfred the Great for a book on cosmography, about 872. The *Roman de la Rose* was sold for about £30; and a homily was exchanged for 200 sheep and five quarters of wheat. Books frequently brought double or treble their weight in gold. In 1400 they sold at prices varying from £10 to £40 each.

Bookbinding is supposed to have begun about 650 A. D., the earliest to be bound being the book of St. Cuthbert. A Latin Psalter was bound in oak boards in the ninth century. Velvet was the covering in the fourteenth century, and silk soon after. Vellum was introduced early in the fifteenth century; and leather came into use about the same time.

Minimum Weights of Produce.— The following are minimum weights of certain articles of produce, according to the laws of the United States:—

	Per Bushel.		Per Bushel.
Wheat,	60 lbs.	Dried Apples,	26 lbs.
Corn, in the ear,	70 "	Clover Seed,	60 "
Corn, shelled,	56 "	Flax Seed,	56 "
Rye,	56 "	Millet Seed,	50 "
Buckwheat,	48 "	Hungarian Grass Seed,	50 "
Barley,	48 "	Timothy Seed,	45 "
Oats,	32 "	Blue Grass Seed,	44 "
Pease,	60 "	Hemp Seed,	44 "
White Beans,	60 "	Salt (see note below).	
Castor Beans,	46 "	Corn Meal,	48 "
White Potatoes,	60 "	Ground Pease,	24 "
Sweet Potatoes,	55 "	Malt,	38 "
Onions,	57 "	Bran,	20 "
Turnips,	55 "		
Dried Peaches,	33 "		

Salt.— Weight per bushel as adopted by different states ranges from 50 to 80 pounds. Coarse salt in Pennsylvania is reckoned at 80 pounds, and in Illinois at 50 pounds per bushel. Fine salt in Pennsylvania is reckoned at 62 pounds, in Kentucky and Illinois at 55 pounds per bushel.

Railroad Statistics.

Compiled from "Poor's Manual of Railroads of the United States."

Mileage of Railroads	195,886.90
Second Tracks and Sidings	70,105.45
Total Track	265,992.35
Steel Rails in Track	246,811.60
Iron Rails in Track	19,180.75
Locomotive Engines, Number	39,729
Cars, Passenger	27,144
" Baggage, Mail, etc	8,667
" Freight	1,409,472
Total Cars	1,445,283
Liabilities.	
Capital Stock	$5,978,796,249
Bonded Debt	6,035,469,741
Unfunded Debt	312,225,536
Current Accounts	456,798,012
Sinking and Other Funds	143,670,983
Total Liabilities	$12,926,960,521
Assets.	
Cost of Railroad and Equipment	$10,717,752,155
Other Investments	1,976,548,412
Sundry Assets	390,112,441
Current Accounts	223,616,024
Total Assets	$13,308,029,032
Excess of Assets over Liabilities	$381,068,511

Miles of Railroad Operated	194,974.96
Passenger Train Mileage	391,543,708
Freight " "	505,468,619
Mixed " "	20,812,985
Total	917,825,312
Passengers Carried	600,485,790
Passenger Mileage	17,789,669,925
Tons of Freight Moved	1,084,066,451
Freight Mileage	148,959,303,492
Traffic Earnings.	
Passengers	$360,702,686
Freight	1,126,267,652
Miscellaneous	125,478,488
Total Traffic Revenue	$1,612,448,826
Net Earnings	520,294,727
Receipts from Other Sources	68,368,814
Total Available Revenue	$588,663,541
Payments.	
Interest on Bonds	$215,191,176
Other Interest	7,327,334
Dividends on Stock	132,162,935
Miscellaneous	36,235,397
Rentals—Interest	39,127,204
Dividends	24,724,348
Miscellaneous	22,586,953
Total Payments	$477,355,347
Surplus	$111,308,194

The Public Lands of the United States.

The following is a tabular statement showing the number of acres of public lands surveyed in the following land States and Territories up to June 30, 1901; also the total area of the public domain remaining unsurveyed within the same, etc.

Land States and Territories.	Area. Acres.	Area. Square Miles.	Number of Acres of Public Land Surveyed Up to June 30, 1897.	Total Area of Public and Indian Lands Remaining Unsurveyed, including the Area of Private Land Claims.	Land States and Territories.	Area. Acres.	Area. Square Miles.	Number of Acres of Public Lands Surveyed Up to June 30, 1897.	Total Area of Public and Indian Lands Remaining Unsurveyed, including the Area of Private Land Claims.
Alabama....	32,657,920	51,028	32,657,920	......	Nevada......	70,336,640	109,901	36,793,765	33,542,875
Arkansas....	33,543,680	52,412	33,543,680	......	N. Dakota...	44,910,080	70,172	38,222,690	6,687,390
California...	99,969,920	156,203	76,721,643	23,448,277	Ohio.........	26,062,720	40,723	26,062,720	......
Colorado....	66,348,160	103,669	61,946,310	4,401,850	Oregon......	61,277,440	95,746	46,058,414	15,219,026
Florida.....	35,072,640	54,801	30,835,559	4,237,081	S. Dakota....	49,206,400	76,885	44,114,973	5,091,427
Illinois......	35,842,560	56,004	35,842,560	......	Utah........	52,541,440	82,096	19,080,408	33,461,032
Indiana.....	22,950,400	35,860	22,950,400	......	Wisconsin...	35,274,880	55,117	35,274,880	......
Iowa........	35,646,080	55,697	35,646,080	......	Washington.	42,746,880	66,792	27,495,664	15,251,216
Idaho.......	53,293,440	83,271	19,182,221	34,111,219	Wyoming...	62,433,280	97,552	54,373,346	8,059,934
Kansas......	52,382,720	81,848	52,382,720	......	Alaska.......	368,103,680	575,162	2,236	368,101,444
Louisiana...	29,055,360	45,399	27,175,212	1,880,148	Arizona......	72,792,320	113,738	18,179,451	54,612,869
Michigan...	36,819,200	57,530	36,819,200	......	Indian Ter...	19,658,880	30,717	19,658,880	......
Minnesota...	51,198,080	79,997	47,483,366	3,714,714	N. Mexico...	78,428,800	122,545	50,934,429	27,494,371
Mississippi..	29,685,120	46,383	29,685,120	......	Oklahoma...	24,774,400	38,710	24,695,192	79,208
Missouri.....	43,795,840	68,431	43,795,840	......					
Montana....	93,593,600	146,240	33,939,743	59,653,857	Total......	1,809,539,840	2,827,406	1,110,642,478	* 698,897,362
Nebraska....	49,137,280	76,777	49,087,856	49,424					

* This estimate is of a very general nature, and affords no index to the disposable volume of land remaining nor the amount available for agricultural purposes. It includes Indian and other public reservations, unsurveyed private land claims, as well as surveyed private land claims, in the districts of Arizona, California, Colorado, and New Mexico; the sixteenth and thirty-sixth sections reserved for common schools; unsurveyed lands embraced in railroad, swamp land, and other grants; the great mountain areas; the areas of unsurveyed rivers and lakes, and large areas wholly unproductive and unavailable for ordinary purposes.

Present Population of the States and Territories.

CENSUS OF 1900.*

States and Territories.	Population.	States and Territories.	Population.	States and Territories.	Population.
Alabama	1,828,697	Maryland..............	1,188,044	Rhode Island...........	428,556
Alaska..................	63,592	Massachusetts..........	2,805,346	South Carolina..........	1,340,316
Arizona................	122,931	Michigan...............	2,420,982	South Dakota...........	401,570
Arkansas...............	1,311,564	Minnesota..............	1,751,394	Tennessee..............	2,020,616
California..............	1,485,053	Mississippi.............	1,551,270	Texas.................	3,048,710
Colorado...............	539,700	Missouri...............	3,106,665	Utah..................	276,749
Connecticut............	908,420	Montana...............	243,329	Vermont...............	343,641
Delaware..............	184,735	Nebraska..............	1,066,300	Virginia...............	1,854,184
District of Columbia....	278,718	Nevada................	42,335	Washington............	518,103
Florida.................	528,542	New Hampshire.........	411,588	West Virginia...........	958,800
Georgia................	2,216,331	New Jersey.............	1,883,669	Wisconsin..............	2,069,042
Idaho..................	161,772	New Mexico............	195,310	Wyoming..............	92,531
Illinois................	4,821,550	New York..............	7,268,894	Hawaii................	154,001
Indiana................	2,516,462	North Carolina.........	1,893,810	Indian Territory........	392,060
Iowa...................	2,231,853	North Dakota...........	319,146	Indian Reservations ...	134,476
Kansas.................	1,470,495	Ohio..................	4,157,545	In Mil. & Nav. service..	91,219
Kentucky...............	2,147,174	Oklahoma..............	398,331		
Louisiana..............	1,381,625	Oregon................	413,536	Grand Total.......	76,303,387
Maine..................	694,466	Pennsylvania...........	6,302,115		

* The United States census of 1890 is tabulated on page 671.

The Language of Gems.—*Amethyst.*—Peace of mind. Regarded by the ancients as having the power to dispel drunkenness.

Bloodstone.—I mourn your absence. Worn by the ancients as an amulet or charm, on account of the medicinal and magical virtues it was supposed to possess.

Diamond.—Pride. Awarded supernatural qualities from the most remote period down to the middle ages. Has the power of making men courageous and magnanimous. Protects from evil spirits. Influences the gods to take pity upon mortals. Maintains concord between husband and wife, and for this reason was held as the most appropriate stone for the espousal ring.

Emerald.—Success in love. Mentioned in the Bible as worn in the breastplate of the High Priest as an emblem of chastity.

Ruby.—A cheerful mind. An amulet against poison, sadness, evil thoughts. A preservative of health. Admonishes the wearer of impending danger by changing color.

Sapphire.—Chastity. Procures favor with princes. Frees from enchantment. Prevents impure thoughts.

Topaz.— Fidelity. Calms the passions.

Turquoise.— Success and happiness. Preserves from contagion.

Garnet.—Fidelity in every engagement.

Onyx.— Reciprocal love.

Opal.— Pure thoughts.

Pearl.— Purity and innocence.

Public Lands Vacant July 1, 1901.

States and Territories.	Surveyed Land.	Unsurveyed Land.	Total Area, Acres.
Alabama	312,630	....	312,630
Alaska	*	367,983,506	367,983,506
Arizona	11,615,248	37,155,806	48,771,054
Arkansas	3,224,128	....	3,224,128
California	34,052,596	7,996,412	42,049,008
Colorado	34,719,759	4,396,055	39,115,814
Florida	1,299,704	160,070	1,459,774
Idaho	11,680,089	30,795,087	42,475,176
Kansas	1,085,315	....	1,085,315
Louisiana	254,317	65,018	319,335
Michigan	462,157	....	462,157
Minnesota	1,967,285	2,172,908	4,140,193
Mississippi	195,980	....	195,980
Missouri	281,727	....	281,727
Montana	19,138,446	46,664,861	65,803,307
Nebraska	9,926,670	....	9,926,670
Nevada	29,667,377	31,654,848	61,322,225
New Mexico	41,108,508	14,480,616	55,589,124
North Dakota	11,973,738	4,982,753	16,956,491
Oklahoma	4,653,605	....	4,653,605
Oregon	23,642,364	10,141,659	33,784,023
South Dakota	11,471,138	397,866	11,869,004
Utah	10,830,242	31,685,613	42,515,855
Washington	5,613,943	6,299,221	11,913,164
Wisconsin	230,813	....	230,813
Wyoming	42,769,587	4,887,309	47,656,896
Total	312,177,366	601,919,608	†914,096,974

* The unreserved lands in Alaska are mostly unsurveyed and unappropriated.

† This aggregate is exclusive of Ohio, Indiana, Illinois, and Iowa, in which, if any public land remains, it consists of a few small isolated tracts. It is also exclusive of military and Indian reservations, reservoir sites, and timber reservations, and tracts covered by selections, filings, railroad grants, and claims as yet unadjudicated, a part of which may in the future be added to the public domain.

Railroad selections made during the fiscal year ended June 30, 1897, were, in acres: Arizona, 91,518.95; Arkansas, 7,024.14; California, 42,579.52; Colorado, 108,877.71; Florida, 281.29; Idaho, 86,526.60; Kansas, 55,770.65; Louisiana, 165.84; Minnesota, 52,698.93; Mississippi, 42,371.55; Montana, 46,318.85; Nebraska, 639.92; Nevada, 647,-898.54; North Dakota, 1,313.81; Oregon, 13,766.86; Utah, 46,657.62; Washington, 114,868.55; Wisconsin, 29,552.21; Wyoming, 149,632.69; Total, 1,538,464.23.

Indebtedness of the States and Territories

Geographical Divisions.	Total Combined Debt* Less Sinking Fund.	Per Capita of Combined Debt.	
	1900.	1900.	1890.
North Atlantic	$467,968,615	$26.89	$37.28
Maine	$15,600,777	$23.60	$35.81
New Hampshire	8,148,362	21.64	31.10
Vermont	3,785,373	11.39	13.54
Massachusetts	81,550,027	36.42	51.55
Rhode Island	13,042,117	37.75	46.91
Connecticut	23,703,478	31.76	35.33
New York	201,763,217	33.64	43.06
New Jersey	49,333,589	34.14	43.66
Pennsylvania	71,041,675	13.51	25.03
South Atlantic	165,107,113	18.64	22.10
Delaware	$2,919,084	$17.32	$16.17
Maryland	42,175,408	40.46	44.31
Dist. of Columbia	19,781,050	85.86	126.66
Virginia	50,837,315	30.70	30.09
West Virginia	2,532,460	3.32	2.65
North Carolina	11,117,445	6.87	12.83
South Carolina	13,295,637	11.55	14.25
Georgia	20,272,095	11.03	12.74
Florida	2,176,619	5.56	9.89
North Central	320,238,281	14.32	14.17
Ohio	$71,065,386	$19.35	$16.59
Indiana	24,442,631	11.15	9.28
Illinois	41,841,649	10.94	15.07
Michigan	16,941,928	8.09	7.36
Wisconsin	10,440,580	6.19	9.19
Minnesota	26,050,929	20.01	14.51
Iowa	11,275,319	5.90	5.01
Missouri	51,557,568	19.24	27.79
North Dakota	3,842,790	21.03	3.57
South Dakota	6,613,707	20.11	8.82
Nebraska	15,536,772	14.67	16.56
Kansas	40,629,022	28.47	15.97
South Central	138,255,311	12.60	16.14
Kentucky	$19,432,885	$10.46	$9.09
Tennessee	29,543,843	16.71	26.42
Alabama	18,930,867	12.51	14.26
Mississippi	6,011,347	4.66	4.88
Louisiana	33,335,497	29.80	45.60
Texas	20,172,063	9.02	7.34
Arkansas	10,828,809	9.60	13.37
Western	43,641,122	14.41	13.85
Montana	$2,918,893	$22.09	$19.54
Wyoming	1,647,381	27.14	9.88
Colorado	8,411,027	20.41	18.67
New Mexico	2,831,538	18.44	.71
Arizona	2,937,971	49.28	9.33
Utah	767,501	3.69	.81
Nevada	1,337,501	29.23	22.48
Idaho	1,594,333	18.89	7.05
Washington	3,145,658	9.00	3.19
Oregon	2,479,860	7.90	4.86
California	15,569,459	12.89	19.18
Total	$1,135,210,442	$18.13	$22.40

Bartholdi's Statue of Liberty.—The figure of this statue, which is made of repoussé, or hammered work—that is, thin sheets of copper beaten into shape and fastened about an iron skeleton—is 110 1-2 feet high and weighs 100,000 pounds. The uplifted torch, however, is raised 26 feet, and adding to this the pedestal, the tip of the torch is raised 220 feet from the ground. The pedestal is of stone, 82 feet high. Some idea of the enormous proportions of the statue may be given from the fact that the forefinger is 8 feet long and 4 feet in circumference at the second joint. The head is 14 feet high, and 40 persons can stand in it.

The Great Wall of China runs from a point of the Gulf of Liaotung, an arm of the Gulf of Pechili, in Northeastern China, westerly to the Yellow river, thence makes a great bend to the south for nearly one hundred miles, and then runs to the northwest for several hundred miles to the Desert of Gobi. Its length is 1,500 miles. For the most of this distance it runs through a mountainous country, keeping on the ridges, and winding over many of the highest peaks. In some places it is only a formidable rampart, but most of the way it is composed of lofty walls of masonry and concrete, or impacted lime and clay, from twelve to sixteen feet in thickness, and from fifteen to thirty or thirty-five feet in height. The top of this wall is paved for hundreds of miles, and crowned with crenelated battlements and towers thirty to forty feet high. In numerous places the wall climbs such steep declivities that its top ascends from height to height in flights of granite steps. An army could march on the top of the wall for weeks and even months, moving in some places ten men abreast.

Most Northern Point Reached by Arctic Explorers.— The following table shows the furthest points of north latitude reached by Arctic explorers up to and including the Nansen expedition:—

Year.	Explorers.	North Latitude.		
1607.	Hudson.	80d.	23m.	00s.
1773.	Phipps (Lord Musgrove).	80d.	48m.	00s.
1806.	Scoresby.	81d.	12m.	42s.
1827.	Parry.	82d.	45m.	30s.
1874.	Meyer (on land).	82d.	09m.	00s.
1875.	Markham (Nare's expedition).	83d.	20m.	26s.
1876.	Payer.	83d.	07m.	00s.
1884.	Lockwood (Greely's party).	83d.	24m.	00s.
1893-96.	Nansen.	86d.	13m.	36s.

The distance from the farthest point of polar discovery to the pole itself is 3 deg. 46 min. 24 sec., or in round numbers, 260 miles, which is only about thirty miles greater than the distance from New York to Washington, by the line of the Pennsylvania railroad, over which the traveler rides in about five hours. But this polar radius, though only 260 miles in extent, is covered by ice gorges and precipices of incredible difficulty; and frost is so severe that no instrument of human invention can measure its intensity, and it blisters the skin like extreme heat.

The greatest progress that has ever been made across these wildernesses of storm, of fury and desolation, was at the rate of five or six miles in a day, the explorers often necessarily resting as many days as they had before traveled miles in a single day, debarred by the obstacles that they had encountered.

The Highest Mountains.

	Feet.
Mount Everest, India	29,002
Dapsang, Thibet	28,278
Kuchin-Junga, India	28,156
Sorata, Andes	25,380
Aconcagua, Chile	22,422
Illimani, Bolivia	21,780
Chimborazo, Ecuador	21,420
Arequipa, Peru	20,320
Kilima-Njaro, East Africa	19,600
Mt. Logan, Canada	19,500
Cotopaxi, Ecuador	18,880
Elbruz, Russia	18,526
Demavend, Persia	18,500
Tolima, Columbia	18,069
Kenia, East Africa	18,045
Mt. St. Elias, Alaska	18,010
Popocatepetl, Mexico	17,784
Orizaba, Mexico	17,380
Ararat, Turkey	17,260
Mt. Brown, Canada	16,000
Mt. Blanc, France	15,810
Mt. Hooker, Canada	15,700
Monte Rosa, Italy	15,208
Mt. Whitney, California	14,898
Mt. Ranier, Washington	14,444
Mt. Shasta, California	14,440
Long's Peak, Colorado	14,271
Pike's Peak, Colorado	14,147
Mauna Loa, Hawaii	13,600
Fremont's Peak, Wyoming	13,576
Mt. Wrangel, Alaska	12,066
Teneriffe, Canaries	12,000
Mt. Hood, Oregon	11,934
Simplon, Alps	11,542
Mt. Miltseen, Morocco	11,400
Mt. Hermon, Palestine	11,000
Mt. Lebanon, Syria	11,000
Olympus, Turkey	9,745
Etna, Sicily	9,652
St. Gothard, Alps	9,080
Mt. Sinai, Turkey	8,593
Ymesfield, Norway	8,543
Roraima, Venezuela	7,874
Mt. Kosciusko, Australia	7,176
Peak of Pico, Azores	7,013
Mt. Mitchell, North Carolina	6,711
Mt. Washington, New Hampshire	6,288
Itacolumi, Brazil	5,740
Mt. Marcy, New York	5,467
Mt. Katahdin, Maine	5,385
Mt. Hecla, Iceland	5,000
Ben Nevis, Scotland	4,368
Vesuvius, Italy	3,948

Height of Loftiest Volcanoes of the World.

Name of Volcano.	Height in feet.	Where Located.
Sahama	23,000	Peru.
Llullaillac	21,000	Chile.
Arequipa	20,500	Peru.
Cayambi	19,813	Ecuador.
Cotopaxi	19,500	Peru.
Antisana	19,200	Ecuador.
San Jose	18,150	Chile.
Mt. St. Elias	17,900	Alaska.
Popocatepetl	17,884	Mexico.
Orizaba	17,370	Mexico.
Altar	17,126	Ecuador.
Sangai	17,120	Ecuador.
Klintcheoskaia	16,512	Kamtschatka.
Iztacihuatl	15,700	Mexico.
Toluco	15,500	Mexico.
Shasta	14,400	United States.
Fujiyama	14,000	Japan.
Mauna Kea	13,953	Sandwich Islands.
Mauna Loa	13,760	Sandwich Islands.
Teneriffe	12,236	Canary Islands.
Mt. St. Helen's	12,000	United States.
Mt. Hood	11,225	United States.
Peak of Tahiti	10,895	Friendly Islands.
Mt. Etna	10,874	Sicily.

Three of the best known volcanoes of the world, Vesuvius, 3,978 feet; Hecla, 3,970 feet, and Stromboli, 3,000 feet, are of much less elevation than many others altogether unfamiliar.

Capacity of the Largest Churches and Halls.

St. Peter's Cathedral	Rome	54,000
Cathedral of Milan	Milan	37,000
St. Paul's Church	Rome	32,000
St. Paul's Cathedral	London	25,000
Church of St. Petronio	Bologna	24,000
Cathedral of Florence	Florence	24,000
Cathedral of Antwerp	Antwerp	24,000
Mosque of St. Sophia	Constantinople	23,000
St. John's Lateran	Rome	22,000
Cathedral of Notre Dame	Paris	21,000
Cathedral of Pisa	Pisa	13,000
Church of St. Stephen	Vienna	12,000
Church of St. Dominic	Bologna	12,000
Church of St. Peter	Bologna	11,400
Cathedral of Vienna	Vienna	11,000
St. Peter's Cathedral	Montreal	10,000
Madison Square Garden	New York	8,433
Auditorium	Chicago	8,000
Academy of Music	Philadelphia	2,862
Theater Carlo Felice	Genoa	2,560
Boston Theater	Boston	2,972
Covent Garden	London	2,684
Academy of Music	New York	2,526
Music Hall	Boston	2,585
Alexander Theater	St. Petersburg	2,332
Opera House	Munich	2,307
San Carlos Theater	Naples	2,240
Imperial Theater	St. Petersburg	2,160
Grand Opera	Paris	2,090
La Scala	Milan	2,113
St. Charles Theater	New Orleans	2,178
Opera House	New Orleans	2,052
Grand Opera House	New York	1,883
Booth's Theater	New York	1,807
McVickar's Theater	Chicago	1,790
Ford's Opera House	Baltimore	1,720
Opera House	Berlin	1,636

Foreign-born Population.— The following table shows the origin of the foreign-born population.

England*	909,092	France	113,174
Wales	100,079	China	106,688
Scotland	242,231	Switzerland	104,069
Ireland	1,871,509	Holland	81,828
Total United Kingdom	3,122,911	Mexico	77,853
Germany	2,784,894	Cuba and West Indies	23,256
Canada and New-foundland	980,938	Hungary	62,435
Sweden	478,041	Belgium	22,639
Norway	322,665	Portugal	15,996
Russia	182,644	Spain	6,185
Italy	182,580	South America	5,006
Poland	147,440	Other Foreign Countries	54,385
Denmark	132,543		
Austria	123,271	Total	9,249,547
Bohemia	118,106		

*Includes Great Britain, not specified.

The Five Wits.— An old and curious standard of mentality is that which credits mankind with having "five wits": common wit, imagination, fantasy, estimation, and memory.

1. *Common wit* is that inward sense which judges what the five senses simply discern: thus the eye sees, the nose smells, the ear hears, and so on, but it is "common wit" that informs the brain and passes judgment on the goodness or badness of these external matters.

2. *Imagination* works on the mind, causing it to realize what has been presented to it.

3. *Fantasy* energizes the mind to act in accordance with the judgment thus pronounced.

4. *Estimation* decides on all matters pertaining to time, space, locality, relation, and so on.

5. *Memory* enables the mind to retain the recollection of what has been imparted.

Bell Time on Shipboard.

Time, A. M.		Time, A. M.		Time, A. M.	
1 Bell,	12.30	1 Bell,	4.30	1 Bell,	8.30
2 Bells,	1.00	2 Bells,	5.00	2 Bells,	9.00
3 "	1.30	3 "	5.30	3 "	9.30
4 "	2.00	4 "	6.00	4 "	10.00
5 "	2.30	5 "	6.30	5 "	10.30
6 "	3.00	6 "	7.00	6 "	11.00
7 "	3.30	7 "	7.30	7 "	11.30
8 "	4.00	8 "	8.00	8 "	Noon

Time, P. M.		Time, P. M.		Time, P. M.	
1 Bell,	12.30	1 Bell,	4.30	1 Bell,	8.30
2 Bells,	1.00	2 Bells,	5.00	2 Bells,	9.00
3 "	1.30	3 "	5.30	3 "	9.30
4 "	2.00	4 "	6.00	4 "	10.00
5 "	2.30	1 Bell,	6.30	5 "	10.30
6 "	3.00	2 Bells,	7.00	6 "	11.00
7 "	3.30	3 "	7.30	7 "	11.30
8 "	4.00	4 "	8.00	8 "	Midnight

On shipboard, for purpose of discipline and to divide the watch fairly, the crew is mustered in two divisions; the Starboard (right side, looking toward the head) and the Port (left). The day commences at noon, and is thus divided: Afternoon Watch, noon to 4 P. M.; First Dog Watch, 4 P. M. to 6 P. M.; Second Dog Watch, 6 P. M. to 8 P. M.; First Watch, 8 P. M. to Midnight; Middle Watch, Midnight to 4 A. M.; Morning Watch, 4 A. M. to 8 A. M.; Forenoon Watch, 8 A. M. to noon. This makes seven Watches, which enables the crew to keep them alternately, as the Watch which comes on duty at noon one day has the afternoon next day, and the men who have only four hours' rest one night have eight hours the next. This is the reason for having Dog Watches, which are made by dividing the hours between 4 P. M. and 8 P. M. into two Watches. Time is kept by means of "Bells" although sometimes there is but one Bell on the ship.

Pawnbroker's Sign, Origin of.—It is generally held that the three golden balls used by pawnbrokers as a sign were adopted from the armorial bearings of the Medici family of Italy by the Lombard merchants, among whom were several representatives of that family. This sign was used in London in very early times by some of those merchants who had emigrated from Italy and established the first money-lending establishments in England.

Indian Folklore.— As a specimen of the folklore of our own aborigines none can surpass in interest the story of Hiawatha, the prophet-teacher, son of Mudjekeewis (*the west wind*) and Wenonah, daughter of Nokomis. He represents the progress of civilization among the North American Indians. Hiawatha first wrestled with Mondamin (*maize*), and, having subdued it, gave it to man for food. He then taught man navigation; then he subdued Mishe Nahma (*the sturgeon*), and taught the Indians how to make oil therefrom for winter. His next exploit was against the magician Megissognon, the author of disease and death; having slain this monster, he taught men the science of medicine. He then married Minnehaha (*laughing water*), and taught man to be the husband of one wife, and the comforts of domestic peace. Lastly, he taught man picture-writing. When the white man came with the gospel, Hiawatha ascended to the kingdom of Ponemah, the land of the hereafter. Among many other accomplishments, when Hiawatha put on his moccasins, he could measure a mile at a single stride.

> He had moccasins enchanted,
> Magic moccasins of deer-skin;
> When he bound them round his ankles
> At each stride a mile he measured!
> —LONGFELLOW, *Hiawatha*, iv.

Barber's Pole.— The spiral red stripe on a barber's pole is said to symbolize the winding of a ribbon or bandage around the arm of a patient upon whom the barber had operated in the capacity of surgeon. In former times, when the operation of bleeding was extensively practiced, blood-letting formed a part of the duties of a barber.

Caste Among the Hindoos.— Caste is a term applied to the division into social classes in India. To each of these classes certain pursuits are limited by the Laws of Manu, B. C. 960. 1. The *Brahmans* or sacerdotal class, which "issued from the mouth of Brahma."

2. The *Chuttree* or military class, which "sprang from the arm of Brahma."

3. The *Baïs* or mercantile class, which "sprang from the thigh of Brahma."

4. The *Sudras* or servile class, which "sprang from the foot of Brahma."

The *Pariahs* and *Chandalas* are nobodies, or worse, for it is pollution to be touched by such "scum of the earth."

American Flags.—It is related that the flag which was raised at Cambridge, January 2, 1776, by Washington, was composed of thirteen red and white stripes, with the crosses of St. George and St. Andrew emblazoned on the blue canton in place of the stars. This flag was also carried by the fleet under command of Commander Esek Hopkins, when it sailed from the Delaware Capes, February 17, 1776. In the following year, June 14, 1777, the continental Congress passed a resolution "That the flag of the United States be thirteen stripes, alternate red and white; that the Union be thirteen stars, white on a blue field, representing a new constellation." How or by whom the idea of the star was first suggested is uncertain, although there are some who ascribe it to John Adams, while others claim the entire flag was borrowed from the coat of arms of the Washington family. In this flag the stars were arranged in a circle, although no form was officially prescribed. It is supposed that the first display of the National flag at a military post was at Fort Schuyler, on the site of the village of Rome, Oneida county, N. Y. The fort was besieged early in the month of August, 1777, and the garrison were without a flag. So they made one according to the prescription of Congress, by cutting up sheets to form the white stripes, bits of scarlet cloth for the red stripes, and the blue ground for the stars was composed of portions of a cloth cloak belonging to Capt. Abraham Swarthout, of Dutchess county, N. Y., and the flag was unfurled August 3, 1777. Paul Jones, as commander of the "Ranger," to which he was appointed, June 14, 1777, claimed that he was the first to display the stars and stripes on a naval vessel. It is probable that the flag was first unfurled in battle on the banks of the Brandywine, September 11, 1777, the first battle after its adoption. It first appeared over a foreign stronghold, June 28, 1778, when Captain Rathbone, of the American sloop of war "Providence," captured Fort Nassau, New Providence, Bahama Islands. John Singleton Copley, the American painter, claimed to be the first to display the flag in Great Britain. On the day when George III. acknowledged the independence of the United States (December 5, 1782), he painted the flag in the background of a portrait of Elkanah Watson. To Captain Mooers, of the whaling ship "Bedford," of Nantucket, is doubtless due the honor of first displaying the stars and stripes in a port of Great Britain. He arrived in the Downs with it flying at the fore, February 3, 1783. When Vermont and Kentucky were added to the Union of States, the flag was altered, the number of stripes and stars being increased from thirteen to fifteen. In 1818 a new flag, having thirteen stripes and a star for every state, twenty at that time, was devised by Capt. Samuel C. Reed, and this has remained the form of the United States flag.

Harbors.— San Francisco may fairly claim to have the most capacious natural harbor of any of the world's great trading marts. It is also one of the very safest. It is entered through the Golden Gate, a passage a mile wide, and thirty-five feet deep at low tide — admitting the largest ships afloat without danger of grounding. The landlocked bay, of which this harbor is part, is fifty miles long, and averages five miles in width. There all the shipping of the entire globe could anchor in perfect safety. Port Philip Bay, the chief harbor of Victoria, Australia, is larger than the bay of San Francisco, being about thirty-eight miles long by thirty-three broad, but its very breadth, with its surroundings, leaves it exposed to storms from certain quarters. Port Jackson, on which Sydney, New South Wales, Australia, is located, is a magnificent harbor, completely landlocked, extending inland in some places fully twenty miles, and having ample depth of water for vessels of the heaviest burden. The harbors of New York city, Rio Janeiro, Brazil, and Havana, Cuba, are capacious and secure. Next come those of Boston, Norfolk, Va., Portland, Me., Halifax, N. S., Copenhagen, Constantinople, Hong Kong, Yokohama, and Nagasaki. The great ports situated on the banks of rivers, such as London, Liverpool, Glasgow, Lisbon, Philadelphia, New Orleans, Quebec, Shanghai, Canton, Calcutta, etc., are not included in the definition of harbors as here considered.

Bunker Hill Monument.— The corner stone of this monument was laid on the fiftieth anniversary of the battle of Bunker Hill, June 17, 1825, by Lafayette, and the oration was pronounced by Daniel Webster. It is a square shaft of Quincy granite, 221 feet high, 31 feet square at the base, and 15 feet at the top. Inside the shaft is a round, hollow cone, 7 feet wide at the bottom, and 4 feet 2 inches at the top, encircled by a winding staircase containing 224 stone steps, which leads to a chamber 11 feet in diameter immediately under the apex. The chamber has four windows, and contains two cannons, named Hancock and Adams, respectively, which were used in the war. The monument was completed and was dedicated June 17, 1843.

Commune, Paris, was an organized band of Socialists, who attempted to establish a revolutionary government in Paris in 1871. Before they were suppressed by the army of the republic, they became absolute masters of Paris, and committed astrocious acts of cruelty and vandalism. They arrested the Bishop of Paris and other prominent citizens, and imprisoned them. They set fire to the public buildings, and endeavored to destroy the ancient monuments and treasures of art. Among the buildings which were destroyed were the Tuileries, the Palais de Justice, the Palais Royal, and the Hotel de Ville, and the Louvre Gallery was partly burned. The Column Vendome, erected in honor of Napoleon, was one of the first monuments to fall. Darboy, the Archbishop of Paris, Bonjean, President of the Court of Cassation, and others whom they held as hostages, were shot. In short, they seemed to be possessed with a very frenzy of hatred against all government and all order, and wantonly destroyed property and human life. The revolution was finally suppressed on May 27, and 25,000 of the Communists were taken prisoners, some of whom were put to death, while a large number were banished. In justice it must be said that the more intelligent and honest leaders of the Commune were discarded before the most astrocious acts were committed.

Alien Holders of Our Lands.— The following is a table of the leading alien holders of lands in the United States, with amount of holdings in acres: —

An English syndicate, No. 3, in Texas	3,000,000
The Holland Land Company, New Mexico	4,500,000
Sir Edw. Reid and a syndicate, Florida	2,000,000
English syndicate in Mississippi	1,800,000
Marquis of Tweedale	1,750,000
Phillips, Marshall & Co., London	1,300,000
German-American syndicate, London	750,000
Bryan H. Evans, of London	700,000
Duke of Sutherland	425,000
British Land Company in Kansas	320,000
Wm. Wharley, M.P., Peterboro, England	310,000
Missouri Land Company, Edinburgh, Scotland	300,000
Robert Tennent, of London	230,000
Dundee Land Company, Scotland	247,000
Lord Dunmore	120,000
Benjamin Neugas, Liverpool	100,000
Lord Houghton in Florida	60,000
Lord Dunraven in Colorado	60,000
English Land Company in Florida	50,000
English Land Company in Arkansas	50,000
Albert Peel, M.P., Leicestershire, England	10,000
Sir J. L. Kay, Yorkshire, England	5,000
Alexander Grant, of London, in Kansas	35,000
English syndicate, Wisconsin	110,000
M. Ellerhauser, of Halifax, in West Virginia	600,000
A Scotch syndicate in Florida	500,000
A. Boysen, Danish consul in Milwaukee	50,000
Missouri Land Company, of Edinburgh	165,000
Total	20,647,000

To these syndicate holdings, should be added the following: The Arkansas Valley Company in Colorado, a foreign corporation, whose inclosures embrace upwards of 1,000,000 acres; the Prairie Cattle Company (Scotch) in Colorado, upwards of 1,000,000; H. H. Metcalf, River Bend, Colorado, 200,000; John W. Powers, Colorado, 200,000; McDaniel & Davis, Colorado, 75,000; Routchler & Lamb, Colorado, 40,000; J. W. Frank, Colorado, 40,000; Garnett & Langford, Colorado, 30,000; E. C. Tane, Colorado, 50,000; Leivesy Brothers, Colorado, 150,000; Vrooman & McFife, Colorado, 50,000; Beatty Brothers, Colorado, 40,000; Chick, Brown & Company, Colorado, 30,000; Reynolds Cattle Company, Colorado, 50,000; several other cases in Colorado, embracing from 10,000 to 30,000; Coe & Carter, Nebraska, fifty miles of fence; J. W. Wilson, Nebraska, forty miles; J. W. Boster, twenty miles; William Humphrey, Nevada, thirty miles; Nelson & Son, Nevada, twenty-two miles; Kennebec Ranch, Nebraska, from 20,000 to 50,000 acres.

Largest Islands in the World.

	Area. Sq. miles.	Population.
New Guinea	325,000	690,000
Borneo	290,000	1,846,000
Madagascar	228,570	3,000,000
Sumatra	168,000	5,000,000
Great Britain	83,826	29,710,000
Celebes	66,750	4,000,000
Java	50,260	17,500,000
Saghalien (used as a penal settlement only)	47,500	13,500
New Zealand, North Island	44,750	570,000
" " South Island	55,224	
Cuba	45,700	2,000,000
Niphon (Japan)	42,000	27,250,000
Newfoundland	40,200	180,000
Luzon (Philippines)	40,000	4,500,000
Iceland	40,000	72,438
Jesso	35,000	163,355
Ireland	31,874	5,174,836
Hayti or San Domingo	29,830	393,200
Tasmania	26,215	130,541
Ceylon	25,635	3,000,000
Tierra del Fuego	21,260	2,000

Government Salary List.— The salary of the president of the United States is $50,000 a year; the vice-president, $8,000; cabinet officers, $8,000. Senators receive $5,000 and mileage. Congressmen, $5,000 and mileage. The Chief Justice of the Supreme Court receives $10,500; Associate Justices, $10,000. The diplomats get good pay: Ministers to Germany, Great Britain, France, and Russia, $17,500; Ministers to Brazil, China, Austro-Hungary, Italy, Mexico, Japan, and Spain, $12,000; Ministers to Chile, Peru, and Central America, $10,000; Ministers to the Argentine Confederation, Belgium, Hayti, Colombia, Netherlands, Sweden, Turkey, and Venezuela, $7,500; Ministers to Switzerland, Denmark, Paraguay, Bolivia, and Portugal, $5,000; Ministers to Liberia, $4,000. The heads of the government departments receive: Superintendent of Bureau of Engraving and Printing, $4,500; Public Printer, $4,500; Superintendent of Census, $5,000; Superintendent of Naval Observatory, $5,000; Superintendent of the Signal Service, $4,000; Director of Geological Surveys, $6,000; Director of the Mint, $4,500; Commissioner of General Land Office, $4,000; Commissioner of Pensions, $3,600; Commissioner of Agriculture, $3,000; Commissioner of Indian Affairs, $3,000; Commissioner of Education, $3,000; Commander of Marine Corps, $3,500; Superintendent of Coast and Geodetic Survey, $6,000.

In 1893 the Ministers to Great Britain, Germany, and France, were made Ambassadors without increase of pay.

The pay of army officers is fixed as follows: General, $13,500; lieutenant general, $11,000; major general, $7,500; brigadier general, $5,500; colonel, $3,500; lieutenant colonel, $3,000; major, $2,500; captain, mounted, $2,000; captain, not mounted, $1,800; regimental adjutant, $1,800; regimental quartermaster, $1,800; first lieutenant, mounted, $1,600; first lieutenant, not mounted, $1,500; second lieutenant, mounted, $1,500; second lieutenant, not mounted, $1,400; chaplain, $1,500. The navy salaries are: Admiral, $13,000; vice-admiral, $9,000; rear admiral, $6,000; commodore, $5,000; captain, $4,500; commander, $3,500; lieutenant commander, $2,800; lieutenant, $2,400; master, $1,800; ensign, $1,200; midshipman, $1,000; cadet midshipman, $500; mate, $900; medical and pay director, and medical and pay inspector, and chief engineer, $4,400; fleet surgeon, fleet paymaster, and fleet engineer, $4,400; surgeon and paymaster, $2,800; chaplain, $2,500.

The White House.— The residence of the president of the United States is officially known as the Executive Mansion, which means that it is the residence of the head of the executive branch of the government; but it is seldom called, in ordinary talk, either by those who live in it, or by the American people in general, anything but the White House. This is a very unpretentious title, and it is interesting to note how the residence of the president, in a country which is full of white houses, came to bear this simple name as its special property.

The explanation is easily found. The first Executive Mansion at Washington was occupied in 1800. It was built of freestone, and was unpainted; but in 1814 the British army occupied Washington, and burned, with other public buildings, the president's house, leaving it a blackened ruin.

The house was rebuilt on the same site, and the same walls were used in its construction; but they were so discolored by smoke that, on the suggestion of General Jackson, they were painted white, not only to improve their appearance, but in token of the successful defiance of British fire by the American Republic.

The mansion soon became the "White House" in the mouths of the people, on account of its dazzling color, and from that day to this it has been repainted white every ten years. Its name commemorates a patriotic feeling, therefore, as well as serves to describe the appearance of the mansion, for the original coat of white paint was a sort of protest against the vandalism of the British, and every subsequent coat has served to perpetuate the protest.

Eagle as an Emblem.— In ancient mythology the eagle was believed to carry the souls of the dying to their abode on Mount Olympus, and was called the Bird of Jove.

The eagle was first taken as a symbol of royal power by the ancient Etruscans, who bore its image upon their standards. In the year 87 B. C. a silver eagle, with expanded wings, poised on the top of a spear, with a thunderbolt held in its claws, was adopted as the military standard to be borne at the head of their legions by the Romans. At the time of Hadrian a golden eagle was substituted for the silver one. A two-headed eagle was adopted by the Byzantine emperors as a symbol of their control of both the East and the West. The double-headed eagle of Russia was adopted on the marriage of Ivan I. with a Grecian princess of the Eastern empire; that of Austria was first used when the Emperor of Germany took the title of the Roman Emperor. The national standard of Prussia bears a black eagle, that of Poland a white one. Napoleon I. took a golden eagle for his standard, modeled of pure gold, and bearing a thunderbolt, after the pattern of the eagle of the Romans. This standard was disused under the Bourbons, but was restored by a decree of Louis Napoleon in 1852. The eagle was first used on American coins in 1788, on cents and half-cents issued from the Massachusetts mint. It was adopted in the plan of a national coinage as a design upon all gold coins, and on the silver dollar, half dollar, and quarter dollar. The design of an eagle was at one time suggested for the national flag, but was abandoned.

Knighthood, originally a military distinction, came, in the sixteenth century, to be occasionally conferred on civilians, as a reward for valuable services rendered to the crown or community. The first civil knight in England was Sir William Walworth, Lord Mayor of London, who won that distinction by slaying the rebel, Wat Tyler, in the presence of the king. The ceremonies practiced in conferring knighthood have varied at different periods. In general, fasting and bathing were in early times necessary preparatives. In the eleventh century, the creation of a knight was preceded by solemn confession and a midnight vigil in the church and followed by the reception of the Eucharist. The new knight offered his sword on the altar, to signify his devotion to the Church and determination to lead a holy life. The sword was redeemed in a sum of money, had a benediction pronounced over it, and was girded on by the highest ecclesiastic present. The title was conferred by binding the sword and spurs on the candidate, after which a blow was dealt him on the cheek or shoulder, as the last affront which he was to receive unrequited. He then took an oath to protect the distressed, maintain right against might, and never by word or deed to stain his character as a knight or a Christian. Upon the infringement of any part of his oath a knight could be degraded, in which case his spurs were chopped off with a hatchet, his sword broken, his escutcheon reversed, and some religious observances were added during which each piece of armor was taken off in succession and cast from the recreant knight. Knighthood is now generally bestowed by a verbal declaration of the sovereign, accompanied with a simple ceremony of imposition of the sword.

Latin Union was formed in 1865 and originally embraced France, Italy, Belgium, and Switzerland, but was joined by Greece in 1868, Spain in 1871, and subsequently Servia and Roumania. The object of this combination was to regulate the amount of silver to be coined yearly in each country, and to secure a uniform coinage which would be received without discount throughout the Union. The unit of coinage in the Latin Union is the franc, and although it is known in other countries under different names the value is always the same. The perfect decimal system of France is also used. The convenience of this coinage system has led to its adoption by about 148,000,000 people. In 1874 the States, by mutual consent, practically suspended the coinage of silver.

Blue Stockings.— The term "blue stocking" originated in England about a century ago. Its invention is traced to the days of Doctor Johnson and was applied then as now to ladies who cultivated learned conversation, and found enjoyment in the discussion of questions which had been monopolized by men. It is said by Dr. John Doran, who, in his work "A Lady of the Last Century," gave an account of Mrs. Montagu and the "blue stockings" of her time, that in 1757 it was quite the thing for ladies to form evening assemblies, when they might participate in talk with literary and ingenious men. One of the best known and most popular members of one of these societies was said to have been a Mr. Stillingfleet, who always wore blue stockings, and when at any time he happened to be absent from these gatherings it was usually remarked that "we can do nothing without blue stockings"; and by degrees the term "blue stockings" was applied to all clubs of the kind described, and eventually to the ladies who attended their meetings.

Mound Builders.— It is generally believed that the Mississippi valley and the Atlantic coast were once populated by an agricultural and partially civilized race quite different from the nomadic Indians, though possibly the progenitors of some of the Indian tribes, and that, after centuries of occupation, they disappeared — at least a thousand, and perhaps many thousand, years before the advent of Europeans. The theory has been advanced that these people migrated from Asia ; that they passed over Asia to Siberia, across Behring Straits, down the Pacific coast of America from Alaska, and to the Mississippi valley, and down to Mexico, Central America, and Peru. The remains of the Mound Builders, as this vanished people are called, are scattered over most of the states of the central and lower Mississippi valley, along the banks of the Missouri, and on the sources of the Allegheny. They are most numerous in Ohio, Indiana, Illinois, Wisconsin, Missouri, Arkansas, Kentucky, Tennessee, Mississippi, Alabama, Georgia, Florida, Texas, and are found in the western part of New York, and in Michigan and Iowa. These mounds vary greatly in size, and in some instances are very extensive and exceedingly intricate, notably those of the Licking valley, near Newark, Ohio, which cover an area of two square miles; in other localities there are some which reach a height of ninety feet. It is not believed that these people had any written language, as no inscriptions or tablets yet discovered indicate this. Many of these mounds have been found to contain skeletons, numerous implements and ornaments, usually composed of stone, sometimes of copper — in its native state — and occasionally shell and bone; also coarse and rude pottery of curious design. In substantiation of the belief that these people came from Asia, is the fact that in Siberia mounds have been found similar to those in the Mississippi valley.

Vegetable Origins.— Spinach is a Persian plant.

Horse-radish is a native of England.

Melons were found originally in Asia.

Filberts originally came from Greece.

Quinces originally came from Corinth.

The turnip originally came from Rome.

The peach originally came from Persia.

Sage is a native of the south of Europe.

Sweet marjoram is a native of Portugal.

The bean is said to be a native of Egypt.

Damsons originally came from Damascus.

The nasturtium came originally from Peru.

The pea is a native of the south of Europe.

Ginger is a native of the East and West Indies.

The gooseberry is indigenous to Great Britain.

Coriander seed came originally from the East.

Apricots are indigenous to the plains of America.

The cucumber was originally a tropical vegetable.

The walnut is a native of Persia, the Caucasus, and China.

Capers originally grew wild in Greece and northern Africa.

Pears were originally brought from the East by the Romans.

The clove is a native of the Malacca Islands, as is also the nutmeg.

Cherries were known in Asia as far back as the seventeenth century.

Garlic came to us first from Sicily and the shores of the Mediterranean.

Asparagus was originally a wild seacoast plant, and is a native of Great Britain.

The tomato is a native of South America, and it takes its name from a Portuguese word.

Parsley is said to have come from Egypt, and mythology tells us it was used to adorn the head of Hercules.

Apples were originally brought from the East by the Romans. The crab apple is indigenous to Great Britain.

The onion was almost an object of worship with the Egyptians 2,000 years before the Christian era. It first came from India.

Cloves came to us from the Indies, and take their name from the Latin clauvis, meaning a nail, to which they have a resemblance.

The cantaloupe is a native of America, and so called from the name of a place near Rome, where it was first cultivated in Europe.

Lemons were used by the Romans to keep moths from their garments, and in the time of Pliny they were considered an excellent poison. They are a native of Asia.

Slavery in the North.— The first state to abolish slavery within her borders was Vermont, which adopted a plan for gradual emancipation in 1777, before she had joined the Union, and in 1800 slavery in that state had entirely ceased. The new Massachusetts constitution, adopted in 1780, contained a clause declaring that "all men are born free and equal, and have certain natural, essential, and inalienable rights, among which may be reckoned the right of enjoying and defending their lives and liberties," which had the effect of freeing all the slaves, a very small number, then held within the borders of that state. In 1780 there were 4,000 slaves in Pennsylvania, and in that year their gradual emancipation was provided for by legislative enactment. Sixty-four of these were still living in bondage, however, in 1840. Rhode Island and Connecticut followed the example of Pennsylvania, and the former had but five slaves left in 1840, and the latter seventeen. New York passed a gradual emancipation act in 1799, at which time she had upward of 20,000 slaves, and slavery was totally abolished in the state from July 4, 1827. In 1850 there were still 236 persons living in bondage in New Jersey, although the state had adopted the gradual emancipation plan in 1804. The census of 1810 showed that there were no slaves held in Massachusetts, New Hampshire, or Vermont, New Hampshire having emancipated the few slaves held in the state between 1800 and 1810. In Pennslyvania, New York, and New Jersey, large numbers of slaves who could not be held in those states were nefariously sold to Southern slave-dealers by unprincipled owners, notwithstanding the fact that each state had adopted, at the time of emancipation, the most stringent laws regarding the exportation of slaves. By the census of 1860 it was shown that slavery was entirely abolished north of Mason and Dixon's line.

Mardi-Gras.— The Mardi-Gras is the festival preceding the first day of Lent, or Ash Wednesday. Most of the distinctive ceremonies now annually performed in New Orleans were originally introduced by the French population as early as 1827. The day is a legal holiday, and the entire city is for the time ostensibly placed under the control of a king of the carnival, the great "Rex." There are two principal pageants. The first, in the daytime, is the escort of the "beloved Rex," through his favorite city; the other, or night pageant, is known as the "Mystick Krewe of Comus." This has a character altogether unique. The first display was in 1857. On Twelfth night (January 6), the "Knights of Momus" have a display analogous to the Mardi-Gras, but more exclusively burlesque, and in which they satirize the follies of the age. The arrangements for these celebrations come within the control of quite an elaborate organization. The Mardi-Gras is held on Shrove Tuesday, a day of pleasure in most Roman Catholic countries. It is the carnival of the Italians, the Mardi-Gras of the French, and the Pancake Tuesday of former times in England.

Suicides.—In European cities the number of suicides per 100,000 inhabitants is as follows: Paris, 42; Lyons, 29; St. Petersburg, 7; Moscow, 11; Berlin, 36; Vienna, 28; London, 23; Rome, 8; Milan, 6; Madrid, 3; Genoa, 31; Brussels, 15; Amsterdam, 14; Lisbon, 2; Christiania, 25; Stockholm, 27; Constantinople, 12; Geneva, 11; Dresden, 51. Madrid and Lisbon show the lowest, Dresden the highest, figure.

The average annual suicide rate in countries of the world per 100,000 persons living is given by Barker as follows: Saxony, 31.1; Denmark, 25.8; Schleswig-Holstein, 24.0; Austria, 21.2; Switzerland, 20.2; France, 15.7; German Empire, 14.3; Hanover, 14.0; Queensland, 13.5; Prussia, 13.3; Victoria, 11.5; New South Wales, 9.3; Bavaria, 9.1; New Zealand, 9.0; South Australia, 8.9; Sweden, 8.1; Norway, 7.5; Belgium, 6.9; England and Wales, 6.9; Tasmania, 5.3; Hungary, 5.2; Scotland, 4.0; Italy, 3.7; Netherlands, 3.6; United States, 3.5; Russia, 2.9; Ireland, 1.7; Spain, 1.4.

The causes of suicide in European countries are reported as follows: Of 100 suicides: Madness, delirium, 18 per cent.; alcoholism, 11; vice, crime, 19; different diseases, 2; moral sufferings, 6; family matters, 4; poverty, want, 4; loss of intellect, 14; consequence of crimes, 3; unknown reasons, 19.

The number of suicides in the United States, six years, 1882-87, was 8,226. Insanity was the principal cause, shooting the favorite method; 5,386 acts of suicide were committed in the day, and 2,419 in the night. Summer was the favorite season, June the favorite month, and the 11th the favorite day of the month. The month in which the largest number of suicides occur is July.

The number of suicides in twenty American cities in 1897 was as follows: New York, 436; Chicago, 384; Brooklyn, 194; St. Louis, 162; Philadelphia, 146; Boston, 92; Cincinnati, 69; Baltimore, 60; Providence, 16; Cleveland, 54; Washington, 52; Milwaukee, 62; Minneapolis, 34; New Orleans, 40; Buffalo, 23; Pittsburg, 33; Jersey City, 24. Total, with ten smaller cities, 2,014. The same cities in 1896, 1,999; increase 15, or .75 of one per cent. These figures are by Frederick L. Hoffman, in the New York *Spectator* for July 1, 1898.

Facts About the Earth.— According to Clark, the equatorial semi-diameter is 20,-926,202 feet=3,963.296 miles, and the polar semi-diameter is 20,854,895 feet=3,950.738 miles. One degree of latitude at the pole=69.407 miles. One degree of latitude at the equator=68.704 miles.

POPULATION OF THE EARTH BY CONTINENTS.

Continental Divisions.	Area in Square Miles.	Inhabitants. Number.	Inhabitants. Per Sq. Mile.
Africa	11,514,000	127,000,000	11.0
America, North	6,446,000	89,250,000	13.8
America, South	6,837,000	36,420,000	5.3
Asia	14,710,000	850,000,000	57.7
Australasia	3,288,000	4,730,000	1.4
Europe	3,555,000	380,200,000	106.9
Polar Region	4,888,800	300,000	0.7
Total	51,238,800	1,487,900,000	29.0

The above estimate was made by Ernest George Ravenstein, F.R.G.S., the geographer and statistician, and is for 1890.

An estimate of population of the earth, made by Drs. Wagner and Supan, editors of *Bevölkerung der Erde* (Perthes, Gotha, 1891), is as follows: Europe, 357,379,000; Asia, 825,954,000; Africa, 163,953,000; America, 121,713,000; Australia, 3,230,000; Oceanic Islands, 7,420,000; polar regions, 80,400. Total, 1,479,729,400. The estimate of area of the continents and islands by the same authorities is 52,821,684.

Ravenstein's estimate of the earth's fertile region, in square miles, is 28,269,200; steppe, 13,901,000; desert, 4,180,000; polar regions, 4,888,800.

The population of the earth at the death of the Emperor Augustus, estimated by Bodio, was 54,000,000. The population of Europe hardly exceeded 50,000,000 before the fifteenth century.

The area and cubic contents of the earth, according to the data of Clark, given above, are: Surface, 196,971,984 square miles; cubic contents, 259,944,035,515 cubic miles.

Murray (Challenger expedition) states the greatest depth of the Atlantic Ocean at 27,366 feet; Pacific Ocean, 30,000 feet; Indian Ocean, 18,582 feet; Southern Ocean, 25,200 feet; Arctic Ocean, 9,000 feet. The Atlantic Ocean has an area, in square miles, of 24,536,000; Pacific Ocean, 50,309,000; Indian Ocean, 17,084,000; Arctic Ocean, 4,781,000; Southern Ocean, 30,592,000. The highest mountain is believed to be Deodhunga, one of the Himalayas, 29,002 feet. Lord Kelvin estimates the age of the solid earth to be between 20,000,000 and 30,000,000 years, and of the human race the same.

POPULATION OF THE EARTH ACCORDING TO RACE.

(Estimated by John Bartholomew, F. R. G. S., Edinburgh).

Race.	Location.	Number.
Indo-Germanic or Aryan	Europe, Persia, etc.	545,500,000
Mongolian or Turanian	Greater Part of Asia	630,000,000
Semitic or Hamitic	North Africa, Arabia	65,000,000
Negro and Bantu	Central Africa	150,000,000
Hottentot and Bush	South Africa	150,000
Malay and Polynesian	Australasia and Polynesia	35,000,000
American Indian	North and South America	15,000,000
Total		1,440,655,000

The human family is subject to forty-five principal governments. As to their form, they may be classified as follows: Absolute monarchies, China, Korea, Morocco, Persia, Russia, Siam, Turkey; limited monarchies, Austria-Hungary, Belgium, British Empire, Denmark, Germany, Greece, Italy, Japan, Netherlands, Portugal, Roumania, Servia, Sweden and Norway, Spain; republics, Argentine Republic, Bolivia, Brazil, Chile, Colombia, Costa Rica, Ecuador, France, Guatemala, Hayti, Honduras, Mexico, Nicaragua, Orange Free State, Paraguay, Peru, Salvador, San Domingo, Switzerland, Transvaal, United States of America, Uruguay, Venezuela. Besides these, are the undefined despotisms of Central and South Africa, and a few insignificant independent States.

The average duration of human life is about 33 years. One quarter of the people on the earth die before age 6, one half before age 16, and only about 1 person of each 100 born, lives to age 65. The deaths are calculated at 67 per minute, 97,790 per day, and 35,639,835 per year; the births, at 70 per minute, 100,800 per day, and 36,792,000 per year.

Statistics of the Press.—Rowell's American Newspaper Directory reports the number of newspapers published in the United States and Canada as 21,305, divided as follows: Weekly, 15,104; monthly, 2,777; daily, 2,285; semi-monthly, 277; semi-weekly, 515; quarterly, 159; bi-weekly, 58; bi-monthly, 70; tri-weekly, 55—total, 21,305.

Alabama	237	Nevada	30
Alaska	8	New Hampshire	92
Arizona	53	New Jersey	380
Arkansas	260	New Mexico	51
California	668	New York	1,863
Canada	975	North Carolina	254
Colorado	328	North Dakota	168
Connecticut	173	Ohio	1,177
Delaware	41	Oklahoma	191
District of Columbia	76	Oregon	192
Florida	147	Pennsylvania	1,356
Georgia	337	Rhode Island	55
Idaho	84	South Carolina	137
Illinois	1,686	South Dakota	269
Indiana	836	Tennessee	273
Indian Territory	106	Texas	757
Iowa	1,054	Utah	72
Kansas	677	Vermont	73
Kentucky	303	Virginia	238
Louisiana	185	Washington	24
Maine	160	West Virginia	194
Maryland	199	Wisconsin	673
Massachusetts	563	Wyoming	38
Michigan	802		
Minnesota	686	Total	21,305
Mississippi	218		
Missouri	981	Hawaii	23
Montana	87	Porto Rico	8
Nebraska	598	Philippines (in English)	4

The total number of newspapers published in the world at present is estimated at about 50,000, distributed as follows: United States and Canada, 21,305; Germany, 7,000; Great Britain, 9,500; France, 4,500; Japan, 2,000.

Italy 1,500; Austria-Hungary, 1,200; Asia, exclusive of Japan, 1,000; Spain 850; Russia, 800; Australia, 800; Greece, 600; Switzerland, 450; Holland, 300; Belgium, 300; all others, 1,000. Of these more than half are printed in the English language.

The Sacred Number.— Seven was frequently used as a mystical and symbolical number in the Bible, as well as among the principal nations of antiquity, the Persians, Indians, Egyptians, Greeks, and Romans. The origin is doubtless astronomical, or rather astrological, viz., the observation of the seven planets and the phases of the moon, changing every seventh day. As instances of this number in the Old Testament, we find the Creation completed within seven days, whereof the seventh was a day of rest kept sacred. Every seventh year was sabbatical, and the seven times seventh year ushered in the jubilee year. The three *Regalim*, or Pilgrim festivals (Passover, Festival of Weeks, and Tabernacles), lasted seven days, and between the first and second of these feasts were counted seven weeks. The first day of the seventh month was a "Holy Convocation." The Levitical purifications lasted seven days, and the same space of time was allotted to the celebration of weddings and the mourning for the dead. In innumerable instances in the Old Testament and later Jewish writings the number is used as a kind of round number. In the Apocalypse we have the churches, candlesticks, seals, stars, trumpets, spirits, all to the number of seven, and the seven horns and seven eyes of the Lamb. The same number appears again, either divided into half (3½ years, Rev. xiii. 5; xi. 3; xii. 6, etc.), or multiplied by ten — seventy Israelites go to Egypt, the exile lasts seventy years, there are seventy elders, and at a later period there are supposed to be seventy languages and seventy nations upon earth. To go back to the earlier documents, we find in a similar way the dove sent out the second time seven days after her first mission, Pharaoh's dream shows him twice seven kine, twice seven ears of corn, etc.

The Seven Churches of Rev. i.-iii. are Ephesus, Smyrna, Pergamos, Thyatira, Sardis, Philadelphia, and Laodicea.—The Seven Deadly Sins are pride, covetousness, lust, anger, gluttony, envy, and sloth.— The Seven Principal Virtues are faith, hope, charity, prudence, temperance, chastity, and fortitude. — The Seven Gifts of the Holy Ghost are wisdom, understanding, counsel, ghostly strength or fortitude, knowledge, godliness, and the fear of the Lord.

Among the Greeks the seven was sacred to Apollo and to Dionysus, who, according to Orphic legends, was torn into seven pieces; and it was particularly sacred in Eubœa, where the number was found to pervade, as it were, almost every sacred, private, or domestic relation. On the many ancient speculations which connected the number seven with the human body and the phases of its gradual development and formation, its critical periods of sicknesses,— partly still extant as superstitious notions — we cannot here dwell. The Pythagoreans made much of this number, giving it the name of Athene, Hermes, Hephaistos, Heracles, the Virgin unbegotten and unbegetting (*i. e.*, not to be obtained by multiplication), Dionysus, Rex, etc. Many usages show the importance attached to this number in the eyes not only of ancient but even of our own times, and it is hardly necessary to add that the same recurrence is found in the folklore of every race.

Hippocrătēs (B. C. 460-357) divided the life of man into seven ages, a division adopted by Shakespeare.

The Egyptian priests enjoined rest on the seventh day, because it was held to be a *dies infaustus*. In Egyptian astronomy there were seven planets, and hence seven days in the week, each day ruled by its own special planet. The people of Peru had also a seven-day week.

The Persians and Mexicans have a tradition of a flood from which seven persons saved themselves in a cave, and by whom the world was subsequently repeopled.

The seven Champions of Christendom are St. George for England, St. Andrew for Scotland, St. Patrick for Ireland, St. David for Wales, St. Denis for France, St. James for Spain, St. Anthony for Italy.

Maelstrom, The, which means, literally, "grinding stream," is situated on the Norwegian coast, southwest of the Loffoden Isles, and is the most remarkable whirlpool in the world. It runs between the island of Moskenes and a large solitary rock in the middle of the straits. The strong currents, rushing between the Great West Fjord and the outer ocean, through the channels of the Loffoden Isles, produce a number of whirlpools, of which the maelstrom is by far the most dangerous. During severe storms from the west, for instance, the current runs continually to the east at the rate of six knots an hour, without changing its direction for rising or falling tide, and the stream will boil and eddy in such mighty whirls that the largest steamer could hardly contend successfully with the waters. The depth of the whirlpool is only 20 fathoms, but just outside the straits soundings reach from 100 to 200 fathoms. The great danger to vessels is of course not of suction into the heart of the whirlpool, as legends have supposed, but of being dashed to pieces against the rocks.

Lucky Horseshoe.—Most of the houses in the West End of London were protected against witches and evil spirits in the seventeenth century, says John Aubrey, the English antiquary, by having horseshoes fastened to them in various ways. It was the belief that then no witch or evil genius could cross the threshold which was protected by the shoe. The custom of nailing horseshoes, for luck, to all kinds of sailing craft is still, to a certain extent, in vogue, and we all know how fortunate it is considered for anyone to find a horseshoe, the good luck being increased by the number of nails that are attached to the shoe when it is picked up. This superstition can be traced back to about the middle of the seventeenth century, and then we find it lost in the obscurity of the ages.

Godiva, Lady, the wife of Leofric, Earl of Mercia and Lord of Coventry. About 1040 the earl imposed certain onerous services and heavy exactions upon the inhabitants of Coventry, who, in consequence, loudly complained. Lady Godiva, having the welfare of the town at heart, eagerly besought her husband to give them relief; and he, in order to escape from her importunities, said he would grant the favor, but only on condition that she would ride naked through the town. Greatly to her husband's surprise she agreed to the conditions; and on a certain day, after having ordered all the inhabitants to remain within doors and behind closed blinds, she rode through the town clothed only by her long hair. This circumstance was commemorated by a stained glass window, mentioned in 1690, in St. Michael's Church, Coventry; and the legend that an unfortunate tailor, the only man who looked out of a window, was struck blind, has also found commemoration in an ancient effigy of "Peeping Tom of Coventry," still to be seen in a niche of one of the buildings. For many years occasional representations were given of the ride of Lady Godiva, the character being taken by some beautiful woman, clothed, however, in considerable more than her hair, and attended by other historical and emblematic personages. The ceremony has now fallen into disrepute.

Molly Maguires.— The first organization of this name was formed in Ireland, with the object, it is believed, of generally misusing process-servers and others engaged in the prosecution and eviction of tenants, and was composed of young men who, in some localities, assumed women's clothing, blackened their faces, and otherwise disguised themselves. It remained, however, for the American "Mollies" to terrorize whole counties, and leave a blood-red trail behind them in the coal regions of Pennsylvania. To give even a record of the murders and outrages they committed would require an entire volume; but they were numbered by hundreds, and the unfortunate victims were, in most cases, well known and respected men. The American organization was composed of the restless and reckless element drawn to the coal regions through the opening of the coal fields. There is no recorded instance where the disguise of women's clothes was assumed in the United States. Through the efforts of James McParlan, a detective, the secrets of the order were finally revealed, and many of its members were brought to justice.

Natural Storm Signals.— A continuous south wind in most localities will in a few days cause rain, because being warm, dense, and charged with moisture, it is rarefied and cooled by the atmosphere of more northern or elevated sections, and thus its capability of sustaining moisture is lessened. On the other hand, a continuous north wind dispels all rain signs for the time being. Flaky clouds, or low-running ones, from any direction but the north, denote rain or snow. Salmon, leaden, or silvery colored clouds denote falling weather; bright red, clear. When the sunset is followed by bright lances or streaks of light of various hues radiating from the point where the sun disappeared, continuing across the heavens and converging to a common point in the opposite horizon, there exists a storm-cloud in line with the sun, though it may be so distant as to be for a while entirely hidden from view by the rotundity of the earth. If the rays of light are evenly divided north and south of the line between the observer and the radiating point, and continue so until they have faded out, the cloud is approaching. When "heat-lightning" is visible there is a storm-cloud in the same direction, though it may not be seen nor thunder be heard. When the lightning is continuous and very brilliant the storm is a violent one, though the track of the destructive elements may be from 100 to 200 miles away.

Great Bells.— In the manufacture of great bells Russia has always taken the lead. The "Giant," which was cast in Moscow in the sixteenth century, weighed 288,000 pounds, and it required twenty-four men to ring it. It was broken by falling from its support, but was recast in 1654. On June 19, 1706, it again fell, and in 1732 the fragments were used, with new materials, in casting the "King of Bells," still to be seen in Moscow. This bell is nineteen feet, three inches high, measures around the margin sixty feet, nine inches, weighs about 443,732 pounds, and its estimated value in metal alone is at least $300,000. St. Ivan's bell, also in Moscow, is forty feet, nine inches in circumference, sixteen and one half inches thick, and weighs 127,830 pounds. The bells of China rank next to those of Russia in size. In Pekin there are seven bells, each of which is said to weigh 120,000 pounds. The weight of the leading great bells of the world are as follows: "Great Bell of Moscow," 443,732 pounds; St. Ivan's, Moscow, 127,830 pounds; Pekin, 120,000 pounds; Vienna, 40,200 pounds; Olmutz, Bohemia, 40,000 pounds; Rouen, France, 40,000 pounds; St. Paul's, London, 38,470 pounds; "Big Ben," Westminster, 30,350 pounds; Montreal, 28,560 pounds; St. Peter's, Rome, 18,600 pounds.

Population of Great Britain and Ireland.

CENSUS OF 1901.

COUNTIES.	Population.	COUNTIES.	Population.	COUNTIES.	Population.	COUNTIES.	Population.
			ENGLAND.				
Bedford	171,249	Essex	1,085,576	Monmouth	292,327	Surrey	2,008,923
Berks	254,931	Gloucester	634,666	Norfolk	460,040	Sussex	605,052
Bucks	195,534	Hampshire	798,756	Northampton	338,064	Warwick	897,678
Cambridge	190,687	Hereford	114,401	Northumberland	602,859	Westmoreland	64,305
Chester	814,555	Hertford	250,530	Nottingham	514,537	Wiltshire	273,845
Cornwall	322,957	Huntingdon	57,773	Oxford	182,768	Worcester	488,401
Cumberland	266,921	Kent	1,351,849	Rutland	19,708	York	3,585,122
Derby	620,196	Lancaster	4,406,787	Shropshire	239,321		
Devon	660,444	Leicester	433,994	Somerset	508,104	Total	30,805,466
Dorset	202,962	Lincoln	498,781	Stafford	1,234,382		
Durham	1,187,324	Middlesex	3,585,139	Suffolk	384,198		
			SCOTLAND.				
Aberdeen	303,889	Edinburgh	437,553	Linlithgow	64,787	Selkirk	23,339
Argyll	73,166	Elgin	44,757	Nairn	9,291	Shetland	27,755
Ayr	254,133	Fife	218,350	Orkney	27,723	Stirling	141,894
Banff	61,439	Forfar	283,729	Peebles	15,066	Sutherland	21,389
Berwick	30,785	Haddington	38,653	Perth	123,255	Wigtown	32,591
Bute	18,659	Inverness	89,901	Renfrew	268,418	Shipping population	9,583
Caithness	33,619	Kincardine	40,891	Ross and Cromarty	76,149		
Clackmannan	31,991	Kinross	6,980				
Dumbarton	113,660	Kirkcudbright	39,359	Roxburgh	48,793	Total	4,471,957
Dumfries	72,562	Lanark	1,337,848				
			WALES.				
Anglesey	50,590	Carnarvon	126,385	Merioneth	49,130	Radnor	23,263
Brecon	59,906	Denbigh	129,935	Montgomery	54,892		
Cardigan	60,237	Flint	81,727	Pembroke	88,749	Total	1,720,609
Carmarthen	135,325	Glamorgan	860,022				
			IRELAND.				
LEINSTER.		Westmeath	61,527	ULSTER.		CONNAUGHT.	
Carlow	37,723	Wexford	103,860	Antrim	461,240	Galway	192,146
Dublin	447,266	Wicklow	60,679	Armagh	125,238	Leitrim	69,201
Kildare	63,469	MUNSTER.		Cavan	97,368	Mayo	202,627
Kilkenny	78,821	Clare	112,129	Donegal	173,625	Roscommon	101,639
King's	60,129	Cork	404,813	Down	289,335	Sligo	84,022
Longford	46,581	Kerry	165,331	Fermanagh	65,243		
Louth	65,741	Limerick	146,018	Londonderry	144,329	Total	4,456,546
Meath	67,463	Tipperary	159,754	Monaghan	74,505		
Queen's	57,226	Waterford	87,030	Tyrone	150.468		

United States Army Recruiting Requirements.— Applicants for enlistment in the regular army must be between the ages of twenty-one and thirty years, unmarried, of good character and habits, able-bodied, free from disease, and must be able to speak, read, and write the English language. Age for enlistment of citizen soldiery, eighteen to forty-five years, married or unmarried.

Minors are not enlisted, except boys between the ages of sixteen and eighteen who may be needed as musicians and who have the written consent of father, only surviving parent, or legally appointed guardian.

Original enlistments are confined to persons who are citizens of the United States, or who have made legal declaration of their intention to become citizens thereof.

For infantry and artillery the height must be not less than five feet four inches, and weight not less than 120 pounds and not more than 190 pounds.

For cavalry the height must be not less than five feet four inches and not more than five feet ten inches, and weight not to exceed 165 pounds.

All soldiers receive from the Government (in addition to their pay) rations, clothing, bedding, medicines, and medical attendance. The following is the rate of pay as now established:—

Grade.	Pay per Month.	Pay per Year.	Pay per 3 Years.
Privates—Cavalry, artillery, and infantry	$13	$156	$468
Field Musicians—Cavalry, artillery, and infantry	13	156	468
Wagoners—Cavalry, artillery, and infantry	14	168	504
Artificers—Artillery and infantry, saddlers and farriers, cavalry	15	180	540
Corporals—Cavalry, artillery, and infantry	15	180	540
Sergeants—Cavalry, artillery, and infantry	18	216	648
First Sergeant of a company—Cavalry, artillery, and infantry	25	300	900
Chief Trumpeter of cavalry	22	264	792
Principal Musician—Artillery and infantry	22	264	792

ARMY PAY TABLE.

GRADE.	Pay of Officers in Active Service. Yearly Pay.					Pay of Retired Officers. Yearly Pay.				
	First 5 Years' Service.	After 5 Years' Service.	After 10 Years' Service.	After 15 Years' Service.	After 20 Years' Service.	First 5 Years' Service.	After 5 Years' Service.	After 10 Years' Service.	After 15 Years' Service.	After 20 Years' Service.
		10 p. c.	20 p. c.	30 p. c.	40 p. c.					
Major-General	$7,500	....	....	....	....	$5,625	....	....	....	....
Brigadier-General	5,500	....	....	....	....	4,125	....	....	....	....
Colonel	3,500	$3,850	$4,200	*$4,500	*$4,500	2,625	$2,887	$3,150	$3,375	$3,375
Lieutenant-Colonel	3,000	3,300	3,600	3,900	*4,000	2,250	2,475	2,700	2,925	3,000
Major	2,500	2,750	3,000	3,250	3,500	1,875	2,062	2,250	2,437	2,625
Captain, mounted	2,000	2,200	2,400	2,600	2,800	1,500	1,650	1,800	1,950	2,100
Captain, not mounted	1,800	1,980	2,160	2,340	2,520	1,350	1,485	1,620	1,755	1,890
1st Lieutenant, mounted	1,600	1,760	1,920	2,080	2,240	1,200	1,320	1,440	1,560	1,680
1st Lieutenant, not mounted	1,500	1,650	1,800	1,950	2,100	1,125	1,237	1,350	1,462	1,575
2d Lieutenant, mounted	1,500	1,650	1,800	1,950	2,100	1,125	1,237	1,350	1,462	1,575
2d Lieutenant, not mounted	1,400	1,540	1,680	1,820	1,960	1,050	1,115	1,260	1,365	1,470

* The maximum pay of Colonels is limited to $4,500, and of Lieutenant-Colonels to $4,000.
The pay of non-commissioned officers is from $18 to $34 per month, and of privates $13 per month.

United States National and International Salutes, with Cannon. Salute to the Union.— This is one gun for each state, and is commemorative of the Declaration of Independence. It is fired at noon of the Fourth of July, at every military post, and on board commissioned naval vessels belonging to the United States.

The National Salute, 21 guns. This is the salute for the national flag, the President of the United States, presidents of foreign republics, or sovereigns of foreign states, visiting the United States.

Vice-President of the United States, American and foreign ambassadors, 19 guns.

The President of the Senate, Speaker of the House of Representatives, Members of the Cabinet, the Chief Justice, a Congressional Committee, Governors within their respective states or territories, Viceroy or Governor General of provinces belonging to foreign states, General of the Army, Admiral of the Navy, and same ranks in foreign armies and navies, 17 guns.

American or foreign Envoys, or Ministers Plenipotentiary, Assistant Secretaries of the Navy or War, Lieutenant General, or a Major General commanding the army, and corresponding ranks in the navy, and foreign armies and navies, 15 guns.

Ministers-Resident accredited to the United States, Major General, Rear Admiral, and corresponding ranks of foreign armies and navies, 13 guns.

Chargés d'Affaires, Brigadier General, Commodore, and corresponding ranks in foreign armies and navies, 11 guns.

Consul Generals accredited to the United States, 9 guns.

Salutes are only fired between sunrise and sunset, and not on Sundays, except in international courtesies. The national colors are always displayed at the time of saluting. The salute of the flag is the only salute which is returned, and this must be done within twenty-four hours. United States vessels do not return salute to the flag in United States waters if there is any fort or battery there to do it, nor do United States vessels salute United States forts or posts.

If there are several batteries or forts within sight or six miles of each other, one of them is designated as the saluting fort, and returns all salutes of foreign men-of-war. In New York, Castle William, on Governor's Island, is the saluting fort.

Washington Monument. — Notwithstanding the fact that the plan of a monument to General Washington was approved by Congress in the latter part of December, 1799, nothing was done in the matter until 1833, when an association of prominent persons undertook the raising of the needed funds by subscription, and on July 4, 1848, had so far succeeded in their undertaking that the corner stone of a monument was laid, and during the succeeding eight years the shaft was carried to a height of 156 feet. The work was then suspended, at first for lack of funds, then because of the Civil War, and finally because the foundations were believed to be insecure. In 1876 Congress undertook the completion of the monument. The base was first strengthened, and the work of rebuilding the shaft was resumed in August, 1880, and was finished August 9, 1884. The shaft is 555 feet high, and the entire height of the monument, including the foundations, is 592 feet. The base is 55 feet 1½ inch square. At 500 feet above the ground the monument has four sides, each of which is 35 feet wide. Its area at this point is that of a comfortable six-room house, each room of which might be 12x16 feet. This square forms the base of the pyramidal top which runs from it 55 feet until it terminates in a metallic point. This point is constructed of the largest piece of aluminium ever made. The stones of which the monument is constructed are great blocks of crystal marble from Maryland, and in some cases are 9 feet long, 2 feet thick, and 3 or more feet wide. There are more than 18,000 of them. The foundation is built of Potomac gneiss, and is 81 feet square at the base. One hundred and eighty-one "memorial stones" have from first to last been contributed for use in the monument; but many were considered unworthy of a place, and one sent by Pope Pius IX., in 1855, was stolen during the Know-Nothing agitation, and was broken into pieces and thrown into the Potomac river. The monument was dedicated with imposing ceremonies on February 22, 1885. Its cost was about $1,500,000, which was raised partially by an appropriation by Congress and partially by private subscription. It is 30 feet higher than any other work of man except the lofty iron Eiffel Tower erected in Paris for the great Exposition of 1889.

Origin of Visiting Cards.—As is the case in many other instances, we owe the invention of visiting cards to the Chinese. So long ago as the period of the Tong dynasty (618-907), visiting cards were in common use in China, and that is also the date of the introduction of the "red silken cords" which figure so conspicuously on the engagement cards of that country. From very ancient times to the present day the Chinese have observed the strictest ceremony with regard to the paying of visits. The cards which they use for this purpose are very large, and usually of a bright red color. When a Chinaman desires to marry, his parents intimate that fact to a professional "match-maker," who thereupon runs through a list of her visiting acquaintances, and selects one whom she considers a fitting bride for the young man; and then she calls upon the young woman's parents, armed with the bridegroom's card, on which are inscribed his ancestral name and the eight symbols which denote the day of his birth. If the answer is an acceptance of the suit, the bride's card is sent in return; and should the oracles prophesy good concerning the union, the particulars of the engagement are written on two large cards, tied together with the red cords.

Average Annual Temperature in United States.

Place of Observation.	Average Temperature.	Place of Observation.	Average Temperature.
Tucson, Arizona,	69	Salt Lake City, Utah,	52
Jacksonville, Florida,	69	Romney, West Virginia,	52
New Orleans, La.,	69	Indianapolis, Indiana,	51
Austin, Texas,	67	Leavenworth, Kansas,	51
Mobile, Alabama,	66	Santa Fe, New Mex. Ter.,	51
Jackson, Mississippi,	64	Steilacoom, Wash.,	51
Little Rock, Arkansas,	63	Hartford, Connecticut,	50
Columbia, S. Carolina,	62	Springfield, Illinois,	50
Ft. Gibson, Indian Ter.,	60	Camp Scott, Nevada,	50
Raleigh, N. Carolina,	59	Des Moines, Iowa,	49
Atlanta, Georgia,	58	Omaha, Nebraska,	49
Nashville, Tennessee,	58	Denver, Colorado,	48
Richmond, Virginia,	57	Boston, Massachusetts,	48
Louisville, Kentucky,	56	Albany, New York,	48
San Francisco, Cal.,	55	Providence, R. I.,	48
Washington, D. C.,	55	Detroit, Michigan,	47
St. Louis, Missouri,	55	Ft. Randall, Dakota,	47
Baltimore, Maryland,	54	Sitka, Alaska,	46
Harrisburg, Pa.,	54	Concord, N. H.,	46
Wilmington, Delaware,	53	Augusta, Maine,	45
Trenton, New Jersey,	53	Madison, Wisconsin,	45
Columbus, Ohio,	53	Helena, Montana,	43
Portland, Oregon,	53	Montpelier, Vermont,	43
Ft. Boise, Idaho,	52	St. Paul, Minnesota,	42

Gems Symbolic of the Months.—January, the jacinth or hyacinth, symbolizing constancy and fidelity.

February, the amethyst, symbolizing peace of mind and sobriety.

March, the bloodstone or jasper, symbolizing courage and success in dangerous enterprise.

April, the sapphire and diamond, symbolizing repentance and innocence.

May, the emerald, symbolizing success in love.

June, the agate, symbolizing long life and health.

July, the carnelian, symbolizing cure of evils resulting from forgetfulness.

August, the sardonyx or onyx, symbolizing conjugal felicity.

September, the chrysolite, symbolizing preservation from folly, or its cure.

October, the aquamarine, opal, or beryl, symbolizing hope.

November, the topaz, symbolizing fidelity and friendship.

December, the turquoise or ruby, symbolizing brilliant success.

Some doubt exists between May and June, July and August. Thus some give the agate to May and the emerald to June; the carnelian to August, and the onyx to July.

Flying Dutchman, The, is the name given by sailors to a phantom ship, supposed to cruise in storms off the Cape of Good Hope. According to tradition, a Dutch captain, bound home from the Indies, met with long-continued head winds and heavy weather off this cape, and refused to put back, as he was advised to do, swearing a very profane oath that he would beat round the cape if he had to beat there till the Day of Judgment. He was taken at his word, and doomed to beat against winds all his days. His sails are believed to have become threadbare, and his ship's sides white with age, and himself and crew reduced almost to shadows. He cannot heave to nor lower a boat, but sometimes hails vessels through his trumpet, and requests them to take letters home for him. The superstition had its origin, probably, in the looming or apparent suspension in air of some ships out of sight — a phenomenon sometimes witnessed at sea, and caused by unequal refraction in the lower strata of the atmosphere.

Age of Animals.— The exact age attained by animals other than those domesticated it is, of course, impossible to ascertain. It is believed, however, among East Indians, that the elephant lives about 300 years, and instances are on record of the animals having been kept in captivity as long as 130 years, their ages being unknown when they were first taken from the forest. Camels live from 40 to 50 years; horses average from 20 to 30, oxen about 20, sheep 8 or 9, and dogs from 12 to 14 years. The age of a whale is ascertained by the size and number of the laminæ of certain organs in the mouth, formed of a horny substance commonly called whalebone. These laminæ increase yearly, and, if the mode of computation be correct, it is known that whales have attained to the age of 400 years. Some species of birds attain a great age. The swan has been known to live 100 years, and it is recorded that the raven has exceeded that age. Parrots have been known to live 80 years. Pheasants and domestic poultry rarely exceed 12 or 15 years. Among fishes and animals that live in the water great age is often attained. The carp has been known to live 200 years. Common river trout have been confined in a well 30 and even 50 years, and a pike was caught in 1497 in a lake near Heilbronn, in Swabia, with a brass ring attached to it recording that it was placed in the lake in the year 1230.

Principal Navies of the World.[a]

CLASS OF VESSELS.	Great Britain.		France.		U. S.		Germany.		Russia.		Italy.		Japan.	
TYPE.	Blt	Bldg	Blt	Bldg	Blt	Bldg	Blt	Bldg	Blt	Bldg	Blt	Bldg	Blt	Bldg
Battle Ships, First Class	49	13	20	6	13	12	14	6	12	12	12	9	6	4
Battle Ships, Second Class	4	—	9	—	1	—	4	—	2	—	—	—	—	—
Battle Ships, Third Class	2	—	1	—	—	—	12	—	1	—	5	—	—	—
Coast Defense Vessels	2	—	14	—	15	1	11	—	13	—	—	—	2	—
Cruisers, Armored	24	17	10	13	2	11	2	4	6	3	5	1	8*	6
Cruisers, Protected, First Class	21	—	7	—	3	—	2	—	6	4	—	—	—	—
Cruisers, Protected, Second Class	51†	2	16	—	12	5	8	—	4	2	5	—	10	2
Cruisers, Protected, Third Class	32‡	7	17	—	2	1	10	2	—	—	11	1	7	1
Cruisers, Unprotected	10	—	1	—	11	—	20	—	3	—	—	—	9	—
Scouts	—	8	—	—	—	1	—	—	—	—	—	—	—	—
Torpedo Vessels	34	—	16	—	—	—	2	—	8	—	14	—	1	—
Torpedo Boat Destroyers	112	34	14	23	16	—	32	6	8	6	14	2	17	2
Torpedo Boats	85	5	247	43	33	4	93	—	150	7	145	8	63	18
Submarines	5	14	15	33	3	5	—	1	—	2	1	2	—	—

* Including two vessels purchased from the Argentine for $7,500,000, Dec. 31, 1903.
† Including three partially protected. ‡ Including one partially protected.

Relative Order of War Ship Strength.[a]

AT PRESENT.		As would be the case were vessels building now completed.	
Nation.	Tonnage.	Nation.	Tonnage.
Great Britain	1,516,040	Great Britain	1,867,250
France	576,108	France	755,757
Germany	387,874	United States	616,275
Russia	346,458	Germany	505,619
United States	294,405	Russia	458,432
Italy	258,838	Italy	329,257
Japan	243,586	Japan	253,681
Austria	93,913	Austria	149,833

a Compiled April 1st, 1905.

A LIST OF THE FIGHTING SHIPS OF THE U. S. NAVY.

ABBREVIATIONS.—(I.H.P.) Indicated horse power. Hull: (S.) Steel, (S.W.) Steel, wood sheathed. Propulsion: (T.S.) Twin Screw, (Tr.S.) Triple Screw, (S) Screw

FIRST CLASS BATTLESHIPS.

NAME.	Displacement.	I. H. P.	Hull.	Propulsion.	Speed.	Keel laid.	Completed.	Cost.	Batteries. Main, No. Guns	Sec'dary, No. Guns	Torpedo Tubes.
Alabama	11,565	11,366	S.	T. S.	17	1896	1900	$2,650,000	18	30	4
Connecticut	16,000	16,500	"	"	18	1903	Bldg	4,212,000	24	50	4
Georgia	14,948	19,000	S.W.	"	19	1901	"	3,590,000	24	42	4
Idaho	13,000	10,000	S.	"	17	1904	"	2,995,500	20	32	2
Illinois	11,565	12,898	"	"	17	1897	1901	2,595,000	22	28	4
Indiana	10,288	9,738	"	"	16	1891	1895	3,063,000	16	30	4
Iowa	11,340	12,105	"	"	17	1893	1897	3,010,000	18	34	4
Kansas	16,000	16,500	"	"	18	1904	Bldg	4,165,000	24	50	4
Kearsarge	11,540	11,954	"	"	17	1896	1900	2,250,000	22	34	4
Kentucky	11,540	12,318	"	"	17	1896	1900	2,250,000	22	38	4
Louisiana	16,000	16,500	"	"	18	1903	Bldg	3,990,000	24	50	4
Maine	12,300	15,580	"	"	18	1899	1902	2,885,000	20	24	2
Massachusetts	10,288	10,403	"	"	16	1891	1896	3,063,000	16	30	3
Minnesota	16,000	16,500	"	"	18	1903	Bldg	4,110,000	24	50	4
Mississippi	13,000	10,000	"	"	17	1904	"	2,999,500	20	32	2
Missouri	12,240	16,000	"	"	18	1900	1903	2,885,000	20	24	2
Nebraska	14,994	19,000	S.W.	"	19	1902	Bldg	3,733,600	24	42	4
New Hampshire*	16,000	16,500	S.	—	18	Projctd	—	4,400,000	24	42	4
New Jersey	14,918	19,000	S.W.	T. S.	19	1902	Bldg	3,405,000	24	42	4
Ohio	12,508	16,000	S.	"	18	1899	1904	2,899,000	20	24	2
Oregon	10,242	11,111	"	"	17	1891	1896	3,222,810	16	30	3
Rhode Island	14,932	19,000	"	"	19	1902	Bldg	3,405,000	24	42	4
Vermont	16,000	16,500	"	"	18	1904	"	4,179,000	24	50	4
Virginia	14,948	19,000	"	"	19	1902	"	3,590,000	24	42	4
Wisconsin	11,564	12,609	"	"	17	1897	1901	2,674,950	18	28	4

* Three others of the same type projected for the building program of 1905-06.

SECOND CLASS BATTLESHIP.

Texas	6,315	8,610	S.	T. S.	18	1889	1895	$2,500,000	8	22	—

ARMORED CRUISERS.

Brooklyn	9,215	18,769	S.	T. S.	22	1893	1896	$2,986,000	20	23	—
California	13,680	23,000	S. W.	"	22	1902	Bldg	3,800,000	18	48	2
Colorado	13,680	23,000	S.	"	22	1901	"	3,780,000	18	48	2
Maryland	13,680	23,000	"	"	22	1901	"	3,775,000	18	48	2
Montana	14,500	23,000	—	—	22	Projctd	—	4,400,000	20	44	4
New York	8,200	17,401	S.	T. S.	21	1890	1893	2,985,000	18	14	2
N. Carolina	14,500	23,000	—	—	22	Projctd	—	4,400,000	20	44	4
Pennsylvania	13,680	23,000	S. W.	T. S.	22	1901	Bldg	3,890,000	30	48	2
S. Dakota	13,680	23,000	S.	"	22	1902	"	3,750,000	18	48	2
Tennessee	14,500	22,500	"	"	22	1903	"	4,035,000	20	48	4
Washington	14,518	22,500	"	"	22	Projctd	—	4,035,000	20	58	4
W. Virginia	13,680	23,000	S. W.	"	22	1901	Bldg	3,885,000	18	48	2

ARMORED RAM.

Katahdin	2,155	5,068	S.	T. S.	17	1891	1896	$930,000	4	—	

MONITORS, SINGLE TURRET. HARBOR OR COAST DEFENSE.

Arkansas	3,200	3,235	S	T. S.	12.03	1899	1902	$960,000	6	11	
Florida	3,200	3,235	"	"	12.4	1899	1903	925,000	6	11	
Nevada	3,200	3,228	"	"	13.03	1899	1903	962,000	6	15	
Wyoming	3,200	3,218	"	"	12.37	1899	1903	975,000	6	11	

MONITORS, DOUBLE TURRET. HARBOR OR COAST DEFENSE.

Amphitrite	3,960	1,060	Iron	T. S.	10.5	1874 Rebuilt	1895	†	6	13	
Miantonomoh	3,990	1,426	"	"	10.5	1874 Rebuilt	1891	†	4	9	
Monadnock	4,005	3,000	"	"	12	1875 Rebuilt	1896	†	6	8	
Monterey	4,084	5,244	S.	"	13.6	1889	1893	$1,628,905	4	12	
Puritan	6,060	3,700	Iron	"	12.4	1875 Rebuilt	1896	†	10	20	
Terror	3,990	1,600	"	"	10.5	1874 Rebuilt	1896	†	8	8	

† Appropriation to complete Monitors, $3,178,046.

A List of the Fighting Ships of the U. S. Navy.—*Continued.*

UNARMORED STEEL VESSELS.

PROTECTED CRUISERS.

NAME.	Displacement.	I. H. P.	Hull.	Propulsion.	Speed.	Keel laid.	Completed.	Cost.	Batteries. Main, No. Guns	Batteries. Sec'dary, No. Guns
Albany	3,769	7,400	S. W.	T. S.	20	—	1900	—	10	20
Atlanta	3,000	4,030	S.	S.	15.60	1883	1886	$617,000	8	13
Baltimore	4,413	10,064	"	T. S.	20.09	1887	1890	1,325,000	18	16
Boston	3,035	4,309	"	S.	15.6	1883	1887	619,000	8	13
Charleston	9,685	21,000	"	T. S.	22	1902	Bldg	2,740,000	14	56
Chattanooga	3,200	4,700	S. W.	"	16.5	1900	"	1,039,000	10	15
Chicago	5,000	9,000	S.	"	18	1883	1889	889,000	18	14
Cincinnati	3,213	10,000	"	"	19	1890	1894	1,100,000	11	13
Cleveland	3,200	4,700	S. W.	"	16.5	1900	1903	1,041,000	10	15
Columbia	7,375	18,509	S.	Tr. S.	22.8	1890	1894	2,725,000	11	17
Denver	3,200	4,700	S. W.	T. S.	17.47	1900	1904	1,080,000	10	15
Des Moines	3,200	4,700	"	"	16.5	1900	1904	1,065,000	10	15
Galveston	3,200	4,700	"	"	16.5	1901	Bldg	1,027,000	10	15
Milwaukee	9,700	21,000	S.	"	22	1902	"	2,825,000	14	56
Minneapolis	7,375	20,862	"	Tr. S.	23.07	1891	1894	2,690,000	11	17
Newark	4,098	8,869	"	T. S.	19	1888	1891	1,248,000	12	23
New Orleans	3,769	7,500	S. W.	"	20	—	1898	—	10	20
Olympia	5,870	17,313	S.	"	21.68	1891	1895	1,796.000	14	24
Philadelphia	4,410	8,815	"	"	19.67	1888	1890	1,350,000	12	18
Raleigh	2,210	10,000	"	"	19	1889	1894	1,100,000	11	13
San Francisco	4,068	9,913	"	"	19.52	1888	1891	1,428,000	12	16
St. Louis	9,700	21,000	"	"	22	1902	Bldg	2,740,000	14	56
Tacoma	3,215	4,700	S. W.	"	16.5	1900	1904	1.041,000	10	15

UNPROTECTED CRUISERS.

NAME.	Displacement.	I. H. P.	Hull.	Propulsion.	Speed.	Keel laid.	Completed.	Cost.	Main, No. Guns	Sec'dary, No. Guns
Detroit	2,103	5,227	S.	T. S.	19	1890	1893	$612,500	10	11
Marblehead	2,089	5,451	"	"	18.4	1890	1894	674,000	10	13
Montgomery	2,089	5,580	"	"	19	1890	1894	612,500	10	10
Reina Mercedes	3,090	3,700	—	—	17	—	—	—	—	—

AUXILIARY CRUISERS.

NAME.	Displacement.	I. H. P.	Hull.	Propulsion.	Speed.	Keel laid.	Completed.	Cost.	Main, No. Guns	Sec'dary, No. Guns
Buffalo	6,000	3,600	S.	S.	14.5	1892	1894	$575,000	6	8
Dixie	6,145	3,800	"	"	16	1893	1894	575,000	8	11
Panther	3,380	—	—	—	13	1889	1890	375,000	6	8
Prairie	6,620	3,800	Iron	S.	14.5	1890	1891	575,000	8	12
Yankee	6,225	3,800	Iron	"	12.5	1892	1893	575,000	8	10

GUNBOATS.

NAME.	Displacement.	I. H. P.	Hull.	Propulsion.	Speed.	Keel laid.	Completed.	Cost.	Main, No. Guns	Sec'dary, No. Guns
Bancroft	839	1,213	—	—	14	1891	1893	$250,000	4	10
Bennington	1,710	3,436	Iron	T. S.	17	1888	1891	490,000	6	10
Castine	1,777	2,199	S.	"	16	1891	1894	318,500	8	7
Concord	1,710	3,405	"	"	16	1888	1891	490,000	6	8
Don Juan de Austria	1,136	1,500	Iron	S.	14	—	1892	180,000	4	8
General Alava	1,115	770	S.	"	10	—	—	—	—	5
Helena	1,397	1,988	"	T. S.	15	1894	1897	280,000	8	11
Isla de Cuba	1,125	2,700	"	"	16	—	1888	215,000	4	8
Isla de Luzon	1,125	2,700	"	"	16	—	1888	215,000	4	8
Machias	1,177	2,046	"	"	15	1891	1893	318,500	8	8
Nashville	1,371	2,536	"	"	16	1894	1897	280,000	8	9
Petrel	892	1,095	"	S.	11	1887	1889	247,000	4	8
Topeka	2,300	2,000	—	—	16	—	1882	170,327	6	9
Wilmington	1,392	1,894	S.	T. S.	15	1894	1897	280,000	8	10
Yorktown	1,710	3.392	—	—	16	1887	1889	455,000	6	10

COMPOSITE GUNBOATS.

NAME.	Displacement.	I. H. P.	Hull.	Propulsion.	Speed.	Keel laid.	Completed.	Cost.	Main, No. Guns	Sec'dary, No. Guns
Annapolis	1,060	1,227	Compo	S.	13	1897	1897	$227,700	6	7
Dubuque	1,085	1,000	S. W.	T. S.	12	1903	Bldg	—	6	8
Marietta	1,000	1,054	Compo	"	13	1897	1897	223,000	6	7
Newport	1,000	1,008	"	S.	12	1897	1897	229,400	6	7
Paducah	1,085	1,000	S. W.	T. S.	12	1903	Bldg	355,000	6	8
Princeton	1,100	800	Compo	S.	12	1898	1898	230,000	6	7
Vicksburg	1,000	1,118	"	"	13	1897	1898	299,400	6	7
Wheeling	1,000	1,081	"	T. S.	12	1897	1897	219.000	6	7

DYNAMITE GUNBOAT.

NAME.	Displacement.	I. H. P.	Hull.	Propulsion.	Speed.	Keel laid.	Completed.	Cost.	Main, No. Guns	Sec'dary, No. Guns
Vesuvius	929	3,795	S.	T.-S.	21	1887	1890	$350,000	3-15in. dymte	5

DESPATCH BOAT.

NAME.	Displacement.	I. H. P.	Hull.	Propulsion.	Speed.	Keel laid.	Completed.	Cost.	Main, No. Guns	Sec'dary, No. Guns
Dolphin	1,486	2,253	S.	S.	16	1883	1885	$315,000	2	9

A List of the Fighting Ships of the U. S. Navy.—*Continued.*

TORPEDO BOAT DESTROYERS, TORPEDO BOATS AND SUBMARINES.

NAME.	Launched.	Length.	Beam.	Draught.	Hull.	Propulsion	Displacement.	I. H. P.	Speed.	Cost.	Armament. Guns.	Torpedo Tubes.	Maximum Coal Supply.
		Ft. In.	Ft. In.	Ft. In.			Tons.		Knots.				Tons.
DESTROYERS.													
Bainbridge	1901	245-0	23-7	6-6	S.	T.S.	420	8,000	29	$283,000	2 12-pr., 5 6-pr.	2	139
Barry	1902	"	"	"	"	"	"	"	"	"	" "	"	"
Chauncey	1901	"	"	"	"	"	"	"	"	"	" "	"	"
Dale	1900	"	"	"	"	"	"	"	28	260,000	" "	"	"
Decatur	1900	"	"	"	"	"	"	"	"	"	" "	"	"
Hopkins	1902	244-0	24-6	6-0	"	"	408	7,200	29	291,000	" "	"	150
Hull	1902	"	"	"	"	"	"	"	"	"	" "	"	"
Lawrence	1900	242-3	22-3	6-2	"	"	400	8,400	30	281,000	" "	"	115
Macdonough	1901	"	"	"	"	"	"	"	"	"	" "	"	"
Paul Jones	1900	245-0	23-7	6-6	"	"	420	7,000	29	285,000	" "	"	139
Perry	1900	"	"	"	"	"	"	"	"	"	" "	"	"
Preble	1901	"	"	"	"	"	"	"	"	"	" "	"	"
Stewart	1902	"	"	"	"	"	"	8,000	29.3	282,000	" "	"	"
Truxton	1901	248-0	23-3	6-0	"	"	433	8,300	30	286,000	" "	"	232
Whipple	1901	"	"	"	"	"	"	"	"	"	" "	"	"
Warden	1901	"	"	"	"	"	"	"	"	"	" "	"	"
TORPEDO BOATS.													
Bagley	1900	157-0	17-0	4-7	S.	T. S.	167	3,920	28	$161,000	3 3-pr.	3	—
Bailey	1899	205-0	19-0	6-0	"	"	235	5,000	30	210,000	4 6-pr.	2	20
Barney	1900	157-0	17-0	4-7	"	"	167	3,920	28	161,000	3 3-pr.	3	—
Biddle	1900	"	"	"	"	"	"	3,910	"	"	"	"	—
Blakeley	1902	175-0	17-6	4-8	"	"	165	3,000	26	159,000	"	"	70
Cushing	1890	138-9	14-3	4-11	"	"	105	1,720	22.5	82,750	3 1-pr.	"	36
Dahlgren	1899	147-0	16-4	4-7	"	"	146	4,200	30.5	194,000	4 1-pr.	2	32
Davis	1898	146-0	15-4	5-4	"	"	132	1,750	22.5	81,546	3 1-pr.	3	—
De Long	1901	175-0	17-6	4-8	"	"	165	3,000	26	159,400	3 3-pr.	"	70
Du Pont	1897	"	17-8	"	"	"	"	3,400	28.58	144,000	4 1-pr.	"	76
Ericsson	1894	149-7	15-6	4-9	"	"	120	1,800	24	113,500	"	"	35
Farrugut	1898	213-6	20-8	6-0	"	S.	273	5,600	30	227,500	4 6-pr.	2	76
Foote	1896	160-0	16-1	5-0	"	T. S.	142	2,000	24.5	97,500	3 1-pr.	3	44
Fox	1898	146-0	15-4	5-4	"	"	132	1,750	22.5	85,000	"	"	—
Goldsborough	1902	194-8	20-5	5-0	"	"	247.5	5,880	30	214,500	4 6-pr.	2	131
Gwin	1897	99-6	12-6	3-3	"	S.	46	850	20.88	39,000	1 1-pr.	"	8
MacKenzie	1898	99-3	12-9	4-3	"	"	65	"	20	48,500	"	"	15.3
Manly	—	—	—	—	"	"	30	250	—	24,250	——	1	—
McKee	1898	99-3	12-9	4-3	"	"	65	850	19.82	45,000	2 1-pr.	2	—
Morris	1898	138-3	15-6	4-1	"	T. S.	105	1,750	24	89,000	3 1-pr.	3	28
Nicholson	1902	174-6	17-0	4-6	"	"	174	3,500	26	165,000	3 3-pr.	"	—
O'Brien	1902	"	"	"	"	"	"	"	"	"	"	"	—
Porter	1896	175-0	17-8	4-8	"	"	165	3,800	28.63	147,000	4 1-pr.	"	76
Rodgers	1896	160-0	16-1	5-0	"	"	142	2,000	24.5	97,500	3 1-pr.	"	44
Rowan	1898	170-0	17-0	5-11	"	"	182	3,200	26	160,000	4 1-pr.	"	60
Shubrick	1899	175-0	17-6	4-8	"	"	165	3,000	26	129,750	3 3-pr.	"	70
Somers	—	149-3¾	17-5	—	"	"	145	1,960	23.5	72,997	——	—	—
Stiletto	—	88-6	11-0	3-0	W.	S.	31	359	18.22	25,000	——	2	4
Stockton	1899	175-0	17-6	4-8	S.	T. S.	165	3,000	26	129,750	3 3-pr.	3	70
Stringham	1899	225-0	22-0	6-6	"	"	340	7,200	30	236,000	7 6-pr.	2	120
T. A. M. Craven	1899	147-0	16-4	4-7	"	"	146	4,200	30.5	194,000	4 1-pr.	"	32
Talbot	1897	96-6	12-6	3-3	"	"	46	850	21.15	39,000	1 1-pr.	"	8.8
Thornton	1900	175-0	17-6	4-8	"	"	165	3,000	26	129,750	3 3-pr.	3	70
Tingly	1902	175-0	"	"	"	"	"	"	"	168,000	"	"	"
Wilkes	1901	"	"	"	"	"	"	"	26.25	146,000	"	"	"
Winslow	1897	160-0	16-1	5-0	"	"	142	2,000	24.5	97,500	3 1-pr.	"	44
SUBMARINES.													
Adder	1901	63-4	11-9	—	S.	S.	120	160	7.8	$170,000	1 Torpedo tube, 5 Whiteh'd T.		
Grampus	Bldg	"	"	—	"	"	"	"	"	"	1 Torpedo tube, 5 Whiteh'd T.		
Holland	1896	54-0	10-3	—	"	"	74	45	8	150,000	1 Dynamite torpedo.		
Moccasin	1901	63-4	11-9	—	"	"	120	160	7.8	170,000	1 Torpedo tube, 5 Whiteh'd T.		
Pike	Bldg	"	11-9	—	"	"	"	"	"	"	1 Torpedo tube, 5 Whiteh'd T.		
Plunger	1902	"	11-9	—	"	"	"	"	"	150,000	1 Torpedo tube, 2 Whiteh'd T.		
Porpoise	1901	"	11-9	—	"	"	"	"	"	170,000	1 Torpedo tube, 5 Whiteh'd T.		
Protector	1892	65-0	11-0	—	"	—	170	250	7.11	—	1 Torpedo tube, 5 Whiteh'd T.		
Shark	1901	63-4	11-9	—	"	"	120	160	7.8	170,000	1 Torpedo tube. 5 Whiteh'd T.		

SUMMARY OF VESSELS IN THE UNITED STATES NAVY.

VESSELS FIT FOR SERVICE INCLUDING THOSE UNDER REPAIR.

First-class battleships,	12
Second-class battleships,	1
Armored cruisers,	2
Armored ram,	1
Single turret, harbor defense monitors,	4
Double turret monitors,	6
Protected cruisers,	18
Unprotected cruisers,	4
Gunboats,	12
Light-draft gunboats,	3
Composite gunboats,	8
Training ship (Naval Academy), sheathed,	1
Special class (Dolphin-Vesuvius),	2
Gunboats under 500 tons,	21
Torpedo boat destroyers,	16
Steel torpedo boats,	35
Submarine torpedo boats,	9
Wooden torpedo boats,	1
Iron cruising vessels, steam,	5
Wooden cruising vessels, steam,	6
Wooden sailing vessels,	4
Tugs,	39
Auxiliary cruisers,	5
Converted yachts,	23
Colliers,	16
Supply and hospital ships,	14
Total,	268

VESSELS UNDER CONSTRUCTION OR AUTHORIZED.

First-class battleships,	12
Armored cruisers,	10
Protected cruisers,	5
Gunboats for great lakes (not begun),	1
Composite gunboats,	2
Steel torpedo boats,	6
Training ships,	2
Training brig,	1
Tugs,	2
Total,	41

VESSELS UNFIT FOR SEA SERVICE.

Iron, single-turret monitors,	5
Wooden cruising vessels, steam,	10
Wooden sailing vessels,	8
Total,	23
Grand total,	332

New York Elevated Railways.—In 1868 an elevated railroad extending a half-mile was constructed on Greenwich street, New York, as an experiment. Three years later the West Side Elevated Railroad Company obtained a charter, but shortly afterward sold its right to the New York Elevated Railroad Company. The new organization proceeded rapidly to erect its roads, and in December, 1879, its rolling stock consisted of 131 locomotives, 292 passenger cars, and 8 service cars. In May, 1879, the road was leased to the Manhattan Railway Company. The Metropolitan Elevated Railroad was first called the Gilbert Elevated Railroad, in honor of its projector, Dr. Rufus H. Gilbert. Although the company obtained its charter in 1872, work was not commenced until March, 1876. In two years it expended $10,300,000 in constructing its lines. In 1879 the road with its rolling stock, consisted of 56 locomotives, 180 passenger cars, and 2 freight cars, was leased to the Manhattan Elevated Railroad Company, which now controls and manages the entire elevated railroad system of New York.

The Famous Connecticut Blue Laws.—These laws, enacted by the people of the "Dominion of New Haven," became known as the blue laws because they were printed on blue paper. They were as follows:—

The governor and magistrates convened in general assembly are the supreme power, under God, of the independent dominion. From the determination of the assembly no appeal shall be made.

No one shall be a freeman or have a vote unless he is converted and a member of one of the churches allowed in the dominion.

Each freeman shall swear by the blessed God to bear true allegiance to this dominion and that Jesus is the only king.

No dissenter from the essential worship of this dominion shall be allowed to give a vote for electing of magistrates or any officer.

No food or lodging shall be offered to a heretic.

No one shall cross a river on the Sabbath but authorized clergymen.

No one shall travel, cook victuals, make beds, sweep houses, cut hair, or shave on the Sabbath Day.

No one shall kiss his or her children on the Sabbath or feasting days.

The Sabbath Day shall begin at sunset Saturday.

Whoever wears clothes trimmed with gold, silver, or bone lace above one shilling per yard shall be presented by the grand jurors and the selectmen shall tax the estate £300.

Whoever brings cards or dice into the dominion shall pay a fine of £5.

No one shall eat mince pies, dance, play cards, or play any instrument of music except the drum, trumpet, or jewsharp.

No gospel minister shall join people in marriage. The magistrate may join them, as he may do it with less scandal to Christ's church.

When parents refuse their children convenient marriages, the magistrate shall determine the point.

A man who strikes his wife shall be fined £10.

A woman who strikes her husband shall be punished as the law directs.

No man shall court a maid in person or by letter without obtaining the consent of her parents; £5 penalty for the first offense; £10 for the second, and for the third imprisonment during the pleasure of the court.

Perpetual Motion.— Perpetual motion is a movement which is not only self-active but also self-creative. A machine which when set in motion would continue to move without the aid of external force and without the loss of momentum until its parts were all worn out, might be said to have solved the perpetual motion problem. But even more is expected of this invention should it ever become practicable, that it shall go on doing work without drawing on any external source of energy, or shall by its movement continually create power. The impossibility of constructing such a machine has long been demonstrated, but still ignorant and ambitious inventors continue to try for it. As early as the year 1775, the Parisian Academy of Sciences refused to receive any further schemes for perpetual motion, regarding it as an impossibility. There was a time when the perpetual motion problem was worthy the attention of a philosopher, just as there was a time when a man might have been justified in doubting whether the earth was a globe.

Grangers, or Patrons of Husbandry, as they are properly called, were organized December 4, 1867, by Mr. O. H. Kelley and Mr. William M. Saunders, both of the Department of Agriculture at Washington. Mr. Kelley was commissioned by President Johnson, in 1866, to travel through the Southern States, and report upon their agricultural and mineral resources. He discovered agriculture in a state of great depression, consequent upon the changes made by the Civil War. There was also at the time serious dissatisfaction among the farmers of the West and Northwest in regard to the alleged heavy rate and unjust discriminations made by railroad companies in their transportation of farmers' products. It was also claimed that middle men exacted exorbitant prices for agricultural implements, etc. Mr. Kelley concluded that an association made up of those who were dissatisfied might be organized on some such plan as the Order of Odd Fellows or Masons. He and Mr. Saunders devised a plan for an organization to be known as the "Patrons of Husbandry," and its branches to be called "Granges," and on December 4, 1867, the National Grange was organized at Washington. In the spring of 1868 granges were founded at Harrisburg, Pa.; at Fredonia, N. Y.; at Columbus, Ohio; at Chicago, Ill., and six in Minnesota. The movement became very popular, and they were, in a few years, organized in nearly every state and territory in the Union. The order has its greatest strength, however, in the Northwestern and Western States.

Facts Worth Knowing.—Proper ages of reproduction 1, length of power of reproduction 2, and periods of gestation 3, in domestic animals:—

	1	2	3 Shortest.	3 Mean.	3 Longest.
	Years.	Years.	Days.	Days.	Days.
Horse	......	12 to 15	....	....	....
Mare	4	10 to 12	287	347	419
Cow	3	10	283	321	340
Bull	....	5	....	....	....
Sow	1	6	109	115	143
Boar	....	6	....	....	....
Ewe	2	6	146	154	161
Ram	....	7	....	....	....
Jackass	....	12 to 15	....	....	....
Ass	4	10 to 12	365	380	391
Goat	2	5 to 6	150	156	163
Slut	2	8 to 9	55	60	63
Dog	....	8 to 9	....	....	....
Cat	1	9 to 10	....	....	....
Cat, female	....	5 to 6	48	50	56

The Longest Rivers in the World.

NAME.	MILES.
AFRICA.	
Nile	3,895
Niger	2,990
Congo	2,700
Zambezi	2,300
Orange	1,152
AMERICA (NORTH).	
Mississippi and Missouri	4,194
St. Lawrence	2,120
Mackenzie	2,120
Saskatchewan	1,918
Rio Grande	1,800
Arkansas	1,514
Columbia	1,383
Ohio and Allegheny	1,265
Red River	1,200
Colorado	1,000
AMERICA (SOUTH).	
Amazon	3,596
Rio Madeira	2,300
Parana	2,211
Rio de la Plata	1,800
AMERICA (SO.)—Cont.	
San Francisco	1,613
Rio Negro	1,650
Orinoco	1,500
ASIA.	
Yenisei	3,688
Hoang Ho	2,812
Lena	2,766
Obi	2,674
Amur	2,673
Euphrates	2,005
Ganges	1,844
Indus	1,613
AUSTRALASIA.	
Murray	3,000
EUROPE.	
Volga	2,351
Danube	1,992
Ural	1,099
Don	1,088
Dnieper	1,020
Rhine	876

Field of the Cloth of Gold was so called from the extravagance and display attendant upon a meeting of Henry VIII. of England and Francis I. of France, in June, 1530. The kings met in the field near the small town of Ardres, in France, which was owned by England, and the meeting was held by the request of Francis I., who desired to gain the friendship of Henry to aid him in his projects for curbing the power of his great rival, Charles V., of Germany. The ceremonial was under the direction of Cardinal Wolsey, and the nobility of France and England vied with each other in the gorgeous decoration of themselves, their banners and tents, and their retinues of followers.

Historic Minor Political Parties.—The minor American parties which have appeared and disappeared during the 19th century of our national life are the following: *Anti-Renters*, a New York party which flourished about 1841. They resisted the collection of back rents on the Van Rensselaer manor near Albany. They had strength enough to defeat Wright, the regular Democratic candidate for governor of New York. *Barn-burners*, New York, 1846, seceders from the Democratic party. They were opposed to slavery extension. *Bucktails*, New York, about 1815; they supported Madison. *Conservatives*, New York and some other states, 1837; paper money Democrats. *Doughfaces*, 1820, Northern members of Congress, who voted in favor of the Missouri compromise. *Hunkers*, New York, a faction of the Democrats favoring the South, the Barn-burners being the other factor. *Know-Nothings*, New York, 1854, opposed to naturalization of foreigners unless they had been twenty-one years in the country. *Loco-Focos*, New York, 1835; a branch of the Democratic party. *Liberal Republicans*, 1872; Republicans who joined with the Democrats in support of Greeley for president. *Temperance*, or Prohibition, from 1830 down, in many states; in favor of preventing or restricting the sale of liquors. *Woman's Rights*, from 1860 down; those who favored granting to women the right of suffrage.

Tax on Commercial Travelers.—The following is a list of places and amount of taxation on commercial travelers: Alabama, $15.50 per year; Arizona, $200 per year; Beaufort, S. C., $10 per visit; Bennettsville, S. C., $1 per visit; Batesburg, S. C., 75 cents per day; Charleston, S. C., $10 per month; Cumberland, Md., $1 per day; Delaware, $25 per year; Deadwood, S. D., $5 per week; Darlington, S. C., $1; East St. Louis, $2 per day; Elkton, Md., per cent. on stock carried; Florida, $25 per year; Hartwell, Ga., $5 per trip; Johnston, S. C., 50 cents per day; Lewistown, Idaho, $5 per trip; Montana, $100 per year for each county; Memphis, Tenn., $10 per week or $25 per month; Mobile, Ala., $3 per day or $7 a week; Natchez, Miss., 25 cents per day; New Orleans, La., $50 per year; Newport, Ky., $1 per month; North Carolina, $100 per year; Nevada, $100 per year; Orangeburg, S. C., $2 per day; St. Matthews, S. C., $1 per day; San Francisco, Cal., $25 per quarter; Texas, $35 a year; Tucson, Arizona, $50 per quarter; Tombstone, Arizona, $10 per day; Virginia, $75 per year; Wilmington, N. C., $3 per day; Washington, D. C., $200 per year; Walhalla, S. C., $1 per day.

Relative Value of Different Foods for Stock.—One hundred pounds of good hay for stock are equal to:—

Articles.	Pounds.	Articles.	Pounds.
Beets, white silesia	669	Lucerne	89
Turnips	469	Clover, red, dry	88
Rye straw	429	Buckwheat	78½
Clover, red, green	373	Corn	62½
Carrots	371	Oats	59
Mangolds	368½	Barley	58
Potatoes, kept in pit	350	Rye	53½
Oat straw	317	Wheat	44½
Potatoes	360	Oil-cake, linseed	43
Carrot leaves (tops)	135	Pease, dry	37½
Hay, English	100	Beans	28

Colored Troops in U. S. Army during the War.

Arkansas	5,526	Maine	104
Alabama	4,969	New Hampshire	125
Connecticut	1,764	New York	4,125
Colorado Territory	95	New Jersey	1,185
Delaware	954	North Carolina	5,035
Dist. of Columbia	3,269	Ohio	5,092
Florida	1,044	Pennsylvania	8,612
Georgia	3,486	Rhode Island	1,837
Iowa	440	South Carolina	5,462
Indiana	1,597	Texas	47
Illinois	1,811	Tennessee	20,133
Kansas	2,080	Vermont	120
Kentucky	23 703	Virginia	5,723
Louisiana	24,052	West Virginia	196
Maryland	8,718	Wisconsin	155
Massachusetts	3,966	At large	733
Michigan	1,387	Not accounted for	5,083
Mississippi	17,869	Officers	7,122
Missouri	8,344		
Minnesota	104	Total	186,017

Amount of Oil in Seeds.

Kinds of Seed.	Per cent. Oil.	Kinds of Seed.	Per cent. Oil.
Rape seed	55	Oats	6½
Sweet almond	47	Clover hay	5
Turnip seed	45	Wheat bran	4
White mustard	37	Oat straw	4
Bitter almond	37	Meadow hay	3½
Hemp seed	19	Wheat straw	3
Linseed	17	Wheat flour	3
Indian corn	7	Barley	2½

Acetylene.—A substance composed of carbon and hydrogen and of remarkable powers. It is produced in large quantities from carbide of calcium, a product of the electric furnace. When water is thrown on this substance it gives off acetylene gas. It was found about 1895, that this gas, when burned in a suitable burner, would give the brightest light of any known gas. When placed under strong pressure acetylene becomes a liquid.

About Ships.—SPEED AND DISTANCE.—The rapidity with which a rapid sailing propelling steamer travels is ascertained by the number of revolutions or movements made per minute in certain portions of the machinery. It is also learned by the dropping of an object attached to a line into the water at the side of the stern of the vessel, which, remaining nearly stationary, allows the operator to know the speed by the number of knots which the line runs out in a certain number of seconds. The drop line, called the log line, contains a small string tied into a knot at a distance of every 47 feet and 3 inches; hence the name "knot."

STEAMSHIP NAMES.—The bow is the extreme forward part of the ship. The stern is the after part. Forward is the forepart of the vessel. Aft is the rear part. Amidships is the central part of the vessel. Starboard is the right side of the ship, looking forward. Port, the left side. The Index Guide gives the following description of sails, namely: The masts are the fore mast, main mast, and mizzen mast. The parts of the masts are the fore mast, fore-top mast, fore-topgallant mast, fore-royal mast, and similarly for the other masts; thus, main mast, main-top mast, mizzen-top mast, etc. Booms are round, heavy wooden spars to which the sails are attached—the jib-boom extending from the bowsprit, the flying jib-boom being attached to, but extending beyond, the jib-boom. The main and mizzen booms are attached to the main and mizzen masts, the spanker boom extends aft from the mizzen mast. Yards are strong, horizontal, wooden spars, extending crosswise the ship, to which the sails are attached along up the masts. The principal sails are the jib and flying jib, long triangular sails extending from the fore-mast to the jib-booms, and along the masts upward from the deck to the try-sail, the fore-course or fore-sail, or fore-top sail, fore-topgallant sail, fore-royal sail, fore-sky sail, and similarly for each of the other masts; thus, main try-sail, main sail, main top-sail, mizzen top-sail, etc., and spanker, the sternmost sail, extending from the spanker boom to the gaff. The ensign or ship's colors are attached to the gaff. Shrouds are the ropes used to sustain the masts and extend from the fore-top to the sides of the ship (the rope ladders). The other ropes used as supports to the masts are designated stays, and are named from that part of the mast to which they are attached, as fore-stay, mizzen-stay, fore royal-stay, mizzen-topgallant-stay, etc. The jib-boom, flying jib-boom, and several of the sails here mentioned, are not required and are not used on the large modern steamers.

Hero and Leander.—Hero was a priestess of Venus. Leander was a youth of Abydos, a famous city on the Asiatic side of the strait of the Hellespont, nearly opposite the city Sestos, on the European coast. At a festival of Venus and Adonis, held at Sestos, Hero and Leander first saw each other, and were immediately inspired with a mutual passion; but Hero's office as a priestess and the opposition of her parents stood in the way of their union. Undaunted by these obstacles, Leander every night swam across the Hellespont to visit his beloved, who directed his course by holding a burning torch from the top of a tower on the seashore. After many meetings Leander was drowned on a tempestuous night, and his body was cast up at the foot of the tower where Hero stood expecting him. Heartbroken at the sight, she flung herself from the tower into the sea, and passed with her lover into the immortality of art and song.

Popular Names of Cities.—The nicknames given to the various prominent cities in the United States are as follows: Brooklyn, N. Y., City of Churches; Boston, Hub of the Universe; Baltimore, Monumental City; Buffalo, Queen City of the Lakes; Chicago, Garden City; Cincinnati, Queen City; Cleveland, Forest City; Detroit, City of the Straits; Hannibal, Bluff City; Indianapolis, Railroad City; Keokuk, Gate City; Louisville, Falls City; Lowell, City of Spindles; New York, Gotham, Empire City; New Orleans, Crescent City; Nashville, City of Rocks; New Haven, City of Elms; Philadelphia, Quaker City, City of Brotherly Love; Pittsburg, Iron City; Portland, Me., Forest City; Rochester, Flour City; St. Louis, Mound City; Springfield, Ill., Flower City; Washington, D. C., City of Magnificent Distances.

Principal Exports of Various Countries.—ARABIA.—Coffee, aloes, myrrh, frankincense, gum arabic.

BELGIUM.—Grain, flax, hops, woolens, linens, laces, various manufactures.

BRAZIL.—Cotton, sugar, coffee, tobacco, gold, diamonds, wheat, and dye-goods.

CANADA, NOVA SCOTIA, AND NEW BRUNSWICK.—Flour, furs, lumber, fish.

CAPE COLONY.—Brandy, wine, ostrich feathers, hides, tallow.

CENTRAL AMERICA.—Logwood, mahogany, indigo, cocoa.

CHILE.—Silver, gold, copper, wheat, hemp, hides, sugar, cotton, fruits.

CHINA.—Tea, silks, nankeens, porcelain, opium, articles of ivory and pearl.

DENMARK.—Grain, horses, cattle, beef, pork, butter, cheese.

EASTERN, WESTERN, AND SOUTHERN AFRICA.—Gold, ivory, ostrich feathers.

EGYPT.—Rice, grain, linseed, fruits, indigo, cotton, sugar.

ECUADOR AND COLOMBIA—Coffee, cotton, indigo, cocoa, fruits, sugar.

FRANCE.—Silks, woolens, linens, cotton, wine, brandy, porcelain, toys.

GERMANY.—Linen, grain, various manufactures of silver, copper, etc.

GREAT BRITAIN.—Woolens, cottons, linens, hardware, porcelain, etc.

GREENLAND.—Whale oil, whalebone, seal skins.

HINDOOSTAN.—Cotton, silks, rice, sugar, coffee, opium, indigo.

HOLLAND.—Fine linens, woolens, butter, cheese, various manufactures.

ITALY.—Silks, wine, oil, grain, fruits.

IRELAND.—Linens, beef, butter, tallow, hides, potatoes, barley.

JAPAN.—Silk and cotton goods, japanware, porcelain.

MEXICO.—Gold, silver, logwood, cochineal, fruits.

PERSIA.—Carpets, shawls, wine, silk, cotton, rice, rhubarb, guns, swords, etc.

PERU.—Silver, gold, Peruvian bark, mercury, sugar, cotton, fruits.

RUSSIA.—Hemp, iron, linen, grain, timber, furs, tallow, platina.

SPAIN AND PORTUGAL.—Silks, wool, wine, oil, fruits, salt.

SWEDEN AND NORWAY.—Iron, steel, copper, timber, fish.

SWITZERLAND.—Watches, jewelry, paper, laces, linen, cotton, and silk goods, etc.

TURKEY.—Grain, fruits, cotton, oil, wines, carpets, muslin, swords.

UNITED STATES:—

EASTERN STATES.—Lumber, beef, pork, fish, cottons, woolens, etc.

MIDDLE STATES.—Flour, wheat, salt, coal, cottons, woolens.

SOUTHERN STATES.—Cotton, rice, tobacco, corn, lumber, pitch, fruits.

WESTERN STATES.—Corn, wheat, lead, coal, iron, salt, lime, beef, pork.

VENEZUELA.—Sugar, coffee, cocoa, cotton, indigo, fruits.

WEST INDIES.—Sugar, rum, molasses, coffee, spice, cotton, indigo, fruits.

What Dynamite is and How it is Made.—Few people know what dynamite is, though the word is in common use. It is a giant gunpowder; that is, an explosive material, varying in strength and safety of handling according to the percentage of nitro-glycerine it contains. Nitro-glycerine, whence it derives its strength, is composed of ordinary glycerine and nitric acid, compounded together in certain proportions and at a certain temperature. Nitro-glycerine, though not the strongest explosive known, being exceeded in power by nitrogen and other products of chemistry, is thus far the most terrible explosive manufactured to any extent. Nitro-glycerine by itself is not safe to handle, hence dynamite is preferred. It is extensively made and consumed in the United States under the various names of Giant, Hercules, Jupiter, and Atlas powders, all of which contain anywhere from thirty to eighty per cent. of nitro-glycerine, the residue of the compound being made up of rotten stone, non-explosive earth, sawdust, charcoal, plaster of paris, black powder, or some other substance that takes up the glycerine and makes a porous, spongy mass.

Nitro-glycerine was discovered by Salvero, an Italian chemist, in 1845. Dynamite is prepared by simply kneading with the naked hands twenty-five per cent. of infusorial earth and seventy-five per cent. of nitro-glycerine until the mixture assumes a putty condition, not unlike moist brown sugar. Before mixing, the infusorial earth is calcined in a furnace, in order to burn out all organic matter, and it is also sifted to free it of large grains. While still moist it is squeezed into cartridges, which are prepared of parchment paper, and the firing is done by fulminate of silver in copper capsules provided with patent exploders.

Nitro-glycerine is made of nitric acid one part and sulphuric acid two parts, to which is added ordinary glycerine, and the mixture is well washed with pure water. The infusion is composed of small microscopic silicious shells which have lost their living creatures. The cellular parts receive the nitro-glycerine and hold it by capillary attraction, both inside and out. The earth is very light. Water is expelled from it by means of a furnace, and then, in the form of a powder, it is mixed with nitro-glycerine. Nitro-glycerine has a sweet, aromatic, pungent taste, and the peculiar property of causing a violent headache when placed in a small quantity on the tongue or wrist. It freezes at 40 degrees Fahrenheit, becoming a white, half crystallized mass, which must be melted by the application of water at a temperature about 100 degrees Fahrenheit.

Confederate Soldiers Surrendered at end of War.—Army of Northern Virginia, 27,805; army of Tennessee, 31,243; army of Missouri, 7,978; army of Alabama, 42,293; army of Trans-Mississippi, 17,686; at Nashville and Chattanooga, 5,029; paroled in Departments of Virginia, Cumberland, Maryland, Alabama, Florida, Tennessee, Texas, etc., 42,189; Confederate prisoners in Northern prisons at the close of the war, 98,802; total Confederate army at close, 273,025. A large and unknown number of Confederate soldiers were not present at surrender.

Costly Mansion.—The largest and costliest private mansion in the world is that belonging to Lord Bute, called Montstuart, and situated near Rothesay, England. It covers nearly two acres; is built in Gothic style; the walls, turrets, and balconies are built of stone. The immense tower in the center of the building is 120 feet high, with a balcony around the top. The halls are constructed entirely of marble and alabaster, and the rooms are finished in mahogany, rosewood, and walnut. The fireplaces are all carved marbles of antique designs. The exact cost of this fairy palace is not known, but it has never been estimated at less than $8,000,000.

Age and Growth of Trees.— An oak tree in three years grows 2 feet 10½ inches. A larch 3 feet 7½ inches; at seventy years it is full grown, and a tree of seventy-nine years was 102 feet high and 12 feet girth, containing 253 cubic feet. Another of eighty years was 90 feet and 17 feet, and 300 cubic feet. An elm tree in three years grows 8 feet 3 inches. A beech, 1 foot 8 inches. A poplar, 6 feet. A willow, 9 feet 3 inches. An elm is fully grown in 150 years, and it lives 500 or 600. Ash is full grown in 100, and oak in 200. The mahogany is full grown in 200 years to a vast size. A Polish oak 40 feet round had 600 circles. An oak in Dorsetshire in 1755 was 68 feet round, two near Cranborne Lodge are 38 feet and 36 feet. There are yews from 10 to 20 feet in diameter, whose age is from 1,000 to 2,000 years. A lime in the Crisons is 51 feet round and about 600 years old. An elm in the Pays de Vaud is 18 feet in diameter and 360 years old. The African baobab is the patriarch of living organizations; one specimen, by its circles, is estimated at 5,700 years old by Adamson and Humboldt. The trunk is but 12 or 15 feet to the branches, and often 75 feet round. A cypress in Mexico is 120 feet round, and is estimated by De Candolle to be older than Adamson's baobab. The cypress of Montezuma is 41 feet round. Strabo wrote of a cypress in Persia as being 2,500 years old. The largest tree in Mexico is 127 feet round and 120 high, with branches of 30 feet. A chestnut tree on Mount Etna is 106 feet round close to the ground, and five of its branches resemble great trees. De Candolle says there are oaks in France 1,500 years old. The Wallace oak near Paisley is nearly 800 years old. The yew trees at Fountain's Abbey are about 1,200 years old. That at Crowhurst 1,500. That at Fortingal, above 2,000. That at Braburn, 2,500 to 3,000. Ivies reach 500 or 600 years. The larch the same. The lime 600 or 700 years. The trunk of a walnut tree 12 feet in diameter, hollowed out, and furnished as a sitting room, was imported from America and exhibited in London. The trunk was 80 feet high without a branch, and the entire height 150 feet, the bark 12 inches thick, and the branches from 3 to 4 feet in diameter. The California pine is from 150 to 200 feet high, and from 20 to 60 feet in diameter. The forests in watered, tropical countries are formed of trees from 100 to 200 feet high, which grow to the water's edge of rivers, presenting a solid and impenetrable barrier of trunks 10 or 12 feet in diameter. The dragon tree is in girth from 40 to 100 feet, and 50 or 60 feet high, and a mimosa in South America is described whose head is 600 feet round.

Mount Etna and Its Eruptions.—Mount Etna is a volcano of Sicily, and has been active from the earliest times. The ancients had a fable that beneath the mountain was buried a mighty giant, Enceladus, whom Jove had hurled from heaven for rebellion, and pinned to earth by tossing a mountain upon him. The flames were the breath of the imprisoned monster, the loud noises his groans, and earthquakes were caused by his efforts to turn over his enormous body. The first recorded eruption of Etna occurred before the supposed date of the Trojan war, but its exact time is not known. Thucydides, the historian, next records three eruptions — one in the year 475 B. C., one in 425, and the third at an earlier date not specified. Since those there have been, down to the present time, seventy-eight outbreaks, many of them harmless. Among the most remarkable of the great eruptions were that of 1169 A. D., when Catania and 15,000 of its inhabitants were destroyed; that of 1527, in which two villages were destroyed and many human beings perished; and two eruptions of 1669, in which 15 villages were destroyed. Many fissures in the earth were made at this time—one twelve miles long, which emitted a most vivid light. Afterward five other fissures opened, from which came smoke and loud noises. The city of Catania, at the foot of the mountain, had built a wall sixty feet high on that side to protect it, but the lava rose until it overflowed the wall and poured a current of liquid fire into the houses. This current flowed onward until it reached the sea, 15 miles distant. It was 600 yards wide and 40 feet deep. Entering the sea, the water was thrown into violent commotion, the noise of its agitation was as loud as thunder, and clouds of steam darkened the air for many hours. The eruption of 1755 was remarkable for an inundation caused by the flow of the hot lava over the snow that covered the mountain. It was imagined at the time that the water was thrown out of the crater. A great eruption took place in 1852, immense clouds of ashes being ejected. From two new openings on the east vast torrents of lava poured out, one of which was two miles broad, and in part of its course 170 feet deep. The outbreak of May, 1879, was violent, the clouds of smoke and showers of ashes being followed by the ejection of a stream of lava 200 feet wide, which desolated large tracts of cultivated land. There were also eruptions in 1883 and 1886, but both subsided before any great damage had been caused. Mount Etna is now 10,868 feet high. It is known that frequent eruptions have broken off large parts of the upper portion of the mountain. Its surface is divided into three distinct regions. The lowest is that of fertile land, producing fruit and grain, which extends 2,000 feet from the base up the mountain side, with a circumference of 92 miles. Above this is a strip nearly 4,300 feet wide, covered with large forests, above which to the mountain top there is only a dreary waste of ashes and hardened lava. In spite of its tragic history, the sides of the mountain have a population of over 300,000 people in 63 small villages and 2 large cities.

Postage Stamps, Language of.—Of late years the postage stamp has been invested with a language of its own. When a stamp is inverted on the right-hand upper corner, it means the person written to is to write no more. If the stamp be placed on the left-hand upper corner, inverted, then the writer declares his affection for the receiver of the letter. When the stamp is in the center at the top it signifies an affirmative answer to a question or the questions, as the case may be; and when it is at the bottom, it is a negative. Should the stamp be on the right-hand corner, at a right angle, it asks the question if the receiver of the letter loves the sender; while in the left-hand corner means that the writer hates the other. There is a shade of difference between desiring one's acquaintance and friendship. For example: the stamp at the upper corner at the right expresses the former, and on the lower left-hand corner means the latter. The stamp on a line with the surname is an offer of love; in the same place, only reversed, signifies that the writer is engaged. To say farewell, the stamp is placed straight up and down in the left-hand corner.

Fabian Policy.—The policy of wearing out the enemy in war by delays, misleading movements, feints of attack, etc., while avoiding open battle, is called the "Fabian policy" from the following circumstance: Fabius Maximus was a Roman General in the second Punic War. Having been appointed just after the Roman army had suffered severe defeat at Lake Thrasymene, he perceived that his disheartened troops and bands of raw recruits could not oppose successfully a trained army flushed with victory and led by their great commander Hannibal. He therefore avoided pitched battles, moved his camp from highland to highland, and tired out the enemy with marches and counter-marches. This he continued until thwarted in his calculations by the impatience of the Roman Senate.

Character by the Month.—Here is an old astrological prediction, said to indicate, with tolerable certainty, the character of the girl according to the month she happens to be born in.

If a girl is born in January, she will be a prudent housewife, given to melancholy, but good-tempered.

If in February, a humane and affectionate wife and tender mother.

If in March, a frivolous chatterbox, somewhat given to quarreling.

If in April, inconstant, not intelligent, but likely to be good-looking.

If in May, handsome and likely to be happy.

If in June, impetuous, will marry early, and be frivolous.

If in July, passably handsome, but with a sulky temper.

If in August, amiable and practical, and likely to marry rich.

If in September, discreet, affable, and much liked.

If in October, pretty and coquettish, and likely to be unhappy.

If in November, liberal, kind, of a mild disposition.

If in December, well proportioned, fond of novelty, and extravagant.

The World's Principal Tin Mines. — Pure tin is an elementary metal, as much so as lead, iron, silver, or gold. The principal tin-producing country is England. The Phœnicians traded with England for tin 1,100 years before the Christian era. There is reason to believe that they got tin from Spain also; but England was depended on for nearly all the tin used in Europe until this ore was discovered in Germany in 1240. It was discovered in Northern Africa in the Barbary States in 1640, in India in 1740, in New Spain in 1782. Tin was mined in Mexico before the Spanish conquest, and used in T shaped pieces for money, and in a bronze composition for sharp tools, the principal mines being at Tasco. Peru has valuable mines of this metal, so have New South Wales, Australia, and Banca, and Malacca in the Malay peninsula. Tin has been discovered in Pennsylvania, Missouri, California, Dakota, and other states of the Union, but not in quantities to tempt capital to engage in mining it, with the exception of Dakota, where the Illinois Steel Mill Company has large interests. The chief tin-producing countries are the following, arranged in the order of importance: England, about 10,000 tons a year; Malacca, about 8,500 tons; Australia, about 6,000 tons; Banca, about 4,000 tons; and Billiton, about 3,000 tons. Both of these last named places are islands of the Dutch East Indies.

St. Valentine's Day.— The custom of sending valentines can, without doubt, be traced, in origin, to a practice among the ancient Romans. At the feast of the Lupercalia, which was held on the 15th of February, in honor of the great god Pan, the names of all the virgin daughters of Rome were put in a box and drawn therefrom by the young men, and each youth was bound to offer a gift to the maiden who fell to his lot, and to make her his partner during the time of the feast. This custom became allied to the name of St. Valentine, probably, only through a coincidence in dates. St. Valentine was a bishop of Rome during the third century. He was of most amiable nature, and possessed remarkable gifts of eloquence, and was so very successful in converting the pagan Romans to Christianity that he incurred the displeasure of the Emperor, and was martyred by his order February 14, A. D. 270. When the saint came to be placed in the calendar, his name was given to the day of his death, and this was made a festival, to offset that of the Lupercalia, and an effort was made to substitute the names of saints for those of girls in the lottery, but naturally without success. Many other customs of mediæval and later times, which have become allied in name to a holy saint of the church, are unquestionably of purely secular, even pagan, origin.

Royal Household. — In all mediæval monarchies of western Europe the general system of government sprang from, and centered in, the royal household. The sovereign's domestics were his officers of state, and the leading dignitaries of the palace were the principal administrators of the kingdom. The royal household itself had, in its turn, grown out of an earlier and more primitive institution. It took its rise in the *comitatus*, described by Tacitus, the chosen band of *comites* or companions who, when the Roman historian wrote, constituted the personal following, in peace as well as in war, of the Teutonic *princeps* or chieftain. In England before the conquest the *comites* were called thegns. After the conquest the most powerful of the king's thegns became officers of the royal household by heredity.

The Stage.

BIRTHPLACES AND BIRTH YEARS OF DRAMATIC AND MUSICAL PEOPLE.

Name.	Birthplace.	Born.
Adams, Maude	Salt Lake City, Utah	1872
Albani, Emma	Chambly, Canada	1851
Aldrich, Louis	Mid-ocean	1843
Alexander, George	Reading, England	1858
Anderson, Mary	Sacramento, Cal	1859
Archer, Belle	Easton, Pa	1860
Arditi, Luigi	Piedmont, Italy	1822
Arthur, Julia	Canada	1869
Bancroft, Sir S. B	England	1841
Bancroft, Lady	England	1840
Bandmann, Daniel E	Cassel, Germany	1839
Bangs, Frank C	Alexandria, Va	1836
Barnabee, H. C	Portsmouth, N. Y	1833
Barrett, Wilson	Essex, England	1846
Barron, Charles	Boston, Mass	1841
Barrymore, Maurice	India	1847
Bateman, Isabel	Cincinnati, O	1854
Bateman, Kate	Baltimore, Md	1842
Belasco, David	San Francisco	1862
Bell, Digby	Milwaukee, Wis	1851
Bellew, Kyrle	London	1845
Bernhardt, Sarah	Paris	1844
Bispham, David	Philadelphia, Pa	1857
Boniface, George C	New York city	1832
Booth, Agnes	Australia	1843
Buchanan, Virginia	Cincinnati, O	1846
Burgess, Neil	Boston, Mass	1846
Burroughs, Marie	San Francisco	1866
Byron, Oliver Doud	Baltimore, Md	1847
Calve, Emma	Aveyron, France	1864
Cameron, Beatrice	Troy, N. Y	1868
Campbell, Mrs. Patrick	London	1864
Carey, Eleanor	Chile, S. A	1852
Cayvan, Georgia	Bath, Me	1858
Chanfrau, Mrs. F. S	Philadelpia, Pa	1837
Clarke, George	Brooklyn, N. Y	1840
Clarke, John S	Baltimore, Md	1835
Claxton, Kate	New York city	1848
Cody, William F	Scott County, Iowa	1845
Coghlan, Rose	Peterboro, England	1853
Coquelin, Benoit C	Boulogne, France	1841
Crabtree, Lotta	New York city	1847
Crane, William H	Leicester, Mass	1845
Daly, Augustin	North Carolina	1838
Daly, Dan	Boston, Mass	1863
Damrosch, Walter J	Breslau, Prussia	1862
Daniels, Frank	Boston, Mass	1860
D'Arville, Camille	Holland	1863
De Belleville, Frederic	Belgium	1853
De Merode, Cleo	Paris	1874
De Reszke, Edouard	Warsaw, Poland	1855
De Reszke, Jean	Warsaw, Poland	1850
De Wolfe, Elsie	New York city	1865
Dickinson, Anna	Philadelphia, Pa	1842
Dixey, Henry E	Boston, Mass	1859
Drew, John	Philadelphia, Pa	1853
Duse, Eleanora	Vigevano, Italy	1861
Eames, Emma Hayden	Shanghai, China	1868
Earle, Virginia	New York city	1873
Ellsler, Effie	Philadelphia, Pa	1858
Eytinge, Rose	Philadelphia, Pa	1837
Fawcett, Owen	London, England	1838
Florence, Mrs. W. J	New York city	1846
Fox, Della	St. Louis, Mo	1871
Frohman, Charles	Sandusky, O	1858
Frohman, Daniel	Sandusky, O	1850
Germon, Effie	Augusta, Ga	1845
Gerster, Etelka	Kaschau, Hungary	1857
Gilbert, Mrs. G. H	Rochdale, England	1820
Gillette, William	Hartford, Ct	1853
Goodwin, Nat C	Boston, Mass	1857
Hackett, James K	Canada	1869
Hading, Jane	Marseilles, France	1861
Hammerstein, Oscar	Berlin, Germany	1847
Harned, Virginia	Boston, Mass	1868
Harrigan, Edward	New York city	1845
Harrison, Maud	England	1858
Hauk, Minnie	New Orleans, La	1853
Haworth, Joseph S	Providence, R. I	1855
Held, Anna	Paris	1873
Herbert, Victor	Dublin, Ireland	1860
Heron, Bijou	New York city	1863
Hill, Charles Barton	Dover, England	1828
Hilliard, Robert S	Brooklyn	1860
Holland, E. M	New York city	1848
Hopper, De Wolf	New York city	1862
Hoyt, Charles H	Concord, N. H	1860
Irving, Isabel	Bridgeport, Conn	1870
Irving, Sir Henry	Keinton, England	1838
Irwin, May	Toronto, Canada	1862
James, Louis	Tremont, Ill	1842
Janauschek, Francesca	Prague, Austria	1830
Jefferson, Joseph	Philadelphia, Pa	1829
Jones, Walter	Springfield, O	1871
Karl, Tom	Dublin, Ireland	1849
Kendal, Mrs. W. H	Lincolnshire, England	1849
Keeley, Mrs. Robert	Ipswich, England	1806
Kelcey, Herbert H. L	London, England	1855
Kellogg, Clara Louise	Sumpterville, S. C	1842
Knowles, Edwin H	Rhode Island	1845
Kopacsy, Julie	Hungary	1871
Langtry, Lily	St. Helens, Jersey (Eng.)	1852
Le Moyne, W. J.	Boston, Mass	1835
Maddern, Minnie	New Orleans, La	1865
Mande, Cyril	London	1862
Mansfield, Richard	Heligoland, Germany	1857
Mantell, Robert B	Ayrshire, Scotland	1854
Marlowe, Julia	Caldbeck, England	1865
Martinot, Sadie	Yonkers, N. Y	1857
Melba, Nellie	Melbourne	1866
Mitchell, Maggie	New York city	1832
Modjeska, Helena	Cracow, Poland	1844
Mordaunt, Frank	Burlington, Vt	1841
Morgan, Edward J	Barnes, Surrey, Eng	1871
Morris, Clara	Cleveland, O	1846
Mounet-Sully	France	1841
Murphy, Joseph	Brooklyn, N. Y	1839
Nevada, Emma	San Francisco, Cal	1857
Nilsson, Christine	Wederslof, Sweden	1843
Nordica, Lillian	Farmington, Me	1858
Olcott, Chauncey	Providence, R. I	1862
O'Neil, James	Ireland	1849
Paderewski, Ignace J	Poland	1860
Palmer, A. M	North Stonington, Ct	1838
Pastor, Tony	New York city	1837
Patti, Adelina	Madrid	1848
Plympton, Eben	Boston, Mass	1850
Ponisi, Madame	Huddersfield, England	1825
Powers, James T	New York city	1862
Rankin, A. McKee	Sandwich, Canada	1844
Reed, Roland	Philadelphia, Pa	1852
Rehan, Ada	Limerick, Ireland	1860
Rhea, Madame	Brussels	1855
Robinson, Frederick	London, England	1832
Robson, Stuart	Annapolis, Md	1836
Roze, Marie	Paris	1846
Russell, Annie	New York city	1864
Russell, Lillian	Clinton, Iowa	1860
Russell, Sol. Smith	Brunswick, Mo	1848
Saleza, Albert	Bruges, France	1867
Salvini, Tommaso	Milan, Italy	1830
Sanderson, Sibyl	Sacramento, Cal	1869
Seabrooke, Thomas Q	Mt. Vernon, N. Y	1860
Sembrich, Marcella	Lemberg, Austria	1858
Skinner, Otis	Cambridgeport, Mass	1857
Smith, Mark	Mobile, Ala	1855
Sorma, Agnes	Germany	1865
Sothern, Edward H	England	1864
Stanhope, Adelaide	Paris, France	1858
Stanley, Alma Stuart	Jersey, England	1860
Stevenson, Charles A	Dublin, Ireland	1842
Stoddart, J. H	Yorkshire, England	1827
Studley, John B	Boston, Mass	1832
Sullivan, Sir Arthur	London	1842
Tearle, Osmond	Plymouth, England	1852
Terry, Ellen	Coventy, England	1848
Thompson, Denman	Girard, Pa	1833
Thompson, Lydia	London, England	1838
Thursby, Emma	Brooklyn, N. Y	1857
Toole, John L	London, England	1833
Tree, Beerbohm	England	1846
Van Dyck, Ernest	Antwerp	1861
Vezin, Hermann	Philadelphia, Pa	1829
Walsh, Blanche	New York city	1873
Warde, Frederick	Wadington, England	1851
Wilson, Francis	Philadelphia, Pa	1865
Willard, E. S	Brighton, England	1853
Wyndham, Charles	England	1841

Vaudeville.— The name Vaudeville is a corruption of Vaux de Vire, the name of two picturesque valleys in the Bocage of Normandy, and was originally applied to a song with words relating to some story of the day. These songs were first composed by one Oliver Basselin, a fuller in Vire; they were very popular, and spread all over France, and were called by the name of their native place (Les Vaux de Vire). As the origin of the term was soon lost sight of, it at last took its present form. The word is now used to signify a play in which dialogue is interspersed with songs incidentally introduced, but forming an important part of the drama.

The Single Tax.— This idea was first formulated by Mr. Henry George, in his book, "Progress and Poverty," in 1879, and has grown steadily in favor. Single tax men assert, as a fundamental principle, that all men are equally entitled to the use of the earth; therefore, no one should be allowed to hold valuable land without paying to the community the value of the privilege. They hold that this is the only rightful source of public revenue, and they would, therefore, abolish all taxation, local, state, and national, except a tax upon the rental value of land, exclusive of its improvements, the revenue thus raised to be divided among local, state, and general governments, as the revenue from certain direct taxes is now divided between local and state governments.

The single tax would not fall on all land, but only on valuable land, and on that in proportion to its value. It would thus be a tax, not on use or improvements, but on ownership of land, taking what would otherwise go to the landlord as owner.

In accordance with the principle that all men are equally entitled to the use of the earth, they would solve the transportation problem by public ownership, and control of all highways, including the roadbeds of railroads, leaving their use equally free to all.

The single tax system would:—

1. Dispense with a horde of taxgatherers, simplify government, and greatly reduce its cost.

2. Give us with all the world that absolute free trade which now exists between the states of the Union.

3. Give us free trade in finance by abolishing all taxes on private issues of money.

4. Take the weight of taxation from agricultural districts, where land has little or no value apart from improvements, and put it upon valuable land, such as city lots and mineral deposits.

5. Call upon men to contribute for public expenses in proportion to the natural opportunities they monopolize, and compel them to pay just as much for holding the land idle as for putting it to its fullest use.

6. Make it unprofitable for speculators to hold land unused or only partly used, and, by thus opening to labor unlimited fields of employment, solve the labor problem, raise wages in all occupations, and abolish involuntary poverty.

Printer's Devil.— The origin of this term is ascribed to the fact that in the early days of printing the apprentice's duties included the inking of the forms with bags containing ink or besmeared with it. In the performance of this work his face and hands became so daubed with the ink that in appearance he suggested the devil. Hence the name.

Bastille.— The famous French prison known by this name was originally the Castle of Paris, and was built by order of Charles V., between 1370 and 1383, as a defense against the English. When it came to be used as a state prison it was provided with vast bulwarks and ditches. The Bastille had four towers, of five stories each, on each of its larger sides, and it was partly in these towers and partly in underground cellars that the prisons were situated. It was capable of containing seventy to eighty prisoners, a number frequently reached during the reigns of Louis XIV. and Louis XV., the majority of them being persons of the higher ranks. The Bastille was destroyed by a mob on the 15th of July, 1789, and the governor and a number of his officers were killed. On its site now stands the Column of July, erected in memory of the patriots of 1789 and 1830.

White House Weddings.— The first wedding to occur in the White House was that of Miss Todd, a relative by marriage of President Madison. Then, in their order, came the weddings of Elizabeth Tyler, a daughter of President Tyler; John Quincy Adams, Jr.; Miss Easten and Miss Lewis, both during General Jackson's administration; Martha Monroe; Nellie Grant; Emily Platt, a niece of President Hayes; and last, President Cleveland.

Dying Sayings of Famous People.

Addison. "See how a Christian dies!" or "See in what peace a Christian can die!"

Anaxagoras. "Give the boys a holiday."

Arria. "My Pætus, it is not painful."

Augustus. "Vos Plaudite." (After asking how he had acted his part in life.)

Beaufort (Cardinal Henry). "I pray you all, pray for me."

Berry (Mme. de). "Is not this dying with courage and true greatness?"

Bronte (father of the authoress). "While there is life there is will." (He died standing.)

Byron. "I must sleep now."

Cæsar (Julius). "Et tu, Brute!" (To Brutus, when he stabbed him.)

Charlemagne. "Lord, into Thy hands I commend my spirit!"

Charles I. (of England). "Remember." (To William Juxon, Archbishop of Canterbury.)

Charles II. (of England). "Don't let poor Nelly starve." (Nell Gwynne.)

Charles V. "Ah, Jesus!"

Charles IX. (of France). "Nurse, nurse, what murder! what blood! Oh, I have done wrong. God pardon me."

Charlotte (the princess). "You make me drink. Pray, leave me quiet. I find it affects my head."

Chesterfield. "Give Day Rolles a chair."

Columbus. "Lord, into Thy hands I commend my spirit!"

Crome (John). "Oh, Hobbima, Hobbima, how I do love thee!"

Cromwell. "My desire is to make what haste I may to be gone."

Demonax (the philosopher). "You may go home, the show is over."—*Lucian.*

Elden (Lord). "It matters not, where I am going, whether the weather be cold or hot."

Fontenelle. "I suffer nothing, but feel a sort of difficulty in living longer."

Franklin. "A dying man can do nothing easy."

Gainsborough. "We are all going to heaven, and Vandyke is of the company."

George IV. "Whatty, what is this? It is death, my boy. They have deceived me." (Said to his page, Sir Walthen Waller.)

Gibbon. "Mon Dieu! Mon Dieu!"

Goethe. "More light!"

Gregory VII. "I have loved justice and hated iniquity, therefore I die in exile."

Grey (Lady Jane). "Lord, into Thy hands I commend my spirit!"

Grotius. "Be serious."

Haydn. "God preserve the emperor."

Haller. "The artery ceases to beat."

Hazlitt. "I have led a happy life."

Hobbes. "Now I am about to take my last voyage—a great leap in the dark."

Hunter (Dr. William). "If I had strength to hold a pen, I would write down how easy and pleasant a thing it is to die."

Irving. "If I die I die unto the Lord. Amen."

James V. (of Scotland). "It came with a lass and will go with a lass" (*i. e.*, the Scotch crown).

Jefferson (of America). "I resign my spirit to God, my daughter to my country."

Jesus Christ. "It is finished."

Johnson (Dr.). "God bless you, my dear!" (To Miss Morris.)

Knox. "Now it is come."

Louis I. "Huz! huz!" (Bouquet says, "He turned his face to the wall, and twice cried 'huz! huz!' (out, out) and then died.")

Louis IX. "I will enter now into the house of the Lord."

Louis XIV. "Why weep ye? Did you think I should live forever?" Then, after a pause, "I thought dying had been harder."

Louis XVIII. "A king should die standing."

Mahomet. "Oh, Allah, be it so! Henceforth among the glorious host of paradise."

Marie Antoinette. "Farewell, my children, forever. I go to your father."

Mirabeau. "Let me die to the sounds of delicious music."

Moody (the actor).

"Reason thus with life,
If I do lose thee, I do lose a thing
That none but fools would keep."—*Shakespeare.*

Moore (Sir John). "I hope my country will do me justice."

Napoleon III. "Were you at Sedan?" (To Dr. Conneau.)

Nelson. "I thank God I have done my duty."

Pitt (William). "Oh, my country, how I love thee!"

Pizarro. "Jesu!"

Pope. "Friendship itself is but a part of virtue."

Rabelais. "Let down the curtain, the farce is over."

Sand (George). "Laissez la verdure." (Leave the tomb green.)

Schiller. "Many things are growing plain and clear to my understanding."

Scott (Sir Walter). "God bless you all." (To his family.)

Socrates. "Crito, we owe a cock to Æsculapius."

Stael (Mme. de). "I have loved God, my father, and liberty."

Thurlow (Lord). "I'll be shot if I don't believe I'm dying."

William III. (of England). "Can this last long?" (To his physician.)

Wolfe (General). "What! do they run already? Then I die happy."

State Flowers.—The following are "State Flowers" as adopted in most instances by the votes of the public school scholars of the respective states:—

California	California Poppy
Colorado	Columbine
Delaware	Peach Blossom
Idaho	Syringa
Indiana	Corn
Iowa	Wild Rose
Maine	Pine Cone and Tassel
Michigan	* Apple Blossom
Minnesota	Cypripedium or Moccasin Flower
Montana	Bitter Root
Nebraska	Golden-rod
Nevada	Sunflower
New York, Rose; State tree	Maple
North Dakota	Golden-rod
Oklahoma Territory	Mistletoe
Oregon	Golden-rod
Rhode Island	Violet
Utah	Sego Lily
Vermont	Red Clover
Washington	Rhododendron

*Adopted by State Legislature, not by public school scholars.

In other states the scholars or State Legislatures have not yet taken action. In Illinois in the vote on the leading State Flower by the pupils of the schools the Rose, Violet, and Golden-rod received the largest number of votes, in the order named, although no state flower was adopted. In Massachusetts the Columbine was strongly urged, but no flower was adopted. In Ohio and Tennessee the Golden-rod is advocated.

Strength of Modern Powders and High Explosives.

Name of Explosive.	Pecentage of Strength.
Perunite B	100.0
Perunite C	91.0
Perunite D	83.0
Explosive gelatine	81.0
Rack-a-rock	79.0
Hellofite	78.0
Nitro-glycerine, best quality	73.0
Nobel's smokeless powder	70.0
Explosive gelatine made from No. 5 nitro-glycerine	68.0
United States Navy gun-cotton	67.5
Fulgurite	67.0
Emmensite	66.0
French nitro-glycerine	63.0
Dynamite No. 1	62.6
Cannonite	62.0
Amide powder	59.0
Progressite	58.5
Tonite	57.0
Bellite	56.0
Oxonite	54.4
Atlas powder, No. 1	54.0
Melinite	49.0
Silver fulminate	48.2
Mercury fulminate	47.5
Rifle powder	35.0
Mortar powder	30.0
Rossel's mixture	89.5
Americanite	82.0
Schnebelite	80.0

Absinthe is a spirit flavored with the pounded leaves and flowering tops of wormwood, together with angelica-root, sweet-flag root, star-anise, and other aromatics. The aromatics are macerated for about eight days in alcohol and then distilled, the result being an emerald-colored liquor. The best absinthe is made in Switzerland, the chief seat of the manufacture being in the canton of Neufchatel. It is chiefly used in France and the United States. The evil effects of drinking this liquor are very apparent; frequent intoxication, or moderate but steady tippling, utterly deranges the digestive system, weakens the frame, induces horrible dreams and hallucinations, and may end in paralysis or in idiocy.

United States Navy Pay Table.

Rank.	At Sea	On Shore Duty.	On Leave or Waiting Orders.
Admiral..........$13,500—For life.	......	......	....
Rear-Admirals	$6,000	$5,000	$4,000
Commodores	5,000	4,000	3,000
Captains	4,500	3,500	2,800
Commanders	3,500	3,000	2,300
Lieutenant-Commanders:			
First four years*	2,800	2,400	2,000
After four years†	3,000	2,600	2,200
Lieutenants:			
First five years*	2,400	2,000	1,600
After five years†	2,600	2,600	1,800
Lieutenants (Junior Grade):			
First five years*	1,800	1,500	1,200
After five years†	2,000	1,700	1,400
Ensigns:			
First five years*	1,200	1,000	800
After five years†	1,400	1,200	1,000
Naval Cadets	500	500	500
Mates	900	700	500
Medical and Pay Directors and Inspectors and Chief Engineers having the same rank at sea....	4,400	......	....
Fleet Surgeons, Fleet-Paymasters, and Fleet-Engineers	4,400	......	....
Surgeons, Paymasters, and Chief Engineers	2,800 to 4,200	2,400 to 4,000	2,000 to 3,000
Chaplains	2,500 to 2,800	2,000 to 2,300	1,600 to 1,900

Warrant officers are paid from $700 to $1,800, and seamen, $228 to $288 per annum.

*After date of commission. †From date of commission.

United States Naval Enlistment.—All applicants for enlistment in the naval service must be of robust frame, intelligent, of perfectly sound and healthy constitution and free from any of the following physical defects: Greatly retarded development, feeble constitution, inherited or acquired; permanently impaired general health, decided cachexia, diathesis or predisposition, weak or disordered intellect, epilepsy or other convulsions within five years, impaired vision or chronic disease of the organs of vision, great dullness of hearing or chronic disease of the ears, chronic nasal catarrh, ozena, polypi or great enlargement of the tonsils, marked impediment of speech, decided indications of liability to pulmonary disease, chronic cardiac affections, large varicose veins of lower limbs, chronic ulcers, unnatural curvature of the spine, permanent disability of either of the extremities or articulations from any cause, defective teeth.

Following are the requirements for the various classes of the service, and monthly wages paid:—

Class.	Age.	Wages.
Landsmen	18 to 25	$16
Ordinary Seamen	18 to 30	19
Seamen	21 to 35	24
Painter	21 to 35	30
Bugler	21 to 35	30
Shipwright	21 to 35	25
Carpenter's mate	21 to 35	40 to 50
Chief yeoman	....	60
Yeoman	....	30 to 40
Musicians	21 to 35	32
Cooks	21 to 35	40
Mess attendants	21 to 30	16
Sailmakers	21 to 35	25
Machinist	....	40 to 70
Boilermaker	21 to 35	60
Blacksmith	21 to 35	50
Firemen	21 to 35	30 to 35
Coal passers	21 to 35	22

Slavery and Serfdom.—Some of the wealthy Romans had as many as 10,000 slaves. The minimum price fixed by the law of Rome was $80, but after great victories they could sometimes be bought for a few shillings on the field of battle. The day's wages of a Roman gardener were about sixteen cents, and his value about $300, while a blacksmith was valued at about $700, a cook at $2,000, an actress at $4,000, and a physician at $11,000.

The number of slaves emancipated in the British Colonies in 1834 was 780,993, the indemnity aggregating, in round figures, $100,000,000. In Brazil, in 1876, there were 1,510,800 slaves, 15 per cent. of the entire population. These were held by 41,000 owners, averaging 37 to each owner. In 1882 the number of slaves was 1,300,000. Owing to the gradual abolition of slavery in Brazil by law, it is expected that it will be entirely obsolete in 1900.

SLAVERY IN THE UNITED STATES.

Year.	Number.	Year.	Number.
1790	697,900	1830	2,009,030
1800	893,040	1840	2,487,500
1810	1,191,400	1850	3,204,300
1820	1,538,100	1860	3,979,700

Serfdom in Russia.—There were 47,932,000 serfs in Russia in 1861, as follows: Crown serfs, 22,851,000; appanage, 3,326,000; held by nobles, 21,755,000. The cost of redemption was, in round numbers, about $325,000,000, as follows:—

Mortgages remitted	$152,000,000	Paid by serfs	$52,000,000
Gov'ment scrip	101,000,000	Balance due	20,000,000

The indemnity to the nobles was $15 per serf. The lands are mortgaged to the state till 1912. The lands ceded to crown serfs are mortgaged only till 1901. The item of "mortgages remitted" is the amount due by nobles to the Imperial Bank and canceled.

AUSTRIAN SERVITUDE (1840).

	Value.
Labor (two days per week)	$175,000,000
Tithe of crops, etc	60,000,000
Male tribute, timber	7,000,000
Female tribute, spun wool	9,000,000
Fowl, eggs, butter	5,000,000
Total	$256,000,000

There were 7,000,000 serfs, whose tribute averaged more than $35 per head, which was, in fact, the rent of their farms. Some Bohemian nobles had as many as 10,000 serfs. The redemption was effected by giving the nobles 5 per cent. Government scrip, and land then rose 50 per cent. in value.

Average Annual Rainfall in United States.

Place.	Inches.	Place.	Inches.
Neah Bay, Wash	123	Hanover, N. H	40
Sitka, Alaska	83	Ft. Vancouver, Wash	38
Ft. Haskins, Oregon	66	Cleveland, Ohio	37
Mt. Vernon, Alabama	66	Pittsburg, Pa	37
Baton Rouge, Louisiana	60	Washington, D. C	37
Meadow Valley, Cal	57	W. Sulphur Springs, Va	37
Ft. Tonson, Indian Ter	57	Ft. Gibson, Indian Ter	36
Ft. Myers, Florida	56	Key West, Florida	36
Washington, Arkansas	54	Peoria, Illinois	35
Huntsville, Alabama	54	Burlington, Vermont	34
Natchez, Mississippi	53	Buffalo, New York	33
New Orleans, Louisiana	51	Ft. Brown, Texas	33
Savannah, Georgia	48	Ft. Leavenworth, Kan	31
Springdale, Kentucky	48	Detroit, Michigan	30
Fortress Monroe, Va	47	Milwaukee, Wisconsin	30
Memphis, Tennessee	45	Penn Yan, New York	28
Newark, New Jersey	44	Ft. Kearney, Neb	25
Boston, Massachusetts	44	Ft. Snelling, Minnesota	25
Brunswick, Maine	44	Salt Lake City, Utah	23
Cincinnati, Ohio	44	Mackinac, Michigan	23
New Haven, Conn	44	San Francisco, Cal	21
Philadelphia, Pa	44	Dallas, Oregon	21
Charleston, S. Carolina	43	Sacramento, California	21
New York City, N. Y	43	Ft. Massachusetts, Col	17
Gaston, N. Carolina	43	Ft. Marcy, New Mex. Ter	16
Richmond, Indiana	43	Ft. Randall, Dakota	16
Marietta, Ohio	43	Ft. Defiance, Arizona	14
St. Louis, Missouri	43	Ft. Craig, New Mex. Ter	11
Muscatine, Iowa	42	San Diego, California	9
Baltimore, Maryland	41	Ft. Colville, Wash	9
New Bedford, Mass	41	Ft. Bliss, Texas	9
Providence, R. I	41	Ft. Bridger, Utah	6
Ft. Smith, Arkansas	40	Ft. Garland, Colorado	6

Tariff.— Import duties, general average:—

	Ratio to Imports. Per cent.		Ratio of Imports. Per cent.
United Kingdom	5½	Belgium	1½
France	6½	Denmark	9
Germany	6	Sweden and Norway	12
Russia	18	Europe	7¼
Austria	5	United States	33⅓
Italy	11	Canada	15
Spain	24	Australia	13
Portugal	26	Brazil	44
Holland	1	Argentine Republic	37

Rabbit's Foot.—The legends of "Br'er Rabbit" among the negroes, his clever devices in outwitting his natural enemies — the dog, fox, and wolf—and thwarting every scheme designed for his own punishment, are almost without number. From these legends of the preternatural sagacity of the living rabbit came the idea that the dead rabbit had certain magic powers. The negroes believe that to carry a rabbit's foot in the pocket is not only a talisman for good luck, but is a specific for diseases. The left hind foot of the rabbit is believed to have the most efficacy, and if it be taken from a rabbit that runs in a graveyard, its supernatural properties are believed to be quite irresistible.

Number of Years Seeds retain their Vitality.

Vegetables.	Years.	Vegetables.	Years.
Cucumber	8 to 10	Asparagus	2 to 3
Melon	8 to 10	Beans	2 to 3
Pumpkin	8 to 10	Carrots	2 to 3
Squash	8 to 10	Celery	2 to 3
Broccoli	5 to 6	Corn (on cob)	2 to 3
Cauliflower	5 to 6	Leek	2 to 3
Artichoke	5 to 6	Onion	2 to 3
Endive	5 to 6	Parsley	2 to 3
Pea	5 to 6	Parsnip	2 to 3
Radish	4 to 5	Pepper	2 to 3
Beets	3 to 4	Tomato	2 to 3
Cress	3 to 4	Egg plant	1 to 2
Lettuce	3 to 4		
Mustard	3 to 4	HERBS.	
Okra	3 to 4	Anise	3 to 4
Rhubarb	3 to 4	Caraway	2
Spinach	3 to 4	Summer Savory	1 to 2
Turnip	3 to 6	Sage	2 to 3

Acquisition of Territory.—The increase in area of the United States, by war and treaty, is shown in the annexed table:—

When.	How.	Whence.	What.	Sq. Miles.
1776 } 1783 }	War	England.	Thirteen original States *a*	820,680
1803	Treaty.	France	Louisiana *b*	899,579
1819	Treaty.	Spain	Florida *c*	66,900
1845	Union.	Mexico	Texas *d*	318,000
1846	Treaty.	England.	Oregon	308,052
1846 } 1848 }	War	Mexico	California and New Mexico *e*	522,955
1853	Treaty.	Mexico	Gadsden Purchase *f*	45,535
1867	Treaty.	Russia	Alaska *g*	580,107
1898	Treaty.	Hawaii	Hawaii	6,740
1898	War	Spain	Porto Rico	3,600
1898	War	Spain	Philippines	120,000
				3,692,148

a Estimated cost of War of Independence, $168,000,000.
b Purchased for $15,000,000. *c* Cost $3,000,000.
d Debt of Texas on admission into the Union, $7,500,000.
e Estimated cost of the Mexican War, $15,000,000.
f Cost $10,000,000. *g* Cost $7,200,000.

The Capital of the United States has been located at different times at the following places: At Philadelphia from September 5, 1774, to December, 1776; at Baltimore from December 20, 1776, to March, 1777; at Philadelphia from March 4, 1777, to September, 1777; at Lancaster, Pa., from September 27, 1777, to September 30, 1777; at York, Pa., from September 30, 1777, to July, 1778; at Philadelphia from July 2, 1778, to June 30, 1783; at Princeton, N. J., June 30, 1783, to November 20, 1783; Annapolis, Md., November 26, 1783, to November 30, 1784; Trenton from November, 1784, to January, 1785; New York from January 11, 1785, to 1790; then the seat of government was removed to Philadelphia, where it remained until 1800, since which time it has been in Washington.

Wireless Telegraphy.—Of the several systems for telegraphing without wires, that devised by Signor Marconi has been most before the public. Early in 1899 messages were successfully sent by this system from South Foreland, England, across the English channel to Boulogne, France, a distance of 32 miles. A full description of the apparatus used and of the experiments themselves was published in a paper by Signor Marconi, read before the Institute of Electrical Engineers of London. In September, 1899, Signor Marconi and several assistants came to America to report the international yacht races off Sandy Hook by wireless telegraphy. Sending apparatus were placed on two steamers which followed the yachts, and receiving apparatus were placed, one on the cable ship *Mackay-Bennett*, anchored near the Sandy Hook lightship, and the other on shore at the Highlands of Navesink. Bulletins of the progress of the races were sent from the following steamers to the receiving stations, and from them by wire to the office of the New York *Herald*. After the yacht races, tests were made by Signor Marconi in conjunction with the Signal Corps of the United States Army and with the Navy Department. The report of the inspecting board in the Navy Department tests was quite favorable to the utility of the system for communicating between vessels at sea.

Since these preliminary tests the system has greatly developed. Vessels communicate with each other at sea. Messages are sent across the ocean and the system is becoming practical as a commercial agent, with great possibilities.

Capacity of Cisterns.

FOR EACH 10 INCHES IN DEPTH.

Twenty-five feet in diameter holds	3059 gallons
Twenty feet in diameter holds	1958 gallons
Fifteen feet in diameter holds	1101 gallons
Fourteen feet in diameter holds	959 gallons
Thirteen feet in diameter holds	827 gallons
Twelve feet in diameter holds	705 gallons
Eleven feet in diameter holds	592 gallons
Ten feet in diameter holds	489 gallons
Nine feet in diameter holds	396 gallons
Eight feet in diameter holds	313 gallons
Seven feet in diameter holds	239 gallons
Six and one half feet in diameter holds	206 gallons
Six feet in diameter holds	176 gallons
Five feet in diameter holds	122 gallons
Four and one half feet in diameter holds	99 gallons
Four feet in diameter holds	78 gallons
Three feet in diameter holds	44 gallons
Two and one half feet in diameter holds	30 gallons
Two feet in diameter holds	19 gallons

The Roman Month was divided into *Calends*, *Nones*, and *Ides*. The Calends always fell upon the first of the month; in March, May, July, and October, the Nones on the 7th and the Ides on the 15th, and in the remaining months, the Nones on the 5th and the Ides on the 13th. The Roman year began with March, and the months corresponded with ours except that their fifth and sixth months were called Quintilis and Sextilis. Afterwards they were changed to July and August in honor of the emperors Julius and Augustus.

The Limits of Vision vary with elevation, conditions of the atmosphere, intensity of illumination, and other modifying elements in different cases. On a clear day an object one foot above a level plain may be seen at a distance of 1.31 miles; one 10 feet high, 4.15 miles; one 20 feet high, 5.86 miles; one 100 feet high, 13.1 miles; one a mile high, as the top of a mountain, 95.23 miles. This allows 7 inches; or, to be exact, 6.99 inches, for the curvature of the earth, and assumes that the size and illumination of the object are sufficient to produce an image.

Mottoes of the States. — *Arkansas. Regnant populi:* The people rule. *California. Eureka:* I have found it. *Colorado. Nil sine numine:* Nothing without the Divinity. *Connecticut. Qui transtulit sustinet:* He who has transferred, sustains. *Delaware.* Liberty and Independence, *Florida.* In God is our trust. *Georgia.* Wisdom, Justice, Moderation. *Illinois.* State Sovereignty and National Union. *Iowa.* Our liberties we prize, and our rights we will maintain. *Kansas. Ad astra per aspera:* To the stars through rugged ways. *Kentucky.* United we stand, divided we fall. *Louisiana.* Union and Confidence. *Maine. Dirigo:* I direct. *Maryland. Crescite et multiplicamini:* Increase and multiply. *Massachusetts. Ense petit placidam sub libertate quietem:* By her sword she seeks under liberty a calm repose. *Michigan. Si quœris peninsulam amœnam circumspice:* If thou seekest a beautiful peninsula, look around. *Minnesota. L'Etoile du Nord:* The Star of the North. *Missouri. Salus populi suprema lex esto:* Let the welfare of the people be the supreme law. *Nebraska.* Popular Sovereignty. *Nevada. Volens et potens:* Willing and able. *New Jersey.* Liberty and Independence. *New York. Excelsior:* Higher. *Ohio. Imperium in imperio:* An empire within an empire. *Oregon. Alis volat propriis:* She flies with her own wings. *Pennsylvania.* Virtue, Liberty, Independence. *Rhode Island.* Hope. *North Carolina. Esse quam videri:* To be, rather than to seem. *South Carolina. Animis opibusque parati:* Ready with our lives and property. *Tennessee.* Agriculture, Commerce. *Vermont.* Freedom and Unity. *Virginia. Sic semper tyrannis:* So be it ever to tyrants. *West Virginia. Montani semper liberi:* The mountaineers are always free. *Wisconsin.* Forward. *United States. E pluribus unum:* From many, one. *Annuit cœptis:* God has favored the undertaking. *Novus ordo seculorum:* A new order of ages. The first named on one side of the great seal, the other two on the reverse.

Barrenness.— One woman in 20, one man in 30 — about 4 per cent. It is found that one marriage in 20 is barren — 5 per cent. Among the nobility of Great Britain, 21 per cent. have no children, owing partly to intermarriage of cousins, no less than 4½ per cent. being married to cousins.

Meteoric Stones.— A meteoric stone, which is described by Pliny as being as large as a wagon, fell near Ægospotami, in Asia Minor, in 467 B. C. About A. D. 1500 a stone weighing 1,400 pounds fell in Mexico, and is now in the Smithsonian Institution at Washington. The largest meteoric masses on record were heard of first by Captain Ross, the Arctic explorer, through some Esquimaux. These lay on the west coast of Greenland, and were subsequently found by the Swedish Exploring Expedition of 1870. One of them, now in the Royal Museum of Stockholm, weighs over 50,000 pounds, and is the largest specimen known. Two remarkable meteorites have fallen in Iowa within the past thirteen years. On February 12, 1875, an exceedingly brilliant meteor, in the form of an elongated horseshoe, was seen throughout a region of at least 400 miles in length and 250 in breadth, lying in Missouri and Iowa. It is described as "without a tail, but having a sort of flowing jacket of flame. Detonations were heard, so violent as to shake the earth and to jar the windows like the shock of an earthquake," as it fell, at about 10.30 o'clock P. M., a few miles east of Marengo, Iowa. The ground for the space of some seven miles in length by two to four miles in breadth was strewn with fragments of this meteor, varying in weight from a few ounces to seventy-four pounds. On May 10, 1879, a large and extraordinarily luminous meteor exploded with terrific noise, followed at slight intervals with less violent detonations, and struck the earth in the edge of a ravine near Estherville, Emmet County, Iowa, penetrating to a depth of fourteen feet. Within two miles other fragments were found, one of which weighed 170 pounds and another thirty-two pounds. The principal mass weighed 431 pounds. All the discovered parts aggregated about 640 pounds. The one of 170 pounds is now in the cabinet of the State University of Minnesota. The composition of this aerolite is peculiar in many respects; but, as in nearly all aerolites, there is a considerable proportion of iron and nickel.

Woman Suffrage.—The constitution of the Colony of New Jersey granted suffrage to all inhabitants, under certain qualifications, irrespective of sex. This act was repealed, however, in 1807. The first Woman's Rights convention was held July 19, 1848, at Seneca Falls, N. Y., and its claims for women were based upon the Declaration of Independence. On October 23, 1850, a National Woman's Rights Convention was held at Worcester, Mass. From that time until 1866 the subject was agitated in America and England, but no decisive action was taken. In the latter year the American Equal Rights Association presented the first petition for woman suffrage to Congress. Two years later (1868) the New England Woman Suffrage Association was formed, and the work of memorializing Legislatures and Congress, holding conventions and circulating documents, began in earnest. By 1870 the agitation had assumed such proportions that the Republican Convention in Massachusetts, held October 5th of that year, admitted Lucy Stone and Mary A. Livermore as regularly accredited delegates. Since then several State conventions have indorsed woman suffrage. December 10, 1869, the Legislature of the territory of Wyoming granted the right of suffrage to women. The same right was granted in 1883 in the territory of Washington but has since been declared unconstitutional. Woman suffrage, limited to school elections or school meetings, has been conferred in the states of Kansas, Washington, Nebraska, New Hampshire, Texas, Vermont, Arizona, the Dakotas, Montana, Colorado, Minnesota, Wisconsin, Massachusetts, New Jersey, Michigan, and New York. In the two latter states the law requires that they be tax-payers. Widows and unmarried women may vote as to special district taxes in state of Idaho if they hold taxable property. In Kentucky any white widow having a child of school age is a qualified school voter; if she has no child, but is a tax-payer, she may vote on the question of taxes. In Oregon widows having children and taxable property may vote at school meetings. Widows, or unmarried women not minors who pay taxes and are listed as parents, guardians, or heads of families, may vote at school meetings in Indiana. They have full municipal suffrage in Kansas, and vote on the sale of liquor in Arkansas and Mississippi. In England, Scotland, and Wales women (unless married) vote for all elective officers, except member of Parliament, on like terms with men. In Ireland women vote everywhere for poor-law guardians; in Dundalk and other seaports, for harbor boards; in Belfast, for all municipal officers. In Sweden their suffrage is about the same as in England, except that they vote indirectly for members of the House of Lords. In Russia women (heads of households) vote for all elective officers and on all local questions. In Austria-Hungary they vote (by proxy) at all elections. In Italy widows vote for members of Parliament. In all the countries of Russian Asia women vote wherever a Russian colony settles. Municipal woman suffrage exists in New Zealand, Victoria, New South Wales, Queensland, and South America. Iceland, the Isle of Man, and Pitcairn Island have full woman suffrage. Tasmania, Sicily, Sardinia, and a host of islands elsewhere, have partial woman suffrage.

Consumption.— Of the total number of deaths, the percentage traceable to consumption in the several states and territories is as follows: Alabama, 9.6; Arizona, 6.1; Arkansas, 6.4; California, 15.6; Colorado, 8.2; Connecticut, 15.1; Dakota, 8.8; Delaware, 16.1; District of Columbia, 18.9; Florida, 8.3; Georgia, 7.9; Idaho, 6.8; Illinois, 10.3; Indiana, 12.6; Iowa, 9.9; Kansas, 7.3; Kentucky, 15.7; Louisiana, 10.4; Maine, 19.2; Maryland, 14.0; Massachusetts, 15.7; Michigan, 13.02; Minnesota, 9.3; Mississippi, 8.8; Missouri, 9.8; Montana, 5.6; Nebraska, 8.8; Nevada, 6.3; New Hampshire, 5.6; New Jersey, 8.9; New Mexico, 2.4; New York, 8.1; North Carolina, 9.5; Ohio, 13.8; Oregon, 12.1; Pennsylvania, 12.6; Rhode Island, 14.6; South Carolina, 9.8; Tennessee, 14.5; Texas, 6.5; Utah, 2.8; Vermont, 16.1; Virginia, 12.2; Washington, 13.2; West Virginia, 13.0; Wisconsin, 10.4; Wyoming, 2.6. Average, 12.0.

Presidents Inaugurated Irregularly. — George Washington, April 30, 1789; James Monroe, second term, March 5, 1821; John Tyler, April 6, 1841; Zachary Taylor, March 5, 1849; Millard Fillmore, July 10, 1850; Johnson, Apr. 15, '65; Hayes, Mar. 5, '77; Arthur, Sept. 20, '81; Roosevelt, Sept. 14, '01.

Women, Myths of the Origin of.— Woman's first appearance has been a fruitful subject of legends. The Phœnician myth of creation is found in the story of Pygmalion and Galatea. There the first woman was carved by the first man out of ivory, and then endowed with life by Aphrodite. The Greek theory of the creation of woman, according to Hesiod, was that Zeus, as a cruel jest, ordered Vulcan to make woman out of clay, and then induced the various gods and goddesses to invest the clay doll with all their worst qualities, the result being a lovely thing, with a witchery of mien, refined craft, eager passion, love of dress, treacherous manners, and shameless mind. The Scandinavians say that as Odin, Vill, and Ve, the three sons of Bor, were walking along the sea beach, they found two sticks of wood, one of ash, and one of elm. Sitting down, the gods shaped man and woman out of these sticks, whittling the woman from the elm, and calling her Ernia. One of the strangest stories touching the origin of woman is told by the Madagascarenes. In so far as the creation of man goes, the legend is not unlike that related by Moses, only that the fall came before Eve arrived. After the man had eaten the forbidden fruit, he became affected with a boil on the leg, out of which, when it burst, came a beautiful girl. The man's first thought was to throw her to the pigs; but he was commanded by a messenger from heaven to let her play among the grass and flowers until she was of marriageable age, then to make her his wife. He did so, called her Baboura, and she became the mother of all races of men. The American Indian myths relative to Adam and Eve are numerous and entertaining. Some traditions trace back our first parents to white and red maize; another is that man, searching for a wife, was given the daughter of the king of muskrats, who, on being dipped into the waters of a neighboring lake, became a woman.

Gotham.— The origin of the name "Gotham," as applied to the city of New York, is contained in a humorous book called "Salmagundi," written by Washington Irving, his brother William, and James K. Paulding, and is used to signify that the inhabitants were given to undue pretensions to wisdom. This definition of the word is taken from a story regarding the inhabitants of Gotham, a parish in Nottinghamshire, England, who were as remarkable for their stupidity as their conceit. The story relates that when King John was about to pass through Gotham toward Nottingham, he was prevented by the inhabitants, who thought that the ground over which a king passed became forever a public road. When the king sent to punish them they resorted to an expedient to avert their sovereign's wrath. According to this, when the messengers arrived they found the people each engaged in some foolish occupation or other, so they returned to court and reported that Gotham was a village of fools. In time a book appeared entitled "Certain Merry Tales of the Mad Men of Gotham," compiled in the reign of Henry VIII. by Andrew Borde, a sort of traveling quack, from whom the occupation of the "Merry Andrew" is said to be derived. Among these tales is the story of "The Three Wise Men of Gotham," who went to sea in a bowl.

Hallows Eve, or Halloween, is the night of October 31st, the eve of All Saints', or Allhallows Day, which is November 1st, and is probably a relic of pagan times or of mediæval superstitions, as it has nothing whatever to do with the church festival. In England and Scotland it is especially selected as the time for trying spells and divinations in love affairs. The superstitious tradition regarding it is that it is the night of all others when supernatural influences prevail; when spirits of the invisible and visible world walk abroad, for on this mystic evening it was believed that the human spirit was enabled, by the aid of supernatural power, to detach itself from the body and wander through the realms of space. There is a similar superstition in Germany concerning "Walpurgis night"—the night preceding the first of May. On this night, the German peasants believe that there is a witch festival, or gathering of evil spirits, on the summit of the Brocken, in the Hartz Mountains, and the malign influence of this convocation was believed to be felt all over the surrounding country. It was an old custom, and still observed in some places, to light great bonfires of straw or brush on that night, to drive away the spirits of darkness supposed to be hovering in the air. Considering that All Saints' Day was originally kept on May 1st, there would appear to be but little doubt that Allhallow eve and Walpurgis night have a common origin, which, doubtless, dates back to the earliest belief in a personal and all-powerful Evil One—the Chaldean's Power of Darkness.

Mammoth Cave, The, is situated in Edmondson County, near Green River, Kentucky, and extends some nine miles. It contains a succession of wonderful avenues, chambers, domes, abysses, grottoes, lakes, rivers, and cataracts. One chamber, the Star, is about 500 feet long, 70 feet wide, and 70 feet high; the ceiling is composed of black gypsum, and is studded with innumerable white points, that by a dim light resemble stars; hence the name. There are avenues one and a half and even two miles in length, some of which are incrusted with beautiful formations, and present a most dazzling appearance. There is a natural tunnel about three quarters of a mile long, 100 feet wide, covered with a ceiling of smooth rock, 45 feet high. Echo River is some three fourths of a mile in length, 200 feet in width at some points, and from 10 to 30 feet in depth, and runs beneath an arched ceiling of smooth rock about 15 feet high; while the Styx, another river, is 450 feet long, from 15 to 40 feet wide, and from 30 to 40 feet deep, and is spanned by a natural bridge. Lake Lethe has about the same length and width as the river Styx, varies in depth from 3 to 40 feet, lies beneath a ceiling some 90 feet above its surface, and sometimes rises to a height of 60 feet. There is also a Dead Sea. The entrance to the cave is reached by passing down a wild, rocky ravine through a dense forest. To visit the portions of this wonderful cave already traversed requires, it is said, 150 to 200 miles of travel.

Yosemite Valley, or, as it is also called, Yohamite, is situated in the eastern portion of California, and is from 8 to 10 miles long, and a little more than a mile wide. In some places the valley is filled with noble oaks; in others it opens out into broad, grassy fields. The natural beauties of this region are of world-wide report. It has pine-covered mountains, towering, with very steep slopes, to the height of 3,500 feet, a precipice, or bluff, in one place rising perpendicularly 3,089 feet above the valley; in another, a rock, almost perpendicular, 3,270 feet high; waterfalls pouring over its sides from heights of 700 to almost 1,000 feet; and one great waterfall broken into three laps, but of which the whole height is 2,550 feet. Of the other waterfalls on the sides of the valley, the Pohono, or Bridal Veil Waterfall, is particularly to be remarked for its beauty, as well as for its height, which is 940 feet, and almost unbroken. The Yosemite Valley was first entered by white men in 1855, but now, like the valleys of Switzerland, has its hotels and guides, and is yearly visited by American and foreign tourists.

Great Eastern, The.—The largest ship in the world, the Great Eastern, was constructed by the Eastern Navigation Company of London. The work of construction commenced May 1, 1854, and the work of launching her, which lasted from November 3, 1857, to January 31, 1858, cost £60,000, hydraulic pressure being employed. Her extreme length is 680 feet; breadth, 82 1-2 feet, and including paddle-boxes, 118 feet; height, 58 feet, or 70 feet to top of bulwarks. She has 8 engines, capable in actual work of 11,000 horse power, and has, besides, 20 auxiliary engines. The ship's history presents a singular series of vicissitudes. She left the Thames September 8, 1859, on her trial trip across the Atlantic; an explosion of steam pipes took place off Hastings; seven persons were killed, and several wounded; and the voyage abruptly came to an end at Weymouth. After a winter spent in costly repairs, the ship started again on June 17, 1860. Leaving Southampton on that day, she crossed the Atlantic in eleven days, and reached New York on the 28th. During the remainder of 1860, and the greater part of 1861, she made many voyages to and fro, losing money by the insufficiency of the receipts to meet the current expenses, and constantly required repairs. In December of the latter year she was used as a troop ship to convey troops to Canada. The years 1862 to 1864 were a blank as concerns the history of the steamer. In 1864 she was employed by the Atlantic Telegraph Company as a cable-laying ship, and continued in such service during 1865 and 1866. In 1867, when the preparations for the Paris International Exhibition were approaching completion, a body of speculators chartered the Great Eastern for a certain number of months, to convey visitors from New York to Havre and back; but the speculation proved an utter failure, there being neither wages for the seamen and engineers, nor profits for the speculators. In 1868 the ship was again chartered by the Telegraph Construction and Maintenance Company. On October 28, 1885, the Great Eastern was sold at public auction for $126,000.

Giant's Causeway.— The name Giant's Causeway is often applied to the entire range of cliffs in the County Antrim, on the northeast coast of Ireland, but it properly belongs to only a small portion of them, which is a platform of basalt in closely arranged columns, from fifteen to thirty-six feet high, which extends from a steep cliff down into the sea till it is lost below low-water mark. This platform is divided across its breadth into three portions, the Little, Middle, and Grand Causeway, these being separated from each other by dikes of basalt. The columns are generally hexagonal prisms, but they are also found of five, seven, eight, and nine sides, in almost every instance being fitted together with the utmost precision, even so that water cannot penetrate between adjoining columns. The name "causeway" was given to the platform because it appeared to primitive imagination to be a road to the water, prepared for giants.

Golden Fleece, The.— According to Greek tradition, Pelias, King of Iolcos, in Thessaly, dethroned the rightful King Æson and endeavored to kill his son Jason, who was, however, saved by his parents, who conveyed him by night to the cave of the centaur Chiron, to whose care they committed him, and then gave out that he was dead. He remained with Chiron until he was twenty years of age and then went to claim his father's crown. Pelias agreed to surrender the kingdom to Jason provided he brought him the golden fleece from Colchis, expecting that he would never attempt it, or, if he did, would surely perish in the rash adventure. One of the myths of the fleece is that Ino, second wife of Athamas, King of Orchomenus, in Bœotia, wished to destroy Phrixus, son of Athamas; but he and Helle were saved by their mother, Nephele, who gave them a golden fleeced ram she had obtained from Mercury, which carried them through the air over sea and land. Helle fell into the sea, and it was named Hellespontus. Phrixus went on to Colchis, where he was kindly received, and sacrificed the ram to Jupiter Phyxius, and gave the golden fleece to Æetes, who nailed it to an oak in the grove of Mars, where it was watched over by a sleepless dragon. Jason, by heralds, announced the great undertaking throughout the land, and all the heroes of Greece flocked to his assistance, and the famous company were called the "Argonauts," from the name of their ship, Argo, which was built for them by Argus, with the aid of Minerva. After a voyage of varied adventure the heroes reached Colchis, and Jason explained the cause of his voyage to Æetes; but the conditions on which he was to recover the golden fleece were so hard that the Argonauts must have perished had not Medea, the king's daughter, fallen in love with their leader. She had a conference with Jason, and after mutual oaths of fidelity Medea pledged herself to deliver the Argonauts from her father's hard conditions if Jason would marry her and carry her with him to Greece. He was to tame two bulls which had brazen feet and breathed flame from their throats. When he had yoked these, he was to plow with them a piece of ground, and sow the serpent's teeth which Æetes possessed. All this was to be performed in one day. Medea, who was an enchantress, gave him a salve to rub on his body, shield, and spear. The virtue of this salve would last an entire day, and protect alike against fire and steel. She further told him that when he had sown the teeth a crop of armed men would spring up and prepare to attack him. Among these she desired him to fling stones, and while they were fighting with one another about them, each imagining that the other had thrown the stones, to fall on and slay them. All of these things were done by Jason, but Æetes refused to give the fleece, and meditated burning the Argo, Jason's vessel, and slaying her crew. Medea, anticipating him, led Jason by night to the golden fleece; with her drugs she put to sleep the serpent which guarded it; and then, taking her little brother Absyrtus out of his bed, she embarked with him in the Argo, and the vessel set sail while it was yet night. They were pursued by Æetes, when Medea killed her brother and threw his body into the sea piece by piece, thus delaying the king, who stopped to gather up the remains, leaving the Argonauts to escape. After many months of toil and numerous trials they at last reached Iolcos, and the Argo was consecrated by Jason, on the Isthmus of Corinth, to Neptune.

The Armed Strength of Europe.

TABLE SHOWING RESOURCES IN THE EVENT OF A GENERAL CONFLICT.

LAND FORCES.

CLASSES.	Germany.	France.	Italy.	Austria-Hungary.	Russia.	Great Britain.*	Turkey.
ACTIVE ARMY AND RESERVE.							
Officers	22,803	22,106	17,600	17,326	27,912	7,786	9,300
Non-com. Officers and Men	1,963,517	1,998,604	652,612	749,868	1,120,602	197,925	192,000
Non-combatants	168,410	34,654	10,000	12,315	42,000	8,145	....
Horses	107,960	112,800	56,700	59,800	162,100	29,000	31,000
Guns	2,864	3,400	1,268	1,624	2,312	720	696
Vehicles	33,400	32,982	14,600	17,000	29,800	....	....
FIRST RESERVE.							
Officers	23,600	19,402	18,424	16,962	18,790	82,652	13,600
Non-com. Officers and Men	2,190,672	1,911,512	592,112	364,800	2,576,840		492,000
Non-combatants	4,201	17,618	3,700	3,211	16,000	....	....
Horses	93,700	83,416	....	23,680	143,816	....	64,000
Guns	1,920	1,680	744	1,200	3,636	....	....
Vehicles	....	3,600	....	....	6,800	....	....
SECOND RESERVE.							
Officers	19,455	18,960	18,940	22,900	18,964	128,612	400,000
Non-com. Officers and Men	992,500	914,600	912,100	497,850	1,372,416		
Horses	....	....	....	....	....	18,000	....
Guns	....	424	....	....	....	....	....
GRAND WAR TOTAL.							
Officers	65,258	60,468	54,964	57,188	65,666	425,120	29,900
Non-com. Officers and Men	5,146,689	4,824,716	2,556,824	1,612,018	5,069,858		1,084,000
Horses	201,660	196,216	68,000	83,480	305,916	4,700	95,000
Guns	4,784	5,504	2,012	2,824	5,948	....	696
PEACE ESTABLISHMENT.							
Infantry	396,782	378,914	130,600	189,320	496,000	146,999	158,800
Cavalry	72,300	72,100	28,200	39,400	121,400	19,361	32,400
Artillery	86,516	83,620	34,800	35,100	112,000	36,977	18,200
Engineers and Train	36,113	27,214	13,860	15,300	34,000	7,900	28,000
Horses	120,300	118,700	59,000	67,000	178,600	29,000	36,000
Guns	2,864	3,400	1,268	1,624	2,312	720	696
TOT. PEACE ESTABLISHMENT.							
Men	591,715	561,848	208,060	279,120	761,400	211,237	237,400
Horses	120,300	118,700	59,000	67,000	178,600	29,000	36,000
Guns	2,864	3,400	1,268	1,624	2,312	720	696

This table does not include fortress guns. * Including regular forces in India and the colonies.

LAND FORCES.

CLASSES.	Spain.	Belgium.	Nether-lands.	Denmark	Greece.	Switzer-land.	Sweden and Norway.	ASIATIC STATES. Japan.	China.	India.†
Infantry	59,600	31,690	43,400	24,470	12,000	120,300	....	101,400	100,000	137,300
Cavalry	9,800	6,213	4,290	2,400	1,200	3,100	....	9,766		38,000
Artillery	15,300	8,740	12,960	9,616	2,800	9,812	....	23,337		24,670
Engineers and Train	6,512	2,600	1,896	1,200	4,100	6,214	....	5,700	....	11,600
Total Active Army	90,212	49,273	62,546	37,686	20,100	129,426	38,840	....	....	....
East Indian Troops	....	....	46,000	....	....	....	....	....	....	....
Sanitary and Administrative Troops	17,600	5,100	4,600	3,200	1,200	4,200	1,600	....	....	....
West Indian Troops	*52,000	....	1,900	1,400	....	....	....	....	....	....
Philippine Troops	17,600	....	....	....	....	....	....	....	....	....
First Reserves	180,000	65,600	53,000	42,000	90,000	81,000	90,000	78,500	500,000	....
Second Reserves	1,000,000	50,000	78,000	48,000	120,000	270,000	125,000	235,000	....	200,000
Total Peace Strength	177,412	54,343	115,046	42,286	21,300	133,626	40,440	140,203	100,000	201,570
Total War Strength	1,357,412	169,943	246,046	132,286	231,300	484,626	225,440	453,703	600,000	401,570

* Remaining in Cuba November 30, 1898. † Including native and white troops.

CONDITIONS OF SERVICE AND AVAILABLE STRENGTH OF POWERS.

Every year the young men who attain the age in which they are available for military service are enrolled, in advance, in every European country. These ages run generally from 21 to 45, and this time is divided up by service; first, in the active army, which answers to our regular establishment; second, in the reserve to the active army; third, in the Landwehr; fourth, in the Landsturm, in which they are never called out, except in time of war, and then for defense of the fatherland only.

Liberty Bell was cast in London in 1752 by order of the Pennsylvania Assembly, for use in their State House. The bell reached Philadelphia the following year, but it cracked without any apparent reason when it was rung to test the sound, and it was necessary to have it recast. This was done by Philadelphia workmen, and in June, 1753, it was again hung in the belfry of the State House. On July 4, 1776, when the Continental Congress declared the colonies independent of Great Britain, the bell was rung for two hours, so the story goes, by the old bellman, who was so filled with enthusiasm and excitement that he could not stop. It was taken down when the British threatened Philadelphia in 1777, and removed to Allentown, Pa., but was returned to the State House in 1778, and a new steeple was built for it. A few years afterward it cracked under a stroke of the hammer, and although an attempt has been made to restore its tone by sawing the crack wider, it has been unsuccessful. During the World's Fair in New Orleans in 1885, the bell was sent there for exhibition. It left Philadelphia, January 24th, in the charge of three custodians appointed by the mayor of the city, who did not leave it day or night until it was returned in June of the same year. The train carrying the bell was preceded over the entire route by a pilot engine. The following words are inscribed around it: "By order of the Assembly of the Province of Pennsylvania, for the State House, in the City of Philadelphia, 1752," and underneath, "Proclaim liberty through all the land unto all the inhabitants thereof—Levit. xxv. 10." Its weight is about 2,000 pounds.

Sizes of Books.—The name indicates the number of pages in the sheet, thus: in a folio book, 4 pages or 2 leaves = 1 sheet; a quarto, or 4to, has 8 pages or 4 leaves to a sheet; an octavo, or 8vo, 16 pages or 8 leaves to a sheet. In a 12mo, 24 pages or 12 leaves = one sheet, and the 18mo, 36 pages, or 18 leaves = 1 sheet, and so on. The following are the approximate sizes of books:—

Royal Folio	19 inches	× 12
Demy	18 "	× 11
Super Imp. Quarto (4to)	15½ "	× 13
Royal 4to	12½ "	× 10
Demy 4to	11½ "	× 8½
Crown 4to	11 "	× 8
Royal Octavo	10½ "	× 6½
Medium 8vo	9½ "	× 6
Demy 8vo	9 "	× 5½
Crown 8vo	7½ "	× 4½
Foolscap 8vo	7 "	× 4
12mo	7 "	× 4
16mo	6½ "	× 4
Square 16mo	4½ "	× 3½
Royal 24mo	5½ "	× 3¼
Demy 24mo	5 "	× 2¾
Royal 32mo	5 "	× 3
Post 32mo	4 "	× 2½
Demy 48mo	3¾ "	× 2¼

Boomerang is an instrument of war or of the chase used by the aborigines of Australia. It is of hard wood, of a bent form; the shape is parabolic. It is about two and a half inches broad, a third of an inch thick, and two feet long, the extremities being rounded. The method of using this remarkable weapon is very peculiar. It is taken by one end, with the bulged side downward, and thrown forward as if to hit some object twenty-five yards in advance. Instead of continuing to go directly forward, as would naturally be expected, it slowly ascends in the air, whirling round and round, and describing a curved line till it reaches a considerable height, when it begins to retrograde, and finally sweeps over the head of the projector and falls behind him. This surprising motion is produced by the reaction of the air upon a missile of this peculiar shape. The boomerang is one of the ancient instruments of war of the natives of Australia. They are said to be very dexterous in hitting birds with it—the birds, being, of course, behind them, and perhaps not aware that they are objects of attack.

United States Census of 1890.

(For Census of 1900 see page 635.)

STATES.	Population.	Square Miles.	Electoral vote
Alabama	1,513,017	52,250	9
Arkansas	1,128,179	53,850	7
California	1,208,130	158,360	8
Colorado	412,198	103,925	3
Connecticut	746,258	4,990	6
Delaware	168,493	2,050	1
Florida	391,422	58,680	3
Georgia	1,837,353	59,475	11
Idaho	84,385	84,800	1
Illinois	3,826,351	56,650	25
Indiana	2,192,404	36,350	13
Iowa	1,911,896	56,025	11
Kansas	1,427,096	82,080	8
Kentucky	1,858,635	40,400	11
Louisiana	1,118,587	48,720	7
Maine	661,086	33,040	4
Maryland	1,042,390	12,210	6
Massachusetts	2,238,943	8,315	14
Michigan	2,093,889	58,915	12
Minnesota	1,301,826	83,365	9
Mississippi	1,289,600	46,810	8
Missouri	2,679,184	69,415	16
Montana	132,159	146,080	1
Nebraska	1,058,910	77,510	6
Nevada	45,761	110,700	1
New Hampshire	376,530	9,305	2
New Jersey	1,444,933	7,815	10
New York	5,997,853	49,170	37
North Carolina	1,617,947	52,250	10
North Dakota	182,719	68,645	2
Ohio	3,672,316	41,060	21
Oregon	313,767	96,030	2
Pennsylvania	5,258,014	45,215	32
Rhode Island	345,506	1,250	2
South Carolina	1,151,149	30,570	7
South Dakota	328,808	79,800	2
Tennessee	1,766,518	42,050	10
Texas	2,235,523	265,780	16
Utah	207,905	82,096	1
Vermont	332,422	9,565	2
Virginia	1,655,980	42,450	10
Washington	349,390	69,180	3
West Virginia	762,794	24,780	5
Wisconsin	1,686,880	56,040	11
Wyoming	60,705	97,890	1
Delaware, Raritan, and New York Bays,		720	..
TOTAL, STATES,	61,908,906	2,634,530	386
TERRITORIES.			
Arizona	59,620	113,020	
District of Columbia	230,392	70	
New Mexico	153,593	122,580	
Oklahoma	61,834	39,450	
Utah	207,905	84,970	
TOTAL, TERRITORIES,	713,344	360,090	
Excluding Alaska, Indian Ter. and Indians..**Grand Total,**	62,622,250		

Strasburg Clock.—The celebrated astronomical clock of Strasburg is in the minster, or cathedral, and was originally designed by an astronomer named Isaac Habrecht, in the early part of the sixteenth century. Previous to this time, in fact as early as 1354, Strasburg had an astronomical clock. It was in three parts. The lower part had a universal calendar, the central part an astrolabe, and in the upper division were figures of the three Magi and the Virgin. At every hour the Magi came forward and bowed to the Virgin; at the same time a chime was played, and a mechanical cock crew. This Clock of the Magi, as it was called, stopped in the early part of the sixteenth century, and was replaced by the clock made by Habrecht, which ran until 1789, when it stopped, and all attempts to put its works in order failed. In 1838 a clockmaker named Schwilgue undertook to remodel the internal machinery, and finished it in 1842. The case of the clock made by Habrecht was retained. A perpetual calendar, forming a ring around a dial thirty feet in circumference, occupies the central part of the lower division of the clock. At midnight, December 31st, the clock regulates itself (for the new year) for 365 or 366 days, as the case may be — even the omission of the bissextile day every 400 years being provided for. The disk within the calendar shows the eclipses of the sun and moon, calculated for all time to come. On one side Apollo points with an arrow to the date and name of the saint for the day. On the opposite side stands Diana, the goddess of night. Above the calendar is a niche in which, on each day, the mythological deity of the day appears—Apollo on Sunday, Diana on Monday, Mars on Tuesday, Mercury on Wednesday, Jupiter on Thursday, Venus on Friday, and Saturn on Saturday. Above this is a dial marking the mean time in hours and quarters, with two genii, one on each side, the one striking the first stroke of every quarter, the other turning over the hourglass at the last stroke of the last quarter. Then follows an orrery, showing the revolution of the seven visible planets around the sun, and, above, a globe giving the phases of the moon. Still above this, in a niche, four figures revolve around the skeleton image of Death, in the center. Childhood strikes the first quarter, Youth the second, Manhood the third, and old Age the last — Death strikes the hour. In a higher niche stands the image of our Saviour. At twelve o'clock the Twelve Apostles pass before Him in line, and He raises His hands to bless them. St. Peter closes the procession, and, as he passes, the mechanical cock on top of the case flaps his wings and crows three times. The left turret of this wonderful clock contains the weights and machinery, and has in its lower part the portrait of Schwilgue, above this the figure of Copernicus, and yet above, the muse Urania. At the foot of the case is a celestial globe, calculated for observation at the latitude of Strasburg. The clock is wound up every eight days. The mythical story of the city fathers of Strasburg putting out the eyes of the clockmaker to prevent his building a similar clock refers to Isaac Habrecht.

Age.—A man's working life is divided into four decades: 20 to 30, bronze; 30 to 40, silver; 40 to 50, gold; 50 to 60, iron. Intellect and judgment are strongest between 40 and 50. The percentages of population to age in various countries are shown thus:—

Country.	Percentage of Population.			Average age of all living, Years.
	Under 20 Years.	From 20 to 60	Over 60.	
United States...	50	45	5	24.9
England........	46	47	7	27.1
Scotland.........	46	45	9	27.4
Ireland	46	43	11	28.6
France	36	52	12	32.2
Germany........	43	49	8	28.0
Italy	44	49	7	27.6
Austria..........	43	50	7	27.7
Greece	48	47	5	25.5
Spain............	42	52	6	27.2
Brazil............	46	45	9	27.3
Belgium	40	50	10	29.7
Holland..........	43	49	8	28.3
Denmark	42	50	8	28.4
Sweden	43	49	8	28.0
Norway..........	43	48	9	28.0

The Americans are the youngest, the French the oldest.

Garter, Order of The, was founded in 1344, some writers say 1350, by Edward III. The original number of knights was twenty-five, his majesty himself making the twenty-sixth. It was founded in honor of the Holy Trinity, the Virgin Mary, St. Edward the Confessor, and St. George. The last, who had become the tutelary saint of England, was considered its special patron, and for this reason it has alway borne the title of "The Order of St. George," as well as that of "The Garter." The emblem of the order is a dark blue ribbon, edged with gold, bearing the motto, *Honi soit qui mal y pense*, in golden letters, with a buckle and pendant of gold richly chased. It is worn on the left leg below the knee. Regarding the adoption of this emblem and motto, the story is that the Countess of Salisbury let fall her garter when dancing with the king, and that he picked it up and tied it round his own leg, but that, observing the jealous glances of the queen, he restored it to its fair owner, with the exclamation, *Honi soit qui mal y pense*. The Order of the Garter, though not the most ancient, is one of the most famous military orders of Europe. It is said to have been devised for the purpose of attracting to the king's party such soldiers of fortune as might be likely to aid in asserting the claim which he was then making to the crown of France, and intended as an imitation of King

Arthur's Round Table. The officers of the order are the Prelate, the Chancellor, the Register, the Garter King of Arms, and the Usher of the Black Rod.

Number of Miles from New York to

Adrian, Mich	775
Akron, Ohio	610
Albany, N. Y	143
Alexandria, Va	238
Algiers, La	1,551
Allegheny, Pa	434
Allentown, Pa	92
Alton, Ill	1,060
Annapolis, Md	222
Ann Arbor, Mich	716
Atchison, Kan	1,368
Atlanta, Ga	1,018
Auburn, N. Y	328
Augusta, Me	407
Augusta, Ga	887
Aurora, Ill	951
Baltimore, Md	188
Bangor, Me	482
Bath, Me	382
Baton Rouge, La	1,320
Belfast, Me	424
Bellefontaine, Ohio	658
Binghamton, N. Y	215
Blackstone, Mass	272
Bloomington, Ill	1,037
Boston, Mass	236
Bristol, R. I	215
Bucyrus, Ohio	632
Buffalo, N. Y	433
Burlington, N. J	74
Burlington, Iowa	1,122
Burlington, Vt	280
Cambridge, Mass	239
Camden, N. J	91
Canandaigua, N. Y	377
Carson City, Nevada	2,800
Chambersburg, Pa	246
Charleston, S. C	874
Charlestown, Mass	235
Chattanooga, Tenn	980
Chicago, Ill	911
Chillicothe, Ohio	645
Cincinnati, Ohio	744
Circleville, Ohio	640
Cleveland, Ohio	581
Columbia, S. C	744
Columbus, Ohio	624
Concord, N. H	308
Covington, Ky	745
Cumberland, Md	364
Davenport, Iowa	1,093
Dayton, Ohio	804
Denver, Col	1,980
Des Moines, Iowa	1,251
Detroit, Mich	679
Dover, N. H	304
Dubuque, Iowa	1,100
Dunkirk, N. Y	460
Elmira, N. Y	274
Erie, Pa	508
Evansville, Ind	1,021
Fall River, Mass	180
Fitchburg, Mass	218
Fort Kearney, Neb	1,598
Fort Wayne, Ind	763
Fredericksburg, Va	296
Galena, Ill	1,083
Galesburg, Ill	1,076
Galveston, Tex	1,900
Georgetown, D. C	228
Hamilton, Ohio	766
Harrisburg, Pa	182
Hartford, Conn	112
Hudson, N. Y	115
Indianapolis, Ind	838
Jackson, Miss	1,498
Jefferson City, Mo	1,210
Kalamazoo, Mich	822
Kansas City, Mo	1,361
Kingston, N. Y	88
Lafayette, Ind	903
Lansing, Mich	785
Lawrence, Mass	262
Leavenworth, Kan	1,385
Lexington, Ky	840
Lexington, Mo	1,354
Little Rock, Ark	1,430
Lockport, N. Y	507
Louisville, Ky	900
Lowell, Mass	261
Lynchburg, Va	404
Macon, Ga	1,121
Madison, Wis	1,049
Memphis, Tenn	1,289
Milledgeville, Ga	1,100
Milwaukee, Wis	996
Mobile, Ala	1,370
Montgomery, Ala	1,193
Montpelier, Vt	454
Nashua, N. H	275
Nashville, Tenn	1,085
New Albany, Ind	903
New Bedford, Mass	181
New Brunswick, N. J	32
Newburgh, N. Y	53
New Haven, Conn	76
New Orleans, La	1,550
Newport, Ky	744
Newport, R. I	162
Norwalk, Conn	45
Omaha, Neb	1,455
Oswego, N. Y	237
Paterson, N. J	17
Peoria, Ill	1,072
Petersburg, Va	378
Philadelphia, Pa	88
Pittsburg, Pa	431
Portland, Me	344
Providence, R. I	193
Quincy, Ill	1,176
Racine, Wis	976
Raleigh, N. C	669
Reading, Pa	128
Richmond, Va	356
Rochester, N. Y	386
Rock Island, Ill	1,093
Rome, N. Y	264
Roxbury, Mass	238
Sacramento, Cal	2,900
St. Joseph, Mo	1,384
St. Louis, Mo	1,084
St. Paul, Minn	1,441
Salem, Mass	252
Salt Lake City, Utah	2,410
San Francisco, Cal	3,038
Sandusky, Ohio	642
Saratoga, N. Y	182
Savannah, Ga	974
Scranton, Pa	142
Springfield, Ill	1,062
Springfield, Mass	138
Springfield, Ohio	828
Staunton, Va	486
Stonington, Conn	143
Syracuse, N. Y	302
Taunton, Mass	210
Tallahassee, Fla	1,190
Terre Haute, Ind	912
Toledo, Ohio	742
Tonawanda, N. Y	463
Trenton, N. J	58
Troy, N. Y	148
Utica, N. Y	237
Vicksburg, Miss	1,542
Washington, D. C	230
Wheeling, W. Va	522
Wilmington, Del	116
Wilmington, N. C	604
Worcester, Mass	192

Number of Miles by Water from New York to

Amsterdam	3,510
Bermuda	660
Bombay	11,574
Boston	310
Buenos Ayres	7,110
Calcutta	12,425
Canton	13,900
Cape Horn	8,115
Cape of Good Hope	6,830
Charleston	750
Columbia River	15,965
Constantinople	5,140
Dublin	3,225
Gibraltar	3,300
Halifax	612
Hamburg	3,775
Havana	1,420
Havre	3,210
Kingston	1,640
Lima	11,310
Liverpool	3,210
London	3,375
Madras	11,850
Naples	4,330
New Orleans	2,045
Panama	2,358
Pekin	15,325
Philadelphia	240
Quebec	1,400
Rio Janeiro	3,840
Round the Globe	25,000
Sandwich Islands	15,300
San Francisco	15,858
St. Petersburg	4,420
Valparaiso	9,750
Washington	400

Patents Issued Since 1852.

Year	Patents and Certificates of Registration Issued						
	Patents	Designs	Reissues	Total Patents	Trade-marks	Labels	Total Certificates
1852	890	109	20	1,019	—	—	—
1860	4,363	183	232	4,778	—	—	—
1870	12,157	737	439	13,333	121	—	121
1880	12,926	515	506	13,947	349	203	552
1890	25,322	886	84	26,292	1,415	304	1,719
1891	22,328	836	80	23,244	1,762	137	1,899
1892	22,661	817	81	23,559	1,737	6	1,743
1893	22,768	902	99	23,769	1,677	—	1,677
1894	19,875	928	64	28,867	1,806	—	1,806
1895	20,883	1,115	59	22,057	1,829	3	1,832
1896	21,867	1,445	61	23,273	1,813	1	1,846
1897	22,098	1,631	65	23,794	1,671	14	1,701
1898	20,404	1,803	60	22,267	1,238	200	1,473
1899	23,296	2,139	92	25,527	1,649	**511**	**2,260**
1900	24,660	1,758	81	26,499	1,721	**737**	**2,551**

NOTE.—The number of patents granted prior to the commencement of this series of numbering (July 28, 1836) was 9957.

The whole number of original patents, including designs, issued up to Jan. 1, 1901, was 698,638.

Scales of Different Thermometers.

Reaumur.	Centigrade.	Fahrenheit.	
80°	100°	212°	Water Boils. (Bar. at 30 inch.)
76	95	203	
72	90	194	
68	85	185	
63½	79½	174	Alcohol Boils.
60	75	167	
56	70	158	
52	65	149	
48	60	140	
44	55	131	
43	53	127	Tallow Melts.
40	50	122	
36	45	113	
34	42½	108	
32	40	104	Fever Heat.
29	37	98	Blood Heat.
28	35	95	
25¾	32¼	90	
24	30	86	
21⅓	26⅔	80	
20	25	77	
19	24	76	Summer Heat.
16	20	68	
13¾	17¼	63	
12	15	59	
10	13	55	Temperate.
8	10	50	Temp. of Spring Water.
5¾	7¼	45	
3⅓	4½	40	
1½	2	35	

0	0	32	Water Freezes,
— 4	— 5	23	
— 5½	— 7	20	Wine Freezes.
— 8	—10	14	
—10	—12½	10	
—12	—15	5	
—14	—18	0	Zero, Fahr.
—16	—20	— 4	
—19	—24	—10	
—20	—25	—13	
—23	—29	—20	
—25	—32	—25	
—28	—35	—31	
—30	—37	—35	
—32	—40	—40	Mercury Freezes.
-103	-130	-200	Pure Alcohol Freezes.

No. Brick Required to Construct any Building.

(Reckoning 7 Brick to each superficial foot.)

Superficial Feet of Wall.	Number of Bricks to Thickness of					
	4 inch.	8 inch.	12 inch.	16 inch.	20 inch.	24 inch
1	7	15	23	30	38	45
2	15	30	45	60	75	90
3	23	45	68	90	113	135
4	30	60	90	120	150	180
5	38	75	113	150	188	225
6	45	90	135	180	225	270
7	53	105	158	210	263	315
8	60	120	180	240	300	360
9	68	135	203	270	338	405
10	75	150	225	300	375	450
20	150	300	450	600	750	900
30	225	450	675	900	1,125	1,350
40	300	600	900	1,200	1,500	1,800
50	375	750	1,125	1,500	1,875	2,250
60	450	900	1,350	1,800	2,250	2,700
70	525	1,050	1,575	2,100	2,625	3,150
80	600	1,200	1,800	2,400	3,000	3,600
90	675	1,350	2,025	2,700	3,375	4,050
100	750	1,500	2,250	3,000	3,750	4,500
200	1,500	3,000	4,500	6,000	7,500	9,000
300	2,250	4,500	6,750	9,000	11,250	13,500
400	3,000	6,000	9,000	12,000	15,000	18,000
500	3,750	7,500	11,250	15,000	18,750	22,500
600	4,500	9,000	13,500	18,000	22,500	27,000
700	5,250	10,500	15,750	21,000	26,250	31,500
800	6,000	12,000	18,000	24,000	30,000	36,000
900	6,750	13,500	20,250	27,000	33,750	40,500
1000	7,500	15,000	22,500	30,000	37,500	45,000

Comparative Yield of Various Grains, Vegetables, and Fruits.

	Lbs. per acre.		Lbs. per acre.
Hops	442	Grass	7,000
Wheat	1,260	Carrots	6,800
Barley	1,600	Potatoes	7,500
Oats	1,840	Apples	8,000
Pease	1,920	Turnips	8,420
Beans	2,000	Cinquefoil grass	9,600
Plums	2,000	Vetches, green	9,800
Cherries	2,000	Cabbage	10,900
Onions	2,800	Parsnips	11,200
Hay	4,000	Mangel-Wurzel	22,000
Pears	5,000		

Yellowstone Park is situated, the greater part, in Wyoming, the remainder partly in Montana and partly in Idaho, and comprises 3,575 square miles. The adaptability of this section of the country to the purposes of a national park was first brought prominently before the public by a company of surveyors who visited the region in the year 1869. In 1870 and 1871 the territory was again explored by scientific expeditions, and the reports of the first visitors were confirmed. The expedition of 1871 was headed by Professor Hayden, and upon his representations an act was passed by Congress, and approved March 1, 1872, by which what is now known as the Yellowstone National Park was "reserved and withdrawn from settlement, occupancy, or sale, and dedicated and set apart as a public park or pleasure-ground for the benefit and enjoyment of the people." This great park contains the most striking of all the mountains, gorges, falls, rivers, and lakes in the whole Yellowstone region. The mountain ranges rise to the height of from 10,000 to 12,000 feet, and are always covered with snow. The banks of the Yellowstone river abound with ravines and canyons, which are carved out of the heart of the mountains through the hardest rocks. The most remarkable of these is the canyon of Tower Creek and Column Mountain, which is about ten miles in length, and is so deep and gloomy that it is called "The Devil's Den." The Grand Canyon, which begins where Tower Creek ends, is twenty miles in length, is impassable throughout, and is inaccessible at the water's edge except at a few points, and its depth is so profound that no sound ever reaches the ear from the bottom. The Park contains a great multitude of hot springs of sulphur, sulphate of copper, alum, etc. There are at least 50 geysers that throw columns of water to the height of from 50 to 200 feet, and the falls of this wonderland are considered marvelous. The altitude of the entire Park is 6,000 feet or more above the sea level.

Aqueducts.—Among modern works the most famous are :—

	Length. Miles.	Million gal's daily.	Cost.
Croton (New York)	41	88	$9,000,000
Madrid	47	40	11,500,000
Marseilles	51	60	2,250,000
Glasgow	34	50	7,775,000
Washington	16	90	———

Rome, in the time of the Cæsars, had nine aqueducts, measuring 249 miles in the aggregate, and with a daily capacity of 320,000,000 gallons, or 200 gallons per inhabitant. The great aqueduct of Peru, built by the Incas, was 360 miles long.

Watches of the Night.— The Jews, like the Greeks and Romans, says the Rev. Dr. William Smith in his "Bible Dictionary," divided the night into watches instead of hours, each watch representing the period for which sentinels or pickets remained on duty. The proper Jewish reckoning recognized only three such watches, entitled the first or "beginning of the watches" (Lamentations ii, 19), the middle watch (Judges vii, 19), and the morning watch (Exodus xiv, 24 ; I Samuel xi, 11). These would last, respectively, from sunset to ten o'clock P. M., from ten o'clock P. M. to two o'clock A. M., and from two o'clock A. M. to sunrise. After the establishment of the Roman supremacy the number of the watches was increased to four, which were described either according to their numerical order, as in the case of the "fourth watch" (Matthew xiv, 25), or by the terms "even," "midnight," "cockcrowing," and "morning" (Mark xiii, 35). These terminated, respectively, at nine o'clock P. M., midnight, three o'clock A. M., and six o'clock A. M.

Walkyries.— The name "Walkyries" is derived from the old Norse *val*, which signifies a heap of slaughtered men, and *kjora*, to choose. In the Scandinavian mythology the Walkyries, also called battle-maidens, shield-maidens, and wish-maidens, are beautiful young women, who, adorned with golden ornaments, ride through the air in brilliant armor, order battles and distribute the death-lots according to Odin's command. Fertilizing dew-drops on the ground from the manes of their horses, light streams from the points of their lances, and a flickering brightness announce their arrival in the battle. They rejoice the glazing eye of the hero with their charming glances, and lead him to Walhalla, where they act as his cup-bearers. Some of the Walkyries spring from elves and other superhuman beings; some, also, are the daughters of princes. They ride generally in companies of three, or of three times three, or four times three, and have the gift of changing themselves into swans. Whoever deprives a Walkyrie of her swan-robe gets her into his power.

Mourning Customs.— From the earliest times the manner of expressing grief at death has differed in different countries. The Hebrew period of mourning was usually seven days; but in some instances, as at the death of Moses and Aaron, it was extended to thirty days. The mourners tore their clothing, cut off the hair and beard, strewed ashes on their heads, and cast themselves on the ground, weeping and smiting their breasts. The Greeks mourned thirty days, except in Sparta, where the mourning period was limited to ten days, and wore coarse black garments, cut off their hair, and secluded themselves from the public gaze. In the event of the death of a great general, the whole army cut off their hair, and also the manes of their horses. The Roman mourning period lasted only a few days; but if the death was that of some great ruler or general, all business was stopped, and the forum and the schools were closed. Among the Fiji Islanders the women are required to burn their bodies on the death of a chief, and in the Sandwich Islands the people go into mourning by knocking out the front teeth and by painting the lower part of the face black. The mourning color among the Romans under the republic was black or dark blue for both sexes, but during the empire the women wore white. In Europe and America the color is black; in Turkey, it is violet; in China, white; in Egypt, yellow; in Ethiopia, brown. It is customary for the courts in all European countries to go into mourning on the occasion of the death of a member of a royal family. The custom of draping buildings on the death of a great man or a hero of national reputation has always prevailed in the United States.

Natural Gas.— The earliest use of natural gas of which there is any record is in China, where for centuries it has been conveyed from fissures in salt-mines to the surface through hollow bamboos and used for burning purposes. There are also places in Asia, near the Caspian Sea, where it is seen to issue from the earth, and a similar phenomenon is to be seen in the Szalatna salt-mine in Hungary. The first discovery of natural gas made in America was in the neighborhood of Fredonia, Chautauqua County, New York, early in this century. In 1821 a small well was bored in the village and the gas was conducted through pipes to the houses and used for illuminating purposes, and, on the occasion of Lafayette's visit in 1824, it is said that the village was illuminated with this gas. Although this discovery was widely known it did not lead to any further experiments, either in the neighborhood or in other places, till fully twenty years after. In the early part of the present century it was found that the wells which were bored for salt in the Kanawha Valley yielded large quantities of gas, but it was not utilized as fuel until 1841. In 1865, a well which was sunk for petroleum at West Bloomfield, New York, struck a flow of natural gas. An effort was made to utilize this, and it was carried in a wooden main to the city of Rochester, a distance of twenty-four miles, in 1870, for the purpose of illuminating the city, but the experiment was a failure. In 1873, a well in Armstrong County, Pennsylvania, was so arranged that the gas could be separated from the water with which it was discharged, and conveyed through pipes to several mills in that vicinity, where it was extensively used for manufacturing purposes for the first time. From that date to the present day the use of natural gas, both for fuel and illuminating, has increased very rapidly, it having been discovered in other parts of Pennsylvania, Ohio, and Indiana.

Associated Press was organized about thirty years ago by the following New York city papers: *Herald*, *Tribune*, *World*, *Times*,

Sun, *Evening Express*, and *Journal of Commerce*, for the purpose of facilitating the collection of news. The general agent of the Association is located in New York, and associate agents in Chicago, Washington, Cincinnati, and other news centers. There is also a complete reportorial staff, and the news collected is used not only by the syndicate of papers, but is transmitted by telegraph tc others in almost every city in the country who have secured the privilege by purchase.

All Fools' Day.— The origin of the custom of April fooling cannot be traced with any degree of certainty. In the literature of the last century there are found many references to it, and yet beyond that it is scarcely possible to go. One suggestion is that the custom of playing tricks on the first day of April was derived from some ancient pagan custom, such as the Huli festival among the Hindoos, or the Roman Feast of the Fools. One fact, however, we do know, and that is that the practice prevails in many countries, under various names, which would seem to indicate that it dates away back to the early history of the race.

Palmistry.—The art of studying the lines in the palm, to discover the character and fortunes of a person, was practiced in ancient India and Greece. The subject was noticed by Aristotle, Pliny, Paracelsus, Albertus Magnus, and Cardan. A work by Johann Hartlieb was published in Augsburg, in 1475. M. le capitaine d'Arpentigny and M. Adrien Desbarrolles are chief modern authorities. L. Cotton's "Palmistry" was published in 1890, and Dr. Francis Galton published his study of "Finger Prints" in 1893.

Pavements.—The Carthaginians are said to have been the first who paved their towns with stones. The Romans, in the time of Augustus, had pavement in many of their streets; the Appian way, a paved road, was constructed 312 B. C. In England there were few paved streets before the time of Henry VII. London was first paved about 1533. It was paved with flagstones between 1815 and 1825. Among modern paving materials are brick, stone, wood, asphaltum, and many kinds of concrete.

Bookkeeping.—The system by double entry, called originally Italian bookkeeping, was taken from the course of algebra published by Burgo, in the fifteenth century, at Venice. John Gowghe, a printer, published a treatise on "Debitor and Creditor," in London, 1543. This was the earliest English work on bookkeeping, and the forerunner of many improved efforts.

Democrats, advocates of government by the people themselves, is a term first adopted by the French republicans in 1790; they termed their opponents *aristocrats*. The name *Democrats* was also adopted by the pro-slavery party in the United States, and the abolitionists were called *Republicans*. Into these two parties a number of smaller ones were absorbed at the presidential election in 1856.

The Twentieth Century began at midnight of December 31, 1900; the year 1901 is therefore the first year of the century. It will contain 25 leap years, and will have 36,525 days, which are equal to 5,218 weeks, lacking one day. It began on Tuesday, and will end on Sunday. February will have five Sundays in 1920, 1948, and 1976.

Sizes of Paper.

FOLDED.

Billet Note	6 x 8	Letter	10 x 16
Octavo Note	7 x 9	Com'rcial Letter	11 x 17
Commercial Note	8 x 10	Packet Post	11½ x 18
Packet Note	9 x 11	Foolscap	12½ x 16
Bath Note	8½ x 14		

Hills in an Acre of Ground.

40 feet apart	27 hills	8 feet apart	680 hills
35 "	35 "	6 "	1,210 "
30 "	48 "	5 "	1,732 "
25 "	69 "	3½ "	3,556 "
20 "	108 "	3 "	4,840 "
15 "	193 "	2½ "	6,969 "
12 "	302 "	2 "	10,890 "
10 "	435 "	1 "	43,560 "

The Wedding Anniversary.

At end of First Year comes the	Cotton Wedding
Second Year	Paper Wedding
Third Year	Leather Wedding
Fifth Year	Wooden Wedding
Seventh Year	Woolen Wedding
Tenth Year	Tin Wedding
Twelfth Year	Silk and Fine Linen Wedding
Fifteenth Year	Crystal Wedding
Twentieth Year	China Wedding
Twenty-fifth Year	Silver Wedding
Thirtieth Year	Pearl Wedding
Fortieth Year	Ruby Wedding
Fiftieth Year	Golden Wedding
Seventy-fifth Year	Diamond Wedding

Pensions.—The total number of pensioners classified and compared for the years 1898 and 1897 are as follow:—

	1898	1897
Widows, Revolutionary soldiers	5	7
Daughters, Revolutionary soldiers	7	9
Survivors of War of 1812	3	7
Widows, War of 1812	2,407	2,810
Survivors, Indian wars, 1832-'42	2,019	2,373
Widows, Indian wars, 1832-'42	4,067	4,288
Survivors, Mexican War	10,012	10,922
Widows, Mexican War	8,143	8,072
Under general laws:		
Army invalids	327,080	336,299
Widows, army	92,545	94,602
Navy invalids	4,833	4,788
Widows, navy	2,300	2,375
Act of June 27, 1890:		
Army invalids	399,366	378,609
Army widows	119,785	110,593
Navy invalids	14,543	13,831
Navy widows	5,944	5,766
Army nurses	655	663
Total	993,714	976,014

Paper Table for Printers' and Publishers' Use.—Showing the quantity of paper required for printing 1,000 copies (including 56 extra copies to allow for wastage), of any usual size book, from 8vo down to 32mo. If the quantity required is not found in the table, double or treble some suitable number of pages or quantity of paper.

No. of Forms.	8vo Pages.	12mo Pages.	16mo Pages.	24mo Pages.	32mo Pages.	1,000 Copies.	
						Rms.	Qrs.
1	8	12	16	24	32	1	2
2	16	24	32	48	64	2	4
3	24	36	48	72	96	3	6
4	32	48	64	96	128	4	8
5	40	60	80	120	160	5	10
6	48	72	96	144	192	6	12
7	56	84	112	168	224	7	14
8	64	96	128	192	256	8	16
9	72	108	144	216	288	9	18
10	80	120	160	240	320	11	
11	88	132	176	264	352	12	2
12	96	144	192	288	384	13	4
13	104	156	208	312	416	14	6
14	112	168	224	336	448	15	8
15	120	180	240	360	480	16	10
16	128	192	256	384	512	17	12
17	136	204	272	408	...	18	14
18	144	216	288	432	...	19	16
19	152	228	304	456	...	20	18
20	160	240	320	480	...	22	
21	168	252	336	504	...	23	2
22	176	264	352	...	...	24	4
23	184	276	368	...	...	25	6
24	192	288	384	...	...	26	8
25	200	300	400	...	...	27	10
26	208	312	416	...	...	28	12
27	216	324	432	...	...	29	14
28	224	336	448	...	...	30	16
29	232	348	464	...	...	31	18
30	240	360	480	...	...	33	
31	248	372	496	...	...	34	2
32	256	384	512	...	...	35	4
33	264	396	528	...	...	36	6
34	272	408	544	...	...	37	8
35	280	420	560	...	...	38	10
36	288	432	576	...	...	39	12
37	296	444	592	...	...	40	14
38	304	456	608	...	...	41	16
39	312	468	...	...	...	42	18
40	320	480	...	...	...	44	

Carrier Pigeons.—That pigeons have been used for a great many years for the transmission of messages is well known, but with what nation the custom originated it is impossible to discover. The Romans used the birds for this purpose, they were in use among the Asiatics, and we have the assertion of the poet Tasso for believing that they were employed during the siege of Jerusalem in 1099; and it is a historical fact that they were used during the crusade of St. Louis, in 1250. Their most remarkable use in modern times was during the siege of Paris, in 1870. In Turkey they have been more generally used than in any other country, and it is said that there the art of training them is carried to its highest perfection. Pigeons intended for this use are taken, when they have acquired full strength of wing, in a covered basket to a distance of about half a mile from their home, and then set at liberty and thrown into the air. If they return home they are then taken to greater distances, progressively increased from forty to fifty miles. When the bird is able to accomplish this flight he may be trusted to fly any distance, overland, within the limits of physical power. It is the general plan to keep the birds in a dark room for some hours before they are used. They are then fed sparingly, but are given all the water they can drink. The paper on which the message is written is tied around the upper part of the bird's leg, or to one of the large feathers of the tail, so as not to impede its flight. The feet are washed in vinegar to keep them from getting too dry, so that the bird will not be tempted to descend to water and thus possibly ruin the message. The rate of flight is from twenty to thirty miles an hour, though the bird has been known to pass over great distances much more rapidly. When thrown up in the air, the pigeon at first flies round and round, as though for the purpose of sighting some landmark that it knows. When this is discovered, it flies toward it, and thence onward to its home.

Emancipation in Great Britain.—The system of slavery was abolished throughout all the British Colonies by act of Parliament in 1833, when a bill was passed which gave freedom to all classes and indemnified their owners with an award of £20,000,000. According to this act, slavery was to cease on August 1, 1834, but the slaves were to continue with their former owners as apprentices for a certain period. This apprenticeship, however, did not work satisfactorily to either side, and complete emancipation took place in 1838. In 1787 the subject of the suppression of the slave trade was agitated in London and received the support of Mr. Pitt, the Prime Minister, and William Wilberforce, a member of Parliament, and in 1791 a bill forbidding the further importation of slaves was offered by Wilberforce in Parliament, but was not passed. The conquest of the Dutch colonies in America by the British led to such an increase in the British slave-trade that in 1805 the traffic was forbidden in the conquered colonies; and in 1806 the friends of emancipation gained still another step by the passage of an act forbidding British subjects to engage in the trade, and the following year a general abolition bill making all slave-trade illegal after January 1, 1808, was adopted by Parliament. This, however, did not have the desired effect, as British subjects still continued the trade under the flags of other nations. So, in 1811, it was made a felony, punishable with imprisonment at hard labor or transportation; and subsequent laws made it piracy, to be punished with transportation for life. From this time until the passage of the Emancipation bill the subject was continually pressed upon the attention of Parliament. Slavery existed in Great Britain in Saxon and Norman times, when the peasantry were sold in the market like cattle for exportation, and were looked upon as mere chattels, to be bought and sold with the land upon which they toiled. In Scotland, even as late as 1780, a law existed which compelled colliers, on entering a mine, to perpetual service there, the right to their labor passing with the mine to an inheritor or purchaser, and their children being in like manner attached to the mine, and forbidden under severe penalty to seek other employment.

Trojan War.— The legend regarding the Trojan war has, undoubtedly, a historical origin, in the fact of the actual destruction of Troy by a Grecian military expedition. About 1194-'84 B. C., according to the traditions, Paris, one of the sons of Priam, enticed Helen, the beautiful wife of Menelaus, King of Sparta, away from her husband, and, at the call of Menelaus all the heroes of Greece flew to arms to avenge this wrong. The Grecian host numbered 100,000 warriors, among whom were Ulysses, Achilles, Ajax, Diomed, and Agamemnon, who, as brother of Menelaus, was chosen to lead the expedition. The siege of the city of Priam lasted ten years. Finally the Greeks, by the device of Ulysses, built an immense wooden horse, in which they concealed a number of their warriors, and left it on the plain in sight of the city, and then retired to their ships as though abandoning the siege. The Trojans, believing that the statue was left as a propitiatory offering to their gods, carried it within their walls, and at night the concealed warriors issued from the horse and opened the gates of the city to their returned comrades, and Troy was sacked and burned. The king and all his sons were killed; in fact, according to the legend, Æneas, and his father, Anchises, and a few devoted followers, were the only ones to escape, and these, after long wanderings by sea and land, finally settled on the shores of Etruria, in Italy. The battles which were fought before the walls of Troy have been immortalized by Homer in the "Iliad."

Bride, Throwing Shoe after. — The custom of throwing a shoe after a departing bride and groom originated so far back in the dim and mystical past that the memory of man stretcheth not back to its beginning. It is by some thought to typify an assault, and is a lingering trace of the custom among savage nations of carrying away the bride by violence. Others claim that it has a likeness to a Jewish custom mentioned in the Bible. Thus, in Ruth, when the kinsman of Boaz gave up his claim to the inheritance of Ruth, and to Ruth also, he indicated his assent by plucking off his shoe and giving it to Boaz. Also, we read in Deuteronomy that when the brother of a dead man refused to marry his widow she asserted her independence of him by "loosing his shoe."

Captain Kidd was born in Scotland, and took to the sea when a mere boy. In 1695 a company composed of leading gentlemen in Great Britain and in the Colonies was formed to make a business of privateering and reap the profits, which were known to be immense. The "Adventure," a galley of 287 tons, quite a large vessel for those days, was purchased, and the command given to Kidd, who sailed with two commissions, one of which empowered him to act against the French, and the other to cruise against pirates. Besides these commissions under the Great Seal, he had the ordinary letters of marque from the Commissioners of the Admiralty. The king was to have one tenth of all the booty, and the rest was to be divided between the shareholders and Kidd in certain specified proportions. A portion was to be appropriated to the crew, who were to receive no regular pay. Kidd left Plymouth April 23, 1696, captured a French fishing vessel off Newfoundland, and in July reached New York, where he remained until September, when he sailed for Madagascar, then one of the strongholds of the buccaneers. In January of the following year he arrived at the island, and in 1698 reports were abroad in England that he had raised the black flag, and orders were dispatched to the effect that he be apprehended should he come within reach. April, 1699, found him in the West Indies, whither he had gone in a vessel called the "Quidah Merchant." This he secured in a lagoon in the island of Saona, near Hayti, and re-embarked in a small sloop named the "San Antonio," for the Colonies of America. He sailed up Long Island Sound to Oyster Bay, after making a landing in Delaware Bay, and there took aboard a New York lawyer named James Emott, whom he afterward sent to Boston to the Earl of Bellamont, who had become governor of the Colonies. Emott was Kidd's advance agent, sent forward to ascertain how the privateersman would be received. While the lawyer was absent on this mission, Kidd buried some bales of goods and treasure on Gardiner's Island. To the inquiries of the New York lawyer Bellamont made evasive answers, and then later induced Kidd to proceed to Boston, where he landed July 1, 1699. Five days later, Kidd, who was examined by the Council, was sent to England, where he was given something of the form of a trial. He was permitted to have no counsel, was not allowed to send for papers or witnesses, and was, of course, found guilty of piracy and of the murder of one of his crew, and was hanged at Execution Dock, with nine of his associates. Bellamont fitted out another vessel to go in search of the "Quidah Merchant," but news came before the search began that the latter had been stripped and burned by the men left with it by Kidd. The treasure which was secured on Gardiner's Island, with what was found with Kidd on the "San Antonio," amounted to $70,000.

Bridge of Sighs is the bridge connecting the palace of the Doge with the state prison in Venice. It was so called because prisoners once having crossed it from the Judgment Hall were never seen again, and it was supposed that many of them were dropped through a trap-door into the dark and deep waters of the canal flowing beneath.

Scarabæus, a peculiar beetle held sacred by the Egyptians. Several mystical ideas were attributed to it; the number of its toes, 30, symbolized the days of the month; the time it deposited its ball, which contained its eggs, was supposed to refer to the lunar month; the movement of the clay-ball referred to the action of the sun on the earth, and personified that luminary. It was supposed to be only of the male sex, hence it signified the self-existent, self-begotten generation, or metamorphosis, and the male or paternal principle of nature. In this sense it appears on the head of the Pygmæan deity Ptah-Socharis Osiris, the Demiurgos, and in astronomical scenes and sepulchral formulas. In connection with the Egyptian notions, the Gnostics and some of the Fathers called Christ the scarabæus. The insect during its life was worshiped and after death embalmed.

Tammany, Society of, or Columbian Order, was formed in 1789, being the effect of a popular movement in New York, having primarily in view a counterweight to the so-called "aristocratic" Society of the Cincinnati. It was essentially anti-Federalist or Democratic in its character, and its chief founder was William Mooney, an upholsterer, and a native-born American of Irish extraction. It took its title from a noted, ancient, wise, and friendly chief of the Delaware tribe of Indians, named Tammany, who had, for the want of a better subject, been canonized by the soldiers of the Revolution as the American patron saint. The first meeting was held May 12, 1789. The act of incorporation was passed in 1805. The Grand Sachem and thirteen Sachems were designed to typify the President and the Governors of the thirteen original States. The society is nominally a charitable and social organization, and is distinct from the general committee of the Tammany Democracy, which is a political organization.

Salutation, Forms of.— The custom of shaking hands, which is the most common among civilized nations, comes undoubtedly from remote barbarism, when two men, meeting, gave each other their weapon hands as a security against treachery or sudden attack. In the East and among the Slavic nations the character of salutations is quite different. Among the Persians, the custom of throwing one's self upon the ground and kissing the feet of the monarch prevails. In China, an inferior upon horseback meeting a superior dismounts and waits until the latter has passed. In Japan the inferior removes his sandals when meeting his superior, crosses his hands by placing the right hand in the left sleeve, and, with a slow, rocking motion of his body, cries out, "Augh! Augh!" (Do not hurt me.) In Siam, the inferior throws himself upon the ground before his superior; the latter sends forward one of his slaves to see whether the former has been eating anything, or carries with him any smell at all offensive. If he does, he is immediately kicked out without ceremony; but if not, the attendant raises him up. In Ceylon, the inferior, on meeting a superior, throws himself upon the ground, repeating the name and dignity of the latter. Among some tribes of the American Indians the custom is to salute by rubbing noses together. This form is also common in the Friendly and Society Islands, where it is returned by each taking the hand of the other and rubbing it upon his own nose and mouth. The Moors of Morocco ride at full speed toward a stranger, as if they intended to run him down, and, on arriving near, suddenly stop and fire a pistol over his head. The Arabians shake hands six or eight times; but if persons of distinction they embrace and kiss several times, also kissing their own hands. In Turkey, it is the custom to place the hand upon the breast and bow to the person saluted. In Burmah, when a gentleman meets a lady or another gentleman he applies his mouth and nose closely to their cheek and draws in a long breath, as if smelling a delightful perfume with both mouth and nose. In the greater portion of Germany it is an act of politeness to kiss the hand of a lady; but this privilege is allowed in Italy only to near relatives, while in Russia it is extended to kissing the forehead. On the European continent, it is usual for men who are intimate friends to kiss one another. The Pelew Island inhabitants grasp either the hand or foot of the one they wish to salute and rub their faces against it; while Yemen persons of rank permit their fingers to be kissed, after long refusal.

Nihilism.—The term "Nihilist" was probably first used by the Russian novelist Turgeneff, and was given to the party now known as Nihilists in derision, because its members sought the destruction of all existing order and government without proposing and apparently without intending to substitute any defined scheme or organization in its place. The earliest advocate of this doctrine was Michael Bakunin, who, as early as 1847, advocated a Russian republic, and in 1868 founded the "International Alliance of Revolution," a secret society having for its object a popular uprising against all monarchical governments. This society was undoubtedly the parent of the many secret organizations that have since sprung into existence throughout Europe. Though Alexander II. introduced a much more liberal policy than any of his predecessors, it came so far short of the desires of the party of progress that the spirit of discontent seemed stimulated, and the existence of a revolutionary conspiracy was proved in 1877, when, after a great trial lasting eighteen months, 135 persons out of 183 arrested were found to belong to such an organization. In 1878, when Vera Sassulitch shot General Trepoff, chief of the secret police, the Nihilists began to attract attention as a really formidable society. Her acquittal was followed by a series of outbreaks and assassinations which were only checked after the Czar himself had fallen at the hands of a Nihilist assassin. The doctrines and objects of the Nihilists must be taken from the declarations of their leaders. Bakunin, in a speech at Geneva in 1868, announced that he was the bearer of a new gospel, whose mission was to destroy the *lie* at the beginning of which was God. Having got rid of this belief, the next *lie* to be destroyed was *right*, a fiction invented by *might* to strengthen her power. "Our first work," he said, "must be destruction of everything as it now exists, the good and the bad; for, if but an atom of this old world remains, the new will never be created."

Bacteria is the name given to certain forms found in animal and vegetable fluids because of their shape, and is derived from a Greek word meaning a club. They are mere points of organized matter, and constitute the lowest form of organic life. They are found in the sap of plants, in the blood of man and of the lower animals, and are abundant in eggs. They bear an important part in healthy as well as morbid processes, in the ripening of fruit as well as decay. They also exist in suspension in the air, and the festering of an open sore is occasioned by the entrance of bacteria from the surrounding air. They also act as powerful organic ferments in the transformation of starch into sugar, of sugar-cane into glucose, etc.

Temperature and Rainfall of Foreign Cities.

Cities.	Mean Annual Temperature.	Annual Average Rainfall, Inches.	Cities.	Mean Annual Temperature.	Annual Average Rainfall, Inches.	Cities.	Mean Annual Temperature.	Annual Average Rainfall, Inches.
Alexandria	69.0	10	Florence	59.2	41	Munich	48.4	....
Algiers	64.3	27	Frankfort	50.0	....	Naples	60.3	30
Amsterdam	49.9	....	Geneva	52.7	32	Nice	58.0	29
Archangel	33.0	....	Genoa	61.1	47	Odessa	48.0	....
Astrakhan	50.1	6	Glasgow	49.8	44	Pará	81.0	71
Athens	63.0	....	Hague	52.0	....	Paris	51.3	22
Bagdad	74.0	....	Hamburg	47.0	....	Pekin	53.0	27
Barcelona	63.0	....	Havana	79.1	91	Port Said	....	2
Berlin	48.2	24	Hong Kong	73.0	101	Prague	50.2	14
Bermuda	72.0	55	Honolulu	75.0	....	Quebec	40.3	....
Berne	46.0	46	Iceland	39 0	30	Quito	60.9	....
Birmingham	48.2	....	Jerusalem	62.6	16	Rio de Janeiro	77.2	29
Bombay	81.3	75	Lima	73 3	....	Rome	60.5	31
Bordeaux	57.0	30	Lisbon	61.4	27	Rotterdam	51.0	23
Brussels	50.0	29	London	50.8	25	San Domingo	81.3	108
Budapest	51.9	17	Lyons	53.0	28	Shanghai	59.0	....
Buenos Ayres	62.8	....	Madeira	66.0	25	Smyrna	60.0	24
Cairo	72.2	....	Madrid	58.2	9	St. Petersburg	39.6	17
Calcutta	82.4	76	Malta	66.0	20	Stockholm	42 3	20
Canton	71.0	39	Manchester	48.8	36	Sydney	65.8	49
Cape Town	62.0	23	Manila	78.4	....	Tobolsk	32.0	....
Cayenne	....	116	Maranham	....	277	Trieste	55.0	43
Cherrapongee*	....	610	Marseilles	58.3	23	Valdivia	52.0	106
Christiania	41.5	....	Melbourne	57.0	29	Valparaiso	64.0	....
Constantinople	56.5	....	Mexico	60.9	....	Venice	55.4	....
Copenhagen	46.6	19	Milan	55.1	38	Vera Cruz	77.0	180
Delhi	77.0	24	Montevideo	62.0	44	Vienna	51 0	19
Dublin	50.1	29	Montreal	44.6	....	Warsaw	56.2	....
Edinburgh	47.1	38	Moscow	40.0	....			

*In Southwestern Assam. It is the wettest place in the world. In 1861 the rainfall there reached 905 inches.
NOTE.—The mean annual temperature of the globe is 50° Fahrenheit. The average rainfall is 36 inches.

Degrees in Freemasonry.

York Rite.

Lodge.

1. Entered Apprentice.
2. Fellow Craftsman.
3. Master Mason.

Chapter.

4. Mark Master.
5. Past Master.
6. Most Excellent Master.
7. Royal Arch Mason.

Council.

8. Royal Master.
9. Select Master.
10. Super Excellent Master.

Commandery.

11. Red Cross Knight.
12. Knight Templar.
13. Knight of Malta.

Scottish Rite.

Lodge of Perfection.

4. Secret Master.
5. Perfect Master.
6. Intimate Secretary.
7. Provost and Judge.
8. Intendant of the Building.
9. Elect of Nine.
10. Elect of Fifteen.
11. Sublime Knight Elect.
12. Grand Master Architect.
13. Knight of the Ninth Arch.
14. Grand Elect, Perfect and Sublime Mason.

Councils of Princes of Jerusalem.

15. Knight of the East or Sword.

Councils of Princes of Jerusalem (Continued).

16. Prince of Jerusalem.

Chapters of Rose Croix.

17. Knight of the East and West.
18. Knight of the Rose Croix de H. R. D. M.

Consistories of Sublime Princes of the Royal Secret.

19. Grand Pontiff.
20. Master Ad Vitam.
21. Patriarch Noachite.
22. Prince of Libanus.
23. Chief of the Tabernacle.
24. Prince of the Tabernacle.

Consistories of Sublime Princes of the Royal Secret (Continued).

25. Knight of the Brazen Serpent.
26. Prince of Mercy.
27. Commander of the Temple.
28. Knight of the Sun.
29. Knight of St. Andrew.
30. Grand Elect Knight, K. H., or Knight of the Black and White Eagle.
31. Grand Inspector Inquisitor Commander.
32. Sublime Prince of the Royal Secret.
33. Sovereign Grand Inspector-General of the 33d and Last Degree.

Cities of the United States, above 25,000.

TWELFTH CENSUS, 1900.

New York, N. Y	3,437,202	Bridgeport, Conn	70,996	Dubuque, Iowa	36,297
Chicago, Ill	1,698,575	Lynn, Mass	68,513	Quincy, Ill	36,252
Philadelphia, Pa	1,293,697	Oakland, Cal	66,960	South Bend, Ind	35,999
St. Louis, Mo	575,238	Lawrence, Mass	62,559	Salem, Mass	35,956
Boston, Mass	560,892	New Bedford, Mass	62,442	Johnstown, Pa	35,936
Baltimore, Md	508,957	Des Moines, Iowa	62,139	Elmira, N. Y	35,672
Cleveland, Ohio	381,768	Springfield, Mass	62,059	Allentown, Pa	35,416
Buffalo, N. Y	352,219	Somerville, Mass	61,643	Davenport, Iowa	35,254
San Francisco, Cal	342,782	Troy, N. Y	60,651	McKeesport, Pa	34,227
Cincinnati, Ohio	325,902	Hoboken, N. J	59,364	Springfield, Ill	34,159
Pittsburg, Pa	321,616	Evansville, Ind	59,007	Chelsea, Mass	34,072
New Orleans, La	287,104	Manchester, N. H	56,987	Chester, Pa	33,988
Detroit, Mich	285,704	Utica, N. Y	56,383	Malden, Mass	33,664
Milwaukee, Wis	285,315	Peoria, Ill	56,100	York, Pa	33,654
Washington, D. C	278,718	Charleston, S. C	55,807	Topeka, Kan	33,608
Newark, N. J	246,070	Savannah, Ga	54,244	Newton, Mass	33,587
Jersey City, N. J	206,433	Salt Lake City, Utah	53,531	Sioux City, Iowa	33,111
Louisville, Ky	204,731	San Antonio, Tex	53 321	Bayonne, N. J	32,722
Minneapolis, Minn	202,718	Duluth, Minn	52,969	Knoxville, Tenn	32,637
Providence, R. I	175,597	Erie, Pa	52,733	Chattanooga, Tenn	32,490
Indianapolis, Ind	169,164	Elizabeth, N. J	52,130	Schenectady, N. Y	31,682
Kansas City, Mo	163,752	Wilkesbarre, Pa	51,721	Fitchburg, Mass	31,531
St. Paul, Minn	163,632	Kansas City, Kan	51,418	Superior City, Wis	31,091
Rochester, N. Y	162,435	Harrisburg, Pa	50,167	Rockford, Ill	31,051
Denver, Col	133,859	Portland, Me	50,145	Taunton, Mass	31,036
Toledo, Ohio	131,822	Yonkers, N. Y	47,931	Joliet, Ill	30,720
Allegheny, Pa	129,896	Norfolk, Va	46,624	Canton, Ohio	30,667
Columbus, Ohio	125,560	Waterbury, Conn	45,859	Butte, Montana	30,470
Worcester, Mass	118,421	Holyoke, Mass	45,712	Montgomery, Ala	30,346
Syracuse, N. Y	108,374	Fort Wayne, Ind	45,115	Auburn, N. Y	30,345
New Haven, Conn	108,027	Youngstown, Ohio	44,885	East St. Louis, Ill	29,655
Paterson, N. J	105,171	Houston, Tex	44,633	Sacramento, Cal	29,282
Fall River, Mass	104,863	Covington, Ky	42,938	Racine, Wis	29,102
St. Joseph, Mo	102,979	Akron, Ohio	42,728	La Crosse, Wis	28,895
Omaha, Neb	102,555	Dallas, Tex	42,638	Williamsport, Pa	28,757
Los Angeles, Cal	102,479	Saginaw, Mich	42,345	Jacksonville, Fla	28,429
Memphis, Tenn	102,320	Lancaster, Pa	41,459	Newcastle, Pa	28,339
Scranton, Pa	102,026	Lincoln, Neb	40,169	Newport, Ky	28,301
Lowell, Mass	94,969	Brockton, Mass	40,063	Oshkosh, Wis	28,284
Albany, N. Y	94,151	Binghamton, N. Y	39,647	Woonsocket, R. I	28,204
Cambridge, Mass	91,886	Augusta, Ga	39,441	Pueblo, Col	28,157
Portland, Oregon	90,426	Pawtucket, R. I	39,231	Atlantic City, N. J	27,838
Atlanta, Ga	89,872	Altoona, Pa	38,973	Passaic, N. J	27,777
Grand Rapids, Mich	87,565	Wheeling, W. Va	38,878	Bay City, Mich	27,628
Dayton, Ohio	85,333	Mobile, Ala	38,469	Fort Worth, Tex	26,688
Richmond, Va	85,050	Birmingham, Ala	38,415	Lexington, Ky	26,369
Nashville, Tenn	80,865	Little Rock, Ark	38,307	Gloucester, Mass	26,121
Seattle, Wash	80,671	Springfield, Ohio	38,253	Joplin, Mo	26,023
Hartford, Conn	79,850	Galveston, Tex	37,789	South Omaha, Neb	26,001
Reading, Pa	78,961	Tacoma, Wash	37,714	New Britain, Conn	25,998
Wilmington, Del	76,508	Haverhill, Mass	37,175	Council Bluffs, Iowa	25,802
Camden, N. J	75,935	Spokane, Wash	36,848	Cedar Rapids, Iowa	25,656
Trenton, N. J	73,307	Terre Haute, Ind	36,673	Easton, Pa	25,238
				Jackson, Mich	25,180

INDEX.

Special dictionaries, such as Dictionary of Authors, Dictionary of Animal, Vegetable, and Mineral Productions, Dictionary of Art, Dictionary of Biography, Dictionary of Medicine, Dictionary of Law and Business Terms, Dictionary of Mythology, etc., are self-indexing and should be consulted in connection with the general index.